THE BULLY PULPIT

DORIS KEARNS GOODWIN

SIMON & SCHUSTER PAPERBACKS

NEW YORK LONDON TORONTO SYDNEY NEW DELHI

Simon & Schuster Paperbacks
A Division of Simon & Schuster, Inc.
1230 Avenue of the Americas
New York, NY 10020

First Simon & Schuster trade paperback edition September 2014

Interior design by Joy O'Meara
Jacket design by Jackie Seow
Jacket art by Getty Images

Manufactured in the United States of America

10 9 8 7

The Library of Congress has cataloged the hardcover edition as follows:

Goodwin, Doris Kearns.
The bully pulpit : Theodore Roosevelt, William Howard Taft, and the golden age of journalism / Doris Kearns Goodwin. — First Simon & Schuster hardcover edition.
pages cm
Includes bibliographical references and index.
1. Roosevelt, Theodore, 1858–1919. 2. Taft, William H. (William Howard), 1857–1930. 3. United States—Politics and government—1901–1909. 4. United States—Politics and government—1909–1913. 5. Progressivism (United States politics)—History—20th century. 6. Press and politics—United States—History—20th century. 7. Republican Party (U.S. : 1854–)—History—20th century. I. Title.
E757.G66 2013b
973.91'1—dc23

2013032709

ISBN 978-1-4165-4786-0
ISBN 978-1-4165-4787-7 (pbk)
ISBN 978-1-4516-7379-1 (ebook)

"The interplay between personality and politics, temperament and leadership is one of the key themes animating Doris Kearns Goodwin's telling books. . . . The same is true of her sprawling new book, *The Bully Pulpit*, which gives us revealing portraits of Theodore Roosevelt and his close friend, handpicked successor and eventual bitter rival, William Howard Taft. . . . She also uses her impressive narrative skills to give us a visceral sense of the world in which Roosevelt and Taft came of age. . . . She creates emotionally detailed portraits of the two men's families, provides an informed understanding of the political forces (conservative, moderate and insurgent) arrayed across the country at the time, and enlivens even highly familiar scenes like Teddy Roosevelt's daring charge up San Juan Hill."

—**Michiko Kakutani,** ***The New York Times***

"In extensive depth, Goodwin examines how each man [Roosevelt and Taft] provided leadership in an era of activism and reform that brought the country closer to its founding ideals. Another Goodwin masterpiece!"

—***The Christian Science Monitor***

"Swiftly moving account of a friendship that turned sour, broke a political party in two and involved an insistent, omnipresent press corps. . . . It's no small achievement to have something new to say on Teddy Roosevelt's presidency, but Goodwin succeeds admirably. A notable, psychologically charged study in leadership."

—***Kirkus Reviews,*** **Starred Review**

"By shining a light on a little-discussed President and a much-discussed one, Goodwin manages to make history very much alive and relevant. Better yet—the party politics are explicitly modern."

—***Publishers Weekly,*** **Starred Review**

"These fascinating times deserve a chronicler as wise and thorough as Goodwin. *The Bully Pulpit* is splendid reading."

—***The Dallas Morning News***

"Goodwin's evocative examination of the Progressive world is smart and engaging. . . . She presents a highly readable and detailed portrait of an era. *The Bully Pulpit* brings the early 20th century to life and firmly establishes the crucial importance of the press to Progressive politics."

—***The Washington Post***

"Doris Kearns Goodwin's exuberant new book, *The Bully Pulpit,* offers a sprawling panorama. . . . Goodwin is a superb storyteller, an author of fascinating narratives that are rich in hard-won detail."

—***The New York Review of Books***

Praise for *The Bully Pulpit*

"If you find the grubby spectacle of today's Washington cause for shame and despair—and, really, how could you not?—then I suggest you turn off the TV and board Doris Kearns Goodwin's latest time machine.... [Goodwin puts] political intrigues and moral dilemmas and daily lives into rich and elegant language. Imagine 'The West Wing' scripted by Henry James."

—*The New York Times Book Review*

"In her beautiful new account of the lives of Theodore Roosevelt and William Howard Taft, historian Doris Kearns Goodwin spins a tale so gripping that one questions the need for fiction when real life is so plump with drama."

—*Associated Press*

"Doris Kearns Goodwin tells this tale with her usual literary skill and deep research.... Goodwin not only sheds light on the birth of the modern political world but chronicles a remarkable friendship between two remarkable men."

—*The Wall Street Journal*

"This sophisticated, character-driven book tells two big stories. . . . This is a fascinating work, even a timely one. . . . It captures the way a political party can be destroyed by factionalism, and it shows the important role investigative journalists play in political life."

—*The Economist*

"Goodwin's account soars. She captures with masterly precision the depth of the Roosevelt-Taft relationship, the slow dissolution and the growing disillusion, the awkward attempts at rapprochement, and then the final break.... It is a story worth telling, and one well told."

—*The Boston Globe*

"A masterpiece of narrative, assembling a vast cast that embraces one of the most consequential eras in American social and political life."

—*The Kansas City Star*

"Pulitzer Prize–winning author Doris Kearns Goodwin has scored again with *The Bully Pulpit*, a thorough and well-written study of two presidents, as well as the journalists who covered them and exposed scandals in government and industry.... Her genius in this huge volume (750 pages of text) is to take the three narratives and weave them into a comprehensive, readable study of the time. . . . *The Bully Pulpit* is a remarkable study of a tumultuous period in our history."

—*St. Louis Post-Dispatch*

ALSO BY DORIS KEARNS GOODWIN

Team of Rivals: The Political Genius of Abraham Lincoln

Wait Till Next Year: A Memoir

No Ordinary Time: Franklin & Eleanor Roosevelt: The Home Front in World War II

The Fitzgeralds and the Kennedys

Lyndon Johnson and the American Dream

Theodore Roosevelt, William Howard Taft,

AND THE

Golden Age of Journalism

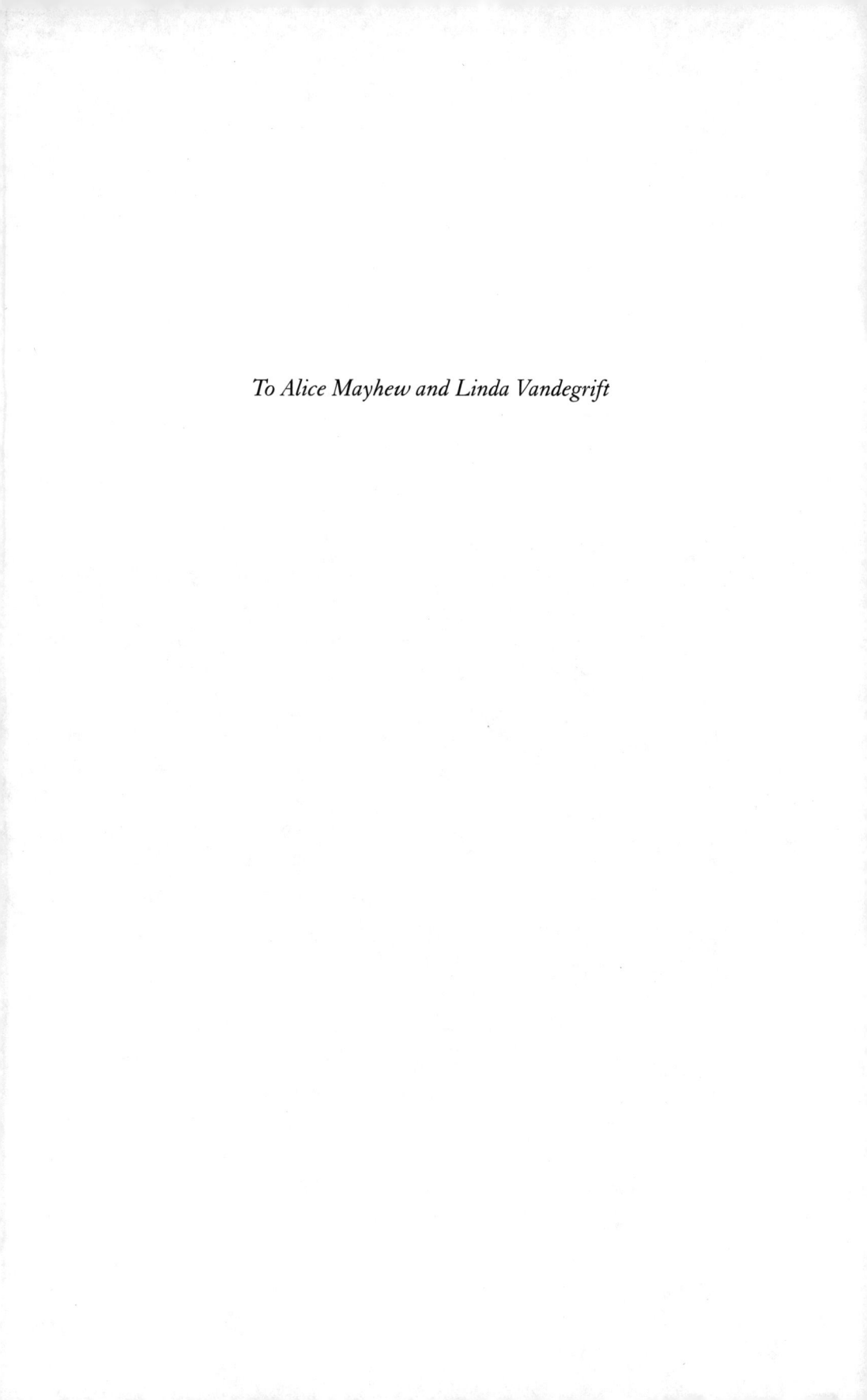

To Alice Mayhew and Linda Vandegrift

CONTENTS

PREFACE

I BEGAN THIS BOOK SEVEN YEARS ago with the notion of writing about Theodore Roosevelt and the Progressive era. This desire had been kindled nearly four decades earlier when I was a young professor teaching a seminar on the progressives. There are but a handful of times in the history of our country when there occurs a transformation so remarkable that a molt seems to take place, and an altered country begins to emerge. The turn of the twentieth century was such a time, and Theodore Roosevelt is counted among our greatest presidents, one of the few to attain that eminence without having surmounted some pronounced national crisis—revolution, war, widespread national depression.

To be sure, Roosevelt had faced a pernicious underlying crisis, one as pervasive as any military conflict or economic collapse. In the wake of the Industrial Revolution, an immense gulf had opened between the rich and the poor; daily existence had become more difficult for ordinary people, and the middle class felt increasingly squeezed. Yet by the end of Roosevelt's tenure in the White House, a mood of reform had swept the country, creating a new kind of presidency and a new vision of the relationship between the government and the people. A series of anti-trust suits had been won and legislation passed to regulate railroads, strengthen labor rights, curb political corruption, end corporate campaign contributions, impose limits on the working day, protect consumers from unsafe food and drugs, and conserve vast swaths of natural resources for the American people. The question that most intrigued me was how Roosevelt had managed to rouse a Congress long wedded to the reigning concept of laissez-faire—a government interfering as little as possible in the economic and social life of the people—to pass such comprehensive measures.

The essence of Roosevelt's leadership, I soon became convinced, lay in his enterprising use of the "bully pulpit," a phrase he himself coined to describe the national platform the presidency provides to shape public sentiment and mobilize action. Early in Roosevelt's tenure, Lyman Abbott, editor of *The Outlook*, joined a small group of friends in the president's library to offer advice and criticism on a draft of his upcoming message to Congress. "He had just finished a paragraph of a distinctly ethical character," Abbott recalled, "when he suddenly stopped, swung round in his swivel chair, and said, 'I suppose my critics will call that preaching, but I have got such a bully pulpit.' " From this bully pulpit, Roosevelt would focus the charge of a national movement to apply an ethical framework, through government action, to the untrammeled growth of modern America.

Roosevelt understood from the outset that this task hinged upon the need to develop powerfully reciprocal relationships with members of the national press. He called them by their first names, invited them to meals, took questions during his midday shave, welcomed their company at day's end while he signed correspondence, and designated, for the first time, a special room for them in the West Wing. He brought them aboard his private railroad car during his regular swings around the country. At every village station, he reached the hearts of the gathered crowds with homespun language, aphorisms, and direct moral appeals. Accompanying reporters then extended the reach of Roosevelt's words in national publications. Such extraordinary rapport with the press did not stem from calculation alone. Long before and after he was president, Roosevelt was an author and historian. From an early age, he read as he breathed. He knew and revered writers, and his relationship with journalists was authentically collegial. In a sense, he was one of them.

While exploring Roosevelt's relationship with the press, I was especially drawn to the remarkably rich connections he developed with a team of journalists—including Ida Tarbell, Ray Stannard Baker, Lincoln Steffens, and William Allen White—all working at *McClure's* magazine, the most influential contemporary progressive publication. The restless enthusiasm and manic energy of their publisher and editor, S. S. McClure, infused the magazine with "a spark of genius," even as he suffered from periodic nervous breakdowns. "The story is the thing," Sam McClure responded when asked to account for the methodology behind his publication. He wanted his writers to begin their research without preconceived notions, to carry their readers through their own process of discovery. As they educated themselves about the social and economic inequities rampant in the wake of teeming industrialization, so they educated the entire country.

Together, these investigative journalists, who would later appropriate Roosevelt's derogatory term "muckraker" as "a badge of honor," produced a series of exposés that uncovered the invisible web of corruption linking politics to business. McClure's formula—giving his writers the time and resources they needed to produce extended, intensively researched articles—was soon adopted by rival magazines, creating what many considered a golden age of journalism. Collectively, this generation of gifted writers ushered in a new mode of investigative reporting that provided the necessary conditions to make a genuine bully pulpit of the American presidency. "It is hardly an exaggeration to say that the progressive mind was characteristically a journalistic mind," the historian Richard Hofstadter observed, "and that its characteristic contribution was that of the socially responsible reporter-reformer."

PERHAPS MOST SURPRISING TO ME in my own process of research was the discovery that Roosevelt's chosen successor in the White House, William Howard Taft, was a far more sympathetic, if flawed, figure than I had realized. Scholarship has long focused on the rift in the relations between the two men during the bitter 1912 election fight, ignoring their career-long, mutually beneficial friendship. Throughout the Roosevelt administration, Taft functioned, in Roosevelt's own estimation, as the central figure in his cabinet. Because it was seen as undignified for a sitting president to campaign on his own behalf, Taft served as the chief surrogate during Roosevelt's 1904 presidential race, the most demanded speaker on the circuit to explain and justify the president's positions. In an era when presidents routinely spent long periods away from Washington, crisscrossing the country on whistle-stop tours or simply vacationing, it was Taft, the secretary of war—not the secretary of state or the vice president—who was considered the "acting President." Asked how things would be managed in his absence, Roosevelt blithely replied: "Oh, things will be all right, I have left Taft sitting on the lid."

Long before Taft's 1908 election, Roosevelt had disclosed his passionate wish that Taft be his successor. There was no man in the country, he believed, better suited to be president, no man he trusted more to carry out his legacy of active moral leadership and progressive reform. Yet, left alone at the helm when Roosevelt embarked on a yearlong African expedition, Taft questioned whether he was suited for the office. For all of Taft's admirable qualities and intentions to codify and expand upon Roosevelt's progressive legacy, he ultimately failed as a public leader, a failure that underscores the pivotal importance of the bully pulpit in presidential leadership.

From the start of his administration, Taft's relationship with journalists was uneasy. He was never able to seek the counsel they offered or harness the press corps to broadcast a coherent narrative concerning his legislative goals. As a former judge, he assumed that his decisions would speak for themselves. Eventually, he recognized the handicap of his inability to engage the press as his predecessor had done, conceding after he left office that he had been "derelict" in his use of the bully pulpit. He had failed to educate the country about his policies and programs. He was simply "not constituted as Roosevelt" to expound upon his thoughts and vent his feelings with the members of the press. It was, Taft came to realize, a matter of temperament.

Finally, my own process of discovery led me to the realization that the story I wanted to tell had three interwoven strands. One was the story of Theodore Roosevelt, whose crusade to expand the role of government in national life required the transformation of the presidency itself. The next strand was the story of William Howard Taft, whose talents and skills played a more significant role in the Roosevelt administration than is generally understood. When Taft attained the presidency, however, he found himself at sea, in large part because he was temperamentally unsuited to make use of the story's third strand—the bully pulpit that had provided the key to his predecessor's success.

As S. S. McClure well understood, the "vitality of democracy" depends on "popular knowledge of complex questions." At the height of *McClure's* success, observed the philosopher William James, the investigative journalists McClure had assembled and their counterparts in other leading magazines had embarked on nothing less than "the mission of raising the tone of democracy," exerting an elevating influence on public sentiment.

It is my greatest hope that the story that follows will guide readers through their own process of discovery toward a better understanding of what it takes to summon the public to demand the actions necessary to bring our country closer to its ancient ideals. "There is no one left," McClure exhorted his readers as he cast about for a remedy to America's woes at the turn of the twentieth century, "none but all of us."

THE BULLY PULPIT

CHAPTER ONE

The Hunter Returns

Theodore Roosevelt receives a hero's welcome in New York on June 18, 1910, following his expedition to Africa.

ROOSEVELT IS COMING HOME, HOORAY! Exultant headlines in mid-June 1910 trumpeted the daily progress of the *Kaiserin*, the luxury liner returning the former president, Theodore Roosevelt, to American shores after his year's safari in Africa.

Despite popularity unrivaled since Abraham Lincoln, Roosevelt, true to his word, had declined to run for a third term after completing seven and a half years in office. His tenure had stretched from William McKinley's assassination in September 1901 to March 4, 1909, when his own elected term came to an end. Flush from his November 1904 election triumph, he had stunned the political world with his announcement that he would not run for president again, citing "the wise custom which limits the President to two terms." Later, he reportedly told a friend that he would willingly cut off his hand at the wrist if he could take his pledge back.

Roosevelt had loved being president—"the greatest office in the world." He had relished "every hour" of every day. Indeed, fearing the "dull thud" he would experience upon returning to private life, he had devised the perfect solution to "break his fall." Within three weeks of the inauguration of his successor, William Howard Taft, he had embarked on his great African adventure, plunging into the most "impenetrable spot on the globe."

For months Roosevelt's friends had been preparing an elaborate reception to celebrate his arrival in New York. When "the Colonel," as Roosevelt preferred to be called, first heard of the extravagant plans devised for his welcome, he was troubled, fearing that the public response would not match such lofty expectations. "Even at this moment I should certainly put an instant stop to all the proceedings if I felt they were being merely 'worked up' and there was not a real desire . . . of at least a great many people to greet me," he wrote one of the organizers in March 1910. "My political career is ended," he told Lawrence Abbott of *The Outlook*, who had come to meet him in Khartoum, the capital of Sudan, when he first emerged from the jungle. "No man in American public life has ever reached the crest of the wave as I appear to have done without the wave's breaking and engulfing him."

Anxiety that his star had dimmed, that the public's devotion had dwindled, proved wildly off the mark. While he had initially planned to return directly from Khartoum, Roosevelt received so many invitations to visit the reigning European sovereigns that he first embarked on a six-week tour of Italy, Austria, Hungary, France, Belgium, Holland, Denmark, Norway, Germany, and England. Kings and queens greeted him as an equal, universities bestowed upon him their highest degrees, and the German Kaiser treated him as an intimate friend. Every city, town, and village received him with a frenzied enthusiasm that stunned the most sophisticated observers. "People gathered at railway stations, in school-houses, and in the village streets," one journalist observed. They showered his carriage with flowers, thronged windows of tenement houses, and greeted him with "Viva, viva, viva Roosevelt!" Newspapers in the United States celebrated Roosevelt's triumphant procession through the Old World, sensing in his unparalleled reception a tribute to America's newfound position of power. "No foreign ruler or man of eminence could have aroused more universal attention, received a warmer welcome, or achieved greater popularity among every class of society," the *New York Times* exulted.

"I don't suppose there was ever such a reception as that being given Theodore in Europe," Taft wistfully told his military aide, Captain Archie Butt. "It illustrates how his personality has swept over the world," such that even "small villages which one would hardly think had ever heard of the United States should seem to know all about the man." The stories of Roosevelt's "royal progress" through Europe bolstered the efforts of his friends to ensure, in Taft's words, "as great a demonstration of welcome from his countrymen as any American ever received."

In the week preceding his arrival in America, tens of thousands of visitors from all over the country had descended upon New York, lending the city's hotels and streets "a holiday appearance." Inbound trains carried a cast of characters "as diversely typical of the American people as Mr. Roosevelt himself . . . conservationists and cowboys, capitalists and socialists, insurgents and regulars, churchmen and sportsmen, native born and aliens." More than two hundred vessels, including five destroyers, six revenue cutters, and dozens of excursion steamboats, tugs, and ferryboats, all decked with colorful flags and pennants, had sailed into the harbor to take part in an extravagant naval display.

An army of construction workers labored to complete the speaker's platform and grandstand seating at Battery Park, where Roosevelt would address an overflow crowd of invited guests. Businesses had given their workers a half-holiday so they could join in the festivities. "Flags floated everywhere," an Ohio newspaper reported; "pictures of Roosevelt were hung in thousands of windows and along the line of march, buildings were draped with bunting."

The night before the big day, a dragnet was set to arrest known pickpockets. Five thousand police and dozens of surgeons and nurses were called in for special duty. "The United States of America at the present moment simulates quite the attitude of the small boy who can't go to sleep Christmas Eve for thinking of the next day," the *Atlanta Constitution* suggested. "And the colonel, returning as rapidly as a lusty steamship can plow the waves, is the 'next day.' It is a remarkable tribute to the man's personality that virtually every element of citizenship in the country should be more or less on tiptoes in the excitement of anticipation."

Shortly after 7 a.m. on June 18, as the bright rising sun burned through the mists, Theodore Roosevelt, as jubilant with anticipation as his country, stood on the bridge of the *Kaiserin* as the vessel headed into New York Harbor. Edith, his handsome forty-eight-year-old wife, stood beside him. She had journeyed halfway around the world to join him in Khartoum at the end of his long African expedition. Edith had found their year-long parting, the longest in their twenty-three years of marriage, almost unbearable. "If it were not for the children here I would not have the nervous strength to live through these endless months of separation from Father," she wrote her son Kermit after Theodore had been gone only two weeks. "When I am alone & let myself think I am done for."

Edith was no stranger to the anxiety of being apart from the man for whom she "would do anything in the world." They had been intimate childhood friends, growing up together in New York's Union Square neighborhood. She had joined "Teedie," as he was then called, and his younger sister Corinne, in a private schoolroom arranged at the Roosevelt mansion. Even as children, they missed each other when apart. As Teedie was setting off with his family on a Grand Tour of Europe when he was eleven years old, he broke down in tears at the thought of leaving eight-year-old Edith behind. She proved his most faithful correspondent over the long course of the trip. She had been a regular guest at "Tranquillity," the Roosevelts' summer home on Long Island, where they sailed together in the bay, rode horseback along the trails, and shared a growing passion for literature. As adolescents, they were dancing partners at cotillions and constant companions on the social scene. Roosevelt proudly noted that his freshman college classmates at Harvard considered Edith and her friend Annie Murray "the prettiest girls they had met" when they visited him in New York during Christmas vacation.

In the summer of 1878, after his sophomore year, however, the young couple had a mysterious "falling out" at Tranquillity. "One day," Roosevelt later wrote, "there came a break" during a late afternoon rendezvous at the estate's summerhouse. The conflict that erupted, Roosevelt admitted, ended "his very intimate relations" with Edith. Though neither one would ever say what had happened, Roosevelt cryptically noted to his sister Anna that "both of us had, and I suppose have, tempers that were far from being of the best."

The intimacy that Edith had cherished for nearly two decades seemed lost forever the following October, when Roosevelt met Alice Hathaway Lee. The beautiful, enchanting daughter of a wealthy Boston businessman, Alice lived in Chestnut Hill, Massachusetts, not far from Cambridge. The young Harvard junior fell in love with his "whole heart and soul." Four months after his graduation in 1880, they were married. Then, in 1884, only two days after giving birth to their only child, Alice died.

A year later, Theodore resumed his friendship with Edith. And the year after that they were married. As time passed, Edith's meticulous and thoughtful nature made her an exemplary partner for Theodore. "I do not think my eyes are blinded by affection," the president told a friend, "when I say that she has combined to a degree I have never seen in any other woman the power of being the best of wives and mothers, the wisest manager of the household, and at the same time the ideal great lady and mistress of the White House."

Their boisterous family eventually included six children. Three of the six were standing next to their parents on the bridge of the ocean liner: twenty-year-old Kermit, who had accompanied his father to Africa; eighteen-year-old Ethel; and twenty-six-year-old Alice, the child born to his first wife.

The girls had joined their parents in Europe. Along the rails of the four upper decks, their fellow passengers, some 3,000 in all, formed a colorful pageant as they waved their handkerchiefs and cheered.

Although wireless telegrams on board the ship had alerted Roosevelt to some of the day's planned activities, he was surprised to learn that President Taft had assigned the massive battleship *South Carolina* as his official escort. "By George! That's one of my ships! Doesn't she look good?" an overwhelmed Roosevelt exclaimed when he saw her gray bulk pulling near. "Flags were broken out from stem to stern in the ceremony of dressing the ship," reported the *Boston Daily Globe*, while "a puff from the muzzle of an eight-pounder" signaled the start of a 21-gun salute, the highest ceremonial honor, generally reserved for heads of state. Sailors clad in blue lined the decks of the warship, as the scarlet-uniformed Marine Band played "The Star-Spangled Banner." The cannon roar of the *South Carolina* was followed by the rhythmic volley of salutes and whistles from the dozen or more additional naval ships in the bay. President Taft had clearly gone to great lengths, Captain Butt proudly noted, "to add dignity to the welcome and to extend a warm personal greeting to his predecessor."

From the deck, Roosevelt spotted the tugboat carrying the reporters whose eyewitness accounts of the spectacular scene would dominate the news the following day. As he leaned over the rail and vigorously waved his top hat back and forth to them, they stood and cheered. To each familiar face, he nodded his head and smiled broadly, displaying his famous teeth, which appeared "just as prominent and just as white and perfect as when he went away." Then, recognizing the photographers' need to snap his picture, he stopped his hectic motions and stood perfectly still.

During his presidency, Roosevelt's physical vigor and mental curiosity had made the White House a hive of activity and interest. His "love of the hurly-burly" that enchanted reporters and their readers was best captured by British viscount John Morley, who claimed that "he had seen two tremendous works of nature in America—the Niagara Falls and Mr. Roosevelt." One magazine writer marveled at his prodigious stream of guests—"pugilists, college presidents, professional wrestlers, Greek scholars, baseball teams, big-game hunters, sociologists, press agents, authors, actors, Rough Riders, bad men, and gun-fighters from the West, wolf-catchers, photographers, guides, bear-hunters, artists, labor-leaders." When he left for Africa, the "noise and excitement" vanished; little wonder that the members of the press were thrilled to see him return.

Shortly after the *Kaiserin* dropped anchor at Quarantine, the revenue cutter *Manhattan* pulled alongside, carrying the Roosevelts' youngest sons, sixteen-year-old Archie and twelve-year-old Quentin, both of whom had remained at home. Their oldest son, twenty-two-year-old Theodore Junior, who was set to marry Eleanor Alexander the following Monday, joined the group along with an assortment of family members, including Roosevelt's sisters, Anna and Corinne; his son-in-law, Congressman Nicholas Longworth; his niece Eleanor Roosevelt; and her husband, Franklin. While Edith anxiously sought a glimpse of the children she had not seen for more than two months, Roosevelt busily shook hands with each of the officers, sailors, and engineers of the ship. "Come here, Theodore, and see your children," Edith called out. "They are of far greater importance than politics or anything else."

Roosevelt searched the promenade deck of the *Manhattan*, reported the *Chicago Tribune*, until his eyes rested on "the round face of his youngest boy, Quentin, who was dancing up and down on the deck, impatient to be recognized," telling all who would listen that he would be the one "to kiss pop first." At the sight of the lively child, "the Colonel spread his arms out as if he would undertake a long-distance embrace" and smiled broadly as he nodded to each of his relatives in turn.

When Roosevelt stepped onto the crimson-covered gangplank for his transfer to the *Manhattan*, "pandemonium broke loose." The ship's band played "America," the *New York Times* reported, and "there came from the river craft, yachts, and ships nearby a volley of cheers that lasted for fully five minutes." Bugles blared, whistles shrieked, and "everywhere flags waved, hats were tossed into the air, and cries of welcome were heard." Approaching the deck where his children were jumping in anticipation, Roosevelt executed a "flying leap," and "with the exuberance and spirit of a school boy, he took up Quentin and Archie in his arms and gave them resounding smacks." He greeted Theodore Junior with a hearty slap on the back, kissed his sisters, and then proceeded to shake hands with every crew member.

Around 9 a.m., the *Androscoggin*, carrying Cornelius Vanderbilt, the chairman of the reception, and two hundred distinguished guests, came alongside the *Manhattan*. As Roosevelt made the transfer to the official welcoming vessel, he asked that everyone form a line so that he could greet each individual personally and then went at the task of shaking hands with such high spirits, delivering for each person such "an explosive word of welcome," that what might have been a duty for another politician became an act of joy. "I'm *so* glad to see you," he greeted each person in turn. The *New York Times* reporter noted that "the 'so' went off like a firecracker. The smile backed it up in a radiation of energy, and the hearty grip of the hand that came down upon its respondent with a bang emphasized again the exact meaning of the words."

When Roosevelt grasped the hand of Joe Murray, the savvy political boss who had first nominated him for the state legislature years before, it must have seemed as if his public life had come full circle. "This takes me back 29 years," he said, "to the old Twenty-first Assembly district when I was getting a start in politics." Earlier he had warmly welcomed Massachusetts senator Henry Cabot Lodge, his closest friend for more than a quarter of a century, and Archie Butt, who had served as his devoted military aide before taking up the same position with President Taft. Jacob Riis, the Danish immigrant whose book, *How the Other Half Lives*, had greatly influenced Roosevelt when he was police commissioner of New York City, received a fraternal welcome and "the broadest of smiles." Roosevelt clasped him with both hands, exclaiming, "O, Jake. I've got so much to tell you." His face grew somber as he glimpsed Beverly Robinson, who conjured memories of McKinley's assassination. "This boy was with me on top of Mount Mary," he mused, "when the sudden news came that I had become President." Nothing, however, could dampen his innate joviality for more than a moment. "Why, hello, Stimson, old sugar trust," he laughed, his eyes twinkling, as he approached Henry Stimson, the government's special counsel in the famous trust case. "Oh, friend, this is good. I can't tell you how I feel," he confided to Frank Tyree, the Secret Serviceman who had protected him loyally for years. On and on he went, his personal greetings for all interspersed with expressions of outright delight: "Fine! Fine! Oh, it's simply great!" "George, this is bully!"

When Vanderbilt suggested it was time to go up to the bridge to acknowledge the thousands of people massed solidly on both the New Jersey and the Manhattan sides of the river, Roosevelt hesitated. "But here are the reporters," he said, turning to the members of the press eagerly taking down his words. "I want to shake hands with them." Indeed, at every stop during the long day, he made sure to deliver a special welcome to the members of the press. "Boys, I am *glad* (emphasis on the glad) to see you. It does me good to see you, boys. I am glad to be back." Clearly, that pleasure was reciprocated. "We're mighty glad to have you back," shouted one exuberant reporter.

From the time reporters had accompanied the Colonel to Cuba—helping transform him and his intrepid Rough Riders into a national icon—Roosevelt had established a unique relationship with numerous journalists. He debated points with them as fellow writers; regardless of the disparity in political rank, when they argued as authors, they argued as equals. He had read and freely commented upon their stories, as they felt free to criticize his public statements and speeches. Little wonder, then, that these same journalists celebrated Roosevelt's return from Africa, flocking to lower Manhattan to welcome him home. For the members of the press, the story of Roosevelt's homecoming was not merely an assignment—it was personal.

Reporters present at the festivities remarked how "hale and hearty" the fifty-one-year-old Roosevelt looked, tanned and extremely fit. "It is true that the mustache, once brown, has grown grayer, but the strong face is not furrowed with deep wrinkles and the crows feet have not changed the expression which is habitual to the man who is in robust health and has a joy in living." After the long African expedition he displayed a leaner physique, but overall, he seemed "the same bubbling, explosively exuberant American as when he left." Archie Butt, however, detected "something different," though at first he could not put his finger on it. After talking with Lodge, the two men speculated that as a citizen of the world, not simply an American, Roosevelt had developed "an enlarged personality," with a "mental scope more encompassing."

At Battery Park, where the *Androscoggin* was due to dock at around 11 a.m., an immense crowd had gathered since early morning, straining for sight of the ship that would bring Roosevelt onto American soil. A reporter captured this mood of anticipation in his story of a stevedore who, in the midst of unloading cargo off another ship, laid aside his hook in hopes of glimpsing Roosevelt. His foreman shouted at him: "You come back here or I'll dock you an hour." The stevedore, undaunted, retorted: "Dock me a week. I'm going to have a look at Teddy."

"There he is!" rose the cry, soon confirmed as a beaming Roosevelt came ashore to a rendition of "Home, Sweet Home" by the Seventy-first Regimental Band. The uplifted cheers that greeted "the man of the hour" as he disembarked were said to exceed the "echoing boom of saluting cannon and the strident blast of steam whistles."

Straightaway, Roosevelt headed from the pier to the speaker's platform. He was in the midst of shaking hands with cabinet members, senators and congressmen, governors and mayors when his daughter Alice cried, "Turn around, father, and look at the crowd." Outspread before him was "one vast expanse of human countenances, all upturned to him, all waiting for him." Beyond the 600 seated guests, 3,500 people stood within the roped enclosure, and beyond them "unnumbered thousands" on the plaza. Still more crammed together on the surrounding streets. It was estimated that at least 100,000 people had come to Battery Park, undeterred by the crushing throngs and the oppressive heat and humidity. From a ninth-floor window of the nearby Washington Building, "a life-size Teddy bear" belted with a green sash was suspended. A large white banner bearing Roosevelt's favorite word, "Delighted," was displayed on the Whitehall Building, where "from street level to skyline every window was open and every sill held as many stenographers and office boys and bosses as the sills could accommodate." Clearly, this was not a day for work!

"Is there a stenographer here?" Roosevelt asked, as he prepared to speak. Assured that one was present, he began, his voice filled with emotion: "No man could receive such a greeting without being made to feel very proud and humble. . . . I have been away a year and a quarter from America and I have seen strange and interesting things alike in the heart of the wilderness and in the capitals of the mightiest and most highly polished civilized nations." Nonetheless, he assured the crowd, "I am more glad than I can say to get home, back in my own country, back among the people I love. And I am ready and eager to do my part so far as I am able in helping to solve problems which must be solved. . . . This is the duty of every citizen but it is peculiarly my duty, for any man who has ever been honored by being made president of the United States is thereby forever after rendered the debtor of the American people." For those who wondered whether Roosevelt would remain active in public life, his brief but eloquent remarks were telling.

The address at Battery Park only served to set off the real celebration. A five-mile parade up Broadway to 59th and Fifth followed, with an estimated 1 million spectators lining the streets. "The sidewalks on both sides of Broadway were jammed with people, from curb to building fronts," the *Chicago Tribune* noted. "There were people in all the windows, people on the housetops, and people banked up in the side streets." As Roosevelt took his place in the open carriage leading the procession, an additional surprise lay in store for him: 150 members of his Rough Rider unit, whom he had led so brilliantly in the Spanish-American War, appeared on horseback to serve as his escort of honor. Beyond the Rough Riders, there were 2,000 additional veterans from that same war who had come to participate in the celebration. The demonstration was "incomparably the largest affair of its kind on record," the Washington, D.C., *Evening Star* claimed, "characteristic of the man himself, the man of superlatives, and of intense moods."

Placards with friendly inscriptions, familiar cartoons, and exhortations for Roosevelt to once again run for the presidency in 1912 hung in shop windows all along the way. At 310 Broadway, an immense Teddy bear stared down an enormous stuffed African lion. At Scribner's, a ten-foot-high portrait of the Colonel in full hunting gear graced the front of the building. Peddlers were everywhere. "You could not move a step," one reporter observed, "without having shoved in your face a remarkable assortment of Teddy souvenirs. There were jungle hats with ribbons bearing the word De-lighted, there were Roosevelt medals, Teddy's teeth in celluloid, miniature Teddy bears, gorgeous flags on canes, with a picture of the Rough Rider, buttons, pins and many other reminders of the Colonel's career." Even along Wall Street, where it was jokingly predicted black crepe would signal Roosevelt's return (given his storied fights with "the malefactors of great wealth"), flags waved and colored streamers were tossed from upper windows.

"Teddy! Teddy! Bully for you, Teddy," the crowd yelled, and he responded with "unconcealed delight" to the gleeful chants. "One could see that he enjoyed every moment of the triumphal progress," the *New York Times* reported, and " those who cheered cheered the louder when they saw how their cheers delighted him." Near the end of the route, a reporter shouted: "Are you tired?" His answer was clear and firm despite the long day, the hot sun, and the perspiration dripping down his face. "Not a bit."

Around 1 p.m., when the parade finally concluded at the 59th Street Plaza, Roosevelt, with tears in his eyes, flashed his dazzling smile and headed toward a private residence for a family lunch. No sooner had the Colonel reached his destination than a frightening storm began. Lightning, thunder, and ferocious winds accompanied a heavy downpour. Uprooted trees littered the ground with fallen limbs. In all, seventeen lives were lost. It seemed the sky had stayed peaceful and blue only for the sun-splashed hours of the celebration for Roosevelt.

"Everyone began talking about Roosevelt luck," Captain Butt observed. While the pelting rain continued, Roosevelt relaxed in the Fifth Avenue home belonging to the grandfather of his son's fiancée and enjoyed a festive meal of chicken in cream sauce with rice while catching up on the news of the day. In the late afternoon, he boarded a special train for his hometown of Oyster Bay, Long Island. Once again, the Roosevelt luck came into play. The severe rainstorm miraculously ceased just as his train pulled in. He was met by "the whole town," complete with a 500-member children's choir, a display of devotion that nearly "swept the former President from his feet as he stepped to the ground." Walking beneath "triumphal arches" constructed by his neighbors, Roosevelt reached a nearby ballpark where grandstands had been raised to seat 3,000 people. There, he spoke movingly of what it meant to be home once more, "to live among you again as I have for the last 40 years." Reporters who had followed Roosevelt since he began shaking hands on the *Kaiserin* that morning marveled at the energy with which he continued to grasp the hands of his neighbors, finding something personal to say to one and all, without revealing "the slightest trace of fatigue in voice or manner."

In their lengthy coverage of the historic day, the press corps brought to light scores of colorful anecdotes. The story they failed to get, however, was the story they wanted above all—Roosevelt's response to the major political issue of the day: the growing disenchantment of progressive Republicans with the leadership of President Taft.

As HIS SECOND TERM NEARED its end, Roosevelt had handpicked from his cabinet the trusted friend he desired to succeed him: William Howard Taft. The two men had first met in their early thirties, when Roosevelt headed the Civil Service Commission and Taft was U.S. Solicitor General. "We lived in the same part of Washington," Taft recalled, "our wives knew each other well, and some of our children were born about the same time." Over the years, this friendship had deepened, becoming what Taft described as "one of close and sweet intimacy." During his first presidential term, Roosevelt had invited Taft, then governor general of the newly acquired Philippine Islands, to serve as his secretary of war. Initially reluctant to leave a post to which his talents were ideally suited, Taft had finally been persuaded to join his old friend's administration as "the foremost member" of his cabinet, his daily "counsellor and adviser in all the great questions" that might confront them.

Roosevelt had thrown all his inexhaustible energy behind the drive to make Taft president. "I am quite as nervous about your campaign as I should be if it were my own," he had told Taft. He had edited Taft's speeches, relayed a constant stream of advice, and corralled his own immense bloc of supporters behind Taft's candidacy. When Taft was elected, Roosevelt reveled in the victory, both delighted for a "beloved" friend and confident that America had chosen the man best suited to execute the progressive goals Roosevelt had championed—to distribute the nation's wealth more equitably, regulate the giant corporations and railroads, strengthen the rights of labor, and protect the country's natural resources from private exploitation.

At the start of Roosevelt's presidency in 1901, big business had been in the driver's seat. While the country prospered as never before, squalid conditions were rampant in immigrant slums, workers in factories and mines labored without safety regulations, and farmers fought with railroads over freight rates. Voices had been raised to protest the concentration of corporate wealth and the gap between rich and poor, yet the doctrine of laissez-faire precluded collective action to ameliorate social conditions. Under Roosevelt's Square Deal, the country had awakened to the need for government action to allay problems caused by industrialization—an awakening spurred in part by the dramatic exposés of a talented group of investigative journalists he famously labeled "muckrakers."

By the end of Roosevelt's tenure, much had been accomplished. The moribund 1890 Sherman Anti-Trust Act had been revived, vast acres of lands had been protected from exploitation, and railroads had been prevented from continuing long-standing abuses. Congress had passed workmen's compensation, a pure food and drug law, and a meat inspection act. Nevertheless, much remained to be done. Roosevelt's legacy would depend upon the actions of his chosen successor—William Howard Taft. "Taft is as fine a fellow as ever sat in the President's chair," Roosevelt told a friend shortly after the election, "and I cannot express the measureless content that comes over me as I think that the work in which I have so much believed will be carried on by him."

While he was abroad, however, Roosevelt had received numerous disturbing communications from his progressive friends. Word that his closest ally in the conservation movement, Chief Forester Gifford Pinchot, had been removed by Taft, left Roosevelt dumbfounded: "I do not know any man in public life who has rendered quite the service you have rendered," he wrote to Pinchot, "and it seems to be absolutely impossible that there can be any truth in this statement." When the news was confirmed, he asked Pinchot to meet him in Europe in order to hear his firsthand account. Pinchot had arrived with a number of letters from fellow progressives, all expressing a belief that Taft had aligned himself with old-line conservatives on Capitol Hill and was gradually compromising Roosevelt's hard-won advances.

Roosevelt found it difficult to believe he had so misjudged the character and convictions of his old friend. On his final day in Europe, he confided his puzzlement to Sir Edward Grey as the two outdoorsmen tramped through the New Forest in southern England in pursuit of the song or sight of several English birds Roosevelt had only read about. "Roosevelt's spirit was much troubled by what was happening in his own country since he left office," Grey recalled. "He spoke of Taft and of their work together with very live affection; he had wished Taft to succeed him, had supported him, made way for him. How could he now break with Taft and attack him?" Yet the concerted voice of his progressive friends was urging him to do precisely that.

All through the spring of 1910, as the date of his return approached, one question had dominated political discourse and speculation: "What will

Mr. Roosevelt do?" Which side would he take in the intensifying struggle that was dividing the Republican Party between the old-line conservatives and a steadily growing number of "insurgents," as the progressive faction was then known. Aware that anything he said would be construed as hurtful or helpful to one side or the other, Roosevelt determined to remain silent on all political matters until he could more fully absorb and analyze the situation. "There is one thing I want, and that is absolute privacy," he told reporters as the day's celebration came to an end. "I want to close up like a native oyster . . . I am glad to have you all here; but . . . I have nothing to say."

THE WEEKS PRECEDING ROOSEVELT'S HOMECOMING had been especially difficult for President Taft. "He looks haggard and careworn," Captain Butt told his sister-in-law, Clara. His characteristic ruddy complexion had faded to a sickly pale, his weight had ballooned to 320 pounds, and his jovial temperament had turned mournful. "It is hard on any man to see the eyes of everyone turn to another person as the eyes of the entire country are turning to Roosevelt," Butt speculated. Nonetheless, Butt acknowledged that Taft's low spirits had little to do with jealousy. Never once had he heard Taft "murmur against the fate" that kept him, "a man of tremendous personality himself . . . in the shadow" of his predecessor. "He is so broad as to show no resentment" of his "secondary role," Butt marveled. Rather, Taft's anxiety stemmed, he thought, from the fact that "he loves Theodore Roosevelt," and the specter of a potential rupture in their friendship was causing great emotional distress.

No shadow of such troubles was in evidence when Taft's presidency began. "He is going to be greatly beloved as President," Roosevelt had predicted. "He has the most lovable personality I have ever come in contact with." A big man with a big heart, clear blue eyes, and a thoughtful nature, Taft was portrayed as "America incarnate—sham-hating, hardworking, crackling with jokes upon himself, lacking in pomp but never in dignity . . . a great, boyish, wholesome, dauntless, shrewd, sincere, kindly gentleman."

The time had come, even Roosevelt's most ardent admirers agreed, for a different kind of leader—a quieter, less controversial figure. Roosevelt, with his fiery temperament, inexhaustible supply of arresting quips, and demagogic appeals, had given powerful voice to the Progressive movement. Now, Roosevelt's journalist friend William Allen White argued, the country needed a man who could "finish the things" Roosevelt had begun, who could work with Congress to consolidate the imperfect statutes and executive orders generated in the tumultuous previous years. Although Taft would "say little," White acknowledged, he would "do much." His mind would not, like Roosevelt's, move "by flashes or whims or sudden impulses," another journalist wrote, but rather with steady efficiency, "in straight lines and by long, logical habit."

Taft agreed with this assessment of the situation he faced. He likened Roosevelt's administration to "a great crusade" that had aroused the people to the need for greater federal regulation of the economy. Now it was the work of his administration to make these expanded powers "permanent in the form of law." In contrast to Roosevelt, a career politician whose "intense desire to reach practical results" had led him occasionally to chafe under "the restraint of legal methods," Taft had trained as a lawyer and a judge, disciplines that had instilled "the necessity for legal method." Roosevelt had ended his presidency "in an ugly fight" with a Congress he had sought to bypass through a direct appeal to the public. With a very different yet complementary temperament, Taft insisted that he must work "with the tools and the men . . . at hand." It was his misfortune to take office at a time marked by a bitter rift within the Republican Party, when progressives viewed compromise with conservatives as treachery.

Taft had not openly sought the presidency. Since his appointment as a superior court judge at the age of twenty-nine, he had aspired to one day become chief justice of the United States. He had moved swiftly up the judicial ladder, becoming U.S. Solicitor General at age thirty-two and a federal circuit judge at thirty-four. When President McKinley asked him to go to the Philippines, it was with the implied promise that he would return to a Supreme Court appointment. When Roosevelt became president, he honored his predecessor's promise, twice offering Taft a position on the Supreme Court. With great reluctance, Taft had declined both opportunities; in the first instance, he felt he could not leave his work in the Philippines unfinished; in the second, his wife and closest adviser, Nellie, persuaded him not to bury himself on the Court at the very moment when, as secretary of war, he was being touted throughout the country as Roosevelt's most likely successor. Indeed, were it not for his wife's White House dreams, Taft would likely never have agreed to a presidential run.

Taft had found little joy in campaigning for the presidency in 1908. He had "great misgivings" about every speech he was forced to make. For months, the thought of his acceptance speech loomed over him "like a nightmare." He feared that his efforts to forge a middle ground on issues would "make many people mad." Unlike Roosevelt, who regularly perused articles about himself and found pleasure in responding to critics, Taft acknowledged that negative press left him "very, very discouraged." After a while, despite Nellie's urgings, he refused to read unfavorable articles altogether. His speeches, Nellie warned, tended to be much too long. "But I am made this way and 'I can do no other,' " he told her. "That is the kind of an old slow coach you married." In the end, with his "campaign manager" (as he called Nellie) by his side to edit his speeches and offer advice, comfort, and encouragement, he won a magnificent victory over William Jennings Bryan.

Taft took office in 1909 with commingled exhilaration and trepidation. "I pinch myself every little while to make myself realize that it is all true," he told a friend. "If I were now presiding in the Supreme Court of the United States as Chief Justice, I should feel entirely at home, but with the troubles of selecting a cabinet and the difficulties in respect to the revision of the tariff, I feel just a bit like a fish out of water." More than a year later, such misgivings had not subsided. When asked if he liked being president, he replied that he "would rather be Chief Justice," for the "quieter life" on the Court would prove "more in keeping with my temperament." However, he reflected, "when taken into consideration that I go into history as a President, and my children and my children's children are the better placed on account of that fact, I am inclined to think that to be President well compensates one for all the trials and criticisms he has to bear and undergo."

Taft well knew how fortunate he was to have a natural politician in his devoted and intelligent wife, one whose superb judgment and political acumen could help him "overcome the obstacles that just at present seem formidable." They had been partners from the earliest days of their married life in Cincinnati. Like Edith and Theodore, Nellie and Will had grown up together in the same city. Their sisters had been "schoolmates," and their fathers, Nellie wrote, had "practiced law at the same bar for more than forty years." Nellie and Will had been friends for six years when their relationship began to deepen into love.

Young Nellie was an unconventional woman. From early adolescence, she craved a more expansive life. She liked to smoke, drink beer, and play cards for money. She was an avid reader with a passion for classical music, a talented writer, and a dedicated teacher. In her early twenties, she had organized a weekly salon, with Will and his brother Horace among the regular participants. Every Saturday night their circle of six or seven friends presented essays and discussed literature and national politics "with such high feeling and enthusiasm," Nellie recalled, that the history of the salon "became the history of our lives during that period." The more time he spent with Nellie, Will told his father, "the deeper grew my respect for her, the warmer my friendship until it unconsciously ripened into a feeling that she was indispensable to my happiness. . . . Her eagerness for knowledge of all kinds puts me to shame. Her capacity for work is wonderful."

For her part, Nellie found in Will a husband who adored her and highly valued her intelligence. Their union provided a channel for her to pursue her intense ambition to accomplish something vital in life. Will also proved a loving father for their three children, Robert, Helen, and Charlie, who were eighteen, sixteen, and eleven when Taft became president. Throughout their marriage, Taft looked to Nellie as a "merciless but loving critic," depending on her advice at every crucial juncture. They labored together over his speeches and discussed political strategy in a manner, one observer recalled, much like "two men who are intimate chums." Their partnership gave Taft confidence that he would learn to navigate the uncharted waters of the presidency.

The *New York Times* predicted that with Nellie Taft as first lady, "the Taft Administration will be brilliant beyond any similar period in America's social history." Over the years, she had established a sterling reputation as a democratic hostess, opening her doors to people from all backgrounds. In the Philippines, she had stunned the conservative military establishment by rejecting their strict segregation of whites and native Filipinos, instead insisting "upon complete racial equality" at the governor's palace. As first lady, she brought the same egalitarian ethos to her position. She spoke out against the unhealthy working conditions of government employees and embarked upon several civic projects. She helped design a beautiful public park along the Tidal Basin where concerts could be held every week during the summer months, and made arrangements to bring the same flowering cherry trees she had admired in Japan to the nation's capital.

Nellie Taft was swiftly becoming one of the most respected and powerful first ladies in history. Then, only ten weeks after the inauguration, terrible misfortune shattered these auspicious beginnings. On board the presidential yacht with her husband and some guests, Nellie suffered a devastating stroke that left her temporarily paralyzed and unable to speak. At the sight of his half-conscious wife, only forty-seven years old, Taft turned "deathly pale." Taft's "great soul," Archie Butt empathized, was "wrapped in darkness." Although Nellie gradually recovered the ability to walk, she would continue to struggle with her speech the rest of her life.

A year after Nellie's stroke, shortly before Roosevelt was due to return to America, Taft sent him a plaintive handwritten letter weighing his accomplishments and failures as president. "I have had a hard time," he confided. "I do not know that I have had harder luck than other presidents but I do know that thus far I have succeeded far less than have others. I have been conscientiously trying to carry out your policies but my method of doing so has not worked smoothly." In closing, he told his old friend, "it would give me a great deal of pleasure if after you get settled at Oyster Bay, you could come over to Washington and spend a few days at the White House."

Taft had been tempted to go to New York and personally welcome Roosevelt home. According to one report in the *Indianapolis Star*, his advisers had suggested that "this demonstration of amity would be appreciated by Col. Roosevelt and would do more than anything else to drive away the suspicion that seems to have gained ground that the relations between the chief executive and his predecessor are strained." Upon reflection, however, Taft concluded that it would diminish the status of the presidential office "if he were to 'race down to the gangplank,' to be the first to shake hands with the former President." He explained to his military aide that he was "charged with the dignity of the Executive" and was determined to "say nothing that will put a momentary slight even on that great office." No matter how much he would rather be Will, welcoming his friend Theodore, he was now *President* Taft. "I think, moreover, that [Roosevelt] will appreciate this feeling in me," he concluded, "and would be the first one to resent the slightest subordination of the office of President to any man."

Instead, he planned a journey of his own that day—a train trip to Villanova, Pennsylvania, to deliver the commencement address at the Catholic university, followed by a visit to the small town of West Chester, and a second commencement address at a celebrated black institution, Lincoln University. "When you are being hammered," Taft explained, "not only by the press, but by members of your own party in Washington, and one feels there isn't anything quite right that he can do, the pleasure of going out into the country, of going into a city that hasn't seen a president for twenty years, and then makes a fuss over him to prove to him that there is somebody that doesn't know of his defects, is a pleasure I don't like to forego."

He boarded the train at Union Station in Washington for a departure to Philadelphia at 7 a.m., the very hour at which Roosevelt's ocean liner reached New York. Before the train left, it was noted that he "read with deep interest the latest news of the homecoming of Col. Roosevelt." Arriving at Philadelphia shortly before ten thirty, he was taken by special locomotive to Villanova, where he was met by a delegation of over five hundred professors and students. The college had arranged to bring all "the members of the faculty, the entire student body and all the townspeople that could get to the station in traps, autos and on foot." As the president stepped from the locomotive, "the Villanova band played 'Hail to the Chief' and the college boys let out one concentrated, prolonged and tremendous yell." Charmed by the rousing welcome, Taft broke into a beaming smile.

The entire visit to Villanova proved a gratifying relief from the besieging trials of the presidency. The commencement exercises took place in the college auditorium, gaily decorated with bunting and flags. Since the auditorium held only 2,500 invited guests, arrangements had been made for Taft to deliver his address outside, so that an overflow crowd of 5,000 people who had been gathering on the grounds since early morning might hear him. "The Roosevelt luck" that graced the former president's celebration in New York with sunny skies did not hold for Taft, however; the sky blackened with thunderclouds just as he was set to start his address, prompting a reluctant decision to speak indoors.

Despite the sudden change, Taft's address was received with enthusiasm. He applauded the Augustinians' missionary work in the Philippines and spoke wistfully of his years as governor general—perhaps the most fulfilling of his political career. An outburst of applause greeted every positive reference to the Catholic Church, and when he finished his speech, the entire audience rose in loud acclamation.

With lifted spirits, Taft boarded a special train to West Chester, home to Republican congressman Thomas S. Butler. Butler had remained loyal to Taft through all the difficult days of his presidency. Now Taft graciously repaid him by making a "flying visit" to the little town to deliver two short speeches extolling his steadfast supporter. "He came to me at the beginning of my administration," Taft said of Butler, "and declared he was going to stand by me to the end—he probably didn't know how much that meant." The townspeople were thrilled to see the president. "Banks, office buildings, residences and the post office were a mass of colors," one correspondent wrote, "while displayed on a number of buildings were the ten foot high letters T-A-F-T."

The president continued on to the campus of Lincoln University, arriving just as "a terrific electrical storm raged overhead." Undeterred, 2,000 people patiently stood on the grounds in the pouring rain without even the protection of umbrellas. "I thank you sincerely for coming out to greet me," he humbly told the cheering crowd. "I understand that it is to the President of the United States, and I accept it as such." In his well-received address, Taft referred to Booker T. Washington as "one of the greatest men of the century" and called on the black community to develop its own educated leaders to help solve the nation's racial problems.

Despite Taft's heartfelt reception all along his route, the press could not resist drawing comparisons between the outright jubilation that marked Roosevelt's sunlit homecoming on the seacoast and the decorous approval accorded the president in the rain-drenched interior. Furthermore, while Roosevelt seemed as fresh and buoyant at day's end as when he disembarked, Taft was "travel-stained" and exhausted when he boarded the train back to Washington. One reporter went so far as to portray the overweight Taft "in a free state of perspiration . . . suffering from so much prickly heat that it pushes his clothes out from him," making it impossible for him to keep his shirt buxom in place. On his way home, Taft read the afternoon newspaper accounts of Roosevelt's homecoming reception, doubtless taking note of the Colonel's remark that he stood "ready and eager" to do his part in solving the country's ills.

When the president reached the White House shortly before ten o'clock, his weariness abruptly vanished with news that his bill to expand the federal government's power to prevent arbitrary increases in railroad rates had passed Congress that day and was awaiting his signature. Even in the worst of times, when bombarded by criticism in insurgent newspapers for his willingness to deal with the conservative bloc in the Congress, Taft had retained "an abiding faith" that if he could secure legislation the country needed, "the credit would take care of itself ultimately." Now, with the passage of his railroad bill, he could allow himself a bit of optimism. In the previous session, he had secured a corporation tax bill, hailed as "the first positive step toward the National supervision of great corporations," as well as an amendment to the Interstate Commerce Act that gave the commission "for the first time, the power to prevent stock-watering."

In addition to the railroad bill, two important progressive measures were about to receive his signature: the first confirmed presidential authority to withdraw millions of acres of land for conservation; the second, a postal savings bill "fought at every step by powerful interests," provided the poor a secure place to deposit their money. That very afternoon, in fact, the lead editorial in the Philadelphia *Evening Bulletin* suggested that Taft "had unquestionably strengthened his position in the public esteem, within the last thirty days," as the country was "beginning to realize more clearly the essential force that lies behind his quiet, persistent methods. . . . His policy throughout has been that of a resolute defender of the public interest who preferred to work without parade or ostentation."

As he went to sleep that night, Taft could take heart that Roosevelt, too, would recognize the necessity that led him to deal with the conservatives. He was working in his own, unspectacular way to accomplish the progressive goals that both shared with equal fervor. That morning, he had dispatched Captain Butt to deliver a second handwritten letter to Roosevelt as he landed in New York. He warmly reiterated the invitation tendered to Roosevelt three weeks earlier, to join him at the White House. Once reunited, despite the swirling tensions and innuendo, they might enjoy the camaraderie of the old days, when, as Roosevelt's sister Corinne recalled, they had so enjoyed one another's company that "their laughs would mingle and reverberate through the corridors and rooms, and Edith would say, 'It is always that way when they are together.' "

The restoration of their old friendship—a matter more in Roosevelt's hands than in Taft's—was not simply a private concern: "No other friendship in our modern politics has meant more to the American people," William Allen White wrote, "for it has made two most important and devoted public servants wiser, kindlier, more useful men."

"The whole country waits and wonders," the *Baltimore Sun* noted in a prescient editorial. Roosevelt "seems to hold the future of his party in the hollow of his hand. Taft looks to him for succor. The Insurgents know if they can win his support the Regulars will be swept away. Old leaders tremble, new aspirants take hope. His decision is important to the country, and even more important to himself. Many another has risen to the heights of popularity to be dethroned in a day. Has Roosevelt reached the pinnacle of his fame, or is he to move forward to fresh conquests? It rests with him. He is at the height of his mental and physical powers. He possesses a great influence over the masses of his countrymen. Such power is a tremendous weapon for good or evil. How will he wield it?"

To understand the complex contours of this consequential friendship, however, we must go backward in time to analyze the similarities in experience that initially drew Roosevelt and Taft together and the differences in temperament that now threatened to split them apart.

CHAPTER TWO

Will and Teedie

"Teedie" Roosevelt, age four, and Will Taft, age seven.

WILLIAM HOWARD TAFT WAS BORN on September 15, 1857, in a two-story yellow brick house in a fashionable neighborhood on Mt. Auburn, one of the hills surrounding Cincinnati. Six days after his birth, his father, Alphonso, proudly noted to a friend: "Louise is getting along astonishing well and the baby is fat & healthy." In the hours after the birth, he explained, Louise "had a fair prospect of milk and on the 3d day the boy had plenty," but a few days later, the infant's "clamorous appetite" necessitated a wet nurse to supplement his mother's milk supply. The plump, ravenous new baby provided welcome relief to his parents. Their first child, Samuel, had been frail from birth and had died of whooping cough at fourteen months, the year before Will was born.

At two months, his mother recorded, Will was "very large for his age, and grows fat every day." Indeed, she noted with amazement and pride, "he has such a large waist, that he cannot wear any of the dresses that we made with belts." While his rapid growth kept her busy making ever larger clothes, she "took great comfort" in his "perfect good health" and his fullness of flesh. "The care of him fills in some measure the void left by Sammy's death," she wrote her mother, "but I am constantly thinking how interesting [Sammy] would be now if he had lived and how pleasant to have two little boys growing up together."

Will's sweet, open nature was evident from infancy. "He spreads his hands to anyone who will take him and his face is wreathed in smiles at the slightest provocation," Louise told her sister, Delia Torrey. His parents admired his cherubic face, "a solitary dimple in one cheek," his eyes "deeply, darkly, beautifully blue." Finding great pleasure and solace in her "healthy, fast-growing boy," Louise happily acquiesced to his insistence "upon being held whenever he is awake," even if she felt her "hands and feet were tied" to the child. "Mother would think it poor management," she confided in Delia, "but I do not understand making him take care of himself." Her torment at losing her firstborn had convinced her that children "are treasures lent not given and that they may be recalled at any time." Parents, she firmly believed, could never "love their children too much."

Louise Torrey came from a line of strong, intelligent women. Her mother, Susan Waters Torrey, had studied philosophy and astronomy at Amherst Academy and possessed a vibrant intellectual curiosity, an interest in antislavery politics, and an appreciation for art. After her marriage to merchant Samuel Torrey, they settled in Boston, where she relished the rich culture and lively debates over the critical issues of the day. To her "great disappointment," her husband, hopeful that country air would improve his health, moved the family to the small town of Millbury, Massachusetts. In Millbury, her spirits plummeted. "She has great mental and physical activity," her daughter Delia noted, "and there is not a man or woman in town with whom she can have any satisfactory intellectual conversation." Lacking any immediate outlet for her talents and energy, she shared the frustration of many educated women in the mid-nineteenth century. "Mother, you know, is very ambitious," Delia dryly wrote Louise, "and ambition in a woman is synonymous with unhappiness."

Resolved to give her daughters opportunity for intellectual development and involvement in a broader world, Susan Torrey exposed Louise and Delia to good literature, lyceum lectures in Boston, theatre in New York. They studied for a time in New Haven, Connecticut, and attended Mount Holyoke College in South Hadley, Massachusetts. Cherishing their freedom, they taught at Monson Academy in Maine, studied music, attended opera, and trav-

eled together through Canada, New England, and New York. Both rejected eligible suitors in favor of their own liberated lives. When one disappointed young man upbraided Delia for willfulness, she retorted: "If 'ladies of strong minds seldom marry,' I suppose the reverse proves true and ladies with weak minds usually do. I prefer to belong to the first class even though it precluded me from marrying."

Louise was twenty-six when she was introduced to forty-three-year-old Alphonso Taft at the home of her uncle, Reverend Samuel Dutton, pastor of North Church in New Haven, a meeting that would alter her existence in an unexpectedly domestic direction. Alphonso had grown up on a small farm in West Townsend, Vermont, the only child of Peter Rawson Taft and Sylvia Howard. "One day in an oat field," he later recalled, he "first told his father of his dream of going to college." The expense would be a hardship for the family, but "to the boy's intense delight," his parents decided to support his education. To help out, Alphonso taught school in Vermont for several years before entering Yale. He made the 140-mile trek from Vermont to New Haven on foot. After graduating Phi Beta Kappa, he taught in a boarding school for two years and then returned to Yale, where he became a tutor and studied law. "He had sacrificed so much and had been so earnest in his pursuit of an education," his youngest son Horace observed, "that everything that he learned in college was sacred in his eyes."

Although Alphonso had initially hoped to practice law in New York, a short stay there changed his mind: "I feel well assured I might make a living in that city, but I dont think it the place for me," he concluded. "I dislike the character of the New York Bar exceedingly. . . . Money is the all in all . . . nothing else brings honor." He decided instead to go west, finding "the Queen City" of Cincinnati a far more congenial place. "There are no such high partition walls here, between different classes," he wrote his mother. "Here & there a family is beginning to stiffen up & assume consequential airs, but they are comparatively few." Perhaps most significant to a man who had striven so hard for his own education, Alphonso found Cincinnati "honourably famous for its free schools," as the visiting Charles Dickens noted, "of which it has so many that no person's child among its population can by possibility want the means of education."

While studying for the Ohio bar, Alphonso clerked in the office of a fellow Vermonter with an established practice. In these early years, he depended for his livelihood on the small sums his parents could send. "I have not spent one dollar," he assured them in 1839, "not a farthing for any amusement, or for anything which was not a matter of immediate, & necessary use." With hard work and untiring discipline, he succeeded in building a successful practice that allowed him to buy the substantial two-story house on Mt. Auburn set back from the street on a stretch of green lawn. There he lived with his first wife, Fanny, an intelligent, scholarly young woman, until tuberculosis took her life at twenty-nine. She left him with two sons, Charley, ten, and Peter, six.

Though Alphonso was seventeen years older than Louise Torrey when they met in New Haven, his handsome face, muscular physique, and abundant energy bridged the years between them. She agreed to marry in 1853 and moved with him to Cincinnati, where she grew to love her "noble husband" with a heart "full of a deep and quiet joy." For his part, Alphonso rejoiced in the affection Louise showed his two older sons, who came to love her as if she were their own mother. "I do feel under the greatest obligation to you, my dear Louise, for the great care and attention you have given to the lads," he wrote to her several years before Will's birth.

Within months of her marriage, Louise confided to Delia that she had "the best husband in the United States." For Delia, the loss of her sister's companionship was devastating. "Oh, Louise, Louise how can I live the rest of my life without you?" she lamented. "I am but half of a pair of scissors." As the months passed, however, the gentle Alphonso made Delia an integral part of her sister's new family.

The family expanded rapidly after Will's birth, eventually containing six children including Charley and Peter. Henry Waters (always called Harry) was born two years after Will, followed quickly by Horace Dutton, and finally by a long-desired girl named Fanny in honor of Alphonso's first wife. As the children grew, good-natured Will remained the center of his parents' affection. "I had more pride in Willie than in all the rest," Louise acknowledged. "Willie is foremost," agreed Alphonso, "and I am inclined to think he will always be so." Rather than displaying the jealousy this favored status might easily have provoked, Will's siblings responded to his "simplicity, courage, honesty, and kindliness"—qualities he shared with his father—with devoted affection. "If flattery or admiration could have spoiled him he would have been ruined before he emerged from childhood," Horace recalled, but "his personality made him a favorite everywhere." The younger brother's fond dedication to Will never wavered. "It was very hard for anybody to be near him without loving him," Horace recollected when he had passed his eightieth birthday.

Even as his family grew and his career flourished, Alphonso Taft was rarely able to relinquish the rigid self-discipline that had enabled him to forge a comfortable existence. "Scarcely a night would pass that he was not bent over a table deep in papers or books he had brought from his office," William's biographer Henry Pringle notes. "We might almost as well ask a train of cars to go out of its course to carry a passenger," Delia lovingly observed, "as to expect Mr. Taft to turn aside from his business for the pursuit of pleasure." To Alphonso, work and family were paramount, and in that order.

Living on the wooded slope of Mt. Auburn with the entire city below "spread out before you like a map" gave the children "the advantages of both city and country," Horace recalled. Left to their own devices, the children rambled and explored. In the nearby pond, "we learned to swim, but not because anybody taught us. . . . We went fishing or on long hikes . . . we had plenty of games, but they were not organized." Looking back years later, Horace wished that they "had been taught to sail, or to rough it," been exposed more to the woods, been challenged by experiences that would have broadened their education. If not adventurous, the life he remembered seemed "wholesome and natural."

Many citizens of Cincinnati, linked to the South through commerce, sympathized with the Confederacy when the Civil War broke out, but Alphonso had long held anti-slavery views. He had been a delegate to the first Republican Convention in 1856, and after Ohio's Salmon Chase failed to secure the presidential nomination in 1860, he supported Abraham Lincoln. He sold government bonds, delivered speeches promoting emancipation, and argued government cases against the Copperhead faction at the request of Secretary of War Edwin Stanton. When news of General Lee's surrender came, "the city fairly blossomed with flags, and everybody turned out to join in a rejoicing which included all parties," Louise told her sister. "Almost every house on Mt. Auburn was lighted to its utmost extent and many were luxuriously ornamented." Hours after the celebration came word of Lincoln's assassination. "The transition from such a jubilee to the unlooked-for calamity of the next morning seemed too great to be believed," she lamented. "The symbols of joy which had been universal were turned into mourning, and the city is draped and creped from one end to the other."

Eight months after the war ended, Alphonso was appointed to fill a vacancy on the Cincinnati Superior Court bench. The following year, he was elected to a full term on the Republican ticket, and two years afterward, he was nominated and elected to the court by both Republicans and Democrats. "He was . . . a born judge," his son Horace proudly remembered. "He had the judicial temperament, the moral courage, the ability and patience."

The most important opinion Judge Taft rendered on the superior court upheld the right of the local school board to prohibit the reading of the Bible in public schools. He argued in a dissenting opinion that "the Constitution of the State did not recognize the Christian religion any more than it recognized the religions of any other citizens of the state" and that "the school board had an obligation as well as a right to keep religious partisanship out of the public schools." Alphonso was forever proud of his opinion, even though it prompted fierce opposition from conservatives.

For Alphonso, nothing equaled the honor of his judicial calling; indeed, he could envision no office higher than a seat on the Supreme Court. "To be Chief Justice of the United States," he told Salmon Chase after Lincoln had announced Chase's appointment to the Court, "is more than to be President, in my estimation." Nonetheless, after six years on the superior court, Alphonso recognized that his judicial salary could not meet the expenses involved in educating his large family. Reluctantly, he resigned his judgeship and returned to private practice. "No leader of the Bar ever left the court feeling that his case had been too difficult or deep for the Judge's understanding and learning," a distinguished lawyer wrote at the time of his resignation. "No beginner at the Bar ever left feeling that the case had been too small and unimportant for the Judge's patience and kindness."

Over the years, Alphonso became increasingly involved in the community life of Cincinnati. As a city councilman, he fought to extend the city line to annex a newly built section so that "rich real estate holders" living there would have to pay "their just share of taxes." He joined future president Rutherford B. Hayes, future Supreme Court justice Stanley Matthews, and lawyer John W. Herron, Nellie's father, as charter members of the Literary Club. And Alphonso and Louise were instrumental in founding the House of Refuge, a progressive reform school designed to return delinquent children to "the path of virtue and integrity." Taking a liberal perspective, Alphonso argued that "these children are unfortunate rather than criminal." Their delinquency, he maintained, was "not the product of nature" but rather of the "cruel circumstances" into which they were born.

At the suggestion of a group of prominent Republicans, Alphonso allowed his name to be put forward as a candidate for governor of Ohio. Though he lost at the convention to his friend Rutherford Hayes, in large part because of widespread opposition to his position on school prayer, his unblemished reputation for being "as honest as the day is long" caught the attention of President Ulysses S. Grant, who brought him into his cabinet. He served first as secretary of war and then as attorney general during Grant's final months in office, where he was seen as a representative of the "reform element" against the "old regime." While he enjoyed his short stint in Washington, he was happy to return to his beloved Cincinnati and resume the practice of law.

Alphonso and Louise supported and expected excellence in their children, pushing them at every level to succeed in their studies. Charley attended Yale and went on to Columbia Law School. Peter followed his brother to Yale, graduating first in his class with the best record ever achieved to that time. The pressure upon Will, his parents' favorite child, to match the sterling records of his older half brothers created anxiety. From his grammar school days, he had to work harder than his fellow students to succeed. His tendency to procrastinate when anxious about assignments further intensified his nervousness. In the afternoons he was frequently seen reading under a tree on the grassy lawn in the front of his house. He was ridiculed by passing neighborhood boys for not playing ball, mocked because he was a "fatty," a "lubber" who could not keep up in their rough-and-tumble games. "If you can't walk," they taunted, "we'll roll you, old butter ball." Refusing to be provoked, he merely smiled and returned to his book.

The desire to please his parents became central to young Taft's temperament and development. At the age of seven he was reading, but his mother had to work with him in "arithmetic and writing." "He means to be a scholar and studies well," Alphonso proudly recorded. "I have never had any little boy show a better spirit in that respect." When he fell to fifth in his class, Alphonso tersely declared: "Mediocrity will not do for Will." By the age of twelve, his last year in grammar school, he ranked first in his class, earning both his school's highest medal and his father's praise. "His average was 95," Alphonso told Delia, "and the nearest to him averaged 85. This was doing uncommonly well, and makes us all very happy." His younger brothers were conscientious students as well, placing second and third in their respective classes. "We felt that the sun shone brighter if we brought home good reports," Horace recalled. Yet each successful performance only fueled higher expectations, giving Will, who drove himself intensely to perform, little peace. Years later, his mother realized the mechanism they had unwittingly fostered: "Love of approval," she acknowledged, became her adored son's "besetting fault."

In the summer of 1869, when Will was eleven, Alphonso and Louise sailed to Europe to join their older sons, Charley and Peter, who were studying and traveling abroad with the aid of $50,000 bequeathed to each upon the death of their maternal grandfather, Judge Phelps. For Charley, Europe proved life-altering, awakening a love of music, art, and theatre that would continue to deepen in the years ahead. Of all the Taft boys, Charley seemed best able to balance study and relaxation. For Peter, the most brilliant yet brittle of the brothers, the desire to meet his father's expectations produced a chronic state of nervous exhaustion, marked by headaches and eye trouble. His family hoped that the year in Europe would restore his spirits.

Will and his younger siblings remained behind during this European sojourn, missing excursions to historical sites in England, Italy, and Germany that would likely have provided far more vivid and spacious lessons than the daily round of class work in their local grammar school. In their letters from abroad, the parents suggested readings that would connect their sons to their various stops along the way. When they reached Liverpool, Louise advised Will to "read up in the Gazetteer and Encyclopedia of this the greatest harbor in the world," trusting that the knowledge his parents were there would "make his geography real & impressive to him." Writing from Rome, where he had visited the supposed site of Julius Caesar's assassination at the base of Pompey's colossal statue, Alphonso re-created for Will the story of Caesar's rivalry with Pompey and the struggle with the senators that led to his death.

In the fall of 1870, Will entered rigorous Woodward High, a public school for college-bound students in downtown Cincinnati. His years there were marked by the same pattern of hard work, procrastination, and an anxiety driven by his need to maintain the family standard of excellence. In his study of Taft's early education, the historian David Burton concludes that Will left high school with "a mastery of fact and a commitment to disciplined study, rather than a sense of an intellectual adventure." Horace Taft, who eventually became a celebrated educator, recalled the learning environment of their childhood home and concluded that "the most conspicuous thing about it was its limitations. My father was very ambitious for all of his children but, like most Americans of that day, thought of education as a school affair and as connected almost exclusively with the school curriculum. . . . We had no music, no art, no mechanical training, and our reading was done with very little guidance." So long as his children worked hard and performed well, Alphonso believed his obligation regarding their education had been met.

The winter of Will's senior year, his brother Charley, who was then practicing law in Cincinnati, married Annie Sinton, the only daughter of the city's wealthiest man, iron king David Sinton. Charley's wedding to Annie Sinton was "the great social event" of the year. Long afterward, Nellie Herron Taft, who was twelve at the time, recalled the excitement of the gala staged at the splendid Sinton mansion situated at the top of her street. A long and happy marriage commenced when the young couple moved into that mansion with Annie's widowed father. Charley would eventually leave the law to become publisher of the *Cincinnati Times*, which merged into the *Evening Star* to form the *Times-Star*, a Taft family holding for the next seven decades. Over the years, Charley accrued considerable wealth that would help provide a foundation for Will's public service career.

Even as a high school student, Will began to develop a progressive sensitivity informed by the feminist teachings of his mother and grandmother. His inclinations for social justice were reflected in a thoughtful essay he wrote during his senior year. "The result of coeducation of the sexes shows clearly that there is no mental inferiority on the part of the girls," he asserted. These views echoed the liberal views of his mother, who was incensed by an article in the *New York Times* suggesting that "from their constitutional peculiarities girls cannot be pushed in school as rapidly as can boys." Moving beyond coeducation, Will argued for woman's suffrage. "Give the woman the ballot, and you will make her more important in the eyes of the world." The right to vote, he optimistically predicted, would beget other benefits. "Every woman would then be given an opportunity to earn a livelihood. She would suffer no decrease in compensation for her labor, on account of her sex. . . . It becomes this country, as a representative of liberty, to lead in this great reform."

Will graduated second in his high school class, with an average of 91, earning him an acceptance at Yale. Still, his father expressed concern about his work habits, citing a teacher who believed the only obstacle to Will's achieving great success was laziness. Despite the affection his parents showered on young Will, the impression remains that he never experienced their love as a steady force, but rather as a conditional reward dependent upon his achievements.

When he entered Yale, Will stood over six feet tall and weighed 225 pounds, quickly earning him the admiring nickname "Big Bill." His affable disposition and genial companionship with students of all backgrounds combined to make him the most popular man in the freshman class. "To see his large bulk come solidly and fearlessly across the campus," one classmate enthused, "is to take a fresh hold on life." Observing him walk through the college auditorium was "like seeing a dreadnaught launched." When the sophomore class challenged the freshmen to a tug-of-war, the freshman team proved seriously outmatched, its members "dragged bodily down the field" until Big Bill entered the fray, anchored the rope, and hauled his classmates back, inch by inch, to victory.

Academics came less easily for Will; he found his courses in Latin, Greek, and mathematics especially difficult. "I begin to see how a fellow can study all the time and still not have perfect [marks]," he warned his father only days after the semester had begun. Nevertheless, when grades were posted after six weeks, his tireless efforts placed him in the first division, where he was joined by his good friend from Cincinnati, Howard Hollister. "It is not more than we expected," Louise told Delia. "Now that the best scholars are in one division, the motive for effort, incited by constant comparison with each other is very strong, inspiring them with unflagging ambition." The added pressure only aggravated Will's distress. There was no respite so long as self-esteem depended on the approval of his parents. "Another week of this 'dem'd horrid grind,' has passed by . . . I am somewhat embarrassed in this first division," Taft confessed to his father. "You expect great things of me but you mustn't be disappointed if I don't come up to your expectations." Despite the worry of such expectations, the fact that Will was able to speak openly to his father about his fears indicates the depth of their relationship.

He did not try out for football, baseball, or crew. His father "had other ideas," Taft recalled years later, insisting he focus solely on his class work. Nor was Alphonso pleased to hear that his social son had been elected president of Delta Kappa and taken into Skull and Bones. "I doubt that such popularity is consistent with high scholarship," he warned. Will disagreed: "If a man has to be isolated from his class in order to take a high stand I dont want a high stand. The presidency of Delta Kap takes none of my time except so much as I spend on Saturday night which I sh'd use any how. There's got to be some relaxation." This brief spark of rebellion was quickly doused as Will settled into a structured regimen that produced the expected academic distinction. Rising at half past six, he studied before breakfast, followed by prayers, morning recitation, lunch, and afternoon recitation until three o' clock. Then he went to the gym for half an hour and studied until his last recitation at five. If he had time before dinner he would stop by the post office in hopes of finding letters from home, and then work until ten or even eleven at night.

"As a scholar, he stood high," a fellow classmate, Herbert Bowen, recalled; more important, "he towered above us all as a moral force." He was the class leader, directing all manner of college activities, from the literary board to the junior prom. He listened sympathetically to the troubles of his fellow students, who regularly sought his counsel. His classmates found him "safe and comforting," always ready to "come up with a cheery bit of wholesome discourse." Without a single dissenting vote, Taft's colleagues affectionately appointed him "father" of their graduating year and long remembered his perpetual smile and rumbling, hearty laugh. In sum, Bowen writes, he "was the most admired and respected man not only in my class, but in all Yale."

Nonetheless, David Burton concludes, "there was little in his academic training at Yale to suggest that learning was exciting for him, a galvanizing experience." Rather, Will was conditioned to regard his subjects "as hurdles to be taken on the way to a degree." When a younger student inquired about setting himself "a course of outside reading" to facilitate a deeper immersion in French and German literature and culture, Will Taft advised: "Don't do it. Get over it. You mustn't try to be too independent, just yet. These University professors have laid out a course, and it's the result of their long experience, while you—well, this is just your first trial at educating anybody. . . . You'd just better stick to the course."

In the spring of his sophomore year, Will delivered an oration on the continued vitality of the Democratic Party, tracing its history from Thomas Jefferson and Andrew Jackson to the present day. Despite his own strong Republican leanings, he could appreciate and praise various Democratic leaders, noting in particular Jackson's "hard common sense which is only acquired by knocking about among the masses." Even at this young age, his biographer observes, "Taft was judicial beyond the comprehensions of a Theodore Roosevelt," who not long thereafter would write a paper at Harvard accusing Jefferson of "criminal folly" and labeling Jackson "a spoilsman before anything else."

Taft would recall one professor above all, the political economist William Graham Sumner, who, he said, "had more to do with stimulating my mental activities than any one under whom I studied during my entire course." Considered one of the most gifted educators of his generation, Sumner lectured to classes packed not only with eager students but with professors from various universities "seeking the secret of his success." An impassioned advocate of laissez-faire and social Darwinism, of property rights and economic freedom, Sumner was an apostle for the gospel of wealth, the reigning philosophy of the Industrial Revolution and the Gilded Age that followed the Civil War.

Sumner passionately rejected concerns about the consolidation of business and the excessive concentration of wealth in the hands of a few, arguing on the contrary that wealthy business leaders like John Rockefeller, Andrew Carnegie, J. P. Morgan, and Cornelius Vanderbilt should be lionized. Through their enterprise, ingenuity, and capital, America had become the world's leading industrial power, capable of building more railroads, producing more oil and steel, manufacturing more clothing, appliances, and consumer goods than any other nation on earth. "If we should set a limit to the accumulation of wealth," he argued, "we should say to our most valuable producers, 'We do not want you to do us the services which you best understand how to perform, beyond a certain point.' It would be like killing off our generals in war."

Will absorbed Sumner's central teaching—that property rights demanded protection against the onslaught of radical theories and socialist ideals. Like Sumner, he argued that "princely profits" represented the just reward for "the men of judgment, courage and executive ability who have conceived and executed the great enterprises." Unlike Sumner, however, he did not place the businessman at "the highest pinnacle of honor and trust." Nor did he regard property rights as absolute, deserving precedence at every turn over human rights. From his father he had learned that the man who devoted himself to his community—"the lawyer who makes man's peace with man; the doctor who makes his peace with Nature; the minister who makes his peace with God"—deserved greater praise than the man who pursued wealth for its own sake. Wealth was honorable only to the extent that it contributed to the well-being of the community.

Honors were showered upon Will Taft during his senior year. His proud father boasted to Delia in late October 1877 that Will had been chosen by his classmates to be class orator, "the greatest prize in college," valedictorian notwithstanding. "He has in this respect surpassed his older brothers," Alphonso noted. "The honor too is of the historical kind which will not be forgotten by his class." He would "have his hands full, however," Alphonso explained, for the chosen student was expected to deliver "a long speech of half an hour to the class, carefully written & committed, & practiced."

Almost immediately, as Will anticipated his performance, anxiety set in. Two months after his selection, with more than five months left to prepare, he so agonized over his insufficient progress that he determined to forgo Christmas vacation in Cincinnati. "We shall regret that Willie cannot come home, but believe he does right in giving time to the great work," Alphonso wrote Delia. "I rely on his strength of purpose, & of intellect to accomplish it all and raise his reputation every time." As spring approached, Will lamented that his oration was "coming on slowly." Though he had settled upon his theme, he had not formulated how to present it. A month later he was still struggling, "finding it rather difficult to adapt its tone to the occasion." Another vacation was spent toiling in New Haven alone.

In the end, young Taft delivered a splendid oration before an overflow crowd at the Battell Chapel. "The sound of approaching music was heard," the *New York Times* reported, "followed by the measured tramp of the Class of '78, as in long line they filed up the aisle and took their places for the last time in their accustomed seats, where they would listen to the address of the Class Orator." No accolade could have pleased Taft more than the comparisons to his father drawn by the *Times*. "The orator in physique, in the method of handling his subject, and in style of oratory, presented some strong resemblances to his distinguished father. The address was characterized throughout by a transparency of thought, a clearness of statement, and an appearance of manly sincerity."

In the weeks before his graduation, Will had grown increasingly alarmed and troubled by news that his brother Peter had suffered a nervous breakdown and been committed to a private hospital for the insane in College Hill, Ohio. "I wish you could get Peter to come to Commencement," he beseeched his father. "We might turn his thoughts back to his college days and ease his mind considerably. President [Noah] Porter asked about him. I told him that we thought he was suffering from some mental disease."

Before his breakdown, Peter had begun practicing law in Cincinnati. There he met and married Tillie Hulbert, daughter of another prominent and wealthy local family. Unfortunately, his marriage did not share the productive harmony of Charley's. The union shortly proved disastrous, and his old anxieties multiplied. "Peter continues so strange," his mother confided to her sister. "He is very cross to Tillie and quarrels about everything in the arrangement of the house. He . . . puts in partitions, buys paper, carpets & furniture and changes the position of everything in the house in opposition to Tillie's wishes." Tormented by a series of ailments, including wild mood swings and a recurrence of the mysterious eye trouble that rendered him unable to read, Peter began the first of several treatments at the sanitarium.

"I am doing my best to be reconciled to the treatment in this institution," he wrote his father. "You have thought it best, and whatever your judgment thinks best I shall obey. But the course here is very hard. The Doctor gives me a kind of tonic that heats my head very much, and makes my mind so sensitive that any exercise of it deprives me of rest at night. . . . You are proceeding on a mistaken theory in my case. What I need is, not to be shut off from you and the family, but to be drawn to you and made to feel your love. . . . It seems to me that I am on a downward path. Whatever is the result of treatment, remember always that I, your son, love you more than I do any living mortal, and I respect your will above all others." Despite the entreaties of both Will and Peter himself, Alphonso decided that Peter should remain in the hospital rather than join the family at Yale.

On June 27, 1878, Will Taft was honored as salutatorian of his class, having surpassed all of his 132 classmates save Clarence Hill Kelsey, who would become a lifelong friend.

Even as he prepared to enter Cincinnati Law School the following fall, much of Will's motivation continued to stem from his father's high expectations rather than from any strong internal drive. Indeed, years later, Taft would credit his father's indomitable will and lofty aspirations in prompting his own achievements. When his father lay dying, he described this enveloping paternal spirit to Nellie: "I have a kind of presentiment that Father has been a kind of guardian angel to me in that his wishes for my success have been so strong and intense as to bring it, and that as his life ebbs away and ends I shall cease to have the luck which has followed me thus far."

Theodore Roosevelt was born thirteen months after Will Taft, on October 27, 1858, in a four-story town house at 28 East 20th Street in Manhattan. "Teedie," as he was nicknamed, was by his own admission "a sickly and timid boy . . . a wretched mite," whose childhood was shaped by an assortment of troubling ailments, the most dangerous of which was asthma. When these agonizing attacks came, he found himself frantically gasping for breath, terrified he would suffocate. "Nobody seemed to think I would live," he recalled. His younger sister, Corinne, remarked on the irony that "Theodore Roosevelt, whose name later became the synonym of virile health and vigor, was a fragile, patient sufferer in those early days of the nursery." His fierce determination to escape an invalid's fate led him to transform his body and timid demeanor through strenuous work; Taft, on the other hand, blessed from birth with robust health, would allow his physical strength and energy to gradually dissipate over the years into a state of obesity.

During the worst of Teedie's asthmatic attacks, when the constriction in his chest made sleep impossible, his father comforted him with "great and loving care." "Some of my earliest remembrances are of nights when he would walk up and down with me," Roosevelt later wrote. "I could breathe, I could sleep, when he had me in his arms." If carrying the gasping child from room to room around the house proved inadequate, Theodore Senior drove him with horse and carriage through the gaslit city streets, hoping that the chill gusts of wind would fill the boy's lungs with air. "My father—he got me breath, he got me lungs, strength—life."

Teedie's father, known as "Thee," was the youngest of five sons born to Margaret and Cornelius Van Shaack Roosevelt, a glass merchant who had amassed a substantial fortune in real estate and banking. Considered "one of the five richest men in New York," C.V.S. hired tutors to educate his sons in the basement study of his imposing brick mansion on Union Square. Instead of enrolling Thee in college, which he feared would "spoil" him, C.V.S. sent him on a Grand Tour of Europe when he turned nineteen. Returning from the year abroad, Thee followed his older brother, James, into the family business. As the years went by, however, his keen sense of social justice began to shift his focus from the firm. Increasingly, he was drawn to philanthropic efforts to improve the lives of the poor at a time when extravagant wealth and abject poverty stood side by side.

In 1853, at age twenty-one, Thee married seventeen-year-old Martha "Mittie" Bulloch, daughter of a high-spirited family from Roswell, Georgia. Mittie had been raised in Bulloch Hall, a white-columned antebellum plantation mansion, where every need was attended to by a dozen slaves. The story of their courtship suggests an intense attraction from the moment they met in Roswell when Mittie was only fifteen. They renewed their acquaintance when she came north to visit relatives in the spring of 1853, and within weeks they were engaged. A southern beauty with delicate features, blue eyes, black hair, and radiant skin, Mittie possessed a quick mind and playful sense of humor. She proved irresistible to a young man raised amid the staid gentility of the Roosevelts' ordered social world.

In June, Thee came to Roswell to meet the members of the large Bulloch clan. "I am trying to school myself to coolly shaking hands with you when we meet—before the family," Thee told her. After his visit, Mittie assured him she was now "confident" of her "own deep love," confessing that "everything now seems associated with you. Even when I run up the stairs going to my own room, I feel as if you were near, and turn involuntarily to kiss my hand to you. I feel, dear Thee—as though you were part of my existence, and that I only live in your being." Her words so thrilled Thee that he felt "the blood rush" to his temples, forcing him "to lay the letter down, for a few minutes to regain command" of himself. "O, Mittie," he declared, "how deeply, how devotedly I love you!" Within four months, the young couple settled into their new 20th Street home, one of two adjoining houses that C.V.S. had purchased for Thee and his brother Robert.

Here, in the eight years that followed, four children were born: Anna, who was nicknamed "Bamie"; Theodore, Elliott, and Corinne. The advent of the Civil War, however, blasted the idyllic days of Thee and Mittie's marriage. While Thee passionately supported the Union cause, Mittie remained loyal to her homeland. Her brother, two stepbrothers, and all the young men she had known in Georgia had enlisted in the Confederate Army. Before the outbreak of war, Mittie's widowed mother, Martha, and her sister, Anna, had left Georgia and moved in with Thee and Mittie. Their plantation eventually fell into the hands of Union soldiers. "If I may judge at all of the embittered feeling of the South against the North by myself," Martha told her daughter, "I would say they would rather be buried in one common grave than ever again live under the same government. I am confident I should." The strain of a divided household took a toll on Mittie's health. "I shudder to think of what she must have suffered," Bamie later said. "I remember that Mother for a long time never came to the dinner table." Unable to bear the inevitable arguments, she withdrew more and more to the sickroom, plagued by an assortment of ills: palpitations, stomach troubles, and debilitating headaches.

Thee suppressed his impulse to volunteer for the Union Army, fearing that it would destroy his fragile wife "for him to fight against her brothers." Reluctantly, he decided to purchase a substitute. Although it seemed the only choice at the time, he "always afterwards felt that he had done a very wrong thing," recalled Bamie, "in not having put every other feeling aside and joined the absolute fighting forces." Thee worked tirelessly on behalf of the Union cause, devoting all his time and abundant energy to the great work of the U.S. Sanitary Commission, the Union League, the U.S. Allotment Commission, and the U.S. Employment Bureau, which found work for soldiers who had lost limbs, yet the decision not to enlist caused an indelible regret.

All four Roosevelt children idolized their father, "the most dominant figure" in their childhood, especially since their mother's fragility absented her from so many of their activities. He was "the most intimate friend of each of his children," Corinne recalled, "and we all craved him as our most desired companion." Theodore described the joyful anticipation when "we used to wait in the library in the evening until we could hear his key rattling in the latch of the front hall, and then rush out to greet him." Bamie was convinced "there was never anyone so wonderful" as her father, while Elliott marveled that "he was one of those rare grown men who seem never to forget that they were once children themselves." He took the children sailing on the swan boats in Central Park and brought them to museums. He tutored them in riding (first on Shetland ponies and then saddle horses) and in tree-climbing, pointing out "the dead limbs" to avoid.

In contrast to Alphonso Taft, who was rarely able to "turn aside from his business for the pursuit of pleasure," the elder Theodore Roosevelt skillfully balanced work and leisure in his family's life. "I never knew anyone who got greater joy out of living than did my father," Theodore declared, "or any one who more whole-heartedly performed every duty." His hard work in both business and philanthropic activities never precluded a rich social life. He reveled in the company of friends at dinner parties, relished a good cigar, danced into the early morning hours, and raced his four-in-hand coach through the streets. While acknowledging the often cruel class divisions that drove Alphonso from New York, he saw the city "not so much for what it was as for what it might become" under enlightened leadership. In an era when assistance to the poor remained mainly in the hands of private charity, Thee developed a sterling reputation for his dedication to improving the lives of tenement children through his work with the Newsboys' Lodging House, the Children's Aid Society, Miss Sattery's School for Italian Children, and the Five Points Mission. "Father was the finest man I ever knew, and the happiest," Roosevelt later told his journalist friend Jacob Riis.

Their father's affection and vitality compelled the Roosevelt children to surmount serious physical ailments. Bamie was deformed at birth by a severe curvature of the spine which gave her a hunchbacked appearance. Elliott was afflicted by what were considered epileptic attacks. Corinne, like Teedie, suffered from asthma, though her illness was not as severe as her brother's. Concern with the children's health prompted Thee to arrange home tutoring rather than send them to school. They were taught the fundamentals of reading, writing, and arithmetic by Mittie's sister, Anna, but their lifelong love of learning, their remarkable wide-ranging intellectual curiosity, was fostered primarily by their father. He read aloud to them at night, eliciting their responses to works of history and literature. He organized amateur plays for them, encouraged pursuit of their special interests, prompted them to write essays on their readings, and urged them to recite poetry. In addition, their mother provided a romantic and engaging perspective on history through accounts of her childhood in the vanished world of plantations, slaves, and chivalrous codes.

Even at a young age, Teedie held a distinct place among his siblings; the asthma that had weakened his body seemed to have inordinately sharpened his mind and sensibilities. "From the very fact that he was not able originally to enter into the most vigorous activities," Corinne noted, "he was always reading or writing" with a most unusual "power of concentration." He especially loved animal stories, adventure tales, and inspiring chronicles of "men who were fearless" in battle. His voracious reading gave him a rich cache of ideas for stories of his own to entertain his younger sister and brother. "I can see him now struggling with the effort to breathe," Corinne recalled, describing her eight-year-old brother's winding serial narratives, "which never flagged in interest for us" though at times they "continued from week to week, or even from month to month."

In the summers, Thee sought a broader field of educational activities for his children in the country, moving the family first to the Hudson Valley, and then to Oyster Bay, in the rambling house called Tranquillity—although Corinne wryly observed that "anything less tranquil than that happy home," crowded with cousins and friends of all the children, "could hardly be imagined." Her friends Edith Carow and Fanny Smith were regular visitors every summer. To Fanny Smith, these summer sojourns to Oyster Bay seemed a blissful round of "riding, driving, boating, picnicking, games and verse-writing—no day was long enough." Fanny was so taken with "the extraordinary vitality and gusto with which the Roosevelt family invested life" that she felt as if they had all been "touch[ed] by the flame of the 'divine fire.' "

In the woodlands surrounding the Roosevelts' summer retreat, young Theodore's avocation as a naturalist took shape. As he roamed the forest trails, he began to observe the birds, listening to their distinctive songs, carefully noting flight patterns, beak and bill shapes, and coloration. When his interest expanded to a wide range of animals, he studied in scientific books, and then took lessons, which his father arranged, from a professional taxidermist. He began to collect, prepare, and mount hundreds of meticulously labeled specimens. Encouraged by Thee, he set about establishing his own "Roosevelt Museum of Natural History," with the fervent aspiration to become the next J. J. Audubon or Spencer Baird.

The expansive education the Roosevelt children enjoyed, with boundaries stretching far beyond the classroom, closely resembled the ideal of learning envisioned by Horace Taft, when he wished that he and his siblings had been exposed to the natural world, to the arts and music, to reading unconfined by pedantic needs and standards. Years later, when Roosevelt was president, he tried to interest Taft in birds and nature. "He loves the woods, he loves hunting," Taft said of Roosevelt; "he loves roughing it, and I don't." On one occasion, when Taft served as Roosevelt's secretary of war, he entered the Oval Office while Roosevelt was speaking with an ornithologist. Taft was anxious to talk about the Philippine tariff bill, but Roosevelt tried to engage Will in his discussion. "Sit down, Will, and we will talk about something more interesting; we'll tell you something about birds," the president exclaimed. Taft responded with a laugh: "I don't believe that you can interest me in natural history, and I don't want you to send me any more such books as you sent me the other day. I read it because you asked me to, and it took me nearly all night. What do I care about dog-wolves, and whether they help she-wolves in procuring food for their young. I don't think I ever saw a wolf, and certainly . . . I am not interested in their domestic affairs."

The same year that Alphonso and Louise traveled abroad, without Will and their younger children, Thee and Mittie took ten-year-old Teedie and the entire family to Europe for a twelve-month journey through England, Scotland, Holland, Germany, Switzerland, Italy, and France. Although Teedie, affectionately known within the family as "a great little home-boy," sorely missed his childhood friends, particularly eight-year-old Edith, his faithful diary entries reveal scores of invigorating adventures. He traversed fields where the Wars of the Roses were fought, inspected the tombs at Westminster Abbey, stood astride the boundary of France and Italy, ascended Mt. Vesuvius, and admired the art treasures of the Vatican.

And always, the children were accompanied by books, allowing Teedie the occasional opportunity to withdraw into his own world. At the end of four months, before the trip was half over, he proudly announced that "we three" (the three younger children, Bamie being considered part of the "big people" world) had read fifty novels. Beyond works of popular fiction, the family carried a small library of classic history and literature, which Thee read aloud to stir discussion.

Although the European voyage answered Thee's hopes "that a real education for his children would be acquired more easily through travel," he feared that Teedie, whose asthma and stomach troubles had necessitated frequent days of bed rest, was becoming too familiar with illness, timidity, and frailty, too prone to retreat into invalidism. When they returned home, he took his young son aside. "Theodore, you have the mind but you have not the body, and without the help of the body the mind cannot go as far as it should," he admonished. "You must *make* your body. It is hard drudgery to make one's body, but I know you will do it." Teedie responded immediately, according to Corinne, giving his father a solemn promise: "*I'll make my body*."

The boy threw himself into a strict regimen of strength and endurance training; week after week, month after month, he lifted weights and pulled himself up on horizontal bars. Methodically, he sought to expand "his chest by regular, monotonous motion—drudgery indeed," first at Wood's Gymnasium and then in the home gym his father constructed on the second floor. The fierce determination that had propelled Teedie to become a serious student of nature, a voracious reader, and a sensitive observer was now directed toward expanding his physical capabilities by refashioning his body. Years would pass before the potential of these labors would be actualized in an adult capacity and physique that made him an exemplar of "the strenuous life."

In the meantime, his physical inferiority made him vulnerable to a humiliating experience that remained fresh in his mind forty years later. In his *Autobiography*, he recounted a stagecoach ride to Maine where he was set upon by two "mischievous" boys, who "proceeded to make life miserable" for him. Attempting to fight back, he discovered that either boy alone could handle him "with easy contempt." The injury to his self-respect was such that he was determined never again to be so helpless. In addition to his regular exercise regimen, he began taking boxing lessons. "I was a painfully slow and awkward pupil," he recalled, "and certainly worked two or three years before I made any perceptible improvement whatever."

Transforming his body was only one step in the psychological struggle against what Teedie shamefully considered his "timid" nature. "There were all kinds of things of which I was afraid at first," he acknowledged, "but by acting as if I was not afraid I gradually ceased to be afraid." As a childhood friend observed, "by constantly forcing himself to do the difficult or even dangerous thing," he was able to cultivate courage as "a matter of habit, in the sense of repeated effort and repeated exercise of will-power."

When Teedie was fourteen, his family went abroad again. Rather than repeat the heady pace of their first sweep through the Continent, they spent an entire winter in Egypt, three weeks in Palestine, two weeks in Lebanon and Syria, three weeks in Athens, Smyrna, and Constantinople, and five months in Germany. None of the children benefited more from this remarkable journey than Teedie, whose romantic nature conjured visions of ancient lives entwined with his own. "We arrived in sight of Alexandria," he wrote in his diary. "How I gazed on it! It was Egypt, the land of my dreams; Egypt the most ancient of all countries! A land that was old when Rome was bright, was old when Babylon was in its glory, was old when Troy was taken! It was a sight to awaken a thousand thoughts, and it did."

In addition to the cultural sites, young Theodore was thrilled by the chance to observe and catalogue exotic species he had hitherto known only in books. This was his "first real collecting as a student of natural history." During their two-month journey along the Nile in a private vessel, staffed by a thirteen-man crew, furnished with comfortable staterooms and a dining saloon, he was able clearly to perceive the habits of these entirely new birds and animals at close range, for finally, he had been fitted with spectacles that corrected his severe nearsightedness. "I had no idea," he later said, "how beautiful the world was until I got those spectacles." In the mornings he and his father would go out shooting along the banks of the Nile, retrieving specimens to be skinned, dissected, preserved with chemicals, and labeled. "My first knowledge of Latin was obtained by learning the scientific names of the birds and mammals which I collected and classified." His early dedication to such pursuits revealed "an almost ruthless single-mindedness where his interests were aroused," one biographer, Carleton Putnam, observed, "suggestive of a purposeful, determined personality."

Summer found the children in Dresden, where their father had arranged for them to live with a German family. Throughout that summer of 1873 and into the early fall, the daughter of the hosts was hired to teach them the German language, literature, music, and art. Teedie was so earnestly focused upon his studies, which occupied six hours of the day, that he asked to extend the lessons further. "And of course," his younger brother Elliott complained, "I could not be left behind so we are working harder than ever in our lives."

In the course of the year abroad, young Theodore had traveled by ship and by train, by stagecoach and on foot; he had stayed in hotels, inns, tents, and private homes. Armed with an innate curiosity and a discipline fostered by his remarkable father, he had obtained firsthand knowledge of the peoples and cultures in Europe, the Middle East, and Africa. Forty years later, Roosevelt remained appreciative of the opportunity afforded him. "This trip," he wrote in *An Autobiography*, "formed a really useful part of my education."

The family returned to a new home at 6 West 57th Street, a stately mansion with a fully equipped gymnasium for the children and a large space set aside in the garret to house Teedie's ever-expanding taxidermy collection. Although the fifteen-year-old's travels abroad had given him an unusually strong foundation in natural science, history, geography, and German, he was, in his own words, "lamentably weak in Latin and Greek and mathematics." If he wished to enter an Ivy League school, he could not compete with students like Will Taft, who had mastered the strenuous program at Woodward High that fully prepared him for Yale. To fill the gaps in Teedie's learning and prepare him for Harvard's rigorous entrance examinations, his father hired a recent Harvard graduate, Arthur Cutler. Under Cutler's tutelage, Teedie worked long hours every day and completed three years of college preparation in two. "The young man never seemed to know what idleness was," marveled Cutler, "and every leisure moment would find the last novel, some English classic or some abstruse book on natural history in his hands."

Elliott also studied under the guidance of a tutor, but lacking his brother's inner motivation and self-confidence, he proved unable to master subjects on his own. Even at thirteen, he worried about his future. "What will I become when I am a man," he plaintively demanded of his father. Acknowledging that Teedie was "much quicker and [a] more sure kind of boy," he pledged that he would "try to be as good . . . if [it] is in me, but it is hard." Desiring perhaps to separate himself from daily competition with his brother, Elliott entreated his father to send him to St. Paul's preparatory school. The summer before his entry, however, he suffered a series of mysterious seizures rooted, doctors believed, in a nervous disorder. Thee decided to postpone St. Paul's, choosing instead to take his son to Europe on a business trip. In Liverpool, Elliott suffered another attack, more severe than any previous incident. "It produced congestion of the brain with all its attendant horrors of delirium," Thee reported to Mittie. Two weeks later, Elliott remained ill. "I jump involuntarily at the smallest sound," he confided in a letter to Teedie, "and have a perpetual headache (and nearly always in low spirits)."

Upon returning home, Elliott resumed working with his tutor, but his hopes were still set on St. Paul's, where, he wrote his father, he "could make more friends" than studying at home. "Oh, Father will you ever think *me* a 'noble boy.' You are right about Teedie he is one and no mistake a boy I would give a good deal to be like in many respects." That fall, Thee agreed to let Elliott go to boarding school, but only a few weeks after arriving, he again fell ill. "During my Latin lesson, without the slightest warning," he told his father, "I had a bad rush of blood to my head it hurt me so that I can't remember what happened. I believe I screamed out." The boarding school experiment ended two months later when he "fainted just after leaving the table and fell down." Teedie was sent to St. Paul's to bring him home. Believing that a vigorous physical regimen would help, Thee sent his son to an Army post in Texas that built up his body but did little to cure his nervous disorder.

Meanwhile, Teedie's systematic effort to prepare himself for Harvard paid off. "Is it not splendid about my examinations," he triumphantly wrote Bamie. "I passed well on all the eight subjects I tried." If he was intellectually prepared for college, however, he lacked the social skills of many of his fellow students. Years of ill health and home schooling had isolated him from regular contact with boys and girls outside his family circle. He entered Harvard at scarcely five feet eight inches tall and only 130 pounds, "a slender nervous young man with side-whiskers, eyeglasses, and bright red cheeks." While Will Taft's sturdy physique, genial disposition, and empathetic manner won immediate popularity at Yale, Theodore Roosevelt took longer to establish a core group of friends at Harvard. He worried initially about the "antecedents" of the people he met, maintaining distance from classmates until he could determine whether their families shared the Roosevelts' station in life.

One contemporary remembers him as "studious, ambitious, eccentric—not the sort to appeal at first." He filled the shelves in his room with snakes and lizards, stuffed birds and animals; the smell of formaldehyde followed him from one class to the next. At a time when indifference toward one's studies was in vogue, Theodore was blatantly enthusiastic. "It was not often that any student broke in upon the smoothly flowing current" of their professors' lectures, one classmate recalled, "but Roosevelt did this again and again," posing questions and requesting clarification until finally one professor cut him short. "Now look here, Roosevelt, let me talk. I'm running this course." He also had a curious habit of dropping into classmates' rooms for conversation; then, rather than joining in, he would retreat to a corner and immerse himself in a book as if seated alone on a tree stump in the middle of the forest. Furthermore, he scorned fellow students who drank or smoked.

"No man ever came to Harvard more serious in his purpose to secure first of all an education," recalled one classmate, Curtis Guild, Jr.; "he was forever at it, and probably no man of his time read more extensively or deeply, especially in directions that did not count on the honor-list or marking-sheet." Whereas Taft discouraged the young Yale student from extracurricular reading, fearful it would detract from required courses, Roosevelt read widely yet managed to stand near the top of his class. The breadth of his numerous interests allowed him to draw on knowledge across various disciplines, from zoology to philosophy and religion, from poetry and drama to history and politics.

"My library has been the greatest possible pleasure to me," he wrote to his parents during his freshman year, "as whenever I have any spare time I can immediately take up a book. Aunt Annie's present, the 'History of the Civil War,' is extremely interesting." From early childhood, he had regarded books as "the greatest of companions." And once encountered, they were never forgotten. Much later, greeting a Chinese delegation when he was president, he suddenly remembered a book about China read many years before. "As I talked the pages of the book came before my eyes," he said, "and it seemed as though I were able to read the things therein contained." Taft was continually amazed at how Roosevelt found time to read, snatching moments while waiting for lunch or his next appointment. "He always carried a book with him to the Executive Office," Taft noted, "and although there were but few intervals during the business hours, he made the most of them in his reading." Charles Washburn, a classmate at Harvard, considered Roosevelt's ability to concentrate a signal ingredient to his success. "If he were reading," observed Washburn with astonishment, "the house might fall about his head, he could not be diverted."

The habits of mind Roosevelt developed early in his academic career would serve him well throughout his life. As soon as he received an assignment for a paper or project, he would set to work, never leaving anything to the last minute. Preparing so far ahead "freed his mind" from worry and facilitated fresh, lucid thought. During the last months of his presidency, aware that he was committed to speak at Oxford University following his yearlong expedition to Africa, he finished a complete draft of his lengthy address. "I never knew a man who worked as far in advance of what was to be done," marveled Taft. "Perhaps I value this virtue more highly because I lack it myself."

While posting honor grades each semester, Roosevelt cultivated a boggling array of social activities. He persevered in the promise to "*make my body*," exercising rigorously day after day. He spent hours in the gym vaulting and lifting weights. He competed for the lightweight cup in boxing and wrestling, rowed on the Charles River, played strenuous games of lawn tennis, and ran three or four miles a day. Like his father, he pursued his chosen pastimes with the same zeal he devoted to his work. He organized a whist club and a finance club at which William Graham Sumner appeared; he wrote for *The Advocate*, joined the rifle club and the arts club, taught Sunday school, and took a weekly dancing class. With his explosive energy "he danced just as you'd expect him to dance if you knew him," a contemporary recalled—"he hopped." And despite this overcharged agenda, he maintained his passionate interest in birds, watching and shooting them in the field during the days, stuffing and labeling them in his room at night.

"His college life broadened every interest," Corinne observed, "and did for him what had hitherto not been done, which was to give him confidence in his relationship with young men of his own age." If he lacked Will Taft's immediate charisma, gradually his classmates could not resist the spell of his highly original personality. "Funnily enough, I have enjoyed quite a burst of popularity," he told his mother after his election into several social clubs, including the Hasty Pudding Club, the D.K.E. Society, and the prestigious Porcellian Club.

Theodore's burgeoning self-assurance and involvement in the Harvard community came at a critical time. He would need all the resilience and support he could muster to cope with a shattering blow during his sophomore year when his forty-six-year-old father came down with a fatal illness. An intense love had continued to bind father and son while Teedie was in college. "As I saw the last of the train bearing you away the other day," Roosevelt had written his son after seeing him off for his freshman year, "I realized what a luxury it was to have a boy in whom I would place perfect trust and confidence who was leaving me to take his first independent position in the world." Teedie's reply reflected his own profound respect and devotion: "I do not think there is a fellow in College who has a family that love him as much as you all do me, and I am *sure* that there is no one who has a Father who is also his best and most intimate friend, as you are mine." With unabashed affection, Teedie addressed his frequent letters to his "darling father" or his "dearest father," and Thee returned the tenderness in kind.

Two months before Roosevelt Senior was taken ill, he had been nominated by President Rutherford Hayes to replace incumbent Chester A. Arthur as

Collector of Customs for the Port of New York. His nomination was seen as a triumph for civil service reformers over New York senator Roscoe Conkling, who had run the port as his special fiefdom for years. The distinguished position required the approval of the U.S. Senate, however, where a fierce battle raged for weeks between the reform element of the Republican Party, represented by Hayes and Roosevelt, and the machine politicians, represented by Conkling and Arthur. In the end, the machine politicians won. The Senate rejected Roosevelt's nomination, insisting instead on the reappointment of Arthur. "The machine politicians have shown their color," a disappointed Thee wrote Teedie. "I fear for your future. We cannot stand so corrupt a government for any great length of time."

Six days after his rejection by the Senate, Theodore Senior collapsed. Doctors diagnosed an advanced stage of bowel cancer. Over Christmas vacation, when Teedie was home, his father seemed "very much better," sparking the false hope that he was beginning to recover. As Teedie was leaving to return to Harvard, he had a conversation with him that he would long remember: "Today he told me I had never caused him a moments pain. I should be less than human if I ever had, for he is the best, wisest and most loving of men, the type of all that is noble, brave, wise & good."

The final days of the forty-six-year-old Thee's two-month bout with cancer produced excruciating pain. His groans reverberated through the house and his dark hair turned gray. Elliott stayed by his father's side, ready to bring a handkerchief drenched in ether to his face. But when he screamed, neither the ether nor the sedatives could still the pain, and the fear in his father's eyes was terrible for the sixteen-year-old boy to behold.

On Saturday, February 9, 1878, the family, who had shielded Teedie from the worsening situation, sent an urgent message for him to come home. He raced to catch the overnight train, but reached New York on Sunday morning to find his father had died late Saturday night. His grief was "doubly bitter," he wrote. "I was away in Boston when the man I loved dearest on earth died." Remembering how his father's devoted strength had comforted him throughout the worst of his childhood attacks, he was filled with unbearable remorse: "I never was able to do anything for him during his last illness."

"The death of Mr. Roosevelt was a public loss," stated the *New York Times*. "Flags flew at half-mast all over the city," reported Jacob Riis. "Rich and poor followed him to the grave, and the children whose friend he had been wept over him." Newsboys from the lodging house, orphans for whom he had found homes, and Italian girls he had taught in Sunday school all grieved for their kind benefactor. "There was truly no end to a life that had been devoted to such philanthropy," Reverend William Adams declared at his funeral, "for the work he had laid out would remain and grow in power long after his death."

"He has just been buried," Theodore wrote in his diary. "I felt as if I had been stunned, or as if part of my life had been taken away; and the two moments of sharp, bitter agony, when I kissed the dear, dead face and realized he would never again on this earth speak to me or greet me with his loving smile, and then when I heard the sound of the first clod dropping on the coffin. . . . " Ten days later, back at Harvard, his loss still struck him "like a hideous dream." Semi-annual examinations offered some distraction to get through the days, but the restless nights were filled with misery. "It has been a most fortunate thing for me that I have had so much to do," he wrote in his diary. "If I had very much time to think I believe I should almost go crazy." He was grateful for the small margin of relief his insular college world offered, realizing that his mother and siblings had nothing to assuage their grief.

Returning home to Oyster Bay that summer was difficult, for "every nook and corner about the place, every piece of furniture about the house is in some manner connected with him." Only frenzied activity managed to keep his sorrow at bay. In late June, however, Theodore confided to his diary a surprising recognition of his own character: "Am leading the most intensely happy & healthy, out of doors life & spending my time riding on horseback, making long tramps through woods and fields after specimens, or else on the bay rowing or sailing—generally in a half naked condition and with my gun along. I could not be happier, except at those bitter moments when I realize what I have lost. Father was himself so invariably cheerful that I feel it would be wrong for me to be gloomy, and besides, fortunately or unfortunately, I am of a very buoyant temper being a bit of an optimist." Nevertheless, the young man remained painfully aware of the magnitude of his loss. His father had been "the only human being to whom I told *everything*," he wrote. "Never failing to get loving advice and sweet sympathy in return; no one but my wife, if ever I marry, will ever be able to take his place."

Perhaps this fundamental loneliness contributed to Theodore's ardent pursuit of seventeen-year-old Alice Hathaway Lee during his junior year at Harvard. He later claimed that when they first met at the home of his college friend, Richard Saltonstall, "it was a real case of love at first sight—and my first love too." Like the first flush of his father's infatuation with Mittie, it seemed as if Theodore's passion for Alice far exceeded his genuine knowledge of her. While his diary is rife with descriptions of her bewitching beauty, scant space is devoted to shared sympathies or interests that might lead to lasting companionship. Within four weeks of their introduction, he vowed "to win her." Seven months later, when he was only twenty, he proposed and initially, she rejected him. He was undeterred.

The campaign he launched to gain Alice's love necessitated a full-blown battle plan. Theodore later told a friend he "made everything subordinate to winning her." Weekend after weekend, he rode his horse six miles to her country home in Chestnut Hill. He took her sledding and skating, read to her, accompanied her on long walks in the woods, and escorted her to dances. He worked to ingratiate himself with her parents and mesmerized her young brother with exciting tales of adventure. Meanwhile, he made every attempt to integrate her into his sphere, introducing her to his friends at the Porcellian and inviting her to join his family for a round of parties in New York. Still, she hesitated to make a commitment at such a young age. Only in the privacy of his diary did young Theodore acknowledge "the tortures" he was suffering. His wooing of Alice had the aspect of an epic quest in which he was the hero, a crusade in which he would succeed or die. "I have hardly had one good night to rest and night after night I have not even gone to bed. I have been pretty nearly crazy over my wayward, wilfull darling."

Finally, in late January of his senior year, she agreed to become his wife, and they set a wedding date for the following autumn. "I am so happy that I dare not trust in my own happiness," he wrote. "I do not believe any man ever loved a woman more than I love her." Captivated by his first love, he believed there was "nothing on earth left to wish for."

Despite the absorption in his engagement, Theodore continued to wrestle and box. He joined a hunting expedition in Maine and had a "royally good time" with his club mates. He completed a thesis on "Equalizing Men and Women Before the Law" that shared the same progressive attitude toward women as Will Taft's senior essay. "As regards the laws relating to marriage there should be the most absolute equality preserved between the two sexes," Theodore wrote. "I do not think the woman should assume the man's name . . . I would have the word 'obey' used not more by the wife than by the husband." Unlike young Taft, however, he was not ready to recommend women's suffrage.

Nor did he neglect his regular class work, applying himself sufficiently to graduate magna cum laude and Phi Beta Kappa, twenty-first in a class that opened with 230 students. Still dividing his classmates according to their family's standing, he boasted that "only one gentleman stands ahead of me." As he approached graduation, he reflected on his college years with self-satisfaction. "I have certainly lived like a prince," he wrote in his diary. "I have had just as much money as I could spend; belonged to the Porcellian Club; have had some capital hunting trips; my life has been varied; I have kept a good horse and cart; I have had half a dozen good and true friends in college, and several very pleasant families outside; a lovely home . . . and to crown all infinitely above everything else put together—I have won the sweetest of girls for my wife. No man ever had so pleasant a college course."

The prospect of marriage altered his long-cherished plan to become a naturalist, a career that would require years of study abroad and was unlikely to provide a substantial income. Instead, he decided to enter Columbia Law School, vowing to "do my best, and work hard for my own little wife."

From that point on, as Carleton Putnam writes, "Natural history was to remain a genuine avocation, but it never loomed again as a feasible career."

By the age of twenty-one, Theodore had known, in his own words, "great sorrow and great joy," and while he believed "the joy has far overbalanced the sorrow," his early suffering had deepened his self-knowledge, intensified his powers of concentration, and heightened his sensibilities.

Both Will and Teedie had the good fortune of growing up as favored children in close-knit, illustrious families where affection and respect abounded. Both inherited from their fathers legacies of honorable and distinguished careers, as well as a commitment to public service and a dedication to the Republican Party. Where Will developed an accommodating disposition to please a living father who cajoled him to do more and do better, Teedie forever idolized a dead father who had paid for a substitute for himself during the Civil War to placate his wife, yet had fostered military and historical tales of heroism in his beloved son.

Will had the stronger physical endowment but the weaker self-control; Teedie the weaker body but the greater strength of will. The enormously powerful Will abused his physical gift; the smaller Teedie, a heroic compensator, toughened and transformed his body. Will tended to stay indoors; Teedie tested himself outdoors, against nature. Taft was easygoing and even-tempered; Roosevelt perpetually in motion, as if to keep self-inquiry at bay.

Will, by temperament warmer and more sociable than Teedie, found common ground with one and all; others instinctively responded to his smiling countenance and kindly demeanor. Teedie was less approachable at first blush, limiting his associations to those who shared his class and station in life.

Where Teedie was an intellectual adventurer with a passion for reading and a wide-ranging curiosity engendered by a broad set of experiences, Will worked methodically, within the defined frameworks outlined by his instructors. The one was self-assured, guided by his own ferocious determination; the other more subject to the entreaties of others, steering his course out of the desire to please. Will was more modest and straightforward; Teedie more boastful and complex. Common to both was a sober good sense and a willingness to work hard that led to high distinction in college and the promise of success as they looked forward to law school.

If there are splendid traits in abundance in the characters of both young men, the one major distinction at this stage is that Teedie had shown he could come through agonizing misfortune. Will had not yet been tested by adversity.

CHAPTER THREE

The Judge and the Politician

Will Taft, rising Cincinnati attorney, in the early 1880s.

FOR WILLIAM HOWARD TAFT, LAW school fortified his life's ambition to become a judge, fixing upon him "a judicial habit of thought and action" that marked the rest of his life as he moved from the bench to the far less congenial world of politics. For Theodore Roosevelt, the study of law merely facilitated his diverse ventures as historian, assemblyman, rancher, civil service commissioner, police commissioner, assistant secretary of the Navy, soldier, governor, and vice president. Each experience would eventually contribute vitally to a memorable presidency.

Cincinnati Law School, where Taft matriculated in 1878, was among the oldest in the country. Situated at that time in the Mercantile Library Building at the city center, it remained an "old style" institution untouched by the modern case method of instruction introduced at Harvard earlier in the decade. While Taft might easily have gained admission to Harvard or Yale, he chose to return to his hometown, to be enveloped by the warmth of his close-knit family. His brothers Charley and Peter were practicing law in his father's firm; Harry was a student at Yale; Horace a senior at Woodward High; and Fanny was still a girl at thirteen. Furthermore, Will's best friend and Yale classmate, Howard Hollister, entered Cincinnati Law in the same class.

For two hours every day, Taft and sixty-six fellow students listened to professors expound broad legal principles derived from standard texts. The curriculum, far less demanding than his courses at Yale, allowed students to work as well as study. Although most law students gained their first practical experience apprenticing in law offices, Taft decided he could learn "more about the workings of the law" as a court reporter for Murat Halstead's local newspaper, the *Cincinnati Commercial*. Once his morning lectures were completed, he began his rounds to the police court, the probate court, the district court, and the superior court. At each venue, he took notes, listed the cases on the various dockets each day, and wrote up short accounts of the half-dozen most compelling cases.

Readers of "The Courts" column followed the cases of a husband suing for divorce after discovering his wife had two husbands; a buxom woman ensnared by a livery-stable keeper who failed to reveal that he suffered from a contagious private disease; a husband alleging that his wife had "struck and scratched him in a vicious manner" and had so ill-treated their children that their lives were endangered. He chronicled criminal trials for larceny, domestic abuse, and assault and battery and followed malpractice suits, contested wills, bastardy cases, contract disputes, and mortgage foreclosures. He wrote in a clear, straightforward style, emphasizing the facts of the cases without embellishment. Usually, he managed to complete these accounts before dinner, allowing him time to relax in the evenings.

In his early twenties, Will found himself the center of a lively set of young friends, enjoying to the fullest the wealth of social activities Cincinnati provided. With a population of 250,000, the "Queen City" had come of age in the 1870s, boasting an array of cultural events that included classical music, opera festivals, theatrical performances, literary societies, and art exhibits. "Washington will remain our political and New York our commercial capital," Murat Halstead predicted in 1878, but cosmopolitan Cincinnati would become "the social center and musical metropolis of America."

Will Taft cut quite a figure in this bustling society: "large, handsome and fair, with the build of a Hercules and the sunny disposition of an innocent child," one local newspaper described him. Women were drawn by his open engaging manner and he, in turn, was completely at ease conversing with them. He listened sympathetically to their concerns, valued their intelligence, and displayed an unself-conscious candor. At dancing parties he sparkled, surprisingly light on his feet. He and his compatriots enjoyed picnics on the Ohio River, sledding parties, debutante balls, nights at the theatre, whist parties, tennis matches, baseball games, and songfests at the beer gardens in "Over-the-Rhine," the German section.

With growing apprehension, Alphonso observed his son's diversions, convinced that without the structured environment that had compelled diligence at Yale, Will was simply marking time. Tensions between father and son only grew when Will went to work in his father's office in the summer of 1879 between his first two years in law school. In late June, Will departed for several days to visit one of his college friends in Cleveland. In his absence, a woman sought legal help in a small case involving the destruction of $300 worth of property. Seeing this as "a capital opportunity" for Will to handle a jury trial with several witnesses to be sworn, Alphonso sent him a letter requesting his immediate return. "I had the case laid over to next Saturday so that you might prepare & try it," he told his son. "I shall be sorry to have you lose it."

The next day, Alphonso wrote again, venting his irritation. Will should disregard the previous letter, for he had "agreed on a settlement of the case . . . a thing which you cd. have done if you had been here, & carried a nice little fee for yourself." Alphonso's exasperation and disappointment were clear. "This gratifying your fondness for society is fruitless," he admonished. "I like to have you enjoy yourself, so far as it can be consistent with your success in life. But you will have to be on alert for business, and for influence among men, if you would hope to accomplish success." Alphonso had not exhausted his censure, for yet a third letter followed the next day. "I do not think you shd make arrangements for a second visit at Cleveland, or for anything, but close application to study and business. There is no day in wk. you will not have as much as you are able to do. You must acquire a mastery of the German Language, as well as of the law and you should be forming valuable business acquaintance, if not political. I do not think that you have accomplished as much this past year as you ought, with your opportunities. You must not feel that you have time enough to while a way with every friend who comes."

Alphonso worried too much. Will finished law school in good standing. Then, heeding his father's advice, he shuttered himself in the law office for the month leading up to the bar examination, combing the shelves of standard legal tomes. Will informed his friends that "he would not be seen in public again until after the tests." He easily passed and was admitted to the bar. His solid work as a court reporter for the *Cincinnati Commercial* had, meanwhile, earned Halstead's esteem and a full-time job offer at a salary of $1,500 a year. Although his calling was to the law rather than journalism, he remained on the newspaper staff through the summer and fall of 1879. There, his coverage of a dramatic embezzlement trial against Cy Hoffman, a Democratic auditor for the city, led to an unexpected opportunity.

Counsel for the defendant in the Hoffman case was the criminal attorney Thomas C. Campbell, head of a political ring said to have dug "its talons deep in the judiciary." Campbell reputedly owned court officers, regularly bribed witnesses and juries, and "was able to secure any verdict" he desired. The Hoffman case took "a sensational turn" when Miller Outcault, the assistant prosecuting attorney, charged that his chief prosecutor, Samuel Drew, had conspired with the unscrupulous Campbell to fix the jury and assure Hoffman's acquittal.

For the idealistic young Taft, the picture of judicial corruption was deeply disturbing. He later acknowledged that he "fell in" with Miller Outcault, providing reports that aided his efforts to expose both the chief prosecutor and the disreputable attorney. The *Cincinnati Commercial* stories about the dramatic proceedings created widespread interest in the case. Large crowds packed the courthouse, spectators "standing upon the railing, desks and chairs" as day after day, Outcault leveled a "nasty torrent of abuse" against both Campbell and his boss. After two weeks of "the bitterest invective" from all parties in this singular "three-cornered fight," the judge was compelled to dismiss prosecutor Drew from the case. Proceedings were suspended until the district court sustained the judge's action. The jury finally received the case but could not reach an agreement; a mistrial was declared.

When Outcault replaced Drew as prosecuting attorney, he offered the post of assistant prosecuting attorney to Will Taft, who had just passed his twenty-third birthday. Nellie Taft later declared that "the experience he had in the rough-and-ready practice in criminal trials, in preparing cases for trial, in examining witnesses, in making arguments to the court and in summing up to the jury, was the most valuable experience he could possibly have in fitting him for trial work at the bar." He prepared indictments for grand juries; he took depositions, interviewed witnesses, and independently conducted a number of criminal trials, including a dramatic murder case. After only four months on the job, Will opened the prosecution's case in the state's second attempt to put the city auditor Cy Hoffman behind bars. Once again, the celebrated criminal defense lawyer Tom Campbell defended Hoffman; once again Campbell secured a hung jury, and suspicions of jury tampering abounded.

Considering the marked contrast of disposition between Taft and Roosevelt, Henry Pringle speculates that "a Theodore Roosevelt might have won renown, glory and headlines in this post of assistant district attorney." He might have publicly pledged to root out the corrupt dealings between officers of the court and the city's political machine, but Will Taft "was no showman, nor was he, to the same extent, personally or politically ambitious." He valued the post solely as a vital contribution to his legal education. "He was on his legs day after day before judge and jury," Horace recalled, and consequently "became so expert in regard to the laws of evidence as to surprise the older lawyers when he mounted the bench."

Although he harbored no political ambitions for himself, Taft took an active role in local Republican politics. During his father's race for governor, he canvassed the city in search of delegates to the state convention and remained involved from that point forward. "I attended all the primaries and all the conventions," he later recalled, "and attempted to do what I could to secure respectable nominees for the party, especially for judicial places." He worked in his ward to defeat disreputable machine candidates "by hustling around among good people to get them out." He never hesitated to attack "the gang methods" whenever he witnessed corruption at the polls, but while attacking their methods, he always stayed "on good terms" with all the various factions. His amiability and reluctance to hold a grudge made him, in the estimation of Republican congressman Benjamin Butterworth, "the most popular young man in Hamilton County."

Beneath Will's benign nature, however, lay a sharp temper, especially where his family's honor was concerned. A weekly tabloid published an anonymous letter ridiculing Alphonso, along with the insidious suggestion that Louise Taft herself had authored the attack. Determined to seek revenge for this slander against both his parents, Will sought out the tabloid's editor, Lester A. Rose. Charley cautioned restraint since Rose "was known to be a bruiser of considerable physical courage and great endurance." Undaunted, Will confronted Rose on a street corner and administered what the newspapers termed a "terrible beating." He reportedly "lifted him up and dashed him to the pavement," executing continuous blows and hammering the man's head against the ground until Rose promised to leave town that very night. The story of the thrashing made news across the country. "The feeling among all classes of citizens," observed the *Bismarck Tribune*, "is that Mr. Taft did a public service and ought to have a medal."

At his father's urging, Will began stumping for Republican candidates in his county. "I want him to accustom himself to speaking from the beginning," Alphonso told Delia Torrey, explaining that as a lawyer, "he is to make speaking a business, & he should do it well." Will was sick with anxiety before his maiden political speech, aghast to see his name, the Hon. William H. Taft, plastered on posters throughout the city. "Don't allow yourself to be discouraged," his father urged him. "It is a great undertaking, but it is the best thing that can happen to you. . . . It will be worth a fortune to you if you can conquer the difficulties & speak well in public. I know it is hard work to get adequate preparation. . . . You will find it difficult to commit literally a long speech. I do not attempt it. You will have your memory helped by notes of the points." Will followed his father's advice, and the speech, which he delivered three times in three different venues, went well. "He finds the farmers make attentive listeners, and he is not embarrassed," Louise noted. "There is every prospect that he will be a first class speaker," Alphonso wishfully predicted, "and a first class lawyer, too."

In January 1882, Taft's popularity with the discordant factions of the Republican Party led Congressman Butterworth to recommend him to President Chester Arthur as Collector of Internal Revenue for the Cincinnati District. The sitting collector, affiliated with a coalition considered unfriendly to the president, had been dismissed. His removal threatened to escalate political strife unless a replacement was found who could mollify all sides. "If you will appoint Will Taft to this important position, everybody will be satisfied," Butterworth told President Arthur. Taft's mother opposed the idea. "I did not wish Will to go into politics," she said. "I wished him to engage in nothing not in the line of his profession." His father, too, questioned the appointment, fearing that Taft was "too young" to lead a staff of more than a hundred employees in the task of collecting over $10 million from the sales of whiskey and tobacco.

Taft later acknowledged that he was offered the post, making him the youngest collector in the country, predominantly because he "had no political enemies." It is likely that this decision to interrupt his emerging legal career was less a function of ambition than of desire to satisfy Congressman Butterworth and President Arthur. Indeed, this unwillingness to disappoint others would continue to shape the course of his professional life. While Taft possessed a highly developed social intelligence, he was less discerning of his own strengths and weaknesses.

Still, it did not take him long to realize that the work was decidedly ill-suited to his temperament. He detested the prominence of the position and could not bear the criticism that inevitably came with the job, acknowledging years later that he was too "thin-skinned" for "public life." Moreover, his moderate reformist tendencies were at odds with the prevailing customs of the day. At a time when civil service reform was still in its infancy, when political patronage, rather than merit, filled the majority of positions, government employees were expected to contribute part of their salaries to the party in power. Horace recalled that when the local Republican Party circulated a subscription list demanding money from each of the department employees, Taft made a contribution in his own name "but announced that he would not look at the subscriptions made by any of his employees." Ruffled party members charged that "he was wrecking the party by the course he followed."

Taft's troubles multiplied during a bitter contest for the congressional nomination in the Second District between Governor Tom Young and Amor Smith. Young sent a letter to Taft demanding the removal of a number of men in the Revenue Department who he claimed were allied with his opponent. Taft refused, resenting the "bulldozer" tone of the letter. The half-dozen men whose removal the governor demanded, he countered, "are among the best men in this District in the energy, skill and faithfulness with which they discharge their duties. If removed they must be simply and solely removed because they would prefer Amor Smith's nomination to yours." As for Young's implied threat to involve President Arthur in the situation, Taft argued that "the popularity of the present Administration in this county has been strengthened by the fidelity with which we have tried to follow the President's moderate course in National Affairs in regard to Civil Service."

In a letter to his father, Taft defiantly declared: "I would much rather resign and let some one else do Tom Young's service and dirty work." In an effort to avoid public dissension, he decided to write to the president directly. "The men whose removal he seeks," Taft told the president, "are such men as practical and conscientious politicians delight to find, men of political power and of ability to discharge their official duties." He promised President Arthur that these employees supported the administration; they simply preferred Smith to Young. Although Governor Young eventually backed down, the disagreeable conflict intensified Taft's desire to resume the practice of law. "I long to get out of politics," he told his father in October 1882, "and get down to business." A month later, after less than a year on the job, he journeyed to Washington and asked the president to accept his resignation. "I am mighty glad he is going to resign," Horace told his mother. With clear admiration for his older brother, he added: "I'll bet one thing & that is they won't get a man in that place very soon who knows more about the law & business of the office than he does or who abstains more carefully from the dirty parts of politics. Will makes fun of me for being so radical theoretical & impractical in my opinions but when it comes to the point I think he is a thorough Civil Service Reformer in practice."

Palpably relieved to be free of political discord, Taft penned a long letter to his father, who was then enjoying a pleasant stint in Vienna as the American foreign minister to Austria-Hungary at the behest of President Arthur. Will happily reported his intent to go into partnership with his father's former law partner, Major Harlan Page Lloyd, a widely respected figure in Cincinnati. "It is the opening of what I hope will be my life's work," he said. "Of course I shall have to work hard but that will agree with me and I shall have that sweetest of all pleasures the feeling of something accomplished, something done in the life that I have marked out for myself." It was a rare moment of insight into his own feelings and desires. Alphonso was gratified to hear that his son was leaving politics "to work at the law, with all his might," he told Charley. "That is his destiny."

By early 1883, Taft was settled in his new job. Charley's wife Annie believed that since leaving the politically embroiled revenue department Will looked "younger by several years." In January, Taft wrote his sister Fanny with evident satisfaction: "I wish you could look in on me now, seated in my cozy library with a cheerful soft coal fire and lots of easy chairs with the familiar old pictures looking down on me from every wall." That summer, he planned to take his first trip abroad to visit his parents. "I hope you will make yourselves comfortable and elegant even if it is a little expensive," he teased them. "You're off on a lark and we are willing to extend your allowance a little to insure your having a good time." But after three months in Europe he was "glad to get home" and resume his law practice. "Will is working well & seems very happy," Major Lloyd reported to Alphonso.

Will and Horace roomed together on the west side of Broadway when Horace, after graduating from Yale, also returned to Cincinnati to study law. Tall, spare, with a refreshing sense of humor, Horace relished politics more than his brother did and would become a fervent advocate for reform. Horace "makes friends wherever he goes," Will reported to his sister, "because his honest good nature and straight forward character shines out of him."

Will also confided in Fanny his hope that his own law practice would "grow large enough in some years to warrant my making an ass of myself in regard to some girl." By his twenty-fifth birthday, however, he confessed that he was "no nearer matrimony than I was when I first went into society. In the loneliness that I sometimes feel stealing over me, the temptation in that direction is strong but with no object to satisfy the feeling, the thought passes like many other castles in the air."

If Will felt he lacked the proper foundation to marry, he was certainly entertaining eligible candidates. When the Opera Festival came to Cincinnati during the first week in February, Taft reported to his mother and sister that he was planning to take a different girl each evening: Nellie Herron on Monday night, Edith Harrison on Tuesday, Miss Lawson on Wednesday, Miss Tomlin on Thursday, Alice Keys on Saturday afternoon, and Agnes Davis on Saturday night. "I see Father shake his head when he reads this list and hear him say that a thorough knowledge of the law is not obtained in that way."

THE REVIVAL OF TAFT'S LEGAL career reignited a clash with his old nemesis: Tom Campbell. A wave of ghastly murders in 1883, including a husband and wife killed for the $30 their bodies would be worth to a dissection class at the medical school, had created panic throughout Cincinnati. And amid this widespread anxiety, a particularly vicious killing of a liveryman on Christmas Eve of 1883 set in motion "a series of events that shook the foundation of Cincinnati."

The prosecution charged that seventeen-year-old William Berner and an accomplice had robbed and killed their employer, William Kirk, by beating him savagely on the head with a blacksmith's hammer and club. They hid the body in a covered wagon, fled with $345, and enjoyed a night of revelry in numerous saloons. When the victim's body was discovered, the pockets of his jacket "were filled with Christmas presents he was taking home to his family." Evidence implicated Berner, who confessed six times to six different people, detailing the planning and execution of the "cold-blooded butchery." Before the trial commenced, Berner, in order to avoid hanging, agreed "to plead guilty to murder in the second degree." The prosecution refused, certain that the evidence for first-degree murder "was absolute and unquestioned," and that the heinous nature of the crime deserved punishment by death.

Tom Campbell was enticed to defend Berner with the hefty fee of $5,000, offered by the father of the accused young man. It proved a sage investment; with the powerfully connected Campbell leading the defense, the jury delivered a shocking verdict. After deliberating but twenty-four hours, they rejected both the first- and second-degree murder charges, finding Berner guilty only of murder in the third degree. Cincinnati residents were stunned and outraged, convinced that the father of the murderer had purchased the verdict through a cunning lawyer who had corrupted the jury. While not the first miscarriage of justice that Cincinnati had witnessed, it was certainly the most infamous.

"The people of Cincinnati are abundantly warned that the law furnishes no protection to life," declared the *Cincinnati Commercial Gazette*. "Justice," the *New York Times* reported, "was poisoned at its source. The peace and safety of society were betrayed by the agency chosen to defend them. It is a terrible fact . . . that money outweighs human life and that the land of the law is palsied by bribes." A number of papers grimly noted that the lower courts in too many cities across the country had "become the mere agents of unscrupulous attorneys, who dictate acquittals or convictions at will. So scandalous and notorious has it become that lawyers now openly boast that they own this or that court."

A mass meeting was held at the Music Hall on March 29, 1884, to protest both the verdict and the corrupting influence of the Campbell organization. Speakers addressed the crowd, and a committee was formed to revise the rules governing the selection of juries. The proceedings were repeatedly interrupted by outbursts of "Hang the jury!," "Hang Tom Campbell!," "Hang Berner!," and a large "boisterous element remained" after the meeting adjourned.

After some excited deliberation, they thronged to the jail, determined to find Berner and deliver by lynching the justice denied by the court. Gathering strength on every corner, the crowd grew to nearly 1,000 by the time it reached the jail. There the mob divided into three groups. The first division stormed the courthouse, ran through the tunnel leading to the jail, and managed to break through the heavy iron doors at the end of the tunnel. The second group shattered the south windows and demolished the chapel on the way to the rotunda. With a heavy ram, the third group battered down the iron entrance to the jail and raced up a winding stairway to reach the cells. But Berner was nowhere to be found; for his safety, he had already been transferred to another jail. In their fury, the mob set the courthouse ablaze.

Order was finally restored with the arrival of the police and the state militia, but in the course of the struggle, forty-five men were killed and more than a hundred injured. Many thousands of dollars of property was lost. The *New York Times* declared it "the bloodiest affair that ever occurred in Cincinnati."

A few weeks later, a grand jury brought an indictment against Tom Campbell for bribing several of the jurors. Taft rightly surmised that it would be impossible "to obtain testimony because the only witnesses of Campbell's rascalities are men who were as deeply implicated in them as he was." Campbell chose for his counsel Joseph Foraker, a rising political ally, and was acquitted by a jury unable to reach a verdict. Taft complained to his father that Foraker had "conducted the defense in a most shystering and ungentlemanly way." In the future, he pledged, "I shall do everything I can against Foraker in every political fight."

The Cincinnati Bar Association, meanwhile, decided to create a committee to prepare sufficient evidence for a disbarment suit against Campbell in the district court. Taft was chosen by the senior members of the bar to serve as junior counsel for the nine-person committee. This appointment, Horace noted years later, "was an extraordinary honor, considering his youth, and was not to be accounted for by smiling good nature." Alphonso worried about the consequences of a direct collision with Campbell and the insidious forces behind him, fearing even for his son's physical safety. Will, however, relished the chance to confront the man who had "thrown the bar of Hamilton County into disrepute." He stridently announced to his father that it was time "for men to have backbone and drive away the scourge that has been such an infliction on this community for so many years. Those who tamely cower in the face of attack I have no use for. I have gone into this thing fully realizing the dangerous enemy we have to encounter."

The committee presented its findings before the district court in July 1884, and a trial date was set for November. Horace proudly recalled that his brother was instrumental in building the case for senior members of the committee. Will had traveled throughout Ohio compiling evidence and interviewing witnesses to document a pattern of disreputable behavior that had persisted for years. While his law practice suffered and his father feared that Campbell's stranglehold on the judicial system would make "a thankless task" of all his endeavors, Will found the work exhilarating.

The intensity of his pursuit drained young Taft of any remnant of zeal for political campaigning. "I find that the Campbell case has robbed politics of any interest for me," he told his father at the start of the 1884 presidential race between Republican James Blaine and Democrat Grover Cleveland. "If I can assist to get rid of Campbell, I think that I shall have accomplished a much greater good than by yelling myself hoarse for Blaine."

As the election neared, however, he succumbed to pressure from Congressman Butterworth and agreed to serve as chief supervisor of elections in the city. He was charged with organizing forces to man the polling places, where intimidation and fraud were rampant, repeat voters numbered in the thousands, and hundreds of men "voted the cemetery." Taft had done his job well. Republicans carried the city and the state, though Cleveland won the presidential election. "Your son Will did splendid service in the campaign," Butterworth informed Alphonso. "He is a magnificent fellow. If he has a flaw in him I don't know where it is. He is not only brainy, but brave, honorable and honest." Despite such accolades, the political world held little appeal for Taft. "This is my last election experience I hope for some years to come," he told his mother.

Campbell's disbarment trial opened before three district court judges on

November 6, 1884, two days after the election. "The investigation," Taft explained to his father, would undertake "to prove acts at the different periods of [Campbell's] professional career to show a consistent course of unprofessional conduct down to the present time." Taft sat beside the senior attorneys who argued the case, providing documents, facts, and affidavits. The trial continued through December, with closing arguments slated for January 5, 1885.

On that crucial day, the senior attorney scheduled to present the prosecution's closing summary fell ill, and William Taft was selected to take his place, "suddenly emerging from obscurity," as Henry Pringle notes, " to play the part of a leading actor." He took the floor for four hours and ten minutes, revealing an absolute mastery of the complex case. Point by point, Taft enumerated the charges against Campbell, reviewing the evidence presented over the previous twenty days. Emphasizing that the members of the Cincinnati Bar Association were "actuated by no other motive than a desire that the profession should be purged of a man whose success in this community threatens every institution of justice that is dear to us or necessary to good governance," Taft offered a powerful concluding summary: "We have presented the case which we think calls for the action of your Honors in saying that the profession must be kept pure. We deny nothing to Mr. Campbell except integrity, and we say that that is the essential, the indispensable quality of a member of the Bar."

On the final day, Campbell took the stand, delivering an impassioned and eloquent plea on his own behalf. "There was not a vindictive word uttered, and one looked in vain for any of the characteristics or manner of speech of the Thos. C. Campbell of one year ago," the *Commercial Gazette* reported. "Tears were welling in his eyes, and there was a look of keen mental suffering upon his face," as he described the pain and humiliation endured "from the first filing of these charges to the present moment." He ascribed the "smoke of suspicion" that shadowed him largely to his active engagement in bitter political wranglings through the years in which "he had blindly made enemies who had multiplied." He acknowledged that "the public had been worked up to the highest pitch of feeling" during the Berner case and that his decision to defend Berner had cost him greatly. He closed with a sentimental flourish, directly impugning Taft as the assassin of his character: "Mr. Taft has said that the relators deny me nothing save integrity. That is like saying, let me wound you just once with a rapier, and I will be merciful and thrust you not through the arm or the leg, but through the heart. Integrity is to a man what chastity is to a woman. When that is gone, all is gone."

Taft anxiously waited week after week while the three judges deliberated. He believed both the reputation of the legal profession and the confidence of the public in the judicial system were at stake. Congressman Butterworth warned that "Tom Campbell controls one of the Judges absolutely and one of the others partially." Nonetheless, few were prepared for the stunning verdict, delivered on February 3, 1885, that exonerated Campbell of all charges save a minor one which merited no suspension from the bar. "It was disastrous and disgraceful," Taft reported to his father. "I am glad to say that this is the universal opinion." Indeed, Butterworth observed that "whatever may be said of the full, clear, complete, technical legal certainty, the moral proof is absolutely overwhelming that Campbell and his ring represent the social, moral, political, legal rot of Cincinnati."

"I am very glad now that I spoke," Taft told his father. "The labor was very great and it is discouraging to have such an ending," he avowed, but "the Public generally and the Bar are disposed to think that we tried the case as well as it could be tried." From his faraway perch in St. Petersburg, Russia, where he had been appointed a second ministerial job, Alphonso agreed. "I was very much pleased with your argument," he assured his son. "I think you must have a great majority of the community on your side; and you will find it will be remembered in your favor. You must not allow yourself to be discouraged by the folly and perverseness if not wickedness of men who have by some accident come into a little brief Authority."

As the weeks went by, Taft managed to recover a measure of optimism. "It is the beginning of an era of reform," he excitedly told his father. "The trial of his case has shorn [Campbell] of that veneer of respectability. . . . Everybody knows he was guilty. He and the Court have gone down together." He also reported a curious shift in his own perception of the matter and the man: "I can hardly explain to you the change in my feeling in regard to him. I have no personal animus toward him. He is no more to me than one of the thieves or bunks men whom I know. He hates me with a perfect hatred but I am indifferent to his feeling toward me."

Taft's satisfaction with his own performance in the case was certainly justified. And in an ironic turn of events, his involvement also aided his judicial ambitions. Taft's unlikely benefactor would be Campbell's ally, Joseph Foraker, who, much to Taft's disgust, became the Republican gubernatorial nominee several months after the trial. "I should not bow my head in tears," Taft confessed, "if the Democratic candidate defeated him." Despite Taft's grave reservations about the "double-faced Campbell man," Foraker won the election and was returned to the governor's office two years later.

In May 1887, during Foraker's second term, a vacancy arose in the Ohio Superior Court when Judge Judson Harmon decided to retire with fourteen months left on his elected term. To Taft's astonishment, Foraker offered to appoint him to fill the temporary vacancy until he could run for a full term. Considering Taft's manifest antipathy toward Foraker, Foraker's choice of a young man who was not yet thirty remains an enigma. In a memoir written after Taft became president, Foraker's wife, Julia, claims that an "instant sympathy" had developed between the two men when Taft, a cub reporter for the *Cincinnati Commercial*, covered cases over which her husband presided. "Foraker liked Taft's smile, liked his agreeable manner, liked his type of mind," she wrote. Foraker also recalled his own prescient respect for the young man after Taft had risen to eminence. Despite his youth, Foraker avowed, he "knew him well enough to know that he had a strong intellectual endowment, a keen, logical, analytical, legal mind, and that all the essential foundations for a good Judge had been well and securely laid."

Taft would surely have denied this "instant sympathy" with a man he roundly disliked. It is more likely that in appointing a young lawyer with Taft's reputation for honesty and sincerity, Foraker sought to mollify reformers who called for the restoration of integrity on the Ohio bench. The *Weekly Law Bulletin* praised the appointment, noting that despite a mere seven years before the bar, Taft was "a very bright young man, who already enjoys great popularity and personal respect." In a letter to Foraker, Taft acknowledged his profound appreciation. "Considering the opportunity so honorable a position offers to a man of my age and circumstances, my debt to you is very great," he wrote. "The responsibility you assume for me in making this appointment will always be a strong incentive to an industrious and conscientious discharge of my duties."

To Taft, who would become the youngest judge in the state of Ohio, this appointment represented "the welcome beginning of just the career he wanted." His work as court reporter, prosecuting attorney, litigator, and counsel for the Bar Association had prepared him well, giving him an intimate acquaintance with varied aspects of the law. The golden chance to sit on the superior court represented the establishment of a judicial career that would eventually lead, after a painful detour as president, to his ultimate destination—chief justice of the United States.

WHEN THEODORE ROOSEVELT TOOK UP the study of law, he was not sure where it would lead, nor whether he even wanted to be a lawyer. Foremost, he was about to be married and had a responsibility, despite the inheritance his father left him, to support his wife and family. Within two weeks of entering Columbia Law School on October 6, 1880, he acknowledged that he had his "hands full attending to various affairs." While mornings were spent in school, his afternoons and evenings were devoted to wedding arrangements. The marriage was scheduled to take place at Chestnut Hill on October 27, his twenty-second birthday. "It almost frightens me, in spite of my own happiness," he revealed in his diary, "to think that perhaps I may not make her happy; but I shall try so hard; and if ever a man love woman I love her."

The wedding was celebrated at noon on a balmy autumn day at the Unitarian church in Brookline before a large crowd, including Theodore's childhood friend Edith Carow. After a sumptuous reception at the Lee mansion, the young couple spent the night in a hotel suite and then headed to Oyster Bay. They remained two weeks at the family's country home, where their every need was attended to by a cook, maid, and groom. "Our intense happiness is too sacred to be written about," Roosevelt asserted in his diary, then proceeded to detail idyllic days spent driving their buggy, roaming through the woods and fields, playing "equally matched" lawn tennis, and reading poetry before blazing fires at night.

On November 17, Roosevelt resumed his law school classes. He set forth shortly after 7:30 a.m. from his mother's house on 57th Street, where he and Alice would spend the winter, to begin the three-mile walk to the four-story law building on Great Jones Street at the corner of Lafayette Place. At Columbia, as at Harvard, he stood out as "an energetic questioner of the lectures," his intensity provoking a mixture of resentment and admiration in his classmates. Though the pleasure he took in his studies is amply expressed in his journal, he was troubled that "some of the teaching of the law books and of the classroom seemed to me to be against justice." He noted critically that "we are concerned with [the] question of what law is, not what it ought to be." Nevertheless, more than 1,000 pages of handwritten notes during his two years of study testify to his diligence, and he impressed professors with his amazingly deft grasp of materials.

During his first year in law school, Roosevelt assumed several positions formerly held by his father on the boards of charitable organizations. Hopeful this philanthropic work might prove fulfilling, he found himself ill-suited to follow in his father's footsteps. "I tried faithfully to do what father had done," he confessed to his reporter friend, Jacob Riis, "but I did it poorly. . . . [I] joined this and that committee. Father had done good work on so many; but in the end I found out that we have each to work in his own way to do our best." Despite his relative youth, Roosevelt demonstrated a confidence and clear-minded assessment of his own interests and capabilities, making him far more successful than Taft in refusing endeavors he found uncongenial.

During this hectic phase of his life, Roosevelt even managed to try his hand as an author. As a senior at Harvard, he had embarked on a project that would become his first published work, *The Naval War of 1812*. His interest in the war had been sparked by a volume in the Porcellian Club library by the reigning British authority on the subject, William James. Angered by the biased, boastful approach of the author, who appeared "afflicted with a hatred toward the Americans," Roosevelt searched out American historians of the war, only to find their accounts equally distorted by jingoism.

With the goal of writing an impartial history, he began research into the official papers and records on both sides of the conflict. By the spring semester of his first year at Columbia, he noted: "I spend most of my spare time in the Astor Library on my 'Naval History.' " In the reading room—"a wonderfully open two-story-high hall surrounded by gilded balconies and books arranged in double-height alcoves"—he pored over official letters, logbooks, original contracts, and muster rolls.

With the same inordinate concentration he gave to law lectures in the mornings, Theodore spent his afternoons at the library compiling figures to compare warring ships in terms of tonnage and guns, and researching the number of officers and men on each side as the war began and ended. He concluded that in most of the battles at sea, the American fleets overpowered the British, but that American historians, desiring to embellish the valor of the commanders, minimized the difference; British historians retaliated with even greater exaggerations. With his fierce utilization of every waking moment, Roosevelt stole time to write both before and after a full round of social engagements, including formal balls, nights at the theatre, large receptions, and more intimate parties. "We're dining out in twenty minutes," Alice lightheartedly complained, "and Teedy's drawing little ships!"

On May 12, 1881, the day after classes ended, Theodore and Alice sailed off on their delayed honeymoon to Europe. His diary tells of joyous days crowded with visits to castles, cathedrals, and museums, with sailing excursions on inland rivers and carriage rides through the Alps. "Alice is the best traveling companion I have ever known," Theodore marveled. "Altogether it would be difficult to imagine any two people enjoying a trip more." But when they reached Zermatt, Theodore pursued a solo adventure: the irresistible challenge of climbing the dangerous Matterhorn. "I was anxious to go up it," he acknowledged to Bamie, "because it is reputed very difficult and a man who has been up it can fairly claim to have taken his degree as, at any rate, a subordinate kind of mountaineer." In the company of two guides, finding the climb "very laborious" but with "enough peril to make it exciting," he reached the summit.

Roosevelt managed to work on his naval history throughout the trip, lugging his books and papers from country to country. "You would be amused to see me writing it here," he told Bamie. "I have plenty of information now, but I can't get it into words; I am afraid it is too big a task for me. I wonder if I won't find everything in life too big for my abilities. Well, time will tell."

Returning home from Europe, he resumed his law courses in early October. "Am working fairly at my law," he reported a few weeks later, "and hardest of all at my book." In early December, he delivered a 500-page manuscript to Putnam's. Recalling this maiden literary voyage, Roosevelt acknowledged years later that some of the chapters "were so dry that they would have made a dictionary seem light reading by comparison." Nonetheless, uniformly favorable reviews hailed his accomplishment, noting flashes of the muscular tone and vigor that would mark his mature prose. "The volume is an excellent one in every respect," noted the reviewer for the *New York Times*, "and shows in so young an author the best promise for a good historian—fearlessness of statement, caution, endeavor to be impartial, and a brisk and interesting way of telling events."

It was an auspicious beginning. He learned early on the rewards attendant upon painstaking research and the meticulous deployment of facts. The boldness with which he challenged entrenched opinion was refreshing to critics, although one reviewer remarked that his running criticisms of the British authority suggested "a comparison with those zealous sailors who 'overloaded their carronades so as to very much destroy the effect of their fire.' "

In the years ahead, even as he turned his prodigious energies and talents to the world of politics, Theodore Roosevelt never stopped writing. Though he may never have realized his dream of writing a book that would rank "in the very first class," he produced a substantial body of excellent work, forty books in all, in addition to hundreds of magazine articles and book reviews. He covered an astonishing range of subjects, including narratives of hunting expeditions, meditations and natural histories on wolves, the grizzly bear, and the black-tailed deer, biographies of public figures, literary essays, commentaries on war and peace, and sketches of birds. His four-volume history of the American frontier would win high praise from the eminent historian Frederick Jackson Turner, who termed it "the first really satisfactory history of the field . . . a wonderful story, most entertainingly told."

Roosevelt's many-sided writings would prove an invaluable resource during his presidency, passionately linking him with hunters, naturalists, bird lovers, historians, biographers, conservationists, educators, sailors, soldiers, and sportsmen. "Everything was of interest to him," marveled the French ambassador, Jean Jules Jusserand, "people of today, people of yesterday, animals, minerals, stones, stars, the past, the future."

THE ROAD THAT WOULD LEAD Roosevelt into public life began at Morton Hall, the "barn-like room over a saloon" at 59th Street and Fifth Avenue that served as the Republican headquarters for the Twenty-first District. That district encompassed both the elegant neighborhoods along Madison Avenue and the more populous tenement sections on the West Side of Manhattan. While Roosevelt had found philanthropic administration ill-suited to his restless temperament, he longed to honor his father and family through his own efforts "to help the cause of better government in New York." When he began inquiring about the local Republican organization, he was warned by his privileged circle that district politics were "low," the province of "saloon-keepers, horse-car conductors, and the like," men who "would be rough and brutal and unpleasant to deal with." Their caution did nothing to deter Roosevelt. "I answered that if this were so it merely meant that the people I knew did not belong to the governing class," he observed, "and that the other people did—and that I intended to be one of the governing class."

In addition to attending the monthly meetings, Roosevelt stopped by in the evenings at the smoke-filled room with its benches, cuspidors, and poker tables that functioned as a club room. "I went around there often enough to have the men get accustomed to me and to have me get accustomed to them," he explained, "so that we began to speak the same language, and so that each could begin to live down in the other's mind what Bret Harte has called 'the defective moral quality of being a stranger.' "

To the machine politicians who represented the tenement population, Roosevelt initially appeared very much an alien. "He looked like a dude, side-whiskers an' all, y' know," one of them commented. Over time, however, as he had done at Harvard, he won over his comrades with the warmth, unabashed intensity, and pluck of his personality. He grew particularly close to Joe Murray, the thickset, red-haired Irish boss with "a fine head, a fighter's chin, and twinkling eyes," the man whom Roosevelt later credited with launching his political career. "He was by nature as straight a man, as fearless and as stanchly loyal, as any one whom I have ever met," Roosevelt wrote in his *Autobiography*.

When Murray determined that the incumbent Republican assemblyman for the Twenty-first District could not hold his seat in the fall elections in 1881, having recently been linked to corruption, he surprised his compatriots by nominating the twenty-three-year-old Roosevelt, unknown to anyone in Morton Hall eight months earlier. The shrewd boss calculated that victory over the Democratic candidate would be assured if the Republican machine mustered its regular totals while Roosevelt mobilized the college-educated men and "the swells" who rarely voted in local elections. Murray's instincts proved correct. On November 1, a list of eminent New Yorkers, including future Secretary of War Elihu Root and Columbia law professor Theodore W. Dwight, heartily endorsed Roosevelt as a man "of high character . . . conspicuous for his honesty and integrity." A week later, Theodore Roosevelt was elected as the youngest member of the New York State Assembly, launching an unprecedented political career, one that would culminate less than two decades later in his becoming the youngest president in the history of the United States.

On January 2, 1882, Theodore Roosevelt was sworn in, along with 127 other assemblymen. "My first days in the Legislature were much like those of a boy in a strange school," he recalled. "My fellow legislators and I eyed one another with mutual distrust. . . . The Legislature was Democratic. I was a Republican from the 'silk-stocking' district." Assemblyman Isaac Hunt, who later became a close friend, would never forget the first time he saw Roosevelt. "He came in as if he had been ejected by a catapult," Hunt recalled. "He pulled off his coat; he was dressed in full dress, he had been to dinner somewhere." With hair parted in the middle, eyeglasses suspended by a silk cord, and elegant gloves, he cut a unique figure.

For the first six weeks, according to Hunt, Theodore Roosevelt was uncharacteristically taciturn. "He was like Moses in the Wilderness," but all the while watching and learning. One night in his private diary, Roosevelt delineated "an analysis of the character of each man in that Legislature." His initial reactions to the other assemblymen revealed that he was still far from overcoming Harte's "defective moral quality of being a stranger." His Republican colleagues, he wrote, were "bad enough, but over half the democrats, including almost all of the City Irish, are vicious, stupid looking scoundrels with apparently not a redeeming trait." The men who belonged to the New York City Tammany Hall Democratic machine, furthermore, seemed "totally unable to speak with even an approximation to good grammar; not one of them can string three intelligible sentences together to save his neck."

Clearly, the Tammany men were as contemptuous of and antagonistic to Roosevelt as he was of them. Tammany lieutenant John McManus, a practical joker nearly twice Roosevelt's size, let it be known that he intended to toss the young upstart in a blanket. Outwardly uncowed, a belligerent Roosevelt confronted McManus: "By God! If you try anything like that, I'll kick you, I'll bite you, I'll kick you in the balls. I'll do anything to you—you'd better let me alone." And he did.

The more serious altercation took place at Hurst's Roadhouse, a popular gathering place for assemblymen and reporters six miles out of Albany. Late one winter afternoon Roosevelt entered Hurst's and was greeted by three jeering bullies, who raucously mocked his appearance and lack of a winter coat. "Why don't your mother buy you an overcoat? Won't Mama's boy catch cold?" A reporter present noted that Roosevelt ignored them until it was clear they would not let up. Finally, he confronted the three. "You—little dude," taunted one, while his companion took a swipe at Roosevelt. "But, quick as lightning, Roosevelt slipped his glasses into his side pocket, and in another second he had laid out two of the trio on the floor. The third quit cold." The story soon made the rounds in the statehouse, along with the significant fact that once the men got off the floor, Roosevelt invited them to join him in a glass of ale.

The lively natures displayed by young Taft and Roosevelt remained with them throughout their lives. The aftermath of their anger, however, was handled very differently. "When Taft gives way to his," one reporter observed, "it is to inflict a merciless lashing upon its victim, for whom thereafter he has no use whatever. With Roosevelt it is a case of powder and spark; there is a vivid flash and a deafening roar, but when the smoke has blown away, that is the end."

Roosevelt quickly determined that his colleagues could be divided into three groups: a small circle of "very good men," fellow reformers like Isaac Hunt, William O'Neil, and Mike Costello, anxious to fight against corrupt political machines, made up the first; the second group, the majority, "were neither very good nor very bad, but went one way or the other, according to the strength of the various conflicting influences acting around, behind, and upon them"; finally, the "very bad men" in both parties, ever susceptible to bribery, made up a rough third of the assembly and were essentially owned by various business interests. Good legislation could be passed only if the conscience of the public was awakened, exerting pressure on the passive majority. Immediately, Roosevelt understood that the most effective means of circumventing the machines and transforming popular sentiment was to establish a good rapport with the press corps.

About thirty reporters from across the state covered the legislature in Albany, where a rigid hierarchy governed their assigned seats. In front-row box seats, facing the assemblymen, sat George F. Spinney of the *New York Times*, Hugh Hastings of the *Albany Express*, H. Calkins of the New York *World,* and A. W. Lyman of the New York *Sun*. Reporters for the *New York Herald*, the *New York Tribune*, and the *Brooklyn Times* sat in the second and third rows. Journalists representing smaller papers were consigned to the bleachers in the back of the chamber. Roosevelt's expansive demeanor, manic energies, and often original, always articulate and quotable statements made him a favorite among the journalists. A mutually productive alliance was forged between these journalists and Roosevelt that would boost his political career at every stage.

The *New York Times* reporter George Spinney took an immediate liking to Roosevelt, calling him a "good-hearted man," with "a good, honest laugh." Spinney, who would later become editor and publisher of the *Times*, was considered then one of the best reporters in the state, lauded for the "vigor, thoroughness and intelligence of his daily dispatches" from Albany. Spinney marveled at the speed with which the rookie assemblyman mastered every aspect of the state legislature. "He grew like a beanstalk," he recalled in a conversation with Assemblyman Hunt forty years later. "He would just stand a man up against the wall and interview him and ask: 'How do you do this in your district and county' and 'What is this thing and that thing.' He went right to the bottom of the whole thing. He knew more about State politics at the end of that first session than ninety percent of them did."

Isaac Hunt himself, described by a contemporary as "a mighty tree that stood out in the forest," had never encountered anyone like Roosevelt. "He would go away Friday afternoon," Hunt remembered, "and Monday he would throw out new things he never had before, just like a child that you see grow from day to day, that is the way he grew. He increased in stature and strength materially all the time." In that first session, Hunt wrote, "I thought I knew more than he did . . . but before we got through, he grew right away from me."

Brooklyn Eagle reporter William C. Hudson, who resided at the same hotel as Roosevelt, was boggled by the young legislator's early morning routine. "It was Roosevelt's habit to come into the breakfast room with a rush, copies of all the morning papers he could lay his hands on under his arm, and, seating himself, to go through those papers with a rapidity that would have excited the jealousy of the most rapid exchange editor. He threw each paper, as he finished it, on the floor, unfolded, until at the end there was, on either side of him, a pile of loose papers as high as the table for the servants to clear away. And all this time he would be taking part in the running conversation of the table. Had anyone supposed that this inspection of the papers was superficial, he would have been sadly mistaken. Roosevelt saw everything, grasped the sense of everything, and formed an opinion on everything which he was eager to maintain at any risk."

Roosevelt's prodigious learning curve was tested after only two months in Albany, when he took a leading role in the battle to impeach a corrupt state supreme court judge, Theodore Westbrook. The battle pitted Roosevelt against a similar insidious alliance to the one Taft had uncovered in the Campbell debacle in Cincinnati. In December 1881, shortly before Roosevelt was sworn in, the *New York Times* had published a nine-column piece condemning Judge Westbrook's collusion with the notorious Wall Street financier Jay Gould in an elaborate scheme to gain control of the elevated railway system in New York. "We went after him with yards of space," recalled Spinney, who conducted several phases of the investigation.

Over the years, the swashbuckling Gould had amassed railroads, steamship lines, telegraph companies, and newspapers in a series of well-planned raids, stitching together an empire that stretched from coast to coast. In 1881, he moved to appropriate the Manhattan Elevated Railway Company, one of the first outfits to engineer and develop a steam-powered rapid-transit system for the city. A burdensome lawsuit devised by Gould's accomplices was brought against the company, forcing it into receivership. Judge Westbrook, who had been Gould's legal counsel, was selected to preside over the bankrupt company. Holding court in Gould's private offices, Westbrook issued a series of onerous rulings calculated to panic stockholders into throwing their shares on the market, depressing the stock to almost nothing. At that point, the Gould syndicate began buying. Once Gould had gained control of the valuable property, Judge Westbrook mysteriously decreed the company solvent, and the stock rose sharply. This simple, perfidious maneuver cost thousands of innocent stockholders their life savings.

The comprehensive account of this stock-jobbing scheme created a stir in the newspaper world. At issue, the *Brooklyn Eagle* proclaimed, were not simply the transgressions of a justice who "prostituted" himself, but the fact that the "State Government in all its branches" has prostrated itself before the robber barons. "These things show where the wealth of the country is going; they show that the farmer, the artisan, and the merchant are sweating their lives out to enrich a little coterie of blooded knaves who regard their fellowmen as the spider does the fly or the wolf the sheep." If the charges were substantiated, the *Auburn* (New York) *Advertiser* argued, nothing less than Westbrook's impeachment would restore the "dignity and respect" of the state supreme court. "Officials should be taught that they are the servants of the people," chided the *Times*, "not of rings and cliques." All agreed that Westbrook could not "remain silent under the severe arraignment of the *Times*."

In fact, that is precisely what Westbrook did; his strategic silence on these charges had nearly extinguished interest in the entire matter when Theodore Roosevelt picked up the case in March 1882. Isaac Hunt had prompted Roosevelt's involvement after a second, unrelated article appeared in the *New York Herald* accusing Judge Westbrook of a flagrant abuse of power and conflict of interest. He had appointed receivers for defunct insurance companies and granted excessive fees to select lawyers (including his cousin and son) who handled the cases. Hunt suggested that Roosevelt introduce a resolution to investigate Judge Westbrook. Roosevelt agreed to consider the action "but would not take it up until he was sure there was evidence sufficient to warrant such a resolution."

Recalling the Westbrook article in the *New York Times* three months earlier (as he seemed to remember anything he had read), Roosevelt approached the city editor, Henry Loewenthal, and asked to examine the corroborating evidence behind the December exposé. The editor later described "an energetic young man" who "questioned and cross-questioned him" throughout the entire night. George Spinney, who had worked for Loewenthal before becoming the Albany correspondent, heard that "the presses in the basement were finishing that day's edition in the early morning hours, when the young Assemblyman emerged with an armful of ammunition" that included an incriminating letter in which Judge Westbrook told Gould, "I am willing to go to the very verge of judicial discretion to serve your vast interests."

On March 29, 1882, Roosevelt rose from his seat in the assembly. Noting that the newspaper charges made against Westbrook in relation to the Manhattan Elevated Railway Company had "never been explained or fairly refuted," he offered a resolution empowering the Judiciary Committee to begin an investigation. This bold action created a sensation in the chamber. "By Jove!" Hunt recalled. "It was like the bursting of a bombshell." Supporters of Westbrook and Gould quickly rallied, demanding a debate that automatically tabled the motion and threatened its indefinite postponement. The next day an editorial in the *New York Times* praised Roosevelt's resolution: "Mr. Roosevelt correctly states that these charges have never been explained or fairly rebutted. . . . Those who believe that Judge Westbrook has been unjustly assailed ought to welcome so good a chance of vindicating his character."

A week later, Spinney recalled, "Roosevelt suddenly interrupted the humdrum routine, with the demand that all business be laid aside and his resolution of investigation be taken up." The move was "so unexpected and so sudden that dilatory tactics were out of the question." When Roosevelt began to speak, "the House, for almost the only time during the session grew silent." Though Roosevelt was not then an accomplished speaker, he delivered his speech "slowly and clearly and his voice filled the chamber, abominable as were its acoustics. A frequent gesture of his determination was the resounding blow of his right fist as he smacked it in the palm of his left hand."

"The men who were mainly concerned in this fraud," Roosevelt began (alluding to Jay Gould, Russell Sage, and Cyrus Field), "were men whose financial dishonesty is a matter of common notoriety," requiring of the judiciary extreme efforts to assure the appearance of probity. Instead, the judge answered petitions in the offices of one of the trio of investors and held court in the office of another who was "nothing but a wealthy shark." To address one aspect of the case, Westbrook appointed a man who was employed by Jay Gould. Every decision was rendered to enable Gould and his conspirators to seize control of the railway at a baldly manipulated bargain price. "We have a right to demand that our judiciary should be kept beyond reproach," Roosevelt ardently continued, "and we have a right to demand that if we find men against whom there is not only suspicion, but almost a certainty that they have had collusion with men whose interests were in conflict with the interests of the public, they shall, at least, be required to bring positive facts with which to prove there has not been such collusion; and they ought themselves to have been the first to demand such an investigation."

"Beyond a shadow of doubt," Spinney believed, "a vote at that juncture would have insured the passage of his resolution." But former Governor Thomas Alvord took the floor and filibustered until the scheduled adjournment at two o'clock in the afternoon. Speaking in "disjointed sentences and fragmentary thoughts," Alvord advised the rookie assemblyman to find proof for his accusations rather than stoop to "slanderous utterances or newspaper stories," because "human reputation and human characters were too sacred to be trifled with."

Though Roosevelt was temporarily outmaneuvered by veteran opposition, "the day's proceedings," Spinney observed, "made the youngest member of the Assembly the most talked of man in the State." That night, from his room at the Kenmore Hotel, Roosevelt wrote to Alice with no small gratification: "I have drawn blood by my speech against the Elevated Railway judges, and have come in for any amount both of praise and abuse from the newspapers. It is rather the hit of the season so far, and I think I have made a success of it. Letters and telegrams of congratulation come pouring in on me from all quarters. But the fight is severe still."

Roosevelt's speech to the assembly garnered widespread coverage, as he well knew it would. "Mr. Roosevelt has a most refreshing habit of calling men and things by their right names," the *Times* editorialized, "and in these days of judicial, ecclesiastical and journalistic subserviency to the robber barons of the Street it needs some little courage in any public man to characterize them and their acts in fitting terms. There is a splendid career open for a young man of position, character and independence like Mr. Roosevelt."

Not surprisingly, Jay Gould's New York *World* castigated him in equal measure. "Before any official shall be subjected to the vexation and discredit of an investigation, some responsible person or association must prefer a charge accompanied with allegations of wrong-doing." Yet in this instance, the *World* complained, "an inexperienced legislator gets up [from] his seat and recites in a somewhat intemperate speech sundry hearsay charges against Judge Westbrook based upon statements published in a newspaper."

Roosevelt dismissed these attacks, according to Hunt, shedding criticism "like water poured on a duck's back." He held his ground, even when an old family friend gently insisted that while "it was a good thing to have made the 'reform play,' " he should not "overplay" his hand. "I asked," Roosevelt recalled, "if that meant I was to yield to the ring in politics. He answered somewhat impatiently that I was entirely mistaken (as in fact I was) about there being merely a political ring," for the "inner circle" was, in truth, a miasma, an enormous knot of "big businessmen, and the politicians, lawyers, and judges who were in alliance with and to a certain extent dependent upon them, and that the successful man had to win his success by the backing of the same forces, whether in law, business, or politics."

The day before the House adjourned for Easter recess, Roosevelt was again frustrated in his attempt to bring the issue to a vote. During the break, however, newspapers continued to headline the story. "By the time the Legislature came back again," Hunt explained, "the Legislators had evidently heard from their home folks, because the vote was overwhelmingly in favor of the investigation." This first skirmish awakened Roosevelt to the massive persuasive capacity of the press to stir public resolve and exert pressure on otherwise unassailable insiders.

The investigation was entrusted to the Judiciary Committee which, over the course of seven weeks, conducted hearings in both New York and Albany. Despite an accumulation of damaging evidence, a majority declared that Judge Westbrook's behavior, although indiscreet, did not warrant impeachment. Hunt later alleged that three decisive votes in favor of impeachment were lost in the middle of the night when the legislators were offered $2,500 each to sign the majority report. When the Judiciary Committee's decision was announced, Hunt recalled, Roosevelt "was dancing and jumping about and full of fire and full of fury and full of fight."

"Mr. Speak-ah! Mr. Speak-ah," he called out, with a strident plea for his colleagues to accept the minority report calling for impeachment: "To you, members of the Legislature of the greatest commonwealth in this great Federal Union, I say you cannot by your votes clear the Judge. He stands condemned by his own acts in the eyes of all honest people. All you can do is to shame yourselves and give him a brief extension of his dishonored career. You cannot cleanse the leper. Beware lest you taint yourselves with his leprosy."

Roosevelt's dramatic exhortation brought "deathless silence" to the chamber, but the assembly nonetheless voted on May 31, 1882, to accept the majority report exonerating the judge. "It was apparent to those familiar with politics," Spinney concluded, "that every wire that could be pulled in both the dominant political parties to prevent impeachment was stretched to the tautest."

"The action of the Assembly last night in voting to exonerate Judge Westbrook is simply disgraceful," declared the *New York Herald*. "We venture the assertion that the entire Bench and nine-tenths of the Bar of the State are convinced that Judge Westbrook ought to be impeached." The *New York Times* titled its editorial "A Miscarriage of Justice"; the *Brooklyn Eagle* called the vote "an open avowal of contempt for public sentiment, for public intelligence and common honesty." The *Buffalo Express* quoted from Roosevelt's speech, and predicted that the young man's indictment expressed "the general verdict."

Though Roosevelt's first joust at entrenched corruption had failed, he emerged as a champion of reform both within the assembly and in the court of public opinion. Hunt maintained that Roosevelt "won his spurs in that fight." While he had been derided as "a society man and a dude" prior to the Westbrook debate, he was now "looked upon as a full-fledged man and worthy of anybody's esteem." When the session came to a close in early June, claimed Spinney, "Roosevelt's name was known to every nook and corner of the State."

"I ROSE LIKE A ROCKET," Roosevelt remembered, proudly noting his reelection the following November with "an enormous majority" despite a Democratic sweep in the state elections. As a further sign of his swift and brilliant ascent, when the legislature convened in January 1883, his Republican colleagues selected him, the youngest member of the New York State Assembly, as their minority leader. Thereafter, he acknowledged, "I immediately proceeded to lose *my* perspective . . . I came an awful cropper, and had to pick myself up after learning by bitter experience the lesson that I was not all-important."

"My head was swelled," he conceded, looking back upon his self-indulgent behavior in the aftermath of such sudden fame. "I would listen to no argument, no advice." In that second session, Hunt recalled, Roosevelt became "a perfect nuisance," interrupting the business of the House in a manner "so explosive, and so radical and so indiscreet" that even fellow reformers worried that he was becoming "a damn fool." When contesting an issue, "he yelled and pounded his desk," firing back "with all the venom imaginary." Without restraint he castigated the New York *World* "as a paper of limited circulation and unlimited scurrility"; he denounced the "rotten" Democratic Party, belittling the political lineage that ran "down the roll from Polk, the mendacious, through Pierce, the Copperhead, to Buchanan, who faced both ways." His colorful language invariably made headlines, spurring him to progressively more outlandish outbursts. His antics kept his name in print, but he finally acknowledged that he was "absolutely deserted" and lamented that "every bit of influence I had was gone. The things I wanted to do I was powerless to accomplish."

This grim, isolate reality prompted a radical reassessment: "I thereby learned the invaluable lesson that in the practical activities of life no man can render the highest service unless he can act in combination with his fellows, which means a certain amount of give-and-take between him and them." Restraining his histrionic rhetoric and making overtures to his fellow legislators, Roosevelt was able to establish common grounds of agreement. "I turned in to help them, and they turned to and gave me a hand," he reflected, "and so we were able to get things done."

Roosevelt's developing sensibilities did not initially embrace the cause of labor seeking greater protection against the abusive onslaughts of the flourishing industrial order. Rather, he regarded union leaders as "exceedingly unattractive persons," and considered the majority of labor bills introduced in the legislature "foolish." The reigning laissez-faire doctrine—inculcated at Harvard as well as Yale, and accepted categorically by those within his privileged circle—had "biased" him, he later acknowledged, "against all governmental schemes for the betterment of the social and industrial conditions of laborers." With unexamined confidence, he voted against increasing the minimum wage to 25 cents an hour, spoke in opposition to a bill that would limit streetcar conductors to twelve-hour workdays, and fought against legislation to raise the salaries of New York's policemen and firemen.

When the Cigar-Makers' Union introduced a bill to prohibit the manufacture of cigars in tenement houses, Roosevelt presumed from the outset he would vote against it. He had always believed that tenement owners had an absolute right to do as they wished with their own property. As he examined more closely the conditions leading to the bill, however, he began to question his inherited resistance to social legislation.

The labor leader Samuel Gompers had long considered the production of cigars in unsanitary tenements "one of the most dreadful, cancerous sores" on the city of New York. Realizing that the only hope of eradicating a system that employed nearly 10,000 people lay in exposing the "actual character of the evils," he conducted a personal inspection of the tenements, gaining entrance in the guise of a book agent peddling copies of Charles Dickens. Gompers made detailed notes of his observations and published comprehensive reports of his findings. He discovered that the capitalists who owned the tenement factories demanded grueling hours from their workers, mainly Jewish immigrants, and charged absurd rents for their filthy, ill-ventilated apartments.

In one tenement house, fifteen families crowded into three floors. Fathers, mothers, and children were at work stripping, drying, and wrapping cigars from six in the morning until midnight. In the yard, "a breeding ground of disease" with "no drain to a sewer," lay large mounds of decaying tobacco. Another building housed ninety-eight people from twenty families, with several families living and working together in one room. Everywhere piles of tobacco and fetid tobacco scraps littered the floors, filling the air with an overwhelming stench. The hallways were so "dark and gloomy" that even at midday it seemed like night.

Roosevelt was shaken by these reports. He agreed to accompany Gompers on an inspection tour, pledging that "if the conditions described really existed he would do everything in his power to secure the passage of the bill." He admitted that he was "a good deal shocked" at what he found. While a few of the tenements provided living space for the workers apart from the sweatshops, the "overwhelming majority" had no separate accommodation. He long remembered one tenement in which five adults and several children were confined to a single room for sleeping, eating, and making cigars. "The tobacco was stowed about everywhere, alongside the foul bedding, and in a corner where there were scraps of food." After two additional forays into this dark underworld, Roosevelt was "convinced beyond a shadow of doubt" that the manufacture of cigars in tenement houses "was an evil thing from every standpoint, social, industrial and hygienic." Though the proposed bill was "a dangerous departure from the laissez-faire doctrine in which he thoroughly believed," he championed its passage and joined a group of supporters urging Governor Grover Cleveland to sign it.

Once the bill became law in March 1883, the cigar makers straightaway brought suit, arguing their right to hold property, guaranteed by the state constitution, was violated by the new regulations. The case, *In re Jacobs*, eventually made its way to the New York Court of Appeals, where the justices declared that the law indeed deprived the cigar makers of their "fundamental rights of liberty . . . without due process of law." Furthermore, the court argued, the legislation did not constitute a legitimate use of the state's police power to regulate behavior detrimental to the public welfare, for tobacco was in no way "injurious to the public health." On the contrary, it was "a disinfectant and a prophylactic."

"It was this case," Roosevelt later said, "which first waked me to . . . the fact that the courts were not necessarily the best judges of what should be done to better social and industrial conditions." While the justices were well intentioned, they interpreted law solely from the vantage point of the propertied classes. "They knew nothing whatever of tenement house conditions," he charged, "they knew nothing whatever of the needs, or of the life and labor, of three-fourths of their fellow-citizens in great cities." In the years that followed, the court's defense of free enterprise in this case would be repeatedly cited to block governmental regulation of industry. "It was," Roosevelt observed, "one of the most serious setbacks which the cause of industrial and social progress and reform ever received."

Roosevelt soon demonstrated his broadening perspective as a legislator in the fight for civil service reform. Members of the Democratic Party he had lately termed "rotten" now became his allies in the construction of a civil service bill that would, he said, "do for the City of New York what the Pendleton bill has done for the United States. Its aim is to take the civil service out of the political arena, where it now lies festering, a reproach and a hissing to all decent men, and the most terrible source of corruption." Recognizing Roosevelt's ability to galvanize the reform element in the assembly, Governor Grover Cleveland summoned him and promised that "he would deliver the Cleveland Democrats in the House" if Roosevelt would corral his own faction. The deal was struck and genuine civil service reform came to New York.

Easily winning a third term in November 1883, when the Republicans recaptured a majority in the assembly, Roosevelt announced he would run for Speaker. With the Republican bosses lined up against him, he calculated that his "only chance lay in arousing the people in the different districts." Never one for half-measures, Theodore Roosevelt campaigned tirelessly. He sent out letters to potential supporters and personally visited dozens of assembly members, traveling by horse, train, or on foot to remote villages and towns. His open pursuit of the post dismayed his patrician circle of friends, who insisted that "the office should seek the man and not the man the office." Roosevelt countered that "if Abraham Lincoln had not sought the Presidency he never would have been nominated."

Though his spirited campaign failed to break the hold of the machine, Roosevelt's attempt to run independent of patronage from the bosses reinforced his leadership of the burgeoning reform element. His autonomy, he later maintained, enabled him "to accomplish far more than [he] could have accomplished as Speaker." Selected as chairman of the influential Committee on the Cities, Roosevelt promptly introduced a series of bills aimed at dismantling the dominion of the Tammany Hall machine. The primary measure would invest greater power in the mayor rather than the aldermen, who were solely "the creatures of the local ward bosses." To enlist public backing in the struggle to reorganize city government, Roosevelt launched investigations into various city departments, reaping headlines with dramatic exposés of venality and abuse of the public trust. "I feel now as though I had the reins in my hand," he assured Alice in January 1884.

Years later, George Spinney fondly recalled that despite the punishing work hours Roosevelt kept, he found time for festive dinners and shared pints of ale with reporters and colleagues where conversation and song stretched into the early morning hours. Spinney would never forget the "great night" when Roosevelt challenged him for the title of amateur boxing champion. With the entire assembly watching, Spinney, taller and heavier than Roosevelt, conceded after three rounds that "he'd had enough." Amid general good cheer, Roosevelt was declared victor.

Every weekend, Roosevelt hastened home to be with his wife, who was expecting their first child in mid-February 1884. A year earlier, Theodore and Alice had moved from his mother's house to a comfortable brownstone on West 45th Street. In diary entries, Roosevelt extolled the pleasure of being "in my own lovely little home, with the sweetest and prettiest of all little wives—I can imagine nothing more happy in life than an evening spent in my cozy little sitting room before a bright fire of soft coal, my books all around me."

Confident that this baby would be the first of many, Theodore bought a spectacular piece of property on Oyster Bay and hired an architect to build a country home amid the fields and forests that had fostered his imagination and spurred his passion for nature. During their weekends together, the young couple spent hours poring over the architect's designs for the spacious ten-bedroom house entirely skirted by a porch. He proposed to christen their nest "Leeholm," in honor of Alice. "How I did hate to leave my bright, sunny little love," Theodore lamented in early February after their weekend had drawn to a close. "I love you and long for you all the time, and oh *so* tenderly; doubly tenderly now, my sweetest little wife. I just long for Friday evening when I shall be with you again."

During the winter months, Theodore decided to sublet his little brownstone and move back to his family's spacious home on West 57th Street. There, his mother, his unmarried sister Bamie, and a host of family servants could watch over Alice while he was in Albany. His sister Corinne, married two years earlier to Douglas Robinson and mother to a baby boy, had also returned to the family home for the winter season. Clearly, Alice would not lack loving support in Theodore's absence.

On Monday afternoon, February 11, with the arrival of the baby imminent, Theodore left for Albany to attend to several city bills then in progress. Alice had assured him that while she "hated" to see him leave, she was "feeling well." The doctor did not expect her labor to begin until Thursday at the earliest. In fact, her gravest concern lay with Mittie, who had suffered for several days with what appeared to the family a severe cold, but which the doctor suspected might be typhoid.

"I do love my dear Thee so much," Alice told him. "I wish I could have my little new baby soon." Twenty-four hours later, at 8:30 p.m. on Tuesday evening, February 12, she gave birth to a healthy eight-and-three-quarter-pound girl. According to the handwritten account that Mittie's sister Anna kept for the child to read when she grew up, Alice was thrilled that her baby was a little girl. A nurse took the newborn to be washed and dressed before returning her to her mother, who cradled and kissed her.

Roosevelt received the welcome news in a telegram from New York the following morning. Isaac Hunt would long recall the joyful scene in the assembly that morning when all present congratulated him on the news. "He was full of life and happiness." Despite an ambivalent report that his mother was "only fairly well," Theodore had no reason to suspect her condition was anything out of the ordinary.

The family at 57th Street, however, was rapidly becoming aware of considerable cause for worry. The attending doctor recognized the symptoms Alice was developing as signs of acute Bright's disease, perhaps resulting from an infection that had inflamed her kidneys. Alice could easily have attributed the complications of the disease—back pain, vomiting, puffiness of the face, and distention of the body—to her advanced pregnancy. By the time the diagnosis was made, fluid had likely accumulated in Alice's lungs, restricting her ability to breathe.

Mittie, meanwhile, slipped in and out of consciousness. The enervating advance of what was indeed acute typhoid racked Theodore's mother with high fever, diarrhea, vomiting, and a worsening dehydration. As in many cases, the disease had progressed "somewhat insidiously," with early symptoms of headache, lassitude, and feverishness that gave way to prostration, delirium, internal hemorrhage, and a "coma vigil" when less than a day of life remained.

A second telegram was dispatched to Albany, advising Theodore to come home at once. The thickening fog that stalled the progress of his train ride to New York mirrored his despair. For nearly two weeks, New Yorkers had endured a string of what the *Times* called "suicidal" days, "dark, foggy, depressing, and dismal." Visibility was drastically diminished in the pervasive fog, which stalled traffic on the river and railways when signals became invisible. Ferryboats were unable to run; horses jostled one another on the streets; the elevated railway ran off its tracks. "There is," the *Times* remarked, "something suggestive of death and decay in the dampness that fills the world, clings to the house door, drips from the fences, coats the streets with liquid nastiness, moistens one's garments, and paints the sky lead-color."

The fog that forced Theodore's train to creep along also delayed the return of Corinne and Douglas Robinson from a brief visit to Baltimore. Elliott met them at the door. "There is a curse on this house!" he said. "Mother is dying, and Alice is dying, too." It was nearly midnight when Theodore finally reached home. Racing up to the third floor, he found Alice in a state of semiconsciousness. He held her gently, refusing to leave her side, until he was informed that if he wished to see his mother one last time, he had better come downstairs. At three o'clock that morning, surrounded by her children, Mittie died. She was only forty-nine. Returning to the third floor, Theodore once more enfolded his wife in an embrace. By two o'clock that dismal St. Valentine's Day afternoon, twenty-two-year-old Alice Lee Roosevelt was also dead. Roosevelt's private diary for that day contains a single, desolate entry. Beneath a large X he wrote: "The light has gone out of my life."

"Seldom, if ever, has New York society received such a shock," observed the New York *World* when word spread that Roosevelt's wife and mother had died in a single day. When the news of the twin deaths reached Albany, the assembly took an action "wholly unprecedented in the legislative annals of the State or country," voting unanimously to adjourn until the following

Monday evening in recognition of "the desolating blow" suffered by its revered colleague. One assemblyman after another rose to show Roosevelt that he had companions in grief. "It has never been my experience to stand in the presence of such a sorrow as this," said one speaker. Isaac Hunt's voice filled with affection as he spoke of his "particular friend." He called upon his colleagues to appreciate "the uncertainty of human life" and use their remaining hours "to improve the opportunities of the present—to act well our part upon this stage of action." Witnessing the overwhelming emotions in the chamber, one reporter stated that "no sadder meeting of the Legislature has ever been held."

Theodore remained "in a dazed, stunned state" throughout the double funeral at the Fifth Avenue Presbyterian Church and the burial at Green-Wood Cemetery in Brooklyn. "He does not know what he does or says," observed his former tutor, Arthur Cutler. "I fear he sleeps little, for he walks a great deal in the night," Corinne told Elliott, "and his eyes have that strained red look."

Six years earlier, his father's death had taught Theodore that frantic activity was the only way to keep sorrow at bay. "If I had very much time to think," he had said then, "I should almost go crazy." Now he determined to return to the assembly as soon as possible. "I shall come back to my work at once," he told one friend. "There is now nothing left for me except to try to so live as not to dishonor the memory of those I loved who have gone before me."

He returned "a changed man," Hunt recalled. "From that time on there was a sadness about his face that he never had before." When Hunt tried to console his friend, he soon discovered that Theodore "did not want anybody to sympathize with him. It was a grief that he had in his own soul." He recorded his pain only in his private diary, and even there the account was spare: "We spent three years of happiness greater and more unalloyed than I have ever known fall to the lot of others. For joy or sorrow my life has now been lived out."

Roosevelt's inability to express and share his grief over the loss of his wife finally locked into an obsessive refusal to speak of her at all. As planned, he allowed the baby to be christened Alice, but in letters to his sister Bamie, with whom the child had gone to live, he referred to her simply as "Baby Lee." "There can never be another Alice to me," he confessed to a friend, "nor could I have another, not even her own child, bear her name." Almost all his love letters to Alice from Harvard were destroyed, along with most of the pictures and mementoes of their courtship. To dwell on the loss, he believed, was "both weak and morbid."

Roosevelt had at first been thrilled to realize that his baby shared her birthday with Abraham Lincoln, one whose high and profound character he considered without parallel. Yet the manner in which his hero had dealt with the death of his ten-year-old son Willie from a typhoid epidemic that swept Washington in 1862 could hardly have differed more from Roosevelt's response to the loss of his wife and the needs of their child. Rather than dispose of all reminders and mementoes, Lincoln cherished every vestige of his son's life: a painting by the child adorned his mantelpiece; he spent hours leafing through a scrapbook in which Willie had followed the various battles of the war; and he told countless stories about his son to visitors and friends. Believing that the dead continue only in the minds of the living, Lincoln willfully maintained an intense connection with his dead son. In starkest contrast to Lincoln's fervent determination to consecrate a part of his daily life to his child is Roosevelt's systematic suppression of his wife's memory. Indeed, Roosevelt's *Autobiography*, written three decades later, failed even to recognize that his first wife had ever lived. And years later, when his niece had lost her fiancé, he likewise advised her "to treat the past as past, the event as finished and out of her life. . . . Let her never speak one word of the matter, henceforth."

UPON HIS RETURN TO ALBANY, Roosevelt immersed himself in the long hours of work. The routine of the daily sessions and the camaraderie of his fellow legislators worked to mitigate his misery, just as the circumscribed world of Harvard had offered refuge from the pain of his father's death. "We are now holding evening sessions and I am glad we are," he told Bamie; "indeed the more we work the better I like it." In the weeks that followed, his Committee on the Cities conducted a series of dramatic investigations, and eventually nine reform bills were reported to the floor. He was able to secure passage of the most vital of these, including his bill to diminish the scope of the machine-controlled Board of Aldermen by centralizing responsibility in the hands of the mayor. The brilliant cartoonist Thomas Nast celebrated Roosevelt's success in a *Harper's Weekly* caricature of the young Republican legislator holding out reform bills to receive the signature of Democratic governor Grover Cleveland. Entitled "Reform Without Bloodshed," the cartoon juxtaposed the bipartisan "Law and Order" triumph in New York with the corruption warping Cincinnati's legal system. Cincinnati's woes were illustrated by headlines announcing the deadly riots and destruction in the wake of the shocking verdict in William Berner's murder trial.

Yet Roosevelt was thwarted in other reform measures, according to

William Hudson of the *Brooklyn Eagle*, because his bills were badly constructed. Cleveland felt compelled to veto them, certain they would embroil the state in "prolonged and expensive litigation." Roosevelt was furious. "You must not veto those bills," he told Cleveland. "I can't have it, and I won't have it." The governor could not be dissuaded. "As debate is his strong point," an editorialist observed of the young Roosevelt, "so parliamentary procedure is his weak one." Too often, the critique concluded, he dives into legislative waters "without considering whether broken bottles or blue water are below him. With more attention to these necessary preliminaries and several years' additional experience, he will be fitted for the larger field of national politics."

That involvement in national politics, however, came sooner than even Roosevelt anticipated. During the weeks before the Republican Convention in June 1884, he had joined a group of reformers that included a new friend, Massachusetts state legislator Henry Cabot Lodge. The reformers backed the presidential candidacy of George F. Edmunds, an honorable but little-known senator from Vermont, over the two leading contenders, President Chester Arthur and James Blaine. While Arthur's admirable performance as president in the wake of Garfield's assassination had surprised reformers, Roosevelt could never forgive the man who had defeated his father for the collectorship. And Blaine, to his mind, was "by far the most objectionable, because his personal honesty, as well as his faithfulness as a public servant, are both open to question."

At the convention, Roosevelt and the small band of reformers fought tirelessly to bring in votes for Edmunds, but in the end widespread popular support for Blaine carried the nomination. "Our defeat is an overwhelming rout," Roosevelt admitted to Bamie. The choice of Blaine "speaks badly for the intelligence of the mass of my party," he ruefully continued. "It may be that 'the voice of the people is the voice of God' in fifty one cases out of a hundred; but in the remaining forty nine it is quite as likely to be the voice of the devil, or, what is still worse, the voice of a fool." Still, he concluded, "I am glad to have been present at the convention, and to have taken part in its proceedings; it was a historic scene."

"Although not a very old man, I have yet lived a great deal in my life," the twenty-six-year-old Roosevelt confided to a reporter friend during the Edmunds campaign, "and I have known sorrow too bitter and joy too keen to allow me to become either cast down or elated for more than a very brief period over any success or defeat." Despite an almost pathological reticence in his personal life, it seemed the recent devastating losses had put the vagaries of politics into perspective.

His three terms in the New York State Assembly had provided Roosevelt with considerable reason for pride and satisfaction in his accomplishments. He had led the fight against Judge Westbrook and been instrumental in the passage of both the cigar bill and civil service reform. He had steered landmark governmental reform bills through his committee and on the floor. Passion and pridefulness might have occasioned some arrogant foolishness, but his perceptiveness and diligence allowed him to develop broader, more effective strategies in the wake of these mistakes. His rigorous honesty and independence inspired adulation in young reformers, and old-timers began to treat him with grudging respect.

The assembly had proved a "great school" for Roosevelt. He had learned to cooperate with colleagues far removed from his patrician background, even those he had initially dismissed as "stupid looking scoundrels" and illiterate thugs. He had come a long way from the Harvard prig who found it necessary to ascertain if a prospective friend's social standing was equal to the status of his own family. "We did not agree in all things," he later said of his colleagues, "but we did in some, and those we pulled at together. That was my first lesson in real politics. . . . If you are cast on a desert island with only a screwdriver, a hatchet, and a chisel to make a boat with, why, go make the best one you can. It would be better if you had a saw, but you haven't. So with men."

Though he insisted that he would stay in public life only if he could remain true to his principles, his singular success in the rough-and-tumble world of the state assembly revealed a temperament supremely suited for politics, strife, and competition. He thrived in the cauldron, functioning best when dramatic moral issues were at stake. He fought with gusto against fraud and corruption, delivering speeches studded with bold and original turns of phrase. "Words with me are instruments," Roosevelt said, and so they were—instruments to galvanize the emotions of the people in spirited battles for reform. "There is little use," he liked to say, "for the being whose tepid soul knows nothing of the great and generous emotion, of the high pride, the stern belief, the lofty enthusiasm, of the men who quell the storm and ride the thunder." When his critics fought back, he relished the fight, believing that "only through strife, through hard and dangerous endeavor," would victory be won.

TAFT STEADFASTLY SHUNNED THE VERY spotlight Roosevelt craved. He preferred to fight his battles from the inside, trusting logic, reason, and the careful recitation of facts. A conciliator by nature, Taft was never comfortable when called upon to deliver partisan diatribes at political rallies. Though reluctant to stir controversy, or give avoidable offense, Taft was not ready to compromise his principles for approval or expediency. He had demonstrated quiet courage in his fight against Tom Campbell and his refusal to fire conscientious workers simply because of their political preferences.

William Taft's amiable disposition and jovial countenance, evident from his earliest days, earned the goodwill and cooperation of family, friends, and colleagues alike. Within the family, Horace recalled, his brother often assumed the role of mediator. His keen perception and empathy allowed him to resolve the little conflicts that inevitably arose among parents and siblings. In his professional world, Taft's skill in developing relationships proved vital to his ascent. He established a rapport with a diverse cadre of mentors, from Murat Halstead and Miller Outcault to Benjamin Butterworth, Major Lloyd, and finally, Joseph Foraker.

Always plagued by procrastination and insecurity, Taft struggled to turn this intuitive emotional intelligence inward to access his own desires and use that knowledge to steer his life and career accordingly. Had he been able accurately to analyze the root of his unhappiness in the collector's office, he might have understood that his temperament was not suited for the turbulent world of politics. He detested political gamesmanship, found no pleasure in giving speeches, and chafed at public criticism. Yet, just as his desire to please Benjamin Butterworth had led him to take the collector's job, so, in the years ahead, his anxiety to please Nellie Herron—the complex woman who would become his wife—would eventually lead him away from his beloved law into the often scathing vortex of political life.

CHAPTER FOUR

Nellie Herron Taft

Nellie Herron, ca. 1886, the year she married William Howard Taft.

EIGHTEEN-YEAR-OLD NELLIE HERRON was enjoying her debutante season when she was introduced to twenty-two-year-old Will Taft. "It was at a coasting party," she wrote years later, recalling a merry gathering where young people went sledding down a steep snow-covered Mt. Auburn hill. Though their parents were acquainted and their younger sisters, Maria and Fanny, were close friends, Nellie and Will had not met before this festive night. "Tall and slender with fine gray eyes and soft brown hair," Nellie was described as handsome rather than beautiful, with a smile that "lights up her whole countenance."

Nellie was the fourth of eleven children born to Harriet Collins and John Herron. She was raised with five sisters and two brothers, while three other siblings had died in infancy. Although her mother, Harriet, was born in

Lowville, New York, a hamlet in the Adirondack foothills, the family was connected with a larger world of culture and politics. Harriet's father, Eli Collins, had served in the New York State Assembly and the U.S. Congress before his sudden death when she was eleven. Six years later, Harriet moved to Ohio to reside with her older brother. There, she met and married twenty-six-year-old lawyer John Herron.

John Herron had been a Miami University of Ohio schoolmate of future president Benjamin Harrison. When Herron opened his law practice in Cincinnati, he shared an office with another man who would be president, Rutherford B. Hayes. "Quite like living my college life over again," Hayes recorded in his diary. "We sleep on little hard mattresses in a little room cooped off from one end of our office." The lifelong friendship that developed between Herron and Hayes would eventually include their wives, Harriet and Lucy. Years later, Harriet said of Lucy that she "had no other friend with whom there has been such freedom of intimacy, none other so ready to respond with generous sympathy." This bond between the two couples would play a significant role in shaping Nellie Herron's ambitions.

When Hayes became governor of Ohio in 1869, he nominated his good friend Herron to the superior court. Herron hungered for the post but could not afford to relinquish his law practice. His wife's hankering for high society and insistence on private schooling for their children meant that he was forced "to go for money and leave glory to others." Hayes tried again a few years later. "I wish I could accept it. I may never have such another chance," Herron replied. "Like other things when I want them, I can't get them. And when I can get them I can't take them. At present I haven't one dollar coming in from a single investment that I have made & so I must look to my profession to support my family."

While Nellie remembered the three-story gray brick house where she grew up as "not particularly distinguished," she took pride that her home shared the same street as the Sinton mansion where Will's brother Charley and Annie Taft lived. Nellie marveled at the elegant facade of the white colonial dwelling; its Doric portico and bay windows, set amid "green lawns and finely kept shrubbery," reminded her of the White House.

At "The Nursery," as the exclusive Miss Nourse's school was known, Nellie excelled. A voracious reader, she carried a book everywhere she went. She read in the afternoons after completing her household chores, read at night in the quiet of her room and on rocky beaches during summer vacations. "A book," Nellie confided in her diary, "has more fascination for me than anything else." She possessed a sensibility for the beauty of language. Reading aloud with her girlfriends, she was attracted to the sound of words and the rhythms of passages. The curriculum at The Nursery included literature, history, science, music, French, German, Latin, and Greek, a comprehensive course of study to prepare students for entry into the best colleges. Nellie yearned to continue her education when she graduated, hoping especially to study music, which she considered "the inspiration of all my dreams and ambitions." While her brothers departed for Harvard and Yale, however, Nellie was informed that her father could not afford to send her to college. Instead, she was expected to "come out" into society and find herself a good husband.

Nellie was sixteen in 1877 when she accompanied her parents on a week-long visit to the White House at the invitation of Rutherford and Lucy Hayes. The president and first lady planned to celebrate their silver wedding anniversary among the friends who had stood with them at their marriage in 1852. The invitation included the prospect of a christening ceremony for the Herrons' seven-week-old baby in the Blue Room. The child had been named Lucy in honor of Harriet's closest friend. Harriet was reluctant at first to accept, protesting that "her baby has no fine clothes fit for such a place . . . & that she herself has only the same dresses that she had last March, hasn't bought a stitch since & hasn't time now to do it, even if she had any money to pay for them." But John insisted, and Nellie was thrilled to be included.

"I feel very much complimented that you should have remembered me in the preparations for the holiday festivities," Nellie wrote her "Aunt Lucy." "I have been in some doubts as to whether it would do for me to emerge from the chrysalis of school girl existence even for a short time into the butterfly life of young ladyhood, but the temptation has proved too strong for me, and it will give me great pleasure to accept your invitation."

Because Nellie had yet to make her official debut, she was not included at the anniversary dinner in the East Room attended by cabinet officers, generals, and justices of the Supreme Court. She could hear the music of the Marine Band from her room and spy the elegant gowns amid the splendor of the Blue, Red, and Green parlors, "profusely decorated with choice flowers from the conservatory." Hayes stated in his diary that Nellie brought "the house alive with laughter, fun, and music."

She was so elated by the visit that she rapturously confided to "Uncle Rutherford" that she intended "to marry a man who will be president." With a smile, Hayes replied: "I hope you may, and be sure you marry an Ohio man." Thirty years later, even as her husband sat in Roosevelt's cabinet, the allure of that first stay at the White House had not dimmed. In interviews with journalists, she recalled every detail. "Nothing in my life," she confessed, "reaches the climax of human bliss, which I felt as a girl of sixteen, when I was entertained at the White House." The vision of that expansive world spurred her sense of purpose. "She was intoxicated by what she saw and heard there," observed one reporter, "the bigness and breadth of the life."

For as long as she could remember—Nellie revealed in her diary—she had dreaded the prospect of leaving school, turning eighteen, and "coming out" into society. In the fall before her first season, she and her best friend, Alice (Allie) Keys, shrank from the prospect of becoming young women according to the traditional rituals, obliged to "receive attentions and offers and to wait around calmly to see if any future life will adjust itself." When the season drew to a close the following spring, though, she noted with surprise that she had "exceedingly" enjoyed herself in the "perfect whirr of gaiety" of the young Cincinnati set. She and her girlfriends Allie, Agnes, Laura, and Mary "stuck valiantly to each other" as they joined their male friends at Gilbert and Sullivan operettas, theatre parties, poker games, and German dances at Clifton Hall.

As summer came, her mood shifted. The cumulative months without intellectual or purposeful activity had grown enervating. "I am blue as indigo," she wrote on July 13, 1880, from a hammock at Yellow Springs, Ohio, a popular summer resort where she was vacationing with her family. "We are all rusticating up here, doing absolutely nothing, and I am reduced to a queer state of mind. . . . I am sick and tired of my life. I would rather be anyone else, even some one who has not some advantages I have and I am only nineteen. I feel often as if I were fifty." She yearned to "be busy and accomplish something." Even her attempts to pursue musical instruction were stymied. While she practiced diligently on her own to become a more accomplished pianist, she required guidance and lessons to achieve genuine virtuosity—lessons that cost more than her father would pay to accommodate what he considered simply a pastime.

"I would much rather give up some of the dresses I am getting," she wrote, "but Mama thinks I must have them." Harriet was determined that her daughters should "enjoy all the comforts and privileges of the wealthy class," even if John had to work long hours and weekends to stay out of debt. Nellie's biographer Carl Anthony conjectures that "a repressed nervousness" was instilled in the young woman by the chronic strain of the family's drive to maintain their place in a circle of greater wealth and privilege.

"I am beginning to want some steady occupation," she confided in her diary. "I read a good deal to be sure . . . but I should have some occupation that would require active work moving around—and I don't know where to find it. I believe my greatest desire now is to write a book. . . . I do so want to be independent."

Nellie's stifled energy and curiosity were quickened by the arrival of "that adorable Will Taft" at Yellow Springs. "Unfortunately I did not recover from my surprise and delight soon enough," she wrote Allie, "to make that impression which I would have wished." Will's solicitous, chivalric nature made a great effect upon Nellie. She was touched when he offered to cut up the meat for her six-year-old sister at a picnic on the Fourth of July, and charmed when he helped the women over brooks as they tramped through the woods the following day. "We had a lovely walk," she reported, and at an evening dance, Will "was enchanting as ever. You see what a splendid chance I had at Will, but alas!" she noted regretfully, "he strikes me with awe."

Later that summer, Nellie accompanied her father to Rhode Island's Narragansett Pier, where she was joined by several friends. Though her days were filled with tennis, croquet, and sailing, she could not rouse herself from her "stupid state." The thrill of forbidden activities provided some respite from her torpor. She hid in the rocks at dusk to smoke cigarettes with her girlfriend Sallie, gambled at cards, and drank milk punches laced with whiskey late at night.

As fall approached, convinced that her rebellious unconventional nature would forever preclude a great success in society, Nellie pledged to devote five or six hours a day to the piano. She begged her mother to intercede with her father and facilitate the music lessons she craved. She realized, however, that no decision could be made until her parents returned from a two-month trip with the president and first lady to California, a historic voyage that marked the first visit by a president to the west coast. Nellie was left behind with her four younger siblings to take charge of the household, to dust and tidy, sew and darn, set the table for dinner, and wash the dishes. "I have not read one good book, novel excepted, but Schiller's Life by Carlyle," she complained.

Nellie gained some leisure time when her parents returned, but the music lessons never materialized. Desperate for a measure of genuine intellectual engagement, she enrolled in less expensive chemistry and German classes at the University of Cincinnati. Her spirits lifted. She relished her studies and joined a walking club that included Annie Taft, several of her girlfriends, John Mack, and Howard Hollister, Will's best friend. "He is very sympathetic," Nellie wrote of Hollister. Seated next to him at a supper following one of their hikes, she was "all afire" when he launched into a sentimental debate on the glory of dying for one you loved. Being "exceedingly romantic" herself, Nellie leapt into the conversation. Then, suddenly overcome by self-consciousness, she worried that he was simply drawing her out to "make fun" of her. "Make fun of you," he exclaimed. "Why Miss Herron there is no one whose good opinion I value as much as yours."

After a brief flirtation, Nellie and Howard settled down to become good friends. "I am perfectly delighted in the hope that a very ordinary love affair may perhaps have become what I always longed for," she wrote in her diary, "a warm friendship between two quite congenial people—which is very rare, and so much more to be desired than the other. . . . Such a friendship is infinitely higher than what is usually called love, for in it there is a realization of each other's defects, and a proper appreciation of their good points, without that fatal idealization which is so blind. . . . From my point of view a love which is worthy of the name should always have a beginning in the other, and should this friendship turn into something higher it is a blessed happiness."

Nellie counseled Howard through a tumultuous relationship with her friend Agnes Davis while he, in turn, supported Nellie's struggle to find purpose in her life. In her diary, she recorded diverting evenings in the German section of town where they "drank beer and ate Wiener Wurst." Mixing with laborers and merchants in raucous beer halls might be unsuitable behavior for a society girl, but Nellie loved the atmosphere. Indeed, the fact that such surroundings "greatly horrified" her proper friends intensified her pleasure. "There being something Bohemian about it which delighted me," she wrote, "I really felt quite like a comrade & man."

In the spring of 1883, contrary to her mother's wishes, Nellie accepted an offer to teach in a private school for boys. "Do you realize you will have to give up society, as you now enjoy it," Harriet reminded her. "Certainly late hours and dancing parties do not promote the patience and physical endurance required by a teacher. And then is it quite the thing for a young girl in your position to teach in a boys school—and where there are no other ladies? . . . I shrink from thinking of you as making your own way in the world in any inconsequential manner." Nellie was shaken by the opposition that her mother expressed in "two dreadful letters." Though several friends admired her decision, the majority questioned her "queer taste." Disconcerted by her inability to "get along as other girls do," she was determined to move forward, envisioning a future as headmistress of a school. "Of course a woman is happier who marries, if she marries exactly right, but how many do," she reasoned. "Otherwise I do think that she is much happier single, and doing some congenial work."

Harriet Herron's conviction that her daughter's decision would inhibit her social life proved unfounded. In fact, Nellie's occupation bolstered her confidence and buoyed her mood, making her a far more engaging companion. Her insecurity in Will Taft's presence evaporated as he joined her regular circle of friends. On numerous occasions, she accompanied Will and Howard Hollister to concerts and German dances at Clifton Hall, returning the hospitality with whist parties at her house. "The meeting at Miss Herron's was a great success," Will told his sister Fanny, describing an evening of cards, supper, charades, and games. "We made the Herron mansion ring with the merry peals of the young ladies and the harsher but joyous tone of the men until the hands of the clock were pushing us home by pointing towards two o'clock."

Sustained by this new sense of direction, Nellie no longer found the long summer days depressing. In July 1883, she joined Allie and a group of their friends at "Sea Verge," the Keys' summer mansion at Little Boar's Head in North Hampton, New Hampshire. Alongside the customary swimming and sailing, tennis and card games, she and Allie determined to embark on an ambitious reading program. They resolved daily to read aloud fifty pages of Henry Buckle's three-volume *History of Civilization in England*; they shared "long and very tough" readings of John Stuart Mill, and immersed themselves in German and Italian. To "repair" their "exhausted intellects," they took long walks through the countryside, picked berries, read a little poetry, and watched the tide break around the rocks. In the evenings they plunged into the bracing water of the North Atlantic to stimulate their appetites before dinner.

Returning to her teaching job in the fall, Nellie struggled with her mother's increasingly strident opposition. "Mamma thinks I am wrong," she told her diary. "I hope that I am not . . . I should be a miserable apathetic woman without an interest in life unless I bettered myself now while I am young and courageous and engaged in some real work. The usual pottering which an unmarried woman calls work would never satisfy me." Still, she could not easily disregard her mother's admonition that a society girl entered the workforce at her peril. "Why should I take life so hard? Other people seem to get through all right without inconvenient ideas," she lamented. "All week I have been in that state when my eyes fill with tears at the least provocation," she admitted, "and I take refuge in silence."

Despite these private misgivings, Nellie was self-possessed and animated among her friends, emerging as the leader of their social circle. The Saturday night salons she hosted, anticipated by her coterie the week long, offered an enlivening combination of entertainment and intellectual pursuits. The regulars included Allie Keys, Will Taft and his brother Horace, Howard Hollister, Agnes Davis, and Maria Herron, Nellie's younger sister. The group selected a different topic each week and the members of the salon were expected to prepare for discussion with all the reading and research they could muster. For the session on the French Revolution, Will read Thomas Carlyle's *The French Revolution, a History*; when the topic was Russia, he read Donald MacKenzie's *Russia*. When Rousseau, Cavour, Edmund Burke, Matthew Arnold, and Isaac Newton were selected as subjects, he scoured the public library for their works. The Yale graduate who had refused to read outside the course curriculum suddenly found himself inspired.

"Nellie Herron has made a great success of her salon," Will reported to his sister. "I feel as if I had really profited greatly by the reading which I have done for it. The pleasure of it has grown as we go on. I value the friendships which have grown out of it very highly. Nobody is absent when he can help it." Indeed, forced to travel out of town one Saturday, Will sent Nellie roses to express his regret at missing "that sweet school of Peripatetic philosophy in which I am an humble but enthusiastic disciple."

Writing of one salon session, focused on Edmund Burke, Will wryly remarked to his mother that the discussion became "very heated especially between the men, who knowing less about the subject than the ladies, are naturally more certain of their position." Burke was not the only topic to stir dissension among these passionate young people; in the aftermath of a debate on slavery, the volatile mixture of historical inquiry and individual points of view left Will much chagrined. "I am not satisfied at all with my bearing in the slavery discussion," he wrote to Nellie. "I deeply regret that my manner was such as to leave the impression on your mind that I held your suggestions or arguments lightly or regarded them with contempt. . . . So far as holding your opinions lightly, I know no one who attaches more weight to them or who more admires your powers of reasoning than the now humbled subscriber."

The attachments forged in the salon deepened as the friends consoled each other in difficulties and together celebrated triumphs. The group spent weekends together at the Keys' mansion in Walnut Hills and escorted each other to the regular Thursday German dances. The girls organized card parties and picnics for which the men provided both the punch and the repast. They put on amateur theatricals for charity. Nellie long remembered the burlesque production of *Sleeping Beauty* in which Will played the beautiful princess, while Horace, who had fallen in love with Nellie's sister, Maria, performed as Puck.

With increasing frequency, Nellie's name appeared in Will's letters to his family in Vienna. He lauded her as "the only notable exception" among superficial society girls who viewed "a suitable marriage as a proper ending of their social career." He proudly relayed the news that she had been offered a teaching position at Miss Nourse's school, declaring that she deserved "the greatest credit" for persevering despite censure from friends and family alike. "It is easy enough to talk about woman's widening her sphere and being something more than an ornament or a housekeeper but it is not so easy in the present state of society for her to act on that theory."

In the summer of 1884, Will was invited to spend a long weekend with Nellie and Allie at Sea Verge, the summer mansion at Little Boar's Head. During those sunlit days, filled with picnics, swims, and ventures into Boston, Will first began to recognize the central place Nellie had come to hold in his life. "After awhile I found myself deferring to her opinion in everything I did or said," he later told Allie. "Finally what she thought became of much more importance to me than what I thought myself."

Largely to gain Nellie's approbation, Will began to carry a book as a matter of course. "Trollope is a great favorite of mine because of the realistic every day tone which one finds in every line he writes," he told her. "His heroes have failings human character is heir to, and we like them none the less on that account." He became increasingly solicitous of Nellie's happiness. When the German opera festival was in town, he accompanied her to hear *Tannhäuser*, admitting to his mother that while "my own appreciation of Wagner is not intense . . . [I] shall derive most if not all of my pleasure from her enjoyment of the music."

Eager to acknowledge Nellie's own desire to accomplish something worthy, he spoke with disdain of two wealthy acquaintances whose chief literary nourishment was drawn from stock reports. "It seems to me that with their money and opportunities they could do so much good in this country where we are in such need of disinterested public work that their listlessness and idleness is little better than a sin. . . . If all the wealthy were of their kind I should become a communist." He found validation for the more progressive ideals he and Nellie shared in reports from the East that "young men of wealth who do not have to devote their time to making a livelihood, are taking an interest in politics." This is "a good augury," he maintained, for it would infuse a generation's political life with a growing zeal for public service. He was likely referring directly to Theodore Roosevelt and Henry Cabot Lodge, whose reform efforts on behalf of George Edmunds were then making news.

By winter, he later confessed, "I was wakened to the fact that I loved her." The truth of his feelings struck him "with overwhelming force," and in late April 1885, he finally asked her to marry him. The proposal stunned Nellie, who feared that his precipitous declaration would compromise a friendship that had become vital to her. Moreover, she feared that marriage would destroy her hard-won chance to accomplish something worthy in her own right. She turned him down and told him never to speak of it again.

Undeterred, Will remained certain that in time he could bring her to love him as he loved her. Only five days later, he penned a long letter, assuring her that the hesitation she felt about the institution of marriage was perfectly understandable. "I never have been certain that marriage was the happier state for women. I know it is for a man. Then too a mistake with him does not involve his entire life. With a woman a mistake is worse than death for in marriage she gives her all." During a long walk a few days after that, he pressed his case, following up with another heartfelt letter. "I love you Nellie," he declared. "I love you for all that you are. I love you for your noble consistent character . . . for all that you are, for all that you hope to be. . . . Oh how I will work and strive to be better and do better, how I will labor for our joint advancement if only you will let me. You will be my companion, my love and my life."

Her initial resistance to his entreaties only confirmed his admiration and intensified his own determination. "My love for you grew out of a friendship, intimate and of long standing," he noted, methodically laying out his appeal. "That friendship of course was founded on a respect and admiration for your high character, your sweet womanly qualities and your intellectual superiority over any woman I know and for that quality in you which is called sympathy but I call it self forgetting companionableness. . . . Much as I should love to have you love me now and say so now, there is proud satisfaction I feel in that such a heart as yours can not be won in a moment."

Finally, Nellie agreed to an engagement. Far from curtailing her ambitions, she sensed that marriage to a man of Will's enlightened temperament would create enhanced opportunities for them both. With her direction and support, he could be her emissary to the wider world she craved. "You know," she told her mother soon after the engagement, "a lot of people think a great deal of Will. Some people even say that he may obtain some very important position in Washington." Although her ambitions for her fiancé had a worldly aspect, Nellie clearly expected far more from him and from herself than mere status and stability.

Will was ready to shout the news of their betrothal from every street corner. Nellie insisted that it remain a secret from all but their parents until she was ready for a public announcement. Forced to maintain a pretense of mere friendship before Howard, Allie, Horace, and all his friends, Will had to content himself with long letters to his parents, who were still in Europe. "The more I knew her," Will told his father, "the deeper grew my respect for her, the warmer my friendship until it unconsciously ripened into a feeling that she was indispensable to my happiness. . . . I know you will love her when you come to know her and will appreciate as I do her noble character and clear cut intellect and well informed mind. She has been teaching for three years and has been no expense at all to her father. She has done this without encouragement by her family who thought the work too hard for her because she chafed under the conventionalities of society which would keep a young lady only for evening entertainments. She wanted something to do in life. . . . Her eagerness for knowledge of all kinds puts me to shame. Her capacity for work is wonderful."

That summer of 1885, when Nellie left for the Adirondacks with her family, Will experienced an unfamiliar sense of desolation. "Your sweet smile today as you stood on the stoop, I shall carry in my memory as something to console me with your absence," he wrote only hours after she departed. "And now Nellie I fold you in my arms and imprint on your lips the kisses I was cheated out of by Fate today." Solace came in the form of the daily letters he wrote. "The only real pleasure I take is in writing you," he told her, "and in the hope, so often in vain, that the mail carrier's appearance inspires in me. When I don't get a letter I read all the old ones over again." His familiar surroundings only exacerbated his restless loneliness. Everywhere he went—the library, the homes of their friends, the corner of Pike and Fifth—heightened his awareness of her absence. "It is the one who stays at home that feels the parting. New scenes, new interests, quickly dispel the pleasant sadness of the parting for the one who leaves."

To mollify his impatience for her return, he narrated the minutiae of the day without her, filling pages with political news, gossip about their friends, and images of the life they would lead once they were married. "I long to settle down in a home of our own," he told her, adding, "we must continue the salon." Nellie's father had promised them a plot of land in Walnut Hills, where they planned to construct their home. "I shall have the greatest pride in entertaining my classmates, Bonesmen, under our roof where you and they can know each other." Although Will's vision of domestic bliss included social entertainment, it focused on the bond of marriage. His letters conjured evenings seated "comfortably and cosily before a bright fire," reading and talking "with such demonstrations of affection as the unruly husband can not restrain." While he acknowledged that his ideal might seem "commonplace" or "prosaic," he fondly anticipated a married life resembling those depicted in Victorian novels, "where the husband was working hard, materially assisted and buoyed up by the earnest sympathy and intelligence of the wife."

He repeatedly assured Nellie that he would strive to make himself worthy of her. He had labored diligently in college to satisfy his parents; now he would persevere and please his wife. "His temperament," one insightful journalist later reflected, "requires settled authority." With Nellie to replace his father's role of "guide, counsellor and friend," he would find far greater success than he could ever have secured on his own. "You are becoming responsible for the actions of two persons now," he frankly admitted to Nellie. "I feel a weight lifted from my shoulders." While they might never be wealthy, they would build a rich life together. With her encouragement, he promised to overcome his reluctance and exact suitable payment for his legal work. "It is hard for me to learn to charge a fee without apologizing for its amount," he confessed. "That is one of the defects in my character you must remedy. You must stiffen me in the matter of fees." He pledged that theirs would be "an equal partnership. You earn half of everything that comes in just as much as if you wrote the briefs or honeyfugled a jury. You may write the briefs, who knows?" He proudly reported that "business had been brisker" and that he had "done twice as much work" in the months since their engagement, a circumstance which his partner Major Lloyd attributed directly to Nellie's influence.

He conceded a natural tendency toward laziness and procrastination, a condition Nellie's influence was certain to remedy in order to make him "a good and just member of society." Indeed, just two weeks before his proposal, he had delivered "a very hastily prepared paper before the Unity Club on Pontifical Rome," which, he acknowledged, did him "no credit." Horace agreed. "As usual," he told his mother, "he put the thing off until he had only two or three days to prepare it and then he had to toil like a slave. I told him I thought it would be a lesson worth a fortune to him if he were to make one complete & ignominious fizzle at this early period of his life from want of preparation. He did not do it this time but it was enough to serve as a warning. His was the best piece of the evening, but that is not saying much and he might have done much better. He has a wonderful power of work when he once gets started and the only danger is in his trusting to it too much." Will's own recognition of these deficits, and of the corresponding drive in Nellie's character, contributed to his profound admiration for the woman he loved and to his deep-seated reliance upon her judgment and resolve.

Will joined Nellie in the Adirondacks for two weeks in early August 1885. "Each day has found Nellie and me on the lake and in the woods," he joyously reported to his mother. "She sews or sketches while I read aloud to her. We finished *Their Wedding Journey* by Howells and have begun *The Mill on the Floss* by George Eliot." At summer's end, Nellie finally assented to make public the engagement.

"I knew you would be delighted to hear," Will wrote to Allie Keys. "Didn't

I know that you were hoping for this for so many months? Didn't I tingle to my finger tips with gratitude to you for the many little schemes which you concocted to help me on in my suit, you little conspirator. . . . Oh, Alice, you do know the prize I have won . . . that no more perfect character than Nellie's is among all our friends. You know what a constant source of comfort and strength she is to everyone who seeks it from her. . . . She has already made me a better man. My ideals of life are higher and I believe my purpose to attain them is stronger. Certainly there could not be given to a man a stronger motive for upright consistent, hardworking and kindly living than the approval and intelligent sympathy of such a wife."

"How much I appreciate your confidence in me," Allie elatedly replied, "your telling me so much of what is in your heart. To have had either you or Nellie marry anyone I did not know or even did not love would have been hard for me, but I should have been happy in your happiness and tried not to be selfish. But to have you marry one another is such a joy to me that the sky has been bluer and the sunlight brighter ever since I heard. Yes, Will, I do know her, and it makes me so happy to think that some one is to have her who appreciates what she is who has known her long enough to understand her, for I do not think she is soon known or easily understood. . . . You and Howard—you have been the two best new friends I ever had, and I hope and believe I shall never lose you." Allie's fervent wishes were soon realized: she and Howard became engaged, and the two couples would remain devoted friends to the end of their lives.

Certainly, Will and Nellie's match met with resounding approval from friends and family. "What a pair you will be!" Horace told Will. "In all my acquaintance she is the girl I would have picked for you long ago & ever since and you are the one I would have chosen for her." Indeed, it had appeared for a time that the two brothers might marry two Herron women, but Horace could not persuade Nellie's beautiful sister Maria to accept his proposal of marriage. Nevertheless, their lives would intersect frequently in the years ahead.

In late February 1886, Nellie and Allie traveled east together for two weeks. In New York, they stayed with Allie's wealthy Aunt Phoebe, mistress of Sea Verge, the summer home where Will first realized the depths of his feelings for Nellie. The two old friends enjoyed their time together, walking around the city, shopping for books and clothes. They perused furniture stores and curiosity shops, looking for tables, sideboards, lamps, and etchings for their new homes. From Cincinnati, Will wrote frequently to Nellie, describing his daily routine in detail only a lover would not find exhausting. "I went to the gymnasium today wholly because of you," he proudly reported. "It was

Washington's birthday and I felt lazy," he admitted, but the thought of his fiancée mobilized him. Four days later, he returned to the gym, though he acknowledged, "I have given up weighing myself each day. 'A watched pot never boils,' and I shall try to surprise myself by waiting until you get home before I weigh again."

Proceeding to Washington, Nellie selected her wedding dress, "a superbly-fashioned satin robe with embroidered front." Pining at home, Will tried to inject some levity into his letter: "I hope you will think of me tomorrow when you take your Sunday afternoon walk along the beautiful streets of Washington. I wonder, Nellie dear, if you and I will ever be there in any official capacity? Oh yes, I forgot, of course we shall when you become Secretary of the Treasury." A few days later he wrote again, musing on the ten short months which had affected a sea change in both their lives since she had finally accepted his proposal: "The parlor is unchanged, the street is unchanged, the new custom house as it was then, but to me they all wear a different look, so different indeed that I almost forget how they did look before you made silent promise to be mine. . . . In that ten months we have had very few differences of any kind."

Nellie Herron and William Taft were married on June 19, 1886, in the parlor of the Herron house on Pike Street. Alphonso and Louise, who had returned from Europe the previous October, were present to celebrate their son's marriage. Maria Herron and Fanny Taft served as bridesmaids. Horace was his brother's best man. After what the *Cincinnati Enquirer* described as "a brilliant reception," the young couple traveled to New York and prepared to embark for Europe and the honeymoon Nellie called "my first taste of the foreign travel of which I had always dreamed."

Aboard ship, they read aloud from Oliver Goldsmith's *Vicar of Wakefield* and the collected poems of Coleridge and Shelley in preparation for their visit to the English countryside. They visited Shakespeare's house in Stratford-on-Avon, reveled at the sight of Gladstone's Welsh castle in Hawarden, and dined in English country inns. Nellie pored through reports of parliamentary speeches by Gladstone and Parnell and hungered to hear live orations and debates. They continued through Scotland, Holland, and France, managing to travel for a hundred days on "just one thousand dollars," thanks to Nellie's unremitting budget.

They returned to a home still under construction in Cincinnati and spent their first month living with Will's parents. Nellie developed a strong attachment to Alphonso, whom she considered "gentle beyond anything I ever knew . . . one of the most lovable men that ever lived." Both Alphonso and Louise, she wrote, "had created a family atmosphere in which the children breathed in the highest ideals, and were stimulated to sustained and strenuous intellectual and moral effort in order to conform to the family standard." She marveled at the "strong minds, intellectual tastes, wide culture and catholic sympathies" that generated the loving yet rigorous environment of the Taft household.

In January 1887, Nellie and Will moved into their redwood-shingled home overlooking a splendid stretch of the Ohio River and the lush hills and valleys on both the Ohio and Kentucky sides. The library, lined with bookshelves of solid walnut, housed Will's accumulating legal texts, which he would continue to accrue until he had proudly amassed a catalogue of scholarly volumes that was estimated among the foremost in the country.

No sooner were the newlyweds settled in their new home on McMillan Street than Will was surprised by Governor Foraker's decision to appoint him to the bench. Hurrying home to share the astonishing news with his wife, he tried to appear casual. "Nellie," he coyly questioned, "what would you think if I should be appointed a Judge of the Superior Court?" "Oh, don't try to be funny," Nellie answered. "That's perfectly impossible." A twenty-nine-year-old, she reasoned, would never receive an appointment over much more experienced lawyers. Quickly realizing that Will was not teasing, she was stunned and gratified by "the honour which came to us so unexpectedly." Horace was thrilled. "Wasn't it immense," he wrote Nellie. "How does his Honor bear it? You'll have to help him work with a vengeance now Nellie. Tie wet towels around his head. You & I know what kind of a judge he will make. We can afford to let the world find out."

Nellie's elation soon gave way to misgivings, however, as she reflected that the appointment "was not a matter for such warm congratulation after all." Indeed, the more she considered his new post and colleagues, the more unsettled she felt. "I saw him in close association with men not one of whom was less than fifteen years older than he, and most of whom were much more than that. He seemed to me suddenly to take on a maturity and sedateness quite out of keeping with his actual years and I dreaded to see him settled for good in the judiciary and missing all the youthful enthusiasms and exhilarating difficulties which a more general contact with the world would have given him. . . . I began even then to fear the narrowing effects of the Bench." For the young woman who had hoped her husband's career would carry them both to an exciting life in Washington, the superior court in Cincinnati assumed the aspect of a stumbling block rather than a stepping-stone.

Nevertheless, Nellie grudgingly acknowledged that her husband "did not share this feeling in any way. His appointment on the Superior Court was to him the welcome beginning of just the career he wanted." Upon completion of Will's interim appointment, Foraker successfully backed him for election to a full five-year term. This ballot marked Taft's only bid for elected office until he became a candidate for president of the United States. He flourished as a judge, proud to sit on the bench where his father had once presided. He immersed himself in work entirely suited to his temperament, enjoying legal research and finding precedents for a broad range of cases covering contracts, wills, trademarks, suits for libel and negligence, disputes between the rights of property and the rights of labor. His profound satisfaction and facility in his vocation were evident to all.

Will Taft's most significant action as a superior court judge was a ruling in 1890 that addressed the balance of power between the burgeoning labor movement and industrial interests. The case involved a secondary boycott, a sanction intended to punish one business by wielding pressure against another business unrelated to the original cause of grievance. In this instance, the Bricklayers' Union had declared a boycott against the contracting firm of Parker Brothers on grounds that the company had discriminated against its members. The union called on all suppliers of the firm's building materials to honor the boycott. When the Moore Lime Company continued to supply Parker Brothers, the union declared it would no longer use lime supplied by Moore's. Moore's & Co. sued the Bricklayers' Union for damages caused by the secondary boycott. Their suit was upheld by the lower court in Hamilton County, which awarded a verdict of $2,250 to the plaintiffs. When *Moore's & Co. v. Bricklayers' Union et al.* reached the superior court on appeal, Taft sustained the lower court decision, affirming that a secondary boycott against a firm with whom there was no dispute was illegal. His decision was upheld by the Ohio Supreme Court. Decades later, it remained a leading case on the law of secondary boycotts.

While his decision worked to limit the power of organized labor, Taft revealed a sympathy for the rights of workers that his more conservative colleagues did not share. He was careful to underscore the union's prerogative in withdrawing its members from Parker Brothers; when the union turned on an unrelated company, however, it had exceeded its legal bounds. Though Taft refused to condone the union's action in this case, he argued strongly for a laborer's "right to work for such wages as he chooses, and to get as high a rate as he can." He maintained that an individual "may lawfully notify his employers of his objection and refuse to work," and concluded that "what one workman may do . . . many may combine to do."

Taft sought to delineate union rights at a hazardous time in Cincinnati, when the memory of a violent general strike was still raw. Calling for an eight-hour day, 32,000 Cincinnati workers had joined workers in other cities in a crippling general strike commencing on May Day, 1886. Singing a version of the *Marseillaise*, they marched through the city, brandishing Springfield rifles and red flags. For days, "no freight moved in or out of the city; garbage went uncollected; laundresses, streetcar conductors, waitresses and machinists cooperated in shutting down the city." The militia was called out and the workers returned to their posts, but the horror of the strikers' "revolutionary fervor" had impressed itself upon Cincinnati's propertied classes. It was in this context that Taft, in his judicial sphere, tried to balance the rights of labor with the rights of capital.

NELLIE'S CAREFUL ALLOCATION OF WILL'S $6,000 annual salary allowed the couple to furnish their new home and still save enough to fund a second trip to Europe the following summer. With the house fully settled, Nellie returned to work, taking a teaching position at the kindergarten recently opened by Miss Nourse to serve the children of the poor. Earlier in the decade, Louise Taft had served as the first president of the Cincinnati Free Kindergarten Association. In the 1880s, Ohio laws had forbidden public funding of education for children younger than six. Public kindergartens would eventually be established, but meanwhile Louise and a group of her friends helped raise money to open a series of charity kindergartens. "If the little ones who wander neglected in our streets are to be reached," she proclaimed, "private benevolence must come to the rescue. We therefore appeal to the friends of education and humanity to help us in this effort." The first kindergarten was established in 1880, followed by others, including Miss Nourse's school. There, Nellie devoted herself to teaching, experimenting with colored balls, cylinders, cubes, and spheres to convey concepts of number, color, and geometric forms to younger children. Determined to allow her young charges every avenue she could devise to quicken their understanding and facilitate its expression, she explored all manner of mediums, hoping to engage them through music, art, and play.

The first serious breach in the close-knit Taft family occurred in early June 1889. Following a divorce from his wife Tillie, the mental condition of Peter, Will's older brother, had seemed much improved. He resumed his law practice and appeared to be leading a quiet life, devoting his leisure time to his young son, Hulbert. His agitation and paranoia gradually returned, however, rendering him incapable of work. He complained that mysterious forces "were conspiring against him," preventing the medicine from taking effect. Throughout his illness, his father's support never wavered. "You may rely upon one thing," Alphonso lovingly assured him, "and that is that my heart is always with you." The deterioration of Peter's mind was accompanied by a progressive wasting of his body, most likely from consumption. Though the family knew he was unwell, his death early that summer came as a shock.

The funeral was conducted at the home of Charles and Annie. One of Peter's Yale classmates delivered the eulogy, recalling the halcyon days when Peter achieved "the highest rank in scholarship ever reached at Yale," bringing "lasting honor on himself, his family, his class." Annie found solace in the knowledge that young Hulbert was able to hear "what sort of a man his father was."

"Poor Peter!" Harry Taft wrote to his father, remembering the brother who was once "the sunniest of us all." In the end, he reflected, "his was a sad life and while I had hoped that life near the old home would add much to his comfort and perhaps to his happiness, it could never have restored him to what he was and perhaps the Lord has done wisely to remove him." Harry had moved to Manhattan after his marriage to Julia Smith, daughter of a wealthy lawyer from Troy, New York. He had begun his legal career at Simpson, Thacher, & Barnum but had recently joined Cadwalader's, a leading corporate law firm that would eventually bear his name. His absence from Cincinnati contributed to an increasing sense of distance at the dispersal of the Taft family.

Will worried about the impact of Peter's death on his father, who was still suffering from the effects of typhoid pneumonia contracted in St. Petersburg. The disease had thickened Alphonso's lungs and affected the right ventricle of the heart, making it difficult for him to breathe. In recent months, he had seemed to improve, but the trauma of Peter's death brought on a marked deterioration in his health. "Every time the telephone rings I am fearful lest it be a sudden summons," Will confided to Horace.

Horace, meanwhile, harbored anxiety and a measure of guilt that he had added to his father's sadness. Disconsolate after Maria Herron refused his marriage offer, he had abandoned Cincinnati and the practice of law, which he had never enjoyed, for a teaching position in Kansas City. "My chief regret about it," he acknowledged, "came from my father's disappointment, for his heart was set on my going on in the law." He had taught in Kansas City only briefly when he was offered a faculty position at Yale, where he conceived the plan of founding a boys' school. The year after Peter's death, he opened a private school in a redbrick house in Watertown, Connecticut, instructing ten boarders and seven day students. In those early years, Horace taught nearly all the classes himself; but in time the institution, known as the Taft School, would become a prestigious preparatory school, boasting a distinguished faculty and more than five hundred students.

On September 10, 1889, Nellie gave birth to an eight-pound son christened Robert Alphonso to carry the patriarch's name into the next generation. "Nellie took the pain bravely," Will reported to his father. "It is a treat to see how happy she is." Will was ecstatic at the arrival of his first son. "On the whole, sitting as I do judicially in this case, I am obliged to give judgment for those who contend that the boy is one of the most remarkable products of this century," he jauntily pronounced. "I have been accused of the unjudicial conduct of rushing out into the street after the boy came and yelling, 'Hurrah!' For a man is born unto me." As Will only presided in court on Tuesdays and Saturdays, he was able to spend prolonged stretches at home, surrounded by the books of his own library, writing opinions. Horace heckled him over this arrangement with a friendly jibe: "I suppose you wish me to deny the report that you adjourn Court whenever Robert Alphonso has the colic. I am trying to keep it out of the papers."

These were happy days for Taft. A *New York Times* correspondent, analyzing his work on the bench, noted: "He breathes good will and suggests mental, moral, and physical wholesomeness. Yet, with all his pleasant informality and his frequent laughter, he has a dignity of manner and carriage that commands respect and attention." In his opinions, he presented the facts and his well-reasoned conclusions in a cogent, if sometimes verbose style. Ohio court records reveal that his thorough, thoughtful decisions were "upheld by the State Supreme Court to a gratifying extent."

Taft's equanimity and penchant for research deeply impressed his two older colleagues, Judges Hiram Peck and Frederick E. Moore. When the death of Stanley Matthews left a vacancy on the Ohio Supreme Court in 1889, they joined other Ohioans in recommending their thirty-two-year-old colleague Taft to President Benjamin Harrison, despite his youth and mere two years on the bench. Governor Foraker concurred, assuring Harrison that Taft's appointment "would be satisfactory to an unusually high degree to the Republicans of this state and no Democrat could justly criticize it." From New Haven, Horace reported a conversation with Will's classmate John Porter, now editor of the *Hartford Post*. His well-connected friends in Washington called Taft's prospects "pretty hopeful." Porter had recently spoken with Congressman

Butterworth, who suggested that Will, if passed over for the supreme court, should run for governor. Horace was less enthusiastic about that possibility, much preferring that his brother become "a fine old Justice."

When President Harrison visited Cincinnati that August, Taft joined the welcoming party at the train. Asked later if he had noticed Taft, Harrison replied: "O Yes, what a fine looking man he is. What a fine physique he has." Although Taft dined with the presidential party that night at the city's leading hotel, the Burnet House, he had no opportunity to speak with the president again. He reported to his father that his "chances of going to the Moon and of donning a silk gown at the hands of President Harrison are about equal. I am quite sure if I were he, I would not appoint a man of my age and position to that Bench." Taft felt some disappointment yet small surprise when, in December 1889, Harrison nominated circuit court judge David Brewer, a twenty-eight-year veteran on the bench.

Harrison had not forgotten the imposing young man. A month later, when U.S. Solicitor General Orlon Chapman suddenly died from pneumonia, Harrison nominated William Howard Taft for the prestigious post of chief barrister for the government. "It is a great event in your career, & you should accept without hesitation," Alphonso counseled from San Diego, where he and Louise were spending the winter. Louise was also enthusiastic. Alphonso had been certain the news would leave him sleepless, she wrote, "but it was I who lay awake . . . it is so hard not to be with you in this excitement." She too emphasized the importance of the appointment—not just for Will but for Alphonso as well, whom the news had imbued with "a new interest in life."

For Nellie, the appointment offered a chance to realize her goals both for herself and her husband. "I was very glad," she later wrote, for it offered Will "an opportunity for exactly the kind of work I wished him to do; work in which his own initiative and originality would be exercised and developed." They would escape the confining world of the Cincinnati Superior Court, where Will fraternized with much older men and dinner conversations too often focused on tedious legal questions. Moreover, she fondly anticipated life in the capital, where her husband's eminence would gain admission to an exciting world of cabinet officials, congressmen, and senators, and where she would attend White House receptions, observe legislative debates, and discuss the vital topics of the day. She was immediately willing to find and furnish a new house, leave behind supportive parents and relatives, and uproot their small son from his routine—all in search of a more fulfilling and exciting existence.

Only Will was reluctant. As solicitor general, he would argue cases as an advocate, standing to present "one side of a case" rather than weighing evidence and rendering judgment, temperamentally a far more congenial role. In his early days as a lawyer, arguing before the court had quickly become his least favorite aspect of the job; his affinity was for administering justice with fairness and integrity. Moreover, he was "entirely unfamiliar with the rules of practice" before the federal court, and had "very little familiarity" with federal statutes. And he knew he would have little time to orient himself. Straightaway upon his arrival, a backlog of cases to be argued would greet him. Furthermore, he took no pleasure in the prospect of leaving behind the close friendships and comfortable life he had built in Cincinnati.

"Go ahead, & fear not," his father advised. "You will have a full library at your service, in your own room, with messengers to get the books, besides Assistant Atty Generals to examine law points & make briefs for you; and you will have a short hand reporter take down & write out with type writing what you wish to have written." He continued to encourage and prod his reluctant son in a string of letters. "To a large extent the legal field of inquiry will be new," Alphonso wrote, "but you can master it, as you have mastered other things." His mother agreed: "You have learned the duties of a Judge so soon you can certainly hope to acquire those of an advocate." Alphonso was intent on stamping out any doubt his son might experience, faced by a change of such magnitude. "I believe you are equal to it," the father proclaimed with confidence, "although I do not believe the experiment has ever before been tried with so young a man. I receive more compliments than I know what to do with for having such a son. I try to behave with becoming modesty. . . . We are intensely proud of you."

The formidable combination of his father's high expectations and his wife's desires proved irresistible for Taft. He wrote to President Harrison, accepting the position. His confirmation was celebrated with a "brilliant reception" at the Lincoln Club. Four days later, Taft set out alone on a sleeper train for Washington, determined to find proper lodging before Nellie and the baby joined him.

Nellie's depiction of Will's anxiety upon reaching the nation's capital evinces a novelist's empathy: "He arrived at six o'clock on a cold, gloomy February morning at the old dirty Pennsylvania station. He wandered out on the street with a heavy bag in his hand looking for a porter, but there were no porters. Then he stood for a few moments looking up at the Capitol and feeling dismally unimportant in the midst of what seemed to him to be very formidable surroundings. . . . He was sure he had made a fatal mistake in exchanging a good position and a pleasant circle at home, where everybody knew him, for a place in a strange and forbidding city where he knew practically nobody." Nellie's account clearly reveals, beneath her insistence that he establish himself in Washington, a compassionate knowledge of her husband's nature. She relates that he dropped his bag off at the Old Ebbit House and walked to the Department of Justice for his swearing-in. Then he went to examine his office, where he "met the most dismal sight of the whole dismal day. His 'quarters' consisted of a single room, three flights up." Nor was the busy hive of assistants his father had forecast waiting to greet him. The sole shorthand reporter on the premises did not work for Taft. He was a telegrapher in the chief clerk's office and could only take Taft's dictation when not engaged in his primary duties. "Altogether it must have been a very disheartening outlook," Nellie wrote. "He wondered to himself why on earth he had come."

Taft's mood brightened considerably once Nellie arrived with Robert. They happily settled into a rented three-story town house at 5 Dupont Circle, which was easily affordable on his yearly salary of $7,000. "It is not a large house, but it is very pleasantly situated," Taft told Judge Peck, "with an outlook on a delightful little park, and is very convenient to the street cars, which are constantly passing to and fro in front of the house." His satisfaction with both their temporary home and the neighborhood, "one of the nicest and most convenient in the City," is evident in a letter to his father: "Our house is what is called a swell front, so that we are able from the front windows to look up and down the street and get such a view and so much light as to make the three front rooms of the house charming. The front room on the first floor is a reception room; the front room on the second floor is a library and sitting-room and the guest room is on the third floor immediately back of the nursery." The dining room was completed with a new table and eight new mahogany chairs, a Chippendale sideboard, and a new rug. For Will, the most important feature of the house was the sanctuary of a large library, lined with shelves sufficient to accommodate his treasured law books. "I find that without a place to work, it is difficult to work. I look forward with the greatest pleasure to the use of my books at night at home."

The most fortuitous and enduring aspect of the new Taft residency, however, lay neither in cheerful accommodations nor access to the city center. Rather, 5 Dupont Circle stood only 1,000 feet away from the modest house at 1820 Jefferson Place which Theodore Roosevelt, newly appointed member of the Civil Service Commission, and his second wife, Edith Carow, had rented, and where they had come to live just two months earlier. The proximity of those two addresses in northwest Washington, both within walking distance of the White House, would give rise to the legendary friendship between Theodore Roosevelt and William Howard Taft.

CHAPTER FIVE

Edith Carow Roosevelt

Edith Carow in 1885, a year before her marriage to the widower Theodore Roosevelt.

IN THE DESOLATE MONTHS AFTER Alice Lee's death, Theodore Roosevelt could never have conceived that within two years he would be secretly engaged to his childhood friend Edith Carow. Retreating to the "vast silent spaces" and "lonely rivers" of the Badlands following the tumultuous Republican Convention in the summer of 1884, he remained certain that his allotment of domestic bliss was "lived out." The ecstatic love he had shared with Alice came only once in a lifetime. His own capacity for passionate feeling was exhausted, he believed, and he resolved never to dishonor the wife he had loved more than "any man ever loved a woman." With an inexorable romantic idealism, he resigned himself to a bleak and isolate existence.

Leaving his four-month-old daughter with Bamie, who had sold the family's New York town house and moved into her own home at 689 Madison

Avenue, Theodore sought refuge from sorrows both personal and public. Privately, memories of his wife haunted every corner of the city. In the political arena, his support of the failed reform candidate against the triumphant machine nominee, James Blaine, had diminished his prospects and informed his decision not to run for a fourth term in the New York State Assembly.

He had fallen in love with the rugged landscape surrounding the Dakota Territory's Little Missouri River during a hunting trip the previous September. He had hoped to return with "the head of a great buffalo bull" to hang in the home he and Alice were building in Oyster Bay, but while there, he had decided to invest in two open-range cattle ranches, the Elkhorn and the Chimney Butte. His purchase of 1,400 head of cattle for $85,000 reduced by more than half the sum his father bequeathed to him. He went into partnership with two local cowboys, Bill Merrifield and Sylvane Ferris, and convinced William Sewall and Wilmot Dow, two wilderness guides he had hunted with in Maine, to join the enterprise. As his vision of family happiness died with Alice, he seriously considered a career as a full-time rancher, residing and writing in the West, with only occasional visits back east.

When he first returned to the Badlands in the summer of 1884, the austere landscape seemed to mirror his melancholy. "The plains stretch out in deathlike and measureless expanse," he wrote. "Nowhere, not even at sea, does a man feel more lonely than when riding over the far-reaching, seemingly never-ending plains." In the "noontide hours" of a scorching summer day, he remarked, "there are few sounds to break the stillness." With every living thing immobile in the stifling heat, he heard only the "soft, melancholy cooing of the mourning-dove, whose voice always seems far away and expresses more than any other sound in nature the sadness of gentle, hopeless, never-ending grief."

Just as he had frantically thrown himself into his labors in the assembly to alleviate the immediate anguish of Alice's death, so he now immersed himself in the daily work of the ranch. He was often on his horse sixteen hours a day, riding after stray horses, hunting game, joining his men in the "hardest work," that of "the spring and fall round-ups, when the calves are branded or the beeves gathered for market." During roundups that covered over two hundred miles in four to five weeks, the cook began "preparing breakfast long before the first glimmer of dawn." Shortly after three o'clock the men were roused from sleep and the day's toil delegated. "These long, swift rides in the glorious spring mornings are not soon to be forgotten," Theodore marveled. "As we climb the steep sides of the first range of buttes, wisps of wavering mist still cling in the hollows of the valley; when we come out on top of the first great plateau, the sun flames up over its edge, and in the level, red beams the galloping horsemen throw long, fantastic shadows."

Relentless physical activity served him well. "Black care," he wrote, "rarely sits behind a rider whose pace is fast enough." Once, constant activity had assuaged the pain of his father's death; now, he hoped that by occupying every minute of his waking day, he could simply outride his depression. A two-week hunting trip in September, he reported to Bamie, had provided "enough excitement and fatigue to prevent over much thought"; he had "at last been able to sleep well at night."

Thirty miles north of Medora, he had a spacious ranch house built to share with his friends, Sewall and Dow, and eventually their wives. "The story-high house of hewn logs is clean and neat, with many rooms," he wrote, "so that one can be alone if one wishes to." The central room featured a massive stone hearth with trophy heads gazing down from the walls and buffalo robes covering the couches. His own chamber held a rubber tub for bathing and rough shelves for his favorite books—"Parkman and Irving and Hawthorne and Cooper and Lowell"—along with a growing assortment of volumes sent from New York by his devoted sister.

As the months passed and Roosevelt started to recover himself, he approached *Century* magazine with the idea of presenting a series of sketches highlighting hunting experiences on the Great Plains. In fits and starts at first, he began to compose during breaks in his work. Before long, he was writing steadily before "the flickering firelight" of the enormous fireplace. Organizing his manuscript around the different game he hunted—black-tailed deer, antelope, bull elk, buffalo, and grizzly bear—he fused a naturalist's interest in the unique characteristics of each animal with a hunter's thrill of the chase.

Daily labor on the ranch had given Roosevelt an acute awareness of the natural cycles and unique pleasures each season held. On summer evenings, he relaxed in his rocking chair on the wide porch of the ranch house, reading in the shade of the cottonwood and enjoying the "cool breeze" from the nearby river. As the crisp autumn temperatures began to transform the landscape, he particularly savored the long days in the saddle, whether hunting or rounding up cattle. "Where everything before had been gray or dull green there are now patches of russet red and bright yellow," he noted. "The clumps of ash, wild-plum trees, and rosebushes in the heads and bottoms of the sloping valleys become spots of color that glow among the stretches of brown and withered grass."

Even when the winter days "dwindled to their shortest" and the yapping wailing songs of coyotes echoed through the "never-ending" nights, Roosevelt took comfort in the camaraderie of housemates gathered round the fireplace to read, relax, or play chess. Soon enough, spring brought earlier daybreak to the Badlands and his morning rides took on "a charm all their own," the bleached landscape becoming "a vivid green, as the new grass sprouts and the trees and bushes thrust forth the young leaves." On those clear mornings, he thrilled to the sounds of "bird songs unknown in the East"—the lilting melodies of the Missouri skylark, the "rich, full notes" of the white-shouldered lark-bunting, the tuneful sweetness of the lark-finch. The green thickets and groves encircling his ranch house teemed with the songs of hermit thrushes and meadowlarks. This quickening of life in the Badlands awakened a corresponding energy in Theodore Roosevelt.

As his fits of depression subsided and publication of his book, *Hunting Trips of a Ranchman*, drew near, Roosevelt's thoughts turned east, toward the home and the people he had left behind. Memories of joyful days spent with his childhood friend Edith Carow increasingly intruded on his consciousness. The desire to renew their old and deep friendship, however, was coupled with a surge of guilt and anxiety when he contemplated anything that might compromise Alice's memory. This thought lay on his conscience like a crime, and he instructed his sisters, who were still close to Edith, that she never be present during his visits. He traveled to New York in July 1885, when his book was published to excellent reviews. This work "will take a leading position in the literature of the American sportsman," the *New York Times* reported. "Mr. Roosevelt writes most happily, tells naturally what he sees and does."

Roosevelt remained in New York that summer, living for the first time in his recently finished country home at Oyster Bay, the planning and design for which had filled many happy hours with Alice. Completed and furnished under Bamie's devoted supervision, the rambling twenty-two-room Queen Anne house stood atop a hill, surrounded by forests and grassy clearings, commanding a clear view of the Long Island Sound. Returning to Cove Neck must have recalled vivid memories of childhood summers at nearby Tranquillity, where "no day was long enough" to contain the myriad pursuits of Roosevelt's lively family and friends.

Replicating those crowded childhood days, Bamie orchestrated a steady stream of houseguests to Oyster Bay, including Corinne's childhood friend Fanny Smith. Fanny found Theodore's new house, which he rechristened "Sagamore Hill," as enchanting as she had once found Tranquillity. The Roosevelt homestead again became a social hub, but Theodore now assumed the central position his father had once occupied. "Especially memorable," Fanny recalled, "were the battles, ancient and modern, which were waged relentlessly on the white linen tablecloth with the aid of such table-silver as was available." Stunned by Theodore's "familiarity with historical details of long past centuries," Fanny admiringly noted that he made her "feel that Hannibal lived just around the corner." Roosevelt's Aunt Annie and her husband had recently completed a country house accessible to his by a dirt path through the woods, and nearby lived his cousin Dr. West Roosevelt, who had accompanied him to Maine when he first met Bill Sewall. Despite this renewed consolidation of the Roosevelt clan, Theodore managed to avoid one old friend. Although Edith had spent a week with Aunt Annie at "Gracewood" earlier that summer, she was noticeably absent from the group that gathered at Theodore's new home.

These summer weeks were the most extended time Theodore had spent with his daughter, Alice, who was now nearly eighteen months old. Under Bamie's loving guardianship, Alice had emerged as a lively, blond, blue-eyed toddler. Indeed, the warmth and affection that bound Bamie and her niece could not have been stronger if they were mother and child. "She was the only one I really cared about when I was a child," Alice later remembered. Though crippled by curvature of the spine and seriously overweight, Bamie seemed to Alice marvelously larger than life, "a great big handsome man of a woman . . . but oh so attractive!" Even as a young child Alice observed that Bamie "had an extraordinary gift with people." Her numerous friends adored her and felt completely at ease in her presence. Had "she been a man," Alice believed, "she would have been the one to be President."

Roosevelt returned to the Badlands in late August, but two months later he was back in New York. He arrived at Bamie's Madison Avenue town house, where he routinely stayed while visiting the city, to find Edith Carow about to depart. Whether Theodore's failure to signal his impending return or her delay in taking leave of Bamie brought about the reunion, long-hidden feelings surfaced before day's end. Less than three weeks later, the two were secretly engaged. "You know all about me darling," Edith told Theodore. "I never could have loved anyone else. I love you with all the passion of a girl who has never loved before."

THE RESURRECTION OF HER RELATIONSHIP with Theodore offered Edith the prospect of happiness and security that had eluded her since childhood. Her father, Charles Carow, became an alcoholic after his family's once-thriving shipping business fell into bankruptcy. The seventh of eight children born to wealthy merchant prince Isaac Quentin Carow, Charles had lacked no privilege growing up in his family's St. Mark's Place mansion. He dwelled in a world of private tutors, dancing lessons, and access to New York's most exclusive clubs. At twenty-five, he had just begun work at Kermit & Carow, the family firm, when his father suddenly passed away.

Charismatic and eligible, Charles Carow seemed a perfect match for Gertrude Tyler. At nineteen, she had lately returned from two years in a fashionable Parisian girls' school. Gertrude's father, Daniel Tyler IV, had graduated from West Point and served in the Army before amassing a fortune in iron manufacturing. Following his marriage to Emily Lee, they moved to the sumptuous mansion in Norwich, Connecticut, where Gertrude was raised.

Intent that she become a poised and well-bred young lady, Gertrude's father had insisted she attend boarding school in Paris. On the Continent, in contrast to America, he assured her, she would "find great attention paid to deportment and manners." She would be schooled in "matters of carriage, such as walking, entering a room, sitting down and rising"; comportment that would signify a proper upbringing. "Do not my dear Gertrude undervalue or despise these matters," he admonished. "They are important and it will be my pride to know and feel that both your mind and manners are formed on good and true standards. Now is the time for you to finish an education, mental and physical which will make you an ornament to society." While Gertrude was often homesick and could not bear to spend the Christmas season abroad, she pledged to work hard at music lessons, study of French, and riding lessons. "Do not doubt," she promised her mother, "that I shall do everything in my power to improve the advantages that you and Father have given me."

Encountering Gertrude in New York soon after her return, Charles pursued her avidly. On March 7, 1859, he formally declared his intentions to her father: "My dear Sir, I have to ask of you the greatest favor that one man can ask of another. I have won Gertrude's heart. Will you give me her hand?" The wedding took place two months later in the Christ Episcopal Church in Norwich, Connecticut, followed by a brilliant reception in the Tyler mansion.

The couple's first child, a boy, died at six months. Then, the year the war began, the Carows welcomed their first daughter, Edith. Gertrude's father rejoined the Army as a general, while Charles remained in New York endeavoring to steer the family shipping business through an abrupt decline precipitated by the Civil War. He had inherited the family enterprise on the brink of a crisis that made "the risk of sailing under the American flag . . . so great as to divert a large share of the carrying trade into foreign bottoms." Buffeted by drastic financial reverses, Charles began drinking heavily and gambling. Soon he was no longer able to afford his own home and the family was forced to move in with his widowed sister, Ann Eliza Kermit. As the war came to an end, the Carow's second daughter, Emily, was born in Ann's large town house at 12 Livingston Place near Union Square.

When Charles was not drinking, he was an affectionate husband and an effusive, doting father. "My dear little girl," he wrote Edith when he and Gertrude left to visit the Tylers in Norwich, "Papa hopes his dolly has been very good since he has been gone. . . . Papa & Mamma always say, before they go to sleep, 'God bless little Edie,' and again before they get up in the morning." From the time she was young, Charles had sought to communicate to his "precious little monkey" his fascination with the theatre and love of literature. Edith proved an apt pupil. "Almost the first thing I remember," she later told Theodore, "is being told about Sinbad the Sailor when I was a tiny girl and used to climb up on my father's knee every evening and beg him to 'spin me a yarn.' " As her father read aloud from the *Arabian Nights*, "a new world" opened up, "full of glowing Eastern light and colour." Her early exposure to such frightful and wonderful stories spurred "a passion for fairy tales" later concisely distilled into her own verse: "Oh fairy tales, my fairy tales / Fantastic, weird and wild / I love you with a changeless love / A mother gives her child."

When father and daughter were apart, Charles urged her to write him her thoughts and feelings without the monitor of self-consciousness, without worry over corrections. "I got your letter about 3 o'clock yesterday," he wrote. "It was so nice & long. No matter about the spelling when you write to me. Say what you want to say and don't lose time thinking how to spell the words. If I want I can beat you with a big stick when you come back—so just write whatever comes into your head." When they were together, he took Edith on long walks, pointing out various wildflowers and teaching her to know them by color, shape, and habitat. This shared pursuit fostered an interest in the natural world that remained with her the rest of her life.

When Charles Carow was drinking, however, recrimination and tension permeated the household. Gertrude began to suffer bouts of melancholy coupled with a mysterious series of nervous disorders. Still, the Carows managed to maintain a public facade of elegance and ease, spending their winters in New York with Mrs. Kermit and their summers at General Tyler's country estate in New Jersey. Gertrude's finishing school lessons in proper carriage and deportment helped her conceal private anxiety behind a veneer of propriety. And she imparted these lessons to her uncommonly poised little girl, Edith.

Edith was a toddler when she first met Theodore Roosevelt. The Kermit house on Livingston Place stood directly behind the 14th Street mansion of Theodore's grandfather, Cornelius Van Schaak Roosevelt. Edith and Corinne

Roosevelt were almost exactly the same age and they soon became, in Corinne's words, "pledged friends." Edith's earliest memories revolved around the Roosevelts' 20th Street household, where she frequently played with Corinne and developed a particular affection for Teedie, three years her senior. Far less did she enjoy their visits to her own house, where she anxiously struggled to hide her "old and broken toys."

When she was five, Edith was invited to join the Roosevelt children in the home school taught by Mittie's sister, Annie Gracie. Years later, Edith fondly recalled "the school room, the children around the table, and dear Mrs. Gracie training clumsy little fingers to write and teaching the earliest lessons in the primer." She and Teedie cherished an illustrated children's magazine called *Our Young Folks*, a compilation of stories, poems, and illustrations by celebrated writers and artists, including Harriet Beecher Stowe, Winslow Homer, Henry Longfellow, and Charles Dickens. Later, "at the cost of being deemed effeminate," Roosevelt confessed an early fascination with "girls' stories," such as *Little Men* and *Little Women* and *An Old-Fashioned Girl*. His ability to focus and withdraw into a book was equaled only in his friend, Edith Carow. "I think imagination is one of the greatest blessings of life," Edith later wrote, "and while one can lose oneself in a book one can never be thoroughly unhappy."

Thoughts of Edith provoked an intense yearning in Teedie during his family's yearlong trip to Europe. "It was verry [*sic*] hard parting from our friend," he confided in his diary. Six months into the Grand Tour, when the family was in France, he dramatically revealed to his diary that a glance at Edith's picture provoked "homesickness and longings for the past which will come again never, alack never." Edith eagerly awaited his return, promising to keep all Teedie's letters so they could read them over back in New York and relive his adventure together.

Edith's parents considered sending Edith to school when Mrs. Gracie's lessons ceased during the Roosevelts' time abroad. In the end, they decided to postpone her entry until the following fall, fearful she was already damaging her eyes by constant reading. "Whenever they see a book in my hands," she told Corinne, "they give me no peace till I lay it down."

Edith was nine years old when a bankruptcy warrant was issued against her father's estate. The *New York Times* followed the proceedings for weeks, reporting creditor meetings and the auction sale of several ships, including the *Edith*, named after his daughter. Charles quickly realized he had no choice but to seek more frugal living arrangements. That summer, his family moved with Aunt Kermit to a more modest house on West 44th Street.

The Carows' reduced means did not prevent them from enrolling Edith in Miss Comstock's renowned private school for girls at West 40th Street. Nor did Gertrude scrimp on the stylish clothes her daughter required to join her classmates for regular forays to the symphony or theatre. Miss Comstock, headmistress of the fashionable school, was a formidable figure to the young girls. Edith's schoolmate Fanny Smith described the "terrifying charm" of that "impressive-looking woman with flashing dark eyes and clear-cut features." The curriculum included history, languages, arithmetic, zoology, botany, poetry, drama, and literature. Edith proved to be a diligent and exceptional student. "When I come home, I study my lessons, and when I think I know them I read," she told Corinne, who was still being schooled by private tutors. "I like my composition class very much," she confided, and "I am trying hard for the Arithmetic and Department prizes and hope to get them."

At Miss Comstock's, Edith developed a lifelong devotion to drama and poetry. "I have gone back to Shakespeare, as I always do," she would write to her son Kermit seven decades later. "Usually the Historical plays, or *Hamlet* or *Macbeth*. *Lear* is too tragic. This time I read *As You Like It*. There can be nothing more delightful! I believe if it were lost I could write it out." She could memorize and recite numerous poems, including John Milton's *Lycidas* in its entirety, and was able to quote extensively from Wordsworth, Coleridge, and other Romantic poets.

Edith also cultivated a defensive air of detachment during her schooldays, declining to participate in the costumed tableaux and girlish gossip that so fascinated her classmates. Her beloved books often took precedence over friends, leading schoolmates to reproach her for "indifference." Years later, Edith explained that her aloofness was simply "a trick of manner" to obscure her own perceived defects. While it may have deprived her of camaraderie, her tactic succeeded in establishing the distance and mystery that prevented humiliation. "Girls," one of her fellow classmates observed, "I believe you could live in the same house with Edith for fifty years and never really know her."

Edith's friendship with the Roosevelt family remained her lodestar, helping her navigate a troubled girlhood as her father became more and more unstable and her mother descended into hypochondria and depression. When the Roosevelts returned from their first trip abroad, Edith joined Corinne, Theodore, and Elliott in a weekly dancing class taught by the demanding Mr. Dodsworth. The dance lessons were "the happiness of many New York children of those years," Edith remembered. A half century later Edith could still recall her pride as she and Corinne, "the only two who had satisfied our difficult and critical teacher," were called onto the floor to dance the minuet all alone. Fanny Smith never forgot the pleasure of belonging to that "little group of girls and boys wearing special badges and pledged either definitely or otherwise only to dance with one another."

During the summers at Tranquillity, Edith was a regular houseguest. In particular, she excelled in the word games the young people loved to play, " 'Consequences,' 'Truth,' and nearly always 'Crambo,' when each one would draw from a hat a folded question and from another hat a word, and then in the few minutes allotted would answer the question in verse which should include the word we had drawn." In the afternoons, "the happy six" would row across the bay: Theodore with Edith, Elliott with Corinne, their cousin West Roosevelt with Fanny, whom he "much worshipped." They would carry their books to the woods and read aloud to one another. At picnic lunches near Cooper's Bluff, they recited their favorite poems. "In the early days," Fanny recalled, "we all delighted in Longfellow and Mrs. Browning and Owen Meredith." Later, they turned to Swinburne, Kipling, Shelley, and Shakespeare.

The Roosevelts celebrated Edith's birthdays as if she were a member of the family. "I cannot believe that my sweet little fair, golden-haired friend, whom I have loved since she was three years old is really fifteen today," Aunt Gracie wrote. Edith was included in small family dinners and visits to the theatre. On New Year's Day, 1877, she stood by Corinne's side to receive guests. At dancing parties, continuing the partnership begun under Mr. Dodsworth's tutelage, she regularly paired off with Theodore. At one of Aunt Gracie's sociables, Corinne and a friend deliberately wandered into the "dimly and suggestively lit" morning room "for the express purpose of interrupting Thee and Edith, who had gone there for a cosy chat." The party was "far too merry," Corinne chided, "for a sentimental tete-a-tete."

Theodore's departure for Harvard produced the first unraveling in the close-knit circle of family and friends. Refusing to let their cherished scholarly and social coterie vanish with him, Corinne and Edith formed a literary society in which Corinne served as president and Edith as secretary. The group, which included Fanny Smith, Maud Elliott, and Grace Potter, expected members to contribute original poems and short stories to be read aloud and criticized at weekly meetings. As secretary, Edith was charged with copying and organizing the submissions into a "Weekly Bulletin."

Edith personally produced dozens of poems, short stories, and essays, which she carefully preserved in her papers. The Roosevelt family biographer Betty Boyd Caroli observes that in her writings for this intimate circle, "Edith revealed about as much about herself as she ever permitted anyone to see."

Her poem entitled "My Dream Castles," written during Theodore's freshman year at Harvard, suggests the lonely distance she maintained despite her inclusion in the Roosevelt household. While she might join in their games and celebrations, loving friendship and charity could not entirely ease an outsider's sense of loss, of alienation:

To my castles none may enter
But the few
Holding to my inmost feelings
Love's own clue.
They may wander there at will
Ever welcome finding still,
Warm and true.

Only one, one tiny room
Locked they find,
One thin curtain that they ne'er
Gaze behind.
There my lost ambitions sleep,
To their tear-wept slumber deep
Long consigned.

This my lonely sanctum is;
There I go
When my heart all worn by grief
Sinketh low.
Where my baseless hopes do lie
There to find my peace, go I.
Sad and slow . . .

Romantic longing and a self-dramatizing nostalgia resonate in her words, an elegy for the warm companionship of the dream family she feared would be left behind with their childhoods. In another poem, "Memories," she once again reveals the profound anxiety of a melancholy girl confronting adulthood at the end of her day:

I sit alone in the twilight
In the twilight gloomy grey
And think with a sad regretting
For the days that have passed away.

Both Corinne and Fanny recognized a superior quality in Edith's writings. "She reads more and writes better than any girl I know," Corinne noted in her diary. For Corinne, whose literary ambitions would drive her to become an accomplished poet, this was not easy to admit. Indeed, she often found Edith's criticism of her work overwhelming and her personality inscrutable. Still, she could not help loving best of all her "clever" friend, "tall and fair, with lovely complexion and golden hair." She confided in her journal: "I have a feeling for Edith which I have for no one else, a tender kind of feeling. I am always careful of her and then I know quite well that I love her much more than she does me in fact."

In the spring of Theodore's freshman year, Theodore Senior brought a small party of young people to visit him at Harvard, including Bamie, Corinne, and Elliott, along with Edith Carow and Maud Elliott. "What fun we did have," Corinne remembered, describing lively lunches and dinners with her brother and his friends, Johnny Lamson and Harry Jackson. They played hide-and-seek, attended the theatre, and enjoyed long carriage rides through the surrounding countryside. Edith and Theodore again found themselves partners, riding in one carriage, while Corinne and Maud were paired with Lamson and Jackson.

"The family all went home, leaving me disconsolate," Theodore recorded in his diary. "The last three days have been great fun." Arriving in New York, Edith immediately wrote to Theodore, echoing his sentiment. She had "enjoyed to the utmost" every moment of "three perfectly happy days." Theodore admitted to Corinne that he had never seen "Edith looking prettier; everyone, and especially Harry Chapin and Minot Weld admired her little Ladyship intensely, and she behaved as sweetly as she looked."

Edith's cherished relationship with Theodore remained constant in the following months, as did her friendship with Corinne. When Theodore Senior lay dying, Corinne confided her grief and frustration to her oldest friend. "Oh Edith, it is the most frightful thing to see the person you love best in the world in terrible pain, and not be able to do a thing to alleviate it." The following summer, Edith joined Theodore and Corinne at Oyster Bay as the Roosevelt children tried to distract themselves from the sorrow of the patriarch's death.

In his diary, Theodore described days spent sailing with Edith or rowing with her to the harbor where the steamboats from the city landed. He wrote of "spending a lovely morning with her" driving to Cold Spring Harbor to pick water lilies.

The next day, August 22, 1878, he took Mittie, Elliott, Corinne, and Edith on a long sail, followed by tea at his cousin West's house. The mysterious severance in their relationship occurred that same evening. In his diary, Theodore merely notes: "Afterwards Edith & I went up to the summer house." What transpired there would become the subject of much speculation by Roosevelt's family and friends. Some postulated that Edith had refused Theodore's offer of marriage, although her intense devotion makes such a scenario unlikely. Furthermore, an initial refusal would hardly have deterred Theodore, who would shortly prove his tenacity in his courtship of Alice. Corinne suggested a different reason, indicating that her dying father had expressed concern about Theodore's intimacy with Edith, given Charles Carow's fiscal and temperamental instability. If Theodore discussed the issue with Edith that night, he might well have triggered the volatility that he would obscurely explain to Bamie as a clash of tempers "that were far from being of the best." This, too, is mere conjecture. Neither Edith nor Theodore ever talked about what happened.

We know only that eight weeks later, Theodore met Alice Hathaway Lee, fell in love "at first sight," and launched the spirited campaign "to win her" that concluded successfully in the winter of 1880. Before the engagement was announced in mid-February, Theodore wrote to Edith. Years later, Corinne spoke of the "shock" Edith experienced when she heard the news. The summer months that year must have been lacerating for Edith; another woman would be Theodore's constant companion, displacing her on morning drives to Cold Spring, afternoon sailing and rowing excursions, and private evening tête-à-têtes in the summerhouse.

Edith was long accustomed to mastering her private sorrows. She schooled herself to participate in the engagement and wedding festivities of the man she adored. Arriving at the Brunswick Hotel in Boston two nights before the marriage, she crowded into an upstairs chamber with Fanny and Grace, while the Roosevelt family occupied two suites downstairs. "We had great fun," Fanny recorded in her diary. They explored the town and shared meals at a large table, where "wild spirits" prevailed. The next morning, Edith, Grace, and Fanny drove to the church together. At the reception following the ceremony, Edith reportedly "danced the soles off her shoes."

Her brave attempt to affect gaiety was not the only trial Edith would face. The death of Mrs. Kermit, with whom Edith had lived since she was a small child, was soon followed by the final days of her gentle grandfather, General Tyler. Initially, she continued to see a great deal of Corinne, Fanny, and Aunt Gracie, who held a weekly sewing class for the girls once their formal schooling ended. Soon, however, she found herself quite forsaken as both Corinne and Fanny became engaged. Edith and Fanny served together as bridesmaids at Corinne's wedding. "All yesterday I thought of nothing but you from morning to night," she explained to her oldest friend. "I do not mean I was sad or grieving for that would be impossible when I know how happy you are going to be, but I kept realizing that you were leaving your old life behind, and if we live to be ninety years old we can never be two girls together again."

In 1883, yet another death seemed to complete the disintegration of Edith's support system. Charles Carow, his body weakened by decades of drinking, collapsed and died that spring. He left his wife and daughters without sufficient means to maintain their accustomed life. Recognizing that they could live abroad more cheaply than in New York, Gertrude made plans for an extended sojourn in Europe with Edith and Emily. While rumor circulated that Edith might marry "for money," such gossip proved groundless. Even as more and more of her friends were engaged or married, Edith maintained her solitude. As the circle of her friends diminished, she sought consolation in her treasured books, keeping a careful record of the hundreds of volumes she completed. During this desolate period, Edith purportedly held on to the belief that "someday, somehow, she would marry Theodore Roosevelt." She certainly never anticipated the grim coincidence that left Theodore's wife and mother dead on the same day. Though Edith joined the family at the funeral service and frequently saw Corinne, Bamie, and Aunt Gracie in the months that followed, there is no evidence that she and Theodore connected until their chance encounter at Bamie's house in October 1885.

THEODORE WAS REMARKABLY ALTERED FROM the young man Edith had last seen. Months laboring under the Badlands sun had hardened his body and bronzed his skin, but he had the same bright eyes, the same splendid smile. Edith herself had become a handsome young woman, still "the most cultivated, best read girl" he knew. In the days that followed, he became a regular visitor, enlivening the parlor of her 36th Street town house. Perhaps their old friendship and mutual losses quickened the relationship. On November 17, 1885, they pledged themselves to marry. The engagement opened a world of joy for Edith, an emergence from five years of bleak nightmare. If the love Theodore developed for Edith lacked the extreme sentimental idealism of his love for Alice, their complex, ever-strengthening bond would sustain a mature and lifelong growth and happiness.

The early months of his reunion with Edith, however, were clouded by Theodore's Victorian belief that second marriages "argued weakness in a man's character." He insisted upon a sufficient interval before informing anyone, even their families, about their intention to marry. Acutely aware of the importance of appearances, Edith decided to accompany her mother and sister to Europe that spring as planned, allowing time to elapse before any public announcement of the engagement. In the meantime, they felt there was nothing wrong with two old friends keeping company during the winter social season. Once again, Edith joined the Roosevelts at the Essex County Hunt Ball, theatre parties at Aunt Annie's, and dinners at Bamie's. Respecting their secret even in his private diary, Theodore never wrote out Edith's full name, though the capital E appears day after day, reflecting the extensive time they spent together.

In the spring of 1886, Edith sailed to Europe and Theodore returned to the Badlands. In New York, he had begun work on a biography of Missouri senator Thomas Hart Benton, which he hoped to complete at his ranch beside the Little Missouri River. Though separated by nearly 5,000 miles, the couple sustained their relationship month after month through the exchange of long letters. In early June, just five weeks after Edith's arrival in London, she had already received seventeen letters from Theodore and written almost as many in return. "How fond one is of old letters and how one prizes them," Edith had written in her composition book at Miss Comstock's. "I never wish to destroy even a note." Though she cherished each word, the intensely private Edith would one day burn nearly their entire correspondence from this period. Only one full letter remains—the same letter in which she declared to Theodore that she loved him "with all the passion of a girl who has never loved before."

Written from London on June 8, 1886, this letter made the strength of Edith's feelings for Theodore abundantly clear, even as she appealed to him to be patient while she tried to put her "heart on paper." Never having troubled much about her appearance, Edith admitted she was suddenly anxious "about being pretty" in order to please him. "I perfectly love your description of the life out west for I almost feel as if I could see you and know just what you are doing, and I do not think you sentimental in the least to love nature; please love me too and believe I think of you all the time and want so much to see you."

Edith's diffident and beseeching tone disappears the moment she turns to literature, whether expressing her fascination with Coleridge's *Kubla Khan* or noting the "digging" required to excavate meaning from Browning's poems. Her critique of the lead singer's performance in a production of *Carmen*, which she had heard the previous night, displays a confident, acerbic wit: "He is middle aged, ugly and uninteresting with not enough voice to redeem his bad acting. His one idea of making love is to seize the prima donna's arm and shake her violently. I am so glad it is not your way."

As ever, books remained a medium through which Theodore and Edith connected and interpreted the larger world. Like Edith, Theodore filled pages of his letters with talk of authors and their creations. He had carried *Anna Karenina* with him during this trip west and told Corinne that he "read it through with very great interest." Although he considered Tolstoy "a great writer," he found his work deeply unsettling. "Do you notice how he never comments on the actions of his personages? He relates what they thought or did without any remark whatever as to whether it was good or bad, as Thucydides wrote history—a fact which tends to give his work an unmoral rather than an immoral tone, together with the sadness so characteristic of Russian writers."

Roosevelt read this novel of multiple marriages, broken marriages, and an assortment of adulteries at a time when the nature of marriage and remarriage, its moral and ethical reverberations, was of signal importance to the newly betrothed widower. From its very first sentence—"Happy families are all alike; every unhappy family is unhappy in its own way"—Tolstoy's *Anna Karenina* confronted Theodore in an intensely personal fashion and his comments upon it illuminate his own nature more brightly than Tolstoy's novel.

"I hardly know whether to call it a very bad book or not. There are two entirely distinct stories in it," he observed. The history of Levin and Kitty "is not only very powerfully and naturally told, but is also perfectly healthy. Annas most certainly is not, though of great and sad interest; she is portrayed as being a prey to the most violent passion, and subject to melancholia, and her reasoning power is so unbalanced that she could not possibly be described otherwise than as in a certain sense insane. Her character is curiously contradictory; bad as she was however she was not to me nearly as repulsive as her brother, Stiva." Roosevelt's revulsion at Tolstoy's infantile, pathetic, endearing *bon vivant*—his categorical interpretation of healthy relationships versus unhealthy relationships—reveals a deep-seated disgust with physical and moral slackness that would remain with him for the rest of his life.

While he continued to enjoy the simple, invigorating routine of his life at the ranch, with long days free to read and write, ride and hunt, his engagement to Edith provided a welcome sense of clarity about his future. He began to muse on the satisfactions and exhilaration of political life that he had abandoned in New York. He contemplated an offer from Mayor William Grace to assume the presidency of the Board of Health, but it ultimately fell through. Still, he admitted to Henry Cabot Lodge in August, "I would like a chance at something I thought I could really do."

In late August and early September, Roosevelt accompanied his ranching partner Bill Merrifield on a hunting trip in Idaho. When he returned, he was appalled to find that news of the engagement had leaked into the social columns of the *New York Times* and that Bamie, assuming the report must be unfounded gossip, had demanded a retraction. Theodore faced the difficult and necessary prospect of revealing the truth to his sister after months of deceit.

"Darling Bamie," he wrote on September 20, 1886, "On returning from the mountains I was savagely irritated by seeing in the papers the statement that I was engaged to Edith Carow; from what source it could have originated I can not possibly conceive. But the statement itself is true. I am engaged to Edith and before Christmas I shall cross the ocean and marry her. You are the first person to whom I have breathed one word on the subject." He proceeded to reiterate his condemnation of second marriages. "You could not reproach me one half as bitterly for my inconstancy and unfaithfulness, as I reproach myself," he maintained. "Were I sure there were a heaven my one prayer would be I might never go there, lest I should meet those I loved on earth who are dead. No matter what your judgement about myself I shall most assuredly enter no plea against it. But I do very earnestly ask you not to visit my sins upon poor little Edith. It is certainly not her fault; the entire blame rests on my shoulders." He was particularly anxious that his family never question their long history of affection toward Edith, that none should mistake her in any fashion for a schemer or interloper.

"As regards yourself, my dearest sister," he continued, "I can only say you will be giving me the greatest happiness in your power if you will continue to pass your summers with me. We ourselves will have to live in the country almost the entire year; I thoroughly understand the change I will have to make in my life. As I have already told you, if you wish to you shall keep Baby Lee, I, of course paying the expense. . . . I will explain everything in full when I see you. *Forever your loving brother*." This arrangement for the child of his previous marriage would prove more problematic than he anticipated.

His plans to return home were delayed by troubles at the Elkhorn ranch. A calamitous drop in the price of cattle had persuaded Sewall and Dow that the ranch was no longer a viable operation. "It looked to me as if we were throwing away his money," Sewall reported, deeply distressed by the prospect of failing his friend Roosevelt. The two men and their wives reluctantly returned to Maine, later reflecting that despite "all of the hardships and work it was a very happy life [they] had lived all together," indeed, "the happiest time" they had ever known.

Roosevelt, too, never forgot his years in the Badlands. Though he would ultimately lose a sizable portion of his fortune when a blizzard decimated his cattle herd, he considered his experience with "fellow ranchmen on what was then the frontier" to be "the most educational asset" of his entire life, instrumental to his success in becoming president. "It is a mighty good thing to know men, not from looking at them, but from having been one of them," Roosevelt explained. "When you have worked with them, when you have lived with them, you do not have to wonder how they feel, because you feel it yourself." Just as his daily work in the assembly had taught him to live down "the defective moral quality of being a stranger" among colleagues with whom he initially had little in common, so his years in the Badlands taught him "to speak the same language" as men who spent their days herding cattle, roping steer, and hunting game in the open country. Men who routinely faced danger and hardship recognized no superiority in social class or family background. His ranching days enabled him "to interpret the spirit of the West," fostering a genuine national perspective foreign to most eastern politicians.

With his wedding planned for December 1886, however, Theodore returned to the city and his preparations for a renewed life with his oldest friend. Immediately upon his arrival in New York, he "was visited by a succession of the influential Republicans of the city to entreat [him] to take the nomination for Mayor." He understood that it was "of course a perfectly hopeless contest," since Democrats outnumbered Republicans by 50,000 votes. Nevertheless, he agreed to make the sacrificial three-week run, knowing that it would elevate his stature within the party.

The race pitted twenty-eight-year-old Roosevelt against both the Democratic candidate, Abraham Hewitt, a socially conscious industrialist, and the independent labor candidate Henry George, a radical, whose hugely popular book *Progress and Poverty* had become a bible for reformers. In powerful prose that struck a chord throughout the country and made the book one of the top ten best sellers in American history, George argued that the "enormous increase in productive power" during the previous decades had not diminished poverty nor lifted "the burdens of those compelled to toil." On the contrary, the progress that accompanied the Industrial Revolution had produced ever harsher lives for the masses of the people. He contended, in opposition to the social Darwinists, that "the want and injustice of the present social state are not necessary." The gap between the rich and the poor was not a consequence of unchanging natural laws or the survival of the fittest, but of environments made by man and changeable by man. Under the right laws, George insisted, "a social state is possible in which poverty would be unknown."

Roosevelt responded that "the mass of the American people are most emphatically not in the deplorable condition of which you speak, and the 'statesmen and patriots of to-day' are no more responsible for some people being poorer than others than they are for some people being shorter, or more near-sighted, or physically weaker than others. If you had any conception of the true American spirit you would know we do not have 'classes' at all on this side of the water. . . . Some of the evils of which you complain are real and can be to a certain degree remedied; others, though real, can only be gotten over through the capacity for steady individual self-help which is the glory of every true American, and can no more be done away with by legislation than you could do away with the bruises which you received when you tumbled down, by passing an act to repeal the laws of gravitation."

"The best I can hope for is to make a decent run," Roosevelt conceded in a letter to Fanny Smith Dana. "The simple fact," he explained, alluding to a famous painting, "is that I had to play Curtius and leap into the gulf that was yawning before the Republican party." As the days progressed, however, with George firing up audiences across the city, Roosevelt worried that the gulf into which he had leapt was even deeper than he had first thought. He feared that many of his "should-be supporters" in the Republican Party would desert him in the end, voting for Hewitt to prevent the election of a radical mayor. Nonetheless, he committed to the campaign with his customary zeal. From sunup to sundown, tirelessly canvassing the city, he roused audiences with his fighting spirit, heartily shook endless hands, and freely granted interviews to reporters. He brought overflow crowds to their feet, pledging, "I am a strong party man myself [but should] I find a public servant who is dishonest, I will chop his head off even if he is the highest Republican in this municipality."

Friends and family were thrilled to see Roosevelt again step into the public arena. "It is such happiness to see him at his very best once more," Bamie wrote to Edith in London. "Ever since he has been out of politics in any active form; it has been a real heart sorrow to me, for while he always made more of his life than any other man I knew, still with his strong nature it was a permanent source of poignant regret that even at this early age he should lose these years without the possibility of doing his best and most telling work . . . this is the first time since the [assembly] days that he has enough work to keep him exerting all his powers. Theodore is the only person who had the power except Father who possessed it in a different way; of making me almost worship him."

Despite the excitement generated by Roosevelt's return to public life, the Democratic candidate, Abraham Hewitt, won the election. Moreover, since thousands of Republicans voted for Hewitt in fear of the radical George, Roosevelt came in a distant third. Nonetheless, the press praised Roosevelt for a spirited campaign. "Fighting is fun for him, win or lose," the New York *Sun* editorialized.

Three days after the election, Theodore set sail for England, accompanied by his faithful sister Bamie. Three weeks later, on December 2, 1886, he married Edith Carow in a simple ceremony at St. George's Chapel in London. Theodore and Edith swiftly departed for a three-month honeymoon that would take them across England, France, and Italy. Typically, even as they explored Florence, Venice, and Paris, Theodore managed to complete a half-dozen articles on ranching life for the *Century* magazine. "I read them all over to Edith," he reported to Corinne, "and her corrections and help were most valuable to me."

During these halcyon days, Edith realized hopes and longings harbored since she was a girl. More than a decade after her honeymoon, she claimed to "remember them all one by one, and hour by hour." Her marriage to Theodore commenced what appears to have been a rich sensual life. Many years later, her biographer Sylvia Morris reports, Edith amazed a granddaughter by openly mentioning "that wonderful silky private part of a woman." When the Roosevelts returned home in March 1887, Edith was already three months pregnant.

The young couple returned from this idyllic interlude to face complications in uniting their daily lives. When Edith learned that Theodore was planning to leave three-year-old Alice in Bamie's care, she surprised him with powerful opposition, insisting they incorporate the little girl into their new household. Edith's reaction created a painful dilemma for Theodore, who well knew the devotion his childless older sister had shown her "blue-eyed darling." "I hardly know what to say about Baby Lee," he uncomfortably informed Bamie. "Edith feels more strongly about her than I could have imagined possible." For Bamie, the loss was devastating. "It almost broke my heart to give her up," she confessed. Although she maintained her composure, conceding that it was best for Alice to be with her father, she avoided further emotional attachments for some time thereafter.

The situation must have been terribly confusing for Alice, whose happiest memories revolved around Bamie's warm and loving home, where "the lovely smell of baking bread coming from the kitchen" heralded "the pleasure of English-style afternoon tea with piping-hot Earl Grey's tea and lots of paper-thin bread and butter." Alice never forgot the wrenching and bewildering day Theodore returned with his new wife: "I in my best dress and sash, with a huge bunch of pink roses in my arms, coming down the stairs at my aunt's house in New York to meet my father and my new mother."

The small child was expected simultaneously to transfer her affections to a new mother and pray each night for her "mother who is in heaven," though her father kept steadfastly mute about the beautiful woman who had been his first love. "In fact," Alice lamented, "he never ever mentioned my mother to me, which was absolutely wrong. He never even said her name . . . I think my father tried to forget he had ever been married to my mother. To blot the whole episode out of his mind. He didn't just never mention her to me, he never mentioned her name, to *anyone*. . . . He obviously felt tremendously guilty about remarrying. . . . The whole thing was really handled very badly. It was awfully bad psychologically."

Edith, too, had to adjust her conception of domestic bliss to the new realities of married life. As mistress of Sagamore Hill, she had envisioned a quiet life in the country with her husband and children, filled with books, writing, and a few like-minded friends. Unlike her husband, she was not a naturally gregarious person. "Where she was reserved," Theodore's cousin Nicholas Roosevelt recalled, "he overflowed with exuberance and enthusiasm." Their divergent natures would require both Theodore and Edith to balance private family life and public pursuits, necessitating compromise and cooperation.

Initially, Theodore focused intently upon his new wife. She happily recalled "rowing over to a great marsh, filled with lagoons and curious winding channels," reading aloud from Browning and Matthew Arnold. The household seemed complete when she gave birth to a son, Theodore Junior, on September 12, 1887. "She was extremely plucky all through," Theodore reported to Bamie. "I am very glad our house has an heir at last!"

For a time, the placid existence suited Theodore. After completing his book on Senator Benton, he had embarked on a short biography of founding father Gouverneur Morris and was beginning research on what would be his major work, *The Winning of the West*. "I have a small son now," he wrote to a friend, "and am settling down more and more to country life for all but a couple of months of the year. My literary work occupies a good deal of my time; and I have on the whole done fairly well at it; I should like to write some book that would really take rank as in the very first class, but I suppose this is a mere dream."

It was not long, however, before his abundant energy and expansive nature required an outlet that tranquil family life could not provide. Even his conception of domestic satisfaction included a continuous stream of houseguests arguing over books or politics at dinner, hiking together in the woods, enjoying canoe races and competitive games of tennis or polo. He assumed that his entire family, which had always been a kind of self-contained universe, would spend weeks together in his rambling home.

For a time, Edith tried to isolate her new household and create a more secluded family life. "Theodore," she would quietly say, "I think this winter we've seen a great deal of Douglas and Corinne and I don't think we'll ask them down for a little while—yet. We may ask them later." At first he would agree: "Very well, very well, Edie, we'll have them later." But soon he "put his foot down" and insisted upon opening their home to the company, stimulation, and activity he needed. Clearly, two very different temperaments had to be reconciled. Edith later acknowledged to Theodore Junior that it had been a great "temptation" to withdraw from society, but "Father would not allow it." Slowly, she began to open her house to her husband's family and friends, while wisely turning the drawing room into her sanctuary, "the place where she kept her own books and treasures." In this elegant room, furnished with bookcases, chairs, and sofas that had been in her family, she found the privacy she craved. Children and guests were told to knock and await permission to enter.

The accommodations Edith made in her manner of life at Sagamore Hill were insignificant beside the transformations occasioned by her husband's impulsive move to Washington, D.C., to become a member of the Civil Service Commission. The 1888 presidential campaign between Benjamin Harrison and Grover Cleveland had revived his interest in politics. A loyal Republican, he had agreed to stump for Harrison, traveling through the Midwest for twelve days, speaking before large crowds, discovering once again the pride and pleasure an enthusiastic audience could bestow. His reintroduction to national politics was "immense fun," he told Henry Cabot Lodge, who would join him in Washington as a new congressman from Massachusetts.

When Republicans captured both the presidency and the U.S. Congress, Roosevelt hoped he might be appointed assistant secretary of state. Despite intense lobbying by his friends, however, the new secretary, James Blaine, was hesitant to have a man of "Mr. T.R.'s temperament" in such an important post. "I do somehow fear that my sleep at Augusta or Bar Harbor would not be quite so easy and refreshing," Blaine admitted, "if so brilliant and aggressive a man had hold of the helm."

After absorbing this disappointing news, Roosevelt finally received word that President Harrison would offer him the less exalted post of civil service commissioner, where he would be charged with enforcing the 1883 Pendleton Act, mandating that one quarter of all federal jobs be filled by competitive examination rather than party affiliation. Roosevelt's family and friends cautioned against accepting the post, believing it beneath his talents, but Roosevelt leapt at the chance to return to political life.

For Edith, pregnant with their second child after a miscarriage the previous summer, the move to Washington signaled an unwelcome disruption of domestic order. Politics held scant interest for her compared with an abiding love of literature, a passion she could share with her husband while he was at work writing. Moreover, as the manager of the family's finances, she worried that his meager annual salary of $3,500 would not cover both the rental in Washington and the maintenance of Sagamore Hill. To economize, Roosevelt decided to stay with Henry Cabot Lodge until Edith could join him after the baby's birth in October.

Whereas Edith dreaded the long separation from her husband, Roosevelt was thrilled to be actively involved in the ferment of the capital. Within minutes of his arrival at the commission offices in the City Hall building, it was clear that he would bring impetus and authority to his new role. Matthew Halloran, who served as a certification clerk for thirty-five years, recalled his first indelible glimpse of Roosevelt. The morning quiet was instantly shattered by his ringing introduction: "I am the new Civil Service Commissioner," he proclaimed, his energetic, penetrating voice and brusque demeanor setting his new staff scrambling. "Have you a telephone? Call up the Ebbit House. I have an engagement with Archbishop Ireland. Say that I will be there at ten o'clock." His appearance had immediate effect. "I jumped up with alacrity," Halloran recalled. "Behind large-rimmed eye-glasses flashed piercing blue-gray eyes, Theodore Roosevelt impressed me as a fine specimen of vigorous manhood. The dazzling smile with its strong white teeth, which was later to become famous all over the world, is still a most vivid recollection. It seemed to mirror the wholesomeness and geniality of the man and it put me wholly at ease. . . . Our friendship and my admiration for him began at that moment."

Indeed, it seemed that a favorable impression of the new commissioner was widespread. In an editorial praising Roosevelt's appointment, the *Decatur* (Illinois) *Republican* observed, "He is equally at home in the drawing rooms of New York or Paris, in the halls of legislation or amid the exciting scenes of a national convention, and when he plays the cowboy on the ranch in Montana he is as far from a tenderfoot as when he takes up the pen to paint in glowing language the glories of a sunset in the Rockies or describes in a magazine article the interest of a fight with the hungry coyotes of the plains." The legend of this intrepid young man and his multifarious talents was beginning to grow.

Theodore spent most of the summer in Washington, with only occasional weekend visits to Sagamore Hill. "It has been a hopeless kind of summer to look back on," Edith wrote in mid-August, "and all I can think of are the times you have been here; our lovely rows and that long drive and our drives to and from the station. . . . My darling you are all the world to me. I am not myself when you are away. Do not forget me or love me less."

On October 10, 1889, Edith gave birth to a second son. She named him Kermit, carrying forward the name of her Aunt Kermit and her father's old mercantile house, Kermit & Carow. Two months later, she finally joined her husband in their newly rented town house at 1820 Jefferson Place. "Edie has occasional fits of gloom," Theodore reported to Bamie on January 4, 1890, "but the house is now getting to look very homelike and comfortable, such a contrast to when I was alone in it! I can hardly realize it is the same place; and I am thoroughly enjoying the change."

So IT WAS THAT THE spring of 1890 saw both the Roosevelts and the Tafts settled in the same Washington neighborhood. Both men had accepted positions in the capital that were far from their ideal vocations, though Roosevelt stepped into his job as commissioner with characteristic verve, while Will approached the role of solicitor general with trepidation. Their two wives also responded very differently to the prospect of life in Washington. Nellie had been an active proponent of the move, undeterred by the idea of uprooting her growing family in order to expand her experience and influence alongside her husband. Edith shuddered at the tumult and social demands of the city, a disruption imposed on the family circle she had waited so long to establish. In many ways, the two women complemented and balanced their respective partners. Nellie spurred Will Taft to greater confidence and action, her expectations and support driving him to greater engagement in the important work of the time. Edith, meanwhile, worked to restrain the impetuous will that drove her husband to ceaseless activity.

Despite—or perhaps because of—their dissimilar natures, Theodore Roosevelt and William Taft would forge a historic friendship. Nellie and Edith, despite their proximity and clear parallels in their interests and upbringings, never made a deep connection. In fact, their commonalities were far more superficial than their disparities. Both had grown up in the shadow of wealthier, more eminent families and had eventually married into them. The social ambitions that dictated private schools, proper wardrobes, and advantageous marriages for both girls were internalized in very different ways. Nellie, exposed to the scintillating world of national politics and society as a girl, was determined to marry a future president (or create one of the man she married).

She had watched her father sacrifice personal ambitions and satisfaction for material comfort and longed to find personal fulfillment, a more vivid and expansive existence. Edith, on the other hand, who had seen the dissipation of her family's empire in the hands of an alcoholic father, craved security and domestic coherence above all else.

Both women were scholars after their fashion. Each had avidly pursued her education, read widely for pleasure, and developed her closest friendships in a circle with similar literary inclinations. For Nellie, literature was a way to engage the larger world, to explore the social issues of the day; reading and writing were intensely personal pursuits for Edith, a way to isolate herself and create a private world to share with those she let in. When Edith married, she believed that she and Theodore could withdraw and build a life centered on books and family, sustained by reading and writing. Nellie, whose relationship with Will evolved in the heated discussions of her salon, agreed to a marriage she believed would expand the boundaries of her existence and her opportunities for involvement and impact.

Nellie always chafed at the conventions that circumscribed her role in the world. The same iconoclastic impulse that drove her to sneak cigarettes or dance in German beer halls made her ache to pursue higher education, as her brothers had, or to find purpose as a pioneer in early childhood schooling despite the opposition of her family. Seeing nothing but ennui in the "favorable" matches that were the crowning achievement for women of her time and station, she sought something different in her union with Will Taft. Solicitous and respectful, he accepted and needed her as a partner in public as well as in domestic pursuits. In London on her honeymoon, she was thrilled to hear Gladstone speak in Parliament. In Cincinnati, she savored newspapers and enjoyed discussions of current events. She was elated that they would now find themselves in Washington, at the epicenter of American political life.

Edith desperately longed for the staid home life that Nellie was fighting to escape. She sought always to make the Roosevelt home a refuge for herself and her family. "A very long way after her husband and children," one friend observed, "came a small group of chosen friends." Like Nellie, she was accomplished and competent, pursuing her intellectual passions while astutely managing her household. She did not, however, share her new neighbor's interest in the social and political agendas that dominated the consciousness of Washington, D.C. While Edith and Nellie lacked a basic affinity and understanding, the unique support each woman gave her husband was indispensable, allowing William Taft and Theodore Roosevelt to find common cause and succeed in ways neither could have alone.

CHAPTER SIX

The Insider and the Outsider

Theodore Roosevelt, U.S. Civil Service Commissioner, ca. 1889.

"WASHINGTON IS JUST A BIG village, but it is a very pleasant big village," Theodore Roosevelt reported in the 1890s. Accustomed to the clamor of New York, "where everything throbs with the chase for the almighty dollar," Roosevelt must have been amazed to find that in the nation's capital, "pleasure takes precedence over work." Government officials enjoyed unhurried breakfasts, arriving at their desks between nine and ten, often leaving the office by four. Even Roosevelt, with his singular disciplined drive, managed to quit work early four or five afternoons each week for a game of tennis or jog through Rock Creek Park before heading off to a dinner party.

To illustrate the marked atmospheric contrast between the two cities, the writer Frank Carpenter observed that in New York, "a streetcar will not wait for you if you are not just at its stopping point. It goes on and you must stand there until the next car comes along. In Washington people a block away signal the cars by waving their hands or their umbrellas. Then they walk to the car at a leisurely pace, while the drivers wait patiently and the horses rest." While the capital might lack "the spirit of intense energy" that animated New York, Carpenter concluded that Washington, with its broad, clean streets and fine marble buildings (and its shanties generally hidden from view), offered "the pleasanter place in which to live."

Roosevelt and Taft apparently met within days of Taft's arrival in town, possibly through their mutual friendship with Congressman Benjamin Butterworth. "Common views and sympathies," Taft recalled, made them immediate allies, particularly in the cause of "Civil Service reform." Roosevelt had been chagrined to find that many influential senators, congressmen, and cabinet officials "hated the whole reform and everything concerned with it and everybody who championed it." For sixty years, politicians in both parties had been complicit in a spoils system where officials (postal carriers, typists, stenographers, and clerks) were appointed, promoted, or fired according to their politics rather than their merit. Uprooting that system would prove a far more strenuous endeavor than Roosevelt had realized when he accepted the post of civil service commissioner.

In William Howard Taft, however, Roosevelt recognized a staunch comrade, a steadfast advocate of advancement due not to cronyism but to competence. Indeed, Taft had been willing to resign his post as revenue collector rather than bow to demands that he fire the best men in his department due to their political affiliations. This experience had given Taft some intimation of the hardships his new friend would face. "It will be a long, hard, discouraging struggle," Taft acknowledged during Roosevelt's tenure as commissioner, "but the right *must* win."

In the mornings, Roosevelt and Taft would often walk together to work. Although a streetcar stopped at nearby Farragut Square, they preferred to go on foot, as did most Washingtonians of the time. "One of the first observations that a New-Yorker makes on coming to Washington," the *New York Times* recorded, "is the difference in the way people walk. Here they usually walk slowly, deliberately always, and one rarely sees the rushing, hurrying, preoccupied walking that lends so much life to New York streets." The two friends soon became familiar figures as they strolled along Connecticut Avenue. More than half a foot shorter and 70 pounds lighter than Taft, Roosevelt busily scanned "everything and everybody" as he pursued a lively conversation. Taft trudged more ponderously, focused intently upon his companion. Taft reached the Justice Department first, which stood one block from the White House, opposite the northern front of the Treasury Department. Roosevelt continued ten blocks east to his destination, Judiciary Square, where the Civil Service Commission was housed.

Increasingly, they relied upon one another for advice and camaraderie, often meeting for leisurely lunches. Roosevelt did most of the talking, finding scant pleasure in his food, while Taft relished generous portions. Whether "absorbed in work or play," one reporter observed, Roosevelt "would eat hay and not know it," whereas Taft savored his meals with care. Profound differences in manner and metabolism never diminished the delight they found in each other's company.

"Externally Taft is everything Roosevelt is not," commented the journalist William Allen White. "Roosevelt's mental processes are quick, intuitive and sure," while "Taft grapples a proposition, wrestles with it without resting and without fatigue until it is settled or solved." Taft had no interest in hunting, boxing, or playing polo, no affinity for the often violent contests of strength and endurance, those manifestations of male prowess that so obsessed Roosevelt. His one passion was for the game of golf, which Roosevelt found excruciatingly dull and slow. Nonetheless, White concluded, the two had no sooner become acquainted than "they established one of those strong friendships that may be established only by men whose exteriors form such antipathetical sutures that they unite by a spiritual affinity."

From the outset, each man recognized the rare character and unique talent of the other. "Mr. Taft," a *Boston American* reporter expounded, "is the kind of man you would expect to find in the president's office of a bank if you went in to start an account. His appearance would give you confidence in the bank. You would say to yourself, 'This man will not let the bank fail if he can possibly help it.' " His kind and ingenuous nature was instantly apparent, inspiring the trust and amity of all he encountered. "If the boat were sinking, and he could swim and you couldn't, you'd hand him your $50,000—if you had it—saying, 'Give this to my wife,' and she'd *get* it."

"One loves him at first sight," Roosevelt acknowledged of Taft. "He has nothing to overcome when he meets people. I realize that I have always got to overcome a little something before I get to the heart of people. . . . I almost envy a man possessing a personality like Taft's." Taft, Roosevelt said, "can get along with some men that I can't get along with." While Roosevelt had difficulty suppressing his contempt and irritation toward men he did not like, Taft's "good nature, his indifference to self, his apparently infinite patience, enables him to get along with men, however cold or acerb or crotchety."

A reporter well acquainted with both men noted that Taft possessed "a capacity, indeed, for personal intimacy which a self-centered man like Roosevelt never could have." Perhaps, he suggested, "Roosevelt could see that sweetness of character in Mr. Taft and he could admire it, as we so often admire the faculties we do not possess." Taft felt a similar wonder at Roosevelt's aggressive self-confidence. His friend's talent for publicity, delight in confrontation, and rousing rhetorical manner were gifts he would never share.

ROOSEVELT WOULD NEED ALL THESE attributes and more if he hoped to win his war against the entrenched spoils system. "Each party profited by the offices when in power," Roosevelt explained, "and when in opposition each party insincerely denounced its opponents for doing exactly what it itself had done and intended again to do." Although long aware that corruption was endemic in the country's political and judicial systems, Roosevelt was sustained by his sometimes overweening belief in the rectitude of his cause and the prospect of a rousing struggle. "For the last few years politics with me has been largely a balancing of evils," he explained to a friend, "and I am delighted to go in on a side where I have no doubt whatever, and feel absolutely certain that my efforts are wholly for the good; and you can guarantee I intend to hew to the line, and let the chips fly where they will."

For Roosevelt, civil service reform presented a historic opening to ensure that "the fellow with no pull should have an even chance with his rival who came backed; that the farmer's lad and the mechanic's son who had no one to speak for them should have the same show in competing for the public service as the son of wealth and social prestige." Allowing party officials to ensconce unqualified friends and kinsmen in public positions, he argued, was not merely "undemocratic"; it ensured inefficient public service that impacted the poor and vulnerable most of all. The smug axiom "To the victor belongs the spoils" was a "cynical battle-cry" he denounced as "so nakedly vicious" that no honorable man could condone it.

Roosevelt's crusade prompted immediate attention from reporters in Washington. Although he was only one of three commissioners, he soon became the public face of the Civil Service Commission. "Yes, TR is a breezy young fellow," a New York *Sun* correspondent commented with patronizing approbation, "and we do not find fault with him because he fancies that he knows it all. The quality of self-confidence is not bad in youth. We rather like to see it, for it indicates usually the possession or the motive power which makes a man aggressive and enterprising. He works more vigorously if he is sure that he is nearer right than other people, and has no misgivings as to his ability to accomplish his ends. The self distrustful, self-critical young man, who is always looking for direction from somebody else, and in whom what the old phrenologists used to call the bump of approbativeness is out of proper proportion, is pretty sure to be left behind in the race."

From the start, Roosevelt understood that public opinion was the single most effective prod for recalcitrant party leaders in the cabinet and the Congress. "Until he began to roar," his biographer Henry Pringle maintained, "the merit system had been a subject that interested a small fraction of the intelligent minority" whom powerful politicians could safely afford to ignore. In order "to secure proper administration of the laws," the task before Roosevelt was nothing less than "to change the average citizen's mental attitude toward the question." In order to battle this entrenched spoils system, it was necessary to instill something of his own sense of outrage into the people, to popularize the reformist cause and foment change from the bottom up.

In his campaign to muster publicity and elicit indignation, Theodore Roosevelt adapted techniques that had served him well in the New York State Assembly, and developed new tactics he would perfect in the years ahead. For his opening salvo, he launched an on-the-spot investigation into the New York Customs House, where rumors indicated that clerks were leaking examination questions to favored party candidates for a fee of $50. When he determined the identity of the guilty clerks, Roosevelt issued a scathing report demanding their dismissal and prosecution. Headlines and editorials broadcast his message across the country, serving notice that civil service law was "going to be enforced, without fear or favor."

Roosevelt's investigation into the New York Customs House furnished evidence that despite the new regulations prohibiting mandatory contributions to the party in power by government employees, party leaders were still demanding "so-called voluntary contributions" from low-level clerks and stenographers as the price for retaining their positions. An identical tithing system had incensed Taft in Ohio, prompting party officials to claim "he was wrecking the party by the course he followed." Cannily appealing to the sympathy and sentiment of his audience, Roosevelt observed that "to a poor clerk just able to get along the loss of three per cent of his salary may mean just the difference between having and not having a winter overcoat for himself, a warm dress for his wife or a Christmas tree for his children."

Straightaway, it was evident to Roosevelt that the corruption he had observed in New York was rampant nationwide, a blight far exceeding the resources of his own staff. To conduct the investigations necessary to expose illegal practices across the country, he cultivated a network of progressive journalists and editors "to point out infractions of the law in their localities."

Recognizing that the foundation of his unwelcome campaign of reform depended on sound information, Roosevelt took especial care to confirm the accuracy of the reports he received.

From Lucius Burrie Swift, editor and publisher of the crusading *Civil Service Chronicle*, he learned that the Indianapolis postmaster, William Wallace, a good friend of President Harrison's, had made a number of irregular appointments that violated civil service standards. "Give me all the facts you can," Roosevelt implored Swift. "I have to be sure that every recommendation I make of any kind or sort can be backed by the most satisfactory evidence. It would be irritating if it were not amusing to see the eagerness with which so many of the people here in power watch to catch me tripping in any recommendation, and their desire to find me making some recommendation, whether for removal or indictment, which I cannot sustain." Initially, Wallace's indignant response generated headlines, but the charges were ultimately verified. "We stirred things up well," Roosevelt gloated to his friend Lodge, "but I think we have administered a galvanic shock that will reinforce [Wallace's] virtue for the future." His hopes were realized. In fact, the newspaper exposure did chasten the Indianapolis postmaster; within two years, his administration was deemed "a model of fairness and justice."

Buoyed by this early success, Roosevelt turned his spotlight on Milwaukee, where informants claimed that Postmaster George Paul was systematically manipulating examination scores in order to appoint favored party members. Evidence in hand, Roosevelt issued a blistering public report and demanded Paul's removal from office. "If he is not dismissed, as we recommend, it will be a black eye for the Commission," Roosevelt told Lodge, "and practically an announcement that hereafter no man need fear dismissal for violating the law; for if Paul has not violated it, then it can by no possibility be violated." Roosevelt's report and the ensuing publicity infuriated President Harrison's postmaster general, John Wanamaker. He charged that Roosevelt was overstepping his authority, intruding on matters that were the province of his own department. A wealthy contributor to Harrison's campaign fund, Wanamaker fully adhered to the time-honored spoils system and harbored contempt for civil service reformers. Wanamaker appealed to the president, who forged a weak compromise by accepting Paul's resignation. "It was a golden chance to take a good stand," Roosevelt lamented, "and it has been lost."

The apparent rebuff from President Harrison did not deter Roosevelt from initiating another, more controversial investigation into violations and irregularities in the Baltimore Post Office. On the basis of information supplied by Charles Bonaparte, a civil service reformer who would one day become a member of his own cabinet, Roosevelt charged officials with using postal appointments as "a bribery chest." Wanamaker countered by conducting his own investigation, submitting the results to a committee in the House of Representatives. Wanamaker's report absolved the employees of any wrongdoing and accused Roosevelt of pursuing an inquisition both "unfair and partial in the extreme." Roosevelt countered by publishing an open letter to Postmaster General Wanamaker, whom he called the "head devil" of the spoilsmen, demanding that he renounce the "gross impertinence and impropriety" of his statements.

The escalating hostility between Roosevelt and Wanamaker delighted the press. "It is war, open, avowed, and to the knife," *The Washington Post* reported. The *New York Times* could "not remember an instance in the history of our Government" when one member of a president's administration made "statements so damaging to the character of another officer of the Government of still higher rank."

Critics assailed Roosevelt's tactics, recommending that he "put a padlock on his restless and uncontrollable jaws." *The Washington Post* claimed that he spoke "like a person suffering from an overdose of nerve tonic," expressing their scorn with savage clarity: "He came into official life with a blare of trumpets and a beating of gongs, blared and beat by himself. He immediately announced himself the one man competent to take charge of the entire business of the Government. To his mind every department of the Government was under the management of incompetent and bad men. He said to himself, to his barber, to his laundryman, and to all others who would listen to his incoherent gibberish: 'I am Roosevelt; stop work and look at me.' For a short time he had clear sailing. As he sailed he took in wind. As he took in wind he became more puffed up. As he became more puffed up he became insolent, arrogant, and more conceited."

As Roosevelt continued to commandeer center stage, relationships with his fellow commissioners, once quite amicable, grew increasingly contentious. He complained to Lodge that Charles Lyman was "utterly useless . . . utterly out of place as a Commissioner," and that Hugh S. Thompson, though an "excellent" fellow, lacked the fortitude to pursue enemies of civil service with the necessary zeal. He much preferred to proceed unilaterally. "My two colleagues are now away and I have all the work of the Civil Service Commission to myself," he told his sister Bamie. "I like it; it is more satisfactory than having a divided responsibility; and it enables me to take more decided steps."

More troubling than friction within the commission was Roosevelt's deteriorating relationship with President Harrison. "I have been continuing my civil service fight, battling with everybody," he groused to Bamie, " the little gray man in the White House looking on with cold and hesitating disapproval." Never once throughout his service in the Harrison administration was Roosevelt invited to dine at the White House. Despite the president's "high regard" for the young commissioner's abilities, he was often irked by Roosevelt's uncompromising, aggressive temperament. "Roosevelt seemed to feel," Harrison remarked, "that everything ought to be done before sundown." Rumors abounded that Roosevelt would be removed. With most of the influential newspapers supporting him, however, and with public indignation about violations of the civil service law at an inflamed pitch, Harrison dared not take action.

Although Roosevelt's impetuous offensives frayed personal relationships, his public triumph over Postmaster General Wanamaker was soon complete. After hearing testimony from both sides, the House committee concluded that incontrovertible evidence backed up every single charge of fraud and misconduct. "Mr. Roosevelt is a regular young Lochinvar," the Boston *Evening Times* remarked. "He isn't afraid of the newspapers, he isn't afraid of losing his place, and he is always ready for a fight. He keeps civil-service reform before the people and as the case often is, his aggressiveness is a great factor in a good cause."

To HER GREAT SURPRISE, EDITH Roosevelt found that she thoroughly enjoyed Washington. Through her husband's friendship with Massachusetts congressman Henry Cabot Lodge, she entered a circle of literary-minded men and women whose engaging conversations centered on the books, art, and music that she loved. "Cabot has been a real comfort to her," Theodore reported to Bamie. "He is one of the few men I know who is as well read as she is in English literature, and she delights to talk with him." Edith also developed a close relationship with Nannie Lodge, a charming woman guided by a quick mind and a warm heart. Both women loved poetry and could recite Shakespeare "almost by heart." The Lodges and the Roosevelts lived close enough to easily frequent each other's homes. "You know, old fellow," Roosevelt confided to Lodge, "you and Nannie are more to me than any one else but my own immediate family."

Together with the Lodges, Theodore and Edith were frequent guests at the Lafayette Square town house of the historian Henry Adams. The distinguished group that congregated there included the Lincoln biographer John Hay and his wife, Clara; Senator Don Cameron with his exquisite wife,

Elizabeth; the sculptor Augustus Saint-Gaudens; and the Winthrop Chanlers. Adams felt an immediate fondness for Edith, who struck him as especially "sympathetic." His encouragement and admiration put her quickly at ease in the group's discussions of literature, drama, and poetry. "Her taste in books and judgment of their merit *qua* literature were always far more reliable than were Theodore's," noted a town house regular.

"Edith is really enjoying Washington," Roosevelt reported to Bamie. "One night we dined at Cabots to meet the Willy Endicotts; another night I gave a dinner to some historical friends; last evening we went to the theatre, and a supper afterwards with John Hay. . . . Of course Hay was charming, as he always is; and Edith enjoyed it all as much as I did." She had even developed a small taste for talk of political events, so long as she could rely on her inner circle for company and conversation. At a breakfast hosted by Secretary of State James Blaine, she was delighted to find herself seated between Elizabeth Cameron and Clara Hay. Her deepening friendships did much to assuage Edith's dread anxiety of Washington's social world. New Year's Day entailed an exhausting series of calls on the wives of government officials, but she was heartened by the company of Nannie Lodge. "Nannie has been a dear about sending me her carriage & this afternoon I have found courage to go out & pay hundreds of calls."

While Edith made an effort to overcome her natural reserve, her husband happily immersed himself in the social whirl of the nation's capital. The Roosevelts hosted casual dinners that made an enduring impression on their circle of friends. "Sunday-evening suppers where the food was of the plainest and the company of the best," Margaret Chanler recalled. "Theodore would keep us all spellbound with tales of his adventures in the West. There was a vital radiance about the man—a glowing, unfeigned cordiality towards those he liked that was irresistible." Edith was "more difficult of access. . . . Just as the camera is focused, she steps aside to avoid the click of the shutter." Despite this elusive quality, "one felt in her a great strength of character, and ineluctable will power."

During those first years in Washington, the Roosevelts successfully established themselves among the city's social and intellectual elite. "Edith and I meet just the people we like to see," Theodore told Bamie. "We dine out three or four times a week, and have people to dinner once or twice; so that we hail the two or three evenings when we are alone at home, and can talk and read. . . . The people we meet are mostly those who stand high in the political world, and who are therefore interested in the same subjects that interest us; while there are enough who are men of letters or of science to give a pleasant and needed variety."

Rudyard Kipling, whom Theodore had first met at the Cosmos Club in New York, was a guest on a number of occasions. Kipling later described that first encounter when he "curled up" on a chair across from Roosevelt "and listened and wondered until the universe seemed to be spinning around and Theodore was the spinner." If Roosevelt initially resented Kipling's "tendency to criticise America," he nonetheless recognized the author's "genius" and found the man himself "very entertaining."

Roosevelt sometimes worried that his political career suffered as he devoted time and attention to his social pursuits. After two years, his war on the spoils system had produced singular successes but little systemic change. While he had managed to reduce the practice of forcing salary contributions from government clerks, he had not "succeeded in stopping political assessments outright." He had "harassed the wrong-doers" who manipulated examination results without eliminating the endemic corruption that fueled the practice.

If Roosevelt fretted that his gains had been modest, he had accomplished more than any of his predecessors in the Civil Service Commission. Through his dramatic investigations of unscrupulous officials, his alliances with reformist journalists and immense skill in generating publicity, he had alerted Americans to the flagrant iniquities of the spoils system. The process Roosevelt had set in motion by shining the light of publicity on these practices would prove crucial in any attempt to create a system of government based upon good work rather than political influence.

Taft embarked upon his tenure in Washington with a very different style of leadership; meticulous habits and an affable disposition helped him build accord among colleagues and superiors at every level, including the executive.

Recalling their time together in Washington, Roosevelt wryly conceded Taft's success in gaining Harrison's cooperation while he so "got on Harrison's nerves," that his very presence set the president's "fingers drumming on the desk before him as though it were a piano." Roosevelt marveled that despite Taft's ability to foster cooperation among all manner of men, "he was always a man of highest ideals."

William Howard Taft's stolid demeanor prevented the sort of aggressive, confident debut in Washington that Roosevelt had enjoyed. He confessed to his father that his first oral argument before the Supreme Court had left him despondent. "I did not find myself as fluent on my feet as I had hoped to," he explained. "I forgot a great many things I had intended to say." He worried that his deliberate speaking style would fail to capture the justices' attention.

"They seem to think when I begin to talk that that is a good chance to read all the letters that have been waiting for some time, to eat lunch, and devote their attention to correcting proof, and other matters that have been delayed until my speech," he grumbled. While the solicitor general's position might offer great "opportunities for professional experience," he doubted his own ability to capitalize on those opportunities. "I find it quite embarrassing to change from the easy position of sitting on the bench to the very different one of standing on your legs before it," he told one friend, "and I do not find myself at home as I hoped to do in presenting one side of a case at Court." Called to make a quick business trip home, he was delighted to spend "a few days in Cincinnati, which it seems to me I left ten years ago, such a change has come over my mode of life."

"Don't be discouraged," his father counseled. "I have no doubt that you will soon come to understand them & their ways perfectly, & that they will be as anxious to hear what you have to say, as you will to say it." His mother also tried to assuage his anxieties. "Members waste their eloquence in the House and the Senate on empty benches or disorderly parties who never listen," she reminded him. Taft assured his parents that he remained steadfastly "philosophical," stoically framing his lack of immediate success as "the strongest reason for . . . having this experience and improving it." Indeed, he acknowledged, "the very fact that I find it difficult, and not particularly agreeable is evidence that the medicine is good for me."

His second appearance before the Court gave him "somewhat more satisfaction" and made him feel "more at home." Unfortunately, his speaking style, at least in his own estimation, seemed to exert "the same soporific power" on the justices. He refused to be discouraged, declaring he would "gain a good deal of practice in addressing a lot of mummies and experience in not being overcome by circumstances."

The sudden death of his predecessor the previous January had left him with a "rather overwhelming" workload; nearly a dozen unfinished cases had to be argued before the Court that spring of 1891. Midnight often found him still methodically reading through briefs, looking up precedents, drafting opinions, and editing proofs in his home library. His hard work secured victories in his first eleven cases. But even then, he could not share Roosevelt's sanguine outlook. "Each time a case of mine is now decided, I look for defeat," he anxiously wrote. "It is my turn. It ought to come, and doubtless will." In fact, of seventeen cases argued in his first year, Taft was gratified to find he had won fifteen. "So," he told his father, "you see that Fortune has been good to me on the whole."Although reluctant to proclaim his own accomplishments, he concluded that "the year's experience has been valuable." He no longer considered "the inattention of the judges" a personal affront. "Everyone suffers the same way," he realized. "It is the custom of the Bench." As he mastered his initial insecurities, Taft appreciated that his position had opened an entirely "new field of federal practice, law and decisions, with which I had no familiarity before."

Perhaps even more central to his success, Taft had "made some very valuable acquaintances" in his year's time. "It would be difficult for the Department of Justice to be organized with officers who are pleasanter to get along with than it has been since I have been here," he happily reported. "The Attorney General [William Miller] is a very satisfactory man to work under. . . . I like him very much, and am conscious that he has been in every way considerate of me."

While Roosevelt reveled in any opportunity to exercise sole power in the absence of his fellow commissioners, Taft took no pleasure in suddenly assuming the role of attorney general. "The novelty of it wore off in just about a day," he admitted, "and no man will be happier than I shall be when he returns to his desk." In the following months, as Attorney General Miller suffered recurring intestinal attacks, Taft became more comfortable wielding authority. But he was careful not to overstep or compromise his relationship with Miller. "The first duty of a subordinate," he strongly believed, "is courteous respect to his superior officer."

Taft's regard for the attorney general went beyond mere professional courtesy. On one occasion, Miller fell ill while his wife was out of town and Taft proposed that he stay overnight: "I shall sleep in a room next to his," he related to Nellie. "I know what it is to be attacked in the stomach at night all alone, and even though I could probably do no good the fact of the presence of a friend is reassuring."

Taft's kind and ingenuous nature defined not only his bond with Miller but a growing intimacy with President Harrison, one of Miller's closest friends. Visiting the attorney general's household, Taft often found the president himself relaxing in the parlor. In the course of their conversations, Harrison in turn found Taft so amiable that he issued an open invitation to call on him at the White House "every evening if convenient." Louise was delighted to learn of the proffered hospitality, regarding the unusual invitation "as not only a great compliment, but as a great privilege."

Furthermore, Taft was happy to note that by year's end he had "come into exceedingly pleasant relations with the Supreme Court," the bench he one day ardently hoped to join. He developed a genuine friendship with Justice John

Harlan and, at Harlan's request, agreed to write a short sketch of his life for publication in a commemorative history of the Supreme Court. "It has been a work of considerable labor, because it involved an examination of a great many cases," Taft related to his father. "However, Judge Harlan has been very kind to me, and I feel as if anything I could do for him was only repaying the friendly interest he has taken in me." Indeed, the trust and affection generated by Taft's good nature made him welcome in the city's most eminent company. He became a regular whenever the attorney general hosted dinners for members of the Supreme Court.

Taft was equally popular among his subordinates and immediate colleagues, quickly earning the confidence and friendship of the assistant attorneys general. His administrative skills enabled him to organize the department's functions in a manner that expedited everyone's work. Under his predecessors, business had been "scattered over the Department," but Taft had methodically taken control of the docket. "Every paper that comes to the Department with reference to Supreme Court business comes to me," he proudly explained to his father. "I have a general idea of all the cases that are to be argued in the Supreme Court." Taft's dedication earned him great esteem in the capital, and word spread that he was "the heaviest weight intellectually of any men in the Department of Justice."

For Nellie, life in Washington settled into a gratifying routine. She had been in town only six weeks when she received her first invitation to a White House dinner for the Supreme Court. "There were fifty at the table," Taft reported to his father, "and it made a very brilliant assemblage." The company included a number of senators and congressmen from the judiciary committees of both Houses, as well as the justices themselves. Nellie's seatmate was "exceedingly conversational and pleasant, and Nellie had a good time," Taft continued, immersing himself in the details of this social landscape. "You may tell Mother that Nellie's dress which she got in Paris she had made over in New York, and that it is exceedingly becoming to her." News of the festivities elicited great excitement in Cincinnati. "Do write me details," Nellie's friend Agnes Davis implored. "I feel so proud of our Cin. friends."

Nellie was back at the White House for the traditional reception on New Year's Day 1891, where the Marine Band's performance must have evoked memories of her first visit as a young girl. "In the East Room," *The Washington Post* reported, "the electric lights were used for the first time, the twelve great crystal suns set in the center of as many medallions on the ceiling gleaming with white light." In the Red Parlor and the Blue Room, government officials and their wives mingled until the invited guests moved into the private dining room for lunch. "She had a very pleasant time," Taft told his father, "and met a great many people—all the diplomats, and most of the prominent officials." Later that afternoon, she stood in the receiving line at a party hosted by the attorney general and his wife. Days later, the Tafts attended a reception hosted by Vice President Levi Morton for the president and the cabinet. Nellie and her husband had established a place in the bright constellation of Washington that she had yearned for since childhood.

The house on Dupont Circle was large enough to accommodate guests, allowing Nellie to entertain her parents, her sister Maria, Taft's brothers and sisters-in-law, and a number of her old friends from home. "Tom Mack is with us now," Taft reported in January 1891, "and he and Nellie go every day to the Senate and House to hear the debates. They have been quite interesting during the past few days." Finally, Nellie Herron Taft was privy to the intellectual and political discourse at the summit of Washington's society.

The Roosevelts and Tafts were frequent guests at the home of Ohio congressman Bellamy Storer and his wealthy wife, Maria Longworth. Nellie and Edith both shopped at the Center Market, considered a Washington institution. On market day, the two women joined "throngs of buyers of all classes of society, fashionable women of the West End, accompanied by negro servants, mingling with people of less opulent sections." They made the rounds of the carts, selecting fresh fruits and vegetables, fish, chicken and other meats. "The true Washingtonian," the historian Constance Green wrote, "regarded marketing in person as much a part of well-ordered living as making calls or serving hot chocolate to morning visitors."

Curiously, despite a constant proximity, the bond between these two impressive women "never ripened into intimacy." In fact, Nellie later confessed to her younger son that "I don't like Mrs. Roosevelt at all. I never did."

DURING HIS SECOND YEAR AS solicitor general, Taft extended his string of victories in three celebrated cases. In the first, he successfully defended the constitutionality of the McKinley tariff, which raised duties on imports competing with American products. His second case, in which he convinced the Supreme Court to sustain Speaker Thomas Reed's new method of counting a quorum, had profound implications for partisan politics in the legislative process. Reed's procedure ended the old practice that demanded a voice vote rather than a simple tally of "those who were actually present in the room" to establish a quorum. This traditional method, in place since the first Congress, had enabled the minority party to prevent the transaction of business by simply hiding in the cloakrooms and refusing to answer the roll call. Reed's new rule, unanimously affirmed by the Court, greatly increased the power of the Speaker, allowing him to push through sweeping legislation.

Taft's most resounding triumph involved a dispute between Great Britain and the United States over fishing rights in the Bering Sea. Initially, the international attention focused on the case disconcerted Taft. "I suppose I ought to feel that it is a great privilege to take part in it," he confessed, "but I look forward with considerable trepidation to making an argument orally before that court in a case which will be so conspicuous." If Taft had gained confidence in the quality of his preparation, he remained uneasy about his oratorical skills. In such an important case, the work was customarily divided between the attorney general and the solicitor general. But another episode of Miller's chronic illness left Taft responsible for the entire brief, a task he welcomed: "I do not object to this, at all, because I like the work," he told his father. In the end, his conscientious planning and competent presentation yielded a unanimous ruling in the government's favor. His three significant victories, announced at the same time, made headlines across the country.

Taft's pleasure in his success as solicitor general was magnified by the joy he knew it would bring to his father. In 1890, the elder Tafts had moved to California, hoping the climate would improve Alphonso's diseased lungs. For a time, it seemed his health had improved, but he soon began to suffer from a range of ailments, including asthma and bladder infections. "Your letters are what we live upon here," Alphonso told his son. "Your success has been wonderful." Despite his exhaustion at the end of each working day in Washington, Will took the time to write to his father, describing his cases in detail. "I am greatly exhilarated by your letters," returned Alphonso wistfully. "They carry back 14 years when I was able to act a man's part & enjoy life as it passed."

In November 1890, Charley Taft traveled to the west coast to spend a week with their father. "The morning is his best time," he reported to Will. "But the afternoon tires him out with pain and suffering. He is ready to go to bed at eight o'clock. His power of enduring suffering is wonderful. I could see traces of pain on his features during the afternoons, when he sits in his chair, but he never complained at all." Louise confirmed Charley's report. "Except when he is actually suffering his happy temperament surmounts all discouragements preserving a cheerfulness equal to Mark Tapley's," she explained, alluding to the irrepressible servant in Dickens's *Martin Chuzzlewit* who sought out all manner of obstacles to surmount and miseries to transcend, and yet maintained a joyful aplomb. While Alphonso's body deteriorated, his mind remained sufficiently lucid to find pleasure when his wife read to him. "What a resource is a cultivated mind!" Louise told her son. "What can people do when old and sick without intellectual resources. I can always entertain him."

Nothing mattered more to Alphonso in his last days, Charley reported, than the accomplishments of his boys—and Will's foremost. "Can you not in your long summer vacation of next year come & see us?" Alphonso beseeched Will. "Think of it, & the fate of one old man who has to be across the continent from the best children in the world."

In early May 1891, Will received word that his father had begun to hemorrhage internally and little time remained. He left work immediately and traveled by train to California. Though doctors had given up any hope for recovery by the time Will arrived, the chance to be with his father at the end was a gift that Theodore had been denied. "His vitality is fighting with death," Will recounted to Nellie ten days later. "Each day might end his life and yet he has breathed on." No longer able to take nourishment, Alphonso had lost some 75 pounds; still, his body clung to life. Only Will could persuade him to take anything to drink: "He seems to trust me. After I had given him some brandy he looked up at me in the sweetest way and said to me 'Will I love you beyond expression.' "

A few mornings later, before Will had risen, Alphonso asked the nurse to fetch his "noble boy." Agonizingly short of breath, he struggled to tell his son that "he ought to have avoided this by suicide." Three days later, with Will by his side, Alphonso Taft died. He was eighty years old.

The funeral was held in the old Taft home on Mt. Auburn. In Washington, the Justice Department flag was flown at half-mast, though Taft rejected the attorney general's proposal to close the department on the day of the funeral. Appreciative of the honor, Taft nonetheless insisted he did not want the general public to be inconvenienced.

All four sons returned to Cincinnati for the funeral. Taft worried that Charley and Annie, who had recently lost their twelve-year-old son David to typhoid fever, could scarcely absorb this new grief. "I trust you may never have this experience to go through," Charley had written Will. "It takes one's heart right out of a person." For the rest of the Taft children, life was proceeding more smoothly. Harry's law business was growing and Julia had given birth to a son. Horace's school was beginning to prosper and he had fallen in love with Winifred Thompson, a teacher in New Haven. Fanny was happily settled in California, having married her father's doctor, William Edwards. And Nellie had returned from Washington pregnant with her second child.

After the funeral, Nellie remained in Cincinnati with her family to await the birth of the baby. Taft returned alone to Washington, well aware that he made a "ludicrous" picture as he raced to catch the train at the Cincinnati station without the benefit of his wife's management. Apparently, Taft had forgotten to safety-pin his drawers to his trousers, and as he began to run, his drawers "began to work themselves clear down into the legs of the trousers and [his] legs were thus shackled so as to prevent any rapidity of movement." To close this comic vignette, just as the train departed the platform, he somehow managed to climb aboard.

Taft returned to a city that was gradually emptying as women and children escaped the insufferable summer heat and humidity, leaving the men behind. With Edith and the children at Sagamore Hill, Theodore and his British diplomat friend, Cecil Spring Rice, roomed together. "Springy and I have had a pleasant time," Roosevelt told Bamie. "He is a good fellow; and really cultivated; in the evenings he reads Homer and Dante in the originals! I wish I could. . . . Of course I miss Edith and the children frightfully. But it is pleasant to be engaged in a work which I know to be useful and in which I believe with all my heart." In July, they moved into Lodge's vacant house while Cabot and Nannie were abroad. "We are just as comfortable as possible," Roosevelt informed Lodge, "and are excellently taken care of by nice black Martha; and we think very gratefully of our absent host and hostess."

On August 1, 1891, Nellie gave birth to a daughter, Helen. Twelve days later, Edith gave birth to Ethel. "I see that I got ahead of Mrs. Roosevelt and feel quite proud," Nellie remarked to Will.

Without the domestic order imposed by the presence of wives and children, the men who worked through the long Washington summer established an intimate camaraderie. With Springy's "nervous and fidgety" assistance, Theodore hosted several dinners, proudly reporting to Lodge that no guest had yet died. In Nellie's absence, he invited Will to one of these bachelor meals. On this occasion, the invitation to Taft revealed an affectionate and casual humor: "Can you dine with me, in the *most* frugal manner Friday night at 8 o'clock. . . . No dress suit—I haven't got any."

At the time of their dinner, Roosevelt was wrestling with the headlong deterioration of his brother Elliott's mental health, a situation that echoed Taft's painful experience with his brother Peter. Elliott had gone to work for his Uncle Gracie's real estate firm, but heavy drinking and mental instability prevented him from contributing to the enterprise. At twenty-three, he had married the socialite Anna Hall. She bore him three children—Eleanor, Elliott Junior, and Hall—but the responsibilities of fatherhood never slowed his drinking. "It is a perfect nightmare about Elliott," Theodore had informed Bamie. "Elliott must be put under some good man, and then sent off on a sea voyage, or made to do whatever else he is told. Half measures simply put off the day, make the case more hopeless, and render the chance of public scandal."

The disgrace Roosevelt feared surfaced that summer. One of Elliott's maids, Katy Mann, threatened to file suit against him, claiming that he was the father of her newborn child. Theodore initially counseled against giving in to blackmail, but changed his mind when the family determined the likely truth of her story. "He is evidently a maniac, morally no less than Mentally," Theodore gravely declared to Bamie. "How glad I am I got his authorization to compromise the Katy Mann affair!" When negotiations stalled and Theodore learned new details of Elliott's increasingly violent behavior at home, he secured Anna Hall's consent to have him institutionalized. His petition to declare his brother legally insane made headlines the very week of his dinner with Taft. ELLIOTT ROOSEVELT DEMENTED BY EXCESSES, proclaimed the *New York Herald*. Two days later, Elliott retaliated in an open letter to the *Herald* "emphatically" denying he was "a lunatic or that any steps have been taken to adjudge him one." Theodore was beside himself. "The horror about Elliott broods over me like a nightmare," he told his sister.

In the end, Elliott agreed to seek a cure for his alcoholism and the family withdrew their petition to declare him insane. The treatment failed, as did several other interventions. Two years later, suffering from delusions, Elliott "jumped out of the parlor window of his house, had a seizure and died." Just as the Tafts had sought solace in memories of the time when Peter was "the sunniest" child in the family, so Theodore found "great comfort" in the realization that he no longer had to dwell on his brother's degradation: "I only need to have pleasant thoughts of Elliott now," he reflected. "He is just the gallant, generous, manly boy and young man whom everyone loved."

While Theodore rarely talked with anyone about his private sorrows, the public nature of the struggle, combined with Taft's empathetic nature raises the possibility that he was able to discuss some portion of the situation with his friend. In a letter to Bamie, Roosevelt spoke of another dinner party in his home that included Taft, "of whom we are really fond." At such gatherings, one observer noted, Taft's "merry blue eyes, his heavy mop of dark-brown hair, and the cherubic look of his big face, conspired with his soft, sibilant, self-deprecatory voice" and booming laugh to make him an ideal companion.

WILLIAM TAFT'S WIDESPREAD POPULARITY IN Washington would prove an invaluable resource when he sought one of nine new circuit court judgeships created by Congress to relieve congestion in the courts. At thirty-four, Taft was young for the prestigious appointment, the second highest in the nation's judicial system. The reduction in pay from his salary as solicitor general mattered little to Taft when he considered that a seat on the Sixth District's court of appeals would put him "in the line of promotion" for the Supreme Court. His old friend Howard Hollister and Yale classmate Rufus Smith both worked tirelessly to build support for the appointment. They "have stirred up matters in my behalf in Cincinnati," he gratefully observed, "so that a great number of letters have come from the leading members of the bar there."

The affinity Taft had developed with Attorney General Miller and Justice Harlan served him well when the two men wholeheartedly endorsed him for the post. In a joint interview with the president, Harlan called Taft "the man whom . . . of all others, you should appoint"; Miller agreed, telling Harrison that he believed Taft possessed "in an eminent degree the judicial faculty" and that his "age was such as to secure to the people of the circuit a great many years of hard work." Justice Henry Billings Brown affirmed that he "would be very glad" if Taft received the appointment. Despite such resounding, prestigious endorsements, Taft remained "entirely philosophical" about his chances, aware that the number of qualified candidates was "legion." The Sixth District covered Ohio, Michigan, Tennessee, and Kentucky, each state offering a favorite son to compete for the position. Indeed, the flood of applicants to the new judicial posts necessitated a nine-month selection process, stretching from March until December. Though Alphonso Taft had been thrilled by the possibility of his son's appointment, he did not live to hear who had received the coveted post.

As the Tafts awaited a decision, Nellie endeavored to discourage Will from actively pursuing the post. She had finally secured the life she had long desired and dreaded a return to the staid, tranquil existence in Cincinnati. Just as she had objected to his superior court appointment years earlier, fearing he would be "settled for good," she now resisted a promotion that would keep him "fixed in a groove for the rest of his life" among colleagues "almost twice his age." Since her life was now completely bound to his, she insisted that she should weigh in on the decision.

Taft was disheartened to find his wife "very much opposed" to a course of action he ardently desired. After five years of marriage, his love for her transcended the passion of courtship days. "It seems to me now," he told her, "as if more completely than ever, we have become one." He was alarmed by her warning: "If you get your heart's desire My darling it will put an end to all the opportunities you now have of being thrown with bigwigs." And he was disquieted when she spoke of her great affection for Washington and her qualms that outside her family there was "hardly a soul" in Cincinnati she cared to see. "You will regard my failure to get the Circuit Judgeship as only another stroke of good luck and perhaps you may be right, though I can not think so," he acknowledged. "In any event my Darling, we can be happy as long as we live, if we only love each other and the children that come to us."

Such assurances notwithstanding, the long delay as President Harrison made up his mind was as tense for Nellie as it was for Will. Though the prospect ran counter to her own desires, she realized how deeply her husband was invested in the appointment. Each week a different rumor surfaced heralding a different name for the post, though Will remained the top candidate. "I hate that you should be disappointed," Nellie cautioned him. "It would be very easy for the Pres. to change his mind, even if it had been made up." The years of their marriage had only served to intensify her own devotion to Will. While she had left him craving the slightest expression of affection during their courtship days, her letters during their recent summer separation were filled with tenderness.

"I am not a bit happy without you," she confessed. "I love you ever and ever so much." Every day they were apart, she penned a letter to him and was disappointed when he missed a day in replying, reminding him that "when we were first married you often wrote twice a day." She felt his anxiety acutely, commingled with her own reluctance to embrace his hopes.

Perhaps the satisfaction she had found in motherhood had given Nellie a measure of equanimity as she faced an uncertain future. She wrote at length about the doings of their children. When Robert was a year old, she noted that he was "simply crazy about people—will go to any one and even run into their rooms if he sees the door open. The moment he sees anyone he knows, he sets up a shout at the top of his voice, which makes him a great favorite." She declared him "the dearest child that ever was," happily noting his devotion toward baby Helen as well as herself.

Nevertheless, her husband remained the primary focus of her love and concern. His eating habits and lack of exercise were constant sources of worry for her. When colleagues praised him, Nellie reveled in the accolades. "I seem to care much more that people should like and appreciate you than that they should care about me," she admitted. And whatever the situation, she never stopped giving him clever and frank counsel. "Don't make your brief too long, dearest," she admonished on one occasion. "The court will appreciate it much more if they don't grow weary over reading it. Many a good thing is spoiled by there being too much of it."

On December 16, 1891, the president announced his nominations for the nine new judgeships. His nomination of William Howard Taft for the Sixth District won widespread approbation. "The press notices have been as flattering as anyone could desire," Harry wrote to his brother. *The Washington Post* called Taft "one of the most popular officials in public life," citing a senior Ohio judge's opinion that "no man could have been named who would be more acceptable to the bar of that circuit." Horace teased that he could no longer afford to keep sending Will telegrams with each new success his brother achieved, but earnestly assured him that he was ideally suited for the post: "Aside from your especially liking the work and being fitted for it, there has always seemed to me a dignity about the office and a chance for fine service. . . . Somehow Father's brave & conscientious career on the bench always pleased me more than any other part of his professional or public life."

Taft viewed the return to his home city of Cincinnati with great high spirits. "One of the sweetest things connected with the appointment," he wrote Howard Hollister, "is the pleasure I anticipate in coming back to our old associations," to renew "the enthusiastic affection and intimacy which we had during our college days, and after. When we are in Cincinnati together, we must see as much of each other as possible." Suppressing her disappointment, Nellie dutifully packed up the house on Dupont Circle and moved back with the children. Taft remained in Washington for three additional months as solicitor general until the Senate confirmed the nominations on March 17, 1892. "I feel so good over the confirmation and the prospect of seeing you and the babies that I could hurrah for joy," he enthusiastically told Nellie.

Once established in his new post, Taft did not forget the kind support he had received in Washington. He wrote with warm appreciation to Attorney General Miller. "The two years which I have spent under you in Washington have been full of pleasure and profit to me. No man ever received more considerate treatment from another than I have from you. . . . Our relations have refined into affectionate friendship and I shall cherish the memory of it always. . . . I know to whom I owe my present appointment to the Bench. But for you, I should not have attained what has been my life's ambition and I am deeply grateful."

LIKE NELLIE, EDITH HAD BECOME accustomed to Washington and was loath to relinquish the "pleasant life" she had built, which seemed likely when the Democrat, Grover Cleveland, defeated Benjamin Harrison in 1892. Roosevelt handed in his resignation, but Cleveland did not immediately accept it. "Our places are still uncertain," she told her sister Emily. She wished that her husband could be "elected by the people" to Congress, rather than dependent on presidential whim for his position and livelihood. She feared, however, this was "a dream never to be realized." It was an anxious time for Theodore as well; they had stretched their finances during their stay in the capital, and his inheritance was dwindling. "He is now in one of his depressed conditions about the future," Edith remarked, "and says the children will have reason to reproach him for not having insisted upon taking a money making profession." Edith understood that such histrionics were essentially "nonsense," a mere diversion from his true concerns. Theodore revealed his deeper troubles to Bamie, insisting that he had no permanent prospects in the political world, where he believed he "could do most." With overdetermined fatalism, he consigned himself to more modest pursuits: "But I shall speedily turn back to my books and do my best with them; though I fear that only a very mild & moderate success awaits me."

Decisions about the future were happily postponed when Cleveland asked Roosevelt to stay at his post for another year or two. News that "the moving spirit of the Commission" would remain was certain to be "received with joy by all reformers, and with equal dismay by spoilsmen throughout the country," the New York *Evening Post* observed. "Through the Harrison Administration, he pursued the spoilsmen 'with a sharp stick,' although they belonged to his own party, and he will not be any easier with them now that he will have to deal with Democrats."

In fact, despite the Democratic administration, the ensuing months brought contentment to the Roosevelts. Theodore got along better with Cleveland than he had with Harrison. Edith happily reported to Bamie that they had finally been invited to a White House dinner. "It was practically a family affair," she noted, and she was "certainly glad to dine once at the White House." Increasingly, however, Edith was occupied by the demands of her growing family. That spring of 1894, she gave birth to her fourth child, named Archibald Bulloch in honor of Theodore's maternal relatives.

The pleasant routine of life in Washington was interrupted in the fall when Roosevelt was approached by the New York Republican bosses to run for mayor. In contrast to his earlier token run, this time the Republicans stood a good chance of winning in both the city and the state. Theodore was elated by the sudden turn of events, he told Lodge, which renewed his "hope of going on in the work and life for which I care far more than any other." But Edith recoiled from the uncertainty, believing "they simply could not afford to take the chance," and asking, "What if Theodore resigned his commissionership in order to run and then lost the election?" Furthermore, she was alarmed that a costly campaign might drain their already diminished resources when their growing family required more stability. And in addition, she hated to leave her good friends for "big, bustling New York."

Edith did not argue with her husband; she simply withdrew "into one of her reserved and disapproving silences, that often, Bamie knew, had more of a disturbing effect on Theodore than anything she said." Both Corinne and Bamie urged their brother to run. In the end, the weight of Edith's opposition and the difficulty of funding the campaign led him to decline the offer. The bosses turned to William L. Strong, a reform-minded businessman, who ran and won on a fusion ticket of Republicans and anti-Tammany Democrats.

Contemplating his lost opportunity, Roosevelt fell into a profound depression. "The last four weeks, ever since I decided not to run, have been pretty bitter ones for me," he admitted to Lodge. "I would literally have given my right arm to have made the race, win or lose. It was the one golden chance, which never returns; and I had no illusions about ever having another opportunity. . . . At the time, with Edith feeling as intensely as she did, I did not see how I could well go in; though I have grown to feel more and more that in this instance I should have gone counter to her wishes and made the race anyhow. It is not necessary to say to you that the fault was mine, not Edith's; I should have realized that she could not see the matter as it really was, or realize my feelings."

Edith was horrified when she fathomed the magnitude of her husband's disappointment. "I cannot begin to describe how terribly I feel at having failed him at such an important time," she confided to Bamie. "He never should have married me, and then would have been free to take his own course quite unbiased. I never realized for a minute how he felt over this, or that the mayoralty stood for so much to him . . . if I knew what I do now I should have thrown all my influence in the scale with Corinne's and helped instead of hindering him. You say that I dislike to give my opinion. This is a lesson that will last my life, never to give it for it is utterly worthless when given—worse than that in this case for it has helped to spoil some years of a life which I would have given my own for."

Both Edith's fierce self-reproach and Theodore's despondent conviction that he had botched his sole opportunity in life, his "one golden chance," proved overwrought. Though his political path might be more circuitous, Roosevelt's restless drive would hardly allow him to retire from public life. The following spring, he was on his way to New York to accept Mayor Strong's offer to serve as police commissioner, a job that would utilize all his intrepid energies.

CHAPTER SEVEN

The Invention of *McClure's*

S. S. McClure *(left)* and John S. Phillips *(right)*, in the offices of *McClure's* magazine, 1895.

IN THE MID-1890S, THE GENTEEL world of patrician reformers and civil service enthusiasts that Taft and Roosevelt initially typified had begun a seismic shift. Widespread discontent with the industrial order, building for over a decade, threatened now to flare into open revolution. The growth of colossal corporations in the aftermath of the Civil War had produced immense, consolidated wealth for business owners, but the lives of the working people, western farmers and eastern factory workers alike, had become increasingly difficult. "We plow new fields, we open new mines, we found new cities," Roosevelt's mayoral rival, Henry George, observed; "we girdle the land with iron roads and lace the air with telegraph wires; we add knowledge to knowledge and utilize invention after invention." Yet despite such vaunted progress, he declared, "it becomes no easier for the masses of our people to make a living. On the contrary, it is becoming harder."

The captains of industry, George acknowledged, had fueled unprecedented innovations: "the steamship taking the place of the sailing vessel, the railroad train of the wagon, the reaping machine of the scythe." To confirm the positive changes wrought by the Industrial Revolution, he continued, one need only visit "the great workshops where boots and shoes are turned out by the case with less labour than the old fashioned cobbler could have put on a sole; the factories where, under the eye of a girl, cotton becomes cloth faster than hundreds of stalwart weavers could have turned it out with their handlooms." With this transfiguring mechanization and the development of mass production, however, "the gulf between the employed and the employer is growing wider; social contrasts are becoming sharper; as liveried carriages appear, so do barefooted children."

Far from heralding an age of plenty, these wondrous savings of time and labor served only to diminish the ability of many Americans to procure the goods they needed to sustain their families. So long as the frontier remained open, restless Americans could escape hardships by moving west, lured by promises of free land and equal opportunity. By the 1890s, this option had withered. As Frederick Jackson Turner observed in a seminal paper delivered during the American Historical Association meeting in Chicago in 1893, the frontier had closed, and a distinctive phase of American history had thereby come to an end.

A mood of rebellion began to spread among the laboring class. The late eighties and nineties witnessed an unprecedented number of violent strikes in the nation's factories, mines, and railroads. The combination of meager wages for twelve-hour working days in unsafe, unsanitary conditions had spurred millions of workers to join unions. "It was a time of strikes and riots, pitting troops against desperate workers," the historian Frank Latham observed, "of tense meetings where businessmen talked fearfully of 'a coming revolution.' "

In the year 1886 alone, more than 600,000 workers walked out on strike, disrupting thousands of businesses and railroad lines for weeks at a time. At the McCormick Reaper plant in Chicago, police were called in to break up a confrontation between strikers and scabs. In the brutal clash, four workers were killed. On May 4, a group of anarchists gathered in Chicago's Haymarket Square to protest those deaths. The peaceful demonstration turned violent when police ordered the protesters to disperse. A bomb thrown into the officers' formation killed eight policemen and four protesters and wounded more than seventy others.

Although police never determined who threw the bomb, they promptly arrested eight anarchists, several of whom had not even attended the demonstration. At their trial, the judge ruled that the anarchists' belief in violence made them as guilty as the murderous bomb thrower. Four were put to death by hanging, the others sentenced to jail. Citing an unprecedented miscarriage of justice, Illinois governor John Peter Altgeld pardoned the remaining prisoners. History has vindicated Altgeld, but the pardon was widely condemned at the time.

News of the Haymarket riot reached Roosevelt at his ranch north of Medora. Drawing no distinction between the strikers and the anarchist protestors, Roosevelt railed against the breakdown of law and order. "My men here are hardworking, laboring men, who work longer hours for no greater wages than many of the strikers; but they are Americans through and through," he told Bamie. "I believe nothing would give them greater pleasure than a chance with their rifles at one of the mobs. When we get the papers, especially in relation to the dynamite business they become more furiously angry and excited than I do. I wish I had them with me, and a fair show at ten times our number of rioters; my men shoot well and fear very little."

While some union supporters regarded the condemned anarchists as heroes, Roosevelt judged them the "foulest of criminals, the men whose crimes take the form of assassination." He denounced Governor Altgeld, along with all those who followed Leo Tolstoy's collectivist longings, Edward Bellamy's Utopian socialism, and Henry George's "wild and illogical doctrines," men who mistakenly believed "that at this stage of the world's progress it is possible to make every one happy by an immense social revolution, just as other enthusiasts of similar mental caliber believe in the possibility of constructing a perpetual-motion machine."

In 1893, the most serious depression the nation had yet experienced settled over the land. The downturn began when the railroads, having borrowed heavily from banks, rashly expanded their operations beyond current demand. More than seventy overbuilt railroads fell into bankruptcy, compromising banks unable to recoup their loans. Scrambling to shore up capital, these institutions called in the loans of all their borrowers. Small businesses and heavily mortgaged farmers unable to cover their notes followed railroads into bankruptcy. As the economic situation deteriorated, frightened depositors rushed to withdraw funds and hundreds of insolvent banks were forced to close their doors. Within twelve months, more than 4 million jobs had been lost. At the nadir of this collapse, nearly one in four workers was unemployed. Jobless men begged for food; homeless families slept on streets; farmers burned their crops rather than send them to market at a loss. Millions feared that in the wreckage of the Gilded Age, democracy itself would crumble.

AMID SUCH PANGS OF RAMPANT anxiety and latent insurrection, *McClure's* magazine was born. This acclaimed muckraking journal would play a signal role in rousing the country to the need for political and economic reform, animating the Progressive movement with which Theodore Roosevelt's name would forever be linked.

The descriptions of thirty-six-year-old Samuel S. McClure, the magazine's founder, bear an uncanny resemblance to accounts of Theodore Roosevelt himself. McClure was termed a "genius," with "a highly creative mind, and a great deal of excitable energy." He impressed all who knew him as a prodigious character, "a vibrant, eager, indomitable personality that electrified even the experienced and the cynical." His frenetic style, though, made him often appear "a bundle of tensions, keyed up, impetuous, impatient, impulsive." While Roosevelt's tumultuous energy elicited comparison to that force and marvel of nature, Niagara Falls, McClure, ever threatening to erupt in "a stream of words," was likened to a volcano. Indeed, McClure cut such a compelling figure that novelists as varied as Robert Louis Stevenson, Willa Cather, Upton Sinclair, William Dean Howells, and Alice Hegan Rice all incorporated him as a character in their fiction.

McClure was capable of wild bursts of creative productivity, episodes during which his mind tumbled from one idea to the next while he prowled the room "like a caged lion." Rudyard Kipling later recalled that his first conversation with McClure "lasted some twelve—or it may have been seventeen—hours." But such euphoria was often punctuated by periods of exhaustion and depression when he could not bring himself to eat, sleep, or concentrate. For months at a time, he was forced into sanitariums, where he was kept in total isolation, on continuous bed rest.

Born the same year as Taft, on a struggling farm in County Antrim, Northern Ireland, Sam McClure faced obstacles unimaginable to Roosevelt or Taft. The first of four sons, he was raised in a stone house with a dirt floor and a straw-covered roof. His father, Thomas, was a rough carpenter; his mother, Elizabeth, worked the fields of their farm. While the coddled childhoods enjoyed by Roosevelt and Taft were calculated to launch them on the road to achievement, the pain and penury of McClure's early life make his convoluted journey to success more unexpected and striking.

Even as a toddler, Sam displayed unusual curiosity, a fierce precocity that convinced his parents to send him to school when he was only four years of age. "That was the first important event in my life," he later wrote. "It was then that I first felt myself a human entity." Teachers recognized his astonishing aptitude and were soon furnishing materials suited for boys twice his age. "For a long while," he recalled, "I was convinced that long division was the most exciting exercise a boy could find." Several times each year, a large box of new books was delivered to his school. For a child whose family possessed a scant three works—the Bible, *Pilgrim's Progress*, and Foxe's *Book of Martyrs*—the experience of "opening those boxes and looking into the fresh books that still had the smell of the press, was about the most delightful thing that happened during the year." Weekends often found the boy depressed; the excitement of his studies "seemed to die down" the moment he returned home.

Sam was seven when his father fell through an open ship's deck where he worked and suffered a fatal head injury. His death left the family destitute, bereft of the small wages his carpentry work had provided. Sam "began for the first time to be conscious of the pressure of poverty." His mother returned temporarily to her father's home as the family debated how to divide the four boys among relatives. Determined to keep her sons together, Elizabeth used her remaining funds to purchase steerage passage across the Atlantic. From Quebec, she shepherded her children to Indiana, where two of her brothers and a married sister with six children had settled. For a time, she stayed with her sister, but the home proved too small to accommodate four additional children. In desperation, she moved with her boys into an empty room in a commercial building undergoing repairs. Before long, the owner evicted them; twice more, they were forced to move until, finally, she found a home for her children by marrying a struggling local farmer, Thomas Simpson.

Sam and his brothers spent so many hours toiling from planting until harvest on his stepfather's farm that they could attend school only during the winter months. Furthermore, the county school was unable to accommodate Sam's searching intellect. Hearing of "a kind of 'arithmetic' in which letters were used instead of figures," the avid pupil asked his teacher to tutor him in algebra. The teacher "had never studied it and had no text-book." The years passed slowly for Sam until, at fourteen, he learned of a new high school opened in Valparaiso. Straightaway, his mother decided that to have a chance in life, he must venture out on his own. If he could find work to pay for room and board, Sam had her blessing to leave. He departed that very day with one dollar in his pocket.

Learning that Dr. Levi Cass was Valparaiso's wealthiest citizen, Sam knocked on his door and inquired if he could exchange work for room and board. Cass accepted the enterprising young man, but his terms were not especially generous: in return for food and a basement room, Sam was expected to build up the fires before dawn, feed the livestock, and do the household laundry. Once the school day was over, a second round of arduous chores left him only a few hours late in the evening to study. In his cellar room, he recalled, "I used to waken up in the night and cry from the sense of my loss." It was in these straitened circumstances that Sam initially suffered "attacks of restlessness," when he "simply had to run away for a day, for half a day, for two days," a compulsion he "seemed to have no control over." Indeed, he acknowledged forty years later, "I have had to reckon with it all my life." Sam persevered in his schooling for two years, until his stepfather's death from typhoid fever forced his return home to help his mother manage the farm.

Sam and his brothers worked the farm well, producing a profit for the first time in years. Still, his mother wanted her eldest son to continue his education. Her brother Joseph Gaston was studying at Knox College in Galesburg, Illinois, about two hundred miles away. In September 1874, as Taft traveled east to Yale, McClure headed west to Galesburg. Upon his arrival, he was informed that his prior fragmentary schooling would require the completion of three full years at Knox Academy before he could even begin college. The news did not deter him. "I was seventeen," he recalled, "and it was a seven years' job that I was starting upon, with fifteen cents in my pocket." Finally realizing the opportunity to pursue a serious education, he "felt complete self-reliance." Once again, he had to work hard for room and board but managed to keep up with his studies, moving toward the day when he would become a freshman at the college.

At seventeen, a shock of blond hair over his forehead and blue eyes bright and clear, the painfully thin Sam had reached his full height of five feet six inches. One classmate remarked that he had "never seen so much enthusiasm and life in such a small carcass." All his subjects interested him, Greek and mathematics most of all. "Everything went well with me until Friday night," he recalled, when the "blank stretch" of the weekend rendered him disconsolate. Without the focal point of classes, he felt lonely and isolated.

During his second preparatory year, Sam fell in love with eighteen-year-old Harriet Hurd, considered by many "the most beautiful and gifted girl in town." The willowy, blue-eyed daughter of Knox College's star professor, Albert Hurd, Hattie, as she was called, was then a sophomore in the college. A brilliant student, she would graduate at the top of her class with the highest academic record ever obtained at Knox. "Don't cry for the moon," the kindly wife of the town's minister told Sam. Hattie had been her father's assistant since childhood, working by his side as he gathered geological specimens and prepared materials for his classes in science, religion, and Latin. Professor Hurd, a graduate of Middlebury College, had studied under Louis Agassiz at Harvard before embarking upon a long and distinguished career at Knox. A commanding figure in Hattie's life, Professor Hurd adamantly opposed his daughter's relationship with an impoverished immigrant. The professor's opposition seemed to embolden rather than discourage Sam. "My feeling for her," he later recalled, "became a despairing obsession, as fixed as my longing to get an education had been."

From the start, Hattie was drawn to Sam's peculiar intensity. After a series of furtive meetings and a surreptitious exchange of romantic letters, she agreed to a secret engagement. Torn between her father's implacable disapproval and her adoration for Sam, she repeatedly broke the engagement, only to realize that she couldn't resist the magnetism of Sam's personality. But when she graduated from Knox and prepared for graduate school in Canada, her father forbade Hattie to disclose her destination to Sam. Secrecy was the price for her continued education. "You mustn't write to me or expect to hear from me, as long as I am dependent on my father," she told Sam. "If I should bring his displeasure on me it would kill me. Oh, Sam, it is very hard to bear." For nearly four years, all communication in this odd and fervent relationship ceased.

Sam immersed himself in his studies, eventually graduating second in his college class. More important, he developed lifelong friendships with two classmates, John S. Phillips and Albert Brady, that one day would be instrumental to the success of *McClure's* magazine. Sam was closer to John Phillips, the quiet, steady, and intellectual son of a respected local physician and a relative of the abolitionist Wendell Phillips. Phillips, McClure proudly noted, "was easily the best read student in the college, a boy with a great natural aptitude for letters." At Phillips's house, McClure first encountered a copy of *Scribner's*, the sophisticated literary magazine that would soon become the *Century*. Returning numerous times to his friend's home, he was thrilled to read the new serialized novel by William Dean Howells, *A Modern Instance*, from start to finish.

Sam McClure's enterprising spirit and unique knack for finding partners with complementary abilities was already evident. In the summer between his junior and senior years, the young man canvassed the Great Lakes region, peddling microscopes with Albert Brady, the son of the editor of the *Davenport* (Iowa) *Daily Times*. Enabled by Brady's shrewdness, the two Knox students bought microscopes wholesale at $25 each and turned them at a profit. McClure would later credit this experience of traveling through villages and knocking on doors with fostering a "close acquaintance with the people of the small towns and the farming communities, the people who afterward bought *McClure's Magazine*."

In his senior year, McClure was chosen as editor-in-chief of the student newspaper. His unconventional working style both troubled and amazed his colleagues on the paper. "He works by fits and starts," a fellow student noted; "weeks, almost months go by, and he does no work to amount to anything and then crowds all into a few days and nights." With Phillips providing daily editorial support and Brady as the advertising virtuoso, the publication produced quality articles and successfully solicited an abundance of advertising from local businesses. In the years ahead, observed the journalist Ray Stannard Baker, this same triumvirate would be responsible for the triumph of *McClure's*. While McClure provided the foundation work of creative genius, the magazine would never have realized its historic status without the insightful editing of Phillips and the business acumen of Albert Brady. "The three together," Baker marveled, "who had been friends since their college days—made the perfect publishing organization."

After an absence of four years, Hattie returned briefly to Galesburg in 1881. She had completed her graduate training and was preparing to depart for Massachusetts, where she had accepted a teaching position at Abbott Academy in Andover. A chance encounter with Sam apparently summoned old feelings, and the young couple recommitted themselves to one another. "My present and future are completely changed," Sam told her. "My soul is filled with love and peace and joy." Although she soon left for Massachusetts, they revived their secret correspondence. Sam filled his letters with grandiose intentions, entertaining various careers as diplomat, philosopher, and writer/publisher. As the date of his June graduation approached, however, Hattie's letters stopped coming. Sensing that something was wrong, Sam consulted Phillips, who recommended that he head for Massachusetts the moment his graduation ceremonies ended. A letter from Hattie arrived just after Sam left Galesburg. "Mr. McClure," it formally declared, "I have come to the unalterable conclusion that I have not and never can have any respect or affection for you . . . I wish never to meet you again."

Once again, Hattie had succumbed to pressure from her father, who vowed that he "would never receive [McClure] as his son-in law," and that if Hattie chose to marry him, he would never be allowed into the house. Everything about McClure was anathema to Professor Hurd, who objected to "his personal appearance, his bearing, his address," adding for good measure that he found Sam "conceited, impertinent, meddlesome." In sum, he concluded, "I regard it as a misfortune that you ever made his acquaintance." Forced to choose between her father and Sam, Hattie could not betray her father. Unaware of the reception that awaited him, McClure knocked on the door where Hattie was staying. Told that she did not wish to see him, he refused to leave the parlor until she finally came down. "I do not love you," she said flatly, adding icily, "and I never can. Please be good enough to return to me any of my letters that you may still have."

"This dismissal," McClure recounted later, "I accepted as final." With no definite plans and no place to stay, he took a train to Boston, where the offices of the Pope Manufacturing Company were located. This company had recently produced a newfangled sensation with the Columbia Roadster, America's first bicycle. The owner, Colonel Albert Pope, had purchased advertising space in Sam's student publication, furnishing him with an opening to meet the entrepreneur. Finding McClure's enthusiasm and determination irresistible, Pope put him in charge of the bicycle rink where beginners came to learn how to ride. Although McClure himself had never ridden a bicycle, he was soon teaching others to operate the unwieldy contraption with a high front wheel nearly twice the size of the rear wheel.

When Pope revealed to McClure his determination to publish a magazine devoted to bicycling, fire was touched to kindling. On the basis of his experience at the *Knox Student*, McClure convinced Pope that he could edit the magazine Pope envisioned, to "weave the bicycle into the best in literature and art." Just at this time, McClure received a fortuitous letter from his friend John Phillips, who was struggling to plot his own future career. "You are the surest fellow I ever saw," Phillips wrote McClure. "You always alight on your feet. I wish I had one half your push and business ability. Great Heavens, I wish I was with you. If you think I can make a living . . . I'll come." So Phillips joined McClure as co-editor of the *Wheelman*, as the surprisingly professional, illustrated monthly magazine was titled.

Reviews of the new magazine, which included short stories, articles, and book reviews, were positive; the *Nation* rated it "among the most attractive of the monthly magazines." While Phillips ran the office, McClure took to the road, hoping to persuade New England writers such as Oliver Wendell Holmes, Harriet Prescott Spofford, and Thomas Bailey Aldrich to barter articles for a new bicycle. "I was in the big game, in the real business of the world," he recalled. "Up to this time I had always lived in the future and felt that I was simply getting ready for something. Now I began to live in the present."

Wheelman was the first professional enterprise into which McClure poured his astounding energy. Ascending the steps to that office at 597 Washington Street in Boston, he bid a final farewell to his youthful self. "When I have passed that place in later years," he recalled in his autobiography in a haunting passage, "I have fairly seen him standing there—a thin boy, with a face somewhat worn from loneliness and wanting things he couldn't get, a little hurt at being left so unceremoniously. When I went up the steps, he stopped outside; and it now seems to me that I stopped on the steps and looked at him, and that when he looked at me I turned and never spoke to him and went into the building. I came out with a job, but I never saw him again, and now I have no sense of identity with that boy."

McClure had not seen Hattie since her brutal rejection; then, as he worked hard to produce *Wheelman* in the fall, she reached out to him, insisting that she had deceived him because she simply "*could not*" bring herself to disobey her father. "I felt that you would take nothing as a reason for our separation," she endeavored to explain, "as long as you believed that I loved you—and so I gave you, falsely, the only reason that I knew would be valid in your eyes . . . I perjured myself . . . I loved you then, and love you still." In September 1883, they were quietly married, with John Phillips serving as McClure's best man. Sam and Hattie began their married life in Boston, but only three months later, when Sam was offered a position as an editorial assistant with the prestigious *Century* magazine, they moved to New York.

The following summer, after the birth of the first of his four children, Sam found himself increasingly restless in his new job. He yearned for independent control of some venture and finally hit upon an idea he shared with Roswell Smith, the editor of the *Century*. He proposed that the *Century* underwrite a Literary Associated Press, a syndicate that would purchase stories and articles from well-known authors and then sell them at reduced rates to numerous newspapers for simultaneous publication, usually in their new Sunday supplements. "I saw it, in all its ramifications, as completely as I ever did afterward," McClure later explained, "and I don't think I ever added anything to my first conception." Roswell Smith liked the idea but thought it unsuitable for his magazine. He offered McClure "a month's vacation with full pay" to see if he could launch the project on his own, with the opportunity to return to the *Century* should the venture fail.

In a matter of weeks, McClure's syndicate was up and running. His first sale was a short story by the popular writer Hjalmar H. Boyesen, which he bought for $150 and promptly sold to a sufficient number of newspapers to make "a handsome profit." He then utilized the proceeds to send a thousand circulars to editors across the nation. This flyer explained how "a dozen, or twenty, or fifty newspapers—selected so as to avoid conflict in circulation—can thus secure a story for a sum which will be very small for each paper, but which will in the aggregate be sufficiently large to secure the best work by the best authors."

The syndicate grew so steadily that by 1887, his biographer Peter Lyon estimates, McClure was "distributing fifty thousand words a week to well over one hundred newspapers." John Phillips, after three years in graduate school, first at Harvard and then in Leipzig, Germany, once again joined his friend and assumed responsibility for the daily management of the syndicate, a role for which he was "much better fitted" than McClure. "He had an orderly and organizing mind—which I had not," McClure acknowledged. "I usually lost interest in a scheme as soon as it was started, and had no power of developing a plan and carrying it out to its least detail, as Mr. Phillips had." With his trusted friend at the helm, McClure was free to travel "from one end of the country to the other" and eventually "from one end of Europe to the other—always seeking new material, and always, like the retriever, coming back with a treasure-trove in his teeth."

"McClure was a Columbus among editors," proclaimed the writer and critic Jeannette L. Gilder. "I doubt if there is any man in his profession who has to his credit the discovery of more big writers." At the time, three principal literary journals—*Century*, *Atlantic*, and *Harper's*—had a stranglehold on America's literary market. They were defenders of everything "dignified and conservative in the magazine world." Young writers, particularly those who embraced the new realistic style scorned by established critics, had difficulty publishing their stories. McClure gave them a chance. "My qualifications for being an editor," he explained, "were that I was open-minded, naturally enthusiastic, and not afraid to experiment with a new man."

McClure, who had adopted the designation "S. S." rather than Sam, is credited with introducing Robert Louis Stevenson, Rudyard Kipling, J. M. Barrie, and Arthur Conan Doyle to American readers. "He secured the best writers in the world," one reviewer noted. "He had the discernment in some cases and the good luck in others to establish connections with rising authors at the happy moment when they were about to step across the threshold of fame. He helped them and they helped him. His treatment of them was both honorable and generous." McClure noted proudly that he had purchased Kipling's work "before the name of Kipling had been printed in a newspaper in this country." After reading one of Conan Doyle's short stories, McClure promptly purchased a dozen Sherlock Holmes mysteries at the bargain price of $60 apiece. "To find the best authors," he boasted, "is like being able to tell good wine without the labels."

The McClure syndicate serialized *The Quality of Mercy*, a novel by the controversial champion of realism, William Dean Howells; they printed stories by Thomas Hardy and Émile Zola which shocked genteel readers, and published a series of polemics by William Morris on socialism, Hamlin Garland on wheat farmers, and Henry Harland on life in the slums of New York's Jewish East Side. Even as he provided a platform for new voices and radical topics, McClure filled the preponderance of his pages with stories and poems from established writers and more staid articles on standard subjects of interest—religion, adventure, travel, Abraham Lincoln, and the Civil War.

By the early 1890s, the success of the McClure syndicate was assured. "I propose to down *all* competition, and in a short time I can dominate the *world* in my line," he bragged headily. "My blood is like champagne." Such unqualified success, however, seemed a harbinger to the restlessness that had plagued him since childhood, the compulsive drive to stave off depression through ceaseless activity. He felt compelled to tackle something new lest depression, always waiting in the wings, resume center stage. In 1892, he and Phillips began discussing the creation of a new low-priced, high-quality illustrated magazine. "I would rather edit a magazine," McClure told Hattie, "than be President of the United States a hundred thousand times over."

Conventional wisdom held that 35 cents was the lowest price a publisher of a quality magazine could charge and still anticipate "a reasonable profit." At 35 cents, a magazine was necessarily targeted to the "moneyed and well-educated classes," a parameter which kept the contents "leisurely in habit, literary in tone, retrospective rather than timely, and friendly to the interests of the upper classes." McClure's resolve to put a quality magazine "within reach of all who care about good literature" at 15 cents per copy was tantamount to revolution.

New technology made his rash endeavor to compete with publications like the *Century* or the *Atlantic* feasible. "The impregnability of the older magazines," McClure explained, "was largely due to the costliness of wood-engraving. Only an established publication with a large working capital could afford illustrations made by that process." Photo engraving was the innovation that fundamentally altered the printing industry. At a fraction of the cost of wood engraving, the new process allowed publishers "to make pictures directly from photographs, which were cheap, instead of from drawings, which were expensive."

McClure envisioned a new magazine containing four sections: "The Edge of the Future" would feature interviews in which scientists such as Thomas Edison or Alexander Graham Bell discussed their recent inventions; "Human Documents" would showcase portraits of famous people at different ages;

"The Real Conversations" would present one distinguished person interviewing another; and the final section would offer short stories initially drawn from the best fiction already published in the syndicate, thereby costing him almost nothing to reprint. McClure hoped to use syndicate profits to support the new magazine until it could stand on its own. One of his trips west to garner support for the magazine included a visit to Davenport, Iowa, where he reconnected with his Knox classmate Albert Brady and persuaded him to come on board as his advertising manager.

For all his plans, McClure could not have anticipated the Panic of 1893, the run on the banks, and the burgeoning unemployment that bankrupted some newspapers and forced others to slash expenses. In this climate, the syndicate became one of the first things struggling newspapers jettisoned. "There was certainly never a more inopportune time to launch a new business," McClure lamented. He had little personal capital to invest in the venture, having paid syndicate authors handsomely and incurred heavy expenses searching out new world-class writers. He had built up an invaluable asset, however: "the good will of thousands of people"—friends, fellow editors, and writers. Phillips persuaded his father to place a mortgage on his Galesburg home, bringing in $4,500; Conan Doyle invested $5,000; Colonel Pope supplied $6,000; and the geologist Henry Drummond, whose articles would frequently appear in the new journal, invested $2,000 and volunteered an additional loan of $1,000.

The first issue, appearing on the stands in June 1893, received uniformly favorable reviews. "It is not often that a new periodical begins its career with prestige enough to make its success a certainty from the very first number," noted the *Review of Reviews*, but "the wisest judges concede it a place among the winners." The *Providence Journal* rated the magazine "no little of a triumph," applauding its freshness and originality: "It is not an imitation of anything existing in this country." The Philadelphia *Public Ledger* placed it in the "front rank at once," while the *Atlanta Constitution* hailed it as "unusually brilliant." From Theodore Roosevelt came a letter of congratulations on "the first issue of your excellent magazine."

McClure immediately understood that his magazine must have "a unity" beyond a mere compilation of freelance articles suiting the individual tastes of miscellaneous authors. He dreamed of creating a full-time staff of writers who would be guaranteed salary and generous expense accounts. The job of staff writer was a new concept; in years to come, McClure would claim he himself "almost invented" it—a justifiable assertion at a time when few magazines subsidized their writers. He wished a writing staff to collaborate with him and with each other, treating mutually agreed-upon topics "in line with the general attitude of the publication." He wanted "to deal with important social, economic and political questions, to present the new and great inventions and discoveries, to give the best in literature," and above all, to become "a power in the land . . . a power for good."

Indeed, the ultimate success of *McClure's*—its literary worth, its major contributions to Progressive era reforms, and its significant role in the rise of Theodore Roosevelt—can be directly traced to the prodigiously gifted writing staff McClure assembled. Along with the nucleus consisting of Ida Tarbell, Ray Stannard Baker, Lincoln Steffens, and William Allen White, the *McClure's* staff intermittently included Burton Hendrick, Mark Sullivan, George Kibbe Turner, Will Irwin, Willa Cather, Stephen Crane, and Frank Norris. This talented pool of writers produced hundreds of influential pieces which played a major role in shaping public discourse around the most pressing economic and social issues of the day.

IDA MINERVA TARBELL, THE FIRST to join McClure's stable of writers, became the "mother hen" of the group. The story of the first meeting between McClure and Tarbell in the summer of 1892 would be told and retold in the years ahead. McClure had briefly stopped in Paris on one of his whirlwind tours in search of material for his new magazine. Thirty-four and unmarried, Tarbell had been living on the Left Bank for twelve months, struggling to support herself with freelance articles for American newspapers. Her free hours were spent in the manuscript room of the Bibliothèque Nationale researching the life of Mme Roland, a celebrated figure in the French Revolution. One of her newspaper articles, "The Paving of the Streets of Paris by Monsieur Alphand," had landed on McClure's desk. "This girl can write," McClure told Phillips. "I want to get her to do some work for the magazine." The piece, he later said, "possessed exactly the qualities" he desired—a clear narrative style alive with human interest, sound judgment, and trustworthy facts.

Tarbell was then lodging in a boardinghouse on an obscure, crooked street "unknown to half the *cochers* of Paris." Yet, somehow, McClure managed to locate the place one Monday evening, "bareheaded, watch in hand, breathless" from racing up the eighty steps to her fourth-floor chamber. "I've just ten minutes," he gasped; "must leave for Switzerland tonight to see [John] Tyndall." Those minutes stretched to nearly three hours as McClure regaled her with childhood tales in Ireland, his struggles at Knox College and desperate pursuit of Hattie, his creation of the syndicate and friendship with Phillips. Finally, he laid out his plans for the new magazine and her involvement in it.

Captivated by his "outrightness, his enthusiasm and confidence," Tarbell, in turn, confided her own experiences, her hopes and ambitions.

Though less extreme than McClure's, Ida's history was shaped by an equally fierce resolution to succeed. The oldest of four children, she was born the same year as McClure and raised in northwestern Pennsylvania, where the discovery of oil had transformed wilderness areas into bustling cities and towns. Her father, Franklin Tarbell, was making "more than he could ever have dreamed" as an independent oil producer. Titusville, where Franklin built a substantial home for his growing family, was flourishing, "confident of its future," boasting graded roads, handsome homes, college preparatory high schools, and a newly built opera house. "Things were going well in father's business," Ida recalled; "there was ease such as we had never known, luxuries we had never heard of."

For the local oilmen, who drilled the wells and sustained a booming local economy, it seemed there was "nothing they did not hope and dare." The triumph of optimism in Titusville was destined to end, however: "Suddenly, at the very heyday of this confidence, a big hand reached out from nobody knew where, to steal their conquest and throttle their future." That mysterious hand belonged to none other than John D. Rockefeller, as Tarbell would boldly elucidate years later in her chronicle of the history of the Standard Oil Company for *McClure's* magazine—the landmark series that would affirm her reputation as the leading investigative journalist of her day.

At the time, all that Ida's father and his colleagues knew was that the railroads arbitrarily doubled their published rates for carrying petroleum—crude and refined—to the east coast, a huge inflation heralding ruin for the entire region. The local oilmen eventually discovered that Rockefeller had forged an alliance between the railroads and a small group of privileged refiners. His "big scheme" enabled those in the newly formed South Improvement Company to receive secret rebates on every barrel shipped, while outside companies would be charged increased rates to make up for the insiders' discount. This deal, meant to destroy small competitors, Tarbell later explained, "started the Standard Oil Company off on the road to monopoly."

The local producers joined together to retaliate. "There were nightly antimonopoly meetings," Ida recalled, "violent speeches, processions; trains of oil cars loaded for members of the offending corporation were raided, the oil run on the ground." The tensions of these confrontations were reflected in the Tarbell household. Franklin Tarbell no longer entertained his family with "the funny things he had seen and heard during the day" or relaxed with an after-dinner cigar to the music he loved. If the machinations behind the conflict were "all pretty hazy" to young Ida, she gleaned enough from her father's conversation to comprehend that "what had been undertaken was *wrong*." From that painful, disruptive period, she wrote, "there was born in me a hatred of privilege"—in this case, the powerful oilmen preying on the independents, but eventually "privilege of any sort."

As her father fought against monopoly, her mother struggled with a painful "readjustment of her status in the home and in society." Esther Tarbell, Ida later wrote, "had grown up with the Woman's Rights movement." She had taught for a dozen years before her marriage and had planned on "seeking a higher education." Had she remained single, Ida believed, "she would have sought to 'vindicate her sex.' . . . The fight would have delighted her." But after marriage she "found herself a pioneer in the Oil Region, confronted by the sternest of problems," which compelled the investment of her energies into the well-being of her family. Witnessing her mother's frustration, Ida determined early on that she "would never marry." She was certain that having a husband and children would thwart her freedom and curtail her nascent ambition. At fourteen, she fell to her knees and entreated God to prevent her ever marrying.

Captivated by the natural world, Ida had spent the long afternoons of her childhood wandering around the countryside to gather leaves and plant specimens in her area, "classifying them by shapes, veins, stalks, color." She began her high school years already intent upon a career as a biologist. Graduating at the top of her class at Titusville High, she enrolled in Allegheny College in Meadville, Pennsylvania, in the fall of 1876, the same year that Roosevelt matriculated at Harvard. At eighteen, Ida had reached her commanding height of five feet ten inches. She was not considered pretty. Her nose and ears were too big, but her "luminous eyes" indicated unusual sensitivity and intelligence.

As the sole woman in the freshman class, and one of four in the entire college, she felt herself "an invader." But in the college library she found "the companionship there is in the silent presence of books." Though she may have been "shy and immature," Ida was a tenacious student, and she had the good fortune of studying under "a great natural teacher," Jeremiah Tingley, the chair of the science department. Like Professor Hurd, Tingley had studied under Louis Agassiz and absorbed the celebrated scientist's "faith in observation and classification, as well as his reverence for Nature." Sensing Ida's enthusiasm and native intelligence, he took particular interest in her progress. Coupled with her own fierce drive, this support helped her excel once again. "She would arise at four A.M. and get to work studying," a classmate recalled.

"She was never satisfied with anything less than perfection . . . but she was no grind. She was too interested in people."

After graduation, Ida taught for two years at Poland Union Seminary in Poland, Ohio, hoping to save enough money to "go abroad and study with some great biologist." But her wages were low, and two years later she had managed to save nothing to further her dream of studying in Europe. She returned to Meadville, where she took a temporary job annotating articles for *The Chautauquan*, the official publication of the recently founded Chautauqua Institution, a summer camp that provided Bible studies and lectures on science, the arts, and humanities. What began as a temporary assignment became a full-time job as she rose to become managing editor of *The Chautauquan*, discovering in the process a great fascination with storytelling and the delineation of character. "My early absorption in rocks and plants had veered to as intense an interest in human beings," she reported. "I was feeling the same passion to understand men and women, the same eagerness to collect and classify information about them . . . I recognized that men and women were as well worth notes as leaves, that there was a science of society as well as of botany."

She and her colleagues on the liberal monthly magazine were "ardent supporters" of the inclusive labor organization the Knights of Labor and their fight for an eight-hour workday. "We discussed interminably the growing problem of the slums, were particularly strong for cooperative housing, laundries and bakeshops," she recalled. She came to the conclusion that "a trilogy of wrongs" was responsible for the maldistribution of wealth: "discriminatory transportation rates, tariffs save for revenue only, and private ownership of natural resources."

"My life was busy, varied, unfolding pleasantly in many ways, but it also after six years was increasingly unsatisfactory," she later wrote. "I was trapped—comfortably, most pleasantly, most securely, but trapped." While she stayed up nights working out several ideas for a novel, her days were occupied with the myriad demands of editing the magazine. Furthermore, the design she had brought to the "disorderly fashion" in which the editor-in-chief, Dr. Theodore L. Flood, had formerly managed the magazine was never truly credited. Inevitably, she found herself "secretly, very secretly, meditating a change." She envisioned herself in Paris, researching and writing a biography of Mme Roland, an alluring character she had included in a series of sketches for *The Chautauquan* on women of the French Revolution. Though she still had little money saved, Ida aspired to earn a living writing articles on Parisian life for several of the newspaper syndicates in the United States.

Dr. Flood was stunned when Ida revealed that she was leaving for Paris. "How will you support yourself?" he demanded. When she replied that she would make her way by writing, his retort was memorably cruel and condescending. "You're not a writer," he announced. "You'll starve." Flood struck deep-seated anxieties in Ida about her vocation as a writer, yet she would not be deterred. She persuaded two of her friends from *The Chautauquan* to join her, and the three set sail for Europe in August 1891. After searching several days for affordable lodgings, they found a boardinghouse in the Latin Quarter run by Mme Bonnet, a cheerful, welcoming landlady. Though their rooms were tiny, they shared a salon with an amiable group of Egyptian students. Before long, they had developed close friendships.

Ida set to work immediately, outlining a series of articles on the daily life of Paris. She astutely guessed that people back home would want to know the very things she herself was curious about: what Parisians did for entertainment; what they ate and drank; how the city preserved the beauty of its parks and sidewalks; whether it was safe for women to walk the streets at night. For an article on the poor, she worked for a time in a soup kitchen. She haunted the shops in the Jewish section for a story on Parisian Jews. "There were a multitude of things I thirsted to know," Ida wrote. "And if I could get my bread and butter finding out, what luck! What luck!"

"There were few mornings that I was not at my desk at eight o'clock," she remembered; "there were few nights that I went to bed before midnight, and there was real drudgery in making legible copy after my article was written." On weekends, she allowed time for expeditions to the cathedrals and the museums, as well as Versailles and Fontainebleau. Before seven weeks had passed, she had sent a dozen articles to various papers at home but had heard nothing in return. It seemed as if Dr. Flood's prediction would prove correct. Finally, in early November, she received her first check, from the *Cincinnati Times-Star*, the paper edited by Will Taft's brother Charles. "It was not much, $6.00," she reported to her family. "How the doctor would scorn it! But I was glad to get it because it's a start."

In the meantime, she and her friends managed to enjoy their "bohemian poverty." They dined two nights a week with Mme Bonnet, who provided "a good dinner of 6 courses with cider and wine for 40 cents." These were "happy evenings," Ida recalled, "for the Egyptians loved games, tricks, charades, play of any sort." They found a local restaurant that catered to Americans and offered a noonday meal for 23 cents. "Think of us," she wrote home, "going into a place where there is sawdust on the floor, a bar in one corner, every table with wine and many men smoking cigarettes, but there are lots of ladies, American artists, and then everybody does it." For their remaining meals, they pledged to spend only 12 cents to offset the expense of the dinners, buying "not a morsel more" than they absolutely required—"a single egg, one roll or croissant, a gill of milk, two cups apiece of café au lait, never having a drop left in the pot."

Winter came early to Paris that year. "It is the most heartless weather I ever experienced," she told her family. "It is clear and dry but the wind cuts like a knife." With only one little heating grate in the room where she wrote, she sat at her desk with one shawl wrapped around her legs, another over her head, and a hand stove to keep her feet warm. At night she wore everything but her sealskin coat to bed. Still, she was convinced that no one in Paris was having more fun. "It isn't money after all that makes the best of things," she assured them.

A breakthrough came in December when *Scribner's* accepted a piece of short fiction pending her agreement on several changes. "I think after 'mature deliberation' for about 1/50 of a second that I'll allow the changes to be made," she excitedly told her parents. "That it has been accepted at all is a tremendous encouragement to me. It gives me heart and hope." *Scribner's* paid $100 for the story, nearly the amount she had brought to cover her passage to Europe and her first months in Paris. "What excitement in our little salon when I showed my companions that check!" Her success freed her to attend courses at the Sorbonne on French history and literature, to spend time at the library going through the papers of Mme Roland, relax with friends in the cafés, and buy a new pair of shoes.

In the months that followed, more and more newspapers accepted her articles. "Writing $5 and $10 articles" was admittedly "an awful slow way of making one's living," but Ida had proved Dr. Flood wrong and banished her own doubts. She was a working woman, living in a city she adored, surviving on her own as a published writer.

McClure's invitation to join him as he launched his new magazine intrigued Ida, but she was unwilling to leave for New York before her research on Mme Roland was complete. She happily agreed, however, to contribute freelance articles from Paris once the magazine was under way. His mission that summer evening in 1892 accomplished, McClure suddenly jumped to his feet. "I must go," he said. "Could you lend me forty dollars? It is too late to get money over town, and I must catch the train for Geneva." As it happened, Ida had exactly that sum stashed in a drawer, saved for a long-awaited vacation. "It never occurred to me to do anything but give it to him," she recalled, though the next day she suffered "some bad moments," fearing he would "simply never think of it again." The following day, a forty-dollar check was sent from McClure's office in London.

Work for the new magazine opened up a broad new world of intellectual adventure. She studied microbe theory and interviewed Louis Pasteur in his home, examined the psychology of legerdemain, investigated the new Bertillon system of criminal identification, surveyed public health practices in French cities, and secured contributions from Émile Zola, Alphonse Daudet, and Alexandre Dumas. McClure was thrilled with her work. "We all hope you are not planning to get married and cut short your career," he told her. "All of the articles which you have sent to us recently are most admirably done . . . I have always liked your work, as you know, but of late you have been surpassing yourself."

The only snag in this propitious arrangement was that McClure had no money to compensate her efforts. Despite rave reviews, the new magazine was struggling to survive in the midst of the severe depression. Indeed, the situation at home was so bleak, Esther Tarbell informed her daughter, that people were "actually starving by hundreds and thousands." The alarming circumstances had convinced her mother that "monopolies are fearful evils," a plague to confront by peaceful means or "by force, if it must be."

Irrepressible Ida, "on the ragged edge of bankruptcy," nonetheless insisted she was "gay as a cricket." She continued to believe in McClure. "The little magazine is sure to live," she assured her family; "they are honest and energetic and young and they'll pull through." Her prediction proved on the mark. Month by month, *McClure's* circulation continued to increase. In April 1894, McClure returned to Paris, this time securing Ida's commitment to begin full-time work on the magazine in the fall. But first she would spend the summer with her parents in Titusville, where she hoped to complete her book on Mme Roland.

Tarbell had been home for only six weeks when she received an urgent wire from McClure, begging her to come to New York. An intense fascination with Napoleon Bonaparte had recently swept Europe and McClure believed that America, too, would be captivated anew by the French emperor. McClure had made connection with Gardiner Green Hubbard, father-in-law to Alexander Graham Bell and owner of a valuable collection of Napoleon portraits. McClure secured Hubbard's permission to reproduce the portraits alongside a short biography of Napoleon by an English author, Robert Sherard. The illustrated series, set to begin in November, had been heavily promoted. When the manuscript arrived, Hubbard found the tone "so contemptuously anti-

Napoleon" that he withdrew permission to let his pictures accompany the text. In desperation, McClure turned to Ida.

Though the task of producing the first installment in six weeks seemed impossible, Ida agreed to try. She left at once for Washington, where she was given a suite in Hubbard's magnificent country estate on Woodley Lane, not far from Roosevelt's modest Dupont Circle home. In addition to Hubbard's immense library, she had access to the State Department archives, which held printed copies of all Napoleon's official correspondence. Granted a desk at the Library of Congress, Tarbell was able to summon books and pamphlets from what turned out to be an exceptional collection covering the Napoleonic era.

Despite her embarrassment at constructing "biography on the gallop," Ida not only met the deadline but produced a work of quality. When the seven installments were completed, the *New York Press* hailed the series as "the best short life of Napoleon we have ever seen." From the reigning Napoleon expert came the welcome, heartening comment: "I have often wished that I had had, as you did, the prod of necessity behind me, the obligation to get it out at a fixed time, to put it through, no time to idle, to weigh, only to set down. You got something that way—a living sketch." An additional benefit of her accomplishment was Scribner's agreement to publish her book on Mme Roland.

On the strength of the Napoleon series, the circulation of *McClure's* doubled, reaching nearly 100,000 by publication of the final installment. Even before it was finished, McClure conjured another series for Tarbell—a short life of Abraham Lincoln. "His insight told him that people never had had enough of Lincoln," explained Tarbell later; he was certain that thirty years after Lincoln's death, hundreds of people remained whose reminiscences were still untapped. Characteristically, once having conceived of the project, McClure "could think of nothing but Lincoln, morning, noon, and night."

"Out with you," he ordered Ida. "Look, see, report." Before her departure, she called on John Nicolay, whose monumental biography had recently been serialized in the *Century*. Nicolay greeted her coldly. He assured her that he and his co-author John Hay had discovered "all there was worth telling of Lincoln's life." She would be well advised "not to touch so hopeless an assignment." When the *Century*'s editor, Richard Watson Gilder, was questioned about his opinion of *McClure's* magazine, he scoffed: "They got a girl to write a Life of Lincoln."

Nicolay's disdain influenced her "plan of campaign." Rather than start her inquiry "at the end of the story with the great and known," she would begin "in Kentucky with the humble and unknown." She would trace Lincoln's life chronologically, through the little towns and settlements where he had lived and worked. Tarbell's approach unearthed scores of people who had known him in those early days. She scoured local histories, probed court records and newspaper clippings. Combining the skills of an investigative reporter with those of a detective, artist, and biographer, she coaxed reluctant people and jogged their memories with the hard evidence she had discovered. McClure covered all her expenses and kept her on salary during the three-year period of her research and writing. She completed her project in a charming Washington boardinghouse on I Street between Ninth and Tenth, a lodging shared by Massachusetts senator and Mrs. George Hoar. McClure scrutinized multiple drafts of every installment, assuring that the narrative retained its momentum.

The series proved a popular and critical triumph. "It is not only full of new things," the *Chicago Tribune* wrote, "but is so distinct and clear in local color that an interest attaches to it which is not found in other biographies." When the first installment appeared, *McClure's* circulation increased by 40,000 copies to 190,000. A month later, it reached a quarter of a million, exceeding both the *Century* and *Harper's Monthly*.

With the completion of the Lincoln series, McClure brought Tarbell to New York as the desk editor of the magazine. The publication was then housed on the sixth floor of the Lexington Building on 25th Street. Working in the office each day, Tarbell soon understood the critical role that John S. Phillips, whom they called "JSP," played in the success of the magazine. If McClure was the wind in the sails, with "great power to stir excitement by his suggestions, his endless searching after something new, alive, startling," the stabilizing ballast was the steady, unflappable Phillips. "Here's a man," Tarbell wrote, "who knows the power of patience in dealing with the impatient." Phillips lived in the city during the week so that he could be available day and night; on weekends, he joined his wife, Jennie, and their small children in Goshen, New York, a small town in the foothills of the Catskills. It was said in the office "that Sam had three hundred ideas a minute, but only JSP knew which one was not crazy."

"I found the place so warmly and often ridiculously human," Tarbell remembered. Her genial temperament allowed her to get on "capitally" with the brilliant but volatile art director, August Jaccaci, whose towering fits of anger "came and went like terrible summer thundershowers." She developed a lifelong friendship with Viola Roseboro, the cigarette-smoking, wisecracking former actress in charge of reading the thousands of unsolicited manuscripts that arrived month after month. Without doubt, Ida was enamored with McClure himself. Years later, she remembered how his blue eyes "glowed and sparkled" when the peripatetic publisher prowled the newsroom spouting a tumult of thoughts and projects, any one of which might harbor "a stroke of genius."

For Ida Tarbell, the most alluring aspect of *McClure's* was "the sense of vitality, of adventure, of excitement," the feeling of "being admitted on terms of equality and good comradeship" with an extraordinary group of people. They perched on one another's desks, they lunched together at the Ashland House, they drank together after hours. Each was an integral component of a team that was creating what would soon become the most exciting and influential magazine the country had ever seen.

THE NEXT "PERMANENT ACQUISITION" TO join Ida Tarbell on McClure's writing staff was Ray Stannard Baker. Baker had spent six years reporting for the *Chicago Record*, a publication he proudly called "an honest paper" that played "no 'inside game,' but wanted to tell the truth, whatever it might be." His distinguished work at the *Record* included an extensive and memorable series on the growing tension between labor and capital. Baker had always enjoyed talking with "farmers, tinkers, blacksmiths, newsdealers, bootblacks, and the like," and firmly believed that "every human being has a story in him—how he has come to be what he is, how he manages, after all, to live, just to live."

At the age of twenty-seven Baker felt he had exhausted the possibilities of the newspaper format. He craved "a wider field of activity," a vehicle for in-depth research, a space for longer stories of lasting "import and value." An avid reader of *McClure's* from its inception, he had quickly become "a devoted admirer." The magazine's long and thoroughly researched articles, he noted with admiration, "were not merely about people . . . the people seemed to be there in person, alive and talking." The innovative publication, in his opinion, was simply "something fresh and strong and living in a stodgy literary world." After reading Tarbell's series on Lincoln, Baker sent *McClure's* a proposal for an article on his uncle, Colonel Lafayette C. Baker, the Secret Service member who had led the party that captured John Wilkes Booth. Tarbell promised to give it serious attention, and within days of its arrival, the piece was accepted for immediate publication. Intuiting that Baker might be a good fit for the magazine, McClure suggested that he come to New York and discuss ideas for further contributions.

"To say that I was awed at having a letter from the founder and editor of such a magazine was to put it mildly," Baker related a half century later. Soon he received a letter from John S. Phillips with an enclosed "pass" on the New York Central Railroad. "It took my breath away," he remembered. "So this was the magical way they did things in New York." Of that first foray into New York, he related that "Mr. McClure had suddenly dashed off to Europe, as was his custom, but I had long and delightful talks with John Phillips and August Jaccaci, the art director, and Ida Tarbell and others of the staff. I went out with them to the jolly table at the old Ashland House where they lunched together, a spot that still glimmers bright in my memory. It all seemed like a marvelous new world, with a quality of enthusiasm and intellectual interest, I had never before encountered. Even with S. S. McClure absent, I suppose I was in the most stimulating, yes intoxicating, editorial atmosphere then existent in America—or anywhere else."

In the months that followed, Baker submitted a half-dozen additional articles to *McClure's* while continuing to work at the *Chicago Record*. When the coveted invitation to join the *McClure's* staff finally arrived, he accepted at once, though he would miss his cohorts at the *Record*. "It 'breaks me all up' to leave after having been so long and so intimately connected with the paper," he told his father. "I suppose the regret is natural and that it will wear off as I bend to other work. I hope so." Once in New York, he never looked back. "This is a magnificent old town," he assured his father. "I never worked so hard in my life as I am doing now." He got along exceedingly well with the entire *McClure's* staff. "I like them and they like me," he proudly noted.

Baker was "a capital team worker," Tarbell recalled. "He had curiosity, appreciation, a respect for facts. You could not ruffle or antagonize him. He took the sudden calls to go here when he was going there, with equanimity; he enjoyed the unconventional intimacies of the crowd, the gaiety and excitement of belonging to what was more and more obviously a success. He was the least talkative of us all, observant rather than garrulous, the best listener in the group, save Mr. Phillips. He had a joyous laugh which was more revealing of his healthy inner self than anything else about him."

Baker's cheerful, balanced temperament could likely be traced to a devoted father and a peaceful childhood in the frontier village of St. Croix, Wisconsin. The oldest of six sons, he shared his father's love for "fishing and hunting" amid "the forests and the swift rivers and the lumber camps." Joseph Stannard Baker, his father, had been educated at Oberlin and the University of Wisconsin. An honored member of the Secret Service during the Civil War, he married Alice Potter, a minister's daughter from Lansing, and became the "resident agent" of a timber-rich swath of Wisconsin Territory owned by absentee landlords.

"Ours was a house of books," Ray fondly recalled, noting with pride that his father's library was the largest in the entire county. Every night, Baker would read aloud to his boys. "How well I remember the little gatherings just before bedtime," Ray later wrote, "the lamp in the middle of the table, the book, whatever it was, open before him and the small audience, tousle-headed, with grimy legs drawn up under them, sitting with mouths open and eyes fixed upon the reader's face! Whatever Father did, he did with gusto." Baker's animation and expressive voice made him "a prodigious story-teller, the best I ever knew. . . . We teased incessantly for stories and it was not unusual in the earlier days, for my father to have a roomful of people for his audience."

Ray was still a child when his father gave him a silver dollar for completing *Pilgrim's Progress*. No further bribery was ever required to fuel his passion for all manner of tales. By the time he was eleven, the boy loved nothing more than entering "into the lives and sorrows and joys" of others through books. "My reading was always a kind of living," he explained later, "a longing to know some man or men stronger, braver, wiser, wittier, more amusing, or more desperately wicked, than I was, whom I could come to know well and sometimes be friends with."

The eldest child and his father's favorite, Ray was expected to help shape the behavior of his younger siblings. Both in the classroom and at home he strove to be worthy of that trust. He was the top student in his grammar school class, performed household chores without complaint, and diligently participated in Sunday school classes. When his mother's ill health briefly forced her into a sanitarium, Ray assumed responsibility for provisioning the household with food and supplies. For a time after her return, her condition seemed to improve, but the year Ray turned thirteen, Alice Baker died. Ray would never forget the shock of witnessing his father's grief: "It went through me like the thrust of a sharp knife: it was more terrible than anything else that had happened. My father, that strong man, that refuge of safety and fearlessness, my father shaken with weeping."

After only one year in high school, Ray passed the entrance examinations for college, allowing him to enter Michigan Agricultural College (later Michigan State) as a fifteen-year-old freshman. Like Ida Tarbell, Ray enjoyed the invaluable benefit of an inspired botany professor, William Beal, yet another acolyte (like Professors Hurd and Tingley) of Harvard's Louis Agassiz. Ray's first experience in Professor Beal's laboratory made an indelible impression. Instructed to study a single plant specimen for several days under a compound microscope, he initially deemed the assignment "a great waste of time" when he could simply research the specimen in a botany text and enumerate its characteristics. Baker soon came to understand that Beal wanted his students to learn by investigating for themselves, by compiling "details and facts before principles and conclusions." Beal, he would come to realize, taught "the one thing I needed most of all to know. This was to *look* at life before I talked about it: not to look at it second-hand, by way of books, but so far as possible to examine the thing itself." The friendship he developed with his professor and mentor would last a lifetime; indeed, Baker would eventually marry Beal's daughter, Jessie. And Beal's methodology would serve as Baker's lodestar throughout his long journalistic career.

The personable Baker was well liked in college. He stood five feet ten inches tall, with handsome features: blue eyes behind round spectacles, a straight nose, and a cleft chin. The intent scholarship that kept him at the top of his class did not preclude joining a fraternity, playing rugby, or serving as editor-in-chief of the school newspaper. He was a leader in student government and was selected to deliver one of the commencement orations.

That his father hoped he would return to St. Croix after college, learn the land business, and ultimately become his partner was long understood. "When the time comes I shall give you advice," his father told him, "but I shall never attempt to force or urge you into any position or calling which is at all distasteful to you." Tears filled young Ray's eyes as he read those words, and he resolved "never to fail" his beloved father; upon graduation, he dutifully returned home to apprentice in Baker's office. Sadly, he soon discovered that he "was not adapted to a business life." He traveled with his father, keeping the books and bank accounts, but "did not *live* in it, as one must do if he is to be happy and truly successful in any employment." Despite his efforts, he found his occupation increasingly distasteful: "I felt as though I were being crowded back into a kind of cocoon from which I had long ago worked free, and flown."

Ray consoled himself by writing poems and stories and by recording thoughts in a journal, a habit he would continue all his life. Decades later, he wrote of the tremendous importance this private chronicle held for him: "Experience soon fades, thought degenerates into musing, even love may presently wither, but the honestly written expression, hot from the penpoint, of the contents of one's mind, its observations, desires, doubts, faith, ambition, and the like, becomes at length a kind of immortality." Ray endured two cheerless years in the office until his brother Harry, who found the land business far more congenial, replaced him. Harry's decision to join their father freed Ray to continue his education.

Having enrolled in the University of Michigan Law School in Ann Arbor, Ray soon found himself drawn instead to courses in the English department.

A gifted professor, Fred Newton Scott, became his mentor. Unlike traditional surveys of the literary canon, Scott's seminar focused on a limited number of writers, subjecting their works to in-depth literary criticism. The progressive young professor believed, as did Howells and the realist school, that authors had a social responsibility to address the problems of their era. The test of a writer's work, he told his students, must be its contribution to the "good working order" of society as a whole.

Baker signed up for a second seminar with Scott called "Rapid Writing," one of the country's earliest college programs to teach journalism. The popular class required that students pick one newspaper to follow daily and focus on a particular subject. Baker chose the *Chicago Record*, concentrating on the struggles between laboring men and employers in that city. Immersed in coverage of the fight to establish workers' rights in the new industrial order, he began to question the laissez-faire economic principles inherited from his Republican father. Though he already had read Henry George's *Progress and Poverty*, the book's remedy—a single tax on land—was "anathema" to his father, whose very livelihood was founded upon the ownership of land. Ray was still trying to reconcile these conflicting ideas when he encountered Professor Scott.

Numerous stories in the *Chicago Record* that semester reflected the growing tension between labor and capital, as well as an economic stagnation that signaled the impending depression of 1893. Every morning, Ray read and analyzed news articles and editorials, writing his own reports "with the greatest fervor," eagerly anticipating Scott's exacting appraisals. "For the first time in my life I was getting honest and direct criticism," he recalled, "and it was like a draught of clear water to a thirsty spirit."

By the semester's close, Baker realized that his desire to study law had evaporated, and he was certain his future lay in journalism. "I did not make this break-away without many hesitations," he admitted. "I knew how disappointed my father would be." Unable to confront Joseph, he set out for Chicago, ostensibly seeking summer employment as a reporter, though in actuality he already hoped to make journalism his career. When he presented himself to the editor of the *Chicago Record*, Baker was told that there were no regular openings, but he could await possible assignments in the city room. After many weeks, his opportunity arrived. The regular labor reporter was out on a story one afternoon when word came that the waiters in a popular restaurant had gone out on strike. Baker received the assignment. When he turned the article in, the assistant night editor delivered words he would never forget. "Great stuff, Baker," he exclaimed, "great stuff." With bolstered confidence, Baker canvassed the neighborhoods of Chicago. His explorations resulted in a series of human interest stories, "glimpses, street scenes, common little incidents of the daily life of a great city, which could be treated more or less lightly or humorously." Pleased with Baker's work, the *Record* offered him a regular position that fall.

But in December 1892 he received an urgent summons from his father. Baker's hearing, damaged in the war many years earlier, was deteriorating into deafness. It was Harry's turn to enroll in college courses, and he needed his oldest son to come home. Ray tried to convince his father that his aspirations as a writer were neither pretentious nor frivolous, but his father's needs prevailed and Ray found himself back in St. Croix. For nearly a year, he remained to assist his father until Harry's winter break allowed a return to Chicago.

The depression was taking a grim toll on the city that winter. Baker was welcomed back to the *Record* to cover the plight of the unemployed. "There are thousands of homeless and starving men in the streets," he told his father. "I have seen more misery in this last week than I ever saw in my life before." This destitute urban population was unlike anything he had encountered. While there were "plenty of people on the frontier who were poor," he noted, they had means of subsistence. "Land was to be had almost for the asking, logs were at hand for their houses, all the streams were full of fish, and all the hills full of game. . . . There was everywhere plenty of work." The city offered no such opportunities. "The miserable living conditions, the long hours, the low wages, the universal insecurity, tended to tear down the personality, cheapen the man."

As Harry prepared for the spring semester, Baker appealed once again to his oldest son. Ray had promised to return home "in the event of absolute necessity" to protect the family business, but leaving the newspaper would force him "to begin all over again at the bottom of the ladder" when he returned to Chicago. Moreover, he insisted, "there is no use in trying to run a business with your heart elsewhere." While reluctant to return, he reassured his father of his loyalty: " I shall regard it as my first duty, whatever may happen to see that your business is protected and I think every one of the six boys feels in the same way." Realizing his son's devotion to his chosen vocation, Baker relented. Ray should remain in Chicago, and he would manage at home.

Supplied with a typewriter for the first time, Ray was sent to Massillon, Ohio, in mid-March 1894 to cover a crusade that would become known as Coxey's Army. The fiery reformer Jacob Coxey planned a massive march on Washington to demand a government-sponsored public works program to put thousands of unemployed men to work building roads. Baker's first articles reflected his paper's editorial stance against the march—venting concern that a horde of vagrants and derelicts would wreak havoc as they marched through the countryside en route to the capital.

Yet as Baker trudged alongside the men, his attitude shifted. "I began to know some of them as Joe and Bill and George," he related. "I soon had them talking about their homes in Iowa and Colorado and Illinois and Chicago and Pittsburgh—and the real problems they had to meet." These were not "bums, tramps, and vagabonds" but "genuine farmers and workingmen," driven in a time of depression by their inability to "earn a living." Baker's sympathetic articles brought hundreds of additional recruits to Coxey's Army and revealed to him the incredible "power of the press." Skeptics had predicted that the Army, outfitted with supplies for only a few days, would soon disintegrate. But at each scheduled stop "there appeared an impromptu local committee, sometimes including the mayor and other public men, with large supplies of bread, meat, milk, eggs, canned goods, coffee, tea."

Following Coxey's improbable army was "a grand adventure" for Baker and his fellow correspondents. Crossing the Allegheny Mountains, they found themselves in snow at least a foot deep. Although some marchers with ragged boots dropped out, the majority persevered, and at last, six weeks after they began, the motley Army reached Washington, D.C. Massive crowds thronged the streets as the procession headed toward the Capitol. Senators and congressmen looked on from the Capitol portico. A large mounted police guard awaited and, as the marchers spilled onto the lawn, Baker reported, "the police seemed to lose their heads completely as they dashed into the crowds on their horses and slashed out with their clubs." Coxey gained the Capitol steps and was beginning to address the crowd when he was arrested for trespassing and roughly carried away.

"Coxey's eventful march from Massillon to the marble steps of the national Capitol closed today in riot and bloodshed," Baker recorded, leaving in its wake public works bills "no nearer passage than they were a month ago." A remark by a Massachusetts politician reflected the widespread hostility to the reforms among legislators. "The bill," he claimed, "was immoral, for unemployment was an act of God." With the arrest of Coxey, the Army "vanished in thin air," and with it, hope for a political solution to unemployment. It would take the Great Depression of the 1930s to convince the New Deal Congress that Coxey's approach had merit.

Immediately upon his return to Chicago, Baker was sent to Pullman, Illinois, the model town founded by the railroad industrialist George M. Pullman, developer of both the sleeping car and the dining car and president of the Pullman Palace Car Company. Baker had read rhapsodic descriptions of the experimental community where Pullman's workers lived in Pullman-owned homes, shopped in Pullman stores, and worshipped in Pullman churches. He had long wanted to meet the "benevolent-looking, bearded man," but he arrived in Pullman in 1894 to discover a scene of "the wildest confusion." Three thousand factory workers were striking to protest substantial wage cuts. The company argued that it was losing money in the hard times, but workmen pointed out that regular dividends were still being paid out to stockholders. Indeed, it was later proved that the company's dividend payouts were in excess of $2 million annually, while profits held steady at $25 million per year.

The Pullman workers appealed for support to the American Railway Union (ARU), headed by Eugene Debs. Initially reluctant to help, Debs was finally convinced by reports of the excessive prices workers were forced to pay for rent, utilities, and food; the predatory hold of the Pullman monopoly must be broken. Baker took an immediate liking to Debs, believing him unselfishly committed to the cause. The ARU gave the company five days to arbitrate a settlement, but Pullman declared that there was "nothing to arbitrate." He insisted that "workers have nothing to do with the amount of wages they shall receive; that is solely the business of the company." The powerful union responded with a boycott of all Pullman cars, disrupting railroad traffic across the nation. When railroad managers attempted to replace the strikers with non-union men, riots broke out.

The managers then requested and received a federal injunction against the boycott, ostensibly on grounds of protecting the delivery of mail. Despite the injunction, the boycott continued until President Grover Cleveland, over the objection of Illinois governor Altgeld, sent in federal troops, thereby escalating the violence. Trains were overturned and fires started. The federal troops opened fire. Dozens were killed and wounded. Debs was jailed for ignoring the injunction. By the end of August 1894, more than three months after it had begun, the strike collapsed with nothing gained for the workers.

Baker well understood that mobs could not run amok, "putting the torch to millions of dollars' worth of property," yet his feelings of support remained firm for the striking workers whose stories he had come to know. Clearly, Joseph Stannard Baker did not share his son's empathy for the strikers. "It does seem to me as if the laboring classes were possessed of the devil," he wrote in early July. "I believe in the free application of rifle balls, grape and canister to mobs." Ray held his ground. Asked to testify before a federal panel that fall, he asserted that he was "in the midst of the mob" when the violence began and that "at no time" did he witness the involvement of a member of the railway union or a striker. On the contrary, the men who overturned the cars were "toughs and outsiders." Moreover, when the federal troops arrived, they fired into the crowd with no warning, killing and wounding innocent spectators. While most of the newspapers blamed the strikers and created the impression that the federal troops had saved Chicago from anarchy, Baker carefully recounted what he had observed.

The young journalist believed that his "honeymoon as a newspaper reporter ended with the Pullman strike." He "had been wonderfully fortunate" to that point, he realized: "I had been able to work on subjects that interested me profoundly ever since my days in the university—the new problems of unemployment and the relationships of labor and capital." But in the aftermath of the protracted and distressing Pullman strike, even those editors sensitive to labor issues sensed that their readers "were profoundly relieved to have the trouble ended," no longer wishing to hear about labor's struggles. Baker found himself covering murders, fires, and robberies. He felt that he was stifling.

The dramatic 1896 campaign between Democrat William Jennings Bryan and Republican William McKinley provided a welcome diversion. After witnessing Bryan's famous "Cross of Gold" speech at the Chicago Wigwam, Baker concluded that the candidate was "the greatest popular orator [he] had ever heard." Though his father vociferously derided Bryan and his Populist followers, Baker was deeply impressed when he went to see him at the Palmer House. "The essential impression he made," Baker later recalled, "was one of deep sincerity." McKinley won a convincing victory, claiming every state outside the West and the South, and Baker found himself once again covering "the commonplace" rather than "the spectacular."

Two years earlier, Ray had married Jessie Beal, with whom he had corresponded since their college days. He was feeling "somewhat low" as he contemplated how he might support his wife and new child on his newspaper salary and doubted if he "was getting anywhere at all as a writer." At this stressful juncture, the fortuitous offer from S. S. McClure prompted elation. "Suddenly and joyously" Ray Stannard Baker was transported to a world "full of strange and wonderful new things," and he was "at the heart of it, especially commissioned to look at it, hear about it, and above all, to write about it."

TWENTY-NINE-YEAR-OLD WILLIAM ALLEN WHITE, EDITOR of a small country newspaper in Emporia, Kansas, ironically came to the attention of S. S. McClure through a scathing anti-Populist editorial that he would later disavow when he became an ardent progressive. "What's the Matter with Kansas?," written in the heat of the election between McKinley and Bryan, ridiculed his home state for endorsing Bryan's "wild-eyed" rhetoric that pitted the rich against the poor and was sure to drive out capital and extinguish the possibility of progress. "That's the stuff!" he jeered. "Give the prosperous man the dickens! Legislate the thriftless man into ease, whack the stuffing out of the creditors. . . . Whoop it up for the ragged trousers; put the lazy, greasy fizzle, who can't pay his debts, on the altar, and bow down and worship him."

White's editorial was republished in dozens of newspapers throughout the country. The sardonic tone caught the fancy of Mark Hanna, McKinley's campaign manager, who had it reprinted and distributed "more widely than any other circular in the campaign." Speaker of the U.S. House of Representatives Tom Reed, without even knowing White's name, sent a laudatory note to the editor of the little paper. "I haven't seen as much sense in one column in a dozen years," he declared. Suddenly, the rotund, florid young man who had labored at his obscure midwestern newspaper became a national figure.

McClure jotted down the name William Allen White; some weeks later, having also read a small volume of short stories White had recently published, he brought the young man to New York. "I had seen cities," White later recalled, "Kansas City, St. Louis, Denver, Chicago, but even in 1897 the New York sky line as I ferried across to the Twenty-third Street slip, made my country eyes bug out with excitement."

At first sight, White was totally smitten too by the *McClure's* staff. McClure himself seemed "a powerhouse of energy," a dynamo "full of ideas," who "talked like a pair of scissors, clipping his sentences, sometimes his words." White's mother, Mary Ann Hatton, they discovered, had been Professor Hurd's student at Knox College. And White connected at once with "fellow midwesterner" John Phillips, who invited him, along with Ida Tarbell, to a "gorgeous dinner" at a cozy restaurant way uptown. "These people knew Rudyard Kipling," he noted with amazement. "They knew Robert Louis Stevenson. . . . The new English poets were their friends."

McClure's original staff members, for their part, were enchanted by the country editor with "the smile of a roguish little boy" and "the eyes of a poet." Tarbell liked "his affection and loyalty for his state, his appreciation and understanding of everything that she does—wise and foolish." Baker relished White's "love of life" and contagious "high spirits." McClure deluged him with concepts for new magazine pieces, and Phillips helped him distinguish the fool's gold from the gold. Before leaving New York, White pledged to send the lion's share of his future stories and articles to *McClure's*. They reciprocated his good faith, urging him to "call on them whenever he needed help," a promise kept when he mentioned he was trying to raise $5,000 to pay for a new home. *McClure's* magazine instantly remitted White a check for all construction costs, plus an additional $1,000.

"The McClure group became for ten or fifteen years my New York fortress, spiritual, literary and, because they paid me well, financial," White later wrote. McClure "was always Sam to me and John Phillips was always John, Miss Tarbell was always Ida M., and Jaccaci was always Jack. And I loved them all. There was no New England repression in our relations. They were cordial to the point of ardent. . . . They talked the Mississippi Valley vernacular. They thought as we thought in Emporia about men and things. They were making a magazine for our kind—the literate middle class. This group had real influence."

Baker was struck with admiration that White "never yielded to the temptation" of leaving Emporia, "the country and the people he knew best." He frequently visited New York, "stayed as long as he wanted to stay . . . worked out plans for new articles and stories, and then went back to Kansas." Yet the rapport and fellowship with the McClure group profoundly influenced his thinking: the provincial editor became cosmopolitan; the young conservative a progressive.

William Allen White's youthful conservatism was nourished by the comfortable world of his childhood. His family lived in "the best house" in the small central Kansas town of El Dorado, where his father, a successful doctor and shopkeeper, enlarged the family fortunes by operating the town's grandest hotel and speculating in real estate. "I look back upon my boyhood there in the big house," White later said, "with a sense of well-being." The "White House," as it was called, boasted eleven rooms and a wraparound porch designed "to get a breeze from every angle." Dr. White was elected to the city council and later served as mayor. He was "somebody," White later said, fostering William's "sense of belonging to the ruling class."

His college-educated mother was thirty-six when she married forty-eight-year-old Doc White. Will, their only surviving child, was, by his own account, terribly spoiled. His "devoted and adoring" parents "bowed down" to accommodate his every desire. "In that Elysian childhood," he recalled, "I was shielded from pain and sorrow and lived, if ever a human being did live, in a golden age." In his local school, everyone liked him. "He was so good-natured," one classmate recalled, "they could not do otherwise." Summer days were spent diving and going fishing in the nearby river; autumn promised hunting in the surrounding woods; the onset of winter meant setting traps for birds and game, and ice-skating on the frozen river. It was a boy's paradise, one that later he would work to faithfully re-create in nostalgic fiction.

White's house, like Baker's, was filled with books, and every night his mother read to him. "I remember as a child sitting in the chair, looking up to her while she read Dickens and George Eliot, Trollope, Charles Reed, and the Victorian English novels. My father, I remember, used to growl a good deal at the performance, and claimed that if my mother read to me so much I would never get so I would read for myself. But his prediction was sadly wrong. It was to those nights of reading and to the books that my mother had always about the house that I owe whatever I have of a love for good reading."

Dr. White was a gentle and jovial man, fond of entertaining guests in his spacious house. Will particularly remembered those cheerful evenings when his family hosted friends, neighbors, and frequently "distinguished citizens—the politicians of the time, the governors, congressmen, senators, and judges who came to the town on their political pilgrimages." The doctor's geniality and the whirl of his social and professional activity obscured a chronic illness: Dr. White was suffering from severe diabetes, and after a two-week illness in the fall of 1882, he died. Will was fourteen. The entire town attended the funeral, with crowds of mourners converging on the house and congesting the surrounding sidewalks and streets. "I was not without my pride," White recalled, "looking back as we made the turn half a mile from home and headed for the East Cemetery, to see the long line of carriages and wagons and carts still moving into the procession on Main Street."

Upon his high school graduation, White enrolled in the College of Emporia, sixty miles away. There he first encountered the new literature of realism through the serialization of William Dean Howells's *A Modern Instance,* the same novel McClure had devoured at John Phillips's home. "Here," White recalled, "was a novel different from the Dickens I adored." The young freshman "read it and reread it" that spring, feeling that "a new door" had opened. When he returned home that summer, White got a job with the local paper, the *El Dorado Democrat*. His responsibilities were limited to sweeping floors, doing odd jobs, and helping the typesetters, but he was enchanted by the world of journalism, certain he had found his "life's calling."

The following year, White transferred to the University of Kansas, and his mother rented out their El Dorado house so she could "establish a home" for her beloved son in Lawrence. White thoroughly enjoyed his years at the university, where he developed a lifelong friendship with his political science professor, Dr. James H. Canfield. A gifted teacher who taught history, sociology, and economics as well as political science, Canfield encouraged "a babble of clamoring voices" in classes built on discussion rather than lectures. In these classes, White first understood the inequities wrought by the high protective tariff, the standard of the Republican Party. In the years ahead, Canfield encouraged White to read books on socialism and to follow the works of the Progressive economist Richard Ely, father of Reform Darwinism. Ely argued that what businessmen claimed to be the "natural laws" of economics were in fact tools "in the hands of the greedy and the avaricious for keeping down and oppressing the laboring classes." Had White focused more on his schoolwork, he might have absorbed more of Canfield's philosophy, but he readily acknowledged that his extracurricular passions—his social life and after-hours work for the *Lawrence Journal*—consumed far more time and attention than his classes. "As I look back at it, classroom pictures blur in my memory of the university," White wrote. "Fraternity meetings are clear; political excursions are etched deeply; parties, little dances, picnics and what, in the student nomenclature of the time, was called 'girling,' I recall vividly. Also, I was downtown much of the time writing my news items for the Lawrence Journal, taking my copy for the Weekly University Courier to the printer, covering local events for the St. Louis and Kansas City papers." He found himself cutting class after class and realized he had somehow "ceased to be a student and had become a reporter." Failing to pass a required mathematics exam for the third time, he left the university without a degree.

Despite his mother's chagrin, she accompanied William back to El Dorado, where he went to work at the *El Dorado Republican*. Though his father had been a Democrat, White had by this time adopted his mother's allegiance to the Republican Party, a commitment he would ardently maintain throughout his life. Charged with generating local stories and editorials, the twenty-two-year-old reporter found himself in the midst of the Populist uprising.

The boom times that had accompanied White's childhood years had vanished for the majority of Kansas farmers, who found themselves caught between usurious interest rates on debts to eastern bankers and the predatory, monopolistic practices of both the grain elevator companies that stored their crops and the railroads that carried them to market. In many sections of the West and Midwest, where only one elevator company or railroad served the area, farmers were forced to pay whatever price these companies demanded. "We have three crops," a Nebraska newspaper editor lamented, "corn, freight rates, and interest. The farmers farm the land, and the businessmen farm the farmers."

The grim hardships endured by farming families galvanized the so-called Grangers movement. They successfully pressured state legislatures to regulate exorbitant elevator and railroad rates, but these laws were swiftly challenged in the courts, where corporate influence was pervasive. The Grangers secured a spectacular, albeit temporary, triumph in the 1877 case of *Munn v. Illinois*. The U.S. Supreme Court confirmed the constitutionality of an Illinois state law regulating excessive elevator rates. The Court agreed that Illinois was simply exercising its "police power" to regulate private property "affected with a public interest." Nine years later, however, in *Wabash, St. Louis & Pacific Railway Co. v. Illinois*, the Supreme Court effectively reversed its decision. The justices denied the state's regulatory power in a case concerning inflated railroad rates on grounds that only Congress had the right to dictate commerce between states. In the years that followed, the Court would remain an uncompromising barrier to state regulation of business in the public interest.

Responding to the public outcry that followed the *Wabash* decision, Congress filled the regulatory void in 1887 by passing the Interstate Commerce Act, which created an Interstate Commerce Commission (ICC) to ensure that railroad rates were "reasonable and just." The practice of granting rebates to favored big shippers, which essentially destroyed smaller competitors, was outlawed. But the legislation did not authorize the commission to set specific rates, a fatal omission that allowed railroad barons to challenge the ICC rulings in the courts at every turn, thereby rendering the law largely ineffective. In time, railroad executives actually found the law useful. "It satisfies the public clamor for a government supervision of railroads," one corporate lawyer, Richard Olney, wrote, "at the same time that the supervision is almost entirely nominal."

Though widespread bitterness against the concentration of economic power led to the passage of the Sherman Anti-Trust Act in 1890, that law likewise remained a paper tiger while the trusts continued to grow. "Liberty produces wealth, and wealth destroys liberty," Henry Demarest Lloyd wrote in *Wealth Against Commonwealth*, an influential 1902 indictment of the trusts. "The flames of a new economic evolution run around us, and we turn to find that competition has killed competition, that corporations are grown greater than the State . . . and that the naked issue of our time is with property becoming master, instead of servant."

In 1890, the Farmers' Alliance, which had succeeded the Grangers, successfully fielded slates of radical candidates in the West and Midwest. Mary Lease, a formidable proponent of reform, traveled around Kansas on behalf of Alliance candidates. "Wall Street owns the country," she charged. "It is no longer a government of the people, by the people and for the people, but a government of Wall Street, by Wall Street and for Wall Street." She angrily dismissed claims that the farmers' troubles stemmed from a surfeit of produce. "Overproduction!—when 10,000 little children, so statistics tell us, starve to death every year in the United States, and over 10,000 shop-girls in New York are forced to sell their virtue for the bread their niggardly wages deny them!"

Buoyed by successes in the midterm elections of 1890, the Farmers' Alliance sent delegates to a national convention in Omaha, Nebraska. There, in 1892, a new party, the People's or Populist Party, was born. "We meet in the midst of a nation brought to the verge of moral, political and material ruin," the platform began. "The fruits of the toil of millions are boldly stolen to build up colossal fortunes for a few, unprecedented in the history of mankind." The Populists called for a graduated income tax to shift the heavier burden to the wealthy, a silver standard to facilitate an easier discharge of their debts, and a federally administered system of postal savings banks where people could safely deposit their earnings. To circumvent the collusion of corporate interests and political bosses who, in turn, controlled the state legislatures, they demanded a constitutional amendment to elect U.S. senators by a direct vote of the people, as well as new techniques—the initiative and the referendum—which would enable voters to directly initiate or reject legislation.

Realizing the necessity of a coalition with more urban areas, organizers of the largely agrarian party tried to appeal to industrial workers. The platform endorsed labor's fight for an eight-hour day and opposed the use of Pinkerton guards as strikebreakers. Finally, arguing that "the railroad corporations will either own the people or the people must own the railroads," the Populists called for government ownership of the railroads. Though their 1892 presidential candidate, James Weaver, proved unable to unify support beyond the western states, the Populist message remained a rallying point for America's working poor.

At first, the ruling classes—the bankers, the businessmen, and the lawyers—paid little attention to the members of the Farmers' Alliance and the new Populist Party. "We prideful ones," White later admitted, "considered the Alliance candidates as the dregs of Butler County society; farmers who had lost their farms, Courthouse hangers-on . . . political scapegraces." White wrote stinging editorials to ridicule the uprising, convinced that the grassroots movement was "demagogic rabble-rousing" without any tie to reality. "A child of the governing classes, I was blinded by my birthright," he later acknowledged. When the local Populists burned him in effigy, he proudly noted that their actions served only to aggrandize his standing with the local leaders of the Republican Party.

Like White, Theodore Roosevelt dismissed the members of the Farmers' Alliance as "pinheaded, anarchistic crank[s]" and castigated the Populists as grandstanding demagogues. While Tarbell sympathized with the Populists' outcry against monopoly after experiencing her father's struggle with Standard Oil, and while Baker came to know personally the members of Coxey's Army, the Pullman strikers, Governor Altgeld, and William Jennings Bryan, Roosevelt categorically denounced them all as "representatives of those forces which simmer beneath the surface of every civilized community, and which, if they could break out, would destroy not only property and civilization but finally even themselves."

For genteel reformers like Theodore Roosevelt and William Howard Taft, "good government," not economic reform, was the benchmark. "The 'best citizens,' " White explained, "were supposed to desire honest men in office, men who would not take bribes, men who would appoint high-minded men as their subordinates, men who would look after the public interests, see that public charities were well supported." The appearance of the Farmers' Alliance, "the first wave of the shock troops of a revolution that was to gather force as the years went by," reported White, "all this did not disturb either the Spring Chickens or their parents at the high-five clubs, the formal dances at the opera house given for the firemen, and the town charities."

White's jeering editorials against the Populists attracted widespread notice and prompted a job offer from the *Kansas City Journal*, a conservative Republican paper. During the next three years, from 1892 to 1895, he wrote for the *Journal* and then for the *Kansas City Star*. During these tumultuous years, as "the black hand of despair" fell over the countryside, he remained, by his own admission, "a supercilious young Pharisee, blinder than a bat to the great forces that were joining issue in our politics, forces that would be in combat for fifty years." Although his attacks on the Populists did not abate, he also began to write short stories based on his early life in Kansas that would eventually attract the attention of Sam McClure.

In 1895, having married schoolteacher Sallie Lindsay, White decided to quit big city life and return to the small town of Emporia, with its population of 15,000, a Main Street and college, and simple neighborly life. Intent on becoming his "own master," White purchased the *Emporia Gazette*, a local paper with a circulation of less than five hundred. He hoped to streamline the paper's production and dedicate most of his time to writing poetry and fiction. Most important, he told a skeptical city friend at the time, "I want to live and work some place where I can sit down with the mayor on the edge of the sidewalk and we can let our feet hang off and can discuss local politics and the state of the nation and what we must do to be saved till it's time to go home to dinner."

In his very first editorial for the *Gazette*, White spelled out a manifesto that would define the rest of his life. "The new editor hopes to live here until he is the old editor," he began. "He hopes always to sign 'from Emporia' after his name when he is abroad, and he trusts that he may so endear himself to the people that they will be as proud of the first words of the signature as he is of the last words." The young idealist would make good on his pledge, living out his years in his beloved country town, even as he became "the best-known and most often quoted country journalist in the United States."

While White never capitulated to Sam McClure's repeated invitations to relocate to New York, the warm friendships he developed with McClure, Phillips, Tarbell, and Baker fundamentally altered his social and political attitudes. He began to understand the profound inequities that had produced the Populist uprising: how the growth of colossal corporations had strangled competition in one field after another; how these corporations blatantly wielded their power through venal politicians, widening the gap between the rich and the poor. Belatedly but surely, he came to recognize that Bryan's platform in 1896 "was the beginning of a long fight for distributive justice, the opening of a campaign to bring to the common man . . . a larger and more equitable share in the commonwealth of our country."

THE FINAL MEMBER OF THE celebrated quartet at the heart of *McClure's* was Lincoln Steffens. As a police reporter for the New York *Evening Post*, Steffens covered Theodore Roosevelt's activities as police commissioner. Early on, McClure had identified Roosevelt as a man of unusual potential: he "seems big from here," McClure confided to Phillips, indicating his resolve to cultivate a connection with a public figure "just our size." Aware of Steffens's intimacy with Roosevelt, the editor hoped to secure that conduit to New York's dynamic commissioner by adding Steffens to his staff.

When first approached by *McClure's*, Steffens was reluctant to abandon the newspaper industry and the reputation he had built as "one of the best journalists New York ever had." A long lunch with Phillips, followed by a visit to the bustling *McClure's* office, began to conquer his hesitancy. McClure was out of town, but Steffens met with the rest of the staff and was particularly captivated by the art director, August Jaccaci. "Jaccaci probed me hard, took me to his home, talked with and drew me out," he recalled. "That was his way. He could not be a friend; he had to be a lover." Their discussions convinced Steffens that the format of a monthly magazine would allow him to "tell the whole, completed story," providing time and space for details and implications he could not explore in a daily newspaper. That conversation "clinched" the deal.

Arriving at *McClure's*, Steffens later recalled, was "like springing up from a bed and diving into the lake—and life." S. S. McClure's sheer, irrepressible drive astounded Steffens. "He was a flower that did not sit and wait for the bees to come and take his honey and leave their seeds," observed the new staff writer. "He flew forth to find and rob the bees." Tensions invariably arose when McClure returned from his trips and assembled the staff to allocate new assignments gleaned from his travels. It was Ida Tarbell, Steffens recalled, who helped sort things out. Time and again, she managed to placate the staffers, to avoid battles, and find a path "to compromise and peace."

Tarbell in turn came to consider the "young, handsome, self-confident" Steffens "the most brilliant addition to the McClure's staff." Though "incredibly outspoken" and "never doubtful of himself," he demonstrated a disconcerting ability to analyze events and detect the underlying patterns, illuminating "the relations of police and politicians, politicians and the law, law and city officials, city officials and business, business and church, education, society, the press." Tarbell found it "entirely in harmony with the McClure method of staff building that this able, fearless innocent should be marked for absorption."

More reserved by nature than the cocksure Steffens, Ray Baker acknowledged they would not likely have been friends had they not been "associates in the same enterprise, eagerly engaged in similar tasks, meeting familiarly every day, discussing ideas and projects." Nevertheless, the more he worked with Steffens, the greater his respect and affection grew. Staff luncheons and dinners, visits to each other's homes, confidences shared, and letters exchanged combined to "make up the texture of a long friendship." Baker thought of Steffens "as a kind of Socratic skeptic, asking deceptively simple questions . . . striving first of all to understand." Indeed, his biographer Robert Stinson observes that throughout Steffens's long career, "his most consistent pose was that of a student." Projecting an earnest, unbiased, and questioning nature, he was able to gain the confidence and elicit the secrets of his subjects.

The qualities that made Steffens a first-rate reporter—his immense curiosity and self-assurance, his social ease and storytelling gifts—were perceptible even in his youth. "My story is of a happy life," he observed in his famous *Autobiography*, beginning with a childhood surrounded by doting parents and three affectionate younger sisters. His mother, Elizabeth Symes, was a cheerful, quick-witted, warmhearted woman who adored him. His father, Joseph, owned a successful business dealing in "paints, oils and glass." Later, as vice president of the California National Bank, president of the Board of

Trade, and a Republican stalwart, he would become a leading figure in Sacramento, California. The "palatial residence" where Lincoln was raised was subsequently turned into the governor's mansion.

Both intrepid and inquisitive, eight-year-old Steffens quickly capitalized on his newfound freedom when his parents gave him a pony. He could explore the countryside so long as he returned home in time for dinner. "If I left home promptly after breakfast on a no-school day and right after school on the other days," Lincoln recalled, "I could see a good deal of the world." His questing, precocious nature attracted a various and colorful assortment of acquaintances. He befriended a bridge-tender who let him follow along as he walked the tracks to extinguish the burning coals spewed by passing locomotives. In the course of their conversations, the bridge-tender shared his dreams of striking it rich as a gold miner. Watching an artist render a drab, leached-out river channel, he saw the scene transformed by small choices of color and light. Hanging out at the racetrack, the boy struck up a relationship with a jockey who dampened his ardor for horse racing by confiding that the races were frequently fixed—so that those "in on the know" would realize "big killings." A friendly page at the state capitol took him to the smoke-filled committee rooms and hotel apartments where legislators and lobbyists hammered out compromises on the price to be paid for votes in a particular piece of legislation. "Bribery! I might as well have been shot," he lamented. "Nothing was what it was supposed to be."

Organized schooling frustrated young Lincoln's quest for knowledge and information. Though he read more books than were required, he resisted the standardized curriculum that he perceived as irrelevant to his experience. Graduating at the bottom of his class from grammar school, he was sent to a military boarding school to remedy the problem. When he still failed the entrance examinations for the University of California at Berkeley, he required an additional year at "the best private school in San Francisco" and the aid of a private tutor in order to matriculate.

In his autobiography, Steffens blithely claimed that the enormous liberties he enjoyed as a child had not made him one of those boys "brought up to do their duty," boys for whom the American educational system was designed. Knowledge at Berkeley, he complained, was "stored in compartments, categorical and independent." He resented the requirements in higher mathematics, wishing only to pursue his passion for philosophy. "No one," he insisted, "ever brought out for me the relation of anything I was studying to anything else." Then, during his junior year, when a history professor demanded research in original documents, he discovered that the past was not a list of dates to be memorized but a series of questions to be continually debated. By the time he graduated from college, Steffens believed himself finally prepared to be a genuine student, an authentic intellectual, and decided to pursue graduate study in Europe.

"My father listened to my plan, and he was disappointed," Steffens recalled. The older man had harbored hopes that his son would take over the business: "It was for that that he was staying in it. When I said that, whatever I might do, I would never go into business, he said, rather sadly, that he would sell out his interest and retire." Facing the same irreconcilable demands of familial duty and personal desire that had plagued Baker, Lincoln Steffens was considerably more self-indulgent. He later postulated that having received love "so freely" as a child, he had never learned to reciprocate. Not until his own son was born, as Steffens approached sixty years old, did he feel any intimation of what unconditional love required.

A three-year interlude in Europe allowed Steffens to continue his philosophic study of man and society, first in Germany, then France, and finally in England. Through the works of Marx and Engels, he was exposed to the idea that the state had a responsibility to foster social welfare. He studied music and art, psychology and philosophy, attending lectures if and when he chose. He spent his days reading in cafés, wandering through museums, attending concerts, playing cards, drinking beer, and debating politics and philosophy with fellow students.

European social and sexual mores offered Steffens greater latitude to pursue unconventional relationships as well. In Leipzig, he became involved with Josephine Bontecou, a liberated woman ten years his senior. The daughter of a wealthy New York surgeon, she was studying psychology and anatomy to further her ambitions as both a scientist and a novelist. "She stands next to me as my equal in all respects," he wrote at the time. "She will have a life and a life's work of her own." After a clandestine marriage in London, concealed to ensure his father would continue sending remittances, the two moved together to Paris. They found lodgings in the Latin Quarter where Ida Tarbell struggled to maintain her meager but exciting livelihood during those same months. Steffens savored a carefree intellectual existence for the better part of a year until summoned by his father's letter: "My dear son: When you finished school you wanted to go to college. I sent you to Berkeley. When you got through there, you did not care to go into my business; so I sold out. You preferred to continue your studies in Berlin. I let you. After Berlin it was Heidelberg; after that Leipzig. And after the German universities you wanted to study at the French universities in Paris. I consented, and after a year with the French, you had to have half a year of the British Museum in London. All right. You had that too. By now you must know about all there is to know of the theory of life, but there's a practical side as well. It's worth knowing."

So at last, determined to heed his father's edict to find work and support himself, Steffens crossed the ocean, landed in New York, and found employment as a reporter. Armed with a letter of introduction from a friend of his father's to Joseph B. Bishop, an editor at the New York *Evening Post*, he was given a chance to prove himself "on space" in an unsalaried position that paid by the word once a piece was accepted for publication. Within weeks, he made good. Assigned to interview the partner of a stockbroker who had suddenly disappeared, he soon gained the man's confidence: "I told him the story of my life; he told me his," Steffens later related. Before long, he learned that the missing banker had absconded with all the firm's funds. More work quickly followed this successful investigation, and soon Steffens was put on salary.

"I came to love New York," he wrote. "In the course of a few months I had visited all parts of the city, called on all sorts of men (and women), politicians, business men, reformers; described all sorts of events, fires, accidents, fights, strikes, meetings. It was happy work for me." Suddenly, "science and philosophy, like the theaters and books, seemed tame in comparison with the men and women, the unbelievable doings and the sayings of a live city." Like Baker and Tarbell, whose early enthusiasm for science gave way to a fascination with human beings, Steffens had found his calling, a focus for his diverse intellectual interests in journalism.

Just as the Panic began during the winter of 1892–93, the city editor assigned Steffens to cover Wall Street. He was directed to develop relationships with leading financiers that would allow the conservative *Evening Post* to explain insolvent banks and railroads in "cool, dull, matter-of-fact terms," rather than resort to the fearmongering and sensationalism practiced by competing papers. Recognizing that the Panic of 1893 "was a dismal time of radiating destruction" for millions of people, Steffens nevertheless noted that "it had its bright side, inside; it was good for the bears." From the sidelines of the Stock Exchange, he dispassionately witnessed "the wild joy" of men who shorted stocks and "rejoiced in the ruin." In later years, he would come to despise "successful men who seize such opportunities," but "the practices of big business" were still a mystery, and he "was not thinking in those days; life was too, too interesting, the world as it was too fascinating, to stop to question."

Steffens gained a reputation as "the gentleman reporter," one who could be relied upon to present the news with "accuracy and politeness." In a letter to his father, he proudly described the close relationships he had cultivated with the big bankers. They "confide in me," he reflected, "saying they know I will report them accurately and without exaggeration." The equanimity and clarity of his writing was gaining notice. "Above all," he confessed to his father, "I want that you should be convinced that you were right in giving me the long training of college and that I am worthy of your long, patient help to a son who did not ever seem worth it all."

In November 1893, a challenging new assignment inspired both elation and unease: "The Evening Post has never given any space to police news: fires, suicides, murders, and other crimes," Steffens explained to his father. "Now I am to be tried." He would be head of a new *Post* police bureau, "with an office on Mulberry Street across the street from Police Headquarters, fitted up with a desk, bookcase, paper racks and telephone, and an assistant and a boy." From the outset, Steffens understood that he faced "beastly work, police, criminals and low-browed 'heelers' in the vilest part of the horrible East Side amid poverty, sin and depravity," but he regarded the challenge with eager anticipation. "Will it degrade me? Will it make a man of me? Here is my field, my chance."

Dr. Charles H. Parkhurst, a respected minister, was responsible for the *Post*'s decision to cover the activities of the police department. Head of the Society for the Prevention of Crime, Parkhurst had undertaken an investigation into the relationship between Tammany Hall and the police force. He exposed a system of ubiquitous bribery and coercion that governed all aspects of municipal operation: appointments, promotions, liquor licenses, protection for houses of prostitution, gambling operations, and saloons operating illegally on Sundays. Long opposed to the Tammany regime, the *Post* editors were delighted to document Parkhurst's findings in full detail.

Parkhurst's allegations forced the state legislature in Albany to authorize its own investigating commission, headed by Republican state senator Clarence Lexow. The hearings of the Lexow Committee splashed headlines throughout the state, ultimately revealing a system of corruption even more widespread than Parkhurst had guessed. The shocking revelations produced a surge of support for reform candidates, precipitating the defeat of Tammany in the 1894 elections, the triumph of reform mayor William L. Strong, and the choice of Theodore Roosevelt as the new police commissioner. By the time Roosevelt arrived in New York, Steffens had learned a great deal about the workings of the police department, insights he readily shared in return for access to the new commissioner and his department. A complicated friendship was born that would give Steffens the unique perspective he would bring to *McClure's*, where the "Big Four"—Ida Tarbell, Ray Baker, William Allen White, and Lincoln Steffens—would become the heart of the muckraking movement.

Unlike McClure, who had become acquainted with the crueler side of American prosperity through a childhood scarred by poverty and instability, the Big Four were the children of prominent and enterprising businessmen. Each of them had encountered the corrosive effects of the industrial system. Ida Tarbell had witnessed the economic ruin of her father and his fellow independent oil producers at the hands of an all-powerful monopoly. Ray Stannard Baker, in his dedicated pursuit of the human stories behind the Chicago labor conflicts, had developed a sympathetic attitude toward the workingman's struggles that set him apart from his father's laissez-faire views. Lincoln Steffens had absorbed radical social ideas during his intense interdisciplinary studies in Europe and would bring an open, inquisitive, analytic mind to his work as police reporter. Even William Allen White, despite a coddled, conservative upbringing, had begun to recognize injustices in the farming and freight industries that had crippled the regional economy and compromised a community he cared for deeply.

All four were extraordinary, independent thinkers. Tarbell defied the conventions of her gender, steadfastly refusing the path of marriage and braving poverty and alienation to pursue her ambitions as a writer. Baker, too, resisted the pressure of social and familial expectation, declining to make his father's business his own life's work. Steffens's difficulty in conforming to a normal course of study allowed him to develop the rigorous and comprehensive understanding of human nature that rendered networks of power transparent. White's passionate devotion to his state's progress may have assumed a pugnacious form in the blistering editorials that brought him into prominence, but that same devotion led him to a progressive metamorphosis as he came to see the neglected underside of the new industrial order.

Each of the four journalists was deeply influenced by a teacher. Both Tarbell and Baker had pursued studies in biology, learning investigative principles and procedures they would later apply to human society. Steffens had discovered the joy of working with original documents and the exhilarating freedom when one is allowed to question established authorities. White had found a mentor whose influence would continue to grow in the years ahead. All passionately believed, with S. S. McClure, that "a vigilant and well-informed press, setting forth the truth," could become "an infinitely greater guard to the people than any government officials." The new fusion of journalism, literature, exposé, and human interest that emerged in the pages of *McClure's* would turn the microscope on humanity, on the avarice and corruption that stunted the very possibility of social justice in America.

This revolutionary cadre of writers would soon play a vital role in Theodore Roosevelt's political future as well, helping to generate the critical mass of public sentiment to implement progressive policies. Though the *McClure's* team had not yet articulated a distinct progressive agenda, their novel, vivid, and fearless explorations of the American condition would sound a summons and quicken the Progressive movement.

CHAPTER EIGHT

"Like a Boy on Roller Skates"

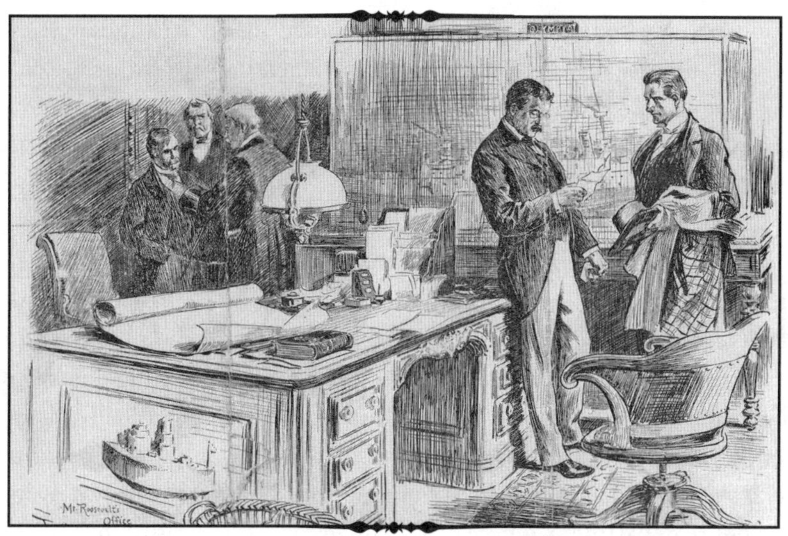

Theodore Roosevelt at work in the Navy Department,
Harper's Weekly, May 7, 1898.

ON MAY 6, 1895, LINCOLN Steffens was relaxing with fellow reporters on the front steps of the newsmen's building across the street from police headquarters when a shout from veteran police reporter Jacob Riis heralded the story of the day. Theodore Roosevelt had been sworn in as police commissioner earlier that morning at City Hall. Accompanied by the three other board members, he was approaching his new headquarters at 300 Mulberry Street in the heart of Little Italy.

As the foursome came into view, Steffens noted that the new commissioner surged past the other gentlemen, "head forward, jaw set and looking straight and sharp out of his big round glasses." Roosevelt greeted Jacob Riis, a friend of several years, with exuberance. "Hello, Jake," he exclaimed, then continued to race up the stairs, signaling for all reporters to follow. "T.R. seized Riis, who introduced me," Steffens recalled, "and still running, he asked questions: 'Where are our offices? Where is the board room? What do we do first?' "

As agreed, the first order of business was to elect Roosevelt president of the four-man board (comprising two Republicans—Roosevelt and Frederick D. Grant, son of General Ulysses S. Grant—and two Democrats—West Pointer Avery D. Andrews and lawyer Andrew D. Parker). With this accomplished, Roosevelt pulled Riis and Steffens aside into his office. "It was all breathless and sudden," Steffens recalled in *The Autobiography*, "but Riis and I were soon describing the situation to him, telling him which higher officers to consult, which to ignore and punish; what the forms were, the customs, rules, methods. It was just as if we three were the police board."

Roosevelt could not have found two more valuable tutors than Jacob Riis and Lincoln Steffens. For nearly twenty years, Riis had covered police activities for the *New York Tribune* and the *Evening Sun*. An immigrant from Denmark, he had landed at Castle Garden the same year that the cosseted eleven-year-old Roosevelt docked in Manhattan after his family's Grand European Tour. For three years, Riis had scraped together a living doing everything from carpentry and peddling to hunting and trapping. Finally, he found an opportunity to pursue his "life-work" in journalism, initially serving for several years as a general reporter. At the age of twenty-eight, he was assigned to the police department, where he remained for most of his professional life. "Being the 'boss reporter' in Mulberry Street," Riis later wrote, was "the only renown I have ever coveted or cared to have." The years spent covering fires, murders, and robberies in the immigrant slums fostered a keen awareness of the devastating conditions confronting families in these tenement districts. "The sights I saw there," he recalled, "gripped my heart until I felt that I must tell of them, or burst, or turn anarchist, or something."

In newspaper exposés, Riis described overcrowded, unsanitary tenements with insufficient light and air, often the properties of absentee owners who neglected "repairs and necessary improvements." Riis had witnessed these conditions in the course of his daily work as a police reporter. Although he documented the same criminal incidents that fellow journalists covered, his perspective was unique. "Only Riis wrote them as stories, with heart, humor, and understanding," Steffens remarked, and "beautiful stories they were . . . for Riis could write." When he narrated a suicide, fire, or outbreak of disease, Jacob Riis took down every detail of the building or the city block where it occurred, relentlessly pursuing the negligent landlords, holding them responsible for the abhorrent conditions and threatening further stories until the problems were redressed. "Why," he asked, "should a man have a better right to kill his neighbor with a house than with an axe in the street?" "The remedy," he concluded, "must proceed from the public conscience."

How the Other Half Lives, Riis's first book, was published in 1890. This visceral account traced the daily struggles he witnessed in the Italian tenements, the Jewish quarters, and the Bohemian ghetto. Riis guided readers to fetid corners of the city they had never visited—to Mulberry Bend, Bandit's Roost, and Bottle Alley. The catchy title, Riis modestly acknowledged, had contributed to the book's phenomenal success. "Truly, I lay no claim to eloquence," he noted, "so it must have been the facts." Humility notwithstanding, readers were captured by the power and empathy of the writing. "I cannot conceive how such a book should fail of doing great good, if it moves other people as it has moved me," wrote the critic James Russell Lowell. "I found it hard to get asleep the night after I had been reading it."

Theodore Roosevelt had read *How the Other Half Lives* while he was civil service commissioner. Calling it "both an enlightenment and an inspiration," he was convinced the book would "go a long way toward removing the ignorance" of comfortable New Yorkers about the hardships confronting their less fortunate neighbors. Furthermore, he was hopeful that Riis's disclosures would help engender a new spirit of reform. Roosevelt found the tone of the writing particularly admirable, lauding the manner in which Riis revealed social ills without stridency, never descending into "hysterical" negativity or "sentimental excess."

When intrigued by the work of a writer or journalist, Roosevelt often endeavored to establish a personal connection; he called on Riis at the *Evening Sun*. Finding him out of the office, Roosevelt left a card, with a succinct message that he had read the book and "had come to help." Riis had long tracked Roosevelt's progress from his days as a young silk stocking legislator "exposing jobbery, fighting boss rule," and "rattling dry bones" disinterred from the city's closets. "I loved him from the day I first saw him," Riis later wrote. Over the course of Roosevelt's tenure as police commissioner, this affection and mutual respect would intensify until Roosevelt regarded Riis as "one of my truest and closest friends."

Roosevelt later recalled "two sides" of his role as police commissioner: first, the daily work of managing the police department; second, the opportunity to use his position, which also encompassed membership on the health board, to make "the city a better place in which to live and work for those to whom the conditions of life and labor were hardest." To comprehend the practical possibility for real change, Roosevelt relied on Jacob Riis. "He had the most flaming intensity of passion for righteousness," Roosevelt recalled.

Never a "mere preacher," he was among the few whose convictions proved a touchstone to action. In Riis, Roosevelt found a man "who looked at life and its problems from substantially the same standpoint" as he did: a moderate reformer seeking to rectify social ills through moral conviction and suasion.

Roosevelt's relationship with the intellectual Lincoln Steffens was more complex. They shared an irrepressible self-confidence, an immense curiosity, a driving ambition, and a sharp intelligence. Later, as Steffens entertained more radical ideas and began to question capitalism itself, Roosevelt lost patience with him. During the decade of Roosevelt's boggling ascent from commissioner to governor and then president, however, they enjoyed a rich friendship that benefited both men substantially. After only four months' acquaintance, Roosevelt gave Steffens an enthusiastic letter of recommendation. "He is a personal friend of mine; and he has seen all of our work at close quarters," Roosevelt assured Horace Scudder, the editor of the *Atlantic Monthly*. "He speaks at first hand as an expert."

While Steffens later acknowledged that he might have overstated his influence in claiming that he and Riis functioned as working members of Roosevelt's police board, he maintained that the statement had truly reflected his "state of mind." So willing was Roosevelt to bring the two journalists into his inner circle, so candid was he in admitting ignorance about his new job, that both men naturally assumed the aura of "wise" mentors to the newcomer.

Steffens had begun his job on the police beat with the simplistic belief that if good men replaced dishonest men at the top of the organization, corruption would be defeated. Only after two years—through numerous days spent with the crusading Dr. Parkhurst and months of coverage devoted to the sensational Lexow Committee hearings documenting the relationship between Tammany Hall and the police department—would Steffens fathom a vast entrenched system of police corruption that would not yield so easily to reform.

Steffens's initial interviews with Dr. Parkhurst began with a series of deceptively innocent questions, a technique that developed into his mode of operating. For what reason, when gambling enterprises and houses of prostitution were illegal, did the police officers of the law allow them to exist? Why were some saloons permitted to stay open beyond the designated hours while others were not? "With astonishment" Steffens learned that pervasive, systematic bribery allowed those businesses willing to pay Tammany Hall's substantial monthly charge to operate unmolested, while those who refused to furnish protection money were closed down.

New police recruits were forced to pay Tammany a fixed fee for their appointments. The fee was well beyond the means of most, but every officer understood he would make the money back with plenty to spare once inside the system. Policemen who secured the confidence of Tammany were promoted, though each advancement required hefty additional fees. "One police captain," Steffens told his father, "has confessed to having paid $15,000 for his promotion and said that, though he had to borrow the money," he was able to repay his debt within two years. With each higher rank a policeman attained, his percentage of the blackmail fund grew. Superintendent Tom Byrnes had amassed what was then a sizable fortune of $350,000, while his chief inspector, Alec "Clubber" Williams, could not explain the unusual size of his bank account when forced to testify before the Lexow Committee.

Observers would later credit Steffens's success as a journalist to his "supreme gift of making men tell—or try to tell—him the truth." He always seemed able to coax people to "explain themselves," even when their explanations implicated rather than vindicated them. After the Lexow Committee hearings, Steffens approached Captain Max Schmittberger, a pivotal witness who had made "a clean breast" of everything. As the two men became friends, Schmittberger explained how, as an "honest" young policeman, he had been drawn into "the whole rotten business." The substance of these long conversations would prove most instructive when Steffens later recounted them with Roosevelt. Immersed so gradually in the venality of the department, Schmittberger never realized the shamelessness of his actions until the Lexow Committee called upon him to testify. After many hours with Schmittberger, Steffens concluded that he was "on the square," a decent man entangled in a crooked system. He persuaded Roosevelt to keep him on the force, a decision resulting in both a trusted ally and an insider who could teach the new commissioner things he could never have learned alone.

Joseph Bishop, the *Evening Post*'s editorial writer to whom Steffens had initially carried his letter of introduction, noted that Roosevelt opened the battle for reform wielding the same weapons he had used in his previous fights against corruption: "full publicity, strict enforcement of the law, and utter disregard of partisan political considerations." Like Steffens, Bishop was "in almost daily confidential conference" with Roosevelt during his tenure as police commissioner. "There began between him and myself," Bishop recalled a quarter century later, "a close personal friendship which continued unbroken throughout his career, growing steadily in mutual confidence and affection with time."

At his first press conference, Roosevelt announced that henceforth appointments and promotions would be made on merit alone: "No political influence could save a man who deserved punishment and none could win an unworthy promotion." The police force had heard such rhetoric before, but they soon began to realize the unique weight of Roosevelt's pledge. Within three weeks of his swearing-in, he summoned Superintendent Byrnes and Inspector Williams to his office and forced them to resign. These stunning departures broadcast clearly that the reform police board "would spare no man" in its campaign to root out corruption.

Genuine reform, however, hinged upon the patrolmen on the beat. Riis suggested that Roosevelt accompany him on a series of unannounced inspections between midnight and sunrise to determine whether the officers on the beat were faithfully safeguarding their designated posts. Concealing his evening clothes beneath a long coat and donning a floppy hat to obscure his face, Roosevelt set out with Riis at 2 a.m. from the steps of the Union League Club. Over the next three to four hours, they would follow a route mapped out in advance by the veteran reporter to encompass a dozen police patrol areas. If he found an officer dutifully patrolling his beat, Roosevelt patted him on the back; but those whom he discovered sleeping or enjoying a meal at an all-night restaurant were summoned to appear before him as soon as the department opened that morning. One startled policeman was chatting with a prostitute when Roosevelt confronted him and asked him to account for himself. Not recognizing the commissioner of the New York City Police, the officer belligerently replied: "What's that to you? Shall I fan him, Mame?" The woman nodded in agreement. "Sure, fan him to death."

The police reporters all attended the morning roundup when the delinquent men appeared before the commissioner. "A sorrier-looking set of men never came to police headquarters," Steffens reported in the *Evening Post*. The New York *Sun* provided details of the new commissioner's midnight forays with the dramatic headline: "Roosevelt on Patrol: He Makes Night Hideous for Sleepy Policemen." Under Bishop's guidance, the editorial page praised the "patrolman hunt" as "the beginning of a new epoch." Roosevelt continued his surprise inspections on subsequent nights with different companions, including Steffens, the celebrated reporter Richard Harding Davis, and the novelist Hamlin Garland.

These predawn missions attracted press attention across the country. "Police Commissioner Roosevelt finds that he can secure more information in one night," observed the *San Antonio Daily Light*, "than he would in a year in broad daylight." As tales of his unorthodox maneuvers spread, Roosevelt became an alluring subject for cartoonists, spawning caricatures of startled policemen cowering at the sight of an enormous set of teeth and round, metal-rimmed eyeglasses. "A pair of gold-mounted spectacles is a mark of authority more to be feared in police circles," one reporter quipped, "than the biggest badge that ever glittered on a uniformed coat." Roosevelt relished seeing his caricature. "Few men," he remarked, "live to see their own hieroglyph."

"These midnight rambles are great fun," Roosevelt admitted to Bamie, "though each meant my going forty hours at a stretch without any sleep." Riis and Steffens guided him through sections of the city he had never explored. "It is one thing to listen in perfunctory fashion to tales of overcrowded tenements," Roosevelt conceded, "and it is quite another actually to see what that overcrowding means, some hot summer night, by even a single inspection during the hours of darkness." Progress was slow, but with the attention Roosevelt helped focus on conditions in the most abject neighborhoods, the city eventually "tore down unfit tenements, forced the opening of parks and playgrounds."

Conversations with Riis and Steffens convinced Roosevelt that the only way to pry out what Riis described as "the tap-root" of corruption in the police force was through strict enforcement of the law requiring that saloons be closed on Sundays. Passed by the state legislature nearly four decades earlier to satisfy rural constituents, the Sunday law had warped into a massive vehicle of police and political blackmail. In more than 10,000 saloons operating in the city, owners and managers understood that so long as they continued to make monthly payments to the police and politicians, they were free to flout the statute on the Lord's Day, often the most lucrative day of the week. If they refused or fell out of favor with Tammany, they were promptly shut down and arrested for violating the law.

Roosevelt fully anticipated the political fallout of rigorously enforcing a law both unpopular and immensely lucrative. "The corrupt would never forgive him," remarked Steffens, "and the great mass of the people would not understand." For the workingmen of the city, the saloon was a place to drink with friends, play cards, and shoot pool on their only day off. Roosevelt sympathized with the statute's critics, allowing that it "is altogether too strict." Until the legislature changed the law, however, he was responsible for enforcing it fairly and squarely. Still, he deliberated long and hard before taking action. "Is there any other way," he implored Steffens and Riis, "to do the work I was sent here to do?" Assured that no alternative existed, he resolutely targeted June 23, 1895, to commence a new policy of regulation that would harbor "no protected class."

Each Sunday proved dryer than the one before. By the third Sunday in

August, Roosevelt and Riis combed the city and discovered more than 95 percent of the saloons shut down. Those that took the risk of remaining open operated "to a most limited extent," with no money changing hands for the privilege. "The tap-root" of corruption had been extracted. "The police force became an army of heroes," Riis noted, at least "for a season."

As expected, Roosevelt's uncompromising enforcement policy drew forth violent resentment. "I have never been engaged in a more savage fight," Roosevelt told Lodge. Vitriolic telegrams flooded his office: "You are the biggest fool that ever lived"; "What an ass you have made of yourself"; "You have wrecked the Republican Party." Reports surfaced that a box containing dynamite had been sent to the commissioner's office. Though it proved a hoax, "the next bomb," warned the *World*, "will be deposited in the ballot-box in November and be loaded with popular indignation at his uncalled-for, unjust, discriminating, oppressive and superlatively foolish execution of the Sunday excise law." Rumors circulated that both the Republican bosses and Mayor Strong were dissatisfied with the new commissioner. "Roosevelt is like a boy with his first pair of skates," one prominent Republican boss lamented, "and the Republican Party is sure to be held responsible for what he does."

"This was a fight after Roosevelt's own heart," remarked Joseph Bishop. When he received a mocking invitation to what promised to be a massive parade protesting his policy, the commissioner astounded the organizers by accepting. Along the parade route more than 150,000 cheering people were gathered, standing "in windows, on steps and poles and wagons, and even lampposts. . . . There were gilded floats, decorated and peopled in a manner most pleasing to the eye," reported the *World*, "and long lines of men in shining uniforms and all the glitter and splendor of mounted paraders." As more than 30,000 marchers paraded along Lexington Avenue, there was Roosevelt, the signal object of derision, smiling and waving for hours from the reviewing stand.

The commissioner "laughed louder than any one else" as the scathing banners and placards came into view: "Send the Police Czar to Russia"; "Rooseveltism is a farce and a humbug." Sighting one banner emblazoned with the words: "Roosevelt's Razzle Dazzle Reform Racket," he asked the bearer if he could keep the banner as a souvenir. "Certainly," replied the man. "That is the best yet," Roosevelt chuckled, pointing to a wagon entitled "The Millionaire's Club." The float sported three gentlemen in frock coats and tall hats, with one bearing "a striking resemblance to Theodore Roosevelt." The trio sipped champagne at a "private club," while at the rear of the wagon a mock arrest of a beer-drinking laborer was staged. "That is really a good stroke," Roosevelt burst forth with admiration.

Even the New York *World*, which had been "shrieking with rage" against Roosevelt, conceded that the crowd was delighted by his appearance: "It looked almost as if the whole affair were in his honor, and the long lines to whom he bowed, took off their hats in salute." All along the way, marchers shouted, "Bully for Teddy!" and "Teddy, you're a man!" His ability to turn the tables, to relish his protracted self-mockery in public, was compressed into the headline of a Chicago newspaper: "Cheered by Those Who Came to Jeer."

Good feelings soon faded, however, when Roosevelt announced that, despite his thorough enjoyment of the festivities, "a hundred parades . . . would not make me change the position I have taken." As the November 1895 elections approached, Roosevelt feared that his unpopular stance on the Sunday closing law might usher in a revival of Tammany. The Republican bosses "are on the verge of open war with me," Roosevelt told Lodge, adding that Mayor Strong "has actually been endeavoring to make me let up on the saloon, and impliedly threatened to try to turn me out if I refused! It is needless to say that I told him I would not let up one particle; and would not resign either." The city elections confirmed Roosevelt's worst misgivings. The Tammany slate routed the Republican slate, and the Republican bosses placed the blame squarely on Roosevelt's uncompromising policy. Rumblings from the state legislature in Albany suggested machinations afoot to sweep him out of his job.

Open dissension in the bipartisan police board multiplied Roosevelt's woes. "Thinks he's the whole board," grumbled Democrat Andrew Parker. "He talks, talks, talks, all the time," Parker complained to the *Evening Post*'s Joseph Bishop: "Scarcely a day passes that there is not something from him in the papers about what he is doing . . . and the public is getting tired of it. It injures our work." In defense of his friend, Bishop replied, "Stop Roosevelt talking? Why you would kill him. He has to talk. The peculiarity about him is that he has what is essentially a boy's mind. . . . I don't know as he will ever outgrow it. But with it he has great qualities . . . inflexible honesty, absolute fearlessness and devotion to good government." Parker "said nothing further," Bishop recalled, "and we parted rather coldly." Parker's hostility toward Roosevelt eventually congealed into hatred, and the structure of the bipartisan board allowed him to paralyze Roosevelt's further ambitions for reform. Not surprisingly, the newspapers delighted in the running feud, likening the battle between Roosevelt and Parker to "armed combat."

During these trying days, Roosevelt's growing family provided indispensable respite. "His wife and children gave him," one friend observed, "a kind of spiritual bath that sent him back to the city refreshed and ready for what might come." Roosevelt spent two or three nights in town at Bamie's pied-à-terre on Madison Avenue, but during the rest of the week he commuted by bicycle and train from the loving home Edith had created at Sagamore Hill. Their five children, now ranging in age from eleven to two, inhabited a world far removed from the intrigue and animosity of his public career. "Their gay doings, their odd sayings," one family friend, Hermann Hagedorn, remarked, "cleansed him of the smoke and the grime of the battle."

When forty-year-old Bamie stunned the family by announcing her engagement and marriage to naval officer William S. Cowles, Theodore and Edith rented her Madison Avenue apartment for the winter months. While Edith preferred the domestic seclusion of Sagamore Hill, city life allowed her to provide the children with wider social and cultural opportunities, including lessons at Mr. Dodsworth's, the dance school she had adored as a young girl.

Despite the restorative presence of his family, Roosevelt seemed "overstrained & overwrought" to Lodge, who confided in Bamie that Theodore's "wonderful spring and interest in all sorts of things is much lowered. He is not depressed but he is fearfully overworked & insists on writing history & doing all sorts of things he has no need to do. He has that morbid idée fixe that he cannot leave his work for a moment else the world should stop."

The 1896 presidential contest between McKinley and Bryan provided a welcome outlet, allowing Roosevelt to leave behind his multitude of problems in the city, traveling through the state and country to stump for the Republican nominee. While he had passionately hoped that his friend Speaker Tom Reed would be the candidate, he campaigned vigorously for the Republican ticket. He retained serious reservations about McKinley, whom he considered to have "a chocolate éclair backbone," but convinced himself that the Republican fight against the Democrats was crucial for the soul of America. If victory came to Bryan and the mob of populists and socialists "who want to strike down the well-to-do, and who have been inflamed against the rich," the United States would face "years of social misery, not markedly different from that of any South American Republic."

Beyond his overwrought dread of a Democratic triumph, Roosevelt also determined that lending his energetic voice to McKinley's campaign represented his best hope for regaining the confidence of the Republican bosses. He spoke before huge audiences everywhere he went. "The halls were jammed," he reported to Bamie, "people standing in masses in the aisles." His adventures in New York, captured in stories, headlines, and cartoons across the nation, had made him a compelling, national figure. Roosevelt capitalized on this interest and his efforts did not go unrecognized. "He gave all of his time, all of his energy, and all of his towering ability to the work of the campaign," recalled Republican National Committee member Albert B. Cummins.

McKinley's victory resulted in Roosevelt's appointment as assistant secretary of the Navy, providing a graceful exit from his mounting troubles as police commissioner. His departure left both Riis and Steffens downcast. Indeed, Jacob Riis considered the two years he spent with Roosevelt on Mulberry Street "the happiest by far" of his entire career. "Then was life really worth living," he recalled, confessing that once Roosevelt departed, he "had no heart in it." Beyond his personal despondency, Steffens for his part feared that "reform was beaten." And in short order, "Tammany did come back."

Still, the impact of Roosevelt's vigorous tenure would not be forgotten. "The end of the reign of Mr. Roosevelt is not the end of Rooseveltism," Steffens wrote in the *Evening Post*, predicting that his impress would exert "an active influence in the force for a generation at least, till the youngest 'reform cop' is retired." Even after Roosevelt became a national hero during the Spanish-American War and was elected governor of New York, Steffens deemed his controversial reign as police commissioner "the proudest single achievement of his life," insisting that no other challenge "called for so much courage, energy, labor or brain and will power." Steffens would also leave Mulberry Street in short order to serve as editor of New York's oldest newspaper, the *Commercial Advertiser*, yet the relationship established with Roosevelt would flourish in the years ahead.

Just as Roosevelt's three years in the New York Assembly had taught him to work with colleagues far removed from his cloistered patrician background, so his two years as police commissioner in New York City had deepened and broadened his outlook on social and economic issues. Jacob Riis had introduced him to the realities of immigrant life in the slums, though Roosevelt found it hard to relinquish his conception of the poor as people who had "failed in life." He had walked through ill-ventilated, dilapidated tenements where wealthy landlords used every legal device to evade regulation and responsibility. Observing this widespread failure to rectify conditions, Roosevelt recalled, "I became more set than ever in my distrust of those men, whether business men or lawyers, judges, legislators, or executive officers, who seek to make of the Constitution a fetish for the prevention of the work of social reform."

The mentoring of Riis and Steffens and the intimate exposure to the hardships confronting the city's poor had begun to work a marked change in Roosevelt, loosening the "steel chain" of conservative opposition to government intervention in the economic and social processes that had been his birthright.

The frenetic pace and stress of Roosevelt's years as New York police commissioner stand in perfect counterpoint to William Howard Taft's ruminative, congenial eight-year-tenure on the circuit court. Two decades later, Nellie would reflect that Taft savored his work on the federal bench "more than any he has ever undertaken," more than his years as governor general of the Philippines, secretary of war, or president. "Perhaps it is the comfort and dignity and power without worry I like," Taft told his brother Horace.

Life on the circuit ideally suited a man of Taft's gregarious temperament. Traveling to Cleveland, Toledo, Memphis, Nashville, Detroit, and Louisville, he quickly made friends in every city that comprised the Sixth District. Though he missed Nellie and the children when he was away from Cincinnati, he delighted in the camaraderie of the circuit. His daily letters home describe a continuous round of banquets and receptions hosted by leading members of the bar, as well as invitations to private clubs. "I have been in court every day from nine until five o'clock and I have been out every night to dine and have not tumbled into bed any night before twelve o'clock," he wrote to Nellie from the Russell House in Detroit, concluding, "I have had no trouble with sleeping except for want of time." In Memphis, he described a ball at the Tennessee Club, a meeting of the Shakespearean circle, and a banquet he attended. "The Bar here is said to be the finest in the circuit," he told Nellie. "Certainly it is a most delightful body of men." He was equally enchanted by three evenings at the palatial Lake Shore home of the Cleveland industrialist Mark Hanna. "They have eight bedrooms besides those required for his family," he explained to his wife, "and he gives house parties lasting a week when he has twenty or twenty five guests at a time."

In these most agreeable settings, Taft was totally at ease, sharing stories, drinks, and conversation. While Roosevelt's indomitable, often contentious nature stirred discord with colleagues at both the Civil Service Commission and the police board, Taft enjoyed warm professional relationships from the outset, bonding effortlessly with his fellow circuit justices, William R. Day and Horace H. Lurton, both of whom would eventually sit on the Supreme Court—the former appointed by Roosevelt, the latter by Taft himself.

No one on the circuit was more widely respected or better loved than Taft. "He is absolutely the fairest judge I have ever seen on the bench," a fellow attorney remarked. Countless stories circulated of his kind and even-handed actions in the courtroom. When a prosecuting attorney persistently hectored a witness who had already disclosed his shame of being illiterate, Taft brought a quick end to the attorney's line of questioning: "Stop that!" he admonished. "You have brought out that this man cannot read; that is enough. I will not have you humiliate this witness any further, because it has no relation to the case." In another incident, an inexperienced lawyer had filed a badly drawn petition on behalf of a young girl whose foot had been severed in a railroad accident; Taft edited the document himself, knowing that otherwise the railroad attorney would easily secure a dismissal of the case.

The work itself was intellectually challenging, requiring him to reach decisions and write opinions on far-reaching issues regarding labor strikes, injunctions, workplace injuries, street railways, and monopolies. He was allowed the time necessary to study cases thoroughly, reviewing precedents and refining his positions. Most important, he was able to draft, revise, and edit his decisions "over again and again" until he had honed the language to his satisfaction. His opinions earned the admiration of lawyers across the nation, building a reputation that bolstered his dream of one day sitting on the Supreme Court.

Presiding on the bench through the turbulent 1890s, Taft was called upon to adjudicate a number of highly controversial cases that shadowed the rest of his career. The most noteworthy, *In re Phelan*, had boiled over from the 1894 Pullman strike. While the strike stirred turmoil in Chicago, Frank Phelan, an authorized representative of Eugene Debs, arrived in Cincinnati to organize railway employees in Ohio and Kentucky for a general boycott of all Pullman trains. With the Cincinnati Southern Railroad nearly paralyzed by the boycott, the company's manager successfully petitioned the court for an injunction, enjoining Phelan from inciting workers—who themselves had no grievance against the Pullman Company—to join a strike preventing the flow of interstate traffic. When Phelan defied the injunction and union members continued to stop trains, Taft issued a warrant for his arrest.

Taft told Nellie, who had taken the children to Canada for that summer of 1894, that the case worried him more than any other. Each day, newspapers carried sensationalized accounts of the tumult in Chicago, claiming that mobs were "holding that city by the throat." Like Roosevelt, Taft feared that demagogic leaders had resolved "to provoke a civil war" and that some of the agitators would have to be killed "to make an impression." Dozens of marshals were posted throughout Cincinnati in anticipation of similar violence. When news broke of Phelan's arrest, Taft received death threats. His decision was loudly denounced at raucous meetings held throughout the city, and his courtroom was ominously crowded with strikers. "I hate the publicity that this brings me into," he complained to Nellie, explaining that his days were occupied "trying to say nothing to reporters."

The mayor of Cincinnati and the chief of police tried to persuade Taft to draw out the trial until the tumult and bloodletting in Chicago had subsided, but with Phelan under arrest and his sympathizers packing the court "to suffocation," Taft's sense of duty obliged him to move the case forward. After hearing the arguments on both sides, he spent two long nights writing his opinion, just managing, he told Nellie, to have "the last sentence copied when twelve oclock struck, the time fixed for its announcement." Attired in the silk judicial robe he donned for important occasions, Taft took almost an hour to read out his long opinion.

At the core of his argument lay the same distinction he had drawn in *Moore's & Co. v. Bricklayers' Union* between a legal strike and an illegal secondary boycott. He began by emphasizing that the employees of the railroad "had the right to organize into or to join a labor union which should take joint action as to their terms of employment." With strong language, he clearly delineated the vital role of unions in industrial society: "It is of benefit to them and to the public that laborers should unite in their common interest and for lawful purposes," Taft began, further explaining that "if they stand together, they are often able, all of them, to command better prices for their labor than when dealing singly with rich employers. . . . The accumulation of a fund for the support of those who feel that the wages offered are below market prices is one of the legitimate objects of such an organization." Furthermore, Taft recognized the legitimacy of union leadership and their right to maintain solidarity. He explained that officers of a union might order members "on pain of expulsion from their union, peaceably to leave the employ of their employer because any of the terms of their employment are unsatisfactory."

Had Phelan arrived in Cincinnati to protest a wage cut by the Cincinnati Southern and "urged a peaceable strike," Taft maintained, "the loss to the [railroad] would not be ground for recovering damages, and Phelan would not have been liable to contempt even if the strike much impeded the operation of the road." In this case, however, "the employees of the railway companies had no grievance against their employers." Nor did they have cause to obstruct the Pullman Company, which had nothing to do with their compensation or working conditions. Phelan, therefore, had conspired to bring about an illegal boycott. Taft found him guilty and sentenced him to six months in jail.

Lost in the ensuing uproar, Taft's clear and forceful defense of labor's right to strike was perhaps the most definitive pronouncement on the subject to that date. Nine years later, when the Wabash Railroad issued an injunction against the striking Brotherhood of Railroad Trainmen and Firemen, the labor union relied on Taft's statement on labor rights to dissolve the injunction and win their case.

Yet Taft's failure to explicate his decision more fully to reporters and his refusal to court public opinion left him vulnerable to charges of an anti-union bias. As police commissioner, Theodore Roosevelt had faced similar accusations from labor leaders following repeated arrests of union picketers involved in violent scuffles with employers and scabs. Unlike Taft, however, Roosevelt had responded with aplomb, realizing that such charges must not go unanswered. At the suggestion of Jacob Riis, Roosevelt had invited union leaders to meet at a beer hall and speak to him, not "as Police Commissioner, but just as plain 'me.' " During a three-hour exchange of views, Roosevelt had insisted that no genuine friend of labor could condone violence. When the marathon session came to a close, the union audience "applauded him to the echo."

While Taft lacked Roosevelt's political savvy and press connections, his advocacy for the workingman and desire for an even-handed policy in a rapidly industrializing nation made his nascent progressivism increasingly evident. Following the Phelan controversy, two additional railroad cases demonstrated Taft's support for the cause of labor. The swift expansion of railroads in the last quarter of the nineteenth century had generated a shocking increase in accidents causing death or severe physical harm to industrial workers. Statistics revealed that annually "one railroad worker in every three hundred was killed on the job," while one out of fifty American laborers sustained an injury. In an era when courts consistently favored property rights over individual rights, railroad employees found it nearly impossible to recover damages. Under the doctrine of assumed risk, railroad attorneys successfully argued that employees assumed all risk of injury, even if railroad negligence was involved. In some cases, railroads demanded that employees sign formal contracts releasing the company from liability in the event of injury or death.

In the case of *Voight v. Baltimore*, Taft held the Baltimore Railroad liable for permanent injuries to a worker. Although the man had signed a contract agreeing to hold the railroad harmless, Taft held that this document did not divest the company of responsibility to employees in the case of negligence. The conservative Supreme Court reversed Taft's ruling, citing the sanctity of contract, but he would later be vindicated when in 1908 President Theodore Roosevelt signed a law specifically outlawing such oppressive contracts.

Taft further challenged the doctrine of assumed risk in the *Narramore* case. A recently passed Ohio law required railroads to install safety devices that would protect workers from getting caught in guard rails and frogs—switch mechanisms that allowed a train to cross from one track to another. One brakeman was working on the tracks when his foot became stuck in an unsecured frog. Unable to escape as the train approached, he suffered horrific injuries, including the loss of one leg. The federal district court heard his case, but refused damages on grounds that Narramore had assumed the risk when he continued to work despite his knowledge that the frogs lacked safety devices. Taft reversed the lower court decision, arguing that any safety law would be "a dead letter" if companies were permitted to defend themselves in this way. In the years ahead, injured employees successfully cited Taft's ruling, allowing them to receive damages when the hazards of their employment resulted from a corporation's failure to meet safety regulations.

Of William Taft's hundreds of rulings in the 1890s, the most consequential involved an anti-trust suit against the Addyston Steel and Pipe Company, which had joined with five other cast-iron pipe manufacturers to fix prices under a contract of association. Since the 1890 passage of the Sherman Anti-Trust Act, corporations had openly defied the law's restrictions against combinations in restraint of trade. Anti-trust suits brought in pro-business state courts were invariably lost, and monopolies continued to grow. In the 1895 *Knight* case, the Supreme Court delivered what seemed a death knell to the Sherman Act, refusing to break up a sugar company that controlled 98 percent of the country's sugar refineries.

When Taft received the government's case against the Addyston Company combination on appeal in 1898, it was widely assumed that he would follow the lower court's ruling and dismiss the suit. Instead, he held that the association was indeed an attempted monopoly designed "to give the defendants power to charge unreasonable prices." Taft's order for the association's dissolution made national news, emboldening those who fought to stay the growth of colossal combinations. The *New York Times* headlined the importance of the decision: "Iron Pipe Trust Illegal: The First Case in Which Manufacturing Combination Had Been Found Guilty." Enumerating the facts of the pipe case, the New York *World* suggested that "precisely the same things are true of hundreds of other trusts, and they can be smashed if the people's attorneys and the courts will do their duty." Still, there was little concerted action against monopolies until 1902, when President Roosevelt brought suit against the Northern Securities Company, a giant holding company combining three railroads in an attempt to control rail prices throughout the Northwest. Roosevelt's suit relied, in part, on Taft's opinion in the *Addyston Pipe* case.

These were productive, invigorating years for William Taft, who also agreed to serve as dean of the new Cincinnati Law School, where he was teaching two courses. "The deanship is going to involve considerable work," he told Nellie, "but I think I can systematize it." He was elected president of the Cincinnati Civil Service Reform Association and was overjoyed to be made a trustee of Yale College, where he regularly presided over reunions with his fellow Bonesmen. Indeed, the only drawback of his burgeoning reputation was the increasing number of invitations to deliver speeches at banquets and meetings.

"I wish I could make a good speech," he confided to Nellie before a banquet in Memphis, "but I fear it must be desultory and haphazard." Another disappointing performance in Grand Rapids, he confessed with chagrin, had left "a bad taste in my mouth but I am used to that." Nellie tried to buoy his confidence, reminding him that whenever he spent time in preparation, he invariably found "something to say that is worthwhile." When he agreed to address the annual meeting of the American Bar Association in Detroit at the end of August 1895, he promised Nellie that he would work on the speech for an hour every day and would submit drafts to her throughout the summer. "I shall use you as my merciless but loving critic," he assured her. Still, when he saw "the prominent names" of the other speakers, including Supreme Court justice David Brewer and Harvard professor James Thayer, it made him "tremble lest I shall make a fizzle of mine."

That same summer, Horace spent a month with his brother at Murray Bay in Canada, where Will and Nellie had expanded a small cottage into "a happy summer home." The little resort village of Murray Bay, situated on the St. Lawrence River one hundred miles north of Quebec, had become a gathering place for the entire Taft clan. In the early days, Charles Taft recalled, the "whole cargo of Tafts," twenty-one in all, shared a six-room house, with thin partitions dividing the rooms. Eventually each of the brothers had purchased or rented cottages of their own, all within easy walking distance of one another, the golf course, the tennis courts, the river, the hills, and the small village.

Horace recalled that although Taft's weight had ballooned by 1895 to 280 pounds, he maintained a preposterous schedule with unflagging vitality: "He played eighteen holes on a very hilly golf course in the morning, came home, ate his lunch, read his mail, and then went down to a tennis court, where he played a rather elephantine game," after which he went rowing on the river until it was time for a picnic supper. One night, Horace found Howard Hollister, Will's old friend, stretched out on the sofa. Asked about plans for the next day, Hollister laughingly replied, "The Lord knows. I doubt whether I shall live till tomorrow. I have been following Bill around today." Provided his weight did not become so onerous as to impede his activities, Taft was able to jest about it. Horace remembered sitting with Harry and Will in an overcrowded theatre with narrow seats. "Horace," Will said, "if this theater burns, it has got to burn around me."

During these years, Nellie Taft, originally reluctant to leave Washington, had immersed herself in the civic life of Cincinnati. She instituted a current events salon where she and her friends studied the administration's Hawaiian policy and the Chinese exclusion question, reading congressional debates and legal briefs. She attended the theatre regularly, took music lessons, and published an essay on Schumann. She also resumed her leadership role in promoting access to early education for the city's children, an advocacy that resulted in the kindergarten movement.

Despite her eclectic pastimes, Nellie found time to undertake the enormous project of founding the Cincinnati Symphony Orchestra, which gave its first concert series in 1895, with nationally recognized Frank Van der Stucken conducting. Previous orchestral associations had failed, but with the permanent dedication of a new Music Hall, Nellie was determined to create a symphony orchestra to rival those in Boston and New York. As president of the Orchestral Association, she raised funds, organized committees to sell subscriptions and advertising space, and negotiated contracts for the conductor and musicians, working with their labor union to protect local musicians against foreign imports. She even managed to persuade the major railroads to offer reduced rates for out-of-town passengers attending concert performances and inaugurated a series of free summer concerts.

Taft was immensely proud of Nellie's work with the orchestra. He kept up with every detail, encouraging her through difficult days and exulting at her great success. "My love for you, Dear, grows each year," he remarked. "This is not the enthusiasm of the wedding journey but it is the truth deliberately arrived at after full opportunity for me to know." He ardently defended Nellie when her mother charged that she fancied herself "the new woman," citing her unseemly public pursuits and the fact that she had borne but two children (though a third, named after Taft's brother Charley, would be born in 1897). Yet, in some ways, Nellie Taft did represent the new woman. She continued to frequent German beer halls, enjoyed smoking, played cards for money, followed the Cincinnati Reds baseball team, and was among the first in her hometown to wear a short skirt. "It is so delightful that I shall live in it," she told Will. "It makes me feel very young and frisky to be so unencumbered." Her manner may have seemed unorthodox to some, but the mutual affection and admiration she shared with her husband allowed her to pursue diverse interests even as she raised healthy, intelligent, confident children.

During his fruitful years on the bench, Taft's friendship with Roosevelt continued to grow. While still civil service commissioner, Roosevelt visited Cincinnati to deliver a lecture and attend a dinner at the St. Nicholas Hotel in honor of their mutual friend Bellamy Storer. During his stay, Roosevelt collaborated with Taft to create the Civil Service Reform Club in Cincinnati, to which Taft was elected president. In the years that followed, Taft worked hard to nominate and elect candidates committed to reform. The two men also met in Washington and New York for lunches, dinners, and long conversations about advancing their reform cause. On one trip to New York, Taft was disappointed when a previous engagement prevented him from dining with Roosevelt. "I should have much preferred to go to the R's," he wrote to Nellie, "because I wanted to have a full political talk with R."

The vision of reform shared by Roosevelt and Taft was still far removed from the Populists' call for fundamental economic change. Yet their experiences as police commissioner and circuit judge had awakened both to the harsh circumstances confronting the nation's working poor and sensitized them to the avarice and power of industrial interests. As social and economic issues increasingly consumed each man's attention, both were beginning to question the laissez-faire doctrine that had guided them since their days in college.

Neither Roosevelt nor Taft could have anticipated that an insurgent rebellion against Spanish rule on the small island of Cuba would soon redirect their energies, and alter both their destinies.

THE POST OF ASSISTANT SECRETARY of the Navy proved difficult to secure for Theodore Roosevelt. Taft and Lodge lobbied intensely for his appointment and were joined in their campaign by Maria Storer, a prominent Washington socialite whose husband, Bellamy, had contributed $10,000 to a private fund so that McKinley could retire his debts. The new president was hesitant to appoint the young New Yorker. "I want peace," he told Maria Storer, "and I am told that your friend Theodore—whom I know only slightly—is always getting into rows with everybody. I am afraid he is too pugnacious." When Taft pressed Theodore's case, McKinley remained unconvinced. "The truth is, Will, Roosevelt is always in such a state of mind," he replied. Roosevelt's friends refused to give up. "Judge Taft, one of the best fellows going, plunged in last week," Lodge reported to Roosevelt. He enlisted the help of both John Addison Porter, his fellow Bonesman at Yale, who would soon become the president's secretary, and Myron T. Herrick, one of the president-elect's closest Ohio friends. "Give him a chance to prove that he can be peaceful," Maria Storer begged. McKinley finally relented, though Taft later speculated that "more than once, when [Roosevelt] was joining with those who demanded war with Spain and almost attacking the Administration for not declaring it, I think McKinley wished he had been anywhere else than where he was."

Even before assuming his post in the Navy Department, Roosevelt had insisted that he "would rather welcome a foreign war." He feared that Americans had lost their "soldierly virtues" in the race for material gain and were becoming "slothful, timid," and sedentary. "The victories of peace are great; but the victories of war are greater," he maintained. "No merchant, no banker, no railroad magnate, no inventor of improved industrial processes, can do for any nation what can be done for it by its great fighting men." While McKinley, who had "seen the dead piled up" at Antietam, prayed for peace, Roosevelt, who had never seen combat, absurdly romanticized war. "Every man who has in him any real power of joy in battle," he blithely wrote, "knows that he feels it when the wolf begins to rise in his heart; he does not shrink from blood and sweat, or deem that they mar the fight; he revels in them, in the toil, the pain and the danger, as but setting off the triumph." No sooner had Roosevelt settled into his office in the Navy Department than he "became convinced" that war with Spain over Cuba was imminent.

For more than two years, Cuban freedom fighters had engaged in a guerrilla war against their Spanish occupiers. Spanish authorities had retaliated by imposing martial law throughout the island, incarcerating nearly a third of the Cuban population in unsanitary concentration camps without sufficient food, water, or medical treatment. Led by William Randolph Hearst and Joseph Pulitzer, yellow journals carried daily, often exaggerated reports of Spanish treachery that aroused humanitarian outrage. These concerns combined with economic interests in the island to fuel jingoist sentiment in favor of intervention. In November 1897, Roosevelt confided to a friend that he recommended going to war with Spain "on the ground of both humanity and self-interest," also citing "the benefit done to our people by giving them something to think of which isn't material gain."

Working under the elderly Navy secretary, John Davis Long, Roosevelt did everything in his power to prepare the U.S. Navy for war. During the long summer months when his boss vacationed in New England, Roosevelt exercised a "free hand" to purchase guns, ammunition, and supplies. He generated war plans, scheduled additional gunnery drills, stocked distant supply stations with coal, consulted Captain Alfred Mahan about the need for new battleships, and succeeded in having Admiral George Dewey placed in command of the Asiatic Fleet. "I am having immense fun running the Navy," he boasted to Bellamy Storer.

Henry Pringle notes that "it is not easy to draw a line between Roosevelt's anxiety to build up the navy, which was legitimate preparedness, and his lust for war." In a comical stream of letters, Roosevelt repeatedly urged Secretary Long to prolong his vacation. "There isn't the slightest necessity of your returning," he told Long on June 22, 1897. "Nothing of importance has arisen." More obviously solicitous a fortnight later, he wrote again: "You must be tired, and you ought to have an entire rest." Three weeks later, he recommended that Long "stay there just exactly as long as you want to. There isn't any reason you should be here before the 1st of October." If Long had any thought of ending his vacation, Roosevelt reminded him that he was fortunate to avoid Washington and the hottest summer in memory.

In January 1898, McKinley agreed to station the battleship USS *Maine* in Havana Harbor as "an act of friendly courtesy" to the Cuban people. Steadfastly, however, he continued to resist mounting pressure for intervention. Then, on February 15, the *Maine* exploded, killing 262 Americans. Though the cause of the explosion was never determined with certainty, Roosevelt immediately labeled the sinking "an act of dirty treachery on the part of the Spaniards," declaring that as prelude to war, he "would give anything if President McKinley would order the fleet to Havana tomorrow."

THE VERY MORNING AFTER THE explosion of the *Maine* in Havana Harbor, Ida Tarbell was scheduled to meet with Army chief General Nelson Miles, the subject of a planned *McClure's* article. Upon hearing the news, she assumed her appointment would be canceled. "It seemed as if the very air of Washington stood still," she recalled. But when she arrived at his office, she was surprised to find that "the routine went on as usual." She would long admire "the steadiness of General Miles" during those troublesome hours, as orderlies periodically interrupted their interview to deliver updated casualty reports.

In the weeks that followed, Tarbell "vacillated between hope that the President would succeed in preventing a war and fear that the savage cries coming from the Hill would be too much for him." While Roosevelt derided McKinley's insistence upon a thorough investigation, Ida respected the president's "suspension of judgment" until it could be determined if the blast was an accident or sabotage. Her esteem for McKinley's restraint was matched by her disgust at Roosevelt's "excited goings-on," which she witnessed during her frequent appointments with General Miles—the departments of War, Navy, and State then being housed together in the Old Executive Office Building. While others worked with steadfast composure to address the crisis, Roosevelt "tore up and down the wide marble halls," she contemptuously recalled, "like a boy on roller skates." War had not yet been declared, yet "already he saw himself an important unit in an invading army."

Though Tarbell was later drawn to the compelling energy of Roosevelt's "amazing" personality, her initial assessment of his unseemly, overwrought avidity for war was wholly accurate. "I am more grieved and indignant than I can say at there being any delay on our part in a matter like this," he told his brother-in-law, William Sheffield Cowles. "A great crisis is upon us, and if we do not rise level to it, we shall have spotted the pages of our history with a dark blot of shame." He had no patience with President McKinley, whose "weakness and vacillation" he considered "even more ludicrous than painful." He summarily rejected all who argued against intervention, dismissing any possibility of legitimate objection. "The only effective forces against the war are the forces inspired by greed and fear," he categorically proclaimed, "and the forces that tell in favor of war are the belief in national honor and common humanity."

As Tarbell feared, the "warlike element" on the Hill, the yellow press, and an aroused public sentiment exerted a combined pressure that proved "too much" for McKinley to resist: "He steadily grew paler and thinner, and his eyes seemed more deep-set than ever," she noted. On April 11, 1898, he finally summoned Congress to authorize armed intervention in Cuba. Two weeks later, the United States formally declared war against Spain. Later that same day, Secretary Long cabled Admiral Dewey to "proceed at once to Philippine Islands," using "utmost endeavor" to attack the Spanish fleet.

That Dewey was equipped to win the famous Battle of Manila Bay was largely due to Roosevelt's exertions months earlier. As acting secretary, he had ordered the squadron to Hong Kong at the beginning of the year. "Keep full of coal," Roosevelt had cabled Dewey when Long was out of the office: "In the event of declaration of war Spain, your duty will be to see that the Spanish squadron does not leave the Asiatic coast." Indeed, Taft later asserted, "if it had not been for Theodore Roosevelt, we would never have been in a position to declare war, for it was he and only he who got from Congress sufficient ammunition to back any bluff we might make with actual play."

The war marked a turning point in the lives of Roosevelt and Taft, and signaled a transformation in the nature of *McClure's* magazine. "In all its earlier years," Tarbell explained, the publication had sought "to be a wholesome, enlivening, informing companion for readers." It strove to provide "an eager welcome" to newly discovered fiction writers and poets, introducing recent inventions in science, while illuminating "the best of the old" in its extended series on Napoleon, Lincoln, and the Civil War. In the spring of 1898, however, McClure jettisoned plans for the June issue to create a special war edition, which, in the months ahead, led to "a continuous flow of war articles." Tarbell was assigned to cover McKinley's White House, Baker to analyze how the press reported the war, and White to gauge the heartland's response to the president's call for 125,000 volunteers. Stephen Crane and Frank Norris were recruited as correspondents from the warfront. "The editors of *McClure's* Magazine, in common with thousands of other American citizens, have to face new conditions and new interests," McClure told his readers. "We hope to obtain a record that will have absorbing human and dramatic interest," he explained, "and one that will prove to be of permanent historical value."

The shift from historical research to current affairs had a profound effect upon Ida Tarbell. She had contemplated returning to Paris after completing her Lincoln series, but realized, she later wrote, that she "could not run away to a foreign land" and become "a mere spectator." Her new assignment allowed an intimate perspective on the hard choices confronting McKinley: "I was learning something of what responsibility means for a man charged with public service," she recalled, "of the clash of personalities, of ambitions, judgments, ideals. And it was not long before I was saying to myself, as I had not for years, You are a part of this democratic system they are trying to make work. Is it not your business to use your profession to serve it?" While others inflamed public sentiment with sensational reports, Tarbell relied upon documentary evidence and dozens of interviews with cabinet officers, White House staff members, congressmen, and senators; using these sources Tarbell analyzed the pressures brought to bear upon McKinley in those two months between the destruction of the *Maine* and his decision to intervene. She revealed a president who struggled gallantly for a peaceful resolution until he was finally overwhelmed by the popular call for war. Her absorbing portrait of the political and psychological strains on a president in wartime created an enduring new model of political journalism.

McClure's also afforded Ray Baker the opportunity for a novel investigation of the newspaper industry itself—a definitive analysis of the unprecedented torrent of news generated by the Cuban conflict. This extensive war coverage, which vastly increased newspaper circulation, was considered "a triumph of the new journalism." College-educated reporters and writers with literary ambitions vied to be dispatched as correspondents. Newspapers spent anything necessary to scoop their rivals. Baker calculated the daily costs incurred by publications that maintained scores of correspondents in both Cuba and Florida: he added up rental fees for the private vessels carrying messages from Havana to Key West; he discovered covert signals indicating the receipt of important intelligence; he followed waiting cabs from the wharf to offices where the messages were cabled to New York; he computed the expense of every transmitted word. "It is a little short of stupendous, the amounts of money being spent in getting up a newspaper which sells for a penny," he told his father. In fact, Arthur Brisbane, the editor of the *New York Evening Journal*, later remarked that had the war not come to a swift conclusion, his paper and many other major dailies would have collapsed into insolvency.

In "When Johnny Went Marching Out," William Allen White described the nationalistic zeal that swept the country with the declaration of war. "Populists stopped watching the money power, Republicans ceased troubling themselves over repudiation, Democrats forgot the deficit," he observed. The indelible marks of regionalism were all but obliterated as northerners and southerners joined to fight under the same flag. "A simple but great emotion, that of patriotic joy, was stirring the people," White felt, "and they moved as men move under stress of strong passion." Children who once staged skirmishes between cowboys and Indians now waged war against the Spanish, adopting "Remember the Maine!" as their rallying cry. Immense crowds greeted the trains rushing soldiers to the front: "Everywhere it was flags: tattered, smoke-grimed flags in engine cabs; flags in buttonholes; flags on proud poles; flags fluttering everywhere."

While *McClure's* special war issue mirrored popular fascination with the Spanish conflict, a concluding article, "The Cost of War," sounded a compelling cautionary note. The generation who lived through the Civil War, the journalist George Waldron tellingly observed, "have not been the most ardent to join in the clamor for war. They know the havoc it wrought, and are not eager to repeat the experience. The thousands slain in battle, the tens of thousands afflicted with wounds which often resulted in death after days of agony, the losses of relatives and friends, the anxious waiting for news, the want and distress of body and mind following in the train of warfare, all have left impressions so vivid that thirty-three years of peace have not sufficed to wear them away." And beyond the social and emotional toll, Waldron calculated that the financial outlay of the Civil War "would have bought the freedom of every slave, and left enough to pay all the peace expenses of the Federal Government for half a century. The divided nation expended money enough during the struggle to supply every man, woman and child with ample food for the entire four years."

This balance of vivid, responsible war coverage and comprehensive analysis made *McClure's* one of the most respected magazines in the country. With a circulation now approaching 400,000, the pressroom and bindery had to operate "day and night" to meet increased demand. The advent of the Spanish-American War fueled the magazine's evolution toward a new role, a crucial engagement in American society. "Having tasted blood," Tarbell recalled, "it could no longer be content with being merely attractive, readable. It was a citizen and wanted to do a citizen's part."

DURING THE WINTER AND EARLY spring of 1898, as the country moved inexorably toward war, Edith Roosevelt was gravely ill. She had never recovered from the birth of her fifth child, Quentin, the previous fall. "For weeks we could not tell whether she would live or die," Roosevelt told a friend. Finally, in early March, doctors diagnosed a massive abscess in a muscle near the base of her spine. A dangerous operation was performed that would require many weeks of slow recovery. During this same spring, ten-year-old Theodore Roosevelt, Jr., underwent treatment for what appeared to be "kind of a nervous breakdown."

Despite the fragility of his family, Roosevelt later acknowledged, he could not forgo the opportunity to go to Cuba. "You know what my wife and children mean to me," he told Archie Butt, "and yet I made up my mind that I would not allow even a death to stand in my way; that it was my one chance to do something for my country and for my family and my one chance to cut my little notch on the stick that stands as a measuring-rod in every family. I know now that I would have turned from my wife's deathbed to have answered the call."

Roosevelt was offered a position as colonel but wisely requested to serve as a lieutenant colonel under his friend Leonard Wood, an Army surgeon and Medal of Honor recipient. The press found the story of the so-called Rough Riders irresistible from the start—a volunteer regiment in which cowboys, miners, and hunters served on an equal footing with Ivy League graduates, Somerset Club members, polo players, tennis champions, and prominent yachtsmen. And no journalist was better suited to cover Theodore Roosevelt and his colorful regiment than Richard Harding Davis, a war correspondent so legendary "that a war hardly seemed a war if he didn't cover it."

Indeed, at the outset of the war, Richard Harding Davis enjoyed far wider recognition than Theodore Roosevelt himself. The son of the feminist novelist Rebecca Harding Davis, thirty-four-year-old Richard was a man of many talents—an award-winning correspondent, best-selling fiction writer, successful playwright, and editor of *Harper's Weekly*. His handsome face and athletic physique had adorned countless magazine covers as Charles Dana Gibson's ideal exemplar of masculine beauty. "We knew his face as we knew the face of the President of the United States," the novelist Booth Tarkington remarked, "but we infinitely preferred Davis's. . . . Of all the great people of every continent, this was the one we most desired to see."

Roosevelt and Davis first met in New York in 1890. After reading "Gallegher," the short story that made Davis a household name, Roosevelt invited the young author to dinner at his sister's Madison Avenue home. Two years later, they encountered each other at a dinner party hosted by members of the British legation. This time, a caustic interchange was sparked by Roosevelt's recent *Cosmopolitan* essay deriding rich Americans who evinced a "queer, strained humility" toward Englishmen and failed to take pride in their own statesmen, soldiers, and scholars. Rebuked by Davis, who affected an aristocratic British accent and admired British customs, Roosevelt later reported the testy exchange to his friend James Brander Matthews. "He apparently considered it a triumphant answer to my position to inquire if I believed in the American custom of chewing tobacco and spitting all over the floor," Roosevelt noted sarcastically, continuing to insist that "I did; and that in consequence the British Minister, who otherwise liked me, felt very badly about having me at the house, especially because I sat with my legs on the table during dinner."

Any resentment either man might have harbored swiftly dissipated in the first days of the Spanish-American War. No public figure of the time understood better than Roosevelt the importance of cultivating reporters. As with Steffens and Riis, Roosevelt granted Davis unusual access. Writing from the headquarters of the Rough Riders, Davis assured his brother that his situation was "absolutely the very best . . . nothing they have they deny us." Davis realized from the start that the Rough Riders were likely to provide the most picturesque story of the war. "This is the best crowd to be with—they are so well educated and so interesting," he reported to his father. "To-day a sentry on post was reading 'As You Like It,' and whenever I go down the line half the men want to know who won the boat race." Indeed, he concluded, "being with such a fine lot of fellows is a great pleasure."

Roosevelt also forged a relationship with the *New York Journal*'s best known correspondent, Edward Marshall. The two men had met in New York when Roosevelt was police commissioner and Marshall was Sunday editor of the *New York Press*. In 1893, Marshall served as the secretary of the

Tenement House Commission, which brought him into close contact with Roosevelt. Like Davis, Marshall managed to write successful novels, short stories, and plays in his spare time. For a time, he edited the Sunday *World*, but when the war broke out, William Randolph Hearst engaged him as a war correspondent.

Both Davis and Marshall accompanied the Rough Riders during their first engagement at Las Guásimas, a confusing ninety-minute battle conducted in a dense tangle of tall grass and twisted brush. Las Guásimas was situated at the intersection of two trails on the way to Santiago de Cuba, an inland town where the Spaniards were known to be concentrated. As the Rough Riders made their way along the steep trail, they encountered fierce fire from an enemy they could not see. Within minutes, a half-dozen men were killed and nearly three dozen wounded. Marshall recorded a defining moment as Roosevelt "jumped up and down," his "emotions evidently divided between joy and a tendency to run," as he awaited Wood's order to lead his troops across a cut wire fence and into a thicket on the right.

Marshall's description continues to recount Roosevelt's pivotal transformation from idealistic, romantic warmonger to composed, levelheaded soldier: "Ushering a dozen men before him, Roosevelt stepped across the wire himself, and from that instant, became the most magnificent soldier I have ever seen. It was as if that barbed-wire strand had formed a dividing line in his life, and that when he stepped across it he left behind him . . . all those unadmirable and conspicuous traits which have so often caused him to be justly criticized in civic life, and found on the other side of it, in that Cuban thicket, the coolness, the calm judgment, the towering heroism, which made him, perhaps, the most admired and best beloved of all Americans in Cuba."

Before long, a bullet tore through Marshall's spine. "He was suffering the most terrible agonies," Davis recalled, yet he "was so much a soldier to duty that he continued writing his account of the fight until the fight was ended." Doctors doubted Marshall would live. He suffered permanent paralysis and the amputation of one leg but survived to write the regimental history of the Rough Riders and to be presented with a medal for valor by Theodore Roosevelt. Davis, too, was honored with a medal for bravery under fire. In the midst of the ambush, the intrepid reporter had picked up a carbine and begun firing at the Spaniards. "If the men had been regulars I would have sat in the rear," Davis explained to his family, "but I knew every other one of them, had played football, and all that sort of thing, with them, so I thought as an American I ought to help." When the Spanish finally retreated, Roosevelt promised to make Davis a captain in his unit, informing the Associated Press that "no officer in his regiment . . . had 'been of more help or shown more courage' " than Richard Harding Davis.

The Las Guásimas skirmish prepared Roosevelt for the decisive battle of the conflict the following week. Large Spanish forces were massed along the ridgeline of two large hills. The Rough Riders were ordered to march on Kettle Hill, while the regulars attacked San Juan Hill. With Roosevelt in the colonel's customary position at the back of the column, the troops advanced slowly under a hail of bullets. Mounted on horseback, Roosevelt suddenly charged toward the front, rallying his men and propelling them onward. When he reached the head of the regiment, he was a short distance from the Spanish rifles. "No one who saw Roosevelt take that ride expected he would finish it alive," Davis reported. "As the only mounted man, he was the most conspicuous object in the range of the rifle-pits. . . . It looked like foolhardiness, but, as a matter of fact, he set the pace with his horse and inspired his men."

Watching Roosevelt "charging the rifle-pits at a gallop and quite alone," Davis marveled, "made you feel that you would like to cheer. He wore on his sombrero a blue polka-dot handkerchief . . . which, as he advanced, floated out straight behind his head, like a guidon." Roosevelt's dauntless leadership, and the unit's remarkable esprit de corps, galvanized the men to storm the hill with near-reckless abandon. The Spaniards were forced to retreat.

Jacob Riis was at his Long Island home when the morning paper blared the Rough Riders' triumph. For days, he and his wife had rushed to get the paper, eager to confirm that their friend Roosevelt was alive and well. At last, on the Fourth of July, the anxiously awaited report arrived, detailing the successful charge under a hail of Spanish fire. "Up, up they went in the face of death," the story read, "men dropping from the ranks at every step. The Rough Riders acted like veterans. It was an inspiring sight and an awful one. . . . Roosevelt sat erect on his horse, holding his sword and shouting for his men to follow him" until they gained the summit at last.

"In how many American homes was that splendid story read that morning with a thrill never quite to be got over," mused Riis. Taking their cue from Davis's account, the newspapers portrayed a battle in which Roosevelt "had single-handedly crushed the foe." He quickly found himself the most popular man in the nation. The war burnished Davis's reputation as well; critics reckoned his writings among the very best of the war. "Except for Roosevelt," Davis's biographer Arthur Lubow observes, "no one had a better war." The Spanish surrendered thirteen days later. By the middle of August, four months after the war began, Roosevelt and his Rough Riders were on their way to a triumphal homecoming.

Jacob Riis was with Edith Roosevelt in Montauk, Long Island, when the ship bearing the Rough Riders came into shore. Although Edith had fully recovered from her operation, she had lived in constant anxiety, steeling herself against possible loss. "These dreadful days must be lived," she told Corinne in June, "and whatever comes Theodore and I have had more happiness in eleven years than most people in long lives." She understood that she must show strength "for the sake of the children," resolutely assuring her husband, "I do not want you to miss me or think of me for it is all in a day's work." Never again, after her unfortunate efforts to dissuade him from an 1894 mayoral run, would Edith interfere in her husband's career decisions. Only with his safe return could she acknowledge the terror she had suffered.

As the bedraggled troops marched down the pier—some limping, others on stretchers, a number stricken with yellow fever—reporters noted that Roosevelt "looked the picture of health," the only man disembarking who "gave no evidence of having passed through the tortures of the Cuban campaign." He "bubbled over with spirits," the *World* observed. Asked how he felt, Roosevelt responded with characteristic verve: "I'm in a disgracefully healthy condition. I feel ashamed of myself when I look at the poor fellows I brought with me." He momentarily fell silent, then added: "I've had a bully time and a bully fight. I feel as big and strong as a bull moose. I wish you all could have been with us."

S. S. McClure, who had identified Roosevelt as a man to watch more than a year before the battle at San Juan heights, was now especially eager to pursue an extended biographical piece on the returning hero. The first editor to commission an in-depth profile, McClure chose Ray Baker for the task.

Like Ida Tarbell, Baker had felt misgivings about the war, initially remaining hopeful that "the sober judgment" of the people would prevail over the yellow journals "to keep the nation from any bloodshed." Before long he found himself swept up in the adventure of the war. "War excitement here runs a great deal higher than it does at any other place I've seen," he reported to his father from New York. "Bulletins are displayed all over the city and the street before them is always filled with jostling crowds." He clearly recollected "the thrill" when he was asked to write a series of war articles, including the character sketch of Theodore Roosevelt.

Baker had met Roosevelt briefly twice before, at the Hamilton Club in Chicago and again at Roosevelt's Mulberry Street office in New York. "It was the personality of the man that chiefly attracted me," he recalled. Never before had he encountered such vitality or such inimitable "concentration of purpose." Entering Roosevelt's large office in the police department as a previous visitor departed, Baker noted with astonishment that "in the few seconds that I took to reach his desk," Roosevelt had picked up a book about the culture of Sioux Indian tribes and appeared totally engrossed in the work. "It is surprising," Roosevelt explained, "how much reading a man can do in time usually wasted."

Researching the Roosevelt piece, Baker spent substantial time with his subject. Roosevelt invited him to the "roomy, comfortable house" at Sagamore Hill, where the host's "prowess as a hunter" was abundantly evident "in the skins of bears and bison, and the splendid antlers of elk and deer." More impressive to a man of Baker's scholarly and artistic bent, the library was "rich" with works of history and literature, and the wide front veranda afforded "a view unsurpassed anywhere on Long Island Sound." The two men spoke at length about Roosevelt's childhood, his days in the legislature, his experiences in the Wild West, and the challenges he faced in the Civil Service Commission and police department. Roosevelt expressed his growing disgust for the predatory rich, "the mere money-getting American, insensible to every duty, regardless of every principle, bent only on amassing a fortune."

From Oyster Bay, Baker journeyed with Roosevelt to Camp Wikoff in Montauk, where the Rough Riders were still in quarantine to prevent a further outbreak of yellow fever. "I talked with a number of officers and troopers in Mr. Roosevelt's regiment," Baker wrote, "and I found their admiration for their colonel to be boundless. 'Why, he knows every man in the regiment by name,' said one. 'He spent $5,000 of his own money at Santiago to give us better food and medicine.' "

The finished article profiled "a magnificent example of the American citizen of social position, means, and culture devoting himself to public affairs." In every phase of Roosevelt's life, Baker detected a "rugged, old-fashioned sense of duty," the legacy of a civic-minded father who "had great strength and nobility of character, combined with a certain easy joyousness of disposition." In Roosevelt, Baker discerned a "rare power of personal attraction," a man possessed of "immense vitality and nervously active strength." Writing to his father as he completed the piece, the journalist predicted that Roosevelt could well be "president of the United States within ten years."

"I want to thank you for the article in 'McClure's,' " Roosevelt wrote Baker. "It has pleased me more than any other sketch of my life that has been written, and especially because of the way in which you speak of my father." In the years ahead, the friendship between the politician and reporter would have significant consequences for progressive policy. "I was to write about him many times afterward," Baker later reflected, "not always so uncritically." Nevertheless, Roosevelt generally took the reporter's criticisms in good stride. Personal loyalty was "one of his finest characteristics," Baker observed. "Once a friend with him, always a friend, and a warm friend, too."

In the months that followed, Baker was commissioned to write on a staggering array of subjects. McClure had an intuitive feel for "what was really interesting to people," Baker recalled. And nothing fascinated the reading public more at the end of the nineteenth century than the spectacular "outpouring of marvelous new inventions and scientific wonders"—the automobile, the incandescent lightbulb, the moving picture, the radio, the phonograph. His peregrinations even took Baker on a voyage to the bottom of the sea, in the most amazing invention "since the days of Jonah"—a submarine boat. He visited automobile manufacturers to assess two competing vehicles: the electric car and the gasoline-powered car. The electric vehicle, Baker concluded, was much quieter, "simpler in construction and more easily managed." Acknowledging that it "could run only a limited distance without recharging," he envisioned a string of festive roadhouses where car owners could relax as their batteries charged.

McClure's uncanny sense for "the new," Baker believed, bordered on genius. No sooner had he got wind of an Italian inventor experimenting with wireless telegraphy than he dispatched Baker to Signal Hill, Newfoundland. There, Baker was among the first to witness Guglielmo Marconi's historic reception of signals from across the Atlantic. Straightaway, Baker produced "the first fully verified account of the new invention and its revolutionary possibilities." Informed that the world's largest steamship was under construction by the Hamburg-American line, McClure sent Baker to Germany. There he remained for six months and completed twelve additional articles, including a long interview with the illustrious German biologist Ernst Haeckel, who was "one of the few thinkers of Europe who supported the theories set forth in 'that extravagant book,' the *Origin of Species*."

Yet, although Baker continued to invest great effort in crafting thorough and polished articles, he was becoming unraveled and despondent. "My life was being ordered," he felt, "not by myself, but by other people; not for my purposes, but for theirs." His reputation was steadily growing, but the focus that gave meaning and clarity to his work had begun to elude him. "I have been spreading too much, trying to do the impossible," he explained. "It seemed to me that I was no longer doing anything of any account. I was not more than half alive." Broken in health and profoundly depressed, Baker decided to resign from *McClure's* and move with his family to the countryside.

There, he hoped to commence work on a serious novel that would tackle the struggle between capital and labor, an issue of vital interest since his first days as a reporter.

Baker's colleagues at *McClure's* fought hard to prevent his departure. Ida Tarbell repeatedly reminded him of McClure's "affectionate interest" and warm feelings. "I cannot think for a moment of your severing your connection with our house," John Phillips told him. "I believe that you can do better than you have ever done and I believe that we can help you to that end." McClure raised his salary by a large margin, made the increase retroactive, and proposed that he take a long break with his wife and young family at the magazine's expense. He encouraged Baker to recover himself fully, urging, "Do only what you yourself want to do, get well physically, and we'll talk it over when you get back." The generosity "quite bowled me over," Baker wrote. "What good friends they were."

Intent on getting "as far away as possible from New York," Baker withdrew to the Santa Catalina Mountains in Arizona. "At first," he recalled, "the desert wastes, the great bare mountains, the wild and rocky arroyos seemed forbidding and even hostile." In time the rugged beauty of the desert exerted a restorative power. Riding for hours in the warm winter sun "across bare ridges and open spaces," Baker enjoyed a "sense of freedom" unknown since his childhood. He delighted in the sight of jackrabbits bounding before him, small desert creatures darting into their holes, birds sheltering under the cacti. For the first few weeks, he deliberately refrained from writing, opting for more physical pursuits. "I rode or tramped to weariness every day. I ate prodigiously. I slept soundly."

As his mind cleared and his strength returned, Baker tried to make sense of his breakdown. "I began again to write in my neglected notebooks, trying to understand what all the things I saw and thought and felt might really mean," he recorded. There could be no return, he realized, to the pioneer days of his youth. The frontier had vanished in a teeming urban landscape marked by a fierce battle for survival, voracious competition, and a hurried pace of life. "This being true, what am I to do about it?" he mused. "What is my function as a writer in a crowded world," he wondered, endeavoring to reconcile his artistic inclinations with popular demands—"that is, a writer not wishing merely to amuse people, but in the practice of his art, to make them see and think."

Reviewing his own inclinations and abilities, Baker determined that he was "not a leader, not an organizer, not a preacher, not a businessman," and probably not a novelist. "*I was a reporter*," he reflected. "I had certain definite gifts for seeing, hearing, understanding, and of reporting afterward what I had seen and heard and, so far as might be, what I understood." This realization hastened his return to *McClure's*, where he focused his journalistic skills on the economic issues that interested him most intensely, employing his gifts "to help people understand more clearly and completely" how they might "live together peaceably." True to his ambition, in the years that followed, Ray Baker would produce a series of landmark articles on labor and capital that would play a pivotal role in shaping public sentiment toward the development of a progressive public policy.

LINCOLN STEFFENS, WHO HAD NOT yet left the *Commercial Advertiser* for *McClure's*, joined the throng of friends and reporters at Montauk to greet Roosevelt upon his return from Cuba. They buttonholed Roosevelt, Steffens reported, and "one by one they whispered to him: 'You are the next Governor of New York.' " Drawing Steffens aside, Roosevelt sought his gauge of the situation. "Should I run?" Aware that the Colonel was debating aloud rather than posing a question, Steffens nevertheless offered a resounding "yes" and, furthermore, predicted victory.

Political conditions in New York were not so simple, as Roosevelt well understood. Without the support of Senator Thomas Collier Platt, head of the state Republican machine, he would never secure the Republican nomination. Although Platt detested reformers like Roosevelt, the powerful old boss was in a bind. The party's image was seriously damaged in the aftermath of an exposé of corruption in the current Republican administration in Albany. The hero of San Juan was perhaps the antidote, the sole candidate who could save the party from defeat in the fall.

Steffens and his reformer friends in the Citizens' Union and the Good Government Clubs believed Roosevelt could outwit the Republican machine by running as an independent. Two leading reformers made the pilgrimage to Montauk to offer Roosevelt the independent nomination. "Take an independent nomination, and the machine will have to support you," they maintained. "You are of us, you belong to us. If you don't, you are a ruined man." With the machine weakened, reformers believed that this was the moment to crush Platt. "He's down now," they crowed. "One more blow will end him." Steffens himself had long since forsworn allegiance to either party, convinced both were irredeemably dishonest. "I am not a Republican," he told his father. "I am also not a Democrat. I am a mugwump or independent." He believed that the independent vote represented the best hope for dismantling the system of governmental corruption, perpetuated by machine control of both the

Democratic and Republican parties. If Roosevelt won as an independent, his victory would fundamentally alter the political culture of New York.

Roosevelt disputed Steffens's analysis. Even in the unlikely event of victory without the organization's endorsement, he would still have to work with the legislature in order to accomplish anything, and the legislature was absolutely controlled by the machine. "I'm a practical man," he insisted. If the Republican nomination were offered to him, he confided to Steffens, he would happily accept and work to reconcile disillusioned independents with the Republican Party, proving that "good public service was good practical politics." His goal was "to strengthen the party by bettering it," to build a decent progressive record for the good of both the state and the Republican Party.

Never content until he had exhausted every angle of a matter, Steffens pressed Roosevelt for further elaboration. Would he approach Platt or wait for the boss to make an overture? "What's the difference?" Roosevelt countered: "Can you see how it matters whether I call on Platt or Platt calls on me? I can't." He had small patience for points of etiquette: "I have to see the leaders. I want to, anyway. . . . I mean to go as far as I can with them. Of course I may have to break away and fight, and in that case I will fight hard, as they know." To the question of whether he would initiate a meeting with Platt, Roosevelt replied confidently. "Yes I'll see him now," he told Steffens, "and I'll see him after election; I'll see him when I'm governor."

Accordingly, on September 17, 1898, four days after the Rough Riders were mustered out of service, Roosevelt went to meet with Platt at the Fifth Avenue Hotel. Emerging from their session, Platt announced that he would support Roosevelt for the nomination. Later the same day, a machine spokesman declared that "Roosevelt most positively will not accept the independent nomination" for governor. "Oh, what a howl there was then!" Steffens recalled. Reformers felt betrayed, certain that a deal had been struck, that in return for Platt's endorsement, Roosevelt had agreed to reject the independent nomination. Rumors surfaced that the Colonel had bowed before the boss. One newspaper suggested that he had "received with becoming meekness the collar that marks him serf and regular, and that all talk of a people's candidate is rubbish." Democrats leaped at the opportunity: "Rough Rider Roosevelt made a charge up the backstairs of the Fifth Avenue Hotel," the Democratic paper jeered, adding that on this occasion, unlike his famous charge up San Juan Hill, "he was taken prisoner."

Platt relished being portrayed as "the master mind playing with the simple foolish soldier, who could lead a regiment into the jaws of death, but could not alone stand up against a domineering politician." Asked what had transpired in the meeting, the old boss cryptically remarked that "the conversation was interesting and satisfactory." Realizing that these "damning words" would convince independents that a sordid deal had indeed been struck, Roosevelt invited Steffens to his sister Corinne's Madison Avenue house for a confidential conversation. "He was pacing, like a fighting man, up and down the dining room," Steffens recalled. "His pride up, his jaw out, and his fist clenched," Roosevelt insisted that no deals had been made, no concessions exacted outside a reasonable promise to consult regularly with the organization and consider their views concerning decisions and appointments. Repeatedly, he emphasized that not "one iota of his independence" had been yielded.

The following day, *Commercial Advertiser* readers perused "an inspired account" of the secret meeting with Platt. Steffens revealed that "no one asked or even suggested to the Rough Rider" that he reject the independent nomination, a decision which was the Colonel's alone. Upon shaking hands with Platt, Steffens reported, Roosevelt made his position clear. "Before you say anything, Mr. Platt," he declared, "let me say this: that if I accept the nomination of the Republican organization I will stand with the ticket. Any support that is not for the rest of the ticket I will not seek, and an independent nomination of myself without my colleagues I will refuse. Now I am ready to listen." Roosevelt had concluded, Steffens explained, "that he would be unable to accomplish as much as he would wish unless he had a majority of the legislature. To insure that, he must do all in his power to discourage separate tickets that would divide the Republican vote for legislators."

While Steffens's account of the meeting satisfied some independent reformers, many who would naturally have been Roosevelt's allies sulked on the sidelines and refused to help in the canvass. Grudgingly admitting that they would probably have to vote for him against Augustus Van Wyck, the Democratic candidate chosen by Tammany Hall boss Richard Croker, they remained disaffected. "It is hard," they complained, "and we cannot advise others to follow our example."

Encumbered by such grumbling, doubt, and rancor, the campaign got off to a cold start. "It looked as though defeat were ahead of Mr. Roosevelt," Steffens reported, "and he was bitterly disappointed." Unwilling to accept failure without putting forth his utmost effort, Roosevelt demanded a statewide push. Machine leaders, who customarily controlled the entire campaign, initially resisted his requests; candidates rarely took the stump on their own behalf. Amid troubling reports of widespread apathy in the final weeks, however, the bosses realized that "the Rough Rider personally would have to win it, for he alone would be able to warm the rank and file to enthusiasm. So Mr. Roosevelt was allowed to go his way."

"He stumped the State up and down and across and zigzag," Steffens wrote, "speaking by day from the end of his special train and at night at mass meetings, in the towns and cities." Immense crowds greeted his train at every station along the way. "The fire and school bells rang," the *New York Times* reported, "and the children were dismissed from the schools so that they could see the hero of San Juan. Cannon fired and a band played, while the people cheered." Some spectators were disappointed, puzzled by their first impression of the Colonel. Newspaper accounts of his startling exploits in Cuba had led them to imagine a colossus, "seventeen feet high and his teeth a foot long." Nevertheless, his old friend William O' Neil reflected, when Roosevelt began to speak, his "presence was everything. It was electrical, magnetic." Before he was done, listeners discovered "that indefinable 'something' which led men to follow him up the bullet-swept hill of San Juan."

Jacob Riis joined Roosevelt as the train sped home from the western part of the state during the final night of the canvass. Over a belated midnight supper, they debated the "probable size" of the impending triumph or defeat. Riis predicted a Roosevelt victory margin of more than 100,000 votes. Roosevelt was less sanguine, believing that if he won, it would be by a mere "ten or fifteen thousand votes." While they sat together at the table, a knock was heard on the door, "and in came the engineer, wiping his oily hands in his blouse, to shake hands and wish him luck." Roosevelt rose, grabbing the engineer's hands with eagerness. "I would rather have you come here," he assured the man, "than have ten committees of distinguished citizens bring pledges of support." Roosevelt, Riis noted with admiration, was "genuinely fond of railroad men, of skilled mechanics of any kind, but especially of the men who harness the iron steed and drive it with a steady eye and hand through the dangers of the night." The engineer's enthusiasm seemed to Riis "an omen of victory."

When the votes were tallied the following day, Roosevelt's forecast proved more accurate than Riis's projection of sweeping victory. He had been elected governor by a relatively narrow margin of fewer than 18,000 votes.

As Steffens contemplated Roosevelt's successful campaign, he recalled the yardstick set forth by his reform-minded political science professor at Berkeley. "Young gentlemen," he had told the class, "you can get the measure of your country by watching how far Theodore Roosevelt goes in his public career." An honest man trying to work in a dishonest system, Roosevelt would never survive the machine politicians, the professor mournfully predicted.

CHAPTER NINE

Governor and Governor General

Governor Roosevelt at work in Albany, New York, ca. 1900;
Governor General Taft at his desk in Manila, ca. 1901.

A FOOT OF SNOW COVERED THE streets of Albany on January 2, 1899, the day Roosevelt was inaugurated as governor of New York. The thermometer registered several degrees below zero, but the bright sun and jingling sleigh bells lent a jubilant air to the thousands gathered at the statehouse. "There never was such a mass of people out to see a Governor installed," the New York *World* reported. In the assembly chamber where the ceremony would take place, "the desks and seats of the members had been removed, and in their places were hundreds of camp chairs for the accommodation of the audience."

"A deafening outburst of applause" greeted Roosevelt as he reached the flag-draped platform. He "stood for a moment in stern-faced dignity," one journalist observed, "but the cheers continued, and then, like a sunburst the familiar Roosevelt smile broke forth." His gaze was drawn to the Ladies' Gallery where Edith and his six children stood, the boys desperately flapping both hands to attract his notice. When he threw his family a kiss, the "touch of human nature" spurred another round of thunderous applause.

Roosevelt's brief inaugural address sketched out the creed he would follow as governor. "He is a party man," a *New York Tribune* editorial remarked, one who "intends to work with his party and be loyal to it in all things that belong to it." Nevertheless, he made it clear that he would "never render to party what belongs to the State, and the State is the first consideration." Addressing fellow reformers who demanded renunciation of Boss Platt and the machine, Roosevelt emphasized that nothing would be accomplished "if we do not work through practical methods and with a readiness to face life as it is, and not as we think it ought to be." Yet Mr. Platt would have to accept that "in the long run he serves his party best who helps to make it instantly responsive to every need of the people."

"It was a solemn & impressive ceremony," Edith told her sister Emily, confessing, "I could not look at Theodore or even listen closely or I should have broken down." That afternoon, she stood by her husband's side to greet more than 5,000 guests attending the festive reception in the executive mansion. But as soon as her public duties were fulfilled, she escaped to her room, where she could quietly read, write letters, and keep her diary. For this inordinately private woman, who seemed "physically to cringe" in the glare of "the public searchlight," the prospect of life in Albany was intimidating. Reporters had already intrusively chronicled every aspect of the "general exodus" that carried "Mrs. Roosevelt, Miss Roosevelt, and the five little Roosevelts, the governesses, the nurses, the maid and the coachman, the mongrel but gentlemanly dog Susan, a new French Bulldog El Carney, the war horse Texas, and the other horses and the pony, as well as the guinea pigs" from Oyster Bay to the governor's three-story mansion. Fanny Smith, who visited her old friend soon after her arrival, noted that Edith, "usually an extremely calm and self-controlled person," paced "nervously up and down the room."

Faced with the imposing task of transforming the cavernous governor's mansion into a comfortable family home, Edith was understandably anxious. After securing the admittance of twelve-year-old Theodore Junior and ten-year-old Kermit to a local boys' academy, she established a schoolroom in the basement for the younger children, Ethel and Archie. A nursery was created for little Quentin, a governess hired for fifteen-year-old Alice, and a third-floor billiard room remodeled to become the gymnasium. A competent staff orchestrated drawing-room receptions, musical entertainments, and large dinner parties, but Edith remained ill at ease on such elaborate occasions. She much preferred the sort of dinner parties and literary discussions she had once enjoyed with her intimate Washington circle. "If only I could wake up in your library," she told Henry Cabot Lodge, "how happy I would be." Edith soon began to adjust to her new role, however, just as she had settled into her new home. "Edith will never enjoy anywhere socially as much as she enjoyed Washington, nor make friends whom she cares for as much as she did for you and a few others," Roosevelt confided to Maria Storer, "but she enjoys the position here greatly and has made some very good friends and is altogether having an excellent time. She is picking up in health and is looking very pretty."

In February, a candid photograph of Edith appeared in newspapers. The image reveals a slender woman of medium height, dressed in plain but "perfect taste." Although she had steadfastly refused interviews and declined to furnish a photograph for publication, reporters considered her neither "haughty, nor excessively modest." She simply disliked personal publicity and proved as intractable as her husband once "her mind is made up." Despite her habitual reticence, she never made reporters feel unwelcome in her home. Her family life was just not an appropriate subject for their stories. "Everything about her speaks of grace," an Iowa journalist remarked. "There's honor even among reporters, or at least there's gratitude," another explained. "We knew Mrs. Roosevelt's wish to keep herself and the children out of the papers, and after her courtesy to us we were glad to respect that wish."

Yet she was always prepared to entertain reporters and friends with humorous stories about the new governor. In a special scrapbook, she meticulously assembled every caricature relating to her husband, whether they "represented him as riding a hobby-horse or dispensing peanuts in paper bags from a corner stand." While other wives were known to burn papers and magazines that burlesqued their husbands, Edith had perfect confidence in Theodore's good humor and relished the laughter they shared over the cartoons.

NEWSPAPER READERS SOON LEARNED THAT Theodore Roosevelt was unlike any governor New York had known. He arrived in his office long before the usual hour of nine o'clock to begin the baffling task of sorting through his mail. Three or four hundred letters arrived each morning, a far larger volume than any previous governor had contended with. At 10 a.m., his official day commenced, with an hour reserved for assemblymen and senators, followed by rapid-fire meetings with political delegations, members of his administration, and individual petitioners. Roosevelt was "ever on his feet" during these sessions, ranging restlessly as he talked, laughed, or scowled. He punctuated sentences with his fists, "filling the entire room with his presence." The stately desk, where his staid predecessors had "judicially" received visitors, might as well have been removed, one observer noted, for "it hardly knows the Governor."

Despite Roosevelt's often combustible and seemingly impulsive nature, he maintained a schedule so precise that he could reliably meet an individual slated for 12:20 to 12:25 and conclude business just in time to usher in his 12:25 appointment. Visitors were encouraged to "plunge at once" into their subject, for the governor deftly yet positively closed the interview after the allotted time. Roosevelt's official day ended at 5 p.m., though he frequently remained in his office until seven o'clock. Once the governor departed the capitol for the short walk to the executive mansion, he was "not to be disturbed" unless by an emergency. "These evening hours," wrote a correspondent who profiled the governor, "are set apart for his literary work, his reading and social converse with his family, the Roosevelt youngsters having a decided claim, even in the midst of the most pressing affairs of the State."

Honoring his promise to regularly consult organization leaders, Roosevelt soon announced that he would visit New York City every weekend during the legislative session to meet with Boss Platt and Benjamin Odell, chairman of the Republican State Committee, an announcement that incensed staunch reformers. The New York *Evening Post*, an influential independent paper which had supported Roosevelt's bitter fight against Tammany Hall as police commissioner, now decried his willingness to "touch Platt both politically and socially." Never had a governor "so belittled the dignity of the office," opined the *Albany Argus*: "Imagine for a moment William Seward, Samuel Tilden or Grover Cleveland running down to New York, like a capitol district messenger boy, to bring back the orders of some party boss."

While Roosevelt absorbed attacks from Democratic papers with equanimity, he could barely contain his fury at "the irrational independents and the malignant make-believe independents" who remained aloof, never engaging genuine political issues for fear of sullying themselves. These "solemn reformers of the tom-fool variety," Roosevelt complained, stridently assumed that any contact with the bosses indicated some "sinister" collusion. "I have met many politicians whom I distrust and dislike," he told a friend, "yet there are none whom I regard as morally worse than the editors of the *Post*." His indignation was aggravated by a conviction that the *Post*'s denunciation might cause some of his friends, the sincere reformers as opposed to the lunatic fringe, to misconstrue his actions.

Once again Roosevelt reached out to Steffens, proffering what the reporter termed "an understanding." Steffens would meet the governor each Friday afternoon when he arrived in Manhattan for his weekly consultation with the bosses, keeping "in close touch with him all the time he was there," and escorting him to the train station for his return to Albany on Sunday evening. "I was to know all the political acts he was contemplating, with his reasons for them," Steffens recounted. By sharing the full context of each decision and appointment before it became public, Roosevelt trusted that Steffens would credit and document the complex, pragmatic maneuvering behind an ethical and effective approach to leadership. Roosevelt's trust was well placed. Steffens kept the governor's confidences until he determined a course of action, providing an authoritative account of the decision-making process for the *Commercial Advertiser.* "T.R. was a very practical politician," Steffens recalled, "and it was partly from watching him sympathetically that I lost some of my contempt for politicians and practical men generally."

Steffens was not the sole journalist to whom Roosevelt granted such inside access. The governor understood that however courteously he might handle Platt and the organization, he would inevitably clash with them on a range of salient issues. When the battles began, he would need the persuasive power of the press to marshal public sentiment for his reformist agenda. Only by "appealing directly to the people," by "going over the heads" of party leaders, did he have any chance of pushing significant reform through the legislature.

To that end, Roosevelt soon declared that he would hold two press conferences each day he was in town. His unprecedented announcement thrilled the twenty-five statehouse correspondents, who quickly labeled the morning session "the séance" and the afternoon session "the pink tea." The governor generally opened these informal conferences "with a smile and nearly always with a joke, generally at his own expense." In the course of fifteen minutes, one reporter marveled, he would explain his objectives and the rationale behind them. He outlined his "future movements" and intentions regarding various controversial issues, clearly indicating which statements were on the record and which were simply shared confidences, not meant for publication. These lively forums impressed the journalists with "the wonderful mental activity of the man." With his "marvelous fund of general information to draw upon," Roosevelt never haltingly answered or appeared at a loss.

One of Roosevelt's first acts as governor was to convene a meeting with Jacob Riis and three leading trade unionists to determine the most constructive labor legislation to sponsor. The labor leaders agreed that while some new laws were in order, workers would most benefit from the application of laws that already had been enacted to cover maximum hours of work, sweatshop conditions, prevailing wages, and safety requirements. In too many instances, such laws had been put on the books simply to satisfy public demand; as soon as publicity and interest faded, they became dead letters, and companies did as they pleased.

To dramatize these flagrant violations, Roosevelt requested that Riis accompany him one day on a series of surprise visits to tenement sweatshops, ostensibly under the supervision of state inspectors. "I think that perhaps if I looked through the sweatshops myself," Roosevelt told Riis, "we might be in a condition to put things on a new basis, just as they were put on a new basis in the police department after you and I began our midnight tours."

Riis never forgot the appalling conditions they unearthed during their inspection tour. "It was on one of the hottest days of early summer," he recalled. "I had picked twenty five-story tenements, and we went through them from cellar to roof, examining every room and the people we found there." In building after building, the minimum requirements for licensing home work—"no bed in the room where the work was done, no outsider employed, no contagious disease, and only one family living in the rooms"—were found wanting or neglected entirely. As soon as the tour concluded, Roosevelt proceeded to the factory inspector's office. "I do not think you quite understand what I mean by enforcing a law," he admonished, insisting that inspectors "make owners of the tenements understand that old, badly built, uncleanly houses shall not be used for manufacturing in any shape." Day's end found Riis spent but Roosevelt percolating with new ideas and eager for extended discussion over a good meal. Immediately, he would increase the number of tenement inspectors, and when the legislature convened the following winter, he would successfully introduce a bill to revise the code of tenement house laws.

Years later, Roosevelt recalled his labor record as governor with satisfaction. Although his effort to pass an employers' liability act failed, he did manage to obtain "the grudging and querulous assent" of the bosses for legislation establishing an eight-hour day for state employees, limiting the maximum hours women and children could work in private industry, improving working conditions for children, hiring more factory inspectors, and mandating air brakes on freight trains. At a time when laissez-faire attitudes reigned, even such limited measures represented considerable progress.

Roosevelt also took pride in a remarkably innovative conservation record. Within weeks of taking office, he invited an old friend, the architect Grant La Farge, along with the head of the U.S. Forestry Division, Gifford Pinchot, to spend the night at the governor's mansion. Pinchot, like Roosevelt, had been born into a moneyed New York mercantile family but had chosen to dedicate his life to public service. A devoted naturalist and wilderness enthusiast, he had studied forestry conservation in France after graduating from Phillips Exeter Academy and Yale College. The tall, confident thirty-three-year-old brought great originality and ambition to his position when McKinley appointed him to head the Forestry Division.

Pinchot's visit with Roosevelt was unforgettable from the outset: "We arrived just as the Executive Mansion was under ferocious attack from a band of invisible Indians," he wrote in his autobiography, "and the Governor of the Empire State was helping a household of children to escape by lowering them out of a second-story window on a rope." After rescuing his young pioneers, Roosevelt settled down to a long evening of food, drink, and conversation, punctuated by a spirited boxing match in which Pinchot "had the honor of knocking the future President of the United States off his very solid pins," though the governor emerged victorious from the wrestling contest that concluded their visit. The alliance established that night would play a central role in future conservation policy.

In the months that followed, Roosevelt convinced the state legislature to preserve tens of thousands of forested acres in the Catskills and the Adirondacks. He appointed a single superintendent to replace the five-man Fisheries, Game and Forest Commission, which had become a haven for machine spoilsmen. He created the Palisades Park and used his bully pulpit to promote awareness of the state's unique natural resources and the pressing need to conserve them. Roosevelt's second annual message, the historian Douglas Brinkley argues, "was the most important speech about conservation ever delivered by a serious American politician up to that time." Pinchot committed whole passages to memory "as if it were the Gettysburg Address," while ornithologists considered its call for the protection of endangered birds "the tipping point for the Audubon Movement."

"I need hardly say how heartily I sympathize with the purposes of the Audubon Society," Roosevelt maintained, expressing his profound emotional investment in the matter. "When the bluebirds were so nearly destroyed by the severe winter a few seasons ago, the loss was like the loss of an old friend, or at least like the burning down of a familiar and dearly loved house. . . . When I hear of the destruction of a species I feel just as if all the works of some great writer had perished; as if we had lost all instead of only part of Polybius or Livy." This lifelong sympathy proved instrumental in preserving natural lands and wildlife habitat in his state and would become a driving force to protect the entire nation's wilderness.

THE GOVERNOR WAS INITIALLY SURPRISED that on many issues, even those involving labor and conservation, he "got on fairly well with the machine." Indeed, his endeavors to placate Platt through weekly pilgrimages to the city seemed so successful that he was unprepared for "the storm of protest" when he came out in favor of a new franchise tax on corporations. Until this moment, Roosevelt acknowledged, he had "only imperfectly understood" the intricate web linking the Platt machine to the corporate world. Unlike other political bosses, Senator Platt "did not use his political position to advance his private fortunes." He lived simply and had few interests beyond the powerful network he had meticulously constructed and nurtured over the decades. To keep control of the political organization he required regular revenue from the corporate world "in the guise of contributions for campaign purposes" and donations for "the good of the party." These sums were distributed to his select candidates for the state legislature with the "gentlemen's understanding" that they could be counted upon for important votes, particularly when an issue touched upon the corporations that fueled the machine. The public had small awareness and less understanding of this threat that Roosevelt labeled the "invisible empire."

For decades, the state of New York had granted exclusive franchises to corporations to operate immensely lucrative electric street railways, telephone networks, and telegraph lines. These franchises, often secured by outright bribery, had been awarded with no attempt to obtain tax revenues from the corporations in return. After investigating the issue, Roosevelt concluded "that it was a matter of plain decency" for these corporations to pay their share of taxes for privileges worth tens or even hundreds of millions. In fact, a bill to tax such franchises had previously been introduced by John Ford, a Democratic state senator from New York City. The measure "had been suffered to slumber undisturbed" in the machine-dominated assembly until the governor's surprise announcement brought the issue "into sudden prominence."

At their next breakfast meeting, Platt furiously warned Roosevelt that the Ford bill would never be permitted to pass. If he persisted in pushing it forward, the governor risked an open break with the machine. This "radical legislation," Platt argued, had no serious public support "until you sprang forward as its champion." In its stead, Platt suggested that a joint legislative committee "consider the whole question of taxation," with the obligation to report back the following year. Realizing that the tax bill had dim prospects for success without Platt's support, Roosevelt agreed to postpone consideration until the commission issued its report. Reformers recognized the commission as a cynical effort to kill the bill and roundly derided the governor for bending to the subterfuge of the machine. "The time to tax franchises is now, not next year," goaded the *Tribune*. "Roosevelt Stops Franchise Tax," the *Herald* blared.

Stung by the swarm of criticism from reformers, Roosevelt altered his approach, explaining to reporters that despite his reservations about the Ford bill, he would like to see it become law. Well aware of the blackmailing power Tammany Hall would gain, he was particularly concerned by the provision allowing cities to determine tax assessments instead of the state. Nevertheless, a flawed bill was better than none, and Roosevelt concluded that if he "could get a show in the Legislature the bill would pass, because the people had become interested and the representatives would scarcely dare to vote the wrong way." Through a complicated series of maneuvers, the bill was finally brought to a vote in both chambers just before the legislative session ended. While many Republicans in the lower chamber heeded Platt's directive to vote against the measure, Roosevelt secured enough Republican support that, combined with a heavy Democratic vote, he was able to produce a majority.

"It was said to-day," Steffens declared in the *Commercial Advertiser*, "that many of the men who supported the measure have been threatened with political destruction by the party leaders for their action in the matter. These men may rest assured," Steffens knowingly asserted, "that they will have the sympathy and support of the governor for their courage in openly declaring themselves. He appreciates courage."

Asked how the tax would affect his company, the counsel for one affected corporation was blunt: "Right in the solar plexus," he replied. In the days that followed, the stock market suffered a significant drop. "You will make the mistake of your life if you allow that bill to become a law," Platt warned Roosevelt at the close of a bitter letter. He promised the governor that an ugly confrontation was imminent unless Roosevelt summoned that "very rare and difficult quality of moral courage not to sign" the bill after endeavoring to pass it. "When the subject of your nomination was under consideration, there was one matter that gave me real anxiety," Platt noted. "I had heard from a good many sources that you were a little loose on the relations of capital and labor, on trusts and combinations, and indeed, on those numerous questions which have arisen in politics affecting the security of earnings and the right of a man to run his own business in his own way, with due respect of course to the Ten Commandments and the Penal Code. Or, to get at it even more clearly, I understood from a number of business men, and among them many of your own personal friends, that you entertained various altruistic ideas." In Platt's lexicon, Roosevelt clearly understood, *altruistic* meant "Communistic or Socialistic." The governor, Platt acknowledged, had lately adjourned a legislative session that "created a good opinion throughout the State." Then, "at the last minute and to my very great surprise, you did a thing which has caused the business community of New York to wonder how far the notions of Populism, as laid down in Kansas and Nebraska, have taken hold upon the Republican party of the State of New York."

"I do not believe that it is wise or safe for us as a party to take refuge in mere negation and to say that there are no evils to be corrected," Roosevelt countered. "It seems to me that our attitude should be one of correcting the evils and thereby showing that, whereas the populists, socialists and others really do not correct the evils at all, or else only do so at the expense of producing others in aggravated form, that we Republicans hold the just balance and set our faces as resolutely against improper corporate influence on the one hand as against demagogy and mob rule on the other." Their disagreement on this salient issue troubled him, he confessed to Platt, especially since "you have treated me so well and shown such entire willingness to meet me halfway." Nevertheless, he firmly believed that the Republican Party "should be beaten, and badly beaten, if we took the attitude of saying that corporations should not, when they receive great benefits and make a great deal of money, pay their share of the public burdens."

Corporate representatives descended on Roosevelt, warning that if he signed the bill, "under no circumstances could [he] ever again be nominated for any public office, as no corporation would subscribe to a campaign fund if [he] was on the ticket." Refusing to be bullied, yet well aware that a break with the organization would be fatal, Roosevelt made one concession. Before signing the bill, he told Platt, he would call a special legislative session and try to pass an amendment that would substitute a state board of assessors for local authorities. He also agreed to hold a hearing with corporate representatives and solicit suggestions for additional improvements in the bill. In the event the extra session produced amendments that would weaken the tax, however, he would simply sign the Ford bill in its present form.

"Some of the morning newspapers repeat the expression of astonishment that Governor Roosevelt has consulted the attorneys of corporations," Steffens reported in the *Commercial Advertiser*. "Some yellow minds cannot seem to understand that the governor is willing to fight the corporations to make them do right and yet be ready to negotiate just terms of peace—nay to fight for the corporations against wrong." In fact, when Roosevelt learned that corporations in some communities had already paid local taxes, he agreed to an amendment providing that "any taxes already payable for public rights could be deducted from the franchise valuation."

The passage of this amendment, along with the shift to state assessors, allowed Platt to make the best of a difficult situation when Roosevelt signed the bill. "Persistent efforts have been made by the Democratic newspapers," the boss told reporters, "to have it appear that there are serious divisions in the Republican Party." Such claims he blithely dismissed: "All agreed," he now maintained, "that franchises were a proper and necessary subject of taxation." While the original bill had been "carelessly drawn and thoughtlessly enacted," these "just and reasonable" amendments enabled Platt and his organization to save face and support the bill.

"Passage of the amended franchise tax bill is a distinct personal triumph for Governor Roosevelt," the *Commercial Advertiser* asserted in its lead editorial. "By exercise of tact and by concessions where no sacrifice of principle was involved, the governor achieved his ends. His integrity of motive and his eagerness to prevent party rupture were so apparent that Republican legislators were left no choice but to support him."

In the summer of 1899, following his successful push for the franchise tax, Roosevelt prepared to head west to New Mexico for the first reunion of his beloved Rough Riders. "Would you let me ask a great favor," he wrote William Allen White several weeks before the trip, "and that is that you should try to join me on the train and ride three or four hours with me. There is very much that I have to talk over with you. As you know, you have got the ideas of Americanism after which I am striving."

White and Roosevelt had met two years earlier during the reporter's first journey to the east coast at the invitation of Sam McClure. Before proceeding to New York, White spent a few days in the nation's capital, where he was informed that "a young fellow named Roosevelt" in the Navy Department had read his famous editorial and book of short stories about Kansas and was eager to meet him. White was deeply impressed by his first glimpse of the man who would become a close friend, confidant, and correspondent: "a tallish, yet stockily built man, physically hard and rugged, obviously fighting down the young moon crescent of his vest; quick speaking, forthright, a dynamo of energy, given to gestures and grimaces, letting his voice run its full gamut from base to falsetto." Roosevelt seemed, White's description concluded, "to be dancing in the exuberance of a deep physical joy of life."

"We walked from the Navy Department under the shade of the young trees that lined the streets that Summer day to the Army and Navy Club, had lunch, talked and talked, and still kept talking," White recollected. Roosevelt was just then beginning to comprehend "the yearnings" of America's working poor for social and economic justice, "to see clearly that our problems were no longer problems of production, but problems affecting the distribution of wealth and income." For White, still adhering to conservative predilections, Roosevelt's progressive ideas were a revelation. "He sounded in my heart the first trumpet call of the new time that was to be," White recalled, stressing that such notes represented "youth and the new order" and "the passing of the old into the new." The young journalist was overcome by "the splendor" of Roosevelt's personality. "I had never known such a man as he," White wrote more than a quarter of a century after Roosevelt's death, "and never shall again."

Roosevelt for his part felt an immediate kinship with the ebullient writer. Both men were blessed with confidence and energy, both ready to engage in the political and ideological contests that would define their country. While the rotund White had no interest in the physical challenges and trials that Roosevelt adored, preferring to spend his leisure time reading poetry or playing piano, his nimble, perceptive mind perfectly matched Roosevelt's, and they shared a vigorous style of speaking and writing. Doubtless, Roosevelt also recognized that the celebrated journalist was an influential leader of middle-class opinion. "Between his newspaper editorials, magazine articles and a growing list of books," one historian suggests, "White could claim one of the largest audiences of any writer in America at the turn of the century."

Following their initial encounter, the two men had continued to exchange letters, articles, and books. Roosevelt purchased an out-of-town subscription to the *Emporia Gazette*, and sent his new friend a copy of his recently published work, *American Ideals and Other Essays*. "I read it with feelings of mingled astonishment and trepidation," White recalled, confessing that "it shook my foundations, for it questioned things as they are. It challenged a complacent plutocracy."

By the time Roosevelt's train steamed through Kansas en route to New Mexico that summer of 1899, White was working "with the zeal of a converted disciple" to help his friend become president in 1904—assuming that McKinley would run again in 1900. Paul Morton, vice president of the Santa Fe Railroad, had offered Roosevelt his private car so the governor and his invited guests (including White and H. H. Kohlsaat, publisher of the *Chicago Times-Herald*) could relax and talk. On short notice, White had done his utmost to ensure that reporters and enthusiastic supporters greeted Roosevelt's train at every stop.

In Topeka, 3,000 people gave the New York governor "a rousing reception." At the Newton station, "cannon boomed, whistles were blown and the crowd cheered." In Kansas City, men wore cards in their hatbands promoting Roosevelt in 1904. The largest audience gathered in White's hometown of Emporia. "No public man who has come into Kansas during the last ten years has stirred as much personal enthusiasm as Roosevelt," White's *Emporia Gazette* proclaimed. Roosevelt made a short fighting speech that roused supporters. "Governor Roosevelt may be said to be an Eastern man with a Western temperament," the *Kansas City Star* noted. "His sympathy with the people of the Transmississippi country and the power he has displayed in appealing to their fancy marks him as a person of unusual breadth." Despite a mere forty-eight hours' notice of his arrival, White rhapsodized, Roosevelt "had a larger crowd at the Kansas stations than McKinley had with the state central committee back of him. Reporters with both trains concede this. . . . There is no man in America today whose personality is rooted deeper in the hearts of the people than Theodore Roosevelt."

Kohlsaat, who had never met Roosevelt before, was stunned by the fervor of the crowds. On travels with his close friend McKinley, he had witnessed nothing comparable to the New York governor's reception. The night the train left Emporia, he and Roosevelt stayed up talking until midnight. Roosevelt was curious to learn about Kohlsaat's relationship with McKinley. For seven years, Kohlsaat proudly noted, McKinley did not once give a speech to the nation "without either wiring, telephoning, or writing me, and sending me his speeches to read before delivering them." When Kohlsaat the next day begged pardon for having sounded arrogant, Roosevelt put his mind at ease: "Do you know what I thought after I went to bed?" Roosevelt asked. "I wondered if you would do the same thing for me."

Delighted to find that Roosevelt welcomed his advice, Kohlsaat suggested that he issue a pledge of support for McKinley's renomination. McKinley's friends, he had learned, were irritated by premature talk of the governor's presidential ambitions. Recognizing the value of Kohlsaat's counsel, Roosevelt immediately telegraphed the president, "telling of the sentiment he had found in the West for his renomination," and provided a similar statement to the press for publication. Shortly afterward, Roosevelt received a telegram from President McKinley inviting him to the White House. "Oh mentor!" Roosevelt addressed Kohlsaat. "Was my McKinley interview all right? . . . Didn't we have a good week together?"

Roosevelt wrote a warm letter to White as well, expressing deep gratitude for their trip together. His absolute trust in White allowed him to share his hopes and intentions unguardedly. Even in that summer of 1899, White recalled, "we were planning for 1904." Before they parted, White promised to send Roosevelt a map analyzing the strengths of various factions in each western state, helping to determine which political leaders should be approached—and by whom. Meanwhile, he assured the governor that the trip through Kansas was already "bearing great fruit," as evidenced by laudatory clippings from Kansas newspapers that White enclosed. He recommended that Roosevelt send a personal note to each editor and publisher he met along the way. "All of these men have endorsed you emphatically since your departure, and spoke of you not only as possibility, but as probability for 1904," White assured him, adding that a personal acknowledgment "would convince those men of their wisdom."

Increasingly, White began to identify the trajectory of Roosevelt's success with nothing less than the nation's prospects. "When the war with Spain broke out, I wanted to go the worst kind [of way]," White confided to Roosevelt, "but my wife was sick and I felt that my first duty was to her. Then when your regiment had such remarkable success and when you came home and were made governor and acquitted yourself so admirably, I formed a great desire to help you to be president of the United States. It has seemed to me that if I could perform some service for you that would land you in the presidency, I would perform as great a service for my country as I could perform upon the battlefield."

In the years that followed, the two men exchanged more than three hundred letters. White reacted to Roosevelt's speeches and Roosevelt religiously read White's stories and articles as they appeared. "I think the 'Man on Horseback' almost your strongest bit of work," he wrote, in response to White's tale of an honest man corrupted by wealth as he builds a street railway empire and, in the process, loses his idealistic son. "There is a certain iron grimness about the tragedy with its mixture of the sordid and the sublime that made a very deep impression on me," Roosevelt told his friend. After finishing another of White's stories about a populist senator who hammers away at trusts and money power while building his own fortune through shady deals, Roosevelt penned a 2,000-word reply. "You are among the men whose good opinion I crave and desire to earn by my actions," he frankly avowed. "I rank you with, for instance Judge Taft of Cincinnati and Jim Garfield of Cleveland, and with the men whom I am trying to get around me here, men of high ideals who strive to achieve these ideals in practical ways, men who want to count for decency and not merely to prattle."

ROOSEVELT WAS PARTICULARLY INTRIGUED BY White's views on the problem of the trusts, finding himself "in a great quandary what position to advocate about them." His struggle for the franchise tax had sensitized him to the "growth of popular unrest and popular distrust" over the increasing concentration of power in large corporations. He told Lodge he was "surprised to find" that many workingmen who had supported McKinley and the Republicans in 1896 now insisted that William Jennings Bryan was "the only man who can control the trusts; and that the trusts are crushing the life out of the small men." He feared that so long as Republicans failed to develop a cogent policy regarding trusts, those workers who suffered "a good deal of misery" would gravitate toward "the quack," whose dangerous remedies would undo the benefits of the Industrial Revolution.

In the months that followed, Roosevelt consulted a variety of experts to develop a reasonable proposal for regulating the trusts, which he intended to present in his second annual message to the legislature when it reconvened in January. When a draft of the message was completed, he sent it to his old friend Elihu Root, a successful corporate lawyer who had just joined McKinley's cabinet as war secretary. Root's vehement opposition to the franchise tax measure had strained their friendship for a time, but he was "such a good fellow," Roosevelt told Lodge, "that I was sure it would not last, and now I think every shade of it has vanished." Root read the draft carefully, making a number of changes to tone down the governor's rhetoric and moderate his condemnation of those who amassed their riches "by means which are utterly inconsistent with the highest rules of morality." Roosevelt gratefully accepted most of Root's suggestions. "Oh, Lord! I wish there were more of you," he wrote; "you have the ideas to work out whereas I have to try to work out what I get from you and men like you."

The lengthy message, delivered on January 3, 1900, opened with praise for the legislative achievements in the previous year, taking special note of the passage of the franchise tax law. More remained to be done to address the state's industrial problems. "In our great cities there is plainly in evidence much wealth contrasted with much poverty and some of the wealth has been acquired or is used in a manner for which there is no moral justification," Roosevelt said. Then, taking heed of Root's advice, he carefully qualified this indictment, noting that "wealth which is expended in multiplying and elaborating real comforts, or even in pleasures which produce enjoyment at all proportionate to their cost will never excite serious indignation."

"We do not wish to discourage enterprise," Roosevelt stressed; "we do not desire to destroy corporations; we do desire to put them fully at the service of the State and the people." He acknowledged that anti-trust legislation vengefully designed to punish the mere acquisition of wealth would be destructive but insisted that it would be "worse than idle to deny" the existence of abuses "of a very grave character." Consequently, "we must set about finding out what the real abuses are, with their causes and to what extent remedies can be applied."

"The first essential," Roosevelt maintained, "is knowledge of the facts, publicity." Such exposure would open the trusts to investigation for "misrepresentation or concealment regarding material facts" and reveal a corporation's involvement in "unscrupulous promotion, overcapitalization, unfair competition, resulting in the crushing out of competitors" or the "raising of prices above fair competitive rates." He recognized that "care should be taken not to stifle enterprise or disclose any facts of a business that are essentially private" but insisted on the state's right to protect the public from monopoly and even from the "colossal waste" of resources in "vulgar forms of social advertisement." With the facts in hand, measures—including taxation—could be devised to regulate the trusts. Most immediately, Roosevelt reiterated, "publicity is the one sure and adequate remedy which we can now invoke."

Advocating "the adoption of what is reasonable in the demands of reformers" as "the surest way to prevent the adoption of what is unreasonable," Roosevelt hoped to propel "the party of property" toward a more "enlightened conservatism." The bosses had no interest in Roosevelt's musings about a transformed Republican Party. On the contrary, Tom Platt and Benjamin Odell considered the message, even with Root's modifications, dangerously provocative toward business. Odell warned that Roosevelt's call to increase publicity surrounding corporate activities would spur manufacturers to leave New York State. Tensions with the party bosses escalated further when the governor threw his support behind a bill that would compel corporations to disclose information on "their structure and finance."

To Roosevelt's great disappointment, the public did not rally behind the bill. The danger of the trusts, apparent to farmers and wage earners, had not yet penetrated the consciousness of middle-class America. In three years' time, Ida Tarbell and her fellow muckrakers would reach that important audience through their narrative abilities, putting faces and names to the giant corporations, shining a bright light on the sordid maneuvers that were crushing independent businessmen in one sector after another, dramatizing the danger in a way the voting population could no longer ignore. In 1900, however, the trusts remained amorphous entities, arousing vague apprehension but insufficient outrage to exert pressure on the political machines operating as their protectors. And in the absence of public demand, it was not difficult for Platt to prevent the legislature from acting on Roosevelt's proposal.

DISSENSION BETWEEN PLATT AND ROOSEVELT continued to intensify. The three-year term of the state's superintendent of insurance was coming to a close in February 1900. Lou Payn, the current superintendent, was Platt's "right-hand" man. His reappointment was a foregone conclusion. Reading newspaper reports of Payn's cozy relationships with the very companies he was supposed to oversee, Roosevelt issued an announcement that he would seek a new superintendent. Straightaway, the party countered with a statement that Payn would continue at his post "no matter what the opposition to him may try to do." At a contentious breakfast, Platt "issued an ultimatum" to the governor, warning "that if he chose to fight," he would most certainly lose, for "under the New York constitution the assent of the Senate was necessary not only to appoint a man to office, but to remove him from office." There was no need to remind Roosevelt who controlled the senate. "I persistently refused to lose my temper," he recalled. "I merely explained good-humoredly that I had made up my mind."

Though he steadfastly refused to consider Payn's reappointment, Roosevelt moved to conciliate the organization. At the next breakfast meeting, he gave Platt a list of good machine men and told him to select any name on it. Still, Platt refused to compromise. While independent newspapers endorsed Roosevelt's decision to remove Payn, they criticized his attempt to mollify Platt. "Why does he not fight in the open?" the *Evening Post* queried. "He could openly say that he found a rogue in office whom all the powers of political corruption in both parties were banded together to keep there, and that he, the people's Governor, must appeal to the good citizens to sustain him in his fight against the whole confederate crew. That would be real war, and how the people would volunteer for it! That would be raising a standard to which honest men could repair. But what sort of banner is it on which the chief insignia are muffins and coffee devoured by Roosevelt and Platt, sitting cheek by jowl?"

The impasse persisted until Roosevelt, with the help of a newspaper investigation, uncovered a loan of more than $400,000 that Payn had received from a trust company controlled by an insurance firm under the superintendent's jurisdiction. Unwilling to risk a scandal and extended scrutiny, Platt finally capitulated. He agreed to the nomination of Francis Hendricks, one of the men on Roosevelt's list, whom the governor considered "thoroughly upright and capable."

"I have always been fond of the West African proverb: 'Speak softly and carry a big stick; you will go far,' " Roosevelt exultantly told a friend. "If I had not carried the big stick the organization would not have gotten behind me." At the same time, he pointed out, had he "yelled and blustered," he would not have been able to muster 10 votes in the senate for Hendricks's nomination. Indeed, following the righteous recommendations of the *Evening Post* "would have ensured Payn's retention" and facilitated "a very imposing triumph for rascality."

"The outcome of the Payn contest is a complete vindication of the governor's way of accomplishing results," Steffens's *Commercial Advertiser* declared. "Could the governor have accomplished any more than he has if he had declared open war on the organization?" The *Evening Post* remained dissatisfied. Although Hendricks's appointment promised an "honest administration of the Insurance Department," the *Post* declared, the governor should have selected his own man "without consulting the organization, and he could thus have dealt the Republican machine such a blow as it has never suffered. The moral courage of the Governor at Albany was not equal to the physical courage of the Colonel before Santiago."

Roosevelt's stormy relationship with Senator Platt troubled him far less than the perpetual hail of invective from fellow reformers. "Could they assail such a man more viciously and persistently than they have assailed him?" the *Commercial Advertiser* queried in his defense. "Are they not making it possible for the politicians to say: 'We gave the reformers a governor who secured reforms and who would not do what we wished him to do: they fell upon him because he did not get reforms in *their* way, not because he did not get reforms.' Why not simply choose one of our own machine men from here on in? They surely won't attack him more fiercely than they have Roosevelt."

Even as he excoriated "the dogs of the *Evening Post*" for their attacks, Roosevelt preserved his friendship with the *Post*'s longtime editorial writer, Joseph Bucklin Bishop. "I value you too much to go into recrimination," he wrote to Bishop in the wake of another derogatory *Post* editorial. "Now, I have a proposal to make. Wouldn't you like to come up here and meet some of the 'wild beasts'?" During his weekends in New York, Roosevelt encouraged

Bishop to visit at Bamie's Madison Avenue town house so they could air their disagreements. "I will explain to you the merits of the police bill, if it passes," he suggested, "and you shall explain to me its demerits, if it fails." Their lively correspondence mollified rancor that might have hardened into lasting hostility. After being quoted that he was uncertain which he regarded "with the most unaffected dread—the machine politician or the fool reformer," Roosevelt hastily assured Bishop that he was "emphatically not one of the 'fool reformers.' "

In late 1899, after sixteen years at the *Post*, Bishop made the wrenching decision to leave the newspaper. His standing there had deteriorated after he declined to follow "positive orders to suppress the truth" concerning Roosevelt's accomplishments. "The policy of the *Evening Post*," he was informed, "is to break down Roosevelt." Consequently, Roosevelt was thrilled when Bishop joined Steffens at the *Commercial Advertiser*. "You are about fourteen different kinds of a trump," Roosevelt told him. "I thank Heaven for the Advertiser continually." With both Bishop and Steffens writing for the well-regarded paper, Roosevelt now had two advocates who might promote vital support among the practical reformers.

In the months that followed, the friendship between Bishop and Roosevelt deepened. Roosevelt sought Bishop's advice on speeches, appointments, and legislation. He invited him to stay overnight in the governor's mansion, met with him regularly over meals in Manhattan, and exchanged letters two or three times a week. "Good Lord, what an interesting correspondence we have had at times!" Roosevelt remarked. Their friendship remained strong even when Bishop publicly disagreed with the governor and told his readers why. "I need not tell you that no criticism of yours can alter in the least my affectionate regard for you," Roosevelt assured Bishop. "You have shown yourself a friend indeed, and above all, when you differ I know you differ because you honestly think you must."

Roosevelt's ability to countenance criticism in the interest of friendship also marked his relationship with the humorist Finley Peter Dunne. Dunne's weekly columns in the *Chicago Times-Herald*, featuring his adopted persona, the irreverent Irish bartender Martin Dooley, placed him among the nation's most popular and influential literary figures. Dunne later recalled that his "first acquaintance with Col. Roosevelt grew, strangely enough, out of an article that was by no means friendly to him." In the fall of 1899, a copy of *The Rough Riders*, Roosevelt's wartime memoir, came across Dunne's desk. "Mr. Dooley's" book review in *Harper's Weekly* mocked Roosevelt's propensity for placing himself at the center of all the action: "Tis Th' Biography iv a Hero be Wan who Knows. Tis Th' Darin' Exploits iv a Brave Man be an Actual Eye Witness," Mr. Dooley observes. "If I was him, I'd call th' book, 'Alone in Cubia.' " Three days after this satirical assessment amused readers across the country, Roosevelt wrote to Dunne: "I regret to state that my family and intimate friends are delighted with your review of my book. Now I think you owe me one; and I shall exact that when you next come east you pay me a visit. I have long wanted the chance of making your acquaintance."

"I shall be very happy to call on you the next time I go to New York," Dunne replied. "At the same time the way you took Mr. Dooley is a little discouraging. The number of persons who are worthwhile firing at is so small that as a matter of business I must regret the loss of one of them. Still if in losing a target I have, perhaps, gained a friend I am in after all." The humorist never had to make the choice he feared; he continued to lampoon the nation's premier target without losing Roosevelt's friendship. "I never knew a man with a keener humor or one who could take a joke on himself with better grace," Dunne recalled. For years, Roosevelt told and retold the story of meeting a charming young lady at a reception: "Oh, Governor," she said, "I've read everything you ever wrote." "Really! What book did you like best?" "Why that one, you know, *Alone in Cuba*."

In June 1900, as Roosevelt's first term as governor began to wind down, Lincoln Steffens wrote a lengthy political analysis for *McClure's*. He described Roosevelt's tenure as "an experiment"—a test to determine whether a leader could serve both the party machine and the good of the state, whether he could simultaneously maintain his ideals and get things done. Steffens vividly depicted the fights over the insurance commissioner and the franchise tax, both of which ended in Roosevelt victories. It remained unclear, however, whether the Roosevelt experiment itself would succeed. Despite an ostensible truce between the governor and Boss Platt, wrote Steffens, "the organization doesn't like Mr. Roosevelt as Governor, neither does 'Lou' Payn, neither do the corporations. The corporations cannot come out openly to fight him; they have simply served notice on the organization that if he is renominated they will not contribute to campaign funds."

Publicly to deny the popular governor a second term would cast the organization in a starkly negative light. The "obvious solution," Steffens predicted, "would be to promote" Roosevelt to "the most dignified and harmless position in the gift of his country"—the vice presidency. "Then everybody could say, 'We told you so,' for both the theorists and the politicians have said that it is impossible in practical politics to be honest and successful too." This astute piece, together with several of Steffens's previous articles on Roosevelt, initially attracted Sam McClure's attention. "Your TR article is a jim-dandy," McClure told Steffens, resolving then and there to bring him from the *Commercial Advertiser* to his own publication. "I could read a whole magazine of this kind of material. It is a rattling good article."

Roosevelt first became aware of Platt's unwelcome "solution" in late January 1900, when three high-ranking representatives from the Republican National Committee came to Albany. They cautioned that he "would be tempting Providence to try for two terms" as governor, emphasizing the near certainty that he would "hopelessly" lower his standing "with either the independents or the party men" before a second term was out. Only "great luck," they claimed, had enabled him to get by thus far "without cutting [his] own throat." On the other hand, the vice-presidential nomination was a fait accompli if he decided within the next few weeks. Disconcerted by the drift of the conversation, Roosevelt informed the committeemen that he had absolutely no interest in the position. The vice presidency, he told Platt the next day, is "not an office in which a man who is still vigorous and not past middle life has much chance of doing anything. As you know, I am of an active nature." He had "thoroughly enjoyed being Governor" and strongly desired a second term. "As Governor," Roosevelt added, "I can achieve something, but as Vice-President I should achieve nothing."

Henry Cabot Lodge questioned Roosevelt's rationale, concurring with the committeemen that his friend was "tempting Providence" by remaining in New York. He would be wiser to accept the political haven of the vice presidency, "the true stepping stone . . . either toward the Presidency or the Governor Generalship of the Philippines." Roosevelt conceded that "in New York with the republican party shading on the one hand into corrupt politicians, and on the other hand, into a group of impracticables . . . the task of getting results is one of incredible difficulty, and the danger of being wrecked very great." Nevertheless, this very challenge rendered the work both more important and absorbing. He could not bear to be a mere "figurehead," with no other task than presiding over the Senate.

Moreover, he confided to Lodge, "the money question is a serious one with me." As governor, he made $10,000 a year and was "comparatively well paid, having not only a salary but a house which is practically kept up all winter." Between the remnant of his inheritance and the few expenses in Albany, he had been able to save money for the first time in years. For Edith, perpetually worried about family finances, this stability was a great "comfort," especially since their older children would soon start private school. The vice president's salary was $2,000 less and no house was provided. Furthermore, the Roosevelts would be expected to entertain as lavishly as their predecessors, men frequently selected based on their resources and affinity for the social side of the office. Even if his family lived simply, Roosevelt concluded, the position "would be a serious drain" for him, causing both him and his wife "continual anxiety."

In addition, Roosevelt did not perceive the vice presidency as a likely avenue to the White House; a student of history, he was well aware that over sixty years had passed since a sitting vice president had been elected to the presidency. His chances in 1904 would be far better if he served as governor of the most populous state in the Union than if he languished in "oblivion" as vice president.

Despite these objections, Roosevelt reasoned, "if the Vice-Presidency led to the Governor Generalship of the Philippines, then the question would be entirely altered." That post was the one he desired above all others, even a second gubernatorial term. From the moment the United States acquired the islands as a provision of the treaty in 1899 ending the Spanish-American War, Roosevelt had coveted the job of creating a new government in a Philippines free of Spanish tyranny. The vigorously paternal leadership he envisioned would "prove to the islanders that [his country] intended not merely to treat them well, but to give them a constantly increasing measure of self-government" until they could "stand alone as a nation."

During the acrimonious Senate debate over ratification of the peace treaty, Roosevelt had expressed nothing but contempt for anti-imperialists who justly argued that acquisition of the Philippines would signal "a violent departure from the established traditions and principles of our republic." They are "little better than traitors," Roosevelt flatly told Lodge, while his public rhetoric made the alternatives stridently clear. "We shall be branded with the steel of clinging shame if we leave the Philippines to fall into a welter of bloody anarchy," he proclaimed, "instead of taking hold of them and governing them with righteousness and justice, in the interests of their own people even more than in the interests of ours."

Serving as the civilian leader on the islands "would not be pleasant," Roosevelt told Maria Storer, "for I should have to cut myself off from my family," who would surely not relocate to the war-torn Philippines. Yet he considered the task "emphatically worth doing" and was increasingly convinced that "the chief pleasure really worth having for any man is the doing well of some work that ought to be done." Moreover, Roosevelt's evolving doctrine of sacrifice and satisfaction applied to nations as well as individuals. In a widely quoted speech delivered in Chicago in April 1900, he insisted that "if we shrink from the hard contests where men must win at hazard of their lives and at risk of all they hold dear, then the bolder and stronger peoples will pass us by, and win for themselves the domination of the world. . . . It is only through strife, through hard and dangerous endeavor, that we shall ultimately win the goal of true national greatness."

McKinley had assured Lodge that Roosevelt was "the ideal man to be the first pioneer Governor" but explained that the appointment would not be made until American troops stationed in the Philippines suppressed the native uprising that had followed the treaty. Known as the Philippine Insurrection, that conflict had erupted when the Filipinos learned, after decades of fighting for independence, that they had been betrayed into exchanging the rule of Spain for American occupation. With 35,000 additional troops authorized by Congress, Roosevelt projected that within two years the rebellion would be crushed, a necessary step before the United States could execute its avowedly beneficent intentions. As governor of New York, he would be free to instantly resign and assume the pioneering post, whereas he would be irreversibly "planted" in the vice presidency for four years. Although he hated to counter Lodge's judgment on a matter of such importance, Roosevelt decided to "declare decisively" that he did not want the post of vice president.

Lodge reluctantly accepted Roosevelt's decision but warned that if he attended the Republican Convention in June, continued refusal in the face of popular clamor for his nomination would damage his future prospects. "There are lots of good men who are strongly for you now who will not like it," Lodge cautioned. Though Roosevelt acknowledged his friend's admonitions, he was constitutionally incapable of forgoing involvement. He allowed himself to be chosen as one of four delegates-at-large from New York and made plans to bring Edith, Corinne, and her husband, Douglas, to Philadelphia.

Three weeks before the convention opened, Judge Alton Brooks Parker was a guest of the Roosevelts at the governor's mansion. Over dinner, Edith expressed her excitement over her first national convention. "You will have the most wonderful time of your life," Judge Parker promised. "You will see almost all the Republican Senators and Members of Congress, many of them with brilliant careers in the public service. And . . . you will see your handsome husband come in and bedlam will at once break loose, and he will receive such a demonstration of applause from the thousands of delegates and guests as no one else will receive. . . . Then, some two or three days later, you will see your husband unanimously nominated for the office of Vice-President."

"You disagreeable thing," Edith interrupted. "I don't want to see him nominated for the vice-presidency." Parker, who regarded Edith highly, instantly regretted his words when he saw how "very anxious" she was that his "prophecy should not come true." For Edith, the vice presidency foretold only burdensome expenses and a stilted social life filled with formal receptions and idle chatter. Most important, she and Theodore had had more time together in the gubernatorial mansion than they had in years. She was by his side when he made his rounds to local fairs and Pioneer picnics. "I really think she enjoyed it as much as I did," Roosevelt proudly reported to Lodge after an eight-day stretch of "the county fair business." Sagamore Hill beckoned when the legislature adjourned in summer and was close enough to Albany to provide a romantic escape, even in the fall.

Judge Parker joined the Roosevelts at another dinner party a few days after his disconcerting conversation with Edith. "You gave my wife a bad quarter of an hour the other night," Roosevelt told him. "Did you mean all you said to her?" Parker replied that he meant "every word," adding that Roosevelt's only possibility of evading the vice-presidential nod was to avoid Philadelphia altogether and deliver elsewhere a categorical refusal of the nomination.

By the time the convention opened in late June, Roosevelt was no longer certain how to proceed. As he pondered his future, his doubts grew: even if he secured the gubernatorial nomination for a second term, there was at least "an even chance" that he would be beaten. And even if he did win, he could easily "come a cropper" with any subsequent misstep that would signal "in all probability the end of any outside ambition." Nevertheless, he continued to prefer the hazardous pursuit of a second term to being buried alive in the vice presidency.

The moment Roosevelt arrived in Philadelphia, the stampede for his nomination began—just as Lodge and Judge Parker had predicted. Entering the crowded lobby of the Hotel Walton around 6 p.m., he was met by "vociferous applause" and thunderous cries of "Teddy, Teddy, Teddy." When the raucous crowd launched into a chorus of "There'll Be a Hot Time in the Old Town Tonight," journalists noted, "Roosevelt blushed, doffed his hat and bowed his acknowledgments as he recognized the tune played after his charge up San Juan Hill."

He had scarcely finished breakfast the following morning, the *New York Tribune* reported, when "he had reason to suspect that something of importance affecting his political fortunes had happened in the course of the night": one state delegation after another "invaded" his room, announcing that he was their unanimous choice for vice president. Throughout the western states, where Roosevelt was regarded as one of their own, the enthusiasm was overwhelming. Corinne was with her brother when the Kansas delegation arrived. "Round and round the room they went," she recalled, chanting, "We want Teddy, We want Teddy, We want Teddy," to the accompaniment of "fife, drum and bugle." Similar demonstrations of support came from California, Colorado, the Dakotas, and Nevada.

The bosses of the eastern states followed suit. To a man, they pledged the full support of their delegations. Platt had done his work well. The only resistance had come from the conservative party chairman, Ohio's Mark Hanna. "Don't you realize," Hanna famously objected, "that there's only one life between this madman and the White House?" In the end, even Hanna conceded that Roosevelt would add more strength to the ticket than any other candidate. "There is not a man, woman, or child in the hotels of Quakertown tonight," the *Washington Times* reported, "who does not believe that TR is to be nominated as President McKinley's running mate."

"These fellows have placed me in an awful position," Roosevelt complained. "If I refused it, people will say that 'Roosevelt has a big head and thinks he is too much of a man to be Vice-President.' " Lodge had little patience with Roosevelt's continued reluctance: "If you decline the nomination," he informed his friend, "you had better take a razor and cut your throat."

Roosevelt eventually resigned himself to the inevitable nomination. The next morning, "the sun shone brightly" for the first time in several days as the formal proceedings began. When the chair recognized Roosevelt to second McKinley's nomination, "the magic" of his personality "sent the multitude into convulsions of enthusiasm." From the gallery, Edith watched her husband stride toward the platform amid "the sea of waving, cheering humanity." The jubilation continued while Roosevelt commanded the stage. "He made no acknowledgements, no salutations to the plaudits, but like a hero receiving his due, calmly awaited the subsidence of the tumult." His expression relaxed only once, the *New York Tribune* correspondent remarked, "when he caught a glimpse of his wife in the gallery and waved his hand to her." At last, with his uplifted hand, the demonstration subsided.

Finally, Roosevelt addressed the adoring crowd: "We stand on the threshold of a new century big with the fate of mighty nations," he proclaimed. "We face the coming years high of heart and resolute of faith that to our people is given the right to win such honor and renown as has never yet been vouchsafed to the nations of mankind." It was not a speech, observed one reporter, "of rounded periods, such as Senator Lodge could deliver, nor did it have the fervor or the rich metaphor of the Wolcotts and Dollivers." Nevertheless, no other speech proved "so effective, none so full of character and none which found so responsive an audience. It carried everything before it, and old campaigners sighed that such energy was beyond them."

Once the frenzy of the convention had waned Roosevelt admitted to a friend that he felt "a little melancholy." While he "should be a conceited fool" not to appreciate such resounding support, the thought of four years in the restrictive office of the vice presidency remained abhorrent. "His friends were in despair," Jacob Riis wrote, "his enemies triumphed. At last they had him where they wanted him."

His family shared Roosevelt's aversion to the prospect. "Oh, how I hate this Vice Presidency," Corinne told Fanny Parsons. "Poor Edith feels it tremendously too." Indeed, Edith admitted to Emily that she "had hoped to the last moment that some other candidate would be settled upon." Her only comfort was the prospect that her husband might "get the rest that he sadly needs and for the next four years he will have an easy time."

While Theodore Roosevelt tried to reconcile himself to the unhappy combination of events resulting in his nomination as vice president, William Howard Taft would embark on the most gratifying period of his long public career. In late January 1900, a telegraph boy knocked on the door of the consultation room at the circuit court in Cincinnati. He handed Judge Taft a telegram, summoning him to the White House for "important business" with President McKinley. "What do you suppose that means?" he excitedly asked Nellie that evening. She had no answer. Had there been an opening on the Supreme Court, the summons might have foretold his long-desired appointment to the bench, but no vacancy then existed.

Secretary of War Elihu Root and Navy Secretary Long had joined McKinley in the Oval Office when the president informed Taft that he intended to appoint him to a new Philippine Commission, charged with formulating a civilian code for governance. "He might as well have told me," Taft remembered, "that he wanted me to take a flying machine." Taft protested that he was not the right man for the task. He was emphatically not an expansionist and had been "strongly opposed to taking the Philippines," believing the United States should not take on a responsibility "contrary to our traditions and at a time when we had quite enough to do at home." Such objections were "beside the question," McKinley countered; now that the Philippines had fallen to the United States, "it behooved the United States to govern them until such time as their people had learned the difficult art of governing themselves."

Taft agreed that once the islands were occupied, we were "under the most sacred duty to give them a good form of government" but insisted he was not the man best equipped for that important responsibility. He did not speak Spanish, which would hamper easy relationships with the Filipino people. Furthermore, he was loath to relinquish his long-cherished lifetime appointment as a judge. "Well," said McKinley, "all I can say to you is that if you give up this judicial office at my request you shall not suffer. If I last and the opportunity comes, I shall appoint you." Long confirmed that the president was speaking of a place on the Supreme Court. "Yes," McKinley assured him, "if I am here you'll be here."

War Secretary Root offered the decisive argument. "You have had a very fortunate career," he told Taft. "You are at the parting of the ways. Will you take the easier course, the way of least resistance . . . or will you take the more courageous course and, risking much, achieve much?" Taft asked for a week to ponder the matter with his wife and brothers.

On the overnight train heading back to Cincinnati, Taft "didn't sleep a wink." Root's words about courage frequented his thoughts, and the president's implied promise of a Supreme Court appointment beckoned powerfully. Despite his mounting excitement, Taft was certain that the long distance and "the atrocious climate of Manila" would not prove a happy prospect for Nellie. Unlike Roosevelt, he could not imagine a protracted absence from his family. By the time he reached home, his countenance was "so grave" that Nellie "thought he must be facing impeachment."

Will explained the president's proposal to his wife, doubtful she would consider joining him. Much to his surprise, Nellie never hesitated: "Yes, of course," she exclaimed, the opportunity gave her "nothing but pleasure." She later admitted that perhaps she should have given the prospect of moving three children under ten years old more than 8,000 miles from home more consideration, but her excitement overcame all anxiety. "I knew instantly," she recalled, "that I didn't want to miss a big and novel experience."

Taft's brothers echoed Nellie's enthusiasm. "You can do more good in that position in a year than you could do on the bench in a dozen," Horace maintained, acknowledging, "I hated to have us take the Philippines, but I don't see how in the world we can give them up." Harry agreed, certain that both Will and Nellie would profit "the rest of [their] lives" from "the educational effect of the experience." Harry added that his brother should ask to be made president of the commission so he "could have a voice in selecting some of [his] colleagues."

Three days later, Taft wrote to Root, accepting the post with the stipulation that he be made head of the commission, "responsible for success or failure" of the venture. Root readily agreed; he and McKinley had assumed that Taft would be granted that authority. Notwithstanding, Taft's resignation from his beloved bench was, Nellie believed, "the hardest thing he ever did."

News of Taft's appointment must have disquieted Roosevelt, who nurtured a slim hope that "the Philippines business" could wait a few years, that the fighting would not abate before he was in a position to serve as the first governor general. Though Taft's appointment to the presidency of the commission did not ensure that McKinley would make him civilian governor when hostilities ended, Roosevelt undoubtedly realized that Taft was now the obvious and logical choice.

The two men had kept in close contact over the years, and Taft remained a loyal friend. At the close of "a very hard month" in the governor's office, Roosevelt had found solace in an encouraging letter from Taft. "Need I tell you how your letter pleased me, and how much touched I was by it?" he wrote back, explaining that he had endeavored to follow Taft's counsel and "make the good of the State [his] prime consideration, and yet not follow any impractical ideas." Still, Roosevelt noted, it was "not always easy to strike the just middle," and he inevitably made mistakes. "The thing I should most like," he revealed to Taft, "would be to have someone here just like yourself to advise with." In a letter to their mutual friend Maria Storer, Roosevelt wistfully reiterated his affection and respect: "I wish there was someone like [Taft] here in New York, for I am very much alone. I have no real community of principle or feeling with the machine. So far I have gotten along very well with them, but I never can tell when they will cut my throat." For his part, Taft habitually tracked Roosevelt's battles closely and had wholeheartedly rejoiced in his "final triumph" over Lou Payn.

Though Roosevelt received news of Taft's appointment with ambivalence, his happiness for his friend soon overcame any personal disappointment. "Curiously enough," Roosevelt told him, "I had just written you a note, but I will tear it up, for now I see that you are going on the new Philippine Commission. . . . You are to do a great work for America, and of all the men I know I think you are best fitted to do it."

While Will traveled to Washington to discuss the composition of the commission with the president and the secretary of war, Nellie began to prepare for the odyssey ahead. "That it was alluring to me I did not deny to anybody," she happily remembered. "I read with engrossing interest everything I could find on the subject of the Philippines." Meanwhile, within eight weeks, she managed to vacate their house, store their belongings, and pack for shipment what they would need. "Robert was ten years old, Helen eight, while Charlie, my baby, was just a little over two. It did not occur to me that it was a task to take them on such a long journey, or that they would be exposed to any danger through the experience," she recalled matter-of-factly.

In mid-April 1900, the five commission members and their families, along with a translator, five secretaries, a stenographer, and an Army surgeon, gathered in San Francisco to board the *Hancock* and begin their two-week journey to the Philippines. "We soon became well acquainted, as people do on shipboard," Nellie recalled, "and proceeded at once to prove ourselves to be a most harmonious company." This close-knit group, with whom Nellie would spend "the most interesting years" of her life, included a former Confederate general, "one of the ablest lawyers in Tennessee"; a New England judge who had served as chief justice of Samoa; a professor from the University of Michigan who had been on two scientific expeditions to the Philippines; and a historian from the University of California who had written on politics and economics. Nellie relished "the bonds of friendship" that developed over drinks, meals, political discussions, and continuous rounds of cards. They learned Spanish together and shared books on British colonization and the history of the Philippines. And their children became fast friends.

No sooner had the *Hancock* landed in Manila Bay than the complexity of Taft's mission was immediately apparent. "The populace that we expected to welcome us was not there," recalled Taft, "and I cannot describe the coldness of the army officers and army men who received us any better than by saying that it somewhat exceeded the coldness of the populace." The Filipinos' lack of faith in the advent of the blue-ribbon commission was unsurprising. Brutal fighting still raged in scattered regions of the islands. Further, reports circulated of water torture and other cruelties practiced by American soldiers against the Filipinos, and condescending suggestions that the Filipinos were not yet fit for self-government roused deep resentment.

Taft had expected to be met by General Arthur MacArthur, who had occupied the Philippines for nearly two years and was serving as military governor. But MacArthur was nowhere to be seen. The general regarded the commission's arrival with displeasure, for it compromised the absolute authority he had exercised in the governance of the islands. According to the president's new instructions, the military governor would retain executive powers until the termination of hostilities, while the new Philippine Commission would become the legislative body. Taft and his colleagues had authority to appropriate money, determine taxes, create political departments, and establish courts. MacArthur bluntly informed Taft that he regarded the appointment of the commission "as a personal reflection on him, and that while he was of course obliged to submit to [its] presence there, he resented it nevertheless."

In his first public statement, Taft appealed to the people of the islands, declaring that the commission's arrival signaled a better day and presaged the beginning of the end of military rule. "We are civil officers. We are men of peace. We are here to do justice to the Philippine people, and to secure to them the best government in our power," he reassured them, explaining that the people would retain "such a measure of popular control as will be consistent with stability and the security of law, order and property." He promised to build schools and roads, to open clinics and improve harbors, to establish a system of justice based on the American model, and eventually to create a political structure run by the Filipinos. He explained that "the field" of his work could not yet include those regions where insurgents remained active. Once the rebels laid down their arms they could rely "on the justice, generosity, and clemency of the United States" to accord them "as full a hearing upon the policy to be pursued and the reforms to be begun, as to anyone."

Harper's Weekly deemed Taft's address "the precise kind of speech" demanded by the situation, suggesting that when a man like Taft made promises, he could be believed. "He is not a New York politician who would sacrifice his soul for office; he is not an anxious member of Congress who would promise anything to get a second term," *Harper's* maintained, heartily endorsing Taft and his agenda. "He is Judge Taft and when we say that he is Judge Taft, we mean to imply that he represents all that is best in American manhood, involving integrity of character, a sane mind, and the loftiest of motives."

As chief executive, General MacArthur occupied the official Malacañan Palace. Left to secure his own housing, Taft finally settled on a comfortable house with a wide veranda overlooking Manila Bay. A central hall separated the large dining room from several roomy bedrooms, and a drawing room was located over the carriage entrance. Three more large downstairs chambers and baths, which Nellie allocated to the children, were equipped with "high canopied and mosquito-netted" beds. The Spanish furniture was "very fine," and electric ceiling fans cooled every room. The house staff included "the cook, the number one boy, the number two boy and the laundryman." The cook, Nellie happily noted, could be given word as late as six or seven o'clock that Taft had eight people coming to dinner and "a perfect dinner would be served." Though their house staff were far outnumbered by the several dozen servants at the Malacañan, the Tafts came to love what Nellie affectionately termed their "homely and unpalatial abode."

Each morning, a coach driven by two horses carried Taft to the old capitol building on Cathedral Plaza in the Walled City, where both military and civilian headquarters were lodged. MacArthur and the military occupied most of the building, forcing the commission to work in tight quarters. Nonetheless, Taft was contented so long as he had space for the large library of books on civil law, history, and government that he had purchased for $2,300 before leaving the States. Taft generally began his workday reading the newspapers and writing letters. At ten o'clock on Mondays, Wednesdays, and Fridays, the commission held executive sessions to hammer out legislation on banking and currency, the courts, public works, civil service, health, and education. The five members were charged with designing—from the foundation up—a new colonial government for a population of nearly 7 million. Once the proposed legislation was drafted, public hearings would be held to solicit contributions from the Filipino people. On Tuesday, Thursday, and Saturday mornings, the door was opened for anyone "who wish[ed] to see them." At one o'clock, Taft drove back to the house for lunch and a Spanish lesson, before returning to preside over the commission's afternoon session. Not until six or seven o'clock would he and a fellow commissioner set out on foot for their homes. "The walk is about two miles and a half and the exercise we get is very good for us," he told his mother-in-law. Dinner was "rather a formidable" affair at which they often entertained guests. Nellie and her sister Maria "put on low-necked gowns" and Will changed into more formal attire. "We begin with soup, have fish, not infrequently an entrée, and the roast and dessert and fruit," he reported in loving detail. Lest his mother-in-law chide him for gaining weight, he rationalized that "in this climate one's vital forces are drawn upon by work so much that one's appetite is very strong at meals."

Taft's "policy of conciliation," his strategy of reaching out to the Filipino people, aroused undisguised antipathy within the insulated regime MacArthur had established. Upon hearing that Taft had referred to the Filipinos as "our little brown brothers," the soldiers promptly composed a marching song "which they sang with great gusto and frequency," climaxing with the jeering refrain: "He may be a brother of William H. Taft, but he ain't no friend of mine!" Believing that it would take ten years to pacify the islands, MacArthur considered Taft's desire to provide education and involve the populace in government as both wrongheaded and ultimately hazardous. As the British colonialists understood, such policies could only lead to "agitation and discontent and constant conspiracy."

The military, Taft sorrowfully reflected, was determined to treat the Filipinos as "niggers." Nellie shared his dismay. "It is a great mistake to treat them as if they were inferiors," she told her husband, "and it really surprises me that the powers that be do not insist upon a different policy." Nellie deplored MacArthur's refusal to entertain anyone in the palace "except a select military circle," and condemned his abhorrence of "even small gestures of social equality among the different races in the Philippines."

In defiance of the established order, Nellie "made it a rule from the beginning that neither politics nor race should influence [their] hospitality in any way." Though her dining room seated only twelve in comfort, she could host parties for hundreds of people in her spacious garden. "We always had an orchestra," she recalled, "and the music added greatly to the festive air of things, which was enhanced too, by a certain oriental atmosphere, with many Japanese lanterns and a profusion of potted plants." While Nellie's insistence "upon complete racial equality" marked a spirit of tolerance far ahead of military attitudes, her guest lists were nonetheless drawn from a narrow segment of the population—educated Filipinos of "wealth and position"—the very class Taft hoped to enlist in the new government.

Although Taft's annual salary of $17,500 was more than he had ever earned, he had to pay his own considerable expenses and could barely sustain his household and lifestyle. Once again, his brother Charley came to his rescue, sending an unexpected $2,500 check. "To say that I was overcome and struck dumb by your generous present is inadequate," Will responded. "Nothing ever diminishes the ardor and enthusiasm of your loyalty to the family." Nellie, too, committed her resources to further her husband's goals, spending a small inheritance she had received to pay for receptions and dinners.

Meanwhile, the Philippine Commission made steady progress. The members revised the Spanish tax code, which had burdened the poor while "giving [the] wealthy comparative immunity." They built a series of schools throughout the islands and brought five hundred recent college graduates from America as teachers. These idealistic young educators, deemed by one historian "precursors of the Peace Corps," arrived carrying "baseball bats, tennis rackets, musical instruments, cameras and binoculars." Under Taft's guidance, the commission built roads, railways, and hospitals, improved harbors and ports, and instituted extensive legal reforms.

Nellie worked side by side with her husband. Upon arrival, he had encouraged her to "enter upon some work of public importance like the organization of a Philippine Orchestra and Philippine bands." She needed no further prompting. Drawing on her love of music and organizational experience, she helped create the Philippine Constabulary Band. Led by an African-American captain, comprised of musicians from all over the islands, the celebrated band would achieve international renown and win a coveted prize at the St. Louis

World's Fair in 1904. While Taft worked on regulatory measures to improve sanitation, Nellie decided her personal cause should be the reduction of infant mortality in Manila. To that end, she instituted an educational campaign on good nutrition and launched a highly successful program to provide the city's children with sterilized milk, a campaign credited with saving many lives. In all her endeavors, she advocated respect for the native culture. When the Army engineers, "in the interest of efficiency and sanitation," threatened to demolish "the medieval walls of the old city of Manila," Nellie successfully campaigned to protect this cherished historical monument.

Taft was immensely proud of his wife. He likened her activism to that of Lady Curzon, who had accompanied her husband to India and achieved worldwide fame for championing women's health. On the eve of their fourteenth anniversary, Will gave Nellie a handwritten note. "I wish to record the fact that it was the most fortunate [day] of my life and every year only confirms me more strongly in that opinion," he wrote. "Every year I feel more dependent on you . . . and every year, my darling, I love you more." Nellie had never been happier. She had welcomed her new living situation "with undisguised surprise and pleasure." The children flourished in their new environment. Bob and Helen were enrolled in one of the new public schools, where they had met "congenial companions." In the evenings and on weekends, they lived outside. In the year-round warm weather, they raced their little ponies on the Luneta, the public stretch of sandy beach bounded on both ends by bandstands, where "everybody in the world came and drove around and around the oval, exchanging greetings and gossip." Two-year-old Charlie, nicknamed "the tornado" for his high-spirited whirl of activity, was petted and simply adored.

Each passing month bolstered Taft's confidence. His judicial training proved indispensable as he labored to draft legislation and regulations. His kind generosity and inclusive style of leadership won the regard of his fellow commissioners. The Filipino people, too, were attracted to the warmth of his personality and his willingness to embrace the native culture. After much practice and intent studying of a diagram indicating the various movements, he and Nellie learned to execute the rigodon, the complicated national dance of the Philippines, "an old fashioned quadrille" that required "graceful and somewhat intricate but stately figures." Observing Taft's impressively large frame, spectators marveled at his surprising agility. This gentle giant, one reporter noted, attended scores of state balls, "literally dancing and smiling his way into the hearts of the people." Indeed, his "unusual size," which required a double rickshaw, created an aura of "superiority."

As Taft became better acquainted with the people of the Philippines, he grew increasingly confident that he would deliver "a good government" and "prosperous" economy to the islands. While he doubted that independence could soon be granted to an illiterate, and in his words, an "ignorant, superstitious people," he trusted that the enlightened colonial rule of the United States would gradually prepare them for self-government. His success depended on McKinley's election, which would ensure consistent support as he constructed new political, educational, and economic institutions. "Not that I am an expansionist," he told a friend, "for I have not changed my mind on that general subject, but only that in the situation into which events have forced us, the Democratic policy of abandonment of these Islands was impossible."

Taft was tremendously heartened by the news of Roosevelt's vice-presidential nomination. The administration had "a good deal to carry" after being in power for four years, he told his brother Charles. Mistakes had "doubtless" been made, and the Democratic nominee, William Jennings Bryan, still enjoyed a formidable following among the working class. Roosevelt's name on the ticket, he explained, added "a following of hero worshippers who [would] give life and vitality to the campaign." Charles agreed, hopeful that Roosevelt would "draw in line all the younger element of the country."

"I could wish that you had continued Governor of New York to do the work thoroughly you have so well begun," Taft told Roosevelt after the Republican National Convention, "but the national election is the more important and you were right to make the sacrifice. The situation here is much more favorable than I had been led to suppose. The back of the Insurrection is broken and the leaders are much discouraged and anxious, most of them, for peace." The remaining insurgents, he claimed, were "restrained from surrender by nothing now but the possibility of Bryan's election." By joining the Republican ticket and rendering "success most probable," he believed Roosevelt "was performing a great service not only to the people of his own country but to the Filipinos as well."

In a warm reply to his friend, Roosevelt acknowledged his regret at forgoing a second gubernatorial term but maintained his satisfaction if he should prove "any help to the ticket this year." Nonetheless, he added wistfully, "I had a great deal rather be your assistant in the Philippines . . . than be vice-president."

Roosevelt's immense contribution to the Republican ticket was beyond question. Telling Mark Hanna that he was "as strong as a bull moose" and should be used "up to the limit," Roosevelt carried the entire campaign on his shoulders. "No candidate for Vice-President in the whole history of this

Republic ever made such a canvass," Boss Platt acknowledged. While McKinley remained at the White House, Roosevelt became "the central figure, the leading general, the field marshal." Breaking every record, "he traveled more miles, visited more States, spoke in more towns, made more speeches and addressed a larger number of people than any man who ever went on the American stump."

Surrounded by his wife and children on November 6, 1900, Roosevelt waited for the results at Sagamore Hill. Throughout the evening, scattered messages arrived from the telegraph operator at the railroad station three miles away. Around ten o'clock, a newspaper correspondent knocked on the door, bringing news of a smashing Republican victory. On the other side of the world, Will and Nellie were on their "tiptoes with excitement." The time difference of thirteen hours between the United States and the Philippines exacerbated their anxiety. "We lived through the day knowing that the United States was asleep, and went to bed just about the time the voters began to go to the polls," Nellie recalled. Finally, just before lunch the next day, a War Department cablegram announced the eagerly anticipated result: "McKinley."

"My dear Theodore," Will saluted his friend in a celebratory letter, "the magnificent victory in the states of the Far West and in New York is eloquent testimony to the good which you have done. The party for whom you made a great sacrifice will not forget it. I have no doubt that you will be the nominee in 1904." Taft felt personal gratitude toward Roosevelt, for McKinley's election allowed him to continue his work, a mission which had come to mean more than he had ever imagined when he reluctantly resigned from the bench.

As Taft had predicted, insurgent activity began to decrease once Bryan's defeat confirmed America's resolve to remain in the Philippines. "Hardly a day passed that did not bring news of the capture or surrender of insurgent officers," Nellie recalled. "The attitude of the native is completely changed," Taft told his brother, "and he is looking around to get in on the 'band wagon.' " By early January 1901, he believed that the momentum had shifted in favor of peace. "The leaders in Manila," he told Senator Lodge, "are hastening to form a party called the 'Federal Party,' which is pushing and pressing for peace and which will have an organization in every province and town in the Islands before many months have passed." The time had come, he continued, to prepare for the transition from General MacArthur and the military authority to the civilian commission. "Their methods of doing things are so very different from ours," he mordantly remarked, "and the people will welcome a change."

To ready the Philippine Commission for full control and responsibility, Taft organized a two-month expedition to the southern provinces, where open hearings would be held to explicate new municipal codes that specified a Filipino governor in every province. Nellie insisted on accompanying the commission. "Of course," Taft told his brother Charles, Nellie would not leave the children behind, so they came along as well. In the end, all the wives and children of the commission were included in the foray, comprising a party of sixty on the Army transport ship. The cluster of wives and children "greatly pleased" the Filipinos, Nellie noted, making the visits far more festive. "Much to the disgust of the military authorities present," she remembered with satisfaction, "we assumed the friendliest kind of attitude."

The desire of the provinces to substitute civil government for military rule was "manifest on every side," Taft reported to his brother Horace. In each provincial capital, "the streets were crowded with men, women and children waving flags and shrilly cheering." Bands playing "The Star-Spangled Banner" and "A Hot Time in the Old Town Tonight" led the commission to the public hall where daylong hearings were held. "Spectacular" festivities followed the working day, Nellie recalled; torchlight parades, fireworks, six-course banquets, and balls celebrated their progress. Altogether, she later wrote, it was "a singular experience, an expedition perhaps unique in history, with which was ushered in a new era, not to say a new national existence, for the people of the Philippine Islands."

At long last, in late February 1901, Congress passed the Spooner Amendment that declared the Insurrection over and called for the transfer of power from military to civilian authorities. Taft informed Roosevelt that he had been selected as the first governor general. "The responsibilities of this position, I look forward [to] with a great deal of hesitation," he confided. "The pitfalls are many and the territory to be traversed is almost unknown." Still, he admitted, "there is a natural gratification in taking control of things."

Roosevelt would have given a great deal to change places with his friend. "I envy you your work," he told Taft eight days after he was sworn in as vice president, bemoaning his own situation. "More and more it seems to me that about the best thing in life is to have a piece of work worth doing and then to do it well." The lull in Roosevelt's customary frenetic activity allowed time for painful reflection: "I did not envy you while I was Governor of New York," he wrote, "nor while I was on the stump last fall taking part in the campaign which I believed to be fraught with the greatest consequences to the Nation; but just at present I do envy you. I am not doing any work and do not feel as though I was justifying my existence."

Roosevelt similarly registered his discontent in a letter to Maria and Bellamy Storer; neither McKinley nor Mark Hanna, he wrote, "sympathize with my feelings or feel comfortable about me, because they cannot understand what it is that makes me act in certain ways at certain times, and therefore think me indiscreet and overimpulsive." Though the president was "perfectly cordial," Roosevelt insisted, "he does not intend that I shall have any influence of any kind, sort or description in the administration from the top to the bottom." Roosevelt longed for some active enterprise in Cuba or the Philippines, but the president had no interest in sending him where real work might be done. The vice presidency "ought to be abolished," he told his friend Leonard Wood. "The man who occupies it may at any moment be everything; but meanwhile he is practically nothing. I do not think that the President wants me to take any part in affairs or give him any advice."

When Congress adjourned for nine months in the spring, suspending the vice president's sole constitutional responsibility of presiding over the Senate, Roosevelt retired to Oyster Bay. "I am rather ashamed to say," he wrote Taft at the end of April, that I do "nothing but ride and row with Mrs. Roosevelt, and walk and play with the children; chop trees in the afternoon and read books by a wood fire in the evening." Despite this peaceful existence, Roosevelt admitted to "ugly feelings," aware that he was "leading a life of unwarrantable idleness."

Taft tried to buoy his friend's spirits with the prospect of a presidential bid in 1904. "I look forward with great confidence to your nomination for President at the next convention," he declared, "and I sincerely hope it may be brought about. Four years in the Vice-Presidential chair will save you from a good many hostilities that might endanger such a result, while the prominence of the position keeps you continually to the front as the necessary and logical candidate." But to Roosevelt it seemed more likely that Taft would get the nod. "I doubt if in all the world there has been a much harder task set any one man during the past year than has been set you," he observed, praising Taft's work under such trying circumstances: "In spite of all the difficulties you have done well, and more than well, a work of tremendous importance. You have made all decent people who think deeply here in this country feel that they are your debtors. . . . It has paid after all, old man."

On the Fourth of July, 1901, William Howard Taft was inaugurated as governor general of the Philippines. The spectacular ceremony featured "music, fireworks, gold lace and glitter, dancing and feasting and oratory." A pavilion had been erected in Cathedral Plaza, the large square in the center of the Walled City, to accommodate the celebration. It was "an occasion of great dignity and interest," Nellie happily remembered. "Americans and Filipinos, all in gala attire, were pressed close together . . . the plaza below was thronged with Filipinos of every rank and condition, in all manner of bright *jusis* and calicos; while above the crowd towered many American soldiers and sailors in spic-and-span khaki or white duck." General MacArthur, who would be departing Manila the next day, stood by as the Filipino chief justice administered the oath of office to Taft. Resplendent in a "crisp white linen suit," Taft appeared "larger even than his natural size."

In his inaugural address, Taft hailed the transfer of authority from the military to the civilian commission as "a new step" toward "Permanent Civil Government on a more or less popular basis." He announced that three leading Filipino citizens would be added to the five-member commission and that educated Filipinos would have voices both in the legislature and in the governance of the provinces. In time, as Stanley Karnow and James Bradley observe, the flaws in Taft's attempt to construct a democracy "from the top down" would become clear. Reliance upon the elite, refusal to sanction any opposition to the Federal Party, and the policy of granting suffrage to a select minority further entrenched the existing "feudal oligarchy," thereby expanding "the gap between rich and poor." On this inaugural day, however, Taft's forthright speech elicited "the wildest of cheering, and the playing of national airs." Such a manifestation "of popular approval," one correspondent noted, "indicates an auspicious beginning for the administration of the new governor."

The next morning, the Tafts relocated their household to the historic Malacañan Palace. "In some ways we regretted that the move was necessary," Nellie recalled, "for we were very comfortable in our 'chalet.' " Until they occupied the palace where MacArthur had presided the Filipinos would not "be convinced that civil government was actually established." Despite her reservations, "the idea of living in a palace . . . appealed to my imagination," Nellie acknowledged. Set on twenty beautifully landscaped acres of trees, flowers, and fountains, the palace stood on a bend in the Pasig River, with windows open all around. There were about twenty rooms on the first floor, "all of them good sized and some of them enormous, and it took a great many servants to keep the place in order," Nellie noted, recollecting the impressive space in detail: "The great living-rooms open one into another, giving a fine perspective, and they lead, through a dozen different doorways, on to a splendid, white-tiled verandah which runs out to the bank of the Pasig." There were a half-dozen houses on the grounds for secretaries and assistants.

Barely established at the palace, Nellie placed an immediate announcement in the newspapers stating that she would hold a reception every Wednesday, open to everyone on an equal basis. Her receptions were soon thronged with "Army and Navy people, civilians of every occupation," and "American school teachers." Never before had the military mixed socially with the islanders, so

Nellie had to cajole the Filipinos to attend "by asking many of them personally and persistently." In short order, she proudly remarked, "there began to be as many brown faces as white among our guests." But Nellie refused to confine herself to the company at the palace and was eager to explore the native culture: she attended local parties and dances, often accompanied by a group of young Army officers, including Archie Butt. Stationed in the Quartermaster Department, Captain Butt was "a great society beau in Washington, and was said to be the handsomest man there," Nellie told her mother. "You would be amused to see Maria and me frisking around with youths years younger than we are, and dancing cotillions with the best of them," she boasted. "Of course the position gives us a great deal of attention which I for one would never have otherwise," she added, "and of course we feel we might as well make the best of it while we have the opportunity."

When news of the triumphant inauguration reached the United States, Roosevelt wrote a long letter to Taft. "It seems idle to keep repeating to you what a lively appreciation not only I but all the rest of us here have of what you are doing. But when you are so far away. . . . I do want you to understand that you are constantly in the thoughts of very many people, and that I have never seen a more widespread recognition of service among men of character than the recognition of the debt we owe you."

Though he rejoiced in his friend's success, Roosevelt was less sanguine about his own prospects. "Here everything is at slack water politically," he continued, addressing Taft's expressed hope for a Roosevelt presidency in 1904. "I should like to be President, and feel I could do the work well," he acknowledged, but "it would be simply foolish for me to think seriously of my chances of getting the office, when the only certain feature of the situation is that my own State will be against me. . . . If the convention were held now, my hold is still so strong both in the west and in New England that I might very well get the nomination without regard to New York. But my present position is one in which I can do absolutely nothing to shape policies, and so looked at dispassionately, I cannot see that there is any but the very smallest chance of my keeping enough hold even to make me seriously spoken of as a candidate." Considering the circumstances, he told Taft, "you are of all the men in this country the one best fitted to give the nation the highest possible service as president. . . . Sometime I want to get the chance to say this in public."

Utterly frustrated and increasingly dispirited, Roosevelt even made plans to begin law school again in the fall, figuring that two additional years of coursework would enable him to pass the bar examinations and launch a legal practice. He also inquired about the possibility of becoming a professor of history at a university. "Of course, I may go on in public life," he reckoned, "but equally of course it is unlikely, and what I have seen of the careers of public men has given me an absolute horror of the condition of the politician whose day has passed; who by some turn of the kaleidoscope is thrown into the background; and who then haunts the fields of his former activity as a pale shadow of what he once was."

On September 6, 1901, that kaleidoscope shifted in a way Roosevelt never anticipated. A young anarchist walked up to shake hands with President McKinley at the Pan-American Exposition in Buffalo. Removing a revolver screened by a handkerchief, the assassin fired two shots into McKinley's chest. Eight days later, the wounds proved fatal. Theodore Roosevelt, at forty-two years of age, became the youngest president in the history of the country.

CHAPTER TEN

"That Damned Cowboy Is President"

"1902 Finds the Helm in Safe Hands," an illustration in *Puck* magazine, Jan. 1, 1902.

THE SHIP OF STATE IS on its way to unknown ports," the *Nation* declared portentously, warning that the assassination of President McKinley had "violently altered the natural course of events." When Roosevelt took the oath of office on September 14, 1901, questions abounded, unsettling conservatives and reformers alike. "What changes will he make?" "What does the future hold in store?" "Will he continue the policy mapped out by his predecessor?"

Conservatives, who had utterly dominated the Republican Party for three decades, feared the impulsive young president would prove a "bucking bronco," upsetting the alliance between business and government that had delivered unparalleled prosperity at the turn of the century. Reformers hoped Roosevelt's vigorous leadership would refashion the Republican Party into the progressive force it had been under Abraham Lincoln, endeavoring to spread prosperity beyond the wealthy few to the common man.

Comforting themselves that Roosevelt remained a loyal Republican despite occasional fights with the party bosses, conservatives maintained that his "first great duty" was to carry on the policies of the slain president. Throughout the latter part of the nineteenth century, presidents had been captive to their parties: not only did nominations require the approval of party machines, but party platforms also dictated policy preferences. Furthermore, the partisan press became the central organ for mobilizing voters. Recognizing this long-standing subordination of any personal agenda, the New York *Sun* predicted that the new president's actions would "not depend on the possible vagaries of an individual judgment." The Wall Street tycoon Henry Clews made a similar assumption. "The conservative policy of Mr. McKinley has become so settled in the minds of the people," he pronounced, "that it matters not who becomes his immediate successor. . . . No one will dare to experiment or to deviate from such a course of administration."

Throughout his career, Roosevelt had struggled to reconcile party allegiance with the drive to address social problems, a balancing act that became more difficult as the troubling aspects of industrialization intensified. While he considered himself conservative in relation to the Populists, he believed that his party was in thrall to reactionaries who so "dreaded radicalism" that they "distrusted anything that was progressive." Precisely such men dominated both chambers of Congress, Roosevelt lamented. He would work to "push" them forward but recognized that genuine progress would require a direct appeal to the people, "the masters of both of us." To reach the general public, he would enlist the new breed of independent journalists, without whose "active support," he later acknowledged, he "would have been powerless."

Initially he understood the necessity of caution. Warned that the stock market might crash unless he reassured Wall Street that he and his predecessor were "one in purpose," Roosevelt issued a solemn pledge: "In this hour of deep and terrible bereavement, I wish to state that I shall continue absolutely unbroken the policy of President McKinley for the peace, prosperity, and the honor of the country."

Even as he publicly vowed to preserve a comfortable conservative agenda, Roosevelt signaled journalists that a new political era was imminent. On his very first day in the White House, he invited managers of the Associated Press, the Scripps-McRae Press Association (now the United Press), and the New York *Sun* to his office. It was "an unusual request," one historian noted, "for in those days, presidents rarely convened journalists to discuss public matters."

He proposed an unprecedented accessibility, agreeing to "keep them posted" on each evolving plan and policy if they, in return, promised never to "violate a confidence or publish news that the President thought ought not to be published." These parameters established, Roosevelt informed them that despite his public endorsement of the status quo, the Constitution had provided for his succession. "I am President," he bluntly maintained, "and shall act in every word and deed precisely as if I and not McKinley had been the candidate for whom the electors cast the vote for President."

That evening, presiding over his first dinner party as president, Roosevelt openly avowed his intention to differentiate himself from McKinley. A small party had gathered in the modest N Street residence of his sister Bamie and her husband, Will Cowles, where Roosevelt boarded during his first week to allow the grieving Ida McKinley a measure of time to move out of the executive mansion. Two guests, William Allen White and the young president of Columbia University, Nicholas Murray Butler, joined the family. White vividly recalled sitting "pop-eyed with wonder" at the edge of his chair while Roosevelt spoke "with a kind of dynamic, burning candor" about his plans. Though accustomed to Roosevelt's indiscreet talk, White had assumed he would "be different" in his new office, only to find that "he was absolutely unchanged."

The president worried openly that his pledge to follow in McKinley's footsteps, compelled by dire economic predictions, would "embarrass him sorely in the future." He might have forestalled a stock market crash, but if he pursued McKinley's policies to the letter, would it not "give the lie to all he had stood for?" During a "cataract solo of talk" that left White astonished, Roosevelt's thoughts turned to his political future. Should he secure a second term, he would be only fifty years old when it came to a close. "Imagine me as an ex-President, dedicating buildings and making commencement speeches," he mused. The prospect of being "the old cannon loose on the deck in the storm" terrified him. Of more immediate concern, he would likely face Republican Committee chair Mark Hanna in 1904. A powerful adversary much like Boss Platt, Hanna threatened to derail Roosevelt's aspiration for a second term.

White was delighted when conversation turned to Platt, on whom he was gathering material for a long profile in *McClure's.* Roosevelt had promised his assistance, and the two men had planned to meet at Oyster Bay before McKinley's assassination brought them both to Washington. The profile of the New York boss was part of a series White had projected for the magazine. Roosevelt had read White's two earlier pieces on William Jennings Bryan and Tammany boss Richard Croker with great enthusiasm. "Here you are living in a small town out in Kansas, not accustomed to the conditions of life in a seething great city, pay a somewhat hurried visit to New York," he marveled, "and yet you sketch Croker as no one in New York, so far as I know, could sketch him. . . . I immensely admired your Bryan; but then I can entirely understand how you knew Bryan. When it comes to Croker it almost seems as if you must have divined it."

White had interviewed Boss Platt in his downtown office, "a frowzy little cubbyhole that had not been tidied up for years." He had talked with his lieutenants, searched out his rivals, and scoured newspaper files. He believed his study of the Platt machine would have national resonance because its "story of intrigue, corruption and the sordid amalgamation of plutocratic self-interest and political power was typical of American politics in the North at that time." In White's mind, Roosevelt was to be commended for wanting a tough story "about his own party printed" and for believing that "the more people knew" about the corrupt alliance binding big business and elected officials, "the sooner they would wreck the machines." By this time, White was convinced the "untrammeled" greed of the great industrial captains must be checked. He left the dinner that night loaded with ammunition for his profile on Platt.

Lincoln Steffens, who joined William Allen White in Washington the following day, recounted his own exhilaration on learning that Roosevelt would assume the presidency. "We reformers went up in the air when President McKinley was shot, took our bearings, and flew straight to our first president, T.R. And he understood, he shared, our joy." The White House offices, Steffens recalled, "were crowded with people, mostly reformers," amid whom the president "strode triumphant." Despite Roosevelt's attempts to mute his ebullience while Washington and the nation mourned, "his joy showed in every word and movement." When the day's work was done, he grabbed White and Steffens: "Let's get out," he exclaimed, propelling the two men into the streets. "For better than an hour, he allowed his gladness to explode. With his feet, his fists, his face and with free words he laughed at his luck. He laughed at the rage of Boss Platt and at the tragic disappointment of Mark Hanna; these two had not only lost their President McKinley but had been given as a substitute the man they had thought to bury in the vice-presidency. T.R. yelped at their downfall. And he laughed with glee at the power and place that had come to him."

By the time White returned to Emporia to write his profile, he had thoroughly imbibed Roosevelt's resentment toward Platt. "Unconsciously, or perhaps consciously, I used my best and most burning adjectives in that article expressing my scorn of Senator Platt and his machine, and contempt for the things it represented," White later recalled. "It was a bitter piece." Although he warned the editors at *McClure's* that he was afraid it might be "too scorching," they were proud to publish it.

The piece vividly delineated the origin of the Platt machine. Twenty years earlier, every business had maintained its own lobby in Albany, an expensive and often inefficient way of influencing the state legislature. Platt made it his business "to bring order out of confusion," centralizing power in his own hands. He first persuaded corporations to contribute generously to the state central committee rather than field individual lobbyists, and then allocated the money to elect the machine's slate of candidates. Over time, Platt built up a majority of legislators absolutely beholden to his organization. Corporations thrived under the Platt regime; it cost less to support the state committee than to keep individual lobbies. Furthermore, since Platt took none of the money for himself, "there were no longer stories of individual corruption, of bribes and scandals." But the people of New York bore the cost of the system that worked so seamlessly for both the corporations and the politicians. "What we call popular government," White concluded, "is abrogated by purchase of privileges."

White's analysis of the workings of the machine was unsparing but deadly accurate; his portrait of Platt, however, was gratuitously savage. He described the New York boss as an earthworm, "boring beneath the roots of local self-government by cities and States, burrowing silently yet with incalculable power, loosening the soil, sagging foundations." He portrayed a soulless man devoid of any "moral nature," loyal only to his machine and its corporate sponsors; a man transformed into "a machine himself—hard, impulseless, cunning, cute but witless, immovable, inexorable, grinding."

Enraged, Platt immediately declared his intention "to haul both author and publisher into court to answer the charge of criminal libel," threatening that his lawyers had already begun preparing their complaint. "I will get that fellow's scalp if it is the last thing I ever do," he seethed, vowing to employ all his resources "to bring about the punishment of this man." Moreover, White and *McClure's* would not be his only targets. Through depositions, he promised to unearth every one of White's sources, exposing those "who told him the lies," and proceeding equally against them. Suspecting that Roosevelt himself was one of White's sources, he stormed into the president's office, demanding that the journalist be forever barred from the White House. "No friend of mine," Platt insisted, "can be a friend of that man." Wisely, Roosevelt denied having read the article but promised to do so.

"I am perfectly heartbroken at the whole business," White revealed to

Roosevelt, " not for myself, but for the embarrassment to you. I thought I was doing a service to good government in the United States by writing the article. I still believe that I was right, but I seem to have been right at a terrible cost to you." The distraught journalist queried how he might "straighten this business out" but forwarded a second letter to the president's secretary without waiting for an answer. The second letter was to be shown to Senator Platt or made public, as Roosevelt saw fit. "Not one syllable, hint, or inference escaped President Roosevelt's lips while I was a guest in the White House, which might have been used in any way to the discredit of Senator Platt," White asserted. "My opinion of Senator Platt was formed, not by President Roosevelt, but by careful study of conditions in New York politics. Many of my conclusions are probably foreign to those, which everyone knows are held by the president."

Roosevelt thanked White for the potentially mollifying letter, nevertheless insisting he had no intention of letting Platt's indignation dictate his friendships. He sought to ease White's anxiety over their relationship by insisting, "The only damage that could come to me through such articles would be if you refused to continue to champion me!"

No sooner had *McClure's* publicly declared that "they would welcome the suit," claiming to possess a wealth of additional information relating to the boss and his machine, than Platt decided not to go forward. But the incident took a heavy toll on White. He suffered "a kind of nervous collapse," and though he felt "perfectly well physically," he could no longer bear to write, or even to read the papers. "My nerves are gone," he told the editors at *McClure's*, explaining his failure to submit another article that was overdue, admitting that "to as much as dictate this letter throws me in a perspiration." His doctor recommended a protracted rest: "I must leave the state and go to the mountains . . . I am very sorry that I have thrown you all out so." The staff of *McClure's* supported him during the five-month recuperation; equally steadfast during this nadir of White's career was Theodore Roosevelt. White would not forget either.

"Probably no administration has ever taken such a curious hold upon the people as that of Theodore Roosevelt," remarked the longtime White House usher Irwin (Ike) Hoover. "While he is in the neighborhood," one critic grudgingly conceded, "the public can no more look the other way than the small boy can turn his head away from a circus parade followed by a steam calliope."

Indeed, Roosevelt's initial months as chief executive were less remarkable for significant political accomplishments than for his impact on the public consciousness. "The infectiousness of his exuberant vitality made the country realize there was a new man in the White House," observed Mark Sullivan, "indeed, a new kind of man. His high spirits, his enormous capacity for work, his tirelessness, his forthrightness, his many striking qualities, gave a lift of the spirits to millions of average men." Among admirers and opponents alike, the president's outsized personality compelled attention.

Newspapers invariably contrasted the vigorous young president with his staid predecessor, a Civil War veteran from a previous generation. "Where Mr. McKinley was patient, cautious, tactful, a very good listener, mindful of the little things which go to put a visitor at ease," observed Walter Wellman of the *Chicago Record-Herald*, "Roosevelt is impetuous, impatient and wholly lacking in tact." When dealing with public officials, Wellman noted, Roosevelt "is so full of energy that he simply runs over. He has no patience with long speeches or extended explanations. He cuts people off in the middle of sentences, tells them he knows all about it, and very often announces his decision before the caller has more than fairly started with his little say. . . . He wants action, action all the time. But he rarely gives offense, and never means to do so." Fortunately, the new president had always tolerated, and even relished, humor at his own expense. It was said that he had "a right good laugh" when told of an epigram circulating widely in Washington: "President McKinley listened to a great many people and talked to but few. President Roosevelt talks to a great many men and listens to nobody."

Roosevelt's frenetic yet disciplined schedule mesmerized the press corps. In a piece for *McClure's*, Lincoln Steffens described a breathless day begun when the president "darts into the breakfast-room with a cheerful hail to those already there," then rushes to his office before the official workday starts to tackle his voluminous correspondence, dictating "one letter after another" to his secretary, "his voice and face reflecting vividly the various emotions which guided his words." From 10 a.m. to 12 p.m., except on cabinet days, the second-floor reception room was crowded with senators, congressmen, Army and Navy officials. "The room is a large one, chairs and sofas are set all about it; but they are filled," Steffens noted, "and many persons are standing."

At noon, the doors opened to ordinary citizens, "an overflowing stream" of people eager to see the most colorful president in their memory. For an hour, Roosevelt moved speedily around the room, giving each person a dazzling smile and a warm handshake. The press of visitors, a *New York Times* reporter observed, never seemed "to try the President's strength or impair his good temper."

At one o'clock, Roosevelt generally excused himself from the crowd for his midday shave. During the "barber's hour," reporters were allowed audience, permitted to question—or more likely listen—as the president expounded upon any number of subjects while the barber desperately tried to ply his trade. "A more skillful barber never existed," newspaperman Louis Brownlow observed, describing how "the President would wave both arms, jump up, speak excitedly, and then drop again into the chair and grin at the barber, who would begin all over." Only "when the barber bent over the presidential head and began to shave the lower lip," Steffens noted, "did he quiet down, giving reporters a few moments to pose their questions."

Lunchtime was always a lively affair, featuring all manner of guests rarely seen in the White House—"Western bullwackers, city prize fighters, explorers, rich men, poor men, an occasional black man, editors, writers." If an article or book piqued Roosevelt's interest, the author received an invitation to lunch. "Whether the subject of the moment was political economy, the Greek drama, tropical fauna or flora, the Irish sagas, protective coloration in nature, metaphysics, the technique of football, or postfuturist painting," the British statesman Viscount Lee remarked, Roosevelt "was equally at home."

Late afternoon was devoted to exercise—a horseback ride or boxing match, a raucous game of tennis or a strenuous hike along the cliffs in Rock Creek Park. Dragging visitors and friends through the wooded sections of the park, Roosevelt had one simple rule: You had to move forward "point to point," never circumventing any obstacle. "If a creek got in the way, you forded it. If there was a river, you swam it. If there was a rock, you scaled it, and if you came to a precipice you let yourself down over it." Journalists delighted in portraying these late afternoon rambles. Jacob Riis described a route that could be traced by the "finger-marks" on "gripped fences, telegraph-poles and trees," where Roosevelt's exhausted companions struggled to follow. Stories multiplied about "this or that general or ambassador or cabinet officer who had dropped out and fallen by the way."

The French ambassador Jules Jusserand left a celebrated account of his first walk with the president. After presenting himself at 1600 Pennsylvania Avenue "in afternoon dress and silk hat, as if we were to stroll in the Tuileries Garden or in the Champs Elysées," he soon found himself in the countryside, following Roosevelt "at breakneck pace" through fields and over rocks. When they approached a broad stream, he assumed the race had finally ended. "Judge of my horror when I saw the President unbutton his clothes and heard him say, 'We had better strip, so as not to wet our things in the Creek.' Then I too, for the honor of France, removed my apparel, except my lavender kid gloves." To be without gloves, he insisted, "would be embarrassing if we should meet ladies."

Reporters soon discovered that the hour when the president returned from these excursions and commenced the daily task of sorting his correspondence was "by far the best time to see him." The *New York Times* reporter Oscar King Davis marveled at Roosevelt's "amazing facility for carrying on a conversation while he was going over the mail. He would glance over a letter, make an addition or alteration with his pen, and sign his name at the same time that he was keeping up a steady fire of talk about whatever subject happened to be under discussion."

Finally quitting his office and the company of his reporter friends, Roosevelt returned to the mansion, where he could relax and dress for dinner. There, in the family quarters, he was "allowed to become again husband, father and playmate." He talked over the day's events with his wife, read to the children or, more often, engaged them in physical games. "I play bear with the children almost every night," he wrote, "and some child is invariably fearfully damaged in the play; but this does not seem to affect the ardor of their enjoyment."

Under Edith's guidance, a vital domesticity returned to the presidential residence. "It was the gloomiest house," she recalled, "with the shadow of death still over it, and a house in which an invalid [McKinley's wife] had lived, why it didn't seem as if the air from Heaven had blown through it." She opened windows, rearranged rooms, brought in fresh flowers, had new carpet laid, and replaced the heavy canopied beds in the children's rooms with their familiar white bedsteads from Oyster Bay.

Not since Willie and Tad Lincoln scampered through hallways and played hide-and-seek in closets had there been such a din in the old mansion. The children, ranging in age from three to seventeen, unabashedly made the White House their own. They dashed across its wooden floors on roller skates. They hid live reptiles in sofa cushions, walked upstairs on stilts, waded through the fountains on the landscaped grounds, and coaxed their pony to ride the elevator to the second-floor bedroom when seven-year-old Archie was sick. "Places that had not seen a human being for years were now made alive with the howls and laughter of these newcomers," observed Ike Hoover. The Roosevelt family has "done more to brighten and cheer the White House than a whole army of decorators," the *Atlanta Constitution* asserted, "and the merry prattle of children echoing through the corridors and apartments impart a homelike atmosphere which every caller is quick to notice and appreciate."

WHILE THE REPUBLICAN ESTABLISHMENT HARBORED misgivings about McKinley's successor, William Howard Taft was certain that Roosevelt possessed every needful quality to be a good president from the outset. In letters home, he rebutted charges of Roosevelt's "impulsiveness and lack of deliberation," citing the fortitude, honesty, and intelligence that characterized his friend's interactions with all manner of men over a wide-ranging career.

Saddened that McKinley had not lived to see "the consummation" of Taft's own endeavors in the Philippines, he nevertheless trusted that Roosevelt would provide the same steadfast support. "In so far as the work in the Philippines was concerned," Nellie noted, "my husband knew where the new President's sympathies were and he had no fears on that score." A week after McKinley's death, *Outlook* magazine published an extraordinary article by Theodore Roosevelt entitled "Governor William H. Taft." Written a month earlier by then Vice President Roosevelt, the extravagantly laudatory article prompted Horace to tease Will that "only a strenuous man like Teddie would put it so strongly in print, unless the subject of the article happened to be dead."

"I dislike speaking in hyperbole," Roosevelt began, "but I think that almost all men who have been brought in close contact, personally and officially, with Judge Taft are agreed that he combines . . . a standard of absolute unflinching rectitude on every point of public duty, and a literally dauntless courage and willingness to bear responsibility, with a knowledge of men, and a far-reaching tact and kindliness." Indeed, Roosevelt observed of his old friend, "few more difficult tasks have devolved upon any man of our nationality during our century and a quarter of public life than the handling of the Philippine Islands just at this time; and it may be doubted whether among men now living another could be found as well fitted as Judge Taft to do this incredibly difficult work."

Roosevelt's support would prove essential for Taft in the weeks that followed as one crisis after another threatened the relative peace and prosperity of the Philippines. Although most of the insurrectionists had surrendered their arms, a brutal uprising in late September 1901 stunned the town of Balangiga on the island of Samar, where a small garrison of American soldiers had set up an outpost at the request of the local mayor. Unbeknownst to the Americans, this request had been a cunning ploy to isolate the troops where they would be vulnerable to a surprise assault.

In the days preceding the ambush, throngs of what appeared to be local mothers and grandmothers in black mourning clothes had assembled at the local church, bearing small caskets said to hold the bodies of their dead children claimed by a recent cholera outbreak. Instead, the coffins held machetelike weapons, and the black-clad figures proved to be guerrilla fighters. Shortly after the church bells rang at 6 a.m. on Sunday morning, September 27, hundreds of insurrectionists suddenly charged into the mess hall and fell upon the unarmed soldiers. One sergeant was decapitated as he sat gripping his breakfast spoon; a private was immersed in the vat of boiling water used to clean utensils. Most of the others were hacked to death. Of seventy-four members of the unit, only twenty escaped with their lives.

"It was a disaster so ghastly in its details," Nellie recalled, "so undreamed of under the conditions of almost universal peace which had been established, that it created absolute panic." As a result, she remembered, attitudes toward the islanders shifted: "Men began to go about their everyday occupations in Manila carrying pistols conspicuously displayed, and half the people one met could talk of nothing else but their conviction that the whole archipelago was a smouldering volcano and that we were all liable to be murdered in our beds any night."

Army officials were quick to place blame for the massacre on Taft's "silly talk of benevolence and civilian rule [and] the soft mollycoddling of treacherous natives." General Jacob W. Smith ordered four companies into Samar with the directive to take "no prisoners. I wish you to kill and burn, the more you kill and burn the better you will please me. I want all persons killed who are capable of bearing arms." When requested to provide a minimum age under which residents of Balangiga might be spared, the general stated clearly: "Ten years." This reprehensible order would eventually lead to Smith's court-martial.

The Samar massacre made headlines in the States: "Disastrous Fight," cried the *New York Tribune*; "Slaughtered by Filipinos," accused the *Houston Daily Post*. The news of "the first severe reverse" in many months prompted a delegation of congressmen to visit the Philippines. Taft called for calm, stressing that the Samar tragedy did not characterize and should not reflect upon the entire Filipino people. "One of the Republicans has made an ass of himself by denouncing the Filipinos as savages and utterly unfit for anything good," Taft told his brother Charles. Contrary to the fearmongering circulated by the military, Taft maintained, "in all other parts of the Islands there is entire peace." If violence escalated, he argued, the military, having roused the native population "to such a pitch of enmity," would bear the blame. At each of the five hundred military posts strung throughout the islands, Taft lamented, they imposed themselves with a dangerous disregard for local communities. "Officers take the good houses in the town and the soldiers live in the church, the 'convento' (which is the priest's house), the schoolhouse or the provincial building," he reported, adding that property owners "are paid an arbitrarily fixed rent and are very fortunate if they get their rent."

The troubles that beset the Philippines were compounded when a highly contagious viral disease called rinderpest laid waste to three quarters of the island's draft cattle. Without these sturdy animals to plow the fields, "a dreadful depression in agriculture" resulted. With the spread of hunger, roving outlaw bands—in a phenomenon known as "ladronism"—preyed on their neighbors. And making matters worse, rats carrying the plague continued to multiply despite an extensive eradication campaign by the new Board of Health. "Altogether," the usually optimistic Taft understated, "we have not passed through the happiest months of our lives out here."

On October 1, Nellie and two of the commissioners' wives departed for a trip to China. That very afternoon, Taft fell seriously ill with what doctors mistakenly diagnosed as dengue fever. He remained bedridden for ten days, and when he returned to work, severe rectal pain prevented him from sitting. At the same time, a fungal infection developed in his groin. "While I have none of Job's comforters," Taft told Horace with grim humor, "I have many of his troubles." On October 25, doctors finally discovered a large perineal abscess, most likely caused by the invasion of bacteria into his system. With gangrene spreading, an immediate operation was necessary. As Taft was carried from the palace on a stretcher, his terrified ten-year-old daughter Helen burst into tears. Taft dispatched a telegram to Nellie: "Come dear am sick." When the ether was administered, he later joked, he deliriously wished that he could "hire a hall and make a speech." A large incision drained the cavity and removed the infected flesh. His doctors worried that the gangrenous tendency and blood poisoning had not been stopped in time, but they became more optimistic as the wound began to heal. The next day, Taft telegraphed Nellie again: "Much better don't shorten trip."

Confined to bed for several weeks, Taft secured an order from Washington appointing commission member Luke Wright as vice governor. This step provided him "peace of mind," assuring that his duties would not be neglected while he convalesced. No sooner had he resumed work than he immediately fell ill again, requiring a second operation. Roosevelt and Root decided that Taft should return to the United States until he was thoroughly recovered and rested. The Filipinos feared they would never see their friend and trusted advocate again. As Taft made ready to depart, he spoke to the large native crowd that surrounded the governor's palace to bid him anxious farewell, promising them he would return as soon as he was well.

WHILE TAFT ENDURED THE MOST discouraging period in his experience as viceroy, Roosevelt worked busily to draft his State of the Union address. Scheduled for early December when the legislature convened, his message would provide the first indication of his position on the most critical issue of the day—how best to address the massive trusts that were rapidly swallowing up competitors in one field after another. The period following McKinley's first election has been labeled "the high summer of corporate influence." Hundreds of small railroads, steamship companies, tobacco firms, copper industries, and collieries consolidated into single corporations that controlled as much as three quarters of the production in their particular fields.

In the year and a half since Roosevelt had failed to secure legislation to regulate the trusts in New York State, corporate consolidation had produced more than a thousand new mergers, including the creation of the world's most colossal trust, United States Steel. And every passing week heralded new combinations, stirring fear in small businessmen and consumers alike. Across the country, mergers brought absentee ownership, disregard for working conditions, higher prices, and lower wages.

Roosevelt believed the future of the Republican Party would be determined by its willingness to confront this malignancy. "I intend to work with my party and to make it strong by making it worthy of popular support," he told Joseph Bucklin Bishop. Despite this resolve, he saw clearly that an open denunciation of the Republican alliance with big business would set the bosses against him. They would deny him the presidential nomination in 1904, just as they had prevented his run for a second term as governor. Moreover, without the support of Republican leadership in Congress, he had no chance of passing even the mildest legislation to regulate the trusts.

The U.S. Senate presented the most powerful obstacle to any progressive reform. Because senators at the time were elected by state legislatures rather than by popular vote, the majority of senators owed their positions to their state machines. These organizations, William Allen White observed, were in thrall to the business interests that filled their coffers through campaign contributions or blatant bribery. In a number of states, the bosses made themselves senators; in others, wealthy individuals purchased their seats outright.

In a scathing editorial, the *New York Times* suggested that a millionaire could buy a Senate seat "just as he would buy an opera box, or a yacht, or any other luxury in which he can afford to indulge himself." In some instances, the *Times* reported, "the sale takes the form of open bribery of the legislators"; more often, the Senate seat was "simply the satisfaction of a 'claim' acknowledged by the leaders of the party and created by large contributions to the Party treasury." A widespread biting anecdote captured the popular view of the Senate: One night, Frances Cleveland, wife of the president, was awakened by a noise in the house. "Wake up," she nudged her husband. "There are robbers in the house." President Cleveland set her mind at ease. "There are no robbers in the House," he reassured her, "but there are lots in the Senate."

Five men comprised the inner circle in the Republican-controlled Senate. Sixty-four-year-old Mark Hanna had only recently joined the Senate after a long and successful business career dealing in coal, iron ore, shipping, and street railways. Architect of McKinley's two victorious campaigns, Hanna had earned the title of "national boss" of the Republican Party. Cartoons and editorials depicted a bloated capitalist, a tool of Wall Street, and a representative of the trusts; though more sympathetic to labor than most capitalists, Hanna had become an emblem of "the liaison between big business and government." Under his influence, not a single anti-trust suit had been prosecuted in two years, even as consolidation escalated beyond anything previously imagined. "In the final analysis," Lincoln Steffens succinctly charged, Hanna's methods "amount to the management of the American people in the interest of the American businessman for the profit of American business and politics."

Much like Platt, Hanna viewed Roosevelt as fundamentally unstable, a political hazard. "I told William McKinley it was a mistake to nominate that wild man at Philadelphia. I asked him if he realized what would happen if he should die," Hanna fumed. "Now look, that damned cowboy is President of the United States!" Early on, Roosevelt was convinced that he would eventually have to wrest party control from Hanna, but if an open break occurred, he told Steffens, "it would be a great calamity to the party and therefore to the public." To assail the powerful Hanna machine, the New York *World* noted, "would be as foolhardy as for a mill hand to fling himself upon a whirling buzz-saw."

Accordingly, Roosevelt reached out to the older man, expressing hope that they might one day share an intimacy similar to the one Hanna had enjoyed with McKinley. In addition, he requested a conference to solicit Hanna's counsel on political strategy and the upcoming message. "Go slow," Hanna cautioned. "It would not be possible to get wiser advice," Roosevelt graciously responded. Such patience would not cost Roosevelt, Mark Sullivan noted, for "his was the rising star; Hanna's was falling."

In addition, Roosevelt sought out the "Big Four," a group of veteran senators who commanded the power to pass, block, or kill any legislation: Nelson Aldrich of Rhode Island, John C. Spooner of Wisconsin, William B. Allison of Iowa, and Orville Platt (no relation to the New York boss) of Connecticut. Aldrich, the leader of the group, had become a multimillionaire through investments in street railways, banking, oil, gas, electricity, and rubber. Elected to the Senate in 1881 after two terms in the House, he was considered the most influential Republican legislator on the Hill. As chairman of the Finance Committee, he wielded absolute control over legislation on tariffs and trusts. Furthermore, Aldrich's only daughter, Abby, had married John D. Rockefeller, Jr., only son of the Standard Oil tycoon.

To each of these influential conservative leaders, Roosevelt made an expansive overture, similar in tone to his September 30 note to Senator Spooner: "I hope to keep in closest touch with you and to profit by your advice in the future as I have profited by it in the past." At regular intervals, he solicited their suggestions, inviting them to the White House for confidential conversations. As he drafted sections of his message, Roosevelt read them aloud to Hanna and the Big Four, appealing to them as valued mentors. He also included members of his cabinet in these sessions, inviting a frank discussion. The press described "a very pretty scene, this young president sincerely and earnestly placing his thoughts before his older counselors and begging them to criticize wherein they thought he was wrong."

Journalists noted in early November that Roosevelt had "made more progress in the preparation of his message to Congress than any of his predecessors ever did so far in advance." This lengthy process allowed him to write the entire message personally rather than simply compile sections submitted by various department heads, as was customary. As page after page accumulated, curiosity about the contents escalated. No subject attracted more interest than the trusts. "Many scribes with many minds, writing for many papers, are guessing and philosophizing as to what the president's message will and will not contain," one newspaper commented, concluding that "the only real thing anybody can guess or predict about with an approximation to truth is that it will be Roosevelt's message and nobody else's."

From the start, Roosevelt determined that he would not retreat "one hair's breadth" from the position on the trusts that he had established in his gubernatorial message, his vice-presidential acceptance speech, and the address he had delivered at the Minnesota State Fair five days before McKinley was shot. "More and more it is evident," he had declared that day in Minneapolis, "that the State, and if necessary, the Nation, has got to possess the right of supervision and control as regards the great corporations." He had repeatedly emphasized the need for corporations to deliver public reports to the government on their capitalization, profits, and financial structures. Now, he intended to highlight that recommendation in his annual message by calling for a cabinet-level Department of Commerce and Industries, an agency empowered to examine the workings of the big corporations.

Orville Platt warned Roosevelt that if Congress passed a law "going so far as to force corporations doing an interstate business to make reports to United States officials," it would likely be ruled unconstitutional. Hanna insisted that the proposition would only "furnish ammunition to the enemy in a political contest" and that "even the labor unions were not greatly interested in corporate control."

Roosevelt held his ground, even after a contentious session with his friends George Perkins and Harvard classmate Robert Bacon, both of whom were partners in J. P. Morgan's firm. While he remained "very fond" of both men, Roosevelt confided to a relative that they argued "like attorneys for a bad case, and at the bottom of their hearts each would know this . . . if he were not the representative of a man so strong and dominant a character as Pierpont Morgan." Not only did they encourage the president "to go back on" his previous demands for disclosure, but Perkins apparently suggested that he "do nothing at all, and say nothing except platitudes; accept the publication of what some particular company chooses to publish, as a favor, instead of demanding what we think ought to be published from all companies as a right." As the historian Eric Goldman observes, the practice of "not prying into business affairs was accepted as part of a prevailing laissez-faire."

Just as Abraham Lincoln would exorcise his frustrations in "hot letters" he would put aside unsent, Roosevelt confined his rancor to private diatribe and followed it with a public letter for Douglas Robinson (Corinne's husband) to share with the two men. "I much enjoyed the visit from Perkins," he amiably wrote. "I am particularly desirous to see him and Bacon as often as possible."

To Paul Dana, conservative editor of the New York *Sun*, Roosevelt spoke more directly. In mid-November, Dana wrote a long, critical letter to Roosevelt admonishing that "the proposition that the Federal Government shall lay its hand on business corporations is revolutionary. . . . It would open the door to an unlimited increase of the powers of the Federal Government." Adding to his argument, Dana insisted that "there is no authority of public opinion for the demand for trust legislation. . . . I deny the political right of the Republican successor of President McKinley to undertake it." Roosevelt acknowledged Dana's warnings but had no intention of altering his course. "Your letter causes me concern," he replied, "to ask me to alter my convictions as to the proper course to be pursued about these big corporations is much like asking me to alter my convictions about the Monroe Doctrine and the need of building a navy. . . . You have no conception of the revolt that would be caused if I did nothing."

On the morning of December 3, 1901, Roosevelt's completed message, totaling more than 20,000 words, was carried to the House and the Senate to be read out by a clerk, as had been the custom since Thomas Jefferson sent the message in writing. "A hush immediately fell over the body as the clerk began in clear, firm, and distinct tones to read the opening paragraphs," the *Washington Times* reported, observing that "he did not read in the usual singsong monotone, but with emphasis and expression." The recitation took about two hours, but "there was interest in every line, and members of both houses listened with unusual attention." The assembled legislators generally received such messages "with scant courtesy," the Washington correspondent for the *Chicago Record-Herald* noted, retiring to the "allurement of the smoking-room or restaurant. To-day they sat still."

The message opened with an emotional denunciation of McKinley's assassin, "a professed anarchist, inflamed by the teachings of professed anarchists." Such men, "who object to all governments, good and bad alike," only sabotaged progress, Roosevelt declared. This impassioned opening introduced Roosevelt's agenda of moderate, reasoned reform. His tempered approach toward curbing the abuses of industrialism, he asserted, would prove the surest way to combat the alarming rise in anarchism, socialism, and demagoguery.

In the long sentences of the president's message, semicolons followed by "yet" or "but" separated clauses that balanced each side of an issue, reflecting Roosevelt's characteristic "on the one hand, on the other" style of crediting antagonistic views. "The captains of industry who have driven the railway system across the continent, who have built up our commerce, who have developed our manufactures, have on the whole done great good to our people," he proclaimed, "yet it remains true . . . there have been abuses connected with the accumulation of wealth." Repeatedly, he employed this rhetorical display of evenhandedness: "To strike with ignorant violence" at the great trusts "endangers the interests of all . . . and yet it is also true that practical efforts must be made to correct those evils." If he had no patience for those who resorted "to hatred and fear" to denounce the trusts, Roosevelt made it clear that he shared the "wide-spread conviction" that certain invidious practices were "hurtful to the general welfare." While he stopped short of advocating prohibition of the trusts, he demanded that they be "supervised and within reasonable limits controlled."

Roosevelt's strategic deliberations provoked a stinging parody from Finley Dunne's Mr. Dooley: "Th' trusts, says [Roosevelt], are heejoous monsthers built up be th' inlightened intherprise iv th' men that have done so much to advance progress in our beloved counthry. On wan hand I wud stamp thim undher fut; on th' other hand not so fast."

Although Roosevelt's carefully balanced propositions invited accusations of equivocation, the rhetoric of his message allowed him to set the stage for reform without immediately alienating corporate interests. Conservative critics, soothed by language touting the benefits of capitalism and condemning the populist call for the total destruction of the trusts, missed the true implications of Roosevelt's central argument concerning the federal government's responsibility to regulate corporations in the public interest. "It is no limitation upon property rights or freedom of contract," he noted, "to require that when men receive from government the privilege of doing business under corporate form," they assume an obligation to the public. Through the creation of a new Department of Commerce, the government would merely exercise its duty "to inspect and examine" corporate finances as a means to determine whether regulation or taxation was necessary. Should Congress determine that "it lacks the constitutional power to pass such an act," Roosevelt recommended that an amendment to the Constitution "be submitted to confer that power."

Public attention immediately following his message focused on the trusts. Yet Roosevelt had also outlined his plans for the welfare of wageworkers, reciprocity agreements, railway rebates, forest preserves, irrigation of arid lands, and the isthmian canal—as well as his ideas for reorganizing the Army and expanding the Navy. At the close of his address, he returned to the tragedy of McKinley's death, acknowledging the expressions of sympathy and grief "from every quarter of the civilized world" that had touched "the hearts" of every American.

Generally, both the public and the press received Roosevelt's address well. "No other message in ten years past has been read by so many American citizens," claimed *The Independent*. The tenor of the State of the Union was viewed as "characteristic of the man; self-assertive, determined, honest, patriotic, permeated with the spirit of progress." Despite widespread approbation, newspapers remained "skeptical of any important outcome from the president's recommendations regarding trusts," convinced that Roosevelt's primary goal at this juncture was his own nomination and election. "He knows very well that no man can secure the Republican nomination over the trusts," one Indiana paper editorialized. The trusts understood the proposals as mere theatre to satisfy reformers. While it was "refreshing" to see "a bold man struggling with the devil-fish of party intrigue," until the middle-class confusion about corporate consolidation galvanized a demand for positive action, the conservative powers in Congress would have no trouble in preventing Roosevelt's proposals from even reaching the floor.

THE FINANCIAL WORLD WAS STAGGERED on February 19, 1902 when Roosevelt announced the government's intention to bring an anti-trust suit against the Northern Securities Company. This giant holding company had recently merged the rail and shipping lines of James Hill, J. P. Morgan, and Cornelius Vanderbilt in the Northwest with those of E. H. Harriman, the Rockefellers, and the Goulds in the Southwest. Consummated during Roosevelt's watch, this vast new combination, first reported on at length by Ray Baker, touched a nerve in the president.

Baker, who had worked for months on a series of articles profiling the nation's tycoons, was well positioned to cover the spectacular merger. He had returned to New York from his sojourn in Arizona reenergized and eager to tackle the unsettling issues of labor and capital that had preoccupied him since his college days. He felt that he "had come to see and know the workers' side" as he covered the Pullman strike for the *Chicago Record*, conversing at length with Eugene Debs and spending long weeks with a number of other labor leaders. "I knew, or thought I knew, the powerful incentives for organization behind their movements," he wrote, "and their demands for more wages and more freedom." Realizing he must also develop an understanding of "the business and financial side," Baker was thrilled when McClure suggested a series focused on the captains of industry. While he did not consider these articles to be "revolutionary" or "crusading," his research shaped an evolving conception of capitalism's dazzling strengths and troubling weaknesses.

Baker's first article, on J. P. Morgan, published in October 1901, portrayed a Wall Street giant who controlled "a yearly income and expenditure nearly as great as that of Imperial Germany, paid taxes on a debt greater than that of many of the lesser nations of Europe, and by employing 250,000 men, supported a population of over one million souls, almost a nation in itself." While Baker acknowledged that the powerful private banker was "an expert financial doctor," who had rescued the American economy from panic on three separate occasions, he withheld judgment on whether Morgan had employed that "unquestioned genius to the highest purpose."

The alarming dimensions of Morgan's empire were delineated in a second, follow-up article that analyzed the structure of the United States Steel Corporation. This immense enterprise, the first billion-dollar corporation in the world, had been conceived the previous April when J. P. Morgan, Andrew Carnegie, and the leaders of nine other steel companies merged to avoid a ruinous, competitive war. Many of these men, Baker concluded, "were unquestionably forced" into consolidation "against their will." The resulting corporation produced "more than a quarter of the entire [steel] production of the world" and dictated "the destinies of a population nearly as large as that of Maryland or Nebraska." To enumerate its corporate possessions glazes the mind: more than 18,000 coke ovens, 80 blast furnaces, six giant railroad companies, and 115 steamships. "It is difficult to convey any adequate idea of the magnitude of the Steel Corporation," Baker concluded. "Nothing like this has ever been seen before."

Baker's research for these two articles on J. P. Morgan provided clear perspective on the machinations behind the formation of Northern Securities. The merger, Baker explained, stemmed from a costly quarrel the previous spring: two rival railroads that controlled the overwhelming majority of railroad lines in their respective regions had fought for control of a third railroad. In the aftermath, under the leadership of J. P. Morgan, "the contestants gathered themselves together, counted their losses, smoothed over their difficulties," and forged a gargantuan new holding company. On November 13, 1901, Northern Securities became "the second largest corporation in the world," behind only U.S. Steel. With tens of thousands of miles of track spanning the continent and hundreds of ships, Baker declared it "absolute dictator in its own territory, with monarchical powers in all matters relating to transportation."

"None outside the golden coterie know all the details," Baker observed, presciently adding, "the future will find one of its great problems in deciding how big a business enterprise must become before the public is entitled to know the full details of its management." It appeared certain that "the same dozen or more men" would own "nearly all the great railroads of America and the greatest industries besides." Indeed, with this new combination in place, a person might journey "from England to China on regular lines of steamships and railroads without once passing from the protecting hollow of Mr. Morgan's hand." Would the day come, Baker mused, "when an imperial M will repose within the wreath of power?" The implication that these few men were "more powerful than the people, more powerful than Congress, more powerful than the government," observed Mark Sullivan, "presented to Roosevelt a challenge such as his nature would never ignore."

Roosevelt asked his attorney general, Philander C. Knox, if an anti-trust suit against Northern Securities could be sustained. A brilliant lawyer who had enjoyed a successful career in Pittsburgh, Knox calculated the odds for several weeks before reporting to Roosevelt that he believed an anti-trust suit based on the Sherman Anti-Trust Law could be won. Roosevelt kept his decision to proceed from everyone else in his cabinet, including Elihu Root, his closest adviser. Root did not share "the view that Taft and I take about corporations," he later explained to a journalist friend. The unexpected announcement that the government was in the process of preparing a bill "to test the validity of the merger" appeared "like a thunderbolt from a clear sky." Many commentators feared the outbreak of "a wholesale war on industrial trusts."

"Not since the assassination of President McKinley has the securities market been compelled to face news for which it was wholly unprepared," declared the *New York Herald*, under headlines announcing a precipitous fall in stock prices. Financiers could not fathom how Roosevelt lacked the courtesy to provide advance notice. He was, after all, one of them: a Harvard man, a member of their clubs. "If we have done anything wrong," J. P. Morgan complained in a hastily arranged meeting with the president three days later, "send your man to my man and they can fix it up." An agreeable resolution was impossible, Roosevelt countered. "We don't want to fix it up," Knox confirmed, "we want to stop it." Turning to Roosevelt, Morgan inquired if U.S. Steel was in jeopardy. "Certainly not," Roosevelt replied, "unless we find out that in any case they have done something that we regard as wrong." Roosevelt remarked to Knox after Morgan's departure: "That is a most illuminating illustration of the Wall Street point of view. Mr. Morgan could not help regarding me as a big rival operator."

Morgan's partners were appalled at the lack of recognition for their substantial contribution to American progress. "It really seems hard," James Hill complained, "that we should be compelled to fight for our lives against the political adventurers who have never done anything but pose and draw a salary." Members of New York's legal community were scathing in their opinion of Knox, calling him "an unknown country lawyer from Pennsylvania." When these words reached the president, his response was curt: "They will know this country lawyer before this suit is ended."

For a quarter of a century, Roosevelt later observed, "the power of the mighty industrial overlords of the country had increased with giant strides, while the methods of controlling them, or checking abuses by them on the part of the people, through the Government, remained archaic and therefore practically impotent." The anti-trust suit "served notice on everybody that it was going to be the Government, and not the Harrimans, who governed these United States." At the same time, Roosevelt's actions clearly demonstrated to powerful Republican leaders "that he was President in fact as well as in name."

Roosevelt next turned his attention to the beef trust. Allegations had surfaced in the press that the big beef packers, led by Armour & Co. and Swift & Co., had agreed to parcel out territories and fix prices, resulting in a sharp cost increase for families purchasing meat. The advent of refrigerated freight cars had diminished the advantage once held by local butchers, facilitating consolidation among the big national firms. Labeling the beef trust "an atrocious conspiracy of greed against need," one New York newspaper challenged anyone to deny "that such absolute control by a few men over the food supply of a nation is in the highest degree hostile to the public welfare." After the Justice Department investigated the matter, Roosevelt directed Knox to bring suit against the beef trust. "This is the right course," the *World* editorialized, "and the president has proved himself, as he did in directing the similar suit against Northern Securities Co., to be wiser and more resolute than leaders of his party in Congress, who sit supinely in the path of a rising storm of popular indignation and refuse to do anything to 'disturb the business' of protecting monopolies by law!"

For all the accolades that attended his confrontations with these massive combinations, Roosevelt considered the Sherman Act a blunt instrument that might prove "more dangerous to the patient than the disease." In the hands of zealots, unable or unwilling to distinguish *good* trusts that yielded efficient operations, lower prices, and better service, from *bad* trusts that used predatory tactics to gain monopoly, artificially depress production, and extort unreasonable prices, the Sherman Act might destroy the very prosperity it was intended to foster. Roosevelt far preferred the approach recommended in his annual address—new legislation enabling the national government to examine corporate records and determine what remedies, if any, were needed. Nevertheless, "with the path to effective regulation blocked by a stubborn, conservative Congress," the historian George Mowry observes, "the only way for Roosevelt to bring the arrogant capitalists to heel was through the judicious use of the anti-trust laws."

For Nellie and Will Taft, the winter of Roosevelt's skirmishes with the trusts marked "a period of bereavement and protracted illnesses." During the long sea voyage from Manila to San Francisco, doctors discovered that Taft's incision was not healing properly. It was "opened and drained," but months of bed rest the previous fall had weakened his knees and ankles, making it painful for him to stand for any protracted time. To compound matters, Nellie was suffering from what was later diagnosed as malaria. In San Francisco, they were informed that their cross-country trip on the Union Pacific would be interrupted by a severe snowstorm in the Midwest. Having received word that her mother was seriously ill, Nellie insisted on moving forward nonetheless. In Utah, a catastrophic blizzard froze water pipes and broke the train's heating system. Wrapped in blankets, they pressed eastward. Even after enduring these hardships, they were too late: in Omaha, Nellie received a telegram bearing the news that her mother had died the previous day.

Taft remained with Nellie and the children in Cincinnati until he had to leave for Washington to testify before the Senate Committee on the Philippines. From the moment he arrived in the capital, Taft was surrounded by affectionate support. War Secretary Elihu Root and his wife insisted that he board with them during his stay, which eventually stretched to thirty days. No sooner had Taft reached their home on Rhode Island Avenue than the president called with plans to join them that evening. Taft was pleased to find Roosevelt "just the same as ever," writing to Nellie that it was hard "to realize that he is the President. He greatly enjoys being President and shows not the slightest sign of worry or hard work in his looks or manner." Scarcely a night passed for Taft without an invitation to dine with the Roosevelts, the Lodges, the Hays, or the Hannas.

Despite his warm reception in Washington, Taft worried about the hearings. Called by Massachusetts senator George Hoar, an eloquent anti-imperialist who insisted on exposing the truth of events in the Philippines, the proceedings would likely be exhausting and unproductive. "If General Chafee is right," Hoar proclaimed, referring to the Civil War veteran who served as the military governor of the Philippines, "there is not a man in those islands who is not conspiring against the government and eager for liberty." The day before the hearings convened, Taft wrote to his brother Horace, playfully requesting "compassion and merciful judgment, when you shall read of the condemnation to which I shall probably be subjected by anti-imperialists and our democratic brethren. Please do not deny the fact that you are still my brother, though a mortified one."

Yet throughout a long week of testimony Taft acquitted himself exceedingly well, drawing a sharp line between the military's negative estimates of the Filipino people and his own more hopeful perspective. "I have much more confidence in the Filipino and his loyalty than have a good many of the military officers," he assured them. Asked by Democratic senator Joseph Rawlins if the country was not "flying in the face" of Asiatic culture and tradition by imposing a republican form of government, he expressed his conviction that such difficulties could be successfully negotiated. In the course of his governorship, Taft said, he had developed "somewhat intimate relations" with the Filipino people and was certain that the overwhelming majority wanted peace and a stable government.

Taft told the committee, as he had told McKinley, that he had not supported the idea of occupying the Philippines, "but we are there." America's primary responsibility, he maintained, must be to help the Filipinos achieve self-rule, slowly inducting them into the political process. Eventually a determination would be possible regarding the future of the Philippines—whether they should apply for statehood, declare full independence, or perhaps develop a commonwealth connection to the United States similar to that of Canada or Australia to Great Britain. He called on Congress to reduce the tariff on Philippine imports and to establish a popularly elected assembly to constitute a lower branch of the government while the Philippine Commission continued to comprise the upper branch. Taft understood that some senators considered this policy "too progressive and too radical," but he believed it would provide "a great educational school" in the art of democracy.

When pressed about instances of military brutality against the Philippine insurgents, he admitted "that cruelties have been inflicted; that people have been shot when they ought not to have been," and that soldiers had employed water torture to extract information from insurgents. Courts-martial had been ordered to address these abuses. He insisted, however, that the military had largely exercised uncommon "compassion" and "restraint."

"Following his appearance," one reporter noted, "not a speaker on either side but paused a moment to pay at least some small tribute to the man." By speaking freely and openly, Taft "had taken his fellow-citizens into his confidence on the dangers and the doubtful points of our 'experiment' as well as on its rosier aspects." In return, he had earned their confidence "in his sincerity and his ability to meet the task in hand." Extremely pleased, Elihu Root assured Taft that if he continued his great service to the Philippines for another year or more, "there was not anything in the gift of the President" that would be withheld.

The pleasure of Taft's stay in Washington was cut short when doctors determined that yet another operation was required to remove a deep abscess that had developed in the aftermath of his previous surgery. The news that he would be confined to his bed for three weeks left him feeling downcast: "I have been hacked and cut and curetted and etherized so much and have lain so long in bed that a continuance of all this for the better part of a month I do not welcome and should deeply regret if it delayed my return." Nonetheless, he submitted gamely to a third operation in six months, and this time happily recorded that "the cure seems to be complete."

Contemplating his return to the Philippines, Taft decided to stop first in Rome, where he hoped personally to negotiate some solution to the perplexing problem of the Spanish friars, a situation that had plagued him from his first days in the islands. To the Filipino people, Taft understood, the friars represented "the crown of Spain, and every oppression by the Spanish government was traced by them to the men whose political power had far outgrown that exercised by them as priests." Over the years, these clerics had come to operate as political bosses, acquiring 400,000 acres of the best agricultural lands and assuming despotic power over the police, the civil government, and the schools. Once the revolution began, he wrote, they "had to flee for their lives. Fifty of them were killed and three hundred of them were imprisoned." If they should return and attempt to reclaim title to the land, he feared violence would break out. Roosevelt and Root deputized Taft to inform the Holy See that the United States would purchase the lands for a fair price so long as the hated friars never returned to the archipelago. The land would then be redistributed among the poor Filipino farmers.

"What a splendid thing it will be to go to Rome," Nellie exclaimed when she learned of her husband's strategic mission. In the weeks before the planned trip, her own health had improved. Blood tests revealed a reduction in her malarial infection and her spleen had returned to normal. But just before they were scheduled to sail, Robert contracted scarlet fever, making departure impossible for Nellie and the children. "What a disarrangement of our plans!" Taft lamented. "And more than this what a trial for Robert and you."

Louise Taft was in Millbury, Massachusetts, when Will called to explain her grandson's illness and to bid her goodbye. Realizing that Nellie could not travel, Louise offered to accompany her son. Nellie, despite her own disappointment, was relieved that Will would have the comfort and assistance of his mother during the trip. "Within twenty-four hours," Nellie recalled, "the intrepid old lady of seventy-four packed her trunks and was in New York ready to sail." In the years since Alphonso's death, Louise had astonished her family with her unflagging activity. "She went wherever she liked," Nellie noted with admiration, "and it never seemed to occur to her that it was unusual for a woman of her age to travel everywhere with so much self-reliance." Until Nellie arrived in Rome with the children more than a month later, Louise managed affairs with "an energy and an enterprise" that overwhelmed her son with "pleasure and pride."

Several factors complicated Taft's mission. He had to take care throughout the process that his dealings with the Pope never implied diplomatic recognition, which would violate America's separation of church and state and incur the hostility of Protestants. At the same time, he sought to defuse Catholics' fears that he was antagonistic to the Church. His initial meeting with the Pope, still "lively as a cricket" and "bubbling with humor" at eighty-two, went better than he could have hoped. Most significantly, Taft noted, he secured the pontiff's promise to meet all questions "in a broad spirit of conciliation," though the details were left to a group of cardinals who proved far less accommodating. Weeks went by before the cardinals finally issued a statement on June 21, 1902. The Church would consent to sell its property in the Philippines, but would not withdraw the friars currently in residence. With this unsatisfactory conclusion, negotiations were suspended.

When Taft at last prepared to sail for the Philippines, word arrived that a cholera epidemic had struck Manila. He decided Nellie and the children should remain in Europe for an additional month, hoping that by then the outbreak "would have run its course." Writing to Nellie from the steamer, he confessed feeling apprehensive about his reception in Manila. "I don't know how the people will take the result of my visit to Rome. Then they are not in very good humor about the strict cholera regulations . . . I may land with a few handshakings and a dull thud." He regretted her absence but trusted she would soon join him and her indispensable support would help him surmount all difficulties. "I can not tell you what a comfort it is to me to think of you as my wife and helpmeet," he declared. "I measure every woman I meet with you and they are all found wanting. Your character, your independence, your straight mode of thinking, your quiet planning, your loyalty, your sympathy when I call for it (as I do too readily) your affection and love (for I know I have it) all these Darling make me happy only to think about them."

To his amazement, Taft's arrival triggered what was said to be the grandest demonstration of popular support ever recorded in the history of the Philippines. Thirty thousand Filipinos had come from the hills and neighboring provinces to welcome Taft home. Whistles sounded and bells rang as soon as his vessel was spied. From the harbor to the palace, his carriage was met by cheering crowds. Triumphal arches and flags decorated the streets. Children tossed flowers and released doves into the air as Taft went by.

In his speech at the palace, Taft told the people "in a straightforward way of his experiences in Washington and Rome." Though negotiations with the Vatican had been suspended, "the sale of church lands to the government was assured," and he was confident that an agreement to remove the friars would eventually be worked out. Taft took comfort that the natives had clearly interpreted his visit to Rome "as a real effort on the part of the United States to do something which could not have been for any other benefit than the benefit of the Filipino people." Visibly moved, he promised to work unremittingly for the people of the islands. So "universal, earnest, and enthusiastic" was the response, reporters noted, that it left no doubt that Taft had earned "a proud position in the hearts of the Filipino people."

Theodore Roosevelt as a Harvard sophomore in 1878. Never content to sit still and listen, he constantly posed questions in class until one professor cut him short: "Now look here, Roosevelt, let me talk. I'm running this course."

2

Known to his admiring Yale classmates as "Big Bill," Taft's affable disposition made him one of the most popular men on campus. His fellow students elected him class orator in 1877, an honor considered "the greatest prize in college."

3

Young Will Taft, perched on a gatepost in the foreground, grew up with four brothers and one sister in this substantial, two-story yellow brick house in a fashionable neighborhood of Cincinnati.

4

When the Roosevelt family returned from a yearlong tour of Europe and the Mediterranean in 1873, they moved into a stately mansion on West 57th Street in Manhattan that boasted a magnificent library, pictured, and a fully equipped gymnasium.

5

6

Intimate childhood friendships flourished between Edith Carow *(above left, seated on the ground)* and the Roosevelt siblings Teedie, Corinne, and Elliott *(left to right)* during their vacations at Tranquillity *(below),* a beloved summer retreat on Long Island. Teedie and Edith's adolescent romance came to an abrupt end in August 1878. Just eight weeks later the young Harvard student met Alice Hathaway Lee. For Teedie, pictured here *(above right)* with Alice *(seated)* and Corinne, "it was a real case of love at first sight."

7

8

As young girls, both Edith Carow and Nellie Herron hungered for intellectual stimulation. Edith formed an all-girl literary society (*above*) with Teedie's sister, Corinne (*seated center*), while Nellie Herron, shown below to the left of twenty-six-year-old Will Taft, organized a lively Saturday night debate society among her circle of friends. Taft's brother Horace is at far right and Nellie's sister Maria at far left (*standing*). Nellie's salon flourished for three years. "Nobody is absent when he can help it," Taft enthusiastically remarked.

9

Seen here as a twenty-four-year-old New York State legislator, Roosevelt found the state assembly to be a "great school" for learning the rough-and-tumble of politics and how to cooperate with colleagues far removed from his patrician background.

11

The years Roosevelt spent visiting this Badlands cabin *(above)* and working as a cattle rancher *(below left)* would become critical to his evolving public image—as in this 1889 cartoon *(below right)*, where Thomas Nast emblazons Roosevelt as a cowboy in the popular imagination.

12

13

As New York City police commissioner, Roosevelt, seen here in his office on Mulberry Street circa 1896, would traverse the city streets at night. Concealing his evening clothes beneath a long coat, he made a series of surprise inspections, checking if policemen on the beat were faithfully safeguarding their posts. He was accompanied on some of these night rambles by Lincoln Steffens *(right)*, then an enterprising crime reporter for the New York *Evening Post*, but who later joined the celebrated team at *McClure's* magazine.

Samuel S. McClure, the indomitable and visionary founder of *McClure's* magazine, faced obstacles unimaginable to Roosevelt or Taft. Raised in poverty in northern Ireland in the thatched cottage shown below, McClure emigrated to America as a young child. Though penniless, his charismatic personality and extraordinary mental abilities earned him a place at Knox College in Galesburg, Illinois. He is pictured here as an undergraduate circa 1878.

16

17

18

19

20

21

In 1893, McClure *(top left)* launched the magazine that would become the engine of progressive reform. At the time he headed the magazine, McClure was capable of wild bursts of creativity, punctuated by periods of exhaustion and depression. His staff, considered by many the most brilliant gathering of journalists ever assembled, included Ida Tarbell *(top right)*, Ray Stannard Baker *(bottom left)*, and William Allen White *(bottom right)*, as well as Lincoln Steffens.

22

24

23

"I am having immense fun running the Navy," Assistant Secretary Roosevelt boasted from his office in the Navy Department *(top)*. While President McKinley vacillated about intervening in Cuba, TR could not contain his excitement at the prospect of conquest, as this 1898 cartoon suggests *(bottom)*. A more skeptical Ida Tarbell *(center right)*, covering the developing story for *McClure's*, derided Roosevelt's martial enthusiasm as that of "a boy on roller skates." Even before war had been declared, she wrote, Roosevelt "saw himself an important unit in an invading army."

25

26

27

Far from dreading the challenge of moving her three children over 8,000 miles from home, Nellie Taft—shown here *(top)* en route to Manila—"knew instantly" that she "didn't want to miss a big and novel experience." At the Malacañan Palace *(center)*, she blazed a trail by opening her guest lists to Filipinos and Americans on an equal basis. "Neither politics nor race," she insisted, "should influence our hospitality in any way." In Albany, Edith Roosevelt turned a cavernous governor's mansion *(bottom)* into a comfortable home for her six children, adding a nursery, a schoolroom, and a gymnasium.

28

Will and Nellie Taft seated in the Philippine governor's residence circa 1901 with their children, four-year-old Charlie *(standing in rear)*, ten-year-old Helen *(seated)*, and twelve-year-old Robert *(standing at right)*.

29

Governor Taft in 1902, somewhat awkwardly riding a carabao, the breed of water buffalo relied upon by Filipino farmers to till fields and haul timber.

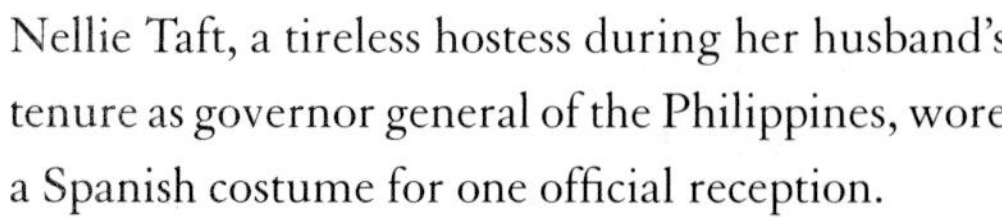

Nellie Taft, a tireless hostess during her husband's tenure as governor general of the Philippines, wore a Spanish costume for one official reception.

30

31

32

After his widely publicized Rough Rider heroics in Cuba, Roosevelt—as seen in this *Harper's Weekly* cartoon from 1900 *(above left)*—was an obvious choice for vice president on the Republican ticket. Stumping for McKinley *(above right)*, Roosevelt became "the central figure, the leading general, the field marshal" of the entire Republican campaign; yet the prize of victory was a do-nothing office that Roosevelt himself believed "ought to be abolished." On September 6, 1901, the kaleidoscope turned: an assassin's bullet made him at forty-two years of age the youngest president in the country's history. Roosevelt is pictured below in 1901, conferring with reporters shortly after McKinley was shot.

33

34

35

During whistle-stop speaking tours across the country in 1902 and 1903, Roosevelt began to test the phrase "the square deal"—the slogan that would come to characterize his entire domestic program. After visiting a majestic grove of giant sequoias in California, he exhorted an audience "to protect these mighty trees, these wonderful monuments of beauty."

36

Roosevelt's inauguration: After weeks of cloudy skies and heavy snow, the morning of March 4, 1905, broke "blue, flecked with lazily floating white clouds."

37

To audiences who gathered at the Capitol to watch him take the oath of office, the new president appeared "supremely happy." Roosevelt's election, the journalist William Allen White predicted, was a clear signal that "the Republican party has turned the corner and is now on a new road."

President Roosevelt's dynamic, often collaborative, relationship with a rising class of progressive journalists resulted in a wave of public enthusiasm for political and social reforms. "The Crusaders," a cartoon from the February 21, 1906, edition of *Puck* magazine, portrays Ida Tarbell, Ray Stannard Baker, Lincoln Steffens, S. S. McClure, and others as medieval knights in shining armor, with shields and weapons, waving banners emblazoned with the names of their publications, crusading against corruption and injustice.

Back in the United States, Taft's visit to Rome met with less enthusiasm. "I am in the worst hole politically I have ever been in my life," Roosevelt confided to his newspaper friend Herman Kohlsaat. "The whole Catholic Church is on my back." Though every intelligence from the Philippines established "what a lecherous lot of scoundrels the Spanish friars are," Roosevelt privately railed, Catholics maintained that these reports were "simply propaganda to establish Protestant missions in the Philippines." If such "calumnies" did not cease, the president was cautioned, Catholics would join en masse to thwart his nomination in two years' time.

"As things have turned out, it has probably been unfortunate that we got you to stop at Rome," Roosevelt wrote Taft, lamenting that the Catholic uproar had "rather complicated the political situation" at home. Perhaps, he suggested, they should "let this whole matter go and simply administer the civil government, leaving the friars and other ecclesiastical bodies to get along as best they can."

Taft responded vehemently. "While the result of the visit to Rome may have been bad in the United States," he told Roosevelt, "I do not state it too strongly when I say that the visit to Rome has done us a great deal of good in this country." Taft's letter persuaded the president to continue talks with the Vatican, which eventually produced an agreement. The United States paid $7.5 million for the lands, which were divided into small parcels and sold to natives, creating a new landowning class. Though the Spanish friars were never formally withdrawn, their power dwindled with the appointment of priests and bishops from other countries. Under Taft's deliberate leadership, a solution had been found that eased tensions and, in the end, finally satisfied the islanders, the administration, and the Catholic Church alike.

On July 1, 1902, Speaker David Henderson delivered a rousing speech to his colleagues, flattering them before they adjourned that "no house of representatives since the adoption of the Constitution had done so much work as this one." The Speaker's laudatory words "touched a responsive chord" among the members, who saluted both their Speaker and themselves with unrestrained emotion. "While the cheering and applause were still in progress," one reporter noted, "the members on the floor began singing 'My Country, Tis of Thee.' It was taken up by the correspondents in the press gallery, and soon the vast hall was ringing" as spectators joined in for "The Star-Spangled Banner" and other patriotic tunes. The mood of jubilation culminated when General

Charles Hooker of Mississippi, a Confederate veteran who had lost his arm in the war, "took his place by the side of the speaker, and together they sang 'Dixie.' "

Roosevelt's assessment of the work done by the 57th Congress was far less sanguine. Nonetheless, he was delighted by the passage of the bill providing $170 million to acquire land and begin construction of the Panama Canal. "By far the most important action I took in foreign affairs during the time I was President," he later reflected, "related to the Panama Canal." He also took "a keen personal pride" in the Newlands Reclamation Act, which set aside revenue from the sale of western public lands into a national fund for the construction of dams and irrigation projects. The act was structured to enable small farmers to settle previously arid lands. "I regard the irrigation business as one of the great features of my administration," he remarked at the time.

Congress also appropriated more than half a million dollars for badly needed renovations to the White House. Despite its thirty-one rooms, the mansion did not provide comfortable living quarters for a family, especially a large one like the Roosevelts'. The entire first floor, except for the family dining room, was used for state functions; the second floor was divided between a private wing and executive offices, including the president's office, the Cabinet Room, and the telegraph room. The family quarters consisted of only five bedrooms and lacked both closet space and sufficient bathroom facilities. The kitchen was outmoded, and the floors throughout "trembled when one walked on them."

Previous presidents had failed to persuade Congress that a thorough renovation was necessary. The Roosevelts alone, Sylvia Morris writes, "had the determination, in spite of criticism, to forge ahead with the long-overdue changes." The plans, drawn up by the architect Charles McKim, called for the construction of a new West Wing office building connected to the main house by a colonnade, freeing up the old second-floor spaces for conversion into extra bedrooms, bathrooms, and sitting rooms—as well as a boudoir, a library, and a den. The demolition and major renovations were scheduled during the summer months, allowing Edith and the children to escape to Oyster Bay. Roosevelt had originally planned to remain in the White House but was finally persuaded to move into a large town house on Lafayette Square.

Despite his satisfaction with the Canal bill, the Reclamation Act, and the successful appropriations for the White House renovation project, Roosevelt was sorely disappointed by the failure of Congress to take action on the signal economic issue of the day: the trusts. The call to establish a Department of Commerce with the power to demand information and determine necessary regulation of corporate trusts had been at the center of Roosevelt's first annual message. While the bill was debated at the committee level, Republican opposition prevented any real progress. Meanwhile, the Democratic attack on the trusts gathered momentum, heightening Roosevelt's anxiety that Republicans would pay at the polls for their failure to address the issue.

Senators obligated to the sugar trust also had managed to kill a reciprocity bill designed to reduce the tariffs on Cuban exports, including raw sugar, by 20 percent. The reduction of duties, Roosevelt argued in a special message, would boost the young republic's economy and simultaneously open Cuba's markets to the United States. "I ask that the Cubans be given all possible chance to use to the best advantage the freedom of which Americans have such right to be proud," he exhorted, "and for which so many American lives have been sacrificed." Despite his plea, no action was taken. "Their conduct will return to plague them later," Joseph Bishop predicted.

With the adjournment of Congress, Roosevelt headed to Oyster Bay for a six-week vacation with his family before launching a campaign swing to generate popular enthusiasm for Republicans in the upcoming midterm elections. The failure of the Republican Congress to take action on corporate regulation and reciprocity issues had furnished Democrats with powerful proof, despite Roosevelt's anti-trust initiatives, that the Republican Party was "in alliance with the trusts and with all the great monopolies of every description which are preying upon the country." By appealing directly to the people and lending his personal prestige to the fight for trust regulation, Roosevelt hoped to save his party from defeat in November.

Traveling by train and open carriage, accompanied by dozens of reporters, he opened his campaign in New England. In each of the six states, he delivered speeches focused predominantly on the trust issue, emphasizing the distinction between his own reasonable call for oversight of federal regulation of trusts and the Democratic crusade to eradicate all trusts in a manner that would "destroy all our prosperity." Roosevelt understood that many looked back with nostalgia on the pre-industrial era, when "the average man lived more to himself," when "the average community was more self-dependent," and when the gap between rich and poor was less glaring. He conceded that cities could never provide "the same sense of common underlying brotherhood" as country living, but argued that the modern industrial society had substantially raised "the standard of comfort" for most people. Efforts to turn backward he considered not only futile but also wrongheaded. Lending "a sympathetic ear" to "the unfocused discontent" he encountered, Roosevelt forged a powerful connection with his audience and then hammered home his core message: the national government must assume "full power" over the giant trusts and that power must "be exercised with moderation and self-restraint."

From Rhode Island, Connecticut, and Massachusetts, to Vermont, New Hampshire, and Maine, the president was met with overwhelming fervor. "The booming of cannon, the clanging of church bells, the tooting of whistles, the braying of brass bands and the cheering of thousands" marked his progress. When he delivered his prepared speeches in the major cities, "factories shut down, stores put up their shutters, flags were hoisted and the people were out in their holiday clothes." There was not a single moment, observed reporters, "when the streets were not crowded and people were not cheering themselves hoarse." As the train moved from city to city, thousands gathered at local railroad stations to glimpse their vibrant young president. Indeed, it seemed to one journalist that "small towns turned out their entire population."

The heady atmosphere of Roosevelt's tour abruptly ceased on the final day of his New England campaign when a speeding trolley car crashed headlong into the open carriage carrying Roosevelt and his party from Pittsfield, Massachusetts, to Stockbridge. The impact overturned the carriage and hurled its occupants to the ground. The president, his private secretary George Cortelyou, and Governor Winthrop Murray Crane of Massachusetts were thrown clear of the wreck, but Roosevelt's favorite Secret Service agent, William Craig, was caught under the wheels of the rushing trolley car and torn apart. "It was a dreadful thing," Roosevelt grimly observed; "the car was coming at such a terrific speed that I felt sure all in the carriage would be killed." The crowd hastened toward the spot where Roosevelt lay, but despite a blackened eye and deep bruises on his jaw and leg, he insisted that he required no help. "I'm all right," he said. "Some of the others are badly hurt. Look after them." When he saw the body of his loyal guard he dropped on his knee. "Poor Craig," he muttered over and over, "too bad, too bad." Still, he insisted that his tour through Stockbridge, Great Barrington, and Bridgeport, Connecticut, should proceed. Seated in a new carriage, he gave the mounted guard somber instructions: "Gallop ahead, tell the people everywhere along the line that Craig has been killed and I wish no cheering." Edith rushed to meet her husband at Bridgeport and take him back to Oyster Bay, where he remained for only one day before departing on a weeklong campaign swing through Tennessee, West Virginia, and North Carolina.

Returning to Sagamore Hill, Roosevelt convened a "memorable conference" (with Senators Aldrich, Spooner, Hanna, Allison, and Lodge) to resolve how he should handle the divisive issue of tariffs during his upcoming western tour. The Republican establishment viewed the high Dingley tariff, passed during McKinley's first administration, as sacrosanct—the key to the country's economic prosperity. Yet in recent years sharply rising consumer prices had produced growing demand for downward revision of the tariff. Capitalizing on this discontent, Democrats argued that high tariffs not only inflated prices but effectively sustained the hated trusts. The destruction of both trusts and tariffs would be the rallying cry of their fall campaign.

Complicating matters further, the tariff issue threatened to divide the president's own party between western Republicans, who clamored for relief from the highest tariff in history, and eastern manufacturers, who insisted on continued protection. At a state convention in the Republican stronghold of Iowa, a resolution had passed that linked tariffs to trusts and called for the elimination of tariffs on any product manufactured by a monopolistic trust. "The tariff must be revised, for it is barbarous, extortionate, damnable," the *Chicago Record-Herald* journalist Walter Wellman wrote to Roosevelt, insisting, "I want to see you take the lead. It is the biggest work to be done in the country today." Should Republicans launch the fall campaign without lowering the tariff, he warned, "hell will be to pay."

Though Roosevelt found this point of view congenial, he also recognized the "dynamite" in tariff reduction. Tinkering with tariff policy might well produce "a panic or something approaching to it, with consequent disaster to the business community and incidentally to the Republican party." Moreover, Senators Aldrich and Hanna made it clear that if a reciprocity treaty could not pass the protectionist Senate, more general tariff revision had absolutely no chance of success. "As long as I remain in the Senate and can raise a hand to stop you," Mark Hanna pointedly told him, "you will never touch a schedule of the tariff act." Bowing to reality, Roosevelt promised the senators gathered at Oyster Bay that he would "make no attempt to revise the tariff at the coming session of Congress," though he would continue to speak out about the trusts. "I do not wish to split my own party wide open on the tariff question," he conceded, "unless some good is to come." The implications of Roosevelt's retreat on this issue would be far-reaching.

Certain that he carried an unwelcome tariff message to western audiences, Roosevelt anticipated "a three weeks' nerve-shattering trip." He soldiered on from Cincinnati to Detroit to Logansport, Indiana, where the sentiment for downward revision of the tariff was particularly strong. The president's references to the tariff, the *New York Times* editorialized, sound "like that of a man treading a path selected for him by others, not chosen by himself, and pursued only because the situation seemed to require it." His words were absorbed by crowds "in comparative silence" after the noisy acclaim that had greeted his earlier speeches. "There are a good many worse things than the possibility of trolley-car accidents in these trips!" Roosevelt darkly quipped.

Unfortunately, the injuries he sustained in the collision proved far more agonizing than tariff complications. He had tried to ignore the continued pain in his leg but was noticeably limping by the time he reached Logansport. A visit to the hospital revealed "a threatening abscess" that required immediate surgery. The abscess was lanced and a miniature pump attached to drain the bloody serum. Refusing anesthesia, Roosevelt climbed onto the operating table and turned to the doctors with a smile. "Gentlemen, you are formal; I see you have your gloves on." The surgeon jested in answer: "It is always in order to wear gloves at a president's reception." If Roosevelt muttered in pain under his breath a few times during the procedure, he reportedly "said nothing that was distinct except to ask for a glass of water before the needle was removed." Carried out on a stretcher, he received strict orders to stay off his leg for several weeks, forcing cancelation of his remaining campaign itinerary.

As renovations to the executive mansion were still not complete, he was taken to the temporary White House at Lafayette Square. "Tell it not in Gath, but really I have enjoyed this nine days' seclusion," he told Senator Orville Platt the following week. "I see Mrs. Roosevelt all the time, as she has come on here to take care of me. I read everything from *Pendennis* and *Our Mutual Friend* down to the last study of European interests in Asia. I do not have to see the innumerable people whom there is no object in seeing, but whom I would have to see if I were not confined to my room with my leg up, and I am able to do all the important work."

Capitalizing on his enforced leisure, Roosevelt appealed to Herbert Putnam, the librarian of Congress, for books that would feed his wildly eclectic intellectual appetites—a history of Poland or something on early Mediterranean races. "Exactly the books I wished," he told Putnam several days later. "I am now reveling in Maspero and occasionally make a deviation into Sergis' theories about the Mediterranean races. . . . It has been such a delight to drop everything useful—everything that referred to my duty—everything, for instance, relating to the coal strike and the tariff, or the trusts, or my power to send troops into the mining districts, or my duty as regards summoning Congress—and to spend an afternoon in reading about the relations between Assyria and Egypt; which could not possibly do me any good and in which I reveled accordingly."

By early October 1902, the coal strike to which Roosevelt referred had become "the most formidable industrial deadlock in the history of the United States." The previous spring, more than 140,000 anthracite coal miners had gone on strike in Pennsylvania to protest low wages, harsh working conditions, and long hours. While the five-month-old strike had caused no serious problems during the hot summer months, panic was setting in as cold weather approached. Coal was then the chief fuel source for heating homes, schools, and businesses. By September's end, schools in the Northeast began closing due to the shortage. Hospitals and government buildings were threatening to shut their doors. Confrontations in the coal fields were becoming increasingly violent, and mobs commandeered coal cars as they trundled through villages and small towns. An all-out social war seemed imminent.

John Mitchell, the charismatic president of the United Mine Workers (UMW), believed that if the American people could truly see "the sorrows and the heartaches of those who spend their lives in the coal mines," they would sympathize with the strikers' decision to stop work. To "the average magazine or newspaper reader," however, the lives of those "who delve in the bowels of the earth; removed from the sight of their fellow-beings," remained as darkly hidden as the work itself, while the hardships generated by their strike were too immediately apparent.

Some years earlier, Sam McClure had tried to expose the suffering of the industry's workers, commissioning the realist author Stephen Crane to write a piece entitled "In the Depths of a Coal Mine." Crane described a sinister system that brought children "yet at the spanking period" into the mines as breaker boys. There, they worked ten hours each day, separating out pieces of slate and other impurities from streams of coal speeding by on conveyor belts. Earning 55 cents a day, a breaker boy rarely set foot in a schoolhouse. His highest ambition was to rise to door-boy, then mule-boy, laborer, miner's helper, and finally full-fledged miner. If he reached that zenith, having survived "the gas, the floods, the 'squeezes' of falling rocks, the cars shooting through little tunnels, the precarious elevators," and the peculiar miner's lung disease, he started "on the descent, going back to become a miner's helper, then a mine laborer, now a door-boy; and when old and decrepit, he finally returns to the breaker where he started as a child."

In most collieries, mining families were forced to rent their shacks from the company and buy their food, clothing, and supplies in the company store, invariably at higher costs than outside the compound. It was a proverbial saying that "children were brought into the world by the company doctor, lived in the company house or hut, were nurtured by the company store, baptized by the company parson, buried in a company coffin, and laid away in the company graveyard." Since mine owners generally paid employees in company-printed scrip instead of cash, workers had little recourse but to pay the exorbitant prices the company demanded. Just such conditions led to the founding of the United Mine Workers Union in 1890.

The wave of consolidation that created trusts in steel, oil, and beef had produced a massive coal trust during this same period. The process of combination had begun when coal-carrying railroads began purchasing coal fields. Quickly, they utilized their control over freight rates to destroy independent coal operators, "reaping the reward" of monopolistic power over both production and transportation. While mine owners and operators of earlier eras had lived near the coal fields, gathering some understanding of the miners' situation, the railroad presidents and financiers who now controlled the industry shared no personal connection with their workers. Skilled in high finance, they had little experience with labor unions and scant comprehension of public relations. In the months preceding the strike, the miners had agreed to accept a 5 percent wage increase, a raise which would have amounted to $3 million annually against the operators' estimated profit of $75 million. The operators, represented by George Baer of the Philadelphia & Reading Railroad, flatly refused, confident that public opinion would drive the strikers back to work, crushing the union and Mitchell in the process.

The operators badly miscalculated; as the strike entered its fifth month, opinion had turned in favor of the miners, largely due to the contrasting public impressions of Mitchell and Baer. In early August 1902, Lincoln Steffens had drawn a profile of the compelling young UMW president for *McClure's*. A telling anecdote in his article illustrated the near-mystical hold Mitchell exercised over the miners, many of them immigrants who barely spoke English: "When President McKinley was shot, and the news spread to the coal region, the workmen gathered into a mob, crying, 'Who shot our President?' They dispersed when they learned that it wasn't President Mitchell who was shot."

Subsequent coverage confirmed Mitchell's stature with the workers and the public at large. "No better strike leader than John Mitchell has ever emerged in any time of industrial strife," Walter Wellman remarked. Throughout the summer, Mitchell conducted himself with impressive dignity, never resorting "to bitterness or retort." He allowed pump men and firemen to continue at work protecting the mines. He agreed to meet with anyone at any time to discuss potential areas of agreement, publicly declaring readiness to compromise.

Whereas Mitchell welcomed arbitration, George Baer refused even to meet with the labor leader and flatly denied Mitchell's right to speak for the anthracite miners in the various collieries. To the wealthy, college-educated railroad president, Mitchell "was only a common coal-miner, who had worked with his hands for 15 years, and was now a labor agitator." Any negotiation, Baer felt, would unduly recognize a mere rabble-rouser.

In response to a citizen's plea for compromise, Baer wrote: "I beg of you not to be discouraged. The rights and interests of the laboring man will be protected and cared for—not by the labor agitators, but by the Christian men to whom God in His infinite wisdom has given the control of the property interests of the country, and upon the successful Management of which so much depends." When Baer's correspondent submitted this rejoinder to the newspapers, the railroad president's overweening arrogance was mocked in editorials across the country. "The doctrine of the divine right of kings was bad enough, but not so intolerable as the doctrine of the divine right of plutocrats," remarked one Boston paper. "It will take a load from the consciences of many earnest people to have this authoritative declaration that God, through the kindness of the coal operators, will be able to manage this strike in accordance with the dictates of infinite wisdom," jeered the *New York Tribune*. "But if the medium's acquaintances really are spirits acquainted with the heavenly mysteries why, oh why, do they on earth talk such egregious nonsense?"

In the Northeast, where people suffered the effects of the strike most keenly, opinion began turning against the Republicans, whom many continued to regard as henchmen of the trusts despite Roosevelt's bold action against Northern Securities. "The coal business here is getting rapidly worse," Lodge wrote from Massachusetts. "If no settlement is reached it means political disaster in New England and especially in this state," he warned. "The demand that the Government take the coal fields is rising louder all the time. It is a perilous cry. When the cold weather comes it will be far worse. You have no power or authority of course, that is the worst of it. Is there anything you can appear to do?" Roosevelt himself was increasingly frustrated. "I am at my wit's end how to proceed," he admitted. "Of course, we have nothing whatever to do with this coal strike and no earthly responsibility for it," he wrote to Hanna. "But the public at large will tend to visit upon our heads responsibility for the shortage in coal precisely as Kansas and Nebraska visited upon our heads their failure to raise good crops in the arid belt, eight, ten or a dozen years ago."

In discussions with Attorney General Knox, Roosevelt was told that he had "no warrant" to intervene. The Constitution provided no precedent for a president to mediate disputes between labor and management. He was warned "that he would almost certainly fail if he tried; and that he would injure his prestige and perhaps sacrifice his political future if he essayed to step outside the role of his constitutional duties." Roosevelt would not be confined by precedent or bound by fear of failure. He held to what he called "the Jackson-Lincoln theory of the Presidency; that is, that occasionally great national crises arise which call for immediate and vigorous executive action, and that in such cases it is the duty of the President to act upon the theory that he is the steward of the people, and that the proper attitude for him to take is that he is bound to assume that he has the legal right to do whatever the needs of the people demand, unless the Constitution or the laws explicitly forbid him to do it."

On October 1, 1902, he sent identical telegrams to the coal operators' board of directors and to the union representative, John Mitchell. Both factions were invited to Washington to discuss "the failure of the coal supply, which has become a matter of vital concern to the whole nation." This singular request from the president captivated newspapermen and magazine writers across the nation.

"For the first time in the history of the country," Walter Wellman wrote, great corporate leaders and union leaders would join "the President of the United States to talk over their differences face-to-face." The large crowd gathered in front of the temporary White House on Lafayette Square earlier that morning was increasing with each passing hour. Confidence spread that an end to the menacing coal strike was near at hand. Reporters eagerly followed the arrival of the parties, contrasting the "luxurious private cars" that carried the six coal operators to the nation's capital with "the smoking car of a night train" that transported Mitchell and his three district presidents to Union Station, whereupon they "trudged down Pennsylvania Avenue, their grips in their hands, stopping at a cheap hotel." Likewise, the elaborate carriages, staffed by footmen in "plum-colored livery," that deposited the coal barons at Roosevelt's door illustrated a sharp disparity with the common streetcars that bore the union representatives from their hotel. Nonetheless, once in the president's presence, both parties met as equals.

Theodore Roosevelt greeted his guests warmly, explaining that he could not rise from his chair, for his leg was still healing after his recent carriage accident. As the gentlemen took their seats, the president opened the meeting with a graceful statement acknowledging the existence of "three parties affected by the situation in the anthracite trade—the operators, the miners, and the general public." He spoke, he assured them, "for neither the operators nor the miners, but for the general public." Rather than adjudicate "respective claims," he would appeal to their shared "patriotism, to the spirit that sinks personal considerations and makes individual sacrifices for the general good."

No sooner had the president finished than Mitchell "literally jumped to his feet." In a voice "clear as a bell," he reiterated his willingness to negotiate with the operators at any time. If they were unable to reach a resolution by themselves, he would willingly abide by the decision of an impartial tribunal that the president might appoint, even if the ruling denied the miners' claims. Mitchell's dramatic statement took both the operators and the president by surprise. "I had not expected such an offer as this," Roosevelt admitted. Turning to the operators, he asked: "What have you gentlemen to say to this proposition?" After a swift consultation, President George Baer stood up. "We cannot agree to it. We cannot agree to any proposition advanced by Mr. Mitchell," he emphatically asserted. "Very well," said the president. "I shall ask you, then, to return at three o'clock and I wish you would present at that time your various positions in writing so we may discuss them."

When they reconvened, tension in the room quickly escalated. Rather than engage in open discussion, the coal barons read a series of typewritten statements that accused the strikers of criminal behavior, including the murder of hundreds of non-union men willing to work the mines during the strike. "The duty of the hour is not to waste time negotiating with the fomenters of this anarchy," Baer declared. Roosevelt was stunned by what he considered the "extraordinary stupidity and bad temper" of the operators, who "did everything in their power to goad and irritate Mitchell," resorting to "insolent" words that were "insulting to the miners and offensive to me." Roosevelt told Mark Hanna that after the operators belittled the union officials, "they insulted me for not preserving order" by sending federal troops to protect their property "and attacked Knox for not having brought suit against the miners' union as violating the Sherman Antitrust Law." Through it all, he marveled, "Mitchell behaved with great dignity and moderation." Not one of the operators, he remarked, "appeared to such advantage as Mitchell," who "towered above" them all. Roosevelt later admitted that after one operator referred to the union as "a set of outlaws," he wanted to take him "by the seat of the breeches and nape of the neck and chuck him out of that window." With great difficulty he managed to keep his anger in check.

Realizing that the operator's high-handed belligerence would negate any direct negotiation, Roosevelt finally repeated Mitchell's proposition that they submit the conflict to a presidential tribunal. Again they refused "to have any dealings of any nature with John Mitchell." Roosevelt was intensely irritated by their stubborn disdain. "If this is the case," he concluded, "I can see no necessity for detaining you gentlemen further."

"Well, I have tried and failed," Roosevelt told Mark Hanna. "I feel downhearted over the result both because of the great misery made necessary for the mass of our people, and because the attitude of the operators will beyond a doubt double the burden on us who stand between them and socialistic action." Worse still, when the coal barons provided an account of the failed conference to the press, they reveled "in the fact that they had 'turned down' both the miners and the President."

The operators' exultation was short-lived. Roosevelt had made arrangements for a stenographer to record the entire proceedings, and when the statements of both parties were released to the press, public opinion turned sharply against them. While a small number of papers endorsed the operators' view that the public had no rights in the situation and insisted that Roosevelt's "uncontrollable penchant for impulsive self-intrusion" had made "a sorry mess" of the negotiations, the majority held the coal barons totally responsible for the failed Washington conference and the continuing strike. Furthermore, their insolent defiance of the president did not compare favorably with Mitchell's "respectful, placable, and patriotic spirit."

Public condemnation of the operators' intractable behavior fortified Roosevelt as he contemplated a more extreme step. With "ugly talk of a general sympathetic strike" beginning to spread, he considered the situation nothing short of "a state of war." He warned Attorney General Knox and Secretary of War Root that he was considering an action that "would form an evil precedent" but felt "obliged to take it rather than expose our people to the suffering and chaos which would otherwise come." Knox and Root were free to disavow the action he was contemplating, but he had made up his mind. He believed that the operators and their colleagues on Wall Street were "absolutely out of touch with the big world," and the president could not remain idle as "misery and death" threatened masses of the American people.

His undisclosed strategy was to ready "a first-rate general" and 10,000 regular Army troops to enter the coal fields with instructions "to dispossess the operators and run the mines as a receiver" for the government until a settlement could be reached. He secured the agreement of his selected general, John M. Schofield, to pay "no heed to any authority, judicial or otherwise," besides the president in his role as "Commander-in-Chief." According to this stratagem, if "the operators went to court and had a writ served on him, he would do as was done under Lincoln, simply send the writ on to the President." This intrepid plan illustrated one of Roosevelt's favorite maxims: "Don't hit till you have to; but, when you do hit, hit hard."

Whether the president would have implemented this unorthodox design is not clear. "Theodore was a bit of a bluffer," Elihu Root observed. But Mark Sullivan had discussed the measure with Roosevelt on a number of occasions and believed he was prepared to follow through: "The one condition Roosevelt's spirit could not endure," he remarked, "was any situation in which individuals or groups seemed able to defy or ignore the people as a whole and their representative in the White House."

The question proved moot. Secretary Root devised a way to resolve the issue that would not humiliate the mine owners or require massive federal intervention. Certain that public opinion had finally convinced the coal barons to negotiate so long as they did not have to deal directly with union representatives, Root proposed that he travel to New York and meet with J. P. Morgan. If anyone could bring the operators to the table, he believed, it would be the original architect of the coal trust. Morgan's financial genius had unified the railway owners and coalmen together in the gargantuan combination that now controlled 80 percent of the anthracite coal market. Root would make it clear that in speaking with Morgan, he acted independently, without instructions from the president. Roosevelt enthusiastically approved the plan.

Taking the midnight train to New York, Root met with Morgan for five hours on his yacht, the *Corsair*. Together, they composed a memorandum that Morgan carried to the Union Club, where the mine owners were holding a meeting. The memo called for the president to establish an Arbitration Commission, virtually identical to the proposition Mitchell and then Roosevelt had suggested at the Washington conference. In this instance, however, J. P. Morgan was advocating the measure—not John Mitchell—allowing the owners to maintain the fiction that they were not negotiating with representatives of organized labor. "It was a damned lie," Root later said, but it opened the door to a settlement. To his credit, Morgan intervened at this critical juncture, for only eight months earlier he had considered Roosevelt's suit against Northern Securities as a personal attack. The financier's willingness to help the president "was one of the crowning moments of his life," one journalist remarked, observing, "there was to be no littleness in this great hour."

Despite this breakthrough, immediate difficulties emerged over the composition of the panel. The owners insisted that the Arbitration Commission be comprised of five members chosen from specific categories: an officer of the military or naval Engineer Corps, an expert mining engineer unconnected with coal, a Pennsylvania judge, a businessman familiar with mining and selling coal, and an eminent sociologist. Both Roosevelt and Mitchell immediately recognized the pointed absence of a labor representative in this configuration. After a series of hurried meetings with Morgan's men, Bacon and Perkins, Roosevelt hit upon a solution. "Suddenly," he recollected, "it dawned on me that they were not objecting to the thing, but to the name. I found they did not mind my appointing any man, whether he was a labor man or not, so long as he was not appointed *as* a labor man." Roosevelt promptly appointed Edgar E. Clark, the head of the Brotherhood of Railway Train Conductors, to the "eminent sociologist" slot. While the owners "would heroically submit to anarchy rather than have Tweedledum," Roosevelt noted with amusement, "yet if I would call it Tweedledee they would accept with rapture."

Once the owners further agreed to expand the commission to include Bishop L. Spalding of Baltimore, Mitchell brought his miners back to work, peacefully concluding the nation's most serious strike. For three months the commission heard complaints from both sides: the operators presented evidence that strikers had not only threatened but used violence to prevent willing miners from working; the miners spoke of the oppressive hardships of the industry. The Arbitration Commission ultimately awarded the miners a retroactive wage increase of 10 percent as well as a reduction in daily work hours, from ten to nine.

"The American people will not soon forget their debt to Mr. Roosevelt," the *Washington Post* editorialized, proclaiming, "More glorious than winning a battle is this triumph of peace." Both Republican and Democratic journals concurred that the strike "was won by popular sentiment, controlled by the people's chief." Acting as "the people's attorney," William Allen White summarized, Roosevelt had defined the public interest in the previously *private* struggle between labor and capital. Understanding that the laissez-faire philosophy retained a powerful appeal, he had patiently waited through five months of the strike until the "steady pressure of public opinion" accompanying the onset of cold weather created space for his unprecedented call to bring the two sides together. And after the failed conference, he wisely allowed outrage over its published transcript to build until the public was primed to sustain radical measures it would have roundly rejected but months earlier. Though he "was all ready to act" if final negotiations failed, Roosevelt was thrilled when a less disruptive solution prevailed. "It is never well to take drastic action," he later commented, "if the result can be achieved with equal efficiency in less drastic fashion."

Flush with victory, Roosevelt agreeably shared credit for the successful settlement. "My dear sir," he addressed J. P. Morgan, "If it had not been for your going into the matter I do not see how the strike could have been settled at this time . . . I thank you and congratulate you with all my heart." With the coal operators, Roosevelt was less generous. "May Heaven preserve me," he told Bamie, "from ever again dealing with so wooden-headed a set."

ROOSEVELT SPENT NOVEMBER 4, 1902, the day of the midterm elections, at Sagamore Hill. "Mother and I took a walk," he told Kermit, "accompanied by all six dogs, whom we both of us feel are real members of the family." And the election results that evening brought an invigorating day to a satisfying conclusion. In early October, when his risky intervention appeared "doomed to failure through the obduracy of the capitalists," there was widespread conviction that "the new Congress would be overwhelmingly Democratic." But Republicans had defied the midterm curse and retained control of both Houses of Congress. Commentators credited the president's successful settlement of the coal strike with saving "many thousands of votes."

Returning to Washington after the midterms, the president was finally able to move back into the renovated White House. All summer long, Edith had worked with the architects, attending to "a steady stream of little problems"—sorting through "fabric swatches by the dozen, samples of wallpaper, and samples of rugs," selecting sofas, tables, and curtains, poring over detailed plans for every bedroom and bath, designing a garden for the children and a tennis court for her husband. The renovations garnered widespread praise. "If Roosevelt had never done anything else," a Washington insider remarked, "the metamorphosis of the White House from a gilded barn to a comfortable residence that he has accomplished would entitle him to his country's gratitude."

Roosevelt credited Edith's perseverance and instinct for tasteful comfort. A girlhood marked by relocation from one temporary abode to another as her father's resources diminished had shaped what one historian shrewdly identifies as a "remarkable coping mechanism," an ability "to make a home on short notice, then pick up her tent and start again." She had reappointed the executive mansion with the same aptitude and flair that had once transformed their tiny rented town house in Washington and the cavernous governor's mansion in Albany.

Edith never sought recognition for her work. "She is an old-fashioned type of woman who feels that no lady should make herself conspicuous," her secretary Isabella Hagner James explained. "By nature and inclination she should probably have had a life of sheltered seclusion," Hagner James later observed in her memoir, but when devotion to her husband necessitated a public presence, "never did a woman carry herself with more gentle dignity and charm." She was "at home" for the cabinet officers' wives every Tuesday morning in the library, entertained hundreds of governmental officials at afternoon teas, and hosted formal dinner parties with uncommon grace. As Jacob Riis understood, however, "the chief end of her life" lay not in her public duties but in "companionship with husband and children."

The president deserved credit for at least one aspect of the new West Wing building. "For the first time in history," reporters gratefully noted, the president had "set apart a room adjoining his own office for the exclusive use of the press." Formerly crowded together at one end of the general waiting room, journalists now enjoyed immediate access to the president and a room furnished with a large oak table, chairs, and telephones. "The public man who now escapes an interview will have to be a sprinter," one journalist happily remarked.

Taking stock of his first fifteen months in office, Roosevelt told Maria Longworth Storer in early December that he had achieved as much as he "had any right to hope or expect." Though occasionally forced to subordinate his own desires to what was possible "under the given conditions," he found comfort in the knowledge that Abraham Lincoln had often done the same.

With each passing month, the president's hold on the American people grew stronger. "It is very curious," Roosevelt told his newspaper friend Joseph Bucklin Bishop, "ever since I have been in the Presidency I have been pictured constantly as a huge creature with enormous clenched teeth, a big spiked club, and a belt full of pistols—a blustering, roaring swashbuckler type of ruffian, and yet all the time I have been growing in popularity. I don't understand it at all." To Bishop, the reason was perfectly clear: "All the cartoonists at heart liked him, and there was seldom or never anything bitter or really unfriendly in their portrayals of him; they were uniformly good-natured."

Caricatures even transformed his failure during a mid-November bear hunt into a triumph, conjuring an image of the president steadfastly refusing to shoot a small bear furnished for the occasion. As renditions of the original Clifford Berryman cartoon proliferated, the bear dwindled in size until he appeared as a tiny cub, prompting toy store owners to market stuffed bears in honor of Teddy Roosevelt. Soon the Teddy bear became one of the most cherished toys of all time.

Roosevelt's burgeoning public favor augured well for the 1904 presidential race, although no vice president had ever been elected in his own right after succeeding to the presidency as a consequence of his predecessor's death. "I'd rather be *elected* to that office than have anything tangible of which I know," he avowed. Nevertheless, he continued to fear that the Republican establishment would prevent his nomination. "*They* don't want it," he flatly stated, "Hanna and that crowd." Indeed, each time he riled business interests—as with his anti-trust suit or intervention in the coal strike—Hanna's name invariably arose. "I do not think Mr. Roosevelt can win," Alabama senator John Morgan predicted in late November. "I do not believe the wiser heads of the Republican Party want him as the nominee. The trouble is they cannot keep him where they can rely on him. Every now and then he bucks and runs off. They have to lasso him and haul him back." Newspapers reported that "the monied interests" were determined to prevent his election, even if it meant contributing "liberally" to the opposition party.

Delegations pledged to Mark Hanna were considered especially likely in the South, where Roosevelt's quiet attempt to include blacks in party councils had stirred fierce opposition. In addition, southern Republicans had never forgiven Roosevelt for the unprecedented dinner invitation extended the previous fall to the black educator Booker T. Washington. At the time, the vehement reaction in the South had stunned and saddened Roosevelt. Newspaper editorials throughout the region decried the president's attempt to make a black man the social equal of a white man by sharing the same dinner table. "Social equality with the Negro means decadence and damnation," announced one southern official. "The action of President Roosevelt in entertaining that nigger will necessitate our killing a thousand niggers in the South before they will learn their place," declared South Carolina's Ben Tillman. For disaffected Republicans in both North and South, Mark Hanna promised deliverance from Roosevelt's wrongheadedness.

All these factors weighed on the president's mind as he prepared his second annual address. Delivered on December 2, 1902, the message reiterated his call for Congress to create a Department of Commerce with broad powers of supervision over the big corporations. The tone of his message, "not nearly so strong as it was expected to be," proved a great disappointment to reformers. "The plain people," Roosevelt insisted, "are better off than they have ever been before." The majority of the great fortunes were "won not by doing evil, but as an incident to action which has benefited the community as a whole." Although abuse and misconduct were undeniable, he urged, "let us not in fixing our gaze upon the lesser evil forget the greater good." Those who sought removal of the protective tariff "as a punitive measure directed against the trusts," he argued, put the entire nation's productivity in jeopardy.

"It appears that the vested interests of the country have succeeded in scaring the President," one Washington correspondent asserted, "preventing him from expressing in his usual forcible style his convictions." The *Cincinnati Enquirer* deemed it "a very lame message for a president who is chiefly celebrated for his strenuosity," and further lamented that it read "like a surrender to the party leaders who control the senate and house." Other commentators were equally unimpressed. "A milk and water communication," charged the *Indiana Democrat*, "from a man whose chief aim is the presidential nomination two years hence."

Even the more moderate reviews were not optimistic that Roosevelt's message heralded any fundamental progress. "We are bound to believe that Mr. Roosevelt's heart is in his policy of regulating the trusts, yet even here he is singularly vague and inconclusive," editorialized the New York *Evening Post*, predicting that "the result of such an uncertain trumpet can not lead to any serious preparation for battle."

In the clamor following the president's message, few perceived that Roosevelt's ideals were always moderated by his pragmatism. Until the Republican establishment felt threatened by an aroused and targeted public opinion, he knew there was little chance of securing legislation to regulate the trusts. His tepid message revealed a conviction that popular outrage was not yet sufficient to threaten the Big Four, those powerful senators who continued to block his path to significant reform.

More than any president since Abraham Lincoln, Theodore Roosevelt was able to shrewdly calculate popular sentiment. He read daily excerpts from scores of newspapers, probed the eclectic assemblage of visitors and guests frequenting the White House, and tested his ideas on reporters. Over time, he developed an uncanny ability to gauge the changeable pulse of the American public. His experience in bringing the suit against Northern Securities and mediating the Pennsylvania coal strike had evinced the signal role that the press could play in rallying the public support essential to achieve substantial reform—just as Ray Baker's series on J. P. Morgan's "monarchical powers" and Stephen Crane's description of the inhumane, abusive practices of the coal barons had proven pivotal in alerting the public to the menace of increasingly concentrated monopolies.

In order to aggressively pursue redress for the abuses and inequity of the industrial age, the president would need to ride a seismic shift in national consciousness. He would need an instrument capable of reaching into the homes of workers, teachers, shopkeepers, and small business people across the country—an instrument that would not just explain but vividly illustrate the human and economic costs of unchecked industrial growth and combination. The complex and sometimes contentious partnerships that Roosevelt had forged with investigative journalists would soon illuminate corruption, as if by heat lightning, and clarify at last a progressive vision for the entire nation.

CHAPTER ELEVEN

"The Most Famous Woman in America"

Ida M. Tarbell, in her office at *McClure's*, 1904.

ROOSEVELT'S FLAGGING HOPES OF CONFRONTING the trusts, purging corrupt political machines, and checking abuses by both capital and labor were rekindled by the January 1903 publication of *McClure's* magazine. In this celebrated issue, the "groundbreaking trio" of Tarbell, Steffens, and Baker produced three exhaustive, hard-hitting investigative pieces that ushered in the distinctive new period of journalism that would later be christened "the muckraking era." First off, Ida Tarbell revealed the predatory, illegal practices of Standard Oil; Lincoln Steffens then exposed the corrupt dealings of Minneapolis mayor Albert "Doc" Ames; and finally, Ray Baker described the complicity of union members manipulating and deceiving their own fellow workers.

The convergence of these three powerful exposés prompted S. S. McClure to attach an unusual editorial postscript to his January issue, exhorting readers to take action against corruption in every phase of industrial life. "Capitalists, workingmen, politicians, citizens—all breaking the law, or letting it be broken," McClure accused, sparing no one in his sweeping denunciation:

> Who is left to uphold it? The lawyers? Some of the best lawyers in this country are hired, not to go into court to defend cases, but to advise corporations and business firms how they can get around the law without too great a risk of punishment. The judges? Too many of them so respect the laws that for some "error" or quibble they restore to office and liberty men convicted on evidence overwhelmingly convincing to common sense. The churches? We know of one [Trinity Church in Manhattan], an ancient and wealthy establishment, which had to be compelled by a Tammany hold-over health officer to put its tenements in sanitary condition. The colleges? They do not understand. There is no one left; none but all of us.

"A lesser editor might have hesitated . . . to print three such contentious papers—arraignments of industry, labor, and government—all in one issue," observes Peter Lyon, McClure's biographer, but McClure was resolute. His exceptional sensitivity to the interests of the American public convinced him that people would not shrink from the truth, however dispiriting. He believed, as Steffens later observed, that "shameful facts, spread out in all their shame," would "set fire to the American pride," that when people fully realized the corrosive national affliction wrought by unchecked industrialism, they would seek remedies. Yet even the remarkably prescient McClure could not have predicted the extraordinary response his exposés would soon receive from readers across the country.

The January 1903 issue sold out within days, faster than any previous issue. The revelatory articles became a leading topic of conversation in cities and towns across the country. With such incriminating information in the hands of *McClure's* vast middle-class audience, one historian observes, "for the first time considerable numbers of small businessmen and white-collar workers were joining factory hands and farmers in a restless questioning." Elated, McClure considered the January issue "the greatest success we have ever had." Editorials in one newspaper after another praised the quality of the research, the dramatic structure of the narratives, the careful documentation. "Of course, every magazine from time to time had published able articles dealing with some phase of wrong and suggesting some needed reform," the *New York World* noted. "What Mr. McClure did was to make this work systematic and persistent, to describe realities with absolute frankness, to avoid preaching, and to let the facts produce their own impression upon the public conscience."

In the months that followed, the circulation of *McClure's* continued to climb as the three writers pursued their investigations. Tarbell's Standard Oil series eventually stretched over a three-year period; Steffens's studies of corrupt political machines in a dozen cities and states generated fourteen articles and two books; and Baker produced more than a dozen seminal articles on labor and capital. Baker later attributed the tremendous impact of these meticulously researched exposés to the fact that they finally verified years of "prophets crying in the wilderness, and political campaigns based upon charges of corruption and privilege which everyone believed or suspected had some basis of truth, but which were largely unsubstantiated." The solid reputation of *McClure's* and its gifted stable of writers assured millions of Americans they could trust what they were reading.

The success at *McClure's* persuaded editors and publishers at a dozen leading magazines—including *Collier's*, *Cosmopolitan*, *Everybody's*, *Leslie's*, *Pearson's*, and *Hampton's*—to launch similar forays into investigative journalism. Like McClure, these publishers began to funnel substantial resources into the extensive research necessary for such in-depth studies, promoting a new breed of investigative reporter dedicated to extensive fact-finding and analysis. Their disclosures of the corrupt linkages between business, labor, and government educated and aroused the public, spearheading the Progressive movement that would define the early years of the twentieth century. "It is hardly an exaggeration to say that the Progressive mind was characteristically a journalistic mind, and that its characteristic contribution was that of the socially responsible reporter-reformer," historian Richard Hofstadter observed. "Before there could be action, there must be information and exhortation. Grievances had to be given specific objects, and these the muckraker supplied. It was muckraking that brought the diffuse malaise of the public into focus."

Years of preparatory work and investigation preceded the publication of *McClure's* landmark January 1903 issue. As early as the spring of 1899, when few middle-class journals would broach the subject, McClure was already endeavoring to determine how the increasingly vital, complex issue of trusts might engage a wide audience. The English journalist Alfred Maurice Low suggested to McClure that if a single trust were traced from its origin through its "gradual rise and growth," an examination of whether malfeasance, wage curtailment, or price inflation had abetted its development would prove "full of intense human interest." McClure enthusiastically agreed. "The great feature is Trusts," he told John Phillips, and the magazine that treats this "great question" will inevitably develop "a good circulation." While Phillips embraced McClure's idea, he insisted the project not be assigned to Low, a reputed sensationalist; better to trust one of their own staff, one trained to rely on substantiated fact rather than overwrought rhetoric.

The McClure team initially considered targeting the sugar or beef trusts, but neither seemed conducive to an extended series. McClure soon struck another approach to the pernicious problem. Several years earlier, after a short story in a small magazine by Frank Norris had attracted his interest, McClure had brought the struggling young author from California to New York, providing him a steady salary to read manuscripts in the mornings, leaving the afternoons free for his own writing. Norris shared McClure's conviction that writers held a responsibility to the public—not simply to entertain but to address contemporary problems such as corporate avarice and economic injustice. "The Pulpit, the Press, and the Novel," Norris argued, "these indisputably are the great moulders of public opinion and public morals to-day."

One morning, Norris appeared in McClure's office with an idea for a sprawling trilogy chronicling the struggle between wheat growers and the railroad trust. The first book, to be called *The Octopus*, would center on an actual incident in the San Joaquin Valley, where scores of local farmers, dispossessed by the Southern Pacific Railroad, had engaged in a violent altercation with railroad agents that left seven people dead. Both McClure and Phillips were attracted by the young novelist's idea, for in this protracted, harrowing fight against one railroad, the larger struggle of the people versus the trusts would play out. McClure pledged to pay Norris's salary while he returned to the west coast to muster all research materials necessary to begin the novel.

The dramatic saga of *The Octopus* interweaves the stories of a dozen or more men and their families. Struggling to draw a good harvest from the arid land, these hardworking people are compromised and oppressed at every turn by the maddening, predatory policies of the railroad: ruinous increases in highly inflated shipping rates for wheat and hops are announced; arbitrary routing decisions require urgently needed agricultural equipment to travel non-stop past the town and then return at extra cost; greed and peculation make a mockery of the state commission board, supposedly designed to administer fair rates. Meanwhile, the implacable railroad rolls on, leaving behind "the destruction of once happy homes, the driving of men to crime and of women and girls to starvation and ruin." As the lives of the novel's central group of characters are shattered, a powerful fuse is lit against "the iron-hearted Power, the monster, the Colossus, the Octopus."

Published two years later, Norris's novel garnered spectacular reviews. "*The Octopus* is a work so distinctly great that it justly entitles the author to rank among the very first American novelists," claimed *The Arena*. "It is a work that will not only stimulate thought: it will quicken the conscience and awaken the moral sensibilities of the reader, exerting much the same influence over the mind as that exerted by Patrick Henry." Although the widely acclaimed and prodigiously gifted Norris would never complete his trilogy—a ruptured appendix ended his life at the age of thirty-two—*The Octopus* was an unmitigated success for both McClure and its young author.

Indeed, Sam McClure seemed to be moving from one triumph to another. The circulation of the magazine had topped 400,000, the syndicate was turning a profit, and his talented staff of writers, editors, and contributors was considered among the country's very best. But even this catalogue of accomplishments could not satiate his restless ambition for long. "The string of triumphs had to be prolonged," his biographer observes, "for only so would McClure get what he most needed: a steady supply of affection, admiration, and flattery."

Just when all his enterprises were proceeding successfully, McClure overreached, committing his company to purchase the prestigious publishing house Harper & Brothers. Negotiated in a burst of manic energy, the deal would bring five additional magazines under McClure's management (including *Harper's Monthly* and *Harper's Weekly*), as well as a second syndicate service, a second book press, and a lecture bureau. Troubles mounted immediately: Frank Doubleday, angry at his marginalization, broke up the association of Doubleday & McClure. Additional responsibilities for *McClure's* staff stole time and attention from the magazine at the heart of the empire. Most crucially, the capital needed to sustain the purchase was never properly in place. Reluctantly, and at enormous expense, McClure was forced to withdraw from the contract six months after it was signed.

The failed deal crushed McClure, precipitating a nervous breakdown in April 1900 that propelled him to Europe to undergo the celebrated "rest cure" devised by an American physician, S. Weir Mitchell. Prescribed for a range of nervous disorders, the rest cure required that patients remain isolated for weeks or even months at a time, forbidden to read or write, rigidly adhering to a milk-only diet. Underlying this regimen was the assumption that "raw milk is a food the body easily turns into good blood," which would restore positive energy when pumped through the body.

This extreme treatment was among the proliferating regimens developed in response to the stunning increase in nervous disorders diagnosed around the turn of the century. Commentators and clinicians cited a number of factors related to the stresses of modern civilization: the increased speed of communication facilitated by the telegraph and railroad; the "unmelodious" clamor of city life replacing the "rhythmical" sounds of nature; and the rise of the tabloid press that exploded "local horrors" into national news. These nervous diseases became an epidemic among "the ultracompetitive businessman and the socially active woman."

While McClure had endured troubling mood swings for years, this depressive episode was the most disturbing, transforming even his love for his work into "the repulsion that a seasick man feels toward the food he most enjoys in health." His manic drive had finally sapped him of his strength. "I had never thought of such a thing as economy of effort. When I had an idea, I pursued it; when I wanted anything, I went ahead and got it." By crossing the ocean and committing himself to exclusive sanitarium in France and Switzerland, he hoped to recover the will and vitality that had sustained him since the penniless days of his youth.

Not surprisingly, the steady diet of milk and tedium did little to restore McClure. After six months in the famous spa towns of Aix-les-Bains and Divonne-les-Bains, he felt more enervated than when he left New York. "When I get rested I become very restless, but no place I plan to go interests me for many hours," he admitted. "A walk of a few blocks tires me terribly. Riding in a cab tires me. I cannot see any of the beautiful things here," he complained, lamenting that he had become "half hopeless & half comatose." Although he tried to remain optimistic, observing that "perhaps my condition is normal & this is the way one gets over brain exhaustion," he confessed to feeling doubtful about the state of his recovery. "I sometimes think that it is like taking off a leaky roof before putting on a new one, for a while the condition is worse than ever."

In October, unable to tolerate the isolation, McClure persuaded a nurse to accompany him to Paris to secure the most recent edition of his magazine. Finding little of timely interest in its pages, he fired off a furious critique to Phillips, accusing him of attempting to destroy the magazine. No sooner was the letter posted than he tried to retrieve it. "I am simply heart-broken to have caused you such grief," the contrite McClure told Phillips, assuring him, "You are the most wonderful friend & comrade a man ever had. Destroy the Paris letter. It was the expression of jangled nerves & a crazy brain. . . . In my mad scramble which in one way or another seems to have existed all my life, I have sacrificed much that is most important . . . I feel hopelessly sad to have caused you such terrible & useless pain. I really ought to have died some time ago . . . I wish you would remember the good things about me & forget all the bad."

But in April 1901, exactly one year after leaving for Europe, McClure unaccountably returned to the office bursting with ideas for future articles. "The great issue," he continued to believe, "was the phenomenon of the trusts." He was now even more strongly convinced that "the way to handle the Trust question was, not by taking the matter up abstractly, but to take one Trust, and to give its history, its effects, and its tendencies." If neither the sugar trust nor the beef trust would suffice, perhaps John D. Rockefeller's Standard Oil, "the Mother of Trusts," would serve as the subject of their investigations. As "the creature largely of one man," Standard Oil was perfectly suited to the biographical approach that had proved so successful with Napoleon and Lincoln. The story of the world's wealthiest man would beguile the public into the more complicated exposition of his corporation and the hitherto esoteric question of the trusts. No one, McClure perceived, was better situated to engage that subject than Ida Tarbell, who "had lived for years in the heart of the oil region."

Tarbell initially hesitated, though no subject so captured her imagination. As a child, she had witnessed the anguish the "big trust" had caused in its early development, and "the unfairness of the situation" had troubled her deeply. As a young woman, she had begun a novel focused on the period when "the bottom had dropped out" of the Allegheny oil region. She never completed the work, however, realizing that "there must be two sides to the question." If she hoped to write a work of history rather than propaganda, she would now have to "comprehend the point of view of the other side." She recognized the difficulties, even hazards, this undertaking would present, for Standard Oil officials were notoriously close-mouthed. Even in her hometown of Titusville, she found that men and women were unwilling to talk, fearing "the all-seeing eye and the all-powerful reach of the ruler of the oil industry." In search of telling, intimate details like those at the core of her Lincoln series, she encountered only the same terse warning: "They will get you in the end." Her own father tried to dissuade her. "Don't do it, Ida," he admonished; "they will ruin the magazine." Finally she was tantalized by "the audacity of the thing"—just as when McClure had challenged her to complete the first installment of Napoleon's life in one month's time.

By early September 1901, Ida Tarbell had read everything from articles extolling the growth of trusts to *Wealth Against Commonwealth*, Henry Demarest Lloyd's passionate diatribe against monopolies. Already she had outlined an extensive series that would detail the history of Standard Oil from its earliest days to the present. Phillips was enthusiastic, but only McClure, then in Switzerland, could approve a project of such magnitude. "Go over," Phillips told Tarbell, "show the outline to Sam, get his decision." McClure was thrilled to hear from Tarbell. "Come instantly," he wrote back, suggesting that she stay for several weeks and travel with him to Lucerne and the Italian lakes; "I want a good time." Hattie, too, welcomed Ida's arrival, knowing her soothing influence upon McClure's anxious temperament.

When Tarbell reached Lausanne, Switzerland, in early October, McClure was so overjoyed that he begged her to remain in Europe so they could spend the winter together in Greece. "You've never been there. We can discuss Standard Oil in Greece as well as here," fancifully adding, "if it seems a good plan you can send for your documents and work in the Pantheon [*sic*]." The image of the proper Miss Tarbell, seated at a desk cluttered with papers and documents in the middle of the ancient marble building, struck him as incongruous and hilarious.

Ida happily agreed to join Sam and Hattie. From their first meeting in Paris nearly a decade earlier, she had never stopped loving this brilliant, creative, hectic, exasperating man. In his expansive moods, no one was better company. While he could be irritable and demanding with others, he was invariably kind and loving toward Ida. "I lean on you as no other," he confided to her. "In all great & noble qualities you are peerless to me."

In mid-October, Sam, Hattie, and Ida set out together for Greece by way of the Italian lake region and the cities of Milan and Venice. As usual, the voluble McClure found interest in everything he saw, frequently jotting down notes for future articles. Before reaching Greece, he decided to stop at Salsomaggiore, an exclusive resort spa in northern Italy. There, enjoying relaxing treatments of mud and steam (and conversing with Cecil Rhodes, who had just returned from his exploits in South Africa), the editor and his writer came to an agreement on the shape of her project. So ebullient was McClure that he encouraged Ida to return to New York at once, postponing Greece for another time. Immediately, she set to work on what would become a twelve-part history of the Standard Oil Company—the magisterial series that would spur popular demand to dismantle the rapacious trusts and ensure her legacy as one of the most influential journalists of all time.

When McClure returned to the office a month later, he assembled the entire staff and bombarded them with suggestions for future articles. "It was always so when he came back from a trip," Steffens recalled. His valise was stuffed with "clippings, papers, books, and letters," ranging over the "world-stunning" subjects he wanted his staff to pursue. Some of these "history-making schemes" were brilliant, Steffens acknowledged, but "five out of seven" were foolish, requiring the staff to "unite and fight" against the "wild editor." Only Ida Tarbell could sift through the ideas that tumbled from his mind with patience and respect. Time and again, she tactfully placated both Sam and the staffers, finding "a way to compromise and peace." Unfortunately, Tarbell was in Titusville researching the early chapters of her story when McClure arrived this time, and the office meeting degenerated into a string of fiery confrontations.

Further fueling these tensions, McClure abruptly decided to switch Samuel Hopkins Adams from the syndicate to managing editor of the magazine; such staffing shifts had become a habit with McClure, but this change proved particularly unsettling. The move produced a violent protest from the art director, August Jaccaci, who charged that Adams was "absolutely incompetent to do this job." The accusation ignited "an epic spat" between Jaccaci and McClure: "Fists were hammered down on desks. Unforgiveable words passed." The manuscript reader Viola Roseboro left the room in tears. Mary Bisland, an editor on the syndicate, wrote a distressed letter to Tarbell, begging her to return before something terrible happened. Another tempest provoked yet another distressed letter to Tarbell. Her response provides insight into the peculiar dynamic at the heart of the revolutionary magazine and an acute and intimate assessment of its founder and animating force: "Things will come out all right," Tarbell assured the staff. McClure "may stir up things and interfere with general comfort but he puts the health of life into the work at the same time." More important, Tarbell urged them to remember that "the inimitable nature of McClure's genius greatly outweighed the inconveniences resulting from his eccentricities."

> Never forget that it was he & nobody else who has created that place. You must learn to believe in him & *use* him if you are going to be happy there. He is a very extraordinary creature, you can't put him into a machine and make him run smoothly with the other wheels and things. We don't need him there. Able methodical people grow on every bush but genius comes once in a generation and if you ever get in its vicinity thank the Lord & *stick*. You probably will be laid up now and then in a sanatarium [*sic*] recovering from the effort to follow him but that's a small matter if you really get into touch finally with that wonderful brain.
>
> Above all, don't worry. What you are going through now we've all been through steadily ever since I came into the office. If there was

> nothing in all this but the annoyance and uncertainty & confusion—that is if there were no results—then we might rebel, but there are always results—vital ones. The big things which the magazine has done always come about through these upheavals. . . . The great schemes, the daring moves in that business have always been Mr. McC's. They will continue to be. His one hundredth idea is a stroke of genius. Be on hand to grasp that one hundredth idea!

For Ida Tarbell, McClure's directive to approach the trust issue through a narrative history of Standard Oil proved that "one hundredth idea"—a true stroke of genius. Her investigations were fortuitously timed. In an era of heightened, yet unfocused, public concern over increasing corporate consolidation, the growth of the first great industrial monopoly provided a dramatic blueprint for comprehending how "a particular industry passes from the control of the many to that of the few."

Tarbell began her customary search for primary sources, a task facilitated by the fact that numerous state and federal authorities had been investigating Standard Oil since its founding. Defendants' testimony in court, she noted, exhibited "exactly the quality of the personal reminiscences of actors in great events, with the additional value that they were given on the witness stand; and it was fair, therefore, to suppose that they were more cautious and exact in statement than are many writers of memoirs." Traveling to Washington, New York, Pennsylvania, Ohio, and Kansas, Tarbell patiently scoured so many thousands of pages of depositions and testimony that she almost lost her eyesight. She culled old files from defunct newspapers, transcribed single-spaced congressional reports, examined a large collection of pamphlets published during various controversies, and studied pages of statistics provided by the Interstate Commerce Commission.

Such vigorous inquiry soon revealed that critical memos and reports had vanished from the record. Informed that Standard had destroyed them, Tarbell refused to give up, convinced that if a document had been printed, it would eventually "turn up." Usually, she was right. In the archives of the New York Public Library, she found the sole remaining report of an obscure thirty-year-old investigation; all the other copies had curiously disappeared. After reaching out to the lawyers and plaintiffs who had conducted the cases, she gradually found everything she needed. "Her sources of information," McClure proudly noted, "were open to any student who had the industry and patience to study them."

As the immense scope of her project became evident, Tarbell realized she would need an assistant in Cleveland, where Rockefeller had gotten his start and established the early headquarters of Standard Oil. She wanted someone who was not only clever and curious but who would also "get his fun in the chase" and "be trusted to keep his mouth shut." In John M. Siddall she found the ideal comrade. "Short and plump, his eyes glowing with excitement," the twenty-seven-year-old reporter manifested such exuberance during their first interview that she "had a sudden feeling of alarm lest he should burst out of his clothes." Tarbell later reflected that she "never had the same feeling about any other individual except Theodore Roosevelt." In the months that followed, she found the partnership "a continuous joy"; eventually the entire *McClure's* staff looked forward to "Sid's" lengthy letters, fascinated by the revealing statistics he compiled or the curious details he had unearthed of Rockefeller's day-to-day existence in the city where he lived and worked, Cleveland. Their alliance, Tarbell's biographer Kathleen Brady writes, "was as illustrious a meeting as that of Holmes and Watson. Only in this case, each was to be Sherlock and no leap of deduction, only clear evidence, was allowed."

Such evidence could only be gathered through methodical, painstaking research. "Someone once asked me why I did not go first to the heads of the company for my information," Tarbell explained to an interviewer. "This person did not know overmuch of humanity I think, else he would have realized instantly that the Standard Oil Company would have shut the door of their closet on their skeleton. But after one had discovered the skeleton and had scrutinized him at a very close range, why then shut the door? That is the reason I did not go to the magnates in the beginning."

Although Tarbell never did secure an interview with the reclusive Rockefeller, she established a warm relationship with Henry H. Rogers, a Standard Oil partner who staunchly believed in the firm and wanted to present his perspective to the public. Learning of the impending series in *McClure's*, Rogers sent word to Sam McClure through their mutual friend, Samuel Clemens (Mark Twain), offering to meet with Tarbell at his home at 26 East 57th Street. "I was a bit scared at the idea," Tarbell later acknowledged. Previous attempts to arrange personal meetings with company executives had either proven unsuccessful or rendered little beyond generic policy statements: "I had been met with that formulated chatter used by those who have accepted a creed, a situation, a system, to baffle the investigator trying to find what it all means." Despite her prior frustrations, she was eager for another chance. "It was one thing to tackle the Standard Oil Company in documents . . . quite another thing to meet it face to face."

Rogers immediately put her at ease. Sixty-two years old, with "a heavy shock of beautiful grey hair," he struck Tarbell as "by all odds the handsomest and most distinguished figure in Wall Street." Decades later, she could still recall his features: his "aquiline" nose, "blazing" eyes, and the white mustache partially obscuring his mouth, which she imagined to be "flexible, capable of both firm decision and of gay laughter." As they began to converse, Tarbell discovered that Rogers had once lived close to her childhood home in a white house on a neighboring hillside. "Oh, I remember it," Tarbell exclaimed; "the prettiest house in the world, I thought."

They reached an amicable agreement that day to continue their conversation in a regular series of meetings: Tarbell would share with Rogers her evidence concerning the controversial aspects of Standard's history; he, in turn, would offer "documents, figures, explanations, and justifications—anything and everything which would enlarge [her] understanding." From the start, Tarbell made it clear that her own judgment would supersede his on all points. Their talks remained friendly; when the debate grew tense or unproductive, one or the other would simply change the subject. For Tarbell, the interchange proved invaluable, helping her construct work of "unimpeachable accuracy."

The rigorous editing process at *McClure's* and the constant support of her colleagues were both vital to the excellence of Tarbell's finished work. Early on, when she was "deep into appalling heaps of documentary stuff," Jaccaci wrote her in Titusville to assure her that the immense jumble of research "will clear up little by little and you will begin to see the possibilities of your story." And throughout the process, McClure offered reassurance, reading her early letters from the field, counseling her not to "hurt your health or hurt the work by speed." She should not feel compelled "to write on the monthly demand of a magazine," he insisted, for "this work will turn out to be our great serial feature for next fall." This regular exchange of letters sustained Tarbell while she was "separated so completely" from the office colleagues with whom she had shared daily meals and conversation.

By late May 1902, ten months after she began, Ida had completed a rough draft of the first three articles. She wrote to Phillips, then recovering from an illness at his summer home in Duxbury, Massachusetts. She hoped to send the articles and, if he was feeling well enough, plan a visit to discuss them. "They are in such shape that you can see the character of the material and the treatment I propose," she explained. "I want very much to have your criticism and judgment. It is certainly a great deal more to me than anybody else's." Indeed, her deep respect for Phillips's opinion led her to delay publication until she could answer his concerns.

Viola Roseboro marveled at Tarbell's willingness to accept harsh criticism from both Phillips and McClure. Both expected to "be satisfied and thrilled; they pounded her and her stuff to make the best of it page by page," Roseboro recalled. Tarbell absorbed the barrage and never flinched. She kept revising, cutting, organizing, and rewriting to meet their demands that she move the narrative forward and strip the text of inessential material. Finally, when she felt "moderately comfortable" with her opening articles, she decided to put the work aside for her regular summer vacation—hoping to return with clearer perspective and renewed intensity. "It has become a great bugbear to me," she confessed to Siddall. "I dream of the octopus by night and think of nothing else by day, and I shall be glad to exchange it for the Alps."

Tarbell's first installment explores the birth of the oil industry in the region where she was raised. The "irrepressible energy" of the pioneers who settled "this little corner of Pennsylvania" transformed the landscape and created an entire commercial machine. Scores of small businesses flourished: refineries were necessary to distill the oil, storage tanks to hold it, barrels to carry it, and teamsters to haul it to shipping points on the river or the railroad. In twelve years, as hamlets became towns and towns became cities, the region metamorphosed "from wilderness to market-place." The residents "boasted that the day would soon come when they would refine for the world."

As Tarbell's story unfolds, she describes how the enterprising individuals whose energy and independence brought such prosperity to the region finally proved no match for the regimented power of Standard Oil. Her narrative plainly documents how the ascendancy of the company was aided at every stage by discriminatory railroad rates and illegal tactics—bribery, fraud, criminal underselling, and intimidation. While Tarbell acknowledges John D. Rockefeller's "genius for detail" and admires his rare strength "in energy, in intelligence, in dauntlessness," she demonstrates compellingly that he would never have achieved his monopoly without special transportation privileges. At a time when Rockefeller and his partners in Cleveland held only one tenth of the refining business in the county, he certified to the railroads that he had control of the industry. Providing his organization cheaper rates than their competitors, he argued, was in their interests. "You will have but one party to deal with," he inveigled. "Think of the profits!" And so, swayed by the prospect of avoiding rate wars and enduring the "wear and tear" of securing quotas, the railroad owners entered into clandestine contracts providing Rockefeller with substantial rebates from the published prices.

With this insider deal granting him rates far below those of competitors, and simultaneously kicking back "the extra hundred percent" that outsiders were now forced to pay, Tarbell described how Rockefeller "swooped down" on the independent oil men in Cleveland. "There is no chance for anyone outside," he announced, "but we are going to give everybody a chance to come in. You are to turn over your refinery to my appraisers." Resistors soon found they could not compete against the lower freight rates Standard enjoyed. Within three months, twenty-one of the twenty-six refiners in Cleveland had sold their assets to Standard.

Rockefeller next laid siege to the Oil Creek refiners. "They were there at the mouth of the wells," noted Tarbell. "What might not this geographical advantage do in time?" In her suspenseful installment, "The Oil War of 1872," Tarbell chronicles the defiant struggle of independents when they learned freight rates would suddenly double. More than 3,000 people gathered at the Opera House in Titusville to protest the ruinous rate inflation. It had long been understood that since "the railroad held its right of way from the people," it must "be just to the people, treating them without discrimination," regardless of the volume of business. The Creek oilmen formed a Petroleum Producers Union, demanding investigations by state and federal authorities, and instituted a series of lawsuits. Unlike Rockefeller they had neither the patience nor the capital for protracted litigation. In the end, "from hopelessness, from disgust, from ambition, from love of money," the majority of the local oil producers "gave up the fight for principle" and succumbed to Standard Oil.

Nevertheless, a few intrepid independents refused to submit. "To the man who had begun with one still and had seen it grow by his own energy and intelligence to ten, who now sold 500 barrels a day where he once sold five, the refinery was the dearest spot on earth save his home," Tarbell explained. Where persuasion and simple coercion failed, Rockefeller resorted to more iniquitous tactics. Tarbell uncovered a system of espionage by which Standard bribed railroad agents to access confidential shipping records, detailing "the quantity, quality, and selling price of independent shipments."

Information in hand, Rockefeller knew exactly how much to undercut prices in a particular region to guarantee the elimination of small competitors. One woman testified that "her firm had a customer in New Orleans to whom they had been selling from 500 to 1,000 barrels a month, and that the Standard representative made a contract with him to pay him $10,000 a year for five years to stop handling the independent oil and take Standard oil!" If undercutting the refiners proved insufficient, retailers were directly threatened. Indeed, grocery stores selling oil refined by independents were themselves hounded and harassed to the point that their businesses failed. Of all the machinations that enabled Rockefeller to build his monopoly, Tarbell found these measures the most insufferable. "The unraveling of this espionage charge, the proofs of it," she later said, "turned my stomach against the Standard in a way that the indefensible and robust fights over transportation had never done. There was a littleness about it that seemed utterly contemptible compared to the immense genius and ability that had gone into the organization."

By 1887, Tarbell writes, Rockefeller "had completed one of the most perfect business organizations the world has ever seen, an organization which handled practically all of a great natural product." With "competition practically out of the way, it set all its great energies to developing what it had secured." Most important, Rockefeller now had the power to control prices. Rather than use this domination and the efficiencies of scale to reduce costs, Standard Oil sought to maximize profits. Wherever competition was extinguished, Tarbell maintained, the consumer paid more. Under investigative duress Standard would temporarily reduce prices, only to jack them up in the same area once the scrutiny ceased. "Human experience long ago taught us," she warned, "that if we allow a man or a group of men autocratic powers in government or church, they use that power to oppress and defraud the public."

Throughout her series, Tarbell acknowledged Standard Oil's "legitimate greatness" and recognized the extraordinary business acumen of John D. Rockefeller: "Plants wisely located—The smallest detail in expense looked out for—Quick adaptability to new conditions as they arise—Economy introduced by the manufacture of supplies—Profit paid to nobody—Profitable extension of products and by-products—A general capacity for seeing big things and enough daring to lay hold of them." Nevertheless, she concludes, while "these qualities alone would have made a great business . . . it would not have been the combination whose history we have traced."

Tarbell's final assessment of Rockefeller's practices and unethical maneuvering is unsparing: He began his ascent by flouting the common law to secure favorable rates from the railroads, allowing him to drive his rivals out. "At the same time he worked with the railroads to prevent other people getting oil to manufacture, or if they got it he worked with the railroads to prevent the shipment of the product. If it reached a dealer, he did his utmost to bully or wheedle him to countermand his order. If he failed in that, he undersold until the dealer, losing on his purchase, was glad enough to buy thereafter of Mr. Rockefeller." In the end, "every great campaign against rival interests which the Standard Oil Company has carried on has been inaugurated, not to save its life, but to build up and sustain a monopoly in the oil industry."

In her closing paragraph, Tarbell issues a challenge: "And what are we going to do about it?" Echoing McClure's celebrated editorial, she exhorts her readers, the American public, to take action. "For it is OUR business," she insists, "we, the people of the United States, and nobody else, must cure whatever is wrong in the industrial situation, typified by this narrative of the growth of the Standard Oil Company."

"YOU ARE TODAY, THE MOST famous woman in America," McClure told the forty-five-year-old Tarbell six months after her sensational series appeared. "People universally speak of you with such a reverence that I am getting sort of afraid of you," he bantered. For the accolades were imposing: A journalist for *The Outlook* proclaimed her "a Joan of Arc among moderns," crusading "against trusts and monopolies." Another journalist declared her "The New Woman," a powerful and independent agent of social change. "At least one American takes rank with the leading biographers and historians of the old world," the *Lowell* (Massachusetts) *Sun* remarked, and "women are proud to know that one is a woman, Miss Ida Minerva Tarbell." The *Los Angeles Times* called her "the strongest intellectual force among the women of the United States," while the *Washington Times* maintained that she had "proven herself to be one of the most commanding figures in American letters."

Tarbell was invited to speak at numerous colleges, clubs, and law schools. Members of the Twentieth Century Club were reportedly enthralled to hear "the woman who talks like a man," while a Missouri newspaperman described an audience enthralled by the tall, stately woman, "so feminine as to appear décolleté in order to make her assault more effective!" Yet, despite her immense professional achievement, influence, and acclaim, Ida Tarbell was the only person in her office not invited to the first annual publishers' dinner. Newspapermen had met annually for several years, but this was the first such official assemblage of magazine publishers and editors together with writers and public officials. President Roosevelt served as the keynote speaker, and the men-only guest list included cabinet and Supreme Court members as well as prominent senators and congressmen. "It is the first time since I came into the office that the fact of petticoats has stood in my way," Ida confessed to Ray Baker, "and I am half inclined to resent it."

The emergence of humorous commentary surrounding "Miss Tarbell" and her exploits only served to underscore her growing popularity. *The Washington Post* facetiously suggested "that Mr. Rockefeller would be glad to pay the expense if some man should win Miss Ida Tarbell and take her on a leisurely tour of the world for a honeymoon." The *Chicago Daily Tribune* noted that "Miss Ida Tarbell goes calmly on jabbing her biographical hat-pin into Mr. Rockefeller." Even on Broadway, the season's biggest hit, *The Lion and the Mouse*, featured a thinly veiled Tarbell character as the mouse that frees the lion Rockefeller from "the net of avarice." The play's young female author enters the magnate's household under the guise of writing a benign biography. In fact, she seeks documents that will clear her father of unjust corruption charges leveled by the Rockefeller character. Once inside, she successfully clears her father's name, changes "Rockefeller's disposition from sordid to benevolent," and, in a final melodramatic twist, is wooed by the tycoon's son!

The *McClure's* series that had inspired this theatrical parable was read and discussed across the nation. Most important for Tarbell, the reaction from critics was overwhelmingly positive. They applauded her "accumulation of facts," stunning "in their significance," her "intimate style," and her ability to tell a complex story "remarkable for being nearly all plot." With each installment, she left the reader "in a state of lively suspense" as to what might follow. Above all, she was praised repeatedly for the fairness of her presentation. "She never rants," one critic observed. "She never howls and waves her arms."

Rockefeller's defenders argued that by focusing her dramatic analysis on one personage, Tarbell ignored the conditions that made consolidation inevitable in scores of industries, including meatpacking, grain elevators, and railroads. Similarly, she failed to acknowledge that rebating was not confined to Standard Oil; it was, on the contrary, "an almost universal practice." Although her work might be "excellent journalism and very good drama," Gilbert Montague wrote in the *Boston Evening Transcript,* "Miss Tarbell does not seem to have guessed the larger bearings of the movement she describes. . . . She prefers to attribute the course of events to a single pervasive, mysterious personality."

It was the "mysterious" Rockefeller, however, who made the series so wildly popular; the story of his life and the creation of his company provided a narrative spine, on which Tarbell could flesh out a more complex and vivid subject. In her portrait of Rockefeller, Tarbell stressed the duality of his nature, presenting "a quiet, modest church-going gentleman, devoted to Sunday school picnics, golf, and wheeling," yet simultaneously "willing to strain every nerve to obtain special and illegal privileges from the railroads which were bound to ruin every man in the oil business not sharing them with him." When she began her series, one newspaper observed, "Rockefeller was known only as a shrewd businessman who had built up an immense business, with a great name for generosity to educational institutions. Now there are very few sane men who would take Rockefeller's millions if his tarnished reputation must go along with them."

As her narrative progresses, Tarbell's indignation at Rockefeller seems to grow, and her language sometimes slips into the same metaphors for soulless mechanical power that cheapened White's portrait of Boss Platt. She describes his eyes "as expressionless as a wall," notes the "downward" droop of "his mouth," his "cruelest" and "most pathetic" feature, and the repellent puffiness of his cheeks. More than a touch of personal vindictiveness colors her representation of Rockefeller as she describes how his pursuit of money renders him no longer "a human man" but rather "a machine—a money machine—stripped by his overwhelming passion of greed of every quality which makes a man worthy of citizenship."

Far more telling insight lies in her argument that "were Mr. Rockefeller the only one of his kind he would be curious, interesting, unpleasant, but in no way vital. . . . But Mr. Rockefeller is not the only one of his kind. He is simply the type preeminent in the public mind of the militant business man of the day." In the end, she insists, there could be "no cure" for the problem of the trusts without "an increasing scorn of unfair play—an increasing sense that a thing won by breaking the rules of the game is not worth the winning. When the businessman who fights to secure special privileges, to crowd his competitor off the track by other than fair competitive methods, receives the same summary disdainful ostracism by his fellows that the doctor or lawyer who is 'unprofessional,' the athlete who abuses the rules, receives, we shall have gone a long way toward making commerce a fit pursuit for our young men."

Though Rockefeller never directly responded to Tarbell's attacks, his friends and associates vented their displeasure by denying McClure membership to the Ardsley Country Club, perched above the Hudson River twenty miles north of Manhattan. Although no protests had been lodged against McClure before the publication of Tarbell's series, he suddenly found himself blackballed through the collusion of board members "closely allied to the Standard Oil interests," including John D. Archbold, William Rockefeller, and Charles Schwab. Such persecution did nothing to subdue McClure's enthusiasm for Tarbell's writing. "Your monumental work on the Standard Oil will never be forgotten," he assured her. In a special editorial, he touted her series as "one of the most remarkable pieces of work ever published in a magazine." Since he fervently believed that it was "up to magazines to rouse public opinion," he was inordinately proud of the fact that her series had mobilized popular sentiment against the trusts as no other writing had done before.

McClure once claimed "that the two things of which he is proudest are, first, that he was the founder of McClure's Magazine; second, that he was the discoverer of Miss Tarbell." Certainly, the peculiar and intimate partnership that they developed was vital to both. McClure may have been more visionary, more in tune with the public's shifting interests, but Tarbell possessed a far sturdier temperament, a relentless work ethic, and the ability to mediate conflict. "You cannot imagine how we all love and reverence you," McClure told her shortly after the launch of the Standard Oil series. "What you have been to me no words can tell." For her part, Tarbell repeatedly proclaimed McClure's manic bursts of energy "the most genuinely creative moments of our magazine life." Nor did she ever forget that he was instrumental in every phase of her journey from obscure expatriate writer to foremost journalist in the nation.

As members of the House and Senate assembled in the winter of 1903, a newspaper in Oshkosh, Wisconsin, predicted that Ida Tarbell's sensational exposure of Standard Oil had finally generated enough pressure to compel congressional action against monopolies. The Republican Party, another western paper editorialized, "must stand by the people or yield to the demands of the corporations." While big business had been "a tower of strength" to the majority party for years, growing indignation demanded that some anti-trust action be taken—the "only question being as to how long the shrewd and cunning agents of the trust can manage to delay this outcome." Indeed, the stalling commenced as soon as Congress convened.

Republican leaders in the Senate spread the word that there would be "no time for anti-trust legislation at this session." The subject, they argued, was too complex for the short session that would end in early March: ill-considered legislation might lead to financial panic; much wiser to wait until the longer session the following year. On the other side of the aisle, Democrats called for radical proposals that stood little chance of passing constitutional muster.

"I pass my days in a state of exasperation," Roosevelt told his son Kermit, "first, with the fools who do not want any of the things that ought to be done, and, second, with the equally obnoxious fools who insist upon so much that they cannot get anything." Emboldened by public support, Roosevelt was determined to prevent the 1903 Congress from playing "the ancient and honorable bunko game" of letting legislation "fall between the two stools" of the House and Senate, with no time left in conference committee to harmonize their differences. "The party had promised antitrust legislation," he maintained, "and it was the party's duty to do something towards fulfilling its obligations." Summoning the leaders of both branches together, he threatened to exercise the president's constitutional power to call an extra session "on extraordinary occasions" unless his anti-trust proposals were brought to the floor before adjournment. "While I could not force anyone to vote *for* these bills," he explained to a friend, "I felt I had a right to demand that there should be *a vote* upon them."

The administration's anti-trust program in 1903 was comprised of three elements: a measure to strengthen existing laws against discriminatory railroad rebates; a bill to expedite legal proceedings against suspected trusts; and of particular interest to the president, a revived proposal to create a cabinet-level Department of Commerce with regulatory powers over the large corporations.

The first measure, sponsored by Congressman Stephen Elkins of West Virginia, rode the crest of popular fury against what had become known as "Rockefeller's rebates." That single word, "rebate," one editorial observed, dominated Tarbell's chronicle of Standard Oil; every successful step Rockefeller took to "corner the oil interests of the country" could be traced to the secret freight rates he obtained from the railroads. For years, farmers and small businessmen had argued that current laws failed to protect them against discriminatory rebating practices. The Elkins bill was designed to remedy weaknesses in the existing regulations, such as the provision that made only railroad agents actually granting the rebates liable to prosecution: under the new bill, corporations would be held responsible for the acts of any of their officers or agents, and failure to follow published rates would subject both railroads and shippers to heavy fines. The courts would be granted increased powers to secure transaction records, demand testimony, and provide summary judgment.

Although secret opposition to the Elkins bill remained, the impact of Tarbell's investigation, Roosevelt told a friend, meant that "no respectable railroad or respectable shipping business can openly object to the rebate bill." By 1903, the railroads themselves actually favored ending cash rebates, which cost them millions of dollars each year in lost revenue. Furthermore, the most powerful corporations offered no objection; as *The Washington Post* noted, they had already "grown beyond any effects the enforcement of the legislation might have." Even with the ban on secret rebates, there remained myriad ways the trusts could exact special concessions from the railroads. The Elkins bill swiftly passed both Houses, promising, in Roosevelt's words, to throw "the highways of commerce open on equal terms to all who use them." The legislation represented small but pragmatic advancement in pursuit of "equal rights for all; special privileges to none."

Growing public sentiment against monopolies also fueled a bill to expedite prosecutions under the Sherman Anti-Trust Act. Initially, this proposed bill to grant anti-trust suits precedence on court calendars had met with what Roosevelt termed "violent opposition"; now, in the face of public rancor, it was "rather sullenly acquiesced in." When the bill passed both Houses with little debate, William Allen White triumphantly declared that "the subconscious moral sense of the people has come to a distinct realization of the fact that crimes are as possible in what we call high finance as they are in lower quarters."

While the trusts reluctantly yielded on the expedition bill, they brought the full force of their influence against the president's proposed Department of Commerce and Labor. The idea of consolidating the various bureaus and offices overseeing immigration, lighthouses, shipping, fisheries, and the census provoked no outcry. When Senator Knute Nelson of Minnesota introduced an amendment crafted by the administration to establish a Bureau of Corporations within the department, however, fierce opposition erupted. Invested with substantial powers to investigate the internal operations of corporations engaged in interstate commerce, the prospective bureau embodied Roosevelt's conviction that publicity was "the first essential" to determine whether individual trusts were guilty of "unfair competition," "unscrupulous promotion," or "overcapitalization." The amendment would provide the bureau with authority to compel testimony, and to subpoena books, papers, and reports. At his discretion, the president could use these findings to determine whether anti-trust laws were being violated and to induce Congress to pass additional regulatory measures to remedy the abuses uncovered.

Long accustomed to operating without effective oversight or federal regulation, corporate interests regarded the prospective Bureau of Corporations as the harbinger of a stifling socialism. "The Standard Oil Company has always regarded anti-trust laws, anti-rebate laws, and such things, as harmless, though, at times annoying," the *Wall Street Journal* explained, "but publicity hurts. And the company will always, at all times, and in all ways, fight publicity." Determined to kill the new bureau, officials of the trusts descended on Washington for private meetings with their loyal allies on Capitol Hill.

Roosevelt's failure the previous year had taught him to carefully monitor every stage of the bill's movement through Congress. Night after night, he convened meetings with leaders of the Senate and the House, impressing on the Speaker, the ranking committee members, and the majority leader that the Nelson amendment was essential to redeem the party's pledge to take action on the trusts. These sessions required all the president's finesse, the press reported, for there was "a disposition in some quarters" to resent his meddling in legislative affairs.

Realizing that he would benefit from the broadest possible consensus, Roosevelt sought to cultivate warm connections with a number of Democrats. Attending the wedding of Missouri's Democratic senator Francis Cockrell's daughter, the president "joked with the girls, shook hands with the matrons and exchanged 'jollying' remarks with the young and old men." At the celebratory breakfast, he announced with sly wit that he could never reside in Missouri, however splendid that state might be: "I think so much of Sen. Cockrell and admire him so greatly that I don't see how I could keep from voting for him, and as he is a Democrat you know that would never, never, do."

"I have been worked until I could hardly stand," the notoriously tireless Roosevelt grumbled to Kermit, "some days twelve hours and over absolutely without intermission." But in fact, his days were not without respite—almost every afternoon he managed the diversion of some mode of exercise. Singlestick, a form of swordplay in which competitors wield wooden sticks, had become his latest obsession. General Leonard Wood, Roosevelt's favorite opponent, bested the president on various occasions, leaving him with a swollen arm, a bruised forehead, and once, a deep cut on his right wrist that required him to shake left-handed at the next White House reception. A comic diagram in the *Minneapolis Journal* pinpointed the numerous injuries Roosevelt had sustained during sundry activities, humorously labeling him "The Most Wounded President in the Nation's History."

When multiplying bruises precluded more singlestick jousts, he rode a horse along snowy streets or split wood for exercise. If his exertions as a woodsman did "not suffice," the *Boston Traveler* quipped, "he might try his hand at lopping off a few of the trust privileges." And indeed, that formidable energy was funneled into a single objective—persuading Congress to pass his pet anti-trust bill.

Saturday, February 7, 1903, would prove critical in the struggle for the Bureau of Corporations. Roosevelt's demeanor, as he discussed literature and international events with the French ambassador Jules Jusserand, revealed nothing of the ruse under way for that evening. As darkness descended, he called together members of the three press associations. Insisting that the source of the information must remain confidential, Roosevelt confided that he had secured proof that John D. Rockefeller was personally orchestrating an underhanded campaign to sabotage the Nelson amendment. A half-dozen senators, he claimed, had received telegrams bearing John D. Rockefeller's signature, with "peremptory" instruction indicating that the corporation was "unalterably opposed" to the bill, and it "must be stopped." The message, one paper reported, was clear: "We own the Republican party and it must do our bidding."

The offending telegrams, Roosevelt assured the assembled journalists—without giving them the exact wording or showing the actual telegrams—had only redoubled his determination to establish the Bureau of Corporations. Unless Congress enacted a satisfactory bill by the March 4 adjournment, he would surely insist on the extra session previously threatened. As anticipated, word of Rockefeller's imperious telegrams inspired headlines and editorials across the country and produced "a decided sensation" on Capitol Hill. One senator after another hastily denied receiving a Rockefeller telegram, "for fear," one Wisconsin paper suggested, that "somebody might think they had intimate relations with the great octopus."

Rockefeller's purported tactic should have occasioned "no surprise," one newspaper sardonically noted: "It is pretty much his senate, anyway. Most of the members of the once august body were elected on a pro-trust understanding, and Deacon John is simply insisting upon fulfillment of the bargain mutually entered into." For years, he and his fellow industrialists had filled Mark Hanna's coffers, the editorial concluded, and Rockefeller was now simply "claiming the privileges he paid for, nothing more."

To combat the pending legislation, Standard Oil sent three of its top lawyers to the Arlington Hotel in Washington. There, they would combine with congressional allies to prepare an emasculating amendment if the bill could not be killed outright. "This is no more than is done every day by managers and attorneys of great business enterprises," the *Los Angeles Times* acknowledged. Companies routinely sent representatives to the nation's capital in an effort to shield themselves from unfavorable legislation. The appearance of the Standard attorneys amid the outrage sparked by Ida Tarbell's exposé and the Rockefeller telegram scandal, however, seemed certain to "inflame the agitator element" in Congress and possibly spur even more radical legislation. "Grasping the whole situation at a glance," Senator Aldrich "wheeled the trio of counsel promptly to right-about," sending them back to New York the next morning.

JUBILANT, ROOSEVELT BOASTED THAT "FROM the standpoint of constructive statesmanship," he considered the Department of Commerce and Labor, with its Bureau of Corporations, "a much greater feat than any tariff law." Well aware of the importance of sharing credit for the victory, he wrote a warm note to

Speaker David Henderson, who had finally conceded that Republicans must take action against the trusts. "Taken as a whole," Roosevelt told him, "no other Congress of recent years has to its credit a record of more substantial achievement for the public good than this over the lower house of which you presided. I congratulate you and it." To head the new department, he chose his private secretary and trusted friend, George Cortelyou, and selected James Garfield, the son of the former president, for Commissioner of Corporations.

After failing for years both as governor and president to pass legislation regulating corporations, Roosevelt had finally succeeded because "a great many people had been thinking and talking" about the problem of the trusts, and "a certain consensus of opinion" had been reached. Ida Tarbell's series had helped foment and articulate a conscious desire for reform in every village, township, and city. In John D. Rockefeller, she had furnished a human face for the bewilderingly intricate and multifaceted problem of the trusts—thereby giving the president an identifiable target that he brilliantly exploited to mobilize public sentiment behind his legislative program.

With the passage of the rebate bill and the expedition bill and the establishment of the Department of Commerce, Roosevelt was convinced that he had "gotten the trust legislation all right," that Democrats could no longer wield the trust issue against his party. Although some charged that even these measures combined were "not sufficiently far-reaching," even these critics acknowledged that Congress had exceeded expectations. Moreover, this trio of bills would provide the basis to determine what further action might be necessary.

Perhaps no forum better illustrated the progressive direction of public opinion than William Allen White's scorecard for the 57th Congress. The country editor who had ridiculed calls for governmental intervention only a few years earlier now heralded Roosevelt's three anti-trust measures as a major step toward rectifying laissez-faire economic policy. He predicted that "no single legislative act since the Missouri Compromise" would impact American business as much as the Department of Commerce and Labor. "Thousands of interests that have known no Federal regulation and control," he wrote, "will be welded to the Government hereafter, and can only grow and develop under the hands of Congress and the President." Some might fear that the country was taking "a step toward socialism," he concluded, but "if so, well and good; the step will not be retracted."

CHAPTER TWELVE

"A Mission to Perform"

"Bigger Than His Party," a Roosevelt cartoon in *Puck* magazine, May 7, 1902.

ON THE MORNING OF APRIL 1, 1903, Roosevelt embarked in high spirits upon the longest tour ever taken by a president—a nine-week transcontinental journey by train that would cover 14,000 miles across twenty-four states and territories. Freed from the vexations of dealing with Congress, he jauntily doffed his hat and waved to the hundreds of cheering well-wishers gathered at the Sixth Street station to see him off. As he boarded the train, he turned to offer parting advice to George Cortelyou, whom he had appointed head of the new Department of Commerce and Labor. "Look out for the trusts," he chuckled. "I hate to leave you here alone with those dreadful corporations, but I can't very well help it. Be careful of them and don't let them hurt you while I am away."

The specially equipped train, reportedly among "the handsomest ever placed on the tracks by the Pullman Company," consisted of six cars. The lush, mahogany-finished *Elysian* would be the president's home throughout the trip. This "traveling palace" boasted three state rooms, a kitchen staffed by expert chefs, a private dining room, an observation parlor, quarters for the servants, and a rear platform from which to address crowds gathered at little stations along the way. The remaining cars included spacious quarters for the president's guests, stenographers, and Secret Service crew, a sleeping car housing reporters and photographers, and a dining car.

Invited to accompany the presidential party, the naturalist John Burroughs described the train's progress north and west through Maryland, Pennsylvania, Illinois, Wisconsin, the Dakotas, and Montana. The president "gave himself very freely and heartily to the people," he noted, his arrival sparking a festive spirit in each village and town. Whenever Roosevelt spotted a group of men or women waving from a distance, he raced out to lift his hat and return the greeting. He never saw such exchanges with the public as inconvenient or intrusive. Burroughs recalled an occasion when the president was lunching as the train passed by a small schoolhouse where the teacher had ushered her students outside. Clutching his napkin, Roosevelt raced to the platform. "Those children," he said, "wanted to see the President of the United States, and I could not disappoint them. They may never have another chance."

Recognizing that people would come "to see the President much as they would come in to see a circus," Roosevelt also surmised that in many small towns the train—rather than the president—was the marquee attraction: "The whole population of the plains now looks upon the Pullman sleepers and dining cars," he told John Hay, "just as Mark Twain describes the people along the banks of the Mississippi as formerly looking at the Mississippi steamers." Nonetheless, he was convinced that "besides the mere curiosity there was a good feeling behind it all, a feeling that the President was their man and symbolized their government and that they had a proprietary interest in him."

Jostled by frantic crowds as he made his way to crude bandstands erected along the route, Roosevelt never betrayed impatience or irritation. Since active campaigning by a presidential candidate was still considered distasteful, this extended tour represented his best chance to gain "the people's trust" before the coming election. Determined to connect with the people, Roosevelt radiated nothing but delight as he accepted an array of bizarre gifts that included an infant badger, a lizard, a horned toad, a copper vase, an Indian basket, two bears, a horse, and a gold inlaid saddle. Through it all, Roosevelt maintained good humor and gratitude. In Butte, Montana, when presented with a foot-high three-handled silver loving cup capable of holding sixteen pints of beer, he graciously exclaimed, "Great heavens and earth!"

Before embarking on the tour, Roosevelt had prepared a half-dozen policy speeches, each addressing a specific issue—the trusts, the tariff, the Navy, the Philippines, and the Monroe Doctrine. "These were not epoch-making addresses," William White explained. Neither "particularly original" nor profound, they were structured with two simple goals in mind: to outline his policies in straightforward language and to establish an emotional rapport with his audiences.

The further he moved from "the thick of civilization," the more expansive and at ease the president appeared. When he talked informally to "rough-coated, hard-headed, gaunt, sinewy farmers and hired hands," Roosevelt proudly told John Hay, he was "always sure of reaching them" with simple language that his Harvard friends would judge "not only homely, but commonplace." Despite "all the superficial differences," he remarked, "down at bottom these men and I think a good deal alike, or least have the same ideals."

Newspapermen began to compile the aphorisms they termed "Roosevelt Gems"—pithy sayings about citizenship, character, and ordinary virtues that he repeated time and again to the great pleasure of his audiences: farmers in Aberdeen, South Dakota, whistled approval when he declared that no law could ever be framed to "make a fool wise or a weakling strong, or a coward brave." They cheered when he compared the qualities desired in the best kind of public servant to those displayed by a good neighbor or a trustworthy friend—"a man who keep[s] his word and never promise[s] . . . what he knows cannot be done." Oregonians nodded in approval when he affirmed, "I do not like hardness of heart, but neither do I like softness of head." Indianans cheered the now familiar Roosevelt adage "Speak softly and carry a big stick." Such "sudsy metaphors," which reportedly dripped "like water from a clothesline," reached the hearts of citizens at every stop along the way.

It was during this western tour that Roosevelt began to test the phrase "a square deal"—the slogan that would come to characterize his entire domestic program. In a speech the previous summer he had called for "a square deal for every man, great or small, rich or poor." Now, he began to flesh out what this really meant for particular segments of the populace. In Arizona, he spoke of the Indians in his regiment: "They were good enough to fight and to die, and they are good enough to have me treat them exactly as square as any white man. . . . All I ask is a square deal for every man." In Montana, he expressed a similar sentiment about the black troops who fought beside him in Santiago. Still later, he elaborated on the concept, applying it to his policy regarding labor and capital. The appeal of the slogan was immediately evident; even advertisers along the president's route appropriated his phrase, headlining "A Square Deal" in their copy. A real estate company in Butte, Montana, began its pitch with Roosevelt's words: "We must treat each man on his worth and merits as a man. We must see that each is given a square deal, because he is entitled to no more and should receive no less."

Reaching Yellowstone, Roosevelt bid a temporary farewell to the newspapermen, who were instructed to stay behind. Accompanied by John Burroughs, he intended to relax for two weeks, to watch birds and simply observe rather than hunt game—the herds of elk, antelope, and black-tailed deer. Roosevelt had stayed with the older man in his log cabin three years earlier, striking Burroughs then as "a great boy," filled with inexhaustible energy. "He climbed everything on the place," the naturalist recalled with mixed awe and dread. "He shinned up tree after tree, running his arms into every high-hole's and woodpecker's nest, while I stood on the ground below shuddering and waiting for him to fall." Their stay at Yellowstone convinced Burroughs that the presidency had altered Roosevelt little: he remained "a man of such abounding energy and ceaseless activity that he sets everything in motion around him wherever he goes. . . . Nothing escaped him, from bears to mice, from wild geese to chickadees, from elk to red squirrels; he took it all in, and he took it in as only an alert, vigorous mind can take it in."

These invigorating days in Yellowstone and a subsequent camping trip in the magnificent forests of Yosemite with the founder of the Sierra Club, John Muir, deeply impressed Roosevelt and informed the tone of his speeches during the remainder of the trip. Turning from trusts and the tariff, he increasingly focused on the importance of preserving the country's national heritage from exploitation. He arrived at the Grand Canyon as a great contest was raging over whether to preserve the landmark as a national monument or open it up to mining for precious metals. "Leave it as it is," he urged his countrymen. "The ages have been at work on it, and man can only mar it. . . . Keep it for your children, your children's children and for all who come after you, as one of the great sights which every American . . . should see." Deeply moved by this "great wonder of nature," the president resolved to ensure the designation of the Grand Canyon as a national park. "If Roosevelt had done nothing else as president," Douglas Brinkley has observed, "his advocacy on behalf of preserving the canyon might well have put him in the top ranks of American presidents."

When the presidential party reached the California coast, Roosevelt took a special detour on a narrow-gauge road into the San Lorenzo Valley, home to a majestic grove of giant sequoias. "I am, oh, so glad to be here," he exclaimed. "This is the first glimpse I have ever had of the big trees." At Stanford University the next day, he exhorted his audience "to protect these mighty trees, these wonderful monuments of beauty." It seemed a desecration to turn "a tree which was old when the first Egyptian conqueror penetrated to the valley of the Euphrates" into house siding or decks or porches. While many would hold that practical progress should trump aesthetic value, Roosevelt argued, "there is nothing more practical, in the end, than the preservation of beauty, than the preservation of anything that appeals to the higher emotions in mankind."

The vital role of these massive redwoods, "the great monarchs of the woods," was confined neither to their commercial value nor to their natural beauty. The primary object of his overall forest policy, Roosevelt insisted, was "not to preserve forests because they are beautiful—though that is a good in itself—not to preserve them because they are refuges for the wild creatures of the wilderness—though that too is a good in itself," but rather, to conserve them in order to guarantee "a steady and continuous supply of timber, grass, and above all, water" that would foster the growth of prosperous communities. Contrary to the prevailing view, Roosevelt foresaw that our natural resources were not inexhaustible. Destructive lumbering practices had already "seriously depleted" the forests. In clear language, he delineated the causal connection between forest protection and water conservation: forests absorb water and slow the melting of snow in the spring; they prevent the rain from "rushing away in uncontrollable torrents"; they "regulate the flow of streams." In every watershed, forests help determine the amount of available water that can transform a wasteland into "a veritable garden of Eden."

In speech after speech, Roosevelt lauded the passage of the 1902 Reclamation Act, which, for the first time, made substantial federal funds available to construct dams, reservoirs, and other irrigation projects in the West. Intended to open "small irrigated farms to actual settlers, to actual home-makers," the legislation stipulated that tracts of land larger than 160 acres would be ineligible for federally sponsored irrigation. In this way, the government sought to ensure that speculators would not commandeer the program's benefits. "We do not ever want to let our land policy be shaped so as to create a big class of proprietors who rent to others," Roosevelt asserted. America's forests and waters must "come into the hands, not of a few men of great wealth, or into the hands of a few men who speculate in them, but be distributed among many men, each of whom intends to make him a home on the land."

Of the five irrigation projects under way in the spring of 1903—in Colorado, Montana, Wyoming, Nevada, and Arizona—the most prominent was a huge masonry arch dam in Arizona's Salt River Valley. When Charles Walcott, director of the U.S. Geological Survey, announced on April 18 that the government had selected the Salt River Valley for its first big enterprise, a banner headline in the *Arizona Republican* hailed the decision: THE DAY OF DELIVERANCE IS AT HAND. The reservoir created by the project, later christened the Roosevelt Dam, would be, excepting the work being done on the Nile, "the greatest in the world." Designed to irrigate 200,000 acres, the dam promised to "make the community near Phoenix [with a population then of 25,000] one of the most prosperous in the country."

The estimated cost of the five projects would total $7 million, which settlers would then repay to the government over a ten-year period. Once completed, Roosevelt predicted, these irrigation projects would more profoundly impact the entire western region over the next half century than "any other material movement whatsoever." He could already envision "a new type" of settler throughout the West who could build homes, roads, businesses, schools, and places of amusement, populating bustling towns and cities that might one day contain "a million inhabitants." Moreover, an arable, enticing West could alleviate some of the social evils caused by overcrowding in the East.

Century magazine suggested that Roosevelt's decision to highlight issues of conservation, irrigation, and preservation would have an "educational effect upon the people," fostering a new determination to protect "the western wonderlands," expand national parks, and institute a sustainable, scientific approach to managing the nation's wilderness areas. Any action to safeguard forest lands was usually delayed until the end of a president's term, the journalist noted, but Roosevelt would not hesitate "to throw the full force of his influence" behind legislation that would halt "the ruinous waste of the great national forests."

From California, the president's train headed north to Portland, Oregon, and Seattle, Washington, before veering east for the long trip home. Roosevelt had delivered 265 speeches, once addressing nine crowds in a single day. He had participated in countless parades, endured long banquets (and gained 11 pounds), met with all manner of local officials, dedicated monuments, and attended military reviews. Sustained by the enthusiastic reception all along his travel route, he returned, according to Edith, "as fresh and unworn as when he left."

Roosevelt had scarcely settled into the White House when reports surfaced of possible governmental corruption over the Salt River reservoir. Objections and accusations swirled around the choice of Salt River for the government's inaugural project. During congressional debates over the Reclamation Act, talk of making desert lands in the public domain "blossom like a rose" abounded; ultimately, the government hoped to open these revitalized lands to individual settlers at a small cost under the Homestead Act. Yet given that almost all the land in the Salt River Valley was already in private hands, such settlements represented a glaring problem. For twenty years, private funds had irrigated the valley; unlike the four smaller projects, this reservoir would "irrigate no public lands, but only those in private ownership, vastly increasing, of course, their value." Indeed, the irrigated lands would likely quadruple in value when the government completed its work. To further complicate matters, some of the tracts—undoubtedly held by speculators—covered upward of 10,000 acres, many times the established limit of 160 acres. Opportunities for corruption seemed boundless.

As Roosevelt struggled to address the complex situation in Arizona, he turned to Ray Baker for insight and counsel. Ever since Baker's early biographical sketch had caught his attention, Roosevelt had followed the reporter's career, occasionally sending him short notes commending his "excellent" work. He had read Baker's now famous January 1903 article on the brutality between union men and the scabs who had continued to work during the coal strike, and gauged the public reaction to Baker's gripping investigative piece. Despite his firm support of trade unions, Roosevelt strongly believed that members who engaged in violent acts such as Baker described should be held accountable. "We intend to do absolute justice to every man," he repeatedly proclaimed, "whether he be capitalist or wageworker, union man or nonunion man."

While Baker shared this conviction, he had initially hesitated when McClure suggested he study the violence perpetrated against non-striking miners. He was loath to provide "ammunition for mere stupid opposition to all labor organizations" or to compromise the labor leaders he had come to know and respect over the years. Furthermore, the coal strike had erupted during his second leave of absence from the magazine as he began long-postponed work on his novel exploring the nation's grave social and economic plight. Baker had finally moved from New York to East Lansing, a quiet hamlet near the campus of Michigan State College where his father-in-law still taught biology. He calculated that his savings would last at least a year. The change delighted his wife tremendously, drawing their three children close to their grandparents and reuniting her with childhood friends.

Baker would "never . . . forget the feeling of joyful independence" as he settled into his new home and commenced work on his novel. On his study wall, he hung portraits of Walt Whitman, Leo Tolstoy, and his own father. He tacked favorite quotations to the back of the desk, which, he noted with satisfaction, was "the first desk I ever had that was big enough . . . where I could spread out my elbows and work as long as I wanted to without interruption."

"I actually thought my future was settled!" Baker recalled of the brief respite. "I did not count sufficiently upon S. S. McClure." Eager to keep his gifted young reporter, McClure had contacted him in October 1902 as the coal strike was escalating. The magazine, he generously proposed, would pay a weekly stipend throughout the year, while Baker would have to work only six months. The rest of the year he would be free to pursue his own writing, which *McClure's* would publish on liberal terms. "So the serpent in my new Eden!" Baker ruefully jested, the proposition too tempting to reject.

Baker had just arrived at the magazine's New York office when he received word that McClure wanted him in Wilkes-Barre, Pennsylvania, where the coal strike was coming to an end. McClure himself had traveled to the coal region shortly after his summer vacation in Europe, joining dozens of reporters, writers, and publishers gathered to cover the historic strike. Recognizing that the press was saturated with stories about the terrible coal-field conditions that had precipitated the five-month strike, McClure sought a different aspect of the story. Despite the abysmal conditions, some miners had kept on the job, refusing to support their fellow strikers, even at the risk of violent reprisal. "What sort of men were they?" McClure pondered. The story of "the scabs" was yet untold, and McClure felt that no one was better suited to investigate the matter than Ray Baker.

When they met at the Hotel Sterling at the corner of River and Market Streets, the buoyant McClure presented his idea to Baker. The young writer was less sanguine, explaining his concern that so long as public opinion "was generally hostile to labor unionism," it must be emphasized that the strikebreakers' plight was "only one aspect of a highly complex problem." But the longer he considered the proposal, the more curious he grew about the 17,000 out of roughly 140,000 miners who persisted in working. Baker had always been intrigued by the motivation of the few who went against the many, and in the end, to McClure's delight, he agreed to stay in the coal region for a month or more to talk with these men and learn why they refused to support the union.

With the same exacting impartiality that marked his investigation of the Pullman strike, Baker sought out people on all sides of the "scab" issue. He talked with the miners in the kitchens of their homes and descended with them down the shafts into the mines, taking note of the "low wages, company houses, company stores, poor schools, wretched living conditions" in the collieries. He sat in on union meetings where "the scabs" were bitterly denounced and interviewed John Mitchell, whom he found "singularly steady-headed" in the wake of the turbulent strike. In hotel suites thick with cigar smoke, he discussed the conflict with fellow writers and radical leaders, including Henry D. Lloyd and Clarence Darrow. Armed with a range of opinions, he spent weeks with scores of non-striking miners, talking with them and their families, eliciting their perspectives of the realities that led to their decision to continue working even under such treacherous conditions.

"What men I met during those fiery weeks!" he recalled. "What stories they told me: what dramas of human suffering, human loyalty, and human fear." McClure was thrilled with Baker's letters from the field. "Don't, my dear boy, be afraid of space," he urged; "we can give this thing all the space it requires, all the articles it requires. I am glad you have struck such a rich mine." A week later, McClure wrote again. The New York *Sun* had devoted two columns that day to a sermon delivered in Brooklyn on the subject of "the feuds in the coal-fields, the bitterness between union and non-union men, the uncompromising hatred" opening "wounds that only death can heal." Baker's subject had "become the most important question of the day," McClure reassured him. "I am going down to go over the material with you yourself," he added. "You have done magnificently!"

Baker completed his piece, which McClure titled "The Right to Work," just in time for inclusion in the landmark issue. At Baker's insistence, an editor's note preceded the piece to clarify the magazine's support for labor unions. Although the magazine would continue to advocate for the nation's workingmen, the editor explained, the public "is beginning to distinguish between unionism and the sins of unionists, as it is between organized capital and the sins of capitalists." By illuminating the individual lives of the strikebreakers, Baker also stressed in his opening, he intended neither to challenge "the rights of labor to organize" nor to question "the sincerity of the labor leader." Instead, he simply wanted to offer a detailed "series of case histories" exploring why these men "continued to work in spite of so much abuse and even real danger."

The story of John Colson dramatically illustrated the divisive impact of the strike within mining families. An engineer from the small town of Gilberton, Pennsylvania, Colson enjoyed "the best position at the colliery." Although not a member of the union, he initially went out with the strikers. But with no prospect of a settlement after several months, he took a job at a distant colliery while his wife remained at home with the children. The moment spies determined that Colson had gone back to work, his wife was targeted for retaliation: stores would not serve her; former friends repudiated her in the streets; neighbors pelted her with rocks. When she tried to move, no teamster would help her. A mob finally tracked down Colson himself, beating him so badly that he was mistakenly listed among those murdered during the strike. After talking with Colson and his wife, Baker went to visit Colson's elderly parents in Mahonay City, four miles away. Mrs. Colson spoke with pride of her sons, all miners, all union members who had faithfully maintained the strike. She discussed her eldest son, John, reluctantly. "He might better be dead," she declared, "for he's brought disgrace on the name. He deserved all he got. He wasn't raised a scab." Never again would the family acknowledge him. "The strike," Baker wrote, "had wholly crushed all family feeling."

Baker's reporting illustrated how, all too often, lifelong friendships, like familial bonds, became casualties of the conflict. A strong believer in unions, one miner, Hugh Johnson, nonetheless considered this strike, the second in two years, a bad idea. Although he voted against it, he remained out with the strikers until he could no longer afford to pay his family's living expenses. As soon as he returned to work, troubles began: his daughter was fired from her job as a teacher, his son harassed at school, and his wife prevented from buying food and supplies at the local stores. One night, a mob chased and threatened to kill him. "All these things," Baker observed, "were done by his neighbors and friends, among whom he had lived an honorable life for years."

As the strike dragged on, the level of violence escalated. One telling example involved James Winstone, a respected community leader. Winstone, too, had argued against the strike but stayed out to support his fellow workers. Informed that he did not qualify for assistance from the union relief fund because he owned property, Winstone finally returned to work. In late September, only a few days before the strike was settled, he was clubbed to death by three longtime neighbors. Such stories, Baker insisted, constituted "only a few among scores, even hundreds, of similar tragedies of the great coal strike."

Baker returned to East Lansing after completing the article "on fire with the wealth of new material, new characters and, above all, new understandings of the human elements" involved in the labor struggle. He happily anticipated sitting at his desk to work on his novel "gloriously all winter long." As January turned to February, however, he found it increasingly difficult to concentrate. Clippings arrived from all over the country praising his article. "Everything has borne out the truthfulness and value of the article you wrote," McClure congratulated him. His case histories had dramatized a vital aspect of the conflict—the price paid by non-striking miners—better than anything else written. McClure sought to entice him with the prospect of an entire series on labor.

Baker found himself making scant headway on his novel, unable "to write fiction when the world seemed literally on fire with critical, possibly revolutionary, movements in which [he] was deeply interested." Putting the fiction aside, he returned to New York, where "a powerful new interest, a common purpose" was energizing the *McClure's* office. The enthusiasm generated by the magazine's critical and popular success was palpable. "I doubt whether any other magazine published in America ever achieved such sudden and overwhelming recognition," Baker proudly remarked. "We had put our fingers upon the sorest spots in American life."

The staff members at *McClure's* had always worked closely, even while pursuing diverse interests. Now that their respective investigations into the problems of modern industrial society substantially overlapped, they eagerly read one another's works, often suggesting further lines of inquiry. Tarbell's disclosures of John D. Rockefeller's illegal activities resonated with Steffens's endeavor to trace political corruption to the captains of industry. Tarbell looked to Steffens for an understanding of the invisible web that linked businessmen to politicians, politicians to judges. Indeed, the intensity of these reciprocally informing projects and the sense of camaraderie in a momentous cause affected Baker profoundly. "I have wondered," he later wrote, "if there could have been a more interesting editorial office than ours, one with more of the ozone of great ideas, touch-and-go experimentation, magic success." This rare formula, he noted, owed as much to rigorous and honest feedback as to affectionate support. "We were friends indeed, but we were also uncompromising critics of one another." Forty years later, Baker still considered John Phillips "the most creative editor" he had worked with in his entire life. "He could tell wherein an article failed and why," he recalled; "he could usually make fertile suggestions for improving it; he was willing to give the writer all the precious time he needed for rewriting his story."

The office itself, now situated just east of the Flatiron Building on 23rd Street, reflected the collaborative ardor of McClure's staff. The walls in the hallway were a mosaic of original artwork designed for pages of the magazine. Mementoes from individual articles decorated each writer's office. They even had special names for one another: McClure was "the Chief," Steffens was "Stef," and Ida M. Tarbell was affectionately dubbed "I-dare-m." In her office, she proudly displayed a framed note from Finley Peter Dunne: "Idarem—She's a lady but she has the punch." No one, Baker said of Tarbell, lived "so warmly in the hearts of her friends." Never had he known "a finer human spirit," "so generous, so modest, so full of kindness, so able, so gallant—and yet with such good sense and humor."

The exhilarating atmosphere in the office persuaded Baker to accept the Chief's suggestion and embark upon a series of labor articles. "Why bother with fictional characters and plots," he told himself, "when the world was full of more marvelous stories that were true: and characters so powerful, so fresh, so new, that they stepped into the narratives under their own power?"

THE PRESIDENT'S REQUEST FOR BAKER's help in uncovering possible corruption in Arizona reached the reporter in Chicago, where he was researching the first of five lengthy articles on various aspects of the labor problem. As the celebrated series unfolded, Roosevelt would frequently reach out to Baker for advice and counsel on labor issues. In the summer of 1903, as Roosevelt labored to assess the contentious Salt River situation, he recalled a more obscure series on the Southwest Baker had written for the literary *Century* magazine the previous year. Like Roosevelt, Baker recognized the transformative potential of irrigation. Using language close to Roosevelt's heart, Baker described riding through miles of desert with "no sign of living creatures," only to discover a green stretch of well-watered acreage "with rows of rustling cottonwoods, the roofs of home, and the sound of cattle in the meadows. A wire fence was the dividing line: on this side lay the fruitless desert; on the other green alfalfa, full of blossoms and bees, brimming over the fences." The sight, Baker proclaimed, "was something to stir a man's heart." "My dear Mr. Baker," Roosevelt wrote on June 25, explaining his dilemma and soliciting Baker's guidance. "As you know, I am especially concerned over the irrigation project. At times I hear rumors of crookedness in connection with the Government irrigation work, especially in Arizona. I have been utterly unable hitherto to get any definite statement in reference thereto. It has occurred to me that you may be able privately to tell me something about this."

Baker swiftly responded, promising to share all the information gleaned concerning the Salt River project. He had, in fact, returned to Arizona earlier that spring, contemplating another irrigation article. Moreover, he had been present at the meetings when Charles Walcott of the U.S. Geological Survey delivered his decision in favor of the Water Users Association in Salt River, and had spent time on an alfalfa ranch in order to "get at the exact sentiment of the people." Though he had witnessed no overt corruption, Baker had little doubt that something was wrong; promoters of the Water Users Association, "backed by the government officials," relied on "overbearing" methods that were "suspicious in the extreme." He assured the president that he would gladly call at the White House when he returned to Washington the following week.

"I suppose that the Government officials you speak of must be in the Geological Survey," Roosevelt replied, adding that "in public life as in private life a man of the very highest repute will occasionally go wrong." Still, he recognized that accusations and rumors are readily fabricated, and in such cases "it is most desirable that their falsity be shown." Some criticism of Walcott was undoubtedly political—fueled by Republicans upset with projects recommended in Democratic states, as well as senators and congressmen in the Rocky Mountain region furious over the choice of Arizona (still a territory without representation in Congress). Regardless of the origins, Roosevelt insisted that if Walcott "or any other Government official has gone wrong in Arizona I am more anxious than any other man can be to get at it." He requested that Baker do him the favor of stopping first to see Gifford Pinchot at the Forestry Division and then joining him for lunch at Oyster Bay. "If there is any kind of ground for believing in fraud of any sort by Government officials," he concluded, "I want to consult with you as to the best way of setting men to work so as to be sure of our getting the proof."

Baker was thrilled by the prospect of working closely with the president either to uncover corruption or to dispel malicious career-destroying rumors. "I was so eager to help," he recalled, "that I got together a large package of notes and memoranda—also maps and pictures—and a veritable article of several thousand words on which I spent several days of hard work, setting forth in detail the exact situation in the Salt River Valley as I had seen it." He took another day to compile a memorandum on the coal fields, just in case Roosevelt ventured to discuss labor issues as well. "I was determined to be fully prepared," he explained, "to give the President of the United States several hours of sound enlightenment and instruction!"

Baker's study of the situation in Arizona convinced him that the government's choice of the Salt River Valley was perfectly justified. "If ever men worked miracles," he wrote, it was in Salt River. Sustained by private capital, neighbors had cooperated for decades to dig ditches and build canals in order to divert water. From inhospitable desert, they had wrested three cities replete with electric lights, fine hotels, schools, and churches—all shaded by mature trees and bordered by thriving and productive "orchards of oranges, almonds, olives, and figs." After seven years of insufficient rainfall and reckless deforestation, however, the "implacable desert" was closing in again: homes were reluctantly abandoned as orchards died, fields withered, and land values plummeted. Without the infusion of vast government capital to build a great reservoir, this once-thriving valley would perish. Baker carefully considered how two related factors complicated the situation: vast tracts of land were already under private ownership, and unscrupulous developers might lure more people into the valley than the water project could supply.

On the morning of July 15, Baker boarded a train at Long Island City. En route to Oyster Bay, where the president was spending the summer, he ran into an old Chicago acquaintance, Herman Kohlsaat, publisher of the *Record-Herald*. Treasury Secretary Leslie Mortimer Shaw and Charles J. Bonaparte, a noted attorney who was investigating postal fraud for the Justice Department, also joined them aboard the train. Upon arrival, the four men crowded into a horse-driven public carriage for the three-mile journey to Sagamore Hill.

"The President lives very simply," Baker informed his father. "I thought as I drove over from the station what some modern German or English worthy might say on entering the president's grounds & seeing no guards or military anywhere about." A maid ushered the guests into the library to wait for the president. "Robust, hearty, wholesome, like a gust of wind," he soon burst in, wearing knee-length breeches and an old coat.

The company at lunch included members of the Roosevelt family and the president's old friend Jacob Riis. Theodore Roosevelt, Baker observed, "takes an extraordinary interest in life, gets pleasure out of everything. His mind seems to leap upon every question with boundless enthusiasm." The president first addressed the alleged postal corruption, assuring Bonaparte that he desired an exhaustive investigation. "I don't care whom it hurts," he assured Baker; "we must get to the bottom of these scandals." Shifting the conversation to Arizona, he reiterated that his irrigation development must benefit the individual settler rather than the wealthy landowner or speculator. Baker understood the difficulty of realizing this intention, but a recently promulgated regulation promised to guide the project in that direction. The government had announced that landowners possessing more than 160 acres must put their extra acreage "on the market at reasonable prices" or receive no water from the reservoir.

Unaware of these developments, Roosevelt suddenly turned to Baker: "Who is the chief devil down there in the Salt River valley?" Baker was momentarily unsure how to respond to such a query. When he hesitated, "the President burst into a vigorous, picturesque, and somewhat vitriolic description of the situation, implying that if he could catch the rascals who were causing the trouble he would execute them on the spot." Baker was taken aback by Roosevelt's simplistic diatribe, "but when I tried to break into the conversation—boiling inside with my undelivered articles and memoranda (one of which I tried to draw from my pocket)—the President put one fist on the table beside him, looked at me earnestly, and said: 'Baker, you and I will have to get together on these subjects.' "

Startled by Roosevelt's pugnacity, Baker and the guests adjourned to the library after lunch. "As the time drew near for leaving," Baker recollected, "I began to wonder when the President would ask me for the information upon which I had spent so much time and hard work. I had my heavy brief case in hand when I went up to say good-bye—and my grand plans for enlightening the Government of the United States vanished in a handshake."

Despite the self-deprecatory tone of this account, Baker's meticulous research, later passed on to Gifford Pinchot, eventually proved invaluable. His conclusion that government agents were doing everything possible to carry out the president's purposes in a complex situation cleared Charles Walcott of suspicion. In a letter to Baker, Pinchot expressed great satisfaction that Baker had arrived at his vindicating assessment despite his initial suspicions.

Several months later, Theodore Roosevelt received an advance copy of Baker's exposé on the corrupt relationship between Sam Parks, the powerful boss of New York's builders' union, and the Fuller Company, the leading contractor in the city. The president quickly penned a long note to the reporter: "I am immensely impressed by your article. While I had known in rather a vague way that there was such a condition as you describe, I had not known its extent, and as far as I am aware the facts have never before been brought before the public in such striking fashion."

Lincoln Steffens had provided Baker with the basis for this first extended study of the role labor racketeering played in the rise of the trusts. Investigating municipal corruption in Chicago and New York, Steffens had unearthed evidence that large building contractors were colluding with corrupt labor bosses to force smaller contractors out of business to eliminate competition. When he shared this material with his colleague, Baker spent months pursuing his own investigation. This research culminated in the stunning charge that the Fuller Construction Company was providing a regular salary to the union leader.

In "The Trust's New Tool—The Labor Boss," Baker focused on one disturbing question: While the great building strike of 1903 paralyzed construction through all of Manhattan, why did one firm, the Fuller Construction

Company, keep on building? In answer, Baker laid out evidence that for years, the Fuller Company had paid Sam Parks to look after *its* interests.

Baker traced Parks's ascent from railroad brakeman to bridge-builder, from "walking delegate" of the Housesmiths' and Bridgemen's Union to undisputed boss of the Board of Building Trades. The board, comprised of the walking delegates who represented workmen in each of three dozen unions affiliated with the building industry, was designed to protect the interests of its members. In theory, Sam Parks was simply a paid agent for his union, receiving the same salary as an ordinary workman in his trade. In reality, Baker tracked him "riding about in his cab, wearing diamonds, appearing on the street with his blooded bulldog, supporting his fast horses, 'treating' his friends." How reminiscent, Baker grimly observed, "of the familiar, affluent aldermen or police captains of our cities building $50,000 residences on salaries of $1500 or less." Indeed, the more he studied the situation, the more parallels emerged between Sam Parks and the Tammany chief Richard Croker.

A half-decade earlier, the Fuller Construction Company had arrived in New York from Chicago; "starting with no business at all," it had swiftly risen to become the "greatest construction company in the world, with the largest single building business in New York, and important branches in Chicago, Baltimore, and Philadelphia." Behind the Fuller Company, Baker found a familiar cast of characters—Charles Schwab represented the steel industry; Cornelius Vanderbilt the railroad industry; and James Stillman, president of Rockefeller's bank, the financial industry. "A gigantic hand had reached into New York," Baker observed, echoing Tarbell's description of Standard Oil's stranglehold on the oil region, "the hand of the Trust."

Baker's article also detailed the events ultimately leading to Parks's arrest. "Curiously enough," he remarked, "the Fuller Company brought Sam Parks from Chicago when it came." The flamboyant labor boss proved helpful in a variety of ways. Offering no explanation to fellow union members, he unilaterally called strikes designed to cripple Fuller's independent competitors. "Worse still," Baker observed, "strikes were often accompanied by a demand for money" before they could be settled. Rumors of blackmail, bribes, and pocketed spoils had circulated for years before District Attorney William Travers Jerome finally indicted Parks. In discovery, Jerome learned that Parks had approached the Hecla Iron Works, threatening to call a strike unless he was paid $1,000. After the company balked, the ensuing strike lasted for several weeks, costing the company $50,000 and keeping over a thousand men out of work. Only when Hecla agreed to Parks's extortion—paying double the amount originally demanded—did the walkout end. When the $2,000 check surfaced, endorsed by Parks and cashed by the Fuller Company, the district attorney finally had sufficient grounds to arrest the labor boss.

Roosevelt told Baker that his exposé illustrated with graphic urgency "the need of drawing the line on *conduct*, among labor unions, among corporations, among politicians, and among private individuals alike!" The president noted sardonically that "the organs of Wall Street men of a certain type are bitter in their denunciations of the labor unions, and have not a word to say against the iniquity of the corporations. The labor leaders of a certain type howl against the corporations, but do not admit that there is any wrong ever perpetrated by labor men." Baker's even-handed investigation and subsequent critique of both labor and capital dovetailed with Roosevelt's own approach. The president invited Baker to the White House to discuss the matter further. "When I get back East again," Baker replied, "I shall be more than pleased to accept your invitation." Roosevelt's commendation, he continued, made him "feel more strongly than ever that there is here a great duty to perform; to bring out these conditions clearly and fairly and above all, truthfully." Furthermore, he added, "Mr. McClure is giving me the best medium in this country to do so."

McClure and Phillips were delighted with the widespread commentary engendered by Baker's labor pieces. The *Wall Street Journal* printed a fierce editorial condemning corporate corruption and demanding change: "When the corporations have their paid agents in the trade unions as they have their paid agents in the legislatures, and in the executive councils of great parties, the necessity for reform in corporate management is clear. . . . The only way the trusts and the labor unions can hope to stand long without harsh restrictive legislation is to play square with the people." And when Harvard professor John Brooks publicly endorsed Baker's analysis, college students across the country flocked to hear the man considered "the greatest reporter" in the country.

"You have gone into a splendid field of material and you are getting the mastery of it," Phillips wrote to his rising star, claiming that "before you are through with this you will know more than any one else about labor questions in America." Steffens congratulated Baker on the greatest triumph "a man can have with a pen," maintaining that the Parks piece had "made both sides see themselves as they are." He confessed his own difficulty in writing after reading Baker's article, finding himself oppressed by a "yellow streak" of jealousy that left him "burning with shame." He finished with a question at once rueful and admiring: "Ever catch yourself at mean thinking? I guess not. I envy you your perfect honesty."

Baker followed up this success with "The Lone Fighter," a biographical piece on the union leader Robert Neidig, who had worked for years to combat

Parks's pernicious influence. Initially, his struggle seemed futile; just as the political bosses kept their power because only a small minority of the public attended party primaries, so despotic union leadership endured when but a small percentage of union members attended meetings. The majority, Baker explained, "were tired at night and wanted to go home and play with their babies." Neidig, a steel builder with a wife and children, decided early on to take his union responsibilities in earnest. He never missed a meeting and gradually built up a following. At election time, however, Parks exercised the full power of his corrupt machine. "We hear of repeaters and purchased votes," Baker reported, "even of fraudulent ballots and fraudulent counts." Neidig was "threatened with personal violence, with loss of his job, and even with expulsion from the union." Nothing, it seemed, could break the labor boss's hold on the union, not even his indictment.

Nevertheless, Neidig refused to abandon his efforts to build an honest union, and Baker's detailed revelations about Parks helped turn the tide. "The 'lone fighter' is not alone," one correspondent observed, "when there are other lone fighters to act at the same time with him." One union member confessed to Baker that before reading the article, he had considered Parks "a true and faithful officer of our Union" and repeatedly supported him in elections. He considered Baker's piece "by far the best exposition of the causes of the present Labor troubles" and recommended that it "be placed in the hands of workingmen" everywhere.

Robert Neidig gratefully assured Baker that his "splendid" exposé had "done more to weaken Parks and Parksism than any article that has been published." Within the union itself, its impact had been tremendous. Members finally understood "the wrong that had been done them" and were ready to take action. "To you belongs a large part of the credit," Neidig commended, concluding that "an excellent prospect" now existed of overthrowing Parks and reorganizing "the Union on a sound and honest basis."

"My present work interests me very deeply," Baker reported to his father. "It seems almost as if I had a mission to perform—to talk straight out on a difficult subject." With justifiable pride, he noted that between his own work and that of Tarbell and Steffens, his magazine was "probably doing more now in stirring up the American people than any other publication ever did before."

CHAPTER THIRTEEN

Toppling Old Bosses

The 1904 *Puck* cartoon "More Rough Riding" shows President Roosevelt galloping the GOP elephant through a crowd of opponents.

ROOSEVELT TRIED TO PROLONG HIS 1903 summer vacation, recognizing that once he returned to the capital, there would be "mighty little letup to the strain." It was "as lovely a summer as we have ever passed," he told Corinne, "the happiest, healthiest, most old-fashioned kind of a summer."

Of all the Roosevelt children, only nineteen-year-old Alice was absent, choosing to spend most of July and August with her fashionable friends in Newport, Rhode Island. This decision rankled her father, who expressed distaste for her wealthy companions at the exclusive resort community. "I suppose young girls and even young men naturally like a year or two of such a life as the Four Hundred lead," he fretted to a friend, perhaps mindful of his own youthful snobbery in preferring to associate only with other gentlemen at Harvard. "But I do not think anyone can permanently lead his or her life amid such surroundings and with such objects, save at the cost of degeneration in character," he added, revealing how far his attitudes had changed. "I have not a doubt that they would mortally object to associating with me—but they could not possibly object one one-hundredth part as much as I should to associating with them. . . . For mere enjoyment, I would a great deal rather hold my own in any congenial political society—even in Tammany."

The rest of the children blissfully entertained themselves, their siblings, and their cousins with picnics, hikes, and sailboat rides. Fifteen-year-old Ted Junior and thirteen-year-old Kermit were delighted to be home from boarding school at Groton. Eleven-year-old Ethel, who had boarded during the week at the National Cathedral School, happily assumed the role of "little mother" to her younger brothers, Archie and Quentin. "She is a great comfort to them," Roosevelt contentedly remarked, "and they are great comforts to her."

Nothing Edith accomplished as first lady compared with the uncomplicated joy of long summer days with her husband at their family home. Edith "looks so young and pretty," Theodore beamed to Emily Carow. Both relished this time alone, riding horses together through the woods, carrying lunches and books with them on picnic excursions, and rowing to the end of Lloyd's Neck, where they "watched the white sails of coasters passing up and down the Sound."

Their tranquil family escape came to an end with the season. As soon as Roosevelt returned to Washington, he was bombarded by delegations of party officials, senators, and congressmen. Only thirteen months remained until the presidential election. "Whether I shall be re-elected, I have not the slightest idea," he admitted. "I know there is bitter opposition to me from many different sources. Whether I shall have enough support to overcome this opposition, I cannot tell." While large and enthusiastic crowds at every stop of his summer tour confirmed the president's unprecedented popularity, the American people did not control the nomination process in these days before the direct primary. Machine politicians and party bosses—the very men Roosevelt had opposed throughout his career—determined the candidates, and their selections were then endorsed by the very same financial interests he had antagonized during his two years as president. The public might applaud his anti-trust policies and his intervention in the coal strike, but the big businessmen whose contributions sustained the Republican Party had become, in Roosevelt's words, "determined foes."

"The whole country breathed freer, and felt as if a nightmare had been lifted when I settled the anthracite coal strike," Roosevelt explained to the British historian George Otto Trevelyan, but although public memory of the crisis quickly dissipated, "the interests to which I gave mortal offense will make their weight felt as of real moment." Roosevelt had not forgotten how the same web of political and financial interests had stymied his hope for a second gubernatorial term after he had defied the party with his franchise tax bill and his stubborn refusal to retain Boss Platt's corrupt friend, Lou Payn, as superintendent of insurance. Then, Republican bosses had retaliated by attempting to bury him in the vice presidency; now, he feared, they would deny him the nomination for president.

Roosevelt understood perfectly that party leaders would vastly prefer the Republican Party chairman Mark Hanna, "flesh of their flesh, bone of their bone," who had cemented the party's alliance with the corporations. Hanna had only to "pass the word along," William Allen White observed, and within ten days "the politicians in the Republican party would leave the president." While Roosevelt had successfully established some of his own men in various state positions, the national organization remained firmly in Hanna's control.

The president's best hope lay in the fact that "reform was in the air." All over the country, White noted, "little Roosevelts were appearing in city halls, county courthouses, statehouses and occasionally were bobbing up in Congress." In Toledo, Republican reformer Samuel Jones had been elected mayor over the determined opposition of the Hanna machine. In Cleveland, Hanna's nemesis, reform Democrat Tom Johnson, was serving a second term as mayor. A newly formed Municipal Voters' League in Chicago, led by Republicans William Kent and George Cole, was engaged in a bitter fight against the entrenched corruption fostered by Charles T. Yerkes, the tycoon whose life Theodore Dreiser later fictionalized in his *Trilogy of Desire*. Republican Robert La Follette of Wisconsin had defied the machine to become governor by waging "war on the railroads that ruled his state."

THESE ROUSING STORIES WERE DRAMATICALLY told in Lincoln Steffens's spectacular series on municipal and state corruption: "Shame of the Cities" and "Enemies of the Republic." Focusing national attention on these local battles, Steffens inspired reformers in other cities to address the corruption that plagued every level of government. His series played a significant role in toppling old bosses, bringing a new generation of Roosevelt-type reformers to positions of power in cities and states across the nation.

As ever, the idea for the acclaimed series had originated with Sam McClure. Returning to the office in late 1901 after several months abroad, McClure encountered Steffens, then serving as managing editor, seated at his desk. "You may be an editor," McClure huffed dismissively, "but you don't know how to edit a magazine. . . . You can't learn to edit a magazine here in this office. . . . Get out of here, travel, go—somewhere. . . . Buy a railroad ticket, get on a train, and there, where it lands you, there you will learn to edit a magazine."

With McClure's support, Steffens embarked on an odyssey. For the better part of three years, he called on people in St. Louis, Minneapolis, Pittsburgh, Chicago, Philadelphia, New York, Cleveland, and Madison. "My business is to find subjects and writers, to educate myself in the way the world is wagging, so as to bring the magazine up to date," he explained to his father. "I feel ready to do something really fine."

Following up on McClure's persistent interest in political corruption, Steffens interviewed city editors, political bosses, crusading district attorneys, and reformist mayors. In each city, he uncovered an invisible web of power linking political bosses to both the criminal world below and the business community above. His investigations convinced him that the misgovernment of American cities would furnish abundant material for a fascinating series, featuring portraits of the bosses and the men who were fighting to expose their corruption. "If I should be entrusted with the work," he told Tarbell, "I think I could make my name." His conjecture proved accurate: *The Shame of the Cities*, the six-part series that began in late 1902, made him an international celebrity.

Everywhere he went during his first weeks of travel, the same questions stirred conversation. Everyone was speculating on the future of a young district attorney named Joe Folk and the investigations he had undertaken in St. Louis. His curiosity aroused, Steffens took a train to St. Louis and, in a lobby corner of the Planters Hotel, met with the idealistic district attorney who was just beginning to lay bare pervasive corruption within the Democratically controlled city council and Board of Aldermen. Mistakenly assuming Folk would be "safe," the Democratic bosses had nominated this "smiling, even-tempered man of thirty-three" for the district attorney post.

The story Folk told fascinated Steffens from the start. An obscure notice in a local newspaper first caught the attorney's eye: a sizable quantity of cash had been deposited in a respected St. Louis banking house with the intention "of bribing certain assemblymen to secure the passage of a street railway ordinance." Folk decided to follow up on the report, even though "no names were mentioned." Suspecting that the legislation in question was a recent bill benefiting the Suburban Railway Company, he pieced their scheme together and issued dozens of subpoenas to assemblymen, councilmen, and the employees and management of Suburban Railway. Evaluating his list to determine who would most likely fold under pressure, he summoned the company president, Charles H. Turner, and the lobbyist rumored to have brokered the deal, Philip Stock.

Turner and Stock were notified that they had three days to cooperate. Facing indictment for bribery and prosecution "to the full extent of the law," they both "broke down and confessed." The ordinance in question, Turner told Folk, would have increased the value of his company by $3 million. To secure its passage, he had first approached Colonel Edward Butler, the longtime boss of St. Louis. When Butler demanded $145,000 to distribute among the assembly members, Turner hired Stock on his promise to get the bill passed for a mere $75,000. As swiftly as that amount was deposited into the bank, the legislation proceeded smoothly. A court decision quickly overturned the franchise ordinance, however, and the Suburban Railway Company refused to turn over the money, claiming it had not secured the franchise. Legislators threatened to sue Turner and Stock, insisting that the money "was theirs because they had done their part."

During this contentious interchange, the newspaper leak occurred. The testimony of Turner and Stock led to numerous confessions, along with the convictions of eighteen municipal assembly members. Folk's investigation eventually revealed that a precise schedule of bribery had been devised, specifying the price of obtaining wharf space, a side track, a switchway, a grain elevator, and so on. "So long has this practice existed," Steffens was told, the members had "come to regard the receipt of money for action on pending measures as a legitimate perquisite of a legislator."

Indefatigable Folk would not be content until he felled "the greatest oak" in this forest of corruption. Colonel Butler, the man who had been saved from indictment in the Suburban scandal simply because he had demanded more money than the company would pay, had controlled nominations and elections in the city for years, becoming a multimillionaire through his schemes. "It was generally understood that he owned Assemblymen before they ever took the oath of office," Steffens wrote, giving him absolute control of legislation and the power to negotiate with businessmen seeking regulations, rulings, or ordinances. When Folk found two members of the Board of Health willing to testify that Butler had promised each of them $2,500 to sign off on a garbage contract, he put the swaggering boss on trial. Folk uncovered documents proving that once the contract was approved, Butler was due to receive over $200,000. In a dramatic closing statement before the jury, Folk argued that the state itself was on trial: "Missouri, Missouri. I am pleading for thee, pleading for thee." Colonel Butler was convicted and sentenced to three years in prison.

After hearing Folk's account, Steffens contacted McClure and Phillips to inform them that he had found an article for the magazine and the person to write it—a local reporter named Claude H. Wetmore. The subject thrilled McClure, but when the first draft arrived, he was displeased that names and places, essential to authenticate and validate the story, had been omitted. Under McClure's guidance, Steffens drafted a new version of the article so that every statement was a matter of record. The names of legislators who fled the state were accompanied by details of their eventual arrests and confessions. A comical anecdote emerged of one House of Delegates member "so frightened while under the inquisitorial cross-fire that he was seized with a nervous chill; his false teeth fell to the floor, and the rattle so increased his alarm that he rushed from the room without stopping to pick up his teeth, and boarded the next train." Satisfied with the revision, McClure proposed the evocative title "Tweed Days in St. Louis." The article, with Wetmore and Steffens listed as co-authors, was a smashing success, prompting the publisher to build an entire series around municipal corruption that would accompany Ida Tarbell's work on corporate corruption.

A newspaper article condemning malfeasance in Minneapolis drew McClure's attention, prompting him to focus Steffens's next project on the Minnesota city. There, testimony before the grand jury had revealed a system of police corruption similar to that Steffens had witnessed in New York during the days of the Lexow Commission. In return for police protection, a host of illegal establishments that included gambling operations, unlicensed saloons, and opium dens paid regular weekly fees. These spoils were divided between the Democratic mayor, his henchmen, and the police captains, all carefully recorded in ledgers each week. After befriending Hovey C. Clarke, the courageous foreman of the grand jury, Steffens received permission to photograph pages from these ledgers. "Your article is certainly a 'corker,' " McClure enthused after reading the first draft. "We'll call it 'The Shame of Minneapolis,' " indicating the piece should be framed as a colossal battle between one crusading individual and the corrupt establishment. "You have made a marvelous success of your Minneapolis article," he assured Steffens. "We fellows are so busy pushing things through that we don't stop to tell each other how much we think of each other's work. But I take this moment to tell you."

The piece, printed in the famous January 1903 issue, made headlines across the country. "Mr. Steffens's stirring story should be read everywhere," advised *Outlook* magazine, "for it strikes at the very heart of both of the twin stupidities which dull the conscience of American municipalities—the optimism which says that all is so good that nothing need be done, and the pessimism which says that all is so bad that nothing can be done." The *Arizona Republic* ardently proclaimed that by exposing corruption in St. Louis and Minneapolis, *McClure's* magazine was "doing a public service," prodding people to conclude that similar corrupt networks were in scores of other cities not yet "overtaken by a wave of reform."

Steffens giddily recalled a train ride during which he overheard men in the washroom and dining car exclaiming over his story and his writing. The article was a surpassing success: "The newsstand had exhausted the printed supply; subscriptions were coming in; and the mail was bringing letters of praise." Citizens across the country invited him to their localities, promising scandals more sordid than those described in Minneapolis and St. Louis. He proudly told his father that as he entered a New York gentleman's club, members stood and applauded. With lavish promises, a London editor had tried to woo him from *McClure's*, while a cigar manufacturer even asked permission to christen a cigar after him, with his portrait on the box lid.

Flush with success, Steffens was anxious to scientifically test his "dawning theory" that corruption originated from the top, not the bottom, that it "was not merely political; it was financial, commercial, social." He suspected that in every case, the web of corruption radiated out from the captains of industry—the big businessmen running gas and electric companies, street railways, and other public service corporations—who would do anything necessary to acquire lucrative franchises and privileges.

Wary of "philosophical generalizations," McClure feared that Steffens would invariably tint his observations or arrange facts to confirm his theory that businessmen were always to blame. He insisted that Steffens present "facts, startling facts" that would involve the reader one step at a time in his detective work. While Steffens chafed to move on to Chicago or Philadelphia, McClure insisted he return to St. Louis to pursue the story in more detail. "The disagreement became acute," Steffens recalled; "it divided the office." At moments like this, Ida Tarbell was indispensable. "Sensible, capable, and very affectionate, she knew each one of us and all our idiosyncrasies and troubles," he noted. She would sit the fractious parties down, "smiling, like a tall, good-looking young mother, to say, 'Hush, children.' " A compromise was reached: Steffens would return to St. Louis, "stick to facts," and only afterwards proceed to any city he desired.

McClure's stipulation that Steffens must follow up in St. Louis proved most fortuitous. In the months since the first article had appeared, a series of events revealed the corruption in Missouri to run far deeper than either Folk or Steffens had suspected. When Colonel Butler's conviction reached the Missouri Supreme Court on appeal, the decision was reversed. All the aldermen cases were overturned as well. Steffens discovered that over the years Butler had directed the nominations not only of legislators but also of justices on the very bench that heard the graft cases on appeal. Indeed, the presiding justice publicly called for Folk to leave Missouri, implying that his exposures were ruining the reputation of the state. More dispiriting still, when the next election arrived, the citizens of St. Louis blithely kept the Butler ring in power. All the felons were back in the assembly, undaunted by the initial round of convictions.

Though McClure was again delighted with the substance of Steffens's article, he was less impressed with its structure. "Your narrative lacks force," he chided, suggesting that the tale should move forward with inexorable momentum and culminate in the shocking circumstance that Butler and the convicted aldermen remained in office, continuing to enact laws and reap profits. "I am telegraphing you to come East," McClure added, insisting, "You must be here with me when you are working out the article." The finished installment, which McClure entitled "The Shamelessness of St. Louis," once again proved a stunning success. The pride and conscience of St. Louis had finally been kindled; on the city streets, 200,000 people sported "Folk for Reform" buttons. "Your article is bearing fruit," Folk told Steffens, observing, "Every number of your March edition has been sold here and there is still a great demand for them." Finally, people rallied to support Folk's cause. Throughout the city, Folk Clubs were organizing. "The State is commencing to speak," Folk happily reported. "The permanent remedy is in the hands of the people and someday they will apply it. I believe the public conscience is more alive to the situation today and the cause of civic righteousness brighter than for many years."

"I must tell you how tremendously I am pleased with your achievements," McClure generously reassured Steffens in June 1903. "I know of no young man who has such a splendid opportunity of work in front of him as you have." Furthermore, the publisher grandly instructed his reporter to inform Folk that he was "the candidate of McClure's Magazine at the present moment for President in 1908." McClure's closing remark revealed his awareness of the massive influence his publication exerted on the American conscience: "I believe," he flatly told Steffens, "we can do more toward making a President of the United States than any other organ."

After St. Louis, Steffens traveled to Pittsburgh, Philadelphia, Chicago, and New York, perfecting the interview technique that allowed him to elicit a great deal of information by sharing the little he already knew. He regaled Pittsburgh's boss with tales of how his counterparts in Minneapolis worked.

He delighted reformers in Chicago with stories of how Folk had uncovered corruption in St. Louis. He spent hours "just chew[ing] the rag" with the old boss of Philadelphia, fascinated by his rise to power. In conversations with a couple of "wise guys" in Minneapolis, he described the famous burglars and con men he had known in New York. "Thieves, politicians, business men, reformers, and our magazine readers," he commented, "all assumed that I had what I was trying to get: knowledge." His demeanor shrewdly implied that he already knew their secrets, he explained, so "they might as well talk." Steffens's gift of drawing out his subjects soon became the stuff of legend. William Randolph Hearst considered Lincoln Steffens "the best interviewer he ever met," and the New York *World*'s Herbert Bayard Swope "looked up to him as a demi-god."

As Steffens expanded the scope of his inquiry, he became increasingly convinced that corruption in municipal politics was not "a temporary evil" engendered by the need for profitable new transportation and electrical facilities in explosively thriving young cities. Older cities, too, were rife with such dishonesty. Nor could it be attributed to Republicans or Democrats or to the presence of large immigrant populations under the sway of political bosses. Philadelphia, with the largest native population of any major city, suffered an epidemic of corruption. In every city, he now confidently argued, business interests were responsible. He had documented them "buying boodlers in St. Louis, defending grafters in Minneapolis, originating corruption in Pittsburgh, sharing with bosses in Philadelphia, deploring reform in Chicago, and beating good government with corruption funds in New York." Corruption, it seemed, was the hallmark of the age—an age in which "public spirit became private spirit, public enterprise became private greed."

When the articles were collected into the book entitled *The Shame of the Cities*, Steffens was hailed as a moral prophet come to save the republic from sin and a worthy descendant of abolitionist agitator William Lloyd Garrison. Across the country, Lincoln Steffens was lionized as "a new kind" of journalist altogether. "Instead of having his news and his editorial on separate pages," one critic noted, "Steffens welds the two into one so that the fact and the meaning and the portent of it strike you simultaneously." According to *The Outlook*, Steffens had "correctly diagnosed the characteristic disease" of the age—"the itch to make a little more money by illegitimate means than can be made by legitimate industry." Rather than examine the abstract political and legal structures of city charters, William Allen White observed, Steffens had ventured "into the wards and precincts of the towns and townships of this land [in order to] bring in specimens of actual government under actual conditions." These articles, another critic remarked, "have done more to awaken the American conscience to civic duty than anything else written in many years."

Immediately upon completing his series on the cities, Steffens embarked on an equally ambitious study of the states. Wherever he had sought to track "the political corruption of a city ring," he had found that "the stream of pollution" was part of a statewide watershed. Although he could have chosen "almost any State," Missouri seemed the logical starting point. As Joe Folk had learned when his cases were overturned, "the System was indeed bigger than St. Louis; it was the System of Missouri." The state constitution prescribed a governor, a legislature, and a judiciary, he remarked, but "this paper government has been superseded by an actual government"—a network of legislators, bosses, and party leaders answering to the state's major industries.

In addition, an investigation in Missouri would bolster Joe Folk's bid for governor on the Democratic ticket. He would be "appealing his case to the people" on a bold platform "that corruption is treason; that the man, who, elected to maintain the institutions of a government by the people, sells them out, is a traitor; whether he be a constable, a legislator, a judge, or a boss, his act is not alone bribery but treason."

Returning a third time to St. Louis, Steffens again joined with Folk to reveal a sweeping bribery scheme that stretched from the president and agent of the Royal Baking Powder Company, to the House and Senate combines, to the lieutenant governor. Published under the title "Enemies of the Republic"—another one of McClure's "brilliant reductions of a complex situation to slogan size"—the article prompted a new round of vehement editorials across the country. Crediting Folk's work as district attorney, the *New York Times* called Steffens's piece "a striking article" that illuminated the situation "with the utmost plainness," implicating "prominent men in politics and in business" in "specific instances of bribery, defining the purposes, and stating the amounts, the givers, the takers." The *Times* concluded by calling on the public to condemn such pervasive dishonesty. "When Americans really agree that corruption is treason," the editors argued, "the traitors will be punished, not legally alone, but as [Benedict] Arnold was, by the insufferable and blasting scorn of his fellow-men."

Folk's fight for the Democratic nomination tore the state wide open, but Steffens's articles had built the district attorney into such a heroic figure that the party did not dare reject him. "Your last article was magnificent and came in just in time to be of tremendous service," a grateful Folk told Steffens. "You ought to be here and see how the people can run things when they take a mind to," he observed, having witnessed the effect of the article on the public; "my faith in the plain people has not been misplaced." They had achieved a stunning victory, Folk happily noted, "when one thinks of the mighty power arrayed on the other side, the great corporations, the boodlers, the gamblers, a gigantic political machine, every professional politician in the State." This "bloodless political revolution," he continued, could never have been accomplished without the indefatigable work of Steffens and the support of McClure.

After Missouri, Steffens pursued investigations in five other states. In Wisconsin, he told the story of "Fighting Bob" La Follette. Soon after La Follette's election as governor, it became clear that his real adversaries were the corrupt leaders in his own Republican Party, who had "fixed" the legislature to kill his reform measures and "discredit him with defeat." The failed legislative session taught La Follette that he had to outmaneuver the bosses, creating an organization of his own to beat the system and install trustworthy men in the legislature. This conflict was still raging when Steffens arrived in Wisconsin. "To have you turn your searchlight on Wisconsin politics is better than anything our guardian angel could do for us—on earth at least," La Follette's wife, Belle, confided to the reporter.

Appearing a month before the election, Steffens's article applauded the young reformer's struggle against an entrenched system, asserting that his "long, hard fight" offered the people of Wisconsin a chance to make their government work for the common good rather than private interests. "La Follette's people think it has turned the scale in his favor," Steffens informed his father, "but the other side is howling at it and at me. It has sold out the magazine already." Governor La Follette not only won reelection but finally "met a friendly legislature," comprised of men who had "gone through the fire" with him and would readily enact his reform measures to regulate the railroads, institute the direct primary, address workmen's compensation, and establish tax reform. "No one will ever measure up the full value of your share in this immediate result," an exultant La Follette wrote Steffens. During reelection campaigning, La Follette witnessed the impact of Steffens's article "everywhere," even "out on the farms, away back among the bluffs and coulees of the Mississippi," noting a distinct "difference" in his reception before and after its publication. "The article settled things," he said. "It was like the decision of a court of last resort."

"The President has been very interested in your articles," Roosevelt's secretary informed Steffens on August 24, 1903. "He wishes to inquire if you cannot come down here some time to see him." A week later, Steffens joined Roosevelt for lunch at Oyster Bay, renewing a friendship somewhat chilled by Steffens's frequent carping that the president compromised too readily with conservatives in his efforts to move legislation forward. Throughout his complicated relationship with Roosevelt, Steffens worked to maintain his distance "as a political critic," keeping personal affection separate from professional judgment. For his part, Roosevelt managed to overcome his occasional irritation with Steffens in order to maintain a mutually advantageous alliance.

During lunch, the two men spoke of Joseph Folk and his great fight against the Missouri bosses. Shortly thereafter, Steffens followed up with a letter urging the president to meet with the young reformer. "He is a Democrat, but only as you are a Republican, and in motives and purposes you and he would be in perfect accord," the journalist reassured him, adding, "you can get from him a great deal of information about essential facts, and all honestly given. Mr. Folk has gotten no little of his inspiration from you." Roosevelt readily agreed to send a letter of invitation to the young district attorney through Steffens. "I wonder if you realize what a fundamental gratification such a letter will be to this man who has gone a long while along a lonely road with all big men against him," Steffens appreciatively replied to the president.

When Folk appeared at the White House, Steffens related to his father, "he and the President, Democrat and Republican, became confidential at sight, and the President thanked me for bringing Folk to his notice." Writing to a Missouri Republican, Roosevelt later proclaimed that though Folk headed the Democratic ticket, his nomination represented "a complete destroying of the old corrupt machine, and the success of the movement for honesty and decency." He assured the politician that "it would be better for the republicans to endorse his nomination instead of making any nomination against him." Such a step would not only demonstrate "a spirit of true citizenship," the president continued, but would "be wise policy on our part."

The Missouri Republicans ignored Roosevelt's advice, choosing to nominate Cyrus P. Walbridge, a conservative businessman who had been mayor of St. Louis. Although concern for the general Republican ticket in Missouri kept Roosevelt from publicly supporting Folk, he refused to endorse Walbridge and was delighted when William Allen White penned a ringing editorial endorsement of Folk in the *Emporia Gazette*. In plain language, White charged that those who voted against the honest Democrat Folk would be voting "with the boodlers, and their victory, whether it is republican or what not, will be in reality a victory for boodle." He reminded Missouri's citizenry that "parties are means for good government and not its ends," insisting that "it is better to be a bolter to a party than a traitor to a state." White's editorial made headlines across the nation and threw Missouri Republicans into what *The Washington Post* described as "a state of violent excitement, to use a mild phrase."

Folk ran a superb campaign, gaining enough votes from independents and reform-minded Republicans to override the corrupt Democratic machine and win the election by over 30,000 votes. "It must make you feel good," Folk later wrote Steffens, "to know the important part you had in bringing about these results." He reiterated the profound obligation he felt toward the reporter and his magazine for their role in the upset victory.

Folk was not alone in recognizing the publication's growing influence. *McClure's*, the monthly periodical *Arena* proclaimed, was "one of the greatest moral factors in America." Having "discovered that the first step toward curing an evil is to make it known," the magazine had become "a powerful exponent of the national revolt against corrupt and oppressive methods in business, in finance and in government." Month after month, its pages contained "must-read" pieces, spurring a national conversation on contemporary issues.

Just a few years earlier, one critic observed, *McClure's* was "distinctly literary in its character, and its content was given over exclusively to reviews, essays, stories and poems." Both format and function had since undergone a dramatic and influential metamorphosis: "The daily newspaper gives the facts as they occur from day to day, with editorial comment thereon, but it is left for the magazine to come along afterwards with a summary of these facts and their relation to one another." When vital issues were treated with depth and insight, people began "thinking for themselves, and a thinking people, if honest, will seldom go wrong in the end."

AWARE OF *MCCLURE'S* BURGEONING POLITICAL clout, Roosevelt invited Sam McClure himself to lunch at the White House on October 9. Steffens joined them for dinner, and the three men talked until midnight. Roosevelt offered to furnish the sources and documents for a potential series of articles outlining his struggles with the trusts and the unions. In the end, however, McClure preferred to continue with Steffens's series on corruption, focusing on a pitched battle being fought in Ohio between a group of young reformers and the Old Guard, led by Mark Hanna. Steffens was energized by the prospect, recognizing that Hanna remained the sole person who could snatch the nomination from Roosevelt—and that if he succeeded, the Republican Party would turn its back on reform.

A preliminary skirmish against Hanna earlier that spring had turned to Roosevelt's advantage. Stirring up trouble, Ohio's senior senator Joseph Foraker had introduced a resolution endorsing Roosevelt's 1904 candidacy at a state convention assembled to nominate candidates for state office in 1903. The development placed Hanna in a bind. As Republican National Convention chairman, he did not want to preclude all other candidacies—including his own—at such an early date, yet he would need administration support to promote his bid for a second Senate term in the fall. In light of his position, Hanna told Roosevelt he felt obliged to oppose the premature endorsement. He did not think it proper for a state convention to "assume the responsibilities" of the following year's national convention. "When you know all the facts," he concluded, "I am sure that you will approve my course." Roosevelt delayed his reply for twenty-four hours. Seeking advice from friends, he ultimately decided that "the time had come to stop shilly-shallying" and inform Hanna that he "did not intend to assume the position, at least passively, of a suppliant to whom he might give the nomination as a boon."

"Your telegram received," Roosevelt finally responded. "I have not asked any man for his support. I have had nothing whatever to do with raising this issue. Inasmuch as it has been raised of course those who favor my administration and my nomination will favor endorsing both and those who do not will oppose." Roosevelt's curt message left Hanna little choice. "In view of the sentiment expressed," Hanna telegraphed back, "I shall not oppose the endorsement of your administration and candidacy by our State Convention."

The publicized exchange of telegrams humiliated Hanna. "It was surrender, unequivocal and certain," declared a California paper. Headlines across the country proclaimed the older man's loss of power: "Hanna Backs Down to Roosevelt and Takes Water Like a Swan"; "Hanna Obeys the President's Wishes." Roosevelt tried to mitigate the sting with a personal letter. "I hated to do it because you have shown such broad generosity and straightforwardness in all your dealing with me," he told the senator, proceeding to offer justifications for his actions. "I do not think you appreciated the exact effect that your interview and announced position had in the country at large. It was everywhere accepted as the first open attack on me." Before closing, he confirmed his intention to attend the wedding of Hanna's daughter in Cleveland a few weeks later and expressed hope that the two of them could have "a real talk—not just a half hours chat" while he was there.

But the damage was already done. The tense interchange had intensified Hanna's reluctance to publicly endorse Roosevelt's candidacy, fueling supporters' confidence that Hanna would eventually announce his own candidacy.

That fall, Hanna launched "the most arduous and exciting stumping tour of his career," rallying the conservative Ohio base behind his chosen slate of candidates for the state legislature. The results were "an overwhelming personal victory" for Hanna, assuring his own reelection to the Senate. The landslide victory, "almost unique in American politics," constituted proof that Hanna was once more "Boss of the Republican party" and Roosevelt "a discredited leader."

"There is alarm in the Roosevelt camp," a Canton, Ohio, newspaper reported. The spectacular showing by Hanna's conservative wing of the party in the Ohio elections, coupled with the defeat of Roosevelt's reform ticket in New York, appeared to signal "the turning point" in the president's career: "Unless Mr. Roosevelt can retrieve his fortunes in a Napoleonic manner," the Omaha *Evening World-Herald* predicted, "the dual elections in Ohio and New York will mark the time that saw the tide begin to ebb from Theodore Roosevelt." The president himself was particularly disturbed by reform mayor Seth Low's defeat in New York. "The wealthy capitalists who practice graft and who believe in graft alike in public and in private life, gave Tammany unlimited money just as they will give my opponent," he grimly told a friend.

Reports multiplied of telegrams and letters of support arriving "by the bushel" in Hanna's office, beseeching him to rally Republican opposition to Roosevelt and build a steady, conservative platform that would foster prosperity and cultivate the pro-business policies begun under McKinley. "It is agreed by leaders of the party that the distinguished gentleman may now have the nomination for the asking," one editorial stated flatly, further suggesting that "Roosevelt may well be apprehensive. The vast following of McKinley will be found back of the Ohio Senator and this together with his own strength will certainly be potent enough to overcome any opposition at the national convention of his party in 1904."

Compounding these difficulties, a campaign financed by the corporations to discredit the president began to gain traction. The Union Pacific's E. H. Harriman dispatched hundreds of letters claiming that Roosevelt had "lost his popularity in the far west" and suggesting that without that region's support, he would be a weak candidate. Criticism of Roosevelt converged on "the general idea that he [was] impulsive, erratic and not to be counted on." Stories were circulated to emphasize his dangerously irresponsible, capricious nature. One disgruntled southerner, still aghast at Roosevelt's dinner invitation to Booker T. Washington, relayed an anecdote of particularly maniacal behavior. "We have a wild boy in the White House," he dismissively observed, painting the president as incompetent and immature: "The other day Roosevelt set out in his yacht from Oyster Bay in the teeth of a hurricane and against warning and advice, and nearly wrecked the vessel before he got to safety; and as he paced up and down the plunging deck and the wild winds blew his coat-tails over his head, there in his pocket was a six-shooter, just as if he were still a boy playing a game out on the plains!"

Rumormongers speculated that Senator Lodge was now "worried lest Hanna should come out at the eleventh hour as a candidate, and wrest the nomination." Roosevelt himself was said to fear that there was "a plot brewing" designed to "rob him of the prize at the last moment." White House lunch guests were reportedly queried about whether there was "any prospect of Hanna getting the delegates" in their respective states, a line of questioning that indicated genuine apprehension on Roosevelt's part.

Amid this discord, Lincoln Steffens's foray into Ohio politics could not have been more fortuitous for Roosevelt. The reporter explained to his father that he was "hoping to get Hanna," and that by unmasking the powerful Ohio boss, he might affect the presidential election just as he had transformed the prospects of Joseph Folk. "If I am to have so much influence," he wrote, "I want to make it a power for the possible and worth while." Before embarking on this project, he would return to the capital "for a short confab with the President." To be sure, "Roosevelt may be beaten," Steffens warranted, "but he will not be beaten without some pretty stiff fighting," and in that battle for reform, he added, with both accuracy and characteristic grandiosity, "we expect to deal some of the heaviest blows."

Steffens spent five weeks in Ohio talking with newspaper editors, politicians, bosses, and citizen groups in Cleveland, Toledo, Columbus, and Cincinnati. "Hanna is my villain this time," he informed his father in late January 1904. Acknowledging that the piece was "pretty rough" on the senator, he nevertheless maintained that "it's true and may do good." Hanna might have considered himself "above the danger mark," added Steffens, but a close examination of his career revealed many troubling, even criminal aspects.

The piece depicted Hanna as a businessman who had entered politics for the sole purpose of gaining special privileges for his street railway system. To secure advantages, Steffens explained, Hanna systematically "degraded the municipal legislature" through campaign contributions and outright bribery. Success only inflamed his ambitions. "He wanted to have a President," Steffens wrote, so he engineered the "spontaneous demand" for William McKinley and backed him with the largest campaign fund ever raised. Then Hanna resolved to become a U.S. senator. Since the votes were cast by the state legislature in 1898, Steffens reported, "legislators were kidnapped, made drunk and held prisoners," bribed and threatened with revolvers; in the end, unsurprisingly, Hanna emerged victorious. Steffens concluded that the system Hanna established in Ohio was "government of the people by politicians hired to represent the privileged class . . . the most dangerous form of our corruption." And this malignant operator "was the choice of big business and bad machine politics for President of the United States."

Steffens had nearly completed the first draft of his exposé when Hanna was stricken with typhoid fever. While his doctors hoped for a full recovery, they admitted that "the senator's advanced age and rheumatic conditions [made] the case a more serious one than in a younger man." When Roosevelt was informed of Hanna's illness, he walked over to the Arlington Hotel, where the senator and his wife occupied a large suite. "For some inexplicable reason, this affected him very much," Roosevelt told Elihu Root. After the president left, Hanna asked for paper and pen. "My Dear Mr. President," he wrote. "You touched a tender spot, old man, when you called personally to inquire after me this a.m. I may be worse before I can be better, but all the same, such 'drops' of kindness are good for a fellow." Always gracious at such times, Roosevelt quickly responded: "Indeed, it is your letter from your sick bed which is touching—not my visit. May you very soon be with us again, old fellow, as strong in body and as vigorous in your leadership and your friendship as ever."

Hanna's condition unexpectedly worsened in the days that followed. His temperature shot up to 104 degrees. He developed a congestive chill and the doctors administered strychnine to stimulate his heart. More than fifty correspondents and dozens of congressmen and senators crowded the lobby of the hotel, awaiting news. Steffens also waited, Hanna's precarious condition having left the fate of his article hanging. "The illness of Hanna leaves me in the air," he reported to his father. For a short time, the old senator seemed to rally, asking if the barber could come in to give him a shave. "Today he is better," Steffens wrote on February 14. Although the crisis seemed to have passed, the fever had not yet crested. "Tomorrow," Steffens predicted, "should decide his fate." Indeed, the following day Hanna's pulse rate dropped precipitously, and that evening, after "a brave struggle," he died at the age of sixty-six.

Without Mark Hanna, pundits agreed, "all talk of any real opposition to the nomination of President Roosevelt seems to have ended." Lacking the voice of a potent conservative leader to challenge the incumbent, open resistance to Roosevelt within the party crumbled.

"Of course, Hanna's death knocks out Steffens' article entirely," the managing editor Albert Boyden told Ray Baker. "It's tough luck!" After six months passed, however, Steffens found a way to revive the story. While his material on Hanna would provide the sordid backdrop of Ohio's boss rule, his focus shifted to the fierce contest in the state between a new generation of reformers and the Old Guard. Calling his piece "A Tale of Two Cities," he dramatically juxtaposed two municipal governments: Cleveland was led by Tom Johnson, the street railway tycoon turned radical reformer; and Cincinnati remained in thrall to George Cox, a corrupt party boss and longtime ally of Mark Hanna. Cleveland, he concluded, was "the best-governed city in the United States, Cincinnati, the worst."

Steffens's lengthy analysis appeared in the midst of Tom Johnson's uphill campaign for a third term as mayor. The well-documented and admiring portrait of Johnson's tenure, one observer noted, "appeared just in the nick of time to turn the tide." The reform mayor won reelection by the largest margin he ever achieved and attributed much of his success to Steffens. "My feeling for you, my dear old fellow," Johnson wrote the reporter, "is stronger than that of blood."

That same year, machine politicians were defeated in a number of cities. "The day of the American boss is past," proclaimed the *Baltimore Herald*. "Few men in the country," declared another publication, "have done more to bring to pass last Tuesday's defeat of municipal bosses than S. S. McClure and Lincoln Steffens." Letters of praise flooded the *McClure's* office. "To you, more than any one individual," one writer told McClure, "belongs much of the credit for this week's rout of the grafters. You were one of the first to grasp the real significance of the evil and to inaugurate its comprehensive exposure." It was a rapturous moment for Sam McClure, who had a protective passion for his magazine "very much like what the lioness has for her cubs."

"The story is the thing," McClure responded, when asked to account for the achievement of his publication. "When Mr. Steffens, Mr. Baker, Miss Tarbell write they must never be conscious of anything else while writing other than telling an absorbing story." As his authors began their research, he explained, they knew they had months—or even years—to complete the investigation and "mold it into a story palpitating with interest." The magazine's reputation as an instrument of reform, he insisted, was "due solely to its effective method of telling the truth, of giving stories vital interest." Had his writers begun with preconceived notions, they could not have so persuasively carried readers through their own process of discovery nor produced such visceral reactions to the unfolding narratives. "We were ourselves personally astonished, personally ashamed, personally indignant at what we found," Baker recalled, "and we wrote earnestly, even hotly." The more the public learned, the more engaged people grew by every facet of the complicated struggle for reform. "Month after month," Baker remarked, "they would swallow dissertations of ten or twelve thousand words without even blinking—and ask for more."

If corrupt businessmen, politicians, or labor leaders took offense to the detailed scrutiny of their motives and means, the *Minneapolis Tribune* noted, their hostility should be considered both "a medal of honor" and "an inspiration," irrefutable evidence "that something is being accomplished." Many decades hence, *The Independent* predicted, "when the historian of American literature writes of the opening years of the century, he will give one of his most interesting chapters to the literature of exposure, and he will pronounce it a true intellectual force."

CHAPTER FOURTEEN

"Thank Heaven You Are to Be with Me!"

President Roosevelt with members of his cabinet;
Secretary of War Taft is seated at the far left.

As *McClure's* writers labored to expose corruption and monopoly, William Howard Taft was too immersed in the knot of difficulties he faced in the Philippines to keep abreast of this transformative time in his own country. Letters from his brother Horace suggest Taft's isolation in the islands but also make clear *McClure's* essential role in keeping the public informed of key political developments at home. "You have been out of the country, and unless you have read the articles in the New York Times and in McClure's," Horace Taft cautioned his brother, "you will not appreciate how much of a stirring there is in the big cities where the worst corruption is. The progress in Chicago is remarkable and most gratifying." Reformers had "absolutely cut off" the spoils system, he explained, ending all manner of illegal privileges for the trolley companies and the railroads.

No one felt Taft's absence more during this period of profound change than

Theodore Roosevelt. With the Northern Securities case moving slowly toward the Supreme Court, Roosevelt wanted Taft to be a member of the Court when the time for decision came. He believed that "it would be impossible to overestimate the importance" of the suit. If Northern Securities was allowed to stand, the national government would be rendered impotent to control the big corporations. Monopolies would continue to grow, stifling competition and crushing small businessmen. Failure would diminish the presidency, confirming the Morgans and the Harrimans as the true rulers of the country.

Roosevelt's appointments to the Supreme Court would therefore prove critical. Indeed, he told a friend, he would hold himself "guilty of an irreparable wrong to the nation" if he failed to nominate men who shared his understanding of the great questions raised by the industrial age. To fill the first vacancy that arose, he had appointed Oliver Wendell Holmes, chief justice of the Massachusetts Supreme Court, whose sympathies with the labor movement were well known. "The labor decisions which have been criticized by some of the big railroad men and other members of large corporations," Roosevelt remarked at the time, "constitute to my mind a strong point in Judge Holmes' favor." When the appointment was announced, it garnered "the hearty approval of the laboring people of the country," as well as "no small amount of praise from the Republican organs."

A second spot on the Supreme Court opened when Judge George Shiras announced that he would retire on January 1, 1903. Roosevelt considered it "of utmost importance" to replace the conservative Shiras with the right man. He could not afford to make a mistake. Under these circumstances, the president immediately settled on his old friend Taft. He not only admired Taft above any other figure in public life, but he knew that Taft's views on economic matters paralleled his own. Like Roosevelt, Taft was dismayed by what he termed "the blindness and greed of the so-called captains of industry." He had little patience with "the unconscious arrogance of conscious wealth and financial success," yet he recognized the necessity of guiding "the feeling against trusts and the abuses of accumulated capital, in such a way as to remedy its evils without a destruction of the principles of private property and freedom of contract." Moreover, Taft's reasoning in the *Addyston Pipe* decision had encouraged reformers hoping to revitalize the Sherman Act.

Three months before Shiras's retirement, Roosevelt informed Taft of his intention to nominate him for the Supreme Court: "I hesitated long, for Root felt you should not under any circumstances leave the islands, and I was painfully aware that no one could take your place; but I do think it of the very highest consequence to get you on the Supreme Court. I am not at all satisfied with its condition—let us speak this only with bated breath and between you and me. I think we need you there greatly."

The telegram disconcerted Taft. "All his life," Nellie recalled, "his first ambition had been to attain the Supreme Bench. To him it meant the crown of the highest career that a man can seek, and he wanted it as strongly as a man can ever want anything. But now that the opportunity had come acceptance was not to be thought of." From Taft's perspective, the timing of Roosevelt's request could not have been worse. "Great honor deeply appreciated but must decline," he telegraphed. "Situation here most critical . . . Cholera, rinderpest, religious excitement, ladrones, monetary crisis, all render most unwise change of Governor. . . . Nothing would satisfy individual taste more than acceptance. Look forward to the time when I can accept such an offer, but even if it is certain that it never can be repeated I must now decline."

"I am disappointed of course," the president returned, "that the situation is such as to make you feel it unwise for you to leave, because exactly as no man can quite do your work in the islands, so no one can quite take your place as the new member of the Court. But, if possible, your refusal on the ground you give makes me admire you and believe in you more than ever. I am quite at a loss whom to appoint to the bench in the place I meant for you. Everything else must give way to putting in the right man."

Before five weeks had passed, however, Roosevelt sent an emphatic letter reopening the question, pushing Taft to accept the Court appointment with what Nellie termed "unanswerable" finality. "I am awfully sorry, old man," Roosevelt explained, "but after faithful effort for a month to try to arrange matters on the basis you wanted I find that I shall have to bring you home and put you on the Supreme Court. I am very sorry. I have the greatest confidence in your judgment; but after all, old fellow, if you will permit me to say so, I am President and see the whole field. The responsibility for any error must ultimately come upon me, and therefore I cannot shirk this responsibility or in the last resort yield to anyone else's decision if my judgment is against it." In closing, Roosevelt informed his friend that he would promote Commissioner Luke Wright to the position of governor general once Taft was appointed to the Supreme Court.

While this second request was en route to the Philippines, the president had a long talk with Taft's brother Harry. The two had become good friends when Roosevelt served in New York as police commissioner and governor. He now called on Harry to persuade his brother to return to Washington. "He is extremely anxious that you accept the appointment," Harry wrote to Taft, laying out Roosevelt's reasoning at length. "He does not belittle the importance of the problems which you have to contend with, but he feels that there are questions pending here which have to be solved by him which are of even greater importance and perhaps of almost equal difficulty. . . . He evidently thinks he has secured the right man in Holmes and now seeks you, because, as he remarked to me, you will approach all the industrial questions without fear of the affect [*sic*] upon yourself of the influence of either J. P. Morgan or of the labor leaders." Harry also reported an interesting talk on the matter with Elihu Root. Root considered Taft "the surest candidate as Roosevelt's successor, at the end of his second term," and therefore "could not be enthusiastic about your going on the Bench."

Despite Roosevelt's design in urging his letter, Harry admitted that he agreed with Root. "Of course, we all know how you have cherished the ambition to receive this appointment," he acknowledged, "but when it is within your grasp, it is natural to reflect as to whether you want to make that choice, particularly when your career in the Philippines and the reputation you have made there has opened up before you so many alluring possibilities." He added that there was "some diversity of view" within the family: Charley favored acceptance, knowing his brother had long coveted the post, while their mother, Aunt Delia, and Horace remained opposed. "I shall be satisfied with your decision," he assured his brother in closing.

To Taft, as to Nellie, the president's letter seemed unanswerable. The request "really leaves me no option, so far as I can see, but to give up here and go to Washington," he told Charley. The *Washington Times* reported that "within a few months" Taft would resign as governor of the Philippines to take a place on the Court. Nellie "heaved a sigh of resignation" and began making plans for their departure. Still, she recalled, her husband "could not resist the temptation to hazard one more protest."

"Recognize soldiers duty to obey orders," he telegraphed Roosevelt on January 8, 1903. "Before orders irrevocable by action, however, I presume on our personal friendship even in the face of your letter to make one more appeal." Taft proceeded to lay out his argument one final time: "No man is indispensable," he reasoned. "My death would little interfere with progress, but my withdrawal more serious. Circumstances last three years have convinced these people controlled largely by personal feeling, that I am their sincere friend and stand for a policy of confidence in them and belief in their future and for extension of self-government as they show themselves worthy. Visit to Rome and proposals urged there assure them of my sympathy, in regard to Friars, in respect of whose far-reaching influence they are morbidly suspicious. Announcement of withdrawal . . . will, I fear, give impression that change of policy is intended, because other reasons for action will not be understood. My successor's task thus made much heavier." Nevertheless, Taft concluded, "if your judgment is unshaken, I bow to it."

With little confidence that his request would be considered, Taft sadly informed his colleagues of his impending departure. The announcement spurred an overwhelming response and precipitated one of the "proudest and happiest" moments William Taft had experienced. As January 10 dawned, he and Nellie awakened to the din of band music, as 8,000 Filipinos gathered in front of the Malacañan Palace, urging the governor to stay. Stretched out for blocks, with "flags flying," the ranks of people carried handmade signs and placards printed in "all sizes and all colours," some in English, some in Spanish, still others in Tagalog, but all bearing the same message: WE WANT TAFT.

Taft listened in glad surprise as one speaker after another hailed his virtues and accomplishments. "This is a spontaneous demonstration of affection for our Governor," the first speaker announced. The orator who followed, a former insurrectionist, declared that all the hardships facing the islanders ranked "as nothing compared with the evil effect caused by [Taft's] impending departure. . . . The Filipino people trust that the home government will not tear from their arms their beloved governor upon whom depends the happy solution of all Philippine questions." When the speeches concluded, journalists reported, "the thousands of people who filled the grounds of the palace broke into a cheer for the governor."

News of the popular demonstration soon reached Washington, along with hundreds of cables from Taft's colleagues, citizen committees, the Filipino Bar Association, and individuals throughout the archipelago, all urging Roosevelt to reconsider. Three days later, a welcome cable arrived in Manila: "All right stay where you are. I shall appoint some one else to the Court. ROOSEVELT." A more personal letter followed a few days later. Roosevelt admitted he was still "very sorry" Taft would not be joining the Court but assured his friend that all would be well. "In view of the protests from the Philippine people," he conceded, "I do not see how I could take you away."

AFTER HIS STRUGGLE TO PERSUADE Roosevelt that he must remain in the Philippines, William Taft resumed work "with renewed vigour and strengthened confidence." A host of challenges remained, but he was optimistic that the connections he had forged among the Filipino people would allow them to make progress. Absorbed in his daily tasks, Taft found immense gratification in "working for other people and attempting to win their confidence and finally in a measure succeeding." His genuinely cordial temperament was infectious, enabling him to create an effective, collegial team. "I was not a month with Judge Taft until I was shaking hands with everyone I met and greeting them with a laugh," remarked one staff member, noting with admiration that he "never saw anyone who could so thoroughly dominate everybody about him and saturate them, as it were, with his own geniality."

Roosevelt himself continued to laud the many gifts that his friend brought to the difficult task of governing the Philippines. "There is not in this Nation," Roosevelt told an audience, "a higher or finer type of public servant than Governor Taft." Secretary of War Elihu Root, who collaborated with Taft on all issues relating to the Philippines, concurred. He assured Henry Taft that his brother possessed "a personality which made [him] nothing but friends" and that "no man in the country had recently exhibited such unusual ability, both administrative and legislative." When good-natured telegrams between Taft and Root subsequently appeared in newspapers, their obvious camaraderie delighted readers. Taft had cabled Root a description of a long trip to a beautiful resort in the Benguet mountains. "Stood trip well. Rode horseback twenty-five miles to five thousand feet elevation." Root, knowing Taft's weight exceeded 300 pounds, cabled back: "How is the horse?" With typical good humor, Taft released Root's cable to the press, along with his praise for the horse—"a magnificent animal," he told Root, "gentle and intelligent and of great power. He stood the trip without difficulty."

With Nellie and the family happily situated at the palace, Taft envisioned a tenure of at least two years, time in which he could construct the foundation for Filipinos to elect their own assembly and achieve a greater degree of sovereignty. But another letter from the president on March 27 soon disrupted this prospect. "You will think I am a variety of the horse leech's daughter," Roosevelt began, alluding to the biblical parable in which a blacksmith's perpetually dissatisfied daughter demands ever more of him. Twice before, Roosevelt had asked Taft to return home; twice he had reluctantly acquiesced to Taft's resolve to remain in the islands. This third request was an imperative.

"The worst calamity that could happen to me (personally and) officially is impending," Roosevelt informed Taft, "because Root tells me that he will have to leave me next fall." The secretary of war had originally joined McKinley's cabinet, remaining on the understanding that he would return to his legal practice once new governments had been established in Cuba and the Philippines. The time to depart, Root insisted, had now come. For Roosevelt, the alarming prospect of losing "the wisest, the most surefooted, the most farseeing" member of his administration could be remedied only by recalling Taft to take his place. "I wish to heaven that I did *not* feel as strongly as I do about two or three men in the public service, notably Root and you," the president told his friend. "But as I *do*, I want to ask you whether if I can persuade Root to stay until a year hence, you cannot come back and take his place."

Recognizing the depth of Taft's nation-building commitment, Roosevelt assured his friend that he would not have to abandon his cause. "As Secretary of War you would still have the ultimate control of the Philippine situation," he insisted, "and whatever was done would be under your immediate supervision." Beyond this enticement, Roosevelt felt he had arrived at the point in his presidency where Taft's judicious guidance was indispensable. "Remember too the aid and comfort you would be to me," he urged, "as my counsellor and adviser in all the great questions that come up." While he respected Taft's repeatedly expressed desire to complete his work in the Philippines, he needed him at home. "If only there were three of you!" Roosevelt concluded. "Then I would have one of you on the Supreme Court . . . one of you in Root's place as Secretary of War . . . and one of you permanently Governor of the Philippines. No one can quite take your place as Governor; but no one of whom I can now think save only you can at all take Root's place as Secretary."

This time, although he reiterated his concerns, Taft realized that the president's summons left no room to maneuver. "In view of your desire that I shall be in Washington expressed thus three times, I should feel reluctant to decline again," he replied, "but the change you propose is full of difficulties for me." He endeavored to explain the problem of extricating himself from his Filipino colleagues, particularly after his recent pledge to remain with them. While continued supervision of Philippine policy as secretary of war made the prospect of departure more palatable, Taft maintained that he had "no knowledge of army matters and no taste for or experience in politics." Moreover, the weight of Roosevelt's expectations left him uneasy: "I cannot but be conscious that were I to come to Washington, you would find me wanting in many of the respects in which you are good enough now to think I might aid you." Taft hoped the president would grant him several weeks to talk things over with Nellie and consult his brothers before supplying "a definite answer."

Much as Nellie enjoyed her life in the Philippines, she counseled Will to accept. She had argued strongly against the Supreme Court appointment but had long envisioned an active role for her husband at the highest level of government. The proffered cabinet post, she reflected, fell precisely "in line with the kind of work I wanted my husband to do, the kind of career I wanted for him." Further, Taft's health had become an increasing priority for Nellie; he had already endured two serious illnesses and was currently suffering from amoebic dysentery, a plague throughout the tropics. At the same time, the children were reaching ages when their education had to be given serious consideration. Thirteen-year-old Robert was scheduled to leave for Horace's boarding school in Watertown, Connecticut, later that summer. In three years, he would be prepared to enter the Yale Class of 1910, as his father had proudly "prophesied on the day of his birth." For Nellie and Will, the separation of 8,000 miles from their eldest son was painful to consider.

In a letter to his brothers, Taft acknowledged the difficulty of refusing the president but expressed serious reservations. "If I were to go, I should have to be in the midst of a presidential campaign, which would be most distasteful to me, for I have no love of American politics," he explained. "In addition, I do not see how I could possibly live in Washington on the salary of a Cabinet officer." Cabinet members were expected to entertain lavishly, but their $8,000 salary was far below his compensation as governor general. "My life insurance policy amounts to nearly $2000 a year," he protested, "and I should very much hate to go there and live in a boarding house." On the other hand, if his dysentery did not improve, doctors were likely to recommend his departure from the Philippines in any case.

Taft's mother, intensely anxious about her son's physical condition, urged his return. Indeed, given these growing health concerns, the family was unanimous in advising that Will accept the post. "I should prefer really not to have you get into politics here," Charles admitted, "but under the circumstances I do not see how you can decline the offer." Horace regretted that his brother would have to give up so "great a work" but feared that remaining in the islands would permanently damage Will's health. If acceptance of the secretaryship seemed inconsistent so soon after declining the Court appointment, Harry reasoned, the control he would retain over Philippine policy considerably mitigated this concern. Reassured by the support of his family, Taft wrote a long letter to Roosevelt indicating acceptance. Yet the letter was so circuitous that his intentions remained somewhat inscrutable. Conceding that the president's "earnest desire ought to be controlling," he nevertheless continued to stress his "great reluctance" to desert the Filipino people.

While Taft's indecision over the cabinet appointment may have been difficult to decipher, there was no equivocation over his personal devotion to Theodore Roosevelt. Taft's letter cited recent "intimations that the trust people, and possibly some of the machine politicians, are looking about for someone to center upon in opposition to your nomination" and noted that his own name had been bandied forth. "This is absurd," he declared, because "my loyalty and friendship for you and my appreciation of the manner in which you have stood behind me . . . are such that it would involve the basest ingratitude and treachery for me to permit the use of my name in any way to embarrass your candidacy." Upon receipt of this puzzling letter, Roosevelt dispatched a telegram to Harry Taft, who assured the president that it should be treated as an acceptance. Roosevelt was thrilled, sending Taft a forthright reply: "You don't know what a weight you have taken off my mind."

The president also worked to ease his friend's qualms over maintaining a proper Washington lifestyle. "It would really add immensely to my pleasure as an American to have you, who will be the foremost member of my Cabinet in the public eye, live the simplest kind of life," he wrote. "I hope you will live just exactly as you and I did when you were Solicitor General and I Civil Service Commissioner." Charley Taft, anxious that his brother should face no hardship in his removal to Washington, provided more tangible support. He gave Will 1,000 shares of Cleveland Gas Company stock worth $200,000 and proffered an additional $10,000 a year so that Taft "should feel independent of everybody and able to do as [he] pleased politically or in any other way." The proposal, Will gratefully replied, "struck me all in a heap: The love you manifest, the possibilities you open and the burdens you take away fill my heart with a joy moderated only by a feeling that I do not deserve it and that I cannot sufficiently requite it."

With the matter settled at last, only the timing and details of Taft's return to America remained. "The President is very much gratified," Harry relayed to Will; "he told me that he expected that you would be the strong man of the Cabinet and he should lean upon your counsel and advice." Root was impatient to depart but had agreed to stay until year's end. "Now that it is decided that you are to go," Harry continued, "we think that you might as well take the step at once." But Taft held his ground, promising to return in early January 1904. Despite his lifelong resolve to "keep out of politics," it seemed he would now be thrust in headlong, in the midst of a presidential campaign. Nonetheless, he admitted, the task ahead excited him.

And Roosevelt was unabashedly thrilled to finally have Taft on board, exclaiming, "Thank Heaven you are to be with me!"

"I have an additional and selfish reason for wanting you here," he confessed, as he looked toward the upcoming presidential campaign. "I shall have to rely very much upon you—upon your judgment and upon your making an occasional speech in which you put my position before the people. I should like you to be thoroughly familiar with this position in all its relations; and such familiarity you can only gain by close association with me for some length of time—in other words, by being in the Cabinet." The mood of the country had changed in Taft's absence, he explained. "When you come back I shall have much to tell you."

When William Taft finally reached Washington at 4 p.m. on January 27, 1904, exhausted from a four-week journey by ocean liner and transcontinental train, he was astonished to discover that President Roosevelt had sent the 15th Cavalry to meet him. Escorted to a waiting carriage by a dozen officers in full uniform, Taft was "too amazed for words" when a bugler sounded the call for a hundred cavalry horses to begin their march to the War Department. As the station crowd cheered, journalists marveled that the elaborate ceremony—befitting a tribute to "a sacred potentate" from some faraway land—was unprecedented for an American citizen not yet even sworn in as secretary of war.

The rumpled traveler had barely settled into his rooms at the Arlington Hotel before having to depart for a reception honoring Elihu Root. The evening "was most enjoyable," Taft reported to Nellie, who was still in California with the two younger children. All the members of the Supreme Court and the cabinet were in attendance, and the president stayed for hours to celebrate both his outgoing and incoming war secretaries.

Journalists gleefully contrasted the easygoing new cabinet member, affectionately known as "Big Bill," with his staid predecessor, whom few would dare address by his first name, if indeed they could correctly pronounce it. "Two men were never born who are more unlike," the *Washington Times* observed. "One is the reserved, dignified, scholarly type, admitted by all persons who know him. The other is the hail-fellow well met, with unlimited brain power and the fortunate gift of being able to make a friend of every man who comes near him."

Roosevelt was sad to see Root go, he told his eldest son, but "Taft is a splendid fellow and will be an aid and comfort in every way." Edith worried that Taft was "too much like" her husband to deliver the same detached advice that Root had always provided. Roosevelt did not share his wife's reservations. "As the people loved Taft, so did Roosevelt," Mark Sullivan observed, recalling that "whenever Roosevelt mentioned Taft's name, it was with an expression of pleasure on his own countenance." Moreover, he instinctively perceived in Taft's steady composure "a needed and valuable corrective to his own impetuosity."

On February 1, Taft was sworn in as secretary of war, the position once held by his father. His brothers Harry and Charley stood by his side, along with Annie Taft. "It was good for sore eyes to see them," Will told his wife. Horace had fallen ill that week and "felt like crying" when he realized he could not join his brothers for the ceremony. After their father's death, the devotion and support among the Taft brothers had only strengthened.

It was quickly evident that Taft's innate diplomacy and administrative acumen would bring a jovial, effective leadership to the department. If his spirit of camaraderie, "democratic manner," and "breezy informality" occasionally irritated Army officers, they, too, eventually succumbed to his authentic affability. "I'm mighty glad to see you," he exclaimed as he grasped officers by the shoulders, determined to overcome barriers in Washington as he had done in Manila. As Taft traversed the halls of the War Department, one reporter noted, "he found time to extend a hearty welcome to colored messengers he had known for years." At 320 pounds, his large frame invariably commanded attention. "He looks like an American Bison, a gentle, kind one," the newspaper editor Arthur Brisbane observed of Taft's benign, substantial presence.

Having arrived in Washington at the height of the social season, Taft was bombarded by dinner invitations. A brilliant stag affair at Root's house was followed by the Gridiron Dinner, a Yale Club reception in his honor, a Judiciary Dinner, a cabinet dinner at the new Willard, a formal military banquet, and a White House reception. "I went down behind the Pres. & Mrs. R with Mrs. Shaw [wife of the treasury secretary] and we cut a wide swath," he told Nellie. "Mrs. Shaw is about as big as I am."

Hardly a day passed that Taft did not lunch at the White House, join the Roosevelt family for dinner, or consult privately with the president in the early morning or late evening. "The President seems really to take much comfort that I am in his cabinet," he informed Nellie. "He tells me so and then he tells people so who tell me. He is a very sweet natured man and very trusting man when he believes in one." Aware that Nellie still reserved judgment, he was careful to add: "I hope you will agree with me when you have fuller opportunities of observation."

Despite his hectic schedule, Taft managed to compose long letters to Nellie, detailing choice anecdotes about Washington's social drama: he gossiped over Mrs. Root's disdain when the first lady invited the "coarse and brazen" divorced wife of ex-Senator Wolcott to the White House; explained that Senator Hale of Maine had been dubbed "the Chief of the Pawnees because he has a pleasant habit of putting his hand on the knees of ladies whom he affects, under the dining table"; and recounted the various exploits of nineteen-year-old Alice Roosevelt—her late night partying, unchaperoned motor rides, brazen public smoking and betting on racehorses. She was known to keep a pet snake in her purse, hide small flasks of whiskey in her long gloves, and play poker with men. Will told Nellie that he had consulted Mrs. Lodge, who had also heard "a great deal of criticism of Alice Roosevelt's manners and rather rapid life," and was "much troubled" about it.

"Isn't there anything you can do to control Alice?" a friend asked Roosevelt. "I can do one of two things," he famously replied. "I can be President of the United States, or I can control Alice. I cannot possibly do both!"

When Nellie elected to spend several months in the California sun before traveling east, Taft was bereft. "I do not feel that I am living at all in your absence," he repeatedly lamented; "all that happens to me, all the work I do, every speech I make are all by the way. They are not permanent steps of progress. I am just marking time till you shall come on and real life shall begin again."

He had little time to brood. Roosevelt "loaded tons of work" on his newly appointed secretary and it seemed "the harder he was pushed the better work he did." William Taft became the "veritable pack horse for the Administration," a "trouble-shooter" with duties that extended beyond military matters and the Philippines. The president chose him to supervise the Isthmian Canal Commission, charged with constructing the Panama Canal, and consulted him regularly on labor and capital issues. And, as he had promised, Roosevelt would rely upon Taft heavily for speeches and advice during the presidential campaign. As one reporter observed: "Wherever a tension needed the solvent of good-will, or friction the oil of benevolence; wherever suspicion needed the antidote of frankness, or wounded pride the disinfectant of a hearty laugh—there Taft was sent."

Taft was "extremely popular both in the senate and the house," one Iowa newspaper reported. "He spends more time at the capital than all the other members of the cabinet," the journalist remarked, noting that he had become "an intermediary between the executive and congress, familiar with both ends of Pa. Ave, and as well liked at one end as the other."

Not surprisingly, Taft remained deeply engaged in the progress of the Philippines. Throughout his tenure as war secretary, he maintained close contact with Luke Wright, his successor as governor general, and with dozens of former colleagues in the islands. "Things have quieted down very much since your departure," one friend told him, "and we are all taking a much-needed rest, including the old-fashioned clock that stood in your office, which stopped on the day of your departure and has refused persistently, though much coaxed, to tick."

Taft spent a great deal of his time in February and March on the Hill, testifying and lobbying for a bill to subsidize the construction of a much-needed railroad system in the Philippines. Consultation with railway leaders in New York and a study of Britain's experience with colonial railroads had convinced Taft that capitalists were loath to invest "so far from home," especially where a tropical climate's long rainy season and dense vegetation complicated their prospects. If the Philippine government were authorized to guarantee 5 percent interest on bonds issued for construction, however, he was confident that vital infrastructure projects would be undertaken.

Taft first secured Speaker Joseph Cannon's approval of the railroad bill, knowing its passage in the Republican-controlled House would then be ensured. "All in favor will please say Aye," the powerful Speaker declared when the railroad bill came up for a vote. "There was a gentle piping of 'aye' on the Republican side." When the Speaker called for those opposed, there was "a thunderous burst of 'No!' " from the Democrats. "The 'noes' seem to make the most noise," Cannon brusquely concluded, "but the 'ayes' have it and the bill is passed."

Opposition in the Senate, where individual members could easily block a bill, proved more formidable. "I have been working with Democratic members," Taft told Nellie. "I have been as pretty to them as I can be but it may be love's labor lost, still more flies can be won with molasses than vinegar and I shall continue to coddle them, even if they go back on me." Through Taft's dogged efforts, the bill finally passed, though not until the following congressional session.

Taft's endeavor to secure congressional support for tariff reduction on Philippine products proved far less successful. Reduced tariffs were essential to the future prosperity of the islands, Taft repeatedly argued, insisting furthermore that reducing excessive import taxes was a matter of basic justice. An Indiana editorial concurred: since the United States had undertaken to govern the Philippines, "it would seem to be taking an unfair advantage of a poor, defenseless people" to levy an "exorbitant tax on their business relations with us" in order to satisfy "a few protected interests." Within the Congress, however, allies of the sugar and tobacco industries vowed to use any parliamentary tactic necessary to prevent a tariff reduction bill from reaching the floor.

"I can see in the opposition," Taft complained to Roosevelt, "the fine Italian hand of our dear friend Aldrich of Rhode Island. Whenever there is anything which is likely to injure the tobacco, sugar or silver mining interests under the so-called trust arrangements, that very able and deft manager of the Senate appears long enough in Washington to disturb the even tenor of projected remedial legislation." Lyman Abbott, as editor of *The Outlook*, offered pithy commiseration: "The interest of dollars is more powerful than the interest of conscience."

To Taft's dismay, Roosevelt defended the Senate leader. "You are unjust to Senator Aldrich," he chided Taft. Though the president often differed radically with Aldrich and the other members of the Big Four, he insisted that "taken as a body, they [were] broad-minded and patriotic, as well as sagacious, skillful and resolute." Such words offered scant consolation for Taft; the Senate's inner circle would effectively block any legislative action on the Philippine tariff reduction until Taft himself became president.

On March 14, 1904, as word spread that the Northern Securities merger decision was imminent, an immense crowd gathered outside the Supreme Court. For Roosevelt, the outcome loomed with enormous implications for his party, as well as the nation. If the Court sustained the administration's argument that the colossal merger represented a monopoly that restricted trade, the victory would demonstrate a fundamental shift in the Republican Party's relationship with the trusts.

Inside the chamber, seating was filled to capacity. Dozens of senators and congressmen jockeyed for space in the section normally reserved for families of the justices. At the government bench, Attorney General Knox and Secretary Taft sat side by side, their expressions marked by "nervous expectancy." Nearby, ranks of powerful corporate lawyers had assembled. At the back of the chamber, more than fifty newspapermen, "paper and pencil in hands," readied to race to the telegraph wires the moment the ruling came down. "It required but little effort of imagination," one reporter noted, "to see in the vast background millions of American citizens awaiting the outcome of this judicial battle against daring financiers."

The crowd stood as the Court crier opened the session with the traditional cry: "Oyez, Oyez, Oyez." The spotlight on the Supreme Court likely conjured conflicting emotions in William Taft, who would have been among the justices had he accepted the president's appointment offer. That seat was now occupied by Justice William Rufus Day, Taft's good friend and former colleague on the Ohio bench. The moment Roosevelt had appointed Day, Taft realized that "being an Ohio man, and coming from the same court" foreclosed any chance that he might succeed to the bench in the near future. "Of course this is something of a disappointment," he had acknowledged to Joseph Bishop at the time, but maintained, "I am sure it would have made no difference if I had known definitely that this was the alternative." When Bishop shared that excerpt from Taft's letter with the president, it only confirmed Roosevelt's admiration. "How eminently characteristic of Taft those extracts are!" he exclaimed. "What a fine fellow he is!"

As Justice John Harlan began to read the Court's 5–4 opinion, papers reported, "everyone was alert for the significant sentence which should disclose the attitude of the majority." They did not wait long. "No scheme or device could more certainly come within the words of the [Sherman Anti-Trust Act]," Harlan immediately pronounced, "or more effectively and certainly suppress free competition between the constituent companies." Echoing the warning Baker had issued when the giant merger first became public, the Court cautioned that if no limits were placed on railroad mergers and more "holding companies" combined, "a universal merger" might be reached, and "a single man might thus control . . . and sway the transportation of the entire country." With this unambiguous declaration, "it was all over," the *Boston Daily Globe* recorded, recounting how "a score of eager men jumped for the exit and disappeared from the chamber to the waiting wires. Wall Street had lost. The government had won."

Taft enjoyed a moment of personal triumph when Harlan explicated the principles and precedents informing the majority decision. Central among the cases he cited was Taft's decision in *Addyston Pipe and Steel*. "If Congress can strike down a combination between private persons or private corporations that restrains trade among the States in iron pipe," Harlan argued, clearly they were empowered "to strike down combinations among stockholders of competing railroad carriers."

Oliver Wendell Holmes, Roosevelt's first appointee to the Court, proved "the surprise of the day" when he joined the other three dissenting justices. Known as "the friend of the common people" and "the champion of labor," Holmes delivered a stinging rebuttal, claiming that "while the merger was undoubtedly taken with the intention of ending competition between the two railroads," the Sherman Act—as currently constructed—did not apply to a transaction of this kind. Roosevelt was stunned by Holmes's dissent. "I could carve out of a banana a judge with more backbone than that," he angrily charged. Years later, Holmes agreed that the Northern Securities case had derailed his nascent friendship with Roosevelt. "We talked freely later," he recalled, "but it was never the same."

Roosevelt's frustration with Holmes did not diminish his absolute pleasure in the verdict. Upon receiving the news, the president "put aside all else to express his satisfaction" to every caller at the White House. The impact of this decision on Roosevelt's political stature could "hardly be exaggerated," the New York *World* editorialized. "People will love him for the enemies he has made. It cannot now be said that the Republican Party is owned by the trusts. It cannot now be said that Mr. Roosevelt is controlled by them." Minnesota governor Samuel Van Sant went so far as to claim the decision meant "more to the people of the country than any other event since the civil war." The government's triumph, the *Minneapolis Times* declared, had confirmed that "no man, however great, is greater than the law." From that moment, Roosevelt's reputation as the great "trust-buster" was confirmed.

Even as he savored his dramatic victory, Roosevelt nevertheless made clear that the government would not "run amuck." While the nation possessed the right and responsibility to regulate corporations, he maintained, "this power should be exercised with extreme caution." The Northern Securities suit should not be construed as the opening volley of a populist campaign to destroy all big corporations simply because they were big. In fact, Roosevelt viewed the organization of capital as a natural outcome of industrialization and welcomed the lower prices and efficient service made possible by combination. "If a corporation is doing square work I will help it so far as I can," he insisted. But at the same time, he asserted, "if it oppresses anybody; if it is acting dishonestly towards its stockholders or the public, or towards its laborers, or towards small competitors—why, when I have power I shall try to cinch it." With characteristic rhetorical balance, the president made it clear he would abide neither the excesses of "the selfish rich" nor the resentful outrage of the "lunatic fringe."

As he worked to implement this vision for genuine but evenhanded reform into public policy, the president was relieved to have William Howard Taft at his side. The approaching campaign would require powerful advocates for Roosevelt's election and for his progressive agenda. With his affable nature and tempered approach, the new secretary of war would be Roosevelt's indispensable complement.

CHAPTER FIFTEEN

"A Smile That Won't Come Off"

The 1904 Republican National Convention in Chicago, with Mark Hanna's portrait visible above the speaker's platform.

WHEN ROOSEVELT UPROOTED TAFT FROM the Philippines to make him a pivotal figure in his Washington cabinet, he had warned his friend that he would lean on him heavily. In an era when it was still considered undignified for candidates to stump heavily on their own behalf, Taft would serve as a campaign surrogate, clarifying and promoting Roosevelt's positions. As the president had feared when he called Taft home, the mood of the country was becoming increasingly unstable. In the opening months of the 1904 election year, tensions between labor and capital had escalated to a dangerously volatile point.

No single incident illustrates the severity of this instability better than the Colorado labor wars, a series of conflicts that pushed the region to the brink of revolution. In the spring, labor violence in Colorado threatened to unbalance the carefully calibrated middle ground Roosevelt had forged in his dealings with unions and management. A continuous round of strikes by the Western Federation of Miners had roiled the region for over a year. The previous November, James Peabody, Colorado's conservative Republican governor, had declared martial law and urged Roosevelt to send federal troops to quell the disturbances. Strikers, he reported, had shut down mining activity across most of the state and were threatening a range of other businesses. The safety of Colorado's citizens and the security of their private property were in peril. After consulting with his cabinet, Roosevelt sent a telegram to the governor. While he understood the difficult conditions, he explained that he had "no lawful authority" to intervene unless the situation amounted to "an insurrection . . . beyond the power of the civil police and military forces of the State to control."

As the violence escalated, Ray Baker traveled to Colorado and began researching the history of "corruption & bribery on the part of the corporations & violence on the part of the strikers. I am going to go for them hard," as he told his father. Upon hearing that Baker was preparing an article on the Colorado labor strife, Roosevelt invited him to the White House. Throughout their lunch, Baker wrote his wife, Jessie, the president "had a pad of paper at his hand" and "asked me much in detail about conditions in the West."

As Baker labored to complete his 10,000-word article, "The Reign of Lawlessness: Anarchy and Despotism in Colorado," he sought Roosevelt's permission to quote from a statement in their private correspondence. "I believe in corporations," Roosevelt had written. "I believe in trade unions. Both have come to stay and are necessities in our present industrial system. But where, in either the one or the other, there develops corruption or mere brutal indifference to the rights of others . . . then the offender, whether union or corporation, must be fought." With the president's blessing, Baker used the quote to headline his argument that both capital and labor had broken the law in Colorado, equally contributing to the pervasive disorder and destruction.

Tracing the chronology of the conflict from the 1890s, Baker began with the Western Federation strikes in Cripple Creek, which successfully obtained "everything the men wanted," including higher wages, closed shops, and an eight-hour workday. But in both Colorado City and Denver, Baker noted, a number of mills remained "open shops," and Telluride mill owners refused to grant an eight-hour day. Federation leaders ordered all 3,000 men out in a "sympathetic strike," exercising a nearly "autocratic" authority over their statewide membership, a majority of whom were reluctant to strike. As union mines shut down across the state and unionized workers instigated violent altercations with non-union men in the smelting plants, public opinion began to turn against the Western Federation. Seizing this opportunity to break the union altogether, mine owners called on the governor to bring in state troops and keep the non-union mines open.

The governor needed little persuasion, Ray Baker reported, for he unabashedly "sided with the mine owners" in an effort "not merely to prevent violence, but *to break the strike*." The state militia arrested union members "without charges," suspending the writ of habeas corpus. Soldiers "entered and searched" private homes without warrants, and a local newspaper was shut down after its editor "criticized the methods of the soldiery."

"One of the great underlying reasons for the existing struggle," Baker determined, "was the demand for an eight-hour day in the smelters and mills of Colorado." In 1899, the state legislature had passed a law restricting work in extremely hazardous occupations to eight hours. After Colorado's supreme court declared the law unconstitutional, the unions sponsored an amendment to the state constitution. Passed by a large majority, the measure mandated that the legislature enact an eight-hour law. When lawmakers assembled, however, lobbyists from the Smelter Trust, controlled by John D. Rockefeller, descended upon the capitol. An eight-hour day would require three shifts instead of two, cutting profits. Money for bribes was plentiful. Despite the clear mandate, the legislature ended its session without having acted on the eight-hour law.

Little wonder, Baker mused, that after years of struggling for this legislation, the unions "were discouraged, even desperate." Nonetheless, he emphasized, the chaos in Colorado was the work of all parties: unions had utilized violent means to drive scabs from work; military forces had become despotic; corporations had bribed legislators; and the legislature itself had defied "the will of the people." Only public outrage and pressure could hope to stem the corruption and violence.

In mid-April, Baker sent an advance copy to Roosevelt. "I have endeavored in this article to set down the truth with absolute frankness, no matter who it hit," he wrote the president, "and if the truth were ever needed, it is needed today in Colorado." Baker's investigation and analysis drew widespread praise throughout the country. *The Arena* called it "the most masterly, exhaustive and on the whole judicially impartial account of the reign of anarchy in Colorado." The evenhanded stance evidenced in the Roosevelt quote Baker cited also occasioned favorable comment. "This language is not calculated to please either the extremists on the side of capital, or the extremists on the side of labor," the *Wall Street Journal* asserted, "but it commends itself to the sober thought of the great mass of people, who, while believing in the right of capital and labor to organize, hold that neither capital nor labor shall be permitted to exercise a power of monopoly." Roosevelt not only read the piece but had it circulated among officials in the Commerce and Labor Department.

On June 6, the long-simmering tensions in Colorado ignited. At two o'clock that morning, twenty-five miners who had just completed a shift in defiance of the union's strike waited at the Cripple Creek station for the 2:15 a.m. train. Suddenly, a massive charge of dynamite detonated near the tracks, rocking the depot. Over a dozen men died instantly in the blast and more were gravely injured. The Western Federation of Miners was blamed for the "dastardly crime." News of this fatal explosion, destructive enough to render the dead unidentifiable by doctors and family members, quickly led to rioting. The governor called out the militia, and soldiers roamed the streets arresting anyone who uttered "the least anarchistic expression." Under orders of the state national guard, more than one hundred union miners were corralled onto a special train and banished from Cripple Creek. Among the thousands who thronged the station, one reporter observed, were "wives and sisters, fathers and mothers of the deported men, and the scenes were affecting."

The Western Federation appealed to the president, "in the name of law and order," pressing him to investigate "the terrible crimes that are being perpetrated in Colorado." The union's plea placed Roosevelt in a difficult position. "Having refused to send them in at the request of one side," he explained, "we are now asked to send them in at the request of the other." Exasperated by inaction, Roosevelt dispatched an investigative team to Colorado. "If it becomes necessary for me to act, or merely lay before Congress a statement of what has occurred, I want to know fully the exact facts," he told labor commissioner Carroll Davis Wright.

Commissioner Wright later informed Ray Baker that his article had served as "the basis of the government investigation in Colorado," which likewise traced the origin and history of the region's labor struggles and analyzed the same incidents, also attributing to both sides responsibility for the confrontation. Reading Wright's preliminary report, Roosevelt concurred with Baker that Governor Peabody had exacerbated the situation, intervening not simply "as the representative of law, order and justice" but "as the supporter and representative of the capitalist against the laborer." Nevertheless, the president believed the miners had erred, leaving strike decisions to an autocratic inner circle and using violence to accomplish their goals. The report validated Roosevelt's initial reluctance to interfere, providing abundant evidence that would justify his decision to Congress and to the public. Once the president had transmitted the final report to the House and the Senate, he again invited Baker to lunch. "He was most gratifyingly complimentary about my work," Baker informed his father. The president's response, he maintained, confirmed that his article "had been absolutely correct & fair."

The turbulence in Cripple Creek eventually subsided, though many of the deported miners never returned. In Telluride, the strike ended when the mine owners finally agreed to an eight-hour day. Governor Peabody was forced out of office, and the state legislature passed a state law limiting working hours for dangerous occupations, including work in mines, smelters, and reduction mills.

As the Republican National Convention opened in Chicago on June 21, 1904, Roosevelt was confident that, "barring a cataclysm," he would secure the nomination. The old bosses who still controlled the delegations might engage in "a great deal of sullen grumbling," but their hope of mounting a successful opposition had died with Marcus Hanna. Rather than "the thunderous demonstration usually attendant upon political conventions," newspapers described "a lifeless gathering," a "sober and unhysterical" affair. An enormous portrait of Hanna had been positioned above the speaker's platform and the first mention of the former chairman's name provoked a wild outburst. Although the majority of the delegates would be voting for Roosevelt, they made it clear from the outset that they supported him "because they had to." Had there been a "shadow of the chance" that any member of the conservative Old Guard could win the presidency, the majority would have "embraced it gladly."

More than any other writer covering the convention, William Allen White perceived the significance of the Republicans' peevish mood. Despite the empty seats, lack of enthusiasm, and "mechanical" twenty-minute cheer when Roosevelt's name was put into nomination, White nevertheless concluded that the convention was the "most successful gathering" in more than a generation. He recognized that "the puppet show" in Chicago was not an accurate reflection of national sentiment: the American people were exerting their will—and the people wanted Roosevelt. "It makes little difference whether the politicians cheered for Roosevelt twenty-three minutes or twenty-four hours," White insisted. Politicians and political machines were "dangerous" only if the people remained passive, but let a reformer like Roosevelt gain public confidence, and "the service of the politicians" would be at his command. "There is no boss so powerful that he can overcome the people."

White believed that this spirit of rebellion, the push to realize "a better world," was fueled by "a new element in political life"—the appearance of progressive newspapers and magazines urging the country to move forward. A decade earlier, men who called for a more equitable distribution of wealth were castigated as socialists or bomb-hurling anarchists. Now reformers were everywhere: small businessmen sought to regulate railroads, merchants demanded new laws to regulate the trusts, skilled laborers were striking for higher wages and shorter hours. All these agents of change, he concluded, now looked to Roosevelt "to speak and act for his times."

The appointment of George Cortelyou to replace Mark Hanna as campaign manager and chairman of the Republican National Committee confirmed that the embattled party needed Roosevelt far "more than he needed the party." A former newspaperman of modest background, Cortelyou had served as private secretary to Cleveland, McKinley, and Roosevelt before becoming head of the Department of Commerce and Labor. Roosevelt's support for Cortelyou drew immediate opposition from "professional politicians," who correctly sensed that they "were losing their grip of power." With his reputation for honesty and dedication, Cortelyou represented a younger, forward-thinking generation that was "taking control of the party," and conservatives "could not bear to abdicate without leaving a monumental growl behind them." Roosevelt moved swiftly to quash the opposition. "People may as well understand that if I am to run for President then Cortelyou is to be Chairman," he told a Massachusetts businessman and politician. "I will not have it any other way," he stated with finality. "The choice of Cortelyou is irrevocable." Delegates were left with no alternative but to ratify Roosevelt's selection.

Roosevelt was less successful in dictating the Republican Party platform. While it largely mirrored the president's public actions and statements on foreign policy, the Panama Canal, trusts, and labor, observers noted that it reflected a difference of opinion on the tariff. Roosevelt argued that failure to revise the tariff would put "a formidable weapon in the hands of our opponents," yet the platform espoused the principle of protectionism as "a cardinal policy of the Republican party." As Roosevelt predicted, the Democrats seized on the issue to proclaim that a Republican victory would herald "four years more of trust domination, of high prices to the consumer and of low prices to the producer." Nevertheless, Roosevelt hesitated to push the issue, fearful that a tariff battle would pit westerners anxious for relief against the eastern industrial and financial establishment, thereby creating a disastrous schism in the party.

Nor did Roosevelt contest the selection of Indiana senator Charles Fairbanks as vice president. Although he far preferred Illinois congressman Robert Hitt, "of all men the pleasantest to work with," he accepted the "cautious, slow, conservative" Fairbanks as a concession to the Old Guard. Since his own experience as vice president had convinced him that the office was essentially powerless, there was no need to take a stand. Paramount was winning his party's presidential nomination.

Seated with his family on the south veranda of the White House, Roosevelt received news of his unanimous nomination. They had just finished lunch when his private secretary, William Loeb, brought the anticipated telegram. After "affectionate congratulations" from his wife and children, Roosevelt returned to his office, where members of the press, many of whom he considered "his personal friends," had convened. The president was "in exceptionally good humor" as he handed out cigars, joking that the stern prohibitionist Carrie Nation would not approve. The AP reporter described the scene: "With genial raillery he chatted with one; exchanged comments on men or things with another; laughed heartily at a cartoon of himself to which his attention was drawn; sketched in a free-hand way incidents of the convention; recalled some interesting situations, personal and political; and in conclusion again thanked his friends for expressions of their congratulations."

When the Democrats assembled in St. Louis two weeks later, the party's conservative wing had clearly regained control. Though William Jennings Bryan remained the heartfelt choice of the rank and file, the professional politicians were starved for victory. After two consecutive defeats with Bryan, party leaders turned to a "gold Democrat," Judge Alton B. Parker. Bryan's repeated calls for using silver rather than gold as the standard unit of currency value had pleased western debtors who would benefit from inflation but had angered eastern creditors whose money would be devalued. Democratic bosses hoped Parker could both retain Bryan's liberal base in the West and win back eastern conservatives who had broken with the party on the gold issue.

Covering the Democratic Convention for *Collier's*, William Allen White portrayed Bryan as "the hero of the occasion, even though he did not triumph." Though deafening yells and "epileptic spasms" greeted Bryan's every appearance, the delegates had vowed not to let sentiment rule a third time. "They were like men who had been stark mad," observed White, "and the fear of it coming back was in their hearts." Bryan managed to keep the platform from endorsing gold, but the overwhelming vote for Parker's nomination signaled that his "eight-year reign was over." The platform roundly denounced trusts and protectionism as "robbery of the many to enrich the few," demanded large reductions in public spending, decried executive usurpation of legislative functions, called for Philippine independence, and advocated direct election of U.S. senators.

The nomination voting was completed shortly before midnight on Friday, July 8. The reporters gathered in Parker's hometown of Esopus, New York, were disappointed to learn that the judge had retired with orders that he not be awakened. As a result, the nominee was not apprised of his victory until returning from his regular morning swim in the Hudson River. Asked for a statement, Parker replied that he would wait until he received official notification. The delay provided time for a shrewd strategic maneuver: at noon, he dictated a telegram to be read before the convention adjourned, informing delegates that he regarded "the gold standard as firmly and irrevocably established." If his views on this issue "proved to be unsatisfactory to the majority," he should feel it his duty "to decline the nomination." The convention moved swiftly to adopt a resolution stating that the currency question did not appear in the platform simply because it was no longer "an issue at this time." The gold standard would not be challenged, they assured Parker, leaving nothing to prevent him from accepting the nomination.

Parker's move "was most adroit," Roosevelt acknowledged. "He is entitled to hearty praise, from the standpoint of a clever politician," the president observed, adding that the maneuver had gained for Parker "all of Cleveland's strength without any of Cleveland's weakness, and made him, on the whole, the most formidable man the Democrats could have nominated." William Taft disagreed, predicting that the success of Parker's machination would be short-lived, unlike the rift within the party it had perpetuated. He assured Roosevelt that Parker "was stronger the morning the telegram was published than he ever will be again." Nevertheless, Roosevelt fretted that he now faced "a hard and uphill fight" in the general election.

According to his habit, Theodore Roosevelt sought to harness anxiety through action. He had begun crafting his acceptance speech immediately after his nomination, but now he turned to it with a vengeance, determined to sharpen its tone. "I always like to do my fighting in the adversary's corner," he told Lodge. The speech, delivered on July 27 from the sun-splashed veranda at Sagamore Hill, "was received with immense enthusiasm" by the assembled crowd. "It is just such a statement as we should expect Theodore Roosevelt to make," the *Minneapolis Journal* editorialized: "terse, luminous, logical, convincing." His defense of Republican policy, said another paper, was "characteristically forceful," and his satirical commentary on the Democratic Party, noted Lodge, was "keen and polished as a Japanese sword blade."

Parker's acceptance speech had no such luster. Between bouts of heavy rain, the Democratic candidate held forth for forty minutes from the soaked lawn of his Esopus country home. Parker's flat style and lack of oratorical experience were immediately apparent; he "used few gestures," failed to distinguish his positions from Roosevelt's, and mustered no "bugle call." The most vigorous applause reportedly followed his closing declaration that, if elected, he would not run for a second term. Roosevelt was relieved that his rival's "shifty and tricky" gambit had failed to "straddle" the factions within the Democratic Party. Perhaps, Roosevelt told Lodge, Taft's assessment had been correct from the start.

Characteristically, Roosevelt began drafting his formal letter of acceptance weeks before its early September publication date, ensuring ample time for consultation with his advisers. Taft attended numerous breakfasts, lunches, and midnight discussions to dissect each section. "His opponents may attack the letter," Taft told Nellie, "but they will not say it is lacking in snap or ginger." Seeking a broad sounding board, Roosevelt also circulated drafts to Root, Lodge, Knox, Hay, Garfield, and the civil service reformer Lucius Swift—requesting merciless critiques. "I went at the letter hammer and tongs," Swift told his wife, "and got in a good many points."

Published on September 12, Roosevelt's letter received widespread praise. "Remarkable," the *New York Times* declared, "astonishingly able." *The Washington Post* observed that he had constructed "a veritable keynote for the stump," in which signal Republican objectives were championed with "enough spirit to arouse the partisan masses." The letter's strength, Taft told Roosevelt, was "the challenge contained in every line of it to the Democrats to be specific in their charges and to deal with facts." He maintained that if Parker produced a letter of acceptance akin to his tepid speech it would be glaringly apparent just "how little real ammunition the Democrats have."

The lackluster piece Taft anticipated from the Democratic candidate did not materialize. Parker's 6,000-word letter presented a spirited attack against centralized government at home and imperialism abroad, along with a robust call for tariff reform and further trust regulation. Republicans frankly acknowledged that now "the issues of the campaign would be more squarely joined." The *New York Times* deemed Parker's letter "a great paper." Though not designed to stir "the yells of crowds," it would appeal "to men who think," presenting "a first-rate test of the people."

Roosevelt conceded that Parker had cleverly managed to engage disparate factions of his party, giving "heart to his supporters" and halting "the downward movement of his campaign." At such moments, Roosevelt sorely longed to "take the offensive in person" and face his Democratic challenger on the stump. "I could cut him into ribbons if I could get at him in the open," he wrote to Kermit. "But of course a President can't go on the stump and can't indulge in personalities." His only option was to "sit still" and trust that his cabinet officials, traversing the country on his behalf, could make the case for his election.

Given William Howard Taft's marked aversion to preparing and delivering public speeches, he surprised even himself by emerging as the most sought-after speaker on the campaign trail. "It seems strange that with an effort to keep out of politics and with my real dislike for it, I should thus be pitched into the middle of it," he told his close friend Howard Hollister. Yet, in letters to Nellie, he confided his irritation at the extent to which "mere political discussion" dominated cabinet meetings. "I suppose it is natural," he lamented, "but it seems to me to be undignified." Nevertheless, as the campaign heated up, he settled into his role as spokesman for the administration. "I rather think I am to do more work than any other member of the cabinet," he noted with pride, "but I don't object to that."

Regardless of his engagement, Taft struggled with his inveterate tendency to procrastinate. Preparing for his first major speech during Harvard's commencement, where he and former Democratic secretary of state Richard Olney would square off on the Philippine issue, he confessed to his brother Charley that he was "right down to almost the last day in the preparation, as is usual with me." The night before departing for Cambridge, he reviewed the speech with the president and James Garfield. The president anticipated that the address would stand as "a great public document." Garfield too rated it "a masterly argument," recording in his diary that he considered Taft "a truly great man."

William Taft presented his speech to the Harvard Law School alumni at Sanders Theatre, presided over by Chief Justice Melville Fuller and Harvard president Charles W. Eliot. For two hours in the morning, Taft simply but clearly recounted the history of America's relationship with the Philippines, beginning with the war against Spain and the decision to exert sovereignty over the islands. He argued that American policy promoted "the Philippines for the Filipinos" and would eventually prepare the people to govern themselves. To promise independence before educating the populace, as many Democrats and independents urged, Taft believed would be a mistake.

Olney's rebuttal openly acknowledged that Taft had rightly earned "the general admiration" of the islanders "by the justice and skillfulness of his rule, and by the tact, patience and humanity of his dealings" with the Filipino people. He insisted, however, that the United States must not "sacrifice American lives and American treasures indefinitely and without stint for the education and elevation of Filipinos." The Constitution did not authorize the government to "turn itself into a missionary to the benighted tribes" or "to tax the toiling masses of this country for the benefit of motley groups of the brown people of the tropics." Simply, continued occupation of the Philippines represented a departure from the traditions and interests of the United States.

Despite their opposing views, both speakers remained impeccably civil. "Their differences," the *Cincinnati Enquirer* observed, "were, of course, stated in terms that prevented any exhibition of acrimony. When such men as Taft and Olney meet, the public can expect enlightenment on high ground." Olney's presentation was "a good thing," the *Enquirer* added, for it allowed "the young men of Harvard to have an opportunity to hear both sides of the question. Otherwise Secretary Taft might have hypnotized them, for they love him."

Taft was emboldened when his first campaign appearance generated nothing but positive notices. "I fired my gun at Cambridge and was pleasantly disappointed to find how well received it was," he drolly wrote to Roosevelt.

Will, Nellie, and the children soon departed Cambridge for their summer home on Murray Bay. Having spent the previous two summers in the Philippines, Taft was overjoyed at their return to this "magical place," where his brothers and their families could readily gather for picnics, trout fishing, and daily rounds of golf. "The air is bracing and delightful," Taft wrote to Roosevelt at Oyster Bay early in July. "I feel a boyish feeling—I'd like to jump up and down and shout." Nellie and the children planned to remain in Murray Bay until late September, but campaign and cabinet duties required Will's return to Washington at the end of July.

In August, Taft delivered two more impressive speeches on the Philippines, one in St. Louis and the other at Chautauqua. Increasingly confident in his area of expertise, Taft nevertheless remained anxious about a campaign appearance in Montpelier, Vermont, at the end of August. "The next ten days I must devote myself to the preparation," he told his wife. For better than twenty years, Taft had not given a purely political speech, and feared he was "a bit rusty on general politics." Indeed, he mused, "the Bench disqualifies one in this respect."

Roosevelt was particularly eager for Taft to speak in Vermont, where the September state elections were considered an important indicator of the vote in the presidential contest. Though the Green Mountain State generally leaned Republican, "the size of her majority" was thought to portend "the trend of public opinion." Rather than presenting an overview of Republican policies, Taft chose to focus on Roosevelt's leadership, mounting a spirited defense against repeated charges that the president was a bully, whose dictatorial demeanor toward Congress transgressed the constitutional separation between executive and legislative powers. "When Theodore Roosevelt is attacked for being a strong-headed tyrant, obstinate in his pride of opinion, and failure to listen to argument, I am in a position to know," he reassured his audience of more than 1,500 Vermonters. "In all my experience I never have met a man in authority with less pride of opinion," he asserted. "I have never met a man who was so amenable to reason, so anxious to reach a just conclusion, and so willing to sacrifice a previously formed opinion." Rather than a litany of clichéd tributes, Taft's vivid, personal testimony concerning the president's nature and character won the interest and enthusiasm of his listeners.

"It was a success," he told Nellie, proudly relaying that he was "told by many that it was thought to be the best political speech delivered in Vermont." The press concurred: "It would be difficult to praise it too highly," one Pennsylvania paper editorialized. "Judge Taft had already attained a high reputation as a jurist and executive officer." Now, he had established himself "as a political orator of the first rank. . . . Probably no member of the President's cabinet will prove more effective in defense and support of his administration." Published in its entirety in the *Boston Transcript*, Taft's speech promised to become "a text-book for Republican orators and writers." Most important, the Vermont vote proved a "glorious" triumph for Republicans, with a larger margin than anyone had predicted. "I am pleased as Punch about Vermont," Roosevelt exclaimed to Taft, adding that the unforeseen magnitude should "cut off some of the money supply of our adversaries."

Taft next proceeded to Portland, Maine; Roosevelt had received "a rather gloomy letter" from Senator Eugene Hale about Republican prospects in the state and hoped that Taft's presence could help energize support. Buoyed by positive reactions, Taft prepared himself "to speak without notes" for the first time. Despite initial anxiety that his memory might fail and leave him floundering, his performance went smoothly.

Taft continued north to Murray Bay for a final two weeks of vacation before the true rigors of the campaign began. To his "great surprise," a large contingent of Murray Bay residents appeared at his house on the night of his forty-seventh birthday. A torchlight parade escorted him to the Bay's largest house, where they feasted and drank, danced the Virginia reel, sang songs, presented gifts, and proposed toasts.

Taft wrote to Roosevelt every other day during his vacation, planning future speeches, exchanging political gossip, discussing Parker's campaign. "Mrs. Taft says that you must be bored by the number of letters that I write you," he jested; "now that I have my Secretary with me you may expect more." Ease and camaraderie mark their correspondence from this period as they discussed matters both personal and political: Roosevelt complained freely about their mutual friend Maria Storer; Taft described a new diet requiring him to refrain from drinking all liquids with his meals; Roosevelt cursed the "infernal liars" in the independent press—"the New York Times, Evening Post, Herald"—with their outrageous claims that he had sent "a corruption fund" to influence the vote in Vermont; Taft recounted "playing golf every day in air that is as invigorating as dry champagne without any evil after effect."

Upon his return to Washington in late September, Taft was immediately dispatched to Ohio, Rhode Island, Connecticut, New York, and New Jersey. "Do not in any speech take any position seeming in the least to be on the defensive," Roosevelt cautioned. "Attack Parker. Show that his proposals are insincere; his statements lacking in candor, and disingenuous. Announce that we have not the slightest apology to make; that we intend to continue precisely as we have been doing in the past; that we shall not abandon building up the navy and keeping up the army, or abandon rural free delivery, or irrigation of the public lands. Either Parker is insincere, or else he must propose to abandon these works and other works like them in order to economize."

On October 1, Taft opened the Republicans' Ohio campaign with a day-long extravaganza in Warren's public square that featured marching bands, songs, and large delegations from neighboring Cleveland, Youngstown, and Akron. With nearly 2,000 people in attendance, the campaign kickoff was considered "the most auspicious in years." Sharing the platform with the state's governor and two U.S. senators, Taft delivered the keynote address. Following Roosevelt's directives, he targeted Parker directly, saving his most stinging condemnation for the gross distortions and outright lies the Democratic candidate had spread about the administration's expenditures in the Philippines. "After reading the statements of Judge Parker concerning the Philippines," Taft repeatedly avowed, "I sometimes wonder whether I was ever there."

Taft would have welcomed Nellie's company on the campaign trail, but she had to settle the family into their new house at 1904 K Street in Washington and prepare the children for school. In daily letters, she related her progress in unpacking cartons of furniture, carpeting floors, setting up beds, working with carpenters, and arranging books in the library. With Robert attending Horace's boarding school in Watertown, Connecticut, only the two younger children remained at home. Thirteen-year-old Helen joined Ethel Roosevelt at the National Cathedral School. Seven-year-old Charlie was enrolled in the local public school, where he became great friends with Quentin Roosevelt. "I hope Charley's first day in school was a success," Taft wrote from Indiana. "I can remember mine. It was not."

As the campaign ground on, Taft's yearning to be home with his wife and children intensified. "I wish I could get on the train and go right to you now," he told Nellie early in October. With each passing day, he grew wearier of presenting the same speech. In Indianapolis, the crowd grew restless, some departing early as he held forth for nearly two hours. "I don't think my style of speaking is calculated to hold the curious," he admitted to Nellie, "but the audience which remained was most attentive." She "could not but smile," Nellie replied, when he mentioned the length of the speech. "If you confine it to an hour," she suggested, "I think people will stay."

A tense situation developed in mid-October, when a delegation of cigar and tobacco manufacturers, irate at Taft's proposed reduction of the tariff on Philippine tobacco, threatened "to control cigar makers enough to defeat Roosevelt in N.Y., Conn, Missouri and almost everywhere else." Enlisting the support of labor organizations in the cigar trade, they petitioned Congress and approached the president, "just at the anxious time when everything assumes distorted proportions." That same day, Taft wrote to the president. "I feel sure you would not wish me to retract anything on that subject," he began, adding that he would willingly cancel his appearances in affected states that might "emphasize the issue." If the president felt it necessary, Taft concluded, he would retire from the cabinet rather than back down on the principle.

"Fiddle-dee-dee!" Roosevelt responded, quickly dismissing Taft's resignation talk as "nerves, or something." While there was certainly no sense in exacerbating the issue by dwelling on the tobacco tariff, the New England states were precisely where his talent was most necessary. With this reassurance, Taft continued his grueling schedule but grumbled to his wife that the issue confirmed his resolve that he "would not run for President if you guaranteed the office. It is awful to be made afraid of one's shadow."

As SUMMER ADVANCED INTO FALL, the struggles between labor and capital increasingly defined the campaign. Democrats sought to contrast Roosevelt, "a man who never needed to do a day's work," and Parker, "a man who has always had to work to maintain himself and his family." This emblematic opposition sought to distinguish "the party of aristocracy and oligarchy" from "the party of liberty and equality." Democratic newspapers predicted that the rank and file of labor would vote in record numbers against Roosevelt. "It is the culmination of many grievances which union labor has against the party and its leaders," judged one paper. In Pennsylvania, Old Guard Republican senator Boies Penrose had "utterly ignored" union demands relating to construction of the state's new capitol. In the Rocky Mountain states, the bitterness of union miners against conservative Governor Peabody threatened to supply Parker with such overwhelming labor support that Republicans were reportedly conceding the region to Democrats. The rising cost of living fueled these complaints of the working class, undercutting Republican campaign strategies of a "full dinner pail" that had once helped McKinley.

All the while, Roosevelt was hammered by party conservatives for being too friendly with labor. Day after day, the New York *Sun* savaged him for his actions in the coal strike, his temerity in inviting labor men to dinner at the White House, and his honorary membership in the Brotherhood of Locomotive Firemen. "He is on the side of the men who are every day seeking to overthrow the Constitution," the *Sun* stridently charged. "He has joined their organizations, espoused their creed, received their leaders at his dwelling and in his official residence; and as President of the United States has welcomed their delegates." Simultaneously, Roosevelt lamented that populist publications reviled him for breaking bread with the great corporate heads.

As this antagonism intensified, Ray Baker began drafting a piece for *McClure's* to dissect each candidate's point of view on the labor issue. He read every one of Judge Parker's decisions addressing unions and corporations, discovering that "without exception," they were "strongly favorable to the contentions of labor." In one case, Parker had declared that "the state has a right to limit the hours of employment for bakers to sixty a week"; in another instance, he stated "that cities must pay the 'prevailing rate of wages' "; in still another, he ruled in favor of the closed shop.

Baker expected a discussion of labor issues when he was invited to spend the afternoon with the judge at Esopus. "Personally he is a most attractive man—a good type of the comfortable country gentleman," Baker told his father. "I was disappointed in finding him so apparently uninformed on labor affairs, though, of course, his mode of life has given him little opportunity of coming into contact with the great vital forces of the industrial conflict." Indeed, beyond his judicial decisions, Baker was unable to decipher coherent underlying principles governing Parker's approach to the paramount issue of the day.

In contrast, when Baker requested from Roosevelt a clarification of what many considered a contradictory position on the labor issue, Roosevelt promptly produced a nearly 2,000-word reply. "I cannot help feeling," the president testily responded, "that the people who have been 'confused by my action in the various labor cases,' must be of such limited brain power that nothing in the world will make my position clear to them." To comprehend his stance, he insisted, one need only study his words and actions over time. If such "creatures" remained confused, he continued, "I hardly think it will be possible to set them right; for they must be people who do not understand that when I say I wish to give a square deal to every man I mean just exactly that, and that I intend to stand by the capitalist when he is right and by the laboring man when he is right, and will oppose the one if he goes wrong just as fearlessly as I should oppose the other." Those offended by his dinner invitations to labor leaders should understand that the White House door would always swing open for labor leaders "just as easily" as "for the big capitalists, but *no* easier."

In this striking letter, Roosevelt proceeded to articulate his actions in the coal strike, the eight-hour day, the Colorado situation, immigration law, and convict labor. The basic principles and convictions Roosevelt so aggressively outlined spurred Baker to reread carefully all of the president's speeches and writings on the subject of labor. "I am perfectly astonished," he wrote to Roosevelt, "though I thought myself pretty well informed before—at the number and definiteness and breadth of your declarations on the labor question, as well as the record of your acts since your early days in the Legislature. And if I, who represent, perhaps the average busy American, am astonished, I believe a great many other people will be."

Before the election, Baker's article, entitled "Parker and Roosevelt on Labor: Real Views of the Two Candidates on the Most Vital National Problem," appeared in *McClure's*. Without any direct exposition or elaboration from Parker, Baker had relied on the judge's reasoning in the applicable half-dozen cases he had presided over. On the other hand, with access to a lifetime of Roosevelt's statements and decisions, Baker could present "a clear idea of the labor platform upon which he stands." Beginning with Roosevelt's early success as a state legislator against sweatshop conditions in tenement cigar factories, Baker demonstrated that, unlike Old Guard Republicans, the president was "a thoroughgoing believer in labor organization." In contrast to radical

Democrats, however, Roosevelt recognized that "there is no worse enemy of the wage-worker than the man who condones mob violence in any shape, or who preaches class hatred."

The time and attention Roosevelt had devoted to the journalist's request proved most rewarding. The *Los Angeles Times* observed that Baker's "thorough and painstaking" methods provided *McClure's* vast middle-class audience with a clear, illuminating portrait of the president's fair-minded and long-standing attitudes toward labor.

WITH ONLY WEEKS REMAINING UNTIL the election, Roosevelt recognized that while "the bulk of the voters" would "oppose or support" him based on his three years in office, "a sufficient mass of voters" remained who might yet be swayed by a dramatic turn in the campaign. Mid-October delivered just such a development, when the discovery of immense corporate contributions to the Republican Party suddenly threatened to compromise Roosevelt's hopes for victory. "The steady advance in the influence of money in our public life," decried a *New York Times* editorial, works "as a poison on the minds and hearts of men." Such toxicity was abundantly clear, the *Times* added, "when a man of Mr. Roosevelt's native scorn for corruption can be the willing, the eager beneficiary of funds paid into his campaign chest through his former secretary and former cabinet officer [Mr. Cortelyou] with the undisguised hope that it will be repaid in favors to the subscribers."

Lincoln Steffens called on Roosevelt at the White House to suggest that the issue could be lanced if he were to return all corporate contributions and look instead to small donations from the general public to fund his campaign. An informed public of small contributors "would make the millions feel that it was their government, as it is; and that you and your administration were beholden to the many, not to the few." Such a change, Steffens believed, would herald a new era in election politics. "If we must have campaign contributions, this is the way to raise them," he concluded. "If you would start this method now you really would begin a tremendous reform."

Roosevelt "most emphatically" rejected the premise of Steffens's argument, insisting that he already felt "beholden to the many more than to the few." Whether an individual or corporation contributed one dollar or one hundred thousand dollars would never sway him to sponsor legislation or take executive action. It was "entirely legitimate to accept contributions, no matter how large," he contended, so long as "they were given and received with no thought of any more obligation on the part of the National Committee or of the National Administration than is implied in the statement that every man shall receive a square deal."

In the end, Roosevelt willingly received hundreds of thousands of dollars from executives in dozens of corporations, including J. P. Morgan's banking house, New York Central Railroad, Standard Oil, General Electric, and International Harvester. Only when apprised of a check for $100,000 from the Standard Oil Company, "the Mother of Trusts," did Roosevelt draw the line. He instructed Cortelyou to return the money immediately: "In view of the open and pronounced opposition of the Standard Oil Company to the establishment of the Bureau of Corporations, one of the most important accomplishments of my Administration, I do not feel willing to accept its aid." So long as other "big business corporations" believed that the country's well-being could "only be secured through the continuance in power of the republican party," however, he deemed their contributions "entirely proper."

Roosevelt's justification did not satisfy the editorial board of the *New York Times*. "The fact that the chief beneficiary of the process is blind to its gross impropriety," declared the *Times*, "and can see in it only a means to the promotion of the welfare of the Nation dependent beyond question upon his attainment of the Presidential office by election shows how insidious and how irresistible has been the demoralization." The general unseemliness of large corporate contributions made little impact on the campaign, however, since it was widely known that corporations habitually "contributed to both campaign funds."

The scandal that did catch the public's attention and threatened to derail Roosevelt's campaign was the far more lethal accusation that the president and George Cortelyou were engaged "in a conspiracy to blackmail corporations." Judge Parker and fellow Democrats charged the Republicans with extortion—using detailed information on violations obtained from the newly created Bureau of Corporations "like a big stick with the threat of prosecution if a fat contribution to the republican campaign [was] not made." Democratic newspapers insinuated that "the prostitution of an entire federal department to the use of a campaign committee was cleverly planned and carefully executed." First, the papers accused, Roosevelt had appointed Cortelyou head of the cabinet department overseeing the new bureau; then, having amassed the necessary information, Cortelyou was made chairman of the Republican National Committee.

Roosevelt's advisers were divided over how to respond. Initially, Cortelyou and Garfield were reluctant to dignify the infamous accusation with a rejoinder. Taft disagreed. "I don't see why Cortelyou does not deny it but he keeps mum," he wrote Nellie. "Of course Parker cites no evidence to sustain his charge and Cortelyou's position is that until he does so, he is not called upon to answer. But I think it would be better to make a short denial."

Roosevelt concurred with Taft that the charges must be refuted, but resolved, against all precedent, to answer them personally. "I am the man against whom Parker's assaults are really directed and I am the man who can give the widest publicity to the denial," he told Cortelyou. "I should feel an intolerable humiliation if I were beaten because infamous charges had been made against me and good people regarded my silence as acquiescence in them." In characteristic fashion, Roosevelt drafted the statement himself, submitting it to his advisers for criticism. Revised speech in hand, he asked Garfield to take the midnight train to New York and confer with Cortelyou and Root.

All reservations concerning the propriety of the president's personal involvement in the fray vanished when, in an inflammatory speech on November 3, five days before the election, Parker labeled Cortelyou's fund "Blood Money." From the rear of his train in Meriden, Connecticut, Parker spoke "without notes for the first time since the campaign began." The Democratic candidate, reporters suggested, was stirred from his usual reticence by the loud enthusiasm of the immense crowd of 5,000. "His eyes flashed, his clenched hand swung above his head and his voice rang out with a vigor that betrayed his emotion," as he declared that all other issues of the campaign were now subsumed by one great question: "whether it is possible for interests in this country to control the elections with money." Parker scornfully claimed that when "every trust in this country, including the Standard Oil Trust, is doing its best to elect the Republican ticket," it becomes the duty of the American people to determine "once and for all, whether money or manhood suffrage shall control." He described how Cortelyou had exploited his cabinet position to blackmail the trusts for campaign contributions. "This country," he pledged in closing, "shall not pass into the hands of the trusts." The crowd responded "with a thundering cry that lasted until the train drew out of sight."

At ten o'clock the following night, William Loeb summoned members of the press to the White House, where he handed them the president's signed statement. The "direct and fierce" tone of this letter "became the common news of the hotels and streets in a few moments," prompting a flurry of discussion among politicians and the press. "The gravamen of these charges," Roosevelt began, "lies in the assertion that corporations have been blackmailed into contributing," and that in return, "they have been promised certain immunities or favors." Such accusations leveled without any evidence were "monstrous," he maintained. "If true, they would brand both of us forever with infamy, and inasmuch as they are false, heavy must be the condemnation of the man making them." He unequivocally dismissed the charge that Cortelyou had used intelligence gleaned from his cabinet position to coerce contributions as "a *falsehood*" and the insinuations that pledges were offered for contributions as "a *wicked falsehood*." All these allegations, the president flatly concluded, were "*unqualifiedly and atrociously false*."

In the wake of Roosevelt's vigorous and categorical rebuttal, Parker seemed to backpedal, claiming that "he had made no criticism of the President, but had simply called attention to a 'notorious and offensive situation.' " Nor, in response to Roosevelt's direct challenge, did he offer to substantiate his earlier claims. "Parker fails to furnish proofs," headlines blared in response. The president's public rebuttal, Garfield happily observed, "has knocked Parker flat."

The outcome delighted Roosevelt. "Parker's attacks became so atrocious," an ebullient Roosevelt told Kermit, "that I determined—against the counsel of my advisors—to hit; and as I never believe in hitting soft, I hit him in a way he will remember. In spite of loud boasting he made no real return attack at all, and I came out of the encounter with flying colors."

As election day approached, Roosevelt's anxiety escalated. He confessed to his sister Corinne that "he had never wanted anything in his life quite as much as the outward and visible sign of his country's approval." Elevated to the presidency as a result of "a calamity to another rather than as the personal choice of the people," he longed "to be chosen President on his own merits by the people of the United States." Should his campaign end in rejection, he consoled himself in moments fraught with tension that he had enjoyed "a first class run." And if, in defeat, he "felt soured at not having had more, instead of being thankful for having had so much," it would signal "a small and mean mind."

Late on the morning of November 8, Roosevelt cast his vote in Oyster Bay. A crowd of "home folk" greeted him at the train station with flags and banners. Arriving at the polling place, he "sprang briskly from the carriage and ran up the stairs." As soon as his ballot was cast, he caught the 1:14 train back to Washington, reaching the White House at 6:30 p.m. Not expecting returns for several hours, Roosevelt tried "not to think of the result, but to school [himself] to accept it as a man." He had scarcely crossed the threshold when news arrived that he had carried doubtful New York with "a plurality so large as to be astonishing." By the time he sat down with his family at dinner, sufficient returns had been received from key precincts in various states to suggest "a tremendous drift" in his direction.

After dinner, the president joined a group of intimate friends and members of his official family in the Red Parlor to await further results. While Taft had not yet returned from voting in Cincinnati, Nellie and the wives of the other cabinet members were present. Eleven-year-old Archie, "fairly plastered with badges," carried telegrams from the telegraph operator to his father, who read them aloud. At 9 p.m., a personal telegram arrived from Judge Parker conceding the election. It was "the greatest triumph I ever had had or ever could have," Roosevelt wrote, "and I was very proud and happy."

An hour later, Roosevelt greeted the Washington correspondents in the executive mansion office. Following an animated discussion in which he made "no attempt to conceal his gratification," the president leaned back in his chair and dictated a statement to his secretary. "So quiet was everyone in the room," one correspondent noted, "that one could hear the clock tick on the mantel shelf" as he read his startling pronouncement.

> I am deeply sensible of the honor done me by the American people in thus expressing their confidence in what I have done and have tried to do. I appreciate to the full the solemn responsibility this confidence imposed on me, and I shall do all that in my power lies not to forfeit it. On the 4th of March next I shall have served three and one half years and the three and one half years constitute my first term. The wise custom which limits the President to two terms regards the substance and not the form, and under no circumstance will I be a candidate for or accept another nomination.

Roosevelt's statement was not an impulsive gesture made in a moment of delirious joy; he had considered renouncing a third term weeks earlier but decided to wait for the election results lest it seem "a bid for votes." From his first days in office, critics had disparaged Roosevelt's single-minded focus on his own advancement. Such negativity sharpened during the campaign as opponents charged that he would "use the office of President to perpetuate [himself] in power." His simple pledge in the wake of the election-day triumph silenced all such criticism.

"I feel very strongly," Roosevelt explained to the British historian George Trevelyan, that "a public man's usefulness in the highest position becomes in the end impaired by the mere fact of too long continuance in that position." Even if custom had not frowned upon a third term, he maintained, "it would yet be true that in 1908 it would be better to have some man like Taft or Root succeed me in the presidency, at the head of the Republican party, than to have me succeed myself. In all the essentials of policy they look upon things as I do; but . . . what they did and said would have a freshness which what I did and said could not possibly have; and they would be free from the animosities and suspicions which I had accumulated, and would be able to take a new start."

When all the votes were finally tallied, Roosevelt had achieved "the greatest popular majority and the greatest electoral majority ever given to a candidate for President." He had won all the northern states, carried the western states previously claimed by Bryan, and added a totally unexpected coup in Missouri, breaking the Democratic Party's enduring hold on the South. "I am stunned by the overwhelming victory we have won," Roosevelt confessed. "I had no conception that such a thing was possible."

Everyone in the administration, Taft told his brother Charley, "has had a smile that won't come off since the election." William Taft could well take particular satisfaction in his own vital contribution to the victorious campaign. Personal letters and newspaper articles recorded his tireless efforts and powerful speeches in defense of administration policy. "The document that gave the most force to the Roosevelt campaign," journalist Murat Halstead told Taft, "was your utterance on the Philippines on the stump—that had the air and the dignity and the conclusiveness of a decision handed down by the Supreme Court." Howard Hollister proudly noted that his old friend had generated "thousands of votes" by standing "fearlessly" on the issues, making "a contribution much greater probably than you would be willing to admit." Characteristically, Taft refused to take credit, replying to all who congratulated him that "the victory is so overwhelming that I cannot think that anything that was done in the way of speaking had any particular effect." Above all, he insisted, the success was "a tribute to the personal popularity of the President."

Notwithstanding the general elation surrounding the historic election, Taft issued a public warning to the Republican Party: "It is no unheard of thing to have a majority as large and sweeping as this followed by a defeat equally emphatic at the next Presidential election." Without a candidate as compelling and charismatic as Roosevelt, it was very possible that the country would have voted Democratic; the Republican Party must not "diminish in any way the care with which the public interests must be protected." His timely admonition met with widespread approval. "Unless the Republican party is wise and liberal toward all legitimate and right demands of the people in the social and economic controversies which are going on," one respondent agreed, "we must expect sweeping radical victories during the next few years."

For those who hoped to see a more progressive Republican Party, Roosevelt's surprise decision to forgo a third term seemed "pregnant with promise" of a vigorous future for reform. Now that he was "absolutely independent of all party bosses and party machines," the *Minneapolis Journal* predicted, "Theodore Roosevelt is likely to make the administration of 1905–9 one of the two or three most resplendent and beneficial in the history of the republic." The *St. Paul Globe* endorsed this sanguine assessment, proclaiming that if Roosevelt stayed true "to the best that is in him," he could "become one of the great presidents in our history." Even his harshest critics had "nothing but praise" for Roosevelt's declaration. It was "to his everlasting honor," the New York *Sun* proclaimed, that "in the hour of his triumph," the president chose to make his second term his last.

Though he reveled in the acclaim that accompanied his declaration, Theodore Roosevelt would come to bitterly regret his action, later reportedly telling a friend that if he could rescind the pledge, he would willingly cut off his hand at the wrist.

CHAPTER SIXTEEN

"Sitting on the Lid"

"I have left Taft sitting on the lid," Roosevelt remarked before departing on a western tour, prompting this April 5, 1905, cartoon in the *Washington Times*.

AFTER WEEKS OF CLOUDY SKIES and heavy snow, the morning of March 4, 1905, broke "blue, flecked with lazily floating white clouds"—the day Theodore Roosevelt was inaugurated president in his own right. Washingtonians happily remarked that once again "Roosevelt luck" had brought "Roosevelt weather." For the tens of thousands lining the streets to watch the president's carriage pass from the White House to the Capitol, "the morning sun gave brilliancy and luster to the fluttering mass of flags and banners."

Roosevelt appeared "supremely happy," waving and bowing as a record-breaking crowd hailed him with "the roar of the ocean upon a rockbound coast." The galleries were filled inside the Senate chamber, where Charles

Fairbanks prepared to take the vice-presidential oath. Raucous cheers broke out when Roosevelt arrived. Stepping onto the floor, he at once scanned the gallery for Edith and the children; spotting them, he did not wave "furtively, nor half-heartedly, nor as if he were afraid someone might see this evidence of his domestic affection but with demonstration frank and full." His demeanor proclaimed simply: "This, my dear wife and children, is the proudest moment of our lives."

Hundreds of spectators perched in trees, crowded on rooftops, and lined the wings of the Capitol building as the president stood before the vast multitude and delivered "a friendly little homily on the duties of the nation and citizen," betraying nothing of the "truculent note" that often marked his speeches. "Much has been given us, and much will rightfully be expected from us," he told the crowd. "We have become a great nation, forced by the fact of its greatness into relations with the other nations of the earth. . . . Our relations with the other powers of the world are important, but still more important are our relations among ourselves." The Industrial Revolution, Roosevelt maintained, had generated both "marvelous material well-being" and the "care and anxiety inseparable from the accumulation of great wealth"—creating a host of problems that government had the responsibility to address. He spoke with characteristic "earnestness," one reporter wrote, stressing every word with such force that it seemed "as if he would like to get hold of each individual person in his audience and pound home the truths which he believes he is uttering, till the wretched man should be forced to admit the error of his ways and agree with the speaker."

Editorialists predicted "tempestuous doings" now that Roosevelt was president in his own right rather than by the happenstance of assassination. Backed by a massive popular mandate, he would no longer be held in check by the conservative bloc in Congress. "The Republican party has turned the corner and is now on a new road," William Allen White proclaimed. "It is hard to believe that the party that eight years ago was advocating the policy of 'hands off' is now ready to lay hands on capital, and such rough hands, too, when capital goes wrong. 'The old order changeth, yielding place to the new.' "

Turbulent events would indeed follow, but first the newly elected president embarked on a two-month vacation trip through the Southwest and the Rocky Mountain region. A Rough Riders reunion in Texas began the hiatus, followed by a five-day wolf-hunting expedition in Oklahoma and a three-week bear hunt in Colorado. "Everybody rejoices that he is to have some time for recuperation," an Ohio newspaper editorialized. "Only the bears and the mountain lions have occasion for regret." On the morning of April 4, cheered by well-wishers at the Pennsylvania Railroad Station, Roosevelt stepped onto a "handsomely fitted" train consisting of a private car, a Pullman sleeper, and a buffet car. He looked, one reporter noted, "like a small boy let out of school," rejoicing that he would soon enter wild country beyond the reach of official duties and office seekers.

Along the route, Roosevelt followed his customary procedure, emerging onto the platform at every stop to shake hands and deliver brief remarks. It was "much more pleasant than ordinarily," he told his son Kermit, because the presidential race was over and he was finally "free from the everlasting suspicion" a candidate invariably arouses. Even in the traditionally Democratic strongholds of Louisville, Austin, and Dallas, flags waved, cannons thundered, and tens of thousands greeted him with "wild enthusiasm."

Clearly, these hunting expeditions not only afforded Roosevelt a most "genuine pleasure" but provided the opportunity for revitalization. In Oklahoma, he was "in the saddle eight or nine hours every day" helping to track and kill eleven wolves: "It was tremendous galloping over cut banks, prairie dog towns, flats, creek bottoms, everything," he exulted. "One run was nine miles long and I was the only man in at the finish except the professional wolf hunter." In Colorado, he was "up at daybreak" and refused to stop until the sun set, keeping his "little band of huntsmen" in constant motion. As always, Roosevelt found the intense physical trial invigorating; while his face was "roughened by wind and sun and snow," he felt healthier than he had for months.

Reporters questioned how any pressing matters arising in his absence would be handled. "Oh, things will be all right," he emphatically responded. "I have left Taft sitting on the lid." The vivid phrase instantly inspired cartoons and commentary. One widely reprinted caricature depicted Taft wielding a big stick while seated on the lid of a boiling cauldron. Even his impressive bulk appears scarcely able to stem the "grave and exacting problems of the highest interest"—Panama, Santo Domingo, Venezuela, and Morocco—threatening to burst forth. In another cartoon, an outsized Taft spans three chairs. He is firmly planted on the widest, the "Chair of the President," but his legs extend on either side, occupying both the "Chair of the Sec'y of State" and the "Chair of the Sec'y of War."

In the absence of both President Roosevelt and Secretary of State John Hay, who was on a long cruise attempting to recover his health, official Washington considered Taft "acting President" and "the real head of all executive departments." Little mention was made in the press of the sitting vice president, Charles A. Fairbanks, as the press focused all attention on Taft. Reporters noted "the unusual sight" of "foreign diplomats going to the War Department instead of to the State Department to conduct business." Such a proliferation of responsibilities might well have intimidated a weaker man, an Ohio paper commented, but "William Howard Taft is a very large man, mentally and physically."

Panama soon emerged as the most pressing of the trouble spots threatening to boil over. Taft had been 8,000 miles away in November 1903 when Roosevelt sent U.S. ships to support a Panamanian uprising against Colombia. Recognition was swiftly granted to the newly formed Republic of Panama, and a treaty was negotiated that guaranteed Panamanian independence. In return, the United States was allowed to purchase land to build a canal. "I took the Canal Zone," Roosevelt later boasted.

When word first arrived at the *McClure's* office "that Roosevelt had snitched Panama," Viola Roseboro remembered, "there were gasps," accompanied by "amusement and excitement." Ida Tarbell, however, "was very grave." Tarbell considered the president's seizure of the Canal Zone "a dishonorable outrage," according to Roseboro. Ida "got a line on Teddy that she never lost sight of." While she considered him "a delight and a wonderful person and of great value to the country," Tarbell could not overlook the despotic side of Roosevelt's leadership. "You cannot conceive of Lincoln's trifling with his conscience," she had admonished, "even for the sake of an international canal."

Taft had also been absent during the fierce senatorial debate surrounding the treaty that granted the United States permanent rights to a ten-mile strip in exchange for $10 million and a significant annual payment. Assuming responsibility for overseeing the Panama Commission shortly after his return, Taft proved a quick study. "He had an enormous capacity for mastering official detail," one historian observed, "content that the overall direction came from his superior." Under Taft's command, the commission was authorized to establish official guidelines for the Canal Zone; make all engineering, construction, and sanitary contracts; acquire private lands; tabulate all monies spent; and institute a civil service system. This complex supervisory job was "really enough to occupy the whole time of any average executive," Taft's biographer maintains, yet it was just one among the many tasks that fell to Secretary Taft during these "crowded years."

As construction of the Canal got under way in the fall of 1904, a wave of popular discontent swept through Panama. Panamanians began to suspect that the United States intended to establish "an independent colony" within their country, compromising their own sovereignty and economic well-being. A small band of soldiers threatened to seize power. Endeavoring to defuse tensions, Roosevelt dispatched Taft to the isthmus.

Conscious of the need to project goodwill and friendship, Taft asked Nellie to accompany him. Their arrival in Colón, Nellie recalled, felt like coming home. "The whole atmosphere and surroundings, the people, the language they spoke, the houses and streets, the rank earth odours and the very feel of the air reminded me so strongly of the Philippines as to give me immediately a delightful sense of friendly familiarity with everything and everybody," she later wrote. They remained in Panama for two weeks. During the day, Taft held private conferences with Panamanian officials; in the evenings, he and Nellie socialized at receptions, dinners, and balls. As in the Philippines, Taft charmed the local citizens with his surprising skill on the dance floor. Finally, an agreement was forged that encompassed a range of political and economic issues. Panamanian citizens greeted the published text with delight. As small boys hawking newspapers shouted "Extras" from every street corner, Nellie recalled, "excited groups stood about here and there wreathed in smiles and talking with great animation. Everybody seemed wholly satisfied and wherever we went we were met with cheers and cries of 'Viva!' "

A number of problems regarding the construction of the Canal required attention before Roosevelt returned from his hunting trip. A serious dispute had arisen between John Wallace, the chief engineer, and William Gorgas, the chief sanitary officer. Wallace remained highly skeptical of his colleague's work to contain the spread of mosquitoes on the theory that the insect transmitted yellow fever. Castigating Gorgas's ideas as merely "experimental," Wallace failed to carry out safety protocols that recommended mosquito-proof screens in all government offices. When a virulent outbreak of yellow fever sent a majority of American workers retreating back to the States, Gorgas demanded greater independent authority from both Wallace and the commission. "Here again I must trust your judgment," Roosevelt wrote to Taft from Glenwood Springs, Colorado. Taft wisely threw his support to Gorgas and eventually called for Wallace to resign.

With equal insight and acumen, Taft resolved conflicts in Santo Domingo that threatened U.S. interests in Morocco and Venezuela. "You are handling everything just right," Roosevelt praised him on April 8. Two weeks later, Roosevelt again assured Taft he was "keeping the lid on in great shape!" Each letter expressed unconditional confidence and support: "You are on the ground," he reiterated, "you see the needs of the situation, and I shall back up whatever you do." Invariably, Roosevelt's letters reflect profound respect and gratitude for his friend's service. "I wish you knew Taft, whom I have had acting as Secretary of State as well as Secretary of War in Hay's absence," he told George Trevelyan. "To strength and courage, clear insight, and practical common sense, he adds a very noble and disinterested character. I know you would like him. He helps me in every way more than I can say." And to John Hay, Roosevelt confided: "Taft, by the way, is doing excellently, as I knew he would, and is the greatest comfort to me."

Roosevelt finally returned to Washington on May 12; six weeks later, Taft left for a journey of his own—a three-month cruise to the Philippines and the Far East. Recalling his pledge that the Filipino people would always remain first in his heart, Taft had been troubled by reports from Dr. Pardo de Tavera, one of the three Filipino members of the Philippine Commission. When Taft had departed two years earlier, Tavera wrote, "everything was in good order and every Filipino was confident in the future," but the commission had since lost its "Pole star"—the policy of working together with the Filipino people to shape their destiny. Under Luke Wright, Taft's successor, "discontent [was] general, resentment profound and well-founded." Tavera implored Taft to return to the islands for a visit. The Filipino people regarded the former governor general as "the only man who can and will reestablish justice and liberty here."

Convinced that he must return to assess the situation in person, Taft assembled a party of eighty people to accompany him, including seven senators, twenty-three congressman, and a dozen journalists. His guest list was inclusive and bipartisan, embracing Democrats and Republicans, pro–tariff reduction men and "standpatters," strong supporters of the administration's policy and fierce opponents alike. He hoped that firsthand experience of the islands' rich potential and personal encounters with the Filipino people would beget a more supportive attitude toward legislation to reduce tariffs, build railroads, and speed agricultural development. "I doubt if so formidable a Congressional representation ever went so far," he proudly noted.

Not long after Taft's party embarked for Southeast Asia, Secretary of State John Hay lost his long battle with illness. "Just heard sad news," Taft cabled Roosevelt, wondering if he should postpone his journey and return to Washington. "If it were not that I feel so keenly the great importance of having you in the Philippines," Roosevelt replied, "I should have been tempted to keep you over here, for I shall miss you greatly." He informed Taft that he would likely ask Elihu Root to take Hay's place. Although he confided to Lodge that he "hesitated a little between Root and Taft," noting that Taft was "very close" to him, the prospect of having both men by his side left "no room for doubt." Taft dispelled any qualms Roosevelt might have felt, urging the president to appoint Root to the premier post. "My dear fellow," Roosevelt replied, "I could say nothing higher of you than that it was just exactly characteristic of you, I do not believe that you will ever quite understand what strength and comfort and help you are to me."

Under the sway of Taft's amicable leadership, everyone who had joined the expedition got along surprisingly well. "I do not think that I have ever known any one with the equanimity, amiability, and kindliness of Mr. Taft," Alice Roosevelt reported. "During all that summer, I never once saw him really cross or upset. He was always beaming, genial, and friendly, through all his official duties, and the task of keeping harmony among his varied and somewhat temperamental army of trippers." In the evenings, guests enjoyed formal dances, sleight-of-hand performances, mock trials, and pillow fights. "The party has been a very jolly one," Taft related to Roosevelt, "and Democrats and Republicans have joined alike in praising the fine weather and really delightful voyage."

Friends and family had warned Taft that dealing with Alice—or "Princess Alice," as she had been dubbed by the press—would prove challenging; despite such admonitions, he found her unspoiled and delightfully forthright. "She is quite amenable to suggestion and I have seen nothing about the girl to indicate conceit or a swelled head," he told Nellie, who had elected to spend "a quiet summer in England" with the children following their hectic year. At times, she could be "oblivious to the comforts of other people," he explained, but considering "what she has gone through and who she is," the young woman managed to make herself extremely popular with the entire party. Nevertheless, he remained troubled by Alice's flamboyant flirtation with Nicholas Longworth, a worldly thirty-five-year-old congressman from Cincinnati with a reputation for numerous dalliances.

Taft was aware that Alice and Nick had been seeing one another before the cruise. He had heard stories about the "fast set" to which they belonged. "She seems to be so much taken up with Nick," he reported to Nellie, that she "pays little attention to anybody else." They took meals together, sat side by side on deck, and partnered on the dance floor, where Alice reportedly "looked almost unreal in her clinging gown, which matched the sea. As she glided through the dance, her long, spangled scarf wound itself around her, serpent like." Noting that the young couple appeared to revel in conversations "usually confined to husband and wife," Taft finally confronted Alice. "I think

I ought to know if you are engaged to Nick," he suggested in a gently paternal manner. Alice cryptically replied: "More or less, Mr. Secretary, more or less."

The arrival of the Taft party in Manila on August 4 inspired widespread celebration. Guns boomed and thousands filled the streets as the official delegation progressed to the Malacañan Palace for the welcoming ceremony. From the outset, Taft was determined to remedy the growing animosity between the Filipino people and the current insular government. The policy of the Roosevelt administration, he reiterated at every stop, was "the Philippines for the Filipinos. If the American officials were not in sympathy with this policy," he assured the islanders, "they would be recalled." While he continued to believe the Filipinos needed to prepare for independence, Taft officially announced that the long-anticipated popular assembly would be established in April 1907. The Filipino people, the *New York Tribune* reported, greeted this definitive proclamation with great enthusiasm.

Informed that the colonial administration considered Filipino families not "of sufficient rank to entertain Senators and Congressmen," Taft decided that he and Alice would move immediately from the palace to the home of a Filipino member of the commission, Benito Legarda. "I knew no way, but the direct way," he explained, "to show that we had no sympathy with the apparent desire to exclude Filipino hosts from those who should entertain the party." At a "very handsome ball" hosted by the Legardas, Taft and Alice delighted the Filipinos by joining in the native rigadon square dance. Taft had taken care to practice the complex steps with Alice and several other young ladies during the long ocean voyage. A number of similar receptions in the homes of local citizens went "a long way in cementing friendships."

Lodging with the Legardas also allowed Taft to meet with scores of disaffected Filipinos who would never have visited him at the palace with Governor General Wright present. "All day long," one observer recorded, "the great hall was occupied, the men sitting by the open windows disposing of one long cigar after another." Hearing their grievances, Taft reluctantly concluded that the majority of the commission—including the governor general—were "utterly lacking in the proper spirit" toward the native population. "They seem to think it does not make much difference whether they have the support of the Filipinos or not," he lamented. "To me it makes every difference in the success of the government." Indeed, he wrote to Nellie, many Filipinos insisted that if only the Tafts returned to Manila, they would soon "restore the old condition of things." The current situation was dispiriting, for it necessitated the removal of the governor general and possibly two other commission members, whom he considered friends.

Taft and his entourage "made the round" of the archipelago, traveling by small boats, bamboo rafts, carriages, and on horseback. They surveyed agricultural conditions where sugar, hemp, and rice were grown, meeting with tradesmen, government officials, educators, manufacturers, and farmers. Correspondents who accompanied the party noted "a happy sea change" in the attitudes of several protectionist congressmen, particularly Sereno Payne, chairman of the House and Ways Committee, and General Charles Grosvenor of Ohio. "It is already apparent," the *Tribune* editorialized, "that Sec. Taft's plan of enlarging the political and mental horizons of leading men of both parties as respects Philippine questions is working out admirably." Several legislators personally expressed their amazement and gratitude to Taft. "It was a great trip and cannot be otherwise than helpful to the Government," one member told him. "I never realized until this journey the magnitude of the Philippine problem, nor did I realize your devotion to the cause. I have heard a great many speeches made in my time, but never heard a series of better ones than were made by you while touring the islands. It is a miracle that so large a party was so harmonious, and the credit is due to your example."

Although Taft's primary mission was to the Philippines, the expedition also made stops in China and Japan, where Taft secretly met with Japan's prime minister, Taro Katsura. Undisclosed for the next twenty years, this meeting would have lasting consequences for the region. Long-standing hostilities between Russia and Japan had flared into war over competing territorial interests in Korea and China. Roosevelt had closely followed the evolution of this conflict, hoping he might mediate between the two warring powers. From the start, he had sympathized with Japan's desire to oversee affairs in Korea, to keep a strong hold on Port Arthur, and to return Manchuria to China. Still, he recognized that mounting Japanese victories would expand the imperial government's demands, upsetting the balance of power in the Far East. He was delighted, therefore, when Taft contacted him in late April to affirm that the Japanese were interested in having the U.S. president facilitate peace talks. In fact, Roosevelt was so enthusiastic that he curtailed his hunting expedition by a week to commence dialogue with the Japanese and Russian ministers.

Concealing the fact that the Japanese had initiated the process, Roosevelt sent identical letters to both sides. He requested that they "open direct negotiations for peace," offering his services "in arranging preliminaries as to time and place of meeting." When both the belligerents agreed, Roosevelt received accolades: "It is recognized all the world over as another triumph of Roosevelt the man," the *New York Tribune* editorialized. "It was America alone that assumed the responsibility. It is to America alone that the world will give the credit."

As preparations for a peace conference in Portsmouth, New Hampshire, began, Taft sailed into Yokohama, where his party received "a demonstrative welcome." Fireworks heralded the arrival of the ship, and thousands of citizens lined gaily decorated streets. From the harbor city, Taft journeyed to Tokyo for his confidential talk with Count Katsura. Taft assured Katsura that while he did not officially speak for the president, he was certain of Roosevelt's position. Katsura made it clear that "Korea being the direct cause of our war with Russia," it was "of absolute importance" that after the war, Japan should control Korea "to the extent of requiring that Korea enter into no foreign treaties without the consent of Japan." In return, Taft sought assurance that Japan did "not harbor any aggressive designs whatever on the Philippines."

Having reached agreement on both points, Taft informed Katsura that without the U.S. Senate's consent, the president could not enter into a formal alliance or even "a confidential informal agreement." Nevertheless, he expressed certainty that the two countries were in such fundamental accord on the issues discussed that the conversation could be treated "as if" a treaty had been signed. Taft promptly telegraphed a memo of the entire exchange to the president. "If I have spoken too freely or inaccurately or unwittingly," he concluded, "I know you can or will correct it." Roosevelt immediately dismissed his concerns, replying, "Your conversation with Count Katsura absolutely correct in every respect. Wish you would state to Katsura that I confirm every word you have said."

On August 5, accompanied by the sound of booming guns, the peace envoys from Russia and Japan met with the president aboard the presidential yacht *Mayflower*, anchored in Oyster Bay. After a buffet lunch served with cold white wine, the envoys proceeded to the U.S. Naval Base at Portsmouth. In the days that followed, agreements on Korea, Port Arthur, and Manchuria were reached with relative ease. Japan's insistence on some form of compensation from Russia threatened to torpedo the conference. The Russian envoys took the position that Russia had neither been conquered nor could be considered "prostrate in the enemy's hands." Therefore, they argued, Japan had no right to extract an "indemnity." Increasingly frustrated with mediating the dispute, Roosevelt confided to Kermit, "I am having my hair turned gray by dealing with the Russian and Japanese negotiators." In the end, the president persuaded the Japanese that prolonging the war simply to secure money would lose international support. A peace treaty was finally signed on

September 5, 1905, earning Roosevelt praise at home and abroad, as well as the Nobel Peace Prize.

DESPITE SUCH INTERNATIONAL TRIUMPHS, PRESSING and complex domestic issues threatened the solidarity of the Republican Party. Once again, Taft had barely returned when he was recruited to suture the wound. Taft's three-month odyssey ended at 3:27 p.m. on October 2, 1905, when he stepped onto the platform at Union Station, appearing "hearty and vigorous" as he greeted colleagues with a big smile and a warm handshake. That evening, he dined with the president and first lady, along with Root, Garfield, and a few family friends. "We had a most interesting dinner," Garfield told his wife. "Mr. Taft is full of interesting accounts of the Orient."

Taft had little time to reacquaint himself with affairs in his department before he was called upon to deal with a troubling situation in Ohio. Factional disputes there threatened the reelection of Republican governor Myron Herrick. Earlier that summer, Lincoln Steffens had published his electrifying report contrasting Democrat Tom Johnson's principled governance of Cleveland with the venal mismanagement of Cincinnati's Republican boss Tom Cox. The piece revealed how Cox had become a millionaire twice over through corrupt alliances with traction companies, banks, and railroads. "The city is all one great graft," Steffens charged. "The reign of Cox is a reign of fear."

The exposé had created a sensation in Ohio. Although Cox claimed it was "full of falsehoods," the tale sparked public outrage and engendered bitter conflict within the Republican Party. Those beholden to the old machines dominated by corporations and political bosses inevitably opposed the progressive drive toward popular rule and governmental regulation. The growing split within the Republicans opened the door to Democrats, who successfully likened Governor Herrick's management of the state to Cox's grip on the city. In fact, they intimated that the governor had become "subservient" to Cox and his crowd, a participant in the systemic graft. "The stampede from Herrick is growing like a wild fire," one Ohio paper reported, "and so consuming is the anti-Cox, anti-bossism flame, that the disaffected thousands say they will vote the democratic ticket from top to bottom this year."

Believing that Ohio's gubernatorial race could influence the fortunes of the entire Republican Party, Roosevelt dispatched Taft to deliver a speech on Herrick's behalf. When Steffens learned of this step, he wrote an impassioned letter to the president, imploring him not to help the governor. "Governor Herrick is not a bad man," conceded Steffens, "he is simply weak. He is one of those men who can do dishonest things honestly." State politics could not be separated from Cincinnati's municipal situation, he insisted, arguing that the growing effort to vanquish Cox—whose candidates were on local ballots that accompanied the gubernatorial election—would be thwarted by the president's push to keep Republicans "in line" behind Herrick.

Caught in this hazardous political knot, Taft devised what newspapers called "a most adroit and ingenuous" speech. Voicing support for Herrick, whom he believed to be a decent man, he leveled a fierce barrage of criticism at the Cox regime. Public condemnation of Cox was "not pleasant" for Taft, particularly given that his brother Charley owned and edited the *Cincinnati-Times*, "the official organ" of the Cox regime. "Any pain you feel at the expressed difference of opinion between us finds a corresponding deep regret in my heart," Taft told Charley on the eve of his speech, "for I love you Charley as I love no one except my wife and children." Nevertheless, he felt bound to declare his opposition to Cox and his corrupt lieutenants.

Delivered before an overflowing audience in Akron, Ohio, the speech was termed "the most severe rebuke" ever suffered by the powerful boss. Accustomed to criticism leveled by his Democratic opponents and the progressive press, Cox now faced censure "from so prominent a Republican, a member of the president's cabinet." In straightforward language, Taft likened "Cox and Coxism" to "a curse" upon the people of Hamilton County, "a local despotism" designed for the financial benefit of the boss, his cronies, and the big corporations. He described the political machine's "distressing effect" on aspiring young Republicans, who were forced to submit "to the tyranny of the boss" or abandon public service altogether. If he were to vote in the upcoming race, Taft acknowledged, he would "vote against the municipal ticket nominated by the Republican organization."

Despite his condemnation, Taft "made clear the difference between Herrick—the clean-living, trusted and honored businessman and efficient executive of the State—and the foul boss of Cincinnati." While he refused to endorse the Republican ticket in Hamilton County, Taft declared that he would happily vote for Governor Herrick and hoped others would do the same. If he believed his visit to Ohio would perpetuate the Cox machine, Taft assured his listeners, he would never have come. But it would be unfair to abandon "a governor who has done well by his State and his party."

Although Taft had sought to rally support for Herrick, newspapers focused on his "scathing denunciation" of Cox, which fell upon the city and state "like the explosion of a bomb." Excerpts from the speech were carried in more than six hundred papers. Dozens of editorials and letters commended

Taft for his honesty and courage. "We had about come to the conclusion that there wasn't a man in Ohio who dared call his soul his own without the permission of George Cox," one Ohio citizen wrote. "You are the only man who can lead this city out of the slough of despond," another remarked. "You have done more good for your own town by that speech than you have any idea of," Taft's close friend Howard Hollister wrote. "The weakness and cowardice of a great many of our principal men have been a chief trouble here, and now they are encouraged to come out and talk and act like men. I hear it everywhere."

The elections that fall brought a crushing defeat for the Cox machine. But Taft's hope that voters would split their tickets, voting Democratic in the local election and Republican in the gubernatorial race, proved vain: John Pattison, the Democratic candidate for the governorship, defeated Myron Herrick by a wide margin. "Do not concern yourself about the stories that are afloat that you caused my defeat," Herrick graciously told Taft. "I know my friends and know you to be one whom I love and respect."

Buoyed by the demise of the Cox machine, young Republicans in Cincinnati formed a new Republican Club with a progressive agenda. Led by Howard Hollister, they called on members to stand unequivocally against bossism and machine politics and advocate a platform that included national regulation of railroads and tariff revision. At Hollister's request, both Taft and Roosevelt accepted honorary memberships in the "Roosevelt Republican Club." Only such clear dissociation from corrupt and self-serving elements of the Republican Party, Hollister argued, could "disabuse the public mind of the growing feeling of domination of the party by the corporations and money making commercial politicians."

As Theodore Roosevelt had surmised, the struggle against corruption and consolidation in Ohio reflected a burgeoning movement across the country. And the president was acutely aware of the difficult balance he would have to strike in order to realign his party without compromising the nation's prosperity. In the winter of 1905, a dramatic "Oil War" in the state of Kansas illuminated this intensifying conflict, captivating the interest of the entire country. "Kansas is in the clutches of the Standard Oil Company," the *Hutchinson News* reported, "and is howling for relief."

A year earlier, spectacular deposits that surpassed the total volume of the Pennsylvania oil fields had been discovered in Kansas and the Indian Territory in Oklahoma. "On the instant," Ida Tarbell recalled, "Kansas went oil-mad, practically every farmer in the state dreamed of flowing wells." The Standard

Oil Company immediately began furnishing tanks, building refineries, and constructing pipelines. Independent producers were placated with the promise that they would receive market price for their oil. Only when Standard had a total lock on refining and transportation, William Allen White explained, did the company "put on the screws." A barrel of oil that had yielded a dollar and eighteen cents in 1904 had dropped to thirty-seven cents a year later. With control of both in-state refineries and all the pipelines, Standard Oil had effectively become "the only transporter and buyer" of the region's crude oil, with power to set whatever price it chose.

Popular anger fueled the successful gubernatorial campaign of Kansas Republican Edward Hoch, who challenged the Republican machine with a platform calling for construction of "a first-class" state refinery that would force Standard "to be reasonable." In his inaugural address, Hoch proposed a series of additional measures to regulate the oil trade, including one to make pipelines common carriers, rendering them subject to the same state supervision as railroads. When the upper house passed the bill for the state refinery, Standard retaliated by boycotting Kansas oil entirely, leaving the producers "without a market" and throwing "a large number of men out of work." Standard's despotic tactics backfired when public recognition that the giant company "was *punishing* Kansas" generated such outrage that the refinery bill sailed through the lower chamber. Borne on a wave of defiance, the legislation even garnered support from conservatives, who felt the measure smacked of socialism. "Scare Kansas! Well, we'll see about that!"

At the White House, telegrams poured in, urging the president to protect the state "from oppression of the Standard Oil trust." Congressman Philip Campbell of southeast Kansas introduced a resolution requesting an investigation into "the unusually large margin" between the price of Kansas crude oil and the market price of refined products. It was "hardly a secret," one Kansas newspaper suggested, that the situation in Kansas presented President Roosevelt with the opening he was seeking to move against "the mother of all trusts." Indeed, some observers speculated that the resolution was instigated by the administration.

After discussing the situation with the Kansas representative, Roosevelt in February 1905 announced that he had directed Bureau of Corporations director James Garfield to undertake "a rigid and comprehensive review" of Standard Oil's methods of operation, "especially in the Kansas field." Garfield planned to travel to Kansas the following month to oversee a team of fifty special agents, ensuring a thorough investigation of the trust's practices. The president clearly understood, Campbell maintained, that this was the "most important investigation of the kind which has been undertaken." Although passage of the House resolution brought Standard's boycott in Kansas to an end, the fundamental problem of monopoly lingered.

Two days after the president's announcement, Ida Tarbell wrote to John Phillips: "What would you think of an article on Kansas & the Standard Oil Company?" Having spent nearly four years studying Standard Oil, Tarbell remained vitally interested in the company's activities. Her twenty-four-part magazine series had been republished as a two-volume book the previous November to great acclaim. One critic predicted it would "rank as one of the most complete and authoritative contributions to economic history written in the last quarter century." Miss Tarbell's study, another wrote, "is to the present time the most remarkable book of its kind ever written in this country." The oil war in Kansas promised to furnish a new and vital postscript.

When she wrote her proposal, Tarbell had returned home to Titusville to be with her father, who was suffering from stomach cancer. His death on March 1 had suddenly "darkened" her world, for he had "built himself into every crook and cranny" of her childhood home—indeed, of the entire town. Her family at the magazine did their best to console her. "I have thought a great deal of you in your sorrow," S. S. McClure wrote from Switzerland when the news reached him. "There are times when your face expresses a singular pathos & sense of suffering & I know how sad & heartbroken you have been." He hoped she found some solace in the fact that her father had seen "with his own eyes" how she had used her substantial gifts to dignify the Tarbell name.

Not long after the funeral, Ida left for Kansas, exhibiting what McClure termed her "pathetic & characteristic" impulse relentlessly to immerse herself in work. Though she set out "with a heavy heart," the monthlong journey proved to be "as exciting" as any she had undertaken. Independent oilmen hailed her arrival as the coming of "a prophet," certain that she would reveal Standard's "unfair and illegal methods" in Kansas to "all the world." Local journalists trailed her throughout the state, taking her picture and printing her remarks. Embarrassed by her celebrity, she told Albert Boyden she hoped "to Heaven . . . all the foolishness" published about her would not be taken seriously in the office. "Believe nothing," she entreated them, "until I have a hearing!"

Straightaway, Tarbell called on the governor. Initially skeptical about his plan for a state refinery, she came away convinced that the project would be "a good thing," and serve "as a measuring stick" for the public to determine the real costs of refining. In the long run, however, Standard's control over oil transport had to be addressed. "Build your own pipe line," she urged the oil producers; "build it to the seas." In addition, she recommended that they pressure Congress to pass a law "making all pipelines common carriers," subject to regulations that would ensure fair play.

Soon afterward, Tarbell joined Governor Hoch and Congressman Campbell at "the biggest mass meeting of oil producers ever known." Diffident when asked to speak before 3,000 people, she composed a letter to be delivered at the convention. She challenged Kansas "to play the oil game as well as the Standard Company plays it," but "with due regards for the rights of men, something the Standard has never done."

Next, Tarbell embarked on a ten-day field trip through the countryside to gauge for herself the extent of the new oil fields. Traveling by a two-horse open carriage over primitive roads, she encountered the worst dust storm in many years. Her driver, bellowing to be heard over the rising wind, roared: "Jehoshaphat! Wrap your head up." Even after the storm passed, Ida was unable to bathe for ten days because dust had seeped into the water supply, producing "a muddy liquid quite impossible to drink and hopeless for cleansing." Undeterred, she continued her mission. "The wonder is that discomfort doesn't count out here," she explained to John Phillips. All hardships were eclipsed by the contagious excitement of the farmers, by the promise that every little town would become "a world's center," every well "a gusher." One weekend, Tarbell crossed the Oklahoma border to see the oil fields in the Indian Territory. Everywhere she went, crowds gathered, bands serenaded her, and people gave her flowers and candy. In the "new town of Tulsa," she was "paraded up and down" the main thoroughfare. At the request of a local citizen in Muskogee, she "submitted to five sittings for her picture." From early morning until midnight, she was called upon to make little speeches.

Needful of respite, Tarbell spent a leisurely weekend in Emporia with William and Mary White. She had taken the "city-shy" boy "by the hand" when he first ventured into New York and had always appreciated "his affection and loyalty for his state." She was delighted now to see his home, his place of work, and his beloved town. In Emporia, Tarbell agreed to address a group of students at a chapel. "The new thing which Kansas has put in the fight against the evils of Standard monopoly," she told them, "is an ethical question. Here people say they oppose Standard's methods because they are wrong." Kansas was not merely motivated by the monopoly's impact on business—"Standard had never met with this spirit in any of its previous fights." After her departure, White wrote an editorial echoing her conviction that the problem with Standard Oil was "as much a moral issue as it is a financial one." The machinations Standard employed—bribing legislatures, tampering with juries, purchasing judges—constituted "the real danger to the country." Yet, he concluded, "because it is a corporation and has neither soul nor body," Standard had largely managed "to escape the vengeance which the law . . . would surely have visited upon natural persons guilty of similar practices."

As Tarbell passed through Kansas City on her way to New York, she stopped for a brief visit to express her gratitude and admiration for the state's spirit. She found that spirit so compelling that she extended her visit. "I stayed and stayed, and even now I am reluctant to return to the east," she later explained, describing how the nature of this fight set it apart: "The Kansans are not fighting now for the money they can make. They are not fighting because their oil doesn't market well. They're fighting because a monopoly, a trust, has sought to come into their state and dictate to them where their products shall go and what shall be paid for their products. It's the fight for justice and right."

In a two-part article, Tarbell argued that "if one wants a neat demonstration, complete to the last detail, that the Standard Oil Company is to-day, as always, 'a conspiracy in restraint of trade,' he should go to Kansas"; there, the company continued to perpetuate "exactly what it did" three decades earlier in Pennsylvania—crushing independents, fixing prices, operating pipelines as private fiefdoms, and colluding with railroads. Her revelations produced a growing demand for official action. If her charges proved accurate, the *Wall Street Journal* commented, "we take it that Commissioner Garfield will be honest enough to report the fact, and if the fact is reported, we believe that the administration is courageous enough to prosecute even the Standard Oil Company."

Early on, Garfield had decided to take on the daunting task of expanding the scope of his investigation beyond Kansas, to encompass Standard's methods of operation nationwide. He traveled to "nearly all of the great fields" and talked with hundreds of producers, refiners, and railroadmen. Special agents were dispatched throughout the United States and even to Europe. Garfield's wife, Helen, was anxious about the investigation. "Do read Ida Tarbell's McClure article," she urged her husband. "It is very cleverly written—I feel that the man and those in the ring will lie to you just as she says they have lied all along." She needn't have worried; not only had Garfield read the piece, he had borrowed Tarbell's collection of relevant sources and documentary evidence. "I shall try to find the truth," he reassured his wife.

Garfield's report was published in two parts. The first concluded that Standard Oil had continued to receive the same "unjust and illegal" preferences from the railroads outlined in Tarbell's exhaustive series and that these rebates, bribes, and kickbacks had facilitated development of the trust's extensive pipeline system. The second outlined the monopolistic position of Standard Oil in the petroleum industry. Roosevelt transmitted the first report to the Congress with a special message: "All the power of the government will be directed toward prosecuting the Rockefeller trust." Commentators agreed that the report, endorsed by the president, constituted "the most severe arraignment of a corporation" ever issued from such "a high official source."

"Garfield's Report Causes Sensation," blasted the *Laredo* (Texas) *Times*. "Makes Almost as Good Reading as Ida Tarbell's Magazine Articles." Indeed, public commentary invariably referenced Tarbell's earlier work. "All that Ida Tarbell told in McClure's Magazine is being reaffirmed," one newspaper remarked; another termed the report "a vindication" of her methods, validated now by the official seal. If the commissioner "can prove all he says," Tarbell herself told a reporter, "he has rendered one of the most important public services in the history of the country."

The Justice Department prepared two lines of attack corresponding to Garfield's report: the first alleged illegal rebates under the Elkins Act of 1903; the second charged "conspiracy in restraint of trade" based on violation of the Sherman Anti-Trust Act. "If my report affords the basis for making these prosecutions successful I shall be mightily pleased," Garfield wrote to Helen. While "conspiracy and monopoly" were difficult to prove, the rebate case promised to be relatively straightforward.

Judge Kenesaw Mountain Landis, a colorful jurist who would later become the first commissioner of baseball, presided over the first case, in which the government charged Standard of Indiana with receiving illegal rebates from the Chicago & Alton Railroad. On the day the ruling was handed down, hundreds of would-be spectators were denied entrance to the overcrowded courtroom. The ruling, which found Standard guilty of accepting rebates on 1,462 carloads of oil, required nearly two hours to read. Landis rendered the judgment with a series of dramatic "sledgehammer blows," drawing applause on two occasions for his condemnation of Standard's corrupting influence on its employees and the nation as a whole. Never before, one court reporter noted, had a judicial sentence featured such inflamed rhetoric.

Although the guilty verdict surprised few, the size of the resulting fine stunned the company and the country. For each of the 1,462 carloads of oil that had enjoyed an illegal rebate, Landis levied the highest possible fine, $20,000, generating a spectacular cumulative total of $29,240,000. Commenting on the hefty charge, Mark Twain drolly remarked that the sum evoked the bride's proverbial astonishment on the morning after her wedding: "I expected it but didn't suppose it would be so big."

Ida Tarbell optimistically declared that the decision presaged the "beginning of the end" for the "giant octopus." For thirty-five years, Rockefeller's corporation had absorbed small fines as the cost of doing business; this "Big Fine," she hoped, would mark the moment when Standard "must either conform" to "fair dealing" or face ruin. Despite such predictions, John D. Rockefeller remained sanguine about his company's prospects. He was on a golf course when word of the judgment reached him. "Judge Landis," he complacently predicted, "will be dead a long time before this fine is paid." Rockefeller's prophecy was confirmed eleven months later when Appeals Court Judge Peter Grosscup overturned the decision on a technicality. "It's nothing more than we expected," the Standard attorneys smugly proclaimed. Roosevelt publicly derided Grosscup's ruling as "a gross miscarriage of justice," further proof of "too much power in the bench."

His momentary frustration aside, Roosevelt remained optimistic about the administration's second and more trenchant line of attack. Six months after the publication of the Garfield Report, the attorney general filed suit in St. Louis, charging Standard Oil of New Jersey and its five dozen subsidiaries with conspiracy to monopolize the oil industry in violation of the Sherman Anti-Trust Act. With this prosecution, the *Des Moines Daily News* observed, "the government [had] finally attacked the very citadel of the Standard Oil Company." Again, reports invariably cited Tarbell's work as both inspiration and template for the government's case. "The petition of the US government for an injunction dissolving the Standard Oil Company of New Jersey reads like a chapter from Ida Tarbell," one commentator asserted. "Every essential charge made by Miss Tarbell in her exposé," another suggested, was "repeated and put into the form of a legal allegation," substantiating her crusade against bribery and spying, sham independent companies, preferential relationships with the railroads, and interlocking boards of directors. In sum, the editorial continued, "the person who more than any other started the government attack on the biggest trust in the world was Ida Tarbell."

This time, the federal court found in the government's favor. Two years later, in a decision that stunned the business world, the Supreme Court affirmed the lower court's ruling. The High Court condemned Standard Oil, "not because it is a trust, but because it has an infamous record," and delivered a warning to "every trust that is tempted to oppress and destroy." A few short weeks later, the Court drove the point home with a similar judgment against the American Tobacco Company. Standard Oil was given six months to dissolve. Once again, Rockefeller was in the middle of a golf game when the news arrived. "Buy Standard Oil," he curtly responded. Even when the corporate "octopus" was divided into thirty-eight parts, Standard Oil of New Jersey preserved its identity, eventually morphing into Exxon; Standard Oil of New York incorporated as Mobil; and Standard Oil of Indiana evolved into Amoco.

While Roosevelt exulted in each of his anti-trust victories, he continued to regard the judicial system as an ineffective arena for controlling giant corporations. For the Department of Justice simultaneously "to carry on more than a limited number" of major suits was "not feasible," and protracted delays meant that "even a favorable decree may mean an empty victory." Regulation, he believed, promised a far better remedy. "The design should be to prevent the abuses incident to the creation of unhealthy and improper combinations," he argued, "instead of waiting until they are in existence and then attempting to destroy them by civil or criminal proceedings."

Unlike anti-trust proceedings, federal regulation required approval in the House and Senate, where conservative Republicans remained a dominant force. After failing to defeat the Bureau of Corporations, this reactionary bloc was determined to prevent Roosevelt from miring the party and the country in policy it considered tantamount to socialism. "The fundamental idea on which our government was founded," conservatives argued, "was that the functions of the federal government were strictly limited, and that all regulations which most closely affect the lives of the people should be left in the hands of state and municipal bodies." Roosevelt's regulatory ideas would "extend the power of the federal government" to an unlimited degree. "Are we to have a national government as highly centralized as that of France or Germany?" opponents ominously queried, warning, "That is what we certainly shall have if we find no way of checking the tendencies in government of which Theodore Roosevelt is so conspicuous and enterprising an exponent."

CHAPTER SEVENTEEN

The American People Reach a Verdict

Roosevelt's looming visage frightens the U.S. Senate in a Feb. 7, 1906, cartoon from *Puck*, entitled "The Latest Thing in Nightmares."

INCREASINGLY FRUSTRATED IN THE WINTER of 1905 by the bickering in Washington and the rancor within his own party, Theodore Roosevelt ranted to a friend that "there are several eminent statesmen at the other end of Pennsylvania Avenue whom I would gladly lend to the Russian Government, if they cared to expend them as bodyguards for grand dukes whenever there was a likelihood of dynamite bombs being exploded!" His sardonic suggestion targeted the coterie of conservative Republican senators who opposed his signature plan to regulate the railroads.

The cost to both his party and the country would be immense, he believed, if "the people at large" perceived "that the Republican party had become unduly subservient to the so-called Wall Street men—to the men of mere wealth, the plutocracy." It would result in "a dreadful calamity," Roosevelt told a conservative friend, to see the nation "divided into two parties, one containing the bulk of the property owners and conservative people, the other the bulk of the wageworkers and the less prosperous people generally; each party insisting upon demanding much that was wrong, and each party sullen and angered by real and fancied grievances."

In the struggle to avert this calamitous future, nothing was more essential, Roosevelt believed, than railroad regulation. His first address to Congress following his election victory had indicated his belief in the primacy of the issue. "Above all else," he declared, "we must strive to keep the highways of commerce open to all on equal terms." The most critical piece of legislation the country needed was an act to give the Interstate Commerce Commission the power to regulate railroad rates that gave an "unreasonable" advantage to the trusts.

As the battle lines formed that winter, S. S. McClure decided that the magazine's next series would concentrate on the railroads. His staff had already concluded that many of the country's gravest problems, from state and municipal corruption to the ascendancy of the trusts, could be traced to the railroads. Whereas earlier modes of transportation (the wagon roads and waterways) had been available to all on an equal basis, a small circle of private owners now controlled the transportation network essential to all commerce. This exclusive circle could effectively determine the fortunes of cities, towns, and companies, the futures of entire industries. Both the Grangers and the Populists had called for governmental regulation of the railroads, but despite the passage of the 1903 Elkins Act, the industry had remained essentially unregulated.

Ida Tarbell's study of Standard Oil had convinced her that Rockefeller had employed discriminatory freight rates as the primary instrument in his campaign to crush independent competitors. "Until the transportation problem is settled and settled right," she warned, "the monopolistic trust will be with us, a leech on our pockets, a barrier to our free effort." Steffens, too, had discovered that in every city and state he had explored, "the story was always the same": corruption "came from the top"—from the men who owned streetcar lines in the cities and railroads in the states. New Jersey's dominant railroad had "seized the government," and the Southern Pacific Railroad had become "the actual sovereign" of California. Like his colleagues, Baker's own countrywide investigations had persuaded him that "the Railroad problem is pretty nearly the basic problem of our life: and we know little or nothing about it!"

Having completed his labor series, and "eager for more dragons to slay," Ray Baker was thrilled to be chosen for the assignment. By supplying "the real facts," the nation's reporters could shape that essential discussion. The journalist, he passionately believed, is the "true servant of democracy." This new project on the railroads, he told his father, would be "far more important than anything [he had] ever done." Baker started by examining everything he could gather on the subject—pamphlets, congressional reports, local investigations, scholarly studies, and court testimonies. He read accounts of La Follette's titanic fight against the railroads in Wisconsin and sought guidance from experts on the railroad industry.

Upon learning that Baker had begun his investigation, Roosevelt invited him to Washington. Baker promptly replied that he hoped to take up the railroad problem "in some big, important, and impressive way." On January 28, 1905, Baker joined the president for a "simple and most informal" family lunch, after which the two men engaged in a private conversation. By this time, Baker had gained "a pretty good grip on the railway problem" and shared with the president a detailed outline of his planned series. Central was the argument that railroads were public highways that must be accessible to all on fair and equal terms. They should no longer enjoy peculiar charter rights from the government—including the right of eminent domain and the right to charge tolls.

For his part, Roosevelt was confident he could steer a bill through the House, where the members felt the direct pressure of growing agitation against the railroads. "His chief trouble," he told Baker, would be the Senate, where members were sent by the state legislatures and many owed their seats to corporate interests. His best chance lay in mobilizing the public so that the Senate could no longer refuse to act. Nevertheless, he urged the reporter to be fair; an analysis couched in demagogic rhetoric would not be trusted. "My job is not to assess blame on anyone," Baker countered. "I am trying to get at the facts and report them as truthfully as I can."

"It was altogether the most interesting meeting & talk with him that I ever had," Baker told his father. "I think he likes to get these things first hand." The president had asked Baker "to consult" with him often during the course of his research, promising to enable the magazine's effort to clarify the complex problem for the general public. "Facilities have been given me here as never before," Baker proudly noted, "the Inter State Commerce people even offering me a desk & stenographer, with full admission to all their published documents & letters. It certainly shows how . . . a greater care for truth & fairness, which I have tried to attain in my articles, gets hold of people."

Two days after meeting with Baker, Roosevelt began his own campaign for railroad regulation with a major speech before the Union League Club in Philadelphia. "Neither this people nor any other free people," he declared, "will permanently tolerate the use of the vast power conferred by vast wealth, and especially by wealth in its corporate form, without lodging somewhere in the government the still higher power of seeing that this power, in addition to being used in the interest of the individual or individuals possessing it, is also used for and not against the interests of the people as a whole." Calling again for a public tribunal with "power over rates," he argued once more that only the national government could "keep the great highways of commerce open alike to all on reasonable and equitable terms."

The next day, Roosevelt met with Baker for another luncheon discussion. He admonished the journalist once again to beware of demagogues, emphasizing that the web of corruption linking politicians and corporations was "due quite as much to the blackmailing demands of legislators as to the offered bribes of businessmen." That evening, Baker wrote a long passage in his notebook enumerating the obstacles to passing desperately needed railroad regulation. While it was certainly possible that some legislators were paid by corporations to oppose unwanted bills, the congressional failure to address the disease was more complex. In recent years, the country had witnessed "an enormous industrial development," marked by the growth of "railroads, trusts & inventions." Although these unprecedented changes required new thinking about the relationship of business and government, Baker reasoned, a "legislative lag" clearly existed. Laws generated fifty years earlier, rooted in laissez-faire philosophy, remained on the books. "Once let an idea really penetrate the mind of a people," as this ethic of non-interference in private enterprise had done, and it would require a massive educational effort to remove it. If he and his fellow journalists could enable the public to re-envision the role of government, Baker noted, there would be "no further difficulty in regulating the trusts & the railroads."

Yet encouraging a new way of thinking demanded time and hard work, and Baker was still in the early phase of his research when Congress took up the question of railroad regulation during its short session in the winter of 1905. An administration-backed bill granting the ICC power to regulate railroad rates passed the House, but the Senate deliberately scheduled its hearings after Congress had adjourned on March 3, ending any chance for the legislation to pass. Assessing his defeat, Roosevelt concluded that his influence had been stunted: once he relinquished the chance to run for a third term, the opposition concluded he "need not be regarded as a factor hereafter." Still, he believed that if the necessity for regulation could be "clearly drawn" in the months ahead, the Senate would eventually bow to public feeling.

Sentiment did indeed begin to shift, but not in the direction Roosevelt desired. Troubled by the passage of the regulatory bill in the House, the railroads launched a sweeping propaganda campaign to turn the country against regulation. Lengthy hearings before the Senate Interstate Commerce Committee provided the opening salvo. Organized by senators sympathetic to the railroads, the six-week proceeding featured a witness list stacked to thwart regulatory efforts. Over two thirds of the witnesses, one reporter from Utah noted, "were either friendly toward or in fear of the railroads and testified accordingly." One after another, railroad executives argued that Roosevelt's bill was misguided at best and unconstitutional at worst. They pointed out "how delicate and difficult a task it was to adjust a freight-rate, how it required long practical experience," intimating that disaster would follow if the government "should meddle" in the complex business. "Any tinkering with rates would raise Cain with stocks," one railway head warned. "It would mean a general unsettling of affairs."

Forced to travel to Washington at their own expense, the few witnesses who spoke in favor of regulation were mocked and labeled as agitators. Railroad king James J. Hill likened the commotion over regulation to "an attack of 'pink-eye' or the grippe," which would eventually run its course. Members of the Senate committee did nothing to stop such belittling attacks. Congressmen who had voted for Roosevelt's bill in the House were blacklisted from receiving any further free passes. Not surprisingly, newspapermen attending the hearings were influenced by the strength of the opposition, and the national coverage soon turned sharply negative. A prominent Republican senator claimed that the president was looking for a way out, that he had finally realized his ill-considered foray into this arena might "throw the country into a panic."

To counter rumors that he had ceded the possibility of reform, Roosevelt dispatched Taft to a conference of three hundred railway executives meeting at the Willard Hotel. Vehemently reinforcing the administration's commitment to regulation, Taft spoke of the certain advent of railway rate legislation, warning that "if the railway men of the country were wise they would aid and not hinder it." The industry must recognize, he insisted, "that railroads are a public institution—an institution which must be regulated by law. You cannot run the railroads as you would run a private business. You must respond to the public demand."

Taft's words were greeted with "absolute silence," until Stuyvesant Fish, president of the Railway Congress, jumped to his feet and exhaustively countered Taft's arguments. The laws already on the books were sufficient to deal with any difficulties, he declared, arguing that the action proposed would cause more harm than good. When he took his seat amid great applause, Taft respectfully asked: "May I have fifteen minutes to reply?" His rebuttal rendered an even more forceful defense of the necessity for a tribunal with powers to revise unfair rates. Taft's words, "driven directly into the ears of the men who are most determined that there shall be no railroad legislation," created "a sensation." Observers understood that the secretary's address "had been carefully prepared, and prepared with the intention of causing exactly the impression that was caused."

The following day, Roosevelt endorsed Taft's speech by flatly stating that his own stance on the subject of the railroads "could not have been better expressed." Railroad magnates needed to understand that it was "essential, in the interests of the public," that the government assume a regulatory power over them. Furthermore, he vowed that if this power were awarded, it would be exercised with justice to both the captains of industry and the American people. Roosevelt repeatedly stressed that "the spirit of demagoguery" must not dictate legislative policy. "If we attack unjustly the proper rights of others because they are wealthy," he was careful to maintain, "we shall do ourselves just as much damage as if we permitted an attack upon those who are poor, because they are poor." He recognized that "the rock of class hatred" was "the greatest and most dangerous rock in the course of any republic." But the time for action had come. If Congress refused to advance the administration's moderate proposal, more radical demands would inevitably gain momentum.

Convinced now of the president's resolve, editorials predicted "a fight to the finish between the railroads and the administration." Nonetheless, *The Washington Post* reported, "an impression prevailed during the summer that the railroad interests were making such a campaign . . . that there was very grave doubt of any legislation of that character passing in the coming Congress."

BY SUMMER'S END, BAKER HAD completed his research and commenced writing a six-part, 50,000-word series, entitled "The Railroads on Trial." To herald the upcoming articles, McClure published a lengthy editorial announcement claiming that "the vitality of democracy" depended on "popular knowledge of complex questions." With regulatory legislation that would impact the entire nation under debate in Congress, the public needed to understand how railroads determined differential rates, whether they conspired to stifle competition, how goods were classified, and how private cars and midnight tariffs operated. The American people, not economists and sociologists, would ultimately have to assess whether a few great men, "like the barons of old," had become "more powerful than the sovereign himself."

Mindful of the president's earlier request to look over his railroad articles before publication, Baker wrote in early September to ask if Roosevelt still wanted to review his first installment, scheduled to appear in the November issue. "Yes, I should greatly like to see the proof," Roosevelt assured him the very next day. "I have learned to look to your articles for real help. You have impressed me with your earnest desire to be fair, with your freedom from hysteria and with your anxiety to tell the truth." Baker later recalled his trepidation after sending off the piece, aware that the president's "approval might be the measure of the usefulness of the entire series [he] had planned." If Roosevelt found his arguments compelling, Baker could employ "the incomparable sounding board of the White House" in his endeavor to educate the public. Five days later, Baker was elated and much relieved by Roosevelt's response: "I haven't a criticism to suggest." Indeed, the president graciously acknowledged, "you have given me two or three thoughts for my own message."

In clear, powerful language, Baker explained how, despite the Elkins Act that barred cash rebates, the railroads still managed to build in special rates. They had devised a schedule that favored products carried by the trusts through clever classification of goods and commodities. "In the early days of the Railroad," Baker pointed out, "the Rate was fixed exactly as it was on a turnpike—a regular toll, for so many miles, so much of a charge." As railroads had begun to consolidate, however, the small circle of controlling owners adopted the principle of "charging what the traffic will bear," providing preferential treatment to the trusts while forcing exorbitant rates on small shippers. When great clients like the Armours, the Rockefellers, or the Morgans desired special privileges, they were easily arranged—given that such families generally sat on the boards of these very same railroads.

Although "the fundamental purpose of all law," Baker argued, "is to do justice between strong and weak, between large and small," the railroads and the trusts had conspired "to build up and enforce the old favoritism to the strong." For the first time, Baker boldly suggested that railroad rates had become the fulcrum of a new political contest that set "a progressive party seeking to give the government more power in business affairs" against "a conservative party striving to retain all the power possible in private hands."

In thanking the president for reviewing his proofs, Baker took the occasion to warn him that the mood in the Midwest had become highly volatile; failure to pass regulatory legislation, he predicted, would foment "violent agitation" and calls for radical action. "The country was never at a more critical point in its career," the reporter observed, nor had it "ever had a better opportunity of handling its problem correctly. I wish, Mr. President—and you will pardon my freedom—that there were a Taft for the Bureau of Commerce and Labor. To my thinking there is no more important place now in the gift of government."

A few weeks later, Baker was amazed to receive a letter from the president, containing a "strictly confidential" partial draft from his annual message dealing with the corporations. "Will you give me any comments," Roosevelt asked, "which your experiences teach you ought to be made thereon?" In eight weeks, the president would deliver his State of the Union speech, and Baker reflected solemnly upon "the seriousness of the responsibility" granted to him. "I knew perfectly well how little I really knew about the complicated problems involved in the new legislation," he later wrote; "but then, who was there at that time who did?"

The reporter carefully weighed Roosevelt's language. Heartened by the president's willingness to make railroad regulation his first priority, he found the tone of the draft message disappointing: "It was too general, there was too much of the President's favorite balancing of good and evil." Baker applauded Roosevelt's drive to empower the Interstate Commerce Commission to revise the disputed freight rates but deplored his proposal to limit the Commission's authority to merely prescribing a maximum rate limit. "I was terribly afraid that he was plumping for a solution that, while it might help a little, and look good politically, would fail to reach the heart of the matter," Baker recalled.

The research for Baker's second article, which detailed all manner of new rebate chicanery, had convinced him that the trusts didn't care what the rate was, so long as they enjoyed a better rate than everyone else. The differential provided their advantage and allowed them to crush their competitors. Beyond their clever freight classification schemes, railroads had implemented a host of "cunning devices"—including private cars, refrigerator charges, elevator allowances, underweighing of freight, and variable tariffs. Such measures were specifically designed to lower rates for the great shippers in beef, oil, and steel while raising them "for the farmer, the small struggling manufacturers and shippers." Believing he had gained a comprehensive understanding of the railroad conspiracy, Baker felt compelled to tell the president plainly that his approach was misguided.

"I have asked myself over and over," Baker wrote to Roosevelt on November 11, expressing his doubts "whether the power to fix a maximum rate, which you suggest, will touch this specific case of injustice." He had determined that it would not. The "evil power" of the trusts, he explained, lay in their ability to compel the railroads to give them a lower rate than everyone else. The problem therefore was "*not* a maximum rate but a minimum rate." The only solution was to allow the governmental tribunal to "fix a *definite* rate."

Roosevelt replied immediately, agreeing that "it would be better if the Commission had the power to fix a definite instead of a maximum rate." His attorney general had warned him, however, that fixing a definite rate might be unconstitutional. While the maximum rate might not alleviate all problems, he concluded, "we should have first a law that is surely constitutional." Baker persisted, reiterating in a second letter that merely limiting the maximum rate would not mitigate the terrible inequity in the entire system. "Is there not, then, some practical way," he entreated, "for reaching the real abuse?" Quoting the abolitionist Wendell Phillips's remark on historic reforms, Baker challenged the president's objection: "If they do not succeed with the Constitution, then they must succeed without it."

There followed "a long and rather heated correspondence" between the two men, spurred by a four-page letter from the president. "I think you are entirely mistaken in your depreciation of what is accomplished by fixing a maximum rate," Roosevelt declared, arguing that "the insistence upon having only the perfect cure often results in securing no betterment whatever." Furthermore, he added, "the railroads have been crazy in their hostility to my maximum rate proposition, and evidently do not share in the least your belief that nothing will result from it." In additional exchanges, Roosevelt branded Baker's continued fear that the proposed measure would prove insufficient "simply absurd." He ended the correspondence with a reminder that "it was Lincoln, not Wendell Phillips and the fanatical abolitionists, who was the effective champion of union and freedom." Confronted by Roosevelt's strident tone, Baker was certain that his "suggestion would come to nothing."

"What was my surprise," Baker later recalled, "when I read the message in its final form as delivered to Congress, to find that the President had inserted a paragraph, almost in my own words, regarding the regulation of minimum rates." After calling upon Congress to grant an impartial tribunal authority to set "a maximum reasonable rate" when an existing rate was deemed "unreasonable and unjust," Roosevelt laid out a far more comprehensive proposal: "It sometimes happens at present not that a rate is too high but that a favored shipper is given too low a rate. In such cases the commission would have the right to fix this already established minimum rate as the maximum; and it would need only one or two such decisions by the commission to cure railroad companies of the practice of giving improper minimum rates." Finally, he urged Congress to grant the ICC supervision of private-car lines, elevator allowances, refrigerator charges, and industrial roads—all the devices Baker had exposed as subtle mechanisms of discrimination.

ON JANUARY 4, 1906, COLONEL William Hepburn, chairman of the Interstate and Foreign Commerce Committee, reported the administration-backed railroad bill to the floor of the House. As Roosevelt had outlined in his annual message, the bill gave the ICC the authority to determine a "just and reasonable" maximum for disputed rates. Though it was essentially a moderate bill, it nonetheless challenged "the most hoary tenet of free private enterprise"—the right to independently set prices according to supply and demand.

While Speaker Joseph Cannon could have easily exercised his absolute control over House procedure to prevent the bill from reaching the floor, he had allowed it to move forward. In exchange, the president had agreed to preserve the protective tariff—an issue the Old Guard considered even more vital than railroad regulation. Popular resentment toward the railroads was such that once the bill reached the floor, the outcome was clear. The overwhelming vote to pass the Hepburn bill on February 8 "was in many ways the most spectacular piece of politics ever witnessed at the Capitol," *The Washington Post* remarked, noting that a bill vitally affecting over $15 billion of property had passed "without the addition of a single amendment."

The following day, Roosevelt invited Ray Baker to join him during his afternoon shave. Baker professed his belief that "this railroad legislation was the most important of the President's administration" but "only a first step" toward broader reform. His investigations throughout the West had convinced the journalist that the public was moving beyond the president's position, even pushing for "governmental ownership of the railroad." Roosevelt vehemently disagreed, twisting so abruptly toward Baker that the barber had to flinch quickly to avoid cutting the president's chin. "I do not represent public opinion: I represent the public," Roosevelt passionately countered, insisting, "I must represent not the excited opinion of the West but the real interests of the whole people." Those interests would be ill served, he curtly rejoined, by turning the operation of the railroads over to government employees, for "he knew better than anyone else could how inefficient & undependable" they were. The Hepburn bill, Roosevelt insisted, would address most of the problems. Rather than speculate on future steps, he must focus on the U.S. Senate, where he faced perhaps the climactic struggle of his administration.

A battle royal was predicted between the president and the conservative senators, led by Nelson Aldrich. Public pressure precluded an outright assault on the bill, yet Aldrich and his colleagues remained confident that they could produce a final bill "so whittled down" by amendments "as to be practically worthless." Roosevelt was clearly prepared for such tactics: "They are making every effort to have some seemingly innocent amendment put in," he explained to Kermit, "which shall destroy something of what I am endeavoring to accomplish."

To forestall these inevitable efforts to gut the bill, Roosevelt declared unequivocally that he wished the Senate to pass the Hepburn bill without amendments. His statement produced "great indignation among the conservative senators." The chief executive, they insisted, had no business meddling in their deliberations. His presumptuous intervention showed a woeful disregard of the Senate's historic role "as a check upon the half-baked and demagogic bills passed by the lower house."

Roosevelt's push to get the bill unamended through the Senate Interstate Commerce Committee rested on the leadership of Iowa's junior senator, Jonathan Dolliver. A young progressive, Dolliver worked doggedly to produce a majority vote and deliver what would become the Dolliver/Hepburn bill to the floor. Of the eight Republicans, he won the support of three—all from the West where agitation for railroad control was most intense. Combined with five Democrats who had long favored regulatory control, they formed the slim majority Dolliver needed to bring the bill to the floor.

Conceding that he had lost in committee, Aldrich deftly contrived a deal with the Democrats: He would give Benjamin Tillman, the ranking Democrat from South Carolina, the honor of leading the fight on the floor in Dolliver's place. In turn, Democrats agreed to report the unamended bill "without prejudice," thereby allowing amendments to be freely offered during debate on the floor. This gambit astonished even the most seasoned journalists. The fact that Roosevelt's "most outspoken opponent" was "put in charge of the administration's pet measure," one Ohio paper remarked, was "considered so audacious a piece of irony that it has made the country gasp." Fully aware that Republicans controlled nearly two thirds of the Senate, Tillman himself "scarcely had time to pinch himself to see if he were really awake."

The loyal Dolliver, who had justifiably assumed he would lead the fight, was humiliated. Worse still, the president confronted a truly awkward dilemma. During Roosevelt's first term, the hot-tempered, foul-mouthed, and slovenly Tillman, known as "Pitchfork Ben," had engaged in a fistfight with a colleague on the Senate floor. In the aftermath, Roosevelt had publicly withdrawn Tillman's invitation to a state dinner, incurring the senator's abiding animosity. The two men had not spoken since. Aldrich calculated that with the irascible Tillman as floor leader, Roosevelt's influence on the legislative process would be severely diminished. The press agreed. Roosevelt now suffered the indignity, declared the *Charleston* (South Carolina) *News and Courier*, of seeing his signal legislation "confided to the care of a man who is not only not of his own party, but one who entertains a personal antagonism toward him." The president's "old enemies" in the Republican Party, the *Indianapolis News* observed, seemed determined not only to defeat his legislation but also to "show at the same time that the President is not after all a formidable figure."

In the following weeks, pro-railroad Republicans took to the floor, proposing a range of amendments designed to shatter the commission's authority. They were particularly intent upon a provision granting the courts broad power to relitigate the commission's revised rates, essentially leaving the pro-railroad judiciary as the true arbiter of rates.

Roosevelt nevertheless remained hopeful that the Hepburn bill would emerge intact, trusting that "public opinion may be relied upon to keep the Senate straight." By the spring of 1906, public outrage over the railroads had indeed reached a crescendo. Hundreds of magazines and newspapers followed every aspect of the debate, clearly outlining what was at stake. These publications, one editorialist observed, were "never better," and "never more influential," than in their joint effort to foster an informed public opinion "compounded of knowledge, discrimination and judgment."

In March, Baker published the most consequential piece in his railroad series, an exposé of the techniques the railroads employed to malign and falsify the Hepburn bill. Acknowledging the right of the railroads, "in common with all other citizens, to present facts and arguments to the people," Baker proceeded to reveal the multifarious devices of the railroads' lavishly funded propaganda campaign. A team of agents determined whether newspaper editors were "good" or "bad" on the issue of the railroads, then distributed free passes to those adjudged favorably inclined, while subjecting those deemed unfriendly to underhanded personal attacks. In one instance, a former city newspaperman was hired to write a pamphlet posing as a representative of farmers against regulation. In another scheme, small newspapers were supplied with free reading supplements seeded with attacks on Roosevelt's railroad legislation. Subsidized pamphlets spread the rumor that if railroad discriminations were outlawed, separate Jim Crow cars for Negroes would be forbidden. If all such "ordinary devices" to co-opt the press failed, then the railroads purchased newspapers outright.

Baker's description of this onslaught of covert railroad propaganda acquainted more than half a million men and women with the true methods of the anti-regulatory campaign. "It is a little startling," one magazine editorialized, "to read how the railroad combines first to rob the country of millions, and then to use a portion of this fund stolen from the people to corrupt the sources of information and thus try to perpetuate their robbery through a blinded public opinion." New subscriptions and letters commending Baker poured in to *McClure's*. A Mississippi farmer wrote that "after plowing all day," he and his boys had read the entire piece aloud. If he had the funds, he told Baker, he would send a copy to every family in the country. "Every member of Congress," he added, "should have a chance to read this able presentation of the question between the people and the railroads." One Wisconsin resident telegraphed *McClure's* that he considered Baker's article "worth all the publication will cost me for the next ten years." The sensational article heightened public demand for regulation, much as the publication of the Standard Oil telegrams had done during the battle over the Bureau of Corporations.

To the dismay of Senator Aldrich, who had counted on Roosevelt's pride to prevent any overture to the man he loathed, the president soon made it clear that he "was of course entirely willing to see Mr. Tillman personally," or meet with any other party empowered to act on Tillman's behalf. "I did not care a rap about Mr. Tillman's getting credit for the bill, or having charge of it," he later recalled. "I was delighted to go with him or with anyone else just so long as he was traveling my way." Still unwilling to set foot in the White House, Tillman asked former senator William E. Chandler to serve as intermediary.

After a series of White House sessions with Chandler, Roosevelt agreed to support a Tillman-endorsed amendment that limited judicial review to a simple determination of whether the commission's rate revision procedures were fair. By moving "to the left of his original position," the president hoped to fashion a majority comprising both Republican progressives and Democratic populists. "The fight on the rate bill is growing hot," Roosevelt told Kermit, explaining his ongoing efforts to save it: "I am now trying to see if I cannot get it through in the form I want by the aid of some fifteen or twenty Republicans added to most of the Democrats."

"As for Tillman," William Allen White wrote in the *Emporia Gazette*, "no member of the President's own party could have pressed the bill more vigorously at all times. He demanded that all other state business be stopped until a rate bill was passed, and he kept the senate an hour earlier and an hour later than it was accustomed to sit." Handed the greatest responsibility of his career, Benjamin Tillman had determined, he said, to "pocket my pride and lay aside my just indignation" in order to aid the president in securing "a good railroad law." No better illustration of "the mysterious ways of Providence and politics" could be found, *The Washington Post* commented, than the alliance of "the pitchfork and the big stick."

Roosevelt would gladly have signed Tillman's more radical revision of the Hepburn bill if his new coalition of progressive Republicans and Democrats had produced sufficient numbers to override the conservative Republican bloc. But in the end, a number of southern senators balked, deeming the bill a violation of states' rights, and Tillman could not deliver enough Democratic votes to make it work. Roosevelt was left with no choice but to revert to the original Hepburn bill, which had simply assumed the constitutional guarantee of due process. Despite such setbacks, Roosevelt remained satisfied with this formulation. "The great object," he insisted, "was to avoid the adoption of any of the broad amendments."

But in order to forge a majority on the original bill, he would have to mollify moderate Republicans who feared that unless the courts were directly vested with judicial review, the bill might be held unconstitutional. To win over this reluctant bloc, Roosevelt called on two Old Guard senators, William Allison of Iowa and John Spooner of Wisconsin. Both had long been staunch lieutenants to Nelson Aldrich, and both were assumed to be supporters of his bid to emasculate the bill. The political landscape was shifting, however; in Iowa and Wisconsin, the momentum to regulate the railroads had reached a frantic pitch and the two senators understood that ignoring their constituents on this issue would put their Senate seats in grave jeopardy.

Allison and Spooner's unexpected cooperation with Roosevelt made headlines. Two of the original Big Four, this "little knot of men" had ruled the upper branch in harmony for years. Nelson Aldrich found the break with Allison especially painful, for he relied upon Allison's masterful knowledge of parliamentary procedure. "Everybody is now watching with eagerness to see which of the two great Senate chieftains will demonstrate superior generalship," commented the *New York Times*. From his post at the *Emporia Gazette*, William Allen White noted that Aldrich appeared befuddled over the fact that he could "neither control the legislation of the upper branch affecting financial interests nor count upon the men he regarded as allies." This rupture in the Senate oligarchy was widely regarded as "symbolic of the new popular alignment all over the country in preparation for the coming contest between the forces of amalgamated capital and those of popular will and sentiment."

Straightaway, Allison devoted himself to fashioning his own amendment to the Hepburn bill, which stipulated the right to judicial review of ICC rulings—but cleverly leaving the scope of that review undetermined. The ambiguous language of the Allison amendment allowed the senator to forge a majority. Although Roosevelt had hoped to limit the court's review to a determination of procedural fairness, he recognized that this compromise provided the only chance of passage. Once the amendment was accepted, Roosevelt later told White, "Aldrich and his people really threw up their hands." Their chance to obtain a broad review provision had been eliminated. Indeed, when the Hepburn bill finally reached the Senate floor for a vote, Aldrich and a number of his older colleagues were noticeably absent. The bill passed by an overwhelming vote on June 29, 1906.

"No given measure and no given set of measures will work a perfect cure for any serious evil," Roosevelt reminded critics of the compromised bill. Though flawed, the president maintained that the Hepburn Act represented "the longest step ever yet taken in the direction of solving the railway rate problem." The legislation not only brought the railroads under federal control; it "lifted the idea of nationality to a point never before reached." The authority granted the Interstate Commerce Commission became clearer in the months that followed as the first case involving rate revision reached the Supreme Court. By declining to review the specific facts, the High Court defined the scope of judicial review in favor of Roosevelt and the progressives.

The president enjoyed widespread credit for the passage of the bill, exhibiting, one Democratic newspaper remarked, "the politician's gift of knowing when to fight, and, as well, when to surrender." Roosevelt had sought a Republican majority for the original Hepburn bill; when his efforts were subverted by the leader of his own party, he had reached out to the Democrats; when that failed to produce a majority, he returned to his original provision, altered only slightly by Allison's amendment. Even Benjamin Tillman grudgingly acknowledged that "but for the work of Theodore Roosevelt, we would not have had any bill at all."

However astute Roosevelt proved in dealing with Congress, he would doubtless have failed to secure a meaningful bill without a galvanized public behind him. The combined efforts of Baker and his fellow journalists had generated a widespread demand for reform. "Congress might ignore a president," the *Fort Wayne* (Indiana) *Weekly Sentinel* observed, "but could not ignore a president and the people."

A letter discovered among Baker's papers testifies to the impact of investigative journalism on the passage of the Hepburn Bill: "It is through writers like yourself, Mr. Steffens and Miss Tarbell that the country as a whole is beginning to understand. In the future your influence on the life of the Republic will be held to be greater than that of the men who now rule our Senate and our House." Baker had reflected on their accomplishment and his growing confidence in the nation's future in a January letter to his father: "This crusade against special privilege in high places is real war, a real revolution," he wrote. "We may not have to go as far as you did, when you fought out the slavery question with powder & blood. At the present, when any of us is wounded we bleed nothing but ink. But ink may serve the purpose."

Upton Sinclair, the young novelist and friend of Ray Baker and Lincoln Steffens, helped instigate the next battle in the crusade against special privilege. Sinclair thought very highly of the dramatic factual stories in *McClure's* that mobilized public opinion but reproached his comrades for failing to endorse the panacea of socialism. At the age of twenty-four, Sinclair had concluded with certainty that socialism was the answer to the country's ills; his experience of reading a socialist pamphlet in 1902, he later said, "was like the falling down of prison walls about my mind."

Thus, unlike the members of the McClure team, Sinclair was not struggling to discover remedies for specific ills. "Perhaps it'll surprise you," he wrote to Baker during the railroad struggle, "but we socialists don't agree with your rebate agony. The quicker the concentration of wealth is completed the better it suits us. . . . The point all you reforming folks seem to miss is that you are locking the stable doors after the horse is gone. *The trusts are formed. The big shipper has got the money*. Also with the money he's bought the government."

By twenty-five, Sinclair had already published two obscure novels when the editor of a popular socialist weekly, *Appeal to Reason*, offered to pay $500 for the right to publish his next fiction project in serial form. He quickly chose the "wage slavery" of industrial-era workers as his subject. The young socialist decided to set his novel in the Chicago stockyards, where an unsuccessful strike by workers in the meatpacking plants had aroused his sympathy. Dazzled by the brilliance of Frank Norris and a small cadre of writers devoted to realism, Sinclair took up residence in Packingtown, the stockyard district. For seven weeks, he recalled, "I sat at night in the homes of the workers, foreign-born and native, and they told me their stories, one after one, and I made notes of everything." Wandering around the yards during the day, he noted, "I was not much better dressed than the workers, and found that by the simple device of carrying a dinner pail I could go anywhere." Passing into rancid, hazardous places that outsiders rarely frequented, he watched with amazement as scraps of meat that were later sold to the public were swept from floors infested with rats and covered in human spit. The pressure to produce profits dictated that nothing was allowed to go to waste: condemned hogs were rendered into lard;

moldy meats were "dosed with borax" and ground into sausage; spoiled hams were pumped with chemicals to mask a smell "so bad that a man could hardly bear to be in the room with them."

After a month of watchfulness, Sinclair had collected the data but not yet conceived the protagonists for his novel. One Sunday afternoon, he chanced to attend the rollicking traditional wedding celebration of a young Lithuanian couple. Standing transfixed with his back to a wall as the festivities unfolded around him, Sinclair found his characters amid the whirl of music and dance—"the bride, the groom, the old mother and father, the boisterous cousin, the children, the three musicians, everybody."

The Jungle tells the story of the young couple and their extended family as they immigrate to Chicago in pursuit of plentiful jobs, decent wages, and the fulfillment of the American dream. No one subscribes more completely to the idea that decency and hard work will earn a place in America than the central character, Jurgis Rudkus. Confident in his ferocious strength and determination to provide for his family, Jurgis immediately lands a job. He is "the sort of man the bosses like to get hold of. . . . When he was told to go to a certain place, he would go there on the run. When he had nothing to do for the moment, he would stand round fidgeting, dancing, with the overflow of energy that was in him." Filled with optimism, Jurgis saves every cent to buy a home for his wife and children: "He would work all day," Sinclair wrote, "and all night too, if need be; he would never rest until the house was paid for and his people had a home."

Before long, the predatory machine of Packingtown begins to corrode Jurgis's optimism and assurance. For years, glib salesmen had counted upon the ignorance of the immigrants. If a single payment was missed, the house was lost, along with everything paid into it. Indeed, Sinclair observed, the houses "were sold with the idea that the people who bought them would not be able to pay for them." The unscrupulous salesman could always count on a new wave of immigrants, clamoring desperately for jobs and needful of food and housing.

The meatpacking plants grind up workers as surely as they grind up hogs and cattle. Sinclair details the brutal hours of work with no compensation for injury and little hope of evading the diseases legion in unsanitary surroundings. During the holiday "speeding up" on the slaughtering floor, Jurgis is hurt. Finally able to return to work, he discovers that his job has been given to another man. Once "fresh and strong," Jurgis becomes "a damaged article" his bosses no longer want. At once vividly individual and representative of an entire beleaguered class, Sinclair's characters are callously denied any real hope of a livelihood or future. The devastation of the entire family has been set in motion, their tragedy engendered not through personal failure but through the savage capitalist system that pits man against man. When his young wife and then his son die, Jurgis is crushed in body and spirit. Finding himself at a socialist rally, he is at last spiritually reborn, awakened to revolution.

After five publishers rejected Sinclair's manuscript outright, Doubleday finally considered publication. "The revelations in the story were so astounding," the *New York Times* reported, "that the publishers commissioned a lawyer to go to Chicago to make a personal investigation of the author's representations." When the attorney's report corroborated Sinclair, Doubleday agreed to move forward. In February 1906, as he nervously awaited official publication, Sinclair sent two advance copies to Ray Baker. One was autographed to the journalist; the second, Sinclair hoped, Baker might deliver to the White House and present to President Roosevelt.

The book created an immediate sensation. Although some reviews criticized the contrived socialist epiphany of the ending, millions of readers found Sinclair's cast of characters and the grotesque details of the meatpacking industry compelling. "Not since Byron awoke one morning to find himself famous," observed the New York *Evening World*, "has there been such an example of world-wide fame won in a day by a book as has come to Upton Sinclair."

James Garfield was the first in the White House to read the book. "Hideous," he termed the story, "but not more so than the place," which he had visited during the Bureau of Corporations' investigation of the beef trust. Sinclair, he wrote in his journal, had produced "a terrible and I fear too true account of the lives of many miserable men & women among the working class in our big cities." During a long walk with the president, Garfield described at length his response to the book.

Intrigued by Garfield's reaction, Roosevelt finished reading the novel and invited the author to the White House during the first week in April. Although he proceeded to disparage the socialist diatribe tacked on to the conclusion, Roosevelt assured Sinclair that "all this has nothing to do with the fact that the specific evils you point out shall, if their existence be proved, and if I have power, be eradicated."

By the time Sinclair arrived for lunch on April 4, a Department of Agriculture investigator was en route to the stockyards with an order from the White House to evaluate the novelist's charges. Sending a representative of the very agency that had failed properly to inspect the plants, Sinclair objected, "was like asking a burglar to determine his own guilt." His objections prompted Roosevelt to dispatch two additional investigators with no official ties to the department. He chose two well-respected men: Commissioner of Labor Charles P. Neill and Assistant Secretary of the Treasury James Bronson Reynolds. Sinclair was delighted, though he feared the investigators would focus on the diseased meats rather than the working conditions in the yard. "I have power to deal with one and not with the other," Roosevelt responded.

As the investigation got under way, the *Chicago Tribune* ran a series of articles citing "on excellent authority" that the president's team had already debunked the overwhelming majority of Sinclair's charges and claiming that Roosevelt intended to castigate the novelist in an upcoming speech. In a state of panic, Sinclair barraged the president with letters, a telegram, and a phone call. Roosevelt patiently explained that the newspaper story was simply fabricated. "It is absurd to become so nervous over such an article," he admonished. "Hundreds such appear about me all the time, with quite as little foundation." Chastened, Sinclair maintained that he "should never have dreamed of writing," except it seemed incomprehensible that a journalist "with a reputation to protect" would dare to disseminate false information in such an "explicit and positive way." Roosevelt immediately assuaged Sinclair's anxiety. "I understand entirely how you felt. Of course you have not had the experience I have had with newspapers. . . . Meanwhile, we will go steadily ahead with the investigation."

In fact, Roosevelt's inspectors found stockyard conditions comparable to those Sinclair had portrayed. Initial reports told "of rooms reeking with filth, of walls, floors, and pillars caked with offal, dried blood, and flesh, of unspeakable uncleanliness." These findings were more than sufficient to convince Roosevelt to take action. On May 22, Indiana senator Albert Beveridge introduced a White House–backed bill to institute a rigid federal inspection program covering all phases of the meatpacking industry, from animal slaughter to sausage and canned meat production. If products were "found healthful and fit for human food," a government label indicating "inspected and passed" would be attached; if not, the meat products would be marked "inspected and condemned."

Roosevelt warned Senate leaders friendly to the packers "that unless effective meat inspection legislation were enacted without loss of time," he would make the report public. Although he had no desire to harm the packing industry or the livestock producers, if the meatpackers moved to kill the legislation, he would feel compelled to expose the sickening work conditions. Fearing adverse publicity even more than the regulation, the packers retreated. Without "a dissenting vote" the Beveridge bill passed the Senate three days after it was introduced.

While Roosevelt was satisfied, Upton Sinclair remained disappointed by the bill's quick passage. To release the report, he told the president, would give the public "a shock it will never get over," prompting true, enduring reform through "an enlightened public opinion." Disregarding Roosevelt's directive to remain patient while the House took up the Senate bill, Sinclair leaked his information from the report to the *New York Times*. "I sincerely hope that the disturbance I have been making has not been an annoyance to you," he told the president. "I had to make up my mind quickly." Exasperated, Roosevelt wrote to Frank Doubleday: "Tell Sinclair to go home and let me run the country for awhile."

The legislation, meanwhile, foundered in the House Agricultural Committee, chaired by the wealthy stockbreeder James Wadsworth, a strong proponent of the beef trust. One after another, witnesses were paraded before the committee to argue that while isolated problems might exist, "conditions were as clean and wholesome as in the average restaurant, hotel and home kitchen. That there were offensive odors was natural—one ought not to expect to find a rosebud in a slaughtering house." A series of emasculating amendments was prepared, one negating the "mandatory character" of inspection and granting packers the right of court review.

"I am sorry to have to say," Roosevelt informed Congressman Wadsworth, "that it seems to me that each change is for the worse and that in the aggregate they are ruinous, taking away every particle of good from the suggested Beveridge amendment." Because the packers and their representatives had reneged, producing only "sham" legislation, the president felt he was not "warranted" any longer in holding back the unfinished Reynolds-Neill Report.

On June 4, the president transmitted what he called a "preliminary" report to Congress. "The conditions shown by even this short inspection," he avowed, were "revolting." His investigators had determined that "the stockyards and packing houses are not kept even reasonably clean, and that the method of handling and preparing food products is uncleanly and dangerous to health." Federal legislation was imperative to prevent continued abuses. If Congress failed in its responsibility, the full report would be made public.

Released to the newspapers, this preliminary assessment produced a national uproar. The *New York Post* captured the public mood in a sardonic jingle:

Mary had a little lamb,
And when she saw it sicken,
She shipped it off to Packingtown,
And now it's labeled chicken.

Faced with public outrage and disgust, the House could no longer keep the bill "chloroformed in the committees." The most egregious of Wadsworth's provisions were eliminated and the measure was sent to a conference committee. In the end, a fairly comprehensive meat inspection bill emerged. "We cannot imagine any other President whom the country has ever had, paying any attention at all to what was written in a novel," the New York *Evening Post* remarked. "In the history of reforms which have been enacted into law," Beveridge proudly noted, "there has never been a battle which has been won so quickly and never a proposed reform so successful in the first contest."

THE MOMENTUM OF THE RAILROAD regulation fight and the meat inspection amendment propelled the passage of a third important bill—the Pure Food and Drug Act—producing a historic session of congressional reform. Crusaders like Dr. Harvey Wiley, chief chemist in the Department of Agriculture, had battled unsuccessfully for over a decade to secure federal legislation requiring proper labels on food and drugs. In the absence of such regulation, adulterated food products and bogus medicines flooded the market. Conservatives lampooned Wiley as "chief janitor and policeman of the people's insides." In the Senate, Nelson Aldrich emerged as the most vocal opponent of regulatory measures. "Are we going to take up the question as to what a man shall eat and what a man shall drink," he scornfully asked, "and put him under severe penalties if he is eating or drinking something different from what the chemists of the Agricultural Department think it is desirable for him to eat or drink?"

Pressure for reform began to build, however, with the publication of two groundbreaking articles in *Collier's* magazine. Interested in commissioning an investigative piece on the patent medicine industry, the editor of the *Ladies' Home Journal*, Edward Bok, reached out to S. S. McClure to find a writer capable of painstaking research. McClure introduced Bok to Mark Sullivan, a recent graduate of the Harvard Law School. Sullivan's article proved too technical and too extensive for the *Ladies' Home Journal*, but Bok brought it to *Collier's*, where it attracted widespread attention.

Sullivan's research yielded some stunning discoveries. The Lydia E. Pinkham Company, a celebrated patent medicine firm, advertised its numerous compounds for ailing women beneath the kindly and intelligent visage of Mrs. Pinkham—offering the promise that she would personally answer letters and dispense advice to inquiring customers. When Sullivan traveled to her hometown of Lynn, Massachusetts, and learned that she had been dead for over two decades, he took a picture of the inscription on her headstone: "Lydia E. Pinkham. Died May 17, 1883."

Less grimly humorous but far more pernicious was the young journalist's revelation that a secret clause had been written into the advertising contracts of thousands of newspapers across the country. At that time, patent medicines provided the largest source of advertising revenue for newspapers, and this clause stipulated that the contract would be canceled if material detrimental to the industry appeared anywhere in the paper. From William White, who had refused to take patent medicine ads in the *Emporia Gazette*, Sullivan obtained an original copy of the contract form.

The success of Sullivan's piece prompted *Collier's* to commission a ten-part investigative series on the patent medicine industry modeled after *McClure's* exposés. In fact, the writer of the series, Samuel Hopkins Adams, had been on *McClure's* staff before moving to *Collier's*. Adams procured experts to test more than two hundred patent medicines, a great majority of which were revealed as either "harmless frauds or deleterious drugs": an ointment containing clay and glycerin was marketed as a cancer cure; a pink starch and sugar pill promised to remedy paralysis; Isham's Spring Water claimed rheumatism would vanish within days. Even more worrisome, many concoctions were found to contain significant quantities of alcohol and narcotics, potentially leading the unwary toward addiction. Laboratories claiming to test these medicines turned out to be fraudulent or nonexistent.

For the first time, public pressure impelled a bill regulating food and drugs "to run the gauntlet of the upper house in safety." After reaching the House, however, "it slept. And it slept." For four months, Speaker Joe Cannon refused to bring the legislation to the floor for a vote. Finally, the national uproar over diseased meat forced his hand. On June 30, 1906, reformers were at last able to celebrate the passage of the Pure Food and Drug Act. The bill "would not have had the slightest chance" of surviving in the House, Senator Beveridge observed, had it not been for "the agitation" generated by the meat inspection amendment. This landmark bill authorized the federal government to examine the contents of processed food and patent medicines, forbade the sale of adulterated or misbranded food and drugs, and required that every package and bottle be properly labeled.

"DURING NO SESSION OF CONGRESS since the foundation of the Government," the *New York Times* proclaimed, "has there been so much done, first, to extend the Federal power of regulation and control over the business of the country, and second, to cure and prevent abuses of corporation privileges." Had Congress accomplished even one of the three major steps toward railroad regulation, meat inspection, or food and drug oversight, one midwestern paper observed, the first session of the 59th Congress would have been historic. Taken together, these three monumental measures marked "the beginning of a new epoch in federal legislation—governmental regulations on corporations and the invocation of the police power, so to speak, to stay the hand of private greed" and protect the general welfare.

No sooner had journalists illuminated a problem than the fight to secure a remedy had begun. By the spring of 1906, it was virtually certain that Congress would pass measures to regulate the railroads and the food and drug industry; only the timing and nature of those regulations remained to be determined. "For pass them they must," McClure's biographer noted. "That verdict had already been reached by the people."

The momentum of the progressive agenda continued with an employer's liability law for the District of Columbia; the Antiquities Act that granted the president authority to declare national monuments on federal lands; and statehood bills for Arizona and New Mexico. Conservatives railed against "the most amazing program of centralization" ever enacted, and Wall Street warned that Roosevelt was only "sowing the seeds" of revolution. But the American people overwhelmingly agreed with the president's declaration that this Congress had accomplished "more substantive work for good than any Congress has done at any session since he became familiar with public affairs."

Even Democratic newspapers "reluctantly" acknowledged the unprecedented efficacy of the 59th Congress and the remarkable leadership of the president. "The public confidence has been greatly restored in our law-makers," observed the *Detroit Free Press*, "inasmuch as strongly reformative measures have been adopted in the face of tremendous private interests, the sole spur necessary being an insistent public demand, clearly defined."

Yet even as he gloried in the moment, Theodore Roosevelt sensed that he would never again achieve this magnitude of success in directing domestic policy. "I do not expect to accomplish very much in the way of legislation after this Congress, and perhaps after this session," he wistfully confided to Kermit. "By next winter people will begin to think more about the next man who is to be President; and then, too, by that time it is almost inevitable that the revulsion of feeling against me should have come. It is bound to come some time, and it is extraordinary that it has not come yet."

CHAPTER EIGHTEEN

“Cast into Outer Darkness”

In this 1906 cartoon, *Puck* portrays “The Muck Rakers”—including Ida Tarbell and Ray Stannard Baker—in the aftermath of Roosevelt’s celebrated “Muckraking-Man” speech.

TO *MCCLURE’S* MATCHLESS TEAM OF journalists, the legislative record of the 59th Congress represented not a fait accompli, but the first successful skirmishes in a much larger war on the corrupt consolidation of wealth and power. “Signs everywhere now show a great moral awakening,” Baker told his father, “the cleaning out of rotten business & still more rotten politics. But we’ve only begun!” For the first time, Baker explained, “men were questioning the fundamentals of democracy, inquiring whether we truly had self-government in America, or whether it had been corrupted by selfish interests.” Most important, he continued, “this questioning came not alone from what one might call the working class,” but from middle America as well.

Investigative journalism, one historian has observed, had “assumed the proportions of a movement,” exerting an influence on the American consciousness “hardly less important than that of Theodore Roosevelt himself.” Magazines like *McClure’s* had become so politically significant that William Allen White quipped it was as if we had “Government by Magazine.” During these heady days, Finley Peter Dunne’s Irish bartender Mr. Dooley waxed poetic on the power of the printed word, noting that it had the strength “to make a star to shine on the lowliest brow” or to “blacken the fairest name in

Christendom." A mere three years before, Dooley explained, John D. Rockefeller had enjoyed the reputation of undiluted success and civic rectitude, until, "lo and behold, up in his path leaps a lady with a pen in hand and off goes John D. for the tall timbers." More astonishingly, Dooley marveled, the same few years had seen a work of fiction rout the beef trust, and Ray Baker's lead pencil produce "a revolution" in Congress, and "when a state [wanted] to elect a governor or a city a mayor," it turned not to professional politicians but to Lincoln Steffens. "Yes," decried Mr. Dooley, "the hand that rocks the fountain pen is the hand that rules the world."

To outsiders, the solidarity of McClure's enterprise appeared impregnable. By 1906, Sam McClure was considered among the ten most important men in America. His gifted writers operated more like an intimate team, an extended family, than the staff of a magazine. For Ida Tarbell, now in her twelfth year at *McClure's*, the magazine provided freedom, security, and comradeship. "Here was a group of people I could work with, without sacrifice or irritation," Tarbell later reflected in her autobiography. "Here was a healthy growing undertaking which excited me, while it seemed to offer endless opportunity to contribute to the better thinking of the country." Ray Baker felt the same way, recognizing the "rare group" McClure had assembled—all "genuinely absorbed in life, genuinely in earnest in their attitude toward it, and yet with humor, and yet with sympathy, and yet with tolerance." The magazine was "a success," Lincoln Steffens recalled. "We had circulation, revenue, power. In the building up of that triumph we had been happy, all of us; it was fun, the struggle."

In the spring of 1906, however, just when "the future looked fair and permanent," Ida reminisced, "the apparently solid creation was shattered and I found myself sitting on its ruins." Ray Baker's memoir registers similar grief and disbelief: "The institution that had seemed to me as permanent as anything could be in a transitory world—I mean *McClure's Magazine*—seemed to be crumbling under my feet." The schism that ended *McClure's* glorious era shocked the publishing world and devastated the staff.

Although McClure's team had long been accustomed to the rapid mood swings that drove Sam McClure into alternating periods of manic energy and pathological torpor, his creative wizardry had always compensated for his mercurial behavior. "Never forget," Ida Tarbell had counseled every time McClure riled the office with one of his outbursts, "that it was he & nobody else" who built the magazine, that all "the great schemes, the daring moves," the ideas that had propelled his writers' series and, finally, the writers themselves to national acclaim originated with him.

But in recent months the frenetic shifts from one grandiose plan to another had become more frequent, the melancholy periods infinitely darker. These radical vacillations in temperament compelled months of bed rest and even destroyed McClure's interest in the work he had always adored. While still capable of brilliance, McClure exhibited increasingly erratic behavior that took a cumulative toll on his colleagues. One of Sam McClure's escapades in the summer of 1903 had marked the first in a series of troubling events that became distressingly emblematic of the way his compulsions began to compromise the accomplishments and aspirations of his friends and colleagues at the magazine.

McClure had invited Ida to join him and his wife, Hattie, at Divonne-les-Bains, the popular spa town in eastern France on the border of Switzerland. Worried that her grinding work on the Standard Oil project was impacting her health, McClure hoped she would join them for the entire summer season. "You are infinitely precious to me," he told Ida. "I dreamed about you last night," he revealed, and "awoke this morning very anxious about you." If she found the pace of the series pressing her, he would gladly rein it in. "The truth is you have taken the forward place in my heart of all my friends," he wrote. "I want to live near you & be much with you during the coming years."

The prospect of a European vacation with Sam delighted Ida, but her work kept her in New York until July. In her absence, McClure invited a young poet, Florence Wilkinson, and a newly wed couple, Alice and Cale Rice, to accompany him to London and France. Wilkinson, a tall, dark-haired beauty, conducted poetry classes at her Greenwich Village studio. Four of her poems, at Sam's direction, had recently appeared in *McClure's*. The inclusion of Wilkinson's slight romantic verse in a magazine that had published the poetry of William Butler Yeats and A. E. Housman puzzled the staff, who suspected that their editor's fascination with the girl betrayed his usually impeccable judgment. The Rices would become well-known writers, but at the time Alice Hegan Rice had published her first novel and her husband had produced two slim volumes of poetry.

In London, McClure had arranged luxurious accommodations and memorable entertainment for his young friends, including a dinner at the Vagabondia with a circle of illustrious writers and an evening of theatre in the box of Bram Stoker, the author of *Dracula*. After arranging British publishers for the three aspiring writers, McClure brought them to Divonne. A week later, while Hattie stayed behind seeking relief for her rheumatism, the ever restless McClure set out with Wilkinson and the Rices for Chamonix and Mont Blanc. At the Hôtel du Paris, he selected a suite for the Rices on the second floor, while he and Florence Wilkinson stayed on the third. By the time Florence left the group for Bellagio, the intimacy that had developed between McClure and the young poet was apparent to the Rices.

When Ida Tarbell joined McClure and the Rices in the Swiss village of Gletsch, the newly organized traveling party set forth on a walking tour of the Alps. In the course of three weeks, they trekked from the valley of the Rhône to Lucerne and Zurich, and then on to the Engadine Valley in Italy, stopping at small inns along the way. Their "rollicking adventure," Alice Rice recalled, was directed by McClure, their "buccaneer leader," who "went through life like a tornado carrying everything in its wake." Reaching San Moritz in the late afternoon as fashionable carriages paraded along the thoroughfare, McClure was so exhilarated by the beauty of the mountain scene that he "lost his head completely," challenging Cale to scale a hill and then somersault down its slope. "So," Alice remembered, "to the utter amazement of the summer residents, taking their afternoon drive, two wild Americans came catapulting down the hillside, landing in the promenade almost under their horses' feet."

During that "never-to-be forgotten" European tour, Alice Rice and her husband forged a lifelong friendship with Ida Tarbell. Toward the end of their journey, the young couple, in all likelihood, confided the intimacy they had witnessed between Florence and Sam. Tensions grew until Ida could barely contain her tears when they parted, and McClure rightly feared that he had diminished himself in her eyes. "I have felt terribly sad since you left," he lamented in a subsequent letter. "I have no friend like you & I cannot endure to have hurt you & forfeited any of your confidence," he added, begging her forgiveness and promising never to "take another party to the Alps *of any kind*, just my family & you and other of my associates."

Ida's real distress was not driven by prudish disdain for his amorous entanglements; instead, she feared that Sam McClure's recklessness could tarnish the magazine with hypocrisy. In article after article, *McClure's* had exposed immoral businessmen and politicians. The authority of its painstaking investigations rested on the integrity of the writers and editors. Clearly, public scandal involving the magazine's charismatic founder would be a valuable weapon for those seeking to demean all their efforts.

After returning to New York that fall of 1903, Ida had shared her apprehensions with John Phillips. When Sam departed alone for a two-month European stay in November, they feared he planned to meet with Florence. His letters home revealed a mood of exultation: "I feel sure of myself as I haven't for many years. I am stronger on this trip than I was any time in ten years," he wrote from Berlin. Sam's buoyant tone persisted as he traveled through Germany and back to London. "I am so much keener & sharper than ever," he boasted. "I feel my vision broadened and feel strong physically and mentally." When McClure suddenly embarked on a solo holiday in the Appalachian Mountains in the spring, Tarbell and Phillips were convinced the sojourn was engineered to meet his lover.

In May 1904, the office erupted into turmoil when McClure directed the poetry editor, Witter Bynner, to purchase yet another of Florence's verses, this time a lover's poem that seemed directed to McClure himself. McClure composed a letter announcing its imminent publication by the magazine. He then asked Bynner to present the announcement to Miss Wilkinson personally, accompanied by a lavish arrangement of fresh flowers. When Tarbell and Phillips learned of these instructions, they upbraided Sam "like a naughty child." By this time, Hattie had learned about the affair, and turbulent days followed. A chastened McClure swore he would finally end the relationship and apparently informed Florence that they must sever all communication.

A week later, Sam left for Europe with his wife. Upon reaching Divonne, Hattie wrote Ida that something "very terrible" had come up during the ocean voyage: Sam had confessed to the existence of numerous letters written to Florence over the previous year. Immediately realizing "all the possibilities implied in that circumstance," Hattie urged her husband to have John Phillips retrieve his correspondence, but Sam "was wild at that idea." Instead, he sent off another letter to Florence, requesting the return of all his correspondence. "As the time approached when an answer could be expected," Hattie confided to Ida, Sam "fell into a terrible condition. He lost flesh, nearly a pound a day for nearly a week." Every day, he fretfully awaited the postman.

"I have so much to do right for," the overwrought McClure confessed to Ida during this interval. "I couldn't bear to lose you, not to speak of John or the others. . . . I am now at the bottom. I can go no further nor feel any sadder . . . I am about to take the desperate, but sure cure. Three weeks, in bed & milk." Realizing that their friend was ill equipped to resolve the situation, Tarbell and Phillips decided they must intervene. The awareness of extant letters exchanged between the illicit lovers confirmed their worst fears. "The Lord help us!" Ida exclaimed. Concluding that they must approach Florence Wilkinson directly, Ida considered visiting the Finger Lakes, where Florence was spending the summer. There, Ida would "make an appeal for courage," hopeful that the young woman would return the letters and refuse further contact with Sam. "I fear I would be hard on her," she admitted to John, as they considered their options, "but I will honestly try to put that out of my mind and help the girl if she will let me." In the end, Ida decided it might be wiser for Phillips to make the appeal, since it was "quite natural" that Florence should "feel resentment" toward her. The shy Phillips agreed to undertake the unpleasant task, meeting with Florence in upstate New York, where he secured her promise to return the letters and refrain from further communication with McClure.

Although Florence initially kept her part of the bargain, Sam could not keep his. "I have received six or seven letters and two cable messages," Florence informed Phillips. The letters, she told him, "I have returned mostly sealed as they came. It hurts me more than words can say." She had indeed sent a packet containing all McClure's correspondence, but Florence could not bear to reject unopened all his new letters. "I think his health is suffering unnecessarily under the strain of absolute silence," she wrote. "I think, too, he is in an agony of doubt as to my feelings toward him. I wish he could know that I love him as well as ever—though I am never to see him." Despite Phillips's concerns, she desperately wished to post one letter assuring Sam that "the love by itself is not wrong." Phillips should understand that "it was not humanly possible for his side to snap off so suddenly," though she would do her utmost to ease the situation.

McClure's longtime friend and London office manager Mary Bisland reported to Ida that Sam could not stop talking about Florence, protesting that he had been "wretched & restless" since the separation and insisting that he had "not the very vaguest idea of giving her up," though he feared she was now determined to end the affair. At times, McClure seemed to listen to reason, making "very solemn promises" to Hattie that he would devote himself to her and that she would once again work in the office by his side. But such pledges alternated with dark declarations that he would leave New York for a year or more, perhaps never to return. "He said he was a hurt animal who wanted to crawl into a hole and hide forever," Hattie sadly told Ida. "My heart is broken to see how weak he is. . . . He must learn over again to live with me and do right."

Yet even during his most depressed days in Europe, McClure never failed to follow every detail of the magazine's progress, continuing to provide valuable input. Writing to Tarbell in June 1904, he captured the vision articulated in recent articles: "The struggle for possession of absolute power which you find in your work among capitalists & Steffens finds among politicians & Baker finds among labor unions, is the age-long struggle & human freedom has been won only by continual & tremendous effort." Much as he admired Steffens's articles on corruption, he warned Phillips that they were "full of dynamite, far & away the most terrible stuff we can handle." Steffens "must never be rushed," he further cautioned, and his use of invective must be carefully curtailed. In the article on Wisconsin, for example, Steffens had accused Senator John Spooner of bribing state legislators to obtain his Senate seat. "Unless Spooner was elected by bribery, we must clear him," McClure instructed. "Either he or the magazine must be cleared." The article on Nelson Aldrich would be equally "sensational" and "must be very understated and very accurate." Compounding his unease, McClure intuited that the atmosphere at the magazine had become less collegial. He feared that with each writer "working in his own little cubicle, in his own little field," each would fail "to get the inspiration or the information that would vitalize his work, from other departments."

His perceptions were by and large astute, but Sam McClure also fired off a series of ill-tempered critiques that upset staffers in New York. They bristled at his particularly high-handed indictment of an internal advertisement extolling the magazine's growing reputation. "The man who is responsible for this advt is relieved from further ad writing absolutely," McClure haughtily ordered, complaining, "Why in the name of ordinary decency and modesty do we have to vaunt ourselves like this, saying we are the best. . . . We act like a spoiled, over-petted and over-praised, but ill-bred small boy." He implored Hattie to write a separate letter conveying to everyone in the office the depth of his displeasure. Henceforth, he demanded, not a single ad should be run without his express approval. Put to bed under doctor's orders to begin the dreaded milk cure yet again, Hattie reported, he had asked her to read some of the magazine's recent short stories, which she had concluded were "very poor, trashy, empty things . . . far below the old McClure standard." Future stories, he then insisted, should be sent to Divonne so Hattie could determine if they seemed "unworthy." Phillips patiently answered Sam's diatribes, but he began to wonder if his oldest friend would ever be healthy enough to return to full-time work.

Hattie's determination to forgive her husband's past indiscretions was severely tested in July 1904 when she received a shattering letter from Miss Wilkinson. Florence had learned that she was not the only "other" woman in Sam's life. Her "dearest" friend, Edith Wherry, had revealed her own romantic relationship with McClure, which had apparently developed after the fateful European vacation. Florence had written Hattie in a fit of jealous anger, intending to injure Sam in his wife's eyes. The distressing missive spurred Sam into belated recognition that he would have to take control of a quickly deteriorating situation. "Yesterday," he wrote to Phillips, "Mrs. McClure received a letter from Florence that brought about a condition that resulted in my making a complete finis to the terrible affair & I have so written Miss W. You have done nobly & Miss Tarbell but now the matter is finished absolutely. . . . There is no possible chance for further troubles."

McClure managed to convince his wife that Miss Wherry's confession was a mere figment of the young girl's imagination, and the troubled couple headed home with a commitment to resume their marriage. While Hattie admitted that her heart was still "wrung with the anguish of it all," she told Sam that she was willing to leave everything in the past now that he had ended his "strange wanderings."

Back home, Sam professed his resolve to abandon all distraction and philandering, insisting to Ida Tarbell that her devoted efforts had "saved" him. He was so "horrified at the awful course of the past year or two" that he dared not dwell on it, fearing he would "never again be first" in her esteem and affections. If he were unable to regain her confidence, he told her, that alone would serve as lasting "punishment" for all he had done. Despite his contrition, there remained a disagreeable postscript to the Wherry episode. When Sam was in Chicago months later, Edith Wherry sent a manuscript to Hattie with the alarming title "The Shame of S. S. McClure, Illustrated by Letters and Original Documents." Miss Wherry claimed that she was determined "to live henceforth in truth & honor." Accordingly, "the wall of lies" which had sheltered her liaison with Sam must be razed. Hattie brought the explosive manuscript to the office, seeking the counsel of Tarbell and Phillips. An urgent telegram was dispatched, urging McClure's immediate return to New York. When he arrived the next day, the staff drew up a plan of financial compensation to suppress the manuscript.

McClure's return to the magazine seemed to revive him. Bursting with new concepts, he proposed that Steffens embark on an investigation of life insurance companies and that Tarbell take on the U.S. Senate, predicting that "the whole future" of the country would be determined by "that most powerful ruling body." During a trip through the Midwest in the summer of 1905, he stopped in Emporia to visit William Allen White and reported that he himself was "getting along splendidly" in both "his work and learning" and that he was poised "to do greater editing than ever before."

Relieved to witness the lift in McClure's spirits, Phillips and Tarbell nevertheless mistrusted his leadership after the enervating months of crises. Not only did Tarbell ignore his suggestion to study the Senate; she had also, McClure sorrowfully noted, neglected to write to him during his travels. "I thought when I came back," he told her, "I could stand the years of waiting until I earned your confidence and regained my place with you & Mr. Phillips." Now, McClure feared that things "would never be the same," and that realization placed "a heavy, heavy load" on his heart. "My mind constantly dwells in the past & more especially the first four years of the magazine," he plaintively confided to Ida. "They were the golden years of my life . . . I often dream of being back with you all. I feel also how much I have done to destroy the most precious possession of my life."

Impelled by a feverish desire to reclaim the affection and respect of his colleagues, McClure spent days and nights developing an elaborate plan for a new monthly companion magazine to *McClure's*. Transported by manic excitement, the publisher convinced himself that it would be "the greatest periodical ever published in America." Once his staff understood the brilliance of the scheme, he exulted, they would acknowledge that he was "a stronger and more productive man than ever." In late November 1905, he sent the finished prospectus to Tarbell. He was sharing "a tremendous secret," he wrote, which he hoped would mollify any anxieties she might continue to harbor.

McClure's Universal Journal, the second monthly he envisioned, would be larger than the current magazine, attracting the most famous novelists and short story writers in the world and featuring serious articles about current issues. Single copies would cost but five cents, one third the price of *McClure's* magazine. The lower price would be accomplished by utilizing less expensive paper and relying on pen-and-ink illustrations instead of costly copperplate engravings. McClure predicted a net yearly income of $2 million and proposed to found the company by issuing nearly $13 million in stock. The staff of *McClure's* would manage both the current magazine and the new journal.

But Sam McClure's extravagant ambitions were not confined to the publishing world. The new monthly would be affiliated with four interlocking, profitable enterprises that would help solve pressing social problems: a People's Bank; a People's Life Insurance Company; a People's University to issue textbooks on all subjects and develop correspondence courses; and a Universal Library to supply the public with affordable copies of great works of literature no longer covered by copyright. In addition to these boggling schemes, McClure planned to purchase 1,000 acres of land upon which to build a model community with affordable housing.

Far from being intrigued, Ida Tarbell considered McClure's grandiosity a manifestation of his illness, a manic projection that eclipsed the gratification of real accomplishment. His compulsion to "build a bigger, a more imposing House of McClure" would only jeopardize the magazine to which she had devoted her best years. *McClure's Universal Journal* would inevitably compete for the same readers as *McClure's* magazine, diminishing the value of her stock in the magazine and destabilizing the entire enterprise. Most troubling of all, whether the product of megalomania or the most beneficent of motives, McClure's scheme of consolidating different enterprises under the same roof echoed the very trusts against which she and her colleagues had waged war. Her instincts told her that this was "the plan which was eventually to wreck his enterprises."

When John Phillips saw McClure's prospectus, he understood more clearly than Tarbell that the company's finances would never support a venture of this magnitude. As the largest minority stockholder and managing editor during Sam's repeated absences, Phillips had "all the different branches of the work in his hand"—the advertising department, the editorial section, the book publishing arm, the printing press, the art department. Over the years, Sam's traveling expenses had been a continuing drain on the treasury. In his expansive moods, the publisher would impulsively purchase twice as many articles as the magazine could possibly use. He had signed deals to extend the company's operations that ultimately had to be abandoned at heavy cost. He had rewarded his writers and artists with money and generous gifts. Though the magazine itself continued to flourish, the company was under stress.

For more than a decade, the steadfast Phillips had anchored the magazine. While Sam wandered through Europe, the quiet editor remained at his desk from early morning until late at night, managing the business details and working intimately with each of the writers. Ray Baker later said that he had never known an editor "who had so much of the creative touch, a kind of understanding which surprised the writer himself with unexpected possibilities in his own subjects." An "uncompromising" critic, Phillips told his writers exactly why their articles did not work, often recommending remedies and suggesting "felicities of expression which the author would have liked to think of first." William Allen White declared that without Phillips, the staff "would not know where to go or what to do."

The dynamic between Phillips and McClure had been established for a quarter of a century: when McClure was editor-in-chief of the college newspaper, John kept the paper running while Sam disappeared for days at a time; in Boston, Phillips edited the bicycling magazine, the *Wheelman*, while Sam traveled around New England in search of writers and ideas; in the early days of their New York syndicate, Phillips managed operations while McClure crossed the ocean to meet with Kipling, James Barrie, and Conan Doyle. When they were young, John had so admired Sam's energy, his "push and business ability," that he would readily have changed places with him. As Sam's mood swings intensified over the years, Phillips willingly assumed more and more of his partner's responsibilities. Finally Phillips's vaunted patience snapped—the combined impact of the Wilkinson affair, the vituperative letters from Divonne, and Sam's preemptive hiring of a high-salaried art director for the new venture proved too much.

After that rash hiring decision, Tarbell and Phillips quickly resolved to work in tandem and persuade McClure to abandon his scheme. During the Wilkinson crisis, the two had formed a close bond. Faced with this new catastrophe, they spent many hours together, strategizing over lunches in the city and dinners in each other's homes. The affection and trust Tarbell had once reserved for McClure was now claimed by Phillips. "He is certainly the rarest and most beautiful soul on earth," she told Albert Boyden, *McClure's* managing editor. In mid-January 1906, craving respite from the office maelstrom, Tarbell joined John and Jennie Phillips on a trip to Kansas, Colorado, and the Grand Canyon. In Emporia, they stayed with William Allen White, who accompanied them for the remainder of the trip.

"It has been a glorious trip," Tarbell wrote cheerfully to Boyden. Their buoyant mood was soon spoiled when they received a series of letters forwarded from the office indicating that "the Chief" had defied their objections and moved ahead in their absence to incorporate the McClure's Journal Company. Phillips "as usual is an angel & has written [McClure] a beautiful letter," Tarbell reported to Boyden, but conditions in the office had reached a "diabolical" stage, requiring a unified action to stop the madness.

McClure informed Phillips that his letter had come the very morning that the new journal's art director arrived at the office. The distraction "thoroughly unfitted me for the work with him," Sam peevishly objected. "I'm engaging upon a tremendous task, a noble and splendid one. I have the greatest idea for a periodical ever invented, and am entering upon an enterprise that will benefit everyone also tremendously, and nothing but a large recovery of my original calmness of mind, and what at one time was unruffable good nature, will enable me to stand what are really petty and useless annoyances and opposition." As "one of the most successful business organizers in this country," he continued, "it never occurred to me that having founded one business I could not found another." McClure went on to assert that his mind was "settled." He would not only launch *McClure's Universal Journal*, but would create a weekly magazine in the near future. Phillips, McClure suggested, had "a tendency to look upon the dark side of things." He recommended that his oldest friend take a two-year paid vacation to gain perspective on his "ridiculous" concerns.

Additional letters from anxious staff members soon reached the vacationers, pleading with them to return before the enterprise suffered irreparable damage. "All S.S. wants is sympathy and a recognition of his genius," Dan McKinley wrote. Their editor, he continued, "feels he is not master in his own shop; he feels that his opinions and ideas are no longer considered worthy of serious thought." Albert Boyden acknowledged that those who remained in the office could no longer cope with the situation. "I wish we did have the brains and wisdom and patience to work it out without you," he wistfully wrote, "but we have not."

By the time the entire staff reconvened in New York, Phillips had reached a desperate resolution: If he could not persuade McClure to abandon his vainglorious scheme, he would resign. "It was a momentous decision for a man of forty-five to make," Phillips wrote in an unpublished memoir. "The impelling reasons were personal, almost spiritual . . . I felt that I could not submit to being wrenched into courses and proposed undertakings that would arouse inner dissension with no prospect of peace. As soon as the decision was made, there was a great calm, a serene contentment."

When McClure learned of Phillips's decision, he summoned Tarbell to his office and demanded to know whether "anybody else is going." She informed him that she, too, would resign. Staying on without Phillips, she insisted, "would be like living in a house with a corpse." At the prospect of her desertion, McClure broke down. "You, too, Ida Tarbell," he accused. Tarbell recorded in her diary that night that as McClure railed against their departure and reiterated his abiding love for her, all she could think of was "Napoleon at Fontainebleau." Her attempts to explain to McClure that for Phillips it was a question of "his own soul"—that it was no longer possible "to live in such humiliation as he has had to endure"—failed to penetrate his hysteria. Finally, she wrote, McClure "sprang up & flung his arms around me & kissed me—left weeping & I sat down sobbing hysterically but am more convinced than ever that we are right."

In the immediate aftermath of their declared intention to resign, a compromise was nearly reached. Phillips and Tarbell agreed to stay if McClure would "democratize" the management of the magazine by creating a board of directors and putting a portion of his stock into a trusteeship administered by Tarbell, Phillips, Steffens, and Baker. When McClure acquiesced, the three of them went off for an awkward lunch together. McClure returned to the office looking "cheerful" for the first time in weeks. An agreement was drawn up.

Then, just as swiftly as McClure had agreed, he changed his mind. The notion that the magazine had become an institution "beyond the ability of one man" to run, he now told Phillips, was "utterly absurd." Though he traveled a great deal, such excursions had always proved invaluable to the magazine. "My facilities for getting to know public opinion and the opinion of able thinkers is vastly greater than it was ten years ago," he insisted. "The management of this magazine is probably not one-thousandth as difficult as Abraham Lincoln's job; but Lincoln could never have managed his job had it not been for the extraordinary facilities that went with his position for sensing public opinion."

The more he contemplated the matter, the more he realized it would be "utterly impossible" for him to accept a lesser role in the magazine. "When you read history," he proclaimed, "you find that kings who have come to the end of their tether, as a rule would suffer death rather than give up part of their power." By grandiose analogy, he would rather sell his majority interests than relinquish control. Tarbell and Phillips immediately offered to purchase his *McClure's* stock. Even as this new document was generated, however, McClure again rescinded the decision. "I cannot leave the magazine," he declared to Tarbell. "I would soon lose my mind." Discussion then shifted to the possibility that he would buy out both Phillips's and Tarbell's stock, enabling them to start their own magazine.

Throughout these negotiations and reversals, Albert Brady's brother Curtis recalled, "the entire office was embroiled in the turmoil." Members of the staff "were compelled to take sides whether or not they wished to do so, but some did it secretly—afraid to express their opinions aloud. It was not unusual to see small groups of men, with their heads together, speaking in undertones, and then busy themselves when someone else came along." It soon became clear that the majority of the staff backed Phillips and Tarbell, including Steffens, Baker, Boyden, and John Siddall.

Explaining his decision to resign in a letter to his father, Steffens observed that McClure had been away for months, "playing and getting well." Then, upon his return, he had embarked upon "a big, fool scheme of founding a new magazine with a string of banks, insurance companies, etc., and a capitalization of $15,000,000. It was not only fool, it was not quite right." Indeed, it seemed "a speculative scheme," designed to extract money from investors that would never be repaid, much like the schemes *McClure's* magazine had been reporting on over the years. "Having built up *McClure's,* given it purpose and character, and increased its circulation so that it was a power as well as a dividend-payer," Steffens maintained, "we did not propose to stand by and see it exploited and used, even by the owner."

During this tumultuous period, Ray Baker had been absent from the office completing his railroad articles. Warned of the situation by a stream of alarming letters, he confided to his wife on March 9 that McClure had "become so utterly unbalanced & unreasonable that he is almost past working with." A week later he grimly concluded that "dynamite, nitroglycerine & black powder" had been laid and could not be defused. When the time came, Baker decided to join his departing associates, who, as he told his father, "are not only my friends, but who have contributed largely to whatever success I have attained." The departure left him painfully adrift: "I was left with no certainty, at the moment anyway, of continuing to do the work to which I was most deeply devoted; I was lost in a fog of contention and antagonism." Recalling the discord years later, Baker acknowledged that "in the afterlook these ills seem trivial enough: at that time, they were all but catastrophic."

As RUMORS SPREAD ABOUT THE impending breakup at *McClure's*, many in the press mistakenly attributed the schism to a memorable address that President Roosevelt delivered that same spring. Exasperated by a sensationalist attack on the U.S. Senate in a magazine owned by his hated political rival, William Randolph Hearst, Roosevelt denounced investigative journalists as muckrakers, bent on relentless negativity and dispiriting exploitation of the nation's ills. "In Bunyan's *Pilgrim's Progress*," he began, "you may recall the description of the Man with the Muck-rake, the man who could look no way but downward." Bunyan's muckraker, he suggested, "typifies the man who in this life consistently refuses to see aught that is lofty, and fixes his eyes with solemn intentness only on that which is vile and debasing."

The coincidence of this speech and the first reports of dissension at the magazine led reporters to speculate that McClure had responded to the president's denunciation of muckraking with a decision to soften future exposés. According to such accounts, Tarbell, Steffens, and Baker, unwilling to accept the change in policy, had deserted to form their own magazine. McClure unequivocally rejected reports that Roosevelt's speech had in any way "affected his views of what a magazine ought to be." *McClure's*, he insisted, would continue to "report the activities of contemporary life," as it had always done. Nonetheless, the lingering implication that the editor had planned "to muzzle his writers" exacerbated McClure's distress.

"The Treason of the Senate," the explosive series that aroused Roosevelt's ire, was conceived by William Randolph Hearst, who had long targeted the trust-dominated Senate in his newspapers. During Hearst's short career as a Democratic congressman from New York and throughout his failed presidential run in 1904, the flamboyant publisher had agitated for a constitutional amendment stipulating popular election of senators. A democratic process, he argued, should replace the current system of election by state legislatures. The 1905 purchase of his first monthly magazine, *The Cosmopolitan*, provided an ideal forum to continue his campaign. He offered David Graham Phillips, the best-selling progressive novelist, a handsome price and substantial research help to undertake an investigation of the Senate's betrayal of the public interest. The first of nine monthly installments appeared in March 1906, just as Roosevelt was battling to secure Senate approval of his signature bill to regulate the railroads.

"Treason is a strong word," the David Graham Phillips series began, "but not too strong, rather too weak, to characterize the situation in which the Senate is the eager, resourceful, indefatigable agent of interests as hostile to the American people as any invading army could be, and vastly more dangerous; interests that manipulate the prosperity produced by all, so that it heaps up riches for the few." In the course of the series, Phillips would sketch individual biographies of eighteen Republican and three Democratic senators. Each portrait revealed "a triangulation" between the senator's eagerness to assist corporations, the increase of his personal wealth, and the expansion of his influence in Washington. Though criticism of the Senate's hostility to progressive reform was not new, the scathing language and focused attack on the most powerful Republican leaders (including Lodge, Aldrich, Elkins, and Knox) attracted widespread attention. The circulation of *The Cosmopolitan* doubled overnight. Throughout the country, small daily and weekly newspapers reprinted individual articles. "Little wonder," the historian George Mowry observes, "that Theodore Roosevelt feared a general discrediting of his party, the national legislature, and indeed the administration if the effects of such charges were not somehow dissipated."

New York senator Chauncey Depew, who had nominated Roosevelt for governor in 1898, was targeted in the first piece. "For those who like the sight of a corpse well beaten up," one newspaper editorialized, this "mean" portrait deserved "the championship belt." Under a picture of Depew, the caption announced: "Here is the archetypal Face of the Sleek, Self-Satisfied American Opportunist in Politics and Plunder." Railroad barons Cornelius and William Vanderbilt were identified as the men who first enlisted Depew in "personal and official service. . . . And ever since then have owned [him] mentally and morally." Throughout the article, charges of "boodler" and "robber" were leveled, alongside the labels "coward" and "sniveling sycophant."

Although he never accused Depew of outright venality, Phillips argued that the New York senator, like many of his colleagues, was thoroughly beholden to the campaign contributions of the special interests.

The tone of the piece appalled Roosevelt. He told his journalist friend Alfred Henry Lewis that while he had the "heartiest sympathy and commendation" for responsible attacks on corruption, "hysteria and sensationalism" would fail to produce "any permanent good," and the country would conclude that "the liar is in the long run as noxious as the thief." The series produced outrage in the conservative press. *The Critic* accused Phillips of "sowing the seeds of anarchy." The New York *Sun* asserted that debasing an institution created by the founding fathers was tantamount to "playing with matches in dangerous proximity to a powder magazine." Speaking in defense of the Senate, Henry Cabot Lodge declared: "Slander and misrepresentation directed against individuals are not of much importance, but wise institutions and free systems of government, painfully wrought, tried in the fires of sacrifice and suffering, should endure."

Concerned that the "epidemic of Congress-baiting" would jeopardize his regulatory program, Roosevelt devised a clever counterstroke. On March 17, 1906, at the annual dinner of the Gridiron Club, an informal assembly of reporters, editors, cabinet officials, and leaders in business and academia, Roosevelt delivered his own piece of propaganda. After a series of humorous skits, the president spoke without notes for forty-five minutes, railing against "muckrakers," who saturated magazines and newspapers "with sensational articles," dredging all that was bleak and corrupt while "ignoring at the same time the good in the world." He had initially planned to indict David Graham Phillips, but Elihu Root persuaded him that a personal attack would only fuel the writer's celebrity. By avoiding a direct condemnation of the "Treason" series, however, Roosevelt inadvertently left the audience speculating about his intended targets.

In truth, the president's attack on the muckrakers reflected more than momentary anger at Hearst and David Graham Phillips. His exasperation with the proliferation of increasingly sensational and shoddily investigated exposure journalism had been slowly building. Although "the masters" at *McClure's* typically invested months and even years of careful research in their studies, a host of less meticulous and principled "imitators" had followed in their wake. In the competition for "hot stuff," politicians and businessmen were being "tried and found guilty in magazine counting rooms before the investigation is begun." The carefully documented quest for truth had been supplanted by slapdash, often slanderous accusations. Even when the articles rested on solid documentary evidence, Roosevelt feared that an incessant fixation on corruption had begun "to produce a very unhealthy condition of excitement and irritation in the public mind," leading to an "enormous increase in socialistic propaganda."

As usual, Peter Dunne's Mr. Dooley trenchantly captured public agitation. There once was a time, the Irish bartender opined, when reading popular magazines calmed the mind. Readers came away feeling that life was a "glad, sweet song." Indeed, one could drape his "watch on the knob" on an unlocked door, confident it would be there in the morning. Now, however, a reader turning the pages of any magazine would discover that "everything has gone wrong." Corruption and double-dealing today were so rampant that "the world is little better," Dooley concluded, "than a convict's camp." Roosevelt "immensely" enjoyed Mr. Dooley's outlook. "I get sick of people who are always insisting upon nothing but the dark side of life," he told Dunne. "There are a lot of things that need correction in this country; but there is not the slightest use of feeling over-pessimistic about it."

National fatigue with the ubiquitous literature of exposure had already set in when Roosevelt spoke to the Gridiron Club. "The public cannot stand at attention with its eyes fixed on one spot indefinitely," the literary critic Edwin E. Slosson shrewdly observed. "It is bound to get restive, and seek diversion in other interests." A Wisconsin municipal court judge expressed the resentment of many: "It is getting so nowadays that the man or corporation that accumulates property to any extent is made the subject of these attacks." Nor, a fellow Wisconsin citizen observed, should a man be considered "a criminal simply because he holds a public office."

THE MORNING AFTER THE GRIDIRON speech, Lincoln Steffens called on the president. "Well," Steffens reproached, "you have put an end to all these journalistic investigations that have made you." Roosevelt insisted that he had not intended a general indictment of legitimate reporters like Steffens. He was simply defending "poor old Chauncey Depew" against a terribly unfair portrait in the Hearst press. Steffens remained unconvinced, correctly sensing the president's growing impatience with the never-ending exposés—even as he relied on them to mobilize public opinion.

In fact, on several occasions the previous year, Roosevelt had directly criticized Steffens for his tendency to "repeat as true unfounded gossip of a malicious or semimalicious character." It was "an absurdity," he had scolded Steffens, to claim that Senator Aldrich was "the boss of the United States."

Such a preposterous claim carried "a sinister significance," for "[we] suffer quite as much from exaggerated, hysterical, and untruthful statements in the press as from any wrongdoing by businessmen or politicians." Roosevelt had also decried Steffens's characterization of Postmaster General Henry C. Payne as the ringleader of a corrupt effort to fix legislators and thereby destroy Governor La Follette's legislative program. "Poor Payne is sick either unto death or nigh unto death," Roosevelt had complained to Lodge, two days before Payne died. "This attack on him in *McClure's Magazine* by Steffens was, I think, the immediate cause of breaking him down; and I am convinced that it is an infamously false attack."

Nevertheless, Steffens had continued to enjoy unusual access to the White House. When he arrived in Washington to investigate whether the corruption uncovered in city and state governments extended to the federal level, Roosevelt offered to help. The president provided the celebrated journalist with a card inscribed: "To any officer or employee of the Government, Please tell Mr. Lincoln Steffens anything whatever about the running of the government that you know (not incompatible with the public interest) and provided only that you tell him the truth—no matter what it may be—I will see that you are not hurt. T. Roosevelt."

The resultant syndicated series, however, nettled Roosevelt. To Steffens, the signal question America faced could not be answered with the passage of railroad regulation or food and drug laws, but only with fundamental change to the corrupt system that invested special interests with undue power at the expense of the people. "I'd rather make our government represent us than dig the canal; the President would rather dig the canal and regulate railway rates. So he makes his 'deal' with the speaker and I condemn it."

Roosevelt was especially angered by reformers' accusations that he was too compromising in his efforts to remedy the abuses of capitalism. "In stating your disapproval of my efforts to get results," he wrote Steffens, "which of course must be gotten by trying to come to a working agreement with the Senate and House and therefore by making mutual concessions, you have often said or implied that I ought to refuse to make any concessions, but stand uncompromisingly for my beliefs, and let the people decide. As a matter of fact I have come a great deal nearer getting what I wanted than, for instance, Governor La Follette."

Roosevelt grumbled that Steffens and his friends failed to understand the requisites of practical leadership—a sense of when to move forward, when to hold back, when to mobilize the public, when to negotiate behind closed doors. Leadership that led to genuine progress depended upon an acute sense of timing, a feel for both the public and the congressional pulse. Yet in recent months it had seemed that crusading writers were intent on usurping his authority, creating the intolerable impression that rather than "summoning," Roosevelt "was being dragged."

All these frustrations had informed Roosevelt's decision to castigate the "new journalism" at the Gridiron Club Dinner. Remarks at the informal club meeting were traditionally off the record, but word of the president's dramatic condemnation "spread like wildfire," along with speculation that he was referencing progressive writers such as Lincoln Steffens, Ray Baker, David Phillips, and Upton Sinclair. When Roosevelt announced his intention to reiterate his Gridiron message in a public address, Baker was dumbfounded, concerned that "such an attack might greatly injure the work which we were trying honestly to do." He finally decided to write a frank letter to the president. "I have been much disturbed at the report of your proposed address," Baker began. "Even admitting that some of the so-called 'exposures' have been extreme, have they not, as a whole, been honest and useful? and would not a speech, backed by all of your great authority, attacking the magazines, tend to give aid and comfort to these very rascals" whose activities were being exposed by hardworking journalists? Moreover, he warned, "the first to stop the work of letting in the light and air will be those who have been trying honestly to tell the whole truth, good and bad, and leave the field to the outright ranters and inciters."

Roosevelt was undeterred. "One reason I want to make that address," he replied the next day, "is because people so persistently misunderstand what I said." The president confided in Baker that "Hearst's papers and magazines" were his intended target and promised his speech would clarify that he abhorred "the whitewash brush quite as much as of mud slinging."

Roosevelt delivered his formal "Muckrake Man" address on April 14, 1906. That he seriously considered Baker's concerns is evident in his carefully measured speech. He cautioned that his words must not be distorted, insisting "at the risk of repetition" that the fight against corruption and exploitation must continue. Every word of reproach against the crusading journalists was counterbalanced with a word of commendation. He termed their investigations "indispensable," yet explained that when muckrakers penned "sensational, lurid and untruthful" articles, they became "potent forces for evil." In the end, however, Roosevelt's vivid portrait of the muckraker eclipsed his positive remarks about investigative journalism. His speech was widely received as an indiscriminate attack on all reform journalists.

Commentators reflected that the president could not publicly speak "upon a question which is shaking the country from center to circumference without exercising a powerful influence upon one side of the other." And despite his "almost nervous dread" of misinterpretation, Roosevelt had "put into the hands of every trust magnate, every insurance thief, and every political corruptionist a handy weapon which will be used unconscionably for their defense." All such interests, one journal predicted, would "now plead not guilty, point to the 'muck rake' and seek shelter behind the portly figure of the President."

Baker read the speech as a profound betrayal. He noted sadly that while Roosevelt had indeed employed his "familiar balance of approval and disapproval," he had failed to distinguish between the sensationalist yellow press and the responsible journalists. "He did not 'think it worthwhile' to acknowledge the service of those men who had been striving to tell the truth, honestly and completely, whose work he had repeatedly approved, and for whose help he had again and again expressed his appreciation," Baker later wrote. Instead, the indelible image of the muckraker "classed all of us together."

Baker's alarm proved well founded: *McClure's* magazine, the most illustrious journal, was "singled out" for a devastating satire in *Life* magazine. Each of the writers of "McSure's" magazine—Ida Tarbarrell, Ray Standard Fakir, Sinkem Beffens—was viciously mocked in turn. "I'm giving my whole life to breaking the butterfly of a John Rockefeller upon the wheel of my ponderous articles," Tarbell/Tarbarrell was quoted as saying. "He's got too much money. If that isn't a shame, I'd like to know what a shame is!" In another scathing send-up, Steffens/Beffens humbly submitted to a supposed interview: "I'm not really great. I'm only eminent, unparalleled, superlatively remarkable." Pondering such achievement, the interviewer highlighted Steffens's process: "With only his suit-case and his gold rake studded with diamonds, he can take the morning train for an unknown city, rake off in a few hours the thick slime of municipal corruption and have a shame-shrieking article ready for McSure's by night."

"These satirical jabs cut [Baker] deeply," his biographer claims. "The bubble of devoted public service that had developed around his work had been irreparably punctured." Deeply demoralized to find his name among those "cast into outer darkness," Baker would never forgive Roosevelt. "I met the President many times afterward and there were numerous exchanges of letters," he recalled, "but while I could wonder at his remarkable versatility of mind, and admire his many robust human qualities, I could never again give him my full confidence, nor follow his leadership."

In the wake of the president's speech, morale among conservatives and corporate interests rallied. The New York *Sun* proclaimed that the muckrakers' era of exposure had come to an end: "It was a great day while it lasted, but it became too hot. The Muck-rakers worked merrily for a time in their own bright sunshine, and an unthinking populace applauded their performance. Now there are few to do them reverence." It was said, only partly in jest, that "rebaters and bribers" were "beginning to walk abroad with the old smile," sensing that "the tidal wave of magazine reform" was finally abating.

Progressives mounted an impassioned defense of the magazine crusaders. One supporter argued that these journalists numbered among "the loftiest and purest of living patriots, who have taken their professional and political lives in their hands that they might serve as 'soldiers of the common good.' " Their "long, laborious work" had initiated the "inspiring movement" for honest government; no fair-minded citizen could deny the "astonishingly great" influence of Ida Tarbell, Lincoln Steffens, or Ray Baker. "The day will come," one sympathetic commentator correctly predicted, "when the 'muck rake' will be borne through the streets as a triumphant emblem of reform," when the epithet "muckraker" would become "a badge of honor."

ON MAY 11, 1906, FOUR weeks after the president's speech, the *New York Times* confirmed that Phillips, Tarbell, Steffens, Baker, and Boyden were leaving *McClure's*. Furthermore, it was understood that the five journalists were "quietly planning to start a magazine venture of their own." After weeks of turmoil, McClure had finally agreed to buy out Phillips and Tarbell, whose combined stock was worth $187,000. He also promised each of them six months salary at full pay. "I am certain that it is not in my power at the present time adequately to reward them for their services, which no money could pay for," McClure told a business associate. "They leave me retaining my deepest love and affection and esteem and confidence. I think I may say that it is the greatest tragedy thus far of my life to lose them." With Baker and Steffens, he was equally generous, continuing their salaries while they completed work on already contracted projects. "I wish you all good fortune," he told Baker. "I have always enjoyed working with you and your work has been very successful in the magazine, and I am very sorry to lose you." Moved by his publisher's remarkable magnanimity, Steffens observed: "There was nothing mean about S. S. McClure."

In the aftermath of the schism, McClure lost not only his star writers but his partner, managing editor, and three top business executives as well. While some in the publishing world wondered if he could survive the loss of the inimitable team that had given the magazine "its chief features of life and popularity," Sam McClure proved surprisingly resilient in the face of catastrophe. Necessity compelled him to abandon his "colossal scheme" and focus all his energies on rebuilding the magazine. "I have really to look after almost every department," he told Hattie, "and am getting up material for the fall prospectus. I am standing it splendidly; I rarely get tired." Without Phillips to maintain daily operations, he could no longer escape responsibility and found himself "working harder" than ever before. In the office by 8 a.m., McClure remained at his desk long past midnight, sustaining himself on "three or four quarts of milk a day." After midnight, he retired to an apartment on a floor above the magazine's offices to read "masses of manuscripts," including portions of an autobiography by Mark Twain which his syndicate had agreed to publish.

In a matter of weeks, McClure managed to assemble an almost completely new roster of talent. Of the original team, only the poetry editor Witter Bynner, the manuscript reader Viola Roseboro, and Albert Brady's younger brothers—Curtis, Oscar, and Ed—remained. To replace Ida Tarbell, he relied upon Willa Cather, a little known fiction writer who would become a world-class novelist. He hired Will Irwin, a distinguished reporter from the New York *Sun*, as managing editor. Two first-rate investigative reporters, George Kibbe Turner and Burton Hendrick, joined the staff full time, along with Ellery Sedgwick, the future editor of the *Atlantic Monthly*. "The very name, *McClure's Magazine*, had an irresistible attraction for any young man," Sedgwick explained. Much as Tarbell, Baker, and Steffens had described their Chief in happier years, Sedgwick was mesmerized by McClure's "burning force," explaining how "everyone about him caught fire and he would inflame the intelligence of his staff into molten excitement."

Though his eager new writers lacked the renown of the original team, McClure reasoned that before long he would "be able to repeat the process" that had made Tarbell, Steffens, and Baker household names. The newly constituted group did indeed produce a number of significant investigations in the months that followed; but the tenor of the magazine, reflecting the temper of the nation, had changed. Even before Roosevelt delivered his "Muckrake Man" speech, McClure had sensed that public interest in the parade of public and private misbehavior was waning. "To go on now with the heavy exposure articles," he told his stockholders, "would not convert those who disagree with us, and those who agree with us don't need conversion."

Furthermore, the new staff members brought differing sensibilities and strategies to *McClure's*. Although Ellery Sedgwick had applauded the early efforts of the crusading journalists, he believed the time had come "to halt and to think soberly." Too many editors, he charged, had lost "all sense of responsibility" in the race for circulation. Ida Tarbell's replacement, Willa Cather, also had a profound influence on the magazine's direction. She edited a superb series on the Christian Science founder Mary Baker Eddy; but Cather's real genius lay in literature, in historical narratives rather than accounts of present-day political struggles and economic analyses. Consequently, while the quality of fiction and poetry in *McClure's* remained high, the impact of the investigative pieces diminished. *McClure's* was not alone; a similar shift took place in popular publications across the country, a literature "of distraction" gradually replacing the literature of "inquiry."

If "an exhilarating sense of excitement and adventure" permeated the revivified magazine in the early months, it was not long before McClure's mercurial temperament produced unbearable tensions within the newly organized staff. As managing editor, Will Irwin found it impossible to deal with the endless intrigues McClure manufactured. "As a curb on genius," he acknowledged, "I was not a success." Sedgwick reported that "the staff worked under some natural law of desperation. The chief was forever interrupting, cutting every sequence into a dozen parts." The dynamic had become frustrating: "A week in the McClure office was the precise reversal of the six busy days described in the first chapter of Genesis. It seemed to end in a world without form and void. From Order came forth Chaos." In fifteen months, both Sedgwick and Irwin were fired.

McClure soldiered on. For years, the fiction and poetry that he scouted and commissioned would continue to set the literary standard for American magazines. He published early stories by Damon Runyan and Joseph Conrad, introduced A. E. Housman's *Shropshire Lad* to the American public, and provided a forum for the new work of William Butler Yeats and Moira O'Neill. The company eventually foundered, hampered by the costs of buying out the departing writers and constructing a new printing plant on Long Island. Forced to economize, McClure could no longer continue his penchant for liberal spending to attract the most gifted writers. Nor could he afford to keep his book publishing arm, which he sold to Doubleday, Page & Company. The magazine never recovered the strength or influence it had exerted during its heyday.

Public disenchantment with sensationalist journalism and Theodore Roosevelt's dramatic caricature of the muckrakers may have conspired to diminish the stature and power of *McClure's*. The real corrosion of the magazine's intensive energy happened from within, however, precipitated by the same force that had made the enterprise great: the outsized personality and manic power of S. S. McClure himself.

THE SHIFTING PUBLIC MOOD ALSO presented difficulties for Phillips and the rest of the departing team. They had initially planned to launch their own venture, but when *The American Magazine*, a monthly "of good reputation," was offered for sale, they pooled their resources to meet the $400,000 price tag. At the time, *The American* was "just about holding its own, financially." By re-creating the publication as a writer's magazine, built upon their own good names, they hoped to raise the circulation and "make it profitable within a comparatively short time."

"All of us had plunged into the enterprise with astonishingly little regard for the future," Baker recalled. "No one of us had much money: we put into the common fund all we had and more." In addition, the friends decided to heavily cut their own paychecks until they turned a profit. If the magazine failed, Baker acknowledged, he stood "to lose everything." Still, he told his father, there was nothing "so dizzily stimulating" as building a new enterprise, "resting in complete confidence upon one's friends, devoted to what one considers high purposes, each sacrificing to the limit for the common cause."

For Steffens, too, trepidation mingled with excitement. "I feel as if I were at the crisis of my life," he wrote. "We are buying an old magazine which we propose to make the greatest thing of the kind that was ever made in this world—sincere, but good-natured; honest, but humorous; aggressive, but not unkind; a straight, hard fighter, but cheerful." Though Ida Tarbell seemed to Baker "the most dauntless of the adventurers," she fully recognized what was at stake. Each of them had "seen something in which they deeply believed go to pieces," she recalled. All of them "had been too cruelly bruised to take anything lightly."

William Allen White followed his friends to *The American Magazine*. Though not party to the bitter final months in the *McClure's* office, White had nevertheless determined long before that despite Sam McClure's "spark of genius," the magazine's stability and success had always relied upon the ballast of John Phillips. White chose to help finance the *The American* but maintained that he bore absolutely no ill will toward McClure or his magazine, where he had received "nothing but the kindest treatment." Indeed, even as he cast his lot with the new venture, he reached out to McClure. "You may draw on me whenever you will for whatever you will," he assured the editor.

Everyone recognized that creating cohesion, building a trusting yet playful atmosphere, would foster the success of *The American*. When Phillips and Tarbell persuaded Finley Peter Dunne to join the group, Baker was thrilled: "Everything amused him! We were youthful and dead in earnest—and he was wise." Dunne proved himself a great companion, who "loved so much to talk" that he could entertain his office mates for hours. "He had a wide knowledge of men and their ways," Tarbell recalled. Whenever conflict arose within the team, "Mr. Dooley" could be relied upon to lighten the heavy mood. As managing editor, Albert Boyden "made it his business" to foster camaraderie among his writers and contributors at the new magazine. At his fourth-floor walk-up on Stuyvesant Square, he hosted regular dinners for a revolving group of novelists, artists, politicians, and scientists. "What talk went on in that high-up living room!" Tarbell recalled. "What wonderful tales we heard!"

The press assumed that with "all the muckrakers muckraking under one tent," *The American Magazine* would provide "a helpful experiment" to determine whether the public appetite for exposure journalism had truly atrophied. "Their muck-raking has been of the convincing rather than the frenzied variety and they have reputations for literary honesty to be maintained," the Omaha *Evening World-Herald* observed. "This is undoubtedly the most notable combination that has ever launched any publication." The Boston *Journal of Education* expressed certitude that the pioneers of authentic investigative journalism would produce an outstanding magazine.

Although the new publishing team proudly proclaimed that they would "not be deterred by adjectives or phrases," their first public announcement nevertheless reflected anxiety about the shift in popular sentiment: "We shall not only make this new *American Magazine* interesting and important in a public way, but we shall make it the most stirring and delightful monthly book of fiction, humor, sentiment and joyous reading that is anywhere published. It will reflect a happy, struggling, fighting world, in which, as we believe, good people are coming out on top. There is no field of human activity in which we are not interested. Our magazine will be wholesome, hopeful, stimulating, uplifting, and above all, it will have a human interest on every page."

The statement provoked a wave of positive commentary in the press, accompanied by pointed advice. "Reformers need relaxation," *The Outlook* observed, "and it has sometimes seemed of late as if, in his endeavor to secure greatly needed righteousness, the ardent and patriotic American might lose his ability to be at ease in a world in which there are so many sources of pleasure as well as of pain." William Allen White, whose cheerful temperament had never really suited him for muckraking, offered similar counsel. "It seems to me the great danger," he told Phillips, "is that of being too Purposeful. People will expect the pale drawn face; the set lips and a general line of emotional insanity. You should fool 'em."

In the end, the new enterprise suffered not from a surfeit of purpose but from a lack of direction. Pressure to fill pages in the early months led to a publication without the focused passion and clear vision of the old *McClure's*. "We are editing in a very funny way," Boyden acknowledged. "We rush in every good thing every month and trust to the Lord to send more." Phillips implored each writer "to look into his literary cupboard" for half-finished work and send it pell-mell to New York. Consequently, those early issues comprised a miscellany: Tarbell submitted articles on Abraham Lincoln and John D. Rockefeller as she began a long series on the tariff; White contrasted Emporia and New York in one article, and the altruistic and egoistic spirit of man in another; Steffens profiled William Randolph Hearst and produced admiring portraits of several prominent progressives or "Upbuilders," including the timber fraud prosecutor Francis Heney and the idealistic millionaire Rudolph Spreckels; and Baker, while investigating the problem of race in America, contributed a long series of articles on the pastoral joys to be found outside the nation's growing cities.

The country life series proved a much-needed tonic for Ray Baker's life and career. "Utterly beaten down with weariness" following the disintegration of *McClure's*, he had returned to the "safe haven" of his country home in East Lansing, still a small village surrounded by farmhouses and "stretches of wilderness." Just as the rugged Arizona landscape had once provided solace during an earlier period of depression, so Michigan's "natural beauties" now absorbed his attention. For hours each day, he split cordwood, mulched fruit trees, and planted shrubs. Such "hard physical work" began to restore his body and mind.

When he received Phillips's request to rummage his literary cupboard, Baker turned to the private journals he had been keeping for nearly a decade. In these pages, he had recorded not only his thoughts on politics and economics but daily observations of rural life. Reading over these entries, he conceived the idea of a fictional alter ego: an educated, successful man who had abandoned his frenetic city life for the rigors and simple pleasures of life on a farm. When Baker sat down to organize his thoughts, memories of his childhood in the frontier town of St. Croix and winters working as a schoolteacher in small Michigan farming communities mingled with his recent experiences in East Lansing. Writing "more easily" than ever before, Baker completed six potential installments for the magazine in three weeks. Anxious that the portrait of country life would confound readers accustomed to his hard-hitting investigative journalism, he chose to solicit an opinion of his new work using the pen name "David Grayson." Swearing Phillips and the staff to secrecy, he mailed out the manuscript with a note: "Take care of my child." Though he later acknowledged how "ridiculous" his request must have appeared, this more intimate mode of writing was "something utterly different" from his previous successful work. Finally, after restless days spent rambling through the countryside, the editorial judgment from Phillips arrived by telegraph: "Manuscript a delight. Bully boy. Send more chapters."

The David Grayson stories instantly resonated with the reading public. Fan letters arrived by the thousands. "You have sublimated the *real* but commonplace experiences of life that we all enjoy," one admirer wrote, "but never take the time or have the talent to write about." David Grayson clubs sprang up in all sections of the country. Women dreamed of marrying a gentleman like David Grayson, a philosopher-farmer with a well-stocked library who had found happiness and peace in growing things, farm auctions, country fairs, schoolhouse meetings, and neighborly conversations. "David Grayson is a great man," Lincoln Steffens told Baker. "I never had realized there was in you such a sense of beauty, so much fine, philosophic wisdom and, most wonderful of all—serenity." Under such titles as *Adventures in Contentment* and *Adventures in Friendship*, the collected Grayson stories continued for decades, filling six books that sold over 2 million copies. Not until years later, when he discovered that imposters were presenting lectures and readings across the country under the name of David Grayson, did Baker finally claim Grayson's work as his own.

While Phillips delighted in the acclaim given the Grayson stories, he had advised Baker even before the series began that "people will be expecting something from you over your own name—something that is timely and notable and distinguished." The industrious Baker had no sooner completed his first Grayson installments than he embarked for San Francisco in early August 1906. There, he documented the aftermath of the devastating earthquake and fire of the previous spring before embarking on what critics considered his best magazine journalism, a "pioneer" study of "the Negro in American life."

His interest had been awakened by two previous articles on lynching he had produced for *McClure's*. Baker traveled extensively throughout the South and the North, talking with people, gathering statistics, reading local papers, and assembling data. Everywhere, he worked "to get at the *facts*," to create a dispassionate portrait of African-American life, of racial prejudice and Jim Crow, of southern moderates and northern philanthropists. Three decades later, in preparing *An American Dilemma*, Gunnar Myrdal relied on Baker's twelve-part series as "a major source." Still, this new work could not match the concrete impact of his earlier series on labor and the railroads. "The Riddle of the Negro" provided only the nebulous hope that "a clear statement of the case" would nudge Americans toward substituting "understanding and sympathy for blind repulsion and hatred." One Pennsylvania newspaper observed matter-of-factly that *The American* was "reporting the negro problem with no effort to solve it." The issue of race in America, the *Bedford Gazette* agreed, was simply "too complex to solve." In the first decade of the twentieth century, a fair-minded discussion of the racial problem represented a significant step forward. The issues containing Baker's series sold throughout the country. "Your work has been a wonderful thing for us," Tarbell assured Baker, "and I am proud of you." Phillips appreciatively told Baker that people everywhere were talking about his articles on race, with the consensus that they were "the best things running now in any magazine."

If Baker contributed disproportionately to the first issues of the new magazine, Lincoln Steffens seriously disappointed his colleagues. Initially inspired by the idea of a writer's magazine, Steffens soon chafed at the "consensus editing," allocation of space, demand for proof against libel, and hurried deadlines. "It does not matter," Phillips told Steffens, "how hard you work and write, if we don't get the material into the magazine when it needs it." The new magazine simply did not have the working capital *McClure's* had enjoyed to cover false starts or years of travel and research. Frayed by the production schedule, Boyden had little patience with Steffens's constant complaints that his articles were given less space in *The American* than they had been granted in *McClure's*. "You are crazy, Stef," Boyden testily replied, enclosing a comparison to show the griping was unfounded. Meanwhile, Boyden reminded Steffens, he had failed to answer a request for pictures to accompany one of his articles. "We don't need any sleeping partners in this concern," Peter Dunne grumbled.

Steffens shot off a resentful letter to Phillips, enumerating his grievances. "It is very difficult for me to write calmly after receiving a letter such as yours," Phillips responded. "It seems to me not only unsympathetic but unmanly. It repudiates all the terms of our association in its tone and its temper. It seems to me that you cannot stand on the threshold and speak spitefully through the door: that you should either come in or go out. . . . I could very easily by comparison show that you have had more out of this magazine than anybody else in proportion to what you have put in." Indeed, he pointed out, the magazine was covering not only Steffens's traveling expenses but those of his wife and her elderly mother. Most disappointing of all, Phillips rebuked his longtime friend and colleague, "you haven't confidence in us, and that is everything!"

Steffens remained oblivious to the vexation of the other staff members. He had money, celebrity, lecture invitations, and a new seaside estate near Cos Cob, Connecticut. "My husband has become famous," Josephine Steffens reflected sadly, "but at a high price." Steffens had issued a sanctimonious ultimatum to his partners: "Either I am to write as I please without being edited; or I quit." Six months later, he resigned from the magazine. At the time of his departure, Steffens argued that he must sell his stock in order to meet expenses while he sought a new position. His partners agreed to buy him out, further diminishing the working capital of the new enterprise.

Through all the hurly-burly at *The American*, Ida Tarbell remained the same stabilizing force she had always been at *McClure's*. Only later did she acknowledge how disorienting the transition had been. "I know now I should not have taken it as well as I did (and inwardly that was nothing to boast of) if it had not been cushioned by an engrossing personal interest," she recalled. Although her New York apartment had served as her "writing headquarters" for years, Ida had yearned for a country home. During the turbulent spring of 1906, she finally purchased an old farmhouse situated on forty acres of land in Redding Ridge, Connecticut. Initially, she planned to use the abandoned property as a retreat, doing only the most necessary maintenance. But soon she was tempted to start "borrowing and mortgaging" to fix the roof and wallpaper the rooms, taking on extra freelance work to pay for furniture, rugs, and antiques. Before long, Tarbell turned her energies to the land: she pruned apple trees, planted crops, created a new orchard, and bought chickens, a cow, a pig, and two horses. Ever practical, she reallocated money set aside for an evening gown to purchase some much-needed fertilizer for the garden. Encouraged by the warmth and camaraderie of her rural neighbors, she learned what Baker had already discovered—that "the most genuine of human dramas" could be found in the trials and triumphs of the surrounding countryside.

"All this was good for me," Ida reflected of her rural homemaking, "but while it was good for me it was not so good for my work on the magazine." Preoccupied with the engaging task of furnishing her new home, she found her research on the tariff increasingly tedious. By pursuing the subject in her first big series for *The American*, she had hoped to expose the special interests that lay behind the complicated schedules for wool, iron ore, coal, sugar, or flax. She loathed protectionism and intended to "get into the fight" for revision. Nevertheless, after months in Washington studying every issue of the

Congressional Record since the Civil War, Tarbell could not render the subject engaging or alive. Though she talked with senators and congressmen who had taken part in earlier tariff struggles, the debates that appeared "so important" to her were "a dead issue to them."

Tarbell's six-part series, "The Tariff in Our Times," ran from December 1906 through June 1907, with three additional installments published two years later. Critics lauded the "comprehensive and careful accumulation of chronological information," but most found the cumulative effect uninspiring. Tarbell dealt "exhaustively (and at times exhaustingly)" with events, one reviewer noted, yet the whole remained "invertebrate." She was the first to admit that her early installments lacked "vitality" and that she relied too heavily on "secondhand" material. The series had no "cohesive force," William Allen White told her candidly. "It is not written around the progressive narrative; it continues but doesn't get anywhere, there is no beginning, climax and end." It seemed to White that the project required exactly what McClure had prescribed as Tarbell researched the Standard Oil Company: "a central figure" that would "hold the reader." While Tarbell's series would eventually build momentum during the fiery debates over the Payne-Aldrich Tariff in 1909, her initial contribution did little to buoy the struggling fortunes of *The American Magazine*.

On July 1, 1907, Tarbell wrote a long letter to Bert Boyden offering her assessment of the magazine's first year. Something was missing, she conceded, "a certain hustle, ingenuity—a generalizing effort such as we used to get out of S.S. It's a talent—a genius, and we haven't it in the staff."

Uncannily, Ida Tarbell received a letter that same day from her old friend and former Chief. "I dreamed of you," McClure told her. "I thought I was telling you how I found out that by speaking slowly & calmly and acting calmly I found I had much greater influence on people (I am actually doing this) & I thought that I was standing by your chair & you drew me down & kissed me to show your approval. When you disapproved of me it nearly broke my heart," he confided, offering a final touching confession: "I never cease to love you as I have for many, many years. I wish you had not turned away."

39

The Roosevelt children, ranging here from five to nineteen years of age, unabashedly made the White House their own. Not since Willie and Tad Lincoln scampered through the halls had there been such a din in the executive mansion. "Places that had not seen a human being for years were made alive by the howls and laughter of these newcomers," observed the chief usher at the White House.

40

The Tafts, shown here circa 1904, traded their exotic life in the Malacañan Palace for a house on K Street in Washington. Their daughter Helen joined Ethel Roosevelt at the National Cathedral School, and seven-year-old Charlie became great friends with Quentin Roosevelt.

41

"Thank Heaven you are to be with me!" Roosevelt exclaimed in 1903, when Taft agreed to return home from the Philippines and become his secretary of war. The president knew that he could rely on Taft, pictured here at his desk in the War Department and on the telephone, as "a needed and valuable corrective to his own impetuosity."

42

43

The 1906 schism that ended *McClure's* magazine's glorious era shocked the publishing world. John Phillips, Ida Tarbell, Albert Boyden *(seated left to right)*, Ray Stannard Baker, and John Siddal *(standing left to right)* were no longer able to continue working with the mercurial S. S. McClure. Together they pooled their talents and resources to buy *The American Magazine*, which they recast as a writers' collective. "This is undoubtedly the most notable combination that has ever launched any publication," one journal commented.

44

After deciding not to seek a third term, Roosevelt told journalists that "he would crawl on his hands and knees from the White House to the Capitol" to secure the election of Taft *(left)* as his successor.

45

Turning the candidate's oversized physique into a metaphor for his inability to take Roosevelt's place, one cartoonist showed Taft vainly trying to stuff himself into Teddy's Rough Rider garments.

A cartoon from 1907 captured the president's determination. Its caption has Roosevelt asking: "Uncle Sam, can't you take him for my third term?"

46

Charley Taft's colonial mansion in Cincinnati, with its white pillars and sweeping green lawns, provided a perfect setting for his brother Will to officially accept his nomination as the Republican presidential candidate on July 28, 1908.

During the election campaign Roosevelt watched over Taft, one political correspondent observed, "like a hen over her chickens." Exultant over Taft's victory, Roosevelt is pictured here with his old friend at the White House on the morning of the new president's inauguration.

49

Defying inaugural tradition, Nellie decided to do what "no President's wife had ever done"—accompany her husband from the Capitol to the White House on March 4, 1909. "That drive was the proudest and happiest event of Inauguration Day," she recalled. "I was able to enjoy, almost to the full, the realization that my husband was actually President of the United States."

As first lady, Nellie, pictured *(above)* with Taft and his military aide Captain Archie Butt (*far left*), introduced a series of Friday afternoon garden parties that quickly became, as one reporter observed, "the most popular form of official hospitality yet seen in Washington." But only ten weeks into her husband's administration, Nellie's career as a social leader in Washington was cut short by a devastating stroke that permanently robbed her of the ability to speak intelligibly. She spent months recuperating in a seaside mansion in Beverly, Massachusetts *(below)*. Surrounded by "parklike lawns" and adjacent to a country club, this residence was a favorite retreat of President Taft and quickly became known as "the Summer White House."

52

Roosevelt displayed no interest in what critics called "devil wagons," far preferring his horses *(left)*, but Taft *(below)* fell in love with automobiles "on the first whirl." As president, Taft converted the White House stables into an oversized garage for his collection of motorcars.

53

54

Taft exercised regularly while in the White House and worked with doctors to improve his diet, yet his weight remained a constant issue, affecting both his health and energy level, and skewing the public's perception of him. The bathtub *(left)*, easily holding four workmen, was specially designed to accommodate his huge frame.

55

Despite Roosevelt's caution that the working class looked upon golf as a "rich man's game," Taft loved nothing more than to spend the afternoon on the green.

56

Taft better served his public image when, on June 9, 1910, accompanied by the ever present Archie Butt, he threw out a ceremonial first pitch at a Washington Nationals game, establishing a tradition that has continued ever since.

57

In April 1910 Roosevelt met with the deposed forester Gifford Pinchot on the Italian Riviera. After receiving a full briefing from Pinchot about his battles with Taft over conservation, Roosevelt for the first time expressed open disappointment at the course of his successor's presidency.

58

The anguish that Taft (shown here signing a bill) felt over Roosevelt's disapproval would be temporarily dispelled by the nearly complete triumph of his administration's legislative agenda. "We never had such a towering wood pile of work from the congressional saw mill," one newspaper editorial observed.

59

When Roosevelt returned from Africa, he established a base of operations at the offices of the weekly public affairs magazine, *The Outlook*.

60

On August 23, 1910, Roosevelt boarded a private railroad car secured by *The Outlook* to begin a speaking tour through the West. One political question was on every reporter's mind: "On which side will the Colonel now align himself? What changes have taken place in his philosophy?"

61

Before every speech President Taft was beset by grave misgivings, acutely aware that his texts remained "infernally long" despite his efforts to prune his words. "Never mind if you cannot get off fireworks," Nellie consoled him. "That is not your style, and there is no use in trying to force it."

When he threw his hat into the ring in the 1912 race for the presidential nomination, Theodore Roosevelt's personal popularity had never been higher. Drawing enthusiastic crowds, he scored impressive victories in states where direct primaries were held.

"If they are anxious for a fight, they shall have it," thundered Roosevelt during the 1912 Republican campaign. Crowds cheered Roosevelt as if he were a boxer, urging him to attack Taft: "Hit him between the eyes!" and "Put him over the ropes!" Political cartoonists were quick to seize on the phenomenon, as in this cartoon of prizefighter Roosevelt working over a Taft-shaped punching bag.

Despite his popularity with rank-and-file Republicans, Roosevelt failed to capture his party's support for president at the Republican National Convention in Chicago in June 1912. The old system prevailed, and Taft was nominated to pursue a second term. The disappointed candidate is shown here arriving in New York after the convention with Edith Roosevelt at his side, firmly resolved to form a third party.

64

On October 14, 1912, a would-be assassin shot at Roosevelt while he campaigned in Milwaukee. The candidate's bundle of notes for his speech, stored in his coat, helped save his life: the bullet penetrated no farther than the ribcage, and Roosevelt, though in pain, was able to deliver his speech on schedule. Returning home after the shooting, he descends from the train in Oyster Bay, assisted by aides and doctors.

65

In later years, the members of the old *McClure's* magazine staff gathered to celebrate their birthdays. For Tarbell *(seated between Willa Cather and Will Irwin)*, these gatherings represented the "unbreakable quality in friendship" that healed old wounds. "We sat enthralled as in the old years while Mr. McClure (*at left*) enlarged on his latest enthusiasm, marveling as always at the eternal youthfulness in the man, the failure of life to quench him."

Theodore and Edith Roosevelt shared an enduring love affair over three eventful decades of marriage. They are pictured here in 1917, two short years before Roosevelt's death at age sixty. He repeatedly declared that she remained as pretty as on the day he married her.

67

In 1921, William Howard Taft finally achieved his life's ambition when he was appointed chief justice of the Supreme Court of the United States. The position was perfectly suited to his temperament: no professional assignment ever made him happier.

68

CHAPTER NINETEEN

"To Cut Mr. Taft in Two!"

This Mar. 18, 1906, cartoon, "Reinforcing the Bench," shows Roosevelt using a "Big Stick" to persuade Taft to take a seat on the Supreme Court bench.

IN EARLY JANUARY 1906, WHILE attending a party in the New Jersey home of his Yale classmate John Hammond, William Howard Taft received a long-distance phone call from the president, informing him that Associate Justice Henry Billings Brown planned to announce his retirement when he turned seventy years old. Brown deemed his weakening eyesight "a gentle intimation" that the time had come "to give place to another." Knowing that duty alone had led Taft to decline the appointment three years before, Roosevelt was delighted to present him with the open seat. Taft was disposed to claim the honor, though Nellie and other friends and advisers begged him to decline, insisting that he "would be shutting the door on any further political advancement" when he was considered "the logical candidate for president in 1908." Since no commitment was required until March, the matter rested until Justice Brown formally announced his decision.

In the interim, Taft focused on pushing the Philippine tariff bill through Congress. The legislation was designed to substantially lower rates on products imported from the islands, an allowance that Taft believed was absolutely critical to the future of the Philippine economy. For two consecutive years, the bill had fallen victim to the powerful sugar and tobacco lobbies and their "standpatter" allies, as the protectionist bloc in Congress was known. But with the help of Democratic votes in late January 1906, it passed the House by an overwhelming vote of 257 to 71. Lauding the victory, Taft happily noted that several key members of the Ways and Means Committee had shifted their stance after touring the islands with his congressional delegation the previous summer.

When the bill proceeded to the Senate, Taft testified for two full days before the Senate Committee on the Philippines, hopeful that "the tremendous vote" in the House would sway the upper chamber. Connecticut senator Frank Brandegee led the opposition, arguing that Taft was "sacrificing" American economic interests for his "sentimental" desire to aid the Filipinos. "I do not believe," the senator maintained, "that we are under any obligations whatever to the Filipino people to open our markets." Taft was furious with Brandegee, privately labeling him "an infernal ass." Despite Taft's persistent efforts, the protectionist bloc managed to kill the bill in committee. "We suffered a very serious blow," Taft related to his Filipino friends, "but I am not despairing." Several publications had pledged to reveal those who had conspired in "smothering" the tariff legislation, so he remained hopeful the bill would eventually reach the Senate floor.

When Justice Brown officially announced his retirement on March 8, the press immediately began speculating that Taft would not only replace Brown but soon thereafter—if seventy-three-year-old Melvin Fuller retired during Roosevelt's term—assume the position of chief justice. Had the tariff bill passed that spring, Taft later remarked, he would "undoubtedly have accepted," but he informed Roosevelt in early March that he was too deeply occupied by critical matters in both the Philippines and Panama to consider the position. At Taft's suggestion, the president offered the post to Philander Knox; when Knox declined, however, Roosevelt renewed the pressure on Taft.

Roosevelt foresaw that over the coming decades, as the federal government confronted the social and economic stresses born of the industrial age, the Court "would have as important decisions to face as [it] had in the days of Marshall." Roosevelt had discussed the matter at length with Henry Cabot

Lodge, who had impressed upon him the absolute necessity of Taft taking the appointment. The Court desperately needed "a big man—one who would fill the public eye and one in whom the public had confidence." With five of the nine justices in their late sixties or seventies, the current Court was clearly "running down." At such a critical juncture, the president claimed, he had no higher duty than to put the best man on the bench. On the following Friday, he intended to announce his nomination of William Howard Taft.

Before the decision was made public, Taft requested time to confer with his brothers in New York. He also confided to Roosevelt that Nellie "bitterly opposed" the appointment; in fact, she had warned that very morning that to accept would be "the great mistake of [his] life." Roosevelt promised to meet with her personally and "explain the situation" before he made anything official. To accommodate such a discussion, Nellie remained behind for a noon meeting with President Roosevelt rather than join her husband on the 9 a.m. train to New York for the family council.

Before boarding the train to New York, Taft sent an explanatory note to Roosevelt outlining Nellie's position. He had repeatedly assured his wife, he told Roosevelt, that he was so engaged in his cabinet duties and the management of his "three great trusts"—the Philippines, Panama, and the U.S. Army—that he "had concluded to stick to it and not seek at your hands or accept any appointment to the Bench." Despite this resolve, he trusted that the president could better weigh the cost of losing him in the cabinet against "the crying need for putting strength in the Supreme Court." If the president determined he could be most beneficial on the bench, he would "of course yield." Even as he declared his preference for remaining in the cabinet, Taft appeared tortured by second doubts and hopeful the president might decide the matter for him.

Conflicting counsel produced during Taft's conference with his brothers did little to clarify the situation. Charles thought he should take the nomination, so long as it was clearly understood (as Roosevelt had already promised) that he would be appointed to the chief justiceship once Fuller retired. Horace, long Nellie's closest ally in advocating against a judicial career, was adamantly opposed, believing that his brother stood an excellent chance of becoming president. Moreover, Horace argued, "quite apart from the Presidency," it would be a shame to have his "personality removed from politics." For his part, Harry found talk of the presidency flattering but felt that Taft was better suited to be chief justice.

When Taft returned to Washington the next morning, he found a remarkable letter from the president awaiting him. After conversing with Nellie the previous morning, Roosevelt believed he had misconstrued his friend's desires. All along, Roosevelt confessed, he had thought that Taft wanted the Court appointment and that all the president's urgings toward that end were consequent with Taft's deepest inclinations. But in the wake of his discussions of the matter with Nellie, he had resolved to leave the decision completely up to Taft himself. "My dear Will," he wrote, "it is preeminently a matter in which no other man can take the responsibility of deciding for you what is right and best for you to do. Nobody could decide for me whether I should go to the war or stay as Assistant Secretary of the Navy . . . whether I should accept the Vice-Presidency, or try to continue as Governor." In each defining situation, he concluded, "the equation of the man himself" must be "the vital factor."

Roosevelt proceeded to offer his heartfelt advice, carefully considering each of his friend's prospects. In the first place, he stated flatly, he considered Taft not only "the best man" to become the next president but the "most likely" to receive the Republican nomination and win the general election. (While Roosevelt held Elihu Root in equal esteem, he recognized that the conservative lawyer's long corporate ties made him unavailable as a candidate.) "The good you could do in four or eight years as the head of the Nation would be incalculable," Roosevelt asserted, adding that "the shadow of the presidency falls on no man twice, save in the most exceptional circumstances." Naturally, no election is guaranteed, the president qualified, adding that he hoped that Taft's "sweet and fine nature" would not "be warped" if he should fail. But even if the presidency did not materialize, Taft would enjoy "three years of vital service" in the cabinet and would certainly be "one of the great leaders for right in the tremendous contests" that lay ahead.

"First and infinitely foremost," Roosevelt wrote, stressing the benefits of assuming a place on the bench, at only forty-eight-years of age, Taft would have "the opportunity for a quarter of a century to do a great work as Justice of the greatest Court in Christendom (a court which sadly needs great men) on questions which seem likely vitally and fundamentally to affect the social, industrial and political structure of our commonwealth"; secondarily, declining this opportunity to join the Court would diminish or foreclose Taft's chance to serve as chief justice, for in order to fill the current vacancy with some other "big man," like Elihu Root, the president might have to utilize the option of the top post.

"Where you can fight best I cannot say, for you know what your soul turns to better than I," Roosevelt acutely observed in closing. "You have two alternatives before you, each with uncertain possibilities, and you cannot be sure that whichever you take you will not afterwards feel that it would have been better if you had taken the other. But whichever you take I know that you will render great and durable service to the Nation for many years to come."

Taft was deeply moved by Roosevelt's generous and candid endeavor to help him work through the momentous decision he faced. The letter was "all I could expect and more," he told Nellie. If forced to decide immediately, he would accept, he explained to Horace—otherwise he might well jeopardize his chance at the chief justiceship. He would talk with the president, he concluded, and ask to defer the decision, allowing him to continue the tariff fight until Congress adjourned in July. Displaying decisiveness in contrast to Taft's dilatory nature, Roosevelt agreed to release a statement explaining that since Brown would not retire until June and the Court not resume work until October, he had decided to postpone his nomination.

Throughout that spring, newspapers speculated on Taft's prospects. It was a "somewhat unusual experience," the New York *Sun* observed, "to possess a public servant whose usefulness and versatility are so generally recognized" that half his supporters hoped he would remain in politics, while the other half preferred to see him on the Supreme Court. Sadly, the *Sun* remarked with broad humor, it was "impossible, under the Constitution and laws, to cut Mr. Taft in two!" While the natural ambition of "the big, jovial, brainy" Taft might incline him toward the bench, the *Hutchinson* (Kansas) *News* suggested, he had now "tasted power," and perhaps an "easy berth" on the Court was no longer so appealing.

As early as the summer of 1906, editorials in Republican newspapers began touting Taft as the only man capable of defeating the Democratic front-runner, the charismatic William Jennings Bryan, in the upcoming presidential election. "He has done big things," the *Kansas City Star* noted, "is magnetic and popular" and "would come nearer to carrying forward the Roosevelt policies than any other Republican." The *Journal of Commerce* observed that "no American" stood higher "in the eyes of his countrymen" than the popular secretary of war. Day after day, Taft received letters begging him to look toward the presidency instead of the Court. "I do not see in the horizon any man in the Republican ranks except yourself who would give us good assurance of carrying the country," *Outlook* publisher Lyman Abbott urged. "For the love of Mike, do not go to the Supreme Bench," another friend pleaded; "there are certain lucky individuals who have a happy faculty of appealing to the imagination and the heart of the general public . . . and you are one of these lucky people."

Though Taft disavowed any desire for the presidency, the prospect inevitably informed his decision to refuse the Court nomination. In a lengthy letter to Roosevelt in mid-July, he insisted that while the bench remained his ultimate preference, the timing was once again wrong. News that Congress had adjourned without passing the tariff bill had produced "a most gloomy" spirit in the Philippines, and remaining in the cabinet would allow him to continue his fight in the next session. "P.S.," he humbly continued. "Please don't misunderstand me to think that I am indispensable or that the world would not run on much the same if I were to disappear in the St. Lawrence River, but circumstances seem to have imposed something in the nature of a trust on me." (Roosevelt eventually nominated Attorney General William Moody to fill the vacant seat.) In a second postscript, Taft contritely confessed that Nellie thought it "an outrage" to inflict such a long letter upon such a busy man!

"Now, you beloved individual," the president replied from Oyster Bay, "as for your long letter I enjoyed it thoroughly." At Sagamore Hill, he explained, he had plenty of time to read and relax; indeed, after only three weeks on vacation, he was "rather shocked" to discover how easily he had adapted. "Ten years ago I got uneasy if I was left with leisure on my hands," Roosevelt remarked, "and if I had no mental work I wished to be riding, chopping, rowing, or doing something of that kind all the time. Now I am perfectly content to sit still." Writing again a few weeks later, he exclaimed: "By George, I am as pleased as Punch that you are to stay in the Cabinet!"

Relieved to have the Court decision behind him, Taft happily anticipated a two-month vacation with Nellie and the children at Murray Bay. There, he intended to continue the diet and exercise regimen that had enabled him to lose over 75 pounds during the previous eight months, reducing his weight from 330 to 254 pounds. During this period, he had faithfully maintained a rigorous, doctor-prescribed diet that excluded sugar, fats, milk, cheese, cream, egg yolks, and bread. He was allowed only grilled fish, lean meat, egg whites, clear soup, salads, vegetables, some fruits, gluten biscuits, and sugarless wine. At his heaviest, Taft had been forced to send away for a new bathroom scale; those available in Washington, he told Charles, were "boys" scales, registering no more than 250 pounds. Having reached a manageable weight by July, he discovered that his new physique was "not an inexpensive luxury." His tailor had to completely reconstruct "twenty pairs of Trousers . . . twenty Waist Coats . . . two Prince Albert Coats . . . and five Sack Coats!" Horace was thrilled by his brother's progress: "It is the best thing you have done for many a day." Given his "infernally healthy" constitution, Horace jested, there was now "no reason why [you] should not live to be a hundred."

During the summer in Murray Bay, Taft's customary day began at 7 a.m., with dictation to his private secretary Wendell W. Mischler. Still in his twenties when he joined the secretary of war Taft, Mischler would remain with Taft until his death. At nine o'clock, Taft joined his family for breakfast, then returned to work for another hour. Generating responses to the five thick batches of mail that arrived by train or steamship each day required three hours in the early morning and two more in the late afternoon. In the interim, Taft relished outdoor activities and socializing with his family—golf games with his brothers, trout fishing and rambles along the rocky shore, tennis and picnics with Nellie and the children. In one golf respite, Taft happened upon fellow Murray Bay vacationer Justice John Harlan "jumping up and down to coax a ball in that was hovering on the very edge of the first hole." Having no luck, Harlan called over to Taft: "Come on! You jump. That will do the business." The casual atmosphere of Murray Bay allowed Taft to dress in comfort, saving his "city clothes" for Sunday church. Without fancy dinners or formal receptions to attend, he could easily adhere to his diet. The nation's problems seemed to recede with each passing day, and friends and family could almost "see youth returning to him."

By the second week in August, as he began preparation for a major political speech, Taft's equanimity started to unravel. The chairman of the Republican State Committee had asked him to give the keynote address at an event in Maine early that September to open the party's midterm campaign. In a letter from Oyster Bay, Roosevelt underscored the importance of the speech. Taft organized his presentation around four topics: the legislative goals of Congress, questions surrounding labor unrest, the trusts, and the tariff. The first three issues gave him little trouble. He agreed wholeheartedly with Roosevelt's regulatory legislation, his position on labor, and his anti-trust initiatives. But he strongly wished to call for a downward revision of the tariff, a step that Roosevelt feared would split the party in two.

Taft's long struggle with conservative Republicans over the Philippine tariff had awakened him to the larger inequity of the entire domestic tariff structure—a system that created immense advantages for eastern manufacturers and massive corporations over western farmers and small business. He believed the tariff represented the "only weakness" in the Republican Party, and he wanted to address the problem publicly. Nonetheless, he remained well aware that he would be regarded as a spokesman for the administration, promising Roosevelt that he would revise his remarks if the draft seemed "too outspoken." Nellie had read an "outrageously long" early draft, which she deemed reminiscent of a "dull" opinion from the bench. He had compressed the entire speech. "One's wife is mighty useful under circumstances like this," he proudly acknowledged to Roosevelt.

"It's a bully speech," encouraged Roosevelt in reply. He was confident that Taft had safely navigated the tariff issue by stating that revision would be possible only when popular sentiment within the party crystallized. Personally, he did not believe that reform would be realized before the presidential election. Yet, if the Republicans were victorious, they would probably have to present a plan for revision immediately afterward. "I neither wish to split the Republican party," Roosevelt wrote, "nor to seem to promise something Congress would not do." In fact, he suggested that Taft show the speech to the conservative party leaders, Speaker Cannon and Charles Littlefield.

On the evening of September 5, 3,000 people gathered at the Alameda Opera House in downtown Bath, Maine, to hear Taft deliver "the first big Administration speech of the campaign." The audience enthusiastically cheered Taft's passionate defense of regulatory reforms and anti-trust initiatives. The president's historic work to strengthen the federal response to long-standing abuses, Taft declared, "is the issue of the campaign, its only issue; its only possible issue." Only when he turned to the tariff did Taft diverge from his central message. "With a frankness that is almost startling," *The Washington Post* observed, the likely 1908 Republican nominee voiced his opposition to the conservative "stand-pat attitude" of both the president and the Speaker of the House, proclaiming "that his party must face tariff revision squarely and unhesitatingly."

Reaction in the press was overwhelmingly favorable. The New York *Sun* called Taft's speech "the frankest, the ablest and the most manly and engaging deliverance that has ever come from any member of Mr. Roosevelt's Cabinet on any subject." The solicitor general, Henry Hoyt, told Taft that he had "never made a sharper speech," lauding it as "honest & courageous all the way through," and adding, "All of us in our hearts agree with you about tariff revision." Taft was delighted by the public praise but most anxiously awaited Roosevelt's response. "It is the great speech of the campaign," Roosevelt telegraphed him, "and I cannot imagine the people failing to recognize it as such." Taft humbly replied: "A man never knows exactly how the child of his brain will strike other people."

TAFT'S PLAN TO EXTEND HIS tranquil vacation at Murray Bay through September was abruptly cut short by turmoil in Cuba. Revolutionary forces, angered by electoral fraud during the 1905 presidential campaign, had taken control of most of the island outside of Havana, leaving President Tomás Estrada Palma in a precarious situation. Though the treaty ending the war with Spain had bound the United States to respect Cuban sovereignty, the Platt Amendment stipulated that the United States retained power to take action whenever necessary to safeguard the independent status of the island nation, and to support "a government adequate for the protection of life, property and individual liberty."

"In Cuba what I have dreaded has come to pass," Roosevelt told George Trevelyan on September 6: "A revolution has broken out, and not only do I dread the loss of life and property, but I dread the creation of a revolutionary habit, and the creation of a class of people who take to disturbance and destruction as an exciting and pleasant business." On September 13, President Estrada Palma claimed he could not "prevent rebels from entering cities and burning property" and secretly requested the landing of U.S. troops "to save his country from complete anarchy." Roosevelt confided to Ambassador Henry White that he was "so angry with that infernal little Cuban republic that I would like to wipe its people off the face of the earth. All that we wanted from them was that they would behave themselves," he added petulantly, "and be prosperous and happy so that we would not have to interfere."

The following day, Roosevelt summoned Taft and Assistant Secretary of State Robert Bacon to a conference at Oyster Bay. The two men would travel to Cuba "as intermediaries," Roosevelt decided, hoping to effect a peaceful solution. From Oyster Bay, Taft took the train to Washington, where he conferred with the judge advocate general to determine whether congressional approval was necessary if the president decided to send troops. The judge advocate general, Taft told Roosevelt, believed the treaty authorized presidential action without congressional approval. Nevertheless, Taft wished to get Attorney General Moody's opinion. Roosevelt adamantly directed him not to consult Moody. "If the necessity arises I intend to intervene," he explained, "and I should not dream of asking the permission of Congress. That treaty is the law of the land and I shall execute it." His decision was in the interest of the country, he added, essential to "give independence to the Executive in dealing with foreign powers." Furthermore, he was certainly "willing to accept responsibility to establish precedents which successors may follow."

When Taft and Bacon reached Havana, they met with President Estrada Palma and the leaders of his Moderate Party. Not a single delegate from the Liberal Party, which represented Cuba's less privileged, was present. Pushing for intervention to sustain their power, Estrada Palma and his supporters were dismayed when Taft refused to act before meeting with rebels in the field to fully evaluate the situation. The secretary of war had not traveled to Cuba intent on using American power to suppress the insurgents; he had come as an arbitrator hoping to reconcile differences peacefully.

Taft's "informal, straightforward and kindly manner," one reporter noted, "created a strong and favorable impression." Even as he privately lamented "the utter unfitness of these people for self government," Taft listened patiently to representatives from both sides. Reviewing the evidence regarding the 1905 election, he concluded that complaints of wholesale fraud were "well founded." To orchestrate a compromise, he suggested that if insurgents "laid down their arms and dispersed to their homes," a temporary executive acceptable to both sides would be appointed, the disputed legislative seats would be vacated, and planning would begin for a new election. The liberals agreed, but the moderates promptly sabotaged the possibility. Rather than accept the compromise terms, Palma announced that he, his cabinet, and every moderate congressman would resign, "leaving nothing of the Government."

Meanwhile, the fierce skirmishes outside Havana continued. Having nearly routed government forces in the countryside, the rebels stood poised to enter the capital. "The insurgents are all about Havana," Taft told Nellie nervously. "I don't know that I can save bloodshed." One insurgent encampment was situated only 1,200 yards from the house where Taft was staying. The rapidly shifting situation required William Taft to take decisive action without explicit guidance from the president. "Things are certainly kaleidoscopic," Roosevelt telegraphed. "I must trust to your judgment on the ground." The tense days during this standoff proved "the most unpleasant" Taft had ever experienced. "I am in a condition of mind where I can hardly do anything with sequence," he confessed to Nellie, adding, "I would give a great deal to talk it over with you." Unable to sleep, he found himself awake at three in the morning, watching a severe thunderstorm build and roll over Havana Bay. Were it not for Nellie and his family, Will reflected, he would not be sorry if one of the bolts flashing in the sky struck him dead.

After a week of rancorous negotiation, Taft finally brokered a four-point plan. President Estrada Palma would remain in office long enough to officially request American intervention. The United States would set up a provisional government, with Taft as the initial temporary governor general. The insurgents, secure in America's pledge that new elections would be held, would begin to disarm. And to keep the peace, American forces would land in Cuba. Taft wisely emphasized that this provisional government would "be maintained only long enough to restore order and peace and public confidence." The Cuban Constitution would remain in full force and Cuba's flag would continue to fly over government buildings. Once elections were held, the U.S. military would be withdrawn.

Taft anticipated that his course of action would be criticized back at home but took solace in the fact that "all parties here seem to be delighted." A resolution without further bloodshed and war, he assured Nellie, would "go a long way to make such attacks futile." A telegraph from Oyster Bay confirmed Taft's judgment: "I congratulate you most heartily upon the admirable way you have handled the whole matter," Roosevelt wrote, adding that he was "especially pleased with the agreement which the revolutionary committee signed."

As soon as the accord became public, the rebels began to disarm. Taft promptly cabled Nellie to join him in Havana, knowing her presence would bring him "great comfort." He planned to remain in Havana for several weeks, until Charles E. Magoon, the former governor of the Panama Canal Zone, could relieve him as governor general. Eager for adventure, Nellie decided instantly to go. Accompanied by Robert Bacon's wife, she sailed from Norfolk on a steamer escorted by a battleship and three hundred Marines. "For the first time in my life I felt as if we were actually 'going to war,' " she recalled. Her ceremonious reception as "the first lady of the land" was reminiscent of her days in Manila. On the day after their arrival, Nellie Taft and Mrs. Bacon hosted a splendid gala at the palace, with a guest list comprising more than three hundred Cubans from both sides of the dispute. "Everybody seemed to be especially happy and festive after the month of gloom," Nellie recalled, "and the pretty white gowns, the gay Cuban colours and the crisp smartness of American uniforms mingled together in the great rooms with quite brilliant effect." Once Magoon was sworn in as governor general, the Tafts made plans to depart Havana. "Upon my word you seem to have handled everything in a most masterly way," Roosevelt commended his secretary of war as he wrapped up his stay in Cuba. "I doubt whether you have ever rendered our country a greater service."

As the Tafts prepared to embark from the Havana dock on October 13, Magoon reported, "the shore of the Bay was lined with thousands of cheering people, all available water craft was pressed into service to escort the ships to the mouth of the harbor, the forts exchanged salutes with the vessels." Nellie recalled a widely printed cartoon depicting poor Magoon seated "in agony on a sizzling stove labeled 'Cuba,' while Mr. Taft appeared in the distance in a fireman's garb carrying a long and helpful-looking line of hose." Indeed, the political situation on the islands was far from resolved, and preparation for the new elections proved unexpectedly complex. In the end, Magoon would struggle for over two years to complete a new census and revise the electoral laws; not until early 1909 were national elections finally held. After the election, Magoon finally relinquished control to a newly elected liberal administration and the U.S. troops sailed for home.

Though many critics opposed the very concept of intervention in Cuban affairs, Taft's role in the crisis was generally praised. "Merely to record the movements and missions of the Secretary of War requires a nimble mind," the New York *Sun* remarked. Most men would have considered it "a labor of Hercules" to negotiate peace in the midst of a revolution: Taft—accustomed to settling volatile dilemmas from Manila to Panama, from Ohio to Maine—simply threw "a change of clothing into a traveling bag" as if he were setting forth on a holiday and "returned to his War Department duties." Taft himself presented a far less jaunty picture of his struggle to implement peace in Cuba: "If mental worry kept me down I should have lost 50 pounds in this crisis," he revealed to Charles. Instead, having sought comfort in food during "those awful twenty days," he had gained back 15 or 20 pounds, necessitating yet another alteration of his wardrobe.

TAFT SCARCELY HAD TIME TO unpack before Roosevelt dispatched him on a three-week speaking tour through a dozen states in advance of the midterm elections. "The paramount issue," a midwestern editorial observed, was "whether the president shall be sustained during the remaining two years of his term by a republican congress." No one could present a better case for the Roosevelt administration than William Howard Taft, the most prominent cabinet member, "the jolly good fellow" most likely to secure the next Republican nomination.

All 5,000 seats at the Lyric Stage in Baltimore were filled, and hundreds more people stood in the back and packed the galleries when Taft stepped to the podium. Though he spoke for an hour and three quarters, defending the measured use of federal power to correct abuses of the industrial system, not one person rose to leave. "This is rather contrary to your theory that no audience can stand more than an hour," he teased Nellie, conceding wryly that a few might have "sneaked out saying to themselves that a man who has the egregious vanity to think he can entertain an audience for more than an hour ought not to be encouraged." In Cleveland, Danville, Decatur, Omaha, and Pocatello, Taft addressed similarly enthusiastic crowds. Seven thousand people thronged to hear him speak in Boise, Idaho, where he was met with sustained applause: "Hats were thrown up in the air, women stood up on the chairs and waved their handkerchiefs."

"The notices have all been favorable," Nellie informed him from home. Nonetheless, she was concerned that he seemed unable to forgo mention of the tariff, sparking an antagonism within the Republican Party that could cost him the nomination. Taft acknowledged the legitimacy of her political estimate but felt so strongly on the issue he would wage the fight notwithstanding. Furthermore, he hoped his wife wouldn't get "the blues" when he explained that despite feeling more "at home" with his audiences, he still found scant enjoyment in the political game and wished she could "put aside any hope in the direction of politics."

Despite her husband's protestations, Nellie was unwilling to relinquish the prospect of a Taft presidency. In Roosevelt, she found a powerful ally, though she continued to fear that he coveted another term for himself. On Saturday, October 27, with Taft in transit from Pittsburgh to Cleveland, Roosevelt invited Nellie to lunch at the White House. He confessed his concern to her, explaining that some Kentucky supporters had told him that Taft had flatly "turned them down" when they approached him about setting up an organization of support, maintaining that he was "not a candidate." If Taft could not be "more encouraging," Roosevelt continued, it might "become necessary for him to support someone else." When Roosevelt mentioned Charles Evans Hughes, the New York attorney who had successfully investigated the life insurance industry and was now running against William Randolph Hearst for governor, Nellie grew annoyed by the tone of conversation. "I felt like saying 'D—— you, support who you want, for all I care,' " she confessed to her husband, "but suffice it to say I did not."

"I think what the president is anxious to do," Taft cannily speculated to his wife after considering her account of the White House luncheon, "is to stir you up to stir me up to take more interest in the Presidential campaign, with a broad intimation that if I did not take more interest he would not." Taft also posted a letter to the president conveying his understanding that Roosevelt might have to support a Hughes candidacy. "If you do," Taft assured the president, "you may be sure it will awaken no feeling of disappointment on my part." In fact, Taft confirmed, his recent travels had convinced him that "the strong feeling" he had encountered everywhere was not for him, but for the renomination of Roosevelt himself. The people did not want a "substitute," he explained; they wanted a third term.

Taft, meanwhile, continued to speak before spirited crowds. In some states, he spoke seven or eight times a day as his train moved from city to city. Despite the frenetic pace, he took the time every few days to update Roosevelt on local and state issues. "I am immensely interested in your account of the campaign," Roosevelt responded. "I take the keenest pride in what you are now doing. Three cheers for 'offensive partisanship'!"

When the votes were tallied on November 6, Roosevelt was tremendously pleased. Republicans had expected significant losses in the midterm elections following their landslide victory two years before. Instead, the party retained a strong majority in the House, losing only twenty-eight seats, and actually added four seats in the Senate. "Our triumph at the elections has certainly been great," Roosevelt wrote to Kermit. His party's hold on Congress, he believed, would make the last two years of his term "very, very much easier than they otherwise would have been." Roosevelt readily acknowledged his debt to Elihu Root and especially to the dutiful William Howard Taft. "I am overjoyed," he told his secretary of war, enthusiastically praising Taft's efforts as he added, "I cannot sufficiently congratulate you upon the great part you have played in the contest." He was particularly pleased by Governor Frank Gooding's reelection in Idaho and the defeat of the "scandal-mongering" William Randolph Hearst in New York—a victory he considered nothing less than a triumph for civilization. "By George," he confided to Taft, "I sometimes wish I was not in the White House and could be on the stump."

Two days after the election, the president and first lady embarked on a long-anticipated trip to Panama. "I'm going down to see how the ditch is getting along," Roosevelt shouted from the deck of the yacht set to carry him from the nation's capital down the Rappahannock River to the sea, where he would board the warship *Louisiana*. The "ditch," one reporter explained, referred to the massive artificial lake under construction on the Isthmus of Panama that promised to rival "the pyramids . . . the Colossus of Rhodes [or] the hanging gardens of Babylon." Roosevelt began the six-day sail in "particularly good spirits," delighted to be taking an unprecedented step in the history of the presidency—leaving the country to visit a foreign land. Indeed, when his trip was first announced, "a large portion of the public gasped," anxious that "such a jaunt would be contrary to law." The public was assured, however, that "modern inventions" would enable the president to keep abreast of the nation's business "no matter where he may be."

Roosevelt's three-day visit to Panama was packed with "a little of everything." Wishing to judge the progress of the construction firsthand, the president climbed atop a steam shovel and barraged the operator with dozens of questions about his work. He traveled by train to several excavation sites, observed drilling machines at work, and watched as dynamite charges were detonated. He met with laborers, toured their sleeping quarters and bathrooms, and listened to their complaints. He even dropped by the workers' mess rooms, insisting that he sample the food they were served. Overall, the *New York Tribune* reported, the president came away "well pleased with what he saw," and the men were well pleased to see him.

Although the Tafts had been invited to join the president and Edith on the Panama trip, Taft had already arranged to follow his western political tour with a weeklong inspection of half a dozen Army bases in Nebraska, Oklahoma, Illinois, Kansas, and Texas. At each base, he was received with elaborate ceremony. "Not in the history of the post at Fort Sill has there been accorded to an officer of the war department a larger reception," one reporter remarked. At Fort Leavenworth, "several thousand school children waved flags; whistles were blown, church bells rung and hundreds of cannon crackers were fired." After a final stop at Fort Sam Houston in San Antonio, Taft settled down for the long train ride home. "One trouble about travel," he wrote Nellie, "is that with nothing particular to do on the cars, meals assume an undue importance." And, indeed, Taft's extensive travels had prompted him to add 15 more pounds to his girth.

WHEN TAFT ARRIVED AT HIS War Department office shortly after his return, he found himself thrust in the midst of a firestorm. During his lengthy absence from Washington, the president had made a unilateral decision on a matter he would normally have discussed with his secretary of war. Roosevelt had issued a sweeping presidential order discharging without honor an entire battalion of black soldiers for an incident three months earlier in Brownsville, Texas.

Racial tensions in the small southern city had been building since late July 1906, when the battalion first arrived at Fort Brown from Nebraska. Local papers had denounced the government's decision to transfer the troops to a region where privileges granted in the North "would certainly be denied them." A series of minor confrontations had taken place: black soldiers were forced off the sidewalk, hit with revolver butts, and denied access to public bars. Rumors of a black soldier assaulting a white woman in her home circulated. Then, just past midnight on August 14, a group of soldiers had allegedly entered town and fired into buildings, killing a saloonkeeper and so grievously injuring the chief of police that his arm was later amputated. Eyewitnesses produced contradictory accounts: some claimed that the townspeople had fired first; others pointed to "colored soldiers in khaki and blue shirts" as the aggressors. No one could identify any of the individual soldiers, all of whom had returned to their barracks immediately after the shootings.

With Taft en route to Cuba when the first official account reached Washington, Roosevelt took charge, ordering the inspector general of the Army to investigate the incident. Six days later, Major Augustus Blocksom wired an initial report. Even while acknowledging that racial prejudice had motivated townspeople to heap abuse upon the enlisted men, he nevertheless discounted the report that the citizens had fired first, blaming an unidentified group of about "nine to fifteen" soldiers for initiating the raid. Interviews with battalion members had failed to disclose the identities of those involved. Blocksom therefore recommended that if the soldiers continued to obstruct the investigation by refusing to cooperate, they should be collectively "discharged from the service." Because the townspeople of Brownsville remained "in a state of great nervous tension," with civilians patrolling the streets with guns "openly at night," he suggested the battalion be temporarily transferred to Fort Reno, Oklahoma. "It is very doubtful," the *Brownsville Herald* observed, "whether our people would ever tolerate the presence of negro soldiers here again."

Roosevelt accepted Blocksom's recommendation to remove the troops, ordering the inspector general, Ernest A. Garlington, to Fort Reno to conduct further interviews with the enlisted men. When Garlington arrived on October 18, he called the troops into formation on the Parade Grounds and read them an ultimatum from the president: If they continued to conceal the names of those involved in the raid, they would be discharged en masse. When not a single man broke rank, Garlington recommended that the entire battalion be dishonorably discharged at once. Although "this extreme penalty" undoubtedly meant that men with "no direct knowledge" of "who actually fired the shots" would be found guilty, because they stood together, he argued, "they should stand together when the penalty falls."

Taft was on the campaign trail in early November when Roosevelt accepted Garlington's recommendation. The president directed that all 167 men be dishonorably discharged from the Army, a status that not only prevented them from reenlistment but barred them from any civil service position. The battalion included several Medal of Honor winners, soldiers with a quarter of a century of distinguished service, and men who had fought beside Roosevelt in the Spanish-American War. To prevent negative publicity, the order was deliberately delayed until after the midterm elections.

When the order was finally revealed, telegrams and resolutions condemning the president's "despotic usurpation of power" flooded both the White House and the War Department. "Deep resentment" percolated in the black community, where Roosevelt had once been lionized for opening "the door of hope" by inviting Booker T. Washington to dinner and publicly fighting to confirm several high-level black appointees. The decision was deemed "a truckling to sectional prejudice" and a bid by the president to capitalize on newfound popularity in the South in the wake of his wildly successful trip through the region. "Once enshrined in our love as our Moses," one black preacher lamented, Roosevelt "is now enshrouded in our scorn as our Judas."

Reading through the pile of telegrams and petitions on the Saturday of his return, Taft consented to meet Mary Church Terrell—a leading black educator, graduate of Oberlin College, and member of New York's Constitutional League. All she wanted, Mrs. Terrell informed the secretary, was for him "to withhold the execution of that order" until a trial could be set to determine "the innocent ones." With "a merry twinkle in his eye," she recalled, Taft responded with gentle irony: "Is that *all* you want me to do?" She "realized for the first time what a tremendous request" she had made, Terrell explained, and "how difficult it would be to change the status of the soldiers' case." Still, there was something in Taft's "generous-hearted" manner that made her believe he would do what he could.

That very day, Taft cabled Roosevelt—then en route from Panama to Puerto Rico—that he intended to "delay the execution of the order" until he received a response. He did not think the president fully realized "the great feeling that has been aroused on the subject," or the negative impact on Army morale and racial relations. Taft always believed it better to reconsider a case when a decision raised serious questions. "If a rehearing shows that the original conclusion was wrong, it presents a dignified way of recalling it; and if it does not, it enforces the original conclusion."

Upon learning that Taft had delayed the order, reporters speculated that the terms of the soldiers' discharge might be modified. Taft publicly remarked that he would prefer honorable discharges, which would allow eventual reinstatement and access to the Soldiers' Homes. Furthermore, he questioned the president's legal power to preclude employment in the civil branch. The *New York Times* reported that the incident had placed such "a severe strain upon the relations between the President and his Secretary of War" that a new appointment to the cabinet might be required.

Taft heard nothing from Roosevelt over the weekend. On Monday, he left Washington for a daylong meeting at Yale, where he had been elected to the Yale Corporation. When he returned on Tuesday afternoon to find that there was still no response to his cable, he met with William Loeb, Roosevelt's private secretary. Loeb showed him a letter the president had written to Massachusetts governor Curtis Guild, Jr., just before leaving for Panama. "The order in question will under no circumstances be rescinded or modified," Roosevelt had declared. "There has been the fullest and most exhaustive investigation of the case." Viewing this document, Taft sadly concluded that he no longer had a right to delay the order. The next morning, a telegram from Roosevelt confirmed that he remained inflexible: "Discharge is not to be suspended," he wrote. "I care nothing whatever for the yelling of either the politicians or the sentimentalists. The offense was most heinous and the punishment I inflicted was imposed after due deliberation."

Criticism of the Brownsville order mounted into early December. When Congress convened on December 3, the conservative Republican senator Joseph Foraker introduced a resolution calling for a full investigation into the matter. Foraker's inquiry, which proposed to study whether the president's order overstepped his authority, provoked what the *New York Times* characterized as a "fighting mad" reaction from Roosevelt. Foraker had been among the most outspoken opponents of Roosevelt's railroad legislation; consequently, his resolution was seen as a blatant political maneuver to wrest control of the Republican Party from Roosevelt, Taft, and the progressives. "It is impossible to admit that he could be sincere in any belief in the troops' innocence," Roosevelt testily asserted.

In a letter to Congress "tingling with indignation," Roosevelt insisted that "he was not only acting well within his constitutional rights, but that it was his duty to strip the uniform" from "murderers, assassins, cowards and the comrades of murderers." The discrimination that the soldiers had endured at the hands of the townspeople offered no "excuse or justification for the atrocious conduct." Indeed, the president asserted that dismissal was "utterly inadequate"—had the murderers been identified and found guilty, they would have been executed. Several days later, Roosevelt underscored his defiant stand, informing reporters that he would "fight to the last ditch" rather than abandon his order. If Congress should adopt legislation to reinstate the soldiers, he would veto it. If the legislation passed over his veto, he would find another means to prevent the soldiers' reenlistment. "Not even the threat of impeachment proceedings," one paper remarked, "would deter him from the stand pat course he had decided to follow."

Roosevelt's strident response provoked both anger and sorrow in the black community. The Suffrage League of Boston predicted that his "extraordinary language" would likely incite "race hatred and violence" against 10 million innocent Negro citizens. The *Washington Bee* declared that "the colored man [would] be deceived no more," for Roosevelt, "intoxicated with peevishness and vindictiveness," had made it evident that he was no friend to their cause. "We shall oppose the renomination of Theodore Roosevelt," the *Bee* concluded, "or anyone named by him."

Though he maintained his public bravado, Roosevelt gradually softened his position, sending a new round of investigators to Brownsville to ask further questions. At Taft's urging, he even revoked the provision barring soldiers from civil jobs with the government. Eventually, he allowed individual soldiers to apply for reinstatement, though the burden to prove innocence concerning the raid and the raiders' identities lay with each applicant. Regardless of these concessions, Roosevelt's handling of the Brownsville affair became a permanent scar on his legacy. Six decades later, the U.S. Army finally "cleared the records" of all 167 soldiers "dishonorably discharged" in what had proved to be the "only documented case of mass punishment" in the institution's history.

Privately, Taft continued to believe that had he been present in Washington during the Brownsville incident, he might have prevented the president from issuing his draconian order. In other difficult situations, he had successfully mollified Roosevelt's pugnacity. Nevertheless, once the order was promulgated, Taft never wavered in his public support for the president. When Richard Harding Davis applauded his "courage and good judgment" in ordering the delay, Taft demurred, telling the reporter his action had "been misunderstood." Because of his absence at the time of the original decision, he maintained to Davis, he had simply not been aware of the facts or of the extensive investigation the president had already carried out.

Only his innermost circle was privy to Taft's continuing anxiety. "This Brownsville matter is giving me a great deal of trouble," he confessed to Howard Hollister, adding plaintively that he sometimes wished himself "out of it all" and engaged in "some quiet occupation which did not involve crimination and recrimination." William Taft understood that his chance for the Supreme Court had come and gone, that "when a man has got his face pointed in one direction the only manly way to do is to keep on and take the mud that is thrown." He fully recognized the futility of agonizing over lost possibilities, he assured Hollister, "but the difficulty with worry is that it does not disappear with argument."

CHAPTER TWENTY

Taft Boom, Wall Street Bust

On Dec. 11, 1907, *Puck* paired this image of Roosevelt struggling to launch Taft's ponderous candidacy with the caption: "How the Diabolo Can I Keep This Going Till Nomination Day?"

DURING THE SECOND SESSION OF the 59th Congress, which stretched from December 3, 1906, to March 4, 1907, Theodore Roosevelt's long-standing apprehension over his waning influence on domestic legislation proved justified. Of the nearly five dozen measures the president had recommended in his annual December address, only a small number were given "favorable consideration"—the rest were rejected outright or simply "passed over in silence." Reporters considered the session "an uneventful and poor spirited affair," despite the passage of two important measures that had been held over from the previous session: a bill banning corporate contributions in federal elections and legislation preventing railroads from "knowingly" working their employees for more than sixteen consecutive hours. Aside from these two achievements many critical bills were blocked by the conservative Republican leadership: the Philippine tariff law, a child labor law for the District of Columbia, the eight-hour workday bill, a national inheritance tax, a progressive income tax, and a federal licensing law for corporations.

In addition, Roosevelt was deeply frustrated by new threats to his hard-won conservation measures. On February 25, 1907, the Senate passed an amendment to the Agricultural Appropriations Act, rescinding the president's executive power to designate national forests in six western states. Thereafter, only an act of Congress could create a forest reserve, leaving "some sixteen million of acres," Roosevelt later contended, "to be exploited by land grabbers and by the representatives of the great special interests." Because a veto of the entire agricultural bill was not politically viable, Roosevelt and his chief of forestry, Gifford Pinchot, devised an ingenious remedy. With six days remaining before the bill would be signed, Pinchot mobilized his office to work round the clock, some employees toiling forty-eight hours without interruption to draft proclamations placing all 16 million acres into forest lands. No sooner was each proclamation completed than Roosevelt signed an executive order withdrawing the land from development. Through these orders, nearly three dozen new national forest reserves were designated in the American West, including Rainier and Cascade in Washington and Oregon, Bear Lodge in Wyoming, and Lewis and Clark in Montana. Only with the amendment rendered meaningless did Roosevelt sign the agricultural bill. "Opponents of the Forest Service," Roosevelt later boasted, "turned handsprings in their wrath."

Though he was pleased with this successful maneuvering, the president was painfully aware that his strength on Capitol Hill remained seriously compromised by his renunciation of a possible third term. Each passing day emboldened conservative members of Congress to challenge the administration's programs and policies. Looking ahead to the election, Roosevelt feared that if the reactionary wing of his party successfully nominated and elected one of their own, they would work to dilute or even repeal his historic regulatory bills and, in the end, gut his achievements and demolish his legacy.

Of paramount importance was a successor who would sustain and advance his agenda, and there was no man he trusted more to uphold the progressive cause than William Howard Taft. Reporters were fascinated by "the deep, unbroken friendship" the two shared, "like unsophisticated schoolboys when together," one journalist expounded, "each apparently under the spell of a romantic affection, a strong, simple sense of knightly companionship in the great field of moral errantry and patriotic adventure." Roosevelt knew he would have to proceed carefully to help his friend get elected. "I am well aware," he told William Allen White, "that nothing would more certainly ruin Taft's chances than to have it supposed that I was trying to dictate his nomination." Nevertheless, he defiantly continued, "it is preposterously absurd to say that I have not the right to have my choice as regards the candidates for the Presidency, and that it is not my duty to try to exercise that choice in favor of the man who will carry out the governmental principles in which I believe with all my heart and soul."

To that end, Roosevelt launched a private campaign of persuasion, engineering a boom of support for Taft's candidacy. In personal letters and meetings, he repeatedly insisted that he would "do all in his power" for Taft, though he could say nothing in public. To visitors, he extolled Taft's "boundless courage," emphasizing his absolute freedom from "any possible corrupting or beguiling influence." In off-the-record conversations with journalist friends, he swore that "he would crawl on his hands and knees from the White House to the Capitol" to secure Taft's election, but if they quoted him, he warned, he would disavow any such statement. A ditty in the *Kansas City Times* compressed the president's stance perfectly:

IMPARTIAL MR. ROOSEVELT
Says Roosevelt: "I announce no choice,
To no man will I lend my voice,
I have no private candidate,
I care not whom you nominate—
Just so it's Taft."

Indeed, the ferocity of Roosevelt's desire for a Taft presidency far exceeded the candidate's own. Taft's declaration of his candidacy was so tepid, so lacking in conviction that it sounded as if he had decided *not* to run: "I wish to say," he began, "that my ambition is not political; that I am not seeking the presidential nomination, that I do not expect to be the Republican candidate." Still, he avowed, "I am not foolish enough to say that in the improbable event that the opportunity to run for the great office of President were to come to me, I should decline it, for this would not be true." This tentative announcement prompted speculation that an unwilling Taft had "been drawn into the maelstrom of Presidential politics," finally yielding to "the persistent pleading of the President and strong personal friends." Even after announcing his candidacy, Taft indicated a preference for working "behind the scenes" and pursuing his duties "irrespective of politics." He found the prospect of soliciting support repugnant and "was very much averse" to burdening his friends with requests for assistance. William Taft, observed a *Chicago Tribune* reporter, seemed to have "an almost morbid fear of being placed in the attitude of struggling for the Presidency."

Initially, Taft's reluctance appeared a winning quality, evidence that the office should seek the man rather than the man the office. "Taft is not a politician in the sense that he is a wire-puller and a seeker of power," commended *The Washington Post*, "but as a natural statesman and leader, he draws all men to him. Let him appear at a public reception, let him make a speech before a large audience, let him attend a private gathering and when he leaves, at least fifty percent of the people will be his friends." The *New York Times* too observed that while Taft might be ignorant of "the little details of politics, the methods of juggling a ward primary, and of playing horse with a caucus," he nevertheless commanded "a bigger, broader kind of politics . . . the kind that is frank and open."

Taft's peculiar diffidence over his presidential hopes also freed him to take a principled stand when faced with trouble brewing in Ohio. In late March 1907, Roosevelt's nemesis, the reactionary senator Joseph Foraker, openly assailed Taft's candidacy, declaring his intention to challenge Taft for the endorsement of the Republican State Committee. The press predicted that a state committee endorsement of Foraker for president could prove crippling to Taft's candidacy. Foraker "may cause trouble," Roosevelt acknowledged to Kermit, adding that in Ohio, the senator was already mustering "the fight against Taft, and incidentally against me."

When Foraker issued his statement, Taft was in the middle of a three-week trip to Panama, Cuba, and Puerto Rico. Speaking on his brother's behalf, Charles Taft accepted Foraker's challenge, suggesting that the question of Ohio's endorsement be put before the voters in a primary. "This is a direct contest between the friends of the Administration of President Roosevelt and his opponents," he argued, relaying Taft's readiness to let the voters decide: "We are willing to submit it to the Republican voters of Ohio and the sooner the better." Nellie found the confrontation unsettling and concurred with the president that Taft "had nothing to gain" from heeding Foraker's challenge and "much possibly to lose."

The decision to call Foraker's bluff, however, soon proved wise. Foraker understood that Roosevelt and Taft enjoyed more support among Ohio's voters and realized that if he manipulated an endorsement from the state committee and subsequently lost to Taft in an open primary or convention, he might jeopardize his Senate seat. Through intermediaries, he therefore offered to endorse Taft for president in exchange for his support in the approaching senatorial contest. Taft flatly refused. "I don't care for the Presidency if it has to come by compromise with Senator Foraker," Taft told Arthur Vorys, his Ohio campaign manager. As "a question of political principle," declared Taft, he could never strike a bargain to endorse a man who had consistently opposed the policies and programs of the Roosevelt administration. Furious, Foraker warned that henceforth, Taft should meet him in the political arena "with a drawn sword in his hand."

In a long letter to Roosevelt, Taft acknowledged that affairs in Ohio had "become somewhat acute." The state committee was scheduled to meet in late July, and Foraker might have sufficient votes to defeat a resolution endorsing Taft's nomination. Still, Taft insisted, he had no regrets. "Rather than compromise with Foraker, I would give up all hope for the Presidency," he stated. "I must explain to you that the Ohio brand of politics the last twenty years has been harmony and concession on the subject of principle to the last degree, provided it secured personal preferment and division of the spoil in a satisfactory way." If Foraker hoped to win, Taft concluded, the senator would have to engage in "a stand-up fight."

Roosevelt's reply demonstrated an admiration for his friend's character that far eclipsed any misgivings over his political acuity. "While under no circumstances," Roosevelt wrote, "would I have advised you to take the position you have taken in refusing to compromise with Foraker on the lines that the local politicians want, yet, now that you have taken it, I wish to say that I count it as just one of those fine and manly things which I would naturally expect from you, and I believe you are emphatically right."

Steeled for defeat when the state committee met to select candidates at the end of July, Taft enjoyed a stunning victory. The committee not only voted 15 to 6 to endorse Taft for president; they also refused to back Foraker in the Senate race. "I am hopeful that it will have a very good effect in other states," a relieved Taft told Howard Hollister. Foraker's political career came to an unceremonious end the following September, when William Randolph Hearst released letters suggesting he had received bribes from Standard Oil. Foraker later argued that the money was simply compensation for legal services, but the damage was done; he withdrew from the Senate race and never served in public office again.

DESPITE HIS VICTORY IN OHIO, Taft found the bitter struggle dispiriting. While Roosevelt reveled in the fight, urging his chosen successor to deliver a "mauling" to Foraker, Taft possessed no such bellicose spirit and could never forget that his "first substantial start in public life" was due to the early kindness of the now disgraced senator. The politics of personal destruction held no relish for a man "born with an instinct to be personally agreeable." Reporters described Will Taft as "the kindest man they [had] ever known in public life." Perhaps better than any other, Louise Taft understood the strengths and weaknesses of her favorite child. Asked what she thought of her son's presidential candidacy, she confessed that she shared Will's reluctance. "A place on the Supreme bench, where my boy would administer justice, is my ambition for him," she admitted. "His is a judicial mind, you know, and he loves the law." Though Taft had proven himself in the Philippines, Cuba, and Panama, the mother knew her son's disposition and the toll that political discord exacted. "Uneasy lies the head that wears a crown," she warned him when he declared his candidacy, shrewdly discerning that "Roosevelt is a good fighter and enjoys it, but the malice of the politicians would make you miserable."

As the months passed, public enchantment with Taft as the reluctant politician began to wane. "He wins the hearts of individuals, but he does not fire the heart of the sovereign multitude," observed reporter James Creelman of the weakening Taft boom. Taft's reluctance to passionately embrace his political ambition began to shift from a sign of moral strength to an indication of weakness: "The country respects and trusts his ability and integrity, but its attitude is that of passive recognition and approval, not the head-long affection that brings power to a political leader of the first rank." Why this "statesman of stainless name, unshakeable independence and creative and administrative abilities" had stirred "so little enthusiasm in the American people" had initially seemed a mystery to Creelman. The explanation, he finally suggested, lay in "the fact that the Secretary of War is not dowered with a political order of mind and is almost wholly devoid of political ambitions." The *New York Times* concurred, adding that people will not flock to a candidate who "can scarcely be said to have waved his standard and asked people to flock to it."

Though Taft had robustly stumped for Roosevelt, he did little in his own behalf to invigorate his popularity. As a candidate in his own right, Taft was expected to emerge as more than the genial defender and chief spokesman for the administration. Correspondents covering the campaign inevitably demanded the headline-generating phrasemaking and charismatic demeanor they had come to expect from Roosevelt. When Taft was criticized as not "fitted to say things that attract attention," his campaign manager urged him to include anecdotes and striking figures of speech in his oratory. "I am not sure that I can make the epigrams that you are hunting for," Taft responded disconsolately, turning to his habitual self-deprecating humor as he continued. "The truth is you have a pretty old horse to run and you've got to take me as I am." Before each address, he was beset by grave misgivings, acutely aware that his drafts remained "infernally long" despite all efforts to prune his words. "Never mind if you cannot get off fireworks," Nellie consoled him. "It must be known by this time that that is not your style, and there is no use in trying to force it. If people don't want you as you are they can leave you, and we shall both be able to survive it."

More problematic to critics than Taft's speaking style was his failure to present a political figure independent from Theodore Roosevelt. On tariff reduction, the sole issue on which he had publicly been at odds with Roosevelt's policy, he now softened his stance and repeated the president's view that "revision must wait until after the election." Though he did not echo Roosevelt's "ferocious denunciation" of business, Taft positioned himself squarely behind the anti-trust and regulatory policies designed to prevent corporate abuses and deflate "swollen fortunes." He passionately defended the railroad rate bill, the food and drug legislation, and the recent conservation measures. He called for a strengthened employer's liability law, a progressive income tax, and an inheritance tax. With only a few "minor exceptions," Taft proclaimed his "complete, thorough, and sincere sympathy" with Roosevelt's policies. The New York *Sun* carped that "there is not an original note" in any of Taft's speeches, jeering that "his ample corporeal capacity receives and contains all that Roosevelt has been, and is, and hopes to be."

Taft expressed bafflement at the press's surprise concerning his sympathy with Roosevelt's policies. "I am much amused at the attitude of the New York papers," he told Horace. "Did they suppose I was coming out to attack Roosevelt's policies? Did they suppose I had stayed in the Cabinet thus long and disapproved of them?" But even some of Taft's ardent backers wished that he would endeavor to set himself apart. "Is it possible," Taft asked one concerned supporter, "that a man shows lack of originality, shows slavish imitation because he happens to concur in the views of another who has the power to enforce those views? Mr. Roosevelt's views were mine long before I knew Mr. Roosevelt at all." He would not, he insisted, "be driven from adherence to those views" by unjust, nonsensical criticism.

Nonetheless, by midsummer of 1907, Taft's candidacy had stalled. A lingering problem, one supporter admitted, lay in "the feeling of uncertainty as to the President's real intentions." So long as the merest possibility remained that Roosevelt might rescind his pledge and run for a third term, many Republicans would not commit to anyone else. "The President is a hero in the eyes of the people," as a friend expressed this concern to Taft, "and they will not surrender his leadership unless they are compelled to." Particularly in the western states, a "well defined movement" had emerged "to force the nomination of Roosevelt." Straw votes taken in the Nebraska and South Dakota legislatures revealed "an almost unanimous sentiment for Roosevelt," and Kansas was reportedly poised to send a Roosevelt delegation to the convention whether he agreed to run or not. "It's hard to write snappy Taft stuff when every damned man I meet gives three cheers for Roosevelt and refuses to talk of any other candidate," another frustrated advocate acknowledged. "Nearly every man who says a good word for Taft doesn't want his name used for fear he may offend Roosevelt. . . . It's a plain, unabridged truth that 90 percent of the Taft sentiment I have found is second-hand or remnant Roosevelt sentiment."

Nellie Taft had never been able to shake her intuitive apprehension that Roosevelt would change his mind about his own candidacy. As calls for a third term gathered steam and newspapers began to suggest circumstances under which the president might enter the race, her concern escalated. While running would be an "almost grotesque" betrayal of his friendship with Taft, the New York *Sun* speculated, the president would doubtless "welcome a situation in which his candidacy might seem inevitable, demanded by the patriotic and imperative clamor of the entire nation." With sardonic, incisive humor, the editorial inquired: "May not the imaginative mind assemble conditions and considerations under which Mr. Taft will seem the victim of it all and also the appointed sacrifice to an illustrious Necessity?" The *Sun*'s piece further unsettled Nellie, who expressed her misgivings to Will: "How they hate him & they go farther than I in insinuating that this is all part of his scheme to get himself nominated as the only man," she wrote, anxiously explaining how easily her husband could be labeled "a martyr and a scapegoat."

In all likelihood, had Roosevelt not declared against a third term on the eve of his overwhelming victory in 1904, he would have pursued a third term. His White House years had been the most fulfilling of his life. Only forty-nine years old and in splendid health, Roosevelt was proud of his work and eager to expand his legacy. He reportedly boasted that he "could get the nomination by simply holding up [his] little finger." Even as he warmed to the popular clamor for a third term, Roosevelt suspected that many of those who called for his reelection "would feel very much disappointed" if he actually ran, and would conclude that he had fallen "short of the ideal they had formed" as to the integrity of his character and the credibility of his word.

Roosevelt told one Cincinnati reporter, Gus Karger, that his decision not to run was an unregrettable "personal sacrifice" so long as Taft secured the nomination. "But I do not wish to have made it in vain," he clarified, "by paving the way to the selection of a successor not in sympathy with the policies of this administration." In case Taft's canvass failed to take off, however, he would not foreclose the possibility of his candidacy. Moreover, Roosevelt argued, while a public reiteration of his vow not to run would rally support for Taft in the West, it might damage his cause in the East, and particularly in New York. Once he irrevocably stated that he would not join the race, he could no longer keep the party organization there from openly backing Governor Hughes. At least "for the moment," Roosevelt convinced himself—and Taft—that saying nothing was "the wisest course." Meanwhile, third-term proponents continued their vocal campaign; by late August, the odds in favor of Roosevelt's renomination had grown "shorter."

"Political affairs are kaleidoscopic," Roosevelt warned his secretary of war on September 3, 1907. Though he still claimed that Taft was "the man upon whom it was most desirable to unite," he acknowledged that his assessment might alter as the race evolved. Support for New York governor Hughes was growing; Treasury Secretary George Cortelyou was still hoping to run; Cannon and Fairbanks remained live possibilities. This unsettled situation made him "a little nervous," Roosevelt admitted to Taft, adding that it was "a matter of real difficulty to prevent certain people declaring for [him]." Taft of all people, he assumed, would appreciate "that the first thing to be considered was the good of the nation and the next thing the good of the party." After that, "any personal preference," he portentously concluded, "must come in the third place."

Just as Roosevelt's support for Taft showed distinct signs of faltering, Taft, ironically, began to feel more sanguine about his campaign. A three-week swing through the heartland and the Far West had gone surprisingly well. "So far as I am able to judge," he reported to Charles, "the trip I have made through the west has helped me." On a sweltering summer day in Columbus, more than 20,000 people had gathered to hear him speak. "It was as great a meeting as they ever had in Ohio," Taft happily noted. In Kentucky, he had spoken to "a fine audience of 4000 people"; in Oklahoma, an immense hall "was filled to suffocation"; and in Denver, he was greeted by "every politician in the state and every state officer." Not only had Taft's formal speeches gone more smoothly, but he had also become increasingly comfortable waving and making brief remarks to the crowds clustered at train stations along his route. "Personal contact," he acknowledged, "does a great deal." His clear blue eyes and famous smile, the *New York Times* reported, made all who met the man "feel glad and sociable and sincere."

Buoyed by his warm reception everywhere he traveled, Taft took Roosevelt's ominous musings in stride. "Nellie was out of patience with the President's letter," he told Charles, "but I understand exactly his state of mind. Under the hammering of the New York papers, and the disposition to press Hughes on, he has become a little more discouraged," Taft explained, claiming, "I don't think he knows as much about the matter as I do, for I have crossed the country and been in all parts of it." Regardless of his current optimism, he promised his brother that he was "not getting into a situation where a failure to get the nomination" would render him "bitter or indeed disappointed." Rather, he assured Charles, "I think that in your general earnestness and zeal on my behalf, a defeat would be more disappointing to you than to me."

The day before his scheduled departure for a long-promised visit to the Philippines, Taft responded to Roosevelt's letter. "I fully understand the difficulties of your position, and exactly how you feel in respect to the candidacy of myself and the others," he began; "I have been, however, agreeably surprised to receive the expressions of good will which I found in the trip across the Continent." Acknowledging that "one hears the things he likes to hear," he had found overwhelming evidence of "affirmative support" across the nation. Nonetheless, he was "prepared to learn at any time" during his Pacific journey that his "boom" had "busted." Whatever the outcome, Taft insisted, he would remain grateful "for the great compliment you have paid me in taking an interest in the matter, and for making my boom at all possible."

WILL AND NELLIE, WITH TEN-YEAR-OLD Charlie in tow, sailed for the Philippines on September 13. Taft met with officials in Japan and China for several weeks before heading to Manila. The former governor general was scheduled to open the first Philippine Assembly. Taft had long considered creation of a popularly elected assembly a vital step toward eventual Filipino sovereignty. Though the Philippine Commission still exercised executive powers, the new assembly would have the "right to initiate legislation" or "to modify, amend, shape, or defeat legislation proposed by the Commission." As "the first parliament ever freely elected in Asia," the historian Stanley Karnow explains, the assembly "was a tribute to the liberalism of U.S. colonial rule," but "American democracy it was not." Only those who owned land, paid taxes, and demonstrated literacy were allowed to vote.

Taft feared he would encounter "a chill" upon reaching Manila rather than the exuberant welcome of two years earlier. Since that time, the movement for independence had gained momentum, casting an unfavorable light on his prediction that it would take generations to prepare the people for self-rule. But his misgivings proved unfounded. "The enthusiasm of the welcome," he related to Charles, exceeded anything he had experienced before, "and it was the more delightful in that it was unexpected." The reception was particularly gratifying, he added, because it showed that the "common people," along with the "wealthier classes," celebrated his role in creating the National Assembly.

He began his address by frankly admitting that he had not changed his mind about the duration required to achieve genuine sovereignty, but conceded that the question would be determined largely by the success of the new assembly. He wisely acknowledged that the United States, unused to the undertaking of colonial rule and lacking a "trained body of colonial administrators and civil servants," had made serious missteps. Adventurers and military men unsuited "by character or experience" for the serious work of public service had delayed effective government in the islands. In addition, he lamented the dilatory pace of American investment and roundly criticized the U.S. Congress for failing to reduce the tariff on the major Philippine exports of tobacco products and sugar. Yet, despite these obstacles, he believed the islands had made great advancements: hundreds of thousands of Filipino children were attending school; sanitation services and general public health had significantly improved; and a judicial system was now in place. Furthermore, he noted, miles of new roads and street railways had been built, a civil service had been established, and the problems with the Catholic Church had been largely settled. Taft ended his oration by extending his "congratulations upon the auspicious beginning of your legislative life" and conveying his "heartfelt sympathy in the work which you are about to undertake."

At the Inaugural Ball, Taft once again won hearts with his graceful execution of the complex national dance, the rigadon. Will and Nellie attended a "thousand and one events" in the days that followed, inspecting projects that had been completed since their last visit and renewing old friendships and acquaintances at a succession of dances, parties, and banquets. "Everybody," Nellie happily noted, "was glad to see us." The Tafts remained in the Philippines from mid-October through the first week of November, far removed from the stock market collapse that threatened both Roosevelt's legacy and Taft's candidacy.

In October, a series of difficulties on Wall Street escalated into what later became known as the Roosevelt Panic of 1907. Stock prices had been slumping since the previous March; in July and August, a number of companies, including a mining firm and a major street railway company, fell into bankruptcy. As industrial production slackened toward summer's end, experts calculated that stock market losses approached $1 billion. Wall Street blamed Theodore Roosevelt's "crusades against business" for the decline, arguing that his excessive regulation had paralyzed the economy. "By slow and insidious degrees," the *Sun* editorialized, "he has upset the public confidence, arrayed class against class, and fomented mistrust and hatred." The *New York Times* concurred, tracing the country's ills to the administration's "deep-seated, undiscriminating hostility" to business. By "going up and down the country, planting the doctrine of discontent," another critic charged, Roosevelt had "sowed the wind, and we will reap the whirlwind." Union Pacific Railroad president E. H. Harriman, a lifelong Republican, bitterly claimed that he would "take Bryan or Hearst rather than Roosevelt. We cannot be worse off than we are now with that man in the White House."

In a defiant rejoinder, Roosevelt dispensed with his characteristic even-handed rhetoric. He stridently railed against "certain malefactors of great wealth," who conspired "to bring about as much financial distress as they possibly can in order to discredit the policy of the government, and thereby to secure a reversal of that policy so that they may enjoy the fruits of their own evil-doing." These plutocrats, he charged, would even "welcome hard times or a panic" to install "a safe type" in the White House. "They are as blind to some of the tendencies of the time, as the French noblesse was before the French Revolution." Those business interests that shrank from regulation, the president suggested, should examine their own operations. He was "responsible for turning on the light," he noted proudly, not "for what the light showed." Curiously, Roosevelt omitted all mention of the muckraking journalists who had proven so instrumental in illuminating industrial abuses.

As summer turned to early fall, Roosevelt continued to frame the downturn as "a temporary period of weakness," part of a worldwide contraction after a period of great prosperity. Unwilling to cancel his agenda, he left Washington on September 29 to deliver a series of speeches in the West, a trip that would culminate in a ten-day bear hunt in northeast Louisiana. Yet, while Roosevelt hunted bear, the bear market savaged Wall Street and the financial crisis deepened.

In early October, banking moguls F. Augustus Heinze and Charles W. Morse drove up copper prices in an attempt to corner the market. Their sensational failure—and the resulting depression of stock value—might have remained an isolated incident if news had not leaked that their costly speculation had been funded by the stately Knickerbocker Trust Company, the second largest investment bank in New York. Spooked by rumors that the venerable institution might fail, investors stood in queues outside the bank doors from dawn till dusk attempting to reclaim their funds. On the afternoon of October 22, the Knickerbocker ran out of money and was forced to shutter its offices. Three weeks later, the bank's president, Charles T. Barney, committed suicide. Evidence that the respected firm had abandoned sound banking practices to gamble with customers' deposits shattered confidence in other financial institutions. In the days that followed, customers rushed to retrieve money, some standing all night on the sidewalks, others sleeping in the vestibules. Reports indicated that "hardly a bank or trust company" was spared, as the Panic threatened to compromise the nation's entire financial structure.

In the absence of a centralized banking system, seventy-year-old J. P. Morgan served as "a one-man Federal Reserve." The magnificent library at his Madison Avenue house was designated "Panic Headquarters." Surrounded by rare books, Renaissance paintings, and exquisite tapestries, Morgan and his partners met with a carefully selected group of leading bankers. Day after day, often late into the night, this financial cabal monitored the precarious situation, transferring monies from one bank to another, declaring which institutions to save and then raising sufficient funds to rescue them. Within two days the bankers had pledged nearly $10 million.

As Roosevelt hurried back to Washington, Treasury Secretary George Cortelyou took a day train to New York. Meeting with Morgan's group that evening, he promised that the government would add $25 million to the bankers' fund to be distributed at Morgan's discretion. "It was an extraordinary transference of power to a private banker," the biographer Ron Chernow observes. The next day, reporters noted that immense bags of bank securities were delivered to the U.S. subtreasury and J. P. Morgan's headquarters. This quick action saved dozens of banks and trust companies, including the venerable Trust Company of America.

Despite these efforts to stabilize the banking system, stock prices continued to tumble. On Thursday, October 24, the president of the New York Stock Exchange broke the news to Morgan that his brokers no longer had the cash to continue trading. Determined to avoid a shutdown that would likely precipitate the wholesale collapse of financial institutions across the city, Morgan called an emergency meeting. Less than thirty minutes had elapsed before a messenger brought word that Morgan's group had pledged $25 million to keep the exchange open. Elated at this reprieve, exuberant stockbrokers hooted and cheered, hailing J. P. Morgan as "the Man of the Hour." The crisis had proven that Morgan "was still the chief among the country's financiers," the New York *Evening Mail* observed, "the one leader who could inspire the confidence of the multitude and command the resources of the nation."

Just as one firestorm was contained a new blaze erupted. On November 1, Morgan learned that Moore & Schley, a leading brokerage house, was on the verge of bankruptcy. Understanding that the firm's failure "would bring down a few more stories of the tottering financial pyramid," Morgan evolved an ingenious plan. The troubled brokerage house owned a large stake in the Tennessee Coal and Iron Company (TC&I), one of the few significant combinations to escape the grip of United States Steel. In a meeting with U.S. Steel's chairman, Judge Elbert Gary, Morgan proposed that U.S. Steel purchase TC&I, exchanging its own solid bonds for TC&I bonds to redeem Moore & Schley. As a precondition, Gary insisted on Roosevelt's assurance that the purchase would not trigger an anti-trust suit. "Can you go at once?" Morgan demanded.

That evening, Judge Gary and Henry Clay Frick took the overnight train to Washington. Meeting with the president at eight o'clock the following morning, the two U.S. Steel representatives maintained that "under ordinary circumstances they would not consider purchasing the stock," which was priced "somewhat in excess" of the firm's true value. Nevertheless, they believed it was "to the interest of every responsible businessman" to avoid a "general industrial smashup." Roosevelt assured them that he "felt . . . no public duty" to file suit under the Sherman Anti-Trust Act.

The announcement of the deal not only saved Moore & Schley; it also helped restore confidence in the market. But when the terms of the TC&I purchase were made public, Roosevelt came under heavy criticism. John Moody, a respected financial analyst, termed the $45 million purchase price "the best bargain . . . ever made in the purchase of a piece of property"; the coal and iron ore deposits alone, he estimated, were worth "hardly less than $1 billion." Some suspected that Roosevelt had been hoodwinked into legitimizing U.S. Steel's bid to "swallow up a lively competitor, while wrapping itself in the cloak of public spirit."

Roosevelt adamantly denied such charges. "The Nation trembled on the brink," he contended, justifying his decision by pointing to the speed and volatility of the financial markets: "Events moved with such speed that it was necessary to decide and to act on the instant, as each successive crisis arose."

A decision had been necessary before the stock market opened that morning. "I would have showed myself a timid and unworthy public servant, if in that extraordinary crisis, I had not acted precisely as I did." In the years ahead, however, the contentious decision would open a painful rift in Roosevelt's friendship with William Howard Taft.

Although the immediate danger of the financial panic subsided, a general malaise began to seep into every sector of the economy, costing laborers their jobs and farmers their livelihood. "Whether I am or am not in any degree responsible for the panic, I shall certainly be held responsible," Roosevelt grumbled to his physician, Dr. Alexander Lambert. "The big moneyed men" had long since "reached a pitch of acute emotional insanity," he told Kermit. That anger-fueled hysteria would begin to infect even friends and supporters, he suspected, "because when the average man loses his money he is simply like a wounded snake and strikes right and left at anything, innocent or the reverse, that presents itself as conspicuous in his mind."

"From all sides," Ida Tarbell observed, "the business world, the press, leaders of public opinion—there came such a berating of the President as a man has rarely had to endure." No longer simply a "destroyer of credit," Roosevelt had now become an "assassin of property." From Kansas, William Allen White wrote to cheer his friend. "I feel personally hurt by all this abuse that is being heaped on you," he began. "The whole system is bending its energy to turn back the clock, and the prayers and the assistance of every good American should be with you in this crisis." Roosevelt found some consolation in White's words but remained pessimistic about his prospects. "I care a great deal more for such a letter as you have written to me than I do for the attacks that are being made upon me," he replied. "If there is much depression, if we meet hard times, then a great number of honest and well-meaning people will gradually come to believe in the truth of these attacks, and I shall probably end my term of service as President under a more or less dark cloud of obloquy. If so, I shall be sorry, of course; but I shall neither regret what I have done nor alter my line of conduct."

On the morning of November 16, Ray Baker arrived at the White House for a scheduled discussion about his series on race in America. Instead, when Baker noticed a thin red pamphlet called *The Roosevelt Panic* on the president's desk, the conversation quickly turned to the economy. Wall Street, Roosevelt explained, had circulated this incendiary tract "to destroy his program of reform." For two hours, Roosevelt shared his vantage on the troubling situation. "It looks now," he told Baker, "as though there would be let down in business throughout the country for some time to come. I shall be blamed for it: my enemies will make capital of it. It is probable that before next summer I shall be the bête noir of the country." While still hopeful for Taft's nomination, the president feared that "the country at the next election would have to choose between an extreme radical like Bryan and a republican reactionary; that in either event the moderate reform movement which he advocates would be lost sight of." Continuing the conversation with Baker the next morning, Roosevelt repeatedly insisted that "the fight must be carried through." The idea of either a reactionary or Bryan as the next president, Baker observed, seemed to set "his fighting blood to running!" The journalist departed with a growing conviction that Roosevelt was seriously considering another run. "A man may sometimes have to jeopardize his own soul," the president had cryptically commented, "when the interests of the country are at stake."

And in truth, Roosevelt was still brooding over the prospects of another term. "I hate for personal reasons to get out of the fight here," he told one friend. "I have the uncomfortable feeling that I may possibly be shirking a duty." The leader who quits "the fight before it is finished" deserves little respect, he confided to another supporter. Nevertheless, he countered, a political leader "must understand the temper and convictions of the people." And while he believed he could win the Republican nomination, Roosevelt had misgivings about the general election. Nothing would be more humiliating than to break his word and then lose.

The time had come, Roosevelt finally decided, to make clear that he would not seek a third term under any circumstance. On the evening of December 11, he released an unusually succinct statement: "On the night after my election I made the following announcement." Verbatim, he repeated his pledge renouncing a third term and concluded with an equally curt finality: "I have not changed and shall not change the decision thus announced."

Roosevelt's proclamation arrived "like a clap of thunder out of the clear sky," the *National Tribune* reported. "Washington has been throbbing with political gossip ever since." Derisive speculation abounded among the president's critics: "I suppose he has come to the conclusion that it would not be worthwhile for him to run," Democratic senator Tillman charged, stridently observing that "the pitiful condition into which he and Cortelyou have got things shows that he could not be elected." Although Roosevelt would undoubtedly "do his utmost to name the man who [would] carry out his policies,"

William Randolph Hearst noted, only time would tell whether the popularity he once enjoyed or the rejection he currently endured would prove more potent for his chosen candidate.

In Republican circles, commentary focused primarily on Taft's brightening prospects. With Roosevelt "definitely and positively out of the Presidential race," party leaders were free "to come out squarely for Taft." California senator Frank Flint insisted that the state had been for Taft "all along" and could now openly declare its support. Kansas senator Chester Long concurred, calling Taft's candidacy "the only one worth considering."

As the political world debated Taft's future, Will and Nellie crossed the Atlantic on the SS *President Grant*. They had cut short their round-the-world tour upon receiving news that Taft's mother was critically ill. Louise Taft had been in splendid health until the previous summer, when she developed an acute inflammation of the gall bladder. Before his departure for the Philippines, Taft had stopped at the old family mansion in Millbury, Massachusetts, where his mother and her sister Delia resided together. Doctors considered Louise's condition serious, yet Will and his brothers were convinced that her cheerful nature and her "strength, constitution and courage" would carry her through. She remained mentally clear and for a time seemed to be "on the road to recovery." On her eightieth birthday in September, Annie Taft reported, "her cheeks were as rosy as a young girl's and she was happy as a child at seeing us. There was something marvelous about the youthfulness of her face." As winter approached, however, she "slowly but steadily" lost ground. On December 4, Charles telegraphed Will in St. Petersburg that the end was near. "Still have hope that she will survive until you arrive," Charles wrote two days later, but Taft's ship had left Hamburg, Germany, when he received word that his mother was dead.

When the SS *President Grant* arrived at Quarantine in New York, a courier handed Taft a confidential letter from the president. "I hope you will say nothing for publication until you see me," Roosevelt cautioned. "Things have become somewhat intricate and you want to consider well what steps you are to take before taking them," he explained. "A great many of your ardent supporters became convinced that your canvass was being hurt by the refusal of many people to accept my declination as final, and that numbers of people who were sincerely attached to you, but who were even more devoted to me, did not come out for you because they thought I was still a possibility . . . I therefore decided to make one more public statement."

Neither politics nor strategy were foremost on William Taft's agenda. No sooner had he landed than he made plans for an immediate trip to Cincinnati.

"I was very much pained not to be able to come here to attend the funeral," he told a friend. Missing the final "epoch" in his mother's life had left him with a terrible "sense of something wanting," a loss he hoped to mitigate by laying "a wreath on her grave and [calling] on her old friends." While his mother's death represented "a great change" for the entire family, he took solace in the knowledge that through eight decades, she had lived according to her own design, never riddled by a longing "for something else." Ever a force "to be reckoned with," Louise Taft had been a formative power within her own family, just as she had helped shape every community in which she lived. And although she would not see the new chapter that was beginning for her son William, Louise Taft had never doubted his devoted and amiable soul.

CHAPTER TWENTY-ONE

Kingmaker and King

In this Aug. 1, 1906, *Puck* cartoon—"The Crown Prince"—Theodore Roosevelt wears an emperor's garb and holds aloft his chosen successor: an infant Taft.

BY THE TIME HE RETURNED to Washington in the early winter of 1908, Taft found that the push for his nomination had "caught its second wind and straightened out for the home-stretch." In the wake of Roosevelt's reaffirmation that he would not run again, William Nelson of the *Kansas City Star* informed Taft that the state now regarded him "as its first and only choice"—a resolution in his favor had gone through "with a whoop." Furthermore, the Colorado State Committee endorsed Taft unanimously, and a poll among likely Michigan delegates showed him trouncing the field by a two to one margin.

Buoyed by the show of widening support, Taft began to actively engage in his campaign for the first time. On the eve of a Republican State Committee meeting in West Virginia, he assured Governor William Dawson that his endorsement would be a decisive blow, clinching not only West Virginia but neighboring states as well. "If you could bring this about," he encouraged the governor, "I shall be everlastingly grateful." He solicited activists for information on the political climate in their regions and responded to encouraging editorials with handwritten notes, telling the publisher of the *St. Paul Pioneer Press and Tribune* that the "friendly tone" of a recent editorial had made his "whole day and week brighter."

Increasingly comfortable at the podium, Taft responded to questions with "rapid-fire" retorts and "witty sallies." Asked at Cooper Union in New York why "a blacklisted laborer" should not "be allowed an injunction as well as a boycotted capitalist," he replied succinctly: "He should be. Were I on the bench I would give him one quickly." Explaining his preference for capitalism over socialism, Taft wryly observed that he did not trust a governmental committee "to determine the worth" of a lawyer, doctor, carpenter or judge—unless, of course, he himself was a member of that committee. Only once did Taft's words come back to haunt him. To the daunting question of what those unable to find work during the recession might do, he had earnestly answered, "God knows. . . . They have my deepest sympathy. It is an awful case when a man is willing to work and is put in this position." Critics seized upon the phrase "God knows" to suggest Taft's want of empathy for the laboring class. Nonetheless, when the long question-and-answer session came to an end, "it was the general verdict that the Secretary was entitled to the referee's decision, and when the gong rang the crowd swarmed into the ring to grasp the victor's hand."

By late January, New York governor Hughes was the sole remaining candidate with a national following who could potentially challenge Taft for the Republican nomination. Taft's supporters urged him to fight Hughes for the New York delegates, but Taft insisted that a nasty struggle in the governor's home fort would ultimately hurt Republican chances in the fall. This decision drew praise from party leaders, but Roosevelt continued to worry that Hughes was a threat. Aware that the governor intended to deliver a major campaign speech on January 31, Roosevelt deliberately chose that same date to present a special message to Congress. The president's words proved to be so "blistering," so "genuinely sensational," that they stole headlines from Hughes's "sane and sound" address.

Roosevelt's anger over the legislature's persistent refusal to act on his recommendations had been mounting for weeks. When the Supreme Court ruled the 1906 Employers' Liability Act unconstitutional in early January, the president was irate, calling it "a matter of humiliation to the Nation" that an employee who suffered an accident "through no fault of his own" would not be protected. "In no other prominent industrial country in the world," he charged, "could such gross injustice occur." He challenged Congress to enact a new liability law and take up his additional regulatory measures without delay. Any implication that such regulations had precipitated the recent panic was wrongheaded, he maintained; in fact, as far as individual blame could be ascribed, the collapse was "due to the speculative folly and flagrant dishonesty of a few men of great wealth, who seek to shield themselves from the effects of their own wrongdoing by ascribing its results to the actions of those who have sought to put a stop to the wrongdoing."

While critics accused Roosevelt of "prostituting his high office and the machinery of government in order to play petty and mean politics against Hughes," the substance of his speech garnered widespread approval. "It hurls defiance at a legislature that thought in its folly that the day of Roosevelt was done," the *Denver Post* observed, contending that "it appeals beyond Congress to the hearts of the American people." The *Boston Daily Globe* also praised the president's "sledgehammer eloquence," while the *Chicago Tribune* rated it "one of America's great state papers." Even those who considered its tone incongruous with "the preconceptions of presidential dignity" acknowledged that the message had caught everyone's attention. "It has maddened my enemies," Roosevelt told Kermit, but "I believe it has helped Taft's nomination."

A New York *World* cartoon aptly illustrated the strategic timing of the president's address: Hughes is pictured trying to deliver his speech while Roosevelt beats an enormous bass drum, drowning out the governor's words. Delighted by the image, Taft wrote to the *World* editor and requested the original caricature. "It records something which may prove to be an epoch in the campaign," he explained. "I should like very much to have it as a part of my memorabilia." By spring, the president noted with satisfaction that "the Hughes boom has collapsed," and Taft's nomination was all but "settled."

Still, Roosevelt continued to monitor every aspect of the campaign, counseling and comforting Taft through the inevitable vicissitudes. In March, for instance, a subordinate in his Columbus campaign office released a statement declaring that Taft would prove more acceptable to the business community than his predecessor. The statement reprinted a series of quotes from the *Wall Street Journal* touting Taft as deliberative and measured in his nature and training—a needful antidote to the impulsive, intemperate president. Both Taft's temperament and his record, the *Journal* had suggested, boded "distinctly against any conclusion that he would continue Mr. Roosevelt's methods." Taft immediately repudiated the release and fired the employee, but the incident continued to disturb him. "Good heavens, you beloved individual," Roosevelt placated him, "you'll have any number of such experiences," though not "as many as I have had; and, unlike you I have frequently been myself responsible!"

Far more troubling, Taft confided, was the "painful experience" of finding himself "held up to execration" as an enemy of the black race for his role as secretary of war during the Brownsville incident. From his abolitionist father, Taft had inherited a deep sympathy and support for the rights of the freed slaves. Indefatigably, he had worked in the Philippines "to oppose the color caste." Yet regardless of his record of combating inequality, scores of traditionally Republican black leaders now considered him "a menace" and declared they would "never, never" support him. While some in Taft's camp suggested he distance himself from the president by publicly discussing his attempt to delay the order, Taft refused; loyalty trumped political advantage. Roosevelt finally took action himself, issuing a formal statement claiming "entire responsibility for the dismissal of the negro troops" and absolving Taft of any role in the decision. As news of Roosevelt's statement spread through the black community, resistance to Taft's nomination dissipated. "We are satisfied," declared the editor of a popular black newspaper, that "President Roosevelt was responsible for the discharge of the soldiers and we believe that Mr. Taft had nothing at all to do with it."

In late spring, however, speaking at Grant's Tomb on Decoration Day, Taft inadvertently instigated his own controversy when he referred to the Civil War general's predilection "for strong drink," which had forced his resignation from the Union Army. Intended as a tribute to the "wonderful resolution, strength of character, and military genius" that allowed Grant to triumph over adversity, Taft's address sought to project a fallible exemplar for young people rather than a mythical figure, "painted as perfect without temptation." Whatever his intention, many veterans perceived Taft's depiction of Grant as a desecration: "I trust you will have the grace to go and hang yourself rather than attempt to belittle a nation by running for the presidency," the commander of the New Hampshire Sons of Veterans histrionically suggested. Across the country, outraged veterans accused Taft of insulting "the mighty dead" and warned that they would not forget his "heartless" remarks on election day. When Roosevelt and Taft reconvened, the president stood "at mock attention," solemnly exclaiming, "Viva Grant." He advised Taft not to fret: "It is not going to hurt you. I have got the public accustomed to hearing the truth from statesmen or politicians, whichever we might be termed, without it changing the destinies of the nation."

The president's confidence, it seemed, was well founded; such stumbles did little to stay the momentum of Taft's campaign. "All opposition to Taft has died down and he will be nominated easily," Roosevelt assured a friend at the end of May. The surge of support in recent months represented "an astonishing achievement for Mr. Taft," the *Chicago Evening Post* observed, affirming the candidate's ability to evade the many snares that had beset his campaign. "We doubt whether the history of the country has ever recorded a more remarkable feat by a presidential candidate than this utter routing of each and every anti-convention attack upon him."

Roosevelt's satisfaction with the progress of Taft's campaign as summer arrived could not mask his chagrin that Congress had refused to act on his proposals for a second straight year. "Congress is ending, by no means in a blaze of glory," the president complained to Whitelaw Reid, ambassador to Great Britain. The reigning conservatives in the House and Senate, he grumbled, "felt a relief that they did not try to conceal at the fact that I was not to remain as President." While a few significant measures had passed—including a revised employer liability act and a child labor bill for the District of Columbia—the core of Roosevelt's progressive recommendations had again been ignored. With "practical unanimity," journalists referred to the session as the "do nothing Congress."

In his frustration, Roosevelt failed to appreciate that conservatives were emboldened not only by his impending departure but also by the diminished power of the muckraking journalists, whose popular exposures of corporate abuse had played a collaborative role in pressuring Congress to act. Nor did the president acknowledge that his celebrated address castigating muckrakers had "crystallized" a nascent sentiment of disfavor toward the new journalism. Two years after Roosevelt's diatribe, a survey of leading monthlies revealed a sharp decline in the fiery investigative pieces that had fueled public demand for reform. "The noon of the muckraker's day is past," one Iowa newspaper declared. "Look upon these magazines now," observed the *New York Times*. "Read them from cover to cover. Where are the muckrakers?" Magazine publishers were acutely sensitive to capricious public sentiment, the *Times* concluded: "Like the manufacturers of print cloth and summer silks," they were "prepared to offer any pattern the reader desires. We judge that quiet patterns are now in favor."

While the country sought respite from grim catalogues of wrongdoing, members of the old *McClure's* team struggled with their vacillating feelings toward Theodore Roosevelt and the Square Deal. William Allen White remained the most passionate champion of the president. Embarking on a biographical sketch of Taft for the May issue of *The American Magazine*, White first consulted with Roosevelt. "Don't hold the knife edge of your balance so perfectly poised in this piece that your readers won't see your bias," Roosevelt had counseled him. White needed little prompting, for he had developed a genuine affection for Taft after spending several days with him on a train from Kansas City to Washington. In the weeks that followed, the two men continued to correspond as White sought to fill in details of Taft's career. In lengthy letters to White, Taft meticulously credited every mentor and benefactor who had helped facilitate his success. "The meanest man in the world," he remarked, "is the man who forgets the old friends that helped him on an early day and over early difficulties."

The resulting piece portrayed Taft as an "amiable giant," who had triumphed through the warmth of his personality, his "prodigious capacity for hard, consecutive work," and his judicial instinct to grapple with every issue "without resting and without fatigue until it is settled or solved." No political figure was better suited than Taft to pursue Roosevelt's "unfinished business," White argued, to push nearly a dozen pending anti-trust suits through the courts, to resolve the imperfections in recently enacted epoch-making laws. "The times demand not a man bearing promises of new things," White concluded, "but a man who can finish the things begun . . . who, with a steady hand, and a heart always kind and a mind always generously just, can clean off the desk." The piece delighted Roosevelt. "It would be impossible to get two men of fairly strong character and fairly marked individuality who would agree more closely," he responded to White, "unless it is either one of us and Taft!"

Ida Tarbell had long shared White's fascination with Roosevelt, though she found his pugnacity and relish for war distasteful. "I wabble terribly whenever I see him face to face," she confessed to Baker. "He seems so amazing." She had genuinely exulted in his crusade against the trusts, sharing his conviction that the government had a right and a duty to regulate corporations "for the sake of democracy." Roosevelt was "in the right," she insisted; "corporations exist not for themselves, but for the people." As Tarbell immersed herself in the tariff issue, however, she began to suspect that the president was a "less amazing" figure than she had initially imagined. Having envisioned Roosevelt as "the St. George" who would marshal popular support for downward tariff revision after the 1907 Panic, she was sorely disappointed by his unwillingness to risk Republican Party unity. Still, Tarbell remained a proponent of the Square Deal, trusting that investigation, legislation, regulation, and judicial proceedings could right the wrongs of the industrial world.

By 1908, Lincoln Steffens had arrived at very different conclusions. Steffens no longer trusted that the Square Deal could solve the nation's gross inequities of wealth and power, believing that more radical measures were necessary, including public ownership of corrupt railroads and trusts. "I certainly am socialistic," he told his sister, "but I'm not a Socialist." In the June issue of *Everybody's*, he published an article comparing the leadership styles of Theodore Roosevelt, Taft, and La Follette. Although he praised Roosevelt for galvanizing the public and predicted that Taft would faithfully follow his predecessor's regulatory course, he argued that La Follette alone was fighting against the system itself.

Roosevelt responded to Steffens with a 2,000-word rebuttal. "You contend," he began, "that Taft and I are good people of limited vision who fight against specific evils with no idea of fighting against the fundamental evil." After a quarter of a century in politics, Roosevelt observed, he had found that change was realized by "men who take the next step; not those who theorize about the 200th step." He pointed out that "it was Lincoln," not Wendell Phillips, who "saved the Union and abolished slavery." Indeed, history suggested that those, like La Follette, who fought "the system in the abstract," accomplished "mighty little good." Roosevelt closed by suggesting that Steffens visit the White House to continue their dialogue. Steffens replied that they had always argued about politics with such "mutual understanding" and "genuine affection" that he now felt closer to the president than to many who shared his own views.

By the final year of Roosevelt's presidency, Ray Baker too had come to question his leadership style, though he still continued to regard him as "the most interesting personality" in the country. In a 1908 article for *The American Magazine*, Baker located the source of the president's strength in what the philosopher William James termed "the art of energizing"—the ability to command ordinary talents to an extraordinary degree. Whereas most people never tapped their "vast stores of hidden energies," Baker contended that Roosevelt succeeded through "the simple device of self-control and self-discipline, of using every power he possesses to its utmost limit—a dazzling, even appalling spectacle of a human engine driven at full speed." Despite being an "ordinary shot," he had practiced methodically to become a world-class hunter. Lacking the succinct poetic clarity of Lincoln's literary genius, he had nonetheless produced an astonishingly versatile body of work. While preaching simple homilies and banal maxims, he had nonetheless reached the hearts of his countrymen and given the people voice.

After a decade of observation, however, Baker had reached a less flattering assessment of the president: "Roosevelt never leads; he always follows. He acts, but he acts only when he thinks the crowd is behind him. . . . Upon all the great issues which he has championed, the country was prepared before he entered the arena." Though he had pushed his agenda "valiantly and fearlessly," Baker argued, the times now demanded a thinker—someone who could deal with the unjust tariff structure and the underlying conflict between the rich and the poor, who could formulate a "European system of comprehensive social insurance to protect the injured, the sick and the aged."

Baker's musings provoked a lively correspondence with Roosevelt. "I think you lay altogether too much stress," Roosevelt told the reporter, "upon your theory that everywhere and at all times political thought divides itself into two opposing forces," driving what Baker had called "the fundamental conflict between the few and the many." In the South, Roosevelt pointed out, the tension between the races reached "immeasurably farther" into the souls of men than any struggle between the poor and the rich. Although he believed in "equal opportunities for all," he decried the inflammatory and unprofitable language of class warfare, which impeded the moral struggle to improve "man as a man."

"I wish as much as you do that we had reached the stage in our civilization where we could avoid the hatred and demagogy of ignorance and class strife," Baker promptly replied. In the present situation, he maintained, class action by unions and parties seemed indispensable. Would "any amount of effort to improve the Russian Jewish tailor of the East-side—as a man—make much headway," he wondered, "unless there is a determined effort to change his environment and the institutions which help to make him poor, downtrodden, outcast?"

One evening, less than a week after this exchange of letters, the two men talked at the White House until midnight, and for the first time in their long acquaintance, the ever exuberant president struck Baker as a weary man. Roosevelt disclosed his plans to spend a year big game hunting in "the wilds of Africa" when his term ended. "The best thing I can do is to go entirely away," he told Baker, "out of reach of everything here." He admitted that he believed his time had come and gone; that he was "through." When Baker suggested that "the people might not be through with him," the president responded "with a curious finality, a sort of sadness" unlike anything Baker had heard from him.

"New issues are coming up," Roosevelt acknowledged. "People are going to discuss economic questions more and more; the tariff, currency, banks. They are hard questions, and I am not deeply interested in them; my problems are moral problems, and my teaching has been plain morality." Never, Baker later reflected, had he seen the president "in a more human mood."

ROOSEVELT'S WISTFUL DEMEANOR ON THE eve of the Republican National Convention in June 1908 in Chicago revealed residual misgivings about his ironclad pledge to forgo a third term. "When you see me quoted in the press as welcoming the rest I will have after March the 3d take no stock in it," he informed his military aide Archie Butt. "I have enjoyed every moment of this so-called arduous and exacting task." For all seven years of his tenure, he proudly told George Trevelyan, he had "*been* President, emphatically," utilizing "every ounce of power there was in the office." At times, he was plagued by "ugly qualms" about "abandoning great work" simply to be true to his word. Yet, if he did answer the call to run again, he feared that even those who had spurred him on would suffer a shock of "disappointment" at an unseemly quest to hold the office "longer than it was deemed wise that Washington should hold it."

Roosevelt was not the only one preoccupied by the tantalizing prospect of a third term. As Chicago began "to throb with the confusion and excitement of arriving throngs" in preparation for the convention, "a stampede" for Roosevelt remained a distinct possibility. "Taft has nothing to fear from any combination of opponents," *The Washington Post* remarked. "The only man who can defeat him is Pres. Roosevelt." In journalistic circles, the odds of a stampede to nominate Roosevelt at the first mention of his name proved "an unfailing topic for conjecture, and the explosive possibility of its injection at the psychological moment" was widely anticipated. Any large political gathering, the *San Francisco Chronicle* observed, can easily become "a mob, ready to accept what psychologists call 'suggestion.' "

As expectations began to mount, two antithetical factions enhanced the likelihood of a Roosevelt stampede. For progressive and moderate Republicans who "in their heart of hearts" preferred Roosevelt to anyone else, hope remained that if actually nominated, the president would feel compelled to accept the honor despite his repeated refusals. The agenda of the second group was far more calculating; for Taft's reactionary opponents, known as "the Allies," "a stampede" would be the "last card" in their effort to break Taft's majority on the first ballot. By pushing for a third term, they hoped "to create a diversion against Taft and weaken him as a candidate." If the president then refused to accept the nomination—as they anticipated—the door would open for a second or third ballot to nominate one of their own: Cannon, Knox, or Fairbanks.

The sky was "full of sunshine" on June 16, the first day of the convention. The band played patriotic airs as delegates found their seats on the floor and spectators piled into the galleries. Barely audible above the din, the presiding officer's tribute to "the glories of the party" did not seem designed "to set the blood tingling." Toledo mayor Brand Whitlock observed a restlessness in the gallery reminiscent of "that expectant interest in which multitudes view an animal trainer at work; down in their hearts the secret human wish, or half-wish, that the animals may turn and eat the trainer." The analogy, he said, served only to point out that "the spectators longed for something to happen. But nothing happened."

The agenda for the second day of the convention promised to sate the crowd's desire for excitement. Though Will and Nellie remained in Washington with their seventeen-year-old daughter Helen and ten-year-old son Charlie, the rest of the Taft clan descended upon Chicago. Two hours before the convention proceedings opened at 10 a.m., William Howard Taft arrived at his War Department office. His quarters at the Old Executive Building included a large reception room for visitors, an adjoining space for his secretary and two clerks, and a private office with a desk, couch, and several comfortable chairs. Electricians equipped the office to receive telegraph messages directly from the convention hall, and a long-distance telephone line allowed Frank Hitchcock, Taft's national campaign manager, to reach him from the floor of the Coliseum. To relieve his anxiety, Taft "plunged into the business of the day," reviewing routine matters with his secretary. When a photographer arrived and suggested that he pose expectantly by the telephone, Taft balked. "I do not sit at the telephone," he laughed, explaining that "telephone messages are taken by somebody else. I'll not do anything unnatural." Nellie arrived at noon, taking a seat at her husband's desk, while young Charlie stationed himself in the anteroom with the telegraph operator, ready to carry incoming messages to his mother. She read each dispatch aloud to the assembled gathering of associates and friends as Taft paced restlessly in and out of the office, intermittently occupying an easy chair by the window. Dozens of newspapermen and clerks gathered in the outer reception room.

At 1:30 p.m., the convention chairman Senator Henry Cabot Lodge approached the podium to deliver the keynote address. For half an hour, the senator held the 14,000 attendees rapt with a powerful critique of the Democrats and a stirring defense of Republican policies, carefully avoiding any mention of Theodore Roosevelt. When he finally introduced "the magic name," Lodge unleashed "a wild, frenzied uncontrollable stampede for Roosevelt." The point of Lodge's speech that touched a "burning fuse to dry powder" was the simple observation that to the great dismay of "vested abuses and profitable wrongs," the president had "fearlessly enforced the laws," becoming "the best abused and most popular man in the United States today." Delegates and spectators "exploded with a roar," clapping, whistling, stamping their feet. "Hats, fans, umbrellas, flags, newspapers, arms, coats were waved, flapped, brandished, jiggled" while the audience chanted: "Four Years More. Four Years More."

When Lodge attempted to continue, his words were drowned in "volleys of cheers" that echoed from floor to ceiling. "It seemed," one journalist remarked, "as if the roof would blow off." This disruption was merely "a trifle compared with what followed." After someone threw a four-foot Teddy bear into the air, delegates began tossing it from one state to another. "Each time it appeared above the heads of the delegates," *The Washington Post* reported, "it was a signal for another outburst." The convention was "on the verge of a good natured riot" when a national committeeman from Oklahoma captured and sat on the bear, successfully resisting all attempts to snatch it away.

Bulletins describing these outbursts on the convention floor understandably produced anxiety for the little group assembled in Taft's office. Fortunately, Taft had departed to meet with Secretary Root about an official matter just before the pandemonium erupted, but Nellie was unnerved. Her anxiety was somewhat mollified when Frank Hitchcock called from the floor assuring everyone that he was "not at all alarmed." The Taft delegates would remain firm.

Back in Chicago, the wild ovation persisted for a record forty-nine minutes, ceasing only when Lodge returned to the podium, wresting the crowd's attention "by the force of his personality" and the impact of his words. "That man is no friend to Theodore Roosevelt," he proclaimed, "who now, from any motive, seeks to urge him as a candidate for the great office which he has finally declined. The President has refused what his countrymen would gladly have given him; he says what he means and means what he says, and his party and his country will respect his wishes as they honor his high character and great public service." Aware that Lodge was the president's designated spokesman—and that he carried a letter confirming Roosevelt's refusal in case of his nomination—the gathering accepted the senator's words "as the voice of the President." The convention quieted; the possibility of the stampede, feared by some and desired by many, had come and gone.

Nellie was still seated at the desk receiving bulletins when Taft returned to the office. After learning of the excitement, he walked over to the White House, where the president and first lady were preparing for a horseback ride through Rock Creek Park. William Loeb, Roosevelt's secretary, remarked that the convention had simply needed "to blow off steam" before moving forward. Archie Butt had never seen Roosevelt more ebullient. Flattered by the emotional outpouring, the president recognized that the convention had paid him the highest possible compliment without forcing a decision that threatened both his party's prospects and the credibility of his word. Taft, too, was smiling. A reassuring telegram had arrived from Frank Hitchcock: "The cheers for Roosevelt today, will be for Taft tomorrow."

When the convention opened the following day, Nellie resumed her customary position at her husband's desk. Charlie happily continued serving as messenger, and Miss Helen Taft, scheduled to attend Bryn Mawr College in the fall, joined the group as the nominating speeches for favorite sons were set to begin. Journalists remarked on the solidarity of the Taft family, particularly noting Nellie's unusual role as one of her husband's "best advisers" in every aspect of the campaign. A *San Francisco Chronicle* reporter described the atmosphere in the room as "electric with excitement [and] suppressed nervous tension."

Nellie strove to remain calm as she relayed reports of the enthusiastic cheering that greeted Ohio congressman Theodore Burton's nominating speech for Taft. Delegates stood on their chairs as a large banner bearing Taft's picture was carried through the aisles, waving their hats and flags to a chorus of "Taft, Taft, Taft." A burst of good-natured laughter greeted a pair of ample trousers adorning a flagpole brandished by a member of the Texas delegation: "As pants the hart for cooling streams," they intoned, "so Texas pants for Taft!" To better view the animated demonstration, Charles Taft climbed a stepladder on the edge of the Ohio delegation. His "beaming smile" revealed pride and pleasure in the accomplishments of a younger brother whom he had mentored and supported since the death of their father. Though less protracted than the frenzy unleashed by Roosevelt's name on the previous day, the exuberant response buoyed the spirits of Taft's supporters.

By late afternoon, visitors inundated Taft's inner office, with reporters streaming in and out. Just before the balloting was set to begin, Nellie was handed a bulletin causing her to turn "white as marble." A large lithograph of Roosevelt had been carried onto the stage, she relayed to the gathering, and once again the audience had erupted into a frenzy that made it impossible for Chairman Lodge to restore order. "Scarcely a word was spoken," one correspondent noted. "Men who ordinarily are not affected by nervousness hung over the telegraph instrument as though their lives depended upon the words which the stolid telegrapher was ticking out." Silence prevailed for nearly fifteen minutes, until the next bulletin announced that twenty-six Massachusetts delegates had voted for Taft. No one could fathom how the roll call had reached Massachusetts until it was discovered that even as the demonstration continued unabated, Lodge had somehow proceeded with the vote. "Pay no attention to the crowd," he shouted to the clerk, declaring, "I shall not have the president made by a Chicago mob." Seven states managed to cast their votes before the mayhem finally subsided. "The scene was absolutely unique in American history," one correspondent noted, "the voting being taken during a terrific uproar in behalf of a man whose name was not before the convention."

Shortly before five-thirty, a telegram arrived declaring that the press associations had "flashed" the nomination of William Howard Taft. Her eyes "aglow with excitement," Nellie read the news to the assembled throng. "Bubbling over with happiness," she rose to embrace her husband, who "laughed with the joy of a boy." A "football rush" followed as Taft's colleagues in the War Department arrived en masse to extend their congratulations. Moments later, a bulletin confirmed that the nomination was declared unanimous, and Secretary of State Root appeared to accompany Taft to an appointment at the War College. "You know how happy I feel over this," Root told the new nominee. " I do," Taft replied, giving the secretary "a resounding whack on the back." The nominee warned Root that they would face a delay as he shook hands with the assembled reporters. "It will be a long time before you will be able to shake the newspapermen," Root quipped. Taft cordially greeted "the boys" in turn but declined to make a statement. "Words don't frame themselves for me now," he humbly insisted, "but I don't deny that I am very happy."

Roosevelt was engaged in a tennis game with Assistant Secretary of State Robert Bacon when he received word of Taft's nomination. He had prepared a formal statement, which he directed his secretary to release straightaway to the press. "The country is indeed to be congratulated upon the nomination of Mr. Taft. I have known him intimately for many years and I have a peculiar feeling for him, because throughout that time we have worked for the same object with the same purposes and ideals. I do not believe there can be found in the whole country a man so well fitted to be president."

That evening, against a backdrop of music and fireworks, Taft addressed hundreds of his neighbors and friends from his doorstep. "A great honor has fallen upon me today to lead a great political party in the contest that is to come," he solemnly acknowledged. He then turned to Nellie, "the real ruler of the family," acknowledging that "no greater need of approval could be desired." Reminded that his nine o'clock reception at the White House would begin in two minutes, he hastened off on foot in that direction. But when the crowd thwarted his progress, he was forced to recruit the Army Band's wagon. "Does this outfit belong to any one?" he inquired. "Everything belongs to you to-night," he was assured. He promptly jumped into the wagon and proceeded to the White House, where his old friend, the proud kingmaker, awaited.

The convention completed its business the following day, nominating the conservative New York congressman James Sherman for vice president. Neither Roosevelt nor Taft was particularly happy with the choice of "Sunny Jim." They had hoped to add a progressive from the West to the ticket, but when Albert Beveridge, Herbert Hadley, Jonathan Dolliver, and A. B. Cummins all refused, they had left the decision to the delegates. The platform approved by the delegates was equally unsatisfying. At Taft's insistence, it called for a special session to revise the tariff and create a postal savings bank system, but it diluted an anti-injunction plank and blamed Democrats for the failure to act on progressive measures, exonerating the Republican majority. While Senators La Follette and Beveridge expressed "disappointment," William Allen White defended the convention's work in an editorial. "We can't get all we desire," he maintained. "A party is no place for a crank. If he cannot compromise and go forward he should flock alone."

"THE NEXT FOUR MONTHS ARE going to be kind of a nightmare for me," Taft confessed to a friend shortly after the convention. Each morning he awakened "with a certain degree of nervous uneasiness of what may appear in the newspaper," he explained, and though he could handle attacks "manufactured out of whole cloth," those blending truth and falsehood were more troubling.

To fortify himself, Taft planned to spend July and August at the Homestead, a celebrated resort hotel in Hot Springs, Virginia, where he could work, relax, and replenish his energies for the fall campaign. Situated atop the Blue Ridge Mountains, a short horseback ride from waterfalls and ancient woodlands, the Homestead boasted a majestic high-ceilinged lobby, a wide veranda surrounding the entire building, and an eighteen-hole golf course. Nellie, Will, and Charlie occupied the Presidential Suite, with a private balcony overlooking the grassy links. In addition, a five-room office suite had been configured, providing two private chambers for the nominee, along with a reception area and workspace for his secretary and clerk. In the days that followed, dozens of senators, congressmen, cabinet officials, and members of the Republican National Committee made the train trip to Hot Springs. Overnight, the little town became the focus of national attention, just as Oyster Bay had been seven years earlier.

Despite the many diversions offered by the luxurious Homestead, Taft kept to a rigorous schedule. Typically awakened at seven by his Filipino valet, he favored a spare breakfast of dry toast and a single soft-boiled egg. By 8:30 a.m., he was bathed, shaved, and settled in his office, where he read and signed responses to more than 1,500 congratulatory notes in addition to general correspondence of nearly 150 letters every day. By ten, he was out on the eighteen-hole golf course with one or two invited guests. By 2 p.m., he had returned to his office, meeting with party leaders to determine strategy for each region of the country. In the late afternoon, he would devote several hours to working on his acceptance speech, scheduled for late July. At seven thirty, he and Nellie went to dinner in the public dining room with their visitors, before settling on the wide veranda that served as the "favorite promenade" for hotel guests.

The week after the Tafts arrived in Hot Springs, the Democratic Party held its convention in Denver. After the defeat of their previous nominee, conservative Judge Alton Parker, the party once again turned to the progressive hero William Jennings Bryan. Their platform demanded the passage of bills Roosevelt had failed to push through the Republican Congress—an eight-hour day, a general employers' liability act, a progressive income tax, and a child labor law. They further advocated the direct election of senators, a public record of campaign contributions, a federal guarantee of bank deposits, and a law removing tariff protection for the products of any corporation with a market share over 50 percent.

The Democratic platform, Taft confided to Roosevelt, left him in a quandary over his own acceptance speech, for while he disagreed vehemently with some of their pledges, he approved many of them. "We will be able to riddle it," Roosevelt assured him in reply. A few days later, the president forwarded specific suggestions on how to "slash savagely" at Bryan and his platform. After working steadily for another week, Taft sent his first draft to Roosevelt. "Both of the first two paragraphs should certainly be omitted," Roosevelt replied, but aside from a weak section on bank deposits, he found the remainder of the address "admirable." He added in closing: "I think that the number of times my name is used should be cut down. You are now the leader."

While Taft's continued desire for the counsel of the country's "most accomplished politician" was understandable, his "extraordinarily frank announcement" that he intended to bring his final draft to Oyster Bay for Roosevelt to review provoked scorn and concern. "I have the highest regard for the president's judgment," he told the press, justifying his apparent deference to Roosevelt's opinion, "and a keen appreciation of his wonderful ability for forceful expression." Editorial writers universally lambasted "the spectacle of Candidate Taft hurrying to Oyster Bay to submit his speech of acceptance." The *New York Times* likened his action to that of "a schoolboy about to submit his composition to the teacher before he read it in school," and observed that despite great admiration for Roosevelt, people would like their next president to demonstrate "an existence independent of his late chief." The New York *Sun* described the visit as a "humiliating pilgrimage," further evidence that Taft was "but the puppet of the White House Punch and Judy manipulator." Although the copy of the speech that Taft's secretary released to the press after Roosevelt's review revealed few substantial changes, the episode was "not calculated to inspire confidence in Republican breasts."

From New York, Taft traveled to his brother Charley's Cincinnati home, where the official notification ceremony and acceptance address would take place. The stately colonial mansion, with its white pillars and sweeping green lawns, provided a perfect setting for the festivities. Workers had constructed a platform and two temporary porches flanking the imposing entrance to accommodate members of the notification committee and distinguished visitors. A flagpole erected on the south lawn flew a silk flag which the local citizens had donated to honor Taft's visits to Cincinnati. The spacious grounds afforded standing room for nearly 1,500 spectators. "What we thought originally would be merely a formal affair, attended by a few people," Charley explained to a relative, "has developed into a big demonstration." Thousands streamed into Cincinnati from neighboring states to attend the open-air concerts, fireworks, receptions, and marching band performances that accompanied the main event. A large, enthusiastic crowd greeted Taft at the Cincinnati train station with an enormous banner bearing the words NO PLACE LIKE HOME. Charles was first to grasp his brother's hand, and they proceeded "arm in arm" to a waiting carriage. On the drive to the Pike Street home where he intended to spend a quiet weekend with Nellie before Tuesday's big event, Taft appreciated the city's "holiday attire"—flags waving, houses draped with bunting, streets adorned with colorful streamers.

On July 28, the designated Notification Day, "the booming of cannon" announced a two-hour parade through the city. From the reviewing stand, Taft was gratified to observe Democrats marching side by side with Republicans in a show of bipartisanship for their favorite son. The formal ceremony began at noon, with the head of the notification committee delivering the official announcement that the Republican Party had selected William Howard Taft "as its candidate for president—the highest honor that can be conferred by this constitutional republic." Taft "smiled cordially and looked as much astonished as he could be." And when his turn came to speak, the audience erupted in warm applause.

Disregarding Roosevelt's admonishment, Taft opened with a tribute to the president's "movement for practical reform," touting his leadership in securing long-overdue regulatory legislation over corporate behavior, the railroads, the food and drug industry, and the conservation of natural resources. These laws, Taft argued, offered a far more constructive avenue for curbing corporate abuses than Democratic proposals to dismantle large corporations simply because they were big. The Republican approach "would compel the trusts to conduct their business in a lawful manner," while Bryan and the Democrats would simply "destroy the entire business in order to stamp out the evils which they have practiced."

Having commended the high standard of morality set by Roosevelt's agenda, Taft was careful to delineate a policy of his own. "The chief function of the next Administration," he pledged, "is distinct from, and a progressive development of, that which has been performed by President Roosevelt. The chief function of the next Administration is to complete and perfect the machinery by which these standards may be maintained, by which the lawbreakers may be promptly restrained and punished, but which shall operate with sufficient accuracy and dispatch to interfere with legitimate business as little as possible. Such machinery is not now adequate." Furthermore, he expressed his personal support for two issues that conservative delegates had refused to sanction in the Republican Party platform: a progressive income tax and the direct election of senators.

After the official hour-long address, Taft spoke informally to friends and fellow citizens, expressing the gratitude and wonder he and Nellie felt at the spectacular reception. "Popular elections are uncertain," he concluded, "but whatever betide me as a candidate, we can never be deprived of the joy we feel at this welcome home." An elated Nellie added her own remarks: "Hasn't it been glorious!" she exclaimed. "I love public life. To me this is better than when Mr. Taft was at the bar and at the bench, for the things before him now and in which he takes part are live subjects."

After a luncheon party at the Country Club, the Tafts ended their long day on the *Island Queen*, escorted up the Ohio River by more than 150 smaller boats, "all ablaze with illumination." From the steamer's deck, Will and Nellie witnessed a magnificent display of fireworks. Three days later, the glow of his home city's "tremendous outpouring" remained with Taft. "No matter what may happen," he reflected to Roosevelt, "the joy we felt at our reception in Cincinnati was unalloyed."

"I congratulate you most heartily," the president wrote. "The speech is a great success and has achieved exactly the purposes you sought to obtain. Of course, the *Sun*, *Times*, and *Evening Post* are dreadfully pained at your having praised me," he gleefully observed, "or rather, as they phrase it, having submitted to my insistence that you should praise me. I am glad they did not see your speech before I got at it." In its revised form, Taft's speech garnered a positive response. The *Wall Street Journal* called it "an exceedingly able and shrewd political document." Though "not brilliant in the Roosevelt and Bryan sense," nor studded with "telling phrases," the *Journal* declared, it increased "the popular faith in Mr. Taft's fitness for the high office" and perfectly positioned him "in the middle of the road, avoiding alike the extreme of eastern conservatism and the extreme of western radicalism."

Relieved that his acceptance speech was behind him, Taft returned to Hot Springs for the month of August, intending to focus on a rigorous regime of dieting and exercise. By limiting his food consumption and walking three or four hours each day over the formidable fairways of the golf course, he hoped to shed the 50 pounds he had gained during the previous year. "I play golf just as I would take medicine," he conceded to reporters, and after a brief stint of this hiking and golfing regimen under the hot sun, he proudly reported to Roosevelt that he had already lost inches in his waist. Taft's other planned activity, trail riding, had to be abandoned after the ankles of his saddle horse proved too weak to carry his weight. "No man weighing 300 pounds has any business on a horse's back," declared the president of the Massachusetts Society for the Prevention of Cruelty to Animals upon reading of the animal's collapse, callously griping, "if he must ride let him use an automobile or an elephant." One Taft supporter offered to donate a 3,500-pound workhorse, one so large that "a special stall" would be built to accommodate the massive creature. Undeterred, Taft continued his daily exertions on the links.

With little hard news to report, correspondents resorted to detailed accounts of Taft's golf game, creating the unfortunate impression that the candidate engaged in little beyond recreation. The *Tribune* reporter, at least, observed that he played golf as he did "everything else, with the same steadiness and poise, and same equable temper, never becoming discouraged by any obstacle and never losing his temper or his nerve as a result of a bad play."

The rash of golfing anecdotes vexed Roosevelt. "It would seem incredible that anyone would care one way or the other about your playing golf," the president complained to Taft, but he had "received literally hundreds of letters from the West protesting about it." Because the working class looked upon golf as a "rich man's game," Roosevelt cautioned his friend to suppress future reports about his golf game. Nor should he even permit himself to be photographed on the golf course, for "the American people regard the campaign as a very serious business." Taft insisted that he was working "very hard" but acknowledged that appearances could be misleading.

As the general election drew near, Roosevelt continued to hover about Taft "like a hen over her chickens." Early on, Taft had pledged to make public all campaign contributions as soon as the election was over. Realizing such transparency might paralyze large donors, Taft told the president that he was "willing to undergo the disadvantage in order to make certain that in the future we shall reduce the power of money in politics." Republican fund-raising did, in fact, suffer. "I must tell you plainly," Taft's treasurer George Sheldon protested, that your pledge has "tied my hands and at least one of my legs and I am well nigh helpless." The nominee caused further consternation when he refused a $50,000 check from William Cromwell, a friend who had donated despite the knowledge that his contribution would be on public record. Taft told Cromwell he could not accept such a large sum from anyone outside his own family. Though he realized the gift was prompted by "nothing but the purest friendship," he feared its size would be "misunderstood." Roosevelt disagreed. "I have always said you would be the greatest President," he chided Taft, "but really I think you are altogether oversensitive. If I were in your place I should accept that contribution of Cromwell's with real gratitude." Taft finally agreed to accept a $10,000 check, with the understanding that the amount could be increased if necessary.

Facing a host of difficulties even before the traditional Labor Day opening for the fall campaign, Taft confessed to Roosevelt that he felt somewhat chagrined about his chances. "Don't get one particle discouraged," Roosevelt assured him; "you have exactly the right attitude of mind in the matter. In 1904 I never permitted myself to regard the election as anything but doubtful." In truth, Taft had reason to worry. Williams Jennings Bryan had become a far more formidable candidate since his previous runs in 1896 and 1900. In those earlier campaigns, the Chicago journalist Walter Wellman noted, many had viewed Bryan as "a dangerous man—revolutionary, socialist, and by some, almost an anarchist." But with the rise of Theodore Roosevelt and the progressive wing of the Republican Party, many policies championed by the Democratic candidate had become law. "No longer an outcast," Bryan pronounced himself a more legitimate heir to Roosevelt than Taft, promising that a Democratic majority would break the stranglehold of Republican conservatives on Congress.

Taft's political strategists were initially reluctant to send their candidate on a speaking tour, preferring to run a front-porch campaign from his brother's home in Cincinnati. They feared that Taft "would be placed at a disadvantage appearing on the stump against the gifted Nebraskan." Once again, Taft's principles collided with their strategy. "If the candidate does not go out and work himself," he told Roosevelt, "the subordinates in the ranks are not liable to tear their shirts, whereas the personal presence of the man at the head will have an encouraging and stimulating effect." At Taft's direction, party strategists designed a strenuous tour, focused mainly in the West and Midwest, where Bryan was gaining substantial momentum.

Fearing that Taft would be too reticent on the stump, Roosevelt barraged him with incessant advice. "Do not *answer* Bryan; attack him!" he counseled in early September, adding, "Don't let *him* make the issues." A week later, the president resumed. "Hit them hard, old man," he encouraged, offering a slew of new suggestions: "Let the audience see you smile *always*, because I feel that your nature shines out so transparently when you do smile—you big, generous, high-minded fellow. Moreover let them realize the truth, which is that for all your gentleness and kindliness and generous good nature, there never existed a man who was a better fighter when the need arose." Taft promised to confront Bryan directly, but he remained reluctant to launch an uncharacteristic, dramatic offensive. "I cannot be more aggressive than my nature makes me," he told a concerned supporter. "That is the advantage and the disadvantage of having been on the Bench. I can't call names and I can't use adjectives when I don't think the case calls for them, so you will have to get along with that kind of a candidate."

"I am not very pleased with the way Taft's campaign is being handled," Roosevelt complained to his son-in-law, Nicholas Longworth, adding, "I do wish that Taft would put more energy and fight into the matter." Constitutionally incapable of remaining on the sidelines, Roosevelt decided "to put a little vim into the campaign" with a series of public letters. The first of these missives challenged Bryan's claim that he, rather than Taft, was the president's "natural successor." "The true friend of reform," Roosevelt clarified, "is the man who steadily perseveres in righting wrongs, in warring against abuses, but whose character and training are such that he never promises what he cannot perform . . . and that, while steadily advancing, he never permits himself to be led into foolish excesses." William Howard Taft "combines all of these qualities to a degree which no other man in our public life since the Civil War has surpassed," he ardently insisted. "For the last ten years," he added, "I have been thrown into the closest intimacy with him, and he and I have on every essential point stood in heartiest agreement, shoulder to shoulder."

Bryan's further assertion that Roosevelt's views aligned more closely with the Democratic platform than with the agenda of his own Republican Party prompted a fiery exchange between the two men. "You say that your platform declares in favor of the vigorous enforcement of the law against guilty trust magnates and officials," Roosevelt noted, "and that the platform upon which Mr. Taft stands makes no such declaration. It was not necessary. That platform approved the policies of this administration." He pointed out that under Grover Cleveland, the last Democratic president, not a single anti-trust case was instituted—nor was action taken to stop rebates. Deeds, he argued in a further exchange, were far more important than words.

Roosevelt's fiery declarations put Bryan on the defensive, and spurred the sluggish Republican campaign. Bryan "walked into a trap," Taft gratefully told Roosevelt, "and that gave you an opportunity, at his instance, to hit him, two or three blows between the eyes." Throughout the West, Taft added, Bryan's "claim to be the heir of your policies is now the subject of laughter and ridicule rather than of serious weight."

Ascribing "the revival in the Republican campaign" to his pugnacious friend, Taft overlooked his own winning impression made at every stop. The "Taft Special," which carried him to twenty-one states in forty-one days, consisted of four cars: a private car for the nominee and his guests, a dining car, a sleeping car for the newspapermen, and a baggage car. Addressing friendly crowds at each city and town along the whistle-stop tour, Taft "proved to be a good deal more of a speaker than most of those present had counted on hearing." While he was in no sense "a professional entertainer," one reporter remarked, his words displayed such openness and were uttered with such conviction that "he strengthened himself in the hearts of his hearers." Audiences invariably came away persuaded that Taft was "on the level," that he told "the truth about himself," and stated his thoughts without equivocation. "That man has a fine face," one spectator enthused. "I would trust him anywhere." As the crowds continued to grow, Taft became more confident in his oratory. "I have been in real touch with the people," he proudly observed. "They have come to see me and hear me in numbers far beyond my anticipation, and what seems of even more importance, they have responded to what I have had to say in a way that I could feel their sympathy."

"You are making such a success with your speeches," Nellie wrote from

New York where she was busy settling her children into their various schools. For weeks, she had been nettled by gossip that Roosevelt was disappointed by Taft's inability to generate campaign momentum. Now, these sanguine reports of the whistle-stop tour left her "treading on air." The president, she informed her husband, had requested a meeting with her: "I can't imagine what Teddy wants," she wrote, " but probably only to complain of some thing." Nellie was mistaken. In fact, the president was growing more confident about Taft's prospects in the general election. Recognizing that Taft's speaking tour had invigorated the campaign, he simply wanted to share his enthusiasm with her. Nellie "had a most delightful time," Will wrote afterward to Roosevelt. "You gave her courage and hope."

Expressing a similar optimism to Kermit in late October, Roosevelt wrote that the political outlook had "changed materially for the better." He was now certain, he told his son, that Taft would be elected. To everyone's relief, the speaking tour had succeeded "tremendously," an achievement for which Roosevelt did not hesitate to take credit—forgetting that Taft had done yeoman work in both his 1904 and 1906 campaigns. Archie Butt told of his amusement at the president's skewed recounting of how he transformed Taft from a soporific lecturer into a popular draw: "I told him he simply had to stop saying what he had said in this or that decision," for at that point people "promptly begin to nod. I told him that he must treat the political audience as one coming, not to see an etching, but a poster. He must, therefore, have streaks of blue, yellow, and red to catch the eye, and eliminate all fine lines and soft colours. I think Mr. Taft thought I was a barbarian and a mountebank at first, but I am pleased to say that he is at last catching the attention of the crowd."

Such indiscretions invariably filtered into Taft's camp, fueling resentment at the president's condescending and potentially damaging self-aggrandizement. Taft's supporters had long felt that Roosevelt "was keeping himself too much in the limelight," creating the impression that Taft was incapable "of standing on his own feet." Always gracious, Taft assured Roosevelt that he did not know who had spread rumors that his people were rankled by the president's active role. Personally, he had been "very touched" by Roosevelt's speechmaking advice and "delighted" by everything done to support him.

Nellie joined Taft in Buffalo on the last day of his speaking tour. In western New York, Pennsylvania, and Ohio, they were met by "monster" crowds brimming with enthusiasm. Reporters noted that Nellie "seemed to enjoy it immensely." They reached Cincinnati at 8 a.m. on November 3, spending the day at Charley's home before going to vote in the afternoon. In preparation for receiving the election returns, Charley had converted the veranda into a telegraph room with wires directly connected to the national Republican headquarters in New York, Western Union, the Associated Press, and the United Press.

The extended family and friends gathered in the large drawing room, surrounded by the exquisite art collection Charles and Annie had assembled during their sojourns in Europe. Newspapermen who had traveled with the candidate on the whistle-stop tour joined them. Gus Karger, the *Cincinnati Times* reporter who had served as Taft's publicity agent during the campaign, read out the returns. Early reports from Massachusetts, Connecticut, New York, and Maryland soon indicated a magnificent victory for William Howard Taft.

The excited candidate paced throughout the evening, "exhibiting the finest specimen of that smile which the campaign had made famous." At 8:45 p.m., he finally agreed to make a statement: "Just say that everything looks favorable," he directed modestly. Nellie was more forthcoming, exclaiming, "I was never so happy in my life." Though Taft's popular margin was only half the size of Roosevelt's 1904 victory, he carried twenty-nine of the forty-six states, beating Bryan by over a million and a quarter votes. Later that night, Taft delivered a short speech with his distinctive, self-effacing sincerity: "I pledge myself to use all the energy and ability in me to make the next Administration a worthy successor to that of Theodore Roosevelt," he said. "I could have no higher aim than that."

At the White House, Archie Butt reported, Roosevelt "was simply radiant over Taft's victory, and made no attempt to disguise it," interpreting the victory as a vindication of his own policies. When the conversation turned to Taft's struggle to lose weight through golf and horseback riding, the president offered pithy advice: "If I were Taft, I would not attempt to take much exercise. I would content myself with the record I was able to make in the next four years or the next eight and then be content to die."

Taft addressed his very first letter as president-elect to his friend and mentor Theodore Roosevelt. "My selection and election are chiefly your work," he told him. "You and my brother Charley made that possible which in all probability would not have occurred otherwise." In later years, Roosevelt would express resentment at being yoked with Taft's brother as a joint benefactor, heedless that Charles's decades of financial support had enabled Will to sustain a career in public service. At that moment, however, Roosevelt responded with unalloyed joy. "You have won a great personal victory as well as a great victory for the party," the president wrote, "and all those who love you, who admire and believe in you, and are proud of your great and fine qualities, must feel a thrill of exultation."

CHAPTER TWENTY-TWO

"A Great Stricken Animal"

First Lady Nellie Taft, posed in formal attire at the White House, ca. 1909.

HENRY ADAMS, SCION OF TWO presidents and an acute student of American political life for nearly seven decades, called William Howard Taft "the best equipped man for the Presidency who had been suggested by either party during his lifetime." A prominent New Yorker argued that Taft was "the greatest all around man" ever to reach the White House. As Congressman James E. Watson noted, "he had served with great success in every subordinate post he had occupied."

From his early days as solicitor general to his governor generalship of the Philippines to his tenure as secretary of war, Taft had proved himself reliable, hardworking, and loyal. On those rare occasions when he disagreed with a superior, he kept his dissent private. Nor had he objected when credit for his achievements was extended to others. "The most difficult instrument to play in the orchestra is second fiddle," a celebrated conductor once noted, yet for nearly two decades, Taft had performed with unfailing mastery.

Whether the skills of this exemplary subordinate were the requisite skills to lead a nation remained the only unanswered question. Ray Baker suggested that sometimes the second fiddler may be a more accomplished musician than the first, "but he could not fill the first fiddler's place. He has not the audience-sense; he does not know how to handle men; he has not the ability to beat disharmonies into harmonies." As leadership scholars observe: "Not everyone was meant to be No. 1."

Within hours of his election triumph, Taft was already anguished that his nature was ill-suited to his new role. He "spoke like a man," one insider noted, "whose job had got him down even before he tackled it." In one of his first statements, Taft predicted that his friends and acquaintances would soon "shake their heads and say 'poor Bill.' " Not long afterward, he responded to confident remarks on the prospects of his administration with "a trembling fear" that in four years' time, he would "be like the man who went into office with a majority and went out with unanimity."

Yet with each substantial step in his successful career, Taft had overcome similar waves of grave doubt and anxiety. As solicitor general, despite fearing in his first days that the demand for a one-sided argument would prove incompatible with his temperament, he had quickly developed into an effective advocate, winning a large majority of the government's cases. When initially approached to govern the Philippines, he had protested that he was not the right man for the job. He left that position with an international reputation as a successful administrator. "Sitting on the lid" as acting president during Roosevelt's two-month vacation, he had deftly defused a number of potentially explosive situations. And painfully aware of his deficiencies as a campaigner, he had nevertheless bested all rivals to win both the Republican nomination and the general election. Through all these challenges Taft had relied on the guidance of a superior; now, for the first time, he was truly on his own.

FACED WITH THE COMPLICATED TASK of shaping a cabinet, Taft sought escape. He traveled first to Hot Springs, Virginia, and then to Augusta, Georgia, where he stayed for six weeks in a comfortable cottage adjacent to the luxury Bon Air Hotel, widely celebrated for its "splendid 18 hole golf course and the handsomest clubhouse in the South." While Nellie thought the location too remote to accurately gauge the tenor of Washington, Taft insisted on "getting away for a complete rest." He defiantly proposed to spend his time sleeping and playing golf. Clearly, there was much preparatory work for the presidency, but Taft's dilatory nature took hold and he refused to consider a single appointment until he was "good and ready." In the interim, he would do his part "to make golf one of the popular outdoor exercises" in the country.

Each evening, groups of leading citizens vied to entertain the Tafts. A committee in Atlanta decorated the city with flags and bunting in preparation for the president-elect's appearance at an elaborate "possum and taters" banquet. Newspapers described a specially constructed cage that housed each arriving batch of twenty possums until a hundred were gathered to feed six hundred guests. Featuring vaudeville acts, songs, and the release of doves, the gala evening was ranked the most brilliant event ever held in Atlanta, marking "a social epoch" in the history of the new South. A cartoon of Taft as Billy Possum prompted a toymaker to patent a new stuffed animal. But expectations that Billy Possum would rival the Teddy bear in popularity were swiftly dashed when the stuffed creature, resembling "a gigantic rat," caused children to cry.

Taft's sojourn at the Bon Air Hotel provided a happy respite, enabling him to enjoy "the honor without the responsibilities of the office." For the first time in months, the entire family was together: Robert and Helen arrived from Yale and Bryn Mawr, and the families of Charles and Harry Taft stayed for several weeks, along with Taft's good friend John Hays Hammond. Splendid weather afforded long hours on the golf links, daylong fishing excursions, and automobile rambles around the countryside. "He is so genial, so companionable, so gentlemanly," a woman remarked, "that one is apt to forget that he is the President-elect."

By postponing cabinet decisions, however, Taft inadvertently fueled speculation and rumor. Conventional wisdom suggested that after repeated pledges to support Roosevelt's policies, the new president would retain most of his predecessor's cabinet. Taft had even conveyed a message to Roosevelt for his cabinet colleagues: "Tell the boys I have been working with that I want to continue all of them. They are all fine fellows, and they have been mighty good to me. I want all them to stay just as they are."

In the months that followed, Taft began to recognize the necessity of establishing an independent identity, particularly after the barrage of criticism that accompanied his "humiliating pilgrimage" to Oyster Bay to consult Roosevelt on his acceptance speech. Throughout the campaign, Taft had stressed the very different challenges that would confront his own prospective administration. Roosevelt, Taft repeatedly explained, had launched a successful crusade against the abuses of industry and "aroused the people to demand reform." Now, Taft said, the time had come to perfect the necessary regulatory machinery and to craft amendments that would ensure proper enforcement. To accomplish these ends, a different sensibility and "different personnel" might be required.

Notwithstanding, the first man invited into Taft's cabinet was Roosevelt's trusted secretary of state, Elihu Root. In the cabinet's premier post, Root would provide the anchor in Roosevelt's absence. Looking back on his achievement in the Philippines, the president-elect attributed much of his success to the detailed instructions, goals, and framework Root had furnished. "I merely followed the way opened up by Root," he insisted. Indeed, after his election, Taft went so far as to tell an audience that the administration was topsy-turvy: Root "ought to be Pres.-elect," he insisted, "and I ought to be a prospective member of *his* Cabinet. Because I know how to serve under him." Such sentiments cannot be simply construed as extravagant humility or an odd, self-disparaging humor. Rather, like his chronic procrastination, they connote tentativeness, a want of confidence arising from underlying insecurity. Root was sorely tempted to accept Taft's offer. "I would rather stay here than do anything else," he told a friend, but "between rheumatism and the climate and the incessant and wearisome pressure of social duties I am satisfied that it would mean a complete breakdown of Mrs. Root's health."

With Root out of the running, Taft turned next to another intimate of his predecessor, Henry Cabot Lodge. Though "touched and gratified," Lodge nonetheless felt that he could be of greater service to the country by remaining in the Senate. After conferring with Roosevelt, Taft finally offered the post to former attorney general Philander Knox, then a Pennsylvania senator. "Knox called on me last night," Roosevelt informed Taft several days later. "I had a long talk over his accepting the position of Secretary of State and I am confident that he will do so." Five days later, Knox sent a telegram confirming his acceptance. Taft told Roosevelt he was planning to invite Knox to Augusta, hoping to secure guidance on his remaining choices. There, Knox would be joined by Taft's campaign chair, Frank Hitchcock, slated to become postmaster general. "Ha ha!" Roosevelt jested. "*You* are making up your Cabinet. *I* in a lighthearted way have spent the morning testing the rifles for my African trip. Life has compensations!"

Taft's initial assurance that he would retain the entire cabinet proved particularly troublesome when he subsequently decided to replace Luke Wright as secretary of war. When Taft had resigned his own cabinet post the previous July after securing the Republican nomination, Roosevelt had wanted Wright,

Taft's successor as governor general in the Philippines, to replace him. Worried that Wright would decline a term of only nine months, Roosevelt had asked Taft if he could offer the "inducement" of a longer tenure should he win the election. Taft had confirmed that he "would be more than pleased to continue Wright," and Roosevelt could relay that message. Once Taft had the choice in his hands, however, he hesitated, concerned that Wright was not "decisive" enough and tended "to let questions settle themselves without mental action by him." Instead, he selected another southern Democrat, Jacob Dickinson. While rethinking a key appointment was surely Taft's prerogative, he exacerbated the awkward situation and irritated Roosevelt by failing to inform Wright until mid-February 1909, just weeks before the inauguration.

In the end, no appointment would have more far-reaching consequences for Taft's administration than his decision to replace Interior Secretary James Garfield with Richard Ballinger. Roosevelt had pushed to retain Garfield from the outset. "I didn't have to be hit with a club ten times a day to understand the workings of his mind," Taft later remarked. No two young men in the Roosevelt administration had been closer to the president than Garfield and Gifford Pinchot. Pinchot had driven Roosevelt's conservation fight; Garfield had served for seven years, first as civil service commissioner, then as head of the Bureau of Corporations, and finally as secretary of the interior, where he worked closely with Pinchot. A "peculiar intimacy" bonded the trio, Roosevelt reflected, "because all three of us have worked for the same causes, have dreamed the same dreams, have felt a substantial identity of purpose."

Garfield had every reason to believe that Taft would ask him to stay. As one of Taft's staunchest supporters during the fight for nomination and election, Garfield had delivered scores of speeches in Ohio and chaired the convention in Columbus that provided an early boost to Taft's candidacy. Furthermore, Garfield was connected with Taft personally as well as politically: he and his wife, Helen, socialized with Will and Nellie, dining at each other's houses and vacationing together. Their son, John, attended Horace Taft's school in Connecticut. The press assumed that Garfield would not only stay on in Taft's cabinet, but would likely become an important member of the new president's inner circle.

Yet almost immediately after his election, Taft began searching for someone to replace Garfield. Although Taft considered Garfield an accomplished bureau chief, he did not think him "big enough" for a cabinet position. He was convinced that Pinchot dominated Garfield, and did not relish the thought of Pinchot running the Interior Department in addition to the Forest Service. While he recognized Pinchot's vital role in securing Roosevelt's conservation legacy, Taft believed that some of his executive policies and land withdrawals had not merely strained but broken existing law. Geographic representation also weighed heavily in Taft's rationale. Garfield hailed from Ohio, the state of the president-elect himself, while the West Coast clamored for someone to represent their interests.

Taft's choice, Richard Ballinger, had been a reform mayor in Seattle before joining the Roosevelt administration as head of the Land Office, where he was regarded as an ardent conservationist and an excellent administrator. By the time Ballinger returned to his Seattle law practice in 1908, Garfield was deeply impressed with his work. "He has done admirably," he noted, "& leaves with a reputation for ability, industry & fairness." When first approached to join Taft's cabinet, Ballinger regretfully declined, citing "limited personal means" and the promise to his wife that they would remain in Seattle. After further conversations, however, he was finally persuaded.

Had Taft taken Garfield into his confidence early on, perhaps explaining the necessity of geographical balance, he might have avoided future conflict, but instead he said nothing. Beyond his initial choice of Knox and Hitchcock, Taft remained silent regarding further appointments until he could assemble a complete cabinet. In late December, rumors circulated that Garfield was "out of the running," leaving the interior secretary in an embarrassing position. "I am utterly at sea," Garfield recorded in his journal on January 11, observing with frustration, "if he wishes me to stay he should ask me soon—if not he surely owes it to me, because of our relations during many years & close association recently, to frankly tell me so." When no announcement was forthcoming by late January, the press speculated that Garfield might be chosen after all and attributed the delay to the difficult process of constructing a balanced, cooperative cabinet, a particular challenge for "a genial, agreeable man, averse to making enemies or disappointing ambition." Yet the longer Taft withheld selections, the more anxious Garfield grew. "Rumors & more rumors but he says nothing," he reported, calling Taft's procrastination "an astounding condition of affairs & wholly without reasonable explanation."

Garfield was not the only former Roosevelt cabinet officer bewildered and exasperated by Taft's inaction. Gossip filled the vacuum; word spread that Taft had "completely changed his mind," deciding "to keep no one" associated with his predecessor so that his administration could stand on its own merits. While Roosevelt publicly defended Taft's right to choose his own men in his own way, he advised the president-elect to inform those he did not intend to reappoint immediately. "They will be making their plans, and less than two months remains, and I do not think they ought to be left in doubt," Roosevelt told Taft. "Of course I am perfectly willing to tell them if you will write me to do so."

"I think I ought to do it myself," Taft replied, yet he continued to wait more than two weeks before sending a half-dozen letters simultaneously. Each began with the same stilted phrase: "The President has thought that you were entitled to the notice of my cabinet plans insofar as to advise you that in the list of my cabinet I have not been able to include your name." The recipients, all formerly Taft's intimate colleagues, were understandably hurt by this impersonal and awkward manner of address. In the end, despite the fact that two additional members of Roosevelt's cabinet—George Meyer and James Wilson—joined Secretary of State Philander Knox in the new administration, the overriding impression was of "a clean sweep" of Roosevelt's team.

"T.R.'s Trusty Aides All to Walk Plank," announced the *Cleveland Press*. "Taft Seems Bent Upon Dumping His Old Associates in his Cabinet." Taft asserted that he had simply examined each position and carefully considered the best men to comprise the new administration. "I have my own record to make," he maintained, "and my own place to secure in the confidence of the country." Proponents of Roosevelt's agenda, however, began to question the president-elect's strategy: "If Taft is going to fire all his old associates in the Roosevelt administration, how is he going to make good his pledge to carry on the Roosevelt policies? Why, if he intends to finish the Roosevelt program, does he get rid of all the men trained in the Roosevelt school?" In addition, Roosevelt supporters voiced concern over the preponderance of corporate lawyers in the new cabinet.

Roosevelt himself could not help but feel "a little cast down" by Taft's dealings and decisions as he assembled his cabinet. Still, he continued to profess belief in his old friend. "They little realize that Taft is big enough to carve out his own administration on individual lines," he told Archie Butt. "I predict a brilliant administration for him. I felt he was the one man for the Presidency, and any failure in it would be as keenly felt by me as by himself or his family." While Taft's "system may be different," the president predicted, "the results will be the same."

After announcing his cabinet choices, Taft wrote a long letter to Roosevelt. "People have attempted to represent that you and I were in some way at odds during this last three months," he explained, "whereas you know and I know that there has not been the slightest difference between us." Indeed, the two men had spent many hours together during the transition. Through conversations and correspondence, Taft had kept Roosevelt informed on each cabinet decision and had shared an early draft of his inaugural address. "How could I but be delighted with your Inaugural?" Roosevelt responded. "It is simply fine in every way . . . and it marks just exactly what your administration will be."

Taft's final letter to Roosevelt before he assumed the presidency expressed "renewed appreciation" for his old friend's "breadth of soul and mind and magnanimity." Roosevelt replied with an equal warmth and affection. "Your letter," he wrote, "[was] so very nice—nice isn't anything like a strong enough word, but at the moment to use words as strong as I feel would look sloppy."

Roosevelt made no secret of his reluctance to leave office. "If I had conscientiously felt at liberty to run again, and try once more to hold this great office," he acknowledged, "I should greatly have liked to do so and to continue to keep my hands on the levers of this mighty machine." In his last annual message to Congress, he had firmly declared that he felt "none of the weariness of public life" which seven tumultuous years might well have produced. Although conservative leaders in the House and Senate had successfully blocked most of his proposals for two straight years, Roosevelt remained undaunted. In a sweeping "valedictory message" of more than 21,000 words, the outgoing president expounded "his whole social philosophy" and urged Congress to "carry into effect the new spirit of democracy," reinforcing federal power to address "present day" social and economic problems.

"He is as voluminous as ever," the *New York Tribune* remarked. If only "a fraction" of the laws that Roosevelt advocated were passed, another reporter observed, "they would commit the country to a course of new experiments and make over the face of the social creation." He wanted authority over telegraph and telephone companies, along with railroads, placed in the hands of the Interstate Commerce Commission. He called for greater regulation of interstate corporations, prohibition of child labor, enforcement of an eight-hour workday, strengthening of workmen's compensation, the establishment of a postal savings system, and an inheritance tax. "The danger to American democracy lies not in the least in the concentration of administrative power in responsible and accountable hands," he argued. "It lies in having the power insufficiently concentrated, so that no one can be held responsible to the people for its use." What might have been interpreted as "an infringement upon liberty" before the Industrial Revolution and the rise of massive corporations "may be [the] necessary safeguard of liberty today." Within this new industrial context, he criticized the courts for ruling unconstitutional various state laws designed to remedy social problems, "arrogat[ing] to themselves functions which properly belong to legislative bodies."

Finally, Roosevelt rounded on Congress. For two decades, the executive departments had deployed members of the Secret Service to ferret out land frauds, violations in anti-trust laws, and, on rare occasions, illegal actions perpetrated by senators or congressmen themselves. The previous year, however, Congress had passed an amendment preventing the Secret Service from pursuing such investigations. Incensed, Roosevelt charged that no one but members of the criminal class could benefit from such an amendment; clearly, "Congressmen did not themselves wish to be investigated."

Roosevelt's comments provoked a "storm of censure" from Republicans and Democrats alike. Senator Aldrich introduced a resolution challenging the president to produce evidence of congressional misbehavior, while Senators Bailey and Tillman huffily defended the "self-respect and integrity" of fellow legislators. Adamantly refusing to retract his charge, Roosevelt fired off a 6,000-word response that targeted specific members of the Congress, including Minnesota representative James Tawney and Senators Tillman and Bailey. "Pandemonium broke loose," the *Times* reported. In return, Congress took a rare measure not utilized since Jackson's presidency, reprimanding Roosevelt with an overwhelming 212–35 vote to reject his message "on the ground that it lacked due respect."

Despite such overwhelming resistance, Roosevelt held fast to his position. "Congress of course feels that I will never again have to be reckoned with and that it is safe to be ugly with me," he confided to Kermit, admitting, "I am not having an easy time." Even as he acknowledged that "it is a President's duty to get on with Congress if he possibly can, and that it is a reflection upon him if he and Congress come to a complete break," he nevertheless insisted that he must continue to "fight hard" on the issue of corruption—a touchstone of his presidency—or "be put in a contemptible position." Although this bitter struggle ended his days in Washington on a disagreeable note, he took pride that he had exercised his presidential powers "right up to the end."

DURING THE FINAL WEEKS OF the Roosevelt administration, a mood of sadness enveloped the White House. "I have never seen so much feeling in evidence in all my life," Archie Butt observed as this vital stage in the lives of both the president and his colleagues drew to a close. As the chief military aide, the forty-three-year-old Captain Butt had developed an intimate relationship with both the president and first lady. His warmth, flair for conversation, and love of books had made him a welcome companion at Sagamore Hill and scores of White House lunches and dinners. A graduate of the University of the South in Tennessee, Archie had worked as a journalist for nearly a decade before volunteering for service during the Spanish-American War. Remaining in the military, he had served in the Quartermaster Department in the Philippines, Cuba, and Washington before Roosevelt brought him to the White House. Butt had begun his duties "believing thoroughly in the real greatness" of the president, and the weeks and months spent with the family had not altered his original judgment. He had traveled with the Roosevelts on overnight trips, joined them for horseback rides, tennis games, and scrambles through Rock Creek Park—always assuming "his duties with a boyish delight and a relish for all the gay doings of the White House."

Archie Butt had grown especially close to Edith Roosevelt. "She is perfectly poised and nothing seems to annoy her," the forty-three-year-old bachelor told his mother, lauding Edith's "ever-softening influence" on her volatile husband. Even while drawing a protective curtain around her family, Edith had unfailingly carried out social obligations with natural elegance. Formerly, Butt remarked, the "smart element" of society had been "wont to sneer" at the garish nature of public entertainments at the White House. Under Edith Roosevelt, however, functions were smaller, less frequent, and more formal; guests were required to present cards, and soon, smart society clamored for invitations. Edith's Friday evening musicales attracted the nation's finest performers, including Ignace Jan Paderewski, the concert pianist, and the young cellist Pablo Casals. "If social affairs have thus become less democratic, they have also become more dignified," remarked one reporter. "Were we living in the days of chivalry," Butt confessed with grandiose nostalgia, "I could easily believe myself in the role of knight for a mistress so gentle, so sweet, and so altogether lovely."

"The ball rolls faster as it nears the bottom," Captain Butt observed as the Roosevelt administration drew to a close in early February. The White House calendar was "filled every minute" with brilliant but melancholy events—the last Army and Navy reception, the last meeting with the diplomatic corps. Several of the ministers and ambassadors "actually wept as they said goodbye," Butt recounted. The wife of the Japanese ambassador "could not say a word, but burst out crying, and the Ambassador was not much better." Later that same afternoon, Edith Roosevelt finally "had a good cry" of her own, but when the president attempted to comfort her, he "broke down himself."

For his final public journey, Roosevelt chose to deliver a speech at Knob Creek Farm in Kentucky, birthplace of his hero Abraham Lincoln. He had ordered his train route withheld from the newspapers, fearing he would be met with diminished enthusiasm as his presidency neared its end. "For the first hour there were no yells," Archie Butt recorded, and Roosevelt looked forlorn as he gazed out at calm streets and empty platforms. Before long, however, the train schedule leaked. Suddenly, throngs materialized at every spot along the way: families and children stood at tiny intersections; in larger towns, thousands assembled to wave and cheer, wishing their president a final farewell. "He jumped from his seat as readily for a half-dozen people at a road crossing as he would for a crowd at a station," Archie Butt marveled. At one point, Roosevelt rushed to the platform to greet a single woman in a field, prompting recollection of an earlier trip when "he found himself waving frantically at a herd of cows." With deadpan mirth, Roosevelt remembered that he had "met with an indifferent, if not a cold, reception."

On March 1, Roosevelt hosted perhaps the most colorful official luncheon on record. "The papers have made a good deal of fun of my tennis cabinet," he playfully observed, "but they have never known how extensive or what a part it has played in my administrations. It will be gathered together to-day for the first time." Thirty-one members of this fabulously eclectic "tennis cabinet"—Roosevelt's hunting companions, sparring partners, tennis mates, and fellow rock climbers—would attend. In order that "various elements" of this informal cabinet might "get acquainted," the president told Archie Butt to seat them "irrespective of rank." Jules Jusserand, the French ambassador, and cabinet members James Garfield, Truman Newberry, and George Meyer should enjoy the company of "the wolf hunters and the 'two-gun' men." Needless to say, this convergence of disparate worlds made quite an impression: "Is there any other man," Mme Jusserand exclaimed, who "could have had on one side of him the Ambassador of a great country and on the other a 'desperado' from Oklahoma?" Throughout the lunch, Roosevelt spoke of his relationship with each of the men in turn. According to Archie Butt, "there was not a dry eye around all that table."

The Roosevelts chose to spend March 3, 1909, their last night in the White House, with the Tafts. Arriving in the late afternoon, Will and Nellie were escorted to a bedroom suite on the second floor, later designated the Lincoln Bedroom. "It was a curious occasion," Alice Roosevelt Longworth recalled. "There were the Tafts, about to take over, obviously being tactful, soft pedaling their natural elation." For everyone else, "like an obscuring fog, was the inevitable melancholy of saying good-by, of closing the door on great times; the interest, the personal associations, the power—all over, gone." Even Archie Butt, who would remain at his post with the new president, "was frankly emotional," and Elihu Root was in such "low spirits" that tears brimmed from his eyes.

"The dinner would have been hopeless," Archie Butt remarked, "had it not been for the President," who lightened the mood with one entertaining story after another. Regardless of Roosevelt's efforts, everyone seemed relieved when the meal ended. In customary fashion, couples separated, the men going to the president's upstairs study while the women congregated in the library. Sometime after 10 p.m., Taft rose to keep his promised appearance at a Yale smoker in his honor at the Willard Hotel. His departure brought the evening to an end, leaving only Theodore, Edith, Nellie, and Captain Butt. "Mrs. Roosevelt finally arose," Butt wrote, "and said she would go to her room and advised Mrs. Taft to do the same. She took her hand kindly and expressed the earnest hope that her first night in the White House would be one of sweet sleep."

Taft remained at the smoker until midnight, his late return to the White House provoking a widely read spoof in the New York *Sun* the next day. A fictional dispatch portrayed a weary Taft trudging upstairs, whereupon a servant announced that the president awaited him. And there before him stood Roosevelt, broadsword in hand. "Thought you'd like a short bout before turning in," Roosevelt offered. "Here, get this mask and these pads on. Here are the gauntlets." Taft barely had time to don his equipment before Roosevelt struck three decisive blows. "Now we'll have a little wrestling," he suggested, and "as if by magic, the mattress was spread." Almost instantly, Taft was on his back. Exulting in triumph, Roosevelt asked the servants to set up the rings and parallel bars. For thirty minutes, they took turns until Roosevelt mercifully declared himself the clear victor. Finally, at 3 a.m., the *Sun* fancied, "the two athletes went to bed!"

In fact, by the time Taft returned to the White House, the Roosevelts had long since retired. Only Nellie, too excited to sleep, had waited up. For weeks, she had been preoccupied with the inaugural festivities and everything had been meticulously arranged—everything except the weather. A soggy wet snow had been falling all day. The storm was supposed to end by morning but the wind gusting over the water "shunted it back angrier than before" and the nation's capital found itself "bound hand and foot" by the worst blizzard since 1888. Gale winds howled, tree limbs cracked under the weight of the heavy snow, and streets were covered with a slick slush. "It was really very serious," Nellie recalled. "Railroad and telegraphic communications were paralyzed all along the Atlantic Coast."

ON MARCH 4, INAUGURAL DAY, the president and president-elect met for an early breakfast. "The storm will soon be over," Roosevelt sardonically predicted. "As soon as I'm out where I can do no further harm to the Constitution it will cease." Taft suggested a different, if equally portentous interpretation. "You're wrong," he told his old friend. "It is my storm. I always said it would be a cold day when I got to be President."

The Street Department was already hard at work clearing snow from Pennsylvania Avenue, but there was no time to remove the "yellowish, slimy, shoe-penetrating mush" from the sidewalks. In front of every structure with windows on the street—"candy stores, pawnbrokers' shops, undertaking parlors, Chinese restaurants, machine shops"—carpenters had been busy all week long building seats which the owners planned to sell at a premium. By midmorning, melancholy enveloped the proprietors of the small shops along the parade route. With wet snow still blanketing the city, prices began to plummet. Seats expected to garner five dollars sold for one; sandwiches priced at a dime could be had for three cents. Despite the severe conditions, people "stood three deep on both sides of Pennsylvania Avenue," prepared to cheer and wave as the carriage bearing the president and president-elect moved slowly toward the Capitol. Unfortunately, hardly a glimpse of the two could be seen through the windows, for a driving snow had forced the coachmen to close the top of the carriage.

At the Capitol, more than 10,000 hearty souls waited to take their seats in the open stands to witness the inaugural ceremony. Inside, the Inaugural Committee debated whether to move the ceremony to the Senate chamber for the first time since President Jackson's second inaugural. Reluctant to disappoint the eager crowd, Taft fought to keep the ceremony on the Capitol Plaza. "If so many spectators could endure the cold merely to see the sight," he argued, "he certainly could endure it." The president-elect relented only when advised that the elderly chief justice and several members of Congress and the diplomatic corps might be imperiled by the exposure. The disheartening news was blared to the expectant crowd through megaphones: "All exercises will be conducted in the Senate chamber, and no one will be admitted there unless he has a ticket." No longer an open, public ceremony, the inaugural was attended by members of Congress, high government officials, Supreme Court justices, and ambassadors.

Cheers erupted when Roosevelt and Taft entered, walking "arm in arm" down the aisle. "Hale and hearty as Mr. Roosevelt looked," the *Sun* reported, "he was dwarfed by Mr. Taft's generous proportions." Appropriately, William Howard Taft took the oath of office on the same Bible used for decades to swear in Supreme Court justices. Then, speaking in "a slow, distinct voice, which carried to the furthest reaches of the chamber," he delivered his inaugural address. "For the first time in a century," correspondents observed, the assembled guests could actually hear the president's words.

While he felt the "heavy weight of responsibility" to preserve and enforce regulatory reforms initiated by "his distinguished predecessor," Taft simultaneously reassured those businesses companies "pursuing proper and progressive business methods." He pledged to secure amendments to both the anti-trust and interstate commerce laws that would make a distinction between "legitimate" combinations "and those formed with the intent of creating monopolies and artificially controlling prices." Pressing Roosevelt's agenda, he urged Congress to pass new conservation laws, consider a graduated inheritance tax, establish a postal savings bank system, and provide added protections to members of the working class. "The scope of a modern government," he maintained, "has been widened far beyond the principles laid down by the old 'laissez faire' school of political writers, and this widening has met popular approval." Finally, stepping into uncharted territory for his party, Taft called for a downward revision of the tariff and announced that he was summoning Congress into special session on March 15 for this purpose.

When Taft finished, Roosevelt jumped up and climbed the steps to the raised platform. "The new president turned to meet him," reporters observed, "with a smile that irradiated his face; the departing president grinned all over." Then, "with hands on each other's shoulders," they talked for several minutes. "God bless you, old man," Roosevelt exclaimed, calling his address "a great state document." Witnesses of the emotional scene "applauded like mad."

Rather than ride together back to the White House, as custom dictated, the two men parted. Months earlier, Roosevelt had decided to go straight from the inaugural ceremony to Union Station. There, he bid adieu to thousands of well-wishers with a short, heartfelt speech. A band played "Auld Lang Syne" and, amid "deafening" cheers, Roosevelt and Edith departed for Oyster Bay.

Since Roosevelt had abandoned tradition, Nellie followed suit, deciding to do what "no President's wife had ever done"—accompany her husband from the Capitol to the White House. "Some of the Inaugural Committee expressed their disapproval," she recalled, "but I had my way and in spite of protests took my place at my husband's side." Although a bitter wind still scoured the streets, the snow had stopped and the new president insisted the carriage top remain open. Drawn by four horses, the carriage elicited "a continuous cheer" from the thousands of visitors unable to witness either the oath of office or Taft's address. "Three cheers for the first lady," a voice shouted along their route. Seeing his wife's radiant smile, Taft took up the cheer himself and soon the entire crowd was hailing the first lady. "That drive was the proudest and happiest event of Inauguration Day," Nellie recalled. "My responsibilities had not yet begun to worry me, and I was able to enjoy, almost to the full, the realization that my husband was actually President of the United States."

Newspapers predicted the genial new president would usher in an "era of good feelings." Taft "has no enemies of his own making; he is not taking over any of the enemies of his predecessor," observed Walter Wellman. The change of administration signaled "peace and reassurance" rather than the atmosphere of "vituperation and denunciation" that had marked the final months of Roosevelt's tenure. While progressives trusted Taft to continue his mentor's work, conservatives took comfort that "judicial poise had succeeded erratic temperament," that decisions would now be made with deliberation, not drama. "Never did any man," the *Sun* editorialized, arrive at the White House "with such universal good will."

Already questioning his own competence for the nation's highest office, Taft found such grand expectations unnerving. Asked a week after his inauguration how he liked being president, he confessed that he remained disoriented. "I hardly know yet. When I hear someone say Mr. President, I look around expecting to see Roosevelt, and when I read in the headlines of the morning papers that the President and Senator Aldrich and Speaker Cannon have had a conference, my first thought is, 'I wonder what they talked about.' So you can see that I have not gone very far yet."

Roosevelt's departure for Africa on March 23 signaled opportunity as well as anxiety for Taft. For years, Archie Butt observed, Taft had "been living on the steam of Theodore Roosevelt," propelled by the outsized personality and ambition of his friend and chief. "He will have to find his own fuel now," Butt conjectured, "and, like a child, will have to learn to walk alone. There is not the slightest doubt in my mind that he will learn to walk alone and will walk possibly all the better but it is going to be a readjustment just the same."

Initially, Captain Butt had hesitated to accept Taft's offer to remain in the White House, fearing he would not be able to serve the new president with the same devotion he continued to feel toward his predecessor. "The influence of Mr. Roosevelt over those around him is masterful and his friends become fanatical, e.g. to wit—I," he told his sister Clara. He had great admiration and liking for Taft, however, and considered Nellie "an intellectual woman and a woman of wonderful executive ability." He had been in the Philippines when Taft was governor general and had seen how the Filipino people had responded to the warmth and openness of the big man's personality. While

Butt acknowledged at the start that he missed Roosevelt's "marvelous wit," he found his new chief a most enjoyable companion. "He is essentially a gregarious animal," Butt reflected. "He likes to have someone in the car with him when he is reading or studying, and if he is at work, he works better if he has someone in the room with him."

Despite Taft's initial reservations, his first two months in office augured well for the new administration. Early on, he decided that his White House would be open to all: he would not, like Roosevelt, compile a "list of undesirables"; there would be no "abrupt and stormy attacks" on fellow politicians. Reflecting on the animosity between the president and Congress that had consumed the country since the previous December, Taft resolved to end such recrimination. "I hope that I shall never be called upon ever to say anything in disparagement of Senators and members of the House. I have no desire to belittle them."

As governor general of the Philippines, Taft had welcomed every political group at Malacañan Palace, making it "a rule never to pay any attention to personal squabbles and differences." He hoped to institute the same policy as president. Aware that access to the White House was an enormous political asset, Taft announced a series of a half-dozen formal dinner parties designed to unify "all the warring factions" in the House and Senate. "I am rather proud of these lists," he told Archie Butt. "I do not believe there were given six dinners at the White House where more thought has been expended than on these six." He was careful to include Senator Joseph Bailey, despite the fact that just a month earlier the Texas Democrat had pronounced Taft wholly unsuited for the presidency. And Bailey appeared to appreciate the gesture. "I have come to pay my tribute and respects to a most agreeable personality," Bailey declared at the event. Taft also lifted Roosevelt's ban on Senator Tillman of South Carolina and invited dozens of rank-and-file congressmen who had not previously attended a White House dinner. Where Roosevelt had dispensed White House invitations "to pay for favors already performed and loyalty which had been proven," Taft hoped his magnanimity would induce future cooperation.

The volatile guest list for the first of these affairs, which included Old Guard Republicans and their progressive antagonists, northern Democrats and southern Populists, created "the liveliest interest" in the capital. Fortunately, one reporter noted, ladies had been invited to keep these "belligerent Congressmen apart." Even with their mollifying influence, some suggested, the situation might "require all of President Taft's diplomacy to keep things going smoothly." In the end, good food, good wine, and the music of the Marine

Band made the first dinner a notable success, setting an agreeable precedent for the five events planned for the future. "It is undoubtedly Mr. Taft's purpose to conciliate," observed a northwestern paper. "He doesn't like discord. He thinks it will be possible to get all the good men of the country together on a common platform—the Roosevelt men and the anti-Roosevelt men."

During the weeks that followed, reporters kept a tally of "the undesirables" once again "finding their way" to the White House. Democratic senator Augustus Bacon of Georgia was "pleased as a boy" with his first invitation in seven years. Senators Hale, Aldrich, Payne, "and a lot of other ungodly standpatters" were again welcomed in the president's home, as were the most fervent Roosevelt men. Rather than wielding the "big stick through the press" to prod legislative action, Taft hoped that "personal appeal," reasoned arguments, and a spirit of hospitality would prevail.

Reporters too delighted in the "startling contrast" evident in Taft's method of handling the hundreds of audience-seekers from that of his predecessor. Senators, congressmen, and all manner of officials appeared during the morning hours between ten and twelve. To expedite matters, Roosevelt had kept his door open, entertaining a dozen or more callers simultaneously with his snappy banter, sending them "on their way out almost before they realized they were in." One visitor described his experience as being "caught in a strong draught." Taft possessed none of Roosevelt's "terminal facilities." He invited callers individually into his office, closed the door, and reportedly made everyone feel "so much at home" that they were inclined to linger all morning. At the pace he conducted business, Archie Butt worried, Taft would "be about three years behind" on the final day of his term.

Taft extended the window for callers an additional hour and a half, interrupting the flow of visitors only to take his lunch. Unlike Roosevelt, who famously invited people from all walks of life to his table, Taft generally ate alone. Forever struggling to lose weight, he limited his midday meal to an apple or a glass of water. One visitor, having reportedly waited three hours to see him, was finally invited into the president's office with an unceremonious greeting: "I am glad you have come in," Taft told him, "but you will have to wait until I have had my luncheon." When the weary caller asked how long it would be, Taft's only reply was to pick up a pitcher of water and pour himself a glass. When he finished drinking, he returned to his desk: "Now I am through, what do you want to tell me?"

Meetings with governmental officials and lawmakers often stretched until five o'clock, after which Taft, like Roosevelt, took time to exercise. "There the resemblance ended," one White House correspondent remarked. Roosevelt took strenuous hikes or played in vigorous tennis matches; Taft much preferred a leisurely round of golf. As a horseman, Roosevelt "jumped hurdles, forded creeks, and sought out unused bridle paths," another reporter noted, while the new president trotted "along the river front or around the ellipse." Before long, even these placid forays were replaced by late afternoon spins in one of the three new White House automobiles. Roosevelt had displayed no interest in what critics called "devil wagons," but "Taft fell in love with them on the first whirl." In short order, he converted the stable, which had held Roosevelt's "jumpers, pacers, and calipers," into an oversized garage for his Model M steam touring convertible (capable of seating seven passengers); a Pierce Arrow Limousine; and a Baker Queen Victoria electric, which Nellie learned to drive.

Diverted by their superficial differences in style, the journalists initially failed to recognize a far more consequential contrast between the two men—their differing attitudes toward the press. More than any previous president, Theodore Roosevelt had treated journalists as intimates; covering the White House had been "a reporter's paradise" for seven years. "No president ever lived on better terms with the newspapermen than did Roosevelt," reporter Gus Karger proclaimed. He inquired after their families, shared confidential anecdotes, and discussed their latest projects. Throughout his day, whether he was being shaved, signing documents, or traveling from place to place, he gave them unheard of access to his comings and goings. Most important, as one historian wrote, "he made the White House hum with activity, and in the process, gave the correspondents who covered him the best ongoing story in generations." Now, that colorful story had come to an end. "There will be some one at the White House whom you will like more than me," Roosevelt had predicted during his final meeting with the press corps, "but not one who will interest you more."

As secretary of war, Taft had enjoyed an easy rapport with members of the press, who frequented his office to secure gossip, information, and anecdotes. "It was a favorite occupation for the correspondents," Oscar King Davis recalled, "to 'go Tafting' "—to meet with the secretary in the late afternoon for "a half-hour or so of very pleasant conversation which often furnished a good deal of news." Always "a good scout," Taft had spoken frankly, and depended on reporter friends to protect his occasional indiscretions. In his first weeks as president, however, Taft discovered that "casual remarks" made headlines, and quickly recognized "the necessity of care" in everything he disclosed. Rather than hold informal daily discussions with members of the press, he would see individual journalists by appointment only. Nonetheless, the new president promised to meet with the entire group of correspondents on a weekly basis. Before he discontinued these press conferences, the White House reporters developed a genuine affection for "the big, good-humored man who had taken the place of the strident, dynamic Roosevelt."

Taft was beginning to create "his own atmosphere," Archie Butt remarked in late April. "People are forgetting that he is the residuary legatee, and his smile, good nature, and evenness of temper are winning hearts to him." The press and the public seemed to have reached a similar verdict about the new occupant of the White House. "Roosevelt made good with the people; and Taft promises to do likewise," one reporter noted. "Take it all and all," another concluded, "Washington is mighty happy in these opening days of the Taft administration."

IF TAFT PROFESSED TO BE "a fish out of water" in his new office, Nellie was finally entirely in her element. The new president frequently touted his wife's strengths, maintaining that without her guidance, he would never have sought and never gained the presidency. "I am no politician," he told a gathering in Georgia shortly after his election. "There," he proudly indicated Nellie, "is the politician of the family. If she had only let me alone, I guess I should now be dozing on the Circuit Court bench." Her acumen, he insisted proudly, had facilitated every critical step of his career. Indeed, he held that without her "tact and diplomacy," he would never have succeeded in the Philippines. Now he had faith that Nellie would "share the responsibilities" of his new office and once again prove instrumental in surmounting the "formidable" challenges he would face.

Journalists latched onto Taft's narrative, emphasizing Nellie's decisive role in her husband's political ascendancy. Their comradeship, the *Ladies' Home Journal* observed, was "like that of two men who are intimate chums." A portrait emerged of an ambitious wife who championed her viewpoints "with almost masculine vigor," while Taft assumed "his most judicial attitude." Article after article highlighted Nellie's role in her husband's choice to leave the Cincinnati Superior Court to become solicitor general, and then to relinquish his federal judgeship and become governor general of the Philippines. "Yes," Nellie acknowledged, "it is true that I urged Mr. Taft to give up his position on the bench and return to politics. I felt that while he honored and loved his legal position more than all else in his career, he might spend the younger years of his life in a wider field." Again, reporters observed, Nellie's "judgment prevailed" when Taft turned down Roosevelt's third offer for the Supreme Court to test the waters for the presidency. A week after his victory, Nellie was asked if she studied politics. "Indeed, I do," she replied in her usual forthright manner. "I have studied the situation gravely and I think I understand it well."

"Few women have gone into the White House so well equipped to meet the exactions" of the first lady's position, remarked the *New York Times*. As the governor general's wife, she had already served in a similar capacity; she acutely understood the importance of getting out among the people, appreciated the ceremonial aspects of her role, and was well versed in the rules of etiquette required for her position. Her knowledge of Spanish, French, and German enabled her to speak freely with the diplomats and natives of numerous countries. "You make me feel truly at home when you converse with me in French," Ambassador Jusserand told her. Nellie's extensive travels had provided her with myriad stories and anecdotes to entertain such dignitaries. The new first lady was "never at a loss for conversation," a reporter for the *New York Tribune* wrote. "Never within the recollection of Washingtonians of today," claimed another correspondent, had a first lady shown herself so conversant "on any subject of contemporaneous interest." Asked how she found time "to keep up so thoroughly" with world events, Nellie rejoined with droll simplicity: "By reading the daily papers."

His first interview with Nellie Taft left the *Ladies' Home Journal* reporter George Griswold Hill "impressed with her dignity." He remarked upon her unusual acuity and shrewd insight into people and situations. "She surveys the man or woman presented to her with a look so calm and deliberate," Hill observed, "that strangers sometimes are wont to describe her as cold." Beneath her "cloak of composure," however, Hill discerned a charming and sensitive woman. A *New York Times* reporter was similarly taken with the clever new first lady: "Her smile has the charm of intelligence," he reported, "that quick flash of recognition, distinct from the frozen, automatic smile peculiar to many women in official life."

As the president's wife, Nellie announced early on, she considered herself "a public personage" and would "cheerfully meet any demands the position [made] upon her." Her statement revealed a far different temperament from that of her predecessor. Even after seven years as first lady, Edith Roosevelt had remained "unwilling to look upon herself otherwise than as a private individual." Believing that "a woman's name should appear in print but twice—when she is married and when she is buried," Edith had refrained from publicly voicing political opinions and routinely declined interview requests. In a rare portrait piece, entitled "Mrs. Roosevelt: The Woman in the

Background," Mabel Daggett portrayed Edith Roosevelt as an intensely private and traditional wife and mother. She "presents none of the restless new woman attributes," Daggett wrote. "She throbs for no reforms. She champions no causes." Surrounded by her boisterous family, Edith was described as "a happy woman," adored by her husband. Edith Roosevelt, Daggett concluded, would intentionally "step out into history as one of the least known" first ladies.

Before she took up residence in the White House, Nellie Taft made it clear she would play a far different role. In December 1908, she agreed to become honorary chair of the Women's Welfare Department of the National Civic Federation (NCF)—a progressive organization founded to better the working lives of wage earners employed in government and industry positions. No previous first lady had taken "a commanding lead" in promoting controversial programs to improve public welfare. At the annual meeting, Nellie delivered a well-received speech calling for investigations into the working conditions of female employees in federal and state departments, post offices, public hospitals, and police stations. "She plainly showed," one attendee noted, "that she has brains and used them without in any sense being aggressive or pedantic." During the NCF banquet at the Waldorf-Astoria in New York the following evening, she was observed "in animated conversation" with the union leader Samuel Gompers. Not all Washingtonians approved of Nellie's unconventional activism. A traditionalist, Archie Butt predicted that Nellie would "make a fine mistress of the White House," but only if she would refrain from speaking publicly about "the betterment of the working girl class," and focus instead upon "the simple duties of First Lady."

Public policy affecting working women was not the only issue on which Nellie expressed a strong opinion. Asked about granting suffrage to women, she answered with her usual directness: "The woman's voice is the voice of wisdom and I can see nothing unwomanly in her casting the ballot." In fact, Nellie fervently rejected traditional restrictions on a woman's role in society, insisting that intellectual development in no way diminished her capabilities in the home. Nothing in a college education, she maintained, "makes a girl either unfit for domestic obligations or masculine in her tastes." Some women were "not called on to preside over a home," and for those who did marry and have children, education would "make them great in intellect and soul." Her daughter Helen, she noted with pride, had chosen to take "a full college course" at the National Cathedral School, then secured a prestigious scholarship to Bryn Mawr College. While Nellie appreciated "the distinct advantages for a young girl in the social life of the White House," she fully supported her daughter's decision to pursue her education elsewhere. With her progressive views, one reporter noted, Mrs. Taft had "endeared herself to that class of women who are sometimes slightingly referred to as 'strongminded.' "

Despite Captain Butt's concern, Nellie's political activities did nothing to interfere with her duties as mistress of the White House. In fact, the new first lady had ambitious plans to make the national capital the hub of American cultural life. The White House, she argued, belonged to the people, and she would conduct social affairs there "on a plane of the highest and broadest democracy." She hoped that Washington would someday supplant New York as the "real social center" of the country. In the capital, she envisioned "a national society" comprised "of the best people in the land, a society not founded on the dollar, but on culture, art, statesmanship." No other city, she maintained, "is more beautifully laid out or has more natural charm during the months given over to official and social life." New Yorkers reacted with scorn, calling the first lady's idea "as absurd as it is impracticable," insisting that New York "has been, and always will be the mecca of culture and wealth in our land."

Undeterred, Nellie embarked on her first major project. With the coming of spring, inspired by the Luneta, the popular municipal park in the heart of Manila where all classes of the citizenry could gather for outdoor concerts, she worked with a landscape architect to transform the south side of Washington's Tidal Basin into "one of the most famous esplanades of the world." She enlisted her husband to persuade Congress that $25,000 should be appropriated to beautify the area—to plant trees, improve both the bridle path and the roadway, build an octagonal wooden bandstand, and install hundreds of comfortable benches. During her travels in the Far East, Nellie had fallen under the enchantment of Japanese cherry trees. Discovering that "both the soil and climate" of Washington were suitable for their growth, she purchased 100 trees from nurseries around the country; when her plans became public, the mayor of Tokyo sent an additional 2,000 young cherry trees to Washington.

On April 17, the president and first lady officially dedicated "Potomac Park" with the first in a series of White House–sponsored public concerts to be held every Wednesday and Saturday afternoon from five to seven. Hours before the first notes of the inaugural concert, "vehicles of every description" began to arrive—"horse drawn victorias and landaus, electric and gasoline motor cars, taxicabs and nearly every type of carriage." Men and women on horseback lined the winding bridle path and thousands of pedestrians settled on the lawn near the river. All told, 10,000 people representing "every walk of life" had gathered in the new park.

Vigorous cheers greeted the president and first lady as they arrived in an open electric landaulet. They smiled and bowed "right and left," stopping frequently to speak with friends and acquaintances. The entire cabinet was present, along with dozens of ambassadors. "Everybody saw everybody that he or she knew," Nellie marveled, "and there was the same exchange of friendly greetings that had always made the Luneta such a pleasant meeting place." Though Nellie had taken pains to ensure that her municipal park would "acquire the special character" she so desired, she could hardly have envisioned the future of Potomac Park and the cherry blossom festival that one day would draw millions of visitors to the nation's capital.

In May, Nellie also introduced a series of Friday afternoon garden parties. After developing a "very strong liking" for open-air festivities in the Far East, she decided the south grounds of the White House would provide a perfect setting for similar events. The Marine Band was stationed on the lawn, a large refreshment tent was situated under the trees at the rear of the mansion, and iron benches were scattered around the grounds. The invitations, issued each week to more than five hundred people, asked men to attend in white "short coats, flannel trousers and straw hats," while women wore white dresses and carried "bright colored parasols." The president and first lady stood on a knoll to receive their guests, who were free to "roam at will in the private grounds of the President and sip tea and punch and eat sandwiches and ices under the historic trees." These picturesque gatherings, one reporter observed, "are as informal as any entertainment given in the name of the President and his wife can be." Nevertheless, they quickly became "the most popular form of official hospitality yet seen in Washington."

Taft expressed his immense pride in Nellie's accomplishments to Archie Butt. "It was a difficult thing for her to give any individuality to her entertainments following so close on the Roosevelt administration, which was so particularly brilliant," he acknowledged, but she had clearly managed to do so. Butt was equally impressed that she had managed to distinguish herself. "She possesses a nature which I think is going to unfold and enlarge itself as it adjusts itself to new and broader surroundings," he told his sister. "She really looks ten years younger since she entered the White House, and I think she has become more gracious and kinder toward all the world."

It was evident to all that the vivacious and self-possessed first lady would continue to be instrumental in all the new president's endeavors. "The complete social success of the Taft administration has been fully established," the *Kansas City Star* observed on May 16. "In the ten weeks of her husband's Administration," the *New York Times* agreed, "Mrs. Taft has done more for society than any former mistress of the White House has undertaken in as many months."

On May 17, Nellie and William Taft hosted a small party on the presidential yacht, the *Sylph*. The guests included Attorney General George Wickersham and his wife; her sister Lady Hadfield and husband; the steel baron Sir Robert Hadfield; and Archie Butt. The *Sylph* set sail on the Potomac, heading toward Mt. Vernon, where a special tour of President Washington's home had been arranged. Nellie was talking with the attorney general when she suddenly grew faint and collapsed.

Crushed ice was pressed to her forehead and wrists, and the first lady "seemed to revive," Butt recalled, but she remained only "half conscious" and "did not speak." Taft raced to her side as the ship turned back and a message was dispatched directing Dr. Matthew Delaney to meet them at the White House. "The trip back seemed interminable," Butt recalled, because "no one could do anything." When they reached the White House, Taft and Butt each took one of Nellie's arms and "practically carried" her inside.

Nellie's right side was paralyzed, the right side of her face had fallen, and she remained unable to speak. Taft was devastated—he "looked like a great stricken animal," Archie Butt sorrowfully remarked. Never had he "seen greater suffering or pain shown on a man's face." The symptoms, Taft anxiously told his son Robert, indicated "a lesion in the brain." After examining Nellie, however, Dr. Delaney concluded that "because she could hear all right," she had suffered in all likelihood "a mere attack of nervous hysteria rather than a bursting of a blood vessel in the brain." With extended rest, he reassured the president, her symptoms might disappear.

The last of the six congressional dinners was scheduled for that very evening. Recognizing his obligation "in the face of sorrow," Taft circulated among his guests with a forced smile and friendly demeanor. "But what a dinner!" Butt observed. "Every mouthful seemed to choke him, yet he never wavered." He was "fighting her battle, for it would humiliate her terribly to feel that people were commiserating with her." While the men smoked cigars, Taft hastened to his wife's room and consulted with her doctor. Told that she had fallen peacefully asleep, he rejoined the party. The night was balmy, allowing the guests, as Nellie had planned, to move to the East Terrace. There, electric lights, covered with red paper and colorful flowers, created an atmosphere of enchantment. "The beauty of the scene cut the President like a knife," Butt sadly noted, who likewise recognized the hand of the stricken first lady in every carefully orchestrated detail.

After sixteen hours of sleep, Nellie finally awakened. "Her old will and determination asserted itself," Archie remarked, as she immediately tried to get out of bed and walk. By late afternoon, Taft reported to Robert, she had regained partial "control of her right arm and her right leg," though she remained mute. The doctor expressed his continued confidence that the paralysis of her vocal chords was temporary. The White House released a statement insisting there was "no cause for alarm." The first lady was simply enduring a "nervous attack"—the label then given to a range of amorphous afflictions brought on by exhaustion. Newspaper reports attributed the collapse to Nellie's "ceaseless and strenuous efforts to aid her husband." Her exertions, the *St. Louis Post Dispatch* suggested, were "more than one person could stand up under and she went to pieces."

Of the true severity of Nellie's illness and disability, the public remained uninformed. In his initial diagnosis, Dr. Delaney had failed to discern the serious stroke she had suffered. A blood vessel had burst in the area of her brain that controlled language and speech, producing what Taft later described as aphasia—the loss or partial loss of the ability to speak. While she remained alert and clearly comprehended verbal communication, she was unable to express her thoughts and ideas in words. Two weeks after her stroke, Nellie could venture hesitantly out of her bedroom and walk around the second floor. "She only comes into the corridor," observed Butt, "when she can do so without running any danger of seeing anyone." At the end of May, she remained unable to project her own thoughts into language, though she could "repeat almost anything" said to her. Nevertheless, the doctor remained optimistic, predicting it "merely a question of time and rest and practice until she regains her speech entirely."

Taft mobilized the entire family to help with Nellie's rehabilitation. Helen came home from Bryn Mawr to be with her mother, and Nellie's sisters—Eleanor More, Lucy Laughlin, and Jennie Anderson—took turns living in the White House. The stroke had not destroyed Nellie's ability to read or listen, so Helen spent hours reading aloud to her mother, then encouraging her to repeat the same passages. Very gradually, Nellie began to speak on her own, though her words were often jumbled and indistinct. At times, she tended "to say the opposite of what she meant" or speak with undue emphasis. "She gets pretty depressed about talking," Helen reported to her brother Robert in mid-June. "She tries very hard but it seems to be such an effort that I hate to make her." Eventually, the first lady learned to deliver stock phrases such as "Glad to see you," but complex expressions remained difficult and enunciation was a struggle. Consonants at the beginning of words presented a particular impediment. The housekeeper, Elizabeth Jaffray, recalled "scores of times" when Taft sat with Nellie, "his hands over hers, saying over and over again:

'Now, please, darling, try and say "the"—that's it, "the." That's pretty good, but now try it again.' "

"No one knows how [the president] suffers over his wife's illness," Butt lamented. "As the weeks go by and there does not seem to be any permanent improvement, his hope sinks pretty low." Despite an outward show of optimism, Taft slowly began to acknowledge "the tragedy" which had befallen his marriage, his family, and his presidency. In Nellie's presence, he remained resolutely cheerful, determined to buoy her spirits and make her laugh. But beneath this bright veneer, Butt detected "a world of misery in his mind." Whenever he was left alone, Taft would sit by the window, "simply looking into the distance."

Before her illness, Nellie had discovered an ideal summer home for the family in Beverly, Massachusetts. On July 3, the president and first lady, accompanied by Nellie's sister Eleanor, Dr. Delaney, and Captain Butt, boarded the *Colonial Express* to "take up their residence" in the seaside community. The grand house stood amid "parklike lawns, shrubs, trees and flower-beds" that lent "an English beauty to its surroundings." One porch faced the sea; the other looked to Beverly Cove. The three children could walk to the Montserrat Club to play tennis, swim, and enjoy all manner of social activities, and two excellent golf courses were close by—the Myopia Club and the Essex Club. But what should have been a relaxing retreat for the first family became a period of enforced inactivity for Nellie. Although the doctor now conceded that it would "take quite a time" for her to recover, he believed she would be immeasurably strengthened by "two months of entire rest." Newspapers reported that the first lady would be kept "in seclusion," that no visitors would be entertained, and that the Secret Service would "keep intruders away."

The president himself was able to stay in Beverly for only twenty-two hours, just long enough to get Nellie settled. He was needed in Washington, where the special session of Congress called to revise the tariff was culminating in a nasty battle. "The great tug will begin," he remarked as he returned to the White House, "and one of the crises of my life will be on." The tariff struggle would indeed become a defining event in Taft's young presidency, but the true crisis had already transpired. His eloquent and independent wife, the partner who had attended to every detail in the opening days of his administration, was permanently incapacitated. The fierce and loving voice that had counseled and prodded Taft to every achievement and consoled him through every insecurity and difficulty was silent.

CHAPTER TWENTY-THREE

A Self-Inflicted Wound

President William Howard Taft.

PRESIDENT TAFT WELL UNDERSTOOD THE political hazards of his pledge to pursue tariff reform. For more than a decade, the Republican establishment had trumpeted the reigning tariff structure as the engine of American prosperity, the key to the nation's burgeoning industry. Protectionism had become a central tenet of conservative Republican ideology. While Theodore Roosevelt had sympathized with progressive claims that high tariffs strengthened monopolies and artificially inflated prices, he had persistently evaded the issue, aware that a tariff battle would create a dangerous schism within the Republican Party, pitting western farmers against eastern manufacturers. During the final years of his administration, however, newly elected western progressives had passionately assailed the unjust advantages that the tariff granted the industrial East at the expense of their agrarian region.

As Taft took office, the battle could no longer be postponed. Sensitized to the inequities of the tariff system by his long and futile efforts to reduce the Philippine tariff, the new president was prepared to take the lead. Of all the members of Roosevelt's cabinet, Taft had espoused the most consistently progressive views on the tariff, tenaciously advocating for revision. Duties, he argued, should be levied simply to "equal the difference between the cost of production abroad and at home." When excessive duties were built into the tariff structure through the influence of powerful corporations, the system served only to spur monopoly, guarantee disproportionate profits, and raise prices for consumers. At Taft's insistence, the Republican platform "unequivocally" called for a "special session of Congress" to revise the tariff.

With the Old Guard still entrenched in both Houses, the president faced formidable opposition. Genuine downward revision, reporters predicted, would only be achieved by an "uprising and demonstration of popular opinion" similar to that which had propelled railroad regulation, meat inspection, and the Pure Food and Drug Act. To prompt them to take action, conservative Republican leaders would have to conclude that nothing short of "cataclysm" would result if they failed to alter their policy.

As the tariff struggle began in earnest in the spring of 1909, no journalist was better positioned to clarify the convoluted tariff system for the public—and expose the economic disparities and suffering wrought by that system—than Ida Tarbell. Two years of research and writing had convinced her that the tariff represented "the greatest issue before the people—the question of special privilege, and unequal distribution of wealth." She launched a passionate crusade "to humanize" the issue by dramatizing the tariff's role in consolidating wealth and imposing serious hardships on working Americans.

That spring, Tarbell published two influential articles in *The American Magazine* that framed the arcane tariff schedule as a simple moral issue. In "Where Every Penny Counts" and "Where the Shoe Is Pinched," she demonstrated how manufacturers' profits had ballooned under the protective tariff even as the wages of ordinary Americans failed to keep pace with the rising cost of living. Protectionists claimed it hardly mattered if "this or that duty made an article cost a cent or two more at retail," she observed; in fact, a cent or two clearly did make "a material difference" in the lives of "the vast majority of American families," who subsisted "on $500 or less a year." To support a family on an average wage of six or eight dollars a week, Tarbell pointed out, a man "must think before he buys a penny newspaper and he must save or plan for months to get a yearly holiday for the family at Coney Island." Faced with such limited choices, she continued, "there is practically no possibility of a nest egg, or of schooling for the children beyond fourteen years of age." Illness inevitably resulted in "debt or charity" for those in such dire circumstances, and "the accumulation of those things which make for comfort and beauty in a home is out of the question." For working-class families, "every penny added to the cost of food, of coal, of common articles of clothing means simply less food, less warmth, less covering."

Tarbell trenchantly illustrated this reality in her second article on the "vital importance" of shoes. For the average working-class family, she explained, the cost of buying and mending shoes made up more than a quarter of their total outlay for clothing. One could do without a hat, extra trousers, or a dress, she maintained, but not without footwear. "It was hard enough for the poor to buy shoes ten years ago before the Dingley tariff," she argued, "but with every year since it has been harder." In the last decade, the price of ordinary shoes and boots had risen 25 percent. "Why should shoes increase in cost?" she asked, pointing out that "they ought to decrease, such has been the extraordinary advance in shoe machinery and in methods." The answer, Tarbell demonstrated, lay in the duties on hides and thread—fees that benefited the Beef Trust, the United Shoe Company, and the Leather Trust at the expense of the consumer. For years, legislators had acquiesced to these duties in return for campaign contributions and support for their local machines.

"At a time when wealth is rolling up as never before," Tarbell concluded, "a vast number of hard-working people in this country are really having a more difficult time making ends meet than they have ever had before." Because wage increases were not keeping pace with the escalating cost of living, the workingman was left to feel that "no matter how much he earns he will still have to spend it all in the same hard struggle to get on, that there is no such thing for him as getting ahead." By focusing on workaday living and highlighting the immediate rather than dwelling on the abstract, Tarbell's articles proved a revelation for many. "I never knew what the tariff meant before," the pioneering social reformer Jane Addams told her.

Despite the heightened awareness spurred by Ida Tarbell's thoughtful explications, President Taft still struggled to transform that growing public sentiment into political capital. The first skirmish in the tariff battle followed immediately upon his election. During the campaign, western proponents of reform had focused their ire on Speaker Joseph Cannon, high priest of protectionism and special interests in the House. The seventy-two-year-old Speaker held the House in an autocratic grasp: no bill could reach the floor without his approval; no member could be recognized to speak without his consent. Deploying his power to appoint all Republican committee members and their chairs, he routinely rewarded conservatives and punished progressives. Conceding Cannon's strength, Roosevelt had repeatedly bargained with him, pledging to preserve the protective tariff in return for Cannon's cooperation in allowing anti-trust and regulatory legislation to reach the floor. During the 1908 presidential campaign, however, the tariff issue had caught fire. "Cannonism" had become a successful rallying cry in western districts, prompting the ouster of a half-dozen Old Guard supporters. After the election, a rebellious group of thirty progressive Republicans initiated a revolt, hoping to assemble a majority capable of unseating the Speaker, or at least curtailing his powers when Congress convened in mid-March 1909.

Taft seriously considered backing these "insurgents," as Cannon's foes became known. He had "never liked" the Speaker, considering him a vulgar reactionary who consistently opposed "all legislation of a progressive character." Writing to Roosevelt immediately after his victory, Taft spoke of the movement to defeat Cannon's nomination. "If by helping it I could bring it about I would do so," he explained, "but I want to take no false step in the matter." Roosevelt cautioned against hasty action: "I do not believe it would be well to have [Cannon] in the position of the sullen and hostile floor leader bound to bring your administration to grief, even tho you were able to put someone else in as Speaker." Elihu Root was even more vehemently opposed to any intervention by Taft, counseling that "it would be very unfortunate to have the idea get about that you wanted to beat Cannon and are not able to do it."

Nonetheless, Taft remained "very much disposed to fight." Replying to Root, he cited a speech Cannon had recently delivered in Cleveland that seemed to repudiate the Republican platform's pledge to revise the tariff. "In our anxiety to get votes," Cannon had reportedly stated, "we sometimes put in our platform things that are not orthodox." Such "cynical references" to platform promises could prove "enough to damn the party if they are not protested against," Taft told Root: "I am willing to have it understood that my attitude is one of hostility to Cannon and the whole crowd unless they are coming in to do the square thing. If they don't do it, and I acquiesce, we are going to be beaten; and I had rather be beaten by not acquiescing than by acquiescing. You know me well enough to know that I do not hunt a fight just for the fun of it, but Cannon's speech at Cleveland was of a character that ought to disgust everybody who believes in honesty in politics and dealing with people squarely."

To better gauge the odds of defeating Cannon, Taft consulted leading Republican editors and state officials across the country, asking them how their local congressmen would likely vote on the issue. "A new irrepressible conflict has begun in earnest," the *New York Times* reported, "a conflict which has been threatening every session of Congress for the last four years, but which Mr. Roosevelt has never been able to make up his mind to undertake." The *Times* predicted "a desperate fight in all probability, for Speaker Cannon and the close friends around him are not quitters. It will leave deep scars and ensure a warfare that probably will endure throughout the Taft administration."

Roosevelt continued to caution against alienating Cannon. In a barrage of "urgent telegrams and letters," he informed Taft that Minnesota congressman James Tawney was "very anxious" to arrange a direct conversation between the president-elect and the Speaker. Roosevelt stressed the importance of the interview, adding that he would provide "a full statement of the facts" on Cannon as soon as Taft returned to Washington from Hot Springs.

As speculation in the press intensified, a delegation of Cannon's friends made a pilgrimage to Hot Springs to assure Taft that Cannon would "support genuine tariff revision" and "not stand in the way of carrying forward" the new president's legislative program. He was shown a full text of Cannon's Cleveland speech, which gave an "entirely different impression" from the troubling excerpt he had read. In fact, the Speaker had promised that within "a hundred days," Congress would pass a new tariff law. This new law would not be "perfect," Cannon explained, but it would be "the best revenue law ever written."

Meanwhile, Taft had received disheartening responses to his inquiries regarding the insurgents' prospects. On the east coast, Cannon's support was unshakable; even in Kansas, a center of progressivism, five of eight congressmen stood with the Speaker. Taft was forced to concede that unless he personally went after Cannon "hammer and tongs," using all the powers of his presidency to fashion a majority, Cannon would be reelected. And even if he prevailed, he would be left with the "factious and ugly Republican minority" that Roosevelt had warned of. In the end, Taft resolved to work through the existing party machinery to accomplish the passage of his legislative proposals.

In itself, Taft's decision to relinquish the effort to oust the Speaker would have aroused little criticism; the mistake that would haunt his presidency, however, was his public declaration of surrender from Hot Springs, which immediately eliminated any advantage over Cannon. Moreover, as Taft's biographer Henry Pringle observes, the public concession "sent a chill of discouragement over the valiant but futile band of House insurgents." After a subsequent meeting with Cannon and Republican members of the Ways and Means Committee, Taft had further dispirited reformers by expressing full confidence in the conservative leadership's promise "to prepare an honest and thorough revision of the present tariff." All hope of unseating Cannon vanished. When Congress convened on March 15, 1909, the Speaker easily won reelection.

Perhaps it was inevitable that Taft's temperament—his aversion to dissension and preference for personal persuasion—would ultimately lead him to work within the system rather than mobilize external pressure from his bully pulpit. But his conciliatory approach left his administration and the American people at the mercy of Joseph Cannon, "the most sophisticated" politician in the country, "the most familiar with every subterranean channel of politics, the most cunning in its devious ways, the most artful in the tricks of the craft."

PROGRESSIVES NEVERTHELESS REMAINED HOPEFUL THAT the new president would provide vital leadership to combat the special interests controlling the congressional tariff-making process. On March 16, 1909, they waited expectantly for the president's message, which would signal the start of the special session. Theodore Roosevelt had used this forum as a powerful tool to focus public attention on his legislative agenda, spending weeks preparing each message. He had dictated "page after page, taking a theme and working it up, his mind glowing with the delight of expression." Though no one anticipated such a definitive or provocative communication from William Howard Taft, his decision to speak about the tariff in his first presidential message augured well. "The Senate and House were crowded," Robert La Follette recalled. "The attention was keen everywhere. The clerk began to read. At the end of two minutes he stopped. There was a hush, an expectation that he would resume. But he laid aside the paper."

As realization spread that the clerk was finished, one journalist reported, "statesmen almost fell out of their chairs." The presidential message, expected to be "historic," contained only 340 words. In truth, Taft had composed the entire text in fifteen minutes that morning. The address sounded "no clarion call to the people" and made "no allusion, direct or indirect, to the question of what kind of changes should be made." He simply and straightforwardly called on Congress to "give immediate consideration" to the tariff. Having already discussed the principles upon which revision "should proceed," Taft believed it unnecessary to reiterate his position. Without an inherent "flair for the dramatic" and hoping he might "avoid the bitter feuding with Congress that had marked Roosevelt's last days in office," he had chosen to launch his administration with "no loud noises, no explosions, no disturbances of the atmosphere."

Taft understood, he later said, that it was vital for a president to communicate "the facts and reasons sustaining his policies." Cultivating good relations with the press afforded "a great advantage" to a leader. Nevertheless, he confessed, from his first days in office he was "derelict" in his use of the bully pulpit. The weekly press conferences he had promised soon became a chore. "There was none of the give and take, the jokes, and the off-the-record comments" that had characterized Roosevelt's interactions with the journalists. Before long, Taft discontinued the weekly sessions, attributing his discomfort with the press to his years on the bench, where he was unaccustomed to freely expanding upon his positions. "When the judgment of the court was announced," he explained, "it was supposed that all parties in interest would inform themselves as to the reasons for the action taken."

Many of the reporters were eager to help him, Taft later acknowledged, "but they properly complained that I did not help them to help me." In the spring of 1909, William Allen White, Ray Baker, and Ida Tarbell all signaled their readiness to support and publicize tariff revision, postal savings, and the rest of the president's progressive agenda. "If ever at any time I may serve you in any way," White wrote after the inaugural, "kindly let me know." Taft thanked him for his offer, and the two men exchanged a few letters, but the president never found a way to properly utilize the Kansas editor. "I am not constituted as Mr. Roosevelt is," he explained to White, "in being able to keep the country advised every few days of the continuance of the state of mind in reference to reforms. It is a difference in temperament. He talked with correspondents a great deal. His heart was generally on his sleeve, and he must communicate his feelings. I find myself unable to do so. After I have made a definite statement, I have to let it go at that, until the time for action arises."

Baker, too, hoped to assist the president's endeavor to revise the tariff. "I knew what a hard fight he had ahead of him, and I wanted to help him, in my own small way, if I could, with my pen," the journalist remembered. Baker had become increasingly disillusioned with Roosevelt's failure to confront the issue. "Although the tariff storm was steadily rising," he lamented, "Roosevelt said not so much as a single word on the subject. Though the issue was driving his party straight upon the reefs, he offered no counsel, suggested no remedy. He left the brunt of the storm for poor Mr. Taft to meet." Now that the new president had made tariff reform his signature issue, Baker was anxious to meet with him and see how he might aid the cause.

An interview was arranged not long after the special legislative session had commenced. The Cabinet Room was filled with people waiting to see the president. Emerging from his private office, Taft asked that Baker "remain to the last," so they would have an opportunity to talk. "I had liked him on previous occasions when I had met him," Baker recalled. Now, watching "his frank, free, whole-hearted way of greeting his visitors," his expansive manner of draping "one of his great arms over the shoulder of a congressman," the journalist liked him "better than ever." Entering the private office where he had previously met with Roosevelt, Baker was struck immediately by the contrast. The small room had formerly exuded "the air of a quiet study." Books of history, works of fiction, and volumes of poetry had been strewn upon the table, "a riding crop and a tennis racket leaning in the corner." Now, Taft had transformed the study into a staid law office: "On all sides of the room were cases filled with law-books, nothing but law books." The shift in decor was "not without significance," Baker concluded, revealing "the legal mind" of the new occupant, a temperament desiring "everything carried forward quietly; according to the rules of the court," without "emotional appeals" to the public.

Initially fearful that the new president's "dislike for publicity" would prevent him from mobilizing public opinion to pressure Congress, Baker was "impressed" by "the perfect freedom" with which Taft discussed the tariff. "He outlined his position with a degree of frankness and earnestness that left in my mind no doubt of his essential sincerity," Baker remarked, noting that the president evinced an "easy optimism" that admitted no doubt about the eventual outcome. "I went away from the White House that day fully convinced that Mr. Taft not only would do what he said he would, regarding the tariff, but that he *could* do it." In the wake of this encouraging visit, however, Taft never called on Baker as the battle dragged on and the prospects for significant revision diminished.

No journalist fathomed the history of corporate efforts to evade downward tariff revision better than Ida Tarbell. As the special session was getting under way, she published a revealing article called "Juggling with the Tariff" that used the example of the wool schedule to illustrate the arcane tariff-making process. "Fifty years ago wool was disposed of in perhaps fifty words, which anybody could understand," she wrote; "to-day it takes some three thousand, and as for intelligibility, nobody but an expert versed in the different grades of wools, of yarns, and of woolen articles could tell what the duty really is." If Congress actually relied on such "disinterested experts," the process might nevertheless produce a decent tariff; instead, Tarbell explained, "Congress consults the wool-growers, the top-maker, the spinner and the weaver, and these gentlemen, being particularly human, each asks for an amount which will give him the advantage in the business—and he who is cleverest gets it."

Not surprisingly, those who secured the desired duties also happened to be the largest campaign contributors to the congressmen and senators on the relevant committees. "Mr. Taft is right," she declared, laying out a blueprint of necessary proceedings for reform: "What is wanted in making the present bill is evidence—evidence of the cost of production here and abroad, gathered not by the interested, but by the disinterested, not by clerks, but by experts. When provision has been made for obtaining that, the first step toward putting an end to the present tariff juggling will have been taken."

Throughout the spring, Tarbell remained hopeful that the new president's leadership would help secure the first genuine revision. She considered William Howard Taft "one of the most kindly, modest, humorous, philosophical of human beings." At a cabinet dinner shortly after the election, she found herself seated next to him. "There was something very lovable about the way the President talked of his election—not at all of any pride or pleasure he had taking the place," but rather of the deep pleasure it had afforded his family. With her warm feelings toward Taft and passion for tariff reform, Tarbell would undoubtedly have supported the president in much the same way Baker had helped Roosevelt during the battle for railroad regulation—sharing extensive research, providing advance copies of upcoming articles, and collaborating through subsequent conversations. Yet there is no record that the president ever followed up their dinner meeting with correspondence or an invitation to the White House.

THE LEGISLATIVE BATTLE PLAYED OUT in three acts. Deliberations began in the House and moved on to the Senate, culminating in a conference committee to reconcile the bills produced by each chamber. Early on, Cannon and Aldrich advised Taft to wait until the final conference committee stage to exert his influence. Trusting that the two men would honor the party's pledge to revise the tariff downward, Taft agreed "to keep his distance" from the congressional deliberations. If adjustments were necessary, he could make a personal appeal afterward, persuading each side to do what was best for both party and country.

"I have got to regard the Republican party as the instrumentality through which to try to accomplish something," he explained to William Allen White, when cautioned that public sentiment in the West had turned against the traditional party leadership. Indeed, the resentment against Cannon and Aldrich was so strong, another friend warned, that "no matter what tariff bill passes, or what you do, you are bound to be soundly abused." Taft remained imperturbable in the face of such admonitions. "I am here to get legislation through," he countered, "not to satisfy particular parts of the country."

Taft considered the Payne bill, passed by the House on the evening of April 9, "a genuine effort in the right direction," though reductions were "not as great" as he anticipated. The bill put hides, oil, coal, tea, and coffee on the free list and reduced the duties on lumber, scrap iron, and a host of other items. To Taft's disappointment, the controversial wool schedule was not changed. The combination of "the Western wool growers and the Eastern wool manufacturers," he lamented, rendered it "impossible" to get lower duties "through either the Committee or the House." The bill also made what the president considered "inappropriate" increases in food, spices, mustard, gloves, and hosiery. Despite these shortcomings, the free trade *Evening Post* judged the Payne bill "a more enlightened and promising measure than any tariff ever fathered by the Republican party." For the first time, the *Post* acknowledged, "the forgotten consumer is given a thought."

If the Senate retained all the reductions in the House bill and struck out the higher rates on food, hosiery, and gloves, Taft told the *New York Times*, the final product "would be satisfactory to him." He would not engage in a struggle with Congress "at this early stage." The measure had passed the House with an almost straight party-line vote of 217 to 161, a good omen for Republican unity. Now it was "up to the Senate"—or, as many believed, to a single senator. "The House makes the tariff," the *New York Press* quipped. "Senator Aldrich, pretty much single-handed, remakes it."

Taft had reason to be skeptical of Nelson Aldrich. He had witnessed the Senate leader's machinations during Roosevelt's fight to regulate the railroads and blamed Aldrich for the repeated failure to reduce the tariff on imports from the Philippines. Initial reports from the Finance Committee indicated that the senator had crafted hundreds of amendments to the House bill, the great majority cleverly constructed to raise, not lower, duties. "I fear Aldrich is ready to sacrifice the party, and I will not permit it," Taft told his secretary, George Meyer. Even more troubling, Aldrich soon openly revealed his antagonism to the president's agenda. On April 22, a scant two weeks after the Senate had taken up the Payne bill, Aldrich stood on the Senate floor and asked, "Where did we ever make the statement that we would revise the tariff downward?" This was the time when Taft should have summoned the press and upbraided Aldrich and his reactionary allies. But whereas Roosevelt spoiled for dramatic fights, public confrontation was not in the new president's disposition. "There is no use trying to be William Howard Taft with Roosevelt's ways," he conceded.

While Taft hesitated to challenge Aldrich openly, La Follette, Beveridge, Nelson, and a small group of progressive Republicans mobilized for a major intraparty battle against the Senate leader. Aware that Aldrich had abundant experience in devising obscure classifications for each of the 4,000 duties in the tariff schedule, they agreed to concentrate on a few major products. For efficiency, they divided the daunting research: Dolliver chose cotton, La Follette selected wool, A. B. Cummins focused on metal and glass, and Joseph Bristow tackled lead and sugar. Time was short, for Aldrich was determined to move the bill through the upper chamber as quickly as possible. "It has been tariff, tariff, all the time, literally morning, noon and night," Lodge reported to Roosevelt, complaining, "I have never been so worked in my life." It was often past midnight when the insurgents left their offices, only to continue sifting through hundreds of pages of material at home until the small hours of the morning. On weekends, they gathered in Albert Beveridge's apartment, sharing information and discussing strategy.

In private meetings, Taft encouraged the insurgents to "go ahead, criticize the bill, amend it, cut down the duties—go after it hard," promising, "I will keep track of your amendments. I will read every word of the speeches you make, and when they lay that bill before me, unless it complies with the platform, I will veto it." Had the president truly followed the devastating critique presented in the insurgents' extended speeches, he would have been far better equipped to influence the final shape of the bill. At the close of a harried day, however, Taft wanted nothing more than to provide Nellie with comfort and companionship, patiently working to help her regain her speech. By June, he confessed to a group of woolen manufacturers that he was "bewildered by the intricacies of the tariff measure" and would have more confidence if he possessed "more technical knowledge."

The Senate debate dragged on, becoming increasingly bitter and unprofitable. The insurgents blasted Aldrich and his lieutenants as "reactionary tools of the trusts and eastern corporations"; the Senate leader, in turn, accused the insurgents of treachery to the Republican Party. During one savage indictment of the cotton schedule, Aldrich attempted to bolt from the chamber. "The Senator will not turn his back upon what I have to say here without taking the moral consequences," Dolliver shouted at him. Taft worried that the insurgents were becoming "irresponsible," exposing the party's rift to the nation, and making compromise impossible.

Aldrich himself, the shrewdest and most discerning political animal in the Senate, knew precisely where to yield and where to hold fast. He bartered reductions on some schedules for increases in others, confident that in the end, the bill would emerge essentially his own. William Howard Taft was the only real obstacle that Aldrich faced. The president possessed the power to mobilize public opposition, use patronage as a club, and ultimately to withhold his signature from a bill. Accordingly, Aldrich set to work on the good-natured Taft. He spent relaxing mealtime hours repeatedly assuring him that the final tariff bill would be worthy of his support. On a number of items, Aldrich acknowledged, the Senate had restored duties cut by the House. When the bill reached the joint committee, however, he promised to "confer" with the president, assuring him that his suggestions would carry "great influence." Knowing Taft's enduring allegiance to the Philippines, he guaranteed that the islands would finally see the reductions Taft had long advocated. Moreover, he claimed to accept the president's plan for a tariff commission composed of experts who would furnish objective information during future debates. Most importantly, the senator pledged that once the tariff was settled, he and his lieutenants would cooperate to move forward the rest of the legislative program outlined in Taft's inaugural address relating to trusts, interstate commerce, postal savings, and conservation—all considered vital to the "general carrying out of the Roosevelt policies."

By early summer, as the futility of the insurgents' struggle on the Senate floor grew increasingly apparent, newspapers called on the president to intervene. "Mr. Taft is not proving a courageous captain," the *New York American* charged, extending the metaphor to suggest a purloined presidency: "His course was clearly charted and the prospect at the outset was for a quick and fair voyage. But he has surrendered the command to Senator Aldrich, and the latter, as was to be expected, is steering the vessel into pirate-infested seas." The president's sympathizers argued that it was premature "to form definite conclusions until results begin to show," suggesting that Taft's benign temperament and beaming smile might well "cloak a determination as unrelenting as Mr. Roosevelt's own."

In mid-June, Taft finally abandoned his "hands off" approach to the legislature, sending a special message to Congress on an issue intimately connected to tariff reduction. To balance the projected loss of federal revenue resulting from overall reductions, some additional form of taxation would be necessary. The House had proposed an inheritance tax, but the Senate roundly objected "on the ground that the States—some thirty-six of them—had already adopted inheritance taxes, and this would be a double tax." Hoping to resolve this contentious standoff, Taft called on Congress to pass both a tax on corporations and a constitutional amendment establishing an income tax. In principle, the president supported the progressives' preference for a bill to impose an immediate federal income tax. But in practice, he feared that the conservative Supreme Court, which had ruled the measure unconstitutional just a decade earlier, would refuse to "reverse itself," exposing the Court to severe criticism at a time when its reputation was "already at a low ebb." A constitutional amendment granting Congress power to levy an income tax would settle the question for good.

As he pursued his tax agenda with Aldrich, Taft engaged in "some pretty shrewd politics." He met individually with members of the Finance Committee and "committed them separately" to both tax propositions before dispatching his message to Congress. The corporate tax, he persuasively argued, would simultaneously provide needed revenue and empower the federal government to oversee the transactions of a wide range of corporations. It would "go a great way" toward securing the protection from "illegitimate schemes" and anti-trust violations that Roosevelt had long hoped to provide. During their previous conversations, Aldrich had reluctantly accepted the corporation tax, thinking that Taft had been persuaded to drop the income tax amendment. But with the president's support, Congress passed both measures. "Just when they thought they had him sleeping," Archie Butt observed, "he showed them he was never so alive in his life." Later that summer, the states began ratification of what would eventually become the sixteenth constitutional amendment; the process was completed before Taft's term came to an end.

With the revenue question resolved, the Senate's tariff bill passed just before midnight on July 8 by a margin of 9 votes. The Senate bill made some reductions that the House had neglected, but also restored duties on hides and raw materials and left intact the controversial wool and cotton schedules. The Democratic vote along party lines was expected; that ten Republican senators followed La Follette in joining the Democrats made headlines. These dissenting votes revealed the very party split Theodore Roosevelt had feared, and long carefully avoided, further complicating matters for Taft.

As the conference committee began its deliberations, Taft remained hopeful that he could persuade the dozen conferees to combine the best elements of both bills in a final product that both progressives and conservatives could support. Newspapers across the country called on the president to take charge. "Congress has had its inning," the *Baltimore Sun* observed. "It is now the President's inning, and he has the masses of the people behind him." The *Boston Journal* declared it time for the president "to make good," calling the proceedings "the greatest crisis of his career as Chief Magistrate." The final tariff legislation, press reports agreed, would be a defining moment in his young presidency. "If he allows a bill to come from conference which disappoints the country," the *Journal* concluded, "he will have forfeited a large share of the stock of popular confidence with which he was invested when he became President."

In the days that followed, Butt observed, Taft "used the White House as a great political adjunct." He invited Payne to dinner one night and Aldrich the next; both men dined with the president the following evening, then retired to the terrace where they continued their conversation until long after midnight. The president put his yacht "at the disposal of the conferees in the hope that they might take a comfortable trip down the Chesapeake and adjust some matters under the influence of such a favorable environment." He took breakfasts with the insurgents, lunches with the standpatters, and late evening automobile rides with Speaker Cannon.

Throughout these intensive negotiations, Taft found time for almost daily letters to Nellie. He was "longing" for her company, he assured her, and would proceed to Beverly the moment the tariff struggle ended. In the interim, he was "delighted" that Bob and Helen had arrived. "I hope that you will feel more like making the effort to talk with them than you have heretofore," he cajoled tenderly, "because it is practice that brings about the changes you seek." The pace of recovery might be frustrating, he acknowledged, but he predicted that progress would come "by jerks." Meanwhile, she was fortunate to enjoy the cooling onshore wind. "Last night was as hot a night as I have ever passed in Washington," he told her. "I slept in three beds, and changed because each time I waked up I found myself so bathed in perspiration that the bed was uncomfortable."

Taft's stream of letters, continuing through July and into the second week of August, provide insight into his strategy during the final stage of the tariff battle. The newspapers, he explained, had overstated the increases in the Senate bill, leading the public to view "the Senate bill as a very bad bill, and the House bill, by contrast as a good one." The primary difference between the two, he told Nellie, lay in the Senate's treatment of raw materials. If he could make the conferees return raw materials and hides to the free list and reduce the lumber rates, he believed he could "reconcile the country to the view that a substantial step downward has been taken."

On July 16, Taft made his first public move to influence the legislative process. Since he had called Congress into special session four months earlier, the president had patiently allowed lawmakers to work their will. Now, as tensions escalated within the conference committee, he issued a forceful statement that "he was committed to the principle of downward revision." Unless he was presented with evidence that the producers of oil, coal, or hides were unable "to compete successfully, without reduction of wages, then they did not need a duty and their articles should go on the free list." He understood that such action might hurt politicians in specific districts, but "with the whole people as his constituency," the president was obliged to provide a "broader point of view." The insurgents were "jubilant." Republican senator Bristow of Kansas commented that the president's statement "greatly strengthens the hands of the progressives." Congratulatory messages flooded the White House and newspapers predicted that the final product would be "the Taft tariff bill—not the Payne or the Aldrich, or the Payne-Aldrich bill."

Nellie was relieved to hear that her husband had intervened at last. "I see today you made a statement as to what you were going to stand for," she wrote. "I hope you won't have to come down much on it dear." While Nellie's handwriting remained poor, her desire to support her husband was fiercely conveyed. Indeed, as the trials of Taft's presidency commenced in earnest, the loss of her acute judgment and indomitable presence was a source of sorrow and frustration for both of them. For the first time in their marriage, Nellie was distracting Will from the difficulties he faced rather than offering sound guidance and solace.

The tariff situation, Taft acknowledged to his brother Horace, was "a good deal more of a muddle than the papers make out." Despite repeated promises to follow the president's lead in the conference proceedings, Aldrich refused Taft's request to commit himself "in writing" concerning free hides and raw materials. Although Taft had developed genuine respect for the Senate leader during the eighteen-week ordeal, he understood that he was dealing with "an expert and acute politician" and that he might "be deceived." He was particularly worried about the cotton schedule of duties. "Aldrich insists that it is not an increase," he confided to Nellie, "but I fear he is not borne out by the facts." Meanwhile, Speaker Cannon threatened to defeat the entire bill unless the conferees agreed to the House-sponsored duties on gloves and hosiery. Apparently, Aldrich explained to Taft, the Speaker felt he "owed his victory" to the glove manufacturer Lucius Littauer, "and therefore it was a personal matter with him" to keep the measure intact. The Speaker's blatant demand outraged Taft. "It is the greatest exhibition of tyranny that I have known," he declared. "Aldrich and I continue to be good friends although we differ somewhat, but he is a very different man from the Speaker."

On July 28, Taft sent an ultimatum to the conference committee, insisting that he would not sign any bill that did not contain both the free raw materials agreed upon by the House and the Senate reductions in gloves and hosiery. "They have my last word," he told Archie Butt, before departing for a round of golf followed by a dinner party. Ten minutes into dinner, Butt recorded, "the message came by phone from the White House that the conferees had agreed and had accepted the rates as laid down by the President. For a moment, Taft remained perfectly silent, staring incredulously at the paper before him." Then, smiling broadly, he shared his satisfaction: "Well, good friends, this makes me very happy." When the round of congratulations ended and the party drew to a close, Butt accompanied Taft to the White House. "There was no one waiting for him," Butt observed. He was "lonelier in his victory than he had been in his fight."

On the afternoon of Thursday, August 5, the president arrived to sign the Payne-Aldrich bill. The sun was shining on the Capitol; the president wore a "cut away suit" and carried "a straw hat in his hand," appearing "fairly radiant" to the assembled spectators. Cabinet officers along with members of Congress filled the president's chamber, where Taft's relief and good humor were evident to all. "Do you think I ought to adjourn Congress before I sign it?" he joked. "I certainly do not," Aldrich replied, as the audience broke into laughter.

For weeks, correspondents had speculated about the possibility of a presidential veto. Progressives, still desperately unhappy with the bill despite the last-minute improvements, had called upon Taft to reject this version and start over in the full session the following year. Well aware that he "could make a lot of cheap capital" and "popularize [himself] with the masses with a declaration of hostilities toward Congress," Taft felt that such an action "would greatly injure the party." Moreover, he was delighted by many aspects of the bill, including the reduced duties on raw materials, the formation of the tariff commission, the corporate tax, the income tax amendment, and the free trade provision for the Philippines. At this juncture, he had worked too hard and too long with congressional leaders to turn against them.

At six minutes after five o'clock, the president signed the Payne-Aldrich bill. Three minutes later, he appended his signature to a companion bill that established free trade with the Philippines, fulfilling a promise made long before. "A broad smile of satisfaction overspread his face," one reporter observed, "and he wrote his name with a flourish not in evidence when he signed the other bill."

In the midst of the ceremony, Butt recorded, "a terrific thunderstorm broke out." The room suddenly darkened. "Heavy black clouds rolled up, and the electric lights had to be turned on. Peals of thunder and vivid flashes of lightning came from the sky." Correspondents straightaway declared the storm a portent, auguring the "storm of protest" that would inevitably follow as the public understood the disappointing limitations of the bill. The measure was not "perfect," Taft admitted in a public statement, but it nevertheless represented "the result of a sincere effort on the part of the Republican party to make a downward revision and to comply with the promises of the platform." Later that night, he celebrated with cigars and wine at a White House dinner. "Practically all the prominent figures in the tariff fight" attended, the *New York Times* noted—"except the 'insurgents' in both branches of Congress." Trusting that the animosities of the debate would soon be forgotten, the president expressed sincere thanks to every member who had helped steer the measure through "its long and stormy journey."

Public reaction to Taft's role in the passage of the tariff bill was mixed. The *New York Tribune* offered a positive assessment, claiming that his "patient leadership" had "borne fruit in the many material concessions forced from the Senate," easing the way "for intelligent and fair-minded tariff legislation in the future." The *New York American* was less optimistic; while conceding that the president had made the final bill "less shocking," it insisted that slight improvements to a bad bill did not relieve him of his obligation to carry out his party's pledge. A tariff law that retained and even increased duties on "the necessities of the common people," such as cotton and wool, many editorials proclaimed, could only be judged an "empty victory." Most agreed that the president had "vindicated his personal sincerity," but the fact that "he erred in his strategy" could not be denied. It was "his own fault," the *New York Times* charged, that the final result had fallen short of his promised reform. "It is clear that he made the mistake of holding aloof too long; that he waited until after the horse was stolen before locking the stable door."

THE DAY AFTER SIGNING THE bill, Taft departed for Beverly. He planned to spend five relaxing weeks with Nellie and the children before embarking on a two-month tour of the West. As the presidential train pulled into tiny Montserrat Station on the edge of town, Taft was thrilled to see Nellie waiting to greet him. The train had barely "come to a standstill," a reporter for the *New York Times* noted, "before he ran down the steps of the observation platform," pushing his way through the "enthusiastic" crowd to reach his wife. He embraced her with kisses "which could be heard by everyone present." While the president and his family motored to their seaside cottage, members of the White House staff drove to the office suites arranged at the Board of Trade building in Beverly. Once Taft escaped to the Myopia Hunt Golf Course that afternoon, the *Baltimore Sun* correspondent discerned an unmistakable message in his expression: "If anybody says the word tariff to me within the space of several days he will get hit with a golf stick."

Taft soon settled into a pleasant routine. After working with his secretary or meeting with visitors in the morning, he played a round of golf, returned to his papers and documents in early afternoon, and then gave "the rest of the day" to Nellie. He sat with her on the veranda, telling stories "to make her forget her illness," and when breezes cooled the late afternoons, he accompanied her on long drives in the countryside and along the shore. Seated beside his wife in the back of the open touring car, Taft directed the chauffeur to travel "over every beautiful road," trying each day "to find some new and pleasant route." They always returned from these forty- or fifty-mile excursions by seven-thirty, when their children joined them for "the family dinner hour" and everyone exchanged stories about the day's activities.

Taft watched the weeks slip by with growing dread, aware that at the end of his holiday his 13,000-mile western tour would commence. "If it were not for the speeches, I should look forward with the greatest pleasure to this trip," he told Captain Butt. "But without the speeches there would be no trip, and so there you are." During the Beverly respite, Taft had hoped to prepare four basic speeches, but as the end of August approached, he had not drafted a single one. "I would give anything in the world if I had the ability to clear away work as Roosevelt did," he confessed. "I have never known any one to keep ahead of his work as he did. It was a passion with him. I am putting off these speeches from day to day, and the result will be that I shall have to slave the last week I am here and get no enjoyment out of life at all." Three days before the trip began, Taft was still unprepared. "I do not know exactly what to say or how to say it," he told a friend. "I shall stagger through the matter some way, but not in any manner, I fear, to reflect credit on the Administration."

Before Taft set out on his trip, he explained to reporters that he hoped to "take the people into his confidence regarding the tariff contest." He would travel from the Alleghenies to the Rockies, where rebellion against the Republican Old Guard and the tariff was "rampant." He was optimistic that straightforward conversation with his critics might "prepossess them in favor of his standard." He would readily acknowledge that "the bill was unsatisfactory in many ways," but insisted that "it was the best he could obtain from the Congress under the circumstances." A future fight for deeper reductions loomed, for Taft believed that the American people had "learned a great deal about the tariff" and were prepared to elect new representatives pledged to remedy the "shortcomings" in the present bill. Most important, Taft believed this comprehensive tour would allow him to engage directly with "tens and hundreds of thousands" of his "fellow citizens," creating a "personal touch" between people in all sections of the country and their president.

In his strategy to realize this ambitious agenda, Taft stumbled badly from the outset. He opened his speaking tour at a black-tie banquet sponsored by the Boston Chamber of Commerce. The audience of nearly 2,000 included "cabinet members, diplomats, congressmen, clergymen and distinguished business leaders." The diners greeted him with hearty applause, but soon settled into a "grim silence" when he announced that he would refrain from any tariff discussion in order "to leave something" for future audiences. He chose instead to expound upon the Monetary Commission, appointed by Congress in the wake of the 1907 Panic. Chaired by Nelson Aldrich, the commission was leaning toward "a central bank" with sufficient reserves to meet future financial crises. The president characterized Aldrich as "one of the ablest statesmen in financial matters in either house," a leader eager "to crown his political career" with the creation of "a sound and safe monetary and banking system." While Aldrich would one day be credited as the "Father of the Federal Reserve Banking System," he was then regarded throughout the West as a servant of special privilege and the chief architect of the disappointing tariff bill. Taft's inept decision to lionize the senator in his very first speech cast a shadow on his tour before it had even started.

The president's train traveled from Boston to Illinois, making short stops along the way. Reaching Chicago that evening, he spoke at Orchestra Hall, where the massive crowd gave him a hearty reception. At Milwaukee the next day, he detailed his plans for postal savings legislation and dedicated a building in La Crosse before moving on to Winona, a small Minnesota city on the banks of the Mississippi, where he finally delivered his first statement on the tariff.

The choice of Winona, home to Representative James Tawney, was dictated, one correspondent noted, by Taft's "omnipresent good nature . . . his most endearing trait." Minnesota was a "hotbed of insurgency." Tawney, chairman of the Appropriations Committee, was the only member of the ten-person state delegation who had voted for the Payne-Aldrich tariff bill. The legislation was so unpopular in Minnesota that Tawney was in danger of losing his seat in the next election. Republican leaders in the House had implored the president to present a strong defense of Tawney's vote in the congressman's home district.

Though Taft knew that his first major speech on the tariff would be widely reported, he continued to procrastinate on the necessary preparation. The day before the scheduled address, he confessed his anxiety to Nellie: "Hope to be able to deliver a tariff speech at Winona but it will be a close shave." On the train from La Crosse to Winona, he finally settled down in his private stateroom to work. He had "a mass of facts and figures before him," along with a lengthy statement prepared by Representative Payne. Two stenographers stood ready to take dictation. A draft was completed when the train reached Winona at eight o'clock that evening, but there was no time to solicit comments or make revisions. "Speech hastily prepared," he telegraphed Nellie, "but I hope it may do some good."

Speaking for over an hour, Taft touted the bill's merits and admitted its faults, particularly acknowledging its failure to reduce the wool schedule. Had he left the matter there, promising to revisit the tariff in the next congressional session, the speech would have stirred scant criticism. Instead, the president pressed on with a clumsy argument to vindicate the embattled Tawney. "What was the duty of a Member of Congress," he asked, who favored more dramatic reform but realized the genuine benefits of compromise? Taft was "glad to speak" in support of Tawney's decision to vote for the bill. In certain situations, party members had to "surrender their personal predilections" for the sake of unity. He would not criticize those Republican legislators who felt the divide between their desired course and the current bill "so extreme" that they "must in conscience abandon the party." In the end, however, he concurred with Representative Tawney that party unity trumped specific reductions "in one or two schedules." Party solidarity was essential to establishing the broader regulatory package that would "clinch the Roosevelt policies." This lumbering argument was effectively a reprise of Taft's earlier justification for his own decision against a veto. The real self-inflicted wound occurred in his twenty-four-word verdict on the bill itself: "On the whole," he concluded, "I am bound to say that I think the Payne tariff bill is the best bill that the Republican party ever passed."

This succinct, ill-considered statement made headlines across the country, obscuring the more nuanced argument presented in the president's address. By stating "without hesitation" that the bill represented the Republicans' signal legislative achievement, the *New York Times* charged, William Taft "has decided to abandon the cause of tariff reform." A majority of editorials echoed this view. "Western Republicans have made up their minds that they are not going to be ruled by New England," the *St. Paul Pioneer Press and Tribune* observed. "Instead of softening the antagonism between the two factions of his party, he has very clearly intensified it." His blundering Winona speech, the *Indianapolis Star* declared, proved that the president was "out of touch with American public sentiment on the tariff question." Even Horace Taft concurred with his brother's critics. "I did not write to you about it," he told

Will, "because my secretary is a lady and no language that suited the speech could be dictated. I will swear at you about it when I see you."

In Minnesota, Taft's "commendation" of Tawney was widely interpreted as an effort to undermine insurgent members of the state delegation. This surge of public resentment rekindled a sharp nostalgia for Taft's predecessor. "Theodore Roosevelt's good fortune has not deserted him," the *New York Times* observed. "The stars in their courses seem to fight for him. If he still cherishes an ambition to return to the White House, the path has been opened to him by President Taft, and no thoroughfare could be more inviting or easier to travel." If Roosevelt were to return and proclaim the tariff a failure to honor his party's pledge, the *Times* added, there would be no way of staying "the overwhelming demand" for his renomination in 1912. In actuality, Roosevelt fully endorsed the Payne-Aldrich tariff. "You have come out as well as we could hope on the tariff question," he told Lodge in a private letter. Like Taft, he regarded the corporate tax as a critical achievement, for it permanently established "the principle of national supervision." When Lodge lauded the critical role Nelson Aldrich had played in the passage of the bill, Roosevelt offered no objection. "I never appreciated his ability so fully before," Lodge wrote, calling Aldrich "a man of real power and force." Roosevelt replied that he was not "surprised" by Lodge's admiration, noting that his own interchanges with Aldrich gave him "a steadily higher opinion of him." Roosevelt remained, of course, 10,000 miles away in "the wilds of Africa." None of these comments became public, and western insurgents continued to enshrine him as the exemplar of true reform, projecting their dissenting views of the tariff onto the former president.

Despite the onslaught of criticism, Taft trusted that the public would ultimately recognize his Winona speech as a "truthful statement." Indeed, he insisted, compromise was "the only ground upon which the party [could] stand with anything like a united force and win victories." He remained convinced that the insurgents would relent when Congress convened in December, and began work on his proposed reform package to strengthen control over corporate interests. In Iowa and California, he delivered rousing speeches designed to regain the confidence of the reformers. "Of course we want prosperity," Taft assured them, "but we wish prosperity in such a way . . . so that everybody will get his share, and that it shall not be confined to a few who monopolize the means of production or the means of transportation, and thus prevent that equality of distribution which we all like to see."

Indeed, it appeared the hostility might dissipate as the crowds grew in size and enthusiasm along the president's route. Nearly 7,000 people cheered him at the Armory in Portland; in Phoenix, he spoke "practically to the entire town of 20,000 people"; at the Seattle Exposition grounds, 80,000 poured through the gates. "Winning Taft Smile Spreads Radiance," the local paper in Albuquerque declared. "Taft's personality again has stood him in good stead," chimed the *Chicago Tribune*. "The distrust has faded." It was clear to those inside his administration that the president's desire to connect with the citizenry was unfeigned. He "really and sincerely likes people," Archie Butt observed. "He likes different types and he enjoys studying them. Whereas most people in his position try to avoid handshaking," the president "will stop a dozen times on his way in and out of a room to shake hands with anybody who calls to him."

Scarcely absent from Taft's side for the duration of the tour, Butt felt "more real affection" for the new chief than ever before. He noticed that Taft showed anger only on a few occasions when he had been savaged in newspaper editorials. Incensed, Taft gave instructions to stop sending him such clippings, particularly from the free trade *New York Times*. "They are prompted by such wild misconceptions and such a boyish desire to point the finger of scorn, that I don't think their reading will do me any particular good," he wrote, "and would only be provocative of that sort of anger and contemptuous feeling that does not do anybody any good." He assured Nellie that he could not have misread the friendly support he encountered everywhere. "Whatever their judgment as to particular things I have done," he told his wife, "I certainly up to this time have their good will, and that is a considerable asset."

Near the end of his transcontinental journey, Taft remarked that he had "enjoyed every moment of the trip." When people wondered how he endured the long days, filled with "266 speeches and 579 formal dinners, luncheons and breakfasts," he said it was a matter "of temperament, one of taste, and possibly one of disposition." For a person like him, who loved meeting with people and hearing about their lives, the trip was "as stimulating as champagne." When his train pulled into Union Station on the evening of November 10, an enthusiastic crowd, including members of his cabinet, was there to welcome him home. "Well, I'm back again," he announced with a broad smile, "feeling just as well as when I went away or even feeling better."

Behind the ebullience and the cheerful faces that greeted Taft when he stepped off the train, however, tensions were brewing that would prove calamitous for the new president's administration. Taft's optimism was soon punctured by the realization that his inner circle was "full of despair and predicting all sorts of evil"—harboring personal and political wounds that Taft's honorable nature had small hope of suturing.

CHAPTER TWENTY-FOUR

St. George and the Dragon

This cartoon, "An Off Day in the Jungle," imagines how Roosevelt, on safari in Africa, heard the news that Gifford Pinchot had been ousted from the Forest Service.

DURING TAFT'S FIFTY-SEVEN-DAY ABSENCE FROM Washington, a latent animosity between Chief Forester Gifford Pinchot, Roosevelt's closest ally in the conservation crusade, and Interior Secretary Richard Ballinger, Taft's choice to replace Garfield, flared into open discord. The conflict quickly escalated beyond the confines of "a mere personal squabble" into "a matter of state." With Roosevelt's allies falling in behind Pinchot, and Taft defending Ballinger, the controversy would pit the East of America versus the West, corporate interests against public rights, developers against conservationists—until all the divisive factions at play in the confrontation between Pinchot and Ballinger were framed as the opening volley in the battle for the 1912 presidential nomination. Noting the great dissatisfaction among progressives with the administration's actions on both conservation and the tariff, the *New York Times* cited the comment that if Roosevelt toured the country upon his return from Africa, "there would be such a fire behind him by the time he got across the continent that nothing could stand in front of it."

Contention over the regulation of waterpower had initially set Ballinger and Pinchot at odds. Near the end of his term, President Roosevelt had delivered a dramatic message to Congress on the future of hydroelectric power: America, he pronounced, was on the verge of a momentous development—the electrical transmission of waterpower over large distances. Although supplies of oil, gas, and coal would eventually be exhausted, hydroelectric power offered a source of renewable energy. The industry was "still in its infancy," yet Roosevelt warned that an "astonishing consolidation" had already occurred. Thirteen large corporations, led by General Electric and Westinghouse, controlled more than one third of the waterpower then in use. Unless potential power sites still owned by the government were leased to developers on terms consistent with "the public interest," the hydroelectric industry would follow the path of the oil industry: a great monopoly would develop, eradicating competition and dictating the price citizens paid for electricity in their homes and businesses. "I esteem it my duty," Roosevelt had concluded, "to use every endeavor to prevent this growing monopoly, the most threatening which has ever appeared, from being fastened upon the people of this nation."

With time running out on his administration, Roosevelt, together with Garfield and Pinchot, had come up with a plan. Acting without congressional authorization, Garfield issued executive orders to withdraw from private development more than 1.5 million acres of land situated along sixteen rivers in half a dozen western states. These protected lands included hundreds of thousands of acres with little connection to waterpower sites, but "there was no time," Pinchot explained, "to make detailed surveys." Under the pressing circumstances, the blanket withdrawal assured safety for the actual power sites. Roosevelt later justified these withdrawals, along with other controversial executive actions, arguing that the president "is the steward of the people, and that the proper attitude for him to take is that he is bound to assume that he has the legal right to do whatever the needs of the people demand, unless the Constitution or the laws explicitly forbid him to do it."

Within three weeks of assuming his post as the new interior secretary, Richard Ballinger restored the vast majority of Garfield's withdrawals to the public domain. A lawyer and former judge, Ballinger believed that the previous administration had acted illegally in making wholesale withdrawals without congressional authorization or even the requisite data to determine potential locations for hydroelectric development. Once the proper surveys were completed, he would ask Congress for legislation to protect the actual sites. Meanwhile, conservation efforts should not restrict legitimate development in the states of the Far West. Developers and businessmen in that region had long excoriated Roosevelt's conservation policies as a socialistic threat to "traditional western individualism." So many tracts of public land had been temporarily withdrawn from settlers and private developers, one critic sarcastically noted, "that a man could ride from the Missouri River to the Pacific Ocean and his horse need not once step a hoof outside government land."

While Taft considered himself a Roosevelt conservationist and recognized the vital work of Garfield and Pinchot, he fundamentally agreed with Ballinger's insistence that problems had to be resolved "on the basis of law." He would never endorse the cavalier attitude that "the end justified the means." In Taft's estimation, the "sweeping declaration of executive authority" used to justify the withdrawals misconceived "the entire theory of the Federal Constitution" which delegated specific powers to each of the three branches. "It is," he declared, "a very dangerous method of upholding reform to violate the law in so doing; even on the ground of high moral principle, or of saving the public." The Constitution granted Congress "the power to dispose of lands, not the Executive." Indeed, Taft believed that Roosevelt's conservation reforms would have been "further along" had he "taken a different way."

Ballinger's restoration orders provoked indignation among progressives, who feared that monopolies would grab thousands of invaluable water sites before the completion of the surveys. "Stop Ballinger," pleaded an editorial in the *Des Moines Daily News*. "Mr. Taft stop him! In the name of justice, if he is blind, see for him! If he is callous, feel for him! If he is without power to estimate the awfulness of this crime, think for him!" While more conservative commentators lauded the shift away from Roosevelt's "cowboy methods," progressives, educated by the former president to both the importance of conservation and the treachery of monopoly, reacted with outrage. "Attention! Land Thieves and Natural Resource Grabbers," the *Tacoma Times* announced: "Game is Soft Again." Under Roosevelt, the *Tacoma Times* declared, "any doubt about the power of the chief executive to make withdrawals of public land was resolved in favor of the people." Taft's administration had resolved the doubt "in favor of the predatory interests."

Gifford Pinchot was on an extended speaking tour in the West when Ballinger reversed Garfield's withdrawals. Returning to Washington in April 1909, he discovered "what was going on" and immediately called on President Taft. Largely uninvolved with conservation efforts during his years in the cabinet, Taft regarded Pinchot as an exemplary public servant but possessed of a fanatical strain, all too ready to attribute evil motives to anyone who opposed his ideas. Furthermore, Taft believed that Pinchot's intimacy with Roosevelt had endowed him with power far beyond his official responsibilities as the head of a single bureau in the Department of Agriculture. For two days running, Taft listened closely as Pinchot "protested as vigorously as [he] knew how against Ballinger's action," explaining why the restorations threatened public interest. "To his honor," Pinchot later said, Taft called in Ballinger and directed him to halt any further restorations and again re-withdraw any such "lands as were actually valuable for water-power purposes." Greatly relieved, Garfield maintained that Pinchot's intervention had forestalled disaster.

But Ballinger's concessions under pressure from the president did little to allay Pinchot's suspicions or satisfy the progressive press. "Everything is not yet altogether serene," the *Springfield* (Massachusetts) *Republican* reported. It remained to be seen whether the waterpower trust had capitalized on the "golden opportunities" provided by Ballinger's original restoration orders. In the absence of facts, rumors abounded. In May, the Philadelphia *Press* reported that "five million acres of publicly owned land" were being turned over to corporate interests. The continuing antagonism between Ballinger and Pinchot provided fodder for drastic speculation: some papers predicted that Ballinger would have to resign, others that Pinchot was on his way out. The future seemed equally murky to the protagonists themselves: "Was Conservation really in danger?" Had the president "gone over to the Old Guard?"

In early August, the controversy came to a head at the National Irrigation Conference in Spokane, Washington. As thousands of delegates from across the country poured into the Armory to discuss and debate reclamation, forests, waterways, and conservation, journalists predicted an open clash between Pinchot and Ballinger, both of whom were among the speakers. On August 9, the day before Pinchot was set to speak, the staff correspondent for the United Press released a sensational attack on Ballinger, claiming the secretary had used "one excuse or another" to delay Taft's re-withdrawal order, enabling General Electric, Guggenheim, and Amalgamated Copper to grab a total of 15,868 acres in Montana, including power sites worth millions upon millions of dollars. "This is a true story," the reporter contended, "of how the birth right of a great state" was lost to monopoly. "Richard Achilles Ballinger, stand up!" demanded the *Spokane Press* the next day. "You are accused of grave misadministration of your high office." Through Ballinger's actions, the state of Montana has been "eternally delivered into the hands of the power trust," the indictment continued. "President Taft cannot do anything about it now."

These spectacular charges set the stage for Gifford Pinchot's speech, which was widely construed as a direct attack on the embattled secretary. "The purpose of the Conservation movement," Pinchot declared at the outset, "is to make our country a permanent and prosperous home for ourselves and for our children and for our children's children." Pinchot "threw down the gauntlet" before Ballinger, stating "unequivocally" that a great waterpower trust was "in process of formation," aided by "strict construction" of the law, which inevitably championed "the great interests as against the people." The struggle over waterpower, he contended, was simply another chapter in "the everlasting conflict" between "the few" and "the many." This statement unleashed "a storm of applause," as did Pinchot's testimonial to Theodore Roosevelt. "I stand for the Roosevelt policies because they set the common good of all of us above the private gain of some of us," he reiterated, "because they recognize the livelihood of the small man as more important to the nation than the profit of the big man. . . . And I propose to stand for them while I have the strength to stand for anything." When he finished, the 1,200 delegates "cheered him for fully five minutes," clapping their hands and stomping the floor in "the wildest reception" accorded to any of the conference speakers. Later that day, Pinchot wrote to inform Taft of the "deplorable fact" he had just discovered, that monopolies had seized valuable waterpower sites in Montana "after the restoration and before the second withdrawal."

The delegates looked with "breathless interest" to Richard Ballinger's response to both the newspaper charges and Pinchot's speech. When the interior secretary stood at the podium the next day, he merely read a "routine dissertation on public-land matters," as if "the conflict" with Pinchot and the furor over his policies "had never been born." Furthermore, he declined to remain for questions after his prepared remarks, as every other speaker had done. "He picked up his hat," one reporter noted, "hustled into a waiting automobile, and hurried to his hotel." Former California governor George Pardee openly denounced Ballinger's decision to flee. "I have been in public office and have been criticized," Pardee derisively observed. "I do not object to it. A public official should be willing to be criticized. An agent of the people of this country should be called to account." Raucous cheers broke out in the hall along with rhythmic shouts of "Hit 'em again."

The United Press reporter who broke the story pressed Ballinger for an interview at his hotel. Refusing to "grant an audience," Ballinger finally agreed to talk by phone. "The dope you put out is all wrong and false," he began. When the reporter claimed to have records and maps substantiating the charges, Ballinger grew testy. "I'll have no conference with you," he responded, terminating the call. When another reporter "questioned and quizzed" the secretary about his actions, Ballinger became equally truculent. "See here. You don't understand this thing," he bellowed. "You are hindering the development of the West."

"Mr. Ballinger's silence is not reassuring," the *San Francisco Call* editorialized. "The country wants to know whether Ballinger is secretly fighting the policy of conservation." When Ballinger eventually put out a statement, he simply repeated that his decisions were fully warranted and his actions unreasonably maligned. "Gross misrepresentations have been sent out," he declared. "Criticisms have been pretty severe from some quarters, but knowing that I am absolutely right in the position I have taken, I have paid no attention to them. In time it will be shown beyond a doubt that my course has been absolutely right." In both his private and public life, Ballinger maintained, he had "always believed" in the tenet of "nonpublicity," confident that his actions would be vindicated "by the results accomplished."

Ballinger was, in fact, eventually able to prove that the Montana land grab story was riddled with error from start to finish. Only four tracts of 40 acres each were actually involved in the restoration, a total of 158.63 acres. Reporting the figure of 15,863 acres, the correspondent had misplaced the decimal point. Moreover, detailed surveys revealed that not a single valuable water site was contained in the restored land. Two of the tracts "did not touch the river at all," the third "touched the river only in its extreme corner," and the fourth had never been included in the Garfield withdrawals. Finally, not one of these entries had moved to actual patent. Pinchot eventually acknowledged that he had been mistaken when he charged that "monopolists had grabbed off" valuable waterpower sites in Montana. By then Ballinger had lost the public battle; the impression that he had betrayed Roosevelt's conservation policies was widespread. The controversy between Pinchot and Ballinger had "assumed a certain symbolic importance," with the chief forester advocating for the public and the interior secretary representing the corporations.

THE DISPUTE OVER WATERPOWER WAS soon "completely overshadowed" by dramatic developments in what was called the Cunningham coal scandal. Pinchot brought such grave allegations against the interior secretary that it was "taken for granted" that "either one side or the other must make good," leaving the other in abject humiliation. Capturing headlines for months, the scandal and ensuing congressional investigation would eventually become "the driving wedge," which "slowly but surely" created an unbridgeable "chasm" between William Howard Taft and Theodore Roosevelt.

Details of the coal case, "a slumbering volcano" in the Interior Department over the previous three years, first became public at the same Spokane conference that escalated the waterpower story. Louis R. Glavis, a twenty-seven-year-old field investigator for the General Land Office in the Interior Department, had approached Pinchot in desperation, fearing that the department, under pressure from Ballinger, was on the verge of handing over 5,000 acres of potentially rich coal land to a syndicate headed by a Seattle developer, Clarence Cunningham.

As the special agent assigned to investigate the validity of land claims in Alaska, Glavis had gradually accumulated evidence suggesting that Cunningham, acting as the agent for a group of wealthy clients, had acted illegally when he staked his thirty-three claims. The Alaska land laws, designed to protect small farmers and prevent monopoly, limited each individual to 160 acres. Individual settlers, who paid small fees for the land, were required to prove they were acting "in good faith," on their own behalf, when they staked claims for land. From the outset, Glavis believed, the Cunningham group had agreed to consolidate their claims "into one property," which would be "operated for the joint benefit of all." Indeed, he had uncovered a document proposing to give a Morgan-Guggenheim Company half the stock in return for $250,000 in cash investments to develop the coal property. Before completing his investigation, however, Glavis had been pulled from the case. Upon learning that the Land Office had scheduled a hearing on the Cunningham claims, half of which lay within the Chugach National Forest, he had turned to the chief forester for help.

Most troubling of all, Glavis reported, Ballinger had been "closely identified" with the members of the Cunningham group at various stages of the claims process. When Ballinger was land commissioner, he had shared all departmental correspondence on the case with Cunningham and had, at one point, actually ordered the claims to patent, pulling back only after an urgent telegram from Glavis. Then, in the summer of 1908, after leaving his post as land commissioner and returning home to Seattle, Ballinger had met with members of the Cunningham group, who had retained him as their "legal representative" before the government. Ballinger's actions, Glavis continued, flouted a three-decades-old ruling that no government employee could "act as counsel, attorney, or agent for prosecuting any claim against the government" within two years of leaving employment. Finally, when Ballinger returned to public service as interior secretary, he had urged the department to decide the Cunningham claims without further delay.

After hearing Glavis's account, Pinchot dispatched an urgent letter to Taft.

"I advised him to lay the whole matter before you without delay," he told the president. Immediate action was in order, Pinchot warned, because "many persons" already knew of "various parts" of the story and it would soon become "impossible to prevent its becoming public." Before Glavis even reached the "Summer Capital" in Beverly, in fact, sensational articles began to appear. "Ballinger Mixed in Alaska Frauds," headlined the *Salt Lake Tribune.* The fact that Ballinger had accepted fees from Cunningham during the year between his service as land commissioner and his return to Washington as secretary drew particular attention. Glavis reportedly had "a whole trunk full of documentary evidence" that would lead to the indictment of Ballinger and several other high officials in the Interior Department. It was later revealed that the publicity wing in the Forest Service had leaked these reports.

When Glavis met with the president on August 18, he handed him a detailed statement on the coal case and his allegations against Ballinger. The following day, Taft discussed the charges with Attorney General George Wickersham, who was vacationing nearby. Wickersham reviewed the Glavis statement and "made notes upon his reading." The two men talked again the following afternoon and determined that Taft should forward the Glavis report to Ballinger and request a written reply. The president instructed Ballinger to answer each of the charges, "especially concerning [his] relation as counsel to the persons interested in the Cunningham coal claims." Taft "quite distinctly" recalled that Ballinger had told him the previous year that because of his "professional relation" with the Cunningham group, he had turned the case over to Assistant Secretary Frank Pierce; beyond that, he remembered little else about the situation. He would appreciate a written explanation "as full as possible." Taft also requested written statements from Frank Pierce and the chief of Field Service, H. H. Schwartz, under whom Glavis had worked.

The Interior Department officials responded quickly, providing a vigorous defense of Ballinger. Pierce insisted that Ballinger "has had nothing to do with these Cunningham cases since he became Secretary," adding that any "blame or criticism . . . should fall upon [him] and not upon the Secretary." Schwartz asserted that Glavis's decision to seek help from the Forestry Department was utterly unnecessary: at that juncture no one in the Interior Department was suggesting "issuance of patents, but only expedition of hearings." And based on the evidence already accumulated, the hearings would likely have resulted in an adverse decision to the claimants.

Meanwhile, Ballinger continued to toil over his own response. Asked about the allegations by the press, he remarked only that he intended "to kill some snakes." On September 4, he completed his 10,000-word document, taking up each one of the Glavis charges in turn. Before becoming land commissioner, Ballinger testified, he had no personal knowledge of the Cunningham claims, though as a twenty-year resident of Seattle he had developed friendships and acquaintances with a number of the claimants. He acknowledged that at one point he had clear-listed the claims, based upon a favorable report from another special agent. Upon receiving Glavis's telegram, however, he had acted immediately to stop the patents. The patents were still being held up when he left the land commissionership.

Ballinger did concede that in the summer of 1908, Cunningham had come to his house simply to complain of his treatment by Glavis. Cunningham told Ballinger that at one of his meetings with Glavis, he had allowed the agent to read a journal documenting each stage of the claims process. He claimed that Glavis had stolen one of the pages, which he was using out of context to demonstrate an illegal intent to consolidate. Cunningham argued that Glavis had interpreted the document incorrectly. When Cunningham learned that Ballinger would soon travel east, he asked him to carry an affidavit to Interior Secretary Garfield presenting his point of view. Ballinger gave the affidavit to Garfield, but the secretary told him that the claims would never be upheld unless the group was willing to apply under a recent law that forgave early signs of consolidation but severely limited the amount of money that could be raised to develop the property. Ballinger advised Cunningham accordingly. For his services and traveling expenses, Ballinger reported, he received $250. Since he had never been retained as a "legal representative," he argued, there had been no violation of the long-standing rule which, at any rate, applied only to monetary claims against the government. Furthermore, he labeled the charge that he had furnished Cunningham with departmental correspondence relating to the case a pure fabrication.

On Labor Day, September 6, Ballinger hand-delivered his written statement to Beverly, along with "several satchels full of documents." Oscar Lawler, the assistant attorney general assigned to the Interior Department, accompanied him. They joined the president for lunch at the Myopia Hunt Club, where Taft was scheduled to present victory cups for the annual horse show before a crowd of 5,000. That evening, Ballinger and Lawler conferred with the president for several hours. Taft later reported that he stayed up until three o'clock, "reading the answers and exhibits." When he reconvened with Ballinger and Lawler the following evening, the president had already determined that the Glavis report contained no hard evidence that Ballinger was dishonest, disloyal, or incompetent. "The cruel injustice which has been done to [Ballinger] makes me indignant," Taft declared. He told Lawler that he "was very anxious to write a full statement of the case," explaining his reasoning to the public. But because he was scheduled to leave in one week for his two-month tour around the country and still had a half-dozen speeches to write, he asked Lawler to prepare a draft statement "as if he were president."

The following Sunday, Wickersham and Lawler returned to Beverly with Lawler's draft. Taft asked Wickersham to spend the rest of the day reviewing the entire record. He continued to work on his own statement, using Lawler's draft as a starting point. After a second reading, Wickersham told Taft that he saw nothing in the record to incriminate Ballinger. Finding Wickersham "in substantial accord" with his own views, Taft completed his own statement and directed the attorney general to embody his notes and oral statement in a written analysis, to be filed with the documents. He should date the analysis prior to the publication of the president's statement, Taft continued, to demonstrate that his decision had been buttressed by the attorney general's "summary of the evidence and his conclusions."

Taft issued his statement on September 13, in the form of an official letter to Ballinger, which he furnished to the press as he boarded the train to begin his 13,000-mile journey. Having examined the documents, Taft wrote, he had concluded that the Glavis charges embraced "only shreds of suspicion without any substantial evidence to sustain his attack." Though he believed that "Glavis was honestly convinced of the illegal character of the claims in the Cunningham group, and that he was seeking evidence to defeat the claims," the record revealed an inordinate delay on his part. The claimants were entitled to a speedy hearing, which was all the Interior Department had requested. As for the charges against Ballinger himself, it was clear that since becoming secretary, he had "studiously declined to have any connection whatever with the Cunningham claims." Glavis was aware of this fact, Taft charged, along with several other pieces of exculpatory evidence, but "in his zeal to convict," he had not provided "the benefit of information" that might place the suspect transactions in a different and more favorable context. A subordinate who believes "his chief is dishonest," Taft asserted, has a responsibility "to submit that evidence to higher authority"; an employee who levels charges founded only on "suspicions" and "fails to give to his chief the benefit of circumstances within his knowledge that would explain his chief's action as on proper grounds," however, can no longer be trusted. He therefore granted Ballinger's request for "authority to discharge Mr. Glavis" for disloyalty to his superior officers in "making false charges against them."

By his own standards of jurisprudence, the president's precipitous decision to declare Ballinger innocent and Glavis guilty was seriously flawed. Taft had provided Glavis no chance to respond to Ballinger's countercharges, or even to see the documents upon which they were based. He had judged Glavis guilty of "misrepresentation," "suppression," and "culpable delay," without "an opportunity to be heard in his own defense." The president of the United States had questioned the young investigator's integrity, condemned his character, and broadcast his severance from public service to the nation at large.

The press greeted the president's statement as a victory for Ballinger and a defeat for Pinchot, who had pushed Glavis forward. "The Ballinger adherents threw their hats in the air and shouted that it is all over," the *New York Tribune* reported. "The Pinchot camp remained grimly silent and muttered threats in strict confidence." Correspondents speculated that Pinchot's resignation was imminent. Yet the chief forester's departure was the last thing Taft wanted. He fully understood that the public would interpret Pinchot's exit as evidence of the administration's opposition to Roosevelt's conservation policies.

To forestall "hasty action" on Gifford Pinchot's part, Taft wrote him a warm, personal letter. "My Dear Gifford," he began, "I write this to urge upon you that you do not make Glavis' cause yours." His decision to uphold Ballinger and discharge Glavis, he explained, was reached only after a careful study of documents Pinchot had never seen and carried no adverse judgment on his chief forester; on the contrary, "I have the utmost confidence in your conscientious desire to serve the Government and the public," and "I should consider it one of the greatest losses that my administration could sustain if you were to leave it." When a public servant had been so "unjustly treated," as Ballinger, he wrote, "it is my duty as his chief, with the knowledge I have of his official integrity and his lack of culpability, to declare it to the public." In the name of "teamwork," he hoped Pinchot and the members of the Forest Service would refrain from further public argument with the Interior Department. "It is most demoralizing," the president concluded, "and subversive of governmental discipline."

After several conferences with Taft, Pinchot agreed to remain at his post. The president, in turn, promised to issue a statement of support for Pinchot to counter the reigning impression that "in holding Ballinger up," he was condemning his chief forester. "Never at any time," Taft said, had he "intended to reflect upon Mr. Pinchot." He also authorized publication of an excerpt from his personal letter, in which he assured the forester that he would deem his resignation "one of the greatest losses" his administration could endure. Pleased that a temporary truce had been established, Taft was nevertheless apprehensive, certain that Pinchot remained "as fanatical" as ever "in his chase after Ballinger." He feared Pinchot had reached "a state of mind" that would "lead to a break" at some point. "He is looking for martyrdom," Taft told Wickersham, "and it may be necessary to give it to him; but I prefer to let him use all the rope that he will."

Taft's instincts were correct. Pinchot had no intention of relinquishing the fight. Indeed, he was already engaged in a conspiracy to deliver the Glavis report to leading muckraking magazines. "I have been thinking this miserable business over," Assistant Forester Overton Price had written Pinchot three days after the president's dismissal of Glavis, "and this is the way I see the thing. . . . First, the most effective publicity possible to the Glavis side, and the Garfield side, of the case, preferably, in a special issue of a clean national magazine. . . . Second, a congressional investigation with an honest man at the head of it. . . . Third, a President discredited by the people and by the man who made him President." Pierce promised that he would attend to all the work himself, without directly implicating Pinchot. "Don't let them cloud the issue by laying yourself open to any charge of direct insubordination. . . . I can do a great deal without getting fired; that isn't your job. You have got a much bigger job."

In the weeks that followed, Overton Price and Alexander Shaw, the Forest Service's legal officer, spent many hours with Glavis, determining how best to publicize his allegations. Price and Shaw later conceded that "as employees of subordinate rank" in the Agricultural Department, they were engaged in highly "irregular" conduct. Nevertheless, they believed that by exposing the head of the Interior Department, they would forestall the "grave and immediate danger" of losing invaluable public lands. In September, Price and Shaw met for six hours with Garfield, "going over in detail" every aspect of the Glavis report. Shaw then aided Glavis to transform his bureaucratic report into an accessible and engaging publishable article. As they prepared the piece, the Forest Service leaked more material to the press, stimulating further criticism of the interior secretary. Such machinations within his administration were not lost on William Taft. "Pinchot has spread a virus against Ballinger," he told Nellie, "and has used the publicity department of his bureau for the purpose. He would deny it, but I can see traces in his talks with many newspapermen on the subject, who assume Ballinger's guilt, and having convicted him treat any evidence showing that he is a man of strength and honesty as utterly to be disregarded."

In late October, Glavis was introduced to Norman Hapgood, the publisher of *Collier's*. Another magazine had offered $3,000 for the piece, but Glavis refused payment for work he considered a public duty. Hapgood "read the article that night and accepted it the next day," proceeding immediately with plans for publication. No attempt was ever made to contact Ballinger or anyone within the Interior Department to verify the details or documents underlying the allegations.

Published in *Collier's* on November 13, the Glavis article renewed "the newspaper frenzy" that had temporarily subsided in the aftermath of Taft's September statement. The piece was carefully phrased throughout; Glavis later claimed he never intended to depict Ballinger as venal—he simply wanted to stop the exploitation of Alaska coal lands. Yet the headline blatantly placed Ballinger at the center of a ring of corruption. "The Whitewashing of Ballinger," read the streamer. "Are the Guggenheims in Charge of the Department of the Interior?" Section headings within the article extended the implication: "A Leak in the Land Office," "Ballinger Pushes Trial When Government Is Not Ready," "The Alaska Coal Lands Are in Danger in Ballinger's Hands." The potential purchase of coal lands by the Morgan-Guggenheim syndicate, which was already in possession of vast copper mines, smelters, steamship lines, and railroads in the West, raised the specter that one company would control all "the natural resources of Alaska."

With this invocation of monopoly, "the muckrake periodical press took off in full cry." Glavis was likened to Ida Tarbell, a dogged investigator fighting to expose corruption at the highest levels. While some of the ensuing articles reflected serious research, others, as Roosevelt had warned in his celebrated rebuke of the "Muckrake Man," simply repeated the most sensational rumors as fact. A piece by John Matthews in *Hampton's* charged that Taft himself was "a party to the conspiracy." Citing "circumstantial evidence," Matthews concocted the tale of a deal purportedly conceived at the 1908 Republican Convention, which would allow J. P. Morgan "on behalf of the Morgan-Guggenheim combination to name the Secretary of the Interior," with the assurance that once Ballinger was in place, "the Alaska coal grants" would be approved.

Ballinger refused to give a detailed statement in response to such distortions and outright slander. Instead, he launched a virulent attack on "literary apostles of vomit," who "imagine they can invent calumnies and pure fabrications so rapidly as to preclude reply." He labeled Matthews's charges "so asinine" they did not merit a rejoinder. "I have felt so thoroughly conscious of the justice of my position," he told the editor of the *Spokesman-Review*, "that I have felt assured that the public would ultimately understand the truth without the necessity of my entering upon a campaign of publicity." Taft, too, shied from the controversy, maintaining that both Ballinger and Pinchot were committed to Roosevelt's conservation policies, despite their divergent approaches to carrying them out.

When Ballinger released his first annual report to Congress on November 29, the chorus of outrage seemed to still. The report displayed a liberal stance on every issue, garnering widespread praise from conservationists. Even Pinchot and Garfield conceded that Ballinger had come out "in favor of all the things we fought for." While Pinchot dismissed Ballinger's motivation as "the goodness of a bad boy recently spanked," he predicted that "the whole controversy will pass quietly away, with the net result that Ballinger is forced completely over on to the Conservation side," leaving "the Administration . . . stronger for Conservation than it otherwise would have been."

More than anyone, Taft wanted the contentious ordeal to end. Ballinger, however, saw only one route to restore his honor and reputation: a full congressional inquiry into the activities of both his department and the Forest Service. For months, he had silently gathered ammunition, evidence that not only vindicated his own actions but implicated Pinchot and his subordinates in manufacturing malignant attacks. Aware of Taft's reluctance, Ballinger told the president "that the situation had become intolerable to him." Unless Taft consented to a congressional investigation, he would resign.

Friends and family urged the president to accept Ballinger's resignation and move on, but Taft felt compelled to defend his beleaguered cabinet official. Aware that an inquiry would prolong the struggle, overshadow his legislative program, and potentially compromise his administration, he nevertheless insisted that he would be "a coward or a white-livered skunk" if he deserted "an honest man" who had been subjected to venomous newspaper attacks. He had hoped that "the whole affair was a tempest in a teapot which soon would simmer down." Instead, leaked information fueled sensational headlines. Faced with Ballinger's ultimatum, the president agreed to the request for a congressional probe.

On December 23, after a series of conferences at the White House, Richard Ballinger sent a letter to Washington State's Republican senator Wesley Jones, demanding a complete investigation into the charges leveled against him. He petitioned that "any investigation of the Interior Department should embrace the Forest Service," as there was "reason to believe that the pernicious activity of certain of its officers has been the inspiration of these charges." Later that day, Senator Jones introduced a resolution asking the government "to transmit to Congress any reports, statements, papers, or documents" relating to the Glavis charges and the president's letter of exoneration. A special investigative committee, comprising six members from each House, was convened.

Pinchot's supporters feared that "all the power of the administration" would be deployed to secure "a packed investigating committee," groomed from the start to "glaze over the evidence against Ballinger," punish members of the Forest Service for leaking government files, and discredit Pinchot "before the people." A Washington "insider" warned Robert Collier that he had acquired "secret information" suggesting that once the committee had "whitewashed" Ballinger, the interior secretary would sue *Collier's* "for a million dollars on the ground of slander." Collier called Pinchot, Garfield, Hapgood, and Henry Stimson, Garfield's legal adviser, to an "emergency council of war" in New York. They agreed that Glavis needed an experienced lawyer to represent him at the hearing. Hapgood suggested Louis Brandeis, the prominent Boston attorney (and future Supreme Court justice). *Collier's* proposed to pay the jurist $25,000 "to conduct the defense." Brandeis readily accepted, beginning at once to pore over thousands of pages of documents.

Gifford Pinchot pursued a more public defense, delivering a speech in New York that attracted unprecedented attention. Framing his struggle with Ballinger as a battle "between special interests and equal opportunity," the chief forester declared conservation "a moral issue," a question of social justice. "Is it fair that thousands of families should have less than they need, in order that a few families should have swollen fortunes at their expense?" he asked. Pinchot, Taft told Horace with grave irritation, was "out again defying the lightning and the storm." While Ballinger was "busily engaged" in the practical endeavor of "drafting laws" to protect the public lands from exploitation, Pinchot was "harassing the wealthy" and "championing the cause of the oppressed." The outcome of this battle within the administration was undecided, however. "Will Pinchot remain the St. George and Ballinger the dragon?" Taft worriedly mused. "I don't know. Let us see."

In January 1910, with the congressional investigation imminent, the *National Tribune* reported that both "the Ballingerites and the Pinchotites" were stockpiling ammunition. The Pinchotites were initially expected "to be on the defensive," working to deflect evidence that the Ballinger camp had gathered "to prove them as plotting against the Interior Department and as furnishing material for the muckraking magazines." When the time came for Ballinger's cross-examination, however, the Pinchotites were projected to gain advantage. "It will be a hot old political time," the *Tribune* predicted, relishing the controversy. "It remains true today as it was in the days of [the Roman emperors]," *Current Literature* observed, "that a gladiatorial combat is the quickest way to ensure tremendous public interest."

Surmising that the Ballingerites would "bring out, piece by piece, various bits of testimony" to shine "the worst possible light" on the Forest Service's involvement with Glavis, Pinchot decided "to lay our hand on the table, tell in advance all the facts, and assign the exact reasons for everything that had been done." He requested a report from Price and Shaw detailing their involvement in the release of "official information" about Ballinger and the Cunningham case. On January 5, three weeks before the hearings, he transmitted their report, along with his own commentary, to Senator Dolliver, Republican chair of the Committee on Agriculture and Forestry. Pinchot acknowledged that Price and Shaw had violated "the rules of official decorum" but argued that "their breach of propriety" was insignificant in comparison with "the imminent danger that the Alaska coal fields still in government ownership might pass forever into private hands with little or no compensation to the public." Appeals through official channels had failed. A final petition to the White House had been derailed by Taft's "mistaken impression of the facts," resulting in his decision to remove Glavis, "the most vigorous defender of the people's interests." Both Price and Shaw had "acted from a high and unselfish sense of public duty," intentionally choosing "to risk their official positions rather than permit what they believed to be the wrongful loss of public property."

Archie Butt was with Taft when news of Pinchot's letter to Congress reached the White House. "One trouble is no sooner over in this office than another arises," Taft declared in frustration. Though he regarded the letter "as a piece of insubordination almost unparalleled in the history of the government," the president realized that by dismissing Pinchot, the man most pivotal in securing Roosevelt's conservation legacy, he risked alienating Roosevelt himself. "I believe [Taft] loves Theodore Roosevelt," Butt attested, "and a possible break with him or the possible charge of ingratitude on his part is what is writhing within him now." Taft told Butt that no decision "had distressed him as much." As he weighed the consequences that afternoon, he looked to Butt "like a man almost ill." Discussing the matter with his cabinet, Taft learned that Pinchot had not cleared his letter with his boss, Agriculture Secretary James Wilson. The president sent for Senator Root, who initially warned against firing Pinchot. An examination of the correspondence, however, changed Root's mind: "There is only one thing for you to do now, and that you must do at once," he advised. Later that night, Taft directed Wilson to fire Pinchot, Price, and Shaw.

"The plain intimations in your letter," Taft wrote Pinchot, "are, first, that I had reached a wrong conclusion as to the good faith of Secretary Ballinger." Yet Pinchot "had only seen the evidence of Glavis, the accuser," and had no knowledge of the documentary evidence submitted to the White House. "Second," the president continued, Pinchot suggested that without public exposure, "the Administration, including the President," would have patented "fraudulent claims" to Alaska's rich coal lands. "I should be glad to regard what has happened only as a personal reflection, so that I could pass it over and take no official cognizance of it. But other and higher considerations must govern me." The people "placed me in an office of the highest dignity and charged me with the duty of maintaining that dignity and proper respect for the office on the part of my subordinates. . . . By your own conduct you have destroyed your usefulness as a helpful subordinate."

After this painful decision, Butt reported, Taft "looked refreshed and even fairly happy." The Washington papers generally agreed that the president "could have followed no other course," for Pinchot's letter "was too flagrant an offense to be overlooked." Pinchot, one editorial suggested, was "suffering from the same malady that overtook Mr. Glavis, a swollen idea of his own importance." It seemed initially that Pinchot's dismissal would precipitate little furor. In fact, Taft's own message on conservation policy two weeks later garnered universal praise. "Quite as admirable a message as Mr. Pinchot could have written," pronounced the New York *World.* The *New York Tribune* found the address "peculiarly satisfactory," noting Taft's "specific and practical" promotion of "new legislation to govern the disposal of the public lands." It was evident from his tone, *The Outlook* agreed, that Taft remained fully committed to "the Roosevelt policies." Furthermore, the appointment of Henry Graves to replace Pinchot clearly demonstrated Taft's commitment to preserve the nation's forests. Graves, the head of the Yale School of Forestry, was "a personal friend of Mr. Pinchot" and a widely respected conservationist.

Theodore Roosevelt was in the Congo when a runner brought him news of Pinchot's dismissal. "I cannot believe it," he wrote Pinchot. "The appointment in your place of a man of high character, a noted forestry expert, in no way, not in the very least degree, lightens the blow." Roosevelt would refrain from any overt criticism of his successor, but he offered Pinchot his sincere support and hoped later to discuss the whole matter in detail. "I do wish that I could see you. Is there any chance of your meeting me in Europe?" Overjoyed to hear from Roosevelt, Pinchot decided to set off as soon as he had completed his testimony before Congress.

First, however, the former forester was determined to use the hearings to vindicate his actions and crush Richard Ballinger. After his dismissal, hundreds of supportive letters and telegrams arrived from across the country urging him to continue the fight. "The people have faith in you, by the million," one telegram read. Freed from the constraints of office and all duties as a subordinate, Pinchot became "general-in-command of the anti-Ballinger forces." Together with Garfield and Collier, he spent hours with Louis Brandeis, helping to prepare Glavis for the witness stand and reading through the mass of material provided by the administration for documents that would buttress their case. Glavis handled himself well on the stand. The *National Tribune* reported that he had presented his case "in the most convincing way." For those anticipating fireworks, however, the early phase of the inquiry proved "a keen disappointment." In the absence of hard evidence of corruption on Ballinger's part, the investigation seemed to show "the existence of a quarrel rather than a scandal."

Public interest in the hearings heightened when Gifford Pinchot took the stand. He "opened with a heavy volley," flatly charging that Ballinger had "been unfaithful to his trust, disloyal to the President and an intentional enemy to the conservation policy." Had the interior secretary not been checked by "the public clamor against him," invaluable public lands would have been lost forever to the special interests. "The imperative duty before this country," Pinchot declared, "is to get rid of an unfaithful public servant." After this impressive start, however, he failed to substantiate his dramatic charges. Taft was relieved. "Pinchot has distinctly discredited himself by his thundering," he told Horace, "and then falling down altogether in respect to his specifications." Horace agreed that Pinchot had "proven nothing at all."

After Pinchot left the stand, the hearings became "so tedious," the *Arizona Republic* editorialized, "that auditors are unable to remain awake." The public was quickly becoming bored with the complex issue and even with Louis Glavis, "of whom it had never heard before and of whom perhaps it will never hear again." The "waning interest," the paper predicted, would soon take the controversy off the front page. "Besides the baseball season is fairly under way," and "the public eye" is turning toward Reno, Nevada, where "The Battle of the Century" was scheduled to take place: the heavyweight fight between the challenger, African-American Jack Johnson, and the reigning champion, Jim Jeffries.

Many years later, Louis Brandeis acknowledged that they had not unearthed anything "really decisive" at that point in the investigation. He returned once again to the mountain of documents that the Taft administration had delivered to Congress. The committee had requested the data upon which the president had based his September 13 decision to exonerate Ballinger and dismiss Glavis, and Brandeis focused particularly on the attorney general's 85-page report, dated September 11. Brandeis read the detailed report "ten, fifteen, twenty times," and "saw that it was not a hastily thrown together patchwork but a carefully prepared unit," so meticulously compiled that it seemed unlikely to have been generated in the brief interval after Taft met with Glavis. Brandeis "was certain that something was wrong, but he had to prove it." In several instances, he finally discovered, the report referenced facts and events that were not known or did not take place until weeks after September 11. The administration was claiming a document that did not exist at the time as the basis for the president's decision.

Brandeis revealed his discovery to *Collier's* Norman Hapgood and asked the editor to come to the hearings on April 22. On that day, Brandeis called Ballinger's assistant Edward Finney to the stand. He had designed a line of questioning that would make Finney realize that the predating had been discovered and asked Hapgood to monitor the expression on Finney's face during the proceedings. At lunch, Hapgood confirmed that Finney had appeared cognizant of his peril; Brandeis sharpened his questions when the session resumed, finally introducing into the record incidents mentioned in the September 11 report that had not yet occurred. He intimated that the document had been prepared after the fact "to make it appear" as if Taft had possessed more substantial documentary evidence when he passed judgment. Prevented by the rules of the investigation from issuing a subpoena to Wickersham, Brandeis leaked the story to the press. Attorney General Wickersham initially refused comment but eventually wrote to Congress that he had, indeed, backdated the report.

As the *National Tribune* observed, backdating documents was common practice in government. Had administration officials acknowledged the actual chronology when they sent the documents to the Congress, "there probably would have been no unfavorable comment." Their failure to do so invited speculation that they had falsified records in a deliberate attempt to deceive Congress and the country. The revelation revived interest in the hearings, accentuating "an attitude of suspicion" toward Ballinger, Wickersham, and Taft himself.

If the lengthy Wickersham report had not served as the basis for Taft's decision, Brandeis queried, what did? It turned out that the lawyer had known the answer for months, though he had bided his time before springing his discovery of the Lawler memo. In February, Brandeis had met with twenty-four-year-old Fred Kerby, one of the two stenographers who had taken Lawler's dictation. After the publication of Taft's celebrated letter the previous September, Kerby had "noted the similarities between the two documents," recognizing sections with identical wording.

Kerby agreed to meet Garfield and Brandeis at Pinchot's house, where he recounted the facts about preparing the memo. He recalled that Lawler, "in constant consultation" with various interior officials, including Ballinger, had written and revised the memo a half-dozen times. It was midnight on Saturday when the final version was completed. The rough drafts were "laid in the grate and a match put to the pile." Lawler placed the final memo "in his brief case" and joined Ballinger in the secretary's carriage. The two men then drove together to the station, catching the "Owl" to New York, where Wickersham would receive the memo to bring to Beverly. Kerby, still employed at the Interior Department and newly married, "asked that, if possible, they avoid calling [him] to testify." Brandeis promised that he would try to "get the facts into the record through cross-examination of Ballinger and thus compel production of the Lawler document."

In early March, Brandeis sent a letter to the attorney general and the Interior Department, requesting production of "the so-called memorandum prepared by Mr. Lawler at the request of the President." Department officials claimed they had searched the files, but it could not be found. A second request in April met with a similar response. Brandeis suspected that they were deliberately withholding the memo, aware that it might cast a shadow on the fairness of Taft's decision to exonerate Ballinger and dismiss Glavis.

When Ballinger took the stand, Brandeis directed a series of questions designed to extract information about the Lawler memo. Brandeis noted that in Ballinger's opening statement he had failed to mention that Lawler had accompanied him to Beverly. When Ballinger claimed he did not consider it "of any material moment," Brandeis pressed him further, asking if it was "not a matter of moment in view of the part that [Lawler] subsequently played?" Ballinger continued his evasive responses as Brandeis turned his questions to the contents of his companion's briefcase. Under repeated questioning, Ballinger said that Lawler had "a grip with some clothes in it," but he wasn't sure what else it contained. Finally, he acknowledged that Lawler had brought the president a memorandum, covering "a sort of resume of the facts." Ballinger appeared intensely nervous as the cross-examination persisted, his foot beating "a restless tattoo on the floor." At one point, he turned in anger toward Brandeis, calling his line of questioning "an insult." Ballinger refused any further questions that bore on the president's actions.

Having "exhausted all channels" to introduce the Lawler memo, Brandeis returned to Fred Kerby. Fully aware that he would compromise his career, Kerby agreed to give a public statement describing the preparation of the memo. In his written statement, Kerby explained that he had known of

Lawler's instructions to prepare a memo which Taft could use as a draft for his own opinion. He identified "certain portions" of the president's published letter that had been drawn from Lawler's draft, though the passages he cited were not substantial. He never suggested that Lawler had actually dictated the president's letter. To the contrary, he said that the draft had been "specifically" prepared in triple space to leave room for revision. The headlines accompanying the young stenographer's statement told a different story, however: "Ballinger Accused of Preparing Taft's Letter of Exoneration," announced the *Washington Times*. "President's Statement Giving Secretary Clean Bill Almost Identical in Verbiage with Notes in Shorthand Note Book which was Ordered Destroyed."

When the story broke on the afternoon of May 14, Taft was on the golf course. Ballinger and Lawler went at once to Wickersham's office, where they suddenly "found" the missing Lawler memo and sent it to the committee. This unexpected discovery "a few minutes after the Kerby story was printed, will go down in history," the *Washington Times* charged, "as one of the most remarkable coincidences of all time." Few questioned Ballinger's immediate dismissal of Kerby, but the secretary was widely criticized for his venomous public statement that charged the young stenographer with "treachery" and claimed that he was "unworthy" of public trust.

On Sunday, Taft finally took up the matter personally. He wrote a public letter to Senator Knute Nelson, chair of the investigating committee, describing in full detail the circumstances under which he had prepared his September 13 letter. He acknowledged that he had, indeed, asked Lawler for a draft statement, but insisted that the resulting memo "did not state the case in the way [he] wished it stated." It was filled with criticisms of both Pinchot and Glavis, which the president "did not think proper or wise to adopt." In the end, while he found the references to the documents helpful, he incorporated only a few general statements. "The conclusions which I reached were based upon my reading of the record," Taft maintained, "and were fortified by the oral analysis of the evidence and the conclusions, which the attorney general gave me." Desiring to have a full record of the circumstances reach the public, he had asked Attorney General Wickersham to incorporate his findings into "a written statement," backdated to September 11 and filed with the record. Occupied with other matters, Wickersham had not completed his analysis and summary until late October.

The press praised both the president's "manly" assumption of responsibility for the predating of the attorney general's summary and his characteristic candor in narrating "the sequence of events from his meeting with Glavis to his exoneration of Brandeis." A line-by-line comparison of the Lawler memo and Taft's letter corroborated the president's testimony that he had used only a few "unimportant" statements from the memo. "There was absolutely nothing wrong," the *Chicago Record-Herald* observed, "in instructing a subordinate to prepare an opinion." Nor was it questionable to use that opinion as a first draft, as was "done every day in public and private offices." Nonetheless, the press generally agreed that "the people who had charge of the management of the Ballinger-Pinchot investigation for the administration" had "simply blundered to the limit." Why did Wickersham wait to acknowledge the predating "until he was cornered?" Why was Ballinger so evasive on the witness stand? Why was the Lawler memo initially withheld from the committee? Why did Wickersham go to such lengths to conceal it? Why, if Kerby simply stated the facts that Taft himself later acknowledged, did Ballinger "fly into a rage" and call him a traitor? Each incident "came as a startling revelation," observed the *San Antonio Light and Gazette*; taken together, they "shattered the last vestige of confidence in the good faith" of those involved. Many were also dismayed by the serial dismissals of those who opposed the administration: first Glavis; then Pinchot, Price, and Shaw; and now Kerby.

When the hearings came to a close in late May, "the puzzled, unsatisfactory verdict" was that Interior Secretary Ballinger had "done nothing illegal." *The Washington Post* observed that "not a single fact has been produced to show that he was even derelict in duty, much less corrupt." Yet, as dozens of editorials pointed out, that finding could not restore the public confidence he had lost. "Rightly or wrongly," a midwestern newspaper declared, "the great mass of the American people have come to look upon him with deep distrust."

Reflecting widespread sentiment, the *Indianapolis Star* called on Ballinger to resign. "His presence in the cabinet is a drag upon the administration," the *Emporia Gazette* concurred. "He cannot be blind to the extraordinary courage which his chief has displayed in standing by him." He should voluntarily lift "the burden" which the president had "carried long and unflinchingly." *The Outlook* asserted that Ballinger could no longer "be regarded as a trustworthy custodian" of the public lands.

An indignant Ballinger announced that he had no intention of stepping down. He had done nothing wrong and therefore was fully "justified in remaining at the head of his department." Charley Taft tried to convince his brother to let Ballinger go, but the president refused. "Life is not worth living and office is not worth having," Taft maintained, "if, for the purpose of acquiring the popular support, we have to do a cruel injustice or acquiesce in it." The press, he believed, had "unjustly persecuted" a good man. The storm of criticism had "broken" Ballinger's health. He looked two decades older than when he joined the cabinet. Taft deemed it his presidential duty to stand by his controversial interior secretary until Ballinger himself chose to leave.

Nine additional months would pass before the secretary decided to resign. During that time, Taft and Ballinger finally succeeded in securing congressional support for a measure granting the president legal authority to withdraw public lands from private development. Backed by the new law, Taft's withdrawals in four years "almost equaled that of Roosevelt" in seven. Conservationists hailed Taft's appointment of Walter Fisher, head of the National Conservation League, to replace Ballinger. "His entrance into the Government service will unquestionably meet with strong public approval," Gifford Pinchot said. "I speak with confidence for we have been working together for years."

The damage to the president's political fortunes had been done, however. While some respected the loyalty the president had shown to his cabinet secretary, progressives believed that Taft should have dismissed Ballinger at the first sign of unfaithfulness to conservation causes. A president had "no right," they argued, to put his own feelings above "the public welfare." The bitter struggle had consumed the attention of the country for more than a year. Reformers' faith in the president, already weakened by the tariff struggle, had plummeted. The split in the Republican Party appeared irreparable.

"Is the Republican Party Breaking Up?"—Ray Baker's provocative title—headlined the first in a series of influential articles in *The American Magazine* in the winter and spring of 1910, designed both to chronicle and aid the growing insurgent movement within the party. For nearly three weeks, Baker traveled through what he called "the skirmish lines in the Insurgent territory—Minnesota, Iowa, Kansas, Wisconsin and Indiana." He met with the rebels who had fought against the tariff and criticized Ballinger—Murdock of Kansas, Cummins and Dolliver of Iowa, La Follette of Wisconsin, Clapp of Minnesota. Plans were evolving to run insurgent candidates against conservative Republicans in every district, even if the intraparty struggle ended up rewarding Democrats.

By wresting power from the Old Guard, the progressives aimed to regulate the economy in the interests of the many as opposed to the interests of the few. Although Roosevelt had occasionally "dragooned" the Congress into supporting progressive policies through outside pressure, the party organization remained in conservative hands. Western insurgents intended to finish the job Roosevelt had begun. The conflict within the Republican Party was no longer regional. When Baker traveled to New England, which gave "at first a decided impression of political quietude," he discovered that insurgency, while less developed in the East than in the West, was "following close behind."

From New England, he proceeded to Washington, just in time to witness the insurgents' unexpected triumph over Speaker Cannon. After failing to unseat Cannon the year before, the insurgents had regrouped around a resolution to divest the Speaker of his autocratic grip on the party. Capitalizing on a moment during a sparsely attended all-night session, George Norris of Nebraska introduced a resolution to rescind the Speaker's authority to appoint the Rules Committee. Instead, the entire House would elect the members of this most powerful body. The long debate that followed was "tense and dramatic." Everyone understood that Joseph Cannon was "fighting the fight of his life for his political future and the integrity of the party machinery." On the afternoon of March 19, Cannon "met his Waterloo." Forty-three insurgent Republicans cooperated with 150 Democrats to pass the resolution. Though Cannon would retain his position, his reign would never again be absolute.

"A real revolution is underway," an emotional Baker told his father, "and it will not stop until government by trusts & special interests is wiped out." In the months that followed, Baker continued to popularize the progressive cause. In a "case study" of Rochester, New York, home of the theologian Walter Rauschenbusch, a towering figure in the Social Gospel movement, Baker "noted with pleasure the existence of a strong religious element working successfully within the reform movement." This progressive uprising gave John Phillips what he had long been searching for—a central focus for the magazine. "We are naturally the insurgent magazine," he told William Allen White, "and we want to make The American Magazine more and more expressive in this movement." He hoped that White would help sustain the movement for reform by following Baker's lead with a series of "vigorous, stirring" political articles. He encouraged White to do anything possible to make the magazine "the organ and mouthpiece of the great liberal movement. This seems to me our opportunity."

White responded immediately to Phillips's request. Kansas was host to a dramatic battle for control of the statewide party. As precinct leader and state committeeman, White had been lining up insurgent candidates to run against standpatters at every level. He believed the Republican Party was doomed unless it changed from within. White strove to vividly articulate for readers the insurgents' vision of what the Republican Party stood for, even as he endeavored to gain control of the political machinery—through the institution of direct primaries, the initiative, the referendum, and the recall. Only an informed and empowered populace could truly win the battle to regulate and control capital in the interests of the country as a whole.

Ida Tarbell, too, lent her "powerful pen" to the insurgent cause. Unlike White, she never engaged directly in politics. Profoundly disappointed by the Payne-Aldrich tariff, which she considered "as hopeless a failure as a tariff could well be," she embarked on a new series designed to reveal how "the same old circus, the same old gilded chariots, the same old clowns" had managed once again to hoodwink America. Her only solace, she later wrote, came from the "rousing challenge" Republican progressives had issued to the Old Guard. She was thrilled by their new style of debate, which, her colleague Ray Baker noted, replaced "the hazy generalities on the advantages of a protective tariff" with a detailed presentation of facts and evidence akin to the muckrakers' investigative skills. During the long legislative struggle, Tarbell asserted, these insurgents had "crystallized into one of the most vigorous and intelligent fighting bands that had been seen for many years in Congress." Their struggle would be fierce, she knew. Political pandering to special interests did not end with the tariff; the same intellect that "argues and fights for a Ballinger" is furious when a railroad rate is questioned and "can be counted on to support anybody's privilege." It was against these "ways of thinking," prevalent in every realm of life, that progressives were fighting.

John Phillips heralded Tarbell's critique of the recent tariff-making process with a trenchant editorial: "The popular judgment of the Payne-Aldrich Tariff Bill grows more severe with each passing month," his piece began. "It is a bogus revision, and every man of sense knows that we will get no permanent settlement of this matter until a genuine, searching, informed revision has been made. He knows that by shirking this duty the Taft Administration has lost the country years of time. Here is the real basis of the anti-Taft sentiment—the good reason for insurgency."

While united in their support of the insurgents, the magazine's team differed in their opinion of William Howard Taft. John Phillips had been ambivalent about the new president from the beginning. "I thought that Taft might stand still," the editor remarked in September 1909. "I didn't think he'd go backwards." Five months later, Phillips observed that disappointment with Taft had kindled a newfound respect for Roosevelt, even among those who had "opposed him." The fact that the former president had never even tried to revise the tariff nor spoken out once against Cannon's regime "mattered little to the insurgents." His "crusading spirit" trumped any details of his actual policy. Tarbell had been more hopeful about Taft at the start, but turned against him with a vengeance when he signed the flawed Payne bill and then compounded his mistake by proclaiming it the best tariff ever passed. "Taft is done for, I fully believe," she told White. "Not a man of discernment, but what shakes his head over him."

William Allen White was slower than his colleagues to abandon faith in the president, still hoping in the spring of 1910 that Taft would succeed in getting his legislative agenda through Congress. White reminded Taft that the insurgents had been his allies in the fight for regulatory reform and postal savings banks. "But they will not work with Senator Aldrich and Mr. Cannon," he warned. "So an unhappy situation has arisen. The people have begun to confuse you with the leadership." Taft responded to White as he did to previous suggestions that he break with the Republican leadership. The idea that he could make enemies of the men with power over the fate of his legislative program made no sense. "I have confidence in the second judgment of the people based on what is done rather than what is proclaimed or what is suspected from appearances," he asserted, "and if I can make good in legislation, I shall rely on fair discussion to vindicate me."

On May 21, 1910, three weeks before Theodore Roosevelt's scheduled return from his African adventure, President Taft invited William Allen White to lunch. News of the invitation sparked hope among insurgents, who felt Taft had "foolishly and needlessly linked his fortunes" with men and influences at odds with the need for action. If the president truly listened to White, he would realize that the best chance of securing his legislative program lay with the growing band of insurgents, not the regulars.

"I could not have asked more courtesy, more consideration, more cordial hospitality," White reported after the meeting. For the first time in months, Taft told White, Nellie "had come to the table at the White House." The first lady had listened with attention, although it seemed to White that she suffered from "a curious amnesia." The reporter repeatedly tried "to steer the conversation" toward the insurgency, but Taft refused to take the bait. The two men talked of art and architecture, of movements in Europe and "everything under the sun but politics." They moved to a sunny porch after lunch and continued to talk. "We had a most amiable time," White reported, but he departed with the dispiriting conviction that he had come on "a fool's errand."

Of all the journalists at that time, Ray Baker had the most profound understanding of Taft's character and personal style. In January 1910, as the Ballinger hearings were getting under way, he began research for a lengthy assessment of the embattled president. "I trust you are gathering some gorgeous material on Taft," Phillips wrote. "The time is getting ripe. Everybody comes in with the same story"—they sense that the White House is occupied by "a jelly fish" incapable of real leadership. "The material is rich, and is getting richer. Somebody is going to make a bomb out of it one of these days," the editor predicted; "we want to be the fellows in charge of the fireworks." Refusing to succumb to pressure, Baker in "The Measure of Taft" produced a remarkably balanced piece, which revealed the president's considerable strengths along with his troubling weaknesses.

He began by noting that despite the progressives' disenchantment, the people by and large regarded the president with warmth. "There is one thing of which no popular criticism of a public man can wholly rob us," Baker maintained, "and that is our own vivid personal impression of him. We like him, personally, or we don't like him." And the public liked Taft. They appreciated the simple pleasure he took in walking about town, stopping in stores to chat with proprietors, visiting friends in their homes and hotels. They applauded his decision to hold receptions for visiting schoolchildren. While congressmen complained that he was wasting too much time shaking hands with the never-ending groups that deluged Washington during Easter break, Taft was adamant: "If these young visitors want to see the President, it is virtually their right." People everywhere were taken with his humble and accessible manner. "A mighty cheer swept across the crowd" at the Nationals' ballpark when the president, "with his good, trusty right arm," threw out the first ball for the first time in history and then chose to sit with ordinary fans instead of heading for the presidential box. "All his life long, Mr. Taft has been thus impressing the men he met with the charm of his personality," Baker noted. "Men have liked him instinctively, and they have not only liked him, but they have admired and respected his high ideals."

But the same "personal charm" that had propelled Taft to the presidency ultimately proved "dangerous" to him, Baker concluded. For far too long, his amiable nature had kept him from the rough-and-tumble of politics, from the need to fight for himself and his convictions. Had he come into the White House when McKinley first arrived, "when the Republican party stood like the Rock of Gibraltar," he might have sailed through his term "with smiling serenity"; instead, he found himself embroiled in a war within his party that threatened to rupture friendships and divide families. "In a war," Baker proclaimed, "the chief thing is to *fight*." The temperate Taft was ill-equipped to take up arms.

The most alarming trait Baker discerned in the president was his inability to accept honest criticism. Taft acknowledged that twelve years on the bench, the one place relatively "free from severe criticism by the press," had done little to prepare him for the onslaught from newspapers and magazines. Rather than accept that "criticism may spring from an honest difference in principles," the president sought to discredit the publications, implying that their critiques sprang from self-interest or malice. They were angry at him, he insisted, for proposing to increase second-class postal rates and for failing to lower the tariff on wood pulp, both measures that would hurt their bottom line.

Taft's loyal supporters further amplified this defensive, even paranoid stance toward the press. One proponent argued that the magazine writers had been "arrayed against" the administration "from the first," disseminating poison with their insidious literary tricks. This diatribe drew a powerful response from Sam McClure. Though McClure's empire was merely a "skeleton" of what it had once been, his words still carried weight. "In the first place," McClure argued, "the administration did not have the magazines against it from the start." On the contrary, the press was "eager to support him." Indeed, *McClure's* had sent George Kibbe Turner, one of its best writers, to the White House to conduct a wide-ranging interview with the president. The resulting piece, which attracted a large readership, was presented entirely in Taft's words, affording him an open platform to explain his views on every contentious subject. "I have trained most of the successful writers, on public questions, for the magazines in this country, and I know their methods and their quality as probably no other man living," McClure justifiably stated; no journalists could be found who "write with greater sincerity or who are more eager to get the truth." Taft's troubles, McClure concluded, stemmed from his own actions: first, the tariff and the Winona speech had spread across the landscape "like a frost"; then "the Alaska business" had begotten the president's relentless defense of Ballinger, "an unnecessary struggle against the people's wishes."

Roosevelt had learned little of Taft's troubles while he was in Africa. He had received an earful from Gifford Pinchot, however, when the latter came to see him on the Italian Riviera in mid-April. Pinchot arrived at Roosevelt's villa in the early morning, remained for lunch, and then accompanied the former president on a long trek over the Maritime Alps. Months earlier, Pinchot had enumerated Taft's failings in a letter, condemning the new president's decision to surround himself with corporate lawyers, his alliance to Cannon and Aldrich, his surrender of executive powers to Congress, and, most damningly, his appointment of Richard Ballinger. "We have fallen back down the hill you led us up," Pinchot had written, "and there is a general belief that the special interests are once more substantially in full control of both Congress and the Administration."

Pinchot carried with him a half-dozen letters from fellow progressives, all confirming his own estimate of Taft. Senator Dolliver spoke with sadness of his "disappointment" that the president had "lost the opportunity and wasted the prestige" Roosevelt had bequeathed him, warning that the corporate tyranny would triumph "unless a way could be found to overthrow the present management in Congress which is now the guardian of the President's opinions." Albert Beveridge provided a devastating narrative of Taft's first year as president. "The people at first received the President with good expectations," he informed Roosevelt, "then with tolerance, then with faint distrust, then with silent opposition and now with open and settled hostility." More telling than such general criticisms, however, was Pinchot's personal story of his acrimonious struggle with Ballinger. "We had one of the finest talks we have ever had," Pinchot eagerly relayed to Jim Garfield. Reporters, noting Pinchot's smile when he returned to his hotel, declared that "no event in Roosevelt's entire trip" held more political significance than this day-long conference.

In a grim letter to Henry Cabot Lodge that same day, Roosevelt expressed his first open disappointment in the course of his successor's presidency: "You do not need to be told that Taft was nominated solely on my assurance to the Western people especially, but almost as much to the people of the East, that he would carry out my work unbroken; not (as he has done) merely working for the same objects in a totally different spirit, and with . . . a totally different sense from that in which both I and the men who acted under my word understood it." Many now believed, Roosevelt lamented, that he had "deceived them." Still, "a good chance" remained that Taft could recover. "Everybody believes him to be honest, and most believe him to be doing the best he knows how." But for the moment at least, the former president would follow the course Lodge had prescribed and "keep absolutely still about home politics."

In preparation for Roosevelt's mid-June homecoming, Ray Baker wrote an ominous speculative piece entitled "The Impending Roosevelt." "As the fight deepens both sides are seen listening sharply for the first clashing sounds of the returning warrior," Baker noted. "He is more popular now than he was when he sailed for Africa." Despite his absence from the political scene for over a year, Theodore Roosevelt remained "the most interesting, amusing, thrilling figure in America." Would he endorse the Taft administration? Would he join the insurgent rebellion? "One thing may be set down as absolutely certain," Baker concluded. "Roosevelt will act. Roosevelt always acts. . . . And when he acts no stage smaller than that of the nation will serve him; he is of continental size."

CHAPTER TWENTY-FIVE

"The Parting of the Ways"

This "Bronco Buster" cartoon illustrates the jolt Roosevelt received when Democrats made huge gains in the 1910 midterm elections.

THE PROSPECT OF THEODORE ROOSEVELT'S return to American soil on June 18, 1910, left William Howard Taft fraught with anxiety. He was perplexed, he confided to Archie Butt, why Roosevelt had never once written to him during his travels. The letter Butt had hand-delivered as the former president left for Africa in March 1909 more than a year earlier remained unanswered. Roosevelt had never acknowledged the farewell gift that accompanied the letter. Butt, who had helped Taft choose the present—a gold ruler extendable to eight inches at one end, with a pencil affixed to the other—was bewildered. "There is no doubt that he received it?" Taft asked. "None whatever," Butt assured him. "I gave it to him, and he held it up for the press men to see and sent his thanks by me and said he would answer it on his way over."

Unaccountably, a copy of a telegram from Roosevelt to Taft, written aboard the SS *Hamburg* on the day he sailed, remains in Roosevelt's own papers. "Am deeply touched by your gift and even more by your letter," Roosevelt had written. "Everything will surely turn out all right, old man." Perhaps, Butt speculated, "Roosevelt did write and gave the letter to someone to mail," who then kept it "as a souvenir." Perhaps Taft, expecting a letter, had forgotten receipt of the telegram. Either way, Taft waited stubbornly for the Colonel to reciprocate the correspondence and was deeply hurt when no letter came.

The lack of communication between the two men became public when Taft was forced to deny a newspaper report that Roosevelt had sent him a letter strongly endorsing the accomplishments of his administration. Upon further questioning, Taft had to admit that, in fact, he had "received no letters" from Roosevelt over the past year and a quarter. This was particularly striking, the *Indianapolis Star* noted, since "the colonel has kept up a pretty steady correspondence with many other persons." Indeed, all social connection between the two families seemed to have cooled. Taft found it hard to understand why Edith Roosevelt had remained "singularly silent during all the time of his wife's illness."

Taft was not the only party harboring hurt feelings. Roosevelt was angered by reports from home suggesting that family members had not been accorded proper treatment from the White House under Mrs. Taft. Edith complained that although eighteen-year-old Ethel had been invited to a garden party during a visit to Washington, the first lady apparently had not done enough to recognize her. Alice and Nick Longworth had received a number of dinner invitations, but Alice felt slighted, believing she should have been asked to greet the guests at the head of the receiving line. The haughty young woman interpreted such minor omissions as a deliberate intent on the first lady's part "to let the setting sun know its place." The Roosevelt children, Butt observed, were convinced that Taft occupied the presidency "solely as a result of their father's predetermination to put him there," placing the new president and his first lady under a special obligation to the entire Roosevelt family. Taft fully appreciated the central role Roosevelt had played in his election, but felt that he had done all he could, given Nellie's serious illness, to accommodate the family. "Everything which is done by either side is misconstrued," Archie Butt told his sister-in-law; the fact that such "petty personal jealousies" could tarnish the long-standing friendship between Roosevelt and Taft seemed to him inexplicable. Further aggravating matters, Roosevelt could not fathom why no "word of welcome" from the White House awaited him when he came out of the jungle and met with scores of correspondents and friends in Khartoum.

When Taft finally decided at the end of May to swallow his pride and write once more to Roosevelt, he described the painful calamity of Nellie's collapse openly. Her inability to speak, he confided, had been "nearly complete" for a prolonged period, requiring that everyone be "as careful as possible to prevent another attack." While she had slowly recovered her physical strength, Taft explained, a year later Nellie still could only "speak a formula of greeting" at large receptions. Dinners and social events that called for conversation had to be circumvented. On the political front, he acknowledged that "the Garfield Pinchot Ballinger controversy" had brought him "a great deal of personal pain and suffering," but he preferred not to "say a word" about the complex dispute. "You will have to look into that wholly for yourself," he told Roosevelt, "without influence by the parties if you would find the truth." Despite these personal and political difficulties, Taft hoped that his old friend would soon find time for an extended visit to the White House.

Concerned that his letter might not reach Roosevelt before he sailed from Europe, Taft made the decision to send Archie Butt to meet the *Kaiserin* in New York, where he might deliver a duplicate copy, along with a shorter note of welcome. To placate any wounded egos, Butt suggested to the president that Nellie also write her own note to Edith. That accomplished, Butt ventured, "you and Mrs. Taft have left nothing undone." If Edith, "not understanding Mrs. Taft's condition," did not feel that enough consideration had been given to her children, then this kindly explanatory note would straighten out the perceived neglect. To Butt's delight, Nellie agreed, though he privately worried that "when women get at cross purposes it is hard to get them straightened out again."

As an official representative of the president, Archie Butt was among the first to board the *Kaiserin*. "Oh, Archie, but this is fine," Roosevelt said, warmly clasping the hand of his former military aide. Archie dutifully delivered Taft's two letters to Roosevelt, explaining that the first was a duplicate of one previously sent, and the second a note of welcome. Roosevelt said he had received and answered the first letter just before setting sail from England, but opened the second one at once and read it through. "Please say to the President that I greatly appreciate this letter and that I shall answer it later," he replied. Butt then told Roosevelt about Nellie's stroke "and how she dreaded to see anyone whom she had known in the past." He trusted his account would explain why the first lady had not entertained the Roosevelt clan more expansively. Roosevelt said only "that he had heard much that had distressed him."

When Edith Roosevelt came in, Archie presented her with Nellie's letter, which she quickly tucked into her handbag. Distracted by the arrival of Alice and Kermit, Edith seemed to forget the correspondence—an oversight confirmed in a subsequent conversation with Archie Butt. Inviting Archie to Oyster Bay in July, Edith pointedly quipped, "if the master will let you off," adding, "Remember me to the President although you brought me no word." Archie reminded her that he had given her a letter; "she looked startled for a minute," only then recalling the note in her handbag. "Of course I will answer it," she recovered. "I appreciate it even if it has come a little bit late."

Archie caught the midnight train from New York and reached Washington in time for breakfast with Taft, providing a full account of his interactions with the Roosevelts. "I feel it is due largely to you that yesterday has passed off as it has," Taft said. "I want you to know that I am grateful." Butt learned that when Taft came back from his trip to Villanova the previous night, he had found Roosevelt's response to his first letter. In Butt's judgment, the response was "courteous," though it lacked the warmth that had characterized the friendship between the two men. "I am of course much concerned about some of the things I see and am told," Roosevelt wrote, "but what I have felt it best to do was to say absolutely nothing." Several days later, Taft received a second letter from Roosevelt thanking him for his "kind and friendly words of welcome." Nonetheless, he still avoided any commitment to a visit with his old friend. "Now, my dear Mr. President," Roosevelt wrote, "your invitation to the White House touches me greatly, and also what Mrs. Taft wrote to Mrs. Roosevelt. But I don't think it well for an ex-President to go to the White House, or indeed to go to Washington, except when he cannot help it." Overall, the feel of the letter disheartened both Taft and Butt. Former presidents, of course, frequently returned to the capital.

Taft's distress over Roosevelt's coolness was temporarily dispelled a week later by the nearly complete triumph of his administration's legislative agenda. Even in the face of intense "factional wrangling," the 61st Congress produced a splendid record, passing "more general legislation than any preceding session for many years." There had been many "dark days" during the winter and spring, the *New York Tribune* remarked, when almost everyone "lost faith" in the president's "ability to control and lead the dissident forces he had been called upon to command." Surprising many, the insurgents and the regulars had come together to enact a series of "strongly progressive" laws. "Taft a failure? Taft not effective?" one editorial remarked, aping the rhetoric of skepticism that had plagued Taft early on. "We never had such a towering wood pile of work from the congressional saw mill."

A new railroad bill bolstered the power of the Interstate Commerce Commission to initiate action against rate hikes, created a "special Commerce Court" to expedite judgments, and brought telegraph and telephone companies under the authority of the Interstate Commerce Act. These provisions strengthened federal control of railway rates, the historic program Roosevelt had begun. Publicizing campaign contributions both before and after congressional elections was mandated; individual statehood for Arizona and New Mexico granted; a Bureau of Mines created to improve the hazardous conditions in the mining industry; and money appropriated for the Tariff Board "to ascertain the difference in the cost of production, at home and abroad."

Passage of the postal savings bank bill, granting people of small means (who had generally hoarded their cash in fear of bank runs) the guarantee of the U.S. Treasury, was considered Taft's "crowning achievement." For nearly four decades, the big banks, stirring the specter of socialism, had defeated the idea of post office banks. "I am not in favor of having the government do anything that private citizens can do as well or better," Taft had repeatedly argued during his transcontinental trip the previous fall, but "the laissez-faire school, which believes that the government ought to do nothing but run a police force," had long fallen out of favor. When the bill finally passed, Taft declared, "I am as pleased as Punch," proudly touting it as "one of the great Congressional enactments. It creates an epoch."

The insurgents rightly took credit for adding amendments that improved each of these laws, but Taft deserved equal praise for corralling support from "Old Guard" Republicans, who at last fulfilled the promises they had made during the bitter tariff fight to support the rest of his legislative program. "When people come to write history fifty years from now," a *New York Times* reporter observed, "they might give credit to the worth of a plain-minded gentleman whose head wasn't thoroughly filled from the beginning with himself, but who really and honestly tried to enact into legislation the things he himself had written into his party's platform." Charley Taft was delighted by his brother's legislative success, writing to tell him, "I always had faith that it would come out that way, but it is a satisfaction to see it in black and white. . . . The record is immense; the accomplishments are tremendous."

Accompanied by Archie Butt and several of his cabinet members, Taft went to the president's room in the Senate on Sunday night, June 26, to sign the remaining bills before Congress adjourned. Members of both Houses "congratulated him on the fact that the measures on which he had been most insistent had been passed." He was "in a jovial mood," the *Washington Times* reported, "and seemed greatly pleased with the way the session was ending." Happy for his chief, Archie noted that "the only incident which marred the closing hours" was that not a single insurgent senator "came in to pay his respects or to say good-bye." Particularly in light of the party's legislative success, Taft was baffled by their continued hostility over the tariff struggle and the Ballinger-Pinchot episode. When the president had finished signing, he told Butt he was not ready to return to the White House, asking him to prepare the car "to take a joy ride." Soon, Archie wrote, they were "humming through the Soldiers' Home and down through the park." The following day, tired but happy, Taft left for his home in Beverly, where Nellie had settled for the summer.

UNLIKE TAFT, ROOSEVELT WAS INCAPABLE of extended periods of leisure; he rested at Sagamore Hill for a single day before heading to Manhattan to take up his duties as contributing editor to the weekly public affairs magazine *The Outlook*. Before leaving for Africa, he had signed a $12,000 annual contract with the publisher, Dr. Lawrence Abbott. *The Outlook* had appointed a three-room suite for Roosevelt: an office for his secretary, a waiting room for visitors, and a private room for the Colonel. Through a hidden wall, Roosevelt could escape to a side elevator without entering the main hall. Overall, the suite's "mahogany furniture, polished floors, and rich rugs" provided a "magnificence unusual for an office building."

Sorting through the 5,000 letters he had received during his absence, Roosevelt issued a statement expressing his "very real gratitude" to the many letter writers, along with his "real regret" that he could answer only "a small proportion." Asked by the newspapermen when he would comment on the current political situation, he declared that he would "not make a speech for two months" and that even then, his commentary would be "non-political." Indeed, he insisted, "I don't know that I will ever make a political speech again." Would he care to qualify that statement? one reporter queried. "Yes," Roosevelt laughingly said. "I won't say never."

And indeed, before a week had passed, Roosevelt had broken his resolve in dramatic fashion. Encountering New York governor Charles Evans Hughes at his thirtieth Harvard Reunion, Roosevelt was soon talking animatedly about how he could offer political support. Their discussion, observers noted, was "marked by frequent gestures"; Roosevelt repeatedly "brought his clenched fist down on the palm of his other hand." Throughout his governorship, Hughes had fought the party bosses, finally deciding to accept Taft's proffer of a Supreme Court seat rather than run for another term; but before leaving office, he hoped to pass a historic bill shifting the power of nomination from the party machine to the people. After listening to Hughes, Roosevelt impetuously agreed to back the governor's direct primary bill.

To substantiate his pledge, Roosevelt sent a telegram to the New York County Committee chair, Lloyd Griscom, roundly endorsing the direct primary bill. "I believe the people demand it," he maintained, and "I most earnestly hope that it will be enacted into law." With this action, Roosevelt "plunged into the very thick of the political controversy." He had taken "the helm and become the State leader in the approaching campaign." The Colonel's advocacy, the *New York Tribune* editorialized, "is likely to prove the most potent factor in determining the fate of that measure."

During Roosevelt's reemergence into the political arena, he carefully limited his contact with William Howard Taft. After spending the night at Henry Cabot Lodge's summer home in Nahant, Massachusetts, a small town only ten miles from Beverly, Roosevelt, most likely at Lodge's suggestion, called on the president at the Summer White House. Archie Butt and Secret Service agent Jimmy Sloan were on the porch when the big touring car carrying Roosevelt and Lodge arrived. Hearing the commotion, the president came outside. "Ah Theodore, it is good to see you," he said. "How are you, Mr. President," Roosevelt replied. "This is simply bully." Taking hold of Roosevelt's shoulders, Taft implored him to drop the formal title, but Roosevelt refused: "You must be Mr. President," he insisted, "and I am Theodore." Taft took Roosevelt's arm and led him to a wicker table on the veranda overlooking the water.

But despite Taft's efforts to revive their former cordiality, the atmosphere remained "strained," Archie Butt lamented. When the butler took drink orders, Roosevelt, who rarely drank anything stronger than wine, blurted out that "he needed rather than wanted a Scotch and soda." Assuming that the president and the Colonel would wish to talk in private, Butt was informed by Lodge that Roosevelt did not want "to be left alone with the President." Taft tried to set Roosevelt at ease, assuring him that he would "do all in his power" to help pass the direct primary bill in New York. When Nellie and Helen Taft joined the group, Roosevelt, aware of Nellie's condition, refrained from directing any questions to her. To alleviate the awkwardness, Taft asked Roosevelt to share stories about his recent encounters with the European kings and queens. Roosevelt happily obliged, regaling the little group with an hour of anecdotes until it was time to leave.

As Roosevelt and Lodge prepared to depart, Lodge proposed that they agree upon a statement for the swarm of two hundred journalists anxiously waiting for them at the gate. If the president did not object, Roosevelt suggested, he would simply say it had been "a most delightful afternoon." Taft readily agreed. "With nothing on which to hang a story," Archie Butt later observed, the reporters used their imaginations to concoct a compelling tale. "From beginning to end it was a love feast," one account ran; the warmth of their meeting was proof "that their friendship is of the stuff that endures," said another. "Just Like Old Times," the *New York Times* reported, fancifully adding that "for a full minute," the two old friends stood "with hands upon each other's shoulders, while evident delight shone in every line of their smile." The continuing "peals of laughter" and "slaps on the back," the *Times* concluded, made it abundantly clear that "rumors of coolness between them" were unfounded. Both men knew that such a convivial encounter was far from the truth. The self-conscious meeting had painfully exposed the widening rupture in their once intimate friendship. The *Times* did, however, get one detail right: when Roosevelt was asked when he intended to return for a second visit, he replied, "I don't know that I shall."

UNPLEASANT NEWS GREETED ROOSEVELT WHEN he got back to Sagamore Hill. That afternoon, the boss-controlled New York Senate, "in swift and emphatic fashion," had defeated the direct primary bill. "It is Mr. Roosevelt who is beaten," declared the New York *World*, while the *New York American* exulted that "for the first time in seven years the triumphant career of Theodore Roosevelt has had a serious backset." *The Literary Digest* predicted that "those who know the Colonel have little doubt" that such a "slap in the face" would propel him "back into the arena prepared for war." The prognosticators proved correct. "They made the fight on me," Roosevelt declared, "and I've got to vindicate myself."

Not surprisingly, Roosevelt's path to achieving vindication pitted him directly against the Old Guard Republican bosses who controlled the state machine. Fearing that reactionary forces would dominate the state convention that fall, Lloyd Griscom urged Roosevelt to run for the post of temporary convention chair. More powerful than its name suggested, the temporary chairman would deliver the keynote speech, exert influence over the platform, and play an important role in nominating the party's slate of candidates. A longtime acquaintance of Taft's, Griscom shortly afterward informed the president that Roosevelt had agreed to run. "It did not occur to me that any one would oppose" Roosevelt's candidacy, Taft later said. At Griscom's request, he sent a telegram to Vice President James Sherman the next day. The conservative New Yorker had been the party's choice, not Taft's, for the second spot. Taft instructed Sherman by telegram to tell the party bosses that they must avoid division at all costs, urging them to hold "a full conference" with Roosevelt and make "reasonable concessions with reference to platform and candidates."

Not until the following day did Taft learn that the Old Guard had decided to run its own candidate. Sherman attempted to enlist Taft's support behind an alternative candidate, such as Elihu Root. "Don't you know," Sherman cautioned, "that [Roosevelt] will make a speech against you and the Administration, and will carry the convention and prevent an endorsement, and take the machinery out of the hands of your friends?" When asked where he would "stand in such a fight," Taft momentarily wavered. Instead of using his influence to prevent opposition to Roosevelt, he simply said he should not be dragged into the battle. During the formal meeting of the Republican State Committee the next day, the bosses proposed the vice president as their candidate for temporary chair. With this clever move, they insinuated that Sherman had the backing of the administration. Griscom, who had not expected the vote that day, was taken aback. As a result, the panel chose Sherman by a 20–15 vote.

When Roosevelt received the news at the *Outlook* office, "he fumed and refused to believe the report." Later that afternoon, he issued a statement openly aligning himself with the progressive faction against the machine. "He was glad," he wrote, that the "State leaders had taken the course they did because it showed that he had tried to bring about harmony, and having failed to do so, he was now able to go in and fight for all he was worth." Indeed, he threatened he would take the fight to the floor of the convention, where the delegates had the power to overturn the committee choice. Bravado notwithstanding, Roosevelt was distressed by the newspaper reports. "Old Guard Is Jubilant," blared the *New York Times*. "The prestige of the former President has received several hard knocks" in the weeks since his return, the *Times* added, but this was "the heaviest blow yet."

When reports spread that Taft had conspired with the party bosses to bring about his defeat, Roosevelt was incensed. Apparently, several committee members had changed their votes after being erroneously told that Taft had endorsed Sherman's candidacy. As word reached the president that Roosevelt was planning to make a statement charging him "with treachery," Taft was beside himself. Unable to sleep, he would wander downstairs each morning at 5 a.m. to glean the latest from the newspapers. "No one knows just what

Mr. Roosevelt is going to do," Archie Butt observed, "and everyone about Beverly seems to be sitting over a volcano except the news paper men—and they, of course, fatten on what kills other people."

Though reluctant to respond to newspaper stories, Taft finally decided to issue a formal statement flatly denying that he had "ever expressed a wish to defeat Mr. Roosevelt" or "taken the slightest step to do so." On the contrary, he had sent the telegram to the New York leaders urging "the necessity for the fullest conference with Mr. Roosevelt." He was "indignant" to find that his request had been ignored. The *Washington Herald* reported that Roosevelt "was very glad to see President Taft's statement."

"As the waters of excitement recede," Butt reported to his sister-in-law, Clara, "it is evident that the last few days have left their permanent mark on the President. He looks ten years older." Taft admitted that he was "profoundly grieved" to learn that Roosevelt had thought, even for a moment, that he was capable of such treachery. "His whole attitude toward me since his return has been unfriendly," he told Archie, complaining that if Roosevelt felt disappointed, "the proper thing for him to have done was to give me the opportunity to explain my position and to thrash it out as we had done many times in the past." Archie Butt himself was equally disconsolate, fearing that the incident had further diminished the chances for reconciliation. "They are now apart," he lamented, "and how they will keep from wrecking the country between them I scarcely see."

LATE THAT SUMMER, COLONEL ROOSEVELT boarded a private railroad car secured by *The Outlook* to begin a three-week speaking tour through sixteen states, including Kansas, Nebraska, the Dakotas, and Minnesota. As he headed west for his first public appearances since returning from Africa, one political question was on everyone's mind: "On which side will the Colonel now align himself? What changes have taken place in his philosophy?" A resounding answer came on August 31, in Osawatomie, Kansas, as Roosevelt spoke at a ceremony dedicating the John Brown Memorial Park. The festive occasion, which brought more than 30,000 people, resembled that of "a county fair," with fireworks, a drum and fife corps, vendor booths, and food stands. Climbing onto a kitchen table that doubled as a speaking platform, Roosevelt delivered the most radical speech he had ever made, placing him ipso facto in "the front rank" of the insurgent forces. Entitled "The New Nationalism," the speech had gone through several drafts, with language and ideas provided by Gifford Pinchot, William Allen White, and *The New Republic*

editor Herbert Croly, whose recent book, *The Promise of American Life*, had attracted Roosevelt's attention.

"The New Nationalism puts the national need before sectional or personal advantage," Roosevelt proclaimed. Such an approach, he explained, "regards the executive power as the steward of the public welfare. It demands of the judiciary that it shall be interested primarily in human welfare rather than in property." While he still stood for "the square deal," he now recognized that "fair play under the present rules of the game" was not enough; the rules themselves had to be "changed so as to work for a more substantial equality of opportunity and of reward for equally good service."

For this generation, Roosevelt maintained, "the struggle for freedom" demanded a fight for popular rule against the special interests. Though "every special interest is entitled to justice," he declared, "not one is entitled to a vote in Congress, to a voice on the bench, or to representation in any public office." To drive these "special interests out of politics," he called for the direct primary and for laws forbidding corporations from directly funding political objectives. "Every dollar received should represent a dollar's worth of service rendered—not gambling in stocks," Roosevelt further contended, calling for both an income tax and an inheritance tax on large fortunes. Finally, he pressed for new laws regulating child labor and women's work, enforcing better working conditions, and providing vocational training. "No matter how honest and decent we are in our private lives," he concluded, "if we do not have the right kind of law and the right kind of administration of the law, we cannot go forward as a nation."

As the crowd thundered its approval, Kansas governor Walter S. Stubbs jumped on the table. "My friends," he exclaimed, "we have just heard one of the greatest pronouncements for human welfare ever made. This is one of the big moments in the history of the United States!" Seated amid the emotional crowd, Gifford Pinchot was overjoyed, later declaring to Roosevelt that he was "the leader to whom all look." Headlines in progressive papers trumpeted Roosevelt's "Advanced Insurgent Stand," suggesting that the insurgent movement would now be "materially strengthened." During the remainder of his western tour, Roosevelt was repeatedly greeted with "frenzied applause" and "overpowering demonstrations of affection and devotion." No man in the present generation, one reporter suggested, "has ever been honored with so magnificent a tribute."

Whereas westerners ecstatically embraced Roosevelt's new radical stance, easterners reacted with "consternation and horror." The New York *Sun* called the New Nationalism doctrine "more nearly revolutionary than anything that ever proceeded from the lips of any American who has held high office in our Government." Conservative commentators warned against "this new Napoleon," who threatened to destroy the constitutional separation of powers. Steering clear of such incendiary labels, moderate and even some liberal Republicans criticized Roosevelt for making only "slight mention" of the president during his strenuous tour, regarding "his silence" as a "most adroit form of attack," ultimately designed to diminish Taft and raise his own prospects for 1912.

Reading reports of Roosevelt's speeches, Taft was genuinely disturbed. "He is going quite beyond anything that he advocated when he was in the White House," he told his brother Charley, "and has proposed a program which it is absolutely impossible to carry out except by a revision of the Federal Constitution. He has attacked the Supreme Court which came like a bolt out of a clear sky, and which has aroused great indignation throughout the country on the part of conservatives." Writing in a similar vein to Horace, he reported that Roosevelt's "wild ideas" had "frightened every lawyer" and startled every decent "conservative" in the East. Horace was saddened to see lines being drawn that positioned his brother "on the other side of the fence" from moderate progressives, making it seem as if he were defending the Old Guard and expounding the "kind of politics" he had always fought against. While Taft's positions had not materially changed since his days as a cabinet officer, Horace worried that many "good men fighting against machine politics" now regarded him as a member of the opposition.

Taft believed that with each "riotous reception" Roosevelt received, "his reasons for thinking I would not do as a candidate in 1912" had multiplied. "His present mental condition," he told Horace, "rejects me entirely and I think he occupies his leisure time in finding reasons why he is justified in not supporting me." He had heard from several sources, he told Charley, that Roosevelt was still angry over the fact that "I dared to include you in the same class with him as assisting me in my canvass for the presidency. I venture to think that swell-headedness could go no further than this." Gossipmongers exacerbated Taft's concerns, reporting letters they had seen in which Roosevelt described him as utterly unfit for the presidency, suggesting that he must be challenged for the nomination.

Archie Butt watched and worried as Taft's bitterness toward his predecessor grew; loyal to both men, Archie found the prospect of an open rupture heartbreaking. Taft sympathized with his aide's dilemma, observing, "I know how it distresses you, Archie, to see Theodore and myself come to the parting of the ways." Recognizing that it pained Archie to listen to conversations critical of Roosevelt, Taft greatly admired the "dignified silence" he maintained. "Your silence will never be misconstrued by me," Taft promised. With each passing month, he had come to rely more and more on Archie. "He told me," Archie recorded in September, "that he always loved to see me come and hated to see me go." Archie's reflections make clear that this feeling was reciprocated. "In many ways," Archie wrote, "he is the best man I have ever known, too honest for the Presidency, possibly, and possibly too good-natured or too trusting or too something on which it is hard just now for a contemporary to put his finger, but on which the finger of the historian of our politics will be placed."

Nellie, too, had grown increasingly dependent on Archie Butt. Though she had learned to communicate her thoughts and make her wishes known to family members, she remained incapable of conducting "a connected conversation with strangers." When the British ambassador and his wife called on the president and first lady, Butt served as "the buffer" between Nellie and Mrs. Bryce, enabling the flow of conversation whenever Nellie came "to a standstill." During a garden party when she "became separated" from the president, Butt again came to her rescue; being on her own, she told her son Robert, "was pretty awful," until Archie escorted her back to the mansion. After a series of fainting spells, Nellie's doctor advised her to reduce the rigorous schedule of musicales and garden parties she had planned for the 1910 social season. She refused, preferring, he interpreted, "to die in harness" rather than "remain in the background as an invalid." Assessing the full social schedule planned for the coming winter and spring, Helen Taft decided to assist her mother at the White House rather than return to Bryn Mawr in the fall.

Within the family circle, Nellie became less anxious about her inability to articulate her thoughts. On the contrary, she tended to blurt out whatever came to her mind without the restraint she had characteristically exercised. During a luncheon conversation, for example, she suddenly mentioned Mabel Boardman, head of the American Red Cross and a longtime family friend. Speaking with excessive emphasis, she told her husband he would never marry Miss Boardman. If he became a widower, she predicted, he would desire "something young and prettier."

Unsurprisingly, much of the first family's conversation in the months following Roosevelt's return centered on divining what he might do. After reading an account of Roosevelt's opposition to Ballinger, Nellie offered a prescient comment to her husband: "I suppose you will have to fight Mr. Roosevelt for the nomination, and if you get it he will defeat you. But it can't be helped. If possible you must not allow him to defeat you for the renomination. It does not make much difference about the reelection." Taft agreed with Nellie's assessment, surmising early on that Roosevelt would indeed challenge him in 1912. Numerous newspapers suggested that he should "step out of the way" for the former president, but he believed that "having once been nominated and elected," he was under obligation to his supporters to run for renomination—even if he faced certain defeat, which he would accept "like a gentleman."

RETURNING FROM HIS WESTERN TOUR in early September, Roosevelt had only two weeks to prepare for battle against Sherman and the Republican bosses at the state convention. The state party was "on the Eve of one of the bitterest factional fights" in a generation, and Roosevelt's contest with Sherman for the temporary chair stood at the center of the proceedings. The great underlying issue, Boss William Barnes declared, is "whether the Republican Party is to remain the party of conservatism or be carried away with radicalism."

Roosevelt felt that the conflict was beneath him. "Twenty years ago I should not have minded the fight in the least," he told Lodge. "It would have been entirely suitable for my age and standing. But it is not the kind of fight into which an ex-President should be required to go." Nonetheless, he confessed, "I could not help myself." Lloyd Griscom admitted to Roosevelt that he was having trouble rounding up votes for him among "good honest" party loyalists, who sympathized with his opposition to the bosses but were upset with his seeming hostility toward the president. A meeting with Taft to demonstrate they were "on good terms," Griscom advised, would be helpful. Roosevelt readily agreed, recognizing that a show of unity might "turn the scale" in a contest as close as this promised to be.

Griscom arranged a luncheon in New Haven, where Taft was attending a meeting of the Yale Corporation. After a general conversation with Griscom and Taft's newly appointed private secretary, Charles Norton, Taft and Roosevelt were left alone. Roosevelt later said he "made a point of being as pleasant as possible," but Taft saw beneath the mask, later divulging to Archie that he felt Roosevelt was "not genial and quite offish." Taft recognized immediately that Roosevelt was strategically waiting to bring up the New York situation so he could later claim that the president "had spoken first." His calculation worked. As the meeting drew to a close, Taft volunteered that he hoped Roosevelt would beat the bosses and was glad to offer his assistance.

Unlike Taft, his secretary was willing to engage in the political game, creating what Roosevelt considered a "very irritating experience." Norton, "a little too slick for genuine wisdom," told the newspapermen that the Colonel had requested the meeting to stave off trouble in New York and needed the president's backing. Roosevelt's opponents jumped on the story as a signal that he was worried about his chances at the convention. At once, Roosevelt put out a statement "emphatically" denying that he had sought the meeting or asked anything of Taft. At Roosevelt's bidding, Griscom followed up with a statement declaring that the meeting was his idea. Regardless of these attempts to reformulate the story, Roosevelt complained to Lodge, a general perception remained that he had come "to beg for assistance"—for this, he blamed Taft as well as Norton. As a result, Archie Butt lamented, Roosevelt and Taft grew "farther apart than ever."

The auditorium at the Saratoga town hall was jammed with 7,000 men and women on September 27 when Roosevelt came down the aisle. His appearance provoked a round of "riotous cheers" as delegates and spectators "shrieked and yelled and waved their hats and bonnets." When Vice President Sherman arrived shortly afterward, "the scene was repeated," setting the stage for a divisive public battle. The Old Guard had selected Colonel Abraham Gruber, "a little roly-poly" man, to deliver the attack against Roosevelt. Unable to make his way through the crowd, Gruber was "practically lifted over the heads of the army of humans and passed up to the platform." Labeling Roosevelt "an enemy of the nation" and a threat to "public safety," Gruber's mean-spirited diatribe provoked such deafening "catcalls" that he could not continue until Roosevelt jumped up, shouting, "I ask a full hearing for Col. Gruber."

Roosevelt's supporters were anxious when the balloting began, but he emerged victorious, receiving 567 votes against Sherman's 445. In a conciliatory speech intended to unify Republicans, Roosevelt listed the accomplishments of the last Congress, giving credit to Republican lawmakers and "to our able, upright, and distinguished Pres. William Howard Taft." Once installed as temporary chair, Roosevelt mustered the votes to get his fellow progressive Henry Stimson the nomination for governor and to pass a fairly progressive platform, including a plank calling for direct primaries. Parts of the platform disturbed him—including the endorsement of Taft in 1912 and approval of the tariff—but he believed that he had come out as well as possible.

While Roosevelt was at Saratoga, Taft was hosting a four-day sleepover for the members of his cabinet at the White House. Having spent the summer in Beverly, the president wanted to catch up on each department's work and make plans for his annual message. "The house party has been a great success," he reported to Nellie. "We have had a jolly time on the one hand, and we have been very hard working on the other." Normally, the unique situation of a cabinet house party would have attracted considerable newspaper attention, but all eyes—including those of the president and his cabinet—were directed to Saratoga and Roosevelt's fight against the Old Guard. "Bulletins were brought to the President as they arrived," Archie reported, and everyone "spent most of the day hearing and discussing the news from New York." On the day the platform was approved, Taft wrote to Nellie in Beverly, commenting, "I hope you saw the proceedings of the Saratoga Convention and the very satisfactory resolutions endorsing your husband. Roosevelt made a speech praising me also, which must have gone a little hard with him, but which indicated that he found it necessary." Overall, Taft's White House party was a distinct success, as evinced by a gracious note that George Wickersham wrote to Nellie: "We had a delicious table and nothing was lacking but the actual presence of its mistress to make the White House a perfect place of abode. It was a charming idea of the President to invite the Cabinet to stay there with him. It has served to draw us more together and to unite us absolutely in an enthusiastic love and admiration of our Chief."

Taft's surmise that necessity, not desire, had compelled both Roosevelt's speech and his acceptance of the tariff plank proved correct. Throughout his long career, Roosevelt had accepted the need for compromise. Though unhappy about the tariff plank, he believed he "should have lost everything" had he demanded its elimination. Hard-line insurgents fiercely disagreed with Roosevelt's flexibility. Gifford Pinchot refused to back the ticket, considering endorsement of the tariff offensive and objecting to Roosevelt's characterization of Taft as upright. Roosevelt fired back at progressive ideologues, defending Taft's honor even while questioning his leadership. "I think it absurd to say that Taft is not upright," though he may be a failed leader. To complaints by William Kent, a Republican congressman from California, that Stimson "was not radical enough," Roosevelt countered: "Among all men who are prominent here, Harry Stimson is the only man who is anywhere near as radical as I am." In a letter to his son Theodore Junior, Roosevelt poured out his frustrations: on the one hand, he pointed out, the traditional elements of the Republican Party—club members, big business, and Wall Street—"have been nearly insane over me." Yet, at the same time, "the wild-eyed radicals do not support us because they think we have not gone far enough. I am really sorry to say that good Gifford Pinchot has practically taken his place among the latter," he noted, finally recognizing the rigidity of Pinchot's views.

A week after the convention, Roosevelt reconnected with Ray Baker, inviting him to lunch at Oyster Bay. "I had one of the freest talks with him I ever had," Baker recorded in his journal. "Much of our talk covered the Saratoga fight. I told him frankly that I had thought that a defeat there on the platform would have been better for him than an organization victory." Appealing to

Baker as "a reasonable exponent of the extreme left wing of the party," Roosevelt defended his actions and "spoke exultantly" of Stimson's candidacy. When the discussion turned to Taft, he made it clear that "they had wholly parted company," fixating again on the letter Taft had written after his election, thanking both Charley and himself in equal measure! His pride clearly wounded, he proceeded to describe the humiliating reports that followed his meeting with Taft in New Haven. "It happened once: but never again! Never again!" When Baker asked if he intended to be a candidate in 1912, he answered frankly, "I don't know." At the present, he maintained that he was "not seeking a nomination," but "circumstances might force me to be a candidate."

After another conversation at the *Outlook* office two days later, Baker told Roosevelt that his words on the tariff lacked his "usual moral punch," that he "would have stood higher with the country" if he had fought against the tariff plank. "He took it all in very good part," Baker wrote, considering this ability to endure criticism "one of his finest characteristics." Nevertheless, the reporter was beginning to believe that Roosevelt would ultimately fail in his attempt to play "the old game" of serving "both party & principle." The tide was simply moving too fast for someone "trying to be both radical & conservative."

As summer turned to fall, Roosevelt spent his days and nights on the campaign trail, trying to keep the Republican Party unified for the midterm elections. He stumped for both progressives and conservatives—for Beveridge in Indiana, then Henry Cabot Lodge in Massachusetts. He traveled first to Georgia, Alabama, and Arkansas, and then to Missouri, Illinois, and Iowa. "I am being nearly worked to death," he admitted to Bamie in early October. "I only hope I can last until election day." In mid-October, he returned to his native state for the final push. Rallying huge audiences, his charismatic self had become the central issue of the campaign, leaving Henry Stimson in his shadow.

As the election neared, Republican prospects across the country darkened. After more than a decade of Republican rule, the people were frustrated by the cost of living, tired of high tariffs, and resentful of machine politics. When Democrats won an "unprecedented" victory in the October state elections in Maine, commentators predicted the midterms would result in a Democratic landslide.

"If Mr. Roosevelt can save New York while neighboring States are captured by the opposition," the *Springfield Republican* declared, "his own national leadership and influence will take on a finality unapproached even in his own career." If he triumphs, the *New York Times* agreed, "it will be practically impossible to prevent his seizing the nomination to the Presidency in 1912."

Republicans had expected to lose ground during the midterm elections, but when the votes were totaled on November 8, the strength of the Democratic victory "stunned Washington." Democrats gained control of the House by a margin of nearly 60 votes, reduced the Republican majority in the Senate by ten seats, and elevated Democratic governors to power in twenty-six of the forty-eight states. In New Jersey, former university president Woodrow Wilson vanquished Republican Vivian Lewis by one of the widest margins in the state's history. In New York, the entire state ticket lost, including Henry Stimson and his own congressman, Charles Cocks. In Connecticut and Massachusetts, Democrats Simeon Baldwin and Eugene Foss easily trounced their opponents. In Ohio, Democrat Judson Harmon handily defeated Warren Harding. "The Democratic party in November of 1910," one historian has observed, "stood rehabilitated in the eyes of the country."

Despite the clear national trend, journalists interpreted the New York result as a "crushing rebuke" to Theodore Roosevelt. Had he kept his initial vow of silence after returning from Africa, one commentator observed, "defeat would have come to his party but a great cry for him as the only compeller of victory would have been heard." Instead, he had alienated the Old Guard at Saratoga, assumed personal control of the state party, and thrown his full weight behind the losing candidate, Henry Stimson. With the thrashing he took on his home turf, the *New York Times* declared, Roosevelt's "New Nationalism has been pitched into its grave." And beyond New York, there seemed "to be a fatal quality in his endorsement," one editorial observed, for "nearly every man whom he lauded in different parts of the country has been defeated," while the men he "singled out for vituperation" were "triumphantly elected."

Sensing blood, Roosevelt's opponents moved in for the kill. "The trail that Mr. Roosevelt has traveled for the last ten weeks can be traced by the battered wrecks of Republican hopes," declared the New York *World*. This "tremendous overthrow," proclaimed the *New York Herald*, "makes complete the defeat of his plans to make himself the next nominee for the Presidency and places upon a man once President a humiliation such as has never before been known by any one who has essayed the role of national leader of his party." Theodore Roosevelt, the New York *Evening Post* editorialized, is seen as "the chief architect of disaster. He has demonstrated that there are thousands of Republicans who will not vote for him or his nominees or his novel doctrines."

Roosevelt acknowledged that he had experienced "a smashing defeat" in New York, with troubling reverberations across the land. He recognized that he had lost support on all sides of the political spectrum: progressives claimed he had not been radical enough; conservatives charged he was too radical. Westerners condemned his failure to break with the administration, while easterners berated his unwillingness to endorse Taft. The time had come, he understood, for a new leader, "one who has aroused less envenomed hatred," to take up the causes he had championed. "The American people," he reluctantly admitted to William Allen White, "feel a little tired of me."

The decisive routing and overwhelming negative press hit the proud former president hard. On the weekend after the election, the journalist Mark Sullivan called on Roosevelt at Sagamore Hill. When Sullivan rose to leave after a good talk, Roosevelt pleaded: "Don't go. The time will come when only a few friends like you will come out to see me here." Roosevelt was still "in a most depressed state of mind" when Lloyd Griscom stopped by weeks later. "All his old buoyancy was gone," Griscom related to Archie Butt. "He really seemed to him to be a changed man." Regardless of his falling-out with Roosevelt, Taft was deeply affected when Archie shared Griscom's description of Roosevelt's isolation at Oyster Bay. "The American people are strange in their attitudes toward their idols," he mused. They lead them on and then "cut their legs from under them," simply "to make their fall all the greater." Given their former intimacy, he understood how hard it must be for Roosevelt "to feel everything slipping away from him, all the popularity, the power which he loved, and above all the ability to do what he thought was of real benefit to his country."

As president and head of the Republican Party, Taft was, of course, more responsible than anyone else for the magnitude of the Republican loss. "It was not only a landslide," he acknowledged, "but a tidal wave and holocaust all rolled into one general cataclysm." As early as the previous January, he had predicted that the "whole drift" of public sentiment was turning toward the Democrats. "Sooner or later I fear we have got to turn the government over to this element and let it demonstrate its incapacity to govern the country," he reflected, believing that only then would Republicans come back into power. When everyone in his inner circle "took a whack at the Colonel," placing all the blame "for the national disaster" on him, Taft cut the conversation short. "Roosevelt did not help the ticket very much," he said, "but I am inclined to think that even had he remained in Africa the result would have been the same."

Three days after the election, Taft headed for Panama to monitor progress on the building of the Canal. "The warmth of the tropics is in our veins again," Archie noted with delight. The balmy climate led Taft to express a similar release from anxiety: "What difference does it make to a man how Ohio went, when he can look at this scene and feel its warmth? Oh how it takes me back to the Philippines!" At every meal during the trip, Taft told nostalgic anecdotes of his time as governor general. "It is always back to the Philippines he likes to go when he reminisces," Archie observed. "The scenes which he pictures" and the events he describes "seem more real than any of the more recent years here in Washington."

While Taft was away, Roosevelt visited Washington to give a speech about his African safari to the National Geographic Society, inspect the collection of specimens he had sent to the Smithsonian, and meet with old friends. Though he knew the first lady was in New York, he stopped at the White House to pay his respects and leave his calling card. Greeted affectionately by the servants and employees, all of whose names he remembered, he expressed enthusiastic approval of the significant renovations Taft had made to the West Wing.

To accommodate the increased White House staff—which now numbered thirty clerks, in addition to the regular cadre of messengers and security guards—Congress had approved a budget of $40,000 to double the office space from six to twelve rooms. Positioned directly "in the center of the new addition" was a handsome new oval-shaped office for the president, replacing what had been a "severe rectangular room." As the former president entered the new Oval Office, he was informed that he was standing on what had been the site of the tennis court, where he and his playmates had spent many happy hours. "Oh, yes," he said wistfully, "the old tennis court."

The shared sense of loss created by the midterm rout engendered a brief period of rapprochement between Roosevelt and Taft. At Archie Butt's urging, Taft wrote to Roosevelt in November 1910, expressing his regret that he had missed his friend's visit to Washington. If he were coming back for the Gridiron Dinner, he added, "it would gratify me very much if you would come to the White House and stay with me." Roosevelt replied with more warmth than he had shown since his return. "You are a trump to ask me to come to the White House, and I should accept at once if I were going to the Gridiron dinner. But I am not going; I have repeatedly refused." Even while declining the invitation, Roosevelt proceeded to ask Taft about Panama and share his concerns about the California legislature, which was about to pass anti-Japanese legislation.

Taft wrote back the next day detailing the progress on the Canal, which was scheduled for completion in July 1913, at which time both of them would be "private citizens," able to go together to see the work begun by one and finished by the other. Roosevelt replied appreciatively, "I have always felt that the one thing for which I deserved most credit in my entire Administration was my action in seizing the psychological moment to get complete control of Panama. Incidentally, it was one of the things for which I was most attacked." And Taft wrote yet again, sending an advance copy of his annual message and letting Roosevelt know that he had discussed the California situation with his cabinet. "I have read your Message with great interest," Roosevelt replied. "There is nothing for me to say save in the way of agreement and commendation."

This cordial exchange of letters continued through the winter. "I see signs of the clouds which have been hanging over the President and Colonel Roosevelt breaking up," Archie happily observed, knowing that he was responsible for many small gestures that had helped to smooth "the rough edges." On Christmas Day, he showed the president a mahogany settee in the Red Room which Edith Roosevelt had purchased for the White House during her husband's first year as president. Sentimentally attached to the sofa because her children had "kneeled on it to look at the circus parades passing up and down Pennsylvania Avenue," Edith had hoped to take it with her to Sagamore Hill. A government bureaucrat summarily denied her request on the ground that it belonged to the White House. Hearing the story from Archie, Taft had the old sofa shipped to Oyster Bay as a New Year's gift, along with a letter, telling Edith he had purchased a substitute, thus making her old sofa his "to bestow by exchange." Both Theodore and Edith were touched by the thoughtful act. If the small sofa "brings the two families closer together," Archie remarked with his unerring emotional intelligence, "then it will indeed be worth preserving in a museum."

CHAPTER TWENTY-SIX

"Like a War Horse"

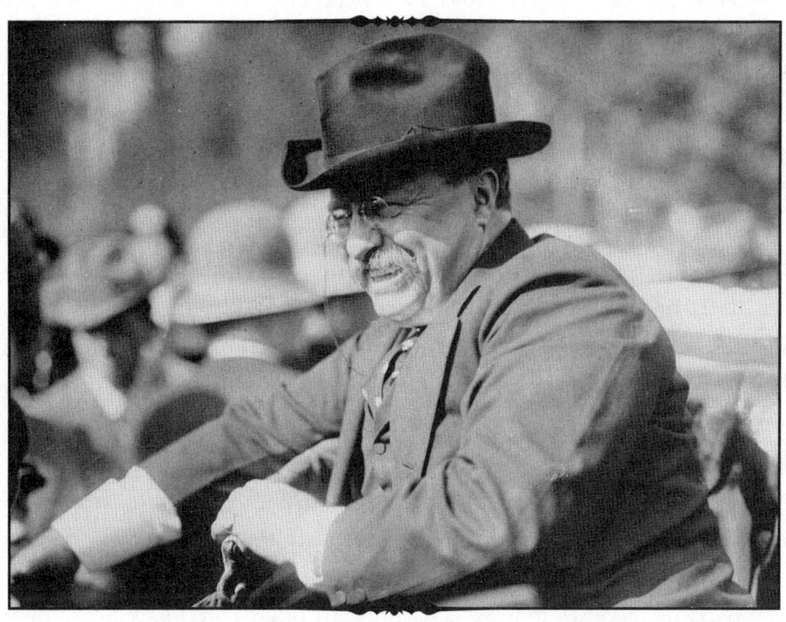

In the winter of 1911, Ray Stannard Baker observed that Roosevelt seemed poised to fight for a third term, "like a war horse beginning to sniff the air of distant battles."

WHILE TAFT AND ROOSEVELT RETREATED to nurse their wounds, Senator La Follette and his dedicated band of insurgents pressed their advantage, confident in their vision for the future of the Republican Party. In states where radicals controlled the nominating slates and platforms, William Allen White pointed out, Republicans had triumphed; in conservative states "where they compromised and pow-wowed and pussy-footed," Republicans had met defeat. "I cannot get Roosevelt to see this," White lamented. "He thinks compromise is the only thing and he is going to be everlastingly crucified by the American people unless he gets this compromise idea out of his head."

On January 21, 1911, La Follette hosted a gathering of progressive leaders at his Washington home. In the prior weeks he had called for the formation of a new organization that would redeem the party and restore popular rule long subverted by the special interests that controlled caucuses, nominating conventions, and the Republican Party organization. The National Progressive League promised to fight for a series of propositions: direct elections of U.S. senators; direct primaries to replace party caucuses; direct election of delegates to the party's national convention; and state constitutional amendments to provide for the initiative, referendum, and recall. The charter membership was impressive—"nine U.S. Senators, six governors and thirteen Congressmen." Nearly every leading progressive spokesman had signed on, including James Garfield, Gifford Pinchot, Louis Brandeis, Ray Baker, and William Allen White. The creation of the national organization spurred numerous states to set up their own Progressive Leagues.

In short order, a Progressive Federation of Publicists and Editors was founded. Its membership list, the *New York Times* remarked, was like "a roll call" of muckraker journalists, including S. S. McClure, Norman Hapgood, George Kibbe Turner, and Lincoln Steffens. La Follette was particularly thrilled to have the support of Lincoln Steffens. After leaving *The American*, the journalist had embarked on a series of disparate projects, among them a study of Boston's city government generously financed by the progressive merchant Edward Filene. A leader of the Good Government Association, Filene had engaged Steffens as "a sort of pathologist" to analyze the historic roots of Boston's corruption. During the two years Steffens lived on Beacon Hill, he had remained in close touch with La Follette. Their correspondence reveals an intimate friendship, different in kind from the mutually advantageous relationship Steffens had forged with Roosevelt. "I am hungry to see you," La Follette had written after a short absence. "How soon can you come to Washington and stay with us for a week?"

Despite their comprehensive reform agenda, the Washington press interpreted the activities of the National Progressive League as "an anti-Taft movement," designed to boost La Follette's prospects for the presidential nomination. "Nothing," the *Springfield Republican* agreed, "could be more reasonable than the supposition that the League will be in the thick of the fight over the Republican presidential nomination of 1912." Observers claimed that La Follette now had "a much larger following in the West than Roosevelt" and that he would be the "decided beneficiary if the Progressive League takes root and advances its schemes for direct nominations and popular government."

Before the inaugural meeting of the National Progressive League, La Follette had tried to enlist Roosevelt as a charter member. "Now, Colonel," La Follette had asked, "can't you consistently give this movement the benefit of your great name and influence?" The two men had never become friends. La Follette considered Roosevelt an opportunist who adapted his positions to accommodate public sentiment, while Roosevelt regarded the Wisconsin senator as "an extremist," with a "touch of fanaticism." Yet at this juncture, both men recognized the value of a show of cordiality. "That is a mighty nice letter of yours," Roosevelt replied, "and I appreciate it to the full." He heartily agreed with the league propositions, the Colonel told La Follette, though he considered them "merely a means and not an end." Nothing in the charter spoke of the economic issues he cared most deeply about—corporate control, the regulation of wealth, or the working conditions of the laboring man. Nevertheless, he intended to give the league his full support, not by joining but by endorsing its principles in *The Outlook*. After the midterm fiasco, he was "very anxious not to seem to take part prominently in any political movement."

On March 8, 1911, Theodore Roosevelt embarked on a six-week train trip through the South and the Southwest that he presumed would be his last extensive speaking tour. He dreaded the daily grind of ceremonies, speeches, and dinners, worrying how he would be received. To friends and family members, Roosevelt claimed he did "not care a rap" about the "fairly universal" criticism directed toward him. "Such a revulsion was bound to come," he said. "The present feeling may wear itself out, or it may not. If it does, and I regain any influence and can use it to good purpose, I shall be glad; and if it does not, I shall be exceedingly happy here in my own home and doing my own work." In any case, he would proceed with his tour, honoring commitments made shortly after his return from Africa.

To Roosevelt's amazed delight, he was met everywhere with crowds as immense and adoring as any he had ever encountered. Eight thousand cheering spectators filled the Armory in Atlanta; 30,000 greeted him in Tacoma, Washington; and the applause from the Minnesota legislature was "as uproarious as in the days of yore." Though he appeared "heavier and slightly grayer," correspondents marveled at his continued ability to withstand rigorous days "without the slightest sign of tiring and without once deviating from the spirit of utmost good humor." Cities vied with one another to honor him. In Spokane, "all traffic was suspended; streetcars were stopped," and "every window, curbstone, cornice and even lofty roofs held their quota of cheering admirers." The Commercial Club in Portland was transformed into an African jungle, complete with live monkeys, parrots, and cockatoos. In Arizona, he formally dedicated the Roosevelt Dam, marking the completion of the immense reclamation project begun during his presidency. "If there could be any monument which would appeal to any man, surely it is this," he declared. "And I thank you from the bottom of my heart for the honor."

As the trip wound to a close, the Washington State *Leavenworth Echo* remarked, Roosevelt's "abiding popularity" would force opponents to revise the "ill-concealed delight" with which they had recently predicted his demise. "To borrow the humor of Mark Twain," the piece continued, "his political death appears to have been very much exaggerated." Indeed, "not another man since the death of Abraham Lincoln could have aroused one-half the popular enthusiasm that his recent trip around the United States created."

ROOSEVELT RETURNED HOME FROM HIS tour to find that the president had engineered a resurgence of his own. For months, Taft had been working quietly on a plan he hoped would convince the American people that despite the complications of the Payne-Aldrich bill, he was a steadfast "low tariff and downward revision man." The previous summer, Taft had initiated negotiations with Canada for a reciprocity agreement that would eliminate or drastically lower tariffs on both sides of the border. In January 1911, negotiators had surprised Washington by announcing a sweeping agreement to be implemented by "concurrent legislation" in Congress and the Canadian Parliament rather than by treaty—requiring a two-thirds vote in the Senate. By providing free trade in agricultural products and reduced tariffs on manufactured goods, the agreement promised to halt the rising cost of living, a major source of public dissatisfaction.

An hour after the old Congress adjourned on March 4, Taft called for the new Congress to meet in special session a month later and consider the reciprocity legislation. Taft liked his chances with the new Congress, which ordinarily would not have convened until December, knowing that Democrats, long opposed to the Republican policy of protectionism, would enjoy a majority in the House and enlarged representation in the Senate. "At one stroke," the monthly periodical *Current Literature* observed, "the Taft administration has altered the whole aspect of political affairs in America, reversed political predictions, confused party ranks and stirred into quick activity industrial and commercial bodies all over the country." And "for the first time since he entered the White House," the writer added, "President Taft now assumes, in the mind of the people, the post of a real leader." No longer "following the lead of President Roosevelt or Senator Aldrich, or Senator La Follette, or any other man," William Taft was "striking out a policy of his own." Expressing similar optimism, the *New York Times* declared that not for a decade had there been such a "well-considered and heroic" break with the "stupid, sordid, greedy" policies of previous administrations. "Beyond all question he has the country behind him."

In contrast to the 1909 tariff fight, the president was clearly unwilling to "sit still and await results." Leaders of the House and Senate were summoned for "breakfast, lunch and dinner." Taft invited a group of ten senators for a "week-end sail" on the luxurious presidential yacht, the *Mayflower*. He composed a series of speeches, setting forth clear arguments for reciprocity. Tariffs were originally designed, he pointed out, to accommodate differences in the cost of production at home and abroad. Yet, between Canada and the United States, "linked together by race, language, political institutions and geographical proximity," there was essentially nothing to equalize. Given this situation, "the productive forces" of both countries should be allowed to operate freely.

Taft adroitly kept Theodore Roosevelt informed at every development, securing his invaluable support. Before he announced the agreement, the president had written a long letter to the Colonel, explaining his reasoning in full. "What you propose to do with Canada is admirable from every standpoint," Roosevelt had replied. "I firmly believe in Free Trade with Canada for both economic and political reasons." While it might "damage the Republican Party for awhile," he continued, it would "surely benefit the party in the end." That spring, Roosevelt "vigorously advocated" the reciprocity legislation in public speeches as well as private correspondence. Beyond the economic advantages, he argued, "it should always be a cardinal point in our foreign policy to establish the closest and most friendly relations of equal respect and advantage with our great neighbor on the North."

When debate opened in the House and Senate, Taft told Charley, he "expected the insurgents not only to support the bill but to claim that I was only trailing after them, and coming to their view." Lower tariffs had been the insurgents' rallying cry. Their passionate opposition to the Payne-Aldrich bill had launched them to national prominence: "Give us something," they had repeatedly argued, "which will decrease the cost of living and save the poor from starvation." The reciprocity agreement promised to address this underlying issue, but it placed the progressives in a serious, unanticipated bind. The majority of insurgents came from midwestern agricultural states. While public sentiment overwhelmingly favored reciprocity, farmers were among the special interests passionately opposed, fearing that free admission of Canada's agricultural products would reduce the demand for food products at home. Unwilling to antagonize their constituents, the insurgents led the attack against the bill.

The adage "politics makes strange bedfellows" was never more clearly illustrated than in the curious alliance that coupled insurgents with conservative "standpatters," who viewed reciprocity as the compromising breach in "the entire citadel of protection." The independent press, which had long admired the fighting spirit of the insurgents, now charged them with hypocrisy. "Washington grows weary of the insurgents," the *National Herald* declared. "This is something more than inconsistency." The "valiant little insurgent band" had shown themselves just "as selfish" as the Old Guard. Many of the derogatory comments were directed at Robert La Follette, who announced his candidacy for the Republican nomination in the midst of the reciprocity struggle. As the Wisconsin senator repeatedly sought to delay consideration of the popular bill, he was denounced for "trying to manufacture an issue for the Presidential campaign."

On April 21, 1911, the House passed a comprehensive reciprocity bill with strong Democratic support. Two months later, the Senate followed suit. Taft was thrilled, believing the legislation would signal the arrival of "a great epoch" for the country. The *Washington Times* agreed. "Today will be an important date in tariff history," the paper remarked; tariff duties, having reached their high point, would finally "descend on the other side." After the vote, Taft "extended his formal thanks to the Democrats," acknowledging that without their aid, "reciprocity would have been impossible."

Meanwhile, discussion of the legislation in the Canadian Parliament had descended into "hysteria." Conservative opponents issued dire warnings that reciprocity would inevitably lead to Canada's annexation by the United States. During the struggle in Congress, opponents had deliberately raised the specter of takeover, going so far as to introduce a resolution calling for negotiations to begin. Taft immediately reassured Canadian officials that no one in the administration had any thought of annexation. "Canada is now and will remain a political unit," he declared. Roosevelt underscored the president's efforts with an emphatic attack on the "bad faith" and "mean spirit" of those members of Congress who "sought to bar the path" to reciprocity by "pretending to look towards the annexation of Canada." With the Canadian debate spinning out of control, Liberal prime minister Sir Wilfrid Laurier decided to dissolve Parliament and take the case for reciprocity to the people in a September election. The great majority of Canadians, he believed, appreciated the tremendous economic advantages reciprocity would bring.

Taft's success with reciprocity had significantly altered the political landscape. The president "has gained remarkably in public estimation," one editorial observed, while "the insurgents have sagged steadily." Taft further consolidated his position when he offered to bring Henry Stimson into his cabinet as secretary of war. Stimson sought advice from Roosevelt, who "strongly urged" him to take the post and do everything possible to help the president. "If two years ago [Taft] had done some of the things he has done now, he would probably have saved himself from nine tenths of the blunders he has made," Roosevelt remarked. Nevertheless, the Colonel had no intention of supporting Taft or anyone else for the nomination. Henceforth, he intended to keep "as much aloof from politics as possible."

WILL AND NELLIE WOULD LATER look back on June 19, 1911, as the happiest day of their White House years. Nellie had never forgotten the sense of wonder she experienced as a sixteen-year-old when she accompanied her parents to Washington for the elaborate festivities surrounding the silver wedding anniversary of Rutherford and Lucy Hayes. As her own silver anniversary approached that June, she began to coordinate an equally grand party that "would be remembered through life by all who were fortunate enough to be present."

The mansion and the gardens would be illuminated with 10,000 colored lights and hundreds of Japanese lanterns. Spotlights were positioned on the nearby rooftops to beam down on the fountains and the lawns. Weather permitting, the reception would be held on the South Lawn, followed by dinner and dancing in the East Room. Invitations were sent to all the members of official Washington: the cabinet, members of Congress, Army and Navy officers, the diplomatic corps, and many other distinguished guests. To give the affair "a unique distinction," Nellie invited the relatives of all former presidents—including kinsmen of Abraham Lincoln, Ulysses S. Grant, James Garfield, Grover Cleveland, Benjamin Harrison, and Theodore Roosevelt. All told, 5,000 invitations were issued.

On May 11, five weeks before the grand event, Nellie and Will went to New York to attend a banquet at the Hotel Astor. Watching over Nellie as Taft spoke, Butt noted how much her health seemed improved, "how truly pretty she was." After the dinner, the president and first lady, accompanied by the newly promoted Major Butt, went to Harry and Julia Taft's apartment, where they planned to spend the night. "For nearly an hour," Butt recalled, they enjoyed "Scotch and soda" and pleasant conversation before retiring. In the middle of the night, Archie heard Taft's voice in the hallway, shouting for help.

Nellie had suffered another stroke, "similar to the first one" though "less severe." Once again, she was unable "to articulate clearly or to find her words," Helen told her brother. Though her slow, hard-won progress was wiped away and "the defect in her speech" made her shrink from seeing anyone outside her family, Nellie refused to stay in bed. News that the first lady had "suffered a serious breakdown" brought "genuine regret and sympathy" from people across the country, along with speculation that the anniversary party would be canceled.

Determined to realize her dream, Nellie spent hours each day practicing a series of stock phrases she could use for the receiving line. She found the perfect dress for the occasion—a heavy white satin gown embroidered with silver flowers, fitted for her slender figure. Should the weather prove inclement, she outlined plans to move the entire party indoors. The president, too, was obsessed with "every detail," walking through the mansion and the grounds day after day to ensure that everything was "finished on time."

At 9 p.m., buglers trumpeted the start of the grand march, officially opening the anniversary celebration. Preceded by dozens of military aides clad in "immaculate white" and followed by the members of the cabinet, the president and first lady walked down the stairway to the sounds of Mendelssohn's "Wedding March." "A mighty shout went up" as they passed, a correspondent reported. "President Taft smiled and dimpled and bowed, and Mrs. Taft smiled and bowed, and everybody smiled." The applause continued as the couple made their way to the enclosed arbor, where Archie Butt stood ready to present each of the 5,000 guests to the president and first lady. Nineteen-year-old Helen remained close by, ready to take her mother's place at the first sign of trouble, but Nellie stayed on the receiving line until "the last hand was shaken."

Finally, Taft escorted the first lady to the mansion, where she relaxed on the portico to watch the dancing in the East Room while he returned to the garden. The president "skipped lightly from group to group," a Washington correspondent observed, "bringing personal messages of hospitality, enjoying himself to the fullest." He expressed his pride in Nellie's fortitude to all. She had stayed by his side "from start to finish," despite his repeated efforts "to make her sit down and save her strength." It appeared she thoroughly enjoyed herself, and that, above all, made him "happy as a boy."

THE PRESS TOOK NOTICE OF the conspicuous absence of Theodore and Edith Roosevelt at the silver anniversary party. Two weeks earlier, when Taft and Roosevelt attended the Jubilee celebration for Baltimore's Cardinal Gibbons, no hint of discord was evident as the two old friends "chatted, laughed and behaved just as they used to when Mr. Roosevelt was in the White House and Mr. Taft was Secretary of War." Roosevelt had promised they would try to attend the anniversary party, but at the last minute he declined. In the interim, a troubling incident had intervened, bringing an end to the temporary period of rapprochement between the two men. Elaborating on the visible rapport at Baltimore, "misguided friends" of the president had inspired an Associated Press story suggesting that Roosevelt had finally decided to endorse Taft, having determined that "under no circumstance" would he allow his own name to go before the convention. A "mutual friend" of both men had purportedly brought word of Roosevelt's endorsement to the White House. "This is the best political news Mr. Taft has received in many months," remarked the *Hartford Herald*, "and it comes to him in a manner that leaves no doubt as to its authenticity."

Asked to "affirm or deny" the report, Roosevelt simply answered, "I have made no such statement to the Associated Press or any paper. That is all I have to say." Taft's supporters hoped he would leave it at that, but as the hours went by, the Colonel became increasingly irritated. This was "too much like a repetition" of the New Haven incident, where he had been put in the embarrassing position of seeming to beg for Taft's aid. In his next go-round with the press, he flatly labeled the endorsement report "an unqualified falsehood." Still angry a week later, Roosevelt wrote to the editor of the Philadelphia *North American*. "It was outrageous for the Associated Press to fake that statement," he insisted. These vehement denials, the *Chicago Daily Tribune* declared, "threw a bombshell in political circles." While the disclaimer was "hailed with jubilation by the progressives," it engendered "considerable chagrin" among Taft's friends.

Resentment between the two men deepened later that summer when Roosevelt came out in striking public opposition to a peace project Taft had carefully developed. On August 4, after months of negotiation, representatives from the United States, England, and France gathered in the Oval Office to sign a comprehensive arbitration treaty. They had forged an agreement that every contentious issue that might arise, even those matters relating to national honor, would be "subject to arbitration." Taft believed that if the treaty emerged relatively intact from the Senate, it would be "the great jewel" of his administration, "the greatest act" of his tenure as president.

"The ideal to which we are all working," he declared, "is the ultimate establishment of an arbitral court to which we shall submit our international controversies with the same freedom and the same dependence on the judgment as in the case of domestic courts." No longer would "the interests of the great masses" be sacrificed to "the intrigues of statesmen unwilling to surrender their scepter of power." While he would never "minimize" the debt owed to the nation's soldiers, "when the books are balanced, the awful horrors" of war "far outweigh the benefits that may be traced to it." As the photographer prepared to capture the historic signing, Archie Butt deftly rearranged the president's desk so that a large photo of Nellie would be visible. "She meant so much in his life at all crucial times that I wanted her represented at this scene," Archie wrote.

Even before the treaty was signed, Roosevelt had positioned himself against the idea that countries could arbitrate questions of national honor. "No self-respecting nation," he wrote in *The Outlook*, "no nation worth calling a nation, would ever in actual practice consent to surrender its rights in such matters." Acquiescence, he maintained, would be tantamount to watching a man slap your wife and then depending upon an arbitrator to settle the matter. Archie Butt was "greatly disappointed" with Roosevelt's article. He considered the analogy puerile, "unworthy" of the man he revered. "For the first time," in discussion with Taft, he openly criticized his "old chief." Roosevelt had not yet exhausted his strident proclamations, however. When the president of the National Rifle Association wrote a scathing editorial criticizing Taft's "mushy" concern with "the horrors of war," Roosevelt expressed wholehearted approval. Roosevelt particularly savored the line which claimed that "death was not a dreadful thing. To me there is something unspeakably humiliating and degrading in the way in which men have grown to speak in the name of humanity of death as the worst of all possible evils. No man is fit to live," he asserted, "unless he is ready to quit life for adequate cause."

That September, as the Senate continued to debate the treaty, Roosevelt published a second article on the subject in *The Outlook*. "It is one of our prime duties as a nation to seek peace. It is an even higher duty to seek righteousness," he began. After detailing the treaty's numerous defects, he concluded that "there are some questions of national policy and conduct which no nation can submit to the decision of any one else." A president's willingness to countenance such outside arbitration "would be proof positive that he was not fit to hold the exalted position to which he had been elected."

Taft was not surprised by Roosevelt's bellicose attitude. "I am afraid the old fellow has made a grave mistake in this," he told Butt. "The fact of the matter is, Archie, the Colonel is not in favor of peace. He thinks that there are many worse things than wars, and he thinks war and a warlike spirit keeps up the virility of a people. He's a fighter, and he doesn't believe in peace."

ON SEPTEMBER 15, AFTER CELEBRATING his fifty-fourth birthday with Nellie at the summer house in Beverly, President Taft boarded a special train to begin a two-month swing through the West. "The White House is once more on wheels," the *New York Tribune* reported. "The official address of the nation's head has again become 'Pres. Taft, en route.' " The presidential train was equipped with "every comfort that modern transportation by rail affords," including bathtubs, dining cars, drawing rooms, and "real beds" rather than conventional bunks. Though Taft likened delivering speeches to "taking medicine or standing a surgical operation," he had worked hard to prepare a series of talks on the major issues of the day, including peace and arbitration, the Tariff Board, conservation, the trusts, and reciprocity.

The first week of the trip proceeded smoothly. At the state fair in Syracuse, New York, he was greeted with "bright skies and a holiday crowd." At every stop in Pennsylvania and Michigan, people approached him with eager smiles. Even those "thought to be unfriendly" listened with respect to his speeches. "Go ahead, old man," they seemed to say. "We're going to see to it that you get a square deal." It comforted Taft that his speeches were "reported in full" in the papers of every city, allowing him to put his "case before the people."

As September 21 approached—the date on which the Canadian election would determine the fate of the reciprocity agreement—an anxious mood enveloped the train. "The bets seem to be so strongly in favor," Horace told his brother, "but the election has been so extraordinary and seems to have roused the people so deeply that it is hard to feel sure of anything." On the evening before the vote, Montreal was reportedly "ablaze with red fire and patriotism; alive with cheering thousands, and echoing with the oratory of the opposing hosts."

At a banquet in Kalamazoo, Taft was handed a telegram with the dismal results: "Laurier government and reciprocity beaten." By "an overwhelming majority," Canadians had thrown the Liberal government out of office. Pundits were "dumbfounded"; analysts concluded that the verdict was against "the bogey of annexation" rather than an actual "unfriendliness to reciprocity." The idea of "an Imperishable Canada" had won the day for the Conservative Party, leaving the prospect of free trade "dead as a ducat." The result was difficult for Taft to absorb. "We were hit squarely between the eyes," the president acknowledged. "I am very greatly disappointed." The extra session was "for naught," the *National Tribune* observed. After "toiling up the hill . . . we are back where we started, and possibly a little worse off." The New York *Evening Post* judged the outcome "a terrible blow" for Taft, perhaps "a fatal hurt." The *Boston Traveler* wryly observed that "it was very unkind of those Canadians to deprive President Taft of his best argument for reelection just when he needed it most."

Taft remained disconsolate for days, though he gamely pushed on with his impossible schedule, eventually covering twenty-eight states, making two hundred stops, and delivering nearly four hundred speeches. In Archie Butt's estimation, Taft's peace and arbitration talks, designed to spur public demand for the Senate to pass the treaties, were "by all odds" his best and most successful. Yet, even as his passionate appeals reached audiences, the Senate was busily crafting amendments to render the treaties impotent.

The rest of Taft's speeches, "dry and full of statistics," were not well received. Crowds often drifted off before he finished. "As I see him sometimes laboring to interest an audience and failing to do so," Butt lamented, "I feel so sorry for him I could almost cry." Correspondents generally deemed the trip a failure. And while people came "to see him and hear his voice," there was "no sign" that public opinion had shifted in his direction. "The Taft trip has proved," William Allen White proclaimed, "that he cannot regain the people's confidence, that he cannot know their language, and that he cannot hold their allegiance."

During the dispiriting days on his tour, Taft found comfort in food; by the time he returned home, he weighed 332 pounds. Butt worried constantly about the state of the president's health. His tendency to fall asleep during carriage rides or even in the midst of conversations had markedly increased. In church, where long sermons provoked drowsiness, Butt kept a watchful eye. If he saw the president's head beginning to nod, Butt would fall into a coughing spell to wake him up. Such discretion was not always possible; on one occasion, Butt recorded, "I had not suspected that he was falling asleep until I heard an audible snore, and then I punched him, and he woke with such a start as to attract the attention of everybody around him." After returning to the White House, Taft acknowledged to Aunt Delia that he was "too heavy," and intended to begin a new diet. "You will see I am not very ambitious," he confessed, "when I say that I shall be entirely satisfied if I can get down to three hundred pounds."

Roosevelt delivered a harsh assessment of the president's tour. "I absolutely agree with everything you have written about poor Taft," he told California's progressive governor Hiram Johnson in late October. "When he started on this trip I still had some flickering hope that when he got out into the West, among the people who are heading the new movement . . . he would become infected with the spirit and would rise to a higher level than that on which he has carried on his presidency, but I am afraid it simply is not in him." Taft's problem, Roosevelt elaborated, was not that he had "gone wrong," but that he had stayed put while the country was moving ahead. "He never thinks at all of the things that interest us most," Roosevelt continued; "he does not appreciate or understand them." While he had been an exemplary lieutenant, serving the public well as governor general of the Philippines and as secretary of war, he appeared oblivious to the monumental changes taking place in his own country. "As for my ever having any enthusiasm for Taft again, it is utterly impossible," Roosevelt concluded. Nonetheless, "I shall support him if nominated because I do not believe that there is any ground for permanent hope in the Democratic Party."

The train of events that altered Roosevelt's perspective about the nomination began on October 27, his fifty-third birthday. Banner headlines across the country that day announced the Taft administration's anti-trust suit against the U.S. Steel Corporation, its allied holdings, and its officials, including J. P. Morgan, John D. Rockefeller, Andrew Carnegie, Judge Gary, George Perkins, and Henry Frick. Labeling U.S. Steel "a gigantic monopoly, acting illegally in restraint of trade, and attempting to stifle competition," the Justice Department sought "the dissolution" of the corporation's seventeen "constituent companies" and its twenty "subsidiaries." Citing a history of illegal actions, the government focused particularly on the acquisition of Tennessee Coal and Iron Company—the transaction President Roosevelt had sanctioned during the Panic of 1907. If the president had understood the facts of the situation, the petition read, he would have understood "that a desire to stop the panic was not the sole moving cause, but that there was also the desire and purpose to acquire control of a company that had recently assumed a position of potential competition of great significance."

This reference to the former president's decision generated a series of unflattering bylines: "Roosevelt Was Deceived"; "Roosevelt Fooled"; "Ignorance as a Defense." In essence, the *Philadelphia Record* observed, Roosevelt had "been named as a co-respondent in the Government's suit to divorce the Steel Corporation and Tennessee Iron. He cannot be indicted and fined; he cannot be enjoined and dissolved. But all the same he is on the defensive and on trial, and he is smarting as he has seldom smarted before. . . . Mr. Taft has kicked him on the shins and hustled him into the witness box for cross-examination." For those convinced that Roosevelt had exceeded his authority and facilitated an illegal merger, the government's brief promised vindication: "This is an official statement," the *St. Louis Post-Dispatch* rejoiced, "that, as president, Theodore Roosevelt was concerned in a lawless act."

Roosevelt was livid. "What I did was right," he truculently declared to a New York lawyer. "I would not only do it again under like conditions if I had the power, but I should esteem myself recreant to my duty if I failed to do it again." At the time, the crisis had spread rapidly and was threatening to destabilize the entire economy. "It was not a question of saving any bank or trust company from failure," he insisted; "the question was of saving the plain people, the common people, in all parts of the United States from dreadful misery and suffering; and this was what my action did." Moreover, the government's implication that he "was misled" by inaccurate facts was simply "not correct." The steel men had told "the truth" when they explained that the acquisition of Tennessee Coal would not produce a monopoly. U.S. Steel was not a monopoly then, nor was it one now. Indeed, Roosevelt pointed out, the market share controlled by U.S. Steel in 1911 was less that it had been in 1907.

The Colonel was particularly infuriated by the perceived hypocrisy of his successor. "Taft was a member of my cabinet when I took that action," he stressed. "We went over it in full and in detail, not only at one but at two or three meetings. He was enthusiastic in his praise of what was done." Any objections "should have been made instantly, or else from every consideration of honorable obligation never under any circumstances afterwards." While Taft might not have personally perused the final brief that cited Roosevelt's action, the Colonel's "own conception of the office of President is that he is responsible for every action of importance that his subordinates take." Roosevelt told his sister Corinne he could "never forgive" Taft for allowing this injustice. That it had "been done without his knowledge" was "the worst feature of the case."

Never content to remain in a defensive position, Roosevelt used the incident to launch a searing attack on the administration's entire anti-trust policy. During his three years in office, Taft had actually instituted more anti-trust suits than his predecessor. The Steel Corporation was simply the latest in a long series of enterprises—including the Electrical Trust, the Bath-Tub Trust, and the Tobacco Trust—that had "felt the heavy hand of the Government laid upon them." With Taft's wholehearted support, Attorney General Wickersham had "embarked upon a regular program of prosecutions and dissolutions and reorganizations." The Department of Justice had become a "juggernaut rolling over the trusts," winning one case after another. Earlier that fall, Wickersham had predicted that "probably one hundred additional corporations would be called to account under the Sherman Act, that their guilty officials would go to jail."

Though Roosevelt had gained great popularity as the nation's "trust-buster," Taft found himself the subject of constant criticism for pursuing the same objective. "The times have changed," one newspaper observed. Public expectation had moved beyond "old fashioned" trust busting, preferring government regulation designed to prevent the formation of monopolies in the first place. Litigation after the fact took on an aura of mean-spirited persecution. Roosevelt's indictment of Taft's anti-trust policy was perfectly timed to catch the shifting current in public opinion.

During his first years in the White House, Roosevelt explained in his *Outlook* article, corporations had viewed the Anti-Trust Law and the Interstate Commerce laws as "dead letters." He had instituted suits against Northern Securities and Standard Oil "because it was imperative to teach the masters of the biggest corporations" that they "would not be permitted to regard themselves as above the law." And when these corporations were truly "guilty of misconduct," these suits resulted in "a real and great good." He had never proceeded against corporations simply because they were big, but on evidence of "unfair practices." Moreover, he had expanded regulatory powers for the Bureau of Corporations as a better solution.

The Taft administration, by contrast, he argued, was apparently determined "to break up all combinations merely because they are large and successful." An endless "succession of lawsuits" threatened "to put the business of the country back into the middle of the eighteenth century." The "sharp practice" of corporate lawyers would inevitably delay decisions for years, ensuring insufficient punishment for the guilty and substantial harm to "the innocent." The job of controlling monopolies belonged to the federal executive, not the courts.

Roosevelt's first significant attack on the president made headlines: "Taft Wrong, Says Roosevelt"; "Colonel Finds Taft Policy Bad"; "Roosevelt Takes Issue with Taft." The entire edition of *The Outlook* immediately sold out and the publisher reprinted "tens of thousands" of copies to meet the overwhelming demand. "Roosevelt's broadside was the only topic of discussion today," reported the *Chicago Daily Tribune*. Progressive Republicans were thrilled that Roosevelt had finally declared publicly against Taft. More conservative Republicans, frightened by the Osawatomie speech, found comfort in the Colonel's carefully reasoned position on trusts. The *New York Times* reported "a striking revival of Roosevelt talk," and the *National Tribune* told of "a thousand questions" raised concerning his availability as a candidate. Roosevelt himself later credited the trust article for "bringing [him] forward for the Presidential nomination." The turbulence surrounding this piece, he believed, had lifted "a strong undercurrent of feeling" for him "to the surface."

In late November and early December 1911, public excitement for Roosevelt's candidacy began to develop "in an almost astonishing fashion." A poll taken by three leading Ohio papers revealed that of more than 16,000 Republican voters questioned, nearly three out of four supported Roosevelt, with the remaining votes scattered between Taft and La Follette. Nebraska Republicans announced that Roosevelt's name would be included on their presidential primary ballot. "Events in all parts of the country," a Pennsylvania paper observed, "point to a growing and irresistible demand on the part of his countrymen that Colonel Roosevelt again enter public life."

Though Roosevelt coyly continued to disclaim any intention of candidacy, his refusal to issue "a flat-footed denial" kept his name everywhere in contention. His sudden resurgence produced "anxious days" for La Follette, whose campaign was finally gathering steam. Earlier that fall, *The American Magazine* had begun publishing a ten-part series by the Wisconsin senator entitled "The Autobiography of an Insurgent." Written with the assistance of Ray Baker, the series proved immensely popular, generating support for both progressivism and its most notable champion. In mid-October, a Progressive Conference in Chicago had given La Follette its "almost unanimous" endorsement for president. At an Insurgents' Club dinner that fall, Gifford Pinchot had enthusiastically come out for La Follette, labeling him "the logical successor to Roosevelt." The mere mention of the senator's name had provoked "loud and prolonged applause." Yet, so long as Roosevelt's candidacy remained a possibility, however remote, La Follette found it challenging to raise funds or build a national organization.

On November 26, Ray Baker joined a small group of La Follette supporters for a dinner meeting at the senator's Washington home. "Will Roosevelt be a candidate? That is the great question," Baker recorded in his journal. If Roosevelt did run, Baker acknowledged, he would draw away much of La Follette's following, though the senator was "bearing the heavy brunt & toil of the work of making the progressive campaign." They would have to reach some resolution, for if both men "split the progressive vote," Taft might well "slip in." John Phillips was concerned that Roosevelt was playing a deft political game by "encouraging La Follette and the Progressives" with the idea of eventually moving in "and appropriating the goods." Conceding that Roosevelt remained one of the most "extraordinary, vital and energetic" people he had ever known, Phillips nonetheless considered Roosevelt's candidacy a powerful "setback for the Progressive or Liberal Movement."

Two weeks later, Baker traveled to New York to sound out the Colonel. Roosevelt still insisted that he was not a candidate, but he seemed to Baker "like a war horse beginning to sniff the air of distant battles." Roosevelt revealed "with evident delight" that two delegations, one from New Hampshire and the other from Ohio, had recently come to visit. Both were unhappy with Taft, but neither was prepared to support La Follette. Unless Roosevelt decided to run, both delegations would end up backing Taft. The conversation between Baker and Roosevelt continued as they walked from the *Outlook* office to the Long Island train station. "Fully a third of the people we met in the hurrying crowds," the journalist remarked, "recognized him & turned toward him or whispered to their companions." Roosevelt kept moving forward, shouldering his way through the crowded streets "as if he were in a football scrimmage." In parting, Baker reminded Roosevelt that the first presidential primaries were three months away. "Come to see me again in January," Roosevelt responded. Their conversation left it "absolutely plain" to Baker that "if the demand is loud and long enough, and if the prospects seem right . . . he will certainly jump into the game."

That same week, after lunching with her father at Oyster Bay, Alice Longworth carried a cryptic message to Archie Butt. "Now, Butt," Alice began, "you know that we are all devoted to you. Father looks upon you as a son, almost. Certainly I have never known him to be fonder of anyone outside his own family than he is of you, so you must understand what he meant when he told me to give you this message." Then she hesitated, afraid that Archie would not want to hear her out, but the major insisted she continue. "Alice, when you get the opportunity," Roosevelt had requested of his daughter, "tell Archie from me to get out of his present job. And not to wait for the convention or election, but do it soon."

CHAPTER TWENTY-SEVEN

"My Hat Is in the Ring"

In this Feb. 1912 cartoon, Roosevelt's hat dwarfs all the others tossed in the "Presidential Ring."

"THE COLONEL IS MUSSING UP the whole Progressive situation with his 'To be or not to be,' " fretted Lincoln Steffens in January 1912. "He won't make a statement. He talks to us privately, but not convincingly; at least not to all of us," he wrote to a friend, resolving that in all probability, Roosevelt "simply isn't clear himself. He's undecided; wabbles and, of course, the Taft side makes the most of it. La Follette is bully. He is for the cause, not himself, and wants to act, at once, and in the best interest of ultimate results." In truth, Roosevelt was far closer to a decision than Steffens realized. Continuing to insist that he would neither "seek the nomination" nor take a single step to secure it, Roosevelt softened his tone and told supporters that if "a genuine popular demand" for his nomination indicated conviction that he was "the man to do the job," he would "of course" accept.

"Events have been moving fast," Roosevelt told Michigan governor Chase Osborn in mid-January, noting that "it is impossible for me much longer to remain silent." Osborn was among more than half a dozen governors who were strongly urging him to run. In response, Roosevelt told Osborn he had come up with a plan: If the governors who had privately encouraged him would sign a joint public letter declaring their desire for him to run, he would answer their demand with an announcement of his candidacy. Roosevelt delegated the task of drafting the letter to Frank Knox, chairman of Michigan's state central committee; after the Colonel added several lines emphasizing that the governors were acting "not for his sake, but for the sake of the country," Knox was dispatched to secure the signatures.

Meanwhile, Roosevelt's friends began working surreptitiously to undermine La Follette's campaign. A convention of Ohio progressives, expected to endorse La Follette, decided on a last-minute substitute resolution that pronounced the Wisconsin senator "the living embodiment of progressive principles," but declined to express a preference "for a single candidate." La Follette was furious at his campaign manager for agreeing to the compromise.

On the night of January 22, La Follette spoke at Carnegie Hall before an overflow audience; crowds lining the streets had waited hours for the doors to open. "Carnegie Hall never held a bigger nor a more enthusiastic audience," the *New York Times* reported. Seated on the platform were more than two hundred Insurgents' Club members, including Gifford and Amos Pinchot, Ray Baker, Lincoln Steffens, and Francis Heney. The passionate orator "got on good terms with the audience at once and never lost it," the New York *World* observed. Afterward, a group of La Follette's friends gathered at the Plaza Hotel for dinner. The celebratory mood quickly dissipated when the conversation turned to Theodore Roosevelt. Earlier that day, the Pinchot brothers had gone to see the former president and were now convinced that the Colonel would run. They worried that if La Follette remained in the race, the two men would divide the progressive vote. William Allen White had already switched his allegiance to Roosevelt, arguing in the *Emporia Gazette* that only the former president could save the Republicans from massive defeat. "Roosevelt or bust!" he proclaimed. Perhaps the time had come, La Follette's friends suggested, for him to withdraw.

The senator could no longer suppress his rage that Roosevelt had been using him as "a stalking horse" all along, testing President Taft's political strength. "When Roosevelt left the White House," La Follette charged, "he had 1916 firmly in his mind." Yet the wild reception as the Colonel toured the country had "fired his blood. There were the old-time crowds, the music, the cheers. He began to think of 1912 for himself. It was four years better than 1916." Regardless of Roosevelt's ambitions, La Follette insisted, he would continue his own campaign.

A week later, during a "painful" conference at the senator's Washington home, the Pinchots redoubled their efforts to persuade La Follette to end his candidacy. The Pinchot brothers were among his most fervent supporters before Roosevelt's name surfaced, and La Follette viewed their entreaties as a bitter betrayal. He told them he would persevere, even if he had to "fight alone," even if he carried only Wisconsin. "When I gave my ultimatum, refusing to abandon the field," La Follette later said, "Gifford Pinchot left my house and never crossed the threshold again." The next morning, La Follette ordered his manager to release a statement: "Senator La Follette never has been and is not now a quitter," the communiqué read, concluding, "He will be there until the gavel falls in the convention announcing the nominee."

For La Follette, trouble soon piled on trouble. Although mentally and physically exhausted, he was scheduled to speak on February 2 in Philadelphia at the annual banquet of the Periodical Publishers' Association. There, he would join an impressive roster of speakers, including New Jersey's new governor Woodrow Wilson, California governor Hiram Johnson, and Philadelphia mayor Rudolph Blankenburg. But five days before the event, doctors diagnosed his thirteen-year-old daughter with tuberculosis in three glands near her jugular vein. An operation to cut off the affected tissue was scheduled for the morning after the banquet. La Follette considered withdrawing from the engagement but feared his failure to show would signal an intention to withdraw from the race.

La Follette arrived late, set to give the banquet's closing speech. Wilson had earlier delivered the evening's best speech, humorous, charming, and short. Before taking the stage at ten o'clock that night, La Follette "took a great gobletful of whiskey and swallowed it neat, as a stimulant." He had prepared a provocative message for the magazine publishers—a warning that the same "money power" that had gained domination over the newspaper industry in recent decades was now threatening to corrupt independent periodicals through "the centralization of advertising." After their staunch efforts to illuminate corruption, he trusted they would "not be found wanting" before this "final test." They alone promised "to hold aloft the lamp of truth, lighting the way for the preservation of representative government."

Had La Follette focused his speech solely on this challenge to magazine journalists, he might have found an appreciative audience; instead, he began with a long historical lecture on how corporate interests had seized control of the newspapers, reducing journalists to hirelings "who no longer express honest judgments and sincere conviction," writing only "what they are told to write." La Follette encountered a response significantly less sympathetic than he might have hoped. In the enervating days preceding the banquet, he had neglected to inquire about the composition of the audience of eight hundred people. This particular annual dinner had been specifically calculated "to bring together the newspaper and magazine publishers." For the first time, newspapermen made up a significant portion of the guests.

La Follette immediately alienated his listeners by announcing that he would read his speech and give it out for publication, since he was "frankly sick of being eternally misquoted." His voice grew "acid and raucous" as he berated the newspapermen as instruments of the "predatory interests." Dumbfounded at first, the audience quickly grew angry. Scores of newspapermen simply rose and left. La Follette "shook his fist at them," roaring: "There go some of the fellows I'm hitting. They don't want to hear about themselves." When another guest leaned over to whisper a comment to his neighbor, the senator pointed "his dagger-like forefinger" at the man, accusing him of accepting bribes from the trust, and hollered: "You've got to listen to me and hear the facts for once!" Attempting to return to his text after each of these fiery outbursts, La Follette repeatedly lost his place, rereading long passages he had already read. During the first two hours, he repeated one section seven times.

As midnight approached, La Follette's secretary, seated directly behind him, desperately tried to get him to stop. Increasing numbers left the room, and those who remained began to applaud with contempt, in hopes of bringing the interminable harangue to an end. "You can't drown me out!" he defiantly shouted, threatening with renewed belligerence, "If you don't shut up and listen I'll talk all night!" By the end of the ordeal, the *New York Times* reporter sardonically noted, he "was denouncing the empty chairs" and "calling the abandoned cups and cigar stubs minions of the trust." At twelve-thirty he collapsed in his chair, "with closed eyes and his chin sunk on his chest."

This humiliating episode was heartbreaking to Baker. He had expected La Follette to deliver "the greatest speech of his career—the speech with which he hoped to win the East." Instead, the gifted orator had utterly lost control of himself and his emotions. "To those of us who were there and who were La Follette's friends," Baker grimly recalled, "it was a tragedy beyond tears."

Rumors circulated that La Follette had suffered a nervous breakdown and headed for a sanitarium. Dispirited and exhausted, he was nevertheless not only able to attend his daughter's operation the following morning but also, after "a short rest," return to the Senate. The damage to his campaign, however, proved irreparable. As he later acknowledged, his supposedly "shattered health" provided a pretext for hundreds of his supporters who wanted to "switch to Roosevelt" but would have felt guilty doing so. In a dramatic statement that captured headlines, Gifford Pinchot announced that he was abandoning La Follette, whose "ill health" compromised the progressive cause. "I shall," he declared, "hereafter advocate the nomination of Colonel Roosevelt, whose duty I believe it is to take up the leadership of the progressive movement."

As La Follette and his wife, Belle, endured the gloomy days that followed, a gracious letter from Sam McClure provided a singular bright spot. "I want to let you know how much I sympathize with you and the Senator," McClure assured Belle, adding that he had "listened with eager interest to all that he said." Indeed, *McClure's* had recently published a seven-part series, the "last great series" Sam McClure would publish, exploring the increasing "concentration of capital in the hands of a few men" on Wall Street—the very "money power" theme at the center of La Follette's botched address.

The senator's speech, McClure told Mrs. La Follette, had simply started too late and lasted too long, preventing the crowd from giving it the "justice" it deserved. "Your letter," Belle replied, "was very helpful to me, and to Mr. La Follette." At its core, the speech had a powerful message, but her husband had been unable to deliver it due to his overwrought emotions. "I think in his state of over strain and exhaustion," she explained, "the hostility he felt in his audience must have caused him to lose all self possession. Of course, he realizes what it means and suffers accordingly . . . I shall always remember your kindness and think of you as a friend."

"Poor Senator La Follette," Roosevelt wrote to his publicity chief, newspaperman John Callan O'Laughlin, after the debacle, attempting to justify his own late entrance into the race. "It is perfectly silly of him to feel hurt at me, and I wish you could bring out the fact that I have done absolutely nothing, that if ever there was a perfectly spontaneous and genuinely popular movement, this has been one . . . each and every one of [the governors] wrote to me out of a clear sky, saying that he was for me. Between ourselves, in more than one case I did not even know the Governor's name until he wrote me." Roosevelt's protest was somewhat disingenuous. While the movement for his candidacy may have begun spontaneously, the Colonel was orchestrating every detail of how and when to respond publicly to the round-robin letter he himself had initiated. Having received an invitation to speak before the Ohio Constitutional Convention in Columbus two months earlier, he decided to use the occasion to present his platform before giving a formal answer to the governors' request.

By delaying his entry into the race, Roosevelt had similarly destabilized Taft's position. "The trouble with the Colonel" had long overshadowed the White House "like a big, black cloud." Throughout the early winter, Taft continued to hope that Roosevelt would ultimately decide against running. Otto Bannard, a friend to both men, believed that "the whole plan" was to effect Taft's voluntary withdrawal, that if Roosevelt had to face the "handicap" of taking the nomination from a sitting president, he would not run. Indeed, Taft had not been happy in the presidency and seriously dreaded the prospect of open conflict with his old friend. Moreover, if he deferred to Roosevelt, he might have another shot at the Supreme Court. But the dignity of the presidency—and his duty to the people who elected him—ultimately prevented such a move. "I hate to be at odds with Theodore Roosevelt, who made me President," he told Horace, to which he made an important addendum: "of course, he made me *President* and not *deputy*, and I have to be President; and I do not recognize any obligation growing out of my previous relations to step aside and let him become a candidate for a third term when he specifically declined a third term."

The period of uncertainty weighed with particular gravity on Archie Butt. "My devotion to the Colonel is as strong as it was the day he left," he told Clara, but "I would not ask to be relieved from the President now if my whole life was at stake." Day in and day out, Butt had been a constant companion to the president. Taft "is so honest, so big, and tries to be so just," Butt said of his boss, "that it is hard for the people to get a proper perspective of him." The affection, even love between the two men was mutual. "A President sees but very few people continuously in a confidential way," Taft explained, "and his Aide has to be with him all the time." For three years, Archie Butt had shared moments of sadness, anxiety, and joy. "I very much doubt whether I have ever known a man," Taft declared, with such an empathetic gift "to put himself in the place of another, and suffer and enjoy with that other, as Archie Butt."

A few weeks after the mysterious warning from Alice Roosevelt that he should leave the White House soon, Archie received an open invitation from Edith Roosevelt to join the family at Oyster Bay. He wrote back to propose a visit the last Sunday in January, when he would be in New York with the president. "Delighted," Edith responded by telegram. "Will expect you to lunch." Despite the tensions of the upcoming election, Archie did not conceal such correspondence from Taft, telling the president he would like to accept the invitation. "Go by all means," Taft replied. "It will cheer them, and I know will make you happy."

The visit, Archie recorded with delight, was "like a leaf out of an old book." Logs were "glowing" in every fireplace; dogs were running "all over the house," and the Colonel and Mrs. Roosevelt "were just the same dear people." Archie sat with Edith by the fire for some time before the Colonel arrived. "We settled down to an old-time gossip," Butt recalled, "Mrs. Roosevelt asking a hundred questions and I tripping up myself in my haste" to tell the latest stories of her Washington friends. Hearing their laughter, Roosevelt charged into the room, urging them to repeat their entertaining conversation. At lunch, Butt angled for some indication of Roosevelt's plans, but the Colonel never "mentioned the president" nor "even asked about him," leaping instead "from subject to subject with the agility of a flying squirrel."

"It is all a mystery to me," Archie told Taft later that night, "but the fact that he would not send a message to you by me was significant." No longer hopeful that Roosevelt would not run, Taft grew "more bitter every hour" about his former friend. "The clash which must follow between these two men is tragic," Archie lamented. "It is moving now from day to day with the irresistible force of the Greek drama, and I see no way for anything save divine Providence to interpose to save the reputation of either should they hurl themselves at each other."

WHEN ROOSEVELT ARRIVED IN COLUMBUS, Ohio, on February 21, 1912, to deliver the speech heralded as his platform should he run for president, an enormous crowd of "cheering spectators" provided "a boisterous reception." Sustained applause greeted his entrance to the rotunda and continued as he took his seat. His face, the president of the constitutional convention declared by way of introduction, was "more familiar than the face of the man in the moon."

"We Progressives believe," Roosevelt began, "that human rights are supreme over all other rights; that wealth should be the servant, not the master, of the people." All those who sought reform were engaged in an epic battle "on behalf of the common welfare," a fight to ensure that the people's wishes, rather than the special interests, propelled governmental decisions. "Unless representative government does absolutely represent the people it is not representative government at all," he proclaimed. An advocate of "pure democracy," he fully embraced the campaign to put additional "weapons in the hands of the people," including direct primaries, the initiative, and the referendum.

To the dismay of the Pinchot brothers, Roosevelt then proceeded to deploy his characteristic "balanced statements": progressives must treat capital with the same justice as labor; they must "encourage legitimate and honest business," even as they attacked "injustice and unfairness and tyranny in the business world," and above all, he maintained, they must understand that "methods for the proper distribution of prosperity" were worthless "unless the prosperity is there to distribute." He renewed his call for federal laws to regulate child labor and women's working conditions, establish an income tax, and secure workmen's compensation—all measures that many moderate Republicans could support.

Near the end of his speech, however, Roosevelt introduced a radical proposal that demolished any prospect of securing support from a broad party base. "When a judge decides a constitutional question, when he decides what the people as a whole can or cannot do, the people should have the right to recall that decision if they think it wrong," he insisted. Time and again, he had witnessed "lamentable" judicial decisions by state courts, which had declared laws designed to secure better conditions for laborers unconstitutional. It was "foolish to talk of the sanctity of a judge-made law," he pointed out, when such cases were often the product of a divided bench, with "half of the judges" fervently condemning the outcome. "If there must be a decision by a close majority," Roosevelt suggested, "then let the people step in and let it be *their* majority that decides."

The "damaging effect" of Roosevelt's recall speech was soon evident. The proposition that "a plebiscite or popular referendum" could overturn "the highest appellate tribunals in the states," the New York *Sun* argued, had "revolutionary" consequences for the framework of America's government—creating nothing less than a "Court of the Crowd, with supreme jurisdiction." Acknowledging that Roosevelt had not included Supreme Court decisions in his proposal, the editorial predicted that such a policy would eventually compromise the highest court in the land as well. Why require the long, cumbersome procedure to secure a constitutional amendment? While the *Sun*'s opposition was predictable, many papers followed a similar line of reasoning. The Colonel's proposed judicial recall, declared the *St. Louis Republic*, revealed "Mr. Roosevelt's incapacity to grasp a legal proposition." The *World* characterized the speech as Roosevelt's attempt to "out demagogue all other demagogues." With this address, the *New York Times* predicted, the former president had effectively removed himself from his party, rendering his nomination impossible.

Beyond this outcry in the press, Roosevelt's inflammatory speech estranged him from several of his closest allies. "Theodore has gone off upon a perfectly wild program," Elihu Root told a friend, admitting that he had "been feeling very sad about [Roosevelt's] new departure." His fellow cabinet member Oscar Straus shared Root's consternation. Roosevelt had shown him a draft of the speech a week before, and Straus was appalled by the judicial recall proposition. His attempt to discuss the issue with Roosevelt, however, had been summarily rebuffed. "That was so unlike the Roosevelt I knew," Straus added, "that I was quite disappointed and somewhat taken aback."

While Straus kept his objections private, Henry Cabot Lodge felt compelled to declare his disapproval publicly. "I am opposed to the constitutional changes advocated by Colonel Roosevelt," he told the *New York Times*. Though the two men had been "close and most intimate friends" for three decades, he could not remain silent when "the sanctity of the judiciary" was under attack. "I have had my share of mishaps in politics but I never thought that any situation could arise which would have made me so miserably unhappy as I have been during the past week," Lodge wrote to Roosevelt, following his public statement. "I knew of course that you and I differed on some of these points but I had not realized that the difference was so wide." Roosevelt replied the next day: "My dear fellow, you could not do anything that would make me lose my warm personal affection for you."

The swirling controversy only reinforced Edith Roosevelt's chagrin over her husband's decision to engage in what would undoubtedly prove a ferocious fight with Taft for the nomination. The previous six months had not been easy for her. In September 1911, riding "at a gallop" with Theodore, she had been thrown on the hard macadam road when her favorite horse suddenly "swerved and wheeled." The concussion and dislocation of three vertebrae that resulted required three weeks of bed rest. "She is very much shattered," Roosevelt confided to a friend a month later. Her convalescence had just begun when Theodore seriously started to entertain the idea of running. "Politics are hateful," Edith despaired in a letter to Kermit. "Father thinks he must enter the fight definitely . . . and there is no possible result which could give me aught but keen regret." Three days after the Columbus speech, Edith and her daughter Ethel sailed to South America. "At the worst of it I was forced to be away," she wrote a friend, admitting that "in all my life I was never more unhappy."

Few were more vexed by Roosevelt's determination to run than his son-in-law, Congressman Nicholas Longworth, whose family had known the Tafts for decades. In her memoir Alice recorded "the quandary" her husband faced: "On the one hand his friendship with Mr. Taft and the fact that he came from

Mr. Taft's own district; on the other his affection for and his admiration of Father, made his position almost intolerable. I have never been so sorry for any one." Roosevelt sympathized with Nick's uncomfortable position. "Of course you must be for Taft," he told Nick on the eve of his announcement. Still, his son-in-law found the situation painful, particularly as Alice grew "single-minded in enthusiasm" for her father's campaign, evincing more emotion and interest in politics than ever before. This newfound political passion stirred domestic strife: at dinner parties with members of Nick's family, Alice fought back whenever they criticized her father. "I got furious," she confided in her diary after one unpleasant exchange. "Poor Nick angry—Says I must 'shut up.' "

If family and friends were foiled by Roosevelt's decision, the Colonel himself embraced the looming battle with gusto. "It is not the critic who counts," he had famously preached upon his return from his African safari, "not the man who points out how the strong man stumbles, or where the doer of deeds could have done better. The credit belongs to the man who is actually in the arena, whose face is marred by dust and sweat and blood; who strives valiantly; who errs, and comes short again and again, because there is no effort without error and shortcoming; but who does actually strive to do the deeds; who knows the great enthusiasms, the great devotions; who spends himself in a worthy cause."

Indeed, his exuberance for battle manifested itself three days before his planned announcement, when he answered a question about his intentions with a spontaneous declaration: "My hat is in the ring." The tradition of "shying the hat" went back to a time when men either fought in a ring "with bare knuckles" or flung a hat at a rooster that would only fight when goaded. The former president's reference to fisticuffs and cockfighting, the New York *Evening World* commented, undoubtedly heralded "some brutality in the contest."

On Sunday evening, February 25, Roosevelt's New York office released the governors' request that "in the interests of the people as a whole," the Colonel should respond affirmatively to the "unsolicited and unsought" demand that he enter the race. "I deeply appreciate your letter," Roosevelt publicly replied, affirming, "I will accept the nomination for President if it is tendered to me, and I will adhere to this decision until the convention has expressed its preference."

That same night, before news of his decision had become public, Roosevelt attended a Porcellian Club Dinner and a meeting of the Harvard Overseers, after which he went to the home of his old college friend, Judge Robert Grant. At Roosevelt's request, Grant had invited another college friend, the historian William Roscoe Thayer, and William Allen White to dinner. While Roosevelt showed "no signs" of agitation about the upcoming struggle, his friends expressed misgivings about his decision to run and the backlash from the Columbus speech. White continued to believe that public sentiment stood "overwhelmingly" with Roosevelt but doubted whether the political system was "flexible enough to register that sentiment." If presidential primaries existed across the nation, he was confident Roosevelt would win, but the convention system had myriad ways of thwarting public desire. Grant believed Roosevelt was making "an unnecessary and possibly fatal blunder" by challenging a sitting president instead of waiting for an open field four years later. And Thayer begged him, "for the sake of his own future, not to engage in a factional strife which might end his usefulness to the country."

The Colonel blithely deflected their arguments with animation and good humor. Never losing his composure when Thayer as a historian defended the judiciary and argued that Roosevelt's platform would "destroy representative government" in favor of "the whims of the populace," Roosevelt countered that he could identify nearly four dozen senators who obtained their offices through the influence of Wall Street. "Do you call that popular, representative government?" he queried in response. And when Grant wondered if he would have the backing of party leaders, Roosevelt acknowledged that he had "none of them; not even Lodge." Instead, he counted on a cadre of young leaders, like Governor Robert Bass of New Hampshire.

As the lively conversation broke up around midnight, Grant made one final attempt to dissuade Roosevelt from running, emphasizing that people would think him disloyal to the president. About to retire to the guest room upstairs, Roosevelt angrily declared: "What do I owe to Taft? It was through me and my friends that he became President. I had him in the hollow of my hand and he would have dropped out." To illustrate his point, he withdrew his pocketknife from his pocket, balanced it in the palm of his hand, then let it clatter to the floor.

THE PRESIDENT, THE FIRST LADY, and a few guests, including Archie Butt, were at dinner in the White House when a messenger brought Roosevelt's letter declaring his candidacy. Reading it aloud to those at the table, Taft remarked that it was more definite than he had expected. Assuming it would be laden "with conditions and explanations," he was surprised to find a clear "rallying cry to the Progressives." Nellie turned to her husband. "I told you so four years ago, and you would not believe me," she chided. Her husband gave a good-natured laugh. "I know you did, my dear, and I think you are perfectly happy now. You would have preferred the Colonel to have come out against me than to have been wrong yourself."

Archie was less able to make light of the revelation, tossing in his bed that night unable to sleep. A week earlier, with the president's blessing, he had made plans for a short European vacation with his good friend, the painter and sculptor Frank Millet. Archie had driven himself "like a steam engine" through the continuous round of dinners and receptions marking the winter social season, and now felt "tired all the time." They were planning to sail on the *Berlin*. "If the old ship goes down," he wrote his sister-in-law, Clara, "you will find my affairs in shipshape condition."

As he lay in his bed that night, Archie had second thoughts about the trip. "It seems to me that the President will need every *intime* near at hand now. If we are ever to be of any real comfort to him, this is the time," he reflected. "I can see he hates to see me go, and I feel like a quitter in going." That morning, he canceled his sailing orders and told the president of his intention to remain in Washington. "He would not hear of it," Archie told his Aunt Kitty, "and insisted on my going on the ground this was the only time I could get away."

On Saturday, March 2, Archie Butt sailed for Europe. He hated "to leave the Big White Chief," he told Clara, but he'd be back in six weeks, returning to the White House in plenty of time to support the president during "the fight of his life for the nomination."

"By a strange coincidence," *The Washington Post* reported, both Taft and Roosevelt opened their national headquarters on the same day. The Taft men commandeered twelve luxurious rooms in the Raleigh Hotel, while two blocks away, the Roosevelt headquarters occupied the tenth floor of the Munsey Building. To head his campaign, the Colonel chose Montana senator Joseph M. Dixon, an energetic young man with "a very pleasant and winning personality, easy manners, and attractive address." Taft selected Illinois congressman William Brown McKinley, chairman of the Republican National Committee. No relation to the assassinated president, McKinley had made a fortune in traction corporations before entering Congress in 1905. For both campaigns, major financial backers helped furnish "the sinews of war." Roosevelt would enjoy the support of two multimillionaires—Frank Munsey, the publisher of newspapers and magazines, and George Perkins, who had departed the house of Morgan "to devote himself to public affairs." Taft could rely on traditional Republican Party stalwarts, including the financiers Otto Bannard and Chauncey Depew. And once again, Charley Taft contributed handsomely to his brother's campaign.

As the battle for the nomination began, Taft was immensely relieved that the Colonel's radical Columbus speech provided the opportunity to distinguish his own position "without indulging in any personal attack." Though he agreed with many of the Colonel's proposals on capital and labor, he had felt that the initiative and the referendum were problematic and was "unalterably opposed" to "the recall of judicial decisions." In a letter to Charley, he noted that Roosevelt had "stirred up a veritable hornet's nest of disapproval." The issues were now "sharply defined," clearing "the political atmosphere wonderfully." Meeting with Roosevelt's friend Henry White in early March, Taft vowed that his campaign would remain a battle of ideas. Indeed, he hoped that "when all this turmoil of politics had passed," he and Roosevelt "would get together again and be as of old."

Speaking in New York, Boston, and Toledo in the late winter and early spring, Taft deployed a series of metaphors to illuminate the inherent dangers in subjecting judicial decisions to "the momentary passions of a people." In one late winter speech, he warned that judicial recall would topple "the pillars of the temple." In subsequent addresses that spring, the president warned that such action threatened to smash "the ark of the covenant" and that it laid "the axe at the foot of the tree of well ordered freedom." Defending his beloved judiciary, Taft found his voice. At the State House in Boston, he enjoyed the most "genuine ovation" of his speaking career. "One cannot adequately describe," he told Charley, "the manner in which my speech was received without using extravagant expressions."

"Taft has behaved with dignity and amiable forbearance since the announcement," Roosevelt's friend Judge Grant told the historian James Ford Rhodes at the end of March, noting that he had "become almost an idol, even in circles where a few months ago he was reviled." If Taft triumphed, Grant continued, it would be "on the crest of the wave of revolt from and denunciation of Roosevelt." In recent weeks, suspicion that Roosevelt had not granted the president "quite the square deal seems to have taken hold of the public mind," and "the abuse" of the Colonel in the New York and Massachusetts newspapers had been "overwhelming and bitter."

When the election year opened, only one eastern state—New Jersey—and five western states—Wisconsin, Nebraska, Oregon, North Dakota, and California—made use of the direct primary. Everywhere else, delegates would be selected at district and state conventions, where local machines and the power of federal patronage gave the president a decided advantage.

Taft's campaign had already established control of most southern state conventions before Roosevelt formally entered the race. Fearful that the region's running totals would make Taft's lead appear impregnable before delegates from the rest of the country were selected, an enterprising Roosevelt supporter organized groups of men to contest the results of conventions throughout the South. Even if it was later determined that legitimate Taft majorities existed, the newspapers would be forced to list the results as contested rather than straight Taft victories. When rumors reached Roosevelt that bribes were being employed, he wrote his overenthusiastic organizer that while he was "absolutely sure that there was not a particle of truth" to the accusations, he nonetheless wanted "assurance" that no "improper" tactics were being used "to influence any man."

At state conventions in the North and West, brutal altercations broke out, swiftly dispelling Taft's hope for a high-minded campaign based on the issues. In Michigan, Taft's forces secured a victory after what one newspaper described as "the worst riots that ever occurred in a political gathering in the state." More than 1,800 men arrived at the Bay City Armory to claim 1,400 seats. The Taft men, the *New York Times* reported, were admitted first and filled the hall "despite the frantic efforts of the Roosevelt men to gain entrance through side doors, windows, and the basement." With the aid of the state militia, delegates without proper credentials were "seized bodily" and thrown to the back of the crowd. Eventually, four hundred Roosevelt supporters were admitted, and "then the fireworks began." When the chairman of the Taft delegation attempted to open the meeting, the Colonel's men "set up a roar," making it impossible for him to continue. One Roosevelt advocate rushed the platform only to be flung backward, landing atop the newspapermen's table. More than a hundred men joined the fight before police "charged on the combatants and restored order with their clubs." The Roosevelt faction promptly selected their own delegates before leaving the hall, "yelling and jeering at their foes." The Taft faction then moved forward with the regular order of business.

Violence erupted at conventions in many other states as well, including Missouri and Oklahoma. In the third Missouri district, the Taft contingent, positioned at the only open door with "clubs and baseball bats," prevented Roosevelt supporters from entering. Pandemonium broke out in Oklahoma City when a Roosevelt man wearing a Rough Rider outfit entered the hall on a horse and "rode down the aisle to the rostrum." Before an hour had passed, a series of "dynamite explosions" shook the convention hall. A few weeks later, at a district convention in Guthrie, Oklahoma, a Roosevelt supporter held a loaded gun to the head of the chairman of Taft's delegation. He wanted to be fully prepared, he declared, in case "any chicanery" occurred. Before the "all-night session" came to a close, one delegate had "dropped dead" from an apparent apoplexy.

EVEN BEFORE OFFICIALLY THROWING HIS hat in the ring, Roosevelt realized that his only chance for the nomination lay in expanding the direct primary beyond the half-dozen states that had adopted the system. In his letter to the governors, he had voiced his "hope that so far as possible the people may be given the chance, through direct primaries, to express their preference as to who shall be the nominee." Initially led by La Follette and his band of insurgents, the movement for direct primaries had been slow to catch on. Two years earlier, Roosevelt had unsuccessfully tried to persuade the New York state legislature to change its nominating system. As a presidential candidate, however, he transformed the "sluggishly moving cause" into "a torrential crusade."

"Get the Direct Primary for Your State," proclaimed a Roosevelt supporter in *Collier's Weekly*, alerting constituents that "the Presidential primary means that you can go to the polls (if you are a Republican) and say whether you want Taft or Roosevelt. If you don't do the choosing the bosses will." Roosevelt operatives pressured legislatures in one state after another to change their rules. "Don't let the politicians tell you it is too late," the progressive journalist Mark Sullivan proclaimed. "The Presidential primary can be got for every State if the people demand it."

The call for a popular voice in party nominations was a delicate issue for the Taft campaign. While the president's strength lay in the old convention system, the political climate made public opposition to direct primaries awkward. Nor did Taft oppose the concept in principle; he told Horace that he had "no objection at all" to Republican primaries, so long as the law provided safeguards to prevent Democrats from voting. Meanwhile, his managers did everything possible to prevent states from adopting primaries. "Legislatures are being dragooned, officeholders are being set at work," the *Washington Times* reported, "and big business is using its influence at every point." Challenged to explain why Taft's campaign organizers were leading the fight, William McKinley flatly stated. "I do not favor changes in the rules of the game while the game is in progress. To propose the recall of conventions in the midst of the campaign is contrary to the dictates of fair play." It appeared the campaign would progress smoothly, Taft assured Horace, if he could "only keep my people from talking too much."

Roosevelt sounded the central theme of his own campaign in a speech at Carnegie Hall on March 20. Every seat was occupied; the speaker's platform was jammed with chairs; women in evening gowns crowded the upper boxes. Five thousand people had to be turned away. Roosevelt "waved his hand energetically" to stop the "wild cheers" that greeted him as he entered, but the demonstration only escalated when someone in the back began the singsong refrain: "What's the matter with Roosevelt?" To which the crowd chanted: "He's all right!" At last, the audience reluctantly quieted and Roosevelt began to speak.

"The great fundamental issue now before the Republican party and before our people can be stated briefly," he thundered, posing the rhetorical question: "Are the American people fit to govern themselves, to rule themselves, to control themselves? I believe they are. My opponents do not." Declaring that he stood by the sentiments in his Columbus speech, Roosevelt adroitly folded his proposal for the recall of judicial decisions into the larger issue of popular rule. Any attack on his proposal, he maintained, was in effect "a criticism of all popular government," grounded in "the belief that the people are fundamentally unworthy."

For the first time, the *New York Times* reported, Roosevelt proceeded to pour "ridicule" on the president, deriding his misguided interpretation of the principles of American government. Unlike Abraham Lincoln, who believed in "government of the people, by the people, for the people," Roosevelt charged that Taft ostensibly held that "our government is and should be a government of all the people by a representative part of the people," the very definition of "oligarchy." Where progressives trusted that the entire voting republic would rule correctly most of the time, Taft rested his hope in the courts—"a special class of persons wiser than the people." In recent years, Roosevelt pointed out, these very courts had proved "the most serious obstacles" to social justice—repeatedly striking down legislation designed to better the working conditions of ordinary citizens. "Our task as Americans is to strive for social and industrial justice, achieved through the genuine rule of the people," he urged. "We, here in America, hold in our hands the hope of the world." The destiny of "our great experiment" would mean nothing, he warned, "if on this new continent we merely build another country of great but unjustly divided material prosperity," rather than a genuine democracy based on "the rule of all the people."

As spring commenced, vigorous efforts by the Roosevelt campaign to spread the direct primary system had succeeded in Pennsylvania, Massachusetts, Maryland, Ohio, South Dakota, Illinois, and New York, bringing the number of participating states to thirteen. The New York struggle resulted in multiple litigations regarding the format of the ballot and the placement of the delegates' names, but the primary was finally set for March 26. In Illinois, the *Chicago Tribune* led a successful campaign to force the reluctant governor to call a special legislative session to pass the bill. With primaries scheduled nearly every week between mid-March and early June, the first presidential campaign conducted under this new system generated widespread interest and high emotions.

The primary season opened on March 12 in North Dakota, where Robert La Follette still "had his fighting clothes on," determined to prove that he was the sole progressive in the race. Roosevelt, he charged, was merely a "switch engine" that ran on "one track, and then on another." Aware that La Follette was generating widespread enthusiasm, Roosevelt's managers published a last-minute appeal in newspapers across the state: "Today's primary crucial. On the returns," the statement advised, "will depend whether Col. Theodore Roosevelt is to be further considered as a factor in the fight for the nomination."

In Washington, Alice Roosevelt Longworth waited anxiously. After placing repeated telephone calls to her father's campaign manager, she finally received the "very bad news" that La Follette had beaten Roosevelt by a margin of 58 percent to 39 percent. Though Taft garnered but a miserable 3 percent of the vote, Roosevelt had predicted that if he did not win, "the East will construe it not as a defeat for Taft but as a defeat for me." *The Washington Post* confirmed Roosevelt's assessment: "The small vote count for President Taft means very little, as he was not fighting for recognition of the primaries as were Roosevelt and La Follette." Moreover, Taft could not anticipate much support in a state on the Canadian border, where many farmers still resented his advocacy for reciprocity. "In a nutshell," the *Post* concluded, the outcome in North Dakota "is decidedly embarrassing to Roosevelt, encouraging to La Follette and the subject of mixed amusement and satisfaction to Taft."

A week later, Roosevelt suffered a far more significant loss when Taft crushed him by a margin of eight to one in New York's "first trial of the new primary law," securing eighty-three out of ninety district delegates. "They are stealing the primary election from us," Roosevelt protested. It was evident that "an entire breakdown of the election machinery" in New York had occurred. Litigation by both the Taft and Roosevelt campaigns had delayed getting the ballots to the printer. In some districts, they arrived only after the polling had closed; in others, the long ballots had been so badly folded that the bottom section bearing the delegates' names became detached. Despite these technical difficulties, the press reported "the indisputable fact" that Taft had scored a decisive victory over Roosevelt.

The day after the New York primary, Roosevelt boarded a train to begin a weeklong swing through the West in anticipation of the Illinois primary. Having studied the returns from New York, he reached Chicago "in a fighting mood." Discarding his prepared speeches, he "raised the cry of fraud," claiming that the Taft men in New York "had cheated the people out of their will by the grossest corruption" since "the days of Tweed." Had he simply been unable to gain support for his political philosophy, the Colonel maintained, he "should be sorry" but would not complain. "If the politicians subvert the will of the people," however, he would "have a great deal to say." Buoyed by immense crowds yelling "Teddy, Teddy, hooray for Teddy," Roosevelt escalated his rhetoric against bosses, machines, and William Howard Taft. "Our fight," he claimed, "is the biggest fight the Republican Party has been in since the Civil War." Before a packed Decatur crowd, he linked Taft directly to Republican William Lorimer, who would soon be expelled from the Senate for bribing members of the Illinois state legislature to obtain his Senate seat. Generating wild applause, he proclaimed: "As an American citizen, it is a shock to me to see the name of Lincoln desecrated by its use as a mask for Mr. Lorimer."

"Easter came on April seventh that year," Alice Roosevelt recalled, "but all that I could think of was the Illinois primary, two days off." A loss in Illinois after his humiliating New York defeat would cripple the Roosevelt movement. But before midnight on April 9, it became clear that Roosevelt had won a sweeping victory, "carrying every district in the State but one, and electing fifty-six of the fifty-eight delegates." His campaign secretary, Oscar King Davis, later designated April 9 as "the day on which the Roosevelt 'band wagon' got its real start, and from then on there was a rush to get aboard it." Well aware that he had benefited from widespread anti-Lorimer sentiment, Roosevelt claimed the stunning victory as "a stinging rebuke to the alliance between crooked business and crooked politics." As he headed toward Pennsylvania, where voters would go to the polls in four days, he wore his broadest smile. "We slugged them over the ropes," he told supporters. The outcome was almost "too good to believe," Alice Roosevelt recorded in her diary. "How wonderfully happy I am."

A somber mood enveloped the Taft camp. Taft confided to Howard Hollister that the Illinois defeat had "given his campaign a heavy jolt." More frustrating than the loss itself, Taft told his friend, was the unjust way that the Lorimer issue had been used to debase him. Roosevelt knew that Taft had never supported Lorimer; indeed, he and the Colonel had exchanged letters, working together to determine how they might persuade a reluctant Senate to expel one of its own. Despite the blow suffered in Illinois, Taft assured Hollister, the campaign could easily "recover by a good result in Pennsylvania."

On Saturday, April 13, the people of Pennsylvania crushed Taft's hope "for turning the avalanche of sentiment" that Roosevelt had unleashed. "It was long after midnight," the *Washington Times* reported, "before the weary managers quit bringing their discouraging telegrams and Mr. Taft sought a few hours rest." By Sunday morning, it was clear that Roosevelt had achieved another staggering triumph, gaining sixty-eight of seventy-six delegates. After hearing the final tally, Taft wrote a long letter to his brother Horace. "One of the burdens that a man leading a cause has to carry is the disappointment that his friends and sympathizers feel at every recurring disaster," he began. With every unfavorable report in the papers, that load grew heavier. "I felt more sorrow at Nellie's disappointment and yours, and that of all who have become absorbed in the fight on my behalf than I did myself," he explained. Nevertheless, he assured his brother, he had no plans to withdraw. Nor did he intend to "make any personal attacks on Roosevelt." If Roosevelt persisted in his "lies and unblushing misrepresentations," however, he could not prevent his campaign managers "from pointing out his mendacity."

"I wish I could help," Horace replied. "I can't manage to think of much else. I don't see how you stand it. I don't mind a licking. I can get used to anything. But the continued uncertainty is hard to bear." No matter the eventual outcome, Horace told his brother, William Taft would never lose the affection and respect of "the thinking men," the men who understood the fight being waged for the Constitution. Hoping to cheer his brother, Horace recounted a conversation with Taft's eldest son, Robert, who had "never loved him so much" and expressed certainty "that his place in history is sure if he never does another lick."

"The stampede is on," the *Pittsburgh Press* proclaimed. "Those who have been led to believe that Roosevelt has been fighting a lost cause will have to change their minds. Theodore Roosevelt is stronger today than he has been at any time since his hat was cast into the ring." Optimism reigned too at Roosevelt's headquarters in Washington. "Of course, Pennsylvania settles it," *Chicago Tribune* correspondent Cal O'Laughlin wrote to Roosevelt on April 14. "I am absolutely convinced that you will be nominated hands down at Chicago," noting with satisfaction that "the gloom around the White House to-day was so thick, it could be cut with a knife."

KEEPING ABREAST OF THE INCREASINGLY bitter nomination struggle from abroad, Major Butt decided to cut his vacation a little short, "anxious to be home," where he could offer comfort and companionship to his beleaguered Chief.

On April 10, 1912, he boarded the White Star Line's palatial new ocean liner, RMS *Titanic*, for her maiden crossing of the North Atlantic.

On Monday morning, April 15, the press reported that the *Titanic*, carrying more than 2,300 passengers and crew, had struck a giant iceberg. The first reports erroneously suggested that the great ship had been "held afloat by her water-tight compartments" and was "slowly crawling" toward Halifax. Relieved to hear that "all onboard had been saved," Taft went to see the comedy *Nobody's Widow* at Poli's Theatre that evening. Learning at around 11 p.m. that the ship had actually gone down in the early morning hours, "he looked," one reporter observed, "like a man that had been stunned by a heavy blow." He rushed back to his office, where he closeted himself in the telegraph room to read the latest bulletins. Shortly before midnight, he dispatched a telegram to the White Star offices in New York: "Have you any information concerning Major Butt? If you communicate at once I will greatly appreciate." The response offered little reason for optimism. There was "no definite information" available. Before returning to the mansion, Taft instructed the telegraph operator to bring him the most recent news regardless of how late it arrived.

The days that followed would drive Taft down into a profound state of grief. By early Tuesday morning, White Star officials had compiled a list of over seven hundred survivors, mainly women and children, who had been loaded into lifeboats and taken aboard the nearby *Carpathia*. At noon, the *Washington Times* reported, the president's telegraph operator received a message from the White Star office, expressing their profound "regret that Major Butt's name" was not to be found on any list of survivors. "Even with the list of the rescued made public," the press reported, "Washington found it hard to realize that the President's military aide, the tall, stalwart, light-hearted man who won such popularity, who knew pretty nearly everybody in the Capital, and was loved by all of them is really dead." The White House canceled all social activities as "news of the disaster swallowed up all such temporary minor considerations as politics and official business."

Both the president and the first lady were "greatly depressed," *The Washington Post* reported; "in fact, the entire White House staff was plunged into sorrow." With tears in his eyes, Taft told callers he considered Archie a member of his family and felt "his loss as if he had been a younger brother." To his friend Mabel Boardman, Taft confessed that it was impossible to believe he would never see Archie again. "I miss him every minute," he wrote; "every house, and every tree, and every person suggests him. Every walk I take somehow is lacking his presence, and every door that opens seems to be his coming."

As survivors began talking about their ordeal, Taft absorbed stories about

Archie's last hours. Marian Thayer, a Philadelphia Main Liner whose husband had perished on the ship, sent a heartfelt letter to the president. "In my own grief I think often of yours," she told him, "and feel I must write to tell you how I spent the last Sunday evening with Major Butt." She had dined with Archie at a small dinner party in honor of the *Titanic*'s captain, Edward J. Smith, and could not forget "how devoted he was to you and what a lovely noble man he was!" Archie had told Mrs. Thayer about the scores of letters he had written to his mother and his sister-in-law over the recent years and shared his hope that if published posthumously, this correspondence might leave "his mark and memorial of truth to the world." He admitted that he was "very nervous" about returning home, Marian confided to Taft, knowing that the nomination battle between "you and someone else he loved but I do not" was in full swing. "Oh, how he loved you" she added, "and how frightfully you will miss his care—such a true, devoted, close more-than-friend."

According to reports, Archie had been in the smoking room enjoying a game of cards at 11:40 p.m. when the *Titanic* hit the iceberg. "A slight rocking of the ship" followed, but the passengers remained unaware of danger until forty minutes later, when a steward announced: "The captain says that all passengers will dress themselves warmly, bring life preservers and go up to the top deck." Over the next two hours, as water continued to flood the vessel, women and children were lowered into lifeboats. Mrs. Henry Harris, wife of the celebrated theatrical producer who died on board, recalled that Archie Butt had been "the real leader" during the rescue operation. A male passenger who survived by jumping at the last moment told reporters: "My last view of Major Butt—one that will live forever in my memory—was of that brave soldier coolly aiding the officers of the boat in directing the dis-embarkation of the women from the doomed ship." Even before the limited survivor list and the testimony of witnesses reached him, William Taft was grimly certain of his companion's fate: "After I heard that part of the ship's company had gone down, I gave up hope for the rescue of Major Butt, unless by accident. I knew that he would certainly remain on the ship's deck until every duty had been performed and every sacrifice made."

Theodore Roosevelt was on a whirlwind speaking tour through the West when the tragic news of the disaster reached him. From Lindsberg, Kansas, he "paid tribute" to his former aide. "Major Butt was the highest type of officer and gentleman. He met his end as an officer and gentleman should, giving up his own life that others might be saved. I and my family all loved him sincerely." For Alice Roosevelt, who was especially close to Archie, the loss was particularly painful. "I can't believe it," she repeatedly recorded in her diary. "I can't believe it."

Taft immediately prepared for the journey to Augusta, Georgia, where he would speak at the memorial service in his devoted aide's hometown. Shops were closed, flags flew at half-mast, and thousands gathered around the Grand Opera House hoping to hear the president speak. "Everybody knew Archie as Archie," Taft began. "I cannot go into a box at a theater; I cannot turn around in my room; I can't go anywhere without expecting to see his smiling face or to hear his cheerful voice in greeting. The life of the President is rather isolated, and those appointed to live with him come much closer to him than anyone else." Before reaching the end of his prepared remarks, he broke down and could not finish.

Heavyhearted, Taft endeavored to return to "a rush of activities" in preparation for the April 30 Massachusetts primary, which the press had deemed "the Gettysburg of the Republican presidential test." If the president could not win the Bay State, "the very heart of the section where he is supposed to be the strongest," commentators noted, "the curtain will ring down on his candidacy." Fully aware of the stakes, Taft decided to buck the tradition that kept sitting presidents from campaigning on their own behalf, announcing that he would deliver his message "in person" to the people of Massachusetts.

For weeks, Taft's campaign advisers had argued that it was "absolutely essential" for him to "open fire" on the former president. Taft had refused, believing it undignified "to get down into the ring of crimination and recrimination." The walloping he suffered in Illinois and Pennsylvania, however, persuaded him that the time had come to answer Roosevelt's charges. His campaign announced that Taft would "explode a bomb" that would level Roosevelt's false accusations. When he finished drafting his speeches, Taft circulated them to his cabinet at an "all night" session. Apparently, one Washington correspondent reported, "the President's idea of severity was not as strong as that of some of his advisers." Informed of the proposed attack, Roosevelt laughed. "Frightful," he mockingly replied.

The president's train reached Springfield, Massachusetts, in the early afternoon of April 25. Speaking in a half-dozen small towns en route to Boston, where he would deliver his principal address that evening, Taft revealed acute discomfort at the need to defend himself "against the accusations of an old friend," whom he "greatly admired and loved," a man who had helped make him president. "This wrenches my soul," he admitted. If the fight were purely personal, he would have remained silent, but it was his duty to represent "the cause of constitutionalism," and he could not allow Roosevelt's false charges to go unanswered. When he arrived at South Station, he learned that an immense crowd had already filled the new Boston Arena, with thousands more packed into Symphony Hall. Anticipation that he would deliver a fighting speech had revitalized his supporters.

"Mr. Roosevelt," Taft began, claims to believe "that every man is entitled to a square deal. I propose to examine the charges he makes against me, and to ask you whether in making them he is giving me a square deal." With emotion in his voice, "throwing aside official reserve," Taft proceeded to tell "the cold, naked truth about Theodore Roosevelt," presenting hard evidence to counter each of his rival's major accusations. He began by producing a transcript to prove that he had never stated, as Roosevelt repeatedly claimed, that "our Government is and *should be* a government of all the people by a representative part of the people." In fact, he had pointed out that major segments of the population remained voiceless, while "the people" included only adult males, since women were not allowed to vote. Nor had he ever been a supporter of the disgraced Senator Lorimer, as Roosevelt well knew. To prove his point, Taft read out the letter to the Colonel in which he had suggested a joint strategy for removing Lorimer from the Senate. Yet another letter revealed Roosevelt's dishonorable opportunism: while the reciprocity agreement was being hammered out with Canada, Roosevelt had written to tell Taft that it was "admirable from every standpoint." Yet facing the opposition of angry farmers, the Colonel had hastily revised his position. Taft pushed relentlessly onward, refuting each of eleven accusations Roosevelt had made against him in the course of the campaign.

Nearly two hours had passed before Taft reached his peroration, which included "a solemn warning to the American people" regarding "the danger of a third presidential term." Mr. Roosevelt, he stated, "is convinced that the American people think that he is the only one to do the job." Though Roosevelt had never articulated "exactly" what that job entailed, the ambitious plans outlined in his Columbus platform could not possibly be completed in four years. "We are left to infer, therefore, that 'the job' which Mr. Roosevelt is to perform is one that may take a long time, perhaps the rest of his natural life. There is not the slightest reason why, if he secures a third term, and the limitation of the Washington, Jefferson, and Jackson tradition is broken down, he should not have as many terms as his natural life will permit." Taft concluded with an ominous question, implying the full danger of granting Roosevelt an unprecedented third term: "If he is necessary now to the Government, why not later?"

The audience, which had "loudly cheered" Taft throughout the entire speech as "each item was submitted to the square deal balance and found wanting," received his final words "with a storm of endorsement." As his advisers had urged, William Taft had finally struck back. "He had cause for exhilaration," his biographer remarked, but "weariness and depression were the only sensations he felt." Informed that evening that several hundred bodies, recovered from the icy waters near the site where the *Titanic* went down, were being taken to Halifax, Taft had dispatched an Army official to the city wharf "to scrutinize" every victim, "in the hope of recovering" the body of Archie Butt. After his speech at the Arena, Taft stopped at Symphony Hall to meet the overflow crowd. It was after midnight by the time he returned to his private car. Spent, he "slumped over," and despite the presence of a journalist, "began to weep."

In sharp contrast, Theodore Roosevelt was in great spirits as he prepared his own Boston speech, scheduled for delivery at Mechanics Hall the very next night. "If they are anxious for a fight they can have it," he blasted, as he flung aside his earlier draft to respond to Taft's allegations. Incited by his belligerent tone, "the crowd was keyed up" from the start. They stamped in unison, shouting: "Hit him between the eyes! Soak him! Put him over the ropes!" The Colonel did not disappoint, delivering what the *New York Times* called a "merciless denunciation" of his former friend, "flaying the President in one scathing sentence after another." With each thrust Roosevelt delivered, the audience "howled with delight," spurring him onward. Roosevelt dismissed Taft's square deal comment out of hand. "Taft has not only been disloyal to our past friendship, but he has been disloyal to every canon of decency and fair play," he countered. "He only discovered I was dangerous to the people when I discovered he was useless to the people." Insisting that a gentleman's unpardonable sin is to publish a letter marked "confidential," the Colonel claimed that the president was guilty of "the crookedest kind of deal." Categorically, he stated, "I care nothing for Taft's personal attitude toward me."

"This is our first presidential campaign under the preference primary plan," the *New York Times* editorialized two days later. "We hope it may be our last. The spectacle presented by the fierce fight for the nomination is one that must be amazing to foreigners, it is one that should bring a blush of shame to the cheek of every American." The old system, the *Times* continued, under which candidates were "content to await the action of the convention" and appeal to the people in a formal acceptance speech, "was a rational, a seemly procedure." Under this new system, "we are no longer a people, but a mob."

On April 30, the Massachusetts voters granted Taft a narrow victory, but six days later, Roosevelt captured Maryland, and the following week California. Then came the battle for Ohio, which brought both men to the Buckeye State for ten days of hard campaigning. Traveling thousands of miles by train from one corner of the state to the other, Taft and Roosevelt sometimes found themselves playing "rival matinees in the same towns." With each passing day, the tone of the campaign degenerated further. Roosevelt called the president a "puzzlewit" and a "fathead," while Taft railed against his rival's egotism. "You'd suppose there was not anybody in the country to do this job he talks about but himself," the president ridiculed. "It's I, I, I, all the time with him." Robert La Follette, having traveled to Ohio after a surprisingly good showing in California, joined in the bitter attacks, focusing most of his ire on Roosevelt. While some people found "the spectacle of a President and ex-President hurling personal abuse at each other" unseemly, "the attacks of one on the other won the loudest applause everywhere."

"It is about as painful for me as it possibly could be," Taft confessed as the contest in Ohio drew near. "At least, if it is settled against me, it will be finally settled," he told his Aunt Delia. "I have had a long and, I hope, an honorable career, and one in which good fortune has been with me at many crises. If now, fortune is to desert me for a time or permanently, it is my business to stand it, and I hope I have the courage to do so." Roosevelt, by contrast, found pleasure in every aspect of the campaign. He reveled in the sight of the enormous crowds that greeted him at every stop; he enjoyed going after his rival, bantering with the press, talking with local officials. "He is having a perfectly corking time," one reporter noted, "and has said so a dozen times."

On May 21, a jubilant Roosevelt carried the state of Ohio by a margin of 55 percent to 39 percent of the popular vote. Beating Taft in his own state had "settled the contest," he predicted. "It will be hopeless to try to beat us" at the convention. A week later, Roosevelt carried both New Jersey and South Dakota, bringing the primary season to an end. In nine of the thirteen states where direct primaries had been held, Roosevelt had won overwhelming victories. Taft had carried only New York and Massachusetts. La Follette had secured North Dakota and Wisconsin. The total popular vote for Roosevelt stood at 1,214,969, while Taft secured 865,835 votes and La Follette 327,357.

"I have had so many jolts," the despondent Taft told Horace—bespeaking a battering far beyond the political arena, to intimate his sorrow over the ugly estrangement from Theodore Roosevelt and a profound grief for his lost companion Archie Butt—"that I am not worrying over it."

CHAPTER TWENTY-EIGHT

"Bosom Friends, Bitter Enemies"

"His Back to the Wall," a June 3, 1912, *New York World* cartoon, dramatizes the tumultuous battle between Taft and Roosevelt for the Republican presidential nomination.

TO OBSERVERS ACROSS THE NATION and even overseas, it was clear an unprecedented challenge to President Taft was well under way. "A month ago practically every impartial observer believed that Mr. Roosevelt had no chance," *The Times* of London noted as the primary season drew to an end. "Now, however, it is admitted on all hands that he has a chance." As Republicans completed preparations to meet in Chicago in mid-June to choose their nominee for president, William Jennings Bryan predicted that the Republican National Convention of 1912 would be "the most exciting ever held in the history of the country." Not only were the main contenders "once bosom friends" who had become "bitter enemies," but the country had "never before" witnessed a fight for the nomination between a president and an ex-president.

"Each side makes confident assertions," one correspondent for the *New York Tribune* remarked, "but each side secretly is scared stiff." Roosevelt steadfastly maintained that the people had already spoken. The vast majority of primary voters had chosen him, furnishing a significant percentage of the 540 delegates he needed to secure the nomination; the convention, he confidently asserted, would "not dare to oppose the will of the majority," because to do so "would mean ruin to the Republican Party." The president, however, had far greater support in states where party organizations retained control of the selection process. Taft believed he had accumulated enough delegates in non-primary states to win at Chicago. In truth, neither campaign arrived in the Windy City with enough votes to take the nomination on the first ballot. "No man in this city, nor any man in this hemisphere," the *Tribune* reporter figured, "knows absolutely who will be nominated for President."

Before the convention could begin its proceedings, the Republican National Committee had to settle disputes over 254 seats. These contested seats represented more than half the votes necessary for victory and the turbulent nomination fight had generated scores of rival delegations. Meeting in Chicago twelve days before the convention, the committee was charged with determining the legitimacy of the competing claims. Lawyers from both sides were prepared with detailed affidavits, but there, the New York *Sun* noted, resemblance to a civilized courtroom setting would likely end. Emotions were running high, the paper declared, and "the lawyers and witnesses and contestants are liable to break out into fisticuffs and thump each other around the committee room." There were "some contests, of course, Roosevelt ought to win," Taft acknowledged, but he believed the vast majority of the disputes brought by the Colonel's campaign had been intended merely to generate publicity. Most important, the National Committee comprised loyal Taft supporters whom Roosevelt would not be able to "frighten or bulldoze."

To Roosevelt's detriment, the first contests to be decided were from the South, where Taft had legitimately secured most of the delegates before his opponent even entered the race. The Roosevelt campaign had never expected to win these contests; indeed, they had been instituted simply to keep Taft's delegate count from appearing insurmountable before the northern primaries commenced. When these early cases came before the committee, even Roosevelt's men voted to seat the Taft delegates, conceding that in most instances "the contestants had failed to make out a case."

In Oyster Bay, Roosevelt followed the hearings with dismay, anxious that decisions in Taft's favor would begin to sound all too "familiar." In one Alabama district where Roosevelt had a reasonable case for seating two of his delegates, the committee nonetheless assigned the two places to Taft, confirming his fears. Roosevelt issued a fierce denouncement of the decision, charging that men had "been sent to the penitentiary for less reprehensible election frauds than the theft of that delegation." The Colonel's bombastic statement succeeded in riveting public attention on the actions of the National Committee. While the public outcry stiffened the spine of his supporters, it simultaneously hardened the attitudes of the Taft committeemen. On subsequent rulings in critical contests in Washington, Indiana, Texas, and California, the committee divided along straight partisan lines, with thirty-nine members consistently voting for Taft's delegates, fourteen for Roosevelt's.

Even impartial observers agreed that in the cases of Washington and Indiana, the committee's decisions complied with "neither justice nor logic." In Washington, the first primaries ever held in Spokane, Tacoma, and Seattle favored Roosevelt by two-to-one and sometimes ten-to-one margins. Overwhelming support in these populous areas should have secured him a majority of the state's fourteen delegates; but when evidence of fraud and "irregularities" in the city primaries surfaced at the hearings, the National Committee decided it had no choice but to stand by the proceedings of the state party organization, which had selected Taft. In Indiana, the committee "reversed itself," declining to examine a series of questionable district primaries in which Taft had emerged the clear victor. Though Roosevelt's team demonstrated that repeat voting had occurred and that some Indianapolis ballots had not been counted, the committee claimed that it was too late to relitigate the election results.

The National Committee's decision to award the majority of the Texas delegates to Taft represented what many considered the most glaring violation of "fair play." Texas was the sole southern state where the leader of the state party, Cecil Andrew Lyon, was a Roosevelt man. Lyon had accompanied the Colonel on his hunting trip in 1905 and remained a personal friend. At the state convention, Lyon engineered a solid victory for Roosevelt. The committee acknowledged that the Roosevelt delegation had been legally chosen according to party rules but claimed that the rival Taft delegation, selected at a rump convention, had greater popular support. Seating the Taft delegation, the committee argued, was an important step toward eliminating "boss rule" in the state of Texas. California was one of the last contests the committee considered. The hearing should have been simple: the California legislature had passed a primary law calling for delegates to be elected at large. Roosevelt, who had won the state by a margin of 77,000 votes, argued he was entitled to all twenty-six of the state's delegates. Taft had carried one district—the

4th congressional district of San Francisco. The committee gave the two San Francisco seats to Taft.

The rhetoric from both campaigns grew more vitriolic with each passing day. Taft's campaign manager, William McKinley, claimed that the Roosevelt forces were taking "desperate measures" to forestall the inevitability of Taft's nomination on the first ballot. It was "common knowledge," McKinley asserted, that several Negro delegates from the South had been "brazenly approached" by Roosevelt men "with offers of money" to switch their allegiance to the Colonel. "I dare them to name any of our men involved in bribery," Senator Joseph Dixon retorted. "McKinley is like a cuttlefish," he added, "that muddies the water that its own hideousness may not be seen."

Of the 254 seats, the National Committee finally awarded 235 to Taft and only 19 to Roosevelt. While most analysts agree that Taft rightfully won the great majority of the southern contests, which yielded over 150 delegates, the 100 remaining seats are subject to debate. Roosevelt likely deserved to win somewhere between thirty and fifty. Even with fifty additional delegates, however, he would have been short of a majority. Still, with the help of La Follette's delegates, Taft's nomination on the first ballot might be prevented—and then, anything was possible.

As the committee hearings wound to a close, Roosevelt's campaign managers decided that they must do something "to crystallize the public spirit, to force public indignation, or arouse enough public sentiment to compel the nomination of Roosevelt." The temporary roll of delegates established by the National Committee still had to be sanctioned by the convention's Committee on Credentials and voted upon by the delegates as a whole. Aware that time was running out, Senator Dixon prevailed upon Roosevelt to take the unprecedented step of coming to Chicago in person.

Roosevelt needed little encouragement. On June 14, he and Edith drove together to his *Outlook* office in New York. Reporters noted that "he seemed in a gay mood," sporting "a new sombrero, with a five-inch brim." The old hat he had worn when he gave his controversial Columbus speech, he quipped, "had been kicked around the ring enough to warrant a new one." The Colonel sequestered himself in his office for several hours before appearing in the lobby with a prepared statement: "A small knot of professional politicians," he charged, were trying "to steal" the right of the people "to make their own nomination." The rank and file of Republican voters, having clearly expressed their will in the primaries, were "not in the mood to see their victory stolen from them."

On the day Roosevelt boarded the *Lake Shore Limited* bound for Chicago, the president issued a brief statement from the White House. "All the information I get is that I will be nominated on the first ballot with votes to spare," Taft announced. He had remained silent during the proceedings of the National Committee, leaving Washington correspondents to chronicle his social life: a trip with Nellie to present diplomas to Annapolis cadets; a sail on the *Mayflower* to Hampton Roads; a dinner for Guatemala's minister of foreign affairs; an evening party on Capitol Hill; and a golf game at Chevy Chase.

While Taft remained tight-lipped, his campaign spokesmen made headlines, depicting Roosevelt's journey to Chicago as "an undeniable admission of defeat." Recalling the Colonel's assertion that he would not go unless it proved "absolutely necessary," William McKinley claimed that the trip represented "the last hope of a lost cause." New York boss William Barnes issued an acid personal attack: "Mr. Roosevelt's departure for Chicago was inevitable. Undignified as it is, and impotent as it will prove to be, its chief interest lies in the disclosure of the mania for power over which Mr. Roosevelt has no control."

The people of Chicago greeted the arrival of Theodore Roosevelt quite differently; word that Roosevelt was en route drove the city "plum crazy" with excitement. Ordinary business was suspended as tens of thousands made plans to celebrate Roosevelt's arrival. In the Loop district, one reporter observed, "there wasn't an office boy on the job." It seemed that "everyone had lost a grandmother and had failed to show up for work." Scuffles erupted in hotel lobbies as Roosevelt delegates routinely cried out "thief" at men sporting Taft badges. Armed with megaphones, Roosevelt supporters belted out songs for "Teddy," only to be met with "jeers and hoots" by equal numbers of Taft men. A bartender at one of the leading hotels offered a special "campaign drink" garnished with a lemon peel cut to resemble a Rough Rider hat. The circumference of the cocktail glass symbolized the political ring into which the Colonel had metaphorically flung his hat. Patrons who kept the lemon peel in the glass as they consumed the gin and vermouth concoction were Roosevelt men; those who discarded it supported Taft.

Hours before Roosevelt's train arrived at La Salle Station, three bands and an immense crowd, waving "Teddy" flags and wearing Roosevelt buttons, had gathered at the railway yards. "The sight of the Colonel, teeth agleam, romantic headgear, burly arms waving greetings, was catalytic," reported Mark Sullivan. "A mob, shouting, laughing, cheering, shoving, engulfed the police and took Roosevelt to its bosom." Thousands of screaming men and women lined the streets as the former president rode in an open car to the Congress Hotel. So frenzied was the crowd in the lobby that it took a team of five men using "football tactics" to propel Roosevelt to the elevator.

No sooner had the Colonel reached the quiet of his room than he clambered from a window onto a balcony over Michigan Avenue, anxious to satisfy the expectations of the waiting crowd. "His appearance was the signal for a roar," the *New York Times* reported. Smiling broadly and waving his hat, he initiated the wild acclaim of the people for several minutes before leaning over the stone railing to speak. "Chicago is a mighty poor place in which to try and steal anything," he roared. "Give it to 'em, Colonel," the crowd thundered in return. "Knock 'em out." In answer to their entreaties, he went directly after the president. "The receiver of stolen goods is no better than the thief," he fiercely pronounced. "The people will win. We have won in every State where the people could express themselves 3 to 1 and sometimes 8 to 1. This is a naked fight against corrupt politicians and thieves and the thieves will not win."

Before Roosevelt went to dinner that night, a newspaperman asked whether he was prepared "to stand up to the rigors of what lay ahead." His answer provided the enduring symbol of his campaign. "I'm feeling like a bull moose," he replied, invoking the antlered king of the northern woods whose supposed instinct "to gore his antagonist" reflected Roosevelt's combative mood. "He is essentially a fighter," Elihu Root said of his old friend, "and when he gets into a fight he is completely dominated by the desire to destroy his adversary." The bull moose icon captured the imagination of the American people. Images of the massive creature suddenly appeared on posters and placards all across the country, while button manufacturers desperately tried to keep up with demand. The Teddy bear had been supplanted by a far more imposing and belligerent mascot.

The following Monday, June 17, Roosevelt "put in one of the busiest days of his life—a very frenzy of activity, which amazed and startled even his close associates." He met with streams of supporters, interviewed Taft delegates who might be persuaded to change their minds, conferred with the seven governors, and talked with reporters, all the while continuing to draft the address he would deliver that evening to a mass audience. It was evident, a *Chicago Daily Tribune* reporter marveled, that the Colonel had not lost any of his "magnetism." And he had retained the gift for making every caller feel that he was "at that moment the exact person of all the world's population he loved and most desired to see."

More than 20,000 people clamored for tickets to hear Roosevelt's final speech of the nominating campaign. His managers had reserved the Auditorium, advertised as "the largest theater in the United States west of the Alleghenies," though, in actuality, it seated only 4,200. At 6 p.m., police shut down all the surrounding streets, allowing only ticket holders to enter the cordoned area. Hundreds of eager bystanders without tickets deployed all manner of "ingenious" schemes to gain entrance: women claimed their husbands and children were already inside; men insisted they were members of the glee club or the platform committee. All were steadfastly denied by the police. Every seat was filled long before Roosevelt arrived. An organist played patriotic tunes while the audience sang along. "A great roar" greeted the Colonel's entrance, and the "avalanche of applause" continued for nearly five minutes. At last, Roosevelt stretched out his arms and began delivering what critics considered not only "the most moving speech of his career" but "one of the most dramatic speeches ever made."

He had decided to run, Roosevelt explained, only when "convinced that Mr. Taft had definitely and completely abandoned the cause of the people and had surrendered himself wholly to the biddings of the professional political bosses and of the great privileged interests standing behind them." He entreated those still backing Senator La Follette to join with him, for he had honestly earned "the overwhelming majority" of the votes of the Republican progressive vote, and he alone could win the fight against Taft. He then set forth two maxims: first, those delegates "fraudulently put on the temporary roll by the dishonest action of the majority of the national committee" must be barred from voting; second, if they were allowed to participate, then progressives would not be bound by the actions of the convention.

Buoyed by the thunderous approval of the crowd, Roosevelt rolled toward his final call to arms. "A period of change is upon us," he proclaimed, warning that "our opponents, the men of reaction, ask us to stand still. But we could not stand still if we would; we must either go forward or go backward. . . . It would be far better to fail honorably for the cause we champion than it would be to win by foul methods the foul victory for which our opponents hope. But the victory shall be ours, and it shall be won as we have already won so many victories, by clean and honest fighting for the loftiest of causes. We fight in honorable fashion for the good of mankind; fearless of the future; unheeding of our individual fates; with unflinching hearts and undimmed eyes; we stand at Armageddon, and we battle for the Lord."

The hall erupted in tumultuous, sustained applause. "There is no question," William Allen White observed, "that the psychology of the situation, the enthusiasm of the crowds, the lonesomeness at Taft headquarters and the energy of the Roosevelt workers all point to Roosevelt's nomination." Still, White reflected, "it is delegates rather than psychology that make nominations."

By the commencement of the Republican National Convention on June 18, the atmosphere was so tense that "extraordinary preparations" were made "to preserve the peace." More than 1,000 policemen were deployed to the Coliseum, a massive stone structure "two squares in length and one in width," capable of seating more than 12,000 people. "Passions have been unloosed, anger has been unbridled," *The Washington Post* reported. "It is almost incredible to hear at a national convention the question seriously discussed if there will be firearms used and whether blood will be shed, but one can hear this at every step in the frightful jam and welter in the hotel lobbies."

In the comfort of the White House that morning, Taft was detached both physically and emotionally from the turmoil in Chicago. "Whatever happens," he wrote to Horace, "I shall be glad to have the strain over." With each passing month, the gulf between Taft and Roosevelt had grown. Taft had long considered himself a moderate progressive, aligned almost perfectly with the sentiments and policies of his old friend. In the throes of the brutal campaign, however, he had withdrawn increasingly from more progressive ideas. "If I am nominated, I shall have to take my stand as the representative of the conservative, sober, second thought of the people of the United States," he told one friend. "I may go down to defeat if a bolt is started by Roosevelt," the president acknowledged to another, "but I will retain the regular organization of the party as a nucleus about which the conservative people who are in favor of maintaining constitutional government can gather."

Before convening his cabinet at ten that morning, Taft spoke by long-distance telephone to his campaign team. McKinley and Charles Hilles were hopeful that they had the votes from the temporary list of delegates to win the crucial election of the convention's presiding officer, known as the temporary chair. Taft's candidate was New York senator Elihu Root, perhaps the shrewdest decision of his entire campaign. William Allen White described the sixty-seven-year-old Root as the "most learned, even erudite, distinguished, and impeccable conservative," a "calm, serene, and sure" leader, capable of dominating any gathering. Indeed, Roosevelt himself had once described his former secretary of state as "the ablest man that has appeared in the public life of any country in any position in my time." Such praise came before Elihu Root had backed William Taft through the bitter primary season. Now, Roosevelt announced his blistering opposition to Root's candidacy for the chairmanship, declaring: "Mr. Root stands as the representative of reaction. He is put forward by the bosses and the representatives of special privilege. He has ranged himself against the men who stand for progressive principles." Roosevelt's vituperative charges, Root's biographer observes, "were cruel thrusts at an old friend and Root felt them."

In an equally canny move, the Roosevelt team chose Wisconsin governor Francis McGovern as their candidate for the chairmanship. A few weeks earlier, Roosevelt had asked Dixon to "think over whether it would not be (a good play) wise to have McGovern of Wisconsin Permanent Chairman." Not only was Wisconsin's popular governor "a fine fellow," but "our choice of him would emphasize, as nothing else would, the fact that we wish all Progressives to stand together." Three days later, Roosevelt approached McGovern directly: "I assume that you will make the nominating speech for La Follette. And this would leave all the La Follette men at entire liberty to stand by him." If McGovern then ran for chair with the backing of the Roosevelt team, the progressives would present "a united front." When McGovern agreed, Roosevelt was delighted, hoping that "state pride" would lead La Follette's twenty-six delegates to support the selection of McGovern for chair.

At noon, Republican national chair Victor Rosewater called the convention to order. Rosewater had been designated to take charge of the proceedings until the election of the chair. But before Rosewater had the chance to call for nominations for the position, Roosevelt's floor leader, Missouri's Herbert Hadley, rose and motioned that seventy-two of the most fiercely contested Taft delegates, fraudulently included in the temporary roll by the National Committee, should be replaced by "honestly elected" Roosevelt delegates.

The method by which the Roosevelt team arrived at the figure of seventy-two remains a matter of conjecture. Three years later, a disaffected former intimate of the Colonel informed Taft that Hadley had approached Roosevelt, suggesting a determined fight on twenty-four or twenty-eight seats that had clearly been stolen from them in states such as Texas, Washington, California, and Indiana. Roosevelt, "with characteristic emphasis and energy," immediately tripled that figure, knowing how many votes he needed to control the convention.

Hadley's motion to bar participation of the seventy-two contested delegates brought great cheers from Roosevelt supporters. After silence was restored, Indiana's James Watson, a Taft spokesman, insisted that Hadley's motion "was not in order, on the ground that the convention itself had no chairman as yet," and therefore could not take up any business. Rosewater allowed forty minutes of debate on the motion before rendering the critical ruling that Hadley's motion was, indeed, out of order, and straightaway opened nominations for the chairmanship. As expected, Root's nomination was greeted with cheers from

Taft's supporters while McGovern drew equal enthusiasm from the Roosevelt side. A wave of surprise swept the hall, however, when La Follette's manager, Walter Houser, stood and forcibly insisted that McGovern's candidacy was "not with La Follette's consent." La Follette, he continued, would strike no deal whatsoever with Roosevelt. Houser's words propelled La Follette boosters to their feet, waving a large banner bearing the words: "We'll heed not Taffy's smile / Nor Teddy's toothsome grin / For it's La Follette once, La Follette twice / And La Follette till we win!" It seemed, the *New York Tribune* observed, that La Follette preferred "to see Senator Root elected rather than to see Colonel Roosevelt win the initial contest of the convention." Roosevelt's failure to reconcile with La Follette would prove costly.

So raucous was the atmosphere in the hall that nearly three hours passed before the voting was completed. When Rosewater announced that Root had defeated McGovern by a narrow margin of 558 to 501, pandemonium erupted. Pennsylvania's William Flinn marched up onto the platform, jabbed a finger at Root, and screamed out: "Receiver of stolen goods!" This brazen accusation prompted a series of fistfights that would have escalated into wholesale rioting without police intervention. Root approached the speaker's table to deliver his keynote address, apparently unperturbed by "the sweating wrathful faces in the pit." Marveling at the senator's comportment, William White reflected that "hundreds of [Root's] outraged fellow Republicans, men who had once been his friends, were glaring at him with eyes distraught with hate." Still, White observed, "Root's hands did not tremble, his face did not flicker."

That afternoon, in lieu of an anxious White House vigil for convention bulletins, Taft and Nellie had motored to the ballpark to attend a Nationals baseball game. When the president entered the stadium, the exuberant crowd of more than 20,000 "loudly cheered him for five minutes, the men throwing their hats into the air and the women waving their handkerchiefs." In a brief speech, Taft congratulated the team on their astonishing record—winning sixteen games in a row—before settling into his box to enjoy the action. So absorbed did he become in the game, which the Nationals won, that he never called for any updated bulletins. Returning to the White House, he discovered, to his great satisfaction, that Elihu Root had defeated Francis McGovern.

Roosevelt, meanwhile, had monitored every twist and turn of the proceedings by wire and telephone. All afternoon, hundreds of supporters had gathered in the Florentine Room of the Congress Hotel, where news from the convention floor was relayed by telephone to a man with a megaphone. "It was his duty," one journalist for the *New York Times* recorded, "to shout out the various incidents of the Colonel's triumphant progress" to those packing the room and the noisy throng assembled in the hallways and the lobby below. "There were frequent cheers from the crowd," the *Times* reporter wrote, "but as it progressed and the tide began to fall, threatening to leave the Colonel stranded on the political sands, the megaphone man lost his enthusiasm and his voice." When word spread that Roosevelt "had lost his preliminary skirmish," the crowd "fell silent."

The Colonel "remained in seclusion" for a short time while he and Dixon debated their next move. Later that night, he called a meeting of his delegates. Infusing them with his own energy and defiance, he "urged them to stand by him" as he resumed the fight to purge the tainted delegate roll once the convention came to order the following morning.

As delegates and spectators gathered for the second day of the convention, June 19, "electricity filled the air." The Coliseum was "a powder mine." With the chairman in place and the convention open for business, Hadley once again moved to replace the seventy-two contested Taft delegates with Roosevelt men. Chairman Root allowed three hours of debate on the motion. Watson, speaking for the Taft campaign, persuasively countered Hadley's motion, insisting that the full convention had "no knowledge" and was "in no temper to pass upon these contests." Evaluating the merits of the National Committee's controversial decisions belonged finally to the Committee on Credentials, which would be officially appointed later that day. After conferring with Hadley, Watson announced that a compromise had been reached and that Hadley would "consent to refer the resolution to the Committee on Credentials." The news thrilled Republicans on both sides of the bitter divide. A Pennsylvania delegate dashed to the stage, shouting, "Hadley, the next president of the United States," triggering a boisterous Hadley demonstration. Delegations marched about the hall exulting in the sudden possibility of a compromise candidate who might unite the party.

Just as suddenly, the spell was broken. An attractive young woman in a white dress, with a "radiant and infectious smile," stood up in the gallery blowing kisses and waving a large Roosevelt poster. The band began playing; shouts of "Teddy, Teddy, Teddy" rose from every corner in the hall. The woman made her way to the floor, escorted through the aisles "with the Roosevelt State delegations and placards falling in line." For forty-two minutes, the crowd followed her lead. Regardless of whether, as some speculated, this lady had been cued to begin blowing kisses and rallying support for the Colonel, the emotional Roosevelt demonstration ended the prospect of bringing Hadley to the stage as a compromise candidate.

When Root finally restored order, Hadley stood up, returning the convention's focus to the delegate confirmation process for the contested seats. While both he and Root agreed that "no man can be permitted to vote upon the question of his own right to a seat in the convention," Hadley stridently argued that the entire group of contested delegates should be barred from determining the composition of the vital Credentials Committee. Root, however, adhering to congressional parliamentary procedure, maintained that "the rule does not disqualify any delegate whose name is on the roll from voting upon the contest of any other man's right, or participating in the ordinary business of the convention so long as he holds his seat." This pivotal ruling, which allowed all the contested delegates to participate in the makeup of the Credentials Committee, essentially delivered control of the convention to Taft.

The committee members began their deliberations that night. Outnumbered thirty-one to twenty-one, the Roosevelt men soon realized that the Taft contingency had no intention of relitigating the National Committee's seating decisions. It was evident that most, if not all, of the contested delegates from the temporary roll would retain their seats, thereby providing Taft a clear majority. At midnight, a message arrived from the Colonel himself. "We are requested to go at once to the Florentine room of the Congress hotel," California's Francis Heney shouted, dismissively observing, "We can't get a square deal here." Back at the hotel, rebellious delegates and regular party members debated whether to bolt. While talk of a new party had been in the air since the convention opened, they now faced the difficult reality of engineering a split and financing a new creation. Suddenly the "prospect of leaving party lines, even to support Colonel Roosevelt," did not seem "half as attractive" as from "some miles further away." If the prospective members were "to be anything other than ridiculous figures in their state campaigns," this new party would require "time and money and effort," with money the paramount resource.

Amos Pinchot would long recall "the moment when the third party was born." At two o'clock in the morning, Roosevelt's inner circle gathered in his bedroom suite. "A dozen were seated around the table, the rest in armchairs or leaning against the wall," Pinchot wrote. "Roosevelt was walking rapidly up and down in silence." All eyes were on Frank Munsey and George Perkins, who whispered together in the corner. Without the financial support of these two wealthy men, there was little hope that a new party could be organized in time for the fall election. "Suddenly, the whispered talk ceased," Pinchot recollected, as both Munsey and Perkins "moved over to Roosevelt, meeting him in the middle of the room. Each placed a hand on one of his shoulders, and one, or both of them, said, 'Colonel, we will see you through.' " Munsey, the more effusive of the two magnates, added: "My fortune, my magazines and my newspapers are with you."

Returning to the conference room, Roosevelt read a short announcement to his delegates and supporters. If the convention refused to purge the tainted roll, the Colonel had resolved to "lead a fight for his principles in defiance of any action of the regular Republican convention." He expressed his thanks "to those who had come thus far in his fight, but who might not care to continue with him further." He would release these men, parting from them "on terms of friendship and undiminished gratitude." Those who chose to stay, he invited to participate in the birth of a new party. "Grizzled veterans wiped tears from their eyes," observed a reporter for the *Washington Times*, "making no effort to conceal their emotions."

As word spread that Roosevelt might come in person to deliver a statement that next day, the convention hall was "jammed to its fullest capacity." Minutes after Root gaveled the convention to order, Taft's floor leader called for a recess, explaining that the report of the Credentials Committee was not ready. A later four o'clock session lasted only a minute because the committee was still not ready. After this second delay, the convention was adjourned until the following day. Leaving the hall, delegates and spectators "gathered in knots," trying to piece together what was happening. Word circulated that men on both sides had revived the search for a compromise candidate—perhaps Cummins or Hughes or Hadley. It was rumored but later denied that Taft had agreed "to withdraw his candidacy providing Colonel Roosevelt would do the same." Details of the dramatic midnight session in Roosevelt's suite gradually began to surface—foremost Roosevelt's pledge to continue fighting if the Credentials Committee refused to seat his "honestly elected" delegates.

The mayhem in Chicago attracted unprecedented attention in the press. Correspondents covered every reversal, every sensational, rancorous moment, with relish. Reporters from dozens of national and regional publications were busy "politicking, filing correspondence, intriguing, pretending they were making a president." Sam McClure, who had come to the convention on his own, "stood on the edges" of the clusters of journalists, feeling "like a cipher." He had been "shorn" as editor of his once celebrated magazine a month earlier when his accumulated debt had finally forced him to lease and then sell

McClure's. The buyer had originally promised to retain McClure as editor, but the final deal left S.S., in his own words, "unhorsed." He had come to Chicago in search of work. At the convention hall and in the lobbies of the hotels, the fifty-five-year-old McClure met up with scores of old friends. For the first time in his life, observing the hurly-burly of the convention, Sam McClure found himself on the periphery of the action.

At noon on Friday, June 21, after two straight nights with little sleep, the Credentials Committee was finally ready to issue state-by-state reports on the contested seats. Proceeding alphabetically with Alabama, the committee chairman announced that the majority had voted to sustain the original decision of the National Committee and seat the two Taft delegates. A minority report introduced by the Roosevelt members was immediately voted down by a safe Taft majority. "A storm of hisses and booing" broke out, but Root swiftly restored order, calling on Arizona and then Arkansas. As one state after another voted to seat the Taft delegates, a voice from the gallery rose from the din: "Roll the steamroller some more!" As each new case was decided in favor of Taft's delegates, "a thousand toots and imitation whistles of the steamroller engine pierced the air." Bedlam followed as the galleries "caught the spirit," rhythmically shouting "Toot Toot" and "Choo Choo." The police removed a man who interrupted the proceedings by repeatedly crying: "All aboard." As he was escorted out, he grinned and waved, provoking "a great uproar." The convention was adjourned until the following day when, amid "a chorus of shrieks, whistles, groans and catcalls," the remainder of the states followed suit, granting Taft all seventy-two contested delegates.

With Taft's nomination on the first ballot virtually guaranteed, Henry Allen, a Roosevelt delegate from Kansas, asked to read a statement from the Colonel. "The Convention has now declined to purge the roll of the fraudulent delegates," Roosevelt's announcement began. "This action makes the convention in no proper sense any longer a Republican convention, representing the real Republican Party, therefore I hope that the men elected as Roosevelt delegates will now decline to vote on any matter before the Convention. . . . Any man nominated by the Convention as now constituted would be merely the beneficiary of this successful fraud." Roosevelt's inflammatory words provoked near riot on the convention floor. Taft delegates physically attacked Roosevelt delegates; brawls erupted throughout the galleries. Although police stopped dozens of scuffles, they were unable "to keep track of them all."

It was nearly 7:30 p.m. on Saturday night before the roll call for the nomination began. At 9:28 p.m., William Howard Taft was officially proclaimed the victor, with 561 votes. Three hundred forty-four Roosevelt delegates had followed the Colonel's request, designating themselves "present but not voting." An additional 107 delegates insisted on following the command of their primaries, casting their votes for Roosevelt. Of the remaining votes, La Follette received 41, Senator Cummins 17, and Justice Hughes 2.

THE WHITE HOUSE WAS so quiet on the night the convention concluded, one reporter remarked, that "no one would have suspected that under the same roof was the man who had been named as candidate of the ruling party." During the balloting, Taft had been with Nellie and their children in the living quarters. Young Charlie Taft was once again in charge of carrying the up-to-date bulletins from the telegraph office. Reporters noted that the fourteen-year-old was "all grin" when word came that his father had secured a majority vote for the nomination. But unlike the "electric" excitement that had filled the room four years earlier, when Nellie had sparkled with happiness and Taft had "laughed with the joy of a boy," both the president and first lady clearly understood that the divisive convention had rendered Republican chances for election in November almost impossible. "No Republican convention ever adjourned," observed the *New York Tribune*, "leaving so many sores and with so little prospect that the wounds would be healed."

"I am not afraid of defeat in November," Taft repeatedly said in the days that followed his nomination. He believed he had already achieved the victory he wanted by preventing Roosevelt from taking over the Republican Party and moving it in an incomprehensibly radical direction that threatened to upset the constitutional separation of powers and destroy "the absolute independence of the judiciary." In the course of the campaign, he had come to regard Roosevelt as "a real menace to our institutions." The central issue "at stake," he declared in his first public statement after his nomination, "was whether the Republican party" would remain "the chief conservator" of the country's constitutional guarantees. His victory, he proudly noted, had "preserved the party organization as a nucleus for conservative action."

THE ROOSEVELT DELEGATES HAD BEGUN their exodus from the Coliseum even before the finalization of Taft's nomination. A "mass meeting" had been called at Orchestra Hall a short distance away to begin the process of forming a new national party. Great applause greeted Edith and the Roosevelt children as they took their seats in a box near the platform. News that conservative Vice President James Sherman had been renominated added to the "delight" of the

Roosevelt men, who had worried that Taft might try to bolster the Republican ticket by selecting a progressive for the second spot. As they waited for the various state delegations to arrive from the convention, the audience joined in a spirited rendition of "America." When the California delegation paraded into the hall bearing its distinctive Golden Bear banner, the crowd erupted with "wild enthusiasm." A new round of cheers began a few minutes later when the Ohio delegation entered the room. "Here comes Texas," screamed a man in the audience as the Lone Star delegation marched in, followed in short order by Oklahoma. Similar waves of cheering met each of the delegations as they entered the room, creating a jubilant atmosphere.

California governor Hiram Johnson opened the formal proceedings of the new Progressive Party. "We came here," he declared, "to carry out the mandate of the people to nominate Theodore Roosevelt. By a fraud he has been robbed of that which was his. We, the delegates free and untrammeled, have come here to nominate him tonight." After a nominating resolution was unanimously passed, a notification committee composed of representatives from twenty-two states escorted Roosevelt into the hall. "The people leaped to their feet with a shout and for five minutes there was pandemonium," the *New York Tribune* reported. Another demonstration ensued when Roosevelt mounted the stage to declare his acceptance. He charged supporters to go home, "find out the sentiment of the people," and then reconvene a few weeks later at "a mass convention" to nominate "a progressive candidate on a progressive platform" that would truly represent people in all sections of the country. "If you wish me to make the fight I will make it," he promised, "even if only one State should support me. The only condition I impose, is that you shall be free when you come together to substitute any other man in my place if you deem it better for the movement and in such case I will give him my heartiest support."

The enthusiasm that had sustained the Roosevelt Progressives all week reached a peak that evening at Orchestra Hall. That a split party had little prospect for victory in November seemed irrelevant to the exuberant crowd, though not to former Republican senator Chauncey Depew, who offered a widely quoted comment as the 1912 Republican National Convention came to a close. "The only question now," he said, "is which corpse gets the most flowers."

DURING THE LAST WEEK OF June, as Democrats gathered in Baltimore to choose their nominee for president, reporters asked Roosevelt for his thoughts on the leading contenders—Speaker Champ Clark and New Jersey governor Woodrow Wilson. "I'm in the fight for an independent Republican party," Roosevelt defiantly declared, "and whatever the Democrats do will make no difference with me." Bluster aside, Roosevelt knew he had a much greater chance of victory if the Democrats chose the more conservative Clark over Wilson, who had emerged as a Progressive champion. "Pop's been praying for Clark," Kermit Roosevelt disclosed, revealing a Roosevelt far from indifferent to the outcome.

Like the Republicans, the Democrats quickly evidenced party discord in their own battle to appoint the temporary chair. Clark, with the backing of Tammany Hall, won that "first skirmish," but progressives refused to accept his nominee, overturning the result when the time came to choose a permanent chair. "Everybody's doing it. Doesn't it remind you of Chicago?" Roosevelt gleefully asked reporters. When the balloting began for the nomination, Clark took an early lead, reaching a majority vote on the tenth ballot. Democratic Party rules required a two-thirds vote for victory, however; by the fourteenth ballot, the momentum had shifted to Wilson. Sixteen ballots later, Wilson held a slight majority, but it was not until the forty-sixth ballot, eight turbulent days after the Democratic National Convention opened, that the New Jersey governor finally secured the nomination. The suspenseful events in Baltimore had transfixed the nation's attention. All week long, William White reported, "the country was standing around the billboards of newspapers in great crowds," waiting for the latest news from that city.

Throughout the dramatic ordeal, Wilson appeared impassive. "You must sometimes have wondered why I did not show more emotions as the news came in from the convention," he told reporters when word of his victory finally arrived, "and I have been afraid that you might get the impression that I was so self-confident and sure of the result that I took the steady increase in the vote for me complacently and as a matter of course. The fact is that the emotion has been too deep to come to the surface."

Wilson's nomination immediately affected Roosevelt's campaign prospects. Chase Osborn, one of the seven governors who had originally urged the Colonel to run, announced that he intended to support New Jersey's Democratic governor. With a progressive in the field, he explained, there was "no necessity for a new political party." The president of Minnesota's Progressive League agreed with Osborn, declaring that his organization would back Wilson. To illustrate that Wilson's appeal crossed party lines, his campaign cited more than 2,000 letters from Republicans pledging support. "Warmest congratulations from a Roosevelt Progressive Republican, who will vote for Wilson," one Californian had written. "I most gladly leave my old party—the party of my father—and join your cause," declared a lawyer from West Virginia.

Robert La Follette was delighted to support Woodrow Wilson. Still consumed with anger toward Roosevelt for projecting his personal ambition for a third term onto "a strong and rapidly growing" Progressive movement within the Republican Party, La Follette insisted that he would devote his days to "exposing the Roosevelt fraud." Calling the Colonel's primary battle "the most extravagant in American history," La Follette vowed to travel through the West, convincing farmers and laborers alike that "men notoriously identified with the Steel Trust and the Harvester Trust" were among Roosevelt's chief financial backers. Wilson gratefully acknowledged La Follette's support, lauding the Wisconsin senator as a courageous leader—"taunted, laughed at, called back, going steadfastly on."

"If Wilson had been nominated first," Roosevelt privately conceded, he might never have initiated the movement for a third party. "But it was quite out of the question," he told a friend, "after having led my men into the fight, that I should then abandon them." Now, supporters would conclude that he "was flinching from the contest," that he "was not game enough to stand punishment and face the possibility of disaster." Moreover, Roosevelt contended, while Wilson might be an "excellent man," supporting him "would mean restoring to power the Democratic bosses in Congress and in the several States, and I don't think that we can excuse ourselves for such action."

The die was cast. On July 7, Roosevelt's campaign manager Senator Dixon released "a call to the people of the United States," designating August 5 for a convention in Chicago of the newly formed National Progressive Party in Chicago. Each state was asked to send a bloc of delegates equal to the total of its senators and representatives, selected by whatever method the state leaders desired. The call urged all those in all sections of the country who believed in "a national progressive movement" to rally together "to secure the better and more equitable diffusion of prosperity," and to "strike at the roots of privilege" in both industry and politics.

Sixty-three prominent Republicans in forty states signed the declaration, but to Roosevelt's chagrin, many of his once most fervent supporters held back. Those who were running for office faced a difficult choice: forsake their hero or join an untested party with little time to develop the machinery to get out the vote. In the end, Montana senator Joseph Dixon was the only senator or governor up for reelection who took the leap of joining the Progressive Party. Senators Cummins, Hadley, Borah, and Nelson declared their opposition to Taft but declined to desert the Republican Party, promising instead to reform it from within. These defections both saddened and irritated Roosevelt, who believed the national cause should hold precedence. "I feel that Cummins naturally belongs to us," he lamented to one friend, while confessing to another, "I greatly regret that Hadley was so foolish as not to come with us."

Carefully observing Roosevelt's efforts to establish his "Bull Moose" party—the name the newspapers gave to the new organization—Taft felt the Colonel's campaign was "sagging." With a trace of sympathy, he remarked to Nellie that the Colonel was "up against now what I have always had to contend against, to wit, the selfishness of local candidates, and he is feeling the effects I suppose of a tendency to regularity that a third party always has to fight." Nonetheless, Taft predicted, Roosevelt was "such a persistent talker" that he would compel "the courage of his followers." Though he believed Roosevelt "utterly unscrupulous" at times, Taft marveled at his "method of stating things, and his power of attracting public attention."

Despite the historic dominance of the two-party system, the Colonel remained confident that once "the object and purposes of his campaign" were made clear, many voters would "be won over," in particular, those "holding back for a nicer definition of his aims." During the final two weeks in July, Roosevelt canceled public appearances and refused visitors, closeting himself "hour after hour" in his private study at Sagamore Hill to prepare both the planks of the new party's platform and the keynote address he would deliver on August 5, the first day of the convention. Fully aware that "a great measure of his party's success" would depend upon "the strength and solidity" of its principles and platform, he promised that his speech would represent "the greatest effort of [his] life."

When he finished the first draft of the platform, Roosevelt took a single day off, amusing reporters with his characteristically frenetic style of relaxation: "Got up with the sun; worked in the library until breakfast; took Mrs. Roosevelt for a long walk toward Cold Spring Harbor; rowed about twelve miles; went horseback riding after luncheon and played six sets of tennis on his return." The next morning, he was back at his desk, reinvigorated, to complete his projected 15,000-word keynote speech on schedule.

In the wake of the contentious Republican National Convention, President Taft wisely decided that "simplicity" should be "the distinguishing feature" of his notification ceremony, scheduled for August 1. There would be none of the fireworks, open-air concerts, booming cannons, parades, or decorated streets that had made Cincinnati so festive four years earlier. Marked by "unusual informality," the ceremony would be held in the White House, with only four hundred persons in attendance—primarily cabinet officials, members of Congress, and prominent Republican figures. During the last week in July, Taft worked "an average of sixteen hours a day" on his acceptance speech, designed as a defense of the Republican Party, the Constitution, judicial independence, private property, and civil liberty. "Roosevelt proposes to give out a radical platform that will startle some people," he told his Aunt Delia, recognizing exactly where he stood in the current political landscape. "Wilson says that his letter of acceptance is going to be radical, so between the two I have no part to play but that of a conservative, and that I am going to play."

The notification ceremony took place at noon in the East Room. The seats had been positioned in a semicircle around a raised platform. Stationed in the adjoining hallway, the Marine Band played patriotic airs. Warm applause greeted Nellie as she walked in and took her seat on the dais. Shortly thereafter, President Taft, accompanied by members of the Notification Committee, entered "amid loud shouts and handclapping." Following tradition, the chair of the Notification Committee, Elihu Root, delivered the official news of Taft's nomination.

In his brief remarks, Root referred to the turmoil surrounding the contested delegates. Speaking with force and authority, Root assured the president that as the convention's presiding officer, he had followed "long-established and unquestioned rules of law governing the party" at every step along the way. "Your title to the nomination is as clear and unimpeachable as the title of any candidate of any party since political conventions began." Root's testimonial provided tremendous comfort to Taft, who worried that Roosevelt's continued "harping" on the seating of delegates had persuaded people that his campaign had "committed great frauds," and that he had, in effect, stolen the nomination.

Taft accepted the nomination on behalf of a Republican Party "through which substantially all the progress and development in our country's history in the last fifty years has been finally effected." Our party, he declared, stands for "the right of property" and "the right of liberty," for institutions that have "stood the test of time," and for an economic system that rewards "energy, courage, enterprise, attention to duty, hard work, thrift, and providence" rather than "laziness, lack of attention, lack of industry, the yielding to appetite and passion." While he hoisted the conservative banner, Taft also spoke with genuine pride of the progressive legislation passed in recent years—the railroad legislation, the postal banking system, workers' compensation, an eight-hour day for all government contracts, and, most recently, the Children's

Bureau, the first federal agency dedicated to the social welfare of children. Even as the Republican Party protected the traditions of the past, he argued, it must remain sensitive to the shifting views of the role of government. "Time was," he explained, "when the least government was thought the best, and the policy which left all to the individual, unmolested and unaided by the government, was deemed the wisest." As industry consolidation and wealth disparity grew apace, however, it was "clearly recognized" that the government had a responsibility "to further equality of opportunity in respect of the weaker classes in their dealings with the stronger and more powerful." In sum, Taft did not intend to take the country backward, but rather to protect it against the demagogic proposals of his adversaries.

Asked to comment on Taft's speech, Roosevelt initially told reporters he preferred to answer the president in his own upcoming address at the Progressive Party Convention. "On second thought," he proved "unable to restrain himself," derogating Taft's words as "fatuous, inadequate, conservative," and ignorant of all "the live issues."

CHAPTER TWENTY-NINE

Armageddon

A Nov. 16, 1912, *Harper's Weekly* cartoon distilled the election's outcome: In the original caption, Taft, as the GOP elephant, says to his opponent, Bull Moose Roosevelt: "Well, you've helped rip me apart and 'downed' yourself! Now I hope you're satisfied!"

AS MEMBERS OF THE PROGRESSIVE Party began filling Chicago's hotels in preparation for the August 5, 1912, opening of the "Bull Moose Convention," journalists remarked that "no man could go through the lobbies" without confronting a gathering of people that "looked less like the average Republican or Democratic Convention than anything you ever saw." There was "not a saloon-keeper in the crowd"; the delegates were younger and more earnest than the usual convention goers. Petticoats were everywhere. Hundreds of social workers, suffragettes, and advocates for working girls' rights had enlisted in the new party. "Instead of forcing your way through a crowd of tobacco-stained political veterans," the *New York Times* observed, "you raise your hat politely and say, 'Pardon me, Madam.' "

A sense of "great adventure" was in the air, William Allen White observed in the *Boston Daily Globe*, despite the certainty of "a convention seemingly without contest or climax, a convention apparently devoid of chance or speculation." No one questioned who the nominee would be or how it would come about. There would be "no dead places" in the convention hall, "no blocks of delegates seated with arms folded, with faces set and sullen while other delegates behaved like dancing dervishes." There was little dissent on any major issue; almost everyone believed in the Social Gospel. They had come to Chicago as crusaders, "satisfied that they were in the right."

Roosevelt had already contrived his response to the only issue that threatened this near-perfect accord. Though the new party embraced a number of Negro delegates from the North ("more, in fact," he noted, "than ever before figured in a National convention"), there would not be a single Negro delegate from the South. The Colonel had given southern progressives permission to send solely white delegations. Hoping to break into the "Solid South," he had persuaded himself that true justice would only come to Negro residents of old Confederate states by enlisting the efforts of "high-minded white men." Roosevelt's policy "was riddled with contradictions and paradoxes," as the historian John Gable succinctly observes. "He wanted to establish the New Nationalism on a nationwide basis by using a sectionalist approach; he sought to bring an end to racism by a racist strategy." When word of Roosevelt's "lily-white" delegations leaked, discord surfaced among party members attending the convention. But once Roosevelt made it clear that he absolutely would "not budge," the issue quickly faded from discussion. It was evident to all that Roosevelt himself was "the whole show," the rhyme and reason for the new party.

Once again, Chicago went mad with Theodore Roosevelt's arrival. The streets were blocked, all work came to a halt, and the sidewalks were filled with thousands of people. Standing in the rear of an open automobile as he made his way to the same hotel suite where he had stayed during the Republican Convention, Roosevelt was buoyant: "My friends," he proclaimed, "it is a great pleasure for me to be in Chicago again, and this time at the birth of a new party and not at the death of an old party." Reaching the Congress Hotel, he settled in to work on his all-important speech. He had deliberately scheduled his address before the platform was voted on, informing delegates that he would accept their nomination only if the party's agenda corresponded to the views he intended to outline in his "Confession of Faith."

When Roosevelt stepped onto the stage of the Coliseum, he received perhaps one of "the greatest personal demonstrations that has ever been given a man in public life." Seasoned reporters were long accustomed to staged political rallies. Over the years, they had witnessed "hundreds of men marching about with signs and banners, and shouting themselves hoarse"; but this display of genuine emotion was unprecedented. The men and women gathering in Chicago had left past affiliations behind, having decided to "cast their lots together" under the banner of a fledgling movement. They signaled their collective identity with a unique "battle flag"—a red bandanna, chosen to represent "the plain people," the heart of the country. Every man wore the party's emblem around his neck; every woman had one around her wrist. One delegate had even fastened a red bandanna around the neck of a stuffed bull moose, strategically placed at the front of the auditorium.

Roosevelt "stood smiling in the center of the storm," waving his bandanna at friends in various delegations. Twenty thousand voices spontaneously rose in "The Battle Hymn of the Republic," the assembled crusaders finding courage and unity in the stirring words and soaring melody. During the nearly hour-long demonstration, Roosevelt's managers invited a procession of people onto the platform to shake hands with the Colonel. When Jane Addams was led to the stage, the delegates "sprang to their feet and yelled," offering a moving tribute to the settlement house worker who had committed her life to helping the poor and the underprivileged. "I have been fighting for progressive principles for thirty years," she said. "This is the first time there has been a chance to make them effective. This is the biggest day of my life."

When it seemed that the ecstatic tumult would never end, Roosevelt looked toward his wife, seated in a box near the stage. While Edith had dreaded her husband's entry into the race, she knew that once he had committed himself to the fight, he had to carry it through. Noting her "jovial smile and bright eye," Roosevelt beamed. He took off his hat and hailed her, inspiring the delegates to follow suit. Then, en masse, they gave homage to the former first lady, doffing their hats and cheering with abandon. "Mrs. Roosevelt shrank into her chair," Richard Harding Davis reported. "Her confusion, her pleasure, her distress, were as pretty as was the compliment the men strove to pay her. Before their onslaught of good will and admiration she blushed and looked like a young girl." The cheering continued unabated until she rose from her seat and bowed to the crowd. "That curtsy she made," exclaimed a correspondent who had covered the Roosevelt family since their days in Albany, "was the most prominent part I ever saw Mrs. Roosevelt take in public life!"

At last, the crowd composed itself enough for Roosevelt to speak. "At present," he began, "both the old parties are controlled by professional politicians in the interests of the privileged classes." Together, they would forge a new Progressive Party, based on "the right of the people to rule." Though the delegates cheered the familiar litany of progressive proposals to establish popular sovereignty through presidential primaries, direct election of senators, and the publication of campaign contributions, they reserved their most sustained applause for the Colonel's pledge to secure women the right to the vote. "In most cases where men applaud the mention of woman suffrage, they do it with a grin," one reporter remarked, but at this convention, "old men and young men alike got up on their chairs, yelled like wild Indians and waved anything available and portable."

Each new reform that Roosevelt projected, the *New York Times* noted, even the most radical, "fell on willing ears"—the call for "a living wage," the prohibition of child labor, federal regulation of interstate corporations, a graduated inheritance tax, an eight-hour workday for women, new standards for workmen's compensation, and, finally, a system of social insurance designed to protect citizens against "the hazards of sickness . . . involuntary unemployment, and old age" to which employers and employees would both contribute. "Surely there never was a fight better worth making than the one in which we are engaged," Roosevelt proclaimed. "Whatever fate may at the moment overtake any of us, the movement itself will not stop." He closed his two-hour address with the same stirring lines he had uttered seven weeks earlier in Chicago: "We stand at Armageddon, and we battle for the Lord."

The following day, the platform—"a purely Rooseveltian document," embracing everything the Colonel wanted—was approved. Nominations followed for the presidency. Jane Addams was among those who seconded Roosevelt's nomination, marking "the first time a woman ever had made a seconding speech in a national convention of a big party." After Roosevelt's unanimous election, the delegates chose California governor Hiram Johnson as the vice-presidential nominee. When the two men entered the hall, "wave upon wave of emotion swept over the audience." And when Roosevelt, equally moved, began to speak, "his voice trembled and he seemed to forget all the little tricks" he commonly deployed when trying to reach an audience. He simply thanked the delegates from the bottom of his heart, saying, "I have been President and I measure my words when I say I hold it by far the greatest honor and the greatest opportunity that has ever come to me to be called by you to the leadership for the time being of this great movement."

"The Bull Moose party has attained more strength & following than I thought possible at first," Ray Baker recorded in his journal not long after Roosevelt's powerfully emotional speech. "It includes no small number of high idealistic sincere men. Its platform is excellent. I can accept the planks nearly every one. A great figure in it is Miss Addams. It has aroused in some quarters almost a fanatical interest." Despite—or perhaps because of—his allegiance to the new party's principles, Baker could not shake a sense of disenchantment with its presidential nominee. "It is odd to me—as though the scales had suddenly fallen from my eyes," he reflected, "to see how different I regard T.R. from what I did a few years ago. There was no more enthusiastic & earnest admirer of him than I was. I felt that he was doing a great work—as I still believe he did do—the work of a great moral revivalist." But at this juncture, Baker believed, the Progressive movement needed a steadier hand, a leader "great enough to forget himself" in service of the cause. Roosevelt's titanic persona, the reporter lamented, "obscures everything," reducing the campaign to a referendum on his personal popularity rather than a discussion of vital reform issues.

In the end, Baker's concern over Roosevelt's distracting cult of personality was strong enough to shift his political allegiance. "As for me," Baker declared that August, "I shall vote for Wilson. I distrust the old party behind him & some of the things it stands for, but I have great confidence in the man and in the faction of the party (the progressive-Bryan faction) which he represents. And I like his clear, calm way of putting things." Baker had first encountered Woodrow Wilson two years earlier as he prepared an article on the forerunners of the 1912 campaign. "I left Princeton," he recalled years later, "convinced that I had met the finest mind in the field of statesmanship to be found in American public life." After that striking first impression, Baker followed Wilson's "meteoric career" with great interest; "overjoyed" by Wilson's subsequent nomination for the presidency, Baker "even dared to make speeches" on the Democratic nominee's behalf.

William Allen White had initially shared Baker's concerns, believing that the Progressive Party would be diminished if conceived as "a personal party." He had advised Roosevelt against bolting from the Republicans, preferring that he remain an "ace" for the future, when the new party had developed more fully. On a personal level, White found Wilson "a cold fish," with "a highty tighty way." The hand Wilson extended when the two men first met felt "like a ten-cent pickled mackerel in brown paper—irresponsive and lifeless." Nevertheless, White recognized that Wilson "had done a fine liberal job" as governor of New Jersey and would most likely make a good president.

Once Roosevelt mortgaged his own future to the new party, however, White never looked back. He quit his post as Republican national committeeman, joined the Progressive Party, and resolved to do everything possible for his hero and the Progressive cause. Playing a central role on the platform committee, White spent "four days and the better part of three nights" at the Congress Hotel in the week prior to the convention, drafting and reworking every section of the document before the delegates arrived. "Our social philosophy," he proudly remarked, could be "simmered down" to a single phrase—"using government as an agency of human welfare!"

Witnessing Roosevelt during the heady days of the Bull Moose Convention, White was impressed anew with his old friend's remarkable vitality—"He seemed full of animal spirits, exhaustless at all hours, exuding cheer and confidence." The rage that had consumed the Colonel during the Republican National Convention seemed transformed into ebullience with the birth of the new party: "What if he was a little obvious now and then as he grabbed the steering wheel of events and guided that convention not too shyly?" White later reflected, explaining, "I felt the joy and delight of his presence and, knowing his weakness, still gave him my loyalty—the great rumbling, roaring, jocund tornado of a man."

While White was transfixed by Roosevelt's performance during the Bull Moose Convention, his colleague Ida Tarbell was stuck in Europe. "It makes me crazy to get back," she wrote to Bert Boyden. "Of course T.R. is a wonder. But what about those Negro delegates? It looks to us here like a suicidal operation. But of course nothing he does counts." Though Tarbell had long been ambivalent about Roosevelt, she believed the financial and industrial powers arrayed against him were "a thousand times more dangerous than he." Months earlier, she had written to John Phillips suggesting that the magazine ought to address the widespread fearmongering that equated Roosevelt's pursuit of a third term with a slide into absolute monarchy. "Why stop with a third term?" opponents repeatedly warned. "The same reasons will apply for a fourth term, or for any number of terms." Without term limits, they argued, Roosevelt would simply stay in power for life. "We've got a King now," Tarbell parried, "this Wall Street—petty boss—Tammany—High Protection crowd. It's a <u>real</u> king—not a possible one like T.R. It's not one man; it's a tight combine of men. It's not impulsive, generous, full of human faults, but always for the human right." The priority, implored Tarbell, must be to destroy "this very able alliance that's got us all in its grip . . . that must be made clear. Then if T.R. needs to be batted a bit—we can do it." *The American Magazine* never ran a specific piece to counter criticism of "King Roosevelt," but John Phillips, Albert Boyden, John Siddall, and Finley Peter Dunne all finally supported Roosevelt and the Progressive Party.

Another of McClure's old team, Lincoln Steffens, was less well disposed toward Theodore Roosevelt when the campaign season opened. Months earlier, the two men had crossed swords over the sensational trial of two union leaders, the brothers John and James McNamara, who had been accused of setting off a bomb at the Los Angeles Times building. The blast, directed at the anti-union newspaper publisher Harrison Gray Otis, killed twenty-one workingmen and injured one hundred others. Labor leaders across the country rose to the defense of the two union men. Steffens publicly defended the brothers, labeling the bombing an act of "social revolution" rather than a crime. Roosevelt was disgusted by such a justification. "It seems to me that Steffens made an utter fool of himself," he told a California friend. "Murder is murder," he proclaimed in an *Outlook* editorial, "and the foolish sentimentalists or sinister wrong-doers who try to apologize for it as 'an incident of labor warfare' are not only morally culpable but are enemies of the American people, and, above all, are enemies of American wage-workers."

But even fierce disagreement with Roosevelt over the culpability of the McNamara brothers did not prevent Steffens from sympathizing with both the Progressive Party and the Colonel's continuing struggle against the titans of Wall Street. "It looks like Wilson out here," the journalist reported to his brother-in-law after canvassing a wide range of opinion; "all the interests are determined to beat T.R. at any rate. They have given up Taft, and they don't care for Wilson, but the man they hate is the Bull Moose and they are bound to beat him if they can. It's personal, you see."

EARLY ON, WILLIAM TAFT MADE it clear that he had no plans to engage in "a whirlwind campaign." Though he planned to deliver a few prepared speeches in Washington or Beverly, he would observe the time-honored precedent that "a President who is a candidate for reelection should remain at home and leave it to the judgment of the people to decide whether or not his record of achievement" deserved a second term. He believed "in his heart" that he had executed his office with dignity and fairness, endeavoring in a judicial manner to decide all issues on their merits without regard to personal advantage. He had revitalized an aging Supreme Court by appointing a staggering six justices to the bench—all distinguished lawyers, half of them Democrats. Most important, Taft's countrymen had enjoyed four years of peace and prosperity under his administration. While the federal government could not bid "the rain to fall, the sun to shine, or the crops to grow," Taft remarked, it could, by pursuing wrongheaded policies, "halt enterprise, paralyze investment," or cause "hundreds of thousands of workingmen" to lose their jobs. William Taft trusted that "the negative virtue of having taken no step to interfere with the coming of prosperity and the comfort of the people is one that ought highly to commend an administration, and the party responsible for it, as worthy of further continuance of power."

Taft's campaign managers accepted his refusal to go on the stump, but worried that both Roosevelt and Wilson would dominate the headlines while their candidate seemed detached from the battle. Without active leadership from the White House, RNC chairman Charles Hilles found it difficult to raise funds, engage surrogate speakers, or keep the public's attention on the president. "It always makes me impatient," Taft confided in Nellie, "as if I were running a P. T. Barnum show, with two or three shows across the street, as if I ought to have as much advertising as the rest." When advisers suggested that he replicate the aggressive demeanor of the Bull Moose, he circuitously declared: "I couldn't if I would and I wouldn't if I could."

Clearly, the campaign had savagely exacerbated existing tensions between Taft and Theodore Roosevelt. "As the campaign goes on," Taft told Nellie, "it is hard for me to realize that we are talking about the same man as that man whom we knew in the Presidency." As for his "personal relations" with his erstwhile friend, Taft bluntly added, "they don't exist." Seriously hurt by the rift, Taft preferred to recall his old friend and mentor as almost a separate person from the belligerent, insult-hurling foe against whom he currently contended. He now looked upon Roosevelt simply "as an historical character of a most peculiar type in whom are embodied elements of real greatness, together with certain traits that have now shown themselves in unfitting him for any trust or confidence." Taft was particularly incensed by the open contempt Roosevelt displayed both toward him personally and for the nation's highest office. When an audience member solicited comment on the president, Roosevelt mockingly replied: "I never discuss dead issues." Before another audience, he repeated a variation of this jest, observing that all the old Republican bosses were shifting allegiance to Wilson, recognizing that the president "was a dead cock in the pit." Nor, Roosevelt elaborated, was the Republican platform even "worthy of serious discussion," given that it was adopted at a convention "organized by theft."

The fall campaign was already in full swing before the president yielded to his supporters' pleas. Standing before an audience of 2,500 cheering Republicans on the lawn of his summer home in Beverly, he delivered a spirited attack on Roosevelt's third party. One issue stood above all others, he declared, eclipsing the traditional partisan wrangling between Republicans and Democrats over the tariff and the trusts—the issue of "the preservation of the institutions of civil liberty as they were handed down to us by our forefathers." Splitting away from the Republican Party, a third party had been created "merely to gratify personal ambition and vengeance." In the pursuit of votes, this new party had employed "every new fad and theory, some of them good, some of them utterly preposterous and impracticable, some of them as Socialistic as anything that has been proposed in the countries of Europe"; all had been stuffed into the Progressive platform. Taken together, the president warned, these reforms suggested "an entire willingness to destroy every limitation of constitutional representative government." So long as Republicans remained true to their heritage, he predicted, this radical movement would surely fail. "The great bulk of our people are not emotional, undiscriminating, superficially minded, non-thinking, or hero worshipping," he asserted; "they have the virtue of second sober thought."

Expanding on the same theme two days later at the Beverly Republican Club, Taft predicted that the secession of the third party would prompt a "new vitality" among traditional Republicans. "We know that we are a better set of men than we are now called by those who were very glad at one time to be known as leading Republicans. No student of history can deny that the grandeur of this Nation, and the height that it has reached among the Nations during the last sixty years, has been due to the guidance, and the force, and the energy, and the enterprise of the Republican Party."

WELL AWARE FROM THE OUTSET that the Republican split made victory in November "very improbable," Roosevelt nevertheless resolved to give every ounce of his energy to the campaign. He embarked upon an unprecedented speaking tour, covering forty states in every region of the country, including the solid Democratic South. He planned to travel by train, making whistle-stops at hundreds of small towns along the way. Although he anticipated a "deluge of travel and dust and howling and irritated fatigue," he would willingly invest "a tremendous amount of very hard work" so long as there was "a chance" of victory. In addition to three or four prepared addresses each day, he agreed to appear on the train's rear platform wherever a crowd assembled, to ride in parades, attend banquets, and meet with local committeemen. "I am perfectly happy," he told his British friend Arthur Hamilton Lee, "for I have never in my life been in a movement into which I could enter as heartily as into this."

The Colonel opened his campaign in Providence, Rhode Island. Journalists noted with amazement that even in this "boss-ridden" and "rock-ribbed" Republican state, immense crowds welcomed him. The 7,000 cheering people who thronged the streets, mostly workers from the textile mills and nearby shops, were markedly different from the usual Republican crowds. Speaking that evening to an overflow audience at Infantry Hall, Roosevelt decried the "rule of the bosses," beseeching his listeners to help establish "the rule of the people" in its place. Echoing the crusading spirit of the Progressive Convention, the audience launched into "The Battle Hymn of the Republic" and "Onward, Christian Soldiers." A massive banner above the speaker's rostrum bore the legend: "We stand at Armageddon and we battle for the Lord." Buoyed by his enthusiastic reception, Roosevelt predicted that Progressives could triumph anywhere "if they could get the people to realize what they were trying to accomplish."

Governor Wilson had initially hoped to confine his campaign appearances to a few well-prepared speeches. "My private judgment," he told a *Washington Times* correspondent, "is that extended stumping tours are not the most effective method of conducting a campaign. You must remember that I am governor of New Jersey and that I must keep in touch with the business of the State." He hoped to reach the public through a reasoned discussion of the issues and a clear explication of his political philosophy. He had no appetite for the kind of whistle-stop tour that would require him to stand on a train platform and shout extemporaneous remarks to a boisterous crowd.

Convinced from the beginning that Taft would run third, Woodrow Wilson viewed Roosevelt as his chief adversary. "I am by no means confident," he admitted to a friend. "He appeals to their imagination; I do not. He is a real, vivid person, whom they have seen and shouted themselves hoarse over and voted for, millions strong; I am a vague, conjectural personality, more made up of opinions and academic prepossessions than of human traits and red corpuscles." The Colonel's headlong campaign would demand sustained exertion. "I haven't a Bull Moose's strength," Wilson reflected, "as Roosevelt seems to have."

Despite his reservations, Wilson eventually agreed to make an extensive tour of the Midwest during the month of September, followed by a second trip "as far west as Colorado" in October. The governor "had, in reality, only one speech to make," Baker observed, and "he made it again and again." He urged listeners to envision a more expansive future for themselves and their country. He delivered his words with "such consummate skill as an orator" that each audience came away convinced that the candidate had spoken directly to their hopes and needs. "Wilson was a new personality in American public life," Ray Baker explained. "He profited by antithesis. He had the unfamiliar glamour, to the popular eye, of the scholar, the thinker, the historian. There had been enough heat in politics; what was needed now was light. Wilson was expository rather than denunciatory. He was asking the country to look at its problems: he was not offering panaceas." With disarming honesty, the candidate repeatedly stated: "I do not want to promise heaven unless I can bring it to you. I can only see a little distance up the road."

Positive responses from both audiences and the traveling press corps bolstered the governor's confidence. Speaking at Boston's Tremont Temple on September 27, he relaxed enough to offer a playful barb at Roosevelt's expense: "Suppose you choose the leader of the third party as President. Don't you think he will be pretty lonely? Not that he'll mind it, because I believe he finds himself rather good company." Wilson's lighthearted ribbing of Roosevelt's majestic ego underscored a serious point—without a majority party behind him in Congress, the Colonel would likely find it difficult to get anything done.

Retiring to the Copley Plaza Hotel after his speech, Wilson discovered that President Taft was in the banquet hall for a dinner address to the International Congress of Chambers of Commerce. The governor sent word that he would be "very glad of the opportunity" to meet with the president before the evening ended. Shortly before midnight, a meeting was arranged in a private suite on the fifth floor. "I hope the campaigning has not worn you out," Taft remarked. "It has been quite a hard week," the governor acknowledged. Indeed, his voice had gotten "a bit husky" from overuse. "Well," Taft cordially responded, "there are three men that can sympathize with you, Mr. Bryan, Mr. Roosevelt, and myself." The mutual regard between Taft and Wilson was evident as the conversation continued. "It was a very delightful meeting," Wilson told reporters waiting in the corridor. "I am very fond of President Taft."

The natural warmth President Taft showed to Governor Wilson reflected an odd tranquility about the election. While Taft occasionally detected "currents of air" that seemed to be "blowing in the right direction," he acknowledged to friends that he would "probably be defeated." Winning the nomination had been the all-important victory—and not simply because he had bested Roosevelt. He had long believed that a loss at the convention would have been regarded as a personal rejection, whereas defeat in the fall election reflected a more general reverse for the party. "I seem to think that we have won what there was to fight about, and that what follows is less important," he told Nellie without a trace of defensive rationalization.

Nellie shared her husband's equanimity. "I wanted him to be re-elected, naturally," she later wrote, "but I never entertained the slightest expectation of it and only longed for the end of the turmoil when he could rest his weary mind and get back into association with the pleasant things of life." In the aftermath of Nellie's stroke, her close family circle had sustained her. Her children were thriving: Robert was an editor of the *Harvard Law Review*; Helen would soon be returning to Bryn Mawr; and irrepressible Charlie was getting excellent grades at the Taft School in Connecticut, where Horace kept a watchful eye over him. As the election approached, Nellie remained in Beverly, content to be removed from the political fray. "She is in a condition where defeat will not disappoint her, if at all," Taft reported to Horace. "I am glad to say she is in a happy frame of mind."

As THE BULL MOOSE CANDIDATE headed west through Iowa and North Dakota to Oregon and California, he continued to attract huge crowds; nonetheless, his managers fretted that he "was going stale," repeating tired arguments about the Republican Convention, the collusion of business and politics, and the dangers of vesting too much power in the courts. Instead of "rehashing" these matters, they pressed him to engage Woodrow Wilson directly. To prepare for such a confrontation, Roosevelt commenced to study the governor's record, receiving daily briefings on his speeches and closely following his rival's campaign. A select group at Roosevelt's headquarters prepared a lengthy report that outlined Wilson's positions on every question—from the minimum wage and woman suffrage to labor and the trusts. From that point forward, remarked Roosevelt's publicity chief, Oscar King Davis, "it was Wilson, Wilson, Wilson, all the time in the private car, and nothing but Wilson and his record in the Colonel's talks."

Roosevelt launched the "first direct assault" on his Democratic opponent in San Francisco, with what the *New York Times* deemed the "most important speech of his campaign since his 'Confession of Faith.' " His criticism addressed the fundamental role of the government in a democratic society. "Mr. Wilson is fond of asserting his platonic devotion to the purposes of the Progressive Party," Roosevelt began, "but such platonic devotion is utterly worthless from a political standpoint because he antagonizes the only means by which those purposes can be made effective." Roosevelt claimed that "the key to Mr. Wilson's position" could be found in a single line he had recently voiced in New York: "The history of liberty," Wilson had stated, "is the history of the limitation of governmental power, not the increase of it." Such an understanding, Roosevelt charged, was a reincarnation of the old "laissez faire doctrine," which, if restored, would mean "the undoing of every particle of social and industrial advance we have made." Under Wilson's theory of limited governmental power, Roosevelt charged, "every railroad must be left unchecked, every great industrial concern can do as it chooses with its employees and with the general public; women must be permitted to work as many hours a day as their taskmasters bid them." By contrast, his own party would build on laws recently established to protect the nation's consumers and workers. His "New Nationalism" proposed "to use the whole power of the Government to protect all those who, under Mr. Wilson's laissez-faire system, are trodden down in the ferocious, scrambling rush of an unregulated and purely individualistic industrialism."

Of course, the single line excerpted from Wilson's address did not represent the full measure of the candidate's thinking about governmental power. In other speeches, Wilson articulated his conviction that "freedom to-day is something more than being let alone." In the modern industrial world, he explained, laws were needed to ensure "fair play." In keeping with the traditional Democratic philosophy Wilson insisted that these laws should emanate from state capitals, not Washington. He understood that the expansion of federal power was anathema to the southern base of the Democratic Party, where states' rights safeguarded segregation. Despite his more progressive personal views, Wilson could not abandon his party's historic commitment to the Jeffersonian ideal of a smaller, less expansive federal government.

Roosevelt's "declaration of war" against his opponent's concept of limited national government prompted Wilson to articulate a more positive strategy to expand the nation's prosperity. In a speech at Indianapolis, he called upon his countrymen to "open again the fields of competition, so that new men with brains, new men with capital, new men with energy in their veins, may build up enterprises in America." While Roosevelt accepted trusts as inevitable and strove, through centralized federal power, to regulate them in the interests of the public, Wilson argued that the very size of the corporations posed a problem. He called upon the American people "to organize the forces of liberty in our time to make conquest of a new freedom."

Wilson's "New Freedom" slogan caught on, providing a counterpoint to Roosevelt's "New Nationalism." Expanding on his theme as the campaign progressed, Wilson argued that "the wealth of America" lay in its small businesses, its towns and villages. "Its vitality does not lie in New York, nor in Chicago," he asserted; "it will not be sapped by anything that happens in St. Louis. The vitality of America lies in the brains, the energies, the enterprise of the people throughout the land; in the efficiency of their factories and in the richness of the fields that stretch beyond the borders of the town." By reinforcing the anti-trust law and by "abolishing tariff favors" and "credit denials," he would return genuine free enterprise to America.

Never one to shy from a fight, Roosevelt delighted in the escalating policy debate with Wilson, vigorously defending his regulatory approach and claiming that Wilson's proposal to break up big corporations defied the realities of modern life. Drawing on his own experience, he pointed out that when the Supreme Court dissolved Standard Oil, the company simply "split up into a lot of smaller companies," which continued to operate "in such close alliance" that they remained, in effect, under Standard's control. The result was higher prices for the consumer and even lower wages for the workers. Only the owners had benefited: "The price of the stock has gone up over 100 percent," Roosevelt observed, "so that Mr. Rockefeller and his associates have actually seen their fortunes doubled by the policy which Mr. Wilson advocates and which Mr. Taft defends." Little wonder, the Colonel sardonically concluded, that Wall Street prayed for either Wilson or Taft's policies in preference to his own commitment to put all these companies under a powerful Federal Commission.

By early October, it was "becoming more and more plain that the fight was between Wilson and Roosevelt," Oscar Davis remarked. "Taft was steadily fading into the background." The Republican Party receded as both front-runners directed their energies to the task of distinguishing the New Freedom from the New Nationalism. The two doctrines "were as close as fraternal twins" compared with the platform embraced by the Socialist Party candidate, Eugene Debs. On the presidential ballot for a fourth time, Debs maintained that the capitalist system was "utterly incapable" of dealing with the problems of the industrial age. His Socialist Party platform called for "the collective ownership" of transportation and communication, of land (wherever it was practical), and of the banking system. To ensure more direct democracy, the Socialist platform proposed the abolition of the U.S. Senate, the elimination of the president's veto power, and the removal of the Supreme Court's power to declare laws passed by Congress unconstitutional.

On the night of Monday, October 14, Roosevelt was scheduled to deliver a speech to a large Milwaukee audience. Two days earlier, as a bitter wind blew through the open flaps of "a mammoth tent" on Chicago's west side, he had shouted himself so hoarse that he could barely speak beyond a whisper. But over the emphatic resistance of Dr. Scurry Terrell, his throat specialist, Roosevelt insisted on honoring his commitment to the people of Milwaukee—which included participating in a parade through the city streets, a banquet at the Gilpatrick Hotel, and a public address. "I want to be a good Indian," he declared.

An open touring car stood in front of the hotel, waiting to convey the Roosevelt party to the Auditorium after dinner. Roosevelt entered first, followed by Henry Cochems, head of the Progressive Party's speaker's bureau. Gathered on the opposite curb, the crowd started clapping and cheering. Roosevelt acknowledged the ovation by standing and doffing his hat. At that moment, a man at the front of the crowd raised a large pistol and fired. "It was point-blank range," Oscar Davis observed, "and almost impossible to miss." As the bullet hit the right side of the Colonel's chest, he lurched and collapsed on the seat. Just as the man with the pistol prepared to fire a second shot, Roosevelt's stenographer, Elbert Martin, leapt on the assailant. A former football player, Martin quickly disarmed the man and began to strangle him. "I wasn't trying to take him prisoner," Martin later admitted, "I was trying to kill him." The inflamed crowd spurred him on, shouting, "Lynch him," "Kill him." In the midst of the chaos, Roosevelt struggled to his feet and called out to Martin, "Bring him here," he ordered, "don't hurt him." The stenographer grudgingly obeyed, dragging the man toward the car. Roosevelt lifted his would-be assassin's head to look directly at his face. "What did you do it for?" he asked, but marking the dead expression in the man's eyes, he added, "Oh, what's the use. Turn him over to the police."

Falling back on his seat once again, Roosevelt ordered the chauffeur to go straight to the Auditorium, against the insistence of Dr. Terrell, who demanded that they stop first at the emergency room of the hospital to have him examined. "You get me to that speech," Roosevelt shouted. Only when they reached the green room in the Auditorium did Roosevelt allow the doctor to look closely at the wound, which was located just under his right nipple. "It was bleeding slightly," Oscar Davis noted, "the blood-spot on his white shirt being about the size of a man's hand." Unable to determine where the bullet had lodged, Dr. Terrell again demanded a thorough hospital examination. "It's all right," Roosevelt said, inhaling deeply several times. "I don't get any pain from this breathing." And with a handkerchief secured to his chest as a bandage, he headed for the stage.

When told of the shooting, the audience cried out in shock, but Roosevelt quieted them down. "It's true," he informed them, "but it takes more than that to kill a bull moose." He withdrew his spectacles and his speech from the inside pocket of his coat. The speech had been typed on fifty heavy sheets of paper folded in half to fit into his breast pocket. Seeing the hole the bullet had ripped through the pages, and the dented spectacle case, Roosevelt suddenly understood "how narrowly he had escaped." Indeed, the bullet would have gone "straight into his heart" if it had not been deflected upward by the buffering combination of his thick manuscript and metal eyeglass case; instead, it struck the fourth rib on the right side, fracturing the bone but coming to a halt.

Roosevelt had spoken for about half an hour when Oscar Davis, standing at the side of the stage, noticed that the color had drained from his face and he was "laboring very hard to go on." He approached, suggesting that the Colonel bring the speech to a close. "No, sir," Roosevelt replied, with a ferocious expression. "I will not stop until I have finished." Though "his heart was racing," he ignored the "knifelike pain in his ribs" and continued to speak for an additional hour. Finally reaching the last page of the script, he turned to Dr. Terrell and murmured, "Now I am ready to go with you and do what you want."

While Roosevelt was being examined at Milwaukee Hospital, police interrogated the attacker, John F. Schrank. A thirty-six-year-old former saloonkeeper from the East Side of Manhattan, Schrank produced a written manifesto that described a dream in which President McKinley had risen from his coffin and indicted Roosevelt as his murderer. He told police that he had first begun "to think seriously" of Roosevelt "as a menace to his country" when he heard the Colonel shout "Thief" at the Republican Convention and announce his decision to run for a third term on a new party. "Any man looking for a third term ought to be shot," Schrank declared. He was fully persuaded, he added, "that if Colonel Roosevelt was defeated at the fall election he would again cry 'Thief!' and that his action would plunge the country into a bloody civil war." Schrank confessed that he had followed Roosevelt to Charleston, New Orleans, Atlanta, and Chattanooga with the intention of shooting him, but the right opportunity had never presented itself.

At Milwaukee Hospital, Roosevelt was in good spirits, joking with doctors as they examined the wound and took X-rays to reveal the location of the bullet. The decision was made to transfer him to Mercy Hospital in Chicago, where chest surgeons would determine if they needed to operate to remove the bullet. "There are only three possible dangers," Roosevelt explained to reporters when he reached Mercy Hospital, "pleurisy, pneumonia, and blood poisoning. If we can get safely past these three there isn't a thing in the world to prevent me from resuming my campaign."

President Taft was at the Hotel Astor in New York to attend a banquet in honor of his cabinet when the head of the Associated Press approached his table with news of the shooting. "All over the room conversation died down," the *New York Tribune* reported; "whispers of 'Roosevelt!' and 'Impossible!' were heard." The dinner guests got up from their tables to rush to the telephones. Later that night, Taft issued a short statement to the press, and the following morning he sent a sympathetic telegram to Roosevelt. Woodrow Wilson offered to suspend his campaign while his opponent remained hospitalized, but Roosevelt swiftly declined his offer: "The fight should go on to its conclusion, just as it would in case of battle," he argued, "even though the commanding general might be struck down."

Edith Roosevelt had been enjoying a musical comedy in New York when she received word of the attack on her husband. She left the theatre and straightaway made arrangements to travel to Chicago the following day, accompanied by Theodore Junior, Ethel, and the family doctor, Alexander Lambert. "It's the best news I've heard since I got here," Roosevelt said. Edith took command as soon as she reached the hospital, consulting with the medical staff, limiting visits, and making sure that her husband followed the doctors' orders. "He has been as meek as a lamb since the Boss arrived," noted the *New York Times* correspondent. Despite Roosevelt's pleas to let more people into his room, she insisted that he needed rest. "This thing about ours being a campaign against boss rule is a fake," he said with chagrin. "I never was so boss ruled in my life as I am at this moment."

By the following Saturday, doctors determined that the danger of infection was past, that the bullet was lodged "outside of the rib" and could most likely "be allowed to live there permanently." The Colonel's color and appetite had returned, though his broken rib continued to make it painful to breathe. So long as he remained "in absolute quiet" for several days, the hospital medical staff agreed to release him after the weekend. By Monday morning, he was cleared to leave. An ambulance transferred him to his railroad car, where he slept and read until the train reached New York.

"I am in fine shape," he reported to Bamie a few days later. Though his wound remained "open" and the doctors would not allow him to return to the campaign trail, the indomitable Colonel still hoped to make one final appearance at Madison Square Garden at the end of October, the week before the election.

The shooting forced the cancelation of scores of campaign events, yet the dramatic attack upon the stalwart and stoic former president had rekindled the nation's empathy, and speculation swirled about how it might reshape the election. "Encouraging reports are coming in from all over," Ethel Roosevelt noted to Bamie; "things look better for us than they ever have." While immense crowds continued to cheer Governor Wilson at every stop of his final campaign tour, a Democratic speaker at an Oakland rally articulated the worst fears of the Wilson camp. "The bullet that rests in Roosevelt's chest has killed Wilson for the Presidency," he said. Taft recognized the difficulty of anticipating the political impact of such an event. With his usual equanimity, he took a more philosophical approach to the furor. "What effect the incident will have on the election," he remarked, "is difficult to conjecture."

Special precautions were taken to protect Roosevelt from "the rush of the crowd" as he made his way to Madison Square Garden on October 30 to deliver his "farewell manifesto." At dinner with Edith and Dr. Lambert earlier that evening, the Colonel had expressed surprise that the simple journey to the city had fatigued him, but he "looked to the excitement of the moment to carry him through." Aware that his voice had not "regained its accustomed power," he was anxious to begin speaking as soon as he took the stage. Catching sight of him, however, the audience of 16,000 poured forth a spontaneous and emotional tribute for forty-two minutes, despite Roosevelt's best efforts to dampen the crowd.

"Perhaps once in a generation," Roosevelt at last began, "there comes a chance for the people of a country to play their part wisely and fearlessly in some great battle of the age-long warfare for human rights." Perhaps less dramatic than the struggles their fathers and forefathers had faced, the battle for social justice was "well-nigh as important." If the problems created by the industrial age were left unattended, Roosevelt cautioned, America would eventually be "sundered by those dreadful lines of division" that set "the *haves*" and the "*have-nots*" against one another.

"We know that there are in life injustices which we are powerless to remedy," Roosevelt acknowledged, "but we know also that there is much injustice which can be remedied." The Progressive Party, he pledged, would harness the "collective power of the people through their governmental agencies" to move the country forward. "We propose to lift the burdens from the lowly and the weary, from the poor and the oppressed," he asserted. "We propose to stand for the sacred rights of childhood and womanhood. Nay, more, we propose to see that manhood is not crushed out of the men who toil, by excessive hours of labor, by underpayment, by injustice and oppression. . . . Surely, there never was a fight better worth making than this." And, finally, contemplating this cause so much larger than any individual, Roosevelt concluded: "Win or lose I am glad beyond measure that I am one of the many who in this fight have stood ready to spend and be spent."

Throughout, his face and manner had revealed strain, but the voice was "as clear as a bell." Those who had witnessed scores of earlier appearances felt they heard "a new Roosevelt" on this night, free from "the old violence and the old sarcasm." He uttered not a single word against his opponents, focusing his remarks solely on the principles for which the Progressive Party stood. Even his nemesis, the New York *Sun*, praised his lyrical and passionate presentation, lauding the "good taste" he exhibited in avoiding the "temptation to misuse an unparalleled opportunity for self-exhibition."

On the Friday before the election, President Taft sat down with New York *World* reporter Louis Seibold for an extended interview. Aware that his chance for outright victory was small, Taft nevertheless hoped to outpoll Roosevelt. A frank discussion of the circumstances surrounding his break with Roosevelt, the reporter suggested, might help to influence public opinion. Taft was "in excellent spirits," Seibold later recalled. The lengthy conversation, transcribed by the president's stenographer, was scheduled to run the following day—not only in the *World* but in newspapers across the country through release to the Associated Press.

When he entered the presidency, Taft explained, he had been "anxious to carry out the promises of the platform," but he was hindered by long-developing factions within the Republican Party. Asked by Seibold if Roosevelt had "fomented" these factions, Taft cast no blame. "No," he replied, "the party naturally divided itself." The rupture was caused by a widening division between eastern manufacturing interests, desiring a high protective tariff, and western farmers, calling for serious tariff reductions. He had moved "in the right direction" when he signed the Payne Bill, but "the genius of publicity," the president admitted, was an attribute he never possessed. "The training of a Judge is something that leads you to depend upon the opinion published and the decree entered as speaking for themselves," he reflected, endeavoring to justify his lack of engagement with the press. As a result, he never properly educated the country about the benefits of the tariff bill, the corporation tax, or any of the other measures he was proud to have passed.

When the reporter sought Taft's comment on anything "beyond the personal ambition of Mr. Roosevelt" that had propelled the former president into the race, Taft demurred. There had been "personalities enough in the preconvention campaign," he cryptically remarked. Under Seibold's persistent probing to explain the bitterness of Roosevelt's commentary during the primary contest, Taft eventually offered a benign explanation: "Mr. Roosevelt is so constituted that it is impossible for him to go into a controversy without becoming personal." Roosevelt had once told him that in every fight he strove to "get close up to a man," attacking "not only the man's argument but the man himself. He could not ascribe to the man differing from him radically any other than an improper motive."

Would Roosevelt have entered the race if he had foreseen "the wrecking of the Republican party," Seibold wondered. "I can not tell," Taft replied, loath to publicly ascribe malicious motives to his adversary. "I don't think he went deliberately into it that way," noting that Roosevelt was not "a planner" but simply a man who "acts from day to day." Taft himself remained "in a philosophical state" as he considered the upcoming election. "I have had to be. The experience I have had in the Presidency has made me so," he explained, "and what I am very hopeful is that whatever happens, the country will go on to ultimate happiness."

After the interview, Seibold was told he could have the transcript upon its completion, but later that afternoon he received word that the president wanted time to make "minor corrections." Taft invited the reporter to join him on the evening train to New York, as the presidential party traveled to attend the funeral of Vice President James Sherman, who had died from heart disease two days earlier. Seibold agreed but emphasized the practical need to get the interview into production; "space was being saved in every newspaper." Still Taft procrastinated, insisting that he needed time for edits, and furthermore wanted to consult Root and Wickersham when the train reached New York. "I'm afraid that's too late," Seibold warned. "But Roosevelt was my closest friend," Taft objected.

The interview never ran.

On election eve, Taft arrived in his home city of Cincinnati following a twenty-eight-hour train ride from New York. He had chosen a "leisurely" route through Ohio, allowing him to greet and visit the friendly crowds gathered at train stations along the way. He refrained from mentioning politics, indulging instead in pleasantries about the prosperous economy and local events. Upon reaching Cincinnati, he went directly to his brother Charley's mansion, where he would receive election returns among family and friends. Nellie had not made the trip, choosing instead to accompany Helen and young Charlie to New York, where the Republican National Committee chairman had arranged a small dinner party.

On election day, November 5, Taft reportedly "slept late, ate a good breakfast, smiled profusely and acted generally as though some sixteen million men were not voting on the subject of his political fate." At noon, he motored to his regular polling place on Madison Road, stopping first to visit Nick Longworth, who was in a tight race to retain his congressional seat. The polling place was crowded, but the president "stood in line and waited his turn," chatting with friends and posing for pictures. After casting his vote, he spent a quiet afternoon at his brother's Pike Street house.

Roosevelt passed "a busy morning" catching up on his voluminous correspondence; at noon, he motored to the small firehouse in Oyster Bay where he traditionally cast his vote. Accompanied by his gardeners, coachman, and chauffeur, he was greeted with cheers from "a crowd of villagers." After signing the register, he headed toward the booth. "Here goes another Bull Mooser vote," a man shouted, eliciting a broad smile from the Colonel. That afternoon, Theodore and Edith took "a long ramble in the woods" before returning to dress for dinner and prepare for the election returns.

After a final campaigning push the night before the election, Woodrow Wilson returned home to Princeton, thrilled to be back with his family on election day. "He felt like a boy out of school on a lark," he told reporters that morning, relieved that for once "he didn't have to jump out and make a speech somewhere." After breakfast, Wilson walked to his polling place at the Chambers Street fire station. Directly across the street stood the boardinghouse where he had lived more than three decades earlier when he came to Princeton as a college freshman. Wilson had spent the better part of his life in Princeton, Ray Baker noted, and he knew "every nook and corner of the old town." After casting his vote, the governor had lunch with his wife and daughters, answered letters, posed for press photographs, and took a walk through the countryside with his secretary and an old friend.

The small dinner party at Wilson's home that night, the *New York Times* reported, "was much in the nature of a celebration, for every minute or two it was interrupted by messages from the telegraph room, every one of which brought news that the tide was running strongly in the Governor's favor." Before long, such bulletins made it clear to both the president and the former president that neither man could win the election. By the time Taft and Roosevelt each sat down for dinner, "an air of gloom and despondency" pervaded Pike Street and Sagamore Hill alike.

Official word of Governor Wilson's victory was confirmed after 10 p.m. via telegraph. Ellen Wilson delivered the welcome news to her husband, who stood talking to friends before a bright fire in the parlor. "My dear," she said, kissing him, "I want to be the first to congratulate you." The bells atop historic Nassau Hall began to ring, and soon several thousand Princeton students arrived at Wilson's house, waving flags and carrying torches. Speaking with "great emotion, even with tears in his eyes," Wilson told the students that he understood the serious challenges he faced. "I look almost with pleading to you, the young men of America, to stand behind me, to support me in the new administration."

Wilson had achieved an immense victory in the Electoral College. He captured forty of the forty-eight states, bringing him 435 electoral votes; Roosevelt took six states, producing 88 votes; Taft won only Vermont and Utah, for a total of 8 electoral votes. The popular vote was somewhat less emphatic. Wilson won nearly 6.3 million votes, compared to 4.1 million for Roosevelt, and a little short of 3.5 million for Taft. Eugene Debs secured over 900,000 votes, the highest total the Socialist Party had ever reached. The split between Taft and Roosevelt had clearly hurt both men: their combined vote exceeded Wilson's by nearly 1.3 million. And together, they had captured over 50 percent of the electorate, leaving only 41.9 percent with the new president, Woodrow Wilson.

At 11:30 p.m., President Taft sent a warm congratulatory telegram to Governor Wilson, extending his "best wishes for a successful Administration." By then, it was already clear that Taft had suffered an overwhelming defeat, coming in third. Four years earlier, he had celebrated victory with dozens of jubilant friends. On that auspicious night, "several thousand of his fellow townsmen with blatant horns and red fire thronged about the mansion." On this night, "the streets were deserted and the only persons in the vicinity were the policemen on guard around the house."

As news of Wilson's victory came over the wires, Roosevelt sent word to the press that he would receive them at eleven o'clock. "They went in rather more subdued than usual," the *New York Times* reported, "filled with a great curiosity to see just how he was taking the defeat." He was seated at his desk, "with a log wood blaze shining softly from the big fireplace," when the group of journalists arrived. "Now old friends," Roosevelt remarked, "I'm really glad to see you." He then proceeded to recite from memory the telegram he had sent to the president-elect: " 'The American people, by a great plurality, have conferred upon you the highest honor in their gift. I congratulate you thereon.' " After finishing, he laughed softly and said: "That's all."

NOT SURPRISINGLY, ROOSEVELT WAS HIT harder by the defeat than the president, who appeared to make a quick recovery. As Taft boarded the train for his return to Washington, he "chatted as gaily as he did before the election," appearing to reporters as if "a great load had been taken from his shoulders." He acknowledged that while he had been "hopeful" that he might secure victory in a close election, he had not been "so hopeful" that he had experienced "any shock of real disappointment." To a lifelong friend he humbly explained his composure: "The people of the United States did not owe me another election. I hope that I am properly grateful for the one term of the Presidency which they gave me, and the fact that they withheld the second is no occasion for my resentment or feeling of injustice." Most important, he reflected to another friend: "As I look back over the record of the administration, I feel very well satisfied that a great deal was accomplished which will be useful to the people in the future, and that, after all, is the only real satisfaction one gets out of any public service."

Although Roosevelt had been realistic about his chances, he was deeply unsettled by the magnitude of the loss. In the two weeks following the attempt on his life, there had been such an outpouring of "popular feeling," Edith explained to Kermit, that Progressive leaders felt victory might truly be possible—not only for Roosevelt but for the party. When the election returns were fully counted, the Progressives actually captured just a single governorship and a dozen congressional seats. The Democrats not only increased their majority in the House but also seized control of the Senate for the first time in nearly two decades. "There is no use disguising the fact that the defeat at the polls is overwhelming," a disappointed Roosevelt wrote his British friend Arthur Hamilton Lee, allowing that he "had expected we would make a better showing." Several days later, his assessment appeared darker as he told Gifford Pinchot: "We must face the fact that our cutting loose from the Republican Party was followed by disaster to the Progressive cause in most of the States where it won two years ago."

Only in time would Roosevelt's perspective on the defeat grow more sanguine. "It was a phenomenal thing to be able to bring the new party into second place and to beat out the Republicans," he told Henry White that November, recognizing the remarkable achievement of an association that had, in a mere three months, managed to gather more support than a sitting president, and defeat a political party that had held sway over national politics for fifty years.

In the aftermath of the election, Roosevelt reiterated to reporters his view that "the leader for the time being is of little consequence, but the cause itself must triumph, for its triumph is essential to the wellbeing of the American people." Rather than a rationalization to assuage the bitterness of his loss, his statement would prove remarkably prescient. Although the Progressive Party met defeat, the progressive causes would continue to influence American politics for years to come. Within the coming decade alone, three signal amendments would be added to the Constitution: the Sixteenth, giving the national government the power to levy a progressive income tax, without which many of the New Deal's social programs might not have been possible; the Seventeenth, providing for the popular election of U.S. senators; and the Nineteenth, finally granting American women the right to vote.

While William Howard Taft had embraced the role of the conservative during the presidential race, he, too, had long since rejected the laissez-faire philosophy that had dominated politics since the Civil War, committing himself instead to the core progressive belief that government had a responsibility to remedy social problems, improve working conditions, safeguard public health, and protect our natural heritage. Though the two men had strikingly different temperaments—Roosevelt's original and active nature at odds with Taft's ruminative and judicial disposition—their opposing qualities actually proved complementary, allowing them to forge a powerful camaraderie and rare collaboration. There was a time, at the height of their careers, when Theodore Roosevelt and William Howard Taft stood shoulder to shoulder as they charted a different role for the U.S. government that would fundamentally enlarge the bounds of economic opportunity and social justice.

EPILOGUE

ON MAY 26, 1918, SIX years after the election that ended his presidency and fractured his party, William Howard Taft arrived for a conference at Chicago's Blackstone Hotel. As Taft was retiring to his room upstairs, the elevator operator informed him that Colonel Roosevelt was presently seated alone in the dining room. "I hear he's leaving right away," the young man remarked. Taft did not hesitate. "Then I'll ask you to take me back downstairs," he responded.

After the White House, Taft had become the Kent Professor of Constitutional Law at Yale, a position that offered intellectual engagement, the camaraderie of a cherished college campus, and the freedom to lecture around the country. Roosevelt had found his own solace through a combination of writing, public speaking, and intense physical activity. The election no sooner behind him, he had begun work on his autobiography. Completing that project within ten months, he embarked on an expedition to explore the River of Doubt, an uncharted tributary of the mighty Amazon. Returning home, he occupied himself writing dozens of articles and delivering scores of speeches each year. He had stopped at the Blackstone Hotel on his way to Des Moines, where the following day he was scheduled to deliver three speeches.

Over the years since the contentious 1912 election, mutual friends and political allies had repeatedly tried to reunite Roosevelt and Taft, but their infrequent meetings had been neither "cordial" nor "intimate," marked by what Taft deemed "armed neutrality." In 1915, they had both served as honorary pallbearers at the funeral of Yale professor Thomas Lounsbury. Taft made the first overture, extending his hand to Roosevelt. "How are you, Theodore?" he asked. The Colonel merely "shook hands silently without smiling," and "no further communication passed between them." A year later, in early October 1916, Elihu Root had arranged for the two men to appear at a Union League Club reception for Republican presidential nominee Charles Evans Hughes. Organized with the goal of "cementing the union of Progressives and Republicans" against Woodrow Wilson, Republicans hailed the event as a "Big Love

Feast." Though Roosevelt's presence was calculated to symbolize his return to "the Republican fold," Taft told Nellie they simply "shook hands with a Howdy do and that was all."

Only when grave illness hospitalized Roosevelt in early February 1918 did the possibility open for a genuine reconciliation. Learning that the Colonel was enduring an operation to remove a fistula much like the ordeal he had suffered through when he was governor general, Taft sent him a sympathetic telegram. "I know something of the pain and discomfort he is passing through," Taft wrote to Nellie, adding that from "the tone of the dispatches," he suspected that Roosevelt's condition was far more serious than his own had been. In fact, the Colonel had never recovered from malaria contracted during his expedition to the River of Doubt, leaving him prone to fever and infection. During this most recent bout of fever, a rectal abscess had developed, along with abscesses in both ears. The surgery to remedy these conditions proved successful, but persistent fever and severe nausea required him to remain in the hospital for almost a month. His first communication was a telegram to Taft. "Am rather rocky, but worth several dear Men," he jested. "Greatly touched and Pleased by Your Message."

This written exchange, the first in six years, led Roosevelt to send Taft a draft of a speech he would deliver in late March. An indictment of Wilson's handling of America's participation in World War I, the piece was entitled "Speed up the War and Take Thought for After the War." It criticized the administration for "sluggishness in making war," and called "for longer hours of work in war plants" as well as for "universal military training—to be continued after the war." Taft wholeheartedly concurred with Roosevelt's critique of Wilson's wartime leadership. He carefully read the draft and made two recommendations. "I have embodied both of those suggestions," Roosevelt wrote in response. "I think them capital. I am rather ashamed I never thought of them myself, and I am malevolently pleased that neither Root nor Lodge thought of them!"

These cordial exchanges renewed Taft's optimism that Roosevelt might finally be ready to reconcile. Hurrying across the Blackstone's dining room, which was bustling with nearly a hundred diners, he spotted the Colonel at a small table by the corner window. "Theodore!" he exclaimed. "I am glad to see you!" Roosevelt rose from his seat and grasped Taft's shoulders. "Well, I am indeed delighted to see you. Won't you sit down?" All across the room, customers rose from their dinners and waitstaff paused, "recognizing the significance of the meeting." Suddenly, the chamber erupted into applause. *New York Tribune* reporter John Leary, who was traveling with Roosevelt, heard the loud ovation from the lobby. Joined by curious members of the hotel staff, he started up the stairs leading to the dining room. Encountering a patron who had witnessed the hoopla, he asked what had incited the outburst. "T.R. and Taft's got together," the man explained. "They're holding an old-home week."

"By Godfrey, I never was so surprised in my life," Roosevelt later told Leary. "I no more thought of him being in Chicago than in Timbuctoo. But wasn't it a gracious thing for him to do?" There was so much commotion when they first greeted each other, he explained, that he could hardly hear what Taft was saying. "I don't mind telling you how delighted I am," Roosevelt added. "I never felt happier over anything in my life. It was splendid of Taft."

The two men talked together "like a pair of happy schoolboys" until Roosevelt had to depart to catch the night train to Des Moines. "Taft was beaming," one witness reported, "and Colonel Roosevelt, leaning half across the table, was expressing himself very earnestly." Meeting Leary on the way out, Taft could not disguise his elation. "Isn't he looking splendid?" he said. "I never saw him looking much better." Asked about the nature of their conversation, Taft simply replied that they "discussed patriotism and the state and welfare of the Nation." His smile suggested that a far more important exchange had occurred. Describing the meeting a week later to Henry Stimson, Roosevelt confided that at long last they had "completely renewed the old friendly relations."

Seven months later, on Christmas Day, 1918, after a six-week hospital stay for a severe attack of inflammatory rheumatism, Theodore Roosevelt returned to convalesce at Sagamore Hill. Though delighted to be back in his beloved home, he was still in considerable pain. Doctors predicted a full recovery, but Edith hired a nurse to attend to his medical needs and contacted James Amos, the black valet who had served Roosevelt in the White House. Her husband, she explained to Amos, would not allow "anyone else" to help, but they understood that it might be difficult for him to come. Amos never hesitated. He packed a suitcase and made arrangements to remain by Roosevelt's side as long as he was needed.

By the following Sunday morning, January 5, 1919, Roosevelt "seemed better again." Comfortably situated in "the warmest room in the house," the large bedroom that had once been the children's nursery, he dictated letters and proofread an editorial for *Metropolitan* magazine, calling on the country to give women the right to vote. "There should be no further delay," he emphatically stated. The war was over. The time had come to focus on domestic issues. "It is an absurdity to longer higgle about the matter."

Together, Edith and Theodore passed "a happy and wonderful day," she later recalled. He had long treasured the view of the water from that corner room, and "as it got dusk, he watched the dancing of waves & spoke with happiness of being home and made little plans for me. I think he had made up his mind," she wrote, "that he would have to suffer for some time to come and with his high courage had adjusted himself to bear it. He was very sweet all day."

At around ten o'clock that night, Theodore told Edith he felt a curious "sensation of depression about the chest," almost as though his heart were preparing to stop. "I know it is not going to happen," he assured her, "but it is such a strange feeling." Edith called their family physician, Dr. George Faller, who "examined him carefully, found no indication of anything wrong with heart and lungs, and after giving him a slight stimulant, left him." While Edith prepared to retire, Amos helped Roosevelt get settled for the night. The Colonel remained for a short time on the sofa before turning to his valet. "James, don't you think I might go to bed now?" Amos took off Roosevelt's robe and "had almost to lift him into bed." Edith returned to give her husband a good night kiss, after which Roosevelt said, "James, will you please put out the light?"

Edith came to check on her husband shortly after midnight, and again two hours later. Finding him in a "peaceful slumber," she departed for her room. Amos rested in a chair not far from the bed. Shortly before four o'clock, the valet was alarmed by the sound of "irregular breathing." Roosevelt's respiration "seemed to stop," he later said. "Then it resumed again and paused again." Amos rushed to summon the nurse and alerted Mrs. Roosevelt. By the time Edith reached his room, Theodore was dead. Doctors later confirmed that Roosevelt had died in his sleep from a coronary embolism. "Death had to take him sleeping," Vice President Thomas Marshall cabled from Washington, "for if Roosevelt had been awake, there would have been a fight."

Ray Baker, Ida Tarbell, and William Allen White were all in Paris on separate assignments covering the Armistice and the Versailles Peace Conference when news of Roosevelt's death reached Europe. Their "brave little adventure" in creating a writer's magazine dedicated to serious public issues had failed. Relentless money troubles had forced John Phillips to sell *The American Magazine* to a big publishing house, which pressured the writers to satisfy advertisers' demands for popular pieces. "The test of the stories," Baker lamented, became not whether they were "good literature" or important contributions to national discourse, but whether they would attract 600,000 readers. Prize contests were introduced, along with stories of romance and marriage. Baker had been tempted to leave in 1912, when the new publishers demanded that he remove a sentence critical of the business community. Loyalty to his colleagues had kept him on board for three additional years until he could no longer abide the way his literary ambitions were continuously "strangled by commercial considerations" and finally resigned. In short order, Tarbell, Phillips, and White also resigned.

White and Tarbell had been sent to Paris by the *Red Cross Magazine*, where John Phillips was now the editor. Ray Baker was serving President Wilson as press liaison, assigned to give daily briefings to over one hundred American correspondents who had journeyed overseas to report on the peace conference. Tarbell observed that Baker managed his demanding job with such "absolute fairness" that even "the tongues of some of the most bumptious" journalists were "silenced." The three old colleagues had taken rooms in the Hôtel de Vouillemont, located just off the Place de la Concorde not far from the headquarters of the American Peace Commission. "There were hours when it seemed like a gathering in the office of the old *American Magazine*," Tarbell recalled, "so natural and intimate it was."

White was at breakfast when he read of Theodore Roosevelt's death in the Paris *Herald*'s morning edition. "Again and again I looked at the headlines to be sure that I was reading them correctly," he recalled. Just then, Ray Baker arrived, carrying the same paper. "Ray, Ray, the Colonel is dead—Roosevelt!" White cried. "Yes, Will," Baker responded, sadly embracing him. "It's a great blow. We are all sorry." Soon Ida Tarbell joined them, White recalled, and the three "sat down to talk it all over, and get used to a world without Roosevelt in it."

William Howard Taft was among the five hundred guests invited to attend Roosevelt's private funeral service, held in the modest Episcopal church in Oyster Bay. "It was my father's wish," Archie Roosevelt explained, "that the funeral service be conducted entirely by those friends among whom he had lived so long and happily." After their fortuitous meeting at the Blackstone Hotel, Roosevelt and Taft had resumed their old habit of intimate, friendly correspondence, sending each other drafts of speeches, commenting on articles, sharing thoughts on the central issues of the day. Visiting Roosevelt in the hospital in late November, Taft had discovered with delight that they were in essential accord on the need for a league of nations to enforce the postwar peace. Snow had fallen the morning that Theodore Roosevelt was laid to rest, but the sun had come out by the time Taft arrived at the church. "You're a dear personal friend," Archie said, taking him by the hand and directing him to a pew in the front. Though the half-hour service had "no pomp, no ceremony," no singing or music, its very simplicity, one mourner observed, made it "profoundly impressive."

The village bells tolled as mourners followed the casket up the hill to the gravesite where "a mound of flowers hid the freshly-turned earth." According to an old "widow's custom," Edith Roosevelt attended neither funeral nor burial. Though she would live to the age of eighty-seven, she had lost the only man she would ever love, the man, she had told Theodore, she loved "with all the passion of a girl who had never loved before."

As Theodore Roosevelt's casket was lowered into the ground, "an isolated figure" stood "quite apart from the others," William Howard Taft, softly crying. "I want to say to you," Taft later told Roosevelt's sister Bamie, "how glad I am that Theodore and I came together after that long painful interval. Had he died in a hostile state of mind toward me, I would have mourned the fact all my life. I loved him always and cherish his memory."

AT NOON ON OCTOBER 3, 1921, sixty-four-year-old William Howard Taft finally secured the position he had long desired "as strongly as a man can ever want anything." The death of Chief Justice Edward White the previous May had created a vacancy that President Warren Harding was happy to fill with the former chief executive. In a ceremony witnessed by Nellie and dozens of old friends, Taft took the judicial oath "to administer justice without respect to persons, and do equal right to the poor and to the rich." Reporters noted that "the famous Taft Smile" was irresistible as friends and colleagues "rushed up to congratulate him." After the ceremony, Taft and Nellie joined the other justices and their families at a White House reception. "This is the greatest day of my life," the new chief justice of the United States declared.

"The people of the United States greet Mr. Taft in his new role," *The Washington Post* editorialized the following day. "Their good wishes will not be inspired solely by their abiding faith in his wisdom and justice, but also by the fact that they like him personally. His popularity throughout the country has grown from the day, nearly ten years ago, when the fortunes of political warfare went overwhelmingly against him and, instead of permitting defeat to sour his nature or crush his spirit, he accepted his lot philosophically and with a smile."

The public trust was not misplaced. Under Taft's able leadership, "antiquated" court procedure was streamlined, "speeding up" and greatly improving the delivery of justice throughout "the whole system of federal courts." And through his "great skill and patience," Taft finally secured from Congress the funds to construct a separate building for the Supreme Court, allowing the justices to move from the "old Senate chamber" to the classic marble structure that graces Washington today. As Taft had always suspected, the position of chief justice was more suited to his mind and temperament than the presidency had ever been. Fulfilled at work and happy at home, he embarked upon a successful regime of diet and exercise, bringing his weight down to less than 250 pounds, a reasonable weight for a man of his stature and proportions. Years of obesity, however, had already damaged his health. On February 3, 1930, escalating heart trouble forced his resignation from the job he had loved more than any other. "We call you Chief Justice still," Justice Oliver Wendell Holmes wrote a week later on behalf of his colleagues, "for we cannot give up the title by which we have known you all these later years and which you have made so dear to us . . . you showed us in new form your voluminous capacity for getting work done, your humor that smoothed the tough places, your golden heart that brought you love from every side and most of all from your brethren whose tasks you have made happy and light."

Just over a month after he left the bench, on March 8, 1930, William Howard Taft was dead. Nellie Taft, whose catastrophic illness had left her husband bereft of his most valuable ally and altered his presidency in ways the public never comprehended, would live thirteen years more, dying just short of her eighty-second birthday.

During the 1920s and the 1930s, the members of the original *McClure's* magazine staff continued to celebrate each other's birthdays. Such was the "unbreakable quality in friendship," Ida Tarbell marveled, that despite the bitter 1906 split, the core group could not be permanently alienated. "You pick up at the day when the friendship was—not broken but interrupted," she observed. Year after year, the "old Crowd" would convene, reviving "a hundred, yes a thousand memories" of the days that had proved the most fulfilling of their lives—the idealistic time when they genuinely believed, in Ray Baker's words, that they were "saving the world." Sustained by passion and optimism, they "muck-raked never to destroy, but with utter faith in reason and progress"; they "criticized in full confidence that, once understood, evils would be speedily corrected." None of them had truly realized, Baker later acknowledged to Lincoln Steffens, how "hard-boiled" the world really was.

At each of these collective birthday celebrations, Sam McClure, then in his seventies and eighties, was "the star of the evening." He would recount his personal history with such charm—his impoverished youth, his marriage to Hattie when his weekly salary was only twelve dollars, his eventual triumph "storming the sacred citadels in the publishing business"—that his listeners were riveted as if the tale were novel. His "old fire" flared up, Tarbell was happy to see. "We sat enthralled," she wrote, as McClure "enlarged on his latest enthusiasm, marveling as always at the eternal youthfulness in the man, the failure of life to quench him."

After John Phillips was unable to attend one of these gatherings, Tarbell wrote to tell him how much he had been missed, how they all realized that he was the one, during all those years, who had kept the *McClure's* "flame steady and lasting." Revisiting "that wonderful adventure we all had together," Phillips confessed to Ray Baker, was "almost like a physical pain—not because of you and me and so on. But because of this country, and because those sincere attempts, to do something in reporting and interpretation of what was good and sound and progressive, seemed lost and forgotten." Still, he hoped that other "times of awakening" lay ahead, that a new generation of journalists would be drawn to the work that "seemed once almost a mission and a call."

ACKNOWLEDGMENTS

At the outset, I wish to acknowledge my debt to a remarkable circle of biographers and historians whose studies of Theodore Roosevelt, William Howard Taft, the muckraking journalists, and the Progressive era provided the background I needed to begin thinking about this project.

Dedicated staff members of numerous libraries have provided invaluable help in my search for primary sources and pictures. I particularly want to thank Joshua Caster, Heather Cole, Wallace Finley Dailey, Zachary Downey, Mary Haegert, E. Ray Henderson, Isabel Planton, Jane Westenfeld, and Cherry Williams.

In Massachusetts, I am grateful to the Theodore Roosevelt Collection at Houghton Library, Harvard University; the Sophia Smith Collection at Smith College, Northampton; and the Jones Library at Amherst. In Ohio, the Cincinnati History Library and Archives at the Cincinnati Museum Center, and the William Howard Taft National Historical Site, National Park Service. In Washington, D.C., the Manuscript Division of the Library of Congress. In Pennsylvania, the Pelletier Library, Allegheny College, Meadville. In New York, the Rare Book and Manuscript Library at Columbia University. And in Indiana, the Lilly Library at Indiana University, Bloomington.

Each of the past seven summers, I have participated in the intern program at Harvard's Institute of Politics, working with a truly wonderful group of students, including Alex Burns, Welton Blount, Samuel Jacobs, Arjun Ramamurti, Sam Barr, James McAuley, and Amanda McGowan. For reading all or parts of the manuscript, I wish to thank Lindsay Hosmer Goodwin, John Hill, Beth Laski, and Frank Phillips. I am grateful to Gary Zola for squiring me through Taft's Cincinnati, and to Paul Grondahl for guiding me through Roosevelt's Albany.

I am especially indebted to Michelle Krowl and Camille Larson for their phenomenal work in searching through the archives at the Library of Congress, where the treasure trove of primary materials that form the bedrock of this book is housed—letters, diaries, newspaper articles, periodical pieces, memoirs, office files, and pamphlets.

My longtime agent Binky Urban gave her wholehearted support to this project from simply the germ of an idea to its completion. There is no one better.

And I owe more than I can express to Beth Laski, my manager, my publicist, my great friend. It is impossible to imagine my life without her.

There is no way this project would have been completed on time without Nora Titone. She worked with me on *Team of Rivals* and then went on to write a wonderful book on Edwin and John Wilkes Booth. She returned these last ten months to help in a thousand ways, tying together all the loose ends with an attention to detail that is simply astonishing. With good cheer and endless enthusiasm, she is an absolute joy to work with. She is a true champion.

How lucky I have been that Simon & Schuster has been my publisher for more than a quarter of a century. Even as I list the following names, I feel as if I am listing members of my family: Jonathan Karp, Carolyn Reidy, Richard Rhorer, Jackie Seow, Joy O'Meara, George Turianski, Gina DiMascia, Julia Prosser, Stephen Bedford, W. Anne Jones. For managing the voyage during these last hectic months, I am particularly grateful to Ann Adelman, my incomparable copy editor; to Jonathan Cox, Alice Mayhew's indefatigable assistant; and to Lisa Healy and Irene Kheradi, who finally brought the book home.

And of course, there is no one like Alice Mayhew, my editor, counselor, and guide, to whom I proudly dedicate this book. She saw the story I wanted to tell from the start, offering critical advice and ideas at every stage. She has been my indispensable partner throughout my writing career. She is a publishing legend. She is my treasured friend.

This book is also dedicated to my research assistant, Linda Vandegrift. We have worked together for nearly thirty years. Every book has benefited greatly from her extraordinary talent, organizational skills, and unfailing good judgment; but from the start, this story engaged her heart and mind more than any other. She became a true collaborator, without whom the book would simply not have been possible.

And finally, words cannot fully convey my gratitude to my husband, Richard Goodwin, and our best friend, Michael Rothschild, who read every draft of every chapter, providing loving and constructive ideas, comments, and criticisms at every step along the way of this seven-year journey.

NOTES

Abbreviations used in the notes:

Names

AB	Archibald Willingham Butt
ARC	Anna Roosevelt Cowles
ARL	Alice Roosevelt Longworth
CRR	Corinne Roosevelt Robinson
DCT	Delia Chapin Torrey
EKR	Edith Kermit Carow Roosevelt
HCL	Henry Cabot Lodge
HHM	Harriet Hurd McClure
HHT	Helen Herron Taft
IMT	Ida Minerva Tarbell
JSP	John Sanborn Phillips
LS	Lincoln Steffens
LTT	Louise Torrey Taft
MAH	Marcus Alonzo Hanna
RBH	Rutherford Birchard Hayes
RHD	Richard Harding Davis
RLF	Robert M. La Follette
RSB	Ray Stannard Baker
TR	Theodore Roosevelt
TR, JR.	Theodore Roosevelt, Jr.
UBS	Upton Beall Sinclair
WAW	William Allen White
WHT	William Howard Taft
WW	Woodrow Wilson

Journals and Collected Works

LTR: Theodore Roosevelt, Elting E. Morison, John M. Blum, and John J. Buckley, eds. *The Letters of Theodore Roosevelt.* 8 vols. Cambridge, MA: Harvard University Press, 1951–54.

NYT: *New York Times*

WTR: Theodore Roosevelt and Hermann Hagedorn, eds. *The Works of Theodore Roosevelt.* 24 vols. New York: Charles Scribner's Sons, 1923–26.

Papers and Collections

AB Letters: Archibald Willingham Butt Letters, Manuscript, Archives, and Rare Book Library, Emory University

ARC Papers: Anna Roosevelt Cowles Papers (MS Am 1834.1), Theodore Roosevelt Collection, Houghton Library, Harvard University

ARL Papers: Alice Roosevelt Longworth Papers, 1888–1942, Manuscript Division, Library of Congress, Washington, DC

CPT Papers: Charles P. Taft Papers, Manuscript Division, LC

CRR Papers: Corinne Roosevelt Robinson Papers (MS Am 1785–1785.7), Theodore Roosevelt Collection, Houghton Library, Harvard University

Derby Papers: Ethel Roosevelt Derby Papers (*87M-100, etc.), Theodore Roosevelt Collection, Houghton Library, Harvard University

Dunne Papers: Finley Peter Dunne Papers, Manuscript Division, LC

Garfield Papers: James Rudolph Garfield Papers, Manuscript Division, LC

Ida Tarbell Papers: Ida Tarbell Papers, Sophia Smith Collection, Smith College, Northampton, MA

IMTC: The Ida M. Tarbell Collection, Pelletier Library, Allegheny College, Meadville, PA

KR Papers: Kermit and Belle Roosevelt Papers, Manuscript Division, LC

LS Papers: Lincoln Steffens Papers, Rare Book & Manuscript Library, Columbia University in the City of New York

McClure MSS: Samuel Sidney McClure Manuscripts, The Lilly Library, Indiana University, Bloomington, IN

O'Laughlin Papers: John Callan O'Laughlin Papers, Manuscript Division, LC

Phillips MSS: John Sanborn Phillips Manuscripts, The Lilly Library, Indiana University, Bloomington, IN

Pinchot Papers: Gifford Pinchot Papers, Manuscript Division, LC

Pringle Papers: Henry F. Pringle Papers, Manuscript Division, LC

RBH Papers: Rutherford Birchard Hayes Papers, Manuscript Division, LC

RSB Papers: Ray Stannard Baker Papers, Manuscript Division, LC

RSB Papers II: Ray Stannard ("David Grayson") Baker Papers, The Jones Library, Amherst, MA

Taft-Karger Corr.: William H. Taft and Gustav J. Karger Correspondence, Cincinnati History Library and Archives, Cincinnati Museum Center

TRC: Theodore Roosevelt Collection, Houghton Library, Harvard University

TRJP: Theodore Roosevelt, Jr. Papers, Manuscript Division, LC

TRP: Theodore Roosevelt Papers, Manuscript Division, LC

White Papers: William Allen White Papers, Manuscript Division, LC

WHTP: William H. Taft Papers, Manuscript Division, LC

PREFACE

Page

xi “He had just finished”: Lyman Abbott, “A Review of President Roosevelt’s Administration: IV—Its Influence on Patriotism and Public Service,” *Outlook*, Feb. 27, 1909, p. 430.

xii “a spark of genius”: William Allen White to Charles Churchill, Aug. 9, 1906, William Allen White Papers, Manuscript Division, LC.

xii “The story is the thing”: “Interview with S. S. McClure,” *The North American* (Philadelphia), Aug. 15, 1905.

xii “muckraker . . . a badge of honor”: Patricia O’Toole, *When Trumpets Call: Theodore Roosevelt after the White House* (New York: Simon & Schuster, 2005), p. 30.

xiii “It is hardly an exaggeration”: Richard Hofstadter, *The Age of Reform: From Bryan to F.D.R.* (New York: Alfred A. Knopf, 1955), pp. 186–87.

xiii “Oh, things will be all right”: *Van Wert* [OH] *Daily Bulletin*, April 5, 1905.

xiii “derelict”: WHT, “Personal Aspects of the Presidency,” *Saturday Evening Post*, Feb. 28, 1914.

xiv “not constituted”: William Howard Taft to William Allen White, Mar. 20, 1909, White Papers.

xiv “vitality of democracy . . . complex questions”: S. S. McClure, “The Railroads on Trial: Editorial Announcement of a New Series by Ray Stannard Baker,” *McClure’s* (October 1905), p. 673.

xiv “the mission of raising”: William James, *Memories and Studies* (New York: Longmans, Green & Co., 1911), p. 323.

xiv “There is no one left . . . none but all of us”: S. S. McClure, “Concerning Three Articles . . . and a Coincidence That May Set Us Thinking,” *McClure’s* (January 1903), p. 336.

CHAPTER ONE: The Hunter Returns

Page

1 ROOSEVELT IS COMING HOME: *Boston Daily Globe*, June 16, 1910.

1 “the wise custom” . . . take his pledge back: Herman H. Kohlsaat, *From McKinley to Harding: Personal Recollections of Our Presidents* (New York: Charles Scribner’s Sons, 1923), pp. 137–38; *Oshkosh* [WI] *Daily Northwestern*, Nov. 9, 1904; *NYT*, Nov. 8, 1904.

2 “the greatest office . . . every hour”: Oscar S. Straus, *Under Four Administrations: From Cleveland to Taft* (Boston: Houghton Mifflin, 1922), p. 251.

2 “dull thud . . . break his fall”: Archibald W. Butt to “My Darling Mother,” June 19, [1908], in Lawrence F. Abbott, ed., *The Letters of Archie Butt, Personal Aide to President Roosevelt* (Garden City, NY: Doubleday, Page & Co., 1924), p. 42.

2 “impenetrable spot”: Elmer J. Burkett, “Theodore Roosevelt,” *The Independent*, June 9, 1910, p. 1270.

2 “Even at this moment”: TR to John Appleton Stewart, Mar. 19, 1910, in Elting E. Morison, ed., *The Days of Armageddon, 1909–1914*, Vol. 7 of *The Letters of Theodore Roosevelt* [hereafter *LTR*] (Cambridge, MA: Harvard University Press, 1951–54), p. 59.

2 “My political career . . . engulfing him”: Lawrence F. Abbott, *Impressions of Theodore Roosevelt* (Garden City, NY: Doubleday, Page & Co., 1923), p. 53.

2 a six-week tour . . . Kings and queens: *Baltimore Sun*, June 18, 1910.

2 “People gathered . . . viva Roosevelt!”: Lawrence F. Abbott, “Mr. Roosevelt in Europe,” *Outlook*, June 4, 1910, pp. 249–50.

2 “No foreign ruler . . . class of society”: *NYT*, June 10, 1910.

2 “I don’t suppose . . . all about the man”: AB to Clara, April 19, 1910, in Archibald Willingham Butt, *Taft and Roosevelt: The Intimate Letters of Archie Butt, Military Aide,* Vol. 1 (Garden City, NY: Doubleday, Doran & Co., 1930), p. 332.

3 “royal progress . . . American ever received”: “A Welcome to Mr. Roosevelt from the President of the United States,” *Outlook*, June 18, 1910, p. 342.

3 “a holiday appearance”: *Evening Tribune* (Marysville, OH), June 19, 1910.

3 “as diversely typical . . . native born and aliens”: Editorial, *Evening Star* (Washington, DC), June 18, 1910.

3 More than two hundred vessels: *NYT*, June 17, 1910.

3 “Flags floated . . . draped with bunting”: *Evening Tribune*, June 19, 1910.

3 The night before . . . special duty: *NYT*, June 17, 1910; *Philadelphia Inquirer*, June 18, 1910.

3 “The United States . . . excitement of anticipation”: *Atlanta Constitution*, June 15, 1910.

3 “If it were not . . . I am done for”: Edith Kermit Carow Roosevelt to Kermit Roosevelt, April 7, 1909, KR Papers.

4 “would do anything in the world”: Edith Kermit Carow to TR, June 8 [1886], in Sylvia Jukes Morris, *Edith Kermit Roosevelt: Portrait of a First Lady* [hereafter *EKR*] (New York: Coward, McCann & Geoghegan, 1980), p. 86.

4 They had been intimate childhood . . . broke down in tears: TR, *Diaries of Boyhood and Youth* (New York: Charles Scribner’s Sons, 1928), p. 13.

4 a regular guest at “Tranquillity”: David McCullough, *Mornings on Horseback* (New York: Simon & Schuster, 1981), pp. 142–43.

4 “the prettiest girls they had met”: Morris, *EKR*, p. 53.

4 mysterious “falling out” . . . at the estate’s summerhouse: Carleton Putnam, *Theodore Roosevelt: The Formative Years, 1858–1886* (New York: Charles Scribner’s Sons, 1958), pp. 170, 556.

4 The conflict . . . “his very intimate relations”: TR to ARC, Sept. 20, 1886, TRC.

4 “both of us had”: TR to ARC, Sept. 20, 1886, TRC.

4 his “whole heart and soul”: TR, Personal Diary, Jan. 25, 1880, TRP.

4 “I do not think . . . mistress of the White House”: TR to Maria Longworth Storer, Dec. 8, 1902, in Elting E. Morison, ed., *The Square Deal, 1901–1903*, Vol. 3 of *LTR*, p. 392.

5 their fellow passengers, some 3,000: *NYT*, June 19, 1910.

5 massive battleship *South Carolina*: *Boston Daily Globe*, June 19, 1910.

5 “By George!”: *Washington Post*, June 19, 1910.

5 “Flags were broken out . . . an eight-pounder”: *Boston Daily Globe*, June 19, 1910.

5 "to add dignity": AB to Clara, June 19, 1910, in AB, *Taft and Roosevelt*, Vol. 1, pp. 394, 400.
5 "just as prominent": *Evening Bulletin* (Philadelphia), June 19, 1910.
5 he stopped his hectic motions: *NYT*, June 19, 1910.
5 "love of the hurly-burly . . . and Mr. Roosevelt": Arthur R. Colquhoun, "Theodore Roosevelt," *Living Age*, May 28, 1910, p. 519.
5 "pugilists, college presidents . . . noise and excitement": Edward G. Lowry, "The White House Now," *Harper's Weekly*, May 15, 1907, p. 7.
6 the Roosevelts' youngest sons . . . Nicholas Longworth: *Chicago Tribune*, June 19, 1910.
6 Eleanor Roosevelt; and her husband, Franklin: Joseph L. Gardner, *Departing Glory: Theodore Roosevelt as ex-President* (New York: Charles Scribner's Sons, 1973), p. 170.
6 Roosevelt busily shook hands: *Boston Daily Globe*, June 19, 1910.
6 "Come here, Theodore . . . anything else": AB to Clara, June 19, 1910, in AB, *Taft and Roosevelt*, Vol. 1, p. 399.
6 "the round face": *Chicago Tribune*, June 19, 1910.
6 "to kiss pop first": *Atlanta Constitution*, June 19, 1910.
6 "the Colonel spread his arms . . . pandemonium broke loose": *Chicago Tribune*, June 19, 1910.
6 "there came from the river": *NYT*, June 19, 1910.
6 "everywhere flags": *Atlanta Constitution*, June 19, 1910.
6 executed a "flying leap" . . . with every crew member: *Fort Wayne* [IN] *Sentinel*, June 18, 1910.
7 "an explosive word . . . meaning of the words": *NYT*, June 19, 1910.
7 "This takes me back . . . tell you how I feel": *Chicago Tribune*, June 19, 1910.
7 "Fine! Fine!": *NYT*, June 19, 1910.
7 "George, this is bully!": *Boston Daily Globe*, June 19, 1910.
7 Roosevelt hesitated . . . "shake hands with them": *NYT*, June 19, 1910.
7 "Boys, I am *glad*": *NYT*, June 19, 1910.
7 "We're mighty glad": *Washington Post*, June 19, 1910.
8 Reporters . . . remarked how "hale and hearty": *Evening Tribune* (Marysville, OH), June 19, 1910.
8 "It is true": *Evening Bulletin* (Philadelphia), June 19, 1910.
8 "the same bubbling": *Boston Daily Globe*, June 19, 1910.
8 detected "something different . . . more encompassing": AB to Clara, June 19, 1910, in AB, *Taft and Roosevelt*, Vol. 1, p. 396.
8 "You come back here . . . a look at Teddy": *Washington Post*, June 19, 1910.
8 "There he is!" . . . "Home, Sweet Home": *NYT*, June 19, 1910.
8 "the man of the hour": *Washington Post*, June 19, 1910.
8 "echoing boom": *Boston Daily Globe*, June 19, 1910.
8 "Turn around . . . all waiting for him": *Washington Post*, June 19, 1910.
8 "unnumbered thousands" . . . surrounding streets: *Boston Daily Globe*, June 19, 1910.
9 "a life-size Teddy bear": *NYT*, June 19, 1910.
9 "Delighted": *NYT*, June 18, 1910.
9 "from street level to skyline": New York *Sun*, June 19, 1910.
9 "Is there a stenographer": *Evening Tribune*, June 19, 1910.
9 "No man could . . . the American people": *Washington Post*, June 19, 1910.
9 A five-mile parade . . . lining the streets: *Evening Post* (Washington, DC), June 18, 1910.
9 "The sidewalks": *Chicago Tribune*, June 19, 1910.
9 Rough Rider unit . . . escort of honor: *Boston Daily Globe*, June 19, 1910.
9 "incomparably the largest": *Evening Star*, June 18, 1910.
9 Placards with friendly . . . front of the building: *Chicago Tribune*, June 19, 1910.
10 "You could not move": New York *Evening Post*, July 18, 1910.
10 "the malefactors of great wealth": *St. Louis Times*, June 19, 1910.
10 "Teddy! Teddy!": *Washington Post*, June 19, 1910.
10 "unconcealed delight . . . Not a bit": *NYT*, June 19, 1910.
10 with tears in his eyes: *Boston Daily Globe*, June 19, 1910.
10 a frightening storm: *Chicago Tribune*, June 19, 1910; *Los Angeles Times*, June 19, 1910.
10 "Everyone began talking": AB to Clara, June 19, 1910, in AB, *Taft and Roosevelt*, Vol. 1, p. 402.
10 a festive meal: AB to Clara, June 19, 1910, in ibid., p. 401.
10 The severe rainstorm . . . "to the ground": *Washington Post*, June 19, 1910.
10 "triumphal arches": *NYT*, June 19, 1910.
10 "to live among you again": *Washington Post*, June 19, 1910.
11 "the slightest trace of fatigue": *NYT*, June 19, 1910.
11 "We lived in . . . sweet intimacy": William Howard Taft, "My Predecessor," *Collier's*, Mar. 6, 1909, p. 25.
11 "the foremost member": TR to WHT, June 9, 1903, in *LTR*, Vol. 3, p. 486.
11 his daily "counsellor": TR to WHT, Feb. 14, 1903, in ibid., p. 426.
11 "I am quite as nervous": TR to WHT, Sept. 19, 1907, in Elting E. Morison, ed., *The Big Stick, 1905–1907*, Vol. 5 of *LTR*, p. 796.
11 When Taft was elected . . . a "beloved" friend: TR to WHT, Aug. 2, 1906, in ibid., p. 341.
12 "Taft is as fine a fellow": TR to Arthur Hamilton Lee, Dec. 20, 1908, in Elting E. Morison, ed., *The Big Stick, 1907–1909*, Vol. 6 of *LTR*, pp. 1432–33.
12 "I do not know any man": TR to Gifford Pinchot, Jan. 17, 1910, Pinchot Papers.
12 asked Pinchot to meet him in Europe: TR to Gifford Pinchot, Mar. 1, 1910, Pinchot Papers.
12 all expressing a belief . . . Roosevelt's hard-won advances: Albert J. Beveridge to Gifford Pinchot, Mar. 24, 1910; Jonathan P. Dolliver to Gifford Pinchot, Mar. 25, 1910, TRP.

12 On his final day: TR to Trevelyan, Oct. 1, 1911, in *LTR*, Vol. 7, p. 415.

12 "Roosevelt's spirit was much troubled": Edward Grey, *Twenty-five Years, 1892–1916* (New York: Frederick A. Stokes Co., 1925), Vol. 2, pp. 93–94.

12 "What will Mr. Roosevelt do?": *Advocate* (Newark, NJ), June 19, 1910.

13 the intensifying struggle . . . dividing the Republican Party: Ray Stannard Baker, "The Measure of Taft," *The American Magazine* (July 1910), p. 362.

13 "There is one thing": *NYT*, June 19, 1910.

13 "He looks haggard and careworn": AB to Clara, Jan. 7, 1910, in AB, *Taft and Roosevelt*, Vol. 1, p. 254.

13 faded to a sickly pale: AB to Clara, Easter [n.d.], 1910, in ibid., p. 312.

13 "It is hard . . . murmur against the fate": AB to Clara, Easter [n.d.], 1910, in ibid., p. 313.

13 "a man of tremendous . . . to show no resentment": AB to Clara, Feb. 9, 1910, in ibid., p. 278.

13 his "secondary role": AB to Clara, Feb. 13, 1910, in ibid., p. 281.

13 "he loves Theodore Roosevelt": AB to Clara, Jan. 7, 1910, in ibid., p. 254.

13 "He is going to be": AB, Dec. 10, 1908, in Abbott, ed., *Letters of Archie Butt*, Vol. 1, pp. 232–33.

13 "America incarnate": William Allen White, "Taft: A Hewer of Wood," *The American Magazine* (April 1908), p. 20.

13 a man who could "finish the things" . . . would "do much": Ibid., pp. 31, 32.

14 "by flashes or whims . . . long, logical habit": "Six Months of President Taft," *The World's Work* (September 1909).

14 "a great crusade . . . in the form of law": George Kibbe Turner, "How Taft Views His Own Administration," *McClure's* (June 1910), p. 211.

14 "intense desire . . . for legal method": WHT, "My Predecessor," *Collier's*, Mar. 6, 1909, p. 25.

14 Roosevelt had ended his presidency: TR to Kermit Roosevelt, May 10, 1908, in TR, Kermit Roosevelt, and Will Irwin, eds., *Letters to Kermit from Theodore Roosevelt, 1902–1908* (New York: Charles Scribner's Sons, 1946), p. 242.

14 "with the tools": "Six Months of President Taft," *The World's Work* (September 1909).

14 He had "great misgivings": WHT to HHT, Aug. 11, 1907, WHTP.

14 acceptance speech . . . "like a nightmare": WHT to TR, July 12, 1908, TRP.

14 He feared . . . "make many people mad": WHT to HHT, Aug. 13, 1907, WHTP.

14 negative press left him "very, very discouraged": *Nevada State Journal*, Mar. 23, 1910.

15 refused to read unfavorable articles: AB to Clara, Nov. 14, 1909, in AB, *Taft and Roosevelt*, Vol. 1, p. 206.

15 "But I am made this way": WHT to HHT, Aug. 15, 1907, WHTP.

15 his "campaign manager": *Syracuse* [NY] *Herald*, June 14, 1908.

15 "I pinch myself": WHT to Henry A. Morrill, Box 29, Pringle Papers.

15 "would rather be Chief Justice . . . to bear and undergo": AB to Clara, Mar. 4, 1910, in AB, *Taft and Roosevelt*, Vol. 1, p. 294.

15 "overcome the obstacles": WHT to Henry A. Morrill, Box 29, Pringle Papers.

15 Their sisters had been "schoolmates . . . forty years": Helen Herron Taft, *Recollections of Full Years* (New York: Dodd, Mead & Co., 1914), p. 7.

15 "with such high feeling . . . during that period": Ibid., p. 11.

15 "the deeper grew my respect": WHT to Alphonso Taft, July 12, 1885, WHTP.

16 a "merciless but loving critic": WHT to Nellie, June 28, 1895, WHTP.

16 "two men who are intimate chums": Betty Boyd Caroli, *First Ladies* (New York: Oxford University Press, 1987), p. 130.

16 "the Taft Administration will be brilliant": *NYT*, Mar. 4, 1909.

16 insisting "upon complete racial equality": Carl Sferrazza Anthony, *Nellie Taft: The Unconventional First Lady of the Ragtime Era* (New York: HarperCollins, 2005), p. 148.

16 Taft turned "deathly pale": AB to Clara, May 17, 1909, in AB, *Taft and Roosevelt*, Vol. 1, p. 88.

16 "great soul . . . wrapped in darkness": AB to Mrs. John D. Butt, June 8, 1909, in ibid., p. 101.

16 "I have had a hard time . . . at the White House": WHT to TR, May 26, 1910, TRP.

17 "this demonstration of amity . . . with the former President": *Indianapolis Star*, June 12, 1910.

17 "charged with the dignity . . . to any man": AB to Clara, June 16, 1910, in AB, *Taft and Roosevelt*, Vol. 1, p. 389.

17 "When you are being hammered": WHT, Speech, Mar. 22, 1910, Series 9, reel 567, WHTP; *Nevada State Journal*, Mar. 23, 1910.

17 he "read with deep interest": *Evening Star* (Washington, DC), June 18, 1910.

17 all "the members of the faculty . . . tremendous yell": *The North American* (Philadelphia), June 19, 1910.

18 gaily decorated . . . 2,500 invited guests: *Evening Bulletin* (Philadelphia), June 18, 1910.

18 "The Roosevelt luck" . . . decision to speak indoors: *Philadelphia Inquirer*, June 19, 1910.

18 the entire audience rose: *The North American*, June 19, 1910.

18 a "flying visit": *Evening Bulletin*, June 18, 1910.

18 "He came to me": *Evening Star* (Washington, DC), June 18, 1910.

18 "Banks, office buildings": *Philadelphia Inquirer*, June 18, 1910.

18 "a terrific electrical storm": Ibid.

18 "I thank you sincerely for coming": WHT, "Speech at Lincoln University, June 18, 1910," WHTP.

18 "one of the greatest men" . . . nation's racial problems: *Evening Star* (Washington, DC), June 19, 1910.

18 the press could not resist drawing comparisons: *The North American*, June 19, 1910.

19 Taft was "travel-stained": *New York Herald*, June 19, 1910.

19 exhausted when he boarded the train: *Fort Wayne* [IN] *Journal-Gazette*, June 19, 1910.

19 "in a free state of perspiration": *Galveston* [TX] *Daily News*, June 19, 1910.

19 "ready and eager": *Waterloo* [IA] *Times-Tribune*, June 19, 1910.

19 his bill . . . was awaiting his signature: *New York Herald*, June 19, 1910.

19 "an abiding faith . . . take care of itself ultimately": WHT to R. L. O'Brien, June 28, 1910, in Donald F. Anderson, *William Howard Taft: A Conservative's Conception of the Presidency* (Ithaca, NY: Cornell University Press, 1973), p. 218.

19 "the first positive step": "Six Months of President Taft," *The World's Work* (September 1909).
19 "for the first time, the power": George Kibbe Turner, "How Taft Views His Own Administration; An Interview with the President," *McClure's* (June 1910), p. 215.
19 a postal savings bill "fought at every step": *Evening Bulletin* (Philadelphia), June 18, 1910.
19 a secure place to deposit their money: WHT to William B. McKinley, Aug. 20, 1910, WHTP.
19 Taft "had unquestionably strengthened": *Evening Bulletin* (Philadelphia), June 18, 1910.
20 "their laughs would mingle": AB to Clara, June 15, 1912, in AB, *Taft and Roosevelt*, Vol. 2, p. 813.
20 "No other friendship": William Allen White, "Taft: A Hewer of Wood," *The American Magazine* (April 1908), pp. 23–24.
20 "The whole country waits and wonders": *Baltimore Sun*, June 18, 1910.

CHAPTER TWO: Will and Teedie

Page
21 "Louise is getting . . . clamorous appetite": Alphonso Taft to Increase N. Talbot, Sept 21, 1857, WHTP.
21 "very large . . . made with belts": LTT to DCT, Nov. 8, 1857, WHTP.
22 "took great comfort . . . boys growing up together": LTT to Susan Torrey, November [n.d.], 1857, WHTP.
22 "He spreads his hands . . . dimple in one cheek": Henry F. Pringle, *The Life and Times of William Howard Taft* [hereafter *Life and Times*] (New York: Farrar & Rinehart, 1939), Vol. 1, p. 3.
22 "deeply, darkly, beautifully blue": LTT to DCT, November [n.d.], 1857, WHTP.
22 "healthy, fast-growing boy": Alphonso Taft to DCT, Dec. 13, 1857, WHTP.
22 "upon being held . . . take care of himself": LTT to DCT, November [n.d.], 1857, WHTP.
22 children "are treasures . . . too much": LTT to Susan Torrey, Feb. 6, 1860, WHTP.
22 To her "great disappointment" . . . town of Millbury, Massachusetts: Horace Dutton Taft, *Memories and Opinions* (New York: The Macmillan Co., 1942), p. 3.
22 "She has great mental . . . synonymous with unhappiness": Ishbel Ross, *An American Family: The Tafts, 1678 to 1964* (Cleveland, OH: World Publishing Co., 1964), p. 18.
23 "If 'ladies of strong minds' ": Ibid., p. 24.
23 "One day in an oat field . . . college was sacred in his eyes": Taft, *Memories and Opinions*, pp. 4–5.
23 "I feel well assured": Alphonso Taft to Frances Phelps, Oct. 9, 1838, WHTP.
23 "There are no such high . . . comparatively few": Alphonso Taft to Sylvia Howard Taft, Nov. 15, 1838, WHTP.
23 "honourably famous": Charles Dickens, *American Notes*, Vol. 11 of *The Writings of Charles Dickens* (New York: Houghton Mifflin, 1894), p. 514.
23 "I have not spent": Alphonso Taft to Peter Rawson Taft, Mar. 30, 1839, WHTP.
24 her "noble husband . . . quiet joy": LTT to DCT, Jan. 4, 1854, WHTP.
24 "I do feel under": Pringle, *Life and Times*, Vol. 1, p. 13.
24 "the best husband": Ross, *An American Family*, p. 20.
24 "Oh, Louise": DCT to LTT, Jan. 18, 1854, WHTP.
24 "I had more pride": LTT to Samuel Torrey, June 6, 1866, WHTP.
24 "Willie is foremost": Alphonso Taft to Samuel Torrey, Oct. 16, 1872, WHTP.
24 "simplicity, courage": Taft, *Memories and Opinions*, p. 5.
24 "If flattery or admiration": Ibid., p. 106.
24 "It was very hard": Ibid., p. 115.
24 "Scarcely a night": Pringle, *Life and Times*, Vol. 1, p. 6.
25 "We might almost as well ask": DCT to LTT, Jan. 17, 1859, WHTP.
25 "spread out before you like a map": Alphonso Taft to Frances Phelps, Nov. 12, 1838, WHTP.
25 "the advantages of both . . . or to rough it": Taft, *Memories and Opinions*, p. 13.
25 "wholesome and natural": Ibid., p. 16.
25 "the city fairly blossomed . . . one end to the other": LTT to Anna Torrey, April 18, 1865, WHTP.
25 "He was . . . a born judge": Taft, *Memories and Opinions*, p. 11.
26 "the Constitution of the State": S. B. Nelson & Co., *History of Cincinnati and Hamilton County, Ohio; Their Past and Present, Including . . . Biographies and Portraits of Pioneers and Representative Citizens, Etc.* (Cincinnati: S. B. Nelson, 1894), p. 189.
26 "the school board": Martha Willard, "Notes for a Biographer," unpublished MS, 1935, p. 92, WHTP.
26 "To be Chief Justice": Ross, *An American Family*, p. 47.
26 "No leader of the Bar . . . patience and kindness": Taft, *Memories and Opinions*, p. 11.
26 "rich real estate holders": Lewis Alexander Leonard, *Life of Alphonso Taft* (New York: Hawke Publishing Co., 1920), p. 48.
26 "the path of virtue and integrity": Ibid., p. 54.
26 "these children are unfortunate . . . cruel circumstances": Ibid.
26 his unblemished reputation . . . "the day is long": *NYT*, March 8, 1876.
26 "reform element . . . old regime": Murat Halstead to Alphonso Taft, Mar. 7, 1876, WHTP.
27 a "fatty": Bessie White Smith, *Boyhoods of the Presidents* (Boston: Lothrop, Lee & Shepard Co., 1929), p. 251.
27 a "lubber": Pringle, *Life and Times*, Vol. 1, p. 20; Eugene P. Lyle, Jr., "Taft: A Career of Big Tasks, His Boyhood and College Days," *The World's Work* (July 1907).
27 "If you can't walk": Smith, *Boyhoods of the Presidents*, p. 251.
27 At the age of seven . . . "arithmetic and writing": Ross, *An American Family*, p. 40.
27 "He means to be a scholar": Ibid.
27 "Mediocrity will not do": Pringle, *Life and Times*, Vol. 1, p. 22.
27 "His average was 95": Alphonso Taft to DCT, Dec. 24, 1869, WHTP.
27 "We felt that the sun": Taft, *Memories and Opinions*, p. 11.

27 "Love of approval": AB to Clara, Aug. 10, 1910, in AB, *Taft and Roosevelt,* Vol. 2, p. 472.

28 "read up in the Gazetteer . . . impressive to him": LTT to Anna Torrey, July 18, 1869, WHTP.

28 Alphonso re-created for Will: Alphonso Taft to WHT, Aug. 1, 1869, WHTP.

28 "a mastery of fact": David H. Burton, *The Learned Presidency: Theodore Roosevelt, William Howard Taft, Woodrow Wilson* (Rutherford, NJ: Fairleigh Dickinson University Press, 1988), p. 91.

28 "the most conspicuous": Taft, *Memories and Opinions*, p. 26.

28 "the great social event": Ross, *An American Family*, p. 58.

28 the splendid Sinton mansion: HHT, *Recollections of Full Years*, p. 4.

29 the *Times-Star*, a Taft family holding: Ross, *An American Family*, p. 67.

29 "The result of coeducation": WHT, "Woman Suffrage," 1874, WHTP.

29 "from their constitutional peculiarities": LTT to DCT, Aug. 16, 1874, WHTP.

29 "Give the woman the ballot . . . this great reform": WHT, "Woman Suffrage," 1874, WHTP.

29 the only obstacle . . . was laziness: Pringle, *Life and Times*, Vol. 1, p. 21.

29 Will stood over six feet . . . nickname "Big Bill": David H. Burton, *Taft, Roosevelt and the Limits of Friendship* (Madison, NJ: Fairleigh Dickinson University Press, 2005), p. 21.

29 "To see his large bulk . . . a dreadnaught launched": Edward H. Cotton, *William Howard Taft: A Character Study* (Boston: Beacon Press, 1932), p. 21.

29 "dragged bodily" . . . to victory: Oscar King Davis, *William Howard Taft, the Man of the Hour; His Biography and His Views on the Great Questions of Today* (Philadelphia: P. W. Ziegler Co., 1908), p. 40.

29 "I begin to see": WHT to Alphonso Taft, Sept. 12, 1874, WHTP.

29 "It is not more": LTT to DCT, Oct. 22, 1874, WHTP.

30 "Another week of this . . . your expectations": WHT to Alphonso Taft, September [n.d.], 1874, WHTP.

30 His father "had other ideas": WHT, "College Athletic," *American Physical Education Review* (April 1916), p. 225.

30 "I doubt that such popularity": Pringle, *Life and Times*, Vol. 1, p. 35.

30 "If a man has to be isolated": WHT to LTT, Nov. 4, 1874, WHTP.

30 settled into a structured regimen: WHT to Alphonso Taft, Oct. 1, 1874, WHTP.

30 "As a scholar . . . moral force": Herbert Wolcott Bowen, *Recollections, Diplomatic and Undiplomatic* (New York: F. H. Hitchcock, 1926), pp. 52–53.

30 He was the class leader: Herbert S. Duffy, *William Howard Taft* (New York: Minton, Balch & Co., 1930), pp. 5–6.

30 "safe and comforting": Lyle, "Taft: A Career of Big Tasks . . . ," *The World's Work* (July 1907).

30 appointed him "father" of their graduating year: Cotton, *William Howard Taft, a Character Study*, p. 4.

30 "was the most admired": Bowen, *Recollections, Diplomatic and Undiplomatic*, p. 53.

30 "there was little . . . way to a degree": David H. Burton, *William Howard Taft, in the Public Service* (Malabar, FL: Robert E. Krieger Publ. Co., 1986), p. 6.

31 "a course of outside reading . . . stick to the course": Lyle, "Taft: A Career of Big Tasks . . . ," *The World's Work* (July 1907).

31 "hard common sense": WHT, "The Vitality of the Democratic Party, Its Causes," Pringle Papers.

31 "Taft was judicial . . . before anything else": Pringle, *Life and Times*, Vol. 1, p. 44.

31 "had more to do with stimulating": Ibid., p. 34.

31 Considered one of the most gifted . . . "secret of his success": Dumas Malone, ed., *Dictionary of American Biography* (New York: Charles Scribner's Sons, 1935), Vol. 9, p. 218.

31 Sumner was an apostle: Robert Green McCloskey, *American Conservatism in the Age of Enterprise: A Study of William Graham Sumner, Stephen J. Field and Andrew Carnegie* (Cambridge, MA: Harvard University Press, 1951), pp. 30–32.

31 "If we should set a limit": Ibid., p. 50.

31 he argued that "princely profits": WHT, "The Right of Private Property," *Michigan Law Journal* (August 1894), p. 223.

32 "the highest pinnacle": McCloskey, *American Conservatism in the Age of Enterprise*, p. 83.

32 "the lawyer who makes": WHT, "The Professional and Political Prospects of the College Graduate," in Harry Clark Coe and William Howard Taft, *Valedictory Poem and Oration Pronounced Before the Senior Class in Yale College, Presentation Day, June 25, 1878* (New Haven, CT: Morehouse & Taylor, 1878).

32 "the greatest prize in college": Pringle, *Life and Times*, Vol. 1, p. 41.

32 "He has in this . . . & practiced": Alphonso Taft to DCT, Oct. 21, 1877, WHTP.

32 "We shall regret that . . . reputation every time": Alphonso Taft to DCT, Dec. 16, 1877, WHTP.

32 "coming on slowly": WHT to Alphonso Taft, Mar. 11, 1878, WHTP.

32 "finding it rather difficult": WHT to Alphonso Taft, April 14, 1878, WHTP.

32 "The sound of approaching music . . . manly sincerity": *NYT*, June 26, 1878.

33 "I wish you could get": WHT to Alphonso Taft, April 14, 1878, WHTP.

33 "Peter continues so strange . . . to Tillie's wishes": LTT to DCT, Jan. 22, 1878, WHTP.

33 "I am doing my best . . . above all others": Peter Rawson Taft to Alphonso Taft, April 19, 1878, WHTP.

33 "I have a kind of presentiment": WHT to HHT, May 10, 1891, WHTP.

34 "a sickly and timid boy": TR to Edward S. Martin, Nov. 26, 1900, in Elting E. Morison, ed., *The Years of Preparation, 1898–1900*, Vol. 2 of *LTR*, p. 1443.

34 "Nobody seemed to think": New York *World*, Nov. 16, 1902.

34 "Theodore Roosevelt, whose name": Corinne Roosevelt Robinson, *My Brother, Theodore Roosevelt* (New York: Charles Scribner's Sons, 1921), p. 1.

34 "great and loving care . . . walk up and down with me": TR to Edward S. Martin, Nov. 26, 1900, in *LTR*, Vol. 2, p. 1443.

34 "I could breathe": Lincoln Steffens, *The Autobiography of Lincoln Steffens* (New York: Harcourt, Brace & Co., 1931), p. 350.

34 "My father": Ibid.

34 "one of the five richest": Nathan Miller, *The Roosevelt Chronicles* (New York: Doubleday & Co., 1979), p. 117.

34 feared would "spoil" him: New York *World*, Feb. 11, 1878.

35 "I am trying to school": Theodore Roosevelt, Sr., to Martha Bulloch Roosevelt, June 10, 1853, TRC.

35 now "confident . . . only live in your being": Martha Bulloch Roosevelt to Theodore Roosevelt, Sr., July 26, 1853, in CRR, *My Brother*, pp. 13–14.

35 "the blood rush . . . I love you!": Theodore Roosevelt, Sr., to Martha Bulloch Roosevelt, Aug. 3, 1853, in ibid., p. 15.

35 "If I may judge": Martha Elliott Bulloch to Susan West, Nov. 16, 1861, TRC.

36 "I shudder to think": AB to Clara, January 8, 1909, in Abbott, ed., *Letters of Archie Butt*, p. 279.

36 Thee suppressed . . . "absolute fighting forces": Anna Roosevelt Cowles, "The Story of the Roosevelt Family," unpublished MS, n.d., CRR Papers.

36 "the most dominant figure": CRR, *My Brother*, p. 9.

36 "the most intimate friend": Ibid., p. 7.

36 "we used to wait": TR, *An Autobiography* (New York: Charles Scribner's Sons, 1920), p. 8.

36 "there was never anyone": ARC, "The Story of the Roosevelt Family," CRR Papers.

36 "he was one of those rare": McCullough, *Mornings on Horseback*, p. 31.

36 He tutored them . . . "the dead limbs": CRR, *My Brother*, p. 8.

36 "turn aside from his business": DCT to LTT, Jan. 17, 1859, WHTP.

36 "I never knew anyone": TR, *An Autobiography*, p. 9.

36 "not so much for what it was": Theodore Roosevelt, Sr., to Martha Bulloch Roosevelt, Sept. 28, 1873, TRC.

37 improving the lives of tenement children: TR, *An Autobiography*, p. 10; CRR, *My Brother*, pp. 4–5.

37 "Father was the finest man": Jacob A. Riis, *Theodore Roosevelt: The Citizen* (New York: Grosset & Dunlap, 1907), p. 446.

37 to arrange home tutoring . . . Mittie's sister, Anna: TR, *An Autobiography*, pp. 12–13.

37 their mother provided: Ibid., p. 4; ARC, "The Story of the Roosevelt Family," CRR Papers.

37 "From the very fact . . . power of concentration": William Draper Lewis, *The Life of Theodore Roosevelt* (Philadelphia: John C. Winston Co., 1919), p. 36.

37 "men who were fearless": TR, *An Autobiography*, p. 27.

37 "I can see him now . . . month to month": CRR, *My Brother*, pp. 1–2.

37 "anything less tranquil": Ibid., p. 89.

38 "riding, driving . . . the 'divine fire' ": Frances Theodora Parsons, *Perchance Some Day* (New York: Privately printed, 1951), pp. 26, 29.

38 "Roosevelt Museum of Natural History": TR, *An Autobiography*, p. 14.

38 "He loves the woods": WHT, "My Predecessor," *Collier's*, Mar. 6, 1909, p. 25.

38 "Sit down, Will . . . domestic affairs": Edward George Lowry, "The White House Now," *Harper's*, May 15, 1909, p. 7.

38 "a great little home-boy": CRR, *My Brother*, p. 45.

39 He traversed fields . . . of the Vatican: TR, *Diaries of Boyhood and Youth*, pp. 18–19, 150, 181; CRR, *My Brother*, pp. 46, 49.

39 "we three": TR, *Diaries of Boyhood and Youth*, pp. 63, 109.

39 "that a real education": Kathleen Mary Dalton, "The Early Life of Theodore Roosevelt," PhD diss., Johns Hopkins University, 1979, p. 188.

39 "Theodore, you have the mind . . . *I'll make my body*": CRR, *My Brother*, p. 50.

39 to expand "his chest": Ibid.

39 "the strenuous life": Ibid.

39 two "mischievous" boys . . . "perceptible improvement whatever": TR, *An Autobiography*, pp. 27–28.

40 his "timid" nature: Parsons, *Perchance Some Day*, p. 28.

40 "There were all kinds of things": Edward Wagenknecht, *The Seven Worlds of Theodore Roosevelt* (New York: Longmans, Green & Co., 1958), p. 3.

40 "by constantly forcing": Parsons, *Perchance Some Day*, p. 28.

40 "a matter of habit": TR, *An Autobiography*, p. 32.

40 "We arrived in sight of Alexandria": TR, *Diaries of Boyhood and Youth*, p. 276.

40 "first real collecting": TR, *An Autobiography*, p. 19.

40 a private vessel . . . thirteen-man crew: McCullough, *Mornings on Horseback*, p. 123.

40 "I had no idea": TR, *An Autobiography*, p. 18.

40 "My first knowledge": Ibid., p. 19.

40 "an almost ruthless single-mindedness": Putnam, *Theodore Roosevelt: The Formative Years*, p. 99.

41 "And of course": CRR, *My Brother*, p. 80.

41 "This trip . . . formed": TR, *An Autobiography*, p. 19.

41 "lamentably weak in Latin": Ibid., p. 21.

41 "The young man never": Putnam, *Theodore Roosevelt: The Formative Years*, p. 127.

41 "What will I become . . . but it is hard": McCullough, *Mornings on Horseback*, p. 144.

42 "It produced congestion": Theodore Roosevelt, Sr., to Martha Bulloch Roosevelt, Nov. 9, 1874, in ibid., p. 145.

42 "I jump involuntarily": Elliott Roosevelt to Theodore Roosevelt, Sr., Nov. 22, 1874, in ibid., p. 146.

42 "could make more friends . . . in many respects": Elliott Roosevelt to Theodore Roosevelt, Sr., Mar. 6, 1875, in Joseph P. Lash, *Eleanor and Franklin* (New York: W. W. Norton & Co., 1971), p. 7.

42 "During my Latin lesson": Ibid.

42 "fainted just after leaving": Ibid., p. 8.

42 "Is it not splendid": TR to ARC, July 25, 1875, in Elting E. Morison, ed., *The Years of Preparation, 1868–1898*, Vol. 1 of *LTR*, p. 13.

42 "a slender nervous young man": Donald G. Wilhelm, *Theodore Roosevelt as an Undergraduate* (Boston: J. W. Luce & Co., 1910), p. 31.

42 He worried initially: TR to CRR, Nov. 26, 1876, TRC.
42 "studious, ambitious": Henry F. Pringle, *Theodore Roosevelt: A Biography* (New York: Harcourt, Brace & Co., 1931), p. 33.
42 "It was not often . . . again and again": Paul Grondahl, *I Rose Like a Rocket: The Political Education of Theodore Roosevelt* (New York: Free Press, 2004), p. 45.
42 "Now look here, Roosevelt": Wilhelm, *Theodore Roosevelt as an Undergraduate*, p. 35.
43 he would retreat to a corner: Ibid., p. 24.
43 "No man ever came": Ibid.
43 "My library has been": TR to Theodore Roosevelt, Sr., and Martha Bulloch Roosevelt, Feb. 11, 1877, in *LTR*, Vol. 1, p. 26.
43 "the greatest of companions": Wagenknecht, *Seven Worlds*, p. 44.
43 "As I talked the pages": Frederick S. Wood, *Roosevelt as We Knew Him: The Personal Recollections of One Hundred and Fifty of His Friends and Associates* (Philadelphia: John C. Winston Co., 1927), p. 361.
43 "He always carried a book": Wagenknecht, *Seven Worlds*, p. 46.
43 Roosevelt's ability to concentrate . . . "not be diverted": Charles Grenfell Washburn, *Theodore Roosevelt: The Logic of His Career* (Boston: Houghton Mifflin, 1916), p. 3.
43 Preparing so far ahead "freed his mind": Straus, *Under Four Administrations*, p. 256.
43 finished a complete draft: Ibid., pp. 255–56.
43 "I never knew a man": WHT, "My Predecessor," *Collier's*, Mar. 6, 1909, p. 25.
44 exercising rigorously day after day: TR, *Diaries of Boyhood and Youth*, pp. 355–56, 363.
44 "he danced just as you'd expect": Putnam, *Theodore Roosevelt: The Formative Years*, p. 166.
44 "His college life broadened": Lewis, *Life of Theodore Roosevelt*, p. 51.
44 "Funnily enough": TR to Martha Bulloch Roosevelt, Oct. 8, 1878, in *LTR*, Vol. 1, p. 34.
44 "As I saw the last of the train": Grondahl, *I Rose Like a Rocket*, pp. 41–42.
44 "I do not think": TR to Theodore Roosevelt, Sr., Oct. 22, 1876, in *LTR*, Vol. 1, p. 18.
45 The Senate rejected Roosevelt's nomination: *NYT*, Oct. 30 & Dec. 4, 1877; *Galveston* [TX] *Daily News*, Dec. 13, 1877.
45 "The machine politicians": Dalton, "The Early Life of Theodore Roosevelt," p. 282.
45 an advanced stage of bowel cancer: McCullough, *Mornings on Horseback*, p. 181.
45 "very much better": TR, *Diaries of Boyhood and Youth*, p. 364.
45 "Today he told me": TR, Personal Diary, Jan. 2, 1878, TRP.
45 His groans reverberated: Elliott Roosevelt, unpublished MS, n.d., TRC.
45 his dark hair turned gray: Putnam, *Theodore Roosevelt: The Formative Years*, p. 148.
45 Elliott stayed by his father's side: Elliott Roosevelt, undated memorandum, TRC.
45 His grief was "doubly bitter . . . dearest on earth died": TR to Henry Davis Minot, July 5, 1880, TRC.
45 "I never was able": TR, Personal Diary, June 20, 1878, TRP.
45 "The death of Mr. Roosevelt": *NYT*, Feb. 13, 1878.
45 "Flags flew . . . wept over him": Riis, *Theodore Roosevelt: The Citizen*, p. 447.
45 "There was truly no end": *NYT*, Feb. 12, 1878.
46 "He has just been buried": TR, Personal Diary, Feb. 12, 1878, TRP.
46 still struck him "like a hideous dream": Ibid.
46 "It has been a most fortunate thing": TR, Personal Diary, Mar. 11, 1878, TRP.
46 "If I had very much time": TR, Personal Diary, Mar. 6, 1878, TRP.
46 "every nook and corner": TR, Personal Diary, June 6, 1878, TRP.
46 "Am leading the most intensely": TR, Personal Diary, June 21, 1878, TRP.
46 "the only human being": TR, Personal Diary, April 18, 1878, TRP.
46 "it was a real case": TR, Personal Diary, Jan. 30, 1880, TRP.
46 he vowed "to win her": TR, Personal Diary, Jan. 25, 1880, TRP.
47 "made everything subordinate": TR to Henry Davis Minot, Feb. 13, 1880, in *LTR*, Vol. 1, p. 43.
47 mesmerized her young brother: Pringle, *Theodore Roosevelt: A Biography*, p. 42.
47 "the tortures" he was suffering: TR, Personal Diary, Jan. 30, 1880, TRP.
47 "I have hardly had": Ibid.
47 "I am so happy": TR, Personal Diary, Jan. 25, 1880, TRP.
47 "I do not believe": TR, Personal Diary, Mar. 11, 1880, TRP.
47 "nothing on earth left to wish for": TR, Personal Diary, July 29, 1880, TRP.
47 a "royally good time": TR, Personal Diary, June 28, 1879, TRP.
47 "As regards the laws": Richard Welling, "Theodore Roosevelt at Harvard," *Outlook*, Oct. 27, 1920, p. 367.
47 "only one gentleman": TR to ARC, Oct. 13, 1879, in *LTR*, Vol. 1, p. 42.
47 "I have certainly lived": TR, Personal Diary, May 5, 1880, TRP.
48 "do my best, and work": TR, Personal Diary, Mar. 25, 1880, TRP.
48 "Natural history was to remain": Putnam, *Theodore Roosevelt: The Formative Years*, p. 179.
48 "great sorrow and great joy . . . overbalanced the sorrow": TR to Henry Davis Minot, July 5, 1880, TRC.

CHAPTER THREE: The Judge and the Politician

Page

50 "a judicial habit of thought and action": Francis E. Leupp, "Taft and Roosevelt: A Composite Study," *The Atlantic Monthly* (November 1910), p. 650.
50 an "old style" institution: Pringle, *Life and Times*, Vol. 1, p. 49.
51 "more about the workings of the law": Burton, *The Learned Presidency*, p. 96.
51 "struck and scratched him": *Cincinnati Commercial*, Nov. 6, 1878.
51 to complete these accounts before dinner: Pringle, *Life and Times*, Vol. 1, p. 53.

51 "Washington will remain . . . metropolis of America": Daniel Hurley and the Cincinnati Historical Society, *Cincinnati: The Queen City* (Cincinnati, OH: Cin. Hist. Soc., 1988), p. 73.
51 "large, handsome and fair": Pringle, *Life and Times*, Vol. 1, p. 61.
52 "a capital opportunity . . . to have you lose it": Alphonso Taft to WHT, July 1, 1879, WHTP.
52 "agreed on a settlement": Alphonso Taft to WHT, July 2, 1879, WHTP.
52 "This gratifying your fondness": Alphonso Taft to WHT, July 2, 1879, WHTP.
52 "I do not think": Alphonso Taft to WHT, July 3, 1879, WHTP.
52 "he would not be seen in public": Pringle, *Life and Times*, Vol. 1, p. 52.
53 a salary of $1,500 a year: Ibid., pp. 53–54.
53 "its talons deep in the judiciary": Duffy, *William Howard Taft*, p. 10.
53 "was able to secure any verdict": *NYT*, Mar. 30, 1884.
53 took "a sensational turn": *Cin. Com.*, Dec. 7, 1880.
53 he "fell in" with Miller Outcault: WHT to WAW, Feb. 26, 1908, White Papers.
53 "standing upon the railing": *Cin. Com.*, Dec. 14, 1880.
53 "nasty torrent of abuse": *Cin. Com.*, Dec. 11, 1880.
53 "the bitterest invective . . . three-cornered fight": *Cin. Com.*, Dec. 9, 1880.
53 to dismiss prosecutor Drew: *Titusville* [PA] *Morning Herald*, Dec. 16, 1880.
53 "the experience he had": HHT, *Recollections of Full Years*, p. 9.
54 "a Theodore Roosevelt might . . . personally or politically ambitious": Pringle, *Life and Times*, Vol. 1, p. 55.
54 "He was on his legs": Taft, *Memories and Opinions*, p. 110.
54 he canvassed the city . . . remained involved: WHT to WAW, Feb. 26, 1908, White Papers.
54 "I attended all . . . on good terms": Ibid.
54 "the most popular young man": LTT to DCT, Jan. 26, 1882, WHTP.
54 "was known to be a bruiser": Duffy, *William Howard Taft*, p. 7.
54 a "terrible beating": *Petersburg* [VA] *Index and Appeal*, April 22, 1879.
54 "lifted him up and dashed him": Lyle, "Taft: A Career of Big Tasks," *The World's Work* (August 1907).
54 "The feeling among all": *Bismarck* [ND] *Tribune*, April 26, 1879.
54 "I want him to . . . do it well": Alphonso Taft to DCT, Oct. 17, 1880, WHTP.
55 aghast to see his name . . . throughout the city: LTT to DCT, September [n.d.], 1880, WHTP.
55 "Don't allow yourself": Alphonso Taft to WHT, Sept. 10, 1880, WHTP.
55 "He finds the farmers . . . not embarrassed": LTT to DCT, September [n.d.], 1880, WHTP.
55 "There is every . . . first class lawyer, too": Alphonso Taft to DCT, Oct. 17, 1880, WHTP.
55 "If you will appoint": Taft, *Memories and Opinions*, p. 111.
55 "I did not wish": LTT to DCT, Jan. 26, 1882, WHTP.
55 Taft was "too young": Ibid.
55 collecting over $10 million: Lyle, "Taft: A Career of Big Tasks," *The World's Work* (August 1907).
55 "had no political enemies": WHT to WAW, Feb. 28, 1908, White Papers.
55 He detested the prominence of the position: WHT to Alphonso Taft, June 4, 1882, WHTP.
55 too "thin-skinned" for "public life": James David Barber, *The Presidential Character: Predicting Performance in the White House* (Englewood Cliffs, NJ: Prentice-Hall, 1985), p. 152.
56 "but announced . . . the course he followed": Taft, *Memories and Opinions*, p. 111.
56 the "bulldozer" tone of the letter: WHT to Alphonso Taft, July 24, 1882, WHTP.
56 "are among the best . . . in regard to Civil Service": WHT to Thomas Young, July 29, 1882, WHTP.
56 "I would much rather resign": WHT to Alphonso Taft, July 24, 1882, WHTP.
56 "The men whose removal . . . down to business": WHT to Alphonso Taft, Oct. 28, 1882, WHTP.
56 "I am mighty glad . . . Reformer in practice": Horace Taft to LTT, Sept. 5, 1882, WHTP.
57 "It is the opening": WHT to Alphonso Taft, Oct. 28, 1882, WHTP.
57 "to work at the law": Alphonso Taft to Charles P. Taft, Jan. 10, 1883, WHTP.
57 "younger by several years": Annie Sinton Taft to Alphonso Taft, May 6, 1883, WHTP.
57 "I wish you could look": WHT to Frances L. Taft, Jan. 26, 1883, WHTP.
57 "I hope you will make": Ross, *An American Family*, p. 71.
57 "glad to get home": WHT to LTT, Oct. 5, 1883, WHTP.
57 "Will is working well": H. P. Lloyd to Alphonso Taft, Dec. 13, 1883, WHTP.
57 "makes friends wherever": WHT to Frances L. Taft, Jan. 6, 1882, WHTP.
57 "grow large enough": Ibid.
57 he was "no nearer matrimony": WHT to LTT, Sept. 10, 1882, WHTP.
58 a different girl each evening: WHT to LTT, Feb. 2, 1883, WHTP.
58 "I see Father shake his head": WHT to Frances L. Taft, Feb. 11, 1883, WHTP.
58 A wave of ghastly murders: Hurley, *Cincinnati: The Queen City*, p. 90.
58 "a series of events": Ibid., p. 92.
58 "were filled with Christmas presents": *NYT*, Mar. 30, 1884.
58 "cold-blooded butchery": Duffy, *William Howard Taft*, p. 10.
58 "to plead guilty . . . absolute and unquestioned": Ibid.
58 Cincinnati residents were stunned: *NYT*, Mar. 31, 1884.
58 "The people of Cincinnati": Pringle, *Life and Times*, Vol. 1, p. 85.
58 "Justice": *NYT*, Mar. 31, 1884.
59 "become the mere agents": *Elyria* [OH] *Republican*, April 10, 1884.
59 "Hang the jury! . . . boisterous element remained": *NYT*, Mar. 30, 1884.
59 the mob divided into three groups: Ibid.
59 Berner . . . transferred to another jail: Pringle, *Life and Times*, Vol. 1, p. 87.

59 "the bloodiest affair": *NYT*, Mar. 30, 1884.
59 "to obtain testimony": WHT to Alphonso Taft, May 10, 1884, WHTP.
59 "conducted the defense": WHT to Alphonso Taft, June 15, 1884, WHTP.
59 "I shall do everything": WHT to Alphonso Taft, May 10, 1884, WHTP.
60 "was an extraordinary honor": Taft, *Memories and Opinions*, p. 112.
60 fearing even for his son's physical safety: WHT to Alphonso Taft, May 10, 1884, WHTP.
60 "thrown the bar": WHT to LTT, April 21, 1884, WHTP.
60 "for men to have backbone": WHT to Alphonso Taft, May 10, 1884, WHTP.
60 his brother was instrumental: Taft, *Memories and Opinions*, p. 112.
60 "a thankless task": Alphonso Taft to WHT, May 21, 1884, WHTP.
60 "I find that the Campbell . . . hoarse for Blaine": WHT to Alphonso Taft, June 15, 1884, WHTP.
60 "Your son Will did splendid": Benjamin Butterworth to Alphonso Taft, Jan. 5, 1885, WHTP.
60 "This is my last election": WHT to LTT, Oct. 26, 1884, WHTP.
61 "The investigation": WHT to Alphonso Taft, Nov. 23, 1884, WHTP.
61 "suddenly emerging": Pringle, *Life and Times*, Vol. 1, p. 89.
61 "actuated by no other motive . . . member of the Bar": *Cin. Com. Gazette*, Jan. 6, 1885.
61 "There was not a vindictive word . . . all is gone": *Cin. Com. Gaz.*, Jan. 8, 1885.
62 "Tom Campbell controls": Benjamin Butterworth to Alphonso Taft, Jan. 5, 1885, WHTP.
62 exonerated Campbell of all charges: *Cin. Com. Gaz.*, Feb. 4, 1885.
62 "It was disastrous": WHT to Alphonso Taft, Feb. 8, 1885, WHTP.
62 "whatever may be said": Benjamin Butterworth to Alphonso Taft, Jan. 5, 1885, WHTP.
62 "I am very glad now . . . it could be tried": WHT to Alphonso Taft, Feb. 8, 1885, WHTP.
62 "I was very much pleased": Alphonso Taft to WHT, Mar. 3, 1885, WHTP.
62 "It is the beginning . . . his feeling toward me": WHT to Alphonso Taft, Mar. 27, 1885, WHTP.
62 "I should not bow my head": WHT to HHT, July 4, 1885, WHTP.
62 "double-faced Campbell man": WHT to HHT, July 10, 1885, WHTP.
63 "instant sympathy . . . his type of mind": Julia B. Foraker, *I Would Live It Again: Memories of a Vivid Life* (New York: Harper & Bros., 1932), p. 305.
63 "knew him well enough": Joseph B. Foraker, *Notes of a Busy Life* (Cincinnati, OH: Stewart & Kidd Co., 1916), p. 237.
63 "a very bright young man": Duffy, *William Howard Taft*, p. 14.
63 "Considering the opportunity": Foraker, *Notes of a Busy Life*, p. 238.
63 "the welcome beginning": HHT, *Recollections of Full Years*, p. 22.
64 "hands full attending to various affairs": TR, Personal Diary, Oct. 18, 1880, TRP.
64 "It almost frightens me": TR, Personal Diary, Oct. 17, 1880, TRP.
64 "Our intense happiness": TR, Personal Diary, Oct. 27, 1880, TRP.
64 "equally matched" lawn tennis: TR, Personal Diary, Nov. 3, 1880, TRP.
64 reading poetry: TR to Martha Bulloch Roosevelt, Oct. 31, 1880, in *LTR*, Vol. 1, p. 47.
64 "an energetic questioner" . . . in his classmates: Putnam, *Theodore Roosevelt: The Formative Years*, p. 219.
64 "some of the teaching": TR, *An Autobiography*, p. 54.
64 "we are concerned": Robert Charles, "Legal Education in the Late Nineteenth Century, Through the Eyes of Theodore Roosevelt," *American Journal of Legal History* (July 1993), p. 247.
64 more than 1,000 pages: Ibid., p. 246.
64 he impressed professors: Putnam, *Theodore Roosevelt: The Formative Years*, p. 219.
64 "I tried faithfully": Riis, *Theodore Roosevelt*, pp. 36–37.
65 a volume in the Porcellian Club library: Ibid., p. 39.
65 "afflicted with a hatred": Hermann Hagedorn, ed., *The Naval War of 1812*, Vol. 6 of *The Works of Theodore Roosevelt* [hereafter *WTR*] (New York: Charles Scribner's Sons, 1926), p. 14.
65 "I spend most of my spare time": TR, Personal Diary, May 2, 1881, TRP.
65 "a wonderfully open": Christopher Gray, "Streetscapes: The Old Astor Library," *NYT*, Feb. 10, 2002.
65 American historians, desiring to embellish: Riis, *Theodore Roosevelt*, pp. 39–40.
65 "We're dining out": Owen Wister, *Roosevelt: The Story of a Friendship, 1880–1919* (New York: The Macmillan Co., 1930), p. 24.
65 "Alice is the best": TR, Personal Diary, May 25, 1881, TRP.
65 "Altogether it would be difficult": TR to CRR, June 16, 1881, in *LTR*, Vol. 1, pp. 48–49.
65 "I was anxious to go . . . to make it exciting": TR to ARC, Aug. 5, 1881, in ibid., p. 49.
66 "You would be amused": TR to ARC, Aug. 21, 1881, in ibid., p. 50.
66 "Am working fairly": TR, Personal Diary, Oct. 17, 1881, TRP.
66 "were so dry": TR, *An Autobiography*, p. 22.
66 "The volume is an excellent one": *NYT*, June 5, 1882.
66 "a comparison with": George T. Temple, "The Naval War of 1812," *The Academy*, July 22, 1882.
66 "in the very first class": TR to S. Van Duzer, in *LTR*, Vol. 1, p. 136.
66 "the first really satisfactory": Frederick Jackson Turner, "The Winning of the West," *The Dial* (August 1889).
67 "Everything was of interest": John A. Gable, ed., *The Man in the Arena: Speeches and Essays by Theodore Roosevelt* (Oyster Bay, NY: Theodore Roosevelt Assoc., 1987), p. 1.
67 the "barn-like room over a saloon": TR, *An Autobiography*, p. 56.
67 "to help the cause": William Roscoe Thayer, *Theodore Roosevelt: An Intimate Biography* (Boston: Houghton Mifflin, 1919), p. 21.
67 district politics were "low . . . of the governing class": TR, *An Autobiography*, p. 56.
67 "I went around there often": Ibid., p. 57.

67 "He looked like a dude": Hermann Hagedorn, *The Boys' Life of Theodore Roosevelt* (New York: Harper & Bros., 1918), pp. 66–67.
67 "a fine head": Ibid., p. 67.
67 "He was by nature": TR, *An Autobiography*, p. 59.
68 the college-educated men and "the swells": Hagedorn, *The Boys' Life*, p. 70.
68 "of high character": Thayer, *Theodore Roosevelt: An Intimate Biography*, p. 30.
68 the youngest president: While John F. Kennedy was the youngest man elected to the presidency, TR was still younger when he assumed the office after McKinley's assassination.
68 "My first days": TR, *An Autobiography*, p. 63.
68 "He came in as if": Hermann Hagedorn, Isaac Hunt, and George F. Spinney, "Memorandum of Conversation at Dinner at the Harvard Club, 27 West 44th Street, New York City, September 20, 1923," p. 42, TRC.
68 "He was like Moses": Ibid., p. 17.
68 "an analysis of the character": Ibid., p. 1.
68 "bad enough": TR, Diary, Jan. 7, 1882, in *LTR*, Vol. 2, p. 1469.
68 "totally unable to speak": TR, Diary, Jan. 24, 1882, in ibid., p. 1470.
69 "By God! . . . let me alone": Hagedorn et al., "Memorandum of Conversation," pp. 84–85, TRC.
69 "Why don't your mother . . . The third quit cold": Ethel Armes, "When T.R. Qualified as a Boxer," unpublished MS, pp. 1–2, TRC.
69 "When Taft gives way": Leupp, "Taft and Roosevelt: A Composite Study," *Atlantic Monthly* (November 1910), p. 649.
69 "very good men . . . very bad men": TR, "Phases of State Legislation," *Century Illus. Monthly Mag.* (April 1885), p. 820.
69 About thirty reporters . . . in the back of the chamber: "Diagrams of Senate and Assembly Chambers," in *Manual for the Use of the Legislature of the State of New York for the Year 1884* (Albany, NY: Weed, Parsons & Co., 1884), n.p.
70 "good-hearted man . . . honest laugh": Hagedorn et al., "Memorandum of Conversation," p. 49, TRC.
70 "vigor, thoroughness": Leupp, "Taft and Roosevelt: A Composite Study," *Atlantic Monthly* (November 1910), p. 649.
70 "He grew like . . . ninety percent of them did": Hagedorn et al., "Memorandum of Conversation," p. 41, TRC.
70 "a mighty tree": *Watertown* [NY] *Daily Times*, May 13, 1939.
70 "He would go away . . . grew right away from me": Hagedorn et al., "Memorandum of Conversation," pp. 40–41, TRC.
70 "It was Roosevelt's habit": William C. Hudson, *Random Recollections of an Old Political Reporter* (New York: Cupples & Leon, 1911), pp. 144–45.
71 Judge Westbrook's collusion: *NYT*, Dec. 27, 1881.
71 "We went after him": Hagedorn et al., "Memorandum of Conversation," p. 13, TRC.
71 Gould had amassed railroads . . . system for the city: Matthew Josephson, *The Robber Barons: The Great American Capitalists, 1861–1901* (New York: Harcourt, Brace & Co., 1964), pp. 194–95, 209.
71 A burdensome lawsuit: Ibid., p. 209.
71 the Gould syndicate began buying . . . rose sharply: *NYT*, Dec. 27, 1881.
71 who "prostituted" himself . . . "the wolf the sheep": *Brooklyn Eagle*, Dec. 30, 1881, reprinted in *NYT*, Dec. 31, 1881, Clipping Scrapbook, TRC.
71 "dignity and respect . . . rings and cliques": *Auburn* [NY] *Advertiser*, Dec. 28, 1881, reprinted in *NYT*, Dec. 30, 1881, Clipping Scrapbook, TRC.
72 "remain silent": *Waterbury* [CT] *Republican-American*, Dec. 28, 1881, reprinted in ibid.
72 Hunt suggested that Roosevelt: Hagedorn et al., "Memorandum of Conversation," p. 1, TRC.
72 "but would not take it up": Ibid., pp. 7–8.
72 "an energetic . . . cross-questioned him": Pringle, *Theodore Roosevelt: A Biography*, p. 71.
72 "the presses in the basement": George F. Spinney, "The Westbrook Scandal," p. 5, TRC.
72 "I am willing to go": TR, *An Autobiography*, p. 75.
72 "never been explained": New York *Evening Post*, Mar. 30, 1882, Clipping Scrapbook, TRC.
72 "By Jove!": Hagedorn et al., "Memorandum of Conversation," p. 9, TRC.
72 "Mr. Roosevelt correctly states": *NYT*, Mar. 30, 1882.
72 "Roosevelt suddenly interrupted . . . grew silent": Spinney, "The Westbrook Scandal," p. 7, TRC.
73 "slowly and clearly": Ibid., pp. 7–8.
73 "The men who . . . demand such an investigation": Ibid., pp. 10–11.
73 "Beyond a shadow . . . to be trifled with": Ibid., pp. 11–12.
73 "the day's proceedings": Ibid., p. 13.
73 "I have drawn blood": TR to Alice Hathaway Lee Roosevelt, April 5, 1882, in Nathan Miller, *Theodore Roosevelt: A Life* (New York: William Morrow, 1992), p. 135.
74 "Mr. Roosevelt has a most refreshing": *NYT*, April 6, 1882, Clipping Scrapbook, TRC.
74 "Before any official . . . in a newspaper": New York *World*, April 12, 1882, Clipping Scrapbook, TRC.
74 "like water poured": Hagedorn et al., "Memorandum of Conversation," p. 16, TRC.
74 "it was a good thing . . . business, or politics": TR, *An Autobiography*, p. 77.
74 "By the time": Hagedorn et al., "Memorandum of Conversation," p. 12, TRC.
74 Hunt later alleged . . . $2,500 each: Hermann Hagedorn and Isaac Hunt, "Conversation Re: Westbrook Affair," unpublished MS, p. 2, TRC.
75 "was dancing and jumping": Ibid., p. 4.
75 "To you, members": Putnam, *Theodore Roosevelt: The Formative Years*, p. 271.
75 "deathless silence": Hagedorn and Hunt, "Conversation Re: Westbrook Affair," p. 4, TRC.
75 "It was apparent": Spinney, "The Westbrook Scandal," p. 24, TRC.
75 "The action of the Assembly": *New York Herald*, June 1, 1882, Clipping Scrapbook, TRC.
75 "A Miscarriage of Justice . . . the general verdict": Quoted in *NYT*, June 2, 1882.
75 "won his spurs . . . anybody's esteem": Hagedorn and Hunt, "Conversation Re: Westbrook Affair," pp. 2, 4, TRC.

75 "Roosevelt's name": Spinney, "The Westbrook Scandal," p. 29, TRC.
75 "I rose like a rocket . . . not all-important": TR to TR, Jr., Oct. 20, 1903, in *LTR*, Vol. 3, p. 635.
76 "My head was": Riis, *Theodore Roosevelt*, p. 58.
76 "a perfect nuisance": Hagedorn et al., "Memorandum of Conversation," p. 26, TRC.
76 "so explosive": Ibid., p. 19.
76 "a damn fool": Ibid., p. 16.
76 "he yelled . . . the venom imaginary": Ibid.
76 "as a paper of . . . rotten": Ibid., p. 4.
76 "down the roll from Polk": TR, Mar. 9, 1883, in Hermann Hagedorn, ed., *Campaigns and Controversies*, Vol. 14 of *WTR*, p. 19.
76 "absolutely deserted . . . powerless to accomplish": Riis, *Theodore Roosevelt*, p. 59.
76 "I thereby learned": TR, *An Autobiography*, p. 85.
76 "I turned in to help": Riis, *Theodore Roosevelt*, p. 59.
76 "exceedingly unattractive persons . . . conditions of laborers": TR, "A Judicial Experience," *Outlook*, Mar. 13, 1909, p. 563.
77 "one of the most dreadful": Samuel Gompers and Stuart B. Kaufman, eds., *The Making of a Union Leader, 1850–1886*, Vol. 1 of *The Samuel Gompers Papers* (Urbana: University of Illinois Press, 1986), p. 172.
77 "actual character of the evils": Ibid.
77 Gompers . . . published comprehensive reports: Samuel Gompers, *Seventy Years of Life and Labor; An Autobiography* (New York: E. P. Dutton, 1925), p. 59.
77 "a breeding ground . . . to a sewer": Gompers and Kaufman, eds., *The Making of a Union Leader*, p. 174.
77 "dark and gloomy" . . . seemed like night: Ibid., p. 176.
77 "if the conditions described": Gompers, *Seventy Years of Life and Labor*, p. 60.
77 "a good deal shocked": TR, "A Judicial Experience," *Outlook*, Mar. 13, 1909, p. 563.
77 "overwhelming majority . . . scraps of food": TR, *An Autobiography*, p. 80.
77 "convinced beyond": TR, "A Judicial Experience," *Outlook*, Mar. 13, 1909, p. 564.
77 "a dangerous departure": Howard L. Hurwitz, *Theodore Roosevelt and Labor in New York State, 1880–1900* (New York: Columbia University Press, 1942), p. 82.
78 "fundamental rights": Ibid., p. 85.
78 "injurious to the public health": *NYT*, Jan. 30, 1884; George F. Spinney, "Memorandum on the Tenement-house Cigar Manufacturing Measure," unpublished MS, n.d., TRC.
78 "a disinfectant": Hurwitz, *Theodore Roosevelt and Labor*, p. 85.
78 "It was this case . . . reform ever received": TR, *An Autobiography*, p. 81.
78 "do for the City": *NYT*, April 10, 1883.
78 "he would deliver": Hagedorn et al., "Memorandum of Conversation," p. 39, TRC.
78 "only chance lay": TR, *An Autobiography*, p. 87.
79 his patrician circle . . . "have been nominated": Ibid., pp. 86–87.
79 "to accomplish far more": Ibid., p. 86.
79 "the creatures of the local ward bosses": Ibid., p. 82.
79 "I feel now": TR to Alice Hathaway Lee Roosevelt, Jan. 22, 1884, in *LTR*, Vol. 1, p. 64.
79 "great night . . . he'd had enough": Armes, "When T.R. Qualified as a Boxer," pp. 1–2, TRC.
79 "in my own lovely": TR, Personal Diary, Jan. 3, 1883, TRP.
80 "How I did . . . be with you again": TR to Alice Hathaway Lee Roosevelt, Feb. 6, 1884, in *LTR*, Vol. 1, p. 65.
80 "hated" to see him . . . "little new baby soon": Michael Teague, "Theodore Roosevelt and Alice Hathaway Lee: A New Perspective," *Harvard Library Bulletin* (Summer 1985), pp. 237–38.
80 Alice was thrilled: Anna Bulloch Gracie, "Account of Alice Roosevelt's Birth, March 25, 1884," TRC.
80 "He was full of life and happiness": Putnam, *Theodore Roosevelt: The Formative Years*, pp. 382–83.
80 "only fairly well": Grondahl, *I Rose Like a Rocket*, p. 129.
80 signs of acute Bright's disease: J. O. Affleck, "Bright's Disease," in T. S. Baynes, D. O. Kellogg, and W. R. Smith, eds., *Encyclopaedia Britannica* (New York: Werner Co., 1898), Vol. 4, pp. 345–46.
81 "somewhat insidiously . . . coma vigil": J. O. Affleck, "Typhus, Typhoid and Relapsing Fevers," in ibid., pp. 678–80.
81 "suicidal . . . and dismal": *NYT*, Feb. 13, 1884.
81 Visibility was . . . off its tracks: *NYT*, Feb. 14, 1884.
81 "There is . . . something": *NYT*, Feb. 13, 1884.
81 "There is a curse": Pringle, *Theodore Roosevelt: A Biography*, p. 51.
81 "The light has gone out of my life": TR, Personal Diary, Feb. 14, 1884, TRP.
81 "Seldom, if ever": New York *World*, Feb. 15, 1884.
81 "wholly unprecedented . . . has ever been held": TR, *In Memory of My Darling Wife, Alice Hathaway Roosevelt, and of My Beloved Mother, Martha Bulloch Roosevelt, Who Died in the Same House and on the Same Day on February 14, 1884* (New York: G. P. Putnam's Sons, n.d.), TRC.
82 "in a dazed, stunned . . . does or says": Putnam, *Theodore Roosevelt: The Formative Years*, p. 390.
82 "I fear he sleeps little": McCullough, *Mornings on Horseback*, p. 286.
82 "If I had very much time": TR, Personal Diary, Mar. 6, 1878, TRP.
82 "I shall come back": TR to Andrew Dickson White, Feb. 18, 1884, in *LTR*, Vol. 1, p. 65.
82 "a changed man . . . in his own soul": Hagedorn et al., "Memorandum of Conversation," p. 68, TRC.
82 "We spent three years": TR, Personal Diary, Feb. 17, 1884, TRP.
82 referred to her simply as "Baby Lee": TR to ARC, various dates, in *LTR*, Vol. 1, pp. 71, 79.
82 "There can never be": TR to Henry Davis Minot, Feb. 21 & Mar. 9, 1884, TRC.
82 "both weak and morbid": TR to CRR, Mar. 7, 1908, in *LTR*, Vol. 6, p. 966.
82 shared her birthday: Grondahl, *I Rose Like a Rocket*, p. 129.

83 an intense connection with his dead son: Doris Kearns Goodwin, *Team of Rivals: The Political Genius of Abraham Lincoln* (New York: Simon & Schuster, 2005), p. 443.
83 "to treat the past": TR to CRR, Mar. 7, 1908, in *LTR*, Vol. 6, p. 966.
83 "We are now holding": Putnam, *Theodore Roosevelt: The Formative Years*, p. 395.
83 "Reform Without Bloodshed": *Harper's Weekly*, April 19, 1884.
84 "prolonged and expensive . . . won't have it": Hudson, *Random Recollections of an Old Political Reporter*, pp. 148–49.
84 "As debate is . . . field of national politics": *Daily Freeman* [n.p.], April 12, 1883, Clipping Scrapbook, TRC.
84 "by far the most objectionable": TR to ARC, June 8, 1884, in *LTR*, Vol. 1, pp. 70–71.
84 "Our defeat is . . . a historic scene": TR to ARC, June 8, 1884, in ibid.
84 "Although not a very": TR to Simon North, April 30, 1884, in ibid., p. 66.
85 a "great school" for Roosevelt: Hagedorn et al., "Memorandum of Conversation," p. 73, TRC.
85 "We did not agree": Riis, *Theodore Roosevelt*, p. 59.
85 "Words with me are instruments": Gable, ed., *The Man in the Arena: Speeches and Essays*, p. 12.
85 "There is little use": Ibid., p. 55.
85 "only through strife": Ibid., p. 42.
86 this intuitive emotional intelligence: Daniel Goleman, *Emotional Intelligence: Why It Can Matter More than IQ* (London: Bloomsbury, 1996), p. 39.

CHAPTER FOUR: Nellie Herron Taft

Page
87 "It was at a coasting party": HHT, *Recollections of Full Years*, p. 7.
87 "Tall and slender . . . her whole countenance": *Washington Post*, May 5, 1907.
88 Harriet moved to Ohio . . . lawyer John Herron: HHT, *Recollections of Full Years*, pp. 5–6.
88 "Quite like living": RBH Diary, Jan. 8, 1850, RBH Papers.
88 "had no other friend": Harriet Collins Herron to RBH, July 8, 1889, RBH Papers.
88 "to go for money": Anthony, *Nellie Taft*, p. 30.
88 "I wish I could accept": John Herron to RBH, Dec. 18, 1875, RBH Papers.
88 "not particularly . . . finely kept shrubbery": HHT, *Recollections of Full Years*, pp. 3–4.
88 "A book . . . has more": HHT Diary, Aug. 23, 1880, WHTP.
89 The curriculum at The Nursery: Anthony, *Nellie Taft*, pp. 28–29.
89 "the inspiration": HHT, *Recollections of Full Years*, p. 7.
89 planned to celebrate their silver wedding anniversary: RBH Diary, Jan. 12, 1878, RBH Papers; *NYT*, Jan. 1, 1878.
89 "her baby has": John Herron to RBH, Dec. 26, 1877, RBH Papers.
89 "I feel very much": Anthony, *Nellie Taft*, p. 31.
89 "profusely decorated": *NYT*, Jan. 1, 1878; *Dubuque* [IA] *Herald*, Jan. 1, 1878.
89 brought "the house alive": Anthony, *Nellie Taft*, p. 32.
89 "to marry a man . . . marry an Ohio man": *Alton* [IL] *Evening Telegraph*, Dec. 2, 1908.
89 "Nothing in my life": *Washington Post*, May 5, 1907.
90 "She was intoxicated": RSB, "The Measure of Taft," *The American Magazine* (July 1910), p. 366.
90 to "receive attentions": HHT Diary, Sept. 5, 1879, WHTP.
90 "exceedingly . . . valiantly to each other": HHT Diary, Mar. 10, 1880, WHTP.
90 "I am blue . . . as if I were fifty": HHT Diary, July 13, 1880, WHTP.
90 "be busy and accomplish something": HHT Diary, Sept. 5, 1879, WHTP.
90 more than her father would pay: HHT Diary, Oct. 21, 1879, WHTP.
90 "I would much rather": Ibid.
90 "enjoy all the comforts": Anthony, *Nellie Taft*, p. 27.
90 "a repressed nervousness": Ibid.
90 "I am beginning": HHT Diary, June 4, 1880, WHTP.
91 "that adorable . . . he strikes me with awe": HHT to Alice Keys, July 5, 1880, WHTP.
91 her "stupid state": HHT Diary, Aug. 17, 1880, WHTP.
91 gambled at cards . . . late at night: HHT Diary, Aug. 17 & 27, 1880, WHTP.
91 the first visit by a president to the west coast: HHT Diary, Aug. 21, 1880, WHTP.
91 Nellie was left behind: HHT Diary, Aug. 28, 1880, WHTP.
91 "I have not read": HHT Diary, Sept. 1, 1880, WHTP.
91 "He is very sympathetic . . . as much as yours": HHT Diary, Jan. 15, 1881, WHTP.
92 "I am perfectly delighted": HHT Diary, Sept. 6, 1883, WHTP.
92 "drank beer . . . like a comrade & man": HHT Diary, Sept. 6, 1883, WHTP.
92 "Do you realize": Harriet Collins Herron to HHT, Mar. 19, 1882, CPT Papers.
92 "two dreadful letters . . . congenial work": HHT Diary, May 5, 1882, WHTP.
93 "The meeting at Miss Herron's": WHT to Frances Taft, Jan. 6, 1883, WHTP.
93 They resolved daily to read aloud: HHT Diary, July 9, 1883, WHTP.
93 "long and very tough": HHT Diary, Aug. 6, 1883, WHTP.
93 "repair" their "exhausted intellects": HHT Diary, Aug. 8, 1883, WHTP.
93 "Mamma thinks": HHT Diary, Sept. 29, 1883, WHTP.
93 "Why should I take": Ibid.
93 "All week I have been": HHT Diary, Oct. 6, 1883, WHTP.
94 "Nellie Herron has made": WHT to Frances Taft, Feb. 28, 1884, WHTP.
94 "that sweet school": WHT to HHT, Mar. 12, 1884, WHTP.
94 "very heated especially": WHT to LTT, Mar. 2, 1884, WHTP.
94 "I am not satisfied": WHT to HHT, Mar. 29, 1884, WHTP.

94 Will played the beautiful princess: HHT, *Recollections of Full Years*, p. 8.

94 "the only notable exception . . . social career": WHT to Frances Taft, Feb. 11, 1883, WHTP.

94 "the greatest credit . . . act on that theory": WHT to LTT, Mar. 2, 1884, WHTP.

95 "After awhile I found": WHT to Alice Keys, Aug. 19, 1885, WHTP.

95 "Trollope is a great favorite": WHT to HHT, Aug. 9, 1884, WHTP.

95 "my own appreciation": WHT to LTT, Mar. 8, 1885, WHTP.

95 "It seems . . . to the fact that I loved her": WHT to Alphonso Taft, July 12, 1885, WHTP.

95 "with overwhelming force": WHT to HHT, June 17, 1885, WHTP.

96 "I never have been certain": Anthony, *Nellie Taft*, p. 73.

96 "I love you Nellie": WHT to HHT, May 10, 1885, WHTP.

96 "My love for you grew . . . won in a moment": WHT to HHT, June 17, 1885, WHTP.

96 "You know": Pringle, *Life and Times*, Vol. 1, p. 108.

96 "The more I knew her": WHT to Alphonso Taft, July 12, 1885, WHTP.

97 "Your sweet smile . . . by Fate today": WHT to HHT, July 2, 1885, WHTP.

97 "The only real pleasure": WHT to HHT, July 16, 1885, WHTP.

97 "It is the one who stays": WHT to HHT, July 4, 1885, WHTP.

97 "I long to settle down": WHT to HHT, July 6, 1885, WHTP.

97 "we must continue the salon": WHT to HHT, July 20, 1885, WHTP.

97 "I shall have the greatest": WHT to HHT, July 6, 1885, WHTP.

97 "comfortably and cosily . . . intelligence of the wife": WHT to HHT, July 5, 1885, WHTP.

98 "His temperament": RSB, "The Measure of Taft," *The American Magazine* (July 1910), p. 366.

98 "guide, counsellor and friend": WHT to Delia Herron, Nov. 1, 1885, WHTP.

98 "You are becoming": WHT to HHT, July 20, 1885, WHTP.

98 "It is hard for me": WHT to HHT, July 11, 1885, WHTP.

98 "an equal partnership": WHT to HHT, July 15, 1885, WHTP.

98 "business had been . . . as much work": WHT to HHT, July 20, 1885, WHTP.

98 "a good and just member of society": Anthony, *Nellie Taft*, p. 73.

98 "a very hastily . . . no credit": WHT to LTT, April 16, 1885, WHTP.

98 "As usual": Horace Taft to LTT, April 19, 1885, WHTP.

98 "Each day has found . . . by George Eliot": WHT to LTT, Aug. 2, 1885, WHTP.

98 "I knew you would be": WHT to Alice Keys, Aug. 16, 1885, WHTP.

99 "How much I appreciate": Alice Keys to WHT, Aug. 31, 1885, WHTP.

99 "What a pair": Horace Taft to WHT, Sept. 2, 1885, WHTP.

99 "I went to the gymnasium . . . I felt lazy": WHT to HHT, Feb. 22, 1886, WHTP.

100 "I have given up": WHT to HHT, Feb. 26, 1886, WHTP.

100 "a superbly-fashioned satin": Anthony, *Nellie Taft*, p. 83.

100 "I hope you will think": WHT to HHT, Mar. 6, 1886, WHTP.

100 "The parlor is unchanged": WHT to HHT, Mar. 10, 1886, WHTP.

100 "a brilliant reception" . . . embark for Europe: Pringle, *Life and Times*, Vol. 1, p. 81.

100 "my first taste": HHT, *Recollections of Full Years*, p. 16.

100 "just one thousand dollars": Ibid., p. 17.

100 "gentle beyond anything . . . catholic sympathies": Ibid., pp. 18–19.

101 home overlooking . . . the Ohio River: Alphonso Taft to WHT, July 5, 1886, WHTP.

101 he had proudly amassed a catalogue: Anthony, *Nellie Taft*, p. 87.

101 "Nellie," he coyly questioned . . . "so unexpectedly": HHT, *Recollections of Full Years*, pp. 21–22.

101 "Wasn't it immense": Horace Taft to HHT, Feb. 4, 1887, WHTP.

101 "was not a matter . . . of the Bench": HHT, *Recollections of Full Years*, p. 22.

102 "did not share this feeling": Ibid.

102 Taft sustained the lower court decision: "Moore's & Co. v. Bricklayers' Union et al.," *Weekly Law Bulletin & Ohio Law Journal*, 23 (Columbus, OH: Capital Printing & Publ. Co., 1890), pp. 665–75.

102 Decades later, it remained: Frederick N. Judson, "The Labor Decisions of Judge Taft," *American Monthly Review of Reviews* (August 1907), p. 213.

102 "right to work . . . combine to do": "Moore's & Co. v. Bricklayers' Union et al.," *Weekly Law Bulletin & Ohio Law Journal*, 23, pp. 668–69.

103 "no freight moved": Hurley, *Cincinnati: The Queen City*, p. 94.

103 the strikers' "revolutionary fervor": Bruce C. Levine, *Who Built America? Working People and the Nation's Economy, Politics, Culture and Society* (New York: Pantheon Books, 1992), p. 73.

103 "If the little ones": *Ohio Educational Monthly & National Teacher*, 43 (1894), pp. 413–14.

103 Nellie devoted herself to teaching: HHT, Diary notebook, Dec. 1887, WHTP.

104 "were conspiring against him": Annie Sinton Taft to Horace Taft, June [n.d.], 1889, WHTP.

104 "You may rely upon": Ross, *An American Family*, p. 81.

104 "the highest rank . . . his father was": Annie Sinton Taft to Horace Taft, June [n.d.], 1889, WHTP.

104 "Poor Peter! . . . wisely to remove him": Henry W. Taft to Alphonso Taft, June 3, 1889, WHTP.

104 "Every time the telephone": WHT to Horace Taft, June 17, 1889, WHTP.

104 he had abandoned Cincinnati: Ross, *An American Family*, pp. 101–02.

104 "My chief regret": Taft, *Memories and Opinions*, p. 60.

105 he opened a private school: Ibid., p. 70.

105 "Nellie took the pain . . . happy she is": WHT to Alphonso Taft, Sept. 10, 1889, WHTP.

105 "On the whole": Ibid.

105 "I suppose you wish": Horace Taft to WHT, Oct. 22, 1889, WHTP.

105 "He breathes good will": Richard V. Oulahan, "William H. Taft as a Judge on the Bench," *American Monthly Review of Reviews* (August 1907), p. 208.
105 "upheld by the State Supreme Court": Pringle, *Life and Times*, Vol. 1, p. 100.
105 "would be satisfactory": Ibid., p. 107.
105 "pretty hopeful . . . a fine old Justice": Horace Taft to WHT, May 7, 1889, WHTP.
106 "O Yes": WHT to Alphonso Taft, August [n.d.], 1889, WHTP.
106 "chances of going": WHT to Alphonso Taft, Aug. 24, 1889, WHTP.
106 "It is a great event": Alphonso Taft to WHT, Feb. 3, 1890, WHTP.
106 "but it was I . . . a new interest in life": LTT to WHT, Feb. 3, 1890, WHTP.
106 "I was very glad": HHT, *Recollections of Full Years*, p. 24.
106 Only Will was reluctant . . . "one side of a case": Peri E. Arnold, *Remaking the Presidency: Roosevelt, Taft and Wilson, 1901–1916* (Lawrence: University Press of Kansas, 2009), p. 77.
107 "entirely unfamiliar . . . very little familiarity": WHT to Alphonso Taft, Feb. 26, 1890, WHTP.
107 "Go ahead, & fear not": Alphonso Taft to WHT, Feb. 1, 1890, WHTP.
107 "You will have": Alphonso Taft to WHT, Feb. 3, 1890, WHTP.
107 "To a large extent": Alphonso Taft to WHT, Feb. 7, 1890, WHTP.
107 "You have learned": LTT to WHT, Feb. 3, 1890, WHTP.
107 "I believe you are": Alphonso Taft to WHT, Feb. 7, 1890, WHTP.
107 a "brilliant reception" at the Lincoln Club: *Sandusky* [OH] *Daily Register*, Feb. 11, 1890.
107 "He arrived at six o'clock . . . why on earth he had come": HHT, *Recollections of Full Years*, p. 25.
108 "It is not a large house": WHT to H. D. Peck, April 26, 1890, WHTP.
108 "one of the nicest": John W. Herron to HHT, April 18, 1890, WHTP.
108 "Our house is what . . . at night at home": WHT to Alphonso Taft, April 18, 1890, WHTP.

CHAPTER FIVE: Edith Carow Roosevelt

Page
109 "vast silent spaces . . . lonely rivers": TR, *An Autobiography*, p. 93.
109 domestic bliss was "lived out": TR, Personal Diary, Feb. 17, 1884, TRP.
109 "any man ever loved a woman": TR, Personal Diary, Mar. 11, 1880, TRP.
109 he resigned himself: Hermann Hagedorn, Interview with William Merrifield, June [n.d.], 1919, TRC.
110 "the head of a great buffalo bull": TR to Alice Lee Roosevelt, Sept. 20, 1883, in H. W. Brands, *T.R.: The Last Romantic* (New York: Basic Books, 1997), p. 158.
110 the Elkhorn and the Chimney Butte: TR, Hermann Hagedorn, and G. B. Grinnell, *Hunting Trips of a Ranchman; Ranch Life and the Hunting Trail* (New York: Charles Scribner's Sons, 1927), p. 10.
110 the sum his father bequeathed: Morris, *EKR*, p. 77.
110 "The plains stretch": TR, *Hunting Trips*, pp. 151–52.
110 "noontide hours . . . hopeless, never-ending grief": Ibid., pp. 309–10.
110 on his horse sixteen hours a day: Hermann Hagedorn, *Roosevelt in the Bad Lands* (Boston: Houghton Mifflin, 1921), p. 156.
110 "hardest work . . . gathered for market": TR, *Hunting Trips*, p. 13.
110 "preparing breakfast": Ibid., p. 327.
110 "These long, swift rides": Ibid., p. 329.
111 "Black care": Ibid.
111 "enough excitement . . . sleep well at night": TR to ARC, Sept. 20, 1884, in *LTR*, Vol. 1, p. 81.
111 "The story-high house": TR, *Hunting Trips*, p. 10.
111 "Parkman and Irving": Hagedorn, *Roosevelt in the Bad Lands*, p. 108.
111 steadily before "the flickering firelight": TR, *Hunting Trips*, p. 305.
111 he relaxed in his rocking chair . . . "cool breeze": Ibid., p. 10.
111 As the crisp autumn . . . rounding up cattle: Ibid., p. 306.
111 "Where everything before . . . withered grass": Ibid., p. 126.
111 "dwindled to . . . never-ending" nights: Ibid., p. 341.
112 gathered round the fireplace . . . hermit thrushes and meadowlarks: Ibid., pp. 305–7, 12.
112 "will take a leading": *NYT*, July 13, 1885.
112 house stood atop a hill: TR, *An Autobiography*, p. 318.
112 "no day was long enough": Parsons, *Perchance Some Day*, p. 26.
112 "Especially memorable . . . just around the corner": Ibid., p. 63.
113 "She was the only one . . . oh so attractive!": Michael Teague, *Mrs. L: Conversations with Alice Roosevelt Longworth* (New York: Doubleday & Co., 1981), p. 10.
113 "had an extraordinary gift": Hermann and Mary Hagedorn, "Interview with Mrs. Nicholas Longworth, November 9, 1954," TRC.
113 Had "she been a man": Hermann and Mary Hagedorn, "Interview with Mr. and Mrs. Sheffield Cowles and Mrs. Joseph Alsop, Jr., November 22, 1954," TRC.
113 the two were secretly engaged: Hermann Hagedorn, *The Roosevelt Family of Sagamore Hill* (New York: The Macmillan Co., 1954), p. 426.
113 "You know all about": EKR to TR, June 8, 1886, Derby Papers, TRC.
113 Her father, Charles Carow: Morris, *EKR*, p. 10.
114 a fortune in iron manufacturing: EKR, *American Backlogs: The Story of Gertrude Tyler and Her Family, 1660–1860* (New York: Charles Scribner's Sons, 1928), pp. 32, 34.
114 "find great attention . . . an ornament to society": Daniel Tyler to Gertrude Tyler, Aug. 14, 1852, in ibid., pp. 86–87.
114 "Do not doubt": Gertrude Tyler to [her mother], Sept. 20, 1852, in ibid., p. 93.

114 "My dear Sir": Charles Carow to Daniel Tyler, Mar. 7, 1859, in ibid., p. 233.
114 "the risk of sailing": John Lynch, *Causes of the reduction of American Tonnage and the decline of navigation interests, being a report of a Select committee made to the House of Representatives of the United States, on February 17, 1870* (Washington, DC: Government Printing Office, 1870), pp. ix–x.
115 "My dear little girl . . . up in the morning": Charles Carow to EKR, May [n.d.], 186[?], TRC.
115 "precious little monkey": EKR, "Second Composition Book," May 18, 1875, TRC.
115 "Almost the first thing . . . light and colour": EKR to TR, June 8, 1886, TRC.
115 "a passion for fairy tales": Ibid.
115 "Oh fairy tales": EKR, "Fairy Tales" in P.O.R.E. Notebook, Jan. 6, 1877, TRC.
115 "I got your letter": Charles Carow to EKR, [n.d.], 1871, TRC.
115 he took Edith on long walks: Sylvia Jukes Morris, "Portrait of a First Lady," in Natalie A. Naylor, Douglas Brinkley, and John Allen Gable, eds., *Theodore Roosevelt: Many-Sided American* (Interlaken, NY: Heart of the Lakes Publ., 1992), p. 64.
116 "pledged friends": CRR, *My Brother*, p. 44.
116 hide her "old and broken toys": EKR, "In Memory of Corinne Roosevelt Robinson," TRC.
116 "the school room": Ibid.
116 *Our Young Folks*: TR, *An Autobiography*, p. 16.
116 "at the cost of . . . girls' stories": Ibid.
116 "I think imagination": EKR to TR, June 8, 1886, TRC.
116 "It was verry": TR, *Diaries of Boyhood and Youth*, p. 13.
116 "homesickness and longings": Ibid., p. 103.
116 "Whenever they see": EKR to CRR, Feb. 1, 1870, Derby Papers, TRC.
116 a bankruptcy warrant was issued: *NYT*, Mar. 1, April 1, & April 27, 1871.
117 "terrifying charm . . . clear-cut features": Parsons, *Perchance Some Day*, p. 20.
117 The curriculum included: Morris, *EKR*, p. 33.
117 "When I come home . . . hope to get them": EKR, "First Composition Book," Nov. 28, 1871, TRC.
117 "I have gone back": EKR to Kermit Roosevelt, Feb. 24, 1938, KR Papers.
117 to quote extensively from Wordsworth: EKR to Theodore Roosevelt, Jr., Mar. 6, 1942, in TRJP.
117 "indifference . . . a trick of manner": EKR to Kermit Roosevelt, Feb. 24, 1938, KR Papers.
117 "Girls . . . I believe": Hagedorn, *The Roosevelt Family of Sagamore Hill*, p. 10.
117 "the happiness of . . . difficult and critical teacher": EKR, "In Memory of Corinne Roosevelt Robinson," TRC.
118 "little group of girls": Parsons, *Perchance Some Day*, p. 36.
118 " 'Consequences,' 'Truth' ": Ibid., p. 35.
118 "the happy six": CRR, *My Brother*, p. 90.
118 whom he "much worshipped": TR, Personal Diary, Aug. 20, 1878, TRP.
118 "In the early days": Parsons, *Perchance Some Day*, p. 30.
118 "I cannot believe": Anna Louisa Bulloch Gracie to EKR, Aug. 6, 1876, TRC.
118 On New Year's Day: CRR, Journal, Jan. 1, 1877, TRC.
118 "dimly and suggestively lit . . . tete-a-tete": CRR, Journal, Jan. 10, 1877, TRC.
118 "Edith revealed": Betty Boyd Caroli, *The Roosevelt Women* (New York: Basic Books, 1989), p. 190.
119 "To my castles . . . Sad and slow": EKR, "My Dream Castles," in P.O.R.E. Notebook, Jan. 27, 1877, TRC.
119 "I sit alone": EKR, "Memories," in P.O.R.E. Notebook, April [n.d.], 1876, TRC.
120 "She reads more": CRR, Journal, Nov. 12, 1876, TRC.
120 her "clever" friend: Ibid.
120 "tall and fair": CRR, Journal, Oct. 6, 1876, TRC.
120 "I have a feeling": CRR, Journal, Nov. 12, 1876, TRC.
120 "What fun we did have" . . . Lamson and Harry Jackson: CRR, Journal, May 10, 1877, TRC.
120 "The family all": TR, *Diaries of Boyhood and Youth*, p. 359.
120 "enjoyed . . . perfectly happy days": EKR to TR, May 29, 1877, Derby Papers, TRC.
120 "Edith looking prettier": TR to CRR, June 3, 1877, in *LTR*, Vol. 1, p. 28.
120 "Oh Edith": Morris, *EKR*, p. 57.
120 days spent sailing with Edith: TR, Private Diaries, Aug. 19, 1878, TRP.
120 rowing with her to the harbor: TR, Private Diaries, Aug. 20, 1878, TRP.
120 "spending a lovely morning": TR, Private Diaries, Aug. 21, 1878, TRP.
121 "Afterwards Edith": TR, Private Diaries, Aug. 22, 1878, TRP.
121 tempers "that were far": TR to ARC, Sept. 20, 1886, TRC.
121 "at first sight": TR, Pocket Diaries, Jan. 30, 1880, TRP.
121 campaign "to win her": Ibid.
121 in mid-February, Theodore wrote: Mabel Potter Daggett, "Mrs. Roosevelt," *The Delineator* (March 1909).
121 the "shock" Edith experienced: Morris, *EKR*, p. 530.
121 another woman would be Theodore's constant: TR, Pocket Diaries, July 1 & 5, 1880, TRP.
121 "We had great fun . . . wild spirits": Parsons, *Perchance Some Day*, p. 43.
121 "danced the soles off": Morris, *EKR*, p. 64.
122 "All yesterday I": EKR to CRR, April 29, 1882, Derby Papers, TRC.
122 might marry "for money": Putnam, *Theodore Roosevelt: The Formative Years*, p. 555.
122 "someday, somehow": Morris, *EKR*, p. 67.
122 "the most cultivated": TR, Personal Diary, Nov. 16, 1879, TRP.
122 "argued weakness": TR to ARC, Sept. 20, 1886, TRC.
123 Respecting their secret even in his private diary: TR, Personal Diary, Feb. 20, 1886; Mar. 5, 6, 9, 10, 12 & 14, 1886, TRP.

123 seventeen letters from Theodore: EKR to TR, June 8, 1886, Derby Papers, TRC.
123 "How fond one is": EKR, "Second Composition Book," May 18, 1875, TRC.
123 "with all the passion": EKR to TR, June 8, 1886, Derby Papers, TRC.
123 "heart on paper . . . so much to see you . . . digging": Ibid.
123 "He is middle aged": Ibid.
124 "read it through . . . as repulsive as her brother, Stiva": TR to CRR, April 12, 1886, in *LTR*, Vol. 1, p. 96.
124 He began to muse on: TR to ARC, June 19, 1886, in ibid., pp. 103–4.
124 an offer from Mayor William Grace: TR to HCL, June 23, 1885, & July 5, 1886, in ibid., p. 91.
124 "I would like a chance": TR to HCL, Aug. 20, 1886, in ibid., p. 109.
125 "Darling Bamie . . . *Forever your loving brother*": TR to ARC, Sept. 20, 1886, TRC.
125 "It looked to me . . . the happiest time": William Wingate Sewall, *Bill Sewall's Story of Theodore Roosevelt* (New York: Harper Bros., 1919), pp. 92, 95.
125 "fellow ranchmen . . . the most educational asset": TR and Ernest Hamlin Abbott, *The New Nationalism* (New York: The Outlook Co., 1909), p. 105.
126 "It is a mighty good": Ibid., p. 105.
126 "to speak the same language": TR, *An Autobiography*, p. 57.
126 "to interpret the spirit": CRR, *My Brother*, p. 150.
126 "was visited . . . perfectly hopeless contest": TR to HCL, Oct. 17, 1886, in *LTR*, Vol. 1, p. 111.
126 "enormous increase . . . compelled to toil": Henry George, *Progress and Poverty* (New York: Cosimo Classics, 2005), pp. 10–11.
126 "the want and injustice . . . would be unknown": Ibid., p. 396.
126 "the mass of": *NYT*, Oct. 24, 1886.
127 "The best I can hope . . . Republican party": TR to Frances Smith Dana, Oct. 21, 1886, in *LTR*, Vol. 1, p. 113.
127 many of his "should-be supporters": TR to HCL, Oct. 20, 1886, in ibid., p. 112.
127 "I am a strong party man": *NYT*, Oct. 28, 1886.
127 "It is such happiness": ARC to EKR, Oct. 23, 1886, Derby Papers, TRC.
128 "Fighting is fun": Edmund Morris, *The Rise of Theodore Roosevelt* (New York: Coward, McCann & Geoghegan, 1979), p. 349.
128 "I read them all": TR to CRR, Jan. 22, 1887, in *LTR*, Vol. 1, p. 119.
128 "remember them all": Morris, *EKR*, p. 105.
128 "that wonderful silky": Ibid., p. 4.
128 "blue-eyed darling": Teague, *Mrs. L: Conversations with Alice Longworth Roosevelt*, p. 13.
128 "I hardly know": TR to ARC, Jan. 10, 1887, TRC.
128 "It almost broke my heart": ARC, "Memoir," p. 3, TRC.
128 she avoided further emotional attachments: Ibid., p. 84.
128 "the lovely smell": Teague, *Mrs. L: Conversations with Alice Roosevelt Longworth*, p. 22.
128 "I in my best dress": Alice Roosevelt Longworth, *Crowded Hours: Reminiscences of Alice Roosevelt Longworth* (New York: Charles Scribner's Sons, 1933), p. 8.
129 "mother who is in heaven": Ibid.
129 "In fact . . . he never ever": Teague, *Mrs. L: Conversations with Alice Roosevelt Longworth*, pp. 4–5.
129 "Where she was reserved": Nicholas Roosevelt, *Theodore Roosevelt: The Man as I Knew Him* (New York: Dodd, Mead & Co., 1967), p. 23.
129 "rowing over": TR to HCL, June 11, 1887, in *LTR*, Vol. 1, p. 128.
129 "She was extremely plucky": TR to ARC, Sept. 18, 1887, in Morris, *EKR*, p. 112.
129 "I have a small son now": TR to Jonas S. Van Duzer, in *LTR*, Vol. 1, p. 136.
130 "Theodore" . . . "put his foot down": Hermann and Mary Hagedorn, Interview with Mrs. Nicholas Longworth, Nov. 9, 1954, TRC.
130 "temptation . . . Father would not allow it": Morris, *EKR*, p. 114.
130 "the place where she kept" . . . permission to enter: *Sagamore Hill National Historic Site Pamphlet* (Lawrenceburg, IN: The Creative Co., 2000), p. 11.
130 "immense fun": TR to HCL, Oct. 19, 1888, in *LTR*, Vol. 1, p. 148.
130 "Mr. T.R.'s temperament . . . hold of the helm": William Henry Harbaugh, *Power and Responsibility: The Life and Times of Theodore Roosevelt* (New York: Farrar, Straus & Cudahy, 1961), p. 74.
131 "I am the new . . . began at that moment": Matthew F. Halloran, *The Romance of the Merit System: Forty-five Years' Reminiscences of the Civil Service* (Washington, DC: Judd & Detweiler, 1929), p. 56.
131 "He is equally at home": *Decatur* [IL] *Republican*, May 16, 1889.
131 "It has been a hopeless": EKR to TR, Aug. 31, 1889, Derby Papers, TRC.
132 "Edie has occasional fits": TR to ARC, Jan. 4, 1890, in *LTR*, Vol. 1, p. 208.
133 "A very long way": Margaret Chanler, *Roman Spring: Memoirs* (Boston: Little, Brown, 1934), p. 203.

CHAPTER SIX: The Insider and the Outsider

Page

134 "Washington is just": TR to ARC, Feb. 11, 1894, in *LTR*, Vol. 1, p. 364.
134 "where everything throbs with . . . precedence over work": Frank George Carpenter and Frances Carpenter, eds., *Carp's Washington* (New York: McGraw-Hill Book Co., 1960), pp. 8–9.
134 managed to quit work early: TR to ARC, June 23, 1893, TRC.
134 "a streetcar will not . . . in which to live": Carpenter and Carpenter, eds., *Carp's Washington*, pp. 8–9.
135 "Common views and . . . Civil Service reform": WHT to Mark Sullivan, July 18, 1926, WHTP.
135 "hated the whole reform": TR, *An Autobiography*, p. 135.
135 "It will be a long, hard": WHT, "Civil Service Reform Applied to Municipal Government," Dec. 28, 1893, WHTP.

135 "One of the first observations": *NYT*, Aug. 30, 1890.
135 Roosevelt busily scanned "everything and everybody": Ibid.
136 "absorbed in work . . . not know it": WAW, "Taft, A Hewer of Wood," *The American Magazine* (April 1908), p. 23.
136 "Externally Taft is . . . settled or solved": Ibid.
136 Taft had no interest . . . dull and slow: WHT, "My Predecessor," *Collier's*, Mar. 6, 1909.
136 "they established": WAW, "Taft, A Hewer of Wood," *The American Magazine* (April 1908), p. 23.
136 "Mr. Taft . . . and she'd *get* it": Lyman Abbott, "William H. Taft," *Outlook*, April 4, 1908.
136 "One loves him": AB to Clara, Dec. 10, 1909, in AB, *Letters of Archie Butt*, p. 233.
136 "can get along": Abbott, "William H. Taft," *Outlook*, April 4, 1908.
136 "good nature": Ibid.
136 "a capacity . . . we do not possess": RSB, "The Measure of Taft," *The American Magazine* (July 1910), pp. 367–68.
137 "Each party profited": TR, *An Autobiography*, p. 131.
137 "For the last few years": TR to James Brander Matthews, July 31, 1889, in *LTR*, Vol. 1, p. 177.
137 "the fellow with no pull": Riis, *Theodore Roosevelt*, p. 106.
137 unqualified friends and kinsmen . . . "undemocratic": TR, "The Spoils System in Operation," in Hagedorn, ed., *Campaigns and Controversies*, *WTR*, Vol. 14, p. 89.
137 "To the victor belongs . . . so nakedly vicious": TR, *An Autobiography*, p. 130.
137 "Yes, TR is a breezy": Reprinted in *Galveston* [TX] *Daily News*, May 21, 1889.
138 "Until he began": Pringle, *Theodore Roosevelt: A Biography*, p. 123.
138 "to secure proper administration": TR, *An Autobiography*, p. 131.
138 "going to be enforced": TR to HCL, June 29, 1889, in *LTR*, Vol. 1, p. 167.
138 "so-called voluntary contributions": *Galveston* [TX] *Daily News*, Jan. 27, 1890.
138 "he was wrecking": Taft, *Memories and Opinions*, p. 111.
138 "to a poor clerk": *Galveston* [TX] *Daily News*, Jan. 27, 1890.
138 "to point out infractions": TR to Lucius Burrie Swift, May 16, 1889, in *LTR*, Vol. 1, pp. 162–63.
139 "Give me all": TR to Lucius Burrie Swift, May 16, 1889, in ibid., p. 162.
139 "I have to be sure": TR to Lucius Burrie Swift, May 7, 1892, in ibid., p. 280.
139 "We stirred things up well": TR to HCL, June 24, 1889, in ibid., p. 166.
139 "a model of fairness and justice": William Dudley Foulke, *Fighting the Spoilsmen: Reminiscences of the Civil Service Reform Movement* (New York: G. P. Putnam's Sons, 1919), p. 53.
139 "If he is not dismissed": TR to HCL, July 28, 1889, in *LTR*, Vol. 1, p. 175.
139 John Wanamaker . . . contempt for civil service reformers: Ibid., p. 171.
139 "It was a golden": TR to HCL, Aug. 8, 1889, in ibid., p. 186.
140 "a bribery chest": *Washington Post*, May 3, 1892.
140 "unfair and partial": TR to John Wanamaker, May 16, 1892, in *LTR*, Vol. 1, p. 281.
140 "head devil" of the spoilsmen: TR to Cecil Spring Rice, May 3, 1892, in ibid., p. 277.
140 "gross impertinence and impropriety": TR to John Wanamaker, May 16, 1892, in ibid., p. 282.
140 "It is war": *Washington Post*, May 26, 1892.
140 "not remember an instance": *NYT*, May 26, 1892, Clipping Scrapbook, TRC.
140 "put a padlock": *Ohio Democrat*, Nov. 27, 1890.
140 "like a person": *Washington Post*, April 29, 1892.
140 "He came into official life": *Washington Post*, May 6, 1890.
140 "utterly useless": TR to HCL, Oct. 19, 1889, in *LTR*, Vol. 1, p. 199.
140 Thompson . . . an "excellent" fellow: Ibid.
140 "My two colleagues": TR to ARC, May 24, 1891, in TR, *Letters from Theodore Roosevelt to Anna Roosevelt Cowles, 1870–1918* (New York: Charles Scribner's Sons, 1924), pp. 117–18.
140 "I have been continuing": TR to ARC, Feb. 1, 1891, in *LTR*, Vol. 1, p. 237.
141 "high regard . . . done before sundown": E. W. Halford, "Roosevelt's Introduction to Washington," *Frank Leslie's Illustrated Weekly*, Mar. 1, 1919, p. 314.
141 the House committee concluded: Joseph B. Bishop, *Theodore Roosevelt and His Time Shown in His Own Letters*, Vol. 1 (New York: Charles Scribner's Sons, 1920), p. 48.
141 "Mr. Roosevelt is": *Evening Times*, Oct. 29, 1890, Clipping Scrapbook, TRC.
141 "Cabot has been a real": TR to ARC, Feb. 12, 1893, TRC.
141 recite Shakespeare "almost by heart": John A. Garraty, *Henry Cabot Lodge: A Biography* (New York: Alfred A. Knopf, 1953), p. 102.
141 "You know, old fellow": TR to HCL, Nov. 1, 1886, in *LTR*, Vol. 1, p. 115.
142 Adams felt . . . especially "sympathetic": Henry Adams to Elizabeth Cameron, May 19, 1889, in Henry Adams and Worthington Chauncey Ford, eds., *Letters of Henry Adams* (Boston: Houghton Mifflin, 1930), Vol. 1, p. 398.
142 "Her taste in books": Chanler, *Roman Spring*, p. 203.
142 "Edith is really enjoying Washington": TR to ARC, Jan. 24, 1890, TRC.
142 "One night we dined": TR to ARC, Jan. 4, 1890, in *LTR*, Vol. 1, p. 208.
142 "Nannie has been a dear": EKR to ARC, Jan. 5, 1891, Derby Papers, TRC.
142 "Sunday-evening suppers . . . ineluctable will power": Chanler, *Roman Spring*, pp. 195, 203.
142 "Edith and I meet": TR to ARC, Feb. 11, 1894, in *LTR*, Vol. 1, p. 364.
143 "curled up . . . Theodore was the spinner": Miller, *Theodore Roosevelt: A Life*, p. 222.
143 "tendency to criticise . . . very entertaining": TR to ARC, April 1, 1894, in *LTR*, Vol. 1, p. 370.
143 not "succeeded in stopping . . . the wrong-doers": *Boston Herald*, Feb. 21, 1893; TR, "Civil Service Reform," in Hagedorn, ed., *Campaigns and Controversies*, *WTR*, Vol. 14, pp. 158–59.
143 "got on Harrison's . . . highest ideals": Abbott, "William H. Taft," *Outlook*, April 4, 1908.
143 "I did not find myself": WHT to Alphonso Taft, April 18, 1890, WHTP.

144 "They seem to think": WHT to Alphonso Taft, May 6, 1890, WHTP.
144 "opportunities for professional . . . case at Court": WHT to Paul Charlton, April 23, 1890, Pringle Papers.
144 "a few days in Cincinnati": WHT to Hiram D. Peck, April 26, 1890, WHTP.
144 "Don't be discouraged": Alphonso Taft to WHT, May 12, 1890, WHTP.
144 "Members waste": LTT to WHT, May 16, 1890, WHTP.
144 steadfastly "philosophical . . . improving it": WHT to Alphonso Taft [n.d.], WHTP.
144 "the very fact": WHT to Paul Charlton, April 23, 1890, Pringle Papers.
144 "somewhat more satisfaction . . . soporific power": WHT to Alphonso Taft [n.d.], WHTP.
144 "gain a good deal": WHT to Alphonso Taft, May 6, 1890, Pringle Papers.
144 "rather overwhelming" workload: WHT to Alphonso Taft, Feb. 26, 1890, WHTP.
144 "Each time a case": WHT to Alphonso Taft, Jan. 23, 1891, WHTP.
144 "So . . . you see": WHT to Alphonso Taft, Feb. 9, 1891, WHTP.
145 "the year's experience has been valuable": WHT to Alphonso Taft, Feb. 14, 1891, WHTP.
145 "the inattention . . . custom of the Bench": WHT to Alphonso Taft, Feb. 10, 1891, WHTP.
145 "new field": WHT to Alphonso Taft, Feb. 14, 1891, WHTP.
145 "made some very valuable . . . considerate of me": Ibid.
145 "The novelty of it": WHT to Charles P. Taft, May 2, 1890, Pringle Papers.
145 "The first duty": WHT to Alonzo Meyers, May 2, 1890, Pringle Papers.
145 "I shall sleep in a room": WHT to HHT, Aug. 27, 1890, WHTP.
145 "every evening . . . a great privilege": LTT to WHT, May 21, 1890, WHTP.
145 "come into exceedingly pleasant": WHT to Alphonso Taft, Feb. 14, 1891, WHTP.
146 "It has been": WHT to Alphonso Taft, Mar. 31, 1891, WHTP.
146 "scattered over . . . in the Supreme Court": WHT to Alphonso Taft, Feb. 14, 1891, WHTP.
146 "the heaviest weight": Alphonso Taft to WHT, Mar. 9, 1891, WHTP.
146 "There were fifty . . . becoming to her": WHT to Alphonso Taft, April 18, 1890, WHTP.
146 "Do write me": Agnes Davis Eckstein to HHT, April 15, 1890, WHTP.
146 "In the East room": *Washington Post*, Jan. 2, 1891.
147 "She had a very": WHT to Alphonso Taft, Jan. 6, 1891, WHTP.
147 "Tom Mack is with us": WHT to Alphonso Taft, Jan. 23, 1891, WHTP.
147 "throngs of buyers": *Illustrated Washington: Our Capital* (New York: American Publ. & Engraving Co., 1890), p. 75.
147 "The true Washingtonian . . . morning visitors": Constance McLaughlin Green, *Washington: A History of the Capitol, 1800–1950* (Princeton, NJ: Princeton University Press, 1963), p. 80.
147 "never ripened into intimacy": Charles Selden, "Six White House Wives and Widows," *Ladies' Home Journal* (June 1927).
147 "I don't like Mrs. Roosevelt": Anthony, *Nellie Taft*, p. 100.
147 "those who were actually": Robert V. Remini, *The House: The History of the House of Representatives* (New York: Smithsonian Books in assoc. with HarperCollins, 2006), p. 248.
148 "I suppose I ought": WHT to Alphonso Taft, Jan. 23, 1891, WHTP.
148 "I do not object": WHT to Alphonso Taft, April 18, 1891, WHTP.
148 "Your letters are": Alphonso Taft to WHT, May 28, 1890, WHTP.
148 "I am greatly exhilarated": Alphonso Taft to WHT, June 6, 1890, WHTP.
148 "The morning is": Charles P. Taft to WHT, Nov. 28, 1890, WHTP.
148 "Except when he is . . . always entertain him": LTT to WHT, April 13, 1891, WHTP.
149 the accomplishments of his boys: Charles P. Taft to WHT, May 21, 1890, WHTP.
149 "Can you not": Alphonso Taft to WHT, Jan. 10, 1891, WHTP.
149 "His vitality": WHT to HHT, May 18, 1891, WHTP.
149 "He seems to trust me": WHT to HHT, May 10, 1891, WHTP.
149 "noble boy . . . avoided this by suicide": WHT to HHT, May 29, 1891, WHTP.
149 did not want the general public to be inconvenienced: *Sandusky* [OH] *Daily Register*, June 4, 1891.
149 "I trust you": Charles Taft to WHT, April 4, 1891, WHTP.
150 a "ludicrous . . . rapidity of movement": WHT to HHT, June 1, 1891, WHTP.
150 "Springy and I": TR to ARC, June 20, 1891, in TR, *Letters from Theodore Roosevelt to Anna Roosevelt Cowles*, p. 118.
150 "We are just as": TR to HCL, July 1, 1891, in *LTR*, Vol. 1, p. 255.
150 "I see that I got ahead": Pringle, *Life and Times*, Vol. 1, p. 120.
150 "nervous and fidgety" assistance: TR to HCL, June 19, 1891, in *LTR*, Vol. 1, p. 253.
150 "Can you dine": TR to WHT, Aug. 19, 1891, in ibid., p. 258.
150 "It is a perfect nightmare": TR to ARC, Jan. 24, 1890, TRC.
150 "Elliott must be put": TR to ARC, May 2, 1890, TRC.
151 "He is evidently": TR to ARC, June 17, 1891, TRC.
151 ELLIOTT ROOSEVELT: Blanche Wiesen Cook, *Eleanor Roosevelt*, Vol. 1: *1884–1933* (New York: Viking, 1992), p. 67.
151 "emphatically . . . adjudge him one": Cited in *Washington Post*, Aug. 22, 1891.
151 "The horror": TR to ARC, Sept. 1, 1891, TRC.
151 "jumped out of the": CRR to ARC, Aug. 15, 1894, ARC Papers.
151 "the sunniest" child: Henry Taft to Alphonso Taft, June 3, 1889, WHTP.
151 "great comfort . . . whom everyone loved": TR to CRR, Aug. 29, 1894, in *LTR*, Vol. 1, p. 397.
151 "of whom we are really fond": TR to ARC, Jan. 7, 1894, in ibid., p. 345.
151 "merry blue eyes": WAW, "Taft, A Hewer of Wood," *American Magazine* (April 1908), p. 24.
152 "in the line of promotion": WHT to Alphonso Taft, Mar. 18, 1891, WHTP.
152 "have stirred up": Ibid.
152 "the man whom . . . years of hard work": WHT to Howard Hollister [n.d.], WHTP.

152 "would be very glad": Ibid.
152 "entirely philosophical . . . legion": WHT to Alphonso Taft, Mar. 18, 1891, WHTP.
152 "settled for good": HHT, *Recollections of Full Years*, p. 22.
152 "fixed in a groove": Ibid., p. 30.
152 "very much opposed": WHT to Alphonso Taft, Mar. 7, 1891, WHTP.
152 "It seems to me now": WHT to HHT, June 1, 1891, WHTP.
152 "If you get your heart's": HHT to WHT, July 18, 1891, WHTP.
153 "hardly a soul": WHT to HHT, July 18, 1891, WHTP.
153 "You will regard my failure": WHT to HHT, May 10, 1891, WHTP.
153 "I hate that": HHT to WHT, July 14, 1891, WHTP.
153 "It would be very easy": Ibid.
153 "I am not a bit happy": HHT to WHT, Aug. 18, 1890, WHTP.
153 "I love you ever": HHT to WHT, Aug. 27, 1890, WHTP.
153 "when we were first married": HHT to WHT, May 23, 1893, WHTP.
153 "simply crazy about": HHT to WHT, Sept. 7, 1890, WHTP.
153 "the dearest child": HHT to WHT, Sept. 1, 1891, WHTP.
153 His eating habits: HHT to WHT, Aug. 18, 1890, WHTP.
153 "I seem to care much more": HHT to WHT, July 13, 1891, WHTP.
153 "Don't make your brief": HHT to WHT, Sept. 21, 1891, WHTP.
154 "The press notices": Henry W. Taft to WHT, Dec. 18, 1891, WHTP.
154 "one of the most popular": *Washington Post*, Dec. 17, 1891.
154 "no man could have been": *Washington Post*, Dec. 20, 1891.
154 "Aside from": Horace Taft to WHT, Jan. 12, 1892, WHTP.
154 "One of the sweetest things": WHT to Howard Hollister, Dec. 21, 1891, WHTP.
154 "I feel so good": WHT to HHT, Mar. 17, 1892, WHTP.
154 "The two years": WHT to William Miller, March [n.d.], 1892, WHTP.
154 relinquish the "pleasant life": EKR to Emily Carow, Mar. 7, 1893, TRC.
154 "Our places are still": EKR to Emily Carow, Mar. 7, 1893, TRC.
155 "elected by the people" to Congress: EKR to Emily Carow, Nov. 14, 1893, TRC.
155 "a dream never to be realized": EKR to Emily Carow, Oct. 16, 1892, TRC.
155 "He is now": Ibid.
155 "nonsense" . . . his true concerns: Ibid.
155 "could do most . . . success awaits me": TR to ARC, Aug. 16, 1893, TRC.
155 "the moving spirit . . . to deal with Democrats": New York *Evening Post*, May 5, 1893, Clipping Scrapbook, TRC.
155 "It was practically": EKR to ARC, Feb. 3, 1894, Derby Papers, TRC.
155 "hope of going on": TR to HCL, Oct. 24, 1894, in TR and H. W. Brands, eds., *The Selected Letters of Theodore Roosevelt* (New York: Cooper Square Press, 2001), p. 96.
155 "they simply could not . . . lost the election?": Lilian Rixey, *Bamie: Theodore Roosevelt's Remarkable Sister* (New York: David McKay Co., 1963), p. 81.
156 "big, bustling New York": EKR to HCL, Oct. 27, 1895, Lodge-Roosevelt Correspondence, Massachusetts Hist. Soc.
156 "into one of her reserved": Rixey, *Bamie*, p. 81.
156 "The last four weeks": TR to HCL, Oct. 24, 1894, in *The Selected Letters of Theodore Roosevelt*, p. 96.
156 "I cannot begin": EKR to ARC, Sept. 28, 1894, Derby Papers, TRC.
156 his "one golden chance": TR to HCL, Oct. 24, 1894, in *The Selected Letters of Theodore Roosevelt*, p. 96.

CHAPTER SEVEN: The Invention of *McClure's*

Page

157 "We plow new fields . . . becoming harder": Cited in Eric F. Goldman, *Rendezvous with Destiny* (New York: Alfred A. Knopf, 1952), p. 32.
158 "the steamship . . . with their hand-looms": Henry George, *Progress and Poverty* (New York: Cosimo Classics, 2005), p. 7.
158 "the gulf between": Cited in Goldman, *Rendezvous with Destiny*, p. 33.
158 in a seminal paper: Frederick J. Turner, "The Significance of the Frontier in American History," in *Annual Report of the Amer. Hist. Assoc. for the Year 1893* (Washington, DC: U.S. Government Printing Office, 1894), pp. 199–227.
158 "It was a time": Frank B. Latham, *The Panic of 1893: A Time of Strikes, Riots, Hobo Camps, Coxey's "Army," Starvation, Withering Droughts and Fears of "Revolution"* (New York: F. Watts, 1971), p. 4.
159 "My men here": TR to ARC, May 15, 1886, in *LTR*, Vol. 1, pp. 100–101.
159 "foulest of criminals": TR, "The Menace of the Demagogue," speech before the American Republican College League, Oct. 15, 1896, in Hagedorn, ed., *Campaigns and Controversies*, *WTR*, Vol. 14, p. 265.
159 "wild and illogical doctrines": TR, "The City in Modern Life," *Atlantic Monthly* (April 1895), p. 556.
159 "that at this stage": TR, "The Menace of the Demagogue," in Hagedorn, ed., *Campaigns and Controversies*, *WTR*, Vol. 14, pp. 264–65.
159 more than 4 million jobs: Latham, *The Panic of 1893*, p. 4.
160 This acclaimed muckraking journal: John Chamberlain, *Farewell to Reform: The Rise, Life and Decay of the Progressive Mind in America* (Chicago: Quadrangle Books, 1965), p. 128.
160 "genius . . . of excitable energy": RSB, *American Chronicle: The Autobiography of Ray Stannard Baker* (New York: Charles Scribner's Sons, 1945), p. 95.
160 "a vibrant, eager": Ida M. Tarbell, *All in the Day's Work: An Autobiography* (Urbana: University of Illinois Press, 2003), p. 119.

160 "a bundle of tensions": Peter Lyon, *Success Story: The Life and Times of S. S. McClure* (New York: Charles Scribner's Sons, 1963), p. 11.
160 "a stream of words": Ibid., p. 14.
160 "like a caged lion": Robert Louis Stevenson and Lloyd Osbourne, *The Wrecker* (London: Oxford University Press, 1954), p. 107.
160 "lasted some twelve": Lyon, *Success Story*, p. 123.
160 "That was the first": Willa Cather and S. S. McClure, *The Autobiography of S. S. McClure* (Lincoln: University of Nebraska Press, 1997), p. 9.
161 "For a long while": Ibid., p. 17.
161 the Bible . . . *Book of Martyrs*: Lyon, *Success Story*, p. 5.
161 "opening those boxes": Cather and McClure, *The Autobiography*, p. 19.
161 "seemed to die down": Ibid., p. 18.
161 "began for the first time": Ibid., p. 27.
161 "a kind of 'arithmetic' . . . no text-book": Ibid., pp. 40–41.
162 "I used to waken": Ibid., p. 28.
162 "attacks of restlessness . . . all my life": Ibid., pp. 57, 59.
162 "I was seventeen . . . felt complete self-reliance": Ibid., p. 62.
162 had "never seen so": Lyon, *Success Story*, p. 13.
162 "Everything went well . . . blank stretch": Cather and McClure, *The Autobiography*, p. 18.
162 "the most beautiful": Lyon, *Success Story*, p. 17.
162 A brilliant student . . . top of her class: Cather and McClure, *The Autobiography*, p. 88.
162 "Don't cry for the moon": Lyon, *Success Story*, p. 17.
163 "My feeling for her": Cather and McClure, *The Autobiography*, p. 96.
163 "You mustn't write": Lyon, *Success Story*, p. 23.
163 "was easily the best": Cather and McClure, *The Autobiography*, p. 134.
163 At Phillips's house . . . William Dean Howells: Harold S. Wilson, *McClure's Magazine and the Muckrakers* (Princeton, NJ: Princeton University Press, 1970), p. 19.
163 "close acquaintance": Cather and McClure, *The Autobiography*, p. 130.
164 "He works by": Wilson, *McClure's Magazine and the Muckrakers*, p. 19.
164 "The three together": RSB, *American Chronicle*, p. 95.
164 "My present": McClure to Harriet Hurd, Dec. 23, 1881, McClure MSS.
164 "Mr. McClure": Lyon, *Success Story*, p. 32.
164 "would never receive": Ibid., p. 39.
164 "his personal appearance . . . his acquaintance": Albert Hurd to Harriet Hurd, April 29, 1883, McClure MSS.
165 "I do not love you": Lyon, *Success Story*, p. 33.
165 "This dismissal": Cather and McClure, *The Autobiography*, p. 143.
165 "weave the bicycle": Lyon, *Success Story*, p. 36.
165 "You are the surest": Ibid., p. 37.
165 "among the most attractive": Ibid., p. 38.
165 McClure took to the road: Wilson, *McClure's Magazine and the Muckrakers*, p. 35.
165 "I was in the big game": Cather and McClure, *The Autobiography*, pp. 150–51.
165 "When I have passed . . . identity with that boy": Ibid., p. 151.
166 "*could not* . . . love you still": Lyon, *Success Story*, p. 39.
166 "I saw it": Cather and McClure, *The Autobiography*, p. 164.
166 "a month's vacation": Jeanette L. Gilder, "When *McClure's* Began," *McClure's* (August 1912), p. 70.
166 "a handsome profit": Ibid.
166 "a dozen, or twenty": Lyon, *Success Story*, p. 57.
167 "distributing fifty thousand": Ibid., p. 74.
167 "much better fitted . . . as Mr. Phillips had": Cather and McClure, *The Autobiography*, p. 181.
167 "from one end of the country . . . in his teeth": Gilder, "When *McClure's* Began," *McClure's* (August 1912), p. 71.
167 "McClure was a Columbus": Ibid.
167 "dignified and conservative": Theodore P. Greene, *America's Heroes: The Changing Models of Success in American Magazines* (New York: Oxford University Press, 1970), p. 63.
167 "My qualifications": Lyon, *Success Story*, p. 94.
167 "He secured the best": "Mr. McClure and His Magazine," *American Monthly Review of Reviews* (July 1893), p. 99.
167 "before the name": J. L. French, "The Story of *McClure's*," *Profitable Advertising*, Oct. 5, 1897, p. 140.
167 purchased a dozen Sherlock Holmes: Cather and McClure, *The Autobiography*, p. 204.
167 "To find the best authors": French, "The Story of *McClure's*," *Profitable Advertising*, Oct. 5, 1897, p. 140.
168 "I propose to down . . . like champagne": Wilson, *McClure's Magazine and the Muckrakers*, p. 55.
168 "I would rather edit": Lyon, *Success Story*, p. 109.
168 "a reasonable profit": *Trenton* [NJ] *Times*, June 14, 1894.
168 "moneyed and well-educated . . . the upper classes": Frank Luther Mott, *A History of American Magazines, Vol. 4: 1885–1905* (Cambridge, MA: Harvard University Press, 1957), p. 2.
168 "within reach of": *Reno* [NV] *Evening Gazette*, July 6, 1893.
168 "The impregnability": Cather and McClure, *The Autobiography*, pp. 207–08.
168 "to make pictures": Ibid., p. 208.
169 "There was certainly": Ibid., p. 211.
169 "the good will of thousands": Gilder, "When *McClure's* Began," *McClure's* (August 1912), p. 72.
169 Conan Doyle invested $5,000: Lyon, *Success Story*, p. 133.

169 "It is not often . . . among the winners": "Mr. McClure and His Magazine," *American Monthly Review of Reviews* (July 1893), p. 99.
169 "no little of a": *Providence* [RI] *Journal*, June 4, 1893, in *McClure's* (August 1893), p. 6.
169 the "front rank at once": *Philadelphia Public Ledger*, June 13, 1893, in ibid.
169 "unusually brilliant": *Atlanta Constitution*, May 1, 1893.
169 "the first issue": TR to McClure, May 29, 1893, McClure MSS.
169 "a unity": Lyon, *Success Story*, p. 129.
169 "almost invented" it: John E. Semonche, *Ray Stannard Baker: A Quest for Democracy in Modern America, 1870–1918* (Chapel Hill: University of North Carolina Press, 1969), p. 76.
169 "in line with": Lyon, *Success Story*, p. 130.
170 "to deal with important": S. S. McClure, "The Making of a Magazine," *McClure's* (May 1924), p. 9.
170 "a power . . . for good": William Archer, "The American Cheap Magazine," *Fortnightly Review* (May 1910), p. 922.
170 the "mother hen": Wilson, *McClure's Magazine and the Muckrakers*, p. 96.
170 "This girl can write . . . exactly the qualities": Cather and McClure, *The Autobiography*, p. 218.
170 "unknown to half . . . enthusiasm and confidence": IMT, *All in the Day's Work*, pp. 118–19.
171 "more than he could ever": Ibid., p. 19.
171 "confident of . . . we had never heard of": Ibid., p. 22.
171 "nothing they did not . . . throttle their future": IMT and David M. Chalmers, *The History of the Standard Oil Company* (New York: Harper & Row, 1966), p. 21.
171 railroads arbitrarily doubled: Kathleen Brady, *Ida Tarbell: Portrait of a Muckraker* (Pittsburgh: University of Pittsburgh Press, 1989), p. 21.
171 His "big scheme": IMT, *All in the Day's Work*, p. 23.
171 "started the Standard Oil": Ibid., p. 219.
171 "There were nightly . . . during the day": Ibid., pp. 23–24.
172 "all pretty hazy . . . privilege of any sort": Ibid., pp. 25–26.
172 "readjustment of her status . . . sternest of problems": Ibid., p. 31.
172 "would never marry" . . . entreated God to prevent her ever marrying: Ibid., p. 36.
172 "classifying them": Ibid., p. 81.
172 "luminous eyes": Brady, *Ida Tarbell*, p. 29.
172 "an invader": IMT, *All in the Day's Work*, p. 40.
172 "the companionship": Ibid., pp. 39–40.
172 "shy and immature . . . reverence for Nature": Ibid., p. 41.
172 "She would arise . . . interested in people": Brady, *Ida Tarbell*, p. 28.
173 "go abroad and study": IMT, *All in the Day's Work*, p. 40.
173 "My early absorption . . . as of botany": Ibid., pp. 80–81.
173 "ardent supporters . . . laundries and bakeshops": Ibid., p. 82.
173 "a trilogy of . . . natural resources": Robert C. Kochersberger, *More Than a Muckraker: Ida Tarbell's Lifetime in Journalism* (Knoxville: University of Tennessee Press, 1994), p. xlvi.
173 "My life was busy": IMT, *All in the Day's Work*, pp. 78–79.
173 "disorderly fashion": Ibid., p. 73.
173 "secretly, very secretly": Ibid., p. 78.
174 "How will you support . . . You'll starve": Ibid., p. 87.
174 "There were a multitude": Ibid., p. 92.
174 "There were few mornings": Ibid., p. 103.
174 "It was not much": Ida M. Tarbell to [Tarbell family], Nov. 13, 1891, IMTC.
174 "bohemian poverty": Brady, *Ida Tarbell*, p. 51.
174 "a good dinner": IMT to [Tarbell family], Dec. 20, 1891, IMTC.
174 "happy evenings": IMT, *All in the Day's Work*, p. 105.
174 "Think of us": IMT to [Tarbell family], October [n.d.], 1891, IMTC.
175 "not a morsel more": IMT to [Tarbell family], Aug. 25, 1891, IMTC.
175 "a single egg": IMT, *All in the Day's Work*, pp. 90–91.
175 "It is the most heartless": IMT to [Tarbell family], November [n.d.], 1891, IMTC.
175 At night she wore everything: IMT to [Tarbell family], Dec. 20, 1891, IMTC.
175 "It isn't money": IMT to [Tarbell family], Dec. 27, 1891, IMTC.
175 "I think after . . . heart and hope": IMT to [Tarbell family], Dec. 7, 1891, IMTC.
175 *Scribner's* paid . . . first months in Paris: IMT to [Tarbell family], Sept. 21, 1891, IMTC.
175 "What excitement": IMT, *All in the Day's Work*, p. 98.
175 "Writing $5 . . . one's living": IMT to [Tarbell family], May 2, 1892, IMTC.
175 "I must go . . . never think of it again": IMT, *All in the Day's Work*, pp. 119–20.
176 "We all hope": McClure to IMT, Mar. 2, 1894, IMTC.
176 "All of the articles": McClure to IMT, Jan. 6, 1894, IMTC.
176 "actually starving . . . by force, if it must be": Esther Tarbell to IMT, Aug. 6, 1893, in Wilson, *McClure's Magazine and the Muckrakers*, p. 67.
176 "on the ragged edge . . . as a cricket": IMT to [Tarbell family], Mar. 16, 1894, IMTC.
176 "The little magazine": IMT to [Tarbell family], [n.d.], 1893, IMTC.
176 "so contemptuously anti-Napoleon": IMT, *All in the Day's Work*, p. 147.
177 "biography on the gallop": Ibid., p. 151.
177 "the best short life": Brady, *Ida Tarbell*, p. 91.
177 "I have often wished": IMT, *All in the Day's Work*, p. 152.
177 "His insight told him": Ibid., p. 161.

177 "could think of nothing": Gilder, "When *McClure's* Began," *McClure's* (August 1912), p. 75.
177 "Out with you": Lyon, *Success Story*, p. 134.
177 "all there was worth . . . so hopeless an assignment": IMT, *All in the Day's Work*, p. 163.
177 "They got a girl": Lyon, *Success Story*, p. 135.
177 "plan of campaign . . . humble and unknown": IMT, *All in the Day's Work*, p. 164.
178 McClure covered all her expenses . . . scrutinized multiple drafts: Brady, *Ida Tarbell*, p. 99.
178 "It is not only": "Miss Tarbell's Life of Lincoln," *McClure's* (January 1896), p. 206.
178 *McClure's* circulation . . . reached a quarter of a million: Lyons, *Success Story*, p. 137.
178 exceeding both the *Century* and *Harper's Monthly*: Brady, *Ida Tarbell*, p. 98.
178 "great power to stir": IMT, *All in the Day's Work*, p. 154.
178 "Here's a man": Ibid., p. 156.
178 "that Sam had three hundred": Brady, *Ida Tarbell*, p. 113.
178 "I found the place": IMT, *All in the Day's Work*, p. 160.
178 allowed her to get on "capitally": IMT to [Tarbell family], Feb. 26, 1893, IMTC.
178 "came and went": IMT, *All in the Day's Work*, p. 159.
178 blue eyes "glowed and sparkled": Ibid., p. 119.
179 "a stroke of genius": Ibid., p. 154.
179 "the sense of vitality . . . good comradeship": Ibid., p. 153.
179 The next "permanent acquisition": Ibid., p. 196.
179 "an honest paper": Semonche, *Ray Stannard Baker*, p. 77.
179 "farmers, tinkers": Ray Stannard Baker, *Native American: The Book of My Youth* (New York: Charles Scribner's Sons, 1942), p. 244.
179 "every human being": Ibid., p. 22.
179 "a wider field . . . import and value": RSB to his father, Jan. 16, 1898, RSB Papers.
179 "a devoted admirer . . . alive and talking": RSB, *American Chronicle*, p. 77.
179 "something fresh": Ibid., p. 78.
179 "To say that I was awed": Ibid., pp. 78–79.
179 "It took my breath . . . or anywhere else": Ibid., pp. 79–80.
180 "It 'breaks me all up' ": RSB to J. Stannard Baker, Feb. 1, 1898, RSB Papers.
180 "This is a magnificent": RSB to J. Stannard Baker, Mar. 25, 1898, RSB Papers.
180 "I like them": RSB to J. Stannard Baker, Sept. 17, 1898, RSB Papers.
180 "a capital team worker . . . anything else about him": IMT, *All in the Day's Work*, pp. 196–97.
180 "fishing and hunting . . . lumber camps": RSB, *Native American*, p. 11.
180 he married Alice Potter . . . "resident agent": Robert C. Bannister, Jr., *Ray Stannard Baker: The Mind and Thought of a Progressive* (New Haven, CT: Yale University Press, 1966), p. 4.
180 "Ours was a house": RSB, *Native American*, p. 38.
181 "How well I remember": Ibid., p. 26.
181 "a prodigious story-teller": Ibid., p. 48.
181 "into the lives and sorrows": Ibid., p. 45.
181 "My reading was always": Ibid., p. 47.
181 Ray assumed responsibility: Semonche, *Ray Stannard Baker*, p. 21.
181 "It went through me": RSB, *Native American*, p. 128.
181 "a great waste of time": Ibid., p. 163.
182 "details and facts": Ibid., p. 164.
182 "the one thing I needed": Ibid., p. 169.
182 well liked in college . . . at the top of his class: Semonche, *Ray Stannard Baker*, pp. 34, 40.
182 "When the time comes . . . successful in any employment": RSB, *Native American*, p. 220.
182 "I felt as though": Ibid., p. 223.
182 "Experience soon fades": Ibid., p. 237.
182 until his brother Harry . . . replaced him: Semonche, *Ray Stannard Baker*, p. 44.
183 "good working order" of society: Bannister, *Ray Stannard Baker*, p. 39.
183 Baker signed up . . . to question the laissez-faire economic principles: Semonche, *Ray Stannard Baker*, p. 50.
183 "anathema" to his father: RSB, *Native American*, pp. 284–85.
183 "with the greatest fervor . . . thirsty spirit": Ibid., p. 255.
183 "I did not make this": Ibid., p. 256.
183 "Great stuff, Baker": Ibid., p. 297.
184 "glimpses, street scenes": Ibid., pp. 291–92.
184 Ray tried to convince his father: RSB to J. Stannard Baker, Dec. 21, 1892, RSB Papers.
184 "There are thousands": RSB to J. Stannard Baker, Dec. 15, 1893, RSB Papers.
184 "plenty of people . . . plenty of work": RSB, *Native American*, pp. 286–87.
184 "The miserable living conditions": Ibid., p. 288.
184 "in the event . . . feels in the same way": RSB to J. Stannard Baker, Jan. 3, 1894, RSB Papers.
185 "I began to know . . . earn a living": Vivian Graff Rosenberg, *Turn of the Century American Journalist, Home-Spun Philosopher, Ray Stannard Baker* (Privately printed, 1977), p. 69.
185 incredible "power of the press": RSB, *American Chronicle*, p. 12.
185 "there appeared": Ibid., pp. 17–18.
185 "a grand adventure": Ibid., p. 27.
185 "the police seemed": Rosenberg, *Turn of the Century American Journalist*, p. 72.
185 "Coxey's eventful march . . . an act of God": Louis L. Snyder and Richard B. Morris, eds., *A Treasury of Great Reporting: "Literature Under Pressure" from the Sixteenth Century to Our Own Time* (New York: Simon & Schuster, 1962), p. 222.

185 "vanished in thin air": RSB, *American Chronicle*, p. 25.
186 "benevolent-looking, bearded": Ibid., p. 35.
186 "the wildest confusion": Ibid.
186 it was later proved . . . $25 million: Pringle, *Life and Times*, Vol. 1, p. 132.
186 the predatory hold of the Pullman monopoly must be broken: RSB, *American Chronicle*, p. 38.
186 "nothing to arbitrate . . . business of the company": Ibid., p. 38.
186 "putting the torch": Ibid., p. 39.
186 "It does seem": J. Stannard Baker to RSB, July 6 & 10, 1894, in Bannister, *Ray Stannard Baker*, p. 51.
186 "in the midst of the mob . . . toughs and outsiders": Testimony of RSB, *Hutchinson* [KS] *News*, Aug. 21, 1894.
187 "honeymoon as a newspaper . . . the trouble ended": RSB, *American Chronicle*, pp. 45–46.
187 "the greatest popular orator": Ibid., p. 62.
187 "The essential impression": Ibid., p. 63.
187 "the commonplace" . . . "the spectacular": Ibid., p. 45.
187 "somewhat low . . . as a writer": Ibid., p. 77.
187 "Suddenly and joyously . . . to write about it": Ibid., p. 84.
187 "What's the Matter with Kansas?" . . . "wild-eyed" rhetoric: WAW, *The Autobiography of William Allen White* (New York: The Macmillan Co., 1946), p. 281.
188 "That's the stuff!": Ibid., p. 282.
188 "more widely than any other . . . in a dozen years": Ibid., p. 284.
188 "I had seen cities . . . English poets were their friends": Ibid., pp. 300–301.
188 "the smile of . . . a poet": Walter Johnson, *William Allen White's America* (New York: Henry Holt & Co., 1947), p. 19.
188 "his affection and loyalty": IMT, *All in the Day's Work*, p. 259.
188 White's "love of life . . . high spirits": RSB, *American Chronicle*, p. 224.
188 "call on them whenever": Lyon, *Success Story*, p. 150.
189 "The McClure group . . . had real influence": WAW, *The Autobiography*, p. 301.
189 "never yielded . . . went back to Kansas": RSB, *American Chronicle*, p. 223.
189 His family lived in "the best house": WAW, *The Autobiography*, p. 69.
189 "I look back upon": Ibid., p. 61.
189 "to get a breeze": Ibid., p. 42.
189 "somebody . . . to the ruling class": Ibid., pp. 61–62.
189 "devoted and adoring . . . bowed down": Ibid., p. 25.
189 "In that Elysian childhood": Ibid., p. 26.
189 "He was so good-natured": Johnson, *William Allen White's America*, p. 10.
189 Summer days were spent . . . a boy's paradise: WAW, *The Autobiography*, pp. 45–46.
190 "I remember as a child": Johnson, *William Allen White's America*, pp. 19–20.
190 "distinguished citizens": WAW, *The Autobiography*, p. 67.
190 "I was not without": Ibid., p. 83.
190 "Here . . . was a novel . . . a new door": Ibid., p. 106.
190 his "life's calling": Ibid., pp. 109, 113.
190 "establish a home": Ibid., p. 136.
190 "a babble of clamoring voices": Ibid., p. 144.
191 "natural laws . . . the laboring classes": Goldman, *Rendezvous with Destiny*, p. 113.
191 "As I look back": WAW, *The Autobiography*, pp. 143–44.
191 "ceased to be a student": Ibid., p. 176.
191 "We have three crops": Latham, *The Panic of 1893*, p. 15.
192 "police power . . . with a public interest": Kermit L. Hall, ed., *The Oxford Guide to the United States Supreme Court Decisions* (New York: Oxford University Press, 1999), p. 203.
192 The justices denied the state's regulatory power: Ibid., p. 321.
192 "reasonable and just": Interstate Commerce Commission Act of 1887 (24 Stat. 379).
192 "It satisfies the public": Gary M. Walton and Hugh Rockoff, *History of the American Economy* (San Diego, CA: Harcourt Brace Jovanovich, 1990), p. 338.
192 "Liberty produces wealth . . . instead of servant": Henry Demarest Lloyd, *Wealth Against Commonwealth* (New York: Harper & Bros., 1902), pp. 2, 494.
192 "Wall Street owns . . . wages deny them!": Mary K. Lease, quoted in Levine, *Who Built America?*, p. 147.
193 "We meet in the midst . . . people must own the railroads": Edward McPherson, *A Handbook of Politics for 1892* (Washington, DC: J. J. Chapman, 1892), pp. 269ff.
193 "We prideful ones": WAW, *The Autobiography*, p. 183.
193 "demagogic rabble-rousing . . . blinded by my birthright": Ibid., p. 187.
193 "pinheaded, anarchistic crank[s]": Miller, *Theodore Roosevelt: A Life*, p. 218.
194 "representatives of those forces": TR, "The Menace of the Demagogue," in *WTR*, Vol. 14, p. 264.
194 "The 'best citizens' ": WAW, *The Autobiography*, p. 191.
194 "the first wave": Ibid., pp. 193–94.
194 "the black hand . . . for fifty years": Ibid., pp. 215–16.
194 becoming his "own master": Ibid., p. 256.
194 "I want to live": Johnson, *William Allen White's America*, p. 76.
194 "The new editor": WAW, *The Autobiography*, pp. 260–61.
195 "the best-known": Johnson, *William Allen White's America*, p. 4.
195 "was the beginning": WAW, *The Autobiography*, p. 286.
195 "seems big . . . just our size": McClure to John S. Phillips, April 21, 1897, Phillips MSS.

195 "one of the best journalists": C. C. Regier, *The Era of the Muckrakers* (Gloucester, MA: Peter Smith, 1957), p. 59.
195 "Jaccaci probed . . . clinched" the deal: LS, *The Autobiography*, p. 358.
196 "like springing up": Ibid., p. 359.
196 "He was a flower . . . compromise and peace": Ibid., pp. 361–64.
196 "young, handsome . . . society, the press": IMT, *All in the Day's Work*, pp. 198–99.
196 "entirely in harmony": Ibid., p. 199.
196 "associates in the . . . long friendship": RSB, *American Chronicle*, p. 221.
196 "as a kind of Socratic": Ibid., p. 221.
196 "his most consistent pose": Robert Stinson, *Lincoln Steffens* (New York: Frederick Ungar, 1979), p. 1.
196 "My story is": LS, *The Autobiography*, p. 3.
196 "paints, oils and glass": Ibid., p. 7.
197 "palatial residence": Justin Kaplan, *Lincoln Steffens: A Biography* (New York: Touchstone, 1974), p. 17.
197 "If I left home promptly": LS, *The Autobiography*, p. 34.
197 befriended a bridge-tender: Ibid., p. 28.
197 "in on the know . . . big killings": Ibid., p. 37.
197 "Bribery!": Ibid., p. 48.
197 "Nothing was what": Ibid., p. 47.
197 "the best private school": Ibid., p. 112.
197 "brought up to do their duty": Ibid., p. 111.
197 "stored in compartments . . . to anything else": Ibid., p. 119.
198 "My father listened . . . his interest and retire": Ibid., p. 128.
198 having received love "so freely": Ibid., p. 77.
198 Not until his own son was born: Kaplan, *Lincoln Steffens*, p. 21.
198 "She stands next": LS to Elizabeth Steffens, Feb. 1, 1891, LS Papers.
198 "My dear son": LS, *The Autobiography*, p. 169.
199 "on space . . . he told me his": Ibid., pp. 172–73.
199 "I came to love . . . a live city": Ibid., pp. 180–81.
199 "cool, dull": Ibid., p. 184.
199 "was a dismal time . . . in the ruin": Ibid., p. 187.
199 "successful men . . . stop to question": Ibid., p. 192.
199 "the gentleman reporter . . . accuracy and politeness": LS to Joseph Steffens, Jan. 18, 1893, in Lincoln Steffens, Ella Winter, Granville Hicks, and Carl Sandburg, eds., *The Letters of Lincoln Steffens*, Vol. 1 (New York: Harcourt, Brace & Co., 1938), pp. 88–89.
200 "confide in me . . . worth it all": LS to Joseph Steffens, Mar. 18, 1893, in ibid., pp. 91–92.
200 "The Evening Post . . . my field, my chance": LS to Joseph Steffens, Nov. 3, 1893, in ibid., pp. 97–98.
200 Long opposed to the Tammany regime . . . were delighted to document Parkhurst's findings: LS, *The Autobiography*, p. 193.
201 "a vigilant and well-informed press": "Interview with S. S. McClure," *The North American* (Philadelphia), August [n.d.], 1905.

CHAPTER EIGHT: "Like a Boy on Roller Skates"

Page
203 Lincoln Steffens was relaxing: LS, *The Autobiography*, p. 257.
203 Jacob Riis heralded . . . of Little Italy: Morris, *The Rise of Theodore Roosevelt*, p. 482.
203 "head forward": LS, "The Real Roosevelt," *Ainslee's Magazine* (December 1898), p. 481.
203 "Hello, Jake . . . "What do we do first?'": LS, *The Autobiography*, p. 257.
204 "It was all breathless": Ibid., p. 258.
204 An immigrant from Denmark . . . the same year: Thaddeus Seymour, Jr., "A Progressive Partnership: Theodore Roosevelt and the Reform Press—Riis, Steffens, Baker and White (Muckrakers)," PhD diss., University of Wisconsin, Madison, 1985, p. 35.
204 his "life-work" in journalism: Jacob A. Riis, *The Making of an American* (New York: Grosset & Dunlap, 1901), p. 197.
204 "Being the 'boss' ": Ibid., p. 202.
204 "The sights I saw there": Ibid., p. 267.
204 neglected "repairs and": Jacob Riis, *How the Other Half Lives: Studies Among the Tenements of New York* (New York: Charles Scribner's Sons, 1890), p. 4.
204 "Only Riis wrote": LS, *The Autobiography*, p. 204.
204 "beautiful stories": Ibid., p. 205.
204 When he narrated . . . the problems were redressed: Ibid., p. 204.
204 "Why" he asked: Riis, *The Making of an American*, p. 349.
205 "The remedy": Riis, *How the Other Half Lives*, p. 4.
205 "Truly, I lay no claim": Riis, *The Making of an American*, pp. 309, 317.
205 "I cannot conceive": JRL quoted in Riis, *The Making of an American*, p. 308.
205 "both an enlightenment": TR, *An Autobiography*, p. 169.
205 "go a long way": TR, "Reform Through Social Work: Some Forces That Tell for Decency in New York City," *McClure's* (March 1901), p. 453.
205 "hysterical . . . sentimental excess": Ibid.
205 read the book and "had come": Jacob Riis, "Theodore Roosevelt," *American Monthly Review of Reviews* (August 1900), p. 182.
205 "exposing jobbery" . . . city's closets: Ibid., p. 181.
205 "I loved him": Jacob Riis, *The Making of an American*, p. 328.

205 "one of my truest": TR, "Jacob Riis," *Outlook*, June 6, 1914, p. 284.

205 "two sides . . . were hardest": TR, *An Autobiography*, p. 170.

205 "He had the most flaming . . . mere preacher": TR, "Jacob Riis," *Outlook*, June 6, 1914, p. 284.

206 "who looked at life": TR, *An Autobiography*, p. 169.

206 "He is a personal friend": TR to Horace E. Scudder, Aug. 16, 1895, in *LTR*, Vol. 1, p. 472.

206 his "state of mind" . . . "wise" mentors: Stinson, *Lincoln Steffens*, p. 143.

206 "With astonishment": LS, *The Autobiography*, p. 248.

207 "One police captain": LS to Joseph Steffens, Dec. 15, 1894, in LS et al., *Letters of Lincoln Steffens*, Vol. 1, p. 107.

207 a sizable fortune of $350,000: Morris, *The Rise of Theodore Roosevelt*, p. 485.

207 Alec "Clubber" Williams . . . the Lexow Committee: LS, *The Autobiography*, p. 252.

207 "supreme gift . . . explain themselves": *NYT*, Aug. 10, 1936.

207 "a clean breast . . . the whole rotten business": LS, *The Autobiography*, p. 273.

207 "on the square": Ibid.

207 "full publicity": Bishop, *Theodore Roosevelt and His Time*, Vol. 1, p. 59.

207 "in almost daily": Ibid., p. 62.

207 "There began between": Ibid., p. 58.

208 "No political influence": LS, "The Real Roosevelt," *Ainslee's Magazine* (December 1898), p. 481.

208 "would spare no man": LS, Scrapbook 1, LS Papers.

208 a route mapped out in advance: Riis, *The Making of an American*, p. 330.

208 those whom he discovered sleeping: New York *Sun*, June 8, 1895.

208 "What's that . . . fan him to death": Pringle, *Theodore Roosevelt, A Biography*, p. 139.

208 "A sorrier-looking set": New York *Evening Post*, June 7, 1895.

208 "Roosevelt on Patrol": New York *Sun*, June 8, 1895, Clipping Scrapbook, TRC.

208 "patrolman hunt . . . a new epoch": New York *Sun*, June 8, 1895, Clipping Scrapbook, TRC.

208 "Police Commissioner Roosevelt": *San Antonio* [TX] *Daily Light*, June 14, 1895.

208 became an alluring subject: Morris, *The Rise of Theodore Roosevelt*, p. 495.

209 "A pair of gold-mounted": New York *Sun*, June 23, 1895.

209 "Few men": Chanler, *Roman Spring*, p. 196.

209 "These midnight rambles": TR to ARC, June 23, 1895, in *LTR*, Vol. 1, p. 463.

209 "though each meant": TR to ARC, June 16, 1895, in ibid., p. 462.

209 "It is one thing": TR, *An Autobiography*, p. 200.

209 "tore down unfit": Riis, *The Making of an American*, p. 344.

209 "the tap-root" of corruption: Riis, *Theodore Roosevelt*, p. 138.

209 "The corrupt would never": LS, "The Real Roosevelt," *Ainslee's Magazine* (December 1898), p. 483.

209 it "is altogether too strict": TR to ARC, June 30, 1895, in *LTR*, Vol. 1, p. 464.

209 "Is there any other way": LS, "The Real Roosevelt," *Ainslee's Magazine* (December 1898), p. 483.

209 harbor "no protected class": TR, *An Autobiography*, p. 191.

210 "to a most limited extent": TR to HCL, Aug. 22, 1895, in TR and Henry Cabot Lodge, *Selections from the Correspondence of Theodore Roosevelt and Henry Cabot Lodge, 1884–1918* (New York: Charles Scribner's Sons, 1925), Vol. 1, p. 165.

210 "The police force became": Riis, *The Making of an American*, p. 329.

210 "I have never been": TR to HCL, July 20, 1895, in *LTR*, Vol. 1, p. 469.

210 "You are the biggest . . . wrecked the Republican Party": Avery Andrews, "Citizen in Action: The Story of T.R. as Police Commissioner," Unpublished typescript, n.d., TRC.

210 Reports surfaced: *The Journal* (New York), Aug. 6, 1895, Clipping Scrapbook, TRC.

210 "the next bomb": New York *World*, Aug. 7, 1895, in Clipping Scrapbook, TRC.

210 Rumors circulated: *NYT*, Jan. 4, 1896, Clipping Scrapbook, TRC.

210 "Roosevelt is like a boy": *Ohio Democrat* (New Philadelphia, OH), July 18, 1895.

210 "This was a fight": Bishop, *Theodore Roosevelt and His Time*, Vol. 1, p. 58.

210 "in windows . . . mounted paraders": New York *World*, Sept. 26, 1895.

210 "laughed louder . . . Certainly": *NYT*, Sept. 26, 1895.

210 "That is the . . . Millionaire's Club": New York *Sun*, Sept. 26, 1895.

210 "a striking resemblance": New York *World*, Sept. 26, 1895.

211 "That is really a good stroke": New York *Sun*, Sept. 26, 1895.

211 "shrieking with rage": TR to HCL, July 20, 1895, in *LTR*, Vol. 1, p. 469.

211 "It looked almost": New York *World*, Sept. 26, 1895.

211 "Bully for Teddy! . . . a man!": *Daily Republican* (Decatur, IL), Sept. 27, 1895.

211 "Cheered by Those": *Chicago Evening Journal*, Sept. 26, 1895, reprinted in *Daily Republican*, Sept. 27, 1895.

211 "a hundred parades": New York *World*, Sept. 26, 1895.

211 "are on the verge": TR to HCL, Oct. 3, 1895, in TR and HCL, *Selections from the Correspondence*, Vol. 1, p. 181.

211 "has actually been endeavoring": TR to HCL, Oct. 11, 1895, in *LTR*, Vol. 1, pp. 484–85.

211 "Thinks he's the whole board": LS, *The Autobiography*, p. 258.

211 "He talks, talks . . . parted rather coldly": Bishop, *Theodore Roosevelt and His Time*, Vol. 1, p. 63.

211 "armed combat": Morris, *The Rise of Theodore Roosevelt*, p. 529.

212 "His wife and children": Morris, *EKR*, p. 163.

212 "Their gay doings": Ibid.

212 "overstrained . . . the world should stop": HCL to ARC, December [n.d.], 1895, in Rixey, *Bamie*, p. 89.

212 "a chocolate éclair backbone": Wister, *Roosevelt: The Story of a Friendship*, p. 50.

212 "who want to strike down": TR to Cecil Spring Rice, Oct. 8, 1896, in *LTR*, Vol. 1, p. 562.

212 "years of social misery": TR to Cecil Spring Rice, Aug. 5, 1896, in ibid., p. 554.

212 “The halls were jammed”: TR to ARC, Oct. 4, 1896, in TR, *Letters from Theodore Roosevelt to Anna Roosevelt Cowles*, p. 194.
213 “He gave all of his time”: Wood, *Roosevelt As We Knew Him*, p. 42.
213 “the happiest . . . really worth living”: Riis, *Theodore Roosevelt*, p. 131.
213 “had no heart in it”: Ibid., p. 151.
213 “reform was . . . did come back”: LS, *The Autobiography*, p. 181.
213 “The end of the reign . . . ‘reform cop’ is retired”: New York *Evening Post*, April 15, 1897.
213 “the proudest single . . . brain and will power”: LS, “The Real Roosevelt,” *Ainslee’s Magazine* (December 1898), p. 480.
213 people who had “failed in life”: Morris, *The Rise of Theodore Roosevelt*, p. 550.
213 “I became more set”: TR, *An Autobiography*, p. 201.
214 loosening the “steel chain”: Goldman, *Rendezvous with Destiny*, p. 85.
214 “more than any he has ever”: HHT, *Recollections of Full Years*, p. 30.
214 “Perhaps it is the comfort”: Pringle, *Life and Times*, Vol. 1, p. 148.
214 “I have been . . . want of time”: WHT to HHT, Dec. 10, 1892, WHTP.
214 “The Bar here . . . body of men”: WHT to HHT, Nov. 26, 1895, WHTP.
214 “They have eight bedrooms”: WHT to HHT, Nov. 21, 1892, WHTP.
214 “He is absolutely”: Lyle, “Taft: A Career of Big Tasks,” *The World’s Work* (September 1907).
215 “Stop that! . . . to the case”: Pringle, *Life and Times*, Vol. 1, p. 126.
215 Taft edited the document himself: Lyle, “Taft: A Career of Big Tasks,” *The World’s Work* (September 1907).
215 “over again and again”: Ibid.
215 “holding that city . . . a civil war”: WHT to HHT, July 9, 1984, WHTP.
215 killed “to make an impression”: WHT to HHT, July 8, 1894, WHTP.
216 “I hate the . . . nothing to reporters”: WHT to HHT, July 4, 1894, WHTP.
216 packing the court “to suffocation”: WHT to HHT, July 11, 1894, WHTP.
216 “the last sentence”: WHT to HHT, July 13, 1894, WHTP.
216 took almost an hour: Ibid.
216 “had the right to organize . . . employment are unsatisfactory”: “Thomas vs. Cincinnati, New Orleans & Texas Pacific Railway Company,” *Federal Reporter*, Vol. 62 (St. Paul: West Publishing Co., 1894), pp. 817–18.
216 “urged a peaceable . . . against their employers”: Ibid.
217 not “as Police Commissioner”: Hurwitz, *Theodore Roosevelt and Labor*, p. 172.
217 “applauded him to the echo”: Riis, *The Making of an American*, p. 333.
217 “one railroad worker”: John Fabian Witt, “Toward a New History of American Accident Law: Classical Tort Law and the Cooperative First-Party Insurance Movement,” *Harvard Law Review* (January 2001), pp. 694–95, 719–20.
217 he would later be vindicated when in 1908: Pringle, *Life and Times*, Vol. 1, p. 139.
218 One brakeman was working: See “Narramore v. Cleveland, Cincinnati, Chicago and St. Louis Railway Company,” *Federal Reporter*, Vol. 96 (1899).
218 “a dead letter”: Pringle, *Life and Times*, Vol. 1, p. 141.
218 injured employees successfully cited: Witt, “Toward a New History of American Accident Law,” *Harvard Law Review* (January 2001), pp. 776–77.
218 “to give the defendants”: Pringle, *Life and Times*, Vol. 1, p. 145.
218 “Iron Pipe Trust Illegal”: Arnold, *Remaking the Presidency,* p. 78.
218 “precisely the same”: New York *World*, Feb. 15, 1898.
219 “The deanship is”: WHT to HHT, July 1, 1897, WHTP.
219 “I wish I could make”: WHT to HHT, Nov. 26, 1895, WHTP.
219 “a bad taste”: WHT to HHT, Nov. 23, 1894, WHTP.
219 “something to say”: HHT to WHT, June 23, 1895, WHTP.
219 “I shall use you”: WHT to HHT, June 28, 1895, WHTP.
219 “the prominent names . . . fizzle of mine”: WHT to HHT, July 13, 1895, WHTP.
219 “a happy summer home”: Mabel Boardman, “The Summer Capital,” *Outlook*, Sept. 25, 1909.
219 “whole cargo of Tafts”: Robert Lee Dunn, *William Howard Taft, American* (Boston: Chapple, 1908), pp. 34, 43.
219 “He played eighteen . . . has got to burn around me”: Taft, *Memories and Opinions*, pp. 107–09.
220 Nellie Taft . . . immersed herself in the civic life: HHT to WHT, Nov. 19, 1892; June 5, 1893; Nov. 11, 16, 20, & 24, 1893; Dec. 4, 1893, WHTP.
220 Nellie found time . . . president of the Orchestral Association: Anthony, *Nellie Taft*, pp. 110–20.
220 “My love for . . . me to know”: WHT to HHT, Feb. 6, 1894, WHTP.
220 fancied herself “the new woman”: WHT to HHT, June 27, 1897, WHTP.
220 “It is so delightful”: HHT to WHT, July 6, 1896, WHTP.
221 “I should have much preferred”: WHT to HHT, Mar. 26, 1896, WHTP.
221 “I want peace”: Mrs. Bellamy (Maria Longworth) Storer, “How Theodore Roosevelt Was Appointed Assistant Secretary of the Navy: A Hitherto Unrelated Chapter of History,” *Harper’s Weekly*, June 1, 1912.
221 “The truth is”: AB, *Taft and Roosevelt*, Vol. 2, p. 441.
221 “Judge Taft”: HCL to TR, Mar. 8, 1897, in TR and HCL, *Selections from the Correspondence*, Vol. 1, p. 252.
222 “Give him a chance”: Storer, “How Theodore Roosevelt Was Appointed . . . ,” *Harper’s Weekly*, June 1, 1912.
222 “more than once”: AB, *Taft and Roosevelt*, Vol. 2, p. 441.
222 “would rather welcome a foreign war”: Wagenknecht, *Seven Worlds*, p. 247.
222 “soldierly virtues . . . slothful, timid”: *NYT*, June 3, 1897.
222 “The victories of peace”: Wagenknecht, *Seven Worlds*, p. 248.
222 “seen the dead piled up”: Evan Thomas, *The War Lovers: Roosevelt, Lodge, Hearst, and the Rush to Empire, 1898* (Boston: Little, Brown, 2010), p. 229.
222 “Every man”: TR, “A Colonial Survival,” in Hermann Hagedorn, ed., *Literary Essays*, Vol. 12 of *WTR*, p. 306.

222 "became convinced": TR, *An Autobiography*, p. 208.
222 incarcerating nearly a third: James Bradley, *The Imperial Cruise: A Secret History of Empire and War* (Boston: Little, Brown, 2009), p. 71.
222 "on the ground of . . . material gain": Pringle, *Theodore Roosevelt: A Biography*, p. 176.
222 exercised a "free hand": TR to ARC, Aug. 21, 1897, in TR, *Letters from Theodore Roosevelt to Anna Roosevelt Cowles*, p. 208.
222 He generated war plans: RSB, "Theodore Roosevelt: A Character Sketch," *McClure's* (November 1898), p. 23.
223 "I am having immense": TR to Bellamy Storer, Aug. 19, 1897, in *LTR*, Vol. 1, p. 655.
223 "it is not easy": Pringle, *Theodore Roosevelt: A Biography*, p. 175.
223 "There isn't the slightest": TR to John Davis Long, June 22, 1897, in *LTR*, Vol. 1, pp. 630–31.
223 "You must be tired": Thomas, *The War Lovers*, p. 174.
223 "stay there just exactly": TR to John Davis Long, Aug. 26, 1897, in *LTR*, Vol. 1, p. 662.
223 fortunate to avoid Washington: TR to John Davis Long, Sept. 15, 1897, in ibid., p. 675.
223 "an act of friendly courtesy": Morris, *The Rise of Theodore Roosevelt*, p. 596.
223 "an act of . . . Havana tomorrow": TR to Benjamin Harrison Diblee, Feb. 16, 1898, in *LTR*, Vol. 1, p. 775.
223 "It seemed as . . . General Miles": IMT, *All in the Day's Work*, pp. 189–90.
223 "vacillated between": Ibid., p. 189.
223 "suspension of judgment": IMT, "President McKinley in War Times," *McClure's* (July 1898), p. 211.
223 "excited goings-on . . . an invading army": IMT, *All in the Day's Work*, pp. 189–90.
224 Roosevelt's "amazing" personality: IMT to RSB, May 3, 1911, RSB Papers.
224 "I am more grieved": TR to William Sheffield Cowles, Mar. 30, 1898, in *LTR*, Vol. 2, p. 804.
224 "weakness . . . ludicrous than painful": "Theodore Roosevelt's Diaries—IV," *Personality* (July 1928), p. 65.
224 "The only effective forces": Bishop, *Theodore Roosevelt and His Time*, Vol. 1, pp. 90–91.
224 "warlike element": IMT, "President McKinley in War Times," *McClure's* (July 1898), p. 221.
224 "too much" for McKinley: IMT, *All in the Day's Work*, p. 189.
224 "He steadily grew paler": IMT, "President McKinley in War Times," *McClure's* (July 1898), p. 223.
224 "proceed at once . . . utmost endeavor": H. W. Brands, *Bound to Empire: The United States and the Philippines* (New York: Oxford University Press, 1992), p. 23.
224 "Keep full of . . . the Asiatic coast": TR to George Dewey, Feb. 25, 1898, in *LTR*, Vol. 1, p. 784.
224 "if it had not been": AB, *Taft and Roosevelt*, Vol. 2, p. 441.
224 "In all its earlier . . . best of the old": IMT, *All in the Day's Work*, pp. 195–96.
225 "a continuous flow of war articles": Ibid., p. 196.
225 "The editors of *McClure's* . . . historical value": "McClure's Magazine in War Times," *McClure's* (June 1898), p. 206.
225 "could not run away . . . to serve it?" IMT, *All in the Day's Work*, p. 195.
225 "a triumph of the new journalism": Hofstadter, *The Age of Reform: From Bryan to F.D.R.*, p. 191.
225 Baker calculated . . . every transmitted word: RSB, "How the News of the War Is Reported," *McClure's* (September 1898), pp. 491–94.
226 "It is a little short": RSB to to J. Stannard Baker, May 1, 1898, RSB Papers.
226 his paper . . . collapsed into insolvency: Thomas, *The War Lovers*, p. 271.
226 "Populists stopped . . . flags fluttering everywhere": WAW, "When Johnny Went Marching Out," *McClure's* (September 1898), pp. 199–203.
226 "have not been . . . entire four years": George B. Waldron, "The Cost of War," *McClure's* (June 1898), pp. 169–70.
227 "day and night": "McClure's Magazine in War Times," *McClure's* (June 1898), p. 206.
227 "Having tasted blood": IMT, *All in the Day's Work*, p. 196.
227 "For weeks we could not tell": TR to Brooks Adams, Mar. 21, 1898, in *LTR*, Vol. 1, p. 798.
227 A dangerous operation: TR to ARC, Mar. 7, 1898, in ibid., p. 790.
227 "kind of a nervous breakdown": TR to William Sheffield Cowles, Mar. 29, 1898, in *LTR*, Vol. 2, p. 803.
227 "You know what": AB to his mother, Oct. 21, 1908, in Abbott, ed., *Letters of Archie Butt*, p. 146.
227 "that a war hardly seemed": Arthur Lubow, *The Reporter Who Would Be King: A Biography of Richard Harding Davis* (New York: Scribner, 1992), front matter.
228 "We knew his face": Ibid., p. 1.
228 "queer, strained humility": TR, "A Colonial Survival," in *WTR*, Vol. 12, p. 301.
228 "He apparently considered . . . table during dinner": TR to James Brander Matthews, Dec. 6, 1892, in *LTR*, Vol. 1, p. 299.
228 "absolutely the very best": Richard Harding Davis and Charles Belmont Davis, *Adventures and Letters of Richard Harding Davis* (New York: Charles Scribner's Sons, 1917), p. 191.
228 "This is the best crowd": Ibid., pp. 195–96.
229 "jumped up . . . Americans in Cuba": Edward Marshall, *The Story of the Rough Riders, 1st U.S. Volunteer Cavalry: The Regiment in Camp and on the Battle Field* (New York: G. W. Dillingham Co., 1899), p. 104.
229 "He was suffering": Richard Harding Davis, *The Cuban and Porto Rican Campaigns* (New York: Charles Scribner's Sons, 1898), p. 163.
229 "If the men . . . 'shown more courage'": RHD and Davis, *Adventures and Letters*, pp. 196–97.
230 "No one who saw": Lubow, *The Reporter Who Would Be King*, p. 185.
230 "charging the rifle-pits": RHD, *The Cuban and Porto Rican Campaigns*, p. 217.
230 "Up, up they went . . . never quite to be got over": Quoted in Riis, *Theodore Roosevelt*, pp. 168–70.
230 "had single-handedly": Lubow, *The Reporter Who Would Be King*, p. 195.
230 "Except for Roosevelt": Ibid.
231 lived in constant anxiety: Morris, *EKR*, p. 181.
231 "These dreadful days": Rixey, *Bamie*, p. 123.

231 "for the sake of the children": Thomas, *The War Lovers*, p. 317.
231 "I do not want": Ibid., p. 279.
231 "looked the picture . . . the Cuban campaign": *NYT*, Aug. 15, 1898.
231 "bubbled over . . . could have been with us": New York *World*, Aug. 6, 1898.
231 "the sober judgment . . . any bloodshed": RSB to J. Stannard Baker, Mar. 8, 1898, RSB Papers.
231 "War excitement here . . . jostling crowds": RSB to J. Stannard Baker, May 1, 1898, RSB Papers.
231 "the thrill": RSB, *American Chronicle*, p. 84.
231 "It was the . . . time usually wasted": Ibid., p. 191.
232 "roomy, comfortable house . . . amassing a fortune": RSB, "Theodore Roosevelt: A Character Sketch," *McClure's* (November 1898), p. 32.
232 "I talked with a number": Ibid., p. 31.
232 "a magnificent example . . . joyousness of disposition": Ibid., pp. 32, 23, 24.
232 "rare power . . . active strength": Ibid., pp. 31–32.
232 "president of the": RSB to J. Stannard Baker, Aug. 30, 1898, RSB Papers.
232 "I want to thank you": TR to RSB, Nov. 4, 1898, RSB Papers.
232 "I was to write": RSB, *American Chronicle*, p. 84.
233 "one of his finest characteristics": RSB, Notebook J, Oct. 6, 1910, RSB Papers.
233 "Once a friend": RSB, "Theodore Roosevelt: A Character Sketch," *McClure's* (November 1898), p. 31.
233 "what was really interesting": Baker, *American Chronicle*, p. 95.
233 "outpouring of marvelous": Ibid., p. 85.
233 most amazing invention "since the days of Jonah": *Sioux Valley News* (Canton, SD), Jan. 5, 1899.
233 "simpler in construction . . . without recharging": RSB, "The Automobile in Common Use," *McClure's* (July 1899), pp. 7, 10.
233 "the first fully verified": Baker, *American Chronicle*, p. 153.
233 "one of the few thinkers": Ibid., p. 110.
233 "My life was being": Ibid., p. 116.
233 "I have been spreading": Ibid., p. 115.
233 "It seemed to me": Ibid., p. 120.
234 McClure's "affectionate interest": IMT to RSB, Sept. 13, 1899, RSB Papers.
234 "I cannot think": Baker, *American Chronicle*, p. 117.
234 "Do only what . . . friends they were": Ibid., p. 123.
234 "as far away as possible": Ibid.
234 "At first": Ibid., p. 124.
234 "across bare ridges . . . sense of freedom": Ibid., p. 125.
234 "I rode or tramped": Ibid., p. 129.
234 "I began again": Ibid.
234 "This being true . . . see and think": Ibid., p. 132.
234 "not a leader . . . live together peaceably": Ibid., pp. 132–33.
235 "one by one": LS, "Theodore Roosevelt, Governor," *McClure's* (May 1899), p. 57.
235 "Should I run?" . . . predicted victory: LS, *The Autobiography*, pp. 342–43.
235 "Take an independent . . . will end him": LS, "Theodore Roosevelt, Governor," *McClure's* (May 1899), p. 58.
235 "I am not a Republican": LS to Joseph Steffens, Oct. 18, 1894, in LS, et al., eds., *Letters of Lincoln Steffens*, Vol. 1, p. 106.
236 "I'm a practical man": LS, *The Autobiography*, p. 346.
236 "good public service . . . by bettering it": LS, "Theodore Roosevelt, Governor," *McClure's* (May 1899), p. 58.
236 "What's the difference? . . . when I'm governor": Ibid., p. 59.
236 "Roosevelt most positively": *NYT*, Sept. 18, 1898.
236 "Oh, what a howl": LS, "Theodore Roosevelt, Governor," *McClure's* (May 1899), p. 58.
236 "received with becoming meekness": *Commercial Advertiser* (New York), Sept. 19, 1898.
236 "Rough Rider . . . taken prisoner": Ibid.
236 "the master mind . . . damning words": Ibid.
237 "He was pacing . . . of his independence": LS, *The Autobiography*, p. 346.
237 "an inspired account": Harry H. Stein, "Theodore Roosevelt and the Press: Lincoln Steffens," *Mid-America* (April 1972), p. 95.
237 "no one asked": *Commercial Advertiser*, Sept. 20, 1898.
237 "Before you say anything": LS, "Theodore Roosevelt, Governor," *McClure's* (May 1899), p. 59.
237 "that he would be unable": *Commercial Advertiser*, Sept. 20, 1898.
237 "It is hard": LS, "Theodore Roosevelt, Governor," *McClure's* (May 1899), p. 60.
237 "It looked as though . . . allowed to go his way": Ibid.
238 "He stumped the State": Ibid.
238 "The fire and school bells": *NYT*, Oct. 27, 1898.
238 "seventeen feet": *Commercial Advertiser*, Oct. 26, 1898.
238 his "presence was everything": William T. O'Neil to J. S. Van Duzer, Nov. 1, 1898, in *LTR*, Vol. 2, pp. 885–86.
238 "that indefinable 'something' ": *Commercial Advertiser*, Oct. 26, 1898.
238 "probable size . . . an omen of victory": Riis, *Theodore Roosevelt*, pp. 204–05.
238 "Young gentlemen": LS, "The Real Roosevelt," *Ainslee's Magazine* (December 1898), p. 484.

CHAPTER NINE: Governor and Governor General

Page

239 the day Roosevelt was inaugurated: *New York Tribune*, Jan. 3, 1899.

239 "There never was such a mass": New York *World*, Jan. 3, 1899.

239 "the desks and seats": *NYT*, Jan. 3, 1899.

239 "A deafening outburst": Ibid.

239 "stood for a moment . . . touch of human nature": *Boston Daily Globe*, Jan. 3, 1899.

240 "He is a party man . . . first consideration": *New York Tribune*, Jan. 3, 1899.

240 "if we do not work . . . of the people": *NYT*, Jan. 3, 1899.

240 "It was a solemn": EKR to Emily Carow, Jan. 3, 1899, TRC.

240 "physically to cringe . . . as well as the guinea pigs": New York *Sun*, Jan. 1, 1899.

240 "usually an extremely . . . down the room": Parsons, *Perchance Some Day*, p. 123.

240 transforming . . . into a comfortable family home: Morris, *EKR*, p. 193.

241 "If only I could wake": EKR to HCL, January [n.d.], 1899, Lodge-Roosevelt Correspondence, Mass. Hist. Soc.

241 "Edith will never enjoy": TR to Maria Longworth Storer, Feb. 18, 1899, in *LTR*, Vol. 2, p. 949.

241 "perfect taste . . . her mind is made up": *Hayward* [CA] *Review*, Feb. 10, 1899.

241 "Everything about her speaks": *Des Moines* [IA] *Daily News*, Dec. 7, 1900.

241 "There's honor even . . . respect that wish": *Lima* [OH] *Daily News*, Mar. 9, 1899.

241 "represented him": *Sandusky* [OH] *Star*, May 24, 1899.

241 "ever on his feet . . . knows the Governor": "A Day with Governor Roosevelt," *NYT Illustrated Magazine*, April 23, 1899.

242 "plunge at once . . . affairs of the State": Ibid.

242 he would visit New York City: *Commercial Advertiser*, Jan. 23, 1899.

242 "touch Platt": New York *Evening Post*, Oct. 2, 1899.

242 "so belittled . . . some party boss": *The Argus* (Albany, NY), Dec. 14, 1899.

242 "the irrational independents": TR to Maria Longworth Storer, Dec. 2, 1899, in *LTR*, Vol. 2, p. 1101.

242 "solemn reformers . . . sinister": TR, *An Autobiography*, p. 288.

242 "I have met many": TR to Lucius Burrie Swift, Feb. 13, 1900, in *LTR*, Vol. 2, p. 1182.

243 "an understanding . . . reasons for them": LS, *The Autobiography*, p. 351.

243 "T.R. was a very practical": Ibid., p. 349.

243 "appealing directly . . . over the heads": TR, *An Autobiography*, p. 280.

243 "the séance . . . information to draw upon": *Commercial Advertiser*, Jan. 16, 1899.

243 workers would most benefit: G. Wallace Chessman, *Governor Theodore Roosevelt: The Albany Apprenticeship, 1898–1900* (Cambridge, MA: Harvard University Press, 1965), p. 202.

244 "I think that perhaps": TR to Jacob Riis, May 2, 1900, in *LTR*, Vol. 2, p. 1284.

244 "It was on one . . . living in the rooms": Riis, *Theodore Roosevelt*, p. 217.

244 "I do not think . . . in any shape": Ibid., p. 219.

244 to revise the code: Janet B. Pascal, *Jacob Riis: Reporter and Reformer* (Oxford: Oxford University Press, 2005), pp. 145–48.

244 "the grudging and querulous": TR, *An Autobiography*, p. 288.

244 legislation establishing an eight-hour . . . considerable progress: Ibid., p. 289.

245 "We arrived just as": Gifford Pinchot, *Breaking New Ground* (New York: Harcourt, Brace, & Co., 1947), p. 145.

245 "had the honor": Ibid.

245 "was the most important": Douglas Brinkley, *The Wilderness Warrior: Theodore Roosevelt and the Crusade for America* (New York: Harper, 2009), p. 356.

245 "as if it were . . . the Audubon Movement": Ibid., p. 358.

245 "I need hardly say . . . Polybius or Livy": TR to Frank M. Chapman, Feb. 16, 1899, in *LTR*, Vol. 2, p. 948.

246 "got on fairly well": TR, *An Autobiography*, p. 290.

246 "the storm of protest": Ibid., p. 298.

246 "only imperfectly understood . . . the good of the party": Ibid., p. 274.

246 "gentlemen's understanding . . . invisible empire": Ibid., p. 275.

246 "that it was a matter": Ibid., p. 298.

246 "had been suffered": Ibid.

246 "into sudden prominence": *NYT*, Mar. 21, 1899.

246 "radical legislation . . . as its champion": Thomas Platt to TR, May 6, 1899, TRC.

246 "consider the whole question": Ibid.

247 "The time to tax": *New York Tribune*, Mar. 29, 1900.

247 "Roosevelt Stops Franchise Tax": Chessman, *Governor Theodore Roosevelt*, p. 139.

247 "could get a show": TR, *An Autobiography*, p. 302.

247 "It was said to-day . . . He appreciates courage": *Commercial Advertiser*, April 28, 1899.

247 "Right in the solar plexus": Ibid.

247 the stock market suffered a significant drop: Chessman, *Governor Theodore Roosevelt*, p. 147.

247 "You will make . . . not to sign": Thomas Platt to TR, May 6, 1899, TRC.

247 "When the subject . . . various altruistic ideas": Ibid.

247 "Communistic or Socialistic": TR, *An Autobiography*, p. 299.

248 "created a good . . . State of New York": Thomas Platt to TR, May 6, 1899, TRC.

248 "I do not believe . . . the public burdens": TR to Thomas Platt, May 8, 1899, TRC.

248 "under no circumstances": Ibid.

248 "Some of the morning newspapers": *Commercial Advertiser* (New York), May 20, 1899.

249 "any taxes": Chessman, *Governor Theodore Roosevelt*, p. 152.

249 "Persistent efforts . . . just and reasonable": *Commercial Advertiser*, May 29, 1899.
249 "Passage of the amended": Ibid.
249 "Would you let me": TR to WAW, May 25, 1899, in *LTR*, Vol. 2, p. 1015.
249 "a young fellow named": WAW, *The Autobiography*, p. 297.
249 "a tallish . . . physical joy of life": WAW, "Remarks at the Theodore Roosevelt Memorial Association, New York, N.Y.," Oct. 27 [n.y.], White Papers.
250 "We walked": Ibid.
250 "the yearnings . . . of wealth and income": Ibid.
250 "He sounded": WAW, *The Autobiography*, p. 297.
250 "youth . . . into the new": Ibid., p. 298.
250 "the splendor . . . never shall again": Ibid., p. 297.
250 "Between his newspaper": Thaddeus Seymour, Jr., *A Progressive Partnership: Theodore Roosevelt and the Reform Press*, (Madison, WI: University of Wisconsin Press, 1985), pp. 159–60.
250 "I read it with": WAW, *The Autobiography*, p. 299.
250 "with the zeal": Seymour, "A Progressive Partnership: Theodore Roosevelt and the Reform Press," p. 163.
251 In Topeka . . . "a rousing reception": *Kansas City Star*, June 24, 1899.
251 "cannon boomed": Ibid.
251 hatbands promoting Roosevelt: Kohlsaat, *From McKinley to Harding*, p. 77.
251 "No public man": *Emporia* [KS] *Gazette*, June 29, 1899.
251 "Governor Roosevelt": *Kansas City Star*, June 26, 1899.
251 "had a larger crowd": *Emporia* [KS] *Gazette*, June 29, 1899.
251 "without either wiring . . . same thing for me": Kohlsaat, *From McKinley to Harding*, p. 78.
251 "telling of the sentiment": Ibid.
251 "Oh mentor!": TR to Herman H. Kohlsaat, Aug. 12, 1899, in ibid., p. 83.
251 "Was my McKinley": Ibid., p. 81.
252 Roosevelt wrote a warm letter to White: TR to WAW, July 1, 1899, in *LTR*, Vol. 2, p. 1028.
252 "we were planning for 1904": WAW, *The Autobiography*, p. 327.
252 "bearing great fruit . . . of their wisdom": WAW to TR, June 29, 1899, White Papers.
252 "When the war": WAW to TR, Aug. 29, 1901, in WAW and Johnson, eds., *Selected Letters of William Allen White*, p. 41.
252 "I think the 'Man' ": TR to WAW, Oct. 28, 1899, in *LTR*, Vol. 2, p. 1091.
252 "You are among the men": TR to WAW, Feb. 6, 1900, in ibid., p. 1169.
253 "in a great quandary": TR to WAW, Aug. 15, 1899, TRC.
253 "growth of popular unrest": TR to Herman H. Kohlsaat, Aug. 12, 1899, in *LTR*, Vol. 2, p. 1045.
253 "surprised to find . . . the quack": TR to HCL, Aug. 10, 1899, in ibid., p. 1048.
253 "such a good fellow . . . vanished": Ibid., p. 1047.
253 "by means which are utterly": Elihu Root to TR, Dec. 13, 1899, in Philip Jessup, *Elihu Root* (New York: Dodd, Mead & Co., 1938), Vol. 1, p. 209.
253 "Oh, Lord!": TR to Elihu Root, Dec. 15, 1899, in ibid., p. 210.
253 "In our great cities . . . remedies can be applied": *NYT*, Jan. 4, 1900.
254 "The first essential . . . which we can now invoke": Ibid.
254 "the adoption of": Ibid.
254 "the party of . . . enlightened conservatism": Chessman, *Governor Theodore Roosevelt*, p. 157.
254 Odell warned . . . leave New York State: Pringle, *Theodore Roosevelt: A Biography*, p. 211.
254 information on "their structure and finance": Chessman, *Governor Theodore Roosevelt*, p. 174.
255 Platt's "right-hand" man: TR, *An Autobiography*, p. 290.
255 "no matter what": *Commercial Advertiser*, Dec. 12, 1898.
255 "issued an ultimatum . . . made up my mind": TR, *An Autobiography*, p. 291.
255 "Why does he . . . cheek by jowl?": New York *Evening Post*, Jan. 19, 1900.
256 "thoroughly upright and capable": TR to Henry L. Sprague, Jan. 26, 1900, in *LTR*, Vol. 2, p. 1141.
256 "I have always . . . triumph for rascality": TR to Henry L. Sprague, Jan. 26, 1900, in ibid.
256 "The outcome of": *Commercial Advertiser*, Jan. 25, 1900.
256 "honest administration . . . the Colonel before Santiago": New York *Evening Post*, Jan. 29, 1900.
256 "Could they assail . . . they have Roosevelt": *Commercial Advertiser*, Jan. 24, 1900.
256 "the dogs of the *Evening Post*": TR to ARC, Feb. 27, 1900, in TR and ARC, *Letters from Theodore Roosevelt to Anna Roosevelt Cowles*, p. 238.
256 "I value you": TR to Joseph Bucklin Bishop, April 17, 1899, in *LTR*, Vol. 2, pp. 989–90.
256 Roosevelt encouraged Bishop to visit: TR to Joseph Bucklin Bishop, Feb. 16, 1899, in ibid., pp. 947–48.
257 "I will explain": TR to Joseph Bucklin Bishop, April 18, 1899, TRC.
257 "with the most unaffected dread": *NYT*, April 12, 1899.
257 "emphatically not one of the 'fool reformers' ": TR to Joseph Bucklin Bishop, April 14, 1899, in *LTR*, Vol. 2, p. 987.
257 "positive orders to . . . to break down Roosevelt": TR to Lucius Burrie Smith, Feb. 13, 1900, in ibid., p. 1182.
257 "You are about fourteen": TR to Joseph Bucklin Bishop, April 13, 1900, TRC.
257 "I thank Heaven": TR to Joseph Bucklin Bishop, May 2, 1900, TRC.
257 "Good Lord": Ibid.
257 "I need not tell you": TR to Joseph Bucklin Bishop, May 4, 1900, in *LTR*, Vol. 2, p. 1286.
257 "first acquaintance": Finley Peter Dunne, "Remembrance of Theodore Roosevelt," Unpublished MSS, Dunne Papers.
257 "Tis Th' Biography": "Mr. Dooley," *Harper's Weekly*, Nov. 25, 1899.
258 "I regret to state": TR to Finley Peter Dunne, Nov. 28, 1899, in *LTR*, Vol. 2, p. 1099.
258 "I shall be very happy": Finley Peter Dunne to TR, Jan. 10, 1900, TRP.

258 "I never knew": Finley Peter Dunne, "Remembrance of Theodore Roosevelt," Dunne Papers.
258 "Oh, Governor . . . *Alone in Cuba*": Elmer Ellis, *Mr. Dooley's America: A Life of Finley Peter Dunne* (New York: Alfred A. Knopf, 1941), p. 146.
258 "an experiment": LS, "Governor Roosevelt—As an Experiment: Incidents of Conflict in a Term of Practical Politics," *McClure's* (June 1900), p. 109.
258 "the organization doesn't": Ibid., p. 112.
258 "obvious solution . . . and successful too": Ibid.
259 "Your TR article": McClure to LS, Mar. 14, 1899, LS Papers.
259 "would be tempting . . . the party men": TR to George Hinckley-Lyman, Jan. 25, 1900, in *LTR*, Vol. 2, p. 1140.
259 Only "great luck . . . own throat": TR to Henry Clay Payne, Feb. 2, 1900, in ibid., p. 1162.
259 was a fait accompli: TR to George Hinckley-Lyman, Jan. 25, 1900, in ibid., pp. 1139–40.
259 "not an office . . . should achieve nothing": TR to Thomas Platt, Feb. 1, 1900, in ibid., p. 1156.
259 "tempting Providence": TR to ARC, Feb. 2, 1900, in ibid., p. 1159.
259 "the true stepping stone": HCL to TR, Feb. 2, 1900, in TR and HCL, *Selections from the Correspondence*, Vol. 1, p. 444.
259 "in New York . . . figurehead": TR to HCL, Feb. 2, 1900, in *LTR*, Vol. 2, p. 1160.
259 "the money question . . . up all winter": TR to HCL, Jan. 30, 1900, in ibid., p. 1153.
259 a great "comfort": EKR to Emily Carow, Oct. 15, 1899, TRC.
260 "would be a . . . continual anxiety": TR to HCL, Jan. 30, 1900, in *LTR*, Vol. 2, p. 1153.
260 languished in "oblivion": Diana D. Healy, *America's Vice-Presidents: Our First Forty-three Vice-Presidents and How They Got to Be Number Two* (New York: Atheneum, 1984), p. 133.
260 "if the Vice-Presidency": TR to HCL, Jan. 30, 1900, in *LTR*, Vol. 2, p. 1154.
260 "prove to the . . . alone as a nation": TR to H. K. Love, Nov. 24, 1900, in ibid., p. 1442.
260 "a violent departure": *Woodland* [CA] *Daily Democrat*, Dec. 29, 1900.
260 "little better than traitors": TR to HCL, Jan. 26, 1899, in *LTR*, Vol. 2, p. 923.
260 "We shall be branded": TR, "Address on the occasion of the presentation of a sword to Commodore Philip, New York," Feb. 3, 1899, in *WTR*, Vol. 14, p. 312.
260 "would not be pleasant": TR to Maria Longworth Storer, Dec. 2, 1899, in *LTR*, Vol. 2, p. 1101.
260 "emphatically worth doing": TR to HCL, January 22, 1900, in TR and HCL, *Selections from the Correspondence*, Vol. 1, p. 437.
260 "the chief pleasure": TR to Fredéric René Coudert, July 3, 1901, in *LTR*, Vol. 3, p. 105.
261 "if we shrink": TR, *The Strenuous Life: Essays and Addresses* (New York: The Century Co., 1902), pp. 20–21.
261 "the ideal man": HCL to TR, Jan. 27, 1900, in TR and HCL, *Selections from the Correspondence*, Vol. 1, p. 440.
261 irreversibly "planted": TR to HCL, Dec. 11, 1899, in ibid., p. 1107.
261 "declare decisively": TR to HCL, Feb. 2, 1900, in *LTR*, Vol. 2, p. 1160.
261 "There are lots": HCL to TR, April 16, 1900, in TR and HCL, *Selections from the Correspondence*, Vol. 1, p. 459.
261 "You will have . . . office of Vice-President": Wood, *Roosevelt As We Knew Him*, pp. 72–73.
262 "You disagreeable thing . . . not come true": Ibid., pp. 73–74.
262 she and Theodore had had more time together: Morris, *EKR*, p. 200.
262 "I really think": TR to HCL, Aug. 28, 1899, in *LTR*, Vol. 2, p. 1062.
262 "the county fair business": TR to Bellamy Storer, Sept. 11, 1899, in ibid., p. 1068.
262 "You gave my wife . . . every word": Wood, *Roosevelt As We Knew Him*, p. 74.
262 "an even chance . . . any outside ambition": TR to ARC, April 30, 1900, in *LTR*, Vol. 2, p. 1277.
262 "vociferous applause . . . Teddy, Teddy, Teddy": *Washington Times*, June 17, 1900.
262 "There'll Be a Hot": *St. Louis Republic*, June 17, 1900.
262 "he had reason . . . invaded" his room: *New York Tribune*, June 18, 1900.
263 "Round and round . . . drum and bugle": CRR, *My Brother*, p. 197.
263 "Don't you realize": TR to William McKinley, addendum, June 21, 1900, in *LTR*, Vol. 2, p. 1337.
263 "There is not a man": *Washington Times*, June 18, 1900.
263 "These fellows have . . . 'Vice-President'": New York *World*, June 18, 1900.
263 "If you decline": Ibid.
263 "the sun shone brightly": New York *Sun*, June 20, 1900.
263 "the magic . . . of the tumult": *NYT*, June 22, 1900.
263 "when he caught": *New York Tribune*, June 22, 1900.
263 the demonstration subsided: *NYT*, June 22, 1900.
263 "We stand on": TR, "Speech Before the Twelfth Republican National Convention, Philadelphia, Pa., June 21, 1900," in *WTR*, Vol. 14, p. 345.
263 "of rounded periods . . . was beyond them": *New York Tribune*, June 22, 1900.
264 "a little melancholy": TR to Henry White, July 7, 1900, in *LTR*, Vol. 2, p. 1349.
264 "should be a conceited fool": TR to HCL, June 25, 1900, in ibid., p. 1340.
264 "His friends were in despair": Riis, *Theodore Roosevelt*, p. 236.
264 "Oh, how I hate": Parsons, *Perchance Some Day*, p. 134.
264 "had hoped to the last": Hagedorn, *The Roosevelt Family of Sagamore Hill*, p. 89.
264 "get the rest": EKR to Emily Carow, June 22, 1900, TRC.
264 a telegraph boy knocked: WHT, "Address before the National Geographic Society," Washington, DC, Nov. 14, 1913, WHTP.
264 "important business . . . suppose that means?": HHT, *Recollections of Full Years*, p. 32.
264 "He might as well": Pringle, *Life and Times*, Vol. 1, p. 160.
264 "strongly opposed": HHT, *Recollections of Full Years*, p. 32.
264 "contrary to our traditions": Pringle, *Life and Times*, Vol. 1, p. 160.
264 "beside the question . . . governing themselves": HHT, *Recollections of Full Years*, pp. 33–34.

265 "under the most sacred": Pringle, *Life and Times*, Vol. 1, p. 160.
265 "Well . . . you'll be here": WHT to Henry W. Taft and Horace Taft, Jan. 28, 1900, Pringle Papers.
265 "You have had": HHT, *Recollections of Full Years*, p. 34.
265 "didn't sleep a wink . . . climate of Manila": Charles E. Barker, *With President Taft in the White House: Memories of William Howard Taft* (Chicago: A. Kroch & Son, 1947), pp. 23–24.
265 "so grave . . . impeachment": HHT, *Recollections of Full Years*, p. 33.
265 "Yes, of course . . . novel experience": Ibid.
265 "You can do more good": Horace Taft to WHT, Jan. 31, 1900, WHTP.
265 "the rest of . . . [his] colleagues": Henry W. Taft to WHT, Jan. 30, 1900, WHTP.
266 "responsible for success or failure": Pringle, *Life and Times*, Vol. 1, p. 161.
266 "the hardest thing he ever did": HHT, *Recollections of Full Years*, p. 35.
266 "the Philippines business": TR to HCL, Feb. 3, 1900, in *LTR*, Vol. 2, p. 1166.
266 "a very hard . . . to advise with": TR to WHT, Jan. 31, 1899, in ibid., p. 927.
266 "I wish there was": TR to Maria Longworth Storer, Dec. 2, 1899, in ibid., p. 1101.
266 rejoiced in his "final triumph": WHT to TR, Feb. 15, 1900, TRP.
266 "Curiously enough": TR to WHT, Feb. 7, 1900, in *LTR*, Vol. 2, p. 1175.
266 "That it was alluring": HHT, *Recollections of Full Years*, p. 33.
267 "Robert was ten": Ibid., pp. 36–37.
267 "We soon became": Ibid., p. 39.
267 "the most interesting years": Ibid., p. 40.
267 "one of the ablest": Ibid., p. 41.
267 a New England judge . . . and a historian: Ibid., pp. 41–45.
267 relished "the bonds of friendship": Ibid., p. 40.
267 "The populace": Pringle, *Life and Times*, Vol. 1, p. 169.
268 "as a personal reflection": WHT, "Address before the National Geographic Society," Washington, DC, Nov. 14, 1913, WHTP.
268 "We are civil officers . . . as to anyone": Press statement enclosed in WHT to Charles P. Taft, June 2, 1900, WHTP.
268 "the precise kind . . . loftiest of motives": *Harper's Weekly* clipping enclosed in Horace Taft to WHT, July 14, 1900, WHTP.
268 "high canopied . . . would be served": HHT, *Recollections of Full Years*, pp. 102–3, 105.
268 "homely and unpalatial abode": Ibid., p. 211.
269 the large library of books on civil law: WHT to Charles Taft, June 23, 1900, WHTP.
269 At ten o'clock . . . "who wish[ed] to see them": WHT to Charles Taft, July 25, 1900, WHTP.
269 At one o'clock . . . foot for their homes: WHT to Harriet Herron, Jan. 19, 1901, WHTP.
269 "The walk is about . . . strong at meals": Ibid.
269 "policy of conciliation": WHT, "Address before the National Geographic Society," Washington, DC, Nov. 14, 1913, WHTP.
269 "our little brown brothers . . . no friend of mine!": HHT, *Recollections of Full Years*, p. 125.
269 "agitation and discontent": Pringle, *Life and Times*, Vol. 1, p. 177.
269 to treat the Filipinos as "niggers": WHT to Charles P. Taft, June 2, 1900, WHTP.
269 "It is a great mistake": HHT to WHT, July 21, 1900, WHTP.
270 "except a select military circle": HHT, *Recollections of Full Years*, p. 109.
270 "even small gestures": Anthony, *Nellie Taft*, p. 141.
270 "made it a rule": HHT, *Recollections of Full Years*, p. 114.
270 "We always had": Ibid., p. 125.
270 insistence "upon complete racial equality": HHT quoted in Anthony, *Nellie Taft*, p. 248.
270 Filipinos of "wealth and position": WHT to HHT, July 8, 1900, WHTP.
270 "To say that": WHT to Charles P. Taft, June 13, 1901, WHTP.
270 spending a small inheritance: Anthony, *Nellie Taft*, p. 141.
270 "giving [the] wealthy": Pringle, *Life and Times*, Vol. 1, p. 194.
270 "precursors of . . . and binoculars": Stanley Karnow, *In Our Image: America's Empire in the Philippines* (New York: Random House, 1989), p. 196.
270 "enter upon some work": WHT to HHT, July 2, 1900, WHTP.
270 Philippine Constabulary Band . . . international renown: Anthony, *Nellie Taft*, pp. 156–57.
271 the reduction of infant mortality in Manila: Ibid., p. 155.
271 "in the interest of": Ibid., p. 154.
271 He likened her activism: WHT to HHT, June 12, 1900, WHTP.
271 "I wish to record": WHT to HHT, June 18 & 19, 1900, WHTP.
271 "with undisguised surprise": WHT to Charles P. Taft, Aug. 31, 1900, WHTP.
271 had met "congenial companions": HHT, *Recollections of Full Years*, p. 217.
271 "everybody in the world": Ibid., p. 98.
271 Charlie, nicknamed "the tornado": Ibid., p. 54.
271 "an old fashioned quadrille": Ibid., p. 166.
271 "literally dancing": Walter Wellman, "Taft, Trained to Be President," *American Review of Reviews* (June 1908).
271 "unusual size . . . superiority": LTT to WHT, July 9, 1900, WHTP.
272 "a good government . . . prosperous" economy: WHT to HHT, June 15, 1900, WHTP.
272 "ignorant, superstitious people": Pringle, *Life and Times*, Vol. 1, p. 173.
272 "Not that I am": WHT to Annie Roelker, Jan. 19, 1901, WHTP.
272 "a good deal to carry . . . to the campaign": WHT to Charles P. Taft, June 30, 1900, WHTP.
272 "draw in line": Charles P. Taft to WHT, June 23, 1900, WHTP.

272 "I could wish . . . Filipinos as well": WHT to TR, June 27, 1900, TRP.
272 "any help . . . be vice-president": TR to WHT, Aug. 6, 1900, in *LTR*, Vol. 2, p. 1377.
272 "as strong as . . . up to the limit": TR to MAH, June 27, 1900, in ibid., p. 1342.
272 "No candidate . . . on the American stump": Thomas Collier Platt and Louis J. Lang, *The Autobiography of Thomas Collier Platt* (New York: B. W. Dodge & Co., 1910), pp. 396–97.
273 Throughout the evening: *NYT*, Nov. 7, 1900.
273 "tiptoes with excitement . . . McKinley": HHT, *Recollections of Full Years*, p. 141.
273 "My dear Theodore": WHT to TR, Nov. [n.d.], 1900, TRP.
273 "Hardly a day passed": HHT, *Recollections of Full Years*, p. 147.
273 "The attitude of the native": WHT to Charles P. Taft, Jan. 29, 1901, WHTP.
273 "The leaders in Manila . . . welcome a change": WHT to HCL, Jan. 7, 1901, WHTP.
274 "Of course" . . . they came along as well: WHT to Charles Taft, Mar. 17, 1901, WHTP.
274 "greatly pleased . . . friendliest kind of attitude": HHT, *Recollections of Full Years*, p. 154.
274 The desire . . . "manifest on every side": WHT to Horace Taft, April 25, 1901, WHTP.
274 "the streets were crowded": HHT, *Recollections of Full Years*, p. 162.
274 "Spectacular" festivities . . . celebrated their progress: Ibid., pp. 162–65.
274 "a singular experience": Ibid., p. 181.
274 "The responsibilities . . . taking control of things": WHT to TR, May 12, 1901, TRP.
274 "I envy you . . . justifying my existence": TR to WHT, Mar. 12, 1901, in *LTR*, Vol. 3, p. 11.
274 "sympathize with . . . top to the bottom": TR to Maria and Bellamy Storer, April 17, 1901, in ibid., p. 56.
275 "ought to be abolished . . . any advice": TR to Leonard Wood, April 17, 1901, in ibid., p. 59.
275 "I am rather . . . unwarrantable idleness": TR to WHT, April 26, 1901, in ibid., pp. 68–69.
275 "I look forward": WHT to TR, May 12, 1901, TRP.
275 "I doubt if . . . old man": TR to WHT, Mar. 12, 1901, in *LTR*, Vol. 3, p. 12.
275 "music, fireworks": *New Castle* [PA] *News*, July 3, 1901.
275 "an occasion of . . . his natural size": HHT, *Recollections of Full Years*, pp. 206–7.
276 "a new step . . . popular basis": WHT, "Inaugural Address as Civil Governor of the Philippines," Manila, July 4, 1901, WHTP.
276 democracy "from the top down": Bradley, *The Imperial Cruise*, p. 121.
276 "feudal oligarchy . . . rich and poor": Karnow, *In Our Image*, p. 198.
276 "the wildest . . . of the new governor": *Daily Northwestern* (Oshkosh, WI), July 5, 1901.
276 "In some ways . . . was actually established": HHT, *Recollections of Full Years*, pp. 211–12.
276 "the idea of living": Ibid., p. 212.
276 "all of them . . . bank of the Pasig": Ibid., p. 213.
276 "Army and Navy people . . . among our guests": Ibid., p. 217.
277 "a great society beau": HHT to Harriet Herron, Sept. 2, 1901, WHTP.
277 "You would be amused": HHT to Jennie Anderson, July 17, 1901, in Phyllis Robbins, *Robert A. Taft, Boy and Man* (Cambridge, MA: Dresser, Chapman & Grimes, 1963), p. 67.
277 "It seems idle . . . to say this in public": TR to WHT, July 15, 1901, in *LTR*, Vol. 3, pp. 120–21.
277 professor of history at a university: TR to Hugo Munsterberg, May 7, 1901, in ibid., p. 72.
278 "Of course, I may": TR to Leonard Wood, Mar. 27, 1901, in ibid., p. 39.

CHAPTER TEN: "That Damned Cowboy Is President"

Page
279 "The ship of state": "President McKinley's Death," *The Nation*, Sept. 19, 1901, p. 218.
279 "What changes": *Washington Post*, Sept. 15, 1901, in Arnold, *Remaking the Presidency*, p. 39.
279 "Will he continue": *Minneapolis Journal*, Sept. 15, 1901.
279 prove a "bucking bronco": Kohlsaat, *From McKinley to Harding*, p. 98.
280 "first great duty": New York *Sun*, Sept. 15, 1901, in Mark Sullivan, *Our Times: The United States, 1900–1925* (New York: Charles Scribner's Sons, 1926), Vol. 2, p. 403.
280 presidents had been captive: See Arnold, *Remaking the Presidency*, p. 3.
280 "not depend on": New York *Sun*, Sept. 15, 1901, in Sullivan, *Our Times*, Vol. 2, p. 403.
280 "The conservative policy": *Boston Sunday Globe*, Sept. 15, 1901.
280 "dreaded radicalism . . . was progressive": TR, *An Autobiography*, p. 351.
280 "push . . . the masters of both of us": Ibid., p. 352.
280 "active support": Ibid., p. 354.
280 "one in purpose": *Atlanta Constitution*, Sept. 14, 1901.
280 "In this hour": *New York Tribune*, Sept. 17, 1901.
280 "an unusual request": George Juergens, "Theodore Roosevelt and the Press," *Daedalus* (Fall 1981), p. 113.
281 "keep them posted . . . not to be published": David S. Barry, *Forty Years in Washington* (Boston: Little, Brown, 1924), p. 268.
281 "I am President": Ibid., p. 267.
281 "pop-eyed . . . burning candor": WAW, "Remarks," Oct. 27 [n.y.], White Papers.
281 "be different . . . absolutely unchanged": Ibid.
281 "embarrass him sorely": Rixey, *Bamie*, p. 172.
281 "give the lie": Ibid.
281 "cataract solo of talk": WAW, "Remarks," Oct. 27 [n.y.], White Papers.
281 "Imagine me": Ibid.
281 "the old cannon": WAW, *The Autobiography*, p. 339.

281 “Here you are”: TR to WAW, Mar. 12, 1901, in *LTR*, Vol. 3, pp. 10–11.
282 “a frowzy little . . . North at that time”: WAW, *The Autobiography*, p. 335.
282 “about his own . . . wreck the machines”: Ibid.
282 “untrammeled” greed: WAW, *Emporia* [KS] *Gazette*, Sept. 7, 1901, cited in Johnson, *William Allen White's America*, p. 127.
282 “We reformers . . . that had come to him”: LS, *The Autobiography*, pp. 502–3.
282 “Unconsciously . . . a bitter piece”: WAW, *The Autobiography*, pp. 339–40.
283 “too scorching”: WAW to August Jaccaci, Oct. 23, 1901, in WAW and Johnson, eds., *Selected Letters of William Allen White*, p. 45.
283 “to bring order . . . purchase of privileges”: WAW, “Platt,” *McClure's* (December 1901), pp. 149–50.
283 an earthworm, “boring . . . inexorable, grinding”: Ibid., pp. 148, 153.
283 “to haul both author”: *Titusville* [PA] *Morning Herald*, Dec. 19, 1901.
283 “I will get”: WAW to John S. Phillips, Dec. 17, 1901, White Papers.
283 “to bring about”: Johnson, *William Allen White's America*, p. 135.
283 “who told him the lies”: New York *World*, Dec. 19, 1901.
283 “No friend of mine”: *Washington Post*, Dec. 18, 1901.
283 “I am perfectly . . . this business out”: WAW to TR, Dec. 17, 1901, White Papers.
284 “Not one syllable . . . by the president”: WAW to George B. Cortelyou, Dec. 18, 1901, TRC.
284 “The only damage”: TR to WAW, Dec. 31, 1901, in *LTR*, Vol. 3, p. 214.
284 “they would welcome”: Johnson, *William Allen White's America*, p. 135.
284 “a kind of nervous . . . you all out so”: WAW to August Jaccaci, Jan. 21, 1902, White Papers.
284 “Probably no administration”: Irwin H. Hoover, *Forty-two Years in the White House* (Boston: Houghton Mifflin, 1934), p. 27.
284 “While he is in”: Sullivan, *Our Times*, Vol. 3, pp. 72–73.
284 “The infectiousness”: Ibid., Vol. 2, p. 399.
285 “Where Mr. McKinley . . . never means to do so”: Walter Wellman, *Chicago Record-Herald*, reprinted in the *Piqua* [OH] *Daily Call*, Nov. 20, 1901.
285 “a right good laugh . . . listens to nobody”: Ibid.
285 “darts into the”: LS, “The Overworked President,” *McClure's* (April 1902), p. 485.
285 “one letter after another”: Parsons, *Perchance Some Day*, p. 141.
285 “The room is”: LS, “The Overworked President,” *McClure's* (April 1902), p. 486.
285 “an overflowing stream”: Ibid., p. 489.
285 “to try the President's”: *NYT*, Sept. 29, 1901.
285 the “barber's hour”: LS, *The Autobiography*, p. 509.
286 “A more skillful”: Louis Brownlow, *A Passion for Politics: The Autobiography of Louis Brownlow: First Half* (Chicago: University of Chicago Press, 1955), p. 399.
286 Only “when the barber”: LS, *The Autobiography*, p. 510.
286 “Western bullwackers”: WAW, *Masks in a Pageant* (New York: The Macmillan Co., 1928), p. 306.
286 “Whether the subject . . . equally at home”: Wagenknecht, *Seven Worlds*, p. 32.
286 “point to point . . . down over it”: Ibid., p. 14.
286 “finger-marks”: Jacob Riis, “Mrs. Roosevelt and Her Children,” *Ladies' Home Journal* (August 1902), p. 6.
286 “this or that general”: AB to his mother, Oct. 10, 1908, in Abbott, ed., *Letters of Archie Butt*, p. 119.
286 “in afternoon dress . . . should meet ladies”: Thayer, *Theodore Roosevelt: An Intimate Biography*, pp. 262–63.
287 “by far the best . . . under discussion”: Oscar King Davis, *Released for Publication: Some Inside Political History of Theodore Roosevelt and His Times, 1898–1918* (Boston: Houghton Mifflin, 1925), p. 128.
287 “allowed to become”: Riis, “Mrs. Roosevelt and Her Children,” *Ladies' Home Journal* (August 1902), p. 5.
287 “I play bear”: TR to Alice Lee Roosevelt, Nov. 29, 1901, in *LTR*, Vol. 3, p. 203.
287 “It was the gloomiest”: “Mrs. Roosevelt's Address,” Oct. 20, 1933, *Roosevelt House Bulletin* (Fall 1933), pp. 2–3.
287 The children . . . pony to ride the elevator: Hoover, *Forty-two Years in the White House*, p. 29; Juergens, “Theodore Roosevelt and the Press,” *Daedalus* (Fall 1982), p. 124; Isabella Hagner James, “Memoirs of Isabella Hagner, 1901–1905,” *White House History: Journal of the White House Historical Association*, No. 26, p. 61.
287 “Places that had not”: Hoover, *Forty-two Years in the White House*, p. 28.
287 “done more to brighten”: *Atlanta Constitution*, Oct. 24, 1901.
287 Taft was certain that Roosevelt: WHT to William C. McFarland, Sept. 20, 1901, WHTP.
288 “impulsiveness and”: WHT to Joseph Bucklin Bishop, Sept. 20, 1901, in Pringle, *Life and Times*, Vol. 1, p. 211.
288 citing the fortitude, honesty, and intelligence: WHT to Elihu Root, Sept. 26, 1901, in ibid.; WHT to Rev. Rainsford, Sept. 20, 1901, Pringle Papers.
288 to see “the consummation”: TR to Joseph Bucklin Bishop, Sept. 20, 1901, in Pringle, *Life and Times*, Vol. 1, p. 210.
288 “In so far as the work”: HHT, *Recollections of a Full Life*, p. 224.
288 “only a strenuous man”: Horace Taft to WHT, Oct. 14, 1901, WHTP.
288 “I dislike speaking . . . incredibly difficult work”: TR, “Governor William H. Taft,” *Outlook* (September 1901), p. 166.
288 Unbeknownst to the Americans: Karnow, *In Our Image*, p. 189.
288 hundreds of insurrectionists suddenly charged: Ibid., p. 190.
289 “It was a disaster . . . in our beds any night”: HHT, *Recollections of a Full Life*, p. 225.
289 “silly talk”: Karnow, *In Our Image*, p. 191.
289 “no prisoners . . . Ten years”: Ibid.
289 “Disastrous Fight . . . Slaughtered by Filipinos”: *New York Tribune*, Sept. 30, 1901; *Houston Daily Post*, Sept. 30, 1901.
289 “the first severe reverse”: *The News* (Frederick, MD), September 30, 1901.

289 "One of the Republicans": WHT to Charles P. Taft, Oct. 15, 1901, WHTP.

289 "in all other parts": WHT to Murat Halstead, Sept. 20, 1901, WHTP.

289 "to such a pitch": WHT to Charles P. Taft, Oct. 15, 1901, WHTP.

289 "Officers take": TR to Horace Taft, Oct. 21, 1901, in Pringle, *Life and Times*, Vol. 1, p. 213.

290 "a dreadful depression": WHT to TR, Sept. 13, 1902, TRP.

290 roving outlaw bands . . . new Board of Health: WHT to Murat Halstead, Sept. 20, 1901, WHTP.

290 "Altogether": WHT to Charles P. Taft, Oct. 15, 1901, WHTP.

290 "While I have none": WHT to Horace Taft, Oct. 21, 1901, WHTP.

290 Helen burst into tears: WHT to Charles P. Taft, Nov. 8, 1901, WHTP.

290 "Come dear am sick": WHT to HHT, Oct. 25, 1901, in Pringle, *Life and Times*, Vol. 1, p. 214.

290 "hire a hall and make a speech": WHT to Charles P. Taft, Nov. 8, 1901, WHTP.

290 "Much better": WHT to HHT, Oct. 26, 1901, in Pringle, *Life and Times*, Vol. 1, p. 214.

290 "peace of mind": WHT to Charles P. Taft, Nov. 8, 1901, WHTP.

290 promising them he would return: James A. Leroy, "Governor Taft's Record in the Philippines," *The Independent*, Jan. 28, 1904, p. 194.

291 "the high summer" . . . Hundreds . . . consolidated into single corporations: George E. Mowry, *Theodore Roosevelt and the Progressive Movement* (Madison: University of Wisconsin Press, 1946), p. 12.

291 "I intend to work": Bishop, *Theodore Roosevelt and His Time*, p. 150.

291 These organizations: WAW, "Platt," *McClure's* (December 1901), p. 150.

291 "just as he would": *NYT*, Jan. 17, 1890.

292 "Wake up . . . lots in the Senate": Lewis L. Gould, *The Most Exclusive Club: A History of the Modern United States Senate* (New York: Basic Books, 2005), p. 10.

292 the title of "national boss": Samuel J. Blythe, "The Passing of the Big Bosses," *Saturday Evening Post*, Feb. 25, 1922, p. 9.

292 "the liaison": Sullivan, *Our Times*, Vol. 2, p. 372.

292 not a single anti-trust suit: Ibid.

292 "In the final analysis": LS, "Great Types of Modern Business & Politics," *Ainslee's Magazine* (October 1901), p. 216.

292 "I told William . . . of the United States!": Sullivan, *Our Times*, Vol. 2, p. 380.

292 "it would be a great": TR to LS, June 24, 1905, in *LTR*, Vol. 4, p. 1254.

292 "would be as foolhardy": New York *World*, Nov. 29, 1901.

292 share an intimacy similar: Sullivan, *Our Times*, Vol. 2, p. 392.

292 "Go slow": Bishop, *Theodore Roosevelt and His Time*, Vol. 1, p. 154.

292 "It would not": TR to MAH, Oct. 16, 1901, in *LTR*, Vol. 3, p. 176.

292 "his was the rising": Sullivan, *Our Times*, Vol. 2, p. 400.

293 "I hope to keep": Nathaniel Wright Stephenson, *Nelson W. Aldrich: A Leader in American Politics* (New York: Charles Scribner's Sons, 1930), p. 175.

293 "a very pretty scene": *Piqua* [OH] *Daily Call*, Nov. 20, 1901.

293 "made more progress": *Decatur* [IL] *Daily Review*, Nov. 2, 1901.

293 "Many scribes": *Daily Nevada State Journal* (Reno, NV), Nov. 21, 1901.

293 "one hair's breadth": TR to Douglas Robinson, Oct. 17, 1901, in *LTR*, Vol. 3, p. 177.

293 "More and more": *Galveston* [TX] *Daily News*, Sept. 3, 1901.

293 "going so far as": Louis A. Coolidge, *An Old-Fashioned Senator: Orville H. Platt, of Connecticut* (New York: G. P. Putnam's Sons, 1910), pp. 445–46.

294 "furnish ammunition . . . in corporate control": Pringle, *Theodore Roosevelt: A Biography*, p. 244.

294 "very fond . . . companies as a right": TR to Douglas Robinson, Oct. 4, 1901, in *LTR*, Vol. 3, pp. 159–60.

294 "not prying into": Eric F. Goldman, "Public Relations and the Progressive Surge, 1898–1917," Institute for Public Relations, Annual Address, Nov. 19, 1965.

294 "I much enjoyed": TR to Douglas Robinson, Oct. 4, 1901, in *LTR*, Vol. 3, p. 160.

294 "the proposition . . . to undertake it": Paul Dana to TR, Nov. 15, 1901, WHTP.

294 "Your letter causes": TR to Paul Dana, Nov. 18, 1901, in *LTR*, Vol. 3, p. 200.

295 "A hush immediately . . . unusual attention": *Washington Times*, Dec. 4, 1901.

295 "with scant courtesy": Bishop, *Theodore Roosevelt and His Time*, Vol. 1, p. 161.

295 "a professed anarchist . . . good and bad alike": TR, "First Annual Message," in Hermann Hagedorn, ed., *State Papers as Governor and President*, Vol. 15 of *WTR*, pp. 84, 81.

295 "The captains of industry . . . reasonable limits controlled": Ibid., pp. 88–89, 90–91.

295 "Th' trusts": Sullivan, *Our Times*, Vol. 2, p. 411.

296 "It is no limitation" . . . touched "the hearts": TR, "First Annual Message," *WTR*, Vol. 15, pp. 91–92, 93, 138.

296 "No other message": "President Roosevelt's Message," *The Independent*, Dec. 12, 1901, p. 2967.

296 "characteristic of the man": *Public Opinion*, Dec. 12, 1901.

296 "skeptical of any . . . over the trusts": *Public Opinion*, Sept. 4, 1901.

296 "refreshing": *Public Opinion*, Dec. 12, 1901.

297 this vast new combination . . . touched a nerve: *New York Herald*, Feb. 20, 1902.

297 "had come to see . . . and financial side": RSB, *American Chronicle*, p. 165.

297 "revolutionary . . . crusading": Ibid., p. 166.

297 "a yearly income . . . the highest purpose": RSB, "J. Pierpont Morgan," *McClure's* (October 1901), pp. 2, 10.

297 "were unquestionably . . . ever been seen before": RSB, "What the U.S. Steel Corporation Really Is, and How It Works," *McClure's* (November 1901).

298 "the contestants gathered . . . the wreath of power?": RSB, "The Great Northern Pacific Deal," *Collier's*, Nov. 30, 1901.

298 "more powerful than": Sullivan, *Our Times*, Vol. 2, pp. 417–18.
298 Roosevelt asked . . . Philander C. Knox: *NYT*, Feb. 20, 1902.
298 A brilliant lawyer: Anita T. Eitler, *Philander Chase Knox, First Attorney-General of Theodore Roosevelt, 1901–1904* (Washington, DC: Catholic University of America Press, 1959), pp. 1–2.
298 "the view that Taft": Pringle, *Theodore Roosevelt: A Biography*, p. 255.
299 "to test the validity": *New York Herald*, Feb. 20, 1902.
299 "like a thunderbolt": *Washington Post*, Feb. 21, 1902.
299 "a wholesale war . . . it was wholly unprepared": *New York Herald*, Feb. 21, 1902.
299 "If we have done . . . a big rival operator": Bishop, *Theodore Roosevelt in His Own Time*, Vol. 1, pp. 184–85.
299 "It really seems hard": Sullivan, *Our Times*, Vol. 2, p. 415.
299 "an unknown country . . . is ended": Bishop, *Theodore Roosevelt in His Own Time*, Vol. 1, p. 183.
299 "the power of the mighty": TR, *An Autobiography*, pp. 423–24.
299 "served notice": Wister, *Roosevelt, The Story of a Friendship*, p. 210.
299 "that he was President": William H. Harbaugh, *Power and Responsibility: The Life and Times of Theodore Roosevelt* (New York: Farrar, Straus & Cudahy, 1961), p. 160.
299 turned his attention to the beef trust: *NYT*, April 15, 1902.
300 "an atrocious conspiracy": New York *World*, April 26, 1902.
300 "that such absolute control": New York *World*, April 30, 1902.
300 "This is the right course": New York *World*, April 26, 1902.
300 "more dangerous to": TR, "Speech in Providence, R.I., August 23, 1902," in *Outlook*, Sept. 13, 1902, p. 113.
300 distinguish *good* trusts . . . from *bad* trusts: TR, *An Autobiography*, p. 433.
300 "with the path": George E. Mowry, *The Era of Theodore Roosevelt* (New York: Harper Bros., 1958), p. 133.
300 "a period of": HHT, *Recollections of Full Years*, p. 233.
300 "opened and drained": WHT to Horace Taft, Jan. 6, 1902, WHTP.
300 their cross-country trip . . . had died the previous day: HHT, *Recollections of Full Years*, pp. 233–34.
301 "just the same . . . looks or manner": WHT to HHT, Jan. 30, 1902, WHTP.
301 without an invitation to dine: WHT to HHT, Feb. 20, 1902, WHTP.
301 "If General Chafee": *Chillicothe* [MO] *Constitution*, Jan. 17, 1902.
301 "compassion and merciful": WHT to Horace Taft, Jan. 30, 1902, WHTP.
301 "I have much more": Henry F. Graff, ed., *American Imperialism and the Philippine Insurrection: Testimony Taken from Hearings on Affairs in the Philippine Islands Before the Senate Committee on the Philippines, 1902* (Boston: Little, Brown, 1969), p. 121.
301 "flying in the face": Ibid., p. 46.
301 "somewhat intimate relations": Ibid., p. 155.
301 "but we are there": Ibid., p. 48.
301 America's primary responsibility: Ibid., p. 37.
302 "too progressive . . . educational school": WHT, "Civil Government in the Philippines," *Outlook*, May 31, 1902, pp. 313–14.
302 "that cruelties have been": Graff, ed., *American Imperialism*, p. 92.
302 uncommon "compassion" and "restraint": Ibid., p. 95.
302 "Following his appearance . . . task in hand": Leroy, "Governor Taft's Record in the Philippines," *The Independent*, Jan. 28, 1904, p. 195.
302 "there was not anything": WHT to HHT, Feb. 24, 1902, WHTP.
302 "I have been hacked": WHT to HHT, Feb. 3, 1902, WHTP.
302 "the cure seems to be complete": WHT to Horace Taft, April 20, 1902, WHTP.
302 "the crown of Spain . . . were imprisoned": WHT, "Civil Government in the Philippines," *Outlook*, May 31, 1902, p. 319.
303 "What a splendid": HHT to WHT, Feb. 24, 1902, WHTP.
303 In the weeks before the planned trip: Anthony, *Nellie Taft*, p. 167.
303 "What a disarrangement": WHT to HHT, April 23, 1902, WHTP.
303 "Within twenty-four hours . . . pleasure and pride": HHT, *Recollections of Full Years*, p. 237.
303 "lively . . . with humor": Pringle, *Life and Times*, Vol. 1, p. 228.
303 "in a broad spirit": WHT to HHT, June 10, 1902, WHTP.
304 Weeks went by . . . negotiations were suspended: Pringle, *Life and Times*, Vol. 1, p. 230.
304 "would have run its course": HHT, *Recollections of Full Years*, p. 250.
304 "I don't know how": WHT to HHT, July 26, 1902, WHTP.
304 "I can not tell": WHT to HHT, Aug. 5, 1902, WHTP.
304 Taft's arrival triggered: *Minneapolis Journal*, Aug. 23, 1902.
304 Thirty thousand Filipinos . . . "the government was assured": *Washington Times*, Aug. 23, 1902.
304 "as a real effort": WHT to TR, Sept. 13, 1902, WHTP.
304 he promised to work unremittingly: *Sandusky* [OH] *Star*, May 24, 1899.
304 "universal, earnest . . . the Filipino people": *Salt Lake Tribune*, Aug. 24, 1902.
305 "I am in the worst . . . calumnies": TR to H. H. Kohlsaat, Aug. 4, 1902, in Kohlsaat, *From McKinley to Harding*, pp. 110–11.
305 "As things have turned out": TR to WHT, July 31, 1902, WHTP.
305 "While the result": WHT to TR, Sept. 13, 1902, WHTP.
305 "no house of representatives . . . they sang 'Dixie' ": *The News* (Frederick, MD), July 2, 1902.
306 "By far the most important": TR, *An Autobiography*, p. 512.
306 "a keen personal pride": TR to Ethan A. Hitchcock, June 17, 1902 in *LTR*, Vol. 3, p. 277.
306 to enable small farmers to settle: TR, *An Autobiography*, p. 396.

306 "I regard": TR to Ethan A. Hitchcock, June 17, 1902 in *LTR*, Vol. 3, p. 277.
306 more than half a million dollars: Abby G. Baker, "The White House of the Twentieth Century," Oct. 22, 1903, *The Independent*, p. 2499.
306 "trembled when one walked": William Seale, *The President's House: A History* (Washington, DC: White House Hist. Assoc., 1988), Vol. 2, p. 657.
306 "had the determination": Morris, *EKR*, p. 242.
306 The plans . . . a library, and a den: *The New North* (Rhinelander, WI), June 12, 1902.
307 "I ask that": *Post-Standard* (Syracuse, NY), June 14, 1902.
307 "Their conduct": Joseph Bucklin Bishop to TR, June 21, 1902, WHTP.
307 "in alliance with the trusts": *The Indianapolis Sentinel*, Sept. 4, 1902.
307 "destroy all our prosperity": TR, "Speech in Fitchburg, Mass., August 23, 1902," *Outlook*, Sept. 13, 1902, p. 120.
307 "the average man . . . standard of comfort": TR, "Speech in Providence, R.I., August 23, 1902," *Outlook*, Sept. 13, 1902, p. 114.
307 "a sympathetic ear . . . unfocused discontent": Leroy G. Dorsey, "Reconstituting the American Spirit: Theodore Roosevelt's Rhetorical Presidency," PhD diss., Indiana University, 1993, pp. 181–82.
308 "full power . . . self-restraint": TR, "Speech in Providence, R.I., August 23, 1902," in *Outlook*, Sept. 13, 1902, p. 115.
308 From Rhode Island . . . overwhelming fervor: *Public Opinion*, Sept. 4, 1902.
308 "The booming . . . their holiday clothes": *Daily Times* (New Brunswick, NJ), Aug. 27, 1902.
308 "when the streets were not": *Boston Daily Globe*, Aug. 24, 1902.
308 "small towns": *Galveston* [TX] *Daily News*, Aug. 24, 1902.
308 William Craig, was caught: New York *World*, Sept. 4, 1902; *Washington Times*, Sept. 4, 1902.
308 "It was a dreadful": New York *World*, Sept. 4, 1902.
308 "I'm all right . . . too bad, too bad": *Washington Times*, Sept. 4, 1902.
308 "Gallop ahead": New York *World*, Sept. 4, 1902.
308 a "memorable conference": Stephenson, *Nelson W. Aldrich*, p. 194.
309 a resolution . . . that linked tariffs to trusts: *Sioux County Herald* (Orange City, IA), Sept. 19, 1902.
309 "The tariff must . . . hell will be to pay": Walter Wellman to TR, April 18, 1902, WHTP.
309 the "dynamite . . . to the Republican party": TR to Nicholas M. Butler, Aug. 12, 1902, in *LTR*, Vol. 3, p. 312.
309 "As long as I remain": Edmund Morris, *Theodore Rex* (New York: Random House, 2001), p. 145.
309 "make no attempt": Stephenson, *Nelson W. Aldrich*, p. 455, n. 54.
309 "I do not wish": TR to Nicholas M. Butler, Aug. 12, 1902, in *LTR*, Vol. 3, p. 312.
309 "a three weeks' ": TR to John Hay, Sept. 18, 1902, in ibid., p. 326.
309 "like that of a man": *Public Opinion*, Sept. 25, 1902.
310 crowds "in comparative silence": "President Roosevelt at Cincinnati," *Outlook*, Sept. 27, 1902, p. 205.
310 "There are a good many": TR to John Hay, Sept. 18, 1902, in *LTR*, Vol. 3, p. 326.
310 "a threatening abscess . . . before the needle was removed": New York *World*, Sept. 24, 1902; *Racine* [WI] *Daily Journal*, Sept. 24, 1902.
310 "Tell it not": TR to Orville H. Platt, Oct. 2, 1902, in *LTR*, Vol. 3, p. 335.
310 books that would feed: TR to Herbert Putnam, Oct. 6, 1902, in ibid., p. 343.
310 "Exactly the books": TR to Herbert Putnam, Oct. 8, 1902, in ibid., pp. 344–45.
311 "the most formidable": Walter Wellman, "The Progress of the World," *American Monthly Review of Reviews* (October 1902).
311 140,000 anthracite coal miners . . . panic was setting in: Sullivan, *Our Times*, Vol. 2, p. 427.
311 "the sorrows": John Mitchell, "The Mine Worker's Life and Aims," *The Cosmopolitan* (October 1901), p. 630.
311 "the average magazine": Ibid., p. 622.
311 "yet at the . . . precarious elevators": Stephen Crane, "In the Depths of a Coal Mine," *McClure's* (August 1894).
311 "on the descent": Mitchell, "The Mine Worker's Life and Aims," *Cosmopolitan*, Oct. 1901, p. 629.
312 "children were brought": Gompers, *Seventy Years of Life and Labor*, p. 154.
312 "reaping the reward": "Progress of the World," *American Monthly Review of Reviews* (November 1902).
312 estimated profit of $75 million: Walter Wellman, "The Inside History of the Coal Strike," *Collier's*, Oct. 18, 1902.
312 "When President McKinley": LS, "A Labor Leader of To-Day: John Mitchell and What He Stands For," *McClure's* (August 1902), p. 355.
312 "No better strike . . . bitterness or retort": "Progress of the World," *American Monthly Review of Reviews* (November 1902).
313 "was only a common": Wellman, "The Inside History of the Coal Strike," *Collier's*, Oct. 18, 1902.
313 "I beg of you": Sullivan, *Our Times*, Vol. 2, p. 426.
313 "The doctrine of the divine": Ibid.
313 "It will take a load": *New York Tribune*, Aug. 22, 1902.
313 "The coal business . . . you can appear to do?": HCL to TR, Sept. 27, 1902, in TR and HCL, *Selections from the Correspondence*, Vol. 1, pp. 531–32.
313 "I am at my wit's": Pringle, *Theodore Roosevelt: A Biography*, p. 269.
313 "Of course, we have": TR to MAH, September 27, 1902, in *LTR*, Vol. 3, pp. 329–30.
314 "no warrant . . . constitutional duties": "Progress of the World," *American Monthly Review of Reviews* (November 1902).
314 "the Jackson-Lincoln theory": TR, *An Autobiography*, p. 464.
314 "the failure of the": TR to John Mitchell, et al., Oct. 1, 1902, in *LTR*, Vol. 3, p. 334.
314 "For the first time": Wellman, "The Inside History of the Coal Strike," *Collier's*, Oct. 18, 1902.
314 "luxurious private cars . . . a cheap hotel": Ibid.
314 footmen in "plum-colored livery": New York *World*, Oct. 4, 1902.
314 "three parties affected . . . general good": Ibid.

315 "literally jumped . . . clear as a bell": Ibid.
315 "I had not expected . . . may discuss them": TR's question and Baer's insolent reply, reported in ibid., are not included in the official transcript, which TR later acknowledged did not include "all the invectives of the operators." See TR to Winthrop Crane, Oct. 22, 1902, in *LTR*, Vol. 3, p. 359.
315 "The duty of the hour": "President Roosevelt and the Coal Strike," *The Independent*, Oct. 9, 1902, p. 2383.
315 "extraordinary stupidity . . . irritate Mitchell": TR to Winthrop Crane, Oct. 22, 1902, in *LTR*, Vol. 3, pp. 360–61.
315 "insolent . . . offensive to me": TR, *An Autobiography*, p. 466.
315 "they insulted me": TR to MAH, Oct. 3, 1902, in *LTR*, Vol. 3, p. 338.
315 "Mitchell behaved": TR to Winthrop Crane, Oct. 22, 1902, in ibid., p. 360.
315 "appeared to such advantage": TR to MAH, Oct. 3, 1902, in ibid., p. 337.
315 "towered above": TR to Robert Bacon, Oct. 5, 1902, in ibid., p. 340.
315 "a set of outlaws": Morris, *Theodore Rex*, p. 160.
315 "by the seat": Wood, *Roosevelt As We Knew Him*, p. 109.
315 "to have any dealings": New York *World*, Oct. 4, 1902.
316 "If this is the case": Ibid.
316 "Well, I have tried": TR to MAH, Oct. 3, 1902, in *LTR*, Vol. 3, p. 337.
316 reveled "in the fact": TR, *An Autobiography*, p. 467.
316 "uncontrollable penchant": Sullivan, *Our Times*, Vol. 2, p. 431.
316 "a sorry mess": *Public Opinion*, Oct. 16, 1901.
316 "respectful, placable": *Public Opinion*, Oct. 9, 1902.
316 "ugly talk . . . would otherwise come": TR to Winthrop Crane, Oct. 22, 1902, in *LTR*, Vol. 3, p. 362.
316 "absolutely out of touch . . . misery and death": TR to ARC, Oct. 16, 1902, in TR, *Letters from Theodore Roosevelt to Anna Roosevelt Cowles*, pp. 252–53.
316 "a first-rate general . . . Commander-in-Chief": Sullivan, *Our Times*, Vol. 2, p. 436.
316 if "the operators went": Bishop, *Theodore Roosevelt and His Time*, Vol. 1, p. 212.
317 "Don't hit till": Wellman, "The Settlement of the Coal Strike," *American Monthly Review of Reviews* (November 1902).
317 "Theodore was a bit": Jessup, *Elihu Root*, Vol. 1, p. 275.
317 "The one condition": Sullivan, *Our Times*, Vol. 2, p. 438.
317 it would be the original architect: Wellman, "The Inside History of the Coal Strike," *Collier's*, Oct. 18, 1902.
317 Root would make it clear: Jessup, *Elihu Root*, Vol. 1, p. 275.
317 "It was a damned lie": Ibid., p. 276.
317 "was one of the": Wellman, "The Settlement of the Coal Strike," *American Monthly Review of Reviews* (November 1902).
317 the composition of the panel: TR to Winthrop Crane, Oct. 22, 1902, in *LTR*, Vol. 3, p. 359.
318 "Suddenly . . . accept with rapture": TR, *An Autobiography*, p. 468.
318 For three months the commission heard: *Public Opinion*, Dec. 18, 1902.
318 "The American people . . . triumph of peace": *Public Opinion*, Oct. 23, 1902.
318 "was won by popular": Ibid.
318 "the people's attorney": WAW, "The President," *Saturday Evening Post*, April 4, 1903.
318 "steady pressure": *Public Opinion*, Oct. 23, 1902.
318 "was all ready to . . . in less drastic fashion": TR, *An Autobiography*, pp. 475–76.
319 "My dear sir": TR to J. P. Morgan, Oct. 16, 1902, in *LTR*, Vol. 3, p. 353.
319 "May Heaven preserve me": TR to ARC, Oct. 16, 1902, in TR, *Letters from Theodore Roosevelt to Anna Roosevelt Cowles*, p. 254.
319 "Mother and I": TR to Kermit Roosevelt, Nov. 6, 1902, in *LTR*, Vol. 3, p. 374.
319 "doomed to failure . . . thousands of votes": "Progress of the World," *American Monthly Review of Reviews* (November 1902).
319 "a steady stream . . . samples of rugs": Seale, *The President's House: A History*, Vol 2, p. 674.
319 designing a garden . . . and a tennis court: Morris, *EKR*, pp. 248, 254.
319 "If Roosevelt had": Ellen Maury Slayden, *Washington Wife: Journal of Ellen Maury Slayden from 1897–1919* (New York: Harper & Row, 1963), p. 46.
319 "remarkable coping . . . and start again": Mac Keith Griswold, "First Lady Edith Kermit Roosevelt's 'Colonial Garden' at the White House," *White House History*, No. 23, p. 5.
319 "She is an old-fashioned": *New York Herald Tribune*, Oct. 30, 1932.
320 "By nature and inclination . . . dignity and charm": Isabella Hagner James, "Memoirs of Isabella Hagner, 1901–1905," *White House History*, No. 26, p. 63.
320 She was "at home" . . . at afternoon teas: *Logansport* [IN] *Journal*, Dec. 13, 1902.
320 "the chief end": Riis, "Mrs. Roosevelt and Her Children," *Ladies' Home Journal* (August 1902), p. 5.
320 "For the first time": *Newark* [OH] *Advocate*, Nov. 10, 1902.
320 immediate access to the president . . . and telephones: *Fort Wayne* [IN] *News*, Nov. 10, 1902.
320 "The public man": *Newark* [OH] *Advocate*, Nov. 10, 1902.
320 "had any right . . . the given conditions": TR to Maria Longworth Storer, Dec. 8, 1902, in *LTR*, Vol. 3, p. 392.
320 "It is very curious . . . uniformly good-natured": Bishop, *Theodore Roosevelt and His Time*, Vol. 1, p. 240.
320 a mid-November bear hunt . . . in honor of Teddy Roosevelt: New York *Sun*, Nov. 15, 1902; *NYT*, Nov. 19, 1902.
321 "I'd rather be *elected* . . . Hanna and that crowd": Pringle, *Theodore Roosevelt: A Biography*, p. 339.
321 "I do not think": *Woodland* [CA] *Daily Democrat*, Nov. 24, 1902.
321 "the monied interests" . . . opposition party: *Ottumwa* [IA] *Daily Courier*, Jan. 9, 1903.
321 the vehement reaction: TR to Lucius N. Littauer, Oct. 24, 1901, in *LTR*, Vol. 3, p. 181.

321 "Social equality": *Public Opinion*, Oct. 31, 1901, p. 556.
321 "The action of President": Ben Tillman, in Dewey W. Grantham, Jr., "Dinner at the White House," *Tennessee Historical Quarterly* (June 1958), p. 117.
321 "not nearly so strong": *Sandusky* [OH] *Daily Star*, Dec. 3, 1902.
321 "The plain people . . . against the trusts": TR, "Second Annual Message," Dec. 2, 1902, in *WTR*, Vol. 15, pp. 140–41, 144.
322 "It appears that": *Indiana* [PA] *Democrat*, Dec. 3, 1902.
322 "a very lame message": *Cincinnati Enquirer*, cited in *Racine* [WI] *Journal*, Dec. 5, 1902.
322 "A milk and water": *Indiana* [PA] *Democrat*, Dec. 3, 1902.
322 "We are bound to believe": New York *Evening Post*, cited in *Racine Journal*, Dec. 5, 1902.

CHAPTER ELEVEN: "The Most Famous Woman in America"

Page
324 "groundbreaking trio": David M. Chalmers, *The Muckrake Years* (New York: D. Van Nostrand Co., 1974), p. 24.
324 "Capitalists, workingmen . . . but all of us": McClure, "Concerning Three Articles in This Number of *McClure's*, and a Coincidence That May Set Us Thinking," *McClure's* (January 1903), p. 336.
325 "A lesser editor": Lyon, *Success Story*, p. 204.
325 "shameful facts . . . to the American pride": *Boston Daily Globe*, May 22, 1904.
325 "for the first time": Goldman, *Rendezvous with Destiny*, p. 74.
325 "the greatest success": Lyon, *Success Story*, p. 206.
325 Editorials . . . praised the quality of the research: *Salt Lake Tribune*, Jan. 4, 1903; *Los Angeles Times*, Feb. 15, 1903.
325 "Of course": New York *World*, cited in *Boston Daily Globe*, May 22, 1904.
326 "prophets crying": RSB, *American Chronicle*, p. 183.
326 "It is hardly": Hofstadter, *The Age of Reform*, pp. 186–87.
326 "gradual rise . . . intense human interest": Wilson, *McClure's Magazine and the Muckrakers*, p. 134.
327 "The great feature is Trusts . . . a good circulation": McClure to John S. Phillips, Sept. 14, 1899, McClure MSS.
327 While Phillips embraced McClure's idea: Wilson, *McClure's Magazine and the Muckrakers*, p. 136.
327 "The Pulpit, the Press": Frank Norris, *The Responsibilities of the Novelist, and Other Literary Essays* (New York: Doubleday, Page & Co., 1903), p. 10.
327 "the destruction of once": Benjamin O. Flower, "The Trust in Fiction: A Remarkable Social Novel, *The Octopus*," *The Arena* (May 1902), p. 547.
328 "the iron-hearted Power": Frank Norris, *The Octopus: A Story of California* (New York: Doubleday, Page & Co., 1910), p. 51.
328 "*The Octopus* is": Flower, "The Trust in Fiction," *The Arena* (May 1902), pp. 547–48.
328 "The string of triumphs": Lyon, *Success Story*, p. 173.
328 McClure overreached: Ibid., p. 166.
328 Frank Doubleday . . . six months after it was signed: Ibid., p. 172.
328 "raw milk is": Ronald F. Schmid, *The Untold Story of Milk: The History, Politics and Science of Nature's Perfect Food: Raw Milk from Pasture-Fed Cows* (Washington, DC: NewTrends, 2009), p. 76.
329 "unmelodious" clamor . . . "rhythmical" sounds: George Miller Beard, *American Nervousness: Its Causes and Consequences; a Supplement to Nervous Exhaustion (Neurasthenia)* (New York: G. P. Putnam's Sons, 1881), p. 106.
329 "local horrors": Ibid., p. 134.
329 "the ultracompetitive": David G. Schuster, "Neurasthenia and a Modernizing America," *Journal of the American Medical Association* 290, Nov. 5, 2003, pp. 2327–28.
329 "the repulsion . . . and got it": Cather and McClure, *The Autobiography*, pp. 254–55.
329 "When I get rested . . . worse than ever": McClure to JSP, Oct. 30, 1900, Phillips MSS.
329 "I am simply heart-broken": McClure to JSP, Oct. 30, 1900, Phillips MSS.
330 "The great issue": Lyon, *Success Story*, p. 190.
330 "the way to handle . . . the oil region": Cather and McClure, *The Autobiography*, p. 238.
330 "the unfairness of the situation": Mary Caroline Crawford, "The Historian of Standard Oil," *Public Opinion*, May 27, 1905.
330 "the bottom had dropped out": IMT, *All in the Day's Work*, p. 204.
330 "there must be two . . . the other side": Crawford, "The Historian of Standard Oil," *Public Opinion*, May 27, 1905.
330 "the all-seeing eye . . . ruin the magazine": IMT, *All in the Day's Work*, pp. 206–07.
330 "the audacity of the thing": Crawford, "The Historian of Standard Oil," *Public Opinion*, May 27, 1905.
331 "Go over": IMT, *All in the Day's Work*, p. 205.
331 "Come instantly . . . a good time": McClure to IMT, Sept. 30, 1901, IMTC.
331 Hattie, too, welcomed: Brady, *Ida Tarbell*, p. 122.
331 "You've never been there . . . in the Pantheon": IMT, *All in the Day's Work*, p. 206.
331 The image . . . incongruous and hilarious: Ibid.
331 "I lean on you": McClure to IMT, Dec. 30, 1901, IMTC.
331 he decided to stop . . . Greece for another time: IMT, *All in the Day's Work*, p. 206.
331 "It was always so . . . wild editor": LS, *The Autobiography*, pp. 363, 361.
332 "a way to compromise": Ibid., pp. 363, 364.
332 "absolutely incompetent . . . words passed": Lyon, *Success Story*, p. 195.
332 Mary Bisland . . . wrote a distressed letter: Ibid., pp. 195–96.
332 "Things will come out . . . that one hundredth idea!": IMT to Albert Boyden, April 26, 1902, in ibid., p. 199.
333 "a particular industry": Mary E. Tomkins, *Ida M. Tarbell* (New York: Twayne Publishers, 1974), p. 60.
333 "exactly the quality": IMT, *All in the Day's Work*, p. 208.

333 almost lost her eyesight: *Atlanta Constitution*, Jan. 11, 1903.
333 "turn up" . . . curiously disappeared: IMT, *All in the Day's Work*, p. 209.
333 "Her sources of information": Cather and McClure, *The Autobiography*, p. 239.
334 "get his fun . . . a continuous joy": IMT, *All in the Day's Work*, p. 209.
334 "was as illustrious a meeting": Brady, *Ida Tarbell*, p. 125.
334 "Someone once asked me": Ibid., p. 126.
334 "I was a bit scared . . . face to face": IMT, *All in the Day's Work*, p. 212.
335 "a heavy shock of . . . the world, I thought": Ibid., pp. 212–13.
335 "documents, figures": Ibid., p. 215.
335 "unimpeachable accuracy": Cather and McClure, *The Autobiography*, p. 240.
335 "deep into appalling heaps . . . of your story": August F. Jaccaci to IMT, Nov. 23, 1901, Phillips MSS.
335 "hurt your health . . . for next fall": McClure to IMT, Dec. 2, 1901, IMTC.
335 "separated so completely": IMT to Harriet Hurd McClure, Nov. 8, 1902, McClure MSS.
335 "They are in such shape": IMT to JSP, May 26, 1902, Phillips MSS.
335 her deep respect for Phillips's opinion: Brady, *Ida Tarbell*, p. 130.
336 "be satisfied and thrilled": Ibid., p. 133.
336 "moderately comfortable . . . for the Alps": IMT to John M. Siddall, June 24, 1902, in ibid., p. 130.
336 "irrepressible energy . . . refine for the world": IMT, "The Birth of an Industry," *McClure's* (November 1902), in IMT and David Mark Chalmers, *The History of the Standard Oil Company* (Mineola, NY: Dover Books, 1966), pp. 18, 17, 1, 16.
336 Rockefeller's "genius for detail": IMT, "The Legitimate Greatness of the Standard Oil Company," *McClure's* (October 1904), in ibid., p. 202.
336 "in energy, in intelligence": Ibid., p. 196.
336 "You will have but one . . . swooped down": IMT, "John D. Rockefeller, A Character Study," *McClure's* (July 1905).
337 "There is no chance": IMT, "The Rise of the Standard Oil Company," *McClure's* (December 1902), in IMT and Chalmers, *History of the Standard Oil Company*, p. 32.
337 Within three months, twenty-one: Ibid., p. 33.
337 "They were there at the mouth": Ibid., p. 27.
337 "the railroad held its right . . . without discrimination": IMT, "John D. Rockefeller, A Character Study," *McClure's* (July 1905).
337 "from hopelessness . . . for principle": IMT, "The Great Consummation," *McClure's* (June 1903), in IMT and Chalmers, *History of the Standard Oil Company*, p. 99.
337 "To the man who had begun": IMT, "The Price of Trust Building," *McClure's* (March 1903), in ibid., p. 66.
337 "the quantity, quality": IMT, "Cutting to Kill," *McClure's* (February 1904), in ibid., p. 123.
337 "her firm had a customer": Ibid., p. 115.
337 Of all the machinations: Ibid., p. 124.
338 "The unraveling of this espionage": IMT, "Speech to Rachel Crothers' Group" [n.d.], IMTC; see also Brady, *Ida Tarbell*, p. 145.
338 "had completed one": IMT, "The Troubles of a Trust," *McClure's* (March 1904), in IMT and Chalmers, *History of the Standard Oil Company*, p. 151.
338 "competition practically out": IMT, "The Price of Oil," *McClure's* (September 1904), in ibid., p. 185.
338 "Human experience": Ibid., p. 194.
338 "legitimate greatness . . . daring to lay hold of them": IMT, "The Legitimate Greatness of the Standard Oil Company," in ibid., p. 196.
338 "these qualities alone": IMT, "Conclusion," *McClure's* (October 1904), in ibid., p. 216.
338 "At the same time": Ibid., pp. 216–17.
338 "every great campaign": Ibid., p. 222.
338 "And what are we going . . . Standard Oil Company": Ibid., p. 227.
339 "You are today . . . afraid of you": McClure to IMT, April 6, 1903, IMTC.
339 "a Joan of Arc . . . against trusts and monopolies": Jeannette L. Gilder, "Some Women Writers," *Outlook*, October 1904, p. 281.
339 "The New Woman": *Logansport* [IN] *Pharos*, July 26, 1904.
339 "At least one American": *Lowell* [MA] *Sun*, June 11, 1904.
339 "the strongest intellectual force": *Los Angeles Times*, Feb. 14, 1906.
339 "proven herself to be": *Washington Times* quoted in "On the Making of McClure's Magazine," *McClure's* (November 1904), p. 107.
339 "the woman who talks": *Boston Daily Globe*, April 7, 1904.
339 "so feminine as to appear": Brady, *Ida Tarbell*, p. 157.
339 publishers' dinner: *Washington Post*, April 8, 1904.
339 "It is the first time": IMT to RSB, April 5, 1904, RSB Papers.
339 "that Mr. Rockefeller": *Washington Post*, July 8, 1905.
340 "Miss Ida Tarbell goes": *Chicago Daily Tribune*, Dec. 31, 1902.
340 "the net of avarice . . . sordid to benevolent": *Washington Post*, Nov. 26, 1905.
340 "accumulation of facts . . . in their significance": *Webster City* [IA] *Tribune*, Nov. 27, 1903.
340 "intimate style": *Outlook*, Oct. 1, 1904.
340 "remarkable for being nearly": *Chicago Daily Tribune*, Dec. 28, 1903.
340 "in a state of lively suspense": *Chicago Daily Tribune*, June 8, 1903.
340 "She never rants": *Webster City Tribune*, Nov. 27, 1903.
340 "an almost universal practice": Chalmers, *The Muckrake Years*, p. 94.

340 "excellent journalism": *Boston Evening Transcript*, Jan. 6, 1904.
340 "a quiet, modest": IMT, "John D. Rockefeller: A Character Study, Part Two," *McClure's* (August 1905), p. 397.
340 "willing to strain": *Fort Wayne* [IN] *Journal-Gazette*, Feb. 9, 1903.
340 "Rockefeller was known": *Alton* [IL] *Evening Telegraph*, Dec. 21, 1904.
341 "as expressionless . . . worthy of citizenship": IMT, "John D. Rockefeller: A Character Study, Part Two," *McClure's* (August 1905), pp. 386, 387, 398.
341 "were Mr. Rockefeller": Ibid., pp. 398–99.
341 "no cure": IMT, "Conclusion," *McClure's* (October 1904), in IMT and Chalmers, *History of the Standard Oil Company*, p. 222.
341 "an increasing scorn": Ibid.
341 board members "closely allied": *Daily Californian* (Bakersfield, CA), April 28, 1904.
341 "Your monumental work": McClure to IMT [n.d.], 1904, IMTC.
341 "one of the most remarkable": "On the Making of McClure's Magazine," *McClure's* (November 1904), p. 107.
341 "up to magazines": Brady, *Ida Tarbell*, p. 139.
341 "that the two things": *Outlook*, Oct. 1, 1904.
342 "You cannot imagine": McClure to IMT, Mar. 18, 1903, IMTC.
342 "the most genuinely creative": IMT, *All in the Day's Work*, p. 199.
342 to compel congressional action against monopolies: *Daily Northwestern* (Oshkosh, WI), Dec. 23, 1902.
342 "must stand . . . a tower of strength": *Logansport* [IN] *Journal*, Feb. 10, 1903.
342 the "only question": *Daily Northwestern*, Dec. 23, 1902.
342 "no time for anti-trust": *New York Tribune*, Jan. 6, 1903.
342 "I pass my days": TR to Kermit Roosevelt, Jan. 17, 1903, in TR et al., *Letters to Kermit from Theodore Roosevelt*, pp. 24–25.
342 "the ancient and honorable . . . the two stools": *Washington Post*, Feb. 19, 1903.
342 "The party had promised": Ibid.
343 an extra session "on extraordinary occasions": U.S. Constitution, art. II, sec. 3.
343 "While I could not force": TR to Lawrence Fraser Abbott, Feb. 3, 1903, in *LTR*, Vol. 3, p. 416.
343 That single word, "rebate . . . interests of the country": *Fort Wayne* [IN] *Journal-Gazette*, Feb. 9, 1903.
343 "no respectable railroad": TR to Lawrence Fraser Abbott, Feb. 3, 1903, in *LTR*, Vol. 3, p. 417.
343 By 1903, the railroads themselves actually favored: Gabriel Kolko, *Railroads and Regulation, 1877–1916* (New York: W. W. Norton & Co., 1970), pp. 94–95.
343 "grown beyond any effects": *Washington Post*, Feb. 8, 1903.
343 "the highways of commerce": TR to Lyman Abbott, Sept. 5, 1903, in *LTR*, Vol. 3, p. 592.
343 "equal rights for all": *Logansport* [IN] *Journal*, Feb. 10, 1903.
344 "violent opposition . . . sullenly acquiesced in": TR to Lawrence Fraser Abbott, Feb. 3, 1903, in *LTR*, Vol. 3, p. 417.
344 "the subconscious moral sense": WAW, "The Balance-Sheet of the Session," *Saturday Evening Post*, Mar. 28, 1903.
344 "the first essential . . . overcapitalization": TR, "First Annual Message," in *NYT*, Jan. 4, 1900.
344 The amendment . . . the abuses uncovered: Arthur M. Johnson, "Theodore Roosevelt and the Bureau of Corporations," *Mississippi Valley Historical Review* 45 (March 1959), p. 576.
344 "The Standard Oil Company": *Wall Street Journal*, Nov. 28, 1903.
345 "a disposition in some quarters": *New York Tribune*, Jan. 8, 1903.
345 "joked with the girls . . . would never, never do": *Logansport* [IN] *Pharos*, Feb. 18, 1903.
345 "I have been worked": TR to Kermit Roosevelt, Feb. 15, 1903, in TR et al., *Letters to Kermit from Theodore Roosevelt*, p. 29.
345 Singlestick . . . required him to shake left-handed: TR to Kermit Roosevelt, Jan. 25, 1903, in ibid., p. 26.
345 "The Most Wounded President": *Minneapolis Journal*, Mar. 7, 1903.
345 rode a horse . . . for exercise: TR to Kermit Roosevelt, Feb. 19, 1903, in TR et al., *Letters to Kermit from Theodore Roosevelt*, p. 30.
345 "not suffice": *Boston Traveler*, quoted in *Hutchinson* [KS] *News*, Feb. 3, 1903.
345 a single objective: Ibid.
345 with "peremptory" instruction: *NYT*, Feb. 10, 1903.
346 "unalterably opposed": *Logansport* [IN] *Pharos*, Feb. 13, 1903.
346 "must be stopped": *Logansport* [IN] *Pharos*, Feb. 10, 1903.
346 "We own the Republican party": Ibid.
346 he would surely insist on the extra session: *Washington Post*, Feb. 8, 1903.
346 "a decided sensation": *NYT*, Feb. 9, 1903.
346 "for fear": *Eau Claire* [WI] *Leader*, Feb. 14, 1903.
346 "no surprise . . . nothing more": *Fort Wayne* [IN] *Journal-Gazette*, Feb. 9, 1903.
346 "This is no more than . . . promptly to right-about": *Los Angeles Times*, Feb. 14, 1903.
346 "from the standpoint": TR to Nicholas M. Butler, Aug. 29, 1903, in *LTR*, Vol. 3, p. 580.
347 "Taken as a whole": TR to David Bremner Henderson, Mar. 4, 1903, in ibid., p. 438.
347 "a great many people . . . consensus of opinion": TR to Nicholas M. Butler, Aug. 29, 1903, in ibid., p. 580.
347 "gotten the trust legislation": TR to Joseph Bucklin Bishop, Feb. 17, 1903, in ibid., p. 429.
347 "not sufficiently far-reaching": *Washington Post*, Feb. 19, 1903.
347 "no single legislative act . . . will not be retracted": WAW, "The Balance-Sheet of the Session," *Saturday Evening Post*, Mar. 28, 1903.

CHAPTER TWELVE: "A Mission to Perform"

Page

348 Roosevelt embarked . . . upon the longest tour: *Boston Daily Globe*, April 2, 1903.

348 "Look out for": New York *World*, April 2, 1903.

349 "the handsomest ever": *Washington Times*, Mar. 31, 1903.

349 This "traveling palace" . . . a rear platform: New York *World*, April 1, 1903.

349 The remaining cars included: *Washington Times*, Mar. 31, 1903.

349 "gave himself very freely . . . have another chance": John Burroughs, *Camping and Tramping with Roosevelt* (Boston: Houghton Mifflin, 1907), pp. 8, 9, 12.

349 "to see the President . . . proprietary interest in him": TR to John Hay, Aug. 9, 1903, in *LTR*, Vol. 3, pp. 550–51, 555.

349 to gain "the people's trust": WAW, "Swinging 'Round the Circle with Roosevelt," *Saturday Evening Post*, June 27, 1903.

349 an array of bizarre gifts: TR to John Hay, Aug. 9, 1903, in *LTR*, Vol. 3, p. 555; "Survey of the World: End of Mr. Roosevelt's Tour," *The Independent*, June 11, 1903.

350 "Great heavens and earth!": *Anaconda* [MT] *Standard*, May 6 & 28, 1903.

350 "These were not epoch-making . . . original": WAW, "Swinging 'Round the Circle with Roosevelt," *Saturday Evening Post*, June 27, 1903.

350 "the thick of civilization . . . the same ideals": TR to John Hay, Aug. 9, 1903, in *LTR*, Vol. 3, p. 548.

350 "Roosevelt Gems": *Daily Journal* (Salem, OR), May 28, 1903.

350 "make a fool wise . . . cannot be done": TR, "Speech in Aberdeen, S.D., April 7, 1903," in TR and Alfred H. Lewis, *A Compilation of the Messages and Speeches of Theodore Roosevelt, 1901–1905,* (New York: Bureau of National Literature and Art, 1906), pp. 263, 265.

350 "I do not like": *Daily Journal* (Salem, OR), May 28, 1903.

350 "Speak softly": *Fort Wayne* [IN] *Journal-Gazette*, April 3, 1903.

350 "sudsy metaphors . . . from a clothesline": WAW, "Swinging 'Round the Circle with Roosevelt," *Saturday Evening Post*, June 27, 1903.

350 "a square deal . . . rich or poor": TR, "Speech at Lynn, Mass., August 25, 1902," in TR and Lewis, *A Compilation of the Messages and Speeches*, p. 74.

350 "They were good enough": TR, "Speech at Grand Canyon, Ariz., May 26, 1903," in ibid., p. 328.

350 the black troops who fought beside him: *Anaconda* [MT] *Standard*, May 28, 1903.

350 he elaborated on the concept: *Atlanta Constitution*, Sept. 8, 1903.

351 "We must treat": *Anaconda* [MT] *Standard*, May 27, 1903.

351 "a great boy . . . waiting for him to fall": *Desert Evening News* (Salt Lake City, UT), Mar. 28, 1903.

351 "a man of such abounding": Burroughs, *Camping and Tramping with Roosevelt*, pp. 4, 80.

351 He arrived at the Grand Canyon: Douglas Brinkley, *The Wilderness Warrior: Theodore Roosevelt and the Crusade for America* (New York: HarperCollins, 2009), p. 527.

351 "Leave it as it is": *Salt Lake Tribune*, May 7, 1903; TR, "Speech at Grand Canyon, Ariz., May 6, 1903," in TR and Lewis, *A Compilation of the Messages and Speeches*, p. 327.

351 "great wonder of nature": *Salt Lake Tribune*, May 7, 1903.

351 "If Roosevelt had done nothing": Brinkley, *The Wilderness Warrior*, p. 528.

351 San Lorenzo Valley, home to: *Evening Herald* (Syracuse, NY), May 12, 1903.

352 "I am, oh, so glad": TR, "Speech at the Big Grove Tree, Santa Cruz, Cal., May 11, 1903," in TR and Lewis, *A Compilation of the Messages and Speeches*, p. 360.

352 "to protect these mighty": TR, "Speech at Leland Stanford, Jr., University, Palo Alto, Cal., May 12, 1903," in ibid., p. 370.

352 "a tree which was old . . . higher emotions in mankind": Ibid., p. 368.

352 "the great monarchs of the woods": Ibid., p. 370.

352 "not to preserve forests": TR, "Speech at the Meeting of the Society of American Foresters, Washington, D.C., March 26, 1903," in ibid., p. 208.

352 "a steady and continuous": *Salt Lake Tribune*, May 30, 1903.

352 already "seriously depleted": TR, "Speech at a Meeting of the Society of American Foresters, Washington, D.C., March 26, 1903," in TR and Lewis, *A Compilation of the Messages and Speeches*, p. 210.

352 "rushing away . . . the flow of streams": "How Our National Forests Conserve Irrigation and Water Power," *Literary Digest*, April 26, 1919, p. 117.

352 "a veritable garden of Eden": *Arizona Republican* (Phoenix, AZ), May 26, 1903.

352 "small irrigated farms": TR, "Speech at Denver, Colo., May 4, 1903," in TR and Lewis, *A Compilation of the Messages and Speeches*, p. 323.

352 "We do not ever": TR, "Speech at Leland Stanford, Jr., University, Palo Alto, Cal., May 12, 1903," in ibid., p. 370.

352 "come into the hands": *Salt Lake Tribune*, May 30, 1903.

353 THE DAY OF DELIVERANCE: *Arizona Republican*, May 19, 1903.

353 "the greatest in the world": *Arizona Republican*, May 26, 1903.

353 "make the community": *Reno* [NV] *Evening Gazette*, May 14, 1903.

353 The estimated cost of the five projects: *The Weekly Gazette* (Colorado Springs, CO), July 23, 1903.

353 "any other material movement": TR, "Speech at Grand Canyon, Ariz., May 6, 1903," in TR and Lewis, *A Compilation of the Messages and Speeches*, p. 327.

353 "a new type . . . a million inhabitants": TR to John Hay, Aug. 9, 1903, in *LTR*, Vol. 3, p. 558.

353 an "educational effect upon . . . great national forests": "The President's Trip and the Forests," *Century Illustrated Magazine* (August 1903), pp. 634–35.

353 Roosevelt had delivered 265 speeches: "Survey of the World: End of Mr. Roosevelt's Tour," *The Independent*, June 11, 1903.

353 "as fresh and unworn": Burroughs, *Camping and Tramping with Roosevelt*, p. 61.

354 "blossom like a rose": *Minneapolis Journal*, July 30, 1903.
354 "irrigate no public lands": *Anaconda Standard*, May 21, 1903.
354 Roosevelt had followed the reporter's career: RSB, *American Chronicle*, p. 170.
354 short notes commending: TR to RSB, Nov. 4, 1898; Feb. 2, 1900, Baker Papers.
354 "We intend to do": TR to George Hoar, Oct. 17, 1902, in *LTR*, Vol. 3, p. 354.
354 "ammunition for mere": RSB, *American Chronicle*, p. 168.
354 Baker had finally moved: Ibid., p. 161.
354 "never . . . forget": Ibid.
355 "the first desk": Ibid., p. 162.
355 "I actually thought . . . serpent in my new Eden!": Ibid., p. 163.
355 "What sort of men": "Interview with S. S. McClure," *The North American* (Philadelphia), Aug. 15, 1905.
355 "was generally hostile": RSB, *American Chronicle*, p. 166.
355 "only one aspect": Ibid., p. 168.
355 the more curious he grew: Ibid., p. 167; TR to Winthrop Crane, Oct. 22, 1902, in *LTR*, Vol. 3, p. 361.
355 Baker sought out people: RSB, *American Chronicle*, p. 167.
356 "low wages": Ibid., p. 163.
356 "singularly steady-headed": Ibid., pp. 166–67.
356 "What men I met": Ibid., p. 167.
356 "Don't, my dear boy": McClure to RSB, Nov. 5, 1902, RSB Papers.
356 "the feuds in . . . death can heal": McClure to LS, Nov. 10, 1902, LS Papers; *NYT*, Nov. 10, 1902.
356 "become the most . . . done magnificently!": McClure to RSB, Nov. 14, 1902, RSB Papers.
356 "is beginning to distinguish": McClure, "Editor's Note," in RSB, "The Right to Work: The Story of the Non-Striking Miners," *McClure's* (January 1903), p. 323.
356 "the rights of labor . . . even real danger": RSB, "The Right to Work," *McClure's* (January 1903), p. 323.
356 "the best position . . . crushed all family feeling": Ibid., pp. 334–35.
357 "All these things": Ibid., pp. 327–28.
357 clubbed to death: Ibid., pp. 330–33.
357 "only a few among scores": Ibid., p. 336.
357 "on fire . . . all winter long": RSB, *American Chronicle*, p. 168.
357 "Everything has borne out": McClure to RSB, Jan. 23, 1903, RSB Papers.
358 an entire series on labor: Ibid.
358 unable "to write fiction": RSB, *American Chronicle*, p. 173.
358 "a powerful new": Ibid., p. 179.
358 "I doubt whether": Ibid., p. 169.
358 "I have wondered": Ibid., p. 99.
358 "We were friends . . . rewriting his story": Ibid., pp. 94–95.
358 "the Chief . . . she has the punch": *Minneapolis Journal*, Feb. 26, 1906.
358 "so warmly . . . good sense and humor": RSB, *American Chronicle*, pp. 98, 99.
359 "Why bother": Ibid., p. 179.
359 a more obscure series: Ibid., pp. 143–45.
359 "no sign of living creatures . . . a man's heart": RSB, "The Great Southwest. III. Irrigation," *Century Illustrated Magazine* (July 1902), p. 361.
359 "My dear Mr. Baker": TR to RSB, June 25, 1903, *LTR*, Vol. 3, p. 504.
359 "get at the exact . . . suspicious in the extreme": RSB to TR [draft letter, n.d.], RSB Papers.
360 "I suppose . . . our getting the proof": TR to RSB, July 4, 1903, in *LTR*, Vol. 3, p. 510.
360 "I was so eager": RSB, *American Chronicle*, p. 170.
360 "I was determined": Ibid.
360 "If ever men . . . implacable desert": RSB, "The Great Southwest. III. Irrigation," *Century Illustrated Magazine* (July 1902), pp. 361–63.
361 the four men crowded: RSB, Notebook, July 15, 1903, RSB Papers.
361 "The President lives": RSB to J. Stannard Baker, July 16, 1903, RSB Papers.
361 "Robust, hearty": RSB, *American Chronicle*, p. 171.
361 "takes an extraordinary interest": RSB to J. Stannard Baker, July 16, 1903, RSB Papers.
361 "I don't care": RSB, *American Chronicle*, p. 172.
361 "on the market at reasonable": *Minneapolis Journal*, July 30, 1903.
361 "Who is the chief . . . get together on these subjects": RSB, *American Chronicle*, p. 172.
362 "As the time drew near": Ibid.
362 Baker's meticulous research . . . cleared Charles Walcott: RSB to Gifford Pinchot, July 17, 1903, RSB Papers.
362 Pinchot expressed great satisfaction: Gifford Pinchot to RSB, July 23, 1903, RSB Papers.
362 "I am immensely": TR to RSB, Oct. 15, 1903, TRC.
362 Investigating . . . Steffens had unearthed evidence: LS, *The Autobiography*, p. 521.
362 Fuller Construction Company was providing: *Wall Street Journal*, Oct. 24, 1903.
363 "riding about in his cab . . . $1500 or less": RSB, "The Trust's New Tool—The Labor Boss," *McClure's* (November 1903), pp. 30–31.
363 "starting with no . . . hand of the Trust": Ibid., pp. 39–40.
363 "Curiously enough": Ibid., p. 41.
363 "Worse still": Ibid., p. 33.
363 Jerome finally indicted Parks: Ibid.
364 "the need of . . . perpetrated by labor men": TR to RSB, Oct. 21, 1903, RSB Papers.
364 "When I get back East . . . to do so": RSB to TR, Nov. 10, 1903, TRC.

364 "When the corporations": *Wall Street Journal*, Oct. 24, 1904.
364 John Brooks publicly endorsed: Semonche, *Ray Stannard Baker*, p. 113.
364 flocked . . . "the greatest reporter": Louis Filler, *The Muckrakers* (Stanford, CA: Stanford University Press, 1993), p. 87.
364 "You have gone": John S. Phillips to RSB, Nov. 10, 1903, RSB Papers.
364 "a man can have . . . your perfect honesty": LS to RSB, Nov. 8, 1903, RSB Papers.
365 "were tired at night": RSB, "The Trust's New Tool—The Labor Boss," *McClure's* (November 1903), p. 34.
365 Neidig . . . built up a following: RSB, "The Lone Fighter," *McClure's* (December 1903), p. 195.
365 "We hear of": RSB, "The Trust's New Tool—The Labor Boss," *McClure's* (November 1903), p. 35.
365 "threatened with": RSB, "The Lone Fighter," *McClure's* (December 1903), p. 195.
365 "The 'lone fighter' ": C. S. Booth to RSB, Dec. 28, 1903, RSB Papers.
365 "a true and faithful . . . hands of workingmen": George O'Kane to RSB, Nov. 1, 1903, RSB Papers.
365 "splendid . . . sound and honest basis": Robert E. Neidig to RSB, Feb. 18, 1904, RSB Papers.
365 "My present work": RSB to J. Stannard Baker, Jan. 31, 1904, RSB Papers.
365 "probably doing more": RSB to J. Stannard Baker, Mar. 27, 1904, RSB Papers.

CHAPTER THIRTEEN: Toppling Old Bosses

Page
366 "mighty little letup . . . kind of a summer": TR to CRR, Sept. 23, 1903, in *LTR*, Vol. 3, pp. 604–5.
366 "I suppose young girls . . . even in Tammany": TR to Edward Stanton Martin, July 30, 1903, in ibid., p. 535.
367 "little mother . . . comforts to her": TR to EKR, Nov. 14, 1903, Derby Papers.
367 "looks so young and pretty": TR to Emily Carow, Aug. 6, 1903, in *LTR*, Vol. 3, p. 544.
367 "watched the white": TR to HCL, Sept. 30, 1903, in ibid., p. 606.
367 "Whether I shall": TR to CRR, Sept. 23, 1903, in ibid., p. 605.
367 "determined foes . . . of real moment": TR to George Trevelyan, May 28, 1904, in *LTR*, Vol. 4, pp. 806–7.
368 "flesh of": WAW, "Seconding the Motion," *Saturday Evening Post*, July 23, 1904, p. 4.
368 "pass the word . . . leave the president": WAW, "The President: The Friends and Enemies He Has Made," *Saturday Evening Post*, April 4, 1903.
368 "reform was . . . bobbing up in Congress": WAW, *The Autobiography*, p. 368.
368 "war on the railroads": LS, *The Struggle for Self-Government* (New York: McClure, Phillips & Co., 1906), p. 79.
368 "You may be an editor": LS, *The Autobiography*, p. 364.
369 "My business is to find": LS to Joseph Steffens, May 18, 1902, in LS et al., eds., *Letters of Lincoln Steffens*, Vol. 1, p. 156.
369 "If I should be": IMT, *All in the Day's Work*, p. 201.
369 Joe Folk and the investigations: "An Exposer of Municipal Corruptions," *The Bookman* (November 1903), pp. 247–48.
369 pervasive corruption: LS, *The Autobiography*, p. 368.
369 "safe . . . man of thirty-three": Johnson and Malone, eds., *Dictionary of American Biography* (New York: Charles Scribner's Sons, 1931), Vol. 3, p. 490.
369 "of bribing . . . no names were mentioned": LS, *The Autobiography*, p. 370.
370 "to the full extent . . . and confessed": Ibid., p. 371.
370 the money "was theirs": Lincoln Steffens, *The Shame of the Cities* (New York: Hill & Wang, 1904), pp. 86, 82.
370 "So long has": Ibid., p. 22.
370 "the greatest oak . . . oath of office": Ibid., p. 39.
370 due to receive over $200,000: Ibid., pp. 88–89.
370 "Missouri, Missouri": Ibid., p. 96.
371 Steffens drafted a new version: LS, *The Autobiography*, pp. 373–74.
371 "so frightened": LS, *The Shame of the Cities*, p. 34.
371 These spoils were divided: Ibid., pp. 48–50.
371 "Your article is": McClure to LS, Nov. 7, 1902, LS Papers.
371 "We'll call it": LS, *The Autobiography*, p. 374.
371 "You have made": McClure to LS, Nov. 10, 1902, LS Papers.
371 "Mr. Steffens's": "Tammany Outdone in St. Louis," *Outlook*, Jan. 10, 1903, p. 106.
372 "doing a public . . . wave of reform": *Arizona Republic* (Phoenix, AZ), Jan. 6, 1903.
372 "The newsstand had": LS, *The Autobiography*, p. 392.
372 a London editor . . . on the box lid: LS to Joseph Steffens, Dec. 13, 1903, in LS et al., *Letters of Lincoln Steffens*, Vol. 1, p. 160.
372 test his "dawning theory": LS, *The Autobiography*, p. 393.
372 "was not merely": LS, *The Shame of the Cities*, p. 9.
372 Wary of "philosophical generalizations": LS, *The Autobiography*, p. 393.
372 McClure feared: McClure to John S. Phillips, Mar. 20, 1903, Phillips MSS.
372 "facts, startling facts": LS, *The Autobiography*, p. 393.
372 "The disagreement became . . . stick to facts": Ibid., pp. 392–93.
373 Butler had directed the nominations: LS, *The Struggle for Self-Government*, pp. 7–8.
373 the presiding justice publicly called: Joseph W. Folk to LS, Mar. 19, 1903, LS Papers.
373 All the felons were back: LS, *The Shame of the Cities*, pp. 98, 100.
373 "Your narrative lacks . . . working out the article": McClure to LS, Jan. 20, 1903, LS Papers.
373 200,000 people sported: LS, *The Shame of the Cities*, pp. 14–15.
373 "Your article is . . . commencing to speak": Joseph W. Folk to LS, Mar. 28, 1903, LS Papers.
373 "The permanent remedy": Joseph W. Folk to LS, April 15, 1903, LS Papers.
373 "I must tell you": McClure to LS, June 17, 1903, LS Papers.
373 "the candidate . . . any other organ": McClure to LS, May 27, 1903, LS Papers.
374 "just chew[ing] the rag": LS, *The Autobiography*, p. 416.

374 "wise guys" in Minneapolis: Ibid., pp. 386, 382.
374 "Thieves, politicians . . . might as well talk": Ibid., p. 386.
374 "the best interviewer . . . a demi-god": Stephen J. Whitfield, "Muckraking Lincoln Steffens," *Virginia Quarterly Review* (Winter 1978), p. 87.
374 not "a temporary evil": LS, *The Autobiography*, p. 413.
374 "buying boodlers": LS, *The Shame of the Cities*, p. 3.
374 "public spirit became": Ibid., p. vii.
374 Steffens was hailed: *New York Tribune*, April 10, 1904.
374 agitator William Lloyd Garrison: *Congregationalist and Christian World*, April 9, 1904.
374 "a new kind" of journalist: "A Master Journalist," *Current Literature* (June 1904), p. 610.
374 "Instead of having": Richard Duffy, "Lincoln Steffens," *The Critic* (May 1904), p. 402.
374 "correctly diagnosed": "The Diagnosis and Cure of Municipal Corruption," *Outlook*, April 16, 1904, p. 917.
374 "into the wards": "William Allen White on Mr. Steffens's Book," *McClure's* (June 1904), pp. 220–21.
375 "have done more": "A Master Journalist," *Current Literature* (June 1904), p. 611.
375 "the political . . . stream of pollution": LS, *The Struggle for Self-Government*, p. 3.
375 "almost any State": Ibid., p. 5.
375 "the System": Ibid., p. 11.
375 "this paper government": Ibid., p. 15.
375 "appealing his case": Ibid., p. 16.
375 "that corruption": Ibid., p. 36.
375 a sweeping bribery scheme: Ibid., pp. 35–36.
375 "brilliant reductions": Kaplan, *Lincoln Steffens*, p. 125.
375 "a striking article . . . of his fellow-men": *NYT*, Mar. 30, 1904.
375 "Your last article . . . bloodless political revolution": Joseph W. Folk to LS, April 17, 1904, LS Papers.
376 "fixed . . . him with defeat": LS, *The Struggle for Self-Government*, p. 108.
376 "To have you turn": Belle La Follette to LS, Aug. 14, 1904, LS Papers.
376 his "long, hard fight": LS, *The Struggle for Self-Government*, p. 118.
376 "La Follette's people": LS to Joseph Steffens, Oct. 2, 1904, in LS et al., *Letters of Lincoln Steffens*, Vol. 1, p. 168.
376 "met a friendly legislature": Thomas Malone, ed., *Dictionary of American Biography* (New York: Charles Scribner's Sons, 1933), Vol. 5, p. 544.
376 "gone through the fire": Robert La Follette to LS, Nov. 14, 1904, LS Papers.
376 "No one will . . . court of last resort": Ibid.
376 "The President has": William Loeb to LS, Aug. 24, 1903, LS Papers.
377 renewing a friendship: *Racine* [WI] *Daily Journal*, Aug. 31, 1903; LS to Joseph Steffens, Oct. 17, 1903, LS Papers.
377 distance "as a political critic": H. H. Stein, "Theodore Roosevelt and the Press: Lincoln Steffens," *Mid-America* (April 1972), p. 98.
377 "He is a Democrat": LS to TR, Sept. 28, 1903, LS Papers.
377 "I wonder if you realize": LS to TR, Sept. 30, 1903, LS Papers.
377 "he and the President": LS to Joseph Steffens, Oct. 17, 1903, LS Papers.
377 "a complete destroying . . . on our part": TR to Thomas Jasper Akins, April 5, 1904, in *LTR*, Vol. 4, p. 771.
377 choosing to nominate Cyrus P. Walbridge: Steven L. Piott, *Holy Joe: Joseph W. Folk and the Missouri Idea* (Columbia: University of Missouri Press, 1997), p. 86.
377 was delighted when William Allen White: WAW to Samuel Adams, Nov. 9, 1904, White Papers.
377 "with the boodlers . . . traitor to a state": *Emporia* [KS] *Gazette*, reprinted in *Chicago Tribune*, July 22, 1904.
378 "a state of violent": *Washington Post*, July 25, 1904.
378 Folk ran a superb campaign . . . 30,000 votes: Piott, *Holy Joe*, p. 89.
378 "It must make you feel": Joseph W. Folk to LS, Nov. 9, 1905, LS Papers.
378 He reiterated the profound obligation: Joseph W. Folk to LS, April 17 & May 22, 1904, LS Papers.
378 "one of the greatest moral": *The Arena* (August 1904), p. 91.
378 "discovered that": New York *World*, reprinted in *Minneapolis Daily Times*, May 16, 1904.
378 "a powerful exponent": *The North American* (Philadelphia), Aug. 15, 1905.
378 "must-read" pieces: Winston Churchill in Semonche, *Ray Stannard Baker*, p. 120.
378 "distinctly literary . . . go wrong in the end": *Daily Northwestern* (Oshkosh, WI), Mar. 8, 1905.
378 for a potential series of articles: LS to Joseph Steffens, Oct. 17, 1903, LS Papers.
378 McClure preferred to continue: Lyon, *Success Story*, p. 222.
379 "assume the responsibilities": Herbert Croly, *Marcus Alonzo Hanna, His Life and Work* (New York: The Macmillan Co., 1912), p. 426.
379 "When you know": MAH to TR, May 23, 1903, TRC
379 "the time had come . . . as a boon": TR to HCL, May 27, 1903, in *LTR*, Vol. 3, pp. 481–82.
379 "Your telegram received": TR to MAH, May 25, 1903, in ibid., p. 481.
379 "In view of": MAH to TR, May 27, 1903, in ibid., p. 481.
379 "It was surrender": *Oxnard* [CA] *Courier*, June 6, 1903.
379 "Hanna Backs Down . . . President's Wishes": *Fort Wayne* [IN] *Journal-Gazette* and *Trenton* [NJ] *Times*, May 27, 1903.
379 "I hated to . . . half hours chat": TR to MAH, May 29, 1903, TRJP.
380 "the most arduous": Croly, *Marcus Alonzo Hanna*, p. 450.
380 "an overwhelming personal victory": *Minneapolis Journal*, Nov. 5, 1903.
380 "almost unique . . . discredited leader": New York *Sun*, Nov. 6, 1903.
380 "There is alarm": *Stark County Democrat* (Canton, OH), Nov. 6, 1903.
380 "the turning point . . . from Theodore Roosevelt": Cited in New York *Sun*, Nov. 6, 1903.
380 "The wealthy capitalists": TR to Nicholas M. Butler, Nov. 4, 1903, in *LTR*, Vol. 3, p. 641.

380 "by the bushel":New York *Sun*, Nov. 6, 1903.
380 "It is agreed": *Stark County Democrat*, Nov. 6, 1903.
380 Roosevelt had "lost his popularity in": *Daily Telegram* (Eau Claire, WI), Dec. 12, 1903.
380 "the general idea . . . out on the plains!": Henry Hoyt to WHT, Oct. 19, 1903, WHTP.
381 "worried lest Hanna . . . getting the delegates": *Davenport* [IA] *Weekly Leader*, Dec. 11, 1903.
381 "hoping to get Hanna": LS to Joseph Steffens, Dec. [n.d.], 1903, in LS et al., *Letters of Lincoln Steffens*, Vol. 1, p. 162.
381 "If I am to have": LS to Joseph Steffens, Dec. 13, 1903, in ibid., p. 160.
381 "for a short confab . . . the heaviest blows": LS to Joseph Steffens, Dec. [n.d.], 1903, in ibid., p. 162.
381 "Hanna is my villain . . . may do good": LS to Joseph Steffens, January 26, 1904, in ibid., p. 184.
381 "above the danger mark": LS to Joseph Steffens, Dec. [n.d.], 1903, in ibid., p. 162.
381 "degraded the municipal": LS, *The Struggle for Self-Government*, p. 165.
381 "He wanted to have a President": Ibid., p. 168.
382 "legislators were kidnapped": Ibid., pp. 179–80.
382 "government of the people": Ibid., p. 168.
382 "was the choice": Ibid., p. 162.
382 "the senator's advanced age": *Minneapolis Journal*, Feb. 5, 1904.
382 "For some inexplicable": TR to Elihu Root, Feb. 16, 1904, in *LTR*, Vol. 4, p. 730.
382 "My Dear Mr. President . . . friendship as ever": *New York Tribune*, Feb. 24, 1904.
382 "The illness of Hanna": LS to Joseph Steffens, Feb. 14, 1904, in LS et al., *Letters of Lincoln Steffens*, Vol. 1, p. 165.
382 the old senator seemed to rally: *Washington Times*, Feb. 12, 1904; *St. Louis Republic*, Feb. 13, 1904.
382 "Today he is . . . decide his fate": LS to Joseph Steffens, Feb. 14, 1904, in LS et al., *Letters of Lincoln Steffens*, Vol. 1, p. 165.
382 after "a brave struggle," he died: James Rudolph Garfield, Diary, Feb. 15, 1904, Garfield Papers.
382 "all talk": *Daily Northwestern*, Feb. 21, 1904.
382 open resistance to Roosevelt: John Morton Blum, *The Republican Roosevelt* (Cambridge, MA: Harvard University Press, 1961), p. 54.
382 "Of course, Hanna's death": Albert Boyden to RSB, Feb. 15, 1904, RSB Papers.
383 "the best-governed": LS, "Ohio: A Tale of Two Cities," *McClure's* (July 1905), p. 293.
383 "appeared just": Brand Whitlock, *Forty Years of It* (New York: D. Appleton & Co., 1914), pp. 168, 167.
383 "My feeling": Tom L. Johnson to LS, Oct. 8, 1908, LS Papers.
383 "The day of the American . . . McClure and Lincoln Steffens": Cited in *Congregationalist and Christian World*, Nov. 18, 1905.
383 "To you, more than": Publicity copy, *McClure's* (November, 1905).
383 "very much like": Kaplan, *Lincoln Steffens*, p. 125.
383 "The story is": "Interview with S. S. McClure," *The North American*, Aug. 15, 1905.
383 "mold it into a story . . . vital interest": *Minneapolis Journal*, Feb. 26, 1906.
383 "We were ourselves": RSB, *American Chronicle*, p. 183.
384 "Month after month": Ibid., p. 184.
384 "a medal of honor . . . being accomplished": *Minneapolis Tribune*, May 16, 1904.
384 "when the historian": "The Literature of Exposure," *The Independent*, Mar. 22, 1906, p. 690.

CHAPTER FOURTEEN: "Thank Heaven You Are to Be with Me!"

Page
385 "You have been . . . absolutely cut off": Horace Taft to WHT, Nov. 2, 1903, WHTP.
386 "it would be impossible": TR, *An Autobiography*, p. 430.
386 "guilty of an irreparable . . . in Judge Holmes' favor": TR to HCL, July 10, 1902, in *LTR*, Vol. 3, pp. 288–89.
386 "the hearty approval": *Logansport* [IN] *Journal*, Sept. 9, 1902.
386 "no small amount of praise": *Daily Californian* (Bakersfield, CA), Sept. 5, 1902.
386 "of utmost importance": TR to WHT, Oct. 25, 1902, TRP.
386 Taft's views on economic matters: TR to HCL, July 10, 1902, in *LTR*, Vol. 3, p. 288.
386 "the blindness and greed . . . freedom of contract": WHT to TR, Nov. 9, 1902, TRP.
386 "I hesitated long": TR to WHT, Oct. 21, 1902, in *LTR*, Vol. 3, p. 358.
387 "All his life": HHT, *Recollections of Full Years*, p. 263.
387 "Great honor deeply": WHT to TR, Oct. 28, 1902, in ibid., p. 264.
387 "I am disappointed": TR to WHT, Oct. 29, 1902, in *LTR*, Vol. 3, p. 372.
387 "unanswerable": HHT, *Recollections of Full Years*, p. 266.
387 "I am awfully sorry": TR to WHT, Nov. 26, 1902, in *LTR*, Vol. 3, p. 382.
387 "He is extremely . . . satisfied with your decision": Henry W. Taft to WHT, Jan. 10, 1903, WHTP.
388 "really leaves me": WHT to Charles P. Taft, Jan. 7, 1903, WHTP.
388 "within a few months" Taft would resign: *Washington Times*, Dec. 9, 1902.
388 "heaved a sigh . . . one more protest": HHT, *Recollections of Full Years*, p. 266.
388 "Recognize soldiers duty . . . I bow to it": WHT to TR, Jan. 8. 1903, TRP.
389 "proudest and happiest" moments: Pringle, *Life and Times*, Vol. 1, p. 245.
389 "flags flying" . . . WE WANT TAFT: HHT, *Recollections of Full Years*, p. 267.
389 "This is a spontaneous . . . all Philippine questions": Ibid., p. 268.
389 "the thousands of people": *Daily Kennebeck Journal* (Augusta, ME), Jan. 12, 1903.
389 "All right stay": TR to WHT, Jan. 13, 1903, in HHT, *Recollections of Full Years*, p. 269.
389 "very sorry . . . take you away": TR to WHT, Jan. 29, 1903, in *LTR*, Vol. 3, p. 413.
389 "with renewed vigour": HHT, *Recollections of Full Years*, p. 269.
389 "working for other people": WHT to William Worthington, Feb. 6, 1904, WHTP.

390 "I was not a month": *Cedar Rapids* [IA] *Evening Gazette*, Jan. 25, 1904.
390 "There is not": TR, "Speech at Fargo, N.D., April 7, 1903," in TR and Lewis, *A Compilation of the Messages and Speeches*, p. 269.
390 "a personality which . . . administrative and legislative": Henry Taft to WHT, Jan. 10, 1903, WHTP.
390 "Stood trip well . . . How is the horse?": *Boston Daily Globe*, Jan. 31, 1904.
390 "a magnificent animal": Pringle, *Life and Times*, Vol. 1, p. 236.
390 "You will think I am . . . to leave me next fall": TR to WHT, Feb. 14, 1903, in *LTR*, Vol. 3, pp. 425–26.
390 "the wisest": Sullivan, *Our Times*, Vol. 3, p. 279.
391 "I wish to heaven . . . questions that come up": TR to WHT, Feb. 14, 1903, in *LTR*, Vol. 3, pp. 425–26.
391 "If only there were": Ibid., p. 426.
391 "In view of your desire . . . a definite answer": WHT to TR, April 3, 1903, TRP.
391 "in line with the kind": HHT, *Recollections of Full Years*, p. 269.
392 "prophesied on the day": WHT to Horace Taft, Aug. 19, 1903, WHTP.
392 "If I were to go . . . live in a boarding house": WHT to Charles P. Taft, Mar. 27, 1903, WHTP.
392 Taft's mother . . . urged his return: Charles P. Taft to WHT, May 8, 1903, WHTP.
392 the family was unanimous: Henry Taft to WHT, June 16, 1903, WHTP.
392 "I should prefer": Charles P. Taft to WHT, May 8, 1903, WHTP.
392 to give up so "great a work": Horace Taft to WHT, May 13, 1903, WHTP.
392 If acceptance of the secretaryship seemed inconsistent: Henry Taft to WHT, June 16, 1903, WHTP.
392 "earnest desire . . . embarrass your candidacy": WHT to TR, April 27, 1903, TRP.
393 "You don't know . . . Civil Service Commissioner": TR to WHT, June 9, 1903, in *LTR*, Vol. 3, pp. 485–86.
393 "should feel independent": WHT to HHT, Feb. 2, 1904, WHTP.
393 "struck me all in a heap": WHT to Charles P. Taft, Feb. [n.d.], 1904, WHTP.
393 "The President is very . . . the step at once": Henry Taft to WHT, June 16, 1903, WHTP.
393 "keep out of politics": WHT to Howard Hollister, Sept. 21, 1903, Pringle Papers.
393 "Thank Heaven": TR to WHT, June 9, 1903, in *LTR*, Vol. 3, p. 486.
393 "I have an additional . . . much to tell you": TR to WHT, Oct. 13, 1903, in ibid., p. 629.
394 "too amazed . . . a sacred potentate": *Davenport* [IA] *Weekly Leader*, Jan. 29, 1904.
394 "was most enjoyable": WHT to HHT, Feb. 1, 1904, WHTP.
394 the president stayed for hours: James Rudolph Garfield, Diary, Jan. 27, 1904, Garfield Papers.
394 affectionately known as "Big Bill": *Cedar Rapids* [IA] *Evening Gazette*, Jan. 25, 1904.
394 "Two men were never": *Washington Times*, Jan. 31, 1904.
394 "Taft is a splendid fellow": TR to Theodore Roosevelt, Jr., Feb. 6, 1904, TRJP.
394 "too much like" her husband: Ibid.
394 "As the people loved . . . his own impetuosity": Sullivan, *Our Times*, Vol. 3, pp. 16, 18.
395 "It was good": WHT to HHT, Feb. 1, 1904, WHTP.
395 "felt like crying": Horace Taft to WHT, Feb. 4, 1904, WHTP.
395 "democratic manner . . . breezy informality": *Washington Times*, Jan. 31, 1904.
395 "I'm mighty glad": *Cedar Rapids* [IA] *Evening Gazette*, Jan. 25, 1904.
395 "he found time": *Washington Times*, Jan. 31, 1904.
395 "He looks like": Sullivan, *Our Times*, Vol. 3, p. 15.
395 bombarded by dinner invitations: WHT to HHT, Mar. 4, 1904, WHTP.
395 "I went down": WHT to HHT, Feb. 12, 1904, WHTP.
395 "The President seems . . . opportunities of observation": WHT to HHT, Mar. 18, 1904, WHTP.
395 "coarse and brazen" divorced wife: WHT to HHT, Mar. 3, 1904, WHTP.
395 "the Chief of the Pawnees": WHT to HHT, April 16, 1904, WHTP.
395 Alice Roosevelt . . . poker with men: Stacy A. Cordery, *Alice: Alice Roosevelt Longworth, from White House Princess to Washington Power Broker* (New York: Viking, 2007), pp. 65–66, 74, 78.
396 "a great deal of criticism . . . much troubled": WHT to HHT, April 5, 1904, WHTP.
396 "Isn't there anything": Hagedorn, *The Roosevelt Family of Sagamore Hill*, p. 186.
396 "I do not feel": WHT to HHT, Mar. [n.d.], 1904, WHTP.
396 "loaded tons of work . . . for the Administration": Arthur Wallace Dunn, *From Harrison to Harding, A Personal Narrative, Covering a Third of a Century, 1888–1921* (New York: G. P. Putnam's Sons, 1922), p. 67.
396 a "trouble-shooter . . . there Taft was sent": Sullivan, *Our Times*, Vol. 3, p. 12.
396 "extremely popular both . . . as the other": *Iowa Postal Card* (Fayette, IA), April 28, 1904.
396 "Things have quieted down": A. B. Fergusson to WHT, Dec. 30, 1903, WHTP.
397 loath to invest "so far from home": *NYT*, Mar. 11 & April 11, 1904.
397 vital infrastructure projects would be undertaken: *Janesville* [WI] *Daily Gazette*, Mar. 25, 1904; *NYT*, April 11, 1904.
397 Cannon's approval of the railroad bill: WHT to HHT, Mar. 31, 1904, WHTP.
397 "All in favor . . . the bill is passed": *Waterloo* [IA] *Daily Reporter*, May 20, 1904.
397 "I have been working": WHT to HHT, Mar. 31, 1904, WHTP.
397 the bill finally passed: *NYT*, Feb. 7, 1905.
397 "it would seem": *Logansport* [IN] *Pharos*, Feb. 2, 1904.
397 allies of the sugar and tobacco industries vowed: *Post-Standard* (Syracuse, NY), Mar. 3, 1904.
397 "I can see": WHT to TR, Jan. 27, 1903, TRP.
398 "The interest of dollars": Lyman Abbott to WHT, Feb. 20, 1903, WHTP.
398 "You are unjust . . . skillful and resolute": TR to WHT, Mar. 19, 1903, in *LTR*, Vol. 3, p. 450.
398 as word spread . . . seating was filled to capacity: New York *Sun*, Mar. 15, 1904.
398 "nervous expectancy": *Boston Daily Globe*, Mar. 15, 1904; *NYT*, Mar. 15, 1904.
398 "paper and pencil . . . against daring financiers": *Boston Daily Globe*, Mar. 15, 1904.

398 "Oyez, Oyez, Oyez": Ibid.
398 "being an Ohio man . . . was the alternative": WHT to Joseph B. Bishop, Jan. 24, 1903, WHTP.
399 "How eminently characteristic": TR to Joseph B. Bishop, Mar. 10, 1903, TRP.
399 "everyone was alert": *Boston Daily Globe*, Mar. 15, 1904.
399 "No scheme or device": *Northern Securities Company v. United States*, 193 U.S. 197 (1904).
399 "holding companies . . . of the entire country": New York *World*, Mar. 15, 1904.
399 "it was all over": *Boston Daily Globe*, Mar. 15, 1904.
399 If "Congress can strike": *Northern Securities Company v. United States*, 193 U.S. 197 (1904).
399 "the surprise of the day . . . champion of labor": *Boston Daily Globe*, Mar. 15, 1904.
399 "while the merger": New York *Sun*, Mar. 15, 1904.
399 "I could carve out . . . it was never the same": Harbaugh, *Power and Responsibility*, p. 162.
399 "put aside all else": *Washington Post*, Mar. 15, 1904.
399 "hardly be exaggerated": New York *World*, Mar. 15, 1904.
400 "more to the people . . . greater than the law": *Public Opinion*, Mar. 24, 1904, p. 356.
400 the great "trust-buster": Hofstadter, *The Age of Reform*, p. 238.
400 "run amuck": *Public Opinion*, Mar. 24, 1904, p. 357.
400 "this power": "Mr. Roosevelt's Platform," *Outlook*, July 2, 1904, p. 481.
400 "If a corporation": TR to RSB, Aug. 27, 1904, in *LTR*, Vol. 4, p. 909.
400 "the selfish rich . . . lunatic fringe": Blum, *The Republican Roosevelt*, p. 60.

CHAPTER FIFTEEN: "A Smile That Won't Come Off"

Page

402 Strikers, he reported . . . were in peril: James H. Peabody to TR, Nov. 16 & 18, 1903, in Carroll D. Wright, *A Report on Labor Disturbances in the State of Colorado: From 1880 to 1904, Inclusive, with Correspondence Relating Thereto* (Washington, DC: Government Printing Office, 1905), pp. 9–10.
402 "no lawful authority . . . to control": Elihu Root to James H. Peabody, Nov. 17 & 19, 1903, in ibid., pp. 9, 11.
402 "corruption & bribery": RSB to J. Stannard Baker, Nov. 18, 1903, RSB Papers.
402 "had a pad . . . conditions in the West": RSB to Jessie Baker, Dec. 3, 1903, RSB Papers.
402 "I believe in": TR to RSB, Oct. 21, 1903, TRP.
402 With the president's blessing: TR to RSB, Nov. 25, 1903, TRP.
402 "everything the men wanted" . . . to stem the corruption and violence: RSB, "The Reign of Lawlessness: Anarchy and Despotism in Colorado," *McClure's* (May 1904), pp. 43–53.
403 "I have endeavored": RSB to TR, April 19, 1904, TRP.
403 "the most masterly": *The Arena* (August 1904), p. 191.
403 "This language is not": *Wall Street Journal*, April 25, 1904.
404 Roosevelt . . . had it circulated among officials: TR to Carroll D. Wright, Aug. 13, 1904, in *LTR*, Vol. 4, p. 891.
404 On June 6 . . . the "dastardly crime": Wright, *A Report*, p. 247.
404 "the least anarchistic expression": *Weekly Gazette* (Colorado Springs, CO), June 9, 1904.
404 "wives and sisters": *Boston Daily Globe*, June 11, 1904.
404 "in the name of law and order": *Reno* [NV] *Evening Gazette*, June 10, 1904.
404 "Having refused": TR to Carroll D. Wright, Aug. 5, 1904, in *LTR*, Vol. 4, p. 883.
404 "If it becomes necessary": TR to Carroll D. Wright, Aug. 13, 1904, in ibid., p. 891.
404 "the basis of": RSB to J. Stannard Baker, Jan. 29, 1905, RSB Papers.
404 "as the representative": TR to Philander C. Knox, Nov. 10, 1904, in *LTR*, Vol. 4, p. 1024.
405 "He was most . . . correct & fair": RSB to J. Stannard Baker, Jan. 29, 1905, RSB Papers.
405 the mine owners finally agreed: Wright, *A Report*, p. 32.
405 Governor Peabody was forced out of office: *New York Tribune*, Mar. 18, 1905.
405 the state legislature passed a state law: *Laws Passed at the Fifteenth Session of the General Assembly* . . . (Denver, CO: Smith-Brooks Printing Co., 1905).
405 "barring a cataclysm . . . sullen grumbling": TR to Kermit Roosevelt, June 21, 1904, in *LTR*, Vol. 4, p. 840.
405 "the thunderous demonstration": *San Francisco Chronicle*, June 22, 1904.
405 "a lifeless gathering": Francis E. Leupp, "The Republican Convention," *Outlook*, July 2, 1904, p. 490.
405 "sober and unhysterical": *New York Tribune*, June 22, 1904.
405 An enormous portrait of Hanna: *New York Tribune*, June 21, 1904.
405 "because they had to": Leupp, "The Republican Convention," *Outlook*, July 2, 1904, p. 489.
405 "shadow of the chance . . . he can overcome the people": WAW, "Seconding the Motion," *Saturday Evening Post*, July 23, 1904, pp. 4–5.
406 this spirit of rebellion . . . to realize "a better world": WAW, *The Autobiography*, p. 88.
406 "a new element . . . for his times": WAW, "Americans Look to Roosevelt to Solve New Perils to Nation," *Chicago Tribune*, Oct. 24, 1904.
406 "more than he needed the party": *Minneapolis Journal*, Nov. 9, 1904.
406 "professional politicians . . . grip of power": Leupp, "The Republican Convention," *Outlook*, July 2, 1904, p. 491.
406 taking control of . . . growl behind them": Ibid.
406 With his reputation for honesty: *New York Tribune*, Nov. 2, 1904.
406 "People may as well . . . irrevocable": TR to George Von Legerke Meyer, June 17, 1904, in *LTR*, Vol. 4, pp. 838–39.
406 "a formidable weapon": TR to Joseph Wharton, Nov. 22, 1904, in ibid., p. 1039.
406 "a cardinal policy": Milton W. Blumenberg, *Official Proceedings of the Thirteenth Republican National Convention: Held in the City of Chicago, June 21, 22, 23, 1904* (Minneapolis: Harrison & Smith Co., 1904), p. 134.
406 "four years more": *Public Opinion*, June 30, 1904, p. 806.
406 Roosevelt hesitated: TR to Nicholas M. Butler, Dec. 2, 1904, in *LTR*, Vol. 4, p. 838.

407 "of all men": TR to Theodore Roosevelt, Jr., May 14, 1904, TRJP.
407 "affectionate congratulations . . . his personal friends": *Post-Standard* (Syracuse, NY), June 24, 1904.
407 "in exceptionally good humor": *Trenton* [NJ] *Times*, June 24, 1904.
407 "With genial raillery": *Post-Standard* (Syracuse, NY), June 24, 1904.
407 "the hero . . . in their hearts": WAW, "The Great Political Drama in St. Louis," *Collier's*, July 12, 1904.
407 "eight-year reign was over": New York *World*, July 13, 1904.
408 "robbery of the many": Milton W. Blumenberg, *Official Report of the Proceedings of the Democratic National Convention Held in St. Louis, Mo., July 6, 7, 8, and 9, 1904* (New York: Press of the Publishers' Printing Co., 1904), p. 148.
408 the nominee was not apprised of his victory: *NYT*, July 10, 1904.
408 "the gold standard . . . decline the nomination": Blumenberg, *Official Report of the Proceedings of the Democratic National Convention*, p. 276.
408 no longer "an issue at this time": *Boston Daily Globe*, July 10, 1904.
408 "was most adroit . . . a clever politician": TR to John Hay, July 11, 1904, in *LTR*, Vol. 4, p. 852.
408 "all of Cleveland's": TR to HCL, July 14, 1904, in ibid., p. 858.
408 "was stronger": WHT to TR, July 16, 1904, TRP.
408 "a hard and uphill fight": TR to HCL, July 14, 1904, in *LTR*, Vol. 4, p. 858.
408 "I always like": TR to HCL, July 14, 1904, in ibid.
408 "was received . . . logical, convincing": *Minneapolis Journal*, July 28, 1904.
409 "characteristically forceful": *Titusville* [PA] *Herald*, July 28, 1904.
409 "keen and polished": HCL to TR, July 29, 1904, in TR and HCL, *Selections from the Correspondence*, Vol. 2, p. 92.
409 "used few gestures": *Washington Post*, Aug. 11, 1904.
409 mustered no "bugle call": *Boston Evening Transcript*, Aug. 27, 1904.
409 would not run for a second term: *Washington Post*, Aug. 11, 1904.
409 "shifty and tricky" gambit: TR to Joseph B. Bishop, Aug. 13, 1904, TRP.
409 failed to "straddle": TR to HCL, August 11, 1904, in *LTR*, Vol. 4, p. 887.
409 Taft's assessment had been correct: TR to HCL, July 22, 1904, in ibid., p. 863.
409 "His opponents may": WHT to HHT, Aug. 18, 1904, WHTP.
409 Roosevelt also circulated drafts: TR to John Hay, July 11, 1904, in *LTR*, Vol. 4, p. 853.
409 "I went at": William Dudley Foulke, *Lucius B. Swift, A Biography* (Indianapolis: Bobbs-Merrill Co. for the Indiana Hist. Soc., 1930), p. 73.
409 "Remarkable": *NYT*, Sept. 27, 1904.
409 "a veritable keynote": *Washington Post*, Sept. 12, 1904.
409 "the challenge contained . . . the Democrats have": WHT to TR, Sept. 14, 1904, TRP.
409 "the issues of the campaign": *Washington Post*, Sept. 27, 1904.
409 "a great paper . . . of the people": *NYT*, Sept. 27, 1904.
410 "heart to . . . his campaign": TR to Joseph B. Bishop, Sept. 28, 1904, TRP.
410 "take the offensive . . . sit still": TR to Kermit Roosevelt, Oct. 26, 1904, in *LTR*, Vol. 4, pp. 992–93.
410 "It seems strange": WHT to Howard Hollister, Sept. 21, 1903, WHTP.
410 "mere political discussion": WHT to HHT, Feb. 2, 1904, WHTP.
410 "I rather think": WHT to HHT, Sept. 27, 1904, WHTP.
410 "right down to": WHT to Charles P. Taft, June 23, 1904, WHTP.
410 "a great public document": TR to HCL, June 28, 1904, in *LTR*, Vol. 4, p. 849.
410 "a masterly argument . . . a truly great man": Garfield Diary, June 26 & Feb. 11, 1904, Garfield Papers.
410 presented his speech . . . at Sanders Theatre: *New York Tribune*, June 29, 1904.
410 Taft simply but clearly . . . "Philippines for the Filipinos": *Cincinnati Enquirer*, June 29, 1904.
411 Olney's rebuttal . . . "for they love him": Ibid.
411 "I fired my gun": WHT to TR, July 3, 1904, TRP.
411 "magical place": *Cincinnati Magazine* (August 1979), p. 72.
411 "The air is bracing": WHT to TR, July 3, 1904, TRP.
411 "The next ten days": WHT to HHT, Aug. 15, 1904, WHTP.
411 "a bit rusty": WHT to HHT, Aug. 3, 1904, WHTP.
411 "the Bench disqualifies": WHT to HHT, Aug. 15, 1904, WHTP.
412 "the size of her": WHT to Horace Taft, Aug. 4, 1904, WHTP.
412 Taft chose . . . a spirited defense: *NYT*, Aug. 28, 1904.
412 "When Theodore Roosevelt . . . previously formed opinion": Ibid.
412 "It was a success": WHT to HHT, Aug. 28, 1904, WHTP.
412 "It would be . . . support of his administration": *Titusville* [PA] *Herald*, July 29, 1904.
412 "a text-book for": Ibid.
412 a "glorious" triumph: WHT to TR, Sept. 7, 1904, TRP.
412 "I am pleased": TR to WHT, Sept. 10, 1904, in *LTR*, Vol. 4, p. 919.
412 "a rather gloomy letter": TR to Eugene Hale, Aug. 4, 1904, in ibid., p. 880.
412 "to speak without notes": WHT to HHT, Aug. 30, 1904, WHTP.
412 "great surprise" . . . proposed toasts: WHT to Howard Hollister, Sept. 16, 1904, WHTP.
413 "Mrs. Taft says": WHT to TR, Sept. 14, 1904, WHTP.
413 Roosevelt complained freely: TR to WHT, Sept. 5, 1904, WHTP.
413 Taft described a new diet: WHT to TR, Sept. 2, 1904, TRP.
413 "infernal liars . . . a corruption fund": TR to WHT, Sept. 10, 1904, in *LTR*, Vol. 4, p. 919.
413 "playing golf": WHT to TR, Sept. 7, 1904, TRP.
413 Taft was immediately dispatched: WHT to TR, Sept. 20, 1904, TRP.
413 "Do not in any speech": TR to WHT, Sept. 29, 1904, in *LTR*, Vol. 4, p. 960.

413 "the most auspicious in years": *Washington Post*, Oct. 2, 1904.
413 "After reading": Ibid.; *Hutchinson* [KS] *News*, Nov. 8, 1904.
413 In daily letters, she related: HHT to WHT, Oct. 3, 4 & 5, 1904, WHTP.
414 "I hope Charley's": WHT to HHT, Oct. 3, 1904, WHTP.
414 "I wish I could": WHT to HHT, Oct. 8, 1904, WHTP.
414 "I don't think": WHT to HHT, Oct. 6, 1904, WHTP.
414 "could not but smile": HHT to WHT, Oct. 7, 1904, WHTP.
414 a delegation of cigar and tobacco manufacturers: *NYT*, Oct. 10, 1904.
414 "to control cigar makers": WHT to HHT, Oct. 8, 1904, WHTP.
414 "just at the anxious time": WHT to HHT, Oct. 10, 1904, WHTP.
414 "I feel sure . . . emphasize the issue": WHT to TR, Oct. 10, 1904, TRP.
414 "Fiddle-dee-dee! . . . or something": TR to WHT, Oct. 11, 1904, in *LTR*, Vol. 4, p. 980.
414 "would not run": WHT to HHT, Oct. 12, 1904, WHTP.
415 "a man who never . . . liberty and equality": *Valentine* [NE] *Democrat*, Oct. 13, 1904.
415 "It is the culmination . . . utterly ignored": *Anaconda* [MT] *Standard*, Oct. 9, 1904.
415 conceding the region to Democrats: Ibid.
415 "full dinner pail": *Atlanta Constitution*, Oct. 18, 1904.
415 "He is on the side": New York *Sun*, July 30, 1904.
415 populist publications reviled him: TR to Joseph G. Cannon, Aug. 3, 1904, in *LTR*, Vol. 4, p. 880.
415 "without exception" . . . the closed shop: RSB, "Parker and Roosevelt on Labor: Real Views of the Two Candidates on the Most Vital National Problem," *McClure's* (November 1904), pp. 41–42.
415 "Personally he is": RSB to J. Stannard Baker, Sept. 8, 1904, RSB Papers.
416 "I cannot help feeling . . . but *no* easier": TR to RSB, Aug. 27, 1904, in *LTR*, Vol. 4, pp. 908, 910–11.
416 "I am perfectly astonished": RSB to TR, Sept. 6, 1904, TRP.
416 "a clear idea . . . preaches class hatred": RSB, "Parker and Roosevelt on Labor," *McClure's* (November 1904), pp. 51–52.
417 "thorough and painstaking" methods: *Los Angeles Times*, Nov. 3, 1904.
417 "the bulk of the voters . . . mass of voters": TR to Kermit Roosevelt, Oct. 26, 1904, in *LTR*, Vol. 4, p. 992.
417 "The steady advance": *NYT*, Oct. 2, 1904.
417 "would make the millions . . . a tremendous reform": LS to TR, Sept. 21, 1905, in LS et al., *Letters of Lincoln Steffens*, Vol. 1, p. 170.
417 "most emphatically" . . . or take executive action: TR to LS, Sept. 25, 1905, in *LTR*, Vol. 5, p. 36.
417 "entirely legitimate": TR to George B. Cortelyou, Oct. 26, 1904, in *LTR*, Vol. 4, p. 995.
418 Roosevelt willingly received hundreds of thousands of dollars: Morris, *Theodore Rex*, pp. 359–60.
418 "In view of the open": TR to George B. Cortelyou, Oct. 27, 1904, in *LTR*, Vol. 4, p. 998.
418 "big business corporations . . . entirely proper": TR to George B. Cortelyou, Oct. 26, 1904, in ibid., pp. 995–96.
418 "The fact that": *NYT*, Oct. 2, 1904.
418 corporations . . . "contributed to both campaign funds": *New York Tribune*, Nov. 1, 1904.
418 "in a conspiracy": *NYT*, Nov. 4, 1904.
418 "like a big stick": *Anaconda* [MT] *Standard*, Oct. 9, 1904.
418 "the prostitution": Ibid.
418 Cortelyou and Garfield were reluctant: Garfield Diary, Nov. 3, 1904, Garfield Papers.
418 "I don't see why": WHT to HHT, Nov. 3, 1904, WHTP.
419 "I am the man": TR to George B. Cortelyou, Nov. 2, 1904, in *LTR*, Vol. 4, pp. 1009–12.
419 to take the midnight train: Garfield Diary, Nov. 3, 1904, Garfield Papers.
419 "Blood Money . . . drew out of sight": *St. Louis Post-Dispatch*, Nov. 4, 1904.
419 "direct and fierce . . . in a few moments": *NYT*, Nov. 5, 1904.
419 "The gravamen of these charges . . . *unqualifiedly and atrociously false*": *NYT*, Nov. 5, 1904 (italics in the original).
420 "he had made no": *Post-Standard* (Syracuse, NY), Nov. 7, 1904.
420 "Parker fails to furnish proofs": TR to William Loeb, Nov. 6, 1904, in *LTR*, Vol. 4, p. 1015.
420 "has knocked Parker flat": Garfield Diary, Nov. 5, 1904, Garfield Papers.
420 "Parker's attacks": TR to Kermit Roosevelt, Nov. 6, 1904, in TR et al., eds., *Letters to Kermit from Theodore Roosevelt*, p. 83.
420 "he had never wanted . . . the United States": CRR, *My Brother*, p. 217.
420 "a first-class run": TR to Rudyard Kipling, Nov. 1, 1904, TRP.
420 "felt soured": TR to Kermit Roosevelt, June 21, 1904, in *LTR*, Vol. 4, p. 840.
420 a crowd of "home folk": *St. Louis Republic*, Nov. 9, 1904.
420 "sprang briskly": *Post-Standard* (Syracuse, NY), Nov. 9, 1904.
420 he caught the 1:14 train: *Washington Post*, Nov. 8, 1904.
420 "not to think of": TR to Kermit Roosevelt, Nov. 10, 1904, in *LTR*, Vol. 4, p. 1024.
420 "a plurality": *Oshkosh* [WI] *Daily Northwestern*, Nov. 9, 1904.
421 "a tremendous drift . . . very proud and happy": TR to Kermit Roosevelt, Nov. 10, 1904, in *LTR*, Vol. 4, p. 1024.
421 "no attempt . . . on the mantel shelf": *Oshkosh* [WI] *Daily Northwestern*, Nov. 9, 1904.
421 "I am deeply sensible": Kohlsaat, *From McKinley to Harding*, p. 137.
421 "a bid for votes": TR to Arthur Von Brisen, Oct. 27, 1904, in *LTR*, Vol. 4, p. 1000; *St. Paul* [MN] *Globe*, Nov. 10, 1904.
421 "use the office": TR, *An Autobiography*, p. 387.
421 "I feel very strongly . . . a new start": TR to George Otto Trevelyan, Nov. 4, 1904, in *LTR*, Vol. 4, pp. 1045–46.
422 "the greatest popular majority": TR to Kermit Roosevelt, Nov. 10, 1904, in TR et al., eds., *Letters to Kermit from Theodore Roosevelt,* p. 84.
422 He had won all . . . unexpected coup: Arthur Wallace Dunn, *How Presidents Are Made* (New York: Funk & Wagnalls, 1920), p. 85.

422 "I am stunned": TR to Kermit Roosevelt, Nov. 10, 1904, in *LTR*, Vol. 4, p. 1024.
422 "has had a smile": WHT to Charles P. Taft, Nov. 17, 1904, WHTP.
422 "The document that gave": Murat Halstead to WHT, April 17, 1905, WHTP.
422 "thousands of votes . . . willing to admit": Howard Hollister to WHT, Nov. 10, 1904, WHTP.
422 "the victory is . . . of the President": WHT to Henry Hoyt, Nov. 12, 1904, WHTP.
422 "It is no unheard of thing . . . must be protected": *Cincinnati Enquirer*, Nov. 11, 1904; *The News* (Frederick, MD), Nov. 11, 1904.
422 "Unless the Republican party": Henry Hoyt to WHT, Nov. 11, 1904, WHTP.
423 "pregnant with promise . . . history of the republic": *Minneapolis Journal*, Nov. 9, 1904.
423 "to the best": *St. Paul Globe*, Nov. 10, 1904.
423 "nothing but praise": *Public Opinion*, Nov. 17, 1904.
423 "to his everlasting honor" . . . his last: New York *Sun*, Nov. 9, 1904.
423 willingly cut off his hand at the wrist: Kohlsaat, *From McKinley to Harding*, p. 138.

CHAPTER SIXTEEN: "Sitting on the Lid"

Page
424 "blue, flecked . . . Roosevelt weather": *Boston Daily Globe*, Mar. 5, 1905.
424 "the morning sun": *Washington Post*, Mar. 5, 1905.
424 "supremely happy . . . moment of our lives": *Boston Daily Globe*, Mar. 5, 1905.
425 "a friendly little . . . truculent note": *Public Opinion*, Mar. 18, 1905.
425 "Much has been given . . . great wealth": TR, "Inaugural Address," March 4, 1905, in *WTR*, Vol. 15, pp. 267–69.
425 characteristic "earnestness": *Boston Daily Globe*, Mar. 5, 1905.
425 "tempestuous doings": See *Public Opinion*, Nov. 24, 1904.
425 "The Republican party": WAW, "The Reorganization of the Republican Party," *Saturday Evening Post*, Dec. 3, 1904.
425 "Everybody rejoices": *Ohio State Journal* (Columbus, OH), cited in *Van Wert* [OH] *Daily Bulletin*, April 5, 1905.
426 a "handsomely fitted" train: *NYT*, April 4, 1905.
426 "like a small boy" . . . office seekers: *Washington Post*, April 4, 1905.
426 "much more pleasant . . . the everlasting suspicion": TR to Kermit Roosevelt, April 14, 1905, in TR et al., eds., *Letters to Kermit from Theodore Roosevelt,* p. 97.
426 "wild enthusiasm . . . genuine pleasure": TR to John Hay, April 2, 1905, in *LTR*, Vol. 4, pp. 1159, 1156.
426 "in the saddle . . . wolf hunter": TR to Kermit Roosevelt, April 14, 1905, in TR et al., eds., *Letters to Kermit from Theodore Roosevelt*, p. 98.
426 "up at daybreak . . . band of huntsmen": New York *Sun*, April 21, 1905.
426 "roughened by wind": TR to Kermit Roosevelt, May 7, 1905, in TR et al., eds., *Letters to Kermit from Theodore Roosevelt*, pp. 99–100.
426 "Oh, things . . . sitting on the lid": *NYT*, April 4, 1905; *Van Wert* [OH] *Daily Bulletin*, April 5, 1905.
426 "grave and exacting problems": *Washington Times* and *Van Wert* [OH] *Daily Bulletin*, April 5, 1905.
426 "Chair of the President . . . Sec'y of War": *Harper's Weekly*, April 15, 1905.
426 "acting President . . . all executive departments": *Van Wert* [OH] *Daily Bulletin*, April 5, 1905.
427 "the unusual sight": *NYT*, April 4, 1905.
427 "William Howard Taft": *Cleveland Leader*, cited in *Van Wert* [OH] *Daily Bulletin*, April 5, 1905.
427 a treaty was negotiated: TR, "Message to Congress," Dec. 3, 1903, in *WTR*, Vol. 15, pp. 202–12.
427 "I took the Canal Zone": Bishop, *Theodore Roosevelt and His Time*, Vol. 1, p. 308.
427 "that Roosevelt had . . . value to the country": Viola Roseboro to Ada Pierce McCormick [n.d.], 1929, IMTC.
427 "You cannot conceive": *Baltimore Sun*, Feb. 22, 1904.
427 "He had an enormous": Burton, *William Howard Taft, in the Public Service*, p. 44.
427 the commission was authorized to establish: TR to WHT, May 9, 1904, in *LTR*, Vol. 4, pp. 788–89.
427 "really enough to occupy": Pringle, *Life and Times*, Vol. 1, pp. 280, 284.
427 "an independent colony": TR to WHT, Oct. 18, 1904, in *LTR*, Vol. 4, p. 986.
428 A small band of soldiers: WHT to Charles P. Taft, Nov. 17, 1904, WHTP.
428 "The whole atmosphere . . . cries of 'Viva!' ": HHT, *Recollections of Full Years*, pp. 284, 287–89.
428 merely "experimental": David McCullough, *The Path Between the Seas: The Creation of the Panama Canal, 1870–1914* (New York: Simon & Schuster, 1977), p. 449.
428 When a virulent outbreak: Ibid., p. 452.
428 "Here again": TR to WHT, April 20, 1905, in *LTR*, Vol. 4, p. 1165.
428 eventually called for Wallace to resign: McCullough, *The Path Between the Seas*, p. 457.
428 "You are handling everything": TR to WHT, April 8, 1905, in *LTR*, Vol. 4, p. 1158.
428 "keeping the lid on": TR to WHT, April 20, 1905, in ibid., p. 1161.
428 "You are on the ground": Ibid., p. 1165.
429 "I wish you knew Taft": TR to George Trevelyan, May 13, 1905, in ibid., p. 1173.
429 "Taft, by the way": TR to John Hay, May 6, 1905, in ibid., p. 1168.
429 "everything was in good": T. H. Pardo de Tavera to WHT, May 6, 1905, WHTP.
429 lost its "Pole star": WHT to TR, Jan. 19, 1905; WHT to HHT, Sept. 24, 1905, WHTP.
429 "discontent": T. H. Pardo de Tavera to WHT, Feb. 5, 1905, WHTP.
429 "the only man who can": T. H. Pardo de Tavera to WHT, May 6, 1905, WHTP.
429 Taft assembled a party of eighty people: WHT to Charles P. Taft, July 24, 1905, WHTP.
429 "I doubt if so formidable": WHT to H. C. Corbin, Mar. 14, 1905, in Pringle, *Life and Times*, Vol. 1, p. 293.
429 "Just heard sad news": WHT to TR, July 1, 1905, TRP.
429 "If it were not" . . . ask Elihu Root to take Hay's place: TR to WHT, July 3, 1905, in *LTR*, Vol. 4, p. 1260.

430 "hesitated a little . . . no room for doubt": TR to HCL, July 11, 1905, in ibid., p. 1271.
430 Taft dispelled any qualms: Ibid., p. 1272.
430 "My dear fellow": TR to WHT, July 6, 1905, in ibid., p. 1261.
430 "I do not think": ARL, *Crowded Hours*, p. 69.
430 "The party has been": WHT to TR, July 13, 1905, TRP.
430 Friends and family had warned Taft: Horace Taft to WHT, Mar. 7, 1905; HHT to WHT, July 13, 1905, WHTP.
430 "She is quite amenable" . . . Nevertheless, he remained troubled: WHT to HHT, Sept. 24, 1905, WHTP.
430 stories about the "fast set": WHT to HHT, Mar. 28, 1904, WHTP.
430 "She seems to be": WHT to HHT, July 31, 1905, WHTP.
430 "looked almost unreal": *Boston Daily Globe*, Aug. 8, 1905.
430 "usually confined to husband": WHT to HHT, Sept. 24, 1905, WHTP.
431 "I think I ought to know . . . more or less": ARL, *Crowded Hours*, p. 88.
431 Guns boomed . . . for the welcoming ceremony: *Galveston* [TX] *Daily News*, Aug. 8, 1905.
431 "the Philippines for . . . would be recalled": *San Francisco Call*, Aug. 12, 1905.
431 The Filipino people: *New York Tribune*, Aug. 13, 1905.
431 "of sufficient rank . . . entertain the party": WHT to HHT, Sept. 24, 1905, WHTP.
431 a "very handsome ball": Ibid.
431 "a long way in cementing": Mabel T. Boardman, "A Woman's Impressions of the Philippines," *Outlook*, Feb. 24, 1906.
431 Lodging with the Legardas: WHT to HHT, Sept. 24, 1905, Taft WHTP.
431 "All day long": Boardman, "A Woman's Impressions," *Outlook*, Feb. 24, 1906.
431 "utterly lacking in . . . of the government": WHT to HHT, Sept. 24, 1905, WHTP.
431 "restore the old condition" . . . considered friends: Ibid.
432 Taft and his entourage "made the round": *New York Tribune*, Aug. 24, 1905.
432 small boats . . . and farmers: Boardman, "A Woman's Impressions," *Outlook*, Feb. 24, 1906.
432 "a happy sea change . . . working out admirably": *New York Tribune*, Aug. 24, 1905.
432 "It was a great trip . . . due to your example": S. Young to WHT, Sept. 11, 1905, WHTP.
432 Taft secretly met . . . lasting consequences for the region: Bradley, *The Imperial Cruise*, pp. 249–50.
432 Roosevelt had closely followed: Howard K. Beale, *Theodore Roosevelt and the Rise of America to World Power* (Baltimore: Johns Hopkins University Press, 1956), p. 242.
432 From the start, he had sympathized: TR to WHT, April 20, 1905, in *LTR*, Vol. 4, pp. 1162–63.
432 he recognized . . . upsetting the balance of power: TR to WHT, April 8, 1905, in ibid., pp. 1158–59.
432 He was delighted . . . facilitate peace talks: WHT to TR, April 25, 1905, TRP.
432 curtailed his hunting expedition: TR to WHT, April 27, 1905, in *LTR*, Vol. 4, p. 1167.
432 Concealing the fact that the Japanese had initiated: TR to HCL, June 5, 1905, in ibid., p. 1202.
432 "open direct negotiations . . . and place of meeting": *Literary Digest*, June 17, 1905.
432 "It is recognized": *New York Tribune*, cited in ibid.
433 "a demonstrative welcome": *Minneapolis Tribune*, July 25, 1905.
433 "Korea being the direct cause . . . without the consent of Japan": WHT to TR, July 29, 1905, TRP.
433 "not harbor any . . . I know you can or will correct it": Ibid.
433 "Your conversation with Count Katsura": TR to WHT, July 31, 1905, in *LTR*, Vol. 4, p. 1293.
433 the peace envoys . . . met with the president: *Newark* [OH] *Advocate*, Aug. 5, 1905.
433 a buffet lunch: Morris, *Theodore Rex*, p. 407.
433 "prostrate in the enemy's hands" . . . extract an "indemnity": *San Francisco Call*, Aug. 12, 1905.
433 "I am having my hair": TR to Kermit Roosevelt, Aug. 25, 1905, in TR et al., *Letters to Kermit from Theodore Roosevelt*, p. 109.
433 In the end, the president persuaded the Japanese: Beale, *TR and the Rise of America,* pp. 255–62.
434 "hearty and vigorous": *Galveston* [TX] *Daily News*, Oct. 3, 1905; New York *Sun*, Oct. 3, 1905.
434 "We had a most interesting": James R. Garfield to Helen N. Garfield, Oct. 3, 1905, Garfield Papers.
434 "The city is all one": LS, "Ohio: A Tale of Two Cities," *McClure's* (July 1905), pp. 310–11.
434 "full of falsehoods": *Lima* [OH] *Daily News*, June 26, 1905.
434 "subservient" to Cox . . . systemic graft: *Washington Times*, Oct. 22, 1905.
434 "The stampede from": *Lima* [OH] *Daily News*, July 24, 1905.
434 "Governor Herrick . . . in line": LS to TR, Aug. 7, 1905, TRP.
435 "a most adroit": *Lima* [OH] *Times-Democrat*, Oct. 25, 1905.
435 Public condemnation . . . "not pleasant" for Taft: WHT to Howard Hollister, Oct. 3, 1905, WHTP.
435 "the official organ": *New Castle* [PA] *News*, July 26, 1905.
435 "Any pain you feel": WHT to Charles P. Taft, July 26, 1905, WHTP.
435 felt bound to declare: WHT to HHT, Oct. 5, 1905, WHTP.
435 Delivered before an overflowing audience: *Washington Post*, Oct. 22, 1905.
435 "the most severe rebuke . . . president's cabinet": *Hamilton* [OH] *Democrat*, Oct. 23, 1905.
435 "Cox and Coxism": *Elyria* [OH] *Republican*, Oct. 26, 1905.
435 "a local despotism": *Washington Times*, Oct. 22, 1905.
435 "distressing effect . . . the Republican organization": Ibid.; Pringle, *Life and Times*, Vol. 1, p. 269.
435 "made clear the difference" . . . others would do the same: *Van Wert* [OH] *Daily Bulletin*, Oct 24, 1905.
435 perpetuate the Cox machine . . . "his State and his party": *Washington Times*, Oct. 22, 1905.
435 "scathing denunciation": *Lima* [OH] *Times-Democrat*, Oct. 25, 1905.
435 "like the explosion": *Newark* [OH] *Advocate*, Oct. 23, 1905.
436 "We had about come": Benjamin Butterworth to WHT, Oct. 26, 1905, WHTP.
436 "You are the only man": Powel Crosley to WHT, Oct. 24, 1905, WHTP.
436 "You have done more good": Howard Hollister to WHT, Oct. 23, 1905, WHTP.

436 But Taft's hope . . . proved vain: LS, *The Struggle for Self-Government*, p. 208.

436 "Do not concern yourself": Myron Herrick to WHT, Nov. 15, 1905, WHTP.

436 a new Republican Club: Howard Hollister to WHT, Dec. 6 & 15, 1905, Feb. 1, 1906, WHTP; *Van Wert* [OH] *Daily Bulletin*, Mar. 14, 1906.

436 "Roosevelt Republican Club": *Van Wert* [OH] *Daily Bulletin*, Mar. 14, 1906.

436 "disabuse the public mind": Howard Hollister to WHT, Sept. 28, 1905, WHTP.

436 a dramatic "Oil War": IMT, "Roosevelt vs. Rockefeller," *The American Magazine* (December 1907), p. 119.

436 "Kansas is in the clutches": *Hutchinson* [KS] *News*, Feb. 2, 1905.

436 "On the instant": IMT, *All in the Day's Work*, p. 244.

437 "put on the screws" . . . a year later: WAW, "The Kansas Conscience," *The Reader* (October 1905), p. 489.

437 "the only transporter and buyer": IMT, "Roosevelt vs. Rockefeller," *The American Magazine* (December 1907), p. 119.

437 "a first-class" state refinery . . . "to be reasonable": IMT, *All in the Day's Work*, p. 249.

437 "without a market . . . men out of work": *Colorado Springs Gazette*, Mar. 13, 1905.

437 "was *punishing* Kansas . . . Well, we'll see about that!": IMT, "Kansas and the Standard Oil Company: A Narrative of Today, Part II," *McClure's* (October 1905), p. 618.

437 "from oppression" . . . refined products: *Atlanta Daily Democrat*, Feb. 20, 1905.

437 "hardly a secret" . . . instigated by the administration: *Hutchinson* [KS] *News*, Feb. 17, 1905.

437 "a rigid and . . . in the Kansas field": *Janesville* [WI] *Daily Gazette*, Feb. 18, 1905.

437 Garfield planned to travel to Kansas: *Syracuse* [NY] *Herald*, June 14, 1908.

438 "most important investigation": *Literary Digest*, Mar. 4, 1905.

438 Although passage of the House resolution: *Waterloo* [IA] *Times-Tribune*, Feb. 21, 1905.

438 "What would you think": IMT to JSP, Feb. 18, 1905, Phillips MSS.

438 "rank as one": *San Francisco Call*, Aug. 12, 1905.

438 "is to the present time": *The Critic*, April 1905, p. 287.

438 "darkened" her world: IMT, *All in the Day's Work*, p. 245.

438 "built himself into": IMT to Jessie Baker, Jan. 1, 1910, RSB Papers.

438 "I have thought" . . . dignify the Tarbell name: McClure to IMT, Mar. 29, 1905, IMTC.

438 "pathetic & characteristic" impulse: Ibid.

438 "with a heavy heart" . . . coming of "a prophet": IMT, *All in the Day's Work*, pp. 245, 247.

438 "unfair and illegal . . . all the world": *Iola* [KS] *Daily Register*, Mar. 15, 1905.

438 Local journalists trailed her: IMT to Albert Boyden, April 4, 1905, IMT Papers.

438 she hoped "to Heaven" . . . "until I have a hearing!": IMT to Albert Boyden, Mar. 20, 1905, IMT Papers.

438 would be "a good thing": *Iola* [KS] *Daily Register*, Mar. 16, 1905.

438 serve "as a measuring stick": IMT, *All in the Day's Work*, p. 249.

438 "Build your own . . . all pipelines common carriers": *Marysville* [OH] *Tribune*, April 20, 1905.

439 "the biggest mass meeting . . . has never done": *Lima* [OH] *Times-Democrat*, Mar. 20, 1905.

439 "Jehoshaphat! . . . hopeless for cleansing": IMT, *All in the Day's Work*, pp. 245–46.

439 "The wonder is . . . a gusher": IMT to JSP, Mar. 28, 1905, Phillips MSS.

439 "new town of Tulsa . . . paraded up and down": IMT, *All in the Day's Work*, pp. 247–48.

439 "submitted to five sittings": *Muskogee* [OK] *Democrat*, Mar. 27, 1905.

439 she was called upon: Albert Boyden to RSB, Mar. 21, 1905, RSB Papers.

439 "city-shy" boy . . . "loyalty for his state": IMT, *All in the Day's Work*, p. 259.

439 "The new thing . . . in any of its previous fights": *Emporia* [KS] *Gazette*, April 3, 1905.

439 "as much a moral issue . . . guilty of similar practices": *Emporia* [KS] *Gazette*, April 10, 1905.

440 "I stayed and stayed": *Marysville* [OH] *Tribune*, April 20, 1905.

440 "if one wants" . . . colluding with railroads: IMT, "Kansas and the Standard Oil Company: A Narrative of Today, Part I," *McClure's* (September 1905), p. 470.

440 "we take it": *Wall Street Journal*, Aug. 26, 1905.

440 "nearly all of the great fields": U.S. Government and James Rudolph Garfield, *Report of the Commissioner of Corporations on the Transportation of Petroleum: May 2, 1906* [hereafter *Garfield Report*] (Washington, DC: Government Printing Office, 1906), p. xix.

440 "Do read": Helen N. Garfield to James R. Garfield, April 13, 1905, Garfield Papers.

440 he had borrowed Tarbell's collection: James R. Garfield to IMT, June 11, 1906, IMTC.

440 "I shall try to find the truth": James R. Garfield to Helen N. Garfield, July 16, 1905, Garfield Papers.

440 "unjust and illegal": *Garfield Report*, pp. xx–xxi.

441 "All the power": *Estherville* [IA] *Enterprise*, May 9, 1906.

441 "the most severe arraignment": *The News* (Frederick, MD), May 12, 1906.

441 "a high official source . . . Ida Tarbell's Magazine Articles": *Laredo* [TX] *Times*, May 9, 1906.

441 "All that Ida Tarbell told": *Alton* [IL] *Evening Telegraph*, May 14, 1906.

441 "a vindication" of her methods: *Estherville* [IA] *Enterprise*, May 9, 1906.

441 validated now by the official seal: *Laredo* [TX] *Times*, May 9, 1906.

441 "can prove all he says": *Boston Daily Globe*, May 5, 1906.

441 "If my report affords . . . conspiracy and monopoly": James R. Garfield to Helen N. Garfield, June 24, 1906, Garfield Papers.

441 On the day the ruling was handed down: *Daily Californian* (Bakersfield, CA), Aug. 3, 1907.

441 "sledgehammer blows": *San Antonio* [TX] *Light*, Aug. 4, 1907.

441 Standard's corrupting influence: *Oakland* [CA] *Tribune*, Aug. 4, 1907.

441 Never before . . . such inflamed rhetoric: *San Antonio* [TX] *Light*, Aug. 4, 1907.

441 Landis levied the highest possible fine: Allan Nevins, *John D. Rockefeller* (New York: Charles Scribner's Sons, 1959), p. 325.

441 "I expected it": Ron Chernow, *Titan: The Life of John D. Rockefeller, Sr.* (New York: Random House, 1998), p. 541.
442 "beginning of the end" . . . or face ruin: *Logansport* [IN] *Journal*, Aug. 11, 1907.
442 "Judge Landis": Daniel Yergin, *The Prize: The Epic Quest for Oil, Money, and Power* (New York: Simon & Schuster, 1991), p. 92.
442 "It's nothing more than we expected": *Emporia* [KS] *Gazette*, July 26, 1908.
442 "a gross miscarriage of justice": *Cedar Rapids* [IA] *Evening Gazette*, Sept. 19, 1908.
442 "too much power in the bench": IMT, *All in the Day's Work*, p. 259.
442 "the government [had] finally": *Des Moines Daily News*, Nov. 19, 1906.
442 "The petition of the US government": *Paducah* [KY] *Evening Sun*, Nov. 15, 1906.
442 "Every essential charge . . . was Ida Tarbell": *Des Moines Daily News*, Nov. 19, 1906.
442 "not because it is a trust": *Indianapolis Star*, May 17, 1911.
442 a similar judgment: Pringle, *Life and Times*, Vol. 2, p. 665.
442 Standard Oil was given six months to dissolve: *Portsmouth* [OH] *Daily Times*, May 16, 1911.
442 "Buy Standard Oil": Chernow, *Titan*, p. 554.
442 Even when the corporate "octopus": Brady, *Ida Tarbell*, p. 158.
443 "to carry on . . . by civil or criminal proceedings": TR, "Seventh Annual Message, December 3, 1907," in *WTR*, Vol. 15, p. 420.
443 "The fundamental idea . . . enterprising an exponent": *Hartford* [CT] *Times*, cited in *Public Opinion*, Dec. 15, 1904.

CHAPTER SEVENTEEN: The American People Reach a Verdict

Page

444 "there are several eminent": TR to Cecil Spring Rice, Feb. 27, 1905, in *LTR*, Vol. 4, p. 1129.
444 "the people at large . . . the plutocracy": TR to Cecil Spring Rice, Dec. 27, 1904, in ibid., p. 1083.
444 "a dreadful calamity . . . grievances": TR to Philander Chase Knox, Nov. 10, 1904, in ibid., p. 1023.
445 "Above all else": TR, "Fourth Annual Message, Dec. 6, 1904," in *WTR*, Vol. 15, pp. 226–27.
445 This exclusive circle could effectively determine: Baker speech, *Boston Daily Globe*, Dec. 17, 1905; *New York Tribune*, Dec. 19, 1905.
445 the industry had remained essentially unregulated: George E. Mowry, *The Era of Theodore Roosevelt, 1900–1912* (New York: Harper & Bros., 1958), pp. 198–99.
445 "Until the transportation problem": IMT, "The History of the Standard Oil Company: Conclusion," *McClure's* (October 1904), p. 671.
445 "the story was always the same": Patrick F. Palermo, *Lincoln Steffens* (Boston: Twayne Publishers, 1978), p. 42.
445 "came from the top": Ibid., p. 42.
445 "seized the government": LS, *The Struggle for Self-Government*, p. 209.
445 "the actual sovereign": LS, *The Autobiography*, p. 564.
445 "the Railroad problem": RSB to J. Stannard Baker, Sept. 14, 1905, RSB Papers.
445 "eager for more dragons": RSB, *American Chronicle*, p. 190.
445 "the real facts . . . servant of democracy": RSB, Notebook [n.d.], 1905, RSB Papers.
446 "far more important": RSB to J. Stannard Baker, Mar. 1, 1905, RSB Papers.
446 Baker started by examining . . . on the railroad industry: RSB, *American Chronicle*, p. 190.
446 Roosevelt invited him to Washington: TR to RSB, Jan. 2, 1905, RSB Papers.
446 "in some big": RSB to TR, Jan. 10, 1905, RSB Papers.
446 "simple and most informal": RSB, Notebook C, Jan. 28, 1905, RSB Papers.
446 engaged in a private conversation: RSB, *American Chronicle*, p. 192.
446 "a pretty good grip": RSB to Albert Boyden, Jan. 12, 1905, RSB Papers.
446 the argument that railroads were public highways: Semonche, *Ray Stannard Baker*, p. 131.
446 "His chief trouble . . . as truthfully as I can": RSB, *American Chronicle*, pp. 192–93.
446 "It was altogether . . . gets hold of people": RSB to J. Stannard Baker, Jan. 29, 1905, RSB Papers.
447 "Neither this people . . . equitable terms": TR, "Speech at the Union League Club of Philadelphia, January 30, 1905," in TR and Lewis, *A Compilation of the Messages and Speeches*, pp. 551–53.
447 "due quite as much": RSB, Notebook C, Jan. 31, 1905, RSB Papers.
447 "an enormous industrial . . . regulating the trusts & the railroads": Ibid.
447 "need not be regarded . . . clearly drawn": TR to Joseph B. Bishop, Mar. 23, 1905, in *LTR*, Vol. 4, pp. 1144–45.
448 "were either friendly": *Truth* (Salt Lake City, UT), June 10, 1905.
448 "how delicate . . . should meddle": RSB, "Railroads on Trial, Part III," *McClure's* (January 1906), p. 327.
448 "Any tinkering with rates": *Truth*, June 10, 1905.
448 "an attack of 'pink-eye' ": RSB, "Railroads on Trial, Part V," *McClure's* (March 1906), p. 543.
448 Congressmen who had voted: *Galveston* [TX] *Daily News*, July 4, 1905.
448 the national coverage soon turned: RSB, "Railroads on Trial, Part V," *McClure's* (March 1906), pp. 544–49.
448 "throw the country into a panic": RSB, *American Chronicle*, p. 197.
448 "if the railway men . . . the public demand": *Sandusky* [OH] *Star-Journal*, May 10, 1905.
448 "absolute silence": *Salt Lake Tribune*, May 10, 1905.
448 Stuyvesant Fish . . . "May I have fifteen minutes": *Sandusky Star-Journal*, May 10, 1905.
449 "driven directly": *Alexandria* [DC] *Gazette*, May 11, 1905.
449 "a sensation": *Fort Wayne* [IN] *Weekly Sentinel*, May 17, 1905.
449 "had been carefully prepared": *Alexandria* [DC] *Gazette*, May 11, 1905.
449 "could not have been . . . of the public": TR, "Speech at the Iroquois Club Banquet, Chicago, Ill., May 10, 1905," in TR and Lewis, *A Compilation of the Messages and Speeches*, pp. 620, 619.
449 "the spirit of demagoguery . . . they are poor": TR, "Speech at the Chamber of Commerce Banquet, Denver, Colo., May 8, 1905," in ibid., p. 616.

449 "the rock of class hatred": TR, "Speech at the Iroquois Club Banquet, Chicago, Ill., May 10, 1905," in ibid., p. 620.
449 "a fight to the finish": *Alexandria* [DC] *Gazette*, May 11, 1905.
449 "an impression prevailed": *Washington Post*, Aug. 20, 1905.
449 "the vitality of democracy . . . than the sovereign himself": S. S. McClure, "Editorial Announcement of a New Series of Articles by Ray Stannard Baker: The Railroads on Trial," *McClure's* (October 1905), pp. 673, 672.
450 Baker wrote in early September: RSB to TR, Sept. 7, 1905, TRP.
450 "Yes, I should greatly like": TR to RSB, Sept. 8, 1905, TRP.
450 "approval might be the measure . . . of the White House": RSB, *American Chronicle*, p. 194.
450 "I haven't a criticism to suggest . . . my own message": TR to RSB, Sept. 13, 1905, in *LTR*, Vol. 5, p. 25.
450 "In the early days . . . what the traffic will bear": RSB, "The Railroad Rate: A Study in Commercial Autocracy," *McClure's* (November 1905), p. 50.
450 families generally sat on the boards: RSB, "Railroads on Trial, Part III," *McClure's* (January 1906), pp. 318–24.
450 "the fundamental purpose . . . in private hands": RSB, "The Railroad Rate: A Study in Commercial Autocracy," *McClure's* (November 1905), pp. 57, 47.
450 "violent agitation . . . in the gift of government": RSB to TR, Sept. 18, 1905, TRP.
451 "strictly confidential . . . to be made thereon?": TR to RSB, Oct. 16, 1905, TRP.
451 "the seriousness . . . at that time who did?": RSB, *American Chronicle*, pp. 197–98.
451 "It was too general": Ibid., p. 198.
451 "I was terribly afraid": Ibid.
451 "cunning devices . . . manufacturers and shippers": RSB, "Railroad Rebates," *McClure's* (December 1905), pp. 185, 180.
451 "I have asked myself . . . fix a *definite* rate": RSB to TR, Nov. 11, 1905, TRP.
452 "it would be better . . . is surely constitutional": TR to RSB, Nov. 13, 1905, TRP.
452 "Is there not . . . succeed without it": RSB to TR, Nov. 17, 1905, RSB Papers.
452 "a long and rather heated": RSB, *American Chronicle*, p. 199.
452 "I think you are entirely": TR to RSB, Nov. 20, 1905, in *LTR*, Vol. 5, p. 83.
452 "the railroads have been crazy": Ibid., p. 84.
452 "simply absurd": TR to RSB, Nov. 22, 1905, in ibid., p. 88.
452 "it was Lincoln": TR to RSB, Nov. 28, 1905, in ibid., p. 101.
452 "suggestion would come": RSB, *American Chronicle*, p. 200.
452 "What was my surprise": Ibid.
452 "a maximum reasonable rate . . . improper minimum rates": TR, "Fifth Annual Message, Dec. 5, 1905," in *WTR*, Vol. 15, pp. 275–76.
453 On January 4, 1906 . . . "just and reasonable": John Ely Briggs, *William Peters Hepburn* (Iowa City: State Hist. Soc. of Iowa, 1919), p. 264.
453 "the most hoary tenet": Blum, *The Republican Roosevelt*, p. 91.
453 to preserve the protective tariff: John M. Blum, "Theodore Roosevelt and the Hepburn Act: Toward an Orderly System of Control," in *LTR*, Vol. 6, Appendix 2, pp. 1561–62.
453 "was in many ways": *Washington Post*, Feb. 9, 1906.
453 "this railroad legislation . . . how inefficient & undependable": RSB, Notebook C, Feb. 9, 1906, RSB Papers.
453 A battle royal: *Public Opinion*, Dec. 9, 1905.
454 "so whittled down": *Public Opinion*, Nov. 11, 1905.
454 "They are making": TR to Kermit Roosevelt, Mar. 4, 1905, in TR et al., eds., *Letters to Kermit from Theodore Roosevelt*, p. 130.
454 "great indignation": *NYT*, Feb. 23, 1906.
454 "as a check": *Current Literature* (March 1906), p. 232.
454 the leadership of Iowa's junior senator: *NYT*, Feb. 24, 1906.
454 agreed to report the unamended bill "without prejudice": *Public Opinion*, Mar. 3, 1906.
454 "most outspoken opponent . . . the country gasp": *Elyria* [OH] *Chronicle*, Mar. 10, 1906.
454 "scarcely had time": *Washington Post*, Feb. 24, 1906.
454 "Pitchfork Ben" . . . a fistfight . . . would be severely diminished: *NYT*, April 5, 1906.
455 "confided to the care": *News and Courier* (Charleston, SC), cited in *Public Opinion*, Mar. 10, 1906.
455 "old enemies": *Indianapolis News*, cited in *Current Literature* (March 1906), p. 233.
455 judiciary as the true arbiter of rates: Blum, "TR and the Hepburn Act," in *LTR*, Vol. 6, pp. 1565–66.
455 "public opinion": TR to John Lee Strachey, Feb. 12, 1906, in *LTR*, Vol. 5, p. 150.
455 "never better . . . discrimination and judgment": "The Evolution of Public Opinion," *The Independent*, June 14, 1906.
455 "in common with all other" . . . "good" or "bad": RSB, "Railroads on Trial, Part V," *McClure's* (March 1906), pp. 535, 548.
455 a former city newspaperman was hired: RSB to TR, Oct. 13, 1905, TRP.
455 small newspapers were supplied . . . purchased newspapers outright: RSB, "Railroads on Trial, Part V," *McClure's* (March 1906), pp. 545, 548.
455 acquainted more than half a million: Semonche, *Ray Stannard Baker*, p. 142.
456 "It is a little startling": *Fairhope Courier* (Des Moines, IA), Mar. 9, 1906, Clipping, RSB Papers.
456 "after plowing all day . . . the people and the railroads": John Gladney to *McClure's*, Mar. 7, 1906, RSB Papers.
456 "worth all the publication": Emmet Zook to *McClure's*, March [n.d.], 1906, RSB Papers.
456 "was of course entirely": TR to William Boyd Allison, May 14, 1906, in *LTR*, Vol. 5, p. 270.
456 "I did not care a rap": TR, *An Autobiography*, p. 436.
456 "to the left of his original position": Blum, *The Republican Roosevelt*, p. 100.

456 "The fight on the rate bill": TR to Kermit Roosevelt, April 1, 1906, in *LTR*, Vol. 5, p. 204.
456 "As for Tillman": *Emporia* [KS] *Gazette*, May 19, 1906.
456 "pocket my pride": Sullivan, *Our Times*, Vol. 3, p. 254.
456 "the mysterious ways": *Washington Post*, Feb. 26, 1906.
457 a number of southern senators balked: Blum, *The Republican Roosevelt*, p. 101.
457 "The great object": TR to William Boyd Allison, May 5, 1906, in *LTR*, Vol. 5, p. 258.
457 Republicans who feared . . . held unconstitutional: TR to HCL, May 19, 1906, in ibid., pp. 273–74.
457 The political landscape was shifting . . . in grave jeopardy: Blum, "TR and the Hepburn Act," in *LTR*, Vol. 6, pp. 1562–63.
457 "little knot of men . . . superior generalship": *NYT*, April 5, 1906.
457 "neither control": *Emporia* [KS] *Gazette*, May 4, 1906.
457 "symbolic of the new": *Public Opinion*, April 21, 1906.
458 this compromise provided the only chance: TR to William Boyd Allison, May 14, 1906, in *LTR*, Vol. 5, p. 270.
458 "Aldrich and his people": TR to WAW, July 31, 1906, TRP.
458 The bill passed: *Salt Lake Tribune*, May 19, 1906.
458 "No given measure": TR to RSB, Nov. 20, 1905, in *LTR*, Vol. 5, p. 84.
458 "the longest step": Blum, *The Republican Roosevelt*, p. 104.
458 "lifted the idea": *Public Opinion*, June 2, 1906.
458 the High Court defined the scope: Blum, *The Republican Roosevelt*, p. 103.
458 "the politician's gift": *The Independent*, May 24, 1906.
458 "but for the work": Ibid.
458 "Congress might ignore": *Fort Wayne* [IN] *Weekly Sentinel*, July 4, 1906.
458 "It is through writers": Elwood Mead to RSB, June 9, 1906, RSB Papers.
459 "This crusade against": RSB to J. Stannard Baker, Jan. 23, 1906, RSB Papers.
459 "was like the falling down": Edmund Wilson, "Lincoln Steffens and Upton Sinclair," *The New Republic*, Sept. 28, 1932.
459 "Perhaps it'll surprise you": UBS to RSB, Dec. 2, 1905, RSB Papers.
459 By twenty-five . . . in serial form: Upton Sinclair, *Autobiography* (New York: Harcourt, Brace & World, 1962), pp. 108–9.
459 the "wage slavery": Anthony Arthur, *Radical Innocent: Upton Sinclair* (New York: Random House, 2006), p. 41.
459 The young socialist decided: UBS, *Autobiography*, p. 109.
459 "I sat at night . . . could go anywhere": Ibid.
460 "dosed with borax . . . in the room with them": Upton Sinclair, *The Jungle* (New York: Modern Library, 2006), pp. 148–49.
460 "the bride, the groom": UBS, *Autobiography*, p. 110.
460 "the sort of man": UBS, *The Jungle*, p. 23.
460 "He would work all day": Ibid., p. 54.
460 "were sold with the idea": Ibid., p. 72.
460 the holiday "speeding up" . . . no longer want: Ibid., p. 136.
461 "The revelations": *NYT*, Jan. 27, 1906; Isaac F. Marcosson, *Adventures in Interviewing* (New York: John Lane Co., 1919), pp. 282–84.
461 Sinclair sent two advance copies: UBS to RSB, Feb. 2, 1906, RSB Papers.
461 "Not since Byron awoke": Upton Sinclair, *My Lifetime in Letters* (Columbia: University of Missouri Press, 1960), p. ix.
461 "Hideous": James Rudolph Garfield, Diary, Mar. 2, 1906, Garfield Papers.
461 "a terrible and I fear": James Rudolph Garfield, Diary, Mar. 3, 1906, Garfield Papers.
461 Roosevelt . . . invited the author: TR to UBS, Mar. 9, 1906, TRP.
461 Although he proceeded . . . "be eradicated": TR to UBS, Mar. 15, 1906, in *LTR*, Vol. 5, pp. 178, 180.
461 "was like asking a burglar": UBS, *Autobiography*, p. 118.
462 He chose two well-respected men: Marcosson, *Adventures in Interviewing*, pp. 285–86.
462 "I have power": TR to UBS, April 9, 1906, TRP.
462 "on excellent authority" . . . intended to castigate the novelist: *Chicago Tribune*, April 10 & 11, 1906.
462 "It is absurd": TR to UBS, April 11, 1906, in *LTR*, Vol. 5, p. 209.
462 "should never have dreamed . . . explicit and positive way": UBS to TR, April 12, 1906, TRP.
462 "I understand entirely": TR to UBS, April 13, 1906, TRP.
462 conditions comparable to those Sinclair had portrayed: *The Independent*, May 31, 1906.
462 "of rooms reeking": *Public Opinion*, June 9, 1906.
462 "found healthful . . . inspected and condemned": *Outlook*, June 9, 1906.
462 "that unless effective": *Chicago Tribune*, May 26, 1906.
462 Without "a dissenting vote" the Beveridge bill passed: *The Independent*, May 31, 1906.
463 "a shock it will never": *NYT*, May 26, 1906.
463 Sinclair leaked his information: *NYT*, May 28, 1906.
463 "I sincerely hope": UBS to TR, May 29, 1906, TRP.
463 "Tell Sinclair": Arthur, *Radical Innocent*, p. 77.
463 "conditions were as clean": *Chicago Tribune*, June 9, 1906.
463 A series of emasculating amendments . . . the "mandatory character": *NYT*, May 29, 1906.
463 "I am sorry": TR to James Wolcott Wadsworth, May 31, 1906, in *LTR*, Vol. 5, p. 291.
463 "sham" legislation: TR to James Wolcott Wadsworth, June 15, 1906, in ibid., p. 299.
463 not "warranted" any longer: TR to James Wolcott Wadsworth, May 31, 1906, in ibid., p. 291.

463 On June 4 . . . a "preliminary" report: James Reynolds and Charles Patrick Neill, *Conditions in Chicago Stock Yards: Message from the President, June 4, 1906. The Roosevelt Policy; Speeches, Letters and State Papers, Relating to Corporate Wealth and Closely Allied Topics, of Theodore Roosevelt, President of the United States* (New York: Current Literature Publ. Co., 1908), Vol. 2, p. 386.

463 "The conditions . . . dangerous to health": Ibid., p. 387.

463 If Congress failed: Ibid., 389.

463 "Mary had a little lamb": Sullivan, *Our Times*, Vol. 2, p. 541.

464 "chloroformed in the committees": Ibid., p. 544.

464 "We cannot imagine": New York *Evening Post*, cited in *The Bookman* (July 1906), pp. 481–83.

464 "In the history of reforms": *Chicago Tribune*, June 30, 1906.

464 "chief janitor and policeman": Sullivan, *Our Times*, Vol. 2, p. 520.

464 "Are we going to take up": Nathaniel W. Stephenson, *Nelson W. Aldrich, a Leader in American Politics* (New York: Charles Scribner's Sons, 1930), p. 234.

464 McClure introduced Bok: Lyon, *Success Story*, pp. 233–34.

464 Bok brought it . . . widespread attention: Mark Sullivan, *The Education of an American* (New York: Doubleday, Doran & Co., 1938), p. 191.

464 Sullivan's research . . . "Died May 17, 1883": Ibid., pp. 187–88.

465 a secret clause . . . an original copy of the contract form: Ibid., p. 189.

465 a ten-part investigative series . . . "or deleterious drugs": Robert Morse Crunden, *Ministers of Reform: The Progressives' Achievement in American Civilization, 1889–1920* (New York: Basic Books, 1982), p. 180.

465 an ointment . . . fraudulent or nonexistent: Samuel Hopkins Adams, "The Great American Fraud," *Collier's Weekly*, Oct. 7, 1905, Jan. 13, 1906, & Feb. 17, 1906.

465 "to run the gauntlet": *Current Literature* (April 1906).

465 "it slept": Sullivan, *Our Times*, Vol. 2, p. 534.

465 On June 30, 1906: William Lamartine Snyder, *Supplement to Snyder's Interstate Commerce Act and Federal Anti-Trust Laws* (New York: Baker, Voorhis & Co., 1906), pp. 136–44.

465 "would not have had . . . the agitation": *Chicago Tribune*, June 30, 1906.

465 This landmark bill: Snyder, *Supplement to Snyder's Interstate Commerce Act*, pp. 136–44.

465 "During no session": *NYT*, June 30, 1906.

466 "the beginning of a new epoch": *Iowa Postal Card* (Fayette, IA), July 12, 1906.

466 "For pass them they must": Lyon, *Success Story*, p. 250.

466 "the most amazing program": Joshua David Hawley, *Theodore Roosevelt: Preacher of Righteousness* (New Haven: Yale University Press, 2008), p. 161.

466 only "sowing the seeds": Benjamin Wheeler to TR, July 1, 1906, TRP.

466 "more substantive work": *Postville* [IA] *Review*, July 6, 1906.

466 Even Democratic newspapers: *The Literary Digest*, July 7, 1906.

466 "The public confidence": Quoted in ibid.

466 "I do not expect": TR to Kermit Roosevelt, June 13, 1906, in TR et al., eds., *Letters to Kermit from Theodore Roosevelt*, p. 149.

CHAPTER EIGHTEEN: "Cast into Outer Darkness"

Page

467 "Signs everywhere": RSB to J. Stannard Baker, Jan. 23, 1906, RSB Papers.

467 "men were questioning": RSB, Notebook: "General Recollection of the Era," RSB Papers.

467 "assumed the proportions": Frank Luther Mott, *A History of American Magazines* (Cambridge, MA: Belknap Press, 1957), Vol. 4, pp. 207, 607.

467 "Government by Magazine": WAW to JSP, May 25, 1908, White Papers.

467 "to make a star to shine . . . that rules the world": Finley Peter Dunne, "Mr. Dooley on the Power of the Press," *The American Magazine* (October 1906). (Dunne's passage has been translated from dialect.)

468 Sam McClure was considered: WAW, *The Autobiography*, p. 386.

468 "Here was a group": IMT, *All in the Day's Work*, p. 254.

468 the "rare group . . . yet with tolerance": RSB, *American Chronicle*, p. 226.

468 "a success": LS, *The Autobiography*, p. 535.

468 "the future looked fair": IMT, *All in the Day's Work*, p. 254.

468 "The institution that had seemed": RSB, *American Chronicle*, p. 213.

468 "Never forget . . . the daring moves": IMT to Albert Boyden, April 26, 1902, in Lyon, *Success Story*, p. 199.

469 "You are infinitely precious . . . during the coming years": McClure to IMT, Mar. 18, 1903, IMTC.

469 Wilkinson . . . conducted poetry classes: Lucy Dow Cushing, ed., *The Wellesley Alumnae Quarterly* (Concord, NH: Wellesley College Alumnae Assoc., 1917), Vol. 2, p. 190.

469 who suspected that their editor's fascination: Lyon, *Success Story*, p. 207.

469 an evening of theatre: McClure to HHM, June 15, 1903, McClure MSS.

469 McClure brought them to Divonne: McClure to HHM, June 11, 1903; Mary Bisland to HHM, July 6, 1903, McClure MSS.

470 he and Florence Wilkinson stayed on the third: Lyon, *Success Story*, p. 256.

470 Their "rollicking adventure . . . under their horses' feet": Alice Hegan Rice, *The Inky Way* (New York: D. Appleton-Century Co.,1940), pp. 65–66.

470 During that "never-to-be forgotten" European tour: Ibid., p. 65; Cale Young Rice, *Bridging the Years* (New York: D. Appleton-Century, 1939), p. 63.

470 Ida could barely contain her tears: McClure to IMT [n.d., Saturday], 1905, IMTC; Brady, *Ida Tarbell*, p. 149.

470 "I have felt terribly sad": McClure to IMT [n.d.], 1903, IMTC.
470 McClure's recklessness could tarnish the magazine: Lyon, *Success Story*, pp. 258–59.
470 they feared he planned to meet with Florence: Ibid., pp. 257–58.
470 "I feel sure of myself": McClure to HHM, Nov. 21, 1903, McClure MSS.
471 "I am so much keener": McClure to HHM, Nov. 29, 1903, McClure MSS.
471 "I feel my vision broadened": McClure to HHM, Nov. [n.d.] 1903, McClure MSS.
471 When McClure suddenly embarked: Lyon, *Success Story*, p. 259.
471 McClure directed the poetry editor: See Florence Wilkinson, "Three Poems," *McClure's* (June 1904), p. 166.
471 upbraided Sam "like a naughty child": Lyon, *Success Story*, p. 260.
471 A chastened McClure swore: Florence Wilkinson to JSP, June [n.d.], 1904, in JSP to IMT [n.d.], 1904, IMTC.
471 something "very terrible . . . for nearly a week": HHM to IMT, June 24, 1904, IMTC.
471 "I have so much to do": McClure to IMT, June 22, 1904, IMTC.
471 "The Lord help us! . . . feel resentment": IMT to JSP, June [n.d.], 1904, IMTC.
472 "I have received six . . . to snap off so suddenly": Florence Wilkinson to JSP, June [n.d.], 1904, IMTC.
472 "wretched & restless . . . idea of giving her up": Mary Bisland to IMT, July 7, 1904, in Lyon, *Success Story*, p. 262.
472 "very solemn promises": HHM to JSP, July 30, 1904, IMTC.
472 "He said he was a hurt animal": HHM to IMT, June 24, 1904, IMTC.
472 "The struggle for possession": McClure to IMT, June 22, 1904, IMTC.
472 "full of dynamite . . . the magazine must be cleared": McClure to JSP, Oct. 15, 1904, Phillips MSS.
473 "sensational . . . very accurate": McClure to IMT, June 22, 1904, IMTC.
473 "working in his own little cubicle": McClure to IMT, Oct. 6, 1904, IMTC.
473 "The man who is responsible": McClure to Albert Boyden [n.d.], 1904, IMTC.
473 "Why in the name of ordinary": McClure to Albert Boyden [n.d.], 1904, IMTC.
473 "very poor, trashy . . . unworthy": HHM to JSP, June 9, 1904, IMTC.
473 Phillips patiently answered: JSP to HHM, Aug. 5, 1904, McClure MSS.
473 she was not the only "other" woman . . . Her "dearest" friend: Florence Wilkinson to HHM, Sept. 25, 1903, McClure MSS.
473 revealed her own romantic relationship: IMT to JSP, Sept. 7, 1904, McClure MSS.
473 "Yesterday": McClure to JSP, July 26, 1904, IMTC.
474 "wrung with the anguish . . . strange wanderings": HHM to McClure, Aug. 26, 1904, McClure MSS.
474 her devoted efforts had "saved" him . . . "punishment" for all he had done: McClure to IMT [n.d.], 1904, IMTC.
474 "The Shame of S. S. McClure . . . the wall of lies": IMT, "Notes of L'Affaire," July [n.d.], 1906, IMTC.
474 the staff drew up a plan: Lyon, *Success Story*, p. 277.
474 "the whole future . . . powerful ruling body": McClure to IMT, Mar. 29, 1905, IMTC.
474 "getting along splendidly . . . than ever before": McClure to HHM, July 5, 1905, McClure MSS.
475 "I thought when I came back . . . heavy heavy load": McClure to IMT [n.d., Saturday], 1905, IMTC.
475 "My mind constantly dwells": McClure to IMT, Mar. 29, 1905, IMTC.
475 developing an elaborate plan: Lyon, *Success Story*, p. 280.
475 "the greatest periodical": McClure to IMT, Nov. 27, 1905, IMTC.
475 "a stronger and more productive man": IMT, *All in the Day's Work*, p. 225.
475 "a tremendous secret" . . . *McClure's Universal Journal*: McClure to IMT, Nov. 27, 1905, IMTC.
475 Sam McClure's extravagant ambitions . . . affordable housing: IMT, *All in the Day's Work*, p. 256; Lyon, *Success Story*, p. 283; Albert Boyden to JSP, Feb. 6, 1906, IMTC.
475 Tarbell considered McClure's grandiosity: IMT, *All in the Day's Work*, p. 257.
475 "build a bigger": Ibid., p. 255.
476 McClure's scheme . . . echoed the very trusts: Ibid., p. 256.
476 "the plan which was eventually": Ibid.
476 "all the different branches": IMT to McClure, Oct. 18, 1904, IMTC.
476 "who had so much of the creative touch": RSB, Notebook, Dec. 1936, RSB Papers.
476 An "uncompromising" critic: RSB, *American Chronicle*, p. 94.
476 "felicities of expression": RSB to F. E. Dayton, Dec. 5, 1936, RSB Papers.
476 "would not know where to go": WAW to JSP, Mar. 17, 1906, in Lyon, *Success Story*, p. 285.
476 John had so admired Sam's energy, his "push and business ability": Lyon, *Success Story*, p. 37.
477 they spent many hours together . . . in each other's homes: JSP to IMT, November [n.d.], 1905, IMTC.
477 "He is certainly the rarest": IMT to Albert Boyden, July 20, 1905, IMTC.
477 "It has been a glorious trip": IMT to Albert Boyden, Feb. 11, 1905, IMTC.
477 a series of letters forwarded: Robert Mather to McClure, Feb. 2, 1906, IMTC.
477 "as usual is an angel" . . . a "diabolical" stage: IMT to Albert Boyden, Feb. 11, 1905, IMTC.
477 "thoroughly unfitted me" . . . his "ridiculous" concerns: McClure to JSP, Feb. 17, 1906, IMTC.
478 "All S.S. wants is sympathy": Daniel McKinley to JSP, Feb. 2, 1906, IMTC.
478 "I wish we did have the brains": Albert Boyden to JSP, Feb. 6, 1906, IMTC.
478 "It was a momentous decision": Lyon, *Success Story*, p. 286.
478 whether "anybody else is going . . . that we are right": IMT Diary, Mar. 22, 1906, IMTC.
478 if McClure would "democratize": Lyon, *Success Story*, pp. 286–87; IMT Diary, Mar. 22, 1906, IMTC.
478 "cheerful" for the first time in weeks: IMT Diary, Mar. 23, 1906, IMTC.
478 "beyond the ability of one man . . . sensing public opinion": McClure to JSP, April 5, 1906, McClure MSS.
479 "utterly impossible": McClure to JSP, April 5, 1906, McClure MSS.
479 "I cannot leave the magazine": McClure to IMT, April 7, 1906, IMTC.

479 "the entire office was embroiled . . . someone else came along": Curtis P. Brady, "The High Cost of Impatience," unpublished typescript, p. 266, McClure MSS.
479 "playing and getting well . . . even by the owner": LS to Joseph Steffens, June 3, 1906, in LS et al., eds., *Letters of Lincoln Steffens*, Vol. 1, p 173.
480 "become so utterly unbalanced": RSB to Jessie Baker, Mar. 9, 1906, in Bannister, *Ray Stannard Baker*, p. 110.
480 "dynamite, nitroglycerine & black powder": Robert William Stinson, "S. S. McClure and His Magazine: A Study in the Editing of 'McClure's,' 1893–1913," PhD diss., Indiana University, 1971, p. 249.
480 "are not only my friends": RSB to J. Stannard Baker, May 3, 1906, RSB Papers.
480 "I was left with no certainty . . . all but catastrophic": RSB, *American Chronicle*, p. 213.
480 "In Bunyan's *Pilgrim's Progress*": TR, "The Man with the Muck-Rake," *Putnam's Monthly* (October 1906), p. 42.
480 The coincidence . . . to form their own magazine: *New York Tribune*, May 11, 1906; *Life*, May 24, 1906.
480 "affected his views of . . . of contemporary life": "Magazines' Heads at War," unidentified newspaper clipping [n.d.], 1906, RSB Papers.
480 planned "to muzzle his writers": Lyon, *Success Story*, p. 294.
480 William Randolph Hearst, who had . . . agitated for a constitutional amendment: Judson A. Grenier and George E. Mowry, introduction, in David Graham Phillips, J. A. Grenier, and G. E. Mowry, *The Treason of the Senate* (Chicago: Quadrangle Books, 1964), p. 20.
481 He offered David Graham Phillips: Ibid., p. 21.
481 "Treason is a strong word": David Graham Phillips, "The Treason of the Senate: I," *The Cosmopolitan* (March 1906), p. 488.
481 Each portrait revealed "a triangulation": Grenier and Mowry, introduction, in Phillips, Grenier, and Mowry, *The Treason of the Senate*, p. 29.
481 The circulation of *The Cosmopolitan* doubled: Ibid.
481 "Little wonder": Ibid., p. 30.
481 "For those who like the sight": *Hutchinson* [KS] *News*, Feb. 22, 1906.
481 "Here is the archetypal Face . . . mentally and morally": Phillips, "The Treason of the Senate: I," *The Cosmopolitan* (March 1906), pp. 489, 588.
481 "boodler . . . sniveling sycophant": *Hutchinson* [KS] *News*, Feb. 22, 1906.
482 Although he never accused . . . contributions of the special interests: Phillips, "The Treason of the Senate: I," *The Cosmopolitan* (March 1906), p. 488.
482 "heartiest sympathy . . . noxious as the thief": TR to Alfred Henry Lewis, Feb. 17, 1906, in *LTR*, Vol. 5, pp. 156–57.
482 "sowing the seeds of anarchy": *The Critic* (June 1906), p. 512.
482 "playing with matches": Quoted in Grenier and Mowry, introduction, in Phillips, Grenier, and Mowry, *The Treason of the Senate*, p. 38.
482 "Slander and misrepresentation": *Public Opinion*, April 7, 1906.
482 "epidemic of Congress-baiting": *Current Literature* (March 1906), p. 231.
482 "muckrakers . . . with sensational articles": *Daily Telegraph* (Atlantic, IA), April 9, 1906.
482 "ignoring at the same time": *NYT*, April 6, 1906.
482 He had initially planned: Grenier and Mowry, introduction, in Phillips, Grenier, and Mowry, *The Treason of the Senate*, p. 34.
482 "the masters" at *McClure's* . . . "imitators" had followed in their wake: Edwin E. Slosson, "The Literature of Exposure," in Filler, *The Muckrakers*, p. 258.
482 "hot stuff . . . before the investigation is begun": *Washington Post*, April 11, 1906.
483 "to produce a very unhealthy . . . socialistic propaganda": TR to WHT, Mar. 15, 1906, in *LTR*, Vol. 5, p. 183.
483 "glad, sweet song . . . than a convict's camp": Mott, *A History of American Magazines, 1885–1905*, Vol. 4, p. 209. (Dunne's passage has been translated from dialect.)
483 "immensely" enjoyed . . . "feeling over-pessimistic about it": TR to Finley Peter Dunne, Dec. 15, 1905, TRP.
483 "The public cannot stand": Slosson, "The Literature of Exposure," in Filler, *The Muckrakers*, p. 258.
483 "It is getting so nowadays . . . holds a public office": *Oshkosh* [WI] *Daily Northwestern*, April 17, 1906.
483 "Well . . . poor old Chauncey Depew": LS, *The Autobiography*, p. 258.
483 Steffens remained unconvinced . . . mobilize public opinion: Ibid.
483 "repeat as true . . . businessmen or politicians": TR to LS, June 24, 1905, in *LTR*, Vol. 4, p. 1254.
484 "Poor Payne is sick": TR to HCL, Oct. 2, 1904, in ibid., p. 965.
484 "To any officer or employee": TR to "Any officer . . . ," Jan. 9, 1906, LS Papers.
484 To Steffens, the signal question: *Syracuse* [NY] *Herald*, Jan. 14, 1906.
484 "I'd rather make our government": LS, *Boston Daily Globe*, Feb. 11, 1906.
484 "In stating your disapproval": TR to LS, Feb. 6, 1906, in *LTR*, Vol. 5, pp. 147–48.
485 rather than "summoning . . . being dragged": Lyon, *Success Story*, p. 250.
485 All these frustrations . . . the "new journalism": *Washington Post*, April 11, 1906.
485 Remarks at the informal club . . . "spread like wildfire": RSB, *American Chronicle*, p. 201.
485 speculation that he was referencing: *Daily Telegraph* (Atlantic, IA), April 9, 1906; *Daily Times-Tribune* (Waterloo, IA), April 14, 1906.
485 "such an attack": RSB, *American Chronicle*, p. 202.
485 "I have been much disturbed": RSB to TR, April 7, 1906, in ibid., pp. 202–3.
485 "One reason I want . . . as much as of mud slinging": TR to RSB, April 9, 1906, in ibid., p. 203.
485 "at the risk of repetition . . . potent forces for evil": TR, "Speech at the Laying of the Corner-Stone of the Office Building of the House of Representatives, April 14, 1906," in TR, *Presidential Addresses and State Papers, April 14, 1906 to January 14, 1907* (New York: Review of Reviews Co., 1910), Vol. 5, pp. 713–15.
486 "upon a question which is shaking . . . portly figure of the President": *Nevada State Journal*, April 22, 1906.
486 "familiar balance of approval . . . classed all of us together": RSB, *American Chronicle*, pp. 203–4.

486 *McClure's* . . . was "singled out": Semonche, *Ray Stannard Baker*, p. 151.
486 "I'm giving my whole life to . . . ready for McSure's by night": Mrs. Woodrow, "A Rake's Progress," *Life*, May 5, 1906, pp. 639–40.
486 "These satirical jabs cut": Semonche, *Ray Stannard Baker*, pp. 151–52.
486 "cast into outer darkness . . . nor follow his leadership": RSB, *American Chronicle*, p. 204.
487 "It was a great day": New York *Sun*, cited in *Literary Digest*, April 21, 1906.
487 "rebaters and bribers . . . wave of magazine reform": Samuel Merwin, "The Magazine Crusade," *Success Magazine* (June 1906), p. 394.
487 "the loftiest and purest": *Nevada State Journal*, April 22, 1906.
487 "long, laborious work . . . astonishingly great": Merwin, "The Magazine Crusade," *Success Magazine* (June 1906), pp. 452, 449.
487 "The day will come . . . emblem of reform": *Nevada State Journal*, April 22, 1906.
487 "a badge of honor": *When Trumpets Call: Theodore Roosevelt After the White House*, p. 30.
487 "quietly planning to start": *NYT*, May 11, 1906.
487 After weeks of turmoil . . . worth $187,000: JSP and IMT to McClure, April 12, 1906, McClure MSS.
487 "I am certain that": McClure to Robert Mather, April 14, 1906, McClure MSS.
487 "I wish you all": McClure to RSB, May 10, 1906, RSB Papers.
487 "There was nothing mean": LS, *The Autobiography*, p. 536.
488 "its chief features of life and popularity": *Riverside* [CA] *Enterprise*, June 23, 1906.
488 Necessity compelled him . . . "colossal scheme": Alice Hegan Rice to IMT, June 14, 1906, IMTC.
488 "I have really to look": McClure to HHM, July 2, 1906, McClure MSS.
488 "working harder": McClure to HHM, June 27, 1906, McClure MSS.
488 "three or four quarts of milk": Lyon, *Success Story*, p. 298.
488 "masses of manuscripts" . . . an autobiography by Mark Twain: McClure to HHM, June 30, 1906, McClure MSS.
488 Of the original team, only . . . remained: Brady, "The High Cost of Impatience," p. 226, McClure MSS.
488 To replace Ida Tarbell . . . editor of the *Atlantic Monthly*: Lyon, *Success Story*, pp. 296–98.
488 "The very name": Ellery Sedgwick, *The Happy Profession* (Boston: Little, Brown & Co., 1946), p. 144.
488 "burning force . . . into molten excitement": Ibid., p. 139.
488 "be able to repeat the process": Lyon, *Success Story*, p. 296.
488 "To go on now": Ibid., p. 294.
489 "to halt and to think soberly . . . of responsibility": *Washington Post*, April 11, 1906.
489 She edited . . . investigative pieces diminished: Robert Cantwell, "Journalism: The Magazines," in Harold Stearns, *America Now: An Inquiry into Civilization in the United States by Thirty-Six Americans* (New York: Charles Scribner's Sons, 1938), pp. 348–49.
489 "of distraction" . . . of "inquiry": Ibid., p. 352.
489 "an exhilarating sense of excitement": Lyon, *Success Story*, p. 296.
489 "As a curb on genius": Will Irwin, *The Making of a Reporter* (New York: G. P. Putnam's Sons, 1942), p. 137.
489 "the staff worked under . . . came forth Chaos": Sedgwick, *The Happy Profession*, p. 142.
489 In fifteen months, both . . . were fired: Lyon, *Success Story*, p. 304.
489 Damon Runyan . . . and Moira O'Neill: Ibid., p. 296; Mott, *A History of American Magazines*, Vol. 4, p. 602.
489 The company eventually foundered: McClure to JSP, Oct. 17, 1906, McClure MSS.
489 Forced to economize: Lyon, *Success Story*, pp. 311–12.
489 Nor could he afford: *Centralia* [WA] *Daily Chronicle*, Dec. 1, 1908.
490 "of good reputation . . . comparatively short time": "Solicitation Letter," July [n.d.], 1906, RSB Papers.
490 "All of us had plunged": RSB, *American Chronicle*, p. 228.
490 stood "to lose everything": RSB to J. Stannard Baker, June 30, 1906, RSB Papers.
490 "so dizzily stimulating . . . for the common cause": RSB, *American Chronicle*, p. 228.
490 "I feel as if I were at the crisis": LS to Joseph Steffens, June 30, 1906, in LS et al., eds., *Letters of Lincoln Steffens*, Vol. 1, p. 174.
490 "the most dauntless": RSB, *American Chronicle*, p. 228.
490 "seen something in which": Tarbell, *All in the Day's Work*, p. 259.
490 "spark of genius . . . the kindest treatment": WAW to Charles Churchill, Aug. 9, 1906, White Papers.
490 "You may draw on me": WAW to McClure, Aug. 27, 1906, McClure MSS.
491 "Everything amused him! . . . loved so much to talk": RSB, *American Chronicle*, p. 225.
491 "He had a wide knowledge": Tarbell, *All in the Day's Work*, pp. 260–61.
491 "made it his business . . . wonderful tales we heard!": Ibid., pp. 261–62.
491 "all the muckrakers muckraking": *The Independent* (Kansas City, MO), July 8, 1906.
491 "a helpful experiment": *Erie* [PA] *Evening Herald*, June 29, 1906.
491 "Their muck-raking has been": *Evening World-Herald* (Omaha, NE), June 30, 1906.
491 "This is undoubtedly the most notable": *Journal of Education* (Boston), July 6, 1906.
491 "not be deterred": "Editorial Announcement," *The American Magazine* (October 1906).
491 "We shall not only make": "Solicitation Letter," July [n.d.], 1906, RSB Papers.
491 "Reformers need relaxation": *Outlook*, July 14, 1906, p. 589.
491 William Allen White . . . offered similar counsel: Johnson, *William Allen White's America*, p. 138.
491 "It seems to me": WAW to JSP, July 6, 1906, White Papers.
492 "We are editing in": Albert Boyden to RSB, Nov. 13, 1906, RSB Papers.
492 "to look into his literary": RSB, *American Chronicle*, p. 228.
492 "Utterly beaten down . . . hard physical work": Ibid., pp. 213–14.
492 "more easily . . . Send more chapters": Ibid., pp. 229, 231–34.

493 "You have sublimated": Ibid., p. 244.
493 "David Grayson is a great man": LS to RSB, July 25, 1906, in ibid., p. 239.
493 Under such titles as: Ibid., pp. 240, 247–48.
493 "people will be expecting": JSP to RSB, July 26, 1906, RSB Papers.
493 a "pioneer" study: Dewey Grantham, Jr., introduction, in Ray Stannard Baker, *Following the Color Line; American Negro Citizenship in the Progressive Era* (New York: Harper & Row, 1964), pp. x, xiii.
493 "to get at the *facts* . . . a major source": Ibid., pp. vii, x.
494 "a clear statement of the case": *Bedford* [PA] *Gazette*, Feb. 22, 1907.
494 "understanding and sympathy": Semonche, *Ray Stannard Baker*, p. 201.
494 "reporting the negro problem": *Bedford* [PA] *Gazette*, Feb. 22, 1907.
494 "too complex to solve": Ibid.
494 "Your work has been a wonderful thing": IMT to RSB, Aug. 9, 1907, RSB Papers.
494 "the best things running": JSP to RSB, May 22, 1907, RSB Papers.
494 chafed at the "consensus editing": Kaplan, *Lincoln Steffens*, p. 164.
494 "It does not matter": JSP to LS, May 11, 1907, LS Papers.
494 "You are crazy, Stef": Albert Boyden to LS, June 18, 1907, LS Papers.
494 he had failed to answer a request: Albert Boyden to LS, April 5, 1905, LS Papers.
494 "We don't need any": John E. Semonche, "The American Magazine of 1906–1915: Principle vs. Profit," *Journalism Quarterly* (Winter 1963), p. 38.
494 "It is very difficult for me": JSP to LS, Feb. 28, 1907, LS Papers.
494 the magazine was covering: Brady, *Ida Tarbell*, p. 183.
495 "you haven't confidence": JSP to LS, Feb. 28, 1907, LS Papers.
495 Steffens remained oblivious . . . near Cos Cob, Connecticut: Peter Hartshorn, *I Have Seen the Future: A Life of Lincoln Steffens* (Berkeley, CA: Counterpoint, 2011), pp. 148–49.
495 "My husband has become famous": Kaplan, *Lincoln Steffens*, p. 160.
495 "Either I am to write": LS to Joseph Steffens, Aug. 27, 1907, in LS et al., eds., *Letters of Lincoln Steffens*, Vol. 1, p. 188.
495 At the time of his departure, Steffens argued . . . the new enterprise: Brady, *Ida Tarbell*, p. 184.
495 "I know now I should not . . . most genuine of human dramas": IMT, *All in the Day's Work*, pp. 262–64.
495 "All this was good for me": Ibid., p. 267.
495 to "get into the fight": Ibid.
496 debates that appeared "so important": Ibid., p. 269.
496 "comprehensive and careful . . . invertebrate": *Life*, Feb. 8, 1912, p. 308.
496 lacked "vitality" . . . "secondhand" material: IMT, *All in the Day's Work*, p. 271.
496 no "cohesive force" . . . "hold the reader": WAW to JSP, June 22, 1907, White Papers.
496 "a certain hustle": IMT to Albert Boyden, July 1, 1907, McClure MSS.
496 "I dreamed of you": McClure to IMT, July 1, 1907, McClure MSS.

CHAPTER NINETEEN: "To Cut Mr. Taft in Two!"

Page

497 while attending a party . . . turned seventy years old: John Hays Hammond, *The Autobiography of John Hays Hammond* (New York: Farrar & Rinehart, Inc., 1935), Vol. 2, p. 532.
497 "a gentle intimation . . . to another": Henry Billings Brown and Charles A. Kent, *Memoir of Henry Billings Brown: Late Justice of the Supreme Court of the United States* (New York: Duffield, 1915), p. 32.
497 "would be shutting the door . . . in 1908": Hammond, *The Autobiography*, Vol. 2, p. 532.
498 In the interim . . . the previous summer: WHT, Professional Diaries [hereafter WHT Diaries], Jan. 22, 1906, WHTP.
498 "the tremendous vote": Ibid.
498 Taft was "sacrificing . . . to open our markets": *New York Tribune*, Mar. 17, 1906.
498 "an infernal ass": WHT to Horace Taft, Jan. 29, 1906, WHTP.
498 "We suffered a very" . . . reach the Senate floor: WHT to Henry Clay Ide, Mar. 17 & 21, WHTP.
498 the press immediately began: *Washington Post*, reprinted in *Syracuse* [NY] *Herald*, Mar. 10, 1906.
498 would "undoubtedly have accepted": WHT quoted in James Creelman, "The Mystery of Mr. Taft," *Pearson's Magazine* (May 1907), p. 529.
498 At Taft's suggestion . . . renewed the pressure on Taft: WHT Diaries, Mar. 10, 1906, WHTP.
498 "would have as important": TR quoted in WHT to TR, Mar. 14, 1906, WHTP.
499 "a big man": WHT Diaries, Mar. 10, 1906, WHTP.
499 "running down" . . . best man on the bench: TR quoted in WHT to TR, Mar. 14, 1906, WHTP.
499 he intended to announce his nomination: *NYT*, Mar. 14, 1906.
499 "bitterly opposed . . . explain the situation": WHT Diaries, Mar. 10, 1906, WHTP.
499 "three great trusts" . . . would "of course yield": WHT to TR, Mar. 14, 1906, WHTP.
499 Charles thought he should take: Charles P. Taft to WHT, Mar. 10, 1906, WHTP.
499 "quite apart from": Horace Taft to WHT, Mar. 13, 1906, WHTP.
499 Harry . . . better suited to be chief justice: Ross, *An American Family*, p. 183.
500 "My dear Will . . . for many years to come": TR to WHT, Mar. 15, 1906, in *LTR*, Vol. 5, pp. 183–86.
501 "all I could expect" . . . until Congress adjourned in July: WHT to HHT, Mar. 15, 1906, WHTP.
501 Displaying decisiveness . . . postpone his nomination: *Racine* [WI] *Daily Journal*, Sept. 24, 1902.
501 "somewhat unusual . . . Mr. Taft in two!": New York *Sun*, Mar. 17, 1906, in WHT Diaries, WHTP.
501 "the big, jovial, brainy" . . . no longer so appealing: *Hutchinson* [KS] *News*, Aug. 21, 1894.
501 "He has done big things": *Kansas City Star*, June 21, 1906; WHT Diaries, June 23, 1906, WHTP.

501 "no American . . . eyes of his countrymen": Clipping, in James Macusker to WHT, July 23, 1906, WHTP.
501 "I do not see": Lyman Abbott to WHT, Aug. 4, 1906, WHTP.
501 "For the love of Mike": Creighton Webb to WHT, May 29, 1906, WHTP.
502 "a most gloomy" . . . such a busy man!: WHT to TR, July 30, 1906, WHTP.
502 "Now, you beloved": TR to WHT, Aug. 2, 1906, in *LTR*, Vol. 5, pp. 341–43.
502 "rather shocked . . . to sit still": TR to WHT, July 21, 1906, in WHT Diaries, WHTP.
502 "By George": TR to WHT, Aug. 20, 1906, in ibid.
502 a rigorous, doctor-prescribed diet: W. E. Zouke Davie to WHT, Oct. 27, 1905, WHTP.
502 a new bathroom scale . . . 250 pounds: WHT to Charles P. Taft, Dec. 3, 1905, WHTP.
502 "not an inexpensive luxury": WHT to HHT, July 15, 1906, WHTP.
502 "twenty pairs of Trousers": Receipt from Owen, Tailor for Men and Women, to Fred W. Carpenter, July 11, 1906, WHTP.
502 "It is the best thing": Horace Taft to WHT, Dec. 13, 1905, WHTP.
503 Taft's customary day: Wendell W. Mischler to [unknown], Aug. 23, 1906, WHTP.
503 Taft relished . . . and the children: Robert Lee Dunn, *William Howard Taft, American* (Boston: Chapple Publ. Co., 1908), pp. 43–44; "Murray Bay," *Cincinnati Magazine* (August 1979), p. 72.
503 "jumping up and down . . . will do the business": Dunn, *William Howard Taft, American*, pp. 44–45.
503 saving his "city clothes": Ibid., p. 32.
503 "see youth returning": Ibid.
503 The chairman . . . to give the keynote: WHT to TR, Aug. 6, 1906, in WHT Diaries, WHTP.
503 In a letter from Oyster Bay: TR to WHT, Aug. 8, 1906, in ibid.
503 Taft organized his presentation: "Mr. Taft on the Present Issues," *Outlook*, Sept. 15, 1906, p. 95.
503 the "only weakness": WHT to TR, Aug. 21, 1906, WHTP.
503 if the draft seemed "too outspoken": WHT to TR, Aug. 28, 1906, WHTP.
503 "outrageously long . . . circumstances like this": WHT to TR, Aug. 28 & 29, 1906, WHTP.
504 "It's a bully speech": TR to WHT, August [n.d.], 1906, in WHT Diaries, WHTP.
504 "I neither wish": TR to WHT, Sept. 1, 1906, in *LTR*, Vol. 5, p. 392.
504 he suggested that Taft show: TR to WHT, Sept. 4, 1906, in WHT Diaries, WHTP.
504 "the first big Administration": *NYT*, Sept. 6, 1906.
504 "is the issue": New York *Sun*, Sept. 6, 1906, in WHT Diaries, WHTP.
504 "With a frankness . . . and unhesitatingly": *Washington Post*, Sept. 6, 1906.
504 "the frankest": New York *Sun*, Sept. 6, 1906, in WHT Diaries, WHTP.
504 "never made a sharper speech": Henry Hoyt to WHT, Sept. 6, 1906, WHTP.
504 "It is the great speech": TR to WHT, Sept. 6, 1906, in WHT Diaries, WHTP.
504 "A man never knows": WHT to TR, Sept. 8, 1906, WHTP.
504 Revolutionary forces . . . a precarious situation: *Newark* [NJ] *Advocate*, Sept. 14, 1906.
505 "a government adequate": Pringle, *Life and Times*, Vol. 1, pp. 305–06.
505 "In Cuba": TR to George Trevelyan, Sept. 9, 1906, in *LTR*, Vol. 5, p. 401.
505 could not "prevent rebels": Consul-General Steinhart to Acting Secretary of War, Sept. 13, 1906, in United States, *Papers Relating to the Foreign Relations of the United States, with the Annual Message of the President Transmitted to Congress December 3, 1906, Part 1* (Washington, DC: Government Printing Office, 1909), pp. 477–78.
505 "so angry with": Cited in Morris, *Theodore Rex*, p. 456.
505 "as intermediaries" . . . a peaceful solution: Bruce A. Vitor II, *Under the Shadow of the Big Stick: U.S. Intervention in Cuba, 1906–1909* (Fort Leavenworth, KS: U.S. Army Command & General Staff College, 2009), p. 12.
505 From Oyster Bay . . . Attorney General Moody's opinion: WHT to TR, Sept. 16, 1906, WHTP.
505 "If the necessity arises": TR to WHT, Sept. 17, 1906, in *LTR*, Vol. 5, p. 514.
505 When Taft and Bacon . . . reconcile differences peacefully: Duffy, *William Howard Taft*, pp. 187–88.
506 "informal, straightforward": *Racine Daily Journal*, Sept. 19, 1906.
506 "the utter unfitness": WHT to HHT, Sept. 20, 1906, WHTP.
506 "well founded . . . to their homes": WHT to Charles E. Magoon, Nov. 22, 1906; TR to WHT, Sept. 21, 1906, both in *LTR*, Vol. 5, p. 418.
506 "leaving nothing of the Government": WHT to TR, Sept. 25, 1906, WHTP.
506 "The insurgents": WHT to HHT, Sept. 23, 1906, WHTP.
506 One insurgent encampment: WHT to HHT, Sept. 22, 1906, WHTP.
506 "Things are certainly": TR to WHT, Sept. 26, 1906, in *LTR*, Vol. 5, p. 426.
506 "the most unpleasant": WHT to HHT, Sept. 27, 1906, WHTP.
506 he found himself awake . . . struck him dead: Ibid.
506 After a week . . . would land in Cuba: TR to WHT, Sept. 30, 1906, in *LTR*, Vol. 5, p. 435.
506 "be maintained only": Vitor, *Under the Shadow of the Big Stick*, p. 31.
506 The Cuban Constitution . . . would be withdrawn: Morris, *Theodore Rex*, p. 461.
507 "all parties here . . . such attacks futile": WHT to HHT, Sept. 30, 1906, WHTP.
507 "I congratulate you": TR to WHT, Sept. 30, 1906, in *LTR*, Vol. 5, p. 435.
507 promptly cabled Nellie . . . "great comfort": WHT to HHT, Sept. 29, 1906, WHTP.
507 "For the first time . . . quite brilliant effect": HHT, *Recollections of Full Years*, pp. 297, 299.
507 "Upon my word": TR to WHT, Oct. 4, 1906, in WHT Diaries, WHTP.
507 "the shore of the Bay": Dunn, *William Howard Taft, American*, p. 182.
507 "in agony on": HHT, *Recollections of Full Years*, p. 301.
508 "Merely to record . . . to his War Department duties": New York *Sun*, Oct. 27, 1906.
508 "If mental worry": WHT to Charles P. Taft, Oct. 4, 1906, WHTP.

508 "those awful twenty days": HHT, *Recollections of Full Years*, p. 295.
508 "The paramount issue . . . the jolly good fellow": *Omaha* [NE] *Daily Bee*, Oct. 31 & Nov. 2, 1906.
508 "This is rather contrary": WHT to HHT, Nov. 4, 1907, WHTP.
509 "Hats were thrown": *Salt Lake Herald*, Nov. 4, 1906.
509 "The notices have all been": HHT to WHT, Oct. 31, 1906, WHTP.
509 she was concerned . . . cost him the nomination: HHT to WHT, Oct. 27 & 29, 1906, WHTP.
509 "the blues . . . the direction of politics": WHT to HHT, Nov. 1, 1906, WHTP.
509 "turned them down . . . I did not": HHT to WHT, Oct. 27, 1906, WHTP.
509 "I think what": WHT to HHT, Oct. 31, 1906, WHTP.
509 "If you do" . . . a "substitute": WHT to TR, Oct. 31, 1906, WHTP.
510 "I am immensely": TR to WHT, Nov. 5, 1906, in *LTR*, Vol. 5, p. 487.
510 "Our triumph . . . would have been": TR to Kermit Roosevelt, Nov. 7, 1906, in TR et al., eds., *Letters to Kermit from Theodore Roosevelt*, p. 487.
510 "I am overjoyed . . . scandal-mongering": TR to John St. Loe Strachey, Oct. 25, 1906, in *LTR*, Vol. 5, p. 468.
510 "By George": TR to WHT, Nov. 8, 1906, in ibid., p. 492.
510 "I'm going down": *Los Angeles Herald*, Nov. 9, 1906.
510 The "ditch . . . gardens of Babylon": *New York Tribune*, Nov. 12, 1906.
510 "particularly good spirits": *Los Angeles Herald*, Nov. 9, 1906.
510 "a large portion . . . where he may be": *San Antonio* [TX] *Daily Light*, Nov. 11, 1906.
510 "a little of everything": *NYT*, Nov. 14, 1906.
510 Wishing to judge . . . about his work: *NYT*, Nov. 17, 1906.
511 He met with laborers . . . "what he saw": *New York Tribune*, Dec. 16, 1906.
511 Although the Tafts . . . Kansas, and Texas: WHT to TR, Nov. 4, 1906, WHTP.
511 "Not in the history": *Ada* [OK] *Evening News*, Nov. 9, 1906.
511 "several thousand": *Emporia* [KS] *Gazette*, Nov. 10, 1906.
511 "One trouble about travel": WHT to HHT, Nov. 16, 1906, WHTP.
511 During his lengthy absence . . . Brownsville, Texas: *Chicago Tribune*, Nov. 21, 1906.
511 "would certainly be denied them": *Brownsville* [TX] *Daily Herald*, Aug. 14, 1906.
511 A series of . . . public bars: United States, *Hearings Before the Committee on Military Affairs, United States Senate, Concerning the Affray at Brownsville, Tex., on the Night of August 13 and 14, 1906* (Washington, DC: Government Printing Office, 1908), Vol. 1, pp. 462–63.
511 Rumors . . . circulated: *Washington Post*, Aug. 15, 1906.
512 "colored soldiers" . . . after the shootings: United States and Ernest A. Garlington, *The Brownsville Affray: Report of the Inspector General of the Army; Order of the President Discharging Enlisted Men of Companies B, C, and D, Twenty-Fifth Infantry; Messages of the President to the Senate; and Majority and Minority Reports of the Senate Committee on Military Affairs* (Washington, DC: Government Printing Office, 1908), pp. 302–03.
512 Major Augustus Blocksom . . . "nine to fifteen": *Washington Post*, Aug. 22, 1906.
512 "discharged from the service": Morris, *Theodore Rex*, p. 455.
512 "in a state . . . openly at night": *Washington Post*, Aug. 22, 1906.
512 "It is very doubtful": *Brownsville Daily Herald*, Aug. 22, 1906.
512 If they continued to conceal: *NYT*, Oct. 18, 1906.
512 "this extreme penalty . . . when the penalty falls": *NYT*, Nov. 7, 1906.
512 The president directed . . . any civil service position: Ibid.; *Cleveland Journal*, Nov. 10, 1906.
512 The battalion included . . . Spanish-American War: *Cleveland Journal*, Nov. 24, 1906.
513 "despotic usurpation of power": *Arizona Silver Belt* (Globe City, AZ), Nov. 11, 1906.
513 "Deep resentment": *NYT*, Nov. 19, 1906.
513 "the door of hope": *NYT*, Nov. 21, 1906.
513 "a truckling": *NYT*, Nov. 19, 1906.
513 "Once enshrined": Ibid.
513 Taft consented to meet Mary Church Terrell: *NYT*, Nov. 18, 1906.
513 "to withhold the execution . . . generous-hearted": Mary Church Terrell, "Taft and the Negro Soldiers," *The Independent*, July 23, 1908.
513 "delay the execution . . . on the subject": Pringle, *Life and Times*, Vol. 1, pp. 324–25.
513 the negative impact: WHT to Louise T. Taft, Jan. 15, 1907, in WHT Diaries, WHTP.
513 "If a rehearing shows": WHT to CPT, Jan. 1, 1907, WHTP.
513 Upon learning that Taft . . . the civil branch: *Cleveland Journal*, Nov. 24, 1906.
513 "a severe strain upon": *NYT*, Nov. 21, 1906.
514 "The order in question": TR to Curtis Guild, Jr., Nov. 7, 1906, in *LTR*, Vol. 5, p. 489.
514 "Discharge is not": TR to WHT, Nov. 21, 1906, in WHT Diaries, WHTP.
514 When Congress convened . . . overstepped his authority: New York *Sun*, Dec. 4, 1906.
514 a "fighting mad" reaction: *NYT*, Dec. 23, 1906.
514 "It is impossible": TR to RSB, Mar. 30, 1907, in *LTR*, Vol. 5, p. 634.
514 "tingling with . . . comrades of murderers": *The News* (Frederick, MD), Dec. 20, 1906.
514 "excuse or justification . . . utterly inadequate": *New York Tribune*, Dec. 20, 1906.
514 "fight to the last . . . decided to follow": New York *Sun*, Dec. 23, 1906.
514 "extraordinary language . . . hatred and violence": *The News* (Frederick, MD), Dec. 20, 1906.
515 "the colored man": *Washington* [DC] *Bee*, Dec. 29, 1906.
515 sending a new round: *Bisbee* [AZ] *Daily Review*, Dec. 30, 1906.
515 At Taft's urging: *Chicago Tribune*, Jan. 15, 1907.
515 Eventually, he allowed: *NYT*, Mar. 12, 1908.

515 "cleared the records": *NYT*, Sept. 29, 1972.
515 Privately, Taft continued: WHT to Charles P. Taft, Jan. 1, 1907, WHTP.
515 "courage and good judgment" . . . already carried out: WHT to Richard Harding Davis, Nov. 24, 1906, WHTP.
515 "This Brownsville matter . . . disappear with argument": WHT to Howard Hollister, Dec. 25, 1906, in WHT Diaries, WHTP.

CHAPTER TWENTY: Taft Boom, Wall Street Bust

Page
516 "favorable consideration . . . in silence": *Fort Wayne* [IN] *Journal-Gazette*, Mar. 7, 1907.
516 "an uneventful and poor": *Post-Standard* (Syracuse, NY), Mar. 5, 1906.
517 a bill banning corporate contributions: *NYT*, Jan. 22, 1907.
517 "knowingly" . . . sixteen consecutive hours: *The Railway Age*, Mar. 8, 1907, p. 323.
517 many critical bills . . . law for corporations: *Fort Wayne* [IN] *Journal-Gazette*, Mar. 7, 1907.
517 "some sixteen million": TR, *An Autobiography*, p. 404.
517 Pinchot mobilized his office . . . into forest lands: Pinchot, *Breaking New Ground*, p. 300.
517 Through these orders: Brinkley, *The Wilderness Warrior*, pp. 677–78.
517 "Opponents of the Forest Service": TR, *An Autobiography*, pp. 404–05.
518 "the deep, unbroken friendship": James Creelman, "The Mystery of Mr. Taft," *Pearson's* (May 1907), p. 530, in WHT Diaries, WHTP.
518 "I am well aware": TR to WAW, July 30, 1907, WHTP.
518 "do all in his power": *Evening Independent* (Massillon, OH), April 23, 1907.
518 "boundless courage . . . beguiling influence": *San Antonio* [TX] *Gazette*, June 25, 1907.
518 "he would crawl": John Callan O'Laughlin, "The Next President," *Outlook*, Mar. 30, 1907, p. 749.
518 he would disavow any such statement: "TR: Press Agent," *Harper's Weekly*, Sept. 28, 1907, p. 1410.
518 IMPARTIAL MR. ROOSEVELT: *Kansas City Times*, April 16, 1907, in WHT Diaries, WHTP.
518 "I wish to say": *Cleveland Leader*, Dec. 29, 1906, in WHT Diaries, WHTP.
518 "been drawn into . . . irrespective of politics": O'Laughlin, "The Next President," *Outlook*, Mar. 30, 1907, p. 747.
519 "was very much averse": WHT to Edward Colston, Mar. 22, 1907, WHT Diaries, WHTP.
519 "an almost morbid fear": O'Laughlin, "The Next President," *Outlook*, Mar. 30, 1907, p. 747.
519 "Taft is not a politician": *Washington Post*, Jan. 27, 1907.
519 "the little details": *Washington Post*, April 25, 1907.
519 The press predicted: *The Independent* (NY), April 4, 1907, pp. 757–58.
519 "may cause trouble": TR to Kermit Roosevelt, April 11, 1907, in TR et al., eds., *Letters to Kermit from Theodore Roosevelt*, p. 188.
519 "This is a direct contest": New York *Sun*, Mar. 31, 1907, in WHT Diaries, WHTP.
519 "had nothing to gain . . . possibly to lose": HHT to WHT, April [n.d., "Easter Sunday"], 1907, WHTP.
519 The decision . . . soon proved wise: WHT to Charles P. Taft, May 8, 1907, WHTP.
520 Through intermediaries . . . senatorial contest: *New York Tribune*, May 11, 1907.
520 "I don't care . . . political principle": WHT to Arthur Vorys, Jan. 20, 1907, WHT Diaries, WHTP.
520 "with a drawn sword in his hand": WHT to Gustav J. Karger, May 14, 1907, Taft-Karger MSS, CMC.
520 "become somewhat . . . a stand-up fight": WHT to TR, July 23, 1907, WHTP.
520 "While under no circumstances": TR to WHT, July 26, 1907, in *LTR*, Vol. 5, pp. 726–27.
520 Steeled for defeat . . . in the Senate race: *New York Tribune*, July 30, 1907, in WHT Diaries, WHTP.
520 "I am hopeful": WHT to Howard C. Hollister, July 31, 1907, WHTP.
520 Foraker's political career . . . in public office again: Pringle, *Life and Times*, Vol. 1, pp. 371–72; *Fort Wayne Journal-Gazette*, Sept. 8, 1908.
521 Despite his victory . . . a "mauling": TR to WHT, Aug. 3, 1907, in *LTR*, Vol. 5, p. 741.
521 "first substantial start": WHT to Joseph B. Foraker, Aug. 24, 1908, in Pringle, *Life and Times*, Vol. 1, p. 371.
521 "born with an instinct": Creelman, "The Mystery of Mr. Taft," *Pearson's* (May 1907), p. 512, in WHT Diaries, WHTP.
521 "the kindest man": Lyle, "Taft: A Career of Big Tasks," *The World's Work* (November 1907).
521 "A place on the Supreme": Unidentified newspaper clipping, Los Angeles, May [n.d.], 1907, in WHT Diaries, WHTP.
521 "Uneasy lies the head": LTT to WHT, Jan. 21, 1907, WHTP.
521 "He wins the hearts . . . devoid of political ambitions": James Creelman, "The Mystery of Mr. Taft," *Pearson's* (May 1907), pp. 511, 505, in WHT Diaries, WHTP.
521 "can scarcely be said": *NYT*, Aug. 18, 1907.
522 "fitted to say things": *Mansfield* [OH] *News*, May 2, 1907.
522 "I am not sure": WHT to Arthur Vorys, Aug. 6, 1907, WHTP.
522 his drafts remained "infernally long": WHT to TR, Aug. 10, 1907, WHTP.
522 "Never mind if": HHT to WHT, Aug. 18, 1907, WHTP.
522 "revision must wait": New York *Sun*, Aug. 20, 1907.
522 "ferocious denunciation . . . and sincere sympathy": *NYT*, Aug. 20, 1907.
522 "there is not": New York *Sun*, Aug. 20, 1907.
522 "I am much amused": WHT to Horace Taft, Sept. 10, 1907, WHTP.
522 "Is it possible . . . adherence to those views": WHT to Charles H. Heald, Dec. 25, 1907, WHTP.
522 "the feeling of . . . are compelled to": Charles Nagel to WHT, May 6, 1907, WHT Diaries, WHTP.
523 "well defined movement": *Cedar Rapids* [IA] *Evening Gazette*, Nov. 8, 1907.
523 "an almost unanimous sentiment": *Chicago Record-Herald*, Mar. 5, 1907, in WHT Diaries, WHTP.
523 "It's hard to write . . . Roosevelt sentiment": C. S. Watts to N. Wright, in Charles P. Taft to WHT, May 21, 1907, WHTP.
523 "almost grotesque . . . an illustrious Necessity?": New York *Sun*, Mar. 31, 1907.

523 "How they hate him": HHT to WHT, Mar. 31, 1907, WHTP.
523 "could get the nomination": Gustav J. Karger to Joseph Garretson, Oct. 30, 1907, Taft-Karger MSS, CMC.
523 "would feel very much . . . they had formed": TR to Kermit Roosevelt, May 15, 1907, in TR, et al., eds., *Letters to Kermit from Theodore Roosevelt*, p. 195.
524 "personal sacrifice . . . this administration": Gustav J. Karger to Joseph Garretson, Oct. 30, 1907, Taft-Karger MSS, CMC.
524 In case Taft's canvass . . . backing Governor Hughes: TR to WHT, Sept. 3, 1907, in *LTR*, Vol. 5, pp. 780–82.
524 "for the moment . . . the wisest course": TR to WHT, Sept. 3, 1907, in ibid., p. 781.
524 by late August . . . had grown "shorter": *Galveston* [TX] *Daily News*, Aug. 31, 1907.
524 "Political affairs . . . in the third place": TR to WHT, Sept. 3, 1907, in *LTR*, Vol. 5, pp. 780–82.
524 "So far as I am able": WHT to Charles P. Taft, Sept. 11, 1907, WHTP.
524 "It was as great": WHT to Charles P. Taft, Aug. 21, 1907, WHTP.
524 "a fine audience of 4000 people": WHT to TR, Aug. 30, 1907, WHTP.
524 "was filled to suffocation": WHT to LTT, Aug. 30, 1907, WHT Diaries, WHTP.
524 "every politician": WHT to TR, Aug. 30, 1907, WHTP.
525 "Personal contact": WHT to Charles P. Taft, Sept. 11, 1907, WHTP.
525 "feel glad": *NYT*, Aug. 18, 1907.
525 "Nellie was out . . . to you than to me": WHT to Charles P. Taft, Sept. 11, 1907, WHTP.
525 "I fully understand . . . my boom at all possible": WHT to TR, Sept. 11, 1907, WHTP.
525 "right to initiate . . . by the Commission": "Address by Wm. H. Taft, Secretary of War, at the Inauguration of the Philippine Assembly, October 16, 1907," in United States and WHT, *Special Report of Wm. H. Taft, Secretary of War, to the President, on the Philippines* (Washington, DC: Government Printing Office, 1908), p. 98.
525 "the first parliament": Karnow, *In Our Image*, p. 238.
526 "a chill . . . wealthier classes": WHT to Charles P. Taft, Oct. 23, 1907, WHTP.
526 He began his address . . . "about to undertake": See WHT, *Special Report . . . on the Philippines*, pp. 86, 89, 102.
526 "thousand and one events": HHT, *Recollections of Full Years*, p. 315.
526 "Everybody": Anthony, *Nellie Taft*, p. 205.
527 stock market losses approached $1 billion: Jean Strouse, *Morgan: American Financier* (New York: Random House, 1999), p. 573.
527 "crusades against business" . . . paralyzed the economy: *Chicago Record-Herald*, Feb. 2, 1907, cited in Pringle, *Theodore Roosevelt: A Biography*, p. 434.
527 "By slow and insidious": New York *Sun*, Dec. 6, 1907.
527 "deep-seated, undiscriminating": *Current Literature* (October 1907), p. 352.
527 By "going up and down": *Current Literature* (December 1907), p. 596.
527 "take Bryan or Hearst": Creelman, "Theodore the Meddler," *Pearson's* (January 1907), p. 4.
527 "certain malefactors": *The News* (Frederick, MD), Aug. 21, 1907.
527 "welcome hard times": TR to William E. Dodd, Jan. 30, 1907, in *LTR*, Vol. 5, p. 575.
527 "They are as blind": TR to William H. Moody, Sept. 21, 1907, in ibid., p. 802.
527 "responsible for turning on": *Current Literature* (December 1907), p. 597.
527 "a temporary period of weakness": TR to Henry L. Higginson, Aug. 12, 1907, in *LTR*, Vol. 5, p. 746.
528 Their sensational failure . . . investment bank in New York: *Current Literature* (December 1907), p. 585.
528 Spooked by rumors . . . shutter its offices: Strouse, *Morgan: American Financier*, p. 577.
528 Evidence that the respected firm: *Current Literature* (December 1907), p. 594.
528 In the days that followed: Ibid., pp. 586–87, 590.
528 "hardly a bank": Ibid., p. 590.
528 "a one-man Federal Reserve": Frederick Lewis Allen, *The Great Pierpont Morgan* (New York: Harper & Row, 1949), p. 265.
528 "Panic Headquarters": Ida May Tarbell, *The Life of Elbert H. Gary: The Story of Steel* (New York: D. Appleton, 1925), p. 199.
528 Within two days the bankers: Jean Strouse, "The Brilliant Bailout," *The New Yorker*, Nov. 23, 1998, p. 69.
528 "It was an extraordinary": Chernow, *The House of Morgan*, p. 124.
528 The next day . . . Morgan's headquarters: *Racine* [WI] *Daily Journal*, Oct. 23, 1907; *Galveston Daily News*, Oct. 24, 1907.
528 On Thursday . . . to keep the exchange open: Strouse, *Morgan: American Financier*, p. 580.
529 "the Man of the Hour": *Literary Digest*, Nov. 9, 1907, p. 676.
529 "was still the chief": Ibid.
529 "would bring down": IMT, *Life of Elbert H. Gary*, p. 196.
529 "Can you go at once?": Ibid., p. 200.
529 "under ordinary circumstances": TR to Charles J. Bonaparte, Nov. 4, 1907, in *LTR*, Vol. 5, p. 831.
529 "somewhat in excess": Mowry, *The Era of Theodore Roosevelt*, p. 218.
529 "to the interest . . . no public duty": TR to Charles J. Bonaparte, Nov. 4, 1907, in *LTR*, Vol. 5, p. 831.
529 But when the terms: Chernow, *The House of Morgan*, p. 128.
529 "the best bargain . . . less than $1 billion": Pringle, *Theodore Roosevelt: A Biography*, p. 444.
529 "swallow up a lively": Allen, *The Great Pierpont Morgan*, p. 261.
529 "The Nation trembled . . . crisis arose": TR, *An Autobiography*, p. 438.
530 "I would have showed": Ibid., p. 442.
530 a general malaise began . . . their livelihood: TR to Cecil Spring Rice, Dec. 21, 1907, in *LTR*, Vol. 6, p. 870.
530 "Whether I am": TR to Alexander Lambert, Nov. 1, 1907, in *LTR*, Vol. 5, p. 826.
530 "The big moneyed men": TR to Kermit Roosevelt, Dec. 8, 1907, in ibid., p. 226.
530 "because when the average": TR to Alexander Lambert, Nov. 1, 1907, in ibid., p. 826.

530 "From all sides": IMT, *Life of Elbert H. Gary,* p. 192.
530 "destroyer of . . . of property": *Literary Digest* (December 1907), p. 594.
530 "I feel personally": WAW to TR, Nov. 22, 1907, White Papers.
530 "I care a great deal more": TR to WAW, Nov. 26, 1907, in *LTR*, Vol. 5, pp. 855–56.
530 "to destroy his . . . blood to running!": RSB to J. Stannard Baker, Nov. 17, 1907, RSB Papers.
531 "A man may sometimes": RSB, Notebook, Nov. 16, 1907, and RSB to J. Stannard Baker, Nov. 16, 1907, RSB Papers.
531 "I hate for personal reasons": TR to Frederic Harrison, Dec. 18, 1907, in *LTR*, Vol. 6, p. 866.
531 "the fight before . . . of the people": TR to Arthur Hamilton Lee, Dec. 26, 1907, in ibid., pp. 874–75.
531 "On the night after . . . gossip ever since": *National Tribune* (Washington, DC), Dec. 19, 1907.
531 "I suppose he has come": *NYT*, Dec. 12, 1907.
531 "do his utmost": Ibid.
532 "definitely and positively": New York *Sun*, Dec. 13, 1907.
532 "to come out squarely": *Sandusky* [OH] *Star-Journal*, Dec. 13, 1907.
532 Frank Flint . . . "all along": *New York Tribune*, Dec. 13, 1907.
532 "the only one worth considering": *NYT*, Dec. 12, 1907.
532 "strength, constitution and courage": Horace Taft to WHT, Aug. 20, 1907, WHTP.
532 "on the road to recovery": Charles P. Taft to Delia Torrey, Nov. 21, 1907, WHTP.
532 "her cheeks were": Anne Taft to WHT, Dec. 20, 1907, WHTP.
532 "slowly but steadily": WHT to Mrs. Samuel Carr, Dec. 24, 1907, WHTP.
532 "Still have hope": Charles P. Taft to WHT, Dec. 6, 1907, WHTP.
532 Taft's ship . . . his mother was dead: WHT Diaries, Dec. 7, 1907, WHTP.
532 "I hope you will say . . . public statement": TR to WHT, Dec. 12, 1907, in *LTR*, Vol. 5, p. 864.
533 "I was very much . . . a great change": WHT to Mrs. Samuel Carr, Dec. 24, 1907, WHTP.
533 "for something else . . . reckoned with": WHT to Therese McCagg, Dec. 26, 1907, WHTP.

CHAPTER TWENTY-ONE: Kingmaker and King

Page

534 "caught its second wind": *The North American* (Philadelphia), June 21, 1908.
534 "as its first . . . with a whoop": William Nelson to WHT, Jan. 22, 1908, WHTP.
534 endorsed Taft unanimously: D. C. Bailey to WHT, Feb. 12, 1908, WHTP.
534 a poll . . . two to one margin: *Van Wert* [OH] *Daily Bulletin*, Feb. 4, 1908.
535 "If you could bring": WHT to William Dawson, Jan. 16, 1908, WHTP.
535 He solicited activists: WHT to Thomas Latta, Feb. 11, 1908, WHTP.
535 "friendly tone . . . brighter": WHT to Tams Bixby, Mar. 26, 1908, WHTP.
535 "rapid-fire . . . witty sallies": *Washington Post*, Feb. 12, 1908.
535 "a blacklisted laborer": Dunn, *William Howard Taft, American*, p. 175.
535 "to determine" . . . of that committee: WHT, "Cooper Union Speech of January 10, 1908," WHTP.
535 "God knows": *Washington Post*, Jan. 11, 1908.
535 "it was the general verdict": *Outlook*, Jan. 18, 1908, p. 108.
535 By late January . . . chances in the fall: WHT to Herbert Parsons, Jan. 23, 1908.
535 so "blistering . . . sensational": Davis, *Released for Publication*, p. 71.
535 "sane and sound" address: Henry C. Ide to WHT, Feb. 2, 1908, WHTP.
536 "a matter of humiliation . . . a stop to the wrongdoing": United States, *Special Message of the President of the United States, Communicated to the Two Houses of Congress on January 31, 1908* (Washington, DC: Government Printing Office, 1908), pp. 2, 26–27.
536 "prostituting his high office": Davis, *Released for Publication*, p. 71.
536 "It hurls defiance" . . . caught everyone's attention: Cited in *Chicago Tribune*, Feb. 2, 1908.
536 "It has maddened": TR to Kermit Roosevelt, Feb. 10, 1908, in TR et al., eds., *Letters to Kermit from Theodore Roosevelt*, p. 231.
536 "It records something": WHT to Frank T. Cobb, Feb. 3, 1908, WHTP.
536 "the Hughes boom . . . settled": TR to Kermit Roosevelt, April 11, 1908, in TR et al., eds., *Letters to Kermit from Theodore Roosevelt*, p. 238.
537 "distinctly against any": New York *Sun*, Mar. 9, 1908, WHTP.
537 Taft immediately repudiated . . . to disturb him: WHT to TR, Mar. 9, 1908, WHTP.
537 "Good heavens . . . myself responsible!": TR to WHT, Mar. 9, 1908, WHTP.
537 "painful experience . . . execration": WHT to Nahum Brascher, Jan. 19, 1908, WHTP.
537 From his abolitionist father: WHT to Robert Barnes, April 26, 1908, WHTP.
537 "to oppose the color caste": "Professor DuBois's Advice," *The Independent*, April 2, 1908, p. 768.
537 "a menace": *Washington Bee*, Dec. 29, 1906.
537 "never, never" support him: "The Negroes and Secretary Taft," *The Independent*, Feb. 13, 1908, p. 374.
537 "entire responsibility": *NYT*, Aug. 8, 1906.
537 "We are satisfied": Ibid.
537 predilection "for strong drink": W. E. Chandler to WHT, June 5, 1908, WHTP.
537 "wonderful resolution": WHT to W. E. Chandler, June 6, 1908, WHTP.
537 "painted as perfect": *Current Literature* (July 1908), p. 10.
537 "I trust you will": Frank H. Challis to WHT, June 2, 1908, WHTP.
537 "the mighty dead . . . heartless": *Los Angeles Herald*, June 2, 1908.
537 "at mock attention . . . destinies of the nation": AB to his mother, June 8, 1908, in Abbott, ed., *Letters of Archie Butt*, p. 23.

538 "All opposition to Taft": TR to Whitelaw Reid, May 25, 1908, in *LTR*, Vol. 6, p. 1036.
538 "an astonishing achievement": *Chicago Evening Post*, April 13, 1908.
538 "Congress is ending": TR to Whitelaw Reid, May 25, 1908, in *LTR*, Vol. 6, p. 1036.
538 "practical unanimity . . . do nothing Congress": *Syracuse* [NY] *Herald*, June 1, 1908.
538 "crystallized" a nascent sentiment: Semonche, *Ray Stannard Baker*, p. 151.
538 "The noon of the muckraker's day": *Waterloo* [IA] *Semi Weekly Courier*, Nov. 27, 1908.
538 "Look upon these . . . now in favor": *NYT*, July 23, 1908.
539 "Don't hold the knife": Johnson, *William Allen White's America*, p. 165.
539 White needed . . . to Washington: WAW to WHT, Jan. 22, 1908, White Papers.
539 In lengthy letters . . . his success: WAW to WHT, Feb. 26, 1908, White Papers.
539 "The meanest man": WHT to Miller Outcault, Mar. 23, 1908, WHTP.
539 an "amiable giant . . . clean off the desk": WAW, "Taft: A Hewer of Wood," *The American Magazine* (April 1908), pp. 19, 23, 31, 32.
539 "It would be impossible": TR to WAW, June 26, 1908, White Papers.
539 "I wabble terribly . . . seems so amazing": IMT to RSB, May 3, 1911, RSB Papers.
539 "for the sake of . . . but for the people": IMT, "Roosevelt vs. Rockefeller," *The American Magazine* (February 1908), p. 434.
539 "less amazing" figure: IMT to RSB, May 3, 1911, RSB Papers.
539 "the St. George": IMT, *All in the Day's Work*, p. 271.
540 "I certainly am socialistic": Palermo, *Lincoln Steffens*, p. 69.
540 Although he praised . . . the system itself: LS, "Roosevelt—Taft—La Follette: On What the Matter Is in America, and What to Do About It," *Everybody's Magazine* (June 1908), pp. 725, 732, 736.
540 "You contend . . . mighty little good": TR to LS, June 5, 1908, in *LTR*, Vol. 6, pp. 1051, 1053.
540 "mutual understanding . . . genuine affection": LS to TR, June 9, 1908, TRP.
540 "the most interesting . . . valiantly and fearlessly": RSB, "The Powers of a Strenuous President," *The American Magazine* (April 1908), pp. 555–56, 559.
541 a "European system": Semonche, *Ray Stannard Baker*, p. 213.
541 "I think you lay . . . man as a man": TR to RSB, June 3, 1908, in *LTR*, Vol. 6, pp. 1047–49.
541 "I wish as much . . . downtrodden, outcast?": RSB to TR, June 8, 1908, TRP.
541 "the wilds of Africa . . . plain morality": RSB, "The New Roosevelt: A Sketch from Life from an Unpublished Letter," *The American Magazine* (September 1908), p. 472.
542 "in a more human mood": Ibid.
542 "When you see me": AB to his mother, May 15, 1908, in Abbott, ed., *Letters of Archie Butt*, p. 7.
542 "*been* President . . . should hold it": TR to George Trevelyan, June 19, 1908, in *LTR*, Vol. 6, pp. 1087, 1086, 1089.
542 "to throb with . . . Pres. Roosevelt": *Washington Post*, June 14, 1908.
542 "an unfailing topic": *Emporia* [KS] *Gazette*, June 16, 1908.
542 "a mob": *San Francisco Chronicle*, June 17, 1908.
542 "in their heart of hearts": *Des Moines Daily News*, June 16, 1908.
542 "a stampede . . . last card": *Washington Post*, June 14, 1908.
542 "to create a diversion": *The North American*, June 21, 1908.
543 "full of sunshine": *Outlook*, June 27, 1908, p. 420.
543 The band played: *Emporia* [KS] *Gazette*, June 16, 1908.
543 "the glories of . . . blood tingling": *New York Tribune*, June 18, 1908.
543 "that expectant interest": *Des Moines Daily News*, June 17, 1908.
543 His quarters at . . . comfortable chairs: *NYT*, March 29, 1908.
543 Electricians equipped . . . the Coliseum: *New York Tribune*, June 18, 1908.
543 "plunged into the . . . do anything unnatural": *Emporia* [KS] *Gazette*, June 18, 1908.
543 Nellie arrived at noon . . . outer reception room: *Washington Post*, June 19, 1908.
544 "the magic name": *Outlook*, June 27, 1908, p. 417.
544 "a wild, frenzied": *Des Moines Daily News*, June 17, 1908.
544 "burning fuse to dry powder": *New York Tribune*, June 19, 1908.
544 "vested abuses . . . United States today": Republican National Convention and Milton W. Blumenberg, *Official Report of the Proceedings of the Fourteenth Republican National Convention: Held in Chicago, Illinois, June 16, 17, 18 and 19, 1908: Resulting in the Nomination of William Howard Taft, of Ohio, for President* (Columbus, OH: F. J. Heer, 1908), p. 87.
544 "exploded with a roar . . . Four Years More": *Outlook*, June 27, 1908, p. 417.
544 "volleys of cheers . . . would blow off": *New York Tribune*, June 18, 1908.
544 "a trifle . . . for another outburst": *Washington Post*, June 18, 1908.
544 "on the verge": *New York Tribune*, June 18, 1908.
544 Fortunately, Taft . . . pandemonium erupted: WHT Diaries, June 17, 1908, WHTP.
544 Nellie was unnerved: Joseph Bucklin Bishop, *Presidential Nominations and Elections: A History of American Conventions, National Campaigns, Inaugurations and Campaign Caricature* (New York: Charles Scribner's Sons, 1916), p. 74.
544 "not at all alarmed": WHT Diaries, June 17, 1908, WHTP.
544 "by the force of his": *Outlook*, June 27, 1908, p. 417.
544 "That man is no friend": RNC and Blumenberg, *Official Report of the Proceedings of the Fourteenth Republican National Convention*, p. 88.
544 "as the voice of the President": *Washington Post*, June 18, 1908.
545 "to blow off steam": *New York Tribune*, June 18, 1908.
545 Archie Butt had never: AB to his mother, June 19, 1908, in Abbott, ed., *Letters of Archie Butt*, p. 39.
545 "The cheers for Roosevelt": *Des Moines Daily News*, June 17, 1908.

545 one of her husband's "best advisers": *Washington Post*, June 19, 1908.
545 "electric with": *San Francisco Chronicle*, June 19, 1908.
545 Nellie strove to remain calm: Bishop, *Presidential Nominations and Elections*, p. 73.
545 "Taft, Taft, Taft . . . beaming smile": *Galveston* [TX] *Daily News*, June 19, 1908.
545 Though less protracted: *Boston Daily Globe*, June 19, 1908.
545 "white as marble": Bishop, *Presidential Nominations and Elections*, pp. 74–75.
545 "Scarcely a word": *San Francisco Chronicle*, June 19, 1908.
546 "Pay no attention": *Galveston* [TX] *Daily News*, June 19, 1908.
546 Seven states managed: *Current Literature* (July 1908), p. 1.
546 "The scene was absolutely": *Galveston* [TX] *Daily News*, June 19, 1908.
546 "flashed . . . aglow with excitement": *Washington Post*, June 19, 1908.
546 "Bubbling over with . . . joy of a boy": *San Francisco Chronicle*, June 19, 1908.
546 A "football rush": *Washington Post*, June 19, 1908.
546 "You know how . . . I am very happy": Ibid.
546 Roosevelt was engaged: *San Francisco Chronicle*, June 19, 1908.
546 "The country is indeed": *Boston Daily Globe*, June 19, 1908.
546 "A great honor . . . to you to-night": New York *Evening World*, June 19, 1908.
547 The convention completed . . . "Sunny Jim": ARL, *Crowded Hours*, p. 151.
547 They had hoped . . . to the delegates: TR to HCL, June 15, 1908, in *LTR*, Vol. 6, p. 1077; WHT to TR, June 15, 1908, WHTP.
547 diluted an anti-injunction plank: *Des Moines Daily News*, June 17, 1908.
547 expressed "disappointment": *Des Moines Daily News*, June 19, 1908; Pringle, *Life and Times*, Vol. 1, pp. 354–55.
547 "We can't get all": *Emporia* [KS] *Gazette*, June 22, 1908.
547 "The next four months": WHT to Charles E. Magoon, July 10, 1908, WHTP.
547 "with a certain degree . . . out of whole cloth": WHT to John Rodgers, July 19, 1908, WHTP.
547 the Presidential Suite . . . secretary and clerk: *Washington Times*, July 12, 1908.
547 In the days . . . seven years earlier: *Fort Wayne* [IN] *Journal-Gazette*, June 19, 1910.
548 Typically awakened . . . settled in his office: *Albuquerque* [NM] *Citizen*, July 21, 1908.
548 more than 1,500 congratulatory . . . letters every day: *Racine* [WI] *Journal*, July 7, 1908; *Bemidji Daily Pioneer* (St. Paul, MN), July 14, 1908.
548 By ten . . . "favorite promenade": *Washington Times*, July 12, 1908.
548 After the defeat . . . over 50 percent: *Greenville* [PA] *Evening Record*, July 11, 1908.
548 The Democratic platform: WHT to TR, July 13, 1908, TRP.
548 "We will be able": TR to WHT, July 13, 1908, WHTP.
548 how to "slash savagely": TR to WHT, July 17, 1908, in *LTR*, Vol. 6, p. 1132.
548 "Both of the first . . . now the leader": TR to WHT, July 21, 1908, in ibid., pp. 1139–40.
548 "most accomplished . . . frank announcement": *NYT*, July 23, 1908.
549 "I have the highest": *Marion* [OH] *Weekly Star*, July 25, 1908.
549 "the spectacle": *New Castle* [PA] *News*, July 24, 1908.
549 "a schoolboy . . . his late chief": *NYT*, July 23, 1908.
549 "humiliating pilgrimage": New York *Sun*, July 24, 1908.
549 "but the puppet": *Pensacola* [FL] *Journal*, July 24, 1908.
549 "not calculated": *New Castle* [PA] *News*, July 24, 1908.
549 The stately colonial mansion . . . distinguished visitors: *Alexandria* [DC] *Gazette*, July 26, 1908.
549 A flagpole: *Piqua* [OH] *Leader-Dispatch*, July 28, 1908.
549 The spacious grounds: *Alexandria* [DC] *Gazette*, July 26, 1908.
549 "What we thought": Charles P. Taft to William Edwards, July 25, 1908, WHTP.
549 NO PLACE LIKE HOME . . . "arm in arm": *New York Tribune*, July 26, 1908.
549 the city's "holiday attire": *Coshocton* [OH] *Daily Age*, July 28, 1908.
549 "the booming of cannon": *Piqua* [OH] *Leader-Dispatch*, July 28, 1908.
549 From the reviewing stand: *Alexandria* [DC] *Gazette*, July 26, 1908.
550 "as its candidate": *Piqua* [OH] *Leader-Dispatch*, July 28, 1908.
550 "smiled cordially": *Alexandria* [DC] *Gazette*, July 26, 1908.
550 "movement for practical reform . . . is not now adequate": WHT, "Speech Accepting the Republican Nomination, July 28, 1908," in *Republican Campaign Text-Book, 1908* (Philadelphia: Dunlap Printing Co., 1908), p. 3.
550 "Popular elections": *Cincinnati Price Current*, July 30, 1908.
550 "Hasn't it been glorious!": Anthony, *Nellie Taft*, p. 215.
550 After a luncheon party . . . "all ablaze with illumination": *Alexandria* [DC] *Gazette*, July 26, 1908.
550 From the steamer's deck: *Piqua* [OH] *Leader-Dispatch*, July 28, 1908.
551 "tremendous outpouring . . . was unalloyed": WHT to TR, July 31, 1908, TRP.
551 "I congratulate you": TR to WHT, July 30, 1908, in *LTR*, Vol. 6, p. 1144.
551 "an exceedingly able . . . western radicalism": *Wall Street Journal*, July 29, 1908.
551 he hoped to shed the 50 pounds: *Waterloo* [IA] *Semi Weekly Courier*, July 7, 1908.
551 "I play golf": *Bemidji* [MN] *Daily Pioneer*, July 14, 1908.
551 after a brief stint . . . in his waist: WHT to TR, July 12, 1908, TRP.
551 "No man weighing 300": *NYT*, Aug. 18, 1908.
551 a 3,500-pound workhorse . . . "a special stall": *NYT*, Aug. 26, 1908.
551 "everything else": *New York Tribune*, Aug. 14, 1908.
551 "It would seem incredible": TR to WHT, Sept. 14, 1908, in *LTR*, Vol. 6, p. 1234.
552 a "rich man's game": *New York Tribune*, Aug. 14, 1908.

552 "the American people": TR to WHT, Sept. 5, 1908, in *LTR*, Vol. 6, pp. 1209–10.
552 "very hard" . . . could be misleading: WHT to TR, Sept. 21, 1908, TRP.
552 "like a hen over her chickens": Charles Willis Thompson, *Presidents I've Known and Two Near Presidents* (Indianapolis: Bobbs-Merrill, 1929), p. 225.
552 "willing to undergo": WHT to TR, July 9, 1908, TRP.
552 "I must tell you": George Sheldon to WHT, Sept. 28, 1908, WHTP.
552 "nothing but the . . . misunderstood": WHT to William N. Cromwell, Aug. 6, 1908, WHTP.
552 "I have always said": TR to WHT, Aug. 7, 1908, in *LTR*, Vol. 6, p. 1157.
552 Taft finally agreed . . . chagrined about his chances: WHT to TR, Aug. 10, 1908, WHTP.
552 "Don't get one particle": TR to WHT, Aug. 24, 1908, in *LTR*, Vol. 6, pp. 1196, 1195.
552 "a dangerous man . . . No longer an outcast": *Fort Wayne* [IN] *Journal-Gazette*, Aug. 8, 1908.
553 "would be placed": *Evening Independent* (Massillon, OH), Oct. 1, 1908.
553 "If the candidate": WHT to TR, Sept. 11, 1908, TRP.
553 "Do not *answer*": TR to WHT, Sept. 1, 1908, in *LTR*, Vol. 6, p. 1204.
553 "Hit them hard": TR to WHT, Sept. 11, 1908, in ibid., p. 1231.
553 Taft promised to confront Bryan directly: WHT to TR, Sept. 14, 1908, TRP.
553 "I cannot be more": WHT to E. N. Huggins, Aug. 11, 1908, WHTP.
553 "I am not very pleased . . . into the campaign": TR to Nicholas Longworth, Sept. 21, 1908, in *LTR*, Vol. 6, pp. 1244–45.
553 the president's "natural successor": *Galveston* [TX] *Daily News*, Sept. 14, 1908.
553 "The true friend . . . shoulder to shoulder": TR to Conrad Kohrs, Sept. 9, 1908, in *LTR*, Vol. 6, p. 1213.
554 "You say that": TR to William Jennings Bryan, Sept. 27, 1908, in *LTR*, Vol. 6, p. 1259.
554 Deeds, he argued: TR to William Jennings Bryan, Sept. 23, 1908, in ibid., pp. 1253–54.
554 "walked into a trap": WHT to TR, Oct. 9, 1908, TRP.
554 "claim to be the heir": WHT to TR, Oct. 3, 1908, TRP.
554 "the revival": WHT to TR, Oct. 9, 1908, TRP.
554 The "Taft Special" . . . forty-one days: *Van Wert* [OH] *Daily Bulletin*, Oct. 6, 1908.
554 consisted of four cars: *Racine* [WI] *Daily Journal*, Sept. 23, 1908.
554 "proved to be . . . a professional entertainer": *Current Literature* (December 1908), p. 621.
554 "he strengthened himself": *Lawrence* [KS] *Daily World*, Oct. 5, 1908.
554 "on the level . . . trust him anywhere": *Evening Independent* (Massillon, OH), Oct. 1, 1908.
554 "I have been in real touch": *NYT*, Oct. 2, 1908.
554 "You are making such . . . treading on air": HHT to WHT, Sept. 24, 1908, WHTP.
555 "I can't imagine": HHT to WHT, Sept. 25, 1908, WHTP.
555 "had a most delightful time": WHT to TR, Oct. 3, 1908, TRP.
555 "changed materially": TR to Kermit Roosevelt, Oct. 24, 1908, in *LTR*, Vol. 6, p. 1318.
555 To everyone's relief . . . "tremendously": TR to HCL, Oct. 21, 1908, in ibid., p. 1314.
555 "I told him he simply": AB to his mother, Oct. 21, 1908, in Abbott, ed., *Letters of Archie Butt*, pp. 143–44.
555 "was keeping himself . . . on his own feet": Hammond, *The Autobiography*, Vol. 2, p. 537.
555 "very touched . . . delighted": WHT to TR, Sept. 14 & Nov. 1, 1908, TRP.
555 "monster" crowds . . . "enjoy it immensely": *Cincinnati Inquirer*, Nov. 3, 1908.
555 They reached Cincinnati . . . in the afternoon: WHT Diaries, Nov. 3, 1908, WHTP.
555 In preparation for . . . the United Press: *Lima* [OH] *Daily News*, Nov. 4, 1908.
556 "exhibiting the finest specimen": Ibid.
556 "Just say that": Ibid.
556 "I was never so happy": HHT to WHT, Nov. 3, 1908, WHTP.
556 Though Taft's popular margin . . . a million and a quarter votes: Pringle, *Life and Times*, Vol. 1, p. 377.
556 "I pledge myself": New York *Sun*, Nov. 4, 1909.
556 "was simply radiant . . . content to die": AB to Clara, Nov. 5, 1908, in Abbott, ed., *Letters of Archie Butt*, pp. 153, 156.
556 "My selection and election": WHT to TR, Nov. 7, 1908, TRP.
556 "You have won": TR to WHT, Nov. 10, 1908, in *LTR*, Vol. 6, p. 1340.

CHAPTER TWENTY-TWO: "A Great Stricken Animal"

Page

557 "the best equipped man": HCL to WHT, June 22, 1908, WHTP.
557 "the greatest all around man": *NYT*, Feb. 28, 1909.
557 "he had served with great": James Eli Watson, *As I Knew Them: Memoirs of James Watson, Former United States Senator from Indiana* (Indianapolis: Bobbs-Merrill Co., 1936), p. 134.
558 "The most difficult instrument": David A. Heenan and Warren G. Bennis, *Co-Leaders: The Power of Great Partnerships* (New York: John Wiley & Sons, 1999), p. 23.
558 "but he could not fill": RSB, "The Measure of Taft," *The American Magazine* (July 1910), pp. 366–67.
558 "Not everyone was meant": Heenan and Bennis, *Co-Leaders*, p. 270.
558 "spoke like a man": Pinchot, *Breaking New Ground*, p. 381.
558 "shake their heads": *Syracuse* [NY] *Herald*, Nov. 6, 1908.
558 "a trembling fear . . . out with unanimity": WHT to Rufus Rhodes, Jan. 2, 1909, WHTP.
558 "splendid 18 hole": *Boston Evening Transcript*, Dec. 17, 1903.
558 While Nellie thought the location: Mowry, *The Era of Theodore Roosevelt, 1900–1912*, p. 233.
558 "getting away for a complete rest": *Piqua* [OH] *Leader-Dispatch*, Nov. 5, 1908.
559 He defiantly proposed: *Fort Wayne* [IN] *Journal-Gazette*, Nov. 8, 1908.
559 "good and ready": *Washington Post*, Jan. 21, 1909.
559 "to make golf": *Syracuse* [NY] *Herald*, Nov. 9, 1908.

559 "possum and taters" banquet: *Atlanta Constitution*, Jan. 4, 1909; *Lima* [OH] *Daily News*, Jan. 1, 1909.
559 a specially constructed cage . . . six hundred guests: *Atlanta Constitution*, Jan. 4, 1909.
559 marking "a social epoch": *Atlanta Constitution*, Jan. 16, 1909.
559 A cartoon of Taft: *Atlanta Constitution*, Jan. 27, 1909.
559 "a gigantic rat" . . . children to cry: Ibid.
559 "the honor without": *Atlanta Constitution*, Jan. 24, 1909.
559 Robert and Helen . . . Bryn Mawr: WHT to Mabel Boardman, Dec. 24, 1908, WHTP.
559 the families of Charles . . . John Hays Hammond: *NYT*, Jan. 11, 1909.
559 "He is so genial": "Mr. Taft's Visit to the South," *The Independent*, Jan. 28, 1909.
559 "Tell the boys": Sullivan, *Our Times*, Vol. 4, p. 321.
559 his "humiliating pilgrimage": New York *Sun*, July 24, 1908.
560 "aroused the people": Pringle, *Life and Times*, Vol. 1, p. 382.
560 "different personnel": WHT to George B. Cortelyou, Jan. 22, 1909, WHTP.
560 "I merely followed": AB, *Taft and Roosevelt*, Vol. 1, p. 345.
560 "ought to be Pres.-elect": *NYT*, Feb. 27, 1909.
560 "I would rather stay here": Jessup, *Elihu Root*, Vol. 2, p. 138.
560 "touched and gratified" . . . in the Senate: HCL to WHT, Dec. 9, 1908, WHTP.
560 "Knox called on me": TR to WHT, Dec. 15, 1908, in *LTR*, Vol. 6, p. 1423.
560 planning to invite Knox . . . his remaining choices: WHT to TR, Dec. 22, 1908, TRP.
560 Frank Hitchcock . . . postmaster general: *Atlanta Constitution*, Jan. 24, 1909.
560 "Ha ha!": TR to WHT, Dec. 31, 1908, in *LTR*, Vol. 6, p. 1454.
561 "inducement . . . to continue Wright": Sullivan, *Our Times*, Vol. 4, p. 320.
561 not "decisive . . . action by him": WHT to Philander C. Knox, Dec. 22, 1908, WHTP.
561 he exacerbated . . . before the inauguration: AB to Clara, Feb. 14, 1908, in Abbott, ed., *Letters of Archie Butt*, p. 338.
561 "I didn't have to be hit": Gustav J. Karger, "Memorandum #5," Mar. 12, 1910, Taft-Karger MSS, CMC.
561 A "peculiar intimacy": TR to Gifford Pinchot, Jan. 24, 1909, TRP.
561 Garfield had every reason . . . to Taft's candidacy: James R. Garfield, Diary, Mar. 3, 1908, Garfield Papers.
561 he and his wife . . . vacationing together: James R. Garfield, Diary, Sept. 3, 1908, Garfield Papers.
561 Their son, John: James R. Garfield, Diary, Mar. 28, 1908, Garfield Papers.
561 The press assumed: *Syracuse* [NY] *Herald*, Dec. 22, 1908.
561 "big enough" . . . the Forest Service: Gustav J. Karger, "Memorandum #5," Mar. 12, 1910, Taft-Karger MSS, CMC.
561 While he recognized . . . represent their interests: Pringle, *Life and Times*, Vol. 1, p. 478.
562 "He has done admirably": James R. Garfield, Diary, Mar. 2, 1908, Garfield Papers.
562 "limited personal means" . . . finally persuaded: Hammond, *The Autobiography*, Vol. 2, p. 543.
562 that Garfield was "out of the running": *Syracuse* [NY] *Herald*, Dec. 22, 1908.
562 "I am utterly at sea": James R. Garfield, Diary, Jan. 11, 1909, Garfield Papers.
562 "a genial, agreeable man": *Jefferson City* [MO] *Tribune*, Jan. 20, 1909.
562 "Rumors & more rumors": James R. Garfield, Diary, Jan. 18, 1909, Garfield Papers.
562 "an astounding condition": James R. Garfield, Diary, Jan. 12, 1909, Garfield Papers.
562 Gossip filled the vacuum: AB to Clara, Jan. 5, 1909, in Abbott, ed., *Letters of Archie Butt*, pp. 271–72.
562 "completely changed . . . to keep no one": James R. Garfield, Diary, Jan. 4, 1909, Garfield Papers.
562 "They will be making": TR to WHT, Jan. 4, 1909, in *LTR*, Vol. 6, p. 1458.
563 "I think I ought": WHT to TR, Jan. 8, 1909, CPT Papers.
563 "The President has thought": WHT to George B. Cortelyou, Jan. 22, 1909, WHTP.
563 The recipients . . . manner of address: James R. Garfield, Diary, Jan. 27, 1909, Garfield Papers.
563 "a clean sweep": Ibid.
563 "T.R.'s Trusty Aides . . . in the Roosevelt school?": *Cleveland Press*, Feb. 11, 1909, clipping in James R. Garfield, Diary, Garfield Papers.
563 "a little cast down": AB to Clara, Jan. 30, 1909, in Abbott, ed., *Letters of Archie Butt,* p. 313.
563 "They little realize": AB to Clara, Jan. 30, 1909, in ibid., p. 314.
563 Taft's "system may be different": AB to Clara, Jan. 11, 1909, in ibid., p. 283.
563 "People have attempted": WHT to TR, Feb. 25, 1909, TRP.
563 "How could I but be": TR to WHT, Feb. 26, 1909, in *LTR*, Vol. 6, p. 1538.
564 "renewed appreciation . . . and magnanimity": WHT to TR, Feb. 25, 1909, TRP.
564 "Your letter": TR to WHT, Feb. 26, 1909, in *LTR*, Vol. 6, p. 1538.
564 "If I had conscientiously": TR to George Otto Trevelyan, Nov. 6, 1908, in ibid., p. 1329.
564 "none of the weariness": *New York Tribune*, Dec. 9, 1908.
564 a sweeping "valedictory message": See *Current Literature* (January 1909), p. 14.
564 "his whole social . . . as voluminous as ever": *New York Tribune*, Dec. 9, 1908.
564 "a fraction . . . the social creation": *Literary Digest*, Dec. 19, 1908.
564 "The danger to American . . . wish to be investigated": TR, "Eighth Annual Message," in *WTR*, Vol. 15, pp. 498, 508, 512, 528.
565 a "storm of censure": *NYT*, Dec. 17, 1908.
565 "self-respect . . . Pandemonium broke loose": *NYT*, Jan. 9, 1909.
565 Congress took a rare measure: Pringle, *Theodore Roosevelt: A Biography*, p. 485.
565 "on the ground": *NYT*, Jan. 9, 1909.
565 "Congress of course feels": TR to Kermit Roosevelt, Jan. 14, 1909, in *LTR*, Vol. 6, p. 1475.
565 "it is a President's . . . up to the end": TR to TR, Jr., Jan. 31, 1909, in ibid., pp. 1498–99.
565 "I have never seen": AB to Clara, Mar. 2, 1909, in Abbott, ed., *Letters of Archie Butt*, p. 376.
566 "believing thoroughly": AB to his mother, April 8, 1908, in ibid., p. 1.

566 "his duties with a boyish": Introduction, in ibid., p. xxiii.
566 "She is perfectly poised": AB to his mother, July 27, 1908, in ibid., p. 75.
566 "ever-softening influence": Ibid.
566 "smart element . . . wont to sneer": AB to his mother, Oct. 19, 1908, in ibid., p. 134.
566 garish nature of . . . clamored for invitations: Mabel Potter Daggett, "Mrs. Roosevelt: The Woman in the Background," *The Delineator* (March 1909), p. 394.
566 Edith's Friday evening . . . Pablo Casals: Morris, *EKR*, p. 236.
566 "If social affairs": Daggett, "Mrs. Roosevelt," *The Delineator* (March 1909), p. 394.
566 "Were we living": AB to Clara, March 2, 1909, in Abbott, ed., *Letter of Archie Butt*, p. 380.
566 "The ball rolls . . . every minute": AB to Clara, Feb. 7, 1909, in ibid., p. 326.
566 "actually wept as . . . broke down himself": AB to Clara, Mar. 2, 1909, in ibid., pp. 376–77.
566 "For the first hour . . . if not a cold, reception": AB to Clara, Feb. 14, 1909, in ibid., pp. 335–36.
567 "The papers have made . . . from Oklahoma?": AB to Clara, Mar. 1, 1909, in ibid., pp. 365–69.
567 "there was not a dry eye": Ibid., p. 368; *Oelwein* [IA] *Daily Register*, Mar. 2, 1909.
567 "It was a curious . . . low spirits": ARL, *Crowded Hours*, pp. 164–65.
568 "The dinner would have been": AB to Clara, Mar. 2, 1909, in Abbott, ed., *Letters of Archie Butt*, p. 378.
568 "Mrs. Roosevelt finally arose": Ibid., p. 380.
568 "Thought you'd like . . . went to bed!": New York *Sun*, Mar. 5, 1909.
568 "shunted it back": *Current Literature* (April 1909), p. 347.
568 "bound hand and foot": *NYT*, Mar. 5, 1909.
568 Gale winds howled: *NYT*, Mar. 4, 1909.
568 "It was really very serious": HHT, *Recollections of Full Years*, p. 328.
568 "The storm will soon . . . got to be President": Ibid.
569 "yellowish, slimy" . . . had for three cents: *NYT*, Mar. 5, 1909.
569 "stood three deep": Ibid.
569 Unfortunately, hardly . . . top of the carriage: Ibid.
569 the Inaugural Committee debated: *Current Literature* (April 1909), p. 348.
569 "If so many spectators": Ibid.; HHT, *Recollections of Full Years*, p. 329.
569 "All exercises will be": *NYT*, Mar. 5, 1909.
569 No longer an open . . . justices, and ambassadors: Ibid.
569 walking "arm in arm": Ibid.
569 "Hale and hearty": New York *Sun*, Mar. 5, 1909.
569 "a slow, distinct voice": *NYT*, Mar. 5, 1909.
570 "For the first time": Ibid.
570 "heavy weight of responsibility . . . met popular approval": William Howard Taft, *Presidential Addresses and State Papers of William Howard Taft, from March 4, 1909, to March 4, 1910* (New York: Doubleday, Page, 1910), pp. 53–56.
570 "The new president . . . each other's shoulders": *NYT*, Mar. 5, 1909.
570 "God bless you . . . state document": HHT, *Recollections of Full Years*, p. 331.
570 "applauded like mad": *NYT*, Mar. 5, 1909.
570 amid "deafening" cheers: *Current Literature* (April 1909), p. 349.
570 "no President's wife . . . my husband's side": HHT, *Recollections of Full Years*, p. 331.
570 "a continuous cheer": *NYT*, Mar. 5, 1909.
570 "Three cheers for the first lady": New York *Sun*, Mar. 5, 1909.
570 "That drive was the proudest": HHT, *Recollections of Full Years*, p. 332.
571 an "era of good feelings": *Current Literature* (April 1909), p. 347.
571 "has no enemies . . . and denunciation": *Los Angeles Times*, Mar. 4, 1909; New York *World*, Mar. 5, 1909.
571 "judicial poise had succeeded": Dunn, *From Harrison to Harding*, Vol. 2, p. 103.
571 decisions would now be made: New York *World*, Mar. 5, 1909.
571 "Never did any man": New York *Sun*, Mar. 5, 1909.
571 "I hardly know yet": AB to Clara, Mar. 11, 1909, in AB, *Taft and Roosevelt*, Vol. 1, p. 9.
571 "been living on . . . just the same": AB to Clara, Mar. 22, 1909, in ibid., p. 27.
571 Captain Butt had hesitated . . . toward his predecessor: AB to Clara, Nov. 30, 1908, in Abbott, ed., *Letters of Archie Butt*, p. 207.
571 "The influence of": AB to Clara, Jan. 5, 1909, in ibid., p. 273.
571 "an intellectual woman": AB to Clara, Nov. 16, 1908, in ibid., p. 173.
572 "marvelous wit": AB to Clara, Mar. 16, 1908, in AB, *Taft and Roosevelt*, Vol. 1, p. 14.
572 "He is essentially": AB to Clara, Mar. 21, 1910, in ibid., p. 308.
572 "list of undesirables . . . stormy attacks": *Oshkosh* [WI] *Daily Northwestern*, April 21, 1909.
572 "I hope that I shall never": AB to Clara, April 15, 1909, in AB, *Taft and Roosevelt*, Vol. 1, p. 308.
572 "a rule never to pay": AB to Clara, Mar. 28, 1909, in ibid., p. 32.
572 "all the warring factions": *Atlanta Constitution*, Mar. 27, 1909.
572 "I am rather proud": AB to Clara, April 24, 1909, in AB, *Taft and Roosevelt*, Vol. 1, p. 60.
572 "I have come to pay": Edward Lowry, "The White House Now," *Harper's Bazaar*, May 15, 1909.
572 Taft also lifted . . . on Senator Tillman: *NYT*, April 25, 1909.
572 invited dozens . . . White House dinner: AB to Clara, April 24, 1909, in AB, *Taft and Roosevelt*, Vol. 1, p. 60.
572 "to pay for favors": AB to Clara, April 27, 1909, in ibid., p. 63.
572 "the liveliest interest . . . things going smoothly": *NYT*, March 27, 1909.
573 "It is undoubtedly": *Oshkosh* [WI] *Daily Northwestern*, April 7, 1909.
573 "the undesirables . . . finding their way": Lowry, "The White House Now," *Harper's Bazaar*, May 15, 1909.
573 "pleased as a boy": AB to Clara, April 8, 1909, in AB, *Taft and Roosevelt*, Vol. 1, p. 44.

573 "and a lot of other": Dunn, *From Harrison to Harding*, Vol. 2, p. 102.
573 the "big stick . . . personal appeal": *Daily Gleaner* (Kingston, Jamaica), April 7, 1909.
573 "startling contrast": *Lawrence* [KS] *Daily World*, Mar. 30, 1909.
573 "on their way . . . terminal facilities": Lowry, "The White House Now," *Harper's Bazaar*, May 15, 1909.
573 "so much at home": *NYT*, April 25, 1909.
573 "be about three years behind": AB to Clara, Mar. 10, 1909, in AB, *Taft and Roosevelt*, Vol. 1, p. 3.
573 "I am glad . . . want to tell me?": Lowry, "The White House Now," *Harper's Bazaar*, May 15, 1909.
573 "There the resemblance . . . around the ellipse": Ibid.
574 "devil wagons . . . pacers, and calipers": *Lawrence* [KS] *Daily World*, Mar. 30, 1909.
574 his Model M . . . Nellie learned to drive: Michael L. Bromley, *William Howard Taft and the First Motoring Presidency, 1909–1913* (Jefferson, NC: McFarland & Co., 2003), pp. 100, 103–4.
574 "a reporter's paradise": Juergens, "Theodore Roosevelt and the Press," *Daedalus* (Fall 1982), p. 114.
574 "No president ever lived": James E. Pollard, *The Presidents and the Press* (New York: The Macmillan Co., 1947), p. 583.
574 "he made the White House": Juergens, "Theodore Roosevelt and the Press," *Daedalus* (Fall 1982), p. 120.
574 "There will be some one": Gustav J. Karger, "Memorandum #3," Mar. 1, 1909, p. 25, Taft-Karger MSS, CMC.
574 "It was a favorite . . . a good scout": Davis, *Released for Publication*, p. 94.
574 "casual remarks . . . necessity of care": *Daily Gleaner* (Kingston, Jamaica), April 7, 1909.
575 "the big, good-humored": Delbert Clark, *Washington Dateline* (New York: Frederick A. Stokes Co., 1941), p. 58.
575 "his own atmosphere . . . hearts to him": AB to Clara, April 27, 1909, in AB, *Taft and Roosevelt*, Vol. 1, p. 68.
575 "Roosevelt made good": *Lawrence* [KS] *Daily World*, Mar. 30, 1909.
575 "Take it all and all": Lowry, "The White House Now," *Harper's Bazaar*, May 15, 1909.
575 "a fish out of water": WHT to Henry A. Morrill, Dec. 2, 1908, Pringle Papers.
575 "I am no . . . Circuit Court bench": L. P. Winter, "Mr. Taft's Visit to the South," *The Independent*, Oct. 9, 1902, p. 178.
575 "tact and diplomacy . . . the responsibilities": *Syracuse* [NY] *Herald*, Mar. 12, 1909.
575 "formidable" challenges: WHT to Henry A. Morrill, Dec. 2, 1908, Pringle Papers.
575 "like that of two men . . . most judicial attitude": George Griswold Hill, "The Wife of the New President," *Ladies' Home Journal* (March 1909), p. 6.
575 Article after article . . . the Philippines: *Milford* [IA] *Mail*, July 16, 1908.
575 "Yes . . . it is true": *Lima* [OH] *Daily News*, Nov. 9, 1909.
575 Nellie's "judgment prevailed": *Milford* [IA] *Mail*, July 16, 1908.
576 "Indeed, I do": *Des Moines Capital*, Nov. 13, 1908.
576 "Few women have gone": *NYT*, Nov. 15, 1909.
576 As the governor general's wife: Hill, "The Wife of the New President," *Ladies' Home Journal*, Mar. 1909, p. 6.
576 "You make me feel": *Oakland* [CA] *Tribune*, Sept. 20, 1908.
576 "never at a loss": *New York Tribune*, May 31, 1908.
576 "Never within the recollection": *Omaha* [NE] *Daily Bee*, Mar. 14, 1909.
576 "to keep up so . . . daily papers": *Ada* [OK] *Evening News*, March 23, 1909.
576 "impressed . . . cloak of composure": Hill, "The Wife of the New President," *Ladies' Home Journal*, Mar. 1909, p. 6.
576 "Her smile has": *NYT*, Nov. 15, 1908.
576 "a public personage . . . private individual": *Syracuse* [NY] *Herald*, Mar. 12, 1909.
576 "a woman's name . . . the least known": Daggett, "Mrs. Roosevelt: The Woman in the Background," *The Delineator* (March 1909), p. 393.
577 to become honorary chair: Mrs. John Hays Hammond, "The Woman's Welfare Department of the National Civic Federation," in Henry R. Mussey, ed., *Proceedings of the Academy of Political Science in the City of New York* (New York: Columbia University Press, 1912), Vol. 2, p. 99.
577 "a commanding lead": *Ada* [OK] *Evening News*, Mar. 23, 1909.
577 controversial programs to improve: Anthony, *Nellie Taft*, p. 250.
577 At the annual meeting . . . police stations: New York *Sun*, Dec. 15, 1908.
577 "She plainly showed": *Ada* [OK] *Evening News*, Mar. 23, 1909.
577 "in animated conversation": *NYT*, Dec. 16, 1908.
577 "make a fine . . . First Lady": AB to [unknown] [n.d.], AB Letters.
577 "The woman's voice": *Des Moines Capital*, Nov. 13, 1908.
577 "makes a girl . . . full college course": *Washington Post*, May 5, 1907.
577 "the distinct advantages": Hill, "The Wife of the New President," *Ladies' Home Journal*, Mar. 1909, p. 6; *Washington Post*, June 24, 1908.
578 "endeared herself": *Ada* [OK] *Evening News*, Mar. 23, 1909.
578 "on a plane": *NYT*, Mar. 14, 1909.
578 the "real social . . . art, statesmanship": *Washington Post*, Nov. 14, 1908.
578 "is more beautifully": *Washington Post*, Mar. 9, 1909.
578 "as absurd . . . wealth in our land": *Washington Post*, Mar. 14, 1909.
578 "one of the most famous": *Hamilton* [OH] *Evening Journal*, April 9, 1909.
578 She enlisted . . . comfortable benches: AB to Clara, April 13, 1909, in AB, *Taft and Roosevelt*, Vol. 1, pp. 51–52; *Kansas City Star*, May 16, 1909.
578 "both the soil and climate": HHT, *Recollections of a Full Life*, p. 362.
578 when her plans . . . to Washington: AB, "1909 Social Diary of Archibald Willingham Butt," WHTP.
578 "Potomac Park . . . every type of carriage": New York *Sun*, April 18, 1909.
578 "every walk of life": *Washington Times*, April 18, 1909.
578 bowed "right and left": *New York Tribune*, April 18, 1909.
579 "Everybody saw . . . special character": HHT, *Recollections of a Full Life*, p. 362.
579 "very strong liking": Ibid., p. 365.

579 "short coats, flannel trousers": *Syracuse* [NY] *Herald*, May 15, 1909.
579 "bright colored parasols": HHT, *Recollections of a Full Life*, p. 368.
579 "roam at will": *Washington Herald*, May 15, 1909.
579 "are as informal . . . seen in Washington": *Kansas City Star*, May 16, 1909.
579 "It was a difficult thing": AB to Clara, May 12, 1909, in AB, *Taft and Roosevelt*, Vol. 1, p. 86.
579 "She possesses a nature": AB to Clara, April 13, 1909, in ibid., p. 54.
579 "The complete social": *Kansas City Star*, May 16, 1909.
579 "In the ten weeks": *NYT*, May 19, 1909.
580 On May 17 . . . President Washington's home: AB to Clara, May 17, 1909, in AB, *Taft and Roosevelt*, Vol. 1, p. 87.
580 Nellie was talking . . . and collapsed: Lewis L. Gould, *Helen Taft: Our Musical First Lady* (Lawrence: University Press of Kansas, 2010), p. 51.
580 "seemed to revive . . . shown on a man's face": AB to Clara, May 17, 1909, in AB, *Taft and Roosevelt*, Vol. 1, p. 88.
580 "a lesion in the brain . . . in the brain": WHT to Robert Taft, May 18, 1909, WHTP.
580 With extended rest . . . symptoms might disappear: AB to Clara, May 18, 1909, in AB, *Taft and Roosevelt*, Vol. 1, p. 92.
580 "in the face . . . like a knife": AB to Clara, May 17, 1909, in ibid., pp. 89–90.
580 "Her old will": AB to Clara, May 18, 1909, in ibid., pp. 91–92.
581 partial "control of her right arm": WHT to Robert Taft, May 18, 1909, WHTP.
581 "no cause for alarm . . . nervous attack": *NYT*, May 18, 1909.
581 "ceaseless and strenuous . . . went to pieces": *St. Louis Post-Dispatch*, June 18, 1909.
581 what Taft later described as aphasia: WHT to TR, May 26, 1910, TRP.
581 "She only comes into": AB to Clara, June 1, 1909, in AB, *Taft and Roosevelt*, Vol. 1, p. 108.
581 she remained unable to project: WHT to Horace Taft, May 28, 1909, WHTP.
581 "repeat almost anything": Helen Taft Manning to Robert A. Taft, May [n.d.], 1909, WHTP.
581 "merely a question of time": Ibid.
581 Taft mobilized . . . to repeat the same passages: WHT to Frances Taft Edwards, June 25, 1909, WHTP.
581 "to say the opposite": Seth Taft, *Going Like 80: A Biography of Charles P. Taft II* (private printing, 2004). Presented to the author by Frances and Seth Taft.
581 "She gets pretty depressed": Helen Taft Manning to Robert A. Taft, June [n.d.], 1909, WHTP.
581 Eventually, the first lady . . . particular impediment: AB to Clara, Jan. 2, 1910, AB Letters.
581 "scores of times . . . 'now try it again' ": Elizabeth Jaffray, *Secrets of the White House* (New York: Cosmopolitan Book Corp., 1927), p. 25.
582 "No one knows": AB to Clara, [Easter] 1909, in AB, *Taft and Roosevelt*, Vol. 1, p. 313.
582 acknowledge "the tragedy": AB to Clara, May 17, 1909, in ibid., p. 89.
582 "a world of misery": AB to Mrs. John D. Butt, June 8, 1909, in ibid., p. 101.
582 "simply looking into the distance": AB to Clara, May 27, 1909, in ibid., p. 99.
582 "take up their residence": AB, "1909 Social Diary of Archibald Willingham Butt," WHTP.
582 "parklike lawns" . . . the Essex Club: Mabel T. Boardman, "The Summer Capital," *Outlook*, Sept. 25, 1909, pp. 176–78.
582 "take quite a time": WHT to Mabel Boardman, June 27, 1909, WHTP.
582 "two months of entire rest": WHT to Frances Taft Edwards, June 25, 1909, WHTP.
582 "in seclusion . . . intruders away": *NYT*, July 7, 1909.
582 "The great tug will begin": WHT to HHT, July 7, 1909, WHTP.

CHAPTER TWENTY-THREE: A Self-Inflicted Wound

Page

583 Protectionism had become a central tenet: Jonathan Lurie, *William Howard Taft: The Travails of a Progressive Conservative* (New York: Cambridge University Press, 2012), p. 103.
583 While Theodore Roosevelt had sympathized . . . inflated prices: RSB, Notebook, Nov. 17, 1907, RSB Papers.
583 During the final years . . . agrarian region: Stanley D. Solvick, "William Howard Taft and Cannonism," *Wisconsin Magazine of History* (Autumn 1964), pp. 51–52.
584 "equal the difference": WHT, "Address Accepting the Republican Nomination for President, Cincinnati, Ohio, July 28, 1908," WHTP.
584 When excessive duties were built . . . prices for consumers: Ibid.; WHT, *Presidential Addresses and State Papers*, pp. 55–56; WHT to Horace Taft, June 27, 1909, WHTP.
584 "unequivocally . . . special session of Congress": RNC and Blumenberg, *Official Report of the Proceedings of the Fourteenth Republican National Convention*, p. 117.
584 "uprising and demonstration . . . cataclysm": *Waterloo* [IA] *Times-Tribune*, Mar. 16, 1909.
584 "the greatest issue" . . . to "humanize": *Washington Times*, June 24, 1910.
584 "this or that duty . . . less covering": IMT, "Where Every Penny Counts," *The American Magazine* (March 1909), pp. 437–38.
585 "vital importance" of shoes: *Atlanta Constitution*, April 25, 1909.
585 "It was hard enough . . . and in methods": IMT, "Where Every Penny Counts," *The American Magazine* (March 1909), p. 440.
585 For years, legislators had acquiesced: IMT, "Juggling with the Tariff: A Sidelight on the Most Lively Question Now Before Congress," *The American Magazine* (April 1909), p. 578.
585 "At a time when . . . getting ahead": IMT, "Where Every Penny Counts," *The American Magazine* (March 1909), p. 439.
585 "I never knew": IMT, *All in the Day's Work*, p. 273.
586 "Cannonism" had become . . . convened in mid-March 1909: Pringle, *Life and Times*, Vol. 1, pp. 402–3; Solvick, "William Howard Taft and Cannonism," *Wisconsin Magazine of History* (Autumn 1964), pp. 52–53.

586 Taft seriously considered backing: WHT to WAW, Mar. 12, 1909, White Papers.
586 "never liked" the Speaker: AB to Clara, April 5, 1911, in AB, *Taft and Roosevelt*, Vol. 2, p. 609.
586 "all legislation of a progressive character": WHT to TR, Oct. 9, 1908, TRP.
586 "If by helping it": WHT to TR, Nov. 7, 1908, TRP.
586 "I do not believe": TR to WHT, Nov. 10, 1908, TRP.
586 "it would be very unfortunate": Elihu Root to WHT, Nov. 23, 1908, in Pringle, *Life and Times*, Vol. 1, p. 405.
586 "very much disposed to fight": WHT to William N. Cromwell, Nov. 22, 1908, WHTP.
586 "In our anxiety": *Salt Lake Tribune*, Nov. 18, 1908.
586 "cynical references . . . with people squarely": WHT to Elihu Root, Nov. 25, 1908, WHTP.
586 To better gauge the odds: WHT to J. N. Dolley, Nov. 23, 1908, and WHT to Frank L. Dingley, Nov. 23, 1908, WHTP.
586 "A new irrepressible . . . Taft administration": *NYT*, Nov. 24, 1908.
587 "urgent telegrams and letters": WHT to Horace Taft, June 27, 1909, WHTP.
587 "very anxious . . . of the facts": TR to WHT, Nov. 28, 1908, in *LTR*, Vol. 6, p. 1389.
587 "support genuine tariff . . . carrying forward": *Waterloo* [IA] *Daily Courier*, Dec. 2, 1908.
587 "entirely different impression": *Washington Post*, Dec. 11, 1908.
587 "a hundred days . . . perfect": *Waterloo* [IA] *Times-Tribune*, Nov. 18, 1908.
587 "the best revenue law": Pringle, *Life and Times*, Vol. 1, p. 403.
587 "hammer and tongs . . . Republican minority": WHT to Joseph L. Bristow, Dec. 5, 1908, WHTP.
587 the mistake that would haunt his presidency: *Waterloo* [IA] *Daily Courier*, Dec. 2, 1908.
587 "sent a chill of": Pringle, *Life and Times*, Vol. 1, p. 407.
587 "to prepare an honest": *Washington Post*, Dec. 11, 1908.
588 All hope of unseating . . . won reelection: *NYT*, Mar. 16, 1909.
588 "the most sophisticated": Sullivan, *Our Times*, Vol. 4, p. 374.
588 "page after page": *Decatur* [IL] *Daily Review*, Mar. 16, 1909.
588 "The Senate and House": Robert M. La Follette, *La Follette's Autobiography: A Personal Narrative of Political Experiences* (Madison, WI: Robert M. La Follette Co., 1919), p. 438.
588 "statesmen almost fell": *Washington Times*, Mar. 17, 1909.
588 expected to be "historic": Claude Gernade Bowers, *Beveridge and the Progressive Era* (Boston: Houghton Mifflin, 1932), p. 334.
588 Taft had composed the entire text: *Decatur Daily Review*, Mar. 18, 1909.
588 "no clarion call": Bowers, *Beveridge and the Progressive Era*, p. 340.
588 "no allusion": *New York Tribune*, Mar. 16, 1909.
588 "give immediate consideration . . . should proceed": WHT, "Message to Congress, March 16, 1909," in WHT, *Presidential Addresses and State Papers*, Vol. 1, p. 69.
588 "flair for . . . days in office": Stanley D. Solvick, "William Howard Taft and the Payne-Aldrich Tariff," *Mississippi Valley Historical Review* (December 1963), p. 428.
588 "no loud noises": *Current Literature* (June 1909), p. 579.
589 "the facts and reasons . . . derelict": WHT, "Personal Aspects of the Presidency," *Saturday Evening Post*, Feb. 28, 1914.
589 The weekly press conferences: F. B. Marbut, *News from the Capital; The Story of Washington Reporting* (Carbondale: Southern Illinois University Press, 1971), p. 171.
589 "There was none": J. Frederick Essary, "Thirty-two Years as a Washington Correspondent," *Editor and Publisher*, May 31, 1941, p. 13.
589 "When the judgment . . . to help me": WHT, "Personal Aspects of the Presidency," *Saturday Evening Post*, Feb. 28, 1914.
589 "If ever at any time": WAW to WHT [n.d.], 1909, White Papers.
589 "I am not constituted": WHT to WAW, Mar. 20, 1909, White Papers.
589 "I knew what a hard": RSB, *American Chronicle*, p. 254.
589 "Although the tariff storm": RSB, "Theodore Roosevelt," unpublished MSS, 1910, RSB Papers.
589 "remain . . . not without significance": RSB, "The Measure of Taft," *The American Magazine* (July 1910), p. 363.
590 "the legal mind . . . dislike for publicity": RSB, "Taft—So Far," *The American Magazine* (July 1909), p. 312.
590 "impressed . . . *could* do it": RSB, "The Measure of Taft," *The American Magazine* (July 1910), pp. 363–64.
590 "Fifty years ago . . . will have been taken": IMT, "Juggling with the Tariff," *The American Magazine* (April 1909), pp. 578–79, 586.
591 "one of the most . . . taking the place": IMT, "William Howard Taft," unpublished MSS [n.d.], IMTC.
591 "to keep his distance": Lurie, *William Howard Taft*, p. 104.
591 If adjustments were necessary: Solvick, "William Howard Taft and the Payne-Aldrich Tariff," *Mississippi Valley Historical Review* (December 1963), pp. 431–33.
591 "I have got to regard": WHT to WAW, Mar. 12, 1909, White Papers.
591 "no matter what tariff bill": William Dudley Foulke to WHT, Mar. 10, 1909, WHTP.
592 "I am here to get": WHT to William Dudley Foulke, Mar. 12, 1909, WHTP.
592 "a genuine effort . . . inappropriate": WHT to Horace Taft, June 27, 1909, WHTP.
592 "a more enlightened . . . given a thought": Cited in *Current Literature* (May 1909), p. 468.
592 "would be satisfactory . . . this early stage": *NYT*, April 21, 1909.
592 "up to the Senate . . . remakes it": *Current Literature* (May 1909), p. 465.
592 Taft had reason . . . from the Philippines: WHT to TR, Jan. 27, 1903, TRP.
592 "I fear Aldrich is ready": AB to Clara, April 4, 1909, in AB, *Taft and Roosevelt*, Vol. 1, p. 41.
592 "Where did we ever": Pringle, *Life and Times*, Vol. 1, p. 429.
592 This was the time: Ibid., p. 430.
592 "There is no use": AB to Clara, Dec. 19, 1909, in AB, *Taft and Roosevelt*, Vol. 1, p. 236.
593 While Taft hesitated . . . against the Senate leader: Mowry, *The Era of Theodore Roosevelt*, pp. 244–45.

593 Aware that Aldrich . . . tackled lead and sugar: Bowers, *Beveridge and the Progressive Era*, p. 339.
593 "It has been tariff": HCL to TR, June 21, 1909, in TR and HCL, *Selections from the Correspondence*, Vol. 2, pp. 337–38.
593 It was often past midnight . . . discussing strategy: Bowers, *Beveridge and the Progressive Era*, pp. 346–48.
593 to "go ahead . . . I will veto it": La Follette, *La Follette's Autobiography*, p. 440.
593 "bewildered by the intricacies": *NYT*, June 9, 1909.
593 "more technical knowledge": WHT to HHT, July 8, 1909, WHTP.
593 "reactionary tools": Mowry, *The Era of Theodore Roosevelt*, p. 245.
593 "The Senator will not turn": Kenneth W. Hechler, *Insurgency: Personalities and Politics of the Taft Era* (New York: Russell & Russell, 1964), p. 121.
593 Taft worried . . . becoming "irresponsible": Bowers, *Beveridge and the Progressive Era*, p. 343.
594 to "confer . . . the Roosevelt policies": WHT to Horace Taft, June 27, 1909, WHTP.
594 "Mr. Taft is not proving . . . pirate-infested seas": *Current Literature* (June 1909), p. 580.
594 "to form definite . . . Mr. Roosevelt's own": Ibid.
594 his "hands off" approach: *NYT*, June 15, 1909.
594 "on the ground that": WHT to Horace Taft, June 27, 1909, WHTP.
595 refuse to "reverse itself": *NYT*, June 20, 1909.
595 "already at a low ebb": *NYT*, June 16, 1909.
595 "some pretty shrewd . . . separately": AB to Clara, June 20, 1909, in AB, *Taft and Roosevelt*, Vol. 1, pp. 124–25.
595 "go a great way . . . illegitimate schemes": George Kibbe Turner, "How Taft Views His Own Administration: An Interview with the President," *McClure's* (June 1910), p. 214.
595 "Just when they thought": AB to Clara, June 20, 1909, in AB, *Taft and Roosevelt*, Vol. 1, p. 125.
595 These dissenting votes revealed: *Current Literature* (August 1909), pp. 3–5.
595 "Congress has had": *Literary Digest*, July 24, 1909.
595 "to make good . . . he became President": Ibid.
596 "used the White House": AB to Clara, Aug. 17, 1909, in AB, *Taft and Roosevelt*, Vol. 1, p. 178.
596 He invited Payne to dinner . . . after midnight: WHT to HHT, July 18, 1909, WHTP.
596 "at the disposal": WHT to HHT, July 17, 1909, in William Howard Taft and Lewis L. Gould, *My Dearest Nellie: The Letters of William Howard Taft to Helen Herron Taft, 1909–1912* (Lawrence: University Press of Kansas, 2011), pp. 46–47.
596 "longing" for her company: WHT to HHT, Aug. 3, 1909, WHTP.
596 "delighted . . . changes you seek": WHT to HHT, July 11, 1909, WHTP.
596 progress would come "by jerks": WHT to HHT, July 18, 1909, WHTP.
596 "Last night was as hot": WHT to HHT, July 13, 1909, in WHT and Gould, *My Dearest Nellie*, p. 39.
596 "the Senate bill . . . has been taken": WHT to HHT, July 11, 1909, WHTP.
596 "he was committed . . . broader point of view": *Decatur* [IL] *Daily Review*, July 17, 1909.
597 "jubilant . . . of the progressives": *Fort Wayne* [IN] *News*, July 17, 1909.
597 Congratulatory messages flooded: *New York Tribune*, July 26, 1909.
597 "the Taft tariff bill": *NYT*, July 18, 1909.
597 "I see today you made": HHT to WHT, July 17, 1909, WHTP.
597 "a good deal more of a muddle": WHT to Horace Taft, July 21, 1909, WHTP.
597 Despite repeated promises . . . "in writing": WHT to HHT, July 11, 1909, WHTP.
597 "an expert and acute . . . be deceived": Solvick, "William Howard Taft and the Payne-Aldrich Tariff," *Mississippi Valley Historical Review* (December 1963), p. 437.
597 "Aldrich insists that": WHT to HHT, July 22, 1909, WHTP.
597 "owed his victory . . . personal matter with him": AB to Clara, July 23, 1909, in AB, *Taft and Roosevelt*, Vol. 1, p. 154.
597 "It is the greatest exhibition": WHT to HHT, July 26, 1909, WHTP.
597 "They have my last . . . in his fight": AB to Clara, July 23, 1909, in AB, *Taft and Roosevelt*, Vol. 1, pp. 163–65.
598 a "cut away suit . . . fairly radiant": *Washington Post*, Aug. 6, 1909.
598 "Do you think . . . certainly do not": *Eau Claire* [WI] *Leader*, Aug. 6, 1909.
598 "could make . . . injure the party": AB to Clara, July 16, 1909, in AB, *Taft and Roosevelt*, Vol. 1, p. 144.
598 "A broad smile": *Eau Claire* [WI] *Leader*, Aug. 6, 1909.
598 "a terrific thunderstorm": AB to Clara, Aug. 6, 1909, in AB, *Taft and Roosevelt*, Vol. 1, p. 170.
598 "Heavy black clouds": *Washington Post*, Aug. 6, 1909.
598 the "storm of protest": AB to Clara, Aug. 6, 1909, in AB, *Taft and Roosevelt*, Vol. 1, p. 170.
599 "perfect . . . branches of Congress": *NYT*, Aug. 6, 1909.
599 "its long and stormy journey": Ibid.
599 "patient leadership . . . in the future": *Literary Digest*, Aug. 7, 1909.
599 made the final bill "less shocking": Ibid.
599 "the necessities of the common people": *Tacoma* [WA] *Times*, Aug. 6, 1909.
599 judged an "empty victory": *NYT*, Aug. 6, 1909.
599 "vindicated his personal . . . in his strategy": *Literary Digest*, Aug. 7, 1909.
599 "his own fault . . . the stable door": *NYT*, Aug. 6, 1909.
599 "come to a standstill . . . enthusiastic": *NYT*, Aug. 8, 1909.
599 "which could be heard": AB to Clara, Aug. 10, 1909, in AB, *Taft and Roosevelt*, Vol. 1, p. 173.
599 While the president and his family . . . in Beverly: *NYT*, Aug. 8, 1909.
600 "If anybody says": *Baltimore Sun*, Aug. 8, 1909.
600 Taft soon settled into: Boardman, "The Summer Capital," *Outlook*, Sept. 25, 1909, p. 177.
600 "the rest . . . forget her illness": AB to Clara, Aug. 10, 1909, in AB, *Taft and Roosevelt*, Vol. 1, p. 173.
600 "over every beautiful . . . pleasant route": *National Tribune* (Washington, DC), Aug. 25, 1909.
600 "the family dinner hour": Boardman, "The Summer Capital," *Outlook*, Sept. 25, 1909, p. 179.

600 "If it were not . . . out of life at all": AB to Clara, Aug. 24, 1909, in AB, *Taft and Roosevelt*, Vol. 1, p. 185.
600 "I do not know exactly": WHT to Nancy Roelker, Sept. 11, 1909, in Anderson, *William Howard Taft*, p. 206.
600 "take the people into": *New York Tribune*, Sept. 10, 1909.
600 "rampant . . . favor of his standard": *National Tribune*, Aug. 25, 1909.
600 "the bill was unsatisfactory . . . under the circumstances": *New York Tribune*, Sept. 10, 1909.
600 A future fight . . . loomed: *NYT*, Sept. 14, 1909.
600 "learned a great . . . shortcomings": *New York Tribune*, Sept. 10, 1909.
600 "tens and hundreds . . . personal touch": WHT, "Speech at the Boston Chamber of Commerce, Sept. 14, 1909," WHTP.
601 "cabinet members . . . and banking system": *Register and Leader* (Des Moines, IA), Sept. 15, 1909.
601 "Father of the Federal": *NYT*, Nov. 19, 1914.
601 Reaching Chicago . . . a hearty reception: *New York Tribune*, Sept. 17, 1909.
601 At Milwaukee . . . first statement on the tariff: *New York Tribune*, Sept. 18, 1909.
601 "omnipresent good nature": Thompson, *Presidents I've Known*, p. 218.
601 "hotbed of insurgency": *Current Literature* (November 1909), p. 480.
601 Republican leaders in the House . . . home district: Thompson, *Presidents I've Known*, p. 218.
601 "Hope to be able": WHT to HHT, Sept. 16, 1909, in Pringle, *Life and Times*, Vol. 1, p. 453.
602 "a mass of facts": *Washington Post*, Sept. 18, 1909.
602 "Speech hastily prepared": WHT to HHT, Sept. 17, 1909, in Pringle, *Life and Times*, Vol. 1, p. 453.
602 "What was the duty . . . Republican party ever passed": William Howard Taft and David Henry Burton, *The Collected Works of William Howard Taft* (Athens: Ohio University Press, 2001), pp. 179, 181, 177.
602 "without hesitation": *NYT*, Sept. 19, 1909.
602 "Western Republicans . . . on the tariff question": All cited in *Literary Digest*, Oct. 2, 1909, p. 511.
602 "I did not write to you": Horace Taft to WHT, Oct. 8, 1909, WHTP.
603 "commendation" of Tawney: *Current Literature* (November 1909), p. 478.
603 "Theodore Roosevelt's . . . overwhelming demand": *Literary Digest*, Oct. 2, 1909.
603 "You have come out . . . national supervision": TR to HCL, Sept. 10, 1909, in TR and HCL, *Selections from the Correspondence*, Vol. 2, p. 346.
603 "I never appreciated . . . power and force": HCL to TR, April 29, 1909, in ibid., pp. 333–34.
603 "surprised . . . opinion of him": HCL to TR, Sept. 10, 1909, in ibid., p. 346.
603 "the wilds of Africa": RSB, Notebook K, June 13, 1908, RSB Papers.
603 "truthful statement . . . win victories": WHT to Robert Taft, Oct. 28, 1909, in Pringle, *Life and Times*, Vol. 1, p. 456.
603 "Of course we want": *NYT*, Oct. 7, 1909.
603 Nearly 7,000 . . . in Portland: WHT to HHT, Oct. 2, 1909, WHTP.
604 in Phoenix . . . through the gates: AB, "Record of the Trip of President Taft," in WHT Diaries, WHTP.
604 "Winning Taft Smile": *Albuquerque* [NM] *Morning Journal*, Oct. 16, 1909.
604 "Taft's personality": *Current Literature* (November 1909), p. 476.
604 "really and sincerely . . . more real affection": AB to Clara, Nov. 14, 1909, in AB, *Taft and Roosevelt*, Vol. 1, p. 205.
604 He noticed that Taft: AB to Clara, Nov. 14, 1909, in ibid., p. 206.
604 "They are prompted": WHT to Frederick Carpenter, Oct. 24, 1909, WHTP.
604 "Whatever their judgment": WHT to HHT, Oct. 24, 1909, WHTP.
604 "enjoyed every moment": WHT, "Speech at Charleston, South Carolina, Nov. 5, 1909," WHTP.
604 "266 speeches": *Current Literature* (December 1909), p. 8.
604 "of temperament": WHT, "Speech at Charleston, SC, Nov. 5, 1909," WHTP.
604 "as stimulating as champagne": *Albuquerque* [NM] *Morning Journal*, Oct. 16, 1909.
604 "Well, I'm back again": *New York Tribune*, Nov. 11, 1909.
604 "full of despair": AB to Clara, Nov. 14, 1909, in AB, *Taft and Roosevelt*, Vol. 1, p. 208.

CHAPTER TWENTY-FOUR: St. George and the Dragon

Page
605 "a mere personal . . . matter of state": *Logansport* [IN] *Reporter*, Nov. 18, 1909.
605 falling in behind Pinchot: AB to Clara, Nov. 14, 1909, in AB, *Taft and Roosevelt*, Vol. 1, p. 203.
605 the opening volley: *New York Tribune*, Nov. 10, 1909.
606 "there would be such a fire": *Current Literature* (December 1909), p. 592.
606 "still in its infancy . . . astonishing consolidation": *New York Daily Tribune*, Jan. 16, 1909.
606 "the public interest": *Emporia* [KS] *Gazette*, April 29, 1909.
606 "I esteem it my duty": *New York Daily Tribune*, Jan. 16, 1909.
606 "there was no time": Pinchot, *Breaking New Ground*, p. 408.
606 "is the steward": TR, *An Autobiography*, p. 464.
606 Within three weeks . . . to the public domain: *Salt Lake Herald*, April 22, 1909.
606 the previous administration had acted illegally: *Washington Times*, April 27, 1909.
607 Once the proper surveys . . . the Far West: *Times-Herald* (Burns, OR), April 3, 1909.
607 threat to "traditional western individualism": Mowry, *The Era of Theodore Roosevelt*, p. 251.
607 "that a man could ride": *Times-Herald*, April 3, 1909.
607 "on the basis of law": WHT to William Kent, June 29, 1909, in Pringle, *Life and Times*, Vol. 1, p. 480.
607 "the end justified the means": *Springfield* [MA] *Daily Republican*, April 30, 1909.
607 "sweeping declaration": Knute Nelson, Louis R. Glavis, et al., *Investigation of the Department of the Interior and of the Bureau of Forestry* [hereafter *Investigation*] (Washington, DC: Government Printing Office, 1911), Vol. 7, p. 4203.
607 "It is . . . not the Executive": WHT to William Kent, June 29, 1909, in Pringle, *Life and Times*, Vol. 1, p. 481.
607 "further along . . . a different way": Ibid., p. 476.

607 "Stop Ballinger": *Des Moines Daily News*, May 2, 1909.
607 "cowboy methods": *Current Literature* (December 1909), p. 592.
607 progressives, educated by . . . treachery of monopoly: *Times-Herald*, April 3, 1909.
607 "Attention! Land Thieves . . . predatory interests": *Tacoma* [WA] *Times*, May 4, 1909.
607 "what was going on": Pinchot, *Breaking New Ground*, p. 409.
608 Taft regarded Pinchot . . . a fanatical strain: WHT to Lawrence F. Abbott, Aug. 31, 1909, WHTP.
608 all too ready to attribute: WHT to HHT, Oct. 3, 1909, WHTP.
608 "protested as vigorously . . . water-power purposes": Pinchot, *Breaking New Ground*, p. 409.
608 Greatly relieved, Garfield maintained: James R. Garfield, Diary, May 8, 1909, Garfield Papers.
608 "Everything is not . . . golden opportunities": *Springfield Daily Republican*, April 30, 1909.
608 "five million acres": Stephen Ponder, " 'Nonpublicity' and the Unmaking of a President: William Howard Taft and the Ballinger-Pinchot Controversy of 1909–1910," *Journalism History* (Winter 1994), p. 114.
608 "Was Conservation . . . the Old Guard?": Pinchot, *Breaking New Ground*, p. 417.
608 "one excuse or another": *Spokane* [WA] *Press*, Aug. 9, 1909.
608 enabling General Electric . . . millions of dollars: *New York Tribune*, Aug. 14, 1909.
608 "This is a true story": *Spokane* [WA] *Press*, Aug. 9, 1909.
608 "Richard Achilles Ballinger . . . about it now": *Spokane* [WA] *Press*, Aug. 10, 1909.
609 Pinchot's speech . . . on the embattled secretary: *NYT*, Aug. 12, 1909.
609 "The purpose of . . . the gauntlet": Pinchot, *Breaking New Ground*, p. 417.
609 "unequivocally . . . in process of formation": *The North American* (Philadelphia), Aug. 11, 1909.
609 "strict construction . . . the many": Pinchot, *Breaking New Ground*, p. 418.
609 "a storm of applause . . . wildest reception": *The North American*, Aug. 11, 1909.
609 "deplorable fact . . . the second withdrawal": Gifford Pinchot to WHT, Aug. 10, 1909, in *Investigation*, Vol. 2, p. 63.
609 "breathless interest . . . never been born": Pinchot, *Breaking New Ground*, p. 419.
609 "He picked up his hat": *Spokane* [WA] *Press*, Aug. 14, 1909.
609 "I have been in": *Seattle Star*, Aug. 12, 1909.
609 "Hit 'em again . . . no conference with you": *Spokane* [WA] *Press*, Aug. 14, 1909.
610 "questioned and quizzed . . . of the West": *Washington Post*, Nov. 18, 1909.
610 "Mr. Ballinger's silence": *San Francisco Call*, Aug. 31, 1909.
610 "Gross misrepresentations": *The Ranch* (Seattle, WA), Sept. 1, 1909.
610 "always believed . . . results accomplished": Richard Ballinger to William Cowles, Dec. 9, 1909, in Ponder, " 'Nonpublicity' and the Unmaking of a President," *Journalism History* (Winter 1994), p. 117.
610 misplaced the decimal point: *New York Tribune*, Aug. 14, 1909.
610 "did not touch . . . its extreme corner": *Investigation*, Vol. 2, p. 719.
610 "monopolists had grabbed off": *National Tribune* (Washington, DC), Mar. 10, 1909.
610 "assumed a certain": Chester Rowell to WHT, Aug. 27, 1909, WHTP.
610 "completely overshadowed": *Washington Times*, Aug. 25, 1909.
610 "taken for granted . . . make good": *Washington Post*, Aug. 26, 1909.
610 "the driving wedge . . . chasm": Mowry, *The Era of Theodore Roosevelt*, p. 258.
611 "a slumbering volcano": *Tacoma* [WA] *Times*, Aug. 24, 1909.
611 in desperation: L. R. Glavis to WHT, Aug. 11, 1909, in *Investigation*, Vol. 2, pp. 4–23.
611 acting "in good faith": Gifford Pinchot to WHT, Nov. 4, 1909, in Vol. 4, p. 1224.
611 "into one property . . . benefit of all": *NYT*, Jan. 2, 1911.
611 to give a Morgan-Guggenheim company . . . coal property: John Lathrop and George Kibbe Turner, "Billions of Treasure: Should the Mineral Wealth of Alaska Enrich the Guggenheim Trust or the U.S. Treasury?," *McClure's* (January 1910), p. 347.
611 "closely identified" with the members: *Washington Times*, Aug. 22, 1909.
611 "legal representative": L. R. Glavis to WHT, Aug. 11, 1909, in *Investigation*, Vol. 2, p. 10.
611 "act as counsel": Louis R. Glavis, "The Whitewashing of Ballinger," *Collier's*, Nov. 13, 1909, p. 16.
612 "I advised him . . . becoming public": Gifford Pinchot to WHT, Aug. 10, 1909, in *Investigation*, Vol. 2, p. 63.
612 "Ballinger Mixed . . . evidence": *Salt Lake Tribune*, Aug. 14, 1909.
612 would lead to the indictment of Ballinger: *Washington Post*, Aug. 26, 1909.
612 It was later revealed: Overton W. Price and A. C. Shaw to Gifford Pinchot, Jan. 5, 1910, in *Investigation*, Vol. 4, p. 1275.
612 "made notes upon his reading": *Titusville* [PA] *Herald*, May 16, 1910.
612 "especially concerning . . . professional relation": WHT to Richard Ballinger, Aug. 22, 1909, in *Investigation*, Vol. 2, p. 64.
612 he remembered little else: Gustav J. Karger, "Conversation with William Howard Taft, March 12, 1910," Taft-Karger MSS, CMC.
612 "as full as possible": WHT to Richard Ballinger, Aug. 22, 1909, in *Investigation*, Vol. 2, p. 64.
612 "has had nothing to do": Frank Pierce to WHT, Sept. 1, 1909, in ibid., p. 188.
612 "issuance of patents": H. H. Schwartz to WHT, Sept. 1, 1909, in ibid., p. 218.
612 "to kill some snakes": *Washington Post*, Sept. 4, 1909.
612 On September 4 . . . left the land commissionership: Richard Ballinger to WHT, Sept. 4, 1909, in *Investigation*, Vol. 2, pp. 66–75.
613 in the summer of 1908 . . . "legal representative": Richard Ballinger to WHT, Sept. 4, 9, & 10, 1909, in ibid., Vol. 2, pp. 68–70, 97, 100.
613 "several satchels": *Oakland* [CA] *Tribune*, Sept. 6, 1909.
613 Myopia Hunt Club: *Indiana* [PA] *Evening Gazette*, Sept. 6, 1909.
613 "reading the answers": *Titusville* [PA] *Herald*, May 16, 1910.
613 "The cruel injustice": WHT to Horace Taft, Sept. 11, 1909, WHTP.

614 "was very anxious . . . the evidence and his conclusions": *Titusville Herald*, May 16, 1910.
614 "only shreds of . . . making false charges against them": WHT to Richard Ballinger, Sept. 13, 1909, WHTP.
615 "misrepresentation . . . in his own defense": These arguments were later made by Louis D. Brandeis on May 5, 1910, in *Investigation*, Vol. 7, pp. 3872–3874.
615 "The Ballinger adherents": *New York Tribune*, Sept. 17, 1909.
615 "hasty action . . . of governmental discipline": WHT to Gifford Pinchot, Sept. 13, 1909, WHTP.
615 "in holding Ballinger up": WHT to Charles Nagel, Sept. 24, 1909, WHTP.
615 "Never at any . . . greatest losses": *Nevada State Journal*, Sept. 26, 1909.
615 "as fanatical . . . after Ballinger": WHT to George Wickersham, Oct. 7, 1909, WHTP.
615 "a state of . . . a break": WHT to Charles Nagel, Sept. 24, 1909, WHTP.
616 "He is looking": WHT to George Wickersham, Oct. 7, 1909, WHTP.
616 "I have been thinking": Overton W. Price to Gifford Pinchot, Sept. 16, 1909, Pinchot Papers.
616 In the weeks . . . publicize his allegations: James R. Garfield, Diary, Sept. 21, 1909, Garfield Papers.
616 "as employees . . . immediate danger": Overton W. Price and A. C. Shaw to Gifford Pinchot, Jan. 5, 1910, in *Investigation*, Vol. 4, p. 1279.
616 "going over in detail": James R. Garfield, Diary, Sept. 21, 1909, Garfield Papers.
616 Shaw then aided Glavis: Norman Hapgood, *The Changing Years, Reminiscences of Norman Hapgood* (New York: Farrar & Rinehart, 1930), p. 182.
616 "Pinchot has spread": WHT to HHT, Oct. 15, 1909, WHTP.
616 "read the article": Hapgood, *The Changing Years*, p. 182.
617 No attempt was ever made: Pringle, *Life and Times*, Vol. 1, p. 498.
617 "the newspaper frenzy": Ponder, " 'Nonpublicity' and the Unmaking of a President," *Journalism History* (Winter 1994), p. 116.
617 "The Whitewashing . . . in Ballinger's Hands": Glavis, "The Whitewashing of Ballinger," *Collier's*, Nov. 13, 1909, pp. 16–18.
617 The potential purchase of coal lands . . . railroads in the West: James L. Penick, *Progressive Politics and Conservation: The Ballinger-Pinchot Affair* (Chicago: University of Chicago Press, 1968), pp. 82–83.
617 "the natural resources of Alaska": Pinchot, *Breaking New Ground*, p. 427.
617 "the muckrake periodical": Mowry, *The Era of Theodore Roosevelt*, p. 257.
617 Glavis was likened to Ida Tarbell: *Fairbanks* [AK] *Daily News-Miner*, Dec. 17, 1909.
617 "a party to the conspiracy": Filler, *The Muckrakers*, p. 333.
617 "circumstantial evidence . . . Alaska coal grants": John Matthews to Gifford Pinchot, Jan. 8, 1910, Pinchot Papers.
617 Ballinger refused to give a detailed statement: *Washington Post*, Nov. 18, 1909.
617 "literary apostles . . . so asinine": Richard Ballinger, "Press Release, Nov. 20, 1909," Pinchot Papers.
617 "I have felt so thoroughly": Richard Ballinger to William Cowles, Dec. 9, 1909, in Ponder, " 'Nonpublicity' and the Unmaking of a President," *Journalism History* (Winter 1994), p. 117.
618 "in favor of all": James R. Garfield, Diary, Nov. 30, 1909, Garfield Papers.
618 "the goodness of a bad": Gifford Pinchot to James R. Garfield, Dec. 4, 1909, Pinchot Papers.
618 "the whole controversy": Gifford Pinchot to Charles R. Crane, Nov. 29, 1909, Pinchot Papers.
618 "that the situation had become": *Washington Post*, Dec. 21, 1909.
618 "a coward . . . an honest man": WHT to Reuben Melville, Dec. 24, 1909, WHTP.
618 "the whole affair": *Washington Post*, Aug. 30, 1909.
618 Faced with Ballinger's ultimatum: *Washington Times*, Dec. 22, 1909.
618 "any investigation . . . papers, or documents": Pinchot, *Breaking New Ground*, p. 443.
618 "all the power . . . before the people": Phillip Wells to William Kent, Dec. 22, 1909, WHTP.
619 A Washington "insider . . . to conduct the defense": Filler, *The Muckrakers*, pp. 334–35.
619 "between special . . . at their expense?": Pinchot, *Breaking New Ground*, pp. 444–45.
619 "out again defying . . . Let us see": WHT to Horace Taft, Dec. 27, 1909, WHTP.
619 "the Ballingerites . . . old political time": *National Tribune* (Washington, DC), Dec. 30, 1909.
619 "It remains true": *Current Literature* (June 1910), p. 588.
619 "bring out . . . worst possible light": *Washington Times*, Jan. 7, 1910.
620 the Forest Service's involvement: Gifford Pinchot to Jonathan P. Dolliver, Jan. 5, 1910, in *Investigation*, Vol. 4, pp. 1283–85.
620 "to lay our hand": Gifford Pinchot to W. K. Kavanaugh, Jan. 20, 1910, Pinchot Papers.
620 "official information . . . of public property": Gifford Pinchot to Jonathan P. Dolliver, Jan. 5, 1910, in *Investigation*, Vol. 4, pp. 1283–84.
620 "One trouble . . . within him now": AB to Clara, Jan. 7, 1910, in AB, *Taft and Roosevelt*, Vol. 1, pp. 253–54.
620 "had distressed him as much": AB to Clara, Jan. 9, 1910, in ibid., p. 256.
620 "like a man almost ill": AB to Clara, Jan. 7, 1910, in ibid., p. 254.
620 "There is only one": AB to Clara, Jan. 9, 1910, in ibid., p. 256.
620 Taft directed Wilson to fire: *El Paso* [TX] *Herald*, Jan. 8, 1910.
620 "The plain intimations . . . a helpful subordinate": WHT to Gifford Pinchot, Jan. 7, 1910, WHTP.
621 "looked refreshed": AB to Clara, Jan. 9, 1910, in AB, *Taft and Roosevelt*, Vol. 1, p. 255.
621 "could have followed . . . to be overlooked": *La Crosse* [WI] *Tribune*, Jan. 8, 1910.
621 "suffering from the same": *Post-Standard* (Syracuse, NY), Jan. 8, 1910.
621 "Quite as admirable . . . public lands": *Literary Digest*, Jan. 22, 1910, p. 128.
621 "the Roosevelt policies . . . friend of Mr. Pinchot": *Outlook*, Jan. 22, 1910, p. 141.
621 "I cannot believe it": TR to Gifford Pinchot, Jan. 17, 1910, Pinchot Papers.
621 "The appointment . . . meeting me in Europe?": TR to Gifford Pinchot, Mar. 1, 1910, Pinchot Papers.
621 "The people have faith": Pinchot, *Breaking New Ground*, p. 457.

622 "general-in-command . . . most convincing way": *National Tribune*, Feb. 3, 1910.
622 "a keen disappointment . . . than a scandal": *Literary Digest*, Feb. 12, 1910, p. 269.
622 "opened with a heavy volley": *National Tribune*, Mar. 3, 1910.
622 had "been unfaithful": *Indianapolis Star*, Feb. 28, 1910.
622 "the public clamor . . . unfaithful public servant": *National Tribune*, Mar. 3, 1910.
622 "Pinchot has distinctly": WHT to Horace Taft, Mar. 5, 1910, WHTP.
622 "proven nothing at all": Horace Taft to WHT, Mar. 9, 1910, WHTP.
622 "so tedious" . . . Jim Jeffries: *Arizona Republican* (Phoenix, AZ), April 18, 1910.
622 "really decisive . . . he had to prove it": Gifford Pinchot, "Interview with Louis D. Brandeis, March 3, 1940," Pinchot Papers.
623 he finally discovered . . . after September 11: Frederick Kerby, "The Inside Story of How a Private Secretary Wrecked an Administration," Unpublished ms [n.d.], enclosed in Frederick Kerby to Gifford Pinchot, Jan. 28, 1941, Pinchot Papers.
623 Brandeis revealed his discovery . . . cognizant of his peril: Pinchot, "Interview with Louis D. Brandeis, March 3, 1940," Pinchot Papers.
623 "to make it appear": New York *Sun*, April 23, 1910.
623 Prevented by the rules . . . leaked the story to the press: *Washington Post*, April 24, 1910.
623 Wickersham initially refused . . . backdated the report: *Newport* [RI] *Daily News*, May 12, 1910.
623 "there probably would": *National Tribune*, May 19, 1910.
623 Their failure to do so . . . Congress and the country: *Le Mars* [IA] *Globe-Post*, May 16, 1910.
623 "an attitude of suspicion": *National Tribune*, May 19, 1910.
623 "noted the similarities . . . match put to the pile": Kerby, "The Inside Story," Pinchot Papers.
624 "in his brief case . . . of the Lawler document": Ibid.
624 "the so-called memorandum": G. W. Wickersham to Knute Nelson, May 14, 1910, in *Investigation*, Vol. 7, p. 4364.
624 "of any material . . . resume of the facts": *Investigation*, Vol. 7, pp. 3862, 3865–66.
624 "a restless tattoo": *New Castle* [PA] *News*, April 30, 1910.
624 "an insult": *Investigation*, Vol. 7, p. 3868.
624 "exhausted all channels": Kerby, "The Inside Story," Pinchot Papers.
625 He identified "certain portions": *Washington Times*, May 14, 1910.
625 "specifically" prepared: *Washington Times*, May 15, 1910.
625 "Ballinger Accused": *Washington Times*, May 14, 1910.
625 the story broke . . . on the golf course: Kerby, "The Inside Story," Pinchot Papers.
625 suddenly "found . . . coincidences of all time": *Washington Times*, May 16, 1910.
625 "treachery . . . unworthy": Ibid.; *Fort Wayne* [IN] *Weekly Sentinel*, May 18, 1910.
625 "did not state . . . a written statement": *Titusville* [PA] *Herald*, May 16, 1910.
625 "manly" assumption: *Waterloo* [IA] *Evening Courier*, May 18, 1910.
625 "the sequence of events": *Fort Wayne* [IN] *Weekly Sentinel*, May 18, 1910.
626 "unimportant" statements: *Washington Herald*, May 15, 1910.
626 "There was absolutely . . . private offices": Cited in *Waterloo* [IA] *Evening Courier*, May 18, 1910.
626 "the people who had": *National Tribune*, May 19, 1910.
626 "until he was . . . fly into a rage": *Waterloo* [IA] *Evening Courier*, May 18, 1910.
626 "came as a startling . . . the good faith": *San Antonio* [TX] *Light and Gazette*, May 16, 1910.
626 "the puzzled . . . done nothing illegal": Stewart Edward White, "The Ballinger Case," *The American Magazine* (March 1910), p. 687.
626 "not a single fact": *Literary Digest*, May 14, 1910.
626 "Rightly or wrongly": *Emporia* [KS] *Gazette*, May 26, 1910.
626 Reflecting widespread sentiment . . . to resign: *Indianapolis Star*, June 10, 1910.
626 "His presence . . . long and unflinchingly": *Emporia* [KS] *Gazette*, May 26, 1910.
626 "be regarded as": "The Ballinger Case: A Review," *Outlook*, June 11, 1910, p. 295.
626 "justified in remaining": *Indianapolis Star*, June 10, 1910.
626 Charley Taft tried . . . the president refused: AB to Clara, May 5, 1910, in AB, *Taft and Roosevelt*, Vol. 1, p. 347.
626 "Life is not worth": WHT to P. A. Baker, May 21, 1910, in Pringle, *Life and Times*, Vol. 2, p. 558.
626 "unjustly persecuted" a good man: AB to Clara, June 22, 1910, in AB, *Taft and Roosevelt*, Vol. 1, p. 408.
627 "broken" Ballinger's health: *Literary Digest*, May 28, 1910, p. 1067.
627 "almost equaled": Paolo E. Coletta, *The Presidency of William Howard Taft* (Lawrence: University Press of Kansas, 1973), p. 98.
627 "His entrance into": Gifford Pinchot, "Statement, March 7, 1911," Pinchot Papers.
627 "no right . . . the public welfare": *Indianapolis Star*, June 10, 1910.
627 "Is the Republican Party" . . . occasionally "dragooned": RSB, "Is the Republican Party Breaking Up? The Story of the Insurgent West," *The American Magazine* (February 1910), pp. 435–39.
628 "at first a decided": RSB, "Is the East Also Insurgent?," *The American Magazine* (March 1910), pp. 579, 587.
628 From New England . . . over Speaker Cannon: Semonche, *Ray Stannard Baker*, pp. 236–37.
628 "tense and dramatic": *Washington Times*, Mar. 19, 1910.
628 "fighting the fight": *Washington Times*, Mar. 18, 1910.
628 "met his Waterloo": *Washington Times*, Mar. 19, 1910.
628 Forty-three insurgent Republicans . . . pass the resolution: Remini, *The House*, p. 275.
628 "A real revolution": RSB to J. Stannard Baker, Mar. 27, 1910, RSB Papers.
628 "case study . . . within the reform movement": Semonche, *Ray Stannard Baker*, p. 238.
628 "We are naturally . . . our opportunity": JSP to WAW, Aug. 9, 1910, White Papers.
628 As precinct leader . . . changed from within: WAW, *The Autobiography*, p. 424.

628 the insurgents' vision: WAW, "The Insurgence of Insurgency," *The American Magazine* (December 1910), p. 171.
629 her "powerful pen . . . could well be": *Washington Times*, June 24, 1910.
629 "the same old circus": IMT, *All in the Day's Work*, p. 272.
629 the "rousing challenge": Ibid., p. 273.
629 "the hazy generalities": RSB, "On the Political Firing Line," *The American Magazine* (November 1910), p. 9.
629 "crystallized into one": IMT, *All in the Day's Work*, p. 274.
629 "argues and fights . . . ways of thinking": IMT, "The Standpat Intellect," *The American Magazine* (May 1911), p. 40.
629 "The popular judgment": JSP, Editorial, *The American Magazine* (September 1910), p. 707.
629 "I thought that Taft": JSP to WAW, Sept. 18, 1909, White Papers.
629 "opposed him": JSP to RSB, Feb. 24, 1910, RSB Papers.
629 "mattered little . . . crusading spirit": Hechler, *Insurgency*, p. 13.
630 "Taft is done for": IMT to WAW, Sept. 29, 1909, White Papers.
630 "But they will not work": WAW to WHT, Feb. 3, 1910, in Johnson, *Selected Letters of William Allen White*, p. 105.
630 Taft responded to White . . . made no sense: WAW to Guy W. Mallon, Jan. 13, 1910, WHTP.
630 "I have confidence": WHT to WAW, Mar. 20, 1909, White Papers.
630 "foolishly and needlessly": *NYT*, April 20, 1910.
630 "I could not have asked . . . steer the conversation": WAW, *The Autobiography*, p. 425.
630 "everything under the sun": WAW to J. Haskel, June 6, 1910, White Papers.
630 "We had . . . a fool's errand": WAW, *The Autobiography*, pp. 425–26.
630 "I trust you are . . . the fireworks": JSP to RSB, Feb. 24, 1910, RSB Papers.
631 "There is one thing": RSB, "The Measure of Taft," *The American Magazine* (July 1910), p. 362.
631 They appreciated . . . homes and hotels: *National Tribune*, Jan. 6, 1910.
631 "If these young visitors": *National Tribune*, Mar. 31, 1910.
631 "A mighty cheer . . . trusty right arm": *Washington Post*, April 15, 1910.
631 "All his life long . . . chief thing is to *fight*": RSB, "The Measure of Taft," *The American Magazine* (July 1910), pp. 364–65, 367–68.
631 "free from severe criticism": WHT, "Speech to the New York Press Club," Mar. 22, 1910, WHTP.
632 "criticism may spring": RSB, "The Measure of Taft," *The American Magazine* (July 1910), p. 369.
632 "arrayed against . . . from the first": Paul Kester to HHT, Sept. 22, 1910, WHTP.
632 "skeleton" . . . still carried weight: Lyon, *Success Story*, p. 322.
632 "In the first place . . . against the people's wishes": McClure to Charles Norton, Oct. 11, 1910, McClure MSS.
632 Pinchot arrived at Roosevelt's villa . . . over the Maritime Alps: *San Francisco Call*, April 12, 1910.
632 "We have fallen back": Gifford Pinchot to TR, Dec. 31, 1909, TRP.
633 "disappointment . . . the President's opinions": Jonathan P. Dolliver to Gifford Pinchot, Mar. 25, 1910, TRP.
633 "The people at first": Albert J. Beveridge to Gifford Pinchot, Mar. 24, 1910, TRP.
633 "We had one of the finest": Gifford Pinchot to James R. Garfield, April 27, 1910, Pinchot Papers.
633 "no event in": *San Francisco Call*, April 12, 1910.
633 "You do not need . . . the best he knows how": TR to HCL, April 11, 1910, in *LTR*, Vol. 7, pp. 71, 70.
633 "keep absolutely still": TR to HCL, Mar. 4, 1910, in ibid., p. 52.
633 "As the fight deepens . . . of continental size": RSB, "The Impending Roosevelt," *The American Magazine* (April 1910), pp. 735, 737.

CHAPTER TWENTY-FIVE: "The Parting of the Ways"

Page

634 He was perplexed: AB to Clara, June 5, 1910, in AB, *Taft and Roosevelt*, Vol. 1, p. 364.
634 a gold ruler: AB to Clara, Mar. 22, 1909, in ibid., p. 25.
634 "There is no doubt . . . his way over": AB to Clara, June 5, 1910, in ibid., p. 364.
635 "Am deeply touched": TR to WHT, Mar. 23, 1909, in *LTR*, Vol. 7, pp. 3–4.
635 "Roosevelt did write": AB to Clara, June 6, 1910, in AB, *Taft and Roosevelt*, Vol. 1, p. 367.
635 The lack of communication . . . accomplishments of his administration: *Mansfield* [OH] *News*, June 15, 1910.
635 "received no letters . . . other persons": *Indianapolis Star*, June 12, 1910.
635 "singularly silent": AB to Clara, Feb. 14, 1910, AB Letters.
635 although eighteen-year-old Ethel . . . to recognize her: EKR to Kermit Roosevelt, May 12, 1909, KR Papers.
635 "to let the setting sun": Nicholas Longworth to TR, April 27, 1910, TRP.
635 "solely as a result": AB to Clara, May 17, 1910, in AB, *Taft and Roosevelt*, Vol. 1, p. 352.
635 "Everything which is . . . personal jealousies": AB to Clara, May 17, 1910, AB Letters.
636 no "word of welcome" . . . in Khartoum: AB to Clara, June 6, 1910, in AB, *Taft and Roosevelt*, Vol. 1, p. 367.
636 "nearly complete . . . would find the truth": WHT to TR, May 26, 1910, TRP.
636 Taft made the decision . . . note of welcome: WHT to TR, June 14, 1910, TRP.
636 "you and Mrs. Taft . . . out again": AB to Clara, June 16, 1910, in AB, *Taft and Roosevelt*, Vol. 1, p. 392.
636 "Oh, Archie . . . answer it later": AB to Clara, June 19, 1910, in ibid., p. 398.
636 "and how she dreaded . . . had distressed him": AB to Clara, June 19, 1910, in ibid., p. 402.
637 "if the master . . . a little bit late": AB to Clara, June 19, 1910, in AB Letters.
637 "I feel it is . . . courteous": AB to Clara, June 19, 1910, in AB, *Taft and Roosevelt*, Vol. 1, pp. 394–95, 403.
637 "I am of course much concerned": TR to WHT, June 8, 1910, in *LTR*, Vol. 7, p. 88.
637 "kind and friendly . . . cannot help it": TR to WHT, June 20, 1910, in ibid., p. 93.
637 Overall, the feel of the letter: AB to Clara, June 24, 1910, in AB, *Taft and Roosevelt*, Vol. 1, p. 411.
637 intense "factional wrangling": *National Tribune* (Washington, DC), June 23, 1910.
637 "more general legislation": *Washington Times*, June 26, 1910.
637 "dark days . . . to command": *New York Tribune*, June 26, 1910.

637 "strongly progressive . . . congressional saw mill": *Eau Claire* [WI] *Leader*, June 25, 1910.
638 a "special Commerce Court . . . at home and abroad": *New York Tribune*, June 26, 1910.
638 Taft's "crowning achievement": *Eau Claire* [WI] *Leader*, June 25, 1910.
638 "I am not in favor": *Los Angeles Herald*, Sept. 18, 1909.
638 "I am as pleased": WHT to [Otto] Bannard, June 11, 1910, in Pringle, *Life and Times*, Vol. 1, p. 519.
638 "one of the great Congressional": WHT to [William B.] McKinley, Aug. 20, 1910, WHTP.
638 The insurgents rightly took credit: *National Tribune*, June 23, 1910.
638 "Old Guard" Republicans . . . the promises: *Eau Claire* [WI] *Leader*, June 25, 1910.
638 "When people come": *NYT*, June 26, 1910.
638 "I always had faith": Charles P. Taft to WHT, July 2, 1910, WHTP.
638 "congratulated him . . . session was ending": *Washington Times*, June 26, 1910.
639 "the only incident . . . through the park": AB to Clara, June 26, 1910, in AB, *Taft and Roosevelt*, Vol. 1, pp. 413–14.
639 he rested at Sagamore Hill . . . *The Outlook*: *Burlington* [VT] *Weekly Free Press*, June 23, 1910.
639 Before leaving for Africa, he had signed: *NYT*, Mar. 11, 1909.
639 a three-room suite . . . "an office building": *Burlington* [VT] *Weekly Free Press*, June 23, 1910.
639 "very real . . . small proportion": "Mr. Roosevelt to The Outlook's Readers," *Outlook*, July 2, 1910, p. 462.
639 "not make a speech . . . I won't say never": *New York Tribune*, June 24, 1910.
639 "marked by frequent . . . his other hand": *NYT*, June 30, 1910.
639 Throughout his governorship . . . direct primary bill: Edmund Morris, *Colonel Roosevelt* (New York: Random House, 2010), pp. 94–95.
640 "I believe the people": *NYT*, June 30, 1910.
640 "plunged into the very thick": *Boston Daily Globe*, June 30, 1910.
640 taken "the helm . . . in the approaching campaign": *NYT*, June 30, 1910.
640 "is likely to prove": *New York Tribune*, June 30, 1910.
640 "Ah Theodore . . . nothing on which to hang a story": AB to Clara, June 30, 1910, in AB, *Taft and Roosevelt*, Vol. 1, pp. 418–20, 431.
641 "From beginning to end": *New York Tribune*, July 1, 1910.
641 "that their friendship": *Washington Post*, July 2, 1910.
641 "Just Like Old Times . . . don't know that I shall": *NYT*, July 1, 1910.
641 "in swift and emphatic fashion": *Boston Daily Globe*, July 1, 1910.
641 "It is Mr. Roosevelt . . . prepared for war": Cited in *Literary Digest*, July 9, 1910, p. 43.
641 "They made the fight": Pringle, *Life and Times*, Vol. 2, p. 563.
641 More powerful than . . . slate of candidates: Lewis L. Gould, *The William Howard Taft Presidency* (Lawrence: University Press of Kansas, 2009), p. 113.
641 "It did not occur . . . platform and candidates": WHT to Lloyd Griscom, Aug. 20, 1910, WHTP.
642 "Don't you know . . . such a fight": WHT to Charles Norton, Aug. 21, 1910, WHTP.
642 Taft momentarily wavered . . . dragged into the battle: AB to Clara, Aug. 17, 1910, in AB, *Taft and Roosevelt*, Vol. 2, p. 479.
642 the panel chose Sherman: Gould, *The William Howard Taft Presidency*, p. 114.
642 "he fumed . . . the heaviest blow yet": *NYT*, Aug. 17, 1910.
642 Roosevelt was incensed . . . endorsed Sherman's candidacy: WHT to Charles P. Taft, Sept. 10, 1910, and WHT to Lloyd Griscom, Aug. 20, 1910, WHTP.
642 "with treachery . . . kills other people": AB to Clara, Aug. 18, 1910, in AB, *Taft and Roosevelt*, Vol. 2, p. 488.
643 "ever expressed . . . conference with Mr. Roosevelt": *Washington Herald*, Aug. 23, 1910.
643 He was "indignant": WHT to Charles Norton, Aug. 22, 1910, WHTP.
643 "was very glad to see": *Washington Herald*, Aug. 23, 1910.
643 "As the waters of excitement": AB to Clara, Aug. 21, 1910, in AB, *Taft and Roosevelt*, Vol. 2, p. 493.
643 "profoundly grieved": AB to Clara, Aug. 18, 1910, in ibid., p. 488.
643 "His whole attitude . . . in the past": AB to Clara, Aug. 19, 1910, in ibid., p. 484.
643 "They are now apart": AB to Clara, Aug. 20, 1910, in ibid., p. 492.
643 "On which side": Amos E. Pinchot, *History of the Progressive Party, 1912–1916* (New York: New York University Press, 1958), p. 115.
643 "a county fair": Robert S. La Forte, "Theodore Roosevelt's Osawatomie Speech," *Kansas Historical Quarterly* (Summer 1966), pp. 195, 196–97.
643 with fireworks . . . food stands: *New York Tribune*, Sept. 1, 1910.
643 Climbing onto a kitchen table . . . "the front rank": *Washington Times*, Sept. 1, 1910.
643 the speech had gone . . . Herbert Croly: Pinchot, *History of the Progressive Party*, pp. 112–13.
644 "The New Nationalism . . . go forward as a nation": Theodore Roosevelt, *The New Nationalism* (New York: Outlook, 1910).
644 "My friends": La Forte, "Theodore Roosevelt's Osawatomie Speech," *Kansas Historical Quarterly* (Summer 1966), p. 197.
644 he was "the leader": Char Miller, *Gifford Pinchot and the Making of Modern Environmentalism* (Washington, DC: Island Press/Shearwater Books, 2001), pp. 235–36.
644 "Advanced Insurgent . . . materially strengthened": *Washington Times*, Sept. 1, 1910.
644 "frenzied applause . . . in our Government": Sydney Brooks, "The Confusion of American Politics," *Fortnightly Review* (October 1910), pp. 648–49.
645 "this new Napoleon": La Forte, "Theodore Roosevelt's Osawatomie Speech," *Kansas Historical Quarterly* (Summer 1966), p. 198.
645 "slight mention . . . form of attack": *National Tribune*, Sept. 8, 1910.
645 "He is going quite beyond": WHT to Charles P. Taft, Sept. 10, 1910, WHTP.

645 "wild ideas" . . . decent "conservative": WHT to Horace Taft, Sept. 16, 1910, WHTP.
645 "on the other side . . . against machine politics": Horace Taft to WHT, Sept. 15, 1910, WHTP.
645 "riotous reception . . . not supporting me": WHT to Horace Taft, Sept. 16, 1910, WHTP.
645 "I dared to include": WHT to Charles P. Taft, Sept. 10, 1910, WHTP.
645 Gossipmongers exacerbated . . . the nomination: AB to Clara, Sept. 17, 1910, in AB, *Taft and Roosevelt*, Vol. 2, pp. 514–15.
645 "I know how . . . misconstrued by me": AB to Clara, September [n.d.], 1910, in ibid., pp. 529–30.
646 "He told me . . . will be placed": AB to Clara, Sept. 17, 1910, in ibid., p. 515.
646 "a connected conversation": AB to Clara, Jan. 2, 1910, AB Letters.
646 "the buffer . . . to a standstill": AB to Clara, Aug. 4, 1910, AB Letters.
646 "became separated . . . pretty awful": Anthony, *Nellie Taft*, p. 280.
646 "to die in harness": AB to Clara, April 14, 1910, AB Letters.
646 "something young and prettier": AB to Clara, Oct. 4, 1910, AB Letters.
646 "I suppose you will have": AB to Clara, July 6, 1910, in AB, *Taft and Roosevelt*, Vol. 2, p. 436.
647 "step out of the way . . . like a gentleman": WHT to Horace Taft, Sept. 16, 1910, WHTP.
647 "on the Eve . . . away with radicalism": *Washington Times*, Sept. 24, 1910.
647 "Twenty years ago . . . on good terms": TR to HCL, Sept. 21, 1910, in *LTR*, Vol. 7, pp. 135–36.
647 unity might "turn the scale": TR to TR, Jr., Sept. 21, 1910, in ibid., p. 133.
647 "made a point of being": TR to HCL, Sept. 21, 1910, in ibid., pp. 135–36.
647 "not genial and quite offish": AB to Clara, Sept. 20, 1910, in AB, *Taft and Roosevelt*, Vol. 2, p. 524.
647 "had spoken first": WHT to HHT, Sept. 24, 1910, WHTP.
647 "very irritating . . . genuine wisdom": TR to HCL, Sept. 21, 1910, in *LTR*, Vol. 7, p. 135.
648 Roosevelt's opponents jumped on the story: *New York Tribune*, Sept. 20, 1910.
648 a statement "emphatically" denying: *Times Dispatch* (Richmond, VA), Sept. 21, 1910.
648 "to beg for assistance": TR to HCL, Sept. 21, 1910, in *LTR*, Vol. 7, p. 135.
648 "farther apart than ever": AB to Clara, Sept. 20, 1910, in AB, *Taft and Roosevelt*, Vol. 2, p. 518.
648 "riotous cheers . . . passed up to the platform": *Washington Herald*, Sept. 28, 1910.
648 "an enemy of the nation . . . public safety": *New York Tribune*, Sept. 27, 1910.
648 "catcalls . . . for Col. Gruber": *San Francisco Call*, Sept. 28, 1910.
648 Roosevelt's supporters were anxious: *Washington Herald*, Sept. 28, 1910.
648 567 votes against . . . 445: Morris, *Colonel Roosevelt*, p. 114.
648 "to our able, upright": *Omaha* [NE] *Daily Bee*, Sept. 28, 1910.
648 "The house party has been": WHT to HHT, Sept. 28, 1910, WHTP.
649 "Bulletins . . . from New York": AB to Clara, Sept. 27, 1910, in AB, *Taft and Roosevelt*, Vol. 2, p. 531.
649 "I hope you saw": WHT to HHT, Sept. 28, 1910, WHTP.
649 "We had a delicious table": George Wickersham to HHT, Oct. 2, 1910, WHTP.
649 "should have lost everything": TR to TR, Jr., Oct. 3, 1910, TRJP.
649 Pinchot refused to back the ticket: TR to TR, Jr., Oct. 19, 1910, in *LTR*, Vol. 7, p. 145.
649 "I think it absurd . . . as radical as I am": TR to William Kent, Nov. 28, 1910, in ibid., p. 176.
649 "have been nearly insane": TR to Theodore Roosevelt, Jr., Sept. 21, 1910, in ibid., p. 133.
649 "the wild-eyed radicals": TR to TR, Jr., Oct. 19, 1910, in ibid., p. 145.
649 "I had one . . . force me to be a candidate": RSB, Notebook, Oct. 5, 1910, RSB Papers.
650 "usual moral punch . . . finest characteristics": RSB, Notebook, Oct. 6, 1910, RSB Papers.
650 "the old game . . . radical & conservative": RSB, Notebook, Oct. 8, 1910, RSB Papers.
650 "I am being nearly worked": TR to ARC, Oct. 7, 1910, TRC.
650 When Democrats won an "unprecedented" victory: *National Tribune*, Oct. 27, 1910.
650 "If Mr. Roosevelt can save": *Literary Digest*, Nov. 5, 1910, p. 775.
650 "it will be practically": *NYT*, Oct. 5, 1910.
651 the strength of the Democratic victory "stunned Washington": *National Tribune*, Nov. 17, 1910.
651 Democrats gained control . . . the forty-eight states: Andrew Busch, *Horses in Midstream: U.S. Midterm Elections and Their Consequences, 1894–1998* (Pittsburgh: University of Pittsburgh Press, 1999), p. 85; Sullivan, *Our Times*, Vol. 4, p. 452.
651 "The Democratic party": Mowry, *Theodore Roosevelt and the Progressive Movement*, p. 156.
651 "crushing rebuke" to Theodore: *NYT*, Nov. 9, 1910.
651 "defeat would have come": *Literary Digest*, Nov. 19, 1910, p. 917.
651 "New Nationalism has been pitched": *NYT*, Nov. 9, 1910.
651 "to be a fatal . . . triumphantly elected": *Literary Digest*, Nov. 19, 1910, p. 917.
651 "The trail that Mr. Roosevelt": *Current Literature* (December 1910), p. 585.
651 This "tremendous overthrow": *Literary Digest*, Nov. 19, 1910, p. 916.
651 "the chief architect": Ibid., p. 917.
651 "a smashing defeat": TR to Arthur Hamilton Lee, Nov. 11, 1910, in *LTR*, Vol. 7, p. 163.
651 He recognized that he had lost support . . . "envenomed hatred": TR to Benjamin Ide Wheeler, Nov. 21, 1910, in ibid., p. 173.
652 "The American people": TR to WAW, Dec. 12, 1910, in ibid., p. 182.
652 "Don't go": Sullivan, *Our Times*, Vol. 4, p. 453.
652 "in a most depressed . . . benefit to his country": AB to Clara, Jan. 19, 1910, in AB, *Taft and Roosevelt*, Vol. 2, pp. 579–81.
652 "It was not only a landslide": AB to Clara, Nov. 9, 1910, in ibid., p. 556.
652 "whole drift . . . govern the country": AB to Clara, Jan. 30, 1910, in ibid., Vol. 1, p. 272.
652 "took a whack . . . would have been the same": AB to Clara, Nov. 9, 1910, in ibid., Vol. 2, p. 555.
652 "The warmth of . . . the Philippines!": AB to Clara, Nov. 11, 1910, in ibid., pp. 556–57.

653 "It is always back . . . here in Washington": AB to Clara, Nov. 24, 1910, in ibid., p. 563.
653 While Taft was away, Roosevelt . . . meet with old friends: *Washington Times*, Nov. 17 & 19, 1910.
653 he stopped at the White House: New York *Sun*, Nov. 20, 1910.
653 To accommodate the increased . . . security guards: *Evening Independent* (Massillon, OH), Oct. 18, 1909.
653 "in the center": William Seale, *The President's House: A History*, Vol. 2 (Washington, DC: White House Hist. Assoc. with the cooperation of the National Geographic Society, 1986), pp. 756–58.
653 "severe rectangular room": *Evening Independent*, Oct. 18, 1909.
653 "Oh, yes": New York *Sun*, Nov. 20, 1910.
653 "it would gratify me": WHT to TR, Nov. 25, 1910, TRP.
653 "You are a trump": TR to WHT, Nov. 28, 1910, WHTP.
653 would be "private citizens": WHT to TR, Nov. 30, 1910, TRP.
653 "I have always felt": TR to WHT, Dec. 8, 1910, WHTP.
654 And Taft wrote yet again: WHT to TR, Dec. 2, 1910, WHTP.
654 "I have read your Message": TR to WHT, Dec. 8, 1910, WHTP.
654 "I see signs of the clouds": AB to Clara, Dec. 26, 1910, in AB, *Taft and Roosevelt*, Vol. 2, p. 570.
654 smooth "the rough edges": AB to Clara, Jan. 7, 1911, AB Letters.
654 On Christmas Day . . . first year as president: AB to Clara, Dec. 26, 1910, in AB, *Taft and Roosevelt*, Vol. 2, p. 570.
654 "kneeled on it to look": AB to Clara, Jan. 7, 1911, AB Letters.
654 "to bestow by exchange": WHT to EKR, Dec. 31, 1910, in Morris, *EKR*, p. 338.
654 Both Theodore and Edith were touched: TR to WHT, Jan. 7, 1911, in *LTR*, Vol. 7, p. 204.
654 "brings the two families . . . in a museum": AB to Clara, Dec. 26, 1910, in AB, *Taft and Roosevelt*, Vol. 2, p. 570.

CHAPTER TWENTY-SIX: "Like a War Horse"

Page

655 "where they compromised . . . out of his head": WAW to Mark Sullivan, Nov. 22, 1910, White Papers.
656 On January 21 . . . the initiative, referendum, and recall: Robert M. La Follette [hereafter RLF] to LS, Jan. 14, 1911, LS Papers.
656 "nine U.S. Senators": *Current Literature* (March 1911).
656 Progressive Federation of Publicists and Editors: Mowry, *Theodore Roosevelt and the Progressive Movement*, p. 173.
656 "a roll call" . . . Lincoln Steffens: *NYT*, Jan. 14, 1911.
656 "a sort of pathologist": Kaplan, *Lincoln Steffens*, p. 167.
656 "I am hungry": RLF to LS, Nov. 6, 1909, LS Papers.
656 "an anti-Taft movement": *National Tribune*, Feb. 2, 1911.
656 "Nothing . . . could be more reasonable": *Current Literature* (March 1911).
656 "a much larger . . . popular government": *National Tribune*, Feb. 2, 1911.
657 "Now, Colonel . . . name and influence?": RLF to TR, Jan. 9, 1911, TRP.
657 La Follette considered Roosevelt an opportunist: RLF, *La Follette's Autobiography*, pp. 215–18.
657 "an extremist . . . fanaticism": TR to TR, Jr., Nov. 21, 1910, TRP.
657 "That is a mighty nice letter": TR to RLF, Jan. 24, 1911, in *LTR*, Vol. 7, p. 214.
657 "merely a means": TR to RLF, Jan. 3, 1911, in ibid., p. 202.
657 "very anxious not to seem": TR to RLF, Jan. 24, 1911, in ibid., p. 215.
657 On March 8, 1911, Theodore Roosevelt embarked: *New York Tribune*, Mar. 7, 1911.
657 "not care a rap": TR to Lady Delamere, Mar. 7, 1911, TRC.
657 "fairly universal . . . my own work": TR to William Dudley Foulke, Jan. 2, 1911, in *LTR*, Vol. 7, p. 196.
657 Eight thousand . . . in Atlanta: *Times Dispatch* (Richmond, Va.), Mar. 9, 1911.
657 30,000 . . . in Tacoma, Washington: *San Juan Islander* (Friday Harbor, WA), April 14, 1911.
657 "as uproarious as": *Bemidji Daily Pioneer* (St. Paul, MN), April 15, 1911.
657 "heavier and slightly grayer": *Seattle Star*, April 7, 1911.
657 "without the slightest sign": *San Francisco Call*, Mar. 24, 1911.
657 "all traffic was . . . cheering admirers": *San Juan Islander* (Friday Harbor, WA), April 14, 1911.
657 The Commercial Club . . . and cockatoos: *Arizona Republican* (Phoenix, AZ), April 4, 1911.
658 "If there could be any monument": *Bisbee* [AZ] *Daily Review*, Mar. 19, 1911.
658 "abiding popularity . . . the United States created": *Leavenworth* [WA] *Echo*, April 14, 1911.
658 "low tariff and downward revision man": WHT to TR, Jan. 10, 1911, TRP.
658 "concurrent legislation": Pringle, *Life and Times*, Vol. 2, p. 587.
658 "At one stroke . . . policy of his own": *Current Literature* (March 1911).
659 "well-considered . . . country behind him": Ibid., p. 6.
659 "sit still and await results": *Washington Times*, Jan. 30, 1911.
659 "breakfast, lunch and dinner": AB to Clara, June 27, 1911, AB Letters.
659 a "week-end sail": *National Tribune*, June 13, 1911.
659 "linked together . . . the productive forces": *Current Literature* (March 1911), p. 4.
659 "What you propose . . . party in the end": TR to WHT, Jan. 12, 1911, WHTP.
659 Roosevelt "vigorously advocated": *Chicago Daily Tribune*, Feb. 23, 1911.
659 "it should always be": Extract from a speech delivered by Theodore Roosevelt in New York City on Feb. 13, 1911, WHTP.
659 "expected the insurgents": WHT to Charles P. Taft, July 22, 1911, WHTP.
659 "Give us something": *New York Tribune*, Jan. 28, 1911.
660 "politics makes . . . citadel of protection": *Current Literature* (March 1911), p. 2.
660 "Washington grows weary . . . as selfish": *Washington Herald*, July 6, 1911.
660 La Follette . . . announced his candidacy: *Washington Times*, June 17, 1911.

660 "trying to manufacture": *Washington Herald*, July 6, 1911.
660 "a great epoch": WHT to Charles P. Taft, July 22, 1911, WHTP.
660 "Today will be . . . have been impossible": *Washington Times*, July 24, 1911.
660 Canadian Parliament had descended into "hysteria": Pringle, *Life and Times*, Vol. 2, p. 597.
660 Conservative opponents . . . negotiations to begin: *Washington Times*, July 24, 1911.
660 "Canada is now": New York *Evening World*, Feb. 15, 1911.
660 "bad faith . . . annexation of Canada": *Chicago Daily Tribune*, Feb. 23, 1911.
661 "has gained remarkably": *Washington Herald*, July 24, 1911.
661 Roosevelt, who "strongly urged" him: Henry L. Stimson and McGeorge Bundy, *On Active Service in Peace and War* (New York: Harper Bros., 1948), p. 28.
661 "If two years ago": TR to James R. Garfield, April 28, 1911, in *LTR*, Vol. 7, p. 246.
661 "as much aloof": TR to TR, Jr., June 20, 1911, in *LTR*, Vol. 2, p. 293.
661 "would be remembered": *National Tribune*, June 22, 1911.
661 The mansion and the gardens . . . many other distinguished guests: *Washington Times*, June 19, 1911.
661 "a unique distinction": *Washington Herald*, June 19, 1911.
661 Nellie invited . . . Theodore Roosevelt: *Salt Lake Tribune*, June 17, 1911.
661 "how truly pretty" . . . shouting for help: AB to Clara, May 14, 1911, in AB, *Taft and Roosevelt*, Vol. 2, pp. 650–51.
662 "similar to the first . . . to find her words": Helen Taft Manning to Robert Taft, May 15, 1911, in Anthony, *Nellie Taft*, p. 304.
662 "the defect in her speech": WHT to Horace Taft, May 25, 1911, WHTP.
662 "suffered a serious . . . regret and sympathy": *Emporia* [KS] *Gazette*, May 18, 1911.
662 Determined to realize . . . her slender figure: *Washington Herald*, June 20, 1911.
662 "every detail . . . finished on time": New York *Sun*, June 19, 1911.
662 aides clad in "immaculate white": *Washington Herald*, June 20, 1911.
662 "A mighty shout . . . everybody smiled": *National Tribune*, June 29, 1911.
662 The applause continued: *Washington Herald*, June 20, 1911.
662 "the last hand was shaken": *National Tribune*, June 29, 1911.
662 "skipped lightly . . . happy as a boy": *Washington Herald*, June 29, 1911.
663 "chatted, laughed . . . Secretary of War": William Manners, *TR and Will: A Friendship That Split the Republican Party* (New York: Harcourt, Brace & World, 1969), p. 192.
663 Roosevelt had promised . . . he declined: William H. Cowles to Henry L. Stimson, June 7, 1911, WHTP.
663 "misguided friends" of the president: *Chicago Daily Tribune*, June 7, 1911.
663 "under no circumstance . . . mutual friend": *Atlanta Constitution*, June 7, 1911.
663 "This is the best political": *Hartford Herald*, June 14, 1911.
663 "affirm or deny . . . like a repetition": *San Francisco Chronicle*, June 8, 1911.
663 "an unqualified falsehood": *NYT*, June 7, 1911.
663 "It was outrageous": TR to Edward A. Van Valkenburg, June 14, 1911, in *LTR*, Vol. 7, p. 286.
663 "threw a bombshell . . . considerable chagrin": *Chicago Daily Tribune*, June 7, 1911.
663 forged an agreement . . . "subject to arbitration": *Salt Lake Tribune*, Aug. 5, 1911.
663 "the great jewel . . . the greatest act": AB to Clara, April 30, 1911, in AB, *Taft and Roosevelt*, Vol. 2, p. 635.
663 "The ideal to which": *San Francisco Call*, Sept. 8, 1911.
664 "the interests of": *New York Tribune*, Oct. 18, 1911.
664 "minimize . . . be traced to it": *Daily Kennebec Journal* (Augusta, ME), May 31, 1911.
664 "She meant so much": AB to Clara, Aug. 4, 1911, in AB, *Taft and Roosevelt*, Vol. 2, pp. 730–31.
664 "No self-respecting nation": TR, "The Arbitration Treaty with Great Britain," *Outlook*, May 20, 1911, p. 97.
664 "greatly disappointed . . . old chief": AB to Clara, May 18, 1911, AB Letters.
664 "mushy . . . for adequate cause": TR to James A. Drain, June 19, 1911, in *LTR*, Vol. 7, p. 287.
664 "It is one of our prime duties": TR, "The Peace of Righteousness," *Outlook*, Sept. 9, 1911, pp. 66, 69, 70.
664 "I am afraid the old fellow": AB to Clara, Sept. 8, 1911, in AB, *Taft and Roosevelt*, Vol. 2, p. 753.
665 On September 15 . . . through the West: *Los Angeles Herald*, Nov. 12, 1911.
665 "The White House is once more": *New York Tribune*, Sept. 17, 1911.
665 "every comfort . . . real beds": *Washington Times*, Sept. 13, 1911.
665 "taking medicine": WHT to Otto Bannard, Sept. 10, 1911, WHTP.
665 he had worked hard . . . and reciprocity: WHT to Charles P. Taft, Sept. 16, 1911, WHTP.
665 "bright skies": *Marion* [OH] *Daily Mirror*, Sept. 16, 1911.
665 "thought to be . . . a square deal": Gustav J. Karger, "Report from Taft's Western Trip," Sept. 1911, Taft-Karger MSS, CMC.
665 "reported in full . . . before the people": WHT to J. C. Hemphill, Nov. 16, 1911, WHTP.
665 "The bets seem to be": Horace Taft to WHT, Sept. 21, 1911, WHTP.
665 "ablaze with red fire": *Washington Herald*, Sept. 20, 1911.
665 "Laurier government": Pringle, *Life and Times*, Vol. 2, p. 598.
665 "an overwhelming . . . to reciprocity": *National Tribune*, Sept. 28, 1911.
665 "an Imperishable Canada": *Times Dispatch*, Sept. 23, 1911.
665 "dead as a ducat": *National Tribune*, Sept. 28, 1911.
665 "We were hit squarely": WHT to Horace Taft, Sept. 26, 1911, WHTP.
666 "for naught . . . little worse off": *National Tribune*, Sept. 28, 1911.
666 "a terrible blow . . . needed it most": Cited in the *Salt Lake Tribune*, Sept. 29, 1911.
666 Taft remained disconsolate . . . four hundred speeches: AB to Clara, Nov. 20, 1911, in AB, *Taft and Roosevelt*, Vol. 2, p. 765.
666 "by all odds" . . . most successful: AB to Clara, Sept. 8, 1911, in ibid., p. 762.

666 "dry and full . . . could almost cry": AB to Clara, Oct. 5, 1911, in ibid., p. 757.
666 "to see him . . . no sign": "The President's Journey," *Outlook*, Nov. 11, 1911, p. 606.
666 "The Taft trip has proved": *NYT*, Oct. 29, 1911.
666 he weighed 332 pounds: Manners, *TR and Will*, p. 210.
666 Butt worried constantly . . . markedly increased: AB to Clara, Nov. 20, 1911, in AB, *Taft and Roosevelt*, Vol. 2, p. 765.
666 "I had not suspected": AB to Clara, Nov. 27, 1911, in ibid., pp. 769–70.
666 "too heavy . . . three hundred pounds": WHT to Delia Torrey, Nov. 29, 1911, WHTP.
667 "I absolutely agree . . . the Democratic Party": TR to Hiram Warren Johnson, Oct. 27, 1911, in *LTR*, Vol. 7, pp. 419–20.
667 Banner headlines . . . Henry Frick: "The Government and the Steel Corporation," *Outlook*, Nov. 4, 1911, p. 547.
667 "a gigantic monopoly": *Manchester Guardian* (UK), Oct. 27, 1911.
667 "the dissolution . . . subsidiaries": *The Independent*, Nov. 2, 1911.
667 "that a desire to stop": *St. Louis* [MO] *Post-Dispatch*, Oct. 28, 1911.
667 "Roosevelt Was Deceived": Manners, *TR and Will*, p. 200.
667 "Roosevelt Fooled": Pringle, *Life and Times*, Vol. 2, p. 670.
667 "Ignorance as a Defense": *St. Louis* [MO] *Post-Dispatch*, Oct. 28, 1911.
667 "been named as a": *New York Herald*, Nov. 18, 1911.
668 "This is an official statement": *Philadelphia Record,* cited in *St. Louis Post-Dispatch*, Oct. 28, 1911.
668 "What I did": TR to Everett P. Wheeler, Oct. 30, 1911, in *LTR*, Vol. 7, p. 430.
668 "It was not a question": TR, "The Steel Corporation and the Panic of 1907," *Outlook*, Aug. 19, 1911, p. 866.
668 "was misled . . . the truth": TR, "The Trusts, the People, and the Square Deal," *Outlook*, Nov. 18, 1911, pp. 650–51.
668 "Taft was a member": TR to James R. Garfield, Oct. 31, 1911, in *LTR*, Vol. 7, pp. 430–31.
668 "should have been . . . his subordinates take": TR to Everett P. Wheeler, Oct. 30, 1911, in ibid., p. 430.
668 "never forgive . . . of the case": AB to Clara, Jan. 15, 1912, in AB, *Taft and Roosevelt*, Vol. 2, p. 813.
668 Never content to remain . . . anti-trust policy: TR, "The Trusts, the People, and the Square Deal," *Outlook*, Nov. 18, 1911, p. 649.
668 "felt the heavy hand": TR, "The Government and the Steel Corporations," *Outlook*, Nov. 4, 1911, p. 574.
668 "embarked upon . . . rolling over the trusts": *National Tribune*, Oct. 19, 1911.
669 "probably one hundred": Pringle, *Life and Times*, Vol. 2, pp. 668–69.
669 "The times have . . . old-fashioned": *National Tribune*, Oct. 19, 1911.
669 "dead letters" . . . harm to "the innocent": TR, "The Trusts, the People, and the Square Deal," *Outlook*, Nov. 18, 1911, pp. 651–52, 653, 656.
669 "Taft Wrong, Says Roosevelt": New York *Sun*, Nov. 17, 1911.
669 "Colonel Finds": *Boston Herald*, Nov. 17, 1911.
669 "Roosevelt Takes Issue": *Chicago Record-Herald*, Nov. 17, 1911.
669 "tens of thousands": TR to Charles D. Willard, Dec. 11, 1911, in *LTR*, Vol. 7, p. 454.
669 "Roosevelt's broadside": *Chicago Daily Tribune*, Nov. 18, 1911.
669 More conservative Republicans . . . position on trusts: Mowry, *Theodore Roosevelt and the Progressive Movement*, pp. 192–93.
670 "a striking revival": *NYT*, Dec. 22, 1911.
670 "a thousand questions": *National Tribune*, Dec. 21, 1911.
670 "bringing [him] forward . . . to the surface": TR to William Bailey Howland, Dec. 23, 1911, in *LTR*, Vol. 7, p. 466.
670 "in an almost astonishing fashion": James R. Garfield to Gifford Pinchot, Nov. 28, 1911, Garfield Papers.
670 A poll taken . . . Taft and La Follette: *New Castle* [PA] *News*, Dec. 8, 1911.
670 Nebraska Republicans . . . primary ballot: *NYT*, Dec. 22, 1911.
670 "Events in all parts": *New Castle* [PA] *News*, Dec. 8, 1911.
670 "a flat-footed denial . . . anxious days": *National Tribune*, Dec. 21, 1911.
670 "The Autobiography of an Insurgent": RSB, Notebook, September [n.d.], 1911, RSB Papers.
670 "almost unanimous" endorsement: James R. Garfield, Diary, Oct. 16, 1911, Garfield Papers.
670 "the logical . . . and prolonged applause": *NYT*, Nov. 28, 1911.
670 La Follette found it challenging: Pinchot, *History of the Progressive Party,*, pp. 42–43.
670 "Will Roosevelt be . . . slip in": RSB, Notebook, Nov. 26, 1911, RSB Papers.
671 "encouraging La Follette . . . Liberal Movement": JSP to WAW, Jan. 5, 1912, White Papers.
671 "like a war horse . . . again in January": RSB, Notebook, Dec. 8, 1911, RSB Papers.
671 "absolutely plain . . . into the game": RSB to RLF, Dec. 8, 1911, La Follette Papers.
671 "Now, Butt . . . but do it soon": AB to Clara, Dec. 4, 1911, in AB, *Taft and Roosevelt*, Vol. 2, p. 776.

CHAPTER TWENTY-SEVEN: "My Hat Is in the Ring"

Page

672 "The Colonel is . . . of ultimate results": LS to Allen H. Suggett, Jan. 24, 1912, in LS et al., eds., *Letters of Lincoln Steffens*, Vol. 1, p. 287.
672 "seek the nomination": TR to Frank Andrew Munsey, Jan. 16, 1912, in *LTR*, Vol. 7, p. 479.
672 "a genuine popular . . . do the job": TR to Herbert Spencer Hadley, Jan. 23, 1912, in ibid., p. 489.
673 he would "of course" accept: TR to Henry Beach Needham, Jan. 9, 1912, in ibid., p. 475.
673 "Events have been moving": TR to Chase Salmon Osborn, Jan. 18, 1912, in ibid., p. 484.
673 If the governors . . . announcement of his candidacy: Ibid., p. 485.
673 "not for his sake": Harold Howland, *Theodore Roosevelt and His Times: A Chronicle of the Progressive Movement* (New Haven: Yale University Press, 1921), p. 210.
673 "the living embodiment . . . a single candidate": *NYT*, Jan. 2, 1912.

673 La Follette was furious: Nancy C. Unger, *Fighting Bob La Follette: The Righteous Reformer* (Chapel Hill: University of North Carolina Press, 2000), p. 201.
673 "Carnegie Hall . . . never lost it": Cited in Belle Case La Follette and Fola La Follette, *Robert M. La Follette, June 14, 1855–June 18, 1925* (New York: The Macmillan Company, 1953), Vol. 1, pp. 388–90.
673 They worried . . . divide the progressive vote: Pinchot, *History of the Progressive Party, 1912–1916*, p. 133.
673 "Roosevelt or bust!": *Chicago Tribune*, Jan. 11, 1912; La Follette, *La Follette's Autobiography*, p. 579.
673 "a stalking horse": Pinchot, *History of the Progressive Party, 1912–1916*, p. 133.
674 "When Roosevelt left . . . better than 1916": *NYT*, Oct. 4, 1912.
674 "painful" conference . . . to "fight alone": Pinchot, *History of the Progressive Party, 1912–1916*, p. 134.
674 "When I gave": Unger, *Fighting Bob La Follette*, p. 202.
674 "Senator La Follette": *Logansport* [IN] *Pharos-Tribune*, Jan. 30, 1912.
674 doctors diagnosed . . . tuberculosis . . . the morning after the banquet: La Follette and La Follette, *Robert M. La Follette*, Vol. 1, pp. 399, 404; Unger, *Fighting Bob La Follette*, pp. 202–3.
674 Wilson had earlier delivered . . . charming, and short: *NYT*, Oct. 21, 1917.
674 "took a great gobletful": WAW, *The Autobiography*, p. 449.
674 "money power . . . what they are told to write": La Follette, *La Follette's Autobiography*, pp. 607–8, 605.
675 "to bring together": La Follette and La Follette, *Robert M. La Follette*, Vol. 1, p. 403.
675 "frankly sick": *NYT*, Oct. 21, 1917.
675 "acid and raucous": Wister, *Roosevelt: The Story of a Friendship,* p. 300.
675 "predatory interests": *NYT*, Oct. 21, 1917.
675 "shook his fist . . . about themselves": Wister, *Roosevelt: The Story of a Friendship,* p. 300.
675 "his dagger-like forefinger . . . facts for once!": *NYT*, Oct. 21, 1917.
675 During the first two hours: *NYT*, Feb. 3, 1912.
675 As midnight approached . . . to get him to stop: Pinchot, *History of the Progressive Party, 1912–1916*, pp. 134–35.
675 "You can't drown . . . minions of the trust": *NYT*, Oct. 21, 1917.
675 "with closed eyes": Pinchot, *History of the Progressive Party, 1912–1916*, p. 135.
675 "the greatest speech . . . tragedy beyond tears": RSB, *American Chronicle*, pp. 267–68.
676 "a short rest . . . switch to Roosevelt": La Follette, *La Follette's Autobiography*, p. 610.
676 "ill health . . . progressive movement": *Washington Herald*, Feb. 19, 1912.
676 "I want to let you know": McClure to Belle Case La Follette, Feb. 6, 1912, McClure MSS.
676 "last great series . . . a few men": Lyon, *Success Story*, p. 326.
676 the "justice" it deserved: McClure to Belle Case La Follette, Feb. 6, 1912, McClure MSS.
676 "Your letter . . . you as a friend": Belle Case La Follette to McClure, Feb. 9, 1912, McClure MSS.
676 "Poor Senator La Follette": TR to John Callan O'Laughlin, Feb. 8, 1912, in *LTR*, Vol. 7, pp. 499–500.
677 "The trouble with . . . big, black cloud": AB to Clara, Dec. 19, 1911, in AB, *Taft and Roosevelt*, Vol. 2, p. 794.
677 "the whole plan . . . handicap": AB to Clara, Dec. 20, 1911, in ibid., p. 798.
677 "I hate to . . . a third term": WHT to Horace Taft, Feb. 15, 1912, WHTP (italics added).
677 "My devotion to the Colonel": AB to Clara, Jan. 13, 1912, in AB, *Taft and Roosevelt*, Vol. 2, p. 812.
677 "is so honest": AB to Clara, Dec. 19, 1911, in ibid., p. 794.
677 "A President sees . . . as Archie Butt": WHT, "Tribute to Major Butt," in Archie Butt and William Howard Taft, *Both Sides of the Shield* (Philadelphia: J. B. Lippincott Co., 1912), pp. vii, x.
678 "Delighted": AB to Clara, Jan. 27, 1912, in AB, *Taft and Roosevelt*, Vol. 2, p. 827.
678 "Go by all means . . . make you happy": Ibid.
678 "like a leaf . . . by me was significant": AB to Clara, Jan. 29, 1912, in ibid., pp. 828–29, 831, 833, 835.
678 "more bitter . . . at each other": AB to Clara, Feb. 14, 1912, in ibid., pp. 843–44.
678 "cheering spectators . . . a boisterous reception": *Marion* [OH] *Daily Mirror*, Feb. 21, 1912.
678 "more familiar than": *Evening Standard* (Ogden City, UT), Feb. 21, 1912.
678 "We Progressives believe . . . in the hands of the people": TR, "A Charter of Democracy," in *WTR*, Vol. 17, *Social Justice and Popular Rule* (New York: Charles Scribner's Sons, 1976), p. 119–20.
679 his characteristic "balanced statements": Pinchot, *History of the Progressive Party, 1912–1916*, p. 141.
679 "encourage legitimate . . . let it be *their* majority that decides": TR, "A Charter of Democracy," in *WTR*, Vol. 17, pp. 124, 125, 139, 142, 146 (italics added).
679 The "damaging effect": *NYT*, Feb. 26, 1912.
679 "a plebiscite . . . supreme jurisdiction": New York *Sun*, Feb. 22, 1912.
679 "Mr. Roosevelt's incapacity" . . . rendering his nomination impossible: Cited in *New York Tribune*, Feb. 22, 1912.
680 "Theodore has gone off": Jessup, *Elihu Root*, Vol. 2, p. 180.
680 "That was so unlike": Straus, *Under Four Administrations*, pp. 310–11.
680 "I am opposed . . . most intimate friends": *NYT*, Feb. 26, 1912.
680 "the sanctity of the judiciary": Garraty, *Henry Cabot Lodge: A Biography*, p. 287.
680 "I have had my share": TR to HCL, Feb. 28, 1912, in TR and HCL, *Selections from the Correspondence*, Vol. 2, pp. 423–24.
680 "My dear fellow": TR to HCL, Mar. 1, 1912, in *LTR*, Vol. 7, p. 515.
680 "at a gallop . . . swerved and wheeled": TR to HCL, Oct. 3, 1911, in ibid., p. 400.
680 The concussion . . . three weeks of bed rest: TR to ARC, Oct. 5, 1911, TRC.
680 "She is very much shattered": TR to William Cowles, Oct. 27, 1911, in TR, *Letters from Theodore Roosevelt to Anna Roosevelt Cowles, 1870–1918*, p. 297.
680 "Politics are hateful": EKR to Kermit Roosevelt, Feb. 11, 1912, in Morris, *EKR*, p. 376.
680 "At the worst of it": EKR to Arthur Lee, April (n.d.), 1912, in ibid., pp. 550–51.
680 "the quandary . . . sorry for any one": ARL, *Crowded Hours*, pp. 185–86.

681 "Of course you must be": TR to Nicholas Longworth, Feb. 13, 1912, in *LTR*, Vol. 7, p. 503.
681 "single-minded in enthusiasm": ARL, *Crowded Hours*, p. 186.
681 "I got furious": Cordery, *Alice*, p. 223.
681 "It is not the critic": TR, "Citizenship in a Republic: An Address at the Sorbonne, Paris, April 23, 1910," in *WTR*, Vol. 13, *American Ideals* (New York: Charles Scribner's Sons, 1926), p. 510.
681 "My hat is in the ring . . . in the contest": New York *Evening World*, Feb. 22, 1912.
681 "in the interests . . . unsolicited and unsought": William Ellsworth Glasscock et al. to TR, Feb. 10, 1912, in *LTR*, Vol. 7, p. 511.
681 "I deeply appreciate": TR to William Ellsworth Glasscock et al., Feb. 24, 1912, in ibid., p. 511.
682 "no signs" . . . the Columbus speech: Robert Grant to James Ford Rhodes, Mar. 22, 1912, in Elting E. Morison, ed., *The Days of Armageddon, 1914–1918*, Vol. 8 of *LTR*, pp. 1456–57.
682 "overwhelmingly . . . register that sentiment": WAW to TR, Feb. 2, 1912, White Papers.
682 "an unnecessary and possibly": Robert Grant to James Ford Rhodes, Mar. 22, 1912, in *LTR*, Vol. 8, pp. 1460–61.
682 "for the sake of his own future . . . popular, representative government?": Thayer, *Theodore Roosevelt: An Intimate Biography*, pp. 352–54.
682 "none of them . . . would have dropped out": Robert Grant to James Ford Rhodes, Mar. 22, 1912, *LTR*, Vol. 8, p. 1457.
682 "with conditions . . . been wrong yourself": AB to Clara, Feb. 25, 1912, in AB, *Taft and Roosevelt*, Vol. 2, p. 850.
683 tossing in his bed that night unable to sleep: AB to Clara, Feb. 26, 1912, in ibid., p. 851.
683 "like a steam engine . . . shipshape condition": AB to Clara, Feb. 23, 1912, in ibid., pp. 847–48.
683 "It seems to me": AB to Clara, Feb. 26, 1912, in ibid., p. 851.
683 "He would not hear of it": AB to Kitty, Feb. 27, 1912, in ibid., pp. 851–52.
683 "to leave . . . for the nomination": AB to Clara, Feb. 23, 1912, in ibid., pp. 847–48.
683 "By a strange coincidence": *Washington Post*, Feb. 15, 1912.
683 The Taft men . . . the Munsey Building: *Indianapolis Star*, Feb. 16, 1912.
683 "a very pleasant and winning": Davis, *Released for Publication*, p. 267.
683 Taft selected . . . William Brown McKinley: *California Outlook* (Los Angeles), Feb. 17, 1912.
683 "the sinews of war": *Indianapolis Star*, Feb. 16, 1912.
683 "to devote himself": Gardner, *Departing Glory*, p. 226.
683 And once again, Charley Taft . . . his brother's campaign: *Mt. Sterling* [KY] *Advocate*, June 19, 1912.
684 "without indulging . . . judicial decisions": *Waterloo* [IA] *Daily Reporter*, Feb. 22, 1912.
684 "stirred up . . . atmosphere wonderfully": WHT to Charles P. Taft, Feb. 28, 1912, WHTP.
684 "when all this turmoil": Pringle, *Theodore Roosevelt: A Biography*, p. 556.
684 "the momentary passions . . . of the temple": *NYT*, Feb. 13, 1912.
684 "the ark of the covenant": "The Ark of the Covenant," *Outlook*, April 20, 1912, p. 847.
684 "the axe at the foot": *Washington Post*, Mar. 9, 1912.
684 "genuine ovation . . . extravagant expressions": WHT to Charles P. Taft, Mar. 20, 1912, WHTP.
684 "Taft has behaved . . . overwhelming and bitter": Robert Grant to James Ford Rhodes, Mar. 22, 1912, in *LTR*, Vol. 8, pp. 1460–61.
684 When the election year opened . . . the direct primary: Sullivan, *Our Times*, Vol. 4, p. 494.
684 Fearful that the region's . . . rather than straight Taft victories: Gardner, *Departing Glory*, pp. 228–29.
685 "absolutely sure . . . influence any man": TR to Ormsby McHarg, Mar. 4, 1912, in *LTR*, Vol. 7, p. 516.
685 "the worst riots": *Washington Herald*, April 12, 1912.
685 "despite the frantic . . . jeering at their foes": *NYT*, April 12, 1912.
685 "clubs and baseball bats": *Jasper* [IN] *Weekly Courier*, Mar. 22, 1912.
685 "rode down . . . dynamite explosions": *NYT*, Jan. 24, 1912.
685 in case "any chicanery" occurred: Mowry, *Theodore Roosevelt and the Progressive Movement*, p. 232.
686 "all-night session . . . dropped dead": *El Paso* [TX] *Herald*, Mar. 15, 1912.
686 his "hope that so far": TR to William Ellsworth Glasscock et al., Feb. 24, 1912, in *LTR*, Vol. 7, p. 511.
686 "sluggishly moving cause . . . crusade": Sullivan, *Our Times*, Vol. 4, p. 492.
686 Get the Direct . . . "people demand it": Ibid., pp. 492–93.
686 "no objection at all": WHT to Horace Taft, Mar. 7, 1912, WHTP.
686 "Legislatures are being": *Washington Times*, Mar. 7, 1912.
686 "I do not favor changes": *Washington Herald*, Mar. 8, 1912.
686 "only keep my people": WHT to Horace Taft, Mar. 7, 1912, WHTP.
687 "waved his hand . . . He's all right!": *NYT*, Mar. 21, 1912; TR to Joseph Moore Dixon, Mar. 21, 1912, in *LTR*, Vol. 7, p. 511.
687 "The great . . . fundamentally unworthy": TR, "The Right of the People to Rule: An Address at Carnegie Hall, New York City, March 20 . . ." *Outlook*, Mar. 23, 1912, pp. 618, 620.
687 "ridicule" . . . principles of American government: *NYT*, Mar. 21, 1912.
687 "our government is . . . rule of all the people": TR, "The Right of the People to Rule," *Outlook*, Mar. 23, 1912, pp. 621, 625.
687 As spring commenced . . . finally set for March 26: *Washington Times*, Mar. 27, 1912.
688 the *Chicago Tribune* led a successful campaign: Davis, *Released for Publication*, p. 273.
688 "had his fighting . . . then on another": Unger, *Fighting Bob La Follette*, pp. 215–16.
688 "Today's primary crucial": *Washington Post*, Mar. 19, 1912.
688 the "very bad news": ARL Diary, Mar. 19, 1912, ARL Papers.
688 Though Taft garnered: Unger, *Fighting Bob La Follette*, p. 216.
688 "the East will construe": TR to William Franklin Knox, Mar. 12, 1912, in *LTR*, Vol. 7, p. 525.

688 "The small vote count": *Washington Post*, Mar. 20, 1912.
688 Taft could not anticipate . . . advocacy for reciprocity: *Washington Post*, Mar. 19, 1912.
688 "In a nutshell": *Washington Post*, Mar. 20, 1912.
688 "first trial of the new primary law": *Atlanta Constitution*, Mar. 27, 1912.
688 "They are stealing": Gardner, *Departing Glory*, p. 231.
688 "an entire breakdown": *Atlanta Constitution*, Mar. 27, 1912.
688 "the indisputable fact": *New York Tribune*, Mar. 28, 1912.
689 "in a fighting mood . . . cry of fraud": *NYT*, Mar. 27, 1912.
689 "had cheated . . . days of Tweed": New York *Sun*, Mar. 28, 1912.
689 "should be sorry . . . since the Civil War": *Chicago Daily Tribune*, Mar. 28, 1912.
689 "As an American citizen": *Decatur* [IL] *Daily Review*, April 8, 1912.
689 "Easter came": ARL, *Crowded Hours*, p. 190.
689 "carrying every district . . . to get aboard it": Davis, *Released for Publication*, p. 280.
689 "a stinging rebuke": TR to Joseph Medill McCormick, April 10, 1912, in *LTR*, Vol. 7, p. 533.
689 "We slugged them": *Washington Times*, April 10, 1912.
689 "too good . . . happy I am": ARL Diary, April 9, 1912, ARL Papers.
689 "given his campaign . . . in Pennsylvania": WHT to Howard Hollister, April 9, 1912, WHTP.
690 "for turning the . . . a few hours rest": *Washington Times*, April 14, 1912.
690 "One of the burdens . . . his mendacity": WHT to Horace Taft, April 16, 1912, WHTP.
690 "I wish . . . does another lick": Horace Taft to WHT, April 16, 1912, WHTP.
690 "The stampede . . . into the ring": *Pittsburgh Press*, April 15, 1912.
690 "Of course, Pennsylvania . . . with a knife": John Callan O'Laughlin to TR, April 14, 1912, John Callan O'Laughlin Papers, Manuscript Division, LC [hereafter O'Laughlin Papers].
690 "anxious to be home": Butt to WHT [n.d.], included in letter from Edward Butt to WHT, Oct. 17, 1918, cited in Anthony, *Nellie Taft*, p. 335.
691 "held afloat . . . slowly crawling": *Washington Times*, April 15, 1912.
691 "all onboard . . . no definite information": *NYT*, April 16, 1912.
691 over seven hundred survivors, mainly women and children: *New York Tribune*, April 16, 1912.
691 "regret that Major Butt's name": *Washington Times*, April 16, 1912; telegram from P. A. S. Franklin to President William H. Taft, April 16, 1912, WHTP.
691 "Even with the list": *Washington Post*, April 17, 1912.
691 "news of the disaster": *Washington Post*, April 16, 1912.
691 "greatly depressed": *Washington Post*, April 19, 1912.
691 "his loss as if he had been": *Washington Times*, April 19, 1912.
691 "I miss him every minute": WHT to Mabel Boardman, April 22, 1912, WHTP.
692 "In my own grief . . . close more-than-friend": Marian Thayer to WHT, April 21, 1912, in Hugh Brewster, *Gilded Lives, Fatal Voyage: The Titanic's First-Class Passengers and Their World* (New York: Crown, 2012), pp. 309–10.
692 "A slight rocking of the ship": Marshall Everett, ed., *The Story of the Wreck of the Titanic: Eyewitness Accounts from 1912* (Mineola, NY: Dover Books, 2011), p. 21.
692 "The captain says": Brewster, *Gilded Lives, Fatal Voyage*, p. 167.
692 "the real leader": *Narka* [KS] *News*, April 26, 1912.
692 "My last view . . . every sacrifice made": *Washington Times*, April 19, 1912.
692 "paid tribute . . . loved him sincerely": *NYT*, April 20, 1912.
693 "I can't believe it": ARL Diary, April 16 & 17, 1912, ARL Papers.
693 "Everybody knew Archie" . . . and could not finish: *NYT*, May 6, 1912.
693 "a rush of activities . . . open fire": *Indianapolis Star*, April 21, 1912.
693 "to get down into the ring": WHT to J. C. Hemphill, April 12, 1912, WHTP.
693 "explode a bomb": *NYT*, April 23, 1912.
693 "all night . . . some of his advisers": *NYT*, April 24, 1912.
693 "Frightful": *NYT*, April 23, 1912.
693 "against the accusations": WHT, "Address at Palmer, Mass., April 25, 1912," WHTP.
693 "greatly admired and loved": WHT, "Address at West Brookfield, Mass., April 25, 1912," WHTP.
693 "This wrenches my soul": *NYT*, April 25, 1912.
694 "the cause of constitutionalism": WHT, "Address at Palmer, Mass., April 25, 1912," WHTP.
694 When he arrived at South Station . . . revitalized his supporters: *Chester* [PA] *Times*, April 26, 1912.
694 "Mr. Roosevelt . . . a square deal": *NYT*, April 26, 1912.
694 "throwing aside . . . Theodore Roosevelt": *Lowell* [MA] *Sun*, April 26, 1912.
694 "our Government is . . . danger of a third presidential term": *NYT*, April 26, 1912.
694 "is convinced that" . . . be completed in four years: WHT, "Address at Boston, Mass., April 26, 1912," WHTP.
694 "We are left . . . why not later?": *NYT*, April 26, 1912.
695 "loudly cheered . . . storm of endorsement": *Lowell* [MA] *Sun*, April 26, 1912.
695 "He had cause": Pringle, *Life and Times*, Vol. 2, p. 781.
695 Informed that evening . . . being taken to Halifax: New York *Sun*, April 26, 1912.
695 "to scrutinize . . . recovering": *Atlanta Constitution*, April 26, 1912.
695 "slumped over . . . began to weep": Pringle, *Life and Times*, Vol. 2, pp. 781–82.
695 "If they are anxious": *NYT*, April 25, 1912.
695 "the crowd was keyed up": *Boston Post*, April 27, 1912.
695 "Hit him between the eyes!": Sullivan, *Our Times*, Vol. 4, p. 485.
695 "merciless denunciation": *NYT*, April 27, 1912.

695 "howled with delight": *Boston Daily Globe*, April 27, 1912.

695 "Taft has not only been . . . attitude toward me": *NYT*, April 27, 1912.

695 "This is our first . . . but a mob": *NYT*, April 28, 1912.

696 "rival matinees": *Washington Times*, May 14, 1912.

696 "puzzlewit . . . fathead": TR to Nicholas Longworth, May 9, 1912, in *LTR*, Vol. 7, p. 541n.

696 "You'd suppose there was not": *El Paso* [TX] *Herald*, May 13, 1912.

696 Robert La Follette . . . after a surprisingly good showing: *Bakersfield* [OH] *Morning Echo*, May 15, 1912.

696 focusing most of his ire: *Washington Herald*, May 13, 1912.

696 "the spectacle of a President": New York *Sun*, May 15, 1912.

696 "It is about as painful . . . courage to do so": WHT to Delia Torrey, May 12, 1912, WHTP.

696 "He is having": *Cleveland Plain Dealer*, May 16, 1912.

696 "settled the contest . . . to beat us": *Emporia* [KS] *Gazette*, May 21, 1912.

696 In nine of the thirteen states: "Appendix B: Republic Primary Results, 1912," in Lewis L. Gould, *Four Hats in the Ring: The 1912 Election and the Birth of Modern American Politics* (Lawrence: University Press of Kansas, 2008), p. 190.

696 "I have had so many": WHT to Horace Taft, May 29, 1912, WHTP.

CHAPTER TWENTY-EIGHT: "Bosom Friends, Bitter Enemies"

Page

697 "A month ago": *The Times* (London), May 23, 1912.

697 "the most exciting . . . never before": *Washington Times*, June 6, 1912.

698 "Each side makes": *New York Tribune*, June 16, 1912.

698 "not dare to oppose": TR to T. R. McAnally, May 24, 1912, in *LTR*, Vol. 7, p. 548.

698 The president, however, had far . . . to win at Chicago: WHT to William Worthington, May 29, 1912, WHTP.

698 "No man in this city": *New York Tribune*, June 16, 1912.

698 "the lawyers and witnesses": New York *Sun*, April 21, 1912.

698 "some contests . . . frighten or bulldoze": WHT to William Worthington, May 29, 1912, WHTP.

698 "the contestants had failed": *Washington Times*, June 7, 1912.

698 all too "familiar": Ibid.

699 "been sent to the penitentiary": *Washington Times*, June 10, 1912.

699 "neither justice nor logic": John A. Gable, *The Bull Moose Years: Theodore Roosevelt and the Progressive Party* (Port Washington, NY: Kennikat Press, 1978), p. 15.

699 two-to-one and sometimes ten-to-one margins: TR, "Thou Shalt Not Steal," *Outlook*, July 13, 1912, p. 574.

699 "irregularities" . . . the committee "reversed itself": Mowry, *Theodore Roosevelt and the Progressive Movement*, p. 239.

699 Though Roosevelt's team demonstrated . . . election results: *Washington Times*, June 10, 1912.

699 Texas delegates . . . "fair play": Sidney M. Milkis, *Theodore Roosevelt, the Progressive Party, and the Transformation of American Democracy* (Lawrence: University Press of Kansas, 2009), p. 109.

699 eliminating "boss rule": Gable, *The Bull Moose Years*, p. 15.

700 gave the two San Francisco seats to Taft: *Salt Lake Tribune*, June 13, 1912.

700 "desperate measures . . . offers of money": Ibid.

700 "I dare them . . . may not be seen": *Washington Times*, June 13, 1912.

700 Roosevelt likely deserved . . . between thirty and fifty: Mowry, *Theodore Roosevelt and the Progressive Movement*, pp. 238–39.

700 "to crystallize": *Chicago Daily Tribune*, June 16, 1912.

700 Aware that time was running out . . . in person: Milkis, *Theodore Roosevelt, the Progressive Party, and the Transformation of American Democracy*, p. 110.

700 "he seemed in . . . stolen from them": *NYT*, June 15, 1912.

701 "All the information I get": *Chicago Daily Tribune*, June 15, 1912.

701 leaving Washington correspondents . . . at Chevy Chase: *New York Tribune*, June 8, 9, 13 & 15, 1912.

701 "an undeniable admission": *Chicago Daily Tribune*, June 15, 1912.

701 "absolutely necessary": Ibid.

701 "the last hope of a lost cause": *New York Tribune*, June 16, 1912.

701 "Mr. Roosevelt's departure": *Chicago Daily Tribune*, June 15, 1912.

701 "plum crazy . . . to show up for work": *Washington Times*, June 15, 1912.

701 cried out "thief": Manners, *TR and Will*, p. 235.

701 songs for "Teddy . . . jeers and hoots": *NYT*, June 15, 1912.

701 a special "campaign drink": Manners, *TR and Will*, p. 235.

701 waving "Teddy" flags . . . at the railway yards: *New York Tribune*, June 16, 1912.

701 "The sight of the Colonel . . . to its bosom": Sullivan, *Our Times*, Vol. 4, pp. 505–6.

701 "football tactics": *NYT*, June 16, 1912.

702 "His appearance was . . . steal anything": Ibid.

702 "Give it to 'em . . . Knock 'em out": New York *Sun*, June 16, 1912.

702 "The receiver of stolen": Manners, *TR and Will*, p. 237.

702 "The people will win": *Washington Times*, June 16, 1912.

702 "to stand up . . . like a bull moose": New York *Sun*, June 16, 1912.

702 "to gore his antagonist": *Cedar Rapids* [IA] *Republican*, June 1, 1912.

702 "He is essentially": Elihu Root to E. S. Martin, Mar. 9, 1912, in Jessup, *Elihu Root*, Vol. 2, p. 180.

702 The bull moose icon: Sullivan, *Our Times*, Vol. 4, pp. 506–7.

702 "put in one of": *New York Tribune*, June 16, 1912.

702 "magnetism . . . most desired to see": *Chicago Daily Tribune*, June 17, 1912.
702 "the largest theater" . . . seated only 4,200: *Chicago Daily Tribune*, June 17, 1912.
703 "ingenious" schemes . . . "avalanche of applause": *Chicago Daily Tribune*, June 18, 1912.
703 "the most moving speech": Sullivan, *Our Times*, Vol. 4, p. 508.
703 "one of the most dramatic": *Washington Times*, June 18, 1912.
703 "convinced that Mr. Taft . . . we battle for the Lord": TR, "The Case against the Reactionaries," in *WTR*, Vol. 17, pp. 205–6, 212–13, 228, 231.
703 "There is no question . . . that make nominations": WAW, Literary MSS, 1912, White Papers.
704 "extraordinary preparations" . . . 12,000 people: *National Tribune* (Washington, DC), June 23, 1912.
704 "Passions have been . . . hotel lobbies": *Washington Post*, June 18, 1912.
704 "Whatever happens": TR to Horace Taft, June 18, 1912, WHTP.
704 "If I am nominated": WHT to Felix Agnus, Feb. 29, 1912, WHTP.
704 "I may go down": WHT to William Worthington, May 29, 1912, WHTP.
704 Before convening his cabinet . . . his campaign team: *New York Tribune*, June 19, 1912.
704 McKinley and Charles Hilles . . . the temporary chair: Sullivan, *Our Times*, Vol. 4, p. 514. Technically, as Sullivan points out, the presiding officer was known as the temporary chair until the final day of the convention, when he became the permanent chair; but to avoid confusion, I am following Sullivan's lead by calling him the permanent chair, or the chair, throughout the story of the convention.
704 "most learned . . . and sure": WAW, *The Autobiography*, pp. 469–70.
704 "the ablest man": Sullivan, *Our Times*, Vol. 4, p. 516.
704 "Mr. Root stands": Ibid., p. 498.
705 "were cruel thrusts": Jessup, *Elihu Root*, Vol. 2, p. 202.
705 "think over whether . . . to stand together": TR to Joseph Dixon, May 25, 1912, in *LTR*, Vol. 7, p. 548.
705 "I assume that . . . a united front": TR to Francis McGovern, May 28, 1912, in ibid., p. 548n.
705 hoping that "state pride" would lead: Sullivan, *Our Times*, Vol. 4, p. 515.
705 At noon . . . "honestly elected" Roosevelt delegates: *New York Tribune*, June 19 & 21, 1912.
705 Three years later . . . "emphasis and energy": Nicholas Butler to WHT, Nov. 12, 1915, Pringle Papers.
705 "was not in order": *New York Tribune*, June 19, 1912.
705 Rosewater allowed . . . out of order: *NYT*, June 19, 1912.
705 Root's nomination . . . the Roosevelt side: Ibid.
706 "not with La Follette's consent": Gardner, *Departing Glory*, p. 248.
706 La Follette . . . would strike no deal whatsoever: *New York Tribune*, June 19, 1912.
706 "We'll heed not": Ibid.
706 "to see Senator Root": *New York Tribune*, June 15, 1912.
706 "Receiver of stolen goods!": Gardner, *Departing Glory*, p. 248.
706 "the sweating wrathful . . . did not flicker": WAW, *The Autobiography*, p. 470.
706 "loudly cheered him": *New York Tribune*, June 19, 1912.
706 their astonishing record: *The Day Book* (Chicago), June 19, 1912.
706 Returning to the White House . . . Francis McGovern: *Washington* (DC) *Herald*, June 19, 1912.
706 "It was his duty" . . . the crowd "fell silent": *NYT*, June 19, 1912.
707 "remained in seclusion . . . stand by him": Ibid.
707 "electricity filled" . . . debate on the motion: *Washington Times*, June 19, 1912.
707 "no knowledge . . . upon these contests": *NYT*, June 20, 1912.
707 "consent to refer . . . Hadley, the next": Ibid.
707 "radiant and infectious . . . falling in line": Sullivan, *Our Times*, Vol. 4, pp. 528, 530.
708 "no man can . . . he holds his seat": RNC and Milton W. Blumenberg, *Official Report of the Proceedings of the Fifteenth Republican National Convention, Held in Chicago, Illinois, June 18, 19, 20, 21 and 22, 1912* (New York: Tenny Press, 1912), p. 160.
708 Outnumbered thirty-one . . . seating decisions: *NYT*, June 20, 1912.
708 "We are requested . . . square deal here": *Chicago Daily Tribune*, June 19, 1912.
708 "prospect of leaving . . . money and effort": *New York Tribune*, June 20, 1912.
708 "the moment when . . . 'we will see you through' ": Pinchot, *History of the Progressive Party, 1912–1916*, p. 165.
709 "My fortune": Stoddard, *As I Knew Them*, p. 306.
709 "lead a fight . . . conceal their emotions": *Washington Times*, June 21, 1912.
709 "jammed to its fullest capacity": *NYT*, June 21, 1912.
709 Minutes after . . . was not ready: *Chicago Daily Tribune*, June 20, 1912.
709 A later four o'clock session . . . the following day: *NYT*, June 21, 1912.
709 spectators "gathered in knots": *Washington Times*, June 20, 1912.
709 "to withdraw . . . honestly elected" delegates: *New York Tribune*, June 21, 1912.
709 "politicking . . . like a cipher . . . shorn": Lyon, *Success Story*, p. 341.
709 his accumulated debt . . . "unhorsed": Ibid., pp. 334–37.
710 "A storm of hisses . . . steamroller some more!": *NYT*, June 21, 1912.
710 "a thousand toots": WAW, *The Autobiography*, pp. 471–72.
710 "caught the spirit . . . Choo Choo": *Evening Standard* (Ogden City, UT), June 22, 1912.
710 "All aboard . . . a great uproar": *NYT*, June 21, 1912.
710 "a chorus of shrieks": *Evening Standard*, June 22, 1912.
710 "The Convention has now . . . this successful fraud": TR to the Republican National Convention, June 22, 1912, in *LTR*, Vol. 7, pp. 562–63.
710 "to keep track of them all": Manners, *TR and Will*, p. 262.

710 It was nearly 7:30 p.m. . . . with 561 votes: *NYT*, June 22, 1912.
711 "present but not" . . . Justice Hughes 2: *New York Tribune*, June 22, 1912.
711 "no one would have suspected": *Washington Herald*, June 23, 1912.
711 the fourteen-year-old was "all grin": Ibid.
711 "electric" excitement . . . "joy of a boy": *San Francisco Chronicle*, June 19, 1908.
711 both the president and first lady . . . almost impossible: WHT to Mabel Boardman, June 23, 1912, WHTP.
711 "No Republican convention": *New York Tribune*, June 23, 1912.
711 "I am not afraid": WHT to Fred Carpenter, June 27, 1912, WHTP.
711 "the absolute independence": *New York Tribune*, June 23, 1912.
711 "a real menace": WHT to Fred Carpenter, June 27, 1912, WHTP.
711 "at stake . . . the chief conservator": *New York Tribune*, June 23, 1912.
711 "preserved the party organization": WHT to Fred Carpenter, June 27, 1912, WHTP.
711 A "mass meeting": Davis, *Released for Publication*, p. 314.
711 Great applause greeted Edith . . . "Here comes Texas": *New York Tribune*, June 23, 1912.
712 "We came here . . . there was pandemonium": Ibid.
712 "find out . . . my heartiest support": *Washington Times*, June 23, 1912.
712 "The only question now": Sullivan, *Our Times*, Vol. 4, p. 531.
713 "I'm in the fight": *New York Tribune*, June 28, 1912.
713 "Pop's been praying": Quoted in *NYT*, July 4, 1912.
713 "first skirmish . . . you of Chicago?": *New York Tribune*, June 26, 1912.
713 When the balloting began . . . finally secured the nomination: Gould, *Four Hats in the Ring*, pp. 92–93.
713 "the country was standing": WAW, *The Autobiography*, p. 478.
713 "You must sometimes": *Times Dispatch* (Richmond, VA), July 3, 1912.
713 "no necessity for": *New York Tribune*, July 4, 1912.
713 "Warmest congratulations . . . join your cause": *Washington Herald*, July 22, 1912.
714 "a strong and rapidly growing": *New York Tribune*, June 29, 1912.
714 "exposing the Roosevelt fraud": *Washington Herald*, July 17, 1912.
714 "the most extravagant . . . the Harvester Trust": *New York Tribune*, June 29, 1912.
714 "taunted, laughed at": Unger, *Fighting Bob La Follette*, p. 232.
714 "If Wilson had . . . abandon them": TR to Alfred Warriner Cooley, July 10, 1912, in *LTR*, Vol. 7, p. 575.
714 "was flinching from . . . of disaster": TR to Chase Salmon Osborn, June 28, 1912, in ibid., p. 566.
714 "excellent man . . . for such action": TR to Chase Salmon Osborn, July 5, 1912, in ibid., p. 569.
714 "a call to . . . roots of privilege": *Washington Times*, July 8, 1912.
714 Senators Cummins, Hadley . . . to desert the Republican Party: *LTR*, Vol. 7, p. 573n.
714 promising instead to reform it from within: Pringle, *Theodore Roosevelt: A Biography*, pp. 565–66.
715 "I feel that Cummins": TR to John C. Kelly, July 10, 1912, in *LTR*, Vol. 7, p. 575.
715 "I greatly regret": TR to William Rockhill Nelson, July 30, 1912, in ibid., p. 583.
715 "sagging . . . courage of his followers": WHT to HHT, July 20, 1912, WHTP.
715 "utterly unscrupulous . . . public attention": WHT to HHT, July 15, 1912, WHTP.
715 "the object and purposes . . . definition of his aims": *Washington Times*, July 8, 1912.
715 "hour after hour . . . and solidity": *New York Tribune*, July 20, 1912.
715 "the greatest effort": *NYT*, Aug. 2, 1912.
715 Roosevelt took a single day . . . "tennis on his return": *Washington Herald*, July 25, 1912.
715 "simplicity . . . unusual informality": *New York Tribune*, July 31, 1912.
716 the ceremony would be held . . . four hundred persons in attendance: WHT to Frances Taft Edwards, Aug. 2, 1912, WHTP.
716 "an average of sixteen": *Washington Herald*, July 29, 1912.
716 "Roosevelt proposes . . . going to play": WHT to DCT, Aug. 1, 1912, WHTP.
716 The notification ceremony . . . "loud shouts and handclapping": *NYT*, Aug. 2, 1912.
716 "long-established . . . political conventions began": WHT and Elihu Root, *Speech of William Howard Taft Accepting the Republican Nomination for President of the United States, Together with the Speech of Notification by Senator Elihu Root, Delivered at Washington, D.C., August 1, 1912* (Washington, DC: Government Printing Office, 1912), p. 3.
716 "harping" . . . stolen the nomination: WHT to HHT, July 15, 1912, WHTP.
716 Taft accepted the nomination . . . "with the stronger and more powerful": WHT and Elihu Root, *Speech of William Howard Taft*, p. 5.
717 Asked to comment . . . Progressive Party Convention: *New York Tribune*, Aug. 2, 1912.
717 "On second thought . . . the live issues": *New York Tribune*, Aug. 3, 1912.

CHAPTER TWENTY-NINE: Armageddon

Page

718 "no man could go": *Washington* [DC] *Times*, Aug. 4, 1912.
718 "looked less like": *NYT*, Aug. 6, 1912.
718 "not a saloon-keeper": William Menkel, "The Progressives at Chicago," *American Review of Reviews* (September 1912).
719 "Instead of forcing": *NYT*, Aug. 5, 1912.
719 "great adventure . . . chance or speculation": *Boston Daily Globe*, Aug. 4, 1912.
719 "no dead places . . . in the right": Richard Harding Davis, "The Men at Armageddon," *Collier's*, Aug. 24, 1912.
719 "more, in fact": *NYT*, Aug. 2, 1912.

719 "high-minded white men": TR, "The Progressives and the Colored Man," *Outlook*, Aug. 24, 1912, p. 911.
719 "was riddled . . . a racist strategy": Gable, *The Bull Moose Years*, pp. 65–66.
719 "lily-white" delegations: *New York Tribune*, Aug. 2, 1912.
719 would "not budge": *NYT*, Aug. 6, 1912.
719 "the whole show": *NYT*, Aug. 7, 1912.
719 Once again, Chicago went . . . thousands of people: *Washington Times*, Aug. 5, 1912.
719 "My friends": Ibid.
719 "Confession of Faith": *New York Tribune*, Aug. 5, 1912.
720 "the greatest personal": *Washington* [DC] *Herald*, Aug. 7, 1912.
720 "hundreds of men . . . cast their lots together": Ernest Hamlin Abbott, "The Progressive Convention," *Outlook*, Aug. 17, 1912, pp. 858–59.
720 "battle flag . . . the plain people": *Emporia* [KS] *Gazette*, June 24, 1912.
720 Every man wore . . . around her wrist: *Washington Herald*, Aug. 6, 1912.
720 a red bandanna around: *NYT*, Aug. 7, 1912.
720 "stood smiling": *Chicago Tribune*, Aug. 7, 1912.
720 Twenty thousand voices . . . soaring melody: *NYT*, Aug. 7, 1912.
720 "sprang to their feet": Davis, "The Men at Armageddon," *Collier's*, Aug. 24, 1912.
720 "I have been fighting": *NYT*, Aug. 7, 1912.
720 When it seemed . . . he had to carry it through: Manners, *TR and Will*, p. 268.
720 "jovial smile and bright eye": *NYT*, Aug. 7, 1912.
720 "Mrs. Roosevelt shrank . . . in public life!": Davis, "The Men at Armageddon," *Collier's*, Aug. 24, 1912.
720 "At present . . . people to rule": TR, "A Confession of Faith," in *Social Justice and Popular Rule*, *WTR*, Vol. 17, pp. 257–58.
721 Though the delegates . . . the right to the vote: *NYT*, Aug. 7, 1912.
721 "In most cases": *NYT*, Aug. 6, 1912.
721 "fell on willing ears": *NYT*, Aug. 7, 1912.
721 "a living wage . . . we battle for the Lord": TR, "A Confession of Faith," in *WTR*, Vol. 17, pp. 268–69, 298–99.
721 "a purely Rooseveltian document": *Washington Herald*, Aug. 8, 1912.
721 "the first time a woman": *Chicago Tribune*, Aug. 7, 1912.
721 "wave upon wave . . . this great movement": *Washington Times*, Aug. 8, 1912.
722 "The Bull Moose party": RSB, Notebook L, Aug. 31, 1912, RSB Papers.
722 "It is odd to me . . . to forget himself": RSB, Notebook M, Aug. 8, 1912, RSB Papers.
722 Roosevelt's titanic persona . . . "obscures everything": RSB, Notebook L, Aug. 31, 1912, RSB Papers.
722 "As for me": RSB, Notebook M, Aug. 8, 1912, RSB Papers.
722 "I left Princeton . . . dared to make speeches": RSB, *American Chronicle*, pp. 273–75.
722 "a personal party" . . . an "ace" for the future: WAW, *The Autobiography*, p. 474.
722 "a cold fish . . . a fine liberal job": Ibid., p. 479.
723 "four days . . . of human welfare!": Ibid., pp. 484–85, 487–88.
723 "He seemed full . . . tornado of a man": Ibid., p. 490.
723 "It makes me crazy": IMT to Albert Boyden, Aug. 23, 1905, Ida Tarbell Papers.
723 "a thousand times": IMT to JSP, n.d., Ida Tarbell Papers.
723 "Why stop with": Harry Pratt Judson, "Mr. Roosevelt and the Third Term," *The Independent*, Mar. 28, 1912.
723 "We've got a King . . . we can do it": IMT to JSP, n.d., Ida Tarbell Papers.
723 *The American Magazine* . . . Progressive Party: RSB, Notebook L, Aug. 31, 1912, RSB Papers.
724 Months earlier . . . injured one hundred others: Robert E. Weir, *Workers in America: A Historical Encyclopedia* (Santa Barbara, CA: ABC-CLIO, 2013), p. 438.
724 an act of "social revolution": *Hawaiian Gazette* (Honolulu), July 23, 1912.
724 "It seems to me": TR to Charles D. Willard, Dec. 11, 1912, in *LTR*, Vol. 7, p. 453.
724 "Murder is murder": TR, "Murder Is Murder," *Outlook*, Dec. 16, 1911, p. 902.
724 "It looks like . . . personal, you see": LS to Allen H. Suggett, Sept. 12, 1912, in *The Letters of Lincoln Steffens*, Vol. 1, p. 308.
724 "a whirlwind campaign": *NYT*, Aug. 13, 1912.
724 "a President who is": *New York Tribune*, July 14, 1912.
724 He believed "in his heart": *NYT*, Aug. 13, 1912.
724 six justices to the bench . . . half of them Democrats: Jonathan Lurie, *William Howard Taft: The Travails of a Progressive Conservative* (New York: Cambridge University Press, 2012), p. 121.
725 "the rain to fall . . . continuance of power": *NYT*, Sept. 29, 1912.
725 "It always makes": WHT to HHT, July 22, 1912, WHTP.
725 "I couldn't if I would": *NYT*, Aug. 13, 1912.
725 "As the campaign . . . trust or confidence": WHT to HHT, Aug. 26, 1912, WHTP.
725 "I never discuss dead issues": *New York Tribune*, Aug. 18, 1912.
725 "was a dead cock": *NYT*, Sept. 18, 1912.
725 "worthy of . . . organized by theft": TR, "A Speech at Grand Forks, North Dakota, 6 September 1912," in TR and Lewis L. Gould, *Bull Moose on the Stump: The 1912 Campaign Speeches of Theodore Roosevelt* (Lawrence: University Press of Kansas, 2008), pp. 75–76.
726 "the preservation of . . . second sober thought": *NYT*, Sept. 29, 1912.
726 "new vitality . . . of the Republican Party": *NYT*, Oct. 1, 1912.
726 Well aware . . . "very improbable": TR to Arthur Hamilton Lee, Aug. 14, 1912, in *LTR*, Vol. 7, p. 598.
726 He embarked upon an unprecedented . . . solid Democratic South: *New York Tribune*, Aug. 13, 1912.

726 "deluge of travel": TR to Ethel Roosevelt, Aug. 21, 1912, TRC.
726 "a tremendous amount": Davis, *Released for Publication*, p. 345.
726 "a chance" of victory: TR to Arthur Hamilton Lee, Aug. 14, 1912, in *LTR*, Vol. 7, p. 598.
726 "I am perfectly happy": Ibid.
727 Journalists noted . . . this "boss-ridden": *Washington Times*, Aug. 17, 1912.
727 "rock-ribbed . . . what they were trying to accomplish": *NYT*, Aug. 8, 1912.
727 "My private judgment": *Washington Times*, Aug. 24, 1912.
727 He hoped to reach the public . . . his political philosophy: *NYT*, Aug. 8, 1912.
727 He had no appetite . . . boisterous crowd: August Heckscher, *Woodrow Wilson* (New York: Scribner, 1991), p. 258.
727 "I am by no means": WW to Mary A. Hulbert, Aug. 25, 1912, in Ray Stannard Baker, *Governor, 1910–1913*, Vol. 3 of *Woodrow Wilson: Life and Letters* (Garden City, NY: Doubleday, Page & Co., 1927), p. 390.
727 "I haven't a": WW to Frank P. Glass, Sept. 6, 1912, in ibid., p. 400.
727 "as far west as Colorado": *American Review of Reviews* (November 1908).
727 "had, in reality . . . skill as an orator": RSB, *Governor, 1910–1913*, p. 377.
728 "Wilson was a new . . . distance up the road": Ibid., p. 391.
728 "Suppose you choose": WW, "How Shall We Use the Government?," in WW and John Wells Davidson, *A Crossroads of Freedom: The 1912 Campaign Speeches* (New Haven, CT: Yale University Press, 1956), p. 295.
728 "very glad of the opportunity . . . fond of President Taft": *NYT*, Sept. 27, 1912.
728 "currents of air . . . the right direction": WHT to Henry Taft, Sept. 18, 1912, WHTP.
728 "probably be defeated": WHT to Gustav J. Karger, Sept. 7, 1912, Taft-Karger Corr., CMC.
728 Winning the nomination . . . a more general reverse for the party: AB to Clara, Nov. 24, 1911, in AB, *Taft and Roosevelt*, Vol. 2, p. 768.
729 "I seem to think": WHT to HHT, July 23, 1912, WHTP.
729 "I wanted him to be": HHT, *Recollections of Full Years*, p. 393.
729 "She is in a condition": WHT to Horace Taft, Nov. 1, 1912, WHTP.
729 "was going stale . . . rehashing": Davis, *Released for Publication*, p. 353.
729 "it was Wilson": Ibid., p. 360.
729 "first direct assault . . . 'Confession of Faith' ": *NYT*, Sept. 15, 1912.
729 "Mr. Wilson is fond . . . advance we have made": TR, "Address at the San Francisco Coliseum, Sept. 14, 1912," in TR and Gould, *Bull Moose on the Stump*, pp. 110–11.
730 "every railroad must": Ibid., p. 113.
730 "to use the whole power": Ibid., pp. 116–17.
730 "freedom to-day . . . fair play": WW and William Bayard Hale, *The New Freedom; A Call for the Emancipation of the Generous Energies of a People* (New York: Doubleday, Page & Co., 1913), p. 284.
730 In keeping with . . . less expansive federal government: Gould, *Four Hats in the Ring*, p. 163.
730 Roosevelt's "declaration of war": *NYT*, Sept. 15, 1912.
730 "open again the fields": John Milton Cooper, *Woodrow Wilson: A Biography* (New York: Alfred A. Knopf, 2009), p. 168.
730 While Roosevelt accepted . . . posed a problem: Ibid., p. 167.
730 "to organize the forces": Ibid., p. 168.
731 "the wealth of America . . . borders of the town": WW, "The Wealth of America: Address at Kokomo, Indiana, October 4, 1912," in Wilson and Davidson, *A Crossroads of Freedom*, p. 333.
731 "abolishing tariff favors" and "credit denials": Wilson and Hale, *The New Freedom*, p. 292.
731 "split up into a lot . . . which Mr. Taft defends": TR, "Speech at the San Francisco Coliseum, Sept. 14, 1912," in TR and Gould, *Bull Moose on the Stump*, pp. 113–14.
731 "becoming more and more plain": Davis, *Released for Publication*, p. 360.
731 "were as close as fraternal twins": Manners, *TR and Will*, p. 268.
731 "utterly incapable" . . . to declare laws passed by Congress unconstitutional: "The Socialist Party Platform: May 12, 1912," in *1900–1936*, Vol. 3 of Arthur M. Schlesinger, Jr., and Fred L. Israel, eds., *History of American Presidential Elections, 1789–1968* (New York: Chelsea House, 1971), pp. 2198, 2200–2.
732 as a bitter wind blew: Davis, *Released for Publication*, pp. 366, 368.
732 "a mammoth tent": *Chicago Daily Tribune*, Oct. 13, 1912.
732 Roosevelt insisted . . . "I want to be a good Indian": Davis, *Released for Publication*, pp. 371–72.
732 An open touring car . . . and began to strangle him: Ibid., pp. 374–76.
732 "I wasn't trying to take him": Thompson, *Presidents I've Known*, p. 148.
732 "Lynch him," "Kill him": *Washington* [DC] *Times*, Oct. 15, 1912.
732 "Bring him here . . . Turn him over to the police": Thompson, *Presidents I've Known*, p. 148.
732 "You get me to that speech . . . pain from this breathing": Davis, *Released for Publication*, pp. 378–80.
733 "It's true": Morris, *Colonel Roosevelt*, p. 245.
733 "how narrowly he had escaped" . . . but coming to a halt: Davis, *Released for Publication*, pp. 381–82.
733 Oscar Davis, standing . . . "until I have finished": Ibid., pp. 383–84.
733 "his heart was racing . . . do what you want": Morris, *Colonel Roosevelt*, pp. 245–46.
733 While Roosevelt was being examined . . . as his murderer: *Chicago Daily Tribune*, Oct. 15, 1912.
733 "to think seriously" . . . the right opportunity had never presented itself: *New York Tribune*, Oct. 15, 1912.
733 At Milwaukee Hospital . . . location of the bullet: *Washington Times*, Oct. 15, 1912.
734 "There are only three possible": Thompson, *Presidents I've Known*, p. 153.
734 "All over the room" . . . to rush to the telephones: *New York Tribune*, Oct. 15, 1912.
734 "The fight should go on": Davis, *Released for Publication*, p. 396.
734 Edith Roosevelt . . . attack on her husband: *Chicago Daily Tribune*, Oct. 15, 1912.
734 She left the theatre . . . Alexander Lambert: *Washington Times*, Oct. 15, 1912.

734 "It's the best news": *Washington Times*, Oct. 16, 1912.
734 "He has been as meek . . . I am at this moment": Thompson, *Presidents I've Known*, p. 151.
734 "outside of the rib . . . live there permanently": EKR to Kermit Roosevelt, Oct. 21, 1912, KR Papers.
734 "in absolute quiet": *Washington Post*, Oct. 20, 1912.
734 By Monday morning . . . until the train reached New York: EKR to Kermit Roosevelt, Oct. 16, 1912, KR Papers.
734 "I am in fine shape": TR to ARC, Oct. 27, 1912, in *LTR*, Vol. 7, p. 632.
734 still hoped to make one final appearance: Ibid.
735 "Encouraging reports are coming in": Ethel Roosevelt to ARC, October [n.d.], 1912, ARC Papers.
735 "The bullet that rests": *NYT*, Oct. 27, 1912.
735 "What effect the incident": WHT to Mabel Boardman, Oct. 17, 1912, WHTP.
735 "the rush of the crowd": *Chicago Daily Tribune*, Oct. 30, 1912.
735 "farewell manifesto": *NYT*, Oct. 30, 1912.
735 "looked to the excitement": New York *Sun*, Oct. 31, 1912.
735 "regained its accustomed power": *New York Tribune*, Oct. 30, 1912.
735 he was anxious to begin speaking: *Washington Post*, Oct. 31, 1912.
735 "Perhaps once in a generation . . . to spend and be spent": TR, "Address at Madison Square Garden, Oct. 30, 1912," in TR and Gould, *Bull Moose on the Stump*, pp. 187, 188, 190, 191–92.
736 "as clear as a bell . . . the old sarcasm": *NYT*, Oct. 27, 1912.
736 "good taste . . . for self-exhibition": New York *Sun*, Oct. 31, 1912.
736 President Taft sat down: Memorandum of Louis Seibold interview, Oct. 26, 1912, WHTP.
736 Taft nevertheless hoped to outpoll: WHT to Horace Taft, Nov. 1, 1912, WHTP.
736 "in excellent spirits" . . . the Associated Press: Pringle, *Life and Times*, Vol. 2, p. 837.
736 "anxious to carry out . . . the country will go on to ultimate happiness": WHT and Louis Seibold interview, Nov. 1, 1912, WHTP.
737 "minor corrections . . . my closest friend": Pringle, *Life and Times*, Vol. 2, pp. 837–38.
737 a "leisurely" route . . . the prosperous economy and local events: *San Francisco Call*, Nov. 5, 1912.
738 Upon reaching Cincinnati . . . a small dinner party: *Washington* [DC] *Herald*, Nov. 5, 1912.
738 "slept late, ate a good breakfast": *Evening World* (New York), Nov. 5, 1912.
738 At noon, he motored . . . his congressional seat: *New York Tribune*, Nov. 6, 1912.
738 "stood in line and waited": *Evening World*, Nov. 5, 1912.
738 "a busy morning . . . Bull Mooser vote": *Washington Times*, Nov. 5, 1912.
738 "a long ramble . . . and make a speech somewhere": *NYT*, Nov. 6, 1912.
738 Wilson walked to his polling place . . . "every nook and corner": RSB, *Governor, 1910–1913*, p. 407.
738 After casting his vote . . . an old friend: *NYT*, Nov. 6, 1912.
738 "was much in the nature": Ibid.
739 "an air of gloom": Ibid.; *Washington* [DC] *Herald*, Nov. 6, 1912.
739 "My dear": *Washington Times*, Nov. 6, 1912.
739 "great emotion . . . the new administration": RSB, *Governor, 1910–1913*, p. 409.
739 Wilson had achieved an immense victory . . . leaving only 41.9 percent: Gould, *Four Hats in the Ring*, pp. 174, 176.
739 "best wishes . . . guard around the house": New York *Sun*, Nov. 6, 1912.
739 "They went in . . . from the big fireplace": *NYT*, Nov. 6, 1912.
739 "Now old friends . . . That's all": *Evening World*, Nov. 6, 1912.
740 "chatted as gaily . . . from his shoulders": *Washington Herald*, Nov. 7, 1912.
740 "hopeful . . . shock of real disappointment": WHT to Horace Taft, Nov. 8, 1912, WHTP.
740 "The people of": WHT to Mrs. Buckner A. Wallingford, Jr., Nov. 9, 1912, WHTP.
740 "As I look back": WHT to Otto Bannard, Nov. 10, 1912, in Pringle, *Life and Times*, Vol. 2, p. 603.
740 "popular feeling": EKR to Kermit Roosevelt, Nov. 6, 1912, KR Papers.
740 "There is no use . . . a better showing": TR to Arthur Hamilton Lee, Nov. 5, 1912, in *LTR*, Vol. 7, p. 633.
740 "We must face": TR to Gifford Pinchot, Nov. 13, 1912, in ibid., p. 642.
740 "It was a phenomenal thing": TR to Henry White, Nov. 12, 1912, in ibid., p. 639.
741 "the leader for the time": *Evening World*, Nov. 6, 1912.
741 the core progressive belief that government . . . our natural heritage: Richard Hofstadter, *The Progressive Movement, 1900–1915* (Englewood Cliffs, NJ: Prentice-Hall, 1963), pp. 3, 4.

Epilogue

Page

743 "I hear he's leaving . . . back downstairs": *New York Tribune*, May 27, 1918.
743 After the White House, Taft had become: Frederick C. Hicks, *William Howard Taft, Yale Professor of Law & New Haven Citizen: An Academic Interlude in the Life of the Twenty-Seventh President of the United States and the Tenth Chief Justice of the Supreme Court* (New Haven: Yale University Press, 1945), pp. 1, 80.
743 he had begun work on his autobiography: Morris, *Colonel Roosevelt,* p. 256.
743 to explore the River of Doubt: Johnson and Malone, eds., *Dictionary of American Biography*, Vol. 8, p. 143.
743 and delivering scores of speeches each year: "Chronology," Appendix IV, in *LTR*, Vol. 8, pp. 1480–94.
743 He had stopped at the Blackstone Hotel: John J. Leary, *Talks with T.R., from the Diaries of John J. Leary, Jr.* (Boston: Houghton Mifflin Co., 1920), p. 200.
743 neither "cordial" nor "intimate": WHT to Gustav J. Karger, April 14, 1915, in Taft-Karger Corr., CMC.
743 "armed neutrality": WHT to Mabel Boardman, April 19, 1915, Mabel Thorp Boardman Papers, Manuscript Division, LC.
743 "How are you . . . between them": William Lyons Phelps, *Autobiography with Letters* (New York: Oxford University Press, 1939), p. 618.

743 "cementing the union": WHT to Gustav J. Karger, Sept. 26, 1915, in Taft-Karger Corr., CMC.
743 a "Big Love Feast": *Daily Capital Journal* (Salem, OR), Oct. 4, 1916.
744 "the Republican fold": *Bridgeport* [CT] *Telegram*, May 29, 1918.
744 "shook hands with": WHT to HHT, Oct. 5, 1916, WHTP.
744 "I know something . . . the dispatches": WHT to HHT, Feb. 9, 1918, WHTP.
744 The surgery to remedy . . . almost a month: Morris, *Colonel Roosevelt,* pp. 517–18.
744 "personally sent . . . by Your Message" TR telegram to WHT, Feb. 12, 1918, WHTP.
744 "sluggishness . . . after the war": TR to WHT, Mar. 4, 1918, in *LTR*, Vol. 8, p. 1294n.
744 Taft wholeheartedly concurred: WHT to TR, Mar. 11, 1918, WHTP.
744 "I have embodied . . . thought of them!": TR to WHT, Mar. 16, 1918, in *LTR*, Vol. 8, p. 1301.
744 "Theodore!" . . . erupted into applause: *New York Tribune*, May 27, 1918.
745 "T.R. and Taft's got together": Leary, *Talks with T.R.*, pp. 201–2.
745 "By Godfrey . . . splendid of Taft": Ibid., p. 204.
745 "like a pair of happy schoolboys": *New York Tribune*, May 27, 1918.
745 "Taft was beaming . . . welfare of the Nation": Leary, *Talks with T.R.*, pp. 202–3.
745 "completely renewed": TR to Henry Stimson, June 5, 1918, in *LTR*, Vol. 8, p. 1337.
745 "anyone else" . . . as long as he was needed: James Amos and John T. Flynn, "The Beloved Boss," *Collier's*, Aug. 7, 1926, p. 40.
745 "seemed better again": CRR, *My Brother*, p. 363.
745 "the warmest room" . . . *Metropolitan* magazine: Morris, *Colonel Roosevelt,* pp. 549–50.
746 "There should be . . . higgle about the matter": *New York Tribune*, Jan. 7, 1919.
746 "a happy and wonderful day": EKR to TR, Jr., Jan. 12, 1919, TRJP.
746 "as it got dusk": Ibid.
746 "sensation of depression": *New York Tribune*, Jan. 7, 1919.
746 his heart were preparing to stop: *NYT*, Jan. 7, 1919.
746 "I know it is not": EKR to KR, Jan. 12, 1919, KR and Belle Roosevelt Papers.
746 "examined him carefully": *New York Tribune*, Jan. 7, 1919.
746 "James, don't you . . . put out the light?": Amos and Flynn, "The Beloved Boss," *Collier's*, Aug. 7, 1926, p. 40.
746 Edith came to check: EKR to Kermit Roosevelt, Jan. 12, 1919, KR Papers.
746 a "peaceful slumber" . . . Theodore was dead: Amos and Flynn, "The Beloved Boss," *Collier's*, Aug. 7, 1926, p. 40.
746 "Death had to take him": Edward Renehan, Jr., *The Lion's Pride: Theodore Roosevelt and His Family in Peace and War* (New York: Oxford University Press, 1998), p. 222.
746 "brave little adventure": Finley Peter Dunne to IMT, [n.d.], IMTC.
746 Relentless money troubles: John E. Semonche, "The American Magazine, 1906–1915," *Journalism and Mass Communication Quarterly* (Winter 1963), pp. 40–42.
747 "The test of" . . . 600,000 readers: RSB, Notebook V, April 14, 1915, RSB Papers.
747 Prize contests . . . and marriage: Semonche, "The American Magazine, 1906–1915," *Journalism and Mass Communication Quarterly* (Winter 1963), p. 43.
747 "strangled by commercial considerations": RSB, Notebook V, April 14, 1915, RSB Papers.
747 White and Tarbell had been sent to Paris: IMT, *All in the Day's Work*, pp. 336–37.
747 Ray Baker was serving President Wilson: WAW, *The Autobiography*, p. 546.
747 over one hundred American correspondents: *Bridgeport* [CT] *Telegram*, Jan. 15, 1919.
747 "absolute fairness . . . intimate it was": IMT, *All in the Day's Work*, p. 350.
747 "Again and again . . . without Roosevelt in it": WAW, *The Autobiography*, p. 551.
747 "It was my father's wish": Morris, *Colonel Roosevelt,* p. 554.
748 Taft had discovered with delight: WHT to Irving Fisher, Dec. 1, 1922, WHTP.
748 "You're a dear personal friend": WHT to HHT, Jan. 9, 1919, WHTP.
748 "no pomp . . . profoundly impressive": "Theodore Roosevelt's Funeral: An Impression," *Outlook*, Jan. 22, 1919.
748 "a mound of flowers": *New York Tribune*, Jan. 9, 1919.
748 "widow's custom": Morris, *EKR*, p. 437.
748 "with all the passion": EKR to TR, June 8, 1886, Derby Papers.
748 "an isolated figure . . . from the others": *Bisbee* [AZ] *Daily Review*, Jan. 9, 1919.
748 "I want to say to you": WHT to ARC, July 26, 1921, in Pringle, *Life and Times*, Vol. 2, p. 913.
748 At noon on October 3, 1921: *Washington* [DC] *Times*, Oct. 3, 1921.
748 "as strongly as a man": HHT, *Recollections of a Full Life*, p. 263.
748 "to administer justice": "Judiciary Oath," U.S. Code, Title 28, Part 1, chap. 21, sect. 453.
748 "the famous Taft . . . greatest day of my life": *Sweetwater* [TX] *Daily Reporter*, Oct. 4, 1921.
748 "The people of the United States": *Washington Post*, Oct. 4, 1921.
749 "antiquated . . . federal courts": Allen Edgar Ragan and Harlow Lindley, *Chief Justice Taft* (Columbus: Ohio State Arch. & Hist. Soc., 1938), p. 104.
749 "great skill . . . old Senate chamber": Robert Post, "The Supreme Court Opinion as Institutional Practice: Dissent, Legal Scholarship, and Decisionmaking in the Taft Court," *Minnesota Law Review* 85 (2011), pp. 1267–68.
749 "We call you Chief Justice": Oliver Wendell Holmes et al., to WHT, Feb. 10, 1930, in Pringle, *Life and Times*, Vol. 2, p. 1079.
749 "unbreakable quality . . . but interrupted": IMT, *All in the Day's Work*, p. 406.
749 the "old Crowd": RSB to IMT, Oct. 30, 1917, IMTC.
749 "a hundred, yes a thousand": IMT to Alice and Cale Rice, Jan. 21, 1933, IMTC.
749 "saving the world": RSB to LS, April 28, 1930, RSB Papers.
749 "muck-raked never to . . . speedily corrected": RSB, Notebook LIV, [n.d.], p. 22, RSB Papers.

750 how "hard-boiled" the world really was: RSB to LS, April 28, 1930, RSB Papers.
750 "the star . . . the publishing business": IMT to Viola Roseboro, Nov. 6, 1937, IMTC.
750 His "old fire": IMT to JSP, Oct. 6, 1937, IMTC.
750 "We sat enthralled": IMT, *All in the Day's Work*, p. 406.
750 Tarbell wrote . . . "flame steady and lasting": IMT to JSP, Oct. 6, 1937, IMTC.
750 "that wonderful adventure . . . a mission and a call": JSP to RSB, Dec. 20, 1920, RSB Papers.

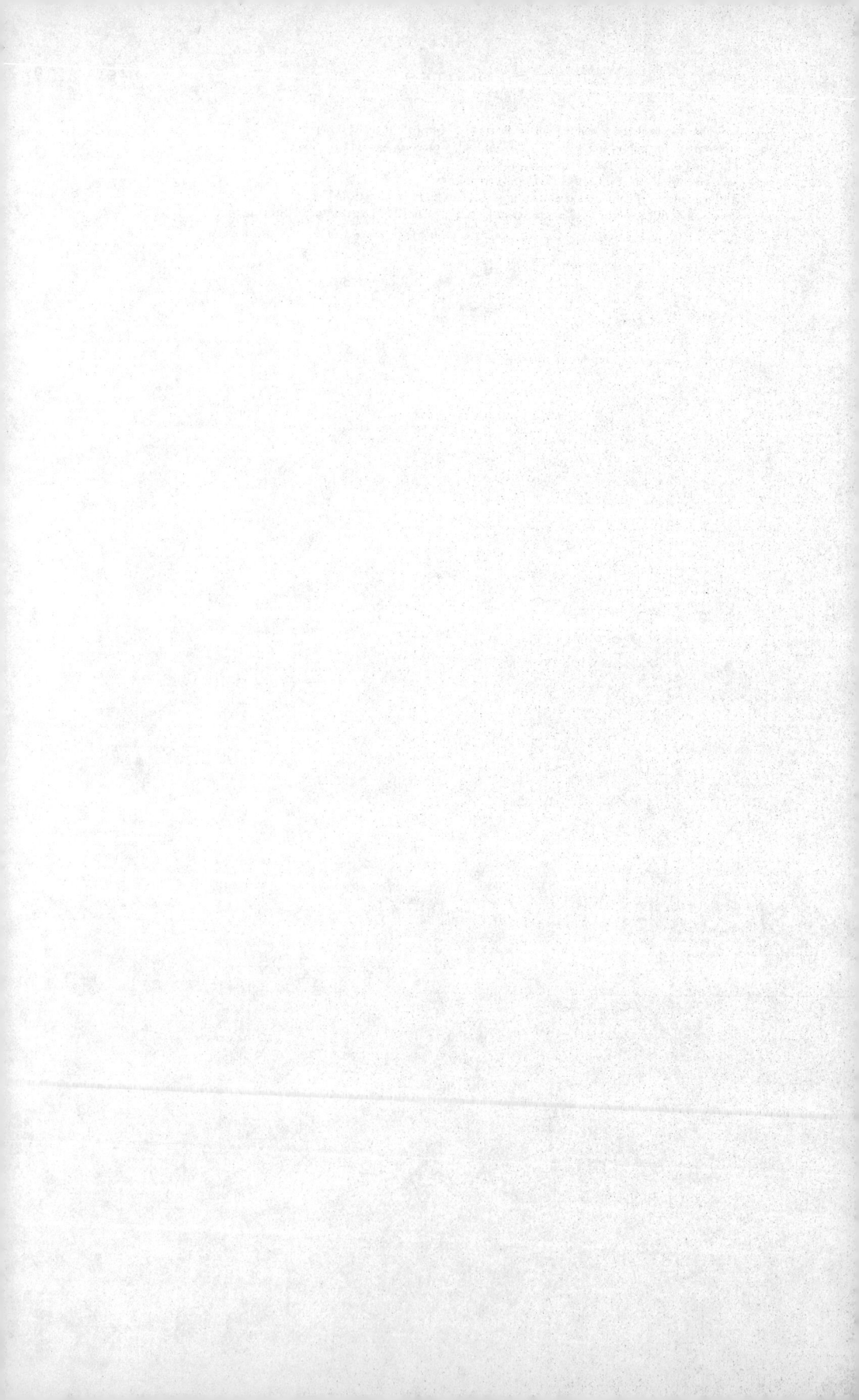

ILLUSTRATION CREDITS 

Numbers in bold roman type refer to illustrations in the inserts; numbers in bold italics refer to book pages.

The Bancroft Library, University of California, Berkeley: **15**

Culver Pictures, Inc.: **54**

Courtesy of the Ida M. Tarbell Collection, Pelletier Library, Allegheny College: ***324***, **19**, **24**, **43**

Kansas State Historical Society: **21**

Library of Congress, Prints and Photographs Division: ***87***, LC-DIG-hec-15220; ***239 (right)***, PR 13 CN 1980: 167 Container (AA) 3; ***557***, LC-DIG-hec-15221; ***583***, LC-USZ62-121727; **25**, LC-USZ62-132301; **30**, PR 13 CN 1980: 167 Container (AA) 4; **38**, LC-DIG-ppmsca-26036; **40**, LC-USZ62-48773; **41**, LC-USZ62-48769; **42**, LC-USZ62-95893; **44**, LC-USZ627757; **49**, LC-USZ62-7634; **50**, LC-DIG-hec-01006; **51**, LC-USZ62-95701; **53**, LC-DIG-hec-01007; **55**, LC-USZ62-53971; **56**, LC-USZ62-10309; **58**, LC-DIG-hec-15169; **61**, LC-DIG-hec-07123; **68**, LC-DIG-hec-15127; *back endpaper*, LC-USZ62-32737

Courtesy, The Lilly Library, Indiana University, Bloomington, Indiana: ***157***, **16**, **17**, **18**, **20**, **66**

Courtesy of Mark Rohling and the Taft Museum of Art, Cincinnati, Ohio: **47**

Theodore Roosevelt Collection, Houghton Library, Harvard University [photographs]: ***1***, TRC-PH-1 560.62; ***21 (left)***, TRC-PH-2 520.11-003; ***109***, TRC-PH-2 570.R67ed-003; ***134***, TRC-PH-2 520.21-001; ***239 (left)***, TRC-PH-2 560.41-020; ***385***, TRC-PH-4 560.52 1906-072; ***401***, Roosevelt R500.P69a-088; ***655***, Roosevelt R560.6.C71; **1**, TRC-PH-2 520.12-003; **4**, TRC-PH-4 560.11-018; **5**, TRC-PH-2 520.11-009; **6**, MS Am 1541.9 (136); **7**, TRC-PH-1 570.1 R67r 1878; **8**, *87M-102; **10**, TRC-PH-1 520.13-003a; **11**, TRC-PH-2 560.14-149; **12**, 520.14-001; **14**, TRC-PH-1 560.22-001; **22**, TRC-PH-2 520.23-007; **27**, TRC-PH-2 560.41-066; **32**, TRC-PH-1 560.41-057; **33**, Roosevelt R500.P69a-050; **34**, TRC-PH-1 560.51 1902-156; **35**, TRC-PH-1 560.51 1903-115; **36**, TRC-PH-1 560.52 1905-002; **37**, TRC-PH-5 560.52 1905-019a; **39**, TRC-PH-3 541.51-001; **48**, TRC-PH-1 560.52 1909-017; **52**, Roosevelt R500.P69a-064; **57**, Roosevelt R500.R67-056; **59**, TRC-PH-2 560.6; **60**, Roosevelt R560.6.C71; **62**, TRC-PH-1 560.7; **64**, TRC-PH-1 560.7; **65**, TRC-PH-1 560.7; **67**, TRC-PH-2 541.9-010; *front endpaper*, TRC-PH-1 560.52 1905-012

Theodore Roosevelt Collection, Houghton Library, Harvard University [political cartoons]: ***203***, TRC-PH-1 560.23; ***279***, ***348***, ***366***, ***444***, ***467***, ***497***, ***516***, ***534***, ***605***, ***634***, ***672***, ***697***, ***718***; **13**, **23**, **31**, **45**, **46**, **63**, preceding illustrations TRC-CT-1

Courtesy of the University of Chicago Library: ***50***, **26**

Courtesy of the U.S. Army Heritage and Education Center: **29**

Courtesy of the William Howard Taft National Historic Site, National Park Service: ***21 (right)***, **2**, **3**, **9**, **28**

INDEX

Page numbers in *italics* refer to illustrations.

Also by Doris Kearns Goodwin

THE BULLY PULPIT

TEAM OF RIVALS

WAIT TILL NEXT YEAR

THE FITZGERALDS AND THE KENNEDYS

LYNDON JOHNSON AND THE AMERICAN DREAM

No Ordinary Time has won the following awards:

Pulitzer Prize for History
Harold Washington Literary Award
New England Bookseller Association Award
The Ambassador Book Award
The Washington Monthly Political Book Award

NO ORDINARY TIME

Franklin and Eleanor Roosevelt: The Home Front in World War II

Doris Kearns Goodwin

SIMON & SCHUSTER PAPERBACKS
New York London Toronto Sydney

SIMON & SCHUSTER PAPERBACKS
Rockefeller Center
1230 Avenue of the Americas
New York, NY 10020

For information about special discounts for bulk purchases, please contact Simon & Schuster Special Sales: 1-800-456-6798 or business@simonandschuster.com.

Designed by Levavi & Levavi
Manufactured in the United States of America

50 49 48 47 46 45 44 43 42

The Library of Congress has cataloged the hardcover edition as follows:
Goodwin, Doris Kearns.
No ordinary time : Franklin and Eleanor Roosevelt : the home front in World War II / Doris Kearns Goodwin.
p. cm.
Includes bibliographical references and index.
1. Roosevelt, Franklin D. (Franklin Delano), 1882–1945. 2. Roosevelt, Eleanor, 1884–1962. 3. World War, 1939–1945—United States. 4. United States—History—1933–1945. 5. Presidents—United States—Biography. 6. Presidents' spouses—United States—Biography. I. Title.
E807.G66 1994 94-28565
973.917'092'2 B—dc20
ISBN-13: 978-0-671-64240-2
ISBN-10: 0-671-64240-5
ISBN-13: 978-0-684-80448-4 (Pbk)
ISBN-10: 0-684-80448-4 (Pbk)

To my sons,

Richard, Michael, and Joseph

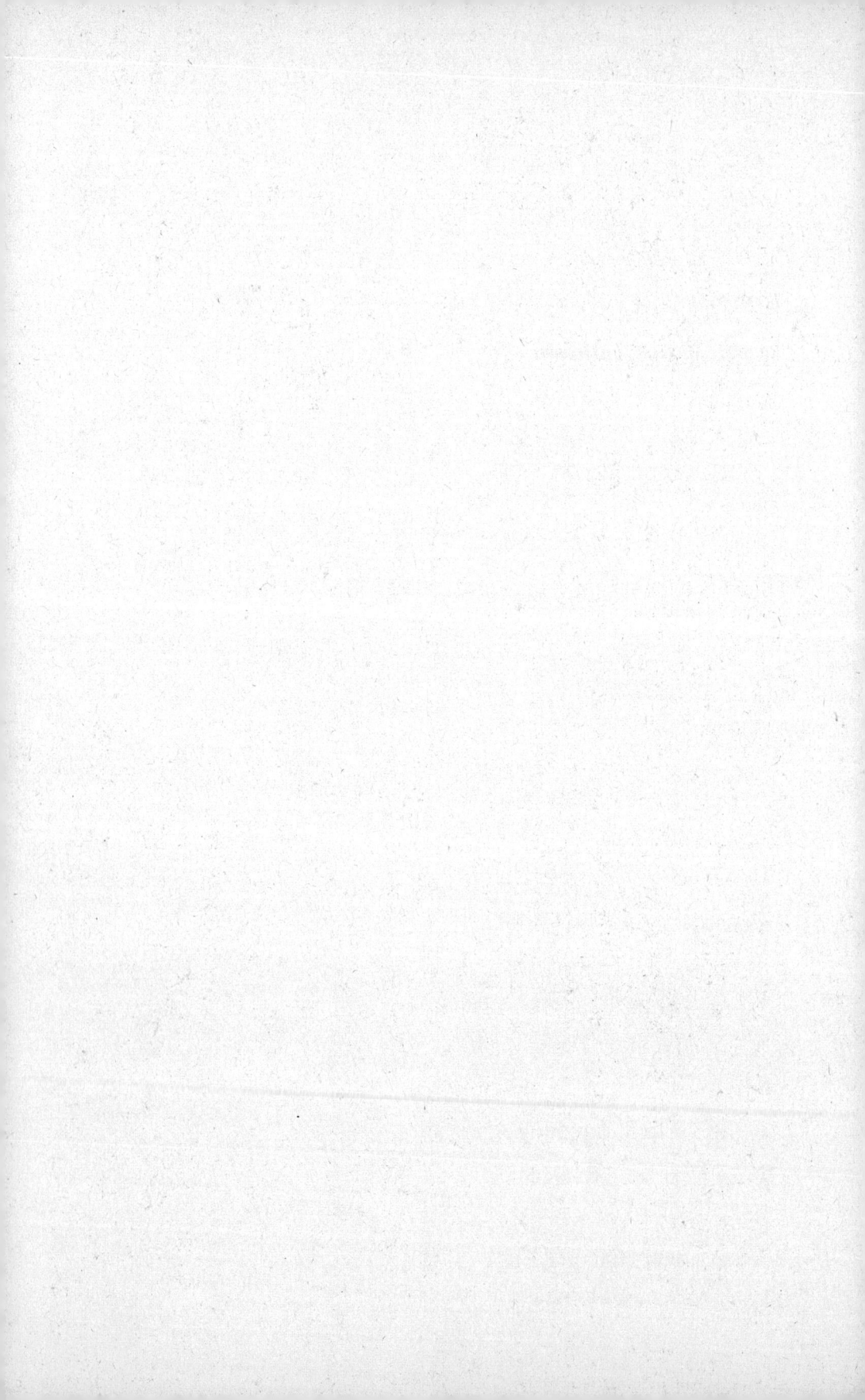

CONTENTS

PREFACE

On May 10, 1940, Hitler invaded Holland, Luxembourg, Belgium, and France, bringing the "phony war" to an end, and initiating a series of events which led, almost inevitably, to America's involvement in history's greatest armed conflict. The titanic battles of that war, the movement of armies across half the surface of the globe, have been abundantly described. Less understood is how the American home front affected the course of the war, and how the war, in turn, altered the face of American life. This book is the story of that home front, told through the lives of Franklin and Eleanor Roosevelt and the circle of friends and associates who lived with them in the family quarters of the White House during World War II.

The Roosevelt White House during the war resembled a small, intimate hotel. The residential floors of the mansion were occupied by a series of houseguests, some of whom stayed for years. The permanent guests occasionally had private visitors of their own for cocktails or for meals, but for the most part their lives revolved around the president and first lady, who occupied adjoining suites in the southwest quarter of the second floor. On the third floor, in a cheerful room with slanted ceilings, lived Missy LeHand, the president's personal secretary and longtime friend. The president's alter ego, Harry Hopkins, occupied the Lincoln Suite, two doors away from the president's suite. Anna Boettiger, the president's daughter, moved into Hopkins' suite when Hopkins moved out. Lorena Hickok, Eleanor's great friend, occupied a corner room across from Eleanor's bedroom. This group of houseguests was continually augmented by a stream of visitors—Winston Churchill, who often stayed for two or three weeks at a time; the president's mother, Sara Delano Roosevelt; Eleanor's young friend Joe Lash; and Crown Princess Martha of Norway.

These unusual living arrangements reflected the president's need to have people around him constantly, friends and associates with whom he could work, relax, and conduct much of the nation's business. Through these continual houseguests, Roosevelt defied the limitations of his paralysis. If he could not go out into the world, the world could come to him. The extended White House family also permitted Franklin and Eleanor to heal, or at least conceal, the incompletions of their marriage, which had been irrevocably altered by Eleanor's discovery of Franklin's affair with Lucy Mercer in 1918. There were areas of estrangement, untended needs that only others could fill.

Encompassed by this small society, Franklin Roosevelt led his nation through the war. Although his role as commander-in-chief has been studied at length, less attention has been paid to the way he led his people at home. Yet his leadership of the home front was the essential condition of military victory. Through four years of war, despite strikes and riots, overcrowding and confusion, profiteering, black markets, prejudice, and racism, he kept the American people united in a single cause. There were indeed many times, as those who worked with him observed, when it seemed that he could truly see it all—the relationship of the home front to the war front; of the factories to the soldiers; of speeches to morale; of the government to the people; of war aims to the shape of the peace to come. To understand Roosevelt and his leadership is to understand the nation whose strengths and weaknesses he mirrored and magnified.

At a time when her husband was preoccupied with winning the war, Eleanor Roosevelt insisted that the struggle would not be worth winning if the old order of things prevailed. Unless democracy were renewed at home, she repeatedly said, there was little merit in fighting for democracy abroad. To be sure, she did not act single-handedly—civil-rights leaders, labor leaders, and liberal spokesmen provided critical leverage in the search for social justice—but, without her consistent voice at the upper levels of decision, the tendency to put first things first, to focus on winning the war before exerting effort on anything else, might well have prevailed. She shattered the ceremonial mold in which the role of the first lady had traditionally been fashioned, and reshaped it around her own skills and commitments to social reform. She was the first president's wife to hold—and lose—a government job, the first to testify before a congressional committee, the first to hold press conferences, to speak before a national party convention, to write a syndicated column, to be a radio commentator, to earn money as a lecturer. She was able to use the office of first lady on behalf of causes she believed in rather than letting it use her, and in so doing she became, in the words of columnist Raymond Clapper, "the most influential woman of her time."

The two stories—that of the Roosevelts and that of America—are woven, in this book, as in reality, into a single narrative, beginning in May 1940 and ending in December 1945. This has required the tools of both history and biography: the effort to illuminate the qualities of Franklin and Eleanor Roosevelt has demanded occasional departures from chronology. Yet the spine of this work is narrative. Most studies of the home front have been arranged topically—production, civil rights, rationing, women, Japanese Americans, etc. But a president does not deal with issues topically. He deals with events and problems as they arise. By following the sequence of events ourselves, it is easier to see the connections between the home front and the war, between the level of production at a particular time and the decisions about where and when to fight, between the private qualities of leadership and the public acts.

And there is also a quality to this period which can only be conveyed through narrative—the sense of a cause successfully pursued through great difficulties, a theme common to America itself and to the family which guided it. "This is no ordinary time," Eleanor Roosevelt told the Democratic Convention of 1940, "and no time for weighing anything except what we can best do for the country as a whole." Guided by this conviction, the nation and its first family would move together through painful adversities toward undreamed-of achievements.

SECOND FLOOR FAMILY QUARTERS*

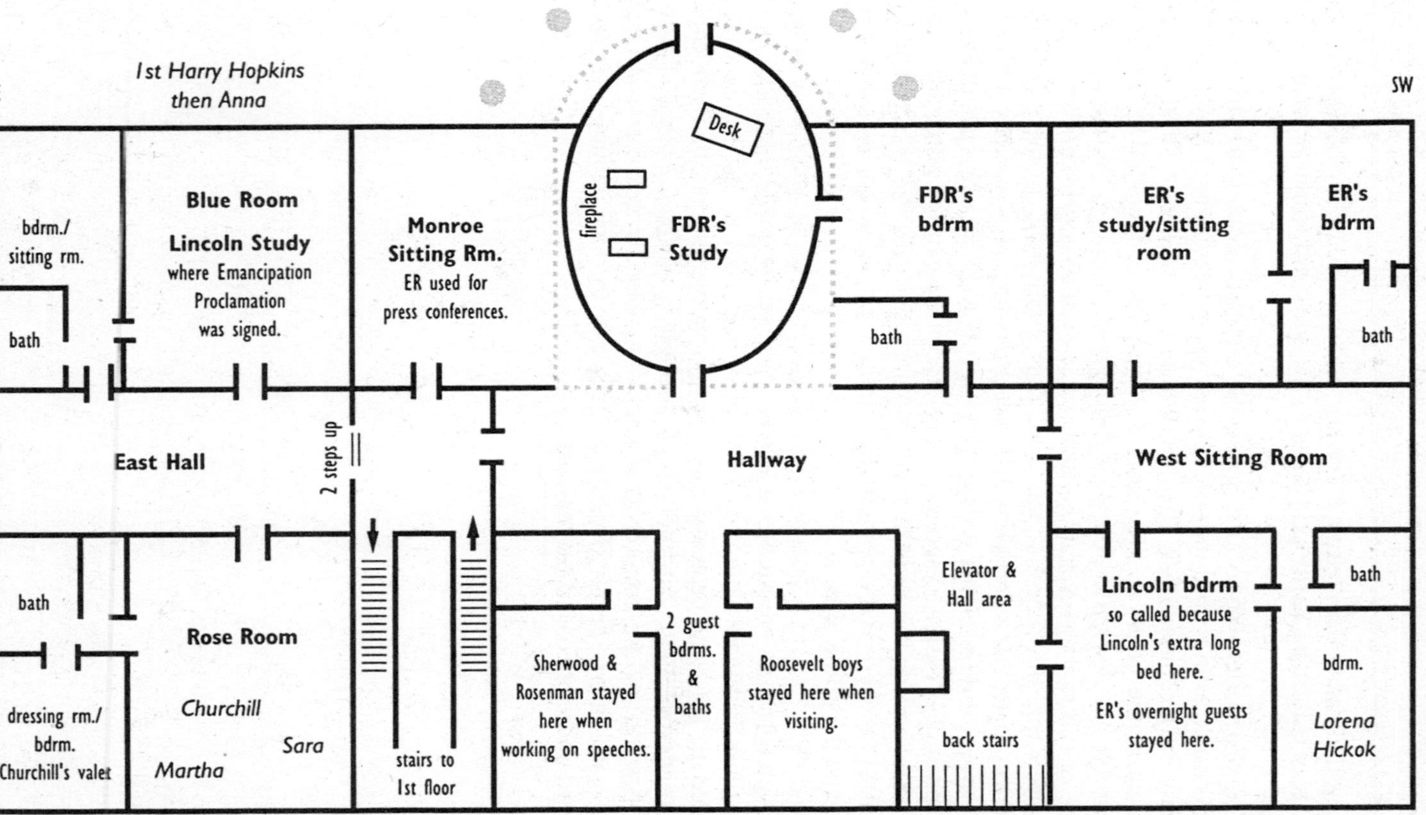

*Missy LeHand's suite was located on the third floor.

CHAPTER 1

"THE DECISIVE HOUR HAS COME"

"All the News That's Fit to Print"

The New York Times.

LATE CITY EDITION

NAZIS INVADE HOLLAND, BELGIUM, LUXEMBOURG BY LAND AND AIR; DIKES OPENED; ALLIES RUSH AID

U.S. FREEZES CREDIT

President Acts to Guard Funds Here of Three Invaded Nations

SHIP RULING TODAY

Envoy Reports to Hull on Germany's Attacks by Air and Land

The International Situation

ALLIED HELP SPED

Netherland and Belgian Appeals Answered by British and French

TACTICS ARE WATCHED

London Thinks Move an Effort to Get Bases to Attack Britain

BRUSSELS IS RAIDED

400 Reported Killed—Troops Cross Border at Four Points

PARACHUTE INVASION

Mobilization Is Ordered and Allied Aid Asked—Luxembourg Attacked

AIR FIELDS BOMBED

Nazi Parachute Troops Land at Key Centers as Flooding Starts

RIVER MAAS CROSSED

Defenders Battle Foe in Sky, Claim 6 Planes as War Is Proclaimed

NAZIS SWOOP ON THE LOW COUNTRIES

Ribbentrop Charges Allies Plotted With the Lowlands

On nights filled with tension and concern, Franklin Roosevelt performed a ritual that helped him to fall asleep. He would close his eyes and imagine himself at Hyde Park as a boy, standing with his sled in the snow atop the steep hill that stretched from the south porch of his home to the wooded bluffs of the Hudson River far below. As he accelerated down the hill, he maneuvered each familiar curve with perfect skill until he reached the bottom, whereupon, pulling his sled behind him, he started slowly back up until he reached the top, where he would once more begin his descent. Again and again he replayed this remembered scene in his mind, obliterating his awareness of the shrunken legs inert beneath the sheets, undoing the knowledge that he would never climb a hill or even walk on his own power again. Thus liberating himself from his paralysis through an act of imaginative will, the president of the United States would fall asleep.

The evening of May 9, 1940, was one of these nights. At 11 p.m., as

Roosevelt sat in his comfortable study on the second floor of the White House, the long-apprehended phone call had come. Resting against the high back of his favorite red leather chair, a precise reproduction of one Thomas Jefferson had designed for work, the president listened as his ambassador to Belgium, John Cudahy, told him that Hitler's armies were simultaneously attacking Holland, Luxembourg, Belgium, and France. The period of relative calm—the "phony war" that had settled over Europe since the German attack on Poland in September of 1939—was over.

For days, rumors of a planned Nazi invasion had spread through the capitals of Western Europe. Now, listening to Ambassador Cudahy's frantic report that German planes were in the air over the Low Countries and France, Roosevelt knew that the all-out war he feared had finally begun. In a single night, the tacit agreement that, for eight months, had kept the belligerents from attacking each other's territory had been shattered.

As he summoned his military aide and appointments secretary, General Edwin "Pa" Watson, on this spring evening of the last year of his second term, Franklin Roosevelt looked younger than his fifty-eight years. Though his hair was threaded with gray, the skin on his handsome face was clear, and the blue eyes, beneath his pince-nez glasses, were those of a man at the peak of his vitality. His chest was so broad, his neck so thick, that when seated he appeared larger than he was. Only when he was moved from his chair would the eye be drawn to the withered legs, paralyzed by polio almost two decades earlier.

At 12:40 a.m., the president's press secretary, Stephen Early, arrived to monitor incoming messages. Bombs had begun to fall on Brussels, Amsterdam, and Rotterdam, killing hundreds of civilians and destroying thousands of homes. In dozens of old European neighborhoods, fires illuminated the night sky. Stunned Belgians stood in their nightclothes in the streets of Brussels, watching bursts of anti-aircraft fire as military cars and motorcycles dashed through the streets. A thirteen-year-old schoolboy, Guy de Liederkirche, was Brussels' first child to die. His body would later be carried to his school for a memorial service with his classmates. On every radio station throughout Belgium, broadcasts summoned all soldiers to join their units at once.

In Amsterdam the roads leading out of the city were crowded with people and automobiles as residents fled in fear of the bombing. Bombs were also falling at Dunkirk, Calais, and Metz in France, and at Chilham, near Canterbury, in England. The initial reports were confusing—border clashes had begun, parachute troops were being dropped to seize Dutch and Belgian airports, the government of Luxembourg had already fled to France, and there was some reason to believe the Germans were also landing troops by sea.

After speaking again to Ambassador Cudahy and scanning the incoming news reports, Roosevelt called his secretary of the Treasury, Henry Morgenthau, Jr., and ordered him to freeze all assets held by Belgium, the Netherlands, and Luxembourg before the market opened in the morning, to keep any resources of the invaded countries from falling into German hands.

The official German explanation for the sweeping invasion of the neutral lowlands was given by Germany's foreign minister, Joachim von Ribbentrop. Germany, he claimed, had received "proof" that the Allies were engineering an imminent attack through the Low Countries into the German Ruhr district. In a belligerent tone, von Ribbentrop said the time had come for settling the final account with the French and British leaders. Just before midnight, Adolf Hitler, having boarded a special train to the front, had issued the fateful order to his troops: "The decisive hour has come for the fight today decides the fate of the German nation for the next 1000 years."

There was little that could be done that night—phone calls to Paris and Brussels could rarely be completed, and the Hague wire was barely working—but, as one State Department official said, "in times of crisis the key men should be at hand and the public should know it." Finally, at 2:40 a.m., Roosevelt decided to go to bed. After shifting his body to his armless wheel chair, he rolled through a door near his desk into his bedroom.

As usual when the president's day came to an end, he called for his valet, Irvin McDuffie, to lift him into his bed. McDuffie, a Southern Negro, born the same year as his boss, had been a barber by trade when Roosevelt met him in Warm Springs, Georgia, in 1927. Roosevelt quickly developed a liking for the talkative man and offered him the job of valet. Now he and his wife lived in a room on the third floor of the White House. In recent months, McDuffie's hard drinking had become a problem: on several occasions Eleanor had found him so drunk that "he couldn't help Franklin to bed." Fearing that her husband might be abandoned at a bad time, Eleanor urged him to fire McDuffie, but the president was unable to bring himself to let his old friend go, even though he shared Eleanor's fear.

McDuffie was at his post in the early hours of May 10 when the president called for help. He lifted the president from his wheelchair onto the narrow bed, reminiscent of the kind used in a boy's boarding school, straightened his legs to their full length, and then undressed him and put on his pajamas. Beside the bed was a white-painted table; on its top, a jumble of pencils, notepaper, a glass of water, a package of cigarettes, a couple of phones, a bottle of nose drops. On the floor beside the table stood a small basket—the Eleanor basket—in which the first lady regularly left memoranda, communications, and reports for the president to read—a sort of private post office between husband and wife. In the corner sat an old-fashioned rocking chair, and next to it a heavy wardrobe filled with the president's clothes. On the marble mantelpiece above the fireplace was an assortment of family photos and a collection of miniature pigs. "Like every room in any Roosevelt house," historian Arthur Schlesinger has written, "the presidential bedroom was hopelessly Victorian—old-fashioned and indiscriminate in its furnishings, cluttered in its decor, ugly and comfortable."

Outside Roosevelt's door, which he refused to lock at night as previous presidents had done, Secret Service men patrolled the corridor, alerting the guardroom to the slightest hint of movement. The refusal to lock his door was related to the president's dread of fire, which surpassed his fear of assassination or of anything else. The fear seems to have been rooted in his childhood, when, as a small boy, he had seen his young aunt, Laura, race down the stairs, screaming, her body and clothes aflame from an accident with an alcohol lamp. Her life was ended at nineteen. The fear grew when he became a paraplegic, to the point where, for hours at a time, he would practice dropping from his bed or chair to the floor and then crawling to the door so that he could escape from a fire on his own. "We assured him he would never be alone," his eldest son, Jimmy, recalled, "but he could not be sure, and furthermore found the idea depressing that he could not be left alone, as if he were an infant."

Roosevelt's nightly rituals tell us something about his deepest feelings—the desire for freedom, the quest for movement, and the significance, despite all his attempts to downplay it, of the paralysis in his life. In 1940, Roosevelt had been president of the United States for seven years, but he had been paralyzed from the waist down for nearly three times that long. Before he was stricken at thirty-nine, Roosevelt was a man who flourished on activity. He had served in the New York legislature for two years, been assistant secretary of the navy for seven years, and his party's candidate for vice-president in 1920. He loved to swim and to sail, to play tennis and golf; to run in the woods and ride horseback in the fields. To his daughter, Anna, he was always "very active physically," "a wonderful playmate who took long walks with you, sailed with you, could out-jump you and do a lot of things," while Jimmy saw him quite simply as "the handsomest, strongest, most glamorous, vigorous physical father in the world."

All that vigor and athleticism ended in August 1921 at Campobello, his family's summer home in New Brunswick, Canada, when he returned home from swimming in the pond with his children and felt too tired even to remove his wet bathing suit. The morning after his swim, his temperature was 102 degrees and he had trouble moving his left leg. By afternoon, the power to move his right leg was also gone, and soon he was paralyzed from the waist down. The paralysis had set in so swiftly that no one understood at first that it was polio. But once the diagnosis was made, the battle was joined. For years he fought to walk on his own power, practicing for hours at a time, drenched with sweat, as he tried unsuccessfully to move one leg in front of the other without the aid of a pair of crutches or a helping hand. That consuming and futile effort had to be abandoned once he became governor of New York in 1929 and then president in 1933. He was permanently crippled.

Yet the paralysis that crippled his body expanded his mind and his sensibilities. After what Eleanor called his "trial by fire," he seemed less arrogant, less smug, less superficial, more focused, more complex, more interesting. He returned from his ordeal with greater powers of concentration and greater self-knowledge. "There had been a plowing up of his nature," Labor

Secretary Frances Perkins observed. "The man emerged completely warm-hearted, with new humility of spirit and a firmer understanding of profound philosophical concepts."

He had always taken great pleasure in people. But now they became what one historian has called "his vital links with life." Far more intensely than before, he reached out to know them, to understand them, to pick up their emotions, to put himself into their shoes. No longer belonging to his old world in the same way, he came to empathize with the poor and underprivileged, with people to whom fate had dealt a difficult hand. Once, after a lecture in Akron, Ohio, Eleanor was asked how her husband's illness had affected him. "Anyone who has gone through great suffering," she said, "is bound to have a greater sympathy and understanding of the problems of mankind."

Through his presidency, the mere act of standing up with his heavy metal leg-braces locked into place was an ordeal. The journalist Eliot Janeway remembers being behind Roosevelt once when he was in his chair in the Oval Office. "He was smiling as he talked. His face and hand muscles were totally relaxed. But then, when he had to stand up, his jaws went absolutely rigid. The effort of getting what was left of his body up was so great his face changed dramatically. It was as if he braced his body for a bullet."

Little wonder, then, that, in falling asleep at night, Roosevelt took comfort in the thought of physical freedom.

• • •

The morning sun of Washington's belated spring was streaming through the president's windows on May 10, 1940. Despite the tumult of the night before, which had kept him up until nearly 3 a.m., he awoke at his usual hour of eight o'clock. Pivoting to the edge of the bed, he pressed the button for his valet, who helped him into the bathroom. Then, as he had done every morning for the past seven years, he threw his old blue cape over his pajamas and started his day with breakfast in bed—orange juice, eggs, coffee, and buttered toast—and the morning papers: *The New York Times* and the *Herald Tribune,* the *Baltimore Sun,* the *Washington Post* and the *Washington Herald.*

Headlines recounted the grim events he had heard at 11 p.m. the evening before. From Paris, Ambassador William Bullitt confirmed that the Germans had launched violent attacks on a half-dozen French military bases. Bombs had also fallen on the main railway connections between Paris and the border in an attempt to stop troop movements.

Before finishing the morning papers, the president held a meeting with Steve Early and "Pa" Watson, to review his crowded schedule. He instructed them to convene an emergency meeting at ten-thirty with the chiefs of the army and the navy, the secretaries of state and Treasury, and the attorney general. In addition, Roosevelt was scheduled to meet the press in the morning and the Cabinet in the afternoon, as he had done every Friday morning and afternoon for seven years. Later that night, he was supposed to deliver a keynote address at the Pan American Scientific Congress. After asking Early to delay the press conference an hour and to have the State Department draft a new speech, Roosevelt called his valet to help him dress.

• • •

While Franklin Roosevelt was being dressed in his bedroom, Eleanor was in New York, having spent the past few days in the apartment she kept in Greenwich Village, in a small house owned by her friends Esther Lape and Elizabeth Read. The Village apartment on East 11th Street, five blocks north of Washington Square, provided Eleanor with a welcome escape from the demands of the White House, a secret refuge whenever her crowded calendar brought her to New York. For decades, the Village, with its winding streets, modest brick houses, bookshops, tearooms, little theaters, and cheap rents, had been home to political, artistic, and literary rebels, giving it a colorful Old World character.

The object of Eleanor's visit to the city—her second in ten days—was a meeting that day at the Choate School in Connecticut, where she was scheduled to speak with teachers and students. Along the way, she had sandwiched in a banquet for the National League of Women Voters, a meeting for the fund for Polish relief, a visit to her mother-in-law, Sara Delano Roosevelt, a radio broadcast, lunch with her friend the young student activist Joe Lash, and dinner with Democratic leader Edward Flynn and his wife.

The week before, at the Astor Hotel, Eleanor had been honored by *The Nation* magazine for her work in behalf of civil rights and poverty. More than a thousand people had filled the tables and the balcony of the cavernous ballroom to watch her receive a bronze plaque for "distinguished service in the cause of American social progress." Among the many speakers that night, Stuart Chase lauded the first lady's concentrated focus on the problems at home. "I suppose she worries about Europe like the rest of us," he began, "but she does not allow this worry to divert her attention from the homefront. She goes around America, looking at America, thinking about America . . . helping day and night with the problems of America." For, he concluded, "the New Deal is supposed to be fighting a war, too, a war against depression."

"What is an institution?" author John Gunther had asked when his turn to speak came. "An institution," he asserted, is "something that had fixity, permanence, and importance . . . something that people like to depend on, something benevolent as a rule, something we like." And by that definition, he concluded, the woman being honored that night was as great an institution as her husband, who was already being talked about for an unprecedented third term. Echoing Gunther's sentiments, NAACP head Walter White turned to Mrs. Roosevelt and said: "My dear, I don't care if the President runs for the third or fourth term as long as he lets you run the bases, keep the score and win the game."

For her part, Eleanor was slightly embarrassed by all the fuss. "It never seems quite real to me to sit at a table and have people whom I have always looked upon with respect... explain why they are granting me an honor," she wrote in her column describing the evening. "Somehow I always feel they ought to be talking about someone else." Yet, as she stood to speak that night at the Astor ballroom, rising nearly six feet, her wavy brown hair slightly touched by gray, her wide mouth marred by large buck teeth, her brilliant blue eyes offset by an unfortunate chin, she dominated the room as no one before her had done. "I will do my best to do what is right," she began, forcing her high voice to a lower range, "not with a sense of my own adequacy but with the feeling that the country must go on, that we must keep democracy and must make it mean a reality to more people.... We should constantly be reminded of what we owe in return for what we have."

It was this tireless commitment to democracy's unfinished agenda that led Americans in a Gallup poll taken that spring to rate Mrs. Roosevelt even higher than her husband, with 67 percent of those interviewed well disposed toward her activities. "Mrs. Roosevelt's incessant goings and comings," the survey suggested, "have been accepted as a rather welcome part of the national life. Women especially feel this way. But even men betray relatively small masculine impatience with the work and opinions of a very articulate lady.... The rich, who generally disapprove of Mrs. Roosevelt's husband, seem just as friendly toward her as the poor.... Even among those extremely anti-Roosevelt citizens who would regard a third term as a national disaster there is a generous minority... who want Mrs. Roosevelt to remain in the public eye."

The path to this position of independent power and respect had not been easy. Eleanor's distinguished career had been forged from a painful discovery when she was thirty-four. After a period of suspicion, she realized that her husband, who was then assistant secretary of the navy, had fallen in love with another woman, Lucy Page Mercer.

Tall, beautiful, and well bred, with a low throaty voice and an incomparably winning smile, Lucy Mercer was working as Eleanor's social secretary when the love affair began. For months, perhaps even years, Franklin kept his romance a secret from Eleanor. Her shattering discovery took place in September 1918. Franklin had just returned from a visit to the European front. Unpacking his suitcase, she discovered a packet of love letters from Lucy. At this moment, Eleanor later admitted, "the bottom dropped out of my own particular world & I faced myself, my surroundings, my world, honestly for the first time."

Eleanor told her husband that she would grant him a divorce. But this was not what he wanted, or at least not what he was able to put himself through, particularly when his mother, Sara, was said to have threatened him with disinheritance if he left his marriage. If her son insisted on leaving his wife and five children for another woman, visiting scandal upon the Roosevelt name, she could not stop him. But he should know that she would not give him another dollar and he could no longer expect to inherit the family estate at Hyde Park. Franklin's trusted political adviser, Louis Howe, weighed in as well, warning Franklin that divorce would bring his political career to an abrupt end. There was also the problem of Lucy's Catholicism, which would prevent her from marrying a divorced man.

Franklin promised never to see Lucy again and agreed, so the Roosevelt children suggest, to Eleanor's demand for separate bedrooms, bringing their marital relations to an end. Eleanor would later admit to her daughter, Anna, that sex was "an ordeal to be borne." Something in her childhood had locked her up, she said, making her fear the loss of control that comes with abandoning oneself to one's passions, giving her "an exaggerated idea of the necessity of keeping all one's desires under complete subjugation." Now, supposedly, she was free of her "ordeal."

The marriage resumed. But for Eleanor, a path had opened, a possibility of standing apart from Franklin. No longer did she need to define herself solely in terms of his wants and his needs. Before the crisis, though marriage had never fulfilled her prodigious energies, she had no way of breaking through the habits and expectations of a proper young woman's role. To explore her independent needs, to journey outside her home for happiness, was perceived as dangerous and wrong.

With the discovery of the affair, however, she was free to define a new and different partnership with her husband, free to seek new avenues of fulfillment. It was a gradual process, a gradual casting away, a gradual gaining of confidence—and it was by no means complete—but the fifty-six-year-old woman who was being fêted in New York was a different person from the shy, betrayed wife of 1918.

• • •

Above the president's bedroom, in a snug third-floor suite, his personal secretary, Marguerite "Missy" LeHand, was already dressed, though she, too, had stayed up late the night before.

A tall, handsome woman of forty-one with large blue eyes and prematurely gray, once luxuriant black hair fastened by hairpins to the nape of her neck, Missy was in love with her boss and regarded herself as his other wife. Nor was she alone in her imaginings. "There's no doubt," White House aide Raymond Moley said, "that Missy was as close to being a wife as he ever had—or could have." White House maid Lillian Parks agreed. "When Missy gave an order, we responded as if it had come from the First Lady. We knew that FDR would always back up Missy."

Missy had come a long way from the working-class neighborhood in Somerville, Massachusetts, where she had grown up. Her father was an alcoholic who lived apart from the family. Her mother, with five children to raise, took in a revolving group of Harvard students as tenants. Yet, even when she was young, Missy's childhood friend Barbara Curtis recalled, "she had a certain class to her. I remember one time watching her go around the corner—our houses weren't too far apart—and my mother looked out the window and called my attention to her. She said, 'she certainly looks smart.' She had a dark suit on to go to high school. She stood out for having a better appearance and being smarter than most."

After secretarial school, Missy had gone to New York, where she became involved in Roosevelt's vice-presidential campaign in 1920. Impressed by Missy's efficiency, Eleanor asked her to come to Hyde Park after the election to help Franklin clean up his correspondence. From the start, Missy proved herself indispensable. When asked later to explain her astonishing secretarial skill, she said simply, "The first thing for a private secretary to do is to study her employer. After I went to work for Mr. Roosevelt, for months I read carefully all the letters he dictated. . . . I learned what letters he wanted to see and which ones it was not necessary to show him. . . . I came to know exactly how Mr. Roosevelt would answer some of his letters, how he would couch his thoughts. When he discovered that I had learned these things it took a load off his shoulders, for instead of having to dictate the answers to many letters he could just say yes or no and I knew what to say and how to say it."

A year later, when Franklin contracted polio, Missy's duties expanded. Both Franklin and Eleanor understood that it was critical for Franklin to keep active in politics even as he struggled unsuccessfully day after day, month after month, to walk again. To that end, Eleanor adhered to a rigorous daily schedule as the stand-in for her husband, journeying from one political meeting to the next to ensure that the Roosevelt name was not forgotten. With Eleanor busily occupied away from home, Missy did all the chores a housewife might do, writing Franklin's personal checks, paying the monthly bills, giving the children their allowances, supervising the menus, sending the rugs and draperies for cleaning.

When Roosevelt was elected governor in 1928, Missy moved with the Roosevelt family to Albany, occupying a large bedroom suite on the second floor of the Governor's Mansion. "Albany was the hardest work I ever did," she said, recalling the huge load she carried for the activist governor without the help of the three assistants she would later enjoy in the White House. By the time Roosevelt was president, she had become totally absorbed in his life—learning his favorite games, sharing his hobbies, reading the same books, even adopting his characteristic accent and patterns of speech. Whereas Eleanor was so opposed to gambling that she refused to play poker with Franklin's friends if even the smallest amount of money changed hands, Missy became an avid player, challenging Roosevelt at every turn, always ready to raise the ante. Whereas Eleanor never evinced any interest in her husband's treasured stamp collection, Missy was an enthusiastic partner, spending hours by his side as he organized and reorganized his stamps into one or another of his thick leather books. "In terms of companionship," Eliot Janeway observed, "Missy was the real wife. She understood his nature perfectly, as they would say in a nineteenth-century novel."

• • •

At 10:30 a.m., May 10, 1940, pushed along in his wheelchair by Mr. Crim, the usher on duty, and accompanied by his usual detail of Secret Service men, the president headed for the Oval Office. A bell announced his arrival to the small crowd already assembled in the Cabinet Room—Army Chief of Staff George Marshall, Navy Chief Admiral Harold Stark, Attorney General Robert Jackson, Secretary of Treasury Henry Morgenthau, Secretary of State Cordell Hull, and Undersecretary Sumner Welles. But first, as he did every day, the president poked his head into Missy's office, giving her a wave and a smile which, Missy told a friend, was all she needed to replenish the energies lost from too little sleep.

Of all the men assembled in the big white-walled Cabinet Room that morning, General George Catlett Marshall possessed the clearest awareness of how woefully unprepared America was to fight a major war against Nazi Germany. The fifty-nine-year-old Marshall, chief of operations of the First Army in World War I, had been elevated to the position of army chief of staff the previous year. The story is told of a meeting in the president's office not long before the appointment during which the president outlined a pet proposal. Everyone nodded in approval except Marshall. "Don't you think so, George?" the president asked. Marshall replied: "I am sorry, Mr. President, but I don't agree with that at all." The president looked stunned, the conference was stopped, and Marshall's friends predicted that his tour of duty would soon come to an end. A few months later, reaching thirty-four names down the list of senior generals, the president asked the straight-speaking Marshall to be chief of staff of the U.S. Army.

The army Marshall headed, however, was scarcely worthy of the name, having languished in skeletal form since World War I, starved for funds and manpower by an administration focused on coping with the Great Depression and an isolationist Congress. Determined never again to be trapped by the corruptions of the Old World, the isolationists insisted that the United States was protected from harm by its oceans and could best lead by sustaining democracy at home. Responding to the overwhelming strength of isolationist sentiment in the country at large, the Congress had passed a series of Neutrality Acts in the mid-1930s banning the shipment of arms and munitions to all belligerents, prohibiting the extension of credits and loans, and forbidding the arming of merchant ships.

Roosevelt had tried on occasion to shift the prevailing opinion. In 1937, he had delivered a major speech in Chicago calling for a "quarantine" of aggressor nations. The speech was hailed by interventionists committed to collective security, but when the press evinced shock at what they termed a radical shift in foreign policy and isolationist congressmen threatened impeachment, Roosevelt had pulled back. "It's a terrible thing," he told his aide Sam Rosenman, "to look over your shoulder when you are trying to lead—and find no one there." He had resolved at that point to move one step at a time, to nurse the country along to a more sophisticated view of the world, to keep from getting too far ahead of the electorate, as Woodrow Wilson had done. The task was not easy. Even the outbreak of war in September had not led to a significant expansion of the army, since the president's first priority was to revise the Neutrality Laws so that he could sell weapons to the Allies. Fearing that larger appropriations for the ground forces would rouse the isolationists and kill his chances to reform neutrality policy, the president had turned a deaf ear to the army's appeals for expansion.

As a result, in 1940, the U.S. Army stood only eighteenth in the world, trailing not only Germany, France, Britain, Russia, Italy, Japan, and China but also Belgium, the Netherlands, Portugal, Spain, Sweden, and Switzerland. With the fall of Holland, the United States would rise to seventeenth! And, in contrast to Germany, where after years of compulsory military training nearly 10 percent of the population (6.8 million) were trained and ready for war, less than .5 percent of the American population (504,000) were on active duty or in the trained reserves. The offensive Germany had launched the morning of May 10 along the Western front was supported by 136 divisions; the United States could, if necessary, muster merely five fully equipped divisions.

In the spring of 1940, the United States possessed almost no munitions industry at all. So strong had been the recoil from war after 1918 that both the government and the private sector had backed away from making weapons. The result was that, while the United States led the world in the mass production of automobiles, washing machines, and other household appliances, the techniques of producing weapons of war had badly atrophied.

All through the winter and spring, Marshall had been trying to get Secretary of War Henry Woodring to understand the dire nature of this unpreparedness. But the former governor of Kansas was an isolationist who refused to contemplate even the possibility of American involvement in the European war. Woodring had been named assistant secretary of war in 1933 and then promoted to the top job three years later, when the price of corn and the high unemployment rate worried Washington far more than foreign affairs. As the European situation heated up, Roosevelt recognized that Woodring was the wrong man to head the War Department. But, try as he might, he could not bring himself to fire his secretary of war—or anyone else, for that matter.

Roosevelt's inability to get rid of anybody, even the hopelessly incompetent, was a chief source of the disorderliness of his administration, of his double-dealing and his tendency to procrastinate. "His real weakness," Eleanor Roosevelt observed, "was that—it came out of the strength really, or out of a quality—he had great sympathy for people and great understanding, and he couldn't bear to be disagreeable to someone he liked . . . and he just couldn't bring himself to really do the unkind thing that had to be done unless he got angry."

Earlier that spring, on at least two occasions, Secretary of the Interior Harold Ickes had brought up the Woodring problem with Roosevelt, suggesting an appointment as ambassador to Ireland as a face-saving gesture. The president did not think this would satisfy Woodring. "If I were you, Mr. President," Ickes replied, "I would send for Harry Woodring and I would say to him, 'Harry, it is either Dublin, Ireland for you or Topeka, Kansas.' The President looked at me somewhat abashed. Reading his mind, I said, 'You can't do that sort of thing, can you, Mr. President?' 'No, Harold, I can't,' he replied."

The confusion multiplied when Roosevelt selected a staunch interventionist, Louis Johnson, the former national commander of the American Legion, as assistant secretary of war. Outspoken, bold, and ambitious, Johnson fought openly with Woodring, bringing relations to the sorry point where neither man spoke to the other. Paralyzed and frustrated, General Marshall found it incomprehensible that Roosevelt had allowed such a mess to develop simply because he disliked firing anyone. Years earlier, when Marshall had been told by his aide that a friend whom he had ordered overseas had said he could not leave because his wife was away and his furniture was not packed, Marshall had called the man himself. The friend explained that he was sorry. "I'm sorry, too," Marshall replied, "but you will be retired tomorrow."

Marshall failed to understand that there was a method behind the president's disorderly style. Though divided authority and built-in competition created insecurity and confusion within the administration, it gave Roosevelt the benefit of conflicting opinions. "I think he knew exactly what he was doing all the time," administrative assistant James Rowe observed. "He liked conflict, and he was a believer in resolving problems through conflict." With different administrators telling him different things, he got a better feel for what his problems were.

Their attitude toward subordinates was not the only point of dissimilarity between Roosevelt and Marshall. Roosevelt loved to laugh and play, closing the space between people by familiarity, calling everyone, even Winston Churchill, by his first name. In contrast, Marshall was rarely seen to smile or laugh on the job and was never familiar with anyone. "I never heard him call anyone by his first name," Robert Cutler recalled. "He would use the rank or the last name or both: 'Colonel' or 'Colonel Cutler.' Only occasionally in wartime did he use the last name alone. . . . It was a reward for something he thought well done."

As army chief of staff, Marshall remained wary of Roosevelt's relaxed style. "Informal conversation with the President could get you into trouble," Marshall later wrote. "He would talk over something informally at the dinner table and you had trouble disagreeing without embarrassment. So I never went. I was in Hyde Park for the first time at his funeral."

As the officials sat in the Cabinet Room, at the great mahogany table under the stern, pinch-lipped stare of Woodrow Wilson, whose portrait hung above the fireplace, their primary reason for gathering together was to share the incoming information from Europe and to plan the American response. Ambassador John Cudahy in Brussels wired that he had almost been knocked down by the force of a bomb which fell three hundred feet from the embassy. From London, Ambassador Joseph P. Kennedy reported that the British had called off their Whitsun holiday, the long weekend on which Londoners traditionally acquired the tan that had to last until their August vacation—"tangible evidence," Kennedy concluded, "that the situation is serious."

Plans were set in motion for the army and navy to submit new estimates to the White House of what they would need to accomplish the seemingly insurmountable task of catching up with Germany's modern war machine. For, as Marshall had recently explained to the Congress, Germany was in a unique position. "After the World War practically everything was taken away from Germany in the way of materiel. So when Germany rearmed, it was necessary to produce a complete set of materiel for all the troops. As a result, Germany has an Army equipped throughout with the most modern weapons that could be turned out and that is a situation that has never occurred before in the history of the world."

• • •

While the president was conducting his meeting in the Cabinet Room, the men and women of the press were standing around in small groups, talking and smoking behind a red cord in a large anteroom, waiting for the signal that the press conference in the Oval Office was about to begin. The reporters had also been up late the night before, so "some were a little drawn eyed," the *Tribune*'s Mark Sullivan observed. "We grouped about talking of—do I need to say? I felt that . . . for many a day and month and year there will be talk about the effect of today's events upon the United States. We shall talk it and write it and live it, and our children's children, too."

The meeting concluded, the president returned to his desk, the red cord was withdrawn, and the reporters began filing in. In the front row, by tradition, stood the men representing the wire services: Douglas Cornell of Associated Press, Merriman Smith of United Press, and George Durno of the International News Service. Directly behind them stood the representatives of the New York and Washington papers. "Glancing around the room," a contemporary wrote, "one sees white-haired Mark Sullivan; dark Raymond Clapper; tall Ernest Lindley . . . and husky Paul Mallon." Farther back were the veterans of the out-of-town newspapers, the radio commentators, and the magazine men, led by *Time*'s Felix Belair. And then the women reporters in flat heels, among them Doris Fleeson of the *New York Daily News* and May Craig, representing several Maine newspapers.

Seated at his desk with his back to the windows, Roosevelt faced the crowd that was now spilling into the Oval Office for his largest press conference ever. Behind him, set in standards, were the blue presidential flag and the American flag. "Like an opera singer about to go on the stage," Roosevelt invariably appeared nervous before a conference began, fidgeting with his cigarette holder, fingering the trinkets on his desk, exchanging self-conscious jokes with the reporters in the front row. Once the action started, however, with the doorkeeper's shout of "all-in," the president seemed to relax, conducting the flow of questions and conversation with such professional skill that the columnist Heywood Broun once called him "the best newspaperman who has ever been President of the United States."

For seven years, twice a week, the president had sat down with these reporters, explaining legislation, announcing appointments, establishing friendly contact, calling them by their first names, teasing them about their hangovers, exuding warmth and accessibility. Once, when a correspondent narrowly missed getting on Roosevelt's train, the president covered for him by writing his copy until he could catch up. Another time, when the mother of a bachelor correspondent died, Eleanor Roosevelt attended the funeral services, and then she and the president invited him for their Sunday family supper of scrambled eggs. These acts of friendship—repeated many times over—helped to explain the paradox that, though 80 to 85 percent of the newspaper publishers regularly opposed Roosevelt, the president maintained excellent relations with the working reporters, and his coverage was generally full and fair. "By the brilliant but simple trick of making news and *being* news," historian Arthur Schlesinger observed, "Roosevelt outwitted the open hostility of the publishers and converted the press into one of the most effective channels of his public leadership."

"History will like to say the scene [on May 10] was tense," Mark Sullivan wrote. "It was not. . . . On the President's part there was consciousness of high events, yet also complete coolness. . . . The whole atmosphere was one of serious matter-of-factness."

"Good morning," the president said, and then paused as still more reporters filed in. "I hope you had more sleep than I did," he joked, drawing them into the shared experience of the crisis. "I guess most of you were pretty busy all night."

"There isn't much I can say about the situation. . . . I can say, personally, that I am in full sympathy with the very excellent statement that was given out, the proclamation, by the Queen of the Netherlands." In that statement, issued earlier that morning, Queen Wilhelmina had directed "a flaming protest against this unprecedented violation of good faith and all that is decent in relations between cultured states."

Asked if he would say what he thought the chances were that the United States could stay out of the war, the president replied as he had been replying for months to similar questions. "I think that would be speculative. In other words, don't for heaven's sake, say that means we may get in. That would be again writing yourself off on the limb and sawing it off." Asked if his speech that night would touch on the international situation, Roosevelt evoked a round of laughter by responding: "I do not know because I have not written it."

On and on he went, his tone in the course of fifteen minutes shifting from weariness to feistiness to playfulness. Yet, in the end, preserving his options in this delicate moment, he *said* almost nothing, skillfully deflecting every question about America's future actions. Asked at one point to compare Japanese aggression with German aggression, he said he counted seven ifs in the question, which meant he could not provide an answer. Still, by the time the senior wire-service man brought the conference to an early close, "partly in consideration of the tired newspaper men and partly in consideration of the President," the reporters went away with the stories they needed for the next day's news.

• • •

While the president was holding his press conference, Eleanor was in a car with her secretary, Malvina Thompson, heading toward the Choate School near the village of Wallingford, Connecticut. Built in the middle of three hundred acres of farm and woodland, with rolling hills stretching for many miles beyond, Choate was a preparatory school for young boys. The students were mostly Protestant, though in recent years a few Catholics had been admitted, including the two sons of Ambassador Joseph Kennedy, Joe Jr. and John Fitzgerald Kennedy.

Like Missy, Malvina Thompson, known to her friends as Tommy, was a fixture in the Roosevelt household, as critical to Eleanor's life as Missy was to Franklin's. Short and stocky, with brown hair and a continual wrinkle in the bridge of her nose, the forty-eight-year-old Tommy had started working for Eleanor when Franklin was governor of New York. She had married Frank Scheider, a teacher in the New York public schools, in 1921 and divorced him in 1939. She had no children. She had her own room in every Roosevelt house: a sitting room and bedroom in the White House, a bedroom in Eleanor's Greenwich Village apartment, and a suite of rooms at Val-Kill, Eleanor's cottage at Hyde Park.

Born of "good old Vermont granite stock," Tommy was smart and tough with a wry sense of humor. "When she walked," a relative recalled, " she gave the impression of saying 'You'd better get out of my way or else.' " Tommy was the person, Eleanor said in 1938, "who makes life possible for me."

During the past seven years in the White House, Eleanor and Tommy traveled more than 280,000 miles around the United States, the equivalent of nearly a hundred cross-country trips. Franklin called Eleanor his "will o' the wisp" wife. But it was Franklin who had encouraged her to become his "eyes and ears," to gather the grass-roots knowledge he needed to understand the people he governed. Unable to travel easily on his own because of his paralysis, he had started by teaching Eleanor how to inspect state institutions in 1929, during his first term as governor.

"It was the best education I ever had," she later said. Traveling across the state to inspect institutions for the insane, the blind, and the aged, visiting state prisons and reform schools, she had learned, slowly and painfully, through Franklin's tough, detailed questions upon her return, how to become an investigative reporter.

Her first inspection was an insane asylum. "All right," Franklin told her, "go in and look around and let me know what's going on there. Tell me how the inmates are being treated." When Eleanor returned, she brought with her a printed copy of the day's menu. "Did you look to see whether they were actually getting this food?" Franklin asked. "Did you lift a pot cover on the stove to check whether the contents corresponded with this menu?" Eleanor shook her head. Her untrained mind had taken in a general picture of the place but missed all the human details that would have brought it to life. "But these are what I need," Franklin said. "I never remembered things until Franklin taught me," Eleanor told a reporter. "His memory is really prodigious. Once he has checked something he never needs to look at it again."

"One time," she recalled, "he asked me to go and look at the state's tree shelter-belt plantings. I noticed there were five rows of graduated size.... When I came back and described it, Franklin said: 'Tell me exactly what was in the first five rows. What did they plant first?' And he was so desperately disappointed when I couldn't tell him, that I put my best efforts after that into missing nothing and remembering everything."

In time, Eleanor became so thorough in her inspections, observing the attitudes of patients toward the staff, judging facial expressions as well as the words, looking in closets and behind doors, that Franklin set great value on her reports. "She saw many things the President could never see," Labor Secretary Frances Perkins said. "Much of what she learned and what she understood about the life of the people of this country rubbed off onto FDR. It could not have helped to do so because she had a poignant understanding. ... Her mere reporting of the facts was full of a sensitive quality that could never be escaped.... Much of his seemingly intuitive understanding—about labor situations ... about girls who worked in sweatshops—came from his recollections of what she had told him."

During Eleanor's first summer as first lady, Franklin had asked her to investigate the economic situation in Appalachia. The Quakers had reported terrible conditions of poverty there, and the president wanted to check these reports. "Watch the people's faces," he told her. "Look at the conditions of the clothes on the wash lines. You can tell a lot from that." Going even further, Eleanor descended the mine shafts, dressed in a miner's outfit, to absorb for herself the physical conditions in which the miners worked. It was this journey that later provoked the celebrated cartoon showing two miners in a shaft looking up: "Here Comes Mrs. Roosevelt!"

At Scott's Run, near Morgantown, West Virginia, Eleanor had seen children who "did not know what it was to sit down at a table and eat a proper meal." In one shack, she found a boy clutching his pet rabbit, which his sister had just told him was all there was left to eat. So moved was the president by his wife's report that he acted at once to create an Appalachian resettlement project.

The following year, Franklin had sent Eleanor to Puerto Rico to investigate reports that a great portion of the fancy embroidered linens that were coming into the United States from Puerto Rico were being made under terrible conditions. To the fury of the rich American colony in San Juan, Eleanor took reporters and photographers through muddy alleys and swamps to hundreds of foul-smelling hovels with no plumbing and no electricity, where women sat in the midst of filth embroidering cloth for minimal wages. Publicizing these findings, Eleanor called for American women to stop purchasing Puerto Rico's embroidered goods.

Later, Eleanor journeyed to the deep South and the "Dustbowl." Before long, her inspection trips had become as important to her as to her husband. "I realized," she said in a radio interview, "that if I remained in the White House all the time I would lose touch with the rest of the world. . . . I might have had a less crowded life, but I would begin to think that my life in Washington was representative of the rest of the country and that is a dangerous point of view." So much did Eleanor travel, in fact, that the *Washington Star* once printed a humorous headline: "Mrs. Roosevelt Spends Night at White House."

So it was not unusual that, on May 10, 1940, Eleanor found herself away from home, driving along a country road in central Connecticut. Months earlier, she had accepted the invitation of the headmaster, George St. John, to address the student body. Now, in the tense atmosphere generated by the Nazi invasion of Western Europe, her speech assumed an added measure of importance. As she entered the Chapel and faced the young men sitting in neat rows before her, she was filled with emotion.

"There is something very touching in the contact with these youngsters," she admitted, "so full of fire and promise and curiosity about life. One cannot help dreading what life may do to them. . . . All these young things knowing so little of life and so little of what the future may hold."

Eleanor's forebodings were not without foundation. Near the Chapel stood the Memorial House, a dormitory built in memory of the eighty-five Choate boys who had lost their lives in the Great War. Now, as she looked at the eager faces in the crowd and worried about a European war spreading once again to the United States, she wondered how many of them would be called to give their lives for their country.

For several days, Eleanor's mind had been preoccupied by old wars. "I wonder," she wrote in her column earlier that week, "that the time does not come when young men facing each other with intent to kill do not suddenly think of their homes and their loved ones and realizing that those on the other side must have the same thoughts, throw away their weapons of murder."

Talking with her young friend Joe Lash that week at lunch, Eleanor admitted she was having a difficult time sorting out her feelings about the war. On the one hand, she was fully alert to the magnitude of Hitler's threat. On the other hand, she agreed with the views of the American Youth Congress, a group of young liberals and radicals whom Eleanor had defended over the years, that the money spent on arms would be much better spent on education and medical care. Her deepest fear, Lash recorded in his diary, was that nothing would come out of this war different from the last war, that history would repeat itself. And because of this sinking feeling, she could not put her heart into the war.

Building on these feelings in her speech to the boys of Choate, Eleanor stressed the importance of renewing democracy at home in order to make the fight for democracy abroad worthwhile. This argument would become her theme in the years ahead, as she strove to give positive meaning to the terrible war. "How to preserve the freedoms of democracy in the world. How really to make democracy work at home and prove it is worth preserving. . . . These are the questions the youth of today must face and we who are older must face them too."

• • •

Eleanor's philosophical questions about democracy were not the questions on the president's mind when he met with his Cabinet at two that afternoon. His concerns as he looked at the familiar faces around the table were much more immediate: how to get a new and expanded military budget through the Congress, how to provide aid to the Allies as quickly as possible, how to stock up on strategic materials; in other words, how to start the complex process of mobilizing for war.

The president opened the proceedings, as usual, by turning to Cordell Hull, his aging secretary of state, for the latest news from abroad. A symbol of dependability, respected by liberals and conservatives alike, the tall gaunt Tennessean, with thick white hair and bright dark eyes, had headed the department since 1933. Hull spoke slowly and softly as he shared the latest bulletins from his embassies in Europe, his slumped shoulders and downcast eyes concealing the stubborn determination that had characterized his long and successful career in the Congress as a representative and senator from Tennessee. In Holland, it was reported with a tone of optimism that later proved unfounded, the Dutch were beginning to recapture the airports taken by the Germans the night before. In Belgium, too, it was said, the Allied armies were holding fast against the German thrusts. But the mood in the room darkened quickly as the next round of bulletins confirmed devastating tales of defeat at the hands of the Germans.

After hearing Hull, the president traditionally called on Henry Morgenthau, his longtime friend and secretary of the Treasury. Just before the Cabinet meeting had convened, Morgenthau had received word that the Belgian gold reserves had been safely evacuated to France, and that much of the Dutch gold was also safe. But this was the extent of the good news Morgenthau had to report. All morning long, Morgenthau had been huddled in meetings with his aides, looking at the dismal figures on America's preparedness, wondering how America could ever catch up to Germany, since it would take eighteen months to deliver the modern weapons of war even if the country went into full-scale mobilization that very day.

Labor Secretary Frances Perkins, the only woman in the Cabinet, tended to talk a great deal at these meetings, "as though she had swallowed a press release." But on this occasion she remained silent as the conversation was carried by Harry Hopkins, the secretary of commerce, who was present at his first Cabinet meeting in months.

For the past year and a half, Hopkins had been in and out of hospitals while doctors tried to fix his body's lethal inability to absorb proteins and fats. His health had begun to deteriorate in the summer of 1939, when, at the height of his power as director of the Works Progress Administration, he was told that he had stomach cancer. A ghastly operation followed which removed the cancer along with three-quarters of his stomach, leaving him with a severe form of malnutrition. Told in the fall of 1939 that Hopkins had only four weeks to live, Roosevelt took control of the case himself and flew in a team of experts, whose experiments with plasma transfusions arrested the fatal decline. Then, to give Hopkins breathing space from the turbulence of the WPA, Roosevelt appointed him secretary of commerce. Even that job had proved too much, however: Hopkins had been able to work only one or two days in the past ten months.

Yet, on this critical day, the fifty-year-old Hopkins was sitting in the Cabinet meeting in the midst of the unfolding crisis. "He was to all intents and purposes," Hopkins' biographer Robert Sherwood wrote, "a finished man who might drag out his life for a few years of relative inactivity or who might collapse and die at any time." His face was sallow and heavy-lined; journalist George Creel once likened his weary, melancholy look to that of "an ill-fed horse at the end of a hard day," while Churchill's former daughter-in-law, Pamela Churchill Harriman, compared him to "a very sad dog." Given his appearance—smoking one cigarette after another, his brown hair thinning, his shoulders sagging, his frayed suit baggy at the knees—"you wouldn't think," a contemporary reporter wrote, "he could possibly be important to a President."

But when he spoke, as he did at length this day on the subject of the raw materials needed for war, his sickly face vanished and a very different face appeared, intelligent, good-humored, animated. His eyes, which seconds before had seemed beady and suspicious, now gleamed with light. Sensing the urgency of the situation, Hopkins spoke so rapidly that he did not finish half of his words, as though, after being long held back, he wanted to make up for lost time. It was as if the crisis had given him a renewed reason for living; it seemed, in reporter Marquis Childs' judgment at the time, "to galvanize him into life." From then on, Childs observed, "while he would still be an ailing man, he was to ignore his health." The curative impact of Hopkins' increasingly crucial role in the war effort was to postpone the sentence of death the doctors had given him for five more years.

Even Hopkins' old nemesis, Harold Ickes, felt compelled to pay attention when Hopkins reported that the United States had "only a five or six months supply of both rubber and tin, both of which are absolutely essential for purposes of defense." The shortage of rubber was particularly worrisome, since rubber was indispensable to modern warfare if armies were to march, ships sail, and planes fly. Hitler's armies were rolling along on rubber-tired trucks and rubber-tracked tanks; they were flying in rubber-lined high-altitude suits in planes equipped with rubber de-icers, rubber tires, and rubber life-preserver rafts. From stethoscopes and blood-plasma tubing to gas masks and adhesive tape, the demand for rubber was endless. And with Holland under attack and 90 percent of America's supply of rubber coming from the Dutch East Indies, something had to be done.

Becoming more and more spirited as he went on, Hopkins outlined a plan of action, starting with the creation of a new corporation, to be financed by the Reconstruction Finance Corporation, whose purpose would be to go into the market and buy at least a year's supply of rubber and tin. This step would be only the first, followed by the building of synthetic-rubber plants and an effort to bring into production new sources of natural rubber in South America. Hopkins' plan of action met with hearty approval.

While Hopkins was speaking, word came from London that Neville Chamberlain had resigned his post as prime minister. This dramatic event had its source in the tumultuous debate in the Parliament over the shameful retreat of the British Expeditionary Force from Norway three weeks earlier. Responding to clamorous cries for his resignation, Chamberlain had stumbled badly by personalizing the issue and calling for a division to show the strength of his support. "I welcome it, indeed," he had said. "At least we shall see who is with and who is against us and I will call on my friends to support me in the lobby tonight."

But the division had not turned out as Chamberlain expected: Tory officers in uniform, feeling the brunt of Britain's lack of preparedness, surged into the Opposition lobby to vote against the government. In all, over thirty Conservatives deserted Chamberlain, and a further sixty abstained, reducing the government's margin from two hundred to eighty-one. Stunned and disoriented, Chamberlain recognized he could no longer continue to lead unless he could draw Labour into a coalition government. For a moment earlier that day, the German invasion of the Low Countries threatened to freeze Chamberlain in place, but the Labour Party refused his appeals for a national government. "Prime Minister," Lord Privy Seal Clement Attlee bluntly replied, "our party won't have you and I think I am right in saying that the country won't have you either." The seventy-one-year-old prime minister had little choice but to step down.

Then, when the king's first choice, Lord Halifax, refused to consider the post on the grounds that his position as a peer would make it difficult to discharge his duties, the door was opened for Winston Churchill, the complex Edwardian man with his fat cigars, his gold-knobbed cane, and his vital understanding of what risks should be taken and what kind of adversary the Allies were up against. For nearly four decades, Churchill had been a major figure in public life. The son of a lord, he had been elected to Parliament in 1900 and had served in an astonishing array of Cabinet posts, including undersecretary for the colonies, privy councillor, home secretary, first lord of the admiralty, minister of munitions, and chancellor of the Exchequer. He had survived financial embarrassment, prolonged fits of depression, and political defeat to become the most eloquent spokesman against Nazi Germany. From the time Hitler first came to power, he had repeatedly warned against British efforts to appease him, but no one had listened. Now, finally, his voice would be heard. "Looking backward," a British writer observed, "it almost seems as though the transition from peace to war began on that day when Churchill became Prime Minister."

Responding warmly to the news of Churchill's appointment, Roosevelt told his Cabinet he believed "Churchill was the best man that England had." From a distance, the two leaders had come to admire each other: for years, Churchill had applauded Roosevelt's "valiant effort" to end the depression, while Roosevelt had listened with increasing respect to Churchill's lonely warnings against the menace of Adolf Hitler. In September 1939, soon after the outbreak of the war, when Churchill was brought into the government as head of the admiralty, Roosevelt had initiated the first in what would become an extraordinary series of wartime letters between the two men. Writing in a friendly but respectful tone, Roosevelt had told Churchill: "I shall at all times welcome it if you will keep me in touch personally with everything you want me to know about. You can always send sealed letters through your pouch or my pouch." Though relatively few messages had been exchanged in the first nine months of the war, the seeds had been planted of an exuberant friendship, which would flourish in the years to come.

• • •

Once the Cabinet adjourned, Roosevelt had a short meeting with the minister of Belgium, who was left with only $35 since an order to freeze all credit held by Belgium, the Netherlands, and Luxembourg had gone into effect, earlier that morning. After arrangements were made to help him out, there began a working session on the speech Roosevelt was to deliver that night to a scientific meeting.

Then Roosevelt, not departing from his regular routine, went into his study for the cocktail hour, the most relaxed time of his day. The second-floor study, crowded with maritime pictures, models of ships, and stacks of paper, was the president's favorite room in the White House. It was here that he read, played poker, sorted his beloved stamps, and conducted most of the important business of his presidency. The tall mahogany bookcases were stuffed with books, and the leather sofas and chairs had acquired a rich glow. Any room Roosevelt spent time in, Frances Perkins observed, "invariably got that lived-in and overcrowded look which indicated the complexity and variety of his interests and intentions." Missy and Harry Hopkins were there, along with Pa Watson and Eleanor's houseguest, the beautiful actress Helen Gahagan Douglas. The cocktail hour, begun during Roosevelt's years in Albany, had become an institution in Roosevelt's official family, a time for reviewing events in an informal atmosphere, a time for swapping the day's best laughs. The president always mixed the drinks himself, experimenting with strange concoctions of gin and rum, vermouth and fruit juice.

During the cocktail hour, no more was said of politics or war; instead the conversation turned to subjects of lighter weight—to gossip, funny stories, and reminiscences. With Missy generally presiding as hostess, distributing the drinks to the guests, Roosevelt seemed to find complete relaxation in telling his favorite stories over and over again. Some of these stories Missy must have heard more than twenty or thirty times, but, like the "good wife," she never let her face betray boredom, only delight at the knowledge that her boss was having such a good time. And with his instinct for the dramatic and his fine ability to mimic, Roosevelt managed to tell each story a little differently each time, adding new details or insights.

On this evening, there was a delicious story to tell. In the Congress there was a Republican representative from Auburn, New York, John Taber, who tended to get into shouting fits whenever the subject of the hated New Deal came up. In a recent debate on the Wage and Hour amendments, he had bellowed so loudly that he nearly swallowed the microphone. On the floor at the time was Representative Leonard Schultz of Chicago, who had been deaf in his left ear since birth. As Mr. Taber's shriek was amplified through the loudspeakers, something happened to Mr. Schultz. Shaking convulsively, he staggered to the cloakroom, where he collapsed onto a couch, thinking he'd been hit in an air raid. He suddenly realized that he could hear with his left ear—for the first time in his life—and better than with his right. When doctors confirmed that Mr. Schultz's hearing was excellent, Mr. Taber claimed it was proof from God that the New Deal should be shouted down!

Harry Hopkins was no stranger to these intimate gatherings. Before his illness, he had been one of Roosevelt's favorite companions. Like Roosevelt, he was a great storyteller, sprinkling his tales with period slang and occasional profanity. Also like Roosevelt, he saw the humor in almost any situation, enjoying gags, wisecracks, and witticisms. "I didn't realize how smart Harry was," White House secretary Toi Bachelder later remarked, "because he was such a tease and would make a joke of everything."

Missy was undoubtedly as delighted as her boss to see Harry back at the White House, though her playful spirit most likely masked the genuine pleasure she took in the company of this unusual man. Once upon a time, after Hopkins' second wife, Barbara, died of cancer, there had been talk of a romance between Missy and Harry. In a diary entry for March 1939, Harold Ickes reported a conversation with presidential adviser Tommy Corcoran in which Corcoran had said "he would not be surprised if Harry should marry Missy." In that same entry, Ickes recorded a dinner conversation between his wife, Jane Ickes, and Harry Hopkins in which they "got to talking about women—a favorite subject with Harry. He told Jane that Missy had a great appeal for him."

Among Hopkins' personal papers, there are many affectionate notes to Missy. During a spring weekend in 1939 when Missy was at the St. Regis in New York, Hopkins sent her a telegram. "Vic and I arriving Penn Station 8. Going direct to St. Regis. Make any plans you want but include us." On another occasion, when Hopkins was in the hospital for a series of tests, he wrote her a long, newsy letter but admitted that "the real purpose of this letter is to tell you not to forget me.... Within a day or two I expect to be out riding in the country for an hour or so each day and only wish you were with me."

The president, Harry, and Missy had journeyed together to Warm Springs in the spring of 1938. "There is no one here but Missy—the President and me—so life is simple—ever so informal and altogether pleasant," Hopkins recorded. "Lunch has usually been FDR with Missy and me—these are the pleasantest because he is under no restraint and personal and public business is discussed with the utmost frankness.... After dinner the President retreats to his stamps—magazines and the evening paper. Missy and I will play Chinese checkers—occasionally the three of us played but more often we read—a little conversation—important or not—depending on the mood."

But if over the years their familiarity had brought Harry and Missy to the point of intimacy, Missy had probably cut it short, as she had cut short every other relationship in her life that might subordinate her great love for FDR. No invitation was accepted by Missy if it meant leaving the president alone. "Even the most ardent swain," *Newsweek* reported, "is chilled at the thought that, to invite her to a movie he must call up the White House, which is her home." At the end of her working day, Missy preferred to retire to her little suite on the third floor, where, more often than not, she would pick up her phone to hear the president on the line, asking her to come to his study and sit by his side as he sorted his stamps or went through his mail.

If this behavior seemed mistaken in the eyes of her friends, who could not imagine how someone so young and attractive, who "should have been off somewhere cool and gay on a happy weekend," would give up "date after date, month after month, year after year," Missy had no other wish than to be with Roosevelt, her eager eyes watching every movement of his face, marveling at his overwhelming personality, his facility for dealing with people of every sort, his exceptional memory, his unvarying good humor. "Gosh, it will be good to get my eyes on you again," Missy wrote Roosevelt once when he was on a trip. "This place is horrible when you are away."

While Franklin was mixing cocktails, Eleanor was on a train back to Washington from New York. For many of her fellow riders, the time on the train was a time to ease up, to gaze through the windows at the passing countryside, to close their eyes and unwind. But for Eleanor, who considered train rides her best working hours, there was little time to relax. The pile of mail, still unanswered, was huge, and there was a column to be written for the following day. Franklin's cousin Margaret "Daisy" Suckley recalls traveling with Eleanor once on the New York–to–Washington train. "She was working away the whole time with Malvina, and I was sitting there like a dumbbell looking out the window, and suddenly Mrs. Roosevelt said to Malvina, 'Now I'm going to sleep for fifteen minutes,' and she put her head back on the seat. I looked at my watch, and just as it hit fifteen minutes, she woke up and said, 'Now Tommy, let's go on.' It was amazing. I was stunned."

Even if Eleanor had reached the White House that evening in time for the cocktail hour, she would probably not have joined. Try as she might over the years, Eleanor had never felt comfortable at these relaxed gatherings. Part of her discomfort was toward alcohol itself, the legacy of an alcoholic father who continually failed to live up to the expectations and trust of his adoring daughter. One Christmas, Eleanor's daughter, Anna, and her good friend Lorena Hickok had chipped in to buy some cocktail glasses for Eleanor's Greenwich Village apartment in the hopes she would begin inviting friends in for drinks. "In a funny way," Anna wrote "Hick," as Miss Hickok was called, "I think she has always wanted to feel included in such parties, but so many old inhibitions have kept her from it."

But, despite Anna's best hopes, Eleanor's discomfort at the cocktail hour persisted, suggesting that beyond her fear of alcohol lay a deeper fear of letting herself go, of slackening off the work that had become so central to her sense of self. "Work had become for Eleanor almost as addictive as alcohol," her niece Eleanor Wotkyns once observed. "Even when she thought she was relaxing she was really working. Small talk horrified her. Even at New Year's, when everyone else relaxed with drinks, she would work until ten minutes of twelve, come in for a round of toasts, and then disappear to her room to work until two or three a.m. Always at the back of her mind were the letters she had to write, the things she had to do."

"She could be a crashing bore," Anna's son Curtis Dall Roosevelt admitted. "She was very judgmental even when she tried not to be. The human irregularities, the off-color jokes he loved, she couldn't take. He would tell his stories, many of them made to fit a point, and she would say, 'No, no, Franklin, that's not how it happened.' "

"If only Mother could have learned to ease up," her son Elliott observed, "things would have been so different with Father, for he needed relaxation more than anything in the world. But since she simply could not bring herself to unwind, he turned instead to Missy, building with her an exuberant, laughing relationship, full of jokes, silliness, and gossip."

• • •

"Stay for dinner. I'm lonely," Roosevelt urged Harry Hopkins when the cocktail hour came to an end. There were few others at this stage of his life that the president enjoyed as much as Hopkins. With the death in 1936 of Louis Howe, the shriveled ex-newspaperman who had fastened his star to Roosevelt in the early Albany days, helped him conquer his polio, and guided him through the political storms to the White House, the president had turned to Hopkins for companionship. "There was a temperamental sympathy between Roosevelt and Hopkins," Frances Perkins observed. Though widely different in birth and breeding, they both possessed unconquerable confidence, great courage, and good humor; they both enjoyed the society of the rich, the gay, and the well-born, while sharing an abiding concern for the average man. Hopkins had an almost "feminine sensitivity" to Roosevelt's moods, Sherwood observed. Like Missy, he seemed to know when the president wanted to consider affairs of state and when he wanted to escape from business; he had an uncanny instinct for knowing when to introduce a serious subject and when to tell a joke, when to talk and when to listen. He was, in short, a great dinner companion.

As soon as dinner was finished, Roosevelt had to return to work. In less than an hour, he was due to deliver a speech, and he knew that every word he said would be scrutinized for the light it might shed on the crisis at hand. Taking leave of Hopkins, Roosevelt noticed that his friend looked even more sallow and miserable now than he had looked earlier in the day. "Stay the night," the President insisted. So Hopkins borrowed a pair of pajamas and settled into a bedroom suite on the second floor. There he remained, not simply for one night but for the next three and a half years, as Roosevelt, exhibiting his genius for using people in new and unexpected ways, converted him from the number-one relief worker to the number-one adviser on the war. Later, Missy liked to tease: "It was Harry Hopkins who gave George S. Kaufman and Moss Hart the idea for that play of theirs, 'The Man Who Came to Dinner.' "

As the president was preparing to leave for Constitution Hall, he remembered something he had meant to ask Helen Gahagan Douglas during the cocktail hour. There was no time to discuss it now, but, stopping by her room, he told her he had an important question for her and asked if she would meet him in his study when he returned. "Certainly," she replied, and he left to address several thousand scientists and scholars at the Pan American Scientific Congress.

"We come here tonight with heavy hearts," he began, looking out at the packed auditorium. "This very day, the tenth of May, three more independent nations have been cruelly invaded by force of arms. . . . I am glad that we are shocked and angered by the tragic news." Declaring that it was no accident that this scientific meeting was taking place in the New World, since elsewhere war and politics had compelled teachers and scholars to leave their callings and become the agents of destruction, Roosevelt warned against an undue sense of security based on the false teachings of geography: in terms of the moving of men and guns and planes and bombs, he argued, every acre of American territory was closer to Europe than was ever the case before. "In modern times it is a shorter distance from Europe to San Francisco, California than it was for the ships and legions of Julius Caesar to move from Rome to Spain or Rome to Britain."

"I am a pacifist," he concluded, winding up with a pledge that was greeted by a great burst of cheers and applause, "but I believe that by overwhelming majorities . . . you and I, in the long run if it be necessary, will act together to protect and defend by every means at our command our science, our culture, our American freedom and our civilization."

Buoyed by his thunderous reception, Roosevelt was in excellent humor when he returned to his study to find Helen Gahagan Douglas waiting for him. Just as he was settling in, however, word came that Winston Churchill was on the telephone. Earlier that evening, Churchill had driven to Buckingham Palace, where King George VI had asked him to form a government. Even as Churchill agreed to accept the seals of office, British troops were pouring into Belgium, wildly cheered by smiling Belgians, who welcomed them with flowers. The change was made official at 9 p.m., when Chamberlain, his voice breaking with emotion, resigned. It had been a long and fateful day for Britain, but now, though it was nearly 3 a.m. in London, Churchill apparently wanted to touch base with his old letter-writing companion before going to sleep.

Though there is no record of the content of this first conversation between the new prime minister of England and the president of the United States, Churchill did reveal that when he went to bed that night, after the extraordinary events of an extraordinary day, he was conscious of "a profound sense of relief. At last I had the authority to give directions over the whole scene. I felt as if I were walking with Destiny, and that all my past life had been but a preparation for this hour and this trial."

"Therefore," Churchill concluded, "although impatient for morning, I slept soundly and had no need for cheering dreams. Facts are better than dreams." He had achieved the very position he had imagined for himself for so many years.

While Roosevelt was talking with Churchill, Helen Douglas tried to prepare herself for the important question the president wanted to ask her. Perhaps, she thought, it was related to her work with the farm-security program, or the National Youth Administration. Both Helen and her husband, fellow actor Melvyn Douglas, were ardent New Dealers, members of the National Advisory Commission for the Works Progress Administration and the California Advisory Commission for the NYA. Earlier that year, they had hosted Mrs. Roosevelt's visit to Los Angeles, accompanying her to the migrant-labor camps in the San Joaquin Valley.

"The day was unforgettable," Helen later recalled. "Soon after we started,

Mrs. Roosevelt spotted a cluster of makeshift shacks constructed of old boards, tarpaper and tin cans pounded flat, one of the ditch bank communities that were commonplace in California then." She asked to stop the car and walked across the field toward some migrants. "One of the bent figures straightened to see who was approaching and recognized her at once. 'Oh, Mrs. Roosevelt, you've come to see us,' he said. He seemed to accept as a natural event of American life that the wife of the President of the United States would be standing in a mucky field chatting with him."

Perhaps the president's question related to something his wife had told him about her journey. To be sure, Helen knew that Roosevelt loved movies and movie people, but not even that knowledge prepared her for the whimsical nature of the question the president posed to her that night.

"OK, Helen," Roosevelt began, his eyes flashing with good humor. "Now, I want you to tell me exactly what happened under the table at Ciro's between Paulette Goddard and Anatole Litvak." The juicy gossip Roosevelt wanted to hear involved the Russian-born director Anatole Litvak and Paulette Goddard, the vivacious brunette actress who was married first to the filmmaker Hal Roach and then to Charlie Chaplin. As Helen Douglas told the story, Goddard and Litvak were having dinner at the elegant nightclub, where the men had to wear tuxedos and the women long dresses, when the urge to make love became so strong that they eased themselves onto the floor under the table. As the moans were heard across the restaurant floor, waiters rushed to the scene with extra tablecloths to cover the sides of the table. Or so the story was told. "I love it, I love it," Roosevelt responded.

Returning to the White House from Union Station just as Helen was finishing her tale, Eleanor heard her husband's laughter and assumed that, as usual, he was with Missy, relaxing at the end of the day. At such times, she later admitted to her son Elliott, she felt terribly left out, wishing that she could let herself go and simply join in the frivolity. But as it was, she knew that if she opened the door she would be driven to talk business, to share the information and insights she had gleaned from her recent trip. Then, if her husband was tired and unresponsive, she would feel hurt and rejected. It had happened this way before. Better to go to her own bedroom and wait until morning to see her husband. "All her life," her niece Eleanor Wotkyns observed, "Eleanor yearned to be more spontaneous, to relax more readily, but in the end how can one force oneself to be spontaneous?"

At ten after eleven that evening, according to the White House usher diary, both Eleanor and Franklin went to bed—Franklin settling into his small bedroom off his study, Eleanor into her own suite of rooms, next to her husband's, in the southwest corner of the mansion. But the separation by night belied the partnership by day—a partnership that would help change the face of the country in the years ahead.

CHAPTER 2

"A FEW NICE BOYS WITH BB GUNS"

At 1 p.m. on May 16, 1940, President Roosevelt was scheduled to address a joint session of Congress. It was the president's first appearance in the House Chamber since the war in Western Europe had begun. Despite the blinding rain falling steadily since early morning, a huge audience had gathered to hear him.

Here, on the floor of the House of Representatives, all the contending forces of American life had gathered over the years to argue their causes—abolitionists versus slaveowners, liberals versus conservatives, unions versus management, farmers versus city-dwellers. On a number of occasions, particularly in the nineteenth century, the debates had descended into physical violence as members brandished pistols, smashed one another's heads with tongs, canes, and brass spittoons, and pummeled each other with fists. The very size of the House Chamber, with large numbers of legislators, clerks, and page boys running from place to place, conspired to produce confusion and chaos.

As one o'clock neared, there was a stir among the audience, an air of expectation. Every face, not knowing for sure where the country was going, wore a look of nervousness. In the Congress in 1940, there were 526 men and five women, nearly three hundred lawyers, two dozen schoolteachers, sixty merchants, twenty bankers and insurance agents, nine newspaper publishers, five dentists, a half-dozen preachers, the owner of the largest cattle ranch in the world, an amateur magician, and a half-dozen or more aspirants to the presidency. There was one Negro.

At 12:59 p.m. the assistant doorkeeper announced the members of the Cabinet. The spectators responded with warm applause. But when the audience caught sight of the president himself, his right hand holding a cane, his left hand grasping the forearm of a Secret Service man, they jumped to their feet, applauding and cheering him as he had never been cheered in the Capitol before, a bipartisan ovation that could only be interpreted as a demonstration of national unity in a time of crisis.

It had been a week no one in the Western world would forget. After only five days of fighting, Holland, with tens of thousands of her citizens said to be dead, had surrendered; the Belgian army was almost totally destroyed, and France, reputed to possess the best army in all of Europe, was being overrun. The Germans seemed to have discovered a radically new style of air-ground warfare that was somehow free from ordinary constraints of time and distance. The speed and destructiveness of Germany's powerful tanks —able to cross rivers and canals as if they were paved boulevards, resisting all fire at normal ranges—were almost incomprehensible. Against these metal mastodons, French Premier Paul Reynaud lamented, the French defenses were like "walls of sand that a child puts up against waves on the seashore." Equally hard to fathom was the effectiveness of Germany's air force, roaring in ahead of advancing columns, bombing communication lines, strafing and terrorizing ground troops to the point of an almost total Allied collapse.

For many in the audience, Roosevelt's dramatic journey to the Hill awakened memories of Woodrow Wilson's appearance before Congress in the spring of 1917, when America entered the Great War. Now, once again, Europe was engaged in an expanding war that threatened to engulf the entire world, and emotions were running high. As the applause continued to swell, the president slowly maneuvered his body up the long ramp from the well of the House to the rostrum.

Standing at the podium, his leg braces firmly locked into place, the president looked at his audience, and an uncharacteristic wave of nervousness came upon him. Absent were both his conspicuous smile and the swaggering way he usually held his head; in their place, a slight slump of the shoulders and a grim expression that matched the gray day. Reporters seated behind the podium detected anxiety in his trembling hands and in the faltering way he tried and failed, not once but twice, to put on his glasses. From the center of the visitors' gallery, where she was seated between Missy and Tommy, Eleanor looked down anxiously, a flush on her cheeks.

The president had cause to feel apprehensive. He knew that both Britain and France were looking to the United States for help. Alone among the democratic nations, the United States possessed the potential resources—the abundance of raw materials, the oil fields, the bauxite mines, the assembly lines, the production equipment, the idle manpower, the entrepreneurial skills, the engineering know-how—necessary to wage technological war on a scale equal to that of Nazi Germany. "I trust you realize, Mr. President," Churchill had written earlier that week, "that the voice and force of the United States may count for nothing if they are withheld too long."

But, as much as Roosevelt wanted to help, he recognized all too well—in a way neither Churchill nor French Premier Paul Reynaud could possibly have imagined—how unprepared America was, both mentally and physically, for war. In Europe, the vision of the New World coming to the rescue of the Old was so alluring that dreams were confused with realities, the boundary between potential and actual production erased, a mobilization that had not even begun considered a *fait accompli.* To harness a nation's economic potential for war was a complex process at any time, but, given the realities of American life in 1940, it seemed an almost impossible task.

• • •

The America over which Roosevelt presided in 1940 was in its eleventh year of depression. No decline in American history had been so deep, so lasting, so far-reaching. "The great knife of the depression," wrote Robert S. and Helen Merrill Lynd in their classic study, *Middletown in Transition,* "had cut down impartially through the entire population, cleaving open lives and hopes of rich as well as poor. The experience had been more nearly universal than any prolonged recent emotional experience in [America's] history. It had approached in its elemental shock the primary experiences of birth and death."

To be sure, the worst days were over—the days when breadlines and soup kitchens were forming in every city, when evicted families were shivering in makeshift tents in the dead of winter and jobless men were bivouacking around wood fires at the railroad tracks. The massive relief programs of the New Deal had stopped the precipitous slide of the first three and a half years, providing an economic floor for tens of millions of Americans.

But the economy had not yet recovered; business was still not producing well enough on its own to silence the growing doubts about capitalism and democracy. Almost ten million Americans, 17 percent of the work force, were without jobs; about two and a half million found their only source of income in government programs. Of those who worked, one-half of the men and two-thirds of the women earned less than $1,000 a year. Only forty-eight thousand taxpayers in a population of 132 million earned more than $2,500 a year.

In his second inaugural, Roosevelt had proclaimed that he saw "one-third of a nation ill-housed, ill-clad, ill-nourished." On this spring day three years later, he could still see abundant evidence of serious deprivation. Thirty-one percent of thirty-five million dwelling units did not have running water; 32 percent had no indoor toilet; 39 percent lacked a bathtub or shower; 58

percent had no central heating. Of seventy-four million Americans twenty-five years old or older, only two of five had gone beyond eighth grade; one of four had graduated from high school; one of twenty had completed college.

Though equal opportunity in a classless society still dominated the rhetoric of the day, the reality was a pyramidal society, a fortunate few at the top and the great mass of citizens stuck at the bottom with few opportunities to move upward on the economic ladder. America was then a predominantly small-town nation, with the majority of citizens living in towns of fewer than twenty-five thousand people. Within these towns, as in the neighborhoods of larger cities, society was stratified along class, racial, and ethnic lines.

"Class membership," historian Richard Polenberg has written of this period, "determined virtually every aspect of an individual's life: the subjects one studied in high school, the church one attended, the person one married, the clubs one joined, the magazines one read, the doctor one visited, the way one was treated by the law, and even the choice of an undertaker."

The American nation had been formed by the continual movement of people from Europe to the New World and then across a hostile continent in a restless, unflagging quest for new opportunity. But now, with the Western frontier closed and every section of America afflicted by depression, most Americans seemed frozen in place, rarely venturing to cross the lines of their county, much less their state.

To be sure, the New Deal, particularly in its exhilarating early days, had profoundly altered the relationship between the government and the people, giving the state final responsibility for the well-being of its citizens. Rejecting the traditional notion that government was the handmaiden of business, the New Deal Congress had enacted an unprecedented series of laws which regulated the securities market, established a minimum wage, originated a new system of social security, guaranteed labor's right to collective bargaining, and established control over the nation's money supply. "It is hard to think of another period in the whole history of the republic that was so fruitful," historian William Leuchtenberg has written, "or of a crisis that was met with as much imagination."

But by 1940, the New Deal revolution had sputtered to an end. The country was weary of reform, and Congress was in full rebellion against the administration's domestic agenda. A bipartisan coalition of conservative Southern Democrats and Republicans had seized the initiative, crushing the president's housing program, slashing appropriations for relief, killing the federal theater project, and eliminating the administration's undistributed-profits tax.

To complicate the situation further, the president's enemies on domestic issues were his friends in foreign policy, and vice versa. Since 1939, most conservative Democrats had supported the president's moves to aid the Allies, while many liberals and Midwestern progressives, fearing that the pull toward war would bring an end to social reform, had joined the isolationist cause.

For the president, there was perhaps additional anxiety in the recognition that the end of the "phony war" defined the beginning of a new presidency for him, one that would be judged by different standards. Roosevelt's old hero Woodrow Wilson was a painful memory in this regard. Wilson, too, had been cheered as never before on that April day in 1917 when he had come to Congress to ask for a declaration of war against Germany. Yet, two years later, after his bruising battle with the Senate over the League of Nations, the cheers had turned to jeers, and his presidency had been destroyed.

• • •

The leadership of the House and Senate—Speaker William Bankhead, House Majority Leader Sam Rayburn, and Senate Majority Leader Alben Barkley—sat behind the president on a marble dais, facing the semicircular rows of seats. In the front row sat the Cabinet—Secretary Woodring gripping the edge of his chair, Secretary Hull holding his chin in his hand, Harry Hopkins slumped in a tense silence. Across the chamber, buddy poppies could be seen on hundreds of lapels, a tribute to the soldiers of World War I who had fought on Flanders Field.

"These are ominous days," the President began in a low, solemn tone, facing a battery of microphones that would carry his words to the world, "days whose swift and shocking developments force every neutral nation to look to its defenses in the light of new factors.... No old defense is so strong that it requires no further strengthening and no attack is so unlikely or impossible that it may be ignored."

Nearly a third of the president's address was devoted to a skillful schoolmasterly description of the flying times from Greenland, the Azores, and the Caribbean Islands to key American cities, to show that, in an age of air warfare, despite the claims of the isolationists, the natural barriers of the Atlantic and Pacific oceans no longer afforded the same protection they had in the past. Deriving strength from the positive reaction to his words, Roosevelt's voice swelled as he warned that Nazi Germany not only had more planes than all its opponents combined, but appeared to have a weekly productive capacity that was far greater than that of its opponents.

How could America respond to this alarming situation? Roosevelt's answer was bold. He asked for appropriations to recruit an additional half-million men for the army, to purchase guns and equipment, to build modern tanks, and to construct naval ships. Then he made a dramatic call for a staggering productive capacity of fifty thousand planes a year, which would in only twelve months put America ahead of Germany, creating an aerial armada second to none in the world. How Roosevelt arrived at the fifty-thousand figure, way beyond the best hopes of his army and navy combined, is still not clear. Some say the giant number—more than ten times the current capacity—was put forth in a conversation with newspaper owner Lord Beaverbrook; others point to a conversation with Secretary Hull. Whatever the source, army historian Irving Holley concludes, "the President's big round number was a psychological target to lift sights and accustom planners in military and industrial circles alike to thinking big."

Speaking later about the fifty-thousand figure, U. S. Steel Chairman Edward Stettinius said it seemed at first "like an utterly impossible goal; but it caught the imagination of Americans, who had always believed they could accomplish the impossible." By laying down the gauntlet in such a sensational way, by projecting on his audience his own faith in the ability of the American people to respond to crisis, Roosevelt seemed to cast a spell upon the members of the House and the Senate, who sprang to their feet and began applauding wildly.

"There are some," Roosevelt concluded, "who say that democracy cannot cope with the new technique of government developed in recent years by a few countries—by a few countries which deny the freedoms which we maintain are essential to our democratic way of life. This I reject." To cope with present dangers, he admitted, the nation requires "a toughness of moral and physical fiber," but these are precisely "the characteristics of a free people, a people devoted to the institutions they themselves have built."

In times of crisis, presidential scholar Grant McConnell has written, the nation, which seemed only an abstraction the day before, suddenly becomes a vivid reality. A mysterious process unfolds as the president and the flag become rallying points for all Americans. At such moments, if the president is able to meet the challenge, he is able to give shape, to organize, to create and recreate the nation.

On May 16, 1940, President Roosevelt met this challenge. When he finished his speech, the voices of the senators and representatives rose in a ringing shout, a sustained ovation whose echoes remained in the chamber after the president had left.

The rain was over, but drops of water still dripped from the trees when the president emerged from the Capitol. At the bottom of the steps, Eleanor took leave of her husband to join a group of young people for lunch at the Powhatan Hotel. The president returned directly to his office, buoyed not simply by the tremendous reception he had received, but even more by his own expression of faith in the dormant powers of democracy, his unalterable belief in the American people.

• • •

Roosevelt "believed that with enough energy and spirit anything could be achieved by man," the philosopher Isaiah Berlin wrote in an essay comparing Roosevelt and Churchill. "So passionate a faith in the future," Berlin went on, "implies an exceptionally sensitive awareness, conscious or self-conscious, of the tendencies of one's milieu, of the desires, hopes, fears, loves, hatreds, of the human beings who compose it, of what are described as 'trends.'" This uncanny awareness, Berlin argued, was the source of Roosevelt's genius. It was almost as if the "inner currents [and] tremors" of human society were registering themselves within his nervous system, "with a kind of seismographical accuracy."

In his imagination on this grim May day, Roosevelt could already envision the construction of hundreds of new factories, fueled by new public-private partnerships, producing planes and tanks and guns, humming with the energies of millions of citizens. On the nation's roads he pictured tens of thousands of American families, their life's possessions in their automobiles, willing to go to wherever the opportunity for work would take them. Little matter that the economy was still depressed and that millions of workers had lost their skills. To the man whose ebullient energy had overcome paralysis, it was natural to believe that the American people, once aroused, would transform the nation, pitching into the work at hand with spirit and resilience. But even Roosevelt could not have imagined that he stood that day on the verge of the most profound transformation in American history.

"There's something that he's got," Harry Hopkins once told Frances Perkins. "It seems unreasonable at times, but he falls back on something that gives him complete assurance that everything is going to be all right that I can't even grasp, that he isn't able . . . to explain to me. I'm just left feeling that it's a ridiculous position he's taken. Why should he be sure that it will be all right?"

No factor was more important to Roosevelt's leadership than his confidence in himself and in the American people. "His most outstanding characteristic is an air of supreme self-confidence," journalist W. M. Kiplinger wrote as the crisis of the European war deepened. "He always gives the impression that to him nothing is impossible, that everything will turn out all right."

The president had a remarkable capacity to transmit this cheerful strength to others, to allow, White House Counsel Sam Rosenman observed, "those who hear it to begin to feel it and take part in it, to rejoice in it—and to return it tenfold by their own confidence." Frances Perkins claimed that "his capacity to inspire and encourage those who had to do tough, confused and practically impossible jobs was beyond dispute." Like everyone else, she said, she "came away from an interview with the President feeling better, not because he had solved any problems . . . but because he had made me feel more cheerful, stronger, more determined."

So it had been in 1933, when, in the midst of the worst days of the Depression, the new president was able to communicate his own strength and assurances to a badly frightened people. Speaking of his first inaugural address, *Collier's* observed that "the new President does not delude himself as to the difficulties that lie before him, and yet he was serenely confident as to the ultimate outcome." By this single speech, Rosenman wrote, Roosevelt accomplished one of the most significant achievements of his presidency: "the renewal of the courage and hope and faith of the American people.

Within a week, more than half a million letters and telegrams were on their way to the White House, expressing faith in him and in his leadership."

Such serenity and strength were precisely the qualities called for in the spring of 1940, as America faced a second national crisis, even more fearful than the first. His belief that dormant energies of democracy could mobilize the nation to meet the Nazi threat was matched only by his own faith in himself. To be optimistic had become his stance in life, so much that, even when he had no reason to be so, he acted upbeat, so as not to disappoint the expectations of everyone around him.

• • •

In the afterglow of the president's triumphant speech, all the leading Republicans—Kansas governor and Republican presidential candidate in 1936, Alf Landon; newspaper publisher Colonel Frank Knox; and New York Governor Tom Dewey—fell into line. Even former President Herbert Hoover was forced to admit, "the President is right." What made this united front more striking was that the president had made no mention in his speech of how the government was going to pay for the new defense program. When reporters queried him, he used the metaphor of "a four alarm fire up the street" which must be extinguished immediately, without worrying about cost. His homely figure of speech evaded the issue and achieved his end. The main thing was to arouse the public to the Nazi threat, and then worry about how to raise the cash.

But the unified alarm about American security, as *Time* magazine pointed out, "was quickly succeeded by alarm over the fate of the GOP in 1940." On second thought, Tom Dewey proclaimed, the fifty-thousand figure was ridiculous. On second thought, Alf Landon stated, the president's message was "tragically late." On second thought, newspaper publisher Frank Gannett said, the message dramatized "the failure of the New Deal to meet and solve the basic problems facing the country."

The expected Republican criticism assumed a darker tone that Sunday night, May 18, when Colonel Charles Lindbergh, the famed aviator, in a nationwide radio address accused the administration of creating "a defense hysteria" and insisted that the United States was not threatened by foreign invasion unless "American peoples bring it on through their own quarreling and meddling with affairs abroad." The only reason we are in danger of becoming involved, he concluded, "is because there are powerful elements in America who desire us to take part. They represent a small minority of the American people, but they control much of the machinery of influence and propaganda. They seize every opportunity to push us closer to the edge."

The isolationists had found their champion. Senator Bennett Clark of Missouri termed Lindbergh's speech "magnificent," and Representative John Rankin of Mississippi called it "the finest advice I have heard in many a day." Senator Gerald P. Nye of North Dakota was glad, he said, "to hear a voice like

Lindbergh's raised in the cause of sanity at this wild moment—a moment engineered by the President."

Lindbergh's scathing critique legitimized congressional fault-finding with the president's popular speech. "During the present Administration," Senator Clark argued, "we have spent in excess of $6 billion on building up the Army and the Navy, and now we are told that we are pitifully unprepared. Simply because an emergency has developed abroad, are we going to turn over lump sums to the same outfit of bunglers that apparently wasted the $6 billion we spent." Two days later, Clark took the floor again. "[Are we going] to pour another billion dollars down the same rat hole?" he asked. (In fact, spread over the years of the Roosevelt administration the $6 billion amounted to less than three-quarters of a billion a year, hardly enough to keep a small army in existence.)

"If I should die tomorrow," Roosevelt told Henry Morgenthau at lunch in a rare moment of blind fury the day after Lindbergh's speech, "I want you to know this. I am convinced Lindbergh is a Nazi." Roosevelt did not anger easily, Eleanor later observed, "but when he did get angry, he was like an iceberg and . . . he could say things that would finish a relationship forever." On the issue of Lindbergh, however, Roosevelt was not alone. "When I read Lindbergh's speech," President Herbert Hoover's Secretary of State Henry Stimson wrote Roosevelt, "I felt it could not have been better put if it had been written by Goebbels himself. What a pity that this youngster had completely abandoned his belief in our form of government and has accepted Nazi methods because apparently they are efficient." Speaking in a more tempered voice, Eleanor told a newspaper reporter she thought the first part of Lindbergh's speech, which analyzed the position of America in the air, was "excellent," but "the last three paragraphs," referring to the sinister elements in America, seemed to her "unfortunate."

Despite the discordant note provided by Lindbergh's blast, the president's skillful speech achieved exactly what he wanted. Before the week was over, the Congress had voted to raise the debt ceiling and to authorize even more monies than the administration had requested. To the army would go a half-billion to train new troops, expedite munitions, and build new tanks and new planes. The navy would receive a quarter-billion to step up its shipbuilding program and to provide all vessels with the latest equipment. Also included in the congressional appropriations was the establishment of additional aviation schools and an increase in the number of pilots from twelve hundred to seven thousand a year.

• • •

Even the most lavish appropriations, however, could not shorten the waiting period of eighteen months projected for the actual delivery of the new tanks, planes, and weapons. The president's optimism about the future was one thing; the reality of America's present state of preparedness—as evidenced by the army's sorry maneuvers currently under way in Louisiana—was quite another.

Under a hot May sun, "on russet roads of sand and clay," the army's "Blue" forces, forty-thousand strong, were on the march in the biggest peacetime maneuver in the history of the United States. The Blues were heading west from Fort Benning, Georgia, to the Sabine Forest in Louisiana to defend their "mythical nation" against a lightning attack by thirty thousand "Red" forces moving east from Texas. (The defenders were given the benefit of more troops.) The war games were intended to serve as a field test of the new triangular divisions, to evaluate the use of horse cavalry against mechanized forces, and to provide practice in advancing large units under danger of air attack.

Through nine months of strenuous training, the soldiers had been living in the field and sleeping on the ground in rain and freezing weather to harden them for this first great maneuver. The supply officers had been preparing nearly as long to accumulate the 177 freightcar-loads of food, 190 tankloads of gas, 10,000 pieces of artillery, 3,500 horses, 1,600 observer stations, and 9,000 civilian volunteers. The games were scheduled to last two weeks and to cost more than a million dollars a day.

The announcement of the war games conjured an image of mock battles with long columns of soldiers running toward each other through the woods, waving flags, shooting blanks, hurling sham explosives into the air. In this glorified image, victory would be accorded to the side that reached a certain goal line first. Anticipating an exciting display of action, men, women, and children lined the Louisiana streets and the Gulf Coast highways to cheer the men on.

In reality, the maneuvers comprised a series of discrete and often invisible exercises—such as penetrating a line, crossing a river, bringing down a plane, or establishing a machine-gun nest on a knoll. At every point, an umpire, with a distinguishing badge on his arm, would determine which side had achieved the advantage. If, for instance, a squadron of Red airplanes came upon a line of Blue trucks moving along the highway in broad daylight, the penalty assessed against the Blues for leaving themselves exposed to "aerial attack" would be severe. Or, if the Blues reached a particular bridge first and could prove they had sufficient explosives to blow it up, then the Reds, upon reaching the "blown-up bridge," would be forced to stay in place until their engineers were able to improvise a new bridge in the same spot. In each instance, an umpire would be on top of the action, record his scores in a small book, and compare with the other umpires that evening to create a pattern of all the advances and losses during the entire day's actions.

"Consider the task," a *Times-Picayune* reporter observed, "faced by the men who shall umpire the war games." Whereas football referees must be on top of every play and watch the movements of twenty-two players on a level playing field, the field of play in the war games included muddy swamps, thick forests, and steep hills, nearly a hundred miles long and fifty miles wide, encompassing nearly seventy thousand players moving an average of 150 miles a day.

On May 10, the first day of the maneuvers, the Red forces, under General Walter Krueger, gained the advantage by surprising the Blues with an early-morning attack. At 4:30 a.m., a column of big armored trucks, their headlights "drilling bright tunnels through the blackness," roared down the back roads of Louisiana, awakening farmers and setting their dogs to howl. At the same time, a squadron of Red bombers attacked the Blue airport at McComb, Mississippi, causing damage to scores of Blue planes. The advance guard of the Blues, led by General Walter Short, had just arrived in the Sabine Forest when the Reds attacked. Exhausted from an overland march from Georgia covering more than six hundred miles, the Blues were no match for the Reds, who won the first encounter decisively. But two days later, the Blue reinforcements arrived at the scene, and the Blues succeeded in penetrating the Red line of resistance. And so it continued for two weeks, as first one side, then the other gained the advantage.

Before the maneuvers officially started, a series of landing accidents destroyed three pursuit planes and so completely damaged the undercarriage of a transport plane that twelve soldiers had to parachute out before it spiraled to the ground. One of the twelve became entangled in his parachute and drowned in the Pearl River. Two days later, Private Harold Vanderbilt of Cove, Arkansas, was killed when he slipped off a log and was crushed under a heavy army truck. That same day, Private Marion Caudell was electrocuted when the radio antennae on his scout car came in contact with a high-tension wire. By week's end, twelve soldiers were dead and nearly four hundred had been admitted to the hospital for injuries and diseases. As the war games progressed, the death toll rose. In a related maneuver, two entire flight crews, eleven men in all, were killed when two army bombers crashed to the earth in the middle of a suburban development.

But the accidents were not the only problem. It was the antiquated equipment, measured against the backdrop of the fast-moving war in Europe, that turned the gigantic maneuvers into a farce. In every critique, inside the army and out, lack of equipment was cited as *the* major problem. Though the morale of the American soldiers was universally praised, it was clear from the shape of the European struggle that courage and daring mattered less than the heavy power of the Germans' revolutionary form of attack—with dive-bombers, artillery, and heavy tanks all tied into one consolidated force. The most glaring weakness the maneuvers revealed was a stunning lack of combat planes. Though the assembly of planes at Barksdale Field was billed as "the greatest concentration of combat planes" ever brought together in the United States, virtually "a sea of planes," the actual total was only four hundred, a mere one day's supply in the current war. Until their opinion was undercut by Germany's shocking use of its air force as the spearhead of its blitzkrieg, the American generals had maintained that the air force was merely an auxiliary force. Consequently, the American army had almost no warplanes. At the end of the maneuvers, General Short admitted that, of the thirty-four missions he had requested of the air corps, only two were accomplished.

Nor were the American ground troops accustomed to shaping their behavior in response to air power. "Too frequently," *The Army & Navy Journal* observed in its critique of the maneuvers, "roads were jammed with motor vehicles closed up bumper to bumper, thus affording excellent targets, not only for artillery fire and air bombing, but also giving the enemy excellent information regarding locations and movements. The occasions when attempt was made to hide vehicles at halts, even in this wooded country, were rare."

Lack of tanks posed a problem almost as troubling as lack of planes. For too many years, high-ranking traditionalists, still believing in the superiority of the horse, had opposed action to upgrade the armored forces. As late as February 1940, even though the Polish cavalry had been dismembered by the German panzers in a matter of minutes, the *Cavalry Journal* was still arguing for the supremacy of the horse. "It is a mistake to persuade the public to attach exaggerated importance to motorization and mechanization," the *Cavalry Journal* contended, "because these can only play a small part in static warfare, which would seem to be the only sort of warfare probable in Western Europe. . . . The idea of huge armies rolling along roads at a fast pace is a dream. Apart from all questions of space and capacity of roads and bridges, rivers and mountains hamper the mass employment of motor vehicles." Besides, "men can keep animals in health and work for indefinite periods without difficulty or outside assistance, but oil and tires cannot like forage be obtained locally."

As a result of such attitudes, though there were acres and acres of land literally covered with the thirty-five hundred horses available for the maneuvers, only 450 tanks participated. And these tanks, Senator Henry Cabot Lodge, Jr., pointed out, were virtually all the tanks the United States had, or about "one finger of the fan-like German advance." When these few tanks were put into action, the results were electrifying. As townspeople watched from porches and roofs, two hundred horses galloped through the streets to their "deaths" in a futile effort to fend off the "slashing, onrushing mechanized brigade." In another exercise, witnesses watched in amazement as a tank brigade roared down an overgrown hill through briars, sumac, and bushes, over ravines where no horse could have crossed. "They were hit on all sides by these red hot bullets but the tanks were immune to rifle fire and small machine gun fire," one observer noted. "I wonder what would have been the effect if we had had on the hillside a unit of horse cavalry, where those red-hot bullets were shooting through the air."

Though cavalry leaders adamantly denied that the motor had made the horse obsolete, General Brees acknowledged that during the maneuvers the infantry and the horse cavalry had tended to become "road-bound"; the infantry was reluctant to detruck and the cavalry stuck to the roads, even when the muddy terrain made forward movement all but impossible.

In addition to numerical superiority, the German tanks were far superior to the American tanks in quality. Whereas the German soldiers sat in comfort and convenience in their heavy vehicles, complete with upholstered seats, shock absorbers, and bumpers, the driver of an American tank, buttoned up in fifteen tons of steel, with virtually no windows, was dependent for sight and direction on signals from the car commander, who sat above him in the turret. And since the clatter of the tank was like "the noise of ten robots tap dancing inside a cement mixer," the business of signaling was no easy matter. Amid such din, the commander in the turret had to rely on foot signals to the driver's shoulder and back. Two kicks meant "Go straight ahead." One kick on the right or left shoulder called for a right or left turn. If the soldier on top was shot, the driver was completely blind. Not surprisingly, soldiers dubbed the American machines "hell buggies."

"The gravity of this situation," Senator Lodge told his colleagues, "consists in the fact that it is almost as difficult to produce tanks as it is to produce planes." To manufacture even one light tank, more than half a dozen time-consuming steps had to be taken, with each part made in a different place: the motor by Continental Aircraft, the armor plate by Diebold Company in Ohio, rubber treads by Goodyear, weapons by Browning, special gears by a variety of firms. Then all the parts had to be sent to Rock Island Arsenal in Illinois to be assembled.

In recognition of the weaknesses revealed by the games, a secret meeting took place in the basement of Alexandria High School on the day the maneuvers ended. At this meeting, Generals Adna Chaffee and John Magruder, commanders of the army's sole tank brigade, and other officers committed to tanks, such as Colonel George Patton, presented their case for an independent armored force. Up to this moment, the tank brigade was under the calvary and infantry divisions, which had deliberately reduced the number of tanks. Pointedly, the chiefs of cavalry and infantry were not invited to the meeting, though they were nearby at the time. The basement conspirators sent their recommendation for an independent branch to Washington. General Marshall responded positively. He withdrew all armor from Cavalry and Infantry and placed it in a new, independent armored force.

American arrogance died during the maneuvers. "Overnight, the pleasant doings in Louisiana became old-fashioned nonsense," *Time* reported. "Against Europe's total war, the U.S. Army looked like a few nice boys with BB guns."

"The fact remains," Senator Lodge asserted, "that our Army today is not what it ought to be." For, if these troops were the cream of the U.S. Army, the best-trained, the most fully equipped, and if they evidenced such great problems, then one could only begin to imagine the situation in the rest of the army.

This was the desolate backdrop to the president's call for arms in his address to the Congress. "What smoldered beneath his words," *Time* observed, "was the warning that the U.S. will have to arm with all its might and main, because the world that is closing in on it is no longer safe for democracy."

• • •

Encouraged by the generally positive reaction to his congressional speech, Roosevelt turned his attention next to the difficult task of translating the idea of preparedness into reality. So complex were the demands of modern warfare, requiring the conversion of existing plants and the creation of new facilities, compelling the transfer of scientific research from objects of peace to weapons of war, demanding new accommodations between business, government, and labor, that dozens of critical policy decisions had to be made.

It was Roosevelt's primary strength that he saw how one decision related to another. The way the government was organized to meet the crisis, for example, would influence the cooperation of industry, the allocation of manpower, and the control of scarce resources. "There were evidently many times when he could truly see it all," Frances Perkins' biographer George Martin wrote, "men, guns, ships, food, the enemy, the Allies."

The first undertaking was to mobilize the business community behind the drive for preparedness. The Congress could provide the money, but it could not build the planes, design the tanks, or assemble the weapons. Without the cooperation of private industry, Roosevelt believed, the massive production effort needed for defense would never get off the ground. The fundamental challenge, as Roosevelt saw the situation that spring, was to bring the proprietors of the nation's chief economic assets—the men who ran the steel mills, the coal mines, the factories, and the automobile plants—into the defense effort as active participants.

It would not be an easy task. For years, business had been driven by an almost primitive hostility to Roosevelt, viewing his zealous support for the welfare state and organized labor as an act of betrayal to his class. Indeed, so incoherent were most businessmen in their rage at Roosevelt that they refused even to say the president's name, referring to him simply as "that man in the White House." The story is told of Howland Spencer, one of Roosevelt's wealthy neighbors, whose anger at the president was so fierce that he exiled himself to the Bahamas through the thirties and forties and only came back after Roosevelt's death.

The hostility had begun in the early days of the New Deal, when business felt steadily encroached upon by the never-ending series of laws which set minimum wages, regulated working conditions, and bolstered unionization. The ill-will had crystallized in 1935, when the Chamber of Commerce formally broke with the president, issuing a vicious denunciation of the New Deal. Roosevelt was wounded by the ferocity of the attack. As he looked back on his first term, he believed he had saved capitalism from itself by tempering its harshest effects. Without the New Deal, he believed, capitalism in America would have been overcome, as it was in Europe, by fascism or communism. Yet, Roosevelt complained, the U.S. Chamber of Commerce appreciated none of this, preferring to castigate him as a traitor to his class.

Roosevelt had responded in kind, lashing out at businessmen as "economic royalists" who were using their economic power to block equality of opportunity for the ordinary citizen in the same way the English Tories had sought to control the lives of the colonists. In the months that followed this outburst, the president's split with business deepened. Indeed, Roosevelt had found in class divisions an important source of political strength. The forces "of organized money are unanimous in their hatred of me," the president told a tumultuous working-class crowd during the 1936 campaign, "and I welcome their hatred. I should like to have it said of my first Administration that in it the forces of selfishness and of lust for power met their match.... I should like to have it said of my second Administration that in it these forces met their master."

As the situation in Europe darkened, the fears of business blazed into hysteria at the prospect of the increased power war would bring to the president. If war came, the president of the American Iron & Steel Institute said, "as certain as night follows day," while we are fighting "to crush dictatorship abroad," we will be "extending one at home." Some businessmen went so far as to suggest that Roosevelt was maneuvering the country into war in order to accomplish his Machiavellian design to install a permanent form of socialism in the United States.

But now, with thousands of people dying at the hands of Hitler every day, Roosevelt decided that the time had come to bring an end to his private war with business, to change his tack and give business a piece of the action, a chance to show whether or not it could truly deliver. "It was a political necessity on the eve of war," the Washington correspondent for *The Nation,* I. F. Stone, wrote at the time, "for a left-centered government in the United States to conciliate the Right by taking some of its representatives into the government. The same process, in reverse, occurred in England, whereby a Conservative government under Churchill conciliated Labor by taking the Bevins and the Morrisons into the Cabinet."

The scheme Roosevelt devised—a seven-member advisory board to be known as the National Defense Advisory Commission (NDAC)—was ingenious. Roosevelt's clever formula was to combine businessmen and New Dealers in equal measure, hopeful that the businessmen would thereby strengthen the faith of the right, while the New Dealers would keep the liberals in line.

For the critical job of directing the actual production process itself, Roosevelt chose millionaire businessman William Knudsen, head of General Motors, a classic example of the self-made man. Born in Copenhagen, Knudsen had come to America at the age of twenty, barely speaking a word of English. He had begun his career in the auto industry as an installer of assembly plants and then moved up the organization to become Henry Ford's production manager. A dispute with Ford led to his becoming vice-president of General Motors, with the task of building a Chevrolet to outsell Ford's Model T. He did this so successfully that he was appointed president of General Motors in 1937, commanding a salary of more than $350,000 a year.

"To many a citizen tired of New Deal–Business baiting," *Time* observed, "Knudsen was a symbol of the hope that business and the New Deal would work together." For his part, Knudsen was thrilled at the chance to serve the country that had served him so well. "I am most happy," he wrote the president after his appointment, "you've made it possible for me to show my gratitude to my country for the opportunity it has given me to acquire home, family and happiness in abundant measure."

In addition to Knudsen, Roosevelt brought in Edward Stettinius, chairman of U.S. Steel, to supervise the production and delivery of raw materials, and Ralph Budd, chairman of the Chicago, Burlington & Quincy, to handle transportation. For seven years, Washington observer Constance Green recorded, these men had formed the core of resistance to the New Deal; "now the captains of industry whom General Hugh Johnson in early NRA days had called 'Corporals of Disaster,' were again honored in Washington." Before the end of the summer, hundreds of businessmen found themselves at the very center of government action, and once they were there, their attitudes toward government control underwent a remarkable change.

Responding to the president's olive branch, the National Association of Manufacturers took out a full-page advertisement in June, pledging its knowledge, skill, and resources to the task of national defense, calling for national unity in the midst of crisis. "In the field of national defense," well-informed sources had been telling business all along, "Roosevelt is a conservative." Now, with Roosevelt's stress on cooperation rather than coercion, business began to believe that maybe this was so, that perhaps, if they put aside their hatred for the regime in power, there just might be "a little something in this saving the world for democracy again."

But, of course, Roosevelt never moved in only one direction at a time. The complex problem he faced was how to reawaken support on the right without instilling anger and discontent on the left. To this end, he gave the New Dealers four of the seven appointments. To handle labor, he brought in labor leader Sidney Hillman. A short, spare man who peered through bifocals and spoke with a marked Lithuanian accent, Hillman had come to America at twenty, the same age as Knudsen, landing in Chicago. He had become a cutter of men's garments at a time when conditions in the clothing industry were intolerable. Leading a revolt among the tailors, Hillman had created the Amalgamated Clothing Workers of America, and then, from the strength of this base, had become John Lewis' right-hand man in building the CIO.

Even more reassuring to the left, the President put Leon Henderson, a noisy New Dealer, in charge of prices. People said of the overweight Henderson that he looked like a Sunday-supplement caricature of a radical, with his wrinkled suits, his curly hair, and his nickel cigar stuck in the corner of his mouth. Born in Millville, New Jersey, and educated at Swarthmore on an athletic scholarship, Henderson had come to Washington to work for the Works Progress Administration. After moving on from there to the Securities and Exchange Commission, he had become a leader in the New Deal attack on business abuse.

To round out this strange amalgam of a commission, Roosevelt brought in University of North Carolina Dean Harriet Elliott to represent consumers, and Federal Reserve Board member Chester Davis to supervise farm products.

Within the NDAC in the months ahead, a fierce battle would rage between the businessmen, who argued that production was best served by industries working freely under the profit system, and the liberals, who believed that a democracy at war should forge wholly new connections between government, business, and labor, moving more in the direction of socialism. "If you are going to war in a capitalist country," Henry Stimson wrote, "you have to let business make money out of the process or business won't work." To the contrary, historian Bruce Catton argued, suppose that liberal bureaucrats instead of industrialists were running the program; perhaps then an entirely different kind of war effort would emerge, one that vested power and responsibility more directly in the workers themselves.

"The conflict was enduring," New Deal economist John Kenneth Galbraith recalled. "My memory of wartime Washington by no means excludes the menace of Hitler and the Japanese. But almost as poignantly it is of the New Dealers' battle with the reluctant business spokesman. . . . At times it seemed that our war with business took precedence over the war in Europe and Asia. There were weeks when Hitler scarcely entered our minds compared with the business types in Washington."

No sooner had the president announced his seven-member advisory commission than the conservative press began demanding that it be given real power and that Knudsen be appointed its "czar." "In private life," the *Kennebunk Journal* observed, "even a peanut stand has to have one boss." It was all voiced in the guise of needing to centralize power for efficiency, but, as liberal commentators pointed out, "the cry for a czar sprang from the desire of big business to take full control of defense and to use defense for its own purposes." In other words, the *New Republic* wryly observed, "let democratic processes abdicate in favor of a business dictatorship. If the lack of a chairman becomes a real problem," the *New Republic* continued, then Leon Henderson "would be the excellent choice."

But the president was not about to abdicate his own leadership of the defense effort to anyone—businessman or New Dealer, conservative or liberal. Spreading power among contending forces allowed Roosevelt to retain undisputed authority in his own hands. When, at the end of the first meeting of the NDAC, Knudsen asked, "Who is my boss?" the president instantly replied, "I guess I am." This reply, more than anything, Budget Director Harold Smith recorded in his diary, "helped to clear the atmosphere." "So long as Roosevelt held the final power over defense," I. F. Stone wrote, "he remained an obstacle to big business attempts to use defense as an excuse for repealing the social reform legislation of the New Deal and weakening the labor movement."

Yet, by refusing to grant Knudsen power proportionate to his responsibility, Roosevelt hobbled the mobilization effort in 1940. The task Roosevelt set for the NDAC was nothing less than the conversion of a peacetime economy to war production, but Knudsen was never given the tools to operate effectively. Roosevelt was being truthful and not truthful at the same time. While claiming that the American people would do anything asked of them provided they fully understood what they were being asked, Roosevelt was afraid of asking too much. Despite the swelling demand for preparedness, he did not trust the people's willingness at this juncture to make sacrifices in order to speed up the mobilization process.

On the contrary, at his press conference announcing the NDAC, he deliberately sought to assure the public that consumer goods would not be restricted. "I think people should realize," he said in answer to a question by Doris Fleeson, "that we are not going to upset, any more than we have to, a great many of the normal processes of life. . . . This delightful young lady will not have to forego cosmetics, lipsticks, ice cream sodas. . . . In other words, we do not want to upset the normal trend of things any more than we possibly can help."

• • •

Even as Roosevelt nursed the relationship between business and government along, he understood clearly that the marriage was "an uneasy one, with both parties meditating extensive infidelities." By playing the role of matchmaker, he risked incurring displeasure from both sides, but since the whole basis of the nation's war-production program depended on cooperation by industry, he was willing to assume that risk.

On Sunday evening, May 26, 1940, Roosevelt carried his appeal for the new partnership to the American people in a special "fireside chat." During his seven years in the White House, Roosevelt had delivered thirteen fireside chats. The first four talks, in the spring and summer of 1933, had focused on the banking crisis, the currency situation, the New Deal program, and the National Recovery Act. Averaging fewer than two chats a year since then, on the belief that less is more, he had delivered his last nationwide radio address on September 3, 1939, on the outbreak of the European war.

The term "fireside chat" had been inspired by Press Secretary Steve Early's statement that the president liked to think of the audience as being "a few people around his fireside." The public could then picture the president relaxing in his study in front of the fireplace and imagine that they were sitting beside him. "You felt he was talking to you," correspondent Richard Strout recalled, "not to 50 million others but to you personally."

In talking on the radio, Roosevelt used simple words, concrete examples, and everyday analogies to make his points. In contrast to the dramatic oratory suitable when speaking to a crowd, Rosenman recalled, "he looked for words that he would use in an informal conversation with one or two of his friends," words the average American could easily understand. Each speech was the product of extensive preparation, having gone through perhaps a dozen drafts before the president was satisfied that he had the talk he wanted.

Roosevelt also paid careful attention to his delivery and to the sound of his voice. When he discovered that the separation between his front two lower teeth was producing a slight whistle on the air, he had a removable bridge made, which he kept in his bedroom in a heart-shaped silver box. On more than one occasion, White House secretary Grace Tully recalled, he forgot to bring the box with him, and "there was a last minute dash" to retrieve the false tooth from his bedroom.

On the evening of this Sunday's broadcast, the president assembled his usual group for cocktails and dinner. Missy was there, along with Hopkins and Rosenman. It was not a relaxed occasion. "There was no levity," Rosenman recalled. "There was no small talk." As the president mechanically mixed drinks, his mind "thousands of miles away," he was reading a series of the most recent dispatches from Europe, all of them depicting a complete rout of the Allied armies. "All bad, all bad," he muttered as he read one report after another.

"The President was worried," Rosenman observed. Everyone was worried. "It was a dejected dinner group." But once the president settled himself in the Diplomatic Cloak Room on the first floor, sitting behind a desk crowded with three microphones, a reading light, and a pitcher of water, his old spirit returned. As the hour of ten o'clock approached, the peak listening hour, he put out his cigarette, arranged his reading copy, and then, on signal, began to speak.

In his mind's eye, Frances Perkins observed, he could actually see the people gathered in their kitchen, their living rooms, their parlors. "He was conscious of their faces and hands, their clothes and homes. . . . As he talked his head would nod and his hands would move in simple, natural, comfortable gestures. His face would smile and light up as though he were actually sitting on the front porch or in the parlor with them. People felt this, and it bound them to him in affection."

"My friends," he began, "at this moment of sadness throughout most of the world I want to talk with you about a number of subjects that directly affect the future of the U.S." He then went on to assure the nation that whatever needed to be done to keep the U.S. secure would be done. We shall build our defenses, he said, "to whatever heights the future may require. We shall build them swiftly, as the methods of warfare swiftly change.

"It is whispered by some," the familiar voice continued, "that only by abandoning our freedom, our ideals, our way of life, can we build our defenses adequately, can we match the strength of the aggressors. . . . I do not share these fears."

On the contrary, though fascism had a tremendous head start in mobilizing for war, Roosevelt had no doubt that American democracy, with its free-enterprise system and its reservoir of mass energy, would win the struggle in the long run. As long as a new relationship between business and government could be forged, success was assured.

Reaching first to the business community, Roosevelt extended an extraordinary promise of governmental cooperation and support. "I know that private business cannot be expected to make all of the capital investments required for expansion of plants and factories and personnel which this program calls for at once. It would be unfair to expect industrial corporations or their investors to do this, when there is a chance that a change in international affairs may stop or curtail orders a year or two hence. Therefore, the Government of the United States stands ready to advance the necessary money to help provide for the enlargement of factories, of necessary workers, the development of new sources of supply for the hundreds of raw materials required, the development of quick mass transportation of supplies. And the details of this are now being worked out in Washington, day and night."

Indeed, even as Roosevelt spoke, officials in the War Department were drafting legislation that would sanction a new "cost plus fixed fee" contract which would allow the government to defray all costs essential to the execution of defense contracts and guarantee the contractor a profit through a fixed fee determined in advance. In other words, the government would assume primary financial responsibility for the mobilization process. At the same time, legislation was being drafted to permit the government to make advance payments of up to 30 percent of the contract price, and to allow defense contracts to be let without the cumbersome procedure of lowest bids. Where private capital was unable to finance expansion because the facilities involved had no demand in peacetime—powder plants, high explosives, bombs—the government would be authorized to construct and operate the plants on its own.

After reaching out to business, Roosevelt turned his attention to his basic constituency—the people at large. "We must make sure in all that we do that there be no breakdown or cancellation of any of the great social gains which we have made in these past years. We have carried on an offensive on a broad front against social and economic inequalities, against abuses which had made our society weak. That offensive should not now be broken down by the pincers movement of those who would use the present needs of physical military defense to destroy it."

There was nothing in the present emergency, he went on, to justify lowering the standards of employment, reducing the minimum wage, making workers toil longer hours without due compensation, or breaking down the old-age pensions. Though businessmen were already arguing for a suspension of New Deal regulations that bore on labor, working conditions, and minimum wages on the grounds that such legislation restricted speedy mobilization, Roosevelt took the opposite tack. "While our navy and our airplanes and our guns may be our first lines of defense, it is still clear that way down at the bottom, underlying them all, giving them their strength, sustenance and power, are the spirit and morale of a free people."

When the president reached this part of his speech, Eleanor, listening from the living room of her Greenwich Village apartment, must have breathed a sigh of relief. She trusted that in her husband's heart he intended, even in the face of war, to preserve the social and economic reforms of the New Deal, but she worried that all the businessmen now swarming around the White House would demand an end to the hated New Deal as the price for their support.

Over the years, Eleanor had come to a distrust of business far deeper than her husband's equivocal attitude. Believing that business inevitably placed priority on the bottom line, she regularly excoriated the blindness of the let-business-alone people whose philosophy was "Take from the bottom, add to the top." "One can't be sure of any corporation," she once wrote, "if a huge sum of money should be placed before it."

When the president's fireside chat came to an end, Eleanor called Joe Lash, who announced that he had liked the last part of the speech, about safeguarding the social advances, best. Chuckling appreciatively, she said she, too, was "glad [the president] had said it—so that it was definitely there."

But the underlying tone of the speech reflected a subtle shift in the president's attitude toward business—a new willingness on the part of government to meet business on its own terms. Beyond the agreement to permit companies to expand their plants at the government's expense, Roosevelt was also considering a variety of alternative measures urged upon him by the business community, including legislation to remove the profit limitations on defense contracts, and new rulings to ease the rigid requirements of antitrust laws.

As each of these issues came to the fore in the months ahead, Eleanor found herself on the side of the New Dealers against her husband. Though she appreciated the president's need to consolidate forces within the United States in order to win the war, she insisted that the war would not be worth winning if the old order of things prevailed.

CHAPTER 3

"BACK TO THE HUDSON"

As the days of May wound to a close, Franklin Roosevelt was faced with one of the most controversial decisions of his presidency: a choice between rearmament at home and aid to the Allies. With France on the verge of defeat, United States military leaders were unanimous in urging Roosevelt to stop supplying the Allies and to focus instead on rearming at home. If the U.S. should later be drawn into a conflict without sufficient munitions on hand, General Marshall warned, "the War Department would naturally and rightfully be subject to the most serious adverse criticism." From London, Ambassador Joseph Kennedy weighed in with a similar analysis, saying it seemed to him that the struggle for England and France was hopeless and "if we had to fight to protect our lives we would do better to fight in our own backyard."

Sobered by the critical reports of the army maneuvers in May, Roosevelt understood only too well how little Americans had in the way of weapons to send to the Allies. But he was determined nonetheless to send whatever he could, even if it meant putting America's own short-term security in jeopardy. "If Great Britain goes down," Roosevelt reasoned, "all of us in the Americas would be living at the point of a gun." The only answer, he believed, in direct contrast to the opinion of his military chiefs, was to bet on the prospect that, if the U.S. did everything in its power to help, the Allies would somehow survive until such time as America could get itself into shape to enter the war.

It was a daring decision. At lunch with Harold Ickes, Roosevelt admitted that he might be wrong in his estimate of Allied strength. "And if I should guess wrong," he said, "the results might be serious." If Britain and France were to fall, the precious American supplies would be taken over by Germany, and the U.S. would be even further diminished in strength. On the other hand, he agreed with the Allied High Command that "one airplane sent to the Allies now will be worth more than ten sent in six weeks and more than 100 sent in six months."

With each day, as the Germans continued their triumphant march through France, the president's bet looked worse and worse. The daily telegrams from Ambassador William Bullitt in Paris reflected an almost hysterical state of mind. "At this moment there is nothing between those German tanks and Paris," Bullitt reported, predicting that there would be communist uprisings and mass butcheries in the city of Paris as the German army drew near. "The Paris police have no weapons except antiquated single shot rifles," he advised on May 28. "Incidentally, we have exactly two revolvers in this entire Mission with only 40 bullets and I should like a few for ourselves."

"This may be the last letter that I shall have a chance to send you," Bullitt wrote Roosevelt on May 30. "In case I should get blown up before I see you again, I want you to know that it has been marvelous to work for you and that I thank you from the bottom of my heart for your friendship."

Bullitt tended by nature to pessimism, but his fears in this instance were fully warranted. After only two weeks of fighting, the French army was disintegrating before the eyes of the British. More than ninety-two thousand soldiers were already dead, and it was clear that the French could not stay in the fight much longer. Meanwhile, the British Expeditionary Force, considered by Churchill "the whole root and core and brain of the British army," was trapped on the beaches at Dunkirk in northern France, its back to the sea. More than sixty thousand British soldiers lay dead, captured, or wounded, and the remaining 350,000, many of them dying from starvation, appeared doomed.

By the morning of May 24, German panzer units were only fifteen miles from Dunkirk. The towering belfry of St. Eloi Church, in the center of the city, was already visible to the German troops. Dunkirk, and the British Expeditionary Force, appeared to be Hitler's for the asking. But then, before the final blow could be struck, the advance of the German panzer troops was suddenly called off. This strange, totally unexpected halt remains incomprehensible—Hitler's first great mistake of the war. Believing it would be best to recover and regroup before bringing the campaign to a final victory, Hitler ordered a three-day rest, just enough time for the Allies to put in place the massive evacuation that became known as the "miracle of Dunkirk."

From Harwich and Margate, from the Narrow Seas to North Foreland, from dozens of little ports on the southern coast of England, a singular armada, made up of every ship known to man, including yachts and trawlers, gunboats and destroyers, motorboats and lifeboats, sailed across the strait to Dunkirk. From there, over a nine-day period, amid blazing ruins, firebombs, and high seas, nearly 340,000 men escaped to England.

As the last of the Allied troops reached the safety of British soil, Churchill delivered a fervent speech to the British Parliament that stirred the souls of the British people and excited the admiration and support of all their Allies. "We shall not flag or fail," Churchill promised. "We shall go on to the end, we shall fight in France, we shall fight in the seas and oceans . . . we shall defend our island, whatever the cost may be, we shall fight on the beaches, we shall fight on the landing grounds, we shall fight in the fields and in the streets, we shall fight in the hills; we shall never surrender, and even if, which I do not for a moment believe, this island or a large part of it were subjugated and starving, then our Empire beyond the seas, armed and guarded by the British Fleet, would carry on the struggle until, in God's good time, the new world, with all its power and might, steps forth to the rescue and the liberation of the old."

Churchill's rousing words bestowed a mythical meaning on Dunkirk that would live in the hearts of Englishmen for generations to come. "So hypnotic was the force of his words," British philosopher Isaiah Berlin has written, "so strong his faith, that by the sheer intensity of his eloquence he bound his spell upon [the British people] until it seemed to them that he was indeed speaking what was in their hearts and minds." If they possessed the courage and determination he perpetually saw in them, it was because he had helped to create it by the intensity of his belief in their qualities. "They conceived a new idea of themselves. They went forward into battle transformed by his words."

The miraculous evacuation produced an upsurge of hope in the American people as well, a renewal of belief that Britain, with the aid of American supplies, might yet defeat Germany. An opinion poll taken the week after Churchill's speech revealed a 43-percent increase in the numbers who favored the sale of planes to the Allies.

But the prime minister understood that wars were not won by evacuations. The nation's gratitude for the army's stunning escape, he cautioned, "must not blind us to the fact that what has happened in France and Belgium is a colossal military disaster." Indeed, the men who returned to England were scarcely an army. In the chaos of the retreat, the BEF had been forced to leave virtually all its heavy equipment behind, including 680 of the 700 tanks it had sent to France, 82,000 scout cars and motorcycles, 8,000 field telephones, 90,000 rifles, and an even greater number of machine guns. In the 9 days of the evacuation, 10 of the nation's 74 destroyers had been sunk and 177 RAF planes had been downed, leaving only 238 aircraft in all of England.

Left in ruins, with a thousand civilians killed, the town of Dunkirk had become a junkyard, with wrecked vehicles, discarded weapons, and abandoned bodies everywhere. A reporter for the *Herald Tribune* described the gruesome scene: "Over a distance of several miles the highway was lined with thousands of Allied trucks and other motorized vehicles. Immense numbers of these had been driven into ditches to prevent their use by the enemy." Along the quays, the chaos was even greater, as motorcycles and trucks and cars were jammed together in every conceivable fashion. "The final jam was completely impossible to disentangle."

These had been Britain's best troops. To these troops, Churchill observed, "all the first fruits of our factories had hitherto been given"—the product of hundreds of thousands of men and women working round the clock. The loss was so calamitous for Britain that it was almost like starting all over again. At that moment, in all of Britain, there were only 600,000 rifles and 500 cannons, many of them borrowed from museums—nowhere near enough to mount an adequate defense against the expected German invasion, much less a second attempt to push the Germans back. "Never," Churchill admitted, "has a nation been so naked before her foes."

• • •

In all the world, only the United States had the ability to resupply the British military. In the middle of May, Churchill sent a "most secret" letter to Roosevelt, promising that, no matter what happened in France, Britain would continue the war alone, and "we are not afraid of that." But in order to keep going, Britain needed help. His immediate needs, Churchill outlined, were forty or fifty destroyers, several hundred airplanes, anti-aircraft equipment, ammunition, and steel.

Roosevelt responded the following day, promising Churchill that he was doing everything in his power to make it possible for the Allied governments to obtain all the munitions on his list, including "the latest type of aircraft." Only the destroyers presented a significant problem, Roosevelt advised, for "a step of that kind could not be taken except with the specific authorization of the Congress," and this was not the right time to make such a move.

In the days that followed, Roosevelt directed his military chiefs to examine Churchill's list of urgent needs and do whatever was needed to send Britain everything they possibly could. He justified his decision on the basis of his own six-month scenario. In this remarkably prescient document, Roosevelt predicted against all odds that by the winter of 1940–41, with the help of the U.S. in supplying munitions, Britain would still be intact, the French government would be resisting in North Africa, and Russia and Japan would still be inactive.

On each of these points, the army and navy chiefs violently disagreed. They doubted that France could survive past the summer; they feared the French could not put up much opposition in North Africa; and they foresaw an invasion of Great Britain in the near future. To their minds, the only answer for the United States was to admit its inability to furnish weapons in quantity sufficient to alter the situation, acknowledge that we were next on the list of victims of the Axis powers, and devote every means to preparing to meet that threat at home.

The army chiefs were particularly disturbed by the president's intention to furnish planes to Britain. Considering the sorry state of the army air force, they believed that virtually anything sent abroad would jeopardize America's national security. "I regret to tell you," Marshall told Morgenthau, whom the president had designated as his representative in securing aid for the Allies, "I do not think we can afford . . . to accommodate the British government." To send even a hundred planes to the Allies, Marshall argued, a mere three days' supply, would set the pilot-training program in America back at least six months. "We have a school at Shreveport," General George H. Brett noted cynically, "instructors, schedules, students, everything except planes."

An even more serious strain was created when the president agreed to send twelve B-17 bombers to Britain. Without mincing words, Marshall pointed out that the B-17 was the only efficient bomber the United States possessed and that we had on hand only fifty-two of them. Releasing twelve would mean losing nearly one-quarter of the United States' supply and "would be seriously prejudicial to our own defensive situation."

Allied requests for guns and ammunition provoked another round of opposition. No further 75mm guns should be released, the chief of army intelligence cautioned. "It would take two years for production to catch up with requirements." Speaking more bluntly, General Walter Bedell Smith warned that if we were required to mobilize after having released guns necessary to this mobilization "and were found to be short in artillery materiel," then "everyone who was a party to the deal might hope to be found hanging from a lamp post."

Still, Roosevelt insisted on sending munitions to Britain, standing firm against the unanimous opinion of his military advisers, key legislative leaders, and his own secretary of war, who continued "to absolutely disapprove of the sale of *any* US military property." On the Senate floor, Senator Nye of North Dakota called for the president's resignation, charging that the Roosevelt policy of aid to the Allies was "nothing but the most dangerous adventurism." That same week, Navy Secretary Charles Edison reported to Roosevelt that Senator David I. Walsh of Massachusetts was "in a towering rage about the sale of Navy stuff to allies. He is threatening to force legislation prohibiting sale of anything. . . . Whole committee in a lather."

"I say it is too risky," Walsh told his colleagues, "too dangerous, to try to determine how far we can go in tapping the resources of our own Government and furnishing naval vessels, airplanes, powder and bombs. It is trampling on dangerous ground. It is moving toward the edge of a precipice—a precipice of stupendous and horrifying depths. . . . I do not want our forces deprived of one gun, or one bomb or one ship which can aid that American boy whom you and I may some day have to draft. I want every instrument. I want every bomb, I want every shell, I want every plane, I want every boat ready and available, so that I can say when and if it becomes necessary to draft him, 'Young man, you have every possible weapon of defense your Government can give you.' "

• • •

"All of Mr. Roosevelt's authority was needed to bludgeon the army officers into quiescence," *The New Republic* reported. At the president's insistence, the War Department searched long-forgotten statutes and determined that, so long as the arms were considered "surplus," it would be legal to sell them to a private corporation, which in turn could sell them to the British. Once this legal device was figured out, and once U.S. Steel was selected as the middleman, Marshall reluctantly agreed, under intense presidential pressure, to approve a long list of equipment for transfer, including 93 bomber planes, 500,000 Enfield rifles, 184 tanks, 76,000 machine guns, 25,000 Browning automatic rifles, 895 75mm guns, and 100 million rounds of ammunition. As he initialed the list, Marshall somewhat righteously observed that he could only define these weapons as surplus after going to church to pray for forgiveness. "It was the only time that I recall that I did something that there was a certain amount of duplicity in it."

At every step, the president's intervention was needed. "I am delighted to have that list of surplus materials," Roosevelt told Morgenthau on June 6. "Give it an extra push every morning and every night until it is on the ships." Since the equipment was scattered in army depots and arsenals across the country, with some tanks and guns at Rock Island, Illinois, others at Schenectady, New York, and still others at San Francisco, California, emergency telegrams had to be dispatched to each of these places, telling the commanding officers to move the selected equipment to a central loading station in Raritan, New Jersey.

Working night and day under strict secrecy, soldiers at each arsenal loaded huge crates of rifles and guns into more than six hundred freight cars headed for Raritan. All along the line, word was flashed to give these freight trains the right of way. In the meantime, a dozen empty British freighters were standing by at Raritan, waiting to take the precious cargo home. By June 11, everything was ready to be loaded, but the transfer could not take place until the contracts had been signed, and Secretary Woodring refused to sign them. Only when the president directly ordered him to sign did Woodring finally execute the documents. Five minutes later, army headquarters called Raritan to say the transfer had been made. "Go ahead and load."

All through that night, hundreds of longshoremen, three huge derricks, and more than twenty barges worked to unload the trains and put the cargo aboard the British ships. The next day, the first British ship, *The Eastern Prince,* sailed to England. So hurried had the loading process been, with stores of weapons simply dumped wherever they could fit, that the unloading process was a nightmare. But Britain assigned its best technical workers to match the right handbooks, and the right range tables to the right field guns, to link the 75mm's with the correct horse poles and straps, to unite the spares with the guns to which they belonged. By the end of June, all twelve ships had sailed to England, carrying seventy thousand tons of equipment which, when new, had been worth over $300 million.

"For weeks," Edward Stettinius later observed, "while England's war factories worked night and day to make up the losses . . . there were few guns in all of Britain that could stop a tank besides the 900 75's from America. The 80,000 Lewis, Marlin, Browning and Vickers machine guns strengthened the defenses of every threatened beachhead and every road leading in from the coast. . . . They went to men who almost literally had no arms at all in the most critical hour of Britain's history since the Spanish armada sailed into the English Channel."

• • •

Surely the negotiations involving the shipment of such massive amounts of equipment could not actually be kept secret, but since nothing had been said officially, no one knew exactly what was going on. The time had come for the president to tell the American people what he was doing. By good fortune, Roosevelt had received an invitation to speak at the commencement exercises at the University of Virginia in Charlottesville on June 10. Since his son FDR, Jr., was graduating from the Virginia Law School that day, the school officials hoped that the president might be enticed to accept their offer. Roosevelt had said he could make no commitment until the last minute, but now, at midnight the night before, he accepted their invitation, intending to use the forum to discuss his commitment to aid the Allies.

As Franklin and Eleanor were getting ready to leave for the train that would take them to Charlottesville that Monday, June 10, the news reached the White House that Italy was entering the war on the side of the Germans. After a week of tense maneuvering in which Roosevelt had tried to keep Italy's dictator, Benito Mussolini, from this explosive expansion of the war, Mussolini had taken the impetuous plunge. If he waited any longer, the Italian dictator feared, France would surrender without his help, and he would lose his chance to share in the spoils.

As Roosevelt perused the State Department's draft of his commencement address, he added a caustic phrase he had seen in a letter from French Premier Paul Reynaud about stabbing one's neighbor in the back. To Roosevelt, it seemed an accurate description of Italy's action. But undersecretary of State Sumner Welles, who had been trying to keep Italy out of the war, argued against using the stab-in-the-back metaphor, claiming it was inflammatory. The president finally agreed; the colorful phrase was deleted from the draft.

But, talking with Eleanor on the three-hour train ride to Charlottesville, the president began to reconsider. He understood the wisdom of the State Department's advice, he told her, but he wanted for once to speak candidly, without holding back out of diplomatic courtesy. Eleanor fully supported him in his desire, encouraging him to reinstate the controversial phrase. "If your conscience won't be satisfied unless you put it in I would put it in," she advised. When the train pulled into Charlottesville, the sentence was back in the text. Feeling altogether satisfied with the speech now, the president waved and smiled at the crowd gathered at the station. A reporter who had traveled with the president's party observed a marked change in Roosevelt's demeanor: whereas he had looked "grave and pale" when he boarded the train in Washington, he now appeared wholly relaxed; "the decision that he had made seemed to strengthen him."

Several thousand persons crowded the Memorial Gymnasium and applauded loudly as the president, in traditional cap and gown, stood at the podium. Speaking slowly and forcefully, Roosevelt uttered the words that would stick in public memory long after the rest of the speech was forgotten. "On this tenth day of June, 1940, the hand that held the dagger has struck it into the back of its neighbor."

Churchill was listening to the president's speech with a group of his officers in the Admiralty War Room at midnight his time. When they heard Roosevelt's angry charge against Italy, Churchill recalled, "a deep growl of satisfaction" spread across the room. "I wondered about the Italian vote in the approaching presidential election; but I knew that Roosevelt was a most experienced American party politician, although never afraid to run risks for the sake of his resolves."

The President's stiff denunciation of Italy captured the imagination of the crowd, but far more important was Roosevelt's ringing public confirmation of America's policy of aiding the Allies. Placing aid to the Allies and America's own military buildup on an equal basis, he told his audience: "We will extend to the opponents of force the material resources of this nation," and at the same time, "we will harness and speed up those resources in order that we ourselves in the Americas may have the equipment and training equal to the task of any emergency and every defense. . . . We will not slow down or detour. Signs and signals call for speed: full speed ahead." There were no disclaimers in Roosevelt's pledge, no qualifying adjectives to diminish the force of his promise to extend "the material resources of this nation" to the Allies.

"We all listened to you," Churchill cabled Roosevelt, "and were fortified by the grand scope of your declaration. Your statement that the material aid of the United States will be given to the Allies in their struggle is a strong encouragement in a dark but not unhopeful hour." Though the amounts involved, in terms of the supplies needed in modern war, were small, they were tremendously important from a strategic and political point of view. For, with the president's pledge at Charlottesville, the British had gained their chief objective—a share in America's vast industrial potential.

The president's pledge, army historians suggest, reflected his "determined faith, not fully shared by the Army staff nor even by General Marshall," that American industry could produce munitions for the Allies in ever-increasing volumes without "seriously retarding" the rearmament program at home. While he appreciated the enormous task involved in converting factory production from household items to weapons of war; while he understood the complications involved in teaching those without the proper experience and skill how to build tanks and planes; while he recognized that millions of people would have to move from locales in which they had long been settled, he believed that, in the end, American industry would come through.

The president returned to the White House that night, "full of the elan of his Charlottesville speech," Assistant Secretary of State Adolf Berle recorded. "He had said for once, what really was on his mind, and what everybody knew; and he could speak frankly, and had done so." It was a liberating feeling. It was "holiday time" for FDR, Jr., as well, who had brought two of his classmates with him back to the White House. At midnight, as Eleanor readied herself for the night train to New York, she found all of them involved in a fiery discussion with Harry Hopkins about world economics. "Though I mildly suggested that a little sleep would do them all good, I left them convinced that the discussion had just begun."

The media were quick to recognize the significance of Roosevelt's talk. "It was a fighting speech," *Time* reported, "more powerful and more determined than any he had delivered since the war began." With this speech, *Time* concluded, "the U.S. had taken sides. Ended was the myth of U.S. neutrality. . . . Ended was the vacillating talk of aiding the Allies; nothing remained now but to get on with the job." Writing in a similar vein, the *New York Post* maintained that Roosevelt "rose to the occasion and gave to the country the pronouncement for which it has waited. . . . The most productive nation in the world has thrown its productive capacity into the scales."

• • •

But when all was said and done, there was nothing "the most productive nation in the world" could do to save France. At dawn on the morning of June 14, German troops entered Paris. Parisians awakened to the sound of German loudspeakers warning that any demonstrations or hostile acts against the troops would be punishable by death. At every street corner decrees were posted: all radio stations were now in the hands of the Germans, all newspapers suspended, all banks closed.

Here and there knots of people stood and watched as thousands of Nazi troops marched in goosestep toward the Arc de Triomphe. Women wept and crossed themselves; the men were grim. At Napoleon's tomb the German soldiers methodically searched the battle flags to remove every German flag they could find—each one symbolizing a lost German battle in the Great War. The German troops swept down the Champs-Elysées, from the Tomb of the Unknown Soldier; past the Gardens of the Tuileries, past the Louvre to the Hôtel de Ville, where they made their headquarters. As the German national anthem blared from every corner, Dr. Thierry de Martel, director of the prestigious American Hospital and a good friend of Ambassador Bullitt's, decided that life under the German occupation would be intolerable. He plunged a hypodermic needle filled with a fatal dose of strychnine into his arm.

When the parade was over, jubilant Nazi soldiers photographed each other before the Arc de Triomphe, at the Tomb of the Unknown Soldier, and in the Gardens of the Tuileries. Racing one another to the top of the Eiffel Tower, a group hauled down the French flag that had flown on the mast atop the tower and replaced it with the German swastika. After the 9 p.m. curfew, Paris, save for the tread of Nazi guards patrolling the city's old cobblestones, fell silent.

A week later, Hitler laid down his terms for an armistice, and, in the same railroad car in a clearing in the woods at Compiègne where the Germans had capitulated to the Allies in 1918, a defeated and humiliated France concluded a truce. After the signing, Hitler ordered that the historic carriage and the monument celebrating the original French victory be conveyed to Berlin. Then, in an attempt to obliterate even the slightest physical memory of Germany's earlier defeat, he ordered that the pedestal of the carriage and the stones marking the site be destroyed. With the French surrender, Adolf Hitler was now the master of Austria, Czechoslovakia, Poland, Luxembourg, Belgium, Denmark, the Netherlands, Norway, and France.

The French collapse produced a sharp drop in American hopes for an Allied victory. By the end of June, only a third of the American people believed Britain would win the war. Though a majority still continued to favor sending aid to the Allies, the level of support was dropping. General Marshall and Admiral Stark were now convinced that they had been right all along. Five days after the surrender, they urged the president to discontinue all aid to Britain at once and transfer most of the fleet from the Pacific to the Atlantic. The president flatly rejected both proposals. In what is considered "one of his most decisive prewar moves," he decreed that aid to Britain would proceed and that the fleet would stay at Pearl Harbor. The positioning of the fleet was of great importance to Churchill, who had told Roosevelt privately he was looking to him "to keep that Japanese dog quiet in the Pacific."

In backing Churchill that critical spring despite the opposition of his military, Roosevelt was placing his faith in the American people. Though he had seen support for the Allies fluctuate with news from abroad, he sensed a significant shift in the public mood. Isolationism still remained a powerful force, but a majority of Americans were beginning to understand that they could no longer escape from commitment, that they had a role to play in the world. For the moment, they were willing to extend themselves only so far; their chief goal in aiding the Allies was to keep the U.S. out of the war. But for now, that was as far as Roosevelt needed or even wanted to go.

• • •

On June 20, after weeks of hesitation, Roosevelt finally resolved the continuing public feud in the War Department. He fired Secretary of War Woodring and announced a sweeping reorganization of his Cabinet. "When the President did decide to get rid of anybody," author John Gunther has written, "he could usually only bear to do so after deliberately picking a quarrel, so that he could provoke anger and then claim that he himself was not to blame." In this case, the quarrel was ready-made in Woodring's refusal to agree to the president's requests for releasing munitions to England.

Woodring's departure was the moment Assistant Secretary Louis Johnson, FDR's faithful ally, had been dreaming of for years. Surely, now, the president would make good on his long-standing promise to elevate Johnson to the high post of war secretary. But, unbeknownst to Johnson, the president had conceived a brilliant plan which left the assistant secretary out in the cold.

The plan called for a reorganization of both the War Department and the Navy Department to make possible a coalition Cabinet. For secretary of war, Roosevelt selected Republican conservative Henry Stimson, the patron saint of the Eastern establishment. At seventy-three, his gray hair cut straight across his broad brow, Stimson had served under every president since William McKinley, working for William Howard Taft as secretary of war and for Herbert Hoover as secretary of state. A graduate of Phillips Academy, Andover; Yale, Skull and Bones, and Harvard Law School, Stimson was as deeply connected to the upper strata of American government and society as any man alive. He was a curious mixture of conservatism and liberalism, known as an excellent manager with an unusual ability to bring out the best in those around him. "Even if I had had any hope that the President would make me Secretary of War," Interior Secretary Harold Ickes recorded in his diary, "I would have had to admit . . . that the Stimson appointment was excellent."

As navy secretary, the President chose Colonel Frank Knox, the *Chicago Daily News* publisher who had been Alf Landon's running mate on the Republican ticket in 1936. Unlike Stimson, Knox had come up the hard way, moving from grocery clerk to gym teacher, from cub reporter to publisher. A colorful figure at sixty-seven, with an open, pleasant face and reddish hair, Knox still cherished the memory of charging up San Juan Hill with Teddy Roosevelt's Rough Riders. As conservative on domestic issues as Stimson, Knox was a forceful speaker, an unsparing critic of the New Deal. Taken together, historian Bruce Catton observed, the appointments were further evidence of "a truce between the New Deal and big business . . . a bit of assurance that the defense effort was not to be a straight New Deal program."

But the domestic views of Stimson and Knox were of secondary importance to the president compared with the fact that both men were ardent interventionists, willing to take their stand against the isolationist tendencies of their own party. Time and again, both men had expressed themselves in support of generous aid to the Allies, on the theory that Nazism and all its implications must be destroyed. And their devotion to public service made them ideal choices for the Cabinet. While some Republicans vigorously protested Roosevelt's "double cross" on the eve of the Republican convention and demanded that Stimson and Knox be read out of the Republican Party, the announcement was generally greeted with approval. "Abroad, these nominations will serve to emphasize the essential unity of America," the *Washington Post* editorialized. "At home, this infusion of new blood should help accelerate the preparedness program."

Vastly pleased by the reactions to his surprise appointments, the president decided to spend the weekend of June 21 at his Hyde Park estate. It was the first time he had been able to enjoy his childhood home since early May. Traveling with Missy and Hopkins and a phalanx of reporters, he boarded his special train at midnight, Friday, at the railroad siding under the Bureau of Engraving and Printing, on 14th Street.

Although the overnight journey to Hyde Park took less than ten hours, hundreds, even thousands of people were involved. For six hours before the president's departure, all rail traffic was deflected from the tracks to be used, so that responsible railroad men could walk every yard of track, inspecting for cracks or broken switches. In the areas adjacent to the tracks, all parked cars were removed, lest they prove hiding places for conspirators. Security agents tested the food and drinks as they were loaded into the dining car. In the Pullman car in front of the president's private car, typewriters and mimeograph machines were installed for his staff. The swirl of activity never stopped, with reporters gathering in the club car until the wee hours of morning, but in the president's compartment the blinds were closed and all was quiet. Roosevelt was sound asleep.

• • •

That same weekend, Hitler decided to celebrate his victory over France with a visit to Paris, his first journey to the city which had enchanted him since his early years as an art student. So closely had he dreamed of Paris that he was certain he could find his way anywhere solely from his knowledge of the buildings and the monuments. Accompanied by a small group of architects and photographers, including Albert Speer, Hitler arrived at Le Bourget before dawn and drove straight to the Opéra, his favorite building. A white-haired French attendant led Hitler's party through the sumptuous foyer and up the great ornamental stairway. When they reached the part of the stage in front of the curtain, Hitler, looking puzzled, told the attendant that in his mind's eye he was certain a salon was supposed to be to the right. The attendant confirmed Hitler's memory; the salon had been eliminated in a recent renovation. "There, you see how well I know my way about," Hitler remarked in triumph to his entourage.

From the Opéra, Hitler was driven down the Champs-Elysées and taken to the Eiffel Tower, the Arc de Triomphe, and Napoleon's tomb. In the tomb, he trembled with excitement and ordered that the remains of Napoleon's son, which rested in Vienna, be transferred to Paris and placed beside those of his father. Minutes later, his mood having shifted, he ordered the destruction of two World War I monuments: the statue of General Charles Mangin, leader of the colonial troops, whose memorial included an honor guard of four Negro soldiers, and the monument to Edith Cavell, the English nurse who became a popular heroine and was executed in 1915 for aiding over two hundred Allied soldiers to escape from a Red Cross hospital in German-occupied Belgium.

As the three-hour tour came to an end, an exhilarated Hitler told Speer: "It was the dream of my life to be permitted to see Paris. I cannot say how happy I am to have that dream fulfilled." That evening, Hitler ordered Speer to resume at once his architectural renovations of Berlin. However beautiful Paris was, Berlin must, in the end, be made far more beautiful. "In the past I often considered whether we would not have to destroy Paris," he confided to Speer. "But when we are finished in Berlin, Paris will only be a shadow. So why should we destroy it?"

• • •

The weather in Hyde Park was "delightfully cool and brilliant" when the president's train pulled into Highland Station that Saturday morning. From the train station it was an easy ride over country roads to Springwood, the president's thirty-five-room estate on the Hudson River. This was the place to which Roosevelt would regularly return when he needed sustenance and peace, the place where he could always relax, no matter what was going on in the world.

Today, as for so many days throughout his fifty-eight years, the president's mother, Sara Delano Roosevelt, was at the door to greet him. Her waist had thickened over the years, but at eighty-five, she was still a handsome woman, with her high forehead, her thick white hair, and her gold lorgnette. Exquisitely dressed in white or black, the only two colors she regularly wore, Sara moved with great distinctness, embodying in her carriage the impression of superiority. But there was warmth in her eyes, and her smile was so startlingly similar to her son's that audiences at movie theaters broke into spontaneous applause when they saw her face.

As the president kissed his mother at the door, reporters recollected that it was just a year ago at the same doorway that Sara Roosevelt had greeted the British monarchs, King George VI and Queen Elizabeth, during their royal visit to Hyde Park. "The weather was much the same as it was on that historic week end last year," one reporter observed, "and the hills across the Hudson River stood out as clearly against the backdrop of the Catskill Mountains to the north but there remained only a memory of the peace which existed in the world at that time."

It is said that, in the weeks before the king and queen arrived, Sara's neighbors along the Hudson had asked her if she was going to redecorate the house. "Of course not," she responded, in her best starchy manner, "they're not coming to see a redecorated house, they're coming to see *my* house."

On the day of the visit, Sara had waited in the library with Franklin and Eleanor for the king and queen. Much to her displeasure, Franklin had prepared a tray of cocktails for the royal visitors. For years, the question of serving alcohol in the Big House had been a point of contention between mother and son—so much so that Franklin had simply gone around his mother by moving his cocktail hour to a secret hiding place in the cloakroom beneath the stairs. The secrecy lent a mischievous air to the gatherings, as journalist Martha Gellhorn recalled. "Shrieks of laughter" would erupt from the cloakroom, she said, "as if we were all bad children having a feast in the dorm at night."

But on this occasion, Franklin had proved as stubborn as his mother, insisting that the alcohol remain in open and ready condition. When the king came into the library, Franklin greeted him with a twinkle in his eye: "My mother does not approve of cocktails and thinks you should have a cup of tea." The king reflected for a moment and then observed, "Neither does my mother." Whereupon the president and the king raised their glasses to one another in an unspoken bond and proceeded to drink their martinis.

There were occasions when Sara's strength failed, when she was tormented by stomach pains or suffered keenly from the heat. At such times, she told her son, she wondered, "Perhaps I have lived too long, but when I think of you and hear your voice I do not ever want to leave you." She thought of him almost all the time, Sara had written Franklin right after his May 16 address to the Congress, "and realize a little of the feelings of responsibility you have, with all the horror of what is going on and the wish to help. I am very proud of the way you keep your head."

There was an extraordinary bond between mother and son. "Nothing," Eleanor observed, "ever seemed to disturb the deep, underlying affection they had for each other."

The president had no special plans for this June weekend beyond rest and relaxation. In the mornings, he slept late; at lunchtime, he lingered longer than usual at the table; and in the afternoons, he took long leisurely rides through his estate and through the surrounding countryside. The unhurried pace was just what he needed to regenerate his energies and refocus his brain. Time and again, Roosevelt confounded his staff by the ease with which, even in the darkest hours, he managed to shake off the burdens of the presidency upon his arrival at Hyde Park, and emerged stronger and more confident in a matter of days.

• • •

"All that is in me goes back to the Hudson," Roosevelt liked to say, meaning not simply the peaceful, slow-moving river and the big, comfortable clapboard house but the ambience of boundless devotion that encompassed him as a child. As the adored only son of a young mother and an aging patriarch, Roosevelt grew up in an atmosphere where affection and respect were plentiful, where the discipline was fair and loving, and the opportunities for self-expression abundant. The sense of being loved wholeheartedly by his parents taught Roosevelt to trust that the world was basically a friendly and agreeable place.

Photographs of Sara Delano, twenty-six years old at the time of his birth, reveal a young woman conscious of her beauty, with lustrous upswept hair, high cheekbones, a long, sleek neck, and large brown eyes. She had spent most of her childhood in a forty-room country estate, Algonac, high above the Hudson River, near Newburgh, New York. There, under the protective wing of her autocratic but loving father, Warren Delano II, she had led a life of elegance and ease, with private tutors, dancing lessons, and trips to the Orient. Her summer days were spent in the country, rowing on the river, riding horseback through the woods, and picnicking on the shore; her winters were divided between social life in Manhattan and the outdoor life of Algonac, complete with sleighrides in the fields and skating on the ponds. It was a tranquil life, producing within Sara the deep sense of privilege and place which she passed on to her son.

Years later, Sara recognized that her parents had deliberately kept from their children "all traces of sadness or trouble or the news of anything alarming." So highly did the Delanos value the outward appearance of tranquillity, Sara proudly recalled, that no one was ever allowed to complain or to cry, even if there was something terribly wrong. At age four, Sara had fallen on the sharp corner of a cabinet. The deep wound was sewed shut with needle and thread. That Sara never flinched or cried drew her father's praise. But in casting a positive light on this aspect of her childhood, Sara failed to appreciate, as her great-grandson John Boettiger, Jr., later put it, that "pain-killing can itself be a lethal act." When she married, she would strive to shelter her son in the same way as her father had sheltered her. "If there remained in Franklin Roosevelt throughout his life," Boettiger, Jr., observed, "an insensitivity towards and discomfort with profound and vividly expressed feelings, it may have been in part the lengthened shadow of his early sheltering from ugliness and jealousy and conflicting interests."

Franklin's father, known as "Mr. James," was nearly twice Sara's age when she married him. Tall and slender with full muttonchop whiskers, he, too, had grown up in an environment of wealth and privilege. Like the Delanos, the Roosevelts defined themselves primarily as country gentlemen, adopting the habits, the hobbies, and the love of the outdoors that characterized the English gentry. Mount Hope, the country estate on which James was born, was twenty miles upstream from Algonac. The Roosevelt family money had been made years before in dry goods, real estate, and trade, primarily the West Indies sugar trade. As a young man, James, after graduating from Harvard Law School, had taken an interest in coal and the railroads, but never was he more content than when he was in the country, hunting, fishing, or riding. At the age of twenty-five, he had married a second cousin,

Rebecca Howland, and the following year a son, James Roosevelt Roosevelt, known as "Rosy," was born. It was, from all accounts, a peaceful marriage, which lasted for nearly twenty-five years, until Rebecca suffered a fatal heart attack.

Four years later, Mr. James was introduced to Sara Delano at a small dinner party hosted by the family of his fourth cousin Theodore Roosevelt. Both James and Sara knew at once that they wanted to marry; the courtship lasted just ten weeks. On October 7, 1880, as the autumn sun was just beginning to set, James took his new bride to Springwood, the rambling house in Hyde Park he had bought two decades earlier, when Mount Hope burned to the ground.

There, at Springwood, in a bedroom overlooking the snow-covered lawn, Franklin Delano Roosevelt was born on January 30, 1882. It was a difficult birth, so difficult that the doctors advised Sara not to have any more children. Unable to produce a large family, Sara focused her prodigious energies on shaping the life of her healthy, handsome son.

"No moment of Franklin's day was unscheduled," Roosevelt biographer Geoffrey Ward has written. "His mother oversaw everything, followed him everywhere. . . . Hers was a loving even adoring autocracy but an autocracy nonetheless," in which the boy's natural longing for a bit of privacy was felt by his mother to be a deliberate shunning of her company. Once, when Franklin was only five years old, his mother noticed that he seemed melancholy. When she asked him why he was sad, he did not answer at first, so she repeated her question. "Then," Sara recalled, "with a curious little gesture that combined entreaty with a suggestion of impatience, he clasped his hands in front of him and exclaimed, 'Oh, for freedom!' "

The incident made Sara wonder if perhaps she was regulating her son's life too closely, but after a short experiment in which he was given no rules for an entire day and allowed to roam at will with absolutely no attention from his mother, Sara reported, he "of his own accord went contentedly back to his routine."

Everything about the boy's childhood seemed structured to make him feel that he was the center of his parents' world. In the early years, Mr. James spent hours every day with his son, teaching him how to row and sail, and skate and sled. Wherever his parents went—whether to visit friends in their carriage or for long walks along the river or to Europe for vacations—Franklin went with them. Surrounded by older people, the young boy developed early on a remarkable ease with adults, an unusual poise, an excellent set of manners which earned him much praise. Relatives consistently remarked on what a "nice child" he was, so adaptable, so uncomplaining, so "bright and pleasant and happy."

Relaxed relationships with children his own age were harder to come by. Most of Franklin's boyhood friends were the children of other River families who were brought to his house to play at scheduled hours and then taken back home. Only with the children of families who worked on his parents' estate did he have what approached spontaneous relationships, and even then everyone involved always knew that the young Roosevelt was ultimately in charge.

An intuitive child, Franklin learned to anticipate the desires of his parents even before he was told what to do. "It never occurred to me," Sara wrote, "to caution him against hazardous undertakings. . . . Franklin had proved himself such a responsible little boy that I never for a moment believed he would undertake anything he was not fully equipped to handle." The mother's confidence built confidence in the son; he rarely disappointed his parents' high expectations. "We never were strict merely for the sake of being strict. We took secret pride in the fact that Franklin instinctively never seemed to require that kind of handling."

Yet one consequence of early adaptation to a parent's wishes is the fear that all the love captured with so much effort is simply admiration for the good manners and the achievements and the good nature, not truly love for the child as he really is. What would happen, the precocious child wonders, if I appeared on the outside as I really am on the inside—sad, angry, rude, jealous, scared? Where would my parents' love be then? The child's fear of exposure can remain in the adult. This would explain Franklin Roosevelt's lifelong tendency to guard his weaknesses and shortcomings as if they were scars, making it difficult for him to share his true feelings with anyone.

As the boy's world widened beyond his house, his sense of confidence deepened. Accompanying Mr. James on daily rounds of his estate, walking with him in the tiny village of Hyde Park, sitting next to him at St. James Church, the boy could not help observing the deferential treatment his father received, the respect accorded the Roosevelts almost as a matter of right. So, too, when he rode in the carriage with his mother as she dispatched food and clothing to the sick and poor, he recognized at once that his family was in the position of having more than enough for themselves so they could give to others. These early observations instilled in the boy the confident belief that the Roosevelts were special people, inheritors of a proud tradition.

When Franklin was eight, his father suffered a serious heart attack that would leave him essentially an invalid for the remaining ten years of his life, unable to play tennis, ride horseback, or even enjoy the long walks in the woods he had once loved so much. More than any other event in Franklin's childhood, his father's heart attack had an indelible impact on the development of his personality. From that point on, the boy's built-in desire to please his parents by being a "nice little boy" was amplified by the fear that if he ever appeared other than bright and happy it might damage his father's already weakened heart. The story is told of a ghastly injury the young boy received when a steel rod fell on his head, leaving an ugly gash in his forehead. Refusing to worry his father, Franklin found a cap to cover the wound and insisted that Mr. James never be told.

In later years, Roosevelt's anxiety to please would become so finely tuned that he would be able to win the hearts and minds of almost everyone he met. "By the warmth of his greeting," Sam Rosenman wrote, "he could make a casual visitor believe that nothing was so important to him that day as this particular visit, and that he had been waiting all day for this hour to arrive. Only a person who really loved human beings could give that impression." It seemed at times as if he possessed invisible antennae that allowed him to understand what his fellow citizens were thinking and feeling, so that he could craft his own responses to meet their deepest needs.

But the desire to please became a two-edged sword in the White House, when the president's lack of candor led to confusion. Wanting to set each caller at ease, he had a habit of nodding his head in agreement. The visitor would leave, mistakenly assuming he had garnered the president's support. "Perhaps in the long run," New Deal adviser Raymond Moley argued, "fewer friends would have been lost by bluntness than by the misunderstandings that arose from engaging ambiguity."

Mr. James' illness brought Sara even closer to her only son, so close that she could not bear to part with him when the time came for him to go to boarding school at Groton. Instead, she kept him home two additional years, not letting him go until he was fourteen. The day before Franklin finally left for school, Sara and he spent many hours together. "We dusted his birds," she wrote in her diary, "and he had a swim in the river. I looked on with a heavy heart." For weeks afterward, Sara could not pass his empty bedroom without breaking down in tears.

Because he started school two years later than most of his classmates, Franklin was always set apart from the rest of the boys. "They knew things he didn't," Eleanor said later. "He felt left out." Unaccustomed to the ordinary give and take of schoolmates, Franklin put his fellow students off. The studied charm that impressed his parents' friends and delighted the faculty at Groton seemed affected to boys his own age. "They didn't like him," Eleanor once said. "They had to give him a certain recognition because of his intellectual ability. But he was never of the inner clique." Resentful at his lack of popularity, yearning to be at center stage as he had been all his life, Franklin turned at times to sarcasm, an unfeeling ribbing of his schoolmates, which only made things worse.

Never once, however, did Franklin admit to his mother, as he would later confess to his wife, that something had gone "sadly wrong" at Groton. On the contrary, blurring the distinction between things as they were and things as he wished them to be, his ever-cheerful letters convinced her that his career at Groton was a great success. "Almost overnight," Sara recorded, "he became sociable and gregarious and entered with the frankest enjoyment into every kind of social activity."

At Harvard College, Franklin faced rejection once more when he was blackballed from the exclusive Porcellian Club, but there was such a variety of things at the college to claim his attention—the rowing crew, the debutante dances, the Hasty Pudding Club, the Fly Club, the student newspaper—that the hurt was less visible. What is more, Franklin was beginning to learn from his success at the *Crimson*—where he was made managing editor and then president—that, if he wanted to assume center stage, he had to create situations where he was the best person to handle a particular job.

During the fall of Franklin's freshman year, his father died. Unable to bear the loneliness of Hyde Park, Sara took an apartment in Boston for the winter so that she could be near Franklin. "She was an indulgent mother," a family friend observed, "but would not let her son call his soul his own." Early on, Franklin had sensed the competition between his interest in other girls and his mother's love. Now it seemed even more important to keep his girlfriends a secret lest his mother feel betrayed. The only way he knew how to fend her off was to become evasive and vague, sharing with her all the unimportant details about his girls while reserving for himself the feelings that really mattered.

Over time, Franklin's evasiveness became a pattern he could never break. "The effort to become his own man without wounding his mother," Ward observed, "fostered in him much of the guile and easy charm, love of secrecy and skill at maneuver he brought to the White House." On occasion, when his deviousness seemed to go beyond the bounds of necessity, it seemed as if he were enjoying subterfuge for its own sake.

So successful was the young Franklin at hiding his emotions that he took his mother and close friends totally by surprise when he announced that he had fallen in love with his fifth cousin Eleanor and intended to marry her. Though Sara had seen Franklin with Eleanor on numerous occasions, she had absolutely no idea the relationship was heading toward marriage.

"I know what pain I must have caused you," Franklin wrote his mother after he told her the shocking news, "and you know I wouldn't do it if I really could have helped it.... I know my mind, have known it for a long time and know that I could never think otherwise... and you, dear Mummy, you know that nothing can ever change what we have always been and always will be to each other—only now you have two children to love and love you—and Eleanor as you know will always be a daughter to you in every true way."

Sara was not so easily assuaged. Reminding Franklin that at twenty-one he was much too young to marry, she exacted a promise from him to postpone the official announcement for a year. In the meantime, she tried to engage his interests elsewhere: first by securing a job for him in London; then, after that failed, by taking him on a Caribbean cruise. But when the trip was over, he was still in love with Eleanor. Sara was desolate. "I am feeling pretty blue.... The journey is over & I feel as if the time were not likely to come again when I shall take a trip with my dear boy...." Sara wrote. "Oh how still the house is...." With unerring intuition, Eleanor apprehended Sara's pain. "Don't let her feel that the last trip with you is over," Eleanor advised Franklin. "We three must take them together in the future. . . ."

As the waiting period drew to a close, Franklin selected an engagement ring at Tiffany's, which he gave to Eleanor on her twentieth birthday. The official announcement, made a few weeks later, produced a round of congratulatory notes. "I have more respect and admiration for Eleanor than any girl I have ever met," Franklin's cousin Lyman Delano wrote. "You are mighty lucky," one of Eleanor's previous suitors told Franklin. "Your future wife is such as it is the privilege of few men to have." But perhaps the letter both Franklin and Eleanor treasured the most was the affectionate note from President Theodore Roosevelt, who offered to give his niece away in marriage.

• • •

If Franklin thought that marriage represented an escape from his mother, he was wrong, for she was unable to back off and he was unable to make her go. Instead, he allowed her to compete with Eleanor for his devotion, build a town house in New York that adjoined his and Eleanor's, retain the purse strings for the family, and share with Eleanor in the task of raising their children.

Over the years, Franklin's failure to separate from his mother would play a major role in undermining his marriage, but for now, as we seek to understand the wellspring of the president's equanimity as he faced the Nazi threat in June 1940, it must be recognized that his mother's unequivocal love for him remained a powerful source of strength all the days of his life. "Reasonable it is to assume," the *Ladies' Home Journal* correctly surmised shortly after Roosevelt moved into the White House, "that much of the President's strength in facing incredible obstacles [was] planted in a childhood presided over by a mother whose broad viewpoint encompasses the art of living."

To be sure, other factors contributed to the president's sublime confidence, chief among them his mental victory over polio, which strikingly confirmed his native optimism. "I think," Eleanor said, "probably the thing that took most courage in his life was his meeting of polio and I never heard him complain. . . . He just accepted it as one of those things that was given you as discipline in life. . . . And with each victory, as everyone knows, you are stronger than you were before."

But in the end, no factor was more important in laying the foundation of the president's confident temperament than his mother's early love. So it was that, as Hitler journeyed triumphantly to Paris, Roosevelt returned quietly to Hyde Park, the locus of his earliest memories, the nest in which his expansive personality unfolded most freely.

CHAPTER 4

"LIVING HERE IS VERY OPPRESSIVE"

As the White House geared the country for war in the spring of 1940, Eleanor became increasingly depressed. For seven years, through days that began at 6 a.m. and ended long after midnight, she had carved out a significant role for herself as her husband's partner in social reform. She believed in what she was doing and knew that her work was respected by millions of people, including, most crucially, her husband. "The President was enormously proud of her ability...," Frances Perkins confirmed. "He said more than once, 'You know, Eleanor really does put it over. She's got great talent with people.' In cabinet meetings, he would say, 'You know my Missus gets around a lot... my missus says they have typhoid fever in that district... my Missus says that people are working for wages way below the minimum set by NRA in the town she visited last week.' "

Now, however, with the president concerned about little but munitions and maneuvers, Eleanor felt a sense of remoteness, a lack of connection to both her husband and the major issue of the day. Robbed of desire, she moved mechanically through her duties; all sense of challenge seemed to have fled. "All that she had worked for over so many years was now in jeopardy," Eleanor's grandson Curtis Roosevelt observed. "She feared that everything would be taken away from her—her value, her usefulness, her role."

"Living here is very oppressive," she confessed to her daughter, Anna, "because Pa visualizes all the possibilities, as of course he must and you feel very impotent to help. What you think or feel seems of no use or value so I'd rather be away and let the important people make their plans and someday I suppose they will get around to telling us plain citizens if they want us to do anything."

Eleanor had an intriguing idea: she would see if she could go to Europe with the Red Cross to help organize the relief effort for refugees. It seemed to her the perfect solution—the chance to relieve suffering and dislocation while at the same time to be right in the thick of things, delivering clothing, blankets, and medical supplies to shelters in bombed-out cities, organizing hot meals for children in schools and canteens, giving first-aid instruction to civilians.

Eleanor had worked with the Red Cross before. While she and Franklin were in Washington during World War I, she had run a canteen at Union Station. Clad in the familiar khaki uniform, she and her fellow volunteers had handed out cups of coffee, newspapers, sandwiches, candy, and cigarettes to trainloads of soldiers en route to army camps and ports of embarkation. "I loved it," she said later. "I simply ate it up." Freed by the war from the social duties she detested, she was able, for the first time in her married life, to spend her days doing work she truly enjoyed.

Indeed, so much had Eleanor loved her work with the Red Cross that summer of 1918 that she had offered her services to go overseas. Many women she knew were working in canteens near the front in France, and she felt that their work was more central to the war. "Yet," she lamented in her memoirs, "I knew no one would help me to get permission to go, and I had not acquired sufficient independence to go about getting it for myself."

Now, twenty-two years later, she was the first lady and she had a plan. On May 12, she was scheduled to accompany her husband on a cruise down the Potomac River on the presidential yacht, U.S.S. *Potomac.* Included in the president's party were Missy, Attorney General and Mrs. Robert Jackson, and the object of Eleanor's campaign, the chairman of the Red Cross, Norman Davis, a white-haired, ruddy-complexioned man of sixty years.

For the president, the *Potomac* offered the perfect escape from both the heat of Washington and the persistent ring of the telephone. Having loved the water since he was a child, he enjoyed nothing more than sitting on the deck, an old hat shading his head from the sun, a fishing rod in his hands. The *Potomac* was not a luxury liner, but a converted Coast Guard patrol boat, rough and ready, tending to roll with the waves, a sailor's boat, with a fair top speed of sixteen knots.

It was a brilliant afternoon, with blue skies and a strong breeze, but even the most perfect day for cruising could not still the anxiety Eleanor felt, the legacy of a frightful childhood experience during a trip to Europe with her parents, when their ship, the *Britannica,* was hit by another ship. The collision beheaded a child and killed a number of other passengers. Amid the "cries of terror," the two-and-one-half-year-old Eleanor clung frantically to the men who were attempting to throw her over the side of the ship into the arms of her father, standing in a lifeboat below. The transfer was eventually accomplished, but a fear of the sea was ingrained in the small child which the adult woman could never fully shake. In the early days of her marriage, knowing how much Franklin loved to sail, Eleanor had made a concentrated effort to conquer her panic, but in recent years, except on special occasions such as this particular cruise, she generally stepped aside and allowed Missy to take her place.

On deck, the president's party gathered in a circular lounge equipped with heavy cushions, easy chairs, and tables. There, as the president relaxed with his fishing rod, Eleanor zeroed in on the chairman of the Red Cross. Davis, a peace-minded idealist who had been appointed to the chairmanship by Roosevelt in 1938 after serving under two previous presidential administrations, listened with genuine interest to Mrs. Roosevelt's proposal, but knew he could not say yes until he talked it over with his fellow Tennessean, Secretary of State Cordell Hull. So the matter rested while the *Potomac* continued its lazy cruise down the river, returning to the Washington Navy Yard after ten o'clock that night.

The following day, Davis discussed Eleanor's proposal with Secretary Hull. The spring of 1940 was a critical period for the American Red Cross. For months, while Germany marched into Czechoslovakia and Poland, Davis had maintained a policy of "extreme circumspection," trying to keep a neutral attitude in the tradition of the International Red Cross. But with the German invasion of Western Europe, all pretense to neutrality was cast aside. At the moment of Eleanor's request, the Red Cross was focusing all its relief efforts entirely on those nations that were being overrun by Germany. If Eleanor were to join the Red Cross in Europe now, she would be placing herself in a dangerous situation.

At another moment, Eleanor was told, it might have worked, but now, because of "the imminence and possibility of a Hitler victory" and because "the capture of a President's wife would be a serious matter," her request was denied.

• • •

Two weeks later, Eleanor suffered an additional disappointment when her young friends in the American Youth Congress turned on her for supporting her husband's call for rearmament. Throughout the 1930s, Eleanor had developed a special bond with the young activists involved with the AYC, an umbrella organization including members of the YMCA, the American League for Peace and Democracy, and the Popular Front. Though she knew that some of the young people belonged to the Communist League, she trusted that the majority were liberals like herself, committed to social reform and collective security. In recent months, her trust had been tested as the AYC, following the flip-flop of Soviet policy in the wake of the Nazi-Soviet pact, had abruptly shifted its stance from pro–New Deal collective security to antiwar isolationism. Still, she refused to give up on her young friends, believing that with her support the liberals would win out.

To this end, she agreed to address the closing session of the Youth Congress at the Mecca Temple on West 56th Street in New York on May 26, 1940. Reaching out to the antiwar crowd, she admitted that she knew all too well how futile war was as a means of solving problems. "You don't want to go to war," she said simply. "I don't want to go to war. But war may come to us." Declaring that England had long "been asleep" and therefore totally surprised by Hitler's onslaught, she told the delegates it was necessary to arm in order to avoid the same crisis. "I think occasionally in the world, you are faced with events over which you have no control." However, she added, her definition of a defense program included, in addition to arms, more and better housing, expansion of the health program, and continuation of work relief until everyone had a job.

The delegates listened in sullen silence, extending only polite applause when she finished. Harlem Representative Vito Marcantonio, who cast the only vote in Congress against the president's defense program, received a standing ovation far exceeding in volume and length that accorded to Mrs. Roosevelt. Describing what he called a "war hysteria" in Congress, Marcantonio charged that the president's defense program was bound to "take us right into the meat-grinder of European battlefields." The only purpose of the war, he went on, as the delegates jumped to their feet, cheering, whistling, and stomping, was to "defend the American dollar and the British pound."

"Poor Mrs. Roosevelt!" *The New York Times* editorialized after her Mecca Temple speech. "After mothering this brood of youngsters . . . harboring them under her wing at White House teas, she suddenly discovers them to be ducklings taking to the water of Communist propaganda as to their natural element. Her scolding did no good. . . . They refused to reconsider their resolution against preparedness."

When Eleanor reached her Village apartment that night, she called Joe Lash, who had been in the audience, to see what he thought of her speech. He answered honestly, saying he didn't feel she had convinced anyone, that even their polite applause "was to demonstrate their views to her rather than to appreciate what she had to say to them." Normally, Eleanor was able to accept criticism as a matter of course, but on this night, gloom crowded in on her. The many small struggles of political life suddenly became too much, and she felt terribly weary.

In the days that followed, emptiness and exhaustion set in. Eleanor's mood became unpredictable, shifting from placid to sullen to stern in a matter of hours. "I really think," a worried Tommy confided to Anna in mid-June, "and this is strictly between you and me, that your mother is quite uncontented.... She has wanted desperately to be given something really concrete and worth while to do in this emergency and no one has found anything for her. They are all afraid of political implications etc. and I think she is discouraged and a bit annoyed about it. She spoke to your father and to H[arry] H[opkins] and Norman Davis. Outside of making two radio speeches for the Red Cross she has not been asked to do anything. She works like Hell all the time and we are busier than ever, but... she wants to feel she is doing something worthwhile and it makes me mad, because she has so much organizing and executive ability she could do a swell job on anything she undertook.... I hate to see her not visibly happy and I feel powerless to do anything about it. She would probably dismember me if she knew I wrote this to you, but I know you are about the only one to whom I could write like this and have it end with you."

Eleanor's dark mood was barely visible to the outside world. To rant or rave, to create a scene, was not her way. Believing that her best recourse was to escape from Washington—"anything that makes me forget the war clouds," she confessed, "is a blessing these days"—she embarked on a series of journeys in late May and early June—a week in New York, an expedition to Appalachia, and then a return trip to New York.

In traveling to Arthurdale, the small homestead community in the hills of West Virginia that she had vigorously supported over the years, Eleanor hoped to buoy her spirits. Considered "Eleanor's baby," Arthurdale was a product of the imagination of the early New Deal, an attempt to relieve the desolation of the hundreds of miners and their families who had been stranded in Scott's Run, West Virginia, when the mines were permanently closed. With Eleanor's backing, the government had advanced the capital for the construction of a school, a community center, and fifty farmhouses, hoping to see under what conditions part-time farming and industrial employment could be combined. Once the structures were completed, fifty families were invited in, on the promise that they would repay the government in thirty years.

But the key to whether the transplanted miners could make a living and repay the government was the successful establishment of an industry within the community to go along with the subsistence farming, and that task had proved more difficult than anyone had anticipated. Fearing that a government-subsidized factory would destroy private industry, Congress had refused to appropriate the funds for the factory, forcing the homesteaders to rely solely on their farms for their livelihood. Eleanor would not be defeated, however, and over the years she had managed to help the homesteaders in a hundred ways: a special grant here, a WPA project there, a government-subsidized nursery school here, a craft shop there.

But during this visit, her energies already depleted, Eleanor came to see the price of her continued support. So dependent on her had the homesteaders become that when their school bus broke down they sent it to the White House garage for repairs. "Deeply disillusioned" at the sight of what she now recognized as a frightful loss of initiative, she admitted to Joe Lash when she returned to New York that "they seemed to feel the solution to all their problems was to turn to government."

In New York, the days were more pleasant. Speaking to an overflowing audience of students at City College, she received a standing ovation. Touring the exhibits at the New York World's Fair, she was met everywhere she went by a huge, friendly crowd, waving to her, throwing out kisses, calling out, "God Bless You." The lights, the attention, the universal murmurs of support were still there, but as soon as she returned to the White House, it all disappeared. The problem was not simply, as she wrote, "the anxiety which hangs over everybody," the exhaustion that comes from "the state of apprehension in which we are living," but, rather, her sense of being cut off from her husband at this critical time.

In the past, Eleanor's trips around the country had been a source of fascination and pleasure to the president, who delighted in the thought-provoking stories she invariably carried back. Over the years, a cherished tradition had evolved. The first night of Eleanor's return, he would clear his calendar so the two of them could sit alone at dinner and talk, so he could hear her impressions while they were still fresh. These long, relaxing talks had become *the* bond between husband and wife, a source of continued enjoyment in one another.

But when Eleanor returned to the White House after her trips to Arthurdale and New York, she was told the president had no time for their traditional dinner. She could join him in his study for a meal, but Harry Hopkins would also be there. At dinner, she tried to engage her husband in a conversation about Arthurdale, but it was clear from the start that his thoughts were following a train of their own. The conversation quickly turned to the war, with Hopkins holding forth at great length. As Eleanor listened to Harry talk, it became obvious that he was far better acquainted with the subject than she was, though how he had learned so much about military matters in such a short time she simply could not fathom. Having little to add, she sat in silence, feeling unwanted and irrelevant.

But Franklin, perhaps feeling the difficulty of Eleanor's position on a night meant for the two of them alone, returned the conversation to domestic affairs and the New Deal. Eleanor took the opening and proceeded to pour out all her worries about the domestic situation, the recent cut in the food allowance for unemployed mothers, a new study on the spread of illiteracy, the civil-liberties questions involved in fingerprinting aliens, the need for greater housing programs and more old-age pensions.

The next day, Eleanor felt, in her own words, "terribly guilty," confessing to Joe Lash that she shouldn't have distracted the president with stuff that didn't relate directly to the international crisis, that he had listened to her late into the night and then worried about all the issues she raised until all hours of the morning.

As guilt and sadness overwhelmed her, Eleanor's feelings of loss focused on Harry Hopkins. Of all the people in the administration, Eleanor felt most closely connected to Hopkins. Indeed, it was her appreciation, back in 1928, for the work this impassioned young social worker had done in New York that had brought Harry to the president's attention in the first place, setting in motion his remarkable career as head of the largest work-relief program in the history of the country, a program that at one point employed more than 30 percent of the unemployed at a cost of $6 billion.

From the start, Eleanor shared with Harry an abiding faith in the unemployed, a belief that they were decent, honest people suffering through no fault of their own, totally deserving of government help. "Both Harry Hopkins and Mrs. Roosevelt were driven during the depression by a sense of urgency," WPA Administrator Elizabeth Wickenden recalled. "They never forgot there were these millions of people who had absolutely nothing, who had once held a steady job and had a sense of self-respect. From their wide travels across the country, they kept in their minds a vivid picture of the lives of these people, and that image drove them to push the government to create as many jobs for as many people as it possibly could."

Under Hopkins' resourceful leadership, the WPA employed two million people a month. It built thousands of schools, libraries, parks, sidewalks, and hospitals. It sponsored murals for the walls of public buildings, and hot lunches for the children of the poor; it put writers to work preparing tourist guides to American cities and states; it supported plays and playwrights and actors and directors. These were the programs that captured Eleanor's heart; it was the WPA sites Eleanor visited most frequently in her tireless trips round the country, bringing back an unrivaled knowledge of the mood of the American people.

To Harold Ickes' criticism that the jobs the WPA created were not permanent, that the only way to relieve unemployment in the long run was to prime the pump by subsidizing private enterprise, Hopkins replied, "people don't eat in the long run. They eat every day. . . . " Regularly attacked in the press as a reckless waster of the taxpayers' money, Hopkins countered: "If I deserve any criticism, it is that I didn't do enough when I had the chance."

Hopkins, Eleanor wrote in her column, "My Day," in 1938, "is one of the few people in the world who gives me the feeling of being entirely absorbed in doing his job well. He seems to work because he has an inner conviction that his job needs to be done and that he must do it. I think he would be that way about any job he undertook." If Eleanor loved someone, a relative of hers once said, she lost her critical faculty entirely and was bound to be disappointed when reality set in. But until that moment, she was able to give herself wholly to love. When Harry's wife, Barbara, was dying of cancer, Eleanor was there. When Harry himself was in the hospital for months at a stretch, Eleanor was there. When Harry's six-year-old daughter, Diana, needed comfort and care, Eleanor brought her to live at the White House, installing her in a bedroom on the third floor, near the sky parlor, and offered to be her guardian should anything happen to her father.

Eleanor's closeness to Hopkins inevitably generated gossip. "Around the White House," the maid Lillian Parks recalled, "there was some talk that Eleanor was romantically inclined toward the gaunt Harry." In journalistic circles, according to Eliot Janeway, the talk took a meaner tone. "In the days before Hopkins discovered Churchill and became resident lapdog he did whatever he could to get in with Roosevelt. Among the fellows in our poker game the great joke was that he even did his duty by Eleanor."

Whatever truth there might be to the gossip, there is little doubt that the bond between Harry and Eleanor was shaped above all by their shared pledge to the poor and the unemployed and their shared belief in the New Deal's restorative powers.

"It was strange," Eleanor later told her son Elliott, "but when I came back from New York that first night of the German invasion, I felt a great sense of foreboding, a fear that the war would get in the way of all the domestic progress we were making. But then, when I saw Harry back in the White House, I felt better, for I knew that he had never been interested in military affairs and that he'd stick with me no matter what happened."

Eleanor was correct in suggesting that Hopkins had little interest in military matters. Rejected from the army in World War I because of a blind eye, he had never fired a gun or fixed a bayonet in infantry drill. His only war experience was welfare work with the Red Cross in Mississippi and Alabama. Furthermore, Robert Sherwood observed, "his New Deal pacifism inclined him emotionally toward a kind of isolationism." Writing to Eleanor on August 31, 1939, the day before the war broke out, Hopkins had said: "The war news is disquieting, but I hope and pray there will be no war. It would seem as though all of civilization were crumbling right under our very eyes."

But now, to Eleanor's mind, Harry had made a devastating turn of 180 degrees in his interests and concerns. He had suddenly transformed himself into an expert on foreign affairs, as if the problems of the sick and the unemployed were no longer of any consequence to him. His total shift from domestic to international concerns was inexplicable to her, suggesting to Eleanor that all along he had been more allied to her husband's concerns than to hers, that their friendship had never meant as much to him as it did to her.

Indeed, Harry Hopkins was so close to the president at this point, Frances Perkins recalled, that he was almost admitted—but not really, since no one ever was—to "a total friendship" with him. Situated in the best guest room in the White House—the large suite that had once been Abraham Lincoln's study, in the southwest corner of the second floor, consisting of one large bedroom with a four-poster bed, a small sitting room, and a bath—Hopkins was available to talk with the president at any hour about anything and everything, about consequential matters and "ordinary fooling," as Hopkins once put it, "passing the time of day and the small talk of people who are living in the same house."

Tommy alluded to Harry's changed position in the White House in a letter to Eleanor's daughter, Anna. "Harry and Missy are thicker than the well-known thieves at the moment," Tommy wrote; "he is staying here and has gone completely over to the other side of the house. If your father does not eat with your mother and any guests, Harry eats with him and Missy and it makes me mad and ready to smack him because your mother was so darn faithful about going to see him when he was sick, agreeing to take Diana if anything happened to him, etc. It seems to me if he had a lick of sense or appreciation, he would make it a real point to spend time with your mother."

During this period, Frances Perkins noticed that Eleanor seemed to be away from the White House even more than usual. She was always going somewhere, Perkins recalled. "It had begun to cause grumbling around, such as 'Where's Mrs. Roosevelt? Why doesn't she stay home? Why doesn't she take care of her husband?' " At one point, Perkins went to see Eleanor. "I really think you ought to be here in the White House more. I say it to you in the warmest kind of friendship. I think it would be better for you and better for the President. The President needs you and needs you here."

Eleanor looked at Perkins and, "with the sweetest smile, sort of twisting her eyes and smiling sweetly, she shook her head and said, 'Oh, no Frances, he doesn't need me any more. He has Harry. . . . He doesn't need my advice any more. He doesn't ask it. Harry tells him everything he needs to know!' "

In the past, Eleanor had been able to work for long stretches without tiring, sleeping only four or five hours a night. But now, as the world around her turned hostile and cold, she had periods of such exhaustion that she found it difficult to get up in the morning. "One day," Tommy reported to Anna, "she didn't come down to breakfast until nearly ten a.m. and I nearly had a fit. I could contain myself no longer, so at 9:30 I went up to see what was wrong. She just decided to stay in bed. I told her to please send out advance notices in the future when she was going to do something so unheard of."

• • •

Eleanor was no stranger to depression. In the months surrounding her husband's first inauguration, in 1933, she had experienced a period of turmoil and loss similar to what she was feeling in the spring of 1940. What she feared then, as she feared now, was the loss of the unique partnership she had forged with Franklin since his paralysis, a partnership that allowed her both an independent existence and the chance to contribute in important ways to his fame and power. As the first lady of New York, she had been able to spend three days a week away from Albany, teaching literature, drama, and American history to the young girls at Todhunter, a private school in Manhattan, while still managing to be her husband's "eyes and ears" in the State Capitol the rest of the week.

But with her husband's nomination to the presidency, she was concerned that her dual existence would come to an end, that she would become a prisoner in the White House, a slave to the superficial, symbolic duties of the first lady. As she saw it, the move to the White House would destroy her working partnership with Franklin and bring an end to any personal life of her own.

She couldn't bear it, she told her friend Nancy Cook in a long letter written on the eve of Franklin's victory at the convention, she just "could not live in the White House." When Nancy showed the indiscreet letter to Louis Howe, his "pale face darkened . . . his lips drew into a thin line, and when he had finished he ripped the letter into shreds, tiny shreds, and dropped these into a wastebasket." Then, according to historian Kenneth Davis, he ordered sternly, "You are not to breathe a word of this to anyone, understand? Not to anyone."

Howe's injunction was respected. The public was never aware of the dismal mood that accompanied Eleanor's journey to the nation's capital. Only a few friends knew how deadened she felt inside, as if all the elements that had rooted her in life and given her a sense of identity were being torn away from her. An accurate gauge of her confusion is her admission in her memoirs that just before the inauguration she tentatively suggested to her husband that, beyond being hostess at the necessary functions, he might like her to do a real job and take on some of his mail. "He looked at me quizzically and said he did not think that would do, that Missy, who had been handling his mail for a long time, would feel I was interfering. I knew he was right and that it would not work, but it was a last effort to keep in close touch and to feel that I had a real job to do."

It was, in retrospect, a terrible idea. Eleanor was much too independent and strong-willed to spend her time simply reflecting her husband's thinking in answering the mail, but at the time Eleanor interpreted Franklin's negative response as a personal rejection. The downward spiral escalated.

"My zest in life is rather gone for the time being," Eleanor had confessed to her friend Lorena Hickok in a grim letter written in the spring of 1933, soon after she had become first lady. "If anyone looks at me, I want to weep . . . ," she continued. "I get like this sometimes. It makes me feel like a dead weight & my mind goes round & round like a squirrel in a cage. I want to run, & I can't, & I despise myself. I can't get away from thinking about myself. Even though I know I'm a fool, I can't help it!"

By the summer of 1933, Eleanor's melancholy had passed. "The times of depression are very often felt as gaps," a psychologist has written, "temporary losses of certainty or identity which leave us feeling empty." Seen in this light, Eleanor's despondency was the intervening period of chaos between the breakup of her old identity as teacher and political activist in New

York State and the establishment of a new identity in the White House. In a remarkably short period of time, with the help of her friends Louis Howe and Lorena Hickok, Eleanor was able to forge a new role for herself, as a new kind of first lady, an activist role never practiced or even imagined before. "Within a few months," one historian has written, "she was more firmly established in the public mind than she had ever been in her native state as a sharply defined personality, a forceful mind, an acutely sensitive conscience, a remarkably strong moral character."

Though Eleanor was able to surmount her particular unhappiness in 1933 by carving out a new role for herself as first lady, the storm which had swept her up in 1933 and again in 1940 had a deeper origin, in the devastating losses she had experienced as a child.

• • •

The story of Eleanor's recurring depressions must begin with her alcoholic father, Elliott Roosevelt. The third of four children born to Theodore Roosevelt, Sr., and Martha "Mittie" Bulloch, Elliott had grown up in a world of privilege: a fashionable town house in Manhattan, a country estate in Oyster Bay, Long Island, private tutors and private schools. In a remarkable household that would produce a president of the United States in the eldest son, Teddy, Elliott was considered the best-looking, the most athletic, the most gregarious, and in many ways the most endearing of them all. But, for reasons that are not easy to understand, Elliott was never able to hold his own in the unrelenting competition that governed everyday life among the talented Roosevelts.

At the age of fourteen, upset by his failure to keep up with his brother Teddy academically, Elliott began having mysterious seizures. "Yesterday during my Latin lesson . . . ," he wrote his father from St. Paul's, "I had a bad rush of blood to my head, it hurt me so that I can't remember what happened." There was some talk of epilepsy, but the attacks were most likely an unconscious mechanism of escape from competitive struggles he could not otherwise endure. An earlier problem with German had produced a similar fainting spell along with a plaintive letter to his father: "Teedee is a much quicker and more sure kind of boy, though I will try my best and try to be good as you if [it] is in me, but it is hard."

Incapable of putting forth the concerted effort needed to stay in school, Elliott wandered off to the Himalayas. Upon his return to New York, he courted Anna Hall, a debutante of such great beauty that her image remained for years in the minds of those who saw her. The stories are legion. The poet Robert Browning was so struck by Anna's looks that he asked if he could sit and gaze at her while she had her portrait painted. Eleanor's cousin Corinne Robinson was so entranced by the sight of Anna, "dressed in some blue gray shimmering material," that the vision stayed with her for the rest of her childhood. But the deepest imprint was on her daughter, Eleanor, who opened her memoirs, written at the age of fifty-five, with the comment that her mother was "one of the most beautiful women" she had ever seen. As a little girl, she added, she was "grateful to be allowed to touch her [mother's] dress or her jewels or anything that was part of the vision."

Elliott Roosevelt and Anna Hall made a dazzling couple. They were invited everywhere, and Anna fell in love. Like so many others, she, too, was affected by Elliott's radiant smile and charming personality. She was nineteen and he was twenty-three when they married. Their happiness was short-lived. The responsibility of marriage and the birth of three children—Eleanor, Elliott Jr., and Hall—served to increase Elliott's anxiety to the point where his casual drinking became heavier and heavier.

When he was not drinking, he was loving and warm, everything Eleanor wanted in a father. "[My father] dominated my life as long as he lived and was the love of my life for many years after he died," Eleanor wrote in her memoirs. One of her earliest recollections is of being dressed up and allowed to come down and dance for a group of her father's friends, who enthusiastically applauded her performance. Then, when she finished, her father would pick her up and hold her high in the air, a moment of triumph for both the father and the little girl. "With my father I was perfectly happy," she recalled. "He would take me into his dressing room in the mornings or when he was dressing for dinner and let me watch each thing he did."

When he was drinking, however, everything changed. The routine of everyday life became impossible to maintain. The household was filled with recrimination. Night after night he would show up too late for dinner, and many nights he failed to show up at all. At one point, he made a servant girl pregnant and a scandal erupted in the newspapers. At times, his drinking led to a melancholy so deep that he threatened suicide. In such moods, he would totally forget the promises he had made to his wife and his daughter only the day before. One afternoon, Eleanor recalled, her father took her and three of their dogs for a walk. As they came up to the door of the Knickerbocker Club, he told Eleanor to wait for a moment with the dogs and he would be right back. An hour passed, and then another, and then four more, and still Eleanor remained at the door, patiently holding the dogs. Finally, her father came out, but so drunk that he had to be carried in the arms of several men. The doorman took Eleanor home.

Still, Eleanor preferred her warm and affectionate father to her cold and self-absorbed mother. At least with her father, she said, she never doubted that she "stood first in his heart," whereas for as long as she could remember she felt that her beautiful mother was bitterly disappointed, almost repelled, by the plainness and the ungainliness of her only daughter. Forced to wear a brace for several years for curvature of the spine, Eleanor recalled that even at the age of two she was "a shy solemn child," completely "lacking in the spontaneous joy or mirth of youth." Moreover, she knew, "as a child senses those things," that her mother was trying to compensate for her lack of beauty by teaching her excellent manners, but "her efforts only made me more keenly conscious of my shortcomings."

Perhaps Anna, having been taught to value beauty and charm as the most important attributes in a woman, did instinctively recoil from her daughter's unattractive looks. But, though Eleanor could never admit it, her father's erratic behavior was the more likely cause of the distance between mother and daughter. Feeling the weight of the world on her shoulders, Anna had little energy left for a stubborn and precocious little girl who kept her father on a pedestal and blamed her mother when her father had to be sent away on various "cures" to various sanitariums. Perhaps, in rejecting Eleanor's fervent love for her father, Anna was rejecting that part of herself that had fallen in love with such an untrustworthy man.

Eleanor slept in her mother's room while her father was away and could hear her mother talking with her aunts about the problem with her father. "I acquired a strange and garbled idea of the troubles which were going on around me. Something was wrong with my father." Eleanor was only seven at the time, too young to understand the intolerable strain on her twenty-eight-year-old mother, a strain that produced in Anna very bad recurring headaches. "I would sit at the head of her bed and stroke her head," Eleanor recalled. "The feeling that I was useful was perhaps the greatest joy I had experienced."

But aside from these dreamy moments serving her mother, Eleanor felt most of the time "a curious barrier" between herself and the rest of her little family. In the late afternoons, she recalled, her mother sat in the parlor with her two brothers. "Little Ellie adored her, the baby [Hall] sat on her lap. . . . [I can] still remember standing in the door, very often with my finger in my mouth—which was, of course, forbidden and I can see the look in her eyes and hear the tone of her voice as she said, 'Come in, Granny.' If a visitor was there she might turn and say: 'She is such a funny child, so old-fashioned, we always call her Granny.' I wanted to sink through the floor in shame, and I felt I was apart from the boys." The painful memory of these afternoons in the parlor remained with Eleanor, reappearing thirty years later in a fictional composition in which she wrote of "a blue eyed rather ugly little girl standing in the door of a cozy library looking in at a very beautiful woman holding, oh so lovingly, in her lap a little fair haired boy."

For most of Eleanor's eighth year, her father remained in exile in Abingdon, Virginia, where her mother and her uncle Theodore had sent him in the hope that the forced separation from his family would motivate him to take hold of himself. "A child stood at a window . . . ," Eleanor wrote in her composition book. "Her father [was] the only person in the world she loved, others called her hard & cold but to him she was everything lavishing on him all the quiet love which the others could not understand. And now he had gone she did not know for how long but he had said 'what ever happens little girl some day I will come back' & she had smiled. He never knew what the smile cost."

On her eighth birthday, Eleanor received a long and loving letter from Abingdon, addressed to "My darling little Daughter." "Because Father is not with you is not because he doesn't love you," he wrote. "For I love you tenderly and dearly. And maybe soon I'll come back all well and strong and we will have such good times together, like we used to have. I have to tell all the little children here often about you and all that I remember of you when you were a little bit of a girl and you used to call yourself Father's little 'Golden Hair'—and how you used to come into my dressing room and dress me in the morning and frighten me by saying I'd be late for breakfast."

These letters, filled only with love for her, Eleanor later wrote, were the letters she loved and kissed before she went to bed. But there were other letters, filled with news of the life he was leading in Abingdon, that inadvertently brought her pain and reinforced her feeling of being an outsider. In these newsy letters he often spoke of riding horseback with a group of little children near where he lived. "I was always longing to join the group," Eleanor later wrote. "One child in particular I remember. I envied her very much because he was so very fond of her."

A month after Eleanor's eighth birthday, her mother contracted a fatal case of diphtheria. Her father was told to return from his exile in Virginia, but Anna died before he was able to get home. "I can remember standing by a window when Cousin Susie told me that my mother was dead," Eleanor later wrote. "Death meant nothing to me, and one fact wiped out everything else—my father was back and I would see him very soon."

When Elliott finally arrived, Eleanor recorded, "he held out his arms and gathered me to him. In a little while he began to talk, to explain to me that my mother was gone, that she had been all the world to him and now he only had my brothers and myself, that my brothers were very young and that he and I must keep close together. Some day I would make a home for him again, we would travel together and do many things. Somehow it was always he and I. I did not understand whether my brothers were to be our children or whether he felt that they would be at school and college and later independent. There started that day a feeling which never left me—that he and I were very close together and some day would have a life of our own together.... When he left, I was all alone to keep our secret of mutual understanding."

The decision was made to send Eleanor and her brothers to their grandmother Hall's while Elliott returned to Virginia. From then on, Eleanor admitted, "subconsciously I must have been waiting always for his visits. They were irregular and he rarely sent word before he arrived, but never was I in the house even in my room two long flights of stairs above the entrance door that I did not hear his voice the minute he entered the front door." During these precious visits, Elliott painted a picture for his daughter of the valiant, gifted, upright little girl he expected her to be, and Eleanor did her best, she later wrote, despite her consciousness of her ugly looks and her many deficiencies, to make herself into "a fairly good copy of the picture he had painted."

The year after her mother died, Eleanor's four-year-old brother, Ellie, also fell ill with diphtheria and died. Though she was a child herself, Eleanor tried to comfort her father. "We must remember," she wrote him, "Ellie is going to be safe in heaven and to be with Mother who is waiting there. . . ."

But then, when Eleanor was ten, the visits and the letters from her father stopped. The years of heavy drinking took their final toll. Suffering from delirium tremens, Elliott tried to jump out of the window of his house, had a seizure and died, at the age of thirty-four. "My aunts told me," Eleanor recalled, "but I simply refused to believe it, and while I wept long . . . I finally went to sleep and began the next day living in my dream world as usual. My grandmother decided we children should not go to the funeral and so I had no tangible thing to make death real to me. From that time on . . . I lived with him more closely, probably, than I had when he was alive."

From the melancholy lives of both her parents, as she would learn again in her own marriage, Eleanor had come to understand that promises were made to be broken, and that no one's love for her was meant to last. The legacy of repeated loss as a child left her prey to the recurring depressions she suffered as an adult. Always waiting in the wings, depression was for Eleanor a dark companion that strode to center stage whenever there were turnabouts in the established pattern of her life.

• • •

But the legacy of Eleanor's childhood also produced resilient strength. No matter how many times her father disappointed her, Eleanor knew, at bottom, that he loved her profoundly, that he had chosen her as his favorite child. And this knowledge was something that neither alcoholism nor death could destroy. "It was her father who acquainted Eleanor with grief," Joe Lash has written. "But he also gave her the ideals that she tried to live up to all her life by presenting her with the picture of what he wanted her to be —noble, studious, religious, loving and good."

"We do not have to become heroes overnight," Eleanor once wrote. "Just a step at a time, meeting each thing that comes up, seeing it is not as dreadful as it appears, discovering that we have the strength to stare it down." So, step by step, Eleanor willed herself to become the accomplished daughter her father had decreed her to be, the fearless woman that would make him proud. Every inch of her journey was filled with peril and anxiety, but she never stopped moving forward. "The thing always to remember," she said, is that "you must do the thing you think you cannot do."

As a young girl trapped in the austere household of her grandmother after her parents died, Eleanor used to hide books under her mattress so she could wake up in the middle of the night to read them, defying her grandmother's edict that she be allowed to read only at set times and in set places. Her passionate reading of Dickens and Scott awakened within her a romantic belief that, no matter how grim everything seemed, there was always some way out.

Hers came when her grandmother sent her away to a boarding school in

London run by an inspired teacher, Mademoiselle Souvestre. From the moment Eleanor arrived at Allenswood and looked into the smiling eyes of the seventy-year-old headmistress, she felt that she was starting "a new life," free from all her earlier troubles. In Mademoiselle Souvestre, Eleanor found the maternal love she had never enjoyed as a child, and in the power of that love, the young girl blossomed. Excelling at everything she did—at her lessons in every subject, at poetry recitations, even at field hockey—Eleanor quickly became "everything" at the school, the most respected student among faculty and students alike. Step by step, Eleanor later said, Allenswood "started me on my way to self confidence." Her three years there, she said, were "the happiest of my life."

Not long after her return to New York, Eleanor began seeing her cousin Franklin at parties and dances. They had first met when they were two and four, but now, fifteen years later, a special bond developed between them. Eleanor was unlike any girl Franklin had met. She was serious and intelligent, free from affectation, and wholly uninterested in the world of debutante balls. Though her interest in philosophy and ethics seemed ridiculous to her cousin Alice Roosevelt, Teddy's daughter, who noted sarcastically that Eleanor "always wanted to discuss things like whether contentment was better than happiness," Franklin was intrigued. He enjoyed her company immensely. He invited her to Campobello in the summer, to dances and football games at Harvard in the fall, and to Hyde Park in the spring, where they rode together in the woods and sat on the porch at twilight reading poetry to one another.

While Franklin completed his studies at Harvard, Eleanor was happily ensconced at the Rivington Street settlement house in New York, where she supervised a class of immigrant children in exercise and dance. From her early childhood, when her father had taken her to a newsboy clubhouse which his father, Theodore Roosevelt, Sr., had started, Eleanor found herself "tremendously interested in all these ragged little boys and in the fact which my father explained, that many of them had no homes and lived in wooden shanties." Her work at the settlement house was tremendously stimulating to her, and she was delighted to feel that she could be of some help.

One afternoon when Franklin was in New York, she asked him to pick her up at the settlement house. Just before they were ready to leave, a young girl suddenly fell ill, and Eleanor enlisted Franklin's help to take the child home. Nothing in Franklin's sheltered life had prepared him for the grating sounds and sour smells of the dilapidated tenement where the young girl lived. "My God," he told Eleanor, "I didn't know anyone lived like that."

How easy Eleanor felt in Franklin's presence! Her awkwardness seemed suddenly to disappear, her old dejection passed away. The inferiority she had always experienced in the presence of men vanished as she came to trust that he thought her better and more interesting than all the other young women in the world. The letters she wrote during the first months of their romance reveal an absolute delight at the experience of falling in love, combined with a fervent wish to be with her lover every moment of the day.

"Though I only wrote last night," she told him one autumn day when she was seventeen, "I must write you just a line this morning to tell you that I miss you every moment & that you are never out of my thoughts dear for one moment. . . . I am so happy. Oh! so happy & I love you *so* dearly."

And she knew that he loved her as she loved him. "It is impossible to tell you what these last two days have been to me," Eleanor wrote after a weekend together at Hyde Park, "but I know they have meant the same to you so that you will understand that I love you dearest and I hope that I shall always prove worthy of the love which you have given me. I have never before known what it was to be absolutely happy."

As the days and months passed, Eleanor recalled, she came to realize that the hours they were together meant the most to her. She was happiest when she was with him. Though she was only nineteen when he asked her to marry him, she was absolutely sure that it was right. "When he told me that he loved me and asked me to marry him, I did not hesitate to say yes, for I knew that I loved him too." A week later, Eleanor was still filled with joy. "I was thinking last night of the difference which one short week can make in one's life. Everything is changed for me now. . . . I am so happy."

Franklin's letters from this period no longer exist. Eleanor burned them —most likely in 1937, Joe Lash speculates, when she was working on her autobiography and found his youthful avowals of constancy unto death too painful and uncomfortable to reread. Yet there is no doubt that he, too, had been caught in the tide of a powerful love. "I am the happiest man just now in the world," he told his mother after Eleanor accepted his proposal, "likewise the luckiest."

• • •

When Eleanor married Franklin, she traded the chance for deeper involvement in social work for the hope of finding happiness as a wife and mother. Six children quickly followed (one of the six died at twenty months). "For ten years I was always just getting over having a baby or about to have another one, and so my occupations were considerably restricted." At one point, she expressed a desire to return to the settlement house, but her mother-in-law dissuaded her on the grounds that she would be coming home with germs that would contaminate her own children.

Forced to remain at home while her husband went to work, Eleanor found her old insecurities returning. So painful was the memory of her own tormented childhood that she approached the task of mothering with little joy. She worried constantly about nutrition, illness, and discipline. Her lack of confidence caught Franklin by surprise. "He had always been secure in every way, you see," Eleanor later said, "and then he discovered that I was perfectly insecure."

It was only after her last child was born, in 1916, and after the crisis provoked by Lucy Mercer, that Eleanor found her identity. Free to define a new role for herself beyond her family, she poured all her pent-up energies into a variety of reformist organizations dedicated to the abolition of child labor, the establishment of a minimum wage, and the passage of protective legislation for women workers. In the process, she discovered she had real talents for organization, leadership, and public life. Her political activities expanded still further after Franklin's paralysis, when he turned to her to keep the Roosevelt name in the public eye while he concentrated on regaining his health. "The polio was very instrumental in bringing them much closer into a very real partnership," Anna observed. "They were finding mutual interests on a totally different level than they had been before."

During Franklin's years as governor and president, the Roosevelts became so deeply involved with one another that they seemed like two halves of a single whole whose lives, as New Deal economist Rexford Tugwell put it, "were joined in a common cause." Her astonishing travels, her strong convictions, her curiosity about almost every phase of the nation's life, from slum clearance to experimental beehives, from rural electrification to country dances, provided fascinating material for endless conversations, arguments, and debates.

Their working partnership involved the creation of a shared emotional territory in which they could relate to each other with abiding love and respect. To be sure, on some occasions, she irritated and even exasperated him, but he never ceased to respect and admire her. Nor did she ever stop loving him. "I hated to see you go . . . ," Eleanor wrote Franklin in the 1930s as he set out on a journey overseas. "We are really very dependent on each other though we do see so little of each other."

Understanding the nature of their relationship, it is not surprising, then, that Eleanor anguished so much in the spring of 1940 over the fear that her partnership would break apart. The husband who had been her close friend would now be more remote, his attention directed to international concerns. The man who loved nothing more than the detailed stories of her travels, now had little time and less inclination to listen to her.

But just as she had surmounted her unhappiness in 1933 and managed to etch a role for the first lady in domestic affairs never before practiced, so now, as the imperatives of war propelled a conversion of the nation, she would slowly come to grips with her depression, rallying her forces once more to effect a transformation of her role to fit the changing times.

• • •

By the end of June, Eleanor had found her first wartime cause in the movement to open America's doors to the refugee children of Europe. With the entire continent under Nazi control, and England living in fear of imminent invasion, the public cry for evacuating as many European children as possible reached a crescendo.

The chance to work on a project that mattered both to her and to the world was a tonic to Eleanor. Into her Greenwich Village apartment she brought together representatives of various relief and charitable agencies —including the American Friends Service Committee, the German-Jewish Children's Aide, and the Committee for Catholic Refugees—to determine what could be done. The refugee crisis seemed the perfect focus for Eleanor's abilities, combining her humanitarian zeal with her organizational skill. Clearly, there was no time to lose.

On the morning of June 20, at a hastily arranged conference at New York's Gramercy Park Hotel, a new umbrella organization was born with Eleanor as honorary chair—the U.S. Committee for the Care of European Children. The purpose of the new committee was to coordinate all the different agencies and resources available in the United States for the care of refugee children. The first goal was to get the State Department to relax its restrictions on the granting of visas; the second, to establish a network of families in the United States willing to care for the children once they arrived.

That evening at Eleanor's apartment, the new committee held its first meeting. A number of members were anxious to have the Republican banker Winthrop Aldrich as chairman. Before endorsing him, Eleanor excused herself and called the president to see what he thought of Aldrich. Roosevelt, who was in his study when she reached him, having dinner with Harry Hopkins, was appalled at the idea. "You know, darling," he told her, wildly overstating his case to make his opposition clear, "he would be the first to welcome Hitler with open arms." Placed in a delicate situation by her husband's sharp reaction, Eleanor quickly composed herself, walked back into the living room, and said in her most disarming manner, "It was kind of Mr. Aldrich to offer to be chairman, but is it not better from the point of view of geography to have someone from the Middle West?" At that, she turned immediately to the Chicago philanthropist and New Deal loyalist Marshall Field; she knew it would be a bother for him, but could he accept? Though caught somewhat off guard, Field gave his assent, and a troublesome problem was averted.

The plight of the refugees, particularly the British children, touched such a responsive chord in the American public that within two days the committee was flooded with thousands of offers of homes. All of these offers had to be confirmed and evaluated, a laborious task which Eleanor willingly shouldered. "I think men are worse than women on committees," Eleanor confided in a letter to her daughter, Anna, "and they do think more of their importance. I hope I'll never think I am of any importance, it makes one so stuffy!"

Moreover, as Eleanor quickly recognized, the task of "finding homes into which to put children when they arrive" was delightfully simple compared with "the horrid legal details" involved in having the children admitted to the country in the first place. From the start, Eleanor understood that visitor visas were the only way to get around the low monthly quotas for immigration which had been set by a xenophobic Congress in the late 1920s. In a radio program on CBS, Eleanor argued for an administrative ruling that would permit refugee children to enter the United States as temporary visitors rather than as immigrants. "The children are not immigrants," she said. "The parents of these children will recall them when the war is over. . . . Therefore [they] should be classified as temporary visitors and not as immigrants. . . . Red tape must not be used to trip up little children on their way to safety."

Since visitor visas were not subject to numerical limitations, the change Eleanor advocated promised to open America's doors to tens of thousands of refugees, and simultaneously to provide an invaluable precedent for saving countless lives in the years ahead. The principal obstacle was the head of the State Department's visa section, Breckinridge Long. A Southerner who proudly traced his roots to the Breckinridges of Kentucky and the Longs of North Carolina, Long was adamantly opposed to the admission of refugees under any circumstances. In a diary filled with invectives against Jews, Catholics, New Yorkers, liberals, and in fact everybody who was not of his own particular background, Long interpreted the widespread desire to admit the British refugee children as "an enormous psychosis" on the part of the American people. "I attribute it to repressed emotion about the war," he recorded in his diary, "the chance finally to DO something, however wrongheaded it may be."

Long had first met FDR during the Wilson administration, when they were both assistant secretaries, Long at State, Roosevelt at Navy. A successful international lawyer, Long had made a sizable contribution to the Democratic campaign fund in 1932 and was rewarded with an ambassadorship to Italy. There, Mussolini and the fascist regime captured his heart until Mussolini's foreign adventures and Italy's invasion of Ethiopia changed his mind. Resigning from the ambassadorship, he returned to the United States, where in January 1940 he was made head of a Special War Problems Division in the State Department, which included the visa section.

Long had come to the unshakable conviction that the admission of refugees would endanger national security, since the Germans were using visitor visas to send spies and foreign agents abroad. Every single one of the now defeated countries, according to Long, had been honeycombed with spies and fifth-column activities. There was some truth to his claims.

But not even Long, whose skill at carrying the security gambit to an illogical extreme boggled the mind, was able to argue that British children were German spies. Moreover, in the summer of 1940, the tide of support for letting the British children into America was so strong, running through every class in American society, that it promised, for a time, to overwhelm the more general antirefugee sentiment that had been prevalent for so many years.

Capitalizing on the moment at hand, Eleanor appealed directly to Franklin, patiently explaining why it was necessary to go over Breckinridge Long's head. For days and weeks, she said, she had been arguing with Long to no avail. The president assured her he would do his utmost, and the next day, in a signal victory for the refugee advocates, Roosevelt ordered Long's boss, Secretary of State Hull, to simplify the procedure so that the British children could come in. A new ruling was issued the following day whereby visitor visas would be issued to British refugee children "upon a showing of intention they shall return home upon the termination of hostilities."

Eleanor was delighted. "I think your mother is really enjoying her work with the refugee committee," Tommy told Anna. "She looks very well and of course, is always happier when she feels she is doing something constructive."

One pressing problem remained: how to get the children here. "The English," Harold Ickes recorded in his diary, "cannot spare warships to convoy bottoms [unarmed merchant ships] bringing in refugee children and it isn't safe to send them except under convoy." Nor was it safe to send American mercy ships into the sub-infested waters. "The very surest way to get America into the war," Long argued, "would be to send an American ship to England and put 2000 babies on it and then have it sunk by a German torpedo." Roosevelt shared Long's fear about sending American ships, but when the pressure to save the British children refused to abate, the Congress took matters into its own hands, passing an amendment to the Neutrality Act which permitted unarmed, unescorted ships to sail to Britain to evacuate British children provided safe conduct was granted by all belligerents.

• • •

While Americans fretted over the plight of British children who were not yet in danger, the people who most urgently needed help were the Jewish refugees from Germany who were trapped in Vichy France. One of the provisions in the French armistice agreement required the Vichy government to return on demand all German citizens named by the German government. As American ships crossed the Atlantic to save the British children, Gestapo agents were on their way to France to round up every German Jewish man, woman, and child they could find. But when Congressman William Schulte of Indiana tried to broaden the use of the visitor visas to any European child under sixteen, his bill was killed before it even reached the floor. The crucial difference, in terms of American public opinion, between the British and the German children was that the British boys and girls were mostly Christian, the German children mostly Jewish.

Throughout the 1930s, as tens of thousands of Jews fled Nazi Germany, Roosevelt worked behind the scenes to let more people in. Estimates show that, in the years between 1933 and 1940, nearly 105,000 refugees from Nazism reached safety in the United States, a record, though limited, that went beyond that of any other country. Only Palestine, which took in 55,000 during these same years, approached the American figure.

But those who were granted refuge were pitifully few compared with those who were trying to flee. "The long pathetic list of refugee ships, unable to find harbors open to them," historian David Wyman argues, "testifies to the fact the world of the late 30s and early 40s was a world without room for the Jews of . . . Europe." The sad saga of the *St. Louis,* which set out from Germany for Cuba in May 1939 with 930 Jewish refugees aboard, was a dramatic case in point. On reaching Havana, the passengers were not allowed to disembark and the ship was turned away. For weeks, as the ship hovered close enough to Miami for the refugees to see the lights of the city, negotiators tried without success to get the U.S. government to provide temporary sanctuary. A telegram to FDR from a committee of the passengers received no reply. The *St. Louis,* memorialized in the movie *Voyage of the Damned,* was forced to sail back to Europe, where many of its passengers eventually died in concentration camps.

Roosevelt was not unsympathetic to the plight of the Jewish refugees. Though anti-Semitism had been part and parcel of the cloistered world in which he and Eleanor had grown up—"The Jew party [was] appalling," Eleanor had written her mother-in-law in 1918 after an evening with Bernard Baruch. "I never wish to hear money, jewels or sables mentioned again"—politics had broadened their attitudes and expanded their sensibilities. During the Roosevelt presidency, though Jews constituted only 3 percent of the U.S. population, they represented nearly 15 percent of Roosevelt's top appointments. Indeed, so prominent were Jews in the Roosevelt administration that bigots routinely referred to the New Deal as the Jew Deal and charged that Roosevelt was himself a Jew. "In the dim distant past," Roosevelt had replied, "[my ancestors] may have been Jews or Catholics or Protestants. What I am interested in is whether they were good citizens and believers in God. I hope they were both."

But it was one thing to sympathize with the plight of the Jewish refugees and quite another to pit his presidency against the xenophobic, anti-Semitic mood of his country in the late 1930s and early '40s. This Roosevelt was unwilling to do. Roper polls confirmed that, though people disapproved of Hitler's treatment of Jews in Germany, the majority of Americans were manifestly unwilling to assist the Jews in practical ways, especially if it meant allowing more Jewish immigration into the U.S. In answer to a question posed in 1938, "What kinds of people do you object to?," Jews were mentioned by 35 percent of the respondents; the next-highest category, at 27 percent, were "noisy, cheap, boisterous and loud people," followed by "uncultured, unrefined, dumb people" at 14 percent and then all other types. The following year, another Roper poll found that 53 percent of the Americans asked believed Jews were different from everyone else and that these differences should lead to restrictions in business and social life.

The desperate situation of the refugees stranded in Europe was brought to Eleanor's attention on June 24, when she hosted a small dinner at her village apartment for her friend Joe Lash and two members of the European underground, Karl Frank and Joseph Buttinger. Buttinger had been head of the underground socialist movement in Austria while Frank had been organizing in Germany. The question was whether Mrs. Roosevelt could do anything for the leading people of the various socialist parties—German, Austrian, Spanish, and Polish. All these people had fought Hitler for years and were now in mortal danger. Buttinger's group had lists of the people who'd been stranded in France and the ones who had moved on to Spain or Portugal. Could she help?

Agreeing at once that she would do what she could, she rose from the table to put in a call to her husband. But if Eleanor expected public support from her husband at this juncture, she was mistaken. For weeks, ever since the Nazi invasion of the Low Countries, the president had been hearing tales of the great success of the Nazis' various infiltration schemes. In Norway, it was said, thousands of Nazi agents, camouflaged as lecturers, refugees, newspapermen, and diplomatic attachés, had infiltrated the country in the months before the invasion. Then, six weeks before the actual seizure, Norway was flooded with German "tourists" who remained on the scene to help the German troops. In Holland, fifth columnists were said to have figured prominently in the Germans' successful parachute landings, signaling to the planes from the ground and then providing the sky troops with Dutch military and police uniforms when they landed.

Addressing the joint session of Congress on May 16, the president had condemned "the treacherous use of the fifth column by which persons supposed to be peaceful visitors were actually a part of an enemy unit of occupation." Ten days later, in his fireside chat, he had used even more forceful language to warn that "today's threat to our national security is not a matter of military weapons alone. We know of new methods of attack, the Trojan horse, the fifth column that betrays a nation unprepared for treachery. Spies, saboteurs and traitors are all the actors in the new strategy. With all that we must and will deal vigorously."

Thus, while Eleanor and other refugee advocates were fighting to liberalize immigration, Roosevelt was moving in the opposite direction. Preoccupied with the question of subversion, he put the State Department to work on tightening restrictions to prevent infiltration of Nazi agents into the United States. Though it was absurd to believe that Jewish refugees, Hitler's principal victims, would somehow become his principal weapons against the United States, the widespread paranoia about foreigners combined with anti-Semitism to cast a net so wide that everyone except the British children was caught in it.

Eleanor reached Franklin in his study, where he was relaxing with Hopkins at the end of a long workday. "He was somewhat impatient and irritated," Lash recorded in his diary, "that it wasn't taken for granted he was already doing all that was possible. He kept bringing up the difficulties while Mrs. Roosevelt tenaciously kept pointing out the possibilities. 'Congress wouldn't let them in. Quotas are filled. We have tried to get Cuba and other Latin American countries to admit them but so far without success.... Can't locate people in France. Spain won't admit even American refugees.' Mrs. Roosevelt interrupted to remind FDR he had always said we could bribe the Spanish and Portuguese governments." There the conversation came to an unsatisfactory end.

When she hung up the phone, Eleanor voiced her inability to understand what had happened to America—the traditional land of asylum, unwilling to admit political refugees. But she said she would take the lists herself and send them to her friend Sumner Welles in the State Department. The European underground should understand it now had a friend at court. In her letter to the State Department the next day, Eleanor said she hoped "the list could be put into the hands of our people in Europe with the request that they do everything they can to protect these refugees. I do not know what Congress will be willing to do, but they might be allowed to come here and be sent to a camp while we are waiting for legislation."

Eleanor's protracted conversation with her husband that evening established the basic pattern their relationship would follow in the years to come. Whereas in the 1930s they had worked side by side in common pursuit of the same goals, now, more and more, she would find herself in the role of the agitator while he remained the politician. On a variety of fronts, she would put pressure on the president when he was tired and would have preferred not to have pressure put upon him. But, as Eleanor's friend Trude Pratt Lash observed, "she had this sense of having to do whatever was humanly possible to do in a difficult time," and nothing, not even her husband, could stop her from trying.

In response to the persistent urgings of Eleanor's committee and other refugee groups, the State Department finally agreed to establish a special procedure to expedite the issuance of visitor visas to political, intellectual, and other refugees in special peril in Spain, Portugal, and southern France. Under this procedure, the President's Advisory Committee on Political Refugees (PAC) would take the first crack at evaluating the lists of names, satisfying themselves as to the purpose for which the refugees sought entry and the manner of their departure from the U.S. at the conclusion of the emergency period. Once the list was approved by the PAC, the consuls abroad were supposed to issue the visas automatically.

It was a summer of high hopes. As long as America and other countries were willing to open their doors to the Jews, the Nazis, at this juncture, were still willing to let them go. Liberal use of visitor visas seemed the ideal solution. "I know it is due to your interest," Karl Frank wrote Eleanor the day after the emergency procedure had been put into operation. Already "many hundreds of people have been granted visitors visas."

"We all know," a grateful Joseph Buttinger told Eleanor, "how decisive your protective word was at a time when it looked as if the rescue action would come to a standstill."

Though still without a sure sense of the shape or direction of her new role in a world torn by war, Eleanor was on her way, beginning once more to believe she still had important tasks to accomplish and that her work would still be acknowledged by others. The depression of that spring was, in fact, part of a healing process, a mourning for the loss of her old relationship with her husband, and the birth pangs of a difficult and ultimately more influential partnership.

CHAPTER 5

"NO ORDINARY TIME"

The president's second term was coming to an end. Ever since George Washington refused a third term, no man had even tried to achieve the office of the Presidency more than twice.

All spring long, Eleanor had tried to push Franklin to make a definite effort to prepare a successor. "Franklin always smiled and said he thought people had to prepare themselves, that all he could do was to give them opportunities and see how they worked out. I felt that he, without intending to do so, dominated the people around him and that so long as he was in the picture, it was very hard for anyone to rise to a position of prominence."

Roosevelt "really meant to develop somebody" who would be a natural successor, Frances Perkins believed, but never quite got around to it. At one point, before Hopkins' health deteriorated, the president did seem to be grooming him for the presidency. Then there was South Carolina Senator Jimmy Byrnes, whom the president liked immensely, but who, Roosevelt felt, would be forever scarred politically by his conversion from Catholicism to Protestantism so that he could marry a wealthy Southern girl. At various times, the president emboldened the hopes of sixty-nine-year-old Secretary of State Cordell Hull, Attorney General Robert Jackson, Federal Security Agency Chief Paul McNutt, and Postmaster General James Farley, the big bald-headed chairman of the Democratic National Committee, who had more friends in more places across the country than any other person in public life. But in the end, he committed himself to no one.

"Perhaps," Perkins admitted, "it wasn't in his nature to do it, so that he was working at cross-purposes with himself, when he was trying to do it." For, at bottom, "he obviously did like being President. It was a full time occupation for all of his energies and talents and anybody is happy and content when fully functioning. Even when the problems are very great, full functioning is such a rare experience that it's quite pleasing."

But the two-term limitation had become a cherished tradition, and Roosevelt knew, as 1940 opened, that he would be asking for trouble if he tried to buck it. In political circles in the winter and early spring, the dominant opinion was that Roosevelt should not run for a third term. "This is a government of law, and not of one man, however popular," Democratic Senator Patrick McCarran said. "No President should seek a third term," West Virginia Senator Rush Holt maintained, "that is, if he believes in the continuation of democracy in this country. Has it come to the place in the glorious history of our great country that we have exhausted all leadership until today our existence depends upon one man in 130 million?"

Coupled with the uncertainties of a bid for re-election, Roosevelt nourished a genuine desire to return to Hyde Park. In a conversation with Senator George Norris, he expressed his weariness. "George, I am chained to this chair from morning till night. People come in here day after day, most of them trying to get something from me, most of them things I can't give them, and wouldn't if I could. You sit in your chair in your office too, but if something goes wrong or you get irritated or tired, you can get up and walk around, or you can go into another room. But I can't, I am tied down to this chair day after day, week after week, and month after month. And I can't stand it any longer. I can't go on with it."

Roosevelt had signed a contract with *Collier's* in January to write a series of articles at an annual salary equal to the $75,000 he received as president. "The role of elder statesman appealed to him," Eleanor said. Throughout much of the winter, his mind had been happily occupied with two building projects at Hyde Park. For years, Roosevelt had wanted a small place of his own where he could write and think in peace away from the bustle of the Big House. At the far end of his property, on a hilltop overlooking the Hudson Valley, he had found the perfect spot to build a small stone cottage, a simple place with a cozy living room, a small kitchen, three bedrooms, and a magnificent porch overlooking the Catskills to the north and rolling wooded fields to the south. "It's perfect, just perfect," he would often say, as he and Missy gradually furnished the place to his own liking, hung the pictures he wanted to see, and chose the books he wanted to read. Some day in the future, Roosevelt imagined, he might even want to live full-time at Top Cottage. So hurt was his mother by his plans for a home away from home, however, that he solemnly promised never to spend a full night there so long as she was alive.

At the same time, he was deeply involved with plans for a presidential library on the grounds of his estate, to house the White House papers and all the other documents of his public life since he first went to the New York State Senate in 1910. Having collected things—stamps, coins, stuffed birds, prints, and books—since he was a child, he took great pleasure in the process of sorting his papers, spending hours at a time with his Hyde Park neighbor Margaret Suckley, whom he had brought on the staff to supervise the transfer. "Every time he came to Hyde Park in the winter and spring of 1940," Miss Suckley recalled, "he brought large gobs of stuff—papers, documents, statues, presents—to be taken to the attic and sorted out for the library." All through the spring, housekeeper Henrietta Nesbitt confirmed, "we were clearing out storerooms, packing and shipping to Hyde Park; in fact, the Roosevelts were closing up."

But after the fall of France, the third-term dialogue shifted. "If times were normal," Senator Elmer Thomas told reporters, "I would not favor a third term for President Roosevelt, [but] I consider 1940 an abnormal year." Arguing along similar lines, Representative Charles Kramer noted that "a speeding car simply cannot change drivers without losing control. No one in the United States is better informed on world affairs than President Roosevelt or so capably qualified to guide us through this critical period. Whether it be the first, second, third or fourth term is not as important as competent leadership."

"I think my husband was torn," Eleanor told an interviewer years later. "He would often talk about the reasons against a third term," but "there was a great sense of responsibility for what was happening. And the great feeling that possibly he was the only one who was equipped and trained and cognizant not only of the people who were involved in the future, and in what was going to happen, but of every phase of the situation."

Candidly, she concluded: "Now, whether that was purely a sense of responsibility, whether there was some feeling of not wanting to leave the center of history . . . no one, I think, could really assess. . . . When you are in the center of world affairs, there is something so fascinating about it that you can hardly see how you are going to live any other way. In his mind, I think, there was a great seesaw: on one end, the weariness which had already begun, and the desire to be at home and his own master; on the other end, the overwhelming interest which was the culmination of a lifetime of preparation and work, and the desire to see and to have a hand in the affairs of the world in that critical period."

While the president was grappling with the perplexing question of whether he should run again or not, Eleanor carefully avoided asking him what he was going to do. She felt she had no right to put pressure on him by saying what she wished he would do. "It was a position of such terrific responsibility," Eleanor explained, "involving the fates of millions where the final decisions always had to be made alone, that the decision of whether or not to run again had to be made by the President himself, uninfluenced."

Eleanor's habitual reluctance to give advice, which extended to her children as well as her husband, had its roots in her sense that "one never knows, one can never be certain that one's advice is correct." At one point, before the German blitzkrieg, she had suggested that "the President might have served his purpose in history and that . . . new leadership was required for the next step ahead." Unless, she cautioned, "the international crisis made him indispensable."

All through her married life, Eleanor had suffered under the domination of her mother-in-law's strong opinions about everything, her haughty inclination to declare what she considered "the straight path," the best and proper thing to do in any situation. Once, after a long evening with Sara and her two sisters, Eleanor remarked to Franklin, "They all in their serene assurances and absolute judgments on people and affairs going on in the world make me want to squirm and turn bolshevik." Determined not to follow in Sara's footsteps, she generally held back her counsel.

"Will the President seek a third term?" reporters asked her repeatedly. "I don't know," she could honestly respond. "I haven't asked him." When reporters tried to get the answer in a different way, by inquiring where she thought she would be after 1940, she replied, "When you have been married as long as I have to a man who has been in public office a long time, you will learn never to think ahead and you will make up your mind to accept what comes along."

But of course she did think ahead, and when she did, she admitted to her old friend Isabella Greenway, she "would not look forward to four years more in the White House with joy." Too much of her day, she felt, was still taken up with the superficial aspects of the first lady's job. Despite her best efforts to focus her energies on a few important issues, "there was no end to the appointments, teas, social obligations." Indeed, in 1939, her secretary recorded that Eleanor received 9,211 tea guests, 4,729 dinner guests, and 323 house guests. It was particularly hard in the busy winter months, when her day was so filled with routine obligations that she couldn't even start working on her mail until after midnight. Staying up regularly until 3 or 4 a.m., she still had to arise at 7 or 8 to begin another long day. If only she could do some work of her own, she remarked, "take on a job and see it through to a conclusion."

There was, however, no room in a world at war for such personal desires.

"At the present moment," Eleanor concluded her letter to Greenway, "what anyone likes or dislikes does not seem very important."

• • •

By refusing to say whether or not he would seek a third term, Roosevelt had effectively paralyzed the political process. By July, leading Democrats were beginning to panic. Believing the time for a decision had come, Democratic National Committee (DNC) Chairman James Farley drove up to Hyde Park on July 9.

Whatever the president decided, Farley was determined not to retreat from the decision he had already taken: to have his own name placed in nomination for the presidency. Though he understood that his candidacy was a long shot at best, he believed someone in the party had to take a principled stand against the third term. The problem with the third term, as Farley saw it, even beyond the risk of shattered tradition, was the fact that having the same man run for president again and again created an inflexible political situation in which ordinary people, particularly younger men and women scattered all around the country, lost interest in politics. When a president is satisfied with the work of the people he's got, he tends not to change them; the turnover is slight and there is little chance for aspiring outsiders to get experience. The young people who ought to be hustling for votes feel everything has already been arranged, and, over time, passion diminishes. Farley was hoping to get Roosevelt to commit himself against running again once and for all.

The journey to Hyde Park took Farley through Rockland County, where he was born and grew to manhood, evoking memories of his parents, his Catholic boyhood, and his years of work in the family's bricklaying business before he entered politics and achieved, as he put it, "greater success than I had dreamed of." Rising steadily through the ranks of the Democratic Party, Farley was in 1928 and 1930 elected secretary and then chairman of the New York State Democratic Committee, where he played a major role in organizing the successful gubernatorial campaigns for FDR. Recognizing Farley's charm and great organizing talent, Roosevelt had chosen him to direct his presidential campaign in 1932 and then had appointed him postmaster general. In 1936, Farley once again directed Roosevelt's tremendously successful campaign, and increased his reputation as a political genius by correctly predicting that the president would carry all but two states. In the past year, however, primarily because of Farley's known opposition to the idea of a third term, relations had cooled to the point where, that very morning, the newspapers had carried a story that Farley would soon resign his Cabinet post to go into private business.

The temperature was ninety-five degrees when Farley reached the president's home. There, still playing the role of the gracious hostess, the president's mother was waiting for him on the broad front porch. Dressed in black lace, she grasped Farley's hand in a warm welcome and then lost no time in asking him if there was any truth to the story that he was thinking of leaving the Roosevelt administration to head the New York Yankees.

"You know," she said, using her hands to emphasize what she was saying in the same way her son did, "I would hate to think of Franklin running for the Presidency if you were not around. I want you to be sure to help my boy."

"Mrs. Roosevelt, you just have to let these things take their course," Farley answered.

But letting things take their course was not in Sara's character. If her son wanted a third term, then everything should be done to make it happen. As Sara and Farley were talking, Harry Hopkins and Missy LeHand came downstairs, and the small party moved into the entrance hall, bordered on one side by a large glass case containing a collection of birds Franklin had shot and stuffed as a boy, on the other by the young man's collection of early-nineteenth-century naval prints.

Since the president was not home from church, Sara led her guests into the spacious living room, which she and her son had designed as a showcase for the family's fifteen thousand leather-bound books, the president's rare coins, and his treasured stamp collection. At the center of the elegant room, flanking the stone fireplace, stood two highback chairs—the one to the left was Sara's; the one to the right, Franklin's; Eleanor was forced to find a chair wherever she could. After all these years, Sara was still the mistress of the house.

Half an hour before lunch, a Chinese gong was tapped, and it was rung once again five minutes before the food reached the table. At the second ring, the banter stopped as Sara led her guests into the dining room, with its heavily carved dark sideboards, and chairs whose leather seats were too well worn for comfort.

At that moment, Eleanor came downstairs. Greeting Farley in the hallway on the way in, she told him she was "both pleased and shocked by the news" in the morning papers that he was leaving politics and going into business. "Of course, I am pleased to have anything happen to you which would be personally beneficial, but I am shocked at the thought you may not direct things in the coming campaign," she said.

Eleanor liked Farley. The jovial party chief was as forthright and simple as Franklin was labyrinthine and complex. Furthermore, she believed her husband was largely to blame for the rift that had grown between the two. Eleanor was still talking with Farley when the president returned from church. Guiding everyone into the dining room, Franklin sat at one end of the table and Sara at the other. In the dining room as in the living room, Eleanor had no seat of her own but simply found a place as best she could—on this occasion, next to Harry Hopkins. "There was a lot of good-natured conversation during the meal," Farley recalled. "Somehow a discussion of Andrew Jackson was raised, during which the President recalled how the hero of New Orleans was attacked on the question of the legality of his wife's divorce. The President's mother pricked up her ears at the mention of divorce, and after listening for a moment or two, turned to me and said: 'My heavens! I didn't know they had such bad things as divorce so long ago.' "

Having had her own way for so many years, Sara tended to say exactly what she thought, speaking in a straightforward, undiplomatic manner. Once, in the middle of a lunch at Hyde Park, a young visitor turned to Eleanor and said, "Mrs. Roosevelt, what is the President going to do about the budget?" Eleanor stopped to think for a moment and at the end of the table Sara suddenly spoke up. "Budget, Budget? What does the child mean?... Franklin knows nothing about the budget. I always make the budget." On another occasion, when the flamboyant governor of Louisiana, Huey Long, was monopolizing the luncheon conversation, Sara glanced at him from head to foot, taking in his striped suit and his polka-dotted tie. Then, in a loud stage whisper, she said to the guest beside her: "That's the reason why I didn't want Franklin to go into politics. He has to deal with such dreadful people."

After lunch, the president asked Farley to join him in his study, a narrow room off the back hall that had been his school room as a boy. The room was small but it contained all the president needed: a comfortable old chair, a big desk, a few mementos of his earlier career, including the placard he had carried for Woodrow Wilson at the Democratic convention in 1916 and the books he wanted near by. "Everything right within reach," he liked to say. From this cluttered room, so unsatisfactory for press conferences that reporters tumbled onto the porch outside, forced to relay the questions and answers back and forth, the president directed the affairs of the nation during the nearly two hundred visits he made to Hyde Park during his presidency. Over the years, Sara had begged him to let her fashion a study befitting his high political office. But he liked the tiny room exactly as it was, the perfect size for his crippled body to maneuver in and manipulate the movements of others.

The midday sun was so hot that before settling down to talk both the president and Farley took off their coats and ties. For the first ten minutes, pictures were taken of the two men smiling and laughing. As soon as the photographers left, however, there was a heavy silence, until the president approached the unpleasant task of admitting to Farley—indirectly, of course—that if the convention nominated him for a third term he would indeed run.

"Jim," the president began, starting off, typically, at the opposite end of what he meant to say, "I don't want to run and I'm going to tell the convention so. You see I want to come up here," he added with a smile, directing his eyes through the open window of his study toward the woods and the Hudson River far below. The house at Hyde Park was at its most beautiful on summer afternoons. It was there under the blossoming trees that he had read as a child, there in the woods that he had first learned to ride a pony, and everything today was just as he remembered it from his boyhood.

Now, Farley was as sentimental as any politician, but, having promised himself that he would not succumb to the president's charm, he cut Roosevelt short. If the president made his wish not to run specific, Farley asserted, the convention would not nominate him. All that was needed was Roosevelt's word. Farley went on to enumerate the reasons he believed a third term would be devastating to the Democratic Party. The president, Farley said, was making it impossible for anyone else to be nominated by refusing to declare his intentions one way or the other.

Mopping his face with a handkerchief, Roosevelt finally asked what Farley would do if he were in the president's place. "In your position," Farley bluntly responded, "I would do exactly what General Sherman did many years ago—issue a statement saying I would refuse to run if nominated and would not serve if elected."

" 'Jim,' Roosevelt said, his right hand clasping the arm of his chair as he leaned back, his left bent at the elbow to hold his cigarette and his face and eyes deadly earnest, 'if nominated and elected, I could *not* in these times refuse to take the inaugural oath, even if I knew I would be dead within thirty days.' "

With this statement, Farley had the information he had come for—Roosevelt was definitely planning to run for a third term. There was a pause, and then Farley resumed the conversation. "Now I am going to say something else you won't like. . . . I am going to allow my name to go before the convention. . . . I feel I owe it to my party."

On hearing the unwelcome news, which smashed his hope to be drafted by acclamation, the president simply nodded, making no attempt to change Farley's mind. When it was clear the discussion was exhausted, Roosevelt thrust out his hand to Farley and said, "Jim, no matter what happens, I don't want anything to spoil our long friendship."

• • •

The weekend before the Democratic convention was set to open in Chicago, the president invited Missy, Dr. Ross McIntire, White House speechwriter Sam Rosenman, and two friends of Missy's, the Bartletts, for an overnight cruise on the *Potomac,* announcing to anyone who would listen that he had absolutely no plans to attend the convention. Despite Farley's intention to "fight" him for the nomination, the president refused to ask the delegates to vote for him, believing that, at the very least, he deserved a spontaneous draft as a show of warmth and affection from the party he had led so well for so many years. At the same time, he knew that he would be stronger in the general election the less anxious he seemed for a third term, which both Washington and Jefferson had refused.

Never leaving anything to chance, the president sent Harry Hopkins to

Chicago. In the troublesome days to come, Roosevelt would insist that Hopkins had been given no authority to act on the president's behalf, that he was simply there to listen and report back to the White House. But once Hopkins got to Chicago and installed himself in a third-floor suite in the Blackstone Hotel with an open wire to Roosevelt in his bathroom, everyone assumed that Hopkins was acting for the president.

From the outset, Harry Hopkins found himself in an untenable position, as bewildered delegates, looking for some word, any word, from FDR, came knocking on his door at every hour of the day. "There was a great deal of news emphasis laid upon the appearance of anybody at Hopkins' headquarters," Frances Perkins recalled. "If anybody turned up there, that was news and in the papers, whereas the regular officers of the convention, even [FDR fund-raiser Frank] Walker and [Bronx boss Ed] Flynn, didn't have as many newspapermen watching their door as watched Hopkins' door." The most glaring contrast was provided by the Farley offices across the street in the Stevens Hotel. DNC Chairman Farley's suite normally would have been the hub of the convention, but so large was Roosevelt's shadow even without an announced intention to run that Farley's rooms remained, in his own words, "as deserted as a church at the setting of the sun." A few delegates came to pay their respects to the big party chief, but even these few, Farley noted, seemed "timidly ill-at-ease."

Since the delegates did not dare to criticize the president directly, "the man who got all the dead cats and overripe tomatoes was Harry Hopkins," reporter Marquis Childs observed. "There was bitterness among the organization leaders at [Hopkins'] presence there," Ed Flynn admitted. "While they had nothing against him personally, in fact a great many of them were fond of him, they felt that he, representing the President, distinctly lowered their prestige. . . . They considered [Hopkins] an amateur."

To be sure, Hopkins' lack of experience did produce mistakes. A seasoned political hand would have called on Farley at once, but Hopkins let several days go by before sending word through a whispered message that he would like the chief to come to his suite. "If Harry Hopkins wants to see me," the proud Farley exploded, "he can see me in the office of the Democratic National Committee where everybody else sees me." The next morning, Hopkins came to call on Farley, but by then Farley was so hurt and angry that nothing was accomplished.

"He threw one leg over the arm of a chair at my desk," Farley recalled. "He looked tired; his eyes were sunk deep in his pallid face; his scanty hair looked as though it had been combed with his fingers. He was restless, constantly fingering a cigarette." The haggard look was familiar, but the difficulty with words was not. "Well," Hopkins finally blurted out, "what I want to say is that whatever you may hear, the Boss wants you to run the campaign."

"Be that as it may," Farley replied, making it clear that he was still determined to have his own name placed in nomination, "I can't discuss it with you."

• • •

The weekend cruise of the *Potomac* might have seemed a rest from the hubbub in Chicago, but on July 13, with Sam Rosenman aboard, it was obvious that the president was intending to work on a message to be delivered to the convention.

During both of the previous conventions, in 1932 and 1936, Roosevelt had relied on Rosenman, a graceful writer and a clear thinker, for help with both the party platform and the acceptance speech. The task at hand now, as Roosevelt explained it to Rosenman on the quiet journey down the river, was a statement to the delegates confirming that he was not actively seeking a third term and that he wanted them to feel free and clear to vote for whomever they wanted. Though Hopkins and Jimmy Byrnes feared that the president's posturing might open the door for someone else to receive the nomination, Roosevelt stubbornly insisted that, unless the convention came to him with an overwhelming show of support, he would refuse the nomination.

As Rosenman set to work on the statement, the president read the newspapers, fished, perused his stamps. "One would never imagine that significant political history was being made," Rosenman observed, "by the calm, thoughtful man" sitting in the stern relaxing with his hobbies. In the evening, after dinner, to his great delight, the president caught a rock bass and an eel. Then, while Missy and her friends adjourned to an upper deck, he rolled up his shirtsleeves and got to work on the brief message that Rosenman had drafted.

Missy tried to turn her mind from the distressing business of the convention. More and more, she saw, her boss was leaning toward a third term. For months, Missy had been living with the happy thought that, when the president's second term was over, she would accompany him to Hyde Park. In Missy's eyes, a friend observed, "Top Cottage was the most cherished spot in all the world, the first home that could truly be hers as well as his." Though she relished the excitement and prestige of her position in the White House, she loved Franklin more. Her whole existence was wrapped up in him, and she knew that, once they were back at Hyde Park, she would have much more time to spend with him alone.

It was now sixteen years since the languid days Missy and Franklin had spent together on the *Larooco* (the seventy-one-foot houseboat he had purchased in 1924, during his convalescence from polio) so he could sun, bathe, and fish in the warm waters off the Florida coast. Four months each winter for three years, Missy had served as Franklin's hostess on the boat, sharing conversations with the guests who regularly came aboard, sitting by his side as he fished off the deck, providing warmth and understanding when the frustrations of his paralysis broke through his cheerful exterior. "There were days on the *Larooco,*" Missy later admitted to Frances Perkins, "when it was noon before he could pull himself out of depression and greet his guests wearing his light-hearted facade."

Eleanor had accompanied Franklin for two weeks during the first winter's cruise, but the aimless days drove her crazy and she hated every minute of the trip. "I tried fishing but had no skill and no luck," she recalled. "When we anchored at night and the wind blew, it all seemed eerie and menacing to me." Far better for everyone concerned, she decided, if Missy stayed aboard while she returned to New York, where she could keep Franklin's name alive by attending meetings, making speeches, and talking with political leaders. Franklin's mother had objected at first to this curious arrangement in which Missy was clearly the "wife" for months at a time, but Eleanor was thankful for the freedom it afforded her to shape her days as *she* wanted them.

The desultory pattern of the years from 1924 to 1927 was such that, after the winter's cruise came to an end, Franklin and Missy moved directly to Warm Springs, Georgia, a resort community where spring water came out of the ground at a soothing eighty-six degrees, winter and summer alike, providing therapy for crippled patients and relaxation for wealthy vacationers. Still searching for the elusive cure that would restore power to his legs, Roosevelt had first journeyed to the little community on the side of a mountain in the autumn of 1924, after hearing that the healing waters had made it possible for a fellow polio victim to walk again.

"Warm Springs was not much beyond the horse-and-buggy stage in those days," recalled Egbert Curtis, manager of the Warm Springs property. "The little whitewashed cottages were dilapidated, and the single hotel in town was pretty run-down, but Roosevelt loved the place the moment he saw it, so much so that he decided to invest money in it, with the idea of sprucing it up and turning it into a national resort."

Eleanor accompanied Franklin on his first visit to Warm Springs, but her reaction to the small Southern town was as negative as her husband's was positive. It was later said that Eleanor began asking questions about the plight of the poor blacks in the town as she rode from the train station the first night; and that once she started asking questions, she never stopped. "We didn't like her one bit," one Southern lady admitted. Between the harsh segregation, the suffocating poverty, the Spanish moss, which she hated, and the sound of the Southern drawl, which grated on her ears, Eleanor could not wait to get away.

It was Missy who stayed by Franklin's side in Warm Springs, as elsewhere, cheering him on as he underwent a daily regimen of exercise in the healing waters, hoping against hope to strengthen his legs to the point where he could walk on his own power again. "I can still remember the day he almost made it," Egbert Curtis recalled. "We had a substitute head nurse that day, a large woman. He braced himself against one wall in the living room, and the nurse walked backward in front of him. Slowly, ever so slowly, he forced his body across the room—one inch at a time, it seemed. He was so drenched with sweat that I was afraid he would collapse from exhaustion. I've always believed that something happened that day, that, while he pretended it was a triumph, the effort to simply inch his way forward was so monumental that this was the moment he knew he would never really walk again. It was not long after this, in fact, that he decided to return to New York and get back into politics, a decision that effectively brought an end to his physical recovery. I remember looking at Missy's face while he was trying to walk. She was in tears."

In the spring of 1927, Roosevelt decided that he had had enough of the pleasant but purposeless existence on the houseboat. The *Larooco,* damaged by a hurricane the previous winter, was sold for junk. "So ended a good old craft with a personality," Roosevelt wrote.

Missy was devastated by the sale of the *Larooco.* The pattern of her life with the man she loved was being disrupted, and there was absolutely nothing she could do about it. That June, she collapsed in her cottage at Warm Springs. It was thought at first to be a mild heart attack, a consequence of the rheumatic fever she had suffered as a child, but though her "heart action quickly improved," as Roosevelt noted in a letter to his mother, she began experiencing alarming bouts of delirium and depression. It was "a little crack-up," secretary Grace Tully later admitted; "a nervous breakdown," in the words of Missy's high-school friend Barbara Curtis.

So severe was Missy's disorientation that the doctor at Warm Springs, Dr. LeRoy Hubbard, ordered her hospitalized and had removed from her hospital room every object that she could use to harm herself. For weeks, while Roosevelt returned to Hyde Park for the summer, Missy remained under the doctor's care. In early July, her brother Bernard LeHand found her greatly improved. "I had a most enjoyable afternoon with Missy on the lawn," he wrote Roosevelt. "She of course has not regained the strength—therefore moves and acts very deliberately and calmly but such an improvement. Just herself—that's all . . . [She] can read. . . . Remembers everything—in detail except for the first eleven day period at the hospital during which time she is hazy on happenings except perfectly conscious of her deliriums. Since the 28 of June has been normal—and it was her own suggestion that visitors be excluded until such time as she was convinced that she had "arrived." Conscious of her own condition . . . She would like her fountain pen. A pencil does not appeal to her, although a pen is really considered a dangerous 'weapon.' I am confident that you will decide to take her to Hyde Park for August."

By November 1927, Missy's strength had returned and she was able to go back to work. The storm had passed. "Except for a few intervals, I never thought of her as unhealthy," Egbert Curtis confirmed. "She was always so cheerful and so vigorous that she made everyone else feel good. What amazed me always was the amount of wit and laughter that flew around in her presence."

But the following autumn, the pattern of Missy's life was jolted again when Roosevelt yielded to pressure and agreed to run for governor of New York. It was October 1928; Roosevelt was in Warm Springs, and the Democratic State Convention was about to convene. New York Governor Al Smith, the Democratic incumbent, had received his party's nomination for president, so the governor's race was up for grabs. Believing that the magic Roosevelt name would generate a large turnout, the Democratic leaders pleaded with Roosevelt to run.

From the beginning, Missy was opposed to his running for governor, believing it would end forever his chances to recover and cut short the time she was able to spend with him. "Don't you dare. Don't you dare," she told him again and again. He seemed at first to agree with her, reckoning that he still needed another year of therapy on his legs.

For days, Roosevelt deliberately stayed out of touch with the party leaders in New York, stealing away for long picnics far out of the reach of the single telephone which stood in the lobby of the old hotel. In desperation, Smith called Eleanor at Hyde Park, imploring her to reach her husband and persuade him to accept the nomination. Eleanor agreed to communicate with Franklin and see if she could get him to talk to Smith. Her message reached him while he was giving a speech in a small town ten minutes from Warm Springs. Franklin returned at once to Warm Springs, where, assisted by Egbert Curtis, he made his way into the phone booth at the old hotel to call Smith. "He was in there a long time," Curtis recalled. "When he finally came out he looked very agitated and was wringing with sweat. 'They want me to run for Governor and that is the last thing I want to do,' he said. I asked if he had accepted. 'Curt, when you're in politics you have to play the game,' he replied."

Roosevelt's decision to run for governor represented a final victory for Eleanor in the long struggle with her mother-in-law provoked by Franklin's polio. Sara was convinced that Franklin should preserve his remaining strength by giving up all thought of a career and settling down at Hyde Park as a gentleman farmer, while both Eleanor and Louis Howe felt strongly that he should resume his political activities and continue to lead a useful life. "My mother-in-law thought we were tiring my husband and that he should be kept completely quiet," Eleanor recalled. "She always thought that she understood what was best particularly where her child was concerned."

"I hated the arguments," Eleanor later admitted, "but they had to happen. I had to make a stand." The struggle over Father's recovery was *the* big issue, Anna observed, against which everything else paled into insignificance. "Father sympathized with mother," Jimmy observed; he was determined to ignore his disability and carry on where he left off. "Ultimately," Jimmy concluded, "he came to admire his wife more than he did his mother."

Within days of Roosevelt's decision, Missy fell ill once again, suffering what was probably a second nervous breakdown. The collapse prevented her from taking part in his successful campaign, but by January she had recovered sufficiently to move into the Governor's Mansion, where, with Eleanor's full support, she was allocated a bedroom of her own on the second floor, right next to FDR's master suite.

• • •

Missy went on to become the most celebrated private secretary in the country. "Marguerite LeHand is the President's Super-Secretary," *Newsweek* announced in an adulatory article written five months after Roosevelt became president. Missy's genius was not simply in doing everything she was asked to do with exceptional skill, but in anticipating the wants and needs of her boss before he knew them himself. She was known to interrupt the most statesmanlike conference on occasion to announce that the time had come for him to take his cough medicine, or to advise him to put on his jacket because of the draft.

"If she thought he was getting pretty tired or stale" from the strain of daily work, Sam Rosenman recalled, "she would arrange a poker game, or invite some guests in whom he liked. He wouldn't know anything about it until maybe six that night. Had she asked he would have said, 'No, I have too much to do.' Acutely sensitive to his moods and feelings, she would know when to bring out the stamps so he could work with them. She would know when to arrange picnics. She was, all in all, fairly indispensable."

"We loved Missy," White House maid Lillian Parks recalled, "because she was so much fun. She could always find the humor in things. They always had bets going and FDR would get up pools and cheat to win before he was found out and had to pay up. She made every day exciting for FDR."

One of the president's sweetest pleasures was to get behind the wheel of his special automobile, which had been designed for him by Ford so that it could be operated by hand levers instead of foot pedals. From all accounts, however, Roosevelt was a dreadful driver, so bad that many of his friends and relatives, including Eleanor, refused to ride with him. But Missy loved nothing more than to accompany him on a late-afternoon spin, sharing his delight as he revved up the motor and left his handicap behind.

At dinner, if Eleanor was away, Missy presided as the president's hostess. "She always did it the right way," the president's cousin Margaret Suckley recalled. "She had great tact. She knew when to escort people in, how to seat a table, and how to keep the conversation going with charm and ease. She was very gracious in handling people." She could get along with anybody, her friend Barbara Curtis remarked, from the king and queen to the butlers and the maids. "Without making a point of it, she had absorbed certain upper-class mannerisms over time."

Though Missy would often have only minutes to change from her secretarial attire to her evening clothes, she took great pride in her appearance.

Her closet was filled with elegant clothes, including, one of her relatives recalled, a few fabulous nightgowns which she liked to wear as evening gowns. "Missy could be the most glamorous woman in the room," Lillian Parks observed, "her chandelier earrings swaying."

But to list all the things Missy did, numerous as they were, is to circumscribe her value in the White House. "Missy was an operator," journalist Eliot Janeway observed. "She was on terms of absolute equality with all the figures she dealt with—[press secretary] Steve Early, [appointments secretary] Marvin McIntyre, [adviser] Sam Rosenman, [speechwriter] Robert Sherwood." Because her judgment of people was so "instinctively sound," the president valued her reactions on everything. Her shrewd observation that a sarcastic passage in a letter "didn't sound like him" smoothed many a ruffled temper. "She was one of the few people who could say 'No' to the President and say it in a way he could take," Rosenman said.

During the 1936 campaign, a turgid speech on finance had been prepared for the president to deliver at Forbes Field. With the speechwriters present, the president started reading the draft aloud. Before he reached the end of the second page, Missy stood up and announced: "By this time the bleachers are empty and the folks are beginning to walk out of the grandstand." As she walked out of the room, everyone burst into laughter. The draft was discarded.

Over the years, Eleanor had come to terms with Missy's primacy in Franklin's working life. "For some reason," Anna's son Curtis Roosevelt mused, "perhaps because Missy came from a lower social class, Eleanor was not threatened by her the way she was with Lucy Mercer."

At the same time, Eleanor knew that, without Missy to attend to Franklin's personal needs, the independent life she had labored to create for herself would be impossible to maintain. "Missy alleviated Mother's guilt," Elliott Roosevelt observed; "knowing Missy was always there allowed Mother to come and go as she pleased without worrying about Father or feeling she was neglecting her wifely duties."

For her part, Missy was ever mindful of the importance of staying close to Eleanor. "This is where Missy was a very, very astute little gal," Eleanor's daughter, Anna, later said. "Dearest ER," Missy wrote Eleanor one Christmas in the mid-1930s, "I have had such a happy year and I hope you know how very much I appreciate being with you—not because of the White House—but because I'm with you. I love you so much. I never can tell you how very much."

Still, there were moments of annoyance and resentment on both sides of this tangled relationship. Nor could it have been otherwise, since both women loved the same man. When Doris Fleeson wrote a long and flattering piece on Missy for *The Saturday Evening Post* which revealed the centrality of Missy's position in the White House, Eleanor resolutely refused to acknowledge that Missy had the slightest influence on the president politically. Only if Eleanor could tell herself that Missy simply did unquestioningly what the president asked her to do, could she accept Missy's role without feeling it intruded on her own role as the president's number-one adviser.

The question whether Missy's love for the president was a physical one has been the subject of many conversations within the circle of Roosevelt's family and friends, and opinion varies widely.

Though physicians examining Roosevelt after his polio attack specifically noted that he had not been rendered impotent by the disease, his son Jimmy believed that "it would have been difficult for him to function sexually after he became crippled," since the sensation in his lower body was "extremely limited." Further, Jimmy argued, he would have been "too embarrassed" to have sex, too vulnerable to humiliation.

Elliott disagreed with his brother's assessment. In a co-authored book written long after both his parents were dead, he alleged that Missy and his father had been lovers. "Everyone in the closely knit inner circle of father's friends accepted it as a matter of course. I remember being only mildly stirred to see him with Missy on his lap as he sat in a wicker chair in the main stateroom [of the *Larooco*] holding her in his sun-browned arms, whose clasp we children knew so well.... He made no attempt to conceal his feelings about Missy." From that point on, Elliott claimed, "it was no great shock to discover that Missy shared a familiar life in all its aspects with father."

"I suppose father had a romance of sorts with Missy," Jimmy countered in his own book five years later, "and I suppose you could say they came to love one another but it was not a physical love.... Elliott makes a lot of Missy being seen entering or leaving father's room in her nightclothes but was she supposed to dress to the teeth every time she was summoned at midnight? This had become her home, too and... none of us thought anything about it at the time. Besides," Jimmy added, "if it had been a physical love, I believe mother would have known—she was very intuitive, you know—and had she thought it was, she would never have accepted the situation as fully as she did. The whole thing was pretty confusing and pretty complex."

Beneath the complexity, however, it is absolutely clear that Franklin was the love of Missy's life, and that he adored her and depended on her for affection and support as well as for work. In Missy's White House papers at the FDR Library, there is preserved a sweet note that captures the warmth and pleasure in their relationship. "From FDR to MAL: 'Can I dine with you? Or will you dine with me?' "

Despite these good times, Missy was ready for a change after eight years in Washington. "I think by 1940 Missy was tired of sharing the president with so many people," a friend observed. At Hyde Park, an ideal existence stretched before her, closer in kind to the happy days on the *Larooco*. Only a few months earlier, it had all seemed possible, but now everything seemed to be pointing to another term in the White House.

The presidential party returned to the White House late Sunday afternoon. The convention was scheduled to open the following day, but the heat in Washington that evening was so oppressive that it was impossible to work. Even the president, who rarely seemed to mind the heat, was so uncomfortable that he decided to watch a movie and retire early, postponing the final editing of his convention statement until morning.

• • •

While her husband sweltered in the heat of the capital, Eleanor was spending the week at Val-Kill, the fieldstone cottage Franklin had built for her on the grounds of the Hyde Park estate, enjoying "the most delightful July weather" she could ever remember, "warm enough in the sun to enjoy drying off after a swim, but cool enough so that even a good walk is not too exhausting."

It was a week Eleanor would long remember, for it marked the beginning of her intimate friendship with Joe Lash, a friendship that would endure until the end of her life, "as close a relationship as I ever knew Mother to have," Eleanor's daughter, Anna, observed. Though they had known each other for six months, the happy days they spent together that week in July, sitting for hours by the pool with their legs dangling in the water, walking through the woods in the late afternoons, and talking on the porch until long past midnight, put their friendship in a new light. From that moment on, the thirty-year-old Lash, young enough to be her son, became part of every plan Eleanor made for the future.

An intense, moody intellectual with brown eyes and black hair, Lash had been swept up by the revolutionary fervor of the 1930s. While still at City College, he had joined the Socialist Party. After receiving a graduate degree in English at Columbia, he had served as national secretary of the American Student Union, a militant popular-front organization committed to radical change in the economic and social order.

Eleanor first met the young student leader in November 1939, when he was called upon to testify before the House Un-American Activities Committee. "It was a confusing time for Joe," his college friend Lewis Feuer recalled. On the one hand, he was still committed to the radical program of change which united liberals, socialists, and communists in the popular front. But with the signing of the Nazi-Soviet pact, which gave Hitler a green light to invade Poland, he had lost his fervor for the popular front and had become increasingly disenchanted with his communist colleagues in the American Student Union, who were, he believed, mindlessly following the Soviet line in calling for an isolationist policy at home. The conflict in loyalties and the ideological crosscurrents revealed in his statement to the committee struck a responsive chord in Eleanor, who sat through the entire proceedings to assure the young people of her moral support. When the testimony was completed, she invited Lash and five of his friends back to the White House for dinner.

"It is funny how quickly one knows about people," Eleanor wrote Lash the following November. "I think I knew we were going to be friends . . . when I looked across the table at you about a year ago!" In the months that followed the hearing, Eleanor kept in touch with Lash, who resigned his position at the American Student Union in early 1940 and was trying unsuccessfully to find another job. "Joe was pretty vulnerable at that point in his life," Feuer recalled. "For ten years he had been a leader in the student movement and now, even though he believed he had done the right thing, he was isolated from his friends and colleagues."

Drifting aimlessly during the spring of 1940, Lash had trouble understanding why someone as powerful and strong as Eleanor would claim a special kinship with him. He recognized they were both fighting for the same goals, for a better order of things to emerge after the war. He shared the belief that the struggle for freedom must be carried on at home as well as abroad, but he could not imagine, in his depressed state, why she enjoyed having him around so much.

But as Eleanor opened up her heart to him that July week at Val-Kill, and shared with him the story of her own private melancholy and the deep convictions of inadequacy she had lived with all her life, Lash came to understand that it was precisely because he was having difficulty that she was drawn to him. "Perhaps . . . my miseries reminded her of her own when she was young. Insecurity, shyness, lack of social grace, she had had to conquer them all and helping someone she cared about do the same filled a deep unquenchable longing to feel needed and useful. Her children had grown up and moved away. The President was immersed in public affairs. She had a compelling need to have people who were close, who in a sense were hers and upon whom she could lavish help, attention, tenderness. Without such friends, she feared she would dry up and die."

There was a simplicity to the days at Val-Kill that Lash found delightful. When he arrived on Sunday, Eleanor met him at the train station in her riding habit. The management of the household was much less formal than the regime at the Big House. "There wasn't a lampshade that wasn't askew," one guest remembered, "and nobody cared if the cups and plates matched." What mattered was the cheerful atmosphere that pervaded every room of the only real home Eleanor had ever known. In the living room by the fire, she finally had a chair of her own, surrounded by a sofa, a set of easy chairs, a piano, and little tables covered with family photographs.

After an informal lunch served family-style, as all meals in the cottage were served, Eleanor led Joe outside for an afternoon swim in the big pool that stood to the left of the cottage, flanked by flowers and surrounded by lawn. At poolside they were joined by Eleanor's friend and former bodyguard from the Albany days, the handsome state trooper Earl Miller, and his fiancée, Simone von Haven.

After dinner, Eleanor and Joe sat together on the porch in the gathering dark and talked till midnight. Had Joe been close to his father? Eleanor wanted to know. The answer was no. His parents were Russian Jews who had ended up in New York City, in a small grocery store in Morningside Heights which kept them so busy that there was little time for family life. Joe was only nine when his father died. She talked with him about philosophy and his plans for the future. She gave him advice. Here was a perceptive and intelligent young man with whom it was easy and pleasant to talk, a sympathetic soul.

In the early days of her marriage, Eleanor had come to understand how absolutely Franklin guarded his weaknesses and vulnerabilities. Sensing this, she had gradually retreated from intimacy. With Lash, however, she felt free to expose her own vulnerabilities. Indeed, it seemed, at times, as if Eleanor were driven to tell her new friend the entire list of her inadequacies, describing in embarrassing detail the stories of her anguished past, sharing with him the terrors of the year she came out into society and had to attend all the balls, admitting that she had never felt comfortable in the Big House and that Mrs. James *still* did not approve of her public activities, on the grounds that she was not doing for Franklin what a wife ought to be doing.

Clearly, the young intellectual filled an emotional need in Eleanor's life. "She was entranced by discussing ideas without worrying about political consequences," Lewis Feuer suggested. "Joe Lash had a strong streak of idealism and a kind of romantic melancholy which she adored. I believe she sort of fell in love with him that summer and began to feel like a young woman again." In a letter written to Joe not long after convention week, Eleanor said: "I'd like you to feel you had a *right* to my love & interest & that my home was always yours when you needed it or anything else which I have. . . ."

For his part, Lash loved Eleanor, needed her, and idealized her as mentor, friend, and soul mate. "She personifies my belief and faith in the possibility of the social democratic way instead of the communist," he wrote in his diary. "At times there is a haunting beauty about her expression and profile," he observed. "Very much like the picture of her mother that adorns the hall." During one conversation, Lash hazarded that a hundred years from then her personal imprint on the nation would be as great as the president's. "Nonsense," Eleanor replied laughingly, "the function of women is to ease things along; smooth them over."

• • •

So it was that the president and his wife were hundreds of miles apart as the delegates assembled in Chicago's sprawling stadium on Monday, July 15. At the White House that evening, Missy played hostess in Eleanor's absence as the president and a small group of guests gathered in the upstairs study to listen to the live radio broadcast of Speaker Bankhead's opening address. At Val-Kill, Eleanor was similarly occupied in her own study, huddled by her radio with Tommy and Joe Lash by her side.

The mood at the convention, commentators noticed, was "strangely subdued." The delegates, so lively and expansive only four years before, had become irritable at the president's refusal to declare himself. They were worried about the popularity of the Republican presidential nominee, liberal businessman Wendell Willkie. They were worried about breaking the tradition of the third term. But there was no one else they could trust to steer the Democrats to victory.

Still, they muttered, if the president wanted a third term, why couldn't he simply come out and say so? "The President could have had anything on God's earth he wanted if he had the guts to ask for it in the open," a group of liberal newspapermen observed. "The people trust him and the people want to follow him; nobody, no matter how whole-souled, can follow a man who will not lead, who will not stand up and be counted, who will not say openly what we all know he thinks privately."

The ugly mood on the floor sent startled convention leaders back to their smoke-filled rooms to figure out what to do. From his private suite, Harry Hopkins placed a series of frantic calls to the president, advising him to drop his coy routine and to tear up the statement he had prepared insisting he did not want to be a candidate. "This convention is bleeding to death," Harold Ickes wired the president, "and your reputation and prestige may bleed to death with it." The only solution, Ickes counseled, with nine hundred "leaderless delegates milling around like worried sheep," was "a personal appearance" by the president.

The president flatly rejected both Ickes' and Hopkins' advice, insistent on "acting out his curious role to the last scene," determined, for the sake of the general election and for the historical record, to make it clear he was not actively seeking an unprecedented third term, demanding that the convention come to him of its own free will. "I have never seen the President more stubborn," Sam Rosenman recalled, "although stubbornness was one of his well-known characteristics."

The president's statement was given to Senator Alben Barkley to read, at the end of the keynote address, on Tuesday night. Barkley was originally scheduled to speak in the early evening, but the proceedings ran so late that it was nearly midnight in Washington before the senator from Kentucky approached the podium. When the president received final confirmation that Barkley was about to speak, he called Eleanor at Val-Kill. Could she listen to the statement and let him know what she thought? Taken by surprise at the whole idea of a statement, Eleanor roused Joe Lash from his bedroom to join her on the porch, where they set up her portable radio.

Alben Barkley was an orator of the old Southern school. He flailed his arms and his face grew red as he worked himself into an oratorical frenzy recapitulating the great achievements of the New Deal. Finally, he came to the climactic moment. "And now, my friends, I have an additional statement to make on behalf of the President of the United States." The president, Barkley said, wished to make clear to the convention that he had "no wish to be a candidate again" and that "all the delegates to this convention are free to vote for any candidate."

There was a moment of uncomprehending silence. In the end, the statement said neither yes nor no. Yet it was what the statement did *not* say that counted: nowhere did the president say that he would refuse to serve if nominated, nor did he officially recognize the power of the two-term tradition. Clearly, Roosevelt was in the hunt. Or was he? The delegates sat for a moment in their seats, uncertain what they were supposed to do. Then, from some loudspeaker not in view, a single booming voice shouted, "We want Roosevelt!" This was all that was needed to ignite the crowd, which picked up the chant and made it their own. "We want Roosevelt." "New York wants Roosevelt." "California wants Roosevelt."

The mysterious voice was later traced to the basement, where Edward Kelly, Chicago's mayor, had planted his "leather-lunged, pot-bellied" superintendent of sewers with a powerful microphone and detailed instructions to begin the stampede as soon as Barkley finished reading the president's statement. However contrived its beginning, the demonstration took on a life of its own. With state banners held aloft, the delegates formed a long parade which wound its way through the aisles, knocking down chairs, surging, singing, screaming. After a short struggle with the Farley contingent, the Massachusetts banner was seized from its holder and carried into the parade. Watching the wild scene from the stage, Farley's eyes were dimmed with tears. A similar struggle with Vice-President John Garner's supporters in the Texas contingent resulted in scores of men rolling on the floor in quest of the banner. And still the demonstration raged.

In the president's moment of triumph, Eleanor shook her head resignedly, knowing now that his nomination was a certainty. She did not see why the presidential statement had had to be made. Naïvely, she had never considered that the delegates to the convention did not feel entirely free to make their own choices regardless of what the president said. But, she admitted when she talked with her husband after the convention finally adjourned, there are times when "even obvious things may have to be said."

• • •

Despite the tumultuous demonstration, the delegates awoke on Wednesday morning feeling rightly that they had been used to serve the president's political purposes. If they were willing to shatter a tradition as old as the country and go down the line for Roosevelt, then, they felt, they deserved at the very least a personal appearance from the president.

"The President has got to come," Frances Perkins was told. "This thing is going to blow up." No matter if the president won the nomination, "he won't have the party back of him." With no prospect of the president's coming to Chicago, the leaderless crowd resembled a restless audience at the performance of a play without its leading man. The mood was definitely sour, Perkins agreed, as she picked up the phone to call the president and urge him to come, "to make a speech, receive a number of delegates and go away—that is, spread light and sweetness over it."

"Absolutely no," the president replied. "I wouldn't think of doing such a thing. I've said I won't go and I won't go. . . . Too many promises will be extracted from me if I go. They'll begin to trade with me. I can't do it."

When Perkins persisted, the president shifted the conversation. "How would it be if Eleanor [came]?" he asked Perkins. "You know Eleanor always makes people feel right. She has a fine way with her." Perkins thought that was an excellent idea. "Call her up and ask her," the president told Perkins. "She's pretty good about this kind of thing. . . . If she says no, tell her what I say, talk with me about it, but I don't want you to tell her that you've talked with me. Don't let Eleanor know that I'm putting any pressure on her."

Perkins reached Eleanor at dinnertime. "Things look black here," she told Eleanor; "the temper of the convention is very ugly. . . . I think you should come." When Eleanor demurred, Perkins insisted, telling her that things were getting worse by the moment, that the delegates would be reassured by her presence and "comforted if she thought what they were doing was right." Still Eleanor balked, although she agreed that she would call the president to talk it over with him.

Listening only to Eleanor's side of the conversation, Tommy thought it would be a terrible move for Eleanor to go. Never before had a first lady addressed a convention; at a time when the sacred two-term tradition was about to be broken, it made little sense, Tommy thought, to break another tradition as well. "I thought it was extremely dangerous," Tommy admitted later to Lorena Hickok. "I did not want to see Mrs. Roosevelt sacrificed on the altar of hysteria."

For his part, Joe Lash could not understand Eleanor's reluctance to go, just as he found it impossible to fathom her hesitancy about another four years in the White House. "For someone like me who loves politics so much," he admitted in his diary, "it is incomprehensible that she wouldn't want to be in Washington much less the White House." Patiently Eleanor explained her reluctance. Suppose she went and gave a speech and said some things the president later said. Immediately "the cry of 'petticoat government' would go up. She would be accused of making up the President's mind and it could get under the President's skin. It would get under anyone's skin."

"Well, would you like to go?" Roosevelt cheerfully inquired, when Eleanor called him, not wanting to ask for help directly if he didn't have to. "No," Eleanor replied, "I wouldn't *like* to go! I'm very busy and I wouldn't like to go at all."

"Well," Roosevelt responded, quickly shifting gears, "they seem to think it might be well if you came out." Then Eleanor asked, "Do you really want me to go?" And so, finally acknowledging that he needed her, he said, yes, "perhaps it would be a good idea."

So, like a good soldier, Eleanor agreed, on the condition that she could call Farley first and see how he felt about it. Knowing there was bad feeling, she later wrote in her memoirs, because "Harry Hopkins has been more or less running things and perhaps has not been very tactful," she was "not going to add to the hard feelings." When Farley heard Eleanor was calling, he was so "overcome with emotion" he was unable at first to speak. At last, he told her it was perfectly all right with him if she came and, from the president's point of view, it was essential. They would delay the vice-presidential nomination until after she had spoken. "Thanks, Jim, I appreciate this. I'll come," she said.

That night, Roosevelt's name was placed in nomination, along with the token candidacies of Farley, Vice-President Garner, Maryland Senator Millard Tydings, and Cordell Hull. The vote was a foregone conclusion: the president received an overwhelming majority of 946 votes on the first ballot. Only 150 votes were cast for all the other candidates. Yet, though the victory was Roosevelt's, the delegates reserved their emotions for the defeated Farley, who mounted the rostrum to speak. "Never had the delegates cheered more heartily," the *Washington Post* observed. "My name has been placed in nomination for the Presidency by a great and noble American," Farley began, referring to the frail but widely respected Virginia Senator Carter Glass, who had risen from his sickbed to deliver the nominating speech. "As long as I live I shall be grateful to [him]." But the time has come, Farley went on, to suspend the rules and declare Roosevelt the candidate by acclamation. The audience cheered and cried as the band struck up "When Irish Eyes Are Smiling" in tribute to the party chief. In her sitting room at Val-Kill, Eleanor sang along in a low voice.

In a revealing statement, Eleanor said that when she heard her husband nominated by acclamation she "felt as though it were somebody else's excitement and that it had very little to do with me." Eleanor was not alone in her sense of alienation. Because of the way the convention had been structured, because Hopkins had pressured the delegates to vote for the president without the presence of the president's assuaging charm, many of the delegates saw their vote as a command rather than a choice. They saw nothing else they could do. And they were right. But they didn't feel good about it.

Though the nomination had not come in the exact form Roosevelt wanted—the "draft" would never be able to shake off the quotation marks surrounding it, since votes had been cast for other candidates—it had been achieved nonetheless, and without the kind of party split that might have hurt the chances for victory in November. All in all, Rosenman recalled, the mood in the president's study that night was one of "general satisfaction and relief."

His nomination secured, Roosevelt turned at once to the vice-presidency. Though it was nearly 3 a.m., he told Chicago Mayor Edward Kelly that his choice was Agriculture Secretary Henry Wallace. Wallace, Roosevelt believed, was a dependable liberal, a good administrator, a deep thinker, and a fervent supporter of aid to the Allies. The response from Boss Kelly was not enthusiastic. To the party leaders in Chicago, Wallace was a babe in the political woods. He had started life as a Republican and only recently switched to the Democratic Party. "The party longs to promote its own," Frances Perkins observed, "and Henry Wallace was not its own. He wasn't born a Democrat.... They would have liked to have had somebody that came right up through the Democratic machine, who owed his whole life to them." But Roosevelt was adamant. Wallace was the man he wanted, he told Kelly, and then he went to bed.

Thursday morning, while the president was having breakfast, Harry Hopkins called to report that things looked bad for Wallace. The opposition was growing by the minute—already there were ten candidates with more votes than Wallace. It would be a cat-and-dog fight, Hopkins warned. "Well, damn it to hell," the president angrily replied, "they will go for Wallace or I won't run and you can jolly well tell them so." Then, turning to Rosenman, he said, "I suppose all the conservatives in America are going to bring pressure on the convention to beat Henry." Well—"I won't deliver that acceptance speech until we see whom they nominate."

By Thursday afternoon, July 18, as Eleanor was in the plane heading for Chicago, the convention had spun out of control. The galleries were packed with placards for a dozen different candidates, including Federal Loan Administrator Jesse Jones, Federal Security Agency head Paul McNutt, Jimmy Byrnes, and Speaker of the House William Bankhead. Everywhere one went, the name of Henry Wallace was met by jeers and catcalls. As Perkins interpreted the unruly situation, the ugliness was the result of Roosevelt's months of silence and the seeming hauteur involved in his failure to appear. "He not only wants to be nominated himself," the delegates seemed to be saying, "he wants to pick his own man. He doesn't want to leave that to the convention. He doesn't want to let us have a runoff here between our political racehorses." But since nobody could afford to show their resentment to the President, it was deflected onto Wallace.

By early evening, as Eleanor's plane was coming in for a landing in Chicago, the president was beginning to get "quite concerned," as Sam Rosenman put it, "about what might happen that night at the Convention." Jim Farley was the first to greet Mrs. Roosevelt as she stepped from the plane in a soft crepe dress and a navy cloth coat. The first lady paused to take some questions from reporters, and then followed Farley into a large sedan, complete with a motorcycle escort and a Chicago police guard of about fifty men.

On the way to the Stevens Hotel, Eleanor told Farley that she would miss him terribly in the upcoming campaign. She said she felt as though she had known him all her life and that she could always turn to him for advice. Thus reassured, Farley confided in her the slights he had experienced at Hopkins' impolitic maneuvers. Having been wounded by Hopkins herself in recent months, Eleanor understood Farley's pain.

Eleanor was brought into the convention hall on Farley's arm, "which was just the way it ought to be," Frances Perkins noted. "They were smiling at each other like obviously close friends." At the sight of the first lady, the entire convention rose to its feet in a rousing cheer. Acknowledging her warm welcome with a smile and a wave of her hand, Eleanor took a seat beside Mrs. Wallace on the platform just as the evening session was about to get under way.

Trouble began immediately. The first lady was scheduled to speak as soon as the nominating speeches for vice-president were finished. From the opening address for Speaker Bankhead, which evoked a demonstration far exceeding the expectations of a "symbolic candidacy," it was clear that the president's nomination of Henry Wallace faced an uphill climb. The situation worsened as names of other candidates were placed in nomination, each to loud, sustained applause. "The rebel yells grew in intensity," *The New York Times* reported, "and there seemed to be a determination, coming out of nowhere, to demonstrate for anybody not picked by the White House."

When the name of Henry Wallace was presented to the convention, the shouts and boos outnumbered the cheers as the delegates rose in rebellion against their president's choice. "It was agony," Frances Perkins recalled. "I shall never forget Henry Wallace's face as he sat there. . . . It was a dreadful thing to go through, terrible. There were catcalls, hisses, all the more vulgar and outward manifestations of dislike and disappointment. I never lived through anything worse. . . . He was listening . . . but his eyes were way off. . . . I remember thinking that his face and posture depicted the kind of suffering that a man in the Middle Ages being tried for some heresy which he couldn't understand might show. The storm was rolling over him and he had to take it. This was certainly nothing he had anticipated."

For Mrs. Wallace, attending her first national convention, the situation was incomprehensible. "Poor Mrs. Wallace was almost out of her mind," Perkins observed. "Her brain was reeling around inside her head. The antagonism and the ill will was a crushing thing, a very hard thing to bear. I remember seeing Mrs. Roosevelt take her hand."

"The noise in the room was deafening," Eleanor recalled. "You could hardly hear yourself or speak to your next door neighbor." At one point, Mrs. Wallace turned to Eleanor and said in understated fashion, "I don't know why they don't seem to like Henry."

How well Eleanor remembered her own discomfort at the first national convention she had ever attended, in Baltimore in 1912! Conventions, Eleanor thought at the time, should be seminars to debate ideas and policies, a "meeting ground of the nation's best minds." Instead, she found a raucous brawl, a fight between Woodrow Wilson and House Speaker Champ Clark that belonged in the gutter. When Clark's daughter was carried aloft through the aisles, arms and legs akimbo, in a procession of support for her father, Eleanor was "frankly appalled." Frustrated and uncomfortable, she left after only one day.

To be sure, Eleanor had traveled a long political road since 1912; the world of politics had become her world as well as her husband's. But the pandemonium at the 1940 convention was unlike any she had seen before. At this stage—as rumors spread that unless Wallace was nominated Roosevelt himself would not accept first place on the ticket—anything seemed possible.

• • •

The scene in the president's study was not a cheerful one. In silence, a large group of staffers listened to the disturbing reports on the radio. A card table had been set up in the middle of the room so the president could relax with a game of solitaire while awaiting his wife's speech and the vice-presidential balloting.

The president's figure, the expression on his face, and the tone of his voice all revealed fierce irascibility. The rebellion had captured the emotions of both the crowd and the commentators, who made it clear that the real target of the anger was not Wallace but the president's arrogance in forcing *his* man upon the delegates. "As the fight got more and more acrimonious," Sam Rosenman recalled, "the President asked Missy to give him a note pad and a pencil. Putting aside his cards he started to write. The rest of us sat around wondering what he was writing. We all felt a great desire to sneak around and read over his shoulders, but none of us succumbed to that temptation."

Finally, after writing in silence for five full pages, the president turned to Sam: "Put that in shape Sam," he said, a strained expression on his face. "Go on Sam, and do as I've told you. . . . I did not want to run and now some of the very people who urged me the most are putting me in the position of an office-hungry politician, scheming and plotting to keep his job. I'm through." He then returned to his game of solitaire.

As Sam walked out of the room into the corridor with the handwritten sheets in his hand, Missy, Steve Early, Pa Watson, and Dr. McIntire followed behind him, demanding to know what it said. At one point, Watson reached out his "hamlike paw and snatched the sheet of paper away from Sam," but Sam got it back and brought it over to a small lamp in the hallway. With Missy and Watson bent over his shoulder, he began to read.

It was a stunning document—a statement to the convention declining the presidential nomination—which he intended to deliver if Wallace lost. Interpreting the battle over Wallace as the conservatives' struggle for the direction of the Democratic Party, Roosevelt's statement argued that "until the Democratic party makes clear its overwhelming stand in favor of liberalism, and shakes off *all* the shackles of control by conservatism and reaction, it will not continue its march of victory." From the beginning of the convention, it claimed, the forces of reaction had been busily engaged in the promotion of discord. Now it was no longer possible to straddle the issue. The time for a fight to the finish had come. Therefore, "I give the Democratic Party the opportunity to make that historic decision by declining the honor of the nomination."

Pa Watson was apoplectic. "Sam, give that damned piece of paper to me—let's tear it up. . . . He's all excited in there now—and he'll be sorry about it in the morning. Besides, the country needs him. I don't give a damn who's Vice-President and neither does the country. The only thing that's important to the country is that fellow in there."

In trying to keep the president from doing something he would soon come to regret, Watson was playing the role normally assigned to Missy. Over the years, she had held up dozens of letters the president had written in anger and pleaded with him the next morning not to follow through. Most of the time, the president's fury had subsided and the letter was thrown away, but if his bad humor remained, she simply put the letter in the drawer of her desk and tried again in another day or two.

This time, however, Missy was absolutely delighted by the sudden turn of events. The poisonous atmosphere at the convention only reinforced her case. It was difficult enough for the president to lead with the country divided on foreign policy; it was impossible without the steadfast support of his own party. She had already seen the toll exacted on Roosevelt by the stress of the eight years; she feared a third term would deplete his energy and destroy his health.

"Fine, I'm glad," she said; the president was doing "the only thing he could do."

In the hallway, Watson continued to argue his case for tearing the paper up, but Rosenman refused. "Pa, I hope he never has to read this speech, but if I know that man inside," if Wallace loses, Roosevelt is going to read it, "and nobody on earth is going to be able to stop him." With this, Rosenman picked up the draft and went to his room to polish it.

When Rosenman returned fifteen minutes later, the president was still playing solitaire. "Pa Watson was almost in tears and looked at me angrily for bringing the sheets back," Sam recalled. "I suppose he had hoped I would run off with them and hide." By now, everyone in the room knew what was happening, and everyone, except Missy, told the president he was making a fatal mistake. But Rosenman knew it was hopeless to try to change his mind, for "if I ever saw him with his mind made up it was that night."

We will never know for sure if Roosevelt truly intended to withdraw or if his statement was simply a ploy. But one thing is certain: once the statement was delivered, events were likely to take on a life of their own, making it difficult for the president to turn things around.

• • •

It was 10:30 p.m. before the state delegates finished their nominating speeches. The plan was to have Mrs. Roosevelt speak first and then proceed with the balloting. But at the last minute, Frances Perkins and Lorena Hickok, the two women most instrumental in getting the first lady to come to Chicago, were overcome with panic. "Oh, she *can't* go now," Eleanor heard the two of them shouting just as FDR fund-raiser Frank Walker reached her chair to escort her to the rostrum. "It's a terrible thing to make her do." By now, the delegates were totally out of control, surging madly up and down the aisles, yelling and screaming. Surely this was not the moment to make history by inviting the wife of a presidential nominee, for the first time ever, to address a major political party conclave.

But Eleanor quietly rose from her chair, and when she reached the rostrum, a majestic silence fell over the tumultuous convention, perhaps the most heartfelt expression of respect and admiration the entire week. She knew before she started that the only hope lay in persuading the delegates to put their personal interests aside at a time when the country was facing one of the most severe challenges in its entire history.

Her words were simple and brief, but the stillness of the listeners testified to their eloquence. She began with an expression of thanks for Jim Farley. "Nobody could appreciate more what he has done for the party, what he has given in work and loyalty." She then moved directly into her message, which pleaded with the delegates to recognize that this was not "an ordinary nomination in an ordinary time," that the president could not campaign as he usually did, because he had to be on the job every minute of every hour. "This is no ordinary time," she repeated, "no time for weighing anything except what we can best do for the country as a whole."

"No man who is a candidate or who is President can carry this situation alone. This responsibility is only carried by a united people who love their country and who will live for it . . . to the fullest of their ability." Without mentioning Wallace, she was reminding the delegates that, if the president felt that the strain of a third term might be too much for any man, and if he believed a particular person was the person best equipped to give him help, then they, in asking him to run again, must respect his judgment.

By the time she finished, the prevailing emotion of the crowd had been transformed. Genuine applause erupted from every corner of the room. Trivial hurts and jealousies subsided as the delegates recalled why they had chosen Roosevelt in the first place. All along, they had simply wanted some sign of appreciation for what they were doing, and now the first lady was giving it to them.

Eleanor's remarkable speech gave the delegates a chance to get their second wind, Alben Barkley said, and it put them in a much better frame of mind. Sam Rosenman agreed. Speaking for the admiring group in the president's study, he said the speech seemed to lift everything "above the petty political trading that was going on and place it on a different level, far removed."

As soon as Eleanor sat down, the balloting began. In the study, the president laid aside his cards and tallied the votes himself. The atmosphere was tense at first, as Bankhead took an early lead, but, with each state that was called, support for the president's choice grew, and by the end of the first ballot, Wallace had garnered a majority of the votes to become the vice-presidential nominee.

The mood in the president's study lightened perceptibly as Roosevelt phoned the convention and announced that he would deliver his acceptance speech within fifteen minutes. But first he asked to be taken into his bedroom to wash his face and change his shirt. The ordeal had taken its toll on the fifty-eight-year-old man, who, Rosenman noted, looked "weary and bedraggled, his shirt wilted from the intense heat." It took him only a few minutes to freshen up, however, and when he came out he was smiling and "looking his usual, jaunty, imperturbable self."

Excepting Missy, the entire group happily accompanied the president to the radio-broadcasting room in the basement. There, at 1:20 a.m. East Coast time, he finally told the convention and the entire nation that he would break the precedent of 175 years and run for a third term. Throughout his entire speech, which would take twenty minutes, Missy was in tears.

Seated before a battery of microphones, in a melancholy voice that sometimes grew emotional, the president gave his reasons both for accepting the nomination and for having kept silent for so long. When he was elected in 1936, he told the delegates, it was his firm intention to turn over the reins of government at the end of his second term. That intention remained firm when the war broke out in 1939. But "it soon became evident" that a public statement at that time announcing that he would not run again "would be unwise from the point of view of sheer public interest." So he waited, and then the German conquest of Europe occurred, and "the normal conditions under which I would have made public a declaration of my personal desires was gone."

"Lying awake, as I have on many nights, I have asked myself whether I have the right, as Commander-in-Chief of the Army and Navy, to call on men and women to serve their country or to train themselves to serve and, at the same time, decline to serve my country in my own personal capacity if I am called upon to do so by the people of my country. . . . Like most men of my age, I had made plans for myself, plans for a private life of my own choice and for my own satisfactions to begin in January 1941. These plans, like so many other plans, had been made in a world which now seems as distant as another planet."

Remarking later on the "painful humbuggery" of this passage, Hedley Donovan, a young *Washington Post* reporter, wrote: "Being highly eligible myself for the other draft, I couldn't grieve too much for FDR's lost private plans." But the speech was just right for the crowd that night, and when it came to the end, the cheering delegates rose as one.

Eleanor was seated on the platform throughout the speech, watching blue searchlights shed their glare on a huge drawing of the president's face hung on the west wall, listening along with everyone else. When her husband's last words came across the loudspeaker, she rose and cheered as the band played "Hail to the Chief." Then, as the weary delegates wandered home to bed, she was driven to the airport to return to Hyde Park.

As the plane began to taxi down the runway, a man came running frantically across the field. The president was on the phone in the hangar, wanting to thank his wife for the excellent job she had done. He was not effusive, Eleanor later recalled. That was not his way, though on several occasions he said to others: " 'Her speech was just right.' I think he thought that people should know by their own feelings when they had done well."

Harry Hopkins was on a second line, also filled with gratitude. When he volunteered that he knew he had made many mistakes, Eleanor frankly agreed. She had seen the hurt on Farley's face. "You young things don't know politics," she said. Then the plane took off.

The next morning, Roosevelt slept soundly until eleven o'clock, but Eleanor, feeling as if "it had all been a dream with a somewhat nightmarish tinge," was up for an early breakfast, though she had slept only a few hours on the flight. "What a schedule she has kept," Joe Lash marveled in his diary. "She was up til 3 a.m. Thursday, had breakfast at 9 a.m., took a plane to Chicago after her broadcast, spent a hot constantly on the go eight hours in Chicago, back to the plane and here for breakfast at 9:30. Now she's taking a bath and will be ready for a full day again which includes a swim, a column, letters, picnic with 30 Hudson Shore Labor School people and dinner with Mrs. James."

In the days that followed, Eleanor was, Tommy told Hick, "swamped with wires and letters of approval" for her speech. "Mrs. Roosevelt stills the Tumult of 50,000," one headline read. But perhaps the letter that meant the most came from Seattle, from her daughter, Anna. "Your speech practically finished me," Anna wrote. "By that I mean you did a wonderful job." She went on to say that the president's speech was very moving, too, although he sounded weary at first, but the point of her letter was to tell her mother how proud she was to be the daughter of such an extraordinary woman. Three days later, Anna wrote again. That morning, Anna related, she had received a letter from Eddie Roddan, a friend who had been at the convention. The letter asserted that "Mrs. Roosevelt *saved* the situation." "We could sense that you had done much more than make a speech, darling, but Eddie's letter makes us very curious to hear the story."

Only one sour note spoiled Eleanor's triumph. Apparently Harry Hopkins was so angry and hurt at what Mrs. Roosevelt had said to him that, Tommy reported, "he is sulking and will not come to Hyde Park." At a luncheon with Jim Farley a week after the convention, Eleanor explained the situation. "Jim, I'm going to tell you something I have discussed with no one but Franklin. Hopkins has complained to Franklin that he didn't like the way I talked to him in Chicago. You will remember I went directly to the Stevens with you and then to the convention, so that I didn't see him. From the Stadium I went directly to the airport. He called me at the airport to say how sorry he was that he did not get to see me. I told him that I was sorry that I didn't get to see him because there were some things I wanted to talk to him about. . . . I told him quite frankly I did not think he had political judgment and that he had helped create an unfavorable situation."

But the final word was Tommy's. "Gosh," she remarked, noting Harry's estrangement, "it seems hard to believe that adults can be so self-centered in a time like this."

For her part, Eleanor deliberately underplayed what she had accomplished. In a remarkably disingenuous column, she reported that the atmosphere in Chicago "was much like the atmosphere one always finds on these occasions. To me, there is something very contagious about the friendly atmosphere brought about by meeting old friends. I was delighted when Mrs. Henry Wallace arrived to sit beside me."

But the delegates at the convention and the people in the White House knew and appreciated the perilous task Eleanor had accomplished. "She is truly a magnificent person," Tommy wrote Hick, "and while you and I have always known that and admitted it, it takes a dramatic thing once in a while to recharge us.... Being too close to the picture very often dulls one's appreciation."

CHAPTER 6

"I AM A JUGGLER"

"I am a juggler," Roosevelt once said. "I never let my right hand know what my left hand does." Throughout his presidency, he repeatedly displayed an uncanny ability to toss a number of balls up in the air and keep them afloat. Whereas critics decried his clever tricks as evidence of manipulation and deception, admirers considered such sleight of hand the mark of a master politician. Never would his juggling act be put to a more severe test than in the summer of 1940, when he had to deal with Britain's urgent request for destroyers, passage of a selective-service bill, the drafting of a controversial tax law, and, influencing all of them, a presidential election.

Almost no one, it seemed, had anything positive to say about life in the nation's capital that summer. Under the strain of a record heat wave which clung to the area for six weeks, flowers wilted, tempers flared, and a general mood of irritation settled over the city. The Capitol building was air-conditioned, but most federal offices and most residential homes in Washington were not. Under normal circumstances, particularly in an election year, when time for campaigning was needed, the politicians would have fled and the wheels of government would have ground to a halt. But this summer, with most of Europe at Hitler's feet, the usual flight from the capital was barred. "I shudder for the future of a country," one congressman commented, "whose destiny must be decided in the dog days."

Air conditioning had recently been installed in six of the White House rooms, including the president's study and bedroom, the first lady's suite, Hopkins' quarters, and Missy LeHand's bedroom on the third floor. But the president's chronic sinus problems were such that he could not work or sleep in an air-conditioned room. Even electric fans seemed to bother him, Sam Rosenman observed, so he would simply take off his coat and tie, roll up his sleeves, and perspire freely.

As he suffocated in the heat, Roosevelt was struggling to find a legal way to make the transfer of the fifty destroyers Churchill had requested in May. There was nothing America could do that would be of greater help to England, Churchill repeatedly emphasized during the summer. More than half the British fleet of destroyers had been sunk or damaged at Dunkirk; eleven more had been damaged in July. Without destroyers to protect its merchant ships from submarines, an island nation which imported every gallon of its oil and half its food could not survive.

Destroyers were also needed, Churchill told Roosevelt, to repel the expected German invasion. On July 16, Hitler had directed his generals to begin a massive air offensive against England with the goal of driving the Royal Air Force out of the skies in preparation for an invasion in mid-September. Night after night, German planes pounded the southern coasts of England, damaging airfields, dockyards, communication lines, and radar stations. (In a single night, the Luftwaffe hit six radar stations, but, not realizing how critical radar was to Britain's defense, the Germans did not pursue the attack.) Meanwhile, hundreds of German barges were moving down the coasts of Europe, convoys were passing through the Straits of Dover, and tens of thousands of German troops were gathering along the northern coasts of France. The Battle of Britain was under way.

The next three or four months would be vital, Churchill cabled Roosevelt on the last day of July. Britain had a large construction program in progress which would produce new destroyers by late fall or early winter. But until that time, only American destroyers could fill the gap. "Mr. President," Churchill concluded, "with great respect I must tell you that in the long history of the world, this is a thing to do now."

Roosevelt agreed. He told his Cabinet on August 2 that "the survival of the British Isles under German attack might very possibly depend on their getting these destroyers." But he faced what seemed an insurmountable obstacle. On June 30, when the Congress adopted the Munitions Program of 1940, which expanded the monies available to national defense beyond the fiscal-year appropriation, Senator David Walsh had attached an amendment stipulating that nothing could be delivered to a foreign government without the certification by Congress that it was surplus material unnecessary to American defense. The stipulation posed a special problem for the transfer of the destroyers Churchill wanted: five months earlier, in an attempt to ward off consigning these same destroyers to a junk heap, Navy Chief Admiral Stark had testified to Congress that they were truly essential to American defense.

During the discussion at the Cabinet meeting, Navy Secretary Frank Knox brought up the possibility of exchanging the destroyers for access to British bases in the Americas, in Newfoundland, Trinidad, Bermuda, and other places. The Cabinet responded enthusiastically to the idea of an exchange, but everyone still assumed, Roosevelt noted after the meeting, that this could not be accomplished without congressional authorization, and that "in all probability the legislation would fail." A majority could be fashioned if members of the Republican minority were brought along, but that seemed unlikely given the bitter divisions that had paralyzed the Congress all summer long over the question of compulsory selective service.

• • •

A bill to create the first peacetime draft in American history had been introduced in both the House and Senate in June. Though no one familiar with the American military situation doubted the necessity of conscription, Roosevelt had been reluctant at first to take a strong stand, believing that aid to Britain had to be given first priority. "It would have been too encouraging to the Axis," he explained to one of his advisers, "too disheartening to Britain, too harmful to our own prestige to make selective service a matter of personal contest with Congress and be defeated."

Arrayed against the draft was a potent combination of isolationists, pacifists, liberals, gold-star mothers, educators, and youth groups. Day after day, black-veiled matrons who called themselves the Mothers of the USA marched in front of the Capitol, vowing to hold a "death watch" against conscription. By the end of July, the opposition had grown so vocal, reporter Mark Sullivan wrote, that "it was said the whole idea of conscription might die, unless Mr. Roosevelt comes to the rescue." War Secretary Stimson agreed: "The President has taken no very striking lead," he recorded in his diary, "and that is reflected in Congress." Indeed, so nervous was Stimson about the military weakness of his country that he found himself waking up at night in a cold sweat.

Finally, on the first Friday of August, Mark Sullivan reported, Mr. Roosevelt the president took precedence over Mr. Roosevelt the candidate. At his weekly press conference, the president endorsed selective service publicly for the first time. Typically, he began the conference by saying he had nothing important to announce. He talked good-humoredly about going to Hyde Park that weekend, then paused, as if this were all he had to say. Instantly the questions began, with a planted inquiry from Fred Essary of the *Baltimore Sun*. "Mr. President," he said, "there is a very definite feeling in Congressional circles that you are not very hot about this conscription legislation and as a result, it really is languishing."

In reply, Roosevelt unequivocally endorsed selective service and urged adoption of the legislation as "essential to national defense." Endorsement of the draft seemed on the surface a risky move for Roosevelt in an election year. "It may very easily defeat the Democratic national ticket—Wallace and myself," Roosevelt predicted in a private letter to a Democratic editor in Illinois. But Roosevelt could sense that public opinion was shifting and that the country was ready to be moved.

While Roosevelt backed the draft, Eleanor continued to argue for a wider form of national service available to both men and women through an expanded National Youth Administration and Civilian Conservation Corps. "To tie it up with military training alone," she wrote in her column in midsummer, "[is to miss] the point of the situation we face today. Democracy requires service from each and every one of us." In Eleanor's view, real national defense meant the mobilization of the country as a whole, so that every individual could receive training to help end poverty and make the community a better place in which to live. When Eleanor told Franklin's friend Harry Hooker this, he said he couldn't believe what he was hearing; that she was a dreamer to believe that either war or poverty could ever be eliminated. Undaunted, Eleanor took the subject up again in a column a few days later, trying to explain why so many young people were in opposition to the draft.

"The way it was written," columnist May Craig warned Eleanor, "it looked as though you shared their views against the draft. Reporters commented you were bucking the old man."

"I am not bucking the President," Eleanor replied, "but would like to see a wider service." Nonetheless, after receiving a memo from her husband telling her in no uncertain terms why the draft was essential, Eleanor made it clear in her next column that her desire for wider service did not mean she was against the draft. The question of selective service, she wrote, "is simply a question of whether or not we are going to get adequate defense against overseas attack. . . . We won't get it if we don't get selective service."

Once she understood how important the draft legislation was to her husband, Eleanor never wavered in her public support for his position. When her pet organization, the American Youth Congress, came out with a sweeping statement against the draft, she characterized it as "stupid beyond belief," and told *The New York Times* it would play "into the hands of the people who would like to see us as unprepared as possible." In reply, AYC head Joseph Cadden, who had spent many evenings at the White House talking with Eleanor, said, "We are all sorry to see Mrs. Roosevelt use angry invective instead of reasoned arguments. . . . We do not feel as Mrs. Roosevelt evidently does, that the supporters of conscription have a monopoly on wisdom when the fate of our democratic insititutions are concerned."

With White House backing, the draft legislation slowly began to move forward in the Congress in early August. But victory was by no means assured. Most observers agreed that the ultimate fate of the bill rested on the stance Republican nominee Wendell Willkie took toward it in his formal acceptance speech, which was scheduled to be delivered in Elwood, Indiana, on August 17. (Though the Republican convention had nominated Willkie in June, he had deliberately waited until August to deliver his acceptance speech, so that it could mark the official beginning of his campaign.) If Willkie came out in opposition to selective service and decided to lead the charge against it, there was little hope for passage. If he endorsed the bill, Senator Hiram Johnson of California predicted, "a dozen timid Democratic Senators and 50 election-conscious Congressmen will be free to support it, since it will no longer be a campaign issue."

"What Wendell Willkie thinks of conscription," the Scripps-Howard Washington correspondent reported in mid-August, "is becoming as much a Washington puzzle as was . . . Mr. Roosevelt's third term intentions."

The man whose views on the draft were so eagerly sought in Washington that summer was one of the most unconventional presidential candidates in the nation's history. A successful businessman, Willkie had no political experience. He had no organization. He had never been a candidate for public office before. He had been a Democrat for most of his life. And his internationalist views were in direct opposition to the powerful isolationist wing of the Republican Party. He had come into the convention with the support of only 3 percent of Republican voters, compared with 67 percent for the odds-on favorite, New York's District Attorney Thomas E. Dewey. But once the delegates came together in Philadelphia, his candidacy took on a life of its own, developing an unstoppable momentum, the *Washington Post* observed, "like nothing a Republican gathering has seen before." From an initial vote of 105 out of 999, Willkie climbed to a stunning victory on the sixth ballot.

Described by journalists as a "shaggy bear," Willkie stood over six feet tall and weighed 220 pounds. After graduating from Elwood High and Indiana University, he had developed an outstanding reputation as a courtroom lawyer for General Tire in Akron, Ohio, and then moved on to New York to become president of a billion-dollar utilities corporation, Commonwealth and Southern. Although in his early years he had been a progressive Democrat, a spirited supporter of Woodrow Wilson's New Freedom, as president of a giant utility company he found himself at fundamental odds with the New Deal's Tennessee Valley Authority. Possessed of charm, wit, and intelligence, he gradually emerged as a supersalesman for business in its fight against governmental interference.

"Nothing so extraordinary has ever happened in American politics," a dazed Harold Ickes wrote. "Here was a man—a Democrat until a couple of years ago—who, without any organization went into a Republican National Convention and ran away with the nomination for President.... No one doubts Willkie's ability. He is an attractive, colorful character, bold and resourceful.... He will be no easy candidate to defeat." The president agreed with Ickes' assessment, believing that the liberal Willkie was "the most formidable candidate for himself that the Republicans could have named."

• • •

It must have been frustrating for Roosevelt, who was accustomed to being the center of the country's attention, to realize that all action on the draft was stalled until Willkie delivered his speech. But with one door closed, Roosevelt managed to open another. On August 13, he convened what Stimson later called "a momentous conference" in the Oval Office with Stimson, Knox, Morgenthau, and Undersecretary of State Welles at which he announced that he had decided to go ahead with the destroyer deal without congressional approval. Though he knew he was opening himself to powerful criticism, he felt he had no other choice. His attempts to reach the Republican minority had failed, and Senator Claude Pepper, who had agreed to sponsor the destroyer bill, had told him the day before that the legislation had "no chance of passing." No one spoke against the president's decision, Stimson recorded in his diary, though "everyone felt it was a desperate situation and a very serious step to take."

In making this extraordinary decision to bypass Congress with an executive agreement, Roosevelt was fortified by a lengthy legal brief which attorney Dean Acheson had published in *The New York Times* on August 11. Acheson argued that the commander-in-chief had the authority to exchange destroyers for bases without congressional approval as long as the net result of the deal produced an increase in America's national security. And the president was the one who kept the accounts. Attorney General Robert Jackson confirmed Acheson's opinion. Referring to the president's twin powers as commander-in-chief of the army and the navy and head of state in relations with foreign countries, Jackson advised Roosevelt that the sweep of these combined powers provided adequate constitutional authority for the president to negotiate the destroyer deal without Congress.

On the basis of this advice, which was what Roosevelt wanted to hear, he decided to complete the deal, and then and only then tell Congress. Later that day, he cabled Churchill the good news that he was ready to transfer the destroyers provided Britain agreed to lease its island bases for ninety-nine years. Churchill accepted the proposal immediately. While the agreement was being negotiated, Roosevelt arranged a hasty summit meeting for August 17 with Canada's Prime Minister Mackenzie King. Roosevelt liked King and knew the Canadian leader would be helpful in working out the details of the transfer. Arrangements were made to hold the meeting in upstate New York so that Roosevelt could inspect the First Army maneuvers in Ogdensburg on the same trip.

But Roosevelt also had a little mischief in mind. By scheduling the summit for the same day as Willkie's acceptance speech, he hoped, he later joked, that he would "steal half the show." He did.

The president arrived in Ogdensburg at noon, accompanied by Secretary of War Henry Stimson. Immediately upon their arrival, a motorcade was formed, consisting of the president's car, five cars for guests, six buses for journalists, and nine trucks for photographers. Wearing a seersucker suit and a Panama hat, the president rode for five hours over a distance of seventy miles to inspect ninety-four thousand soldiers assembled in six divisions. At every crossroad in every hamlet, reporters observed, the presidential motorcade was met by scores of cheering residents, "girls in their prettiest dresses and men in their Sunday suits."

As the motorcade halted before the first of the six divisions massed to greet their commander-in-chief, ten thousand officers and men stood at attention in perfectly formed lines and squares, their field guns slanting skyward under brightly colored regimental banners that had once flown at such historic places as Gettysburg, Big Horn, and Meuse-Argonne. Twenty-one guns sounded a tremendous salute, and the division band played the presidential ruffles and flourishes. "The weather was beautiful, bright and clear and it made a fine sight," the seventy-two-year-old Stimson recorded in his diary. "I wished very much that I was . . . working with the troops instead of sitting in a motor car all day and watching them."

Beneath the impressive show, however, the situation remained desperate. During these exercises, as in the maneuvers the previous May, the troops were so handicapped by lack of equipment that they were drilling with broomsticks instead of machine guns, and driving trucks instead of tanks. More alarming was the condition of the men. Five of the six divisions assembled for these August maneuvers were undertrained, overweight National Guard units from New England, New York, and Pennsylvania. "They haven't got the bodies soldiers must have," one military observer reported. "They haven't got the psychology of the soldier. . . . Just because mechanized divisions race into battle with soldiers jammed into trucks, it doesn't mean that the soldiers are any good if they get out of the trucks with fat under their belts, short-winded and with legs that won't stand up for a hard march."

These troops were volunteers, Lieutenant General Hugh Drum explained to the president during a picnic lunch in the shade of the woods. Many of them had never fired a gun. During the daily marches, they were falling to the ground in great numbers from heat and exhaustion. During a maneuver the previous day, an inexperienced road-construction crew had inadvertently left fifteen dynamite sticks under a roadbed over which the president's train was scheduled to pass a few hours later. Fortunately, the mistake was quickly discovered.

The only answer, General Drum stressed, was conscription. "The voluntary system must be replaced by a national conscription system if we are to succeed. We are wasting our time and ignoring basic lessons of history by discussing volunteers vs. conscription systems. Let us not be blind to the realities. . . . The day when we could put guns into the hands of citizen soldiers, teach the manual of arms and send them to match their spirit and brawn against that of an enemy has passed."

The president could not have asked for better evidence of the need for conscription than the sight of these paunchy National Guardsmen, unaccustomed to life in the open, inexperienced at firing a gun. "The men themselves were soft—fifteen miles a day was about all they could stand and many dropped out," Roosevelt admitted to his newspaper friend L. B. Sheley. "Anybody who knows anything about the German methods of warfare would know that the army would have been licked by thoroughly trained and organized forces of a similar size within a day or two."

As the hour of Willkie's speech approached, an air of anticipation surrounded the presidential party. But in spite of the importance of the speech for the future of the draft, the president stubbornly made a point of being too busy to listen. At 3 p.m., as the broadcast began, one reporter observed, "the radio in the President's car was silent" and Roosevelt listened intently to a lecture by first army officers on the goals of the maneuvers. By not listening to the broadcast, the president was able to tell reporters searching for a reaction that he would have to read the speech first before commenting.

Willkie's speech, delivered under a broiling sun which had sent the mercury well above the hundred-degree mark before noon, was heard by a vast crowd of over two hundred thousand, assembled at Callaway Park, about two miles from the center of Elwood. From all over the Midwest these people had come, in sixty-three special trains, three hundred Pullmans, twelve hundred buses, and sixty thousand cars. By 5 a.m. the day of the speech, the surrounding cornfields looked like a refugee camp, with tens of thousands of men and women camped out on blankets or sleeping in their cars. A majority of the homes of Elwood had been turned into boarding houses, and the one hotel in town was long since filled. Along the main street of the town, storefronts were converted into hot-dog stands and souvenir shops hawking Willkie stamps, license plates, playing cards, bats, pillow cases, and glass tumblers.

As Willkie stepped to the front of the platform, facing a grove of trees under which thirty-five thousand people were sitting, with four times that number standing behind the seats, he received a tremendous ovation. Smiling broadly, sweat dripping from his forehead, he waited for the applause to subside. Then he began. "Today we meet in a typical American town. The quiet streets, the pleasant fields that lie outside, the people going casually about their business, seem far removed from the shattered cities, the gutted buildings and the stricken people of Europe. Instinctively we turn aside from the recurring conflicts over there. . . . Yet . . . instinctively also . . . we know that we are not isolated from those suffering people. We live in the same world as they and we are created in the same image. . . . Try as we will, we cannot brush the pitiless picture of their destruction from our eyes or escape the profound effects of it upon the world in which we live."

With these opening words, Willkie cast his lot against the isolationist sentiment so prevalent in the Midwest. He then went on to say he could not ask the American people to put their faith in him "without recording my conviction that some form of selective service is the only democratic way in which to assure the trained and competent manpower we need in our national defense."

This was exactly what the Roosevelt administration wanted to hear. "Willkie for Draft Training," the headlines would read. But Willkie went even further down the line with the administration, stating that he was in full agreement with the president's policy enunciated at Charlottesville of extending the full material resources of America to the opponents of force.

Even in the domestic section of his speech, where he criticized the New Deal's attack on business, Willkie emphasized that he agreed with the New Deal's minimum wages and maximum hours, with federal regulation of banks and the securities market, and with unemployment insurance and old-age benefits. It was only at the end, when he challenged Roosevelt to a series of debates, that the speech took on a partisan tone.

Listening with May Craig on a car radio, driving back to Hyde Park from New York City, Eleanor was impressed. "He has a good voice and speaks well over the radio," Eleanor observed. "It was a brave speech," Craig agreed. "Willkie is a strong man and he spoke strongly. One thing is certain. We have two unusual men from whom to choose our next leader."

By late afternoon, Roosevelt and Stimson were heading back to the president's train for the summit meeting with Canada's prime minister. The original plan called for the conference to take place in the two small vestibules in Roosevelt's car (one equipped for dining, the other for sitting) while the train remained in the yards at Ogdensburg. But at the last minute Ed Starling, chief of the White House Secret Service detail, noticed two huge gas tanks between the train and the river. Uncomfortable with the situation, Starling had the train moved to the quiet village of Heuvelton, where the president and the prime minister could talk undisturbed late into the night. Along the tracks, fifty National Guardsmen with fixed bayonets patrolled the area, while an army patrol boat stood watch on the St. Lawrence River. Outside the train, as the sun beat down, dozens of laborers worked round the clock, stuffing huge chunks of ice into the train's air-conditioning system.

When MacKenzie King and Jay Moffat, the American minister to Canada, arrived, a round of cooling drinks was served. The president, Moffat noted, was tired but exhilarated from his long drive across the hot country roads inspecting the troops. He wished, he said, that everyone who opposed the draft could see with their own eyes what he had seen that day—the proof that voluntary enlistments would not suffice. "He talked at random about whatever came into his head," Moffat recalled. "His talk on the whole was brilliant and the charm of the man, a happy blend of Chief of State, man of the world, and host, was never more vivid." He was anxious to get the full text of the Willkie speech, for the first reports were fragmentary.

At dinner, Stimson joined the president's party. In the middle of the meal, the text of Willkie's speech came in over the wire. All conversation stopped as the president read the speech. A broad smile came over his face when he reached Willkie's endorsement of both the draft and aid to the Allies. If this was true, the master politician declared, if Willkie was agreeing with the administration on all these issues, then "Willkie is lost." Historians in later years would agree with Roosevelt's instant analysis, considering Willkie's failure to delineate how he differed from the president a fatal blunder. But the men on the train that night were thrilled. Stimson described the speech as "able and courageous," and Moffat called it "a godsend."

The remainder of the evening, Stimson recorded, passed in a happy discussion of the destroyer deal. The president told the Canadian prime minister that he "had originally felt he would require the action of Congress in order to release the destroyers," but that he had decided to go ahead on his own. The two heads of state agreed that, once the agreement was signed, American crews should bring the destroyers to some place in Canada where they could officially be turned over to Britain. "Almost with tears in his eyes," King thanked the president and agreed to telegraph Churchill that night to send British crews to Canada at once to man the ships. Time was of the essence, for, even as Roosevelt and King were meeting, the sky in southern England had become "a place of terror, raining blazing planes, shell splinters, parachutes, even flying boots." And with each passing day, the RAF losses were mounting.

Roosevelt's discussion with King and Stimson lasted late into the night, after which the president and King went to sleep in adjoining compartments. The next morning, at breakfast, Stimson told Moffat that he had gone to sleep much easier as a result of the late-night talks. Indeed, so important was the destroyer deal in Stimson's mind that he dared to profess that "perhaps today would mark the turn of the tide of the war." In talking with Stimson that morning, Moffat observed in the old man a new energy: "the old war horse smelled the smell of battle, and rejoiced. It had given him a new zest in life."

In the days that followed, however, an unexpected obstacle arose when Churchill balked at the idea of announcing the trade publicly. He had no problem turning over his bases for destroyers, but he preferred to see the two transactions as two friends in danger helping each other with gifts rather than "anything in the nature of a contract, bargain or sale." If the bases were seen as payment for the destroyers, he told Roosevelt, "people will contrast on each side what is given and received," and since there was no comparison between the questionable value of the antiquated craft and the permanent strategic security afforded to the U.S. by the island bases, the prime minister would look foolish.

Roosevelt appreciated Churchill's predicament, but he also understood that the only way to win popular approval in America for the deal was to present it as a shrewd Yankee bargain. So Churchill was told that the U.S. Constitution made it impossible for the president to send essential weapons as a gift; the destroyers could only come as a *quid pro quo* in an exchange which added to the security of the United States. With no way out, Churchill agreed to the exchange.

• • •

There remained the problem of announcing the agreement to the Congress and the American public. "Congress is going to raise hell over this," Roosevelt predicted. He had hoped to keep the deal under wraps until the Selective Service Act passed the Congress, but by early September Great Britain's need for the ships was so urgent that he could no longer afford to wait.

The date he chose for the startling announcement was September 3; the place, the tiny vestibule of his private car on the Roosevelt train, forty-five minutes after he had departed from South Charleston, West Virginia, where he was inspecting restoration work being done on a long-abandoned ordnance plant. With no knowledge of the stunning announcement the president was about to make, *New York Daily News* correspondent Doris Fleeson observed that morning that Roosevelt's face had a yellowish tint and that he was irritable, which she interpreted as a sign of fatigue in a man of his genial temperament. After luncheon with the president on the first day out, financier Bernard Baruch confided in TVA head David Lilienthal that the president seemed to be "brooding about something"; his mind wasn't on what they were talking about, and twice he said that "he might get impeached for what he was about to do."

The mystery was solved at noon, when the president called a press conference in the sitting room of his private car. The room comfortably accommodated seven, the *Time* correspondent observed, but "twenty odd jammed in, jostling each other as the train rolled along." He did not have much to tell them, the president announced half-apologetically, his face unable to hide a smile at the enormity of the secret he was about to reveal. What he was going to relate, the president suggested, was "the most important event in the defense of the U.S. since Thomas Jefferson's Louisiana Purchase." He then went on to explain that in return for fifty destroyers he had acquired from the British the right to nine strategic bases. When the president was asked if the Senate needed to ratify the agreement, he said no. "It is all over. It is done." As the reporters raced from the room to file their stories, the drawn shade of the window revealed FDR, "massive-gray-headed; smiling," relieved that the thing was done.

As Roosevelt expected, the news of the deal provoked harsh criticism in Washington. While approving the trade in principle, Wendell Willkie denounced Roosevelt's decision to bypass Congress as "the most dictatorial and arbitrary of any President in the history of the U.S." The *St. Louis Post Dispatch* agreed, noting that Roosevelt had merely informed Congress of the agreement. "Note well the word 'informed.' The President is not asking Congress—the elected representatives of the people—to ratify the deal. He is telling them that it has already been ratified by him. Mr. Roosevelt today committed an act of war. He also becomes America's first dictator."

The news reached the House of Representatives just as the final debate was to begin on the draft legislation. The president's timing stunned even his staunchest supporters. "If Mr. Roosevelt can do what he likes with our destroyers without consulting Congress," Representative Frances Bolton argued in her maiden speech on the floor, "and we give him our boys, God alone knows what he will do with them." When she finished she received a standing ovation.

But as far as Roosevelt was concerned, the end justified the means. If fifty old destroyers which had been collecting rust and barnacles helped turn the tide of battle in Britain's favor, then the risk was worth taking. Churchill agreed, understanding as he did that, beyond the transfer of the ships, the deal represented "a decidedly unneutral act by the U.S." According to every standard of history, Churchill later wrote, the German government would have been justified in declaring war upon the U.S. for the destroyer deal. Explaining the deal to the Parliament, Churchill predicted that, from this moment on, the affairs of the British Empire and the U.S. would inevitably be mixed together, rolling along unstoppably like the Mississippi River. "Let it roll on," he cried, "full flood, inexorable, benignant, to broader lands and developments."

Even as Churchill spoke, the American destroyers, one reporter observed, "their four tunnels raking sharply, canvas caps laced over the black muzzles of anti-aircraft guns on deck, sleek brass-nosed torpedoes nursing dynamite death below decks," were arriving at the entrance to Halifax Harbor, where, "by the long arm of coincidence," Churchill joked, they were met by a British ship, carrying the first batch of British crews.

For days, American sailors had worked to give the ships a fresh coat of paint and stock them with every necessary piece of equipment. The British captains, weary from battle, were overwhelmed by the immaculate condition of the ships and the lavishness of the provisions. "There were coffee makers, china, silver and table cloths in the wardroom," author Philip Goodhart reported, "pencil sharpeners in the cabins while such unaccustomed luxuries as tinned asparagus, corn, chipped beef, clams, instant coffee, tomato juice and pumpkins bulged out of the store cupboards." At ten o'clock on the morning of September 9, the ships were decommissioned by the U.S. Army in a simple ceremony. Before noon, they were on their way to do battle in the Atlantic.

Fortunately for the president, the initial attacks against the destroyer deal were more than balanced by expressions of approval as the advantages to America in gaining the bases became clear. Though his technique was occasionally deplored, Roosevelt was universally praised for his skill in getting the better end of the deal. "We haven't had a better bargain," the *Louisville Courier Journal* exulted, "since the Indians sold Manhattan Island for $24 in wampum and a demi john of hard liquor." "The President's bargain," the *Washington Post* gleefully noted, "was the first major expansion of the American frontier since the Spanish American War."

Popular approval for the destroyer deal strengthened the hand of the president's supporters on conscription, as did rising approval of the draft in the polls, and when the vote was finally taken, first in the Senate and then in the House, the historic legislation passed by a comfortable margin.

• • •

Thus reassured on the twin issues of the destroyers and the draft, a confident and composed president headed for a weekend rest at Hyde Park. The old house was charged with excitement when the president arrived on the morning of September 7. The cause of the excitement was the presence of Crown Princess Martha of Norway. Tall and willowy, full of light and gaiety, the thirty-nine-year-old Martha looked, in the words of reporter Bess Furman, "exactly as a princess should look." Everything in her appearance, from her gray dress and her gold jewelry to her high cheekbones and chiseled mouth, bespoke good breeding. A handsome woman with large brown eyes, long lashes, and a clear complexion, Princess Martha was to become one of the president's most intimate companions.

Martha's birth, in Stockholm, had occasioned a twenty-one-gun salute in both Norway and Sweden to mark the arrival of the granddaughter of Oscar II, king of the combined union of Norway and Sweden. By the time Martha grew up, Norway and Sweden had ended their union, but the blood ties between the dynasties of the two countries remained strong. Martha's father was a Swedish prince, the younger brother of the Swedish King Gustav V. Her mother was a Danish princess, the younger sister of the Norwegian King Haakon VII. Martha was only a child when she met her first cousin and future husband, Prince Olav. As the only son of King Haakon, Olav was Norway's adored "little prince." Songs and poems were written in his honor, and his picture hung on every schoolroom wall. When Olav and Martha became engaged in 1929, Norway went wild with excitement. As the couple rode through the streets of Oslo on their wedding day, they were cheered by tens of thousands of jubilant spectators. The marriage soon produced two princesses, Ragnhild and Astrid, and a prince, Harald, destined one day to follow his father to the throne.

The royal family's reign had been brought to an abrupt end when the Nazis invaded Norway in early April 1940. For two months, the king and the members of the Parliament had bravely resisted German demands for surrender, moving deeper and deeper into the north woods to avoid capture. "I cannot accept the German demands," Haakon told his nation as the infuriated Germans tried to kill him. "It would conflict with all that I have considered to be my duty as King of Norway. . . ." When advancing German troops made it impossible for Haakon to hold out any longer, he and his son fled to London to set up a government in exile, while Princess Martha, concerned about the safety of her children, accepted an offer of asylum from President Roosevelt.

Roosevelt had met both Olav and Martha in the spring of 1939, when the royal couple traveled to the United States to dedicate the Norwegian exhibit at the World's Fair. From the first moment the president saw Martha, dressed in her favorite shades of gray, he was entranced by her good looks and her lively manner. No sooner had they exchanged greetings than the princess asked the president what he thought of the speech Hitler had delivered that morning. All day long, Roosevelt had avoided comment on the speech, claiming that he had not heard it, but now, confronted with a direct question by the princess, he was forced to reply. "It left the door about an inch open," he told Martha in an offhand judgment that would make headlines the following day. To the delight of both Franklin and his mother, the royal couple spent a weekend that spring at Hyde Park, enjoying a festive picnic, a concert by the Vassar College Choir, and a large country dinner.

These carefree days seemed far removed in August 1940, when Martha and her children joined eight hundred American refugees aboard the army transport ship the *American Legion* for the perilous voyage to the United States. Troubled by rumors of a Nazi plan to kidnap the princess and her son, the ship was forced to take a circuitous route from the Arctic port of Petsamo, Finland, down the Norwegian coast, through the mined waters of the North Atlantic into New York. When the ship landed safely, Martha spoke to the press, denouncing Hitler in "brave words" that impressed Eleanor. From the docks in New York, the princess journeyed to Hyde Park, accompanied by her children, her lady-in-waiting, the court chamberlain, and a retinue of servants.

It was clear at once that the president regarded the effervescent princess as a superlative addition to his household. At breakfast, lunch, or dinner, she sat upright in her chair, a never-failing smile on her face, and when the president spoke, she gazed into his face in a girlish, good-humored way. It was amusing to watch her flirt, one witness reported. "Martha would sit and simper and tell him how wonderful and beautiful he was." She would bat her eyes and put on "a little girl act," and the president "seemed to eat it up."

"Nothing is more pleasing to the eye," Roosevelt once observed, "than a good-looking lady, nothing more refreshing to the spirit than the company of one, nothing more flattering to the ego than the affection of one." Roosevelt was a ladies' man by temperament, Jimmy Roosevelt explained, "at his sparkling best when his audience included a few admiring and attractive ladies." Little wonder, then, that the president developed such strong feelings of affection for Martha, who sat by his side, giggling and looking "adoringly" at him. "He seems to like it tremendously," one guest reported, "and there is a growing flirtatious intimacy. . . ."

Anna's daughter, Eleanor Seagraves, a teenager at the time, recalls the spark Martha provided to the Roosevelt household. "She was a lot of fun, and not at all stiff or stuffy. I remember that her lady-in-waiting had a tattoo on her arm." Down-to-earth, practical, and unassuming, Martha had an open, vivacious personality which served her well.

On Saturday evening, September 7, the entire Roosevelt household, including Martha, Sara, Eleanor, and Missy, journeyed to nearby Peekskill for an end-of-summer clambake at the home of the Morgenthaus. "It became a kind of annual event," Henry Morgenthau III explained. "There was beer and brandy and singing. FDR would join in the singing. It was that kind of free, relaxed evening with good food that FDR enjoyed." It was cold that night, Eleanor wrote in her column, "but the big bonfire looked warm and we all wore plenty of warm garments." After dinner, the entire party went into the living room for a square dance. "Mrs. Roosevelt loved to square dance," Morgenthau recalled.

While the Roosevelt party was enjoying the festivities at the Morgenthaus', over six hundred German bombers were coming down in long shallow dives over London, the heaviest attack ever delivered on a single city. More than four hundred people were killed in a matter of minutes, and fourteen hundred were seriously injured. Buses and trains stopped running, the lights went out, and large fires sprang up all over the city. "The London that we knew was burning," one horrified Londoner later wrote—"the London which had taken thirty generations of men a thousand years to build . . . and the Nazis had done that in thirty seconds."

Earlier that week, in what would later prove to be a great tactical error, German Air Marshal Hermann Goering had decided to shift his priorities from daylight attacks on the RAF in southern England to massive night bombings of London. The decision was in part an emotional one, reflecting a desire to retaliate against the British people for the recent bombing of Berlin, which, unbeknownst to the Germans, had resulted from a minor navigational error. Goering also hoped to destroy the will of the British people by disrupting the daily life of their capital.

Goering's shift in tactics came at just the wrong moment. After a month of heavy fighting in the air, the battered RAF Fighter Command was on the verge of exhaustion. The German superiority of numbers was beginning to tell. "A few more weeks of this," journalist William Shirer has written, "and Britain would have no organized defense of its skies. The invasion could almost certainly succeed." The raids on London, which would continue for fifty-seven consecutive nights, gave the RAF a chance to recover, regroup, and regain the upper hand. By mid-October, long after Goering had promised Hitler that the RAF would be driven from the skies, the British Fighter

Command was still in control. The prerequisite for the invasion had not been met, forcing Hitler on October 12 to postpone the preparations for "Sea Lion" until the following spring.

Of course, no one in Britain realized this at the time. On the contrary, the furious attacks on London that began on September 7 and became known as the Blitz seemed to signal just the opposite: that the Nazi invasion was about to begin. Throughout the country, church bells rang and military units were told to be ready to move at an hour's notice. From this night on, *New Yorker* correspondent Molly Panter-Downes has written, there were "no longer such things as good nights. There [were] only bad nights, worse nights and better nights," as Londoners learned to adapt to an entirely new way of life—lining up in the evenings for public shelters, carrying blankets and babies to the vast dormitories in the underground tubes, shifting their sleeping quarters to their basements.

"The amazing part of it," Panter-Downes marveled, "is the cheerfulness and fortitude with which ordinary individuals are doing their jobs under nerve-wracking conditions." Small shopkeepers whose windows had been totally blown apart would hang up "Business as Usual" stickers in the open spaces and exchange jokes and stories with their customers. And everywhere one looked, in the heaps of rubble that had once been homes, offices, and churches, were paper Union Jacks stuck defiantly to the sides of crumbling walls. Londoners suddenly came to realize, reported Ben Robertson, correspondent for the liberal daily, *PM,* that "human character can stand up to anything" if it has to. For the British people, this was indeed, as Churchill had predicted, "their finest hour."

• • •

Sunday morning, September 8, as "a vast smoky pall" hung over London and exhausted firemen struggled to bring the fires under control, President Roosevelt proclaimed a nationwide day of prayer. Accompanied by Mrs. Roosevelt, Princess Martha, and the Countess Ragni Ostgaard, Martha's lady-in-waiting, Roosevelt drove to his family church, the St. James Episcopal Church, an ivy-covered stone building set in a peaceful grove of trees. There, seated between Eleanor and Martha, he heard the minister proclaim: "We are on the brink of the greatest catastrophe of all times. Can the hand of the oppressor be stayed? The President of the United States believes that it can, with God's help. That is why he has called upon us to join today in prayer."

Luncheon that afternoon was a royal affair, as the President brought Martha together with the former empress of the Austro-Hungarian Empire, Zita, and her two young sons, the Archduke Otto of Hapsburg and Archduke Felix. The former empress, who had been safely exiled in Belgium until the German bombs destroyed her asylum, had arrived in the United States in mid-July.

Seated at the head of the table, holding herself erect, the president's mother reveled in the presence of her royal guests. There was something in

Sara's demeanor that suggested her own form of majesty. "Sara was known in some circles as 'The Duchess,' " one family friend explained, "not because she gave orders, but because she had an unconscious air of being considered above all other people. I don't think that she felt anyone was her social equal, except maybe the queen of England, and she wasn't sure about that."

When Sara talked, she spoke with great slowness and distinctness, pronouncing every syllable of every word. Keeping a vigilant watch on the table at large, she was particularly taken with the composure of Martha's children, whose excellent manners reminded her of Franklin's when he was a boy. The children were all fair-haired and good-looking with regular features. Turning her gaze from Martha's children to her own child, his head so like hers, Sara smiled broadly. This was her house, her family, her world, and she was perfectly at ease.

• • •

When Martha left at the end of the weekend the president issued an open invitation to the princess to live at the White House until she found a proper residence for herself and her children. Martha took him up on his generous offer, settling herself into the Rose Suite, on the second floor of the family quarters. There she remained for weeks, joining the president for tea in the late afternoons, sharing his cocktail hour at night, accompanying him on his weekend cruises on the *Potomac*. "She was a special character," Secret Service Agent Milton Lipson recalled, "a real beauty."

"I don't think I will ever be able to express my gratitude for your kindness toward me and my children," Martha wrote the president. "The way you talk to my three little children and make them happy by collecting and finding stamps also makes me very happy."

"There was no question," Jimmy Roosevelt recalled, "that Martha was an important figure in Father's life during the war." Indeed, Jimmy observed, "although historians have never really looked into it, there is a real possibility that a true romantic relationship developed between the president and the princess. Father obviously enjoyed her company. He would kiss her hello when she arrived and goodbye when she left and good night if she stayed over." Martha's ubiquitousness became a source of teasing among the president's aides, who took to describing her as "the president's girlfriend."

Teasing within the White House was one thing, but when reporter Walter Trohan wrote a series of suggestive articles about Princess Martha in the *Chicago Tribune,* Steve Early was furious. "Early tried every way he could to get me to stop writing about Martha," Trohan later recalled, "but I was having too much fun so I just kept doing it. For example, I'd count the number of times Martha had been to Hyde Park in the space of four and five weeks. Then I'd describe her descending the steps of the train in high heels and black silk hose. If you read between the lines, the drift was clear. 'Goddamn it,' Early would say, 'after Eleanor, isn't the president entitled to some feminine interest?' I'd say, 'Isn't Missy enough?' and that would end the conversation, but I'd never ever write anything negative about Missy. I liked her too much."

Eventually, with the help of the president, who drove with her to scout out possible choices, Martha found a magnificent estate to rent, Pook's Hill, a rambling twenty-four-room stone house on 105 acres of wooded land in Bethesda, Maryland. "Martha and her lady-in-waiting were very much elated when we met at tea time," Eleanor reported on September 26, "because they found a comfortable house." Still, Martha continued to visit the White House regularly, often staying overnight, and on a number of occasions the president drove out to Pook's Hill to visit her.

For the most part, Eleanor regarded Martha's flirtatiousness with wry detachment, explaining to a friend that "there always was a Martha for relaxation and for the nonending pleasure of having an admiring audience for every breath." After three decades of watching her husband bask in the glow of admiring females, Eleanor was rather accustomed to the situation Martha created. Knowing that she was unable to play so casually at love, Eleanor looked with both disdain and longing at Martha's coquettishness. "I can't imagine Mrs. Roosevelt even thinking of flirting," Betsey Whitney, Jimmy Roosevelt's first wife, said. Yet, near the end of her life, speaking in a wistful tone, Eleanor told a friend that flirting was the one thing she wished she had learned how to do when she was young.

• • •

If Eleanor managed to take her husband's fondness for Martha in stride, Missy was distraught. Keeping an anxious watch on the president whenever the princess was around, Missy could not help noticing how his spirits soared the moment Martha entered the room. In the past, Missy was the one who had always sat in the place of honor next to the president in his car, a lap robe tucked around them. Now, when the President took his long rides in the afternoon for relaxation, it was Martha who sat by his side.

Once, when Missy was in her late twenties, she was asked by a friend if she ever regretted not being married. "Absolutely not," Missy laughingly replied. "How could anyone ever come up to FDR?" To be sure, there had been a few romances in her life, a dalliance with Eleanor's bodyguard, the handsome state trooper Earl Miller, in the early 1930s, and a more serious romance with William Bullitt a few years later.

It is not clear how these romances started or ended. Earl Miller claims that he deliberately played up to Missy because he could see that Eleanor, whom he loved, was being hurt by Missy's closeness with Franklin. For two years, Miller says, he squired Missy around, taking her out to dinner or the movies in their free time. "Missy had me put on night duty so that I could come to her room [at Warm Springs]," Miller recalls. But the carefree Miller had not counted on Missy's becoming emotionally involved. When she discovered he was simultaneously "playing around with one of the girls in the Executive Office," she took to her bed and cried for three days.

Missy's involvement with Bullitt was more significant. Born into a wealthy old-line Philadelphia family, Bullitt had distinguished himself at Yale as editor of the *Yale Daily News* before embarking on a successful career as a newspaper correspondent and foreign diplomat. In 1933, Roosevelt appointed him ambassador to Russia; three years later, he was made ambassador to France. Outgoing and opinionated, Bullitt had married and divorced two women—Ernesta Drinker, a Philadelphia socialite, and Louise Bryant Reed, widow of the writer John Reed.

The people closest to Missy believed that Bullitt was very much in love with her. The gossip in Missy's home town was that something big was going on. Suddenly the young secretary was sporting beautiful jewelry, all courtesy of Bullitt. "He used to telephone her all the time from Russia, and when he'd come to Washington he'd take her out," Missy's friend Barbara Curtis recalled. "Indeed, at one point he wanted to marry her, but her attraction to Roosevelt was simply too overpowering." This was, Jimmy Roosevelt confirmed, "the one real romance" in Missy's life. "Father encouraged it, feeling, I think she had devoted a lot of her life to him and was entitled to a life of her own."

Others saw Bullitt's interest in Missy in darker tones. "I think Bullitt used Missy as a way of getting access to FDR," Morgenthau's son, Henry III, observed. "He was a great operator, and he led Missy to believe he would marry her when he never intended to." In his diary, Henry Morgenthau, Jr., records a meeting with the president to discuss various candidates for director of the budget. "I was very much amused at Miss LeHand seriously suggesting Bill Bullitt and the President said, quite curtly, 'No, no, he is all wrapped up in international diplomacy and knows nothing about this' to which Miss LeHand answered, 'But he would like to. . . .' "

When Bullitt was in Russia, Dorothy Rosenman recalled, Missy traveled to Moscow to see him, only to find on arriving there that he was involved with a ballet dancer. "I don't know why the engagement ended," Jimmy Roosevelt wrote. "I believe Bill treated her badly. . . ." And from then on, "Missy devoted the rest of her life to father."

The second week of September, Missy celebrated her forty-second birthday at a White House dinner with a half-dozen friends and colleagues, including the president, Harry Hopkins, Grace Tully, and Roberta Barrows. "I remember that she was uncharacteristically quiet that night," Roberta Barrows recalled. "She seemed sad and lonely, as if she were brooding about something." Perhaps, taking stock of her life as she began her forty-third year, Missy was forced to admit to herself that her chances for marriage and children were all but gone.

Over the years, Missy had enjoyed warm relations with the five Roosevelt children. "Nearer my age than Father's," Jimmy Roosevelt remarked, "Missy was a wonderful go-between. I often relied on her judgment as to the best times to approach Father on some delicate matter." In Missy's files at the Roosevelt Library, there are scores of affectionate letters to and from Roosevelt's daughter, Anna, suggesting an almost sisterly relationship. But, as close as Missy was to the Roosevelt children, it was not the same as having a husband and family of her own. In later years, Anna admitted that she hated driving in a car with her father and Missy because Missy automatically took the preferred seat next to him, so that she had to find a seat wherever she could. FDR, Jr., also admitted that he had resented Missy terribly when he was younger. At one point the anger tumbled out. "Are you always so agreeable?" he asked her. "Don't you ever get mad and flare up?" She looked at that moment, FDR, Jr., recalled, "as if she were going to cry."

• • •

There remained one unfinished piece of business before the Congress adjourned in 1940—tax legislation. Though the Congress had imposed new taxes in June in order to raise part of the revenue needed for the defense effort, a more comprehensive tax program was required. Despite the promise of the cost-plus-fixed-fee contracts, private enterprise remained reluctant to convert its plants to defense production until a new tax structure had been put into place.

In mid-July, Roosevelt told business what it wanted to hear. He called for legislation that would permit companies building new plants and equipment to amortize their capital expenses within five years or less. This meant that companies could deduct 20 percent of their capital costs before arriving at the net income on which taxes were paid. At the same time, he proposed repeal of the Vinson-Trammell Act, which held aircraft and shipbuilding manufacturers to a flat 8-and-12 percent profit rate. In its place, he recommended a steeply graduated "excess profits tax" that would apply to all companies, not just airplane manufacturers and shipbuilders.

Liberals were dismayed, believing that Roosevelt was surrendering to what amounted to a strike by capital instead of labor, a deliberate refusal by business to sign any defense contracts until it got the precise tax legislation it wanted. There was truth to these claims. At the August 2 Cabinet meeting where the destroyer deal was discussed at length, Stimson warned Roosevelt that "delay in enacting legislation covering the amortization question was holding up many contracts." Yet, unlike the scattered labor strikes that summer at the Kearney Shipyard, Vultee Aircraft, and the Boeing Company, where the demand for a raise of 10 cents was greeted on Capitol Hill with the cry of "treason," *Nation* columnist I. F. Stone noted, "no such harsh accusation has been made against the aviation companies, though plane contracts to the value of 85 million have been held up by their recalcitrance."

As the probusiness legislation emerged from the House Ways and Means Committee, liberal opposition heightened. It was "a lousy bill," Morgenthau told Roosevelt. Drafted by a lawyer from the Chamber of Commerce, it sponsored "the very kinds of discrimination that the President, and the

Treasury have for so many years opposed." First, Morgenthau warned, the wording of the excess-profits tax would place "a grave handicap on growing business, would give established corporations a near monopoly in their industries." Second, the final version of the amortization scheme was so generous that, in effect, government would be fully responsible for building the plants and equipping them at its own expense, while permitting corporations to make huge profits at practically no risk.

"This is abandoning advanced New Deal ground with a vengeance," Harold Ickes recorded in his diary. "It seems to me intolerable to allow private people to use public capital in order to make a guaranteed profit for themselves. . . . If private citizens won't supply munitions of war at a reasonable profit and take pot luck with the rest of the citizens in the matter of taxation, then the government ought to build its own plants and conscript the necessary managers to run them."

Eleanor agreed wholeheartedly with Morgenthau and Ickes. For months, Joe Lash had been telling her that the administration's defense program evoked no enthusiasm because "there was no clearcut vision of the kind of world that was wanted." What was so discouraging to Lash about the fight of the manufacturers to lift the profit margin of 8 percent was that it meant "we still had the old order of things." If only, Lash urged Eleanor, the president were willing to carry a fight against monopoly, promising that something different would emerge out of the war, then young people would go enthusiastically into battle. Youth wants "battle cries," Lash said, "with which it can go to death exultantly—something worth dying for."

Taking up Lash's hope that a new economic system would emerge out of the war that would place the forces of production at the disposal of all, Eleanor suggested in her column that, while the government was drafting men, it should also "draft such capital as may be lying idle for investment in ways which may be deemed necessary for defense." The best minds in the country, she said, should be occupied with "determining how it can be made equally certain that capital, wherever possible, is drafted for the use of the country in just the way that lives are drafted." In a follow-up column written two weeks later, Eleanor endorsed the controversial Russell-Overton amendment to the September Selective Service Act, which allowed the president to take over uncooperative factories. Responding to Willkie's charge that this provision would "sovietize" American industry, Eleanor wrote: "I, for one, am glad to see some consideration is being given to a draft of industry as well as men."

Eleanor's economic musings provoked a sharp rebuttal from business writer Ralph Robey in *Newsweek.* Claiming that she had been led astray in her thinking, Robey warned that, should her ideas be followed, "that is, should the government start taking over our accumulated supplies of wealth," then "our system of private enterprise will necessarily come to an absolute dead end. There will be no supply of private savings with which to go ahead—no private wealth out of which to make the investment necessary to create jobs—Everything, from top to bottom, will have to be government."

Robey need not have worried, for on the revenue issue the president was listening to Stimson, the War Department, and the conservatives in Congress rather than to Morgenthau, Ickes, or his wife. Stimson, never having been a New Dealer, shared none of Morgenthau's suspicions of big business, nor his urgent desire to protect the principles of tax reform. As Stimson and the War Department saw the situation, the need for production was so great that nothing must be placed in the way of getting started. The War Department was not in the business of social reform; its goal was not to change the nation's industrial pattern but to procure munitions as quickly as possible. "There are a great many people in Congress who think that they can tax business out of all proportion and still have businessmen work diligently and quickly," Stimson wrote. "This is not human nature."

Though Roosevelt did not share Stimson's unqualified enthusiasm for business, he did agree that the primary task at hand was to convert industries of peace into industries of war, and to this end he was willing to give business what it wanted even if it meant capitulating on the tax bill. "I regret to say," Ickes recorded in his diary, "the President is willing to take what Congress will give him and Congress will give him only what big business is willing that he should have."

During a heated session over the legislation on the president's back porch at Hyde Park that summer, Morgenthau reported that Roosevelt sat in his rocker and repeated over and over, "I want a tax bill; I want one damned quick; I don't care what is in it; I don't want to know. . . . The contracts are being held up and I want a tax bill." When Eleanor gamely offered to continue the fight, Morgenthau advised her to back off. "Leave the President alone," he warned. "He is in one of those moods."

But Eleanor was constitutionally incapable of leaving the president alone. On a Sunday night in September, with FDR's economic adviser Charles Taussig as her dinner guest, she renewed her arguments against the tax bill, charging that manufacturers were placing profits before patriotism. The president listened sympathetically, nodding his head in his usual manner, but he remained absolutely firm in his conviction that it was necessary to accept an imperfect law in order to encourage the defense program. Once the legislation went through, he predicted, the mobilization program would get under way. In this prediction Roosevelt was correct, for, when the revenue bill finally passed later that fall, the capital strike came to an end and war contracts began to clear with speed.

Army historians contend that passage of the amortization law was a major turning point in the mobilization process. The rapid-write-off provision converted high tax rates from "a liability into an asset," inducing business "to retain its earnings in the form of expanded plant and equipment." With tax rates at their peak, the historians argue, the success of the amortization privilege "shattered conventional beliefs that high tax rates would inevitably lead to drying up of capital."

But liberals were correct in suggesting that small business would be hurt by the way the tax legislation was structured. As the defense program got under way, military-procurement agencies turned more and more to big business. A study released the following summer indicated that in the first year of the mobilization fifty-six large corporations accounted for three-fourths of the dollar value of all prime contracts. "We had to take industrial America as we found it," War Department Undersecretary Robert Patterson explained. "For steel we went to the established steel mills. For autos we went to Detroit." Large firms had the facilities and experience to handle large orders. "It would have been folly to have ignored the great productive facilities of these concerns and to have placed our business with companies that could not produce."

In the months ahead, as the cries of small businessmen began to be heard on Capitol Hill, new legislation would be enacted to try to increase the relative share of small business in total army procurement. But by then, the basic pattern—the link between big business and the military establishment, a link that would last long into the postwar era and lead a future president to warn against the "military-industrial complex"—was already set. Eager for action—too eager, liberals thought—the president made war production his overriding concern. He could fight only one war at a time. If this priority produced negative consequences for small business, that was a price he was willing to pay.

The 76th Congress had been a tumultuous gathering. So trying were the conditions, observers noted, that, just after the final House vote on conscription, Speaker William B. Bankhead died of a stroke. (He was replaced by Sam Rayburn of Texas.) But in the end, despite the blunders, divisions, and dillydallying, the Congress had granted the president the legislation he needed to begin the process of mobilization, and with it the revitalization of the American economy after a decade of depression.

It was the president's custom each year on the night that Congress was due to adjourn to host a poker game in his study. The game would begin in the early evening, and then whoever was ahead at the moment the Speaker called to say that Congress had officially adjourned would be declared the winner. On this night, Morgenthau was far ahead when the Speaker phoned, but Roosevelt pretended that the call was from someone else and the game continued until midnight, when Roosevelt finally pulled ahead. At this point, Roosevelt whispered to an aide to go into another office and call the study. When the phone rang, he pretended it was the Speaker and declared himself the winner. Everyone was in high spirits until the next morning, when Morgenthau read in the paper that the Congress had officially adjourned at

9 p.m. He was so angry that he handed in his resignation. Only when the president called and convinced him that it was all in good fun did Morgenthau agree to stay. Morgenthau should have realized that Roosevelt was not above a little deception if it helped him win his bets!

CHAPTER 7

"I CAN'T DO ANYTHING ABOUT HER"

When Eleanor accepted A. Philip Randolph's invitation to speak at the Convention of Sleeping Car Porters on September 16, 1940, she set in motion a chain of events that would carry her into the center of a convulsive battle for racial equality in the armed forces. Although few recognized it at the time, this battle would prove a turning point in American race relations. It would stimulate a new spirit of militancy in the black community, a new willingness to protest. The civil-rights movement that would flower in later decades was struggling to be born.

A. Philip Randolph, the man who would lead the movement in the 1940s, was a commanding figure with a handsome face and a voice so resonant that he once considered a career in acting. When he was still in his twenties and living in Harlem, he had founded an independent journal, *The Messenger,* which became an influential voice for radical action among Negroes in America. In 1925, he was asked to organize the overworked Pullman porters, who had been trying without success to form a union since 1900. The odds against the union were great; it took a leader of Randolph's intelligence and ability to counter the Pullman Company's propaganda, threats, and spies. When Randolph succeeded in creating the powerful Brotherhood of Sleeping Car Porters, he became, almost overnight, the most important Negro leader in America.

Eleanor was joined at the dais by Negro leaders Mary McCleod Bethune and Walter White.

The daughter of an illiterate South Carolina sharecropper, the youngest of seventeen children, Bethune was the only one in her family to receive an education. At fifteen, after taking every subject taught at the little missionary school near her home, she was given a scholarship to attend Scotia Seminary in North Carolina. There she became inspired with the vision of founding a school to help other Negroes. Her purpose was realized when she founded a Negro primary school in Florida and then built it into Bethune-Cookman College.

Walter White, by contrast, was born into a middle-class family, the son of a postman in Atlanta. Slender in build with fair skin, blue eyes, and blond hair, White was only one-sixty-fourth Negro. But when his father died from an injury which his son believed was brought about "by his being a colored man," White became a leader of the Negro cause. After graduating from Atlanta University, he wrote for the Negro publication *The Crisis,* conducted investigations of race riots and lynchings, and assumed a permanent position with the NAACP.

Eleanor's presence that evening was a testament to the long journey she had taken from the insulated days of her childhood when she listened to her Southern relatives reminisce about the slaves they had owned on their plantation in Georgia. "I quite understand the southern point of view," she later wrote, "because my grandmother [Martha Bulloch] was a Southerner ... and her sister had a great deal to do with bringing us up when we were small children. . . ." When Eleanor first moved to the segregated city of Washington, D.C., with her young husband, her primary contact was with black household staff members, whom she persisted then in calling darkies and pickaninnies. Her sympathetic comprehension of the Negro situation in America had been a gradual awakening, a product of her exhaustive travels around the country and her developing friendships with Negro leaders, which, one black historian has written, "began to resemble a crash course on the struggle of blacks against oppression."

Though the New Deal never succeeded in giving full justice to the economic needs of black Americans, Eleanor was largely responsible for the steady increase over the years in the numbers of Negroes on public relief and in the funds they earned. When she first began inspecting New Deal programs in the South, she was stunned to find that Negroes were being systematically discriminated against at every turn. Under the Agricultural Adjustment Act (AAA), Negro tenant farmers were the first to be cast off in the wake of the crop-reduction program. Under the National Recovery Act (NRA), Negroes either had to accept less money for the same work performed by whites or risk replacement. Even Eleanor's favorite program, the WPA, was guilty of discrimination. "Is it true," Eleanor queried Harry Hopkins, "that wages for Negroes in regions 3 and 4 (the southern regions) under work relief are lower than those established for white people? It is all wrong to discriminate between white and black men!"

Largely because of Eleanor Roosevelt, black complaints against New Deal programs received a hearing at the White House, and in 1935 the president agreed to sign an executive order barring discrimination in the administration of WPA projects. From that point on, the Negro's share in the New Deal expanded. By the end of the thirties, the WPA was providing basic earnings for one million black families; three hundred thousand black youths were involved in NYA training programs, and another quarter-million were serving in the CCC. Though the Negro's proportionate share in state activity was never as large as it should have been, the cumulative effect of the New Deal programs provided an economic floor for the entire black community. "For the first time," commented a delegation of Negro social workers visiting Hyde Park in the summer of 1939, "Negro men and women have reason to believe that their government does care."

During the thirties, Eleanor's public identification with black causes encouraged the hopes of the black community. In 1938, when confronted with a segregation ordinance in Birmingham, Alabama, that required her to sit in the white section of an auditorium, apart from Mrs. Bethune and her other black friends, she had captured public attention by placing her chair in the center aisle between the two sections. In 1939, she had resigned from the Daughters of the American Revolution (DAR) after it barred the Negro singer Marian Anderson from its auditorium. Over the years, she invited hundreds of Negroes to the White House, had her picture taken with them, and held fund-raising events for Negro schools and organizations. Although these actions may seem purely symbolic now, they must be evaluated in the context of their times. "Blacks in the thirties found them impressive," historian Nancy Weiss has written, "because there had been nothing like them in anyone's memory."

The president was far more cautious than his wife. While Eleanor thought in terms of what *should* be done, Franklin thought in terms of what *could* be done. "I did not choose the tools with which I must work," he told Walter White in the mid-thirties, explaining his refusal to endorse a federal antilynching campaign. "Had I been permitted to choose them I would have selected quite different ones. But I've got to get legislation passed by Congress to save America. The southerners by reason of the seniority rule in Congress are chairmen or occupy strategic places on most of the Senate and House committees. If I come out for the anti-lynching bill, they will block every bill I ask Congress to pass to keep America from collapsing. I just can't take that risk."

Yet, without a federal law, the U.S. government was powerless to intervene against lynchings in individual states. Eleanor refused to give up. Much to the dismay of the president's Southern-born secretaries, Steve Early and Marvin McIntyre, she continued to speak out in favor of an antilynching law.

"They were afraid," Eleanor later explained, "that I would hurt my husband politically and socially, and I imagine they thought I was doing many things without Franklin's knowledge and agreement. On occasion they blew up to him and to other people." During the antilynching campaign, Early complained in writing that Eleanor's friend Walter White had been bombarding the president with telegrams and, "Frankly, some of his messages to the President have been decidedly insulting." Mrs. Roosevelt must understand, Early went on, that, even before President Roosevelt came to the White House, Walter White was "one of the worst and most continuous troublemakers." Undeterred, Eleanor penned a personal note to Early: "If I were colored," she stated, "I think I should have about the same obsession that he [White] has.... If you ever talked to him, and knew him, I think you would feel as I do. He really is a very fine person with the sorrows of his people close to his heart."

Across the country, Eleanor's activism in behalf of blacks engendered scathing comments. "If you have any influence with the President," a New Jersey woman wrote Missy LeHand, "will you please urge him to muzzle Eleanor Roosevelt and it might not be a bad idea to chain her up—she talks too damn much." Throughout the South, she became a symbol of everything wrong with the attitudes of white Northerners toward Southern society. "The South is sick and tired of being treated as a conquered province," Georgia Representative George Cox warned his fellow Democrats, "and if the party which it has cradled and nurtured and supported all these years permits itself to be used as an instrument for its complete undoing then you may depend upon its people finding some other means of protection."

Never once, however, did the president move to curb his wife's activities in behalf of the Negroes. Do you mind if I say what I think, she once asked her husband. "No, certainly not," he replied. "You can say anything you want. I can always say, 'Well, that is my wife; I can't do anything about her.' "

In part, Franklin tolerated Eleanor because she represented the more generous, idealistic side of his own nature, the humanitarian values he himself held but felt unable to act upon in the context of the Southern-dominated Congress. But it was also good politics. While he kept the party intact in the South, Eleanor was building new allies in the North among tens of thousands of migrating blacks who were gaining access to the ballot in urban areas such as New York, Chicago, and Detroit. In the Northern precincts, the same photographs of Eleanor entertaining various black figures that had been circulated throughout the South as proof of White House treachery contributed to a historic shift in the political allegiance of Negroes. Before the Roosevelts came into power, Negroes, still loyal to the party of Lincoln, had consistently voted the Republican ticket. In 1936, blacks swung decisively into the Roosevelt coalition. "I'm not for the Democrats," explained one black who had voted Democratic for the first time in 1936, "but I am for the man." Though the president had taken no specific initiatives in behalf of the Negroes, and had failed to support the antilynching campaign, he had managed, with Eleanor's substantial help, to convey to blacks that the administration was on their side. "When you start from a position of zero," civil-rights leader Clarence Mitchell, Jr., later observed, "even if you move up to the point of two on a scale of 12, it looks like a big improvement."

• • •

By the time of the porters' convention, however, a new and explosive issue —the elimination of discrimination and segregation in the armed forces— had replaced lynching as the dominant concern among Negro Americans.

When the U.S. began to rearm in the summer of 1940, Negro citizens had flocked to recruiting stations by the thousands, only to be met by a series of obstacles. In the regular army of close to a half-million men, there were only forty-seven hundred Negroes, two Negro officers, and three Negro chaplains. There were only four Negro units, the Ninth and Tenth Cavalry and the 24th and 25th Infantry regiments, and only one was receiving combat training. There was not a single Negro in the Marine Corps, the Tank Corps, the Signal Corps, or the Army Air Corps.

As stories of discrimination began surfacing in different parts of the country, the *Pittsburgh Courier* provided front-page coverage and launched a national drive for equal participation in the armed forces. The NAACP followed suit, resolving at its national convention to devote its full energies to the elimination of Jim Crow in the military. Discrimination in the military became for many blacks a symbol of the entire order of racial separation in the South. The struggle for "the right to fight," as it came to be called, mobilized thousands of Negroes who had not been previously involved in civil rights, expanding the ranks of the NAACP and the circulation of the Negro press.

The new mood contrasted sharply with the "close-ranks" strategy articulated by W. E. B. Du Bois during World War I, which had called on Negroes to "forget our special grievances and close ranks shoulder to shoulder with our white fellow-citizens." This time, feeling it was the psychological moment to strike out for their rightful place in American society, Negro leaders were taking an openly aggressive stance.

Through her talks with civil-rights leaders and her correspondence with Negro citizens, Eleanor had achieved a vague understanding of the new mood in the Negro community. In early September, she had received a disturbing letter from a Negro doctor, Henry Davis. "At a time when everyone is excited about increasing the size of the army," he told her, he had been refused an active commission simply because of his dark skin. "I am greatly disappointed and am very much depressed," he admitted, "gradually losing faith, ambition and confidence in myself."

It was not until the porters' convention, however, when she talked at great length with Randolph, that Eleanor came to appreciate the full dimensions of the situation. The discrimination Dr. Davis had experienced, Eleanor was told, was widespread. In Charlotte, North Carolina, a Negro high-school teacher holding a master's degree from Columbia had been severely beaten by white soldiers stationed at a recruiting office when he sought information for his pupils. At the University of Minnesota, Walter Robinson had successfully completed the Civil Aeronautics Authority flight-training program, finishing thirteenth in a class of three hundred. But when he applied for enlistment in the Army Air Corps, he was told that it was useless to complete the application. "There is no place for a Negro in the Air Corps," the lieutenant in charge said. Dr. Winston Willoughby, a Negro dentist, had received an equally peremptory response when he sought a commission in the Dental Corps. "Hell, if you said you were colored I would have saved you a trip," he was told. "There are no colored dentists in the Dental Corps."

The situation in the navy, where four thousand Negroes served, was even more hypocritical. To the extent the navy had opened its doors to Negroes, it was strictly as mess men, assigned to make the officers' beds, serve their meals, clean their rooms, shine their shoes, and check their laundry. Unaware of this depressing situation, many Negroes had been drawn into the navy by false promises, only to find, once they were in, that there was no room for advancement.

The same week as the porters' banquet, fifteen navy mess men aboard the U.S.S. *Philadelphia* had come to a determination to speak up against the intolerable conditions. Led by twenty-five-year-old Byron Johnson, who had joined the navy in 1937 on the promise he would be taught a trade, the fifteen sailors wrote an open letter to the *Pittsburgh Courier*. "Our main reason for writing," the letter began, "is to let all our colored mothers and fathers know how their sons are treated after taking an oath pledging allegiance and loyalty to their flag and country. . . . We sincerely hope to discourage any other colored boys who might have planned to join the Navy and make the same mistake we did. All they would become is seagoing bell hops, chambermaids and dishwashers. We take it upon ourselves to write this letter regardless of any action the Navy authorities may take. We know it could not possibly surpass the mental cruelty inflicted upon us on this ship." Signed Byron Johnson, Floyd Owens, Otto Robinson, Shannon Goodwin, et al.

The navy's reaction to the published letter was swift and severe. The signers were placed in the brig, indicted for conduct prejudicial to good order, and given dishonorable discharges for "unfitness." "I am still 100 percent a loyal American," Byron Johnson stated. "If necessary I'd gladly fight for my country. However, I don't feel we 15 fellows have received a fair deal. Not given an opportunity to defend ourselves at any sort of a trial, we are kicked out of the Navy because we dared express our convictions to the *Pittsburgh Courier*—in a country where free speech is supposed to be every man's privilege."

Despite the punishment exacted, the courageous action of the fifteen mess men, like a small rock tumbling over the side of a mountain, initiated an avalanche of protest that would eventually change the face of the navy. With cynicism and hope existing side by side under the charged conditions of impending war, hundreds of Negro mess men in dozens of ships began to speak up. "Since other mess attendants . . . are putting up such a stiff fight for equality," three Negro sailors wrote from the U.S.S. *Davis* in San Diego, "we feel it only right for us . . . to do our share. . . . Before now, we were afraid of the consequences if we fought naval discrimination, but now that we have outside help which has given us new hope, we are prepared and determined to do our part on the inside to the last man." Signed Jim Pelk, L. Latimore, Raymond Brown. "I understand the plight of these colored sailors," another mess man wrote, "for I am one myself, having quit college to join the Navy. You may publish my name if you feel it necessary to do so. That, of course, would probably mean that I would meet the same fate Byron Johnson and his friends met. But I am fanatical enough about it all to allow that to happen to me, if necessary."

Conditions in the Navy remained unrelievedly bleak, but the new conscription law provided a small ray of hope for the army. During the congressional debate, in response to public pressure about the use of Negro troops, language had been added to the bill, pledging to increase Negro participation in the army to a figure equivalent to the percentage of Negroes in the population, about 10 percent. "In the selection and training of men under this act," the amendment further provided, "there shall be no discrimination against any person on account of race or color." The problem, Negro leaders recognized, was the next sentence in the bill, which promised that "no man shall be inducted for training and service unless he is acceptable" to the army and "until adequate provision shall have been made for shelter, sanitary facilities, water supplies, heating and lighting arrangements, medical care and hospital accommodations." Would the army ever deem large numbers of Negroes acceptable? Could lack of separate shelter and facilities for Negroes preclude their induction?

To obtain answers to these questions, Randolph and White had requested a meeting with the president in early September. Just before she was to speak to the porters, Eleanor learned that the president's secretaries Early and Watson had failed to respond to the request. Making a note to herself to see what she could do, Eleanor walked to the podium. She delivered a passionate pledge to the Negro audience to give her "faith, cooperation and energy" in order to make America a better place, a place where everyone, Negro and white, could live in equality and opportunity. When she finished, her face expressing genuine affection and concern, she received a standing ovation.

Later that evening, from her apartment in Greenwich Village, Eleanor dictated a note to her husband, telling him she had just heard that no conference was ever held on the subject of "how the colored people can participate" in the armed forces. "There is a growing feeling amongst the colored people . . . [that] they should be allowed to participate in any training that is going on, in the aviation, army, navy. . . . I would suggest that a conference be held with the attitude of the gentlemen: these are our difficulties, how do you suggest that we make a beginning to change the situation? There is no use of going into a conference unless they have the intention of doing something. This is going to be very bad politically besides being intrinsically wrong and I think you should ask that a meeting be held."

When Eleanor returned to Washington two days later, she bypassed Early and Watson and confronted the president directly. "She has already spoken to the President," Early informed Watson; "a meeting is to be arranged for next week," with the secretaries of war and navy; Arnold Hill, former secretary of the Urban League; and Walter White and Philip Randolph, Negro leaders. Unable to contain his scorn, Early went on to tell Watson that Mrs. Roosevelt would telegraph the addresses of Hill and Randolph, though the address of Walter White, because he came so frequently to visit Mrs. Roosevelt, was "altogether too well known to [White House usher] Rudolph Forster and others here about."

The president's meeting with the three civil-rights leaders took place at twelve-thirty on Friday, September 27. Navy Secretary Frank Knox and Assistant Secretary of War Robert Patterson were also present. Randolph opened the discussion. "The Negro people . . . feel they are not wanted in the armed forces of the country. They feel they have earned their right to participate in every phase of the government by virtue of their record in past wars since the Revolution, [but] they are feeling . . . they are not wanted now."

The president responded by referring to the War Department's recent pledge to recruit and place Negroes in all branches of the armed forces. "Of course," he emphasized, "the main point to get across is . . . that we are not [as we did] in the World War, confining the Negro to the non combat services. We're putting them right in, proportionately, into the combat services. . . . Which is *something*."

"We feel that is fine," Randolph countered, but only a beginning. Earlier that morning, the three Negro leaders had met in the NAACP office to draw up a memo outlining the steps that would have to be taken to integrate Negroes into the defense program. These actions included selecting officers for army units regardless of race, integrating specialized personnel such as Negro doctors and dentists into the services, broadening opportunities for Negroes in the navy beyond menial services, appointing Negroes to local selective service boards, designating centers where Negroes could be trained for work in aviation, and appointing Negro civilians as assistants to the secretaries of the navy and war.

Although there might be problems in putting white and Negro soldiers together in Southern regiments, the Negro leaders admitted, there was no reason to anticipate insurmountable difficulties in the North. Roosevelt nodded his head in agreement and suggested backing into the formation of mixed units by mixing up replacements. "The thing is we've got to work into this," the president said. "Now, suppose you have a Negro regiment . . .

here, and right over here on my right in line, would be a white regiment. . . . Now what happens after a while, in case of war? Those people get shifted from one to the other. The thing gets sort of backed into."

Encouraged by the president's open-mindedness about the army, Randolph turned to Knox and asked about the prospects for integrating the navy. The secretary spoke bluntly, suggesting that the problem in the navy was almost insoluble. "We have a factor in the Navy that is not so in the Army, and that is that these men live aboard ship. And in our history we don't take Negroes into a ship's company."

"If you could have a Northern ship and a Southern ship it would be different," Roosevelt laughingly observed, "but you can't *do* that." He then went on to suggest putting Negro bands on white ships to accustom white sailors to the presence of Negroes on ships.

At the conclusion of the meeting, the president promised to confer with Cabinet officers and other government officials about the problem and then to talk with the civil-rights leaders again. Vastly encouraged, the Negro leaders awaited further word from the president. Beneath the cordiality of the meeting, however, the armed forces remained unyielding in their opposition to the idea of integration. At this crucial moment in America's history, General Marshall argued, there is no time "for critical experiments which would have a highly destructive effect on morale." Secretary Knox agreed, telling Roosevelt that, if he were asked to desegregate the navy at the same time that he was supposed to create a two-ocean navy, he would have to resign. In his diary that evening, Stimson deplored the strain a "rambunctious" president was putting on the War Department by attempting "to satisfy the Negro politicians who are trying to get the Army committed to colored officers and various other things which they ought not to do."

"I sent [Undersecretary Robert] Patterson to this meeting, because I really had so much else to do," Stimson recorded. "According to him it was a rather amusing affair—the President's gymnastics as to politics. I saw the same thing happen 23 years ago when Woodrow Wilson yielded to the same sort of a demand and appointed colored officers to several of the Divisions that went over to France, and the poor fellows made perfect fools of themselves. . . . Leadership is not embedded in the Negro race yet and to try to make commissioned officers to lead the men into battle is only to work disaster to both. Colored troops do very well under white officers but every time we try to lift them a little beyond where they can go, disaster and confusion follow. . . . I hope for heaven's sake they won't mix the white and colored troops together in the same units for then we shall certainly have trouble."

Stimson's disparaging opinion of the performance of colored troops in previous wars mirrored the official conclusions of the Army War College Report on "Negro Manpower" issued in 1925. "In the process of evolution," the report observed, "the American negro has not progressed as far as other sub species of the human family. . . . The cranial cavity of the negro is smaller than whites. . . . The psychology of the negro, based on heredity derived from mediocre African ancestors, cultivated by generations of slavery, is one from which we cannot expect to draw leadership material. . . . In general the negro is jolly, docile, tractable, and lively but with harsh or unkind treatment can become stubborn, sullen and unruly. In physical courage [he] falls well back of whites. . . . He is most susceptible to 'Crowd Psychology.' He cannot control himself in fear of danger. . . . He is a rank coward in the dark."

In World War I, the report went on, the Negro officer was a failure in combat. "Negro troops are efficient and dependable only so long as led by capable white officers. Under Negro officers they have displayed entire inaptitude for modern battle. Their natural racial characteristics, lack of initiative and tendency to become panic stricken, can only be overcome when they have confidence in their leaders."

Negroes saw a different reality. Proud of the many awards garnered by the few colored regiments that actually did see combat in World War I, Negroes laid the blame on the army for improperly training and equipping the colored troops. "Soldiers who were asked to submit like lambs to segregated training facilities," black opinion held, "could not be expected to perform like lions on the battlefield." If Negroes were given half a chance, civil-rights leaders maintained, their performance would bring glory to both their race and their country.

For seven days, Randolph and White anxiously awaited an affirmative response from the White House, but nothing came. When follow-up telegrams and telephone calls were not returned, White turned in despair to Eleanor, explaining that not getting a reply from the White House put him in a most difficult position with his people. "We did not want to violate the unwritten rule about revealing what had taken place in the conference with the President until the White House had given us authority to do so." With his note to Eleanor, White enclosed the draft of a statement to be issued jointly by the White House and the civil-rights leaders, describing the positive nature of the discussions on September 27. Eleanor promised to get the draft statement into the hands of the proper people, eliciting appreciation from White for her "usual prompt and vigorous action."

Eleanor's intervention prodded the War Department into action, but the resulting statement was not what Eleanor and the civil-rights leaders wanted to hear. Measured against the heightened expectations of the civil-rights leaders, the actual concessions that were granted—the promise that Negro units would be formed in each major branch of the service and the announcement of plans for training Negroes in aviation—seemed minor indeed. Beyond this the War Department would not go, flatly refusing to consider the possibility that Negro officers could lead white troops or that selected Northern regiments could be integrated. "The policy of the War Department," the statement concluded, "is not to intermingle colored and white enlisted personnel in the same regimental organizations. This policy has been proven satisfactory over a long period of years and to make changes would produce situations destructive to morale and detrimental to the preparation for national defense."

The policy statement was disappointing enough in itself, but disappointment turned to fury when, in presenting it to the press, Steve Early gave the false impression that the three Negro leaders had agreed with the wording and countenanced the policy of segregation. This put the three men in an impossible situation; their seeming acquiescence was condemned as betrayal by their own groups. Under the circumstances, they had no choice but to strike back. In a joint public statement of their own, they vigorously repudiated the White House press release as trickery and characterized Roosevelt's official approval of the policy as "a stab in the back of democracy . . . a blow at the patriotism of twelve million Negro citizens." Of all the shabby dealings, *The Crisis* commented, "none is more shameful or indefensible than the refusal to give Negroes a fair chance in the armed forces."

"I am sorry we were forced to take this step," Walter White explained to Eleanor in a personal note. "But the White House announcement left no other alternative." Saddened by the turn of events, Eleanor appealed to her husband to rectify the situation. Roosevelt, appreciating the predicament of the Negro leaders, agreed to issue a statement of his own, deeply regretting the misinterpretation of the earlier statement which had led to the faulty assumption that the Negro leaders had approved a policy of segregation. The president reassured the Negro community that, despite the War Department's affirmation of the status quo regarding the use of Negro officers in current units, there was "no fixed policy" regarding future units. In approving the statement as written, the president explained, he was simply saying that, "at this time and this time only," in the present emergency, "we dare not confuse the issue of prompt preparedness with a new social experiment, however important and desirable it may be."

"Rest assured," Roosevelt told White in a separate letter, "further developments of policy will be forthcoming to ensure fair treatment on a nondiscriminatory basis." Though White and Randolph found Roosevelt's response most reassuring and encouraging, the Negro press continued to pound away at the White House. "We are inexpressibly shocked," the *Crisis* editorialized, "that a President at a time of national peril should surrender so completely to enemies of democracy who would destroy national unity by advocating segregation." In Harlem, thousands of Negroes attended a mass meeting to protest the War Department policy. The White House was besieged with angry letters. "The Negro situation has become more difficult," White House aide Jim Rowe warned the president in the weeks before the election. "Never before has the power of the Negro vote loomed so portentous," the *Pittsburgh Courier* observed, reporting a tremendous growth of pro-Willkie sentiment among Negroes. "It looks as though they are all going against him," Harry Hopkins confided to Farm Security Administrator Will Alexander; "tell me what to do."

What the Negroes wanted at that moment, Hopkins was told, was the promotion of Colonel Benjamin Davis, grandson of a slave, to brigadier general, and the appointment of William Hastie, dean of Howard Law School, as a civilian aide to Secretary Stimson. Change in the structure of the military would only come, Negroes now believed, if strong black men were placed in positions of leadership.

Roosevelt heard the cry of his political advisers. Moving quickly to repair the damage that had been done, he announced the promotion of Colonel Benjamin Davis, commander of the 369th National Guard Regiment in New York, to brigadier general, and the appointment of Dean William Hastie to the War Department. Stimson considered both appointments a terrible mistake. In his diary, he decried the fact that "the Negroes are taking advantage of this period just before the election to try to get everything they can in the way of recognition from the army" and blamed the situation on "Mrs. Roosevelt's intrusive and impulsive folly." And in a letter to Knox the following day, he noted sarcastically that, when he called on the Navy Department the next time with his colored brigadier general, he "fully expected to be met with a colored Admiral."

Stimson's negative attitude was reflected in the president's mail. "Are you crazy appointing a nigger as General in the U.S Army?" an angry man from West Virginia wrote. "It is incomprehensible to normal Americans," an Illinois couple wrote, "for you to appoint a member of the red, yellow or black race to the high rank of Brigadier General." But the Negro press was pleased, calling the twin appointments a major victory "in the fight for equitable participation of colored people in the national defense program." Sending a personal word to the president on the eve of the election, Walter White expressed his thanks "for all you did to insure a square deal for Negroes in the defense of our country."

The irony of the situation was not lost on Eleanor. Had it not been for the inept way the War Department and the White House press office handled the original statement, the appointments that so delighted the Negro community would probably not have been made. Up until this time, Eleanor had believed that, as long as segregated facilities were provided equally to blacks and whites alike, there was no issue of discrimination. But now she was coming to understand that things were not that simple, that "the basic fact of segregation which warps and twists the lives of our Negro population" was itself discriminatory.

• • •

No sooner had the commotion over the president's meeting with the civil-rights leaders begun to subside than Eleanor became embroiled in a fiery argument with the State Department over its refugee rescue operation. In mid-September, she learned from friends on the President's Advisory Committee that the visa arrangements entered into with such high hopes in July had completely broken down. After working indefatigably all summer long, sifting the lists, negotiating with various agencies, and examining affidavits, the PAC had submitted 567 carefully selected names, supported by all the necessary documents, to the State Department. The visa procedure was supposed to move forward automatically from that point on. But somewhere along the line, something had gone wrong; more than three months had passed and only fifteen visas had been issued.

A deliberate policy of obstruction was under way, directed from the top of the State Department, from the man in charge of refugee matters, Breckinridge Long. Working with what one refugee scholar has called "a singleness of purpose and a formidable arsenal of political weapons," Long had successfully devised a series of obstructive tactics that walled out any applicant the State Department wished to exclude. In a secret memo addressed to State Department officials James Dunn and Adolf Berle, Jr., early in the summer, Long had spelled out his plans: "We can delay and effectively stop for a temporary period of indefinite length the number of immigrants into the United States. We could do this by simply advising our consuls to put every obstacle in the way and to require additional evidence and to resort to various administrative advices which would postpone and postpone and postpone the granting of the visas."

On September 28, the day after the president's meeting with Randolph, White, and Hill, Eleanor penned an indignant note to her husband describing the unhappy situation. "Mr. [James] McDonald [chairman of the PAC] is so wrought up about it, he wants to talk to you for about 15 minutes. He would come to Washington, and I promised to help him. Because he feels that their good faith has been impugned and because he also feels that there is something he ought to tell you which makes him extremely uncomfortable [most likely she is referring here to the perceived anti-Semitism of Breckinridge Long] and about which he does not wish to write, he is asking for an appointment. I am thinking about these poor people who may die at any time and who are asking only to come here on transit visas and I do hope you can get this cleared up quickly."

Eleanor's note stirred Franklin to contact Undersecretary Sumner Welles. "Please tell me about this," the president wrote. "There does seem to be a mix-up. I think I must see McDonald." In reply, Welles suggested that the president talk first with Breckinridge Long. A meeting was set for noon, October 3. Long was well armed, carrying fearsome stories purporting to prove that many of the refugees Eleanor and her friends wanted to bring into the country were not refugees at all, but German agents trying to use America's hospitality for their own dark purposes. By playing on the president's fears that spies had infiltrated the refugee stream, Long managed to persuade Roosevelt that the State Department's cautious policy was the only way to go.

"I found that he [Roosevelt] was 100% in accord with my ideas," Long recorded triumphantly in his diary. "The President expressed himself as in entire accord with the policy which would exclude persons about whom there was any suspicion that they would be inimical to the welfare of the

United States no matter who had vouchsafed for them. I left him with the satisfactory thought that he was wholeheartedly in support of the policy which would resolve in favor of the United States any doubts about admissibility of any individual."

When the president met with McDonald the following week, the battle was already lost. Refusing to face the situation head on, Roosevelt spun one diverting story after another until the half-hour was up. When McDonald started condemning and criticizing Long, the president warned him not to "pull any sob stuff." The meeting ended with nothing accomplished.

Still Eleanor refused to give up, bombarding the president with requests for action, but Franklin, preoccupied with the question of Britain's survival, was unwilling to listen. "Something does seem wrong," she insisted in one note. "*What* does seem wrong?" Franklin replied, manifestly annoyed.

• • •

Eleanor's sole triumph during this period was her successful intervention in behalf of eighty-three Jewish refugees who had sailed to America aboard the Portuguese freighter the S.S. *Quanza.* Filled to capacity with 317 passengers, the *Quanza* had steamed into New York Harbor in late August. All those in possession of American visas were allowed to debark. The remaining passengers, refugees who had escaped from occupied France, pleaded with authorities to let them come ashore, too. "Impossible," said the officials, "no one can step onto America soil without the proper papers." The *Quanza* sailed on to Veracruz, hoping to find a more receptive port, but the Mexican authorities ordered the ship to return to Europe. "Complete despair overwhelmed the passengers," one young woman traveling with her parents recalled: Europe to them was "a German concentration camp." Preparing for the return trip, the *Quanza* docked at Norfolk, Virginia, to load up with coal. While the ship remained in the harbor, Jewish organizations appealed to Mrs. Roosevelt for help.

Eleanor was at Hyde Park when she received word of the situation. Convinced that something should be done, she appealed to her husband directly. He agreed to send Patrick Malin, representing the PAC, to Norfolk to see what he could do to secure visas for children, for aliens holding visas from other countries, and for bona-fide political refugees. Working quickly, Malin certified all the documents that were presented to him and construed everybody else to be a political refugee so that the entire ship could disembark.

Long was furious. "I remonstrated violently," he recorded in his diary, "said that I thought it was a violation of the Law . . . that I would not be party to it, that I would not give my consent, that I would have no responsibility for it." But Malin refused to back down. "When he [Long] told me that he felt he could not take responsibility for them," Malin wrote, "I informed him that they were already landing."

"Mrs. Roosevelt saved my life," one passenger affirmed.

• • •

But Eleanor's success was short-lived. Long was soon back in the saddle, cleverer and more treacherous than ever. "The department does not refuse visas," Freda Kirchwey explained in *The Nation.* "It merely sets up a line of obstacles stretching from Washington to Lisbon and on around to Shanghai. . . . It is as if we were to examine laboriously the curricula vitae of flood victims clinging to a piece of floating wreckage and finally to decide that, no matter what their virtues, all but a few had better be allowed to drown." The resulting "record," she concluded, "is one which must sicken any person of ordinary humane instincts."

On November 15, refugee advocate Joseph Buttinger appealed again to Eleanor. Remembering how she had helped in June, he sent her a long memo detailing the various obstacles that were keeping refugees from getting their visas. "It looks again," he pleaded, "as if only your word could once more help us to overcome the barricades and hindrances in this ghastly situation."

Attached to the memo was a chilling two-page letter from a Jewish doctor which detailed a story that would become all too familiar in the years ahead. On Tuesday, October 22, a police officer had appeared at his home in the province of Baden, Germany, and told him he had an hour to pack up whatever could fit in a single suitcase. When the doctor and his family reached the designated assembly point, he learned that "all Jews, not only of the town but of all Baden and the Palatinate had been hit by the same fate." There was a moment of relief when they learned they were not being taken "to dreaded Poland," but conditions in the refugee camp in France where they ended up were far worse than anything they had imagined. Thirteen thousand refugees were living "like criminals behind barbed wire in dark, cold, wet, unhealthy barracks without beds, table or chair." In the first seven weeks, he reported, more than five hundred refugees had died.

At the end of his letter, which somehow made its way to the White House, the doctor pleaded for help. "For us here there only exists one solution, the quick emigration from Europe. All our appeals in that respect have been in vain so far. If the United States continues to work so slowly the number of dead here is going to increase in a most deplorable manner."

When Eleanor sent the material on to her husband, she attached a personal note of her own. "FDR, Can't something be done?" There is no evidence that Roosevelt ever replied to Eleanor's note. "The President's overriding concern was the war," Eleanor's friend Justine Polier explained, "and he probably didn't like to be urged as much as he was in regard to refugees."

At one point, as continued reports of Long's intransigence filtered in, Eleanor flared up angrily at her husband. "Franklin, you *know* he's a fascist," she said over lunch. "I've told you, Eleanor, you must not say that," the president replied, cutting her short with an "unusually cross" tone. "Well, maybe I shouldn't say it," Eleanor countered, "but he is!"

So the battle to save lives by bringing large numbers of refugees into America was lost during the crucial months of 1940, when Germany was still willing to grant exit permits to the Jews. "True, the Nazis wished to be rid of the Jews," historian David Wyman has written, "but until 1941 this end was to be accomplished by emigration, not extermination. The shift to extermination came only after the emigration method had failed, a failure in large part due to lack of countries open to refugees."

Eleanor's failure to force her husband to admit more refugees remained, her son Jimmy later said, "her deepest regret at the end of her life."

• • •

Through the months of September and October, while Willkie was conducting a vigorous campaign in thirty states, traveling by train for 17,300 miles, the president insisted on limiting his trips to war plants and shipyards. In his acceptance speech, he had contended that, with the war raging in Europe, he would have neither the time nor the inclination to campaign for re-election. Yet one look at the crowded schedule the president kept that autumn suggests that under the guise of nonpolitical inspection trips the old politician was alive and well.

On the last day of September, Roosevelt telescoped three "inspections" into six hours. He began his tour at Aberdeen Proving Ground in Maryland, where all guns and their carriages were fully proofed before being issued to troops and all powders, shells, and bombs were tested to check quality and performance. During the previous fifteen months, employment at the proving ground had nearly tripled, and a six-day work week was now in force. Facilities of this nature, designed for use in the actual operation of the army, were known as command facilities. To carry out their expansion—including airfields, army posts, artillery ranges, camps, forts, hospitals, research labs, and a new Pentagon building—the War Department had to acquire unprecedented quantities of land. (Over the next five years, the U.S. government would purchase more than five million acres of land for these command facilities, an area larger than the commonwealth of Massachusetts.)

Seated in an open touring car, the president saw at close range the new types of ordnance, including the new Garand automatic rifle and a new railway howitzer. He witnessed an impressive display of mobile artillery, ranging from eight-inch guns to the antitank cannon, and saw a completely mechanized company exercise over a field with steep hillocks and quagmires. Though the army would continue to experiment with new weapons, he told reporters traveling with him, the point had been reached where the current models could be standardized and carried into mass production.

Driving southward to the Glenn Martin plant in Baltimore, Maryland, where the B-26 twin-engine bomber, "said to be the fastest bomber in the world," was being built, the president saw construction under way for a new building that would eventually accommodate forty thousand workers. The Glenn Martin Company, America's oldest builder of bomber planes, had come close to bankruptcy only a few years earlier, but now, with $400 million worth of orders, it was flourishing. Construction was also under way at Fort Meade, Maryland, which Roosevelt visited after a picnic lunch. Then housing two thousand men, Fort Meade was being enlarged, by an $11-million building program, to serve as a gathering center for twenty-five thousand men at a time.

Everywhere Roosevelt looked, there were signs of a rapidly improving economy. With new army camps and defense plants appearing all across the country, with textile mills running double shifts to fill orders for uniforms and blankets, with shipyards working round the clock, the unemployment rolls were swiftly shrinking—by four hundred thousand in August, by five hundred thousand in September. The eleven-year depression was, at last, coming to an end.

Returning to the White House in an ebullient mood, Roosevelt penned a letter to his son-in-law, John Boettiger. "The main point of these trips which has never yet appeared in print is that the places visited by me—arsenals, Navy yards, private plants, etc.—get a real enthusiasm and speed up production during the days following my visit. It does seem to help."

The following week, the president journeyed to the Midwest to inspect steel plants in Pittsburgh and Youngstown, a government housing project for defense workers at Terrace Valley, and the Wright Field in Dayton, Ohio, where he saw new types of planes, "one knifing through the air and another moving so unbelievably slowly that it seemed to be hung on a wire." Everywhere he went, he was greeted with all the fervor and trappings of an old-fashioned campaign. Schools were dismissed, and more than a quarter-million people lined his route. Still, he refused to acknowledge that he was campaigning. "I have come here today very informally," he said, " on what is essentially a trip to educate myself, to learn about what is happening for national defense."

While the president reveled in the cheering crowds, Eleanor headed to the West Coast to visit her oldest son, Jimmy, who had just been ordered to active duty at Marine headquarters in San Diego, California. Tall, thin, and prematurely balding, Jimmy had married Boston debutante Betsey Cushing soon after his graduation from Harvard. In 1937, after working in the insurance business for seven years, he had joined the White House staff as his father's secretary. He was generally credited with excellent work, but after two years, the stress of the position, coupled with charges in the press that he had used his public office for private gain, proved too much. He suffered a perforated ulcer, had two-thirds of his stomach removed, and was forced to resign. That fall, he moved to Los Angeles to become a film executive with Samuel Goldwyn Productions. The move coincided with the breakup of his marriage and the start of a new romance with Romelle Schneider, the nurse who had cared for him when he was in the hospital.

Twenty-six-year-old FDR, Jr., an officer in the navy reserve, was also affected by the standing order to report to duty. Considered the "golden boy" of the family, with his father's good looks and outgoing personality, FDR, Jr., had distinguished himself in both academics and athletics at Harvard. His marriage to heiress Ethel du Pont was labeled the wedding of the decade. After Harvard, on the advice of his father, he had chosen law in preparation for a career in politics, but now, like so many thousands of young Americans, he had his plans interrupted by the war.

Soon all four of the Roosevelt boys would be in the armed forces: thirty-year-old Elliott would accept a captain's commission in the Army Air Corps, and twenty-four-year-old John would join the navy. Of all the boys, Eleanor was closest to Elliott. "Elliott was the most like her father and brother," Minnewa Bell, his fourth wife, observed. "She had the feeling that Elliott was going to be a drinker. She was closer to Elliott because she worried about him more." Like all the Roosevelt boys, Elliott had gone to Groton, but when the time came to apply to Harvard he had willfully flunked his entrance exams. Unable to get his feet on the ground, he had moved from one career to another and from one woman to another. In 1940, his second marriage was already in trouble.

The youngest son, John, was quieter and more reserved than his older brothers. When he entered Harvard, his father warned the freshman dean that "he has to study to get things done" and "will not be good at assuming or seeking leadership." The only one of the four boys who would never run for political office, John once worked under a pseudonym to avoid the favoritism that was attached to the Roosevelt name. Married at twenty-two to socialite Anne Lindsay Clark, he was a manager at Filene's department store in Boston when he entered active duty with the navy.

The boys' disappointing careers and broken relationships (between the four of them there would be eighteen marriages) devastated Eleanor. "None of them really lived up to the name," Eleanor's friend Abram Sacher observed, "and some of them, in fact, demeaned it" by exhibiting an astonishing lack of sensitivity about using their father's influence to make money. "She didn't know what to do with her sons," Anna's son Curtis Roosevelt admitted. "They were often very rude to their father. At dinner, arguing about politics, particularly FDR, Jr., and Elliott, they were so extraordinarily arrogant with FDR."

Characteristically, and perhaps not without some cause, Eleanor blamed no one but herself. "I don't seem to be able to shake the feeling of responsibility . . . ," Eleanor wrote Hick in the mid-thirties, at the time of Elliott's first divorce. "I guess I was a pretty unwise teacher as to how to go about living. Too late to do anything now, however, & I'm rather disgusted with myself. I feel soiled. . . ."

"She felt that the guilt was all hers," Elliott later wrote, "because she had been unable to extend to us in our nursery days the warmth of love that the young find as necessary as food or drink." Eleanor believed she had failed as a mother because "she was so unsure of herself in the early days." Lacking confidence in her mothering skills, she allowed her ever-confident mother-in-law to take charge of hiring the nurses and setting up the nursery, accepting Sara's intervention both grudgingly and gratefully, cowed by inexperience and fear. "I was not allowed to take care of the children," Eleanor recalled, "nor had I any sense of how to do it."

"At a visceral level," Curtis Roosevelt recalled, "a kid can sense lack of confidence in a parent. My mother, Anna, lacked it. ER lacked it. Sara had it. She was the grande dame. She knew who she was and what she wanted." Even as a great-grandchild, Curtis recalled, he was drawn to that supreme confidence, "like a moth to the flame."

The struggle between the two women was no mere skirmish; it was war. Since Sara was unable to prevent her son's marriage, Eleanor observed in an unpublished article, "she determined to bend the marriage to the way she wanted it to be. What she wanted was to hold onto Franklin and his children; she wanted them to grow as she wished. As it turned out, Franklin's children were more my mother-in-law's children than they were mine."

Granny referred to them as *her* children, Jimmy recalled. She told them, "your mother only bore you, I am more your mother than your mother is." Even as a young boy, Jimmy recognized that this was a cruel thing for his grandmother to say, but he loved her and needed her too much to condemn her: "She was sort of a fairy godmother."

The children remembered Eleanor as a dutiful but preoccupied mother who read to them in bed, heard their prayers, and tried to teach them right from wrong. "It did not come naturally to me to understand little children or to enjoy them," Eleanor confessed. "Playing with children was difficult for me because play had not been an important part of my own childhood."

In contrast to their tangled feelings about their mother, the children would remember for the rest of their lives the adventures they shared with their father. "Franklin loved his small children," Eleanor recalled. "They were a great joy to him; he loved to play with them and I think he took great pleasure in their health and good looks and in their companionship. He made the children feel that he really was their age." On Saturday afternoons, he would "play the most ridiculous baseball games with them and go on paper chases and do all the things that . . . children enjoy." In later years, when their father had less and less time for them, the children tended to romanticize their playful romps, setting their father's spontaneity against their mother's stiffness.

Discipline was always a source of trouble in the Roosevelt household. "I was the disciplinarian, I'm afraid," Eleanor recalled. "[Franklin] found punishing a child almost an impossibility. He just couldn't do it. I remember distinctly once telling Johnny to go upstairs to his room, and just having a feeling that he hadn't gone. I went into my husband's study at Hyde Park and found Johnny sitting in his lap, weeping his heart out on his father's shirt front, and both of them looking equally guilty when I discovered them."

• • •

Although Eleanor anguished over her inability to communicate easily with her sons, she derived priceless comfort from her close relationship with her only daughter, Anna. When Anna was small, however, Eleanor was no more at ease with *her* than with the boys. Anna later told her third husband, James Halsted, that her mother was "very unpredictable and inconsistent in bringing up her children. Inconsistent in her feelings—sweet and lovely one hour and the next hour very critical, very demanding, and very difficult to be with. You could never tell what she really meant." Until Anna entered adolescence, she was closer to her father than to her mother. All the happiest moments of her childhood revolved around him, riding with him on the front of his horse to "the most unexpected spots in peaceful deserted glens deep in the woods," coasting with him down the steep hill behind the house at Hyde Park, where there were sudden bumps and the sled "would take off into the air," walking the mile and a half or so with him to her school in Washington, talking about "all sorts of things I liked to hear about—books I was reading, a cruise we might be going to take. . . ."

Anna was fifteen the summer her father contracted polio. Suddenly the wonderful playmate who had taken long walks with her and sailed with her and done so many physical things was now struggling to walk with heavy steel braces, the sweat pouring down his face. It was "traumatic," Anna later admitted. The situation was aggravated by the fact that Anna was in a new school in New York, much larger than her previous school, and was having trouble making friends. Meanwhile, Eleanor was so consumed in helping Franklin recover that she "did not realize that Anna was in difficulty." Interpreting her daughter's sullenness as typical adolescent behavior, Eleanor failed to appreciate that, with all the focus on Franklin, Anna had become convinced that she no longer mattered to either her mother or her father. "It never occurred to me," Eleanor later admitted, "to take her into my confidence and consult with her about our difficulties or tell her just what her father was going through."

The tension between mother and daughter was finally released late one afternoon that fall. Eleanor was reading a story to her youngest boys when the strain of trying both to nurse her husband and to mother her children suddenly overwhelmed her. She began to cry and she could not stop. Emancipated for the moment from the felt need of remaining in control (the only time in her life she remembered having gone to pieces in this manner), Eleanor flung herself on her bed and sobbed shamelessly for hours. "This outburst of mine had a good result so far as Anna and I were concerned," Eleanor later recognized. "She saw that I was not cold and unfeeling after all. And she poured out her troubles to me, saying she knew she had been wrong in thinking I did not love her. It was the start of an understanding between us."

From that day forward, Eleanor gave Anna her best hours. When Anna returned from her first round of debutante dances, Eleanor waited up for her in case she wanted to talk. Though Anna was blonde and beautiful with marvelous long legs, Eleanor recognized some of her own insecurities in her daughter's awkward presence. One night, they talked until dawn. During these intimate exchanges, Eleanor shared with Anna the sorrows of her own childhood, the buried anger at her mother, the disillusionment with her father.

And then, one night, in the most memorable talk of all, Eleanor told her daughter about Franklin's love affair with Lucy Mercer. "I felt very strongly on Mother's side," Anna recalled. "I was mad—mad at Father" for his having hurt her mother so deeply. "Emotionally from then on I was always closer to my mother than I was to my father."

When Anna's youthful marriage to New York stockbroker Curtis Dall began to fall apart only a few years after they were wed, it was Eleanor who provided understanding and support. Then, when Anna fell in love with John Boettiger, the *Chicago Tribune* correspondent, during the 1932 campaign, Eleanor watched over and protected their love. In the forbidden phase of the romance, while both lovers were still married, Eleanor provided empathy, sanction, and encompassing love. "Eleanor saw in John the nice son she might have had," Anna's son Curtis observed. "He was smart, very good-looking, and knowledgeable about the issues. At the same time, he was very responsive to her, calling her Lovely Lady and flirting with her. It was nice for Anna that her mother and John got along so well."

On the eve of Anna's marriage to John in 1935, Eleanor sent a private letter to John. "I love Anna so dearly that I don't need to tell you that my willingness to let her go speaks much for my trust and love of you," she wrote. She would never interfere, she promised, but she had one last word of motherly advice: "Remember that Anna is I think rather like me, she'd always rather have the truth even if it is painful and never let a doubt or suspicion grow up between you two which honest facing can dispel."

The following year, Anna and John moved to Seattle, Washington, where they had an unusual opportunity to work together on a major West Coast daily—the *Seattle Post-Intelligencer*. At William Randolph Hearst's invitation, John was made publisher and Anna became associate editor of the women's pages. "The Northwest welcomed the Boettigers with bands and fireworks," a reporter from *The Saturday Evening Post* noted. "Crowds met the train at hinterland stations. Seattle threw a big banquet." It was a happy time for the young couple. Under their leadership the *Post-Intelligencer* expanded its circulation, and the two of them became the toast of the town. Glowing features portrayed John, with his "jovial manner, resonant voice and big physique" as a natural-born politician while Anna was likened to movie star

Katharine Hepburn, with her long legs, her figure "as slim and boyish as a schoolgirl," her careless clothes, and her manner of speaking directly.

Eleanor was despondent when Anna left Washington. "Perhaps I needed to have you away . . . ," she wrote, "to realize just how much it means to have you. . . . I have felt sad every time we passed your door." But she was determined not to let the distance diminish their relationship. She wrote to her daughter several times a week, talked to her frequently on the phone, and scheduled her lecture tours so that she could spend a week in Seattle every spring and fall. So, this October, after watching Jimmy drill with his battalion on the evening of October 16, Eleanor flew to Seattle, where she spent the rest of the week with Anna and John in their new home, a sprawling white house on Lake Washington with ten bedrooms and five baths. "I begin to feel really at home in Seattle," a relaxed Eleanor told her readers. "There seems to be an endless flow of conversation that can fill up long hours of time." With the boys, Eleanor confided to Hick, she felt only tolerated, but with her daughter, she felt wanted and needed. "I suppose that is why I enjoy being with Anna and John so often."

• • •

Everything Eleanor heard on her cross-country trip convinced her that the Willkie campaign was gaining momentum. His crowds were growing with each passing day; his polls were steadily rising, and his message was gaining strength and substance. In late September, the Republican challenger had shifted his strategy, adopting a more strident tone. If Roosevelt continued in office, he shouted to audiences at every stop, "you can count on our men being on transports for Europe six months from now." The specter of American boys fighting in Europe opened what one historian has described as a "wide crack in a dam holding back floodwaters of popular emotion." Willkie's polls began to move upward; Roosevelt's victory margin began to shrink.

Eleanor sensed this change in sentiment and predicted that the president would lose unless he took to the road himself in a full-scale campaign. Though she conceded that he was coming into contact with thousands of people through his "inspection trips," she believed there was something fundamentally deceptive about his insistence that these forays to factories and arsenals were not campaign stops. The American people, she argued, did not want to be taken for granted. The president's responsibility was to go to them directly, to outline his positions, to counter Willkie's charges, and to ask for their support.

"Dearest Franklin," she wrote in mid-October. "I hope you will make a few more speeches. It seems to me pretty essential that you make them now as political speeches. The people have a right to hear your say in opposition to Willkie between now and the election."

Harold Ickes agreed with Eleanor. After presenting his arguments to Steve Early, Ickes went in to see Missy. Knowing that Missy had no fear of speaking honestly to the president, Ickes shared with her his worries about the campaign. "I painted her a pretty dark picture," Ickes recorded in his diary. "I asked her frankly whether the President wanted to win and suggested that the way he had been acting I was disposed to doubt whether he did or not. She said that he did... but he didn't like to put himself in a position of making it possible for Willkie, to say that he, Willkie, had smoked him out. I told Missy that in his speech of acceptance the President had said in effect that he would feel free at any time to correct any misrepresentations or misstatements and that certainly Willkie had given him a sufficient basis on this ground to justify his going out on the stump."

Under pressure from both Eleanor and Ickes, the president finally announced on October 11 that he would make five major campaign speeches in the weeks ahead. Following Ickes' suggestion, he justified his departure from his convention pledge by referring to the gross misrepresentations of the Willkie campaign, which required him to counter falsifications with facts. "I will not pretend that I find this an unpleasant duty," he told a cheering crowd at his first speech, in Philadelphia on October 23. "I am an old campaigner and I love a good fight."

The president may have spoken the truth when he said he loved a good fight, but two days later, when CIO chief John L. Lewis delivered a vitriolic personal attack against him in a speech that was broadcast on national radio, he was perceptibly disturbed. The isolationist labor leader had been criticizing the administration for months; he had denounced the creation of the NDAC as a turn to the right and had fought against conscription on the ground that it would deprive labor of all its gains under the New Deal. But few observers predicted that he would actually break with Roosevelt and support Willkie.

At 9 p.m., as Lewis moved up to the microphones to speak, the president was sitting by his radio in his study, accompanied by Harry Hopkins and Grace Tully. Eleanor was at the Olney Inn for dinner with a group of female journalists, including Ruby Black, Martha Strayer, Emma Bugbee, and Bess Furman. It had been a busy day for Roosevelt, starting with a press conference in the morning, various appointments, lunch with Eleanor, a meeting with the Cabinet, a brief appearance at a tea Eleanor had arranged for the National Conference of Negro Women, and a visit to the doctor. He was tired, but with only ten days left before the election and thirty million Americans tuned in to the event, the Lewis speech was too important to miss.

Delivered in a deep baritone voice, rich in rhetoric, Lewis' speech was perhaps the most vigorous attack ever launched against the popular president. He denounced the president as a man whose motivation and objective was *war*. "His every act leads me to this inescapable conclusion. The President has said that he hates war and will work for peace but his acts do not match his words." Indeed, Lewis argued, "the President has been scheming for years to involve us in war."

"Are we," Lewis asked, "to yield to the appetite for power and the vaunting ambitions of a man who plays with the lives of human beings for a pastime? I say no. I think the reelection of President Roosevelt for a third term would be a national evil of the first magnitude. . . . It is time for the manhood and the womanhood of America to assert themselves. Tomorrow may be too late. If not Roosevelt whom do I recommend?

". . . Why, Wendell Willkie, of course . . . a gallant American," a man with a common touch, a man "born in the briar and not to the purple," a man who "has worked with his hands and has known the pangs of hunger." Then Lewis issued a surprising ultimatum. Convinced that the division between Roosevelt and Willkie was so close that labor's vote would carry the election, he told his immense constituency that if Roosevelt was re-elected it would mean that labor had rejected his advice. If that were so, he would have no choice but to resign as president of the CIO. In other words, "sustain me now, or repudiate me." The choice was the public's: a vote for Roosevelt would be a vote against Lewis.

Both Roosevelt and Hopkins were "sad and low" after the speech. Visiting the White House the following morning, labor leader Sidney Hillman said that he had never seen either of them "so thoroughly scared." For Roosevelt, the depth of the hatred so evident in the speech was hard to comprehend. Though the president could understand and accept opposition to his domestic and foreign policies, Lewis' anger ran so deep that it could not be categorized in ordinary terms.

In private conversation, Willkie conceded that Lewis' dislike of Roosevelt was so profound that it was almost pathological. "John never can forget that he came up the hard way," Willkie observed. "The President is very genteel and he is patronizing to John without meaning to be and this drives John wild." Nor could Lewis forget the time he had received an invitation to bring his wife to tea with the president and the first lady. Eleanor was out of town, so Missy served, as she often did, as the president's hostess, but Lewis interpreted Eleanor's absence as a deliberate slight.

Hundreds of telegrams poured into the White House the day after the Lewis speech. In some mysterious way, Lewis' attack had created a powerful counterforce. "We take the liberty of assuring you that John L. Lewis did not speak for us," the New York local of the Amalgamated Clothing Workers wrote; "the attack made by Lewis is a betrayal of the interests and cause of labor." "Paducah labor is for you 100 percent," another telegram read. "Our shirtworkers starved on a dollar a day under Republican rule. Now we have 13 dollar forty hour week and a union. We are all talking and working and voting for you." "Don't let Lewis' speech weaken you," UMW Local #6082 wired. "We are behind you 100 percent." Sensing for the first time that the president might be in trouble, Roosevelt's supporters rallied to his side with passion and conviction. "John L. Lewis has kicked his mother after he had milked her dry," Alex Tunis wrote from West 97th Street in New York. "You are the only President that ever done anything for the miners," a miner's wife wrote from Barnabus, West Virginia. "I don't want to go back to the day before you took office. Them were terrible days for the miners. I hope you and Mrs. Roosevelt continue in the White House as long as you live and I hope you live a long time." Writing in a similar vein, a Minnesota homemaker assured the president that she would never forget that because of him her aged mother's last days were made comfortable, mentally as well as physically. "Old age pensions is only one thing for which you are to be eternally thanked."

Buoyed by stacks of similar telegrams, the president took to the road with a lift in his heart. "I am an old campaigner," he repeated with increasing conviction before every crowd, "and I love a good fight." On October 28, before a capacity crowd of twenty-two thousand at Madison Square Garden, Roosevelt set out to answer the Republican charge that he had been slow in preparing the U.S. for defense. Every seat in the Garden was filled; another thirty thousand people were gathered outside, trying to get in. For seven years, the president began, Republican leaders had blocked every effort to strengthen America's defenses, shouting from the rooftops that our armed strength was sufficient for any enemy. "Great Britain would never have received an ounce of help from us if the decision had been left to [Congressman Joseph] Martin, [Congressman Bruce] Barton and [Congressman Hamilton] Fish." At the first use of the rhythmic sequence "Martin, Barton and Fish," the crowd roared with laughter. When he used it again, they were ready to join in, yelling "Barton" and "Fish" as soon as he said "Martin." By the end of the speech, the crowd was on its feet, yelling, screaming, and laughing.

"The way of the man with his crowds," one reporter wrote, "very great and responsive, roused them as much as anything he said. In every toss of his head, in every lift of a jutting chin, in every crackling, twitting jibe at his opponents, in every gesture and fillip of his speaking, he was as cocky a candidate" as one could imagine. "I have just come from one of the most remarkable experiences of my life," David Lilienthal recorded in his diary at midnight that night. "I sat on the platform not ten feet from the President and heard him deliver a really great speech." When the president first arrived, Lilienthal observed, "his face was gray under the lights and showed the strain of that awful walking. Nothing I have ever seen was like the next few minutes. The President's voice as he spoke was strong, there wasn't a trace of weariness at any time. He seemed to be in fine fettle."

The masterly speech came at the climax of a fourteen-hour day of strenuous campaigning. It was nearly midnight when the president returned to Penn Station to board his special train to Washington. In the confusion of the large crowd that had gathered at the track, Roosevelt's press secretary, Steve Early, was stopped by two policemen, one Irish, the other Negro. They were under orders to keep everyone away from the train. Early tried to push his way through but was shoved back. In the melee, he kicked the Negro policeman, James Sloan, in the groin. When Sloan, a decorated patrolman and father of five who had just returned to duty after an operation for a hernia, had to be taken to the hospital for treatment, the incident became a front-page story in the Negro press. Republicans quickly capitalized on it. Pictures of Sloan recuperating in his bed were handed out in black neighborhoods. "Negroes," the caption read, "if you want your President to be surrounded by Southern influences of this kind, vote for Roosevelt. If you want to be treated with respect, vote for Wendell Willkie!"

Early was reportedly inconsolable, fearing he might have lost the election for the president, but when reporters interviewed Patrolman Sloan at his bedside, the controversy came to an end. "I am a Democrat," Sloan said. "If anybody thinks they can turn me against our great President who has done so much for our race because of this thing, they are mistaken."

• • •

On the 29th of October, the president set in motion the first peacetime conscription in history with a drawing of draft numbers to determine the order of induction. Two weeks earlier, on registration day, all males between twenty-one and thirty-five had been required to present themselves at their local draft boards, where they were each assigned a serial number. Now, on lottery day, the chance selection of numbers stirred in the big fishbowl with a big wooden dipper would determine which of the young men who had registered would be called to leave civilian life for a year's military training, and in what order they would be called.

A number of Roosevelt's advisers had strongly urged him to postpone the lottery until after the election, but he refused. The timing was so bad, Sam Rosenman observed, that "any old-time politician would have said [it] could never take place." It was a brave decision on the president's part to let it happen at this time, Stimson recorded in his diary, "when there is a very bitter campaign being made against it on account of his support of the Draft." But after it was over, Stimson came to believe that the solemn nature of the historic ceremony "served to change the event . . . into a great asset in his favor."

The president's expression was serious as he sat beside Secretary Stimson on the stage of Washington's Departmental Auditorium. Both the large glass fishbowl and the long ladle used to stir the cobalt capsules had been used in World War I to select the men who would go into battle. The strip of yellow linen used to blindfold Secretary Stimson was cut from the covering of the chair used at the signing of the Declaration of Independence. After putting his blindfold in place, Stimson reached his left hand into the large jar, picked up the first capsule he touched, and handed it to the president. "The first number," Roosevelt announced, reading into a battery of microphones carrying his voice across all three radio networks, "is one-fifty-eight."

No sooner had the president spoken then a woman's scream was heard. Seated in the middle of the crowded auditorium, Mrs. Mildred Bell gasped. Her twenty-one-year-old son, Harry, who was supposed to be married the following week, held number 158. Now, suddenly, his future was linked to that of his country. Number 158 was held by some six thousand registrants in different precincts throughout the country, including Cleveland welder Michael Thomson, father of three children; Jack Clardy, a one-armed Negro banjo picker from Charlotte, North Carolina; and unemployed James Cody of Long Island City. In New York, the surnames of those bearing number 158 told a story in themselves: Farrugia, Chan, Re, Weisblum, Tsatsarones, Stoller, Clement. Some were pleased and proud to be the first number called, others said they'd make the best of it, still others were upset at their bad fortune. "This is the first lottery I ever won in my life," several jokingly complained. It took seventeen hours to draw the remaining nine thousand capsules, but when the bowl was finally empty, the order of induction for more than sixteen million men had been established.

Eleanor was in Maine delivering a speech at Colby College while the lottery was taking place. "As I listened to the radio," she wrote Joe Lash, "and heard the draft numbers read, I found myself thinking of you and hoping that your number would not come up. I want you so much to get started along lines which you can follow and develop into great influence and use to others of the younger generation and I would hate to see you packed off for a year of army training. . . . I don't feel the same about my boys, except FDR Jr. whom I would like to see take his bar exam in March."

• • •

Roosevelt was anxious and testy on the day after the drawing. Riding to Boston in his special train for a speech to be delivered that night at the Boston Garden, he was bombarded by messages from frightened Democrats who feared he would lose the election unless he guaranteed to American mothers that their sons were being sent to army camps only to be trained, that they would never have to fight. Seeking to allay these concerns, he decided to include in his speech a pledge that would haunt him again and again in the years ahead. "Very simply and honestly," he said, "I can give assurance to the mothers and to the fathers of America that each and every one of their boys in training will be well housed and well fed. . . . And while I am talking to you fathers and mothers I give one more assurance. I have said this before, but I shall say it again, and again, and again. Your boys are not going to be sent into any foreign wars." In all his previous speeches, he had qualified the pledge that American boys would not fight in foreign wars by adding the phrase "except in cases of attack." The speechwriters had inserted a similar qualification in the draft of the Boston speech, but the president insisted on removing the words. "It's not necessary," he argued. "It's implied clearly. If we're attacked, it's no longer a foreign war."

The president's impulsiveness, Rosenman observed, was to cause him "a lot of headaches later," for his opponents took great pleasure in quoting the categorical pledge he had made in Boston. In her column two days later, Eleanor gently took issue with the disingenuousness of her husband's promise. "Today," she told her readers, "no one can honestly promise you peace at home or abroad. All any human being can do is to promise that he will do his utmost to prevent this country from being involved in war."

• • •

The day was warm for the 5th of November; in the Roosevelt home at Hyde Park, the family was getting ready for the short journey into town to vote in the presidential election. As he always did on election day, Roosevelt stopped to chat with his Hyde Park neighbors before entering the little town hall. Reporters observed nothing in the president's demeanor to indicate concern over the outcome of the election; on the contrary, he seemed "extraordinarily jovial," joking with staff and journalists alike. Yet, underneath his cheery manner, Roosevelt was fully aware that in the latest Gallup poll Willkie's support was almost even with his, making the election too close to call.

Inside the town hall, photographers waited in the balcony overhead to snap a picture of the president as he emerged from behind the green curtains of the voting booth. Standing next to her son in line, Sara stepped up to the table. "What name please?" the election clerk inquired. "Sara Delano Roosevelt," she answered firmly, "and it's been my name for a good many years." In the confusion created by the photographer, Eleanor started to leave the building before she had recorded her vote. Reminded by her husband, she hastily returned to the booth.

During the afternoon, the president made a halfhearted attempt to work on his stamp collection in his study, while Eleanor and Joe Lash went on a long walk through the woods. Eleanor told Lash she hoped that, if the president were re-elected to an unprecedented third term, he "would do all the things he had wanted to do and knew had to be done but had not done because of political considerations."

At six o'clock, Eleanor welcomed about forty family members and friends, including Harry Hopkins, Frances Perkins, and Helen Gahagan, to a buffet supper at her cottage. With a wood fire on the hearth, she moved from one guest to another, putting everyone at ease. Toward nine o'clock, the guests wandered back to the Big House, where they chatted nervously, listened to the radio, and awaited the returns.

Seated apart from all the guests, alone at the mahogany dining table with large tally sheets and a long row of freshly sharpened pencils before him, the president of the United States charted the election results. Occasionally, the door slid open to admit Missy LeHand, carrying the latest totals for the president to add to his tally. As the early returns filtered in, the president's face darkened. In almost every state Willkie was doing far better than Alf Landon had done. Sweating profusely, Roosevelt called Mike Reilly, his Secret Service guard. "Mike, I don't want to see anybody in here," he said. "Including your family?" Reilly asked. "I said anybody," Roosevelt repeated, as he closed the door. It appeared to Reilly that the president had lost his nerve.

By 11 p.m., however, as the votes in the big states of New York, Illinois, Ohio, and Pennsylvania began to come in, showing heavy Democratic majorities, the tide turned toward the president. Nationwide, the votes of labor, Negroes, and the foreign-born were holding up. In the lowest-income districts, the president was winning nearly 75 percent of the votes. The tension in the house began to dissipate. At midnight, a smiling president emerged to greet a jubilant crowd of local Democrats parading across the lawn with torchlights. "It looks all right," the president told his cheering neighbors. "We, of course, face difficult days in this country. But I think you will find me in the future just the same Franklin Roosevelt you have known a great many years. My heart has always been here. It always will be."

Behind the president, as he spoke from the balcony, stood his mother, his wife, and his sons FDR, Jr., and John. Farther back, standing by himself, Harry Hopkins did "a little jig and clapped his fist into the open palm of his left hand as if to say 'we did it.' " When the president finished speaking, the family turned toward the house. "We want Eleanor," the crowd shouted. "We want Eleanor." But Eleanor gestured them away. "What have I to do with it? It's the President they want to hear—not me."

As the president fell asleep that night in his childhood home, he had reached the highest peak of his career. In numbers, it was not a great victory. He had won 54.7 percent to 44.8 percent for Willkie, the smallest plurality since the election of 1916. But he had won, despite the hatred of conservatives and isolationists, despite the attacks of John L. Lewis. He had won something that neither Washington nor Jefferson nor Jackson had ever achieved—a third term as president of the United States.

CHAPTER 8

"ARSENAL OF DEMOCRACY"

"Just how does the President think?" reporter John Gunther once asked Eleanor Roosevelt. "My dear Mr. Gunther," Eleanor replied. "The President never thinks. He decides."

Mr. Gunther's question was on the minds of several Cabinet members in mid-November 1940, when the president seemed unable and unwilling to concentrate his thoughts on a new and disturbing crisis: Great Britain was on the verge of bankruptcy.

The cash reserves of the British treasury, the U.S. was told after the election, were no longer sufficient to pay for the munitions and supplies that Britain had ordered from the U.S.—supplies needed now more than ever. Though Britain's success in repulsing the Luftwaffe had postponed the threatened invasion until spring, the German advantage in war materials was growing and would continue to grow as Germany increasingly moved to supplement its own vast production with that of the industrial countries it had conquered—Holland, Belgium, France, Czechoslovakia. Without American supplies to close the gap, Britain would be defeated in a matter of months.

What to do? The idea of loaning the money to Britain was raised in the Cabinet, but no one believed that Congress would go along, given America's experience with unpaid debts in World War I. During the discussion, the president, Frances Perkins recalled, threw out "a question here and a hint there." Perkins had the feeling that "he was thinking about something, about some way in which the people of the U.S. could assist the British," but he had nothing concrete to offer. The problem seemed insoluble.

In the midst of the crisis, as administration officials were frantically scurrying from one meeting to another, the president suddenly announced that he was leaving Washington for a ten-day sail through the Caribbean on the navy cruiser the U.S.S. *Tuscaloosa.* He told his stunned Cabinet, "All of you use your imaginations" to come up with an answer. To be sure, the exhausted president needed to rest after the wearying campaign. "The more I sleep, the more I want to sleep," he was heard to say. But the timing of the pleasure trip was profoundly disturbing to those who worried about Britain's survival.

"Hope you have a grand trip," Eleanor wired Franklin from Abilene, Texas, as she set forth on a trip of her own—a rigorous lecture tour through the South and the Midwest. Everywhere she went, she kept her eye on the economic and social weaknesses of the nation preparing for war. Driving through the rural sections of Texas, she was saddened to see that, despite the New Deal's housing program, people were still living in shacks, "made of scraps apparently, bits of corrugated iron, even heavy cardboard is used. . . . I cannot help feeling that there should be a better way of meeting this problem." Hearing reports that, of the first million men selected for the draft, almost 40 percent were found physically unfit for military service, Eleanor hoped the sorry figures would "give impetus to the movement for a comprehensive and nationwide health program." And as always, there remained the plight of the Negro, particularly visible in the slums of Chicago and Detroit.

"In every place," Tommy reported to Anna, "the audiences have been capacity audiences and the attention and interest excellent. There is no question that your mother is an idol to the people of this country." Looking over Tommy's shoulder at this point, Eleanor observed, with a flash of self-deprecatory humor, that instead of saying, "your mother is an idol," Tommy should say, "your mother isn't idle."

• • •

Hundreds of people were standing on the dock at Miami when the president, accompanied by a handful of his closest aides, including Harry Hopkins, Pa Watson, and Dr. Ross McIntire, arrived to board the ship. With a happy smile on his face, he waved his hat to the applauding crowd and stood by the rail while the national anthem was played. Horns began to blow as the ship was cast off and continued until the vessel was out of the harbor and steaming into the Atlantic.

The president spent his days with his white shirtsleeves rolled up over his wrestler's arms, talking, fishing and basking in the sun. From the beginning of the trip to the end, the newspapermen who followed faithfully behind on a convoy destroyer had no idea where they were going or how long they would be gone. At Guantanamo Bay the cruiser pulled into the dock for an hour's stop so that a large stock of Cuban cigars could be carried on board. At Jamaica, St. Lucia, and Antigua, the president hosted British colonial officials and their wives at lunch. At Eleuthera Island he was joined by the duke of Windsor. Relaxing evenings were spent on deck cheering boxing matches between black mess attendants, listening to drummer contests between sailors and marines, playing poker, and watching movies—including *Tin Pan Alley,* starring Betty Grable, and *Northwest Mounted Police,* with Gary Cooper and Paulette Goddard.

At designated points along the way, navy seaplanes circled the presidential flotilla and landed alongside the *Tuscaloosa* to deliver the White House mail. Several chatty letters from Eleanor arrived. She was enjoying her trip, she told him, though she was growing weary of the Southern voice. "I think of you as sleeping and eating and I hope getting a rest from the world."

But the world would not go away. From daily news dispatches Roosevelt learned that heavy raids on London had devastated the House of Commons, and that massive bombings of Coventry, Birmingham, and Bristol had so severely damaged dozens of war factories that vital production would be halted for months. At the same time, it was reported that the severity of German submarine sinkings had escalated; in a matter of weeks, seven merchant vessels carrying tons of needed supplies had been sunk. And from Washington came news of the unexpected death of Lord Lothian, British ambassador to the U.S., who had worked unremittingly to strengthen his country's bond with the United States. A Christian Scientist, Lothian had refused treatment for a simple infection that turned toxic.

On the morning of December 9, a seaplane touched down with a letter from Winston Churchill. Having composed it over a period of weeks, Churchill regarded the letter as "one of the most important" he had ever written. "My dear Mr. President," Churchill began. "As we reach the end of this year I feel you will expect me to lay before you the prospects for 1941. I do so strongly and confidently." At the outset, he wanted the president to understand that while Britain could endure "the shattering of our dwellings and the slaughter of our civil population by indiscriminate air attacks," she was facing "a less sudden and less spectacular but equally deadly danger"—economic strangulation. "Unless we can establish our ability to feed this Island, to import the munitions of all kinds which we need, we may fall by the way, and the time needed by the U.S. to complete her defensive preparations may not be forthcoming." He went on to catalogue in detail the losses in production and shipping Britain had sustained from the bombing raids and the U-boat attacks. "Only the United States," he wrote, "could supply the additional shipping capacity so urgently needed as well as the crucial weapons of war."

Last of all, he came to the knotty problem that was on everyone's mind—the problem of finances. "The moment approaches where we shall no longer be able to pay cash for shipping and other supplies. While we will do our utmost and shrink from no proper sacrifices to make payments across the exchange, I believe you will agree that it would be wrong in principle and mutually disadvantageous in effect if, at the height of this struggle Great Britain were to be divested of all saleable assets so that after the victory was won with our blood, civilization saved and the time gained for the United States to be fully armed against all eventualities, we should stand stripped to the bone. Such a course would not be in the moral or economic interests of either of our countries. . . .

"You may be assured that we shall prove ourselves ready to suffer and sacrifice to the utmost for the Cause, and that we glory in being its champions. The rest we leave with confidence to you and to your people, being sure that ways and means will be found which future generations on both sides of the Atlantic will approve and admire."

Churchill's letter had a profound effect on the president, though he said little about it at first. "I didn't know for quite a while what he was thinking about, if anything," Hopkins said later. "But then—I began to get the idea that he was refueling, the way he so often does when he seems to be resting and carefree. So I didn't ask him any questions. Then, one evening, he suddenly came out with it—the whole program. He didn't seem to have any clear idea how it could be done legally. But there wasn't a doubt in his mind that he'd find a way to do it."

The president's "whole program," later to be known as "lend-lease," was the unconventional idea that the United States could send Britain weapons and supplies without charge and then, after the war, be repaid not in dollars but in kind. How Roosevelt arrived at this ingenious idea, which cut through all the stale debates in Washington about loans and gifts, is not clear. "Nobody that I know of," White House speechwriter Robert Sherwood has written, "has been able to give any convincing idea" of how the refueling process worked. "He did not seem to talk much about the subject in hand, or to consult the advice of others, or to 'read up' on it. . . . One can only say that FDR, a creative artist in politics, had put in his time on this cruise evolving the pattern of a masterpiece."

Frances Perkins later described the president's idea for lend-lease as a "flash of almost clairvoyant knowledge and understanding." He would have one of these flashes every now and then, she observed, much like those that musicians get when "they see or hear the structure of an entire symphony or opera." He couldn't always hold on to it or verbalize it, but when it came, he suddenly understood how all kinds of disparate things fit together. Though Stimson could justly complain that trying to follow the president's intuitive thought processes as he moved from one idea to the next in no logical order was "very much like chasing a vagrant beam of sunshine around a vacant room," Roosevelt made up for the defects of an undisciplined mind with a profound ability to integrate a vast multitude of details into a larger pattern that gave shape and direction to the stream of events.

• • •

The president returned to Washington Monday afternoon, December 16, tanned, rested, and in excellent humor. The following day, at his press conference, he puffed hard on his cigarette and then revealed his startling plan. He had heard a great deal of nonsense about finances in the past few days, he began, by people who could think only in traditional terms. Whereas banal minds assumed that either the Neutrality Acts of the late 1930s or the Johnson Act, barring loans to defaulters on World War I debts, would have to be repealed in order to allow loans or gifts to England, he had a much simpler notion in mind—a gentlemen's agreement that eliminated the foolish dollar sign entirely, and allowed England to make repayment in kind after the war.

"Well, let me give you an illustration: Suppose my neighbor's home catches on fire, and I have a length of garden hose four or five hundred feet away. If he can take my garden hose and connect it up with his hydrant, I may help to put out his fire. Now what do I do? I don't say to him before that operation, 'Neighbor, my garden hose cost me $15; you have to pay me $15 for it.' What is the transaction that goes on? I don't want $15—I want my garden hose back after the fire is over. All right. If it goes through the fire all right, intact, without any damage to it, he gives it back to me and thanks me very much for the use of it." And if the hose was damaged by the fire, he could simply replace it.

The president's idea, Frances Perkins observed, "was really based upon very old, primitive and countrified ways of doing things. . . . He could draw very large deductions and large plans from such simple operations which he had observed in his childhood and youth, which were common in the country and seemed natural, like lending hoses or ladders to a neighbor when his house was on fire, and the neighbor would reciprocate when he could." Even if the ladder burned and the neighbor was unable to repay the actual money it cost, then, "the next potato crop he gets, he comes around with a few barrels of potatoes for you." The moral of the story was clear: by sending supplies to the British now, the U. S. would be abundantly repaid by the increase to its own security.

• • •

The following week, the president took his argument for lend-lease to the American people in a fireside chat that would later become known as the "arsenal for democracy" speech. A fierce debate over aid to England was engulfing the nation, on street corners and college campuses, in labor halls and country stores, in corporate boardrooms and family living rooms. In September, a powerful noninterventionist organization, the America First Committee, had been formed. Sixty thousand citizens were already on board, and it was said to be gaining members "like a house afire." America Firsters were convinced that extensive aid to Britain would inevitably drag

America into the war. It was important for the president to find the words that would undercut the opposition and set the tone for the congressional debate that would follow the introduction of the lend-lease bill.

The speech went through seven drafts. Speechwriters Sam Rosenman and Robert Sherwood came to live at the White House for the week. It was Harry Hopkins who suggested the key phrase "arsenal of democracy." Roosevelt, Sherwood recalled, "really enjoyed working on this speech for, with the political campaign over, it was the first chance he had had in months and even years to speak his mind with comparative freedom."

As the appointed hour of 9 p.m. approached, theater owners in New York noted a decided drop in attendance: thousands of people who would otherwise have gone to the movies stayed home to listen to the president's speech. Roosevelt began by telling the nation that there was no hope of a negotiated peace with Germany. "No man can tame a tiger into a kitten by stroking it. There can be no appeasement with ruthlessness." If Britain fell, the "unholy alliance," which now included Japan as well as Germany and Italy, would continue its drive to conquer the world, and then "all of us in all the Americas would be living at the point of a gun."

Next he summoned the American people to become "the great arsenal of democracy" by showing "the same resolution, the same sense of urgency, the same spirit of patriotism and sacrifice as we would show were we at war." This job, he emphasized, "cannot be done merely by superimposing on the existing productive facilities the added requirements for defense." Americans must discard the notion of "business as usual." He admitted that "there is risk in any course we may take," but he insisted that there was less chance of getting into war if the U.S. did all it could to support the nations fighting the Axis.

In arguing for aid to Britain as an alternative to war, Roosevelt crystallized what a large number of his fellow citizens were thinking and feeling. A recent Gallup poll revealed that a clear majority of Americans favored military aid to Britain but 88 percent of those polled said they would vote against American entrance into the war. As long as lend-lease was positioned as a substitute for war, it would gather wide support. "I call for this national effort," the president concluded, "in the name of this nation which we love and honor and which we are privileged and proud to serve. I call upon our people with absolute confidence that our common cause will greatly succeed."

On the night of the fireside chat, the Germans subjected London to the heaviest bombing attack of the war, hoping to counter the effect that Roosevelt's words might produce on British morale. A large part of the old city was destroyed. The ancient Guildhall, seat of the city's municipal government since the days of William the Conqueror, was reduced to a blackened shell, as was the historic house off Fleet Street where Dr. Samuel Johnson had written many of his famous works. Eight Christopher Wren churches and the Central Criminal Court, better known as Old Bailey, were also hit and burned. "The havoc," one reporter wrote, "was comparable only to that wrought in the Great Fire of 1666."

"London has nothing to smile about at the moment," Germany's propaganda minister, Joseph Goebbels, recorded in his diary. The Reichminister was mistaken. At 3:30 a.m., thousands of Londoners were crowded around their radios listening to the president's broadcast. His words, Churchill told Roosevelt the next day, stirred hope and confidence. "When I visited the still-burning ruins today, the spirit of the Londoners was as high as in the first days of the indiscriminate bombing in September, four months ago.

"I thank you for testifying before all the world that the future safety and greatness of the American Union are intimately concerned with the upholding and the effective arming of that indomitable spirit."

• • •

Labor leader Walter Reuther, architect of the historic sit-down strikes in Detroit in the mid-thirties, answered the president's call for an end to "business as usual" with a provocative plan to manufacture war planes in automobile plants. Production of planes, he pointed out, was 30 percent behind schedule and would continue to lag as long as the aircraft industry continued to rely on the "slow and costly methods of hand-tooled custom made production." Though Detroit had mass-produced four million cars the previous year, the combined production of all the airplane manufacturers in 1939 was eighteen hundred planes. "Conventional methods will never bring results in unconventional warfare," Reuther argued.

Reuther's plan was based on the theory that plane- and auto-making were alike at many steps. Instead of building entirely new aircraft plants which could not be put into operation for eighteen months, he proposed adapting existing automotive machinery to aircraft manufacture. "We propose to transform the entire unused capacity of the auto industry into one huge plane production unit."

The plan called for the president to appoint an aviation production board of nine members, three each representing government, management, and labor. The board would have complete authority to supervise and coordinate the mass production of airplanes in the auto industry. Each auto plant would be asked the make the parts it could best manufacture—Buick might put out the crank shafts, Dodge the cylinders, and Hudson the valves—and then two central plants would be used to assemble the planes.

The announcement of the Reuther plan created a sensation in the press. Columnist Dorothy Thompson called it "the most important event" in weeks, and columnist Walter Lippmann claimed the proposal held historic importance because it represented "the first great plan which organized labor had offered in its status not of a hired man but of the responsible partner."

Roosevelt's immediate response was equally positive. "It is well worth our while," he wrote William Knudsen, "to give a good deal of attention to this program." But even before a meeting between Knudsen and Reuther was arranged, the attacks from both the aircraft and the automobile industries began. Though planes and autos were alike to a point, the industrialists argued, the higher degree of precision required to produce a delicately balanced plane demanded special skills, special equipment, and hand-held operations. There was some truth to this argument, but the problem was not insurmountable, as was evidenced by the fact that, under contracts let earlier in the year, the Cadillac plant in Detroit was already at work manufacturing the most precise parts of the Allison engine, while Murray & Briggs were stamping wing parts for Douglas bombers. What was insurmountable was the reluctance of the aircraft industry to cheapen production methods and lower prices at a time when the government was prepared to pay any price for the planes it so desperately needed. A similar reluctance affected the auto industry, which was enjoying its most profitable season in years as the reviving economy allowed Americans to buy some of the comforts they had been unable to afford for so long.

Under the weight of industry's attacks, the excitement about the Reuther plan faded. By the time Knudsen finally sat down to talk with Reuther, the plan was already dead. "Mr. Knudsen and I had met previously on opposite sides of the table," a bitter Reuther told the press after the fruitless meeting. "I thought on this matter of national defense we might sit on the same side. I was mistaken."

The hostile reaction to the Reuther plan had deeper roots than the fear of losing profits. "The fear," correspondent I. F. Stone concluded, "was a fear of losing power, a fear of democracy in industry as instinctive as the fear and hatred kings felt for parliament." Historian Bruce Catton reached a similar conclusion. The problem, he wrote, was that "labor had grown up and had ideas. This wasn't going be be like the last war, with the trade associations running industry and [Samuel] Gompers exhorting the boys not to strike. . . . Labor was coming up to the quarter deck just as if it had a right to be there, making suggestions about how the ship ought to be handled." Treasury Secretary Henry Morgenthau expressed the same sentiment in more succinct terms: "There is only one thing wrong with this proposal," he warned Roosevelt. "It comes from the wrong source."

It would take the attack on Pearl Harbor and American entry into the war to create a receptive audience for Reuther's vision of mass-producing airplanes in automobile plants. But in the meantime, precious time was lost.

• • •

The Christmas holidays found the White House in a state of cheerful confusion, with dozens of houseguests coming and going—some staying only for the night, some for a few days, others for longer stretches. There was Sara Roosevelt, the president's mother, who brought her maid and took up residence in the Rose Suite, the principal guest quarters on the second floor, which the queen of England had occupied during the royal visit in 1939.

There was Crown Princess Juliana of the Netherlands, who arrived with her two little daughters and a retinue of servants. There were Elliott Roosevelt and FDR, Jr., with his wife, infant son, and nursemaid. There was an odd assortment of single men occupying various bedrooms on the third floor, including Eleanor's younger brother, Hall; Franklin's old friend Harry Hooker; and Eleanor's new friend Joe Lash.

Despite the full household, Eleanor managed to slip away for several days to New York, where she lunched with author Ernest Hemingway, whose book *For Whom the Bell Tolls* was currently on the best-seller list; saw Ethel Barrymore in *The Corn Is Green;* enjoyed an excellent production of the opera *Tristan and Isolde;* and finished her Christmas shopping at Arnold Constable, where she bought eighteen dozen pairs of nylon-silk hose and fourteen sets of matching ties and handkerchiefs. In her customary fashion, Eleanor had begun shopping for this Christmas the day after the previous Christmas; she couldn't bear the anxiety of waiting until the last minute, she once told a friend, but preferred to stretch the process over the entire year, taking comfort in the gifts that were accumulating month by month in her special Christmas closet.

The president, White House housekeeper Henrietta Nesbitt reported, was in a happy mood when Eleanor returned. "He was just bursting with news." For weeks, he had been trying to make arrangements to bring Prince Olav to Washington from London as a surprise Christmas present for Princess Martha and the children, and finally everything had been worked out. How was he getting here? Eleanor asked, knowing how difficult it was to secure any form of transportation from Europe. "By clipper," Roosevelt announced. "I arranged it."

Eleanor spent the morning after she returned going over menus with Mrs. Nesbitt. The week before Christmas was a trying time for the household staff. Besides the houseful of guests, there was a special round of parties—a formal reception for the members of the judiciary, a state dinner in honor of Crown Princess Juliana, and a large reception for White House employees and their families. Mrs. Nesbitt did not deal well with added stress. A plain, unimaginative woman of German stock with a stern face and a dark bun pulled tightly at the nape of her neck, Mrs. Nesbitt supervised a staff of twenty-six, including cooks, butlers, ladies' maids, and chambermaids. She was not a professional housekeeper—Eleanor had originally hired her in the mid-twenties to bake pies and strudels for large parties at Hyde Park—but she was thrifty, and Eleanor was determined to keep a tight rein on expenses at the White House.

For years, the president had pleaded with Eleanor to find a new housekeeper to replace Mrs. Nesbitt. All his life, he had loved good food—he was especially fond of quail and pheasant cooked so rare as to be bloody. He loved oyster crabs, out-of-the-way country cheeses, and peach cobbler. But Mrs. Nesbitt maintained that a proper diet consisted of "plain foods, plainly prepared." She served the same simple meals over and over again, to the point where White House guests could predict by the day of the week what they would have for dinner—tongue with caper sauce on Mondays, boiled beef on Tuesdays, roast beef and mashed potatoes on Wednesdays. The word was out that the White House cuisine was impossibly drab, dull, and overcooked.

For the president, who rarely had a chance to eat out in restaurants because of his paralysis, Mrs. Nesbitt was a unique cross to bear. But, true to form, he could not bring himself to fire her. So Mrs. Nesbitt—or "Fluffy," as she was called behind her back—remained at her post, month after month, year after year. Elliott Roosevelt recalled various dinners at the White House when Missy, "always handsome in a dinner gown," would catch the president's eye as some overcooked dish appeared. They would smile knowingly at one another, proceed to eat as much as they could bear, and then rummage up egg sandwiches in the little kitchen off the president's study.

As long as Mrs. Nesbitt remained in charge of the kitchen, her concept of what should be eaten prevailed. She insisted, for instance, on serving Roosevelt broccoli even though he let everyone know that he didn't like it. "Fix it anyhow," she told the cooks; "he *should* like it." Once, when royal guests were dining with the president, the call came to the kitchen for hot coffee. Mrs. Nesbitt sent iced tea instead. "It was better for them," she said.

The housekeeper's personal tastes governed breakfasts as well. "My God!" the president exclaimed one morning to Grace Tully. "Doesn't Mrs. Nesbitt know that there are breakfast foods besides oatmeal? It's been served to me morning in and morning out for months and months now and I'm sick and tired of it!" Later that day, he called Tully in for dictation. Leaning back in his chair, he held in his hand an advertisement for various cereals he had torn from the morning paper. "Corn Flakes! 13 ounce package, 19 cents! Post Toasties! 13 ounce package, 19 cents! Cream of Wheat! two for 27 cents! . . . Now take this gentle reminder to Mrs. Nesbitt."

When Mrs. Nesbitt failed to respond to his gentle reminders, Roosevelt turned to Eleanor. "Do you remember," he asked her in a memo, "that about a month ago I got sick of chicken because I got it (between lunch and dinner) at least six times a week? The chicken situation has definitely improved, but 'they' have substituted sweetbreads, and for the past month I have been getting sweetbreads about six times a week. I am getting to the point where my stomach positively rebels and this does not help my relations with foreign powers. I bit two of them today." Eleanor must have relayed the message, but the sweetbreads kept coming until the president sent Mrs. Nesbitt an ultimatum, telling her he did not want to see sweetbreads again for at least two months!

Unfortunately for the president, Eleanor had absolutely no taste for fine food. Her own cooking was limited to scrambling eggs, and she never thought about what she was eating. To her mind, good conversation created a good meal; the food was secondary. Though she tried to respond to the president's specific requests, the White House food remained, "to put it mildly," frequent visitor John Gunther observed, "undistinguished."

If the food was undistinguished, the company was not. The president loved the bustle of Christmas, the festive atmosphere, the holly that decked the mansion, and the gay conversations. Whether greeting guests on a receiving line or sharing a dinner, he was a genial host, charming and attentive. If the conversation flagged, he could always get it going by asking a question, telling a story, or exchanging a piece of gossip. Clever company and bright conversation stimulated him; talk was his favorite form of relaxation.

This Christmas, the president took added pleasure in the arrival of a new puppy named Fala, a gift from his cousin Margaret Suckley. He had longed for a puppy for years, he told his cousin as he lifted the little Scottish terrier into his arms, but Eleanor did not consider the White House a proper place to bring up a dog. Roosevelt had had pets before, but Fala became his friend in a way no other pet had been. Fala accompanied the president everywhere, eating his meals in Roosevelt's study, sleeping in a chair at the foot of his bed. Within a few weeks of his arrival, the puppy was sent to the hospital with a serious intestinal disturbance. He had discovered the White House kitchen, and everyone was feeding him. When he came home, Roosevelt issued a stern order to the entire White House staff: "Not even one crumb will be fed to Fala except by the President." From then on, Fala was in perfect health.

"In years to come," author William Klingaman has written, "many Americans would remember December 25, 1940, as one of the happiest Christmases of their lives." Though there were terrible problems abroad, the economy at home was showing signs of prosperity for the first time in more than a decade. Factories were working double shifts; the railroads were adding personnel and equipment, steel production was on the rise. Unemployment had fallen by nearly two million since the previous year. People had money now and were spending it. Automobile manufacturers were looking to their biggest year since 1929. Restaurant operators were enjoying a marked increase in business; people were ordering prime steak for the first time in years. Gift buying in department stores that December, *The New York Times* reported, approached "an orgy of spending as if customers were determined to show there was at least one country that enjoyed peace and good will."

For her part, Eleanor seemed more driven than usual, racing from one event to the next, helping Santa Claus hand out toys to seven hundred needy children from the stage of a local theater, attending the annual Christmas party for the Salvation Army, greeting a community chorus of Negro carolers and looking in on a neighborhood celebration at Green's Court, a squalid alley dwelling within sight of the Capitol building. "Here life is not so pleasant," she conceded, "but for another year we may hope for fewer alleys and better places to live in."

• • •

On January 6, 1941, the president was scheduled to present his lend-lease program to Congress in his annual State of the Union Address. While the speech was being drafted, Eleanor was reading *And Beacons Burn Again,* a new book by a British author. It would not be the landed gentry that would save England, the book argued, but the miners and the workers and the people from the slums. "Here is something to make us swell with pride," Eleanor wrote in her column on New Year's Day, "for it proves that our American conception of equality . . . is putting faith in the place it should be, in the strength and capacity of the average human being. Justice for all, security in certain living standards, a recognition of the dignity and the right of an individual human being without regard to his race, creed or color—these are the things for which vast numbers of our citizens will willingly sacrifice themselves."

"Eleanor was forever discussing how the world would look after the war," her friend Trude Pratt Lash later observed, "and finally her ideas took hold in the president's call for four freedoms in his State of the Union." The speech had gone through three or four drafts, Sam Rosenman recalled, when the president suddenly announced "he had an idea for a peroration." He paused, gazed at the ceiling, and then told his secretary to take down his words. As his speechwriters listened, he slowly dictated what would turn out to be the most memorable part of the speech—a call for a world based on "four essential human freedoms": freedom of speech, freedom of worship, freedom from want, and freedom from fear. Eleanor never claimed credit for anything her husband did or said, and there is no way of tracing the direct connection between Eleanor's ruminations about democracy and Franklin's concept of four freedoms, but the link seems obvious.

Eleanor was seated in the president's box next to Missy, Lorena Hickok, and Princess Martha, who was elegantly dressed, reporters noted, in a black coat and silver fox, when Roosevelt entered the House chamber at 2:03 p.m. The speech began on a somber note: "As your President, performing my constitutional duty to 'give to the Congress information of the state of the union,' I find it unhappily necessary to report that the future and the safety of our country and of our democracy are overwhelmingly involved in events far beyond our borders." Because American security depended on defeat of the Axis, he explained, he was asking Congress for authority and funds to continue sending aid to England and other democracies fighting the Axis powers even if these nations could no longer pay with ready cash. "Let us say to the democracies: We Americans are vitally concerned in your defense of freedom."

As the country committed itself to national defense, he went on, it must never forget the goals for which it was fighting: equality of opportunity, jobs for those who could work, security for the needy, the ending of special privilege for the few, the preservation of civil liberties for all. Leaning forward in her seat, Eleanor smiled broadly as she heard these words, and the smile remained on her face as the president presented his vision of a new world founded on four freedoms. Since the beginning of the war, she had challenged her husband to recognize that the concept of a genuine national defense also encompassed better housing, work training, equal opportunity, and expanded health programs. Now, as the president gave eloquent voice to the ideas about democracy that were uppermost in her mind, she was elated.

Curiously, Eleanor's gratification led to a rare lapse of judgment. In the column she wrote the afternoon of the speech, she angrily observed that the Republicans had failed to applaud the president's address. "It looked to me as though those men were saying to the country as a whole, 'we are Republicans first. We represent you here in Congress not as citizens of the U.S. in a period of crisis, but as members of a political party which seeks primarily to promote its own partisan interests.' This is to me shocking and terrifying. There was running through my mind as I watched them, in what would have been an act of childish spite, if it had not been such a serious moment in history, the lines of a song which was popular when I was young: 'I don't want to play in your yard. I don't love you any more.' "

Reaction to Eleanor's comments was swift and savage. Republican Representative Edith Nourse told the House that Mrs. Roosevelt's suggestion that all members applaud "presents a new concept in American constitutional theory. Under our form of government, members of Congress are not elected to applaud the official utterances of the White House, but to frame legislation. The suggestion of a duty to applaud appears to me a dangerous and unwholesome manifestation of war hysteria." Representative Hoffman of Michigan took the argument even further, charging that "the Roosevelts apparently have in some way gotten the idea they are entitled to receive homage and applause as our King and Queen."

• • •

As Roosevelt approached his third inaugural, critics lamented his deviousness, his lack of candor, his capricious experimentation, his tendency to ingratitude. His character flaws were widely discussed—his stubbornness, his vanity, his occasional vindictiveness, his habit of yessing callers just to be amiable. Former aide Raymond Moley believed he had succumbed over the years to the "intensifying and exhilarating effect of power," to the unlovely habit of "telling, not asking," to an "irritable certitude" that led him to ascribe "self-interest or cowardice or subtle corruption or stupidity" to people who questioned his decisions.

But the critics' complaints were submerged by the wave of favorable publicity that accompanied Franklin Roosevelt's historic third term. His hair was thinner and grayer, reporters noted, his face heavier and more deeply lined; yet there was the same captivating smile in his eyes and on his lips, the same bright forehead, the same mannerism of tossing his head before replying to a question. His physical condition, his doctor said, was "the best in many years." As always, he ate heartily and enjoyed a nightly cocktail. His weight was a perfect 187½ pounds, and thrice weekly he continued to swim in the White House pool. Crises, wars, campaigns notwithstanding, he generally managed to sleep eight hours a night, from midnight to eight. "One of the grand things about him is that he can relax," Dr. Ross McIntire said. "In the main he has the ability to put his troubles aside when he shouldn't carry them with him."

The day before the inauguration, *The New York Times Magazine* painted a glowing portrait of a president who still retained an astonishing buoyancy despite the strenuous times. The challenge of war, it was suggested, had added a new dimension to his vitality. "Serious but not grim, concerned but not worried," reporter Charles Hurd wrote, "in confidence and vigor of assurance he is the same man who told the American people, 'The only thing we have to fear is fear itself.' " The article went on to describe the long hours the president worked, the voluminous correspondence he handled, the variety of newspapers he read, and the numbers of conferences he held.

"The Presidency and its problems have nevertheless left their mark on Mr. Roosevelt," the *Times* concluded. "Though he gives the impression of cheerfulness, it is cheerfulness without all the spontaneity associated with the first flush of the New Deal," and though he appears optimistic, "after nearly eight years correspondents have learned that the President does not always reveal his true feelings."

With this concluding assessment Eleanor heartily agreed. Still puzzled, after nearly thirty-five years of marriage, by her husband's inability to share himself openly with anyone, Eleanor remarked to Joe Lash that those final paragraphs of the *Times* piece perfectly captured the frame of mind of the president in the days before his fifty-ninth birthday. He had kept his own counsel for so long, she observed, that it had become "part of his nature not to talk to anyone of intimate matters."

Over the years, many tried to penetrate the president's reticence, but few succeeded. "The President talked so much," Frances Perkins recalled, "and yet, all through this talkativeness, there ran a kind of reserve. I saw him often: he dropped the curtain over himself. He never told you, or anyone else, just what was going on inside his mind—inside his emotions—inside his real intentions in life. . . . I think he never intended to reveal himself."

A week before the inauguration, Supreme Court Justice Felix Frankfurter begged Stimson to see more of the president and seek out opportunities for more talks alone with him. Stimson told Frankfurter he had been keeping away because he did not like to bother him. "Frankfurter said that was wrong," Stimson recorded in his diary, "that he was a very lonely man and that he was rather proud and didn't like to ask people to come to him but that he was sure that he would welcome my approaches, if I would make them."

To be sure, Harry Hopkins provided a companionship that comforted many lonely hours. Night after night, Roosevelt sat in his study with Harry, talking about the war, sharing a meal, exchanging gossip. There were times, Hopkins told the president, when he thought it might be easier if he found a place of his own. But Roosevelt always insisted he stay. "He seems to want to have someone around he can talk to when he wants to," Hopkins recognized, "or not talk to."

But even Harry Hopkins was replaceable. "Each imagines he is indispensable to the President," Eleanor once remarked. "All would be surprised at their dispensability. The President uses those who suit his purposes. He makes up his own mind and discards people when they no longer fulfill a purpose of his."

Still, it must be borne in mind that the president never seemed bothered by the loneliness ascribed to him by others. "He had more serenity than any man I have ever seen," Attorney General Francis Biddle said. "One felt that nothing ultimately would upset him." If friends and family were frustrated by his lack of capacity for intimacy, he regarded it as a strength.

• • •

"Bright-eyed and smiling," Eleanor was "just about the most composed person" during the inaugural festivities, the *Washington Post* observed. Not a trace of the fear so palpable in her at the time of the first inaugural remained. On the contrary, she seemed radiant, full of life, good-humored. Her eight years as first lady had opened up to her a new and irresistible world, filled with extraordinary accomplishment, pride, and prestige. Her old fear of failure, her melancholy, though not entirely disappearing, had substantially abated. In support of her belief that the position of first lady could be used as a power for good, she had committed herself to an astonishing range of activities which had earned her the lasting gratitude of millions of citizens.

Her years as first lady had also brought a positive change in her appearance. She had removed from her hair the ugly black hairnet that had accompanied her for too long in public life. Dressed by day in simple, tailored clothes and by night in elegant gowns, she walked with a more confident step, her naturally high complexion enhanced by a small amount of rouge.

To be sure, the first lady had her own share of critics. The hectic travel and honest talk that made her a heroine in some quarters rendered her vulnerable to attack in others. Columnist Westbrook Pegler called her "Madam President," "Empress Eleanor," and "The Gab." Why couldn't she stay home with her husband, she was frequently asked, "and tend to her knitting as an example for other women to follow"? After visiting the White House on a tour, one woman gave Eleanor unsolicited advice. "Instead of tearing around the country, I think you should stay at home and personally see that the White House is clean. I soiled my white gloves yesterday morning on the stair-railing. It is disgraceful." All these resentments came together in the 1940 campaign in a prominent button: "We don't want Eleanor, either."

Eleanor appeared unruffled by most of her critics. "If I could be worried about mud-slinging, I would have been dead long ago," she said. "Almost any woman in the White House during these years of need would have done what I have done"—become a voice for the poor, the migrants, the Negroes. Though this was certainly not true, Eleanor's insistence that she was only trying to do what others would have done, and did not deserve all the attention she received, only added to her charm.

"She is the President's Number One Adviser on sociological problems," *U.S. News* proclaimed. Many people assumed that the New Deal's domestic program would be abandoned as Roosevelt shifted his focus to war and defense, but "they reckoned without the President's wife. . . . She never lets the President or his administrators think that all is well, that there is time to rest from advancing their liberal objectives. She backs the President's most courageous self. . . . No matter how deeply absorbed he may become in international affairs, she will keep him from forgetting the New Deal."

• • •

A family reunion was arranged at Hyde Park for the weekend before the inauguration. Anna and John had flown in from from Seattle; Elliott was en route from Texas; and FDR, Jr., and Ethel had come up from Washington. "The nearer I draw to Hyde Park, the more excited I become," Eleanor wrote in her column, admitting a particular pleasure at the thought of seeing Anna. "With my daughter I feel the bond that exists with any child, but in addition there has grown between us the deepest understanding such as exists with an intimate friend. John is not just my son-in-law, but one of my dearest friends. I can be serious or I can be gay with Anna and John without any thought of age or generation to divide us."

"It was wonderful to have two full days in the country," Eleanor wrote. "We walked and talked, ate too much, and slept too little which is always the way of family reunions for once conversation starts time slips by unnoticed!"

Sara, too, was in her element, delighted to have her son at home, surrounded by family and friends before the White House claimed him for another four years. For every one of the guests she had a gay smile, but most of her attention, as always, was focused on her brilliant son. "I always have been proud of him and still am," she said.

The dinner table looked resplendent on Saturday night, January 11, 1941, with the president at one end and Sara at the other. In the course of the conversation, Eleanor raised the troubling question of housing under the defense program. During her last trip to the West Coast, she had seen the devastating effects of overcrowding in Washington State, where the navy yard and shipbuilding construction had attracted thousands of workers from all over the country, part of the first wave of what would be the greatest internal immigration in American history. In Bremerton, she noted, every habitable shack and shed had been rented, scores of families were crowded into unsanitary trailer camps, and two thousand children were without schools. "I think we are going to have to be a nuisance about these questions if we are going to be fair to people all over this country," she believed. "What we do now must be with an eye to the well-being of the people who are going to do the work essential to our defense. We have no right to ask them to sacrifice their home life to live in a way not compatible to our way."

In response, the president said he had just appointed Charles Palmer, an Atlanta real-estate man, to head the new Division of Defense Housing, with broad powers to assure speedy construction in connection with rearmament and military-training programs. This was not the response Eleanor wanted to hear. From her own sources she had learned that Palmer's interest in public housing "arose from his desire to rid Atlanta of slums that were depreciating his own holdings." In contrast to Eleanor's belief that "in the long run all housing is defense housing," Palmer had declared that "sociology was no part of his job, that overcrowding would remain the private builder's opportunity." For weeks, Palmer had been under fire in the liberal paper *PM* for his belief that government construction was not needed since the overwhelming percentage of defense housing could be handled by private firms. Now, this was the man the president had chosen to coordinate the government's housing program!

"Would he be sensitive to problems of low-cost housing, schools and the like in defense areas," Eleanor wanted to know. The president became restless, impatient. But, despite the uneasy glances flung at her by Sara, Eleanor persisted, saying "she had heard that Palmer was partial to real estate people." Clearly annoyed at this point, the president agreed to "appoint someone with Palmer to watch for these things." But, Eleanor countered, would that person "have any authority?"

While Franklin and Eleanor were arguing, Sara motioned to the butler to bring the president's wheelchair to the table. Furious at Eleanor's hectoring, Sara stood behind her son and had him shifted to the other end of the table. In the past, Sara's obvious reproof would have left Eleanor distraught—at a parallel family dinner two decades before, Eleanor had collapsed in tears when Sara turned on her about something—but at this point in her life, Eleanor had enough confidence to confront both her husband and her mother-in-law on an issue she considered important. After dinner, Anna, John, and FDR, Jr., all congratulated her on having stuck to her guns.

"My mother-in-law belonged to the established world of the last century," Eleanor once wrote. "She accepted its shibboleths without questioning." To her, "there were certain obligations she as a privileged person must fulfill. She fed the poor, assisted them with money, helped them with medical expenses. This was a form of charity required of her." She simply could not accept the idea that "human beings had rights as human beings"—a right to a decent house, a job, education, human dignity.

The next day, Sara invited the son of Arnulfo Arias, the president of Panama, to dine with the family. He was "a dandyish" young man, Lash observed, whom Sara affectionately called "Robertito." When it was learned that young Arias had bragged to reporters that he was lunching privately with the president, FDR, Jr., told his grandmother she was being taken in. Refusing to acknowledge this, Sara announced that she wanted to invite him to the White House for the inaugural festivities. "It fell to Mrs. Roosevelt," Lash recorded in his diary, "to tell her it could not be done. [Mrs. James] complained that she was never allowed to have any of *her* friends, an obvious dig at the kind of friends Mrs. R. invited."

How far off seemed the early days, when Eleanor had first started to work for the League of Women Voters. At that time, in 1921, she had entered a world of feminist women whose values and behavior were totally foreign to Sara—women who lived with other women; active, accomplished women who did things outside the home; independent women, well satisfied with their lives and convinced that they could not possibly live in any other way.

The apprenticeship of Eleanor Roosevelt had begun with two remarkable League women, Elizabeth Read and Esther Lape. Read, an honors graduate of Smith College, was an accomplished lawyer; Lape, a Wellesley graduate, had taught English at Swarthmore and Barnard and then achieved prominence as a publicist. Brilliant, hardworking, and ambitious, they had found in their love for one another the freedom from conventional marriage that allowed them to live according to their own desires, surrounded by music and books. Eleanor was immediately entranced by the stimulating lives these women led, with discussions of politics and public policy at dinner, and poetry readings after dessert. Their book-lined house in Greenwich Village reminded her of the happy days she had spent at Mademoiselle Souvestre's school in England.

When Eleanor first met Read and Lape, she was still suffering the effects of having discovered her husband's love affair with Lucy Mercer. She sorely lacked confidence. She needed appreciation and she was lonely. She found in Elizabeth and Esther's community of women the strength and encouragement to do things on her own, to explore her own talents, to become a person in her own right. Over the years, the friendships deepened into an intimacy which would continue for the rest of Eleanor's life.

Through her work with the League, Eleanor met two other lifelong friends, Nancy Cook and Marion Dickerman. Cook, a vital, tough-looking young woman, was the director of the Women's Division of the New York State Democratic Party. Dickerman, a tall, soft-spoken scholar whose grim countenance hid a dry wit, was a teacher and vice-principal at Todhunter, an exclusive girls school in Manhattan. Like Elizabeth and Esther, Nancy and Marion lived together in what has been described as a "Boston marriage." Over the years, both women had been actively involved in the long struggle for women's suffrage, the movement to abolish child labor, and the efforts to establish maximum working hours.

There is every evidence that the four women, along with half a dozen others (including Elinor Morgenthau and Caroline O'Day, members of the Women's Division of the New York Democratic State Committee, social worker Molly Dewson, and AP reporter Lorena Hickok), played a substantial role in the education of Eleanor Roosevelt, tutoring her in politics, strategy, and public policy, encouraging her to open up emotionally, building her sense of confidence and self-esteem. In contrast to the distant relationship she had with most of the males in her life at this juncture, her relationship with her female friends was warm and open, frolicsome and relaxed. They kissed and hugged each other when they met; they had pillow fights at night; they wrote long and loving letters when they were apart; they challenged the traditional sense of what was possible.

When Eleanor first came into contact with these bold and successful women, she found herself in awe of the professional status they had acquired. "If I had to go out and earn my own living," she conceded, "I doubt if I'd even make a very good cleaning woman. I have no talents, no experience, no training for anything." But all this would change as Eleanor, encouraged by her friends, began to discover a range of abilities she never knew she had—remarkable organizing skills, superb judgment, practical insight, and astonishing endurance. In the space of two years, with the guidance of her female colleagues, Eleanor emerged as a major force in New York public life, speaking out in behalf of political reform, worker's rights, and children's issues, sought after for statements in newspapers, chosen to serve on all manner of committees. At the same time, she began teaching three days a week at Todhunter, organizing courses in literature, drama, and American history. "She loved it," Marion Dickerman recalled. "The girls worshiped her."

Though Franklin and Louis Howe sometimes joked about Eleanor's "squaws" and "she-men," they both recognized that she was becoming an excellent politician and that her tireless work around the state would inevitably redound to Franklin's credit. Even before polio had crippled Franklin, Howe had encouraged Eleanor to become actively involved in politics. Once the polio struck, Eleanor's ability to stand in for her husband became critical. Moreover, both Franklin and Louis genuinely liked Elizabeth and Esther, Nan and Marion, and found their conversation stimulating and absorbing.

For Sara, Eleanor's transformation was harder to accept. Sara was appalled at the idea of a well-bred woman's spending so much time away from home in the public eye. A woman's place was with her husband and her children. "My generation did not do those things," Sara explained. The more involved Eleanor became in politics, the less time she had to take Sara out to lunch or to pour tea for Sara's friends. "My mother-in-law was distressed and felt that I was not available, as I had been," Eleanor recalled.

Sara often displaced her criticisms onto Eleanor's friends, making them feel uncomfortable whenever they came to visit at Hyde Park, scanning their mannish suits and oxford shoes with disapproving eyes, glaring in bewilderment at their close-cropped hair. To Sara, they all looked alike: unkempt, unconventional, unnatural. Understanding the situation, Franklin suggested that Eleanor and her friends Nan and Marion build a cottage for themselves in the woods so they could have a place of their own to pursue their interests apart from Sara's. "My Missus and some of her female political friends want to build a shack on a stream in the back woods," Franklin explained to Elliott Brown, whom he asked to supervise the project. He then became actively involved in the building of the "shack"—a fieldstone house which eventually grew to accommodate twenty-two rooms.

"The peace of it is divine," a grateful Eleanor told her husband the first summer she spent at Val-Kill, in 1925. From that time forward, though she stayed at the Big House whenever Franklin and the children were at Hyde Park, Val-Kill became Eleanor's home—the first home of her own she had ever had. "Can you tell me *why* Eleanor wants to go over to Val-Kill cottage to sleep every night?" a perplexed Sara once asked one of Eleanor's friends. "Why doesn't she sleep here? This is her home. She belongs here."

The woman who in 1925 had been frightened by the prospect of earning her own living was in 1941 among the highest-paid lecturers in the country, pulling in $1,000 a lecture. Her syndicated column, "My Day," was printed in 135 newspapers, placing her on a par for circulation with Dorothy Thompson, Westbrook Pegler, and Raymond Clapper. And in 1938, the first installment of her autobiography, *This Is My Story,* had been published to widespread popular and critical acclaim. To be sure, as Eleanor recognized better than anyone, her success was due in no small part to the fact that she was the president's wife. Nonetheless, in April 1940, when it was not at all certain that Roosevelt would run for a third term, United Features had renewed her column for five additional years, a clear recognition that she had established herself in her own right.

So, in January 1941, when it fell to Eleanor, seated at the table in Sara's house, to tell her mother-in-law that her young Latin American friend was not welcome in *her* house, the big white house on Pennsylvania Avenue, it was clear that the balance of power between the two dominant women in the president's life had shifted.

• • •

The president was in high spirits on January 20, 1941, as he headed toward the Capitol for his inaugural. The sky was clear, the sun shining, and the Gallup poll showed that his public support had reached a new high of 71 percent. Seated in an open-air car, he flashed his familiar smile and waved his top hat to the thousands of well-wishers who waited for him at every point along the way.

At high noon, the president stood before a cheering crowd on Capitol Plaza and took the oath of office for a third time. Nineteen members of the Roosevelt family witnessed the historic moment, including Sara, Eleanor, and all five children. When he began to speak, the raking winter sun lit up the right side of his face like a cameo. His voice was clear; his gestures were strong; his speech was a summons to the spirit of democracy.

"There are men who believe that democracy . . . is limited as measured by a kind of mystical and artificial fate—that for some unexplained reason, tyranny and slavery have become the surging wave of the future—and that freedom is an ebbing tide. But we Americans know that is not true.

"A nation, like a person," he went on, "has a body which must be housed and fed and clad and a mind which must be educated and informed but it also has something deeper, something more permanent, something larger than the sum of its parts. It is that something which matters most to its future —which calls forth the most sacred guarding of its present. It is a thing for which we find it difficult—even impossible—to hit upon a single, simple word. And yet, we all understand what it is—the spirit—the faith of America."

• • •

The first problem facing Roosevelt after his inauguration was getting the Congress to pass the lend-lease bill. Introduced in the House as H.R. 1776, the controversial legislation authorized the president to transfer munitions and supplies for which Congress had appropriated money to "the government of any country whose defense the President deems vital to the defense of the U.S."

Opponents attacked the bill on two grounds: first, that it granted the president dictatorial powers, "to carry on," in Senator Robert Taft's words, "a kind of undeclared war all over the world"; second, that it would lead America inexorably into war. Administration spokesmen took the opposite tack. By allowing Britain to continue the fight against Germany, they argued, the bill was the last best hope for keeping America out of the war.

The situation the administration faced was tricky: debate was essential to develop a mass base of support, but every day taken up in discussion was another day lost in Britain's desperate struggle to ready itself for the expected invasion. "The lend-lease bill will furnish a bigger test than the merits of the bill itself," Washington correspondent David Lawrence wrote. "It is whether America can make a military decision of tremendous interest to her national safety without taking weeks and weeks to debate the issue."

The hearings began in the House Committee on Foreign Affairs in January, before an overflowing crowd of reporters and spectators. By noontime, all the seats in the high-ceilinged committee room had been taken, and still the curious kept coming; they stood in the corners, sat on the windowsills, and waited in long lines in the corridor outside. The first witness to testify against the bill was the recently resigned ambassador to Great Britain, Joseph Kennedy. For weeks, after an indiscreet interview with *Boston Globe* columnist Louis Lyons which lost him his ambassadorship, Kennedy had been flirting with the isolationists, tantalizing them with the prospect that he would make an open break with the administration and join their crusade against the war. But Roosevelt, knowing his man better than his opponents, had invited Kennedy to the White House for an early-morning talk in mid-January. Relaxing in his bedroom, the president allowed Kennedy to pour out his heart about the miserable treatment he had received from "the boys in the State Department" and "the President's hatchet men." Kennedy told the president he didn't think it was fair to wind up seven years of service in his administration with a bad record. He had gone in for everything the president wanted, and now the time had come to do something for the Kennedy family.

Nodding sympathetically, the president reminisced about the good times the two of them had had together over the years, and told Kennedy that once the lend-lease bill got through he would make sure the country recognized how valuable a public servant Joe Kennedy had been. Disarmed as always by Roosevelt's charm, Kennedy shifted the tone of the statement he had prepared for Congress so substantially that his isolationist friends felt betrayed. Though he said he opposed lend-lease in its present form because the powers of Congress in foreign affairs should be preserved, he came out for complete aid to Britain, parroting the administration's line that aid to Britain was the best means of avoiding war. It was a confusing statement, neither for nor against, exposing Kennedy to criticism from both sides. But Roosevelt, who had feared his former ambassador to England might lead the isolationist charge, was greatly relieved.

A few days after the ambassador's testimony, Anna Roosevelt's husband, John Boettiger, sent Kennedy a friendly note. "Somehow or other," Boettiger wrote, "I feel sure we are all thinking along the same lines and that the Roosevelts, the Kennedys and the Boettigers will be struggling shoulder to shoulder first to keep America out of war, but always to keep America free!" In a somewhat self-pitying reply, Kennedy told Boettiger, "if my statements and my position means that, outside of the ever loyal Boettigers I am to be a social outcast by the administration, well so be it.... At any rate, I am delighted that you and Anna were sweet enough to send a note and I appreciate it more than I can tell you."

Kennedy's delight would have been diminished had he seen the subsequent exchange of letters between Boettiger and the president, occasioned by Boettiger's decision to send his father-in-law a copy of Kennedy's note.

After thanking his son-in-law for sending Kennedy's note, Roosevelt wrote in unusually candid terms: "It is, I think a little pathetic that he worries about being, with his family, social outcasts. As a matter of fact, he ought to realize of course that he has only himself to blame for the country's opinion as to his testimony before the Committees. Most people and most papers got the feeling that he was blowing hot and blowing cold at the same time—trying to carry water on both shoulders.

"The truth of the matter is that Joe is and always has been a temperamental Irish boy, terrifically spoiled at an early age by huge financial success; thoroughly patriotic, thoroughly selfish and thoroughly obsessed with the idea that he must leave each of his nine children with a million dollars apiece when he dies (he has told me that often). He has a positive horror of any change in the present methods of life in America. To him, the future of a small capitalistic class is safer under a Hitler than under a Churchill. This is sub-conscious on his part and he does not admit it. . . . Sometimes I think I am 200 years older than he is!"

Despite the setback of Kennedy's ambivalent statement, the opposition continued its relentless attack against the bill, culminating in a powerful warning from Charles Lindbergh that H.R. 1776 was "another step away from democracy and another step closer to war." Fully expecting this line of attack, the president had two weapons waiting in reserve—Harry Hopkins and Wendell Willkie.

In early January, Roosevelt had sent Hopkins to London to meet with Churchill and obtain a firsthand impression of Britain's resolve and Britain's needs. The journey to London, aboard a Pan American Clipper, had taken five days over a circuitous route. When Hopkins arrived, he was "sick and shrunken and too tired even to unfasten his safety belt." Years later, Churchill's daughter-in-law, Pamela Churchill Harriman, recalled her shock at her first sight of the ill Hopkins, a dead cigarette in his mouth, a weary man in a large overcoat which he never took off.

But the thrill of his mission soon served to revive Hopkins' health. At the welcoming dinner in his honor, the story is told, Churchill, knowing that Hopkins was a social worker with no military background, deliberately directed the conversation to issues of economic and social reform, emphasizing that after the war he planned to modernize Britain's slum cottages with electricity and plumbing. "Mr. Churchill," Hopkins interrupted, "I don't give a damn about your cottagers. I've come over here to find out how we can help you beat this fellow Hitler." When he heard this, Churchill's face lit up; he straightened his shoulders and got up from the table. "Mr. Hopkins, come with me," he said, leading Hopkins to his study.

For the next four hours, Churchill confided the entire direction of his nation's affairs to the president's envoy. "And from this hour," Churchill wrote in his memoirs, "began a friendship between us which sailed serenely over all earthquakes and convulsions. He was the most faithful and perfect channel of communication between the President and me. . . . There he sat, slim, frail, ill, but absolutely glowing with refined comprehension of the Cause. It was to be the defeat, ruin, and slaughter of Hitler, to the exclusion of all other purposes, loyalties, or aims. . . . He was a crumbling lighthouse from which there shone the beams that led great fleets to harbour."

While Hopkins was in England, he spent almost every waking hour with Churchill—journeying with him to Scapa Flow, Scotland; dining together night after night; relaxing at Chequers, Churchill's country home. Proximity to the great man had its effect; Hopkins became an ardent admirer of Churchill and an absolute partisan of Britain's cause. At a small dinner party one evening, Hopkins rose to his feet. "I suppose you wish to know what I am going to say to President Roosevelt on my return. Well, I'm going to quote you one verse from that Book of Books. . . . 'Whither thou goest, I will go and where thou lodgest, I will lodge, thy people shall be my people, and thy God my God!' " Then, in his own words, he added, "Even to the end." When Hopkins sat down, Churchill's doctor, Lord Moran, looked over at Churchill and saw tears streaming down his face.

With their friendship sealed, Hopkins moved to elicit Churchill's help in the lend-lease debate. In early February, Churchill was working on a major speech to be broadcast throughout the world. At Roosevelt's request, Hopkins asked Churchill to skew the speech to American public opinion by promising that lend-lease was the best means to keep the Americans out of the war. Churchill readily complied, weaving Hopkins' suggestions together with a personal note he had just received from the president in the hands of a second envoy—Wendell Willkie. Just before Willkie left for London, Roosevelt, with shrewd insight, had asked him to come to the White House. He gave Willkie a letter of introduction to the prime minister with a verse from Longfellow in his own handwriting. In his speech on February 9, Churchill put the verse to brilliant use.

"In the last war," Churchill began, "the U.S. sent two million men across the Atlantic. But this is not a war of vast armies firing immense masses of shells at one another. We do not need the gallant armies which are forming throughout the American Union. We do not need them this year, nor next year, nor any year; that I can foresee."

"The other day," Churchill continued, Roosevelt had sent him a verse from Longfellow, which he said "applies to you people as it does to us. . . .

"Sail On, O Ship of State!
Sail On, O Union Strong and great!
Humanity with all its fears,
With all the hopes of future years,
Is hanging breathless on thy fate!

"What is the answer that I shall give in your name to this great man, the thrice-chosen head of a nation of 130 million. Here is the answer I will give to Mr. Roosevelt. Put your confidence in us. . . . We shall not fail or falter. . . . Give us the tools and we will finish the job."

When Willkie returned to the States on February 11, he went directly to the Hill to testify in behalf of the lend-lease bill. It was the most important testimony in six weeks of hearings. In a blue suit rumpled from the plane ride, with his hair drooping over one eye and his voice as hoarse as ever, Willkie declared that if we sat back and withdrew within ourselves there was no telling where "the madmen who are loose in the world" might strike next. With flashbulbs popping and twelve hundred people crowded against the marble walls, Willkie predicted that, "if the Republican party makes a blind opposition to the bill and allows itself to be presented to the American people as the isolationist party, it will never again gain control of the American government."

Repeatedly, Willkie found himself at odds with isolationists on the committee, who insisted on going over one by one the critical comments Willkie had made about Roosevelt during the campaign. "He was elected President," Willkie replied. "He is *my* President now." When asked about his prediction that if Roosevelt were elected America would be in the war by April 1941, Willkie smiled and said, "It was a bit of campaign oratory." The chamber burst into goodhearted laughter.

Eleanor, in her column that day, said she was "thankful beyond words" for Willkie's testimony. Her gratitude was not misplaced. The bill sailed through both houses with substantial majorities, and at ten minutes of four on the afternoon of March 11, a smiling Roosevelt signed lend-lease into law. Three hours later, the president declared the defense of Britain vital to the U.S. and authorized the navy to turn over to Britain thousands of naval guns and ammunition, three thousand charges for bombs, and two dozen PT boats. Full of confidence, the president told reporters he had already begun work on a supplemental request of $7 billion to implement lend-lease.

That night, as Big Ben struck midnight, Churchill stood up in Parliament to voice the gratitude of his people toward America for passing what he called "the most unsordid act in the history of any nation." With this act, he declared, "the most powerful democracy has, in effect, declared in a solemn statute that they will devote their overwhelming industrial and financial strength to insuring the defeat of Nazism." Put in simpler terms, a Londoner told journalist Molly Panter-Downes, "Thank God! The tanks are coming."

When Hopkins returned from England, a grateful Roosevelt designated him administrator of the lend-lease program, with a staff of thirty-five. While seventeen rooms were hastily cleared for Hopkins and his staff in the Federal Reserve Building, Hopkins continued to work out of his big bedroom on the second floor of the White House. There, from a card table set in the middle of his room, with documents and papers spilling off chairs and tables, he threw himself into what Pamela Churchill Harriman later called "one of the most massive undertakings in U.S. history."

The appointment provoked mixed reaction within the Cabinet. "The blind side of the President, when his personal friends are involved, seems to be growing blinder," Ickes lamented. "Hopkins has not the ability from any point of view intellectual or physical to carry such a job as this. . . ." Morgenthau, too, had his doubts. "I am just worried sick over it, because Hopkins isn't well enough." But Stimson held a more positive view. "The more I think of it," he recorded in his diary after listening to Hopkins' "thrilling" descriptions of Churchill's leadership and the situation in Britain, "the more I think it is a godsend that he should be at the White House and that the President should have sent him to Great Britain where he has gotten on such intimate terms with the people there. It's a real connection that helps and Hopkins himself is a man that I have grown to appreciate and to respect more and more the more I see him."

In the days that followed Hopkins' return, the president spent many hours with him, soaking up the information Hopkins had gathered while he was in England. In the course of his sojourn, Hopkins had talked with more than three hundred men and women, including all the important leaders of Parliament; he had visited defenses, soldiers, and air forces; he had seen Churchill in action with British crowds. He knew more about Britain's problems than any American. And with Hopkins, as with Eleanor, Roosevelt knew he was receiving a straightforward picture of the situation, an honest and unbiased account, filled with insight, intuition, and human detail.

"Upon his return from England," Marquis Childs wrote in *The Saturday Evening Post,* "Hopkins' friends sensed a change in him. He was more serious, and at the same time more detached, as though he were relieved, happy almost at having found something in which he could abandon his own personal destiny, submerging himself in a task of immeasurable magnitude and immeasurable risk." Reporters began comparing Hopkins to Woodrow Wilson's intimate envoy, Colonel Edward House, and soon, Childs noted, "a spate of invitations fell upon him—to write for syndicates at astronomical rates, to lecture, to talk on the record and off the record, to attend little intimate dinners of important people."

"It tore Eleanor's heart up," Eleanor's friend Martha Gellhorn later said, "that Harry could forget the hungry and unemployed. . . . In the New Deal he had been Eleanor's protégé; now he was FDR's. He was wittier and brighter in the second period but much nicer in the first."

For Roosevelt, the lend-lease triumph was not simply the passage of the bill but the successful education of the American public. When the hearings started, the country was divided down the middle on lend-lease, with 50 percent in favor, 50 percent against. By the time the bill passed, those in favor had risen to 61 percent.

"Yes," Roosevelt prophetically remarked a few days after the bill passed, "the decisions of our democracy may be slowly arrived at. But when that decision is made, it is proclaimed not with the voice of one man but with the voice of 130 million."

With the passage of lend-lease, Goebbels recorded in his diary, "the Führer finally gave his propagandists permission to attack America. It was high time. Now we shall let rip. Mrs. Roosevelt is shooting her mouth off around the country. If she were my wife, it would be a different story."

CHAPTER 9

"BUSINESS AS USUAL"

In celebration of the passage of lend-lease, Roosevelt set off on a ten-day fishing trip to Florida with his usual group of friends—Hopkins, Watson, and Dr. McIntire. Eleanor accompanied him to the train station, kissed him goodbye, and then promptly headed for New York, where she dined at the Lafayette Hotel with friends, went to see the play *The Doctor's Dilemma,* and met with the British War Relief Society. After returning to Washington the next morning, she entertained eighty people in the State Dining Room, visited with financier Bernard Baruch, attended a concert, delivered a lecture on race relations, and spent two hours with a group of Negro pilots who were training at the Tuskegee Institute.

"This house is seething," Mrs. Nesbitt wearily recorded in her diary. "ER back for breakfast, out for dinner, here for supper. In the house she always goes at a dog trot, so fast she bends forward. Somebody said she can give you enough work in five minutes to keep you busy for two weeks. But she drives herself hardest of all."

Eleanor finally joined Franklin at the tail end of his trip, meeting him at Fort Bragg, in the sandy hills of eastern North Carolina. They had only a few minutes together on the train before the motorcade arrived to take them on a three-hour inspection tour of the immense camp, which had originally been designed for twenty thousand men but now held more than sixty-seven thousand.

For nine months, a labor force of 28,500 had worked 24-hour days to triple the size of the camp. They had built a road that stretched 74 miles, a reception center capable of handling 1,000 men at a time, 20 63-men barracks, and a new hospital with 99 interconnected buildings and beds for 1,680 soldiers. When a critical shortage of furnaces threatened to halt construction of the hospital, four railroad locomotives had been brought into the camp on temporary sidings to pump steam into the building. And still the ringing of hammers could be heard everywhere the Roosevelts went.

Eleanor found the 25-mile drive through Fort Bragg "extraordinarily interesting." She heard a general say that "they put up a building of some kind every 32 minutes." She was pleased with the range of activities available to the soldiers—the athletic programs, the recreation centers, the football fields, and the theaters—though she worried about the strain on the small city of Fayetteville, and took note, as always, of the lack of housing for workmen, who were sleeping in trailers, in the back seats of cars, in makeshift tents on the hillsides.

The hurried pace at Fort Bragg could have been seen at any number of spots across the country. In order to train and equip the army of 1.4 million that conscription had decreed, 46 new army camps had to be built. The camps were concentrated along the Eastern Seaboard, in the states of the Old Confederacy, and along the California coast. Ideally, the construction would have been finished before the draftees were inducted, but because funds were not available until the passage of the Selective Service Act in September, the army was struggling to complete the camps even as the troops arrived. The job was monumental: land had to be cleared, hills leveled, valleys filled, trees uprooted, roads surfaced, and drainage systems installed before the construction of barracks, laundries, officers' quarters, and rifle ranges could begin. The building of the new camps required 400,000 men, 908,000 gallons of paint, 3,500 carloads of nails, and 10 million square feet of wallboard.

The frantic schedule had resulted in scores of mistakes. Lacking proper engineering surveys, camps had been built on rocky terrains and swampy soil. "We're building this camp in a sponge," workmen at Camp Blanding in Florida complained. One camp had been located 16 miles from "the worst malaria area in the southeastern United States." Another lacked adequate water supplies and had to be moved. In some cases, confused orders had gone out to put up barracks before roads had been built. In other cases, men were brought in before even the most rudimentary facilities—latrines and kitchens—were available. "If our plans for military campaigns are no more extensive and no better than these constructions," Senator Harry Truman's special committee to investigate the national defense program later concluded, "we are indeed in a deplorable situation."

Each camp was a little city, with a population ranging in size from 40,000 to 80,000, with its own police force, fire department, water sewerage, and transportation system. "But to the new soldier," Lee Kennett has written in his study of the American soldier in World War II, "the camp that would be his home for the next few months was like no city he had known in civilian life." The buildings were all so similar, made with the same "bare, angular, institutional look of the Quartermasters' 700 Series plans," that it was almost impossible to tell them apart. All the intersections looked the same as well; the relentless rectangular layout made it easy to get lost. In the early days of the planning, Eleanor had suggested that "curved streets might make the camps more pleasant places," but the rectangular orthodoxy prevailed. The original intention was to leave the buildings unpainted, but here Eleanor achieved partial success—the structures were painted but the same drab color was used throughout. Whether in Louisiana, Florida, Mississippi, or New Jersey, the camp presented an unwelcoming aspect to the new arrival.

But all these problems paled beside the magnificent achievement of the Quartermaster Corps under General Brehon Somervell. By the spring of 1941, despite the waste and the bungling, despite the obstacles of weather and terrain, all 46 camps were open and functioning, ready to receive the new American army. And when they were finished, Geoffrey Perrett has written in his study of the American army during the war, "they were the best run, most comfortable, most efficient posts [the army] had ever possessed."

Roosevelt was delighted with his inspection tour. Reporters noted his high spirits and suggested that he seemed to be "sitting on the top of the world." Returning to his train, he passed a group of children from a Negro school in Fayetteville. His appearance made a lasting impression. Twelve months later, the school's principal, Edwin Martin, wrote him that the children still recalled "that wave of the hand and that broad smile."

As the train pulled away from the station, the army fired the president's 21-gun salute. "Fala stood with his paws on the window," Eleanor noted in her column, "and as each gun went off, he sniffed the air," a bewildered expression on his face.

• • •

On the night of their return to the White House, the president dined with Missy while Eleanor attended a dinner party at the Women's National Press Club. Special guests included Margaret Mitchell, author of *Gone with the Wind,* which had inspired the biggest movie of the year, and Marjorie Rawlings, author of *The Yearling.* In Eleanor's honor, the women journalists had devised a humorous skit depicting the curious assortment of houseguests Eleanor was constantly inviting to the White House, with members of the club impersonating the president and the first lady. At one point in the make-believe party, which sported a wildly clashing group of guests, an annoyed Franklin approached Eleanor. "You do have the damndest people at the White House, Eleanor," he told her. "Now, Franklin," she replied, "you know I had all the royalties you like, and besides . . ." Eleanor enjoyed every moment, leading the applause.

But even as the members of the press club teased Eleanor about her eclectic guest list, they had no idea that the newest addition to the Roosevelts' unorthodox "family" was one of their own—former AP reporter Lorena Hickok. Miss Hickok, known to everyone as Hick, had moved from New York to Washington in January to become executive secretary to the Women's Division of the Democratic National Committee. Leaving behind a rented apartment in Manhattan and a country house on Long Island, she could not afford to rent an apartment in Washington. Eleanor, understanding Hick's predicament, invited her to stay at the White House until she could sublet her New York apartment.

Hick ended up living in the White House for four years. The little room she occupied was part of the northwest corner suite on the second floor. Two hundred feet from the president's bedroom, this was the room where Louis Howe had once lived. It was originally designed as the dressing room for the larger bedroom next door, but it contained a bed, a dressing table, a desk that jiggled, an old-fashioned commode that served as a night table, and a fireplace. "I never knew any greater comfort or luxury," Hick later said, "than lying in bed and looking into that fire. It was wonderful not to have to carry in logs for it. Twice a day a man came in with logs, poked up the fire, and swept up the ashes."

Eleanor's generosity allowed Hick to keep her beloved country house in Mastic, Long Island. "But that was not the only reason why I stayed at the White House," Hick later admitted. "Although I never told Mrs. Roosevelt I couldn't bear the idea of being in Washington and hardly ever seeing her."

When Hick and Eleanor first became friends in the fall of 1932, the thirty-nine-year-old Hick was at the top of her profession as a journalist. Having worked at the Associated Press in New York for a dozen years, she was the most widely known female reporter in the country, respected for her political savvy, her passionate convictions, and her superb writing style. At poker games with her colleagues, she looked and acted like one of the boys, with her flannel shirt and trousers loosely covering her two-hundred-pound frame, and a cigar hanging from her mouth.

Eleanor that fall was at one of the lowest moments in her life, filled with terror at the thought of moving to Washington and becoming first lady, fearing that everything she had built in the previous decade with the help of her female colleagues would be destroyed.

Now, eight years later, the tables were turned. As Hick was moving into the White House, it was Eleanor who had transformed the position of first lady into one perfectly suited to her remarkable skills, while Hick was depressed and emotionally unstable.

To understand this reversal, one must understand their relationship in the days after Eleanor and Hick first became acquainted. During the last weeks of the 1932 campaign, Hick was assigned to cover Eleanor on a regular basis. "You'd better watch out for that Hickok woman," Franklin had warned his wife. "She's smart." But, the more time they spent together—sharing a drawing room on the presidential train, riding together in an automobile from one event to the next—the more Eleanor began to grasp the vulnerability and need that lay beneath Hick's hard-boiled exterior—a vulnerability that found an answering chord in Eleanor's own sense of weariness and pain.

In the time they spent in each other's company, Hick told Eleanor the story of her childhood days on a poor dairy farm in Wisconsin. Her father was an abusive man who beat her regularly, killed her dog, and crushed her mother's kitten against the house. "There must have been times when he was not angry," Hick later wrote, "times when he was gay, affectionate, perhaps even indulgent with his children, but I do not remember them." After leaving home as soon as she could, Hick put herself through high school by working as a servant in a number of rooming houses. She won every school prize that was offered, then spent two years at Lawrence University before quitting to become a cub reporter.

Her rise through the world of journalism was exceptional. She went from cub reporter at the *Battle Creek Journal* to society editor of the *Milwaukee Sentinel* within the space of a year. From there she moved on to the *Minneapolis Tribune,* where she became the first woman sports reporter and a star feature writer.

In her personal life, Hick had achieved less success. When she was twenty-five, she had fallen in love with a wealthy young woman named Ellie Morse, who was taking English courses at the university and trying to write poetry. For six years, Hick and Ellie lived together in what seemed to be a serene and happy relationship. Then, one day, without warning, Ellie eloped with an old boyfriend, leaving Hick in a ravaged state, certain she would never fall in love again.

Hick's story touched Eleanor profoundly, prompting her to share with the reporter the story of her own wretched childhood. "I am *not* unhappy," Eleanor assured Hick. "Life may be somewhat negative with me, but that is nothing new. I think it was when I was a child & is now a habit. . . ." Eleanor further confided in Hick the catastrophe of her husband's affair with Lucy Mercer and the slow, painful process of reconstructing herself through her work with the League of Women Voters and a dozen other organizations in her home state. But with her husband's move to the White House, she would be forced to leave all her friends behind, forced to invent herself all over again. It was a daunting prospect.

Hick empathized with Eleanor's fears of becoming first lady in a way that other friends did not. And she had the professional experience and political sophistication to help Eleanor figure out how to make the job she feared into one she wanted. It was Hick who suggested that Eleanor consider holding her own press conferences, restricted to female reporters so as to encourage the papers to employ more women. It was Hick who suggested that Eleanor publish a running account of her daily experiences in the form of a column, a suggestion that led directly to Eleanor's enormously popular syndicated column, "My Day." It was Hick who encouraged Eleanor to write frequent magazine pieces and spent hours editing her early drafts. But, far more important, it was Hick who fell madly in love with Eleanor, pursuing her in a way she had never been pursued before.

"Every woman wants to be first to someone in her life," Eleanor later explained to Joe Lash, "and that desire is the explanation for many strange things women do." When Franklin was inaugurated on March 4, 1933, Eleanor was wearing a sapphire ring which Hick had given her just before she left New York. "Hick, darling," Eleanor wrote Hick after the inauguration. "I want to put my arms around you . . . to hold you close. Your ring is a great comfort. I look at it and I think she does love me, or I wouldn't be wearing it!"

Every night of that first week in the White House, as Franklin summoned the Congress into special session and prepared his first fireside chat on the banking crisis, Eleanor had sat in her room writing to Hick, whose work had taken her back to New York immediately after the festivities. "I felt a little as though a part of me was leaving tonight. You have grown so much to be a part of my life that it is empty without you even though I'm busy every minute. . . . My love enfolds thee all the night through."

Hick called Eleanor at the White House the following day. "Oh! how good it was to hear your voice," Eleanor wrote later; "it was so inadequate to try and tell you what it meant. Jimmy was near and I couldn't say Je t'aime and je t'adore. . . . I go to sleep thinking of you and repeating our little saying.

"The nicest time of day is when I write to you," Eleanor assured Hick, pledging that she would kiss Hick's picture since she couldn't kiss her. "Remember one thing always, no one is just what you are to me. I'd rather be with you this minute than anyone else. . . . I've never enjoyed being with anyone the way I enjoy being with you."

For her part, Hick counted the days until she and Eleanor could be together again. Having found the love she had been seeking all her life, she was miserable without Eleanor. "Funny," Hick wrote, "how even the dearest face will fade away in time. Most clearly I remember your eyes, with a kind of teasing smile in them and the feeling of that soft spot just northeast of the corner of your mouth against my lips."

What are we to make of these intimate letters? "While they seem at first glance to be the letters of one lover to another," historian and former Roosevelt Library Director William Emerson observes, "the passionate words were more likely a substitute for the expressions of love Eleanor needed so desperately." Eleanor's friend Trude Lash agrees. "Eleanor had so many emotions stored up inside, that when Hick came along, it was almost like a volcanic explosion. But does that mean that Eleanor acted on her words, that she had a lesbian relationship with Hick? I do not think so."

Hick's biographer, Doris Faber, concedes the amorous phrases but reminds us that personal letters can be terribly misleading unless they are placed in the context of their time. In a ground-breaking study of correspondence between women in Victorian America, the world into which Eleanor was born, Carroll Smith-Rosenberg argues that women routinely used romantic, even sensual rhetoric to communicate with their female friends. At a time when relationships between men and women frequently lacked ease and spontaneity, women opened their hearts more freely to other women, exchanging secrets, sharing desires, admitting fears.

To be sure, the letters possess an emotional intensity and a sensual explicitness that is hard to disregard. Hick longed to kiss the soft spot at the corner of Eleanor's mouth; Eleanor yearned to hold Hick close; Hick despaired at being away from Eleanor; Eleanor wished she could lie down beside Hick and take her in her arms. Day after day, month after month, the tone in the letters on both sides remains fervent and loving.

Yet the essential question for the biographer is not whether Hick and Eleanor went beyond kisses and hugs, a question there is absolutely no way we can answer with certainty. The far more absorbing question, and the one that *can* be answered, is what role the precious friendship played in each of their lives at that particular juncture.

There is every evidence that Hick's love for Eleanor came at a critical moment in Eleanor's life, providing a mix of tenderness, loyalty, confidence, and courage that sustained her in her struggle to redefine her sense of self and her position in the world. For Eleanor, Hick's love was a positive force, allowing her to grow and take wing, write the story of her life the way *she* wanted it to be, even in the White House. Secure in the knowledge that she was loved by the most important woman in her life, Eleanor was able to create a public persona that was to earn the love of millions. "You taught me more than you know & it brought me happiness . . . ," Eleanor later told Hick. "You've made of me so much more of a person just to be worthy of you."

For Hick, the love that had made her so euphoric at the start soon left her wretched and sulking. When she was separated from Eleanor, she felt restless and miserable, able only with the greatest difficulty to concentrate on the work that had once given her such pleasure and prestige. What is more, in drawing so close to Eleanor, Hick had compromised her position as a journalist. "A reporter," Louis Howe once warned Hick, "should never get too close to a news source." Through her friendship with Eleanor, Hick found herself smack in the middle of some of the biggest stories of the First Hundred Days, but it never once occurred to her to share what she was hearing with her office. Her days as a reporter had come to an end before she recognized it.

Willing to submit to anything as long as she could spend time with Eleanor without feeling guilty, Hick resigned her position at AP in the summer of 1933. It was a major miscalculation. Though Eleanor found her a good

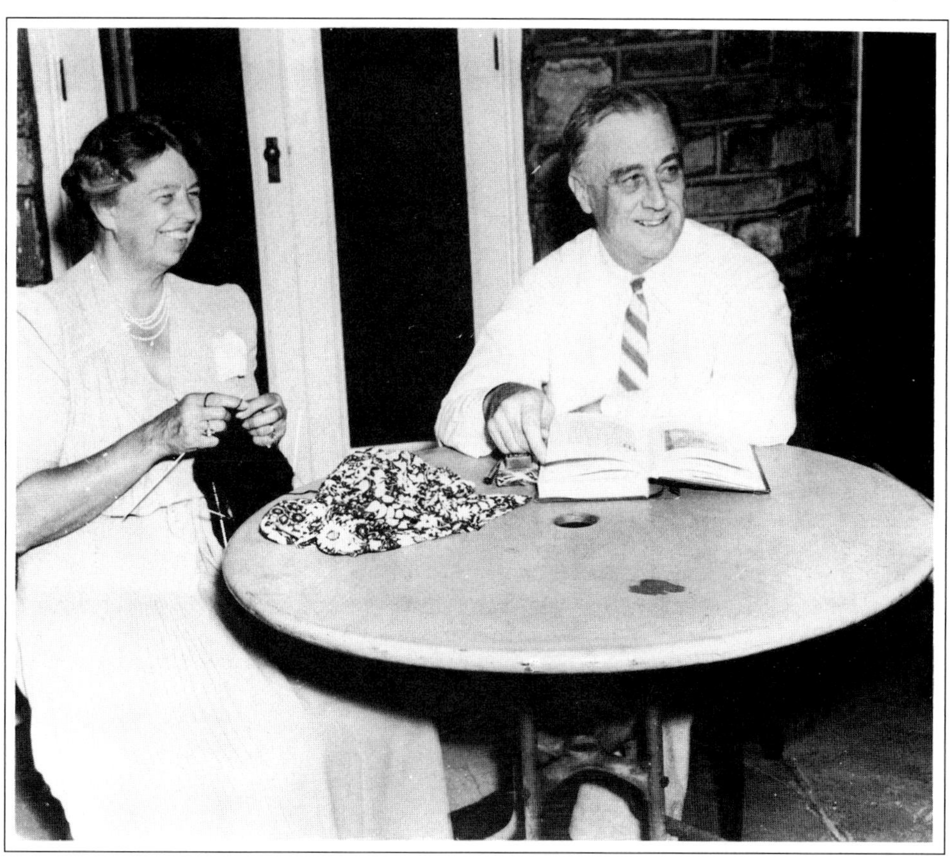

Franklin and Eleanor Roosevelt in a rare moment of relaxation on the south porch of the Roosevelt home at Hyde Park (1).

2

Eleanor was unlike any girl Franklin had met. She was serious and intelligent, free from affectation, and wholly uninterested in the world of debutante balls. The young couple is shown here on the beach at Campobello shortly after their marriage (2) and with their first child, Anna (3).

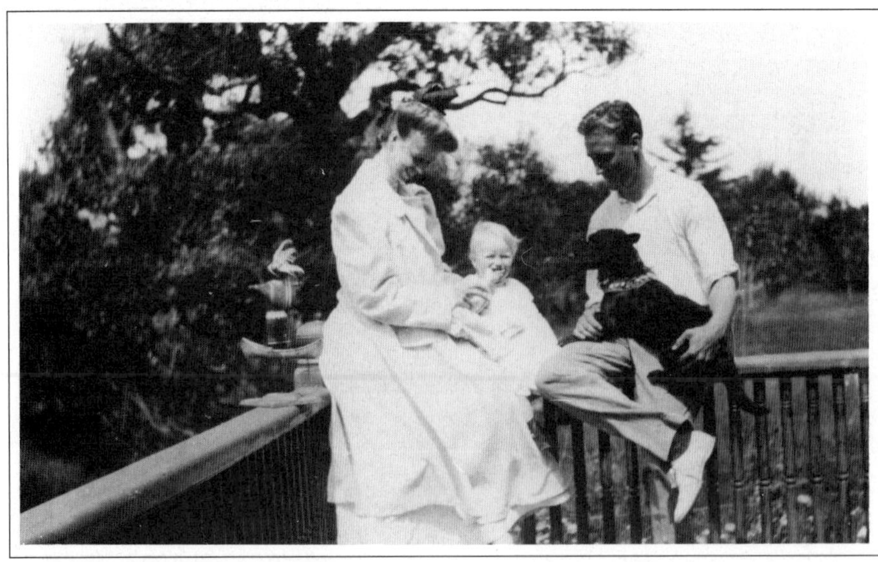

3

4

When Eleanor discovered a packet of love letters from Lucy Mercer (4) in 1918, the bottom, she said, dropped out of her world. Three years later, Franklin contracted polio. During his convalescence he lived for months at a time on a houseboat in Florida with his secretary, Missy LeHand, here to his left along with Maunsell Crosby and Frances Dana De Rahm (5), while Eleanor remained in New York.

5

6

Three generations of Roosevelt women: Anna, Eleanor, and Sara listen to Roosevelt accept the Democratic nomination for a second term (6).

7

8

9

Roosevelt with Harry Hopkins in the second-floor study, the president's favorite room in the White House (7). It was here that he read, played poker, sorted his beloved stamps, and conducted most of the business of the presidency. A door at the rear of the study led to the president's bedroom next door (8). After breakfast, pushed along in his wheelchair by the White House usher, the president headed for the Oval Office (9).

10

11

Eleanor occupied a second-floor suite adjacent to the president's bedroom. Keeping the smaller room as her bedroom (10), she turned the larger room into a sitting room, where she greeted guests and handled her voluminous correspondence (11).

12

The Roosevelt White House during the war resembled a small, intimate hotel. The residential floors were occupied by a series of houseguests, some of whom stayed for years. Harry Hopkins, here with his daughter, Diana, and his wife, Louise (12), occupied a suite in the southeast corner of the second floor. Missy LeHand, pictured here with Roosevelt (13), lived in a cheerful room with slanted ceilings on the third floor.

13

14

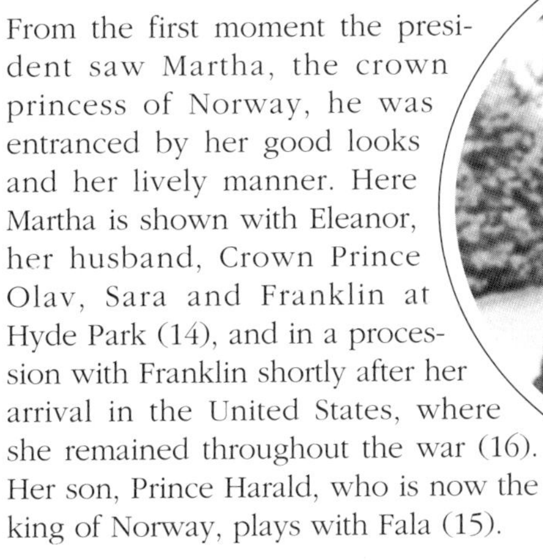

From the first moment the president saw Martha, the crown princess of Norway, he was entranced by her good looks and her lively manner. Here Martha is shown with Eleanor, her husband, Crown Prince Olav, Sara and Franklin at Hyde Park (14), and in a procession with Franklin shortly after her arrival in the United States, where she remained throughout the war (16). Her son, Prince Harald, who is now the king of Norway, plays with Fala (15).

15

16

17

Eleanor had her own entourage, including her secretary, Malvina Thompson, here with Eleanor in England (17), and her friend Lorena Hickok, who lived in the White House for four years during the war, occupying a room across the hall from Eleanor's suite. Hick, as she was called, is shown below with Eleanor and Governor Paul Pearson of the U.S. Virgin Islands (18).

18

19

Knowing that his mother disapproved of his wife's women friends, Franklin built Eleanor a fieldstone cottage of her own on the grounds of the Hyde Park estate. Though Eleanor stayed at the Big House whenever Franklin and the children were at Hyde Park, she considered Val-Kill, here the site of a National Youth Administration Conference, the only real home she had ever known (19).

20

One friend recalled that whenever the president's daughter, Anna, here with her father and her second husband, John Boettiger (20), walked into her father's study, the president's whole face lighted up. The world's problems stopped for a few minutes; he just adored her.

21

All four Roosevelt boys were in the service during the war. Elliott, top left, was in the Army Air Corps; James, top right, was in the marines; while FDR, Jr., bottom left, and John, bottom right, were in the navy (21).

22

23

24

There was an extraordinary bond between the president and his mother. "Nothing," Eleanor observed, "ever seemed to disturb the deep underlying affection they had for each other." Here Sara is driving with Eleanor to Campobello in the summer of 1941 (22), accompanying Franklin after a speech in the U.S. Capitol (23), and standing between Franklin and Eleanor at St. John's Church in 1940 (24).

25

"All that is in me goes back to the Hudson," Roosevelt liked to say. Time and again Roosevelt confounded his staff by the ease with which, even in the darkest hours, he managed to shake off the burdens of the presidency upon his arrival at Hyde Park. Here are Franklin and Eleanor on the porch of Eleanor's house Val-Kill in 1943 (25); the front of the big house in winter (26); Roosevelt speaking to the Roosevelt Home Club at the home of his tenant farmer, Moses Smith, while Eleanor holds their grandchild, Elliott Jr., and Harry Hopkins listens (27).

26

27

After he had polio, Franklin built a cottage in Warm Springs, Georgia, where spring water came out of the ground at a soothing eighty-six degrees, winter and summer, providing therapy for crippled patients and relaxation for vacationers. The simple cottage became known as the Little White House (28).

28

Although it was difficult for Roosevelt to maneuver his leg braces in the narrow pews, he still attended church whenever he could. Franklin and Eleanor leave church after Easter services, April 13, 1941 (29).

job with Harry Hopkins that made use of her writing skills in evaluating WPA projects, Hick reproached herself bitterly for giving up her career, her colleagues, her daily by-lines, her life. "Unwittingly," Eleanor's granddaughter Eleanor Seagraves said, "Hick let herself slip into a role where she lost her old identity and became dependent on my grandmother." No longer a nationally recognized reporter, she found it degrading and hateful to be identified in pictures as Eleanor's secretary or bodyguard. Yet, even if she had wanted to get rid of the love that obsessed her, she could not.

Ironically, as Eleanor, with Hick's considerable help, grew into her role as first lady, the ardor of the friendship diminished. "No question that Hick helped Eleanor get her wings," a Roosevelt relative observed, "but once Eleanor began to fly she didn't need Hick the same way." Surrounded by the love and admiration of thousands, Eleanor no longer required the private reassurances from Hick that had bolstered her in the anxious days before she left New York for Washington. In the beginning of the relationship, it was Eleanor who was jealous of Hick's job and Hick's accomplishments—"I should work as you do, but I can't. I am more apt to disappoint you, dear, than you are to disappoint me"—but before long the lines of jealousy ran the opposite way. Sensing that she needed Eleanor more than Eleanor needed her, Hick became moody and sullen, demanding time with Eleanor alone, apart from Eleanor's family and friends.

Eleanor tried to accommodate Hick's desire for time alone, but, more often than not, she found herself apologizing to Hick for including other people in their plans. First it was Louis Howe. "I know you will be disappointed . . . ," she warned Hick, "but Louis seems so miserable I would feel horrible to tell him I wouldn't look after him that evening. You know I'd rather be with you." Then it was Anna. "I'd rather go alone with you but I can't hurt her feelings. . . ." There were so many others—Nan, Marion, Earl, Esther, Elizabeth. They all needed her, too, and though she understood Hick's "cry from the heart for something all her own," she couldn't turn her back on her old friends.

After each confrontation with Hick, Eleanor felt miserable. "I went to sleep saying a little prayer," Eleanor told Hick. "God give me depth enough not to hurt Hick again. Darling I know I'm not up to you in many ways but I love you dearly."

"I know you have a feeling for me which for one reason or another I may not return in kind, but I feel I love you just the same," Eleanor wrote Hick on another occasion. "You think some one thing could make you happy. I know it never does. We may want something, and when we have it, it is not what we dreamed it would be, the thing lies in oneself."

But over time, Hick's possessiveness wore Eleanor down. "I could shake you for your letter . . . ," Eleanor scolded Hick after Hick had complained of a change of plans. "I know you felt badly & are tired, but I'd give an awful lot if you weren't so sensitive."

The low point came during a trip to Yosemite, when Hick became so jealous of the attention the park rangers were showing Eleanor that she "shouted and stalked like a wild animal." When the trip was over, Hick bemoaned her conduct. "I hope you are having a happy, restful time . . . a happier, more peaceful time than you had with me. Oh, I'm bad, my dear, but I love you so, at times life becomes just one long, dreary ache for you. But I'm trying to be happy and contented."

Driven by Hick's behavior to a pitch of exasperation, Eleanor offered a piece of unthinking advice. "Of course you should have had a husband & children & it would have made you happy if you loved him & in any case it would have satisfied certain cravings & given you someone on whom to lavish the love & devotion you have to keep down all the time."

What exactly did Eleanor mean by suggesting to Hick that if she loved a man her frustrated cravings might have been satisfied? Cravings for what? For women instead of men? Was Eleanor unable to accept that Hick was a lesbian? Was she speaking from ignorance, prejudice, or fear?

For her part, Hick cursed the fate that bound her obsessively to Eleanor and hoped that someday she would be free of it. "It would be so much better, wouldn't it," she repeatedly asked Eleanor, "if I didn't love you so much sometimes. It makes it trying for you."

As Eleanor's passion diminished, her guilt increased. "Of course dear, I never meant to hurt you in any way," Eleanor told Hick in 1937, "but that is no excuse for having done it. It won't help you any but . . . I'm pulling myself back in all my contacts now. I've always done it with my children & why I didn't know I couldn't give you (or anyone else who wanted or needed what you did) any real food, I can't now understand. Such cruelty & stupidity is unpardonable when you reach my age."

Hick's melancholy was still evident in a long letter she wrote Eleanor shortly after the 1940 election. "I'd never have believed it possible for a woman to develop after fifty as you have in the last six years. My God, you've learned to do surprisingly well two of the most difficult things in the world —to write and speak. My trouble I suspect has always been that I've been so much more interested in the person than in the personage. I resented the personage and fought for years an anguished and losing fight against the development of the person into the personage. I still prefer the person but I admire and respect the personage with all my heart. . . . I can think of only one other person who undoubtedly felt about this as I have—or would have felt so, increasingly, had he lived, Louis Howe."

"You are wrong about Louis," Eleanor replied. "He always wanted to make me President when FDR was thro' & insisted he could do it. You see he was interested in his power to create personages more than in a person, tho' I think he probably cared more for me as a person as much as he cared for anyone & more than anyone else ever has! Sheer need on his part I imagine!"

How the words "he probably cared more for me . . . than anyone else ever has" must have hurt Hick, who knew in her heart that no one had ever loved Eleanor more than she. But at this point in the relationship, there was nothing Hick could do.

By the time Hick moved into the White House in 1941, a permanent pain had settled in her heart. Though she had come to accept that she could never mean to Eleanor what Eleanor meant to her, the yearning in her soul was still too powerful to allow her to break away. Accepting Eleanor's invitation was in some ways a self-destructive act, but, by living so close, she rationalized, she would at least have the chance to share an occasional breakfast with Eleanor in the morning or talk with her late at night. It was not enough, but it was better than nothing.

• • •

"A more discouraging agenda could not have been imagined," *U.S. News* suggested, than that which faced the president in early April, when he "settled down in his swivel chair" upon his return from Fort Bragg: "urgent proposals for more aid to Britain"; Allied defeats in the Middle East; "seizure of Axis ships in American ports; expulsion of the Italian naval attaché"; and, perhaps most discouraging of all, news of lagging production and record numbers of strikes.

Though 1940 had been relatively quiet on the strike front, with only 2.3 percent of the workers in the country involved—the lowest percentage since 1932—1941 became a banner year for strikes. One of every twelve workers, the highest percentage since 1919, would go out on strike in 1941, and the number of strikes would be exceeded in history only by 1937 and 1919.

The most severe strains that spring were in the aircraft industry, which was still in the process of being unionized, still fighting a rearguard action against the rights labor had gained in much of the automotive industry. But strikes were also being fought over wages, work conditions, work loads, and jurisdictional disputes. "Some friends of labor are very deeply troubled," columnist Raymond Clapper wrote, "over the fact that labor is working itself into a role of irresponsible obstruction to war production."

Believing that legislation was necessary to prevent strikes altogether, the War Department sought to use the strike statistics as a public-relations weapon. Every week in March and April, the War Department printed bulletins showing how many man days had been lost as a result of the various strikes at Allis Chalmers, Vultee Air, American Car and Foundry, and Motor Wheel. The bulletins also contained a list of critical items affected—light tanks, landing wheels for the P-40 plane, ammunition, blankets, generators, bombs, zinc. The public-relations effort worked. At theaters across the country, audiences loudly booed whenever pictures of strikers were shown on the newsreels.

Eleanor took a different tack, arguing that business caution, not labor excess, was the root of lagging production. She contended that the fear of being left with surplus capacity after the war was still operating as a brake on plans for expansion. As long as the defense agencies were weighted down with wealthy businessmen (dollar-a-year men, as they were called), there was little hope for change. "All these men will be returning to business," Eleanor told Bernard Baruch at lunch. "How can they be expected to crack down on people with whom they will have to do business in the future?"

"I cannot escape the feeling," Eleanor told the readers of her column, "that the tendency so far has been to say that labor must make sacrifices of wages and hours because of necessities of national defense. I have yet to see anywhere a statement that manufacturers and business concerns . . . shall make this same type of sacrifice by cutting profits and reducing the salaries of executives."

Amid these charges and countercharges came the news that the Ford employees in Dearborn, Michigan, had struck for the first time in the thirty-eight-year history of the River Rouge plant, the largest auto plant in the world. The Rouge plant was the capital of the Ford empire. An entirely self-contained twelve-hundred-acre unit, the plant generated enough power to light all the homes in Chicago, used enough water to supply all the families of Detroit, Cincinnati, and Washington combined, and wore out seven thousand mops a month to keep itself clean.

The strike had begun during the night shift in response to the firing of eleven union workers. As word of the firing spread, the men in one department after another began a spontaneous walkout. At midnight, with the strike officially authorized by the UAW-CIO, squads of union members roamed the plant urging workers to leave their jobs. By 3 a.m., almost all the night workers, eight thousand or more, were out in front of the plant, cheering and singing the union song, "Solidarity Forever." In the meantime, union members from the day shift began to arrive by the thousands to barricade the roads leading into the plant.

Ever since 1936, *Newsweek* reported, the UAW-CIO had awaited the chance to crack Ford, "the last unconquered citadel in its campaign to organize the auto industry." In the wake of the sit-down strikes in the mid-thirties, General Motors, Chrysler, Studebaker, Nash, Packard, and Willy had all come to terms with the union. In moments of vanity, owner Henry Ford liked to believe that he was different from all his colleagues, that they had brought their troubles on themselves whereas he had been an ideal employer, so ideal that his employees didn't need a union.

In truth, fear had been the operating force behind the reluctance of the Ford employees to join the union. Over the years, Ford Service Department head Harry Bennett had built a powerful goon squad of three thousand ex-pugilists, ex-jailbirds, fired policemen, and small-time gangsters, whose primary function was to spy on the employees, taking names of any workmen who accepted union leaflets, tearing union buttons off the caps of employees, physically assaulting union organizers. Little wonder that for so many years the union drive at Ford had stalled.

Ford's miserable labor relations complicated the government's position in the defense crisis. The War Department believed that Ford's immense facilities were essential to rapid munitions production, but labor's vociferous complaints were hard to ignore. In the end, the need for mass production won out; on November 7, 1940, the army had awarded Ford a $122-million contract for the production of four thousand plane engines—the largest such order of the arms program. A week later, a second contract had followed, for a mosquito fleet of four-wheel-drive midget cars, able to go anywhere and get there fast.

Labor spokesmen were horrified at the government's decision to reward "union enemy number one." In liberal circles, the Ford contracts were considered a grievous setback which threatened to take away all the rights working people had achieved through a decade of bitter struggle. "Ford is the country's foremost violator of the Wagner Act," *The Nation* decried, referring to the National Labor Relations Act of 1935, which guaranteed collective-bargaining rights and outlawed such management practices as blacklisting union organizers and spying on union members, "a symbol of the determination of big business to remain above the law," and yet the government had chosen to award the company with not one but two contracts.

The first lady shared labor's discontent, telling delegates at an American Student Union Convention that she thought it was "a bad thing to give contracts to uncooperative people." For his part, the president fully appreciated the complexity of the situation, but his first impulse, he told Henry Stimson, was "to let bygone issues go and concentrate on getting Ford to play fair with labor in the future." It was Roosevelt's belief that once Ford accepted large defense contracts change was inevitable; the dynamics of the situation would eventually force Ford into accepting the union. It was with similar reasoning that Roosevelt had expressed the naïve hope to Negro leader A. Philip Randolph that, by putting white and black regiments side by side in the fluid situation of war, the armed forces would eventually back into integration.

In February 1941, Ford's refusal to "play fair" took its toll on the company. Though Ford was the lowest bidder on a large government order for airplanes, the War Department, under strong pressure from labor, felt compelled to reject the bid because management refused even to sign a clause pledging future compliance with the labor laws. "Best news in a long time," I. F. Stone wrote. The decision gave heart to union organizers at Ford, who began a new drive. Emboldened further by a Supreme Court decision that fixed responsibility on Ford for violating the Wagner Act, union leaders succeeded in signing up thousands of workers. The stage was set for the strike that began on the first of April, when Ford fired the union's key organizers.

From the beginning, the historic strike was complicated by racial conflict. Though the overwhelming majority of the workers stood behind the strike, there remained within the plant nearly two thousand nonstriking Negroes who claimed loyalty to Ford and refused to join the union. Stationing themselves on the roof of the main plant, hundreds of Negro employees hurled metal buckets into the crowd of picketers marching peacefully below. At one point in the struggle, two hundred Negroes armed with steel bars and crudely fashioned swords rushed the main gate, engaging in hand-to-hand combat with the strikers. By the second day of the strike, with company agents busily stirring up racial hatred in the streets, the situation had escalated out of control, threatening to produce a full-scale race war. If the violence continued, the Ford Company argued, the government would have to issue an injunction and send troops to end the strike. Ford also claimed to have evidence of a direct connection between the CIO and the Communist Party. The strike, Ford alleged, was part of the communist program to impede America's mobilization.

Fortunately for the strikers, Roosevelt's lines of intelligence stretched beyond Ford's assessment of the situation. From Hyde Park, where she had gone for the weekend, Eleanor sent Franklin a copy of a long memo she had received from civil-rights leader Mary McCleod Bethune. In this memo, Bethune explained that, though it was true that Ford had earned the loyalty of Negroes by employing "more Negroes in skilled and semi-skilled capacities than any other auto manufacturer in the company," the policy was rooted in opposition to the union. Over time, Bethune explained, "the Ford Negro workers have been propagandized very strongly against trade unionism of any kind and it was expected that in any labor dispute these workers would form the backbone of the Ford anti-union forces." Ford's immediate plan, Bethune had learned, was to use these Negro workers as the vanguard of a back-to-work movement sometime after the weekend. If this was attempted, Bethune predicted, it would result in "one of the bloodiest race riots in the history of the country." Bethune closed by saying she was sending this confidential information to Eleanor in the hope that Eleanor would use her influence to prevent an occurrence "which would set race relations back a quarter of a century."

Armed with the information Bethune provided, Roosevelt appreciated the terrible bind in which the Negro workers found themselves, caught between their past loyalty to Ford and their hopes for the future. "It will be a bitter blow to those who look to the future of the Negro in trade union organizations," the *Pittsburgh Courier* observed, "if this most crucial strike is lost by use of Negro scabs."

Refusing to be drawn into the situation on Ford's side, the president articulated a policy of "watching and waiting and watching," intended to give the mediation machinery a full chance to work. Republicans in the Congress had a field day with the Ford strike. "With the help of the President of the U.S., Hitler has closed the Ford plant," Congressman George Dondero argued. "The dictators in Europe ought to be celebrating today." Representative George Shafer of Battle Creek agreed: "I am convinced the President and his utterly incompetent Secretary of Labor have purposely remained inert and silent while the defense program has been sabotaged."

While the Republicans railed against the president for failing to issue an injunction, he was working behind the scenes to bring about a peaceful settlement. With Roosevelt's approval, NAACP head Walter White journeyed to Detroit to address the Negroes in the plant. Speaking from a union car, White urged the Negro workers to reject their role as strikebreakers, to evacuate the plant and stand shoulder to shoulder with their fellow workers. After several tense days, the Negro workers finally agreed to come out of the plant, clearing the way for the negotiations between labor and management to begin.

The fate of the strikers now rested in the hands of two men, the seventy-seven-year-old founder of the company, Henry Ford, and his only son, Edsel. The elder Ford, stooped and diminished by a series of small strokes, had begun to show unmistakable signs of failing powers: forgetfulness, stubbornness, episodes of inattention and drowsiness. His eyes, one Ford employee said, looked as if someone had "dimmed the power behind them." Two decades earlier, Edsel had replaced his father as president of the company. When the old man came into the plant, however, his word was still law. In June 1940, Edsel had committed Ford to build nine thousand Rolls-Royce engines for British Spitfire planes. Henry agreed at first, but when he realized that the company was expected to deal directly with the British, he changed his mind. It was against his isolationist principles to provide war materials to a foreign power. Edsel was humiliated by the sudden turnabout; when William Knudsen asked him to explain, he could only say that his father had made him do it.

On the central issue of the strike, however, Edsel stood his ground against his father. Whereas the elder Ford believed he could bring the fledgling union to its knees by simply refusing to accept its existence, Edsel argued strongly that negotiating with labor was the only path to the future. It was Edsel who convinced his father to allow Ford officials, for the first time in the history of the company, to sit across a conference table from union representatives. "Mr. Ford gave in to Edsel's wishes," Harry Bennett conceded. The union would never have won "if it hadn't been for Edsel's attitude."

As part of the agreement, preparations were made for a company-wide election to determine whom the workers wanted to represent them. Both the CIO and its conservative rival, the AFL, were on the ballot, along with the option of remaining a nonunion shop. When the votes were counted, the CIO had won a smashing victory, taking 70 percent of the vote to 27 percent for the AFL. A mere 2.6 percent had voted to keep Ford a nonunion shop.

The results took Henry Ford totally by surprise. "It was a measure of Henry Ford's contact with reality," his biographer Robert Lacey observed, that he actually cherished the expectation that his men, "in a gesture of confidence and gratitude for his lifetime of laboring on their behalf," would reject both union options and decide to keep Ford a nonunion shop. "It was perhaps the greatest disappointment he had in all his business experience," Ford's production chief, Charles Sorensen, recalled.

After the election, Henry Ford was never the same again. His zest seemed to vanish. When the time came to sit down with the CIO and work out a new contract, he simply caved in—granting the union virtually everything it asked, including wages equal to the highest in the industry, the abolition of the infamous spy system, and reinstatement of all employees dismissed for union activities. Union leaders pronounced the settlement the greatest of all labor victories in their generation.

• • •

Labor's victory at Ford vindicated Roosevelt's faith that the mobilization process would be an agent of positive change. But he also knew that every delay in the defense program was deadly, and that the public was turning against unions with a vengeance. In the House, a bill was introduced providing "treason" penalties for strikes on defense work; in Georgia, the draft board announced it would furnish no more men for the army until the government moved to stop strikes. Trying to steer a middle course, the president promised to take action against unjustified strikes in the defense industry.

Eleanor, unconstrained by her husband's need for balancing opposing sides, became even more emphatic in her support of labor, arguing that the bill to provide the death penalty for strikers was "perfect nonsense." "We ought not to behave as though this question were a case of patriotism," she said. "The strike situation is not so bad. If we take all the hours of man hours lost from the defense program we find there is a loss of only one-tenth of one percent man labor hours in the year so far."

At her press conference on April 7, Eleanor conceded that she had received a great many letters from mothers of service trainees demanding that labor be forced to produce the arms their sons were called to bear. But in the long run, Eleanor argued, maximum productivity could only be attained if the workers were satisfied that their rights and interests were fully respected. Seen in this light, the strike at Ford was not a sinister act to be feared but, rather, an affirmation of the vitality of democracy.

Eleanor's support for labor became more difficult to maintain in the weeks ahead, when a wildcat strike at the North American Aviation plant in Inglewood, California, halted production on desperately needed twin-engine bombers. This time, in contrast to the situation at Ford, a small splinter group with admitted ties to the Communist Party had arrogantly defied both the federal government and the CIO by walking out in the middle of negotiations. "The infamous hand" of the Communist Party "is apparent," UAW labor leader Richard Frankensteen warned. "This is not just a charge on the part of the company management."

With the North American strike, *Time* observed, "Franklin Roosevelt reached a worm-turning point. Having tolerated strikes in defense industry for many months—until the public was fed up and Congress indignant—he either had to put up or curl up."

In a tense mood, Roosevelt signed an executive order directing the secretary of war, with the help of twenty-five hundred federal troops, to take possession of the plant and break the strike. As the uniformed troops marched into the area, the local strike leader, Joe Freitag, issued a defiant call. "The armed forces will not break our strike. Bombers can't be made with bayonets." Freitag was wrong. Only two hours after the army battalions took over, the workers returned, streaming through the gates by the thousands. The strike was over.

• • •

Spring had come to Washington. The cherry blossoms were in bloom. Yet the glacial mood of the capital refused to melt. Accusations filled the air as the mobilization process faltered. Production of planes was 30 percent behind schedule. "Washington rarely ever has been in such confusion as today," Washington correspondent David Lawrence wrote. "The internal situation is becoming almost as grave as the external." Though the president had replaced the NDAC in December with a stronger organization, the Office of Production Management (OPM), headed jointly by former NDAC members William Knudsen and Sidney Hillman, he had not yet developed an organization that could run without him. When he was indisposed or preoccupied with other matters, the wheels seemed to stop moving. "What has not yet been realized," Lawrence continued, "is that it is impossible for the President through the normal peacetime type of organization to carry on war preparations which amount to the same thing as if America were actually at war."

"It took Hitler more than five years to get ready for this war," observed Leon Henderson, the rumpled chief of yet another new organization, the Office of Price Administration and Civilian Supply (OPACS), designed to prevent profiteering and undue price rises. "We've got months, not years in which to prepare." And the battle could only be won "if this nation produces more and faster than any nation has ever produced before."

New Dealers argued that business was intentionally holding down defense production in order to profit from the tantalizing rise in consumer demand for civilian products that was accompanying the military buildup. Business countered that it was doing all it could to expand its defense production in an atmosphere poisoned by labor strife and social-welfare concerns.

The struggle focused that spring on the automobile industry, which was producing new cars in record numbers, "gobbling an intolerable share of scarce raw materials"—80 percent of all rubber, 49 percent of strip steel, 44 percent of sheet steel, 34 percent of lead. While the War Department agonized over America's limited supply of steel, aluminum, and rubber, auto dealers were proudly displaying their shiny new models in showrooms. The new Packard boasted a streamlined shape with fenders integral to the body and a high radiator grill; Willys announced a new price leader, the American Blue Streak Coupe; Chevrolet introduced a new "get away" gear or second speed.

As the new head of OPACS, Leon Henderson was at the center of the controversy. For months he had argued for a sharp curtailment in the production of passenger cars in order to force the industry to divert its men, management, and raw materials from civilian to defense needs. "You can't have 500 bombers a month *and* business as usual," declared Henderson. "We cannot fight a war with convertible coupes," I. F. Stone added, "or overawe a Panzer division with a brigade of statistics on automobile sales."

But Henderson's call for a 50-percent cut in the production of automobiles met unrelenting resistance at the top of the administration, from William Knudsen. The OPM chief argued that a cut of 50 percent would throw the entire industry into chaos, resulting in widespread unemployment and tremendous distress. Moving quickly to outflank Henderson, Knudsen called a press conference on April 17, and announced with great fanfare that he had just concluded a meeting with the leaders of the auto industry. "The entire industry willingly accepted an initial 20 percent reduction in the production of motor vehicles for the model year beginning August 1," Knudsen proudly announced.

It sounded swell, I. F. Stone noted in *The Nation,* but it was in fact a ruse, given that production for the banner year of 1941 was already running more than 20 percent ahead of the previous year, so a cut of 20 percent would merely bring it back to normal. "The problem," Stone continued, "is to turn existing mass-production facilities as rapidly as possible to the production of armament. We are fumbling that problem, and we have no time to fumble." The time had come, Stone concluded, for Knudsen to turn in his resignation. Stimson agreed. "I am afraid," the secretary of war recorded in his diary, "that Knudsen is too soft and slow because of his connection with the auto industry."

Eleanor was in full agreement with Henderson and Stimson; she had argued all along that Knudsen was fatally biased toward industry. Entering the fray, she approached the problem from a different angle, calling on the American people "to begin thinking about doing without various commodities such as new automobiles and aluminum kitchen utensils when present stocks are exhausted." Instead of competing for various articles now, she urged Americans to save their money for the future, for the abundant new cars and refrigerators that would become readily available after the emergency ended. Echoing Eleanor's sentiments, Henderson predicted that Americans would "cheerfully forego the luxury of new automobiles in order to assure adequate mechanized equipment for defense."

Henderson was wrong. In truth, just the opposite phenomenon developed that spring, whereby anxious consumers, afraid that the supply of cars would eventually be curtailed, rushed to the showrooms in greater numbers than ever before. It would take the attack on Pearl Harbor to create the patriotic mood that, along with rationing and a limited supply of civilian goods, stimulated Americans to do precisely as Eleanor suggested—to put their money in government bonds, which could be cashed in for houses and cars and washing machines as soon as the war ended. Indeed, during the war, personal savings would rise to unprecedented levels, laying the foundation for the postwar boom.

But for the time being, in the fractious mood that characterized a still-divided America in the spring of 1941, Eleanor's pleas fell on deaf ears, and the struggle between Henderson and Knudsen continued unabated.

• • •

By the end of April, a tone of weariness and irritation had crept into the president's voice as he tried to juggle the cries of isolationists with Britain's struggle to survive. "The President has on his hands at the present time," Admiral Harold Stark observed, "about as difficult a situation as ever confronted any man anywhere in public life."

With the coming of spring, the Germans had resumed their offensive, and the results were devastating. The first week of April witnessed the invasion of Yugoslavia, heralded by the killing of seventeen thousand civilians in Belgrade within the first twenty-four hours. Eleven days later, the overwhelmed Yugoslavians signed an act of surrender. After Yugoslavia, it took the Germans less than four weeks to conquer neighboring Greece, and to drive British forces in Libya back to the Egyptian border.

While British armies were meeting disaster abroad, Britain's home economy was on the verge of strangulation and collapse. In March and April, German submarines seemed to be roaming the North Atlantic at will; British ships were being sunk at the terrifying rate of three times their capacity to replace them. Imports into Britain had fallen to a volume less than needed to feed the British people or to keep the factories going. Unless the Battle of the Atlantic could be won, there was little hope that the country could survive.

For months, Stimson and Knox had been pressuring the president to ask the Congress for the power to convoy British ships across the Atlantic. Without American intervention "to forcibly stop the German submarines," Stimson told Roosevelt, "the dispatch of additional supplies to Britain was like pouring water into a leaky bathtub." The navy plans called for transferring three battleships, four cruisers, and one aircraft carrier from the Pacific fleet to the Atlantic to serve as escorts for the merchant ships.

Roosevelt knew that everyone was waiting for him to cross the line, and he knew that sooner or later he would cross it. But, for the moment, he refused to take the lead, convinced that convoys would lead to shooting, and shooting would lead to war. Believing that his broad consensus for lend-lease had been forged on the assumption that aid to Britain would prevent, rather than instigate, American entry into war, Roosevelt feared that convoys would shatter the national agreement and force him to carry a divided nation into war. A national poll on the 8th of April confirmed the president's fears. When asked if they supported convoys, 41 percent of the American people were in favor, 50 percent opposed.

The president proposed instead a more limited action—the establishment of an extended patrol system to detect German subs and report their locations to British ships. When it was suggested by the press that these patrols, which the president likened to those used by the pioneers to scout Indians, might in effect be convoys, an aggravated Roosevelt remarked that "one could not turn a cow into a horse by calling it a horse." Yet FDR, Jr., in a confidential letter to his sister, Anna, on April 2, did precisely that when he told her that his destroyer, the U.S.S. *Mayrant,* was going to be part of the new "escort patrol" squadron, "which is the cutest name I can imagine for what I think will be actual convoying before long."

From the German perspective, there was little doubt, as Goebbels wrote in his diary in April, that "the U.S.A. is preparing to make the leap to war. If Roosevelt were not so chary of public opinion, he would have declared war on us long ago."

On Tuesday morning, April 22, a discouraged Stimson went to see the president. Stimson warned his boss from the outset that he was going to speak very frankly and hoped Roosevelt wouldn't question his loyalty and affection. "He reassured me on that point and then I went over the whole situation of the deterioration in the American political situation toward the war that has taken place since nothing happened immediately after the lend-lease victory. I cautioned him on the necessity of his taking the lead and that without a lead on his part it was useless to expect the people would voluntarily take the initiative."

Though Stimson was delighted by the "intimate" nature of his conversation with the president, he remained apprehensive about Roosevelt's lack of leadership. "I am worried," he recorded in his diary, "because the President shows evidence of waiting for the accidental shot of some irresponsible captain on either side to be the occasion for his going to war. I think he ought to consider the deep principles which underlie the issue in the world and [have] divided the world into two camps, [of] one of which he is the leader."

At the very moment when Stimson was talking frankly with the president, Interior Secretary Harold Ickes was baring his own disgruntled soul to Missy LeHand. Ickes was so concerned about the president's lack of leadership that he was considering resigning from the Cabinet. "Knudsen simply is not delivering the goods," he recorded in his diary. "Big business is having altogether too much say about our preparedness program. We are talking about asking working men to give 24 hour service in shifts, but we listen to businessmen talk about 'business as usual.' " In every direction, Ickes believed, there was a growing discontent with the president's leadership. "He still has the country if he will take it and lead it." But people were starting to say, "I am tired of words; I want action."

"I turn to Missy," Ickes wrote in his diary on April 22, "when I feel deeply about how things are going because I not only trust her discretion but have confidence in her wisdom, even if I mistrust her on the subject of Harry Hopkins. I took my hair down and told her exactly how I felt about the situation. I found that she had the same thoughts and the same apprehensions. She knows that he is tired and she appreciates as keenly as anyone the fact that he is relying more and more on the people in his immediate entourage. I told her that I would be perfectly satisfied if he fired everyone else and relied solely on her. She agreed with me that no one could hope to get in from the outside as Felix Frankfurter had suggested. . . . She realizes that something ought to be done to build up public sentiment in the country and remarked caustically that, while we were doing nothing, Senator Wheeler and others were going about making speeches and creating an adverse sentiment."

On Friday, May 2, the president journeyed to Staunton, Virginia, to dedicate the home in which Woodrow Wilson had been born. With Eleanor on the West Coast, Missy accompanied him as the official hostess. It was a rough day for Roosevelt. His stomach was in turmoil, he was running a temperature, and all the color from his face was gone. "FDR looked as bad as a man can look and still be about," the *Time* reporter observed. Though he managed to get through his brief address, the accompanying pleasantries were canceled.

That evening, Dr. McIntire found the president suffering from an intestinal disturbance and severe anemia. His red-blood-cell count, which should have been at five million, had dropped suddenly to 2.8 million. The immediate therapy involved iron injections, two transfusions, and complete rest.

Unaware of her husband's illness, Eleanor was cheerfully ensconced with Anna and John at their home in Seattle. Curiously, when Eleanor had first arrived on the West Coast the week before, she had had a premonition that something was wrong. In her mailbox at the Ambassador Hotel in Los Angeles was a message saying that Washington was calling. "My heart sank," she admitted. "But in a few minutes my husband's calm and reassuring voice announced that he was just calling to give me a little conversation."

The president's illness kept him away from his desk for nearly two weeks. Canceling all appointments, he spent most of his time in his bedroom, accompanied only by Harry and Missy. To be sure, for at least half of that period he was truly sick, but even after his temperature was normal and his intestinal disturbance had cleared itself up, he remained in bed, inaccessible to all but Harry and Missy. At one point during this period of isolation, Robert Sherwood was invited in to talk. Surprised at how healthy Roosevelt seemed, never once coughing or sneezing, Sherwood asked Missy what was going on. Missy smiled and said, "What he's suffering from most of all is a case of sheer exasperation."

Missy knew her man. Frustrated by the contradictory impulses of public attitudes toward the struggle, dismayed at the prospect of carrying a divided country into war, the president was "waiting to be pushed into the situation." Throughout his long political career, Roosevelt had worked hard to fathom the unfathomable force of public opinion. From long experience, he had learned that in a democracy one man alone cannot guide tens of millions of people without following (and shaping, as far as one could) that intangible force called the spirit of the country. He had seen at first hand President Woodrow Wilson's failure to reinforce his foreign policy with public and congressional backing. He had, in effect, made what historian Eric Larrabee has called "a compact with the electorate which he had every reason for wishing to keep." Yet so confused and so volatile was public opinion in the spring of 1941 that Roosevelt was like a man staring into a fog.

By the middle of May, the percentage of people supporting convoys had risen from 41 percent to 55 percent, even though three-quarters of the population believed convoying would eventually put the country into war. At the same time, 79 percent of the people expressed the strong desire to stay out of the fighting; and 70 percent felt the president had either gone too far or was already doing enough to help Britain. Roosevelt recognized that with education he could command a national majority on convoys and even on direct involvement in the war, but he feared that his consensus would quickly vanish if a substantial portion of the people felt that he, rather than a recognized threat to national security, had compelled involvement.

So Roosevelt's bed became the escape he needed to avoid action and deflate pressure. "Missy was exactly right," journalist Eliot Janeway affirmed. "Simply put, the President was in bed because he was in a funk, feeling there was nothing he could do except let the tides fall."

• • •

Eleanor returned from the West Coast on the evening of May 7 in good spirits. Her trip had been a fruitful one, and there was much to tell the president. She had lectured in a dozen places, often following Charles Lindbergh. The questions she received, she believed, reflected his arguments and gave her an insight into the isolationists' frame of mind. She had spent a morning touring one of the new housing projects built under the U.S. Housing Authority; she had talked with a lively group of young men and women involved in a defense-training program sponsored by the NYA; she had spent an afternoon with a group of Negroes at a WPA center for Negro art. And, perhaps of greatest potential interest to the president, she had been taken on a tour of the Boeing Aircraft plant in Seattle, where she witnessed the completion of the first four motor bombers. "Since defense is now the key thing," Lash observed in his diary, "she is determined to learn as much as she can in her detailed human being interest sort of way, just as she had with WPA etc."

But before seeing her husband, Eleanor journeyed to Hyde Park for the weekend. That Sunday was Mother's Day, and Sara needed Eleanor's help in preparing her traditional Mother's Day broadcast to the nation. Speaking from her living room at exactly noon, the president's eight-six-year-old mother characterized 1941 as a year marked with great suffering, "probably the most crucial year in history." Watching Sara's stalwart performance, Eleanor could not help admiring the old lady. "There is no one I know who sets a greater value on the duties and pleasures of motherhood," Eleanor wrote in her column. That same week, Sara traveled to Toronto to raise money for one of her charities. "Isn't she amazing?" Eleanor commented to Anna.

Franklin and Eleanor talked together on the phone several times that weekend, and Eleanor was relieved to discover that he was in good humor, responsive and cheerful, "on the way to being quite well." Anxious to know whether his young trees had survived the early-spring drought, he asked her to make an inspection and report back as soon as she could. Hyde Park in the spring was one of the most delightful places in the world. Eleanor reveled in the sight of the river tumbling past and the sounds of the birds in the woods. When she reported that everything not newly planted seemed unharmed, he was delighted.

Yet no sooner had Eleanor arrived at the White House than the old tensions resumed. Impatient to disclose what she had discovered in her cross-country trip—delays in defense housing, inequities in recreational facilities provided for whites and Negroes, the refusal of certain industries to hire Italians and Germans—she found her husband "very tired and very edgy." What is more, she felt unable to break in on Harry and Missy's territory.

"The situation with Harry, Missy and Pa is funny," Eleanor admitted in a long letter to Anna. "It is a very closed corporation just now. So far I've told him nothing as I didn't think he was well enough to accept any disagreeable facts." But as long as she was away so often, it was inevitable that her husband would turn to others for companionship. It was, after all, Missy and Harry, not Eleanor, who had sat with Roosevelt in his bedroom night after night when he was sick, talking with him, playing cards with him, soothing his frustration.

In the third week of May, the president's energy returned; lethargy gave way to action. "Franklin is much better," Eleanor told Esther Lape, "really looks very well and is now working very hard to catch up with what he missed while he was ill." In the Oval Office, where silence had reigned for more than a fortnight, there was now a welcoming air, with lights burning until well after midnight and a steady stream of visitors.

After weeks of avoiding the press, the president announced that he would deliver a major speech to the nation on May 27. It seemed that everyone was asked to contribute to the draft—Hopkins, Stimson, Welles, Knox, Hull, Berle, Sherwood, and Rosenman. In the meantime, the White House received some twelve thousand letters from all over the country advising the president what to say. It fell to Sherwood and Rosenman, as usual, to collect all the suggestions and then sit with the president to hear what *he* wanted to say. Generally, Roosevelt would dictate his thoughts at the end of the day, until it was time to go to bed. Then the speechwriters would retire to the large table in the Cabinet Room, where, with scissors and paste, they would begin the task of assembling a coherent speech. The following night, after reading the draft, the president would dictate some more, and then his aides would return to the Cabinet Room to start a second draft.

These drafting sessions often lasted most of the night. During the preparations for the May 27 speech, Eleanor told Sherwood and Rosenman that she had seen their lights in the Cabinet Room at 3 a.m., and gently scolded them for working so hard and staying up so late. "If I may say so, Mrs. Roosevelt," Sherwood countered, "you were up rather late yourself." Unperturbed, Eleanor replied, "I was working on my mail," failing to understand why everyone laughed.

The major thrust of the speech concerned the president's decision to declare an unlimited national emergency, a step which, under the law, the chief executive could take only when he believed war to be imminent. With this proclamation came a variety of domestic and international powers which a peacetime president did not possess—including the power to increase the size of the regular army or navy, to place compulsory defense orders in factories or plants, and to assign priority rating to producers and suppliers, directing them to fill defense orders ahead of private orders. In the last hours before the speech, the president began to waver. "There's only a small number of rounds of ammunition left to use," he explained, "unless Congress is willing to give me more. This declaration is one of those few rounds, and a very important one. Is this the right time to use it or should we wait until things get worse—as they surely will?" Ultimately, he decided this *was* the right time.

Just before the president began to speak at 10:30 p.m., the electric meters in power stations across the country began jumping skyward as people everywhere, in cities and remote towns, in mountains and valleys, in mansions and tenements, turned on their radios. "For almost an hour," *The New York Times* reported, "a whole nation here stilled itself to listen to his words."

Speaking in the oppressive heat of the East Room into a bank of microphones before a gathering of representatives of the Pan American Union, the president began by recalling that he had promised the people he would not send their boys to war except in case of attack, then went on to define what was meant by the word "attack." "Some people seem to think that we are not attacked until bombs actually drop in the streets of New York or San Francisco or New Orleans or Chicago. But they are simply shutting their eyes to the lesson that we must learn from the fate of every nation that the Nazis have conquered. The attack on Czechoslovakia began with the conquest of Austria. The attack on Norway began with the occupation of Denmark . . . and the attack on the U.S. can begin with the domination of any base which menaces our security—North or South. . . . We know enough by now to realize that it would be suicide to wait until they are in our front yard. When your enemy comes at you in a tank or a bombing plane, if you hold your fire until you see the whites of his eyes, you will never know what hit you. Our Bunker Hill of tomorrow may be several thousand miles from Boston."

With this broadened definition of "attack," the president justified his decision to add more ships and planes to the American patrols. And beyond that, he promised that "all additional measures necessary to deliver the goods will be taken. Any and all further methods or combination of methods . . . are being devised."

Finally, "I have tonight issued a proclamation that an unlimited national emergency exists and requires the strengthening of our defense to the extreme limit of our national power and authority." In justifying his proclamation, he said that a succession of events had made it clear that "what started as a European war" had developed into "a war for world domination." Indifference to this fundamental fact would "place the nation at peril."

Eleanor was seated in the front row as the president spoke, surrounded on all sides by flags and representatives of all the nations of South and North America. "The atmosphere in the room was one of suppressed and intense excitement," she wrote. "Diplomats are trained to observe the amenities, no matter what they feel, but everybody's face showed some emotion as the evening progressed. I felt strangely detached, as though I were outside, a part of the general public. I represented no nation, carried no responsibility."

But then she looked at her husband's face and, "like an oncoming wave, the thought rolled over me. What a weight of responsibility this one man at the desk, facing the rest of the people, has to carry. Not just for this hemisphere alone but for the world as a whole! Great Britain can be gallant beyond belief, China can suffer and defend herself in equally heroic fashion, but in the end the decisive factor in this whole business, may perhaps be . . . the President of the United States. In my capacity of objective citizen, sitting in the gathering, I felt that I wanted to accept my responsibility and do my particular job whatever it might be to the extent of my ability. I think that will be the answer of every individual citizen of the U.S.A."

Harry Hopkins was in his bedroom, listening to the speech in his old bathrobe. According to Robert Sherwood, Hopkins always preferred to listen to the president's speeches on the radio, so he could imagine himself in the living room of an ordinary family. After the diplomats left, Eleanor came into Harry's room to invite him to join the president in the Monroe Room, where a small group of friends, including songwriter Irving Berlin, were gathered to enjoy a midnight snack. The president seemed completely at ease, laughing and smiling as he listened to Berlin play the piano and sing some of his favorite songs.

This transition from a grim speech to an intimate party with popular music, Rosenman observed, "would have been difficult for most men. For the President, however, those who knew him thought it nothing unusual. It was not callousness or indifference. It was the kind of relaxation that helped him to meet the terrible problems and burdens of the next day, and to live through twelve years of nerve-racking decisions."

The response to the speech was overwhelmingly favorable. More than a thousand telegrams were delivered to the White House that night. "They're 95 percent favorable," the president remarked. "And I figured I'd be lucky to get an even break on this speech."

On the whole, Henry Stimson was pleased with the speech. Though the final draft was not as strong as he had hoped—at the last minute, the president elected not to disclose his plans for transferring part of the fleet to the Atlantic—the proclamation of emergency promised to create a receptive atmosphere down the line, when more drastic steps were needed.

"We listened to father's speech on the train and were greatly thrilled," Anna wrote her mother. "The speech came over beautifully and he sounded well and strong, thank goodness." Listener polls published the next day revealed that the president's speech had set an all-time record in the history of radio. It was estimated that more than sixty-five million people in twenty million homes had heard the talk—70 percent of the total home audience in the U.S. The second-highest rating was also held by the president—his fireside chat on December 29 had been heard by 59 percent of the radio audience. Only one other broadcast had come even close to these figures: the second Louis-Schmeling fight at Yankee Stadium in 1938 had achieved a rating of 57.2 percent. To understand the magnitude of the interest in Roosevelt's words, one need only realize that America's top-ranking radio comedy shows—*Jack Benny, Bob Hope, Fibber McGee and Molly, The Goldbergs, Ma Perkins, Amos 'n' Andy*—were currently garnering what were considered fabulous ratings of 30 to 35 percent.

The speech was heard round the world as well. Goebbels lambasted it in his diary as "demagogic and aggressive." Roosevelt's talk, the propaganda minister believed, was nothing but "beer-hall bragging" that should not be taken seriously. "What can the USA do faced with our arms capacity? They can do us no harm. He will never be able to produce as much as we, who have the entire economic capacity of Europe at our disposal." Nonetheless, Goebbels admitted, Roosevelt's "reckless accusations" against Germany were irritating. "The USA stands poised between peace and war. Roosevelt wants war, the people want peace. . . . We must wait and see what he does next."

CHAPTER 10

"A GREAT HOUR TO LIVE"

The president's return to health at the end of May signaled an end to the hours Missy had enjoyed with him isolated from the world at large. Indeed, no sooner was Roosevelt's vigor restored than he motored to Pook's Hill to spend an afternoon with Princess Martha. Missy was under no illusion that the president fully reciprocated her devotion. She knew, however, that she had been a central presence in his life for twenty years, someone to whom he could always turn for undivided comfort and support. It was most unsettling to watch herself being supplanted by another woman.

As the felt injustice of her position accumulated, "she may have begun," Roosevelt's grandson Curtis Roosevelt surmised, "to face him with emotional demands: Why don't you respond to me, acknowledge me more, give me what I give you? She may have been getting too protective, making demands he couldn't meet. He could never cope with people who started making emotional demands. He didn't like weepy women. He was turned off by people who couldn't fit into his game."

Part of the problem, Elliott Roosevelt observed, was that "Missy was not as relaxing for the President as she used to be." She had become so influential in the Washington community, representing so many people to the president, that she could no longer simply "sit and simper" the way Martha did. For Jim Rowe, Felix Frankfurter, Harold Ickes, and untold others, Missy had become *the* conduit to the president, advising them "when to approach FDR and when to put off a vexing matter until another day." In Missy's files there are numerous requests for her to intervene on behalf of one person or another.

"Some of the people who worked closely in the administration with my husband . . . ," Eleanor Roosevelt later noted, "were brought in through Missy's efforts . . . [presidential adviser] Tom Corcoran, [Ambassador] William Bullitt. . . .

"I think none of them ever meant a great deal to Franklin. I also think they exploited Missy's friendship, believing her more interested in them personally than in what they could contribute to Franklin's work. In that they were mistaken; . . . though occasionally someone fooled her for a time, I always waited for enlightenment to come, with confidence born of long experience."

To make matters worse, Missy was afflicted that spring with insomnia, and the opiates she was taking to combat it were having a bad effect. More and more, her benign temper was punctuated by outbursts of irascibility. The pressure of her job began to get to her. "The president would work night after night," Missy's friend Barbara Curtis remarked, "and she was always right there working with him. He could take it, but I think her strength just didn't hold out to take all that."

"She said quietly one time that he had no idea of the demands he put upon people who were close to him," Barbara's husband, Egbert Curtis, recalled. "Would you do this? Would you do that? And it went beyond some of their powers to keep up."

On June 4, 1941, the dam burst. At six-thirty that evening, the president was relaxing with the members of his White House staff, including Missy, Harry Hopkins, Grace Tully, and Pa Watson, at a party hosted by Harry Somerville, the manager of the Willard Hotel. Mr. Somerville's party, an annual tradition, was normally held at the Willard, but on this evening the event was held at the White House so the president could attend. A piano was rolled in, and Marvin McIntyre played all the songs FDR loved.

Near the end of the dinner, Grace Tully recalled, Missy arose from her chair, saying she felt ill and very tired. Tully urged her to excuse herself and retire to her room, but she insisted on staying until the president left. He did so at 9:30 p.m. and, moments later, Missy let out a piercing scream, wavered, and fell to the floor unconscious. Dr. Ross McIntire and Commander George Fox, the president's physical therapist, took her to her room on the third floor and sedated her.

The doctors seemed to think at first it was some sort of heart trouble or a kind of nervous collapse, much like the ones she had experienced before, brought about in this case by a combination of sleeplessness and overwork. "It was very secret," White House secretary Toi Bachelder remembered. "The fact that she was ill was kept very quiet. Nobody said anything."

The next morning, when White House maid Lillian Parks arrived at the third-floor sewing room across from Missy's bedroom, a distraught nurse was in the hallway just outside Missy's door. "She's gotten up and I can't get her back in bed," the nurse said, asking for help. Parks walked into the room. "Come on, Miss LeHand," she said sternly. "Come get into bed." Responding to the tone of Parks' voice, Missy climbed meekly back into bed, where she remained, stroking Parks' arm, until Dr. McIntire and a second doctor arrived. McIntire told Parks that Missy was utterly exhausted, that she had been working too hard and needed complete rest. Her speech was slightly slurred, but this was attributed to the opiates and the sleeplessness.

Eleanor was in Hyde Park the night Missy collapsed, but as soon as she heard about the situation, she called Maggie Parks, Lillian Parks' mother, who had retired from the White House two years earlier. "Missy loved you," she told Maggie; "would you come back and sit with her at night? She is so lonely."

So Maggie sat through the nights with Missy, listening to her ramblings, her wild callings for FDR, her worries that her work was piling up and that her boss would suffer as a result. "It's sad to love a man so much," Maggie commented to her daughter, believing that "the strain of loving and knowing nothing could come of it" had helped bring about Missy's illness.

Eleanor did not know what to make of Missy's collapse. "Missy is very ill again," she confided to Anna on June 12. "She's been taking opiates and had a heart attack and then her mind went as it does, so now we have three nurses and the prospect of some weeks of illness before we get her straightened out." The following week, Eleanor suggested to Anna that Missy's problem was complicated by "change of life."

In 1941, the superstitions of past ages still retained a firm hold on popular attitudes toward menopause. "Too many women," Maxine Davis wrote in *Good Housekeeping,* "attribute all sorts of ailments—headaches, backaches, worries, depression, bad temper—to the menopause.... Other women nourish the gnawing fear that they'll lose their minds. They can remember Aunt Ida and Mother's horror stories of cousin Edith, who finally had to be committed to an institution."

In Missy's case, the loss of the childbearing function that accompanied menopause may have been the hardest to bear, providing dread confirmation of her failure to marry and build a family of her own. Though she was only forty-three, a monumental door was closing behind her, never to be opened again.

As Missy's feelings of desolation and uncertainty intensified, she began to write a series of agitated, scarcely decipherable letters to people who had been close to her over the years. Passages in these tormented letters were manic descriptions of her love life, fantasies of a world she had never entered. "The letters told of this one being in love with her, and that one wanting to marry her," Anna confided years later to the writer Bernard Asbell. "Everyone realized that she could no longer be trusted with important information. These friends and the family drew together to get the letters out of sight, to hush up Missy's lapse."

For the president, Missy's breakdown was a catastrophe. Day after day he visited her third-floor apartment. As time went by, she seemed to get worse, not better. How many hours Roosevelt had spent with Missy in this comfortable suite, escaping from official guests. There stood the familiar chair and the wooden bookcase he had carved for her years before as a special present; there the familiar desk and the four-poster bed. Nonetheless, everything had changed. On the bed, her head propped high on the pillows, Missy looked like a frightened stranger. Anguished eyes peered at him, instead of the gaze of love he had found for twenty years.

Unable to grieve, unable to accept the fact that Missy was not getting better as she always had before, Roosevelt developed an illness of his own; his throat became infected and he began to run a temperature. Worried about her husband's fever, Eleanor begged him to see an outside doctor. But in a letter to Anna, she admitted that Missy's collapse was the most likely cause of Franklin's illness. "Missy has been worse for the last few days," Eleanor confided, "and that may be at the bottom of much of Pa's trouble."

In retrospect, it is clear that Missy's condition was caused by neither insomnia nor the change of life; her collapse on the evening of June 4 was most likely a small stroke, an undiagnosed warning signal for the major stroke she suffered two weeks later. The naval ambulance arrived at the White House at 9:30 p.m. on Saturday, June 21. The president had spent the afternoon with Princess Martha and had worked through dinner clearing up his correspondence with Grace Tully. He was still at work when Missy was carried out on a stretcher to the ambulance and taken to Doctors Hospital at 35th and I streets.

Since Missy had suffered from rheumatic heart disease as a child—the dread disease which "licks the joints and bites the heart"—it is most likely that her stroke was caused by a cerebral embolism, a clot that was formed in her heart and carried by her blood to her brain. When it reached the narrow blood vessels of the brain, it got stuck, cutting off the blood flow to the brain cells on her left side. The result was the loss of movement in her right arm and leg, and the loss of her ability to speak coherently.

Word of Missy's illness gradually slipped out. "I was distressed to hear from Mother that you have been miserable," Anna wrote Missy. "Please, do be a good girl and get well quickly. Even thinking of the pressure of responsibility and work on you all makes one shudder and the importance of watching one's health becomes greater than ever. Being sick is never any fun—and it's not natural to think of you that way."

"My dear Missy," Sara Roosevelt wrote from Campobello, "I do not like to think of you still in bed, but I believe you and I are cases for bed. I for old age and you for rest to an overworked rather delicate organ. For the autumn perhaps you will come to Hyde Park and rest with me."

For her part, Missy must have been horrified by the breakdown of her body, overwhelmed by a sense of solitude. The doctors held out hope that over time she would be able to relearn the movements necessary for standing and walking, but she was particularly sensitive to the effect of her illness on her speech. She refused most visits, except those of the Roosevelts, who came to see her at Doctors Hospital nearly every week all summer long.

For the president, the visits were unbearable. All his life, he had steeled himself to ignore illness and unpleasantness of any kind, to maintain an attitude of perpetual cheer. So now he would wheel himself into her room, his face set in a wide smile, a series of amusing anecdotes on his lips. But the president's cheery monologues were not what Missy needed to hear. Tired and bewildered, filled with dread and foreboding, she frequently broke into tears. Suddenly Roosevelt had no more stories to tell. He would look at her, smile another smile, and say goodbye.

For Eleanor, who was more accustomed to vulnerability and loss, the visits were easier to handle. She went to see Missy as often as she could, sending her flowers, fruit, presents, and letters. "The strange thing," Elliott Roosevelt observed, "was that Mother was more protective and upset about Missy's illness than Father. He seemed to accept it and go through the loss without its affecting him nearly as much as I would have thought it would have affected him."

To outside observers, Roosevelt's equanimity in the face of Missy's illness seemed disturbingly coldhearted. "Roosevelt had absolutely no moral reaction to Missy's tragedy," Eliot Janeway remarked. "It seemed only that he resented her for getting sick and leaving him in the lurch. This was proof that he had ceased to be a person; he was simply the president. If something was good for him as president, it was good; if it had no function for him as president, it didn't exist."

In a moment of anger at the president after a bitter political fight that summer, Harold Ickes made a similar observation. "As I sat at the Cabinet table yesterday looking at the President," he recorded in his diary, "I felt a clear conviction that I had lost my affection for him . . . despite his very pleasant and friendly personality, he is as cold as ice inside. He has certain conventional family affections for his children and probably for Missy LeHand and Harry Hopkins, but nothing else. Missy, who has been desperately ill for several weeks, might pass out of his life and he would miss her. The same might be true as to Harry, but I doubt whether he would miss either of them greatly or for a long period. When Louis Howe died, so far as appearances, the President was not noticeably affected, although no one has ever had a more devoted friend than Louis Howe."

That Roosevelt made no outward display of his feelings did not mean, however, that he was indifferent to Missy's distress. Indeed, his actions tell a different story. While Missy was in the hospital, he ordered round-the-clock care, absorbed every expense, and wrote each of her doctors personal notes. "No words will ever be able to express to you," he wrote Dr. John Harper, "my very deep feeling of appreciation and gratitude for the outstanding and unselfish services you have rendered in looking after my secretary, Miss LeHand."

In the months that followed the stroke, Missy's condition improved, but ever so slightly. With the help of daily physical therapy, movement began to return to her right leg, and after many weeks of practice she was ready, with the help of a heavy brace and crutches, to start walking again. "The case has been a difficult one, indeed," Dr. Winfred Overholser wrote the president, "but I am encouraged by the progress made in the last few weeks." But such are the mysteries of rehabilitation that the right hand and arm stubbornly resisted any improvement at all, as did the function of speech. Though she was able to understand both spoken and written language, she was unable to speak herself except in simple phrases.

Recognizing that Missy's therapy would take months, if not years (and even when it was completed, there was scant hope that she could return to her demanding job in the White House), Roosevelt worried about what would happen to her if he should die. The only money Missy ever had was her annual salary, which at its peak of $5,000 was half that of the male secretaries. With no savings in the bank and no family money to back her up, there was no guarantee that her medical expenses would be covered.

With this in mind, Roosevelt took a decisive act. He arranged a luncheon with his old friend and legal adviser, Basil O'Connor. At the lunch, he told O'Connor that he wished to alter his will in order to leave half of his estate to Missy. O'Connor fiercely opposed the change, for it involved removing the Roosevelt children as beneficiaries. But Roosevelt insisted. He argued that "the children could care for themselves, but this faithful aide could not."

The new provision was incorporated into Roosevelt's will five months after Missy's stroke. After first directing that half of his estate (which was eventually probated at more than $3 million) be left to his wife, he directed that the remaining half be left "for the account of my friend Marguerite LeHand" in order to cover all expenses for "medical attention, care and treatment during her lifetime." Upon Missy's death, the trustees were instructed to distribute the remaining income in equal shares to his five children.

"I owed her that much," Roosevelt later explained to his son Jimmy. "She served me so well for so long and asked so little in return."

• • •

That June of 1941, a storm was gathering in the black community. Though some progress had been made in opening doors to blacks in the armed forces, discrimination in the mushrooming defense industry continued unabated. All over the country, the new war plants were refusing to hire blacks. "Negroes will be considered only as janitors," the general manager of North American Aviation publicly asserted. "It is the company policy not to employ them as mechanics and aircraft workers." In Kansas City, Standard Steel told the Urban League: "We have not had a Negro working in 25 years and do not plan to start now." And from Vultee Air in California a blanket statement was issued: "It is not the policy of this company to employ other than of the Caucasian race."

The black press abounded with stories of flagrant discrimination. In early 1941, a hundred NYA trainees were sent to Quoddy Village to work in an aircraft factory near Buffalo. One of the hundred was black, and he was the only one not hired, even though he had the best grades of the group. "Negroes who are experienced machinists are being refused employment," the *Pittsburgh Courier* observed, "while white men and boys who have had no training in this work are being hired and trained later."

"What happens," Walter White asked in a long letter to the *New York Post*, "when a Negro who has had excellent training at one of NYC's technical or trade schools applies for one of the thousands of new jobs opening up? He finds the jobs segregated even in New York City. 'Wanted—white Mechanics, tool and die makers, sheet metal workers.' Far less frequently he finds, 'Wanted—colored. Porters, cleaners, janitors.' " Or perhaps, White went on, "the colored applicant is told that he can get a job only if he is a member of the AFL aeronautical workers union, chartered by the International Association of Machinists, whose constitution bans all but white persons from membership."

The fundamental unfairness of the situation led A. Philip Randolph to a radical change in thinking. For years, he and other civil-rights leaders had relied on decorous middle-class pressure applied through letters, telegrams, and conferences with government-department heads. But now, as Randolph witnessed Negroes being "shunted from pillar to post, given the run-around and oft-times insulted when they applied for war jobs to help make our country an arsenal of democracy," he concluded that all these established methods were simply "chloroform for the masses. When the chloroform wears off, the passions of the beast of race prejudice flare up again."

The time had come, Randolph argued, setting the strategic stage for the civil-rights movement of later decades, to mobilize the power and pressure that resided, not in the few, not in the intelligentsia, but in the masses, the organized masses. "Only power," he observed, "can effect the enforcement and adoption of a given policy, however meritorious it may be."

Randolph's shift in strategy had taken concrete form in early 1941. Traveling with his friend and colleague Milton Webster on a long train ride through the deep south to visit the Sleeping Car Brotherhood Divisions, Randolph had suddenly declared that "we ought to get 10,000 Negroes and march down Pennsylvania Avenue and protest against the discriminatory practices in this rapidly expanding economy." There was silence; then Webster asked: "And where are you going to get 10,000 Negroes?" "We can get them," Randolph promised softly.

As the two civil-rights leaders continued their journey through the South, they proposed the idea of a Negro march on Washington at every stop where they could find an audience. "I think the first place we talked was Savannah," Webster recalled. "It scared everybody to death. The head colored man in Savannah opened up the meeting and introduced me and ran off the platform to the last seat in the last row." But as the word began to spread through the Brotherhood, thousands of voices joined in the refrain. For the first time, Randolph later recalled, "the voiceless and helpless 'little men' became articulate. In meeting after meeting, the 'forgotten black man' could rise and tell an eager and earnest crowd about jobs he had sought but never got, about the business agent of the union giving him the brush-off, how he had gone to the gates of the defense plants only to be kept out while white workers walked in, how he cooled his heels in an office and finally was told with a cold stare 'no more workers wanted.' "

Encouraged by the enthusiastic response, Randolph formed a national March on Washington Committee with branches in eighteen cities. Within days, the Sleeping Car Brotherhood was out on the streets, approaching people in churches and schools, shops, and bars, publicizing the march, and raising money to finance the movement. Black newspapers printed Randolph's call to march in banner headlines. "Be not dismayed in these terrible times," Randolph exhorted the black community. "You possess power, great power. The Negro stake in national defense is big. It consists of jobs, thousands of jobs. It consists of new industrial opportunities and hope. This is worth fighting for.... To this end we propose that 10,000 Negroes march on Washington.... We call upon President Roosevelt... to follow in the footsteps of his noble and illustrious predecessor [Lincoln] and take the second decisive step to free America—an executive order to abolish discrimination in the work place. One thing is certain and that is if Negroes are going to get anything out of this National defense, we must fight for it and fight for it with gloves off."

By June, there was every indication that, on the first of July, not ten thousand but perhaps twenty-five thousand Negroes would be streaming into Washington, reporter Murray Kempton wrote, "crying for their rights, to the boundless embarrassment not merely of politicians but of the arsenal of democracy which had forgotten them." Reports of a phenomenal surge of support were beginning to reach the White House—dozens of trains had already been hired from Chicago, Memphis, and Cleveland; thousands of dollars had been raised. "Let the Negro masses speak," Randolph proclaimed. "It will wake up Negro as well as white America."

In the White House, the reaction to the news that the march was gathering force was one of fear and anxiety. All spring long, the president had denied repeated requests from Walter White to discuss the exclusion of Negroes from employment in defense. "The pressures of matters of great importance," Pa Watson had informed White, "is such that it does not seem probable he will be able to comply with your request for a personal conference."

Fortunately, the president had Eleanor to keep him at least somewhat informed about the volatile situation. Her exhaustive travels that spring, which had taken her to various Negro projects, homes, and colleges—including Virginia College for Negroes and Tuskegee Institute, where she had addressed five thousand blacks in the chapel, had brought her to a clear understanding of why the idea of the march had so fully captured the heart and soul of the black community. Speaking to a crowd of nine thousand in early June at St. Paul Auditorium in Minnesota, with hecklers and placards in the audience proclaiming, "Who is President? Eleanor or Franklin?" and "My Day is not your day," she had spurred the black members of the audience to great cheers when she expressed her fervent hope for the time "when there would be no such thing as discrimination against any person in this country."

"Mrs. Roosevelt's coming will be a never to be forgotten event," one of those present, Joseph Albright, wrote the president's secretary Steve Early after her speech in St. Paul. "The praiseworthy manner in which she flayed racial discrimination before the large audience made a profound impression upon us all. . . . Will you express to the President that the opportunity for Negroes out here to see and hear Mrs. Roosevelt has only served to endear him more deeply in our regard and to strengthen our loyalty to his cause."

Eleanor returned to Washington armed with stories about blacks with Ph.D.'s and law degrees finding it impossible to secure work in defense plants except as janitors and cleaners. The stories had an effect upon the president. This was not how a democracy was supposed to work, and he knew it. Nor could he justify the position of the Naval Academy earlier that spring, when it refused to allow its lacrosse team to play against Harvard if a black member of Harvard's team appeared on the field.

On a Sunday in late May, Roosevelt sent a handwritten note to William Knudsen and Sidney Hillman containing a radical suggestion that may well be the first official call for what later became known as affirmative action. "To order taking Negroes up to a certain percentage in factory order work. Judge them on *quality*—the 1st class Negroes are turned down for 3rd class white boys." Two days later, Knudsen replied: "I have talked with Mr. Hillman and we will quietly get manufacturers to increase the number of Negroes for defense work. If we set a percentage it will immediately be open to dispute; quiet work with the contractors and the unions will bring better results."

It was precisely the realization that "quiet work" with contractors would never do the job that had led Randolph to the idea of direct action and mass appeal in the first place. But, however sympathetic the president was to the substance of Randolph's quest, he was vehemently opposed to the idea of tens of thousands of Negroes converging on the streets of Washington. He feared that people would be hurt or killed and that the march itself would set a bad precedent for other groups.

Recognizing that his wife enjoyed much deeper trust and support within the black community than he did, the president turned to her for help, asking her to share his concerns with the black leaders. Eleanor agreed, and wrote a thoughtful letter to Randolph. "I have talked with the President," she began, "and I feel very strongly that your group is making a very grave mistake at the present time to allow this march to take place. I am afraid it will set back the progress which is being made, in the Army at least, towards better opportunities and less segregation. I feel if any incident occurs as a result of this, it may engender so much bitterness that it will create in Congress even more solid opposition from certain groups than we have had in the past.... You know that I am deeply concerned about the rights of Negro people, but I think one must face situations as they are and not as one wishes them to be. I think this is a very serious decision for you to take."

Understanding the spirit in which Eleanor's letter was written, Randolph released it to the *Pittsburgh Courier*. "I am submitting the letter received from Eleanor Roosevelt," he explained, "which expresses an important point of view from not only an influential person but a strong and definite friend of the Negro. There is no question that can rise in the minds of the Negroes about the fact that she is a real and genuine friend of the race."

But Randolph was unable to accept Eleanor's advice, believing as he did that nothing had arisen in the life of Negroes since the Emancipation that had "gripped their heart and caught their interest and quickened their imagination more than the girding of our country for national defense without according them the recognition and opportunity as citizens, consumers and workers they felt justified in expecting." Nothing short of the president's commitment to issue an executive order abolishing discrimination in national defense would warrant calling off the march.

Feeling besieged on every side, Roosevelt called on Aubrey Williams, the liberal head of the National Youth Administration, for help. "When I got into the President's office," Williams recalled, "I saw that he was tired and irritable. I said nothing waiting for him to speak.... He rubbed his eyes and leaned over towards me and said: 'Aubrey, I want you to go to New York and get White and Randolph to call off the march.... The missus is up there and you can get in touch with her...." "Get the missus and Fiorello [LaGuardia] and Anna [Rosenberg, regional director of New York City's Social Security Board] and get it stopped.' "

The meeting took place at City Hall on the morning of June 13. "Mrs. Roosevelt reminded me of her sympathy for the cause of racial justice," Randolph recalled, "and assured me she intended to continue pressuring the President. But the march was something else. Had I considered the problems? Where would all those thousands sleep and eat?" Randolph answered that they would go to hotels and order dinner. "But the attitude of the Washington police, most of them Southerners," Eleanor went on, "and the general feeling of Washington itself are such that I fear that there may be trouble if the march occurs." Randolph listened to Eleanor's concerns but insisted that the movement for the march had touched a chord so deep that he "could not think of calling it off." Furthermore, Walter White added, they had tried all spring to see the president, but each time had been rebuffed. Eleanor assured White and Randolph that "she was definitely in favor of definite action to be taken now," and that she would get in touch with the president immediately, "because I think you are right."

After the meeting, Anna Rosenberg called Pa Watson to report that both Eleanor and LaGuardia agreed strongly that nothing would stop the march "except the President's pressure and direction." It was their joint recommendation that the president invite Randolph and White and the relevant government officials to a meeting in his office.

Roosevelt agreed. He scheduled a White House conference for Wednesday afternoon, June 18. Besides the two civil-rights leaders, he invited Secretary of War Stimson, Secretary of the Navy Knox, OPM heads Knudsen and Hillman, Aubrey Williams, and Anna Rosenberg. Eleanor was unable to attend: she and Joe Lash were on their way to Campobello to get the house in order for the arrival of thirty students for a Student Leadership Institute which Lash was running at the Roosevelt cottage in July.

The president opened the meeting with small talk and then, in typical fashion, turned raconteur, entertaining his audience with political anecdotes. To Roosevelt it seemed so natural that everyone should be fond of hearing his charming stories that he was somewhat taken aback when Randolph broke in. "Mr. President, time is running out. You are quite busy, I know. But what we want to talk with you about is the problem of jobs for Negroes in defense industries."

"Well, Phil, what do you want me to do?"

"Mr. President, we want you to issue an Executive Order making it mandatory that Negroes be permitted to work in these plants."

"Well, Phil, you know I can't do that.... In any event I couldn't do anything unless you called off this march of yours. Questions like this can't be settled with a sledge hammer.... What would happen if Irish and Jewish people were to march on Washington? It would create resentment among the American people because such a march would be considered as an effort to coerce the government and make it do certain things."

"I'm sorry Mr. President, the march cannot be called off."

"How many people do you plan to bring?"

"One hundred thousand, Mr. President."

The astronomical figure staggered belief. Perhaps Randolph was bluffing. Turning to White, Roosevelt asked, "Walter, how many people will really march?" White's eyes did not blink. "One hundred thousand, Mr. President," he affirmed.

Years later, NAACP leader Roy Wilkins suggested that it may well have been a bluff on Randolph's part, but what an extraordinary bluff it was. "A tall courtly black man with Shakespearean diction and the stare of an eagle had looked the patrician FDR in the eye—and made him back down."

Mayor LaGuardia broke the impasse. "Gentleman," he said, "it is clear that Mr. Randolph is not going to call off the march and I suggest we all begin to seek a formula." The president agreed, asking the black leaders to adjourn to the Cabinet Room with the government officials and come up with the kind of order they thought he should issue. Stimson was clearly annoyed. He considered the meeting "one of those rather harassing interruptions with the main business with which the Secretary of War ought to be engaged—namely, in preparing the Army for defense." Knudsen took the position that an executive order was unnecessary; it was his experience that "more can be done through persuasion and education than by force." But Randolph stood firm: "It was not enough to depend on persuasion and education since the process had been proved to be ineffective so far."

The next morning, Joe Rauh, a young government lawyer, was called in by presidential assistant Wayne Coy to draft the actual language of the order. "As Coy was leaving," Rauh recalled, he said: " 'Hey, Joe, if we're doing this don't forget the Poles.' The Roosevelt administration had been under fire for discriminating against the Poles in Buffalo. So Coy wanted me to throw them in as well, which I did, changing the phrase to read forbidding discrimination on grounds of 'race, color, creed or national origin.' "

When Rauh completed his work, the draft was sent to LaGuardia and Randolph, but Randolph was still not satisfied, arguing it was not strong enough. Back it came and back it went, and still Randolph wanted more. "Who is this guy Randolph," Rauh wondered. "What the hell has he got over the President of the U.S.?" Finally, Rauh said, "We've got every piece of constitutional power in this, there's nothing more I can do, but I've got an idea. I'll change it around one more time and then we should send it to Mrs. Roosevelt. Let her read it to Randolph and say: 'Now, I don't want a general critique that this is not strong enough; tell me what should be done.' "

Communicating with Eleanor on the remote island of Campobello was not easy. There was no phone in the cottage, so Eleanor had to walk a half-mile down the road to the home of the island's lone telegrapher, and sit on the steps until a call came through. But at last Eleanor spoke to Randolph, who agreed that the last draft was just great. The struggle was over. In later years, Rauh would come to believe that Randolph was "one of the greatest and most dignified men" he had ever known.

The president signed Executive Order 8802 on June 25. The order called upon both employers and labor unions "to provide for the full and equitable participation of all workers in defense industries, without discrimination because of race, creed, color or national origin." In addition, a five-member commission was set up, the Fair Employment Practices Commission, soon to be known as the FEPC. Chaired by Mark Ethridge, a liberal newspaperman from the South, the FEPC was empowered to investigate grievances, monitor compliance, and publicize its findings.

Randolph was thrilled. "The President has just drafted the Executive Order," he telegraphed Eleanor. "I therefore consider that the proposed Negro March on Washington is unnecessary at this time." The telegram went on to express his warmest thanks for her "fine spirit of cooperation and help in securing this action on the part of the President." There had grown between Randolph and Eleanor a strong bond of affection and respect. Even at the height of the tensions, Randolph had assured Eleanor that "the Negro people have the utmost faith in your great spirit and purity of heart on their question, and we know that whatever position you take is a result of your convictions that it is in the interest of the Negro people."

Rejoicing in the news, Eleanor telegraphed Randolph immediately that she was "very glad that the march has been postponed and delighted that the President is issuing an Executive Order on defense industries. I hope from this first step, we may go on to others."

The response of the black community to the executive order was overwhelmingly positive. It was greeted, the *Negro Handbook* noted, "as the most significant move on the part of the Government since the Emancipation Proclamation." The *Amsterdam News* called it "epochal to say the least," suggesting that, if Lincoln's proclamation had been designed to end physical slavery, Roosevelt's was designed "to end, or at least curb, economic slavery." To be sure, there remained serious concerns about the inadequate budget, the small staff, and the meager enforcement penalties provided, but it was, the National Negro Congress said, "a great step forward" nonetheless.

"Never before in the history of the nation," the *Chicago Defender* observed, had Negroes, from illiterate sharecroppers in Arkansas to college students in Chicago, "ever been so united in an objective and so insistent upon an action being taken." When the President signed the executive order, "faith in a democracy which Negroes had begun to feel had strayed from its course was renewed throughout the nation."

• • •

At dawn of June 22, 1941, in a stunning move that would prove to be a great turning point of the war, Germany invaded Russia. "Now the guns will be thundering," Goebbels recorded in his diary at 3:30 a.m. "May God bless our weapons."

The idea of invading Russia had been an integral part of Hitler's imperial dream for decades. "When we speak of new territory in Europe today, we must think principally of Russia and her border vassal states," he had written in *Mein Kampf* in 1925. "Destiny itself seems to wish to point out the way to us here. This colossal empire in the East is ripe for dissolution. The end of Jewish domination will also be the end of Russia as a state." The Nazi-Soviet pact of 1939 had not changed but simply postponed Hitler's plans.

"The novelty," Hitler's biographer Alan Bullock has written, "lay not so much in the decision to turn east as in the decision to drop the provision he had hitherto regarded as indispensable, a settlement with Britain first." Since the beginning of the war, the Nazi leader had insisted that he could oppose Russia only when he was free in the West. A two-front war had been the nightmare of German generals for a century. But in the last month of 1940, while the struggle in England was still unfinished, Hitler had committed himself to what would turn out to be an irrevocable decision to invade Russia in the spring. The war against Russia, he convinced himself, would be over quickly—in three months at most—and then the final attack on England could begin. "We have only to kick in the door," Hitler told General Alfried Jodl, "and the whole rotten structure will come crashing down."

On the eve of the attack, Hitler dispatched a letter to Mussolini. "Since I struggled through to this decision, I again feel spiritually free," he claimed. "The partnership with the Soviet Union . . . seemed to me a break with my whole origin, my concepts and my former obligations. I am happy now to be delivered from this torment."

"Everything is well prepared. The biggest concentration of forces in the history of the world," Goebbels noted in the last hours before the attack. The propaganda chief was not exaggerating. The Germans had amassed 150 divisions on the Russian border—more than three million men supported by twenty-seven hundred planes, thirty-three hundred tanks and six hundred thousand motor vehicles. "The Führer seems to lose his fear as the decision comes nearer. All the exhaustion seems to drop away."

For months, Britain and the U.S. had sought to warn Soviet leader Joseph Stalin that Allied intelligence reports indicated large numbers of German troops massing in the east. But nothing could shake the Russian dictator's blind hope that his country would somehow escape Hitler's vengeance. Thus the attack, when it came, took the Soviet Union by surprise, catching a large portion of the Soviet air force on the ground, destroying thousands of planes before they could get up into the air. "War is mainly a catalogue of blunders," Churchill observed in his memoirs, "but it may be doubted whether any mistake in history has equaled that of which Stalin and the Communist Chiefs were guilty when they . . . supinely awaited or were incapable of realizing, the fearful onslaught which impended upon Russia."

The Germans invaded Russia on a wide front, driving simultaneously toward Kiev and the Dnieper River in the south and toward the Baltic States and Leningrad in the north. Then the two armies were to make a junction and press on to Moscow. The opening days of the campaign seemed to justify Hitler's optimism. In two weeks' time, German troops had reached the Dnieper, and by mid-July they were in Smolensk, only two hundred miles from Moscow. Hundreds of thousands of Russians were killed in those first few weeks, and over six hundred thousand were taken prisoner. The German troops seemed unstoppable.

The president was asleep when news of the invasion reached Washington, but before the sun rose, lights were on at the State Department. At Chequers, Churchill was also asleep, having given strict orders never to be awakened before eight unless Britain herself had been invaded. At exactly eight, the prime minister's secretary John Colville knocked on Churchill's door. "Tell the B.B.C. I will broadcast at nine tonight," Churchill said. Minutes later, the prime minister's valet, Frank Sawyers, walked from room to room breaking the news. Anthony Eden, Churchill's foreign secretary, who had spent the weekend at Chequers, recalled that when he answered Sawyer's knock he was handed a large cigar on a silver salver. "The Prime Minister's compliments," Sawyers said, "and the German armies have invaded Russia."

Churchill spent the rest of the day preparing for his speech. He wanted his countrymen and the entire world to know that he was absolutely committed to Russia's cause. "I have only one purpose, the destruction of Hitler," Churchill explained to Colville before the speech, "and my life is much simplified thereby. If Hitler invaded Hell I would make at least a favourable reference to the Devil in the House of Commons."

Finished only twenty minutes before delivery, the speech was vintage Churchill—full of passion and conviction. "No one has been a more consistent opponent of Communism than I have for the last twenty-five years. I will unsay no word that I have spoken about it. But all this fades away before the spectacle which is now unfolding.... Can you doubt what our policy will be?... We are resolved to destroy Hitler and every vestige of the Nazi regime. From this nothing will turn us—nothing.... Any man or state who fights on against Nazidom will have our aid.... It follows, therefore, that we shall give whatever help we can to Russia and the Russian people...."

Roosevelt, in contrast, exercised a cautious policy of making haste slowly, keeping in touch with the unfolding events but maintaining a public silence. Indeed, that Sunday evening, he escaped the press by motoring to Princess Martha's estate in Maryland for a long and leisurely dinner. "Perhaps," an irritated Ickes mused, "he was not able to make up his mind as to what our attitude should be. It would be just like him to wait for some expression of public opinion instead of giving direction to that public opinion."

But, in spite of Harold Ickes' impatience, Roosevelt had good reason to move slowly. For one thing, his Cabinet was divided on how to respond to the Russian invasion. Whereas Ickes and Hull believed in giving Russia all possible aid, Stimson and Knox, along with General Marshall and the entire General Staff, were convinced that Russia would be unable to contain Hitler. Scarce American equipment sent in haste to the Soviet Union would simply fall into Germany's hands. Better, Stimson argued, to use "this precious and unforeseen period of respite" to redouble our aid to England and push "with the utmost vigor our movements in the Atlantic theater of operations."

Across the United States, opinion was equally divided. For the isolationists, the Russian invasion simply confirmed the wisdom of keeping America out of the war. The struggle between Nazism and communism is "a case of dog eat dog," Missouri Democrat Bennett Clark argued. "Stalin is as bloody-handed as Hitler. I don't think we should help either one." America should rejoice, isolationist opinion held, in watching two hated dictatorships bleed each other to death. For Catholics, who felt bound by a recent papal encyclical which stated that communism was "intrinsically wrong" and that "no one who would save Christian civilization may give it assistance on any understanding whatsoever," the best action was to do nothing.

On the political left, confusion reigned. For months, following the Nazi-

Soviet pact, communist-leaning organizations had been busily engaged in marching for peace, provoking strikes, and opposing aid to England. With Russia under attack, however, these same forces began to cry out for immediate intervention and massive aid for Russia. Robert Sherwood recalled attending an interventionist rally in Harlem on the Sunday afternoon of the Russian invasion. When he entered the Golden Gate Ballroom, there was a communist picket line in front with placards condemning the Fight for Freedom supporters as "tools of British and U.S. Imperialism." By the end of the rally, the picket line had totally disappeared. "Within that short space of time," Sherwood marveled, "the Communist party line had reached all the way from Moscow to Harlem and had completely reversed itself."

That same day, in a different part of the city, Michael Quill, the left-leaning head of the Transport Workers of New York, was delivering an angry speech denouncing the imperialist war, arguing that the American worker should have absolutely nothing to do with it. In the middle of his speech, he was handed a note informing him that the Nazis had invaded the Soviet Union. Without missing a beat, Quill totally changed direction, arguing that "we must all unite and fight for democracy."

In Campobello, where she sat by her portable radio with her friend Joe Lash and the reporter May Craig, Eleanor was unsure what to make of the news. "Will it be good or bad?" she kept asking. It all depended "on whether the Russians can hold out." But then "where will our Catholics go?" For his part, Lash felt immensely relieved. "It's the event I've been waiting for since the Nazi-Soviet Pact," he admitted in his diary. For two years, Lash had been caught in the crossfire between his peace-oriented leftist friends and his own belief that Hitler had to be fought. But now all those divisions were suddenly healed. Still, Lash worried. "I couldn't believe that Hitler would attack if he wasn't sure of victory."

From morning to night, Eleanor and her friends listened to the radio. Finally, with a little persuasion, Eleanor agreed to call her husband to get more information, using the island's single telephone connection. "He said he thought it would be helpful," Eleanor repeated to Lash, "except for the Catholics." He said "Hitler expected to defeat Russia in two months. . . . We asked whether he would go on radio. Said he wouldn't. Said it was too damn hot.'"

Yet, when the president finally met with the press in his office on June 24, he made it all sound easy. "Of course we are going to give all the aid we possibly can to Russia," he declared with a smile, never for a moment betraying the anxiety he must have felt in deciding to overrule his military advisers and stake everything on the chance that the Red Army could hold out until the onset of winter, much longer than anyone was predicting it could at the time. His only problem, he said, was that he had absolutely no idea what the Soviet government actually needed. Indeed, so scant were the diplomatic reports from Russia that he "probably knew less of what was going on in Moscow at this time than any desk man in a newspaper office."

And even after a specific list was obtained, he emphasized, " we can't simply go to Mr. Garfinkel's [department store] to fill the order."

Still thirsting for firsthand knowledge three weeks later, Roosevelt sent Hopkins on an arduous double mission to London and Moscow. The first leg of his circuitous journey took him to Montreal, to Gander, Newfoundland, and from there to Prestwick, Scotland. By the time he reached Britain, he was seriously ill, but, as usual, he refused to rest, insisting that he be taken immediately to see Churchill. The two men discussed the new landscape created by the Russian invasion. Hopkins assured Churchill that the president wanted Britain to have first lien on all planes, tanks, and munitions, but he needed to know in detail how the British and Russian requests could fit together. When Hopkins left Chequers, he asked Churchill if there was anything he wanted to tell Stalin. "Tell him, tell him," Churchill said, "tell him that he can depend on us. . . . Goodbye—God bless you, Harry."

After a difficult journey seated on a machine gunner's stool near the tail of an unheated PBY plane, the ailing envoy arrived in Moscow and was taken inside the Kremlin through a series of long corridors to meet Joseph Stalin. Hopkins later wrote: "No man could forget the picture of the dictator of Russia . . . an austere, rugged determined figure in boots that shone like mirrors, stout baggy trousers and snug fitting blouse. He wore no ornament, military or civilian. He's built close to the ground, like a football coach's dream of a tackle. He's about five feet six, about a hundred and ninety pounds. His hands are huge, as hard as his mind. His voice is harsh but ever under control. He's a chain smoker, probably accounting for the harshness of his carefully controlled voice. He laughs often enough, but it's a short laugh, somewhat sardonic, perhaps. There is no small talk in him."

Hopkins was elated by his intimate conversation with Stalin. He found the Russian leader intelligent, courteous, and direct. "Not once did he repeat himself. He talked as he knew his troops were shooting—straight and hard. . . . He smiled warmly. There was no waste of word, gesture, nor mannerism. . . . Joseph Stalin knew what he wanted, knew what Roosevelt wanted, and he assumed that you knew."

In four hours of conversation, Hopkins saw no signs of the cruel and ruthless temperament that lay behind Stalin's mask of politeness. Like so many other Americans who met Stalin during the war, Hopkins came away impressed. "There was little in Stalin's demeanor in the presence of foreigners," Russian envoy Charles Bohlen later admitted, "that gave any clue of the real nature and character of the man." Yet this son of an alcoholic who began working as a troubleshooter for Lenin, organizing a series of bank robberies to fill the revolutionary coffers, and eventually rose to the top of the Communist Party, was directly responsible for the deaths of millions of his own countrymen. Through his forced collectivization of the Russian peasants in the twenties and his purge trials of the thirties, which resulted in the execution of every rival Bolshevik figure, Stalin had spread a reign of terror through the entire Russian nation. Hopkins must have had some sense of these events, but Russia was still so embroiled in mystery that he was able, like Churchill, to let the past fade away before the unfolding spectacle of the Nazi invasion.

As Hopkins listened to Stalin talk, even with the thunder of the German army rumbling in the distance, he came away convinced that Russia could and would hold out. However many Russian troops were killed, there were always more to take their place. "I feel ever so confident about this front," Hopkins cabled Roosevelt. "The morale of the population is exceptionally good. There is unbounded determination to win." Stalin admitted that the Soviets had been taken by surprise and that the German army was "of the very best," with "large reserves of food, men, supplies and fuel," but he argued that the Red Army had superiority in numbers of divisions. Moreover, the Germans were already finding that moving mechanized forces through the vast plains and thick forests of Russia was "very different than moving them over the boulevards of Belgium and France."

The primary need of the Russian army, Stalin told Hopkins, was for vast quantities of light anti-aircraft guns to give protection against low-flying planes. The second need was aluminum, to be used in the construction of airplanes. It was this request that convinced Hopkins that Stalin was viewing the war on a long-range basis. "A man who feared immediate defeat would not put aluminum so high on the list of priorities." The third need was machine guns. "The outcome of the war in Russia," Stalin told Hopkins, "would largely depend on . . . adequate equipment, particularly in aircraft, tanks and anti-aircraft." In short, the Soviet Union, like Britain, was depending on America's miraculous mass production to produce the weapons and material needed to win the war.

• • •

Though this sublime faith in America's productive capacity would ultimately be justified, the mobilization effort in the summer of 1941 remained disappointing. There were growing signs of forward movement in a number of different areas, but overall production was still lagging. In July, *Life* devoted a special issue to analyzing America's progress in national defense over the previous year. "The country is awake," *Life* concluded, "though not yet aroused." More than $30 billion had been set aside for defense, yet there was still not a lot to show, since a high proportion of the funds had gone into plant expansion and tooling up.

Among the crucial instruments of war, planes were still a major problem. Though a bottleneck in engines had been cleared up, propellers were now in short supply, and the production process as a whole was nowhere near as fast as it would have to be for the U.S. to catch up with Germany. Production of medium tanks had made excellent progress in 1941—Chrysler's new twenty-eight-ton tank was two months ahead of schedule—but the army still had no heavy tanks. The "brightest spot" in defense was smokeless-powder production, which had been almost nonexistent two years before and was now moving so rapidly that cutbacks might soon be possible. Pride could also be taken in General Motors' AC Spark Plug factory, which had turned from spark plugs to .50-caliber machine guns and was now rifling forty barrels in the time it used to take to rifle one, but production of armor plate was behind schedule, as was production of antitank guns. Surely, *Life* concluded, the defense situation in 1941 was better than it had been in 1940, but, considering the urgency of the crisis, things "should be a lot better."

The president's men refused to acknowledge failure. They defined the first year of the mobilization process as an "educational phase." They likened the president to a baseball promoter who had built a new stadium and a new team from the bottom up and was now waiting to get the rest of the county into the grandstands. Then the game of total defense could really begin.

To be sure, a tooling-up period of six to twelve months was inevitable in the production of complex munitions, but the president could not escape the charge that he lost precious time in 1940 by failing to push business harder toward all-out war production. He had had an election to win and needed to make peace with business in order to win it, but a price had been paid.

Aluminum was a case in point. The previous November, Edward Stettinius, NDAC commissioner for industrial materials, had assured the country that there was more than enough aluminum for everything in sight. For forty-eight years, one monopoly, ALCOA, had been supplying America with 100 percent of all the aluminum it needed, and now, Stettinius claimed, this "good' monopoly was gearing up for the peak load required for the airplane defense program.

Not everyone agreed that ALCOA was a good monopoly. For two years, Thurman Arnold's antitrust division in the Justice Department, "the battered citadel of a romantic lost cause," to use I. F. Stone's words, had been waging war against ALCOA. Arnold's antitrust suit, which had generated thousands of pages of testimony but was still to be decided, had the fervent support of Eleanor Roosevelt, who saw in the struggle the old fighting spirit of the New Deal.

"There never was a monopoly as tight and as agile as ALCOA," observed Arthur Goldschmidt, who was working for Harold Ickes at the time. "First they had patent control, then they moved to control power, then mining. Everything they did was calculated to keep supply down and prices up. They even kept the auto industry—no mean feat—from having scrap, fearing it would lower prices."

Limited supply was damaging enough in peacetime; in wartime, it was catastrophic, for, even as Stettinius was heaping praise on ALCOA's unlimited capacity, ALCOA was unable to fill the defense orders already on its books. "As soon as Roosevelt made his speech calling for fifty thousand planes," Goldschmidt recalled, "I took out a yellow pad and figured out how much aluminum was necessary for each plane, recognizing that bombers take more than fighters. When I totaled up the figures, it was clear that the astronomical amount needed was way beyond what ALCOA was producing." Worse still, since no one at ALCOA was willing to admit this fact in public, the OPM was still discouraging others from entering the field.

It took the creation of the Truman Committee, charged in April 1941 with responsibility for investigating the national defense program, to spur new companies into the field. As one airplane company after another testified at hearings to delays in manufacturing as a result of the shortages of aluminum, the ALCOA men finally had to admit that they simply could not keep up with demand. The government responded to the admission by bringing Reynolds Metal Company into the aluminum business with a generous Reconstruction Finance Corporation loan to finance construction of a large new plant. But invaluable time had been lost. "When the story of the war comes to be written," Harold Ickes testified at the hearings, "if it has to be written that it was lost, it may be because of the recalcitrance of ALCOA."

In July, while Hopkins was in Russia discussing Russia's desperate need for aluminum, the OPM announced a two-week nationwide scrap drive to collect worn-out pots and pans for remelting and reuse. It was estimated that five thousand dishpans, ten thousand coffee percolators, two thousand roasters, and twenty-five hundred double boilers would make one plane. All told, it was hoped that the aluminum gathered from American housewives would make about two thousand planes.

The response was overwhelming. Enthusiastic householders, delighted at the call for service, hauled an astonishing collection of aluminum wares to their village greens—Uncle Mike's coffeepot, Aunt Margaret's frying pan, the baby's milk dish, skillets, stew pots, cocktail shakers, ice-cube forms, artificial legs, cigar tubes, watch cases, and radio parts. Great piles of the precious metal accumulated.

All along, Roosevelt had argued that, once the energies and passions of the American people were aroused, America's home front would win the war. The aluminum drive was the first test of the president's belief, and the people came through with spectacular ingenuity and imagination. In Cleveland, a popular dairy promised one free ice-cream cone to every child who turned in a piece of aluminum. In Tacoma, a police judge declared that every fine assessed during the scrap drive would have added to it one piece of aluminum. In Lubbock, Texas, a likeness of Adolf Hitler was placed in the middle of the courthouse square as a target for the pots and pans hurled by the citizens. In Albany, Mrs. Lehman, wife of the governor, turned in two dozen pieces of kitchenware, including an ice-cream mold. "Many a good dessert has it molded for this family," she said.

But popular success was not matched at the administrative level. In the midst of the drive, Undersecretary of War Patterson discovered to his horror that some quartermaster had ordered dozens of aluminum chairs and brass cuspidors. "He laughed over this," David Lilienthal recorded in his diary, "saying that if you didn't take it as a joke, it would be awful." Worse still, the authorities eventually determined that, though scrap could be remelted for peacetime purposes, only virgin aluminum could be used in the making of planes. Nonetheless, what Roosevelt had stirred up with the great aluminum-scrap drive was nothing less than an exhibition of the dormant energies of a patriotic democracy.

• • •

By the middle of the summer, heartened by the reports Hopkins had cabled from Moscow, the president was fully committed to sending Russia everything she needed as quickly as possible. "I am sick and tired of hearing that they are going to get this and they are going to get that," he told his Cabinet during a forty-five-minute outburst on Friday afternoon, August 1; "the only answer I want to hear is that it is under way."

The president directed his fire mainly at Stimson, who looked "thoroughly miserable," Morgenthau observed. It was, Ickes wrote, "one of the most complete dressings down that I have witnessed." The Russian war had been going on for six weeks, Roosevelt pointed out, and, despite our initial promises, we had done nothing for them. He believed that the War Department and the State Department were giving the Russians a runaround. "Get the planes off with a bang next week," Roosevelt insisted, specifying that 150 pursuit planes be sent along with a smaller number of four-engine bombers. "I want to do all of this at once," he declared, "in order to help their morale."

Stimson thought the attack "highly unfair," arguing that the delay was "due largely to the uncorrelated organization which the President had set up." He had never seen a list of Russian wants, nor had the War Department. The slip-up was not the fault of the War Department, he countered, but of Harry Hopkins' organization. With Hopkins away, there was no one with authority to cover sales to other countries. Furthermore, Stimson insisted, even if the administrative snafus were straightened out, the United States simply did not have the equipment to supply both Britain and Russia. "All of these other people are just hellbent to satisfy a passing impulse or emotion," Stimson remarked in his diary, "and they have no responsibility over whether or not our own army and our own forces are going to be left unarmed or not."

General Marshall heartily agreed with this sentiment. "In the first place," Marshall wrote Stimson, "our entire Air Corps is suffering from a severe shortage. . . . If any criticism is to be made in this matter, in my opinion it is that we have been too generous to our own disadvantage and I seriously question the advisability of our action in releasing the P-40s at this particular time."

But the president refused to back down, saying that "we must get 'em, even if it was necessary to take them from the troops." He was really in a "hoity-toity humor," Stimson wrote, "and wouldn't listen to argument." Ickes was delighted: for the first time in months, he observed, the president seemed tough, alert, and "very much on the ball," finally recognizing that "this was a time to take some risks." Ickes' own view of the Russian aid situation was that "we ought to come pretty close to stripping ourselves, if necessary, to supply England and Russia, because if these two countries between them can defeat Hitler, we will save immeasurably in men and money."

As soon as the Cabinet meeting was over, the president designated Wayne Coy, whom he considered one of his best administrators, to take charge of Russian orders. "We have done practically nothing to get any of the materials they asked for on their actual way to delivery in Siberia," Roosevelt wrote Coy the next morning. "Please get the list and please with my full authority, use a heavy hand—act as a burr under the saddle and get things moving!"

Even with the president's order, it was not easy to get things moving. "Our own Army and Navy were impoverished," Coy later explained. "Congress and the American press were demanding more supplies for the Army then in training." It was only "little by little," Coy wrote, that "there came to be an understanding that Russia's ability to hold off the German hordes gave us greater time to train and equip an Army and Navy and build up military production. As that opinion grew, the Russian supply program grew."

With the signing of the first Moscow protocol in the fall, the U.S. committed itself to a long list of supplies, including trucks, tanks, submachine guns, fighter planes, light bombers, enough food to keep the Russian soldiers from starving, and enough cotton, blankets, shoes, and boots to clothe and bed the entire Russian army. A few weeks later, the president formally declared the defense of the Soviet Union vital to the United States, bringing Russia under lend-lease. A massive aid program, second in size only to the British, was finally under way.

• • •

On August 3, Roosevelt left Washington, supposedly for a midsummer fishing trip in the waters of Cape Cod. "My husband, after many mysterious consultations," Eleanor recalled, "told me that he was going to take a little trip up through the Cape Cod Canal. . . . Then he smiled and I knew he was not telling me all that he was going to do."

"There was nothing about the start of the trip to make us think that it was other than the usual thing," Dr. McIntire recalled. The party consisted only of Pa Watson, naval aide Captain John Beardall, and McIntire—"all tried and true fishermen." To be sure, McIntire noted that Roosevelt seemed particularly excited, but the doctor attributed his lightened mood "to the lift that a vacation at sea always gave him."

"I hope to be gone ten days," Roosevelt wrote his mother in Campobello. "The heat in Washington has been fairly steady and I long to sleep under a blanket for the first time since May. But I am feeling really well and the progress of the war is more conducive to my peace of mind—in spite of the deceits and wiles of the Japs. Do take care of yourself and you will read shortly daily reports from the Potomac."

Before he left, the president made plans to join Princess Martha for a sail in Buzzards Bay, along the coast of Massachusetts, where she was vacationing with her children for the month of August. "I hope this map will be sufficient for you to find us on the cross marked," the princess wrote the president. "It is the second small pier on the right hand side when entering the bay. It belongs to the New Bedford Yacht Club which is a square house with a bright green roof. I am very much looking forward to your visit."

On the morning of the 4th, a clear and sunny day, the president's yacht found the spot, picking up Princess Martha and her brother Prince Carl of Sweden. Nearly twelve months had passed since Martha's arrival in the U.S., and in that time Roosevelt had seen more of this good-natured, pretty woman than of any other person beyond his immediate White House circle. The little party fished, ate lunch on the dock, and fished some more. People sailing small boats that day swore they had seen the president of the United States at the edge of the yacht, dressed in a sport shirt and slacks. "They came back and told their friends," Frances Perkins recalled. "People said they were absolutely crazy and they had dreamed something." At the end of the relaxing day, the *Potomac* headed back to South Dartmouth. As the yacht neared the harbor, the president loaded his royal guests onto a speedboat and personally escorted them to the dock. Then, under a bright moon, the *Potomac* sailed to Martha's Vineyard.

The real adventure began as the *Potomac* came upon a flotilla of American warships—including the heavy cruiser the U.S.S. *Augusta* and five destroyers. On the decks of the *Augusta* were all the principal officers of the U.S. Armed Forces—General George Marshall; Admiral Harold Stark; General Henry Arnold, commander of the U.S. Army Air Force; and Admiral Ernest King, commander-in-chief of naval forces. Transferring to the *Augusta,* the president prepared to begin a secret journey through treacherous seas to a conference off the coast of Newfoundland with Winston Churchill.

On the other side of the Atlantic, Churchill was readying himself for his part of the historic voyage on board a new British battleship, the *Prince of Wales.* On the morning of his departure, Churchill's aide-de-camp found him as excited as a schoolboy. "Churchill probably never had shown so much exuberance and excitement since Harrow," Commander W. H. Thompson wrote. "He bumped over the grass of his country place like a balloon dragged by a hurrying child. He was all smiles and mystic gestures, quick lurches of the head, whispers." Three times that morning, Churchill asked Thompson when they were due to depart, and when the appointed hour finally arrived, he jumped into the waiting car and "flashed his most bewitching smile."

"We are just off," Churchill cabled Roosevelt as the *Prince of Wales* put out to sea. "It is 27 years ago today that the Huns began their last war. We must make good job of it this time. Twice ought to be enough. Look forward so much to our meeting."

Harry Hopkins had flown thirty hours in rough weather from Moscow to the airfield at Archangel, on the White Sea, to the British airbase at Scapa Flow, Scotland, so that he could meet up with the *Prince of Wales* and journey with Churchill to the Atlantic Conference. In the middle of his flight, he realized he had left his satchel of life-sustaining medicines in Moscow, but he refused to turn back, knowing that if he did he would miss his connections with Churchill. Without his daily injections, he became desperately ill. By the time he arrived aboard the *Prince of Wales,* he seemed, Robert Sherwood has written, "at the end of the last filament of the spider's web by which he was hanging on to life." But after eighteen hours of sleep and emergency transfusions, he miraculously revived. In the mornings, he worked on his Russian report; in the afternoons, he sat with Churchill on the deck talking; in the evenings, he and Churchill spent hours playing backgammon for a shilling a game.

Through the entire seven-day trip, Churchill was irrepressibly cheerful. He sang merrily, walked informally about the ship, and for the first time in months read books for pleasure. He was about to meet the legendary president of the United States, and he could no longer contain his excitement. "You'd have thought Winston was being carried up to the heavens to meet God!" Hopkins later said. In his conversations with Hopkins, Churchill struggled to find out what kind of man Roosevelt was underneath. What did the New Deal really mean to him? What did he really think of Germany? Across the Atlantic, Roosevelt was asking Frances Perkins, who had known Churchill as a young man before World War I, a similar set of questions. What kind of fellow was he? Would he keep his word? Was he angry at anybody? Did anger becloud his judgment at times?

Hopkins understood how important it was for the future of both Britain and the U.S. that these two men get along. Knowing both personalities, he could see that they had much in common. They had both learned through long experience, one reporter wrote, that "the longest way around is sometimes the shortest way home. Both had a gift for rhetoric, an instinct for the telling phrase. They were both students of politics and history." But there were differences—Roosevelt, Hopkins believed, was more of an idealist in international affairs; Churchill was still an old-style imperialist. Roosevelt was almost always charming, enjoying gossip and small talk, whereas Churchill tended to be gruff, wasting little time on pleasantries. On the other hand, Churchill was more forthright and open with people than Roosevelt. Hopkins' main concern was that both men, accustomed to being the focus of attention, would continually try to take center stage. He feared their formidable egos would clash. "I suppose you could say," he told CBS correspondent Edward R. Murrow when he first arrived in London to meet Churchill, "that I've come here to try to find a way to be a catalytic agent between two prima donnas." But Hopkins' worries would soon be put to rest. From the moment the two men met, it was clear that they were destined to be not only allies in a common cause but special friends.

On Saturday morning, August 9, the *Prince of Wales,* with her flags flying and her band playing the Sousa march "Stars and Stripes Forever," came within sight of the *Augusta.* "Around us were numerous units big and small from the U.S. Navy," Churchill's aide-de-camp Lieutenant Thompson recalled. "How hungrily Winston Churchill looked over their firepower. How we needed it!" With the naked eye, the figure of Franklin Delano Roosevelt could be discerned standing on the upper deck, supported by his son Elliott. As Churchill boarded the *Augusta,* the crowd stirred and the navy band struck up "God Save the King." Roosevelt remained still for several instants. Then a smile began to run over his face like a rippling wave and his whole expression turned into one of radiant warmth. "I have never seen such a smile," Thompson said. "At last, we've gotten together," Roosevelt said, with that gay and brotherly cordiality which could not help charming the prime minister. "Yes," Churchill nodded, with an equally agreeable elegance of intonation. "We have."

The opening discussion centered on what to do about Japan's increasingly aggressive stance in the Pacific. For more than a year, Roosevelt had been trying to avoid a showdown with Japan, whose expansionist policies under Premier Fumimaro Konoye threatened American interests in the Pacific. To the president's mind, a détente with Japan was essential to gain the time he needed to train the armed forces and mobilize the factories to accomplish the real end of American foreign policy—the destruction of the Hitler menace. Roosevelt believed an early war with Japan would mean "the wrong war in the wrong ocean at the wrong time."

In recent months, an intense struggle had broken out within the Cabinet. Stimson, Morgenthau, and Ickes were convinced that stronger measures—including a total embargo on oil shipments—were required, while Hull insisted that stopping oil would inevitably lead to war. In June, the debate over the oil embargo had assumed political significance at home when Ickes, in his capacity as fuel administrator, was forced to ration oil in New England. "It's marvelous," Morgenthau taunted the president, describing a cartoon just published in the *Washington Star.* "It's got you leaning up against the gas tanks saying sorry, no gas today and . . . it's got a car driving up with a Japanese as a chauffeur and Hull filling the gas tank . . . and Sumner Welles saying, any oil, sir, today?"

Despite the urgings of Morgenthau and Ickes, the president continued to hold out against imposing an embargo, fearing it would simply drive Japan to the Dutch East Indies and that would mean war in the Pacific. "It is terribly important for the control of the Atlantic," Roosevelt told Ickes on the first of July, "for us to help keep peace in the Pacific. I simply have not got enough Navy to go around—and every little episode in the Pacific means fewer ships in the Atlantic."

"The Japanese are having a real drag-down and knock-out fight among themselves," Roosevelt further explained, "and have been for the past week —trying to decide which way they are going to jump—attack Russia, attack the South Seas (thus throwing in their lot definitely with Germany) or whether they will sit on the fence and be more friendly with us. No one knows what their decision will be."

But in mid-July, when forty thousand Japanese troops invaded rubber-rich Indochina and quickly took over the country, the president finally agreed to take retaliatory action. He froze all Japanese assets in the U.S., notified Japan that the Panama Canal would be closed for repairs, and announced that he was cutting off all high-octane, gasoline. Whereas Stimson and Ickes believed that all gasoline—not just high-octane, suitable for airplanes—should be embargoed, Roosevelt preferred to move one step at a time, "to slip the noose around Japan's neck, and give it a jerk now and then."

Churchill was ready at the Atlantic Conference to take a tough line against Japan. He pleaded with Roosevelt to sign a joint declaration warning Japan that any future encroachment in the South Pacific would produce a situation in which the U.S. and Great Britain "would be compelled to take counter measures even though this might lead to war." Roosevelt seriously considered Churchill's proposal, but in the end he settled on a softer, unilateral message, fearing that the strong language of the joint declaration would guarantee war.

Turning to the other side of the world, the two leaders forged a concrete arrangement which finally committed American envoys to escort both British and American ships as far as Iceland. Though Churchill had hoped for more dramatic evidence of American support, he came away convinced that Roosevelt "would wage war, but not declare it and that he would become more and more provocative" in the Atlantic, including forcing an incident at sea with Germany.

But the Atlantic Conference would be remembered by posterity not so much for the strategic commitments that were made as for the Atlantic Charter, a stirring declaration of principles for the world peace to follow "the final destruction of the Nazi tyranny." For some time, Roosevelt had been anxious to lay down a set of broad principles which would guide Allied policy during and after the war. Churchill readily agreed to the idea, eager for any means to identify the policies of the United States and Great Britain. The resulting declaration pledged the two countries to seek no territorial aggrandizement, pursue no territorial changes which did not accord with the wishes of the people concerned, respect the rights of all peoples to choose the form of government under which they would live, commit themselves to free trade, and work for both disarmament and a permanent system of general security.

For both Roosevelt and Churchill, the emotional peak of the conference came on Sunday morning, as Roosevelt boarded the *Prince of Wales* for a religious service, complete with the singing of a dozen common hymns.

Supported by his son Elliott, Roosevelt crossed the narrow gangway from the *Augusta* to the *Wales* and then walked the entire length of the ship to his designated place beside Churchill on the quarterdeck. "One got the impression of great courage and strength of character," *Prince of Wales* Captain W. M. Yool recalled. "It was obvious to everybody that he was making a tremendous effort and that he was determined to walk along the deck if it killed him." Holding hymnbooks in their hands, the two leaders joined in song, with hundreds of British and American sailors crowded together side by side, sharing the same books. "The same language, the same hymns and more or less the same ideals," Churchill mused that evening. "I have an idea that something really big may be happening—something really big."

"If nothing else had happened while we were here," Roosevelt later said, the joint service that sunlit morning "would have cemented us." For one brief moment, human togetherness gained ascendancy. Over the vast ship, so bright and gay with its glittering colors, there was a unity of faith of two people. "Every word seemed to stir the heart," Churchill attested, "and none who took part in it will forget the spectacle presented . . . It was a great hour to live."

• • •

The mood of good cheer at Argentia was dispelled temporarily on the last day of the conference with the arrival of disagreeable news from Washington. Extension of the draft, which most observers assumed would be easily accomplished, had passed the House of Representatives by the razor-edged vote of 203 to 202. The Selective Service Act of 1940 had obligated draftees for a period of only twelve months; the extension called for an additional eighteen. Had a single vote gone the other way, the new army would have melted away, nullifying everything that had been accomplished in the last year.

Opponents castigated the extension as a breach of contract with the draftees, who had been told they would only have to serve one year. General Marshall acknowledged the limiting language of the original bill, but to demobilize now, he argued, would be "to court disaster." In the past two years, the U. S. Army had grown eight times its initial size. It was just now "reaching the point where it could provide the country with an adequate defense." Wholesale release of men would destroy "the battle worthiness of nearly every American division."

At the height of the debate in Congress, while a million draftees in camps across the nation were wondering whether they would be allowed to return to civilian life in a matter of weeks or be forced to remain in the service for another eighteen months, *Life* magazine sent a reporter to Fort McClellan, Alabama, to sample soldier sentiment. After talking to some four hundred privates from five different regiments, the *Life* reporter concluded that morale in the camp was very low.

The most important reason for the low morale was the general sense of uncertainty. "As far as the men can see, the Army has no goal. It does not know whether it is going to fight, or when or where." Lack of equipment was also producing a rising tide of discontent. Whereas draftees had been content to train with stovepipe rifles and cardboard tanks in the early months, they were losing patience with the lack of real weapons. "We came here to learn how to fight a blitzkrieg. Instead, we get close-order drill and kitchen police."

Everywhere one looked, the reporter observed, on walls of latrines, on trucks, on field-artillery pieces, the word "OHIO" could be seen. It stood for "Over the Hill in October," a code name for the massive desertion that was planned for October, once the year's service was up. Most of the citizen soldiers would do nothing so drastic, but their palpable resentment was communicated in letters to their parents, and the parents relayed their sons' sentiments to their congressmen. Stimson acknowledged that morale was slipping. "The absence of any concrete war objective," he explained to the president in mid-August, "coupled with delays in getting their weapons and lack of energy and imagination here and there among their instructors, are being reflected in the spirit of the men and I am seeing letters on the subject."

The rumbles from the army camps undoubtedly contributed to the close margin in the Congress. "Mindful of next year's election," Marshall's biographer Forrest Pogue observed, "members from strongly isolationist areas of the country were weighing their desire to back the Army against their chances of returning to Washington. In most cases, Washington won."

The vote on August 12 came after a long day of fiery debate. The overhead galleries were packed. As soon as the voting began, it became clear that Democrats as well as Republicans were deserting the administration. After the first tally, the House rules allowed those who wanted to change their votes to approach the well below the rostrum and gain recognition from the Speaker, Sam Rayburn of Texas. This continued for some time until Rayburn saw the total become 203 for and 202 against, at which point he quickly proclaimed victory. "On this vote," he shouted, "203 members have voted 'Aye,' 202 members have voted 'No,' and the bill is passed!" A great protest was lodged by Republicans who claimed that the voting was not finished, that there were still changes and additions to be made. But Rayburn said it was too late: the totals had already been announced.

The news of the paper-thin margin, Hopkins recalled, had "a decidedly chilling effect" upon everyone at Argentia, particularly the British. Accustomed to the parliamentary way of thinking, the British regarded the division within the Democratic Party on an issue of such critical importance as a signal of "No Confidence" that would, in their country, result in the fall of a Cabinet. "The Americans are a curious people," a British man in the street commented. "I can't make them out. One day they're announcing they'll guarantee freedom and fair play for everybody in the world. The next day they're deciding by only one vote that they'll go on having an Army."

But Roosevelt was not discouraged. Though it was not a pretty victory, it was a victory nonetheless, and it meant that he could keep the soldiers on duty for another eighteen months. A near catastrophe had been averted. The army was saved.

CHAPTER 11

"A COMPLETELY CHANGED WORLD"

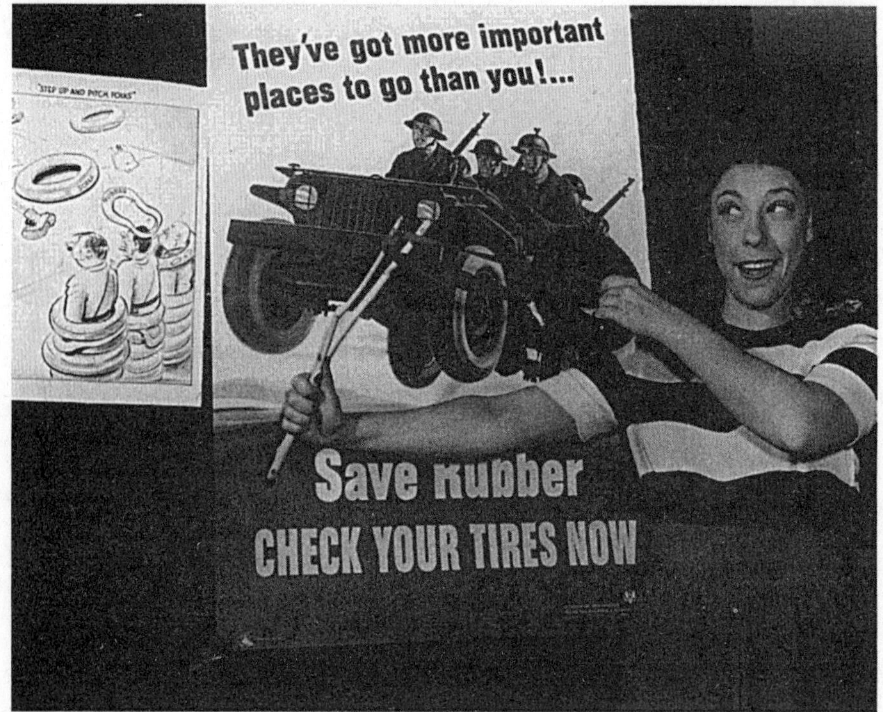

As American relations with Japan moved to a thunderous climax during the fall of 1941, the Roosevelt family suffered a pair of personal losses. In the space of three weeks in September, both the president's mother, Sara, and Eleanor's brother, Hall, died.

At Campobello that summer, Eleanor could see that her mother-in-law was failing. She had suffered a stroke in June and, aside from a few appearances at lunch, had remained in her bedroom all summer long. "I should not be surprised if this were the start of a more restricted life for her," Eleanor had written Anna. Watching Sara's steady decline, Eleanor begged her to engage a trained nurse. Sara stubbornly refused until Franklin wired her, asking if, for his "peace of mind," she would allow a nurse to be hired. "Of course, you are right to have a nurse," Sara quickly replied. "I am sorry you got alarmed. I wish you were here looking out of my window. I am taking off two days in my room, don't be anxious and do keep well, my one and only."

The presence of the nurse buoyed Sara's spirits, and her condition seemed to improve. When the time came for her to close up the cottage, she insisted on walking down the front steps herself. She had to stop halfway down to lean on the banister and catch her breath, but she made it to the back seat of her automobile without assistance.

Eleanor flew to New York in early September to meet Sara upon her return from Campobello and help her get settled at Hyde Park. As the two women sat together at breakfast, Eleanor noticed Sara's pale face and labored breathing. Struck by a sudden premonition that death was imminent, she called Franklin at the White House and told him to come to Hyde Park. As a young child, Eleanor had suffered miserably from not being told that her father was ill until after he died; for years, she had been unable to accept that he was really dead. Now she wanted to spare Franklin such pain.

Impressed by the tone of Eleanor's voice, Roosevelt decided to leave for Hyde Park on the overnight train. Sara was lying quietly in her bedroom with her brother Fred and her sister Kassie at her side when she received word that her son was on his way. "A telegram has just come from the President," the butler announced. "He will be here tomorrow morning at 9:30." Sara brightened perceptibly. "I will be downstairs on the porch to meet him," she said. But when morning came, Sara was too weak to venture downstairs. She did insist, however, on dressing up for her son—she put on an elegant bed jacket edged with lace, and had her hair wound into a braid with a bright-blue ribbon.

Sara's bedroom was in the two-story wing that had been added in 1916, when the house was enlarged to thirty-five rooms. From her window she could see her beloved trees and glimpse arrivals to her house. How delighted she had been over the years to greet the many distinguished men and women who had journeyed to Hyde Park to see her son! To be sure, she was irritated at times, when her unfailing eye discerned cigarette butts in her rose garden or small holes in her Oriental rugs, but she had long since decided that "a mother should be friends with her children's friends," even if some of them were overweight, grubby, chain-smoking newspapermen.

It gave her great comfort to know how much the old house still meant to her son and his children. More than any recent birthday gift, she had enjoyed the scroll presented to her from her grandchildren when she turned eighty. "Although we are now scattered in different places, Hyde Park has been and always will be, our real home, and Hyde Park means you and all the fun you give us there."

During the summer, as her body had begun to fail her, Sara had made herself happy by simply thinking about her son and remembering all the good times they had shared together. "I lie on my bed or sit in a comfortable armchair all day," she told Franklin, but "you are constantly in my thoughts and always in my heart." Sitting in her sunny window, writing little notes to family and friends, she admitted: "I think of you night and day." Indeed, so successful was Sara in conjuring up her son's image that even when they were apart she could picture him with different people in different situations. No sooner, for instance, had she heard the first rumors about the president and the prime minister meeting somewhere on the Atlantic than she could see them in her mind's eye walking up her lawn.

At 9:30 a.m. on Saturday, September 6, just as he had promised, the president pulled into the gravel driveway. Sara was lying on her chaise longue, propped up with pillows, when her son appeared in the doorway. He rolled swiftly toward her, kissed her cheek, and touched her hand with the same warmth he had shown her all his life. "Now that he is back, everything is changed," Sara had written nearly forty years earlier, when Franklin had returned from a trip to Europe. "Such happiness to be together again."

Franklin spent the rest of the morning and most of the afternoon giving his mother the details of his summit meeting with Winston Churchill, telling her what was going on in Washington, talking of old times. At the family dinner that night, everyone agreed that Sara seemed better; it was hoped that the crisis had passed. But at 9:30 p.m., she lapsed into a deep state of unconsciousness from which the doctors were unable to rouse her. A blood clot had lodged in her lung, and her circulatory system collapsed. Franklin returned to her room and sat with her through most of the night, while Eleanor called family and friends to tell them that the end was near.

As dawn came, the dying woman lay motionless. Her face, with its broad brow and high cheekbones, its beautiful mouth and aristocratic lines, was not disfigured by the proximity of death. Finally, just before noon, two weeks before her eighty-seventh birthday, with her son by her side, Sara Delano Roosevelt died.

Less than five minutes later, with no storm, wind, or lightning to prompt it, the largest oak tree on the estate simply toppled to the ground. "The President went out and looked at it," his bodyguard Mike Reilly recalled, "struck, as we all were, by the obvious symbolism." Geologists later explained that, because of the thin layer of earth over the rocky base that surrounded the Hyde Park area, such occurrences were not out of the ordinary. For anyone who had known the president's mother, however, that was never the true explanation.

• • •

In the days that followed Sara's death, *The New York Times* reported, the president "shut himself off from the world more completely than at any time since he assumed his present post." Canceling all appointments, he withdrew into the seclusion of his Hyde Park home. For a time at least, the events of the war were pushed into the background.

"I am so weary, I cannot write," Eleanor scribbled to Hick the day after

Sara's death. "I was up most of last night and I've been seeing relatives all day."

Eleanor was "of course attending to everything," Franklin's half-niece, Helen Robinson, noted in her diary. It was Eleanor who called the undertakers and had the body carried from the second-floor bedroom to the spacious book-lined library, where it would lie in a mahogany coffin beneath the portraits of various Roosevelt ancestors. It was she who met with the Reverend Frank Wilson, the rector at the country church where Sara had worshiped for more than half a century, to plan the burial. "The endless details," Eleanor wearily confessed to her aunt Maude Gray, "clothes to go through, checks, books, papers."

"The funeral was nice and simple," Eleanor wrote. While Reverend Wilson performed the Episcopal rites, Sara's family and friends, servants and tenants sat in the library amid the fine paintings, prints, and antique furniture she had collected over the years. The coffin was then transported in procession three miles north to the churchyard behind St. James. There some three dozen men and women assembled under the towering pines to watch as Sara's casket was lowered into the ground beside her husband, James. The president stood with one hand on the open sedan that had carried him to the church. "He never looked toward the grave," *Washington Post* reporter Amy Porter noted, "nor did he return an anxious glance cast his way by his wife." Finally, with a tolling of church bells and the familiar words "earth to earth, ashes to ashes, dust to dust," the solemn ceremony came to an end.

"I think Franklin will forget all the irritations & remember only pleasant things," Eleanor wrote Maude Gray, "which is just as well." To be sure, as in any parent-child relationship, the irritations were legion. "Don't you think you've had enough of your . . . cocktails for one evening?" Sara would frequently ask. "You promised me you would see [Hyde Park neighbor] Edith Eustis," she reminded Franklin in one of her last letters, "so please telephone her at once." Unable to accept that her son was a grown man even when he was president of the United States, Sara would pester him constantly to wear his rubbers and listen in on his phone calls. "Mama, will you *please* get off the line," a relative once heard the president telling her. "I can hear you breathing. Come on, now." On another occasion, when Sara was eighty-two and Franklin was fifty-six, Sara simply announced to newsmen at Hyde Park that she wasn't going to let her son go to church the next day because he was so far behind on his mail.

Yet, once Sara was gone, as Eleanor predicted, a surge of positive remembrances came to the fore, crowding any disagreeable memories from Franklin's mind. Long to be cherished was the memory of the time when he was quarantined in the Groton School infirmary with scarlet fever. Since no visitors were allowed to enter the quarantined room, Sara had climbed a tall rickety ladder several times a day so she could peer over the window ledge and talk with her son. "At first sight of me," Sara later wrote, "his pale, little face would break into a happy, albeit pathetic smile." Equally treasured was the memory of winter nights at Hyde Park, as he lay sprawled on the floor of the library before the fire, organizing and pasting his stamps while his mother read aloud to him.

The president managed to get through the days without breaking down until, late one afternoon, sorting through his mother's things with his secretary Grace Tully, he discovered a box he had never seen. Inside, with each item carefully labeled in her familiar writing, were his first pair of shoes, his christening dress, his baby toys, a lock of his baby hair, and an assortment of the little gifts he had made for her when he was young. Looking down with a tear-stained face, he quietly told Grace that he would like to be left alone. The tears were so unlike the president's habitual composure, and the dismay depicted on his face was so out of keeping with his usual cheerfulness, that she hurried from the room. "No one on his staff had ever seen Franklin Roosevelt weep," Geoffrey Ward observed. Nothing in his entire life had prepared him to deal with such crushing sorrow.

Eleanor's own emotions were more complex. On the one hand, as she looked at the peaceful expression on Sara's face, with "all the lines smoothed out, and the stark beauty of contour," she could not help respecting "the rich, full, confident life" Sara had led. "She loved her own home and her own place.... She had seen her only son inaugurated as President three times and still felt that her husband was the most wonderful man she had ever known. Her strongest trait was loyalty to the family. If anyone else in the world were to attack a member of her family she would rise to their defense like a tigress.... She had long contemplated this final resting place beside her husband."

Yet there were too many hurts over too many years to allow Eleanor to feel a deep sense of personal loss. "I kept being appalled at myself because I couldn't feel any real grief," Eleanor wrote to Anna, "and that seemed terrible after 36 years of fairly close association." In the early days of her marriage, Eleanor had spent more hours with her mother-in-law than with anyone else, lunching with her, riding with her to visit family friends, taking tea in the late afternoons, absorbing her ideas on everything from decorating to children. But this period was branded on Eleanor's memory as a time of humiliating dependence. "I had so much insecurity in my young life," she later explained. "At first the sense of security that my mother-in-law gave me made me very grateful." But before long, Eleanor felt oppressed by Sara's dominating personality.

The strain of accommodating herself to Sara's wishes finally proved too much for Eleanor. A few weeks after she and Franklin moved into the new house on East 65th Street that Sara had bought for them, Eleanor broke down. "I did not quite know what was the matter with me," she recalled years later, but "I sat in front of my dressing table and wept and when my bewildered young husband asked me what on earth was the matter with me, I said I did not like to live in a house which was not in any way mine, one that I had done nothing about and which did not represent the way I wanted to live. Being an eminently reasonable person, he thought I was quite mad and told me so gently, and said I would feel different in a little while and left me alone until I should become calmer."

Eleanor pulled herself together in short order, but the tension with Sara failed to subside. When Eleanor decided to redecorate her half of the town house, Sara told her not to bother, for "she could make it attractive in half an hour," and, besides, everyone liked *her* house better than her daughter-in-law's. Again and again, Eleanor was stung by Sara's belittling jibes about her clothes, posture, and appearance. "If you'd just run a comb through your hair, dear," Sara would tell Eleanor in front of dinner guests, "you'd look so much nicer."

"What happened would never have happened," Anna mused years later, "if Mother had the self-assurance to stand up to Granny. There would have been separate houses, but Mother didn't know how to stand up at that period." Over the years, a blistering anger formed in Eleanor's heart—directed mainly toward herself, for having submitted for so long to everyone else's wishes but her own. Though she had long since ceased to be dependent on her mother-in-law, it was not until Sara's death that Eleanor fully comprehended how far she had journeyed from the early days of her marriage. "I looked at my mother-in-law's face . . . ," she told Joe Lash, "& understood so many things I had never seen before." Had Sara had her way, Eleanor realized, her daughter-in-law would have lived a quiet life along the Hudson, tending mainly to hearth and home. "She thought that the land was tied with the family forever."

Having achieved a measure of peace in her own feelings about Sara, Eleanor was able to reach out to Franklin in ways she never could before. "Mother went to father and consoled him," James recalled. "She stayed with him and was by his side at the funeral and through the difficult days immediately afterward. She showed him more affection during those days than at any other time I can recall. She was the kind you could count on in a crisis, and father knew that."

A renewed commitment to one another is evident in the communications between husband and wife in the weeks that followed. Knowing that her husband needed her, Eleanor canceled a long-awaited trip to the West Coast so that she could stay in Washington. "Can I have MacKenzie King at Hyde Park on the 31st," Franklin asked his wife, recognizing that, with Sara gone, Eleanor was now the mistress of the house. "Will you let me know?" Then, the following day, confronted with a long letter of sympathy from one of Sara's friends, Franklin sent it on to Eleanor with a personal note: "Do be an angel and answer this for me." Even Henrietta Nesbitt noticed that something was different when she approached Eleanor's bedroom one morning and discovered, to her surprise, that the president was having breakfast with her—"a rare treat for them both," Nesbitt remarked.

Still, Eleanor remained wary of letting herself get too close. "Pa sprang on me today that I had better take Granny's room [which was twice the size of her own Spartan cubbyhole], but I just can't and I told him so," she wrote Anna. "Of course, I know I've got to live there more, but only when he is there and I'm afraid he hasn't realized that and isn't going to like it or understand it. Will you and the boys understand or does it make you resentful?"

To Eleanor's mind, the Big House had taken on the old lady's forbidding personality. The only way to make it her home was to redecorate it. Her first thought was to turn Sara's snuggery into a study for herself. But, as she quickly discovered, the prospect of changing any of the rooms stirred deep anxiety in her husband. He wanted to keep the old house exactly as it was. The only change he supported in the fall of 1941 was a request Sara had made just before she died to rearrange the room in which he was born so that it looked as it had in 1882, the year of his birth. Franklin never flatly rejected Eleanor's plans; such a confrontation would be unthinkable for him. Instead, he waited until Anna came east and then let her know that he wanted absolutely no changes in the house. In other words, Eleanor said after Anna relayed Roosevelt's wishes to her, "Hyde Park is now to be a shrine and it will still not be a home to me."

• • •

The same week that Sara died, Eleanor's brother, Hall, collapsed in his home and was taken to Vassar Hospital in Poughkeepsie, New York. Years of chronic alcoholism had destroyed his liver, "as they told him it would," Eleanor wrote Maude Gray. When Eleanor arrived at her brother's bedside, he begged her to grant him two wishes: to have him moved to Walter Reed Hospital in Washington and to bring him a bottle of gin. The first was easy; with one telephone call, the transfer was arranged. The second was more difficult. Eleanor regarded liquor as her mortal enemy; it had killed her father and destroyed her uncles and her brother. But now that Hall was dying, she wanted to give him as much comfort as possible. Against everything she held dear, she took a bottle of gin from the house at Hyde Park and smuggled it into the hospital.

The boisterous Hall struck everyone as extraordinarily unlike his sister. His features were like hers—a large frame with dark hair and blue eyes—but his face wore the never-failing smile of irrepressible youth, whereas hers invariably wore a look of anxiety and fretfulness. With Eleanor's father, mother, and younger brother Elliott dead, Hall was all she had left of her family, and she loved him deeply, often treating him as a son instead of a brother. When she married, she kept a room for him in her New York town house so he would always feel he had a home.

But, the more responsibility Eleanor undertook, the more self-indulgent and irresponsible Hall became. While he was a dazzling student at Harvard, with an intellect which both Franklin and Eleanor recognized as superior to their own, he was never able to commit himself to a steady line of work, moving from engineering to banking to civil service. He began drinking when he was in his twenties and never stopped. By the time he was fifty, he had divorced twice and was drinking between three-quarters and a whole gallon of expensive wine a day, in addition to gin, rum, and whiskey.

When Hall drank, he became querulous and crude. Curtis Roosevelt, Anna's son, remembers being petrified of his great uncle. "The level of noise was so high," Curtis recalled, "the tone of voice so abrasive, the horseplay a little out of control. I was terrified he'd pick me up, throw me in the air, and then forget to catch me." At formal White House dinners, Elliott Roosevelt recalled, Hall "had a penchant for applying a playful squeeze to a person's knees on the nerve just above the joint. In the middle of the first course, a shriek from Missy rose above the conversation of the fourteen other guests, and she leaped from her chair. We knew that Hall had been up to his tricks again." From her end of the table, Eleanor said softly to her brother, "I wish you wouldn't do those things."

Yet there was no one who could make Eleanor laugh or smile as much as Hall. He radiated charm and seemed to have an inexhaustible talent for having a good time. "There was nothing that made Eleanor happier," Hall's daughter, Ellie Wotkyns, recalled, "than dancing with my father. He was such a wonderful dancer and she loved to waltz with him. When she saw happiness you could almost feel her touching it and liking the warmth of it. I believe, both my aunt and my father were basically unhappy; he hid his unhappiness with a jolly demeanor, she hid hers with hard work. And in the end, she hung on to work as tightly as he hung on to drink."

Eleanor returned to Washington immediately after Sara's funeral so she could be with her brother. Though he was slipping in and out of consciousness and failed to recognize either his live-in companion, Zena Raset, or his daughter, Ellie, he seemed to know Eleanor and her presence served to quiet him. "This watching Hall die and seeing Zena suffer is a pretty trying business," Eleanor wearily confessed to Anna. "It is such an unattractive death, he's mahogany color, all distended, out of his head most of the time and his speech is almost impossible to understand. He moves insistently and involuntarily so you try to hold him quiet and it is really most distressing."

While Eleanor attended her dying brother, Franklin was readying a major speech for delivery to the nation on September 11. He had committed the United States to convoys at the Atlantic Conference, but he had not yet revealed the new policy to the American people. A submarine attack on the U.S.S. *Greer* gave him the incident he needed to mobilize public support behind convoys.

The events surrounding the *Greer* attack were not quite as the president described in his nationwide radio address. He said the German submarine had "fired first upon the American destroyer"; he claimed the *Greer*'s identity as an American ship was "unmistakable." In fact, the *Greer* had deliberately stalked the German sub, having been alerted to its presence by a British plane. The British plane had attacked the U-boat with depth charges while the *Greer* continued in pursuit. The sub fired a few torpedoes, the *Greer* responded with a few depth charges, and the chase came to an uneventful end. There was no positive evidence, the navy told the president, that the sub knew the nationality of the ship at which it was firing.

But the fact that German torpedoes had been fired on an American ship was all Roosevelt needed to reassert the principle of freedom of the seas. "No matter what it takes, no matter what it costs," the president warned the Axis powers, "we will keep open the line of legitimate commerce in these defensive waters. . . . Let this warning be clear. From now on, if German or Italian vessels of war enter the waters, the protection of which is necessary for American defense, they do so at their own peril. . . . When you see a rattlesnake poised to strike, you do not wait until he has struck before you crush him. These Nazi submarines and raiders are the rattlesnakes of the Atlantic."

To implement this warning, the president announced the final decision of the government to convoy British supplies, and a new policy by which the navy would shoot on sight any German raiders that came into our defensive zones. "It was," Stimson wrote, "the firmest statement and the most forward position yet taken by the President." Churchill was exultant. The shooting war in the North Atlantic had begun.

The president's "shoot on sight" policy won the solid support of 62 percent of the American people. "Sentiment on Capitol Hill has changed almost overnight," Washington correspondent David Lawrence reported. The news of the attack led "many a Congressman to say that the American people will not have their ships fired on and that defense of the freedom of seas will once again command substantial support in both houses."

Yet, for all the positive results that the president's depiction of the *Greer* attack produced, an unfortunate precedent was set that would return in later years to haunt the American republic. "Roosevelt's deviousness in a good cause," Senator William Fulbright said after the Gulf of Tonkin incident helped propel escalation in Vietnam, "made it easier for Lyndon Johnson to practice the same kind of deviousness in a bad cause."

• • •

The following weekend, the president brought a dozen guests to Hyde Park, including Crown Princess Martha and her three children, FDR, Jr.'s wife, Ethel, and two grandchildren. Though it was only two weeks since his mother's death, he wanted to fill the Big House with life and laughter once again. On Sunday, Hall's condition worsened. Hall had "suddenly gone very bad," Dr. McIntire informed the president at Hyde Park. "He may not last throughout the afternoon." While Eleanor, who had remained in Washington, hurried to the hospital, the president headed for Highland Station to catch the overnight train to Washington. Hall's condition was so bad when Eleanor reached the hospital that she decided to stay with him through the night. Sleeping fitfully in her clothes, she awoke to find him emitting ghastly noises as he struggled for breath.

This had been a bad day, she admitted to Joe Lash, who had been staying with her at the White House. "My idea of hell, if I believed in it, would be to sit or stand & watch someone breathing hard, struggling for words when a gleam of consciousness returns & thinking 'this was once the little boy I played with & scolded, he could have been so much & this is what he is.' It is a bitter thing & in spite of everything I've loved Hall, perhaps somewhat remissedly [sic] of late, but he is part of me."

"The President returned this morning," Tommy told Anna, "with the Crown Princess and Mme. Ostgaard and Jimmy has the Maurice Benjamins staying here. If anything happens to Hall today or tomorrow, I wonder if they will have the sense to leave. I doubt it."

The end came at 5 a.m. on Thursday morning, September 25. Eleanor was by her brother's side when he died. Exhausted, she returned to the White House before breakfast and went straight to her husband's bedroom. Jimmy was with his father when his mother arrived and was so struck by the intimacy of the scene that followed that he remembered every detail years later. " 'Hall has died,' Eleanor told Franklin simply. Father struggled to her side and put his arms around her. 'Sit down,' he said, so tenderly I can still hear it. And he sank down beside her and hugged her and kissed her and held her head on his chest. I do not think she cried. I think Mother had forgotten how to cry. She spent her hurt in Father's embrace. . . . For all they were apart both physically and spiritually much of their married life, there remained between them a bond that others could not break."

Though Eleanor was grateful that Hall's agony had finally ended, she felt as if she had lost a child, and grieved terribly over the waste of a potentially brilliant life. "My mother-in-law was 86 and she had a great life, full of rich experience," Eleanor observed to her journalist friend Martha Gellhorn. "Hall was just 51 and could have had much more out of life." What bothered her most, Tommy observed, was "the terrible waste of a promising life. If he had some illness from a natural cause, I think she could bear it better."

For hours that night, Tommy recalled, Eleanor dug out old photos and letters from Hall and talked about their childhood. Among the photos was a picture of Hall as a toddler, with blond curls and a little round face. In one of the folders, she found a letter from her father to her grandmother at a sad period of his life, as well as a batch of letters from Hall to her. Reading the letters made her so unhappy that Tommy suggested she burn the entire correspondence and get it out of her life. Eleanor agreed; she lit a fire and slowly fed one letter after another into the flames.

"The loss of someone whom you love is hard to bear," Eleanor observed years later in her memoirs, "but when sorrow is mixed with regret and a consciousness of waste there is added a touch of bitterness which is even more difficult to carry day in and day out. I think it was in an attempt to numb this feeling that I worked so hard at the Office of Civilian Defense that fall."

• • •

The president had created the OCD the previous spring with a broad mandate to enlist men, women, and children as defense volunteers. When her friend Mayor LaGuardia was named director, Eleanor thought she had won her battle for including social service in defense. But in the months that followed, as the OCD remained narrowly intent on signing up air-raid wardens, aircraft spotters, and volunteer fire brigades, Eleanor was disappointed.

At a press conference the week before Sara died, Eleanor had indirectly charged the OCD with failing its mission, declaring that "no government agency as yet had given civilian volunteers an adequate opportunity to participate in the defense effort." Her comments were construed by the press as criticism of LaGuardia's leadership. "There are 135,000,000 people in this country," LaGuardia wrote Eleanor. "The criticism of 134,999,999 wouldn't touch me. Yours did." The mayor went on to suggest that if she really wanted to implement her ideas she should come to work at the OCD as assistant director.

Eleanor was tantalized by LaGuardia's offer. Since her first days in Washington, she had longed for a specific job of her own to focus her energies. With a defined job, she believed, she would finally be able to follow through on her ideas and see the end results of her efforts. Yet, on the eve of accepting the unpaid assistant-directorship, she was overcome with apprehension. This would be the first government job ever held by a first lady; what if she ended up as a target for everyone who wanted to get at the president? What if she and LaGuardia clashed? "I'm worried about the civilian defense job," she confided to a friend, "because I don't want to do it & . . . at this moment I feel very low."

In spite of her fears, Eleanor accepted the offer and promised to report for work at the end of September. She then threw herself wholeheartedly into familiarizing herself with the organization. "I honestly think your mother is going to get a tremendous amount of interest out of the civilian defense job," Tommy wrote Anna. "When she talks about it, there is a gleam in her eye and a sparkle which has been absent for a long time." Indeed, during the black days of watching Hall die, the prospect of the OCD job was the one sustaining hope that kept Eleanor going.

After Hall's burial on Saturday, September 27, at Tivoli, New York, in the Hall family vault, Franklin and Eleanor drove to Hyde Park for the weekend. Unable to sleep, Eleanor came downstairs at 3 a.m. and spent the next three hours mentally organizing the OCD work. At dawn, she began making notes which detailed the goals she hoped to accomplish in her first month on the job. "If I feel depressed," she once said, "I go to work. Work is always an antidote for depression."

For her first day on the job, Monday, September 29, the first lady chose a trim black silk dress with a touch of white at the collar and several strings of pearls. The early-morning air was crisp as she set forth on foot from the White House to the OCD offices at Dupont Circle. It took a good half-hour, even at Eleanor's long-legged pace, but since she did not think she would get exercise any other way, she was determined to walk to and from work. En route, a young woman came up beside her and said: "You are Mrs. Roosevelt and I am from California and I have always wanted to shake hands with you." The encounter buoyed Eleanor's spirits as she approached her ninth-floor office.

Eleanor's office, which she shared with her friend Elinor Morgenthau, who served as her assistant, contained a pair of desks, a gray fireplace, and a red carpet. At a brief press conference that morning, Eleanor pledged that she would be on the job at nine every morning and remain as long as possible. As for the work she would do, she outlined three goals: to give every person wishing to volunteer an opportunity to train for work; to provide meaningful jobs that would be of benefit to the community, such as work in nursery schools, recreational facilities, housing projects, and homes for the aged; and to prepare citizens to meet emergency calls.

Though Eleanor's broad definition of defense would eventually bring her into conflict with the Congress, her early months on the job were productive. She was hard-pressed at times to stay on top of everything, since she was still responsible for a daily column, a weekly radio broadcast, a semi-annual lecture tour, and a vast personal correspondence, but she gloried in the feeling that the OCD job was hers and hers alone. "I am ridiculously busy," Eleanor wrote to Martha Gellhorn, but the tone of the letter suggested that she loved every minute of her frenetic activity.

For his part, Franklin was delighted to see Eleanor so happy and absorbed. "He was glad," Social Security Regional Director Anna Rosenberg laughingly remarked, "to channel her energies into one area so that she would leave him alone in other areas. He knew that she felt frustrated because many of the liberal programs had to be put aside."

"What's this I hear?" Franklin teased Eleanor one morning. "You didn't go to bed at all last night?" Eleanor nodded her head. "I had been working on my mail without regard to the time, and when suddenly it began to get light, I decided it was not worth while going to bed."

With Eleanor abundantly fulfilled by her work, the tensions with her husband eased. Lash records an enjoyable evening in the president's study on the last day of September. Franklin and Harry Hopkins were already sitting down to supper when Eleanor, Lash in tow, dashed in with profuse apologies for being late. To Eleanor's delight, the president had not even noticed the delay. "There is an advantage to a household where everybody is busy," she later observed. The conversation centered for a while on Mayor LaGuardia, with a good deal of spoofing about his childlike fascination with fire engines. From LaGuardia, the conversation shifted to Benjamin Franklin, whose bust by Houdon the president urged Eleanor to take into her bedroom. "You can always say, 'I have Franklin with me,'" he cracked. The president then asked everyone to name four outstanding leaders, including Ben Franklin. His choices, he said, were Franklin, Jefferson, Teddy Roosevelt, and the earl of Orrery, a confidential adviser of Oliver Cromwell, "concerning whose life he knew the most intimate details." Eleanor countered with her choices: Anne Hutchinson, Harriet Beecher Stowe, Emily Dickinson, and Carrie Chapman Catt. All told, Lash concluded, it was "a jolly party."

Two weeks later, on Eleanor's fifty-seventh birthday, the president persuaded her to join him on a cruise down the river. For the occasion, he had invited a small group of her friends, including Tommy, Joe Lash, ballroom dancer Mayris Chaney, and Helen Gahagan. "We all had a very pleasant time," Lash recorded in his diary, "and I think she had a good time in spite of not wanting anyone to mention her birthday." In the afternoon, Eleanor sat in a deck chair and worked on her mail while the president relaxed with his stamps and the guests sat around chatting. But at six-thirty everyone came together for a grand dinner with champagne and a special toast to Eleanor. It was the first time in more than a year, the president affectionately pointed out in his toast, that he had been able to get his wife on his boat, so the occasion merited a special round of applause.

• • •

During the months of September and October, the president was preoccupied with U-boat sinkings in the Atlantic. On the 19th of September, the *Pink Star*, an American cargo vessel, was sunk off Greenland. Included in the lost cargo was enough cheddar cheese to feed more than three and a half million laborers in Britain for an entire week; a supply of evaporated milk which represented a year's production for three hundred cows; and crates of machine tools which required the labor of three hundred workers for four months. Three weeks later, the *Kearney*, one of America's newest destroyers, built in New Jersey at a cost of $5 million, was torpedoed while on patrol near Iceland; and two weeks after that, the destroyer *Reuben James* was sunk, with the loss of over a hundred American sailors.

"I think the Navy are thoroughly scared about their inability to stamp out the submarine menace," Stimson confessed in his diary. "The Germans have adopted new methods of hunting in packs and shooting under water without showing themselves and it is a new deal and it is pretty hard to handle."

Roosevelt understood that lend-lease would fail unless the United States could keep the sea-lanes open. The time had come, he decided, to take the next step—to ask Congress to remove Neutrality Act restrictions that prevented merchant ships from being armed. He had considered going to Congress in July, but when he was warned that a request for revision would provoke a filibuster and jeopardize extension of the draft, he backed off. Opinion was changing, however. In April, only 30 percent of the American people thought that American ships should be armed; by the end of September, the figure had risen to 46 percent; and now, in the wake of the recent sinkings, an overwhelming majority of 72 percent favored arming merchant ships.

Still, it was not easy to get the Congress to act. The revision passed the House by a close margin and then stalled in the Senate, where critics argued that the U.S. was provoking incidents at sea in order to arouse the American public. "If we continue to look for trouble," Senator Robert Reynolds warned, "the probabilities are that we will eventually find it." Was anyone surprised that American ships were being fired on? America Firster John Flynn asked. "American war vessels, under orders of war-like Knox, are hunting down German subs. . . . The American people must realize that . . . they are the victims of a conspiracy to hurry them into the war."

It took eleven days of acrimonious debate before the Senate finally agreed, on November 8, to amend the Neutrality Act to arm merchant ships. The thirteen-vote margin was the smallest the administration had received on any major foreign-policy initiative since the beginning of the war. The closeness of the vote made it clear to Roosevelt that, short of some dramatic event, there was no chance of getting Congress to vote a declaration of war against Germany. "He had no more tricks left," Robert Sherwood observed. "The bag from which he had pulled so many rabbits was empty." His only recourse was to wait on events.

• • •

He did not have to wait for long. The Japanese attack on Pearl Harbor on the 7th of December provided the answer to the president's dilemma.

After Japan's invasion of Indochina in July, Roosevelt had agreed to a policy of sanctions, including an embargo of high-octane oil. Implemented by subordinates while he was away at the Atlantic Conference with Churchill, the limited embargo he had sanctioned had become full-scale. By the time Roosevelt realized that all types of oil had been closed to Japan, it was too late—without seeming weak—to turn back.

Japan could not tolerate the embargo on oil. The crisis strengthened the hand of the military. On October 16, War Minister General Hideki Tojo replaced Fumimaro Konoye as premier, and gave Japanese diplomats until the last day of November to arrange a satisfactory settlement with the United States that would end sanctions; if they failed, war would begin in early December. In the meantime, active preparations were under way for a massive air strike against Pearl Harbor.

The stumbling block in the negotiations was China. Whereas Japan was willing to remove its troops from Indochina and promise not to advance beyond current positions in return for America's lifting of the embargo, she refused to withdraw completely from China. For a time, it seemed that Roosevelt would accept a partial withdrawal of Japanese troops from China, but strong protests from Nationalist Chinese leader Chiang Kai-shek hardened the U.S. position.

While the negotiations dragged on, the president adhered to his customary routine. The weekend that Tojo assumed power in Japan, Roosevelt was at Hyde Park with Princess Martha and Harry Hopkins. Anna and John Boettiger were also there, having flown east from Seattle for a short visit. The weather was crisp and autumnal, and, as always, Roosevelt found an agreeable sense of repose among the familiar surroundings. Driving through the countryside during the day or lying down in the clean linen of his bed at night, with his dog, Fala, at his feet, he must have felt, for a few moments at least, as though the war were far away.

The following weekend, while Eleanor was in New York on OCD business, the president invited Princess Martha to join him for a leisurely cruise on the *Potomac*. The nature of his relationship with Martha at this point is not clear. Neither of the principals ever talked openly about their friendship. The White House usher diaries during this period, however, testify to her frequent presence: Thursday night, November 6, 7:30 to 11:45, dinner with Crown Princess Martha; Saturday, November 15, 1:17, lunch in study with Martha followed by a special showing for the two of them of Walt Disney's new movie, *Dumbo*; Sunday, November 16, 6:20 to 10:50, to Pook's Hill for dinner with Martha; Thursday, November 20, 4:30, swim with Martha, her lady-in-waiting, and her kids, followed by tea in the West Hall and dinner; Tuesday, November 25, 7:30 to 12:00, dinner with Martha. On most of these occasions, Eleanor was traveling on OCD business. Her job was taking her out of town more than she had originally assumed it would, but she felt more fulfilled than she had in years.

At a Cabinet meeting on November 14, Secretary of State Cordell Hull told the president that negotiations with Japan had reached an impasse. The tone of Hull's voice, Frances Perkins later recalled, was "very discouraged and cynical." Hull said he had come to believe that the Japanese diplomats were hypocrities; "they were always being so superficially, excessively polite, showing him such respect, that it made him angry to think that they thought he didn't see through their little ploy." According to Perkins, Hull had "a quaint way of saying quite rough things," which, when added to his inability of saying the "cr" sound because of his lisp, produced a most humorous effect. "If Cordell Hull says Oh Chwist again," Roosevelt confided in Perkins, "I'm going to scream with laughter. I can't stand profanity with a lisp."

In late November, as he had done for nearly two decades, the president planned a journey to Warm Springs to celebrate Thanksgiving with the patients and staff of the polio foundation. This particular trip held special meaning, since Missy LeHand would also be there, having left Doctor's Hospital in early November to continue her convalescence at the rehabilitation center at Warm Springs. The physical condition of her legs had been steadily improving. It was hoped that a return to the little Georgia community she loved would stimulate the return of her speech.

"Just as you move out of one hospital I move into another," Hopkins wrote Missy on November 12, as he entered the Naval Hospital for a round of diagnostic tests to determine why he was experiencing difficulty in walking. "But Harper tells me you are a model patient compared with me. I complain about the food, the nurses and in general leave the impression that I know much more about running the hospital than Navy doctors do. At least now I am relaxed and reading some books. . . . I am delighted at the reports I hear from you and just as soon as I can push my way out of the hospital I am coming down to see you."

When Missy arrived at Warm Springs, she was installed with a private nurse in a little cottage that stood at the top of the hill across from the main complex of the foundation—a cluster of buildings which included a hospital, rehab center, dining hall, auditorium, and treatment pools. To the polio patients who had known Missy over the years, "so quick and full of fun . . . so often running errands for the boss that her path and theirs had many points of intersection," it must have seemed strange to see her now, tired and bewildered from her long train ride, unable to walk, unable to talk. If Warm Springs had brought life and hope back to Roosevelt, perhaps it could do the same for her.

The president was scheduled to leave Washington for Warm Springs on November 19, but the situation at home was so tense—with striking miners paralyzing the entire steel industry—that the trip was postponed. Earlier in the month, on the orders of John L. Lewis, fifty-three thousand United Mine Workers, representing 95 percent of all the men who worked in captive mines owned by steel companies, had gone on strike when the National Defense Mediation Board refused to grant Lewis' request for a union shop, which would have compelled the remaining 5 percent to join the UMW. (Although, true to his word, Lewis had resigned as president of the CIO after FDR's victory, he had remained as president of the UMW.)

"I must say," FDR, Jr., had written Eleanor from the navy, "it's a pretty discouraging and disgusting sight to see a great country blackmailed by a bull-headed rascal like Lewis. . . . I know Pa's knowledge and judgment of not only public opinion but the whole cross-word puzzle show is thoroughly sound. But still, sometimes I wish he'd leave his kind nature in his bunk some morning and roll up his sleeves and really get tough—it would be a wonderful show to watch."

Young Franklin got his wish, for this time the president did get tough, threatening to send in the troops if the miners refused to return to work. "I tell you frankly," Roosevelt pledged, "the government will never compel this 5 percent to join the union by a government decree. That would be too much like Hitler's methods toward labor." Though Roosevelt was not opposed in principle to the idea of a union shop, he believed it had to come about through negotiations between labor and management, not through a government decree. The president's hard line paid off. On November 22, Lewis agreed to compulsory arbitration and the miners went back to work. "We felt a weight off our minds and hearts," Eleanor wrote, "when we knew the coal strike was to be arbitrated. I know what a relief it is for men to go back to work."

With the settlement of the coal strike, the president rescheduled his trip to Warm Springs for November 27. But then, the day before he was set to go, he received word that, in the midst of the continuing negotiations, a Japanese expedition was heading south from Japan. He "fairly blew up," Stimson recorded in his diary, "jumped up in the air, so to speak, and said . . . that changed the whole situation because it was evidence of bad faith on the part of the Japanese."

November 27 was "a very tense, long day," Stimson reported, as news of the Japanese expedition kept coming in. "I have washed my hands of it," Secretary Hull told Stimson. "It is now in the hands of you and Knox." Still, there was no clear understanding of where the expeditionary force was headed. "If the current negotiations end without agreement," Admiral Stark warned the president later that day, "Japan may attack: the Burma Road, Thailand, Malaya, the Netherlands East Indies, the Philippines, the Russian Maritime Provinces. . . . The most essential thing now from United States viewpoint, is to gain time. Considerable Navy and Army reinforcements have been rushed to Philippines but desirable strength not yet been reached. Precipitance of military action on our part should be avoided so long as consistent with national policy. The longer the delay, the more positive becomes the assurance of retention of these Islands as a naval and air base."

The president agreed with Stark about the importance of playing for time. Though he had little hope now that an agreement could be reached, he instructed Hull to send a proposal to the Japanese demanding that Japan leave China and Indochina in return for an American promise to negotiate new trade and raw-materials agreements. The note reiterated what the United States had been saying for months: that Japan could at any moment put an end to the exploding situation by embracing a peaceful course, and that once she did this her fears of encirclement would come to an immediate end.

The following day, the president left for Warm Springs, where he hoped to remain for ten days so that he could celebrate Thanksgiving with the polio patients. Stimson was "very sorry that he went but nobody spoke out and warned him." The presidential train reached the village of Newman, Georgia, about noon on Saturday, November 29. Welcomed by sunny skies and a friendly crowd, Roosevelt decided to ride the remaining forty miles to Warm Springs in an open automobile, waving to the crowds gathered along the way. The newspapermen, arriving at Warm Springs, settled themselves in two cottages, then "had a few drinks and entered into the spirit of a much-needed holiday."

While the others relaxed, the president drove directly to Missy's cottage to say hello, bringing Grace Tully with him. "You had to have at least two people," Egbert Curtis once explained, "so you could talk across Missy to the other person. Suppose I could only say yes, yes, it would be very difficult for you or anybody else to talk with me."

Tully hoped the visit would bolster Missy's spirits, but the president was ill at ease and distracted, too tired and worn, writer Bernard Asbell suggests, to "endure the ordeal of trying to cheer Missy—the old, cheery, talkative, loyal Missy—who could now say without great effort only a single word." He stayed only fifteen minutes before telling Missy he had to return to his own cottage.

No sooner had the president reached the "little White House," as his unpretentious cottage on the edge of a ravine was called, than Secretary Hull phoned to say "the Far East picture was darkening and that the talks in Washington were in such brittle state that they might be broken at any time." The president told Hull to call again after dinner; if things were no better, he would return to Washington.

When Hull called at 9 p.m., he told Roosevelt that he had just finished reading an explosive speech which Premier Tojo was scheduled to deliver the following day. The speech called on Japan, "for the honor and pride of mankind," to take immediate steps to wipe out U.S. and British "exploitation" in the Far East. Hull was convinced that a Japanese attack was imminent; he advised Roosevelt to return to Washington as soon as possible. The president agreed to leave the following day.

On Sunday morning, Grace Tully accompanied the president as he paid a short farewell call on Missy. She was "nearly in tears at losing us so soon," Grace recalled. Accustomed for decades to being at the center of the whirling action, she could only sit back and watch as the presidential party pulled away, leaving her alone in a small cottage in a tiny community in the middle of Georgia.

• • •

Eleanor was in the midst of a press conference on Monday morning, December 1, when the presidential party returned. She had just announced some appointments to the OCD when Franklin's dog, Fala, came running into the room. "That means the President is here," she told reporters, a smile on her face as she leaned down to pat Fala's head.

Tensions with Japan continued to escalate through the first week of December, as the United States awaited Japan's reply to Secretary Hull's note. By Friday's Cabinet meeting, on December 5, Secretary Knox was so agitated, Frances Perkins recalled, that you could see "the blood rush up to his neck and face." Still, the president insisted that the United States keep the option of peace alive. "We must strain every nerve to satisfy and keep on good relations with this group of Japanese negotiators," he told Hull. "Don't let it deteriorate and break up if you can possibly help it."

Toward the end of the meeting, the discussion turned to the whereabouts of the Japanese fleet. "We've got our sources of communication in pretty good shape," Knox assured the president, "and we expect within the next week to get some indication of where they are going."

On Saturday afternoon, December 6, intelligence experts at the War and Navy departments, who had broken the secret Japanese code in July, intercepted a message from Tokyo informing the Japanese ambassador that a fourteen-part response to Hull's ten-point document was on its way. By early evening, the first thirteen parts had been transmitted; the fourteenth part, Tokyo said, would be sent the following morning. When the first thirteen parts were deciphered, a feeling of dread filled the air. It was obvious from the point-by-point rejection of each and every one of Hull's proposals that Japan was refusing all reconciliation; only one glimmer of hope remained—nowhere in the thirteen points had Japan formally broken off negotiations.

The improbable hope of Saturday night was crushed on Sunday morning, December 7, when the fourteenth part of the Japanese message, terminating diplomatic negotiations, arrived. Within minutes, a second message came through, instructing Ambassador Kichisaburo Nomura to deliver the entire fourteen-part reply to Secretary Hull at precisely one o'clock. To Colonel Rufus Bratton, chief of the Far Eastern Section of the War Department, the timing of the 1 p.m. deadline seemed significant. With a sinking heart, he told General Marshall that he feared it might coincide with an early-morning attack somewhere in the Pacific. Marshall acted swiftly, writing a priority dispatch to the various American commanders in the Pacific. "The Japanese are presenting at 1 p.m. EST today what amounts to an ultimatum. Just what significance the hour set may have we do not know, but be on the alert." Uncertain of the security of the scrambler phone, Marshall opted to send his warning by the slower method of commercial telegraph. In order of priority, the warning was to go first to Manila, then to Panama, and finally to Hawaii. By the time the message reached the telegraph station in Honolulu, the attack on Pearl Harbor had already begun.

• • •

Shortly after 7:30 a.m., local time, while sailors were sleeping, eating breakfast, and reading the Sunday papers, the first wave of 189 Japanese planes descended upon Pearl Harbor, dropping clusters of torpedo bombs on the unsuspecting fleet. Half the fleet, by fortunate coincidence, was elsewhere, including all three aircraft carriers, but the ships that remained were tied up to the docks so "snugly side by side," Harold Ickes later observed, "that they presented a target that none could miss. A bomber could be pretty sure that he would hit a ship even if not the one he aimed at." Within minutes—before any anti-aircraft fire could be activated, and before a single fighter plane could get up into the air—all eight of the American battleships in Pearl Harbor, including the *West Virginia*, the *Arizona*, and the *California*, had been hit, along with three destroyers and three light cruisers.

Bodies were everywhere—trapped in the holds of sinking ships, strewn in the burning waters, scattered on the smoke-covered ground. Before the third wave of Japanese planes completed its final run, thirty-five hundred sailors, soldiers, and civilians had lost their lives. It was the worst naval disaster in American history.

Knox relayed the horrifying news to the president shortly after 1:30 p.m. Roosevelt was sitting in his study with Harry Hopkins when the call came. "Mr. President," Knox said, "it looks like the Japanese have attacked Pearl Harbor." Hopkins said there must be some mistake; the Japanese would never attack Pearl Harbor. But the president reckoned it was probably true —it was just the kind of thing the Japanese would do at the very moment they were discussing peace in the Pacific. All doubt was settled a few minutes later, when Admiral Stark called to confirm the attack. With bloody certainty, the United States had finally discovered the whereabouts of the Japanese fleet.

While the president was on the phone with Stark, Eleanor was bidding luncheon guests goodbye. Heading back toward her sitting room on the second floor, she knew by one glance in her husband's study that something had happened. "All the secretaries were there, two telephones were in use, the senior military aides were on their way with messages. I said nothing because the words I heard over the telephone were quite sufficient to tell me that finally the blow had fallen and we had been attacked." Realizing at once that this was no time to disturb her husband with questions, Eleanor returned to work in her room. Earlier that morning, she had begun a chatty letter to Anna which spoke of her plans to come to California for a visit in early January. When she resumed writing after lunch, she told Anna, "the news of the war has just come and I've put in a call for you and Johnny as you may want to send the children East." In the confusion of the first news of Pearl Harbor, it was thought that Japan might attack the West Coast as well. Finally, she drew the letter to a close. "I must go dear and talk to Father."

The first thing Eleanor noticed when she went into her husband's study was his "deadly calm" composure. While his aides and Cabinet members were running in and out in a state of excitement, panic, and irritation, he was sitting quietly at his desk, absorbing the news from Hawaii as it continued to flow in—"each report more terrible than the last." Though he looked strained and tired, Eleanor observed, "he was completely calm. His reaction to any event was always to be calm. If it was something that was bad, he just became almost like an iceberg, and there was never the slightest emotion that was allowed to show." Sumner Welles agreed with Eleanor's assessment. In all the situations over the years in which he had seen the president, he "had never had such reason to admire him."

Beneath the president's imperturbable demeanor, however, Eleanor detected great bitterness and anger toward Japan for the treachery involved in carrying out the surprise attack while the envoys of the two countries were still talking. "I never wanted to have to fight this war on two fronts," Franklin told Eleanor. "We haven't got the Navy to fight in both the Atlantic and the

Pacific... so we will have to build up the Navy and the Air Force and that will mean that we will have to take a good many defeats before we can have a victory."

At Jimmy Roosevelt's home in Washington, the phone rang. The White House operator was on the line telling him his father wanted to talk with him. Jimmy had not yet heard the news of Pearl Harbor. "Hi, Old Man, what can I do for you?" Jimmy asked. "I don't have time to talk right now but could you come right away?" "Pa, it's Sunday afternoon," Jimmy said, laughing, but then, sensing there was something wrong from the tone of his father's voice, he agreed to come at once. "He was sitting at his desk," Jimmy recalled. "He didn't even look up. I knew right away we were in deep trouble. Then he told me. He showed no signs of excitement, he simply and calmly discussed who had to be notified and what the media campaign should be for the next forty-eight hours."

"Within the first hour," Grace Tully recalled, "it was evident that the Navy was dangerously crippled." And there was no way of knowing where the Japanese would stop. The president's butler Alonzo Fields recalls overhearing snatches of a remarkable conversation between Harry Hopkins and the president that afternoon in which they imagined the possibility of the invading Japanese armies' driving inland from the West Coast as far as Chicago. At that point, the president figured, since the United States was a country much like Russia in the vastness of its terrain, we could make the Japanese overextend their communication and supply lines and begin to force them back.

Meanwhile, a little bit at a time, the public at large was learning the news. "No American who lived through that Sunday will ever forget it," reporter Marquis Childs later wrote. "It seared deeply into the national consciousness," creating in all a permanent memory of where they were when they first heard the news.

• • •

Churchill was sitting at Chequers with envoy Averell Harriman and Ambassador John Winant when news of the Japanese attack came over the wireless. Unable to contain his excitement, he bounded to his feet and placed a call to the White House. "Mr. President, what's this about Japan?" "It's quite true," Roosevelt replied. "They have attacked us at Pearl Harbour. We are all in the same boat now."

"To have the United States at our side," Churchill later wrote, "was to me the greatest joy." After seventeen months of lonely fighting, he now believed the war would be won. "England would live; Britain would live; the Commonwealth of Nations and the Empire would live." The history of England would not come to an end. "Silly people—and there were many...," Churchill mused, "—might discount the force of the United States," believing the Americans were soft, divided, paralyzed, averse to bloodshed. He knew better; he had studied the Civil War, the bloodiest war in history, fought to the last inch. Saturated with emotion, Churchill thought of a remark British politician Sir Edward Grey had made to him more than 30 years before. The U.S. was like "a gigantic boiler. Once the fire is lighted under it there is no limit to the power it can generate."

Shortly before 5 p.m., the president called Grace Tully to his study. "He was alone," Tully recalled, with two or three neat piles of notes stacked on his desk containing all the information he had been receiving during the afternoon. "Sit down, Grace. I'm going before Congress tomorrow. I'd like to dictate my message. It will be short."

He began to speak in the same steady tone in which he dictated his mail, but the pace was slower than usual as he spoke each word incisively, specifying every punctuation mark. "Yesterday comma December 7th comma 1941 dash a day which will live in world history . . ."

While the president worked on his speech, Eleanor was across the hall, rewriting the script for her weekly radio broadcast. When she reached the NBC studios at 6:30 p.m., she was joined by a young corporal, Jimmy Cannon, who was scheduled to follow her with a report on morale in the army. Astonished to be in the presence of the first lady, the young soldier fumbled with the clasp on his script. "She leaned over," he later wrote, "gently took it from me and broke the clasp."

"For months now," Eleanor began, "the knowledge that something of this kind might happen has been hanging over our heads. . . . That is all over now and there is no more uncertainty. We know what we have to face and we know we are ready to face it. . . . Whatever is asked of us, I am sure we can accomplish it; we are the free and unconquerable people of the U.S.A."

Corporal Cannon listened to the first lady's cultured voice and then delivered his own message. As she arose to go, he later told a *PM* reporter, she turned to him and said suddenly, as though it had been on her mind all the time she had been there, "The Japanese Ambassador was with my husband today. That little man was so polite to me. I had to get something. That little man arose when I entered the room." Apparently, Eleanor could not get out of her mind the fact the Japanese ambassador was talking to her husband at the very moment when Japan's airplanes were bombing Pearl Harbor.

It is a curious story, for there is no evidence that the Japanese ambassador was at the White House that Sunday. The only explanation is that Eleanor mistook the Chinese ambassador, who had stopped by to see the president shortly after noon, for the Japanese ambassador. Indeed, in the weeks to follow, the inability to tell a Chinese from a Japanese proved so widespread that Chinese consulates took steps to tag their nationals with signs and buttons: "Chinese, not Japanese, please." As angry citizens mistakenly victimized their Chinese allies, *Life* magazine marched into the fray with a rule-of-thumb guide to distinguish "friendly Chinese from enemy alien Japs." The typical Chinese, *Life* argued, "is relatively tall and slenderly built. His complexion is parchment yellow, his face long and delicately boned, his nose more finely bridged." In contrast, the typical Japanese "betrays aboriginal antecedents in a squat, long-torsoed build, a broader, more massively boned head and face, flat, often pug nose, yellow-ocher skin and heavier beard."

At eight-thirty on Sunday night, the Cabinet began to gather in the president's study. A ring of extra chairs had been brought in to accommodate the overflow. The president, Perkins noted later, was sitting silently at his desk; he was preoccupied, seemed not to be seeing or hearing what was going on around him. "It was very interesting," Perkins observed, "because he was always a very friendly and outgoing man on the personal side. He never overlooked people.... But I don't think he spoke to anyone who came in that night. He was living off in another area. He wasn't noticing what went on on the other side of the desk. He was very serious. His face and lips were pulled down, looking quite gray. His complexion didn't have that pink and white look that it had when he was himself. It had a queer gray, drawn look."

Finally, he turned around and said, "I'm thankful you all got here." He went on to say this was probably the most serious crisis any Cabinet had confronted since the outbreak of the Civil War. Then he told them what he knew. "I remember," Perkins later said, "the President could hardly bring himself" to describe the devastation. "His pride in the Navy was so terrific that he was having actual physical difficulty in getting out the words that put him on record as knowing that the Navy was caught unawares.... I remember that he said twice to Knox, 'Find out, for God's sake, why the ships were tied up in rows.' Knox said, 'That's the way they berth them!' It was obvious to me that Roosevelt was having a dreadful time just accepting the idea that the Navy could be caught off guard."

By 10 p.m., congressional leaders had joined the Cabinet in the overcrowded study. The president told the gathering that he had prepared a short message to be presented at a joint session of Congress the following day. The message called for a declaration by Congress that a state of war had existed between Japan and the United States from the moment of the attack Sunday morning. He then went on to describe the attack itself, repeating much of what he had told his Cabinet, including new information that Japanese bombs had also hit American airfields in Hawaii, destroying more than half the planes in the Pacific fleet. Apparently, the planes had been an easy mark, since they were grouped together on the ground, wing tip to wing tip, to guard against subversive action by Japanese agents. "On the ground, by God, on the ground," Roosevelt groaned.

"The effect on the Congressmen was tremendous," Stimson recorded. "They sat in dead silence and even after the recital was over they had very few words." Finally, Senator Tom Connally of Texas spoke up, voicing the question that was on everyone's mind. "How did it happen that our warships were caught like tame ducks in Pearl Harbor?" he shouted, banging the desk with his fist, his face purple. "How did they catch us with our pants down? Where were our patrols? They knew these negotiations were going on. They were all asleep."

"I don't know, Tom," the president muttered, his head bowed, "I just don't know."

Historians have focused substantial time and attention trying to determine who knew what and when before the 7th of December—on the theory that Roosevelt was aware of the Japanese plans to attack Pearl Harbor but deliberately concealed his knowledge from the commanders in Hawaii in order to bring the United States into hostilities through the back door. Unable to swing Congress and the public toward a declaration of war against Germany, critics contend, the president provoked Japan into firing the first shot and then watched with delight as the attack created a united America.

To be sure, Roosevelt was concerned that, if war came, the Japanese should be the ones to initiate hostilities. Stimson records a conversation on November 25 in which the president raised the possibility that Japan might attack without warning. The question Roosevelt asked "was how we should maneuver them into the position of firing the first shot without allowing too much danger to ourselves." But in the discussion, as in all others preceding Pearl Harbor, the reigning assumption was that Japan would attack from the south. Though Pearl Harbor was mentioned once, the previous January, in a report from the U.S. ambassador to Japan, Joseph Grew, to the State Department, it was assumed, again and again, right up to December 7, that the Philippines was the most likely target for Japanese aggression.

Moreover, "without allowing too much danger to ourselves," is the important phrase in the president's conversation with Stimson. Common sense suggests that, if the president had known beforehand about Pearl Harbor, he would have done everything he could to reposition the fleet and disperse the airplanes to ensure minimal damage. For the purposes of mobilizing the American people, one American ship torpedoed by the Japanese at Pearl Harbor would have sufficed. It is inconceivable that Roosevelt, who loved the navy with a passion, would have intentionally sacrificed the heart of its fleet, much less the lives of thirty-five hundred American sailors and soldiers, without lifting a finger to reduce the risk. It is an inquiry that obscures the more important question that Senator Connally posed: "How did it happen that our warships were caught like tame ducks in Pearl Harbor?"

It happened because the U.S. forces at Pearl Harbor were fatally unprepared for war on the morning of December 7. "Neither Army or Navy Commandants in Oahu regarded such an attack as at all likely," Secretary Knox explained to Roosevelt. "Both [General Walter Short and Admiral Husband Kimmel] felt certain that such an attack would take place nearer Japan's base of operations, that is, in the Far East." Lack of readiness characterized every aspect of the base—from the unmanned aircraft batteries to the radar station whose sentries went off duty at 7 a.m. that morning.

A great military base, historian William Emerson explains, takes years of planning and coordination. "The anti-aircraft artillery must be tied into the central command post. The ground observer corps must fill in where the radar system leaves off. People must react to each other with the speed of

Las Vegas croupiers." None of this had yet come together at Pearl Harbor, which had been only a minor naval base until the early summer of 1940, when the decision was made to base the fleet there. "We are operating on a shoestring," Rear Admiral Patrick Bellinger had warned in January 1941, with great deficiencies in planes, equipment, materiel, personnel, and facilities. It was estimated that one effective patrol through 360 degrees, at a distance of eight hundred miles, with necessary relief in planes and pilots, required at least 180 reconnaissance planes. Nowhere near this number was available at Pearl Harbor, nor was there manpower to operate them. Nor, once the attack came, was there adequate anti-aircraft artillery or an adequate number of fighter planes.

But this was not the time for recriminations. "The damage was done," Dr. McIntire said, "and the thing to do was to repair it." Not the least of Roosevelt's strength as a leader was his ability to close his mind against the setbacks of the past and focus instead on making plans. Relief came in action: in perusing troop dispositions with General Marshall, in getting Stimson and Knox to mount guards around defense plants, in placing the Japanese Embassy under surveillance, in putting the final touches on his speech to the Congress.

At a little past 10 p.m., in the middle of the president's meeting with Cabinet and congressional leaders, Missy telephoned from Warm Springs. She wanted to talk with the president. Grace Tully took the call, heard the distress in Missy's voice as her old friend struggled desperately to make herself intelligible. But there was no way Grace could interrupt the president to ask him to speak with Missy. Instead, she typed out a message. "Missy telephoned and wanted to talk with you. She is thinking about you and much disturbed about the news. She would like you to call her tonight. I told her you would if the conference broke up at a reasonable hour—otherwise you would call her in the morning."

Toward midnight, the meeting in the president's study drew to a close; and while every face wore an expression of regret and reproach, there was also relief. For Stimson, it was in the knowledge "that the indecision was over and that a crisis had come in a way which would unite our people." No matter how great the damage, at least, the matter was settled. "You know," Frank Knox whispered to Frances Perkins, "I think the boss must have a great load off his mind. I thought the load on his mind was just going to kill him, going to break him down. This must be a great sense of relief to him. At least we know what to do now."

• • •

"Monday was almost worse than Sunday," Marquis Childs observed. "A merciful kind of shock prevailed under the first impact and now as that wore off, the truth was inescapable." In Washington, the rumors of damage "hovered like a low-hanging gas, spreading the panic that seemed to infect the capital." On the same day as Pearl Harbor, the Japanese had attacked the Philippines, Malaya, Wake Island, Guam, and Hong Kong.

At noon, under heavy security, the president motored from the East Gate of the White House to the Capitol, where, to deafening applause, he delivered a brief but powerful speech. From his first words, commemorating the day that would "live in infamy," to his call upon Congress to declare that, since "the unprovoked and dastardly attack by Japan on Sunday, December 7th, a state of war has existed between the United States and the Japanese Empire," the president's anger and indignation burned through. His head held high, his chin thrust out, Roosevelt roused his audience to a standing ovation when he pledged that "this form of treachery shall never endanger us again. The American people in their righteous might will win through to absolute victory." The Congress responded unambiguously to the president's call; both chambers approved a declaration of war, with only one dissenting vote—that of white-haired Representative Jeanette Rankin of Montana.

Isolationism collapsed overnight. "American soil has been treacherously attacked by Japan," former President Herbert Hoover stated. "Our decision is clear. It is forced upon us. We must fight with everything we have." Senator Arthur Vandenberg of Michigan, who had struggled long and hard against American involvement in the war, phoned the White House to tell the president that "he would support him without reservation." Even Representative Hamilton Fish of New York, one of Roosevelt's severest critics, urged the American people "to present a united front in support of the President." After months of vacillation, confusion, and hesitation, the United States was committed at last to a common course of action.

Amid the surge of patriotism that suddenly enveloped the country, union leaders hastily agreed that there would be "no strikes or lockouts" for the duration of the war. All disputes would be peacefully settled by a new War Labor Board, to be created by the president. "Labor's response to the Axis attack has been splendid and spontaneous," Sidney Hillman reported to the president five days after Pearl Harbor. After a series of conferences with representatives of the CIO and the AFL, Hillman was able to promise Roosevelt "that the outlook for constructive participation by labor in the victory effort is good."

Eleanor had accompanied her husband to the Capitol when he made his speech, but as soon as he was finished, she rushed back to the White House to prepare for an overnight trip to the West Coast. Amid reports that Los Angeles and San Francisco might soon be attacked, she and Fiorello LaGuardia felt the need to strengthen civilian-defense organization and morale. At present, the OCD had a total of 950,000 people enrolled as air-raid wardens, fire-fighting auxiliaries, and medical corpsmen. Now the time had come to assign specific people to specific posts in order to translate plans into action. "Hell, this isn't a pinochle party we're having," LaGuardia said, "It's war."

En route to Los Angeles, the pilot brought Eleanor a wire report that San Francisco was being bombed by the Japanese. When she awakened LaGuardia to tell him the news, he put his head out of the curtains, "looking for all the world like a Kewpie," Eleanor recalled. If the report was true, he said, "we will go direct to San Francisco." The mayor's instantaneous response was so characteristic of him that Eleanor "glowed inwardly." When the report proved erroneous, the mayor and the first lady proceeded as planned to Los Angeles. There they met with the governor of California, the mayor of the city, and the State Counsel of Defense. "I am not here to give you any message," Eleanor said. "I am here to get down to work. I came here to find out from you what are the most helpful things we in Washington can do to help you. Tell me what you found lacking and what you want."

As Eleanor traveled up and down the coast, she bore witness to the growing hysteria directed against aliens and citizens of Japanese descent. Within two hours of Pearl Harbor, FBI agents had begun taking key Japanese leaders into custody. California is "a zone of danger," the *LA Times* proclaimed the day after the attack. It is the duty of alert citizens "to cooperate with the military authorities against spies, saboteurs and 5th columnists." As the panic spread, government officials swooped down upon Japanese banks, department stores, produce houses, and newspapers, locking their doors with giant padlocks. Houses where aliens lived were searched for pictures or documents that might suggest loyalty to the emperor of Japan; drawers and closets were rummaged for anything that might conceivably be used as a weapon. In the process, thousands of radios and cameras were confiscated.

"Rumors were everywhere," recalled Jiro Ishihara, a young Japanese American who was in high school in East Los Angeles at the time. "We'd hear that the person down the street had been picked up for having feudal dolls and that a neighbor had been taken away for having Japanese recordings. So my father burned everything that had the slightest connection to Japan. When you contributed to the Japanese relief fund, you got these magnificent certificates, but they had the imperial seal on them, so we threw them into the fire along with everything else. The hardest problem was a small sword my father had been given when he first came to the States by an old swordmaster in his family. That sword meant a lot to him, so we asked a Jewish friend of ours to hold it for us. It was a terrible time."

Swimming against the rising tide of prejudice and fear, Eleanor had her picture taken with a group of American-born Japanese in Tacoma, Washington. In the statement that accompanied the picture, she warned of unwarranted suspicions against loyal citizens. "Let's be honest," she said. "There is a chance now for great hysteria against minority groups—loyal American born Japanese and Germans. If we treat them unfairly and make them unhappy we may shake their loyalty which should be built up. If you see something suspicious, report it to the right authorities, but don't try to be the FBI yourself."

"We know," Eleanor wrote in her column, "there are German and Italian agents, Japanese as well, who are here to be helpful to their own nations. But the great mass of people, stemming from these various national ties, must not feel they have suddenly ceased to be Americans."

Eleanor's call for tolerance antagonized many Californians. "When she starts bemoaning the plight of the treacherous snakes we call Japanese, with apologies to all snakes," the *Los Angeles Times* proclaimed, "she has reached the point where she should be forced to retire from public life." Undeterred, she continued to speak out: "I think almost the biggest obligation we have today is to prove that in a time of stress we can still live up to our beliefs and maintain the civil liberties we have established as the rights of human beings everywhere."

While Eleanor was on the West Coast, Franklin delivered a fireside chat in which he outlined a program for doubling and quadrupling war production by increasing working hours, establishing factories, and using more available materials for war production. Later that night, Sam Rosenman stopped by to see if the president was still up. As he entered the oval study, he found Roosevelt sitting at his desk, at work on his stamps, smoking a cigarette. "He was all alone," Rosenman remarked. "If Missy had been well she would have been sitting up with him in the study that night. She always did in times of great stress to see whether there was anyone he wanted to call or talk to. . . . The President looked up as I came in and smiled . . . a sad and tired smile."

To be sure, Princess Martha was still available for pleasant companionship —she had dinner with the president two of the six nights Eleanor was on the West Coast—but in moments of crisis like this, calling for work round the clock, there was no substitute for the devoted love and loyalty of Missy LeHand.

• • •

In the days that followed Pearl Harbor, Roosevelt found himself in an awkward situation. He had been telling his countrymen for more than a year that Hitler's Germany was the real enemy. He had expected that Germany would join Japan in declaring war against the United States. But time was passing and still nothing was heard from Berlin. "Was it possible," political scientist James MacGregor Burns has written, "after all Washington's elaborate efforts to fight first in Europe, with only a holding action in the Pacific, that the United States would be left with only a war in the Far East?"

The answer came on December 11, when Adolf Hitler, who viewed America as a decadent democracy incapable of making a sustained commitment to war, delivered a vitriolic speech against Roosevelt and declared war against the United States. "A world-wide distance separates Roosevelt's ideas and my ideas," he began. "Roosevelt comes from a rich family and belongs to the class whose path is smoothed in the democracies. I was only the child of a small, poor family and had to fight my way by work and industry." Whereas National Socialism had led to an unprecedented economic revival in Germany, Hitler claimed, Roosevelt's New Deal had not succeeded in bringing about even the slightest improvement. "This is not surprising if one bears in mind that the men he had called to support him, or rather, the men who had called him, belonged to the Jewish element, whose interests are all for disintegration and never for order." And then, Hitler contended, Roosevelt had provoked war in order to cover up the failures of his New Deal. "This man alone," he thundered, "was responsible for the Second World War," and under the circumstances, Germany "considers herself to be at war with the United States, as from today."

The next day, in response to a written request from the president, the United States Congress unanimously recognized that "a state of war exists between the United States, Germany and Italy."

• • •

When Eleanor returned to Washington on December 15, the capital had moved to a wartime footing. "It seems like a completely changed world," she noted sadly. Previously, casual visitors had been allowed to stroll around the White House grounds during the day. But now sentry boxes, staffed with Secret Service and White House guards, were set up at all the external gates. Only those with official appointments were allowed inside, and only after careful scrutiny. "No more Congressional constituents," Lorena Hickok remarked, "no more government clerks hurrying through the grounds . . . no more Sunday tourists feeding the squirrels, taking snapshots and hanging around the portico hoping someone interesting would come out."

Eleanor chafed at the new restrictions; she particularly disliked the long blackout curtains, "gloomy in winter and hot in the summer," that had been fitted on all the windows. Fires were no longer allowed in the fireplaces, Hick noted wistfully. It was feared that smoke rising from the chimneys would attract enemy bombers. "The house was chill and silent, as though it had died. Even Fala did not bark."

The week after Pearl Harbor, the Secret Service presented the president with a long report of recommended changes to improve White House security. It proposed covering the skylights with sand and tin, camouflaging the house, painting the colonnade windows black, setting up machine-gun emplacements on the roof, and building an air-raid shelter in a subbasement area of the new East Wing. The president rejected most of the suggestions, "with not a little annoyance," though he finally agreed to the construction of a temporary shelter in the Treasury Department, which would be accessed by a tunnel that would run under the street from the White House to the Treasury.

Secret Service agent Milton Lipson recalls sleeping in the shelter at night with a group of fellow agents as they practiced dry runs in the event of a bombing raid. "One of the Secret Service men would sit in a wheelchair, and then we would use our stopwatches to see how long it would take to get the president from the White House to the shelter. We got it down to under a minute." When Morgenthau tried to get the president to visit the shelter, Roosevelt told the Treasury secretary, "Henry, I will not go down into the shelter unless you allow me to play poker with all the gold in your vaults."

Though Eleanor understood the need for protection against a bombing attack, she insisted that the doors of the White House remain open to the American people. "Mrs. Roosevelt is very much annoyed today with Secret Service and indirectly with Morgenthau," Tommy wrote Esther Lape on December 16, "because they insisted she could not have 350 foreign students in the White House for tea. Also because civilian defense counsel here does not want to have the usual lighted community Xmas tree across the street in Lafayette Park because it is so close to White House. In exasperation, Mrs. Roosevelt asked if they were going to take down the Washington monument because an enemy could measure the distance between it and the White House."

CHAPTER 12

"TWO LITTLE BOYS PLAYING SOLDIER"

About 9 a.m. on Monday, December 22, the president's chief butler, Alonzo Fields, was summoned to the president's bedroom. As he reached the door he heard a heated argument. "You should have told me," Eleanor was saying. "Why didn't you tell me? I can't find Mrs. Nesbitt anywhere. If only I had known." At this juncture, the president noticed Fields standing at the door. "Now, Eleanor, all that little woman would do even if she were here is to tell Fields what we can tell him ourselves right now. Fields, at eight tonight we have to have dinner ready for twenty. Mr. Churchill and his party are coming to stay with us for a few days."

"It had not occurred to him," Eleanor bluntly observed in her column, unaccountably venting her anger before the entire country, "that this might require certain moving of furniture to adapt rooms to the purposes for which the Prime Minister wished to use them. Before all the orders were finally given, it was 10 a.m. and I was half an hour late for my press conference."

In point of fact, although the president had known for nearly two weeks that Churchill was coming to Washington, he was not expecting the prime minister until the following day. The original schedule had called for the prime minister, after ten days at sea, to anchor in Chesapeake Bay and then cruise up the Potomac River to Washington. But once he arrived on American soil, Churchill's doctor, Lord Moran, explained, "he was like a child in his impatience to meet the President. He spoke as if every minute counted. It was absurd to waste time; he must fly."

The flight to Washington made a lasting impression on Churchill's aide-de-camp Commander C. R. (Tommy) Thompson. "It was night time. Those in the plane were transfixed with delight to look down from the windows and see the amazing spectacle of a whole city lighted up." Though blackout restrictions had been issued for Washington, they were not yet fully in force; compared with London, the city seemed ablaze with light. "Washington represented something immensely precious. Freedom, hope, strength. We had not seen an illuminated city for five years. My heart filled."

The president was waiting at the airport, propped against a big car, when Churchill's plane landed. Churchill clasped Roosevelt's hand and then introduced him to Lord Moran. "Even in the half-light," Moran later recalled, "I was struck by the size of his head. I suppose that is why Winston thinks of him as majestic and statuesque, for he has no legs to speak of."

Eleanor greeted her guests as they stepped off the elevator on the second floor, inviting Churchill and his aides for a cup of tea. "The President was in his wheelchair," Eleanor's houseguest—an old friend, Mrs. Charles Hamlin—recalled, "and all were laughing and talking and in excellent spirits." Shorter by almost a head than Roosevelt, Churchill wore a knee-length double-breasted coat, buttoned high, in seaman fashion. He gripped a walking stick to which was attached a flashlight for the purpose of navigating London blackouts. "He reminded me of a big English bulldog who had been taught to give his paw," Mrs. Hamlin observed.

At dinner that first night, as at all subsequent dinners, the conversation sparkled, Roosevelt and Churchill vying with one another to assume center stage. Surrounded by guests, including Minister of Aircraft Production Lord Beaverbrook, British Ambassador to the United States Lord Halifax, Secretary and Mrs. Hull, and Undersecretary and Mrs. Welles, the president looked sublimely self-confident. The conversation turned to the president's first meeting with the prime minister, at Argentia. Roosevelt laughingly recalled that the news of the secret meeting had leaked from the British side, not the American. It must have been the British Cabinet, Roosevelt suggested, since, unlike the American president, the prime minister had to get permission to leave the country from his Cabinet. No, Churchill retorted, twinkling his eyes, "It must have been the women."

Over the course of the evening, the conversation developed into a peculiar tug of war. When Roosevelt was at center stage, gaily holding forth, Churchill would slump into silence, his chubby face petulant. Then, after five minutes of surly biding, Churchill would enter the conversation with an unforgettable quip that turned all eyes toward him—at which point the president would once again begin to talk. Finally, just before dinner ended, the president held up his glass of champagne. "I have a toast to offer—it has been in my head and on my heart for a long time—now it is on the tip of my tongue—'To the Common Cause.' "

"At ten o'clock," Eleanor recorded, "the gentlemen left us to consult together, while the ladies made conversation until after midnight, when their husbands returned a bit shamefaced to take them home. . . . I still remember that as time wore on that evening I suddenly caught myself falling asleep as I sat trying to talk to my guests." It is little wonder that Eleanor's head occasionally nodded. In addition to preparing for Churchill's arrival and conducting a press conference at the OCD, her fifteen-hour day found her attending a half-dozen Christmas celebrations for various alley dwellers, putting in an appearance at the headquarters of the Salvation Army, sitting in on a meeting of the American committee for British Catholic relief, and looking in on the Washington premiere of *Adeste Fideles*, a film of Christmas in wartime Britain.

Churchill was installed in the Rose Suite, on the second floor of the family quarters. His valet slept in the adjoining dressing room, and his two secretaries were given the Lincoln study, across the hall. The White House staff had worked all day shifting beds around to accommodate Churchill and his staff. The quiet upstairs hall was turned into the headquarters of the British government, with a flow of messengers carrying secret documents in the old red leather dispatch cases so characteristic of the British Empire. The Monroe Room was emptied of its furniture and transformed into a map room to provide a place for Churchill to hang the large maps that had come with him from England, representing the present strategic situation on land, sea, and air.

Despite the last-minute arrangements, Eleanor lamented, she was unable to give the prime minister all the things he liked to have. In the morning, Churchill confronted the President's butler Alonzo Fields. "Now, Fields," Churchill began, his bare feet sticking out below his long underwear, his crumpled bedclothes scattered on the bed, the floor strewn with British and American newspapers, "we had a lovely dinner last night but I have a few orders for you. We want to leave here as friends, right? So I need you to listen. One, I don't like talking outside my quarters; two, I hate whistling in the corridors; and three, I must have a tumbler of sherry in my room before breakfast, a couple glasses of scotch and soda before lunch and French champagne and 90 year old brandy before I go to sleep at night."

"Yes, sir." Fields nodded, not offended in the least by the prime minister's gruff, straight-talking manner.

In the days that followed, the president and prime minister stayed up talking, drinking brandy, and smoking cigars until 2 or 3 a.m. Accustomed to late hours, Churchill managed to disappear every afternoon for a long nap. "I'll be back," he would suddenly say in the midst of a conversation with Roosevelt. After two hours, during which Roosevelt had remained at his desk in the Oval Office, Churchill would reappear, reinvigorated.

Several times during these late nights, Roosevelt's head nodded. But soon a remark of Churchill's would rouse him, the conversation would resume, and there would be peals of merry laughter. "There is no question," Eleanor observed, "when you are deeply interested it is possible to go on working til all hours of the night. But for the people who have to wait up til you are through it is a deadly performance."

For the better part of three weeks, despite Eleanor's efforts, the late nights continued. "Mother would just fume," Elliott recorded, "and go in and out of the room making hints about bed, and still Churchill would sit there." It almost seemed, Elliott believed, as if Churchill were deliberately goading Eleanor by keeping Franklin up drinking brandy and smoking cigars. Repulsed by the abundant trays of liquor that accompanied Churchill wherever he went, Eleanor went to Franklin, White House maid Lillian Parks recalled, and told him "that she worried about Churchill's influence on him because of all the drinking. FDR retorted she needn't worry because it wasn't his side of the family that had a drinking problem."

On the second day of his visit, the prime minister had joined the president in an extraordinary dual press conference. Wearing a polka-dot bow tie, a short black coat, and striped trousers, he stared imperturbably into space, his long cigar between his compressed lips, as Roosevelt spoke. When the time came for him to speak, reporters in the back of the crowded room called out that they could not see him. Asked to stand, he not only complied, but scrambled atop his chair. "There was a wild burst of applause and then cheering," *The New York Times* reported, "as the visitor stood there before them, somewhat shorter than many had expected, but with confidence and determination written on the countenance so familiar to the world." In answer to questions, Churchill said the most immediate problem was allocating scarce materials to the forces fighting Hitler in various theaters of the world. However, once the great productive power of the United States was turned loose, he predicted, the problem of choosing where and when war supplies should be sent would be eliminated.

In the course of the Arcadia Conference, as the Christmas talks came to be known, the president and prime minister reaffirmed the commitment they had made at Argentia to a strategy of dealing with Germany first. This was now made more difficult for Roosevelt by the overwhelming desire of the American people—strengthened with each new defeat in the Pacific—to take revenge upon Japan. "The news around us is pretty gloomy," Stimson recorded in his diary during Churchill's visit. The Japanese were sweeping through Malaya and the Philippines with astonishing ferocity. On December 12, a force of three thousand Japanese had come ashore on the coast of Luzon, in the Philippines; twelve days later, seven thousand Japanese troops had landed at Lamon Bay; the main Japanese force struck at Lingayen Gulf on the day Churchill arrived in Washington. Within a matter of days, Guam, Wake, and Hong Kong had fallen. In the Philippines, General Douglas MacArthur, General Jonathan Wainwright, and their troops were trapped on the southern tip of the Bataan Peninsula and the rock of Corregidor. These were the battles that held the attention of the American people. It was American territory that was being invaded, and American men who were dying. Nonetheless, Roosevelt never wavered from his resolve to defeat Germany first.

Roosevelt also reaffirmed America's commitment to lend-lease. In an emergency action on the night of Pearl Harbor, the army had stopped the movement of all supplies to Britain and Russia in order to ensure that its own needs would be met. Hitler's propagandists triumphantly announced to the world that America's supply line had been cut off. But at the Arcadia Conference, Roosevelt declared that America's entry into the war would bring an increase, not a decrease, in lend-lease supplies.

In the Soviet Union, the struggle for survival had reached a crucial stage. During seven months of fighting, the Russians had lost more territory than the whole of France, and more people than all the other combatants combined. In September, German troops had reached the outskirts of Leningrad and had cut the city off from communications and supplies. By the end of December, as the siege of Leningrad entered its seventeenth week, more than three thousand Russians were dying of starvation every day. "Even daily air raids no longer make any special impression," survivor Elena Skrjabina recalled. "Everyone is occupied with only one thought; where to get something edible so as not to starve to death."

As the death rate in Leningrad grew, there weren't enough coffins to contain the bodies. "When you leave the house in the morning," Skrjabina recorded in her diary, "you come upon corpses lying in the streets. The corpses lie around for a long time since there is no one to take them away." The first week of January, a friend of Skrjabina's dropped by. "He was always a gay, lively, young man but now he is unrecognizable. He came to find out if the large gray cat which belonged to an actress living in our apartment house was still alive. He was in hopes that the cat had not been eaten since he knew how much the actress adored it. I had to disappoint him. All animals have been eaten, either by occupants of our house or by our agile neighbors."

More than one million people would die in Leningrad before the nine-hundred-day siege came to an end, but in late December 1941, the tide of war in Russia was beginning to turn. As the Russian winter set in, the Red Army unleashed a massive counterattack against the thinly clad German soldiers. (Hitler had refused to issue sufficient winter coats or boots on the ground that the war in Russia was supposed to be over by winter.) In the extreme cold, which reached temperatures of minus forty degrees Fahrenheit, even minor wounds could lead to shock and death. In a single day in December, more than fourteen thousand German soldiers had to undergo amputation as a result of frostbite. Now it was Germany's turn to experience the desperate suffering of war.

While the president and prime minister continued their discussions, the chiefs of staff of both countries met in order to establish a method of unified command. On the American side, the Joint Chiefs were represented by Chief of Staff General George Marshall; Commander General, U.S. Army Air Force, Henry Arnold; Commander in Chief of Naval Forces Ernest King; and Roosevelt's personal military representative, Admiral William Leahy; on the British side by Field Marshal Sir John Dill, Chief of the Imperial General Staff; Chief of Air Staff Sir Charles Portal; Admiral of the Fleet Sir Dudley Pound; and Lord Beaverbrook. The British wanted to create two committees—one in London, the other in Washington—but Roosevelt wanted a single structure, and after what Hopkins called "a hell of a row," he got what he wanted. The war would be run from Washington. A Combined Chiefs of Staff organization was set up, along with a Combined Munitions Board to pool resources and move them from spot to spot around the world.

"Our people are very unhappy about the decision," Lord Moran noted, "and the most they will agree to is to try it out for a month. They were, however, brought back to good humor by the final figures of the production estimates (45,000 aircraft in 1942, 100,000 in 1943; 45,000 tanks in 1942, 75,000 in 1943). I think Winston, more than anyone here, visualizes in detail what this programme means to the actual conduct of the war. He is drunk with the figures."

"We live here as a big family," Churchill telegraphed Labour Party leader Clement Attlee, "in the greatest intimacy and informality, and I have formed the very highest regard and admiration for the President. His breadth of view, resolution and his loyalty to the common cause are beyond all praise."

On Christmas Eve, the prime minister joined the president in the traditional Christmas-tree lighting ceremonies. The president had insisted on having the tree, despite the worries of the Secret Service, though he had agreed to relocate it from Lafayette Park to the southern grounds of the White House. Though the lights would still bring danger, historian William Seale observed in *The President's House*, the Secret Service "could at least better protect the President this way; only those people invited as spectators would pass through the iron fence, while thousands of uninvited would remain outside." For the fifteen thousand citizens who gathered in the clear twilight to hear the two leaders speak, it was a night to remember. A crescent moon hung overhead. In the distance loomed the Washington Monument, its red light burning, and farther south the monuments to Jefferson and Lincoln. Standing at the president's right on the South Portico with the Marine Band playing "Joy to the World," the prime minister smiled broadly as the president pressed the button which set the colored lights of the Christmas tree twinkling. As the crowd roared its approval, the president introduced his "old and good friend" to say a word to the people of America.

The great orator did not disappoint. "Let the children have their night of fun and laughter," he began. "Let the gifts of Father Christmas delight their thoughts, let us share to the full in their unstinted pleasure before we turn again to the stern tasks in the year that lies before us. But now, by our sacrifice and daring, these same children shall not be robbed of their inheritance or denied their right to live in a free and decent world."

For Eleanor, the Christmas holidays were distressing. For the first time in years, not a single Roosevelt child was home for the holidays: all four boys were in the service, and Anna was in Seattle. Joe Lash records in his diary a worrisome telephone conversation with Eleanor during this period. "Her voice did not have the customary ring to it, so I asked her how she was. There was a period of silence. . . . Then we both mumbled something inconsequential and hung up." Sensing something was seriously wrong, Lash jumped into a taxi. "She started to scold me for having come," Lash wrote, "and then confessed she had a hard day and burst into tears. I thought bad things had happened at OCD which shows how little I understand her." She told Lash her melancholy was rooted in the loss of her four boys to the war. "She knew they had to do it, but it was hard. By the laws of chance not all four would return. Again she lost control and wept."

Only one sock hung on the mantel in the president's room. Eleanor had put it there, labeled it for Fala, and filled it with rubber bones and toys. Ten-year-old Diana Hopkins also had a stocking, but it was hung by the fireplace in her father's room. In the absence of children and grandchildren, the president decided to dispense with his traditional reading of Dickens' *Christmas Carol*.

After the Christmas-tree lighting ceremony, the president invited Martha and her husband, Crown Prince Olav (whom the president had once again brought over from England as a present for Martha), to the Red Parlor for tea with Churchill, Lord Beaverbrook, Lord Moran, and Harry Hopkins. In the midst of this festive gathering, Eleanor asked Franklin if he had called Missy in Warm Springs to wish her a merry Christmas. He replied that he had not called her and wasn't planning to. This apparent callousness was something she simply couldn't understand, she told Lash. "She could never get accustomed to his lack of real attachment to people,'" Lash recorded in his diary. "Could never conceive of him doing a reckless thing for a friend because of personal attachment. Said she had to have contact with people she loved to get refreshment and strength for her duties and work. President seemed to have no bond to people. Not even his children. Completely political person."

Yet, though Roosevelt's remoteness was difficult for those who loved him, Eleanor understood that "it kept him from making mistakes," it gave him an inner independence which freed him to make the right decisions for the right reasons, to be "the kind of person the times required."

Surely Missy understood Roosevelt's temperament as well as Eleanor. "He was really incapable of a personal friendship with anyone," she once confided in her friend, writer Fulton Oursler. But it was one thing to accept his remoteness while she herself was a vital participant in his world. It was quite another to sit in her cottage at Warm Springs, waiting for a phone call that never came. Among the possessions she treasured the most was a maroon box containing hundreds of engraved invitations to Marguerite A. LeHand—requests for the pleasure of her company at White House lunches, receptions, dinners; blue ribbons to admit the bearer to the presidential platform at the inaugural ceremonies; special passes to the 1932 Olympic games at Lake Placid; tickets to the Water Carnival at the U.S. Naval Academy; a seasonal pass from the New York State Racing Commission for entry to the Saratoga racetrack. But now the busy and fevered life these mementos represented had been replaced by monastic stillness as Missy sat in her wheelchair, desperately trying to make sense of her ruined life.

Five Christmases earlier, Missy had sent Franklin and Eleanor a sparkling letter, which thanked her boss for giving her such a happy year but ended on an ominous note: "I guess I'm usually too flippant to tell you 'Well done' but it sounds so inadequate somehow. However, you must know how proud I am every time you get something accomplished—which is all the time—just being with you is a joy I can't explain.

"Please let me do things for you—you are the ones who have my love and only real devotion—without that I would have little reason for taking up space, don't you think?"

Unable now to do things for the man she loved, Missy apparently lost faith in her reason for "taking up space." One night, during the 1941–42 holidays, the telephone rang in the home of Dr. C. E. Irwin, medical director of the Warm Springs foundation. It was after midnight, but he dressed and left immediately for Missy's cottage. As the sun was coming up, he returned, frazzled and confused. "I don't know what I'm going to do about Missy," he told his wife, Mabel, shaking his head in disbelief and sadness. "I think she tried to kill herself tonight."

There is no evidence that Franklin and Eleanor were ever told of this suicide attempt in Missy's cottage that night. Not a word was said in the chatty letter Missy's sister Ann Rochon wrote to Eleanor after visiting Missy over the holidays. "Missy and I had a lovely Christmas together and I want you to know how much she enjoyed all the wonderful presents that you and the President sent to her."

• • •

"Xmas was a very sad day for me," Eleanor admitted to her daughter. "I think Pa enjoyed all the officialdom and he did know that much of importance was being accomplished. I wish I could be less personal. It just didn't seem as though anywhere around there was much personal feeling. We didn't bother about stockings and nothing seems to have much zest but I suppose life must be like this till we return to peace!"

Churchill, too, was out of sorts on Christmas Day. Though he was his usual animated self through the afternoon working session, he retreated into silence at the formal dinner. Guests included Martha and Olav, Lord and Lady Halifax, Henry and Elinor Morgenthau. If the president seemed "jolly and care free" to Lord Moran, the prime minister was "silent and preoccupied" as he turned over in his restless mind the speech he was scheduled to deliver the following day before a joint session of Congress.

"He just wasn't having a good time," Morgenthau observed. "You see him on one side of Mrs. Roosevelt and Beaverbrook on the other, and Beaverbrook's face is a map of life, but in Churchill's face there is absolutely nothing. . . . He asked three times to be excused after dinner so, he says, 'I can prepare these impromptu remarks for tomorrow.' "

Of course, the remarks were anything but impromptu. As Churchill fully appreciated, the invitation to a foreigner to speak before a joint session of Congress was "a tremendous occasion." He could remember "nothing quite like it in his time," he told Moran. "The two democracies were to be joined together and he had been chosen to give out the banns. . . . He knew, of course, that some of the senators were not all friendly to the British. Would they perhaps show it? This morning he decided that what he was going to say to them was all wrong. At any rate, he had to finish his speech before he went to bed. He yawned wearily. He would be glad when it was all over. . . . He got up and asked the President to excuse him."

When Churchill left, sheets of music were handed out to the sixty-odd guests, and the president led everyone in singing carols. So astonishing was Roosevelt's appetite for life that evening, Moran marveled, that "it was difficult to believe that this was the man who was taking his nation into a vast conflict."

The prime minister's methods of preparing a speech fascinated Hopkins. Trained by years of vigorous debate in the House of Commons, Churchill liked to think on his feet, dictating his speeches as he paced up and down the room, imagining that a large crowd had already assembled. At various times, he would refer to notes he had made in the preceding days, but most of the phrasing and imagery emerged from his head and his heart, a product, Isaiah Berlin once observed, of his capacity "for sustained introspective brooding, great depth and constancy of feeling—in particular, feeling for and fidelity to the great tradition for which he assumes a personal responsibility." This peculiar pride in the British people had assumed a major role in Churchill's speeches in the dark days of 1940.

Hopkins told Moran, during a long conversation in his bedroom one evening, that it was interesting to hear two great orators with such different methods. When Roosevelt prepared a speech, Hopkins observed, he "wastes little time in turning phrases; he tries to say what is in his mind in the shortest and simplest words. All the time he gives to that particular speech is spent in working out what each individual in his audience will think about it; he always thinks of individuals, never of a crowd."

In contrast, though Churchill had learned by long experience the feel of an audience as a whole, he knew little about their individual lives, their experiences, their aspirations. Churchill, Isaiah Berlin observed, in contrast to Roosevelt, "does not reflect a social or moral world in an intense and concentrated fashion; rather, he creates one of such power and coherence that it becomes a reality and alters the external world by being imposed upon it with irresistible force."

At noon on the 26th, Churchill was still working on his speech when the motorcade arrived at the back entrance of the White House to take him to the Senate Chamber. "Churchill is always quiet before a speech," C. R. Thompson observed. "It is dangerous to speak to him. There is one little ritual between us. I must always ask him whether he has remembered to put his speech glasses in his pocket. He is forgetful of them, and has great difficulty reading typed notes without them. He patted his pocket. Yes, he had them."

Escorted to a small waiting room beside the Senate Chamber, Churchill paced rapidly up and down the room, mumbling whole sections of the speech to himself. Suddenly he stopped and looked directly at Moran, his eyes popping. "Do you realize we are making history?"

Minutes later, Churchill stood at the podium before the crowded chamber, his fingertips under the lapels of his coat, his heavy gold watch chain hanging from the pocket of his striped trousers. "I cannot help reflecting," he began, "that if my father had been American and my mother British, instead of the other way round, I might have got here on my own." The effect of these words was electric; cheers and laughter instantly overwhelmed the entire audience. Then, when the laughter died down, Churchill's voice quieted to a whisper as he spoke of the difficulties ahead in the struggle against the Axis powers.

He warned that the forces ranging against the Allies were powerful, bitter, and ruthless, and that "without doubt there is a time of tribulation before us during which ground will be lost which will be hard and costly to regain." But, with a magnificent confidence that contagiously echoed in repeated ovations, he drove home his central message that "the task which has been set is not above our strength, its pangs and trials are not beyond our endurance." In eighteen months, he pledged, American and British industry would produce results in war power "beyond anything that has been seen or foreseen in the dictator states."

His voice rising to a fury, he condemned Nazi tyrannies, heaped scorn on Mussolini, and questioned the sanity of the Japanese. "What sort of people do they think we are?" he shouted. "Is it possible they do not realize that we shall never cease to persevere against them until they have been taught a lesson which they and the world will never forget?"

At this juncture, David Lilienthal recorded in his diary, the place erupted, "the first sound of blood lust I have yet heard in the war." Overall, it was a masterpiece, Lilienthal concluded, "the color and the imagery of his style, the wonderful use of balance and alliteration and the way he used his voice to put emotions into his words. Why at one point he made a growling sound that sounded like the British lion!"

When Churchill finished, the *Washington Post* reported, there was a moment's silence, and then a mighty roar, as members of the House and Senate, the Cabinet, the Supreme Court, and the galleries were on their feet, clapping and cheering. "They had witnessed a magnificent drama. Now they wanted an encore." With a brilliant gesture, Churchill obliged. He turned, smiled, and then let his fingers shape the letter "V," the brave symbol captive peoples of Europe had engraved on history as a salute to victory. Throughout the chamber, hundreds of arms were raised in a return salute. It was a stunning climax to a speech which the *Post* ranked with Edmund Burke's defense of the American colonies.

When Churchill returned to the White House to join the president at a Cabinet meeting, he was sweating freely but a thrilling sense of mastery possessed him. "I hit the target all the time," he exulted to Moran. The laughter and applause had come just where he expected them. "It was a great weight off his chest," Moran noted in his dairy.

That evening, the president made up his mind that everyone had worked hard enough and needed relaxation, so he provided a movie in the upper hall, *The Maltese Falcon*. For two hours, the president and prime minister, Beaverbrook, and Canada's Prime Minister MacKenzie King watched as Humphrey Bogart's Sam Spade engaged in his memorable quest for a priceless statuette. Since Eleanor had retired to her study to catch up on her mail, her friend Mrs. Charles Hamlin sat in the front row between the president and prime minister. In the end, Mrs. Hamlin later remembered, when Bogart gave up Brigid O'Shaughnessy, the girl he loved, to justice, Mr. Churchill recalled that when he was home secretary a very similar case had come up to him. "It was a tragic case and the man did give up the girl." Churchill seemed very sad at the memory. When the picture was over, Eleanor rejoined the party and found "everyone completely restored to working capacity."

Eleanor watched the developing affection between the president and prime minister with a worried eye. "She saw in Churchill a male tendency to romanticize war," Eleanor's grandson Curtis Roosevelt observed. "She had a memory of Teddy Roosevelt caring about the environment and social progress but then getting totally caught up in the Spanish-American War. And she remembered FDR in Europe after the First World War, knowing he would have traded absolutely everything to be one of the heroic soldiers wounded in battle."

"Nobody enjoyed the war as much as Churchill did," Martha Gellhorn wryly observed. "He loved the derring-do and rushing around. He got Roosevelt steamed up in his boy's book of adventure."

No sooner, for instance, had Roosevelt seen Churchill's mobile map room than he wanted one of his own so that he, too, could visualize the progress of the war. Within days, a sophisticated map room was created on the ground floor of the White House in a low-ceilinged room that had previously been a coatroom for women. Located between the diplomatic reception room and Dr. McIntire's office, it provided easy access for the president when he visited the doctor for his daily massage. "The walls were covered with fiberboard," naval aide George Elsey recalled, "on which we pinned large-scale charts of the Atlantic and the Pacific. Updated two or three times a day, the charts displayed the constantly changing location of enemy and Allied forces. Different shape pins were used for different types of ships, a round-headed pin for destroyers, a square head for heavy cruisers. For the army we had a plastic cover with a grease pencil to change the battle lines as new dispatches came in."

The information was derived from the War and Navy Departments; it was hand-delivered by messenger several times a day and then transferred to the big maps. Special pins revealed the location of the leaders of the Big Three. Churchill's pin was shaped like a cigar, FDR's like a cigarette holder, Stalin's like a briar pipe. Since top-secret dispatches came in at all hours, the map room was manned around the clock by three shifts of officers taken from the navy, army, and air force. Beyond the map-room personnel, access was strictly limited to Roosevelt, Hopkins, Marshall, King, and Leahy.

There was one occasion, however, when Eleanor, passing the map room on her way down the hall, happened to glance inside. There, in front of the brightly colored charts, she saw her husband and Churchill engaged in animated conversation, pointing at different pins in various theaters of the war. "They looked like two little boys playing soldier," Eleanor observed. "They seemed to be having a wonderful time, too wonderful in fact. It made me a little sad somehow."

• • •

On New Year's Day, 1942, the president and the prime minister motored through the countryside of Virginia to lay a wreath on George Washington's tomb at Mount Vernon. On the way down, Eleanor later told her friend Justine Polier, Churchill kept saying, "After the war we've got to form an Anglo-American alliance to meet the problems of the world." And Franklin kept nodding his head and saying, "Yes, yes, yes!" Eleanor said nothing. Unlike Churchill, she did not believe that "we should stress the control of the English speaking people when peace comes." On the contrary, she thought that "all people who believe in democracy" should be included in whatever institution or organization controlled the peace. To focus on Anglo-American control was simply the "old British colonialism in a new form."

Ordinarily, Eleanor would have interrupted immediately, but she was intimidated by Churchill's dogmatic assertions. It seemed to her that once he gave his opinion the matter was concluded. So she sat in silence until she couldn't stand it anymore. "You know, Winston," she finally blurted out, "when Franklin says yes, yes, yes it doesn't mean he agrees with you. It means he's listening." Churchill listened to her stonily, a scowl on his face.

Churchill apparently did not comprehend the highly visible role Eleanor had been playing for nearly ten years as first lady—her public speeches, syndicated column, trips to slums, mines, factories. When Eleanor asked him at a luncheon a few days later what Mrs. Churchill was doing during the war, he puckishly expressed his delight that his wife, and indeed the wives of all his ministers, did not engage in any public activities but stayed at home—

failing to acknowledge the extensive role British women were already playing in the war effort. A strange silence fell on the table as all eyes turned toward Eleanor. But she never "batted an eyelash," according to Sam Rosenman, and the conversation resumed.

"Churchill wasn't very fond of Mother," Elliott Roosevelt recalled. "They were always very polite to each other but they were totally different personalities. She believed in the future and the expansion of democracy everywhere, while he was basically a monarchist at heart."

After lunch on New Year's Day, Lash, Tommy, and Eleanor gathered in Mrs. Roosevelt's sitting room and compared impressions of the president and prime minister. "The Prime Minister has the richer temperament," Lash began, "but the President is a more dependable, steadier man in a crisis." When Lash finished, Tommy clapped her hands and said she and Mrs. Roosevelt felt the same. The president was more hardheaded, they felt. He was less brilliant, but more likely to do the right thing. The president also gave the impression of being more under control, of never letting himself go.

"I like Mr. Churchill," Eleanor wrote Anna, "he's lovable and emotional and very human but I don't want him to write the peace or carry it out."

• • •

During the last week of December, twenty-six nations at war with the Axis had negotiated a declaration of unity and purpose. The document, entitled "A Declaration by the United Nations," pledged the full resources of each signing nation to the fight against the Axis, reiterated adherence to the principles of the Atlantic Charter, and pledged each country not to make a separate peace. It was Roosevelt who had come up with the phrase "United Nations" to express the common purpose that united the Allies.

Accounts vary as to how the president communicated his suggested title to the prime minister. By far the best story was told by Harry Hopkins, who claimed the president was so excited by his inspiration that he had himself wheeled into Churchill's bedroom early one morning, just as the prime minister was emerging from his bath, stark naked and gleaming pink. "Bathtubs," Churchill once said, "were a contrivance that America had foisted upon the British but there was nothing like a hot bath . . . lying back and kicking one's legs in the air—as at birth."

The president apologized and said he would come back at a better time. No need to go, Churchill said: "The Prime Minister of Great Britain has nothing to conceal from the President of the United States!"

The declaration was signed in the president's study at 10 p.m. As the invited guests gathered round, Mrs. Hamlin recalled, "It was as quiet as a church in the study—not a whisper, the only sound came from Fala who was stretched out sleeping heavily—oblivious of the momentous happenings."

The president signed first. Perhaps he should have used the title "commander-in-chief," he remarked. "President ought to do!" Hopkins said dryly.

Then the prime minister signed. Roosevelt looked at the signature. "Hey, ought you not to sign Great Britain and Ireland?" Churchill agreed, amending his signature. Foreign Minister Maxim Litvinov signed next for the Soviet Union, and finally Chinese Ambassador T. V. Soong for China. "Four-fifths of the human race," observed Churchill. "In the room," Lash recorded, "there was a sense of Hitler's doom being sealed."

As Churchill readied his return to England, Hopkins handed him a note to take to his wife, Clementine. "You would have been quite proud of your husband on this trip," Hopkins told Mrs. Churchill. "First because he was ever so good natured. I didn't see him take anybody's head off and he eats and drinks with his customary vigor. If he had half as good a time here as the President did having him about the White House he surely will carry pleasant memories of the past three weeks."

The hectic days and late nights took a toll on Hopkins, however. "His lips are blanched as if he had been bleeding internally," Lord Moran observed, "his skin yellow like stretched parchment and his eyelids contracted to a slit so that you can just see his eyes moving about restlessly, as if he was in pain." Living on sheer will and unquenchable spirit, Hopkins collapsed as soon as Churchill left, checking himself into the Naval Hospital in a state of nervous exhaustion.

When Churchill reached London, an affectionate message from the president awaited him. "It is fun," Roosevelt told Churchill, "to be in the same decade with you."

• • •

"We must raise our sights all along the production line," Roosevelt told the Congress in his State of the Union message on January 6, 1942. "Let no man say it cannot be done." He then proceeded to outline a staggering set of production goals for 1942: sixty thousand planes, forty-five thousand tanks, twenty thousand anti-aircraft guns, six million tons of merchant shipping. "The figures," *U.S. News* reported, "reached such astronomical proportions that human minds could not reach around them. Only by symbols could they be understood; a plane every four minutes in 1943; a tank every seven minutes; two seagoing ships a day." Thoroughly convinced that a dramatic announcement of spectacular goals would both rally the American public and serve notice on the Axis powers that America's vast industrial might would soon be producing munitions for all its Allies in every theater of war, the president had arbitrarily taken a pencil and revised the figures upward on the eve of his speech. When Hopkins questioned the wisdom of reaching so high, Roosevelt jauntily replied: "Oh—the production people can do it, if they really try."

Ironically, while the leaders of industry clung to a more or less static view of the American economy, rooted in prevailing notions of limited annual growth, it was Franklin Roosevelt and his impractical theorists, who never met a payroll, who held to a powerful vision of the country's latent potential, spurred by government spending, to produce more than anyone had ever dreamed possible.

"These figures," Roosevelt told a cheering Congress, "will give the Japanese and the Nazis a little idea of just what they accomplished at Pearl Harbor." Henceforth, Roosevelt said, workers must be prepared to work long and hard to turn out weapons twenty-four hours a day, seven days a week. Henceforth, every available tool, whether in the auto industry or the village machine shop, must be devoted to the production of munitions. "The militarists of Berlin and Tokyo started the war," he concluded, his voice rising. "But the massed, angered forces of common humanity will finish it."

The automobile industry was the first to feel the force of the president's fighting words. The time for persuasion had passed; a complete ban was imposed on the retail sale of new passenger autos and of light and heavy trucks. The order froze all stock in the hands of dealers until January 15. On that date, a program of rationing the 450,000 cars and trucks on hand, plus the two hundred thousand currently on the assembly line, was announced. First call went to the government for lend-lease; the remainder was parceled out to doctors, police, and others whose operations were essential to public health and safety. The drastic action was necessary, Office of Price Administration chief Leon Henderson said, so the entire manufacturing facilities of the auto industry could be brought into the national armaments program.

"In the dealers' holiday-decorated showrooms," *Time* reported, "the stillness of death" prevailed, as forty-four thousand auto dealers and their four hundred thousand employees were laid off. To Eleanor's mind, this human hardship could have been avoided if the big automobile companies had accepted the necessity for conversion earlier. Instead, blindly insisting they could produce great quantities of both cars and planes, they had exposed the workers to a perilous situation.

Taking out her anger and frustration on OPM chief William Knudsen, Eleanor accosted him one afternoon to ask what he intended to do about all the people being thrown out of work. "Mr. Knudsen looked at me like a great big benevolent bear," Eleanor said, "as if to say, 'Now, Mrs. Roosevelt, don't let's get excited.' "

"I wonder if you know what hunger is?" Eleanor countered. "Has any member of your family ever gone hungry?"

Later, when called upon to explain her severity, Eleanor softened her attack. "I said nothing derogatory about anyone and nothing which I would not apply to myself," she argued. "None of us, whether we are government officials or private individuals, can afford to sit back and wait for the development of these problems without feeling the urgency that a group of hungry children in our homes would put upon us."

In truth, the auto industry's reluctance to convert before Pearl Harbor was part of a larger failure of will in the nation as a whole, but Knudsen was the man on the spot, and as a result he was the one to shoulder the blame.

Though Knudsen had been denied power commensurate with his responsibility, the president determined on January 13, 1942, that a shake-up was in order. He announced that former Sears, Roebuck executive Donald Nelson would head a powerful new organization, the War Production Board, which would have "final" decisions on procurement and production. It was the greatest delegation of power the president had ever made.

Knudsen was conducting a meeting when his secretary broke in to convey the news which had just come over the wire. "Look here," Knudsen told a colleague, holding a piece of paper torn from the ticker. "I've just been fired." Knudsen was stunned. The president who had called him Bill and treated him so warmly had not even had the courtesy to explain the shake-up face to face.

In the White House, Hopkins realized that the situation had been handled badly, but he knew from long experience that Roosevelt could never be made to tackle controversy head on. Securing the president's agreement to offer Knudsen a special commission in the army, Hopkins urged Federal Loan Administrator Jesse Jones to see Knudsen that night and persuade him to accept the post. "I have never seen a more disconsolate man," Jones reported. "After dinner he sat at the piano and played and hummed sad tunes as though his heart would break." Jones advised him to accept the presidential appointment, but Knudsen was so hurt he couldn't figure out what to do. Finally, Jones took matters into his own hands. He called the White House and asked for Hopkins. "Knudsen," Jones announced, "will accept a 3 star generalship in the Army," which put him in charge of "promoting production for war." When Knudsen failed to contradict him, Jones knew that the decision—which turned out to be an excellent one for everyone concerned—had been made.

The following day, with everything seemingly settled, the president invited Knudsen to the White House for lunch. At this point, wanting nothing so much as to leave the relationship on good terms, the old master set to work. His abundant charm was everywhere, in his warm greeting when Knudsen walked in, his generous praise of Knudsen's accomplishments, and his good-natured banter about Knudsen in a uniform. By the end of the luncheon, Knudsen said he would take any position the president offered. It was a triumph for Roosevelt. His ingenious maneuvering had produced a new director of war production without permanently alienating the old.

• • •

Gradually, one step at a time, the war was brought home to the American people. The tooling up period was over. The U.S. economy was finally prepared to swing into production on an unprecedented scale. "For more than a year," novelist Winston Estes observed in *Homefront*, "new defense factories and plants had been sprouting up from the landscape as though the ground underneath had been fertilized. And still they continued to appear, larger and more mysterious, turning out arms and munitions in unthinkable quantities." And while the new plants were being built, manufacturing concerns of every imaginable type were moving to convert their old plants to the production of weapons. A merry-go-round factory was using its plant to fashion gun mounts. A corset factory was making grenade belts. A manufacturer of stoves was producing lifeboats. A famous New York toy concern was making compasses. A pinball-machine maker was turning out armor-piercing shells. Despite continuing shortages of raw materials, 1942 would witness the greatest expansion of production in the nation's history.

On January 30, the President signed an Emergency Price Control Bill, which gave Henderson and the Office of Price Administration added, though still not sufficient, power to keep prices down. Under the new legislation, Henderson could impose ceilings on a selective range of consumer items from raw materials to finished goods; he could have violators imprisoned or fined, and he could fix maximum rents in defense areas. At the same time, a preliminary rationing system was established to hold the demand for goods to the available supply.

In the White House, Eleanor tried to set an example for housewives. When the need for parachutes put an end to silk stockings, she wore heavy black cotton stockings instead, announcing that she would do without just like everyone else. When a shortage of sugar was first contemplated, since the army and navy needed alcohol derived from sugar to make smokeless powder, Eleanor promised that the White House would be very careful in the use of sugar, relying on corn syrup and other substitutes wherever possible, replacing desserts with salads, if necessary. Eleanor's comments, Representative Emmanuel Celler of New York charged, provoked a run on sugar, which made sugar rationing inevitable. Without the hoarding brought about by the fear of loss which Eleanor incited, Celler argued, there would never have been a sugar shortage.

"It never crossed my mind," Eleanor rather naïvely said in self-defense, "that you couldn't tell the American people the truth and count on them to behave themselves accordingly. It is perfectly obvious that a housewife who goes out and buys 100 pounds of sugar for herself and puts it away is putting up the price of sugar for herself and her family. It is also obvious that she cannot buy enough pounds of sugar to last her through the war. . . . Sooner or later the hoarder is going to have to face the shortage and it is a lot more chummy to get into the boat with the rest of the citizenry from the start."

• • •

On the war front, everything was going badly. In the Far East, Japan's success was so complete that it surprised even the Japanese. In a matter of weeks, the Empire of the Rising Sun had seized what colonial powers had taken centuries to acquire. Nearly a million square miles of land—including Hong Kong, Thailand, Malaya, Burma, the Dutch East Indies—and a hundred million people had come under Japan's domain. In the Philippines,

General Jonathan Wainwright and his embattled troops were on the verge of defeat.

In the Atlantic, the United States was still losing its battle with the German submarine; merchant ships were still being sunk faster than new ships could be put into service. In the month of January alone, forty-three ships were sent to the bottom of the sea, with a loss of more than a thousand lives. By cutting off the supply line, Hitler was striking at the heart of the American war effort. "We are in a war of transportation," U.S. Maritime Commission Chairman Emory Land confirmed, "a war of ships. It's no damn sense making guns and tanks to be left in the U.S." General Eisenhower, deputy chief of the War Plans Division, admitted that tempers were short. "We've got to have ships and we need them now."

When the situation at sea was at its worst, Lord Moran found Churchill in his London map room. "He was standing with his back to me, staring at the huge chart with the little black beetles representing German submarines. 'Terrible,' he muttered. He knows that we may lose the war at sea in a few months and that he can do nothing about it. I wish to God I could put out the fires that seem to be consuming him."

On Sunday, February 15, the bottom seemed to drop out when Singapore, the symbol of Western power in the Far East, fell to the Japanese. "The news came to a great many people as a shock," Eleanor recorded in her column. "I had talked with the President and he said resignedly that of course, we had expected it, but I know a great many people did not." With food stocks running low and water supplies threatened, General Arthur Percival marched out under a white flag to surrender to the Japanese commander.

"Perhaps it is good for us," Eleanor mused, "to have to face disaster, because we have been so optimistic and almost arrogant in our expectation of constant success. Now we shall have to find within us the courage to meet defeat and fight right on to victory. That means a steadiness of purpose and of will, which is not one of our strong points. But somehow, I think we shall harden physically and mentally as the days go by."

At the center of the storm, the president remained, in presidential assistant William Hassett's recollection, "calm and serene, never impatient or irritable." Through all the bad news from the Far East, through the dark days of the submarine menace, there was "never a note of despair, chin up, full of fight." The years may have drawn lines around his eyes, *New York Times* reporter Anne O'Hare McCormick noted on the occasion of his sixtieth birthday, on January 30, 1942, but "neither time nor the hammer blows of defeat in the Pacific have shaken his steady self-assurance." On the contrary, despite the titanic tasks before him, he is "more at ease in all circumstances, more at home in his position, than any leader of his time. His nerves are stronger, his temper cooler and more even. If he worries, he gives no sign of it." Indeed, McCormick concluded, perhaps because "the uncertainties are resolved and the great debate is over, his mood seems brighter, if anything, than it was a few months ago."

• • •

If the fortunes of the war depended upon American shipping, then the only answer, Roosevelt reasoned, was to build ships and more ships, twice as many as the Germans could sink. In his State of the Union message, Roosevelt had set an incredibly high goal of eighteen million tons for 1942. Now, in the wake of the terrifying sinkings, he raised his sights even higher—to twenty-four million tons. "I realize that this is a terrible directive on my part," Roosevelt admitted to Emory Land, "but I feel certain that in this very great emergency we can attain it."

The crisis in shipping could not have occurred at a worse time. After years of neglect, the U.S. merchant fleet ranked only "fourth in tonnage in foreign trade, fifth in speed and eighth in number of new, first class ocean-going ships." From building fewer than a hundred ships a year, the U.S. Maritime Commission was now charged with building twenty-nine hundred ships right away; from dealing with forty-six shipways, it was now responsible for nearly three hundred; from thinking in terms of one hundred thousand men, it could soon count on more than seven hundred thousand. In peacetime, a shipfitter used to serve a four-year apprenticeship; the training period was now reduced to seven weeks. "It gives you a feeling like holding a hand grenade after removing the pin," Admiral H. L. Vickery admitted.

In attempting the impossible, the government turned to Henry Kaiser, an irrepressible sixty-year-old industrialist who had been involved in the building of Boulder Dam, Grand Coulee Dam, and the Oakland–San Francisco Bridge. Though new to the shipping business, Kaiser was an entrepreneurial genius who instinctively grasped Roosevelt's rule that "energy was more efficient than efficiency." He sent bulldozers to build his first yard in Richmond, California, across the bay from San Francisco on January 20, 1941. Eighty-five working days later, he laid his first keel.

Lavishly spending the government's money, building ships as fast as steel could be found, Kaiser reached for every crane, derrick, and bulldozer he could lay his hands on. He hired workers with little regard for qualifications on the theory that anyone could be trained on the job; he grafted the techniques of mass production to the art of building a ship, replacing riveters with welders to cut weight and save time, using prefabricated bulkheads, decks, and hulls to move the ships off the ways as quickly as possible.

Under Kaiser's leadership, the average time to deliver a ship was cut from 355 days in 1940 to 194 days in 1941 to 60 days in early 1942. With six new yards in operation after only one year in the business, Sir Launchalot, as he was dubbed, had become the pacesetter for the entire shipbuilding industry. The Maritime Commission translated each new record he set into a schedule increase for shipyards across the nation, from Bath and South Portland to Norfolk and Vancouver.

To be sure, the finished product—the Liberty Ship—was an ugly duckling which fell short of traditional shipbuilding standards. It was not fast and it tended on occasion to split in half. But Roosevelt reasoned it was better to have a lot of makeshift ships now—each one capable of carrying 2,840 jeeps, 440 light tanks and three million C-rations—than a fleet of faster, more graceful, more durable ships after the war was lost.

• • •

As the dismal days of February drew to a close, Roosevelt decided to give a fireside chat, his first since Pearl Harbor. The speech was intended to involve the American people in the drama of the war, to lay out for them in the frankest terms the situation the Allies faced. At the same time, he hoped to reassure them that, despite the blackness of the present outlook, victory was bound to come. "No one," Robert Sherwood said, "is as good as the President in fixing the line between keeping up morale and confidence on the one hand and being too optimistic on the other."

Roosevelt told his speechwriters he was going to ask the American people to have a map of the world before them as they listened to him speak. "I'm going to speak about strange places that many of them never heard of—places that are now the battleground for civilization. . . . I want to explain to the people something about geography—what our problem is and what the overall strategy of the war has to be. I want to tell it to them in simple terms of ABC so that they will understand what is going on and how each battle fits into the picture. . . . If they understand the problem and what we are driving at, I am sure that they can take any kind of bad news right on the chin."

Responding enthusiastically to the president's request, American citizens by the thousands raced to their local stores to purchase maps. "The map business is booming," *The New York Times* reported. At C. S. Hammond & Co. on 43rd Street, E. O. Schmidt, the sales manager, had gone to the downtown warehouse on the Saturday morning before the speech and brought two thousand copies of their new atlas back to the store to augment their stock. By nightfall, the entire stock was completely sold. Mr. Schmidt said he had seen nothing like it in the twenty-four years he had been in the business. "Why even last night when I went home, my wife, who has never particularly cared about maps, asked me to put up on the wall a large commercial map I've had for years."

When the president spoke at 10 p.m. on February 23, more than sixty-one million adults (nearly 80 percent of the total possible adult audience) were by their radios, many with their maps spread before them. Speaking in a clear, confident tone, Roosevelt likened the present stage of the struggle to the early years of the Revolutionary War, when George Washington and his Continental Army were faced with formidable odds, recurring defeats, and limited supplies. "Selfish men, jealous men, fearful men proclaimed the situation hopeless." But Washington "held to his course" and a new country was born.

In similar fashion, Roosevelt said, the American people must be prepared to suffer more losses "before the turn of the tide." The months ahead would not be easy. But "your government has unmistakable confidence in your ability to hear the worst without flinching or losing heart." This war, he explained, was "a new kind of war," waged on "every continent, every island, every sea, every air-lane in the world. That is the reason why I have asked you to take out and spread before you a map of the whole earth, and to follow with me the references I shall make to the world-encircling battle lines of the war."

Revealing his own vast knowledge of geography, derived to a large extent from his beloved stamps, Roosevelt patiently described the Allied situation in every part of the world. In this new war, he explained, "the broad oceans which have been heralded in the past as our protection from attack have become endless battlefields." The road ahead would be difficult, but he was certain, he said, that it was only a matter of time until America's productive genius was fully mobilized, capable of giving the Allies "the overwhelming superiority of military material necessary for ultimate triumph."

"From Berlin, Rome and Tokyo we have been described as a nation of weakling-playboys," he concluded. "Let them tell that to General MacArthur and his men . . . Let them tell that to the boys in the flying fortresses. Let them tell that to the Marines!"

The speech was a great success, "even more effective," Sam Rosenman observed, "than the President's first fireside chat back in the dark days of 1933 during the banking crisis." *The New York Times* agreed, hailing the address as "one of the greatest of Roosevelt's career." Success bred the desire for more. Russell Leffingwell, an old friend and a partner at J. P. Morgan, advised Roosevelt that the only way to rouse the people was for him to speak more frequently on the radio.

"Sometimes," Roosevelt replied, revealing a subtle understanding of leadership, "I wish I could carry out your thought of more frequent talking on the air on my part but the one thing I dread is that my talks should be so frequent as to lose their effectiveness. . . . Every time I talk over the air it means four or five days of long, overtime work in the preparation of what I say. Actually, I cannot afford to take this time away from more vital things. I think we must avoid too much personal leadership—my good friend Winston Churchill has suffered a little from this. It must grow more slowly—remembering always that we have only been in the war for three months."

As always, Roosevelt's dominant instinct was to unify the nation. "No one understood better than he," historian Eric Larrabee has written, "the inner dynamics of American strength: how to mobilize it, how to draw on it, how to gauge its limits. Once mobilized, it did not need to be driven; it needed only to be steered."

• • •

If Roosevelt shrewdly understood the strength of America's democracy, he failed miserably to guard against democracy's weakness—the tyranny of an aroused public opinion. As attitudes toward Japanese Americans on the West Coast turned hostile, he made an ill-advised, brutal decision to uproot thousands of Japanese Americans from their homes, forcing them into incarceration camps located in the interior of the country.

The tortuous path to the president's tragic decision, considered by the American Civil Liberties Union "the worst single wholesale violation of civil rights of American citizens in our history," began with a false assessment by the military that the Japanese Americans were a substantial threat to national security. Though there was never any hard evidence brought forward to confirm sabotage on the part of the Japanese Americans, the rumors of shore-to-shore signaling and fifth-column treachery were so widespread that they became accepted as fact. "Two Japs with Maps and Alien Literature Seized," one report read. "Caps on Jap Tomato Point to Air Base," read another. Though the Army's West Coast commander, General John De Witt, admitted that nothing had actually been proved, he proceeded, in a tortured twist of logic, to argue that "the very fact that no sabotage has taken place is a disturbing and confirming indication that such action *will* be taken."

Racism fueled the claim of "military necessity." For fifty years, anti-Japanese sentiment had been embedded in the social structure of the West Coast, producing exclusionary laws and restrictions on alien citizenship. With the attack on Pearl Harbor and the humiliating defeats suffered by the Allies in the Pacific, the explosive force of this hostility was released. Day after day, newspapers headlined vilification against the Japanese, calling them "mad dogs, yellow vermin and nips." The atmosphere of hatred gave license to extremist elements. "California was given by God to a white people," the president of Native Sons and Daughters of the Golden West proclaimed, "and with God's strength we want to keep it as he gave it to us."

"These people were not convicted of any crime," Eleanor wrote years later in a draft of an unpublished article, "but emotions ran too high, too many people wanted to wreak vengeance on Oriental looking people. There was no time to investigate families or to adhere strictly to the American rule that a man is innocent until he is proved guilty."

Economic cupidity also played a significant role. "Originally," Eleanor wrote, the Japanese immigrants "were much needed on ranches and on large truck and fruit farms but as they came in greater numbers, people began to discover that they were not only convenient workers, they were competitors in the labor field, and the people of California began to be afraid." Though Japanese-owned farms occupied only 1 percent of the cultivated land in California, they produced nearly 40 percent of the total California crop. One pressure group, the Grower Shipper Association, blatantly admitted wanting to get rid of the Japanese for selfish reasons: "We might as well be honest," they said, openly coveting the rich farmland of the Japanese.

Had the Japanese Americans been politically organized, they might have countered these pressure groups, but since the first-generation parents, known as the Issei, were prevented by law from voting or becoming citizens, and since the great majority of American-born Nisei were still in school, they provided an easy target.

From every side, Roosevelt was exposed to pressure to act against the Japanese Americans. In California, the entire political establishment—including Governor Culbert Olson and Attorney General Earl Warren—were strongly on the side of evacuation. In the military, all the leading figures—General De Witt, Provost Marshal General Allen Gullion, Henry Stimson, and War Department official John McCloy—argued for internment. By the time the decision was made in mid-February, Francis Biddle, who had replaced Robert Jackson as attorney general in September, was the only significant hold-out, and because he was new to the Cabinet, his opinion held little weight.

In the absence of countervailing persuasive pressures, Roosevelt accepted the "military necessity" argument at face value, directing Stimson and McCloy to do whatever they thought necessary as long as they were as reasonable and as humane as possible. The War Department came back with a blanket order—Executive Order 9066—requiring the forced removal of all people of Japanese descent from any area designated as a military zone. Since the entire state of California, the western half of Washington and Oregon, and the southern part of Arizona were all designated as military zones, the order affected more than a hundred thousand citizens and aliens of Japanese descent.

Though Roosevelt later admitted that he regretted "the burdens of evacuation and detention which military necessity had imposed upon these people," he showed no qualms whatsoever when he signed the order on February 19. "I do not think he was much concerned with the gravity or implications of this step," Francis Biddle observed. "He was never theoretical about things. What must be done to defend the country must be done." Since everything depended, he believed, on winning the war, anything that threatened that prospect had to be dealt with boldly and harshly.

Told to bring only what they could carry, the evacuees were herded into sixteen hastily provided assembly centers at racetracks and athletic fields along the West Coast, while permanent centers further inland were being constructed by army engineers. "We are having quite a problem figuring out just what to take," twenty-six-year-old Charles Kikuchi wrote in his diary. "There is still so much junk around and you know how the Japanese like to hang on to old things. Anyway, we will have to store a lot of it since they will not allow us to take more than the barest of necessities."

In the assembly centers, Berkeley resident Mine Okubo has written, "there was a lack of privacy everywhere. The incomplete partitions in the stalls and the barracks made a single symphony of yours and your neighbor's loves, hates and joys. One had to get used to snores, baby cryings, family troubles." The older women could not bring themselves to stand in line for the communal shower; they bathed in tubs made from barrels instead; they pinned up curtains wherever they could.

"Can this be the same America we left a few weeks ago?" a young architectural draftsman named Ted Nakashima asked. "It all seems so futile, struggling to live our old lives under this useless, regimented life." Born in Seattle, Washington, Nakashima was the third son of Japanese parents who had been in the United States since 1901. His father was an editor, his oldest brother an architect, his middle brother a doctor. Yet all three brothers and their parents were forced to leave flourishing careers behind and spend their days amid the suffocating smell of horse manure in a stall that was only eighteen feet wide by twenty-one feet long.

"The senselessness of all of the inactive manpower," young Nakashima observed. "Electricians, plumbers, draftsmen, mechanics, carpenters, painters, farmers—every trade—men who are able and willing to do all they can to lick the Axis . . . Oddly enough I still have a bit of faith in army promises of good treatment and Mrs. Roosevelt's pledge of a future worthy of good American citizens. . . . What really hurts is the constant reference to we evacuees as 'Japs.' 'Japs' are the guys we are fighting. We're on this side and we want to help. Why won't America let us?"

When the news of Franklin's decision had reached Eleanor, she was shaken. She had witnessed the growing hysteria for weeks and had feared that something like this might happen. But so drastic was the president's order that it took her breath away. To her mind, the guarantees of the Bill of Rights must never be surrendered, even in the face of national disaster. When she tried to speak to her husband about his decision, however, he gave her a frigid reception and said he did not want her to mention it again.

Under ordinary circumstances, Eleanor would have argued her case relentlessly, regardless of the president's reaction, but the weeks that surrounded the evacuation decision found her in the midst of an all-consuming controversy of her own as the Office of Civilian Defense was exposed to irreparably damaging criticism.

• • •

With the coming of war, the activities of the OCD had moved to the forefront of public awareness, bringing Eleanor's philosophical differences with LaGuardia into the open. "I could not help realizing," Eleanor admitted, "that the mayor was more interested in the dramatic aspects of civilian defense—such as whether cities had good fire-fighting equipment—than in such things as building morale." To Eleanor's mind, the stresses and dislocations of war—such as migration, unemployment, housing, and health—were creating social problems as acute, if not so dramatic, as anything to be anticipated from bombing. But, try as she might, she could not turn LaGuardia's focus from the protective side. Eleanor saw that his work as mayor of New York "prevented him from giving his full time to organizing civilian defense. The few group meetings we had left me with an impression of great hurry and a feeling that decisions were taken which were not carefully thought out."

For the president, his desk piled high with somber reports from both the Atlantic and the Pacific, his wife's dispute with the mayor was irritating and disconcerting. "I can't take Eleanor and LaGuardia," he told Anna Rosenberg in confidence. "Each one comes with a story; each one is right; each one comes to me: I cannot cope with it and I want you to try and keep them away from me and reconcile their differences."

But there was no way that anyone could keep Eleanor away from Franklin when she had something to say. By mid-December 1941, she had become convinced that LaGuardia could not handle both the mayor's job and the OCD post. The time had come, she told her husband, for LaGuardia to step down from the OCD in favor of a full-time administrator. The president agreed with Eleanor. "I am brought to the realization by war," he diplomatically wrote LaGuardia, "that by acts of my own I have created for you an almost impossible situation." In the days and weeks before the war, Roosevelt went on, it had probably been possible for LaGuardia to carry both jobs. But as the war made each job more exacting, he realized he was asking something physically impossible of his good friend. Perhaps the best solution was to name a successor at the OCD who could administer the organization full-time. When it was put on this basis, LaGuardia agreed, albeit reluctantly, to step aside in favor of Harvard Law School Dean James Landis.

Rumors spread that Eleanor, too, was about to resign, but she denied them absolutely. The fact was that, with LaGuardia gone, she believed she had a fighting chance to realize her dream for the OCD. But on February 6, 1942, in the Chamber of the House of Representatives, Eleanor's wish was destroyed when two of her appointments to the OCD were subjected to a withering attack. "I rise today to utter a protest against 'boondoggling' in connection with the OCD," Representative Faddis began. "I want the members to take into consideration today the fact that we are paying Melvyn Douglas $8000 a year—as much as we are paying that matchless and heroic soldier, General MacArthur, when he is battling in the forests of the Philippines every day. . . . I call attention to the fact that we are paying this dancer, Miss Chaney, $4600 a year—almost twice as much as the base pay of Captain Colin Kelly [first hero of the war] and he gave his life in defense of this Nation."

When it was learned that both Melvyn Douglas and Mayris Chaney were close friends of Eleanor's, the criticism mounted. "The work of OCD concerns the safety and welfare of the people of this nation," columnist Raymond Clapper wrote. "Yet it has become a kind of personal parking lot for the pets and protégés of Mrs. Roosevelt. . . . How can you have any kind of morale with a subordinate employee, who happens to be the wife of the President, flitting in and out between lecture engagements to toss a few pets into nice jobs, some of them at salaries larger than a brigadier general and a rear admiral gets."

Had the high salaries been attached to work the country deemed essential, the flap would have quickly died down. But in the wake of war, Eleanor's noble ideas about mental health and physical fitness suddenly seemed luxuries, particularly since the real necessities of physical defense—gas masks and helmets—were not being provided in an organized way. Still, Marquis Childs observed, "the storm that burst out," particularly over Miss Chaney's assignment to teach dancing to children, "was far out of proportion to the cause. It became a witch hunt, and once Miss Chaney's status on the payroll was discovered, decency was out the window."

For days, while the men of Bataan were caught in a hopeless siege and Singapore was falling to the Japanese, one congressman after another rose to attack Eleanor Roosevelt and her friends. From both sides of the House, bitter assertions were launched that the country needed bombers, not dancers, and that "parasites and leeches" should be stricken from the payroll. "Mrs. Roosevelt," a woman from Kalamazoo wrote Eleanor, "you would be doing your country a great service if you would simply go home and sew for the Red Cross. Every time you open your mouth the people of this country dislike and mistrust you more."

"I am not in the least disturbed by the latest attack," Eleanor wrote her friend Paul Kellogg, editor of *Survey* magazine. "It is purely political and made by the same people who have fought NYA, CCC, WPA, Farm Security, etc." She would only be sorry, she said, if it lessened the effectiveness of the OCD or hurt the people involved.

But so violent was the newspaper frenzy that followed the congressional outburst that Eleanor found herself, for the first time in nearly ten years as first lady, a target of merciless criticism not only from conservatives but from people who counted themselves her supporters and friends. A woman writing from the Plaza Hotel in New York told Eleanor that she had always greatly admired her energy, ability, and accomplishments, but had now come to believe that, "in these troubled times, you should spend more time with the President. To us he seems a very lonely man, with heartbreaking burdens to carry."

The climax came when the House of Representatives took a direct slap at Eleanor by issuing a ban against the use of civilian-defense funds for "instruction in physical fitness by dancers." Eleanor realized that by staying in the job she was jeopardizing the survival of the OCD. The time had come to resign. "I still believe in all the things we started out to do," she wrote Florence Kerr, director of WPA Community Services Projects, explaining her resignation, "but I know if I stayed longer, I would bring more harm than good to the program."

Furthermore, Eleanor admitted, she had come to the reluctant conclusion that it was impossible for the wife of the president to have an official job with the government. Since no one could ever be sure if she was acting on her own behalf or in the name of the president (a circumstance she and her husband had often employed to great political advantage in an unofficial capacity), she was now, as a public official, being accorded a measure of influence and blame that went far beyond that of the ordinary public servant.

On the evening of February 20, Eleanor held a farewell party for all the people who had worked for her in the OCD. Looking back over her five months, she said, she felt no little pride in what she had accomplished, particularly in broadening the definition of defense to include nutrition, housing, recreation, and medical care. Now that everything was in place, she maintained, it was time to move on.

Yet, no matter what she said about the proper time to go, an aura of defeat clouded Eleanor's resignation. For she knew, and the press knew, that with her departure her dream of the OCD as a people's movement had come to a humiliating end.

• • •

No sooner had Eleanor resigned from the OCD than she became entangled in further controversy—a brutal battle between blacks and whites over the occupancy of a newly built federal housing project in Detroit. The two-hundred-unit development, named the Sojourner Truth project, had been developed for black defense workers by Eleanor's friend at the Federal Works Agency, Clark Foreman, a liberal Southerner who took the position that blacks were as entitled as whites to enjoy the benefits of the public-housing boom necessitated by the war.

Eleanor had repeatedly urged Franklin to use the defense emergency as a lever for replacing the slums of the city with permanent new housing that could still be used after the war ended. There was a chance, she believed, if new neighborhoods could be properly planned and designed, that blacks and whites could live together in peace. But Eleanor's ideas for the future were shattered at every turn by her old nemesis Charles Palmer, the housing coordinator she had vehemently opposed at the time of his appointment.

It was Palmer's position, backed by private real-estate interests, that the federal government should limit its role to the construction of temporary housing. As long as the workers had some sort of shelter while they produced for the war, it mattered little how long the buildings lasted. The Congress agreed. When the House approved a bill authorizing $300 million for new construction, it specified that none of it could be spent for slum clearance.

Even with these restrictions, Clark Foreman had managed to target money for the Sojourner Truth project. Everything proceeded according to plan until word of the project reached the white community in Detroit. Coming at a time when the majority of white workers were living in overcrowded, overpriced apartments, with three shifts to the same "hot" bed, the news provoked an emotional outburst.

The population of Detroit had exploded since 1940, as some three hundred thousand whites and fifty thousand blacks migrated from farmlands in Mississippi, Alabama, Tennessee, and Louisiana in search of employment in war plants. Thousands of workers were sleeping in boxcars, tents, church pews, and jails. Every habitable shed had been rented for all the traffic would bear, and new families were still pouring into Detroit at a rate of five thousand a month.

When white workers heard about the Sojourner Truth project, they demanded the units for themselves and enlisted the support of white residents in the neighborhood where the development was being built. Rudolph Tenerowicz, Detroit's congressman, carried the ball in Washington, successfully prevailing upon the members of the Conference Committee, consisting mostly of Southerners, to add a clause to the FWA's $300,000 appropriations bill specifying that "no money would be released unless the 'nigger lover' [Clark Foreman] was fired and the project converted to white occupancy." The FWA capitulated quickly and dishonorably. That same day, the Detroit housing committee was ordered to redirect its recruitment of prospective tenants from black to white. Minutes later, Clark Foreman "resigned."

Civil-rights leaders reacted with rage. Their first impulse was to contact Eleanor. "Surely you would not stand by and see the Sojourner Truth defense homes that were built for Negroes be taken away from us," Mrs. Charles Diggs wrote from Detroit. Calmly and directly, Eleanor approached the president, emphasizing that both blacks and whites, including Edward Jeffries, Detroit's mayor, and leaders of the UAW, were firmly committed to the position that the blacks should have the project.

Eleanor's intervention prevailed. "After a conference last night with many Negroes from Detroit," Palmer solicitously told her, "it looks as though we are going to get that project straightened out to their entire satisfaction." Two weeks later, the FWA directed the Detroit Housing Committee to begin its selection of black tenants, with occupancy set for the last day of February.

On Saturday morning, February 28, the first twenty-four Negro families, their household goods loaded on trucks and vans, began moving into their new homes. Overnight, seven hundred white pickets, armed with knives, guns, rifles, and clubs, gathered at the entrance to the project. A fiery cross was burning at the site. As the trucks, supported by a crowd of three hundred blacks, tried to cross the picket line, a battle erupted. Before it ended, many people, both black and white, were hospitalized, and 104 were arrested.

The disorder occasioned a great outpouring of Axis propaganda; newspapers in both Germany and Japan carried pictures of the bloody struggle. According to wire reports in Tokyo, Washington had arbitrarily ordered white Detroiters to take Negro war workers into their homes. "Many dead and wounded," Tokyo radio claimed.

Convinced that the government's vacillation had set the stage for the riot, Eleanor rushed headlong into the battle. From here on, she argued, the government must stay its course in behalf of the rights of black citizens. Her pleas did not go unheeded. On April 29, while eight hundred Michigan troops with fixed bayonets stood guard, black tenants were again moved into the Sojourner Truth project, this time without incident. With the situation happily resolved, Eleanor turned her attention to Clark Foreman. It was not fair, she told her husband, that Foreman was being blacklisted simply because he had exhibited the courage to stand up for the rights of black citizens. The president agreed. "What can we do for Foreman?" he wrote his Southern-born aide Marvin McIntyre. "He is not as bad as you think." A few weeks later, a job was found for Foreman in the manpower operation.

Even as Franklin acceded to some of Eleanor's specific requests, he refused to admit that, in so doing, he was planning for the future. When, shortly after the Sojourner Truth riot, Edwin Embree of the Rosenwald Fund pleaded with him to create a wide-ranging commission on race and color, he flatly refused. "Such a commission appears to me at this time premature," he explained. "We must start winning the war with all the brains, wisdom and experience we've got before we do much general or specific planning for the future. . . . I am not convinced that we can be realists about the war and planners for the future at this critical time."

For Eleanor, whose primary concern was the home front, not the war, the present and the future were inextricably linked. Speaking to a group of Washington church women shortly after Pearl Harbor, she had argued, "The nation cannot expect the colored people to feel that the U.S. is worth defending if they continue to be treated as they are treated now." These incendiary remarks, a man from Kentucky angrily wrote, "are probably the most dangerous ever uttered by a woman in your position. . . . Your quarrel in this respect seems to me to be with Providence."

"I am not agitating the race question," Eleanor replied. "The race question is agitated because people will not act justly and fairly toward each other as human beings."

Nowhere was this unjust treatment more obvious, Eleanor believed, than in the navy. The previous year, in response to the vigorous protest by civil-rights leaders against the relegation of Negroes to the position of mess men, the navy had created a committee to analyze the relationship between the "U.S. Navy and the Negro race." The committee held three short meetings before coming to the conclusion that "the enlistment of Negroes (other than as mess attendants) leads to disruptive and undermining conditions."

Pearl Harbor provoked a whole new round of protest. On December 9, the NAACP sent a telegram to Navy Secretary Frank Knox asking whether, "in view of the intensive recruiting campaign then underway, the Navy would accept colored recruits for other than the messman's branch." Answering for the Navy, the Bureau of Navigation (responsible for procurement and assignment of personnel) abruptly replied that "there had been no change in policy and that none was contemplated."

The navy's obstinate refusal to bend unleashed fierce pressure on the White House from black leaders and black newspapers across the land. The clamor and increasing political pressure convinced Roosevelt that something had to give. "I think," he wrote Knox on January 9, "that with all the

Navy activities the Bureau of Navigation might invent something that colored enlistees could do in addition to the rating of messman."

Responding to the president's tone, Knox asked the General Board to submit a plan for taking five thousand Negroes for billets other than as mess men. Two weeks later, the board reported back, concluding in no uncertain terms "that members of the colored race be accepted only in messman branch." The rationale once again was the intimate nature of life on a ship. "Men on board ship live in particularly close association; in their messes one man sits beside another, their hammocks or bunks are close together; in their common tasks they work side by side. . . . How many white men would choose that their closest associates in sleeping quarters, in mess be of another race? General Board believes that the answer is 'few if any' and further believes that if the issue were forced, there would be a lowering of contentment, teamwork and discipline in the service."

The president, much to Eleanor's satisfaction, refused to accept the board's report. In a blistering reply, Roosevelt told Knox that he regarded the report as (a) unsatisfactory and (b) insufficient. "Officers of the U.S. Navy are not officers only but are American citizens. . . . They should, therefore, be expected to recognize social and economic problems which are related to national welfare. . . . It is incumbent on all officers to recognize the fact that about 1/10th of the population of the United States is composed of members of the Negro race who are American citizens. . . . It is my considered opinion that there are additional tasks in the Naval establishment to which we could properly assign an additional number of enlisted men who are members of the Negro race. . . . I [ask] you to return the recommendations of the General Board to that Board for further study and report."

As the General Board reanalyzed the situation, the pressures for change continued to mount. Through February and March 1942, every black newspaper carried the story of black mess man Dorie Miller, whose heroic exploits on the bridge of his battleship at Pearl Harbor earned him the Navy Cross. The example of Miller's heroism became a principal weapon in the battle to end discrimination in the navy. Here was a high-school dropout who raced through flaming oil to carry his captain to safety. Seizing a machine gun left beside a dead gunner, Miller, without any weapons training, began to fire at the oncoming Japanese planes, downing one or maybe two of the enemy aircraft. Only after his ammunition was exhausted, the ship sinking rapidly, did he finally obey the order to abandon ship.

Although Miller's acts of heroism were mentioned in the first navy dispatches, he was referred to simply as "an unidentified Negro messman." The navy, it seems, did not want the first hero of the war to be a black man. That honor was reserved for West Point graduate Colin Kelly, who perished three days later. When Miller's name was finally released in March, the result of a determined effort by the *Pittsburgh Courier,* bills were introduced to accord him the Congressional Medal of Honor, and schools and parks were given his name. But "the greatest honor that could be paid mess attendant Dorie Miller," the NAACP argued, "would be for the U.S. Navy to abolish restrictions against Negro enlistments at once."

Now the navy's General Board had no choice but to capitulate. They issued a second report to Knox, agreeing that blacks could enlist for general service other than mess-man duty—as gunners, clerks, signalmen, radio operators, ammunition handlers, etc.—as long as the training and the units remained segregated. The change in policy was not as broad as civil-rights leaders had hoped for, but it was, the *Pittsburgh Courier* agreed, "a forward step." "Navy broke down a historic barrier," *The New York Times* reported. A door was now open, however slightly.

• • •

Some halting progress was also recorded in removing barriers against Negro labor in war industries. By early 1942, as a result of pressure from the Fair Employment Practices Commission, more than half the defense employees were committed to the principle of using Negro labor in production jobs. In hundreds of cases, Negroes were working in firms which had formerly banned them. In shipyards, Negro employment had risen from six thousand to fourteen thousand in twelve months. In the aircraft industry, which had employed no Negroes in 1940, five thousand were now employed. The gains were small but significant. "I look for an acceleration of this improvement," Roosevelt promised the Fraternal Council of Negro Churches, "as the demand for labor in our war industries increases."

Eleanor possessed less faith in the power of momentum. Without continual pressure, she feared, management would do all it could to shun its responsibility, either by keeping the numbers so small as to afford only token compliance, or by concentrating Negroes in unskilled jobs. And, beyond problems with management, there remained recalcitrant unions and prejudiced workers who threatened to strike when blacks were hired. Eleanor realized that the power of the FEPC was limited by the fact that its ultimate weapon—requesting cancellation of a defense contract—was no weapon at all, since the administration was loath to jeopardize war production. "For the government to terminate an important war contract by reason of the contractor's indulgence in discriminatory employment," one friend of the FEPC admitted, "would be highly impractical."

Still, Eleanor believed in the power of publicity generated by the hearings the FEPC held throughout the country in response to complaints of discrimination. Traveling from coast to coast, she engaged anyone who would listen, even at the risk of courting public displeasure, in a blunt dialogue about the role of the FEPC and the importance of bringing blacks into defense jobs. In the South, a mood of fury and indignation set in as Southern newspapers accused the FEPC "of trying to turn the South upside down under the clock of necessity brought on by the war emergency." With taunting sarcasm, the *Alabama Times* announced that "a bunch of snoopers, two of whom are

Negroes, will assemble in Birmingham to determine whether the South is doing right by Little Sambo."

Believing that the existing Southern order was inherently harmonious, white Southerners rationalized away the rising dissatisfaction in the black community as the product of outside agitation. "Anyone who hears Delta Negroes singing at their work," a cotton trade journal in Tennessee intoned, "who sees them dancing in the streets, who listens to their rich laughter, knows that the Southern Negro is not mistreated. He has a carefree, child-like mentality and looks to the white man to solve his problems and take care of him."

"Don't you think there are enough difficulties," a woman from Winston-Salem wrote the president, "without Mrs. Roosevelt going around over the country stirring up strife between white and colored people? She can't realize the grave danger. . . . So see Mr. President if you can't put a stop to Mrs. Roosevelt stirring up trouble down here telling these people they are 'as good as the white people.' "

Resisting the mounting criticism of her progressive stance on civil rights, Eleanor continued to speak out, and without public objection from the president. Though his sense of what the country would accept on civil rights at particular moments was invariably more cautious, he refused to "put a stop to Mrs. Roosevelt's stirring up trouble." As long as he was persuaded that the advances she advocated corresponded to the general direction in which the American society was moving, and did not interfere with the conduct of the war, he was willing to bend with her current.

• • •

The differences between Franklin and Eleanor on the issue of compulsory national service were harder to reconcile. During the spring of 1942, a fierce debate divided Washington over how best to mobilize the labor force. Without government control in the form of civilian conscription for war work, the military argued, the organizational problems presented by the task of marshaling and directing seventy million people employed in fifteen hundred different trades and occupations in dozens of different defense centers would be insurmountable. In the absence of centralized control, the spontaneous movement of workers, wandering the country to the lure of premium wages, had resulted in too many workers in some areas, too few in others.

Convinced that the government's decentralized approach would never solve the manpower problem in a time of war, Eleanor came down strongly on the side of civilian conscription. "I've come to one very clear decision," she announced in mid-March, after a White House conference on man-power, "namely, that all of us—men in the services and women at home—should be drafted and told what is the job we are to do. So long as we are left to volunteer we are bound to waste our capacities and to do things which are not necessary."

Eleanor's call for civilian conscription provoked a violent outcry, directed to the idea of conscripting women. "This drive to Hitlerize women sets aside the civil and industrial gains of women won after centuries of struggle," the International Woodworkers of America resolved at their national convention. It "breaks down the American home and traditional family life, robs us of the power to safeguard the health and direct upbringing of our children." The press, assuming Eleanor was testing the wind for the administration, went after the plan with a vengeance. "If Mrs. Roosevelt's 'draft us all' plan becomes part of the law," Hugh Johnson wrote in the *New York World Telegram*, "we shall have here a complete Nazi pattern of forced labor."

When the president was asked about his wife's remarks, he noted pointedly that he had not participated in the conference she mentioned. What is more, he did not agree that civilian conscription was necessary. Wary of having the government assume too much power over something as sacred as man's right to a job, he chose instead to rely on indirect persuasion—giving draft deferments to skilled labor in war plants, giving the war industry first call on workers registered with the Employment Service, providing carrots and sticks for peacetime plants to convert to war production. Though admitting the possibility that this less centralized approach might not be sufficient, he wished to move one step at a time, trusting that democracy and momentum would carry the country where it needed to go.

The difference between Eleanor's call for conscription and Franklin's reliance on democratic incentives was deep, and signaled their incompatibility of outlook. The president was temperamentally opposed to the imposition of compulsory discipline upon the rich variety of human relations; Eleanor feared that, in the absence of imposed order and discipline, confusion would result. The confusion Eleanor feared, Roosevelt saw as the necessary price for democracy.

Indeed, the great voluntary migration that would irrevocably alter the face of American society had already begun. Since 1940, more than seven million Americans had moved across county and state lines in search of employment in the burgeoning war-production centers. By the end of the war, more than fifteen million civilians would have moved to different counties. The population patterns of the country would be permanently changed.

The greatest shift was from east to west, as millions of people, drawn by the shipyards and the aircraft plants on the West Coast, flocked to California, Oregon, and Washington. More than half the wartime shipbuilding and almost half the manufacture of airplanes were centered in these three coastal states, whose population would increase by over 34 percent during the war. "It wouldn't take any imagination at all," one migrant to the West Coast observed, "to think that you were going West on a covered wagon and were a pioneer again." California alone saw an enormous increase, of more than two million people. Here, journalist Richard Lingeman perceptively notes, "was the real gold rush in California's colorful history."

A second tide was carrying some six million whites and blacks from the country to the city and from the South to the North. In 1940, according to economists, there were far too many people on the nation's farms to allow a decent living for all. As the war drained the surplus to the cities—to Mobile and Charleston in the South, and Detroit and Chicago in the North —the agricultural depression of the thirties would finally be broken, and the profits of the farmers who remained on the land would reach record highs.

Though the mass exodus of blacks from the South to the North would create severe social problems in Northern cities, "by and large," economist Harold Vatter concludes, "and despite the hard, insecure, impoverished, and discriminating conditions of ghetto life the migration brought material improvement." Economist John Kenneth Galbraith agrees. "Before the war," he points out, "there were 1,466,701 black farm workers in the rural labor force of the Old Confederacy, all, virtually without exception, exceedingly poor. In 1970, there were 115,303."

The bustling movement of so many Americans was a tremendous relief to Roosevelt, coming as it did after the paralysis of the Depression years, when few people had either the psychic or the economic resources to get up and go. The great migrations confirmed his belief: if Americans were given opportunity, they would rise to the challenge.

CHAPTER 13

"WHAT CAN WE DO TO HELP?"

Although public concerns dominated the thoughts and activities of the president and the first lady in the early months of 1942, the Roosevelt White House, where family and friends lived and worked in unusually close quarters, was also the site of the irrepressible renewal of love and desire. In the spring, Missy LeHand returned to her old room on the third floor in the hope of reclaiming her place in the president's heart; Harry Hopkins fell in love with socialite Louise Macy; Princess Martha visited the president again and again; Eleanor seemed obsessed by her relationship with Joe Lash; and the president, as always, seemed to be removed from everybody, in spite of his ever-tolerant, ever-cheerful manner.

In the second week of March, the president had Missy brought from Warm Springs to Washington. The hours she had put in with her therapists were beginning to pay off. Her right leg had improved so that she was able to walk with the use of a brace much like the one the president used. Her arm had not come back, however, nor had her throat condition much improved. Though she understood everything that was said to her, her speech remained almost impossible to understand. Still, there was hope that these faculties would eventually come back, and the doctors had decided that her recovery would be speeded up if she returned to the White House.

Missy reached the familiar gates shortly before 10 a.m. on March 18, and was taken immediately to her third-floor room, where Lillian Parks helped her unpack. Miss Parks recalls that Missy was depressed by the blackout curtains in her windows. White liners were fitted into the curtains so that she would not have to look at black windows.

While Missy was getting settled, the president arrived at the door to welcome her back. He stayed for ten minutes only; he was scheduled to see Admiral King in his office at eleven-fifteen. It was characteristic of Roosevelt to avoid conversation with a string of stories, but, no matter how much he talked, he could not help noticing the deep silences, the sudden shifts of expression, the dark and melancholy eyes. It must have been a somewhat strained meeting, more like a verification of the unbridgeable distance between them than a happy reunion.

For her part, nothing in the world mattered more to Missy than the understanding she had shared with the president. After four months apart, there was undoubtedly comfort in the simple sight of the familiar Roosevelt smile. During the last ten months, she had come to accept some of the inroads that her devastating stroke had made. But now, in the presence of the man she loved, her spirit seemed to gird itself for a renewed attempt to conquer her illness.

Missy's reappearance produced anxious moments for Grace Tully. Tully had replaced Missy as the number-one secretary, working directly with the president on much the same level of competence and reliability. Although she never enjoyed the intimacy, playfulness, and absolute trust Missy had, she had grown accustomed to her new and powerful position. At the same time, Missy was her close friend, and she felt she should involve Missy in the work of the White House as much as she possibly could. Knowing that Missy could read, for instance, Grace brought her the daily decoded messages from the State Department that described what was going on around the world. "I wanted her to feel that she was keeping up with things," Tully said.

The president provided nurses round the clock. They brought Missy her breakfast, wheeled her onto the sun porch for lunch, and kept her company at night. Now and then, Roosevelt would look in on her, but as the weeks went by, even these brief visits became less and less frequent. One night, the story is told, Missy eluded her nurse and made her way, with great difficulty, to the second floor. The door to the president's study was slightly ajar; inside, she saw Franklin laughing and smiling with Princess Martha. Just then, the nurse caught up with her patient and led her back to her room, where for several hours Missy wept.

As the weeks went by, Missy's anxiety increased. To be back in the White House, aware of the president's comings and goings but unable to participate in any real work, proved intolerable. She spent her days waiting for his visits, drifting about the White House like a wandering star in the president's constellation. "She felt there was nothing for her to do," Tully said; "she was getting depressed." Sometimes she had periods of such blackness, Lillian Parks recalled, that she seemed almost bent on destroying herself. At one point, she tried to set herself on fire.

The decision was made, with Missy's concurrence, to send her to Somerville, Massachusetts, to live with her sister, Ann Rochon. Perhaps there, in the shade of the old house on Orchard Street, she could better continue her recuperation. At seven o'clock on Saturday night, May 16, the president stopped by Missy's apartment to say goodbye. He stayed for less than ten minutes. In his study, Princess Martha and Harry Hopkins were waiting. The cocktail hour had begun, to be followed by dinner for three. At the stroke of ten, while the president was still relaxing over coffee with Martha and Harry, the car arrived to return Missy to the Somerville house she had left behind two decades earlier. She would never again return to the White House.

In Washington, Missy LeHand's absence from the president's inner circle was frequently lamented. At a dinner one night at the Rosenmans', Justice Felix Frankfurter noted, the talk turned to the "extraordinarily beneficent role" that Missy had played because of her "remarkable judgment, disinterestedness and pertinacity." Rosenman and Frankfurter agreed that her stroke was "a calamity of world dimensions." Missy, Rosenman said, was "one of the very, very few people who was not a yes-man, who crossed the President in the sense that she told him not what she knew to be his view or what he wanted to hear, but what were, in fact, her true views and convictions."

• • •

Roosevelt absorbed an additional loss that spring when he bade farewell to his mother's house on East 65th Street. The old house held many memories. It was here that he and Eleanor had come to live in the early years of their marriage; here that he had stayed during the first years of his recovery from polio; here that he had visited his mother for nearly four decades. When moving day arrived, Roosevelt drove to New York to go through the house one last time. "Knowing how deeply sentimental the President is," William Hassett recorded, "I felt that his heart was full as he separated himself from a place that held so many associations of life and birth and death, of joy and sorrow." Eleanor's memories of the place were far less positive than Franklin's, but she, too, felt a tug in her heart as she walked through the rooms, crowded with barrels and boxes, for the last time. "Many human emotions have been recorded by many people within the walls of these rooms," she wrote, "and if walls could talk, an interesting book might be written."

Earlier in the spring, Eleanor had found a new apartment at 29 Washington Square, which she intended to occupy whenever she was in New York. Only weeks before Sara died, she had given up her previous Greenwich Village apartment so that she could spend more time with her ailing mother-in-law at East 65th Street. Now that Sara was dead and the twin houses sold, she was free to purchase an apartment of her own.

The Washington Square apartment consisted of seven rooms—a high-ceilinged living room with a wood-burning fireplace and built-in bookcases beneath two windows facing the park's trees and lawns, a dining room, kitchen, three bedrooms, including a master bedroom with a connecting dressing room, a maid's room, and three baths. For Eleanor, who regularly spent a day or two a week in the city, it was a godsend to have a place of her own. "When I am in New York City," she once said, "I feel that I am an unofficial person leading a private life." Yet, even as she valued her independence, she had a private elevator installed just in case the president should ever want to visit. "At last I am settled here," she wrote her aunt Maude Gray on May 9. "It is a nice apartment with a lovely view and perfectly suited to Franklin if he ever comes!"

• • •

"Just a week from tonight you will be out of reach & starting on this new life that I dread so much for you," Eleanor wrote Joe Lash on April 6, as he was about to be inducted into the army. "A little bit of my heart seems to be with you always Joe. You'll carry it round wherever you go & in its place the thought of you will be with me wherever I go.... Sometimes I think if we have *chosen* to love someone, we love them even more than we do the children of our bodies...." Though she loved her own boys deeply, she explained, she had never enjoyed the secure relationship with them that she had with him. "With you I have that feeling of understanding & companionship. Now & then I have moments of that with the boys but it is not the same...."

On April 7, Eleanor threw a large going-away party for Lash at the Hotel Brevoort in New York. "It was a curious affair," Joe's friend Lewis Feuer recalled. "Suddenly a telegram arrived signed by ER saying there'd be a big dinner for Joe at this classy hotel. As the dishes were served, an orchestra of seven or eight came over and serenaded Joe. The dishes were ornate. We were at war. I thought it was in terrible taste. All this sentimentality about Joe going into the service."

On the third floor of the White House, Eleanor set aside a room for Lash to use whenever he was on leave. On her desk she placed an enlarged photo of Lash. "I want to be able to look at you all the time," she explained. In addition, Eleanor told Joe to call her collect at the White House whenever the president was away at Hyde Park, and to "know that her love was there for him always. No other engagement can't be given up, if there is a chance to see you!"

Before he left for his training camp in Miami, Lash gave Eleanor a miniature good-luck horseshoe, which she put on her chain "so it would be always with me as I like having something from you very near me always." Traveling on a train with a bunch of soldiers, she imagined for a moment she had seen his face. "Wouldn't it be fun sometime if you were in the crowd when I looked up?" In the White House, Eleanor waited anxiously for his letters and calls. "Your telegram came," she happily noted. "I could have kissed the telegram. I was so glad to have word from you."

Eleanor was not the central person in Joe's life that spring, however. For more than a year, he had been involved with a fellow worker at the International Student Service, Trude Pratt. The situation was complicated, since Trude was still married to Eliot Pratt, a wealthy man who was threatening to keep the children if she divorced him. During these months, Eleanor was close to Trude as well; indeed, she seemed to fall into the role of matchmaker, much as she had done with her daughter, Anna, and John Boettiger in the heady days of their illicit romance, before their divorces were final. For hours on end, she counseled both Joe and Trude, offering advice, love, and support, providing safe cover for their meetings.

"Of one thing I am sure . . . ," she wrote Lash, perhaps reflecting her own experience, "don't accept a compromise. Trude must be all yours, otherwise you will never be happy.

"Someday I'll tell you why I'm sure that is so, but just now no corroborating history is of interest to you & all the contribution I can think of which is helpful, is to beg you not to accept ½ a loaf of love."

• • •

Perhaps only with Lorena Hickok had Eleanor ever felt the sense of being loved exclusively. In every one of her other relationships, it seemed, she was the third person in the triangle: the outsider looking in at her husband's intense relationship with his mother; the outsider looking in at the love between Esther Lape and Elizabeth Read, between Nancy Cook and Marion Dickerman, between Anna Roosevelt and John Boettiger, between Joe Lash and Trude Pratt, between Franklin and Missy and Martha and Lucy.

It was now more than a year since Hick had moved into the White House, and Eleanor remained intensely loyal to her old friend. "Our friend Hick is still here," Tommy complained to Esther Lape. "The ushers call her 'the enduring guest.'" "She can't pay rent and her income tax and her dentist bill," Tommy chided, "so she has cut out paying rent! . . . Elizabeth will be interested to know that one night when the Hickok was rather mellow and ranting on about how she adored Mrs. Roosevelt etc., etc. she said that if anything happened to her I was delegated to destroy all the letters which Mrs. R. had written her. I accepted the assignment but I did not add that I had already made up my mind on that score."

Whenever Eleanor was free for breakfast, she invited Hick to join her, in the West Hall in winter, on the South Veranda in summer. The two old friends would talk until breakfast was served, and then Eleanor would retire behind *The New York Times,* reading aloud an item here or there. Then, when Hick got home from her work at the Democratic National Committee, usually around 10:30 or 11 p.m., she would stop in Eleanor's sitting room so they could talk a bit while Eleanor was buried in mail. Sometimes, Hick recalled, "if she was out when I came in, she would come into my room and sit on the foot of my bed and talk for a little while." Though the intense feeling had cooled, there remained a strong bond between them; they enjoyed one another's company.

The same spring that Eleanor lost Joe Lash to the army, Hick became involved with Marion Janet Harron. Marion was ten years younger than Hick, a Phi Beta Kappa graduate from the University of California, a judge in the U.S. Tax Court. In the months that followed, her presence at the White House was so frequent that the guards at the gate no longer bothered to ask for her identification.

Eleanor experienced both relief and sorrow as she watched Hick fall in love with another woman. Knowing that her friend was happy lessened her guilt about the pain she had caused when she no longer needed Hick as Hick needed her. Yet, at the same time, there had undoubtedly remained a secret pleasure in knowing how passionately Hick loved her. And now that love had turned to someone else.

• • •

The war would be won, the president said again and again that spring, only if the incalculable force of American democracy could be let loose, if people scattered throughout the land came to feel that their individual skills and talents were an essential part of the common endeavor. A host of separate images prevailed: workers in aircraft factories assembling planes; welders at dockyards building ships; miners in West Virginia digging coal; farmers in Kansas planting crops; pilots at airfields learning to fly; sailors in the Atlantic dodging German submarines; soldiers in the Pacific fighting the Japanese. Roosevelt understood that the challenge was to find a way of binding these men and women together in the shared enterprise of total war.

To this end, he submitted to Congress in late April a seven-point economic program, including heavier taxes, war bonds, wage and price controls, and comprehensive rationing—designed to ensure, as he put it, "an equality of sacrifice." Explaining the program to the people in his second wartime fireside chat, he said that, though not everyone could have the privilege of "fighting our enemies in distant parts of the world," or "working in a munitions factory or a shipyard," there is "one front and one battle where everyone in the United States—every man, woman and child—is in action. . . . That front is right here at home, in our daily tasks.

"To build the factory, to buy the materials, to pay the labor, to provide the transportation, to equip and feed and house the soldiers and sailors and marines, and do all the thousands of things necessary in a war—all cost a lot of money, more money than has ever been spent by any nation at any time in the long history of the world." When the government spends such unprecedented sums, he explained, the money goes into the bank accounts of the people. "You do no have to be a professor of math or economics to see that if people with plenty of cash start bidding against each other for scarce goods, the price of these goods goes up." For that reason, a system of rationing and price control was needed. Henceforth, by the action of what came to be known as the "General Maximum Price Regulation," all prices would be effectively fixed for the duration of the war. The ceiling price of each item would be the highest price charged for that item in March 1942.

To bolster his call for shared sacrifice, he told the story of Captain Hewitt Wheless, a B-17 pilot who came from a small town in Texas with a population of 2,375. Wheless had just been awarded the Distinguished Service Cross for downing seven Japanese planes in a single mission that pitted him against eighteen Japanese zeros. During the lopsided attack, one engine on the American bomber was shut down, one gas tank was hit, the oxygen system was entirely destroyed, the radio operator was killed, the gunner was crippled, and the engineer's right hand was shot off. Still, the fight continued until the Japanese squadron ran out of gas and turned away. With both engines now gone and the plane practically out of control, the B-17 returned to its base and made an emergency landing. "As we sit here at home contemplating our own duties," he concluded, "let us think and think hard of the example which is being set for us by our fighting men."

Ten days later, Captain Wheless stood before a cheering crowd of eighteen thousand Boeing employees in the Seattle plant where the B-17 was produced. For an entire hour, not one rivet gun sounded; the deep boom of the drop hammer was stilled. It was the first time in months that work in the plant had come to a stop, as men in overalls and women in slacks heard a replay of the president's speech over the loudspeaker. When Wheless stepped to the microphone, he made it clear that he owed his life to the B-17, "the Queen of the Sky," and to the workers standing before him. "The men operating the planes don't want all the credit," he told the enthusiastic crowd. "I want to thank you for myself and a lot of other pilots who more or less owe their lives to your design and workmanship. Continue the good work and together we can't lose."

• • •

The continuing need to sustain national morale against the backdrop of military reverses in the Far East led Roosevelt that April to endorse a risky raid on Tokyo by a force of sixteen B-25s under the leadership of Lieutenant Colonel James H. Doolittle. Immediately after Pearl Harbor, the president had told his military chiefs that, despite the distances involved, a way had to be found to carry out a retaliatory raid on Japan. A much-needed lift to American spirits would be achieved, Roosevelt calculated, if a direct blow could be struck at the heart of Japan. Plans were drawn to launch a raid from a ship positioned some six hundred miles from the coast of Japan. It would be the first time heavily loaded bombers had ever taken off from a navy carrier. The question was whether the deck of the largest carrier was large enough to propel a fleet of B-25s.

On April 18, the day of the raid, the sea was rough. Doolittle was the first to take off. As he started his engines, heavy waves broke over the deck, sending cascades of spray along the sides of his twin-engine plane. If the plane was unable to get airborne, it would drop off the deck and be sliced in half by the sharp edge of the bow. At the far end of the carrier, carefully gauging the rise and fall of the deck, the flight-deck officer waved his checkered flag as a signal for takeoff to begin. Doolittle pushed his throttles forward, and the bomber waddled slowly down the deck. Standing nearby, a navy pilot shouted that the plane wasn't going to make it. But the wheels came off the deck just in time, and the plane took off without a hitch. Within an hour, the remaining fifteen planes were also in the air.

Doolittle and his squadron reached Tokyo shortly after noon; they dropped their bombs and then flew on to China. Though the physical damage from the raid was comparatively light, the psychological damage was enormous. The Japanese government had promised the people of Japan that their homeland would never be attacked. The Doolittle raid had shown that the empire was not invulnerable after all. When the news of the raid was broadcast throughout the world, everyone wanted to know where the planes had come from. Delighting in the mystery, Roosevelt smiled broadly. "They came from a secret base in Shangri-la," he said, referring to the mythical land in James Hilton's *Lost Horizon.*

It was the first good news from the Pacific theater. Telegrams of support flooded the White House. "I hope my two boys in the army have a similar opportunity," Mrs. T. J. Dykema of Pittsburgh wrote. "Give us more Doolittles and we will take our chances in the west," James Jordon of Oregon telegraphed. Even Stimson, who had been doubtful about this "pet project" of the president's, agreed the daring raid had had "a very good psychological effect in the country both here and abroad."

Moreover, through a series of strange twists and turns, the Doolittle raid led to the Battle of Midway. As the American bombs fell on Japanese soil, Admiral Isoroku Yamamoto, the commander-in-chief of the Japanese Combined Fleet, who had planned the attack of Pearl Harbor, strengthened his resolve to prevent any future penetration of Japan's perimeter. At his insistence, the decision was made to send an overwhelming force of ten battleships, four aircraft carriers, and seventy destroyers, 185 ships in all, to seize Midway Island, the farthest outpost of the Hawaiian chain.

Had the Japanese fleet been able to catch the much smaller American forces unawares, there is little doubt that Yamamoto would have achieved his aim. But because the navy had broken the Japanese code, Pacific Fleet Commander Admiral Chester Nimitz had an incalculable advantage, allowing him to concentrate his planes, carriers, and men at precisely the right points, waiting to pounce at precisely the right time. Nimitz launched his strike on June 4, 1942, just before the Japanese fleet reached Midway. Catching Yamamoto totally by surprise, the attack destroyed all four Japanese carriers, one heavy cruiser, three battleships, and 372 aircraft; thirty-five hundred Japanese sailors were killed.

The battle at Midway, Admiral King later observed, was a major turning point, "the first decisive defeat suffered by the Japanese Navy in 350 years. It put an end to the long period of Japanese offensive action and restored the balance of naval power in the Pacific." But victory at Midway was offset at Corregidor, where, on May 6, despite a valiant effort to hold out, American troops had been forced to surrender. "With broken heart and head bowed in sadness but not in shame," General Jonathan Wainwright wired the president, "I go to meet the Japanese commander."

The situation looked bleak on the Russian front as well. With the coming of spring, the Germans had launched a vast new offensive to defeat the Red Army. Refreshed and resupplied, the German army was pushing fast toward Leningrad in the north and Rostov and Stalingrad in the south. To ease the pressure, Stalin was demanding a second front in France; only simultaneous offensives in the East and the West, he argued, could vanquish Hitler.

By spring, officials in both Washington and London were engaged in daily discussions over the feasibility of a second front. That a massive concentrated force in Western Europe would be necessary to defeat Hitler was axiomatic to both General Marshall and the new War Plans Division chief, General Eisenhower. For weeks, with the strong backing of Henry Stimson, Marshall and Eisenhower had been arguing against a piecemeal scattering of Allied forces. "We've got to go to Europe and fight," Eisenhower urged, "and we've got to quit wasting resources all over the world—and still worse—wasting time. If we're going to keep Russia in, save the Middle East, India and Burma; we've got to begin slugging with air at West Europe; to be followed by a land attack as soon as possible."

Preliminary plans for a cross-Channel attack were presented to the president at the end of March. The plans called for a massive assault across the Channel by April 1943 (Operation Bolero). A more limited emergency operation (Operation Sledgehammer) was designed for the fall of 1942, to be employed if the Red Army was at the point of imminent collapse. Stimson feared that the president lacked "the hardness of heart" to commit himself wholly to this concentrated effort, which required resisting requests for troops in other theaters of the war. "The same qualities which endear him to his own countrymen," Stimson mused, "militate against the firmness of his execution at a time like this." Marshall, too, was concerned about the president's inability to reject appeals for other good purposes; he had a habit, Marshall observed, "his cigarette-holder gesture," of tossing out new operations in response to new information from troubled areas.

But when Marshall completed his presentation, the president not only endorsed the cross-Channel plan, but decided to send Marshall and Hopkins to London to secure Churchill's agreement. As Hopkins packed his bags, Roosevelt arranged for a naval doctor to accompany him to London to protect him from overexertion, and directed Marshall "to put Hopkins to bed and keep him there under 24-hour guard by army or marine corps" while he got some rest.

Churchill's wife, Clementine, was delighted to see Hopkins once again.

"Oh how glad I am that you are back once more," she told him, "to encourage, to cheer, to charm us. You can't think what a difference it makes to Winston. He is carrying a very heavy load and I can't bear his dear round face not to look cheerful and cherubic in the mornings, as up to now it has always done. What with Singapore and India . . . we are indeed walking through the Valley of Humiliation."

The discussions with Churchill went surprisingly well. For months, Churchill had been arguing against an all-out attack on Hitler's Europe, preferring a series of peripheral operations, in the Mediterranean, the Middle East, and North Africa. But now, as he listened to Marshall and Hopkins, Churchill knew that their arguments for a second front carried the weight of the president's convictions. "What Harry and George Marshall will tell you all about has my heart and mind in it," Roosevelt had wired Churchill. Before the first day's discussions were over, Hopkins had wired an optimistic report to Roosevelt. Churchill's conciliatory mood puzzled Canada's MacKenzie King. "It was not like him to agree, almost as it were, without a fight," King noted. "He may have decided that the time has not yet come to take the field as an out and out opponent of a second front."

Emboldened by Churchill's apparent support for the cross-Channel attack, Roosevelt cabled Stalin to ask if Foreign Minister Vyacheslav Molotov could come to Washington to discuss Allied plans for a second front to relieve the situation in Russia. A delighted Stalin replied that Molotov would come to Washington in three weeks.

While Hopkins was in London, Churchill received a report that Louis Johnson, Roosevelt's emissary to India, was trying, with Roosevelt's knowledge, to negotiate with Gandhi's Congress Party a military agreement that would commit the nationalist forces to join with British defenders to stop Japan's westward advance. In return, the nationalists were asking for some measure of immediate self-government to motivate the Indian people to feel they were defending their own freedom. On hearing the news, Churchill was furious. India was Britain's colony, and no one, not even his great friend Franklin Roosevelt, was going to tell Britain how to resolve the tangled situation. For two hours, Hopkins reported, Churchill walked around the room issuing a string of invectives.

At 3 a.m., long past the time when he was supposed to be in bed, Hopkins was still listening to Churchill. Churchill said that he would be ready to resign on the issue, but that if he did the War Cabinet would simply continue his policy. He then wrote to Roosevelt: "Anything like a serious difference between you and me would break my heart, and would surely deeply injure both our countries at the height of this terrible struggle." Once Roosevelt saw that pressing Churchill on India would do serious damage to Anglo-American relations, he dropped his efforts.

Molotov arrived at the White House on Friday afternoon, May 29. Since Eleanor was in West Virginia for a commencement at the school at Arthurdale, a stag dinner was prepared that evening for Molotov, Roosevelt, and

Hopkins. Two interpreters were also present. To the eyes of the president's butler, Alonzo Fields, Molotov had "an owlish, wise look" on his face, accentuated by his chubby cheeks, his stubby mustache, and his round glasses. On occasion, Fields noted, "his eyes would dart around with the glint of a fox waiting to spring on his prey." The need for continuous translation made conversation difficult, frustrating Roosevelt's desire to get to know Molotov. Moreover, whenever the conversation seemed about to open up, Molotov brought it back to the second front, insistent on securing a definite commitment from the Americans for the cross-Channel attack. So unswerving did Molotov prove, content to sit in his chair for hours on end sticking to his argument, that Roosevelt later nicknamed him "Stone Ass."

During the entire Molotov visit, one State Department official observed, the president and his advisers were "head-down in their desire to make the Soviets happy." Before Molotov arrived, Roosevelt had sent a memo to his Joint Chiefs, declaring that "at the present time, our principal objective is to help Russia. It must be constantly reiterated that Russian armies are killing more Germans and destroying more Axis material than all the 25 united nations put together."

"The fact that the Russians were carrying so heavy a load led to a guilt complex in our relations," Russian envoy Charles Bohlen observed. The guilt increased with the dark picture Molotov painted of the fighting on the Eastern front; in recent weeks, the Russians had suffered devastating defeats at Kharkov and Kerch, and it was clear that Sevastopol could not hold out much longer. The German army was now only eighty miles from Moscow.

Desiring to placate the courageous Russians, who were engaged every hour of every day with Hitler's finest troops, while American and British troops were fighting only on the periphery, Roosevelt asked Marshall, in Molotov's presence, whether "developments were clear enough so that we could say to Mr. Stalin that we were preparing a second front." When Marshall said yes, Roosevelt told Molotov to tell Stalin that "we expect the formation of a second front this year." Though Roosevelt's pledge did not specify when or where the second front would take place, Molotov was jubilant. The ice was broken. The president felt he was actually getting chummy with his Russian visitor.

Molotov was put up in the family quarters, in the room Churchill had occupied across the hall from Hopkins' room. Though Eleanor returned to the White House too late to join the Molotov party for dinner, she conversed with Molotov in her sitting room before going to bed. Earlier in the evening, Molotov had told Hopkins that he wanted to meet Mrs. Roosevelt, and though it was past midnight, Hopkins had brought him to Eleanor's room. Eleanor later remarked that she liked him immediately. She felt he was "an open, warm sort of person." They talked about women in Russia.

The following day, as Molotov greeted members of a Russian plane crew, Eleanor joined Franklin for a review of the Memorial Day parade. As the first soldiers passed, Roosevelt applauded with enthusiasm. Eleanor was glad to see the new types of equipment on exhibit, but in contrast to her husband, who enjoyed the spectacle immensely, she found it difficult to forget that killing was the object of the lavish weapons on display. Indeed, earlier in the month, she had taken public issue with her husband when he called for a series of parades to accompany different groups of draftees to camp. "American boys on their way to war don't love a parade," she had countered. "There's no glamour to this war."

As reports of Roosevelt's meeting with Molotov reached London, along with the implied promise of a "sacrificial landing" in 1942 if the Russians faced imminent collapse, Churchill decided to fly to the United States immediately. For, just as MacKenzie King had suspected, beneath his apparent support for a second front when he talked to Hopkins and Marshall in London, Churchill remained adamantly opposed to the idea of a direct assault on the Continent. Unable to fight off the ghosts of the Somme, where the British had lost sixty thousand men in a single day, he was determined "to go round the end rather than through the center." As he looked around him in the House of Commons, he once told special envoy Averell Harriman, "he could not help but think of all the faces that were not there," the faces of men destined to lead Britain who had never returned from the trenches. To order yet another direct assault on the Continent seemed to Churchill equivalent to consigning a new generation to death on the battlefield.

Churchill arrived at Bolling Field in Washington on June 18, and then flew to Hyde Park the next morning. "The President was on the local airfield," Churchill recalled in his memoirs, "and saw us make the roughest bump landing I have experienced. He welcomed me with great cordiality, and, driving the car himself, took me to the majestic bluffs over the Hudson River on which Hyde Park . . . stands."

For more than an hour, they drove together around the estate. With boyish enthusiasm, Roosevelt jerked the car forward and backward in an attempt to elude the Secret Service. "I confess," Churchill later admitted, "that when on several occasions the car poised and backed on the grass verges of the precipices over the Hudson I hoped the mechanical devices and brakes would show no defects." To reassure Churchill, Roosevelt invited him to "feel his biceps, saying that a famous prize-fighter had envied them." Much to Churchill's relief, the car finally came to a stop at the round driveway in front of the president's house. Lunch was served, and then the two leaders ensconced themselves in Roosevelt's study for a long talk before taking tea at the house of his cousin Laura Delano and dinner at the Big House.

In Washington, Stimson was nervous. "I can't help feeling a little bit uneasy about the influence of the Prime Minister on him at this time. The trouble is WC and FDR are too much alike in their strong points and in their weak points. They are both penetrating in their thoughts but they lack the steadiness of balance that has got to go along with warfare." Stimson was right to worry. Churchill lost no time in expressing his anxiety about the potential bloodbath that a direct assault on the Continent would bring. The president listened carefully, though he stood firm on the need for some action to reduce the pressure on the Russians.

Churchill awakened early Saturday morning. "He surely is an informal house guest," Hassett noted. "He was out on the lawn barefoot and later was seen crossing the passage to Hopkins' room, still barefoot. The President calls him Winston. . . . The Boss has a knack for entertaining guests with a minimum of strain and fussiness both to him and to them. He always pursues the even tenor of his ways whether in the White House, on the train or here at Hyde Park. Never changes his routine; meets his guests at mealtime or when mutually convenient. Otherwise they and he are free to do as they please. If he did it differently, this steady stream of visitors would wear him to a frazzle."

In the morning, the president took the prime minister on a second tour of the estate, stopping first at the library and then at his beloved Top Cottage. After lunch, they settled down to talk in Roosevelt's small study on the ground floor. It was at this time, with Hopkins seated in the corner, that Churchill brought up the subject of "Tube Alloys," the English code name for the project to create an atomic bomb. "We knew what efforts the Germans were making to produce supplies of 'heavy water,' " Churchill recalled, "a sinister term, eerie, unnatural, which began to creep into our secret papers. What if the enemy should get an atomic bomb before we did! . . . I strongly urged that we should at once pool all our information, work together on equal terms, and share the results, if any, equally between us."

There was ample reason for concern. Three months earlier, German Propaganda Minister Joseph Goebbels had received an optimistic report about the latest developments in German science. "Research in the realm of atomic destruction," he recorded in his diary, "has now proceeded to a point where its results may possibly be made use of in the conduct of this war. Tremendous destruction, it is claimed, can be wrought with a minimum of effort. . . . Modern technique places in the hands of human beings means of destruction that are simply incredible. German science is at its peak in this matter. It is essential that we be ahead of everybody, for whoever introduces a revolutionary novelty into this war has the greater chance of winning it."

It was now nearly three years since the president's first discussion with economist and biologist Alexander Sachs about atomic developments. At that momentous meeting in October 1939, Sachs had delivered to the president a letter from Albert Einstein in which the celebrated physicist reported that scientists in Berlin had achieved the fission of uranium atoms and the release of colossal amounts of energy. On the basis of additional work done by Italian émigré Enrico Fermi and Hungarian physicist Leo Szilard, it was possible, Einstein predicted, to set up a nuclear chain reaction which could be harnessed into bombs so powerful that they could blow up entire ports. Though Roosevelt found the discussion interesting, he seemed to hesitate about committing government funds to such speculative research. But after Sachs reminded him of Napoleon's rejection of Fulton when the inventor tried to interest him in the idea of a steamship, Roosevelt agreed to move forward. "Alex, what you are after is to see that the Nazis don't blow us up," Roosevelt said. "This requires action."

Little progress had been made until after the fall of France, when substantial government funds were finally committed to atomic research. British scientists were also experimenting with atomic weaponry, Churchill told Roosevelt, but, with Britain under severe bombing, it was too risky to continue the research on the scale that was necessary. Churchill was delighted when the president said that the United States would assume the major responsibility for the development of the atomic bomb. Two months later, the Manhattan Project, directed by army engineer General Leslie Groves, was launched. By 1945, more than 120,000 people would be employed on the search for an atomic bomb, at a cost of $2 billion.

Atomic research would produce the most dramatic scientific development of the war, but the combined efforts of science, industry, and government would lead to a host of groundbreaking discoveries, including the large-scale production of penicillin to combat infections, the development of plasma, the use of synthetic drugs like Atabrine to substitute for scarce quinine, improved radar, proximity fuses for mines, and the jet engine.

• • •

After dinner at the Big House, where they were joined by Averell Harriman, the president and Churchill left for Highland Station to catch the overnight train to Washington. At the White House, Churchill was installed in the Rose Suite, in the family quarters. "There was something so intimate in their friendship," Churchill's aide Lord Ismay noted. "They used to stroll in and out of each other's rooms in the White House, as two subalterns occupying adjacent quarters might have done. Both of them had the spirit of eternal youth."

After an hour's respite for breakfast and the morning papers, Churchill joined the president and Hopkins in Roosevelt's study. They had just settled down when a secretary handed the president a telegram. It contained the devastating news that on June 21 the British garrison at Tobruk in Libya had surrendered to the Germans, with twenty-five thousand British soldiers taken prisoner. The president handed the telegram to Churchill without a word. "It was a bitter moment," Churchill conceded. For thirty-three weeks, Tobruk had withstood the German siege; now a garrison of twenty-five thousand had laid down their arms to perhaps one-half that number of Germans. "Defeat is one thing," Churchill wrote; "disgrace is another."

There was a moment of silence, and then Roosevelt turned to Churchill. "What can we do to help?" "Give us as many Sherman tanks as you can spare, and ship them to the Middle East as quickly as possible," Churchill replied. The president sent for General Marshall, and within days three hundred tanks and one hundred self-propelled guns were on their way to the Eighth Army in Alexandria. When Eleanor joined her husband and the prime minister at lunch, she was amazed at the spirits of the two men. Though they were obviously stricken by the news, their first reaction was to figure out what could be done. "To neither of those men," she marveled, "was there such a thing as not being able to meet a new situation. I never heard either of them say that ultimately we would not win the war. This attitude was contagious, and no one around either of them would ever have dared to say, 'I'm afraid.' "

In later years, Churchill admitted that the fall of Tobruk was "one of the heaviest blows" he could recall during the war. Not only was the military loss enormous, but the humiliating circumstances of the surrender had substantially damaged the reputation of the British army. Later that night, Lord Moran found him pacing his room, repeating over and over that Tobruk had fallen, crossing and recrossing the room with quick strides, a glowering look on his face. "What matters is that it should happen while I am here," he said. "I am ashamed. I cannot understand why Tobruk gave in. More than 30,000 of our men put their hands up. If they won't fight . . ." He stopped abruptly, fell into a chair, and seemed to pull himself together, recounting for Moran the generosity of the president's immediate response: "What can we do to help?"

The fall of Tobruk increased the importance of the Mediterranean theater in Churchill's mind and cemented his opposition to a cross-Channel attack in 1942. Though Marshall and Stimson continued to press their case, Roosevelt was unwilling to go ahead without the agreement of his friend and partner. The discussion turned instead to a project Roosevelt had been mulling over for weeks as an alternative to the attack on the Continent—an invasion of French North Africa. The smaller-scale invasion would pull German troops from the Eastern front, while at the same time helping to shore up the British position in the Middle East.

Relieved, Churchill threw his weight behind the operation, code-named Gymnast. "I am sure myself that Gymnast is by far the best chance for effective relief to the Russian front in 42," he told Roosevelt. "This has all along been in harmony with your idea. In fact it is your commanding idea. Here is the true second front in 42. Here is the safest and most fruitful stroke that can be delivered this autumn." There remained the unpleasant task of communicating the Gymnast decision to Stalin, who believed, on the basis of the fateful Molotov communiqué, that something much larger was in the works. Churchill volunteered to go to Moscow himself to break the news.

Marshall and Eisenhower remained adamant in their opposition to the president's "secret baby," as Stimson dubbed the plan to invade North Africa, in late October. To use up men and resources in a peripheral action when victory could only be won by a direct assault on the Continent seemed to their minds a fatal mistake. What is more, the operation itself seemed to them more risky than the president realized. Instead of an orderly buildup over many months, "we now had only weeks," Eisenhower wrote. "Instead of a massed attack across narrow waters, the proposed expedition would require movement across open ocean areas where enemy submarines would constitute a real menace. Our target was no longer a restricted front where we knew accurately terrain, facilities and people as they affected military operations, but the rim of a continent where no major military campaign had been conducted for centuries." Still, Roosevelt persisted in going forward, prompting Eisenhower to predict that the day the invasion order was signed would go down as "the blackest day in history."

When he issued the order, against the robust opposition of his advisers, Roosevelt was thinking not only of the negative effect on the Russians if another year were to pass without substantial action on the part of Anglo-American forces; he was also thinking of the negative effect on the American soldiers and the American people if there were no opportunity for U.S. ground troops to be brought into action against Germany in 1942. He had recently received a discouraged letter from FDR, Jr., written from an army base in Hawaii. The most depressing thing, his son had written, was the lack of action. "A lot of these guys aren't having any fun," he wrote, "just tenseness and waiting our turn."

As the leader of a democracy, Roosevelt had to be concerned with the question of morale; the constant challenge he faced, through speeches and actions alike, was to figure out ways to sustain and strengthen the spirit of the people, without which the war could not be won. "We failed to see," George Marshall observed after the war, commenting on the army's opposition to the president's plan for North Africa, "that the leader in a democracy has to keep the people entertained. That may sound like the wrong word but it conveys the thought."

• • •

While Roosevelt and Churchill were together for these June meetings, Hopkins confided in them that he was engaged to be married to Louise Macy, the former Paris editor of *Harper's Bazaar,* a beautiful woman with dark hair worn in a long bob, bright-blue eyes, and a little gap between her two front teeth. She had graduated from the Madeira School in Washington, attended Smith College, and married and divorced a wealthy attorney. "In smart sets from Santa Barbara to Long Island, 'Louie' Macy is popular," *Time* reported. "She radiates good spirits, talks well, laughs easily." From the day Hopkins met her at the home of Averell and Marie Harriman, he seemed reborn emotionally and physically. "Looking better than he has for three or four years," William Hassett noted. "He's gained ten pounds," Eleanor told Anna, "and seems very perky."

There was still a great physical attractiveness in Hopkins—remarkable vitality came through his thinness and his pallor, conveying an image of a far younger, healthier man. Bill Hassett's diaries that spring are filled with references to the passion of Hopkins' romance. "Harry head over heels in love—52—and doesn't care who knows it," Hassett wrote after spending a long weekend with Harry and Louise at Hyde Park. A week later, Hassett noted that Louise had come again to Hyde Park for dinner, "to happiness of HH who languishes in love."

When Hopkins picked July for the wedding, the president suggested that the ceremony be held at the White House. Hopkins was delighted. "It is going to be done very quietly," he wrote Missy, apologizing for not having told her earlier, "and I only wish you could be here. Of all the people I know I should like to have you. When I see you I will tell you how nice she is."

To all outward appearances, the president was happy with the marriage. Louise was exactly the kind of woman he liked; she was gregarious and funny and she relished good-natured gossip. She was a gay addition to the White House "family." Still, Roosevelt must have feared that Hopkins' romance would make him less accessible for cocktails, meals, and conversation. It is unlikely that the president ever voiced these fears to his old friend. It was not his style to be open about his needs. Nor was it necessary, for Hopkins was equally impelled to make sure that his romance did not in any way undercut his friendship with Roosevelt. When the president asked him to continue living in the White House after the marriage, Hopkins never hesitated for a moment.

Plans were made, against Eleanor's better judgment, to rearrange Hopkins' suite to accommodate a wife. Eleanor's chief concern was for Harry's motherless daughter, ten-year-old Diana. "I'm worried about Harry's marriage & Diana's adjustment if they live at the White House," Eleanor admitted to Hick, "but F.D.R. & Harry seem to think it the only way out." In a letter to Esther Lape, Tommy recorded Eleanor's aggravation. "I imagine Mrs. Roosevelt told you about her reaction to the Hopkins family moving into the White House—bag and baggage," Tommy wrote. "This is with no consultation with Mrs. Roosevelt—just a statement of [Hopkins'] plans."

For more than four years, Eleanor had religiously kept the commitment she had made to Harry when his wife died that she would give Diana a home in the White House. "She did everything that you would normally do with a child as a mother," Diana gratefully recalled. "Everything—the manners, the clothes, the exposing one to literature, being sure the homework got done, the reading aloud, having the friends over, the laying on of the birthday party, the 'let your friends use my bathing suit'—and boy you should've seen some of those little 4th grade kids running around in ER's bathing suit—everything, everything except the arms around the body.

"I was a little kid," Diana went on. "I was dying for a mommy and if she had opened her arms and said, 'Come and hop on my lap,' I would've been there in a minute, hugging her around the neck." But Eleanor had told Harry at the start, Diana remembered, that she didn't want to become too close to Diana in a motherly way, because she felt that "someday he would remarry and she didn't want to step into this affection place where a new mother would come along one day and be able to fill it."

Though Eleanor's relationship with Harry had cooled as a consequence of his absorption with the war, she knew she could count on his idealism at critical junctures. But now she feared the influence of Louise's lighter nature, her fascination with wealth and power, her delight in society. "Mrs. Roosevelt and Louise were polar opposites," Diana observed. "Mrs. Roosevelt was the most civic-minded person I have ever known. Politics and idealism controlled her life and everything she did. In contrast, Louie was absolutely apolitical. She was a more feminine, fluffy type of person. She didn't have a political cell in her body." Eleanor's fears were confirmed by the newspaper stories that accompanied Hopkins' engagement. Somewhere along the way, *Time* magazine reported, Hopkins had doffed the reformer's sackcloth and donned a sports jacket. "Hopkins is equally at home now in a relief office or at Newport, at a faculty dinner or in a rich friend's box at the races, with high minded old ladies or with glamour girls."

• • •

Nothing would prove more damaging to Eleanor and Harry's already troubled relationship than the tangled controversy surrounding Odell Waller, a young black sharecropper in Virginia who was convicted of killing his white landlord and sentenced to die at the end of June in the electric chair. Throughout his trial, Waller resolutely maintained that the killing was in self-defense. An all-white jury deliberated only twenty minutes before finding him guilty of first-degree murder. The defense argued that Waller had not received a fair trial since all the men on the jury were selected from a list of citizens who paid a yearly poll tax, a list that excluded almost without exception the poor white and the Negro sharecropper.

To Negroes across the country, Waller became a symbol of oppression, "of Negro toil in the white man's fields, of Negro fate in the white man's courts, of every black body which has swung at the end of a rope from barn or bridge." The injustice was made all the more conspicuous by comparison with a mirror-image case in the same county. R. G. Siddle, a white farmer, shot and killed an unarmed Negro sharecropper during a quarrel. Charged with murder, Siddle was acquitted by an all-white poll-paying jury in less than fifteen minutes.

As news of the Waller case spread, A. Philip Randolph formed a nationwide committee to pressure Virginia's Governor Colgate Darden to grant clemency. On June 16, a two-hour blackout was staged in Harlem; on every street, in every tavern and barbershop, the lights were turned out to protest the Waller verdict. Within a period of several weeks, seventeen thousand letters reached Darden's desk.

Eleanor became involved when Odell Waller sent her a handwritten note from his cell in the Richmond Prison: "I relize [sic] I'm a stranger to you, I have heard lots of people speak of what a nice lady you are and what I can hear is that you believe in helping the poor. . . . I was raised in Virginia on a farm. I never had a chance to make anything not even a good living. I always worked hard but I couldn't get anything out of it. I raised some wheat with a man named Oscar Davis an [sic] he took all of the wheat and I tried to get my share of it he wouldn't let me have the wheat. We got in a quarrel. And I shot him to keep him from hurting me not meaning to kill him. He carried a gun an [sic] I was afraid of him. . . . Please write to the Governor and get him to have mercy on me and allow me a chance. You will never regret it."

Moved by Waller's plea, Eleanor asked the president to intervene. Decisions on clemency were strictly the prerogative of the governor, and presidential action would be considered highly inappropriate. Roosevelt circumvented this dilemma with "a wholly personal and unofficial note" to the governor, signed by "an old friend who just happens to be President." In the note he described a similar case that had occurred when he was governor of New York. A man had shot his neighbor in the midst of an argument after the neighbor advanced against him in a threatening way. Though the jury convicted him of murder in the first degree, Roosevelt had the sentence commuted to life imprisonment and was always glad he had done so.

The president sent a copy of this letter to Eleanor with a covering note which reflected a poignant yearning for praise from his toughest critic. "Dearest Babs. Didn't I do good? Aren't you proud?" Eleanor was thrilled. "It's a grand letter. Thanks." she replied.

Despite the president's letter, Governor Darden decided, after ten hours of testimony at a clemency hearing, to refuse commutation. In desperation, Randolph and Walter White journeyed to Washington the day before the execution to see the president, unaware of the personal letter the president had already sent Governor Darden.

When Randolph's delegation arrived in Washington, Roosevelt was at Hyde Park, a fact that could not be disclosed since the president's comings and goings were kept secret in wartime. Told simply that an appointment was not possible, the group turned, as always, to Eleanor. With only eighteen hours left until the execution, Eleanor tried all day to reach Franklin at Hyde Park. Each time, Harry Hopkins told her the president was unavailable. Roosevelt knew why she was calling and, realizing there was nothing more he could do without making matters worse, was avoiding her calls.

As the hours passed, with Randolph's delegation waiting by the telephone at the NAACP headquarters, Eleanor became frantic. Between the late afternoon and the early evening, she called Hopkins four or five times, begging him to plead her case with the president. Still, the president refused to come to the phone, and Eleanor, Hopkins later remarked, "would not take 'No' for an answer." Finally, Hopkins realized that Eleanor was taking out her anger on him, that she had drawn the conclusion he was not pressing her case with the president adequately. "I felt that she would not be satisfied until the President told her himself, which he reluctantly but finally did . . . that under no circumstances would he intervene with the Governor and urged very strongly that she say nothing about it."

With a heavy heart, Eleanor placed a call to Randolph. She spoke simply and directly. "Mr. Randolph. I have done everything I can do. I have been to the President twice. And the President has said to me this is a matter of laws and not of men and if I go back to the President he will be displeased with me." A young black activist, Pauli Murray, was listening in to the conversation between Mrs. Roosevelt and Mr. Randolph. "There were five telephones in that office, and there were two of us glued to each telephone. I could hear tears in her voice."

The next day, at 8:35 a.m., Odell Waller was strapped into an electric chair at the Virginia penitentiary. "Have you ever thought," he wrote in a final statement, "about some people are allowed a chance over and over again then there are others allowed little chance, some no chance at all. I worked hard from sunup to sundown and it ended in death for me." At 8:45, the prison doctor declared, "Waller's debt to the community has been paid."

Waller's death had a powerful effect upon the Negro community. "We lost the fight to save his life," Randolph told his followers, "but even so we went a step forward. The Negroes are learning to use pressure. We didn't get quite enough pressure to crack this case but we almost did."

Predictably, Eleanor's public support of Waller drew a new round of criticism from white Southerners. "I cannot understand your sympathy for a Negro who murdered a white man," a resident of New Orleans wrote. A Virginian complained that she had watched the papers daily for accounts of Odell Waller. "I am very much disappointed that you do not devote more of your time to the Red Cross, the USO and help win the conflict rather than indulge in creating disorders among Americans. You are helping to make the Negroes uppish and forward."

During this same period, Eleanor received an angry letter from Pauli Murray. Writing in pain and disappointment, Murray suggested that the president had never been as forthright about race as his Republican rival Wendell Willkie, and that there were even times when she doubted that any white man had the capacity to solve the racial problem.

Eleanor was saddened and angry when she read Murray's letter. "I wonder if it ever occurred to you that Wendell Willkie has no responsibility whatsoever. He can say whatever he likes and do whatever he likes and nothing very serious will happen. If he were to be elected President, on that day, he would have to take into consideration the people who are heads of important committees in Congress . . . people on whom he must depend to pass vital legislation for the nation as a whole. For one who must really have a knowledge of the workings of our kind of government, your letter seems to me one of the most thoughtless I have ever read."

Knowing what Pauli Murray did not know and what she could not tell her, that the president *had* sent a letter to the Virginia governor in Waller's behalf, Eleanor judged her criticism totally unfair. Still, she held out her hand to the young militant with the suggestion of a personal meeting to talk things over. When Pauli arrived at the White House, Eleanor went over to her, hugged her, and mentioned Waller right away, saying what a terrible night it had been. "And this just removed all the anger," Murray recalled. "We met as two people—a bond of sympathy—we had been through a painful experience together." During this meeting, a friendship was born which lasted until Eleanor died.

• • •

In the weeks that followed, Eleanor could not shake the feeling that, on the critical night before the execution, Harry Hopkins had deserted her. One night she vented her frustration and anger directly at Hopkins. "She must've said a few very tough things," Diana Hopkins later suggested, and "he was a very frank guy and he must've really said something very tough to her." Eleanor took to her room for days. The White House staff assumed she was sick. "It's the first time I've ever known her to turn her face to the wall," Tommy told Esther Lape. "I was very disturbed." When Eleanor journeyed to New York the following week, she told Esther Lape, "Something happened to me. I have gotten used to people who say they care for me but are only interested in getting to Franklin. But there was one person of whom I thought this was not true, that his affection was for me and I found that this was not true and I couldn't take it." If their relationship had faltered before, it was now broken.

Outwardly, Eleanor's poise and dignity prevailed. She took it upon herself to plan Hopkins' wedding. The ceremony took place in front of the fireplace in the president's study on July 30, 1942. "A very nice affair," Hassett recorded. The fireplace was banked with greens, the president's desk was covered with white flowers, and vases of roses were everywhere. Franklin wore a white linen suit, Eleanor a blue-and-white polka-dot chiffon. "Harry trembled like an aspen leaf throughout the ceremony," Hassett observed, "but managed to fish the wedding ring out of his pants pocket at the proper time." A luncheon for one hundred guests followed.

"After Harry married Louise," Diana Hopkins recalled, "FDR was more lonely than ever before." Though Hopkins was still living at the White House, the relationship was not the same. Of course, Princess Martha was still available for conversation and companionship. Almost every weekend during the spring and early summer of 1942, the usher diaries reveal, the president spent the majority of his leisure time with Martha, either at her Pook's Hill estate, at the White House, or at Hyde Park.

It was a time of loneliness for Princess Martha as well. Though she filled her days with work for Norway—giving speeches about Norway's struggle for freedom, visiting Norwegian marine stations in the U.S.A. and Canada, entertaining Norwegian seamen posted on the East Coast, attending official banquets, hosting special events at the Norwegian Embassy—she was far away from her country, her husband, and her closest friends.

Both were in search of companionship, and they found it in each other. During this period, Diana Hopkins was told, the president would ask Louise Hopkins to chaperone for visits with Martha. "No sooner would Louise return to the White House from her volunteer work as a nurse at Columbia Hospital," Diana recalled, "than there would be a message that the president wanted her to join him for tea with Princess Martha immediately. There was no time even to get out of her uniform. She had to jump in the car and drive with the president to Martha's estate . . . Then they'd get there, and Princess Martha would say, 'Louise, why don't you go and see the children?' And so Louise would go and see the children, and the president and Martha would have tea, and this was one hell of a tough situation for [her]."

• • •

In the summer of 1942, the accustomed rhythms of daily life were disrupted in every factory, business, and home by the institution of rationing and price control. In his April address to the nation, the president had explained that rationing of scarce commodities was the only equitable solution to the shortages brought about by the war, since it prevented those who could pay the most from getting whatever was available and forced those in less fortunate circumstances to go without.

While the machinery for the rationing of consumer goods was being devised and set in motion, the government established a series of regulations at the manufacturing level. To ensure a sufficient amount of cotton and wool to supply the army with more than 64 million flannel shirts, 165 million coats, and 229 million pairs of trousers, the War Production Board mandated a new "Victory" suit for civilians, with cuffless trousers and narrower lapels. Reductions in the amount of cloth allowed also led to shorter, pleatless skirts, rising several inches above the knee, and to the creation of a new two-piece bathing suit.

Women took the loss of pleated skirts and one-piece bathing suits in stride, but when the rubber shortage threatened the continuing manufacture of girdles, a passionate outcry arose. Though government sources tried to suggest that "women grow their own muscular girdles, by exercising," woman argued that "neither exercise nor any other known remedy" could restore aging muscles to their original youthful tautness. Without "proper support from well-fitted foundation garments" to hold the abdomen in place, there was no way, journalist Marion Dixon argued in a contemporary health magazine, that a woman past thirty could keep her posture erect or do physical work without tiring. "Certainly," Dixon concluded, "Uncle Sam does not want American women to wear garments that would menace their health or hamper their efficiency, especially during wartime, when every ounce of energy and effort is needed."

The government heeded the women's cries. Not long after the first public discussion of curtailing girdles, the War Production Board announced that foundation garments were an essential part of a woman's wardrobe, and as such could continue to be manufactured, despite the precious rubber involved!

The first step in developing the rationing system was the creation of a list of essential items in short supply. Each item was then given a price in points, and each man, woman, and child in the country was given a book of stamps. The stamps in each ration book—worth forty-eight points each month, and good for six months—could be spent on any combination of goods, from meat, butter, and canned vegetables to sugar and shoes. When a sale was made, the retailer would collect the points and use them to replenish his stocks. Ration books were priceless possessions, as Mrs. Harold Calvert of Oklahoma City found out when her two children ate all the coupons from her first book and she had to present the damaged book before being issued a replacement.

By and large, American housewives accepted the system of rationing cheerfully. When butter became scarce, they added a yellow dye to margarine to make it look like butter. When sugar was cut back, they substituted corn syrup and saccharin in cakes and cookies. They planted Victory Gardens in their backyards. They saved kitchen fats and exchanged them at the butcher shop for points. There were also black markets in every city—places where scarce goods could be sold outside the normal channels of distribution. For a premium, almost anything could be bought—nylon hose for $5 a pair, cigarettes for 30 cents a pack, boneless ham for twice the ceiling price.

But nothing cut as deeply into the pattern of everyday life as the rationing of tires and gasoline. For millions of Americans who had known that "curious independence," as Marquis Childs put it, which ownership of a motorcar brings, "the untrammeled right to go as far and as fast, or almost as fast, as your money will permit," the most onerous restrictions were those on driving. A draconian order forbidding the sale of new tires anywhere in the country had been issued at the end of December, as Japan moved quickly toward the rubber-rich islands of Malaya and Indonesia. Since tire factories accounted for 75 percent of the country's annual consumption of crude rubber, it was essential to freeze the current supply while a rationing organization could be devised.

By early January 1942, a certificate program had been put into place; if an individual met certain standards of eligibility and could show genuine need, he was issued a one-time certificate that allowed him to buy a new set of tires. Determining who was eligible was a tricky process, as OPA Administrator John Kenneth Galbraith found out when he devised the list of people entitled to buy new tires. Galbraith's first list—which included physicians, war workers, public officials, and others rendering essential services, but failed to mention ministers—produced an immediate explosion, particularly in the rural South. "Roosevelt was outraged," Galbraith recalled, "that anyone could be so casual about both fundamentalist religion and the fundamentals of American politics. Ministers were promptly proclaimed essential."

Rationing of tires was followed by rationing of gasoline, which began on the Eastern Seaboard on the 15th of May, 1942. Though gasoline was not in short supply, the government believed that gas rationing was the only way to save rubber. The decision was made to start with the seventeen Eastern states and then extend the gas rationing westward. Consumers of gas were divided into different classes: the majority of drivers were granted A cards, which entitled them to five gallons a week; B cards were given to war workers, doctors, and others whose vocations required supplemental mileage; X cards were granted to those whose occupations required unlimited mileage.

The misrepresentation of one's status before the gas-rationing board carried a fine of $10,000 and a sentence of ten years in jail. Yet, within weeks, it became clear that thousands of motorists had wangled B or X cards when their work did not truly require them. Those who had willingly accepted A cards were bitter to find their neighbors in a privileged position. Public resentment grew when it became known that members of Congress had been automatically granted X cards. So angry was the outpouring of public sentiment that a resolution was introduced in the Senate requiring members to renounce their claim of special privilege. When the defiant senators defeated the resolution by a vote of sixty-six to two, the public mood darkened. "The very men to whom the whole country looks to set an example and to encourage the public to accept the personal inconvenience," Raymond Clapper wrote, "are doing exactly the reverse. Instead of trying to cooperate they are cackling like wet hens to hold their special privileges."

When Roosevelt realized how badly muddled the gas situation had become, he moved in several directions at once. In mid-June, he initiated a nationwide rubber drive, designed not only to gather precious tons of scrap, but also to instill in the American psyche a sympathetic understanding of the rubber shortage before the inevitable need for extending gas rationing to the country at large came into play. To kick off the drive, he gave a fireside chat. "I want to talk to you about rubber," he told the people, "about rubber and the war—about rubber and the American people." He then proceeded to describe the present shortage, along with the plans for building a new synthetic-rubber industry. "That takes time," he explained, "so we have an immediate need," which the American people could help to fill if they reached into their homes and their yards to recover old rubber tires dumped into basements or garages or still hanging from apple trees for kids to swing on, as well as old garden hoses, rubber shoes, and rubber raincoats. A two-week period from June 15 to June 30 was set aside during which filling-station operators were authorized to take the old rubber in and to pay for it at the rate of a penny a pound.

The response was overwhelming. In the course of two weeks, the nation's stockpile was increased by more than four hundred tons; the average contribution was almost seven pounds for each man, woman, or child. The White House itself was inundated with a motley assortment of rubber items. "Today I am mailing you my old rubber girdle I have cut and torn into strips," Mrs. Meta Kirkland wrote from Santa Ana, California. "I hope I may claim the privilege of being the first to donate personal wearing apparel for the good cause." From Ben Cohen in New York came a package of rubber balls and rubber bones. "On December 7th when the Japs bombed Pearl Harbor, my dog Snuffy went the way of all flesh, a tried and true pal," he wrote. "Our dog was all we had and I trust you don't think me a screwball after you receive my dog Snuffy's toys, these toys are the last of Snuffy's memory." And from the Sixteenth Ward Democratic Club of Reading, Pennsylvania, came a hundred thousand rubber bands collected and formed into a huge ball weighing more than seventy pounds.

Once the rubber drive was completed, the president turned to financier Bernard Baruch and asked him to head a committee to investigate the entire rubber question, to recommend such civilian actions as necessary to ensure an adequate supply of rubber for the armed forces. The choice of "Mr. Facts," as Baruch was dubbed during World War I because of his insistence on finding the facts before he approached any problem, was a master stroke. "The nation waits anxiously these days for the definite report on rubber," *The New York Times* observed in mid-August. "That report may mean the end of auto driving for leisure for the duration and thus drastically change the pattern of American life; but it is believed here that the man in the street will accept the sacrifice once the facts are laid before him. The confidence is due in no small measure to the character and reputation of the man whom the President has named to head the special investigating committee."

Baruch's report, made public in early September 1942, called for a new nationwide gas-rationing system. "Gas rationing is the only way of saving rubber," it concluded. "Every way of avoiding this method was explored, but it was found to be inescapable. The limitation on the use of gas is not due to a shortage of that commodity—it is wholly a measure of rubber saving. Any localized measure would be unfair and futile." The report also called for a reduction in the national speed limit to thirty-five miles per hour and the appointment of a "Rubber Director." "The Baruch report on rubber seems like the first really good job done in Washington since the war began," *The New Republic* noted. *Fortune* concurred. For all the initial confusion and public clamor over the first misguided attempt at rationing, *Fortune* observed, "the Baruch Committee report is supremely an example of the ability of a country and of a government to grow by its own criticism."

As nationwide gas rationing was put into place, pleasure driving virtually ceased. On Sundays, traffic shrunk to a trickle; red and green lights blinked mechanically on and off, but nothing stopped or started. Since Sunday drivers knew they were liable to be stopped by an OPA investigator and asked to explain why their trip was necessary, it was easier to leave the car at home. Citizens learned to walk again. In the months that followed, car pools multiplied, milk deliveries were cut to every other day, and auto deaths fell dramatically. Parties at homes and nightclubs generally broke up before midnight so that people could catch the last bus home.

All in all, pleasures became simpler and plainer as people spent more time going to the movies, entertaining at home, playing cards, doing crossword puzzles, talking with friends, and reading. At the time of Pearl Harbor, William Shirer's *Berlin Diary* stood at the top of the best-seller lists. It was replaced the following spring by Elliot Paul's *The Last Time I Saw Paris* and John Steinbeck's *The Moon Is Down.* Then, in July, "a meteor burst across the publishing skies" as Marion Hargrove's memoir of training camp at Fort Bragg, *See Here, Private Hargrove,* became one of the best-selling books of all time. Americans liked to read, one observer noted, about what their boys were doing at that moment. When the boys went into action, books about the war itself, such as William White's *They Were Expendable,* took center stage.

Once the rubber mess was brought under control, the president turned his focus to the rising cost of living and the threat of inflation. The seven-point stabilization program he had called for in April had not yet passed the Congress. Fearful of constituent reaction in an election year, Congress was reluctant to impose price ceilings on farm products or to levy higher taxes. By summer's end, the entire stabilization program was in jeopardy, as food prices kept rising while wages were fixed. Labor was furious. "You cannot expect the laborer to maintain a fixed wage level if everything he wears and eats begins to go up drastically in price," Roosevelt said in a truculent address that ended with an ultimatum: if the Congress did not act by October 1 to stabilize farm prices, he would act on his own. His war powers enabled him to do so and he intended to use them.

Though Senator Robert La Follette of Wisconsin declared that the president had "placed a pistol at the head of Congress," the threat worked. The Congress passed the necessary legislation at 9 p.m. on October 2, only one day late. That same day, the president appointed Associate Justice James Byrnes of the Supreme Court to a powerful new position as director of economic stabilization. And later that week, the Congress agreed to increase personal and corporate income taxes. The fight against inflation was finally on track.

CHAPTER 14

"BY GOD, IF IT AIN'T OLD FRANK!"

On Thursday night, September 17, 1942, the president and first lady boarded the ten-car presidential train to begin a two-week inspection tour of factories, army camps, and navy yards. It had been a long day. The president had awakened early to bid farewell to Princess Martha, who had been a houseguest for several days. Then, from midmorning through dinner, he was caught in one meeting after another, with congressional leaders, economic advisers, and military men. Now, as he settled down in his oak-paneled private car, which held four staterooms, a comfortable living room, and a dining room large enough to seat twelve, the president was undoubtedly glad to relax.

Franklin Roosevelt was not a man who asked favors of a personal nature easily. Yet, on this occasion, he had made it clear to Eleanor that he wanted her to accompany him on his fortnight's train journey. She had agreed to go as far as Chicago with him; at that juncture, she would have to leave for previously arranged meetings in Washington. Later, perhaps, she could join him again, for the rest of the trip.

Roosevelt had been alone that summer in a way he had not been for years. Weekends at Martha's estate on Pook's Hill had offered him pleasant distraction from the war, but at the end of each working day, he was by himself. Harry Hopkins still lived in the White House, but while his devotion and energy had not wavered, his marriage had dramatically reduced the evenings he and Roosevelt could easily spend together. And, most important, it had become painfully apparent to Roosevelt that summer that he and Missy would never be able to restore their former relationship.

Against certain facts the president was helpless: against Missy's devastating illness; against his mother's death; against Harry Hopkins' falling in love. But with Eleanor, there was still a chance to alter the relationship so they could be together more often, perhaps a chance to open their hearts to one another again. He wanted her with him on the train.

As additional companions on the trip, the president had invited his two unmarried cousins, Laura Delano and Margaret Suckley. When Roosevelt was tired late at night and would see no one else, he enjoyed sitting with Laura and Margaret. "You're the only people I know," he told them once, "that I don't have to entertain." Like Franklin, both Laura and Margaret had been trained from early childhood to present a sunny face to the world, to be pleasant and gracious. "They were just very good company," Anna's daughter, Eleanor Seagraves, recalled. "They were charming, witty, intelligent, and full of fun. After Missy's stroke, they were around all the time."

At fifty-two, Laura Delano, known to family and friends as Polly, was still a beautiful woman. She had a thin face with high cheekbones and an exquisite widow's peak, which she accentuated by dying her hair a blue-white, almost purple shade. "She was the only person I knew on whom that purple hair looked wonderful," Eleanor Seagraves recalled. With her penchant for wearing red velvet slacks and adorning her wrists with five to six bracelets which rustled as she walked, she seemed to bring with her at 9 a.m. the brilliance of the late-night drawing room. Aware of the effect of her looks, she "flirted like mad," Eleanor's niece, Eleanor Wotkyns, recalled, bustling about the president with vivacious charm. The story was told that she had once been in love with the first secretary of the Japanese Embassy, Saburo Kurusu, the scion of a rich Japanese family. "It was quite a scandal," Anna's son Curtis Roosevelt observed, "totally unacceptable to the Delano family. The pressure was too great; the affair was ended, and Laura never married."

By contrast with the flamboyant Laura, Margaret Suckley was quiet and plain, free from the slightest shade of coquetry. Short and thin, with a wry sense of humor and a gentle demeanor, "Daisy" was an intelligent listener, a lover of birds, dogs, and books. It was Daisy who had given the president Fala, the beloved Scottish terrier who accompanied him everywhere. In 1940, the president had put Daisy in charge of sorting through his private papers for the library, a perfect job for this totally discreet woman.

Eleanor had mixed feelings about the Misses Delano and Suckley. Though she was glad to have them along since it gave her the freedom to leave the train at midpoint, as she wished, she had little patience with either the smiling homage they paid the president or the insubstantial nature of their conversation. "Evidently the P[resident] likes women who are not too serious," Tommy wrote Esther Lape. "Laura Delano is no fool, but she has the technique of so many women who appear to be just chatterers." What is more, Laura loved to gossip. "She had a compulsion to be the one who tells things before someone else," Curtis Roosevelt observed. "And while FDR delighted in gossip, Eleanor did not." Nor did Eleanor appreciate Laura's lighthearted humor. After Eleanor met Churchill, the only thing Laura wanted to know was whether he was sexy. Not knowing how to banter, Eleanor simply said, "I just don't know, Laura, I just don't know."

It was the president's wish, he had told his Secret Service aide Mike Reilly before the trip began, to see everything he could from coast to coast without pointless parades and fancy receptions that would only slow up production and prevent him from really absorbing what was going on. The only way to make this possible was to keep the trip "off the record," alerting the plant owners and the governors of all the states at the last possible moment, usually 3 a.m. the day of the president's arrival. Reporters were told they could only write about the trip after the fact.

The first stop was Detroit, where a transformation of historic proportions had taken place. In nine months, the entire capacity of the prolific automobile industry had been converted to the production of tanks, guns, planes, and bombs. Pearl Harbor had accomplished what UAW leader Walter Reuther had envisioned. General Motors was now making complete planes, anti-aircraft guns, aircraft engines, and diesel engines for submarines. Ford was now producing bombers, jeeps, armored cars, troop carriers, and gliders. Chrysler was building tanks, tank engines, army trucks, and mine exploders. The industry that had once built four million cars a year was now building three-fourths of the nation's aircraft engines, one-half of all tanks, and one-third of all machine guns.

Observers accustomed to the "swing-and-duck rivalry" that had existed in Detroit before Pearl Harbor were astonished to note that the Big Three were now "more or less loosely knit," dependent on one another for parts and subassemblies. "Ford is making all-important units for General Motors," journalist Walter Davenport reported in *Collier's* in the summer of 1942, "and the latter is loud in its praise of the lean, dry genius whom it used to pretend to ignore. It's just as if the Brooklyn Dodgers took a few days off and won a few games for the Phillies."

The first stop in Detroit was the Chrysler tank arsenal, the largest arsenal in the world devoted completely to the production of military tanks. Only a year ago, a cornfield had stretched across the site of the huge manufacturing plant, which measured five city blocks wide by two city blocks long, connected by a railroad track extending the full length of the building. As the president entered the plant in an open-top car, the startled workers whooped and whistled. "By God if it ain't old Frank!" one smudge-faced mill operator shouted. The president laughed with delight and waved his hat at the man. Accompanied by Eleanor, Governor Murray Van Waggoner of Michigan, and President K. T. Keller of Chrysler, Roosevelt proceeded to a testing ground where a new M-4 Sherman tank, heavier, faster, and safer than its predecessor, the Grant M-3, was experimenting with a half-dozen difficult maneuvers. An uneasy moment ensued when the powerful tank, after running through a series of muddy depressions, rumbled straight toward the president at considerable speed. Roosevelt's eyes bulged a bit as the driver brought the tank to a standstill about fifteen feet from his car. "A good drive!" the president laughingly remarked. "A good drive!"

At the time of the president's visit, tanks were rolling off the assembly lines at Chrysler, Cadillac, and fifteen other plants at the phenomenal rate of nearly four thousand a month. This extraordinary level of achievement can best be understood by recognizing that Germany, the previous world leader in tank production, was currently producing at a rate of four thousand a *year.* In September, Hitler announced a major expansion in Germany's tank production. The goal he set—eight hundred tanks per month—was less than 15 percent of Roosevelt's objective for 1943!

Later that afternoon, as a bright sun came out from under the clouds, the presidential party arrived at Ford's Willow Run, the big bomber factory named for the willow-lined stream which meandered through the woods and farmland on which the giant plant was built. Boasting "the most enormous room in the history of man," with a system of conveyors designed to bring the parts from manufacturing and subassembly into final assembly, Willow Run had captured the imagination of the public in the early months of 1942. "It is a promise of revenge for Pearl Harbor," exulted the *Detroit Free Press.* "Bring the Germans and Japs in to see it," Ford's production chief, Charles Sorenson, boasted; "hell, they'll blow their brains out." But it had taken longer than expected to build the $86-million plant, to design new fixtures for mass production, to train tool designers, engineers, production men. Only one bomber had come off the assembly line before the president's visit.

When the president and first lady arrived, Ford officials suddenly noticed that old Henry Ford was not in the welcoming lineup. The crusty chief was found in a far corner of the plant, playing with a new machine. Shrugging his shoulders, he reluctantly agreed to join the presidential party. But he was scrunched between the Roosevelts in the back seat, and his face wore a menacing look as he watched the enthusiastic response of his workmen to his old enemy. The president, as always, was enjoying himself thoroughly. Spotting two midgets working high up on the tail section of a half-assembled B-24, where persons of normal height would be unable to fit, he asked to say hello. The two men scrambled down immediately, thrilled at the chance to shake the president's hand.

As Eleanor cast her eyes about the huge L-shaped room, she took great pleasure in the sight of hundreds of women standing side by side with the men. For the first time in the history of the company, women were working on the assembly line as riveters, welders, blueprint readers, and inspectors. Only now, as the first anniversary of Pearl Harbor approached, were officials willing to admit what Eleanor had predicted many months before—that vast numbers of women would be needed as the men went off to war.

"I feel quite certain," Eleanor had insisted in 1941, long before anyone would listen, "that we will use women in many ways as England has done. I think it would save time if we registered women now and analyzed their capabilities and decided in advance where they could be used." The president had reacted positively at first to Eleanor's registration plan, but when he was told by War Manpower Commission chief Paul McNutt that large reserves of unemployed men were still available, he decided against it.

Attitudes toward female employment began changing when the dramatic increase in the armed forces substantially reduced the supply of male workers in war-production centers. The War Manpower Commission reflected this shift in a new statement of policy. "The present number of gainfully employed workers is inadequate to fill even the immediate requirements of the war production program," it stated. "In many areas the lack of adequate housing and transportation facilities compels full use of the local labor supply. These considerations require that substantially increased numbers of women be employed in gainful occupations in war production and essential civilian employment. The recruitment and training of women workers must be greatly expanded and intensified."

The first wave of women war workers had been drawn from women who were already working in lower-paid "feminized" jobs as maids and domestic workers, sewers of clothing, textiles, and shoes. These women needed little convincing to work in defense. Not only was the money substantially higher than anything they could earn elsewhere, but defense jobs were regarded by society as important and valuable. "Finally valued by others," Sherna Gluck observed in her study of women war workers, "they came to value themselves more." In the factory, moreover, there was a sense of sharing, of working together for a common goal.

The second pool of female war workers consisted of young girls, recent high-school graduates. This was the group targeted by the government in its patriotic ads calling on women to do their part in the war, to be "the woman behind the man behind the gun." In magazines and newsreels, Rosie the

Riveter was pictured as a blue-eyed, rosy-cheeked woman with a kerchief on her head, a rivet gun across her lap, and a powder puff in her coverall pocket, the perfect combination of health, strength, and femininity. "Actually what attracted me," Juanita Loveless explained, "was not the money and it was not the job because I didn't even know how much money I was going to make. But the ads . . . 'Do Your Part,' 'Uncle Sam Needs You,' 'V for Victory!' I got caught up in that patriotic 'Win the War, Help the Boys.' The patriotism that was so strong in everyone then."

Eleanor championed the movement of women into the factories. "I'm pretty old, 57 you know, to tell girls what to do with their lives," she said, "but if I were of a debutante age I would go into a factory—any factory where I could learn a skill and be useful." Cautioning girls not to marry too hastily from patriotic fervor, she advised them to get "every bit of preparation they could to expand their horizons and contribute to their country."

For years, there had remained in Eleanor's heart a feeling of sadness for having discarded too quickly, under the pressure of her mother-in-law's negative opinion, the settlement-house work she had loved as a young woman. Now, as new paths were opening up for millions of women who were just starting in life, she was delighted.

Though recruitment of recent students and women already in the work force before the war provided more than half of the women defense workers, the devouring need for war workers eventually led to the recruitment of full-time homemakers as well. For months, Paul McNutt had resisted the move—directing that "no woman with dependent children should be encouraged or compelled to seek employment until all other sources had been exhausted." By the fall of 1942, however, the point of exhaustion had been reached, and the recruitment of homemakers was beginning.

It was dusk when the presidential party left Willow Run. For all the hype, the president observed, Willow Run's production was nowhere near what Ford had promised. Ford's initial difficulties delighted North American Aviation's President J. H. Kindleberger. An outspoken critic of the government's decision to bring automobile companies into the business of building planes, Kindleberger consistently maintained that mass production of airplanes, each one requiring three hundred thousand rivets and one hundred thousand additional parts, was impossible. "You cannot expect blacksmiths to learn to make watches overnight," he sneered. But not long after the president's visit, Willow Run's production would begin to accelerate. By mid-1943, it would produce three hundred bombers a month, and by 1944, when the plant hit its stride, its monthly output would reach six hundred. Army historians argue further that, "if success is measured in terms of more airframe pounds produced with the least cost in dollars and man-hours," Willow Run held a decided margin of superiority over the industry average.

The following morning, Franklin and Eleanor inspected the Great Lakes Naval Training Station, where sixty-three thousand men, supervised by 550 officers, were learning to become radiomen, machinists' mates, aviation metalsmiths, torpedomen, and hospital corpsmen. At Eleanor's request, the president stopped at Camp Robert Small, where the first regiment of Negro naval recruits were being trained as gunners, signalmen, yeomen, and quartermasters. The school had been set up in response to Roosevelt's order the previous spring that Negroes must be trained for a variety of positions beyond that of mess men. As the president and first lady watched, the men went through an obstacle course designed to simulate a real battlefield.

The Negro service school at Camp Robert Small was separate from the main service school at the Great Lakes Naval Training Center, in Waukegan. The pattern of segregation required duplication of mess halls, sick bays, school instructors, housing and recreational facilities. "It was a luxury and a waste of manpower that the Navy could ill afford," Dennis Nelson wrote, but it remained in force, because the majority of white personnel desired it, and because the top officers of the navy still believed that abandoning segregation would at best "adversely affect morale, and at worst, result in serious racial conflict and bloodshed."

• • •

That night, as Eleanor flew back to the capital, the president's train reached the Twin Cities, where he visited the night shift of a cartridge plant that was producing six carloads of small-arms ammunition every day. On the walls, a number of striking posters could be seen. "Keep Sharp—We Have an Axis to Grind," "Fifty Caliber Zippers for Slant-Eyed Gyppers." The morale in the plant was infectious. Turning to General Brehon Somervell, the newly designated chief of the Army Service Forces, the president said, "Brehon, that was grand!"

The work of the Twin Cities cartridge plant had been compromised in recent months by a shortage of copper and brass. Years of experience suggested that brass was the only satisfactory material that could be used in the making of cartridge cases. Brass could be cleaned after firing and used over and over again; brass did not rust; brass was flexible. But so astronomical were the ammunition requirements for both the armed forces and lend-lease that by the summer of 1942 several ordnance plants were operating with less than one week's supply of brass. To alleviate the situation, ordnance plants were experimenting with steel cartridges. The problems at first seemed insurmountable—the inelasticity of steel caused the cases to expand and stick in the chamber after firing—but eventually steel proved a suitable substitute.

From Minnesota, the president's train passed through North Dakota and Montana en route to the West Coast. "Life on the train began to get a little cramped," journalist Merriman Smith reported. "The porters burned incense in the Pullmans as the dirty laundry piled up." But the president's spirits remained high as the train wended its way to Fort Lewis, Washington, an army post just outside Tacoma, and to the Bremerton Navy Yard.

When the president arrived at the Boeing plant in Seattle, he was joined by the Boettigers—Anna, John, and Anna's children, Sistie and Buzz. Roosevelt had not seen his daughter for nearly a year; her last visit to Washington had been in the fall of 1941, following Sara's death. Delighting in Anna's presence, the president was in the happiest frame of mind as his open car moved slowly past long lines of men and women engaged in the complex process of producing the B-17 bomber. Twelve months earlier, the first B-17 had rolled down the runway of Boeing Field. Hundreds of spectators had lined the fences and the roads that day to watch the birth of "The Flying Fortress," as the durable B-17 was named. Since that day, with women constituting nearly half of the work force, Boeing had turned out more aircraft per square foot of floor space than any other plant in the United States, earning the company a "joint Army-Navy E" award for excellence.

No single aircraft would contribute more to the American bombing offensive in Europe than the B-17. Between 1940 and 1945, 12,677 B-17s would be built, equipping thirty-three combat groups overseas. On the ground, the B-17 was a strange-looking creature, its sprouted machine guns extending like the quills of a porcupine. In the air, it commanded universal affection from its pilots. It had an excellent high-altitude capacity and the ability to absorb an exceptional amount of battle damage. "This was an airplane you could trust," B-17 pilots testified again and again. "To me," one bomber-group leader said, "the Flying Fortress was, and always will be, the Queen of the Sky. I owe my life to the Queen."

Standing on the Boeing assembly line that day was Inez Sauer, a married woman with two sons who had left behind her life of bridge parties, golf, and country-club luncheons to work in the factory. "My mother was horrified," she recalled. "She said no one in our family has ever worked in a factory. . . . You don't know what kind of people you're going to be associated with. . . . My father was horrified. He said no daughter of his could work in a factory. My husband thought it was utterly ridiculous."

Sauer's mother warned her that she would never go back to being a housewife, and she was right. Working at Boeing changed Sauer's outlook on life; she joined the union, marched in a labor demonstration, learned to respect people who worked with their hands, and came into contact with blacks for the first time in her life. When the war ended, she decided she could not go back to being a "club woman."

That night, the president had dinner with Anna and John; the next morning, Anna accompanied her father to the Kaiser shipyard in Portland, where she christened a new ship, the U.S.S. *Teal,* whose keel had been laid only ten days earlier, thereby breaking every shipbuilding record. The president sat in his open car at the top of the ramp while the hull plates were burned away with torches to free the ship from its berth. At that instant, Anna, remembering the lessons her father had given her in her youth on how to swing a baseball bat, pulled her arm back and swung the bottle. A resounding crack was heard when the bottle broke against the hull.

As the ship floated calmly in the waters of the river, the crowd of workers and dignitaries exploded in applause. "When we finished one of these beautiful ships," a female worker later recalled, "it was inspiring and thrilling. Once it . . . withstood the test of water your whole body thrilled because you'd done something worthwhile."

The U.S.S. *Teal* was the 576th ship build by the Kaiser shipyards in less than eighteen months, a remarkable record that inspired the president to tell the Kaiser employees that he wished "every man, woman and child" in the country could come to Portland to witness what "a wonderful piece of work" they were doing for their country. "With the help of God we are going to see this thing through together," he concluded, with a smile and a wave of his hand.

Standing beside the president, Henry Kaiser could hardly contain his pride. "Just look at those assembly lines," the heavily built man with the full face exclaimed, as he pointed to the ingenious methods which had allowed him to mass-produce cargo ships at a pace undreamed of before the war. The key to Kaiser's success, one of his associates said, was his imagination. "He can mentally visualize a whole vast, complex problem. He has enthusiasm, creative ability and the happy faculty of being unafraid to delegate responsibility. He will tackle anything he thinks is right and will do it without following any beaten path." When, for example, it was discovered that the largest cranes could not carry the immense superstructure of the ship off the assembly line, it was decided to cut the finished structure into four pieces, take each one off the line, and then weld them back together. It was faster to do it this way, even though it meant slicing the ship apart after it was built.

That afternoon, as the president's train headed south to California, Anna returned to her home in Seattle. "Your father missed you when you left," Margaret Suckley wrote her. "The rest of us were less entertaining." For Anna, the days with her father were filled with wonder. "It was almost too good to be true to have Father out here," she answered Margaret, "and we all felt that he was getting real rest despite the many inspection trips."

In California, the president journeyed to the Douglas Aircraft plant in Long Beach, where bombers and C-54 cargo planes, the largest transport ships currently in production, were being turned out at the phenomenal rate of four hundred per month. As his car entered the air-cooled building, a blackout structure with no windows, the Douglas executives gaped in amazement. Cheers and handclapping followed him through the plant as stunned men and women realized that the man in the green car was truly FDR.

The Douglas plant had been slow to hire women and slow to make them feel welcome when they first arrived. The women were "the lipsticks" or "the dollies" to the men. "The factory's no place for women," the new arrivals were told. "The happiest day of my life," one supervisor said, "will be when I say goodbye to each one of you women as I usher you out the front door." Every day for the first few weeks, as the women walked by the assembly line on their way to the washroom, the men whistled and hooted. When the catcalls continued despite repeated requests to stop, the women took matters into their own hands. As the men streamed out the door for lunch, the women were waiting. Every time a handsome young man walked by, they whistled and shouted. "Look at Tarzan! Isn't his body beautiful!" The men's antics ended abruptly. The women felt better, and production went up. "We may have thought a year ago we could never get along with them," one executive admitted. "Today we know we can never get along without them."

Eleanor rejoined Franklin in Fort Worth, Texas, and they journeyed together to the Consolidated plant, where the longest assembly line in the world was turning out B-24 Liberator planes. Produced in greater quantities than any other American plane, the B-24 would operate over more fronts for a longer period than any enemy bomber. Once again, Eleanor took special pleasure in hearing that women were "doing a swell job, better than they expected." Supervisors reported that women were more patient with detail, more capable of handling the repetitive jobs without losing interest, more eager to learn, less prone to hide their greenness, more willing to ask directions and take instruction. At Consolidated, one supervisor admitted, the production rate shot up immediately in the departments where they used large percentages of women. Mrs. Frances De Witt was one of Consolidated's best lathe operators. "I never did anything more mechanical than replace a blown-out fuse," she said. "But after the war broke out I wasn't satisfied with keeping house and playing bridge." After three weeks of craft school, she was hired by Consolidated. "The foreman asked if I could run a lathe. I said, 'I can, if you'll show me how.' He did, and I've been at it ever since."

"I'll deny it to the end of my days if you use my name," one male executive told a female reporter. "Listen, girl, I'll deny that I ever saw you. But if you want to know how I feel, I'll tell you. . . . If I had my way now, I'd say 'to hell with the men. Give me women.' "

Everywhere she went, Eleanor later reported, the plant managers wanted to know how and where they could get more women. "I hardly saw a man," she said, "who did not speak to me about the need for women in production." Her answer was always the same; she urged that special community services be established to alleviate the burdens on working mothers, and that companies make a firm commitment to the new policy of "equal pay for equal work" recently enunciated by the War Labor Board. In a letter to Joe Lash written from Fort Worth, Eleanor reported that "FDR seemed happy with his trip and much amazed at the increase in women workers. At last he is interested in nursery schools, family restaurants, etc."

For Negro women, the factory offered a respite from domestic servitude. "Had it not been for the war," a black riveter, Sybil Lewis, observed, "I would never have had the opportunity to work in different kinds of jobs and make the kind of money I made." Brought up in a segregated town in Oklahoma, Lewis had begun working at fourteen as a maid, the only job the women in her family had ever held. When the war came, she headed west, riding behind a curtain on a segregated train until she found a job at Douglas Aircraft. Though the jobs Negro women were given were all too often the most grueling and dangerous ones the factory had to offer—working with ammunition and gunpowder, poisonous plastics and acetone, sealing mud and nauseating glue—they relished the camaraderie and better wages of the factory in contrast to the loneliness and low pay of domestic work.

Within the factories and shipyards, prejudice against blacks abounded. The discrimination Sybil Lewis experienced, she later observed, was not "so much about being a woman," but about being a Negro. One white woman spoke for many when she said: "I still don't like to be near them, my mother is the same way. I can't say that the way I feel is right. I suppose it isn't, but I have been taught that way and that is the way I feel." Another woman told reporters she had tried to overcome her negative attitude but could not. "It don't make me no difference how hard I try, I just can't get used to working with niggers. I'll be so glad when this war is over and we don't have to do it no more."

In June, several thousand white workers at Hudson Naval Ordnance in Detroit had gone out on a wildcat strike, shutting down 60 percent of the plant's production, because eight Negro employees, in accordance with seniority rights, had been assigned to machines formerly operated by white men. "You can't expect the plant to adopt a missionary attitude concerning its colored employees," one plant manager said. "We can't buck the whole system. This is a plant and we are forced to produce. We can't produce if our employees are going to hold up production while they fight out the race question."

Still, Eleanor clung to the hope that, with daily contact, attitudes would change, and to some extent they did. "At first I thought I just couldn't do it," one female employee from Texas admitted, "but I wouldn't want to work with nicer people. If every white man could be as nice and polite as that colored man who works with me, he'd have something to be proud of. . . . I always thought colored people were not clean and smelled bad and weren't as good as white people, but these I have worked with at the plant are just as good as anybody." Another white woman, who could barely tolerate the idea of associating with Negroes at the start, found herself respecting and even liking a Negro colleague. "Alice," she told her supervisor in a tone of astonishment, "I said good night to Mary tonight when she left. I actually told a colored girl good night!"

As Eleanor traveled through the South with the president, she was besieged with angry charges from whites about the "Eleanor Clubs" that black servants were supposedly forming in her honor, demanding higher wages, more privileges, and fewer hours. In every town she had visited over the past year, she was told that an Eleanor Club had been formed soon thereafter, committing the Negro cooks and maids to a set of club rules which changed their relationship to their white employers. In Florida, Eleanor was told, a maid stopped bringing in wood for the fire because the other maids in the neighborhood had jumped on her and told her she could not belong to the Eleanor Club if she continued to do extra chores that were not part of the job. In South Carolina, a maid began coming in the front door instead of the back, telling her boss that this was the rule of the Eleanor Club.

"All the Negroes are getting so uppity they won't do a thing," one woman from North Carolina asserted. "I hear the cooks have been organizing Eleanor Clubs and their motto is 'A white woman in every kitchen by Christmas.' " In Louisiana, it was said, a white woman drove to her maid's house and asked her to come do the washing. The maid pointed to a mirror on the wall and said, "You look in that and you'll see your washerwoman. Now you get out of here!" In an army camp in the South, Eleanor was told, a Negro maid working for an officer and his wife had set an extra place for dinner. When she was asked who the place was for, she replied, "In the Eleanor Club, we always sit with the people we work for." In the midst of a fancy dinner party, another story went, the maid refused to continue serving when a derogatory remark about the president was made.

After hearing these stories from one end of the South to the other, Eleanor asked the FBI to investigate whether Eleanor Clubs truly existed, and if so, what they were doing. After a comprehensive field investigation, the FBI concluded definitively that, despite the great sweep of rumors, not a single Eleanor Club actually existed. The answer to the mystery, the FBI observed, lay in the troubles white women were experiencing retaining their Negro servants in the face of the higher-paying factory jobs the war had made available. "It was but logical that the blame was to be placed upon something or somebody," the FBI wrote. And that somebody was Eleanor, considered by many Southerners "the most dangerous individual in the United States today." Eleanor was relieved to receive the FBI report, fearing that such clubs would not advance the cause of the Negro maids. "Instead of forming clubs of that kind," she wrote, "they should enter a union and make their household work a profession."

• • •

While they were traveling together in the South, Franklin approached Eleanor with the idea that they should try once more to live as man and wife. As Jimmy Roosevelt later heard the story, Franklin turned to Eleanor late one night and asked her to stay home more; to commit herself, since civilian travel was restricted anyhow, to their life in the White House; to be his hostess at his cocktail hour, and do things with him on the weekends.

"I think he was really asking her to be his wife again in all aspects," Jimmy observed. "He had always said she was the most remarkable woman he had ever known, the smartest, the most intuitive, the most interesting, but because she was always going somewhere he never got to spend time with her. But now that Missy was gone and his mother was dead and Harry had Louise he was lonely and he needed her."

Franklin's request threw Eleanor into a tumult of conflicting emotions. For years, her most profound yearnings had centered on her husband; for years, there was nothing she would have cherished more than the prospect of intimacy, the chance to create a shared emotional territory in which each could depend on the other for love and support. But over the past decade, the experience of becoming a political force in her own right had brought with it a profoundly different sense of self—of independence, competence, and confidence. If joining her husband now meant giving up the life she had built for herself, it seemed a great deal to ask.

Eleanor told Franklin she would think over his request. She was leaving the train the next morning to fly to the West Coast to visit Anna and John, but when she returned to Washington, they would talk again.

• • •

From Texas, the presidential train turned east, stopping at Camp Shelby, near Hattiesburg, Mississippi, and Camp Jackson in South Carolina, where the president inspected the troops at huge parade grounds. For generations, the buttons on the uniform coats of the officers, as well as the distinctive military insignia, had been made of brass. Brass was considered ideal for ornamental purposes, because it resembled gold when it was polished. But as the supply of copper became inadequate to meet vital ammunition needs, the army was forced to replace its shiny bronze buttons with olive-drab plastic buttons. The shortage of silk, which had been largely imported from Japan, necessitated another change. Though silk had, because of its special weathering and draping qualities, long been the army's material of choice for banners and ribbons for decorations and medals, the army had to accept a rayon substitute.

But far more important than the ceremonial look of the officers was the striking increase in the size of the army. Almost four million men had been added to the army in 1942, bringing the total strength from 1.6 million to 5.4 million. Thirty-seven new divisions had been brought into being. The number of soldiers in the ground arms had doubled; the number in the service branches and the Air Corps had multiplied more than fourfold.

On Thursday, October 1, after traveling two weeks and nearly nine thousand miles, the president returned to Washington, where he reported on his trip at a special press conference. Seated in his shirtsleeves at his desk, smoking a cigarette from a long holder, he was in high spirits as he praised the morale of the American people. Reporters observed "no appearance of strain from the consecutive nights spent on the train." His voice was "smooth and unruffled" as he described his long trip in excellent detail.

The following week, he shared his impressions with the nation in a long, chatty radio address. The main thing, he observed, was that "the American people are united as never before in their determination to do a job and do it well." He went on to describe some of the places he had been, skillfully mingling praise for the positive things he had seen with criticism for employers who were still unwilling to hire women and blacks. "I was impressed by the large proportion of women employed, doing skilled manual labor running machines," he said. "Within less than a year from now, there will probably be as many women as men working in our war production plants." But in some communities, he charged, employers were still reluctant to hire women or blacks or older people. "We can no longer afford to indulge such prejudices or practices," the president concluded. Eleanor could not have been more delighted had she written the speech herself.

True to her word, Eleanor arranged to have dinner alone with Franklin on Friday night, October 9. She recognized that, with Sara and Missy gone, Franklin needed her in ways he hadn't needed her in years. Even before their talk in Fort Worth, she had noted his more frequent invitations to join him for meals. It was clear that he was trying to forge anew the bond that had once held them so close. She, too, was at a peculiar crossroads. In recent months the nature of her relationships with three of her closest friends—Joe Lash, Harry Hopkins, Lorena Hickok—had been altered significantly, leaving her more alone than ever before.

Still, she could not accept her husband's proposal. Too much had happened over the years to allow her to begin again. There were too many hurts to forget.

It was now nearly four decades since their courtship, when Eleanor had believed their life together would be happy and untroubled. Things were much changed. Over the years, the very qualities that had first attracted Franklin and Eleanor to one another had become sources of conflict in their marriage. After initially valuing Franklin for his confidence, charm, and sociability, qualities that stood in contrast to her own insecurity and shyness, Eleanor had come to see these traits as shallow and duplicitous. After being drawn to Eleanor's sincerity, honesty, and high principles, Franklin had redefined these same attributes as stiffness and inflexibility. "She bothered him because she had integrity," Anna Rosenberg observed. "It is very hard to live with someone who is almost a saint. He had his tricks and evasions. Sometimes he had to ridicule her in order not to be troubled by her."

If at first each had found in the other a complementary aspect of something lacking in his or her self, as time went by the tendency developed to disavow and demean the opposite qualities in the other, to be irritated rather than delighted by their differences. "You couldn't find," Anna Boettiger mused, "two such different people as Mother and Father." Whereas Franklin, Anna thought, had "too much security and too much love," with parents and relatives and servants all doting on him, Eleanor seemed forever starved for love.

The hidden springs of Eleanor's insecurity had disrupted her marriage from the very beginning. The honeymoon trip to Europe was not easy. Though there were many good days, filled with marvelous sights and warm companionship, Eleanor found herself ill at ease in the presence of other young tourists. At Cortina, high in the Dolomites, Franklin decided to spend the day climbing a mountain. When Eleanor, having no confidence in her climbing ability, declined to join him, he invited a fellow guest at the hotel, a handsome young woman named Kitty Gandy, to go along.

"She was a few years his senior," Eleanor later explained, "but she could climb and I could not, and though I never said a word I was jealous beyond description." As the day wore on, Eleanor grew more and more restless. By the time the exuberant hikers returned to the hotel, filled with stories of all they had seen, Eleanor had lapsed into an irritable and aggrieved silence—a pattern of behavior that would be repeated hundreds of times in the years to come.

Fear of failure prompted Eleanor again and again to give up too soon on a variety of activities which would have allowed an easy companionship with her husband. After days of practicing golf on her own, she allowed Franklin's teasing remarks about her awkwardness to turn her away from trying to play again. A minor crash into a gatepost kept her from driving for more than a decade. The fear of losing control kept her from enjoying sledding or horseback riding. Terror of the water ruled out the pleasures of swimming and sailing. Nor, for reasons that even she did not understand, did Eleanor ever allow herself to learn enough about Franklin's stamp collection to share the fun of it. "If I had it to do over again," Eleanor confessed years later, "I would enter more fully into Franklin's collecting enthusiasm. I would learn all I could about stamps. Every collector appreciates the real interest of his family in what he is doing."

Even more troubling to the young couple's marriage was Eleanor's lack of ease in social situations. Though she was thoroughly comfortable in serious discussions with older people about politics or philosophy, she found herself incapable of casual conversation with people her own age. "I think I must have spoiled a good deal of the fun for Franklin because of this inability to feel at ease with a gay group," Eleanor admitted. The story is told of the evening she and Franklin went together to a large party. She was so impatient with the small talk that she left early and alone. Arriving at her doorstep without her key, she sat on the stoop, irritable and peevish, until Franklin sauntered in at three in the morning. Once again she had, by her own actions, made herself the wronged one.

Franklin tried on occasion to accommodate his wife's needs. Recognizing how much pleasure she received from her friendship with her aunt Maude Gray, he invited Maude to visit Campobello. "I know what a delight it is to Eleanor to have you," he told Maude, "and I am afraid I am sometimes a little selfish and have had her too much with me in past years and made life a trifle dull for her really brilliant mind and spirit." But on the whole, the ever-cheerful Franklin found Eleanor's manifold insecurities hopelessly bewildering, and though it troubled him to see her unhappy and depressed, he blithely assumed that if he left her alone everything would be all right.

Perhaps, as Franklin hoped, everything would have eventually worked out had Eleanor been able to derive confidence and comfort as a mother. But from the moment the children were born, the rivalry between her and Sara had been transformed into a battle over the children, a battle so fierce that the children ultimately became an additional force pulling Franklin and Eleanor apart.

This was the fertile soil that produced Franklin's affair with the young and beautiful Lucy Page Mercer. As is often the case, the affair was more a symptom of disturbance within the marriage than a disturbance itself. Franklin had married when he was "young and immature," Eleanor's cousin, Corinne Robinson observed, "and had a life sheltered by Mama. Eleanor and Franklin were both smart and had produced many children and on the whole it was a good marriage but it lacked the 'délicieux.' The affair with Lucy provided the danger and excitement that was missing from Franklin's life."

• • •

Lucy had first entered the Roosevelts' lives in the winter of 1914, when Franklin and Eleanor were living in Washington. Pregnant with her fourth child, Eleanor was overwhelmed by the voluminous social invitations to be sifted, accepted, and declined. The protocol was complicated; as assistant secretary of the navy, Franklin held an important social position which had to be maintained at all times. To help her with her correspondence, Eleanor hired Lucy Mercer to assist her three mornings a week.

Though she was only twenty-two, Lucy was well suited for the position. Her father, Carroll Mercer, was descended from a distinguished Catholic family which included the founders of Maryland. Her mother, Minnie, was rated by one social reporter "easily the most beautiful woman in Washington." As a young girl, Lucy was educated in elite private schools, but by 1914 the family had fallen on hard times. Carroll Mercer drank too much; the marriage was in trouble; and there was little money left. Lucy needed the income the job with Eleanor would provide. In return, she brought to her duties the intimate knowledge of Washington society which Eleanor lacked.

Lucy was tall and statuesque, with blue eyes, abundant brown hair, and a rich contralto voice that belonged in the best drawing rooms. The Roosevelt children welcomed the days Lucy came to work. "She was gay, smiling, and relaxed," Elliott recalled. "She had the same brand of charm as Father, and everybody who met her spoke of that—and there was a hint of fire in her warm dark eyes."

From the beginning, Lucy told her friend Elizabeth Shoumatoff, she and Franklin were drawn to one another. "Lucy was a wonderful listener," Anna later observed; "she knew the right questions" to ask; she had a gift of following the hidden meanings within conversations while appearing to be sailing on the surface. She was intelligent and responsive without being judgmental as Eleanor tended to be. Whereas Eleanor would invariably interrupt Franklin with "I think you are wrong, dear," Lucy saw no need to correct his stories, or to redirect the conversation. She enjoyed everything he had to say—light or lofty, silly or serious.

Almost imperceptibly, the story is told, the relationship slid from an affectionate friendship into an affair. Franklin was not by nature one to take great risks in his personal life, but at some point, it seems, he realized that his love for Eleanor and his children was not enough. "Of course he was in love with her," Lucy's close friend Eulalie Salley observed. "So was every man who ever knew Lucy." The need for camouflage gave ordinary conversations an air of mystery and romance which most likely increased Lucy's desirability to Franklin.

Fired by the intrigue, Franklin devised various stratagems to spend time with Lucy. In the late afternoons, they would meet in the hills of Virginia and motor together through the dirt roads and small hamlets of the countryside. Franklin's excursions did not escape the prying eyes of Theodore Roosevelt's daughter Alice Longworth. "I saw you 20 miles out in the country," she teased him. "You didn't see me. Your hands were on the wheel but your eyes were on that perfectly lovely lady." "Isn't she perfectly lovely?" a smitten Franklin replied. For the rest of their days, intimacy and country roads would be so joined that whenever Franklin and Lucy got together they set out for a long ride.

In the summers, with Eleanor and the children in Campobello, Franklin grew bolder; accompanied always by a circle of friends, he brought Lucy sailing with him on the river, to small dinner parties at night, to picnics in the woods. In love, he was determined to do what he wanted. As the months went by, Eleanor noticed the growing attraction between Franklin and Lucy. Nervous about leaving Franklin alone, she kept delaying her departure for Campobello in the summer of 1917. She finally left, but not without chiding Franklin that he seemed almost anxious to have her go. "You were a goosy girl to think or even pretend to think that I don't want you here *all* summer," Franklin wrote from Washington, "because you know I do! But honestly *you* ought to have six weeks straight at Campo, just as *I* ought to. . . ."

The next autumn, Eleanor's suspicions were confirmed. Franklin had returned from an inspection trip to Europe with pneumonia. It was then, while unpacking his trunks, that she came upon the devastating bundle of love letters from Lucy.

• • •

Shortly after the affair ended in 1918, Lucy left Washington to become a live-in governess for the six small children of a wealthy fifty-five-year-old widower, Winthrop Rutherfurd. Rutherfurd was a member of an old and distinguished family which included Peter Stuyvesant of New York and John Winthrop of Boston. An avid sportsman, Rutherfurd divided his days between an elegant town house in New York; an old estate at Allamuchy, New Jersey, surrounded by thousands of acres of deer park and mountain slopes;

and Ridgeley Hall, a winter home in Aiken, South Carolina, just across from the Palmetto Golf Club.

Lucy brought warmth and grace to the Rutherfurd household. Within weeks of her arrival, the children and the father alike had fallen in love with her. And the feeling was mutual; on February 13, 1920, Winthrop Rutherfurd and Lucy became man and wife. Two days later, Eleanor took note of the marriage in a letter to her mother-in-law. "Did you know Lucy Mercer married Mr. Wintie Rutherfurd . . . ?" she asked, in a chatty tone that gave no hint of the immense relief the news of the marriage must have brought.

With the removal of Lucy Mercer, Franklin and Eleanor made a renewed commitment to their marriage. For months thereafter, Franklin tried to do the things he knew would please Eleanor. He took to coming home earlier in the evenings, spending more time with the children, accompanying Eleanor to church. For her part, Eleanor made an effort to enjoy herself at parties, to be the gay companion he so desired her to be. Their life resumed. In appearance, everything was as it had been.

Beneath the surface, however, everything had changed, in both their individual lives and their relations to each other. Franklin's friends believed that his love affair had had a permanent effect upon his personality. "Up to the time that Lucy Mercer came into Franklin's life," Corinne Robinson Alsop observed, "he seemed to look at human relationships coolly, calmly, and without depth. He viewed his family dispassionately, and enjoyed them, but he had in my opinion a loveless quality as if he were incapable of emotion. . . . It is difficult to describe," Corinne said, "but to me it [the affair] seemed to release something in him." Corinne's husband, Joe Alsop, agreed, observing that Roosevelt's disappointment in this great love helped to banish the superficial aspects of his personality; "he emerged tougher and more resilient, wiser and more profound even before his struggle with polio."

Though the discovery of the affair had liberating dimensions for Eleanor, leading her to forge a new sense of herself in the world, the hurt would endure forever, finding expression in sudden flashes of anger, unpredictable changes of mood, immobilizing depressions. "I have the memory of an elephant," she once told a friend. "I can forgive but I cannot forget." Among the belongings on her bedside table when she died in her New York apartment in 1962, seventeen years after her husband had died, was a faded clipping of the poem "Psyche" by Virginia Moore.

> The soul that has believed
> And is deceived
> Thinks nothing for a while,
> All thoughts are vile.
>
> And then because the sun
> Is mute persuasion,
> And hope in Spring and Fall

Most natural,
The soul grows calm and mild,
A little child,
Finding the pull of breath
Better than death . . .
The soul that had believed
And was deceived
Ends by believing more
Than ever before.

Across the top of the clipping, in Eleanor's scrawled hand, was a single notation: "1918."

• • •

In the end, it was yet again Eleanor's inability to forget that proved the stumbling block to her acceptance of her husband's proposal that they live together again as man and wife. Though she still loved him deeply, she was afraid to open herself once more to the devastating hurt she had suffered before.

Nor, after establishing her independence, could she go back to depending on one person for fulfillment and satisfaction. Moreover, she knew that if she stayed at home the lack of productive activity and contacts with new people would be deadly, and she would undoubtedly find herself irritated by the adoring women who surrounded Franklin—Princess Martha, Laura Delano, Margaret Suckley.

When the time came to answer, Eleanor, in characteristic fashion, never mentioned the proposal directly. Instead, she opened the conversation with an impassioned plea for a new war-related assignment that would allow her to move about the country and to travel abroad. She wanted desperately, she said, to be given the chance to visit American troops in England.

It must have been immediately obvious to Roosevelt what his wife was trying to say. With no further discussion, he told her she could travel to England on an extended inspection tour as soon as the proper arrangements were made.

So it happened, in a twist of irony, that the consequence of Franklin and Eleanor's renewed closeness in the summer of 1942 was Franklin's willingness, after months of Eleanor's fruitless pleading, to let her undertake a journey to the war front that would take her thousands of miles away for many weeks. And from Eleanor's excited reaction to the news it was clear that Franklin's attempt to forge a new bond between them had come to a gracious but definite end.

CHAPTER 15

"WE ARE STRIKING BACK"

"I confide my Missus to the care of you and Mrs. Churchill," the president wrote the prime minister just before Eleanor set off on October 21, 1942, for the inspection trip to England she had longed to take for more than two years. "I know our better halves will hit it off beautifully."

It was twilight when Eleanor arrived at London's cavernous Paddington Station, where a large crowd awaited the special train the prime minister had sent to carry her from the coastal city of Bristol. For days, Eleanor's forthcoming visit had provoked much comment in the London press. "After nine years as [first lady]," the *Evening Standard* observed, "she is more popular than at the beginning of her first term." To residents of London's East End, Eleanor's trip was much anticipated. Impressed by stories of her commitment to the poor, they hoped she would visit them to hear their troubles.

As the first lady stepped from the train, a tall and smiling figure in a long black coat and blue-fox furs, she was met by an official welcoming party which included the king and queen, the duke of Kent, Foreign Minister Anthony Eden, and General Eisenhower, who was in London preparing for the Allied invasion of North Africa, which he had been chosen to lead. "We welcome you with all our hearts," the queen said. As Eleanor drove away in the royal Daimler, the conductor on the train on which she had ridden shook his head in wonderment. "Mrs. Roosevelt never stopped talking and writing for one moment," he said. "I've never seen such energy."

At Buckingham Palace, Eleanor was given an enormous suite specially restored for her visit after a German bombing attack. "We are lost in space, Tommy and I," she wrote Hick that evening, "but we have a nice sitting room with a coal fire and a page takes us hither and yon." The signs of war were everywhere. Before dinner the first night, Eleanor was handed her own ration card and assigned a bed in a shelter; the tub in her bathroom bore a five-inch mark above which the water was not allowed to go, and the heat in the palace was off until the first of November.

Anxious to get out among the people, Eleanor drove with the king and queen on a tour of London. "I was struck by the area of destruction in the City," she recorded in her diary. "Street after street of destruction of small shop buildings, with people living over them." The queen told Eleanor that the wrecked houses they were passing had been very bad in the first place, but Eleanor, revealing once again her capacity to imagine herself in other people's shoes, observed that, "no matter how bad they had been, they were the homes of people." In one crowded section of the city, where only a third of the population was left, she noted sadly that "each empty building speaks of a personal tragedy."

Refreshed after a night's sleep, Eleanor went to the Red Cross Club in London, where hundreds of American soldiers gathered to join in conversation, with shouts of "Hi Eleanor" rising from all parts of the packed room. The morale of the boys was good, she observed; their chief complaints related to the slowness of the mail service from home and the lack of warm woolen socks. With only thin cotton socks, their feet were constantly blistered, and this was one of the reasons, they told her, that they had colds. Eleanor promised to see what she could do. "I know you want heavier socks but don't expect this change too soon," she warned. "You know how the Army hates to change." With this remark, which proved her a "regular," the assembled doughboys gave her a standing ovation.

True to her word, Eleanor approached General Eisenhower the next evening. Eisenhower checked with his quartermasters the following day and discovered there were two and a half million pairs of woolen socks waiting in the warehouses. He promised the first lady they would be distributed at once. "I have already started the various commanders on a check-up to see that no man needs to march without proper footgear," he pledged. Feeling useful at last, Eleanor was overjoyed.

In the days that followed, Eleanor was on the go, visiting army camps and talking with women in every line of work. The previous December, over Churchill's resistance, civilian conscription of women had begun, and as a result the British women, even more than their American counterparts, were doing all manner of jobs that had previously been limited to men: repairing trucks, servicing planes, driving tractors, digging ditches, cutting kale, building ships. "I can feel the exhilaration," Eleanor told her readers. "Many of them were hairdressers, typists or housewives once upon a time. They love their new work." In one factory she visited, 80 percent of the workers were women; in the countryside, a female "land army" had been formed to carry out the work of the farmers who had gone off to war; at the Air Transport Auxiliary, women were ferrying new planes from factories to battle stations. "We have not used women as much as you," Eleanor told the British. This was just the sort of thing, she added, that the president would like to know about.

Everywhere she went, Eleanor made a particular effort to visit the day nurseries that had been set up in factories, government buildings, churches, and community centers. As far as she could learn, the British mothers had been reluctant to use the nurseries at first, but the numbers were increasing steadily. Searching for the human details that she knew her husband relished, she questioned teachers, mothers, and children alike, listening attentively as they spoke.

Mrs. Churchill accompanied Eleanor on part of the tour, but the pace was so strenuous that the prime minister's wife found it impossible to keep up. During a visit to the Women's Voluntary Services, a group engaged in the task of distributing clothing sent from America to victims of the bombings, Mrs. Churchill sat down on a marble staircase and waited as her intrepid companion climbed four flights of stairs to chat with the workers. At one point, an English reporter asked Eleanor whether she ever relaxed, slept late, or forgot her obligations. "Not since I can remember," she said. "Why do you ask?" The reporter smiled. "Because I wish you would [rest] now—because *I'm* tired out."

When the touring party reached the countryside, Eleanor climbed on a farm wagon which had only bales of hay for seats; when they arrived at Bovington Airport, she insisted on climbing into a B-17. "I saw every inch of it, even squeezed up into the pilot's seat," she remarked. She looked down into the nose, where the bombardier and the navigator crouched "like animals at bay." She looked past the bomb bays, where the ball-turret gunner was stuffed, "his feet on a level with his ears." She peered into the tail, where the tail gunner rested on his knees. "I found I'm very fat for the pilot's seat," she laughingly noted; "it wasn't made to accommodate an old lady well over 50. I wondered once or twice whether I would ever be able to move forward or backward again."

But it was well worth doing, Eleanor said, even if she got a little muddy and untidy, for it let her feel what each boy in a bombing mission did, and with that image in her mind she could better understand what they were thinking and feeling.

Eleanor enjoyed her time with Mrs. Churchill. She "is very attractive, and has a charming personality—young looking for her age," she noted in her diary, but it was hard to know what she really believed, because she never voiced any opinions publicly. "One feels that she has had to assume a role because of being in public life, and that the role is now part of her, but one wonders what she is like underneath."

She spent a night at Chequers, the prime minister's country home, and dined with the Churchills in London on several occasions. She was particularly amused to see the prime minister with his little grandson, Winston, "who is a sweet baby, and exactly like the PM," she noted. "They sat on the floor and played a game and the resemblance was ridiculous." But tensions between her and Churchill inevitably flared when the conversation turned to politics.

One night, at a small dinner party which included Churchill and his wife, Treasury Secretary Henry Morgenthau, Minister of Information Brendan Bracken, and Lady Limerick of the British Red Cross, the prime minister brought up the subject of Spain. Why couldn't we have done something to help the Loyalists, the antifascist faction in the Spanish Civil War? Eleanor asked Churchill, repeating an argument she had often had with her husband. The prime minister replied that the two of them would have been the first to lose their heads if the Loyalists had won. Eleanor replied that she cared not a whit about losing her head, whereupon the prime minister said: "I don't want you to lose your head and neither do I want to lose mine." At this point, Mrs. Churchill leaned across the table and said, "I think perhaps Mrs. Roosevelt is right." His wife's intervention only increased Churchill's agitation. "I have held certain beliefs for sixty years and I'm not going to change now," he growled. With that he got up, an abrupt signal that dinner was over.

Unaccustomed to having women argue with him in public, Churchill did not know what to make of Eleanor Roosevelt. It was still difficult for him to absorb the extent to which she was an independent force, the most famous woman in America, a person whose opinions were sought after and quoted. Nonetheless, he could see that the British people had fallen in love with her. In his cables to Roosevelt, he described her visit as a triumphant success. "Mrs. Roosevelt has been winning golden opinions here from all for her kindness and her unfailing interest in everything we are doing," he wrote. "We are most grateful for the visit and for all the encouragement it is giving to our women workers. I did my best to advise a reduction of her programme and also interspersing it with blank days, but I have not met with success and Mrs. Roosevelt proceeds indefatigably. . . . I only wish you were here yourself."

Determined to see as many soldiers as she could, Eleanor spent long, tiring days traveling to Red Cross clubs and army camps across the country. "Every soldier I see is a friend from home," she noted in her column, displaying her trademark sincere sentiment, "and I want to stop and talk with him whether I know him or not. When I find we really have some point of contact, it gives me a warm feeling around the heart for the rest of the day."

At an army camp in Liverpool, she inspected a regiment of Negro troops;

she visited their sick bay, cook house, and mess, and was pleased to note that they seemed to be doing very well. Before Eleanor left America, she had heard from several sources that racial tensions were rising in English camps because white Southerners "were very indignant" to find out that the Negro soldiers were not looked upon with terror by English girls. "I think we will have to do a little educating among our Southern white men and officers," she had written Henry Stimson. "It is important for them to recognize that in different parts of the world, certain situations differ and have to be treated differently." Fearful that Eleanor would fan the flames of controversy once she got to England, Stimson had gone to see the president shortly before the first lady was scheduled to leave. In confidence, he asked the president to caution his wife against making any public comment about "the differential treatment which Negroes receive in the United Kingdom from what they receive in the U.S." The president promised to pass the word along, and most likely he did; the only thing Eleanor said about Negroes while she was in England was how well the troops seemed to be.

For Eleanor, a special aspect of her trip was the chance it provided to spend time with her son Elliott, who was stationed with his photo-reconnaissance unit at Steeple Morton, not far from Cambridge. Elliott had come to Buckingham Palace the first night his mother arrived, and the two of them had talked by the fire in her sitting room until 2 a.m. She was delighted to see that her son's snap judgments about the British were being revised in the wake of his growing admiration for the way they were taking the war. Elliott also joined his mother at Chequers, and she journeyed to Steeple Morton to meet his fellow soldiers. After years of worrying about her father's namesake, Eleanor liked the man he was becoming. "He has matured," she wrote Hick, "and will be a good citizen I think."

As Eleanor continued her remarkable ramblings through Bath to Birmingham and back to London, she found herself even more of a celebrity abroad than at home. "The First Lady is receiving the greatest ovation ever paid any American touring Britain," a reporter on the London staff of *Newsweek* observed. "Groups loiter about the American Embassy all day long hoping to catch a glimpse of her. There are spontaneous outbursts of cheers and clapping at stations when she unexpectedly appears."

So positive was Eleanor's press that Hitler's propaganda chief, Joseph Goebbels, felt compelled to issue a directive to all German journalists. "The hullabaloo about Eleanor Roosevelt should be left to die down gradually and should not result in Mrs. Roosevelt's journey being popularized or invested with a certain importance." But Goebbels held no power over the British and American press, which followed Eleanor day after day, quoting her remarks and observations as if she were an elected official in her own right. Back in Washington, Hick was thrilled. "I'm simply delighted with the press you are getting," she wrote Eleanor. "I'm awfully happy about it and so proud of you."

The president, too, was delighted by the success of Eleanor's trip. From

Hyde Park, where he had gone for the weekend before the November off-year elections, he cabled Churchill to thank him for helping to make his wife's visit a triumph. "She has had what I would call an almost unanimously favorable press in this country," Roosevelt proudly announced.

• • •

The 1942 off-year elections took place in an atmosphere decidedly unfavorable to the administration. Polls recorded a general dissatisfaction with the conduct of the war at home and abroad.

Recent news from the Far East had been depressing. In August, the navy had chosen the mountainous island of Guadalcanal for its first offensive in the Pacific. Though the marines had made a successful landing, they soon encountered fierce opposition and were still engaged, two months later, in grisly combat with the Japanese. Losses on both sides were sickeningly high. On the Eastern front, after ten weeks of bloody, hand-to-hand fighting in homes, factories, attics, and cellars, the German drive on Stalingrad was still moving forward. Americans, unaware of Roosevelt's plans for the invasion of North Africa, were frustrated by the apparent lack of movement on a second front.

At home, many people had grievances: farmers complained about walking twenty miles to their county rationing board for a few gallons of kerosene; small businessmen found the burden of regulation heavy; Southern whites viewed the rising racial unrest with alarm; housewives failed to see the war-related necessity of many rationed items; union organizers were upset by the ceilings on wages.

Displeasure with the system of rationing was heightened on October 31, when, just three days before the election, OPA Administrator Leon Henderson announced that, in three weeks' time, coffee would be rationed at the rate of one cup a day for each person over fifteen. The announcement sent a major shock through the country, where eighty-three million Americans considered themselves faithful coffee drinkers, consuming an average of three cups per day. Since coffee had first appeared in seventeenth-century America, when New Amsterdam burghers began to drink it at breakfast instead of beer, it had become an integral part of daily life.

The problem, the OPA tried to explain, was the scarcity of ships: the ships that were being used to haul coffee from Central America and Brazil were needed to carry weapons and soldiers abroad. It all made sense, but the loss was immediate and deeply felt. "So far," a woman from New York wrote, this has been "the wartime measure to have affected one the most."

It was thus an irritated public that went to the polls on Tuesday, November 3. With the pundits predicting a Republican sweep in the Congress, the president was "under no illusions," White House aide William Hassett remarked, "as to the outcome of the result." In Hyde Park, a heavy rain fell as Roosevelt entered the white frame town hall, just off Main Street in the village, to cast his vote. In contrast to other years, when he was accompanied by his wife, his mother, and Missy LeHand, this time, Hassett noted, he was all alone. For Missy, still in her sister's house in Somerville, this was the first election in almost two decades in which she was unable to cast her vote along with the president. Wanting him to know she was there in spirit, she had sent a telegram to Hyde Park earlier that morning: "I am fighting for you."

As the president approached the registration desk to begin the familiar routine, the chairman of the election board, J. W. Finch, peered up over his spectacles. "Name, please?" he asked with a straight face. "Roosevelt," the president replied, with a twinkle in his eye; "I think that's what I said last time." Indeed, he had been saying it for nearly forty years at the same place. "Not so big a vote today," the president observed, upon learning that only 174 of his neighbors had voted so far. "No, a little slow, so far," Finch replied.

The light turnout in Hyde Park was repeated in districts everywhere. The vote proved to be the smallest since 1930, totaling only one-half the number of voters who went to the polls in the last presidential year, 1940. The low turnout favored the Republicans, who picked up forty-four seats in the House, nine seats in the Senate, and a number of governorships. Though the Democrats still retained a slim majority in both houses, there were immediate signs, *U.S. News* reported, "that an unofficial coalition was in the making between anti–New Deal Democrats and Republicans to pluck all budding social reforms from future war legislation."

Though Roosevelt was not happy with the results, he was glad the election was over. "Found the President in high spirits," Hassett recorded on Wednesday morning, "not a trace of the post election gloom which, according to his enemies, should encircle him . . . No bitter word toward anyone." Indeed, at his press conference that Friday he made only one reference to the elections, saying he assumed that "the new Congress would be as much in favor of winning the war as the Chief Executive himself."

• • •

The weekend after the election, the president went to Shangri-la, the presidential retreat in the woods of Maryland, about seventy-five miles from Washington. The rustic camp, built by the Civilian Conservation Corps as a summer camp for boys and girls in the thirties and later known as Camp David, had been fitted out for the president's use in the summer of 1942 after he was told that, with a war on, it was no longer advisable for him to cruise the open waters on his presidential yacht. The retreat consisted of six oak cabins connected by a series of dirt paths. The principal cabin, used by the president and his guests, had a combination living and dining room, a kitchen, four bedrooms, two baths, and a screened-in stone porch at the edge of the woods. Roosevelt chose the name Shangri-la to express his appreciation of the reinvigorating effects of the time he was able to spend in the secret paradise, away from the turmoil and confusion of Washington,

D.C. Settled comfortably on his porch, overlooking the valley, the president was able to relax, arranging his stamps, playing solitaire, reading, talking with friends.

This weekend, however, the president was uncharacteristically tense. His face wore a strained and uneasy look; his buoyancy was diminished. The invasion of North Africa was scheduled to begin on Sunday, November 8, and he was worried. "He knew that it was largely because of his insistence that this invasion was taking place," Sam Rosenman observed, "that on the next day many American lives might be lost," and "he was concerned—deeply." He had ordered the risky endeavor over the opposition of his service chiefs. Aware that he was showing his anxiety, he told Grace Tully simply that he was expecting an important message.

Four thousand miles away, stationed in a command post deep in the tunnels under the Rock of Gibraltar, where the blackness was only partially pierced by feeble electric bulbs and the damp air was stagnant, General Eisenhower was having an equally rough time. This was not the operation he would have chosen; never had anyone undertaken a night landing on a hostile coast so far from home base. Yet, as the commander of the invasion, he was responsible for the lives of the seventy thousand Americans who were steaming through the Atlantic on six hundred ships. Among these was the president's son FDR, Jr., a gunnery officer on the destroyer *Mayrant.* Furthermore, since the convoy was under radio silence, there was no way to tell exactly where it was or if it had been spotted by the menacing line of German submarines that stretched the length of the Middle Atlantic.

Zero hour was sunrise, Sunday morning, November 8, which was Saturday night at Shangri-la. The ever-changing plans called for a three-pronged assault against French North Africa, from Algiers in the mid-Mediterranean to Oran and Casablanca on the Atlantic coast of Africa. Only twelve days out of 365 were fit for debarkation at Casablanca and Oran; the rest of the year, the heavy fifteen-foot-high breakers of the Atlantic surf would make it impossible to land, tossing the ships about like matchwood.

Political ambiguities aggravated the military danger. For months, Roosevelt and his advisers had wrestled with alternative ways to convince the French that the invading force was intended to liberate, not conquer America's former ally. If the Vichy French forces in North Africa opposed the landing with their full strength, a great many lives would be lost and there would be little hope of gaining control. Indeed, aware of the importance of securing some sort of acceptance by the French, Roosevelt insisted that the initial attacks be made by an exclusively American ground force. "The operation should be undertaken on the assumption that the French will offer less resistance to us than they will to the British," he had written Churchill. "We agree," Churchill responded. "We have plenty of troops highly trained for landing. If convenient, they can wear your uniform. They will be proud to do so."

The troops that were heading toward North Africa were carrying with them an astonishing array of material. "This is just to let you know," supply chief General Somervell wrote Eisenhower on the eve of the invasion, "that we have been giving everything we have to outfitting your organization, both here and in England. God knows Ike we wish you the best of luck and outstanding success. The country needs one badly."

In this first encounter with the enemy, the army was determined that American boys have the best equipment their country could give them: the new streamlined Sherman tanks, new multiple gun mounts, amphibious tractors, submachine guns, and a revolutionary rocket launcher named "bazooka" which had so impressed the commander of II Corps, General George Patton, when he first saw it tested, that he demanded it be issued to his troops even though there was no time to teach them how to use it. The ground commanders also insisted on providing each soldier with a staggering supply of items designed to ensure maximum comfort. These included extra wool blankets, sun and dust goggles, dust respirators, mosquito bars, head nets, magnifying glasses, black basketball shoes, rubber boats, bed socks, hip boots, stepladders, and bicycles.

The proliferation of materials had made the loading process in the States a nightmare. At Newport News, Virginia, the central clearing point for the ships, thousands of men were needed to sort through the badly marked crates of stuff that arrived from army supply centers across the land. At one point, twenty-five railway cars were needed just to carry the barracks bags of a single regimental combat team. Unschooled in logistics, inexperienced loaders invariably stored the small-arms ammunition and other cargo needed first in the deepest holds of the ships. Heavy equipment that should have gone into bottom stowage arrived later and was put on top instead.

The chaos of the loading process would be duplicated at the other end, when the time came to unload the ships and send the troops ashore. "It was as though some gigantic overhead scoop full of supplies had suddenly emptied its contents," one military observer noted. "Nothing had been stacked. One box was simply dumped on top of another." Everywhere one looked, there were "boxes, crates, ammunition and gasoline drums piled and scattered."

As the hour of the invasion approached, the tension on the ships mounted. Africa had never seemed so dark and mysterious to the ancient sea-rovers, naval historian Admiral Samuel Morison observed, as she seemed that night to these seventy thousand young men, the great majority of whom had been civilians in 1940 with absolutely no experience at sea.

To make matters worse, the men were so burdened by weapons, ammunition, and equipment—some of the barrack bags were reported to weigh as much as 180 pounds—that they could hardly move, much less run to shore. "I realize," one officer wrote, "that the great American public may not like the idea of their sons going to war without a complete wardrobe akin to the one which Gary Cooper might have in Hollywood, but I also know he can't wrestle it around in North Africa." Indeed, several soldiers were drowned in the landing simply because they were unable to regain their footing after being rolled over by a wave. As the rest of the troops struggled through the surf, more and more stuff was jettisoned. By daybreak, the beaches were strewn with water-soaked bags and ruined equipment.

Had the president been aware of the chaos that attended the American landings, his anxiety would have been even greater. As it was, a thousand times over in that long day, with tense and uneasy eyes, he had glanced at his White House phone, waiting for a call to tell him the invasion had begun. Finally, shortly before 9 p.m., Saturday, November 7, the phone rang. Grace Tully took the call and told the president that the War Department was on the line.

As he reached for the phone, Tully vividly remembered years later, his hand was shaking. He listened intently for several minutes without saying a word. Despite all the difficulties, luck had prevailed. The Atlantic surf was unusually calm. The first wave of landings was accompanied by a minimum of loss. "Thank God. Thank God," the president said. "That sounds grand. Congratulations. Casualties are comparatively light—much below your predictions. Thank God." With a broad smile on his face, he put down the phone and turned to his guests. "We have landed in North Africa," he said. "Casualties are below expectations. We are striking back."

Exultant, the president prepared a message to the nation announcing the successful landing of the American troops. This was the news for which so many had been waiting for so long, General Somervell observed. The U.S. had at last taken the offensive on a large scale. "America is on the march. Not a defensive march. Not a part time campaign. Not a small sector. This is the real thing, the biggest of its kind ever attempted." General George Marshall's wife, Katherine, was in Washington Stadium attending a night football game when the president's announcement came over the public-address system. Suddenly Mrs. Marshall understood why her husband had been so preoccupied. The crowd of twenty-five thousand went wild. "Like the waves of an ocean," she wrote, "the cheers of the people rose and fell, then rose again in a long sustained emotional cry. The football players turned somersaults and handsprings down the center of the field; the crowd went wild. . . . We had struck back."

"*This is it.* Those were the words that raced through the mind of the nation at 9 o'clock on the night of Saturday, November 7th," *Newsweek* observed. "The U.S. had at last taken the offensive on a major scale. In a nation where the sting of defeat had gone deeper than most citizens would admit, this was the best of all possible news. From one end of the country to the other there spread a feeling that now the United States was going to show the world—as it had always done before."

"They followed the North African campaign in the newspapers and on the radio," Winston Estes writes in *Homefront.* "Names of places they dared not try to pronounce became familiar to them. They located a map. They examined action photos in the newspapers." The war had entered their homes.

As if the tide were turning everywhere, the news from the British forces in Egypt was equally positive. At El Alamein, with the help of the three hundred Sherman tanks Roosevelt had sent after the fall of Tobruk, the British Eighth Army, under Field Marshal Bernard Montgomery, had finally gained the offensive. Thirty thousand German soldiers had been taken prisoner; Rommel was in full retreat. All over Great Britain, Eleanor noted in her column, church bells pealed to celebrate the victory. "Now, this is not the end," Churchill told his people. "It is not even the beginning of the end. But it is, perhaps, the end of the beginning."

"Jesus Christ," Steve Early remarked as euphoria swept the land. "Why couldn't the Army have done this before the election!"

In fact, the original date for the attack had been sometime in October, the 30th at the latest. "Please make it before Election Day," Roosevelt had pleaded with Marshall, folding his hands in a mock prayer. But when Eisenhower and his commanders decided to postpone the operation until November 8, five days after the election, Roosevelt didn't say a word. This was a decision that rested with Eisenhower, he told friends, not with the Democratic National Committee.

The euphoria in the States was short-lived. The luck that had accompanied the military phase of the landings disappeared when the politics set in. On the night of the landings, Roosevelt had broadcast a message to the French people in North Africa. "We come among you to repulse the cruel invaders who would remove forever your rights of self government. . . . We come among you solely to defeat and rout your enemies. Have faith in our words. We do not want to cause you any harm."

To buttress America's case that this was a liberation rather than an invasion, arrangements had been made by Roosevelt's man in Algiers, Robert Murphy, for General Henri Giraud, the French general who had recently escaped from a German prison camp, to accompany the American troops and take charge. But when Giraud's arrival was delayed, Murphy turned to the former commander-in-chief of the French navy, Admiral Jean-François Darlan, who happened to be in Algiers visiting a sick son. Darlan had collaborated with the Nazis when the Germans invaded France; now, once again, he bowed to superior force and agreed to cooperate with the American authorities. Though the British did not like the idea of negotiating with a representative of Vichy France, Murphy and Eisenhower believed Darlan could be useful in persuading local French forces to join the Allies. In France, however, the Vichy government, under Marshal Henri Pétain, refused to cooperate. "We are attacked," he announced. "We shall defend ourselves; this is the order I am giving." The confusion was compounded when General Charles de Gaulle, speaking from London for the Free French Forces, bitterly denounced Darlan. "The U.S. can pay traitors but not with the honor of France," he proclaimed. "What remains of the honor of France will stay intact in my hands."

The Darlan deal was vigorously denounced in the United States as well, particularly in liberal circles. "Prostitutes are used," Freda Kirchwey wrote in *The Nation*. "They are seldom loved. Even less frequently are they honored." What appeared to Eisenhower and his commanders as a reasonable military expedient to reduce the fighting by the French was now seen as a serious political error, a form of appeasement. Suddenly, Stimson admitted, "the enormous benefits which that deal brought to us in the immediate laying down of the arms of the French were as nothing compared with the sacrifice in dealing with a member of the Vichy government." In Washington, Henry Morgenthau was apoplectic. "Poor Henry was sunk," Stimson observed. "He was almost for giving up the war which he said had lost all interest for him."

Roosevelt was enraged by the mounting tide of criticism, particularly since it came from those who generally supported him. Sam Rosenman later said he had never seen the president so deeply affected by a political attack. "He showed more resentment and more impatience with his critics throughout this period than at any other time I know about. He so sincerely detested Fascism and Nazism that the charges of undue and unnecessary collaboration with some former Fascists in North Africa were painfully distressing." At times he seemed obsessed by his critics, reading aloud every word of every unfavorable column; at times he refused to talk about North Africa at all, taking escapist pleasure in leisurely dinners and long drives in the country with Princess Martha.

Feeling irritable, Roosevelt decided at week's end, November 13, to take the overnight train to Hyde Park. Though he had to be back in Washington early Monday morning, he knew, with characteristic clearness, that sleeping in his old bedroom would soothe him, as it always did. Accompanied by Harry and Louise Hopkins and Princess Martha, he spent thirty-six hours relaxing over breakfast, talking by the fire, and calling on his cousin Laura Delano, who was convalescing from pneumonia. Despite the frosty temperatures in the Hudson Valley that weekend, he found what he was looking for —warmth, security, and peace of mind.

Returning to Washington with a clear head, he agreed to issue a clarifying statement to the press which removed much of the sting of the criticism. "I have accepted General Eisenhower's political arrangements for the time being," he said. "I thoroughly understand and approve the feeling in the United States and Great Britain and among all other United Nations that in view of the history of the past two years no permanent arrangement should be made with Admiral Darlan. The present temporary arrangement . . . is only a temporary expedient justified solely by the stress of battle."

Meanwhile, the news from the war front was excellent. Both Algiers and Oran were in Allied hands. Allied fighters had driven away German and

Italian dive-bombers. At Casablanca, despite fierce fighting, the U.S. forces had secured their beachheads. The great port of Rabat had fallen. The Allies were plunging into Tunisia. By November 14, a week after the invasion had begun, the Axis forces were in full retreat.

The Allied victory in North Africa, army historians contend, represented the triumph of superior military force, of abundant equipment, weapons, and supplies in the hands of the Allied soldiers. The Desert Fox, Erwin Rommel, would have agreed with this assessment. "The bravest men can do nothing without guns, the guns nothing without ammunition," he once said. "The battle is fought and decided by the quartermasters before the shooting begins."

• • •

"The news from Africa has given the British people a tremendous lift," Eleanor wrote in her column from England. "Everywhere there was a feeling of: 'now we are fighting together.' It seemed to add to the people's courage and was reflected in group after group. The dockers along the Liverpool docks and streets cheered more lustily. One woman said: 'God Bless Your Men; May this be the beginning of the end for old Hitler.' "

By the final days of Eleanor's trip, the soles of her shoes were completely gone, and the newspaperwomen who had followed her for three weeks looked as though they were "about to die." But the trip was an unqualified success. In London, reporter Chalmers Roberts wrote, "Mrs. Roosevelt has done more to bring a real understanding of the spirit of the United States to the people of Britain than any other single American who has ever visited these islands."

There was much debate about how to send her home. Both Churchill and Ambassador John Winant thought it too risky to send her by a commercial flight along the southern route. Her trip had been so publicized that her plane would present a juicy target to the Germans. As the discussions stalled, Roosevelt finally weighed in, telling Churchill to send her as quickly as possible. He wanted her home.

• • •

When Eleanor's plane landed in Washington on November 17, 1942, she saw the Secret Service standing near the waiting cars and, glancing swiftly round, realized, with a tug at her heart, that the president had taken time off to meet her. Her eyes glowed as she stepped from the plane and gave her husband a hug. "I really think Franklin was glad to see me back," she confided in her diary, "and I gave a detailed account of such things as I could tell quickly and answered his questions. Later I think he even read this diary and to my surprise he had also read my columns."

That, after thirty-six years of married life, her husband's simple gesture afforded Eleanor such unconcealed delight, suggests how deeply she still loved him despite the troubles in their marriage. For his part, the president was pleased to have her back, safe and sound and in such high spirits. "I met her at the airport," he cabled Churchill, "and found her well and thrilled by every moment of her visit. My thanks to you and Mrs. Churchill for taking such good care of her."

At noon, Eleanor lunched with Franklin in his office, "which is something I only do on particular occasions," she proudly reported. She gave him the presents she had brought—a shillelagh, a cane from Londonderry, and a tin of Scottish shortbread—and they talked together for more than an hour. That evening, they dined together again, just the two of them, while Eleanor shared with her husband everything she had seen and felt.

Because the war had been brought home to Britain more deeply than it had to the United States, she told her husband, the British people were ahead of us in mobilizing every person to do his part. With women in particular, America was just at the beginning; Eleanor believed there would inevitably be an enormous expansion of the sphere of women's work. The key challenge she saw, after visiting England's day nurseries, was to set up similar programs in America, for "it was useless to expect women to go into factories without making arrangements for care of children."

That Eleanor also shared with her husband her observations on the excellent morale of the Negro troops, who found the prejudice in England much less than in the American South, is suggested by the fact that the president sent a confidential memorandum to Attorney General Francis Biddle that afternoon, asking him to study the constitutional question of universal suffrage. "Would it be possible," he wrote, "for the Attorney General to bring an action against, let us say, the State of Mississippi, to remove the present poll tax restrictions? I understand that these restrictions are such that poor persons are, in many cases, prevented from voting. . . ." Though he cautioned that the issue of race should not be raised, it was clearly a radical suggestion whose implementation twenty-five years later would forever alter the face of Southern political life.

In the days that followed, as Eleanor permitted herself to unwind from her trip, she spent more undistracted time with her husband than she had in months. They dined alone together again in midweek, and on the weekend she traveled with him to Shangri-la. "Quiet day," she recorded, "devoted mostly to reading all the things which had accumulated, from reports to magazines." Surprisingly relaxed, she allowed herself the luxury of spending over an hour and a half having her hair and nails done, something she normally could not stand to do.

It must have been a pleasant interlude for them both, with the president relieved and happy over the course of events in North Africa, and Eleanor jubilant about her trip to England. "It was deeply interesting and I am very glad I went," she wrote her friend Martha Gellhorn. "I did see an enormous amount and I think, with the training which Tommy and I acquired in the past through traipsing around in our own country, we got a great deal of what was underneath as well as what was on top."

But the peripatetic Eleanor was never able to relax for very long; she was home for less than a week when she began traveling again: first to New York overnight, then to Philadelphia to a bond rally for "women in war work," then to Connecticut for a day with the faculty and students at the Connecticut College for Women.

Curiously, years later, when she came to write about her homecoming from England in her autobiography, she mistakenly recalled that the very day she arrived home Franklin had a large dinner for the president of Ecuador. "I should have liked at least one evening to catch up on my family, for I had been away several weeks," she wrote, "but that is a pleasure a public person cannot always count on. Naturally Franklin could make no change in an engagement of this kind which had been arranged weeks before." In fact, the dinner with the president of Ecuador did not take place until a week *after* Eleanor arrived home, and, according to the White House Usher's Diary, Eleanor did not even attend. After taking tea with her husband's foreign visitor, she went off to dine with Joe Lash and then took the overnight train to New York.

In the intervening years, the guilt she may have felt in neglecting her duty as her husband's hostess in favor of a dinner with Joe Lash had been transmuted into anger at officialdom and sorrow for herself. The convoluted memory may also have masked an unwillingness on Eleanor's part to admit that, every time Franklin tried to draw close to her, she invariably moved away.

On Thanksgiving Day, the president and the first lady attended religious services in the East Room. Members of the Cabinet, congressional leaders, and members of the Supreme Court, about two hundred people in all, had been invited for this first-ever service, designed by the president, who personally selected the hymns. Earlier in the week, Eleanor had received a letter from someone asking why the president could not have cut out Thanksgiving entirely this year, adding that there was nothing to be grateful for. "I can think of a thousand things," she countered, "for which I am deeply thankful. I am grateful for the fact that my country is made up of many peoples; that I have an opportunity to show that I really believe that all men are created equal; that our boys whom I love have not fallen; for my husband's strength and for his belief in God."

Though Roosevelt seldom talked about religion, Eleanor was right in recognizing the strength of his belief in God. "His religious faith," Robert Sherwood once observed, "was the strongest, most mysterious force that was in him." Christened an Episcopalian, he had become a warden in the St. James Church in Hyde Park, as his father had before him. Though he did not attend church regularly as president, he drew upon the Bible frequently for inspiration, and greatly enjoyed singing hymns.

For this Thanksgiving service, the president had chosen a few of his favorites: "Faith of our Fathers," "Come, Ye Thankful People Come," and "Battle Hymn of the Republic." The service opened with the president's reading of his Thanksgiving Proclamation, continued with the prayers and lessons from the Book of Common Prayer, and ended with the hymns. It was all well conceived, William Hassett recorded in his diary, "and carried out with dignity and simplicity." The only note of displeasure was voiced by the president later that night. "I selected the hymns, but I couldn't control the singing," he remarked, noting that the Marine Corps band had jazzed up the melodies. "They made a two step out of the Battle Hymn," he noted wryly.

• • •

Three days after Thanksgiving, as ordered by the OPA, coffee rationing went into effect. The order followed a week during which all sales were halted to allow the dealers to make the necessary preparations for the new system. Eleanor promptly announced that the limitation to one cup a person per day would be observed in the White House as well, and that the after-dinner demitasse would be dispensed with. "Personally, whether I drink coffee, tea or hot water, it is all the same to me," she told her press conference. But for millions of Americans who, unlike Eleanor, cared passionately about their coffee, November 29 was "a drab and gloomy day."

By the end of November, government regulations extended into almost every aspect of American life. Shortages of iron and steel prohibited the manufacture of a wide range of consumer items, including electric refrigerators, vacuum cleaners, sewing machines, electric ranges, washing machines and ironers, radios and phonographs, lawn mowers, waffle irons, and toasters. The use of stainless steel was prohibited in tableware. Shoe manufacturers were ordered to avoid double soles and overlapping tips; lingerie makers were limited to styles without ruffles, pleating, or full sleeves.

As the level of public irritation increased, someone had to take the blame, and that someone was OPA Administrator Leon Henderson, the man "who had to step on everybody's toes in order to protect everybody from runaway inflation." Henderson, journalist David Brinkley observed, "was not one of the boys. He was never known to have slapped a back at a Rotary Club luncheon. He was merely a brilliant public servant who took nothing for himself." For Democrats, still smarting from the loss of forty-four seats in the by-election, Henderson was the ideal whipping boy. A powerful bloc of legislators threatened to cut off all OPA appropriations until Henderson was replaced. The word went out: Henderson's days were numbered.

To forestall damage to the OPA, Henderson submitted his resignation. "I have determined to cut my connection with government completely," he wrote the president. "Different times require different types of men. I hope I have been suited to the battling formative period. I am decidedly not adjustable to the requirements of the future as it now begins to disclose its outline." After his resignation, OPA official John Kenneth Galbraith noted, Henderson was "never completely happy again. The public interest had been his mistress, his true love, and now he was cut off from that love. Divorced from public concerns, he did not wholly exist."

Liberals were disconsolate. "We have lost one of the bravest and best of the generals that we possessed," *The New Republic* wrote. "If there was one high ranking leader in government who was right on policy all the way through it was Leon Henderson. He was right on the battle for expansion; right on the steel construction program; right in demanding conversion a year before it was accomplished, right in foreseeing, early, the necessity of adequate price and cost control." To I. F. Stone, Henderson's resignation marked "the second phase of the New Deal retreat, as the alliance with big business in May 1940 marked the first."

The struggle for control of the OPA was accompanied by a struggle over manpower that pitted the military, the War Department, and civilian authorities against one another. In mid-October, War Manpower Commission chief Paul McNutt had come to the president with a plea to combine Selective Service and the U.S. Employment Service under his authority. This was the only way, McNutt argued, to allocate the manpower needed by the armed forces and by essential industry in an orderly manner. The president was sympathetic to the idea of combining both military and civilian manpower under the same supervision, but he knew Secretary of War Stimson was adamant against the idea of the combination and against McNutt, the man who would be king. The whole trouble, Stimson believed, was the softheartedness of the president, who he feared "might quite possibly hate so to hurt the feelings of McNutt he would take McNutt's plan."

Stimson's worries were justified. Though the president delayed the inevitable for a while, offering the manpower job to Ickes one day and then taking it back the next, he finally decided not only to keep McNutt but to give him the authority he needed to accomplish his goals. On December 5, he signed an executive order which centralized all manpower decisions, including selective service, in McNutt's hands. In this way, Roosevelt was able to bridge the gap between the military's desire for compulsory national service and his own desire to keep the job market voluntary as long as possible. With this sweeping order, *The New York Times* observed, McNutt was given "more power over men in this country than anyone has ever exercised before in its history. McNutt may now, in effect, say whether a man is to go into the Army or the Navy, the Marine Corps, Coast Guard, shipbuilding or some other plants or to a farm."

Another key decision was made that fall with the establishment of the Controlled Materials Plan, a bold new vertical system of materials distribution, which finally broke the logjam on raw materials. Designed by a former investment banker, Ferdinand Eberstadt, the CMP brought an end to the continuing battles between contractors for scarce materials. It assured the completion of end products by allotting each contractor the supplies he needed of three critical materials—steel, copper, and aluminum—at the time the contract was signed.

• • •

Eleanor was in New York on December 2, 1942, for the Day of Mourning and Prayer, sponsored by Jewish leaders to focus public attention on the desperate situation of the European Jews. In various synagogues throughout the city, special services were held; in factories and stores, Jewish laborers halted production for ten minutes, and several radio stations went silent.

The Allied world had been aware for months that Jews from all over Europe were being rounded up and deported by train to various "labor camps" in the East, but a new and devastating report from a reliable source had just reached the United States. The report, from German refugee Gerhart Riegner, revealed that a plan had been discussed in the Führer's headquarters to deport all the Jews in German-occupied countries to concentration camps in the East, where they would be "at one blow exterminated in order to resolve, once and for all the Jewish question in Europe." Though officials in the State Department questioned the validity of the report, it did explain the mass killings in Russia, the round-ups in Holland and France, the crowded trains heading toward Poland.

The next morning, sensitized to the situation by the Day of Prayer, Eleanor noticed a small item buried in the paper which filled her, she said, "with horror." In Poland, it was reported, more than two-thirds of the Jewish population had been massacred. News of massive killings in Poland had been leaking out for months, but this was the first time that Eleanor had fully absorbed the enormity of the slaughter. At the beginning of the year, there was only one camp, Chelmno, to which Jews were being deported and killed; by the end of the year, a half-dozen more, including Auschwitz, Belzec, Treblinka, Sobibor, and Birkenau, were in full operation. In the space of twelve months, nearly three million Polish Jews had been murdered.

The Riegner report so terrified Jewish leader Rabbi Stephen S. Wise that he asked for a meeting with the president. The meeting, which included Adolph Held of the Jewish Labor Committee and Maurice Wertheimer of the American Jewish Congress, took place at noon on December 8. According to Held's notes, the president received the group hospitably and immediately launched into a story of his own about his plans for postwar Germany. When the president had finished, Wise read aloud a two-page statement put together by a group of Jewish leaders which stressed that "unless action is taken immediately the Jews of Hitler's Europe are doomed." The group asked the president to issue a warning against war crimes. He readily agreed, and asked the Jewish leaders to draft a statement for him. The meeting drew to a close. Roosevelt had talked 80 percent of the time. "We shall do all in our power to be of service to your people in this tragic moment," he said as he bid the group goodbye.

But all in his power was not very much. In early November, Roosevelt had requested a new war-powers bill that would have given him the power to suspend laws that were hampering "the free movement of persons, property and information into and out of the United States." The intent of the legislation was simply to make it easier for Allied military and industrial consultants to come in and out of the United States, but had it passed it might have opened the gates of immigration to Jewish refugees. Once this was made clear, the bill had no chance. The powerful conservative coalition, strengthened immeasurably by the by-elections, crushed it. "The ugly truth," *Newsweek* observed, "is that anti-Semitism was a definite factor in the bitter opposition to the President's request."

"The question of the Jewish persecution in Europe is being given top news priority by the English and the Americans," Goebbels remarked in his diary that same week. "At bottom, however, I believe both the English and the Americans are happy that we are exterminating the Jewish riff raff."

• • •

A Gallup poll released on December 8 revealed that Eleanor Roosevelt was probably "the target of more adverse criticism and the object of more praise than any other woman in American history." Few Americans, Gallup found, were neutral in their feelings about this powerful woman who had refused to accept the traditional role of a president's wife. Nearly half the people polled were emphatically positive in their approval, pleased with the fact that "she has a personality of her own and doesn't allow herself just to sit at home and do nothing." Her "social consciousness and her efforts on behalf of the poor" drew particular praise, as did her ability "to take a stand on almost any current problem." With equal fervor, however, about two out of five persons expressed strong disapproval of almost everything about her. "She ought to stay at home, where a wife belongs; she is always getting her nose into the government's business; why the way she acts, you'd think the people elected her president; she interferes in things that are not her affair; she is stirring up racial prejudice." With such strong feelings on both sides, the strangest moment came for one field reporter when an old man scratched his head and said, "Never heard of her."

Yet, beneath her public face, beneath the courage, tenacity, and conviction she showed to the world, there remained a striking vulnerability which revealed itself once again during the Christmas holidays. As she raced from one activity to the next, organizing parties for the White House staff and the soldiers who guarded the president, distributing Christmas presents to the poor, attending the children's party of the Kiwanis Club and the tree-lighting ceremony at the Salvation Army, she admitted to Joe Lash that she had come of late years "to dread, not what I do for those I love, but the mass production side & the formal impersonal things I have to do. I'm always with so many people & always so alone inside. . . ."

Still, she kept to her usual back-breaking schedule, even on Christmas Day, which found her, in between church services and luncheon for fifteen at the White House, motoring to Walter Reed Hospital to see the soldiers who had been wounded in the invasion of North Africa. As she went from bed to bed, she was introduced to a young man whose body was so badly burned he could barely speak. The doctor told her he had been a pianist. She said nothing then, but a few weeks later she wrote the commanding officer of the hospital and asked him to tell the soldier whose hands were burned that, as soon as he was able, if he would like to practice on the White House piano, he should feel free to do so. "This was the beginning of a friendship that was to continue until Mrs. Roosevelt's death," the soldier, Hardie Robbins, later recalled. "I didn't know that I would be in the hospital for seventeen months, but after a year's practice on the White House Steinway, Mrs. Roosevelt invited me to lunch with her and the President."

New Year's Eve in the White House was a far more festive occasion than it had been in 1941. As the U.S. approached its thirteenth month of fighting, the president retained, reporters observed, "the same buoyancy of confidence and determination" as he had at his first inaugural. Though America's first year of war had been strenuous, dangerous, and frustrating, it had ended on a triumphant note with the invasion of North Africa.

"Looking back across the year," I. F. Stone wrote, "the President has much with which to be pleased. The task of mobilizing a fairly prosperous and contented capitalist democracy for war is like trying to drive a team of twenty mules, each stubbornly intent on having its own way. Only by continual compromise with the ornery critters is it possible to move forward at all. Examined closely, by the myopic eye of the perfectionist, Mr. Roosevelt's performance in every sphere has been faulty. Regarded in the perspective of his limited freedom of choice and the temper of the country, which has never really been warlike, the year's achievements have been extraordinary."

"At the end of the first year of her intensified war effort," *The New York Times* boasted, "the United States was turning out more war materiel than any other country in the world. She was producing more than Great Britain, more than Russia, more than Germany with all the resources of Europe at her disposal."

To be sure, there was unhappiness and frustration all around. There were complaints that the army was trying to take over the entire civilian economy. War Production Board head Donald Nelson's decision the previous January to leave procurement in the hands of the military, rather than place it in the hands of a civilian agency, was criticized as a sign of weakness. There were concerns about the president's decision in March 1942 that "pending anti-trust suits deemed capable of interfering with war production be dropped and that such suits be avoided as far as possible during the conflict." This action, which brought an end to New Dealer Thurman Arnold's trust-busting division in the Justice Department, was seen by *The New York Times* as "one of the first major indications that the Chief Executive was prepared to subordinate internal social struggles to the prosecution of the war."

And the guardians of small business continued to worry. Despite the passage of the Small Business Act in May 1942, which set up a capital fund of $150 million to finance the conversion of small plants to war work, big business continued to receive the lion's share of military contracts. In 1940, historian John Blum points out, approximately 175,000 companies provided 70 percent of the manufacturing output of the U.S., while one hundred companies produced the remaining 30 percent. By the beginning of 1943, that ratio had been reversed. The hundred large companies formerly holding only 30 percent now held 70 percent of all government contracts.

But with billions of dollars expended on the war effort in 1942, unemployment had virtually ended, and millions of Americans had moved above the poverty line. There was much to celebrate as the year came to an end.

• • •

The New Year's festivities at the White House began with cocktails at seven-thirty, followed by dinner at eight. The Hopkinses, the Morgenthaus, the Sherwoods, and the Rosenmans were there, along with Prince Olav and Princess Martha. Dinner was followed by a private screening of Humphrey Bogart and Ingrid Bergman in *Casablanca.* The film could not have been more appropriate, though few of the guests understood its significance at the time. In ten days, Roosevelt was scheduled to leave for his next secret war conference with Churchill; his destination was Casablanca.

While a mood of good cheer enveloped the White house, Missy LeHand was in a state of despair as she sat alone with her sister in her Somerville house. The first months at home had been difficult. "She would see the news, hear the news, read the news, and it was so hard for her," neighbor Dawn Deslie recalls. "You'd sense the total frustration of someone who'd been at the center of everything and now could not even speak your name." Gradually, Missy had established her own routine. To accommodate her illness, the downstairs den was converted into a bedroom and a full-time nurse was hired. Missy would work with the therapist in the mornings, take rides with friends in the afternoons, and frequently go to the movies at Harvard Square in the evenings.

Still, Missy's heart belonged to the one person who never visited and rarely called. Roosevelt did pen occasional notes to her, but talking with her on the telephone continued to be too painful, wearying, and aching an ordeal. Consumed by his own loss of her working presence, he seemed immune to her incalculably larger hurt. Fate had dealt a nasty turn to both of them, but, whereas Roosevelt had managed to sterilize his memories and suppress his powerful feelings, Missy had only managed to make her memories more vivid and intense.

For hours on end, she would sift through her treasure chest of mementos —the colorful invitations and handwritten notes that served as physical reminders of the glamorous life she had once enjoyed. Over the years, she had kept a signed copy of every major speech the president had delivered. The informal tone of his various signatures revealed the warmth of their relationship. "For Marguerite, who helped to prepare the inaugural," he wrote beside the first inaugural address. "A successful speech though not a gem," he scrawled beside a copy of his Convention Hall speech in Philadelphia in October 1940. "From Who do you think," he teased in sending along another campaign speech that same month. But sorting through mementos of the past must have only reminded Missy of her terrible loss.

"She started crying New Year's Eve about 11:30 and we couldn't stop her," her sister Ann Rochon reported to the president. "And then she had a heart spell and kept calling 'F.D., come, please come. Oh F.D.' It really was the saddest thing I ever hope to see, we were all crying, she was very depressed all through the Holidays and that was the climax. She was expecting you to call Christmas day and when we sat down to dinner her eyes filled with tears and she said 'A Toast to the President's health' and there again in the middle of dinner—another toast to you. She loves your gift and kept saying sweet, lovely, beautiful, I love it. She watches for the Postman every trip. . . . She worries about you all the time."

In the president's study, a round of champagne was served at midnight. The first toast the president offered was his customary one: "To the United States of America." He then added a new toast, which brought a smile to Eleanor's face: "To the United Nations." It meant, she exulted, that "we really are conscious of this bond between the United Nations," a bond that must be strong enough and permanent enough to keep us together in peace as well as war. Eleanor offered the next toast: "To those members of the family and friends who are in other parts of the world and unable to be with us tonight."

The final toast, coming from a man who found it difficult to say what he was feeling at any given moment, was perhaps the most heartfelt. "To the person who makes it possible for the President to carry on," Roosevelt said, as he gestured gently toward Eleanor, an affectionate smile on his face.

CHAPTER 16

"THE GREATEST MAN I HAVE EVER KNOWN"

The President was in high spirits in the early days of 1943. At midnight, January 9, he was set to begin the first leg of a seventeen-thousand-mile top-secret journey to Casablanca for a ten-day meeting with Winston Churchill. The trip promised the drama and adventure upon which his health of spirit depended. He would be the first president in history to fly overseas, the first since Abraham Lincoln to visit his troops in an active theater of war.

The security concerns were agonizing. Casablanca was filled with Vichyites and Axis agents; if the Germans discovered the site of the conference, protection could not be guaranteed. Indeed, it was later determined that the Germans did find out, through a coded message in Berlin, that a summit meeting was taking place at Casablanca, but fortunately, because the word "Casablanca" was translated literally as "white house" instead of the Moroccan city, Hitler assumed the meeting was in Washington.

The more the president's aides fretted over the risk he was taking, the more excited Roosevelt became, his enthusiasm like that of a young child escaping the control of his parents. To preserve absolute secrecy, elaborate deceptions were planned at every point. From Washington, the presidential train headed north as if it were taking Roosevelt and Hopkins on a routine trip to Hyde Park. But once it reached Baltimore, it turned around and came back on a different line, heading south to Miami, where a Boeing Clipper stood ready to carry the travelers across the Atlantic to North Africa. From his window, Roosevelt glimpsed the jungle of Dutch Guiana, the vast Amazon River, and the western rim of the Sahara Desert.

Equally merry, Churchill was heading toward Casablanca in a Liberator bomber. Observing the prime minister's high spirits, Lord Moran noted that, whenever he got away from his red dispatch boxes, he put his cares behind him. "It's not only that he loves adventure; he feels, too, at times that he must 'let up' . . . shed for a little the feeling that there are more things to do in the 24 hours than can possibly be squeezed in." Perhaps, Moran suggested, the president also had that feeling. "It's the instinct to escape, to take a long breath. Besides, neither of them, in a way, have ever grown up."

Not even the crude accommodations on the flight managed to dampen Churchill's mood. In the stern of the unheated bomber, two mattresses were stretched side by side, one for the prime minister, the other for Lord Moran. In the middle of the night, Moran awoke with a start to find Churchill crawling down into the well below. He had burned his toe on the red-hot metal connections of an improvised heating arrangement placed at the foot of his mattress. Hours later, Moran awoke again to discover a shivering prime minister on his knees, trying to keep out the draft by putting a blanket against the side of the plane. "The P.M. is at a disadvantage in this kind of travel," Moran wryly noted, "since he never wears anything at night but a silk vest. On his hands and knees, he cut a quaint figure with his big, bare, white bottom."

The site of the conference was the Anfa Hotel, a creamy-white structure shaded by palm trees, overlooking the Atlantic. For weeks, the soldiers of General Patton's Third Battalion had worked to surround the hotel and its environs with two lines of heavy barbed wire. If anyone so much as approached these lines, he risked being shot by hundreds of American infantrymen stationed on the roofs. Heavy anti-aircraft batteries were deployed throughout the area. Every morsel of food and every drop of liquor to be consumed by the president and the prime minister had been tested by medical officers and then placed under heavy guard. Still, Patton remained feverishly nervous about the whole affair. "I hope you'll hurry up and get the hell out of here," he raged at Dr. McIntire the day of the president's arrival. "The Jerries occupied this place for two years and their bombers know how to hit it. They were around ten days ago and it's a cinch they'll be back."

The president and the prime minister were installed in separate villas fifty yards apart. The president's villa boasted a two-story living room with French windows that looked out on a luscious orange grove, a master bedroom with heavy drapes and a sunken bathtub, and two bedrooms on the second floor: one for Harry Hopkins and the other for Elliott and FDR, Jr., who had been summoned to Casablanca to join their father. The president had also requested the presence of Hopkins' twenty-one-year old son, Robert, who was stationed in Tunisia as a combat photographer. For young Robert, whose parents were divorced when he was seven and who had rarely seen his father while he was growing up, the chance to share daily meals and conversation was a great treat.

Within minutes of the president's arrival, Churchill was at the door, ready for a drink before dinner. As always, the two friends were delighted to see one another. "Father was . . . not a bit tired," Elliott recalled. "He was full of his trip, the things he'd seen." Relief and pleasure were evident in the glow of his eyes and the smile on his face. Here in Casablanca, there was no need to think about Ickes or Stimson or Morgenthau, no need to worry about the nagging concerns of politics.

Through a relaxed, candlelit dinner, the conversation flowed. The talk was of Stalin and the Eastern front. Roosevelt had hoped that Stalin would agree to join the summit, but the Russian leader had cabled that he could not leave his country in the midst of the Battle of Stalingrad. For five months, the German Sixth Army, victors in Belgium and Holland in 1940, had been engaged in savage fighting in and around Stalingrad. In September, Nazi dive-bombers had set fire to large portions of the city, and the German army had rammed its way through the Russian defenses in the northwestern sector. "Stalingrad makes me ashamed," Eleanor had written Hick in October, at the height of the battle, commenting that, in the absence of a second front, the Soviet forces were carrying the brunt of the land fighting against the Germans.

Somehow, the Russians had managed to hang on, however, and in late November, the Red Army had launched a counteroffensive which cut the German army in two, trapping nearly three hundred thousand German soldiers without food, supplies, or ammunition. When Roosevelt and Churchill met in Casablanca, German rations had been reduced to a few ounces of bread a day, and more than ninety thousand German troops had died from starvation. It was now only a matter of days until German Field Marshal Friedrich von Paulus would be forced to surrender his huge German force. "After nearly three and one half years of victories, conquests, advances and the exhilaration of creating fear and uncertainty," British historian Martin Gilbert wrote, "the Germans appeared vulnerable. The inevitability of triumph was gone."

But the price of the Russian victory at Stalingrad was almost incomprehensible. In this single battle, the Russians had lost more than one million men, more than the United States would lose in the entire war. To be sure, American munitions and supplies had played a critical role in the victory. During the last quarter of 1942, the U. S. had sent Stalin 60,000 trucks, 11,000 jeeps, 2 million pairs of boots, 50,000 tons of explosives, 450,000 tons of steel, and 250,000 tons of aviation gas. American vehicles substantially increased the mobility of the Red Army, while American machinery and raw materials helped the Soviet Union maintain its war production despite the losses of great industrial areas to the enemy.

Still, Stalin insisted angrily, the Soviets were enduring a disproportionate loss of life. The time had come for the Allies to bear a larger burden of the fighting. "I feel confident," Stalin wrote Roosevelt on the eve of the Casablanca Conference, "that no time is being wasted, that the promise to open a second front in Europe which you, Mr. President, and Mr. Churchill gave for 1942 or the spring of 1943 at the latest, will be kept."

It was not to be that simple. Again the British chiefs were united in their opposition to a major cross-Channel attack. Instead, they argued in favor of invading Sicily, convinced that victory there would come quickly and easily, hopeful that it might knock Italy out of the war. Once more, General Marshall carried the banner against what he saw as a diversionary campaign in favor of a direct assault before the end of the year on Nazi-occupied Western Europe. But the American chiefs were divided among themselves. Admiral King wanted American forces to keep positive pressure on the Japanese in the Far East, where, after five months of fighting, Japanese resistance at Guadalcanal was finally coming to an end; General Arnold argued for weakening Germany first by heavy bombing from the air.

After four days of intense discussion, Roosevelt opted to go along with the British plan to invade Sicily instead of France in 1943. Though he remained sympathetic to Stalin's request for a major operation to divert German troops from Russia, he concluded that Allied deficiencies in shipping—of cargo boats, tankers, destroyers, and escort vessels—were still too great to allow the cross-Channel attack to proceed. In early 1943, sinkings of merchant ships still exceeded new construction; the United Nations had less tonnage at the end of 1942 than they had at the beginning. The most troublesome shortages were escort vessels and landing craft. Without escort vessels to protect convoys, it was impossible to send American troops to Europe for a second front. "One of the most poignant arguments in favor of invading Sicily," envoy Averell Harriman recalled, "was that the troops to be used were for the most part already in the Mediterranean," obviating the need for ocean transport.

Until the American home front could be geared to peak production in 1943, Roosevelt reasoned, the goals of the war front had to be reduced to intermediate levels. Hopkins was not happy about the decision, preferring to get on with the invasion of France, but both he and Marshall understood that shipping was the major consideration. Beyond Sicily, the two leaders agreed to two offensive operations in the Far East, the seizure of Rabaul, on the island of New Britain, and the invasion of Burma in conjunction with the Chinese.

Now that the major decisions were behind him, Roosevelt left the grounds of his villa for the first time. With General George Patton as his guide, he embarked on a daylong journey to Rabat, some eighty-five miles to the northwest, to visit the troops. Along the way, joined by Averell Harriman, Harry Hopkins, and Hopkins' son Robert, the president enjoyed a picnic lunch with twenty thousand soldiers of General Mark Clark's Fifth Army. After lunch, settled comfortably in an open jeep, he inspected the troops of the Ninth Infantry Division. Robert Hopkins later recalled with pleasure "the faces of the men standing rigidly at attention as they broke into wide grins when they saw who it was inspecting them." One soldier was so excited that he jumped up and down, "like an animated jack-in-the-box, unable to say a word."

To Roosevelt, who roared with laughter when he heard one soldier say, "Gosh—it's the old man himself!" the sight of so many young Americans in good health and high spirits was a tonic for the soul. "Those troops," he told his son Elliott, "they really look as if they're rarin' to go. Tough, and brown and grinning, and . . . ready." Later, he visited Port Lyautey, scene of some of the heaviest fighting during the landings, and placed wreaths on the graves of American and French soldiers.

That night, while the president shared a quiet dinner in his villa with Churchill, FDR, Jr., and Elliott went into town to explore the night life of Casablanca, with its spicy smells and exotic music, its open-air cafés and narrow winding streets, its colorful mixture of fortune-tellers and snake charmers. FDR, Jr., "certainly was in rollicking form," Elliott reported in a letter to his mother, hinting that perhaps too much liquor had been consumed. "I do hope that after this war he can settle down to some kind of work, because if he doesn't I fear that he may waste a brilliant mind like Hall did."

When the boys returned to the villa, the president was still up, anxious to hear all about their evening on the town. "As always," Elliott recorded, "he was envious of our relative freedom, and listened to my story with the greatest gusto."

The president's good mood continued through dinner with the sultan of Morocco the following night. Magnificently dressed in white silk robes, the sultan and his entourage arrived bearing gifts—a gold-painted dagger in a gorgeous teakwood case for the president, and a high golden tiara for the first lady. "One glimpse of the tiara," Elliott laughingly recalled, "and Father gave me a straight-faced sidelong look, and then a solemn wink. The same thought was in both our minds: a picture of Mother presiding over a formal function at the White House with that imposing object perched atop her hairdo."

Seated on the sultan's left, Churchill did not share in the president's good humor. Since Muslim etiquette prevented the drinking of liquor in public, there was no wine served either before or during the meal. This did not set well with the prime minister, who had announced earlier that day, when Hopkins found him drinking a bottle of wine for breakfast, that "he had no intention of giving up alcoholic drink, mild or strong, now or later." Explaining further, he said that "he had a profound distaste on the one hand for skimmed milk, and no deep rooted prejudice about wine," so he had reconciled the conflict in favor of the latter. "He had lived to be 68 years old and was in the best of health, and had found that the advice of doctors, throughout his life, was usually wrong."

Churchill's mood darkened still further as the president led his dinner companions into a discussion of the postwar scene, cheerfully predicting that colonialism would soon be a thing of the past. While the sultan delighted in the prospect of his country's independence, Churchill shifted uneasily in his chair, coughing persistently until the conversation changed. But the mood the president had set had a rhythm of its own, and the conversation soon returned to the forbidden subject of postcolonialism.

In the days that followed, the conferees were preoccupied with the thorny problem of French politics. From the start of the conference, Roosevelt was determined to bring together the warring factions represented by General Henri Giraud, the compromise leader of the French forces in North Africa, and General de Gaulle, the valiant symbol of the French resistance. The president told Churchill that he would produce the bride (Giraud) if Churchill produced the groom (de Gaulle). Giraud's presence was easily arranged, but de Gaulle flatly refused to deal with anyone connected to the Vichy regime. Only when Churchill threatened to stop paying his salary in London did the proud Frenchman agree to come to North Africa.

Yet, once he reached Casablanca, de Gaulle refused to call upon Giraud. Churchill was furious. "Well, just look at him!" Churchill remarked, as de Gaulle stalked down the garden path after a stormy session with British leaders. "His country has given up fighting, he himself is a refugee, and if we have to turn him down he's finished. Look at him! He might be Stalin, with 200 divisions behind his words!"

Finally, Roosevelt decided to intervene, asking de Gaulle to meet him in his villa. "The General was sullen," Mike Reilly noted, "never smiled, and he had that unmistakable attitude of a man toting a large chip on each shoulder. He and the President shook hands, and then everybody left them alone together." Or so it seemed. Behind the drapes, Reilly remained half hidden, his pistol removed from his holster. "I saw before me the President of the United States in a hot argument," the Secret Service chief explained. "The man was six foot three, the President a cripple."

For his part, de Gaulle noticed shadows at the rear of the balcony and saw the curtains moving, but he never said a word, carrying on the conversation as if he and Roosevelt were completely alone. By the end of the session, a breakthrough had been achieved: de Gaulle agreed to sign a memorandum of unity with Giraud. "In human affairs the public must be offered a drama," Roosevelt told de Gaulle. If the news of Casablanca could be accompanied by a joint declaration of the French leaders, even if it concerned only a theoretical agreement stating they both wanted France freed and would consult and collaborate, it would, Roosevelt predicted, "produce the dramatic effect we need."

"Let me handle it," de Gaulle agreed. In his memoirs, the French leader attributes his change of heart to the president's soothing charm. Despite their differences, de Gaulle was convinced that Roosevelt was governed by "the loftiest of ambitions" and that "his intelligence, his knowledge and his audacity gave him the ability . . . to realize them."

The atmosphere chilled the next day, however, when Churchill lost his temper with de Gaulle. "In these days," Lord Moran observed of his boss, "when he is stretched taut, certain people seem to get on his nerves: de Gaulle is one of them." The argument arose just as Giraud was being escorted into the room by Hopkins for a historic handshake with de Gaulle. Reacting quickly, Roosevelt paid no attention to Churchill's diatribe, turning instead to de Gaulle. "Will you at least agree," he said in his kindest manner, "to be photographed beside me and the British Prime Minister along with General Giraud?"

"Of course," de Gaulle replied, knowing full well that serious disputes of substance still remained unresolved. "Will you go so far as to shake General Giraud's hand before the camera?" "I shall do that for you," de Gaulle answered. The picture was snapped, the dramatic moment captured for posterity. In the foreground, a stiff-necked de Gaulle offers his hand to Giraud. In the background is the seated president, his face thrown back in wholehearted enjoyment of the delicious scene.

As the Frenchmen departed, Roosevelt and Churchill remained behind on the lawn to talk with the assembled newsmen. The day was so lovely, with a bright sun and blue skies, and Roosevelt was feeling so gay, that in a spontaneous moment he called for the unconditional surrender of Germany, Italy, and Japan. Churchill was stunned. Though he and Roosevelt had exchanged views on unconditional surrender on several occasions, no final agreement on a text had been reached. Later that evening, Harriman recalled, Churchill was "in high dudgeon. He was offended that Roosevelt should have made such a momentous announcement without prior consultation. . . . I had seen him unhappy with Roosevelt more than once, but this time he was more deeply offended than before. I also had the impression that he feared it might make the Germans fight all the harder."

Roosevelt blithely explained later that getting de Gaulle and Giraud together had been so complicated that it reminded him of Grant and Lee, "and then suddenly the press conference was on, and Winston and I had no time to prepare for it, and the thought popped into my mind that they had called Grant 'Old Unconditional Surrender' and the next thing I knew I had said it."

But the deed was done, and Churchill could not remain angry at Roosevelt for long. With the work of the conference completed, he suggested that he and the president travel together to Marrakesh, the jewel of Morocco, a city which combined a perfect climate, a wealth of ancient monuments, and a unique setting of palm trees against snow-capped mountains.

"Let us spend two days there," Churchill said. "I must be with you when you see the sunset on the snows of the Atlas Mountains." Delighted to stretch his trip a little longer, Roosevelt agreed. The journey by automobile took five hours, with time out for a basket lunch along the way. Driving together along the plain, Roosevelt and Churchill fell into easy conversation, heartily enjoying their last moments of freedom before returning to the burdens that awaited them at home. During the last hour of the journey, the shapes of the mountain peaks began to emerge on the horizon, the palm trees to grow more thickly. At 6 p.m., they reached a spectacular villa, surrounded by a fairyland of fountains and waterfalls, where they were to spend the night.

At the top of the villa stood a sloping tower six stories high with a magnificent view of the snow-capped mountains. It was the view Churchill wanted to share with the president. The steep, winding stairs were too narrow to accommodate Roosevelt's wheelchair, so Mike Reilly and George Fox made a cradle with their hands to carry him step by step to the top, his legs, Moran noted, "dangling like the limbs of a ventriloquist's dummy." At the topmost terrace, the president sat with Churchill for half an hour, gazing at the purple hills, where the light was changing every minute. "It's the most lovely spot in the whole world," the prime minister remarked.

At this moment, Churchill was perhaps at the peak of his wartime power. The conference had ended exactly as he had hoped—with a postponement of the cross-Channel attack and the decision to invade Sicily. Never again, with Stalin's power rising every day, would Churchill enjoy such influence with Roosevelt.

The president's plane was scheduled to leave for the United States the following morning at seven-thirty. Churchill had intended to see Roosevelt off, but after a long evening of food, drink, speeches, and songs, he had trouble getting out of bed. At the last minute, still clad in his red-dragon dressing gown and black velvet slippers, he raced outside to catch the president's car. At the airfield, the photographers begged for a shot. "You simply cannot do this to me," he laughingly remarked, and they obliged, lowering their cameras.

As the president's plane took off, Churchill put his hand on American Vice-Consul Kenneth Pendar's arm. "If anything happened to that man," he said, "I couldn't stand it. He is the truest friend; he has the farthest vision; he is the greatest man I have ever known."

• • •

"Dearest Babs," Franklin wrote Eleanor as he flew back to the States. "All has gone well though I'm a bit tired—too much plane. It affects my head just as ocean cruising affects yours."

Roosevelt hated flying. He vastly preferred the slower pace of ocean travel. "He always used to tell me that clouds were dull," Eleanor explained. "What he loved was the sea all around him, the motion of the waves." Franklin had long tried to convince Eleanor that getting there was half the fun, soliciting her companionship on languid trips by boat and train, but to Eleanor's mind nothing was comparable to flying. Possessed by a deep-rooted horror of wasting time, she always wanted to get where she wanted to go as quickly as possible.

"What do you know!" Franklin excitedly wrote Eleanor as he crossed the northern coast of South America. "Back in the US. Saturday evening and we should get to Washington by 8 p.m. on Sunday [January 31]." Having been away for nearly a month, he seemed eager to see his wife, to tell her all that had happened, to hear her speak, as if the time apart had created a surge of forgotten emotions. Perhaps, on coming home, he indulged himself in the fancy that Eleanor would be there, just as his mother had always been, to welcome him back with warmth, love, and exuberant delight.

But the spell was quickly broken when he arrived in the White House and found a handwritten note from Eleanor: "Welcome home! I can't be here Sunday night as months ago I agreed to open a series of lectures at Cooper Union but I'll be home for dinner Monday night as I don't want you to tell all the story and miss it. . . . I have to be gone again for the day Tuesday but will be back Wednesday a.m. I'm terribly sorry not to be home. I think I will now delay going west til late March. . . . Much love and I am so glad you are back."

That evening, while Eleanor kept her engagement at Cooper Union, the president relaxed in his study with Anna and John, who had arrived in Washington for a winter vacation while he was in Casablanca. The president's animated spirits were so contagious, his stories of the conference so vibrant, that both Anna and John were enthralled. "I'd give my eyeteeth to go along on such a trip," John suddenly announced. "That couldn't be done," the president replied. "And why not?" John ardently persisted. "Why couldn't I?"

"Well," the president countered, "you are not in uniform!" Roosevelt's reply was most likely nothing more than a statement of White House protocol surrounding military conferences, but to young Boettiger, already sensitive about his civilian status, it seemed a personal attack that could not have come at a worst moment.

For months, John had been suffering from bouts of depression, displayed in a sudden ebbing of interest in his work at the *Seattle Post-Intelligencer* and a withdrawal from his wife and family. Anna assumed that she was somehow at fault. "I feared," she later admitted to John, "you were getting tired of something or other about me or in me."

But, unbeknownst to Anna at the time, John's melancholy had deeper roots. Paralyzing doubts about his abilities had surfaced periodically in the course of his marriage, but now, as John entered his fortieth year, they were assuming more powerful proportions than before. Haunted by the knowledge that his position as publisher of the paper was dependent upon his status as the president's son-in-law, John had begun to envision military service as an escape from his depression and pain. The choice was not easy, however, for it meant leaving Anna alone in Seattle to cope with running the paper.

The president's careless comment settled the issue. "I won't say that one remark of his did it," John later admitted, "but it went farther than any or all influences that did make my mind up." The following day, he wrote a letter to his old friend General Eisenhower requesting that he be commissioned in the army and put into service in North Africa.

Anna was crushed. "From the moment you wrote that letter," she wrote, "I began to suffer acutely. I seemed to know all too accurately what it was going to be like when you left." Confused by the rashness of the decision, fearful that his leaving implied a rejection of her, terrified of running the paper on her own, she was nonetheless afraid that if she tried to dissuade him from going he would regret it for the rest of his life and take out his anger on her. "Maybe I was wrong not to have told you all I was thinking and dreading," she later confessed, "but I just couldn't."

Two days later, Eleanor accompanied Anna and John to Union Station, where they boarded a sleeper train to Seattle. "I went to the train and stayed till it pulled out," Eleanor wrote Joe Lash. "Anna seemed to want me." The president was delighted with John's decision to serve, Eleanor went on, but Anna couldn't help feeling resentful. "Happiness is a fragile thing and she fears its shattering. I can't be delighted either. I wish pride compensated fear with me."

"I hated to see you go," Eleanor wrote Anna, "for I know that having John consider going off ends something very close and precious which you two have had. . . . Yet always men have had the urge for adventure and fared forth and the women are always held by 'appendages.' "

• • •

No sooner had the president returned to Washington than his attention was yanked from global strategy to domestic politics. At the War Production Board, a tremendous crisis was brewing. The military had lost faith in the leadership of Donald Nelson, believing him too weak, too nice, and too tolerant. There was merit to the military's claim. Torn between the competing demands of conflicting agencies, Nelson was habitually indecisive. Stimson's diary during this period is filled with recriminations against Nelson's inability to take charge. Returning from a meeting with Nelson, Knox, Ickes,

Navy Undersecretary James Forrestal, and rubber chief William Jeffers, Stimson was irate. "It was a pathetic spectacle. . . . it was like four hungry dogs quarreling over a very inadequate bone—the Army for planes and gas; Navy escort vessels; Ickes octane gas; Jeffers rubber."

In truth, however, the nub of the military's complaint was not directed at Nelson's administrative weaknesses, but at his insistence on civilian control of the production process. The military, geared to think of its own needs first, was forever arguing that too much steel or rubber or manpower was being devoted to civilian activity. Though Nelson listened to the military, he insisted on a balance between civilian and military needs. When newsprint grew short, the army argued for the elimination of comic strips, but Nelson refused. When the army opposed the diversion of scarce labor materials to build housing for war workers in overcrowded cities, Nelson argued that decent housing was essential to maintaining production.

The continued pulling and hauling between military and civilian priorities made for disorderly administration. Stimson was in despair over the "disjointed" conduct of the war. "The President is the poorest administrator I have ever worked under in respect to the orderly procedure and routine of his performance," he confessed to his diary. One evening while Roosevelt was in Casablanca, Stimson unburdened himself to Felix Frankfurter. "He wanted to relieve himself by talking," Frankfurter observed, "for he has had a good many headaches recently"—all of them attributable to bad organization.

Frankfurter told Stimson "he had better make up his mind that orderly procedure is not and never has been the characteristic of this Administration —it has other virtues but not that. . . . he had better reconcile himself to looseness of administration and the inevitable frictions and conflicts resulting therefrom which naturally go against the grain of an orderly, systematic brain like his."

While Roosevelt was in Casablanca, however, the quarrels within the WPB had become so bitter that Congress had stepped into the fray, threatening to replace the strife-torn organization with a new superagency, bringing production, manpower, and supply under one roof. The time had come, Economic Stabilization Director Jimmy Byrnes told Roosevelt, for Nelson to be replaced. First Knudsen had been in trouble, Roosevelt mused, now Nelson. Perhaps businessmen were not as qualified as everyone thought to run complicated government agencies.

There was only one man for the job, Byrnes counseled, one man who would please both the army and the Congress—Bernard Baruch. The decision was not an easy one for Roosevelt; Donald Nelson had been a loyal and devoted chief. But he finally agreed, directing Byrnes to prepare a letter for his signature asking Baruch to become the new chairman of the WPB. Acting with dispatch, for fear that Roosevelt might change his mind, Byrnes drafted the letter immediately and then read it to Baruch later that afternoon.

Baruch was delighted. This was the job he had craved since the war began. He asked only that he have time to check with his doctor the next day, to make sure that, at seventy-three, he was healthy enough to undertake the task. Byrnes was disappointed, fearing the delay would open the door for Roosevelt to back down, which is precisely what Roosevelt did.

Later that night, at supper with Hopkins, Roosevelt began to question his decision. Hopkins told Roosevelt that, by appointing Baruch and giving in to the army, he would look weak. Baruch would emerge the conquering hero, the most powerful man in Washington. Better, Hopkins advised, to let the storm pass and keep Nelson at the post. The president agreed.

This was not the first time Roosevelt had by-passed Baruch. As much as he respected the shrewd financier, Roosevelt did not like him a great deal. "They are too much alike," I. F. Stone keenly observed; "both are charmers. Mr. Roosevelt feels about Baruch as a young married woman does when her mother tries to help her by showing her the right way to handle a maid or a baby. He resented Al Smith's attempt to 'help' him when he first succeeded Smith as Governor and there is reason to believe that he has been irked by Baruch's burning desire to show him how *really* to run a war."

When Baruch arrived at the Oval Office to advise the president of his acceptance, Roosevelt greeted him in his customary genial fashion. "Mr. President, I'm here to report for duty," Baruch said. The salutation went unacknowledged. "It was as though he had not heard me," Baruch recalled. The president then launched into a curious monologue about Middle Eastern politics which lasted until he was called to leave for a Cabinet meeting. "That was the end of it," Baruch later wrote; "neither he nor I ever mentioned the WPB Chairmanship—then or later." The "strange and disagreeable little drama" had come to an end.

• • •

On Friday night, February 5, seeking rest from his strenuous trip and escape from the muddle of Washington, Roosevelt journeyed to Hyde Park for a long weekend, accompanied by Bill Hassett, Pa Watson, and Grace Tully. He slept until ten or eleven each morning, relaxed over leisurely meals, and rummaged through his library. A heavy snowfall had blanketed the lawns and the trees just before his arrival, warming the atmosphere of the Big House. "Most of my time was spent asleep," Roosevelt reported to Anna when he returned to Washington the following Wednesday. "I did as little work as possible—and now I am ready for practically anything."

While Franklin was unwinding at Hyde Park, Eleanor was traveling by train through Connecticut and Massachusetts to Portland, Maine, visiting old friends, naval hospitals and war plants. She left New York on Saturday morning, then spent the day with Esther Lape and Elizabeth Read in Saybrook, Connecticut. Elizabeth was in a miserable state, suffering from cancer and "so far away in her mind" that she could scarcely participate in the conversation. For Eleanor, the only solace came in observing the "constant care and devotion" that Esther generously extended to her lifelong companion. Through most of this "marriage," Elizabeth had subordinated her interests and concerns to Esther's; now Esther was returning that love, dedicating all her energies to her dying friend.

From Connecticut, Eleanor journeyed north to Somerville, Massachusetts. There, on Sunday afternoon, she visited Missy in her home. During the thirties, Eleanor had visited 101 Orchard a number of times. "We got to know Mrs. Roosevelt very well," Missy's next-door neighbor Barbara Dudley recalled, "because, whenever there was a crisis or a big event in the family, she came up to help Missy out. When Missy's mother died, she took over the kitchen. I remember we were imagining that we'd have all kinds of fancy foods, but she made two things only: tomato soup and peanut-butter sandwiches."

Though there was little improvement in Missy's speech, the circulation in her right side was returning. "Where it was just like an icicle," her sister Ann Rochon told Eleanor, "is as warm as the left side now." With three speech lessons a day instead of one, two vigorous massages, and two hours of exercise each morning, there was, Ann reported, "a decided change for the better." What is more, Missy "realizes it and is *so* excited." But, Ann confessed, "Missy worries so terribly about the President."

On reaching Portland at 9 p.m. that Sunday, Eleanor went immediately to the shipyards to talk with women working the graveyard shift. "It was really very dramatic to see the plant at night," Eleanor later wrote, praising the high spirits of the women workers. "Exhibiting her usual energy," the *Portland Press Herald* observed, "Mrs. Roosevelt mounted a platform to speak with several women welders by literally 'walking the plank' which was the only means of ascending the platform erected four feet above the ground." Sitting down beside them, Eleanor asked questions about the nature of their work, the training they had received, how many children they had, how they were being cared for, how the shopping got done.

Now, for the first time, the government was targeting its recruitment ads directly and predominantly at housewives. "The real situation," *Business Week* observed, "is that unless industry draws 2.8 million more [women] away from household or school duties in 1943 . . . production quotas will have to be revised down."

In the ads directed at housewives, the temporary nature of the job was stressed, the idea being that women would come into the factories during the war and then go back home as soon as it was over. "A woman is a substitute," one War Department brochure claimed, "like plastic instead of metal." To ease the transition, the work was presented as similar in kind to the work housewives already knew how to perform. "If you've sewed on buttons, or made buttonholes on a machine," a Labor Department pamphlet urged, "you can learn to do spot welding on airplane parts. If you've done fine embroidery, or made jewelry, you can learn to do assembly on time fuses, radio tubes. If you've used an electric mixer in your kitchen, you can learn to run a drill press. If you've ironed your sheets in an electrical mangle, you can learn to run a blueprint machine. Are you ready?"

The government's vigorous recruitment of women provoked fierce opposition in many quarters. In their lead editorial in April 1943, *Catholic World* argued that "women who maintain jobs outside their homes... weaken family life, endanger their own marital happiness, rob themselves of man's protective capabilities, and by consequence decrease the number of children. The principal evil in women's work is that it alienates the life of the wife from the life of the husband and gives marriage as much permanence as the room sharing of two freshmen at boarding school."

Eleanor took a more practical approach. If the country needed married women to work, as it undoubtedly did, then it was the country's responsibility to preserve home life as much as possible by helping to lighten the housekeeping burdens. Back in September, Eleanor had forecast "a very chaotic situation" unless government stepped in with a comprehensive program which included day nurseries and play schools adjacent to the plants, community laundries, family restaurants organized to provide fully prepared takeout foods for working women, and the provision of transportation for children from their homes to their schools.

Eleanor's early fears were realized in 1943, as the absentee rate among women working in war industries soared, creating havoc on production lines. The major cause, the Women's Bureau argued, lay in "women's outside responsibilities—the difficulty they have in carrying on a full-time job in the factory and also keeping up a family, doing the shopping, marketing and all the other things which must be done if you are to carry on both jobs." Attempts at purchasing food at the close of the day were often fruitless, because stocks were exhausted and the store was ready to close. The result was that homemakers working the day shift had to remain away from work in order to secure food for their families. "No matter how intense a woman's interest in her job may be," the War Manpower Commission observed, "her children must be cared for, the work of running the house falls on her and she must have time for shopping."

In her talks with the women at the South Portland Shipbuilding yard, Eleanor called for a wide range of creative solutions—staggering the opening and closing times of the factories, keeping bank and department stores open at night, encouraging butchers to hold back part of their meat supply until 6 p.m., asking war plants to hire personal shoppers for the women, to take their orders in the morning and have the filled grocery bags waiting at the door at the end of the shift.

For two hours, the women in the Portland plant shared the details of their daily lives with the first lady. She asked about their homes and their families as well as their work. "Shyly they came forward to speak to her," one of the workers, Betty Blakeley reported, following her as she journeyed from one job to the next, joining her in the cafeteria for a midnight snack. For her part, Eleanor was pleased to see how "extremely interested" the women were in their work—one woman drove fifty miles a day to reach the shipyard; another endured an eighteen-mile bus ride each way. All of them loved the experience, the camaraderie of the plant, the pride in a job well done. As she left, she told the women that her trip through the yard had made her very proud of them and "the wonderful way they had taken hold, particularly of the hard and dirty jobs always heretofore assigned to men."

The following week, Eleanor flew to Des Moines, Iowa, to visit the headquarters of the Women's Army Auxiliary Corps. Legislation creating the opportunity for women to serve with the army as clerks, cooks, chauffeurs, airplane spotters, telegraphers, secretaries, and telephone operators had been signed by the president the previous May. The response was overwhelming. Before the first day of registration had come to an end, more than thirteen thousand women had applied—an "infinite variety," *Life* reported, including "college girls and career women, shop girls and stenographers, housewives and widows," girls whose fathers were army men, girls whose husbands were flying planes and driving tanks, girls who had never passed the gates of a military post. Ultimately, 350,000 women would serve as members of the Women's Army Corps and the WAVES (Women Accepted for Voluntary Emergency Service in the Navy).

When she arrived at Fort Des Moines, a little before noon, Eleanor toured the mess hall, the kitchen, and the barracks. There were forty women in each barrack. "Fall out" time was 5 a.m., with reveille at 6 and classes from 8 to 5. The training encompassed calisthenics, map reading, poison-gas identification, military courtesy, airplane spotting, current events, and parade formation. "In our spare time," one young recruit, Ruth Thompson Pierce, wrote her mother, "we have chores. Scrubbing floors, washing windows, policing grounds, and picking up papers. My knees are like two balloons from scrubbing floors." At KP, she later recalled, "gruff army men would give us heavy cast-iron pots to lift, hundred-pound sacks of flour to carry. Then they would stand around laughing. But we refused to cry 'uncle.' It was exhausting and exhilarating and I loved it."

Eleanor relished the sight of so many women from so many different backgrounds working together. Though she imagined that "the lack of privacy must seem hard to the older women," with double-decker bunks and two thousand people eating in the cafeteria at the same time, she marveled at the adventurous spirit of this female "army behind the fighting forces." Standing on a barracks porch in icy weather, she reviewed twenty-eight hundred bundled-up officer candidates and then watched another sixteen hundred pass in review in the Coliseum. With WAAC bands playing at both reviews, it was a memorable occasion. "I am sure that if all people in the country could see it," Eleanor wrote in her column the following day, "they would be as enthusiastic and as full of admiration as I am about the training and the women who take it."

Eleanor's desire to spend time with women war workers brought her a few weeks later to the Kaiser Company shipyard in Portland, Oregon, where women made up 60 percent of the work force. There she talked at length with Henry Kaiser and his son Edgar about the most critical problem women war workers faced—the lack of adequate day care.

In the summer of 1942, the president, at Eleanor's urging, had approved the first government-sponsored child-care center under the Community Facilities Act which had passed Congress the previous year. The Lanham Act, as it came to be known, provided local aid to war-impacted communities for schools, hospitals, water and sewers, and recreational facilities. Since the summer, six additional centers had been funded in Connecticut, Texas, and North Carolina, but the total number of children covered was only 105,000 —"a mere drop in the bucket," one reporter noted, at a time when perhaps two million children needed care.

For months, Eleanor had been calling on private industry to recognize that providing a day-care center was as essential as providing a cafeteria. Until the needs of working mothers with young children could be fully met, she argued, there was no possibility of ensuring a stable work force. But Eleanor's message was not easily accepted by a generation of men and women who believed, as the Minneapolis chief of welfare, John O. Louis, proclaimed, that "the child should be cared for by its own mother; and that only in those instances where inadequacies of physical surroundings, or mental and moral environment make it absolutely necessary, the child be placed outside the home."

"The worst mother is better than the best institution," Mayor LaGuardia argued in January 1943, and few officials publicly disagreed. So prevalent was the theory that mothers belonged at home that Frances Perkins, the sole woman in the Roosevelt Cabinet, felt compelled to speak up against government-sponsored day care. "What are you doing," Perkins asked the chief of the Children's Bureau, Katherine Lenroot, "to prevent the spread of the day nursery system which I regard as a most unfortunate reaction to the hysterical propaganda about recruiting women workers."

Undeterred, Eleanor stepped up her campaign for day care. Whether one felt it advisable or not for women to work, the fact remained that women were working: more than three million new women had entered the work force between 1940 and 1942, and three million more were expected to enter before the war was over, bringing the total of female workers to nineteen million. Furthermore, the profile of the female worker was changing. Whereas the majority of women workers had been young and single, now 75 percent were married, 60 percent were over thirty-five, and more than 33 percent had children under fourteen. Without day care, Eleanor argued, there was a real danger of child neglect.

From war centers across the country, disturbing reports were coming in of makeshift, unsatisfactory solutions to the child-care problem. In one family in Chicago, *Fortune* reported in February 1943, "a 9 year old boy gets up in a cold house, rouses and feeds his 4 year old sister, delivers her to kindergarten on his way to school, takes her home and prepares her lunch, then locks her in the house while he returns to school." In another family in Connecticut, *The Saturday Evening Post* reported, "a woman in the graveyard shift drives her car close to the windows of the place where she is employed and her four children sleep in the automobile." In California, a four-year-old girl is found with a box of matches in her hands. She has been trying to light the gas stove as her mother does. The teenage girl who was supposed to baby-sit for her had not shown up.

"These are not isolated cases," *The Saturday Evening Post* concluded after sending a team of reporters around the country. "You can multiply them and cases like them by the thousands. First let it be understood that this country has long had a serious child care problem never adequately met. Now the industrial upheaval of war is blowing up the child care problem to the proportions of an enormous and thinly stretched balloon."

Believing that child neglect was verging on a national scandal, Eleanor pleaded with Kaiser to create a model child-care center that could serve as a prototype for other wartime industries. Kaiser empathized with Eleanor's concern. More than four thousand of the sixteen thousand women at Swan Island and Oregonship, the two Kaiser shipyards in Portland, were mothers, many with children of preschool age. If a day-care center could be constructed at the shipyard so that the mothers could bring their children before work and stop in to see them during the day, the level of productivity would undoubtedly rise.

Within weeks of Eleanor's visit, under the leadership of young Edgar Kaiser, plans were under way to construct a spectacular day-care center, complete with the newest play equipment, the most sophisticated teaching devices, a cafeteria staffed by nutritionists, and an infirmary staffed by nurses and doctors. With construction costs covered by the U.S. Maritime Commission and operating costs borne by Kaiser, nothing was spared in the attempt to create a wholesome, happy environment for the children.

The Swan Island Center was built in the shape of a wheel, which enclosed a great inner court protected from outside traffic. The spokes were fifteen playrooms, each with long banks of windows on two sides to ensure proper lighting. "It was as nice a building as one could imagine," the center's director, James Hymes, recalled. "The walls were painted in beautiful pastel shades; the chandeliers had a futuristic look, with the letters of the alphabet and elephants painted on them. It was one of those rare settings where the only obstacles, like time, were not man-imposed."

Outstanding teachers were recruited to staff the center, which was open whenever the shipyard was open—six days a week, fifty-two weeks a year. Mount Holyoke graduate Mary Willett was teaching at an exclusive nursery school on the East Coast when she heard about the new center at the Kaiser shipyards. "I could tell immediately that this was something special," she recalled, "a chance to reach children from all different backgrounds at a very early age. I was thrilled when the telegram came offering me a position at $55 a week. How privileged I was to be part of this great experiment!"

When Miss Willett reached the Swan Island Center, the situation was even better than she hoped. The children, ranging from eighteen months to six years, came from farms in Minnesota, Ohio, and Iowa, from city streets in St. Louis, Los Angeles, and Oakland, from Southern towns and foreign lands. "We had Indian children, Mexican children, and black children," she recalled. "I remember one big black woman whose son, Freddy, was in the program. She was so happy to know that, for the first time in Freddy's life, he was not being Jim Crowed."

The Swan Island Center was a head-start program a quarter of a century ahead of its time. One woman came all the way from Louisiana because she heard the program was great for children. And the experience was unique for the teachers as well. "It was without question the highlight of my whole career," Mary Willett lovingly recalled fifty years later.

In its first year of operation, the Swan Island Center served nearly two thousand children. Opened at first only for day and swing shifts, it soon added cots and bedding supplies to accommodate the graveyard shift, keeping its doors open twenty-four-hours a day. During summers and school vacations, it operated a separate program for children from ages six to twelve. An additional program was created for nonenrolled Swan Island families who needed emergency care just for the day, if their usual arrangement broke down. The total cost for full-time care, including food, was 75 cents per child per day, $1.25 for two. And the center went a step further. At the end of the day, tired workers could pick up, at cost, fully cooked dinners to bring home to their families. For this Eleanor was directly responsible. "She had seen a food-service operation in England," Director James Hymes recalled, "and had told Henry Kaiser about it."

The success of the Swan Island Center stimulated war plants and shipyards across the nation to provide day care. It was estimated that each child-care center serving forty mothers made possible eight thousand productive man hours monthly. Slowly, Eleanor was winning her long struggle to make child care recognized as a national problem that required a collective response. Though the needs of working mothers were never fully met, nearly $50 million would be spent on day care before the war came to an end, $3 million for construction of new centers and $47 million for operating expenses. By the summer of 1945, more than a million and a half children would be in day care.

• • •

When Eleanor returned home from her travels in late February, she found that her husband had been sick in bed for a week with an intestinal grippe. In her absence, Margaret Suckley had taken care of him, sharing tea with him in the late afternoon, sitting by his bedside at night, traveling with him to Hyde Park. It happened that Churchill was also confined to his bed that week, suffering from fever and pneumonia. "Oddly enough," *The New York Times* observed, while the papers were full of war maps showing the tides of battle, "the two most important war graphs of the last fortnight were never published. . . . They are the temperature charts of the recent sick rooms in the White House and at 10 Downing Street. . . . It is no exaggeration to say that the doctors' charts were fully as important for the world as any maps in the newspaper."

"I think I picked up sleeping sickness or Gambia fever or some kindred bug in that hell hole of yours called Bathhurst," Roosevelt teased Churchill, referring to the capital of British Gambia, where his plane had refueled en route to Casablanca. "It laid me low—four days in bed—then a lot of sulphadiathole which cured the fever and left me feeling like a wet rag. I was no good after 2 p.m. and after standing it for a week or so, I went to Hyde Park for five days: got full of health in glorious zero weather—came back . . . and have been feeling like a fighting cock ever since. Please, please for the sake of the world don't overdo these days. You must remember that it takes about a month of occasional let-ups to get back your full strength. . . . Tell Mrs. Churchill that when I was laid up I was a thoroughly model patient and that I hope you will live down the reputation in our Press of having been the 'world's worst patient.' "

• • •

As the tenth anniversary of Roosevelt's first inaugural approached, reporters remained astonished by his unruffled demeanor. Amid tumultuous events abroad, turmoil in Congress, and trouble at home, he remained relaxed, good-humored, and self-assured.

The war had cut into many of Franklin's favorite relaxations. The hours before bed that he had used to devote to his stamp collection now went to a study of thick reports about tanks and planes, while the unending pile of work on his desk—four thousand letters a day compared with the four hundred President Hoover received—took away the late-afternoon swims he had so enjoyed in the White House pool.

But still he was able to joke and to laugh. And still he found ways to relax—over cocktails, movies, and cards. At his ritual cocktail hour, the unwritten rule remained that all talk of politics or war must cease. On weekends at Hyde Park, he refused to work until after noon, indulging in long hours of sleep and lazy jaunts through the woods that invariably lifted his spirits.

While Roosevelt continually renewed his energies through relaxation, Adolf Hitler diminished his strength through overwork. "The Fuhrer seems to have aged 15 years during three and a half years of war," Goebbels noted in his diary that same March. "He doesn't get out into the fresh air. He does not relax. He sits in his bunker, fusses and broods." In time, Albert Speer argued, Hitler's tendency to overwork left him "permanently caustic and irritable," unable to absorb fresh impressions, unwilling to listen to criticism.

During the early days of the war, Hitler had taken great pleasure in the ritual of a late-afternoon tea to which, much like Roosevelt's cocktail hour, he invited close associates and friends for relaxed conversation and idle gossip. But as the pressures of war mounted, the hour for tea was steadily pushed back, from four to six to eight to ten. By 1943, Speer noted, Hitler's evening tea did not begin until two o'clock in the morning. While most of Berlin slept, Hitler sat with his aides, recounting tales from his youth or from the early days of struggle. Within this intimate circle, Speer remarked, Hitler's familiar stories "were appreciated as if they had been heard for the first time," but exhaustion took its toll, and no one could "whip up much liveliness or even contribute to the conversation." At the end of the "relaxed" tea, Hitler was more agitated than when it began.

Roosevelt's tenth anniversary in office found Eleanor, in Tommy's judgment, "a bit worn as to patience," still tending to crowd too many engagements into a single day. "Five minutes here and five minutes there are not satisfactory to anyone," Tommy complained in a letter to Esther Lape. But as long as America's boys were dying abroad, Eleanor refused to lighten her load; as long as she was privileged to travel, the least she could do was to visit wounded soldiers in hospitals wherever she went. "I'm completely exhausted after a hospital day," she confessed to Joe Lash, "& I lie awake thinking what we should do in the future for them but one goes on with daily round of life."

Eleanor had promised Lash before he went into the army that she would give up any other engagement if she had a chance to see him. Despite the pressure of an almost inhuman schedule, she kept her promise. No sooner was Lash transferred to weather-forecasting school at Chanute Field than Eleanor journeyed to Urbana, Illinois, to see him.

She arrived at the Hotel Lincoln on Friday night, having reserved room 332 for herself and Tommy and a connecting room for Lash. At 9 p.m., Lash joined Eleanor for dinner in her room. On Saturday, they stayed in the hotel all day long, eating all their meals in their room except for lunch, which they ate in the hotel dining room. Afterward, Lash "stretched out luxuriantly" on the bed for a long nap. "I'm so happy to have been with you," she wrote Joe Lash after she returned to Washington on Sunday. "Separation between people who love each other, makes the reunion always like a new discovery. You forget how much you love certain movements of the hands or the glance in the person's eyes or how nice it is to sit in the same room & look at their back!"

Three weeks later, Eleanor joined Joe Lash again, this time at the Hotel Blackstone in Chicago. Here, too, they stayed in Eleanor's room most of the day. In the afternoon, they went out for a walk; in the evening, Lash was so drowsy that he fell asleep on the bed while Eleanor stroked his forehead. "I loved just sitting near you while you slept . . . ," Eleanor later wrote.

But the pleasures Eleanor derived from her time with Lash were quickly dispelled when she was told by a hotel employee that her room had been bugged. For weeks, it turned out, Lash had been under surveillance by the army's Counter-Intelligence Corps. Mistakenly convinced that he was part of a communist conspiracy, the CIC had been reading his mail and trailing him wherever he went. When the first lady's telegram arrived, inviting him to join her at the Hotel Blackstone, the CIC bugged her room.

Apparently unconcerned about the impropriety of spending two weekends in adjoining rooms with a young serviceman, Eleanor went to see Hopkins as soon as she returned and pleaded with him to find out what was going on. Hopkins took the matter up with General Marshall, who confirmed that Mrs. Roosevelt's room had indeed been bugged. When the president learned that army agents had put his wife under surveillance without presidential authorization, he was furious. Moving quickly to take action against everyone responsible, he ordered an immediate shake-up of the army's intelligence operations, including the disbanding of the CIC. In addition, military orders were drawn up to send Lash overseas, along with his entire group of weather forecasters.

Years later, Lash was still unsure whether the president himself was behind the decision that sent him to the South Pacific. "All the top men who were involved in this affair—the President, Hopkins, Marshall—were preoccupied with decisions that carried the fate of nations and millions of lives," Lash recorded. "They would understandably be impatient with G-2 and its obsession with Eleanor Roosevelt and myself. They may well have decided that, in addition to shaking up G-2, the most expeditious way of getting rid of the Lash problem was to ship me overseas along with a group of fellow student forecasters so it would not seem that I had been singled out for this sanction."

• • •

In March, Eleanor's attention was drawn once again to the struggle for equal treatment in the military. On her desk she found an eloquent plea for help from Henry Jones, a Negro sergeant stationed at Carlsbad Army Air Field in New Mexico. Sergeant Jones described the morale-shattering treatment visited upon Negro soldiers as a consequence of segregated facilities. The Negro men of the 349th Aviation Squadron were "loyal Americans," he began, "ready and willing to do their part to preserve Democracy. For the most part the Personnel of this Squadron is made up of young men who were born and lived in the Northern states where they enjoyed to a large degree the advantages of a democracy. However, the fact that we want to do our best for our country and to be valiant soldiers, seems to mean nothing to the Commanding Officer of our Post as indicated by the fact that 'Jim Crowism' is practiced on the very grounds of our camp."

The sergeant's complaint focused on the Negro soldier's unequal access to recreational facilities and transportation—visible symbols of injustice. At the post theater, with a total capacity of over a thousand seats, only 20 seats, in the last row, were provided for Negroes. At the post exchange, where refreshments were served, Negroes did not have the privilege of eating inside the building. On buses to and from camp, the front seats were reserved for white soldiers; Negro soldiers were either crammed into one small row of seats in the rear or passed up altogether and forced to walk.

"We do not ask for special privileges," Jones concluded, speaking for 121 fellow Negro soldiers whose signatures were attached. "All we desire is to have equality; to be free to participate in all activities, means of transportation, privileges and amusements afforded any American soldier."

After reading Jones' letter, Eleanor wrote a long letter to Henry Stimson describing the conditions at Carlsbad and said she would appreciate it very much if he would request an investigation. Unfortunately, the discrimination at Carlsbad was standard practice throughout the country, since the majority of army camps were located in the South and the Southwest, where strict segregation prevailed.

Most army camps boasted a central post theater, where movies were shown, lectures delivered, and concerts performed. In some camps, as Jones described, Negroes were confined to a few seats in the last row. In other camps, a separate, less adequate space was allocated. "They have a show where the colored go," one GI explained, "and you sit on the outside to see the picture. If it rains there isn't any picture." Observing these unequal arrangements, the singer Lena Horne cut short her tour of army posts. German POWs imprisoned in the U.S., she argued, had a better opportunity to hear her than Negro soldiers.

For Negro soldiers, like Henry Jones, who had lived all their lives in the North, subjection to the Jim Crow laws of the South was intolerable. In almost every Southern city or town, Negro soldiers were restricted to a small area of the city where a few restaurants and lounges were crowded together on a single block. If they tried to go elsewhere, restaurants refused to serve them, merchants evicted them, and townspeople shouted at them.

To many Negroes, army historian Ulysses Lee concluded in his study of Negro troops, "the uncertainty of their status was as damaging to morale as the knowledge of definite restrictions." Since the rules varied widely from post to post and from town to town, each recruit had to find his own way through the maze of shaded meanings. Would he be served if he tried to make a purchase at the main post exchange? Was there a special Negro branch? Was he free to enter the gym, the bowling alley, the theater? Was he allowed to subscribe to a Negro newspaper? Which chair should he use in the barber shop, in the dentist's office? "That's the kind of democracy we are fighting for," Private Laurence Burnett pointedly remarked upon discovering that he had to sit in a colored-only chair at the dental clinic. "It is so foolish it makes me laugh most of the time. I can't sit in a dental chair that a white man has sat in or will sit in in the future!"

When Eleanor heard these stories, she felt like weeping. "What a lot we must do to make our war a real victory for democracy," she said, again and again. From her sitting room on the second floor, she fired off passionate missives to General Marshall asking him to investigate the unacceptable situations described by men like Henry Jones. So large was the flow of Eleanor's letters to Marshall that the general was forced to assign one and later two members of his staff to respond.

Finally, on March 10, 1943, the War Department took corrective action. A directive was issued to all service commands forbidding the designation of any recreational facilities, "including theaters and post exchanges," by race. The new directive required the removal of remaining "White" and "Colored only" signs in the designation of facilities, specifying that, if only one facility existed on a camp, arrangements must be made for its equal use by troops of both races. Though the directive did not touch on transportation, perhaps the most deeply felt problem, and though it did not prevent the continued use of separate facilities as long as they were not designated by racial signs (on many posts, blacks still frequented what had been the colored service club, since it was closest to their barracks, only now it was known as Service Club No. 2), it did establish the principle that Negro troops were to be given equal opportunity to use all the existing facilities provided for the welfare and recreation of soldiers. "The fact that anyone could use any facility," army historians observed, "was enough to turn the tide of Negro soldiers' morale upward." It was a beginning wedge in the desegregation of the armed forces.

Eleanor's special advocacy of Negro troops involved her later that same spring in the fortunes of the 99th Pursuit Squadron, the first unit of Negro combat pilots. The flight program at Tuskegee Air Field had been instituted in March 1941 in response to a legal suit filed by a young black pilot, Yancey Williams, who had been denied admission to the all-white Air Corps. Through 1941 and 1942, the program produced nearly a thousand black combat pilots, but by the spring of 1943 not a single one had been sent into combat. "We were undoubtedly the most highly trained squadron in the US," Louis Purnell, a member of the 99th, later wrote; "the Air Corps brass couldn't decide what to do with us so we flew and flew for nearly a whole year simply to maintain our proficiency." Inspectors had declared the 99th ready for deployment in September 1942, but still nothing happened. "The waiting got tiresome," squadron leader Benjamin Davis, Jr., recalled.

In March, Tuskegee Director Frederick Patterson turned to Eleanor for help. "The program of preflight training is going forward," he explained, "but morale is disturbed by the fact that the 99th Pursuit Squadron trained for more than a year is still at Tuskegee and virtually idle." Eleanor sent a copy of Patterson's letter to Stimson with a cover note of her own: "This seems to me a really crucial situation."

The long period of waiting came to an end on the morning of April 15, 1943, when the members of the 99th boarded a ship en route to North Africa. News of the squadron's departure spread quickly through the Negro press, which had been agitating for months "to get our boys overseas like everybody else." It was a "tremendous moment," Benjamin Davis, Jr., recalled. "All the members of the 99th were beginning to understand the significance of an assignment which went far beyond purely military considerations. If a black fighter squadron could get a good account of itself in combat, its success might lead the way to greater opportunities for black people throughout the armed services."

"As we left the shores of the United States," Davis recalled, "we felt as if we were separating ourselves, at least for the moment, from the evils of racial discrimination. Perhaps in combat overseas, we would have more freedom and respect than we had experienced at home."

The Tuskegee airmen would prove to the world, a Defense Department study later noted, that "blacks could fly in combat with the best of the pilots of any nation." In the course of 1,578 missions over North Africa, Italy, and Germany, the 99th Pursuit Squadron would be credited with shooting down 111 airborne craft and destroying 150 on the ground. Winners of a hundred Distinguished Flying Crosses, the 99th was the only escort group that never lost a single bomber to an enemy fighter.

• • •

On April 13, 1943, Roosevelt was scheduled to leave for a sixteen-day train trip through the deep South and the Midwest to inspect army bases and training camps. It was almost seven months since his last inspection trip, and the commander-in-chief was anxious to take his own measure of the readiness of the American soldier.

Eleanor had intended to accompany her husband on the trip, but when she learned that Anna, agitated by John's imminent departure to North Africa, was on her way to Washington, she decided to stay with her daughter for several days and then join Franklin on the road later in the week. Anna was still finding it hard to accept John's decision to leave the hard plodding job of publishing the paper to her while he opted for a glamorous assignment abroad. "Men are always little boys, I guess," Eleanor told her daughter. Never had the bond between mother and daughter seemed stronger. "I'll always be on hand when you need me," Eleanor promised.

In Eleanor's absence, Laura Delano and Margaret Suckley once again accompanied the president on his trip. Ross McIntire, Steve Early, Grace Tully, and Basil O'Connor were also on the train, though, from what Tommy could gather, Roosevelt spent all his time with Laura and Margaret, "had two meals every day with them and only once or twice had any of the others on the train at meals." Feeling irritated at Laura Delano, whom she considered "an imperious thing," Tommy failed to understand that on trips like this, when he was out among thousands of people all day long, the president needed to relax, and with Laura and Margaret he could say what he wanted and never worry about the consequences.

As usual, Margaret was in charge of the president's dog, Fala. A favorite with the crowds, Fala was invariably greeted by oohs and aahs whenever he emerged from the train for his limbering-up walks. Laura had also brought along a dog, a five-month-old Irish setter. "She had to get off at every stop," Tommy complained, "find a grass stop and wait for the biological functions which she then discussed in detail with anyone who would listen. One night she was off the train and the secret service did not realize it until the train had started. They threw her on and threw the dog after her and were much annoyed."

The president stopped first at the Parris Island Marine boot camp in South Carolina, where two thousand recruits were massed to render honors and be reviewed. After the official ceremonies, the president was driven to the rifle range, where, in the midst of a howling windstorm, he witnessed an elaborate target practice with Garand rifles.

No longer were American soldiers training with broomsticks and stovepipes; no longer did the army look like "a few nice boys with BB guns." By the spring of 1943, after only three years of mobilization, the American army had expanded from fewer than five hundred thousand to 4.3 million, and the president had authorized a total of 7.5 million by the end of the year. Nothing so large had ever been created in such a short time. "Just imagining it and willing it into existence," historian Geoffrey Perrett has written in his study of the American army in World War II, "was a brilliant, thrilling adventure of the spirit."

Nor were the men soft and overweight, as they had been in September of 1940, when the president first witnessed maneuvers in upstate New York. At Fort Benning, Georgia, the next day, the president was told that the men in training had pulled in their belts an average of four inches while adding an inch to their chests and ten pounds of muscle. Driving through the wooded hilly terrain of Fort Benning, the president saw paratroopers leaping from huge transports in groups of eighty-two and watched with interest as officer candidates ducked and dodged through a field alive with tracer bullets and exploding charges.

"Fort Benning is such an immense post," Roosevelt's naval aide William Rigdon wrote in his report of the trip, "and there was so much of interest happening here today, as to create within one the same feeling he would experience in attending his first 5 ring circus." After visiting the Parachute School, Roosevelt visited the Infantry School, where every phase of the complex training of an infantryman was demonstrated. "Even in the Infantry, the ground arm requiring the least technical training," army historian Robert Palmer notes in his study of the procurement of enlisted personnel, "the private had to understand the use of a dozen weapons. He had to acquire at least an elementary knowledge of many things besides: camouflage and concealment; mine removal and the detection of booby traps; patrolling and map reading; and combat intelligence; recognition of American, Allied and enemy aircraft, armored vehicles, and other equipment; the use and disposal of captured equipment; the processing of prisoners of war; first aid, field sanitation, and maintenance of life and health out of doors over long periods and under conditions of extreme difficulty."

Although these facts were understood by the high command of the armed forces, the combination of voluntary enlistment in the navy and the Marine Corps, and priorities established in 1942 which gave the army air force first call on the army's highest-quality men, had left a disproportionate share of the nation's lowest-quality enlistees—in terms of intelligence and education—in the ground forces. By mid-1943, Lieutenant General Leslie McNair, commanding general of the army ground forces, was so worried about the situation, believing that American soldiers were sustaining avoidable casualties because ground troops "did not represent a fair cross section of the nation's manpower," that the priority of air and ground forces was reversed.

At Fort Oglethorpe, Georgia, the following day, the president inspected three companies of WAAC trainees. Standing in formation along the border of the parade field, trim and neat in their khaki summer uniforms, the women were so excited to see the president that they momentarily forgot their military status and broke ranks to wave. The president smiled broadly and waved back. The next day, he enjoyed a hearty meal at Camp Gruber consisting of salad, chili con carne, macaroni, carrots, French-fried potatoes, rolls, and butter. "I don't get as good a meal as that in the White House," he laughingly remarked, referring, of course, to the infamous Henrietta Nesbitt.

Eleanor joined her husband at their son Elliott's home in Fort Worth, Texas, on the morning of April 19. Though Elliott was overseas, the Roosevelts enjoyed the chance to see their daughter-in-law Ruth and their three grandchildren. "This is a lovely restful home," Eleanor noted in her column that day, though everywhere she looked she was reminded of her absent son, who was stationed in Africa. "How many men there are today whose little children will have to learn to know them after their babyhood is over," she remarked. Photographs, books, saddles, and pictures all spoke of her son's interests, but it might be years before he would be home again.

The next day, the president and the first lady headed to Monterrey, Mexico, for dinner with Mexican President and Mrs. Manuel Avila Camacho. Though the visit was not announced until that afternoon, the streets were lined with thousands of people holding flags, flowers, and children. Ever since the president's Good Neighbor Policy in 1933, which declared America's commitment to equality and cooperation among the American republics and called for an abolition of all artificial barriers to trade, Roosevelt had been a popular figure in Latin America. Driving with Mrs. Avila Camacho, Eleanor proudly carried on a small conversation in Spanish, the result of the Spanish lessons she had begun that winter in Washington. At Corpus Christi, Texas, the following day, the president addressed the body of naval cadets and witnessed an impressive aerial show highlighted by an exhibition of dive-bombing in which seaplanes dived to within fifty feet of the water before releasing their dummy bombs over a small yellow float moored in the bay. At each direct hit, the crowd roared with applause. There was also a large contingent of WAVES at the base, and Eleanor was amused to learn that "some of the officers who had been very much opposed to them were now clamoring for more."

On Easter Sunday, the president stopped at Fort Riley, Kansas, one of the oldest military posts in the nation, dating back to 1852. After lunch at the Cavalry School Club, Roosevelt spoke reassuringly to the troops, contrasting this inspection tour with the last one he had made, seven months earlier. "It seems to me that I see in you that intangible thing," he said, "a very definite improvement." Morale was strikingly higher than it had been before. He could see it by watching the faces of the officers and listening to them talk. He could see it by looking at the tough seasoned bodies of the young recruits. He could see it by driving through the grounds of bustling camps where only dirt and mud had existed a short time before. "The Army has gone through growing pains and today the Army is a grown-up unit." Indeed, so impressed was he by the healthy appearance of the men and women he had seen that he had begun, he admitted, to come around to the idea Eleanor had originally backed, of continuing some form of national service even in peacetime.

On returning to Washington, the president met with the press. "His spirits were higher and he looked fresher," reporters noted. He had seen "a picture of America's resources, physical, industrial, agricultural and spiritual," being summoned to "an all out effort" to win the war. "He had traveled many miles in various kinds of conveyances, had felt sun and wind and rain, had eaten turkey, hot dogs, chili and a seven course Mexican dinner, had made talks and been among crowds. But for him, it was fun; it was one of his favorite ways of relaxing."

• • •

In the middle of the president's tour, the White House mail pouch had carried a disturbing letter from Interior Secretary Ickes suggesting that the situation in the Japanese internment camps was rapidly becoming worse. The evacuees, Ickes warned, "who first accepted with philosophical understanding the decision of their Government," were becoming increasingly bitter. "I do not think that we can disregard the unnecessary creating of a hostile group right in our own territory," Ickes wrote.

Troubled by the tone of Ickes' letter, the president asked Eleanor to take a side trip to the Gila River Camp in Arizona before returning to Washington. It was a risky request for Roosevelt to make, knowing as he did the strength of Eleanor's negative feelings about the original order to evacuate. Sending her to check things out would inevitably involve her again in the situation. But there was no one else he trusted as much to bring him back an unvarnished picture of what was going on.

The Gila River Camp, housing twelve thousand people, was one of ten permanent camps built by the War Relocation Authority to house the hundred thousand evacuees. The others included Heart Mountain in Wyoming, Topaz in Utah, Manzanar in California, and Minidoka in Idaho. Set in the middle of the desert, Gila endured temperatures that ranged between 125 degrees in the summer and thirty degrees below in winter. In the summer, one evacuee wrote, "You could not take hold of a doorknob without a handkerchief in hand." On summer nights, the internees all slept out of doors, some between wet sheets, others with wet towels on their heads.

Arriving on April 23, Eleanor was spared the unbearable heat of the summer sun, though she did encounter the swirling dust that left everyone's hair white, mouths gritty, and eyes red. "It chokes you and brings about irritations of the nose and throat," she wrote. For many evacuees, the ever-present dust in the desert camps was enemy number one. "It gets into every pore in the body," one evacuee wrote; "it comes in through every crack in the room of which there are thousands; it comes sifting down from the roof and it gets through your clothes and sticks to your body."

Eleanor was escorted through the camp by Dillon Myer, director of the War Relocation Authority, which oversaw the ten centers. Myer was overwhelmed by Eleanor's energy. She "covered everything in the center of any importance," he wrote, "including all the wards in the hospitals, the schools and all phases of the service activities so that she could report back to the President."

Eleanor came away from her sojourn with increased respect for the ingenuity and endurance of the Japanese Americans. Despite the wind and the dust, the internees had created a productive community. On the land surrounding the camp, they were raising livestock and producing vegetables sufficient to feed the entire camp. A camouflage-net factory was producing far beyond expectations. Within the camp itself, the evacuees had set up their own barber shops, dental offices, newspapers, adult-education courses, movie theaters, and government. In the ten centers as a whole, over 25 percent of the adult population were enrolled in a wide variety of classes, including psychology, English, American history, cabinetmaking, radio repair, auto mechanics, and shorthand, with English and American history the two most popular subjects.

"Everything is spotlessly clean," Eleanor marveled. The people worked on their whitewashed barracks constantly, and "you can see the results of their labors." Handmade screens created a sense of individuality and privacy amid rows of residential blocks that otherwise looked exactly alike. "Sometimes there are little Japanese gardens, sometimes vegetables or flowers bloom. Makeshift porches and shades have been improvised by some out of gunny sacks and bits of wood salvaged from packing cases."

Considerable ingenuity had also been used, Eleanor observed, in planning schools. There were nearly thirty thousand Japanese-American children of school age in the ten centers. Establishing schools for them amid hostile local school authorities had been a major undertaking. Requests to the

University of Arizona for library books and faculty lectures had been regularly rejected. "We are at war," University of Arizona President Alfred Atkinson said, "and *these people* are our enemies." Yet, despite all these problems, a complete school system had been established. In the absence of school buildings, different barracks had been set aside for a nursery school, an elementary school, a high school, and a library. Other barracks, their walls decorated with paper flowers and paintings, had been turned into laundry rooms and recreation centers and mess halls. The food was adequate, Eleanor noted, though the evacuees were in no way being "coddled," as some newspapers charged.

From a superficial point of view, the daily life at Gila seemed bearable. The evacuees had decent shelter, sustenance, and work. But Eleanor had learned from long practice to look below the surface in order to understand the inner life of the institutions she inspected. What was not bearable, she recognized, was the loss of freedom: the barbed-wire fences and the armed guards in sentry towers surrounding the camp; the regulations confining everyone to barracks by nine with lights out by ten; the orders given to the guards to shoot anyone who approached within twenty feet of the fence.

No matter how hard the WRA tried to make the camp look like an ordinary community, it was a penitentiary, imprisoning people who had never been convicted of doing anything wrong. No matter how enthusiastic the teachers, it was impossible to teach the principles of American democracy to citizens and residents whose fundamental rights had been taken away. "To be frank with you," sighed Mrs. Jones, an elementary-school teacher appointed by the WRA, "it embarrasses me to teach them the flag salute. Is our nation indivisible? Does it stand for justice for all? Those questions come up to my mind constantly."

Beyond the loss of liberty, Eleanor recognized, was the breakdown of the traditional family structure. With thousands of people assembled together, parents were unable to exercise the strict control they had once had over their children. "With everyone eating in mess halls," one Gila resident explained, "the family eating pattern was broken up completely. Table manners were forgotten. Conversation was impossible."

In the topsy-turvy world of the camps, the Nisei held the upper hand. "We hold the advantage of numbers," young Charles Kikuchi recorded in his diary, "and the fact we are citizens. Many of the parents who would never let their daughters go to dances before do not object so strenuously now. There can no longer be conflict over types of food served as everybody eats the same thing—with forks. The Nisei as a whole rejoice that they no longer have to attend Japanese language school."

"For the young people, it was an adventure," high-school student Jiro Ishihara observed. "But for the older people it was intolerable. I understood this only much later, when I became a parent myself and realized how hard it must have been for my parents to wake up one day and know that every ritual their life depended upon had been taken away."

"Feel sort of sorry for Pop tonight," Charles Kikuchi wrote shortly after arriving at the camp. "He had his three electric clippers hung on the wall and Tom has built him a barrel chair for the barber seat. It's a bit pathetic when he so tenderly cleans off the clippers after using them. He probably realizes he no longer controls the family group."

The split between the generations had been unwittingly aggravated, Eleanor came to understand, by the War Department's decision on January 28, 1943, to allow the American-born Nisei to enlist in a special unit in the army to be trained for combat. Though the new policy had been enthusiastically embraced by Nisei who rushed to sign up, the despair had deepened on the part of Issei, who were not allowed to volunteer, contributing to the decline in morale Harold Ickes had noted.

Henry Ebihara spoke for many in a poignant letter to Stimson. "I was very happy when I read your announcement that Nisei Americans would be given the chance to volunteer for active combat duty. But at the same time I am sad—sad because under your present laws I am an enemy alien. I am 22 years old, American in thought, American in act, as American as any other citizen. I was born in Japan. My parents brought me to America when I was only two years old. . . . Please give me a chance to serve in the armed forces. How can a democratic nation allow a technicality of birthplace to stand in the way when the nation is fighting to preserve the rights of free men?"

The only answer, Eleanor determined, taking into account all the reasons for the declining morale in the camps, was to relax the exclusion order and allow the Japanese to return to their homes, "to start independent and productive lives again." Dillon Myer agreed. Now that military necessity could no longer be considered a viable rationale, he argued that the time had come to open the doors of the camps.

"To undo mistakes is always harder than not to create them originally," Eleanor observed, "but we seldom have foresight. Therefore we have no choice but to try to correct our past mistakes."

The president listened carefully to Eleanor's report. Though he did not admit that the original decision had been a mistake, he agreed with her that "normal American life is hardly possible under any form of detention" and that "the best hope for the future lies in encouraging the relocation of Japanese Americans throughout the country." But at the same time, he was hearing from Stimson that if he moved too quickly a massive public outcry would result. It was the opinion of the War Department that the recent decline in morale could be traced to the activities of "a vicious, well-organized pro-Japan minority group to be found at each relocation project." The first step, Stimson argued, was to remove these agitators to a separate camp at Tule Lake; then, and only then, could steps be taken to clear the remaining evacuees for release.

The president backed Stimson's decision to segregate the troublemakers, but he promised Eleanor that he would meet with Myer and figure out ways to relax the order so that exit permits could be issued to individual Japanese who had work to do and a place to go. The process was slow and cumbersome, but by the end of 1943, between those who had joined the army and those who had received work permits to leave, nearly one-third of the evacuees had left the camps.

CHAPTER 17

"IT IS BLOOD ON YOUR HANDS"

By 1943, Washington was pretty much like any other boomtown during the war—its population had nearly doubled since 1940, decent housing was impossible to find, uniforms were everywhere, gasoline was scarce, buses were overcrowded, and living costs were high. Most of the newcomers were women, searching for jobs as typists and clerks in the burgeoning federal bureaucracy, which had spread its offices into every available space, into ugly temporary buildings, old schools, apartments and homes, gymnasiums and skating rinks. They were called GGs, or government girls; they came on buses and trains with their suitcases in their hands, to live in huge dormitories specially erected for them; and with their help, journalist David Brinkley wrote, "the federal government created more records in the four years of war than in its entire previous history."

The 11th of May was a soft spring day in Washington. Couples sauntered along the banks of the Potomac; strollers circled the Reflecting Pond. In weather like this, the president would ordinarily have taken the time to enjoy a leisurely ride through the hills of Virginia, but since Prime Minister Churchill was due to arrive that evening for a two-week visit, Roosevelt was forced to spend the entire day at his desk, cleaning up correspondence.

The one break in the day came at 2:30 p.m., when he received an off-the-record visit from the Russian artist Elizabeth Shoumatoff. Madame Shoumatoff had come to paint a portrait of the president, at the request of Lucy Mercer Rutherfurd. Considering the impact Lucy had had on his marriage, and the promise he had made to Eleanor never to see her again, Roosevelt decided to keep Shoumatoff's visit a private matter.

Shoumatoff had met Lucy Rutherfurd six years before in Aiken, South Carolina, when Lucy's stepdaughter, Alice Rutherfurd, had commissioned her to do a portrait of Lucy. Meeting Lucy for the first time was "quite impressive," Shoumatoff recalled. "Very tall, like the rest of her family, exquisitely lovely and gracious, she impressed you not so much by her striking appearance as by the shining quality in her features, particularly in her smile." An acute observer, Shoumatoff noticed that the clothes Lucy wore made her look older than she was, "as if deliberately diminishing the thirty-years difference between herself and her husband.

Winthrop Rutherfurd was seventy-five years old and in frail health when Shoumatoff first met him. Though she had come to draw a portrait of Lucy, Lucy asked her to paint her husband first. "Winthrop Rutherfurd, in spite of his advanced years," Shoumatoff later recalled, "was one of the handsomest men" she had ever painted, "and certainly the most aristocratic." He looked like "an English peer with his chiseled features, sharp eyes, and a sarcastic expression around his mouth." Curiously, Shoumatoff observed, "there was something about his face that vaguely resembled FDR."

Observing the daily routine in the Rutherfurd household during that first meeting, Shoumatoff was struck by the unflagging attention Lucy gave to her husband. "Everything whirled around him; their life was governed by his invalid regime. She never went out in the evenings and completely devoted her existence to making him happy and comfortable." Through nearly two decades of marriage, Lucy had mothered Winthrop's five children (a sixth had died on the eve of their wedding) and given birth to a daughter of her own, Barbara Rutherfurd. Barbara was fourteen, a student at the fashionable Fermate School for Girls in Aiken, when Shoumatoff first met Lucy. Watching Lucy with her extended family, Shoumatoff remarked that she had "seldom seen a mother more beloved and respected than was Lucy by her stepchildren."

For the Rutherfurds, as for most residents of the Aiken winter colony, the social season stretched from mid-October until after the Easter holidays. During these months, the calendar was filled with charity balls, bazaars, and sporting events, including the annual hunt breakfast, the point tournament at the Palmetto Golf Club and the thoroughbred races at the Aiken Mile. Through the twenties and thirties, Winthrop and Lucy Rutherfurd were regulars at all these events; the Rutherfurd name frequently appeared in the society pages of the *Aiken Standard & Review*. Since Winthrop's illness, Lucy had led a quieter life, but the comings and goings of the Rutherfurd children were regularly noted in the local paper. There were stories of athletic achievement—all four boys, Winthrop Jr., John, Hugo, and Guy, were outstanding athletes, champion golfers, tennis players, and scull racers—while Alice and Barbara excelled at horseback riding. There were descriptions of social engagements and debutante balls. The sheer variety of activities the children enjoyed was impressive.

Lucy had been so pleased by the first portrait that she asked Shoumatoff to come to their summer estate, in Allamuchy, New Jersey, to paint a second picture of her husband, with his fox terriers. It was in Allamuchy, Shoumatoff recalled, on a moonlit evening as she and Lucy were driving along the woodland roads, that Lucy first talked of Franklin Roosevelt. Shoumatoff had heard rumors that Lucy and Franklin had enjoyed a romance before Lucy was married, but on this occasion Lucy simply talked about his leadership qualities, "his extraordinary ability to work, his dynamic approach to anything he undertook."

It was not until the spring of 1943, when Shoumatoff was back in Aiken for a series of additional portraits, that the conversation returned to Roosevelt. "You should really paint the President," Lucy told her friend. "He has such a remarkable face. There is no painting of him that gives his true expression. I think you could do a wonderful portrait. Would you do a portrait of him if it was arranged?" Delighted and daunted by the challenge, Shoumatoff was stunned when Lucy called the following morning to say she had telephoned Washington and the president would sit for a portrait in two weeks, on May 11. "I did not understand how the whole thing could have been arranged so quickly," she admitted.

The answer lay in the affection Roosevelt still held for the woman he had once loved. If little by little passion had been extinguished by absence, regret smothered by routine, the memories were still there. The man who had disciplined himself nearly a quarter-century ago to give Lucy up must have felt he had a right to indulge the legitimate wishes of an old friend.

The exact shape of Franklin's friendship with Lucy over time is not easy to fix. Through the twenties and thirties, the only evidence that they ever saw one another is the oft-told tale that Lucy attended Roosevelt's first inaugural as his special guest, half concealed in a limousine on the edge of the crowd. The only other recorded contacts through these two decades are a couple of chatty letters Lucy wrote in 1927, the first congratulating Roosevelt on becoming a grandfather with Anna's first child, the second describing a summer holiday in Europe with the children. As long as Winthrop Rutherfurd was healthy and strong, as long as Missy LeHand guarded the gates to the White House, the risks of further association must have seemed tremendous.

The first hint of a personal meeting is contained in the handwritten version of the White House usher diary for Friday, August 1, 1941. In addition to the typed list of official appointments on the president's schedule each day, a handwritten diary was kept which filled in his movements both before and after the scheduled appointments: his trips to the doctor's office, his exercise time in the pool, his sojourns in the map room, his off-the-record guests. At eight-forty that night, the handwritten diary records a visit by a Mrs. Paul Johnson. "Mrs. Johnson," according to Roosevelt's Secret Service agent, William Simmons, was a coded name for Lucy Rutherfurd. Though we cannot say for sure that the Mrs. Johnson who visited the president on the first of August was indeed Lucy Rutherfurd, the fact that she met with him alone and stayed with him until 11 p.m. and then returned for dinner the following evening and did not leave until nearly midnight underscores that she must have been somebody special in Roosevelt's life.

The timing of the first meeting makes sense. Winthrop Rutherfurd had recently suffered a stroke and was a bedridden invalid. Early in his illness, when he was desperately sick, Lucy had contacted Roosevelt for help, perhaps to gain admission to Walter Reed. The friendship had been renewed. During these same months, Lucy's mother had been placed in the Waverly Sanitarium, in Rockville, Maryland, and her only sister, Violetta, had moved to D.C., giving Lucy other reasons to come to Washington. On Roosevelt's side, the timing was also right. Missy was still in the hospital recovering from her stroke, and Eleanor was in Campobello for the final session of her summer leadership institute.

"Mrs. Johnson" returned to Washington three months later, on November 9, accompanied by her daughter (presumably Barbara Rutherfurd). The two women took tea with the president in the late afternoon, and then Mrs. Johnson dined with him alone in his study. Eleanor was in New York at the time. In December, young Barbara visited the White House on her own, to eat dinner with Harry Hopkins and the president in Roosevelt's study. The following spring, Mrs. Johnson showed up twice for dinner, and then, in October, when Eleanor was en route to England, she returned once more, dining with him one day and taking tea with him the next. Nothing specific is known of the conversation they shared. If the infatuation of their earlier days was still alive, it is not likely that either allowed the other to know.

When Shoumatoff arrived at the president's office that day in May 1943, he greeted her with such friendliness that his hand, she later wrote, seemed to stretch across the entire room. "How is Mrs. Rutherfurd? And how is Barbara?" he asked. Throughout the sitting, he was "very cheerful," talking at length about the royal refugees in the U.S. and the recent visit of the Soviet ambassador to the United States, Maxim Litvinov. As Shoumatoff finished her sketch, she commented that his gray suit and blue tie were too drab for a painting. The president laughed and then suggested that he put on his favorite navy-uniform cape. Perfect, the artist replied, and the portrait was completed. A week later, she returned to Aiken and presented the handsome painting to a "delighted" Lucy.

• • •

Churchill arrived in Washington the evening of May 11, just as the Allied operation in North Africa was coming to a successful conclusion. Two days earlier, the Axis forces in Tunisia had surrendered unconditionally to the Allies.

It had been a long struggle for the Allies, longer than expected. After the first flush of victory in French North Africa, the Allied drive on Tunis had come up against the fierce resistance of reinforced German forces under the leadership of the great "Desert Fox," German General Erwin Rommel. On February 20, at Kasserine Pass, inexperienced American forces had encountered their first blitzkrieg attack by German tanks, artillery, and dive-bombers. Though the Americans fought bravely, they were outmaneuvered by the seasoned German troops: their defense of the pass was ill-conceived, their tanks were under-armed, their equipment was inferior, their training for the removal of mines was inadequate, and their air-ground communications were faulty. The Germans broke through the pass, destroyed a large cache of weapons, and took thousands of American prisoners.

Two weeks after the battle at Kasserine Pass, a telegram addressed to Mrs. Mae Stifle on Corning Street arrived at the Western Union Station in the small town of Red Oak, Iowa, population six thousand. "The Secretary of War desires me to express his deep regret that your son Daniel Stifle . . . is missing in action." Fifteen minutes later, a second telegram arrived, telling Mrs. Stifle that her second son, Frank, was also missing in action. A few minutes later, Mrs. Stifle's daughter, Marie, received word that she had lost her husband, Daniel Wolfe. As the evening wore on, the telegrams kept coming until there were twenty-seven. The Gillespies on Second Street had lost two boys—Charles, twenty-two, and Frank, twenty. Duane Dodd and his cousins, the two Halbert boys, were missing.

The families gathered in the lobby of the Hotel Johnson, next door to the Western Union Station, and tried to make sense of what was happening. Someone recalled seeing something in the papers about a difficult engagement at a place called Kasserine Pass, but it would take weeks for the people of this small town to come to understand that their entire National Guard unit had been destroyed in a single battle. Red Oak had suffered a disproportionate loss, greater than any other town in the United States. Only two years earlier, the members of Company M had marched side by side through the streets on their way to war; now their names were listed side by side on the official casualty list.

Red Oak, Iowa, was the "hometown we dreamed of overseas," one serviceman wrote after the war, "rich and contented, with chicken and blueberry pies on Sundays, for whose sake, some said, we were fighting the war." Looking up the main street, one could see the newly painted store fronts of J. C. Penney and Montgomery Ward, the sandstone structure of the Hudson State Park, and, across the way, the Green Parrot, an ice-cream parlor full of young people. On the road into Red Oak was the Grand Theater, where farmers from surrounding towns brought their children on Saturdays for a double feature. Everyone in this small town knew someone on the list.

By March, the Americans had recovered from their reversal at Kasserine Pass and were pushing forward aggressively. By April, with General Patton in command, American troops had finally joined up with General Montgomery's Eighth Army, having started two thousand miles apart. The Axis forces were driven eastward and trapped in the Tunisian tip, where they surrendered. Nearly a quarter-million Germans and Italians were taken prisoner. The Allied victory in Africa was complete.

The Tunisian victory cast a bright light on the May summit, which became known as the "Trident Conference." Goebbels noted in his diary on the eve of the conference that "the Americans are happy as children to be able for the first time to take German troops into custody. . . . My thoughts often turn to North Africa and to our soldiers. . . . The only comforting thought is the fact that they are falling into the hands of a civilized opponent." For his part, Churchill could not help recalling "the striking change which had taken place in the situation since he had last sat by the President's desk and had heard the news of the fall of Tobruk. He could never forget the manner in which the President had sustained him at that time."

Much had happened in the past year. At Stalingrad, Guadalcanal, El Alamein, and Tunis, the Allies had shown that the Axis powers could be defeated in battle. But, as Martin Gilbert has written, these places "stood on the periphery of the areas under Axis control. The continent of Europe, and the vast island expanses of South East Asia, were still under the military rule of those who had chosen to make war. The Allies, for all their recent triumphs, stood at the edge of immense regions confronted by hugely powerful forces still to be overthrown."

The central issue at the Trident Conference was the timing of the cross-Channel invasion—in particular, what to do with the twenty divisions that would come free when the invasion of Sicily was completed, sometime in August. Once again, the old disagreements emerged. Churchill wanted to use these divisions to invade Italy, postponing still further the cross-Channel invasion; Roosevelt wanted to send them to England to build up the monstrous force that would be needed to invade France in the spring of 1944. In the days ahead, the discussions would become increasingly intense, but first, Roosevelt insisted, it was time to relax with drinks and dinner.

Since Eleanor was en route to New York for a meeting of the Committee for the Care of European Children, the president asked his daughter, Anna, to be his hostess at dinner. Anna had come to Washington earlier in the week to bid farewell to her husband as he sailed overseas to North Africa, and she was thrilled by her father's request. Since her girlhood, she had yearned to be important to her father, to be needed by him. Indeed, the presiding image from her childhood was the memory of her father coming home from work and shutting himself up for hours in a room with cigar-smoking politicians. Forbidden to interrupt or even to peek inside, she could imagine nothing more wonderful than to be invited, as she now was, to take her mother's place in the inner sanctum of her father's political life.

Seated opposite the president, with Hopkins on her left and Churchill on her right, Anna made a striking impression. Her blue eyes shone, her warmth radiated. After dinner, the guests were treated to a preview of an unreleased film, *The Battle of Britain.* It was excellent, Anna told John, "so much so that the PM wept." All in all, Anna enthused, the entire evening was "intensely interesting."

That weekend, the president took Churchill to Shangri-la, along with Eleanor, Anna, Hopkins, and Beaverbrook. As the guests piled into the cars for the two-hour trip to the wooded Maryland retreat, Eleanor insisted that Churchill sit beside Franklin in the back seat while she occupied one of the small front seats. Churchill would have none of this, insisting that Mrs. Roosevelt take her proper place by her husband's side. The conflict of wills went on for three minutes, Churchill recalled, as "the British empire went into action" against the formidable Mrs. Roosevelt. In the end, Eleanor relented, agreeing to sit beside her husband while Churchill sat up front.

As the motorcade approached Frederick, Maryland, Churchill asked if he could see the house of Barbara Frietchie, whose courage in placing a Union flag outside her attic window as the Confederate army marched by inspired John Greenleaf Whittier's poem "Barbara Frietchie." The discussion prompted Roosevelt to quote the famous lines " 'Shoot, if you must, this old gray head, / But spare your country's flag,' she said." When it was clear that this was as far as Roosevelt could go, Churchill chimed in, quoting from memory the entire poem. While his companions were asking themselves how he could do this when he hadn't read the poem for thirty years, Churchill went on to give a brilliant review of the Battle of Gettysburg, along with a lengthy disquisition on Stonewall Jackson and Robert E. Lee.

Eleanor was impressed by Churchill's memory, his wit, and his extensive knowledge. "He is always using quotations & can quote endless poetry," she wrote Lash. She was also impressed by Lord Beaverbrook, who "fell completely for Anna & offered to help her on her paper," yet "none of them," she remarked, with evident pride in her husband's personality, has "the geographic knowledge, nor all around historical knowledge & grasp of the whole picture today which our own raconteur has & he can outtalk them all too which amused Anna & me very much."

On the trip to Shangri-la, the president told Churchill he was looking forward to a few hours with his stamp collection. Later, Churchill sat by his side, watching "with much interest and in silence for perhaps half an hour as he stuck them in, each in its proper place, and so forgot the cares of State." But all too soon, Churchill noted, General Walter Bedell Smith arrived, carrying an urgent message from Eisenhower. "Sadly FDR left his stamp collection and addressed himself to his task."

The evening was great fun, Anna reported to John, though she discovered that "the PM picks his teeth all through dinner and uses snuff liberally. The sneezes which follow the latter practically rock the foundations of the house and he then blows his nose about three times like a fog horn." But the conversation was sparkling, Anna enthused, as Churchill, Roosevelt, and Beaverbrook vied with one another in telling stories. The only unpleasant moment came when Eleanor insisted on telling a story of her own, "which showed all too plainly her dislike for a certain lady [most likely Princess Martha] whom you and I and the boss like!"

In the morning, the president took Churchill fishing in a nearby stream. "He was placed with great care by the side," Churchill recorded, "and sought to entice the nimble and wily fish. I tried for some time myself at other spots. No fish were caught, but he seemed to enjoy it very much, and was in great spirits for the rest of the day."

After the relaxing weekend, the presidential party descended the Alleghenies and returned to Washington, where, Stimson recorded, "a very decided deadlock" arose between the president and the prime minister. "The British are holding back dead from going on with [Operation] Bolero . . . and are trying to divert us off into some more Mediterranean adventures. Fortunately the President seems to be holding out. I talked with Marshall. . . . He seems to be glad to have my backing in the matter because the burden of the whole thing has been falling on him."

The debate went on for days, and the longer it continued, the hotter it became. As the tension mounted, Churchill's mood darkened, shifting from anger to irritation to despair. After one heated session, Lord Moran found him pacing up and down his room, scowling at the floor. "The President is not willing to put pressure on Marshall," Churchill lamented. "He is not in favor of landing in Italy. It is most discouraging. I only crossed the Atlantic for this purpose. I cannot let the matter rest where it is." For his part, Marshall thought Churchill was acting like "a spoiled boy," and Hopkins found him "a little subdued—for Winston that is."

As Churchill got ready to leave, a compromise was achieved: a general resolution was drafted calling on the Allied commander-in-chief "to plan such operations in exploitation of Husky [the Allied invasion of Sicily] as are best calculated to eliminate Italy from the war and to contain the maximum number of German forces." In other words, Roosevelt was willing to consider the possibility of taking action in Italy if and only if he was assured that such action would not detract in any substantial way from the buildup for the cross-Channel attack. This was not the firm commitment to invade Italy that Churchill wanted, but it was a step in the right direction.

Churchill's departure on May 27 brought a collective sigh of relief to the White House staff. As much as everyone revered the prime minister, the president's aide William Hassett observed, he was "a trying guest—drinks like a fish and smokes like a chimney, irregular routine, works nights, sleeps days, turns the clock upside down." Even Franklin, Eleanor observed, who "really likes the PM and believes he can manage him in the end," was utterly exhausted. The morning after Churchill left, Roosevelt took Princess Martha and Harry Hopkins to Hyde Park, where he slept ten hours a day for three days straight until he recovered from Churchill's visit.

• • •

When the president returned to the White House on June 2, he was greeted with the unwelcome news that the nation's coal miners, under the leadership of John L. Lewis, had gone on strike. For months, Lewis had been engaged in a running battle with the War Labor Board to secure an increase of $2 a day for the miners. He had used every weapon in his armory, including the threat to strike, but he had been unable to shake the WLB from its position that any wage increase would violate the "Little Steel" formula promulgated by the president the year before to restrain both wage advances and cost-of-living increases. Under the formula, wage increases were allowed only if necessary to correct serious maladjustments or gross inequities. The ink was scarcely dry on the latest WLB refusal when Lewis and the miners decided to strike.

The effect of the strike—which took five hundred thousand miners off the job and closed more than three thousand mines—was devastating. Without coal to process the iron ore or fire the steel plants, eleven blast furnaces had to be shut down. Steel production faltered. Railroad schedules were cut back for lack of fuel. Production of guns and tanks slowed. The chain of losses reached deep into the national economy.

While Roosevelt considered his options in long meetings with Ickes and Jimmy Byrnes, angry letters poured into the White House from citizens and soldiers at home and abroad. "You must have lace on your pants for allowing John L. Lewis to pull such a stunt," Sophia Carroll wrote from Maryland. "I think you are equally guilty with John L. Lewis for the mess we are in," Esther Morrow wrote. "You babied and petted him until he thinks he is boss also."

Opinion among the GIs was even more damning. Pfc. John Adkins spoke for 90 percent of the soldiers, according to *Stars and Stripes,* when he wrote from North Africa, "While these American boys are over here sweating, bleeding and dying to protect America and even the right to strike, those people back there have the gall to quit their jobs."

"What sort of traitors are those miners?" one marine asked. "I've just come down from the North with a plane load of men who were injured in the Attu fighting. One of them was minus a leg. . . . His entire life is pretty well ruined. Imagine it must be rather bewildering to return from battle . . . to find the defenders of the homefront bargaining for another dollar or two to add to already mountainous wages."

"If I were on the front lines, and a Marine was scared or tired and refused to fight or advance I would have to shoot him," another soldier, John Jaqua, observed. "Unless my sense of values is completely warped, he is doing no more than a laborer who strikes."

As the strike continued, public anger at the miners turned against the labor movement as a whole. Labor spokesmen tried in vain to set the record straight, pointing out that the great majority of labor leaders had kept the no-strike pledge they had given after Pearl Harbor. To be sure, disgruntled employees at various plants had engaged in unauthorized wildcat strikes from time to time. In July 1942, scattered employees at the Detroit diesel-engine division at General Motors, upset because their departments were not included in a pay-raise award, had walked out. A few weeks later, workers at Monroe Auto Equipment brought claims of "speed-up" and walked out when new gears were installed in their machines. Most of these wildcat strikes had been quickly settled, and production had continued with little interruption. But with the country at war, the general public refused to make fine distinctions. By an overwhelming majority, the people believed that strikes should be outlawed.

In the halls of Congress, the protest reached a crescendo. In the second week of June 1943, the House joined the Senate in supporting a bill, the Smith-Connally Act, that imposed drastic penalties and restrictions on any person encouraging a strike in government-owned plants. The bill was a humiliating setback to the entire labor movement. "It is the judgment of the CIO," CIO President Philip Murray wrote Roosevelt, "that this proposed legislation if enacted into law would constitute one of the most serious blows directed against our national war effort and be the equivalent of a major military disaster."

Eleanor told a *New York Times* reporter she was sick at heart about the whole situation. Though she could not condone the stoppage of work in an industry so vital to war production, she knew from her visits to the coal mines in Appalachia that the miners had genuine grievances that badly needed remedying. She had seen the unpainted shanties with muddy yards on muddy streets where the miners lived. She understood the tremendous risks the miners endured—in 1941, 64,764 were killed or injured as a consequence of gas explosions, bad ventilation, defective timbering, and cave-ins. She had witnessed the miners' helpless dependence on high-priced company stores that kept them "in hock" forever by running a tab which was then deducted from their weekly pay checks. "I have seen pay envelopes containing three cents," she said. For all these reasons, she believed that "the settlement of the strike should be brought about in the light of what the miners and their families have lived through for the past ten years. I think they are entitled to some concessions."

Eleanor's opinion was not popular, but the president listened to her words. Despite his fury at John L. Lewis, which led him, in the privacy of the Oval Office, to crack that "he would be glad to resign as President if Lewis committed suicide," he kept a tight rein over his temper in public, allowing the situation to speak for itself. "I understand the devotion of the coal miners to their union," he said, speaking more in sadness than in anger. "Every improvement of the conditions of the coal miners of this country has had my hearty support. And I do not mean to desert them now. But I also do not mean to desert my obligations and responsibilities as President of the U.S. and Commander-in-Chief of the Army and Navy. The first necessity is the resumption of coal mining."

Acting under the cover of his emergency war powers, Roosevelt instructed Ickes to take over the mines in the name of the government. At the same time, he ordered the five hundred thousand miners to return to work, reminding them that they were working for the government "on essential war work and it was their duty no less than that of their sons and brothers in the Armed Forces to fulfill their war duties." Stimson wanted the president to go even further, to tell the miners that they would all be inducted if they refused to go back to work, but for the time being, Roosevelt was hesitant to use induction as a penalty.

While Lewis was deciding how to respond, a telephone call brought one of the striking miners the sad news that his son, who was in the navy, had been killed in the Pacific. "I ain't a traitor," the miner burst out, "damn 'em I ain't a traitor. I'll stay out until hell freezes over. Dickie was fighting for one thing, I'm fighting for another and they ain't so far apart." But on the sixth day of the strike, Lewis ordered his men back to work.

There remained the thorny problem of the Smith-Connally Act, which arrived in the White House pouch for the president's signature in the middle of June. "If I were FDR I wouldn't sign it," Eleanor confided to Joe Lash, "but I'm not enough of a politician to judge the temper of the country." William Hassett agreed. "This is a bad bill, through which, if approved, labor stands to lose its hard won gains."

The War Department argued that the president should sign the legislation. "In spite of imperfections of the bill," Stimson wrote, "it has enough good points on the vital issues of having young men at home perform their duties without discrimination like the soldiers, making it an important moral issue to have the bill passed."

The sentiment of the country was overwhelmingly in favor of the bill. A woman from Sewanee, Tennessee, spoke for many in a stormy letter to the president. "We the people are getting fed up with you and your spineless treatment of labor.... I was one of your ardent admirers when you first went into office but now I can hardly wait for the day you go out of office. Between you and your treatment of labor and Mrs. Roosevelt and the niggers, this is one hell of a place."

The president kept the country and the Congress waiting for the maximum time he could—nine and one-half days plus two Sundays—while he pondered his decision. On June 25, at 3:15 p.m., he sent his answer to the Congress: he had decided to veto the bill. "Let there be no misunderstanding of the reasons which prompt me to veto this bill at this time," he began. "I am unalterably opposed to strikes in wartime. I do not hesitate to use the powers of government to prevent them." He clearly understood, he said, that it was the will of the American people "that no war work be interrupted by strike or lockout." But the American people should realize that, for the entire year of 1942, "99.95 percent of the work went forward without strikes, and that only 5 one-hundredths of 1 percent of the work was delayed by strikes. That record has never been equaled in this country. It is as good or better than the record of any of our Allies in wartime."

He conceded that laws are often necessary "to make a very small minority of people live up to the standards that the great majority of the people follow," but he contended that, far from discouraging strikes, the bill's provisions would stimulate labor unrest.

Eleanor was pleased by the president's veto, as was organized labor. "In vetoing the Smith-Connally bill, President Roosevelt has demonstrated once more," CIO President Philip Murray said, "his sound understanding of the nature of the democracy for which we are fighting and the need for full mobilization of the nation for victory." But the euphoria was short-lived. At 3:30, only fifteen minutes after it had received the president's veto message, the Senate overrode the veto fifty-six to twenty-five. As soon as word of the Senate action reached the House, the members immediately laid aside debate on a Commodity Credit Corporation extension and took up the override. Representative Clifton Woodrum set the tone when he called for "action, not tomorrow, not Monday, but today, so that we can send the message to our boys in the foxholes that the American people are behind them." At 5:28 p.m., the House joined the Senate in the override, and the Smith-Connally Act became law.

Stimson considered the congressional override, only the eighth time in ten years that the Congress had enacted a bill into law over Roosevelt's veto, "a bad rebuff and an unnecessary rebuff.... His administration really is beginning to shake a little and throughout the country there is evident feeling that he has made a mistake in regard to labor."

In a conversation at Hyde Park the following week, Eleanor asked Franklin if he thought "our lack of leadership and discipline in Congress came about because we'd been in power too long." The president replied reflectively. "Perhaps, we certainly have no control. I think the country has forgotten we ever lived through the 30s."

Unchastened by the congressional slap, Lewis struggled on in defense of the miners. Twice again in the months ahead, he ordered his men on strike. Twice again, the president seized the mines. There was more idleness in 1943 due to strikes in the mining industry than in any other. Finally, an ingenious solution was reached whereby the United Mine Workers shifted their focus from a straight pay raise to "portal to portal pay." For years, the miners had suffered under a system which saw their hourly wage begin only when they reached their place of work deep within the mine. The long ride in a metal cart from the top of the mine to the bottom was not considered work. Through Ickes' intervention, an agreement was reached that allowed the miners to be paid "portal to portal," from the moment they entered the mine to the moment they left. Since extra time did not violate the "Little Steel" formula, the solution was approved by the War Labor Board.

"We were thrilled at the news," coal miner Michael Lilly recalled. "Once you entered the coal mines, you were in danger. It was dark from the moment you went in. Anything could happen on the way down. I was always afraid. Now I knew from the moment I got into the cart at the top of the hill the money was kicking in. That eased everything a great deal."

• • •

As Eleanor worked on her column in Hyde Park on Sunday morning, June 20, she was wrapped in gloomy spirits. "The domestic scene," she admitted, referring not only to the coal dispute but to a rash of racial disturbances that had recently broken out, "is anything but encouraging and one would like not to think about it, because it gives one a feeling that, as a whole, we are not really prepared for democracy."

Three weeks earlier, in Mobile, Alabama, a racial incident in the Addsco shipyard had resulted in the loss of ten thousand workers for seven days. "No city in the deep South has felt the war more sharply than Mobile, Alabama," journalist Selden Menefee concluded after a nationwide tour of the United States in the first half of 1943. "Here is an historic town that slept for 230 years, then woke up in two. The population of Mobile's metropolitan area has increased by 60%, from 79,000 in 1940 to an estimated 125,000 in the spring of 1943." Drawn by the magnet of the great shipyards of Mobile, many of the new arrivals were poor whites from the hinterlands. "If these 'poor whites' are full of anti-Negro prejudices, as they are," Menefee observed, "it is because the whiteness of their skins is the one thing that gives them a degree of social status."

The trouble began when a group of skilled Negro welders were upgraded and assigned to work on the same job with white welders. To the white welders, the idea of being forced to work side by side with Negroes was an unacceptable wedge in the time-honored system of segregation. "We realize the fact that they are human beings," Archie Adams wrote in a letter to the *Mobile Register,* but "we don't any more want to work or want our women to work alongside a Negro than you would want to take one into your dining room and sit him down between your wife and mother to eat dinner, or for your wife to invite the cook in for a game of bridge, or take her to the movies."

As the morning shift began, a group of white welders, armed with bricks, clubs, and bars, attacked the Negro welders. "No nigger is goin' to join iron in these yards," one worker shouted. The fighting soon spread to other parts of the yard. Before it ended, eleven Negroes were carried to the hospital. Peace was restored only when the company decided, in a move reluctantly approved by the FEPC, to assign the skilled Negro welders to a separate shipway, where they would not mingle with whites. With vital production heavily curtailed, it seemed the only way to avoid future trouble. But it was clearly a step backward, as Eleanor assuredly understood.

Worse was to come. A few hours after Eleanor finished her cheerless column, while she and Franklin were entertaining Queen Wilhelmina of the Netherlands in the library after dinner, word was received at Hyde Park of bloody rioting in Detroit. The disturbance had begun at Belle Isle, a public park frequented mostly by blacks. By midafternoon, the temperature in Detroit had hit ninety-one and the park was filled to capacity, with a hundred thousand people. As evening approached, the bridge to the mainland was jammed with cars and pedestrians. A few scuffles broke out between whites and blacks. A young white couple was assaulted and robbed of $2 by a group of seven Negroes. Two white girls got into a fight with a Negro girl. One of the white girls knocked the Negro girl down; the Negro girl bloodied the white girl's nose and blackened her eye. A rumor floated that a group of whites had thrown a Negro woman and her baby off the bridge. Shortly after midnight, at a nightclub on Hastings Street, in the heart of "Paradise Valley," the Negro district, a well-dressed Negro carrying a briefcase took the microphone, stopped the music, and announced that fighting was in progress on Belle Isle, that three Negroes had been killed and a Negro woman and her baby drowned. He urged everyone to get guns and cars and join the fight. The rioting spread.

Groups of Negroes came out into the streets, smashing windows, stopping streetcars, stoning whites. Gangs of whites charged into Negro areas, chasing and beating Negroes as they walked down the street. By midnight, four hundred were injured and ten were dead. Later in the morning, a milk driver making his rounds in the Negro district and an Italian doctor answering an emergency call were beaten to death. During the worst hours of the fighting, Governor Harry Kelly of Michigan stubbornly insisted that he could handle the situation with local and state police. Without a request from the governor for federal troops, or certification that state authorities could not control the violence, the president was constitutionally unable to act. It was not until Monday morning, eighteen hours after the rioting had begun, that the governor finally asked for help. The federal troops, thirty-eight hundred strong, arrived at 11 a.m., and by late afternoon peace was restored, but by then death had come to twenty-five Negroes and nine whites, while nearly one thousand were injured.

That night, in Detroit's Receiving Hospital, reporters noted that bleeding Negroes and whites sat side by side, joined by a common bewilderment at the incomprehensible events they had seen. The story was told of a colored woman of light complexion who was beaten to death by colored men who mistook her for a white woman. In another part of the city, white youths had begun to close in on a Negro. Three white sailors stepped in and broke it up. "He's not doing you any harm," one of the sailors said. "Let him alone." "What's it to you?" snapped one of the gang. "Plenty," replied the sailor. "There was a colored guy in our outfit and he saved a couple of lives. Besides you guys are stirring up something that we're trying to stop."

In the days that followed, politicians and reporters sought to understand why the explosion had taken place. To many people in both the North and the South, the answer was clear: Eleanor Roosevelt was "morally responsible" for the riot. "It is blood on your hands, Mrs. Roosevelt," the *Jackson Daily News* declared on June 22. "You have been personally proclaiming and practicing social equality at the White House and wherever you go, Mrs. Roosevelt. What followed is now history." Detroit resident John Lang pointed his finger in the same direction. "It is my belief," he wrote the president, that "Mrs. Roosevelt and Mayor [Edward] Jeffries of Detroit are somewhat guilty of the race riots due to their coddling of negroes."

Eleanor responded with composure. "I suppose when one is being forced to realize that an unwelcome change is coming, one must blame it on someone or something," she replied.

Stimson's initial reaction was to blame "the deliberate effort that has been going on on the part of certain radical leaders of the colored race to use the war for obtaining the ends which they were seeking, and these ends are very difficult because they include race equality to be social as well as economic and military and they are trying to demand that there will be this complete intermixing in the military." But when Stimson saw the pictures in *Life* magazine that showed Negroes being beaten and assaulted by whites, generally young white boys, he told General Somervell he had "come to the conclusion that we have got to do something . . . or there will be real trouble in the tense situation that exists among the two races throughout the country."

The truth was that dozens of causes had coincided to bring about the riots. C. E. Rhetts, special assistant to Attorney General Francis Biddle, spent the first week of July in Detroit, interviewing hundreds of people, including politicians, policemen, FBI agents, labor leaders, civil-rights leaders, and journalists. "Many newspapers and individuals have charged that the enemy fomented this riot," Rhett stated at the beginning of his report. "But though there is no doubt that the riot gave great comfort and some aid to the enemy, no evidence has yet been developed to indicate that he contrived it." On the contrary, Rhett concluded, the riot was the product of the spontaneous combustion of a number of troubling elements.

For one thing, Detroit had grown phenomenally during the previous two years, adding nearly 500,000 people, including 150,000 Negroes, to its population of 2.5 million. As Negroes and whites competed for what little housing, transportation, and recreation was available, the fascist exhortations of radio commentators Father Charles Coughlin and Gerald K. Smith found fertile soil. The Ku Klux Klan took on new life. "The old, subdued, muted, murderous Southern race war," one journalist noted, "was transplanted into a high-speed industrial background." Housing conditions for Negroes, Rhett reported, were "deplorable." Time and again, real-estate investors had blocked any chance for the construction of adequate federal housing, and "the vacillation which characterized the federal government's position in the case of the Sojourner Truth Negro housing project last year did not help."

Trailer camps were everywhere, and with them, as one reporter described it, "a sizable population of delinquent, rootless 'trailer boys'—the cruel, pitiable, negative young savages who are good for riots and fascist putsches." For months, conflicts between whites and blacks in the high school had been on the increase. "Large segments of the negro community hate the police, probably not without reason." All these factors, taken together, created a "highly explosive community."

The riots cast a baleful shadow on the home front, rendering false the image of a united people in time of war. "Like a defective screw in a great machine, though apparently insignificant," Eleanor's friend Pauli Murray warned the president, the problem of race "can literally wreck our national endeavor.... This matter has become a national menace." Civil-rights leaders entreated Roosevelt to address the nation in a fireside chat. "We urge you to go on the radio at the earliest possible moment," Walter White wrote. The only solution to the racial problem, Mary McCleod Bethune observed, is "a straight forward statement and program of action from the President."

For her part, Eleanor believed that the race riots put us "on a par with Nazism which we fight, and makes us tremble for what human beings may do when they no longer think but let themselves be dominated by their worst emotions." In countless memos she had warned her husband about the disgraceful living conditions that accompanied the overcrowded boomtowns. For months, she had worried about rising racial tensions, calling at one point for an interracial conference of Negro and white leaders. Now that the long-anticipated explosion had taken place, she was convinced that the conservative Southern bloc in Congress, which repeatedly refused to better conditions for Negroes, was largely to blame. "Detroit should never have happened," she wrote Trude Pratt, "but when Congress behaves as it does why should others be calmer?"

While Eleanor suffered outwardly, the president reacted calmly, telling reporters at his weekly press conference that he refused to become aroused as long as war production continued at top levels. At one point, a week after the riots, he considered making a nationwide statement about race, but in the end he abandoned the idea. He was convinced, Eleanor told Lash, that "he must not irritate the southern leaders as he feels he needs their votes for essential war bills." Better to wait, he decided, until later in the summer, when he intended to deliver a more general address to the nation on the home front.

The presidential silence on race was not easy for liberals to understand. "Why," *New Republic* writer Thomas Sanction asked, "hasn't Mr. Roosevelt come to us with one of his greatest speeches, speaking to us as Americans, speaking to us as the great mongrel nation ... why hasn't he come to us and talked to us in the simple and genuine language that Lincoln might have used, why hasn't he come waking memories of the old American dream, of live and let live, of a land where all men are endowed with inalienable rights, of a country where all men are created equal?"

• • •

As the riots faded from the national consciousness, the president turned his attention to the invasion of Sicily, which was scheduled to begin in early July. At the end of his working day, Roosevelt frequently visited the map room to follow the buildup of the Allied landing force. By the first week of July, one-third of the invading force, 160,000 men, with six hundred tanks and two thousand landing craft were assembled in Malta, waiting for the weather to clear so they could make their move. At dawn on July 10, the landings began. Despite the high winds, which blew the paratroopers too far inland, Allied forces successfully fought off both Italian and German troops. The Axis, having lost a quarter of a million troops in Tunisia, had only ten Italian divisions and two German panzer units stationed in Sicily at the time of the invasion. Two weeks later, as the invading forces swept toward Palermo, on the western half of the northern coast, Roosevelt headed to Shangri-la with Robert Sherwood and Sam Rosenman to begin work on a major speech to the nation—his first fireside chat on the war since February.

Between the coal strike and the riots in Mobile and Detroit, national morale was suffering. "The whole world is watching our domestic troubles," reporter Edwin James wrote in *The New York Times.* "Our President has said, and often, that we would show the world that a democracy could be made to work at war as well as any totalitarian state. . . . Therefore, much depends on how we run our democracy at war. And we are not running it any too well."

In his speech, Roosevelt wanted to make it clear to the American public that the home front and the war front were one and the same; that the factory worker at home was as crucial to the war as the soldier abroad. If the identity between the two fronts could be reinforced, he believed, morale and productivity would go up. What the home front worker needed was neither to be reprimanded nor flattered; he simply needed information about the relationship between his workaday job and the effort to beat the Nazis. Once he had that information, he could be trusted to do his job.

On July 27, the day before his speech, Roosevelt was asked at his press conference what the talk would be about. "It is going to be about the war," Roosevelt quipped, provoking laughter throughout the room. "Abroad or at home, sir?" one reporter asked. "You know, I hoped you would ask that question just that way," Roosevelt replied, then proceeded to deliver an extemporaneous mini-version of his speech. "There are too many people in this country . . . who are not mature enough to realize that you can't take a piece of paper and draw a line down the middle of it and put the war abroad on one side and put the home front on the other, because after all it all ties in together. When we send an expedition to Sicily, where does it begin? Well it begins at two places practically; it begins on the farms of this country, and in the mines of this country. And then the next step in getting that army into Sicily is the processing of the food, and the processing of the raw material into steel, then the munitions plants that turn the steel into tanks and planes or the aluminum. . . . And then, a great many million people in this country are engaged in transporting it from the plant, or from the field, or the processing plant to the seaboard. And then it's put on ships that are made in this country . . . and you have to escort and convoy with a lot of other ships. . . . Finally, when they get to the other side, all these men go ashore. . . . But all through this we have to remember that there is just one front, which includes at home as well as abroad. It is all part of the picture of trying to win the war."

Roosevelt was in high spirits as he sat before the microphones in the Diplomatic Reception Room at 9:25 p.m. on July 28. As the speech was being put into final form, word had come over the radio that Italian dictator Benito Mussolini had been ousted from power. In the wake of the Allied invasion of Sicily, the Grand Fascist Council had convened, and Mussolini had been summoned to a meeting with King Victor Emmanuel of Italy at which he was told he was being relieved of his offices. When Mussolini was leaving the palace, the king had him arrested and asked Marshal Pietro Badoglio to form a new government.

The stunning news from Italy provided the perfect backdrop to the president's argument that the home front and the war front were inexorably tied together. "The first crack in the Axis has come," he began. "The criminal, corrupt Fascist regime in Italy is going to pieces. The pirate philosophy of the Fascists and Nazis cannot stand adversity."

In contrast, he argued, the productivity of the democracies was "almost unbelievable." The logistical war was entering a new phase. The margin of Allied production over the Axis was now estimated to be three to one. The month of July promised a new peak of 4,560 planes, with a total output of eighty-six thousand expected by the end of 1943, nearly double the output for the previous year.

Production of merchant ships was even more impressive. "This year," Roosevelt proudly observed, "we are producing over 19 million tons of merchant shipping and next year our production will be over 21 million tons. For several months, we have been losing fewer ships by sinkings and we have been destroying more and more U-boats. We hope this can continue. But we cannot be sure." As it turned out, the decline in shipping losses during the spring of 1943 would prove to be permanent. The Battle of the Atlantic was finally being won, releasing a flood of American munitions and troops into the major overseas theaters.

Overall, munitions output in 1943 would be 83 percent greater than in 1942, aircraft tonnage 140 percent higher, merchant ships 100 percent higher, and naval ships 75 percent higher. The United States had come a long way since 1940 and 1941, when the army and navy needed all they could get of everything—tanks, bombs, planes, ships, rifles. Now, with important exceptions—steel, landing craft, and escort vessels—stockpiles were sufficiently high to permit cutbacks.

American ingenuity had also filled the critical gap in the rubber supply after Pearl Harbor, when the Far Eastern plantations that had supplied the United States with 90 percent of its rubber were suddenly lost to Japanese conquest. At that moment, one reporter wrote, when production of all synthetic rubber totaled a mere twelve thousand tons a year, one-fiftieth of American's annual prewar needs, "our very national existence was at the mercy of a dwindling stockpile." But by 1943, production of synthetic rubber had turned the corner. Eighty-three percent of the 308,000 tons of new rubber supplies produced in 1943 would come from synthetic rubber. The first tires concocted by chemists from farm alcohol and petroleum had been released to essential civilian drivers. The crisis had passed.

"To a large degree," army historians have concluded, "the improvement in the military situation [in 1943] was a result of the huge outpouring of munitions from American factories and of ships from American yards. These trends coincided with a basic change that was occurring in the military position of the Anglo-American coalition—the regaining of the strategic initiative."

"We are still far from our main objectives in the war," Roosevelt cautioned. But, compared with the previous year, progress was being made. "You have heard it said," he concluded, "that while we are succeeding greatly on the fighting front, we are failing miserably on the homefront. I think this is another of those immaturities—a false slogan easy to state but untrue in the essential facts. . . . Every combat division, every naval task force, every squadron of fighting planes is dependent for its equipment and ammunition and fuel and food, as indeed it is for manpower, dependent on the American people in civilian clothes in the offices and in the factories and on the farms at home . . .

"The plans we have made for the knocking out of Mussolini and his gang have largely succeeded. But we still have to defeat Hitler and Tojo on their own home grounds. No one of us pretends that this will be an easy matter. . . . This will require far greater concentration of our national energy and our ingenuity and our skill. It's not too much to say that we must pour into this war the entire strength and intelligence and will power of the United States."

Novelist Saul Bellow remembers the exhilarating experience of listening to Roosevelt speak. "I can recall walking eastward on the Chicago Midway on a summer evening. The light held after nine o'clock, and the ground was covered with clover, more than a mile of green between Cottage Grove and Stony Island. The blight hadn't yet carried off the elms, and under them drivers had pulled over, parking bumper to bumper, and turned on their radios to hear Roosevelt. They had rolled down the windows and opened the car doors. Everywhere the same voice, its odd Eastern accent, which in anyone else would have irritated Midwesterners. You could follow without missing a single word as you strolled by. You felt joined to these unknown drivers, men and women smoking their cigarettes in silence, not so much considering the President's words as affirming the rightness of his tone and taking assurance from it."

• • •

The weekend after the president's speech, Eleanor entertained labor leader Walter Reuther and his wife at Val-Kill. She talked with the young couple for several hours, spending the afternoon outside in the sun and then moving onto the porch, where, she wrote, they "watched the sun go down in a brilliant red ball of fire." Reuther had a way of talking about industrial democracy that excited Eleanor. It was his dream to change both labor and management from their narrow pressure-group thinking to create a new form of workplace governance that would draw on the strengths of both sides.

As long as the man behind the machine was viewed as "the worker," standing in a class apart from management, the illusion would persist that he had no ideas to contribute to the successful operation of the plant. As long as management appealed to labor with the same techniques used to sell cigarettes and toothpaste, the immense creative reservoir which lay in the minds of millions of laborers would remain untapped. But if labor could be seen as something more than skill and brawn hired by the hour, if the workers could be given a measure of responsibility for generating new ideas, then there was no limit to the productivity of the American economy.

Reuther's idea centered on the notion of continuing the governmental functions of the War Production Board after the war ended, in a new entity to be called the Peace Production Board. The Peace Board would be charged with the responsibility of administering the nation's industrial effort for the benefit of the greatest number of citizens. Its first task, Reuther suggested, would be to oversee the conversion of aircraft factories into factories for prefabricated housing.

"He is much the most interesting labor leader I've met," Eleanor wrote Anna, "and I hope you meet him. He spent two years with a younger brother bicycling around the world and earning their way. He's been to such out of the way places as Baluchistan, worked a year in Russia. Now he's dreaming dreams of the postwar world and you would find him intensely interesting."

It was typical of Eleanor, when she found someone she liked, to wish that Anna could be there, too. With Anna, Eleanor once explained, she had grown to something different from her love for her boys, "to a mature understanding and sympathy, a feeling that we think and feel alike and can visit each other as friends and companions." For her part, Anna had come to trust her mother's love. She knew, her son Johnny later observed, "she had more of her mother than she had earlier in her life and more than anyone else in the family" and she took pleasure in that. "Darling Mum," Anna wrote after they spent a week together in Seattle, "somehow and no matter how long we have been separated, there is a click when we get together and a continuous clicking until we have to part once more."

So it was that Eleanor, knowing that Anna was having a difficult time at the paper with John away, traveled to Seattle in midsummer. In John's absence, the burden of editing the paper and dealing with the continuing machinations of William Randolph Hearst had fallen on Anna's shoulders. No sooner had John left than Hearst had put in place as associate publisher a man named Charles Lindemann, who Anna believed had "a terrific hatred" for the New Deal, did not like her, and was doing everything he could to ensure that she failed.

Though Eleanor's plane reached Seattle long past midnight, Anna was at the airport waiting. "She looks very thin," Eleanor wrote Lash, "but is making a wonderful effort to meet what is almost an intolerable situation." Working with people she neither liked nor trusted was very difficult for her, Eleanor explained, but "if possible she was going to stick it out."

For Anna, as for thousands of other women whose husbands had gone off to war, there were new burdens and new responsibilities. It was a confusing time. Yet mingled with the weight of obligation there was also a sense of exhilaration. During her first week of editing the paper on her own, Anna could honestly say that, despite the intrigue and the challenge, she loved it. "I'm having the time of my life—calling on all the tact I possess," Anna wrote John, "enjoying making my own decisions and attempting to use my bean for all it's worth." The situation had become more difficult since then, but even so, Anna told John, "You'd be amazed at the timid gal you used to know—who was always hearing spooks in the house and depending on you to defend her from all sorts of imaginary dangers! Now I drive myself alone at any and all times of the day and night, through the worst as well as the best parts of town."

With Eleanor, Anna could talk about her feelings—her pride in her newfound independence, her anger at John for leaving, her daily struggles at the paper. "It is the first time since you left that I've had someone to 'blow-off' to and it's been a very relaxing experience," Anna wrote John. For six peaceful days, Eleanor accompanied Anna to the office in the morning and sat by her side in the afternoon as she banged away on her typewriter. In the evenings, they played badminton, went swimming, and then celebrated the close of the day with an "old-fashioned" cocktail.

The more Anna extended herself to find a life of her own, the closer she felt to her mother. No longer seeing her mother with the eyes of a child, she was able to empathize with Eleanor's lifelong attempt to establish an independent identity. For her part, Eleanor was pleased to be needed. "I think having me here relaxed her because she could talk about all sorts of things she had not felt like discussing with others," she told her son-in-law.

At the same time, Eleanor confided to Anna her own worries about Jimmy and Elliott. Jimmy and his second wife, Rommie, had spent a miserable Fourth of July weekend at Hyde Park. Rommie claimed the president kept mentioning Jimmy's first wife, Betsey Cushing, and snubbed her at every opportunity. Elliott had also spent a weekend at home, but the visit was tense. She and he had such different philosophies, Eleanor told Anna, that she had to be careful around him at all time. "I only like being in close quarters with people whom I love very much," she admitted. "I made the discovery long ago that very few people made a great difference to me, but that those few mattered enormously. I live surrounded by people, and my thoughts are always with the few that matter whether they are near or far."

Eleanor's visit to Seattle served to renew both her own and Anna's spirits, but her absence from Washington exacted a toll on her relationship with her husband. Though she talked with him once while he was in Hyde Park for the weekend with Margaret Suckley, the conversation was distant and he seemed evasive about his plans for the rest of the summer. "It was nice talking with you last night," Eleanor wrote the following day, "but I began to wonder if you were planning to leave for parts unknown very soon. Will you call me . . . and tell me what your plans are? Of course I'll come at once to Washington if you are leaving in the near future."

"I guess one of the sad things in life," Eleanor admitted to Joe Lash, "is that rarely do a man and woman fall equally in love with each other and even more rarely do they so live their lives that they continue to be lovers at times and still develop and enjoy the constant companionship of married life."

• • •

The midsummer weeks of 1943 witnessed expanding activity in the American Jewish community in behalf of the European Jews. During the last days of July, an Emergency Conference to Save the Jewish People of Europe was convened at the Hotel Commodore in New York City. Through three sweltering days, fifteen hundred people listened to an impressive group of speakers, including Mayor Fiorello LaGuardia, writers Dorothy Parker and Max Lerner, and former President Herbert Hoover, offer a range of plans for rescue.

Roosevelt's response to a plea for cooperation was a vague, noncommittal message, read at the end of the conference, which spoke of the government's "repeated endeavors" to save the European Jews and promised that "these endeavors will not cease until Nazi power is forever crushed." Yet, far from making repeated endeavors, the government had attempted very little on the rescue front, and the few actions they had taken, such as the two-power American-British Conference on Refugees which had been held in Bermuda the previous spring, had produced little or no results.

Eleanor sent an equally unsatisfactory message to the Emergency Conference, which revealed complete misunderstanding of the situation. Though she was glad "to be of help in any way," she could not figure out, she said, what could be done at the present time. If, however, a program of action could be formulated, she was certain that the American people, "who have been shocked and horrified by the attitude of the Axis powers toward Jewish people will be more than glad to do all they can to alleviate the suffering of these people in Europe and to help them reestablish themselves in other parts of the world if it is possible to evacuate them."

Contrary to Eleanor's assumption, a program of action already existed and was spelled out in detail by the speakers at the conference. The first step, rescue advocates argued, was to form a governmental agency officially charged with rescuing Jews. With this in place, former President Hoover suggested, additional measures could be taken, including Allied protection and support for those Jews who had escaped to neutral countries, pressure on Palestine to absorb more Jews, and preparations for refugee havens in Africa. Beyond these actions, Mayor LaGuardia observed, the U.S. must open its own doors to increased immigration. "Our own government cannot urge other nations to take the initiative before it takes action of its own."

The stumbling block was not ignorance of what should be done but the absence of sustained will and desire on the part of either the government or the people to do anything at all. Despite Eleanor's claim that the American public was "shocked and horrified" about what was going on, the vast majority of ordinary people had only a vague idea of what was happening to the European Jews. Most American newspapers printed very little about the slaughter of the Jews. If mass killings were mentioned, they were generally presented not as the systematic murder of an entire race of people, but as an unfortunate byproduct of the general ravages of war. Nor could most Americans, growing up in a democratic culture, comprehend the unprecedented scale and savagery of Hitler's determination to obliterate the Jews.

Of course, Roosevelt was privy to far greater information than the ordinary citizen. Though neither he nor anyone else in his administration fully understood the extent of what only much later came to be known as the Holocaust, he had read the Riegner report the previous November. He had met that fall with Rabbi Wise and a delegation of Jewish leaders to talk about the slaughter of European Jews. He had spent nearly an hour in July talking with Jan Karski, a leader in the Polish underground who had traveled to London and Washington at great risk to report on the terrible events he had witnessed in Poland. Disguised as a policeman, Karski had seen the insides of the Belzec concentration camp, on the western border of Poland, where thousands of Jews were being gassed. "I am convinced," Karski told Roosevelt, "that there is no exaggeration in the accounts of the plight of the Jews. Our underground authorities are absolutely sure that the Germans are out to exterminate the entire Jewish population of Europe."

Why, then, did Roosevelt fail to provide leadership on this momentous issue? The answer, some suggest, is that he was wholly absorbed in waging a global war and believed that the only solution to the Jewish problem was the final defeat of Hitler and the rooting out of the Nazi system. To the extent that rescue efforts would divert time, attention, and resources from this ultimate goal, thereby lengthening the war, he could not sanction them. Yet, as David Wyman argues in *The Abandonment of the Jews,* "virtually none of the rescue proposals involved enough infringement on the war effort to lengthen the conflict at all or to increase the number of casualties, military or civilian." In fact, when other humanitarian needs were at issue, when refugees in Yugoslavia and Greece were in desperate straits, transportation somehow materialized, the war effort was bent, and the rescue was achieved. Moreover, the rationale that only victory would save the European Jews ignored the chilling question which *The New Republic* asked that summer: "Will any of these Jews survive to celebrate victory?"

The problem lay in the political landscape. Few in Congress showed concern about saving the European Jews. The majority of church leaders were silent on the issue; the intellectual community remained inert. Even the American Jews, who did more than anyone else to publicize the slaughter and press for action, were hampered by a lack of unity. When the Committee for a Jewish Army first proposed the Emergency Conference, rival Jewish leaders and Rabbi Stephen Wise did everything they could to undermine it. Other Jews, like Roosevelt adviser Sam Rosenman, feared that, if too much attention were paid to the plight of the European Jews, American anti-Semitism would increase. Such divisions weakened the pressure on Roosevelt, allowing him to fall back on his rationale that the most important thing he could do to help the Jews was to win the war as quickly as possible.

In mid-August, Peter Bergson, the organizer of the Emergency Conference, met with Eleanor Roosevelt at Hyde Park. Their conversation deepened Eleanor's awareness of the need for action. In her column the next day, she emphasized that the Jews in Europe had suffered as had no other group. "The percentage killed among them," she wrote, "far exceeds the losses among any of the United Nations." Though still admitting that she wasn't sure what could be done to save them, she predicted that "we will be the sufferers if we let great wrongs occur without exerting ourselves to correct them."

CHAPTER 18

"IT WAS A SIGHT I WILL NEVER FORGET"

August 1943 was a busy month at Hyde Park. There was activity everywhere, movement all day long. On the 12th, Churchill and his daughter Mary arrived at the president's estate to spend the weekend relaxing on the Hudson before the two leaders set off for a weeklong conference in Quebec. As usual, Churchill's visit caused considerable commotion in the Roosevelt household. The timing of the trip was particularly difficult for Eleanor, who was preparing an even longer trip of her own, to the South Pacific to visit American troops. "These last few days at home are busy for me," she confided in Lash, "& having the Churchills won't make it easier but somehow I'll get off!"

The weekend was filled with picnics on the hilltop, with hamburgers and hot dogs barbecued on the grill and watermelon slices for dessert. Knowing this was the first time Mary Churchill had eaten watermelon, the president laughingly admonished her not to swallow any of the pits lest they grow into watermelons in her stomach. Through the entire meal, Sam Rosenman observed, the prime minister enjoyed himself, his cheerfulness revealing "more eloquently" than the official bulletins "how much better we were doing in the war." The president, too, was in a jovial mood—although, as Rosenman commented, "even during the darkest days of the war he never seemed so worried or so downcast as the Prime Minister."

After lunch, the president and the prime minister sat under the trees, talking, laughing, and telling stories. "You know," Churchill told Eleanor, "one works better when one has a chance to enjoy a little leisure now and then. The old proverb all work and no play makes Jack a dull boy holds good for all of us."

Only the stifling summer heat cut into the pleasure of the weekend. On Friday night, Churchill recorded, it was so hot that he could barely breathe. Unable to sleep, he wandered across the back lawn to the bluff overlooking the Hudson River. There he sat for hours, only returning to the Big House, refreshed and relaxed, after the sun had risen.

At dinner Saturday night, Churchill launched into a discussion of "his hopes that the fraternal relationship between the United States and Great Britain would be perpetuated in peacetime." Eleanor, Averell Harriman recorded, was less than enchanted by this idea. "Mrs. Roosevelt seemed fearful this might be misunderstood by other nations and weaken the United Nations concept." The prime minister took just the opposite tack, arguing that the only hope for the United Nations lay in "the leadership given by the intimacy of the U.S. and Britain in working out misunderstandings with the Russians—and the Chinese too." Listening to the lively conversation, Harriman was impressed by the purity of Eleanor's idealism. Churchill was also impressed. Having grown accustomed by now to her spirited interruptions, he was able to enjoy the byplay. She had "a spirit of steel and a heart of gold," he told Harriman later that night.

The next morning, with Churchill en route to Quebec a day early, Eleanor relished the chance to be alone with her husband. As the time for her departure to the South Pacific drew near, she found herself in a tranquil mood, happy for once to sit still and enjoy the summer day. "Your mother is so pleased with herself," Tommy reported to Anna. "She has lost 25 pounds and looks very slim and young and it has not made her face look drawn."

After a leisurely breakfast, Eleanor joined Franklin in his study as he penned letters to General MacArthur and Admiral Halsey in her behalf. Though both men had already been apprised of the first lady's visit, Eleanor was afraid that undue security concerns would keep her from seeing the troops and the battlefields. In particular, she yearned to visit Guadalcanal, where Joe Lash was stationed. Recognizing how much it meant to her to see young Lash, the president paved the way. "She is especially anxious to see Guadalcanal," he told Admiral Halsey, "and at this moment it looks like a pretty safe place to visit." But of course, he added, "I would not have you let her go to any place which would interfere in any way with current military or naval operations—in other words, the war comes first." This was the best Eleanor could hope for, and she was pleased.

Enjoying her husband's company, Eleanor decided to postpone her departure for New York, where she was supposed to appear on a radio show with Mayor LaGuardia to talk about "Unity at Home—Victory Abroad." Hurried arrangements were made to tape the broadcast from Hyde Park. "I spoke from the library," she later wrote, "with my husband listening which was a curious situation, for I have often sat listening to him but I cannot remember when he sat listening to me. The fact that I could speak from there gave us several more hours in the country together and I was happy not to miss the pleasant, leisurely luncheon out of doors and the good talk, which is one of the rare things we enjoy when only a small company is gathered together."

In the late afternoon, Eleanor left for New York and the president returned to Washington. Since he was leaving for Quebec the following day and she was flying out that night to San Francisco en route to the South Pacific, this was the last time they would see one another for nearly six weeks. "The P[resident] was very sweet to her when she left," Tommy reported to Esther Lape. "She left all her jewelry and instructions as to their disposal in case anything happened. It gave me a queer feeling."

Anna, too, was plagued with worry as Eleanor boarded the unheated army bomber that was to take her to the South Pacific. "Darling, it kinda gives me the creeps to think of you heading off into space. Please don't take any more chances than you have to."

• • •

While Eleanor flew west, Roosevelt journeyed north by train, accompanied, as usual, by Harry Hopkins. On Tuesday evening, August 17, a small crowd was gathered in the president's car to celebrate Hopkins' fifty-third birthday. For Hopkins, who was being subjected daily to vicious attacks in the papers, the relaxed celebration was a moment to be cherished. Though controversy had attended Hopkins from the start of his unconventional relationship with the president, the recent spate of criticism had assumed an unusual virulence. In one paper after another, it was charged that the president's closest friend was benefiting in questionable ways from his position of public trust.

One story, told by a Republican congressman on the floor of the House and retold in the papers, held that Lord Beaverbrook had presented Louise Hopkins with a gift of emeralds worth nearly a half-million dollars. Though the story was vehemently denied by Louise Hopkins, who insisted that she did not own even a single emerald, the damage was done. The emerald story was followed by reports of an extravagant dinner for sixty invited guests which Bernard Baruch held at the Hotel Carlton in honor of Harry and Louise. Since the dinner coincided with the publication of an article in

The American magazine in which Hopkins urged the populace to accept rationing as part of the inevitable sacrifice of war, the newspapers took great pleasure in running the dinner menu at the Carlton, complete with caviar and pâté de foie gras, alongside Hopkins' call for sacrifice.

As one attack followed another, Hopkins pondered what to do. The final blow came when the *Chicago Sunday Tribune* published a malicious article which likened him to the Siberian mystic Grigory Rasputin, whose ability to improve the condition of Alexis, the hemophiliac heir to the Russian throne, made him a favorite at the court of Czar Nicholas and Czarina Alexandra. The article featured side-by-side pictures and compared their leering expressions, their clumsy demeanor, and their malevolent influence over their nations. Against the advice of the president, Hopkins decided to sue for libel. "This is a fight in which you would be licked before you could even get started," Roosevelt warned Hopkins. "The whole proceedings would give them a glorious opportunity to pile on smears. . . . What earthly good would it do you to win a verdict and receive damages of one dollar?" Though Hopkins eventually backed down, the hurt remained.

Adding immeasurably to Hopkins' stress that summer was his wife's desire to move out of the White House into a house of their own. Louise was convinced that their lives would never be their own so long as they remained at the president's beck and call in the second-floor suite. Eager to invite her own guests to dinner and to serve her own meals as she thought they should be served, she had begun to look for a house in Georgetown. For Harry, it was a difficult choice, knowing as he did that Roosevelt would not be pleased. But by midsummer, the pressure to move proved irresistible. "Harry and Louise are going to move to their own house," Eleanor reported to Joe Lash, "though P[resident] doesn't like their going."

On the surface, Harry's relationship with the president remained as before, but underneath, the cord of communion was cut. For the president, accustomed to standing at the absolute center of Hopkins' life, his friend's decision to move seemed to suggest an ebbing of affection, a form of abandonment. Though Hopkins postponed the move for five months, a frost descended on their relationship.

When Churchill was at Hyde Park before the trip to Quebec, he had found Hopkins "ailing and fearing he had lost favor with his chief." But in short order "it seemed like old times again," and Churchill delighted in the presence of the straight-speaking Hopkins. So now, as Hopkins relaxed with the president on the train, mixing a round of old-fashioneds to celebrate his birthday, everything appeared for the moment the same as it had always been.

In Quebec on the evening of the 17th, the president and the prime minister stayed in the Citadel, a magnificent fortress that stood above the St. Lawrence River on the heights of Cape Diamond. The aides were quartered in the Château Frontenac, a few miles away, where the official working sessions took place. For five days prior to the arrival of the president and the prime minister, the military experts had been doing preliminary "pick and shovel" work. Now, with both leaders present, the time for decision had come.

The principal business at the Quebec Conference was to decide the date for the cross-Channel attack. Though Churchill was still haunted by his memories of World War I, he knew, Lord Moran claimed, that the time had come to give way. He could delay the decision no longer. As he studied the plans for the invasion, he could not help being impressed by the massive numbers that would be engaged, the tonnage involved. More than once, Moran recalled, he referred to the plan as "majestic."

With the target date set for May 1, 1944, the two leaders turned their attention to the details of the landing—the numbers of landing craft required, the building of synthetic harbors, the extent of shipping necessary. In the midst of these discussions, British Minister of Defense Lord Ismay records a curious conference in Churchill's bathroom. "If a stranger had visited," Ismay wrote, "he might have seen a stocky figure in a dressing gown of many colors, sitting on a stool and surrounded by a number of what our American friends call 'top brass.' While an admiral flapped his hand in the water at one end of the bath in order to simulate a choppy sea, a brigadier stretched a lilo [an inflatable rubber mattress] across the middle to show how it broke up the waves. The stranger would have found it hard to believe that this was the British high command studying the most stupendous and spectacular amphibious operation in the history of the war."

Churchill's apparent change of heart brought relief to Roosevelt and the American high command, but Hopkins feared that the decision was not irrevocable, that Churchill might change his mind again, as he had done the previous year. In a conversation with Moran one morning, Hopkins spoke of Churchill in an uncharacteristically aggressive way. Though Churchill had seemingly thrown in his hand, Hopkins told Moran he was convinced that "Winston's obstinacy, his drawn out struggle to postpone a second front in France has in fact prolonged the war. That if he had been reasonable earlier we might now be in sight of peace." Was Hopkins right? Moran asked himself. "That must remain the riddle of the war."

In the meantime, the news arriving from the Italian front was excellent. On August 17, reports confirmed that, after only thirty-one days of fighting, the island of Sicily was under Allied control. The campaign had succeeded beyond expectations, so much so that Eisenhower was now recommending that the success in Sicily be followed up with an assault on the Italian mainland, beginning September 3. This was, of course, what Churchill had wanted all along, and finally Roosevelt agreed, believing that the plans for Operation Overlord were firmly set.

As the planning for the cross-Channel attack became more detailed, the question of command arose. The president and prime minister had previously agreed that the commander of Overlord should be British, since

Eisenhower had commanded the landings in North Africa. Based on this understanding, Churchill had offered the post to Field Marshal Alan Brooke, chief of the imperial general staff. But now, as the contours of the invasion became clear, Churchill recognized that the Americans would be sending "a very great preponderance" of the troops, five times more than the British. When Roosevelt argued for an American commander on the basis of the numbers, Churchill gracefully agreed. To balance the scale, the Southeast Asian command was established under Lord Louis Mountbatten, with General Joseph W. Stilwell as his deputy.

While in Quebec, the president and the prime minister discussed the atomic bomb. Churchill had agreed the previous year that research and manufacture of the bomb should take place in the United States, but the British felt that the Americans were deliberately keeping them from knowing what was going on. To provide an amicable solution to what was becoming a divisive issue, Roosevelt agreed to sign a joint "tube alloy" memo with Churchill, which ensured full sharing of all the work and promised that no secrets would be withheld on either side. Each nation also promised never to use the bomb against the other and not to use it against a third party without the other's consent.

Stalin provoked the only dark moment at the Quebec Conference. On the sixth afternoon of the summit, a cable arrived from Moscow. "Until now the matter stood as follows," the Russian premier asserted. "The United States and Great Britain made agreements but the Soviet Union received information about the results of the agreements between the two countries just as a passive third observer. I have to tell you that it is impossible to tolerate such situation any longer." Both Roosevelt and Churchill were offended by the tone of the message. "We are both mad," Roosevelt announced as he arrived for dinner that evening. Curiously, Harriman noted, Roosevelt's anger made him gayer than usual; his conversation at dinner sparkled with banter and good cheer. In contrast, Churchill arrived at dinner "with a scowl and never really got out of his ill humor all evening." Stalin, Churchill told Harriman, is "an unnatural man. There will be grave troubles."

When the conference closed on August 25, Churchill followed Roosevelt to Washington for an additional round of talks. As always, Churchill's presence turned the White House upside down, creating havoc for everyone, including Hick, who was forced to vacate her bedroom on the second floor and move upstairs. "I gather she didn't like the third floor," Tommy told Anna. "However, I know your father would have spasms if any of the Churchill party had to go on the third floor and Hick was left on the second. One would think knowing the criticism of Harry's being there that she would take a hint."

"PM's sleeping arrangements have now become quite promiscuous," British Foreign Office Undersecretary Sir Alexander Cadogan noted. "He talks with President till 2 am and consequently spends a large part of day hurling himself violently in and out of bed, bathing at unsuitable moments and rushing up and down the corridors in his dressing gown."

Accustomed by now to Churchill's irregular routine, Roosevelt found refuge at Hyde Park, where he escaped for the weekend while Churchill remained in the White House. But Hopkins had returned from Quebec so exhausted that he had to be admitted to the Naval Hospital for another series of blood transfusions. Although he joked that it was nothing serious, that Quebec and Churchill had simply been "too much for him," he admitted that he was "in pretty bad shape" and remained in the hospital for three weeks.

Before leaving for London, Churchill sent a warm telegram to Eleanor in the South Pacific, telling her that he was sorry she'd been unable to join the presidential party in Quebec but realized that her journey was "of high importance to our common interests and causes."

• • •

In truth, Eleanor was finding her days in the South Pacific grimly depressing. To start, she was traveling without Tommy for the first time in years, having decided that the twenty-thousand-mile trip would be too strenuous for her faithful secretary. But without someone to share the experience, Eleanor was overcome with loneliness. "I feel a hundred years away as though I were moving in a different and totally unattached world," she admitted to Tommy. "I don't like it much."

Everywhere she went that first week, she met with resistance on the part of the top brass, who regarded her trip as a nuisance and insisted on surrounding her with so much protection that she felt cut off from the ordinary soldiers she had come to see. When she landed in New Caledonia and presented Admiral Halsey with the president's letter supporting her desire to go to Guadalcanal, Halsey was blunt: "Guadalcanal is no place for you, Ma'am!" he said. "If you fly to Guadalcanal, I'll have to provide a fighter escort for you, and I haven't got one to spare." Crushed at the thought of having come so far and not being able to see Joe Lash, Eleanor refused to give up, getting Halsey to agree that he would put off his final decision until she returned from New Zealand and Australia.

"In some ways," Eleanor cabled Franklin from Noumea, "I wish I had not come on this trip. I think the trouble I give far outweighs the momentary interest it may give the boys to see me. I do think when I tell them I bring a message from you to them, they like it but anyone else could have done it as well and caused less commotion!"

In a letter to Hick, she revealed her feelings more completely. "I have no zest for travel any more," she admitted. "If it does any good I'll be satisfied. I can't judge at all whether it will accomplish what FDR hoped for or not."

As anxiety crowded in on her, Eleanor stepped up her schedule. On the go from dawn till dusk, virtually without a break, she toured one hospital after another, drove hundreds of miles in an open jeep to talk with soldiers at their camps, gave dozens of speeches to tremendous crowds, pinned her name on the wall maps of Red Cross clubs in every part of Australia and New Zealand, attended large receptions at night, and still managed to write and type a four-hundred-word column every day.

Everywhere she went, wearing the crisp blue-gray summer suit of the Red Cross, Eleanor assured the soldiers she met that they were not forgotten at home. "When I left," she told them, "my husband asked me to give you a message. He said to tell you that every day he goes down to the map room in the White House and notes on the maps where you are and what you are doing. He said to tell you that you have done and are doing a wonderful job. He wants me to give you his deepest admiration and gratitude . . . and now that I have given his message let me add mine. . . ."

"We liked this speech," one soldier said. "Her sincerity permeated every word. I can tell you that after a year of listening to nothing but bassooning top sergeants and officers, it was good to hear a kind lady saying nice things."

Realizing that many of these men would never see their homes and their families again, Eleanor had a hard time concealing her emotions. Every time she grabbed a new hand, one reporter noted, her eyes lit up with a resolute effort to make contact, to project "a genuine impulse of friendship towards the person she is greeting."

Traveling in Queensland, she saw in the distance a convoy of army trucks loaded with troops headed for the battlefront. She insisted that she catch up with them to tell them goodbye and wish them luck. Trudging down the rough road, the *Times* reporter observed, "her shoes dusty and scarred by rocks," she stopped at each truck and spoke to each soldier in full battle dress. "At one point her voice quavered but she quickly recovered and continued on down the line."

Eleanor's indomitable energy staggered the mind of everyone who followed her. "Mrs. Roosevelt literally took New Zealand by storm," wrote Major George Durno, a former newspaperman who had been assigned to her by Air Transport Command. "She did a magnificent job, saying the right thing at the right time and doing 101 little things that endeared her to the people." A friend of Hopkins witnessed an impromptu visit to a Red Cross club with Eleanor leading the way, "followed by a brace of generals and admirals manfully teetering on the edge of collapse." As Eleanor's party swept in, two privates were standing by an electric heater without benefit of trousers. "While management gasped for shame and the entourage gasped for breath, she coolly and graciously chatted with the two boys both paralyzed with amazement and chagrin but thrilled through and through." Everyone in the club was charmed by Eleanor's simplicity and graciousness, Hopkins' friend confirmed, though he himself could not get his mind off the two boys without any pants. "The talk over, Eleanor departed, the management collapsed and the two boys grasped their scorched legs and burst into all sorts of excited exclamation."

As Eleanor's visit continued, Admiral Halsey found himself yielding to her charm, professing total admiration of her dedication and commitment. "When I say that she inspected those hospitals," he reported, "I don't mean that she shook hands with the chief medical officer, glanced into a sun parlor, and left. I mean that she went into every ward, stopped at every bed, and spoke to every patient: What was his name? How did he feel? Was there anything he needed? Could she take a message home for him?" And a promise made was a promise kept. When Sergeant Al Lewis asked her to call his girlfriend, Helen Carl, she would later follow through, provoking the young girl's breathless astonishment on hearing the White House was calling!

Beneath her cheerful exterior, Eleanor found these hospital visits excruciating. Apparently, as soon as she arrived at a hospital or a military base, the word went out that a woman was coming. For reasons of security, it could not be said that this woman was the first lady. Certain that the young men were expecting a beauty queen, Eleanor feared she would be a woeful disappointment. Each time she entered a new ward, she wished she could be changed "in some magic way" from Eleanor Roosevelt, first lady, into "the sweetheart or the wife or sister the men were longing to see." Her anxiety was such that she failed to see what Halsey immediately saw—the joyous impact she made on everyone she met. "Over here," one soldier said, "she was something . . . none of us had seen in over a year, an American mother." Standing beside her, Halsey witnessed the expressions on the faces of the gruesomely wounded boys as she leaned over them, a warm smile on her face. "It was a sight I will never forget."

From Washington, the president cabled Eleanor every few days, letting her know how he was and assuring her that her trip was making "a fine impression" at home, with absolutely "no disagreeable notes." Worried that she was taking on too much, he suggested she cut back a bit. "If I wasn't busy," she replied, "I'd go crazy." When Admiral Jones invited her to spend a relaxing day at his cottage by the sea, she explained that as soon she got home she would rest but she had no right to do so while she was in the war zone.

In her cables to her husband, Eleanor described the spirit of the soldiers, the scourge of malaria, and the stultifying overprotection of the top brass toward her. "I've had so many Generals and Admirals and MPs to protect me that I remind myself of you," she joked.

As her days in Australia wound to a close, Eleanor journeyed to the seaside town of Cairns, where she spent a long evening talking to a group of soldiers. The one thought on the minds of all these boys, she found, was the desire to finish the struggle so they could go "home." Halfway round the world, home had become the goal for which they were all living.

The rich conversations, the soft air, and the sound of the waves breaking against the beach stirred memories of courtship days at Campobello, when she and Franklin walked along the shore, relishing the chance to be alone, sharing their hopes for the future. "How little I ever thought," she mused, "when I wandered on the moonlit beaches on the coast of Maine that I would one day see one in Australia and sit all evening listening to the waves while we talked of America with American men who wanted to know what was going on at home while they fought a war thousands of miles away."

The next day, to her unbounded delight, Eleanor learned that Admiral Halsey had finally agreed she could go to Guadalcanal. A round of official duties was arranged, including a visit to the cemetery where thousands of American soldiers were buried, a tour through several island hospitals, lunch with General Nathan Twining, commanding officer of the Thirteenth Air Force, and dinner with Admiral Halsey. But for Eleanor, the shining moment of the day came at two-thirty in the afternoon, when a note was slipped to her saying that a young man named Joe Lash was waiting for her outside the tent. Ignoring army protocol, she embraced him warmly, an excited smile on her face. They talked for a while and then arranged to meet again in the late afternoon, after her second hospital tour was done. After dinner, Lash came back once more, and they sat on a screened porch and talked until eleven-thirty.

"How I hated to have you leave last night," Eleanor wrote the next morning, and told him that she was reliving every moment they had had together. "When the war is over I hope I never have to be long away from you. It was so wonderful to be with you, the whole trip now seems to me worthwhile. It is bad to be so personal but I care first for those few people I love deeply and then for the rest of the world I fear."

Now that she had covered seventeen islands, New Zealand, and Australia, the time had come to begin her journey home. Admiral Halsey came to say goodbye. "I was ashamed of my original surliness," he admitted later. "She alone had accomplished more good than any other person, or any group of civilians, who had passed through my area."

The Central Solomons campaign was nearly completed by the time Eleanor left, bringing U.S. forces 350 miles nearer Rabaul on the way to the Philippines and, ultimately, to Japan. But, as naval historian Samuel Eliot Morison has observed, the arduous campaign had brought the Americans only one-tenth of the way to Tokyo. If the United States continued hopping from island to island at this pace, it would take almost ten years to reach Japan. It was just at this point, Morison notes, that "leapfrogging" was substituted for "island hopping." Pacific Fleet Commander Admiral Nimitz had provided the first demonstration of the advantages of leapfrogging by skipping inadvertently over Kiska to take Attu. When the Japanese decided to evacuate Kiska a few weeks later, the United States had secured two victories for the price of one. Henceforth, the Combined Chiefs decided, American forces would leapfrog their way to Japan.

As Eleanor settled into her seat for the flight to San Francisco, she thought of all the things she wanted to tell Franklin. Bone-tired but unable to sleep, obsessed with the thought that somehow there must be a way, through fundamental change in the postwar era, to make sense out of all the carnage she had witnessed, she took out her pad and scribbled a series of notes. Her first note took up labor leader Walter Reuther's suggestion about a Peace Production Board. "FDR, should there not be a call on men like those now in the WPB . . . to remain through transition period" to guide the process of converting from war to peace. "FDR, isn't resumption of peacetime industry largely dependent on bank loan policy and possible guarantees by government in same way as was done for conversion to war industry." Other memos urged that legislation providing for jobs and education for veterans should be passed as soon as possible and made known to every American soldier in every part of the world. For, as it was, "men not chief concern anywhere. Officers have too much, men too little."

The president was in Hyde Park with Princess Martha, her children, and Empress Zita of Austria-Hungary when Eleanor reached San Francisco. At a lunch with Martha and Margaret Suckley, Empress Zita suggested that Eleanor would be very tired when she got home. "No," Roosevelt joked, "but she will tire everybody else." His joking aside, Roosevelt was anxious to see his wife. "Hope you come Washington where I arrive Sat. morning or HP if you get to NY early Friday," he cabled her.

Yet, when she called him from the airport in San Francisco, he could not resist teasing her about the extraordinary lengths she had gone to see her friend Joe Lash. "Did you have fun, darling," he asked in a jocular and perhaps slightly jealous tone, "as if she had been on a pleasure jaunt which he had been big-hearted enough to fix up for her." Eleanor was devastated.

The only thing that had kept her going through her long and tiring days was the thought that she was accomplishing what the president had asked her to do. And now he seemed uninterested and unconcerned. As soon as she hung up the phone, she called Anna in Seattle and poured out her disappointments, remarking that "she had never worked harder in her life." Eleanor said she was going to ask her Pacific escort, Major George Durno, to report to the "OM" on the trip, in the hope that he'd tell him how successful it was. "Poor LL," Anna commented to John. ("OM," "Old Man," "Oscar Mann," "LL," and "Lovely Lady" were the codes Anna and John used for the president and the first lady.)

Eleanor arrived back in Washington on September 25. "Pa asked me more questions than I expected," she told Anna, "and actually came over to lunch with me on Saturday [September 25] and spent two hours." In her husband's presence, Eleanor lightened up, telling entertaining stories of her travels, even poking fun at herself. When she first entered the Pacific area, she joked, she overheard an anguished cry. "Oh, no, Eleanor Roosevelt is on the move again." That evening, she continued her tales at a small dinner with the president, Tommy, and Hick. When asked by reporters on Monday if his wife had told him about her trip, Roosevelt laughed. "Yes, she has been talking ever since she got back."

In the days that followed, reporters noted that the first lady seemed exhausted. "They missed her usual warmhearted gusto. Lines of weariness were traced on her face, netting her friendly blue eyes in a delicate web of fatigue. They were eyes that had seen much—perhaps too much." With rest, they assumed, the exhaustion would dissipate. But as September turned to October, her fatigue deepened, accompanied by an escalating sense of anxiety and dread. A paralyzing depression was setting in.

Eleanor's gloom thickened as she found herself subjected to a new round of criticism for her costly "junkets." When Representative Harold Knutsen of Minnesota complained that Eleanor was gallivanting around the world, "while the farmers in my neighborhood can't even get gasoline to work with their farms," dozens of Republicans followed suit. "The outcry in Congress is so great," Eleanor confided in Joe Lash, "that FDR feels I should not use Government transportation or even go on any far trips for awhile."

Imprisoned in the White House, Eleanor moped to the point where her friends became concerned. "[Tommy] is worried about Mrs. Roosevelt," Trude reported to Lash, "and I feel uneasy too. Mrs. R. is strange, often sits and looks absent mindedly into space and then realizes she has not heard a word. . . . Even the President said something after he had in the presence of [Crown Princess of the Netherlands] Juliana tried to get Mrs. R. to invite Juliana to Washington—and only met complete lack of response."

In their letters to each other that fall, Joe and Trude tried to understand what was wrong. Trude attributed Eleanor's depression to "her deep horror at what she saw and the great sadness at the continuing bloodshed and dying." For all her belief in the Allied cause, Eleanor was appalled when she observed firsthand the horror and the ruin which war entails. Nothing in her previous experience had prepared her for the misery she encountered in the hospitals—the mangled bodies, the stomachs ripped by shells, the amputated limbs, the crushed spirits. Only a few photographs of dead American soldiers had appeared in magazines and newspapers since the war began. The bodies shown were always clothed and intact, as if they were sleeping. The Office of War Information, established by Roosevelt in the spring of 1942 to coordinate the dissemination of war information, had so sanitized the war experience that few people on the home front understood what the war was really about.

At home, traveling from one factory to the next, Eleanor had seen the best face of war—the productivity, the camaraderie, the pride of accomplishment. On the assembly line, planes, tanks, and guns stood as shining emblems of American democracy. In the South Pacific, the emblematic quality was gone, and these same planes and tanks assumed their real shape as lethal weapons of destruction. Slowly, Eleanor began to absorb the terrible reality that all that productive genius which her husband's leadership had helped to call forth was directed toward a single, brutal goal—that of killing and maiming the enemy.

For weeks after she returned, Eleanor kept picturing the cemetery in Guadalcanal, "the crosses row on row," the thousands of young men who had died in that faraway place cut off from the world of their family and friends, the poignant way the living troops had countered the anonymity of the dead by hanging their buddies' mess kits on their crosses and carving personal tributes on each one: "A swell pal," "a good guy," "best friends forever."

By the end of 1943, American casualties, though few in number in comparison with the rest of the nations at war, were beginning to mount. The army and army air force counted 117,142 killed, wounded, or missing in action. For the navy and Marine Corps, each engagement carried its own list of casualties: Pearl Harbor, 2,554; fall of the Philippines, 1,383; Battle of Coral Sea, 705; Battle of Midway, 547; Guadalcanal, Tulagi landings, 6,040; Battle of Savo Island, 1,691; Battle of Guadalcanal, 1,460; Sicilian landings, 1,064; Italian landings, 1,688; Battle of the Atlantic, 3,314.

In a letter to FDR, Jr., written shortly after her return, Eleanor admitted that her trip was "emotionally disturbing" and that she was now preoccupied with the thought of bringing the war to a speedy end. "I know and understand your obsession to see the end of this war," young Franklin replied. "But Mummy, we've got to see it through completely this time."

But if Eleanor's eyes had seen too much of war, the roots of her depression were grounded in deeper soil. "I think," Lash wrote Trude, "another and larger part of it has to do with a great inner loneliness." Eleanor's encounter with death and dying had served notice on the life she was leading, the hours wasted in polite conversation, the endless rounds of social obligations. Though she was tied to her husband in a thousand ways and was devoted to Anna and John and to Joe and Trude, she was still the outsider looking in.

• • •

As she had so many times before in her life, Eleanor sought to escape her sadness through unremitting work, through a redoubled effort to ensure that the world that emerged in the postwar era was worthy of the lives that had been lost. "I think the things one dreads sometimes tend to be forgotten as quickly as possible," she wrote, "but this time . . . we must remember the dreadful things and try to see they don't happen again."

In her columns that fall, she spelled out her hopes for the future: legislation to provide education for returning veterans; a governmental agency to deal with the conversion of industry from war to peace; a permanent international organization that could build on the present cooperation between the United Nations; a relief agency to help people all over the world get back on their feet; an interchange of young people among the various nations as a step toward better understanding.

On previous occasions when Eleanor had tried to get her husband to focus on postwar concerns, she had been unable to attract his attention. To the commander-in-chief it seemed presumptuous, even reckless, to ruminate over the challenges of peace while the Axis powers were winning the war. But now, with the turn in the tide, he found himself willing to look toward the future, both at home and abroad.

In the third week of October, Roosevelt asked Congress for early action on a massive program of education and training for returning GIs—an unprecedented program that would later be known as the GI Bill of Rights. The president's message called on the federal government to underwrite the college education of returning veterans for a period of one to four years. "Lack of money should not prevent any veteran of this war from equipping himself for the most useful employment for which his aptitudes and willingness qualify him," Roosevelt said. "I believe this nation is morally obligated to provide this training and education."

In the weeks that followed, Roosevelt called for additional measures to ensure a smooth transition for every returning veteran. He proposed mustering-out pay on a monthly basis to cover the period of time between discharge and the finding of a new job; unemployment insurance if no job could be found; credits toward social security for time in the service; hospitalization and rehabilitation. Taken together, these measures promised American servicemen more support and more opportunity than any other country had ever given its veterans.

Eleanor was pleased. "I'd like to see us pass all legislation for veterans as soon as possible," she told reporters. "It would add to the confidence of the men to have such legislation an accomplished fact."

The president took another forward-looking step that autumn, when he appointed Bernard Baruch to head a newly created unit under War Mobilization Director Jimmy Byrnes to deal with postwar adjustment problems and the conversion of industry from war to peace. The appointment of Baruch was a master stroke. Had anyone else been put in charge of planning the peace, the conservatives on Capitol Hill, who considered the very word "plan" a communist invention, would have had a field day. But so revered was Baruch by Republicans and Democrats alike that all controversy was suppressed. Once again, Eleanor's delight was palpable. "Baruch is still the most comforting person I know," she exulted. Though the structure of the new unit failed to capture the broad-gauged vision of the Peace Production Board proposed by Walter Reuther, it did promise to bring a unified governmental approach to the conversion process.

The autumn of 1943 also witnessed significant progress in planning an international body to organize the peace. In the past, fearful that public debate on the shape of the postwar world would stir up isolationist attacks and undermine the unity necessary to prosecute the war, Roosevelt had vigorously opposed a detailed discussion of how the Allies would organize the peace. His change of heart could be traced to the phenomenal success of Wendell Willkie's book, *One World.* No book in American publishing history had ever sold so fast. Within two months of its publication, sales had reached a million copies. Based on Willkie's travels through Russia, China, and the Middle East, the book was an eloquent plea for international cooperation to preserve the peace. Unless Roosevelt took the lead, Democratic colleagues warned, the Republicans stood poised to capture the postwar issue in the next campaign.

The president found his opening in the Conference of Foreign Ministers' meeting in Moscow that fall. With Roosevelt's encouragement, Secretary Hull engineered a Four Power declaration pledging the United States, Great Britain, the Soviet Union, and China to continued cooperation in a great international organization to be established at the earliest practicable date. Though no details were determined, the assurance of postwar unity provoked rejoicing on the part of the American public.

The president hosted an elaborate ceremony in the East Room in early November to commemorate the signing of an international agreement for a United Nations Relief and Rehabilitation Administration to feed, clothe, and house the world. "The representatives of 44 nations sat around a long table with the President," Eleanor happily observed. "Behind them were their flags. I watched each man go up to represent his country and thought how interesting it was that, before the end of the war, we have the vision this time to realize that there is much work to do and that preparation by the peoples of the United Nations is necessary. . . . It was impressive and F[ranklin]'s short speech clear and good. I feel in the end something great may have begun today."

• • •

The first week of November 1943 found the president and the first lady at Hyde Park. The weather was clear and invigorating, Eleanor exulted, "with a sky so blue" that the stars at night were shining as brilliantly as they did in the real winter months. Basking in the beauty of the cool autumn days, the president finished his work in the early afternoons to allow time for picnics at Top Cottage, motor rides through the countryside, and dinners at Val-Kill.

"Good news comes in from every battlefront," William Hassett recorded on November 1. In Italy, after a successful landing on the mainland to the north of Reggio on September 3, the Allied forces were slowly working their way north up the instep of the Italian boot. The fighting was tougher than expected. Though the new Italian government had surrendered on the first day of the invasion, Hitler's troops were fighting furiously every step along the way. The battle for Salerno had been, army historians contend, "one of the bitterest battles of the war." But by the end of October, Allied forces had seized both Palermo and Naples and were only ninety miles from Rome. In the South Pacific, the U.S. landings on Bougainville, the next hop toward Rabaul, had begun. And in the Eastern front, the Red Army was moving forward again toward Kiev after having been driven back halfway to the Dnieper by a German counterattack.

But for Roosevelt, the most encouraging news of the day was Stalin's agreement, at long last, to meet the Allied leaders at a summit conference in Teheran at the end of November. The first leg of the journey would take the president to Cairo to meet Generalissimo Chiang Kai-shek. From there, he and Churchill would journey together to Teheran to join the Russian leader.

As soon as Eleanor heard about the meeting with Stalin, she pleaded with Franklin to bring her along. Never once had she been present at a summit conference, though her sons Elliott and FDR, Jr., had been invited to both Argentia and Casablanca. "Mrs. R wanted very much to go," Trude reported to Joe. "But the Boss just put his foot down. Absolutely no women." Besides, he had already asked Elliott, FDR, Jr., and John Boettiger to join him, and that was plenty of company. Eleanor was crushed, not simply by the decision itself but by the insensitivity of her husband's attitude. But, in characteristic fashion, she deflected the argument from her own disappointment to the wisdom of dragging FDR, Jr., off his ship, which was leaving for Gibraltar in several days, to return to the United States for repairs after a torpedo attack. Feeling strongly that it would hurt her son's relationship to his men to leave his ship, she was furious when the president insisted that he needed both boys and that was that. An argument followed. "The OM sat all over her," Anna reported to John, "and hurt her feelings."

When Anna heard about the trip, she, too, begged to go, "not just because of the interest of the occasion itself," she told her mother, "but because he'll be seeing my John." Eleanor urged her to send a special-delivery letter asking if she could go. "I'll read him your desire," she promised, "but I fear all females are out."

"The answer was, of course, no!" Anna reported bitterly to John. In no uncertain terms, Roosevelt told his daughter that, under navy rules, no women were allowed on shipboard, so there was no way she could come. "Pa seems to take for granted that all females should be quite content to 'keep the home fires burning,' and that their efforts outside of this are merely rather amusing and to be aided by a patronizing male world only as a last resort to keep some individually troublesome female momentarily appeased."

In the days that followed, Anna's irritation toward her father deepened. In long phone calls with her mother, she worked herself into a fury at the thought that her brothers would be attending their third conference in two years but her only request had been flatly denied. Mother, Anna told John, "goes along very strongly with me in our feeling that OM is a stinker in his treatment of the female members of his family. She pointed out that even though I couldn't have gone with him in the ship that it would have been perfectly possible for me to fly. Of course the uniform angle (lack of it) is obvious; but a R[ed] C[ross] uniform and mission could have solved that!"

Anna's sense of injustice was compounded by fear that John was suffering an emotional breakdown in North Africa. Though his early letters revealed a genuine excitement about taking part in "the big show," his recent letters were filled with self-pity at not having been given anything important to do, despite the assurances he had been given before he arrived that he was really needed. Suddenly he had decided that he could no longer go it alone, that the only way he could contribute to the war effort was if he and Anna could work together as one, either by her obtaining an assignment abroad or his coming home.

In frenzied letters to both Anna and Eleanor, John pleaded for help to come home. "Tell me darling if you can," John asked Anna, "what made me do this thing? Why should I, with YOU, with US and with real and patriotic responsibilities at home, tear off to what at this stage gives smaller promise of real usefulness. . . . What could I possibly gain to weigh against the job I left vacant on the homefront and the pain I bring to you. Has what I have done to US impaired your love for me in any way? So please my beloved, don't try to banish US from your thoughts."

"Neither of us is giving to the war effort separately what we could give jointly," John wrote Eleanor, "and I fully realize now what a tragic error it was in every way to attempt anything different. . . . If amends can be made I will be ever so grateful. . . . I hope you won't think too badly of me."

The problem, Anna explained to John, was that, though her mother was sympathetic to his desire for a transfer, she did not expect her father would understand. Nor could she think of anyone "among the higher ups in Washington who would give serious help and consideration to anything suggested by me or LL. I believe they would be nice and kind and put us both off, believing we were just two sentimental females—this one hungry to get her mate back."

The only hope, Anna believed, was for the two of them to get together somewhere so she could restore his confidence and bring him back to his senses. Otherwise she feared he might do something stupid in his obsession to come home. That was why the trip to Teheran mattered so much to her, and why her father's peremptory refusal hurt so badly.

As Anna's anxiety about John deepened, her own fragile confidence wavered; her pride and pleasure in her work at the paper vanished. She found herself unable to cope with the increasingly bitter political struggles over editorial policy. Sensing her daughter's pain, Eleanor wrote to her almost every day. "I realize how desperately lonely you must be dearest and it worries me for you." Why not, Eleanor suggested, think of coming east for Christmas? The family was intending to spend the holidays at Hyde Park, and it would be wonderful if Anna could join them.

When Eleanor invited Anna to come east that winter, she had no way of knowing that her daughter's visit would lead to her taking a permanent position in the White House as her father's hostess, a move that would nearly destroy the powerful bond between mother and daughter that had been forged over a period of twenty years.

• • •

At 10:30 p.m. on November 11, 1943, a cold and rainy night in Washington, the president boarded the *Potomac* for the first leg of his journey to Cairo and Teheran. "I just saw Pa off with Admiral Leahy, Admiral Brown, General Watson, Dr. McIntire, Hopkins," Eleanor told Anna. "I hated to see Pa go and yet I think it will do much good." The next morning, the president was transferred to the battleship *Iowa* to begin the long voyage through the heavy seas of the Atlantic.

"Everything is very comfortable and I have with me lots of work and detective stories and we brought a dozen good movies," Roosevelt wrote Eleanor the first day of the trip. "Weather good and warm enough to sit with only a sweater as an extra over an old pair of trousers and a fishing shirt . . . It is a relief to have no newspapers! I am going to start a one page paper. It will pay and print only news that really has some relative importance!"

After nine days at sea, the *Iowa* pulled into the naval base at Oran. There the president was greeted by Elliott, FDR, Jr., and Eisenhower. "The sea voyage had done Father good," Elliott observed; "he looked fit; and he was filled with excited anticipation of the days ahead." As it turned out, only Elliott was going on with his father to Cairo. After a week of agonizing, FDR, Jr., had finally decided that he had best go back with his ship. This was, of course, what Eleanor had wanted him to do all along, and she was glad that he had the sense of responsibility to know what was right. She should never have gotten so worked up, she admitted to Joe Lash, "for things always turn out this way."

For security reasons, Eisenhower recommended a night flight from Tunis to Cairo. The president was disappointed. He had wanted to follow the road the battle had taken from El Alamein. But once the plane was in the air, he was excited at the prospect of seeing the Pyramids. He asked the pilot to circle the banks of the Nile at sunrise so he could have a good view. "He was thrilled by the monuments, the Sphinx and the Nile," Secret Service chief Mike Reilly recorded. As he looked at the Pyramids, he observed that "man's desire to be remembered is colossal."

In Cairo, Anna's husband, John Boettiger, and Hopkins' son Robert joined the presidential party. Churchill had arrived the night before, accompanied by his daughter Sarah; Chiang and his wife were settled in a villa nearby. No women allowed, Roosevelt had told Eleanor. Yet here, in plain view for all the photographers to see, were Sarah Churchill and Madame Chiang. Roosevelt must have realized at once that Eleanor would be furious.

She was. No sooner had the first pictures of the conference appeared than she fired off a sarcastic note to her husband. "I've been amused that Madame Chiang and Sarah Churchill were in the party. I wish you had let me fly out. I'm sure I would have enjoyed Mme Chiang more than you did though all the pictures show her in animated conversation with you and [Chiang] wears a rather puzzled look as Winston chews his cigar."

The Roosevelts had hosted the temperamental Madame Chiang at the White House the previous spring. Though Eleanor had grown to like her, the president had found her difficult. "In a queer way," Eleanor told Anna, "I think the men (including FDR) are afraid of her. She is keen and drives her point and wants to nail them down and they squirm." To the Secret Service and the White House staff, she was an insufferable prima donna with an unfortunate habit of clapping her hands whenever she wanted something.

In asking Chiang Kai-shek to Cairo, Roosevelt was less interested in China's military contribution to the Pacific war than in aligning China to the Allied cause in the years ahead. "This will be very useful 25 to 50 years hence," he said, "even though China cannot contribute much military or naval support for the moment." Though Roosevelt was under no illusions about Chiang's ill-trained, ill-equipped troops, he believed it essential to keep China in the war against Japan and was willing to make a number of promises to ensure that result. The sessions were not easy; Chiang, with his wife interpreting, was stubborn and demanding, making promises one day only to reverse himself the next. The British and the Americans were at odds on several points.

"I'm sorry things only went *pretty* well with Chiang," Eleanor consoled. "I wonder if he, Mme or Winston made trouble. The questions are so delicate that the Sphinx must be a relief. . . . I loved your quip about the Congress and the one page paper."

On Thanksgiving Day, troubles and misgivings were cast aside as the president hosted a dinner for Churchill and his daughter, Hopkins and his son, Elliott and John, Anthony Eden, Lord Moran, and Pa Watson. "Let us make it a family affair," he said as he sat high in his chair, carving two enormous turkeys which he had brought from home. "I had never seen the President more gay," Churchill noted.

After dinner, the president lifted his glass. "Large families are usually more closely united than small ones . . . and so, this year, with the peoples of the United Kingdom in our family, we are a large family, and more united than ever before. I propose a toast to this unity, and may it long continue!"

Never one to be outdone, Churchill, too, lifted his glass. "He started slowly," Robert Hopkins recalled. "His sentence used a very unusual construction. He stopped. He seemed lost. There was a long pause. He can't get out of this, I thought. He's an old man, his faculties are failing. Then suddenly he picked out a word so perfect, so brilliant, that everyone broke into spontaneous applause. It was a tour de force."

After dinner, the army band played music and dancing began. Since Sarah was in great demand as the only woman present, Churchill asked Pa Watson, Roosevelt's big, bluff aide, to dance. Watching the odd couple from the sofa,

Roosevelt roared with laughter. All in all, it was a delightful evening, one that would remain a high point in Churchill's mind for years.

Roosevelt arrived in Teheran eager to meet Stalin face to face. All his life he had prided himself on finding common ground with disparate men; so now he looked forward to the challenge of creating a bond with the forbidding, unapproachable Russian premier. He had scarcely settled into his bedroom at the yellow mansion which housed the Soviet Embassy when word came that the marshal was at the door. "Seeing him for the first time was indeed a shock," Mike Reilly recalled. "Stalin sort of ambled across the room toward Roosevelt, grinning." Though he was short, he had the presence of a large man; his mustard-colored uniform boasted such large epaulets that it looked, Lord Moran observed, "as if the tailor . . . had put a shelf on each shoulder and on it has dumped a lot of gold lace with white stars."

"I am glad to see you. I have tried for a long time to bring this about," the president said, evoking hearty laughter on Stalin's part. For thirty minutes they chatted briefly about things they would later talk about at length. "He seems very confident, very sure of himself," Roosevelt remarked to his son Elliott. But when the pleasantries were finished, Roosevelt still felt he was dealing with a complete stranger. He had no idea as Stalin left whether he'd been able to dissipate any of the distrust that lay like a thick fog between them.

The conference convened that afternoon in the embassy's boardroom, an immense chamber with dark tapestries on the walls, large, heavy chairs, and a round oak table made specially for the occasion so that no one would argue about who should be placed at its head. "It was a thrilling experience to see the Big Three sitting round the same table at last," Lord Ismay wrote.

Roosevelt, State Department aide Charles Bohlen observed, "clearly was the dominating figure at the Conference." Ismay agreed: "He looked the picture of health and was at his best . . . wise, conciliatory and paternal." Churchill, by contrast, was suffering from a miserable cold, a bronchial cough and an intermittent fever, though, as always, Ismay noted, "mind triumphed over matter, and he did his full share of talking." As for Stalin, he seemed at first not to be seeing or hearing what was passing about him; he had the air of a man absorbed in his own reflections, doodling wolfheads on his pad with downcast eyes.

It was, at first, the old story. Though Roosevelt thought that at Quebec he had gained Churchill's absolute commitment to the cross-Channel invasion, the prime minister was once again suggesting a host of peripheral possibilities—including the capture of Rome and inducements to get Turkey to enter the war. But this time, Stalin's presence was the deciding factor. Bluntly opposing Churchill's diversionary tactics, Stalin argued that the capture of Rome was irrelevant and the hope for Turkish entry into the war illusory. "If we are here to discuss military matters," Stalin said, "then Russia is only interested in Overlord."

As Stalin took the offensive for Overlord, his eyes grew keener, his voice deepened. "I thank the Lord Stalin was there," Stimson later wrote, after reading the minutes of the conference. "In my opinion, he saved the day. He brushed away the diversionary attempts of the PM with a vigor which rejoiced my soul."

As he watched the balance swing against him, Churchill's mood became somber. Unable to purge himself of his abiding fear that catastrophe would accompany a direct assault on the Continent, he told Lord Moran that he believed "man might destroy man and wipe out civilization," Europe would be left desolate, and he would be held responsible.

His only hope, Churchill believed, was to see Roosevelt alone and to win him back. As soon as the first plenary session was over, Churchill asked Roosevelt if they could lunch together. It seemed a simple request, considering the vast number of lunches these two men had shared, from elegant meals at Casablanca to hot dogs at Hyde Park. But Roosevelt firmly declined the invitation; he feared that Stalin's suspicions would be aroused if he and Churchill were seen alone, conferring in a language the Russians couldn't understand.

Having come to Teheran to accommodate Stalin, Roosevelt was determined to do everything he could to make a personal connection with the Russian leader. The task was proving more difficult than he had imagined. "I had done everything he asked me to do," Roosevelt remarked. "I had stayed at his Embassy, gone to his dinners, been introduced to his ministers and generals. He was correct, stiff, solemn, not smiling, nothing human to get hold of. I felt pretty discouraged."

Finally, Roosevelt conjured a way to break the ice. " 'I hope you won't be sore at me for what I am going to do,' " he warned Churchill as they reassembled at the plenary session. As soon as they sat down, Roosevelt began talking privately with Stalin. "I didn't say anything that I hadn't said before, but it appeared quite chummy and confidential. . . .

"Then I said, lifting my hand up to cover a whisper . . . , 'Winston is cranky this morning, he got up on the wrong side of the bed.'

"A vague smile passed over Stalin's eyes, and I decided I was on the right track. . . . I began to tease Churchill about his Britishness, about John Bull, about his cigars, about his habits. It began to register with Stalin. Winston got red and scowled, and the more he did so, the more Stalin smiled. Finally Stalin broke out into a deep, hearty guffaw, and for the first time in three days I saw light."

Suddenly Roosevelt and Stalin had become a twosome, with Churchill, rather than the marshal, the third man out. "From that time on," Roosevelt exulted, "our relations were personal. . . ."

After a while, Stalin, too joined in the fun of teasing the prime minister. Churchill later claimed that he didn't resent the teasing in the slightest, but it couldn't have been easy, and he may have felt envious as he watched Roosevelt turn his considerable charm toward Joseph Stalin.

More important, Churchill must have realized that, as long as Roosevelt and Stalin stuck together on Overlord, there was nothing he could do to stop the invasion. Bowing to reality, he lent his voice to a unanimous agreement that Overlord would be launched on the first of May. The threesome also agreed, over Churchill's initial objection, to a supporting attack in the south of France. And Stalin promised that, once Germany was defeated, Russia would join the war against Japan.

When these decisions had been reached, the tension snapped. On November 30, Roosevelt and Stalin joined Churchill in a jubilant celebration of the prime minister's sixty-ninth birthday. "There were toasts and more toasts," Hap Arnold recalled. "One speech followed another. Churchill extolled the President, glorified Stalin, then the U.S." Roosevelt toasted the valor of the Red Army. As each toast was made, "Stalin went around the table and clicked glasses with all the military men." Finally, Stalin rose to speak.

"I want to tell you, from the Russian point of view, what the President and the United States have done to win the war. The most important things in this war are machines. The United States has proven that it can turn out from 8,000 to 10,000 airplanes per month. Russia can only turn out, at most, 3,000 a month. England turns out 3,000 to 3,500. . . . The United States, therefore, is the country of machines. Without the use of these machines, through Lend-Lease, we would lose the war."

This was the first time the Soviet government had ever publicly thanked the United States for lend-lease. Except for sporadic releases in the Russian press about the arrival of particular items, the people of Russia had never been officially informed about the relationship between the vast American shipments that were coming into Russia every week and the phenomenal success of the Red Army in rolling back the Germans.

At the time of the Teheran Conference, American factories were supplying the Soviet Union with fully two-thirds of their motor vehicles and one-half of their planes; the United States had sent Russia over five thousand fighter planes in 1943 alone, more than to any other theater of war. American rails were enabling the Russians to rebuild their railroad lines; American communication equipment was making possible the control of military movements; American tires and American oil were keeping Russian trucks moving and planes flying. American explosives were being used in the manufacture of bombs and shells in Russian factories; American seeds were being planted in reconquered farmlands that had been devastated in the fighting. At the same time, American industry was supplying thirteen million Soviet soldiers with their winter boots, their uniforms, and their blankets. And for the larder of the Red Army, the United States was sending millions of tons of foodstuff, including wheat, flour, meat, eggs, and milk.

It was an astonishing story: every week, hundreds of thousands of tons of supplies were being loaded onto freight trains and transferred to one group of ships, which plied their way through the icy waters of the Arctic Ocean to Murmansk and Archangel, while another fleet sailed halfway round the world across the Pacific to Siberia, and a third traveled through the Persian Gulf to the port of Basra. For more than two years, American ships had been sailing the hazardous waters of both the Atlantic and the Pacific to bring their precious cargo to the Russian troops. More than 12 percent of the American convoys had been lost in 1942, with a heavy loss of life. But only now was Stalin willing to express the gratitude of his nation.

Midnight came and went, and the toasts continued. Finally, at 2 a.m., Roosevelt asked for the privilege of the last word. "We have differing customs and philosophies and ways of life," he said. "But we have proved here at Tehran that the varying ideals of our nations can come together in a harmonious whole, moving unitedly for the common good of ourselves and of the world."

The conference drew to a close the following day with a wide-ranging discussion of postwar concerns, including the need for an international body to keep the peace, the fate of the Baltic States, the borders of Poland, and the dismemberment of Germany. At one point, in an exercise that would have infuriated Eleanor had she been there, the three men huddled around a large map of Central Europe blandly drawing new borders for Poland.

The next morning, believing that the conference had been "an important milestone in the program of human affairs," Roosevelt departed for Cairo, where he continued his talks with Churchill. Though everybody was tired, one crucial decision remained. The time had come to choose the commander for the Allied invasion. Roosevelt was leaning toward George Marshall; in a letter earlier in the year to General John J. Pershing, commander of American Expeditionary Forces in World War I, Roosevelt said that, although he considered Marshall the most important figure among the Combined Chiefs, and would hate to lose him, he thought it only fair to give him a chance in the field. "I want George to be the Pershing of the Second World War and he cannot be that if we keep him here."

But, the nearer the decision drew, the more Roosevelt worried about losing Marshall's presence from the Joint Chiefs. Everything had worked so well for so long; to break it up now seemed too risky. Better, he reasoned, to keep Marshall in Washington and give Eisenhower the job. Unable to face Marshall directly, Roosevelt sent Hopkins to feel him out. When Marshall gamely replied that he would go along wholeheartedly with whatever decision the president made, the die was cast. "Well, Ike," Roosevelt jovially announced when they met in Tunis, "you are going to command Overlord."

"Homeward bound," Roosevelt cabled Eleanor on December 9. "I am now on a 12 hour plane trip which I hate. But on the whole it has been a real success. . . . Lots to tell you about and lots and lots of love."

• • •

Tanned by the sun of North Africa, the president returned to the White House in a positive frame of mind. His spirits were raised still further when he found his entire Cabinet, the congressional leaders, and the White House

DRAFT No. 1 December 7, 1941.

PROPOSED MESSAGE TO THE CONGRESS

Yesterday, December 7, 1941, a date which will live in infamy the United States of America was suddenly and deliberately attacked by naval and air forces of the Empire of Japan.

The United States was at peace with that nation and was still in conversation with its Government and its Emperor looking toward the maintenance of peace in the Pacific. Indeed, one hour after Japanese air squadrons had commenced bombing in Oahu the Japanese Ambassador to the United States and his colleague delivered to the Secretary of State a formal reply to a recent American message. While this reply stated that it seemed useless to continue the existing diplomatic negotiations it contained no threat or hint of war or armed attack.

It will be recorded that the distance of Hawaii from Japan makes it obvious that the attack was deliberately planned many days or even weeks ago. During the intervening time the Japanese Government has deliberately sought to deceive the United States by false statements and expressions of hope for continued peace.

1

Shortly before 5 p.m. on Sunday night, December 7, 1941, the president called his secretary, Grace Tully, to his study and began dictating the message he wanted to give to Congress the following day. He signed the declaration of war, which both chambers decisively approved with only one dissenting vote, the same day. (1)

2

3

4

In September 1942, the president and first lady undertook a two-week inspection tour of factories and army camps. The first stop was the Chrysler tank arsenal, the largest arsenal in the world devoted completely to the production of military tanks. In the car with Franklin and Eleanor to the far right is Donald Nelson, War Production Board chief (2). Later that afternoon, at Ford's Willow Run bomber factory, the president spoke with two midgets working high up on the tail section of a bomber where persons of normal height were unable to fit (3). The first shift enters the North American Aviation plant in Inglewood, California (4).

As more and more married women entered the work force, the president, at Eleanor's urging, approved the first government sponsored day-care center. Before the war's end, nearly $50 million was spent on day care. Here Eleanor visits a group of children at a center in Greensboro, North Carolina (5).

5

For the first time in the history of many companies, women worked on the assembly line as riveters, welders, blueprint readers, and inspectors. "If I were of a debutante age," Eleanor said, "I would go into a factory—any factory where I could learn a skill and be useful." At the Douglas aircraft plant in Los Angeles, California, women made up nearly 60 percent of the work force (6,7).

6

7

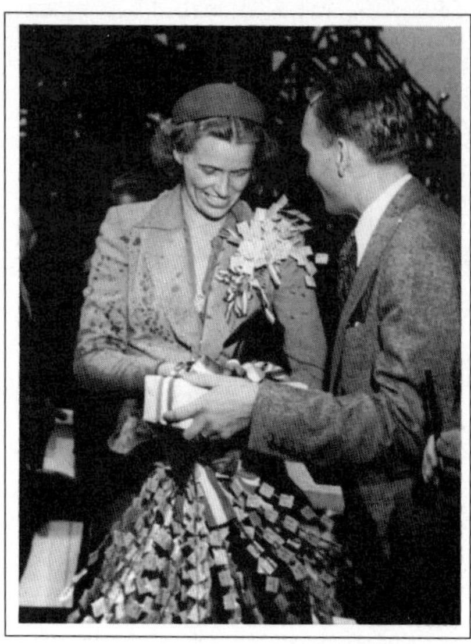

8

Under Henry Kaiser's leadership, the average time to deliver a ship was cut from 355 days in 1940 to 194 days in 1941 to 69 days in early 1942. At top, the president's daughter, Anna, receives a gift from a Kaiser official after christening a merchant ship, the SS *Joseph Teal*, in 1942 (8). Construction of the ship is shown below (9).

9

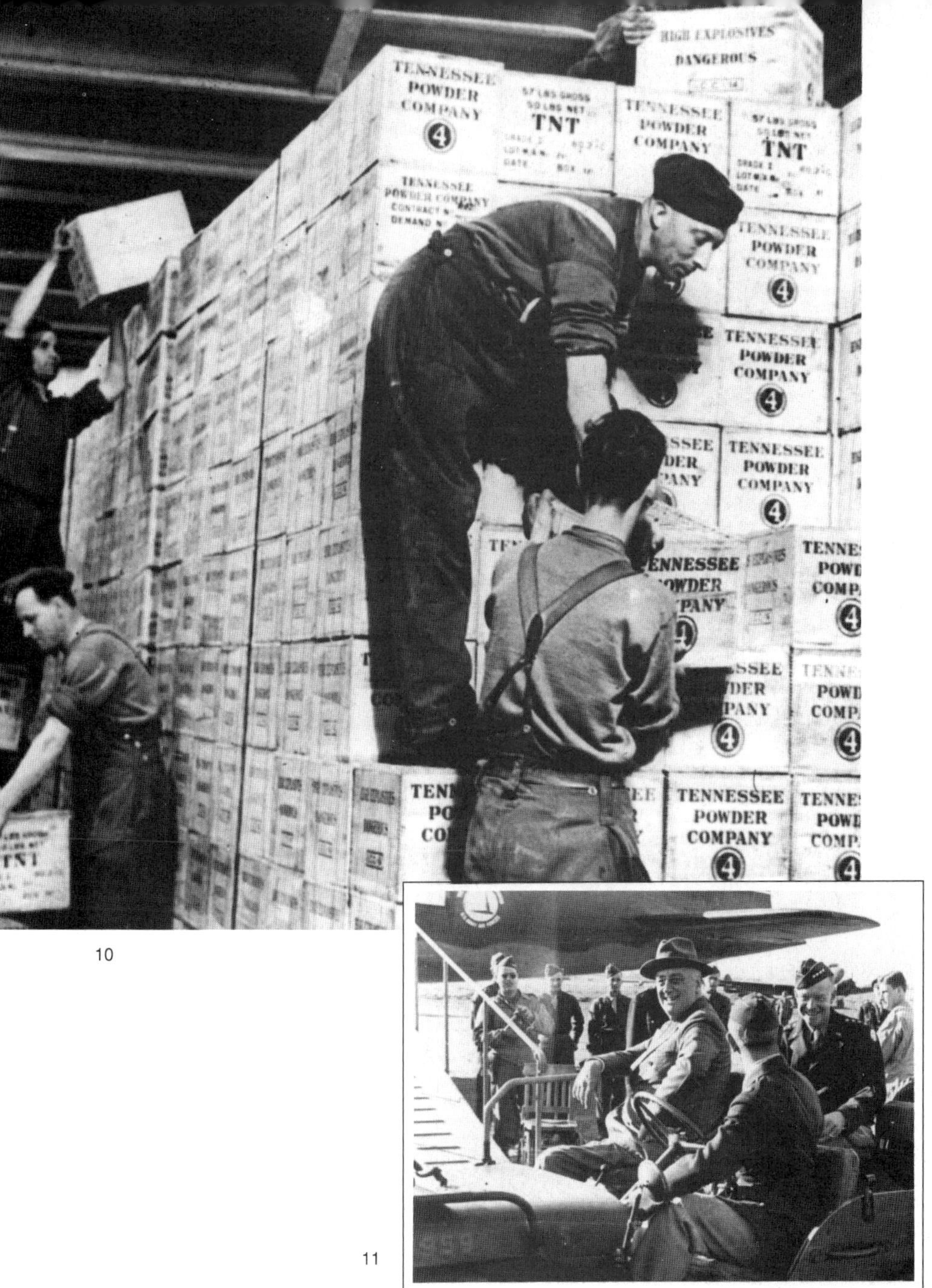

10

11

The miracle of shipbuilding allowed weapons and supplies to reach Europe and Asia. Lend-lease, Churchill once said, was the "most unsordid act in the history of any nation." The boxes of gunpowder above represent the tiniest fraction of the millions of tons of weapons and supplies shipped to Britain and Russia during the war (10). In 1943, American troops began pouring into Europe. Roosevelt inspects U.S. troops with General Eisenhower in Sicily.

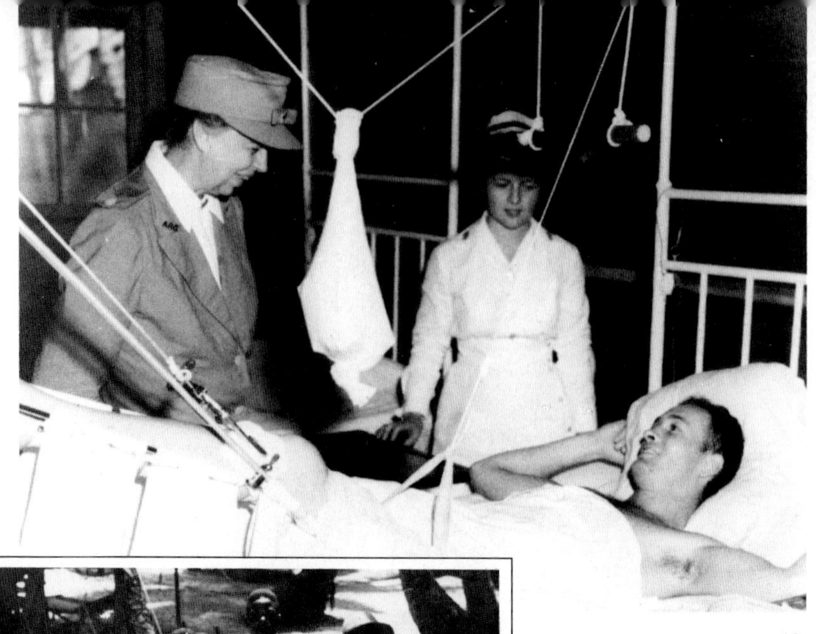

12

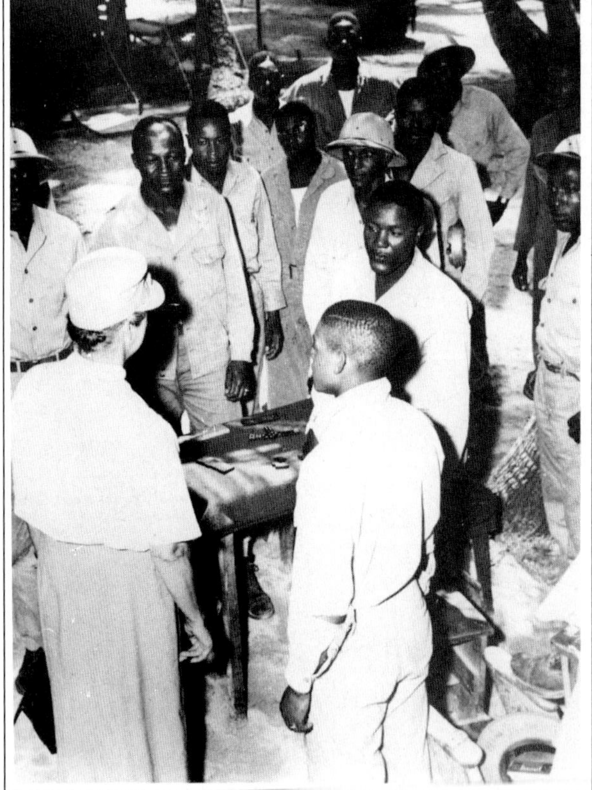

Though Admiral William Halsey was initially opposed to Eleanor's visit to the South Pacific in 1943, he ended up expressing admiration for her dedication and commitment. "It was a sight I will never forget," he said after watching her lean over gruesomely wounded soldiers at the base hospital, a warm smile on her face (12). Below, she addresses Negro troops at Penrhyn Island (13).

13

14

15

The accustomed rhythms of daily life were disrupted in every factory, business, and home by the institutions of rationing and price control. The motion picture industry contributes to the war bond drive with a premiere (14). A woman presents her ration book to the grocer in order to buy sugar (15).

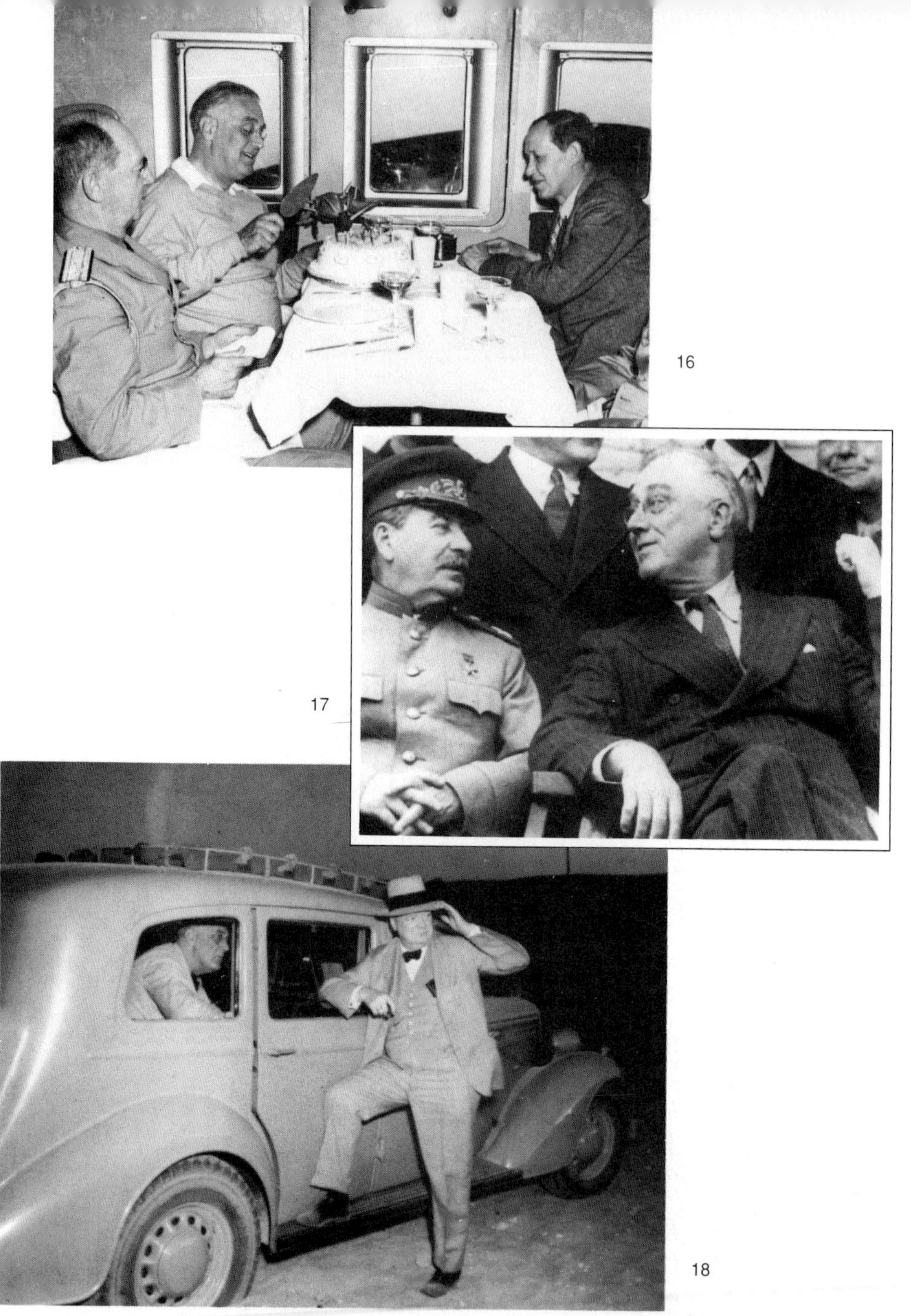

16

17

18

Nineteen forty-three was the year of conferences. Roosevelt celebrates his sixty-first birthday with Harry Hopkins and Admiral William Leahy as he returns from his meeting with Churchill at Casablanca (16). Roosevelt talks with Russian Premier Joseph Stalin at the Teheran Conference, where Stalin publicly thanked the U.S. for lend-lease for the first time (17). Roosevelt and Churchill view the Pyramids in Egypt on their way to Teheran, Iran (18).

19

The second Quebec Conference in 1944, Lord Ismay observed, "was more like the reunion of a happy family" on holiday "than the gathering of sedate Allied leaders for an important conference." Mrs. Churchill is seated between Roosevelt and Churchill; Eleanor talks to Canadian Prime Minister Mackenzie King (19). Returning from the Yalta Conference, Roosevelt talks to Ambassador to England John Winant, while Secretary of State Edward Stettinius confers with Harry Hopkins (20).

20

21

22

Despite widespread worries about Roosevelt's health, the 1944 campaign proved, as one reporter said, that "the old master still had it." By 10 p.m. on election night, the trend was clear: the people of the U.S. had returned FDR to the White House for a fourth term. In these pictures, Roosevelt, adhering to ritual, receives his Hyde Park neighbors on the terrace of his home, as Eleanor and Anna stand behind him (21, 22).

23

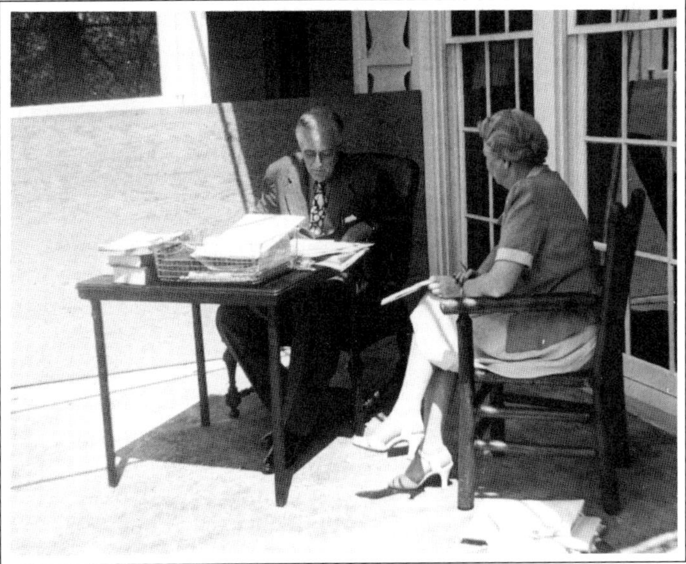

24

"The days flowed peacefully by," Margaret Suckley recalled of the president's last trip to Warm Springs. In the mornings, he would work on his papers at the table before the fireplace (23). In the afternoons, he would work on the terrace with Grace Tully (24).

25

26

Unable to accompany her father to Warm Springs in April 1945, Anna made arrangements for Lucy Mercer Rutherfurd to visit him the second week of his stay. Lucy is shown here with FDR in pictures taken the day before Roosevelt died (25, 26). On April 12, 1945, Roosevelt was sitting for a portrait by Elizabeth Shoumatoff (27) when he suddenly said, "I have a terrific pain in the back of my head," and slumped forward. He never regained consciousness.

27

28

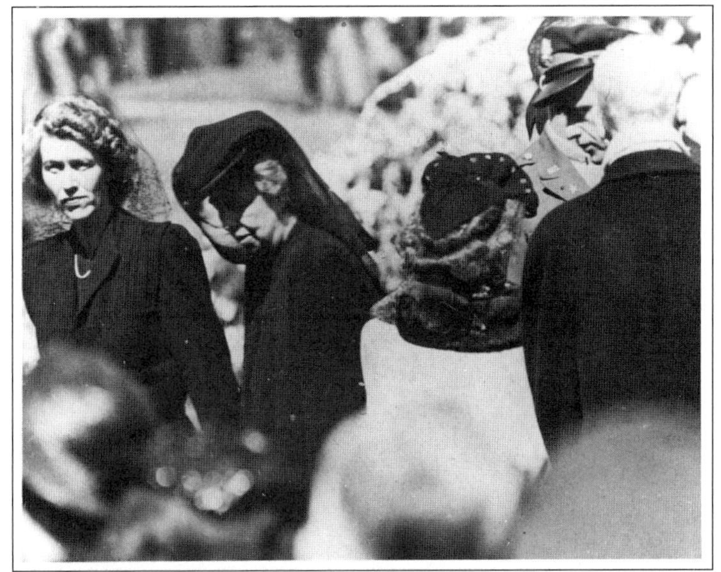

The president's coffin was carried by train from Warm Springs to Washington to Hyde Park, where he is buried in the green hedged garden of his boyhood home. Anna and Eleanor are pictured here at the end of the service. Elliott, in uniform, is partly hidden on the right (28). The riderless horse behind the cortege is the traditional symbol of the fallen leader (29).

29

30

After Roosevelt died, Eleanor found unexpected comfort in the president's dog. Fala accompanied Eleanor on her walks through the woods at Val-Kill, sat beside her chair in the living room, and greeted her at the door when she came home (30).

staff on hand in the Diplomatic Reception Room to welcome him home. "He was in his traveling linen suit," Stimson recorded, "looked very well, and greeted all of us with very great cheeriness and good humor and kindness. He was at his best. Republicans were mixed with Democrats and they all seemed very glad to have him back safe and sound."

The president's good humor did not extend to his wife and daughter. Knowing they were still angry with him for not taking them along on his fabulous trip, he was withdrawn, ill at ease, uncommunicative. "OM was very cool to me that first day," Anna wrote John, "never mentioned you except to answer my questions by saying that you were well." For her part, Eleanor was determined, in recompense for not being invited, to find out everything that had happened at the conference. That evening, to the president's first dinner home in more than three weeks, she invited Trude Pratt and Franklin's old friend Harry Hooker to join Anna and FDR, Jr. "Tonight," she pledged, "we shall ply him with questions."

The dinner that night, Anna reported to John, was "a complete fiasco," as Eleanor "proceeded to push, push, push at OM to relate his experiences," though FDR "wanted to sit leisurely over cocktails and dinner and tell his story in his own way." Instead, "LL rushed him through cocktails and kept hammering at him until his annoyance was so obvious, Frankie and I were wild, could do nothing about it."

Finally, to appease his wife, the president began telling the story of the conference, revealing in rich detail anecdotes about Stalin and Churchill. So intimate, even indiscreet, were these disclosures that Anna felt compelled to interrupt, putting her hand on her father's arm. If any of the stories were to leak from this room, she warned, looking at Mr. Hooker and Mrs. Pratt, "it would be dynamite and could be used by the 'opposition' to ruin all of your most important plans. OM answered 'you're quite right' but LL did not appreciate my crack!"

"Honestly," Anna admitted to John, "LL uses such poor judgment at times. Tommy and I have had long talks about our sweet and wonderful LL's indiscretions in repeating things to such people as Trude. Also Tommy has good evidence that LL's letters to Joe are opened sometimes and that LL is not always discreet in these letters. By that I mean that Tommy worries that LL might repeat to Joe what OM told that night at dinner. It's all kinda tough, because LL is so damn sweet and unselfish, so lovely and sensitive."

Still, Eleanor refused to give up. When the dinner guests departed, she tried to get more out of the president by following him to his room. Her efforts proved fruitless. It was nearly midnight, he had had a long day, and he was exhausted.

The next morning, Anna joined her father for breakfast in his room. Knowing how uncomfortable Eleanor had made him the night before with her relentless quest for details about the conference, Anna deliberately confined her conversation to good-natured gossip about family and friends —the sort of talk FDR loved.

"I finally managed to break the ice," Anna proudly reported to John, with "a good old chin-fest." During their frolicsome talk, Anna provided her father with juicy details about the "sex peregrinations" of her two brothers Elliott and FDR, Jr. Apparently Elliott was involved in a passionate romance with the actress Faye Emerson, and FDR, Jr., had developed a terrific crush on Kay Summersby, General Eisenhower's beautiful young driver.

As it happened, the president had met Miss Summersby in Algiers when he stopped to see Eisenhower. He had sat only one place away from her at dinner one night, and had shared a picnic lunch with her and Eisenhower the following day. An experienced observer of human nature, Roosevelt had come to the conclusion, he confided in Anna, that this attractive young British woman was sleeping with General Eisenhower! Delighting in the intimacy of their conversation, Anna then recalled that Frankie, in the throes of his own passion for the same woman, had remarked that, as beautiful as she was, "the things she had been through [divorce and death of her subsequent fiancé] had made her a bit of a psychopathic case."

Anna's "chin-fest" with her father continued until nearly 10 a.m., when he had to get ready for a meeting with the vice-president and congressional leaders. As he dressed, he was in great spirits. There was nothing he enjoyed more than exchanging gossip. Yet, with Missy gone, the opportunities for lazy, relaxed conversations had greatly diminished. It was good to have Anna home. For her part, Anna was euphoric. "Ever since my talk with OM about Elliott and other things," she exulted to John, "he and I have been on very good terms—closer, I think, than usual."

Roosevelt's chumminess with his daughter coincided with his loss of Harry Hopkins. On December 21, Hopkins finally moved out of the White House into his new home, a charming town house in Georgetown, at 33rd and N. For Harry and Louise, who had felt for months that Eleanor resented their being at the White House, the move was long overdue. "It is the first time I have had Christmas in my own house for years," Hopkins wrote his youngest son, Stephen, who was a marine in the South Pacific, "and Louie made it the pleasantest that I think I ever had in my life."

But for Roosevelt, Harry's departure was distressing. For nearly three and a half years, ever since May 10, 1940, when the phony war was brought to an abrupt end by Germany's invasion of Western Europe, Hopkins had been his constant companion. Night after night, hearing steps by his study door, Roosevelt had looked up to find Hopkins, an intelligent, amused expression on his face. With Missy gone, no one knew better than Hopkins when Roosevelt needed to relax and when he needed to work. Ever ready with a joke, he knew how to hit the exact line between playfulness and seriousness. Now, though he would still occupy a critical position in the administration, the relationship would not be the same.

As when Missy got sick, Roosevelt no doubt tried to tell himself that everything would be all right, that other friends would take Harry's place. And it was true, to a degree. Coincident with Harry's departure, Margaret

Suckley appeared more frequently at the White House, joining the president almost daily for tea or dinner. But, as much as Roosevelt enjoyed talking with her about his papers and his plans for his library, she never grew as close to him as Missy or Harry had been. That space, left open for a while, was only filled when Anna came to live in the White House the following month.

Christmas found the president at Hyde Park with Eleanor, Anna, FDR, Jr., and Johnny. It was the first Christmas the Roosevelts had spent at Hyde Park since 1932, and the first time the children had been back to the old house since Sara died. "I am sure it will seem very strange to them, as it does to practically everyone," Eleanor wrote. "My mother-in-law lived for so many years in the house, that she really seemed a part of it. Her personality seems to go right on living there."

For Anna, it was a wonderful week. Despite the galaxy of MPs and Secret Service men, she still "loved the old place," the thick woods she had wandered through as a girl, "the gently rolling countryside," the traditional reading of Dickens, and the warmth of the carolers. "There's been no snow," she told John, "but it's been cold, clear and dry with all ponds, waterfalls and streams frozen over." Relaxing with her father, she shared breakfast with him in the mornings, sat beside him in his study in the afternoons, and joined him for cocktails at night. It was the beginning of a new intimacy in their relationship.

Indeed, so comfortable did Anna feel with her father at Christmas that she broached the sensitive subject of accompanying him the next time he took an overseas trip. He readily agreed that if she secured a Red Cross uniform and then flew to meet his navy ship it would work. What is more, he said, the "no women on ships" was merely one of many navy rules, "all of which he was responsible for and which he could break if he so wished." This was just what Anna wanted to hear.

• • •

Roosevelt returned to Washington two days after Christmas, and held a casual press conference on December 28. At the end, he let it be known that he wished the press would no longer use the term "New Deal" to describe his administration, for the times had changed and there was no longer a need for the New Deal.

When asked why the slogan was no longer appropriate, he presented a long allegory. "How did the New Deal come into existence?" he asked. "It was because in 1932 there was an awfully sick patient called the United States of America. He was suffering from a grave internal disorder—he was awfully sick—he had all kinds of internal troubles. And they sent for a doctor."

Old Dr. New Deal prescribed a number of remedies—the Federal Deposit Insurance Corporation (FDIC) to guarantee bank deposits; the Home Owners Loan Corporation (HOLC) to save homes from foreclosures; the

Securities and Exchange Commission (SEC) to provide truth in the sale of securities; minimum wages and maximum hours; abolition of child labor; unemployment insurance, social security, and the Wagner Act to protect labor; and the work-relief programs, the PWA, the WPA, the CCC, and the NYA. It was a long, slow process, Roosevelt admitted; "it took several years before those ills, that illness of ten years ago, were remedied.

"But two years ago," the president continued, after [the sick patient] had become pretty well, he had a very bad accident.... Two years ago on the 7th of December, he got into a pretty bad smash-up—broke his hip, broke his leg in two or three places, broke a wrist and an arm. Some people didn't even think he would live, for a while.

" 'Old Doc New Deal' didn't know anything about broken legs and arms," the president said. "He knew a great deal about internal medicine but nothing about this new kind of trouble. So he got his partner, who was an orthopedic surgeon, 'Dr. Win the War,' to take care of this fellow. And the result is that the patient is back on his feet. He has given up his crutches. He has begun to strike back—on the offensive."

In substituting Dr. Win the War for Dr. New Deal, Roosevelt did not intend to diminish the past accomplishments of the New Deal. Indeed, it was of great historic significance that, despite all the changes the war had brought, it had not called into question the basic institutional reforms identified with the New Deal—such as minimum wage, social security, labor protection, market regulation. He was simply saying that, when the times change and the problems change, the slogans should also change.

Reporters agreed. "The New Deal slogan has outlived its vote-getting usefulness at home, " *U.S. News* pointed out. "The things it stood for in the depression-ridden 30s do not attract votes in the war boom 40s. [Today] there are far more jobs than workers. Farm controls have been thrown away. The urge is to grow more food, not less. The effort is to hold wages down, not raise them; to check rising prices, not spur them on. Many of the Government controls now are called irksome.... As a vote-catcher, [the New Deal] has no more allure than a 1932 glamour girl who did not watch her diet."

With full employment, the work programs of the old New Deal were no longer needed. The CCC was the first to go, felled by the hands of Congress. The end of the CCC was followed by the demise of the WPA, which was given "an honorable discharge" by the president himself. The NYA, already reduced to a skeletal training program for young people about to enter war industries, was next.

"The war has finally accomplished most of what the New Deal set out to do," columnist Raymond Clapper wrote in 1943. "The war has given every workman a job at high wages, removed him from dependence on charity, and through rationing has leveled off the upper crust until the rich man cannot buy any more of many things than the poor man. The common man, in other words, is getting a better break through the war than the New Deal was able to give them."

For Eleanor and her liberal friends, the demolition of the old agencies was difficult to watch. Though she realized that much of their work had become unnecessary under changed conditions, she believed that many of the old activities were even more useful in wartime than they had been during the Depression—housing, recreational facilities, maternity care, day care, public health. To Eleanor's mind, the New Deal was more than a description of old programs; it was a rhapsodic label for a way of life representing a national commitment to social justice and to the bettering of life for the underprivileged. And that commitment, Eleanor argued, was every bit as important in 1943 as it had been a decade before.

No one, Eleanor insisted in reply to a question at her own press conference, has laid the New Deal "away in lavender." On the contrary, "the future is going to require not only interest in the needs of our citizens but the needs of the world."

CHAPTER 19

"I WANT TO SLEEP AND SLEEP"

Old Doc New Deal was not dead and buried after all. Confounding critics and supporters alike, the president brought the old doctor back for a triumphant encore in the State of the Union message on January 11, 1944.

Roosevelt began the speech as Dr. Win the War, warning his countrymen against overconfidence, reminding them of the distance that still separated American troops from their objectives in Berlin and Tokyo. "If ever there was a time to subordinate individual or group selfishness to the national good, that time is now," he said, looking ahead to the cross-Channel invasion certain to produce casualty lists in America that dwarfed every engagement that had gone before.

"The overwhelming majority of our people have met the demands of this war with magnificent courage and understanding. They have accepted inconveniences; they have accepted hardships; they have accepted tragic sacrifices. However, while the majority goes on about its great work without complaint, a noisy minority maintains an uproar of demands for special favors for special groups. There are pests who swarm through the lobbies of the Congress and the cocktail bars of Washington, representing these special groups as opposed to the basic interests of the nation as a whole.

They have come to look at the war principally as a chance to make profits for themselves."

To counter these special interests and to concentrate the country's energies and resources on winning the war, the president recommended a series of stringent measures: a tax increase, both to produce revenue and keep inflation down; a renegotiation of war contracts to prevent exorbitant profits; a cost-of-food law; a stabilization statute; and a national-service law. Though he had resisted the pressure to conscript civilians for three years, he had now come to believe that a national-service law would assure that the right number of workers went to the right places at the right times. It would alleviate current labor shortages in copper mines, in ball-bearing plants, in the forge industry, and in factories making B-29s. He understood the burden civilian conscription placed on labor and would not recommend a national-service law, he said, unless the other laws were also passed to keep down the cost of living, share the burdens of taxation, and prevent undue profits.

As Roosevelt reached the climax of his speech, he cast aside Dr. Win the War and became Dr. New Deal once more. "It is our duty now to begin to lay plans . . . for the winning of a lasting peace. . . . We cannot be content, no matter how high the general standard of living may be, if some fraction of our people—whether it be one-half or one-third or one-tenth—is ill-fed, ill-housed and insecure. This Republic had its beginning under the protection of certain inalienable political rights—among them rights of free speech, free press, free worship, trial by jury, freedom from unreasonable searches and seizures. They were our rights to life and liberty.

"As our nation has grown in size and stature, however—as our industrial economy expanded—these political rights proved inadequate to assure us equality in the pursuit of happiness. We have come to a clear realization of the fact that true individual freedom cannot exist without economic security and independence. 'Necessitous men are not free men.' People who are hungry and out of a job are the stuff of which dictatorships are made."

In the modern era, Roosevelt argued, a second Bill of Rights was needed to provide a new basis of security and prosperity for every American regardless of race, color, or creed. That economic Bill of Rights must include: the right to a useful and remunerative job; to earnings sufficient for adequate food and clothing and recreation; to decent housing; to adequate medical care; to protection from the economic fears of old age and unemployment; to a good education.

All these rights were implicit in the programs of the New Deal. But never before had Roosevelt stated them in so comprehensive a manner. Nor had he ever been so explicit in linking together the negative liberty from government achieved in the old Bill of Rights to the positive liberty through government to be achieved in the new Bill of Rights. "For decades," political scientist James MacGregor Burns has written, "the fatal and false dichotomy —liberty against security, freedom against equality—had deranged American social thought and crippled the nation's capacity to subdue depression and poverty. Now Roosevelt was asserting that individual political liberty and collective welfare were not only compatible, but they were mutually fortifying."

Roosevelt's speech thrilled liberals—including Eleanor, who listened to it on a small barracks radio as she visited with a group of WAVES at American University. Still excited the following morning, she reread the message in its entirety, certain that her husband would now turn his vital energies to the building of the new America that would make all the sacrifices of war worthwhile.

It was not to be that simple, of course. By insisting that all his proposals were linked, that national service would not work without a tax increase or reduction of excess profits, Roosevelt left himself hostage to the conservative coalition in the Congress, which was in no mood to hear his plea for higher taxes. Convinced that the administration was using the war to legitimize a redistribution of income, the Congress substituted its own revenue bill, which reduced the administration's proposal to a fleshless skeleton. It canceled the automatic 1-percent increase in the social-security tax, which was to be levied on both wage and salary earners and on employer payrolls; it granted relief from existing taxes; it exempted the lumber industry and natural-gas pipelines from the excess-profits tax. Indeed, so replete was the bill with loopholes for special interests that it raised only $2 billion in revenue, in contrast to the president's call for $10.5 billion.

After much thought, Roosevelt decided to veto the bill, even though he realized he was jeopardizing his program, including national service. "It has been suggested by some," he explained in his veto message on February 22, "that I should give approval to this bill on the ground that having asked Congress for a loaf of bread to take care of this war for the sake of this and succeeding generations, I should be content with a small piece of crust." But this bill, Roosevelt charged, in an uncharacteristic display of bitterness, provides "relief not for the needy but for the greedy." His decision made, Roosevelt set off that evening for Hyde Park. He was "in the best of spirits," William Hassett recorded. To have said exactly what he felt seemed to afford him unfeigned pleasure.

The next afternoon, Hassett chronicled, "hell broke out in the Senate." Majority Leader Alben Barkley, who had faithfully carried the president's banner on Capitol Hill for seven years, stood before his colleagues and formally broke with the president, announcing that he would resign as leader. Speaking before a hushed audience, Barkley accused the president of delivering "a calculated and deliberate assault upon the legislative integrity of every Member of Congress. Other members of Congress may do as they please; but, as for me, I do not propose to take this unjustifiable assault lying down.... If the Congress of the United States has any self-respect yet left, it will override the veto of the President and enact this bill into law, his objections to the contrary notwithstanding." When Barkley finished, he received a thunderous ovation; "practically every senator stood on his feet and clapped," Vice-President Wallace recorded, making it clear that the president's veto would not be sustained.

Word of Barkley's angry speech reached the president in his study at Hyde Park, where he was examining old family papers with Margaret Suckley. He appeared at first to be unconcerned, predicting that the storm would blow over in a few days. "Alben must be suffering from shell shock," he suggested, attributing the outburst to the fact that Barkley was tired and Mrs. Barkley was ill. When Eleanor spoke to the president from Washington later that afternoon, she found him "quite calm over it." For her part, Eleanor questioned the use of the phrase "not for the needy but for the greedy." Such phrases are "tempting," she told a friend, "but I'm not sure of their wisdom."

Later that night, however, in response to an impassioned call from Jimmy Byrnes, Roosevelt agreed to send a conciliatory note to Barkley, saying that he had never intended to attack the integrity of the Congress, that their differences on the tax issue did not in any way affect his confidence in Barkley's leadership, and that he hoped, if Barkley did resign, he would immediately be re-elected. The president's letter set the stage for the events that followed. On February 25, 1944, amid sustained applause, Barkley resigned and was unanimously re-elected. Then, by large margins in both houses, the Congress overrode the president's veto.

At Hyde Park, where he was joined by Eleanor and Anna for the weekend, the president remained serene. "Still no word of bitterness or recrimination," Hassett noted. On Saturday afternoon, in the midst of a snowstorm, he inspected his tree plantings, observing wryly that the passage of the flawed tax bill over his veto had saved him $3,000 in taxes on his income from his lumbering operations. The next morning, he took great delight at the sight of his grandchildren sledding down the big hill behind the house.

The president's equanimity in the face of his congressional defeat can be traced to his awareness that, despite the loopholes in the present bill, the administration's wartime taxation had generally assumed a just and redistributive character. Year after year, against the wishes of the conservative coalition to substitute a regressive sales tax for stepped increases in the personal and corporate income tax, the administration had prevailed both in securing rising rates and in adding millions of new taxpayers to the rolls. The Treasury was able to finance about 44 percent of the total war expenditures of $304 billion through taxation. The rest was secured through war bonds and borrowing. The debt rose from 43 percent of the GNP in 1940 to 127 percent in 1946.

A transformation had also been effected in the method of collecting taxes. Before the war, individuals were always a year behind in their tax payments, since they were called upon to pay taxes in quarterly installments on the income they had earned the previous year. The system had functioned well enough when rates were low and few people paid taxes, but when millions of people, unfamiliar with preparing tax forms, became taxpayers for the first time, change was inevitable. It took the form of "Pay as You Go," a system that withheld taxes from paychecks before the employee even saw the money, allowing everyone to start the new year free from debt. This was "a revolution in American public finance," journalist David Brinkley has written. Since people were paying taxes with money they had never seen, their resistance to the idea of taxation lessened.

So, while everyone else's nerves became jittery, Roosevelt kept his dispute with Congress in perspective. Remaining at Hyde Park for a full week after the great explosion, he managed, Hassett recorded, to confound his enemies by sleeping ten hours a night, though they "supposed he was lying awake nights worrying about their machinations."

While Roosevelt was in Hyde Park that last week of February, the Eighth Air Force, in Europe, was enjoying what later came to be called "the Big Week," seven days of unparalleled success during which thirty-eight hundred bombers dropped nearly ten thousand tons of bombs, which damaged or destroyed more than 70 percent of the German war plants involved in aircraft production. The tonnage dropped in this single week was equal to the total bomb tonnage dropped by the Eighth Air Force in its entire first year of operation. In contrast to "Black October," 1943, when American losses were so devastating, amounting to more than half of the sorties, that pilots had come to accept as a fact that "you would be shot down eventually . . . that it is impossible to complete a full tour of duty," the Big Week pilots enjoyed the critical advantage of new and improved escort planes. These new planes, P-47 Thunderbolt "Jugs," were equipped with droppable fuel tanks that allowed them to fly much faster and farther than ever before.

Though German industry would show remarkable recuperative powers after the bombing of Big Week, the German air force had been permanently damaged. Over six hundred German fighters had been downed, and nearly a thousand German pilots and crewmen had been killed or wounded. "This was a turning point in the air war against Germany," Churchill later wrote. "From now onwards the U.S. 8th Air Force was able to bomb targets in Germany by day with high accuracy and ever increasing freedom." The back of the Luftwaffe had been broken.

• • •

Returning from Hyde Park on the first of March, Roosevelt found to his great delight that Anna had moved from the guest quarters on the third floor to the spacious Lincoln Suite on the second floor, where Harry Hopkins had lived for three and a half years. The move signaled Anna's commitment to stay with her father for the duration of the war, to serve as the hostess of the White House in her mother's absence, to provide the warm, relaxed companionship he had missed since Missy was taken ill.

Neither father nor daughter had imagined this outcome when Anna first arrived for the Christmas holidays. She had originally intended to return to

Seattle in early January, but as the time for her departure approached, she found that her father did not want her to go. In the four weeks she had been at the White House, he had come to rely on her.

"With no preliminary talks or discussions," Anna recalled years later in a published article, "I found myself trying to take over little chores that I felt would relieve Father of some of the pressure under which he was constantly working." Conquering the old fears and insecurities that had previously diminished her personality in her father's presence, she entertained guests at the cocktail hour, arranged the seating at the dinner table, made suggestions on speeches and saw people her father was too busy to see.

"Father could relax more easily with Anna than with Mother," Elliott observed. "He could enjoy his drink without feeling guilty. Though Mother had gotten to the point where she would think she was relaxing, she was always working."

Blessed with a radiant smile and a ribald sense of humor, Anna took pleasure in the same silly hair-down jokes that her father relished. When she and her father were together, the valets recalled, laughter would ring out. "She could tell a great story," her son Johnny Boettiger said; "she loved gossip and when she laughed, it was a real laugh; she threw her head back and let the laugh out."

And she was beautiful, tall and blonde with long, shapely legs, blue eyes, and healthy skin. Eleanor's friend Justine Polier recalled being with the president in his study one morning when Anna came in. "She walked in in her riding boots after a ride. His whole face lighted up; the world's problems stopped for a few minutes. He just adored her."

What would she think, he inquired as she was preparing to leave, about quitting her job at the *Post-Intelligencer* and coming to work for him? For Anna, the timing of the request was perfect. After months of effort, John Boettiger had finally succeeded in securing a transfer from North Africa to the Pentagon. Working in the White House would allow her not only to be with her father on a daily basis, but to be with her husband as well. Yes, Anna agreed, she would love to move into the White House and help him, "but not until I have talked with mother."

Anna's caution was well advised, knowing as she did from conversations with Tommy that her mother had invariably clashed with every woman who had presumed to fill her role as mistress of the White House—with Jimmy's first wife, Betsey Cushing, and with Missy LeHand and Louise Hopkins. "Louise would arrange dinner parties, and seat the table," Anna was told. "Mother would be home. This would annoy the pants off her." This was not ordinary jealousy at work; the threat Eleanor perceived was to her position, not her marriage. Though she cherished her independence and her freedom to travel she did not want anyone taking over her position as mistress of the White House.

Eleanor was very frank with her daughter. If Anna came to stay, "it would be wonderful," Eleanor said. "She personally would love it," but she did not want to go through with her daughter what she had gone through with Louise Hopkins and others in the White House.

Just recently, an awkward situation had developed when, without telling Eleanor, Grace Tully and Franklin had invited Missy to spend the second week of March at the White House. When Eleanor discovered this, she wrote to Missy canceling the invitation. "I was away last week when Grace and Franklin arranged for you to come down on the 7th of March. I am terribly sorry that they did not realize that I want to be here when you come. Therefore, as I have to go on this Caribbean trip, it will be necessary for you to postpone your trip. I am very sorry that they did not consult me before making plans but it is hard to get everyone together."

Though Eleanor's insistence on being home during Missy's visit reflected a valid desire to make sure that Missy was well taken care of while she was there, the postponement was devastating to Missy, coming as it did on the heels of learning that all her things had been removed from her third-floor bedroom and stored in the East Wing attic. "I know that you will realize," Eleanor had written, "that in order to keep your belongings from being harmed by nurses and children and casual guests I have had them temporarily put where they are safe."

Though Eleanor suggested an alternative date in April, Missy refused to reconsider. "I hope you understand," Missy's sister Ann Rochon wrote Eleanor, "that we did everything we possibly could to make her go to Washington this month but she simply wouldn't allow us to talk about it. We felt the change would do her so much good and of course she always considered it home."

When Anna assured her mother that she understood the ground rules, Eleanor embraced her daughter's decision to move to Washington. In February, Anna put her home in Seattle on the rental market. Her first weeks in the White House proved delightful for everyone, including Eleanor. Whenever Eleanor had to travel, she was glad to know, she admitted, there would be "young life in the White House as it makes it a more cheerful place to anyone who happens to stay there." And when she was home, Eleanor took pleasure in Anna's vibrant personality, which "brought to all her contacts a gaiety and buoyance that made everybody feel just a little happier because she was around."

Though Anna was never given an official title or salary, her assignments, she joked, grew "like Topsy, because I was there all the time and it was easy for Father to tell someone to 'ask Anna to do that' or to look over at me and say, 'Sis, you handle that.'" When it became clear to her that she couldn't write fast enough to take accurate notes on all the things her father asked her to do, she taught herself shorthand at night, when the day's work was done. "It was immaterial to me whether my job was helping to plan the 1944 campaign, pouring tea for General de Gaulle or filling Father's empty cigarette case."

"It was an ideal match for both of them," Anna's son Johnny Boettiger observed, "a perfect fit, hand in glove." For the little girl who still adored her father, there was endless pleasure in the observation that he enjoyed her beauty, her laugh, her pretty dress. For the awkward adolescent who had been so worried about making mistakes in front of her father that she fled from the library one day in tears when an armful of books he had handed her slipped from her grasp, there was the chance to deal with him now from a position of strength and confidence, to take pride in the mastery of a job well done. "She is really in finer health and spirits," her husband reported to Jimmy Roosevelt, "than at any time since the war began."

"Anna's day at the White House begins at 6:45 a.m.," *Time* reported in a glowing portrait of the president's daughter later that spring. She took breakfast with her husband and her five-year-old son, Johnny, in the Lincoln Suite; then Major Boettiger went off to the Pentagon while Johnny headed for kindergarten, accompanied by a Secret Service man. For the rest of the day, until 4 p.m., she was at her father's side, "until Johnny comes marching home," at which point she broke off from work for a quick game of Ping-Pong with him or a swim in the White House pool. Then back to the oval study to work, while Johnny, dressed in a little khaki uniform and cap, strolled the White House grounds, a toy wagon under his arm, pursuing his ambition to become a White House guard. An early supper for Johnny was followed by cocktails and dinner with her father. "The President's daughter will preside over social engagements and welcome visitors of state any time Eleanor Roosevelt is off on a trip," *Time* concluded, "but she has made it plain that she will not be [officially] considered an assistant hostess. She has reiterated . . . instructions to the State Department's protocol office: at White House guest dinners, 'Put me anywhere, I'm not official.' "

• • •

The more time Anna spent with her father in the spring of 1944, the more conscious she became of the darkening hollows under his eyes, the loss of color in his face, the soft cough that accompanied him day and night. To her observant eye, his strength seemed to be failing him; he was abnormally tired even in the morning hours; he complained of frequent headaches and had trouble sleeping at night. Sitting beside him in the movies, she noticed for the first time that his mouth hung open for long periods; joining him at his cocktail hour, she saw the convulsive shake of his hand as he tried to light his cigarette; once, as he was signing his name to a letter, he blanked out halfway through, leaving a long illegible scrawl. At first, Anna attributed her father's troubles to the prolonged bout of influenza he had suffered during the winter, but when spring came and he failed to bounce back, she began to worry.

That same spring, Grace Tully noted with alarm that her boss was nodding more frequently over his mail, even dozing off during dictation. "He would grin in slight embarrassment as he caught himself," she recalled, and though she saw "no diminution of clarity or sparkle," she worried nonetheless. In mid-March, former NYA Administrator Aubrey Williams dined with the president in the White House and was "shocked" at how "tired and worn" he looked. Even the ever-faithful Hassett admitted on March 24, "President not looking so well.... This latest cold has taken lots out of him. Every morning in response to inquiry as to how he felt a characteristic reply has been rotten or like hell."

Anna confided her concerns about her father's health to her mother, but Eleanor refused to acknowledge that anything was seriously wrong. "I don't think Mother saw it," Anna told writer Bernard Asbell years later. "She wasn't looking for him to be any different."

If Eleanor failed to see in her husband the alarming changes Anna saw, it was in part because she was hundreds of miles away from him much of the time. In February, she made two extended trips to New York, one to Clarksburg, West Virginia, and one to Pittsburgh. In March, she was in the Caribbean from the 4th to the 28th, inspecting bases and visiting soldiers. And even when she was home, she was so busy—testifying against the deplorable conditions of Negro housing in Washington, D.C.; speaking out against discrimination in the armed forces; calling for the inclusion of women at the peace table—that she had no time simply to sit with her husband and relax.

Even if she had seen her husband more often, it is not clear that Eleanor would have understood what was happening to him. She simply wasn't "interested in physiology," Anna insisted, "that was all there was to it. She seemed to be cerebrating one hundred percent, *all* the time." Having shared so completely in her husband's triumph over polio, "she still believed," as her grandson Johnny Boettiger put it, that "iron will and courage could conquer any illness. Though she was an unusually compassionate woman, she was never patient with illness—her own or anyone else's. This made it hard for her and hard for others."

Reluctant to admit even to herself that Franklin was really sick, Eleanor ascribed his fatigue to psychological factors. For one thing, the spring had brought the disturbing news that Elliott's second marriage, to Ruth Googins, was falling apart. Though Ruth had initially agreed to wait until the war was over to file for divorce, the agreement had broken down, and by the end of March the papers had been filed. "I think the constant tension must tell," Eleanor confided in Joe Lash, "and though [Franklin] has said nothing I think he's been upset by Elliott and Ruth."

Beyond the family problems, there remained in Roosevelt, Eleanor believed, an unspoken anxiety about the forthcoming invasion. "The President hasn't been well," she told her readers in "My Day," "but I think it is probably as much the weariness that assails everyone who grasps the full meaning of war as it is a physical ailment."

Something more than internal stress was at work, however; by the last week of March, Roosevelt's health was deteriorating so steadily that he canceled all appointments and confined himself to his bedroom, taking all his meals on a bed tray with Anna at his side. As always, Roosevelt worked to keep up appearances, summoning his energy to be pleasant. "He is cheerful in spirit," Hassett noted on a day when his temperature reached 104 degrees, "always good natured, none of the ill temper that sick folks are entitled to display."

Though Roosevelt's good spirits fooled reporters and visitors, Anna, who was with him most of his waking hours, could not ignore the discernible signs of trouble. There were too many times in the course of the day when she could see that "the blood was not pumping the way it should through one hundred percent of the body."

After comparing notes with Grace Tully, Anna took it upon herself to summon Dr. Ross McIntire to her quarters to discuss her father's health. A stiff man who zealously guarded his authority as the president's personal physician, McIntire submitted reluctantly to Anna's cross-examination. What was happening to her father? Anna wanted to know. Clearly, something was very wrong. Not to worry, McIntire said. He was recovering from a combination of influenza and bronchitis. A week or two in the sun and he would be his old carefree self again.

McIntire's response did not sit well with Anna. Knowing that McIntire was not a general internist but, rather, an ear-nose-and-throat man chosen to treat her father's chronic sinus condition, Anna feared that his narrow focus had blinded him to larger concerns. "I didn't think," Anna later confessed, that he "really knew what he was talking about." Pushing further, Anna asked if he ever took her father's blood pressure. "When I think it necessary," McIntire replied.

Softening her tone, Anna told McIntire that she was worried. She, too, had seen her father bounce back from many illnesses, but this time he seemed to be losing the struggle. His body seemed to be breaking down little by little. Could McIntire please send the president to the hospital for a thorough checkup? And would he promise not to tell her father that she had suggested it?

• • •

McIntire grudgingly acceded to Anna's request, arranging a checkup for the afternoon of March 28, 1944, at Bethesda Naval Hospital. Anna accompanied her father in the car as the cavalcade headed up Wisconsin Avenue. When they reached the hospital grounds, Roosevelt pointed through the trees to a tall, elegant building. "I designed that one," he told Anna joyfully, fancying a greater contribution to the building than he had really made. Loving architecture as he did, Roosevelt had occasionally submitted drawings for certain public buildings, but there his participation usually stopped. This was probably just as well, for he had a tendency to overlook critical items in his plans, such as closet space and bathrooms.

At the door of the hospital, Anna smiled and waved goodbye. Her mother was returning that same afternoon from her Caribbean tour, and Anna had promised to meet her at the airport. As the president rolled down the corridor in his wheelchair, he waved cheerfully to the patients and the members of the staff who had gathered round to see him. There was nothing in his demeanor to indicate the disturbing symptoms that had brought him to the hospital.

Inside the medical suite, Dr. Howard Bruenn, a young cardiologist, waited anxiously for his famous patient. Bruenn had been told only that the president was not recovering well from a bout of influenza and bronchitis, that a more thorough checkup was needed. "It was a warm day," Bruenn recalled years later, "and I was perspiring a lot. I felt I had a big weight on my shoulders." Having never met the president before, Bruenn had requested from McIntire earlier that day the results of previous heart and chest exams. McIntire wasn't sure he could find them, but when Bruenn pressed him, arguing that without previous results there was no way to make comparisons, McIntire promised to look carefully and send them by messenger if they were found.

The records had not yet arrived as the president was lifted onto the examining table, leaving Bruenn with no comprehension of the patient's history. "I suspected something was terribly wrong as soon as I looked at him," Bruenn recalled. "His face was pallid and there was a bluish discoloration of his skin, lips and nail beds. When the hemoglobin is fully oxygenated, it is red. When it is impaired, it has a bluish tint. The bluish color meant the tissues were not being supplied with adequate oxygen."

At first glance, Bruenn also observed that Roosevelt was having difficulty breathing. The mere act of moving from one side to the other caused considerable breathlessness. Working quickly and methodically, the young doctor put his hands on the president's chest and listened to the sounds of his heart. "It was worse than I feared," he recalled.

The examination revealed that the apex of the heart was much farther to the left than it should have been, suggesting a grossly enlarged heart. If the heart is under increased blood pressure, as Roosevelt's apparently was, one of the first things it does is to increase its size. Bruenn asked his patient to take a deep breath and hold it as long as he could. Roosevelt expelled it after only thirty-five seconds. In the president's lungs, Bruenn heard rales, an abnormal rattling or bubbling sound indicating a dangerous buildup of fluid.

In the midst of the exam, the medical records finally arrived. Bruenn covered the president and excused himself for a moment. Reading swiftly, he noted that high blood pressure had been detected as far back as 1941 (188/105mm). Why McIntire had not called in a heart man earlier was incomprehensible to Bruenn. In the interim, much damage had been done. Roosevelt, Bruenn concluded, was suffering from congestive heart failure. His damaged heart was no longer able to pump effectively. Left untreated, Roosevelt was unlikely to survive for more than a year. And in 1944, the therapy for hypertension was limited.

Bruenn never said a word to Roosevelt of the dark thoughts that were filling his mind. McIntire had instructed him not to volunteer any information to the president. Nor did Roosevelt ask a single question about what Bruenn was finding. On the contrary, throughout the entire exam, Roosevelt chatted genially about a range of topics totally unrelated to his health, and when the exam was finished, he smiled his famous smile and extended his hand. "Thanks, Doc," he said, and then he was gone.

Yet, at some level, Roosevelt must have felt relief in knowing that someone other than he was worrying about what was going on. Though he could not bring himself to ask the questions aloud, he must have harbored terrible fears and frustrations as he found himself unable to sleep at night and too tired to work during the day. At least now something would be done.

At his regular press conference later that afternoon, Roosevelt was asked about his health. Smiling broadly, he said that he had been suffering from bronchitis for the last three weeks but otherwise was fine. He then coughed and patted his chest to demonstrate how it affected him. Asked if he was alarmed by his condition, the president said he'd been told only one of 48,500 cases of bronchitis might develop into pneumonia, so he thought he had a rather slim chance. So effective was Roosevelt's upbeat performance that reporters concluded that his bronchitis had been whipped and that he was feeling fine. "Not only were the President's color and voice better," *The New York Times* observed, "but his spirits were good, too."

When Roosevelt returned to his study after the press conference, Eleanor and Anna were there. Eleanor was in high spirits. Her Caribbean trip had been an unqualified success; her meetings with the soldiers had gone well, and her press coverage had been triumphant. There was much to tell her husband, but first she had a present for him, a souvenir to add to his collection of ships. It was a little model of a jangada, a raftlike native boat used by the fishermen at Recife, Brazil. Pleased with his gift but too tired to talk, now that he no longer needed to perform, Roosevelt retired to his bedroom at seven-thirty.

Dr. Bruenn reported his alarming findings to Dr. McIntire the following day, along with a memorandum of recommendations, including complete bedrest for seven weeks with nursing care, avoidance of tension, digitalis, a change in diet to restrict salt and to lower calories, and the use of an elevated Gatch bed to relieve breathlessness at night. "McIntire was appalled at my suggestions," Bruenn recalled. "The president can't take time off to go to bed," McIntire insisted. "You can't simply say to him, Do this or do that. This is the president of the United States!"

To shore up his position, McIntire called in a team of consultants, including Dr. John Harper, Bruenn's commanding officer at Bethesda, Dr. James Paullin of Atlanta, and Dr. Frank Lahey of Boston. They were shown the

X-rays, electrocardiogram, and other laboratory data, and Bruenn was asked to present his recommendations. The seniors disagreed emphatically with Bruenn's diagnosis; after all, someone said, McIntire had been examining the president for years; it was simply impossible to imagine that Roosevelt had become this gravely ill overnight. As for Bruenn's drastic recommendations, the only one that they supported was the installation of a Gatch bed, which allowed the head to be elevated.

"I was only a lieutenant commander," Bruenn said. "McIntire was an admiral. Harper was my boss. But I knew I was right, so I held my ground." Finally, McIntire agreed to let Paullin and Lahey examine the president later that afternoon; discussions would resume the following day.

After seeing the president, Dr. Paullin announced that he now agreed with Bruenn's diagnosis and would approve a cautious program of digitalization to tone up the heart muscle and strengthen it. "Digitalis was a miracle drug," Bruenn observed later. In 1944, however, it was difficult to calibrate the amount of the digitalis leaf that would produce a therapeutic versus a toxic effect. "The risk," Bruenn admitted, "was that overdosage could lead to nausea, loss of appetite, and further damage to the heart."

Dr. Lahey apparently came away from the exam with a different set of concerns, centered on the president's gastrointestinal tract. It is not clear exactly what worried Lahey, but Dr. Harry Goldsmith of Massachusetts, who has plumbed the question of Roosevelt's health for more than a decade, believes that Lahey may have found an inoperable malignant tumor in Roosevelt's stomach. The cancer may have started, Goldsmith suggests, in a mole over the president's left eye, or in a wen that had been removed from the back of his head earlier in the year and then metastasized to his stomach.

However valid Lahey's line of inquiry may have been, the discussion quickly returned to the president's heart. The doctors finally agreed on a scaled-down version of Bruenn's original recommendations: digitalis would be administered in low doses; a low-fat diet would be instituted; callers would be held to a minimum at lunch and dinner; and the president would be asked to cut his consumption of cigarettes from twenty to ten per day and to limit himself to one and a half cocktails a day. The secret conference was adjourned.

It is not clear how much the president was told of his underlying condition. Though Bruenn was brought in to see the president on a regular basis, he remained under strict orders from McIntire to reveal nothing to Roosevelt. Bruenn assumed that McIntire was talking to the president, but McIntire declared later that he deliberately did not tell Roosevelt what the diagnosis was. It was an extraordinary act of presumption on McIntire's part, depriving Roosevelt of the right to know what was happening to his life.

Shortly after Bruenn's diagnosis, Roosevelt confessed to Eleanor that he was worried. "He suspects the doctors don't know what is the matter," Eleanor admitted to Joe Lash. At one point, suffering pain in his rectal area, he feared there might be a growth. But then the pain subsided and he relaxed. Curiously, during all this time he never once asked his doctors what they knew; day after day, he took his green digitalis pills without asking what they were or why he was taking them; day after day, he had his blood pressure read without asking what it was.

The conspiracy of silence extended to the public. On April 4, 1944, one week after the disconcerting checkup, McIntire blithely assured the press that nothing was wrong, that the president was simply suffering from a case of bronchitis. The results of the checkup were excellent, he claimed. "When we got through we decided that for a man of 62 we had very little to argue about, with the exception that we have had to combat flu plus respiratory complications." McIntire went on to say that all the president needed now was "some sunshine and more exercise."

The digitalis worked. X-rays of Roosevelt's chest taken two weeks after the treatment revealed a significant decrease in the size of the heart and a notable clearing of the lungs. His coughing had stopped, his color was good, his blood chemistries were normal, and he was sleeping soundly at night.

• • •

Although the president was improving, the doctors decided that he needed a period of rest away from the White House, where work inevitably pushed its way into his living quarters, into his upstairs study, even into his bedroom. When Bernard Baruch heard that the president was looking for a place to rest, he offered Hobcaw, his roomy brick mansion situated on a knoll overlooking the Waccamaw River in South Carolina.

Roosevelt, accompanied by Drs. Bruenn and McIntire, Pa Watson, and Admiral Leahy, arrived at the Baruch plantation on Easter Sunday, April 9. In the days before his arrival, the Secret Service had been hard at work building wooden ramps for the front and back staircases, a railing in the fishing pier, and a canvas chute that could, in case of fire, allow the president to slide from his bedroom to the ground.

It was the perfect hideaway. The three press-association reporters who had accompanied the president kept their distance from the mansion, standing by in the Prince Georges Hotel eight miles away just in case something happened. "The Secret Service impressed on us repeatedly to 'stay out of the old man's way,'" Merriman Smith recalled. Though just about every living soul in Georgetown knew "He" was there, Smith laughingly observed, all three reporters went along with the game, giving Roosevelt free rein to do as he pleased day in and day out.

"I want to sleep and sleep," Roosevelt said when he first arrived, "twelve hours a night." In the quiet of Baruch's graceful mansion, surrounded by twenty-three thousand acres of fields, woods, and streams, the president got his wish. He awakened at nine-thirty in the morning and went to bed at nine-thirty at night. In the mornings, he read the papers and worked on his correspondence; on sunny afternoons, he fished from the pier or trolled in the bay; on rainy days, he drove around the estate, stopping to see the elaborate gardens, the deer, and the wild boar. Cocktails were usually served at six, with dinner at seven.

During the second week of Roosevelt's vacation, the mail pouch carried an executive order for the president's signature, directing the secretary of commerce to take possession of the Chicago offices of the mammoth mail-order firm Montgomery-Ward. Since April 12, a strike had been in progress, provoked by the company's failure to comply with the WLB's directive to hold fair elections. The case was a complex one, provoking fiery disagreement within the administration. Stimson argued that, since Montgomery-Ward was not doing war business, the army had no right to stick its nose into the labor situation and extend presidential power far wider than he was sure it ought to be extended. Attorney General Francis Biddle disagreed: since 75 percent of Montgomery-Ward's customers were farmers, and since farmers were engaged in producing food vital to the country's war operations, the army had a responsibility to take over the company.

It is not clear how much Roosevelt focused on the issue, but in the end he sided with Biddle and signed the order sending in the troops. The decision backfired. As steel-helmeted soldiers, bearing guns with bayonets fixed, surrounded the Chicago headquarters, Montgomery's chairman, Sewell Avery, refused to leave his eighth-floor office. There was a moment of hesitation, following which Biddle ordered the soldiers to remove him. Two soldiers locked their hands together to form a seat beneath Mr. Avery; two others steadied him by the shoulders. He struggled slightly and then was lifted bodily into the elevator and onto the street.

The photograph of Mr. Avery being carried from the building—voted by news photographers the best photo of the year—prompted a wave of criticism against Roosevelt. "There is no warrant in the Smith-Connally Act or in the President's wartime powers for this seizure," the *Washington Post* editorialized. "It was the manner in which the troops were used," Walter Lippmann observed, "which has made the affair so notorious." This "great howl" was just what Stimson had feared. In his diary, he lamented the action and predicted "it would be used by [Roosevelt's] enemies as corroborating fear of his seeking autocratic power."

With this single exception, Dr. Bruenn recalled, "the whole period was very pleasant. . . . The president thrived on the simple routine. I had never known anyone so full of charm. At lunch and dinner alike, he animated the conversation, telling wonderful stories, reminiscing with Baruch, talking of current events, pulling everyone in. He was a master raconteur. There was no question about it."

While Roosevelt was at Hobcaw, Anna flew to Seattle to pack up her belongings and get their house ready for occupancy. "Beloved of mine," John wrote her from the White House. "Life is just a mess without you. In some ways I wonder if it is wise for me to confess to you that the whole world—except only you—is like warm flat beer to me and you are excitement and joy and life itself."

"Anna has arranged to bring the children East," Eleanor wrote Franklin from Hyde Park on April 21, "and we will have to open the big house from about the middle of June on. Couldn't you arrange to go up and stay a month at a time and only come back for 2–3 days a month? It would be heavenly for us all." She went on to say she wanted to buy a few things to make the servants' rooms more livable and promised she wouldn't spend much. "May I?" she asked. "Also, if I made a diagram of mama's room so everything could be put back in place could I arrange it as a sitting room with a day bed in case someone had to sleep there?"

The following week, Eleanor and Anna, along with Prime Minister and Mrs. John Curtin of Australia and Costa Rican President Teodoro Picado flew to Hobcaw for lunch with the president. Though there was little time for private conversation, Eleanor noticed with satisfaction that Franklin's color was better and his spirits were high. "I came home feeling that it was the very best move Franklin could have made." The sunshine was working wonders, she decided, predicting that he would return from Hobcaw "in better condition than when he left."

Anna was less sanguine about her father's condition, having talked with Dr. Bruenn after lunch about the long-term effects of coronary disease and the necessity to change her father's White House routine radically. Bruenn also impressed upon Anna the importance of altering Roosevelt's diet—something Eleanor apparently did not understand, for no sooner had she returned to Washington than she sent a bunch of steaks in the mail pouch, hoping the president would enjoy them.

Eleanor's delight in her husband's relaxing days with Baruch would more than likely have been diminished had she known that, on the morning of April 28, at the president's invitation, Lucy Mercer Rutherfurd was heading toward Hobcaw from Aiken, 140 miles away.

A month earlier, at Ridgeley Hall in Aiken, Lucy's ailing husband, Winthrop Rutherfurd, had died, leaving Lucy a widow at the age of fifty-two. Survived by two daughters and four sons, Winthrop was buried at his family's estate in Allamuchy, New Jersey. For Lucy, whose life had revolved around her husband for more than twenty years, it was not an easy time. There were complicated estate problems to solve, worries over the children, and difficult decisions to make. And, for the first time, she was alone.

Lucy arrived shortly before noon, accompanied by her stepdaughter and her stepson's wife. In spite of all she had been through the previous month, she retained her beauty and her charm. She could still reach Roosevelt in a way that no one else could. Lucy's presence at the luncheon that day was officially recorded in a seating chart that remains among the president's papers. This time, perhaps because Mr. Rutherfurd was no longer alive, she is openly listed as Lucy Rutherfurd rather than Mrs. Paul Johnson. The diagram of the table shows that Roosevelt was seated at one end, Baruch at the other, Lucy to the president's right. Other guests included Admiral Leahy and Dr. McIntire, Captain Robert Duncan, and Dr. Bruenn. Years later, Baruch vividly remembered the occasion, in part because he had to give up several of his precious war-ration tickets so that Lucy could make the long drive.

For Roosevelt, Lucy's presence must have provided a delightful tonic, reminding him of his younger self, before his paralysis, before the illness that was now overwhelming him. In Lucy's company he could re-establish continuity with his youth, bringing back in his mind the healthy body in which he had once lived. If his future was disappearing, at least he could relive the happy moments of his past.

During lunch, word came that Navy Secretary Frank Knox had died of a heart attack at the age of seventy. The self-imposed unrelenting pace that marked the life of the energetic Knox had finally taken its toll. Eleanor was in the White House, having lunch with Mrs. Kermit Roosevelt, widow of Teddy Roosevelt's son, when the news came. Assuming that her husband would cut his vacation short and come to Washington for the funeral, she postponed by a week an impending trip to New York, including a half-dozen speaking engagements, so she could be at home when her husband returned.

As it happened, Roosevelt did not return for the funeral, electing to remain in Hobcaw an extra week. Though his health had improved markedly during his stay, he suffered a setback later that afternoon that kept him in bed for several days. Shortly after his lunch with Lucy, he experienced acute abdominal pain, slight nausea, and a throbbing sensation all through his body. Dr. Bruenn tentatively diagnosed gallstones and made arrangements for X-rays as soon as they returned to Washington.

In the meantime, a hypodermic injection of codeine allowed Roosevelt to meet the press at eight that evening to discuss Knox's death. Though Merriman Smith noticed that the color of the president's skin was not particularly healthy, he "seemed in such good spirits" that the reporter thought little of it. When Roosevelt talked of Knox, he revealed little emotion. "That may have been the Roosevelt breeding," Smith observed, "because I've been told people of superior breeding never let their emotions come to the surface publicly." Knox was the first of Roosevelt's wartime Cabinet to die, though four other Cabinet members were in their seventies—Stimson at seventy-six, Hull at seventy-two, and Jones and Ickes at seventy.

Roosevelt explained to reporters that the doctors were keeping him in South Carolina a little longer, "lest his recovery from a bad coughing winter be interrupted." Once the discussion of Knox was out of the way, Smith noted, Roosevelt "chatted gaily," about fishing. He asked the three reporters how they were getting along and, upon hearing that they had to pay $12.50 for a bottle of poor rye at the Prince Georges Hotel, he ordered Pa Watson to serve a round of Baruch's bourbon at once, "lest the reporters feel poorly on their return to the city."

In Washington, Eleanor was disappointed to hear that Franklin had delayed his return until May 7. "You will come home just as I leave which is sad," she wrote, explaining that, because she had switched her appointments around the previous week, she now had to be in New York from the 5th to the 12th. "I hate to be away when you come back!"

It helped, however, to know that Anna would be there, able to take her mother's place in welcoming the president home. Just before Eleanor left, Anna celebrated her thirty-eighth birthday. "Nothing I could give you dear could ever tell you how much I love you," Eleanor wrote in a note accompanying her gifts, "but I hope you and John know what a joy it is to have you near and how much I cherish all our pleasant happy times."

• • •

Roosevelt's return to the White House on Sunday morning, May 7, marked the end of the most complete vacation he had had during his eleven years in the presidency. "I had a really grand time at Bernie's," Roosevelt wrote Hopkins, who was convalescing from an operation at White Sulphur Springs, West Virginia, "slept 12 hours out of 24, sat in the sun, never lost my temper, and decided to let the world go hang."

It had been a rough five months for the president's old friend. In January, Hopkins had entered the hospital with a recurrence of his old intestinal troubles. In February, en route to Florida to recuperate, he had received word from Roosevelt that his eighteen-year-old Marine Corps son, Stephen, had been killed in the Marshall Islands. Then, after his abdominal surgery at the Mayo Clinic in March, he had developed jaundice. Finally, at White Sulphur Springs, he seemed to be getting better.

"It is grand to get the reports of how well you are getting on," Roosevelt wrote, "and I have had a mighty nice letter from [Dr. Andrew] Rivers—couched mostly in medical terms, which, however, I have had translated!

"The main things I get from it are two. First, that it is a good thing to connect up the plumbing and put your sewerage system into operating condition. The second is (and this comes from others in authority) that you have got to lead not the life of an invalid but the life of common or garden sense. I, too, over one hundred years older than you are, have come to the same realization and I have cut my drinks down to one and a half cocktails per evening and nothing else—not one complimentary highball or night cap. Also, I have cut my cigarettes down from twenty or thirty a day to five or six a day. Luckily they still taste rotten but it can be done. The main gist of this is to plead with you to stay away until the middle of June at the earliest. I don't want you back until then. If you do come back before then you will be extremely unpopular in Washington, with the exception of [*Washington Times Herald* Publisher] Cissy Patterson who wants to kill you off as soon as possible—just as she does me. . . ."

"We can all be glad," *The New York Times* editorialized the day after the president returned, that "he has had a chance to enjoy a month of rest and relaxation from the almost overwhelming burdens which his office forces him to carry. He earned every hour of it." Writing in a similar vein, *New*

York Times correspondent Anne O'Hare McCormick remarked that the vacation was "good news for the American people," since Roosevelt would need "all the strength, serenity and fortitude of spirit he could muster" to face the climactic days ahead when Allied armies began pouring into Europe for a fight to the finish.

Hassett found the president "brown as a berry, radiant and happy, insisting he has had a complete rest." But Anna was still worried. Though his color was good and his spirits were high, she could see that he was not his old self. "Anna was afraid," Dr. Bruenn recalled, "that her father would fall back into his old habits now that he was back in the White House. She had read up on cardiovascular disease and she understood how important rest and diet were. She was a great help to me. She became his protector. It was Anna who enforced the new regime."

In the weeks that followed, Anna was by her father's side from the moment he awakened until he went to bed at night, making sure that his workload was kept to six hours a day. "You would find many changes here," Ickes wrote Missy on May 23. "He makes only a few appointments a day—not enough in fact for us to transmit important business—and then goes back to house where he usually lunches alone with Anna. He is supposed to go to bed at 9:30 at night but Anna told me she has difficulty in persuading him to do that. . . . Then he goes away for weekends."

A sampling of the usher diaries for May reveals meetings with Cabinet and congressional leaders in the mornings, lunch with Anna and sometimes Margaret Suckley under the magnolia tree on the southern grounds at 1:30 or 2 p.m., additional meetings in the afternoons, followed by a drive in the countryside or a swim in the pool, cocktails and dinner with Anna and John, bed by 10 or 10:30.

For a man who could not be alone, who relished people as his major source of relaxation, Anna's company was vital. For a while, Princess Martha had been able to take up where Missy and Harry had left off, providing Roosevelt with lively companionship and good cheer. But as Roosevelt's health weakened, his meetings with Martha diminished. Though he continued to see her occasionally during the spring and summer of 1944, their "romance" faded. "With people like Martha," Anna's son Johnny Boettiger speculated, "his performance always had to be on. Surely, it was second nature to him and he loved it, but as his energy decreased, their sparkling conversation left him somewhat depleted. With Anna, who loved to tell stories almost as much as he did, he could sit back and let himself be."

Anna's continuing presence in the White House freed Eleanor to do what she wanted, and "what she wanted," Johnny Boettiger observed, "was to be out on her own. She had an opportunity to develop her character and to enjoy a range of experiences few women had." For Eleanor, being on the road and meeting new people was life itself. "I am always waiting for the day to appear when I shall put on my lace cap and sit by the fire," Eleanor once wrote. "But when I am with a number of young people I become so interested I put off that day a little longer."

Returning home from her trips, Eleanor observed the growing bond between Franklin and Anna with mixed emotions. It was hard for Eleanor to accept that Anna now knew things she did not. In a conversation one day with Eleanor about political possibilities in 1944 and what Roosevelt might think about them, Trude Pratt was struck by Eleanor's wistful comment: "Anna is the only one who would know about that."

The tensions multiplied as the weeks went by. "Anna tried to be as protective as she could with her father's health," Dr. Bruenn observed, "but Eleanor was a different kind of person, more driven, more insistent. She couldn't accept that he was really sick or that he needed to cut down his activities, especially if they related to her concerns. I would sit with the family telling everyone how important it was not to annoy him or upset him at the dinner table but she couldn't stop herself."

Of course, Eleanor drove Franklin no harder than she drove herself; there were just too many things to accomplish, and at some level, even if she couldn't admit it openly, she must have worried that time was running out for both of them. The condition of black Americans remained closest to her heart. It seemed that, the more criticism she received about her advocacy of blacks, the more committed she became. In February, she had attended the opening of the first non–Jim Crow servicemen's canteen in Washington, D.C. When a picture of her appeared in the papers surrounded by a group of white and Negro servicemen and their dates, a bitter controversy flared. "How can anyone," Representative Charles McKenzie of Louisiana argued on the floor of the House, "be a party to encouraging white girls into the arms of Negro soldiers at a canteen dance while singing 'Let Me Call You Sweetheart?' "

"I know, of course, you are bidding for negro votes for your good husband," an "outraged" woman wrote Eleanor, "but isn't it rather a costly price to pay? . . . Would you have enjoyed seeing your daughter Anna being hugged by those negroes. . . . You are the most dangerous woman in America today and may I beg you to stop and think before you are guilty of such a thing again."

Though Eleanor did not doubt her husband's ultimate commitment to racial equality, she believed constant reminders were essential to counter the rising pressures from the conservative coalition in Congress. Her commitment to women required equal vigilance. When she came home from her Caribbean tour, she was upset to find that only men were being sent to an international conference in London on education. She got one woman added at the last moment, but that was not good enough. "Women should be represented in every international conference," she insisted.

When the president was strong and healthy, he had enjoyed and even invited Eleanor's advocacy. "She pushed him terrifically, this I know," Anna admitted. "But you can't ask somebody to be your eyes and ears and then not . . ." Grace Tully recalls a tense moment when Eleanor was cross-examining Franklin at a dinner party. "Mother, can't you see you are giving Father indigestion?" Anna pleaded.

"She couldn't see why," Anna recalled, "at a moment when he was relaxing—I remember one day when we were having cocktails. . . . A fair number of people were in the room, an informal group. . . . I was mixing the cocktails. Mother always came in at the end so she would only have to have one cocktail—that was her concession. She would wolf it—she never took it slowly. She came in and sat down across the desk from Father. And she had a sheaf of papers this high and she said, 'Now, Franklin, I want to talk to you about this.' I have permanently blocked out of my mind what it was she wanted to bring up. I just remember, like lightning, that I thought, 'Oh God, he's going to blow.' And sure enough, he blew his top. He took every single speck of that whole pile of papers, threw them across the desk at me and said, 'Sis, you handle these tomorrow morning.' I almost went through the floor. She got up. She was the most controlled person in the world. And she just stood there a half second and said, 'I'm sorry.' Then she took her glass and walked toward somebody else and started talking. And he picked up his glass and started a story. And that was the end of it.

"Intuitively I understood that here was a man plagued with God knows how many problems and right now he had twenty minutes to have two cocktails—in very small glasses—because dinner was served at a certain hour. They called you and out you went. He wanted to tell stories and relax and enjoy himself—period. I don't think Mother had the slightest realization."

Earlier in the spring, almost as if she were anticipating this terrible moment, Anna had written to John, "I pray I don't get caught in the crossfire between those two." Over the years, Anna had come to understand the pain her mother had endured from being placed in an emotional triangle with her mother-in-law, competing with the older woman for the love of the same man. And she knew about her father's affair with Lucy Mercer. The last thing Anna wanted was to create a situation that would recapitulate her mother's earlier dilemma. But so deep was Anna's pleasure in playing the role of caretaker to her father that there was no way she could give it up, even if it jeopardized her relationship with her mother.

CHAPTER 20

"SUSPENDED IN SPACE"

Through the last days of May and the early days of June, Eleanor observed, everyone seemed to live "suspended in space, waiting for the invasion, dreading it and yet wishing it could begin successfully." In the hush of the moment, Roosevelt tried to maintain a pretense of normal activity, but his secretary Grace Tully noticed that "every movement of his face and hands reflected the tightly contained state of his nerves."

He had done all he could to make sure that the young soldiers who crossed the Channel would have the greatest possible chance of success. From factories in Michigan, Illinois, Indiana, and New York had come the overwhelming majority of the vehicles—the trucks, tanks, armored cars, jeeps, ambulances—that were now carrying the men and supplies to the embarkation posts in southern England. From assembly plants in Ohio, Oregon, and California had come the bombers and the fighter planes that would provide life-sustaining air cover for the invading force. And from shipyards on both coasts had come the largest fleet ever assembled—900 warships in all, including 9 battleships, 23 heavy cruisers, 104 destroyers, and, perhaps most important, from Andrew Higgins in New Orleans had come the landing craft needed to carry the troops onto the beaches. Indeed, so much time had the Allied high command spent worrying about landing craft that Eisenhower once said that, "when he is buried, his coffin should be in the shape of a landing craft, as they are practically killing him with worry."

Yet, with the target date now only days away, there was little either Roosevelt or Eisenhower could do except sit back and wait. "The nearer H hour approached," army historian Gordon Harrison explained in the official army history of the cross-Channel attack, "the more heavily and exclusively the responsibility for the invasion settled on the lower commanders." For the few—Roosevelt, Churchill, Eisenhower, Marshall, Montgomery, and Brooke—would now be substituted the many, "as the battlefield so long seen as a single conceptual problem, becomes a confused and disparate fact—a maze of unrelated orchards and strange roads, hedgerows, villages, streams and woods, each temporarily bounding for the soldier the whole horizon of the war."

Once the order to "go" was given, the chief burden of the fighting would reside with the individual soldier; the advance of each unit would depend in large measure on his courage and skill, on his willingness to jump from the landing craft into water which was sometimes up to his neck, or higher; to wade through the bloodstained waves onto the beach, amid bloated bodies and bullets; and then to walk or crawl up the hill where the vaunted German army was waiting with rifles, mortars, and machine guns. Months of training and experience on other fronts in North Africa or Italy had brought each soldier to this point, but in the hearts of many, fighter pilot and military historian William Emerson admitted, "there was a question of whether we could make it against the big leagues. Till then we'd been fooling around the periphery. Now we were going into the center of things. Beneath the bravado, there was an undercurrent of concern, even fear."

Eisenhower determined that only four days in June provided the combination of conditions necessary for the assault—a late-rising moon for the paratroopers, and, shortly after dawn, a low tide. The invasion was set for Monday, June 5, a month later than originally planned.

Roosevelt had intended to fly to England in early June so that he could be close to Churchill and Eisenhower as the invasion began. When his health prevented the trip, Churchill was sorely disappointed. Even at this late date, the prime minister was still anxious about the whole operation, still oppressed by "the dangers and disasters that could flow from Overlord if the landings should fail." If only Roosevelt were there; then at least some of the tension might be eased. "Our friendship is my greatest stand-by amid the ever-increasing complications of this exacting war," Churchill wrote Roosevelt on June 4, as he journeyed south to be near Eisenhower and the troops. "How I wish you were here."

For his part, Roosevelt decided to spend the weekend in Charlottesville, Virginia, at the home of his military aide Pa Watson. In the quiet of Watson's elegant estate, Roosevelt hoped to prepare a speech to the nation to be delivered once the invasion began. Eleanor was invited to join her husband, but she elected to stay in Washington instead, knowing perhaps that her own anxiety would only contribute to his. For weeks, Eleanor had been unable to sleep through the night. "I feel as though a sword were hanging over my head," she had written in mid-May, "dreading its fall and yet knowing it must fall to end the war."

Several months earlier, Eleanor had received a haunting letter from a woman whose favorite nephew had just been killed while serving in the navy. "It is too bad that you and your husband have not been punished by some deadly disease," the distraught woman wrote. "Maybe though you and your husband will have to look into the faces of the dead corpses of your four sons. . . . God always punishes the wicked in some way." Eleanor published the letter in her column, along with a simple reply. "Neither my husband nor I brought on this war," she wrote, but "I quite understood her bitterness." Now that the target date was drawing near, Eleanor could not free herself from monstrous thoughts of the battlefield, of the dead and the wounded. "Soon the invasion will be upon us," she wrote on June 3; "I dread it."

What is more, Eleanor had no confidence that she could help her husband on this critical speech. The Office of War Information had asked her to prepare a radio speech of her own to be used after the invasion began, but she had declined. It was supposed to be addressed to the mothers of the U.S.A., and she couldn't think of what she wanted to say, she explained to Joe Lash. "I only know I don't want to say any of the things they suggested!"

In Eleanor's absence, Anna and John accompanied Roosevelt to Charlottesville, where the three of them worked together on a draft of the president's speech. Years later, Anna recalled with pleasure the role she and John had played in suggesting that the speech be in the form of a prayer instead of a regular speech. "We all started making our contributions. Father would take a little from all of us and then write it as his own."

That same Saturday, June 3, Eisenhower met with his meteorologists in the Library of Southwick House at Naval Headquarters in Portsmouth. The news was not good. A marked deterioration had taken place in the good conditions originally predicted for June 5. Now Captain J. M. Stagg, senior meteorologist for Supreme Headquarters Allied Expeditionary Force, was saying that June 5 would be overcast and stormy, with high winds and visibility so low that the air force could not be used. And the weather pattern was so unpredictable that forecasting more than a day in advance was highly undependable. With great reluctance, Eisenhower decided to postpone the operation for twenty-four hours.

News of the postponement threw Churchill into "an agony of uncertainty." If the bad conditions continued for another day, Overlord could not be launched for at least another two weeks. Unable to endure the tension, he decided to return to London. In Charlottesville, Roosevelt remained calm, though he, too, elected to return to his nation's capital. In Eleanor's judgment, her husband was better able to meet the tension than many of the others, "because he'd learned from polio that if there was nothing you could do about a situation, then you'd better try to put it out of your mind and go on with your work at hand."

On Sunday night, June 4, Eisenhower met again with his meteorologists. This time Captain Stagg reported a slight improvement in the weather; the rain front was expected to clear in three hours, and the clearing would last until Tuesday morning; later that Tuesday, however, considerable cloudiness was expected to develop. Eisenhower recognized that these conditions were far from ideal but "the question," he said, was "just how long you can hang this operation on the end of a limb and let it hang there." At nine forty-five that night, Eisenhower announced his decision. "O.K., let's go." The invasion would be launched at dawn on the 6th of June. "I don't like it, but there it is," he said. "I don't see how we can possibly do anything else."

On the eve of D-day, a nervous Churchill went to his map room to follow the movement of the convoys as they headed toward the coast of France. "Do you realize," he said to his wife, Clementine, who had joined him before she went to bed, "that by the time you wake up in the morning twenty thousand men may have been killed?"

That same night, Roosevelt went on the air to salute the fall of Rome. "The first of the Axis capitals is now in our hands," Roosevelt said. "One up and two to go!" The Allied struggle to capture Rome had been long and costly, with heavy loss of life. In January, the Germans had pinned down more than 150,000 Allied soldiers to a bridgehead at Anzio on the Tyrrhenian Sea, preventing them from linking up with the main Allied force to the south. It took more than four months of fighting for the Allies finally to break out from Anzio on May 23 and link up with the Allied forces advancing on Rome. Things moved swiftly after that, leading to the capture of Rome in a matter of days. "How magnificently your troops have fought," Churchill telegraphed.

Though Roosevelt knew that thousands of American soldiers were crossing the Channel as he delivered his address, he never tipped his hat, concentrating his remarks on Italy. Shortly after the speech, the president went to bed.

As the clock tolled midnight in Washington, the first waves of young Americans were plunging into the surf. Few had slept the night before, war correspondent Ernie Pyle reported, and many had thrown up their breakfasts, as the invasion turned "from a vague anticipatory dread into a horrible reality." Some, loaded down with gas masks, grenades, TNT, satchel charges, and rifle ammunition, sixty-eight pounds in all, drowned when they first jumped into the water; others were hit by bullets and killed or wounded as they waded in to shore; still others were struck as they scrambled across the beach. Some of the beaches proved easier than others. Omaha was the worst. One infantry company at Omaha lost a quarter of its men in the first forty-five minutes. "I don't know why I'm alive at all," one survivor said. "It was really awful. For hours there on the beach the shells were so close they were throwing mud and rocks all over you. It was so bad that you didn't care whether you got hit or not."

But by 3 a.m., Washington time, when General Marshall called the White House to speak to the president, most of the troops were moving forward, making their way onto the beaches and up the hills. Eleanor was still awake when the call came. Franklin had told her the invasion news before she went to bed, and she became so wrought up she could not sleep. "To be nearly sixty and still rebel at uncertainty is ridiculous isn't it," she chided herself. The White House operator called Eleanor first, knowing she was still up, and asked her to awaken the president. Eleanor entered her husband's room. "He sat up in bed and put on his sweater, and from then on he was on the telephone. . . ."

The official announcement of the invasion came at 3:32 a.m. along with a reading of Eisenhower's order of the day: "Soldiers, sailors and airmen of the Allied Expeditionary Force! You are about to embark upon the great crusade, toward which we have striven these many months. . . . Much has happened since the Nazi triumph of 40–41. . . . Our homefronts have given us an overwhelming superiority in weapons and munitions of war, and placed at our disposal great reserves of trained fighting men. The tide has turned! I have full confidence in your courage, devotion to duty and skill in battle. We will accept nothing less than full victory!"

At 4 a.m., Roosevelt told the White House operator to call every member of the White House staff and ask them all to report to duty at once. One by one the calls were made; only Harry Hopkins, still convalescing in the army hospital in White Sulphur Springs, was excluded from the list. More than anyone else on the staff, Hopkins had deserved to be there that day to share the news of the great invasion he had long supported. Alone in his hospital room, he told his biographer Robert Sherwood, he thought about all the production problems that had challenged the United States in 1939 and 1940, of how the various bottlenecks had been broken and the desperate shortages of strategic materials converted into surpluses. If ever there was a country unprepared for the war, it was the U.S. in 1940. And yet now, only four years later, the United States was clearly the most productive, most powerful country on the face of the earth.

As the news of the invasion reached the American people in the early hours of June 6, church bells tolled, school bells rang, factories sounded their whistles, fog horns blasted. "It is the most exciting moment in our lives," Mayor LaGuardia told reporters. Sporting events were canceled. Retail stores closed. People streamed into the streets. "Outwardly they appeared to be celebrating a victory," *Homefront* author Winston Estes observed, "but underneath all that raucous, uncontrolled excitement, lay a cold fear and a grim anxiety which gnawed at their insides."

"The impulse to pray was overwhelming," historian Stephen Ambrose wrote. People jammed the pews of churches and synagogues in cities and towns throughout the land to sit in silence and pray. "We have come to the hour for which we were born," *The New York Times* editorialized the next day. "We go forth to meet the supreme test of our arms and our souls, the test of the maturity of our faith in ourselves and in mankind."

Roosevelt met with his congressional leaders at 9:50 a.m. and his military leaders at 11:30. The official news was still fragmentary, but by midafternoon, as he lunched with Anna under the magnolia tree, it was clear that the landings had gone pretty well, better than anyone had hoped. Though casualties were high—some sixty-six hundred were recorded that first day alone —they were fewer than expected. The main event of the day was the president's regular press conference at 4 p.m., which drew 180 men and women packed in a solid mass.

"The President was happy and confident," I. F. Stone recorded. "Our faces must have shown what most of us felt as we came in. For he began, after an extraordinary pause of several minutes in which no questions were asked and we all stood silent, by saying that the correspondents had the same look on their faces that people all over the country must have and that he thought this a very happy conference."

"I have just sat in on a great moment in history," a young reporter wrote his mother later that day. "The President sat back in his great green chair calm and smiling, dressed in a snow white shirt with the initials FDR on the left sleeve in blue and a dark blue dotted bow tie. In his hand he held the inevitable long cigarette holder and when he held the cigarette in his mouth it was cocked at the angle they say he always has it when he is pleased with the world."

Still, Roosevelt warned the press against overconfidence. "You just don't land on a beach and walk through—if you land successfully without breaking your leg—walk through to Berlin. And the quicker this country understands it the better."

Later that evening, Roosevelt went on the air to deliver the simple prayer he had prepared in Charlottesville, "a far cry," Rosenman noted, "from the kind of speech Hitler would have made if *his* troops were landing on the beaches of England." The general tone of his voice reflected concentrated, quiet intensity, perfectly matching the mood of the country. He prayed first for "our sons, pride of our Nation. . . . Give strength to their arms, stoutness to their hearts, steadfastness in their faith." He then prayed for the people at home, for strong hearts "to wait out the long travail, to bear sorrows that may come. . . . Give us Faith in Thee," he concluded: "faith in our sons; faith in each other; faith in our united crusade."

As Eleanor listened to her husband, she noted with pleasure that he looked very well and seemed himself again, full of plans for the future. At one moment, he talked of going to England as soon as Hitler was ready to surrender; the next moment, he spoke of Honolulu and the Aleutians. For her part, she had no sense of excitement whatsoever: "All emotion is drained away."

The "hedgerow battles" that followed in the days after the landings were characterized by savage fighting, slow movement, and few geographic gains. Tangled hedges and bushes were ubiquitous in the bocage country surrounding Normandy; everywhere one looked, they boxed in fields and orchards of varying sizes and shapes. "Each hedgerow," army historian Gordon Harrison notes, "was a potential earthwork into which the defenders cut often-elaborate foxholes, trenches, and individual firing pits. The dense bushes atop the hedgerows provided ample concealment for rifle and machine gun positions, which could subject the attacker to devastating hidden fire from three sides.... Each field thus became a separate battlefield."

But if the infantry was temporarily splintered by the dense terrain, Allied air and naval power was practically unopposed. From the larger perspective, the overwhelming weight of Allied arms gradually wore down the defenders. "I cannot say enough for the Navy," Corporal William Preston wrote his father, "for the way they brought us in, for the firepower they brought to bear on the beach. Whenever any of us fired a burst of tracer at a target, the destroyers, standing in so close they were almost ashore, fired a shot immediately after us, each time hitting what we were firing at on the nose." And all this time, Preston marveled, while twenty thousand Allied planes formed a protective umbrella in the sky, "not a single German plane" could be seen. "Nobody doubted now," Hap Arnold recorded, "the meaning of the damage reports, photographs, figures and percentages of the great air attack on the Luftwaffe in the five great days of February."

Three weeks after D-day, one million men had been put ashore, along with an astonishing supply of 171,532 vehicles and 566,000 tons of supplies. "As far as you could see in every direction the ocean was infested with ships," Ernie Pyle observed, but when you walked along the beach, a grimmer picture emerged. "The wreckage was vast and startling." Men were floating in the water, lying on the beach; nearly nine thousand were dead. "There were trucks tipped half over and swamped... tanks that had only just made the beach before being knocked out... jeeps that had burned to a dull gray... boats stacked on top of each other. On the beach lay expended sufficient men and mechanism for a small war. They were gone forever now.

"And yet, we could afford it," Pyle marveled. "We could afford it because we were on, we had our toehold, and behind us there were such enormous replacements for this wreckage on the beach that you could hardly conceive of the sum total. Men and equipment were flowing from England in such a gigantic stream that it made the waste on the beachhead seem like nothing at all, really nothing at all."

Standing amid the wreckage, looking out to sea at the immense armada of ships still waiting to unload, Pyle noticed a group of German prisoners. "They stood staring almost as if in a trance. They didn't say a word to each other. They didn't need to. The expression on their faces was something forever unforgettable. In it was the final, horrified acceptance of their doom."

• • •

Comforted by the news from France, Roosevelt journeyed to Hyde Park for seven days in the middle of June. "Much kidding about his destination," Hassett recorded, "even mentioned possibility of taking me into Catskills for a drinking party." A "Swiss family Robinson" caravan left the Bureau of Engraving terminal at 10 p.m. on a warm Thursday night: Franklin and Eleanor; Martha and Olav and their three children; Tommy, Tully, and White House operator Louise Hackmeister.

"I've unpacked a little and have some photos where I can enjoy them," Eleanor wrote Joe Lash the next morning from her desk in Sara's old bedroom, which she had finally taken over, "but really living here is hard for me—I've made Mama's room pleasant and I can work in it and not feel her presence . . . but over here there is no getting away from the bigness of the house and the multitudes of people. Franklin has a diet. The Crown Princess another and running the house is no joke!" Never from choice would she live in this house, Eleanor had confessed several weeks earlier, for her heart was in the cottage, "but suddenly Franklin is more dependent."

Following the simple routine he treasured so greatly at Hyde Park, the president worked in his library in the mornings, organized picnics along the river in the afternoons, took tea at Laura Delano's, and went to bed early. By the time he returned to Washington, he looked, Hassett recorded, "in the pink of condition."

The morning he returned, June 22, 1944, the president hosted a public ceremony in the Oval Office to celebrate his signing of the GI Bill of Rights. This extraordinary bill, which carried out in full the visionary recommendations Roosevelt had made the previous year, had passed the Senate by a vote of fifty to zero and the House by 387 to zero. Acknowledging the intense gratitude the country felt toward the men and women who had given up months and years of their lives in service to their country, the GI Bill was designed to provide the returning veteran with a chance to command the status, education, and training he could have enjoyed if he had not served in the military.

"There is one great fear in the heart of any serviceman," Eleanor observed in her column, quoting a letter from a young soldier overseas, "and it is not that he will be killed or maimed but that when he is finally allowed to go home and piece together what he can of life, he will be made to feel he has been a sucker for the sacrifice he has made."

The GI Bill responded to that fear by providing special opportunities for veterans: it backed them in their efforts to buy a home or get into business by guaranteeing loans up to $2,000; it authorized those who were unable to find a job to receive $20 a week for fifty-two weeks; it provided construction of additional hospital facilities, and, most far-reachingly, it provided $500 a year for college tuition plus a monthly payment of $75 for living expenses.

In 1940, when the average worker earned less than $1,000 a year and when tuition, room, and board ranged from $453 at state colleges to $979 at private universities, a college education was the preserve of the privileged few. By providing an allowance of what amounted to $1,400 a year, the GI Bill would carry more than two million veterans into colleges and graduate schools at a total cost of $14 billion. In the late forties, veterans would constitute almost 50 percent of the male students in all institutions of higher learning. To accommodate the new students, colleges and universities would vastly expand their physical plants. Scores of new urban campuses would be created. Moreover, under the same provision, another three million veterans would receive educational training below college, and two million would receive on-the-job training. Through this single piece of legislation, the educational horizons of an entire generation would be lifted.

Exceeding all expectations, the GIs would do exceptionally well at school. A *Fortune* survey of the class of '49, 70 percent of whom were veterans, concluded it was "the best . . . the most mature . . . the most responsible, the most self disciplined group of college students in history." Despite overcrowding in housing and the classroom, they were determined to make the most of this extraordinary opportunity. "We were men, not kids," veteran Chesterfield Smith observed, "and we had the maturity to recognize we had to go get what we wanted and not wait for things to happen to us."

"Almost everything important that happened to me later came from attending college," veteran Larry Montrell would write. "I don't know what I would have been if it hadn't been for that." Returning soldier Dan Condren agreed. "I doubt if I would have moved away from the Texas Panhandle. It set a whole new standard of improved education for a large number of people."

A smiling Roosevelt used ten pens to sign the historic legislation, handing the first to Representative Edith Nourse Rogers of Massachusetts, a strong proponent of veterans' rights and benefits. This bill, Roosevelt pledged, "gives emphatic notice to the men and women in our armed forces that the American people do not intend to let them down."

• • •

The American people were far less generous toward the first wave of Japanese Americans who had been given permission to leave the internment camps in the West to work in other parts of the country. In Great Meadows, New Jersey, where a critical shortage of farm labor existed, a farmer by the name of Edward Kowalick had hired a Japanese American named George Yamamoto. Kowalick was delighted with his new employee; the young Japanese American's suggestions saved hours of work in the greenhouse. But once the townspeople of Great Meadows became aware of Yamamoto's presence, trouble began. A mass meeting was called; the following day, a small shed on the farm was burned and a sign reading "One Mile to Little

Tokyo" was placed on the road leading to Kowalick's farm. After two weeks of tension, Kowalick finally agreed to dismiss Yamamoto; the neighbors celebrated by throwing Kowalick a surprise party.

Similar tensions were generated elsewhere. In Chicago, Eleanor learned of another "deplorable incident." A meat packer had employed a half-dozen Japanese Americans to work in his meat plant. The hiring was done in cooperation with the War Relocation Authority. Things went fine until an army colonel came into the plant and ordered the meat packer to get rid of the six workers. The meat packer resisted, but the colonel insisted, and the men were discharged.

At the same time, the number of Japanese Americans serving in the U.S. Army continued to grow, reaching thirty-three thousand. "I've never had more whole-hearted, serious-minded cooperation from army troops," Lieutenant Colonel Farrant Turner said of the all-Japanese 100th Infantry Battalion, which fought with great distinction in Italy and France. The 442nd Regimental Combat Team, which also fought in Italy and France, was known as the "Christmas tree regiment," because it became the most decorated unit in the entire army. In seven major campaigns, the combined 100th and 442nd suffered 9,486 casualties and won 18,143 medals for valor, including almost ten thousand Purple Hearts. In addition, more than sixteen thousand Nisei served in military intelligence in the Pacific, translating captured documents.

At Topaz, Manzanar, Poston, Heart Mountain, and other relocation camps, the parents of fallen heroes accepted the extraordinary honors on behalf of their sons. The color guard turned out as the medals of the dead were pinned on their mothers' blouses. The familiar sadness of the ceremony was multiplied by its setting: a tawdry tar-paper barrack surrounded by strips of barbed wire which denied the parents of the honored soldiers the very freedom for which their sons had died.

The only answer to this hideous situation, Eleanor had long argued, was to close the camps and begin a massive program of education, reminding every American of his commitment to democracy. Harold Ickes agreed with Eleanor. Now that military necessity could no longer be used to justify the incarceration, "the continued retention of these innocent people," he told the president in June, "would be a blot upon the history of this country."

Roosevelt listened to them both, but he refused to be pushed. "The more I think of this problem of suddenly ending the orders excluding Japanese Americans from the West Coast, the more I think it would be a mistake to do anything drastic or sudden," he wrote Edward Stettinius on June 12. (Stettinius was serving as the acting secretary of state in place of the ailing Cordell Hull.) "I think the whole problem for the sake of internal quiet should be handled gradually, i.e., I am thinking of two methods: a) seeing with great discretion, how many Japanese families would be acceptable to public opinion in definite localities on the West Coast, b) seeking to extend greatly the distribution of other families in many parts of the U.S. . . . Dissemination and distribution constitute a great method of avoiding public outcry."

There was some merit to Roosevelt's idea of distribution, but by deciding to wait until after the election to rescind the exclusion order, he bears responsibility for extending what was already one of America's darkest hours.

• • •

An even darker chapter in the history of the world was being written that summer as Hitler, facing defeat in his conventional war against the Allies, redoubled his efforts to exterminate the Jews. In this phase of the Final Solution, more than one million additional Jews were being rounded up from Western and Central Europe and transported by train to Hitler's "vast kingdom" of secret death camps—Auschwitz, Dachau, Birkenau, Treblinka, Belzec, Chelmno—where nearly two million Jews had already been killed.

In May, the UP reported that three hundred thousand Hungarian Jews were being taken from the Hungarian countryside to Auschwitz and Birkenau. In desperation, rescue advocates pleaded with Washington to bomb the railway lines from Hungary to Auschwitz in order "to slow down or stop the deportations."

The request was forwarded to the newly created War Refugee Board, which the president, under strong pressure from Henry Morgenthau, had finally agreed to establish in January 1944. The goal of the board was "to develop positive, new American programs to aid the victims of Nazism while pressing the Allies and neutrals to take forceful diplomatic action in their behalf." If only it had been set up earlier, War Refugee Board Director John Pehle wistfully noted years later, "things might have been different. Finally there was a place where rescue advocates could go; finally there was a claimant agency mandated to aid the victims of Nazism."

In the early days of spring, the WRB had succeeded in getting Roosevelt to issue his strongest statement yet on the issue, accusing Germany of "the wholesale systematic murder of the Jews" and promising the world that Germany's crimes, "the blackest crimes in all history," would not go unpunished by the Allies. In May, Pehle had scored another victory when Roosevelt agreed to establish an emergency shelter for Jewish refugees in an abandoned army camp in Oswego, New York. Both actions, however, as Pehle freely admits, came far too late to make much difference. If America had lent its prestige to the idea of sanctuaries for refugees in 1939–40, when Hitler was still willing to let the Jews go, perhaps other countries would have followed suit. But once extermination replaced emigration, the only hope for rescue lay in military action aimed at stopping the killing process itself.

The request for Allied bombing of the rail lines ended up on the desk of John McCloy, Stimson's assistant secretary. Though McCloy was not an anti-

Semite like Breckinridge Long, he shared some of the stereotypes and prejudices against Jews held by many men of his generation and social milieu, including a suspicion of any information coming from Jewish sources. His answer to the request was a definite no. "The War Department is of the opinion," he wrote, "that the suggested air operation is impracticable," for it would require "diversion of considerable air support" essential for other operations and was of such "doubtful efficacy" that it made no sense.

Pehle refused to give up. The following week, he forwarded another request to McCloy, this time suggesting that the concentration camps themselves should be bombed, so that "in the resultant confusion some of the unfortunate people might be able to escape and hide." Though a large number of inmates would inevitably be killed in such an operation, any action was better than none for a people who were already doomed. What was more, Pehle argued, "if the elaborate murder installations were destroyed, it seems clear the Germans could not reconstruct them for some time."

Once again, McCloy delivered a negative response, arguing that the camps were "beyond the maximum range" of Allied dive-bombers and fighter planes stationed in the U.K., France, and Italy. "The positive solution to this problem," he insisted, repeating the old refrain, "is the earliest possible victory over Germany."

McCloy's argument that the targets were beyond the reach of Allied bombers was not technically true. In fact, long-range American bombers stationed in Italy had flown over Auschwitz several times that spring in search of the I. G. Farben petrochemical plant which was close by. Jan Karski and Elie Wiesel were later given a chance to see some of the aerial reconnaissance photos that were taken on those flights. "It was the saddest thing," Karski recalled. "With a magnifying glass we could actually read the names and numbers of the Hungarian Jews standing on line waiting to be gassed. Yet McCloy claimed the target was too far away."

• • •

Having rallied his energies for D-day, Roosevelt succumbed to exhaustion and melancholy in the weeks that followed. Though he seemed his old self when he appeared in public, his confident smile still masking vulnerability, it was increasingly obvious to those closest to him that his characteristic ebullience had diminished. For this man who adored good food, good liquor, and good conversation, the Spartan regime the doctors had ordered had erased much of the joy of daily life.

And, despite the new diet and the new schedule, he was still suffering from frequent headaches and chronic fatigue, his body no longer able to supply the stamina he needed to get through his appointments. Eleanor confided in Anna that one day he had unexpectedly cried out: "I cannot live out a normal life span. I can't even walk across the room to get my circulation going."

To the members of the White House staff, he seemed curiously withdrawn. Though both politicians and the public expected him to head the Democratic ticket for the fourth time when the party convened in July, he showed no interest whatsoever in the nominating process. His mind seemed preoccupied with intimations of death.

Sam Rosenman recounted a troubling conversation in the Oval Office that summer when the president suddenly turned to him and said that, if the country wanted to build a small memorial to him after he died, he would like it to be situated "in the small park triangle where Constitution and Pennsylvania Avenue cross facing east." Grace Tully recalled an equally disturbing moment, when, in the midst of dictating a letter, the president abruptly switched the subject. "I told Margaret," he mused, "that if anything ever happened to me she is to get Fala. I'm quite sure that Eleanor will be too busy to look after him and he's devoted to Margaret."

Anna tried to cheer her father with light conversation and amusing stories. With Eleanor settled in Hyde Park for the summer, Anna lunched with her father every day under the magnolia tree, joined him at the pool in the afternoon, and dined with him in his bedroom at night. On the one hand, he remained as she had known him as a child, good-natured and uncomplaining. Though he would acknowledge from time to time that he was tired, "it wasn't a complaint," Anna recalled, "it was a statement of fact."

Yet she could not help seeing that he was in fact depressed, and that there was no one with whom he could share his feelings. Though she tried to break his impenetrable façade, the patterns of a lifetime held: the father who had smiled and joked as he was being carried off to the hospital with infantile paralysis was still unable to let his guard down in front of his daughter. Late at night, when she returned to her bedroom suite with John, she railed against "the legacy of self-containment" that had encouraged her father all his life to deny feeling helpless or weak, leaving him forever mistrustful of intimacy.

It was during this period, at some point in late June or early July, that Roosevelt approached his daughter with a whispered request. "What would you think," he is said to have asked, not giving her time to say anything in reply, "about our inviting an old friend of mine to a few dinners at the White House. This would have to be arranged when your mother is away and I would have to depend on you to make the arrangements."

Anna knew at once that the old friend was Lucy Mercer Rutherfurd. And she knew with certainty that her mother would be destroyed if she ever found out. Though the affair had taken place almost three decades earlier, Franklin had promised Eleanor that he would never see Lucy again. "It was almost like a trap in time," Trude Lash later observed. "He couldn't tell Eleanor that he wanted to see Lucy because it was stuck somewhere in the past."

Anna's first reaction was one of anger toward her father for plunging her into an extremely awkward situation. "It was a terrible decision to have to make in a hurry," she later said. Anna had long taken her mother's side in this dispute, sympathizing keenly with the trauma her mother had suffered when she discovered Lucy's letters.

At the same time, Anna knew that her father's strength was failing and she understood how important it would be for him to enjoy some evenings that were, as she put it, "light-hearted and gay, affording a few hours of much needed relaxation." If seeing Lucy again provided the inspiration he needed to assuage his loneliness and buoy his spirits, then who was she to sit in judgment? After all, she herself had fallen in love with her second husband before she was divorced from her first. At thirty-eight years of age, no longer regarding her father from the vantage point of a child, she was learning to accept his weaknesses and enjoy his strengths. If he wasn't perfect, neither was she. "While they were my parents," she later said, "nevertheless they had reached an age where they were certainly entitled to lead their own private lives without having me, of all people, or any of their children say, 'You shouldn't do this' or 'You shouldn't see this person or the other person.' "

Still, it was intolerable to imagine the hurt her mother would experience if she found out. But, as long as the dinners were classified as private engagements not included in the official guest lists, there was no reason to believe that Eleanor would know. "Standards were different in those days," reporter Bob Donovan recalled. "I'm sure there were some reporters, friends of the White House, who knew about Lucy. But none of them ever thought about exposing the situation. The newspaper business in those days was not so damn serious as it is today; it was a hell of a lot more fun. We didn't think we were angels; we knew all the things we were doing; so to point our hand at someone else wouldn't seem sporting!"

Weighing these factors together, Anna told her father she would do as he asked. She would make sure that Lucy came in the back door—the Southwest Gate, across from the Executive Office Building. She would make it understood that the guest list that night was not to be given out. She would, in short, conspire with her father, hoping that her mother would not find out.

Anna arranged for Lucy to visit over the weekend of July 7. It was the first of what would amount to more than a dozen secret meetings between the two old friends over the next nine months. The original plan called for Roosevelt to take Lucy away from Washington to Shangri-la, his mountain hideaway, but with General de Gaulle still in Washington after two days of meetings, the president decided to stay in the White House.

The talks between President Roosevelt and General de Gaulle were intended to ease the tensions between the United States and the French Committee of National Liberation before Allied troops began moving forward into the French interior. Roosevelt wanted to ensure that American soldiers would receive maximum cooperation from the French underground once they finally broke away from the hedgerow country and began advancing toward Paris. But he had resisted giving official recognition to de Gaulle for months, on the grounds the choice should be French, the choice of forty million people, not something foisted on France by an outside power.

The leader of the Free French arrived at the White House on Thursday afternoon, July 6. "He stepped from the automobile," Hassett recorded, "with an air of arrogance bordering on downright insolence, his Cyrano de Bergerac nose high in the air." Roosevelt was waiting at the door, "all smiles and cordiality." There followed a round of official meetings and ceremonies, highlighted by a state dinner on Friday at which the president toasted the health of America's "friend" General de Gaulle and spoke movingly of the common effort to remove every German boot from France, "once and for all."

At eight forty-five that evening, Lucy, having made arrangements to stay with a friend in Georgetown for the weekend, arrived at the White House. It had been a long day for the president, beginning with a press conference that morning at which he announced his decision to recognize the French Committee of National Liberation as the *de facto* authority in France, followed by a luncheon for thirty-six in the State Dining Room at one and a Cabinet meeting at two, but the president remained with his old friend until after eleven.

The final meeting with de Gaulle was completed by noon on Saturday, after which Roosevelt lunched with Anna. Sitting under the grand magnolia tree which had been planted during Andrew Jackson's days in the White House and still boasted huge branches, lemon-scented blossoms, and glossy leaves, Anna agreed to join her father that evening for dinner with Lucy.

At 6:20 p.m. on Saturday, the president called for his car and asked to be driven to 2238 Q Street in Georgetown to call on Mrs. Rutherfurd. After he picked her up at the door, they drove together through the streets of Washington as they had done so many years before. Arriving at the White House, he brought her to his study, where Anna and John were waiting to join them for cocktails and dinner. If Roosevelt experienced a moment of awkwardness when he introduced his favorite child to the woman whose love had nearly destroyed his marriage, he undoubtedly covered it up.

To Roosevelt's delight, the two women liked each other. Anna was immediately impressed by Lucy's "innate dignity and poise which commanded respect." She found Lucy "most attractive and stately" but "warm and friendly" at the same time. For her part, Lucy understood immediately why this beautiful young woman with unbounded vitality, warmth, and humor meant so much to her father.

Anna had not seen Lucy for nearly three decades, but she remembered her clearly. She recalled as a child "feeling happy" whenever Lucy was working in the house. "I liked her warm and friendly manner and smile," Anna later wrote in an unpublished article. For her part, Lucy understood how important it was to Roosevelt that the two of them get along. "Anna is a dear fine person," Roosevelt had written Lucy earlier; "I wish so much that you knew her."

The president's butler, Alonzo Fields, served dinner. "You could sense that this was a special evening," he later recalled. "You could feel that this was someone warm who cared a great deal about him. From then on, every time Lucy came, the president would have no one else but me serve them."

There was much to talk about that night. Across the ocean, London was reeling from a terrifying barrage of Germany's newest weapon, the V-1 flying bomb, a pilotless rocket-powered craft launched from giant concrete bunkers in German-occupied territory in northern France. The V-1 carried more than twelve thousand pounds of high explosives and fell indiscriminately on people and buildings alike. In two weeks, nearly three thousand people had been killed and over ten thousand wounded. Had the V-1 and its even more formidable successor, the V-2 liquid-fuel rocket, been developed earlier in the war, the balance of power might have been fatally tilted against the Allies. But by July 1944, the Allies were moving forward in every sector of the war.

In Normandy, the last German strongholds in Cherbourg had surrendered. On the Eastern front, the Red Army had begun a powerful new offensive that found its troops surging westward into Poland. More than 130,000 Germans had been killed in the last week of June, and sixty-six thousand taken prisoner. And in the Southwest Pacific, after a series of assaults, Allied troops were advancing rapidly along the coast of New Guinea.

Beyond world events, there were memories to share: silly stories Roosevelt loved to tell and retell, "all the ridiculous things," Lucy later wrote, he liked "to say—and do—and enjoy." Years later, Anna's son Johnny Boettiger could easily understand why Anna and Lucy got along so well, and why this meant so much to the president. "The three of them had a capacity for loving humor, for having fun. It wasn't a tight, ironic sense of humor. It was a silly humor that didn't respect the boundaries they all imagined Eleanor would impose."

It was after midnight when Roosevelt retired, but he awakened early the next morning so he could take Lucy on a day trip to Shangri-la. Were Lucy and Roosevelt lovers at this point? It is impossible to know, though, given the state of Roosevelt's health, doubt remains. Still, even if they did not share the same bed, it is reasonable to imagine that there was a pleasing sexuality in their friendship.

Yet, of all the pleasures Lucy gave, perhaps the most important was her willingness and ability to talk to Roosevelt about what was happening to his health. Having nursed her husband through illness for seven years, she must have been highly attuned to the fear and frustration of being inside a body that was breaking down. If Roosevelt was able to talk at all about his fears, about what it was like to be in pain, about the prospect of death, it would have been with Lucy. With everyone else, he had to summon up his energies to be cheerful. But with Lucy, it is possible that he was able to drop his act, to admit his fears and demonstrate his anger.

• • •

While Roosevelt was enjoying the company of Lucy Rutherfurd, Eleanor was in Hyde Park celebrating a noteworthy advance against segregation in the South. That Saturday, July 8, 1944, the War Department issued an order to all commanding generals directing that all "buses, trucks or other transportation owned and operated either by the government or by government instrumentality will be available to all military personnel regardless of race. Restricting personnel to certain sections of such transportation because of race will not be permitted either on or off a post camp, or station, regardless of local civilian custom."

The War Department directive spoke squarely to the primary source of racial tension in the South. Restricted by law to a few seats at the back of the bus, Negro soldiers were often relegated to stand at the bus stop for hours as overcrowded buses passed them by. Where separate buses were provided for Negroes and whites, the "colored" buses usually ran on less frequent schedules, forcing Negro soldiers to watch as dozens of "white" buses containing empty seats drove past.

There were scores of incidents. In Savannah, Georgia, forty-three miles from Camp Stewart, the Greyhound bus terminal had separate ticket windows for whites and coloreds. One employee handled both windows; he regularly made the colored GIs wait until all the whites were taken care of, even if the colored GIs had arrived first. It could take up to twelve hours for the Negro soldier to buy a ticket. Yet, if he was late getting back to camp, he was considered AWOL and issued a service penalty.

In Louisiana, a group of nine Negro GIs boarded a train for transfer from the hospital at Camp Claiborne to the hospital at Fort Huachuca in Arizona. The train was delayed for twelve hours. "The only place that would serve us was the lunch room at the station," one of the nine reported. "But we couldn't eat where the white people were eating. To do that would contaminate the very air of the place, so we had to go to the kitchen. That was bad enough but that's not all. About 11:30 that same morning, about two dozen German prisoners of war came to the lunchroom with two guards. They entered the large room, sat at the table. Then meals were served them. They smoked and had a swell time. As we stood on the outside and saw what was going on, we could scarcely believe our own eyes. There they sat: eating, talking, laughing, smoking. They were enemies of our country, people sworn to destroy all the so-called democratic governments of the world. . . . What are we fighting for?"

Resentments multiplied. In Beaumont, Texas, Charles Rico, a black private, was ordered off a bus because he took a vacant seat in a section reserved for whites. After he left the bus, he was beaten by a white policeman and shot twice through the shoulder and the arm. In Mobile, Alabama, where bus drivers were authorized to carry firearms to enforce local laws and customs, Private Henry Williams, a black soldier, was shot and killed when he walked to the wrong section of the bus. In Montgomery, Alabama, a black nurse, Lieutenant Norma Greene, boarded a bus after a shopping tour in preparation for overseas duty. When she refused to get out of the bus after the driver told her it was a "white" bus, she was so badly beaten that her nose was broken and her eyes were blackened.

"[Negroes] have been instructed to regard themselves as soldiers," warned Truman Gibson, civilian aide to the Secretary of War. "They are not conditioned to withstand the shock of attitudes" to which they are subjected day in and day out. One black corporal, insulted by a conductor, threw a "colored only" sign out the window. He was immediately arrested and carried back to camp as a common criminal. "Honey, I am so hurt inside," he wrote his girlfriend, "so much that I don't really know what to do. . . . Just think I may have to fight some day, but honey what will I be fighting for, surely not the rotten conditions we have to bear down here."

For months, Eleanor had been pushing the War Department to do something about the public-transit situation. Responding to innumerable letters from black soldiers, she had barraged the War Department with questions and comments. She understood, she wrote John McCloy, that, if the bus was privately owned, there was nothing the army could do about it. But if it was an army bus, then it was unconscionable to allow segregation to stand. "These colored boys lie side by side in the hospitals in the southwest Pacific with the white boys and somehow it is hard for me to believe that they should not be treated on an equal basis."

Though the directive of July 8, 1944, covered only government-owned or -operated buses, liberals hailed it as "an important step forward in the fight to abolish discrimination," and the Negro press treated it as a great victory. "Extra! Extra!" the *Baltimore Afro-American* headlined: "US Army Bans Jim Crow." "Here It Is!" the *Pittsburgh Courier* enthused, publishing the full text of the order.

Among Southern whites, not surprisingly, the order provoked a fiery protest. Governor Chauncey Sparks of Alabama warned the White House that its malicious action threatened to break down "the essential principle of race relations in the South." As a consequence, Southern politicians would find it extremely difficult "to hold the south within its traditional democratic allegiance in the years to come."

Once again, Eleanor Roosevelt became the target of Southern criticism. A new round of rumors spread, stories of "Eleanor Tuesdays," days when Negro women supposedly went out into the streets en masse with the goal of knocking Southern white women to the ground. There is no evidence that such days actually existed, but so widespread were the rumors that many white women in the South were afraid to go out of their houses on Tuesdays.

Despite the hysterical overtones of the Southern protest, the War Department refused, this time, to back away from its assertion that all soldiers should be treated alike. "This knowledge," army historians observed, "raised morale higher in many units than the construction of the most elaborate service club." Never, Howard University Dean William Hastie assured John McCloy, "have I seen so much enthusiasm and goodwill generated by a particular bit of official action. . . . I think it means more to the Negro soldier than you can possibly realize."

• • •

Dramatic changes in the navy that summer gave Eleanor further cause for satisfaction. Under James Forrestal, the boyish-looking financier who had succeeded Frank Knox as secretary on May 11, 1944, the navy was taking unprecedented strides toward racial equality. Within weeks of becoming secretary, Forrestal had instituted a series of experiments designed to bring an end to the navy's dismal record in the use of Negro personnel.

The first change was reflected in a memo to the president on May 20. "Up to the present time," Forrestal observed, though the navy had opened its general service ranks to Negroes in 1942, "the majority of Negroes have been employed in the Shore Establishment," performing the arduous, prosaic work involved in handling ammunition and loading ships. To many Negroes, it seemed that they had simply "swapped the waiter's apron for the stevedore's grappling hook." Looking at the situation, Forrestal concluded that precious energy, money, and morale were being wasted by the navy's insistence on separating Negroes and whites. The time had come "to expand the use of Negro personnel by assigning them to general sea duty."

Forrestal's proposal, which Roosevelt readily approved, called for Negroes to make up 10 percent of the crews of twenty-five large auxiliary ships. To the surprise of many, who had to revise their established notions and prejudices about the Negro's proper place, the experiment worked remarkably well. Official navy records indicate that colored personnel were being "successfully absorbed in the ships' companies." The experiment was then extended to smaller vessels, where, against even higher odds, black and white crew members managed, with a minimum of fuss, to work, eat, and sleep together in extremely close quarters.

Forrestal's innovations came none too soon, for, that July, a bloody tragedy at the ammunition depot at Port Chicago in northern California provided unmistakable evidence of the bankruptcy of the navy's old segregation policy. On the night of July 17, more than six hundred men, mostly black, were hard at work loading tons of ammunition, high explosives, and incendiary bombs into the holds of the S.S. *Bryan*. Shortly after 10 p.m., a deafening explosion erupted. The *Bryan* was sundered in pieces, everyone on the pier was instantly killed, the naval base was left in ruins, and the town of Port Chicago was damaged. Two hundred and two blacks were killed, and another 233 injured. "This single stunning disaster," sociologist Robert Allen observed, "accounted for more than 15 percent of all black naval casualties during the war. It was the worst homefront disaster of World War II."

The loss of so many black sailors at once focused public attention on the injustice of racial discrimination in the navy, motivating Forrestal to press even more strongly for equality of treatment for blacks. In the weeks that followed, he moved in several directions at once: assigning white work units to Port Chicago and other ammo depots; stating that he no longer considered practical the establishment of separate facilities and quotas for Negroes who qualified for advanced training; appointing more Negroes to the navy's V-12 program; insisting on Negro admittance to the Naval Academy; and issuing a far-reaching "Guide to Command of Negro Naval Personnel." In this guide, which *Commonweal* regarded as "an outstanding document in the field of race relations," the navy stated for the first time that it accepted "no theories of racial differences in inborn ability, but expects that every man wearing its uniform be trained and used in accord with his maximum individual capacity determined on the basis of individual performance."

The Negro press and liberal spokesmen were exultant, observing that change in the navy was now coming faster and further than anyone had thought possible. "This improvement" was all the more spectacular, *Commonweal* observed, "in that at the beginning of the war the Navy's race policy was considered worse than the Army's."

To Eleanor, the policy changes in both the army and the navy afforded profound gratification. Indeed, had she been given the choice between supplying the relaxation for her husband that Lucy was providing, or summoning her powers to effect a change in the lives of Negro Americans, she would undoubtedly have chosen the latter. After two decades of social activism, Eleanor's commitment to the underdog had become such an integral part of her makeup that it is impossible to imagine her without a cause to fight.

• • •

On Tuesday morning, July 11, five days before the opening of the Democratic convention in Chicago, Roosevelt finally let it be known that he would accept his party's nomination for a fourth term. At his regular press conference, he read aloud a letter he had written to Bob Hannegan, chairman of the Democratic National Committee. In the letter, in a reversal of the famous statement General William Sherman had made when he renounced plans to run for office, he pledged that if the convention nominated him for the presidency he would accept, and that if the people, the ultimate authority, commanded him to serve he would have "as little right to withdraw as the soldier has to leave his post in the line."

"All that is within me cries out to go back to my home on the Hudson River," he went on, "but the future existence of the nation and the future existence of our chosen form of government are at stake."

While the president was making his momentous announcement, Eleanor was in Dayton, Ohio, preparing for a luncheon talk to a group of three hundred WACs at Wright Field. Approached by reporters, she said her husband's decision was news to her. "The President doesn't discuss these things with me. Many people think he does but most often the first I know of some decision is when I see it in the papers."

Eleanor viewed Franklin's candidacy with mixed emotions. On the one hand, she believed her husband's victory was essential for "the good of the country." The thought of the Republican nominee, Governor Thomas Dewey, as president worried her deeply. "Dewey seems to me more and more to show no understanding of the job at home or abroad," she wrote James. And though she realized that her husband had tended to tire more easily in recent months, she was convinced, she told James, that "if elected, he'll do his job well. I feel sure and I think he can be kept well to do it." On the other hand, the thought of another four years of White House life was almost more than she could bear. "I am very conscious of age and the short time in which I have to live as I like," she admitted to Joe Lash, "and I know that it is such selfish thinking that no one has a right to even let it be in one's mind."

There was no such ambivalence on Capitol Hill. When the news reached the Democratic senators, reporter Allen Drury observed, "it was as though the sun had burst from the clouds and glory surrounded the world. Relief, and I mean relief, was written on every face. The meal ticket was still the meal ticket and all was well with the party."

In accepting the nomination in advance of the convention's decision on the vice-presidency, Roosevelt had discarded the club he might have used to drive the convention into naming the running mate he himself wanted. The choice of the vice-president would be left up to the delegates.

"I am just not going through a convention like 1940 again," he explained, recalling the lengths he had gone to ensure the re-election of Wallace. "It will split the party wide open and it is already split enough between North and South, it may kill our chances for election this fall and if it does it will prolong the war and knock into a cocked hat all the plans we've been making for the future."

The president's apparent indifference to the choice of a running mate worried his aides. "He just doesn't give a damn," Pa Watson observed. Had Roosevelt been in good health, his lack of concern about his potential successor would have been understandable. But since he at least suspected that he was unlikely to live out a full term, it remains incomprehensible.

In truth, Roosevelt's mind that summer was moving in a different direction; his dream was to join hands with Republican Wendell Willkie in the creation of a new liberal party that would combine the liberal elements of the Democratic Party, minus the reactionary elements in the South, with the liberal elements of the Republican Party. Since Willkie had been defeated at the Republican convention by the conservative wing of his party, Roosevelt hoped he would be receptive to the idea. "We ought to have two real parties," Roosevelt told his aide Sam Rosenman, "one liberal and the other conservative. As it is now each party is split by dissenters."

To sound Willkie out, Roosevelt dispatched Rosenman to meet with him in New York in early July. "The meeting obviously had to be a complete secret," Rosenman later recalled, "so I had lunch served in a private suite in the St. Regis Hotel." Indeed, Willkie was so anxious lest anyone find out that he stepped into the bedroom of the suite when lunch arrived so the waiter would not recognize him.

Willkie was instantly drawn to the idea. "You tell the President that I'm ready to devote almost full time to this," he said. "A sound liberal government in the U.S. is absolutely essential to continued co-operation with the other nations of the world." Willkie went on to say he would be glad to meet with Roosevelt to discuss the plan more fully but "he was convinced that the meeting should not take place until after the election."

Roosevelt was so pleased with Willkie's positive response that he couldn't wait. On July 13, he dictated a letter asking Willkie to join him as soon as possible for an off-the-record meeting either in the White House or at Hyde Park, "just as you think best." Unfortunately, news of the letter leaked out, causing great embarrassment to both Willkie and Roosevelt. Now there was no choice, Willkie insisted, but to wait until after the election. (Roosevelt's dream of creating a liberal party would never be realized. In the fall, while Willkie was in the hospital for a minor ailment, he had a massive heart attack and died.)

Meanwhile, Roosevelt was up to his usual games, making each person who came to see him feel that he was the one the president wanted. "He said I was his choice," Henry Wallace recorded in his diary after a meeting on July 10, and at lunch later that week, "He drew me close and turned on his full smile and a very hearty hand clasp, saying, 'I hope it will be the same team.' " Yet, at Shangri-la two weeks earlier, Roosevelt had assured Jimmy Byrnes that *he* was the president's choice for vice-president. "You are the best qualified man in the whole outfit," Roosevelt told Byrnes; "if you stay in you are sure to win."

The plot thickened on July 11, when Roosevelt met with the political bosses—DNC Chair Robert Hannegan, Frank Walker, and Ed Flynn—to discuss the vice-presidency. Over dinner and drinks, with everyone in shirt-sleeves because of the oppressive heat, the full list of candidates was examined. Wallace was rejected out of hand. He was too intellectual, too liberal, too idealistic, too impractical, the bosses claimed. If he were nominated, he would cost the ticket from one to three million votes. Byrnes was just as quickly undone; as a lapsed Catholic and a Southerner with segregationist views, he would alienate Catholics and Negroes. Barkley was a good man, but he was too old.

Roosevelt proposed Supreme Court Justice William O. Douglas. Before Roosevelt appointed him to the Court in 1939, Douglas had been a professor of law at Yale and the chairman of the Securities and Exchange Commission, where he led the fight to bring public utilities under federal regulation. He was young and energetic, the president said, and, what was more, he played an interesting game of poker. Despite Roosevelt's obvious enthusiasm for Douglas, no one else picked up the idea. The talk turned then to Senator Harry Truman. He was a good Democrat, he was from the Midwest, his record on labor was good, and, as Flynn observed, "he had never made any 'racial' remarks." Concerned about Truman's age, which no one could pinpoint (he was sixty), Roosevelt sent for the *Congressional Directory* to check his date of birth. But by the time the *Directory* arrived, the conversation had drifted to other subjects. As the meeting broke up, Roosevelt turned to Hannegan and said, "Bob, I think you and everyone else here want Truman."

Pleased with the turn of events, Hannegan asked Roosevelt to put something in writing. Using a pencil, Roosevelt scribbled an unofficial one-line note on the back of an envelope. "Bob, I think Truman is the right man." It was more than Hannegan had hoped to achieve, but, given Roosevelt's propensity for telling each person what he wanted to hear, it was not enough. A day or so later, Roosevelt was again urging both Wallace and Byrnes to run. The decision was still up in the air.

• • •

In the midst of all the confusion, the president set out for California in his private railroad car, the Ferdinand Magellan, on the first leg of a monthlong journey that would ultimately take him to Hawaii for a discussion of Pacific strategy. Boarding the train in Hyde Park, accompanied by Eleanor and Tommy, Pa Watson and Sam Rosenman, Grace Tully and Dr. Bruenn, he ordered the engineers to move slowly so he would not arrive in San Diego until the convention had completed its balloting for the presidential nomination.

Politics could not be avoided altogether, however. When the train reached Chicago, Bob Hannegan came aboard. The president was just finishing lunch with Eleanor and Sam Rosenman. "We excused ourselves," Rosenman recalled, "and left Hannegan alone with the President for about an hour." The convention was convulsed in bloody turmoil, the DNC chair said; unless the president made his wishes known, there was no telling what would happen. Though still reluctant to "dictate" to the convention after his experience in 1940, Roosevelt agreed to sign a letter which said in essence that he would be very glad to run with either Bill Douglas or Harry Truman, since either one "would bring real strength to the ticket."

At the last minute, Hannegan came running back to Grace Tully. "Grace, the President wants you to retype this letter and to switch the names so it will read 'Harry Truman and Bill Douglas.' "

"The reason for the switch was obvious," Tully later observed. "By naming Truman first it was plainly implied by the letter that he was the preferred choice. By that narrow margin and rather casual action did one man rather than another, perhaps one policy rather than another, eventually arrive at the head of the American government in April of 45."

Since the trip was an official secret, there were no scheduled stops, no crowds to address, no questions to answer. Yet, as the armor-plated train slowly wended its way through the steel mills of Indiana and the cornfields of Oklahoma, rumors began to spread. At various stations along the way, the familiar face of Mrs. Roosevelt was seen; on numerous platforms, the president's little dog, Fala, was spotted taking a stretch. These sightings soon dispelled any questions: the president's train was passing through!

"The trip out was slow and peaceful," Tommy reported to Esther Lape. "We did little work, read and played gin-rummy." For Roosevelt, the leisurely pace of the trip was ideal. For him, the train was a small human community, a society of friends whose conversation was all he needed for stimulation.

This was the first occasion in a long while on which Roosevelt and his wife had spent so much relaxing time together. "The slow speed was a good thing for us both," Franklin later wrote her.

The unbroken hours allowed Franklin to share with Eleanor his hopes for the future, evoking a picture of the happiness that would be theirs once the presidency was over. He wanted to take her on a trip around the world, he said. He talked of buying land in the Sahara Desert and of demonstrating to the Arabs the miracles that could be accomplished through irrigation, electrification, and reforestation. "I think it would be fun," he said, "to go and live in the desert for two or three years and see what we could do." He went over all the details of that faraway period—imagining the trip on a slow freighter that would allow them to take in all the sights along the way.

Engrossed as Eleanor must have been in the charm of the conversation, she still felt the need to protect herself, to preserve the physical and emotional space that had grown between them. She could not let him continue without interrupting him, without reminding him that she had hated long sea voyages ever since she was a child. Undeterred, Franklin went on to suggest a happy compromise. If Eleanor preferred, she could travel instead by air, swooping down to meet his freighter at all the locations they wished to visit and explore!

Whereas Franklin would have lingered on the train for several additional weeks, Eleanor couldn't wait to escape. "Mrs. R was impatient at the slow speed and the waste of time," Tommy observed. Work refused to leave her mind, even for these few summer days. "I don't know that I'm being very useful on the trip as there is nothing to do," she wrote Trude Pratt. "FDR sleeps, eats, works and all I do is sit through long meals which are sometimes interesting and sometimes very dull." If Roosevelt sensed his wife's discomfort, it must have been frustrating for him to realize that she alone was immune to his charms. He could regale everyone else with his sparkling conversation, but his wife was bored!

More than likely, Roosevelt remained oblivious to Eleanor's distress.

Though he liked to think he was savoring her presence, he spent almost no time with her alone. "I don't know why we went," Tommy complained, no doubt echoing Eleanor's sentiments, "as there were many cronies on the train so the President would not have been lonesome." Once again, the possibility of real togetherness was opened and closed before either partner fully understood what was going on.

• • •

When the train reached San Diego on July 20, 1944, Franklin and Eleanor were joined by their son Jimmy and John's wife, Anne Clark, who had moved with their children to California when her husband was transferred to the Pacific. Lunch was served at Anne's house in Coronado, and Jimmy hosted a family dinner. After dinner, Eleanor and Tommy left for Los Angeles, where a plane was waiting to carry them back to Washington.

The next morning, while the convention readied itself for the presidential balloting, Roosevelt was scheduled to review an amphibious-landing exercise in Oceanside, California. Just before he was about to leave, he turned "suddenly white," Jimmy recalled; "his face took on an agonized look."

"Jimmy, I don't know if I can make it," he said. "I have horrible pains." Jimmy was so frightened he wanted to call the doctor, but Roosevelt resisted. It was just stomach pains, he insisted, indigestion from eating too fast and not being able to exercise. He'd be all right in a few minutes if only Jimmy would help him out of his berth and let him stretch out flat on the floor for a while. "So for perhaps ten minutes," Jimmy wrote, "Father lay on the floor of the railroad car, his eyes closed, his face drawn, his powerful torso occasionally convulsed as the waves of pain stabbed him. Never in all my life had I felt so alone with him—and so helpless."

Gradually, his body stopped shaking and the color returned to his face. "Help me up now, Jimmy," he said. "I feel better." Minutes later, he was seated in an open car, heading to the amphibious-training base to witness the Fifth Marine's practice invasion—a colossal exercise involving five thousand Marines and three thousand naval personnel. Situated atop a high bluff overlooking the beach below, he watched the smooth unloading of men and equipment from dozens of landing craft of the type recently used in the landings on Guam.

During the afternoon, he received word from the convention chairman, Samuel D. Jackson, that he had been officially nominated for a fourth term as president. Later that night, speaking from the observation car of his train, he delivered his acceptance speech. "What is the job before us in 1944?" he asked. "First, to win the war—to win the war fast, to win it overpoweringly. Second, to form worldwide international organizations... And third, to build an economy for our returning veterans and for all Americans—which will provide employment and provide decent standards of living."

It was not a memorable speech, but the immense crowd filling the Chicago stadium loved it. As the familiar voice came booming through the amplifiers, forty thousand people cheered. Their captain would see them through after all.

Afterward, with Jimmy by his side, a relaxed Roosevelt posed at the table, rereading portions of the speech so a pool of photographers could take pictures. Since there were no processing facilities in San Diego, all the film was flown up to Los Angeles, where the AP agreed to process it and transmit prints to everyone. At the AP, a young editor named Dick Strobel took the film out of the hypo fixing agent and exposed it to light. "There were several negatives to choose from," Strobel later recalled. "In one his mouth was closed; in the other it was open. I chose the one with the open mouth, since it was more obvious that he was talking. I went into my office to write the caption while the darkroom technicians processed the print."

When the picture came out, the photographer, George Skaddings, was appalled. "Hey, you better look at this," he told Strobel. The open mouth made Roosevelt look terrible: his eyes were glassy, his face was haggard, his expression weary. By then, however, it was close to 11 p.m., or 2 a.m. on the East Coast. The papers were yelling for the picture. Strobel decided he couldn't wait any longer to print another negative. "I made the judgment to go with what we had."

The next day, Strobel recalled, "all hell broke loose," as every anti-Roosevelt paper blew the picture up and displayed it prominently. In Washington, the president's press secretary, Steve Early, was furious, and called Skaddings on the carpet. "It's not my fault," Skaddings insisted. "I just shot the picture. Some idiot in L.A. picked it." Early kicked Skaddings off the tour, but the damage was done. The unfortunate photo, which Rosenman insisted bore no resemblance to the man he watched deliver the speech that night, provided Republicans with precisely the ammunition they needed to bolster their argument: the old man was no longer physically capable of being president.

Nominations for the vice-presidency began the next afternoon. Wallace took an early lead, but by the end of the second ballot Truman had emerged the clear-cut victor. Back in Hyde Park, Eleanor was "sick about the whole business." A fervent Wallace supporter, she "had hoped until the last," she wrote Esther Lape, "that Mr. Wallace might have strength enough." It was "bad politics" not to stick to Wallace, as well as "disloyal." Nonetheless, she was much more satisfied with Senator Truman than she would have been with Byrnes or any of the other conservatives who were being considered. Though she did not know Truman, "from all I hear," she wrote, "he is a good man."

• • •

At midnight that Friday, July 21, following a zigzag course in a darkened cruiser, Roosevelt sailed westward from San Diego for Pearl Harbor. "Off in a few minutes," he wrote Eleanor, but suggested he might have to hurry back earlier if the German revolt against Hitler got worse. The day before, a group of German officers led by Lieutenant Colonel Klaus von Stauffenberg had tried to assassinate Hitler. At the last minute, however, the briefcase holding the bomb had been inadvertently pushed to the far side of the room, and Hitler had survived the blast. Roosevelt's trip to Hawaii would go forward as planned.

"Yesterday a.m. Jimmy and I had a grand view of the landing operation at Camp Pendleton," he told Eleanor, "and then I got the collywobbles and stayed in the train in the p.m. It was grand having you come out with me."

A tremendous crowd was gathered at the pier when the president's cruiser pulled in. As far as the eye could see, men in whites were standing at attention at the rails of dozens of navy ships. A rousing cheer went up as the gangplank was lowered to receive Admiral Nimitz and some fifty high-ranking officials. Greeting everyone on the deck of the *Baltimore,* Roosevelt observed that one person was noticeably absent—General Douglas MacArthur. When asked where the general was, Nimitz retreated into an embarrassed silence. MacArthur's plane from Brisbane had landed an hour earlier, but the general had insisted on going to his quarters first to drop off his bag and take a bath. The welcoming ceremony was just about to break up when a shrieking siren was heard, indicating MacArthur's arrival. Stepping out from his limo, wearing his leather flying jacket, MacArthur acknowledged the tumultuous applause and raced up the gangplank.

That evening, the president invited both Nimitz and MacArthur to join him for dinner at the elegant beach estate which had been made available to him during his stay. After dinner, the strategic talks began. Seated before a huge wall map of the Pacific, the president reviewed America's situation, using a bamboo pointer to indicate the islands where battles were still being fought.

For six weeks, the American navy had been engaged in a bitter struggle with the Japanese for the control of Saipan, Guam, and Tinian, three of the Mariana Islands. The battle for Saipan had been particularly bloody—more than fourteen thousand marines had been killed—but on July 9, the island had been secured. Two weeks later, both Guam and Tinian had been captured. These were major victories: with the Marianas under control, the mighty B-29s, the largest aircraft ever produced, would finally have the bases from which they could bomb Japan.

Roosevelt's interest in bombing Japan had never diminished, despite the overwhelming difficulties involved. For years he had followed the B-29 through its production and teething problems, never losing faith in General Arnold's quest for a larger, heavier, and more powerful version of the B-17. "The B-29 was a great gamble," military historian William Emerson observed. "General Arnold had committed $3 billion to its production before a single prototype had even been flown. This was more than the Manhattan Project. But Roosevelt backed him all the way, convinced that a superbomber was the only way to get at Japan offensively."

In mid-June, the first B-29s had taken off from eastern China: their target, the iron- and steelworks at Yawata on Kyushu Island. Though the raid produced little material damage, the boost to American morale was enormous. And now, with the capture of the Marianas, they could launch many more direct raids against Japan.

The question was: where to go from here? Admiral Nimitz proposed a direct assault on Formosa and the Chinese coast, bypassing the Philippines and all the small islands along the way. MacArthur disagreed, pressing for the liberation of the Philippines and the bypassing of Formosa. America, he argued, had a moral responsibility to avenge the crushing defeat of 1942, to liberate the Filipinos and to free the American prisoners of war. If Roosevelt chose to bypass the Philippines, MacArthur warned, "I dare to say that the American people would be so aroused that they would register most complete resentment against you in the polls."

"In such a situation," James MacGregor Burns has observed, "Roosevelt was at his best, skillfully placating both the Admiral and the General, steering the discussion away from absolutes, narrowing the differences." In the end, Roosevelt sided with MacArthur, pledging that America would not bypass the Philippines. "As soon as I get back," he promised the flamboyant general, "I will push on that plan [for liberating the Philippines] for I am convinced that as a whole it is logical and can be done." As a matter of fact, Roosevelt went on, he wished he and MacArthur could swap places, though "I have a hunch that you would make more of a go as President than I would as General in retaking the Philippines."

When the strategy sessions were completed, the president traveled around Oahu, inspecting shipyards, hospitals, training grounds, and airfields. "At one of the hospitals," Rosenman reported, "the President did something which affected us all very deeply. He asked a secret service man to wheel him slowly through all the wards that were occupied by veterans who had lost one or more arms and legs. He insisted on going past each individual bed. He wanted to display himself and his useless legs to those boys who would have to face the same bitterness."

Roosevelt generally allowed himself to be seen in public in only two situations—either standing with his braces locked, or seated in an open car. But here, in the presence of so many young amputees, he was willing to reveal his vulnerability, to let them see that he was as crippled as they. "With a cheering smile to each of them," Rosenman observed, "and a pleasant word at the bedside of a score or more, this man who had risen from a bed of helplessness ultimately to become President of the United States and leader of the free world was living proof of what the human spirit could do."

There was one other occasion when Roosevelt had allowed a group of strangers to witness his infirmity, according to Anna Faith Jones. The occasion was the dedication of a new building at Howard University in 1936. Before the ceremony began, Jones' father, Howard's president, Mordecai Johnson, had asked Roosevelt to allow the students to see that he was crippled. They had been so crippled themselves, Johnson pleaded, if the president let them see him as he was, they could say to themselves, If he can do this, we can do anything. Roosevelt agreed. He let himself be lifted from the car and set down in full public view, and then he proceeded to walk slowly and painfully to the podium.

Rosenman claimed he had never seen the president with tears in his eyes, but that afternoon in Oahu, as he was wheeled out of the hospital, "he was close to them." Later that day, Roosevelt reboarded the *Baltimore* for the final leg of his long journey—a visit to the troops at Adak, a treeless island located off the western coast of Alaska.

CHAPTER 21

"THE OLD MASTER STILL HAD IT"

On Sunday evening, July 30, 1944, while Roosevelt was cruising the Pacific en route to Alaska, Missy LeHand was in the movie theater at Harvard Square with her sister Ann Rochon and her friend Maydell Ramsey. A double feature was playing that night: *The Man from Down Under,* starring Charles Laughton as a World War I veteran who smuggles two orphans back into Australia, and *Rationing,* a light comedy about a small-town storekeeper frustrated by wartime restrictions.

The accompanying newsreel featured images of Roosevelt's acceptance speech, delivered from his railroad car at San Diego. As the story was told to Missy's friend Barbara Curtis, "Missy was shocked at the way he looked and the way his voice sounded." Having not seen his picture for several months, she was unaware of all the weight he had lost, unprepared for the haggard look on his face. Until this moment, she had still envisioned him as the vigorous, well-built man she had last seen the previous spring.

It was raining at 11 p.m., when Missy returned to her Orchard Street home. In her bedroom, she began agitatedly leafing through old pictures, almost as if she were trying to conjure up a substitute image for the one that was now in her mind. In her collection of photos she had a handsome shot of Roosevelt in a striped bathing suit, a charming picture of the two of them sitting together on the porch at Warm Springs, a group shot at a picnic. Suddenly her left arm, which had not moved since her stroke three years earlier, began to move up and down. It seemed for a moment as if she might finally recover her faculties.

But the reprieve was short-lived. Sometime after midnight, Ann heard strange noises coming from her sister's room. Looking in, she saw Missy tremble violently and then slump over. An ambulance was called, and at 2 a.m. Missy was taken to Chelsea Naval Hospital.

There doctors determined that she had suffered a cerebral embolism. Death came seven hours later, shortly after 9 a.m. The death certificate listed auricular fibrillation and rheumatic heart disease as contributing factors to the fatal embolism. She was forty-six years old.

Eleanor was in Hyde Park when the news reached her. She immediately sent a telegram to Missy's sister, offering to come to Boston to be with the family during the funeral. "I am sure that for her, after her long illness, death will be a release," Eleanor wrote in her column. "But those who loved her . . . will feel her loss deeply. She was a member of our family for a good many years."

Roosevelt received the sad news by means of a radiogram to his ship from William Hassett and Steve Early. "Regret to inform you that Miss LeHand died in the Naval Hospital at Chelsea at 9:05 today. . . . Admiral Sheldon [of the Bureau of Medicine and Surgery] said she had attended theater last evening and that the change for the worse was unexpected. . . . Have notified Mrs. Roosevelt and Miss Tully. Await instructions."

A second radiogram followed a few hours later, letting the president know that Mrs. Roosevelt would attend the funeral and that his absence had been carefully explained to Missy's family. "I'm glad F is away," Eleanor confided to Lash, "for he would have felt he had to come and these journeys are always depressing."

A statement was drafted in the White House and issued in the president's name. "Memories of more than a score of years of devoted service enhance the sense of personal loss which Miss LeHand's passing brings. Faithful and painstaking, with a charm of manner inspired by tact and kindness of heart, she was utterly selfless in her devotion to duty."

"Missy's death," Arthur Krock noted in *The New York Times,* "severs a shining link between these grim times and the exciting days when the New Deal and the administration were young. Her influence upon the President was very great and constructive as was Mr. Howe's. Many of the friendliest observers of Mr. Roosevelt since he took office have, after these intimate counselors left the White House, attributed certain acts and words of his that evoked widespread criticism to the loss of their devoted and wise services." Writing in a similar vein, Harold Ickes observed that Missy's disability "constituted the greatest loss that the President has suffered since his inauguration."

Letters of condolence poured into the White House, revealing the extraordinary impact Missy had on all those who had come to know her. "What the devil can a fellow say," Roosevelt's old friend Ralph Cropley wrote, "who was as close to Missy as I was in those days when Missy, Louis Howe and I put up the fight to instill in that head of yours the desire to live? Outside of Eleanor, no one knows more than I what sacrifices Missy made for you. She was one of the grandest persons who ever lived."

"I know how profoundly affected you are by Missy's death," journalist Herbert Swope wrote the president. "I, too, loved Missy. She was a rare person in her loyalty, in her intelligence, her courage and her principles."

Some twelve hundred persons attended the funeral mass at St. John's Church in North Cambridge. Hundreds more stood outside as the president's wife, wearing a blue suit and a black straw hat, arrived to join the LeHand family in the second row. The mourners included James Farley, Former Boston Police Commissioner Joseph Timilty, and Joseph Kennedy. Bishop Richard J. Cushing read the prayers, and the body was lowered into a grave at Mount Auburn Cemetery.

To family and friends in the working-class community of Somerville, Massachusetts, Missy was a celebrity. "She was a real role model in our whole family's history," Missy's grand-niece Jane Scarborough observed. "Her life had glamour, excitement, independence, and mystery. I remember when Elliott Roosevelt's book came out implying a romance between the president and Missy, I asked my aunt [Marguerite Collins] what she thought. 'It would be nice to have some spicy past in our family,' she replied with a smile, 'but I simply don't know.' "

Since her sister Ann's divorce, Missy had supported her two nieces, Barbara and Marguerite. It was Missy who took care of their education and bought their clothes for school. "There was an air of magic about Missy," neighbor Barbara Dudley recalled. "She had the most beautiful jewelry, which Ambassador Bullitt had given her. When I was young, I loved to go into her room with my friends and peek in her bureau drawers. She had magnificent underwear from Paris and sweet-smelling perfume. We'd try everything on and then put it all back into the drawers in exactly the same order, so she'd never know."

In her will, Missy divided her belongings between her two nieces. To Marguerite she gave her mink coat, wristwatch with diamonds, small diamond ring, and, perhaps her most precious possession, the small hanging bookcase that President Roosevelt had made for her. To Barbara went her ermine cape, gold watch, and amethyst earrings given to her by Mr. and Mrs. Roosevelt.

The rest of her things—photographs, appointment books, signed drafts of the president's inaugurals and fireside chats—were packed in an old brown suitcase and kept in her sister's closet. The suitcase ended up in Connecticut, in the attic of Barbara's daughter, Jane Scarborough. Years later, Scarborough dimly remembered seeing what must have been the hanging bookcase that Roosevelt made for Missy. "It was in my brother's attic. We often wondered if there were a story behind it. But no one in our generation had any idea what it was. It was so ugly. I think in the end it went off in a garage sale. I wish I had realized what it meant to Missy."

"You and I lost a very dear friend," Grace Tully would later sympathize with Roosevelt. "And he was about to cry," she recalled, "and so was I, and he said, 'Yes, poor Missy.' But he never liked to talk about those things.... He didn't want to show any emotion."

Missy's death took its toll on him. While he rallied to greet the troops at Adak on August 3, he suffered an attack of angina a week later while standing on the deck of his ship delivering a speech to ten thousand navy-yard workers in Bremerton, Washington. This was the first time in months he had used his braces. Because of all the weight he had lost, they no longer fitted him properly, so that he had difficulty keeping his balance. A sharp wind began to blow. The heavy rocking of the ship compelled him to grasp the lectern with both hands, making it hard to turn the pages of his speech. As he struggled to keep his place, his voice faltered.

Ten minutes into the talk, he experienced an oppressive sensation in his chest which radiated to both shoulders. The constricting pain lasted nearly fifteen minutes, but he managed, sweating profusely, to continue talking, keeping himself upright by gripping the edge of the lectern. When he finished, he returned to the captain's quarters and collapsed in a chair. Dr. Bruenn cleared everyone out, including Anna, who had flown to the West Coast earlier that evening to join her father for the remainder of his trip. Dr. Bruenn took an electrocardiogram and a white blood count. Though no permanent damage was found, the attack was sufficiently frightening to Roosevelt that he agreed to rest completely during the trip home.

• • •

The week the president returned to Washington provided a defining moment in the young life of the Fair Employment Practices Commission. In its first three years of operation, hampered by administrative shuffling, lack of funds, limited power, cumbersome bureaucratic machinery, and continuing congressional attacks, the FEPC had failed to realize the bright hopes of its founders. Lacking the power of enforcement, the agency succeeded, historian John Blum writes, "only when black workers were courageous enough to file complaints and corporate offenders decent or embarrassed enough to comply." In too many situations, it surrendered to pressure. Three times, for instance, hearings on discrimination in the railroad industry were postponed as powerful interests—big business, the railroads, organized labor unions, and the Southern bloc—were brought to bear.

On August 1, 1944, when ten thousand mass-transit employees in Philadelphia went out on strike to protest the upgrading of eight Negro employees to motormen, the FEPC was confronted with "the supreme test" of its history. The Philadelphia Transit Company had always resisted employing Negroes as conductors and operators. The five hundred Negroes who worked in the company were confined to laboring and custodial jobs. After Roosevelt issued Executive Order 8802, on discrimination, in 1941, a group of Negro employees requested the opportunity to compete for platform and clerical positions. They were told that nothing could be done because the company union had a contract specifying that "customs bearing on the employer-employee relationship" could not be changed without the agreement of both sides.

The FEPC had notified both the company and the union in the fall of 1943 that they were violating the president's executive order. Conferences were held and a directive was issued ordering the company to hire and upgrade Negroes. This was the first time the FEPC had ordered an entire city transit system to offer equal opportunity. But both the company and the union refused to honor the directive. The impasse remained until the spring of 1944, when a new union, pledging nondiscrimination, defeated the old company union in elections to represent the transit workers.

Deciding that the time was ripe for bold action, the FEPC pressed the company to comply with the president's executive order. Under duress, the company announced a new round of qualifying examinations, open to anyone, for the position of motorman. William Barber, a young Negro who had started with the transit system as a laborer and worked his way up to welder, was one of fifty who took the exam. "The exam was a written test, math plus some general questions," Barber recalled. "Eight of us passed. I got a ninety-eight, one of the highest scores. I was pretty proud of that, since several of the people taking it had a college education, while I hadn't finished high school."

As August 1, his first day on the new job, approached, William Barber was excited. "I felt like a pioneer as I went out to catch the trolley to the carbarn. I knew it was a big thing. But when I get to the corner there are no trolleys anywhere. Everyone was milling around, wondering what was going on. So I go back home, put on the radio, and hear that the whole system—everything, all the trolleys, buses, and subways—is on strike on account of me and my friends' starting our training as operators."

The night before, as it happened, the old union, sensing a golden chance to regain its former positions, had called a mass meeting to protest the hiring of Negroes. Three thousand workers cheered lustily when union leader Frank Carney shouted: "We don't want Negroes and we won't work with Negroes. This is a white man's job. Put the Negroes back where they belong—back on the roadway." Workers cheered again when John Smith, a training instructor, announced that he would quit his job rather than instruct a Negro trainee.

Handbills distributed to the crowd argued that seniority would be destroyed if Negroes were allowed to be upgraded. "Your buddies are in the Army fighting and dying to protect the life of you and your family and you are too yellow to protect their jobs until they return. Call a strike and refuse to teach the Negroes. The public is with you." Other handbills bore a fabricated message from Franklin to Eleanor. "You kiss the Negroes and I'll kiss the Jews and we'll stay in the White House as long as we choose."

By the end of the emotional meeting, the decision was made to call a strike. It began at 4 a.m. that Tuesday, August 1. By 6 a.m., all streetcars and buses had been stopped, leaving William Barber and thousands of work-bound Philadelphians stranded on street corners. By 10 a.m., the city's subway and elevated lines were paralyzed. "There was one motorman who was late in hearing about the strike," a reporter for *PM* noted; "his was the only car which rattled merrily around the loop at 23rd and Hunting Park. Four cars full of strikers bore down upon it, chased the passengers out and drove the trolley down to the carbarn."

Along every street, long columns of workers could be seen walking or trying to thumb rides with the few cars that were still on the road. The Philadelphia Navy Yard, employer of nearly forty-five thousand workers, developed an emergency transportation system for its employees. But for most of the city's nine hundred thousand war workers, there was no way to get to work. Production of critical war materials, including radar, heavy artillery, heavy ammunition, and incendiary bombs, was halted.

On the third day of the strike, with the fourth-largest war-production center virtually paralyzed, President Roosevelt took decisive action. He issued an executive order authorizing the secretary of war "to take possession and assume control of the transportation systems of Philadelphia Transportation Company." The order called upon the army to operate the streetcars and subways "on the basis of conditions that prevailed before the strike"; in other words, the army was to be guided by the nondiscriminatory policies laid down by the FEPC. In contrast to the situation that had developed during the Addsco strike in Mobile, Alabama, the previous year, where the government seemed to condone the practice of segregation, this time both the president and the FEPC acted to uphold equal opportunity.

Events moved quickly after that. The citizens of Philadelphia turned against the strikers. "In whatever degree the PTC walkout is based upon race prejudice, it is wholly indefensible and thoroughly un-American," the *Philadelphia Inquirer* editorialized. "It represents nothing but insult and injury to millions of Philadelphians." On Saturday morning, August 5, the strike leaders were arrested for violating the Smith-Connally Act. Hours later, five thousand soldiers moved into the city. And at five that evening, an ultimatum was broadcast to all the strikers: unless they returned to work by Sunday at midnight, they would lose their jobs, receive no unemployment, and fall subject to the draft. "The war cannot wait," Major General Philip Hayes declared, "while the employees of this company make up their minds whether they will come back to work or not."

Roosevelt's strong-arm tactics worked. Faced with the choice of work or war, the strikers hurried back to work. By Monday evening, all the bus lines, streetcars, subways, and elevated trains were running at full capacity. The transit strike made headlines across the country, provoking a new round of protest in the South. "In the case of Philadelphia," the *South Carolina Post* wrote, "the trouble can be traced directly back to the FEPC through its arbitrary and inept policies." The *Savannah News* pinned the blame directly on "Mrs. Eleanor Roosevelt's persistent efforts to force social equality on the American people."

The training of the eight Negroes went forward. "The first runs were tough," William Barber recalled. "People spit at me. I almost lost my temper, but I said, No, I'll just take it. I'm setting an example. And gradually things settled down. I remember one day a woman with a bad attitude came in. I called her stop and she missed it. She started screaming at me. 'Look, lady,' I said. 'If you don't leave in one minute, one or the other of us is going to be meeting our maker very soon.' With that, everyone on the bus burst into cheers and the lady shut up."

Negro newspapers were exultant at the turn of events. "The impossible has happened," the *Pittsburgh Courier* declared, "history has been made! Negro Americans are operating Philadelphia Transit Company Trolley Cars on regular passenger runs in various sections of the city." The *Courier* observed that surveys showed that 52 percent of the citizens of the city were in favor of Negroes' operating trolley cars if they were qualified. Over time, the integration of Negro workers into the transit force proved so satisfactory and was so well received by the public that the company opened up additional opportunities for Negro motormen. Philadelphia was the crowning achievement of the FEPC.

More progress followed. By the end of the war, the number of black workers in manufacturing had increased by six hundred thousand, to a total of two million, while those enrolled in unions had risen by seven hundred thousand. The percentage of Negroes employed in war production had risen from 2.5 percent to nearly 10 percent. More important, Negroes had made significant breakthroughs in access to more highly skilled positions as foremen, craftsmen, and operatives. "These changes," observed Robert Weaver, a Negro authority on employment and housing, represented "more industrial and occupational diversification for negroes than had occurred in the 75 preceding years."

Significant increases were also reported in the number of Negroes in government service. In 1938, despite the large Negro population in Washington, D.C., Negroes represented only 8.4 percent of all federal employees; by 1944, their percentage had grown to 19, the number rising from sixty thousand to two hundred thousand. In 1938, nine out of ten Negroes in federal service were custodians; in 1944, the percentage who were custodians had dropped to 40.

"With more and better employment opportunities," Jacqueline Jones wrote in *Labor of Love, Labor of Sorrow,* "black men gained a new measure of self-respect, which, in turn, affected family relationships." One young woman said her father felt "proud and happy" when he went from selling junk and cleaning cesspools to a carpenter's job at a nearby military base.

To be sure, economic necessity, in the form of the growing labor shortage during the war, played as great a role as the FEPC in forcing companies to open their doors to Negroes. But, as Louis Ruchames concluded in his study of Executive Order 8802, the FEPC "brought hope and confidence" into the lives of Negroes. "The government of the United States was now doing something to help them, and in defending that government, and the country it represented, they were defending their own destiny and future."

• • •

On August 20, Roosevelt escaped for the weekend to Hyde Park. There was "a decided nip in the air," Hassett observed, "a reminder of waning summer." The days had more early fall than late summer in them; darkness came sooner; and, Eleanor wistfully noted as she walked through the woods, the first autumn colors were beginning to show in the trees. "I am afraid before long the summer days will come to an end," she wrote in her column, "and all of us will feel that we have to return to our routine occupations."

The Big House was filled with visitors when Roosevelt arrived. "Too many," Hassett observed, "all ages, sexes and previous conditions of servitude—hardly relaxing for a tired man." Assorted children and grandchildren were there, along with Henry Kaiser and his wife, Sam Rosenman, Trude Pratt, and two veterans who had lost their legs overseas. Feeding this multitude was not an easy chore, Hassett noted, made harder by the fact that neither the president nor Tommy was allowed to eat what everyone else was eating. "Mrs. Roosevelt never noticed I didn't eat anything," Tommy complained to Esther Lape. "She is very impatient with the President because he has to stick to a diet."

It was Eleanor's good fortune, but also her undoing in her relations with ailing family and friends, to enjoy excellent health. Not once during the preceding four years had illness forced her to stay in bed, she rarely contracted colds, she almost never suffered from indigestion, and she once boasted that she had never had a headache. "She feels if she ignores anything that is wrong with anyone, it won't exist," Tommy observed.

But even Eleanor could not will away her husband's declining health. "Pa complains of feeling tired and I think he looks older," she admitted to Anna. "I can't help worrying about his heart." To Lash she expressed similar worries about "whatever he had last spring," but in the end, she concluded, as long as "he still feels his experience and equipment will help him do a better job than [Republican nominee Thomas Dewey]," he would go forward.

Eleanor remained at Hyde Park when the president returned to Washington the morning of the 23rd. At noon, as word of the liberation of Paris reached the White House, Roosevelt met with Stimson. "This is a great day," Stimson observed. Parisians came out into the streets by the tens of thousands to welcome their liberators with flags, flowers, and wine. The triumphant news buoyed Roosevelt's spirits. "He was in better physical form than I expected," Stimson noted, "and was very warm and cordial."

Later that same day, Roosevelt was wheeled to the South Portico, where Anna and Lucy Rutherfurd were waiting for him, along with Lucy's daughter, Barbara, and her stepson John. Tea and biscuits were served for a relaxing hour.

A week later, Roosevelt managed to see Lucy again, this time at Tranquility Farms, her summer estate in northern New Jersey. En route to Hyde Park for the Labor Day weekend, Roosevelt had his train rerouted from his traditional B & O route to the Pa-Leigh route, which allowed him to stop at Allamuchy. The unexpected stop took some of the passengers by surprise. Sara's old cook, Mary Campbell, was greatly concerned, Hassett noted, "when we laid over in New Jersey and she expected to wake in Highland," but no one, not even the three press reporters, who hardly looked up from their card-playing when told the train would be delayed for a few hours, sought to find out where the president was going.

Lucy later told her friend Elizabeth Shoumatoff about the pleasure of seeing Roosevelt in her own home, with its mountain lake, deer park, and thousands of acres of land. Prior to the visit, the house was in an uproar, as servants cleaned the rugs and polished the tables. "You'd think the president was coming," one of Lucy's employees commented. "He is," Lucy proudly announced. Lucy had a special phone installed to receive foreign calls, and she listened as Roosevelt talked with Churchill. Churchill was recovering from a bout of pneumonia. He was feeling better, he told Roosevelt that day, and was confident he could get away for their seventh summit conference, planned for Quebec the following week. "I hope you will pardon a further transgression of the Teheran scale," Churchill went on, alluding to the problems he had caused at Teheran by bringing his daughter after Roosevelt had told Eleanor and Anna no women were allowed. "I am planning to bring Mrs. Churchill with me," he said. "Perfectly delighted that Clemmie will be with you," Roosevelt replied. "Eleanor will go with me."

Roosevelt's visit with Lucy lasted only a couple of hours; he returned to the train in time for a late-afternoon arrival at Highland Station. But he had enjoyed his stopover so much that he asked the Secret Service later that night if the Allamuchy run could be used every now and then as an alternate route to Hyde Park. After careful study, the Secret Service concluded it was satisfied with the safety of the new route even though this required going over the Hell's Gate Bridge in New York. Delighted, Roosevelt smiled and said "he didn't believe the bridge would be blown up during his transit."

Eleanor was waiting at the station when her husband arrived. She had prepared a special dinner for the two of them at Val-Kill, away from the bustle of the Big House. In her cottage, without the ghost of her mother-in-law hovering around, she could relax, share a drink with her husband in the dusk, and listen to the familiar sounds of a country evening.

• • •

A week later, Franklin and Eleanor journeyed to Quebec, arriving at Wolfe's Cove twenty minutes earlier than the prime minister. Roosevelt had made sure to arrive first, so that he could be on the platform, along with the American chiefs of staff, to welcome his old friend. "I'm glad to see you," the president boomed as the prime minister, carrying a cane, stepped from the train. "Look," Roosevelt said, waving a hand toward his wife, "Eleanor's here"; by that time, Mrs. Churchill had spied Mrs. Roosevelt and shouted, "Hello there."

The exuberant scene, Lord Ismay observed, "was more like the reunion of a happy family starting on a holiday than the gathering of sedate Allied war leaders for an important conference. . . . To see them together, whether at work or play, was a joy." Eleanor enjoyed the scene as well. "There is something boyish about the PM," she noted, as she watched him with her husband. "Perhaps that is what makes him such a wonderful war leader."

At lunch, Eleanor recalled, a spirited conversation evolved, during which Churchill twitted her about their differences of opinion on various subjects, most notably Franco's Spain. In her column written later that day, Eleanor delighted in the notion that she had reached a point in life where she could disagree with people on certain things and still remain friends. "I assured him I had not changed, and neither had he, but we like each other nonetheless." But, in the days that followed, Churchill insisted on bringing up Spain at every meal. "He talks picturesquely, but I'm tempted to say stupidly at times," Eleanor confided to Joe Lash. At one point, he became "very much upset," asserting that he had never said what she was quoting him as saying, but she refused to pull back, calling on the Morgenthaus, who had been present when he spoke, to back her up.

"I think he likes me," Eleanor wrote Esther Lape, "but I also think that he feels women should be seen and not heard on any subject of public interest." In keeping with Churchill's attitudes—and, indeed, with the prevailing opinion of the day—the women were not allowed to join the men at any of the official sessions of the conference. "The ladies' duties are all social," Eleanor complained to Elinor Morgenthau. "It seems like such a waste of time." Though the hours she spent with Mrs. Churchill were pleasurable—they went shopping together one morning, and one afternoon took a trip into the countryside, where they sipped tea on a rug in a lovely field—she was unable, she wrote, to grow intimate quickly. It would all be insufferable, she told Elinor, "except for the meals with a few people when PM and F are entertaining."

The first plenary session opened on Wednesday, September 13. "Optimism was at its height," army historians record. Allied forces had entered Belgium and Luxembourg and had seized a series of bridges over river and canal lines in Holland. It was believed that the German armies in the west had been so "decisively weakened by the battles since D-day" that they would collapse if momentum could be sustained. The major topic of discussion was how to prevent another war with Germany. Everyone agreed that the German army should be destroyed and the Nazi leaders severely punished, but Treasury Secretary Henry Morgenthau had in recent weeks devised a far more drastic plan that called for turning Germany into an agricultural nation by obliterating the industrial resources of the Ruhr. Though Stimson was "utterly opposed to the destruction of such a great gift of nature," Roosevelt had invited Morgenthau to Quebec to explain his proposal to Churchill.

"I had barely got underway," Morgenthau later recalled, "before low mutters and baleful looks" indicated the prime minister's strong opposition. "After I finished my piece he turned loose on me the full flood of his rhetoric, sarcasm and violence. He looked on . . . the Treasury plan, he said, as he would on chaining himself to a dead German. . . . I have never had such a verbal lashing in my life."

"I'm all for disarming Germany," Churchill said, "but we ought not to prevent her living decently. There are bonds between the working classes of all countries and the English people will not stand for the policy you are advocating. I agree with Burke. You cannot indict a whole nation."

The president sat by, saying very little, waiting for the tempest to pass. It did. The next day, after being told by Privy Councillor Lord Cherwell that the Treasury Plan would save Britain from bankruptcy by eliminating Germany as a competitor, Churchill opened his mind to Morgenthau's ideas. "After all, the future of my people is at stake," Churchill said, "and when I have to choose between my people and the German people, I am going to choose my people."

After further discussion, both Churchill and Roosevelt agreed to sign an extraordinary memo which called for "converting Germany into a country primarily agricultural and pastoral in its character" by "eliminating the war making industries in the Ruhr and the Saar." Morgenthau was thrilled. Invited to join the president for drinks in Roosevelt's suite at the Citadel, he noted, "We haven't had a talk like this since almost going back to the time when he was governor." It was, Morgenthau recalled, "the high spot of my whole career in Government."

But Morgenthau's euphoria was short-lived. When news of the draconian plan leaked to the press, a loud outcry arose within Roosevelt's Cabinet, and the idea quietly died. "I never heard my husband say that he had changed his attitude on this plan," Eleanor later wrote. "I think the repercussions brought about by the press stories made him feel it was wise to abandon [it] at that time. . . ."

The conference turned next to Pacific strategy. Churchill opened the discussion by declaring that Britain now stood ready and willing to send its main fleet to join in the struggle against Japan. Though Admiral King was initially opposed to the idea, not wishing, in the last stages of the war, to surrender America's exclusive jurisdiction over the area, Roosevelt accepted

Churchill's offer without hesitation, welcoming the British fleet "whenever and wherever possible." American plans for the final blow against Japan envisaged an invasion of the Japanese homeland sometime in 1945, after Germany's defeat.

For the after-dinner entertainment that evening, Roosevelt chose *Woodrow Wilson,* a motion-picture biography on the rise and fall of the twenty-eighth president. The film followed in detail Wilson's harsh descent into illness, incapacitation, rejection, and death. It was a curious selection for Roosevelt to make, coming at a time when he was beset with worries about both his own health and his fate at the hands of the electorate. Only hours earlier, Roosevelt had talked with Canadian Prime Minister MacKenzie King about his chances for re-election in November, and King could see that he was really concerned. Churchill was so restless during the film that he walked out halfway through. He was worried enough about his friend; he did not need a historical reminder of presidential illness. Indeed, so concerned was Churchill with Roosevelt's appearance at Quebec that he went to see Dr. McIntire. McIntire, as usual, assured Churchill that Roosevelt was fine. "With all my heart I hope so," Churchill replied. "We cannot have anything happen to that man." When the film ended, sometime after midnight, Roosevelt seemed depressed, Dr. Bruenn noted, and his blood pressure was elevated to 240/130.

When the conference was over, Churchill accompanied Roosevelt to Hyde Park for two days before returning to England. On arriving at the Big House, the prime minister was delighted to learn that Harry Hopkins, who had not been present at Quebec, was coming to lunch. Hopkins' absence from the conference had troubled both Churchill and Mrs. Churchill. "He seems to have quite dropped out of the picture," Mrs. Churchill had written her daughter from Quebec. "I found it sad and rather embarrassing. We cannot quite make out whether Harry's old place in the President's confidence is vacant, or whether Admiral [William] Leahy is gradually moulding into it."

Churchill later recalled a curious incident at lunch. Hopkins arrived a few minutes late, and the president "did not even greet him." Later that afternoon, Hopkins explained to Churchill his altered position. His marriage, his decision to move from the White House, and his own ill-health had induced a decline in the president's favor. "You must know I am not what I was," Hopkins admitted to Churchill. "He had tried to do too much at once," Churchill later said. "Even his fullness of spirit broke under his variegated activities."

"There was no open breach between them," Hopkins' biographer Robert Sherwood observed, "simply an admission that [Hopkins] was no longer physically fit to share the burdens of responsibility for the big decisions of the war." But Hopkins had made remarkable comebacks before, and in the months ahead, he would rally his energies once more to re-establish himself as Roosevelt's chief adviser.

Mrs. Churchill thoroughly enjoyed her days at Hyde Park, the picnics on the lawn, the good talk, the leisurely walks through the woods. This was the first time that she had met Anna. "She is a wonderful combination of yourself and the President," she wrote Eleanor. "She charmed Winston and me with her gay and vivacious personality."

If Mrs. Churchill flourished in the simple routine of Hyde Park, Eleanor was glad when the visit was over. "My time slips away," she lamented to Joe Lash, explaining that she felt like "a glorified housekeeper" with a household that changed every hour. "These are the days when the resentment at the tyranny of people and things grows on me until if I were not a well-disciplined person I would go out and howl like a dog! The Churchills and party came at 11, Harry Hopkins at 12, the Duke of Windsor at 12:15. After lunch I dashed to the cottage and did one column, returned at 3:30, changed all the orders given at 12:30 and walked with Mrs. Churchill for an hour and a half ending up at Franklin's cottage for tea, worked again 5–7:15, dashed home and had Henry and Elinor and [neighbors from Staatsburg] the Lytle Hulls for dinner. Now the mail is done and my spirit is calm and I can enjoy writing to you."

During Churchill's last night at Hyde Park, the conversation turned to the subject of the atomic bomb. The scientists at Los Alamos were now predicting that a bomb, equivalent to thirty thousand tons of TNT, would almost certainly be ready by August 1945. Admiral Leahy, who was present at the conversation, had little confidence in the whole project. He feared that Roosevelt had assumed too great a risk in allocating such huge sums of money to a mere experiment. But the president and the prime minister were hopeful that the bomb "might perhaps, after mature consideration be used against the Japanese, who should be warned that the bombardment will be repeated until they surrender."

Churchill also asked for assurance at this time that nothing would be said to the Russians about the bomb. In earlier conversations, Roosevelt had expressed the feeling that, since the Russians would find out about it sooner or later, they should at least be advised, as a gesture of friendship to an ally, that a bomb was in the making. But Churchill was adamant, and Roosevelt finally agreed in writing that the matter should continue to be regarded as of "the utmost secrecy."

The long days with Churchill were taxing on Roosevelt. "The President under a heavy strain ever since he went to Quebec," Hassett noted, "continuous talking—sat up with Churchill until 1 o'clock this morning. Fortunately part of the strain is eliminated by departure of the Prime Minister tonight." Soon after the Churchills' departure at about 7 p.m., Roosevelt went to bed, leaving word that he wanted "to sleep right through the morning."

• • •

By late September, when the president returned to Washington, Democratic leaders were filled with anxiety. The Republican challenger, Thomas E. Dewey, was running an efficient campaign. The steady barrage of Republican criticism—suggesting that the government was in the hands of tired old men who were destroying free enterprise, coddling labor, regimenting agriculture, and saddling the country with high taxes and dangerous debt—was achieving its desired effect. Dewey was rising in popularity, while Roosevelt was rapidly losing ground.

The president had to prove to the electorate that he possessed the strength and resilience to rise to the Republican challenge. He began by announcing that he would go out on the stump for a series of speeches; his campaign would officially open on the evening of September 23 with an address to the Teamsters Union at the Statler Hotel in Washington, D.C. The announcement was greeted with relief by Democrats, but apprehension soon set in. Was the president up to the task?

There was reason to worry. Roosevelt did not look good. His loss of weight made him seem much older than his sixty-two years. His color was bad. He had not given a major speech since his appearance at Bremerton, when he had suffered the angina attack in the middle of his delivery. Since then, continuing weight loss and lack of exercise had reduced the already frail muscles in his legs and hips to flab, making it almost impossible for him to maneuver on his braces. Within the White House, the consensus was that the president should no longer even try to walk. But Roosevelt refused to give in. On the eve of his Teamsters speech, he called Dr. McIntire into his bedroom. A few minutes later, when Sam Rosenman came into the room with the latest draft of the speech, he found the president "with his braces on walking up and down, leaning on the arm of Dr. McIntire." In spite of the overwhelming volume of work facing him, Rosenman sadly noted, "he was literally trying to learn to walk again!"

Though Roosevelt eventually did manage to regain sufficient use of his legs to allow him to stand up and speak for short periods from the rear platform of his train, he reluctantly agreed to deliver his Teamsters speech from a sitting position. Having worked over the speech through dozens of drafts, he was afraid to let anything interfere with his concentration and delivery.

In the banquet hall that night were gathered all the leading Democrats in Washington, along with the leadership of the International Brotherhood of Teamsters, Chauffeurs and Warehousemen. As the president was introduced, a worried Anna, seated ten yards from the dais at a table filled with family and friends, turned to Rosenman. "Do you think Pa will put it over?" she whispered. "It's the kind of speech which depends almost entirely on delivery, no matter how good the writing—if the delivery isn't just right, it'll be an awful flop." Rosenman told her there was "no doubt in the world he'll get it over fine," covering his own anxiety with a reassuring tone.

The President began smoothly with a joking reference to his advancing age. "Well, here we are together again—after four years—and what years they have been. You know, I am actually four years older, which is a fact that seems to annoy some people. In fact, in the mathematical field there are millions of Americans who are more than eleven years older than when we started in to clear up the mess that was dumped in our laps in 1933."

Roosevelt proceeded, with a voice that purred softly and then struck hard, to ridicule Republicans for trying to pass themselves off every four years as friends of labor after attacking labor for three years and six months. "The whole purpose of Republican oratory these days seems to be to switch labels. The object is to persuade the American people that the Democratic Party was responsible for the 1929 crash and the depression, and that the Republican Party was responsible for all social progress under the New Deal."

"Now," he said, drawing out his words, "imitation may be the sincerest form of flattery—but I am afraid that in this case it is the most obvious common or garden variety of fraud." Indeed, he went on, when he first heard the Republicans blaming the Democrats for the Depression, he rubbed his eyes and recalled an old adage: " 'Never speak of rope in the house of a man who has been hanged.' In the same way, if I were a Republican leader speaking to a mixed audience, the last word in the whole dictionary that I think I would use is that word 'depression.' "

The audience loved it. They howled, clapped, and cheered. One teamster was so excited, Merriman Smith wrote, that he beat the silver tray with a soup ladle, while his colleague at a neighboring table smashed glasses with a wine bottle. At the family table, Anna's smile brightened, and she began to relax. "The Old Master still had it," the reporter from *Time* observed. "He was like a veteran virtuoso playing a piece he has loved for years, who fingers his way through it with a delicate fire, a perfection of timing and tone, and an assurance that no young player, no matter how gifted, can equal. The President was playing what he loves to play—politics."

Then came the climax of the speech, in which he pitted his dog, Fala, against the entire Republican establishment. "These Republican leaders have not been content with attacks on me, or my wife, or on my sons," Roosevelt said in a mock-serious tone. "No, not content with that, they now include my little dog, Fala. Well, of course, I don't resent attacks, and my family doesn't resent attacks, but Fala does resent them. You know, Fala is Scotch, and being a Scottie, as soon as he learned that the Republican fiction writers in Congress and out had concocted a story that I had left him behind on the Aleutian Islands and had sent a destroyer back to find him—at a cost to the taxpayers of two or three, or eight or twenty million dollars—his Scotch soul was furious. He has not been the same dog since. I am accustomed to hearing malicious falsehoods about myself . . . but I think I have a right to resent, to object to libelous statements about my dog."

The audience went wild, laughing and cheering and calling for more. And the laughter carried beyond the banquet hall; it reverberated in living rooms and kitchens throughout the country, where people were listening to the speech on their radios. The Fala bit was so funny, one reporter observed, that "even the stoniest of Republican faces cracked a smile." In closing, the president outlined the tasks ahead: finishing the war as speedily as possible; setting up international machinery to assure that the peace, once established, would not be broken again; reconverting the economy from the purposes of war to the purposes of peace.

As the familiar voice said good night, the audience was on its feet, shouting and applauding. "There were tears in the eyes of many," Rosenman observed, "including his daughter Anna."

"The 1944 campaign was on," *Time* reported, "and Franklin Roosevelt had got off to a flying start. . . . The Champ had swung a full roundhouse blow. And it was plain to the newsmen on the Dewey Special that the challenger had been hit hard—as plain as when a boxer drops his gloves and his eyes glaze."

With his triumphant speech behind him, Roosevelt boarded the overnight train for Hyde Park, where he joined Eleanor and Princess Martha for three days in the crisp country air.

• • •

Still, all indications pointed to a close race, with the president's health a major concern. It was rumored that Roosevelt had suffered a stroke, that he had had a major heart attack, that he had undergone a secret operation for cancer, that he was forced to carry a male nurse around with him for the purpose of emptying his bladder two or three times a day. "Let's not be squeamish," the *New York Sun* declared, "six presidents have died in office." The only counterattack, Roosevelt decided, was to go before as many people as possible so they could make up their own minds about his vigor and health.

The president began his tour in New York City on Saturday, October 21. The plan called for him to drive in an open Packard through four of the five boroughs—Brooklyn, Queens, the Bronx, and Manhattan. If the expected crowds materialized, he could easily see three million people in the course of the day. In theory, the plan was excellent, but the weather refused to cooperate. When the president's train reached Brooklyn at 7 a.m., a cold rain was falling, the tail end of a hurricane. The rain flooded the streets, dashed against the buildings, and beat down on the heads of the sidewalk crowds.

Dr. McIntire pleaded with the president to close the Packard's canvas top, but Roosevelt was adamant. The people had come to see that he was still alive and well, and he was determined to give them what they wanted. Taking off his navy cape, he positioned himself in the rear seat of the car, grinning and waving at enormous crowds whose ardor had not been in any way diminished by the dismal weather. The rain drenched his gray suit, splattered his glasses, and ran down his cheeks, but the president never stopped smiling and the crowds went wild. At Ebbets Field, he received a thunderous ovation as he hoisted himself to a standing position and hobbled toward a lectern positioned behind second base. He had rooted for the

Dodgers for years, he said, flashing his best smile. His radiance in the midst of the storm, Hassett noted, seemed undeniable proof that he was physically up to the job.

He was thoroughly soaked by the time his talk was finished, but he laughingly confided to Anna that Dr. McIntire had arranged to bring the car into a Coast Guard motor pool, where he was able to make a complete change of clothes without leaving the car. The green Packard continued through Queens to the Bronx, then went on to Harlem, Broadway, and the garment workers' district. Huge crowds continued to line the streets; at every stop, hundreds of thousands of people were standing in the pouring rain to catch a glimpse of their president.

In midafternoon, the cavalcade pulled up to Eleanor's apartment at 29 Washington Square, where there was a second complete change of clothes for Roosevelt, a late lunch, and a short rest. Though Eleanor had purchased the apartment more than two years earlier, this was the first time Roosevelt had seen it. As she showed her husband around the tall-ceilinged, gracefully decorated rooms, Eleanor asked if he had noticed that there were no steps leading into the apartment. He nodded happily. Everything had been arranged for his comfort, she noted. There were two rooms connected by a bathroom which could be shut off from the rest of the apartment just in case he ever wanted to stay. Franklin said he liked it very much.

In the library, overlooking Washington Square, drinks were served. Dr. McIntire prescribed a glass of bourbon to warm the president up. Roosevelt gulped it down and asked for a second, and then a third. "It was the only occasion," Grace Tully later recalled, "on which I knew him to have more than a couple of drinks." The bourbon did the trick; after lunch, the president retired to the bedroom for a restful nap.

It is interesting to imagine what Roosevelt might have thought as he looked about the cheerful apartment, observing a part of his wife's life he had not seen before. Did his eyes travel about the rooms, conjuring images of Eleanor with her friends, serving dinner, sipping coffee after a night out at the theater? On her dresser, she kept a few framed pictures: one of the two of them when they were young, one of Anna and John, one of Joe Lash. For two decades, Eleanor had enjoyed an independent life apart from his, and now, for a few moments, he was a witness to that life.

After resting for an hour, the president took a hot bath and dressed for dinner. Mixing a round of cocktails before he left, he seemed almost giddy as he was helped into his car and driven to the Waldorf-Astoria, where two thousand members of the Foreign Policy Association were waiting in the grand ballroom to hear him speak.

The text of the speech was designed to focus on the new postwar organization, but the president was so relaxed at the dais that he began to ad-lib. Spotting Eleanor at a table just below him, he was reminded of a story she had told him in 1933 about a trip she had made to a fourth-grade history class. On the wall, he told the crowd, she had seen "a map of the world with a great big white spot on it—no name—no information. And the teacher told her that it was blank, with no name, because the school wouldn't let him say anything about that big blank space. Oh, there were one hundred eighty to two hundred million people in that space which was called Soviet Russia. And there were a lot of children, and they were told that the teacher was forbidden by the school board even to put the name of that blank space on the map." How much had changed since that time, he noted, now that the Americans and the Russians were fighting together against a common enemy.

Listening from a table in the back of the room, Grace Tully wondered if the president would ever get to the prepared text. Sam Rosenman and Robert Sherwood, who had worked on the speech, were wondering the same thing. But the president was, as always, a pro. Returning to the text, he took up the most important question relating to the new world organization, the question that had destroyed the League of Nations. In an emergency, would it have the authority to commit the United States to the use of armed force without waiting for the Congress to act? The president's answer was an emphatic yes.

"Peace, like war," he said, "can succeed only where there is a will to enforce it, and where there is available power to enforce it. The Council of the United Nations [the name Roosevelt had conceived the first time Churchill visited him in Washington had stuck] must have the power to act quickly and decisively to keep the peace by force, if necessary. A policeman would not be a very effective policeman if, when he saw a felon break into a house, he had to go to the Town Hall and call a town meeting to issue a warrant before the felon could be arrested. So to my simple mind it is clear that, if the world organization is to have any reality at all, our American representative must be endowed in advance by the people themselves, by constitutional means through their representatives in the Congress, with authority to act."

As the president ended his speech, he was given a standing ovation; cheers were still ringing in his ears when he was escorted to a waiting elevator to go to the basement, where, on New York Central tracks, his presidential train was waiting to take him to Hyde Park.

The next morning, Hassett reported, the president was elated to discover that he had "no trace of a cold—not even a sniffle after his exposure in New York." Though two of the three pool reporters and several hardy Secret Service men were fighting bad colds, he was none the worse for the wear. Indeed, far from hurting the president, Eleanor observed, the rainy campaign trip had done him good. "Not for a long time had he been in contact with the crowds, meeting with a lot of people and getting an impression of how they feel," she said. It seemed almost as if Roosevelt had absorbed some of the strength and vitality of the many people who wanted so much to see their president that they were willing to stand in a drenching rain for more than four hours. "Their enthusiasm for him and his feeling of being at one with them," Eleanor observed, "seemed to give him an amount of exhilaration and energy and strength that nothing else did."

Roosevelt's high spirits carried him through the rest of the campaign. At the end of October, he journeyed through seven states in three days, delivering major speeches in Philadelphia and Chicago. Once again he was subjected to rain and icy winds, but once again he emerged, in Hassett's words, "brisk as a bee, brimming with health and spirits."

In the meantime, Eleanor observed, "the news from the Pacific is so startling that one holds one's breath." On October 18, American troops had shelled Japanese defenses on the island of Leyte, the first step in the dramatic battle to regain the Philippines. In contrast to the situation two years earlier, when the invasion of North Africa was launched too late to help the president in the midterm elections, this time Roosevelt was lucky. Two weeks before the elections, the nation awoke to banner headlines announcing that General MacArthur had landed in the Philippines; his famous pledge that he would return had been redeemed. "There were extremely light losses," Roosevelt told his press conference that morning. "The enemy was caught strategically unaware."

Two days before the election, Roosevelt traveled to Boston, where he was scheduled to speak at Fenway Park. The trip evoked in speechwriter Robert Sherwood "painful memories" of the trip four years previously, when Roosevelt promised American mothers that their boys would never be sent into a foreign war. Sherwood asked Roosevelt if he would make a reference to that speech, emphasizing that, once the Japanese had attacked Pearl Harbor, the war was no longer a foreign war. Roosevelt readily agreed. He referred to his 1940 pledge and then added: "I am sure that any real American would have chosen, as this Government did, to fight when our own soil was made the object of a sneak attack. As for myself, under the same circumstances, I would choose to do the same thing—again and again and again." With the repetition of the phrase, the crowd applauded loudly.

On election eve, in Hyde Park, with Anna instead of Missy by his side, Roosevelt assumed his usual place at the dining table, tabulating results. Eleanor was in the living room. She "swirled around among the guests," Merriman Smith noted, "seeing that everybody had cider and doughnuts." It was an odd group, Smith observed, watching Margaret Suckley, Laura Delano, and Marion Dickerman, "arty old ladies in tweed, or evening gowns of two decades before."

By 10 p.m., the trend was clear: the people of the United States had returned Franklin Delano Roosevelt to the White House for a fourth term. Though the election was closer than it had been in 1940, Roosevelt had garnered 53.5 percent of the popular vote and 432 electoral votes, to 46 percent and 99 electoral votes for Dewey. Dewey had carried the Midwest, the mountain states, and the New England states of Maine and Vermont, but Roosevelt had kept the support of the various groups that had supported him in previous elections—labor, Catholics, Jews, Negroes, soldiers.

At midnight, adhering to ritual, the president was wheeled out on his porch to greet the torchlight parade of villagers. Standing by her father's side, Anna gently pulled his old navy cape around his shoulders. The president smiled broadly and waved to his neighbors. "It looks like I'll be coming up from Washington again for another four years," he said. In the big spruce tree to the left of the terrace, he spotted a group of young boys. Seeing them reminded him, he said, of the days when he was young and "sought sanctuary from discipline in the friendly branches of that very tree."

After the neighbors left, Eleanor invited the shivering newsmen and photographers into the house for cider, as everyone waited for a message from the Republican challenger. It was 3:16 a.m., Hassett noted, before "the graceless Dewey" officially broadcast his concession, but he sent no message to the victor. "I still think he is a son of a bitch," Roosevelt remarked as he headed off to bed.

In other years, the Roosevelt boys would have been present on election eve, enjoying the moment with their father, but, like millions of other American families that November, the Roosevelts were scattered, with John and FDR, Jr., in the Pacific, Elliott in Europe, and Jimmy in Hawaii. "Word has just come in that Dewey has conceded," John wrote from an unnamed lagoon somewhere in the South Pacific. "I really missed not being with you at Hyde Park to watch the returns come in as we did four years ago. . . . I hope that at this time four years hence we can all be together again and that this show will be over."

CHAPTER 22

"SO DARNED BUSY"

The postelection period was one of confusion and drift for Eleanor, who felt herself tugged in opposing directions. On one side, she was intensely aware, as her friends reminded her, that she commanded more power and respect than any other woman in the United States. Millions of people, Joe Lash insisted, had voted for her as well as the president, conferring on her a conspicuous position of leadership even though her name had not appeared on the ballot. The challenge, Esther Lape advised, with so much opportunity to accomplish so many things, was to take time to think out the best ways to exercise "the tremendously increased powers that are so peculiarly now yours."

Yet, even as she contemplated new ways to use her remarkable position, Eleanor was plagued by guilt and pulled by the more traditional side of her nature. "Maybe I'd do the most useful job if I just became a 'good wife' and waited on FDR," she wrote to Esther Lape a week after the election. "Anna has been doing all of it that Margaret Suckley does not do but she can't go on doing it.

"If I did I'd lose value in some ways because I'd no longer have outside contacts. I'd hate it but I'd soon get accustomed to it. It is funny how hard it is to be honest with yourself and not be swayed by your own wishes, isn't it."

She found it difficult to make a decision, she admitted to Lape. Though she acknowledged her responsibilities to her husband, she felt "inadequate," fearing there was no longer "any fundamental love to draw on, just respect and affection" and "little or no surface friction." At times, she confessed, she felt "a great weariness and sense of futility in life but a lifelong discipline in a sense of obligation and a healthy interest in people" kept her going, and she guessed that was "plenty to go on for one's aging years!"

The agitation the sixty-year-old Eleanor felt in not knowing what to do was echoed in the hearts of the millions of American women for whom the war had been a major turning point, creating new expectations, new adjustments, new problems. Responding to their country's call, women had poured into jobs previously held by men, performing beyond everyone's expectations as truck drivers, lathe operators, welders, riveters, and stevedores.

At the peak of wartime employment, over nineteen million women were employed, constituting one-third of the civilian labor force. Since five million of the total were new workers, the nature of the female labor force had been transformed. Whereas before the war the bulk consisted of widows, unmarried women, and young wives with no children, now married women with children constituted nearly one-half of the female working population. Not surprisingly, the war industries showed the largest gains: between 1940 and 1944, women's employment in war-related work had risen 460 percent, while female membership in unions had quadrupled.

When these women were asked if they enjoyed working more than staying at home, an astounding 79 percent said yes; of this total, 70 percent were married with children. For some, the best part of work was the sociability of the workplace versus the isolation of domestic responsibilities. For others, the best part was the financial independence, the freedom from having to ask their husbands if they could buy a new dress or clothes for the kids, the knowledge that they were contributing to the family's economic welfare. Still others relished the mastery of new skills, the sense of industry, the pleasure of a job well done. "At the end of the day I always felt I'd accomplished something," welder Lola Weixel recalled. "It was good—there was a product, there was something to be seen."

But now, as the war was winding down, the country was beset with worries. What would happen to women after the war? What would the men find when they came home? Would wives be glad to give up their jobs and return to being homemakers, or would they continue working?

In the summer of 1944, the War Department published a pamphlet entitled *Do You Want Your Wife to Work After the War?* Designed as one of a series of GI pamphlets which officers could use to provoke discussions and forums, the pamphlet tried to impress on its readers that women's roles were changing, but the dominant voices were those that spoke against women's working.

"There are two things I want to be sure of after the war," one soldier in the South Pacific was quoted as saying. "I want my wife waiting for me and I want my job waiting for me. I don't want to find my wife busy with a job that some returning soldier needs and I don't want to find that some other man's wife has my job."

"Where I come from," another soldier wrote, "we don't send our wives to work. If I can't make enough money to support a wife I don't expect to get married. My mother had plenty to do right around the house. . . . I'm for the good old-fashioned way."

As demobilization loomed on the horizon, the image of women as comrades-in-arms was replaced by the image of women as competitors for men. And with this shift came a shift in public opinion. Enthusiastic admiration for Rosie the Riveter was replaced by the prevailing idea that "Women ought to be delighted to give up any job and return to their proper sphere —the kitchen." All of a sudden, in every medium of popular culture, women were barraged with propaganda on the value of domesticity.

Magazines that had once given prominent display to products such as Heinz soup and GE cleaners, which allowed women to fly through their chores at home so they could rush to their work in the factory, now featured menus that took a full day to prepare. Numerous articles appeared linking juvenile delinquency to the absence of a mother at home. Pictures of young children smoking cigarettes were printed as warnings to working mothers. Stories of women such as Liz Eck, a brilliant concert soprano, who was giving up her career because it threatened her marriage, were displayed prominently. Mrs. Eck planned to concentrate on being a wife and mother, she said, because "it's the only lasting happiness a woman can have."

Ignoring poll after poll that suggested that the majority of women wanted to continue working, the women's magazines focused almost exclusively on those women who were ready to quit. "My position is to go," Mrs. Cliff Ferguson was quoted in the June 1944 issue of *Ladies' Home Journal,* "unless of course my man comes back wounded. He wants me home and I want to be there. And we want kids."

"Am I planning to stop work after the war? I'll say I am," Mrs. Irma Stewart told the *Journal.* "It will be grand to get back to normal living again." Camilla Taylor expressed similar sentiments in *Women's Home Companion.* "I really believe I'll do better by my children and husband when I stay home. Anyhow, housework is infinitely more satisfactory than office work. You can't tell me that any job is as worthwhile as creating a home."

Movies and plays followed suit. *Soldier's Wife* was a successful play on Broadway which Eleanor went to see in the fall of 1944. It centered, Eleanor told her readers, on the wife of a GI who "found herself an authoress overnight, but decided that her marriage meant more to her than all the possibilities temptingly held out to her." Perhaps it was meant simply as entertainment, Eleanor wrote, "perhaps no real lesson was intended, but it certainly carries one."

Through her columns and her speeches, Eleanor tried to present a more rounded view of women's work, reminding her audience that different women worked for different reasons. To be sure, the women who were working solely for patriotic reasons would "gladly relinquish their jobs the day war comes to an end," as would women who planned to raise a family as soon as their husbands returned. But, Eleanor predicted, since millions of women were working out of economic necessity, "a good proportion" would undoubtedly remain in the labor market.

The nation could not afford, Eleanor warned, to return to an economy of scarcity in which women and minorities were denied the right to work. "To give anyone who wants to work a chance to work," she said, "it is necessary to envisage a future in which you produce to a maximum and sell to the rest of the world." What the women workers needed, she argued, was the courage to ask for their rights with a loud voice, demanding equal pay for equal work, an expansion of day care, and a proper share in postwar planning. "Women are fully as capable as men," she asserted. "Men and women were meant to work together."

Labor leader Walter Reuther wholly agreed with these sentiments. Speaking to UAW delegates at the first national women's conference in Detroit, he argued that "industry must not be allowed to settle the employment problem by chaining women to kitchen sinks." The solution would come only through planning now for reconversion. He called for the creation of an overall production board, representing labor, management, and government, to work toward peacetime employment and toward meeting the country's needs in housing, transportation, and durable consumer goods. "We must start planning immediately," he urged; "sixty million jobs will not create themselves."

But even as Reuther was speaking, women were losing their jobs with unseemly haste; their layoff rate was 75 percent higher than for men. In some factories, supervisors made a practice of harassing women into leaving—placing them on the midnight shift, reassigning them to undesirable jobs, transferring them to new locations, and closing down day-care centers. In other factories, all pretense was abandoned, as gleeful supervisors handed quit slips to every woman on the line, willingly subjecting themselves to ridicule as cartoonists satirized management's abrupt about-face in its attitudes toward women. In one cartoon, a supervisor is depicted handing a termination notice to a distressed-looking woman. "Now that War is nearly over," he tells her, "so sorry, have suddenly remembered you are incapable of working in factory."

• • •

By the eleventh month of 1944, the layoffs were affecting men as well as women. War production had reached its peak in November of 1943 and was beginning to move downward. At Brewster Aeronautical in Long Island, New York, 13,500 workers had been thrown out of work on three days' notice when the navy suddenly terminated the company's fighter-plane contract.

The navy had no problem with the quality of Brewster's work; on the contrary, the Brewster workers, like the overwhelming majority of their fellow workers, had done their job faster and better than anyone had anticipated. Indeed, so well had the arsenal of democracy lived up to its name that the unimaginable had happened: the country was now making more munitions than were needed to win the war.

The time had come, War Production Board chief Donald Nelson argued, for reconversion to begin, for the government to design measures to ensure a smooth transition to a peacetime economy. As a first step, Nelson proposed to lift restrictions on the use of aluminum, magnesium, and other materials no longer needed for war production, so that small companies whose war work was done could begin building schools, hospitals, railroad equipment, and appliances needed in the civilian economy. Eleanor Roosevelt wholly agreed with this line of thinking. We must begin now, she wrote in her column, to work out the methods "whereby every worker will be assured of a job when his war work comes to an end."

Creating structured programs for workers laid off from defense plants would alleviate the pressures that were leading to chaos in some factories as workers who were still needed to produce wartime goods were anxiously reconverting themselves, moving by the thousands into lower-paying nonwar jobs, hoping to get a jump start on the future before the war came to an end.

But the military refused even to think about reconversion, fearing that if civilian production were allowed to expand, if refrigerators, dishwashers, and automobiles suddenly became available, the populace would think the crisis had passed and would begin to relax, opening the way "for dangerous leakages of materials and manpower." Convinced that the war demanded undivided attention until the job was done, the War Department argued that continuing restrictions on the production of civilian goods was the only means of combating complacency. "Many people seem to believe that this is the time for the seventh-inning stretch," supply chief General Brehon Somervell said, "and while they're stretching, the Nazis are digging in."

To bolster their point of view, the military argued that critical shortages of supplies still remained, despite the astonishing success of the overall production effort. Undersecretary of War Robert Patterson held a press conference with a group of soldiers just returning from France, where intense fighting was still going on. The GIs told stories of infantry units forced into battle without enough shells and grenades, of campaigns stalled and lives lost because of the strict rationing of ammunition. "It's tough to see your buddies get killed and not be able to stop it," one GI said.

These dramatic stories created a "misperception of the problem," Senator James Mead of New York argued, speaking as the new chairman of the Truman Committee on National Defense. "Insufficient production in the United States has not been the cause of shortages of weapons and ammunition at the front. Any shortage has been due, up to now, solely to transportation problems overseas." Donald Nelson agreed. For the military to focus on production shortages instead of on the difficulties of supplying a far-flung army was "one of the most dangerous bits of double talk."

But as historian Bruce Catton has observed, "neither facts nor logic made any impression." The military was not open to argument. Its position was utterly simple: there must be no interference whatsoever with the war effort.

The military found a natural ally in big business, who feared that speedy reconversion would confer advantage on small companies, which, because they were not essential cogs in the war machine, could more easily make the shift to civilian production. What was at stake in the reconversion battle was nothing less than the future of the American economy. The industrial giants were determined to dominate postwar production just as they were dominating production for the war. If small businesses and independent producers were allowed to get a head start in the race for peacetime markets, the established industrial order—in which fewer than one hundred large corporations were producing more than two-thirds of all the goods and services—would be overthrown.

As chairman of the Smaller War Plants Corporation, Maury Maverick put up a valiant fight for small business. Small business needed a head start, Maverick argued, to compensate for the overwhelming preference given to big business in the granting of wartime contracts. Much of the opposition to reconversion, he declared, "was motivated by nothing more lofty than a desire to save the postwar business opportunities for the big manufacturers." But every attempt he made to secure peacetime work for small business or to move forward on reconversion was stymied by the developing military-industrial alliance.

"You know what they're doing to me," Maverick complained, referring to the big-business interests. "They started on the roof, then they took rubber hoses and beat me, on top of the roof, and then they threw me down that chute—you know—and then they threw me down the steps to the third floor, and they kicked me, on that escalator, and I got a leg cut off and both of my ears. . . . I just came out with my life."

Eleanor found herself on Maury Maverick's side, believing that small business must be protected. Her heart ached for every individual thrown out of work by the cutbacks in war production. In conversations and correspondence with Walter Reuther, she explored the idea of creating a pool of machine tools which could be moved around to different factories, allowing war production and civilian production to move forward at the same time.

Roosevelt listened to his wife, but in the debate between Donald Nelson and labor leaders on one side and James Byrnes and the military on the other, he came down on the side of the military, agreeing with Byrnes that the country should not be asked to do two things at once, to pursue an all-out war-production effort while simultaneously releasing materials and facilities for civilian production. Better to risk unemployment in selected areas then to divide the nation's attention at a time when casualties on both fronts were mounting.

The argument over reconversion came to be known as "the war within a war." The fight between the military and the civilian elements, Nelson believed, was one of the most severe fights the government ever witnessed. Byrnes strenuously urged that Roosevelt remove Nelson from his post as war-production chief and replace him with someone sympathetic to the military's point of view. Roosevelt agreed that something had to be done, but, in characteristic fashion, he refused to face the issue head on, electing instead to send Nelson on a special mission to China to determine how China's industrial potential could be strengthened for more effective use against the Japanese. It was a graceful exit but an exit nonetheless, making room for the triumph of the military-industrial interests.

• • •

Late in the afternoon on November 27, after a busy day of engagements, Roosevelt boarded the train for Warm Springs, Georgia, for a three-week vacation at the Little White House. This was his first extended visit to Warm Springs since Pearl Harbor, and he was eagerly looking forward to his traditional Thanksgiving meal with the polio patients.

Eleanor had elected to stay in Washington. Since Laura and Margaret were accompanying Roosevelt, she told Hick, "I don't have to go." She planned instead to celebrate Thanksgiving in Lexington, Virginia, with Joe and Trude Lash. Lash had returned from the South Pacific in October and had married Trude in early November in a simple ceremony in New York City, which Eleanor attended. Their marriage must not have been easy for Eleanor, however close she had grown to Trude. Once again, she was the outsider looking in, wishing the couple well, but knowing that her special relationship with the intense young sergeant would never be the same. "You and Joe were very sweet to let me share your evening after the wedding," Eleanor wrote Trude the next day, "and I am very grateful and love you both very much."

Eleanor's plans for Thanksgiving did not materialize. Shortly before she was ready to leave, she received a letter from Joe telling her he feared her presence would jeopardize his chances for admission to Officers Candidate School. "Mrs. Roosevelt's feelings were hurt as you know they can be," Tommy explained to Esther Lape. "Trude was smart enough to sense this and so they wrote an appeasing letter," in which they begged forgiveness, reinvited her, and admitted that what they had done in disinviting her was wrong, "that no one should weigh love against expediency."

"But the weighing was already done," Tommy shrewdly observed, "and nothing would make ER go now. These brilliant people don't seem to be able to understand ER. If the whole thing had been put on the basis of wanting her no matter the cost, she wouldn't have gone."

"A new LL crisis," Anna confided in John, "brought on by Joe and his gal. It may blow over but for the present it makes for the usual tenseness."

Longing for company, Eleanor filled her calendar with engagements. In the forty-eight hours after her husband left, she met with two Yugoslavians who presented her with a report on the terrible conditions existing among the civilian population in Yugoslavia; hosted a small luncheon for the widow of Presidential Appointments Secretary Marvin McIntyre, who had died in December 1943; entertained a group of veterans from the Naval Hospital; brought the biographer Catherine Drinker Bowen to tea; met with twenty-three students from American University; had cocktails with Hick; dined with nine guests on the South Portico; hosted an evening with British war correspondent William Courtney; and paid a late-night call to Elinor Morgenthau, who was alone for the evening. On returning to the White House at ten-thirty, she worked on her mail until well after midnight, and then began a letter to Trude.

"I am very depressed tonight," she admitted. "Elliott called me from Beverly Hills to say he was going to be married on Saturday. He says he has known the girl, Faye Emerson, by name some time. He told me when here, however, he did not mean to marry til he was home, had a job etc. and I fear it is just another of his quick actions because of loneliness. I've certainly not succeeded in giving my children much sense of backing. I called FDR and told him and he took it calmly. . . . I have a curious kind of numb and dread feeling."

At Warm Springs, Roosevelt saw only a handful of visitors during his entire stay. In the mornings, he slept late, read, and attended to his mail; in the afternoons, he sunned himself on the terrace behind his house, swam in the pool, and rambled about the countryside in his '38 Ford; in the evenings, he sat beside the fieldstone fireplace in his living room, talking with Laura, Margaret, and a few local friends.

Roosevelt loved Warm Springs: the rugged terrain, the climate, the rustic cottage he had designed, "a little house," he once wrote, "flush with the ground in front but in back out over the ravine a porch as high as the prow of the ship. Wonderful for sunsets. A home for all the time I'll spend here."

Many times in the course of his presidency, Franklin had drawn solace from the "little house," but perhaps never more so than on this extended trip. The day after he arrived, Lucy Rutherfurd appeared. Taking up residence in the guest cottage, to the left of the main house, she was an ideal companion, joining Roosevelt on his afternoon drives, sitting by his side on the porch, talking over meals, reading by the fire.

Perhaps, for a few moments, Roosevelt knew the happiness of belonging to someone, of being together, of completing a circuit of emotion. In his fitted auto he drove with Lucy for hours, maneuvering the dusty roads with skill, delighting in the spectacular views, the hills of stately oaks and pines, the fields dotted with mountain laurel and wild azaleas. At times he would slip away from his cottage without the Secret Service, relishing the freedom of the open road.

On Saturday morning, December 2, Roosevelt finished his mail earlier than usual. At noon, he and Lucy drove off together to his favorite picnic retreat, Dowdell's Knob, overlooking the Pine Mountain Valley. The peaceful afternoon long remained in Lucy's mind. "You know," she told Anna months later, "your father drove me in his little Ford up to . . . Dowdell's Knob, and I had the most fascinating hour I've ever had. He just sat there and told me of some of what he regarded as the real problems facing the world now. I just couldn't get over thinking of what I was listening to, and then he would stop and say, 'You see that knoll over there? That's where I did this-or-that,' or 'You see that bunch of trees?' Or whatever it was. He would interrupt himself, you know. And we just sat there and looked."

"As Lucy said all this to me," Anna recalled, "I realized Mother was not capable of giving him this—just listening. And of course, this is why I was able to fill in for a year and a half, because I could listen."

While Franklin was with Lucy, Eleanor was embroiled in a policy struggle in Washington. Before leaving for Warm Springs, Roosevelt had appointed Edward Stettinius to replace the retiring Cordell Hull as secretary of state. Stettinius had asked for and been given authority to appoint his own assistant secretaries. When the appointments were announced, Eleanor was very upset to find that Stettinius had surrounded himself with conservatives, including James Dunn, a wealthy croquet-playing diplomat who had allied himself with General Franco in Spain, and Will Clayton, a former member of the Liberty League and the biggest cotton broker in the world.

After an unsatisfactory phone conversation with Franklin about the situation, Eleanor sat down on the night of December 4 and wrote a long, irritated letter to her husband: "I realize very well that I do not know the reasons why certain things may be necessary. . . . It does, however, make me rather nervous for you to say that you do not care what Jimmy Dunne [*sic*] thinks because he will do what you tell him to do and that for three years you have carried the State Department and you expect to go on doing it. I am quite sure that Jimmy Dunne is clever enough to tell you that he will do what you want and to allow his subordinates to accomplish things which will get by and which will pretty well come up in the long time results to what he actually wants to do.

"The reason I feel we cannot trust Dunne is that we know he backed Franco and his regime in Spain. We know that now he is arguing Mr. [John] Winant and the War Department in favor of using German industrialists to rehabilitate Germany because he belongs to the group which Will Clayton represents, plus others, who believe we must have business going in Germany for the sake of business here.

"I suppose I should trust blindly when I can't know and be neither worried or scared and yet I am both and when Harry Hopkins tells me he is for Clayton etc. I'm even more worried. I hate to irritate you and I won't speak of any of this again but I wouldn't feel honest if I didn't tell you now."

But, of course, she did speak of it again, waiting only twenty-four hours to let him know that she was still very unhappy about the State Department. "Now if Clayton brings down [First National Bank of New York President] Leon Fraser," she sarcastically remarked, "it will be perfect!" Before she closed, however, she noted that she was sending along the first page of a glowing letter she had received about the president's leadership, "one of many which has come breathing faith and admiration and since I am such a pest I thought this might compensate a little!"

The following day, she pressured him on Yugoslavia. Her conversation with the two young Yugoslavians had convinced her that something had to be done to alleviate the desperate situation in that ravaged land, where communist leader Tito's partisans were putting up a brave fight against the German army. She placed a call to Warm Springs. Dr. Bruenn, who had begged Eleanor time and again not to upset her husband, was in the living room when the call came. "She insisted that the president order troops and supplies to the partisans in Yugoslavia, forgetting what I'd said about not pushing him. He kept telling her it was impossible because there were no lines of communication and the Germans were occupying that part. But she kept pushing. He got more and more upset, as did I. She had tunnel vision. Anything interesting to her was paramount."

Italy was next. She was glad, she told her husband, that the United States was officially protesting Churchill's veto of the antifascist Count Carlo Sforza as foreign minister in the new Italian Cabinet, "but," she went on, "are we going to use any real pressure on Winston? I am afraid words will not have much effect."

Beyond dealing with the pressures from his wife, Roosevelt was bombarded with appeals from various members of his Cabinet anxious about their status in the postelection period. At seventy-seven, Stimson feared that the president might want a younger man to finish up with. He hated to be in the position where he might be dragged on beyond the time when the president really wanted him. Through Hopkins, Roosevelt let Stimson know that just the opposite was true: now that Hull was gone, Stimson was the only man of commanding stature in the Cabinet. The president wanted him to go on giving his advice and help as he had always given it.

Burdened with similar worries, Harold Ickes had sent Roosevelt a letter of resignation, hoping for reassurance that his services were still needed. Recognizing what Ickes wanted, Roosevelt penned a flattering letter from Warm Springs, teasing the old curmudgeon that if he said anything more about resigning he would find a Marine Guard from Quantico dogging his footsteps day and night. "Of course I want you to go along at the Old Stand where you have been for 12 years," Roosevelt wrote. "We must see this thing together."

"Your letter," Ickes gratefully replied, "makes me feel all fluttery. To have you write about me as you did is like an accolade to my spirit. No one can be so generous as you and from no one else would what you wrote mean so much."

Despite these intrusions, Roosevelt profited greatly from his days at Warm Springs. Dr. Bruenn was visibly pleased at the improvement in the president's appearance. The color in his skin was normal, and his spirits were high.

Eleanor talked with her husband shortly before he left Warm Springs. She was very sorry, she said, but she could not be in Washington to meet him when he returned. Her aunt Tissie (Elizabeth Hall) had died, and she had to go to New York for the funeral. "He sounds as though his three weeks in Warm Springs, Georgia had given him much enjoyment," she told her readers, "as well as time to think over the world and its affairs. Even if you are always at the end of a telephone wire, and if dispatches and pouches continue to come, still the change of scenery and the concerns of a different community . . . do something to one's mind and spirit."

• • •

On returning home, Roosevelt was greeted by the appalling news that on December 16 the Germans had caught the Allies by surprise with a massive counteroffensive in the Ardennes. Designed to drive the Allies back through Belgium to Antwerp on the North Sea, the daring German move, which became known as the Battle of the Bulge, dispelled Allied hopes for an early end to the war.

Hitler had been at work for months building up the kind of strike force that had served him so brilliantly early in the war. By mid-December, he had amassed more than 2,500 tanks, posted in 10 panzer divisions; in all, 250,000 German soldiers were facing a scant 80,000 Allied troops.

Hitler's audacious plan had been revealed to the German military only four days before the offensive began, when a dozen German generals and field commanders were gathered in a bus in the middle of the night, driven aimlessly around the countryside to make them lose their bearings, and set down at the entrance to an underground bunker which turned out to be the Führer's headquarters. There, from Hitler himself, "hunched in his chair," William Shirer wrote, "his hands trembling, his left arm subject to a violent twitching which he did his best to conceal," they learned for the first time of the mighty offensive intended to recapture the initiative for the Germans.

For ten days, with a thick mist rendering Allied operations in the air virtually impossible, the Germans drove forward, outnumbering and outgunning the unprepared American troops. At the Schnee Eifel in southeastern Belgium, nearly nine thousand Americans were forced to surrender, marking the second-largest single mass surrender in American history (Bataan was the first). For those who had imagined that Germany was essentially defeated, this was a bitter and depressing period.

Through the worst days, Roosevelt remained calm. He followed the course of the attack on the wall charts in his map room, watching somberly as the red pins, signaling German forces, multiplied, forcing the green pins, signaling the United States, into a full retreat. Yet not once, Marshall marveled, did he seek to interfere in any way with Eisenhower's command; not once did he force the Joint Chiefs to explain how this disaster had been possible. He had relied on these men through the entire war, and he would continue to rely on them now. "In great stress," Marshall declared, "Roosevelt was a strong man."

Roosevelt's steadiness in the midst of the crisis kindled gratitude in Stimson as well. "He has been extremely considerate," Stimson recorded in his diary. "He has really exercised great restraint, for the anxiety on his part must have been very heavy."

Eleanor was not as stalwart as her husband. She found the bad news from Europe difficult to absorb. "I cannot help thinking," she wrote, "of the weariness and disappointment of the men who have taken these miles of enemy territory and are now being driven back. Setbacks like these must be expected, but it makes one's heart ache to think of the gloom and disappointment among our soldiers and the news of individual losses, which will come increasingly often knocking at our doors."

By Christmas Eve, the worst of the German attack was over. With the clearing of the fog, the air superiority of the Allies was finally brought into play, and the battle began to turn. In less than a week's time, in what General James Gavin has called "an amazing performance," General George Patton, Third Army commander, was able to move his entire army the fifty miles from the Saar River to Bastogne, positioning himself to attack the Germans from the south. By the middle of January, a month after the beginning of the offensive, the German forces were back to where they had started; the Bulge had been erased.

German losses were shocking—120,000 men killed, wounded, or missing, plus a loss of 1,600 planes, 600 tanks, and 6,000 vehicles. American casualties were also brutal, with 19,000 killed and 48,000 wounded. But the Americans could replenish their infantry and their supplies, whereas the Germans could not. Hitler's wild gamble would cost him greatly; defeat in the West was now inevitable.

• • •

At the height of the Battle of the Bulge, with the army desperate for replacements, a dramatic call went out to all Negro units in the European theater. Representing a major break with traditional army policy, which kept blacks segregated in their own, predominantly service divisions, the call invited Negro soldiers to volunteer as infantrymen and fight side by side with white troops in the front lines. Negro volunteers were promised a six-week training period and then, for the first time, assignment "without regard to color or race to the units where assistance is most needed." Those who answered the call would have "the opportunity of fighting shoulder to shoulder to bring about victory."

The response to the army's appeal was phenomenal. Within a matter of weeks, more than four thousand Negro soldiers had volunteered. Currently serving as truck drivers, construction engineers, stevedores, and longshoremen, the Negro soldiers recognized they were being presented with an opportunity to affirm their competence and courage on the battlefield and to prove that whites and blacks could work together. In one engineering outfit consisting of 186 men, 171 volunteered for combat. "We've been giving a lot of sweat," one Negro ordnance man said. Now the time had come "to mix some blood" with the sweat.

For many volunteers, the chance to move from service units to combat units was the answer to their dreams. Though Negro service troops had played a critical role building bridges, constructing airports, driving trucks filled with food, clothing, and medical supplies through mud, snow, and sleet, Negroes resented seeing such a large percentage of their men (over 90 percent) assigned to the rear lines. "It is hard to identify one's self with fighting a war," one Negro soldier said, "when all one does is dig ditches and lay concrete."

For months, civil-rights leaders and the black press had been protesting the War Department's failure to use Negro soldiers in a combat capacity. Only three Negro divisions had been established, and of these only one, the 92nd, fighting with the Fifth Army in Italy, had seen extensive action on the battlefield. The 93rd had been sent to the South Pacific in 1943, but had participated in few engagements; the Second Cavalry had reached North Africa in early 1944 only to be broken up into service units. "My brother is now serving in the 2d cavalry division," Mrs. Francis Lewis wrote FDR when the conversion took place. He was "trained for a year approximately for combat duty," but now his division has been transformed into a labor unit. Please, she begged, "give our colored soldiers the opportunity to take their rightful place in this democracy."

"It is hard to decide which is more cruel," Lucille Milner observed in *The New Republic,* "this new pattern of murdering the ambition, the skills, the high potential contributions of the gifted Negro or the old pattern of physical brutality."

When asked to justify its position, the War Department had consistently fallen back on the poor records of Negro combat troops in World War I and the inability of the Negroes, as Stimson put it in a statement that became known as the "Negro is too dumb to fight" policy, "to master efficiently the techniques of modern warfare."

"It so happens," Stimson went on, "that a relatively large percentage of Negroes inducted in the Army have fallen within the lower educational classifications," so low that training proved impossible. According to a recent study, Stimson argued, 20 percent of Negroes and 74 percent of whites were rated in grades 1, 2, and 3 (considered the most rapid learners) by army classification tests; whereas 80 percent of Negroes and 26 percent of whites fell into grades 4 and 5 (considered the slowest learners).

No one could argue with Stimson's facts; what he failed to mention was the direct relationship between level of schooling and performance on the test. In the 1940s, almost 75 percent of the Negro registrants came from the poorest regions of the country, the Southern and border states, where educational and economic opportunities were so limited that four out of five Negroes had not completed the fourth grade. Indeed, the performance of whites from these same areas was almost as poor as blacks. Nationwide, of course, whites fared much better, with 41 percent of the white registrants having graduated from high school, compared with only 17 percent of the blacks. These differences in schooling proved to be major determinants of success on the classification tests.

Stimson's statement raised a passionate outcry in the black community. "The consensus," NAACP official Roy Wilkins wrote Roosevelt, was that Mr. Stimson had "offered gratuitous insult" to all Negro soldiers, miserably reflecting "upon the ability and patriotism of Negro citizens generally." What did the Negro soldier think about Mr. Stimson's blanket statement? *The Crisis* asked. "He considers it a vicious attack upon his manhood." But now, in the wake of the Battle of the Bulge, Negro soldiers were finally to be given a chance.

The first twenty-five hundred volunteers assembled in Noynes, France, in early January to begin a six-week course in tactics and weapons. The training was rigorous. When the six weeks were up, officers arrived to take the soldiers to their new assignments. Only then did the Negro soldiers learn that a change had been effected: instead of being integrated on an individual basis, they were to be formed into platoons and then sent into white combat units. Though disappointed by the change, the Negro volunteers remained enthusiastic about their adventure. "They were used to broken promises," Jean Byers shrewdly observed in her study of the Negro soldier, "and were anxious to prove their capabilities."

Within the mixed divisions, blacks and whites ate, slept, and played ball together; they used the same bathrooms and the same showers; they were given a chance to know and respect each other. As they fought their way together across Germany, prejudices would break down.

When told about the plan for integrated platoons, 64 percent of the whites were skeptical. Three months later, 77 percent said their attitudes had become highly favorable. "When I heard about it," a platoon sergeant from South Carolina admitted, "I said I'd be damned if I'd wear the same patch they did. After that first day when we saw how they fought I changed my mind. They're just like any of the other boys to us."

At one point, in the midst of heavy fighting, a black platoon was so decimated that a white squad had to be added to it. "You might think that wouldn't work," the company commander said, "but it did. The white squad didn't want to leave the platoon. I've never seen anything like it."

Treated with equality, the Negro platoons fared brilliantly. "They are aggressive as fighters," one white lieutenant said. "The only trouble is getting them to stop. They just keep pushing."

"I am mighty proud of these men," Lieutenant Robert Trager announced. "I have seen them in action that other soldiers wouldn't go through. I can say truthfully they are the best platoon I have ever led barring none."

Though Negroes were returned to their former segregated units after the Battle of the Bulge was over, the excellent performance of the integrated platoons demonstrated once again the waste and impracticality of segregation. Under the pressure of events, traditional attitudes were slowly shifting. Startling changes had occurred in a short period of time.

• • •

The Christmas holidays found the Roosevelt family together at Hyde Park. Anna and John were there, along with Sistie, Buzz, and Johnny; Ethel DuPont, FDR, Jr.'s wife, had come with their three children; and Elliott had arrived with his new wife, Faye Emerson. She is "pretty, quiet and hard," Eleanor told Hick, "but I don't think she is more than a passing house guest."

On Christmas Eve, Roosevelt sat in his customary place to the right of the fire for his annual reading of *A Christmas Carol*. In the corner of the book-lined library, surrounded by huge piles of presents, the candlelit tree glistened. At Roosevelt's feet, grandchildren of varying ages were sprawled on the rug, listening with noisy delight as the consummate old actor concocted different voices for each character, from the nervous pitch of Bob Cratchit to the bullying tone of Ebenezer Scrooge. "Next year," Eleanor said quietly when the reading was done, "we'll *all* be home again."

On Christmas Day, Elliott accompanied his father on a long drive around the estate to inspect the tree cuttings. Later that night, father and son sat together by the fire in the president's bedroom, talking. "Father spoke to me about Mother in terms I had never heard him use before," Elliott recalled. "You know, he said, 'I think that Mother and I might be able to get together now and do things together, take some trips maybe, learn to know each other again.' He talked at length of his appreciation of her as a person, her strength of character, her value to him. 'I only wish she wasn't so darned busy,' he said. 'I could have her with me much more if she didn't have so many other engagements.' "

After nearly forty years of marriage, Roosevelt still retained an intense admiration for his unusual wife, who, despite her stubbornness, her eccentricities, her moodiness, and her lack of understanding of him, remained, he told Elliott, "the most extraordinarily interesting woman" he had ever known. Thinking back to the polio attack that had nearly ended his life, he could not help remembering how steadfast she had been, how vigorously she had raised her voice against his mother in behalf of a full recovery. And surely their life together since then had been full, dramatic, and memorable.

The next day, Elliott took it upon himself to tell his mother what his father had said. "I was delighted when Mother expressed the same desire, that the day would soon come when their intimidating workloads could be rearranged to give them more time together."

"I hope this will come to pass," Eleanor said, her lips parting in a smile.

CHAPTER 23

"IT IS GOOD TO BE HOME"

As the year 1945 dawned, Roosevelt's health preoccupied his family and friends. On days when his eyes looked bright or his color seemed good or his spirits were high, his colleagues convinced themselves that their beloved chief would see the war to its end after all. "President in gleeful mood," Hassett exulted on January 11, detailing the teasing way in which Roosevelt had characterized the entrance he and Pa Watson had made into the bedroom that morning: "said we tripped in like fashion mannequins and, sitting there in bed, gave an imitation." A few days earlier, Budget Director Harold Smith recorded his own delight in finding that the president was looking "very well" and seemed in good form.

There were other days, however, when his lips were blue and his hands shook, when his mind was unable to focus and his best attempts to rally his energies collapsed in exhaustion. After a Cabinet meeting on January 19, Frances Perkins had an anguished sense of the president's enormous fatigue. "He had the pallor, the deep gray color of a man who had long been ill," she observed. "He looked like an invalid who had been allowed to see guests for the first time and the guests had stayed too long."

Sometimes, Perkins recalled, Roosevelt could go in a matter of hours "from looking pretty well to looking very badly," almost as if the spring of his remarkable vitality had suddenly snapped. His eyes would assume a glassy look, his jaw would slacken, and his mouth would droop. His fatigue at that point was apparently so deep that he was not even aware that he had lost control of the muscles in his face.

There was a story told on Capitol Hill that winter of two senators, Wyoming's Joseph O'Mahoney and Connecticut's Frank Maloney, who came to see the president on successive half-hours. Both were old friends of Roosevelt's, both had been to the Oval Office dozens of times. When O'Mahoney emerged at the end of the first half-hour, Maloney was anxious to know how the president seemed. "He was absolutely terrific," O'Mahoney said. "He told some wonderful stories, he talked about what a pain in the ass a certain person was; he was funny; he was charming; it was just like old times." Reassured by this excellent report, Maloney went in and sat down. Roosevelt looked up but said nothing, his eyes fixed in a strange stare. After a few moments of silence, Maloney realized that Roosevelt had absolutely no idea who his visitor was. A pious Catholic, Maloney crossed himself and ran to get Pa Watson, fearing the president had suffered a stroke. "Don't worry," Watson said. "He'll come out of it. He always does." By the time Maloney returned to the Oval Office, Roosevelt had pulled himself together. Smiling broadly, he greeted Maloney warmly and launched into a spirited conversation.

So the days passed, some good, some bad, as Roosevelt moved toward an unprecedented fourth term.

• • •

On the morning of inauguration day, January 20, 1945, the family quarters of the White House echoed with the sounds of children racing through the corridors, anxious to play outside in the newly fallen snow. Roosevelt had insisted that every grandchild—a baker's dozen in all, ranging in age from two to eighteen—attend the ceremony. He wanted the family all together, Eleanor later recalled, "realizing full well this would certainly be his last inauguration, perhaps even having a premonition that he would not be with us very long. . . ."

The White House "bulged at the corners," Eleanor recalled, with every bedroom, dressing room, and maid's room on both the second and third floors occupied. In order to find space for two grandchildren and their nurse who arrived at the last minute, Eleanor had to give up her own bedroom suite and sleep in the maid's quarters on the third floor. "I was not too comfortable, nor, I fear, too sweet about it," she admitted, but she was determined to honor her husband's request.

Roosevelt had also asked that his eldest son, Jimmy, on whose arm he had leaned through three inaugurations, be granted temporary duty in Washington so that he could be present at this fourth ceremony. Jimmy later recalled standing beside his father that morning as Roosevelt gazed out the window across the snow-covered lawn, watching the children coast down the hill and then race to the top again. Though the gentle slope of the White House lawn could hardly compare with the sledding hill at Hyde Park, Roosevelt delighted in watching his grandchildren enjoy the same simple pleasures he had enjoyed as a child.

Turning his attention to the morning papers, Roosevelt's eye was drawn to the headline story in *The New York Times:* "Housekeeper Rejects Roosevelt's Menu Choice for Luncheon." The story detailed the battle between the president and Mrs. Nesbitt over the president's desire to serve chicken à la king at his inaugural luncheon for two thousand guests. "We aren't going to have that because it's hot and you can't keep it hot for all those people," Mrs. Nesbitt flatly stated, suggesting that her word in this case was law, no matter what her boss desired. She would serve chicken salad instead, along with unbuttered rolls, coffee, and unfrosted cake.

In the weeks before the election, Roosevelt had joked with Anna and Grace Tully that the main reason he wanted to be elected to a fourth term was to be in a position to fire Mrs. Nesbitt! Yet the election had come and gone and the humorless Nesbitt remained at her post, still insisting that her only duty was to produce "plain food plainly prepared," regardless of the president's special desires. If the coffee she sent on the breakfast tray tasted bitter, then he could make his own with a percolator beside his bed. If he had a special craving for the big white asparagus that came in large cans, then his secretaries could search around and find it! As long as Henrietta Nesbitt retained the title of chief housekeeper, she and she alone was in charge.

For his fourth inaugural, Roosevelt dispensed with the traditional ceremony on the Capitol steps, as well as the marching bands, fancy floats, and hundreds of thousands of guests. "Who is there here to parade?" he replied when reporters asked whether there was going to be one. In keeping with the gravity of the moment, he prepared a five-minute speech to be delivered from the South Porch of the White House in front of the smallest inaugural crowd in generations. "Dog catchers have taken office with more pomp and ceremony," Secret Service chief Mike Reilly noted.

"The day was bitterly cold," General Marshall's wife, Katherine, recalled. "The President was pale and drawn, his hands trembled constantly, his voice appeared weak." Yet his message was strong. Grasping the edge of the lectern, he spoke quietly and poignantly of the catastrophic war that was putting America through a supreme test, "a test of our courage, of our resolve, of our wisdom, of our essential democracy. If we meet that test—successfully and honorably—we shall perform a service of historic importance which men and women and children will honor throughout all time."

After the ceremony, the luncheon began. With two thousand guests it was the largest luncheon ever held during Roosevelt's twelve years in the White House. Resting for a moment with Jimmy in the Green Room before facing the throng, Roosevelt was seized by a pain in his chest. "He was thoroughly chilled," Jimmy recalled, "and the same type of pain, though somewhat less acute, that had bothered him in San Diego was stabbing him again. He gripped my arm and said, 'Jimmy, I can't take this unless you get me a stiff drink. You'd better make it straight.' I brought him a tumbler half full of whiskey which he drank as if it was medicine. Then he went to the reception."

As always, the president made a determined effort to remain cheerful in the company of his guests. But he was tired and distracted, and it showed. Mrs. Woodrow Wilson was among the visitors that day; as she looked at the president, she was overcome with anxiety. "Oh, Mrs. Perkins," she cried when she saw the secretary of labor in the corridor, "did you get a good look at the President? Oh, it frightened me. He looks exactly as my husband looked when he went into his decline."

After making a short appearance at the public luncheon, the president retreated to the Red Room, where he relaxed with Princess Martha and a few friends, leaving Eleanor to circulate among the guests. All went smoothly except for one thing: the chickens Mrs. Nesbitt had bought for the chicken salad weren't frozen properly, leaving only a small amount of usable chicken for a salad that was supposed to feed two thousand people. The problem did not go unnoticed. At a party later that night, the toastmaster, George Jessel, began his remarks: "Mrs. Roosevelt, I wish to ask you seriously how it is humanly possible to make chicken salad with so much celery and so little chicken." Eleanor answered candidly, "I do not know, Mr. Jessup [*sic*]. I had a hard time finding any chicken myself." Eleanor's lighthearted response brought the house down.

• • •

Two days after his inauguration, Roosevelt embarked on a strenuous journey to meet Churchill and Stalin at Yalta, a Soviet port on the Black Sea. The secret meeting was intended to review the immediate military situation and to reach agreement on the structure of the postwar world.

The White House buzzed with rumors, if Lillian Parks' memory is to be trusted, that Eleanor "would finally be going with the President on something important"; the maids speculated that, with the sea air and the romance of the high seas, the president and first lady would become intimate once again.

The rumors proved false. Though Eleanor had humbled herself to ask the president if she could go with him on the trip, he had invited Anna instead, making a choice that came out of his own feelings, his need for someone to take care of him, to sit by his side, to preserve his strength—all the things his wife could not do. "If you go," he rationalized to Eleanor, "they will all feel they have to make a great fuss, but if Anna goes it will be simpler," especially since Churchill and Harriman were both bringing their daughters.

"You know," Pa Watson explained to Frances Perkins, who thought it odd that Anna was going instead of Eleanor or one of the boys, "Anna can do things with her father and with other people that the boys can't. They can't manage him. Anna can handle him. She can tell him, 'You mustn't see people.' 'You mustn't do that. It tires you out. You'll be no good tomorrow.' And she can also handle the other people."

For her part, Anna was so thrilled at the chance to meet Stalin and serve as her father's confidante that she refused to acknowledge that she was hurting her mother. Realizing that if her mother went she could not go, she hungrily accepted the rationale that daughters would be simpler than wives. "I wanted desperately to go," she admitted later, "so I just fell in with this, just blocked it out for my own purposes very selfishly."

Eleanor made a valiant effort to rise above her hurt and go about her business, but it was impossible to ignore the bustle of preparations when everyone else seemed to be going—Jimmy Byrnes, Pa Watson, Harry Hopkins, Admiral Leahy, even Ed Flynn, the boss of the Bronx. "I am tired and very depressed tonight," she admitted to Joe Lash the day before the president left. "The next years seem impossible to live through."

The presidential party boarded the U.S.S. *Quincy* in Newport News, Virginia, the morning of the 23rd. Anna later recalled sitting alone with her father on the deck that morning as the ship steamed past the coastline of Virginia. Feeling relaxed and happy, Roosevelt discoursed at length on the various birds that inhabited the Virginia shores. Then, suddenly, he told Anna to look at a particular spot on the shoreline. "Over there," he said casually and without a trace of self-consciousness, "is where Lucy grew up."

"Ocean voyage is certainly the life of Reilly," Anna reported to John that first day, as the great warship cruised the Atlantic in weather that would remain calm the entire week. The gentle roll helped the president sleep until ten or eleven in the morning; at twelve, he lunched with Anna and his male cronies; in the afternoons, he lounged on the deck, enjoying the warm sunshine, sorting his stamps, and reading quietly by himself; at five, cocktails were served on the deck, followed by dinner and a movie. "Oh darling," an exultant Anna wrote John, trying as always to shore him up, "I'm so grateful to you for letting me come—because I know that you would have been of so much more real value."

On the seventh day at sea, January 30, Roosevelt celebrated his sixty-third birthday. He had forgotten the date, he claimed, until a surprise package from Lucy Rutherfurd and Margaret Suckley arrived with his breakfast tray. It contained "a lot of little gadgets," he delighted in telling Anna, including a pocket comb, a room thermometer, and a cigarette lighter that could be used in the wind; they were whimsical gifts, but they signaled affection and intimate knowledge on the part of the givers, and that made him feel good.

That evening, Anna added a surprise of her own, a festive party with five cakes, three of the same size representing the first three terms, then a huge cake representing the fourth term, and finally a tiny cake with a large question mark representing a possible fifth term. She had also engineered the perfect present—a handsome map showing the route to Yalta along with a little message from everyone accompanying him and a brass ashtray fashioned from the case of a five-inch shell that had been fired by the *Quincy* during her first combat engagement at D-day. "Anna made the dinner a gala occasion," Jimmy Byrnes recalled, noting that Roosevelt seemed happy and gay even though he looked tired and worn. "Our birthday dinner," Anna told John, "was a great success. [Roosevelt] won all the money at poker, and seemed to enjoy all our little jokes."

Twenty-five hundred miles away, Eleanor was working on her husband's behalf, making the rounds of the annual birthday balls held to benefit the March of Dimes in its fight against polio. Starting early in the morning with the making of a newsreel, she hosted the traditional birthday luncheon for movie stars in the East Room, met with the trustees of the National Foundation for Infantile Paralysis, toured five balls, returned to the White House to read the president's message of appreciation to the nation, journeyed to the State Department to cut the cake at midnight, and then resumed her tour of the balls until 1 a.m.

Throughout the long day, Eleanor remained, as always, gracious and outgoing, but it was not hard to see her loneliness under the public persona. In the midst of her public duties, she tried to send a personal birthday telegraph to her husband, but the ship was under radio silence because two German submarines had been reported nearby. As it happened, the only communication he received from her that day was an irritated letter she had written four days earlier about the battle that had broken out in Congress over Roosevelt's nomination of Henry Wallace to succeed Jesse Jones as secretary of commerce.

She was sorry she had to bother him about this, she had written, but if he refused to put his prestige behind Wallace, the conservatives would have their way and it would look as if he had nominated Wallace simply to have him beaten. "Of course Jones has behaved horribly," she insisted, "but I guess he's the kind of dog you should have ousted the day after election and given him the reasons."

Tired and sick, anxious about Yalta, Roosevelt did not need to hear this from his wife on his birthday. Though he rarely chose to reveal to anyone the full extent of what he was thinking or feeling, he spoke openly to Anna about his frustrations with Eleanor. It's "a very sad situation," Anna told John: "the only times he has mentioned her to me on this trip have been times when he's griped about her attitudes toward things he's done or people he likes."

As the *Quincy* was steaming east into the Mediterranean, Churchill was flying south to the island of Malta, where he and Roosevelt were scheduled to meet before going to Yalta. The journey began badly, Lord Moran reported: the prime minister was running a temperature and feeling generally out of sorts. Huddled in his greatcoat against the seat of the plane, he looked, his daughter Sarah observed, "like a poor hot pink baby about to cry!" It was a restless night for all; when Churchill awoke the next morning, he was "in the doldrums," turned his face against the wall, and called for Clemmie, who was thousands of miles away.

The war had taken its toll on both partners of the Grand Alliance. Roosevelt's decline was more dramatic, but some of Churchill's vaunted vitality had also been sapped. "It is not the flesh only that is weaker," Moran lamented. "Martin [Churchill's private secretary] tells me that his work has deteriorated a lot in the last few months; and that he has become very wordy, irritating his colleagues in the Cabinet by his verbosity." For four years, Moran noted, Churchill had kept his own counsel, "sharing his secret thoughts with no man." Whereas the president had Harry Hopkins, "someone in whom he could confide," Churchill had no one to whom he could open his heart and unburden his soul. And now, Moran believed, he was paying the price for his long isolation.

Harry Hopkins, meanwhile, was also in bad shape. He had traveled to London for talks with Churchill, then to Paris to confer with de Gaulle, and then to Naples to join Stettinius. "He was so weak," Stettinius recalled, "that it was remarkable that he could be as active as he was. He fought his way through difficult and trying conferences on coffee, cigarettes, an amazingly small amount of food, paregoric and sheer fortitude." On the flight from Italy to Yalta, he was so sick that he lay collapsed in a cot the entire ride.

When the *Quincy* pulled into the Grand Harbor at Valetta, Malta, Churchill came aboard. The president was sitting on the deck waiting for his old friend. Sarah Churchill, who had not seen Roosevelt since Teheran, was shocked at "the terrible change in him," as were most of the members of the British party. But Churchill saw what he wanted to see—the smile, the jaunty cigarette holder, the cloth cap. He wrote Clemmie that night, "my friend has arrived in the best of health and spirits. Everything going well!"

Over the course of the day, Sarah felt better about Roosevelt, her attention drawn from his physical condition to his mental outlook, to his "bright charm" and his "brave expansive heart." Churchill was also struck by the president's high spirits and his friendly manner. "He must have noticed the candle by my bed when we were at the White House," Churchill told Moran, "because there was a small lighted candle at the luncheon table by my place to light my cigar."

That evening, Roosevelt and Churchill dined together on the *Quincy*. At ten-thirty, Anna gently but firmly broke up the party so that her father could rest before his midnight flight to Russia. Minutes later, as Anna was frantically packing, Hopkins and his son Robert arrived at her cabin. "Harry demanded a drink," Anna wrote in her diary, "so I gave him my one bottle. A few minutes after they had left I went to get the bottle and it was gone. Stettinius had confided to me earlier that Hopkins has a return of his dysentery, has been drinking far too much."

When Roosevelt arrived at Luga Airport in Malta, some twenty transport planes were waiting to carry the British and American delegations, totaling nearly seven hundred persons, to the Crimea. The flight was long and cold.

Churchill was standing on the airfield in Saki when the president exited from his plane. Together they inspected the guards of honor, the president sitting in an open jeep, Moran noted, while the prime minister walked beside him, "as in her old age an Indian attendant accompanied Queen Victoria's phaeton."

The drive from the Saki airfield to Yalta was eighty miles. Anna placed herself beside the president "so that he could sleep as much as he wanted and would not have to 'make' conversation." During the drive, Harriman pulled up beside the president's car and told Anna that in about forty-five minutes they would reach a house along the road where Foreign Commissar Vyacheslav Molotov was waiting with vodka, wines, caviar, fish, bread, and butter. With Roosevelt's concurrence, the decision was made not to stop; the drive to Yalta was long and hard enough as it was. The same invitation was issued to Churchill, Anna noted, and that "tough old bird accepted with alacrity." Though Churchill had already eaten lunch in his car, he could see how disappointed the Russians were at the Americans' failure to stop, so he fell on the food and showed by his appetite his appreciation of Molotov's magnificent refreshments. Relaxed and fortified, he returned to his car and proceeded to recite Byron's "Childe Harold" to Sarah for the remainder of the journey to Yalta.

• • •

The Conference was held in Lividia Palace, the former summer home of Czar Nicholas. Situated more than 150 feet above the Black Sea, the fifty-room palace included a main building with two wings, each one built around a separate courtyard, and a turreted tower with Moorish arches. Roosevelt was installed in the czar's bedroom in the left wing; Anna found herself in the opposite wing, "a block and a half away." General Marshall and Admiral King were given suites on the second floor, where the czarina and her five children had lived, while the remaining members of the delegation, including Hopkins, Leahy, Watson, Byrnes, and Harriman, were scattered in various sections of the palace.

The first session of the conference was held on February 4 in the grand ballroom, a rectangular room with arched windows and a huge fireplace. Stalin invited Roosevelt to sit in the presider's chair, closest to the fireplace, while he and Churchill took seats on opposite sides of the round table. With Roosevelt were Hopkins, Leahy, Stettinius, and Bohlen; with Churchill were Anthony Eden, Undersecretary to the Foreign Office Sir Alexander Cadogan, Secretary to the Cabinet Sir Edward Bridges, and British Ambassador Sir Archibald Clark Kerr. With Stalin were Foreign Commissar Molotov, Ambassador to the United States Andrei Gromyko, Soviet Deputy Foreign Minister Andrei Vyshinsky, and Soviet diplomat Ivan Maisky.

The discussion opened with a review of the military situation. For the first time, Stettinius noted, the Russian generals talked from maps, mentioning exactly where their troops were at the moment and making a complete disclosure of their plans for the future. On the Eastern front, Soviet troops had enveloped Budapest, taken Warsaw, driven the Nazis out of Yugoslavia, penetrated Austria and Czechoslovakia, and conquered East Prussia, and were now poised at the Oder River, less than fifty miles from Berlin. On the Western front, General Marshall reported that the Allies had completely recovered from the Battle of the Bulge, had expelled all German forces from Belgium, and were now entering Germany east of St. Vith. Six of the capital cities captured by the Germans in 1939 and 1940 were now liberated: Paris, Brussels, Warsaw, Belgrade, Budapest, and Athens. The war in Europe was slowly coming to an end. When the presentations of the generals were completed, the Big Three agreed to complete collaboration on all future military operations. "This is the first time such a thing has ever been done," Stettinius marveled.

While the first session was going on, Anna was "sitting on tacks." Her father was hosting the formal dinner that evening, and no definite list of invitees had been made up. Harriman kept assuring her "it was quite customary to do things this way," but Anna worried that certain people's feeling would be hurt. Her worries were realized when Dr. Bruenn told her Jimmy Byrnes was having a tantrum and she had better go to his room at once.

"Fire was shooting from his eyes," Anna recorded in her diary that night. He was furious that he had not been invited to the formal session: "Harry H. had been at the Conference—why hadn't he?" And now, Anna wrote, "he was asking me the only favor he would ever ask me in his life: to go and tell FDR that he would not attend the dinner." Knowing that her father would be upset, Anna argued and cajoled for twenty minutes. Many times she was tempted to say, "Okay, who cares anyhow if you do or don't get to the dinner," but she realized that if Byrnes did not go there would be thirteen at the table, "which I knew would give superstitious FDR ten fits. Finally won my argument on the stupid basis of superstition."

The dinner was a success. Stalin, Roosevelt, and Churchill were all in good humor, and the conversation was relaxed and personal. No subject of importance came up until the last half-hour, when the discussion turned to the rights and responsibilities of big powers versus small powers. "Stalin made it quite plain," Bohlen recorded, "he felt the three great powers which had borne the brunt of the war . . . should have the unanimous right to preserve the peace. Said it was ridiculous to believe Albania would have an equal vote with three powers who won war. He would never agree to have any action of any of the great powers submitted to judgment of small powers."

Both Roosevelt and Churchill recognized in Stalin's thought an undercurrent of antagonism to the concept of the United Nations, but little more was said at the moment, and the dinner ended on a pleasant note. "FDR seemed happy about both the Conference and the dinner," Anna wrote. "FDR says Jimmy [Byrnes] made a fine toast. This amused me as J. had told me very firmly that if he went to the dinner as a favor to me, he would not open his mouth!"

"Life is quickly assuming a definite pattern," Anna noted. In the mornings, while the president ate breakfast, worked on his pouch, and dictated responses to America's domestic problems, Anna made the rounds of Harry's room, Steve Early's room, and anyone else she ran into, "to pick up information on the day's plans, what meetings are scheduled outside the big conference, gossip on meetings, etc."

After making her morning rounds, she went into her father's room "to get his version of events and fill him in with any gossip" she had picked up that might be "amusing or interesting" to him. Her talks with Harry, for instance, revealed that Harriman's daughter Kathleen and FDR, Jr., had had a heavy romance two years earlier, and that Hopkins used to carry letters between them.

The plenary sessions convened after lunch and lasted for four or five hours. When he returned to his suite, Roosevelt typically enjoyed a quick rubdown and then dressed for dinner, with people rushing in and out of his study, sometimes at ten-minute intervals. The formal dinners, complete with buckets of Caucasian champagne and thirty or forty standing toasts, were generally lengthy affairs, making sleep a precious commodity.

"Just between you and me," Anna explained to John, "we are having to watch OM very carefully from physical standpoint. He gets all wound up. Seems to thoroughly enjoy it all but wants too many people around and then won't go to bed early enough. The result is he doesn't sleep well. Ross and Bruenn are both worried because of the old ticker trouble."

Dr. McIntire had been telling her for months that everything was going to be all right; that, as long as her father got sufficient rest, he could live a productive life for years to come. But now, at Yalta, Anna had the chance to talk at length with Dr. Bruenn, who gave her a more honest assessment. "I have found out through Bruenn who won't let me tell Ross I know," Anna confided in John, "that this ticker situation is far more serious than I ever knew. And the biggest difficulty in handling the situation here is that we can of course tell no one of the ticker troubles. (Better tear off and destroy this paragraph.)"

"I am using all the ingenuity and tact I can muster to try to separate the wheat from the chaff," she went on, "to keep the unnecessary people out of OM's room and to steer the necessary ones in at the best times. This involves trying my best to keep abreast as much as possible of what is actually taking place at the Conference so I will know who should and should not see the OM."

Harry Hopkins, Anna soon discovered, was in the best position to know what was really going on. Though he was so sick that he spent most of the conference in his bedroom, venturing out only to attend the plenary sessions, his room was a center of activity, with members of all three delegations stopping by to seek his advice. "I wish Harry was in better fettle," Lord Moran recorded in his diary. "He knows the President's moods like a wife watching the domestic climate. He will sit patiently for hours, blinking like a cat, waiting for the right moment to put in his point and if it never comes . . . he is content to leave it to another time."

It was Hopkins who persuaded Roosevelt to side with Churchill instead of Stalin on the issue of giving France a significant role in the occupation of Germany. Though France was a country without an army (Stalin's argument), Churchill was thinking of the future, when the American troops had gone home and Britain was left to contain the might of Russia. At that moment, a strong France would be critical to the overall stability of Europe. Giving France a zone of occupation was thus an important first step. Once Roosevelt was brought to agree with Churchill on this, Stalin was forced to go along.

• • •

Each of the Big Three leaders had different priorities at Yalta. Roosevelt was primarily concerned with reaching an accord on the new international organization and bringing Russia into the war against Japan as quickly as possible. The Joint Chiefs had told Roosevelt it was worth almost any price to secure the Red Army's military assistance in the Far East, where the invasion of Japan was expected to cost a million American casualties. Churchill wanted above all to maintain the British Empire and to keep Europe from being dominated by one power (thus his stance on France). Stalin had little interest in such abstractions; his mind was sharply focused on the borders of Poland, on reparations from Germany, and on various pieces of real estate in the Far East.

At meetings held the previous September with Britain and Russia at the Dumbarton Oaks estate in Washington, D.C., to discuss the framework of a postwar security organization, the United States had outlined a world organization of two houses: a large Assembly and a small Security Council consisting of seven members, four of them permanent—the U.S., Russia, Great Britain, and China. In cases that involved the sending of United Nations forces to trouble spots or mediating international disputes, any one of the Big Four could exercise a veto. However, if one of the Big Four were involved, that country could discuss the problem but could not vote on it. When the Dumbarton Oaks Conference ended, two key issues remained unresolved: the Soviet Union was refusing to go along with the voting procedures in the Security Council, and was insisting on sixteen seats in the Assembly for the sixteen Soviet republics.

At Yalta, Stalin dramatically shifted. He accepted Roosevelt's voting proposals for the Security Council and said he would now be satisfied with two or three extra seats in the Assembly for the republics that had suffered the most during the war—the Ukraine, White Russia, and Lithuania. Churchill was pleased. As long as each member of the Commonwealth had a separate vote, he had no trouble granting Stalin's request for a few extra votes for the Soviet republics.

The issue was not so easy for Roosevelt; firmly committed to the principle of one vote for each member of the Assembly, he found the idea of any extra votes at all abhorrent. Yet, if he refused to compromise with Stalin after the Russian leader had come so far, then the whole structure of the United Nations would be in jeopardy. After struggling for several days, Roosevelt endorsed Stalin's proposal on the condition that, if the United States needed to add two extra votes of its own to satisfy Congress, it could do so.

The Polish problem was to take up more time and generate more heat than any other issue at Yalta, though in many ways, as Averell Harriman observed, "events were in the saddle," and the fate of Poland had already been decided before the subject was even taken up. With Stalin's troops occupying the entire country and a communist regime firmly in place in Warsaw, "it would have taken," Harriman argued, "a great deal more leverage than Roosevelt and Churchill in fact possessed, or could reasonably be expected to apply, in order to alter the situation fundamentally."

Roosevelt was willing to be flexible about Poland's borders—the Soviet plan basically called for the westward movement of the entire country, compensating Russia at Germany's expense—as long as the government itself was free, independent, and strong. "The most important matter," Roosevelt argued in his opening presentation, "is that of a permanent government for Poland . . . a government which would represent all five major parties." Churchill agreed: "I am more interested in the question of Poland's sovereign independence and freedom than in particular frontier lines. I want the Poles to have a home in Europe and to be free to live their own lives there. This is what we went to war against Germany for—that Poland should be free and sovereign."

Now it was Stalin's turn. "The Prime Minister has said that for Great Britain the question of Poland is a question of honor. For Russia it is not only a question of honor but of security." For more than a century, Poland had been the traditional invasion route to Russia; Napoleon had come that way, Hitler had come that way, and the Soviet Union was determined that this would never happen again. Indeed, Stalin threatened, he would continue the war as long as necessary in order to ensure a friendly government in Poland. This was, he concluded, "a matter of life and death for the Soviet State."

Realizing that without a settlement on Poland the Big Three would break up, Roosevelt did what he could in the days that followed to extract concessions from Stalin. He got Stalin to agree that the communist government in Warsaw should be "reorganized on a broader democratic basis" to include the leaders of the exile government in London, and that "free and unfettered elections" would be held soon, perhaps within a month. On paper it looked good, but the critical matter of supervising the elections to ensure that they were truly free remained obscure.

As it was written, the formula was "so elastic," Admiral Leahy complained to Roosevelt, "that the Russians can stretch it all the way from Yalta to Washington without even technically breaking it."

"I know, Bill," Roosevelt wearily replied, "I know it. But it's the best I can do for Poland at this time."

In the end, Roosevelt biographer James MacGregor Burns concludes, Roosevelt's position on Poland resulted not, as many have since charged, from "naïvete, ignorance, illness or perfidy, but from his acceptance of the facts: Russia occupied Poland. Russia distrusted its Western allies. Russia had a million men who could fight Japan. Russia could sabotage the new peace organization. And Russia was absolutely determined about Poland and always had been."

The Polish issue settled, Roosevelt turned back to his original goal: securing Russian help in the war against Japan. The costly invasions of Iwo Jima and Okinawa were about to begin. The American military chiefs believed that the war against Japan would continue at least eighteen months after Germany's surrender. The first test of the atomic bomb was not to take place for another five months. The United States needed Russia's help. It could mean the savings of tens of thousands of American lives.

With all this in mind, Roosevelt negotiated a secret agreement with Stalin in which Stalin pledged to enter the war against Japan within two to three months of Germany's surrender. In return, Roosevelt agreed to legitimize Russian claims in the Far East, including the recovery of southern Sakhalin from Japan, the annexation of Japan's Kurile Islands, the lease of Port Arthur as a naval base, the right to use the international port at Dairen, and a joint share with the Chinese in control over the Manchurian railroads.

High spirits were evident on the part of all three leaders on February 8, when it was Stalin's turn to host the formal dinner. Held at Yusupov Palace, Stalin's sumptuous dinner lasted until 2 a.m., with forty-five standing toasts. Stalin toasted Churchill as "the bravest governmental figure in the world," the courageous leader of a great nation that had stood alone "when the rest of Europe was falling flat on its face before Hitler." In reply, Churchill toasted Stalin as "the mighty leader of a mighty country that had taken the full shock of the German war machine" and broken its back. Stalin then saluted Roosevelt as "the man with the broadest conception of national interest; even though his country was not directly endangered, he had forged the instruments which led to the mobilization of the world against Hitler."

• • •

"We have wound up the Conference, successfully, I think," Roosevelt happily reported to Eleanor as the presidential party left Yalta. "I am a bit exhausted but really all right. It has been grand hearing from you."

Roosevelt's long absence had been hard on Eleanor. Though she had passed the first week pleasantly enough at her apartment in New York, she seemed at loose ends in Washington, feeling far removed from the center of action, waiting every day for mail from her husband and daughter. "LL was really so happy to get a letter from you," John reported to Anna. "She has had so little word. . . . That is somewhat tragic." Anna and John wrote faithfully to one another almost every day—"What a lonesome barn this is," John told Anna the day after she left; "only one night and I am dying"—but Eleanor heard from Franklin only twice.

Matters were not improved when Roosevelt asked Lieutenant A. L. Conrad, a White House courier who had returned early from Yalta, to bring Eleanor a bouquet of flowers. "Lt. Conrad came to lunch," Eleanor reported to Franklin, "and brought the orchids which he said you told him to get me. Many thanks dear but I rather doubt his truth since you wouldn't order orchids [orchids were tremendously expensive at that time of year] and so I suggest you don't forget to pay him!"

But personal hurts seemed secondary, Eleanor conceded, against the momentous events at Yalta. When the official communiqué from the conference came over the wires, Eleanor was pleased to hear that full agreement had been reached on the structure of the new United Nations. This to her was the most important issue at Yalta. "All the world looks smiling!" she told Franklin. "You must be very well satisfied and your diplomatic abilities must have been colossal. I think having the first United Nations meeting in San Francisco is a stroke of genius."

The mood of the American delegation as they boarded the *Quincy* on Great Bitter Lake was one of "supreme exultation" as telegrams of praise flooded in from around the world. Though parts of the protocol remained secret, the published communiqué met the enthusiastic response of opinion leaders everywhere. The fact that agreement was reached on so many subjects, ranging from the United Nations to German reparations to the role of France and the frontiers of Poland, seemed extraordinary. William Shirer labeled the agreements "a landmark in human history"; the *New York Times* editorialized that they seemed "to justify or surpass most of the high hopes placed on this fateful meeting."

"We really believed in our hearts," Hopkins later recalled, "that this was the dawn of the new day we had all been praying for and talking about for so many years."

But as the *Quincy* proceeded westward to Algiers, clouds seemed to settle over the ship. Hopkins was by now so desperately ill that he was unable to leave his cabin. The thought of the nine-day voyage across the Atlantic in rough seas filled him with dread, and he decided to leave the ship at Algiers, rest at Marrakesh for a few days, and then fly back to Washington.

Roosevelt was angered by Hopkins' decision to leave. "Why did Harry have to get sick on me," he muttered, his voice trailing off. He was counting on Hopkins to help with the report on the Yalta Conference, which he had promised to deliver to Congress as soon as he returned. Though Sam Rosenman was scheduled to come aboard and help with the speech, no one but Hopkins knew the full story of what had gone on and what could be revealed.

"The president was good and mad," Harry's son Robert recalled, "so much so that he didn't actually say goodbye when he left. Dad had always rallied before, the president reasoned. Why couldn't he rally now? Besides, the best road to recovery was to keep your spirits up, and the best way to do that was to stay together."

Weary himself, the president was unable to see that Hopkins, who had always been there beside him, loving him and fighting for him, had simply reached the limit of his endurance. All that Roosevelt could see was that Hopkins was leaving him, as Missy had left him before, and Louis Howe before that. Perhaps, if Roosevelt had been able to explain any of those feelings to Hopkins, Hopkins might have stayed on the ship. But the sad truth is that nothing was said, and the two old friends parted with a frosty farewell that proved to be their last.

Two days later, Roosevelt's military aide, the bluff and genial Pa Watson, suffered a cerebral hemorrhage aboard the *Quincy* and died. "One moment he was breathing and the next his pulse had stopped," Anna recorded in her diary. McIntire and Bruenn broke the news to Roosevelt in his cabin while Anna waited and worried outside. "He was very, very upset," Bruenn recalled. "I shall miss him almost more than I can express," Roosevelt said.

"Many in Washington considered Watson merely a jovial companion to the President," Sam Rosenman observed. "He was much more. Like Missy, he had an uncanny instinct for distinguishing between the fake and the genuine in human beings and human conduct.... The President had seen many of his friends die; but in his weakened and tired condition, the death of Watson seemed to have a more depressing effect on him than the death of any of the others."

For days, the president remained in his cabin, withdrawn, quiet, and preoccupied, refusing to work with Rosenman. "It was a sorry ship," Rosenman recalled. It was not until February 26, the day before the *Quincy* was scheduled to land at Newport News, that Roosevelt finally agreed to go over the minutes of the meetings and begin working on the speech. It was "none too soon," Rosenman remarked.

Knowing of Watson's death and Hopkins' illness, Eleanor was nervous as she waited for her husband to come home, fearing that he would be in worse shape than when he left. Yet, to her surprise, when he landed in Washington, he seemed unaccountably well and, in spite of the sorrow, retained some of the exhilaration of the trip, "leading you to forget" for a moment, she said, how tired he was.

"Look at the communiqué from the Crimea," he told Eleanor, "the path it charts! From Yalta to Moscow, to San Francisco and Mexico City, to London and Washington and Paris! Not to forget it mentions Berlin! It's been a global war, and we've already started making it a global peace."

• • •

In the years to come, the rosy assessments that surrounded the initial publication of the Yalta protocol would give way to severe criticism as the Yalta Conference came to be seen by many as a symbol of failure in foreign policy, a series of surrenders to Russia that led inexorably to the Cold War and the loss of Eastern Europe to the communists. Critics, profiting by their knowledge of later events not known to the participants at the time, have focused most of the blame on Roosevelt, a "sick man at Yalta," unfit for the job of negotiating with Stalin.

What is the truth of these claims? It must be agreed at the outset that Roosevelt *was* a sick man at Yalta. It was obvious to anyone who saw him that his strength was waning. "To a doctor's eye," Lord Moran wrote, stunned at the change in the president since Quebec, "he has all the symptoms of hardening of the arteries of the brain in an advanced stage so that I give him only a few months to live." Averell Harriman, who had not seen the president since November, was equally taken aback. "The signs of deterioration seemed to me unmistakable," Harriman later admitted.

Still, the question remains: did Roosevelt's physical condition impair his judgment? There is no simple answer. The Americans who worked with him most closely at the conference—Stettinius, Leahy, Harriman, and Byrnes—are unanimous in their belief that Roosevelt was in full possession of his faculties at all times. Admittedly, Harriman observed, the long conference tired him. "Nevertheless he had blocked out definite objectives which he had clearly in his mind and he carried on the negotiations to this end with his usual skill and perception." Admiral Leahy agreed. "It was my feeling," Leahy later concluded, "that Roosevelt conducted the Crimean Conference with great skill and that his personality had dominated the discussions."

Even Anthony Eden, who was disheartened when he first saw Roosevelt at Malta, later acknowledged that Roosevelt's ill-health did not seem to alter his judgment. To Eden's surprise, Roosevelt not only kept up with Churchill in the round of conferences, but also found time to conduct a whole separate enterprise—negotiations with Stalin over the Far East.

Certainly, if Roosevelt had been in better health, he might have held out longer on a number of detailed points—he might have insisted on stronger safeguards with regard to Poland, he might have kept more ambiguous his commitments to Russia in the Far East, he might have fought harder against the two extra Assembly seats—but in the end, there is no evidence that fine points of language would have made a great deal of difference in the course of events. "If Stalin was determined to have his way," Averell Harriman concluded years later, "he was bound to bend or break the agreements even if they'd been sewn up more tightly." Unless, of course, the people of the United States were willing to go to war with Russia over Poland or Latvia or Lithuania, which Harriman seriously doubted they were.

• • •

At noon on March 1, 1945, Roosevelt went up to the Capitol to address a joint session of Congress. The chamber was filled to overflowing with everyone anxiously awaiting the president's report on the Yalta Conference. In time-honored fashion, the doorkeeper announced the members of the Supreme Court, the members of the Cabinet, and finally the president of the United States. A hush went over the great chamber as the door opened to reveal the president seated in his wheelchair. In all the times the president had addressed the Congress, this was the first time he had ever allowed himself to come down the aisle in his wheelchair. Always before, either supported by the arm of a colleague or leaning on crutches, he had "walked" to the well.

And now, also for the first time, instead of standing behind the lectern in a position above the well, he seated himself in a soft chair in front of a small table on the floor below the dais. "I hope you will pardon me for the unusual posture of sitting down during the presentation of what I want to say," he began, "but I know that you will realize that it makes it a lot easier for me in not having to carry about ten pounds of steel around on the bottom of my legs; and also because I have just completed a fourteen thousand mile trip."

The applause at this point was sustained. Seated in the front row, Frances Perkins found herself close to tears. "It was the first reference he had ever made to his incapacity, to his impediment, and he did it in the most charming way. I remember choking up to realize that he was actually saying, 'You see, I'm a crippled man.' He had never said it before and it was one of the things that nobody ever said to him or even mentioned in his presence. It wasn't done. It couldn't be done. He had to bring himself to full humility to say it before Congress."

For twelve years, Roosevelt had engaged in what writer Hugh Gallagher has felicitously called "a splendid deception." The public had no idea that their president could stand only for short periods of time, that he could walk only when pushed along by the momentum of another person, that he had to be carried up and down steps and helped into bed at night by his valet. Eleanor's young friend Jane Plakias remembered her shock when she first realized the extent of Roosevelt's paralysis. "I was at a picnic at Val-Kill. I saw a car drive up and two big Secret Service agents lifted Roosevelt out of the backseat and carried him into his wheelchair. It never occurred to me he couldn't walk. I never got over that."

There was an unspoken code of honor on the part of the White House photographers that the president was never to be photographed looking crippled. In twelve years, not a single picture was ever printed of the president in his wheelchair. No newsreel had ever captured him being lifted into or out of his car. When he was shown in public, he appeared either standing behind a podium, seated in an ordinary chair, or leaning on the arm of a colleague. If, as occasionally happened, one of the members of the press corps sought to violate the code by sneaking a picture of the president looking helpless, one of the older photographers would "accidentally" block the shot or gently knock the camera to the ground. But such incidents were rare; by and large, the "veil of silence" about the extent of Roosevelt's handicap was accepted by everyone—Roosevelt, the press, and the American people.

But now the energy required to sustain the deception was no longer there. The effect on the listeners was electric. Even though the speech itself was too long and rambling, the reaction to it was overwhelmingly favorable. Freed from the burden of his braces, Roosevelt delivered an intimate, chatty address that sounded, Eleanor noted, as if he were in his private study talking to a small group of friends.

For years, Roosevelt's handicap had been regarded as a badge of courage by those who had worked closely with him, witnessing the extraordinary effort he had to make every day to overcome his physical affliction. And now, for a brief moment, the entire chamber was allowed to see what Roosevelt's colleagues had always seen. But rather than lessening their regard for him, as Roosevelt had always feared it might, this glimpse of Roosevelt's vulnerability only magnified the power and charm of his personality.

"First of all," Roosevelt said, opening the formal part of his speech, "I want to say, it is good to be home." He then went on to discuss the work of the conference, the plans to bring defeat to Germany with the greatest possible speed, the design for the new United Nations. "This time," he insisted, as he outlined the plans for the April 25 meeting in San Francisco, "we are not making the mistake of waiting until the end of the war to set up the machinery of peace. This time, as we fight together to win the war finally we work together to keep it from happening again."

In preparing his address, Sam Rosenman later conceded, Roosevelt made "one of his major mistakes in public relations." He chose, unwisely, to keep secret for the time being that part of the Yalta agreement that granted the Soviet Union three votes in the Assembly. By deciding not to take the American people into his confidence, explaining to them how insignificant a concession this really was, Roosevelt opened himself to sharp attack when the news eventually leaked. Perhaps if Harry Hopkins had been able to work on the speech the mistake would not have been made, but Hopkins was in such terrible condition by the time his plane landed that he was forced to go straight to the Mayo Clinic in Minnesota.

Nevertheless, the speech that day was a great success, and the president, Perkins thought, looked "really well." He had a slight sunburn, which gave his skin color and vitality; his eyes were bright and his voice was strong.

• • •

Roosevelt, of course, was not well. When Canadian Prime Minister MacKenzie King visited the White House in mid-March, he was left with the distinct impression that the president was failing. "He looked much older," King observed, and "I noticed in looking at his eyes very closely that one eye had a clear direct look" while the other one was "not quite on the square."

Nonetheless, after a long talk with Roosevelt on the first evening of his visit, King was reassured. The president and the Canadian prime minister "talked steadily from 8:30 until twenty past 11," when King looked at the clock. "The President said he was not tired; was enjoying the talk." He spoke of Churchill and Stalin, of Yalta and the United Nations. And "on the whole," King concluded, "I found more strength in him than I had expected. In fact, I felt less concerned than I had at the beginning."

It was the conversation at lunch the next day that disturbed King. Word for word, Roosevelt repeated two long stories about Jimmy Byrnes' converting to Catholicism and Winston Churchill's swimming in the ocean that he had told King the night before. King noticed that Mrs. Roosevelt and Anna "seemed a little embarrassed," but nothing was said.

King was not alone in his worries. "I saw the President today," former OPA chief Leon Henderson recorded in his diary a few days later. "And I'm scared." After leaving the government, Henderson had gone into private business, and had not seen the president since 1942. "It wasn't only his appearance as an old man. . . . It wasn't just his preoccupation with other affairs. It was the whole atmosphere of incredibility. . . . It was agonizing to me to see his plain difficulty in conversation. He wandered from topic to topic. I had a horrible vision that he might grow weaker and weaker, that his enemies would trample him underfoot as they did Woodrow Wilson."

The following week, speechwriter Robert Sherwood emerged from a weekly meeting with Roosevelt feeling "profoundly depressed." Never before, Sherwood noted, had he seen the president so unnaturally quiet and even querulous. Never had he found himself "in the strange position of carrying on most of the conversation with him." The only time the president perked up, Sherwood observed, was during lunch on the sun porch, when, "under the sparkling influence of his daughter Anna," he almost seemed to be his old self.

The five-week trip to Yalta had brought Roosevelt closer to Anna than ever before, and the old man reveled in the warmth of his daughter's love. For her part, Anna had returned from Yalta full of self-possession. She had handled her responsibilities extremely well, and her father could not have asked for a better companion. And she had enjoyed herself thoroughly. "The other meetings have all been tiddlywinks compared with this one," her husband, John, happily pointed out. "So you can say fiddlesticks to your brothers."

Though Anna was never given an office in the West Wing (she worked at a desk in her bedroom), never had an official title, and never took a salary, unlike her brother Jimmy, who got $10,000 a year for assisting his father, there was no question, *Life* magazine reported that spring, that Washington considered her the one to call to get through to the Big Boss. First Louis

Howe had controlled access to the throne, later it was Missy, and still later Harry Hopkins. "But for weeks now," *Life* reporter John Chamberlain observed, "the rumor mongers have been busy whispering a new secret: control of access has passed to Anna Roosevelt Boettiger, the long-legged, energetic and handsome eldest child," the "free-speaking, free-cursing" daughter of President Roosevelt. "Anna," Jim Farley once remarked, "has the most political savvy of all the Roosevelt children."

"For purposes of public consumption," Chamberlain concluded, "she may continue to pose as someone simply living in the White House in prolonged transit from and to a newspaper job. But no matter what the White House press agents may say, it is a fair bet that Missy LeHand's shoes have at last found a permanent occupant. Daddy's girl has her work cut out for her, running Daddy."

• • •

A great deal of work had piled up while Roosevelt was at Yalta. On the domestic front, the president's first priority was passage of the National Service Act, which he had once again called upon Congress to enact in his State of the Union speech on January 6, 1945. Having come to believe that a total mobilization of all the country's human resources was needed to bring a speedy end to the war, Roosevelt was now convinced that the "work or fight" bill was essential.

The House had passed the national-service bill in February, but it was stuck in the upper chamber, where a majority of senators bridled at the thought of any further extension of controls over individuals. The Senate delay infuriated Roosevelt. "He seemed to feel," Budget Director Harold Smith reported on March 12, "he did not want to send anything more to the Congress until it had disposed of the manpower issue. . . . He felt [Congress] was kicking the manpower situation around and said that in almost every battle of the war if there had been just a little more in the way of men and materials the result could have been a little more decisively on our side."

But Roosevelt's disappointments at home that spring were more than balanced by victories abroad. In Germany, the Third Army was advancing rapidly toward the Rhine. "Don't tell anyone," General Patton telephoned General Omar Bradley, commander of the Twelfth Army Group, on the morning of March 23, "but I'm across. I sneaked a division over last night. But there are so few Krauts around here, they don't know it yet." And in the Pacific, the Battle of Iwo Jima, begun on February 19, 1945, was finally won. Halfway between Tokyo and the U.S. base on Saipan in the Marianas, the island of Iwo Jima was critical to the United States as a base from which heavily loaded B-29s could bomb Japan. To make Iwo Jima theirs, the U.S. Marines had stormed what was probably the most heavily defended spot per acre of ground in the world. Battling through caves and dugouts forty feet deep, the marines had absorbed terrible losses—more than six thousand were killed and fifteen thousand wounded, representing the greatest number of casualties in a single encounter of the Pacific war to date. But with the taking of Iwo Jima, a great victory was achieved, for American planes could now begin to bomb Japan with their full weight.

Still, the specter of Japan's zeal made it clear that the war in the Pacific would be even longer and bloodier than anyone had projected. Only two hundred of the 20,700 Japanese troops on Iwo's garrison remained alive at the end of the battle; so humiliating was the thought of capture that hundreds, perhaps thousands, committed suicide, some by leaping into the Suribachi volcano.

As reports of the Iwo Jima fighting reached Washington, Stimson met with Roosevelt to discuss the A-bomb project. Apparently several people at the State Department, including Jimmy Dunn, had become alarmed about rumors that the director of the Office of Scientific Research and Development, Vannevar Bush, and Harvard President James Conant had, at extravagant cost, sold the president a lemon. Stimson wanted to assure the president that substantial progress was indeed being made, that "practically every physicist of standing," including four Nobel Prize winners, was engaged on the project. Indeed, "the bomb was expected to be ready for testing in mid summer," Stimson promised, in plenty of time to have a major impact on the Pacific war.

Stimson went on to explain the opposing schools of thought regarding the bomb's use and future control. Though there was no question that America was developing the weapon in order to use it, the question remained: Could a demonstration of the bomb precede the military drop, "with subsequent notice to Japan that [it] would be used against the Japanese mainland unless surrender was forthcoming"?

In a conversation with economist Alexander Sachs the previous December, Roosevelt purportedly agreed with Sachs that the first step should be a nonmilitary demonstration before a team of international scientists. The next step would be a warning, outlining exactly where and when the bomb would be dropped, so civilians could escape. In a similar conversation with Vannevar Bush, Roosevelt questioned whether the bomb should actually be dropped on the Japanese or used simply as a threat. But either option remained premature until the bomb was ready.

Nor was any decision reached with regard to future control, after the war. General Leslie Groves, head of the Manhattan Project, and the military were on one side, wanting the project to remain solely in America's hands; Bush and Conant were on the other, favoring international control and free access to laboratories around the world. Whichever way the president went, Stimson argued, his policy must be in place before the bomb was ready for use. Roosevelt agreed, but nothing more was said. Feeling good about this wide-ranging conversation, Stimson left, never imagining that this was the last time he would see his boss.

• • •

In the middle of March, Lucy Rutherfurd came to Washington for a week. She stayed in Georgetown with her sister, Violetta, and her brother-in-law, William Marbury. The timing of the visit, arranged most likely with Anna's help, coincided with a three-day trip Eleanor was taking to North Carolina to speak to the legislative assembly in Raleigh and attend a conference on "Education in the Mountains" in Montreat, North Carolina.

In preparation for Lucy's arrival on Monday afternoon, March 12, Roosevelt approved a long list of visitors in the morning, including U.S. Ambassador to China Patrick Hurley, Secretary of State Edward Stettinius, U.S. Ambassador to Brazil Adolf Berle, and Budget Director Harold Smith. Smith told the president he looked well but seemed to have lost some weight. "Do you think so?" the president asked, with a look that suggested to Smith that he might be a bit sensitive about the subject.

If Roosevelt was concerned about his appearance for Lucy's sake, his worries were quickly dispelled that afternoon, when he motored to pick her up, for Lucy thought he looked more handsome than ever. While everyone else lamented his extreme thinness, Lucy told her friend Madame Shoumatoff that there was "something about his face that shows the way he looked when he was young," the way he looked when she first fell in love with him. "Having lost so much weight," Lucy said, "his features, always handsome, are more definitely chiseled."

Secret Service agents later recalled riding behind the president's car as he and Lucy headed off for a leisurely drive through the Virginia countryside before returning to the White House for dinner. Seated together in the back seat, sealed by a glass partition from the chauffeur, the two old friends enjoyed a few moments of privacy. For Roosevelt, Hick once observed, motoring was not only a favorite form of recreation, it was almost a necessity, for he had so few ways of getting a change of scene. Watching his excitement as he readied himself to leave on a drive, one visitor recalled that "he was like a little boy going to the circus."

Anna and John joined Lucy and the president for dinner that night in his study. "Never was there anything clandestine about these occasions," Anna later insisted. "On the contrary, they were occasions which I welcomed for my father because they were light-hearted and gay, affording a few hours of much needed relaxation for a loved father and world leader in a time of crisis."

Yet, if nothing underhanded was intended, the fact remained that Lucy's visits were kept strictly secret from Eleanor. "I doubt that father felt he was doing anything wrong in seeing Lucy," Jimmy observed, "but I certainly can understand his keeping it a secret because he believed mother would take it badly and would be hurt."

Lucy came to dinner again the following night, along with Anna, John, and MacKenzie King. King made no specific reference to Lucy in his diary that night, saying only that the dinner that evening was "strictly a family affair," which he "greatly enjoyed." As King got up to leave at nine-thirty,

Roosevelt said that, if there was any way he could help in the prime minister's upcoming election, he would gladly do so. Warmly shaking King's hand, Roosevelt invited him to return any time to the White House, Warm Springs, or Hyde Park. Lucy remained with the president in the study another hour and then Roosevelt went to bed.

The next day, after a busy round of appointments, Roosevelt was wheeled into the sun parlor for lunch with Lucy and Anna. Anna later recalled welcoming these rare, relaxed meals "because I felt the pressure of the war, with constant decisions to be made, must be relegated to the background occasionally." Lucy was "a wonderful person," Anna said, and "I was grateful to her." At seven-thirty that night, Lucy returned, to enjoy a three-hour dinner alone with the president.

When Eleanor came back to the White House on Thursday morning, Lucy's visits stopped. On Saturday, Eleanor and Franklin celebrated their fortieth wedding anniversary at a small family luncheon with Anna, Franklin's old friend and law partner Harry Hooker, and the Morgenthaus. If Anna felt in any way self-conscious about her curious role as go-between for her father and Lucy, she gave no evidence to anyone, remaining open and warm with both her parents. Hassett noted the "complete contrast in the position of the principals to the scene forty years ago when the bride was given away by her 'Uncle Ted,' " who, "in the very hey day of his popularity, stole the whole picture."

That evening, Franklin and Eleanor celebrated again with a small formal dinner in the State Dining Room. The guests included Crown Princess Juliana of Holland; the Dutch ambassador, Alexander Loudon, and his wife, Elizabeth; Assistant Secretary of State Nelson Rockefeller; and Anna and John. The dinner was followed by a movie, *The Suspect,* an Edwardian murder mystery about a man driven to kill his nagging wife. The party dispersed sometime after midnight. "Thus," Hassett observed, "another milestone is passed in the career of an extraordinary man and wife."

Eleanor remained in town until Monday morning, when she left on a four-day trip that would take her to New York and then to Greensboro, North Carolina, to attend a seminar on "The Returning Black Serviceman" at Bennett College and to meet with twenty-five hundred young women at the women's college of the state university. These were just the kind of gatherings Eleanor relished. "This world of young people, especially of young women," she wrote in her column, "is a very exciting world, for in their hands lies so much of the promise of this nation."

With Eleanor away, Roosevelt acted once more, writer Jim Bishop observed, "like a boy on vacation from school." He and Lucy took a long drive together through the countryside on Monday afternoon, dined with Anna and John on Tuesday, and were served tea together in the study on Wednesday. At the Gridiron dinner the following night, just after Lucy's weeklong visit had come to an end, reporter Allen Drury, who had been saddened at first to see how old the president looked, found a definite spark of the old FDR as Roosevelt passed by, "the head going up with a toss, the smile breaking out, the hand uplifted and waving in the old familiar way."

• • •

When Eleanor returned from North Carolina, she was saddened to discover that Hick had packed up her things and moved back to Long Island. Hick had been suffering for several months from diabetes, and the stress of her position at the Democratic National Committee was draining her limited energy. Under doctor's orders, she had quit her job and made arrangements to leave Washington for good.

Before leaving, Hick had penned a long farewell note to Eleanor. "The goodbyes have all been said," Hick wrote, "and presently I shall be on the way out of Washington with two orchids pinned to my shoulder.... With you as an example, I tried awfully hard to do a good job, and most of the time, I think I honestly did give the Women's division the best that was in me. But many times I was irritable and impatient and intolerant. One of the qualities I loved most in you is your tolerance....

"I wish I had the words to tell you how grateful I am for your many kindnesses these past four years. It did two wonderful things—kept me near you and made it possible for me to hang on to my house, which is infinitely precious to me. I shall miss you. Yet I shall feel that you are near. After all these years, we could never drift very far apart. You are a very wonderful friend, my dear." Though Hick's love for Eleanor had not turned into a lasting romance, as Hick had originally hoped, their friendship had remained constant.

Now the curious double life Hick had led while she lived in the White House could be brought to an end. Fearing that the politicians she worked with at the Democratic National Committee would expect her to produce favors for them if they realized she was actually staying at the White House, she had pretended she was living at the Mayflower Hotel. If someone escorted her home from a party, she would say goodbye in the lobby, walk toward the elevators, wait until her escort had departed, and then take a cab to the White House. Her closest friends, including Judge Marion Harron and a few of her former female colleagues, knew of her residence, but never once did a single reporter mention Hick's living arrangements in a story. Her secret was protected.

For Eleanor, Hick's continuing friendship had been invaluable. Never would Eleanor forget that it was Hick who had originally suggested to her that her nightly letters to her friends could be transformed into a newspaper column. Now Eleanor's syndicated column was a daily fixture, appearing six times a week in hundreds of papers in cities and towns throughout the country. Indeed, that same March, as Hick was leaving Washington, the syndicate asked Eleanor to sign up for another five years, until December

1950. She was especially pleased by the length of the contract. Since it carried her two years past the 1948 election, she would finally, she believed, be able to write without the constraints of being first lady.

But if Eleanor's career had been helped by friendship with Hick, Hick's career had suffered. By giving up her identity as a newspaperwoman, Hick later acknowledged, she had paid a terrible price. She was particularly reminded of her loss, she said, when Madame Chiang was at the White House. Eleanor had invited Hick to attend Chiang's joint press conference with the president in the Oval Office. Hick was anxious to meet Chiang but felt compelled to decline the invitation. "The office would be packed," Hick wrote. "Probably not all of the working people could get inside. I could imagine some of my former colleagues muttering, 'What's she doing, taking up room in there. She's no longer a reporter.' "

Yet, even though Hick had surrendered to her passion, she had not lost her pride. Years later, when Eleanor completed the second installment of her autobiography, she sent Hick a draft of the pages covering the first inauguration, including a description of the interview she had given Hick on inaugural day. At the end of the inaugural paragraph, Eleanor had commented: "Later I came to realize that in the White House one must not play favorites." Thinking it sounded as if she had gotten the chance to cover Eleanor Roosevelt just because she was "a nice tame pet reporter," Hick dashed off a letter to Tommy.

"Tommy, I didn't get that story because I was anybody's pet reporter.... In those days (pardon an old lady her conceit) I was somebody in my own right. I was just about the top gal reporter in the country. Forgive me but I was good, I knew it.... I got the story because I earned it.... Maybe I'm being silly. But I just can't let the high spot of my newspaper career—the only thing in my whole life I'm really proud of—fizzle out like a wet firecracker, as though I was a nice tame little girl who was somebody's pet until she learned that she didn't play favorites!"

Eleanor changed the paragraph to read: "Soon after the inaugural ceremonies Lorena Hickok, to whom I had promised an interview, came up to my sitting room. Both my husband and Louis Howe had agreed to the interview because she was the outstanding woman reporter for the Associated Press and they both had known her and recognized her ability in New York."

CHAPTER 24

"EVERYBODY IS CRYING"

On Saturday night, March 24, 1945, after dinner with Crown Princess Martha and Crown Prince Olav, Franklin and Eleanor took the overnight train to Hyde Park, where the president planned to relax, get a lot of sleep, and do a few things at the library. "Hope he responds to good air and quiet," Hassett noted the morning after their arrival.

"Everything is just beginning to grow," Eleanor observed happily. The sight of budding trees and young flowers poking through the ground combined to produce a sense of serenity and a feeling of renewal. On Sunday afternoon, Franklin spoke with Eleanor of something that had long been in his mind. He wanted her to travel with him on April 20 to San Francisco for the opening session of the United Nations, and then, sometime in late May or early June, he wanted her to accompany him to London, Holland, and the front.

They would travel by ship to Southampton and then by train to Buckingham Palace, where they would stay with the king and queen for several days. He owed a return visit to the royal family, he said, and this seemed to be the best time. Then he would like to drive with the king through the streets of London, give an address before the houses of Parliament, and spend time with Churchill at Chequers. He had already told Churchill of his plans, and the prime minister was enthusiastic.

Roosevelt, Churchill predicted, "is going to get from the British people the greatest reception ever accorded to any human being since Lord Nelson made his triumphant return to London. . . . It will come genuinely and spontaneously from the hearts of the British people; they all love him for what he has done to save them from destruction by the Huns; they love him also for what he has done to relieve their fear that the horrors they have been through for five years might come upon them again in increased fury."

After London, they would visit men on the battlefields, call on Queen Wilhelmina in Holland, stay at the Hague, and end up in Paris. So excited was Roosevelt at the thought of the trip that he had been unable to keep it a secret. He had brought it up in recent conversations with MacKenzie King and Frances Perkins and seemed as happy as he had been in months. "I have long wanted to do it," he said to Perkins. "I want to see the British people myself. Eleanor's visit in wartime was a great success. I mean a success for her and for me so that we understood more about their problems. . . . I told Eleanor to order her clothes and get some fine things so that she will make a really handsome appearance."

When Perkins protested that a trip to Europe would be too dangerous, that the Germans would be out to get him, Roosevelt put his hand over his mouth and whispered, "The war in Europe will be over by the end of May." It comforted Perkins, she said later, to know that Roosevelt realized this. "I've always remembered it."

Eleanor listened eagerly to Franklin's plans. When her husband was like this, brimful of ideas, flushed, and triumphant, there was no one like him. Perhaps, in the closeness of the moment, she, too, began imagining the trip in all its splendid detail, erasing the painful knowledge, made even more vivid in recent days, of Franklin's considerable decline.

For the first time, Eleanor sadly noted that weekend, Franklin no longer wanted to drive his own car. He let her drive, which he had never done before, and he let her mix the cocktails, something that would have been inconceivable only a few months earlier. Nor, she observed, was he able to enjoy her usual way of arguing with him on a matter of public policy. In the midst of a heated discussion on peacetime conscription, she "suddenly realized he was upset," that he "was no longer the calm and imperturbable person" who had always goaded her on to vehement arguments. "It was just another indication of the change which we were all so unwilling to acknowledge."

Yet here he was talking with such enthusiasm about plans for the future that she, too, began to believe all these trips would come to pass. Beyond San Francisco and London, he still had dreams of taking her around the world with him, and of spending a couple of years in the Middle East to help bring parts of the desert to life with reforestation, irrigation, proper farming, and conservation.

When Eleanor laughingly suggested that he might like "to enjoy life for a few years without responsibility," without taking on "new and perplexing problems," he turned to her and with very characteristic emphasis said, "No, I like to be where things are growing." His comment reminded her of something he had said years before, when they first visited the Grand Canyon. She thought it "the most beautiful and majestic sight" she had ever seen, but he disagreed. "No, it looks dead," he said. "I like my green trees at Hyde Park better. They are alive and growing."

"That sense of continuing growth and development was always keenly present with him," Eleanor observed. "He never liked to dwell on the past, always wanted to go forward." So now, though she worried about signs of ebbing strength, she took heart in his crazy plans to help straighten out the Middle East and Asia. "Does that sound tired to you?" she said to a friend who had commented on his sunken appearance. "I'm all ready to sit back. He's still looking forward to more work."

While the president was at Hyde Park, relations with Stalin reached a point of crisis. Roosevelt had been trying for weeks to put the best light on the deteriorating situation in Poland, where, in spite of Stalin's solemn agreements at Yalta, the communist regime in Warsaw was refusing to broaden its base or hold free elections. Churchill had been urging Roosevelt to intervene, warning that if forceful action were not taken soon their hopes for democracy in Poland would vanish. Roosevelt had been slow to respond, fearing that a direct confrontation with Stalin on Poland would defeat his larger dream for the United Nations.

But as continuing reports, each more disturbing than the last, filtered in from Harriman and Stettinius, Roosevelt finally agreed with Churchill that the time had come to address Stalin directly. "I cannot conceal from you," Roosevelt cabled Stalin on March 29, "the concern with which I view the developments of mutual interest since our fruitful meetings at Yalta. . . . I must make it quite plain to you that any solution which would result in a thinly disguised continuance of the present Warsaw regime would be unacceptable and would cause the people of the United States to regard the Yalta agreements as having failed."

Though Stalin evaded the issue in an unsatisfactory reply, Churchill was much relieved to know that he and Roosevelt were now acting in concert. "Our friendship," he assured the president, "is the rock on which I build for the future so long as I am one of the builders. I always think of those tremendous days when you devised Lend-Lease, when we met at Argentia, when you decided, with my heartfelt agreement, to launch the invasion of Africa and when you comforted me for the loss of Tobruk by giving me the 300 Shermans of subsequent Alamein fame. I remember the part our personal relations have played in the advance of the world cause now nearing its first military goal."

• • •

When the president returned from Hyde Park the morning of March 29, Grace Tully was saddened to see that his four-day weekend "had failed to erase any of the fatigue from his face." He looked drawn and gray, and the shadows under his eyes seemed to have darkened. "Did you get any rest at Hyde Park?" Tully asked. "Yes, child, but not nearly enough. I shall be glad to get down south."

At four that afternoon, Roosevelt was scheduled to leave for Warm Springs for a two-week rest, accompanied by Laura, Margaret, Tully, and Bruenn. He had packed his "usual leisure time paraphernalia," Tully recalled, "his stamp collection, catalogue and equipment," and was looking forward to the trip. Anna had planned to go, too, but at the last minute her six-year-old son, Johnny, had come down with a serious gland infection and had to be hospitalized at Walter Reed, where he was being administered daily doses of penicillin, a radical new drug still in a stage of experimental use.

Unable to accompany her father, Anna made arrangements for Lucy Rutherfurd to come to Warm Springs the second week of his stay. Knowing this, Franklin gently dissuaded Eleanor from coming. "He was very amusing about it," Eleanor recalled years later. "He loved going to Warm Springs but he said to me that he felt that there were certain things I had to do, and I'd better wait and come down later. He would take two people whom he enjoyed having with him, Margaret Suckley and Laura Delano, and he said, in an amusing way, that he did not have to make any effort with either of them."

The train pulled into the tiny station at Warm Springs at 2 p.m. "The President was the worst looking man I ever saw who was still alive," the station agent recalled. Mike Reilly, too, had an inkling that something was wrong when he went to transfer the president into a car. Normally the process was "pretty simple, despite his 180 pounds and his complete inability to use his legs. He depended entirely upon his hands and arms and shoulders. Usually he'd turn his back to the auto and one of the Detail would lift him. He'd reach backward until his hands had secured a firm grip on each side of the car door, and then he'd actually surge out of your arms into the car and onto the jump seat." But on this day, it took every bit of Reilly's strength to make the transfer, for the president was "absolutely dead weight."

But Reilly took heart in the knowledge that "Warm Springs had saved his life once" and could do so again. "I always felt he looked upon it as a miraculous source of strength and health," Reilly noted. So, when Roosevelt headed toward the Little White House, "it wasn't just a matter of our hoping the trip would help the Boss, we just naturally assumed it would."

By the end of a week in the warm Georgia sun, the old magic seemed to be working. "The days flowed peacefully by," Margaret Suckley recalled, "with FDR getting slowly but steadily more rested. His appetite, too, improved from day to day and his spirits rose as he felt less tired." During the mornings, he would work on his papers and give dictation; after lunch, a nap and a drive through the rolling countryside, where the peach trees were covered with fruit.

On Thursday, April 5, Sergio Osmeña, the president of the Philippines came for lunch. After Osmeña left, Roosevelt held a leisurely press conference in his living room. "He was in fine form," Suckley noted, "and looked so much better than a week ago that we almost forgot he was still not his old self. He looked as though he had put on some weight, and his face looked fuller and much less tired."

"It was a beautiful, tranquil afternoon," Merriman Smith noted; "the President was in a friendly and easy mood." While Fala waddled from one person to the next, sniffing trouser cuffs and wagging his tail, Roosevelt told reporters that he and Osmeña had discussed the war in the Pacific and the not-too-distant day of complete Philippine independence. The relaxed interview was just about over when a reporter abruptly shifted ground, asking Roosevelt to comment on a news leak that Russia was going to get three votes in the United Nations General Assembly.

"That," Roosevelt said, with a roaring laugh, "is not even subtle." But, in the genial atmosphere of his living room, Roosevelt went on to explain how the controversial three-vote situation had come about. "As a matter of fact, the plea for votes was done in a very quiet way. Stalin said to me—and this is the essence of it—'You know, there are two parts of Russia that have been completely devastated. . . . One is the Ukraine, and the other is White Russia. In these sections, millions have been killed, and we think it would be very heartening—would help build them up—if we could get them a vote in the Assembly.' It is not really of any great importance. It is an investigatory body only." With this, Roosevelt drew the conference to an end and went for a nap.

While Franklin was away, Eleanor had much to keep her busy, between her usual rounds of beneficent activities and her commitments to her friends. On the weekend of April 6, she and Tommy went to Hyde Park to begin the process of opening up the Big House for the summer. Franklin called her there that Saturday night but, as she explained in a long, chatty letter the next day, she had been half asleep when he called, having put in a long day unpacking barrels, rearranging china, and clearing off shelves. She ached from the unwonted exercise, she told him, though it had been fun.

"I forgot to tell you," she went on, "that Elinor Morgenthau had a serious heart attack at Daytona, Florida and Henry has been terribly worried. I think Elinor can't stand the war strain and trying not to show it has had an effect on her circulation. . . . I haven't felt sleepy tonight so I've written James, Elliott, and Frankie, Elinor, Rommie and Sisty and now I must go to bed as we leave in the morning and go up to New Hampshire tomorrow night and I'll be in Washington Wed. eve."

"Much love to you dear," she concluded. "I'm so glad you are gaining. You sounded cheerful for the first time last night and I hope you'll weigh 170 lbs when you return."

Unbeknownst to Eleanor, Franklin's good cheer that Saturday night was likely prompted by the knowledge that Lucy Rutherfurd was coming to see him on Monday. Phone logs at the FDR Library reveal that Roosevelt called Lucy in Aiken almost every day while he was at Warm Springs. She was planning to drive to Warm Springs on Monday, April 9, with her painter friend, Elizabeth Shoumatoff. Roosevelt told her he would meet their car in Macon at 4 p.m. The roads were tricky, however, and the two women lost their way, arriving quite late. "Nothing in sight," Shoumatoff observed, no presidential cars, no limousines. "Nobody loves us," Lucy joked, "nobody cares for us." Continuing on toward Warm Springs, they noticed a crowd gathered in front of a corner drugstore in the small village of Greenville. Franklin Roosevelt was sitting in an open car with Margaret Suckley and Fala, drinking a Coca-Cola. Shoumatoff was struck at once by "the expression of joy on FDR's face upon seeing Lucy," and by Lucy's relief in knowing that Roosevelt had not forgotten her after all.

Dinner that night, Shoumatoff recalled, found Roosevelt "full of jokes," basking in the admiration of four women (Margaret and Laura had been invited to join Lucy and her friend). Shoumatoff's eye was drawn to Laura's exotic looks, her bright-blue hair, her striking dinner pajamas, and her "profile as beautiful as a cameo," but Roosevelt, she noted, seemed constantly to address himself to Lucy, in a wide-ranging conversation that moved from Churchill to Stalin to food.

The next morning, while Roosevelt sat on the sun porch working on his papers, Shoumatoff began preliminary sketches for a portrait which Lucy wanted to give to her daughter, Barbara. Even as Shoumatoff sketched, Roosevelt continued joking with Lucy. Watching the affectionate rapport between them, Shoumatoff's photographer, Harold Robbins, whom she had brought along to help her with her work, thought they were like "happy kids enjoying golden days as if there would be no end to them."

In the afternoon, Roosevelt took the four women for a long drive in his open coupe. Along the way, he encountered Merriman Smith riding a horse which he had hired for the afternoon at the village drugstore. "As I reined in the horse," Smith recalled, "Roosevelt bowed majestically to me. His voice was wonderful and resonant. It sounded like the Roosevelt of old. In tones that must have been audible a block away, FDR hailed me with 'Heigh-Ho, Silver!' "

After dinner, Roosevelt gave Lucy a photograph taken when the two of them had first met, when he was assistant secretary of the navy. As Shoumatoff looked at the picture of the handsome young Roosevelt and then at Lucy's "beautiful, slightly flushed face," she felt happy for them. "The quiet and beauty of the place," she later wrote, "the privacy of the surroundings, seemed almost created for the new blossoming of those old memories."

The following day, April 11, Roosevelt was in high spirits as he worked on a draft of his Jefferson Day speech. "I remember so clearly seeing him writing and writing," Suckley recalled years later, "a little bent over the table, Miss Tully waiting by his side, pencil in hand.... Then, when he had finished, I remember distinctly how he came into the room from the porch, a look of great satisfaction on his face, and said, 'Well, I've written much of that speech in my own hand.'"

It was "a good speech," Hassett recorded, fueled, as most of Roosevelt's speeches were, by a striking combination of optimism and belief in the American people. "The only thing we have to fear is fear itself," Roosevelt had said in his famous first inaugural; and now, in the peroration of the last speech he would write, he returned to the same theme. "The only limit to our realization of tomorrow," he wrote, "will be our doubts of today. Let us move forward with strong and active faith."

That evening, Henry Morgenthau, in transit to Washington from Florida, joined Roosevelt and the four women for cocktails and dinner. "I was terribly shocked when I saw him," Morgenthau recorded in his diary. "I found he had aged terrifically and looked very haggard. His hands shook so that he started to knock over the glasses. I had to hold each glass as he poured out the cocktail.... I have never seen him have so much difficulty transferring himself from his wheelchair to a regular chair, and I was in agony watching him."

After two cocktails, Roosevelt seemed to improve. He was in good spirits when he called Anna in Washington to check on Johnny's progress. "He was full of this wonderful barbecue that was coming off the next day," Anna recalled. "The only bad thing about it," he told her, was that he knew ahead of time that he was going to overeat, but he intended to "thoroughly enjoy it."

The conversation at supper was lively and agreeable, though Shoumatoff detected "an encompassing tension" which she attributed to Morgenthau's presence. As soon as the outsider left, "the atmosphere resumed its former easy and pleasant manner." With Roosevelt settled comfortably in an armchair by the fireplace, Shoumatoff volunteered to tell her favorite ghost story about the black-pearl necklace of Catherine the Great. "Upon finishing my story," Shoumatoff recalled, "another was about to be told when Dr. Bruenn and his assistant arrived. The President, like a little boy, asked to stay up longer, but finally consented to retire, telling me he would be ready for my painting the next morning."

"The sky was clear" in Warm Springs on April 12, 1945, Suckley recalled, "with the promise of a hot day." At noon, the president was sitting in his living room with Lucy, Laura, and Margaret while Shoumatoff stood at her easel, painting. Shoumatoff was struck by his "exceptionally good color"; Suckley, too, thought he looked "surprisingly well, and very fine in a double breasted gray suit and crimson tie."

The mail was heavy; a stack of letters and documents awaited the president's signature. Hassett took each paper as it was signed and spread it on a chair for the ink to dry. "Well," Roosevelt teased, "are you through with your laundry yet? Is it all dry?" Among the documents was a letter prepared for the president's signature by the State Department. "A typical State Department letter," Roosevelt laughingly observed. "It says nothing at all." His spirits remained high as he came to a bill just passed by Congress which extended the life of the Commodity Credit Corporation. "There," he boasted to the women as he signed his name with a flourish, "there is where I make a law."

At that moment, Lizzie McDuffie, the president's maid, was walking to the guest cottage to make the beds. Looking through the living-room window, she saw Roosevelt sitting in his chair, laughing and smiling at Lucy. "The last I remember," Lizzie said later, "he was looking into the smiling face of a beautiful woman."

At one o'clock, the butler came in to set the table for lunch. Roosevelt glanced at his watch and said, "We've got just fifteen minutes more." Then, suddenly, Shoumatoff recalled, "he raised his right hand and passed it over his forehead several times in a strange jerky way." Then his head went forward. Thinking he was looking for something, Suckley went over to him and asked if he had dropped his cigarette. "He looked at me," Suckley recalled, "his forehead furrowed with pain, and tried to smile. He put his left hand up to the back of his head and said, 'I have a terrific pain in the back of my head.' And then he collapsed."

Suckley reached for the telephone and asked the operator to find Dr. Bruenn and send him over at once. In the meantime, the president's valet, Arthur Prettyman, and the butler carried the unconscious president into the bedroom. When Dr. Bruenn arrived, he could tell at once that the president had suffered a cerebral hemorrhage. "It was a bolt out of the blue," Bruenn later observed. "A good deal of his brain had been damaged."

Lucy and the other women were still standing in the living room. "The confusion was so great," Shoumatoff recalled. "Nobody seemed to know whether they were coming or going."

"We must pack up and go," Lucy whispered to Shoumatoff. "The family is arriving by plane and the rooms must be vacant. We must get to Aiken before dark." In a few moments, Shoumatoff recalled, she and Lucy were back in the guest cottage, hurriedly tossing their things into suitcases. It was about two-thirty when they left.

In the bedroom, Bruenn did what he could, "which wasn't much," he admitted. He notified Dr. McIntire, who placed an emergency call to Atlanta to Dr. James Paullin, who had been part of the team that examined Roosevelt at Bethesda Naval Hospital the previous year. Bruenn took off the president's clothes and put on his pajamas. By the time Grace Tully reached the house, there were terrible sounds of tortured breathing coming from the bedroom. "All you could hear was breathing," Lizzie McDuffie recalled. "It was kind of like—deep, steady, long gasps."

Tully dropped her head to pray while Hassett went into the bedroom. "His eyes were closed," Hassett recorded, "mouth open—the awful breathing . . . But the Greek nose and the noble forehead were grand as ever. . . . I knew that I should not see him again."

Shortly before three-thirty, Roosevelt's breathing stopped. Dr. Bruenn was on the bed giving him artificial respiration when Dr. Paullin arrived. "We put a shot of adrenaline into his heart," Bruenn recalled—"sometimes that starts the heart up again—nothing worked. And that was it." The president was dead.

• • •

Hassett called the White House to break the news to Press Secretary Steve Early. The two men agreed to say nothing more until Eleanor was told. Dr. McIntire had called her an hour earlier to tell her that Roosevelt had fainted. The doctor was "not alarmed," Eleanor recalled, but suggested she prepare to go to Warm Springs that evening. Should she cancel her speaking engagement at four that afternoon? Eleanor asked. No, McIntire insisted, it would cause great comment if she canceled and then at the last minute flew to Warm Springs.

Arriving at the Sulgrave Club promptly at 4 p.m., Eleanor took a seat between Mrs. Woodrow Wilson and Mrs. Allen Dougherty, chairman of the charity event. Dressed in a soft red suit which one reporter described as "unusually smart," Eleanor delivered a short talk and then returned to the head table to listen as the celebrated pianist Miss Evelyn Tyner played. In the middle of the piece, Eleanor was told she was wanted on the telephone. The message gave her "a quick start," one of the ladies seated nearby later recalled.

Quietly excusing herself, Eleanor went to the phone. Steve Early was on the line. He was "very much upset," Eleanor recalled, and he "asked me to come home at once. I did not even ask why. I knew down in the heart that something dreadful had happened. Nevertheless the amenities had to be observed, so I went back to the party. . . ."

Resuming her place at the head table, Eleanor waited until Miss Tyner's piano piece was completed, joined in the applause, and then rose to say, "Now I'm called back to the White House and I want to apologize for leaving before this delightful concert is finished." The audience gave her a standing ovation and she left the room.

"I got into the car and sat with clenched hands all the way to the White House. In my heart I knew what had happened, but one does not actually formulate these terrible thoughts until they are spoken. I went to my sitting room and Steve Early and Dr. McIntire came to tell me the news."

Anna was at Bethesda Naval Hospital with Johnny when she heard. She had been told by Dr. McIntire earlier in the afternoon that her father had collapsed, but since there was nothing she could do she had returned to the hospital. "I hadn't been there more than about twenty minutes," she recalled, "when the head of the Naval Center Hospital, in Bethesda, came and only said one sentence, 'Mrs. Boettiger, my car's waiting to take you to the White House.' And he'd been told, too, obviously. And that is the way it was done."

When she got back to the White House, Anna went to her mother's sitting room. Eleanor had already changed into a black dress, sent for the vice-president, and cabled her four sons, all in active service. "He did his job to the end," she wrote, "as he would want you to do." In the midst of indescribable confusion, she had the presence of mind to call the hospital in Daytona Beach where Elinor Morgenthau lay ill to ask that the radio be removed from her room lest Elinor hear the news and suffer a setback.

At five-thirty, Vice-President Harry Truman arrived at the White House, not knowing why he had been asked to come. He was ushered into the first lady's sitting room where Eleanor was waiting with Anna, John and Steve Early. Eleanor stepped forward to greet him, placing her arm gently on his shoulder. "Harry," she said, "the President is dead." For a moment Truman was unable to speak. Then, at last, he found his voice to ask if there was anything he could do for her.

In reply, Eleanor said: "Is there anything we can do for you? For you are the one in trouble now." She told Truman she was planning to fly to Warm Springs that night and wondered if it was still proper for her to use a government plane. Truman assured her that it was. Minutes later, Stettinius came to the doorway. With tears streaming down his face, he discussed the plans to assemble the Cabinet and swear in the new president.

By 7 p.m., nearly all the members of the Cabinet were gathered in the Cabinet Room, along with Chief Justice Harlan Stone. "It was a very somber group," Stimson recorded, as he looked at the faces of Morgenthau, Biddle, Ickes, Perkins, and Stettinius. "For with all his idiosyncrasies our Chief was a very kindly and friendly man and his humor and pleasantry had always been the life of the Cabinet meetings. I think every one of us felt keenly the loss of a real personal friend. I know I did. I have never concealed the fact that I regarded his administrative procedures as disorderly, but his foreign policy was always founded on great foresight and keenness of vision, and at this period of great confusion of ideas in this country, the loss of his leadership will be most serious."

Minutes after the swearing in, Eleanor left for Warm Springs. When she appeared at the front portico of the White House, she talked for a few minutes with Anna, who was staying behind to coordinate plans for the funeral service. Heading toward the car, she leaned over to recognize the clustered group of ushers, doormen, and women reporters who stood there. "A trooper to the last," reporter Bess Furman marveled. Then she kissed Anna goodbye and "strode with her usual determined gait to the waiting limo. Silent and alone, she went to her husband."

Harry Hopkins was still at St. Mary's Hospital in Rochester, Minnesota, when he heard the news. Frail as he was, he made plans to fly immediately to Washington. Then, from his hospital bed, he began calling his friends, feeling a desperate need to talk about Roosevelt. "You and I have got something great we can take with us the rest of our lives," he told Robert Sherwood. "It's a great realization because we know it's true what so many people believed about him and what made them love him. The President never let them down. That's what you and I can remember."

"Oh, we all know he could be exasperating," Hopkins went on, "and he could seem to be temporizing and delaying and he'd get us all worked up when we thought he was making too many concessions to expediency. But all of that was in the little things, the unimportant things—and he knew exactly how little and how unimportant they really were. But in the big things—all the things that were of real, permanent importance—he never let the people down."

It was after midnight in London when Churchill heard that Roosevelt was dead. "I felt as if I had been struck a physical blow," Churchill recalled. "My relations with this shining personality had played so large a part in the long, terrible years we had worked together. Now they had come to an end, and I was overpowered by a sense of deep and irreparable loss."

In Moscow, Ambassador Harriman learned of Roosevelt's death at about 3 a.m. local time. He drove to the Kremlin to tell Stalin. The Russian leader appeared "deeply distressed," Harriman recorded, holding the envoy's hand for nearly thirty seconds before asking him to sit and talk. Stalin then questioned Harriman closely about the circumstances of Roosevelt's death and sent a message to the State Department asking that an autopsy be performed to determine if Roosevelt had been poisoned.

As word spread from city to town within the United States, ordinary people, politicians and reporters struggled to come to terms with Roosevelt's death. For the millions who adored him and for those who despised him, an America without Roosevelt seemed almost inconceivable. He was in his thirteenth year as president when he died. Those who had just reached the legal voting age of twenty-one in time for this fourth election had been only nine years old when he took the oath of office for the first time. Schoolgirl Anne Relph remembered riding her bicycle back to the playground after hearing that Roosevelt had died, "and feeling, as a child, that this was going to be the end of the world, because he was the only president I'd ever known. I was almost not aware that there could be another president. He had always been THE PRESIDENT, in capital letters."

Correspondent I. F. Stone was at the *PM* newspaper office in New York when a copy boy ran out of the wire room with a piece of United Press copy confirming the president's death. "That first flash," Stone recalled, "seemed incredible; like something in a nightmare, for down under the horror was the comfortable feeling that you would wake to find it all a dream. The Romans must have felt this way when word came that Caesar Augustus was dead." Journalist Studs Terkel heard the news while he was having drinks in the Stevens Hotel. "Everybody left. I'm walking south on Michigan Boulevard, and I can't stop crying. Everybody is crying." Reporter Jack Altschul was in his office at *Newsday,* "God, there were people in the office who were professed Republicans and may have come from stockbroking families who have never forgiven Roosevelt . . . but I can remember going with some of the guys to the bar where we used to hang out after we put out the new edition, and the guys were crying."

"I am too shocked to talk," Senate Majority Leader Alben Barkley told reporters. "It is one of the worst tragedies that ever happened." Mr. Republican, Senator Robert Taft agreed. "The President's death," he said, "removed the greatest figure of our time at the very climax of his career, and shocks the world to which his words and actions were more important than those of any other man. He dies a hero of the war, for he literally worked himself to death in the service of the American people." And Alf Landon, Republican presidential nominee in 1936 said, "it is tragic he could not have lived to see the fruition of his greatest undertaking."

Even the normally staid *New York Times* was extravagant in its editorial praise. "Men will thank God on their knees a hundred years from now, that Franklin D. Roosevelt was in the White House. . . . It was his hand, more than that of any other single man, that built the great coalition of the United Nations. . . . It was his leadership which inspired free men in every part of the world to fight with greater hope and courage. Gone, now, is this talent and skill. . . . Gone is the fresh and spontaneous interest which this man took, as naturally as he breathed air, in the troubles and the hardships and the disappointments and the hopes of little men and humble people."

• • •

Churchill once said that to encounter Franklin Roosevelt, with all his buoyant sparkle, his iridescent personality, and his inner élan was like opening your first bottle of champagne. Roosevelt genuinely liked people, he enjoyed taking responsibility, and he adored being president. Alone among our modern presidents, he had "no conception of the office to live up to," political scientist Richard Neustadt noted, "he was it. His image of the office was himself-in-office." He did not have the time or the inclination for a melancholy contemplation of the "burdens" of the presidency. "Wouldn't you be President if you could?" he once naïvely asked a friend. "Wouldn't anybody?"

Whether sorting his stamp collection with Missy LeHand at his side, inspecting the troops in the company of his wife, probing the latest Hollywood gossip with Harry Hopkins, enjoying the company of a stylish woman, co-opting a potential rival, delivering a fireside chat, charming a disgruntled Cabinet officer, exchanging repartee with reporters or confidences with Churchill, Roosevelt's ebullience permeated every aspect of his leadership. "Under Roosevelt," historian William Leuchtenburg observed, "the White House became the focus of all government—the fountainhead of ideas, the initiator of action, the representative of the national interest. He took an office which had lost much of its prestige and power in the previous twelve years and gave it an importance which went well beyond what even Theodore Roosevelt and Woodrow Wilson had done. [He] re-created the modern Presidency."

"He was one of the few statesmen in the twentieth century, or any century," the British philosopher Isaiah Berlin wrote, "who seemed to have no fear of the future." Though the United States was miserably unprepared for war in the spring of 1940, Roosevelt never doubted that the American home front would eventually win the war, that the uncoerced energies of a free people could overcome the most efficient totalitarian regime. To his mind, there was no danger too great, no challenge too profound to yield to the combined efforts of the American people. He would provide the framework, the opportunity, and the inspiration, and the people would do the rest.

It was fashionable during the war to decry the chaos and confusion in Washington, the mushrooming bureaucracies with overlapping jurisdictions and inconsistent mandates. Yet it seems, with the luxury of hindsight, that no other form of organization could have produced the triumphs and transformations of Roosevelt's America. Indeed, it was not an organization at all. There was no master plan, no neat division of responsibilities, no precise allocation of burdens. The conduct of the nation during the war mirrored the temperament, the strengths, and the frailties of a single man. A lesser man, a man of smaller ego, would have sought greater control, more rigid lines of responsibility and authority. But Roosevelt never felt that he or his leadership was threatened by multiplicity and confusion. He could try everything; he could move in different directions at the same time; he could let the horses run, never doubting his ability to rein them in should they threaten to become uncontrollable. As long as the home front was big at the base, as long as the great majority of the American people were involved in the production effort, he could afford to let things be confused at the top.

His critics were certain that he would straitjacket the free-enterprise system once the war began. To this day, Franklin Roosevelt remains the symbol of big government and the controlled economy. Yet, under Roosevelt's wartime leadership, the government entered into a close partnership with private enterprise, enabling business to realize its full potential for the first time in many years. Despite the wide variety of government controls, private producers freely negotiated their contracts with the government, and no one was told where to move or where to work. Business was exempted from antitrust laws, allowed to write off the full cost of investments, given the financial and material resources to fulfill contracts, and guaranteed a substantial profit. The leader who had once proclaimed his intention to master the forces of organized money had become their greatest benefactor.

But even as he reached out to business during the war years, Roosevelt insisted on preserving the social gains of the previous decade. His partnership with business was not forged at the expense of American labor. On the contrary, the American workingman during the war enjoyed full employment, generous earnings, new fringe benefits, and a progressive tax code. Union membership expanded by more than six million. In less than half a decade, the Depression, which Roosevelt had fought so vigorously but with limited success, had been ended. Fueling this advance of business and labor was the material reality of an extraordinary, seemingly limitless, flow of weapons and vehicles far in excess of those Roosevelt predictions which had been scorned as "visionary" by economists and businessmen alike. Though Roosevelt had not lived to see the end of the war, his goal of making America "the arsenal of democracy" was abundantly fulfilled before he died. Between 1940 and 1945, the United States contributed nearly three hundred thousand warplanes to the Allied cause. American factories produced more than two million trucks, 107,351 tanks, 87,620 warships, 5,475 cargo ships, over twenty million rifles, machine guns, and pistols, and forty-four billion rounds of ammunition. "There is little doubt," army historians conclude, "that America's outpouring of war materiel rather than an Allied preponderance of manpower was the dominant factor in winning the war."

"The figures are all so astronomical that they cease to mean very much," historian Bruce Catton wrote. "Say that we performed the equivalent of building two Panama Canals every month with a fat surplus to boot; that's an understatement, it still doesn't begin to express it all, the total is simply beyond the compass of one's understanding. Here was displayed a strength greater even than cocky Americans in the old days of unlimited self-confidence had supposed; strength to which nothing—literally nothing, in the physical sense—was any longer impossible."

Roosevelt's success in mobilizing the nation to this extraordinary level of collective performance rested on his uncanny sensitivity to his followers, his ability to appraise public feeling and to lead the people one step at a time. More than any previous president, he studied public opinion: he read a variety of newspapers; he analyzed polls; he traveled the country when he could and dispatched his wife when he could not; he brought in people of clashing temperaments to secure different points of view; he probed visitors at dinner; he tried out his ideas on reporters. But more than diligence was involved. Like any great artist, Roosevelt relied on his own intuition to fit the smallest details and the most disparate impressions into a coherent pattern. He was able to sense what the people were thinking and feeling.

Above all, he possessed a magnificent sense of timing. He understood when to invoke the prestige of the presidency and when to hold it in reserve, when to move forward and when to pull back. "I am like a cat," he once said. "I make a quick stroke and then I relax." He was committed to the

Allied cause from the start of the war, but he understood that he had to bring an isolationist people along little by little, through a combination of decisions, speeches, and events.

He let the reaction to the Nazi invasion of Western Europe build before he addressed the joint session of Congress on May 16, 1940. He let a citizens' group take the lead on the draft in the summer of 1940 while he focused on making the destroyer deal with Britain. Then, when it looked as though the draft would be defeated, he delivered a strong endorsement that carried the bill through. He sat quietly for days on the *Tuscaloosa* after receiving Churchill's urgent plea for help with Britain's financial crisis until he suddenly emerged with the idea of "lending" Britain weapons to be paid back in kind after the war. Then, perfectly sensing just how far the public was willing to go at that moment, he successfully sold the idea of lend-lease to the Congress and the country as America's best alternative to war. He resisted strong pressure to convoy ships in the spring of 1941, believing that convoys would bring America into the war before the American people were ready. Yet, once again perfectly sensing the state of public feeling—in which the growing commitment to the Allied cause was undercut by the fear of sending American boys abroad—he dramatized the grim situation on the seas by declaring an "unlimited emergency," which made it seem that he was moving further than he really was. Determined not to carry a divided country into war, he waited for events to unify the nation. The wisdom of this assessment was confirmed when the extension of the draft passed the House by only a single vote in August 1941. It would take the Japanese attack on Pearl Harbor to shatter isolationism once and for all and create the unified support necessary to win the war.

Roosevelt's sense of timing was also manifest in his actions as commander-in-chief. Once again, he knew when to invoke his powers and when to hold them in reserve. He picked a first-class military team—Marshall, King, Arnold, Leahy—and gave them wide latitude to run the war. Never once, Stimson admiringly remarked, did Roosevelt overturn his commanders' decisions for personal or political motives. Though the Democrats would have been greatly strengthened in the 1942 elections if the invasion of North Africa had occurred a few days earlier, he did not interfere with Eisenhower's decision to begin the landing six days after the election. Through the worst days of the war—the weeks after Pearl Harbor, the early days at Guadalcanal, the Battle of the Bulge—he remained calm and imperturbable, earning the deep respect of every single one of his commanders.

Yet, at critical junctures, he had the courage to force action over the protest of his military advisers, and almost all of these actions had a salutary effect on the war. In 1940, he insisted on giving all aid to Britain short of war, though his military chiefs warned him that he was jeopardizing America's own security in so doing. He brought Russia under the lend-lease umbrella at a time when his military advisers believed Russia had almost no chance of holding out. He encouraged the Doolittle raid on Japan, which inadvertently led to great success at Midway. He personally made the hotly debated decision to invade North Africa, and later granted MacArthur permission to recapture the Philippines. It was Roosevelt who gambled on the production of the B-29 superbomber, decided to spend $2 billion on an experimental atomic bomb, and demanded that the Allies commit themselves to a postwar structure before the war was over.

To be sure, there were errors in Roosevelt's wartime leadership. A precious year was lost in 1940–41, when the mobilization process was not pushed hard enough, when, as Washington lawyer Joe Rauh noted, "the arsenal of democracy was more democracy than arsenal." Indeed, had it not been for the period of borrowed time provided by the heroic resistance of the British and the Russians, the United States might not have been able to overcome the head start of the Axis in time to influence the course of the war. And once the mobilization got under way, he failed to protect small business against the military's tendency to lavish its contracts on the nation's industrial giants. It was during the war years that the links were forged that would lead to the rise of the "military-industrial complex" in postwar America.

One must also concede the failures of vision that led to the forcible relocation of the Japanese Americans, and the lack of a more decisive response to the extermination of the European Jews. Totally focused on winning the war, Roosevelt mistakenly accepted the specious argument that incarceration of the Japanese Americans was a military necessity. In so doing, he deprived tens of thousands of men, women, and children of Japanese descent of their civil liberties, and trampled on values he himself cherished.

Sorting out Roosevelt's actions and inactions with respect to the European Jews is more complicated. He believed that winning the war was the best means of rescuing the Jews. And there was merit to his belief. By the time the news of the systematic murder of the Jews reached the West in mid-1942, it was too late to mount a massive rescue effort short of winning the war as quickly as possible. But Roosevelt's intensity of focus blinded him to a series of smaller steps that could have been taken—the War Refugee Board could have been established earlier and given more authority; the United States could have applied more pressure on Germany to release the Jews and more pressure on neutral countries to take them in; the United States Air Force could have bombed the train tracks and the concentration camps. "None of these proposals guaranteed results," holocaust scholar David Wyman admits. "But all deserved serious consideration. . . . Even if few or no lives had been saved, the moral obligation would have been fulfilled."

But in the end, Roosevelt's strengths far outweighed his weaknesses. Despite confusions and conflicts, clashing interests and disparate goals, the American people were successfully combined in an unparalleled national enterprise. Indeed, at times, it seemed as if Roosevelt alone understood the complex and shifting relationship between the nation's effort at home and its struggle across the globe. "More than any other man," historian Eric

Larrabee concludes in his study of Roosevelt's wartime leadership, "he ran the war, and ran it well enough to deserve the gratitude of his countrymen then and since, and of those from whom he lifted the yoke of the Axis tyrannies. His conduct as Commander in Chief... bears the mark of greatness."

• • •

It was nearly midnight by the time Eleanor reached Warm Springs. She was, everyone commented, calm and composed when she arrived. When she walked into the living room, she embraced her two cousins and Miss Tully. Then she sat down on the sofa and asked each of them to tell her exactly what had happened. Tully recounted her own schedule that day; she had been dressing for lunch when she first heard the president was sick and had been in the living room when he died. Eleanor listened quietly and then turned to Margaret, who described sitting on the sofa crocheting when the president slumped forward in his chair.

Then Laura began to speak, telling Eleanor some brutal truths: Franklin had been sitting for a portrait when he collapsed. The painter was a friend of Lucy Rutherfurd's. Mrs. Rutherfurd was there as well, sitting in the alcove by the windows. The two women had been staying in the guest cottage as Franklin's guests for the past three days.

"It was a malicious thing to do," Eleanor's niece Eleanor Wotkyns later suggested, "but very fitting for her. She was a small, petty woman, jealous all her life of Eleanor's great success. Though she thought herself every bit as smart as Eleanor, she hadn't done a thing in her life except raise red setters and let her chauffeur drive her to dog shows all over the country. This was an act of revenge."

Laura's explanation was that "Eleanor would have found out anyway." Too many people knew the president had been sitting for a portrait when his cerebral hemorrhage struck. Too many people knew that Lucy was there. Still, Laura must have understood how devastating the news would be to Eleanor. Henceforth, thoughts of her husband's final days would be inextricably linked in her mind with thoughts of Lucy Mercer Rutherfurd.

When Laura finished speaking, Eleanor walked into the bedroom to see her husband's body. She closed the door behind her and remained inside —alone with her husband—for more than five minutes. When she emerged from the bedroom, Tully recalled, her eyes were dry and her face was composed. She sat down on the sofa again and questioned Laura further. Had Franklin seen Lucy at other times in recent years? Yes, Laura replied. Lucy had dined at the White House a number of times. Had anyone else been present? Yes, she and Margaret and... Anna. Indeed, Anna was the one who had arranged Lucy's visits.

Eleanor gave no visible sign then or in the days to come of the pain she must have felt on hearing these words. "At a time like that, you don't really feel your own feelings," she explained later. "When you're in a position of being caught in a pageant, you become part of a world outside yourself and you act almost like an automaton. You recede as a person. You build a facade for everyone to see and you live separately inside the facade. Something comes to protect you. I was well prepared for it. My grandmother brought me up to prepare for it, in a social way. I was never permitted as a child to say that I had a headache. I was trained to put personal things in the background."

Then Eleanor returned to the bedroom to select the clothes for her husband's burial—a double-breasted blue business suit flecked with gray, a soft white shirt, and a dark-blue-and-white four-in-hand tie. The president's valet finished dressing the body. He tenderly parted the hair and combed it back. Eleanor nodded her approval, and the body was brought into the living room and placed in a casket. "Oh, he was handsome," Lizzie McDuffie exclaimed. "You wouldn't have thought he had a day's illness."

The next morning, thousands of villagers were gathered at the little railroad station in Warm Springs to say goodbye to their president. They stood in clusters, heads bowed, openly weeping, as a military guard of honor lifted the bronze coffin into the rear car of the presidential train. A special cradle had been erected so the casket could be seen through the window as the train moved slowly eight hundred miles north toward the nation's capital. Hundreds of thousands of people lined the tracks along the way. "They came from the fields and the farms," INS reporter Robert Nixon wrote, "from hamlets and crossroads: and in the cities they thronged by the thousands to stare in humble reverence and awe."

"Men stood with their arms around the shoulders of their wives and mothers," Merriman Smith noted. "Men and women openly wept. Church choirs gathered at the trackside and sang Rock of Ages and Abide with Me." As the train made its way through Georgia's valleys and hills, Smith noticed four Negro women in a cotton field working on a spring planting. They were "kneeling near the edge of the field. Their hands were clasped together in prayerful supplication."

Several times during the long trip, various members of the president's staff walked through the train to the lounge car where Eleanor was seated. Was there anything they could do to help? they wanted to know. Each time, Eleanor thanked them but said there was nothing she needed.

As night fell, the rest of the train was dimmed so the president's catafalque could be seen for miles. "I lay in my berth all night with the window shade up," Eleanor recalled, "looking out at the countryside he had loved and watching the faces of the people at stations, and even at the crossroads, who came to pay their last tribute all through the night."

In the early morning, Eleanor sent for Grace Tully. "Did Franklin ever give you any instructions about his burial?" she asked. "She had difficulty saying that," Tully recalled. "Her eyes welled and her voice broke. It was only momentary. It was the only time during the whole ordeal I ever saw her almost lose her control." Tully recalled for Eleanor a conversation she had had with the president a year before. He had asked to be buried in the green-hedged garden of his ancestral home. He had also placed a memo outlining his wishes in his bedroom safe, asking for a plain white monument containing no carving or decoration, only the dates of his birth and his death. He wanted the monument to be placed on the grave from east to west. He hoped "my dear wife will on her death be buried there also."

Tully went on to recount other requests the president had made, including that Fala be given to Margaret Suckley. He assumed that Mrs. Roosevelt would be too busy to look after him. Unable to hide her disappointment, Eleanor hurried on to the next subject—she needed Tully's help, she said, in drafting a form letter to acknowledge the thousands of condolence messages.

The funeral train crossed the Potomac River and pulled into Union Station. Thousands stood in silence as Anna, Elliott, and Elliott's wife entered the rear car. (FDR, Jr., and John were in the midst of battle and unable to leave their ships; Jimmy was still en route from San Diego.) President Truman and the Cabinet were there, along with General Marshall, Admiral King, and members of Congress. As two military bands played and army bombers thundered overhead, the funeral procession moved down Constitution Avenue to 18th Street, to Pennsylvania Avenue, and finally to the White House.

Never, Truman later wrote, would he forget the sight of so many people in grief. "The streets," recalled General Marshall's wife, Katherine, "were lined on both sides with troops. In back of them could be seen the faces of the crowds. At each intersection the crowds extended down the side streets as far as you could see. Complete silence spread like a pall over the city, broken only by the funeral dirge and the sobs of the people."

The White House was in a state of confusion when the cavalcade arrived at the South Portico. Reporters were jamming the lobby, and the staff members were standing around in tears. The coffin was lifted from the caisson and carried up the front stairs. Eleanor alighted first. She walked slowly by herself into the mansion, her face composed. Whenever she was in trouble, Hick later observed, "she would walk unusually erect with her head held high. She was walking very erect that day."

The coffin was wheeled down a long red carpet to the East Room, where an honor guard was waiting to watch over the body until the funeral service at four that afternoon. "Can you dispense with the Honor Guard for a few moments and have the casket opened?" Eleanor asked White House usher J. B. West. "I would like to have a few moments alone with my husband."

"Please don't let anybody come in," Eleanor instructed as West and two other ushers guarded the doors. "Mrs. Roosevelt stood at the casket," West recalled, "gazing down into her husband's face. Then she took a gold ring from her finger and tenderly placed it on the President's hand. She straightened, eyes dry, and she left the room. The coffin was never opened again."

Now the time had come to confront Anna. Returning to the family quarters, Eleanor asked her daughter to come into her sitting room. Her face was "as stern as it could get when she was angry," Anna recalled. She demanded to know why she had never been told about Mrs. Rutherfurd. Was it true that Mrs. Rutherfurd had been at the White House and that Anna had made the arrangements? Yes, Anna nodded, explaining that one evening, when she was taking notes from her father on things he wanted done, he had mentioned to her that he would like to invite his old friend Mrs. Rutherfurd to dinner. Would she object? he had asked her. She hadn't known how to respond at first, Anna said, but in the end, when she thought of all the burdens her father was facing and of his declining health, she decided it was not up to her to deny him. "It was all above board," she assured her mother. "There were always people around."

"Mother was so upset about everything and now so upset with me," Anna later recalled. Indeed, so intense was the confrontation that Anna feared her mother would never be able to forgive her, and that their close relationship would no longer be the same.

"Mother was angry with Anna," Jimmy acknowledged, "but what was Anna to do? Should she have refused Father what he wanted? She was not in a position to do so even had she wanted to. Accepting the confidence of Father, should she have betrayed him by running to report to Mother every move he made? A child caught between two parents can only pursue as honorable a course as possible. Anna could no more serve as Mother's spy than she could as Father's spy on Mother."

Yet Anna's son Curtis understood some of what Eleanor must have been feeling. "He was her husband," Curtis said. "She was his wife. He was president. She was first lady. And now Anna had walked into the picture and made it possible for Lucy to return to the president's life. It must have seemed an unforgivable act."

• • •

The East Room was filled with flowers at 4 p.m. as the simple service began. Mrs. Roosevelt and the Roosevelt family sat in the front row, across the aisle from President Truman, Mrs. Truman, and their daughter, Margaret. Behind the president's family sat Cabinet members, Supreme Court justices, labor leaders, agency heads, politicians, and diplomats from all the countries of the United Nations, including British Foreign Minister Anthony Eden and Russian Ambassador to the U.S. Andrei Gromyko. "It was the final roll call of the Roosevelt era," reporter Bess Furman noted.

At Eleanor's request, the ceremony began with "Faith of Our Fathers," a hymn the president loved, and closed with the celebrated lines of Roosevelt's first inaugural: "The only thing we have to fear is fear itself." Throughout the service, Eleanor remained dry-eyed, her calmness in sharp contrast to the sobs of those around her. Harry Hopkins, *Time* reported, "stood almost fainting beside his chair, white as death and racked with sobs."

"After everyone left," Secret Service agent Milton Lipson recalled, "Mrs. Roosevelt took a last look at all the flowers and asked us if we'd arrange to have them all taken to a mental hospital. Then, seeing us teary-eyed, she added, 'Oh, of course, if any of you want a souvenir, please help yourself.' I still have my pressed flower."

Later that evening, the funeral train headed north toward Hyde Park, curving along the east bank of the Hudson, the route Roosevelt had taken so many times. "I'll never forget that train trip," Anna recalled. "As usual, the Secret Service had assigned staterooms and berths to each individual. I've never known who assigned it to me but I was given Father's stateroom. All night I sat on the foot of that berth and watched the people who had come to see the train pass by. There were little children, fathers, grandparents. They were there at 11 at night, at 2 in the morning, at 4—at all hours during that long night."

The president's coffin was lifted from the train at the riverfront and placed in a caisson, which was brought up the steep hill by six black-draped horses. Directly behind it walked a hooded horse, its saddle empty, its stirrups reversed—the traditional symbol of the fallen leader. As the cortege made its way up the hill, past the ice pond and the open field, the music started getting louder and louder, with cannons booming until the caisson stopped outside the hedge where a large assembly waited: President Truman and the Cabinet, General Marshall and Admiral King, James Farley and Edward Flynn, congressmen and senators, family and friends.

The four hedge walls of the rectangular garden were lined with West Point cadets in scarlet capes as the president's body was carried to the grave. "The funeral was very beautiful," Trude Lash wrote Joe. "The day was gloriously snappy, very sunny and blue, white lilacs were in bloom," and "the birds were singing."

The president's seventy-eight-year-old pastor, the Reverend George Anthony, recited the familiar lines: "We commit his body to the ground, earth to earth, dust to dust." The West Point cadets raised their rifles and fired three volleys. After each volley, Trude noted, Fala barked, a child whimpered, and then it was over.

As the crowd dispersed, Eleanor remained in the garden. She stood quietly, her head bowed, watching the workmen as they shoveled soil onto her husband's grave. Then, silent and alone, she walked away.

As Eleanor left, Moses Smith, an old tenant farmer on the estate, picked up a bucket and walked over to water a row of young maples. "He wanted me to plant these trees," he said. "I planted them for him. He'll never see them now."

CHAPTER 25

"A NEW COUNTRY IS BEING BORN"

Eleanor returned to the White House immediately after the funeral to begin the task of packing up the family furniture and all the personal possessions that had accumulated over a period of twelve years. She had promised the Trumans she would be out by Friday night, and she intended to keep her word. Monday morning, Henrietta Nesbitt came into Mrs. Roosevelt's bedroom. "She had all her clothes out of wardrobes and over chairs, and was sorting them," Nesbitt recalled. "I was thinking she'd never make it, with all there was to do, but at the same time I knew she would." The next morning, Jimmy Byrnes found her in the president's bedroom, packing books and personal belongings. She saved the president's study, crammed with pictures, models of ships, Currier and Ives prints, and tiny souvenirs from all over the world for last. "My husband was a collector with a great interest in history," she explained to her readers, "so there were many things to go over." Eventually a thousand boxes would be sealed, filling twenty army trucks. She was "a bit keyed up," she admitted to Joe Lash, "because there is so much to do and to think about." Her eyes were tired, one reporter noted, and she was pale, but she worked without pause.

In the midst of the packing, Eleanor took Bess and Margaret Truman on a tour of the White House. "In the years I have been here I have taken many people through," Eleanor wrote in her column that day. "I always have a pride in the beauty of the rooms, their proportions, the woodwork and the historically interesting furnishings which remain the same no matter what individuals may live here. It was good to find Mrs. Truman appreciative of the things that I have loved."

In private, Bess and Margaret Truman were appalled at what they saw: walls streaked with dust and faded along the outlines of all the pictures that had been taken down, shabby furniture badly in need of upholstering, threadbare carpets that hadn't been cleaned in years, draperies that were actually rotting. Eleanor had been so busy that she had not paid much attention to the physical condition of the mansion, leaving untouched a $50,000 congressional allocation for upkeep and repair. "Mrs. Roosevelt was more concerned about people being swept under the national rug due to injustice than she was about someone finding dirt under the White House rug," White House butler Alonzo Fields explained. "The White House upstairs is a mess," Margaret Truman wrote. "I was so depressed." White House usher J. B. West confirmed Margaret Truman's impression. "It was like a ghost house," he recalled. "What little was left in the White House gave it the appearance of an abandoned hotel."

While talking with Mrs. Truman, Eleanor suggested that she hold a press conference that week. Eleanor promised to sit by her side and introduce her to the women reporters. "Do you think I ought to do that?" a worried Bess Truman queried Frances Perkins. "It terrifies me. I don't even think of public affairs."

"No, Mrs. Truman," Perkins replied. "I don't think you ought to feel the slightest obligation to do it. Mrs. Roosevelt is an unusual person. She enjoys it. There certainly isn't anything the press has a right to ask you."

Eleanor Roosevelt was more than "an unusual person"; she was unique. She had seized the power inherent in the position of first lady, to become, in the words of a contemporary reporter, "a Cabinet Minister without portfolio," an influential advocate for social reform. In her efforts to reach a mass audience, she had become the first president's wife to hold regular press conferences, to write a syndicated daily column, to deliver sponsored radio broadcasts, to enter the lecture circuit. She had broken precedent time and again—when she spoke before the Democratic National Convention in 1940, traveled overseas to visit American troops in England and the South Pacific, and journeyed twice to Capitol Hill to testify before congressional committees on the plight of migrant workers and the conditions of life in the District of Columbia. No first lady before had ever become such a public figure. Her breadth of activities created new expectations against which her successors would be measured.

• • •

On her last full day in the White House, Eleanor invited all the members of the Women's Press Corps to a farewell tea in the State Dining Room. She stood at the door shaking each hand warmly as fifty-seven newswomen filed in. "Traces of grief" were etched on her pale features, one reporter noted, "her black costume relieved only by a pearl necklace and the small fleur-de-lis pin."

The newswomen had brought their notebooks. She lifted her hand. It was shaking uncontrollably. "This is a social thing," she said, "not a press conference. If you want to say Mrs. Roosevelt said this or that in conversation, that is your privilege but I do not want to be quoted directly." She talked in a low voice, twisting her tortoiseshell glasses in her hand, telling reporters how much she had enjoyed the press conferences over the years. The experiment begun twelve years earlier had, she believed, been a good thing. Her insistence on having only female reporters at her press conferences had forced newspapers to hire women and enhanced the careers of dozens of women reporters. She now told them that her apartment in New York and her cottage at Hyde Park were all she wanted to take care of. The Big House, she hoped, if the children agreed, would be turned over to the nation.

"Nearly all that I can do is done," Eleanor wrote Hick later that day. "The upstairs looks desolate and I will be glad to leave tomorrow. It is empty and without purpose to be here now." With everything gone that makes a home, she wrote Lash, she couldn't wait to leave. "I never did like to be where I no longer belonged. I am weary and yet I cannot rest. When do you think that will cease?"

Before falling asleep that night in the White House, Eleanor looked out her bedroom window for the last time. "I have always looked out at the Washington monument the last thing at night," she confided to her readers, "and the little red light at the top of it has twinkled at me in friendly fashion."

The next morning, Eleanor had her last breakfast on the sun porch and said goodbye to the office staff and the house staff. "We were all in tears," Mrs. Nesbitt recalled. "There is always a certain emotional strain about the last time for anything," Eleanor wrote in her column. "When you have lived twelve years in a house, even though you have always known that it belonged to the nation, you grow fond of the house itself and fonder still of all the people connected with your life in that house." She rode down in the old cage elevator that morning, she admitted, "with a feeling of melancholy and I suppose something of uncertainty because I was saying goodbye to an unforgettable era" and, from that day forward, "I would be on my own."

As she walked out the door, Eleanor waved to onlooking journalists and "without a backward glance," according to a *Newsweek* reporter, headed for Union Station, where a train was waiting to take her to New York. "Her departure," the *Boston Evening American* noted, "signified the end of an era for a generation which has never known any President but Franklin Delano Roosevelt or any First Lady but Mrs. Roosevelt."

When she reached her Washington Square apartment, Eleanor was exhausted. A cluster of reporters was waiting at the door. She had nothing to tell them. "The story," she said simply, "is over."

• • •

But the story was not over. Indeed, for Eleanor, whose strength of will was never more apparent than in the spring of 1945, a new chapter was beginning. She had passed through difficult days—absorbing not only the death of her husband but the discovery that Lucy Rutherfurd was with him when he died. Yet, as she doggedly resumed her labors—writing her daily column, traveling, and beginning to answer the hundreds of thousands of letters that were sent to the White House after the president's death—she gradually moved toward reconciliation with her husband's memory.

She had fought him on so many issues for so many years, pressuring him when her pressure was neither wanted nor welcome, that the full import of her husband's meaning to the nation had been hidden from her. But now, wherever she went, people—porters at the station, taxi drivers, doormen, elevator men, passengers on the train, riders in the subway—told her how personally bereaved they felt, how much they had loved him, how much they missed him. "I am realizing day by day," she wrote in her column, "how much my husband meant to young people in Washington, to veterans in the service hospitals, to men and women."

"It has warmed my heart," she told her readers, "to discover how many people would stop and speak to me as they left the train, often murmuring only: We loved your husband." On the subway in New York, a man, visibly controlling his emotion, came up to her and said: " 'He was like a friend who came and talked to us every now and then.' These spontaneous outbursts of affection for my husband from casual people whom I have never seen before, are spoken so sincerely that I often wish my husband could hear them himself."

She was stunned, she wrote her aunt Maude Gray as the United Nations Conference opened in San Francisco in late April, by the "upsurge of love" on the part of so many people, and by their realization of how much they had depended on him. "One feels in the San Francisco Conference that a strong hand is missing," she went on. "I am sad that he could not see the end of his long work which he carried so magnificently."

Eleanor confessed to her friends she had not realized until after he was gone how much she, too, had depended on her husband. "I find that mentally I counted so much on Franklin," she wrote Joe Lash, "I feel a bit bereft." The readjustment to being alone, she said, without someone else at the center of her life, was harder than she would have imagined. She was only now beginning to realize, she told Elinor Morgenthau, who was recovering from her heart attack, how much she had relied on "Franklin's greater wisdom," and it left her "without much sense of backing." Moreover, she observed, "I think we had all come to think of him as able to carry the world's problems and now we must carry them ourselves."

Eleanor had decided, even before the funeral train from Warm Springs reached Washington, that if the children agreed, which they eventually did, she would turn the Big House over to the government and make Val-Kill her permanent home. By the fall, the Big House had to be emptied of everything the family wanted—a task requiring hours of sorting and packing. In the midst of her labors, Eleanor took unexpected comfort in Fala's return to the Roosevelt household. Shortly after the funeral, Jimmy Roosevelt had written Margaret Suckley and asked her to send Fala back. "In talking to my sister and brother, we all feel very disappointed that Fala is not staying with Mother," Jimmy wrote. Fala was "part of the family," and it would make Mother "very happy to have him back." Suckley agreed, and Fala came to live at Val-Kill. Soon he and Eleanor became inseparable. Fala accompanied her on her walks through the woods, sat beside her chair in the living room, and greeted her at the door when she came home. "No one was as vociferously pleased to see me as Fala," she noted proudly after a trip to New York. Still, Fala missed the president. When General Eisenhower came to Hyde Park to lay a wreath on Roosevelt's grave, Fala heard the sirens of the motorcade and thought his master was returning. "His legs straightened out" and "his ears pricked up," Eleanor noted; he was hoping to see his master coming down the drive.

• • •

As the war in Europe came to a close, Eleanor was saddened anew that Franklin had not lived to see the triumphant end result of his wearying labors. On April 30, 1945, as the Red Army advanced on Berlin, Adolf Hitler hastily married his mistress, Eva Braun, and then committed suicide with her in his underground bunker. A week later, a newly assembled German government surrendered unconditionally. When Eleanor heard Truman, Churchill, and Stalin proclaim the surrender of Germany on the radio on May 8, she could almost hear her husband's voice making the announcement. "V-E Day was a curious day," she confessed to Maude Gray. "It was sad Franklin couldn't have announced it. I felt no desire to celebrate."

"I cannot help but think today of that little garden in Hyde Park where Franklin Roosevelt lies," Harry Hopkins told reporters the same day. "No man in the world contributed more to victory and freedom, and I believe that the free people of the earth will forever bless his name."

Churchill, too, thought of his friend on V E Day as the bells pealed throughout England and all of London came out into the streets, laughing, cheering, dancing, singing. "It was without any doubt Churchill's day," *New Yorker* correspondent Molly Panter-Downes observed. He was greeted everywhere he went with a roaring enthusiasm that "exceeded by double" anything anyone remembered. But even as he celebrated what he called the greatest day in the long history of England, Churchill's thoughts turned to Roosevelt and to "the valiant and magnanimous deeds of the USA" under his magnificent leadership. These extraordinary deeds, Churchill predicted, "would forever stir the hearts of Britons in all quarters of the world in which they dwell."

Ten weeks later, Churchill was unceremoniously swept out of office when the Labour Party triumphed in the British elections. Having gone to bed on election night believing he had won, he awoke just before dawn "with a sharp stab of almost physical pain"; a subconscious conviction that he was beaten "broke forth and dominated" his mind, he said, only to be confirmed later that day. The news that he had lost was difficult for Churchill to absorb. "It's no use pretending I'm not hard hit," he told Lord Moran. "It would have been better to have been killed in an aeroplane or to have died like Roosevelt."

Now it was Eleanor's turn to recall what Churchill meant to her husband, to the British, and to the Americans. "His place in the hearts of the people of Great Britain is safe for all time," she wrote. "No one in the British empire —nor in the United States—who heard his brave words after Dunkirk will ever feel anything but the deepest respect and gratitude and affection for Churchill, the man and the war leader."

A week after the British elections came the news that an atomic bomb had been dropped on Hiroshima. Eleanor had first learned about the secret weapon in July 1943, when a young physicist working on the project came to see her in her Washington Square apartment. The young man, Irving Lowen, was worried that Germany was pulling ahead of the United States in the search for an atomic weapon. He begged Eleanor to impress upon the president the need to proceed as quickly as possible. The president agreed to see Lowen at Eleanor's urging, but when the young scientist breached security a second time by returning to see Eleanor, he was transferred out of the Manhattan Project.

Eleanor did not question the decision to drop the bomb, believing that it would bring the war to a speedier end, but she "could not help feeling a little sad," she wrote, "when the news came that we had to use our second atomic bomb." She had hoped that "after the first bomb, which was followed by Russia's declaration of war and their prompt entry into Manchuria, the Japanese would decide to accept unconditional surrender and the loss of life could come to an end." It was not until August 15, six days later, that Japan finally surrendered.

The most destructive war in history had come to an end. The best estimates put the number of deaths at an unimaginable 50 million people. The Soviet Union lost 13 million combatants and 7 million civilians. The Germans calculated losses of 3.6 million civilians and 3.2 million soldiers. The Japanese estimated 2 million civilian and 1 million military deaths. Six million Jews had been killed. The number of British and commonwealth deaths is calculated at 484,482. With 291,557 battle deaths and 113,842 nonhostile deaths from accident and disease, the United States suffered the fewest casualties among the major nations.

When the word was flashed on August 15 that the war was over, Eleanor found herself "filled with very curious sensations." Though she was thrilled "to be in a world where peace has come," she had no desire to join the happy throngs on the streets. Recalling the way the people had celebrated when the last war ended, she felt that this time "the weight of suffering which has engulfed the world during so many years could not so quickly be wiped out." Moreover, she admitted to her daughter, "I miss Pa's voice and the words he would have spoken."

• • •

"Now that the war is over," war worker Mary Smith lamented, "I've lost my job—for no other reason apparently except that I am a woman." The bomb was dropped, Frankie Cooper recalled, and a few days later the foreman gathered all the women in the shipyard together. He told them that the first troop ship was coming home from the Pacific and he asked them to take off their welders' caps, let their hair down, and go down to the dock to meet the soldiers. "We were thrilled. We all waved," Cooper said. The next day, all the women were laid off. "It was a shock." At the Kaiser day-care center in Portland, Oregon, schoolteacher Mary Willett experienced a similar jolt. Though her center had cared for two thousand children at its peak and had received national attention for its excellent work, it was permanently closed down and all the teachers were dismissed just two weeks after the war was over.

In her columns that fall, Eleanor tried in vain to stem the tide. She argued on principle that everyone who wanted to work had a right to be productive. She asked industry to face the fact that many women were obliged to work to support their families and that "it was essential they be treated in this respect on a par with the men." She railed against the closing of the child-care centers as a shortsighted response to a fundamental social need. "Many thought they were purely a war emergency measure," she wrote in September. "A few of us had an inkling that perhaps they were a need which was constantly with us, but one that we had neglected to face in the past." She had received a number of letters from women, she reported, appealing to her to help keep the child-care centers open. Some of the women who wrote had husbands who were killed in the war. Others had husbands who were crippled or wounded. For these women, work was the only means of supporting their family. "My whole life and that of my two children," Mrs. Dorothy Thibault wrote, "depends on my working eight hours each day. My little girl is 4 and the boy is 2 and one-half. The care and training they have received in this childcare center is the best possible thing that could have happened to them."

Despite all these problems—despite the layoffs, the insufficient child care, and the postwar elevation of domestic virtues into an ideology—millions of women would refuse to abandon the workplace. Though female jobs in manufacturing fell sharply after the war, the rate of female employment as a whole began climbing steadily upward again in 1947, soon surpassing the wartime peak. "My husband would have been happy if I went back to the kind of girl I was when he married me," Frankie Cooper recalled, "and that was a little homebody there on the farm, in the kitchen. I wasn't that person anymore. . . . I tried it for a couple, three years, but it just didn't work out. . . . I did all the things—churned butter, visited the neighbors, I became president of the PTA—I did all the things, but I wasn't satisfied. I just had that restlessness. . . . I wanted to go back to work."

As women's expectations shifted, divorces multiplied. In 1946, the United States would experience the highest divorce rate in the world, thirty-one divorces for every hundred marriages. Shirley Hackett had supported herself while her husband was away and had become accustomed to an independent life. But the moment her husband returned, she was expected to revert to the role of housewife. When her husband found her writing checks to pay the bills, he asked, "Why do you want to do that? I'm back!" When he saw her changing a tire on the car, he treated her as if she were "insane" to think that she could do such a thing. Troubles developed in the marriage.

War wife Dellie Hahne had a similar experience. "My husband did not care for my independence," she recalled. "He had left a shrinking violet and come home to a very strong oak tree." The marriage lasted only a few years. "I think the seeds of my liberation and many other women's started with the war," she observed. The first intimation Hahne had of the changes that were taking place came when she was invited to a friend's house for Sunday dinner and heard the mother and grandmother talk about which drill would bite into a piece of metal at the factory. "My God, this was Sunday dinner in Middle America and to hear, instead of a discussion of the church service, a conversation about how to sharpen tools—it was a marvelous thing. I remember thinking that these women would never again be the same."

Throughout the war, Eleanor had talked unceasingly about her hopes for the next generation of women, but even she could not have foreseen the myriad ways in which the experiences of women war workers would affect the lives and prospects of their daughters. "Mothers that worked during the war . . . I think they have a less conservative outlook than if they had stayed in the home," Frankie Cooper said. "They traveled . . . met different kinds of people, they listened to different kinds of ideas, they went home with a completely different outlook on life. I think that this rubbed off on their children. You see, the boys that went overseas had their war stories, and the women that were in war work had theirs. And daughters and sons listened to these."

In a *Senior Scholastic* poll of thirty-three thousand girl students taken in 1946, 88 percent wanted a career in addition to homemaking, and only 4 percent chose homemaking exclusively. The war had proved to millions of women, Frankie Cooper observed, that they could do things they'd thought they couldn't, and now they were telling their daughters: "You can do anything you want to. You can be anybody you want to. And you can go anywhere you want to."

The war had made possible, social historian William Chafe has written, what no amount of agitation could achieve. "The content of women's lives had changed, and an important new area of potential activity had opened up to them. Work had proved liberating and once a new consciousness had been formed, there was no going back."

• • •

From the beginning of the war, Eleanor had insisted that the struggle abroad would not be worth winning unless democracy were renewed at home. All along, Franklin had assured her that the mobilization process would be an agent of change, that once the dormant energies of democracy were unleashed, the country would be transformed.

Eleanor had been unable to share in her husband's optimism; she had worried constantly about what America would look like after the fighting stopped, whether the liberal and humane values which had animated the New Deal were being sacrificed to the necessities of war. But in the fall of 1945, as she began traveling around the country again, she realized that the nation had taken even greater strides toward social justice during the war than it had during the New Deal. Indeed, the Roosevelt years had witnessed the most profound social revolution in the country since the Civil War—nothing less than the creation of modern America.

The small-town America, where people clung to their roots, immobilized within their ethnic and income class, had passed into history. Over fifteen million Americans had left their home towns to work in war plants and shipyards and were living in a different state or county from the place of their birth. Twelve million more had entered the armed forces and been flung out over the turbulent globe. More than 20 percent of the entire population had taken part in the great migration. They had moved from the farm to the factory, from the South to the North, from the East to the exploding states of the Western rim. And there would be no return. The habit of mobility, which would prove both liberating and fragmenting, had become ingrained. America had become irrevocably an urban nation.

The war had been both a catalyst of unity and a disrupter of community ties. More than ever, citizens sought their identity not through ethnic bonds, but as Americans. Flagmakers fell months behind in their orders. There was a sharp decline in foreign-language radio broadcasts, and many foreign-language publications went bankrupt. Men and women hastened to become American citizens—almost two million aliens became naturalized during the six years preceding and following the war. Yet this new national identity also threatened the smaller units within which Americans had located themselves, both physically and psychologically. It would prove difficult—perhaps impossible—to re-establish the once-secure ties of neighborhood and community.

No segment of American society had been left untouched. More than seventeen million new jobs had been created, industrial production had gone up 100 percent, corporate profits doubled, and the GNP had jumped from $100 billion to $215 billion. The war had radically changed the shape of the American economy, exerting a profound impact on the everyday lives and expectations of people in all parts of the country. In 1940, only 7.8 million Americans out of 132 million made enough money to pay taxes; in 1945, that figure had risen to nearly 50 million in a population of 140 million. The wartime economy allowed millions of Americans who had been on relief to get back on their feet and start over again. Miners had enjoyed steady employment for the first time in twenty years. Automobile workers had doubled their incomes and expanded their skills. Black sharecroppers had left the rural South for the cities of the North, where, despite terrible racial tensions and a hard destiny, they would find a more abundant life than the one they had left behind.

The society of a few haves and a multitude of have-nots had been transformed. Because of the greatest—indeed, the only—redistribution of income downward in the nation's history, a middle-class country had emerged. Half of the American people—those at the lower end of the compensation scale—had doubled their income, while those in the top 20 percent had risen by little more than 50 percent. Those in the bottom half of earners had seen their share of the country's income increase by 16 percent, while those at the top had lost 6 percent. As a result, social historian Geoffrey Perrett observed, "barriers to social and economic equality which had stood for decades were either much reduced or entirely overthrown."

The foundation of postwar progress had been constructed. When the war ended, pent-up demand—desire matched with money—would fuel a postwar boom. And wartime policies would ensure that business had the capital to meet this demand. They had enjoyed large profits and a tax code which enabled industry to carry forward the paper losses from accelerated depreciation to offset taxes. Thus, industry had a large cushion of capital. They had won a new respect from the government and the electorate. They had benefited from a multitude of technological advances and, even more important, had discovered the intimate relation between technology, research, and growth which, a half-century later, is still a dominating characteristic of the modern economy. The fears of a return to depression—which so preoccupied the political leaders who followed Roosevelt—would never be justified.

The American economy had not merely been revitalized, it had been altered. The old laissez-faire ideal—buyers and sellers conducting transactions in an untrammeled market—was gone forever. The feared socialist order would not materialize. Instead, a new economic order would come into being, one that economists would call "a mixed economy." No longer would government be viewed as merely a bystander and an occasional referee, intervening only in times of crisis. Instead, the government would assume responsibility for continued growth and for fairness in the distribution of wealth. Big government—modern government—was here to stay.

The new responsibilities of government amounted to nothing less than a new relationship between the people and those whom they chose for service, a new understanding, a revised social contract, one framed within the democratic limits of the original understanding, but drastically changed in content.

It may well be true that a social revolution is not possible without war or violent internal upheaval. These provide a unity of purpose and an opportunity for change that are rarely present in more tranquil times. But as the history of other countries and America's own experience after World War I illustrates, war and revolution are no guarantee of positive social change. That depends on the time, the nation, and the exercise of leadership. In providing that leadership, Franklin Roosevelt emerges as the towering public figure of the twentieth century.

• • •

Eleanor Roosevelt added a vital dimension of her own to the achievements of wartime America. At a time when her husband was preoccupied with winning the war, she remained an uncompromising voice in behalf of justice in the allocation of wartime gains. Though the logic of Roosevelt's mobilization program in 1940 dictated a policy of accommodation with anti–New Deal business interests, Eleanor strove with considerable effect not only to maintain the fundamental goals of the New Deal but to further social advance. Many joined her in this effort—civil rights leaders, labor leaders, liberal spokesmen. But her voice in the highest councils of decision was always influential and often decisive.

Eleanor Roosevelt's stand on civil rights, her insistence that America could not fight racism abroad while tolerating it at home, remains one of the affirming moments in the history of the home front during the war. Though she was naïve about many aspects of the racial problem, she was far ahead of the president and the times in her understanding that separate but equal facilities were not enough, that the fact of segregation itself impaired the lives of the Negro population.

She had insisted, against the advice of the White House staff, that the president meet with Negro leaders to discuss what could be done about discrimination and segregation in the armed forces. Progress was slow and incomplete, but these meetings, along with Eleanor's continuing intervention, eventually led to broadened opportunities for Negroes in both the army and the navy. Between 1940 and 1945, the Negro military force had increased in size from 5,000 to 920,000 and the number of Negro officers had grown from 5 to over 7,000. Moreover, whereas almost every Negro soldier in 1940 was confined to a service unit, by war's close Negroes held responsible jobs in almost every branch of the army as artillerymen, tankmen, infantrymen, pilots, paratroopers, doctors, and more. "The Negro was no longer regarded as an Army auxiliary," Jean Byers concluded in her study of the Negro in World War II. "He had at last attained the status of a soldier."

The changes in the navy during the war were even more spectacular. Though the navy still had not succeeded in using every Negro "in accordance with his maximum capacity," since half the Negro sailors still remained in the stewards' branch, great strides had been taken. "The Navy of 1945," Byers concluded, "was hardly recognizable as the Navy of 1941." At the start of the war, the navy considered it unthinkable to allow Negroes to enter its organization on an equal footing with white men; Negro sailors could enlist only if willing to serve as mess men. By 1945, hundreds of Negroes were serving in all manner of posts, as machinists and metalsmiths, radiomen and electricians. In 1941, the navy adhered to a rigid policy of racial segregation; in 1945, the navy officially declared that the integration of black and white sailors was "both possible and desirable." In sum, "the Negro was considered a servant by the Navy in 1941; in 1945, the Negro was acknowledged as a sailor."

More than anyone else in the White House, Eleanor was responsible, through her relentless pressure of War Department officials, for the issuance of the two directives that forbade the designation of recreational areas by race and made government-owned and -operated buses available to every soldier regardless of race. By the end of the war, only one major step was needed to ensure true equality for Negro soldiers, and that step would come in 1948, when President Truman issued Executive Order 9981, ending segregation in the armed forces.

Through her travels and her close ties with Negro leaders, Eleanor made Franklin more aware of the new spirit of militancy that was developing within the Negro community in reaction to continuing discrimination in employment. She played an instrumental role in the negotiations surrounding the threatened March on Washington which led to the creation of the FEPC, the first presidential action on civil rights since the Civil War. She provided access for Negro leaders and ordinary Negro citizens. American Airlines President C. R. Smith recalled that, when he came to the White House one night, "the place was running over with blacks." Smith said to Eleanor: "Looks like we're entertaining most of the blacks in the country tonight." She said: " 'Well, C.R., you must remember that the President is their President also.' " Such moments were all part of a bigger victory—making the federal government more relevant and more responsive to Negro Americans.

Though civil rights remained the great unfinished business of American democracy at the end of the war, Eleanor could take much satisfaction in knowing that the war had been a turning point in the struggle, a watershed experience in which the seeds of the protest movements of the succeeding decades were sown. Looking back on the 1940s, historian Carey McWilliams observed that "more has happened in the field of race relations in this country; more interest has been aroused; more has been said and written; more proposed and accomplished than in the entire span of years from the end of the Civil War to 1940." These years, historian Richard Dalfiume confirms, constitute "the forgotten years of the Negro revolution."

Eleanor was also far ahead of her time in championing the movement of women into the factories. Through her speeches and her columns, she provided a powerful counterweight to the negative attitudes that prevailed in the early years of the war against women working outside the home. She played a central role in securing government funds for day-care centers and in getting local cities and towns to provide after-school programs, takeout foods, and community laundries. If there had been no Eleanor Roosevelt, women would still have gone to work, but the conditions under which they worked would have been far less conducive to the preservation of home life, and their resulting productivity would have been substantially lower.

Eleanor's influence can also be seen in the generally supportive position Roosevelt adopted toward labor during the war despite the rising frustration and anger of Congress and the public against unions and strikes. Her constant reminder that labor should not bear the brunt of sacrifice as the country converted to a war footing, served to counter the powerful voices of the businessmen who flooded into Washington during the war. And her insistence on the importance of planning for the postwar period played an important role in Roosevelt's call for the GI Bill of Rights.

She also had her own share of failures. Her misguided appointments and actions at the Office of Civilian Defense brought about the congressional outburst which blunted her voice and forced her resignation. Her call for tolerance toward the Japanese Americans was lost in the tide of hysteria that followed Pearl Harbor. Her attempts to bring more refugees into the United States met with limited success. Her call for the protection of small business went unheeded. Her hopes for using the defense emergency as a lever for replacing the slums were never realized.

Unsympathetic observers referred to her as "Lady Bountiful," "The Busybody," "The Meddler," and "The Gab." It was said that she was not a systematic thinker, that she had no ability to focus or to set priorities, that her chatty columns qualified as journalism only through her position, that she was the victim of her generous impulses, intervening in behalf of any person in trouble, whether the complaints were justified or not. "Oh, my God, here's another one," officials at the War Department and the State Department would lament when yet another missive from Mrs. Roosevelt would reach them.

Even Eleanor's most ardent admirers in the Roosevelt inner circle admitted that she pushed her husband too hard at the end of the day, when he was tired and needed to relax. "She would come in after he'd been wrestling with major problems all day long and insist that he find a job for some unemployed actor in New York," Anna's daughter, Eleanor Seagraves, recalled. And if he refused to do something she asked, she would come back again and again until it reached the point where he had to tell his aides to keep her away. If he would not meet somebody she thought he should meet, she would simply invite the person to dinner without telling anyone and seat the person next to the president. "I think he let her get away with stuff he wouldn't have," White House aide Jonathan Daniels said, "if he hadn't had that sense of guilt."

It was said jokingly in Washington during the war years that Roosevelt had a nightly prayer: "Dear God, please make Eleanor a little tired." But in the end, he often came around to her way of thinking. Labor adviser Anna Rosenberg had been one of those who criticized Eleanor's unceasing pressure on the president, but years later she changed her mind. "I remember him saying, 'We're not going to do that now. Tell Eleanor to keep away; I don't want to hear about that anymore.' And then 2–3 weeks later he would say, 'Do you remember that thing Eleanor brought up? Better look into it, maybe there's something to it—I heard something to indicate that maybe she's right.' I'm not sure she would have had the opportunity to bring things to his attention unless she pressured him—I mean he was so involved and in retrospect it was never anything for herself. . . . He would never have become the kind of President he was without her."

They made an extraordinary team. She was more earnest, less devious, less patient, less fun, more uncompromisingly moral; he possessed the more trustworthy political talent, the more finely tuned sense of timing, the better feel for the citizenry, the smarter understanding of how to get things done. She could travel the country when he could not; she could speak her mind without the constraints of public office. She was the agitator; he was the politician. But they were linked by indissoluble bonds and they drew strength from each other. "The truth of the matter is that a deep and unshakeable affection and tenderness existed between them," Jimmy Roosevelt said.

On the walls of the president's study hung a charming portrait of Eleanor painted when she was young. "You know, I've always liked that portrait," Franklin told Frances Perkins. "It's a beautiful portrait, don't you think so? . . . You know the hair's just right, isn't it? Lovely hair! Eleanor has lovely hair, don't you think so?" As Perkins listened, she was struck by the "light in his eye," which to her mind signaled "the light of affection." White House aide Isador Lubin also witnessed frequent moments of affection, when the president would kid Eleanor about something in a light way and would "give her a whack on the fanny."

The fact that "certain parts of their marriage were not as happy as one would have hoped," Anna later said, did not mean that Eleanor didn't love Franklin. "She did love Father. There wasn't any doubt." Eleanor's close friend Esther Lape agreed. "I don't think she ever stopped loving him. That was why he always had the ability to hurt her."

"He might have been happier with a wife who was completely uncritical,"

Eleanor observed in her memoirs. "That I was never able to be, and he had to find it in other people. Nevertheless, I think I sometimes acted as a spur, even though the spurring was not always wanted or welcome. I was one of those who served his purposes."

"She had indeed served his purposes," historian Lois Scharf wrote, "but he had also served hers. He furnished the stage upon which her incomparable abilities and human qualities could gain the widest audience and respect. Few Presidents and no other First Ladies have ever used the platform to such effect. In less obvious ways he was her spur as much as she was his." Together they mobilized existing forces "to create a far different political and social landscape than the one that had existed when they entered the White House."

Though years would pass before the full extent of these changes were understood, Eleanor was convinced in the fall of 1945 that "a new country is being born." It seemed to her, she told her son Jimmy, that "a giant transference of energy" had taken place between the president and the people. "In the early days, before Pearl Harbor," she said, "Franklin was healthy and strong and committed to the Allied cause while the country was sick and weak and isolationist. But gradually, as the president animated his countrymen to the dangers abroad, the country grew stronger and stronger while he grew weaker and weaker, until in the end he was dead and the country had emerged more powerful and more productive than ever before."

It was a romanticized view of her husband's leadership, ignoring the many fierce arguments they had had during the war regarding his decision to intern the Japanese Americans, his failure to do more to help the Jews of Europe, his surrender to big business on military contracts, his caution on civil rights. She had brooded over his shortcomings while he was alive, but now she could idealize him as she had idealized her father, and grasp the elements of his greatness—his supreme confidence, his contagious faith, his sense of timing, his political skills. Beneath all, there had been, she could now see, a fundamental commitment to humane and democratic values, a steadiness of purpose, a determination to win the war as fast as possible, a vision of the principles on which the peace would be based, a dedication to better the life of the average American.

"As I look back over the years," she wrote, "I think that I am most grateful for the fact that my husband earned and deserved the love and respect of his countrymen. He cared greatly about his fellow man and they returned his concern with a full measure of affection."

• • •

As Eleanor began to realize the magnitude of her husband's legacy, she also came to terms with Lucy's return to Franklin's life and with Anna's role in making her visits possible. While she was going through her husband's belongings at Hyde Park, she came upon a little watercolor of Franklin that Lucy's friend Madame Shoumatoff had painted. She instructed Margaret Suckley to send the painting on to Lucy.

"Thank you so very much," Lucy wrote Eleanor; "you must know that it will be treasured always. I have wanted to write you for a long time to tell you that I had seen Franklin and of his great kindness about my husband when he was desperately ill in Washington, and of how helpful he was too, to his boys—and that I hoped very much that I might see you again. . . . I think of your sorrow—you—whom I have always felt to be the most blessed and privileged of women must now feel immeasurable grief and pain and they must be almost unbearable. . . . As always, Affectionately, Lucy Rutherfurd."

Later that week, Anna telephoned Lucy. She had not spoken to Lucy since her father's death, but now, perhaps knowing from Margaret Suckley what Eleanor had done, she felt free to call. "Your telephoning the other night meant so much to me," Lucy wrote Anna. "I did not know that it was in me just now to be so glad to hear the sound of any voice—and to hear you laugh—was beyond words wonderful."

> *I had not written before for many reasons—but you were constantly in my thoughts & with very loving and heart torn sympathy & I was following every step of the way. This blow must be crushing to you—to all of you—but I know that you meant more to your Father than any one and that makes it closer & harder to bear. It must be an endless comfort to you that you were* able *to be with him so much this past year. Every second of the day you must be conscious of the void and emptiness, where there has always been—all through your life—the strength of his beloved presence—so filled with loving understanding, so ready to guide and to help. I love to think of his very great pride in you. . . . He told me so often & with such feeling of all that you had meant of joy & comfort on the trip to Yalta. He said you had been so extraordinary & what a difference it made to have you. He told me of your charm & your tact—& of how* everyone *loved you. He told how capable you were & how you forgot nothing & of the little typewritten chits he would find at his place at the beginning or end of the day—reminding him of all the little or big things that he was to do. I hope he told* you *these things—but sometimes one doesn't. In any case you must have known—words were not needed between you. I have been reading over some very old letters of his—and in one he says: "Anna is a dear fine person—I wish so much that you knew her"—Well, now we do know one another—and it is a great joy to me & I think he was happy this past year that it was so. . . . And through it all one hears his ringing laugh & one thinks of all the ridiculous things he used to say—& do—& enjoy. The picture of him sitting waiting for you that night with the Rabbi's cap on his extraordinarily beautiful head is still vivid.*
>
> *Forgive me for writing of things which you know so much better than I—& which are sacred—& should not ever be touched on by a stranger. I somehow cannot feel myself to be that, & I feel strongly that you understand.*

My love to your husband—and to you—Anna darling, because you are his child & because you are yourself.

I am very devotedly & with heartbroken sympathy

Lucy Rutherfurd

Anna kept Lucy's letter in her bedside table for the rest of her life, "showing it," her son Johnny recalled, "only on a few occasions, in privacy, to those for whom she had a special trust and care and to whom she wished to convey something of herself for which she had no words of her own. Perhaps no one other than Lucy could have confirmed the father-love she so treasured, first and to the end, and the depth of her loss." At the same time, Anna's daughter, Sistie, speculated, Lucy's precious letter may have lessened the guilt Anna felt toward her mother. "Perhaps, by revealing what a fine person Lucy was, a person of such innate dignity and poise, the letter justified the quiet arrangements Anna had made to bring Lucy and her father together."

A strain between mother and daughter lasted through the summer and into the fall. The return to Seattle in June had not been easy for Anna and John. A disagreement with publisher William Randolph Hearst led to their severance from the *Post-Intelligencer,* and John was having trouble figuring out what to do. His self-esteem was at a low ebb. For almost a quarter of a century, he wrote Eleanor, he had had "a flood of work" constantly ahead of him, but now he had no specific responsibilities and "he was running scared." The death of FDR marked the end of an era for John, his son, Johnny, observed, the end of an inspired time in which he had lived in the protective shadow of his father-in-law's position. His old feelings of inferiority now returned, creating serious tensions in his marriage.

When Anna came east in mid-October, she was worried about her husband and anxious about the future. Walking with her mother through the Big House, she was close to tears. It was the last time she would ever see the house as she had known it as a child. The government was about to take it over and begin the process of turning it into a museum. "I think it is very hard for her," Eleanor confided in Hick. Later that night, when the conversation turned to John, Anna broke down. Her tears released the remaining tension between mother and daughter, just as Eleanor's tears had released the strain between them two decades earlier, when Anna was an adolescent.

Eleanor assured Anna that all was forgiven between them. She had come to the realization that her daughter had never meant to hurt her, but was only trying to provide a measure of relaxation for her weary father. What is more, she had come to forgive Franklin as well. "All human beings have failings," she later observed, "all human beings have needs and temptations and stresses. Men and women who live together through long years get to know one another's failings; but they also come to know what is worthy of respect and admiration in those they live with and in themselves."

• • •

For the rest of her life, her son Elliott observed, Eleanor "chose to remember only the lovely times they had shared, never the estrangement and pain." She loved to quote word for word the things they had told one another. She kept up the traditions he had established for the family—including the picnic on the Fourth of July and the reading of Dickens at Christmas. Maureen Corr, Eleanor's secretary during the forties and fifties, remembers her "constantly talking about what Franklin did or what Franklin said or . . . how Franklin thought about this or that. And every time she mentioned his name you could hear the emotion in her voice and see the glow in her eyes."

In early December 1945, President Truman telephoned Eleanor in her Washington Square apartment. The first meeting of the United Nations General Assembly was scheduled to open in January in London. Would she be willing to serve as a member of the American delegation? Oh no, she said, she could not possibly do it. She had no experience or background in foreign affairs. Truman refused to be put off. He urged her to think about it for a while and assured her he had no doubt whatsoever about her capabilities. Eleanor debated her decision for days. She considered the United Nations to be the greatest of her husband's legacies, and she longed for the job, but was terrified of failure. Finally, conquering what she called her "fear and trembling," she accepted the position, setting forth on a new journey into the field of universal human rights that would make her "the most admired person in the world"—and an important figure in American public life for nearly two more decades.

In these first months on her own, Eleanor derived constant comfort from a little verse sent to her by a friend. "They are not dead who live in lives they leave behind. In those whom they have blessed they live a life again." These simple lines, she wrote, inspired her to make the rest of her life worthy of her husband's memory. As long as she continued to fight for his ideals, he would continue to live.

AFTERWORD

Harry Hopkins resigned from the government after Roosevelt died. "The time has come," he wrote President Truman, "when I must take a rest." In September 1945, at a White House ceremony, he was awarded the Distinguished Service Medal for what Truman called his exceptional ability in welding the Allies together in World War II. Four months later, in January 1946, Hopkins died. He was fifty-five. "A strong, bright, fierce flame has burned out a frail body," Churchill said on hearing the news.

Lucy Mercer Rutherfurd continued to divide her time between her estates in Aiken, South Carolina, and Allamuchy, New Jersey. In June 1945, she told her friend Elizabeth Shoumatoff that she had burned all of Roosevelt's letters. Three years later, Lucy was diagnosed with leukemia. She died in July 1948, at the age of fifty-seven, and was buried beside her husband at Tranquility Farms in Allamuchy.

Malvina Thompson continued to work for Mrs. Roosevelt until 1953, when she died in a New York hospital from a brain hemorrhage. She was sixty-one.

Crown Princess Martha returned with her husband to Norway after it was liberated in May 1945. In June, King Haakon and the royal family were officially welcomed home with a triumphant celebration. In 1954, Martha died of a liver ailment at the age of fifty-three. The crown prince never remarried. He became king when his father died in 1957, and ruled until his death in 1991. His son, Harald, is now king of Norway.

Winston Churchill settled unhappily into his postwar role as leader of the parliamentary opposition, occupying his days with the writing of his monumental history of World War II. In 1951, the Conservatives were returned to power and Churchill became prime minister a second time. He remained in power until 1955, when ill-health forced his resignation. He suffered a massive stroke in early January 1965 and died two weeks later, at the age of ninety. He was the first commoner to be accorded a state funeral since the duke of Wellington more than a century earlier.

Lorena Hickok eventually moved to a little cottage in Hyde Park, where she remained until her death in 1968, at the age of seventy-five. In her will, she requested that her ashes be scattered among the trees along the Hudson. The funeral home, unaware of her request, placed them on a shelf along with other unclaimed items, where they remained for years, until her sister, Ruby, honored her request.

Joe Lash remained friendly with Eleanor until the end of her life. After Eleanor's death, the Roosevelt children authorized him to write her biography based on her private papers. Published when Lash was sixty-one, the book won the Pulitzer Prize. Lash died in 1987 at the age of seventy-seven.

Anna and John Boettiger bought a newspaper in Phoenix, Arizona, in 1946. When the newspaper failed, John became increasingly depressed. In 1949, he and Anna were divorced. The following year, John committed suicide by jumping from the window of a New York hotel. Two years later, Anna married Dr. James Halsted, a clinical professor of medicine at Albany Medical College. Anna died of cancer in 1975, at the age of sixty-nine.

John Roosevelt died in 1981 of heart failure at New York Hospital. He was sixty-five. The only one of the Roosevelt boys who never ran for elective office, he was a businessman and an investment banker. In 1952, he became a Republican. He was married twice.

FDR, Jr., died of cancer in 1988, on his seventy-fourth birthday. He served three terms in Congress from the Upper West Side of Manhattan. He ran twice for governor of New York, losing the first race to Averell Harriman, the second to Nelson Rockefeller. In 1960, he campaigned for John Kennedy and was appointed undersecretary of commerce. He was married five times.

Elliott Roosevelt died of congestive heart failure in 1990, at the age of eighty. He authored fourteen books, including three biographical works on his family, and a series of mystery novels which cast Eleanor as a detective. In 1962, he moved to Miami Beach, where he served as mayor. He was married five times.

James Roosevelt died in 1991, at the age of eighty-three, of complications from a stroke. In 1950, he won the Democratic nomination for governor of California, but was defeated by Earl Warren. He was elected to Congress four years later from the 26th district in California. He remained in the

House for six terms. In 1972, he played a prominent role in Democrats for Nixon. He was married four times.

Eleanor Roosevelt remained an important political figure until her death in 1962, at the age of seventy-seven. She was a leading force behind the United Nations' Declaration of Human Rights adopted in 1948, a vigorous advocate for the establishment of a Jewish state in Israel, a prominent actor in New York politics, a supporter of Adlai Stevenson, and a founding member of Americans for Democratic Action. During her last years, she was often called "the greatest woman in the world." Mourners at her funeral included President and Mrs. Kennedy, Vice-President Johnson, former Presidents Truman and Eisenhower, Chief Justice Earl Warren, Adlai Stevenson, Frances Perkins, James Farley, Sam Rosenman, and Francis Biddle. She was buried next to her husband in the rose garden at the Hyde Park estate. A plain white marble monument marks the grave. As President Roosevelt wished, it contains no decoration and no inscription except the following:

FRANKLIN DELANO ROOSEVELT

1882–1945

ANNA ELEANOR ROOSEVELT

1884–1962

A NOTE ON SOURCES

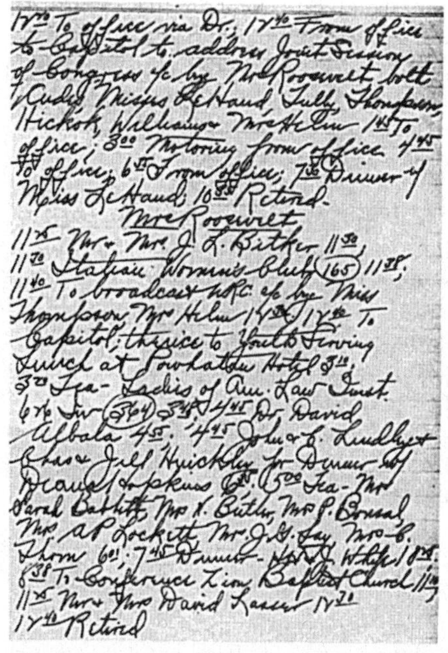

12^{10} To office via Dr.; 12^{40} From office
to Capitol to address Joint Session
of Congress ac by Mrs Roosevelt, both
Aides, Misses LeHand, Tully, Thompson,
Hickok, Williams & Mrs Helm 1^{45} To
office; 3^{00} Motoring from office 4^{45}
To office; 6^{15} From office; 7^{30} Dinner of
Miss LeHand; 10^{55} Retired-
Mrs Roosevelt
11^{25} Mr & Mrs J. L. Bitker 11^{30};
11^{30} Italian Woman's Club (165) 11^{38};
11^{40} To broadcast NBC ac by Miss
Thompson, Mrs Helm 12^{30}; 12^{40} To
Capitol; thence to Youth Serving
Lunch at Powhatan Hotel 3^{10};
3^{30} Tea - Ladies of Am. Law Inst.
[illegible] (364) 3^{45}; 4^{45} Dr David
Albala 4^{55}; 4^{45} John & L. Lindley &
Chas & Jill Hinckley for Dinner w/
Diana Hopkins [illegible]; 5^{00} Tea - Mrs
Sarah Babbitt, Mrs R. Butler, Mrs J. Bruseal,
Mrs A P Lockett, Mrs J. G. Fay, Mrs C.
Thorn 6^{00}; 7^{45} Dinner - [illegible] 8^{25};
8^{38} To Conference Zion Baptist Church 11^{10};
11^{15} Mr & Mrs David Lasser 12^{30}
12^{40} Retired

This book relies predominantly upon a multitude of primary materials: manuscript collections, memoranda, private letters, diaries, memoirs, office files, oral histories, pamphlets, newspapers, periodicals, personal interviews. The White House Usher Diaries proved an especially invaluable guide at the start of the project. These day-by-day, even minute-by-minute chronologies reveal when the president and the first lady awakened, who joined them for meals and meetings, how much time was spent with each visitor, where they went during the day, when they went to bed at night. With these daily chronologies as my base, I searched for personal diaries, letters, oral histories, and memoirs of the people who were with Franklin and Eleanor Roosevelt at particular moments of interest. Eleanor's daily columns also proved essential. Though they ramble from one topic to the next, and often were limited to an account of her daily activities, they do give us an insight into contemporaneous concerns and perceptions.

I treasure the details that emerged from these primary sources: an interview with the president's daughter-in-law revealed the nightly ritual Roosevelt followed as he tried to fall asleep in the middle of the war; a talk with the White House butler produced the unforgettable image of Winston Churchill standing in his long underwear, demanding ninety-year-old brandy in his White House suite every night; an oral history provided the telling description of how the president's face would light up when his daughter, Anna, walked into the room; a diary entry revealed the dramatic scene when the president's mother wheeled him away from the dinner table in order to end an unpleasant discussion with Eleanor; letters to the president asking him to muzzle his wife, chain her up or, at the very least, make her stay at home with her knitting, revealed the depth of animosity felt by some toward her unusual independence.

Some of my favorite details came from the press reports of the time: the woman's scream from the audience as she witnessed the lottery drawing for the draft and realized that her son held the first number drawn; the observation that the president's nervousness before his press conferences resembled that of an opera singer about to go on stage; the likening of Harry Hopkins' weary look to that of "an ill-fed horse at the end of a hard day," the run on maps when Roosevelt announced that he wanted people listening to his fireside chat to follow along with a map spread before them; the sweat dripping from Wendell Willkie's forehead as he delivered his acceptance speech; the trembling of Roosevelt's hands as he stood before a Joint Session of Congress; the image of dozens of laborers working around the clock to stuff huge chunks of ice into the primitive air-conditioning in the president's train; the spontaneous remark when a worker at the Chrysler tank arsenal realized the man in the visitor's car was President Roosevelt—"By God, if it ain't old Frank."

Details such as these can only emerge from research. To remedy gaps in knowledge by fabricating details, even those which may seem inconsequential, is to shift from nonfiction to fiction and is a betrayal of the historian's trust.

Though my story took place more than a half century ago, I was able to talk with scores of people who knew the Roosevelts and the members of their extended family personally. A list of my interviews follows.

INTERVIEWS

Winthrop Aldrich
Bernard Asbell
Carl Ally
Toinette Bachelder
William Barber
Mildred Barker
Roberta Barrows
Eleanor Bartman
Betty Bishop
John Boettiger, Jr.
Dr. Howard Bruenn
Dorothy Butturf
Maureen Corr
Barbara Mueller Curtis
Egbert Curtis
Dawn Deslie
Robert Donovan
Betty Dooley
Jim D'Orta
Dorothy Dow
Barbara Dudley
Virginia Durr
Meg Egeberg
George Elsey
William Emerson
Creekmore Fath
Lewis Feuer
Alonzo Fields
Fran Fremont-Smith
Frank Friedel
Larry Fuchs
John Kenneth Galbraith
David Ginsburg
Rosemary Goepper
Arthur Goldschmidt
Edna Gurewitsch
Kate Roosevelt Haddad
Diana Hopkins Halsted
Elinor Hendrik
Robert Hopkins
James Hymes, Jr.
Jiro Ishihara
Tama Ishihara
Barbara Jacques
Eliot Janeway
Frances Kaplan
Jan Karski
Mary Keyserling
Mary Gaston Kramer
Trude Lash
Michael Lilly
Milton Lipson
Mayris Chaney Martin
Sara McClendon

Henry Morgenthau III
Louise Morley
Kathleen Harriman Mortimer
Robert Nathan
Verne Newton
Thomas P. O'Neill
John Pehle
Ruth Thompson Peirce
Esther Peterson
Jane Plakias
Joyce Ralph
Joseph Rauh
Curtis Roosevelt
Eleanor Wotkyns Roosevelt
Elliott Roosevelt
James Roosevelt
James Roosevelt, Jr.
Jane Scarborough
Eleanor Seagraves
Virginia Shipp
David Smith
Grace Stang
Richard Strobel
Margaret Suckley
Mark Talisman
Walter Trohan
Mary Veeder
Betsey Roosevelt Whitney
Elizabeth Wickenden
Billy Wilder
Mary Willett
Page Huidekoper Wilson

NOTES

ABBREVIATIONS USED IN NOTES

AB Anna Boettiger*
AH Anna Halsted*
ER Eleanor Roosevelt
FDR Franklin Delano Roosevelt
HH Harry Hopkins
JL Joseph Lash
LH Lorena Hickok
MLH Missy LeHand
SDR Sara Delano Roosevelt
WC Winston Churchill
WW Walter White

AM *Atlantic Monthly*
BEA *Boston Evening American*
BG *Boston Globe*
CB *Current Biography*
CR *Congressional Record*
LHJ *Ladies' Home Journal*
MD "My Day" (Eleanor Roosevelt's column)
NR *New Republic*
NYHT *New York Herald Tribune*
NYT *New York Times*
OH Oral History
PC *Pittsburgh Courier*
SEP *Saturday Evening Post*
TIMS *This Is My Story* by Eleanor Roosevelt
TIR *This I Remember* by Eleanor Roosevelt
TP *Times Picayune,* New Orleans, Louisiana
WP *Washington Post*

FDRL Franklin D. Roosevelt Library
OF Office File, Franklin D. Roosevelt Papers
PPF President's Personal File, Franklin D. Roosevelt Papers
PSF President's Secretary's File, Franklin D. Roosevelt Papers

PREFACE

9 living arrangements at the White House: William Seale, *The President's House: A History* (1986), vol. II, pp. 926–28.
10 he could truly see . . . : George Martin, *Madame Secretary: Frances Perkins* (1976), p. 435.
11 "the most influential woman . . .": Joan Hoff-Wilson and Marjorie Lightman, eds., *Without Precedent: The Life and Career of Eleanor Roosevelt* (1984), p. 11.
11 "this is no ordinary time . . .": *WP,* July 19, 1940, p. 1.

* Anna Roosevelt was married to John Boettiger during the war years. She married James Halsted in 1952.

CHAPTER ONE: "The Decisive Hour Has Come"

13 On nights filled with tension: interview with Betsey Whitney.
14 John Cudahy call: *WP,* May 10, 1940, p. 1.
14 German planes in the air: Jay Pierpont Moffat, *The Moffat Papers* (1956), p. 307.
14 "Pa" Watson: *NYT,* July 23, 1939, sect. VI, p. 6.
14 Stunned Belgians: *WP,* May 10, 1940, p. 1.
14 A thirteen-year-old: *Time,* May 20, 1940, p. 18.
14 Bombs were also falling: *Newsweek,* May 20, 1940, p. 18.
14 freeze all assets: *WP,* May 10, 1940, pp. 1, 3.
15 had received "proof": *NYT,* May 10, 1940, p. 1.
15 "The decisive hour . . .": *Time,* May 20, 1940, p. 22.
15 "in times of crisis . . .": Adolf Berle quoted in Moffat, *Papers,* p. 307.
15 Irvin McDuffie: obituary, *NYT,* Jan. 31, 1946, p. 28.
15 "he couldn't help . . .": ER interview, Graff Papers, FDRL.
15 straightened his legs: Hugh Gregory Gallagher, *FDR's Splendid Deception* (1985), p. 163.
15 Description of bedroom: *Collier's,* Sept. 14, 1946, pp. 96–97.
15 Eleanor basket: *NYT,* July 5, 1936, sect. IV, p. 7.
15 "Like every room . . .": Arthur M. Schlesinger, Jr., *The Age of Roosevelt,* vol. II, *The Coming of the New Deal* (1958), p. 511.
16 his aunt Laura: Geoffrey C. Ward, *Before the Trumpet* (1985), pp. 117–18.
16 "We assured him . . .": James Roosevelt, *My Parents: A Differing View* (1976), p. 81.
16 "very active . . .": AH, *OH,* Columbia University.
16 "a wonderful playmate . . .": AH interview, Graff Papers, FDRL.
16 "the handsomest . . .": interview with James Roosevelt.
16 "trial by fire": Joseph P. Lash, *Eleanor and Franklin* (1971), p. 267.
16 "There had been a plowing . . .": *Collier's,* Aug. 24, 1946, p. 12.
17 "his vital links . . .": Arthur M. Schlesinger, Jr., *The Age of Roosevelt,* vol. I, *The Crisis of the Old Order* (1957), p. 407.
17 "Anyone who has gone . . .": Lash, *Eleanor and Franklin,* p. 424.
17 "He was smiling . . .": interview with Eliot Janeway.
17 FDR's morning routine: *New Yorker,* June 16, 1934, pp. 24–25.
18 ER's visit to the city: *MD,* May 9–11, 1940.
18 honored by *The Nation: NYT,* May 2, 1940, p. 18.
18 "distinguished service . . .": *Nation,* May 18, 1940, p. 623.
18 "What is an institution? . . .": ibid.
18 "My dear, I don't care . . .": *NYT,* May 2, 1940, p. 18.
19 "It never seems . . .": *MD,* May 3, 1940.
19 "I will do my best . . .": *NYT,* May 2, 1940, p. 18.
19 "Mrs. Roosevelt's incessant . . .": *Fortune,* May 1940, p. 160.
19 Lucy Mercer: Bernard Asbell, *The FDR Memoirs* (1973), pp. 228–33.
19 "the bottom dropped . . .": Joseph P. Lash, *Love, Eleanor* (1982), p. 66.
19 Story of SDR and divorce: ibid., pp. 66–71; James Roosevelt, *My Parents,* pp. 99–102; AH, unpublished article, box 84, Halsted Papers, FDRL.
20 "an ordeal to be borne": Asbell, *FDR Memoirs,* p. 222.
20 "an exaggerated idea . . .": Geoffrey C. Ward, *A First-Class Temperament* (1989), p. 17.
20 "There's no doubt . . .": Raymond Moley, *The First New Deal* (1966), pp. 273–75.
20 "When Missy gave . . .": Lillian Rogers Parks, *The Roosevelts: A Family in Turmoil* (1981), p. 177.
20 "she had a certain class . . .": Asbell, *FDR Memoirs,* p. 247.
21 "The first thing . . .": *NYT,* June 10, 1934, sect. VI, p. 9.
21 "Albany was the hardest . . .": *SEP,* Jan. 8, 1938, p. 60.
21 "In terms of companionship . . .": interview with Eliot Janeway.
22 poked his head: *SEP,* Jan. 8, 1938, p. 60.
22 George Marshall: *Time,* July 29, 1940, pp. 30–33.
22 "Don't you think so . . .": Leonard Mosley, *Marshall: A Hero for Our Times* (1982), pp. 121–22.

22 pre–World War II army: R. Elberton Smith, *The Army and Economic Mobilization* (1959), pp. 24–35, 119–26.
22 "It's a terrible thing . . .": Samuel I. Rosenman, *Working with Roosevelt* (1952), p. 167.
23 136 divisions: Erwin Rommel, *The Rommel Papers* (1953), p. 3.
23 U.S. merely five divisions: memo, Col. J. H. Burns, Ordnance Dept. Executive, to Assist. Sec. of War, May 10, 1940, Morgenthau Papers, FDRL.
23 almost no munitions industry: Charles J. Hitch, *America's Economic Strength* (1941), p. 67.
23 Marshall trying to get Woodring: Richard M. Ketchum, *The Borrowed Years, 1938–1941* (1989), pp. 537–38.
23 "His real weakness . . .": ER interview, Graff Papers, FDRL.
24 "If I were you . . .": *SEP,* June 5, 1948, p. 90.
24 Louis Johnson: Ketchum, *Borrowed Years,* pp. 537–38.
24 Marshall found it incomprehensible: Forrest C. Pogue, *George C. Marshall: Ordeal and Hope, 1939–1942* (1966), vol. II, p. 23.
24 "I'm sorry . . .": ibid., pp. 93–94.
24 "I think he knew exactly . . .": James Rowe, *OH,* FDRL.
24 "I never heard him call . . .": Robert Cutler, *No Time for Rest* (1966), p. 223.
24 "Informal conversation . . .": ibid., p. 224.
25 Cudahy wired: *Time,* May 20, 1940, p. 25.
25 "tangible evidence . . .": Joseph P. Kennedy to Treasury Dept., May 10, 1940, Morgenthau Papers, FDRL.
25 "After the World War . . .": Military Establishment Appropriations Bill, statement of Gen. Marshall, April 30, 1940, p. 30.
25 ". . . a little drawn eyed . . .": *NYHT,* May 11, 1940, p. 19.
25 "Glancing around the room . . .": *NYT,* Feb. 1, 1942, sect. VI, p. 7.
26 "Like an opera singer . . ."; "all-in": ibid.
26 "the best newspaperman . . .": Betty Houchin Winfield, *FDR and the News Media* (1990), p. 1.
26 On press conferences: John Gunther, *Roosevelt in Retrospect* (1950), pp. 134–39; Samuel I. and Dorothy Rosenman, *Presidential Style* (1976), pp. 330–39.
26 bachelor correspondent: Charles Hurd, *When the New Deal Was Young and Gay* (1965), p. 241.
26 "By the brilliant but simple trick . . .": Schlesinger, *Coming of the New Deal,* p. 566.
26 "History will like to say . . .": *NYHT,* May 11, 1940, p. 19.
26 "Good morning . . .": press-conference typescript, collection of speeches, FDRL.
27 "partly in consideration . . .": *NYHT,* May 11, 1940, p. 19.
27 Choate School: *Choate Catalogue,* 1934–1936, p. 33.
27 Malvina Thompson: Lash, *Eleanor and Franklin,* p. 315; Minnewa Bell, *OH,* FDRL.
27 "good Vermont granite . . .": biographical facts on M. Thompson, LH Papers, FDRL.
27 "who makes life . . .": *NYT,* April 13, 1953, p. 27.
27 ER and Tommy traveled: *Life,* Feb. 4, 1940, p. 70.
27 "will o' the wisp": Elliott Roosevelt and James Brough, *A Rendezvous with Destiny* (1975), p. 71.
28 "It was the best education . . ." . . . "One time . . .": Alfred Steinberg, *Mrs. R* (1958), p. 162.
28 "She saw many things . . .": Frances Perkins interview, Graff Papers, FDRL.
28 "Watch the people's . . .": Steinberg, *Mrs. R,* p. 209.
28 "did not know what . . .": ibid.
29 ER in Puerto Rico: Ruby Black, *ER* (1940), p. 296.
29 "I realized that . . .": *NYT,* April 22, 1937, p. 24.
29 "Mrs. Roosevelt Spends Night . . .": William Leuchtenburg, *Franklin D. Roosevelt and the New Deal* (1963), p. 192.
29 "There is something . . .": *MD,* May 11 and 13, 1940.
29 Near the Chapel: *Choate Catalogue,* p. 35.
29 "I wonder that the time . . .": *MD,* May 9, 1940.
30 Talking with her young friend: Lash, *Eleanor and Franklin,* p. 608; *NYHT,* May 27, 1940, p. 8.
30 Her deepest fear: Lash Diary, May 10, 1940, Lash Papers, FDRL.

30 "How to preserve...": *NYT,* May 11, 1940, p. 23.
30 president opened: Gunther, *Roosevelt in Retrospect,* pp. 131–34.
30 Cordell Hull: *CB,* 1940, pp. 412–15.
30 Belgian gold reserves: memo for Treasury from Butterworth, May 10, 1940, Morgenthau Papers, FDRL.
31 Morgenthau had been huddled: memos of May 10, 1940, activities in Morgenthau Papers, FDRL.
31 "as though she had...": *CB,* 1940, p. 645.
31 HH: *CB,* 1941, pp. 405–6.
31 HH in and out of hospitals: interview with Robert Hopkins.
31 "He was to all intents...": Robert E. Sherwood, *Roosevelt and Hopkins* (1948), p. 10.
31 "an ill-fed horse...": *CB,* 1941, p. 406.
31 "a very sad dog": from "Harry Hopkins: At FDR's Side," documentary written by Verne Newton, FDRL. Hereafter cited HH documentary, FDRL.
31 "you wouldn't think...": *WP,* Oct. 31, 1943, p. 2.
31 "to galvanize...": Marquis Childs, *I Write from Washington* (1942), p. 170.
32 "only a five or six months...": Harold L. Ickes, *The Secret Diaries of Harold L. Ickes,* vol. III, *The Lowering Clouds, 1939–1941* (1954), p. 175.
32 90 percent of America's supply: *Time,* May 20, 1940, p. 73.
32 Reconstruction Finance: Ickes, *Secret Diaries,* vol. III, p. 175.
32 word came from London: ibid., p. 176.
32 "I welcome it, indeed...": Richard Collier, *1940: The World in Flames* (1979), p. 74.
32 Attlee's blunt reply: ibid., p. 76.
33 "Looking backward...": *NYT Magazine,* Sept. 14, 1941, p. 5.
33 "Churchill was the best...": Ickes, *Secret Diaries,* vol. III, p. 175.
33 the two leaders had come to admire: *Churchill & Roosevelt: The Complete Correspondence* (1984), vol. I, p. 6.
33 "I shall at all times...": ibid., p. 89.
33 second-floor study: William Seale, *The President's House,* vol. II (1986), p. 989; Rexford G. Tugwell, *The Democratic Roosevelt* (1957), p. 301.
34 "invariably got that lived-in...": Frances Perkins, *The Roosevelt I Knew* (1946), p. 66.
34 The president mixed the drinks: Rosenman, *Working with Roosevelt,* pp. 150–51.
34 FDR's storytelling: ibid., p. 152.
34 John Taber story: *Time,* May 20, 1940, p. 19.
34 "I didn't realize...": interview with Toi Bachelder.
35 "he would not be surprised...": Ickes Diary, p. 3248, Library of Congress.
35 "Vic and I arriving...": HH to MLH, May 22, 1939, HH Papers, FDRL.
35 "the real purpose...": HH to MLH, Aug. 31, 1939, HH Papers, FDRL.
35 "There is no one here...": Sherwood, *Roosevelt and Hopkins,* pp. 114–15.
35 "Even the most ardent...": *Newsweek,* Aug. 12, 1944, p. 16.
35 "should have been off...": Fulton Oursler, *Behold This Dreamer!* (1964), pp. 424–25.
35 "Gosh, it will be good...": MLH to FDR, Dec. 1936, PPF 3737, FDRL.
36 "She was working away...": interview with Margaret Suckley.
36 "In a funny way...": AB to LH, Dec. 2, 1935, LH Papers, FDRL.
36 "Work had become...": interview with Eleanor Wotkyns.
36 "She could be...": interview with Curtis Dall Roosevelt, son of Anna Roosevelt and Curtis Dall.
36 "If only Mother...": interview with Elliott Roosevelt.
37 "Stay for dinner...": HH documentary, FDRL; David E. Lilienthal, *The Journal of David E. Lilienthal,* vol. 1 (1964), pp. 169–70.
37 "There was a temperamental...": Perkins quoted in Louis W. Koenig, *The Invisible Presidency* (1960), p. 317.
37 "feminine sensitivity": Sherwood, *Roosevelt and Hopkins,* p. 2.
37 borrowed a pair of pajamas: *New Yorker,* Aug. 7, 1941, p. 26.
37 "It was Harry...": Sherwood, *Roosevelt and Hopkins,* p. 173.
37 Helen Douglas story: interview with Billy Wilder.
37 "We come here tonight...": text of speech, *NYT,* May 11, 1940, p. 1.
38 British troops were pouring: *WP,* May 11, 1940, p. 1.

38 "a profound sense . . .": Winston S. Churchill, *The Second World War,* vol. I, *The Gathering Storm* (1948), p. 601.
38 "The day was unforgettable . . .": Helen Gahagan Douglas, *OH,* FDRL.
39 "OK, Helen . . .": interview with Billy Wilder.
39 she felt terribly left out: interview with Elliott Roosevelt.
39 "All her life . . .": interview with Eleanor Wotkyns.

CHAPTER TWO: "A Few Nice Boys with BB Guns"

40 Here, on the . . . : Neil MacNeil, *Forge of Democracy: The House of Representatives* (1963), p. 132.
40 In the Congress in 1940: *NYT,* Jan. 7, 1940, sect. VI, p. 3.
41 The president's arrival: *WP,* May 17, 1940, p. 4; *NYT,* May 17, 1940, p. 10.
41 "walls of sand . . .": Cordell Hull, *The Memoirs of Cordell Hull,* vol. II (1948), p. 769.
41 Absent were both: *NYT,* May 17, 1940, pp. 1, 10; *Charlotte Observer,* May 17, 1940, p. 2.
41 failed to put on glasses: *Time,* May 27, 1940, p. 17.
42 "I trust you realize . . .": WC to FDR, May 15, 1940, *Churchill & Roosevelt: The Complete Correspondence* (1984), vol. I, p. 37.
42 "The great knife . . .": quoted in Carl Degler, *Out of Our Past* (1959), p. 383.
42 employment and tax statistics: *Historical Statistics of the United States Colonial Times to 1957* (1961), pp. 67–73, 713–15.
42 Thirty-one percent: Richard Polenberg, *One Nation Divisible* (1980), p. 19.
43 small-town nation: ibid., p. 17.
43 "Class membership . . .": ibid., p. 16.
43 "It is hard to think . . .": William Leuchtenburg in Harvard Sitkoff, *Fifty Years Later: The New Deal Evaluated* (1985), p. 230.
44 "These are ominous days . . .": transcript of speech, collection of speeches, FDRL.
45 "the President's big round number . . .": Irving Holley, Jr., *Buying Aircraft* (1964), p. 228.
45 "like an utterly impossible . . .": Edward R. Stettinius, Jr., *Lend-Lease* (1944), pp. 12–13.
45 In times of crisis: Grant McConnell, *The Modern Presidency* (1976), p. 4.
45 "believed that with enough . . .": *AM,* Sept. 1949, p. 43.
45 "So passionate a faith . . .": ibid., p. 39.
46 In his imagination: interview with James Roosevelt.
46 "There's something . . . ": Perkins, *OH,* Columbia University.
46 "His most outstanding . . .": W. M. Kiplinger, *Washington Is Like That* (1942), p. 14.
46 "those who hear it . . .": Samuel I. and Dorothy Rosenman, *Presidential Style* (1976), p. 321.
46 "his capacity to inspire . . .": *Collier's,* Sept. 12, 1946, p. 102.
46 "the new President . . .": *Collier's,* March 11, 1933, p. 8.
46 "the renewal of the courage . . .": Rosenman and Rosenman, *Presidential Style,* p. 323.
47 "the President is right": *Time,* May 27, 1940, p. 21.
47 "a four alarm fire . . .": *Newsweek,* May 27, 1940, p. 35.
47 "was quickly succeeded . . .": *Time,* May 27, 1940, p. 22.
47 "tragically late": ibid., p. 21.
47 "the failure of the New Deal . . .": *NYT,* May 17, 1940, p. 10.
47 "a defense hysteria . . .": *Vital Speeches,* vol. 6, pp. 485–86.
47 response to Lindbergh speech: *NYT,* May 21, 1940, p. 12.
48 "During the present . . .": *CR,* 76th Cong., 3rd sess., May 13, 1940, p. 5947; May 15, 1940, p. 6163.
48 "If I should die tomorrow . . .": Ted Morgan, *FDR: A Biography* (1985), p. 523.
48 "but when he did get angry . . .": ER interview, Graff Papers, FDRL.
48 "When I read Lindbergh's speech . . .": Henry Stimson to FDR, May 21, 1940, PSF 106, FDRL.
48 ER told a newspaper reporter: *NYT,* May 21, 1940, p. 12.
48 congressional appropriations: Mark S. Watson, *Chief of Staff* (1950), pp. 166–69.
49 "on russet roads . . .": *Time,* May 21, 1940, p. 18.
49 biggest peacetime maneuver: *NYT,* April 28, 1940, p. 19.

49 Blues were heading: *NYT,* May 7, 1940, p. 8; *TP,* April 27, 1940, p. 4.
49 games were intended: *TP,* April 28, 1940, p. 1; *NYT,* April 28, 1940, p. 19.
49 supplies: *Newsweek,* May 13, 1940, p. 29.
49 announcement of games: *TP,* April 14, 1940, sect. II, p. 6.
49 men, women, and children: *TP,* May 10, 1940, p. 1.
49 discrete exercises: ibid.
49 "Consider the task . . .": *TP,* April 14, 1940, sect. II, p. 6.
50 "drilling bright tunnels . . .": *TP,* May 10, 1940, pp. 1, 3.
50 squadron of Red bombers: *NYHT,* May 10, 1940, p. 7.
50 Two days later: *TP,* May 14, 1940, p. 23.
50 maneuver accidents: *TP,* May 5, 1940, p. 1; May 13, 1940, p. 29; May 15, 1940, p. 27; May 18, 1940, p. 7.
50 By week's end: *TP,* May 19, 1940, p. 15.
50 army bombers crashed: *NYT,* June 18, 1940, p. 3.
50 lack of equipment was cited: *TP,* May 25, 1940, p. 3; *NYT,* May 26, 1940, p. 2.
50 Germans' form of attack: Senator Lodge in *CR,* 76th Cong., 3rd sess., May 27, 1940, p. 6876.
50 "the greatest . . .": *TP,* May 23, 1940, p. 3.
51 General Short admitted: *NYT,* May 26, 1940, p. 2.
51 "Too frequently . . .": *Army and Navy Journal,* June 1, 1940, p. 962.
51 "It is a mistake . . .": *Cavalry Journal,* Jan.–Feb. 1940, p. 35.
51 "one finger of the fan-like . . .": *CR,* May 27, 1940, p. 6877.
51 As townspeople watched: *TP,* May 16, 1940, p. 18.
51 "They were hit . . .": *CR,* May 15, 1940, p. 6135.
51 "road-bound": *NYT,* May 26, 1940, p. 2.
52 "the noise of ten robots . . .": *NYT,* Sept. 8, 1940, sect. VII, p. 26.
52 "The gravity of this situation . . .": *CR,* p. 6877.
52 a secret meeting took place: Christopher R. Gabel, "1940 Maneuvers: Prelude to Mobilization," Ohio State University, given to author by Dr. Gabel.
52 "Overnight, the pleasant doings . . .": *Time,* May 27, 1940, p. 19.
52 "The fact remains . . .": ibid.
53 "What smoldered beneath . . .": ibid., p. 21.
53 "There were evidently . . .": George Martin, *Madame Secretary* (1976), p. 435.
53 "that man . . ."; Howland Spencer: William Leuchtenburg, *Franklin D. Roosevelt and the New Deal* (1963), p. 176.
53 ill-will crystallized: ibid., p. 147.
54 "of organized . . .": Franklin D. Roosevelt, *Public Papers and Addresses of Franklin D. Roosevelt, 1940* (1941), pp. 568–69.
54 "as certain as night follows day . . .": *Journal of Economic History,* Winter 1953, p. 69.
54 "It was a political necessity . . .": I. F. Stone, *Business as Usual* (1941), p. 126.
54 NDAC: *WP,* May 29, 1940, pp. 1, 2; *NYT,* May 29, 1940, pp. 1, 15.
54 William Knudsen: *CB,* 1940, pp. 464–65.
55 "To many a citizen . . .": *Time,* Dec. 23, 1940, p. 14.
55 "I am most happy . . .": Norman Beasley, *Knudsen* (1947), p. 246.
55 Edward Stettinius: *CB,* 1940, pp. 761–62.
55 "now the captains . . .": Constance McLaughlin Green, *Washington* (1963), p. 467.
55 "In the field of national defense . . .": *Journal of Economic History,* Winter 1953, p. 74
55 "a little something . . .": *NR,* June 24, 1940, p. 264.
55 Sidney Hillman: *CB,* 1940, pp. 386–88.
55 Leon Henderson: ibid., pp. 377–79.
56 "If you are going . . .": Stimson Diary, Aug. 26, 1940, Yale University.
56 suppose that: Bruce Catton, *The War Lords of Washington* (1969), p. 121.
56 "The conflict was enduring . . .": John Kenneth Galbraith, *A Life in Our Times* (1981), pp. 108–9.
56 "At times . . .": interview with John K. Galbraith.
56 "In private life . . .": quoted in *Army and Navy Journal,* Nov. 2, 1940, p. 226.
56 "the cry . . ."; "let democratic processes . . .": *NR,* Sept. 30, 1940, p. 446.

57 "Who is my boss? . . .": Smith conference notes, May 30, 1940, Harold Smith Papers, FDRL.
57 "So long as . . .": Stone, *Business as Usual,* p. 129.
57 "I think people . . .": Franklin D. Roosevelt, *Public Papers and Addresses, 1940,* pp. 241–50.
57 "an uneasy one . . .": Catton, *War Lords,* p. 25.
57 fireside chats: Russell D. Buhite and David W. Levy, eds., *FDR's Fireside Chats* (1992), p. xv.
57 "a few people . . .": Betty Houchin Winfield, *FDR and the News Media* (1990), p. 104.
58 "You felt he was talking . . .": ibid.
58 "he looked for words . . .": Rosenman and Rosenman, *Presidential Style,* p. 92.
58 a dozen drafts: ibid., p. 11.
58 "there was a last minute dash . . .": Grace Tully, *F.D.R., My Boss* (1949), p. 100.
58 "There was no levity . . .": Rosenman and Rosenman, *Presidential Style,* p. 196.
58 "The President was worried . . .": ibid.
58 "He was conscious . . .": Frances Perkins, *The Roosevelt I Knew* (1946), p. 72.
58 "My friends . . .": *NYT,* May 27, 1940, p. 12.
59 "cost plus fixed fee": R. Elberton Smith, *The Army and Economic Mobilization* (1959), pp. 280–302; see also Gerald White, *Billions for Defense* (1980).
60 "One can't be sure . . .": Joseph P. Lash, *Eleanor Roosevelt: A Friend's Memoir* (1964), p. 67.
60 "glad [the president] . . .": Lash Diary, May 27, 1940, Lash Papers, FDRL.

CHAPTER THREE: "Back to the Hudson"

61 rearmament versus aid to Allies: Mark S. Watson, *Chief of Staff* (1950), ch. 10 generally.
61 "the War Department . . .": ibid., p. 303.
61 "if we had to fight . . .": Cordell Hull, *The Memoirs of Cordell Hull,* vol. II (1948), p. 766.
61 "If Great Britain goes down . . .": Maurice Matloff and Edwin Snell, *Strategic Planning for Coalition Warfare, 1941–1942* (1953), p. 13.
62 "And if I should . . .": Harold L. Ickes, *The Secret Diaries of Harold L. Ickes,* vol. III, *The Lowering Clouds, 1939–1941* (1954), p. 200.
62 "one airplane sent . . .": *CR,* 76th Cong., 3rd sess., p. 3588.
62 "At this moment . . .": William C. Bullitt, *For the President, Personal and Secret* (1972) p. 416.
62 "The Paris police . . .": ibid., p. 434.
62 "This may be the last . . .": ibid., pp. 440–41.
62 "the whole root and core . . .": Arthur Bryant, *The Turn of the Tide* (1957), p. 5.
62 May 24, St. Eloi Church: Norman Gelb, *Dunkirk* (1989), p. 128.
62 Hitler's first great mistake: Martin Gilbert, *The Second World War* (1989), p. 73.
62 "miracle of Dunkirk": Robert Leckie, *Delivered from Evil: The Saga of World War II* (1987), p. 171.
62 From Harwich and Margate: Hanson W. Baldwin, *The Crucial Years, 1939–1941* (1976), pp. 39–41.
63 nearly 340,000 men escaped: Winston S. Churchill, *The Second World War,* vol. II, *Their Finest Hour* (1949), p. 115.
63 "We shall go on . . .": Winston S. Churchill, *Great War Speeches* (1957), p. 25.
63 "So hypnotic . . .": *AM,* Sept. 1949, p. 41.
63 opinion poll: Richard M. Ketchum, *The Borrowed Years, 1938–1941* (1989), p. 354.
63 "must not blind us . . .": Churchill, *Speeches,* p. 23.
63 chaos of the retreat: General Sir William Edmund Ironside, *Time Unguarded* (1962), p. 354; Gilbert, *Second World War,* p. 86.
63 Left in ruins: Gelb, *Dunkirk,* p. 233.
64 "Over a distance . . .": *NYHT,* June 7, 1940, p. 3.
64 Britain's best troops: Edward R. Stettinius, Jr., *Lend-Lease* (1944), p. 24.
64 "all the first fruits . . .": Churchill, *Finest Hour,* p. 125.
64 only 600,000 rifles: Gilbert, *Second World War,* p. 261.
64 "Never has a nation . . .": Churchill, *Finest Hour,* p. 128.

64 "most secret" letter, FDR's response: letter of May 15, 1940, *Churchill & Roosevelt: The Complete Correspondence* (1984), vol. I, p. 37.
64 FDR directed his military chiefs: John Morton Blum, *From the Morgenthau Diaries* (1965), vol. II, pp. 149–50.
64 violently disagreed: Matloff and Snell, *Strategic Planning,* pp. 14–15.
65 "I regret to tell you . . .": Blum, *Morgenthau Diaries,* vol. II, p. 151.
65 "We have a school . . .": Watson, *Chief of Staff,* p. 307.
65 ". . . seriously prejudicial . . .": Marshall to Woody, June 18, 1940, George Catlett Marshall, *The Papers of George Catlett Marshall,* vol. II (1981), p. 247.
65 "It would take two years . . .": Watson, *Chief of Staff,* p. 311.
65 ". . . found to be short . . .": Matloff and Snell, *Strategic Planning,* p. 17.
65 "to absolutely disapprove . . .": Watson, *Chief of Staff,* p. 304.
65 ". . . dangerous adventurism": *NYT,* June 21, 1940, p. 6.
65 "in a towering rage . . .": Charles Edison to FDR, June 14, 1940, PSF 189, FDRL.
65 "I say it is too risky . . .": *CR,* 76th Cong., 3rd sess., June 21, 1940, pp. 8783–84.
66 "All of Mr. Roosevelt's . . .": *NR,* July 1, 1940, p. 11.
66 Marshall reluctantly agreed: Watson, *Chief of Staff,* pp. 309–10.
66 "It was the only time . . .": Marshall, *Papers,* p. 262.
66 "I am delighted . . .": Philip Goodhart, *Fifty Good Ships That Saved the World* (1965) p. 60.
66 Since the equipment was scattered: ibid., p. 61.
66 Working night and day: Stettinius, *Lend-Lease,* p. 27.
66 "Go ahead and load": Goodhart, *Fifty Good Ships,* p. 62.
66 All through that night; worth over $300 million: H. Duncan Hall, *North American Supply* (1955), p. 138; Goodhart, *Fifty Good Ships,* p. 60.
67 "For weeks . . .": Stettinius, *Lend-Lease,* pp. 28–29.
67 FDR, Jr., was graduating: *BEA,* June 10, 1940, p. 12.
67 news reached the White House: *Time,* June 17, 1940, p. 13.
68 "If your conscience . . .": Stimson Diary, Dec. 29, 1940, Henry L. Stimson Papers, Manuscripts and Archives, Yale University Library. Hereafter cited Stimson Diary, Yale University.
68 "grave and pale . . .": *Time,* June 17, 1940, p. 13.
68 "a deep growl . . .": Churchill, *Finest Hour,* p. 116.
68 "We will extend . . .": *NYHT,* June 10, 1940, p. 13.
68 "We all listened to you . . .": June 11, 1940, cable, *Churchill & Roosevelt Correspondence,* vol. I, p. 43.
68 "determined faith . . .": Stetson Conn and Byron Fairchild, *The Western Hemisphere* (1960), p. 36.
69 While he appreciated: Richard Leighton and Robert Coakley, *Global Logistics and Strategy, 1940–1943* (1955), p. 30.
69 "full of the elan": Adolf A. Berle, *Navigating the Rapids, 1918–1971* (1973), p. 322.
69 "Though I mildly suggested . . .": *MD,* June 12, 1940.
69 "It was a fighting speech . . .": *Time,* June 17, 1940, p. 13.
69 "rose to the occasion . . .": quoted in Ketchum, *Borrowed Years,* p. 358.
69 German troops entered Paris: Gilbert, *Second World War,* p. 94.
69 Parisians awakened: Noel Barber, *The Week France Fell* (1976), pp. 157–66.
70 A week later: *Time,* July 1, 1940, pp. 20–25; Robert Payne, *The Life and Death of Adolf Hitler* (1973), p. 390.
70 Marshall and Stark were convinced: Leighton and Coakley, *Global Logistics,* pp. 19–21.
70 "one of his most decisive . . .": Eric Larrabee, *Commander in Chief* (1987), p. 47.
70 "to keep that Japanese dog . . .": *Churchill & Roosevelt Correspondence,* vol. I, p. 38.
71 fired Secretary Woodring: *NYT,* June 21, 1940, p. 1.
71 "When the President did decide . . .": John Gunther, *Roosevelt in Retrospect* (1950), p. 42.
71 president would make good: Bernard M. Baruch, *Baruch: The Public Years* (1960), p. 277; *Time,* Oct. 19, 1939, p. 16.
71 coalition Cabinet: Geoffrey Perrett, *Days of Sadness, Years of Triumph* (1973), p. 42.
71 Henry Stimson: *CB,* 1940, pp. 766–67.
71 "Even if I had had . . .": Ickes, *Secret Diaries,* vol. III, p. 214.

71 Frank Knox: *CB,* 1940, pp. 461–62.
71 "a truce between the New Deal . . .": Bruce Catton, *The War Lords of Washington* (1969), pp. 23–24.
71 both men had expressed; "double cross": *NYT,* June 12, 1940, pp. 1, 4; *NR,* July 1, 1940, p. 4.
72 "Abroad, these nominations . . .": *WP* quoted in *Army and Navy Journal,* June 29, 1940, p. 1058.
72 For six hours before: Charles Hurd, *When the New Deal Was Young and Gay* (1965), pp. 255–63.
72 Hitler's visit to Paris: Payne, *Life and Death of Hitler,* pp. 390–91; Albert Speer, *Inside the Third Reich* (1970), pp. 171–72.
72 "There, you see . . .": Speer, *Third Reich,* p. 171.
73 ". . . the dream of my life . . .": ibid., p. 172.
73 "In the past . . .": ibid.
73 "delightfully cool and brilliant": *NYHT,* June 24, 1940, p. 4.
73 Springwood: *American Heritage,* April 1987; Clara and Hardy Steeholm, *The House at Hyde Park* (1950), pp. 123–24.
73 Description of SDR: *LHJ,* April 1934, p. 13; *NYT,* Sept. 8, 1941, p. 1; Kleeman notes, Kleeman Papers, FDRL; *Literary Digest*, Feb. 24, 1934, p. 13.
73 "The weather was . . .": *NYHT,* June 24, 1940, p. 4.
73 "Of course not . . .": interview with Margaret Suckley.
74 a tray of cocktails: *TIR,* p. 195.
74 "Shrieks of laughter . . .": Martha Gellhorn, *OH,* FDRL.
74 "My mother . . .": *TIR,* p. 196.
74 "Perhaps I have lived . . .": James Roosevelt, *My Parents: A Differing View* (1976), p. 31.
74 "and realize a little . . .": SDR to FDR, May 21, 1940, box 10, Roosevelt Family Papers Donated by the Children, FDRL.
74 "Nothing ever seemed . . .": Eleanor Roosevelt, *On My Own* (1958), p. 23.
74 On FDR activities during June 21 weekend: *Poughkeepsie Eagle News,* June 21, 1940, p. 11; June 22, 1940, p. 18; *NYHT,* June 22, 1940, pp. 7, 16; June 23, 1940, p. 18; June 24, 1940, p. 4; *NYT,* June 24, 1940, p. 12.
74 "All that is in me . . .": Joseph P. Lash, *Eleanor and Franklin* (1971), p. 116.
75 On Sara Delano and Algonac: Geoffrey C. Ward, *Before the Trumpet* (1985), ch. 2; Rita Halle Kleeman, *Gracious Lady* (1935).
75 "all traces of sadness . . .": Ward, *Trumpet,* p. 85.
75 "pain-killing can itself . . .": John R. Boettiger, Jr., *A Love in Shadow* (1978), p. 29.
75 "If there remained in Franklin . . .": ibid.
75 On James Roosevelt: Ward, *Trumpet,* ch. 1.
76 "No moment of Franklin's day . . .": ibid., pp. 125–26.
76 ". . . with a curious little . . .": Sara Delano Roosevelt, *My Boy Franklin* (1933), pp. 4–5.
76 "of his own accord . . .": ibid.
76 FDR and his father: Kenneth S. Davis, *FDR: The Beckoning of Destiny, 1882–1928* (1971), pp. 70–71.
76 "nice child . . .": Ward, *Trumpet,* p. 145.
76 relationships with children: ibid., pp. 139–42.
77 "It never occurred to me . . .": Sara Delano Roosevelt, *My Boy,* pp. 17–18.
77 "We never were strict . . .": ibid., p. 33.
77 one consequence: Alice Miller, *The Drama of the Gifted Child* (1981), p. 15.
77 Accompanying Mr. James: Ward, *Trumpet,* p. 122.
77 story of steel rod: Geoffrey C. Ward, *A First-Class Temperament* (1989), p. 607.
78 "By the warmth . . .": Samuel I. Rosenman, *Working with Roosevelt* (1952), p. 24.
78 "Perhaps in the long run . . .": *SEP,* Sept. 16, 1939, p. 95.
78 "We dusted his birds . . .": SDR's diary quoted in Ward, *Trumpet,* p. 177.
78 "They knew things . . .": Bess Furman, *Washington By-Line* (1949), p. 272.
78 "They didn't like him . . .": Ward, *Trumpet,* p. 203.
78 "Almost overnight . . .": Sara Delano Roosevelt, *My Boy,* p. 35.
78 FDR at Harvard: Ward, *Temperament,* pp. 258–62.
79 "She was an indulgent mother . . .": Ward, *Trumpet,* p. 245.
79 "The effort to become . . .": Ward, *Temperament,* flap copy.

79 "I know what pain . . .": Franklin D. Roosevelt, *FDR: His Personal Letters,* vol. I (1947), p. 518.
79 "The journey is over . . .": Lash, *Eleanor and Franklin,* pp. 128–29.
80 "Don't let her feel . . .": ibid., p. 130.
80 "I have more respect . . .": ibid., p. 136.
80 "You are mighty lucky . . .": ibid., p. 137.
80 "Reasonable it is to assume . . .": *LHJ,* April 1934, p. 12.
80 "I think probably the thing . . .": ER interview, Graff Papers, FDRL.

CHAPTER FOUR: "Living Here Is Very Oppressive"

81 "The President was enormously . . .": Frances Perkins, *The Roosevelt I Knew* (1946), pp. 69–70.
81 "All that she . . .": interview with Curtis Roosevelt.
82 "Living here is . . .": ER to AB, June 4, 1940, Bernard Asbell, *Mother and Daughter* (1988), p. 118.
82 ER had worked for the Red Cross: *TIMS,* pp. 254–55.
82 "I loved it . . .": Joseph P. Lash, *Love, Eleanor* (1982), p. 67.
82 ". . . I knew no one . . .": *TIMS,* p. 262.
82 *Potomac* offered escape: John Gunther, *Roosevelt in Retrospect* (1950), pp. 89–90.
83 "cries of terror": Joseph P. Lash, *Eleanor and Franklin* (1971), p. 29; see also *TIMS,* p. 7.
83 Norman Davis: *CB,* 1940, pp. 227–29.
83 ER's proposal for Davis: Lash Diary, May 27, 1940, Lash Papers, FDRL.
83 Red Cross in spring of 1940: Foster Rhea Dulles, *The American Red Cross* (1950), p. 346.
83 "the imminence . . .": Lash Diary, May 27, 1940, Lash Papers, FDRL.
84 "You don't want to go . . .": *NYT,* May 27, 1940, p. 1.
84 "been asleep"; "I think occasionally . . .": *NYHT,* May 27, 1940, p. 8.
84 "war hysteria": ibid.
84 "take us right into . . ."; "defend the American dollar . . .": *NYT,* May 27, 1940, p. 13.
84 "Poor Mrs. Roosevelt . . .": *NYT,* May 28, 1940, p. 22.
84 "was to demonstrate . . .": Lash Diary, May 27, 1940, Lash Papers, FDRL.
84 "I really think . . .": Tommy to AB, June 17, 1940, box 75, Halsted Papers, FDRL.
85 "anything that makes . . .": *MD,* May 21, 1940.
85 Arthurdale: *SEP,* Aug. 4, 1934, pp. 5–7, 61–65; Lash, *Eleanor and Franklin,* ch. 37, pp. 393–417.
85 "Deeply disillusioned . . .": Lash Diary, May 27, 1940, Lash Papers, FDRL.
86 City College: Lash Diary, May 10, 1940, Lash Papers, FDRL.
86 "God Bless You": Lash Diary, June 1, 1940, Lash Papers, FDRL.
86 "the anxiety which hangs . . .": *MD,* May 20, 1940.
86 At dinner with FDR and HH: Lash Diary, June 3, 1940, Lash Papers, FDRL.
86 "terribly guilty": ibid.
87 "Both Harry Hopkins . . .": interview with Elizabeth Wickendon.
87 HH's leadership of WPA: Robert E. Sherwood, *Roosevelt and Hopkins* (1948), pp. 67–71, 75–76.
87 "people don't eat . . .": ibid., p. 52.
87 "If I deserve . . .": HH documentary, FDRL.
87 "is one of the few . . .": *MD,* Aug. 22, 1938.
87 If Eleanor loved: interview with Eleanor Wotkyns.
88 "Around the White House . . .": Lillian Rogers Parks, *The Roosevelts: A Family in Turmoil* (1981), pp. 74–75.
88 "In the days before . . .": interview with Eliot Janeway.
88 "It was strange . . .": intervew with Elliott Roosevelt.
88 "his New Deal . . .": Sherwood, *Roosevelt and Hopkins,* p. 11.
88 "The war news . . .": HH to ER, Aug. 31, 1939, HH Papers, FDRL.
88 "a total friendship": Perkins, *OH,* Columbia University.
88 HH's bedroom: Sherwood, *Roosevelt and Hopkins,* pp. 203–4.
89 "ordinary fooling . . .": Perkins, *OH,* Columbia University.

89 "Harry and Missy . . .": Tommy to AB, June 17, 1940, box 75, Halsted Papers, FDRL.
89 "It had begun to cause . . .": Perkins, *OH,* Columbia University.
89 "One day . . .": Tommy to AB, April 1940, box 75, Halsted Papers, FDRL.
90 "could not live . . .": Kenneth S. Davis, *Invincible Summer* (1974), pp. 107–8.
90 "He looked at me quizzically . . .": *TIR,* p. 76.
90 "My zest in life . . .": Lash, *Love, Eleanor,* p. 159.
90 "The times of depression . . . ": Lesley Hazelton, *The Right to Feel Bad* (1984), p. 123.
91 "Within a few months . . .": Davis, *Invincible Summer,* p. 110.
91 Elliott Roosevelt: Lash, *Eleanor and Franklin,* pp. 1–13; David McCullough, *Mornings on Horseback* (1981), pp. 76–79; Edmund Morris, *The Rise of Theodore Roosevelt* (1979).
91 "Yesterday during my Latin . . .": Lash, *Eleanor and Franklin,* p. 7.
91 "Teedee is a much quicker . . .": McCullough, *Mornings,* p. 145.
91 courted Anna Hall: ibid., pp. 248–50. On Anna Roosevelt, see Lash, *Eleanor and Franklin,* pp. 14–20.
91 Robert Browning: Lash, *Eleanor and Franklin,* p. 23.
91 "dressed in some blue gray . . .": Geoffrey C. Ward, *Before the Trumpet* (1986), p. 265.
92 "one of the most . . .": *TIMS,* p. 1.
92 "grateful to be allowed . . .": ibid., p. 13.
92 "dominated my life . . .": ibid., p. 6.
92 "With my father . . .": ibid.
92 When he was drinking: Ward, *Trumpet,* p. 275; Morris, *Rise of Theodore Roosevelt,* pp. 429–30.
92 Knickerbocker Club episode: Lash, *Eleanor and Franklin,* pp. 51–52.
92 "stood first in his heart": *TIMS,* p. 9.
92 "a shy solemn child . . .": ibid., pp. 5–6.
92 "as a child senses . . .": ibid., p. 11.
93 "I acquired a strange . . .": ibid., p. 16.
93 "I would sit . . .": ibid., p. 13.
93 "a curious barrier": ibid., p. 17.
93 "Little Ellie . . .": ibid., pp. 17–18.
93 "a blue eyed . . .": Lash, *Eleanor and Franklin,* p. 33.
93 "A child stood . . .": ibid., p. 729.
93 "My darling little . . .": ibid., p. 42.
94 "I was always longing . . .": *TIMS,* p. 32.
94 "I can remember standing . . .": ibid., p. 19.
94 "Death meant . . .": ibid.
94 "he held out his arms . . .": *TIMS,* pp. 20–21.
94 "subconsciously I must have . . .": ibid., pp. 29–30.
95 "We must remember . . .": Lash, *Eleanor and Franklin,* p. 49.
95 "My aunts told me . . .": *TIMS,* p. 34.
95 "It was her father . . .": Lash, *Eleanor and Franklin,* p. 3.
95 "We do not have to . . ."; "The things always to remember . . .": *American Heritage,* Nov. 1984, p. 18.
95 used to hide books: Alfred Steinberg, *Mrs. R* (1958), p. 32.
95 boarding school in London: *TIMS,* pp. 54–88.
96 "a new life": ibid., p. 65.
96 "started me . . .": Eleanor Roosevelt and Helen Ferris, *Your Teens and Mine* (1961), p. 44.
96 "happiest . . .": Lash, *Eleanor and Franklin,* p. 87.
96 "always wanted to discuss . . .": Michael Teague, *Mrs. L: Conversations with Alice Roosevelt Longworth* (1981), p. 155.
96 Rivington Street settlement: *TIMS,* p. 108; Lash, *Eleanor and Franklin,* pp. 98–99.
96 "tremendously interested . . .": *TIMS,* p. 27.
96 "My God . . .": Eleanor Roosevelt and Ferris, *Your Teens and Mine,* p. 181.
97 "Though I only wrote . . .": Lash, *Eleanor and Franklin,* p. 110.
97 "It is impossible . . .": ibid., p. 109.
97 "When he told me . . .": Eleanor Roosevelt and Ferris, *Your Teens,* pp. 181–82.
97 "I was thinking . . .": Lash, *Eleanor and Franklin,* p. 110.

97 Eleanor burned them: ibid., p. 101.
97 "I am the happiest man . . .": Franklin D. Roosevelt, *FDR: His Personal Letters,* vol. I (1947), p. 518.
97 "For ten years . . .": *TIMS,* p. 163.
97 "He had always been . . .": Geoffrey C. Ward, *A First-Class Temperament* (1989), p. 12.
98 "The polio was very . . .": John R. Boettiger, Jr., *A Love in Shadow* (1978), p. 90.
98 "were joined . . .": Rexford G. Tugwell, *The Democratic Roosevelt* (1957), p. 529.
98 "I hated to see you go . . .": Lash, *Eleanor and Franklin,* p. 345.
99 ER brought together representatives: David S. Wyman, *Paper Walls* (1985), p. 18.
99 June 20 meeting: *NYT,* June 21, 1940, pp. 1, 3.
99 "You know, darling . . .": Lash Diary, June 25, 1940, Lash Papers, FDRL.
99 "It was kind . . .": Lash, *Eleanor and Franklin,* p. 635.
99 "I think men are worse . . .": ER to AB, June 26, 1940, Asbell, *Mother and Daughter,* p. 119.
99 "finding homes . . .": *MD,* July 13, 1940.
100 "The children are not . . .": *NYT,* July 7, 1940, p. 5.
100 "an enormous psychosis . . .": Breckinridge Long, *The War Diaries of Breckinridge Long* (1966), p. 108.
100 On Long: Henry L. Feingold, *The Politics of Rescue* (1970), pp. 131–35.
101 "upon a showing . . .": Wyman, *Paper Walls,* pp. 119–21.
101 "I think your mother . . .": Tommy to AB, July 12, 1940, box 75, Halsted Papers, FDRL.
101 "The English cannot spare . . .": Harold L. Ickes, *The Secret Diaries of Harold L. Ickes,* vol. III, *The Lowering Clouds, 1939–1941* (1954), p. 239.
101 "The very surest way . . .": Long, *War Diaries,* p. 119.
101 Estimates show: Wyman, *Paper Walls,* pp. 169, 211.
102 "The long pathetic . . .": ibid., p. 39.
102 the *St. Louis:* Arthur Morse, *While Six Million Died* (1983), pp. 270–88.
102 "The Jew party . . .": Ward, *Temperament,* p. 252.
102 "In the dim distant . . . ": ibid., p. 254.
102 Roper polls: Daniel Yankelovich, "German Behavior, American Attitudes," talk given in May 1988 at a conference at Harvard on the Holocaust and the Media, sponsored by the Anti-Defamation League, the Harvard Divinity School, the Nieman Foundation, and WCVB-TV, Boston.
102 brought to ER's attention: Lash, *Eleanor and Franklin,* p. 636.
103 president had been hearing tales: Wyman, *Paper Walls,* pp. 188–91; Feingold, *Politics of Rescue,* pp. 128–31.
103 "the treacherous use . . .": *NYT,* May 17, 1940, p. 10.
103 "today's threat . . .": Franklin D. Roosevelt, *Public Papers and Addresses of Franklin D. Roosevelt, 1940* (1941), p. 238.
103 "He was somewhat . . .": Lash Diary, June 25, 1940, Lash Papers, FDRL.
104 "the list could be . . .": Lash, *Eleanor and Franklin,* p. 636.
104 "she had this sense . . .": interview with Trude Lash.
104 PAC: Wyman, *Paper Walls,* pp. 138–48; ER to Welles, Oct. 1, 1940, OF 3186, FDRL.
104 "I know it is due . . .": Lash, *Eleanor and Franklin,* p. 636.
104 "We all know . . .": J. Buttinger to ER, Nov. 15, 1940, OF 3816, FDRL.

CHAPTER FIVE: "No Ordinary Time"

106 "Franklin always smiled . . .": *TIR,* p. 213.
106 "really meant to develop . . .": Perkins, *OH,* Columbia University.
107 "Perhaps it wasn't . . .": ibid.
107 "This is a . . ." *U.S. News,* July 12, 1940, p. 24.
107 "No President . . .": ibid.
107 "George, I am chained . . .": Ted Morgan, *FDR: A Biography* (1985), p. 520.
107 FDR had signed contract: ibid., p. 527.
107 "The role of elder . . .": *TIR,* p. 212.
108 Top Cottage: *NYT Magazine,* Aug. 24, 1941, p. 231; Geoffrey C. Ward, *A First-Class Temperament* (1989), p. 741.
108 "Every time he came . . .": interview with Margaret Suckley.

108 "If times were normal . . .": *U.S. News,* July 12, 1940, p. 24.
108 "a speeding car . . .": ibid.
108 "I think my husband . . .": ER interview, Graff Papers, FDRL.
108 "Now, whether . . .": ibid.
108 ". . . When you are in the center . . .": *TIR,* p. 214.
109 "It was a position . . .": Lash Diary, July 18, 1940, Lash Papers, FDRL.
109 "one never knows . . .": Lash Diary, July 15, 1940, Lash Papers, FDRL.
109 "the President might have . . .": Lash Diary, Feb. 5, 1940, Lash Papers, FDRL.
109 "They all in their serene . . .": Joseph P. Lash, *Love, Eleanor* (1982), p. 74.
109 "Will the President seek . . .": *NYT,* Nov. 4, 1939, p. 18.
109 "When you have been . . .": *NYT,* Nov. 6, 1939, p. 11.
109 "would not look forward . . .": ER to Isabella Greenway, Aug. 20, 1940, ER Papers, FDRL.
109 "there was no end . . .": Lash Diary, Feb. 3, 1940, Lash Papers, FDRL.
109 9,211 tea guests: Joseph P. Lash, *Eleanor and Franklin* (1971), p. 613.
109 "take on a job . . .": Lash Diary, July 17, 1940, Lash Papers, FDRL.
110 "At the present moment . . .": ER to Isabella Greenway, Aug. 20, 1940, ER Papers, FDRL.
110 Meeting with Farley: James A. Farley, *Jim Farley's Story: The Roosevelt Years* (1948), pp. 246–52, unless otherwise indicated.
112 "Mrs. Roosevelt, what is the President . . .": Roland Redmond, *OH,* FDRL.
112 Huey Long story: *NYT,* Sept. 8, 1941, p. 10.
112 FDR's study at Hyde Park: *NYT Magazine,* Aug. 24, 1941, p. 23.
112 "Everything right within reach": *Collier's,* Sept. 14, 1946, p. 96.
113 Hopkins to Chicago: Robert E. Sherwood, *Roosevelt and Hopkins* (1948), pp. 176–77.
114 "There was a great deal . . .": Perkins, *OH,* Columbia University.
114 "as deserted as a church . . .": Farley, *Jim Farley's Story,* p. 260.
114 ". . . dead cats and overripe tomatoes . . .": Marquis Childs, *I Write from Washington* (1942), p. 194.
114 "There was bitterness . . .": Edward J. Flynn, *You're the Boss* (1962), p. 156.
114 "If Harry Hopkins . . .": *Newsweek,* July 22, 1940, p. 15.
114 "He threw one leg . . .": Farley, *Jim Farley's Story,* p. 263.
114 "Be that as it may . . .": ibid.
115 "One would never . . .": Samuel I. Rosenman, *Working with Roosevelt* (1952), p. 208.
115 "Top Cottage was . . .": interview with Egbert Curtis.
116 "There were days . . .": Bernard Asbell, *The FDR Memoirs* (1973), p. 241.
116 "I tried fishing . . .": *TIMS,* pp. 345–46.
116 Missy clearly the "wife": Asbell, *FDR Memoirs,* p. 249.
116 Missy and FDR to Warm Springs: ibid., p. 237.
116 "Warm Springs was not much . . .": interview with Egbert Curtis.
116 "We didn't like . . .": Theo Lippman, Jr., *The Squire of Warm Springs* (1977), p. 91.
116 "I can still remember . . .": interview with Egbert Curtis.
117 "So ended . . .": Elliott Roosevelt and James Brough, *An Untold Story: The Roosevelts of Hyde Park* (1973), p. 230.
117 "heart action . . .": Asbell, *FDR Memoirs,* p. 252.
117 "a little crack-up"; "a nervous breakdown": ibid.
117 "I had a most enjoyable . . .": Bernard LeHand to FDR, July 10, 1927, box 21, Roosevelt Family Papers Donated by the Children, FDRL.
117 "Except for a few intervals . . .": interview with Egbert Curtis.
118 "Don't you dare . . .": Ward, *Temperament,* p. 792.
118 "He was in there . . .": Asbell, *FDR Memoirs,* p. 253.
118 "My mother-in-law thought . . .": *TIMS,* p. 336.
118 "I hated the arguments . . .": James Roosevelt, *My Parents: A Differing View* (1976), p. 78.
118 "*the* big issue": AH interview, Bernard Asbell. Transcript given to author by Professor Asbell.
118 "Father sympathized . . .": James Roosevelt, *My Parents,* p. 78.
119 "Marguerite LeHand . . .": *Newsweek,* Aug. 12, 1933, p. 15.
119 "If she thought . . .": Rosenman, *OH,* Columbia University.
119 "We loved Missy . . .": Lillian Rogers Parks, *The Roosevelts: A Family in Turmoil* (1981), p. 177.
119 "She always did it . . .": interview with Margaret Suckley.

119 "Without making a point . . .": interview with Barbara Curtis.
120 "Missy could be . . .": Parks, *Family in Turmoil*, p. 184.
120 "Missy was an operator . . .": interview with Eliot Janeway.
120 "She was one of the few . . .": Rosenman, *OH*, Columbia University.
120 "By this time the bleachers . . .": Rosenman, *Working with Roosevelt*, p. 113.
120 "For some reason . . .": interview with Curtis Roosevelt.
120 "Missy alleviated . . .": interview with Elliott Roosevelt.
120 "This is where Missy . . .": Asbell, *FDR Memoirs*, p. 255.
120 "Dearest ER . . .": MLH to ER, n.d., box 21, Roosevelt Papers Donated by the Children, FDRL.
120 ER resolutely refused: Eleanor Roosevelt, *My Days* (1938), p. 220.
121 "it would have been . . .": James Roosevelt, *My Parents*, p. 104.
121 "Everyone in the closely knit . . .": Elliott Roosevelt and Brough, *Untold Story*, p. 196.
121 "I suppose father had a romance . . .": James Roosevelt, *My Parents*, p. 104.
121 "From FDR to MAL . . .": Asbell, *FDR Memoirs*, p. 262.
121 "I think by 1940 . . .": interview with Egbert Curtis.
122 "the most delightful . . .": *MD*, July 18, 1940.
122 "as close a relationship . . .": AH, review of Joseph P. Lash, *Eleanor Roosevelt, A Friend's Memoir*, box 36, Halsted Papers, FDRL.
122 "It was a confusing time . . .": interview with Lewis Feuer.
122 "It is funny how quickly . . .": Lash, *Love, Eleanor*, p. 323.
123 "Joe was pretty vulnerable . . .": interview with Lewis Feuer.
123 "Perhaps . . . my miseries . . .": AH, review of Joseph P. Lash, *Eleanor Roosevelt: A Friend's Memoir*, box 36, Halsted Papers, FDRL.
123 "There wasn't a lampshade . . .": tour guide, Val-Kill, Hyde Park, New York.
123 Eleanor led Joe outside: Lash Diary, July 15, 1940, Lash Papers, FDRL.
123 talked till midnight: Lash Diary, July 16, 1940, Lash Papers, FDRL.
124 "She was entranced . . .": interview with Lewis Feuer.
124 "I'd like you to feel . . .": Lash, *Love, Eleanor*, p. 315.
124 "She personifies . . .": Lash Diary, March 24, 1940, Lash Papers, FDRL.
124 "At times there is . . .": Lash Diary, April 22, 1940, Lash Papers, FDRL.
124 "Nonsense . . .": Lash Diary, July 17, 1940, Lash Papers, FDRL.
124 "strangely subdued": *NYT*, July 16, 1940, p. 1.
125 "The President could have had . . .": quoted in Francis Biddle, *In Brief Authority* (1962), p. 142.
125 "This convention is bleeding . . .": Herbert S. Parmet and Marie B. Hecht, *Never Again* (1968), p. 185.
125 "acting out his curious . . .": James MacGregor Burns, *Roosevelt: The Lion and the Fox* (1956), p. 426.
125 "I have never seen . . .": Rosenman, *Working with Roosevelt*, p. 210.
125 ER listening to FDR's statement: Lash Diary, July 16, 1940, Lash Papers, FDRL.
125 Barkley oratory: *Chicago Daily Tribune*, July 17, 1940, p. 2.
125 "And now, my friends . . .": *NYT*, July 17, 1940, p. 1.
126 delegates' response to statement: Burns, *The Lion and the Fox*, pp. 427–28; Farley, *Jim Farley's Story*, pp. 280–81.
126 "leather-lunged . . .": Burns, *The Lion and the Fox*, p. 428.
126 Massachusetts banner seized: Parmet and Hecht, *Never Again*, p. 186.
126 demonstration raged: *NYT*, July 17, 1940, p. 3; *Chicago Daily Tribune*, July 17, 1940, p. 3.
126 "even obvious things . . .": Lash Diary, July 16, 1940, Lash Papers, FDRL.
126 "The President . . .": Perkins, *OH*, Columbia University.
127 "Absolutely no . . .": ibid.
127 "How would it be . . .": *Collier's*, Sept. 7, 1946, p. 25.
127 "Call her up . . .": Perkins, *OH*, Columbia University.
127 "Things look black here . . .": *TIR*, p. 214.
127 "comforted if she thought . . .": Lash Diary, July 16, 1940, Lash Papers, FDRL.
127 ". . . extremely dangerous . . .": Tommy to LH, July 25, 1940, LH Papers, FDRL.
127 "For someone like me . . .": Joseph P. Lash, *Eleanor Roosevelt: A Friend's Memoir* (1964), p. 129.

127 "... 'petticoat government'...": Lash Diary, July 17, 1940, Lash Papers, FDRL.
127 "Well, would you like...": ER interview, Graff Papers, FDRL.
127 "Harry Hopkins has been...": *TIR,* pp. 214–15.
128 "overcome with emotion": Lash Diary, July 17, 1940, Lash Papers, FDRL.
128 "Thanks, Jim...": Farley, *Jim Farley's Story,* p. 283.
128 "Never had the delegates...": *WP,* July 18, 1940, p. 1.
128 ER sang along: Lash Diary, July 17, 1940, Lash Papers, FDRL.
128 "felt as though it were...": *TIR,* p. 215.
128 "general satisfaction...": Rosenman, *Working with Roosevelt,* p. 212.
129 "The party longs...": Perkins, *OH,* Columbia University.
129 "Well, damn it...": Grace Tully, *F.D.R., My Boss* (1949), p. 239.
129 "I suppose all the...": Rosenman, *Working with Roosevelt,* p. 213.
129 convention out of control: *WP,* July 19, 1940, p. 1.
129 "He not only wants...": Perkins, *OH,* Columbia University.
129 "quite concerned...": Rosenman, *Working with Roosevelt,* p. 215.
129 ER arrival: *NYT,* July 19, 1940, pp. 1, 5.
129 Farley confided: Farley, *Jim Farley's Story,* p. 299.
129 "which was just...": Perkins, *OH,* Columbia University.
130 convention rose to its feet: *NYT,* July 19, 1940, p. 4.
130 "The rebel yells...": ibid.
130 "It was agony...": Perkins, *OH,* Columbia University.
130 "Poor Mrs. Wallace...": ibid.
130 "The noise in the room...": ER interview, Graff Papers, FDRL.
130 "meeting ground...": J. William T. Youngs, *Eleanor Roosevelt: A Public and Private Life* (1985), pp. 99–100.
131 scene in president's study: Parmet and Hecht, *Never Again,* p. 194; Burns, *The Lion and the Fox,* p. 429.
131 "As the fight got...": Rosenman, *Working with Roosevelt,* p. 215.
131 "Put that in shape...": Ross McIntire, *White House Physician* (1946), p. 125.
131 "hamlike paw...": ibid.
131 "until the Democratic party...": Rosenman, *Working with Roosevelt,* p. 216.
132 "Sam, give...": ibid., p. 217.
132 "Fine, I'm glad...": ibid., p. 216.
132 "Pa, I hope...": ibid., p. 217.
132 "Pa Watson was almost...": ibid.
132 "Oh, she *can't* go...": ER interview, Graff Papers, FDRL.
133 ER quietly rose: *U.S. News,* July 26, 1940, p. 9.
133 "Nobody could appreciate...": *WP,* July 19, 1940, p. 1.
133 "No man who is...": *NYT,* July 19, 1940, pp. 1, 5.
133 Genuine applause: Lash, *Eleanor and Franklin,* p. 623.
133 "above the petty...": ibid., p. 624.
134 "weary and bedraggled...": Rosenman, *Working with Roosevelt,* p. 219.
134 Missy was in tears: ibid.
134 FDR's acceptance speech: *WP,* July 19, 1940, pp. 1, 6.
134 "painful humbuggery...": Hedley Donovan, *Roosevelt to Reagan* (1985), pp. 20–21.
134 ER on platform: *Chicago Daily Tribune,* July 19, 1940, p. 1.
135 " 'Her speech was...": *TIR,* p. 218.
135 "You young things...": Lash Diary, July 19, 1940, Lash Papers, FDRL.
135 "it had all been a dream...": *TIR,* p. 218.
135 "What a schedule...": Lash Diary, July 19, 1940, Lash Papers, FDRL.
135 "swamped with wires...": Tommy to LH, July 25, 1940, LH Papers, FDRL.
135 "Your speech practically finished...": AB to ER, July 19, 1940, Bernard Asbell, *Mother and Daughter* (1988), p. 121.
135 "Mrs. Roosevelt *saved*...": AB to ER, July 22, 1940, box 59, Halsted Papers, FDRL.
135 "he is sulking...": Tommy to LH, July 25, 1940, Halsted Papers, FDRL.
135 "Jim, I'm going to...": Farley, *Jim Farley's Story,* p. 317.
136 "Gosh. It seems hard...": Tommy to LH, July 25, 1940, LH Papers, FDRL.
136 "was much like...": *MD,* July 20, 1940.
136 "... truly a magnificent person...": Tommy to LH, July 25, 1940, LH Papers, FDRL.

CHAPTER SIX: "I Am a Juggler"

137 "I am a juggler . . .": Ted Morgan, *FDR: A Biography* (1985), p. 550.
138 life in the capital that summer: *NYT Magazine,* July 28, 1940, p. 10.
138 "I shudder for the future . . .": J. Garry Clifford and Samuel R. Spenser, Jr., *The First Peacetime Draft* (1986), p. 175.
138 electric fans bothered him: Samuel I. Rosenman, *Working with Roosevelt* (1952), p. 204.
138 On July 16, Hitler: William L. Shirer, *The Rise and Fall of the Third Reich* (1981), p. 753; Martin Gilbert, *The Second World War* (1989), pp. 107–14.
138 "Mr. President . . .": *Churchill & Roosevelt: The Complete Correspondence* (1984), vol. I, p. 57.
138 "the survival of the British . . .": William M. Goldsmith, *The Growth of Presidential Power,* vol. III, *Triumph and Reappraisal* (1974), p. 1754.
139 "in all probability . . .": ibid.
139 "It would have been too encouraging . . .": Rosenman, *Working with Roosevelt,* p. 225.
139 black-veiled matrons: Clifford and Spenser, *Peacetime Draft,* p. 175.
139 ". . . conscription might die . . .": *NYHT,* April 3, 1940, p. 13.
139 "The President has taken . . .": Stimson Diary, Aug. 1, 1940, Yale University.
139 Stimson's cold sweat: Jay Pierpont Moffat, *The Moffat Papers* (1956), p. 327.
140 press conference: Franklin D. Roosevelt, *Public Papers and Address of Franklin D. Roosevelt, 1940* (1941), pp. 317–21.
140 "It may very easily . . .": FDR to L. B. Sheley, Aug. 26, quoted in Clifford and Spenser, *Peacetime Draft,* p. 204.
140 "To tie it up . . .": *MD,* July 11, 1940.
140 ER a dreamer: Lash Diary, Sept. 18, 1940, Lash Papers, FDRL.
140 "The way it was written . . .": May Craig to ER, Aug. 6, 1940, "The Papers of Eleanor Roosevelt, 1933–1945," Susan Wars and William H. Chafe, eds., University Publications of America, 1986. Hereafter cited ER Microfilm Collection, FDRL.
140 "I am not bucking . . .": ER to May Craig, Aug. 8, 1940, ER Microfilm Collection, FDRL.
140 "is simply a question . . .": *MD,* Aug. 6, 1940.
140 "stupid beyond belief . . .": *NYT,* Sept. 17, 1940, p. 25.
141 "We are all sorry to see . . .": ibid.
141 "a dozen timid . . .": Clifford and Spenser, *Peacetime Draft,* p. 192.
141 "What Wendell Willkie thinks . . .": ibid.
141 "like nothing a Republican . . .": *WP,* June 28, 1940, p. 1.
141 On Willkie: *NYT Magazine,* June 28, 1940, p. 6.
142 "Nothing so extraordinary . . .": Harold L. Ickes, *The Secret Diaries of Harold L. Ickes,* vol. III, *The Lowering Clouds, 1939–1941* (1954), p. 221.
142 "a momentous conference . . .": Stimson Diary, Aug. 13, 1940, Yale University.
142 Acheson had: *NYT,* Aug. 11, 1940, p. 18.
142 Jackson on constitutional authority: Jackson to FDR, Aug. 27, 1940, *Public Papers and Addresses, 1940,* pp. 394–405.
142 cabled WC the good news: *Churchill & Roosevelt Correspondence,* vol. I, pp. 58–60.
143 "steal half the show": Clifford and Spenser, *Peacetime Draft,* p. 200.
143 FDR arrived in Ogdensburg: *NYT,* Aug. 17, 1940, p. 3; Aug. 18, 1940, p. 2.
143 "girls in their prettiest . . .": *NYT,* Aug. 18, 1940, p. 3.
143 "The weather was beautiful . . .": Stimson Diary, Aug. 17, 1940, Yale University.
143 drilling with broomsticks: *NYT,* Aug. 18, 1940, p. 3.
143 "They haven't got the bodies . . .": *TP,* Aug. 20, 1940, p. 7.
143 never fired a gun: *NYT,* Aug. 7, 1940, p. 3.
143 falling to the ground: *NYT,* Aug. 18, 1940, p. 3.
144 "The voluntary system . . .": *NYT,* Aug. 23, 1940, p. 9.
144 "Let us not . . .": *NYT,* Aug. 8, 1940, p. 3.
144 "The men themselves . . .": Clifford and Spenser, *Peacetime Draft,* p. 204.
144 "the radio in the President's car . . .": *NYT,* Aug. 18, 1940, p. 2.
144 Willkie's reception in Elwood: *NYHT,* Aug. 18, 1940, pp. 1, 29; *NYT,* Aug. 18, 1940, p. 35; Clifford and Spenser, *Peacetime Draft,* p. 194; Steve Neal, *Dark Horse: A Biography of Wendell Willkie* (1984), pp. 133–35.
144 "Today we meet . . .": *NYT,* Aug. 18, 1940, p. 33.

145 "He has a good voice . . .": *MD,* Aug. 20, 1940.
145 "It was a brave speech . . .": column from Aug. 21, 1940, paper unidentified, ER Microfilm Collection, FDRL.
145 Starling had train moved: *Time,* Aug. 26, 1940, pp. 11–12.
146 "He talked at random . . .": Moffat, *Moffat Papers,* p. 325.
146 "Willkie is lost": ibid.
146 "able and courageous . . .": ibid., p. 327.
146 "had originally felt . . .": J. W. Pickergill, ed., *The Mackenzie King Record,* vol. I, *1939–1944* (1960), p. 131.
146 "Almost with tears . . .": ibid.
146 "a place of terror . . .": Richard Collier, *1940: The World in Flames* (1979), p. 210.
146 "perhaps today would mark . . .": Moffat, *Moffat Papers,* p. 327.
146 ". . . bargain or sale . . .": *Churchill & Roosevelt Correspondence,* vol. I, pp. 63–64.
147 "Congress is going . . .": Grace Tully, *F.D.R., My Boss* (1949), p. 244.
147 yellowish tint; "brooding about something . . .": David E. Lilienthal, *The Journal of David E. Lilienthal,* vol. 1 (1964), p. 207.
147 "twenty odd jammed in . . .": *Time,* Sept. 16, 1940, p. 11.
147 "the most important event . . .": ibid.
147 "It is all over . . .": Franklin D. Roosevelt, *Public Papers and Addresses, 1940,* p. 379.
147 "massive,-grey-headed . . .": *Time,* Sept. 16, 1940, p. 11.
148 "the most dictatorial . . .": James MacGregor Burns, *Roosevelt: The Lion and the Fox* (1956), p. 441.
148 "Note well the word . . .": reprinted in *NYT,* Sept. 4, 1940, p. 13.
148 "If Mr. Roosevelt can . . .": Clifford and Spenser, *Peacetime Draft,* p. 213.
148 "a decidedly unneutral act . . .": Winston S. Churchill, *The Second World War,* vol. II, *Their Finest Hour* (1949), p. 358.
148 "Let it roll on . . .": ibid., p. 362.
148 "their four tunnels raking . . .": *BG,* Sept. 4, 1940, p. 1.
148 "by the long arm . . .": Churchill, *Finest Hour,* p. 368.
148 "There were coffee makers . . .": Philip Goodhart, *Fifty Good Ships That Saved the World* (1965), pp. 194–95.
149 "We haven't had . . .": excerpts reprinted in *WP,* Sept. 4, 1940, p. 4.
149 "The President's . . .": ibid.
149 "exactly as a princess . . .": Bess Furman, *Washington By-Line* (1949), p. 288.
149 On Martha and family: Patricia C. Bjaaland, *The Norwegian Royal Family* (1986), pp. 22–41.
149 "I cannot accept . . .": Shirer, *Rise and Fall,* p. 705.
150 "It left the door . . .": *NYT,* April 29, 1939, p. 1.
150 royal couple spent weekend: ibid., p. 9.
150 Martha's escape to the U.S.: *Time,* Sept. 3, 1940, p. 28; *Newsweek,* Sept. 9, 1940, p. 19.
150 "brave words": *MD,* Aug. 30, 1940.
150 "Martha would sit . . .": interview with Trude Lash.
150 "Nothing is more pleasing . . .": James Roosevelt, *My Parents: A Differing View* (1976), p. 17.
150 "at his sparkling best . . .": James Roosevelt and Sidney Schalett, *Affectionately, F.D.R.* (1959), p. 22.
151 "adoringly . . .": Joseph P. Lash, *Love, Eleanor* (1982), p. 399.
151 "She was a lot of fun . . .": interview with Eleanor Seagraves.
151 "It became a kind . . .": interview with Henry Morgenthau III.
151 "but the big bonfire . . .": *MD,* Sept. 9, 1940.
151 "Mrs. Roosevelt loved . . .": interview with Henry Morgenthau III.
151 bombers over London: Shirer, *Rise and Fall,* p. 780; *London Times,* Sept. 9, 1940, p. 4; *Newsweek,* Sept. 16, 1940, pp. 22–23.
151 "The London that we knew . . .": Ben Robertson, *I Saw England* (1941), p. 121.
151 Goering had decided: Shirer, *Rise and Fall,* pp. 774–80.
151 "A few more weeks . . .": ibid., p. 777.
152 "no longer such things . . .": Molly Panter-Downes, *London War Notes, 1939–1945* (1971), pp. 98–99.
152 "The amazing part . . .": ibid.

152 "human character can stand . . .": Robertson, *I Saw England,* p. 130.
152 "vast smoky pall": *Newsweek,* Sept. 16, 1940, p. 23.
152 "We are on the brink . . .": *NYT,* Sept. 8, 1940, p. 8.
152 Empress Zita: *NYT,* July 21, 1940, p. 25.
153 "Sara was known . . .": interview with Egbert Curtis.
153 Martha in Rose Suite: Victoria Henrietta Nesbitt, *White House Diary* (1948), pp. 253–54.
153 ". . . a special character . . .": interview with Milton Lipson.
153 "I don't think . . .": Martha to FDR, Aug. 6, 1941, box 21, Roosevelt Family Papers Donated by the Children, FDRL.
153 "There was no question . . .": interview with James Roosevelt.
153 "the president's girlfriend": interview with Roberta Barrows.
153 "Early tried every way . . .": interview with Walter Trohan.
154 "Martha and her lady-in-waiting . . .": *MD,* Sept. 26, 1940.
154 "there was always a Martha . . .": Lash, *Love, Eleanor,* p. 399.
154 "I can't imagine . . .": interview with Betsey Whitney.
154 flirting was the one thing: interview with Eleanor Wotkyns.
154 Missy was distraught . . .: interview with James Roosevelt.
154 "Absolutely not . . .": interview with Barbara Curtis.
154 "Missy had me put . . .": Lash, *Love, Eleanor,* p. 118.
155 William Bullitt: *CB,* 1942, pp. 122–25.
155 "He used to telephone her . . .": interview with Barbara Curtis.
155 "the one real romance . . .": James Roosevelt, *My Parents,* p. 107.
155 ". . . Bullitt used Missy . . .": interview with Henry Morgenthau III.
155 "I was very much amused . . .": John Morton Blum, *From the Morgenthau Diaries,* vol. I, *Years of Crisis, 1928–1938* (1959), p. 134
155 "I don't know why . . .": James Roosevelt, *My Parents,* p. 107.
155 "I remember that she . . .": interview with Roberta Barrows.
155 "Nearer my age than father's . . .": James Roosevelt, *My Parents,* p. 106.
156 Anna admitted: interview with James Roosevelt.
156 "Are you always so agreeable? . . .": Lash Diary, June 4, 1940, Lash Papers, FDRL.
156 In mid-July: John Morton Blum, *From the Morgenthau Diaries,* vol. II, (1965), p. 290.
156 "delay in enacting . . .": Stimson Diary, Aug. 2, 1940, Yale University.
156 "no such harsh . . .": I. F. Stone, *The War Years, 1939–1945* (1988), p. 17.
156 "a lousy bill": Blum, *Morgenthau Diaries,* vol. II, p. 293.
156 "the very kinds of . . .": ibid., p. 295.
157 "a grave . . .": ibid., p. 296.
157 "This is abandoning . . .": Ickes, *Secret Diaries,* vol. III, pp. 210, 295–96.
157 "there was no clearcut . . .": Lash Diary, Aug. 1, 1940, Lash Papers, FDRL.
157 "draft such capital . . .": *MD,* Aug. 6, 1940.
157 "I, for one, am glad . . .": *MD,* Aug. 30, 1940.
157 ". . . should the government . . .": *Newsweek,* Aug. 19, 1940, p. 38.
158 "There are a great . . .": Stimson Diary, Aug. 26, 1940, Yale University.
158 "I regret to say . . .": Ickes, *Secret Diaries,* vol. III, p. 295.
158 "I want a tax bill . . .": Blum, *Morgenthau Diaries,* vol. II, p. 292.
158 "Leave the President alone . . .": Lash Diary, Aug. 5, 1940, Lash Papers, FDRL.
158 "a liability into . . .": R. Elberton Smith, *The Army and Economic Mobilization* (1959), p. 475.
159 A study: ibid., p. 413.
159 "We had to take industrial . . .": ibid., p. 414.
159 Story of poker game: interview with Verne Newton.

CHAPTER SEVEN: "I Can't Do Anything About Her"

161 A. Philip Randolph: *CB,* 1940, pp. 671–73.
162 Mary McCleod Bethune: *CB,* 1942, pp. 79–81.
162 Walter White: ibid., pp. 888–90.
162 "by his being a colored man": ibid., p. 888.
162 "I quite understand . . .": Joseph P. Lash, *Eleanor and Franklin* (1971), p. 522.
162 darkies: ibid.

162 "began to resemble . . .": Harvard Sitkoff, *A New Deal for Blacks,* vol. 1 (1978), p. 60.
162 Under the AAA, NRA: Arthur M. Schlesinger, Jr., *The Age of Roosevelt,* vol. III, *The Politics of Upheaval* (1960), p. 431.
162 "Is it true . . .": ER to HH, July 16, 1935, HH Papers, FDRL.
163 to sign executive order: Sitkoff, *New Deal,* vol. 1, p. 69.
163 Negroes share in New Deal: ibid., pp. 70–74.
163 "For the first time . . .": ibid., p. 83.
163 ER in 1938 in Alabama: ibid., p. 64.
163 ER in 1939 and Marian Anderson: Lash, *Eleanor and Franklin,* p. 525.
163 "Blacks in the thirties . . .": Nancy J. Weiss, *Farewell to the Party of Lincoln* (1983), p. 157.
163 "I did not choose . . .": Walter White, *A Man Called White* (1948), pp. 179–80.
164 "They were afraid . . .": *TIR,* p. 164.
164 "Frankly, some of his messages . . .": Early to Tommy, Aug. 5, 1935, Lash, *Eleanor and Franklin,* p. 518.
164 "If I were colored . . .": ibid., p. 519.
164 "If you have any influence . . .": Meldra Barber to MLH, June 4, 1940, PPF 3737, FDRL.
164 "The South is sick and tired . . .": *CR,* 76th Cong., 3rd sess., Jan. 8, 1940, p. 130.
164 "No, certainly not . . .": Frank Freidel, *Franklin D. Roosevelt: A Rendezvous with Destiny* (1990), p. 246.
164 ER represented the more generous: Schlesinger, *Politics of Upheaval,* p. 435.
164 photos of ER entertaining blacks: Sitkoff, *New Deal,* p. 95.
164 "I'm not for the Democrats . . .": Weiss, *Party of Lincoln,* p. 292.
165 "When you start . . .": ibid., p. 211.
165 Negroes to recruiting stations and figures in services: Jean Byers, "A Study of the Negro in Military Service," War Department Study, June 1947, p. 67, given to the author by Jean Byers Sampson.
165 "forget our special grievances . . .": W. E. B. Du Bois in Richard Polenberg, *War and Society: The United States, 1941–1945* (1972), p. 100.
165 ". . . everyone is excited . . .": Henry Davis to ER, Sept. 9, 1940, forwarded by Tommy to Sec. Stimson on Sept. 19, OF 93, FDRL.
166 Negro high-school teacher; "There is no place . . .": *SEP,* Dec. 14, 1940, p. 61.
166 "Hell, if you said . . .": *PC,* July 13, 1940, p. 3.
166 strictly mess men: Byers, "Negro in Military Service," p. 213.
166 mess men's duties: *PC,* Dec. 28, 1940, pp. 1, 4.
166 drawn into the navy: *PC,* Oct. 5, 1940, p. 1.
166 "Our main reason . . .": ibid., p. 4.
166 "I am still 100 percent . . .": *PC,* Dec. 28, 1940, p. 4.
167 "Since other mess attendants . . .": *PC,* Dec. 7, 1940, p. 4.
167 "I understand the plight . . .": *PC,* Nov. 9, 1940, p. 4.
167 new conscription law: Ulysses G. Lee, *The Employment of Negro Troops* (1966), pp. 69–75.
167 "In the selection . . .": ibid., p. 74.
167 "no man shall be inducted . . .": ibid.
167 "faith, cooperation and energy": *New York Age,* Sept. 21, 1940, p. 1.
167 "There is a growing feeling . . .": ER to FDR, n.d., PSF 177, FDRL.
168 "She has already spoken . . .": Early to Watson, Sept. 19, 1940, OF 2538, FDRL.
168 FDR's meeting with leaders: entire conversation is from *BG,* Jan. 24, 1982, p. A15; *American Heritage,* Feb.–March 1982, p. 24. These articles reveal the contents of tape-recorded conversations at the White House in 1940.
169 "for critical experiments . . .": George Catlett Marshall, *The Papers of George Catlett Marshall,* vol. II (1981), p. 376.
169 ". . . to satisfy the Negro . . .": Stimson Diary, Sept. 27, 1940, Yale University.
169 "In the process of evolution . . .": report, "Employment of Negro Man Power in War," Nov. 1925, FDRL.
170 "Soldiers who were asked . . .": Polenberg, *War and Society,* p. 123.
170 "We did not want to violate . . .": WW to ER, Oct. 4, 1940, ER Microfilm Collection, FDRL.
170 "The policy of . . .": Lee, *Negro Troops,* p. 76.
171 Early gave false impression: press release, Oct. 9, 1940, OF 93, FDRL.

171 "a stab in the back . . .": NAACP release, Oct. 11, 1940, OF 93, FDRL.
171 "none is more shameful . . .": *Crisis,* Dec. 1940, p. 375.
171 "I am sorry . . .": WW to ER, Oct. 12, 1940, ER Microfilm Collection, FDRL.
171 "no fixed policy . . .": FDR statement, OF 93, FDRL.
171 "Rest assured . . .": FDR to WW, Oct. 25, 1940, OF 93, FDRL.
171 "We are inexpressibly shocked . . .": *Crisis,* Nov. 1940, p. 356.
171 "The Negro situation . . .": Jim Rowe to FDR, Oct. 31, 1940, OF 93, FDRL.
171 "Never before . . .": *PC,* Oct. 19, 1940, p. 1.
171 "It looks as though . . .": Will Alexander, *OH,* FDRL.
172 Davis and Hastie: Lee, *Negro Troops,* pp. 79–81.
172 "the Negroes are taking advantage . . .": Stimson Diary, Oct. 22, 1940, Yale University.
172 ". . . a colored Admiral": Stimson Diary, Oct. 25, 1940, Yale University.
172 "Are you crazy . . .": A. P. Allen to FDR, Oct. 25, 1940, OF 93, FDRL.
172 "It is incomprehensible . . .": Mr. and Mrs. Alexander Kirk, Oct. 25, 1940, OF 93, FDRL.
172 "in the fight for equitable . . .": *PC,* Nov. 2, 1940, p. 1.
172 ". . . to insure a square deal . . .": WW to FDR, Nov. 4, 1940, OF 93, FDRL.
172 "the basic fact of segregation . . .": Lash, *Eleanor and Franklin,* p. 532.
173 PAC had submitted 567 names: David S. Wyman, *Paper Walls* (1985), p. 143.
173 only fifteen visas issued: Henry L. Feingold, *The Politics of Rescue* (1970), p. 141.
173 "a singleness of purpose . . .": ibid., p. 136.
173 "We can delay . . .": ibid., p. 173.
173 "Mr. McDonald is so wrought up . . .": ER to FDR, Sept. 28, 1940, OF 3186, FDRL.
173 "Please tell me . . .": FDR to Welles, Oct. 2, 1940, OF 3186, FDRL.
173 "I found that he was . . .": Breckinridge Long, *The War Diaries of Breckinridge Long* (1966), pp. 134–35.
174 "pull any sob stuff": Wyman, *Paper Walls,* p. 147.
174 "Something does seem wrong . . .": ER to FDR, Oct. 10; reply, Oct. 16, 1940; both in OF 3186, FDRL.
174 S.S. *Quanza: NYT,* Aug. 21, 1940, p. 5.
174 "Impossible . . .": Stella K. Hersham, *A Woman of Quality* (1970), p. 40.
174 "Complete despair . . .": quoted in ibid., p. 40.
174 "I remonstrated violently . . .": quoted in Feingold, *Politics of Rescue,* p. 144.
174 "When he told me . . .": Marlin to George Warren, Sept. 27, 1940, OF 3186, FDRL.
174 "Mrs. Roosevelt . . .": Hersham, *A Woman of Quality,* p. 41.
175 "The department does not refuse . . .": *Nation,* Dec. 28, 1940, p. 649.
175 "It looks again . . .": Joseph Buttinger to ER, Nov. 15, 1940, OF 3186, FDRL.
175 "all Jews . . .": this letter attached to ibid.
175 "FDR, Can't something be done?": ER to FDR, Nov. 27, 1940, OF 3186, FDRL.
175 "The President's overriding concern . . .": Justine Polier, *OH,* FDRL.
175 "Franklin, you *know* . . .": ibid.
176 "True, the Nazis . . .": Wyman, *Paper Walls,* p. 35.
176 "her deepest regret . . .": interview with James Roosevelt.
176 Willkie campaign in thirty states: *Time,* Nov. 4, 1940, p. 12.
176 FDR telescoped three "inspections": *NYT,* Oct. 1, 1940, p. 1.
176 unprecedented quantities of land: R. Elberton Smith, *The Army and Economic Mobilization* (1959), p. 441.
177 "said to be . . .": *NYT,* Oct. 1, 1940, p. 14.
177 Glenn Martin plant: *Fortune,* Dec. 1939, pp. 73–76.
177 unemployment rolls: Kenneth S. Davis, *FDR: Into the Storm, 1937–1940* (1991), p. 613.
177 "The main point . . .": FDR to John Boettiger, Oct. 1, 1940, box 7, Halsted Papers, FDRL.
177 the president journeyed to Midwest: *NYT,* Oct. 11, 1940, p. 1; Oct. 13, 1940, p. 1.
177 "one knifing through the air . . .": *NYT,* Oct. 13, 1940, p. 22.
177 Schools dismissed: *Time,* Oct. 21, 1940, p. 15.
177 "I have come here today . . .": *NYT,* Oct. 11, 1940, p. 11.
177 Jimmy: *NYT,* April 23, 1939, p. 3; Ted Morgan, *FDR: A Biography* (1985), pp. 462–66.
178 FDR, Jr.: *NYT,* April 23, 1939, p. 3.
178 "golden boy": interview with Trude Lash.
178 Elliott: Morgan, *FDR,* pp. 458–61.
178 "Elliott was the most like . . .": Minnewa Ball, *OH,* FDRL.

178 John: Morgan, *FDR,* pp. 455–57.
178 worked under a pseudonym: John Gunther, *Roosevelt in Retrospect* (1950), p. 198.
178 "None of them really lived . . .": Abram Sacher, *OH,* FDRL.
178 "She didn't know . . .": interview with Curtis Roosevelt.
178 "I don't seem to be able . . .": Joseph P. Lash, *Love, Eleanor* (1982), p. 159.
179 "She felt that the guilt . . .": Elliott Roosevelt and James Brough, *A Rendezvous with Destiny* (1975), p. 67.
179 "she was so unsure . . .": Lash Diary, Aug. 1, 1940, Lash Papers, FDRL.
179 "I was not allowed . . .": John R. Boettiger, Jr., *A Love in Shadow* (1978), p. 45.
179 "At a visceral level . . .": interview with Curtis Roosevelt.
179 "she determined . . .": Lash, *Love, Eleanor,* p. 56.
179 "your mother only bore you . . .": interview with James Roosevelt.
179 "It did not come naturally . . .": Lash, *Love, Eleanor,* p. 57.
179 "Franklin loved . . .": ER interview, Graff Papers, FDRL.
179 "I was the disciplinarian . . .": ibid.
180 "very unpredictable . . .": James Halsted in Bernard Asbell, *Mother and Daughter* (1988), p. 9.
180 "the most unexpected spots . . .": AH, "What Does It Feel Like to Be the Offspring of Famous Parents?," manuscript, n.d., box 84, Halsted Papers, FDRL.
180 "traumatic": AB interview, Graff Papers, FDRL.
180 "did not realize that Anna . . .": Eleanor Roosevelt and Helen Ferris, *Your Teens and Mine* (1961), p.71.
180 "It never occurred to me . . .": *TIMS,* p. 338.
180 "This outburst of mine . . .": Eleanor Roosevelt and Ferris, *Your Teens and Mine,* p. 70.
181 "I felt very strongly . . .": AH, *OH,* Columbia University.
181 "I was mad . . .": Asbell, *Mother and Daughter,* p. 40.
181 "Emotionally . . . ": AH, *OH,* Columbia University.
181 "Eleanor saw in John . . .": interview with Curtis Roosevelt.
181 "I love Anna so dearly . . .": Asbell, *Mother and Daughter,* p. 68.
181 "The Northwest welcomed . . .": *SEP,* July 8, 1939, p. 25.
181 "jovial manner . . .": ibid.
182 "as slim and boyish . . .": *NYT,* April 23, 1939, p. 21.
182 "Perhaps I needed . . .": Lash, *Love, Eleanor,* p. 232.
182 "I begin to feel . . .": *MD,* Oct. 18, 1940.
182 "I supposed that is why . . .": Lash, *Love, Eleanor,* p. 200.
182 "you can count on . . .": *NYT,* Oct. 25, 1940, p. 1.
182 "wide crack in a dam . . .": Davis, *FDR: Into the Storm,* p. 614.
182 "Dearest Franklin . . .": ER to FDR, Oct. 11, 1940, box 16, Roosevelt Family Papers Donated by the Children, FDRL.
183 "I painted her a pretty dark . . .": Harold L. Ickes, *The Secret Diaries of Harold L. Ickes,* vol. III, *The Lowering Clouds, 1939–1941* (1954), p. 351.
183 "I will not pretend . . .": Robert E. Sherwood, *Roosevelt and Hopkins* (1948), p. 186.
183 Lewis speech: *WP,* Oct. 26, 1940, p. 5.
184 "sad and low . . .": Matthew and Hannah Josephson, *Sidney Hillman: Statesman of American Labor* (1952), p. 488.
184 "John never can forget . . .": notes attached to letter, Charles Michelson to Steve Early, Sept. 29, 1940, PSF 194, FDRL.
184 MLH served as hostess: Bernard Asbell, *The FDR Memoirs* (1973), p. 245.
184 "We take the liberty . . .": Amalgamated to FDR, Oct. 26, 1940, OF 2546, FDRL.
184 "Paducah labor is for you . . .": Oct. 26, 1940, OF 2546, FDRL.
184 "Don't let Lewis' speech . . .": Local #6082 to FDR, Oct. 26, 1940, OF 2546, FDRL.
184 "John L. Lewis has kicked . . .": Alex Tunis to FDR, Oct. 25, 1940, OF 2546, FDRL.
184 "You are the only President . . .": Mrs. Grim to FDR, n.d., OF 2546, FDRL.
185 "Old age pensions . . .": Mrs. L. M. Feirer to FDR, Oct. 26, 1940, OF 2546, FDRL.
185 "I am an old campaigner . . .": Samuel I. Rosenman, *Working with Roosevelt* (1952), p. 238.
185 "Great Britain would never . . .": *NYT,* Oct. 29, 1940, pp. 1, 12.
185 "The way of the man . . .": *BG,* Oct. 31, 1940, p. 1.

185 "I have just come . . .": David E. Lilienthal, *The Journal of David E. Lilienthal,* vol. 1, (1964), p. 223.
185 Early kicking Sloan: *Time,* Nov. 11, 1940, pp. 17–18.
186 "Negroes . . .": Weiss, *Farewell,* pp. 280–81.
186 "I am a Democrat . . .": *NYT,* Nov. 1, 1940, p. 20.
186 "any old-time politician . . .": Rosenman, *Working with Roosevelt,* p. 241.
186 ". . . a very bitter campaign . . .": Stimson Diary, Oct. 29, 1940, Yale University.
186 "The first number . . .": *NYT,* Oct. 30, 1940, p. 1.
186 Mrs. Mildred Bell gasped: *WP,* Oct. 30, 1940, pp. 1, 2.
187 Michael Thomson: *Cleveland Press,* Oct. 30, 1940, p. 1.
187 Jack Clardy: *Charlotte Observer,* Oct. 30, 1940, p. 1.
187 James Cody; "This is the first . . .": *NYT,* Oct. 30, 1940, p. 1.
187 "As I listened . . .": ER to JL, Oct. 30, 1940, Lash Papers, FDRL.
187 "Very simply and honestly . . .": *NYT,* Oct. 31, 1940, p. 14.
187 "It's not necessary . . .": Rosenman, *Working with Roosevelt,* p. 242.
188 "Today . . .": *MD,* Nov. 2, 1940.
188 "extraordinarily jovial": *NYT,* Nov. 6, 1940, p. 2.
188 "What name please? . . .": *WP,* Nov. 6, 1940, p. 2.
188 "would do all the things . . .": Lash Diary, Nov. 5, 1940, Lash Papers, FDRL.
188 buffet supper: *NYT,* Nov. 6, 1940, pp. 1, 2.
188 FDR on election night: Grace Tully, *F.D.R., My Boss* (1949), p. 240; Lash Diary, Nov. 5, 1940, Lash Papers, FDRL; *NYT,* Nov. 6, 1940, pp. 1, 2.
188 "Mike, I don't want . . .": Michael F. Reilly, *Reilly of the White House* (1947), p. 66.
189 "It looks all right . . .": James MacGregor Burns, *Roosevelt: The Soldier of Freedom* (1970), p. 4.
189 "a little jig . . .": *NYT,* Nov. 6, 1940, p. 2.
189 "We want Eleanor . . .": ibid.

CHAPTER EIGHT: "Arsenal of Democracy"

190 "Just how does the President think? . . .": Eric Larrabee, *Commander in Chief* (1987), p. 644.
191 "a question here . . .": Perkins, *OH,* Columbia University.
191 "All of you use . . .": John Morton Blum, *From the Morgenthau Diaries,* vol. II, *Years of Urgency, 1938–1941* (1965), p. 202.
191 "The more I sleep . . .": *U.S. News,* Nov. 29, 1940, p. 20.
191 "Hope you have . . .": ER to FDR, Dec. 2, 1940, box 16, Roosevelt Family Papers Donated by the Children, FDRL.
191 "made of scraps . . .": *MD,* Dec. 3, 1940, box 16, Roosevelt Family Papers Donated by the Children, FDRL.
191 "give impetus to . . .": *NYT,* Dec. 17, 1940, p. 20.
191 "In every place . . .": Tommy to AB, Nov. 18, 1940, box 75, Halsted Papers, FDRL.
192 At Guantanamo Bay, etc.: Robert E. Sherwood, *Roosevelt and Hopkins* (1948), pp. 222–23.
192 "I think of you . . .": ER to FDR, Dec. 4, 1940, box 16, Roosevelt Family Papers Donated by the Children, FDRL.
192 death of Lothian: Richard M. Ketchum, *The Borrowed Years, 1938–1941* (1989), p. 572.
192 "My dear Mr. President . . .": *Churchill & Roosevelt: The Complete Correspondence* (1984), vol. I, pp. 102–9.
193 "I didn't know . . .": Sherwood, *Roosevelt and Hopkins,* p. 224.
193 "Nobody that I know of . . .": ibid.
193 a "flash of almost clairvoyant . . .": George Martin, *Madame Secretary: Frances Perkins* (1976), p. 435.
193 "very much like chasing . . .": Stimson Diary, Dec. 18, 1940, Yale University.
194 "Well, let me . . .": text of speech, Franklin D. Roosevelt, *Public Papers and Addresses of Franklin D. Roosevelt, 1940* (1941), pp. 604–15; also *NYT,* Dec. 18, 1940, pp. 1, 10; *WP,* Dec. 18, 1940, pp. 1, 2.
194 "was really based . . .": Perkins, *OH,* Columbia University.
194 America First Committee: Wayne S. Cole, *America First* (1953), p. 14.

195 "really enjoyed working . . .": Sherwood, *Roosevelt and Hopkins*, p. 226.
195 "No man can tame . . .": Franklin D. Roosevelt, *Public Papers and Addresses, 1940*, p. 638.
195 "unholy alliance . . .": ibid., p. 639.
195 "the great arsenal . . .": ibid., p. 643.
195 recent Gallup poll: George Gallup, *The Gallup Polls: Public Opinion, 1935–1971*, vol. 1, *1937–1948* (1972), p. 255.
195 "I call for this . . .": Franklin D. Roosevelt, *Public Papers and Addresses, 1940*, p. 644.
195 large part of old city destroyed: *London Times*, Dec. 30, 1940, p. 2.
196 "The havoc was comparable . . .": *NYT*, Dec. 31, 1940, p. 1.
196 "London has nothing . . .": Joseph Goebbels, *The Goebbels Diaries, 1939–1941* (1983), p. 222.
196 "When I visited . . .": WC to FDR, Dec. 31, 1940, *Churchill & Roosevelt Correspondence*, vol. I, p. 123.
196 Walter Reuther: *Business Week*, Jan. 17, 1942, p. 60.
196 "slow and costly . . .": Walter Reuther, "A Program for Utilization of the Auto Industry for Mass Production of Defense Plants," attached to letter, Philip Murray to FDR, Dec. 20, 1940, OF 4234, FDRL.
196 "Conventional methods . . .": ibid.
196 "We propose . . .": ibid.
196 "the most important . . .": quoted in I. F. Stone, *Business as Usual* (1941), p. 238.
196 "the first great . . .": ibid.
196 "It is well . . .": FDR to William Knudsen, Dec. 31, 1940, OF 4234, FDRL.
197 Cadillac plant: *Time*, Dec. 30, 1940, pp. 13–14.
197 "Mr. Knudsen . . .": John Barnard, *Walter Reuther and the Rise of the Auto Workers* (1983), p. 78.
197 "The fear . . .": Stone, *Business as Usual*, p. 235.
197 "labor had grown . . .": Bruce Catton, *The War Lords of Washington* (1969), pp. 91–92.
197 "There is only . . .": Morgenthau quoted in Barnard, *Walter Reuther*, p. 78.
197 Christmas holidays at the White House: White House Usher Diaries, FDRL; *MD*, Dec. 20–27, 1940.
198 ER shopping: *NYT*, Nov. 29, 1940, p. 18.
198 "He was just bursting . . .": Victoria Henrietta Nesbitt, *White House Diary* (1948), p. 257.
198 On Mrs. Nesbitt: Elliott Roosevelt and James Brough, *A Rendezvous with Destiny* (1975), p. 47; William Seale, *The President's House*, vol. II (1986), p. 929.
198 "plain foods . . .": Grace Tully, *F.D.R., My Boss* (1949), p. 115.
199 "Fluffy": Seale, *President's House*, vol. II, p. 966.
199 "always handsome . . .": Elliott Roosevelt and James Brough, *An Untold Story* (1973), p. 297.
199 "Fix it anyhow . . .": Lillian Rogers Parks, *The Roosevelts: A Family in Turmoil* (1981), p. 170.
199 "My God! . . .": Tully, *F.D.R.*, p. 116.
199 "Do you remember . . .": FDR to ER, April 29, 1942, box 75, Halsted Papers, FDRL.
199 ultimatum: Nesbitt, *White House Diary*, p. 279.
199 ER's scrambling eggs: Elliott Roosevelt and Brough, *Rendezvous with Destiny*, p. 48.
200 "to put it mildly . . .": John Gunther, *Roosevelt in Retrospect* (1950), p. 92.
200 ER did not consider: *TIR*, p. 118.
200 Fala became FDR's friend: Tully, *F.D.R.*, p. 129.
200 "Not even one crumb . . .": interview with Margaret Suckley.
200 "In years to come . . .": William K. Klingaman, *1941* (1988), pp. 30–31.
200 economy at home: Donald Rogers, *Since You Went Away* (1973), pp. 13–28.
200 "an orgy of spending . . .": *NYT*, Dec. 25, 1940, p. 1.
200 "Here life is not . . .": *WP*, Dec. 25, 1940, p. 1.
201 "Here is something . . .": *MD*, Jan. 1 and 2, 1941.
201 "Eleanor was forever . . .": interview with Trude Lash.
201 "he had an idea . . .": Samuel I. Rosenman, *Working with Roosevelt* (1952), p. 263.
201 ER and guests in FDR's box: *NYT*, Jan. 7, 1941, p. 5.
201 Text of speech: *NYT*, Jan. 7, 1941, p. 4.
202 "It looked to me . . .": *MD*, Jan. 6, 1941.

202 "presents a new concept . . .": *NYT,* Jan. 9, 1941, p. 19.
202 "the Roosevelts apparently . . .": *NYT,* Jan. 11, 1941, p. 3.
202 "intensifying and exhilarating . . .": *SEP,* Sept. 16, 1939, pp. 96, 98.
202 reporters noted: *NYT,* Jan. 19, 1941, sect. VI, p. 3.
203 "One of the grand things . . .": *WP,* Jan. 19, 1941, p. 2.
203 "Serious but not . . ."; ". . . after nearly . . .": *NYT,* Jan. 19, 1941, sect. VI, p. 3.
203 "part of his nature . . .": Joseph P. Lash, *Eleanor and Franklin* (1971), p. 344.
203 "The President talked . . .": Perkins interview, Graff Papers, FDRL.
203 "Frankfurter said . . .": Stimson Diary, Jan. 4, 1941, Yale University.
204 "He seems to want . . .": David E. Lilienthal, *The Journal of David E. Lilienthal,* vol. 1 (1964), p. 169.
204 "Each imagines . . .": Lash Diary, March 20, 1941, Lash Papers, FDRL.
204 "He had more serenity . . .": quoted in Arthur Schlesinger, Jr., *The Crisis of the Old Order, 1919–1931* (1956), p. 407.
204 "Bright-eyed . . .": *WP,* Jan. 21, 1941, p. 1.
204 Pegler called her: Tamara Hareven, *Eleanor Roosevelt: An American Conscience* (1968), pp. 273–74.
204 "and tend to her . . .": J. William T. Youngs, *Eleanor Roosevelt: A Personal and Private Life* (1985), p. 198.
204 "Instead of tearing . . .": Hareven, *Eleanor Roosevelt,* p. 271.
205 "We don't want . . ."; "If I could be worried . . .": *NYT,* Oct. 26, 1940, p. 9.
205 "She is the President's . . .": *U.S. News,* Dec. 20, 1940, pp. 9–10.
205 "The nearer I draw . . .": *MD,* Jan. 10, 1941.
205 "It was wonderful . . . ": *MD,* Jan. 12, 1941.
205 "I always have been . . .": *WP,* Jan. 21, 1941, p. 3.
205 ER raised troubling question: Lash Diary, Jan. 16, 1941, Lash Papers, FDRL.
206 "I think we are going . . .": *NYT,* Jan. 26, 1941, p. 1.
206 On Palmer: Lash Diary, Jan. 16, 1941, Lash Papers, FDRL; *Time,* Feb. 3, 1941, p. 59; *PM,* Jan. 19, 1941, p. 9; March 26, 1941, p. 9.
206 "arose from . . .": *PM,* Jan. 19, 1941, p. 9.
206 "in the long run . . .": *Time,* Feb. 3, 1941, p. 59.
206 Palmer had been under: *PM,* Jan. 19, 1941, p. 9; March 26, 1941, p. 9.
206 "Would he be sensitive . . .": Lash Diary, Jan. 16, 1941, Lash Papers, FDRL.
206 "My mother-in-law . . .": Eleanor Roosevelt, *Tomorrow Is Now* (1963), pp. 64–65.
207 SDR invited: ibid.
207 Elizabeth Read and Esther Lape: Joseph P. Lash, *Love, Eleanor* (1982), pp. 78–82; Blanche Wiesen Cook, *Eleanor Roosevelt,* vol. I, *1884–1933* (1992), pp. 288–301.
207 Nancy Cook and Marion Dickerman: Lash, *Love, Eleanor,* pp. 82–85.
207 "Boston marriage": ibid., p. 82.
208 "If I had to go out . . .": Eleanor Roosevelt and Lorena Hickok, *Ladies of Courage* (1954), p. 262.
208 "She loved it . . .": Lash, *Eleanor and Franklin,* p. 307.
208 "squaws" and "she-men": Cook, *Eleanor Roosevelt,* vol. I, p. 302.
208 "My generation . . .": Rita Halle Kleeman, *Gracious Lady: The Life of Sara Delano Roosevelt* (1935), p. 291.
208 "My mother-in-law . . .": Geoffrey C. Ward, *A First-Class Temperament* (1989), p. 564.
209 "My Missus and . . .": quoted in Kenneth S. Davis, *Invincible Summer* (1974), p. 35.
209 "The peace of it . . .": Ward, *Temperament,* p. 740.
209 "Can you tell me *why* . . .": ibid.
209 Gallup poll: *U.S. News,* Jan. 31, 1941, p. 17.
209 Nineteen members of family: *WP,* Jan. 20, 1941, p. 2.
210 "There are men . . .": *WP,* Jan. 21, 1941, p. 2.
210 "A nation, like a person . . .": ibid., p. 3.
210 "the government . . .": Richard Leighton and Robert Coakley, *Global Logistics and Strategy, 1940–1943* (1955), p. 77.
210 "to carry on . . .": Senator Taft quoted in Charles A. Beard, *President Roosevelt and the Coming of the War, 1941* (1948), p. 67.
210 "The lend-lease . . .": David Lawrence, *Diary of a Washington Correspondent* (1942), p. 92.

210 On Kennedy: Michael Beschloss, *Kennedy and Roosevelt* (1980), pp. 238–41.
211 "Somehow or other . . .": John Boettiger to Joseph P. Kennedy, Jan. 31, 1941, Boettiger Papers, FDRL.
211 "if my statements . . .": Kennedy to Boettiger, Feb. 10, 1941, Boettiger Papers, FDRL.
211 "It is, I think . . .": FDR to Boettiger, Feb. 1941, Boettiger Papers, FDRL.
212 "another step away . . .": Ketchum, *Borrowed Years,* p. 578.
212 "sick and shrunken . . .": Sherwood, *Roosevelt and Hopkins,* p. 234.
212 her shock: interview transcript from HH documentary, FDRL.
212 "Mr. Churchill . . .": ibid.
212 "And from this hour . . .": Winston S. Churchill, *The Second World War,* vol. III, *The Grand Alliance* (1950), p. 21.
212 "I suppose you wish . . .": Lord Moran, *Churchill—the Struggle for Survival, 1940–1965* (1966), p. 6.
213 HH asked WC: Sherwood, *Roosevelt and Hopkins,* pp. 253–55.
213 "In the last war . . .": Winston S. Churchill, *Great War Speeches* (1957), pp. 93–105.
213 "the madmen . . .": *NYT,* Feb. 12, 1941, pp. 1, 6.
214 "He was elected . . .": ibid., p. 1.
214 "thankful beyond words": *MD,* Feb. 11, 1941.
214 "the most unsordid act . . .": *NYT,* March 13, 1941, p. 1.
214 "Thank God! . . .": Molly Panter-Downes, *London War Notes, 1939–1945* (1971), p. 137.
214 "one of the most massive . . .": interview transcript from HH documentary, FDRL.
214 "The blind side . . .": Harold L. Ickes, *The Secret Diaries of Harold L. Ickes,* vol. III, *The Lowering Clouds, 1939–1941* (1954), p. 480.
214 "I am just worried . . .": Blum, *Morgenthau Diaries,* vol. II, p. 232.
214 "The more I think . . .": Stimson Diary, March 5, 1941, Yale University.
215 "Upon his return . . .": *SEP,* April 26, 1941, p. 73.
215 "It tore Eleanor's . . .": Martha Gellhorn interview, *OH,* FDRL.
215 "Yes, the decisions . . .": James MacGregor Burns, *Roosevelt: The Soldier of Freedom* (1970), p. 49.
215 "the Führer finally . . .": Goebbels, *Goebbels Diaries, 1939–1941,* p. 240.

CHAPTER NINE: "Business As Usual"

216 "This house is . . .": Victoria Henrietta Nesbitt, *White House Diary* (1948), p. 261.
216 Fort Bragg: *Fortune,* May 1941, p. 162.
217 labor force of 28,500: *NYT,* Feb. 16, 1941, p. 31.
217 "extraordinarily interesting . . .": *MD,* March 31, 1941.
217 at any number of spots: *Fortune,* May 1941, pp. 58, 62.
217 "We're building . . ."; "the worst malaria . . .": *U.S. News,* Aug. 29, 1941, p. 28.
217 most rudimentary facilities: Ulysses G. Lee, *The Employment of Negro Troops* (1966), p. 43.
217 "If our plans . . .": *U.S. News,* Aug. 29, 1941, p. 28.
218 "But to the new . . .": Lee Kennett, *GI* (1987), p. 42.
218 "curved streets . . .": ibid., p. 43.
218 "they were the best run . . .": Geoffrey Perrett, *There's a War to Be Won* (1991), p. 36.
218 "sitting on the top . . .": *NYT,* March 23, 1941, sect. IV, p. 7.
218 "that wave . . .": Edwin Martin to FDR, March 21, 1942, OF 93, FDRL.
218 "Fala stood . . .": *MD,* March 31, 1941.
218 "You do have . . .": *NYT,* April 2, 1941, p. 14.
219 LH moved to Washington: Doris Faber, *The Life of Lorena Hickock* (1980), pp. 278–79.
219 "I never knew . . .": LH unpublished manuscript, box 1, LH Papers, FDRL.
219 "But that was not . . .": ibid.
220 "You'd better watch out . . .": Faber, *Lorena Hickok,* p. 94.
220 "There must have been . . .": ibid., p. 16.
220 "I am *not* unhappy . . .": Joseph P. Lash, *Love, Eleanor* (1982), pp. 254–55.
221 "Every woman wants . . .": Joseph P. Lash, *A World of Love: Eleanor Roosevelt and Her Friends, 1943–1962* (1984), p. 116.
221 ". . . I want to put . . .": ER to LH, March 7, 1933, box 1, LH Papers, FDRL.
221 "I felt a little . . .": ER to LH, March 5, 1933, box 1, LH Papers, FDRL.

221 "Oh! how good . . .": ER to LH, March 6, 1933, box 1, LH Papers, FDRL.
221 "The nicest time . . .": ER to LH, March 11, 1933, box 1, LH Papers, FDRL.
221 "Funny how even . . .": LH to ER, Dec. 5, 1933, box 1, LH Papers, FDRL.
221 "While they seem . . .": interview with William Emerson.
221 "Eleanor had so many . . . ": interview with Trude Lash.
222 women routinely used: Carroll Smith-Rosenberg, ch. 14 in Nancy F. Cott and Elizabeth H. Pleck, *A Heritage of Her Own* (1979).
222 "You taught me more . . .": Lash, *Love, Eleanor,* p. 211.
222 "A reporter should never . . .": ibid., p. 133.
223 "Unwittingly . . .": interview with Eleanor Seagraves.
223 "No question that Hick . . .": conversation with Anna Seagraves, Eleanor Seagraves' daughter.
223 "I should work . . .": Lash, *Love, Eleanor,* p. 161.
223 ". . . you will be disappointed . . .": ibid., p. 208.
223 "I'd rather go alone . . .": ibid., p. 181.
223 "cry from the heart . . .": Faber, *Lorena Hickok,* p. 180.
223 "I went to sleep . . .": ibid., p. 156.
223 "I know you have . . .": Lash, *Love, Eleanor,* p. 223.
223 "You think some . . .": ibid., p. 240.
223 "I could shake you . . .": ibid., p. 229.
224 "shouted and stalked . . .": Faber, *Lorena Hickok,* p. 177.
224 "I hope you are having . . .": ibid., p. 174.
224 "Of course you should have . . .": Lash, *Love, Eleanor,* p. 218.
224 ". . . if I didn't love you . . .": Faber, *Lorena Hickok,* p. 266.
224 "Of course dear . . .": Lash, *Love, Eleanor,* p. 254.
224 "I'd never have believed . . .": ibid., pp. 277–78.
224 "You are wrong about Louis . . .": ibid., p. 278.
225 Accepting ER's invitation: LH unpublished manuscript, box 1, LH Papers, FDRL.
225 "A more discouraging . . .": *U.S. News,* April 11, 1941, p. 20.
225 strike statistics: Rosa Swafford, *Wartime Record of Strikes and Lockouts, 1940–1945* (1946), p. vii.
225 "Some friends of labor . . .": Raymond Clapper, *Watching the World* (1944), p. 218.
225 War Department's use of statistics: Byron Fairchild and Jonathan Grossman, *The Army and Industrial Mobilization* (1959), p. 60.
226 "All these men . . .": Lash Diary, Feb. 16, 1941, Lash Papers, FDRL.
226 "I cannot escape . . .": *MD,* Dec. 9, 1940.
226 River Rouge plant: *Life,* Aug. 19, 1940, pp. 37–39.
226 "the last unconquered citadel . . .": *Newsweek,* April 14, 1941, p. 35.
227 Ford contracts: *WP,* Nov. 7, 1940, p. 1; *NYT,* Nov. 30, 1940, p. 9.
227 "union enemy . . .": Fairchild and Grossman, *Mobilization,* p. 39.
227 "Ford is the country's . . .": *Nation,* Dec. 14, 1940, p. 595.
227 "a bad thing . . .": *NYT,* Dec. 29, 1940, p. 12.
227 "to let bygone issues . . .": Stimson Diary, Jan. 1, 1941, Yale University.
227 War Department pressed to reject bid: *NYT,* Feb. 6, 1941, p. 11.
227 "Best news . . .": *Nation,* Feb. 8, 1941, p. 147.
227 Supreme Court decision: *Business Week,* Feb. 14, 1941, p. 14.
227 Description of strike: *Detroit News,* April 2, 1941, p. 1; *NYT,* April 3, 1941, pp. 1, 18.
228 "more Negroes . . .": Mary Bethune to ER, April 4, 1941, ER Microfilm Collection, FDRL.
228 "It will be a bitter . . .": *PC,* April 12, 1941, p. 4.
228 "watching and waiting . . .": *NYT,* April 4, 1941, p. 14.
228 "With the help . . ."; "I am convinced . . .": *Detroit News,* April 13, 1941, p. 1.
229 White journeyed: *Detroit News,* April 9, 1941, p. 1.
229 "dimmed the power . . .": Peter Collier and Robert Horowitz, *The Fords* (1987), p. 170.
229 Rolls-Royce: ibid., p. 178.
229 Edsel humiliated by turnabout: Norman Beasley, *Knudsen* (1947), p. 261.
229 "Mr. Ford gave . . .": Robert Lacey, *Ford* (1986), p. 376.
229 votes counted: Charles Sorenson and William Samuelson, *My Forty Years with Ford* (1956), p. 268.
229 "It was a measure . . .": Lacey, *Ford,* p. 377.

230 "It was perhaps . . .": Sorenson and Samuelson, *Forty Years,* p. 260.
230 "treason" penalties: *NYT,* April 2, 1941, p. 1.
230 "perfect nonsense . . .": ibid., p. 14; also *BEA,* April 12, 1941, p. 3.
230 ER's press conference: *NYT,* April 8, 1941, p. 19.
230 "The infamous hand . . .": *Time,* June 16, 1941, p. 15.
231 "Franklin Roosevelt . . .": ibid.
231 with help of federal troops: *NYT,* June 10, 1941, p. 10.
231 "The armed forces . . .": *Time,* June 16, 1941, p. 15.
231 "Washington rarely . . .": David Lawrence, *Diary of a Washington Correspondent* (1942), p. 144.
231 "What has not yet . . .": ibid., p. 141.
231 "It took Hitler . . .": *Fortune,* July 1941, p. 68.
231 "gobbling an intolerable share . . .": *Business Week,* April 26, 1941, p. 19.
232 Packard, Willys, Chevrolet: *Business Week,* Jan. 18, 1941, p. 56.
232 "You can't have 500 . . .": *Fortune,* July 1941, p. 68.
232 "We cannot fight a war . . .": *Nation,* May 3, 1941, p. 519.
232 "The entire industry . . .": Beasley, *Knudsen,* p. 313.
232 "The problem is to turn . . .": *Nation,* May 3, 1941, p. 519.
232 "I am afraid . . .": Stimson Diary, May 29, 1941, Yale University.
232 "to begin thinking . . .": *NYT,* Feb. 18, 1941, p. 1.
232 "cheerfully forego . . .": [James Rowe] to FDR, July 22, 1941, Henderson Papers, FDRL.
233 "The President has . . .": Eric Larrabee, *Commander in Chief* (1987), p. 63.
233 Yugoslavia: Martin Gilbert, *The Second World War* (1989), p. 170.
233 British ships being sunk: Robert Dallek, *Franklin D. Roosevelt and American Foreign Policy, 1932–1945* (1981), p. 260.
233 "to forcibly stop . . .": Stimson Diary, Dec. 19, 1941, Yale University.
233 waiting for him to cross: James MacGregor Burns, *Roosevelt: The Soldier of Freedom* (1970), p. 91.
234 41 percent, 50 percent: Dallek, *Roosevelt and Foreign Policy,* p. 261.
234 "one could not . . .": *U.S. News,* May 2, 1941, p. 22.
234 "which is the cutest . . .": FDR, Jr., to AB, April 2, 1941, box 68, Halsted Papers, FDRL.
234 "the U.S.A. . . .": Joseph Goebbels, *The Goebbels Diaries, 1939–1941* (1983), p. 336.
234 "He reassured me . . .": Stimson Diary, April 22, 1941, Yale University.
234 "I am worried . . .": Stimson Diary, May 23, 1941, Yale University.
234 "Knudsen simply is . . .": Harold L. Ickes, *The Secret Diaries of Harold L. Ickes,* vol. III, *The Lowering Clouds, 1939–1941* (1954), p. 509.
235 "He still has the country . . .": ibid., p. 511.
235 "I turn to Missy . . .": ibid., pp. 487–88.
235 "FDR looked as bad . . .": *Time,* May 19, 1941, p. 16.
235 "My heart sank . . .": *MD,* April 25, 1941.
236 "What he's suffering . . .": Robert E. Sherwood, *Roosevelt and Hopkins* (1948), p. 293.
236 "waiting to be pushed . . .": John Morton Blum, *From the Morgenthau Diaries,* vol. II (1965), p. 254.
236 "a compact with . . .": Larrabee, *Commander in Chief,* p. 42.
236 May percentages: George Gallup, *The Gallup Polls: Public Opinion, 1935–1971,* vol. I, *1937–1948* (1972), pp. 278–80.
236 "Missy was . . .": interview with Eliot Janeway.
236 "Since defense is now . . .": Lash Diary, April 20, 1941, Lash Papers, FDRL.
237 "probably the most crucial . . .": *NYT,* May 12, 1941, p. 15.
237 "There is no one . . .": *MD,* May 11, 1941.
237 "Isn't she amazing?": Bernard Asbell, *Mother and Daughter* (1988), p. 132.
237 "on the way . . .": ibid.
237 everything not newly planted: *MD,* May 10, 1941.
237 "very tired . . .": Asbell, *Mother and Daughter,* p. 131.
237 "The situation with Harry . . .": ibid.
237 "Franklin is much better . . .": ER to Esther Lape, May 23, 1941, ER Microfilm Collection, FDRL.
238 Preparation of speech: Sherwood, *Roosevelt and Hopkins,* pp. 279–80.
238 "If I may say so . . .": Samuel I. Rosenman, *Working with Roosevelt* (1952), p. 279.

238 "There's only a small . . .": ibid., p. 284.
238 "For almost an hour . . .": *NYT,* June 2, 1941, p. 1.
238 Text of speech: *NYT,* May 28, 1941, p. 2.
239 "The atmosphere . . .": *MD,* May 27, 1941.
239 "like an oncoming wave . . .": ibid.
239 ER asked HH to join FDR: Sherwood, *Roosevelt and Hopkins,* p. 298.
240 "would have been difficult . . .": Rosenman, *Working with Roosevelt,* p. 288.
240 "They're 95 percent favorable . . .": Sherwood, *Roosevelt and Hopkins,* p. 298.
240 Stimson was pleased: Stimson Diary, May 27, 1941, Yale University.
240 "We listened to father's . . .": AB to ER, May 29, 1941, box 59, Halsted Papers, FDRL.
240 Listener polls: *NYT,* June 1, 1941, sect. IX, p. 10.
240 "demagogic and aggressive": Goebbels, *Goebbels Diaries, 1939–1941,* p. 240.

CHAPTER TEN: "A Great Hour to Live"

241 "she may have begun . . .": interview with Curtis Roosevelt.
241 "Missy was not as relaxing . . .": interview with Elliott Roosevelt.
241 "sit and simper . . .": interview with Trude Pratt.
242 "when to approach FDR . . .": *SEP,* Jan. 8, 1938, p. 9.
242 "Some of the people . . .": *TIR,* pp. 169–70.
242 "The president would work . . .": interview with Barbara Curtis.
242 "She said quietly . . .": interview with Egbert Curtis.
242 On June 4, 1941: Lillian Rogers Parks, *The Roosevelts: A Family in Turmoil* (1981), p. 186.
242 Missy arose: Grace Tully, *F.D.R., My Boss* (1949), p. 246.
242 "It was very secret . . .": interview with Toi Bachelder.
243 "She's gotten up . . .": Parks, *Family in Turmoil,* pp. 186–87.
243 "Missy loved . . .": ibid.
243 "It's sad . . .": ibid., p. 187.
243 ". . . She's been taking opiates . . .": Bernard Asbell, *Mother and Daughter* (1988), p. 132.
243 "change of life": ibid., p. 133.
243 "Too many women . . .": *Good Housekeeping,* July 1943, p. 30.
243 "The letters told . . .": Bernard Asbell, *The FDR Memoirs* (1973), p. 403.
244 "Missy has been worse . . .": Asbell, *Mother and Daughter,* p. 133.
244 "licks the joints . . .": *Hygeia,* April 1942, p. 270.
244 "I was distressed . . .": AB to MLH, n.d., box 36, Halsted Papers, FDRL.
244 "My dear Missy . . .": SDR to MLH, Aug. 3, 1941, box 10, Roosevelt Family Papers Donated by the Children, FDRL.
245 "The strange thing . . .": interview with Elliott Roosevelt.
245 "Roosevelt had absolutely . . .": interview with Eliot Janeway.
245 "As I sat . . .": Ickes Diary, July 12, 1941, Library of Congress.
245 "No words will ever . . .": FDR to Dr. Harper, Aug. 27, 1941, PPF 3737, FDRL.
246 "The case has been . . .": Dr. Winfred Overholser to FDR, Aug. 28, 1941, PPF 3737, FDRL.
246 "the children . . .": interview with James Roosevelt.
246 Roosevelt's will: copy of last will and testament of Franklin D. Roosevelt, dated Nov. 12, 1941, FDRL.
246 "I owed her . . .": James Roosevelt, *My Parents,* p. 108.
246 "Negroes will be considered . . .": Richard Polenberg, *War and Society: The United States, 1941–1945* (1972), p. 114.
247 "We have not had . . .": The Annals of the American Academy of Political and Social Sciences, Sept. 1942, p. 74.
247 "It is not the policy . . .": *Fortune,* March 1941, p. 163.
247 "Negroes who are experienced . . .": *PC,* Sept. 28, 1940, p. 3.
247 "What happens . . .": *New York Post,* March 6, 1941, n.p.
247 "shunted from pillar . . .": *Chicago Defender,* June 12, 1943, p. 1.
247 "Only power . . .": Jervis Anderson, *A. Philip Randolph* (1973), p. 248.
247 "we ought to get . . .": Murray Kempton, *Part of Our Time* (1965), p. 250.
248 "I think the first . . .": ibid.
248 "the voiceless and helpless . . .": *Chicago Defender,* June 12, 1943, p. 1.

248 "Be not dismayed . . ." "Call to Negro Americans," July 1, 1941, OF 93, FDRL.
248 "crying for their . . .": Kempton, *Part of Our Time,* p. 251.
248 "Let the Negro . . .": Anderson, *A. Philip Randolph,* p. 251.
248 "The pressures of matters . . .": Watson to WW, April 8, 1941, OF 93, FDRL.
249 ER at Virginia College: *PC,* April 12, 1941, p. 3.
249 ". . . when there would be . . .": *NYT,* June 8, 1941, p. 41.
249 "Mrs. Roosevelt's coming . . .": Joseph Albright to Steve Early, June 8, 1941, OF 93, FDRL.
249 Naval Academy refused: Harvard Committee for Democracy and Education to FDR, April 11, 1941, OF 93, FDRL.
249 "To order taking Negroes . . .": FDR to Knudsen, May 25, 1941, OF 93, FDRL.
249 "I have talked with Mr. Hillman . . .": Knudsen to FDR, May 28, 1941, OF 391, FDRL.
250 "I have talked with the President . . .": ER to A. P. Randolph, June 10, 1941, ER Microfilm Collection, FDRL.
250 "I am submitting . . .": *PC,* June 21, 1941, p. 4.
250 "gripped their heart . . .": Randolph to Knudsen, June 3, 1941, OF 391, FDRL.
250 "When I got . . .": John Salmond, *A Southern Rebel* (1983), p. 194.
250 "Get the missus . . .": Joseph P. Lash, *Eleanor and Franklin* (1971), p. 534.
250 "Mrs. Roosevelt . . .": Kempton, *Our Time,* p. 251; Walter White, *A Man Called White* (1948), p. 193.
251 "except the President's . . .": Watson to FDR, June 14, 1941, OF 93, FDRL.
251 "Mr. President, time . . .": Anderson, *Randolph,* p. 256.
251 ". . . What would happen . . .": *Chicago Defender,* June 28, 1941, p. 2.
251 "I'm sorry Mr. President . . .": Anderson, *Randolph,* pp. 256–57.
251 "A tall courtly . . .": Roy Wilkins, *Standing Fast* (1982), p. 180.
251 "Gentlemen, it is clear . . .": Anderson, *Randolph,* p. 258.
252 "one of those . . .": Stimson Diary, June 18, 1941, Yale University.
252 "more can be done . . ."; "It was not enough . . .": quoted in *PC,* June 28, 1941, p. 4.
252 "As Coy was . . .": interview with Joe Rauh.
252 "Who is this guy . . .": Anderson, *Randolph,* p. 259.
252 "We've got every piece . . .": interview with Joe Rauh.
252 "one of the greatest . . .": ibid.
252 "to provide for the full . . .": press release, OF 93, FDRL.
252 "The President has just . . .": Randolph to ER, June 24, 1941, ER Microfilm Collection, FDRL.
253 "the Negro people . . .": Randolph to ER, June 23, 1941, ER Microfilm Collection, FDRL.
253 "very glad that the march . . .": ER to Randolph, June 26, 1941, ER Microfilm Collection, FDRL.
253 "as the most significant . . ."; "a great step forward": Louis Ruchames, *Race, Jobs and Politics* (1953), p. 22.
253 "Never before . . .": *Chicago Defender,* June 25, 1941, p. 2.
253 "Now the guns . . .": Joseph Goebbels, *The Goebbels Diaries, 1939–1941* (1983), p. 424.
253 ". . . new territory in Europe . . .": William L. Shirer, *The Rise and Fall of the Third Reich* (1981), p. 796.
253 "The novelty . . .": Alan Bullock, *Hitler* (1962), p. 651.
254 "We have only . . .": ibid., p. 652.
254 "Since I struggled . . .": Shirer, *Rise and Fall,* p. 851.
254 "Everything is well . . .": Goebbels, *Goebbels Diaries, 1939–1941,* p. 423.
254 "War is mainly . . .": Winston S. Churchill, *The Second World War,* vol. III, *The Grand Alliance* (1950), p. 316.
254 Russians killed: Martin Gilbert, *The Second World War* (1989), p. 218.
254 "Tell the B.B.C. . . .": Churchill, *Grand Alliance,* p. 331.
255 "The Prime Minister's compliments . . .": Martin Gilbert, *Winston S. Churchill,* vol. VI, *'Finest Hour': 1939–1941* (1983), p. 1119.
255 "I have only one . . .": Churchill, *Grand Alliance,* p. 331.
255 "No one has been . . .": ibid., pp. 331–33.
255 "Perhaps he was not . . .": Harold L. Ickes, *The Secret Diaries of Harold L. Ickes,* vol. III, *The Lowering Clouds, 1939–1941* (1954), p. 549.
255 precious and . . .": quoted in William Langer and Everett Gleason, *Undeclared War* (1953), pp. 537–38.

255 "a case of . . ." . . . "no one who would save . . .": Langer and Gleason, *Undeclared War*, pp. 542–43.
256 "tools of British . . .": Robert E. Sherwood, *Roosevelt and Hopkins* (1948), p. 303.
256 Michael Quill: James Loeb, *OH*, FDRL.
256 "Will it be good . . ." . . . "He said he thought . . .": Lash Diary, June 23, 1941, Lash Papers, FDRL.
256 "Of course we are . . .": *NYT*, June 25, 1941, p. 7.
257 HH's double mission: Sherwood, *Roosevelt and Hopkins*, p. 308.
257 "Tell him, tell him . . .": Averell Harriman and Elie Abel, *Special Envoy to Churchill and Stalin, 1941–1946* (1975), p. 73.
257 "No man could forget . . .": Sherwood, *Roosevelt and Hopkins*, p. 344.
257 "Not once did . . .": ibid., p. 343.
257 "There was little . . .": Charles E. Bohlen, *Witness to History, 1929–1969* (1973), pp. 357–58.
258 HH cabled FDR: Sherwood, *Roosevelt and Hopkins*, pp. 333–34.
258 "The country is awake . . .": *Life*, July 7, 1941, p. 17.
259 "educational phase": *Fortune*, April 1941, p. 36.
259 To be sure: ibid.
259 ALCOA: *NR*, Jan. 27, 1941, p. 104.
259 "the battered citadel . . .": I. F. Stone, *The War Years, 1939–1945* (1988), p. 154.
259 "There never was a monopoly . . .": interview with Arthur Goldschmidt.
259 "As soon as Roosevelt . . .": ibid.
260 "When the story . . .": *Time*, July 7, 1941, p. 10.
260 five thousand dishpans: *Woman's Home Companion*, Nov. 1941, p. 120.
260 "Many a good dessert . . .": *NYT*, July 22, 1941, pp. 1, 21.
260 "He laughed over this . . .": David E. Lilienthal, *The Journal of David E. Lilienthal*, vol. 1 (1964), p. 404.
261 "I am sick and tired . . ."; "thoroughly miserable": John Morton Blum, *From the Morgenthau Diaries*, vol. II (1965), p. 264.
261 "one of the most . . .": Ickes, *Secret Diaries*, vol. III, p. 592.
261 "Get the planes off . . .": Blum, *Morgenthau Diaries*, vol. II, p. 264.
261 "highly unfair . . .": Stimson Diary, Aug. 1, 1941, Yale University.
261 "All of these . . .": Stimson Diary, Aug. 4, 1941, Yale University.
261 "In the first place . . .": quoted in Ed Cray, *General of the Army: George C. Marshall, Soldier and Statesman* (1990), p. 198.
261 "we must get 'em . . ."; "hoity-toity humor . . .": Stimson Diary, Aug. 1, 1941, Yale University.
262 "very much on the ball . . .": Ickes, *Secret Diaries*, vol. III, p. 592.
262 "we ought to come . . .": ibid., p. 595.
262 "We have done . . .": *NR*, April 15, 1946, p. 546.
262 "Our own Army . . .": ibid., p. 547.
262 long list of supplies: ibid.
262 "My husband . . .": *TIR*, p. 224.
262 "There was nothing . . .": Ross McIntire, *White House Physician* (1946), p. 130.
262 "I hope to be gone . . .": FDR to SDR, Aug. 3, 1941, PPF 8, FDRL.
263 "I hope this map . . .": Martha to FDR, n.d., box 21, Roosevelt Family Papers Donated by the Children, FDRL.
263 On the morning of the 4th: McIntire, *Physician*, p. 130.
263 "They came back . . .": Perkins, *OH*, Columbia University.
263 On the decks of the *Augusta:* Henry H. Arnold, *Global Mission* (1949), p. 248.
263 "Churchill probably never . . .": W. H. Thompson, *Assignment: Churchill* (1955), p. 224.
263 "We are just off . . .": *Churchill & Roosevelt: The Complete Correspondence* (1984), vol. I, p. 226.
264 ". . . last filament of the spider's web . . .": Sherwood, *Roosevelt and Hopkins*, pp. 347–49.
264 "You'd have thought . . .": ibid., p. 351.
264 "the longest way . . .": *NYT Magazine*, Sept. 14, 1941, p. 5.
264 "I suppose you could say . . .": Sherwood, *Roosevelt and Hopkins*, p. 236.

265 "Around us were numerous . . .": Thompson, *Assignment,* pp. 231–32.
265 "the wrong war . . .": James MacGregor Burns, *Roosevelt: The Soldier of Freedom* (1970), p. 150.
265 "It's marvelous . . .": Blum, *Morgenthau Diaries,* vol. II, p. 375.
265 "It is terribly important . . .": ibid.
265 "The Japanese . . .": ibid.
266 "to slip the noose . . .": Robert Dallek, *Franklin D. Roosevelt and American Foreign Policy, 1932–1945* (1981), p. 274.
266 "would be compelled . . .": Churchill, *Grand Alliance,* p. 390.
266 "would wage war . . .": Gilbert, *Churchill,* vol. VI, p. 1168.
266 "the final . . .": Churchill, *Grand Alliance,* p. 393.
267 "One got the impression . . .": Theodore Wilson, *The First Summit* (1969), p. 109.
267 "The same language . . .": H. V. Morton, *Atlantic Meeting* (1943), p. 114.
267 "If nothing else . . .": Elliott Roosevelt, *As He Saw It* (1946), p. 33.
267 "Every word seemed to stir . . .": Churchill, *Grand Alliance,* p. 384.
267 "to court disaster": *NYT,* July 16, 1941, p. 1.
267 "reaching the point . . .": Forrest C. Pogue, *George C. Marshall: Ordeal and Hope, 1939–1942* (1966), vol. II, p. 147.
267 "the battle . . .": ibid.
268 "As far as the men . . .": *Life,* Aug. 18, 1941, p. 17.
268 "OHIO": ibid.
268 "The absence . . .": Stimson to FDR, Aug. 15, 1941, PPF 20, FDRL.
268 "Mindful of the next . . .": Pogue, *Ordeal and Hope,* p. 152.
268 "On this vote . . .": Alfred Steinberg, *Sam Rayburn* (1975), p. 171.
268 "a decidedly . . .": HH draft article, HH Papers, FDRL.
268 "The Americans . . .": Sherwood, *Roosevelt and Hopkins,* p. 367.

CHAPTER ELEVEN: "A Completely Changed World"

270 suffered a stroke in June: Lash Diary, June 4, 1941, Lash Papers, FDRL.
270 "I should not be . . .": Bernard Asbell, *Mother and Daughter* (1988), p. 134.
270 "peace of mind": FDR to SDR, July 23, 1941, box 10, Roosevelt Family Papers Donated by the Children, FDRL.
270 "Of course, you are right . . .": SDR to FDR, July 23, 1941, box 10, Roosevelt Family Papers Donated by the Children, FDRL.
271 SDR insisted on walking: James Roosevelt and Sidney Schalett, *Affectionately, F.D.R.* (1959), p. 316.
271 ER's sudden premonition: *NYT,* Sept. 9, 1941, p. 8.
271 "A telegram has . . .": Fred Delano to FDR, Sept. 27, 1941, PPF 8, FDRL.
271 SDR dressing up: Geoffrey C. Ward, *A First-Class Temperament* (1989), p. 3.
271 cigarette butts: Michael F. Reilly, *Reilly of the White House* (1947), p. 82.
271 "a mother should . . .": Frances Perkins, *The Roosevelt I Knew* (1946), p. 67.
271 "Although we are now . . .": Rita Kleeman, "Compilation of Material for an Article About Mrs. James Roosevelt," Kleeman Papers, FDRL.
271 "I lie on my bed . . .": SDR to FDR, Aug. 1, 1941, box 10, Roosevelt Family Papers Donated by the Children, FDRL.
272 could see them in her mind's eye: SDR to Monroe Robinson, Aug. 6, 1941, PPF 8, FDRL.
272 "Now that he is back . . .": Rita Halle Kleeman, *Gracious Lady: The Life of Sara Delano Roosevelt* (1935), p. 233.
272 Details of FDR-SDR last meeting: Ward, *Temperament,* pp. 5–6.
272 "The President went out . . .": Reilly, *Reilly,* p. 84.
272 "shut himself off . . .": *NYT,* Sept. 9, 1941, p. 8.
272 "I am so weary . . .": ER to LH, Sept. 7, 1941, LH Papers, FDRL.
273 "of course attending . . .": Joseph P. Lash, *Love, Eleanor* (1982), p. 355.
273 "The endless details . . .": ibid.
273 "The funeral was nice . . .": Asbell, *Mother and Daughter,* p. 136.
273 "He never looked toward . . .": *WP,* Sept. 10, 1941, p. 1.
273 "I think Franklin . . .": Lash, *Love, Eleanor,* pp. 360–61.

273 "Don't you think . . .": James Roosevelt, *My Parents: A Differing View* (1976), p. 31.
273 "You promised me . . .": SDR to FDR, July 14, 1941, box 10, Roosevelt Family Papers Donated by the Children, FDRL.
273 to wear his rubbers: ER interview, Graff Papers, FDRL.
273 "Mama, will you please . . .": interview with Betsey Whitney.
273 Sara simply announced: John Gunther, *Roosevelt in Retrospect* (1950), p. 165.
273 "At first sight . . .": Sara Delano Roosevelt, *My Boy Franklin* (1933), p. 42.
274 sorting through . . .: Grace Tully, *F.D.R., My Boss* (1949), p. 105.
274 "No one on his staff . . .": Ward, *Temperament,* p. 9.
274 "all the lines . . .": *MD,* Sept. 8, 1941.
274 "I kept being appalled . . .": Asbell, *Mother and Daughter,* p. 136.
274 "I had so much insecurity . . .": Lash Diary, Aug. 1, 1940, Lash Papers, FDRL.
274 "I did not quite know . . .": *TIMS,* p. 162.
275 "she could make it . . .": Joseph P. Lash, *Eleanor and Franklin* (1971), p. 303.
275 "If you'd just run a comb . . .": Ward, *Temperament,* p. 175.
275 "What happened would never . . .": AH interview with Bernard Asbell.
275 "I looked at . . .": Lash, *Love, Eleanor,* p. 356.
275 "She thought . . .": *MD,* Sept. 9, 1941.
275 "Mother went to father . . .": James Roosevelt, *My Parents,* p. 113.
275 "Can I have . . .": FDR to ER, Oct. 7, 1941, box 16, Roosevelt Family Papers Donated by the Children, FDRL.
275 "Do be an angel . . .": FDR to ER, Oct. 8, 1941, box 16, Roosevelt Family Papers Donated by the Children, FDRL.
275 "a rare treat . . .": Victoria Henrietta Nesbitt, *White House Diary* (1948), p. 268.
276 "Pa sprang on me . . .": Asbell, *Mother and Daughter,* p. 137.
276 FDR waited until AB came east: Lash Diary, Oct. 23, 1941, Lash Papers, FDRL.
276 "Hyde Park is now . . .": Lillian Rogers Parks, *The Roosevelts: A Family in Turmoil* (1981), p. 241.
276 "as they told him . . .": Joseph P. Lash, *Eleanor and Franklin* (1971), p. 643.
276 she took a bottle of gin: interview with Willliam Emerson.
277 When Hall drank: Eleanor Wotkyns, *OH,* FDRL.
277 "The level of noise . . .": interview with Curtis Roosevelt.
277 "had a penchant . . .": Elliott Roosevelt and James Brough, *A Rendezvous with Destiny* (1975), p. 93.
277 "There was nothing . . .": Eleanor Wotkyns, *OH,* FDRL.
277 "This watching Hall . . .": Asbell, *Mother and Daughter,* p. 137.
277 "fired first upon . . .": *NYT,* Sept. 12, 1941, p. 1.
277 *Greer* had deliberately stalked: Robert Dallek, *Franklin D. Roosevelt and American Foreign Policy* (1981), p. 287.
278 "No matter what . . .": *NYT,* Sept. 12, 1941, p. 4.
278 "It was the firmest . . .": Stimson Diary, Sept. 11, 1941, Yale University.
278 "shoot on sight" policy: *NYT,* Oct. 19, 1941, p. 5.
278 "Sentiment on Capitol Hill . . .": David Lawrence, *Diary of a Washington Correspondent* (1942), p. 206.
278 "Roosevelt's deviousness . . .": Dallek, *Roosevelt and Foreign Policy,* p. 289.
278 "suddenly gone . . .": William Hassett to FDR, Sept. 21, 1941, box 19, Roosevelt Family Papers Donated by the Children, FDRL.
279 ghastly noises: interview with William Emerson.
279 "My idea of hell . . .": Lash, *Love, Eleanor,* p. 357.
279 "The President returned . . .": Tommy to AB, Sept. 24, 1941, box 75, Halsted Papers, FDRL.
279 " 'Hall has died' . . .": James Roosevelt, *My Parents,* p. 113.
279 "My mother-in-law . . .": ER to Martha Gellhorn, Oct. 1, 1941, ER Microfilm Collection, FDRL.
279 "the terrible waste . . .": Tommy to AB, Sept. 24, 1941, box 75, Halsted Papers, FDRL.
279 ER dug out old photos: Joseph P. Lash, *A World of Love: Eleanor Roosevelt and Her Friends, 1943–1962* (1984), p. xviii.
279 "The loss of someone . . .": *TIR,* p. 230.
280 "no government agency . . .": *NYT,* Aug. 26, 1941, p. 5.

280 "There are 135,000,000 . . .": Lash, *Eleanor and Franklin,* p. 642.
280 "I'm worried . . .": Lash, *Love, Eleanor,* p. 355.
280 "I honestly think . . .": Tommy to AB, Sept. 24, 1941, box 75, Halsted Papers, FDRL.
280 "If I feel depressed . . .": *LHJ,* Oct. 1944, p. 43.
281 ER attire on September 29: *WP,* Sept. 30, 1941, p. 10.
281 "You are Mrs. Roosevelt . . .": *MD,* Sept. 29, 1941.
281 ER outlined three goals: *NYT,* Sept. 30, 1941, p. 28.
281 "I am ridiculously busy": ER to Martha Gellhorn, Nov. 10, 1941, ER Microfilm Collection, FDRL.
281 "He was glad . . .": Anna Rosenberg Hoffman, *OH,* FDRL.
281 "What's this I hear? . . .": *TIR,* p. 231.
281 "There is an advantage . . .": Lash Diary, Oct. 5, 1941, Lash Papers, FDRL.
282 "We all had . . .": ibid.
282 *Pink Star:* Franklin D. Roosevelt, *Public Papers and Addresses of Franklin D. Roosevelt, 1940* (1941), p. 399.
282 *Kearney: NYT,* Oct. 8, 1941, p. 1.
282 *Reuben James:* Richard M. Ketchum, *The Borrowed Years, 1938–1941* (1989), p. 605.
282 "I think the Navy . . .": Stimson Diary, Oct. 23, 1941, Yale University.
282 only 30 percent: *NYT,* Oct. 1, 1941, p. 8.
283 majority of 72 percent: *NYT,* Oct. 9, 1941, p. 5.
283 "If we continue . . .": *WP,* Sept. 7, 1941, p. 1.
283 "American war vessels . . .": *NYT,* Oct. 18, 1941, p. 9.
283 Senate finally agreed: *NYT,* Nov. 8, 1941, p. 1.
283 "He had no more tricks . . .": Robert E. Sherwood, *Roosevelt and Hopkins* (1948), p. 383.
283 FDR had agreed to a policy: Dallek, *Roosevelt and Foreign Policy,* pp. 273–75.
283 Tojo replaced Konoye: ibid., p. 303.
284 "very discouraged and cynical . . .": Perkins, *OH,* Columbia University.
284 "Just as you move . . .": HH to MLH, Nov. 12, 1941, HH Papers, FDRL.
285 "so quick and full . . .": interview with Virginia Shipp.
285 FDR's trip was postponed: *NYT,* Nov. 21, 1941, p. 13.
285 "I must say . . .": FDR, Jr., to ER, Nov. 26, 1941, box 57, Halsted Papers, FDRL.
285 "I tell you frankly . . .": Joel Seidman, *American Labor: From Defense to Reconversion* (1953), p. 66.
285 "We felt a weight . . .": *MD,* Nov. 23, 1941.
286 "fairly blew up . . .": Stimson Diary, Nov. 26, 1941, Yale University.
286 "a very tense, long day . . .": Stimson Diary, Nov. 27, 1941, Yale University.
286 "If the current negotiations . . .": Stark to FDR, Nov. 27, 1941, PSF 80, FDRL.
286 FDR instructed Hull: Stimson Diary, Nov. 28, 1941, Yale University.
286 "very sorry that he . . .": ibid.
286 train reached Newman: *NYT,* Nov. 30, 1941, p. 34.
286 "had a few drinks . . .": A. Merriman Smith, *Thank You, Mr. President* (1946), p. 107.
286 "You had to have . . .": Bernard Asbell, *The FDR Memoirs* (1973), p. 400.
287 "endure the ordeal . . .": ibid.
287 "the Far East picture . . .": Tully, *F.D.R.,* p. 249.
287 "for the honor and pride . . .": Cordell Hull, *The Memoirs of Cordell Hull,* vol. II (1948), pp. 1089–90.
287 "nearly in tears . . .": Tully, *F.D.R.,* p. 251.
287 "That means . . .": *NYT,* Dec. 2, 1941, p. 27.
287 "the blood rush up . . ." . . . "Don't let it . . .": Perkins, *OH,* Columbia University.
287 "We've got our sources . . .": ibid.
288 December 6: Forrest C. Pogue, *George C. Marshall: Ordeal and Hope, 1939–1942* (1966), vol. II, pp. 224–27.
288 December 7: ibid., pp. 226–29.
288 "The Japanese are . . .": ibid., p. 229.
288 189 Japanese planes: Vice Admiral Homer N. Wallin, *Pearl Harbor—Why, How: Fleet Salvage and Final Appraisal* (1968), p. 88.
288 "snugly side by side . . .": Harold L. Ickes, *Secret Diaries of Harold L. Ickes,* vol. III, *The Lowering Clouds, 1939–1941* (1954), p. 661.
289 Knox relayed the news: Sherwood, *Roosevelt and Hopkins,* p. 431.

289 "Mr. President . . .": *American Heritage,* Nov. 1989, p. 54.
289 "All the secretaries . . .": *MD,* Dec. 7, 1941.
289 ER returned to work: *TIR,* p. 233.
289 "the news of the war . . .": Asbell, *Mother and Daughter,* p. 139.
289 "deadly calm . . .": ER interview Graff Papers, FDRL.
289 "each report more . . .": ibid.
289 "he was completely . . .": ibid.
289 "had never had . . .": *American Heritage,* Nov. 1989, p. 60.
289 "I never wanted . . ."; "We haven't . . .": ER interview, Graff Papers, FDRL.
290 "Hi, Old Man . . .": interview with James Roosevelt.
290 "Within the first hour . . .": Tully, *F.D.R.,* p. 255.
290 remarkable conversation: interview with Alonzo Fields.
290 "No American who lived . . .": Marquis Childs, *I Write from Washington* (1942), p. 241.
290 ". . . It's quite true. . . .": Winston S. Churchill, *The Second World War,* vol. III, *The Grand Alliance* (1950), p. 538.
290 "To have the United . . .": ibid., p. 539.
291 "He was alone . . .": Tully, *F.D.R.,* p. 256.
291 "Yesterday comma . . .": ibid., p. 256.
291 "She leaned over . . .": *PM,* Dec. 8, 1941, "Amidst Crowded Days" diary in clippings of Mrs. Franklin D. Roosevelt, compiled, edited and executed by A. Cypen Lubitsh, 1943, box 3201, ER Papers. Hereafter cited Scrapbook, ER Papers, FDRL.
291 "For months now . . .": ibid.
291 "The Japanese . . .": ibid.
291 "Chinese, not Japanese, please . . .": *Life,* Dec. 22, 1941, pp. 81–82.
292 "It was very . . ."; "I'm thankful . . .": Perkins, *OH,* Columbia University.
292 "The effect on the Congressmen . . .": Stimson Diary, Dec. 7, 1941, Yale University.
292 "How did it . . ."; "How did they catch . . .": *American Heritage,* Nov. 1989, p. 86.
293 "I don't know, Tom . . .": Francis Biddle, *In Brief Authority* (1962), p. 206.
293 "was how we should . . .": Stimson Diary, Nov. 25, 1941, Yale University.
293 "Neither Army or Navy . . .": Frank Knox, "Report by the Secretary of the Navy to the President," Dec. 14, 1941, PSF 80, FDRL.
293 "The anti-aircraft . . .": interview with William Emerson.
294 "We are operating . . .": Wallin, *Pearl Harbor,* p. 45.
294 "The damage was . . .": Ross McIntire, *White House Physician* (1946), p. 137.
294 "Missy telephoned . . .": Asbell, *FDR Memoirs,* p. 401.
294 "that the indecision . . .": Stimson Diary, Dec. 7, 1941, Yale University.
294 "You know . . .": Perkins, *OH,* Columbia University.
294 "Monday was almost . . .": Childs, *I Write,* p. 242.
295 "the unprovoked . . .": *NYT,* Dec. 9, 1941, p. 1.
295 Rankin: ibid.
295 "American soil . . .": ibid.
295 "he would support . . .": *NYT,* Dec. 8. 1941, p. 6.
295 "no strikes . . .": George Martin, *Madame Secretary: Frances Perkins* (1976), p. 451.
295 "Labor's response . . .": Hillman to FDR, Dec. 12, 1941, OF 4076, FDRL.
295 ER to West Coast: *TIR,* p. 236.
295 "Hell, this isn't . . .": *Los Angeles Times,* Dec. 10, 1941, p. D.
296 "looking for all the world . . .": *TIR,* p. 236.
296 "I am not here to give . . .": *Los Angeles Times,* Dec. 10, 1941, p. D.
296 ". . . to cooperate with . . .": *Los Angeles Times,* Dec. 9, 1941, p. 2.
296 "Rumors were everywhere . . .": interview with Jiro Isihara.
296 "Let's be honest . . .": *NYT,* Dec. 15, 1941, p. 9.
296 "We know there are . . .": *MD,* Dec. 15, 1941.
297 "When she starts bemoaning . . .": Tamara Hareven, *Eleanor Roosevelt: An American Conscience* (1968), p. 167.
297 "I think almost . . ." *Washington Star,* Dec. 17, 1942, Scrapbook, ER Papers, FDRL.
297 "He was all alone . . .": Samuel I. Rosenman, *Working with Roosevelt* (1952), p. 312.
297 "Was it possible . . .": James MacGregor Burns, *Roosevelt: The Soldier of Freedom* (1970), p. 171.

297 Hitler's speech: text in William L. Shirer, *The Rise and Fall of the Third Reich* (1960), pp. 897–900.
298 "a state of war . . .": *New York Times,* Dec. 9, 1941, p. 1.
298 "It seems like . . .": ER to LH, Dec. 11, 1941, LH Papers, FDRL.
298 "No more Congressional . . ."; "gloomy in winter . . .": LH manuscript, LH Papers, FDRL.
298 "with not a little annoyance": William Seale, *The White House: The History of an American Idea* (1992), p. 228.
298 "One of the Secret Service . . .": interview with Milton Lipson.
299 "Henry, I will not . . .": *TIR,* p. 237.
299 "Mrs. Roosevelt is very . . .": Tommy to Esther Lape, Dec. 16, 1941, box 6, Esther Lape Papers, FDRL.

CHAPTER TWELVE: "Two Little Boys Playing Soldier"

300 "You should have . . .": interview with Alonzo Fields.
300 "It had not occurred . . .": *MD,* Dec. 22, 1941.
301 "he was like a child . . .": Lord Moran, *Churchill—The Struggle for Survival, 1940–1965* (1966), p. 11.
301 "It was night time . . .": W. H. Thompson, *Assignment: Churchill* (1955), p. 246.
301 "Even in the half-light . . .": Moran, *Churchill,* p. 11.
301 "The President was . . .": Mrs. Charles Hamlin, "Memories," FDRL; also in *NR,* suppl., April 1946.
301 "It must have been . . ."; "I have a toast . . .": ibid.
302 "At ten o'clock . . .": *TIR,* p. 242.
302 WC was installed: William Seale, *The President's House* (1986), p. 974; Robert E. Sherwood, *Roosevelt and Hopkins* (1948), p. 442.
302 "Now, Fields . . .": interview with Alonzo Fields.
302 "I'll be back . . .": ER interview, Graff Papers, FDRL.
303 "There is no question . . .": ibid.
303 "Mother would just fume . . .": interview with Elliott Roosevelt.
303 "that she worried . . .": Lillian Roger Parks, *The Roosevelts: A Family in Turmoil* (1981), p. 99.
303 "There was a wild burst . . .": *NYT,* Dec. 24, 1941, p. 4.
303 In the course of the Arcadia Conference: Martin Gilbert, *Winston S. Churchill,* vol. VII, *Road to Victory: 1941–1945* (1986), pp. 35–36.
303 "The news around . . .": Stimson Diary, Dec. 25, 1941, Yale University.
303 sweeping through Malaya: Sherwood, *Roosevelt and Hopkins,* p. 453.
304 end of December: Elena Skrjabina, *Siege and Survival* (1971), p. 28.
304 "When you leave . . .": ibid., p. 30.
304 "He was always a gay . . .": ibid., p. 51.
304 one million would die; counterattack: James MacGregor Burns, *Roosevelt: Soldier of Freedom* (1970), pp. 187–88; Martin Gilbert, *The Second World War* (1989), p. 284.
305 "a hell of a row": quoted in Moran, *Churchill,* p. 21.
305 "Our people are very . . .": ibid., p. 24.
305 "We live here as . . .": Winston S. Churchill, *The Second World War,* vol. III, *The Grand Alliance* (1950), p. 608.
305 Christmas Eve: Seale, *President's House,* p. 974; *NYT,* Dec. 25, 1941, pp. 1, 12; *WP,* Dec. 25, 1941, pp. 1, 5.
305 "old and good friend": *NYT,* Dec. 25, 1941, p. 12.
305 "Let the children . . .": *WP,* Dec. 25, 1941, pp. 1, 5.
306 "Her voice did not . . .": Lash Diary, Dec. 26, 1941, Lash Papers, FDRL.
306 for Fala: *Washington Star,* Dec. 26, 1941, Scrapbook, ER Papers, FDRL.
306 "She could never get . . ."; "it kept him . . .": Lash Diary, Jan. 1, 1942, Lash Papers, FDRL.
306 "He was really incapable . . .": Fulton Oursler, *Behold This Dreamer!* (1964), pp. 424–25.
307 "I guess I'm usually . . .": MLH to FDR, n.d., PPF 3737, FDRL.
307 "I don't know what . . .": Bernard Asbell, *The FDR Memoirs* (1973), p. 402.
307 "Missy and I . . .": Ann Rochon to ER, Jan. 1, 1942, PPF 3737, FDRL.
307 "Xmas was a very sad day . . .": Bernard Asbell, *Mother and Daughter* (1988), p. 141.

307 "jolly and care free . . .": Moran, *Churchill*, p. 15.
308 "He just wasn't having . . .": John Morton Blum, *From the Morgenthau Diaries*, vol. III (1967), p. 122.
308 "a tremendous occasion . . .": Moran, *Churchill*, p. 15.
308 "it was difficult . . .": ibid.
308 WC's methods: Sherwood, *Roosevelt and Hopkins*, p. 261.
308 "for sustained . . .": *AM*, Sept. 1949, p. 41.
308 "wastes little time . . .": Moran, *Churchill*, p. 13.
308 "does not reflect . . .": *AM*, Sept. 1949, p. 40.
309 "Churchill is always . . .": Thompson, *Assignment*, p. 253.
309 "Do you realize . . .": Moran, *Churchill*, p. 16.
309 "I cannot help reflecting . . .": text of speech, *NYT*, Dec. 27, 1941, p. 4.
309 "the first sound . . .": David E. Lilienthal, *The Journal of David E. Lilienthal*, vol. 1 (1964), p. 418.
309 "They had witnessed . . .": *WP*, Dec. 27, 1941, pp. 1, 3.
310 "I hit the target . . .": Moran, *Churchill*, p. 17.
310 "It was a tragic . . .": Hamlin, "Memories," FDRL.
310 "everyone completely . . .": *MD*, Dec. 26, 1941.
310 "She saw in Churchill . . .": interview with Curtis Roosevelt.
310 "Nobody enjoyed the war . . .": Martha Gellhorn, *OH*, FDRL.
310 "The walls were covered . . .": interview with George Elsey.
311 "They looked like . . .": interview with James Roosevelt.
311 motored to Mount Vernon: *NYT*, Jan. 2, 1941, p. 1.
311 "After the war . . ." . . . "You know Winston . . .": Justine Polier, *OH*, FDRL.
312 "batted an eyelash": Samuel I. Rosenman, *Working with Roosevelt* (1952), p. 320.
312 "Churchill wasn't very fond . . .": interview with Elliott Roosevelt.
312 "The Prime Minister . . .": Lash Diary, Jan. 1, 1942, Lash Papers, FDRL.
312 "I like Mr. Churchill . . .": Asbell, *Mother and Daughter*, p. 141.
312 best story was told: Sherwood, *Roosevelt and Hopkins*, p. 442.
312 "Bathtubs were a contrivance . . .": Joseph P. Lash, *Roosevelt and Churchill, 1939–1941* (1976), p. 15.
312 "The Prime Minister . . .": Sherwood, *Roosevelt and Hopkins*, p. 442.
312 declaration signed: *NYT*, Jan. 3, 1942, pp. 1, 4.
312 "It was as quiet . . .": Hamlin, "Memories."
312 "President ought to do! . . .": Lash, *Roosevelt and Churchill*, pp. 19–20.
313 "You would have been . . .": Sherwood, *Roosevelt and Hopkins*, p. 478.
313 "His lips are . . .": Moran, *Churchill*, p. 13.
313 "It is fun . . .": ibid., p. 27.
313 "We must raise . . .": *NYT*, Jan. 7, 1942, p. 5.
313 "The figures reached . . .": *U.S. News*, Jan. 10, 1942, p. 15.
313 "Oh—the production people . . .": Sherwood, *Roosevelt and Hopkins*, p. 474.
313 "who never met . . .": Bruce Catton, *The War Lords of Washington* (1948), p. 84.
314 "These figures . . .": *NYT*, Jan. 7, 1942, p. 5.
314 complete ban: *NYT*, Jan. 2, 1942, p. 1.
314 rationing cars and trucks: *NYT*, Jan. 16, 1942, p. 14.
314 Leon Henderson said: *NYT*, Jan. 3, 1942, p. 1.
314 "In the dealers' . . .": *Time*, Jan. 12, 1942, p. 61.
314 "Mr. Knudsen looked . . .": Alfred Steinberg, *Mrs. R* (1958), p. 279.
314 "I said nothing . . .": *MD*, Jan. 14, 1942.
315 Donald Nelson: W. M. Kiplinger, *Washington Is Like That* (1942), pp. 37–38.
315 "final" decisions: *Life*, Jan. 26, 1942, p. 29.
315 "Look here . . .": Norman Beasley, *Knudsen* (1947), p. 341.
315 "I have never seen . . .": Jesse H. Jones, *Fifty Billion Dollars* (1951), p. 272.
315 By the end of the luncheon: Beasley, *Knudsen*, pp. 342–43.
315 "For more than a year . . .": Winston M. Estes, *Homefront* (1976), p. 45.
316 Emergency Price Control Bill: *NYT*, Jan. 31, 1942, pp. 1, 26.
316 ER's promises on use of sugar: *NYT*, Jan. 27, 1942, p. 18.
316 run on sugar: *NYT*, Feb. 10, 1942, p. 13.
316 "It never crossed . . .": *NYT*, Jan. 27, 1942, p. 18.

316 "It is perfectly . . .": *MD,* Jan. 20, 1942.
317 ship sinkings: *U.S. News,* Feb. 27, 1942, p. 15.
317 "We are in a war . . .": *Fortune,* May 1942, p. 68.
317 "We've got to have . . .": Dwight D. Eisenhower, *Crusade in Europe* (1948), p. 22.
317 "He was standing . . .": Moran, *Churchill,* p. 35.
317 "The news came . . .": *MD,* Feb. 16, 1942.
317 "Perhaps it is good . . .": ibid.
317 "calm and serene . . .": William D. Hassett, *Off the Record with F.D.R.* (1958), p. 22.
317 "neither time . . .": *NYT,* Jan. 25, 1942, sect. VI, pp. 3, 24.
318 "I realize . . .": Frederick C. Lane, *Ships for Victory* (1951), p. 144.
318 "fourth in tonnage . . .": *Fortune,* May 1942, pp. 65, 68.
318 "It gives you . . .": ibid., p. 170.
318 Henry Kaiser: *CB,* 1942, pp. 431–35.
318 delivery time cut: *Time,* May 25, 1942, p. 82.
318 Liberty Ship: John Bunker, *Liberty Ships* (1972), p.7.
319 "No one is as good . . .": quoted in Rosenman, *Working with Roosevelt,* p. 5.
319 "I'm going to speak . . .": *NYT,* Feb. 24, 1942, pp. 1, 4.
319 "The map business . . .": *NYT,* Feb. 21, 1942, p. 8.
319 sixty-one million at radios: *NYT,* Feb. 25, 1942, p. 4.
319 "Selfish men . . ." . . . ". . . tell that to the Marines!": *NYT,* Feb. 24, 1942, p. 4.
320 "even more effective . . .": Rosenman, *Working with Roosevelt,* p. 329.
320 "one of the greatest . . .": *NYT,* Feb. 24, 1942, p. 5.
320 "Sometimes I wish . . .": FDR to R. Leffingwell, March 16, 1942, Franklin D. Roosevelt, *FDR: His Personal Letters* (1947), pp. 1298–99.
320 "No one understood . . .": Eric Larrabee, *Commander in Chief* (1987), p. 11.
321 "the worst single . . .": Burns, *Soldier of Freedom,* p. 216.
321 "Two Japs with Maps . . .": Roger Daniels, *Concentration Camps USA* (1970), p. 32.
321 "the very fact that . . .": Carey McWilliams, *Prejudice: Japanese Americans* (1944), p. 109.
321 "mad dogs, yellow vermin . . .": Daniels, *Concentration Camps USA,* p. 31.
321 "California was given . . .": quoted in John Armor and Peter Wright, *Manzanar* (1988), p. 29.
321 "These people . . ."; "Originally . . .": ER, typescript, "For Colliers—Japanese Relocation Camps," attached to packet of information provided by Dillion Meyer to ER, letter stamped May 13, 1943, box 881, ER Papers, FDRL.
321 40 percent of the total: Richard Lingeman, *Don't You Know There's a War On?* (1970), p. 337.
321 "We might as well . . .": Peter Irons, *Justice at War* (1983), pp. 39–40.
322 Issei, Nisei: Francis Biddle, *In Brief Authority* (1962), p. 213.
322 California political establishment: ibid., p. 226.
322 as reasonable and as humane: William Manchester, *The Glory and the Dream* (1975), p. 299.
322 "the burdens . . ."; "I do not think . . .": Biddle, *Authority,* p. 219.
322 "We are having . . .": Charles Kikuchi, *Kikuchi Diary* (1973), p. 49.
322 "there was a lack . . .": Mine Okubo, *Citizen 13660* (1966), p. 36.
323 "Can this be . . ."; "The senselessness . . .": *NR,* June 15, 1942, pp. 822–23.
323 "I could not help . . .": *TIR,* p. 231.
323 "prevented him . . .": ibid.
324 "I can't take . . .": Anna Rosenberg Hoffman, *OH,* FDRL.
324 "I am brought . . .": FDR to La Guardia, Dec. 18, 1941, PSF 12, FDRL.
324 "I rise today to utter . . .": *CR,* 77th Cong., 2nd sess., Feb. 6, 1942, p. 1097.
324 "The work of OCD . . .": *Liberty,* April 7, 1942, Scrapbook, ER Papers, FDRL.
325 "the storm that burst . . .": Marquis Childs, *I Write from Washington* (1942), p. 262.
325 "parasites and leeches . . .": Mrs. A. E. Curtenius to ER, Feb. 11, 1942, box 953, ER Papers, FDRL.
325 "I am not in the least . . .": ER to Paul Kellogg, Feb. 10, 1942, ER Microfilm Collection, FDRL.
325 "in these troubled . . .": Mrs. Ethel Jamison to ER, Feb. 8, 1942, ER Microfilm Collection, FDRL.
325 "instruction in physical . . .": *NYT,* Feb. 7, 1942, Scrapbook, ER Papers, FDRL.

325 "I still believe in . . .": ER to Flo Kerr, Feb. 18, 1942, ER Microfilm Collection, FDRL.
326 Clark Foreman: *Nation,* Feb. 21, 1942, p. 213.
326 none of $300 million for slum clearance: *NR,* Dec. 29, 1941, p. 887.
326 white workers overcrowded: ibid., p. 886.
326 population of Detroit: Walter White, "What Caused the Detroit Riots," unpublished manuscript, p. 1, OF 93, FDRL.
326 migrated from farmlands: *NYT,* July 5, 1943, p. 9.
327 sleeping in boxcars: *NR,* Dec. 29, 1941, p. 886.
327 five thousand a month: *NYT,* Aug. 9, 1942, sect. IV, p. 10.
327 ". . . be released unless . . .": *Nation,* Feb. 21, 1942, p. 213.
327 "Surely you would not . . .": Mrs. Diggs to ER, Jan. 18, 1942, box 850, ER Papers, FDRL.
327 "After a conference . . .": Palmer to ER, Jan. 30, 1942, box 846, ER Papers, FDRL.
327 On February 28: *Detroit News,* March 1, 1942, p. 15; *NYT,* March 1, 1942, p. 40.
327 "Many dead and wounded": *Detroit News,* March 8, 1942, p. 10.
327 On April 29: *NYT,* April 30, 1942, p. 8.
328 ER's attention to Foreman: ER to FDR, April 30, 1942, box 16, Roosevelt Family Papers Donated by the Children, FDRL.
328 "What can we do . . .": FDR to McIntyre, June 26, 1942; reply, July 13, mentioned that McNutt had promised a job; both in OF 4947, FDRL.
328 "Such a commission . . .": FDR to Edwin Embree, March 16, 1942, box 4, OF 93e, FDRL.
328 "The nation cannot . . .": *Washington Star,* Jan. 9, 1942, Scrapbook, ER Papers, FDRL.
328 "are probably the most . . .": R. J. Divine to ER, Jan. 21, 1942, box 1638, ER Papers, FDRL.
328 "I am not . . .": ER to R. J. Divine, Jan. 29, 1942, box 1638, ER Papers, FDRL.
328 "the enlistment . . .": Dennis Nelson, draft ch., "Negro in the Navy," p. 3, OF 93, FDRL.
328 "in view of . . ."; "there had been no . . .": ibid., p. 4.
328 "I think that with all . . .": FDR to Knox, Jan. 9, 1942, box 11, PSF, FDRL.
329 "that members of the colored . . .": Chairman, General Board, to Sec. of Navy, Feb. 3, 1942, box 11, PSF, FDRL.
329 "Officers of the U.S. Navy . . .": FDR to Sec. of Navy, Feb. 9, 1942, box 11, PSF, FDRL.
329 Dorie Miller's exploits: *Texas History,* March 1977, pp. 10–13.
329 "an unidentified Negro . . .": *NYT,* Dec. 21, 1942, p. 5; *NYT,* Feb. 8, 1942, p. 35.
329 Miller's name finally released: *NYT,* March 13, 1942, p. 3; *PC,* March 14, 1942, p. 1.
330 "the greatest honor . . .": *PC,* March 21, 1942, p. 1.
330 second report to Knox: Chairman, General Board, to Sec. of Navy, March 20, 1942, box 11, PSF, FDRL.
330 "a forward step": *PC,* April 8, 1942, p. 1.
330 ". . . historic barrier": *NYT,* April 8, 1942, p. 11.
330 "I look for an acceleration . . .": FDR to Fraternal Council of Negro Churches, Mar. 16, 1942, OF 93, FDRL.
330 "For the government to terminate . . .": Richard Polenberg, *War and Society: The United States, 1941–1945* (1972), p. 117.
330 "of trying to turn . . .": *NYT,* July 2, 1942, p. 44.
330 "a bunch of snoopers . . .": Roi Ottley, *New World A-Coming* (1943), p. 302.
331 "Anyone who hears . . .": Polenberg, *War and Society,* p. 109.
331 "Don't you think . . .": Jessie Lupo to ER, Sept. 2, 1942, OF 93, FDRL.
331 "I've come to one . . .": *MD,* March 10, 1942.
332 "This drive to . . .": *New York Daily News,* May 6, 1942, Scrapbook, ER Papers, FDRL.
332 "If Mrs. Roosevelt's . . .": *New York World Telegram,* March 14, 1942, Scrapbook, ER Papers, FDRL.
332 When FDR was asked: *NYT,* March 14, 1942, p. 8.
332 more than seven million: Lingeman, *Don't You Know,* pp. 67–68.
332 greatest shift: ibid., p. 69.
332 "It wouldn't take . . .": ibid., p. 71.
332 "was the real gold rush . . .": ibid., p. 69.
333 agricultural depression broken: ibid., p. 67.
333 "by and large . . ."; "and despite . . .": Harold Vatter, *The U.S. Economy in World War II* (1985), p. 129.
333 "Before the war . . .": quoted in ibid., p. 129.

CHAPTER THIRTEEN: "What Can We Do to Help?"

334 MLH's right leg had improved: Ross McIntire to FDR, June 1, 1942, PPF 3737, FDRL.
335 MLH was depressed: Lillian Rogers Parks, *The Roosevelts: A Family in Turmoil* (1981), p. 188.
335 "I wanted her to feel...": Bernard Asbell, *The FDR Memoirs* (1973), p. 403.
335 Missy eluded her nurse: interview with James Roosevelt.
335 "She felt there was...": Asbell, *FDR Memoirs,* p. 403.
336 tried to set herself on fire: Parks, *Family in Turmoil,* p. 188.
336 "extraordinarily beneficent role...": Felix Frankfurter, *From the Diaries of Felix Frankfurter* (1975), p. 162.
336 "one of the very...": ibid.
336 "Knowing how deeply...": William D. Hassett, *Off the Record with F.D.R.* (1958), p. 34.
336 "Many human emotions...": *MD,* April 14, 1942.
336 ER's new apartment: *NYT,* April 5, 1942, p. 19.
337 "When I am in New York...": *NYT,* April 16, 1942, p. 16.
337 "At last I am settled...": Joseph P. Lash, *Love, Eleanor* (1982), p. 389.
337 "Just a week from tonight...": ibid., pp. 381–82.
337 "With you I have...": ibid., p. 378.
337 "It was a curious...": interview with Lewis Feuer.
337 "I want to be able..."; "...know that...": ER to JL, May 2, 1942, Lash Papers, FDRL.
337 "so it would be always...": ER to JL, April 22, 1942, Lash Papers, FDRL.
337 "Wouldn't it be fun...": ER to JL, April 18, 1942, Lash Papers, FDRL.
338 "Your telegram came...": ER to JL, May 2, 1942, Lash Papers, FDRL.
338 Trude Pratt: Lash, *Love, Eleanor,* pp. 206–7.
338 "Of one thing...": ibid., pp. 383–84.
338 "Our friend Hick...": Tommy to Esther Lape, Joseph P. Lash, *A World of Love: Eleanor Roosevelt and Her Friends, 1943–1962* (1984), p. xxi.
338 "if she was out...": LH manuscript, LH Papers, FDRL; Doris Faber, *The Life of Lorena Hickok* (1980), p. 283.
339 LH and Marion Harron: Faber, *Lorena Hickok,* pp. 290–91.
339 ER experienced: interview with James Roosevelt.
339 second wartime fireside chat: text in *NYT,* April 29, 1942, pp. 1, 14.
340 "General Maximum Price Regulation": John Kenneth Galbraith, *A Life in Our Times* (1981), p. 165.
340 "As we sit here...": *NYT,* April 29, 1942, p. 14.
340 "The men operating...": Eric Larrabee, *Commander in Chief* (1987), p. 6.
340 Plans for Doolittle raid: Henry H. Arnold, *Global Mission* (1949), pp. 298–99.
340 Details of raid: Duane Schultz, *The Doolittle Raid* (1988), pp. 145–55.
341 Within an hour: ibid., p. 300.
341 "...base in Shangri-la": Hassett, *Off the Record,* p. 41.
341 first good news: Robert E. Sherwood, *Roosevelt and Hopkins* (1948), p. 542.
341 "I hope my two boys...": Mrs. T. J. Dykema to FDR, May 19, 1942, OF 5510, FDRL.
341 "Give us more...": James Jordon to FDR, May 19, 1942, OF 5510, FDRL.
341 "...a very good...": Stimson Diary, April 18, 1942, Yale University.
341 Midway: James MacGregor Burns, *Roosevelt: The Soldier of Freedom* (1970), pp. 225–26; Admiral J. J. Clarke, *Carrier Admiral* (1967), p. 94; Samuel Eliot Morison, *History of United States Naval Operations in World War II,* vol. IV (1960), p. 80.
342 "the first decisive...": Admiral King, 1st Official Report, March 1, 1944, p. 525.
342 "With broken heart...": Burns, *Soldier of Freedom,* p. 227.
342 "We've got to go...": Forrest C. Pogue, *George C. Marshall: Ordeal and Hope, 1939–1942* (1966), vol. II, p. 304.
342 "the hardness of heart...": Stimson Diary, May 27, 1942, Yale University.
342 "his cigarette-holder gesture...": Pogue, *Marshall,* vol. II, p. 306.
342 "...under 24-hour guard...": ibid.
343 "Oh how glad I am...": George McJimsey, *Harry Hopkins* (1987), pp. 247–48.
343 "What Harry and George...": *Churchill & Roosevelt: The Complete Correspondence* (1984), vol. I, p. 441.

343 "It was not like him . . .": J. W. Pickergill, ed., *The Mackenzie King Record,* vol. I, *1939–1944* (1960), p. 38.
343 Louis Johnson trying: Sherwood, *Roosevelt and Hopkins,* pp. 524–25.
343 "Anything like . . .": *Churchill & Roosevelt Correspondence,* vol. I, p. 449.
344 "an owlish, wise look . . .": Alonzo Fields, *My 21 Years in the White House* (1961), p. 100.
344 "Stone Ass": Thomas Parrish, *Roosevelt and Marshall* (1989), p. 276.
344 "head-down in their desire . . .": Charles E. Bohlen, *Witness to History, 1929–1969* (1973), p. 128.
344 "at the present time . . .": FDR to Joint Chiefs, May 6, 1942, box 106, PSF, FDRL.
344 "The fact that the Russians . . .": Bohlen, *Witness,* p. 127.
344 "developments were clear . . .": Averell Harriman and Elie Abel, *Special Envoy to Churchill and Stalin, 1941–1946* (1975), p. 137.
344 "an open, warm . . .": Lash, *Love, Eleanor,* p. 394.
344 Memorial Day parade: *MD,* May 30, 1942.
345 "American boys . . .": *New York Daily News,* May 6, 1942, Scrapbook, ER Papers, FDRL.
345 "to go round . . ."; "he could not help but think . . .": Harriman and Abel, *Special Envoy,* p. 143.
345 "The President was on . . .": Winston S. Churchill, *The Second World War,* vol. IV, *The Hinge of Fate* (1950), p. 338.
345 "I confess that when . . .": ibid.
345 "I can't help . . .": Stimson Diary, June 20 and 21, 1942, Yale University.
346 "He surely is an informal . . .": Hassett, *Off the Record,* p. 67.
346 "We knew what efforts . . .": Churchill, *Hinge of Fate,* p. 341.
346 "Research in the realm . . .": Joseph Goebbels, *The Goebbels Diaries, 1942–1943* (1948), p. 140.
347 "Alex, what you are . . .": Richard Rhodes, *The Making of the Atomic Bomb* (1986), p. 314.
347 By 1945, more than 120,000: Paul S. Boyer, et al., *The Enduring Vision* (1993), p. 909.
347 groundbreaking discoveries: Richard Lingeman, *Don't You Know There's a War On?* (1970), p. 128.
347 "There was something . . .": Hastings Ismay, *The Memoirs of General Lord Ismay* (1960), p. 256.
347 "It was a bitter . . .": Martin Gilbert, *Winston S. Churchill,* vol. VII, *Road to Victory: 1941–1945* (1986), p. 128.
347 "Defeat is one thing . . .": Churchill, *Hinge of Fate,* p. 343.
347 "What can we do . . .": ibid.
348 "To neither of those men . . .": *TIR,* p. 252.
348 "one of the heaviest blows . . .": Churchill, *Hinge of Fate,* p. 343.
348 "What matters is that . . .": Lord Moran, *Churchill—The Struggle for Survival, 1940–1965* (1966), p. 41.
348 "I am sure myself that . . .": *Churchill & Roosevelt Correspondence,* vol. I, p. 520.
348 "secret baby": Stimson Diary, June 21, 1942, Yale University.
349 "we now had only weeks . . .": Dwight D. Eisenhower, *Crusade in Europe* (1948), p. 72.
349 "the blackest day . . .": Captain Harry Butcher, *My Three Years with Eisenhower* (1946), p. 29.
349 "A lot of these guys . . .": FDR, Jr., to ER, May 13, 1942, ER Papers, FDRL.
349 "We failed to see . . .": Larrabee, *Commander in Chief,* p. 9.
349 HH confided: Sherwood, *Roosevelt and Hopkins,* p. 593.
349 "In smart sets . . .": *Time,* July 13, 1942, p. 14.
349 "Looking better . . .": Hassett, *Off the Record,* p. 57.
349 "He's gained ten pounds . . .": Bernard Asbell, *Mother and Daughter* (1988), p. 144.
349 "Harry head over heels . . .": Hassett, *Off the Record,* p. 80.
350 "to happiness of HH . . .": ibid., p. 91.
350 "It is going to be . . .": HH to MLH, July 28, 1942, HH Papers, FDRL.
350 "I'm worried about Harry's . . .": Lash, *Love, Eleanor,* p. 400.
350 "I imagine . . .": Lash, *World of Love,* p. xxiv.
350 "She did everything . . .": Diana Hopkins, *OH,* FDRL.
351 "Mrs. R and Louise . . .": interview with Diana Hopkins Halsted.

351 "Hopkins is equally...": *Time,* July 13, 1942, p. 14.
351 "of Negro toil...": *NR,* July 13, 1942, p. 46.
351 "I relize [sic]...": Odell Waller to ER, June 8, 1942, PSF 143, FDRL.
352 "a wholly personal...": FDR to Darden, June 15, 1942, PSF 143, FDRL.
352 "Dearest Babs...": FDR to ER, June 16, 1942, PSF 143, FDRL.
352 "It's a grand...": ibid. ER wrote note on memo and returned it to FDR.
352 ER tried all day: Parks, *Family in Turmoil,* p. 175.
352 "would not take 'No'...": Ted Morgan, *FDR* (1985), p. 572.
353 "I felt that she would not...": Joseph P. Lash, *Eleanor and Franklin* (1971), p. 671.
353 "Mr. Randolph...": Pauli Murray, *OH,* FDRL.
353 "Have you ever thought...": *Nation,* July 13, 1942, p. 32.
353 "Waller's debt...": *Richmond Times-Dispatch,* July 3, 1942, p. 6.
353 "We lost the fight...": *NR,* July 13, 1942, p. 46.
353 "I cannot understand...": Armand Kreeger to ER, Aug. 6, 1942, box 1638, ER Papers, FDRL.
353 "I am very much...": Winnie Downing to ER, July 5, 1942, box 1638, ER Papers, FDRL.
353 "I wonder if it ever...": ER to Pauli Murray, Aug. 3, 1942, Pauli Murray Papers, FDRL.
354 "And this just removed...": Pauli Murray, *OH,* FDRL.
354 "She must've...": interview with Diana Hopkins Halsted.
354 "It's the first time...": Lash interview with Esther Lape, Lash Papers, FDRL.
354 "A very nice affair...": Hassett, *Off the Record,* p. 95.
354 "Harry trembled...": ibid.
354 "After Harry married...": interview with Diana Hopkins Halsted.
354 work for Norway: Wilhelm Morgenstierne, in *Märtha Norges Kronprincesse 1929–1954* (n.d.), pp. 70–71, courtesy of Neils Justensen, Norwegian Embassy. Translated for the author by Toril Lampert.
355 "No sooner would Louise...": interview with Diana Hopkins Halsted.
355 "Then they'd...": Diana Hopkins Halsted, *OH,* FDRL.
355 "Victory" suit: John Morton Blum, *V Was for Victory* (1976), p. 94.
355 "women grow their own..." ... "proper support...": *Hygeia,* Aug. 1942, pp. 582, 622.
355 "Certainly Uncle Sam...": ibid., p. 624; see also *Business Week,* Sept. 19, 1942, pp. 57–59.
356 ration books: Cabell Phillips, *The 1940s* (1975), pp. 86–87.
356 yellow dye, corn syrup: Lingeman, *Don't You Know,* pp. 244–45; *U.S. News,* Feb. 20, 1942, p. 16.
356 black markets: Blum, *V Was for Victory,* pp. 96–97; *Time,* Dec. 21, 1942, p. 95.
356 "curious independence...": Marquis Childs, *I Write from Washington* (1942), p. 299.
356 order forbidding new tires: *NYT,* Dec. 22, 1942, p. 1.
356 certificate program: Galbraith, *Life in Our Times,* p. 155.
356 "Roosevelt was outraged...": ibid.
357 rationing of gasoline: *NYT,* April 23, 1942, pp. 1, 16.
357 "The very men to whom...": Raymond Clapper, *Watching the World* (1944), p. 199.
357 "I want to talk to you...": *Time,* June 22, 1942, p. 16.
358 "Today I am mailing...": Mrs. Kirkland to FDR, June 13, 1942, OF 150, FDRL.
358 "On December 7th...": Benjamin Cohen to FDR, July 1, 1942, OF 150, FDRL.
358 hundred thousand rubber bands: Samuel Werner and Esther Fisher to FDR, June 27, 1942, OF 150, FDRL.
358 "Mr. Facts": *NYT,* Aug. 16, 1942, sect. VII, p. 5.
358 "The nation waits...": ibid.
358 "Gas rationing...": Rubber Survey Committee Report, Sept. 10, 1942, p. 6, OF 150, FDRL.
358 "The Baruch report...": *NR,* Sept. 21, 1942, p. 336.
358 "...grow by its own criticism": *Fortune,* Nov. 1942, p. 227.
358 Effects of gas rationing: *Time,* May 25, 1942, p. 16.
359 "a meteor burst...": Lewis Gannet, "Books," in Jack Goodman, ed., *While You Were Gone* (1946), pp. 447–63.
359 "You cannot expect...": *NYT,* Sept. 8, 1942, pp. 1, 15.
359 "placed a pistol...": *NYT,* Oct. 3, 1942, p. 1.
359 FDR appointed Byrnes: *NYT,* Oct. 4, 1942, p. 1; Nov. 18, 1942, sect. VII, p. 5.

CHAPTER FOURTEEN: "By God, If It Ain't Old Frank!"

361 made it clear to ER: interview with James Roosevelt.
361 "You're the only . . .": Geoffrey C. Ward, *A First-Class Temperament* (1989), p. 629n.
361 "They were just very good . . .": interview with Eleanor Seagraves.
361 "She was the only person . . .": ibid.
361 "flirted like mad": interview with Eleanor Wotkyns.
361 "It was quite . . .": interview with Curtis Roosevelt.
362 Margaret Suckley: interviews with Winthrop Aldrich, Eleanor Seagraves, Curtis Roosevelt, and Eleanor Wotkyns.
362 Daisy in charge of papers: interview with Margaret Suckley.
362 "Evidently the P[resident] . . .": Joseph P. Lash, *A World of Love: Eleanor Roosevelt and Her Friends, 1943–1962* (1984), p. 3.
362 "She had a compulsion . . ": interview with Curtis Roosevelt.
362 "I just don't know . . .": interview with Eleanor Wotkyns.
362 "swing-and-duck rivalry . . .": *Collier's,* July 11, 1942, p. 110.
362 "Ford is making . . .": ibid.
363 Chrysler tank arsenal: *Machinery,* Dec. 1941, p. 107; "Our Nation at War: Log of the President's Inspection Trip," p. 2, box 61, OF 200, FDRL.
363 "By God if it ain't . . .": A. Merriman Smith, *Thank You, Mr. President* (1946), p. 50.
363 M-4 Sherman tank: *NYT,* May 26, 1942, p. 18.
363 "A good drive! . . .": *NYT,* Oct. 2, 1942, p. 15.
363 tank production in U.S. and Germany: Harry Thomson and Lidas Mayo, *The Ordnance Department: Procurement and Supply* (1960), pp. 239, 255.
363 "the most enormous room . . .": Robert Lacey, *Ford: The Man and the Machine* (1986), p. 391.
363 "It is a promise . . .": ibid., p. 393.
363 Only one bomber: "Our Nation at War," p. 3.
363 Ford in far corner: ibid., p. 394.
364 Spotting two midgets: Ford's News Bureau, press release, Sept. 18, 1942, OF 200, FDRL.
364 women working on assembly line: "Summary of Willow Run Bomber Plant," April 30, 1942, p. 4, OF 200, FDRL; *NYT,* July 11, 1942, p. 16.
364 "I feel quite certain . . .": *NYT,* Feb. 16, 1941, p. 22.
364 "The present number . . .": "Policy on Women," *Manual of Operations: War Manpower Commission,* Oct. 17, 1942, Record Group 86, Woman's Bureau, National Archives, Washington, D.C.
364 "Finally valued by others . . .": Sherna Berger Gluck, *Rosie the Riveter Revisited* (1987), p. xiv.
364 "the woman behind . . .": ibid., p. 11.
365 "Actually what attracted . . .": ibid., p. 135.
365 "I'm pretty old . . .": *BEA,* April 16, 1942, p. 5.
365 "every bit of preparation . . .": *Pensacola Journal,* Feb. 2, 1942, Scrapbook, ER Papers, FDRL.
365 "no woman with dependent children . . .": Chester Gregory, *Women in Defense Work During World War II* (1974), p. 19.
365 "You cannot expect . . .": Lacey, *Ford,* p. 393.
365 "if success is measured . . .": Irving Holley, Jr., *Buying Aircraft* (1964), p. 527.
365 Great Lakes: "Historical Information about the U.S. Naval Training Station, Great Lakes," OF 200, FDRL.
366 "It was a luxury . . .": Dennis D. Nelson, *The Integration of the Negro into the Navy* (1951), p. 29.
366 "Brehon, that was grand!": "Our Nation at War," p. 14.
366 shortage of copper and brass: R. Elberton Smith, *The Army and Economic Mobilization* (1959), p. 28; Constance McLaughlin Green, Harry C. Thomson, and Peter C. Root, *The Ordnance Department: Planning Munitions for War* (1955), p. 488.
366 "Life on the train . . .": A. Merriman Smith, *Thank You,* p. 53.
367 "The Flying Fortress": "Our Nation at War," p. 24.
367 "joint Army-Navy E": *NYT,* Aug. 11, 1942, p. 10.
367 "This was an airplane . . .": Martin Cardin, *Flying Forts* (1968), p. 3.

367 "To me the Flying Fortress . . .": ibid., p. 5.
367 "My mother was horrified . . .": Inez Sauer interview, University of Southern California Collection.
367 Anna christened the U.S.S. *Teal*: *NYT*, Sept. 24, 1942, p. 1.
367 remembering the lessons: AB to Hall Babbitt, Publicity Director, Nov. 3, 1942, box 68, Halsted Papers, FDRL.
368 "When we finished . . .": Lyn Childs in "Rosie the Riveter," PBS Documentary.
368 ". . . With the help of God . . .": "Our Nation at War," pp. 27–28.
368 "Just look at those . . .": *NYT*, Jan. 24, 1943, sect. VII, p. 30.
368 "He can mentally visualize . . .": ibid., p. 30.
368 cut into four pieces: ibid., p. 3.
368 "Your father missed you . . .": Daisy Suckley to AB, Oct. 15, 1942, box 74, Halsted Papers, FDRL.
368 "It was almost . . .": AB to Daisy Suckley, Oct. 23, 1942, box 74, Halsted Papers, FDRL.
368 Douglas Aircraft: *Douglas View*, Sept. 1942, pp. 13–14; *NYT*, June 26, 1942, p. 17.
368 "the lipsticks . . .": *SEP*, May 30, 1942, p. 30.
368 "The factory's no place . . .": Inez Sauer interview, University of Southern California Collection.
369 "Look at Tarzan! . . .": *Aviation*, June 1942, pp. 249–50.
369 Consolidated, B-24: *NYT*, March 16, 1942, p. 1.
369 "doing a swell job . . .": *NYT*, Oct. 15, 1942, p. 25.
369 "I never did anything . . .": *SEP*, May 30, 1942, p. 31.
369 "I'll deny it to the end . . .": quoted in *American Women at War: By 7 Newspaper Women* (1942), p. 13.
369 "I hardly saw a man . . .": *MD*, Oct. 8, 1942.
369 "FDR seemed happy . . .": ER to Lash, Sept. 29, 1942, Lash Papers, FDRL.
369 "Had it not been . . .": Sybil Lewis interview, University of Southern California Collection.
370 not "so much . . .": ibid.
370 "I still don't . . .": *Social Forces*, Oct. 1942, p. 79.
370 "It don't make . . .": ibid.
370 Hudson Naval Ordnance shutdown: *NYT*, June 3, 1942, p. 16.
370 "You can't expect . . .": *Social Forces*, Oct. 1942, p. 81.
370 "At first I thought . . .": ibid.
370 "Alice, I said good night . . .": ibid., p. 80.
370 "Eleanor Clubs": FBI report, OF 93, FDRL.
371 "All the Negroes": ibid.
371 "It was but logical . . .": ibid.
371 "Instead of forming . . .": *LHJ*, Oct. 1942, p. 23.
371 "I think he was really . . .": interview with James Roosevelt.
372 Brass: Erna Risch, *The Quartermaster Corps* (1953), p. 63.
372 silk: ibid., p. 70.
372 1.6 million to 5.4 million: Kent R. Greenfield, Robert R. Palmer, and Bell I. Wiley, *The Organization of Ground Combat Troops* (1947), pp. 209–11.
372 "no appearance of strain . . .": *NYT*, Oct. 2, 1942, p. 1.
372 "the American people . . .": Russell D. Buhite and David W. Levy, eds., *FDR's Fireside Chats* (1992), pp. 240–48.
373 She recognized . . . : interview with James Roosevelt.
373 "She bothered him . . .": Anna Rosenberg, *OH*, FDRL.
373 "You couldn't find . . .": AH interview, Lash Papers, FDRL.
374 "She was a few years . . .": *TIMS*, p. 130.
374 "If I had it to do over . . .": Eleanor Roosevelt and Helen Ferris, *Your Teens and Mine* (1961), p. 186.
374 "I think I must have spoiled . . .": *TIMS*, p. 180.
374 "I know what a delight . . .": Joseph P. Lash, *Eleanor and Franklin* (1971), p. 182.
374 "young and immature . . .": Ward, *Temperament*, p. 415.
375 "easily the most beautiful . . .": ibid., p. 359.
375 "She was gay . . .": Elliott Roosevelt and James Brough, *An Untold Story: The Roosevelts of Hyde Park* (1973), p. 73.
375 "same brand . . .": ibid., p. 82.

375 drawn to one another: Elizabeth Shoumatoff, *FDR's Unfinished Portrait* (1990), p. 16.
375 "Lucy was a wonderful . . .": AH interview, Bernard Asbell. Transcript given to author by Prof. Asbell.
376 "Of course he was in love . . .": quoted in *NYT,* Aug. 13, 1966, p. 23.
376 "I saw you 20 . . .": Lash, *Eleanor and Franklin,* pp. 225–26.
376 "You were a goosy girl . . .": ibid., p. 223.
376 Winthrop Rutherfurd: *NYT,* March 21, 1944, p. 19.
377 "Did you know . . .": Lash, *Eleanor and Franklin,* p. 227.
377 "Up to the time . . .": Joseph P. Lash, *Love, Eleanor* (1982), p. 70.
377 "he emerged tougher . . .": quoted in Lois Schraf, *ER: First Lady of American Liberalism* (1987), p. 56.
377 "I have the memory . . .": Kenneth S. Davis, *Invincible Summer* (1974), p. 93.
377 "Psyche" by Virginia Moore: as quoted in Lash, *Eleanor and Franklin,* p. 245.
378 if she stayed . . . When the time . . . : interview with James Roosevelt.

CHAPTER FIFTEEN: "We Are Striking Back"

379 "I confide my Missus . . .": FDR to WC, Oct. 19, 1942, box 12, Roosevelt Family Papers Donated by the Children, FDRL.
379 "After nine years . . .": as reprinted in *NYT,* Oct. 21, 1942, p. 4.
379 "We welcome you . . .": *BEA,* Oct. 24, 1942, p. 3.
380 enormous suite: *Newsweek,* Nov. 2, 1942, p. 48.
380 "We are lost . . .": ER to LH, Oct. 23, 1942, LH Papers, FDRL.
380 ration card and bed in shelter: *Newsweek,* Nov. 2, 1942, p. 8.
380 "I was struck . . .": ER diary of trip to Great Britain, Oct. 24, 1942, box 2962, ER Papers, FDRL.
380 "Hi Eleanor . . .": *BEA,* Oct. 26, 1942, p. 14.
380 "I have already . . .": Joseph P. Lash, *Eleanor and Franklin* (1971), p. 662.
381 "I can feel . . .": *MD,* Nov. 7, 1942.
381 "We have not used . . .": *BEA,* Oct. 26, 1942, p. 3.
381 Mrs. Churchill sat down: *NYT,* Oct. 29, 1942, p. 25.
381 "Not since I can remember . . .": *NYT,* Oct. 31, 1942, p. 8.
381 "I saw every inch . . .": ER diary of trip, Oct. 29, 1942, box 2962, ER Papers, FDRL.
381 "like animals at bay . . .": Martin Cardin, *Flying Forts* (1968), p. 148.
381 "I found I'm very fat . . .": *NYT,* Oct. 30, 1942, p. 6.
381 She "is very attractive . . .": ER diary of trip, Oct. 30, 1942, box 2962, ER Papers, FDRL.
382 "who is a sweet . . .": ER diary of trip, Oct. 25, 1942, box 2962, ER Papers, FDRL.
382 "I don't want . . .": ER diary of trip, Oct. 27, 1942, box 2962, ER Papers, FDRL.
382 ". . . winning golden opinions . . .": *Churchill & Roosevelt: The Complete Correspondence* (1984), vol. I, p. 655.
382 "Every soldier I see . . .": *MD,* Nov. 5, 1942.
383 "were very indignant . . .": ER to Stimson, Sept. 22, 1942, box 851, ER Papers, FDRL.
383 "the differential treatment . . .": Stimson Diary, Oct. 2, 1942, Yale University.
383 Elliot; "he has matured . . .": ER to LH, Nov. 5, 1942, LH Papers, FDRL.
383 "The First Lady is . . .": *Newsweek,* Nov. 9, 1942, p. 45.
383 "The hullabaloo . . .": Willi A. Boelcki, ed., *Secret Conferences of Dr. Joseph Goebbels* (1970), p. 291.
383 "I'm simply delighted . . .": LH to ER, Oct. 26, 1942, LH Papers, FDRL.
384 "She has had . . .": *Churchill & Roosevelt Correspondence,* vol. I, p. 656.
384 people had grievances: John Morton Blum, *V Was for Victory* (1976), p. 231.
384 Henderson announced: *NYT,* Nov. 1, 1942, sect. IV, p. 12.
384 eighty-three million coffee drinkers: *NYT,* Nov. 29, 1942, sect. IV, p. 8.
384 ". . . the wartime measure . . .": ibid., p. 9.
384 "under no illusions . . .": William D. Hassett, *Off the Record with F.D.R.* (1958), p. 132.
385 "I am fighting for you": MLH to FDR, Nov. 4, 1942, PPF 3737, FDRL.
385 "Name, please? . . .": *NYT,* Nov. 4, 1942, p. 5; Hassett, *Off the Record,* p. 133.
385 light turnout: Herbert Nicholas, ed., *Washington Despatches, 1941–45* (1981), p. 11; *NYT,* Nov. 7, 1942, p. 30.
385 "that an unofficial . . .": *U.S. News,* Nov. 13, 1942, p. 17.

385 "Found the President . . .": Hassett, *Off the Record,* p. 135.
385 "the new Congress . . .": *NYT,* Nov. 7, 1942, p. 30.
385 Shangri-la: Samuel I. Rosenman, *Working with Roosevelt* (1952), pp. 349–50.
386 "He knew that it was largely . . .": ibid., p. 363.
386 showing his anxiety: Grace Tully, *F.D.R., My Boss* (1949), p. 264.
386 Eisenhower having rough time: Dwight D. Eisenhower, *Crusader in Europe* (1948), pp. 96–97.
386 Zero hour: Stimson Diary, Nov. 7, 1942, Yale University.
386 "The operation should be . . .": *Churchill & Roosevelt Correspondence,* vol. I, p. 583.
386 "We agree . . .": ibid., p. 591.
387 "This is just to let . . .": Richard Leighton and Robert Coakley, *Global Logistics and Strategy, 1940–1943* (1955), p. 445.
387 best equipment: ibid., pp. 440–41.
387 "It was as though . . .": ibid., p. 449.
387 never seemed so dark: Samuel Eliot Morison, *The History of United States Naval Operations in World War II,* vol. II, *Operations in North African Waters* (1947), p. 54.
387 "I realize . . .": Leighton and Coakley, *Global Logistics,* p. 452.
388 "Thank God . . .": Tully, *F.D.R.,* p. 264.
388 "America is on the march . . .": quoted in News Bulletins, Nov. 11, 1942, PSF, FDRL.
388 "Like the waves . . .": Katherine Tupper Marshall, *Together* (1946), p. 140.
388 *"This is it . . .": Newsweek,* Nov. 16, 1942, p. 17.
388 "They followed the North African . . .": Winston M. Estes, *Homefront* (1976), p. 129.
389 "Now this is not . . .": Robert E. Sherwood, *Roosevelt and Hopkins* (1948), p. 656.
389 "Jesus Christ . . .": James MacGregor Burns, *Roosevelt: The Soldier of Freedom* (1970), p. 291.
389 "Please make it . . .": Forrest C. Pogue, *George C. Marshall: Ordeal and Hope, 1939–1942* (1966), vol. II, p. 402.
389 "This was a decision . . .": Burns, *The Soldier of Freedom,* p. 290.
389 "We come among you . . .": Rosenman, *Working with Roosevelt,* p. 364.
389 "We are attacked . . .": Pétain quoted in News Bulletin, Nov. 8, 1942, PSF, FDRL.
389 "The U.S. can pay . . .": Charles de Gaulle, *The Complete War Memoirs* (1964), p. 134.
390 "Prostitutes are used . . .": *Nation,* Nov. 21, 1942, pp. 529–30.
390 "the enormous benefits . . .": Stimson Diary, Nov. 16, 1942, Yale University.
390 "He showed more resentment . . .": Rosenman, *Working with Roosevelt,* p. 363.
390 "I have accepted . . .": Sherwood, *Roosevelt and Hopkins,* p. 653.
391 the triumph of superior . . . : George Howe, *Northwest Africa: Seizing the Initiative in the West* (1957), pp. 669–77.
391 "The bravest men . . .": Erwin Rommel, *The Rommel Papers* (1953), p. 328.
391 "The news from Africa . . .": *MD,* Nov. 8, 1942.
391 "about to die": ER diary of trip, Nov. 11, 1942, box 2962, ER Papers, FDRL.
391 "Mrs. Roosevelt has done more . . .": Lash, *Eleanor and Franklin,* p. 668.
391 "I really think . . .": ER diary of trip, Nov. 17, 1942, box 2962, ER Papers, FDRL.
392 "I met her at the airport . . .": *Churchill & Roosevelt Correspondence,* vol. II, p. 7.
392 "which is something . . .": *MD,* Nov. 17, 1942.
392 gave him the presents: *Newsweek,* Nov. 30, 1942, p. 38.
392 "it was useless to expect . . .": *NYT,* Nov. 18, 1942, p. 27.
392 "Would it be possible . . .": FDR to Biddle, Nov. 17, 1942, PSF 76, FDRL.
392 "Quiet day . . .": *MD,* Nov. 21, 1942.
392 "It was deeply interesting . . .": ER to M. Gellhorn, Dec. 1, 1942, ER Microfilm Collection, FDRL.
393 "I should have liked . . .": *TIR,* p. 278.
393 Thanksgiving Day service: Hassett, *Off the Record,* p. 142.
393 "I can think of a thousand . . .": *MD,* Nov. 23, 1942.
393 "His religious faith . . .": Sherwood, *Roosevelt and Hopkins,* p. 9.
394 "and carried out . . .": Hassett, *Off the Record,* p. 141.
394 "Personally, whether I . . .": *NYT,* Nov. 24, 1942, p. 1.
394 "a drab and gloomy day": *NYT,* Nov. 29, 1942, sect. VII, p. 8.
394 "who had to step . . .": I. F. Stone, *The War Years, 1939–1945* (1988), p. 142.
394 "was not one of the boys . . .": David Brinkley, *Washington Goes to War* (1988), p. 133.

394 "I have determined...": Henderson to FDR, Dec. 15, 1942, PSF 151, FDRL.
394 "never completely happy...": John Kenneth Galbraith, *A Life in Our Times* (1981), p. 179.
395 "We have lost...": *NR,* Dec. 28, 1942, p. 847.
395 "the second phase...": Stone, *War Years,* p. 144.
395 McNutt had come: Smith conference notes, Dec. 4, 1942, Harold Smith Papers, FDRL.
395 "might quite possibly hate so...": Stimson Diary, Nov. 7, 1942, Yale University.
395 December 5 executive order: *NYT,* Dec. 5, 1942, p. 1.
395 "more power over men...": *NYT,* Dec. 6, 1942, p. 1.
395 CMP: Blum, *V Was for Victory,* pp. 122–23.
396 Day of Mourning and Prayer: David S. Wyman, *The Abandonment of the Jews: America and the Holocaust, 1941–1945* (1984), p. 71.
396 Riegner report: ibid., pp. 44–45.
396 "at one blow...": Martin Gilbert, *The Second World War* (1989), p. 351.
396 "with horror": *MD,* Dec. 5, 1942.
396 Wise asked for meeting: Arthur D. Morse, *While Six Million Died* (1983), pp. 26–28.
396 "unless action is taken...": Wyman, *Abandonment,* p. 72.
396 "We shall do...": ibid., p. 73.
397 "the free movement...": *NYT,* Nov. 3, 1942, p. 1.
397 "The ugly truth...": *Newsweek,* quoted in Wyman, *Abandonment,* p. 57.
397 "The question of the Jewish...": Boelcki, ed., *Secret Conferences,* p. 240.
397 "the target of more adverse...": *NYT,* Dec. 19, 1942, p. 23.
397 "to dread, not what...": Joseph P. Lash, *Love, Eleanor* (1982), p. 417.
398 "This was the beginning...": *California Pioneer Teacher,* p. 6, Hardie Robbins Papers, FDRL.
398 "Looking back across...": Stone, *War Years,* p. 134.
398 "At the end...": *NYT,* Nov. 15, 1942, p. 3.
398 "pending anti-trust suits...": *NYT,* March 29, 1942, p. 1.
398 "one of the first major...": ibid.
399 approximately 175,000 companies: Blum, *V for Victory,* p. 123.
399 New Year's festivities: Rosenman, *Working with Roosevelt,* pp. 364–65.
399 "She would see the news...": interview with Dawn Deslie.
399 mementos: in the possession of Jane Scarborough.
400 "She started crying...": Ann Rochon to Mr. Pres., Dec. 31, 1942, PPF 3737, FDRL.
400 "To the United..."; "To the person who makes...": Rosenman, *Working with Roosevelt,* p. 364.

CHAPTER SIXTEEN: "The Greatest Man I Have Ever Known"

401 first to fly overseas: ER interview, Graff Papers, FDRL.
401 first since Lincoln: *NYT,* Jan. 27, 1943, p. 6.
402 heading south to Miami: Grace Tully, *F.D.R., My Boss* (1949), p. 208.
402 "It's not only that...": Lord Moran, *Churchill—The Struggle for Survival, 1940–1965* (1966), pp. 86–87.
402 "The P.M. is at a disadvantage...": ibid., p. 86.
402 Description of security: "Log of the Trip of the President to the Casablanca Conference," p. 522, OF 200, FDRL; *NYT,* Jan. 27, 1943, p. 6; Michael F. Reilly, *Reilly of the White House* (1947), p. 149.
402 "I hope you'll hurry...": Ross McIntire, *White House Physician* (1946), p. 149.
403 The president's villa: Elliott Roosevelt, *As He Saw It* (1946), pp. 65–66.
403 "Father was... not a bit tired...": ibid., p. 64.
403 "Stalingrad makes me ashamed...": ER to LH, Oct. 1, 1942, LH Papers, FDRL.
403 "After nearly three...": Martin Gilbert, *The Second World War* (1989), p. 399.
404 60,000 trucks: Robert H. Jones, *The Roads to Russia* (1969), appendix; "14th Report to Congress on Lend-Lease Operations for the Period Ending Dec. 31, 1943," FDRL.
404 "I feel confident...": James MacGregor Burns, *Roosevelt: The Soldier of Freedom* (1970), p. 315.
404 "One of the most poignant...": Averell Harriman and Elie Abel, *Special Envoy to Churchill and Stalin, 1941–1946* (1975), p. 183.

405 "the faces of the men . . .": *Life,* March 8, 1943, p. 51.
405 "Gosh—it's . . ."; "Those troops . . .": Elliott Roosevelt, *As He Saw It,* pp. 106–7.
405 "certainly was in rollicking form . . .": Elliott to ER, Feb. 28, 1943, box 57, Halsted Papers, FDRL.
405 "As always . . .": Elliott Roosevelt, *As He Saw It,* p. 94.
405 "One glimpse of the tiara . . .": ibid., p. 110.
406 "he had no intention . . .": Robert E. Sherwood, *Roosevelt and Hopkins* (1948), p. 688.
406 sultan delighted: Elliot Roosevelt, *As He Saw It,* pp. 110–12.
406 the bride, the groom: Sherwood, *Roosevelt and Hopkins,* p. 680.
406 "Well, just look at him! . . .": Moran, *Churchill,* p. 88.
406 "The General was sullen . . .": Reilly, *Reilly,* p. 157.
406 de Gaulle noticed shadows: Charles de Gaulle, *The Complete War Memoirs* (1964), p. 390.
407 "In human affairs . . .": ibid., pp. 389–92.
407 "In these days . . .": Moran, *Churchill,* p. 87.
407 "Will you at least . . ." . . . "I shall do that . . .": de Gaulle, *War Memoirs,* p. 399.
407 "in high dudgeon . . .": Harriman and Abel, *Special Envoy,* pp. 188–89.
407 "and then suddenly . . .": ibid., p. 188.
408 "Let us spend two days . . .": Winston S. Churchill, *The Second World War,* vol. IV, *The Hinge of Fate* (1950), p. 621.
408 made a cradle: McIntire, *White House Physician,* p. 155.
408 "dangling like the limbs . . ."; ". . . most lovely spot . . .": Moran, *Churchill,* p. 90.
408 "You simply cannot . . ."; "If anything happened . . .": Eric Larabee, *Commander in Chief* (1987), p. 39.
409 "Dearest Babs . . .": Burns, *The Soldier of Freedom,* p. 324.
409 "He always used to tell me . . .": ER interview, Graff Papers, FDRL.
409 "What do you know! . . .": FDR to ER, Jan. 29, 1943, box 12, Roosevelt Family Papers Donated by the Children, FDRL.
409 "Welcome home! . . .": ER to FDR, Jan. 28, 1943, box 16, Roosevelt Family Papers Donated by the Children, FDRL.
409 "I'd give my eyeteeth . . .": John R. Boettiger, Jr., *A Love in Shadow* (1978), p. 238.
410 "I feared you were getting tired . . .": ibid.
410 "I won't say . . .": Bernard Asbell, *Mother and Daughter* (1988), p. 154.
410 "From the moment . . .": ibid.
410 "I went to the train . . .": ER to JL, Feb. 3, 1943, Lash Papers, FDRL.
410 "I hated to see you go . . .": Asbell, *Mother and Daughter,* p. 154.
411 "It was a pathetic . . .": Stimson Diary, Jan. 9, 1943, Yale University.
411 "The President is the poorest . . .": Stimson Diary, March 28, 1943, Yale University.
411 "He wanted to relieve . . .": Felix Frankfurter, *From the Diaries of Felix Frankfurter* (1975), p. 168.
411 Byrnes told FDR: James F. Byrnes, *Speaking Frankly* (1947), pp. 171–73.
412 HH told FDR: Sherwood, *Roosevelt and Hopkins,* pp. 699–700.
412 "They are too much alike . . .": I. F. Stone, *The War Years, 1939–1945* (1988), p. 151.
412 "Mr. President, I'm here . . .": Bernard M. Baruch, *Baruch: The Public Years* (1960), pp. 317–18.
412 "Most of my time . . .": FDR to AB, Feb. 10, 1943, box 62, Halsted Papers, FDRL.
412 "so far away in her mind . . .": Joseph P. Lash, *A World of Love: Eleanor Roosevelt and Her Friends, 1943–1962* (1984), p. 100.
413 "We got to know Mrs. Roosevelt . . .": interview with Barbara Dudley.
413 "Where it was just . . .": Ann Rochon to ER, May 14, 1943, box 1731, ER Papers, FDRL.
413 "It was really very dramatic . . .": *MD,* Feb. 7, 1943.
413 "Exhibiting her usual . . .": *Portland Press Herald,* Feb. 8, 1943, p. 1.
413 "The real situation . . .": *Business Week,* Jan. 9, 1943, p. 72.
413 "A woman is a substitute . . .": Paul Boyer et al., *The Enduring Vision* (1993), p. 914.
413 "If you've sewed on buttons . . .": leaflet, U.S. Department of Labor and Women's Bureau, April 1943, Division of Research, Record Group 86, Women's Bureau, National Archives, Washington, D.C.
414 "women who maintain jobs . . .": *Catholic World,* April 3, 1943, pp. 482–86.
414 "a very chaotic situation . . .": *NYT,* Sept. 2, 1942, p. 12.

414 "women's outside responsibilities . . .": *NYT,* March 6, 1943, p. 10.
414 "No matter how intense . . .": War Manpower Commission, "The Employment of Women: Facing Facts in the Utilization of Manpower," June 1943, Division of Research, Record Group 86, Women's Bureau, National Archives, Washington, D.C.
414 called for wide variety: *NYT,* Sept. 2, 1942, p. 12; *Portland Press Herald,* Feb. 8, 1943, p. 2.
414 "Shyly they came forward . . .": *Portland Press Herald,* Feb. 9, 1943, p. 2.
415 "infinite variety . . .": *Life,* June 8, 1942, pp. 26–27.
415 ER toured: *MD,* Feb. 14, 1943.
415 "In our spare time . . .": interview with Ruth Thompson Pierce.
415 "the lack of privacy . . .": *MD,* Feb. 14, 1943.
415 reviewed twenty-eight hundred: *NYT,* Feb. 15, 1943, p. 1.
415 "I am sure that if . . .": *MD,* Feb. 14, 1943.
415 Lanham Act: *NYT,* Sept. 1, 1942, p. 15.
416 "a mere drop in the bucket": *SEP,* Oct. 10, 1942, p. 106.
416 "the child should be . . .": *Public Welfare,* May 1943, p. 141.
416 "The worst mother . . .": *NYT,* Jan. 26, 1943, p. 16.
416 "What are you doing . . .": Perkins to Katherine Lenroot, June 26, 1942, Children's Bureau 1942; records of the Department of Labor, Record Group 174, National Archives, Washington, D.C.
416 Statistics on female employment: Boyer, *The Enduring Vision,* p. 913.
416 "a 9 year old boy . . .": *Fortune,* Feb. 1943, p. 224.
417 "a woman in the graveyard shift . . .": *SEP,* Oct. 10, 1942, p. 20.
417 "These are not isolated cases . . .": ibid.
417 women at Portland shipyards: *NYT Magazine,* Nov. 7, 1943, p. 20.
417 plans under way: ibid.
417 "It was as nice . . .": interview with James Hymes.
417 "I could tell immediately . . .": interview with Mary Willett.
418 "We had Indian children . . .": ibid.
418 "It was without question . . .": ibid.
418 In its first year: pamphlet, *One Year Anniversary,* n.d., loaned to author by Mary Willett.
418 "She had seen a food-service . . .": interview with James Hymes.
418 nearly $50 million: Margaret O'Brien Steinfels, *Who's Minding the Children? The History and Politics of Day Care in America* (1973), p. 67.
419 "Oddly enough . . .": *NYT,* March 6, 1943, p. 9.
419 "I think I picked . . .": *Churchill & Roosevelt: The Complete Correspondence* (1984), vol. II, pp. 156–57.
419 "The Führer seems . . .": Joseph Goebbels, *The Goebbels Diaries, 1942–1943* (1948), p. 266.
419 "permanently caustic . . .": Albert Speer, *Inside the Third Reich* (1970), p. 294.
420 "were appreciated as if . . .": ibid., pp. 296–97.
420 "a bit worn as to patience . . .": Tommy to Esther Lape, April 6, 1943, box 6, Esther Lape Papers, FDRL.
420 "I'm completely exhausted . . .": Joseph P. Lash, *Love, Eleanor* (1982), p. 457.
420 "stretched out luxuriantly . . .": ibid., pp. 441–42.
420 "I loved just sitting . . .": ibid., p. 449.
421 room had been bugged: ibid., pp. 489–91.
421 "All of the top men . . .": ibid., p. 490.
421 "loyal Americans . . .": Henry Jones to ER, Feb. 3, 1943, attached to ER to Stimson, March 8, 1943, ER Microfilm Collection, FDRL.
422 ER wrote to Stimson: ibid.
422 "They have a show . . .": Philip McGuire, *Taps for a Jim Crow Army* (1983), p. 13.
422 Lena Horne cut tour: Ulysses G. Lee, *The Employment of Negro Troops* (1966), p. 307.
422 "the uncertainty . . .": ibid., p. 30.
422 "That's the kind of democracy . . .": memo to Director of Intelligence, Morale Report on 493rd Port Battalion, June 17, 1943, Record Group, p. 107, National Archives, Washington, D.C.
422 "What a lot we must do . . .": *MD,* July 28, 1943.
423 general forced to assign: Larrabee, *Commander in Chief,* p. 104.
423 "including theaters . . .": Lee, *Negro Troops,* p. 308.

423 "The fact that anyone . . .": ibid., p. 400.
423 "We were undoubtedly . . .": *Air and Space,* Oct.–Nov. 1989, p. 35.
423 "The waiting got tiresome": Benjamin O. Davis, Jr., *Autobiography* (1992), p. 90.
423 "The program of preflight . . ."; "This seems to me . . .": ER to Stimson, April 10, 1943, box 890, ER Papers, FDRL.
424 "tremendous moment . . .": Davis, *Autobiography,* p. 93.
424 "As we left the shores . . .": ibid., p. 94.
424 "blacks could fly . . .": *Black Americans in Defense of Our Nation,* Washington, D.C.: Department of Defense (1990), p. 64.
424 1,578 missions: *Air and Space,* Oct.–Nov. 1989, p. 38.
424 "the hard plodding . . .": ER to FDR, April 1, 1943, box 16, Roosevelt Family Papers Donated by the Children, FDRL.
424 "Men are always little boys . . .": Asbell, *Mother and Daughter,* p. 158.
424 "had two meals every day . . .": Lash, *World of Love,* p. 3.
425 "She had to get off . . .": ibid.
425 army had expanded: Kent R. Greenfield, Robert R. Palmer, and Bell I. Wiley, *The Organization of Ground Combat Troops* (1987), pp. 212–17.
425 "Just imagining it . . .": Geoffrey Perrett, *There's a War to Be Won* (1991), p. xxvi.
425 "Fort Benning is such . . .": "Log of the President's Inspection Trip," April 15, 1943, OF 200, FDRL.
425 "Even in the Infantry . . .": Robert R. Palmer, Bell I. Wiley, and William Keast, *The Procurement and Training of Ground Combat Forces* (1948), p. 2.
426 "did not represent . . .": ibid., p. 4.
426 "I don't get as good . . .": "Log," April 18, 1943.
426 "This is a lovely . . .": *MD,* April 19, 1943.
426 headed to Mexico: *NYT,* April 22, 1943, p. 1.
427 "some of the officers . . .": "Log," April 21, 1943.
427 "It seems to me . . .": "Log," April 25, 1943.
427 "The Army has gone . . .": ibid.
427 "His spirits were higher . . .": *NYT,* April 25, 1943, p. 8; *U.S. News,* April 30, 1943, p. 31.
427 "who first accepted . . .": Ickes to FDR, April 13, 1943, Harold Ickes Papers, Library of Congress, Washington, D.C.
428 camps built by War Relocation Authority: Carey McWilliams, *Prejudice: Japanese Americans* (1944), p. 156.
428 "You could not take hold . . .": Audrie Girdner and Anne Loftis, *The Great Betrayal* (1969), p. 212.
428 "It chokes you . . .": ER, "Japanese Relocation Camps," unpublished manuscript written for *Collier's,* attached to letter, Dillion Myer to ER, May 13, 1943, box 881, ER Papers, FDRL.
428 "It gets into every pore . . .": letter received by evacuee in Granada from another evacuee in Topaz, Feb. 12, 1943, attached to Dillion Myer to ER, May 13, 1943, box 881, ER Papers, FDRL.
428 "covered everything . . .": Dillion Myer, "Autobiography," *OH,* University of California at Berkeley.
428 "Everything is spotlessly clean . . .": *MD,* April 23, 1943.
428 "Sometimes there are little . . .": ibid.
429 "We are at war . . .": McWilliams, *Prejudice,* p. 160.
429 "coddled": ER, "Japanese Relocation Camps."
429 "To be frank with you . . .": McWilliams, *Prejudice,* p. 212.
429 "With everyone eating . . .": interview with Jiro Ishihara.
429 "We hold the advantage . . .": Charles Kikuchi, *The Kikuchi Diary* (1973), p. 81.
429 "For the young people . . .": interview with Jiro Ishihara.
430 "Feel sort of sorry for Pop . . .": Kikuchi, *Diary,* p. 61.
430 "I was very happy . . .": Henry Ebihara to Stimson, Feb. 4, 1943, attached to letter, Dillion Myer to ER, May 13, 1943, box 881, ER Papers, FDRL.
430 "to start independent . . .": ER, "Japanese Relocation Camps."
430 "To undo mistakes . . .": ibid.
430 "normal American life . . .": FDR to Ickes, April 24, 1943, Harold Ickes Papers, Library of Congress, Washington, D.C.

430 "a vicious, well-organized . . .": Stimson to Myer, May 10, 1943, attached to Dillion Myer to ER, May 13, 1943, box 881, ER Papers, FDRL.

CHAPTER SEVENTEEN: "It Is Blood on Your Hands"

432 Washington in 1943: Selden Menefee, *Assignment USA* (1943), pp. 36–40.
432 "the federal government . . .": David Brinkley, *Washington Goes to War* (1988), p. 111.
433 visit from Shoumatoff: Elizabeth Shoumatoff, *FDR's Unfinished Portrait* (1990), pp. 80–81.
433 "quite impressive . . .": ibid., p. 75.
433 "Winthrop Rutherfurd . . .": ibid.
433 "Everything whirled . . ."; "seldom seen . . .": ibid., pp. 76–77.
433 comings and goings of Rutherfurd children: *Aiken Standard & Review,* society page for various issues, 1939–45.
434 "his extraordinary . . .": Shoumatoff, *FDR's Portrait,* p. 79
434 "You should really paint . . ."; "I did not understand . . .": ibid., p. 80.
434 Lucy at inauguration: Elliott Roosevelt and James Brough, *An Untold Story: The Roosevelts of Hyde Park* (1973), p. 282.
434 letters of 1927: Lucy to FDR, April 16 and July 2, 1927, box 21, Roosevelt Family Papers Donated by the Children, FDRL.
435 "Mrs. Johnson": the Usher Diary recorded the dates and times of Mrs. Johnson's visits. Bernard Asbell discovered this information when interviewing William D. Simmons, a Secret Service man. See Bernard Asbell, *The FDR Memoirs* (1973), p. 411.
435 "How is Mrs. Rutherfurd? . . .": Shoumatoff, *FDR's Portrait,* p. 82.
436 Kasserine Pass: George Howe, *Northwest Africa* (1957), ch. XXII, pp. 438–58.
436 Red Oak: *Life,* May 3, 1943, p. 26.
436 "The Secretary of War . . .": *SEP,* Aug. 17, 1946, pp. 15, 71.
436 "hometown we dreamed of . . .": ibid., p. 14.
437 "the Americans are happy . . .": Joseph Goebbels, *The Goebbels Diaries, 1942–1943* (1948), pp. 372, 376.
437 "the striking change . . .": Winston S. Churchill, *The Second World War,* vol. IV, *The Hinge of Fate* (1950), p. 706. Churchill is quoting from a summary of the agreed-upon Anglo-American record of the meeting.
437 "stood on the periphery . . .": Martin Gilbert, *The Second World War* (1989), p. 401.
437 AB hostess at dinner: AB to John Boettiger, May 15, 1943, box 5, Boettiger Papers, FDRL.
438 "the British empire . . .": Churchill, *Hinge of Fate,* pp. 710–11.
438 " 'Shoot, if you must . . .' ": Robert E. Sherwood, *Roosevelt and Hopkins* (1948), p. 729.
438 "He is always using . . .": Joseph P. Lash, *Love, Eleanor* (1982), p. 508.
438 "with much interest . . ."; "Sadly FDR left . . .": Churchill, *Hinge of Fate,* p. 712.
438 "the PM picks his teeth . . .": AB to John Boettiger, May 15, 1943, box 5, Boettiger Papers, FDRL.
439 "He was placed . . .": Churchill, *Hinge of Fate,* p. 713.
439 "a very decided deadlock . . .": Stimson Diary, May 16, 1943, Yale University.
439 "The President is not willing . . .": Lord Moran, *Churchill—The Struggle for Survival, 1940–1965* (1966), p. 104.
439 "a spoiled boy": Stimson Diary, May 25, 1943, Yale University.
439 "to plan such operations . . .": Hastings Ismay, *The Memoirs of General Lord Ismay* (1960), p. 298.
439 "a trying guest . . .": William D. Hassett, *Off the Record with F.D.R.* (1958), p. 169.
439 "really likes the PM . . .": Joseph P. Lash, *A World of Love: Eleanor Roosevelt and Her Friends, 1943–1962* (1984), p. 11.
440 effect of the strike: *NYT,* May 1, 1944, p. 1.
440 "You must have lace . . .": Sophia Carroll to FDR, April 28, 1943, OF 290 #2, FDRL.
440 "I think you are equally guilty . . .": Esther Morrow to FDR, n.d. [April 1943], OF 290 #2, FDRL.
440 "While these American boys . . .": Robert Meyer, Jr., *The Stars and Stripes: Story of World War II* (1960), p. 60.
440 "What sort of traitors . . .": "A fighting man" to FDR, June 1, 1943, Harold Ickes Papers, Library of Congress, Washington, D.C.

440 "If I were on the front lines . . .": John Jaqua to Ernest Jaqua, May 23, 1943; Ernest Jaqua sent a copy of his son's letter to HH, June 1, 1943, HH Papers, FDRL.
441 unauthorized wildcat strikes: Rosa Swafford, *Wartime Record of Strikes and Lockouts, 1940–1945* (1946), pp. 16–17.
441 "It is the judgment . . .": Philip Murray to FDR, June 15, 1943, OF 497b, FDRL.
441 "I have seen pay envelopes . . .": *NYT,* May 9, 1943, p. 6.
441 "he would be glad to resign . . .": Smith conference notes, June 3, 1943, Harold Smith Papers, FDRL.
441 "I understand the devotion . . .": *NYT,* May 3, 1943, p. 4.
442 "on essential war work . . .": *NYT,* June 4, 1943, p. 1.
442 FDR hesitant to use induction: Stimson Diary, June 9, 1943, Yale University.
442 "I ain't a traitor . . .": Rochelle Chadakoff, ed., *Eleanor Roosevelt's My Day* (1989), vol. 1, p. 293.
442 "If I were FDR . . .": Lash, *World of Love,* p. 24.
442 "This is a bad bill . . .": Hassett, *Off the Record,* p. 180.
442 "In spite of imperfections . . .": Stimson Diary, June 25, 1943, Yale University.
442 "We the people . . . ": Mrs. Cravens to FDR, June 26, 1943, OF 407b, FDRL.
442 "Let there be no . . .": text of speech, *NYT,* June 26, 1943, pp. 1, 3.
443 "In vetoing the Smith-Connally . . ."; "action, not tomorrow . . .": ibid., p. 4.
443 "a bad rebuff . . .": Stimson Diary, June 25, 1943, Yale University.
443 "our lack of leadership . . ."; "Perhaps . . .": Lash, *World of Love,* p. 34.
443 More idleness in 1943 in mining: Swafford, *Wartime Record,* p. 33.
443 "portal to portal pay": *Monthly Labor Review,* Dec. 1943, p. 115; see also T. H. Watkins, *Righteous Pilgrim* (1990), pp. 753–59.
444 "We were thrilled . . .": interview with Michael Lilly.
444 "The domestic scene . . .": *MD,* June 20, 1943.
444 "No city in the deep South . . ."; "If these 'poor whites' . . .": Menefee, *Assignment USA,* pp. 51, 56.
444 "We realize . . .": *Mobile Register,* June 3, 1943, p. 8.
444 "No nigger is goin' . . .": Menefee, *Assignment USA,* p. 155.
444 separate shipway: *Mobile Register,* June 8, 1943, pp. 1, 7.
445 rioting in Detroit: Robert Shogan and Tom Craig, *The Detroit Race Riots* (1964); see also accounts in *Detroit Free Press.*
445 "He's not doing . . .": *Detroit Free Press,* June 22, 1943, pp. 1, 2, 8.
446 "It is blood . . .": *Michigan History,* Fall 1969, p. 198.
446 "It is my belief . . .": Lang to FDR, July 29, 1943, OF 93c, FDRL.
446 "I suppose when one . . .": ER to Josephus Daniels, July 23, 1943, ER Microfilm Collection, FDRL. Daniels had sent her a copy of his editorial denouncing criticisms.
446 "the deliberate effort . . .": Stimson Diary, June 24, 1943, Yale University.
446 "come to the conclusion . . .": Stimson Diary, July 5, 1943, Yale University.
446 "Many newspapers and individuals . . .": C. E. Rhett to Biddle, June 12, 1943, OF 93c, FDRL.
446 "The old, subdued, muted . . .": *NR,* July 5, 1943, p. 9.
446 ". . . the vacillation . . .": C. E. Rhett to Biddle, June 12, 1943, OF 93c, FDRL.
447 "a sizable population . . .": *NR,* July 5, 1943, p. 10.
447 "Large segments . . .": C. E. Rhett to Biddle, July 12, 1943, OF 93c, FDRL.
447 "highly explosive . . .": ibid.
447 "Like a defective screw . . .": Pauli Murray to FDR, June 18, 1943, OF 93c, FDRL.
447 "We urge you . . .": WW to FDR, June 21, 1943, OF 93c, FDRL.
447 "a straight forward statement . . .": Bethune to FDR, June 22, 1943, OF 93c, FDRL.
447 "on a par with Nazism . . .": *MD,* July 13, 1943.
447 "Detroit should never . . .": Lash, *World of Love,* p. 32.
447 "he must not irritate . . .": ibid., p. 38.
447 "Why hasn't Mr. Roosevelt . . .": *NR,* July 5, 1943, p. 12.
448 first week in July: Gilbert, *Second World War,* p. 442.
448 "The whole world . . .": *NYT,* June 27, 1943, sect. IV, p. 3.
448 "It is going to be about the war . . .": *NYT,* July 28, 1943, p. 9; Franklin D. Roosevelt, *Public Papers and Addresses of Franklin Delano Roosevelt, 1943* (1950), p. 324.
449 "The first crack in the Axis . . .": text of speech, *NYT,* July 29, 1943, p. 4.

450 "our very national existence . . .": *AM,* Oct. 1943, p. 72.
450 "To a large degree . . .": Richard Leighton and Robert Coakley, *Global Logistics and Strategy, 1940–1943* (1955), p. 601.
450 "We are still far . . .": *NYT,* July 29, 1943, p. 4.
450 "I can recall . . .": Saul Bellow, *It All Adds Up: From the Dim Past to the Uncertain Future* (1994), pp. 28–29.
451 "watched the sun go down . . .": *MD,* Aug. 1, 1943.
451 "He is much the most interesting . . .": Bernard Asbell, *Mother and Daughter* (1988), p. 163.
451 "to a mature understanding . . .": Lash, *Love, Eleanor,* p. 378.
451 "Darling Mum . . .": Asbell, *Mother and Daughter,* p. 150.
452 "a terrific hatred": AB to John Boettiger, June 26, 1943, box 5, Boettiger Papers, FDRL.
452 "She looks very thin . . .": Lash, *World of Love,* p. 41.
452 "I'm having the time . . .": AB to John Boettiger, May 28, 1943, box 5, Boettiger Papers, FDRL.
452 "You'd be amazed at the timid . . .": AB to John Boettiger, Aug. 1, 1943, box 5, Boettiger Papers, FDRL.
452 "It is the first time . . .": AB to John Boettiger, July 16, 1943, box 5, Boettiger Papers, FDRL.
452 "I think having me here . . .": ER to John Boettiger, July 18, 1943, box 26, Boettiger Papers, FDRL.
453 "I only like being . . .": Lash, *World of Love,* p. 43.
453 "It was nice . . .": ER to FDR, July 18, 1943, box 16, Roosevelt Family Papers Donated by the Children, FDRL.
453 "I guess one of the sad things . . .": Lash, *World of Love,* p. 104.
453 "repeated endeavors . . .": *NYT,* July 26, 1943, p. 19.
453 "to be of help . . .": David S. Wyman, *The Abandonment of the Jews: America and the Holocaust, 1941–1945* (1984), p. 145.
454 "Our own government . . .": *NYT,* July 26, 1943, p. 19.
454 "I am convinced . . .": Jan Ciechanowski, *Defeat in Victory* (1947), p. 182.
454 "virtually none of . . .": Wyman, *Abandonment,* p. 337.
455 "Will any of these Jews . . .": quoted in ibid., p. 150.
455 "The percentage killed . . .": *MD,* Aug. 12, 1943.

CHAPTER EIGHTEEN: "It Was a Sight I Will Never Forget"

456 "These last few days . . .": Joseph P. Lash, *A World of Love: Eleanor Roosevelt and Her Friends, 1943–1962* (1984), p. 54.
457 "more eloquently . . .": Samuel I. Rosenman, *Working with Roosevelt* (1952), pp. 387–88.
457 "You know . . .": *MD,* Aug. 16, 1943.
457 "fraternal . . .": Averell Harriman and Elie Abel, *Special Envoy to Churchill and Stalin, 1941–1946* (1975), p. 222.
457 "Mrs. Roosevelt . . .": ibid.
457 "Your mother is so pleased . . .": Tommy to AB, Aug. 11, 1943, box 75, Halsted Papers, FDRL.
457 "She is especially anxious . . .": Franklin D. Roosevelt, *Public Papers and Addresses, 1943* (1950), p. 1439.
458 "I spoke from the library . . .": *MD,* Aug. 15, 1943.
458 "The P[resident] was very sweet . . .": Lash, *World of Love,* p. 55.
458 "Darling, it kinda gives me . . .": AB to John Boettiger, Aug. 11, 1943, box 5, Boettiger Papers, FDRL.
458 gift of emeralds: Robert E. Sherwood, *Roosevelt and Hopkins* (1948), p. 614.
458 denied by Louise: *NYT,* Jan. 8, 1943, p. 6.
458 extravagant dinner: Sherwood, *Roosevelt and Hopkins,* p. 698.
458 publication of article: ibid.
459 final blow: ibid., p. 750.
459 "This is a fight . . .": ibid., p. 698.
459 Eager to invite: Tommy to AB, Sept. 2, 1943, box 75, Halsted Papers, FDRL.
459 "Harry and Louise . . .": Lash, *World of Love,* p. 54.

459 "ailing and fearing . . . ": James MacGregor Burns, *Roosevelt: The Soldier of Freedom* (1970), p. 392.
459 "it seemed like . . .": ibid.
460 "pick and shovel": *NYT,* Aug. 18, 1943, p. 1.
460 haunted by memories, "majestic": Lord Moran, *Churchill–The Struggle for Survival, 1940–1965* (1966), p. 116.
460 "If a stranger had visited . . .": Hastings Ismay, *The Memoirs of General Lord Ismay* (1960), p. 309.
460 "Winston's obstinacy . . .": Moran, *Churchill,* p. 117.
461 "a very great preponderance": Winston S. Churchill, *The Second World War,* vol. V, *Closing the Ring* (1951), p. 76.
461 discussed the atomic bomb: Martin Gilbert, *Winston S. Churchill,* vol. vii, *Road to Victory: 1941–1945* (1986), pp. 470–71.
461 "Until now . . .": Harriman and Abel, *Special Envoy,* p. 225.
461 "We are both mad . . .": ibid., p. 226.
461 "I gather she didn't like . . .": Tommy to AB, Sept. 2, 1943, box 75, Halsted Papers, FDRL.
461 "PM's sleeping arrangements . . .": Sir Alexander Cadogan, *The Diaries of Sir Alexander Cadogan, O.M. 1938–1945* (1972), p. 559.
462 "too much for him . . .": George McJimsey, *Harry Hopkins* (1987), p. 295.
462 "of high importance . . .": ER to FDR, Sept. 6, 1943, box 16, Roosevelt Family Papers Donated by the Children, FDRL.
462 "I feel a hundred . . .": Lash, *World of Love,* p. 62.
462 "Guadalcanal is no place . . .": Joseph P. Lash, *Eleanor and Franklin* (1971), p. 684.
462 "In some ways . . .": Lash, *World of Love,* p. 60.
462 "I have no zest . . .": ibid.
463 "When I left": *NYT,* Aug. 28, 1943, p. 13.
463 "We liked this speech . . .": ibid.
463 "a genuine impulse . . .": J. William T. Youngs, *Eleanor Roosevelt: A Personal and Public Life* (1985), p. 9.
463 "her shoes dusty and scarred . . .": *NYT,* Sept. 13, 1943, p. 21.
463 "Mrs. Roosevelt literally . . .": Lash, *World of Love,* pp. 62–63.
463 "followed by a brace . . .": copy of letter received by Florence Kerr attached to HH to ER, Oct. 19, 1943, box 214, HH Papers, FDRL.
464 "When I say that . . .": Lash, *Eleanor and Franklin,* p. 685.
464 "in some magic way . . .": *TIR,* p. 298.
464 "Over here . . .": *NYT,* Sept. 6, 1943, p. 19.
464 "It was a sight . . .": Lash, *Eleanor and Franklin,* p. 685.
464 "a fine impression . . . ": FDR to ER, Aug. 30, 1943, box 12, Roosevelt Family Papers Donated by the Children, FDRL.
464 "If I wasn't busy . . .": as repeated in ER to Tommy, Sept. 18, 1943, Malvina Thompson Papers, FDRL.
464 "I've had so many . . .": ER to FDR, Sept. 15, 1943, box 16, Roosevelt Family Papers Donated by the Children, FDRL.
465 "How little I ever thought . . .": *MD,* Sept. 12, 1943.
465 "How I hated . . .": Lash, *World of Love,* p. 71.
465 "I was ahamed . . .": Lash, *Eleanor and Franklin,* p. 691.
465 "leapfrogging" substituted: Samuel Eliot Morison, *The Two-Ocean War* (1963), p. 282.
466 "FDR, should there . . .": ER notes, Sept. 22, 1943, box 12, Roosevelt Family Papers Donated by the Children, FDRL.
466 "No, but she will . . .": William D. Hassett, *Off the Record with F.D.R.* (1958), p. 200.
466 "Hope you come . . .": FDR to ER, Sept. 21, 1943, box 12, Roosevelt Family Papers Donated by the Children, FDRL.
466 "Did you have fun . . . ": repeated by AB in AB to John Boettiger, Nov. 11, 1943, box 6, Boettiger Papers, FDRL.
466 "she had never . . .": AB to John Boettiger, Sept. 22, 1943, box 6, Boettiger Papers, FDRL.
466 "Pa asked me . . .": Bernard Asbell, *Mother and Daughter* (1988), p. 169.
466 "Oh, no, Eleanor . . .": *NYT,* Aug. 30, 1943, p. 8.
467 "Yes, she has been . . .": *NYT,* Sept. 29, 1943, p. 23.
467 "They missed her usual . . .": *Time,* Oct. 4, 1943, p. 25.

467 "while the farmers . . .": *NYT,* Oct. 17, 1943, p. 28.
467 "The outcry in Congress . . .": Lash, *World of Love,* p. 84.
467 "[Tommy] is worried . . .": ibid., p. 81.
467 "her deep horror . . .": ibid.
467 "the crosses row on row . . . ": *MD,* Sept. 17, 1943.
467 American casualties: figures provided by the Army History Center and Navy History Center, Washington, D.C.
467 "emotionally . . ."; "I know and understand . . .": FDR, Jr., to ER, Oct. 21, 1943, box 26, Boettiger Papers, FDRL.
468 "I think another . . .": Lash, *World of Love,* p. 81.
468 "I think the things . . .": *NYT,* Aug. 28, 1943, p. 3.
469 "Lack of money . . .": Theodore Mosch, *The G.I. Bill* (1975), p. 32.
469 "I'd like to see . . .": *NYT,* Dec. 18, 1943, p. 12.
469 "Baruch is still . . .": ER to John Boettiger, Dec. 8, 1943, box 6, Boettiger Papers, FDRL.
470 *One World:* Jack Goodman, ed., *While You Were Gone* (1946), p. 452–53.
470 "The representatives of 44 nations . . .": *MD,* Nov. 9, 1943.
470 "with a sky so blue . . . ": ibid.
470 "Good news comes . . .": Hassett, *Off the Record,* p. 218.
470 "one of the bitterest . . .": Robert Coakley and Richard Leighton, *Global Logistics and Strategy, 1943–1945* (1989), p. 192.
470 "Mrs. R wanted very much . . .": Lash, *World of Love,* p. 93.
470 "The OM sat all over her . . .": AB to John Boettiger, Dec. 6, 1943, box 6, Boettiger Papers, FDRL.
471 "not just because of . . .": AB to ER, Nov. 11, 1943, box 57, Halsted Papers, FDRL.
471 "I'll read him your desire . . .": ER to AB, Nov. 6, 1943, box 57, Halsted Papers, FDRL.
471 "The answer was . . .": AB to John Boettiger, Nov. 11, 1943, box 6, Boettiger Papers, FDRL.
471 ". . . Pa seems to take . . .": AB to John Boettiger, Nov. 11, 1943, box 6, Boettiger Papers, FDRL.
471 "goes along very strongly . . .": AB to John Boettiger, Dec. 11, 1943, box 6, Boettiger Papers, FDRL.
472 "Tell me darling . . .": John Boettiger to AB, May 29, 1943, box 5, Boettiger Papers, FDRL.
472 "Neither of us is giving . . .": Asbell, *Mother and Daughter,* p. 165.
472 "among the higher ups . . .": AB to John Boettiger, Sept. 18, 1943, box 5, Boettiger Papers, FDRL.
472 "I realize how desperately lonely . . .": ER to AB, Oct. 10, 1943, box 57, Halsted Papers, FDRL.
473 "I just saw Pa . . .": ER to AB, Nov. 11, 1943, box 57, Halsted Papers, FDRL.
473 "Everything is very comfortable . . .": FDR to ER, Nov. 18, 1943, box 12, Roosevelt Family Papers Donated by the Children, FDRL.
473 "The sea voyage . . .": Elliott Roosevelt, *As He Saw It* (1946), p. 133.
473 "for things always . . .": Lash, *World of Love,* p. 98.
473 "He was thrilled . . .": Michael F. Reilly, *Reilly of the White House* (1947), p. 170.
473 "I've been amused . . .": Lash, *World of Love,* p. 96.
474 "In a queer way . . .": Asbell, *Mother and Daughter,* p. 156.
474 clapping her hands: Lash, *World of Love,* pp. 1–2.
474 "This will be very useful . . .": Frank Freidel, *Franklin D. Roosevelt: A Rendezvous with Destiny* (1990), p. 478.
474 "I'm sorry things only went . . .": ER to FDR, Dec. 5, 1943, box 12, Roosevelt Family Papers Donated by the Children, FDRL.
474 "Let us make it . . .": Churchill, *Closing the Ring,* p. 300.
474 "Large families . . .": Elliott Roosevelt, *As He Saw It,* p. 16.
474 "He started slowly . . .": interview with Robert Hopkins.
474 WC asked Pa Watson: Churchill, *Closing the Ring,* p. 301.
475 "Seeing him . . .": Reilly, *Reilly,* p. 179.
475 "as if the tailor . . .": Moran, *Churchill,* p. 146.
475 "I am glad to see . . .": Charles E. Bohlen, *Witness to History, 1929–1969* (1973), p. 144.
475 "He seems very confident . . .": Elliott Roosevelt, *As He Saw It,* p. 176.
475 "It was a thrilling experience . . .": Ismay, *Memoirs,* p. 337.
475 "clearly was the dominating . . . ": Bohlen, *Witness,* p. 142.

475 "He looked the picture . . .": Ismay, *Memoirs,* p. 338.
475 doodling wolfheads: Bohlen, *Witness,* p. 151.
475 "If we are here . . .": Moran, *Churchill,* p. 147.
476 "I thank the Lord . . .": Stimson Diary, Dec. 5, 1943, Yale University.
476 "man might destroy . . . ": Moran, *Churchill,* p. 151.
476 to see FDR alone: ibid., p. 146.
476 "I had done . . ." . . . "A vague smile . . .": Frances Perkins, *The Roosevelt I Knew* (1946), pp. 83–84.
476 "From that time on . . .": ibid., pp. 84–85.
477 "There were toasts . . .": Henry H. Arnold, *Global Mission* (1949), p. 498.
477 "I want to tell you . . .": *Foreign Relations of the United States: The Conferences at Cairo and Teheran, 1943* (1961), p. 469.
477 American factories were supplying: Fourteenth Report on Lend-Lease for period ending December 31, 1943, pp. 30–33, FDRL.
477 every week: ibid.
478 "We have differing customs . . .": Burns, *Soldier of Freedom,* p. 411.
478 huddled around a map: ibid., pp. 412–13.
478 "an important milestone . . .": *NYT,* Dec. 7, 1943, p. 6.
478 "I want George . . .": Sherwood, *Roosevelt and Hopkins,*p. 760.
478 "Well, Ike . . .": Dwight D. Eisenhower, *Crusade in Europe* (1948), p. 207.
478 "Homeward bound . . .": Lash, *World of Love,* p. 98.
479 "He was in his traveling . . .": Stimson Diary, Dec. 17, 1943, Yale University.
479 "OM was very cool . . .": AB to John Boettiger, Dec. 19, 1943, box 6, Boettiger Papers, FDRL.
479 "Tonight . . .": *MD,* Dec. 17, 1943.
479 "a complete fiasco . . ." . . . "the things she had been through . . .": AB to John Boettiger, Dec. 19, 1943, box 6, Boettiger Papers, FDRL.
480 "I finally managed . . .": ibid.
480 "Ever since my talk . . .": AB to John Boettiger, Dec. 27, 1943, box 6, Boettiger Papers, FDRL.
480 "It is the first time . . .": Henry H. Adams, *Harry Hopkins* (1977), p. 351.
481 first Christmas at Hyde Park since 1932: *NYT,* Dec. 26, 1943, p. 5.
481 "I am sure it will seem . . .": *MD,* Dec. 20, 1943.
481 "loved the old place . . .": AB to John Boettiger, Dec. 27, 1943, box 6, Boettiger Papers, FDRL.
481 "no women on ships . . .": ibid.
481 "How did the New Deal . . .": text of speech, *NYT,* Dec. 29, 1943, p. 8.
482 "The New Deal slogan . . .": *U.S. News,* Jan. 7, 1944, pp. 26–27.
482 "an honorable discharge": *NYT,* Dec. 5, 1943, pp. 1, 32.
482 "The war has finally . . .": Raymond Clapper, *Watching the World* (1944), p. 131.
483 "away in lavender": Lash, *Eleanor and Franklin,* p. 696.
483 "the future . . .": *U.S. News,* Jan. 14, 1943, p. 24.

CHAPTER NINETEEN: "I Want to Sleep and Sleep"

484 "If ever there was a time . . .": text of speech, *NYT,* Jan. 12, 1944, p. 12.
485 ". . . the fatal and false . . .": James MacGregor Burns, *Roosevelt: The Soldier of Freedom* (1970), p. 426.
486 ER who listened: *MD,* Jan. 11, 1944.
486 "It has been . . . relief not for the needy . . .": *NYT,* Feb. 23, 1944, p. 14.
486 "in the best . . ."; "hell broke . . .": William D. Hassett, *Off the Record with F.D.R.* (1958), p. 235.
486 "a calculated and deliberate . . .": *NYT,* Feb. 24, 1944, p. 12.
487 "practically every senator . . .": Henry A. Wallace, *The Price of Vision* (1973), p. 302.
487 "Alben must be . . .": Hassett, *Off the Record,* p. 235.
487 Barkley was tired: Burns, *Soldier of Freedom,* p. 426.
487 "quite calm . . ."; "but I'm not sure . . .": Joseph P. Lash, *A World of Love* (1984), pp. 112–13.
487 call from Jimmy Byrnes: James F. Byrnes, *Speaking Frankly* (1947), pp. 211–12.

487 "Still no word . . .": Hassett, *Off the Record,* p. 237.
487 The Treasury was able: Harold G. Vatter, *The U.S. Economy in World War II* (1985), pp. 104–5.
488 "a revolution in American . . .": David Brinkley, *Washington Goes to War* (1988), p. 218.
488 "supposed he was lying . . .": Hassett, *Off the Record,* p. 238.
488 "the Big Week": Martin Cardin, *Flying Forts* (1968), p. 444; interview with William Emerson.
488 "you would be shot down . . .": Michael Sherry, *The Rise of American Air Power* (1987), p. 157.
488 "This was a turning point . . .": Winston S. Churchill, *The Second World War,* vol. V, *Closing the Ring* (1951), p. 462.
489 "With no preliminary . . .": John R. Boettiger, Jr., *A Love in Shadow* (1978), p. 253.
489 "Father could relax . . .": interview with Elliott Roosevelt.
489 "She could tell . . .": interview with John Boettiger, Jr.
489 "She walked in . . .": Justine Polier, *OH,* FDRL.
489 "but not until . . .": Joseph P. Lash, *Eleanor and Franklin* (1971), p. 699.
489 "Louise would arrange . . .": Bernard Asbell, *Mother and Daughter* (1988), p. 99.
489 "it would be wonderful . . .": Lash, *Eleanor and Franklin,* p. 699.
490 "I was away last week . . .": ER to MLH, Feb. 18, 1944, box 87, ER Papers, FDRL.
490 "I know that you . . .": ibid.
490 "I hope you understand . . .": Ann Rochon to ER, n.d., box 1731, ER Papers, FDRL.
490 "young life in the White House . . .": *MD,* March 4, 1944.
490 "brought to all her contacts . . .": *TIR,* p. 319.
490 "like Topsy . . .": Asbell, *Mother and Daughter,* pp. 175–76.
490 "It was immaterial . . .": ibid., p. 176.
491 "It was an ideal . . .": interview with John Boettiger, Jr.
491 fled from the library: *The Woman,* May 1949, pp. 8, 9.
491 "She is really in finer . . .": John Boettiger to Jimmy Roosevelt, Aug. 15, 1944, box 26, Boettiger Papers, FDRL.
491 "Anna's day at the White House . . .": *Time,* May 29, 1944, p. 18.
491 "He would grin . . .": Grace Tully, *F.D.R., My Boss* (1949), p. 274.
492 ". . . tired and worn": *NYT,* March 26, 1944, p. 35.
492 "President not looking so well . . .": Hassett, *Off the Record,* p. 239.
492 "I don't think mother . . .": Asbell, *Mother and Daughter,* p. 177.
492 "interested in physiology . . .": ibid.
492 "she still believed . . .": interview with John Boettiger, Jr.
492 "I think the constant tension . . .": Lash, *World of Love,* p. 115.
492 "The President . . .": *MD,* April 6, 1944.
493 "He is cheerful in spirit . . .": Hassett, *Off the Record,* p. 240.
493 "the blood was not pumping . . .": Asbell, *Mother and Daughter,* p. 177.
493 comparing notes with Grace: Tully, *F.D.R.,* p. 274.
493 "I didn't think . . .": Asbell, *Mother and Daughter,* p. 177.
493 "I designed that one": Jim Bishop, *FDR's Last Year* (1974), p. 3.
494 "It was a warm day . . .": interview with Howard Bruenn.
494 "I suspected something . . .": ibid.
494 "It was worse . . .": ibid.
494 examination revealed: *Annals of Internal Medicine,* April 1970, pp. 580–81; hereafter cited as Bruenn, "Clinical Notes."
495 "Thanks, Doc": Bishop, *Last Year,* p. 6.
495 "Not only were . . .": *NYT,* March 29, 1944, p. 1.
495 little model: *NYT,* March 31, 1944, p. 38.
495 "McIntire was appalled . . .": interview with Howard Bruenn.
496 "I was only a lieutenant commander . . .": ibid.
496 "Digitalis was a miracle drug . . .": ibid.
496 Goldsmith suggests: *Surgery, Gynecology & Obstetrics,* Dec. 1975, pp. 899–903.
496 "He suspects the doctors . . .": Lash, *World of Love,* p. 118.
497 "When we got through . . .": *NYT,* April 5, 1944, p. 1.
497 Hobcaw: Bernard M. Baruch, *Baruch: The Public Years* (1960), pp. 335–37.

497 "The Secret Service...": A. Merriman Smith, *Thank You, Mr. President* (1946), p. 139.
497 "I want to sleep and sleep...": Bishop, *Last Year,* p. 25.
498 Montgomery Ward strike: *NYT,* April 13, 1944, p. 1.
498 Stimson argued: Stimson Diary, May 4, 1944, Yale University.
498 Biddle disagreed: Francis Biddle, *In Brief Authority* (1962), pp. 315–16.
498 Sewell Avery refused: *NYT,* April 27, 1944, pp. 1, 14; Aaron Levenstein, *Labor Today and Tomorrow* (1945), pp. 1, 2.
498 "There is no warrant...": "Comments on the Montgomery Ward Case," May 11, 1944, box 3, OF 4451, FDRL.
498 "It was the manner...": ibid.
498 "great howl": Stimson Diary, May 4, 1944, Yale University.
498 "Beloved of mine...": John Boettiger to AB, April 10, 1944, box 6, Boettiger Papers, FDRL.
499 "Anna has arranged...": ER to FDR, April 21, 1944, box 16, Roosevelt Family Papers Donated by the Children, FDRL.
499 "I came home...": *TIR,* p. 328.
499 "in better condition...": *NYT,* April 13, 1944, p. 8.
499 Winthrop Rutherfurd: obituary, *Aiken Standard,* March 24, 1944, p. 4; *NYT,* May 21, 1944, p. 17.
499 Baruch vividly remembered: Bernard Asbell, *The FDR Memoirs* (1973), p. 412.
500 acute abdominal pain: Bruenn, "Clinical Notes," p. 548.
500 "seemed in such good spirits...": Smith, *Thank You,* pp. 140–41.
500 "lest his recovery...": ibid., p. 141.
500 "You will come home...": ER to FDR, April 29, 1944, box 16, Roosevelt Family Papers Donated by the Children, FDRL.
501 "Nothing I could give...": ER to AB, May 1, 1944, box 57, Halsted Papers, FDRL.
501 "I had a really grand time...": FDR to HH, May 18, 1944, HH Papers, FDRL.
501 Stephen killed: *NYT,* Feb. 13, 1944, p. 1.
501 "It is grand to get..."; "The main things...": FDR to HH, May 18, 1944, HH Papers, FDRL.
501 "We can all be glad...": *NYT,* May 8, 1944, p. 18.
502 "good news...": ibid.
502 "brown as a berry...": Hassett, *Off the Record,* p. 241.
502 "Anna was afraid...": interview with Howard Bruenn.
502 "You would find...": Ickes to MLH, May 23, 1944, Harold Ickes Papers, Library of Congress, Washington, D.C.
502 "With people like Martha...": interview with John Boettiger, Jr.
502 "what she wanted...": ibid.
502 "I am always waiting...": *MD,* April 18, 1944.
503 "Anna is the only one...": Lash, *Eleanor and Franklin,* p. 700.
503 "Anna tried to be...": interview with Howard Bruenn.
503 "How can anyone...": Margery Truiz to FDR, Feb. 16, 1944, with excerpts from newspaper article, OF 93, FDRL.
503 "I know, of course...": "Outraged" to ER, Feb. 28, 1944.
503 "Women should be represented...": *NYT,* March 31, 1944, p. 38.
503 "She pushed him terrifically...": Asbell, *Mother and Daughter,* p. 176.
504 "Mother can't you see...": Tully, *F.D.R.,* p. 110.
504 "She couldn't see...": Asbell, *Mother and Daughter,* p. 177.
504 "I pray I don't...": AB to John Boettiger, April 7, 1944, box 6, Boettiger Papers, FDRL.

CHAPTER TWENTY: "Suspended in Space"

505 "suspended in space...": ER to FDR, May 2, 1944, box 16, Roosevelt Family Papers Donated by the Children, FDRL.
505 "every movement...": Grace Tully, *F.D.R., My Boss* (1949), p. 265.
505 900 warships: Max Hastings, *Overlord: D-Day and the Battle for Normandy* (1984), p. 80.

506 "when he is buried...": Harry C. Butcher, *My Three Years with Eisenhower* (1946), p. 275.
506 "The nearer H hour..."; "as the battlefields...": Gordon Harrison, *Cross-Channel Attack* (1989), p. 274.
506 order to "go": ibid., p. 284.
506 "there was a question...": interview with William Emerson.
506 "the dangers and disasters..": Averell Harriman and Elie Abel, *Special Envoy to Churchill and Stalin, 1941–1946* (1975), p. 311.
506 "Our friendship...": *Churchill & Roosevelt: The Complete Correspondence* (1984), vol. III, p. 162.
506 "How I wish...": ibid., p. 186.
507 "I feel as though...": ER to Doris Fleeson, May 15, 1944, ER Microfilm Collection, FDRL.
507 "It is too bad...": *MD,* Jan. 6, 1944.
507 "Soon the invasion...": ER to Esther Lape, June 3, 1944, Lape Papers, FDRL.
507 "I only know...": Joseph P. Lash, *A World of Love: Eleanor Roosevelt and Her Friends, 1943–1962* (1984), p. 124.
507 "We all started...": AH interview, Graff Papers, FDRL.
507 Eisenhower met: Stephen E. Ambrose, *The Supreme Commander: The War Years of General Dwight D. Eisenhower* (1970) p. 415.
507 "an agony...": Hastings Ismay, *The Memoirs of General Lord Ismay* (1960), p. 357.
507 "because he'd learned...": ER interview, Graff Papers, FDRL.
508 "the question...": Harriman and Abel, *Special Envoy,* p. 274.
508 "Do you realize...": Martin Gilbert, *Winston S. Churchill,* vol. VII, *Road to Victory, 1941–1945* (1986), p. 794.
508 "The first of the Axis...": Franklin D. Roosevelt, *Public Papers and Addresses of Franklin D. Roosevelt, 1944,* (1950), p. 147.
508 "How magnificently...": *Churchill & Roosevelt Correspondence,* vol. III, p. 163.
508 "from a vague...": Ernie Pyle, *Brave Men* (1944), p. 356.
508 "I don't know why...": ibid., pp. 364–65.
509 "To be nearly sixty...": Lash, *World of Love,* p. 124.
509 "He sat up in bed...": ER interview, Graff Papers, FDRL.
509 "Soldiers, sailors and airmen...": Robert Meyer, Jr., *The Stars and Stripes* (1960), p. 234.
509 HH thought about production problems: Robert E. Sherwood, *Roosevelt and Hopkins,* (1948), p. 807.
509 "...the most exciting moment...": Stephen E. Ambrose, *D-Day* (1994), p. 494.
509 "Outwardly they appeared...": Winston M. Estes, *Homefront* (1976), p. 257.
509 "The impulse to pray...": Ambrose, *D-Day,* p. 495.
510 "We have come...": quoted in ibid., p. 494.
510 "The President was happy...": I. F. Stone, *The War Years, 1939–1945* (1988), p. 236.
510 "I have just sat in...": letter from "The B." to "Mom," June 6, 1944, Reminiscences by Contemporaries, FDRL.
510 "You just don't land...": Franklin D. Roosevelt, *Public Papers and Addresses, 1944,* p. 159.
510 "a far cry...": Samuel I. Rosenman, *Working with Roosevelt* (1952), p. 433.
510 "our sons, pride...": press release, June 6, 1944, attached to "The B." to "Mom," June 6, 1944, Reminiscences by Contemporaries, FDRL.
510 "All emotion...": *MD,* June 6, 1944.
511 "Each hedgerow..."; "I cannot say enough...": Harrison, *Cross-Channel Attack,* p. 284.
511 "I cannot say...": quoted in Annette Tapert, ed., *Lines of Battle: Letters from American Servicemen, 1941–1945* (1987), pp. 160–61.
511 "Nobody doubted now...": Henry H. Arnold, quoted in "The War Reports of General of the Army George Marshall, General of the Army H. H. Arnold, Fleet Admiral Ernest J. King." N.Y.: J.B. Lippincott Co. (1947), p. 67.
511 "As far as you could...": Pyle, *Brave Men,* p. 358.
511 "There were trucks..."... "They stood staring...": ibid., pp. 367–69.
512 "Much kidding...": William D. Hassett, *Off the Record with F.D.R.* (1958), p. 252.
512 "I've unpacked a little...": Lash, *World of Love,* p. 118.
512 "in the pink...": Hassett, *Off the Record,* p. 254.
512 GI Bill of Rights: Theodore Mosch, *The GI Bill* (1975), p. 40.

512 "There is one great fear . . .": *MD,* June 25, 1944.
513 "the best . . . the most mature . . .": Harold G. Vatter, *The U.S. Economy in World War II* (1985), pp. 137–38.
513 We were men . . .": Joseph C. Goulden, *The Best Years* (1976), p. 67.
513 "Almost everything important . . .": quoted in Mark Jonathan Harris, Franklin D. Mitchell, and Steven J. Schechter, *The Homefront* (1984), p. 221.
513 "I doubt if . . .": quoted in ibid., p. 221.
513 "gives emphatic notice . . .": James MacGregor Burns, *Roosevelt: The Soldier of Freedom* (1970), p. 509.
513 Edward Kowalick: memo, newspaper clippings, April 1–23, 1944, Harry Alpert to Philleo Nash, PSF 4245g, FDRL.
514 "deplorable incident": Wilbur La Roe, Jr., to ER, May 27, 1944, attached to Sec. to ER to John McCloy, June 1, 1944, box 919, ER Papers, FDRL.
514 "I've never had more . . .": *NYT,* Feb. 2, 1943, p. 17.
514 "Christmas tree regiment": John Armor and Peter Wright, *Manzanar* (1988), p. 149.
514 seven major campaigns: ibid., p. 148.
514 "the continued retention . . .": Kai Bird, *The Chairman, John McCloy* (1992), p. 171.
514 "The more I think . . .": quoted in Allan R. Bosworth, *America's Concentration Camps* (1967), p. 209.
515 "to slow down . . .": Bird, *Chairman,* p. 211.
515 "to develop positive . . .": Arthur D. Morse, *While Six Million Died* (1983), p. 314.
515 "finally there was . . .": interview with John Pehle.
515 "the wholesale . . .": Morse, *Six Million Died,* p. 337.
516 "The War Department . . .": ibid., p. 358.
516 "in the resultant . . .": Bird, *Chairman,* p. 216.
516 "if the elaborate murder . . .": Morse, *Six Million Died,* pp. 359–60.
516 "beyond the maximum range . . .": Bird, *Chairman,* p. 221.
516 "It was the saddest . . .": interview with Jan Karski.
516 "I cannot live out . . .": Jim Bishop, *FDR's Last Year* (1974), p. 8.
517 "in the small park . . ."; "I told Margaret . . .": ibid., p. 70.
517 "it wasn't a complaint . . .": *The Woman,* May 1949, p. 10
517 "the legacy . . .": interview with John Boettiger, Jr.
517 "What would you think . . .": interview with James Roosevelt.
517 "It was almost . . .": interview with Trude Lash.
517 "It was a terrible decision . . .": AH, *OH,* Columbia University.
518 "light-hearted and gay . . .": AB typescript on Lucy and FDR, box 84, Halsted Papers, FDRL; Hereafter cited as AB on Lucy.
518 "While they were my parents . . .": AH, *OH,* Columbia University.
518 "Standards were different . . .": interview with Robert Donovan.
518 Anna told . . .: AH, *OH,* Columbia University.
519 "He stepped . . .": Hassett, *Off the Record,* p. 259.
519 "all smiles . . .": Charles de Gaulle, *The Complete War Memoirs* (1964), p. 571.
519 America's "friend": Franklin D. Roosevelt, *Public Papers and Addresses, 1944,* pp. 194–96.
519 "innate dignity . . .": AB on Lucy, box 84, Halsted Papers, FDRL.
519 "feeling happy"; "I liked her . . .": ibid.
520 "Anna is a dear fine . . .": Bernard Asbell, *Mother and Daughter* (1988), p. 188.
520 "You could sense . . .": interview with Alonzo Fields.
520 More than 130,000 Germans: Martin Gilbert, *The Second World War* (1989), p. 549.
520 "all the ridiculous things . . .": Asbell, *Mother and Daughter,* p. 188.
520 "The three of them . . .": interview with John Boettiger, Jr.
521 "buses, trucks . . .": Ulysses G. Lee, *The Employment of Negro Troops* (1966), p. 397.
521 separate buses: ibid., p. 322.
521 Camp Stewart: Jean Byers, "A Study of the Negro in Military Service," War Department Study, June 1947, p. 64.
521 "The only place . . .": ibid., p. 68.
521 Charles Rico: *PC,* Aug. 22, 1942, p. 1.
522 Henry Williams: Truman Gibson to Secretary of War, Nov. 17, 1942, Record Group 107, National Archives, Washington, D.C.
522 Norma Greene: ibid.

522 "[Negroes] have been . . .": Truman Gilson to Assistant Secretary of War, May 14, 1943, Record Group 107, National Archives, Washington, D.C.
522 "Honey, I am so hurt . . .": Morale Report of 494th Port Battalion, June 1, 1943, Record Group 107, National Archives, Washington, D.C.
522 "These colored boys . . .": ER to John McCloy, Sept. 29, 1943, ER Microfilm Collection, FDRL.
522 "an important step . . .": *PC,* Sept. 9, 1944, p. 1.
522 "Extra! Extra! . . .": Lee, *Employment of Negro Troops,* p. 398.
522 "the essential principle . . .": *PC,* Sept. 2, 1944, p. 1.
522 "to hold the south . . .": Daniels to Hassett, Aug. 29, 1944, box 7, OF 93b, FDRL.
523 "This knowledge raised . . .": Lee, *Employment of Negro Troops,* p. 400.
523 "have I seen so much . . .": Hastie to McCloy, Sept. 5, 1944, Record Group 107, National Archives, Washington, D.C.
523 "Up to the present . . .": Forrestal to FDR, May 20, 1944, box 84, PSF, FDRL.
523 "swapped the waiter's apron . . .": *Common Ground,* Winter 1947, p. 63.
523 "to expand the use . . .": Forrestal to FDR, May 20, 1944, box 84, PSF, FDRL.
523 "successfully absorbed . . .": Lee Nichols, *Breakthrough on the Color Front* (1954), p. 60.
523 "This single stunning . . .": Robert L. Allen, *The Port Chicago Mutiny* (1989), p. 64.
524 "an outstanding . . .": *Commonweal,* Sept. 21, 1945, pp. 546–48.
524 "This improvement . . .": ibid., p. 546.
524 "as little right . . .": *U.S. News,* July 21, 1944, p. 27.
524 "All that is within . . .": ibid.
525 "The President doesn't . . .": *NYT,* July 12, 1944, p. 12.
525 "the good of the country": Lash, *World of Love,* p. 129.
525 "Dewey seems . . .": James Roosevelt and Sidney Schalett, *Affectionately, F.D.R.* (1959), p. 353.
525 "I am very conscious . . .": Lash, *World of Love,* p. 130.
525 "it was as though . . .": David McCullough, *Truman* (1992), p. 299.
525 "I am just not going . . .": Rosenman, *Working with Roosevelt,* p. 439.
525 "He just doesn't . . .": Sherwood, *Roosevelt and Hopkins,* p. 820.
525 "We ought to have . . .": Rosenman, *Working with Roosevelt,* p. 463.
526 "The meeting obviously . . .": ibid., p. 464.
526 "You tell the President . . .": ibid., p. 466.
526 "just as you . . .": ibid., p. 468.
526 "He said I was . . .": John Morton Blum, *The Price of Vision: The Diary of Henry A. Wallace, 1942–1946* (1993), p. 362.
526 "He drew me . . .": ibid., p. 367.
526 "You are the best . . .": quoted in McCullough, *Truman,* p. 303.
526 would cost the ticket: Rosenman, *Working with Roosevelt,* pp. 444–45.
527 "he had never . . .": Edward J. Flynn, *You're the Boss* (1962), p. 181.
527 "Bob, I think you . . .": Ted Morgan, *FDR: A Biography* (1985), p. 728.
527 "Bob, I think Truman . . .": McCullough, *Truman,* p. 301.
527 "We excused ourselves . . .": Rosenman, *Working with Roosevelt,* p. 449.
527 "Grace, the President . . ."; "The reason for the switch . . .": Tully, *F.D.R.,* p. 276.
528 "The trip out . . .": Tommy to Esther Lape, July 24, 1944, box 6, Esther Lape Papers, FDRL.
528 "The slow speed . . .": FDR to ER, July 21, 1944, box 12, Roosevelt Family Papers Donated by the Children, FDRL.
528 "I think it would be fun . . .": James Roosevelt and Schalett, *Affectionately, F.D.R.,* p. 348.
528 "Mrs. R was impatient . . ": Tommy to Esther Lape, July 24, 1944, box 6, Esther Lape Papers, FDRL.
528 "I don't know that . . .": Lash, *World of Love,* p. 129.
529 "I don't know why . . .": Tommy to Esther Lape, July 24, 1944, box 6, Esther Lape Papers, FDRL.
529 "suddenly white . . ." . . . "So for perhaps . . .": James Roosevelt and Schalett, *Affectionately, F.D.R.,* pp. 351–52.
529 "Help me up . . .": James Roosevelt, *My Parents: A Differing View* (1976), p. 279.
529 "What is the job . . .": Franklin D. Roosevelt, *Public Papers and Addresses, 1944,* p. 204.

530 "There were several negatives . . .": interview with Dick Strobel; see also Rosenman, *Working with Roosevelt,* p. 453.
530 "Hey, you better . . .": interview with Dick Strobel.
530 "I made the judgment . . .": ibid.
530 "all hell broke loose . . .": ibid.
530 "It's not my fault . . .": ibid.
530 "sick about the whole business . . .": Lash, *World of Love,* p. 132.
530 "had hoped until the last . . .": ER to Esther Lape, July 29, 1944, box 5, Esther Lape Papers, FDRL.
530 "From all I hear . . .": ibid.
530 "Off in a few minutes": FDR to ER, July 21, 1944, box 12, Roosevelt Family Papers Donated by the Children, FDRL.
531 "Yesterday a.m. . . .": ibid.
531 noticeably absent: Rosenman, *Working with Roosevelt,* p. 456.
531 leather flying: William Manchester, *American Caesar* (1978), p. 365.
531 "The B-29 was a great . . .": interview with William Emerson.
532 "I dare to say . . .": Manchester, *American Caesar,* p. 369.
532 "In such a situation . . .": Burns, *Soldier of Freedom,* pp. 488–89.
532 "As soon as I . . .": D. Clayton James, *The Years of MacArthur,* vol. II (1975), p. 535.
532 "At one of the hospitals . . .": Rosenman, *Working with Roosevelt,* p. 458.
532 "With a cheering smile . . .": ibid.
532 one other occasion: interview with Anna Faith Jones.
533 "he was close to them": Rosenman, *Working with Roosevelt,* p. 459.

CHAPTER TWENTY-ONE: "The Old Master Still Had It"

534 MLH at movies: *Yankee Magazine,* June 1977, p. 174.
534 "Missy was shocked . . .": Bernard Asbell, *The FDR Memoirs* (1973), p. 404.
534 collection of photos: interview with Jane Scarborough.
535 telegram to Missy's sister: ER to Ann Rochon, July 31, 1944, PPF 3737, FDRL.
535 "I am sure that for her . . .": *MD,* July 31, 1944.
535 "Regret to inform . . . ": memo from Hassett and Early to FDR, July 31, 1944, PPF 3737, FDRL.
535 "I'm glad F . . .": Joseph P. Lash, *A World of Love: Eleanor Roosevelt and Her Friends, 1943–1962* (1984), p. 133.
535 "Memories of more than a score . . .": *NYT,* Aug. 1, 1944, p. 15.
535 "Missy's death . . .": ibid., p. 14.
535 "constituted the greatest . . .": T. H. Watkins, *Righteous Pilgrim* (1990), p. 807.
535 "What the devil . . .": Ralph Cropley to FDR, Aug. 1, 1944, PPF 3737, FDRL.
536 "I know how profoundly . . .": Herbert Swope to FDR, Aug. 1, 1944, PPF 3737, FDRL.
536 funeral mass at St. John's: *BEA,* Aug. 2, 1944, p. 4.
536 "She was a real . . .": interview with Jane Scarborough.
536 "There was an air . . .": interview with Barbara Dudley.
536 In her will: copy in PPF 3737, FDRL.
536 "It was in my brother's . . .": interview with Jane Scarborough.
537 "You and I lost . . .": Asbell, *FDR Memoirs,* p. 404.
537 speech in Bremerton: Samuel I. Rosenman, *Working with Roosevelt* (1952), pp. 461–62.
537 FDR collapsed in a chair: Bruenn, "Clinical Notes," p. 586; Elliott Roosevelt and James Brough, *A Rendezvous with Destiny: The Roosevelts of the White House* (1975), p. 378.
537 "only when black workers . . .": John Morton Blum, *V Was for Victory* (1976), p. 196.
537 Philadelphia transit strike: Louis Ruchames, *Race, Jobs and Politics: The FEPC* (1953), p. 105.
538 "customs bearing . . .": ibid.
538 "The exam was . . ."; I felt like a pioneer . . .": interview with William Barber.
538 "We don't want Negroes . . .": AP dispatch, Aug. 2, 1944, 3:24 p.m., box 8, OF 4245G, FDRL.
538 "Your buddies are in . . .": Ruchames, *Race, Jobs and Politics,* p. 109.
539 "You kiss the Negroes . . .": ibid., p. 117.
539 "There was one motorman . . .": *PM,* Aug. 2, 1944, p. 10.

539 nearly forty-five thousand: *BEA,* Aug. 1, 1944, p. 3.
539 "to take possession . . .": executive order, Aug. 3, 1944, quoted in *NYT,* Aug. 4, 1944, pp. 1, 8.
539 "on the basis of conditions . . .": *NYT,* Aug. 4, 1944, pp. 1, 18.
539 "In whatever degree . . .": *Philadelphia Inquirer,* Aug. 1, 1944, p. 12.
539 "The war cannot wait . . .": *NYT,* Aug. 6, 1944, p. 1.
540 protest in the South: News Items, Aug. 19, 1944, box 8, OF 4245G, FDRL.
540 "The first runs . . .": interview with William Barber.
540 "The impossible has . . .": *PC,* Aug. 19, 1942, p. 1.
540 By the end of the war: Harold G. Vatter, *The U.S. Economy in World War II* (1985), p. 127; Richard Polenberg, ed., *America at War* (1972), p. 107.
540 "These changes . . .": Vatter, *U.S. Economy,* p. 134.
540 Negroes in government: Robert H. Ziegler, *American Workers, American Unions, 1920–1985* (1986), p. 82.
540 "With more and better . . .": Jacqueline Jones, *Labor of Love, Labor of Sorrow* (1985), p. 254.
541 "brought hope and confidence . . .": Ruchames, *Race, Jobs and Politics,* p. 159.
541 "a decided nip . . .": William D. Hassett, *Off the Record with F.D.R.* (1958), p. 266.
541 "I am afraid before long . . .": *MD,* Aug. 24, 1944.
541 "Too many . . .": Hassett, *Off the Record,* p. 267.
541 "Mrs. Roosevelt never noticed . . .": Tommy to Esther Lape, July 24, 1944, box 6, Esther Lape Papers, FDRL.
541 never had a headache: Rex Tugwell, *OH,* FDRL.
541 "She feels . . .": Tommy to Esther Lape, box 6, Esther Lape Papers, FDRL.
541 "Pa complains . . .": ER to AB, Aug. 24, 1944, box 57, Halsted Papers, FDRL.
541 "whatever he had . . .": Lash, *World of Love,* p. 135.
541 "This is a great day . . .": Stimson Diary, Aug. 23, 1944, Yale University.
542 managed to see Lucy again: Jonathan Daniels, *Washington Quadrille* (1968), p. 289.
542 ". . . to wake in Highland": Hassett pages from original diary for Sept. 1, 1944, Hassett Papers, FDRL.
542 "You'd think the president . . .": interview with Grace Stang.
542 "I hope you will pardon . . .": *Churchill & Roosevelt: The Complete Correspondence,* (1984), vol. III, p. 305.
542 "Perfectly delighted . . .": ibid.
542 "he didn't believe . . .": Hassett, *Off the Record,* p. 269.
543 "I'm glad to see you . . .": *NYT,* Sept. 12, 1944, p. 56.
543 "was more like the reunion . . .": Hastings Ismay, *The Memoirs of General Lord Ismay* (1960), p. 372.
543 "There is something . . .": *MD,* Sept. 11, 1944.
543 "I assured him . . .": ibid.
543 "He talks picturesquely . . .": Lash, *World of Love,* p. 140.
543 "I think he likes me . . .": ER to Esther Lape, Sept. 22, 1944, box 5, Esther Lape Papers, FDRL.
543 "The ladies' duties . . .": Lash, *World of Love,* p. 137.
543 "except for the meals . . .": ibid.
543 "Optimism was . . .": Robert Coakley and Richard Leighton, *Global Logistics and Strategy, 1943–1945* (1968), p. 534.
544 "utterly opposed . . .": Stimson Diary, Sept. 6, 1944, Yale University.
544 "I had barely got . . .": John Morton Blum, *From the Morgenthau Diaries* (1967), vol. III, p. 369.
544 "I'm all for disarming . . .": Lord Moran, *Churchill—The Struggle for Survival, 1940–1965* (1960), p. 190.
544 "After all, the future . . .": Blum, *From the Morgenthau Diaries,* vol. III, p. 371.
544 "converting Germany into . . .": ibid., p. 372.
544 "We haven't had a talk . . .": ibid.
544 "the high spot . . .": ibid., p. 373.
544 "I never heard . . .": *TIR,* p. 334.
545 "whenever and wherever possible": James MacGregor Burns, *Roosevelt: The Soldier of Freedom* (1970), p. 519.

545 WC restless during film: Martin Gilbert, *Winston S. Churchill*, vol. VII, *Road to Victory, 1941–1945* (1986), p. 964.
545 "With all my heart . . .": Jim Bishop, *FDR's Last Year* (1974), p. 143.
545 FDR seemed depressed: ibid., p. 139.
545 "He seems to have . . .": Gilbert, *Churchill*, vol. VII, p. 969.
545 "did not even greet him": Winston S. Churchill, *The Second World War*, vol. VI, *Triumph and Tragedy* (1953), p. 142.
545 "You must know . . .": ibid.
545 ". . . no open breach . . .": Robert E. Sherwood, *Roosevelt and Hopkins* (1948), p. 814.
546 "She is a wonderful combination . . .": *Churchill & Roosevelt Correspondence*, vol. III, p. 332.
546 "My time slips away . . .": Lash, *World of Love*, p. 139.
546 bomb ready by August 1945: Gilbert, *Churchill*, vol. VII, p. 969.
546 "might perhaps . . .": ibid., p. 970.
546 "the utmost secrecy": ibid.
546 "The President under . . .": Hassett, *Off the Record*, p. 272.
547 "with his braces . . .": Rosenman, *Working with Roosevelt*, p. 474.
547 In the banquet hall: *Time*, Oct. 2, 1944, p. 21.
547 "Do you think Pa . . .": Rosenman, *Working with Roosevelt*, p. 478.
547 "Well, here we are . . .": Franklin D. Roosevelt, *Public Papers and Addresses of Franklin D. Roosevelt, 1944* (1950), p. 284.
548 "The whole purpose . . ."; "Now, imitation may be . . .": ibid., p. 285.
548 One teamster was so excited: A. Merriman Smith, *Thank you, Mr. President* (1946), p. 155.
548 "The Old Master . . .": *Time*, Oct. 2, 1944, p. 21.
548 "These Republican leaders . . . ": Franklin D. Roosevelt, *Public Papers and Addresses, 1944*, p. 290.
548 "even the stoniest . . .": *Time*, Oct. 2, 1944, p. 22.
548 In closing: Franklin D. Roosevelt, *Public Papers and Addresses, 1944*, p. 291.
549 "There were tears . . .": Rosenman, *Working with Roosevelt*, p. 478.
549 "The 1944 campaign . . .": *Time*, Oct. 2, 1944, p. 22.
549 "Let's not be squeamish . . .": quoted in Jim Bishop, *FDR's Last Year* (1974), p. 157.
549 train reached Brooklyn: Hassett, *Off the Record*, p. 278.
549 Dr. McIntire pleaded: Ross McIntire, *White House Physician* (1946), p. 207.
549 He had rooted for the Dodgers: Hassett, *Off the Record*, p. 279.
550 complete change of clothes: *The Woman*, May 1949, p. 112.
550 first time FDR had seen it: Hassett, *Off the Record*, p. 279.
550 FDR at ER's apartment: *TIR*, p. 337.
550 "It was the only occasion . . .": Grace Tully, *F.D.R., My Boss* (1949), p. 282.
550 "a map of the world . . .": Franklin D. Roosevelt, *Public Papers and Addresses, 1944*, p. 344.
551 Tully wondered: Tully, *F.D.R.*, p. 282.
551 "Peace, like war . . .": Franklin D. Roosevelt, *Public Papers and Addresses, 1944*, p. 350.
551 "no trace . . .": Hassett, *Off the Record*, p. 282.
551 "Not for a long time . . .": *NYT*, Oct. 25, 1944, p. 23.
551 "Their enthusiasm for him . . .": ER interview, Graff Papers, FDRL.
552 "brisk as a bee . . .": Hassett, *Off the Record*, p. 287.
552 "the news from the Pacific . . .": *MD*, Oct. 15, 1944.
552 "There were extremely light . . .": Frank Freidel, *Franklin D. Roosevelt: A Rendezvous with Destiny* (1990), p. 563.
552 "painful memories": Sherwood, *Roosevelt and Hopkins*, p. 829.
552 "I am sure . . . ": ibid., pp. 829–30.
552 "swirled around among . . .": Smith, *Thank You*, p. 159.
552 election results: Harold Gosnell, *Champion Campaigner* (1952), pp. 211–12.
553 "It looks like . . .": Franklin D. Roosevelt, *Public Papers and Addresses, 1944*, p. 414.
553 "sought sanctuary . . .": Hassett, *Off the Record*, p. 294.
553 "the graceless Dewey"; ". . . son of a bitch": ibid.
553 "Word has just come . . .": John Roosevelt to FDR, Nov. 8, 1944, box 20, Roosevelt Family Papers Donated by the Children, FDRL.

CHAPTER TWENTY-TWO: "So Darned Busy"

554 Millions of people: Joseph P. Lash, *A World of Love: Eleanor Roosevelt and Her Friends, 1943–1962* (1984), p. 146.
554 "the tremendously increased . . .": ibid., p. 149.
554 "Maybe I'd do . . .": ibid., p. 150.
554 "If I did I'd lose . . .": ibid.
555 "inadequate" . . . "great weariness . . .": ibid.
555 one-third of civilian labor force: Richard Polenberg, ed., *America at War* (1972), p. 131.
555 79 percent said yes: *LHJ,* June 1944, p. 23.
555 "At the end . . .": Ruth Milkman, *The Dynamics of Gender at Work* (1987), p. 103.
555 "There are two things . . .": *War Department Educational Manual* (1944), p. 1, Record, Group 56, National Archives, Washington, D.C.
556 "Where I come from . . .": ibid., p. 23.
556 "Women ought to be delighted . . .": Frieda Miller, "Women's Conference on War and Postwar Adjustments of Women Workers," Dec. 1–5, 1944, Record Group 86, National Archives, Washington, D.C.
556 "it's the only lasting . . .": George Q. Flynn, *The Mess in Washington* (1979), p. 182.
556 "My position is to go . . .": *LHJ,* June 1944, p. 22.
556 "Am I planning . . .": ibid., p. 23.
556 "I really believe . . .": *Women's Home Companion,* July 1944, p. 24.
556 "found herself an authoress . . .": *MD,* Oct. 20, 1944.
557 "gladly relinquish . . .": *NYT,* April 25, 1944, p. 20.
557 "a good proportion": *NYT,* April 24, 1944, p. 15.
557 "To give anyone who wants . . .": *NYT,* April 25, 1944.
557 "Women are fully as capable . . .": *NYT,* Oct. 12, 1944, p. 42.
557 "industry must not . . .": *NYT,* Dec. 10, 1944, p. 42.
557 layoff rate 75 percent higher: Flynn, *Mess in Washington,* p. 181.
557 "Now that War . . .": Milkman, *The Dynamics of Gender at Work,* p. 141.
557 Brewster Aeronautical: Walter Reuther to ER, July 11, 1944, ER Microfilm Collection, FDRL; *NYT,* May 21, 1944, p. 35.
558 "whereby every worker . . .": *MD,* Sept. 20, 1944.
558 "for dangerous leakages . . .": Bruce Catton, *The War Lords of Washington* (1969), p. 231.
558 "Many people seem . . .": Byron Fairchild and Jonathan Grossman, *The Army and Industrial Manpower* (1959), p. 80.
558 "It's tough to see . . .": Catton, *War Lords,* pp. 267–68.
558 ". . . Insufficient production . . .": ibid., p. 268.
559 "one of the most . . .": Donald M. Nelson, *Arsenal of Democracy* (1946), p. 409.
559 "neither facts nor logic . . .": Catton, *War Lords,* p. 232.
559 "was motivated by . . .": ibid., p. 253.
559 "You know what they're doing . . .": ibid, p. 290.
560 "the war within a war": Nelson, *Arsenal of Democracy,* p. 43.
560 Nelson on mission to China: ibid., pp. 412–13.
560 "I don't have to go": Lash, *World of Love,* p. 151.
560 "You and Joe . . .": ibid., p. 147.
560 "Mrs. Roosevelt's feelings . . .": ibid., pp. 154–55.
560 "But the weighing . . .": ibid.
561 "A new LL crisis . . .": AB to John Boettiger, Nov. 24, 1944, box 6, Boettiger Papers, FDRL.
561 "I am very depressed . . .": Lash, *World of Love,* p. 157.
561 At Warm Springs: Theo Lippman, Jr., *The Squire of Warm Springs* (1977), pp. 15–17.
561 "a little house . . .": ibid., p. 199.
561 Lucy in guest cottage: Lippman, Jr., *Squire,* p. 15.
562 "You know . . .": Bernard Asbell, *The FDR Memoirs* (1973), p. 413.
562 ". . . Mother was not capable . . .": ibid.
562 "I realize very well . . .": ER to FDR, Dec. 4, 1944, box 16, Roosevelt Family Papers Donated by the Children, FDRL.
562 "The reason I feel . . .": ibid.

563 "Now if Clayton . . .": ER to FDR, Dec 5, 1944, box 16, Roosevelt Family Papers Donated by the Children, FDRL.
563 "She insisted . . .": interview with Howard Bruenn.
563 ". . . any real pressure on Winston? . . .": ER to FDR, Dec. 6, 1944, box 16, Roosevelt Family Papers Donated by the Children, FDRL.
563 FDR let Stimson know: Stimson Diary, Dec. 12, 1944, Yale University; Robert E. Sherwood, *Roosevelt and Hopkins* (1948), p. 835.
563 "Of course I want you . . .": FDR to Ickes, Dec. 9, 1944, box 75, PSF, FDRL.
564 "Your letter makes me . . .": Ickes to FDR, Dec. 13, 1944, box 75, PSF, FDRL.
564 visibly pleased: interview with Howard Bruenn.
564 Her aunt Tissie: ER to FDR, Dec. 18, 1944, box 16, Roosevelt Family Papers Donated by the Children, FDRL.
564 "sounds as though . . .": *MD,* Dec. 19, 1944.
564 December 16: Martin Gilbert, *The Second World War* (1989), p. 618.
564 "hunched in his chair . . .": William L. Shirer, *The Rise and Fall of the Third Reich* (1960), p. 1091.
565 "In great stress . . .": Forrest C. Pogue, *George C. Marshall: Organizer of Victory, 1943–1945* (1973), p. 486.
565 "He has been extremely . . .": Stimson Diary, Dec. 31, 1944, Yale University.
565 "I cannot help thinking . . .": *MD,* Dec. 20, 1944.
565 "an amazing performance": Eric Larrabee, *Commander in Chief* (1987), p. 488.
565 casualties: Shirer, *Rise and Fall,* pp. 1095–96.
565 "without regard to color . . .": Ulysses G. Lee, *The Employment of Negro Troops* (1966), p. 689.
566 four thousand volunteered: ibid., p. 693.
566 "We've been giving . . .": Jean Byers, "A Study of the Negro in Military Service," War Department Study, June 1947, p. 165.
566 "It is hard . . .": ibid., p. 89.
566 "My brother is now . . .": Mrs. Lewis to FDR, March 15, 1944, box 6, OF 93, FDRL.
566 "It is hard to decide . . .": *NR,* March 13, 1944, p. 342.
566 "Negro is too dumb to fight": *PC,* March 18, 1944, p. 1.
566 "to master . . ."; "It so happens . . .": Stimson to Congressman Fish, Feb. 19, 1944, *CR,* p. 2007.
567 In the 1940s: Byers, "Negro in Military Service," pp. 16–19.
567 "The consensus . . .": Roy Wilkins to FDR, March 9, 1944, box 6, OF 93, FDRL.
567 "He considers it . . .": *Crisis,* Sept. 1944, p. 290.
567 First volunteers: Byers, "Negro in Military Service," p. 165.
567 "They were used . . .": ibid., p. 167.
567 "When I heard about it . . .": ibid., p. 174.
567 "You might think . . .": ibid., p. 175.
568 "They are aggressive . . .": ibid., p. 170.
568 "I am mighty proud . . .": ibid.
568 "pretty, quiet and hard . . .": Lash, *World of Love,* p. 161.
568 "Next year . . .": Elliott Roosevelt and James Brough, *A Rendezvous with Destiny: The Roosevelts in the White House* (1975), p. 391.
568 "Father spoke . . .": Elliott Roosevelt and James Brough, *An Untold Story: The Roosevelts of Hyde Park* (1973), p. 307.
568 "the most extraordinarily . . .": interview with Elliott Roosevelt.
569 "I was delighted . . ."; "I hope . . .": Elliott Roosevelt and Brough, *Untold Story,* p. 308.

CHAPTER TWENTY-THREE: "It Is Good to Be Home"

570 "President in gleeful . . .": William D. Hassett, *Off the Record with F.D.R.* (1958), p. 309.
570 "very well": Smith conference notes, Jan. 1, 1945, Harold Smith Papers, FDRL.
570 "He had the pallor . . .": quoted in *Collier's,* Sept. 21, 1946, pp. 102–3.
570 "from looking pretty well . . .": Perkins, *OH,* Columbia University.
571 story of two senators: interview with Eliot Janeway.
571 "realizing full well . . .": *TIR,* p. 339; see also ER interview, Graff Papers, FDRL.

571 "bulged at the corners . . .": *TIR,* p. 339.
571 Jimmy later recalled: interview with James Roosevelt.
572 "Housekeeper Rejects . . .": *NYT,* Jan. 20, 1945, p. 1.
572 "We aren't going to have . . .": ibid.
572 joked with AB and Grace: Grace Tully, *F.D.R., My Boss* (1949), p. 115.
572 "plain food . . .": ibid.
572 "Who is there here . . .": Samuel I. Rosenman, *Working with Roosevelt* (1952), p. 516.
572 "Dog catchers have . . .": Michael F. Reilly, *Reilly of the White House* (1947), p. 516.
572 "The day was bitterly cold . . .": Katherine Marshall, *Together* (1946), p. 232.
572 "a test of courage . . .": Franklin D. Roosevelt, *Public Papers and Addresses of Franklin D. Roosevelt, 1945* (1950), p. 523.
572 two thousand guests, largest luncheon: Bess Furman, *Washington By-Line* (1949), p. 312; *NYT,* Jan. 21, 1945, p. 3.
572 "He was thoroughly chilled . . .": James Roosevelt and Sidney Schalett, *Affectionately, F.D.R.* (1959), p. 355.
573 "Oh, Mrs. Perkins . . .": Perkins, *OH,* Columbia University.
573 chickens Mrs. Nesbitt had bought: Victoria Henrietta Nesbitt, *White House Diary* (1948), p. 300.
573 "Mrs. Roosevelt, I wish to ask . . .": Katherine Marshall, *Together,* p. 232.
573 "would finally be going . . .": Lillian Rogers Parks, *The Roosevelts: A Family in Turmoil* (1981), p. 261.
573 "If you go . . .": *TIR,* p. 339.
573 ". . . Anna can do things . . .": Perkins, *OH,* Columbia University.
574 "I wanted desperately . . .": Bernard Asbell, *Mother and Daughter* (1988), pp. 181–82.
574 "I am tired and very depressed . . .": Joseph P. Lash, *A World of Love: Eleanor Roosevelt and Her Friends, 1943–1962* (1984), p. 164.
574 "Over there . . .": Asbell, *Mother and Daughter,* p. 187.
574 "Ocean voyage is . . .": AB to John Boettiger, Jan. 27, 1945, box 6, Boettiger Papers, FDRL.
574 "Oh darling . . .": ibid.
574 "a lot of little gadgets": AB to John Boettiger, Jan. 30, 1945, box 6, Boettiger Papers, FDRL.
574 five cakes: ibid.
575 brass ashtray: *Foreign Relations of the United States: The Conferences at Malta and Yalta, 1945* (1955).
575 "Anna made the dinner . . .": James F. Byrnes, *Speaking Frankly* (1947), p. 22.
575 "Our birthday dinner . . .": AB to John Boettiger, Jan. 31, 1945, box 6, Boettiger Papers, FDRL.
575 radio silence: AB notes on Yalta, Feb. 1, 1945, box 84, Halsted Papers, FDRL.
575 "Of course Jones . . .": Lash, *World of Love,* p. 165.
575 "a very sad situation . . .": AB to John Boettiger, Feb. 6, 1945, box 6, Boettiger Papers, FDRL.
575 WC running a temperature: Lord Moran, *Churchill—The Struggle for Survival, 1940–1965* (1966), p. 232.
575 "like a poor hot pink . . .": Martin Gilbert, *Winston S. Churchill,* vol. VII, *Road to Victory* (1986), p. 1163.
576 "in the doldrums": Moran, *Churchill,* p. 233.
576 "It is not the flesh . . .": ibid., p. 232.
576 "sharing his secret . . ."; "someone in whom . . .": ibid., p. 174.
576 "He was so weak . . .": Edward Stettinius, *Roosevelt and the Russians* (1949), p. 57.
576 "the terrible change in him": Sarah Churchill, *A Thread in the Tapestry* (1967), p. 76.
576 "my friend has arrived . . .": Gilbert, *Churchill,* vol. VII, p. 1167.
576 "bright charm . . .": Sarah Churchill, *Thread in Tapestry,* p. 76.
576 "He must have noticed . . .": Moran, *Churchill.* p. 234.
576 "Harry demanded a drink . . .": AB notes on Yalta, Feb. 2, 1945, box 84, Halsted Papers, FDRL.
577 "as in her old age . . .": Moran, *Churchill,* p. 234.
577 "so that he could sleep . . .": AB notes on Yalta, Feb. 3, 1945, box 84, Halsted Papers, FDRL.
577 "tough old bird . . .": ibid.

577 Relaxed and fortified: Sarah Churchill, *Thread in Tapestry,* p. 78.
577 Lividia Palace: Stettinius, *Roosevelt and the Russians,* pp. 81–82.
577 "a block and a half away": AB notes on Yalta, Feb. 3, 1945, box 84, Halsted Papers, FDRL.
577 Russian generals talked from maps: Stettinius, *Roosevelt and the Russians,* p. 239.
578 "This is the first time . . .": ibid., p. 240.
578 "sitting on tacks . . .": AB notes on Yalta, Feb. 4, 1945, box 84, Halsted Papers, FDRL.
578 "Fire was shooting . . .": ibid.
578 "Stalin made it . . .": Charles Bohlen, minutes, Tripartite Dinner Meeting, 8:30 p.m., William Rigdon Papers, FDRL.
578 "FDR seemed happy . . .": AB notes, Feb. 4, 1945, box 84, Halsted Papers, FDRL.
579 "Life is quickly . . .": AB notes, Feb. 5, 1945, box 84, Halsted Papers, FDRL.
579 "to get his version . . .": ibid.
579 "Just between you and me . . ."; "I have found out through Bruenn . . .": AB to John Boettiger, Feb. 6, 1945, box 6, Boettiger Papers, FDRL.
579 "I am using . . .": ibid.
580 "I wish Harry . . .": Moran, *Churchill,* p. 241.
580 HH persuaded FDR: Robert E. Sherwood, *Roosevelt and Hopkins* (1948), p. 859.
580 Dumbarton Oaks: ibid., p. 854.
581 issue not so easy for FDR: ibid., pp. 855–57.
581 "events were in the saddle": "it would have taken . . .": Averell Harriman and Elie Abel, *Special Envoy to Churchill and Stalin, 1941–1946* (1975), p. 405.
581 "The most important matter . . .": James MacGregor Burns, *Roosevelt: The Soldier of Freedom* (1970), p. 570.
581 "The Prime Minister . . .": ibid.
581 "reorganized on a broader . . .": ibid., p. 572.
582 "so elastic . . .": William Leahy, *I Was There* (1950), pp. 315–16.
582 "I know, Bill . . .": ibid.
582 "naïvete, ignorance . . .": Burns, *Soldier of Freedom,* p. 572.
582 FDR negotiated secret agreement: Stettinius, *Roosevelt and the Russians,* p. 255.
582 forty-five standing toasts: Bohlen, minutes, Tripartite Dinner, William Rigdon Papers, FDRL.
582 "We have wound up . . .": Lash, *World of Love,* p. 168.
583 "LL was really so happy . . .": John Boettiger to AB, Feb. 11, 1945, box 6, Boettiger Papers, FDRL.
583 "What a lonesome barn . . .": John Boettiger to AB, Jan. 23, 1945, box 6, Boettiger Papers, FDRL.
583 "Lt. Conrad came to lunch . . .": Lash, *World of Love,* p. 167.
583 "All the world looks smiling! . . .": ibid., p. 168.
583 mood of "supreme exultation": Sherwood, *Roosevelt and Hopkins,* p. 869.
583 "a landmark . . ."; "to justify or surpass . . .": quoted in Ross McIntire, *White House Physician* (1946), p. 221.
583 "We really believed . . .": Sherwood, *Roosevelt and Hopkins,* p. 870.
583 "Why did Harry . . ."; "The president was good and mad . . .": interview with Robert Hopkins.
584 "One moment he was breathing . . .": AB notes on Yalta, Feb. 20, 1945, box 84, Halsted Papers, FDRL.
584 "He was very, very . . ."; "I shall miss him . . .": interview with Howard Bruenn.
584 "Many in Washington . . .": Rosenman, *Roosevelt and Hopkins,* p. 524.
584 "It was a sorry ship . . ."; "none too soon": ibid., p. 527.
584 "leading you to forget": ER interview, Graff Papers, FDRL.
584 "Look at the communiqué . . .": Elliott Roosevelt, *As He Saw It* (1946), p. 246.
585 "To a doctor's eye . . .": Moran, *Churchill,* p. 242.
585 "The signs of deterioration . . .": Harriman and Abel, *Special Envoy,* p. 389.
585 "Nevertheless he had blocked . . .": ibid.
585 "It was my feeling . . .": Leahy, *I Was There,* p. 321.
585 Eden later acknowledged: Anthony Eden, *The Memoirs of Anthony Eden, Earl of Avon: The Reckoning* (1965), p. 594.
585 "If Stalin was determined . . .": Harriman and Abel, *Special Envoy,* p. 389.
586 first time FDR wheeled down aisle: Perkins, *OH,* Columbia University.

586 "I hope you will pardon me . . .": Rosenman, *Working with Roosevelt,* p. 527.
586 "It was the first . . .": Perkins, *OH,* Columbia University.
587 "accidentally . . .": Hugh Gregory Gallagher, *FDR's Splendid Deception* (1985), pp. 94, 96.
587 Roosevelt delivered: *MD,* March 1, 1945.
587 "First of all . . .": Rosenman, *Roosevelt and Hopkins,* p. 536.
587 "one of his major mistakes . . .": ibid., p. 537.
587 looked "really well": Perkins, *OH,* Columbia University.
588 "He looked much older . . ." . . . ". . . more strength in him . . .": J. W. Pickergill and D. F. Foster, eds., *The Mackenzie King Record,* vol. II, *1944–1945* (1968), p. 325.
588 "seemed a little embarrassed": ibid., p. 329.
588 "I saw the President . . .": Leon Henderson diary, March 13, 1945, Henderson Papers, FDRL.
588 "profoundly depressed . . .": Sherwood, *Roosevelt and Hopkins,* p. 880.
588 "The other meetings . . .": John Boettiger to AB, Feb. 15, 1945, box 6, Boettiger Papers, FDRL.
589 "But for weeks now . . .": *Life,* March 5, 1945, p. 96.
589 "Anna has . . .": quoted in ibid., p. 100.
589 "For purposes of public consumption . . .": ibid., p. 108.
589 "He seemed to feel . . .": Smith conference notes, March 12, 1945, Harold Smith Papers, FDRL.
589 "Don't tell anyone . . .": Omar Bradley and Clay Blair, *A General's Life* (1983), pp. 521–22.
589 more than 6,000 . . . : Robert Meyer, Jr. *The Stars and Stripes: Story of World War II* (1960), pp. 376–78.
590 Only two hundred: Samuel Elliot Morison, *The Two-Ocean War* (1963), p. 524.
590 "practically every physicist of standing . . .": Stimson Diary, March 15, 1945, Yale University.
590 "with subsequent notice . . .": Peter Wyden, *Day One: Before Hiroshima and After* (1984), p. 126.
590 Stimson argued: Stimson Diary, March 15, 1945, Yale University.
591 "Do you think so?": Smith conference notes, March 12, 1945, Harold Smith Papers, FDRL.
591 "something about his face . . .": Elizabeth Shoumatoff, *FDR's Unfinished Portrait* (1990), p. 98.
591 Hick once observed: LH unpublished manuscript, box 1, LH Papers, FDRL.
591 "he was like a little boy . . .": Mrs. Kermit Roosevelt quoted in ibid.
591 "Never was there anything . . .": AH on Lucy.
591 "I doubt that father felt . . .": James Roosevelt, *My Parents* (1976), p. 103.
591 "strictly a family affair . . .": Pickergill and Foster, eds., *Mackenzie King Record,* p. 334.
592 "because I felt the pressure . . .": AB draft letter to the editor concerning column "FDR Romance," n.d., box 84, Halsted Papers, FDRL.
592 "wonderful person . . .": AB to Margaret Suckley, Oct. 28, 1948, box 74, Halsted Papers, FDRL.
592 "I was grateful to her . . .": AB draft letter to the editor concerning column "FDR Romance," n.d., box 84, Halsted Papers, FDRL.
592 "the complete contrast . . .": Hassett, *Off the Record,* pp. 323–24.
592 "Thus another milestone . . .": ibid.
592 "This world of young people . . .": *MD,* March 21, 1945.
592 "like a boy on vacation . . .": Jim Bishop, *FDR's Last Year* (1974), p. 485.
593 "the head going . . .": quoted in ibid., p. 520.
593 LH quit her job: Doris Faber, *The Life of Lorena Hickok* (1980), p. 300.
593 "The goodbyes . . .": ibid., pp. 300–301.
593 LH had pretended: LH unpublished manuscript, box 1, LH Papers, FDRL.
594 "the office would be packed . . .": ibid.
594 "Later I came to realize . . .": LH to Tommy, July 23, 1949, LH Papers, FDRL.
594 "Soon after the inaugural ceremonies . . .": *TIR,* p. 78.

CHAPTER TWENTY-FOUR: "Everybody Is Crying"

595 "Hope he responds . . .": William D. Hassett, *Off the Record with F.D.R.* (1958), p. 326.
595 "Everything is just . . .": Joseph P. Lash, *A World of Love: Eleanor Roosevelt and Her Friends, 1943–1962* (1984), p. 177.
595 He wanted her to travel: ibid., p. 174; J. W. Pickergill and D. F. Foster, eds., *Mackenzie King Record,* vol. II, *1944–1945* (1968), p. 328.
596 "is going to get . . .": quoted in Samuel I. Rosenman, *Working with Roosevelt* (1952), p. 546.
596 "I have long wanted . . ."; "The war in Europe . . .": *Collier's,* Sept. 21, 1946, p. 103.
596 "suddenly realized . . .": *TIR,* p. 343.
597 "to enjoy life . . ." . . . "No, I like . . .": *MD,* April 20, 1945.
597 "the most beautiful . . ." . . . "That sense . . .": ibid.,
597 "No, it looks dead . . .": ibid.
597 "He never liked . . .": ibid.
597 "Does that sound . . .": Joseph P. Lash, *Eleanor and Franklin* (1971), p. 719.
597 "I cannot conceal . . .": *Churchill & Roosevelt: The Complete Correspondence* (1984), vol. III, pp. 595–96.
597 "Our friendship . . .": ibid., p. 574.
598 "had failed to erase . . .": Grace Tully, *F.D.R., My Boss* (1949), p. 356.
598 "Did you get any rest . . .": ibid.
598 "usual leisure time . . .": ibid., p. 358.
598 "He was very amusing . . .": ER interview, Graff Papers, FDRL.
598 "The President was the worst . . .": Bernard Asbell, *When F.D.R. Died* (1961), p. 14.
598 "pretty simple, despite . . .": Michael F. Reilly, *Reilly of the White House* (1947), pp. 226–27.
598 "Warm Springs had saved . . ."; "it wasn't just a matter . . .": ibid.
599 "The days flowed . . .": Margaret Suckley, *OH,* FDRL.
599 "He was in fine form . . .": ibid.
599 "It was a beautiful . . .": A. Merriman Smith, *Thank You, Mr. President* (1946), p. 184.
599 "That is not even subtle": ibid., p. 185.
599 "As a matter of fact . . .": Asbell, *When F.D.R. Died,* p. 28.
599 "I forgot to tell you . . ."; "Much love . . .": Lash, *World of Love,* pp. 181–82.
600 "Nothing in sight . . ."; "Nobody loves us . . .": Shoumatoff, *FDR's Unfinished Portrait* (1990), p. 100.
600 "full of jokes . . .": ibid.
600 "profile as beautiful . . .": ibid., pp. 102–3.
600 "happy kids enjoying . . .": Lillian Rogers Parks, *The Roosevelts: A Family in Turmoil* (1981), p. 262.
600 "As I reined in . . .": A. Merriman Smith, *Thank You,* p. 186.
601 "beautiful, slightly flushed face . . .": Shoumatoff, *FDR's Portrait,* p. 108.
601 "I remember so clearly . . .": Margaret Suckley, *OH,* FDRL.
601 "a good speech": Hassett, *Off the Record,* p. 333.
601 "The only limit . . .": James MacGregor Burns, *Roosevelt: The Soldier of Freedom* (1970), p. 597.
601 "I was terribly shocked . . .": John Morton Blum, *From the Morgenthau Diaries,* vol. III (1967), p. 416.
601 "He was full of this . . .": AH interview, Graff Papers, FDRL.
601 "an encompassing tension . . .": Shoumatoff, *FDR's Portrait,* p. 114.
601 "The sky was clear . . .": Margaret Suckley, *OH,* FDRL.
602 "exceptionally good color": Shoumatoff, *FDR's Portrait,* p. 115.
602 "surprisingly well . . .": Margaret Suckley, *OH,* FDRL.
602 ". . . through with your laundry . . .": Parks, *Family in Turmoil,* p. 263.
602 "A typical State Department letter . . .": Asbell, When *F.D.R. Died,* p. 33.
602 " . . . there is where I make a law": Hassett, *Off the Record,* p. 334.
602 "The last I remember . . .": Asbell, *When F.D.R. Died,* p. 36.
602 "We've got . . ."; "he raised his right hand . . .": Shoumatoff, *FDR's Portrait,* p. 117.
602 "He looked at me . . .": Margaret Suckley, *OH,* FDRL.
602 "It was a bolt . . .": *Navy Medicine,* March–April 1990, p. 13.

602 "The confusion..." ..."We must pack up and go...": Shoumatoff, *FDR's Portrait,* pp. 118–19.
602 "which wasn't much": *Navy Medicine,* March–April 1990, p. 13.
603 tortured breathing: Tully, *F.D.R.,* p. 362.
603 "All you could hear...": Asbell, *When F.D.R. Died,* p. 45.
603 "His eyes were closed...": Hassett, *Off the Record,* p. 335.
603 "We put a shot...": *Navy Medicine,* March–April 1990, p. 13.
603 "not alarmed": *TIR,* p. 343.
603 "unusually smart": Asbell, *When F.D.R. Died,* p. 50.
603 "a quick start": ibid., p. 51.
603 "very much upset...": *TIR,* p. 344.
603 "Now I'm called back...": Asbell, *When F.D.R. Died,* p. 51.
603 "I got into the car...": *TIR,* p. 344.
604 "I hadn't been there...": AH interview, Bernard Asbell.
604 "He did his job...": *NYT,* April 13, 1945, p. 3.
604 presence of mind to call: *Newsweek,* April 23, 1945, p. 40.
604 "Harry, the President is dead...": David McCullough, *Truman* (1992), p. 342.
604 "Is there anything...": ibid.
604 ER told Truman she was planning: ibid.
604 "It was a very somber group...": Stimson Diary, April 12, 1945, Yale University.
605 "A trooper to the last": Bess Furman, *Washington By-Line* (1949), p. 314.
605 "strode with her usual...": *Time,* April 23, 1945, p. 18.
605 "You and I have...": Robert E. Sherwood, *Roosevelt and Hopkins* (1948), p. 880.
605 "Oh, we all know...": ibid., pp. 880–81.
605 "I felt as if...": Winston S. Churchill, *The Second World War,* vol. VI, *Triumph and Tragedy* (1953), p. 412.
605 "deeply distressed": Averell Harriman and Elie Abel, *Special Envoy to Churchill and Stalin, 1941–1946* (1975), p. 440.
605 "and feeling as...": Roy Hooper, *Americans Remember the Home Front* (1992, abridged ed.), p. 228.
606 "That first flash...": I. F. Stone, *The War Years, 1939–1945* (1988), p. 273.
606 "Everybody left...": Hooper, *Americans Remember,* p. 229.
606 "God, there were...": ibid., p. 227.
606 "I am too shocked...": Asbell, *When F.D.R. Died,* p. 117.
606 "The President's death...": ibid., p. 117.
606 "it is tragic...": *BEA,* April 14, 1945, p. 4.
606 "Men will thank God...": *NYT,* April 13, 1945, p. 18.
606 WC said like opening champagne: John Gunther, *Roosevelt in Retrospect* (1950), p. 18.
606 "no conception of the office...": Richard E. Neustadt, *Presidential Power and the Modern Presidency* (1990), p. 136.
606 "Wouldn't you be...": Gunther, *Roosevelt in Retrospect,* p. 49.
607 "Under Roosevelt...": William Leuchtenburg, *Franklin D. Roosevelt and the New Deal* (1963), p. 327.
607 "He was one of the few...": Isaiah Berlin, *Personal Impressions* (1981), p. 26.
608 contributed nearly: compiled from charts in R. Elberton Smith, *The Army and Economic Mobilization* (1959), pp. 9–27; also Geoffrey Perrett, *Days of Sadness, Years of Triumph* (1973), p. 399.
608 "There is little doubt...": Smith, *The Army and Economic Mobilization,* p. 706.
608 "The figures are all...": Bruce Catton, *The War Lords of Washington* (1969), p. 306.
608 "I am like a cat...": James MacGregor Burns, *Leadership* (1978), p. 281.
609 Never once: Stimson Diary, April 14, 1945, Yale University.
609 action over the protest: Eric Larrabee, *Commander in Chief* (1987), p. 15.
609 "the arsenal...": interview with Joe Rauh.
610 "None of these proposals...": David S. Wyman, *The Abandonment of the Jews: America and the Holocaust, 1941–1945* (1984), p. 335.
610 "More than any...": Larrabee, *Commander in Chief,* p. 644
611 calm and composed; Tully recounted her schedule: Tully, *F.D.R.,* p. 366.
611 Laura began to speak: Bernard Asbell, *Mother and Daughter* (1988), p. 186.
611 "It was a malicious thing...": interview with Eleanor Wotkyns.

611 "Eleanor would have . . .": Jim Bishop, *FDR's Last Year* (1974), p. 635.
611 alone with her husband; eyes dry: Tully, *F.D.R.*, p. 366.
611 Had Franklin seen Lucy: Asbell, *Mother and Daughter*, p. 186.
611 "At a time like that . . .": Asbell, *When F.D.R. Died*, p. 155.
612 valet tenderly parted the hair: Bishop, *Last Year*, p. 621.
612 "Oh, he was handsome . . .": Asbell, *When F.D.R. Died*, p. 130.
612 "They came from the fields . . .": *BEA*, April 15, 1945, p. 5.
612 "Men stood with their arms . . .": A. Merriman Smith, *Thank You*, pp. 193–94.
612 "I lay in my berth . . .": *TIR*, p. 345.
612 "Did Franklin ever . . .": Asbell, *When F.D.R. Died*, p. 153.
613 "my dear wife will . . .": Tully, *F.D.R.*, p. 367.
613 Truman later wrote: McCullough, *Truman*, p. 357.
613 "The streets were lined . . .": Katherine Marshall, *Together* (1946), p. 244.
613 White House in state of confusion: Victoria Henrietta Nesbitt, *White House Diary* (1948), p. 309.
613 "she would walk . . .": LH interview, Graff Papers, FDRL.
613 "Can you dispense . . ." . . ."Mrs. Roosevelt stood . . .": J. B. West, *Upstairs at the White House* (1973), p. 56.
614 "as stern as it could get . . .": AB notes attached to letter to JL, Jan. 28, 1972, box 36, Halsted Papers, FDRL.
614 "Mother was so upset . . .": ibid.
614 "Mother was angry with Anna . . .": Asbell, *Mother and Daughter*, p. 186.
614 "He was her husband . . .": interview with Curtis Roosevelt.
614 "It was the final roll call . . .": Furman, *Washington By-Line*, p. 313.
614 "stood almost fainting . . .": *Time*, April 23, 1945. p. 19.
614 "After everyone left . . .": interview with Milton Lipson.
615 "I'll never forget . . .": John R. Boettiger, Jr., *A Love in Shadow* (1978), p. 261.
615 "The funeral was . . .": Lash, *World of Love*, p. 184.
615 watching the workmen: *Time*, April 23, 1945, p. 20.
615 "He wanted me to plant . . .": *BEA*, April 14, 1945, p. 7.

CHAPTER TWENTY-FIVE: "A New Country Is Being Born"

616 "She had all . . .": Victoria Henrietta Nesbitt, *White House Diary* (1948), p. 311.
616 "My husband . . .": *MD*, April 18, 1945.
616 "a bit keyed up . . .": Joseph P. Lash, *A World of Love: Eleanor Roosevelt and Her Friends, 1943–1962* (1984), p. 188.
616 eyes were tired: *Newsweek*, April 30, 1945, p. 24.
616 "In the years . . .": *MD*, April 16, 1945.
617 "Mrs. Roosevelt . . .": interview with Alonzo Fields.
617 "The White House upstairs . . .": David McCullough, *Truman* (1992), p. 373.
617 ". . . like a ghost house . . .": J. B. West, *Upstairs at the White House* (1973), p. 58.
617 "Do you think . . .": Perkins, *OH*, FDRL.
617 "a Cabinet Minister . . .": quoted in Joan Hoff-Wilson and Marjorie Lightman, eds., *Without Precedent: The Life and Career of Eleanor Roosevelt* (1984), p. 11.
618 "Traces of grief . . .": *Newsweek*, April 30, 1945, p. 44.
618 "This is a . . .": ibid., p. 24.
618 "Nearly all that . . .": Lash, *World of Love*, p. 189.
618 "I never did . . .": ibid.
618 "I have always . . .": *MD*, April 20, 1945.
618 "We were all in tears": Nesbitt, *White House Diary*, p. 313.
618 ". . . When you have . . .": *MD*, April 20, 1945.
618 ". . . feeling of melancholy . . .": Eleanor Roosevelt, *On My Own* (1958), p. 1.
618 "without a backward glance": *Newsweek*, April 30, 1945, p. 44.
618 "Her departure . . .": *BEA*, April 20, 1945, p. 5.
619 "The story is over": *Newsweek*, April 30, 1945, p. 44.
619 "I am realizing . . .": *MD*, April 21, 1945.
619 "It has warmed . . .": *MD*, Sept. 9, 1945.
619 " 'He was like . . .' ": *MD*, Nov. 9, 1945.

619 "upsurge of love . . .": Lash, *World of Love,* p. 191.
619 "I find that . . .": ibid., p. 188.
619 "Franklin's greater wisdom . . .": ibid., p. 186.
619 "I think we had . . .": ibid., p. 190.
620 ER had decided: Eleanor Roosevelt, *On My Own,* p. 4.
620 "In talking . . .": Joseph P. Lash, *Eleanor: The Years Alone* (1972), p. 23.
620 "No one was . . .": *MD,* June 9, 1945.
620 "His legs straightened out . . .": J. William T. Youngs, *Eleanor Roosevelt: A Personal and Public Life* (1985), p. 205.
620 "V-E Day was . . .": Lash, *World of Love,* p. 191.
620 "I cannot help . . .": *NYT,* May 9, 1945, p. 18.
620 "It was without . . .": *The New Yorker Book of War Pieces* (1947), p. 474.
620 "the valiant and . . .": Winston S. Churchill, *The Second World War,* vol. VI, *The Grand Alliance* (1953), p. 376.
621 "with a sharp stab . . .": ibid., p. 583.
621 "It's no use pretending . . .": Lord Moran, *Churchill—The Struggle for Survival, 1940–1965* (1966), p. 310.
621 "His place . . .": *MD,* July 29, 1945.
621 ER had first learned: Joseph P. Lash, *Eleanor and Franklin* (1971), pp. 704–7.
621 "could not help . . .": *MD,* Aug. 10, 1945.
621 number of deaths: Martin Gilbert, *The Second World War* (1989), p. 746.
621 U.S. suffered the fewest: information obtained from the Naval Historical Center and the Army Historical Center, Washington, D.C.
622 "filled with very . . .": David Emblidge, ed., *Eleanor Roosevelt's "My Day,"* vol. II, *The Post-War Years, Her Acclaimed Columns, 1945–1952* (1990), p. 28.
622 "to be in a world . . .": Lash, *World of Love,* p. 202.
622 "the weight of suffering . . .": Emblidge, ed., *Eleanor Roosevelt's "My Day,"* p. 28.
622 "I miss Pa's voice . . .": ER to AB, Aug. 14, 1945, box 76, Halsted Papers, FDRL.
622 Now that the war . . .": *Independent Woman,* Oct. 1945, p. 274.
622 "We were thrilled . . .": Frankie Cooper interview, University of Southern California Collection.
622 Though her center: interview with Mary Willett.
622 "it was essential . . .": *MD,* Sept. 7, 1945.
622 "Many thought they . . .": ibid.
622 "My whole life . . .": *Detroit Free Press,* June 14, 1945, Reuther Library.
623 "My husband would . . .": Frankie Cooper interview, University of Southern California.
623 In 1946: Joseph C. Goulden, *The Best Years, 1945–1950* (1976), p. 41.
623 "Why do you want . . .": Mark Jonathan Harris, Franklin D. Mitchell, and Steven J. Schechter, *The Homefront: America During World War II* (1984), p. 231.
623 "My husband did not care . . .": ibid., p. 230.
623 "My God, this was . . .": ibid.
623 "Mothers that worked . . .": Frankie Cooper interview, University of Southern California.
623 *Senior Scholastic* poll: William H. Chafe, *The American Woman: Her Changing Social, Economic and Political Role, 1920–1970* (1972), p. 179.
623 "You can do . . .": Frankie Cooper interview, University of Southern California.
624 "The content of women's lives . . .": Chafe, *American Woman,* p. 195.
624 Over fifteen million: Richard Polenberg, ed., *America at War* (1972), p. 124.
624 more than seventeen million: Polenberg, ed., *America at War,* p. 26.
625 GNP: Goulden, *The Best Year,* p. 92.
625 "barriers to social . . .": Geoffrey Perrett, *Days of Sadness, Years of Triumph: The American People, 1939–1945* (1973), p. 11.
626 between 1940 and 1945: Jean Byers, "A Study of the Negro in Military Service," War Department Study, June 1947, pp. 41, 49.
626 "The Negro was no longer . . .": ibid., p. 50.
627 "in accordance with . . .": ibid., p. 237.
627 "The Navy of 1945 . . .": ibid.
627 "both possible . . .": ibid., p. 238.
627 "the Negro was considered . . .": ibid.
627 "the place was running . . .": C. R. Smith, *OH,* FDRL.

627 "more has happened . . .": Carey McWilliams, *Brothers Under the Skin* (1943), p. 4.
628 "the forgotten years . . .": *Journal of American History,* June 1968, p. 90.
628 "Oh, my God": Anna Rosenberg Hoffman, *OH,* FDRL.
628 "She would come in . . .": interview with Eleanor Seagraves.
629 "I think he let her . . .": Jonathan Daniels, *OH,* FDRL.
629 "Dear God, . . .": Jean Gould and Lorena Hickok, *Walter Reuther: Labor's Rugged Individualist* (1972), p. 345.
629 "I remember him . . .": Anna Rosenberg Hoffman, *OH,* FDRL.
629 "The truth of the matter . . .": James Roosevelt and Sidney Schalett, *Affectionately, F.D.R.* (1959), p. 313.
629 "You know, I've always . . .": Perkins interview, Graff Papers, FDRL.
629 "give her a whack . . .": James Halstead, *OH,* FDRL.
629 "certain parts . . .": AH, *OH,* Columbia University.
629 "She did love . . .": AH interview, Graff Papers, FDRL.
629 "I don't think . . .": Esther Lape interview, Lash Papers, FDRL.
629 "He might have been . . .": *TIR,* p. 349.
630 "She had indeed . . .": Lois Scharf, *ER: First Lady of American Liberalism* (1987), p. 140.
630 "a new country . . .": interview with James Roosevelt.
630 "a giant transference . . .": ibid.
630 "In the early days . . .": ibid.
630 "As I look back . . .": *MD,* Nov. 25, 1945.
631 "Thank you . . .": Lucy Rutherfurd to ER, May 2, 1945, ER Papers, FDRL.
631 "Your telephoning . . .": Lucy Rutherfurd to AB, May 9, 1945, box 70, Halsted Papers, FDRL.
632 "showing it only on . . .": John R. Boettiger, Jr., *A Love in Shadow,* p. 261.
632 "Perhaps, by revealing . . .": interview with John Boettiger, Jr.
632 "a flood of work . . . ": Bernard Asbell, *Mother and Daughter* (1988), p. 191.
632 end of an era: Boettiger, Jr., *Love in Shadow,* p. 263.
632 "I think it is . . .": Lash, *World of Love,* p. 205.
632 "all human beings . . .": *TIR,* p. 349.
633 "chose to remember . . .": Elliott Roosevelt and James Brough, *Mother R* (1977), p. 83.
633 "constantly talking . . .": Maureen Corr, *OH,* FDRL.
633 Truman telephoned ER: Elliott Roosevelt and Brough, *Mother R,* pp. 68–69.
633 "fear and trembling": ibid., p. 69.
633 "the most admired . . .": Garry Wills, *Certain Trumpets: The Call of Leaders* (1994), p. 62.
633 "They are not dead . . .": *MD,* April 25, 1945.

BIBLIOGRAPHY

Manuscripts and Personal Papers

MANUSCRIPT COLLECTIONS CONSULTED AT THE FRANKLIN D. ROOSEVELT LIBRARY

Boettiger, John
Coy, Wayne
Halsted, Anna Roosevelt
Hassett, William D.
Henderson, Leon
Hickok, Lorena
Hopkins, Harry
Kleeman, Rite Halle
Lape, Esther
Lash, Joseph P.
Morgenthau, Henry, Jr.
Rigdon, William
Roosevelt, Anna Eleanor
Roosevelt, Franklin D.
  Collection of Speeches
  Papers Pertaining to Family, Business, and Personal Affairs
  Office File
  President's Personal File
  President's Secretary's File
Roosevelt, James
Roosevelt Family: Papers Donated by the Children
Smith, Harold
Suckley, Margaret

HENRY L. STIMSON PAPERS, MANUSCRIPTS AND ARCHIVES, YALE UNIVERSITY LIBRARY

Oral History Transcripts

ELEANOR ROOSEVELT ORAL HISTORY TRANSCRIPTS, FRANKLIN D. ROOSEVELT LIBRARY

Bell, Minnewa
Corr, Maureen
Daniels, Jonathan
Douglas, Helen Gahagan
Halsted, Diana Hopkins
Halsted, James
Hight, Mr. and Mrs. John
Hirschhorn, Joan Morgenthau
Hoffman, Anna Rosenberg
Lash, Trude
Morgenthau, Henry, II
Murray, Pauli
Polier, Justine
Redmond, Roland

Roosevelt, Elliott
Roosevelt, Elliott, Jr.
Roosevelt, James
Rowe, James
Tugwell, Rexford
Wotkyns, Eleanor

ROBERT D. GRAFF INTERVIEWS, FRANKLIN D. ROOSEVELT LIBRARY
Halsted, Anna Roosevelt
Perkins, Frances
Roosevelt, Eleanor

COLUMBIA UNIVERSITY ORAL HISTORY TRANSCRIPTS
Halsted, Anna Roosevelt
Perkins, Frances
Rosenman, Samuel I.

Books

Acheson, Dean. *Present at the Creation.* New York: Norton, 1969.
Adamic, Louis. *Dinner at the White House.* New York: Harper, 1948.
Adams, Henry H. *Harry Hopkins: A Biography.* New York: Putnam, 1977.
Alinsky, Saul. *John L. Lewis: An Unauthorized Biography.* New York: Putnam, 1949.
Ambrose, Stephen E. *The Supreme Commander: The War Years of General Dwight D. Eisenhower.* Garden City, N.Y.: Doubleday, 1970.
———. *D-Day: The Climactic Battle of World War II.* New York: Simon & Schuster, 1994.
American Women at War, by 7 Newspaper Women. New York: National Association of Manufacturers, 1942.
Anderson, Jervis. *A. Philip Randolph: A Biographical Portrait.* New York: Harcourt Brace Jovanovich, 1973.
Armor, John, and Peter Wright. *Manzanar.* New York: Times Books, 1988.
Arnold, Henry H. *Global Mission.* New York: Harper, 1949.
Asbell, Bernard. *When F.D.R. Died.* New York: Holt, Rinehart & Winston, 1961.
———. *The FDR Memoirs.* Garden City, N.Y.: Doubleday, 1973.
———. *Mother and Daughter: The Letters of Eleanor and Anna Roosevelt.* New York: Fromm, 1988.
Baldwin, Hanson W. *The Crucial Years, 1939–1941.* New York: Harper & Row, 1976.
Barber, Noel. *The Week France Fell.* New York: Stein & Day, 1976.
Barnard, John. *Walter Reuther and the Rise of the Auto Workers.* Boston: Little, Brown, 1983.
Baruch, Bernard M. *Baruch: The Public Years.* New York: Holt, Rinehart & Winston, 1960.
Beard, Charles A. *President Roosevelt and the Coming of the War, 1941.* New Haven, Conn.: Yale University Press, 1948.
Beasley, Maurine H. *Eleanor Roosevelt and the Media: A Public Quest for Self-Fulfillment.* Chicago: University of Illinois Press, 1987.
Beasley, Norman. *Knudsen: A Biography.* New York: McGraw-Hill, 1947.
Bellow, Saul. *It All Adds Up: From the Dim Past to the Uncertain Future.* New York: Viking, 1994.
Berle, Adolf A. *Navigating the Rapids, 1918–1971: From the Papers of Adolf A. Berle.* Edited by Beatrice Bishop Berle and Travis Beal Jacobs. New York: Harcourt Brace Jovanovich, 1973.
Berlin, Isaiah. *Personal Impressions.* Edited by Henry Handy. New York: Viking, 1981.
———. *Washington Despatches 1941–45: Weekly Political Reports from the British Embassy.* Edited by H. G. Nicholas. Chicago: University of Chicago Press, 1981.
Beschloss, Michael. *Kennedy and Roosevelt: The Uneasy Alliance.* New York: Norton, 1980.
Biddle, Francis. *In Brief Authority.* Garden City, N.Y.: Doubleday, 1948.
Bird, Kai. *The Chairman, John McCloy: The Making of the American Establishment.* New York: Simon & Schuster, 1992.
Bishop, Jim. *FDR's Last Year.* New York: William Morrow, 1974.
Bjaaland, Patricia C. *The Norwegian Royal Family.* Tano, 1986.

Black, Ruby. *ER.* New York: Duell, Sloane & Pearce, 1940.

Blum, John Morton. *From the Morganthau Diaries.* Boston: Houghton Mifflin. Vol. I, *Years of Crisis, 1928–1938,* 1959. Vol. II, *Years of Urgency, 1938–1941,* 1965. Vol. III, *Years of War, 1941–1945,* 1967.

———. *V Was for Victory: Politics and American Culture During World War II.* New York: Harcourt Brace Jovanovich, 1976.

Boelcki, Willi A., ed. *Secret Conferences of Dr. Joseph Goebbels: The Nazi Propaganda War, 1939–1943.* New York: E. P. Dutton, 1970.

Boettiger, John R., Jr. *A Love in Shadow.* New York: Norton, 1978.

Bohlen, Charles E. *Witness to History, 1929–1969.* New York: Norton, 1973.

Bosworth, Allen R. *America's Concentration Camps.* New York: Norton, 1967.

Boyer, Paul, Clark Clifford, Jr., Joseph Kett, Neal Salisbury, Harvard Sitkoff, and Nancy Woolch. *The Enduring Vision: A History of the American People.* Lexington, Mass.: D. C. Heath, 1993.

Bradley, Omar, and Clay Blair. *A General's Life.* New York: Simon & Schuster, 1983.

Brinkley, David. *Washington Goes to War.* New York: Knopf, 1988.

Bruenn, Howard J. "Clinical Notes on the Illness and Death of President Franklin D. Roosevelt." *Annals of Internal Medicine,* vol. 72 (April 1970).

Bryant, Arthur. *The Turn of the Tide: A History of the War Years Based on the Diaries of Field-Marshall Lord Alanbrooke.* Garden City, N.Y.: Doubleday, 1957.

Buhite, Russell D., and David W. Levy, eds. *FDR's Fireside Chats.* Norman, Okla.: University of Oklahoma Press, 1992.

Bullitt, William C. *For the President, Personal and Secret: Correspondence Between Franklin D. Roosevelt and William C. Bullitt.* Edited by Orville H. Bullitt. Boston: Houghton Mifflin, 1972.

Bullock, Alan. *Hitler: A Study in Tyranny.* New York: Harper & Row, 1962.

Bunker, John. *Liberty Ships: Ugly Ducklings of World War II.* Annapolis, Md.: Naval Institute Press, 1972.

Burns, James MacGregor. *Roosevelt: The Lion and the Fox.* New York: Harcourt, Brace, 1956.

———. *Roosevelt: The Soldier of Freedom.* New York: Harcourt Brace Jovanovich, 1970.

———. *Leadership.* New York: Harper & Row, 1978.

Butcher, Harry C. *My Three Years with Eisenhower: The Personal Diary of Captain Harry C. Butcher, USNR, Naval Aide to General Eisenhower, 1942 to 1945.* New York: Simon & Schuster, 1946.

Byrnes, James F. *Speaking Frankly.* New York: Harper, 1947.

Cadogan, Sir Alexander. *The Diaries of Sir Alexander Cadogan, O.M., 1938–1945.* Edited by David Dilks. New York: Putnam, 1972.

Cardin, Martin. *Flying Forts.* New York: Meredith Press, 1968.

Catton, Bruce. *The War Lords of Washington.* New York: Greenwood Press, 1969.

Chadakoff, Rochelle, ed. *Eleanor Roosevelt's My Day.* Vol. I, *Her Acclaimed Columns, 1936–1945.* New York: Pharos Books, 1989.

Chafe, William H. *The American Woman: Her Changing Social, Economic and Political Role, 1920–1970.* New York: Oxford University Press, 1972.

Childs, Marquis. *I Write from Washington.* New York: Harper, 1942.

Churchill, Sarah. *A Thread in the Tapestry.* New York: Dodd, Mead, 1967.

Churchill, Winston S. *The Second World War.* Boston: Houghton Mifflin, vol. I, *The Gathering Storm,* 1948. Vol. II, *Their Finest Hour,* 1949. Vol. III, *The Grand Alliance,* 1950. Vol. IV, *The Hinge of Fate,* 1950. Vol. V, *Closing the Ring,* 1951. Vol. VI, *Triumph and Tragedy,* 1953.

———. *Great War Speeches.* New York: Corgi Books, 1957.

Ciechanowski, Jan. *Defeat in Victory.* Garden City, N.Y.: Doubleday, 1947.

Clapper, Raymond. *Watching the World.* New York: McGraw-Hill, 1944.

Clarke, Admiral J. J., with Clark G. Reynolds. *Carrier Admiral.* New York: David McKay, 1967.

Clifford, J. Garry, and Samuel R. Spenser, Jr. *The First Peacetime Draft.* Lawrence, Kan.: University Press of Kansas, 1986.

Coakley, Robert, and Richard Leighton. *Global Logistics and Strategy, 1943–1945.* Washington, D.C.: Center for Military History, 1989.

Cole, Wayne S. *America First: The Battle Against Intervention, 1940–1941.* Madison, Wisc.: University of Wisconsin Press, 1953.

Collier, Peter, and Robert Horowitz. *The Fords: An American Epic.* New York: Summit Books, 1987.

Collier, Richard. *1940: The World in Flames.* New York: Penguin, 1979.

Conn, Stetson, and Byron Fairchild. *The Western Hemisphere: The Framework of Hemispheric Defense.* Washington, D.C.: Office of the Chief of Military History, 1960.

Cook, Blanche Wiesen. *Eleanor Roosevelt.* Vol. I, *1884–1933.* New York: Viking Penguin, 1992.

Cott, Nancy F., and Elizabeth H. Pleck. *A Heritage of Her Own: Towards a New Social History of American Women.* New York: Simon & Schuster, 1979.

Cray, Ed. *General of the Army: George C. Marshall, Soldier and Statesman.* New York: Norton, 1990.

Cutler, Robert. *No Time for Rest.* Boston: Little, Brown, 1966.

Dallek, Robert. *Franklin D. Roosevelt and American Foreign Policy, 1932–1945.* New York: Oxford University Press, 1981.

Daniels, Jonathan. *Washington Quadrille: The Dance Beside the Documents.* Garden City, N.Y.: Doubleday, 1968.

Daniels, Roger. *Concentration Camps USA: Japanese-Americans and World War II.* New York: Holt, Rinehart and Winston, 1970.

Davis, Benjamin O., Jr. *Benjamin O. Davis, Jr., American: An Autobiography.* New York: Plume, 1992.

Davis, Kenneth S. *FDR: The Beckoning of Destiny, 1882–1928.* New York: Putnam, 1971.

———. *Invincible Summer: An Intimate Portrait of the Roosevelts, Based on the Recollections of Marion Dickerman.* New York: Atheneum, 1974.

———. *FDR: Into the Storm, 1937–1940.* New York: Random House, 1993.

Degler, Carl. *Out of the Past: The Forces That Shaped Modern America.* New York: Harper, 1959.

Donovan, Hedley. *Roosevelt to Reagan: A Reporter's Encounter with Nine Presidents.* New York: Harper & Row, 1985.

Dulles, Foster Rhea. *The American Red Cross: A History.* New York: Harper, 1950.

Eden, Anthony. *The Memoirs of Anthony Eden, Earl of Avon: The Reckoning.* Boston: Houghton Mifflin, 1965.

Eisenhower, Dwight D. *Crusade in Europe.* Garden City, N.Y.: Doubleday, 1948.

Emblidge, David, ed. *Eleanor Roosevelt's My Day.* Vol. II, *The Post-War Years. Her Acclaimed Columns, 1945–1952.* New York: Pharos Books, 1990.

Estes, Winston M. *Homefront.* New York: Avon, 1976.

Faber, Doris. *The Life of Lorena Hickok: E.R.'s Friend.* New York: Morrow, 1980.

Fairchild, Byron, and Jonathan Grossman. *The Army and Industrial Mobilization.* Washington, D.C.: Office of the Chief of Military History, 1959.

Farley, James A. *Jim Farley's Story: The Roosevelt Years.* New York: McGraw-Hill, 1948.

Feingold, Henry L. *The Politics of Rescue: The Roosevelt Administration and the Holocaust, 1938–1945.* New Brunswick, N.J.: Rutgers University Press, 1970.

Fields, Alonzo. *My 21 Years in the White House.* New York: Coward-McCann, 1961.

Flynn, Edward J. *You're the Boss.* New York: Collier Books, 1962.

Flynn, George Q. *The Mess in Washington.* Westport, Conn.: Greenwood Press, 1979.

Foreign Relations of the United States. The Conferences at Cairo and Teheran, 1943. Washington, D.C.: U.S. Government Printing Office, 1961.

Foreign Relations of the United States. The Conferences at Malta and Yalta, 1945. Washington, D.C.: U.S. Government Printing Office, 1955.

Foreign Relations of the United States. The Conferences at Washington and Quebec, 1943. Washington, D.C.: U.S. Government Printing Office, 1970.

Foreign Relations of the United States. The Conferences at Washington, 1941–42, and Casablanca, 1943. Washington, D.C.: U.S. Government Printing Office, 1968.

Frankfurter, Felix. *From the Diaries of Felix Frankfurter.* Edited by Joseph P. Lash. New York: Norton, 1975.

Freidel, Frank. *Franklin D. Roosevelt: A Rendezvous with Destiny.* Boston: Little, Brown, 1990.

Furman, Bess. *Washington By-Line.* New York: Knopf, 1949.

Galbraith, John Kenneth. *A Life in Our Times.* Boston: Houghton Mifflin, 1981.

Gallagher, Hugh Gregory. *FDR's Splendid Deception.* New York: Dodd, Mead, 1985.

Gallup, George. *The Gallup Polls: Public Opinion, 1935–1971.* New York: Random House, 1972. Vol. I, *1937–1948.*

Gaulle, Charles de. *The Complete War Memoirs.* New York: Simon & Schuster, 1964.

Gelb, Norman. *Dunkirk: The Complete Story of the First Step in the Defeat of Hitler.* New York: Morrow, 1989.

Gilbert, James. *Another Chance: Postwar America, 1945–1948.* Philadelphia: Temple University Press, 1981.

Gilbert, Martin. *Winston S. Churchill.* Boston: Houghton Mifflin. Vol. VI, *"Finest Hour": 1939–1941,* 1983. Vol. VII, *Road to Victory: 1941–1945,* 1986.

———. *The Second World War: A Complete History.* New York: Henry Holt, 1989.

Girdner, Audrie, and Anne Loftis. *The Great Betrayal: The Evacuation of the Japanese-Americans During World War II.* New York: Macmillan, 1969.

Gluck, Sherna Berger. *Rosie the Riveter Revisited: Women, the War, and Social Change.* Boston: Twayne, 1987.

Goebbels, Joseph. *The Goebbels Diaries, 1942–1943.* Edited by Louis Lochner. Garden City, N.Y.: Doubleday, 1948.

———. *The Goebbels Diaries, 1939–1941.* Edited by Fred Taylor. New York: Putnam, 1983.

Goldsmith, William M. *The Growth of Presidential Power.* Vol. III, *Triumph and Reappraisal.* New York: Chelsea House, 1974.

Goodhart, Philip. *Fifty Good Ships That Saved the World: The Foundations of the Anglo-American Alliance.* Garden City, N.Y.: Doubleday, 1965.

Goodman, Jack, ed. *While You Were Gone: A Report of Wartime Life in the US.* New York: Simon & Schuster, 1946.

Gosnell, Harold. *Champion Campaigner: Franklin D. Roosevelt.* New York: Macmillan, 1952.

Gould, Jean, and Lorena Hickok. *Walter Reuther: Labor's Rugged Individualist.* New York: Dodd, Mead and Co., 1972.

Gould, Joseph C. *The Best Years.* New York: Atheneum, 1976.

Green, Constance McLaughlin. *Washington: Capital City, 1879–1950.* Princeton, N.J.: Princeton University Press, 1963.

———, Harry C. Thomson, and Peter C. Root. *The Ordnance Department: Planning Munitions for War.* Washington, D.C.: Office of the Chief of Military History, 1955.

Greenfield, Kent R., Robert R. Palmer, and Bell I. Wiley. *The Organization of Ground Combat Troops.* Washington, D.C.: Office of the Chief of Military History, 1947.

Gregory, Chester. *Women in Defense Work During World War II: An Analysis of the Labor Problem.* Jericho, N.Y.: Exposition Press, 1974.

Gunther, John. *Roosevelt in Retrospect.* New York: Harper, 1950.

Hall, H. Duncan. *North American Supply.* London: Her Majesty's Stationery Office & Longmans, Green & Co., 1955.

Hareven, Tamara. *Eleanor Roosevelt: An American Conscience.* Chicago: Quadrangle, 1968.

Harriman, Averell, and Elie Abel. *Special Envoy to Churchill and Stalin, 1941–1946.* New York: Random House, 1975.

Harris, Mark Jonathan, Franklin D. Mitchell, and Steven J. Schechter. *The Homefront: America During World War II.* New York: Putnam, 1984.

Harrison, Gordon. *Cross-Channel Attack.* Washington, D.C.: Center for Military History, 1989.

Hassett, William D. *Off the Record with F.D.R.* New Brunswick, N.J.: Rutgers University Press, 1958.

Hastings, Max. *Overlord: D-Day and the Battle for Normandy.* New York: Simon & Schuster, 1984.

Hazelton, Lesley. *The Right to Feel Bad: Coming to Terms with Normal Depression.* New York: Ballantine Books, 1985.

Hershan, Stella K. *A Woman of Quality.* New York: Crown, 1970.

Hitch, Charles J. *America's Economic Strength.* New York: Oxford University Press, 1941.

Hoff-Wilson, Joan, and Marjorie Lightman, eds. *Without Precedent: The Life and Career of Eleanor Roosevelt.* Bloomington, Ind.: Indiana University Press, 1984.

Holley, Irving, Jr. *Buying Aircraft: Materiel Procurement for the Armed Forces.* Washington, D.C.: Office of the Chief of Military History, 1964.

Hoopes, Roy. *Americans Remember the Home Front: An Oral Narrative of the World War II Years in America.* Abridged edition. New York: Berkley Books, 1992.

Howe, George. *Northwest Africa: Seizing the Initiative in the West.* Washington, D.C.: Office of the Chief of Military History, 1957.

Hull, Cordell. *The Memoirs of Cordell Hull.* Vol. II. New York: Macmillan, 1948.

Hurd, Charles. *When the New Deal Was Young and Gay: FDR and His Circle.* New York: Hawthorn Books, 1965.

Ickes, Harold L. *The Secret Diaries of Harold L. Ickes.* Vol. III, *The Lowering Clouds, 1939–1941.* New York: Simon & Schuster, 1954.

Irons, Peter. *Justice at War: The Story of the Japanese American Internment Cases.* New York: Oxford University Press, 1983.

Ironside, General Sir William Edmund. *Time Unguarded: The Ironside Diaries, 1937–1940.* New York: David McKay, 1962.

Ismay, Hastings. *The Memoirs of General Lord Ismay.* New York: Viking, 1960.

James, D. Clayton. *The Years of MacArthur.* Vol. II. Boston: Houghton Mifflin, 1975.

Janeway, Eliot. *The Struggle for Survival.* New Haven, Conn.: Yale University Press, 1951.

Jones, Jacqueline. *Labor of Love, Labor of Sorrow: Black Women, Work, and the Family from Slavery to the Present.* New York: Basic Books, 1985.

Jones, Jesse H., with Edward Angly. *Fifty Billion Dollars: My Thirteen Years with the RFC.* New York: Macmillan, 1951.

Jones, Robert H. *The Roads to Russia: United States Lend-Lease to the Soviet Union.* Norman, Okla.: University of Oklahoma Press, 1969.

Josephson, Matthew, and Hannah Josephson. *Sidney Hillman: Statesman of American Labor.* Garden City, N.Y.: Doubleday, 1952.

Kearney, James R. *Anna Eleanor Roosevelt: The Evolution of a Reformer.* Boston: Houghton Mifflin, 1968.

Kempton, Murray. *Part of Our Time.* New York: Simon & Schuster, 1965.

Kennett, Lee. *G.I.: The American Soldier in World War II.* New York: Charles Scribner's Sons, 1987.

Ketchum, Richard M. *The Borrowed Years, 1938–1941: America on the Way to War.* New York: Random House, 1989.

Kikuchi, Charles. *Kikuchi Diary: Chronicle from an American Concentration Camp.* Urbana, Ill.: University of Illinois Press, 1973.

Kimball, Warren, ed. *Churchill & Roosevelt: The Complete Correspondence.* 3 vols. Princeton, N.J.: Princeton University Press, 1984.

Kiplinger, W. M. *Washington Is Like That.* New York: Harper, 1942.

Kleeman, Rita Halle. *Gracious Lady: The Life of Sara Delano Roosevelt.* New York: Appleton-Century, 1935.

Klingaman, William K. *1941.* New York: Harper & Row, 1988.

Koenig, Louis W. *The Invisible Presidency.* New York: Rinehart, 1960.

Lacey, Robert. *Ford: The Man and the Machine.* Boston: Little, Brown, 1986.

Lane, Frederick C. *Ships for Victory: A History of Shipbuilding Under the US Maritime Commission in World War II.* Baltimore: Johns Hopkins University Press, 1951.

Langer, William L., and Everett S. Gleason. *Undeclared War: 1939–1940.* New York: Harper & Row, 1952–53.

Larrabee, Eric. *Commander in Chief: Franklin Delano Roosevelt, His Lieutenants, and Their War.* New York: Harper & Row, 1987.

Lash, Joseph P. *Eleanor Roosevelt: A Friend's Memoir.* Garden City, N.Y.: Doubleday, 1964.

———. *Eleanor and Franklin: The Story of Their Relationship.* New York: Norton, 1971.

———. *Eleanor: The Years Alone.* New York: Norton, 1972.

———. *Roosevelt and Churchill, 1939–1941: The Partnership That Saved the West.* New York: Norton, 1976.

———. *Love, Eleanor: Eleanor Roosevelt and Her Friends.* Garden City, N.Y.: Doubleday, 1982.

———. *A World of Love: Eleanor Roosevelt and Her Friends, 1943–1962.* Garden City, N.Y.: Doubleday, 1984.

Lawrence, David. *Diary of a Washington Correspondent.* New York: H. C. Kinsey, 1942.

Leahy, William. *I Was There.* New York: McGraw-Hill, 1950.

Leckie, Robert. *Delivered from Evil: The Saga of World War II.* New York: Harper & Row, 1987.

Lee, Ulysses G. *The Employment of Negro Troops: US Army and World War II.* Washington, D.C.: Office of the Chief of Military History, 1966.

Leighton, Richard, and Robert Coakley. *Global Logistics and Strategy, 1940–1943.* Washington, D.C.: Office of the Chief of Military History, 1955.

Leuchtenburg, William. *Franklin D. Roosevelt and the New Deal.* New York: Harper & Row, 1963.

———. *In the Shadow of FDR: From Harry Truman to Ronald Reagan.* Ithaca, N.Y.: Cornell University Press, 1983.

Levenstein, Aaron. *Labor Today and Tomorrow.* New York: Knopf, 1945.

Lilienthal, David E. *The Journals of David E. Lilienthal.* Vol. 1, *The TVA Years.* New York: Harper & Row, 1964.

Lingeman, Richard R. *Don't You Know There's a War On? The American Home Front 1941–1945.* New York: G. P. Putnam's Sons, 1970.

Lippman, Theo, Jr. *The Squire of Warm Springs: FDR in Georgia, 1924–1945.* Chicago: Playboy Press, 1977.

Long, Breckinridge. *The War Diaries of Breckinridge Long: Selections from the Years 1939–1944.* Edited by Fred L. Israel. Lincoln, Neb.: University of Nebraska Press, 1966.

MacNeil, Neil. *Forge of Democracy: The House of Representatives.* New York: David McKay, 1963.

Manchester, William. *American Caesar: Douglas MacArthur, 1880–1964.* Boston: Little, Brown, 1978.

Marshall, George Catlett. *The Papers of George Catlett Marshall.* Vol. II, *"We Can't Delay," July 1, 1939–Dec. 6, 1941.* Edited by Larry Bland. Baltimore: Johns Hopkins University Press, 1981.

Marshall, Katherine Tupper. *Together: Annals of an Army Wife.* New York: Tupper & Love, 1946.

Martin, George. *Madame Secretary: Frances Perkins.* Boston: Houghton Mifflin, 1976.

Matloff, Maurice. *Strategic Planning for Coalition Warfare, 1943–45.* Washington, D.C.: Office of the Chief of Military History, 1959.

——— and Edwin M. Snell. *Strategic Planning for Coalition Warfare, 1941–1942.* Washington, D.C.: Office of the Chief of Military History, 1953.

McConnell, Grant. *The Modern Presidency.* New York: St. Martin's, 1976. Second Edition.

McCullough, David. *Mornings on Horseback.* New York: Simon & Schuster, 1981.

———. *Truman.* New York: Simon & Schuster, 1992.

McGuire, Philip. *Taps for a Jim Crow Army.* Santa Barbara, Calif.: ABC-Clio, 1983.

McIntire, Ross. *White House Physician.* New York: Putnam, 1946.

McJimsey, George. *Harry Hopkins: Ally of the Poor and Defender of Democracy.* Cambridge, Mass.: Harvard University Press, 1987.

McWilliams, Carey. *Brothers Under the Skin.* Boston: Little, Brown, 1943.

———. *Prejudice: Japanese Americans, Symbol of Racial Intolerance.* Boston: Little, Brown, 1944.

Menefee, Selden. *Assignment U.S.A.* New York: Reynal & Hitchcock, 1943.

Meyer, Robert, Jr. *The Stars and Stripes: Story of World War II.* New York: David McKay, 1960.

Milkman, Ruth. *The Dynamics of Gender at Work: Job Discrimination by Sex During World War II.* Chicago: University of Illinois Press, 1987.

Miller, Alice. *The Drama of the Gifted Child.* Translated by Ruth Ward. New York: Basic Books, 1981.

Moffat, Jay Pierpont. *The Moffat Papers.* Edited by Nancy H. Hooker. Cambridge, Mass.: Harvard University Press, 1956.

Moley, Raymond. *The First New Deal.* New York: Harcourt, Brace and World, 1966.

Moran, Lord. *Churchill—The Struggle for Survival, 1940–1965: Taken from the Diaries of Lord Moran.* Boston: Houghton Mifflin, 1966.

Morgan, Ted. *FDR: A Biography.* New York: Simon & Schuster, 1985.

Morison, Samuel Eliot. *The History of United States Naval Operations in World War II.* Boston: Little, Brown. Vol. II, *Operations in North African Waters, October 1942–June 1943,* 1947. Vol. IV, *Coral Sea, Midway and Submarine Action, May 1942–Aug. 1942,* 1960.

———. *The Two-Ocean War: A Short History of the United States Navy in the Second World War.* Boston: Little, Brown, 1963.

Morris, Edmund. *The Rise of Theodore Roosevelt.* New York: Coward, McCann & Geoghegan, 1979.

Morse, Arthur D. *While Six Million Died: A Chronicle of American Apathy.* Woodstock, N.Y.: Overlook Press, 1983.

Morton, H. V. *Atlantic Meeting.* New York: Dodd, Mead, 1943.

Mosch, Theodore R. *The G.I. Bill: A Breakthrough in Educational and Social Policy in the United States.* New York: Exposition Press, 1975.

Moscow, Warren. *Roosevelt and Willkie.* Englewood Cliffs, N.J.: Prentice-Hall, 1968.

Mosley, Leonard. *Marshall: A Hero for Our Times.* New York: Hearst Books, 1982.

Neal, Steve. *Dark Horse: A Biography of Wendell Willkie.* Garden City, N.Y.: Doubleday, 1984.

Nelson, Dennis D. *The Integration of the Negro into the Navy.* New York: Farrar, Straus and Young, 1951.

Nelson, Donald M. *Arsenal of Democracy.* New York: Harcourt, Brace, 1946.

Nesbitt, Victoria Henrietta. *White House Diary.* Garden City, N.Y.: Doubleday, 1948.

Neustadt, Richard E. *Presidential Power and the Modern Presidency: The Politics of Leadership from Roosevelt to Reagan.* New York: Free Press (Macmillan), 1990.

The New Yorker *Book of War Pieces, London, 1939, to Hiroshima, 1945.* New York: Schocken Books, 1947.

Nichols, Lee. *Breakthrough on the Color Front.* New York: Random House, 1954.

Okubo, Mine. *Citizen 13660.* New York: Columbia University Press, 1966.

Ottley, Roi. *New World A-Coming.* Boston: Houghton Mifflin, 1943.

Oursler, Fulton. *Behold This Dreamer!* Boston: Little, Brown, 1964.

Panter-Downes, Molly. *London War Notes, 1939–1945.* New York: Farrar, Straus & Giroux, 1971.

Parks, Lillian Rogers, with Francis Spatz Leighton. *The Roosevelts: A Family in Turmoil.* Englewood, N.J.: Fleet, 1981.

Parmet, Herbert S., and Marie B. Hecht. *Never Again: A President Runs for a Third Term—Roosevelt versus Willkie, 1940.* New York: Macmillan, 1968.

Parrish, Thomas. *Roosevelt and Marshall: Partners in Politics and War.* New York: Morrow, 1989.

Payne, Robert. *The Life and Death of Adolf Hitler.* New York: Praeger, 1973.

Perkins, Frances. *The Roosevelt I Knew.* New York: Viking, 1946.

Perrett, Geoffrey. *Days of Sadness, Years of Triumph: The American People, 1939–1945.* New York: Coward, Cabell & Geoghegan, 1973.

———. *There's a War to Be Won: The United States Army in World War II.* New York: Random House, 1991.

Phillips, Cabell. *The 1940s: Decade of Triumph and Trouble.* New York: Macmillan, 1975.

Pickergill, J. W., ed. *The Mackenzie King Record.* Vol. I, *1939–1944.* Chicago: University of Chicago Press, 1960.

Pickergill, J. W., and D. F. Foster, eds. *The Mackenzie King Record.* Vol. II, *1944–1945.* Toronto: University of Toronto Press, 1968.

Pogue, Forrest C. *George C. Marshall: Ordeal and Hope, 1939–1942.* Vol. II. New York: Viking, 1966.

Polenberg, Richard. *War and Society: The United States, 1941–1945.* Philadelphia: Lippincott, 1972.

———. *One Nation Divisible: Class, Race and Ethnicity in the US since 1938.* New York: Viking, 1980.

———, ed. *America at War: Homefront, 1941–1945.* Englewood Cliffs, N.J.: Prentice-Hall, 1968.

Pyle, Ernie. *Brave Men.* New York: Henry Holt & Co., 1944.

Reilly, Michael F. *Reilly of the White House.* New York: Simon & Schuster, 1947.

Rhodes, Richard. *The Making of the Atomic Bomb.* New York: Simon & Schuster, 1986.

Risch, Erna. *Quartermaster Corps: Organization, Supply and Service.* Vol. 1. Washington, D.C.: Office of the Chief of Military History, 1953.

Robertson, Ben. *I Saw England.* New York: Knopf, 1941.

Rogers, Donald, *Since You Went Away.* New Rochelle, N.Y.: Arlington House, 1973.

Rommel, Erwin. *The Rommel Papers.* Edited by Liddell Hart and Basil Henry. New York: Harcourt, Brace, 1953.

Roosevelt, Eleanor. *This Is My Story.* New York: Harper, 1937.

———. *My Days.* New York: Dodge Publishing Co., 1938.

———. *This I Remember.* New York: Harper & Brothers, 1949.
———. *It Seems to Me.* New York: Norton & Co., 1954.
———. *On My Own.* New York: Curtis Publishing Co., 1958.
———. *Tomorrow Is Now.* New York: Harper, 1963.
——— and Helen Ferris. *Your Teens and Mine.* Garden City, N.Y.: Doubleday, 1961.
——— and Lorena Hickok. *Ladies of Courage.* New York: Putnam, 1954.
Roosevelt, Elliott. *As He Saw It.* New York: Duell, Sloane & Pearce, 1946.
———. *A Rendezvous with Destiny: The Roosevelts of the White House.* New York: Putnam, 1975.
———. *Mrs. R: Eleanor Roosevelt's Untold Story.* New York: Putnam, 1977.
——— and James Brough. *An Untold Story: The Roosevelts of Hyde Park.* New York: Putnam, 1973.
Roosevelt, Franklin D. *FDR: His Personal Letters.* Vol. I, *The Early Years.* Edited by Elliott Roosevelt. New York: Duell, Sloane & Pearce, 1947.
———. *Public Papers and Addresses of Franklin D. Roosevelt.* Edited by Samuel I. Rosenman. 1937–1940, 4 vols. New York: Macmillan, 1941. 1941–1945, 4 vols. New York: Harper, 1950.
Roosevelt, James, with Bill Libby. *My Parents: A Differing View.* Chicago: Playboy Press, 1976.
——— and Sidney Schalett. *Affectionately, F.D.R.: A Son's Story of a Lonely Man.* New York: Harcourt, Brace, 1959.
Roosevelt, Sara Delano. *My Boy Franklin.* As told to Isabel Leighton and Gabrielle Forbush. New York: Long & Smith, 1933.
Rosenman, Samuel I. *Working with Roosevelt.* New York: Harper, 1952.
——— and Dorothy Rosenman. *Presidential Style: Some Giants and a Pygmy in the White House.* New York: Harper & Row, 1976.
Ruchames, Louis. *Race, Jobs and Politics: The FEPC.* New York: Columbia University Press, 1953.
Salmond, John. *A Southern Rebel: The Life and Times of Aubrey Willis Williams.* Chapel Hill, N.C.: University of North Carolina Press, 1983.
Scarf, Maggie. *Intimate Partners: Patterns in Love and Marriage.* New York: Ballantine Books, 1987.
Scharf, Lois. *ER: First Lady of American Liberalism.* Boston: Twayne Publishers, 1987.
Schlesinger, Arthur M., Jr. *The Age of Roosevelt.* Boston: Houghton Mifflin. Vol. I, *The Crisis of the Old Order, 1919–1933,* 1957. Vol. II, *The Coming of the New Deal,* 1958. Vol. III, *The Politics of Upheaval,* 1960.
Schultz, Duane. *The Doolittle Raid.* New York: St. Martin's, 1988.
Seale, William. *The President's House: A History.* 2 vols. Washington, D.C.: National Geographic Society, 1986.
———. *The White House: The History of an American Idea.* Washington, D.C.: The American Institute of Architects Press, 1992.
Seidman, Joel. *American Labor: From Defense to Reconversion.* Chicago: University of Chicago Press, 1953.
Sherry, Michael. *The Rise of American Air Power: The Creation of Armageddon.* New Haven, Conn.: Yale University Press, 1987.
Sherwood, Robert E. *Roosevelt and Hopkins: An Intimate History.* New York: Harper, 1948.
Shirer, William L. *The Rise and Fall of the Third Reich: A History of Nazi Germany.* New York: Touchstone, 1981.
Shogan, Robert, and Tom Craig. *The Detroit Race Riots.* Philadelphia: Chilton Books, 1964.
Shoumatoff, Elizabeth. *FDR's Unfinished Portrait.* Pittsburgh, Pa.: University of Pittsburgh Press, 1990.
Sitkoff, Harvard. *A New Deal for Blacks: The Emergence of Civil Rights as a National Issue.* New York: Oxford University Press, 1978.
———, ed. *Fifty Years Later: The New Deal Evaluated.* New York: Oxford University Press, 1978.
Skrjabina, Elena. *Siege and Survival: The Odyssey of a Leningrader.* Carbondale, Ill.: Southern Illinois University Press, 1971.
Smith, A Merriman. *Thank You, Mr. President: A White House Notebook.* New York: Harper, 1946.

Smith, R. Elberton. *The Army and Economic Mobilization.* Washington, D.C.: Center for Military History, 1959.

Sorenson, Charles, and William Samuelson. *My Forty Years with Ford.* New York: Norton, 1956.

Speer, Albert. *Inside the Third Reich: Memoirs.* New York: Macmillan, 1970.

Steeholm, Clara, and Hardy Steeholm. *The House at Hyde Park.* New York: Viking, 1950.

Steinberg, Alfred. *Mrs. R.* New York: Putnam, 1958.

———. *Sam Rayburn: A Biography.* New York: Hawthorn Books, 1975.

Steinfels, Margaret O'Brien. *Who's Minding the Children? The History and Politics of Day Care in America.* New York: Simon & Schuster, 1973.

Stettinius, Edward R. *Lend-Lease: Weapon for Victory.* New York: Macmillan, 1944.

———. *Roosevelt and the Russians: The Yalta Conference.* Garden City, N.Y.: Doubleday, 1949.

———. *The Diaries of Edward R. Stettinius Jr., 1943–1946.* Edited by Thomas M. Campell and George C. Herring. New York: New Viewpoints, 1975.

Stone, I. F. *Business as Usual: The First Year of Defense.* New York: Modern Age, 1941.

———. *The War Years, 1939–1945.* Boston: Little, Brown, 1988.

Swafford, Rosa L. *Wartime Record of Strikes and Lockouts, 1940–1945.* Washington, D.C.: U.S. Department of Labor, 1946.

Tapert, Annette, ed. *Lines of Battle: Letters from American Servicemen, 1941–1945.* New York: Pocket Books, 1987.

Teague, Michael. *Mrs. L: Conversations with Alice Roosevelt Longworth.* Garden City, N.Y.: Doubleday, 1981.

Thompson, W. H. *Assignment: Churchill.* New York: Farrar, Straus & Young, 1955.

Thomson, Harry, and Lidas Mayo. *The Ordnance Department: Procurement and Supply.* Washington, D.C.: Office of the Chief of Military History, 1960.

Tugwell, Rexford G. *The Democratic Roosevelt: A Biography of Franklin D. Roosevelt.* Garden City, N.Y.: Doubleday, 1957.

Tully, Grace. *F.D.R., My Boss.* New York: Charles Scribner's Sons, 1949.

Vatter, Harold G. *The U.S. Economy in World War II.* New York: Columbia University Press, 1985.

Walker, Turnley. *Roosevelt and the Warm Springs Story.* New York: Wyn, 1953.

Wallace, Henry A. *The Price of Vision: The Diary of Henry A. Wallace, 1942–1946.* Edited by John Morton Blum. Boston: Houghton Mifflin, 1973.

Wallin, Vice Admiral Homer N. *Pearl Harbor—Why, How: Fleet Salvage and Final Appraisal.* Washington, D.C.: Naval History Division, 1968.

Ward, Geoffrey C. *Before the Trumpet: Young Franklin Roosevelt, 1882–1905.* New York: Perennial Library, 1986.

———. *A First-Class Temperament: The Emergence of Franklin Roosevelt.* New York, Harper & Row, 1989.

Watkins, T. H. *Righteous Pilgrim: The Life and Times of Harold L. Ickes, 1874–1952.* New York: Henry Holt, 1990.

Watson, Mark S. *Chief of Staff: Prewar Plans and Preparations.* Washington, D.C.: Office of the Chief of Military History, 1950.

Weiss, Nancy J. *Farewell to the Party of Lincoln: Black Politics in the Age of FDR.* Princeton, N.J.: Princeton University Press, 1983.

Welles, Sumner. *The Time for Decision.* New York: Harper, 1944.

West, J. B., with Mary Lynn Kotz. *Upstairs at the White House: My Life with the First Ladies.* New York: Coward, McCann & Geoghegan, 1973.

White, Gerald. *Billions for Defense: Government Financing by the Defense Plant Corporation During World War II.* University, Ala.: University of Alabama Press, 1980.

White, Walter. *A Man Called White.* New York: Viking, 1948.

Wilkins, Roy. *Standing Fast: The Autobiography of Roy Wilkins.* New York: Viking, 1982.

Wills, Garry. *Certain Trumpets: The Call of Leaders.* New York: Simon & Schuster, 1994.

Wilson, Theodore. *The First Summit: Roosevelt and Churchill at Placentia Bay, 1941.* Boston: Houghton Mifflin, 1969.

Winfield, Betty Houchin. *FDR and the News Media.* Chicago: University of Illinois Press, 1990.

Wyden, Peter. *Day One: Before Hiroshima and After.* New York: Simon & Schuster, 1984.

Wyman, David S. *The Abandonment of the Jews: America and the Holocaust, 1941–1945.* New York: Pantheon, 1984.

———. *Paper Walls: America and the Refugee Crisis, 1938–1941.* New York: Pantheon, 1985.

Youngs, J. William T. *Eleanor Roosevelt: A Personal and Public Life.* Boston: Little, Brown, 1985.

Ziegler, Robert H. *American Workers, American Unions, 1920–1985.* Baltimore: Johns Hopkins University Press, 1986.

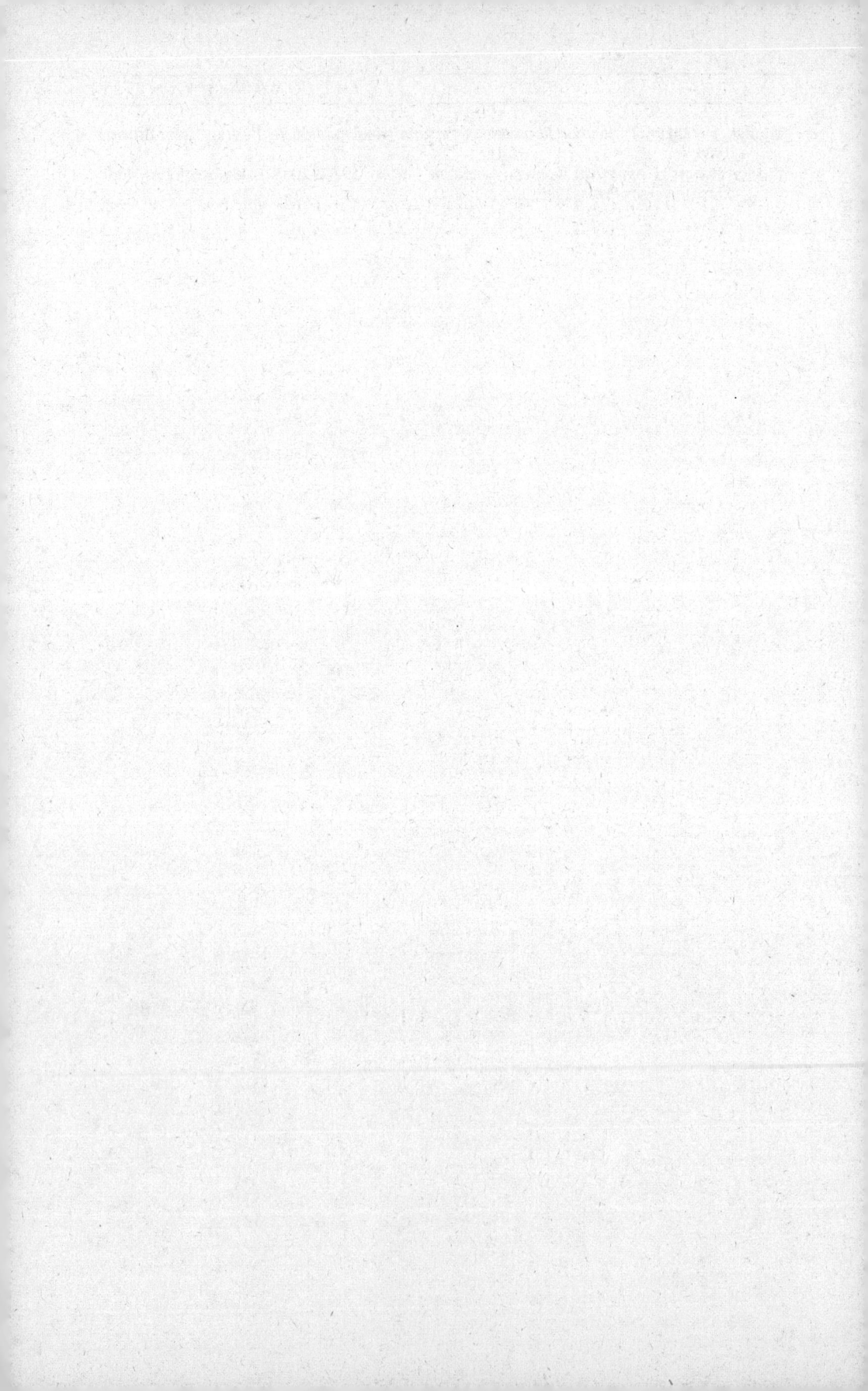

ACKNOWLEDGMENTS

This book would not have been possible without the research help of Linda Vandegrift, my friend and colleague, who labored with me every day from the very start of the project six years ago. Her diligence in digging through archives, her love of detail, and her passion for the subject accompanied me every step along the way. This book is, in many ways, her creation as well as mine.

I wish to acknowledge at the outset my debt to the extraordinary circle of Roosevelt scholars whose histories and biographies educated and inspired me. Their books, listed in the bibliography and acknowledged in my endnotes, provided a foundation for this study. At the Franklin D. Roosevelt Library in Hyde Park, New York, where so much of my research was done, I owe a special thanks to the former director, Dr. William Emerson. His enthusiasm for the idea of studying Roosevelt's leadership of the home front was decisive for me in the early, unfocused months, and as the years went by, he became a mentor and friend, always willing to share so generously his vast knowledge and experience. I am grateful to the entire staff of the Roosevelt library, including its present director, my friend, Verne Newton, Ray Teichman, Bob Parks, Mark Renovitch, Paul McLaughlin, John Ferris, Nancy Snedeker, and Karen Burtis.

I am also grateful to the scores of people I interviewed over the years who gave of their time and their memories without asking anything in return. Several members of the Roosevelt family were especially helpful, including James and Elliott Roosevelt, who are no longer alive, Eleanor Seagraves, and Curtis Roosevelt. Particular thanks to Trude Lash, Henry Morgenthau, Robert Hopkins, Eleanor Seagraves, and Harold Ickes for permission to quote from various letters and papers. Grateful acknowledgement is also made to the University of Southern California for permission to publish excerpts of oral histories of Dan Condren, Frankie Cooper, Shirley Hackett, Dellie Hahn, Sybil Lewis, Larry Mantrell, and Inez Sauer. The University of Southern California retains exclusive ownership of all copyrights to the interviews. I am also grateful to Columbia University for permission to quote from the oral histories of Frances Perkins and Samuel Rosenman and to Yale University for permission to quote from Henry Stimson's Papers. I want to thank Jeanine Derr for conducting research in the National Archives in Washington, Andrew Blankstein for searching through old newspapers at the Library of Congress, and Lulie Haddad for researching the oral histories at Columbia University.

A number of friends and colleagues sustained me in various ways over the long course of this book, including Alfred Checchi, Phyllis Grann, Arnold Hiatt, Michael Rothschild, and Janna Malamud Smith. And I owe a special debt to my agent, Sterling Lord, who was there when I needed him, as he has always been.

At Simon and Schuster, I owe thanks to Lydia Buechler, Terry Zaroff, Frank and Eve Metz, Victoria Meyer, and Elizabeth Stein. In the course of the last six months, as all the pieces of the book were being put together, I relied on Liz Stein for so many things, talking to her nearly every day, that I can hardly imagine doing a book without her warmth, humor, and support. From beginning to end, I was fortunate once again to have Alice Mayhew as my editor. At every stage of the writing, I benefited greatly from her critical intelligence and her broad, penetrating knowledge. She seems to understand intuitively when to leave a writer alone and when to intervene, when to offer criticism and when to simply encourage. She is, as every one of her authors knows, the best there is.

My husband, Richard Goodwin, has been at my side through all my writing life. This book would not be what it is without him. He shared in the shaping of the story, helped me to articulate the larger themes and spent weeks of his time editing the final manuscript. He is my best friend and my most loving and constructive critic.

INDEX

PHOTO CREDITS

Photos in text:

Page 13	© 1940 by *The New York Times.* Reprinted by permission.
Page 61	AP/Wide World Photos
Page 106	UPI/Bettmann Newsphotos
Page 270	Franklin D. Roosevelt Library
Page 360	Franklin D. Roosevelt Library
Page 401	Franklin D. Roosevelt Library
Page 456	Government of New Zealand/FDRL
Page 534	*The Philadelphia Record*
Page 595	Ed Clark, *Life* Magazine © Time Warner
Page 637	Courtesy of The White House

All photos not credited below are from the Franklin D. Roosevelt Library:

Section I

UPI/Bettmann Newsphotos 1, 6, 14, 20, 23, 24, 29
Courtesy Margaret Suckley/FDRL 7
Thomas McAvoy, *Life* Magazine © Time Warner 9
Percy T. Jones/FDRL 15
J. T. Holloway/FDRL 28

Section II

UPI/Bettmann Newsphotos 4, 17, 27, 28, 29
Courtesy Margaret Suckley/FDRL 21, 22
Photos from *FDR's Unfinished Portrait* by Elizabeth Shoumatoff (University of Pittsburgh Press, 1990) 25, 26

PHOTO CREDITS

PHOTOS IN TEXT:

Page 13	© 1940 by *The New York Times.* Reprinted by permission.
Page 61	AP/Wide World Photos
Page 106	UPI/Bettmann Newsphotos
Page 270	Franklin D. Roosevelt Library
Page 360	Franklin D. Roosevelt Library
Page 401	Franklin D. Roosevelt Library
Page 456	Government of New Zealand/FDRL
Page 534	*The Philadelphia Record*
Page 595	Ed Clark, *Life* Magazine © Time Warner
Page 637	Courtesy of The White House

All photos not credited below are from the Franklin D. Roosevelt Library:

SECTION I

UPI/Bettmann Newsphotos 1, 6, 14, 20, 23, 24, 29
Courtesy Margaret Suckley/FDRL 7
Thomas McAvoy, *Life* Magazine © Time Warner 9
Percy T. Jones/FDRL 15
J. T. Holloway/FDRL 28

SECTION II

UPI/Bettmann Newsphotos 4, 17, 27, 28, 29
Courtesy Margaret Suckley/FDRL 21, 22
Photos from *FDR's Unfinished Portrait* by Elizabeth Shoumatoff (University of Pittsburgh Press, 1990) 25, 26

DORIS KEARNS GOODWIN is the author of the critically acclaimed and bestselling *Team of Rivals: The Political Genius of Abraham Lincoln*, in part the basis for Steven Spielberg's major motion picture, *Lincoln*. She was awarded the Pulitzer Prize in history for *No Ordinary Time: Franklin & Eleanor Roosevelt: The Home Front in World War II* and is also the author of the bestsellers *Wait Till Next Year*, *The Fitzgeralds and the Kennedys*, and *Lyndon Johnson and the American Dream*. She lives in Concord, Massachusetts, with her husband, Richard N. Goodwin.

Praise for *Team of Rivals*

Winner of the Lincoln Prize
Winner of The New-York Historical Society Book Prize
Winner of the Barondess/Lincoln Award
Winner of the Bostonian Society's 2006 Bostonian History Award
Finalist for the National Book Critics Circle Award for biography
Finalist for the Los Angeles Times Book Prize in biography

"An elegant, incisive study of Lincoln and leading members of his cabinet that will appeal to experts as well as to those whose knowledge of Lincoln is an amalgam of high school history and popular mythology. . . . Goodwin has brilliantly described how Lincoln forged a team that preserved a nation and freed America from the curse of slavery."

—James M. McPherson, *The New York Times Book Review*

"A brilliantly conceived and well-written tour de force of a historical narrative. . . . Goodwin's contribution is refreshingly unique. . . . Goodwin's emotive prose elevates this tome from mere popular history to literary achievement."

—Douglas Brinkley, *The Boston Globe*

"A sweeping, riveting account. . . . Put simply, Goodwin's story of Lincoln's great, troubled, triumphant life is a star-spangled, high-stepping, hat-waving, bugle-blowing winner."

—*Daily News* (New York)

"Goodwin finds her Lincoln hiding in plain view. He is Lincoln the politician, but one whose political shrewdness ends up being indistinguishable from wisdom. She has written a wonderful book. There is a man in it."

—Garry Wills, *American Scholar*

"Probe[s] the 16th president's personal and public lives with insight, engaging narrative and careful research. . . . When it comes to political complexity and intrigue, Goodwin excels. . . . Riveting political history."

—*Chicago Tribune*

"*Team of Rivals* is one of the most compulsively readable books of history for a general audience to come along in a long time. An engagingly intimate look at Lincoln's private life and public actions, the book convincingly brings to life this man who may have been the most extraordinary individual in American history."

—*The Sunday Oregonian*

"This immense, finely honed book is no dull administrative or bureaucratic history; rather, it is a story of personalities—a messianic drama. . . . Portraits are drawn in spacious detail and with great skill. . . . Goodwin's narrative powers are great."

—*The Washington Post Book World*

"Captivating. . . . Immensely readable. . . . Goodwin . . . is a master storyteller."

—*The Christian Science Monitor*

"Magnificent. . . . Vastly readable. . . . Brilliantly told."

—*The Atlanta Journal-Constitution*

"This is a serious biography that ranges across an immense territory. . . . Goodwin has probed a vast trove of contemporary sources. . . . Her account of the 1860 Republican convention is spellbinding."

—*The New York Observer*

"*Team of Rivals* is well-executed popular history from one of the masters of the genre."

—*The New York Sun*

"Goodwin's gripping narrative propels the reader. . . . Offers fresh perspectives, astute analysis, and sensitive portrayals of her four main characters and a host of lesser ones. *Team of Rivals* is a masterful work of history."

—*The Providence Journal*

"Fascinating. . . . *Team of Rivals* makes us long for men of such integrity, goodness and insight."

—*The Commercial Appeal* (Memphis)

"Splendid . . . *Team of Rivals* tells of a day when men were true leaders."

—*U.S. News & World Report*

"If you think you know all there is to know about Abraham Lincoln, spend some time in the mid-1800s with Doris Kearns Goodwin in her new book, *Team of Rivals.* This masterful and extremely entertaining work shines light on the 16th president's astounding grasp of the subtleties of politics and his mastery of the presidency during the Civil War, adding even more luster to the Lincoln image."

—*The Courier-Journal* (Louisville, Kentucky)

"Goodwin's fine book makes an important contribution to our national understanding of this crucial era."

—*National Review*

"Restores Lincoln to his proper time and place. . . . Goodwin reveals something about Lincoln that's too often neglected: his remarkable capacity for empathy, affection and manipulation. These qualities informed his most critical political decisions."

—*Austin American-Statesman*

"A sweeping survey of Lincoln and his Cabinet that contributes a great deal to our understanding of Lincoln's character and political dexterity. . . . A master storyteller, Goodwin uses the intertwined lives of Lincoln and his key cabinet members . . . to weave a compelling narrative of wartime Washington."

—*American Heritage*

"Meticulous. . . . Goodwin vividly evokes Lincoln's struggles to avoid war, his resolve to fight hard once war became inevitable, and his unflagging effort to hold fast the fragile union."

—*St. Petersburg Times*

"A window into the political life and times of the late 19th century. . . . The book [has] an immediacy and freshness much like the intimacy of Ken Burns' documentary on the Civil War."

—*Chicago Sun-Times*

"Excellent. . . . Lincoln is brought to life beautifully in *Team of Rivals*. . . . Clarifies and preserves Lincoln's legacy with rare skill."

—*The Seattle Times*

"A wonderful book. . . . Goodwin has written a history that is also a good yarn. . . . This book ennobles politics, at least as practiced by Abraham Lincoln. Our democracy could use some ennobling these days."

—*The Sunday Star-Ledger* (Newark, N.J.)

"There is something for just about every reader in this book: the story of Union politics during the Civil War; an insight into how people lived in the 19th century; and riveting prose that will keep you reading."

—*The Roanoke Times*

"Doris Kearns Goodwin has written an enormous book possessed of a friendly grandeur and, against all odds, a considerable freshness."

—*The Atlantic Monthly*

"An intriguing contribution. . . . One of the few books on the Civil War period that presents a rounded portrait of Mary Todd Lincoln."

—*Richmond Times Dispatch*

"Original in conception and brilliant in execution. . . . This is history at full flood, an absorbing narrative. . . . In *Team of Rivals*, the political genius of Abraham Lincoln meets the historical genius of Doris Kearns Goodwin."

—*The Globe and Mail* (Toronto)

"Goodwin illuminates all aspects of the life of Lincoln with a dignity that befits one of the greatest Americans."

—*Pittsburgh Tribune-Review*

"A wonderful book that shows Lincoln clearly by broadening the focus to include his Cabinet. Perhaps just in time to make us envious, Goodwin gives us a portrait of effective democratic government in bad times, led by a political genius. . . . She has written a history that is also a good yarn. . . . This book ennobles politics, at least as practiced by Abraham Lincoln."

—Newhouse News Service

"*Team of Rivals* is fascinating, artfully constructed, beautifully written. It is as fresh as if this were the first book on Abraham Lincoln ever published."

—David Herbert Donald, author of *Lincoln*

"In this majestic work, Lincoln emerges both as a master politician and transcendent moral figure. Goodwin shows Lincoln's White House as it really was: a place of moral courage and triumph, but also intrigue and tragedy. The story of the president and his brilliant, fractious cabinet has never been so beautifully told."

—Michael Bishop, Executive Director, Abraham Lincoln Bicentennial Commission

"What an achievement! It is brilliant in its execution, compassionate in its presentation, and informative in every sense."

—Frank J. Williams, Chairman, The Lincoln Forum

"The book is splendid—I felt like I was at every cabinet meeting, every crisis conference, every hand-wringing visit to the telegraph office, watching Seward relax, Chase puff up, and Lincoln grow into the genius Goodwin asserts in the title. It's a triumph."

—Harold Holzer, author of *Lincoln at Cooper Union* and *The Lincoln-Douglas Debates*

"Nowhere is there a better understanding or more lyrical portrayal of those who served as Lincoln's top advisors. . . . Goodwin provides us with a comparative perspective producing new and compelling insights into Lincoln's personal and public life. Goodwin beautifully captures the infighting, the gossip and the high stakes politics of the Lincoln presidency. . . . Any reader of this book will enthusiastically agree that Lincoln's political genius laid the foundation for Union victory, emancipation and ultimately the Thirteenth Amendment."

—Thomas F. Schwartz, Illinois State Historian

Also by Doris Kearns Goodwin

Wait Till Next Year
A Memoir

No Ordinary Time
Franklin and Eleanor Roosevelt:
The Home Front in World War II

The Fitzgeralds and the Kennedys

Lyndon Johnson and the American Dream

TEAM OF

DORIS KEARNS GOODWIN

Simon & Schuster Paperbacks

RIVALS

THE POLITICAL GENIUS of ABRAHAM LINCOLN

New York London Toronto Sydney New Delhi

SIMON & SCHUSTER PAPERBACKS
An Imprint of Simon & Schuster, Inc.
1230 Avenue of the Americas
New York, NY 10020

First Simon & Schuster paperback edition 2006

Maps © 2005 Jeffrey L. Ward

Book design by Ellen R. Sasahara

Manufactured in the United States of Americ

27 29 30 28 26

The Library of Congress has cataloged the hardcover edition as follows:
Goodwin, Doris Kearns.
Team of rivals : the political genius of Abraham Lincoln / Doris Kearns Goodwin.
p. cm.
Includes bibliographical references and index.
1. Lincoln, Abraham, 1809–1865. 2. Political leadership—United States—Case studies. 3. Genius—Case studies. 4. Lincoln, Abraham, 1809–1865—Friends and associates. 5. Presidents—United States—Biography. 6. United States—Politics and government, 1861–1865. I. Title.
E457.45.G66 2005 973.7092—dc22 [B] 2005044615

ISBN: 978-0-684-82490-1
ISBN: 978-0-7432-7075-5 (pbk)
ISBN: 978-1-4165-4983-3 (ebook)

For Richard N. Goodwin,
my husband of thirty years

"The conduct of the republican party in this nomination is a remarkable indication of small intellect, growing smaller. They pass over . . . statesmen and able men, and they take up a fourth rate lecturer, who cannot speak good grammar."

—The *New York Herald* (May 19, 1860), commenting on Abraham Lincoln's nomination for president at the Republican National Convention

"Why, if the old Greeks had had this man, what trilogies of plays—what epics—would have been made out of him! How the rhapsodes would have recited him! How quickly that quaint tall form would have enter'd into the region where men vitalize gods, and gods divinify men! But Lincoln, his times, his death—great as any, any age—belong altogether to our own."

—Walt Whitman, "Death of Abraham Lincoln," 1879

"The greatness of Napoleon, Caesar or Washington is only moonlight by the sun of Lincoln. His example is universal and will last thousands of years. . . . He was bigger than his country—bigger than all the Presidents together . . . and as a great character he will live as long as the world lives."

—Leo Tolstoy, *The World,* New York, 1909

CONTENTS

MAPS AND DIAGRAMS

INTRODUCTION

In 1876, the celebrated orator Frederick Douglass dedicated a monument in Washington, D.C., erected by black Americans to honor Abraham Lincoln. The former slave told his audience that "there is little necessity on this occasion to speak at length and critically of this great and good man, and of his high mission in the world. That ground has been fully occupied. . . . The whole field of fact and fancy has been gleaned and garnered. Any man can say things that are true of Abraham Lincoln, but no man can say anything that is new of Abraham Lincoln."

Speaking only eleven years after Lincoln's death, Douglass was too close to assess the fascination that this plain and complex, shrewd and transparent, tender and iron-willed leader would hold for generations of Americans. In the nearly two hundred years since his birth, countless historians and writers have uncovered new documents, provided fresh insights, and developed an ever-deepening understanding of our sixteenth president.

In my own effort to illuminate the character and career of Abraham Lincoln, I have coupled the account of his life with the stories of the remarkable men who were his rivals for the 1860 Republican presidential nomination—New York senator William H. Seward, Ohio governor Salmon P. Chase, and Missouri's distinguished elder statesman Edward Bates.

Taken together, the lives of these four men give us a picture of the path taken by ambitious young men in the North who came of age in the early decades of the nineteenth century. All four studied law, became distinguished orators, entered politics, and opposed the spread of slavery. Their upward climb was one followed by many thousands who left the small towns of their birth to seek opportunity and adventure in the rapidly growing cities of a dynamic, expanding America.

Just as a hologram is created through the interference of light from separate sources, so the lives and impressions of those who companioned Lincoln give us a clearer and more dimensional picture of the president himself. Lincoln's barren childhood, his lack of schooling, his relationships with male friends, his complicated marriage, the nature of his ambition, and his ruminations about death can be analyzed more clearly when he is placed side by side with his three contemporaries.

When Lincoln won the nomination, each of his celebrated rivals believed the wrong man had been chosen. Ralph Waldo Emerson recalled his first reception of the news that the "comparatively unknown name of Lincoln" had been selected: "we heard the result coldly and sadly. It seemed too rash, on a purely local reputation, to build so grave a trust in such anxious times."

Lincoln seemed to have come from nowhere—a backwoods lawyer who had served one undistinguished term in the House of Representatives and had lost two consecutive contests for the U. S. Senate. Contemporaries and historians alike have attributed his surprising nomination to chance—the fact that he came from the battleground state of Illinois and stood in the center of his party. The comparative perspective suggests a different interpretation. When viewed against the failed efforts of his rivals, it is clear that Lincoln won the nomination because he was shrewdest and canniest of them all. More accustomed to relying upon himself to shape events, he took the greatest control of the process leading up to the nomination, displaying a fierce ambition, an exceptional political acumen, and a wide range of emotional strengths, forged in the crucible of personal hardship, that took his unsuspecting rivals by surprise.

That Lincoln, after winning the presidency, made the unprecedented decision to incorporate his eminent rivals into his political family, the cabinet, was evidence of a profound self-confidence and a first indication of what would prove to others a most unexpected greatness. Seward became secretary of state, Chase secretary of the treasury, and Bates attorney general. The remaining top posts Lincoln offered to three former Democrats whose stories also inhabit these pages—Gideon Welles, Lincoln's "Neptune," was made secretary of the navy, Montgomery Blair became postmaster general, and Edwin M. Stanton, Lincoln's "Mars," eventually became secretary of war. Every member of this administration was better known, better educated, and more experienced in public life than Lincoln. Their presence in the cabinet might have threatened to eclipse the obscure prairie lawyer from Springfield.

It soon became clear, however, that Abraham Lincoln would emerge the undisputed captain of this most unusual cabinet, truly a team of rivals. The powerful competitors who had originally disdained Lincoln became colleagues who helped him steer the country through its darkest days. Seward was the first to appreciate Lincoln's remarkable talents, quickly realizing the futility of his plan to relegate the president to a figurehead role. In the months that followed, Seward would become Lincoln's closest friend and advisor in the administration. Though Bates initially viewed Lincoln as a well-meaning but incompetent administrator, he eventually concluded that the president was an unmatched leader, "very near being a perfect man." Edwin Stanton, who had treated Lincoln with contempt at their initial acquaintance, developed a great respect for the commander in chief and was unable to control his tears for weeks after the president's death. Even Chase, whose restless ambition for the presidency was never realized, at last acknowledged that Lincoln had outmaneuvered him.

This, then, is a story of Lincoln's political genius revealed through his extraordinary array of personal qualities that enabled him to form friendships with men who had previously opposed him; to repair injured feelings that, left untended, might have escalated into permanent hostility; to assume responsibility for the failures of subordinates; to share credit with ease; and to learn from mistakes. He possessed an acute understanding of the sources of power inherent in the presidency, an unparalleled ability to keep his governing coalition intact, a tough-minded appreciation of the need to protect his presidential prerogatives, and a masterful sense of timing. His success in dealing with the strong egos of the men in his cabinet suggests that in the hands of a truly great politician the qualities we generally associate with decency and morality—kindness, sensitivity, compassion, honesty, and empathy—can also be impressive political resources.

Before I began this book, aware of the sorrowful aspect of his features and the sadness attributed to him by his contemporaries, I had assumed that Lincoln suffered from chronic depression. Yet, with the exception of two despondent episodes in his early life that are described in this story, there is no evidence that he was immobilized by depression. On the contrary, even during the worst days of the war, he retained his ability to function at a very high level.

To be sure, he had a melancholy temperament, most likely imprinted on him from birth. But melancholy differs from depression. It is not an illness; it does not proceed from a specific cause; it is an aspect of one's nature. It has been recognized by artists and writers for centuries as a potential source of creativity and achievement.

Moreover, Lincoln possessed an uncanny understanding of his shifting moods, a profound self-awareness that enabled him to find constructive ways to alleviate sadness and stress. Indeed, when he is compared with his colleagues, it is clear that he possessed the most even-tempered disposition of them all. Time and again, he was the one who dispelled his colleagues' anxiety and sustained their spirits with his gift for storytelling and his life-affirming sense of humor. When resentment and contention threatened to destroy his administration, he refused to be provoked by petty grievances, to submit to jealousy, or to brood over perceived slights. Through the appalling pressures he faced day after day, he retained an unflagging faith in his country's cause.

The comparative approach has also yielded an interesting cast of female characters to provide perspective on the Lincolns' marriage. The fiercely idealistic Frances Seward served as her husband's social conscience. The beautiful Kate Chase made her father's quest for the presidency the ruling passion of her life, while the devoted Julia Bates created a blissful home that gradually enticed her husband away from public ambitions. Like Frances Seward, Mary Lincoln displayed a striking intelligence; like Kate Chase, she possessed what was then considered an unladylike interest in politics. Mary's detractors have suggested that if she had created a more tranquil domestic life for her family, Lincoln might have been satisfied to remain in Springfield. Yet the idea that he could have been a contented homebody, like Edward Bates, contradicts everything we know of the powerful ambition that drove him from his earliest days.

By widening the lens to include Lincoln's colleagues and their families, my story benefited from a treasure trove of primary sources that have not generally been used in Lincoln biographies. The correspondence of the Seward family contains nearly five thousand letters, including an eight-hundred-page diary that Seward's daughter Fanny kept from her fifteenth year until two weeks before her death at the age of twenty-one. In addition to the voluminous journals in which Salmon Chase recorded the events of four decades, he wrote thousands of personal letters. A revealing section of his daughter Kate's diary also survives, along with dozens of letters from her husband, William Sprague. The unpublished section of the diary that Bates began in 1846 provides a more intimate glimpse of the man than the published diary that starts in 1859. Letters to his wife, Julia, during his years in Congress expose the warmth beneath his stolid exterior. Stanton's emotional letters to his family and his sister's unpublished memoir reveal the devotion and idealism that connected the passionate, hard-driving war secretary to his president. The correspondence of Montgomery Blair's sister, Elizabeth Blair Lee, and her husband, Captain Samuel Phillips Lee, leaves a memorable picture of daily life in wartime Washington. The diary of Gideon Welles, of course, has long been recognized for its penetrating insights into the workings of the Lincoln administration.

Through these fresh sources, we see Lincoln liberated from his familiar frock coat and stovepipe hat. We see him late at night relaxing at Seward's house, his long legs stretched before a blazing fire, talking of many things besides the war. We hear his curious and infectious humor in the punch lines of his favorite stories and sit in on clamorous cabinet discussions regarding emancipation and Reconstruction. We feel the enervating tension in the telegraph office as Lincoln clasps Stanton's hand, awaiting bulletins from the battlefield. We follow him to the front on a dozen occasions and observe the invigorating impact of his sympathetic, kindly presence on the morale of the troops. In all these varied encounters, Lincoln's vibrant personality shines through. In the mirrors of his colleagues, he comes to life.

As a young man, Lincoln worried that the "field of glory" had been harvested by the founding fathers, that nothing had been left for his generation but modest ambitions. In the 1850s, however, the wheel of history turned. The rising intensity of the slavery issue and the threatening dissolution of the nation itself provided Lincoln and his colleagues with an opportunity to save and improve the democracy established by Washington, Jefferson, and Adams, creating what Lincoln later called "a new birth of freedom." Without the march of events that led to the Civil War, Lincoln still would have been a good man, but most likely would never have been publicly recognized as a great man. It was history that gave him the opportunity to manifest his greatness, providing the stage that allowed him to shape and transform our national life.

For better than thirty years, as a working historian, I have written on leaders I knew, such as Lyndon Johnson, and interviewed intimates of the Kennedy family and many who knew Franklin Roosevelt, a leader perhaps as indispensable in his way as was Lincoln to the social and political direction of the country. After living with the subject of Abraham Lincoln for a decade, however, reading what he himself wrote and what hundreds of others have written about him, following the arc of his ambition, and assessing the inevitable mixture of human foibles and strengths that made up his temperament, after watching him deal with the terrible deprivations of his childhood, the deaths of his children, and the horror that engulfed the entire nation, I find that after nearly two centuries, the uniquely American story of Abraham Lincoln has unequalled power to captivate the imagination and to inspire emotion.

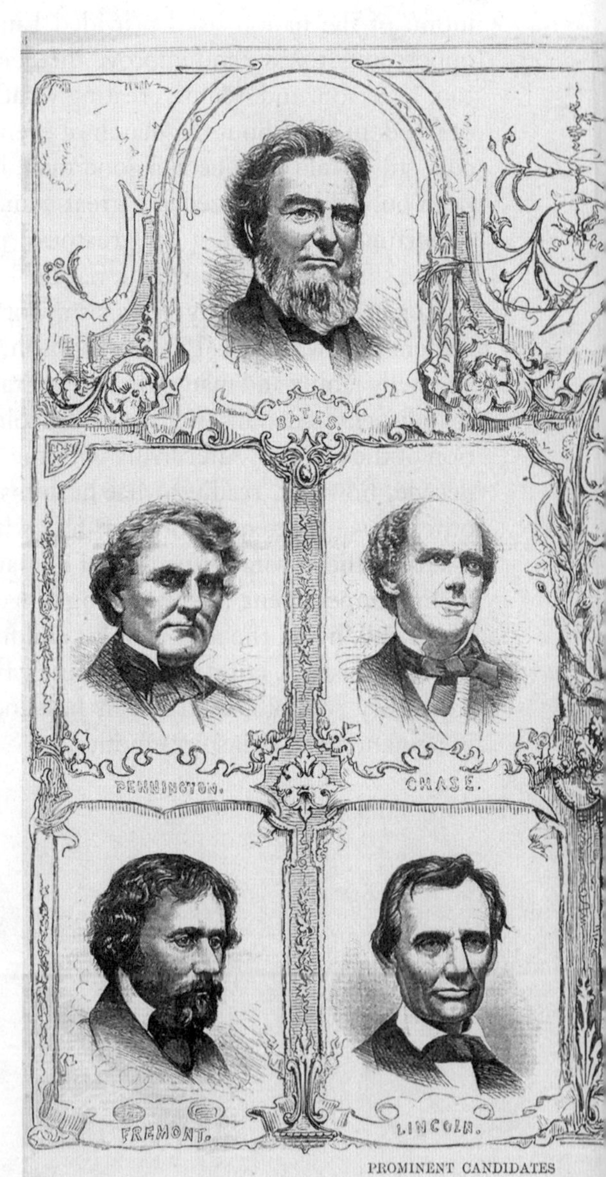

PROMINENT CANDIDATES

PART I

THE RIVALS

R THE REPUBLICAN PRESIDENTIAL NOMINATION AT CHICAGO.—[From Photographs by Brady.]

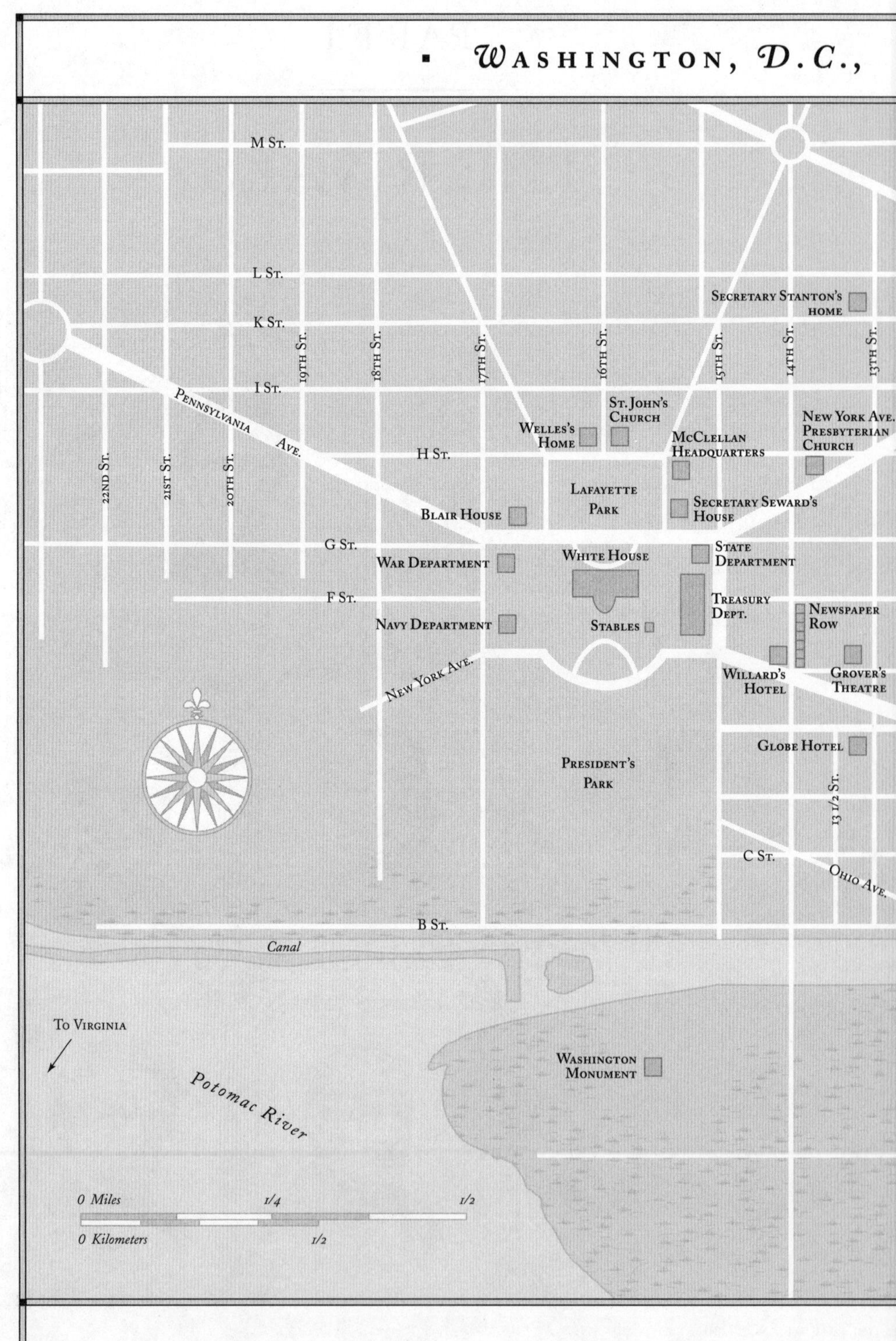

Washington, D.C.,
M St.
L St.
K St.
I St.
H St.
G St.
F St.
B St.
C St.
22nd St.
21st St.
20th St.
19th St.
18th St.
17th St.
16th St.
15th St.
14th St.
13th St.
13 1/2 St.
Pennsylvania Ave.
New York Ave.
Ohio Ave.
Secretary Stanton's home
St. John's Church
Welles's Home
McClellan Headquarters
New York Ave. Presbyterian Church
Lafayette Park
Blair House
Secretary Seward's House
White House
State Department
War Department
Treasury Dept.
Newspaper Row
Navy Department
Stables
Willard's Hotel
Grover's Theatre
Globe Hotel
President's Park
Canal
To Virginia
Washington Monument
Potomac River
0 Miles
1/4
1/2
0 Kilometers
1/2

During the Civil War

To Soldiers' Home and Silver Spring
M St.
Massachusetts Ave.
L St.
K St.
New York Ave.
I St.
North Capitol St.
Mrs. Surratt's Boarding House
Massachusetts Ave.
H St.
12th St.
11th St.
10th St.
9th St.
8th St.
7th St.
6th St.
5th St.
4th St.
1st St.
G St.
3rd St.
2nd St.
Patent Office
Bates's Home
F St.
Petersen House
Ford's Theatre
Post Office Department
Judiciary Hospital
New Jersey Ave.
E St.
Chase-Sprague Mansion
Kirkwood House
D St.
National Intelligencer Newspaper
B.&O. Train Station
Star Newspaper
Pennsylvania Ave.
Louisiana Ave.
Indiana Ave.
Metropolitan Hotel
C St.
National Hotel
B.&O. Railroad
Center Market
B St.
Canal
4 1/2 St.
7th St.
U.S. Capitol
Smithsonian Museum, Library, and Lecture Hall
War Hospitals
Maine Ave.
D.C. Armory
Maryland Ave.
To Navy Yard
Canal
To Long Bridge
To wharves–ferry to Virginia
© 2005 Jeffrey L. Ward

CHAPTER 1

FOUR MEN WAITING

On May 18, 1860, the day when the Republican Party would nominate its candidate for president, Abraham Lincoln was up early. As he climbed the stairs to his plainly furnished law office on the south side of the public square in Springfield, Illinois, breakfast was being served at the 130-room Chenery House on Fourth Street. Fresh butter, flour, lard, and eggs were being put out for sale at the City Grocery Store on North Sixth Street. And in the morning newspaper, the proprietors at Smith, Wickersham & Company had announced the arrival of a large spring stock of silks, calicos, ginghams, and linens, along with a new supply of the latest styles of hosiery and gloves.

The Republicans had chosen to meet in Chicago. A new convention hall called the "Wigwam" had been constructed for the occasion. The first ballot was not due to be called until 10 a.m. and Lincoln, although patient by nature, was visibly "nervous, fidgety, and intensely excited." With an outside chance to secure the Republican nomination for the highest office of the land, he was unable to focus on his work. Even under ordinary circumstances many would have found concentration difficult in the untidy office Lincoln shared with his younger partner, William Herndon. Two worktables, piled high with papers and correspondence, formed a T in the center of the room. Additional documents and letters spilled out from the drawers and pigeonholes of an outmoded secretary in the corner. When he needed a particular piece of correspondence, Lincoln had to rifle through disorderly stacks of paper, rummaging, as a last resort, in the lining of his old plug hat, where he often put stray letters or notes.

Restlessly descending to the street, he passed the state capitol building, set back from the road, and the open lot where he played handball with his friends, and climbed a short set of stairs to the office of the *Illinois State Journal*, the local Republican newspaper. The editorial room on the second floor, with a central large wood-burning stove, was a gathering place for the exchange of news and gossip.

He wandered over to the telegraph office on the north side of the square to see if any new dispatches had come in. There were few outward signs that this was a day of special moment and expectation in the history of Springfield, scant record of any celebration or festivity planned should Lincoln, long their fellow townsman, actually secure the nomination. That he had garnered the support of the Illinois delegation at the state convention at Decatur earlier that month was widely understood to be a "complimentary" gesture. Yet if there were no firm plans to celebrate his dark horse bid, Lincoln knew well the ardor of his staunch circle of friends already at work on his behalf on the floor of the Wigwam.

The hands of the town clock on the steeple of the Baptist church on Adams Street must have seemed not to move. When Lincoln learned that his longtime friend James Conkling had returned unexpectedly from the convention the previous evening, he walked over to Conkling's office above Chatterton's jewelry store. Told that his friend was expected within the hour, he returned to his own quarters, intending to come back as soon as Conkling arrived.

Lincoln's shock of black hair, brown furrowed face, and deep-set eyes made him look older than his fifty-one years. He was a familiar figure to almost everyone in Springfield, as was his singular way of walking, which gave the impression that his long, gaunt frame needed oiling. He plodded forward in an awkward manner, hands hanging at his sides or folded behind his back. His step had no spring, his partner William Herndon recalled. He lifted his whole foot at once rather than lifting from the toes and then thrust the whole foot down on the ground rather than landing on his heel. "His legs," another observer noted, "seemed to drag from the knees down, like those of a laborer going home after a hard day's work."

His features, even supporters conceded, were not such "as belong to a handsome man." In repose, his face was "so overspread with sadness," the reporter Horace White noted, that it seemed as if "Shakespeare's melancholy Jacques had been translated from the forest of Arden to the capital of Illinois." Yet, when Lincoln began to speak, White observed, "this expression of sorrow dropped from him instantly. His face lighted up with a winning smile, and where I had a moment before seen only leaden sorrow I now beheld keen intelligence, genuine kindness of heart, and the promise of true friendship." If his appearance seemed somewhat odd, what captivated admirers, another contemporary observed, was "his winning manner, his ready good humor, and his unaffected kindness and gentleness."

Five minutes in his presence, and "you cease to think that he is either homely or awkward."

Springfield had been Lincoln's home for nearly a quarter of a century. He had arrived in the young city to practice law at twenty-eight years old, riding into town, his great friend Joshua Speed recalled, "on a borrowed horse, with no earthly property save a pair of saddle-bags containing a few clothes." The city had grown rapidly, particularly after 1839, when it became the capital of Illinois. By 1860, Springfield boasted nearly ten thousand residents, though its business district, designed to accommodate the expanding population that arrived in town when the legislature was in session, housed thousands more. Ten hotels radiated from the public square where the capitol building stood. In addition, there were multiple saloons and restaurants, seven newspapers, three billiard halls, dozens of retail stores, three military armories, and two railroad depots.

Here in Springfield, in the Edwards mansion on the hill, Lincoln had courted and married "the belle of the town," young Mary Todd, who had come to live with her married sister, Elizabeth, wife of Ninian Edwards, the well-to-do son of the former governor of Illinois. Raised in a prominent Lexington, Kentucky, family, Mary had received an education far superior to most girls her age. For four years she had studied languages and literature in an exclusive boarding school and then spent two additional years in what was considered graduate study. The story is told of Lincoln's first meeting with Mary at a festive party. Captivated by her lively manner, intelligent face, clear blue eyes, and dimpled smile, Lincoln reportedly said, "I want to dance with you in the worst way." And, Mary laughingly told her cousin later that night, "he certainly did." In Springfield, all their children were born, and one was buried. In that spring of 1860, Mary was forty-two, Robert sixteen, William nine, and Thomas seven. Edward, the second son, had died at the age of three.

Their home, described at the time as a modest "two-story frame house, having a wide hall running through the centre, with parlors on both sides," stood close to the street and boasted few trees and no garden. "The adornments were few, but chastely appropriate," one contemporary observer noted. In the center hall stood "the customary little table with a white marble top," on which were arranged flowers, a silver-plated ice-water pitcher, and family photographs. Along the walls were positioned some chairs and a sofa. "Everything," a journalist observed, "tended to represent the home of a man who has battled hard with the fortunes of life, and whose hard experience had taught him to enjoy whatever of success belongs to him, rather in solid substance than in showy display."

During his years in Springfield, Lincoln had forged an unusually loyal circle of friends. They had worked with him in the state legislature, helped him in his campaigns for Congress and the Senate, and now, at this very moment, were guiding his efforts at the Chicago convention, "moving heaven & Earth," they assured him, in an attempt to secure him the nomination. These steadfast companions included David Davis, the Circuit Court judge for the Eighth District, whose three-hundred-pound body was matched by "a big brain and a big heart"; Norman Judd, an attorney for the railroads and chairman of the Illinois Republican state central committee; Leonard Swett, a lawyer from Bloomington who believed he knew Lincoln "as intimately as I have ever known any man in my life"; and Stephen Logan, Lincoln's law partner for three years in the early forties.

Many of these friendships had been forged during the shared experience of the "circuit," the eight weeks each spring and fall when Lincoln and his fellow lawyers journeyed together throughout the state. They shared rooms and sometimes beds in dusty village inns and taverns, spending long evenings gathered together around a blazing fire. The economics of the legal profession in sparsely populated Illinois were such that lawyers had to move about the state in the company of the circuit judge, trying thousands of small cases in order to make a living. The arrival of the traveling bar brought life and vitality to the county seats, fellow rider Henry Whitney recalled. Villagers congregated on the courthouse steps. When the court sessions were complete, everyone would gather in the local tavern from dusk to dawn, sharing drinks, stories, and good cheer.

In these convivial settings, Lincoln was invariably the center of attention. No one could equal his never-ending stream of stories nor his ability to reproduce them with such contagious mirth. As his winding tales became more famous, crowds of villagers awaited his arrival at every stop for the chance to hear a master storyteller. Everywhere he went, he won devoted followers, friendships that later emboldened his quest for office. Political life in these years, the historian Robert Wiebe has observed, "broke down into clusters of men who were bound together by mutual trust." And no political circle was more loyally bound than the band of compatriots working for Lincoln in Chicago.

The prospects for his candidacy had taken wing in 1858 after his brilliant campaign against the formidable Democratic leader, Stephen Douglas, in a dramatic senate race in Illinois that had attracted national attention. Though Douglas had won a narrow victory, Lincoln managed to unite the disparate elements of his state's fledgling Republican Party—that curious amalgamation of former Whigs, antislavery Democrats, nativists, foreigners, radicals, and conservatives. In the mid-1850s, the Republican

Party had come together in state after state in the North with the common goal of preventing the spread of slavery to the territories. "Of *strange, discordant*, and even, *hostile* elements," Lincoln proudly claimed, "we gathered from the four winds, and *formed* and fought the battle through." The story of Lincoln's rise to power was inextricably linked to the increasing intensity of the antislavery cause. Public feeling on the slavery issue had become so flammable that Lincoln's seven debates with Douglas were carried in newspapers across the land, proving the prairie lawyer from Springfield more than a match for the most likely Democratic nominee for the presidency.

Furthermore, in an age when speech-making prowess was central to political success, when the spoken word filled the air "from sun-up til sundown," Lincoln's stirring oratory had earned the admiration of a far-flung audience who had either heard him speak or read his speeches in the paper. As his reputation grew, the invitations to speak multiplied. In the year before the convention, he had appeared before tens of thousands of people in Ohio, Iowa, Indiana, Wisconsin, Kentucky, New York, and New England. The pinnacle of his success was reached at Cooper Union in New York, where, on the evening of February 27, 1860, before a zealous crowd of more than fifteen hundred people, Lincoln delivered what the *New York Tribune* called "one of the happiest and most convincing political arguments ever made in this City" in defense of Republican principles and the need to confine slavery to the places where it already existed. "The vast assemblage frequently rang with cheers and shouts of applause, which were prolonged and intensified at the close. No man ever before made such an impression on his first appeal to a New-York audience."

Lincoln's success in the East bolstered his supporters at home. On May 10, the fired-up Republican state convention at Decatur nominated him for president, labeling him "the Rail Candidate for President" after two fence rails he had supposedly split in his youth were ceremoniously carried into the hall. The following week, the powerful Chicago *Press and Tribune* formally endorsed Lincoln, arguing that his moderate politics represented the thinking of most people, that he would come into the contest "with no clogs, no embarrassment," an "honest man" who represented all the "fundamentals of Republicanism," with "due respect for the rights of the South."

Still, Lincoln clearly understood that he was "new in the field," that outside of Illinois he was not "the first choice of a very great many." His only political experience on the national level consisted of two failed Senate races and a single term in Congress that had come to an end nearly a dozen years earlier. By contrast, the three other contenders for the nomination were household names in Republican circles. William Henry Seward had been a celebrated senator from New York for more than a decade and governor of his state for two terms before he went to Washington. Ohio's Salmon P. Chase, too, had been both senator and governor, and had played a central role in the formation of the national Republican Party. Edward Bates was a widely respected elder statesman, a delegate to the convention that had framed the Missouri Constitution, and a former congressman whose opinions on national matters were still widely sought.

Recognizing that Seward held a commanding lead at the start, followed by Chase and Bates, Lincoln's strategy was to give offense to no one. He wanted to leave the delegates "in a mood to come to us, if they shall be compelled to give up their first love." This was clearly understood by Lincoln's team in Chicago and by all the delegates whom Judge Davis had commandeered to join the fight. "We are laboring to make you the second choice of all the Delegations we can, where we can't make you first choice," Scott County delegate Nathan Knapp told Lincoln when he first arrived in Chicago. "Keep a good nerve," Knapp advised, "be not surprised at any result—but I tell you that your chances are not the worst . . . brace your nerves for any result." Knapp's message was followed by one from Davis himself on the second day of the convention. "Am very hopeful," he warned Lincoln, but "dont be Excited."

The warnings were unnecessary—Lincoln was, above all, a realist who fully understood that he faced an uphill climb against his better-known rivals. Anxious to get a clearer picture of the situation, he headed back to Conkling's office, hoping that his old friend had returned. This time he was not disappointed. As Conkling later told the story, Lincoln stretched himself upon an old settee that stood by the front window, "his head on a cushion and his feet over the end," while Conkling related all he had seen and heard in the previous two days before leaving the Wigwam. Conkling told Lincoln that Seward was in trouble, that he had enemies not only in other states but at home in New York. If Seward was not nominated on the first ballot, Conkling predicted, Lincoln would be the nominee.

Lincoln replied that "he hardly thought this could be possible and that in case Mr. Seward was not nominated on the first ballot, it was his judgment that Mr. Chase of Ohio or Mr. Bates of Missouri would be the nominee." Conkling disagreed, citing reasons why each of those two candidates would have difficulty securing the nomination. Assessing the situation with his characteristic clearheadedness, Lincoln could not fail to perceive some truth in what his friend was saying; yet having tasted so many disappointments, he saw no benefit in letting his hopes run wild.

"Well, Conkling," he said slowly, pulling his long frame up from the settee, "I believe I will go back to my office and practice law."

• • •

WHILE LINCOLN STRUGGLED to sustain his hopes against the likelihood of failure, William Henry Seward was in the best of spirits. He had left Washington three days earlier to repair to his hometown of Auburn, New York, situated in the Finger Lakes Region of the most populous state of the Union, to share the anticipated Republican nomination in the company of family and friends.

Nearly sixty years old, with the vitality and appearance of a man half his age, Seward typically rose at 6 a.m. when first light slanted into the bedroom window of his twenty-room country home. Rising early allowed him time to complete his morning constitutional through his beloved garden before the breakfast bell was rung. Situated on better than five acres of land, the Seward mansion was surrounded by manicured lawns, elaborate gardens, and walking paths that wound beneath elms, mountain ash, evergreens, and fruit trees. Decades earlier, Seward had supervised the planting of every one of these trees, which now numbered in the hundreds. He had spent thousands of hours fertilizing and cultivating his flowering shrubs. With what he called "a lover's interest," he inspected them daily. His horticultural passion was in sharp contrast to Lincoln's lack of interest in planting trees or growing flowers at his Springfield home. Having spent his childhood laboring long hours on his father's struggling farm, Lincoln found little that was romantic or recreational about tilling the soil.

When Seward "came in to the table," his son Frederick recalled, "he would announce that the hyacinths were in bloom, or that the bluebirds had come, or whatever other change the morning had brought." After breakfast, he typically retired to his book-lined study to enjoy the precious hours of uninterrupted work before his doors opened to the outer world. The chair on which he sat was the same one he had used in the Governor's Mansion in Albany, designed specially for him so that everything he needed could be right at hand. It was, he joked, his "complete office," equipped not only with a writing arm that swiveled back and forth but also with a candleholder and secret drawers to keep his inkwells, pens, treasured snuff box, and the ashes of the half-dozen or more cigars he smoked every day. "He usually lighted a cigar when he sat down to write," Fred recalled, "slowly consuming it as his pen ran rapidly over the page, and lighted a fresh one when that was exhausted."

Midmorning of the day of the nomination, a large cannon was hauled from the Auburn Armory into the park. "The cannoneers were stationed at their posts," the local paper reported, "the fire lighted, the ammunition ready, and all waiting for the signal, to make the city and county echo to the joyful news" that was expected to unleash the most spectacular public celebration the city had ever known. People began gathering in front of Seward's house. As the hours passed, the crowds grew denser, spilling over into all the main streets of Auburn. The revelers were drawn from their homes in anticipation of the grand occasion and by the lovely spring weather, welcome after the severe, snowy winters Auburn endured that often isolated the small towns and cities of the region for days at a time. Visitors had come by horse and carriage from the surrounding villages, from Seneca Falls and Waterloo to the west, from Skaneateles to the east, from Weedsport to the north. Local restaurants had stocked up with food. Banners were being prepared, flags were set to be raised, and in the basement of the chief hotel, hundreds of bottles of champagne stood ready to be uncorked.

A festive air pervaded Auburn, for the vigorous senator was admired by almost everyone in the region, not only for his political courage, unquestioned integrity, and impressive intellect but even more for his good nature and his genial disposition. A natural politician, Seward was genuinely interested in people, curious about their families and the smallest details of their lives, anxious to help with their problems. As a public man he possessed unusual resilience, enabling him to accept criticism with good-humored serenity.

Even the Democratic paper, the *New York Herald*, conceded that probably fewer than a hundred of Auburn's ten thousand residents would vote against Seward if he received the nomination. "He is beloved by all classes of people, irrespective of partisan predilections," the *Herald* observed. "No philanthropic or benevolent movement is suggested without receiving his liberal and thoughtful assistance. . . . As a landlord he is kind and lenient; as an advisor he is frank and reliable; as a citizen he is enterprising and patriotic; as a champion of what he considers to be right he is dauntless and intrepid."

Seward customarily greeted personal friends at the door and was fond of walking them through his tree-lined garden to his white summerhouse. Though he stood only five feet six inches tall, with a slender frame that young Henry Adams likened to that of a scarecrow, he was nonetheless, Adams marveled, a commanding figure, an outsize personality, a "most glorious original" against whom larger men seemed smaller. People were drawn to this vital figure with the large, hawklike nose, bushy eyebrows, enormous ears; his hair, once bright red, had faded now to the color of straw. His step, in contrast to Lincoln's slow and laborious manner of walking, had a "school-boy elasticity" as he moved from his garden to his house and back again with what one reporter described as a "slashing swagger."

Every room of his palatial home contained associations from earlier days, mementos of previous triumphs. The slim Sheraton desk in the hallway had belonged to a member of the First Constitutional Congress in 1789. The fireplace in the parlor had been crafted by the young carpenter Brigham Young, later prophet of the Mormon Church. The large Thomas Cole painting in the drawing room depicting *Portage Falls* had been presented to Seward in commemoration of his early efforts to extend the canal system in New York State. Every inch of wall space was filled with curios and family portraits executed by the most famous artists of the day—Thomas Sully, Chester Harding, Henry Inman. Even the ivy that grew along the pathways and up the garden trellises had an anecdotal legacy, having been cultivated at Sir Walter Scott's home in Scotland and presented to Seward by Washington Irving.

As he perused the stack of telegrams and newspaper articles arriving from Chicago for the past week, Seward had every reason to be confident. Both Republican and Democratic papers agreed that "the honor in question was [to be] awarded by common expectation to the distinguished Senator from the State of New York, who, more than any other, was held to be the representative man of his party, and who, by his commanding talents and eminent public services, has so largely contributed to the development of its principles." The local Democratic paper, the Albany *Atlas and Argus*, was forced to concede: "No press has opposed more consistently and more unreservedly than ours the political principles of Mr. Seward. . . . But we have recognised the genius and the leadership of the man."

So certain was Seward of receiving the nomination that the weekend before the convention opened he had already composed a first draft of the valedictory speech he expected to make to the Senate, assuming that he would resign his position as soon as the decision in Chicago was made. Taking leave of his Senate colleagues, with whom he had labored through the tumultuous fifties, he had returned to Auburn, the place, he once said, he loved and admired more than any other—more than Albany, where he had served four years in the state senate and two terms as governor as a member of the Whig Party; more than the U.S. Senate chamber, where he had represented the leading state of the Union for nearly twelve years; more than any city in any of the four continents in which he had traveled extensively.

Auburn was the only place, he claimed, where he was left "free to act in an individual and not in a representative and public character," the only place where he felt "content to live, and content, when life's fitful fever shall be over, to die." Auburn was a prosperous community in the 1860s, with six schoolhouses, thirteen churches, seven banks, eleven newspapers, a woolen mill, a candle factory, a state prison, a fine hotel, and more than two hundred stores. Living on the northern shore of Owasco Lake, seventy-eight miles east of Rochester, the citizens took pride in the orderly layout of its streets, adorned by handsome rows of maples, elms, poplars, and sycamores.

Seward had arrived in Auburn as a graduate of Union College in Schenectady, New York. Having completed his degree with highest honors and finished his training for the bar, he had come to practice law with Judge Elijah Miller, the leading citizen of Cayuga County. It was in Judge Miller's country house that Seward had courted and married Frances Miller, the judge's intelligent, well-educated daughter. Frances was a tall, slender, comely woman, with large black eyes, an elegant neck, and a passionate commitment to women's rights and the antislavery cause. She was Seward's intellectual equal, a devoted wife and mother, a calming presence in his stormy life. In this same house, where he and Frances had lived since their marriage, five children were born—Augustus, a graduate of West Point who was now serving in the military; Frederick, who had embarked on a career in journalism and served as his father's private secretary in Washington; Will Junior, who was just starting out in business; and Fanny, a serious-minded girl on the threshold of womanhood, who loved poetry, read widely, kept a daily journal, and hoped someday to be a writer. A second daughter, Cornelia, had died in 1837 at four months.

Seward had been slow to take up the Republican banner, finding it difficult to abandon his beloved Whig Party. His national prominence ensured that he became the new party's chief spokesman the moment he joined its ranks. Seward, Henry Adams wrote, "would inspire a cow with statesmanship if she understood our language." The young Republican leader Carl Schurz later recalled that he and his friends idealized Seward and considered him the "leader of the political anti-slavery movement. From him we received the battle-cry in the turmoil of the contest, for he was one of those spirits who sometimes will go ahead of public opinion instead of tamely following its footprints."

In a time when words, communicated directly and then repeated in newspapers, were the primary means of communication between a political leader and the public, Seward's ability to "compress into a single sentence, a single word, the whole issue of a controversy" would irrevocably, and often dangerously, create a political identity. Over the years, his ringing phrases, calling upon a "higher law" than the Constitution that commanded men to freedom, or the assertion that the collision between the North and South was "an irrepressible conflict," became, as the young Schurz noted, "the inscriptions on our banners, the pass-words of our combatants." But those same phrases had also alarmed Republican moderates, especially in the West. It was rhetoric, more than substance, that had stamped Seward as a radical—for his actual positions in 1860 were not far from the center of the Republican Party.

Whenever Seward delivered a major speech in the Senate, the galleries were full, for audiences were invariably transfixed not only by the power of his arguments but by his exuberant personality and, not least, the striking peculiarity of his appearance. Forgoing the simpler style of men's clothing that prevailed in the 1850s, Seward preferred pantaloons and a long-tailed frock coat, the tip of a handkerchief poking out its back pocket. This jaunty touch figured in his oratorical style, which included dramatic pauses for him to dip into his snuff box and blow his enormous nose into the outsize yellow silk handkerchief that matched his yellow pantaloons. Such flamboyance and celebrity almost lent an aura of inevitability to his nomination.

If Seward remained serene as the hours passed to afternoon, secure in the belief that he was about to realize the goal toward which he had bent his formidable powers for so many years, the chief reason for his tranquillity lay in the knowledge that his campaign at the convention was in the hands of the most powerful political boss in the country: Thurlow Weed. Dictator of New York State for nearly half a century, the handsome, white-haired Weed was Seward's closest friend and ally. "Men might love and respect [him], might hate and despise him," Weed's biographer Glyndon Van Deusen wrote, "but no one who took any interest in the politics and government of the country could ignore him." Over the years, it was Weed who managed every one of Seward's successful campaigns—for the state senate, the governorship, and the senatorship of New York—guarding his career at every step along the way "as a hen does its chicks."

They made an exceptional team. Seward was more visionary, more idealistic, better equipped to arouse the emotions of a crowd; Weed was more practical, more realistic, more skilled in winning elections and getting things done. While Seward conceived party platforms and articulated broad principles, Weed built the party organization, dispensed patronage, rewarded loyalists, punished defectors, developed poll lists, and carried voters to the polls, spreading the influence of the boss over the entire state. So closely did people identify the two men that they spoke of Seward-Weed as a single political person: "Seward is Weed and Weed is Seward."

Thurlow Weed certainly understood that Seward would face a host of problems at the convention. There were many delegates who considered the New Yorker too radical; others disdained him as an opportunist, shifting ground to strengthen his own ambition. Furthermore, complaints of corruption had surfaced in the Weed-controlled legislature. And the very fact that Seward had been the most conspicuous Northern politician for nearly a decade inevitably created jealousy among many of his colleagues. Despite these problems, Seward nonetheless appeared to be the overwhelming choice of Republican voters and politicians.

Moreover, since Weed believed the opposition lacked the power to consolidate its strength, he was convinced that Seward would eventually emerge the victor. Members of the vital New York State delegation confirmed Weed's assessment. On May 16, the day the convention opened, the former Whig editor, now a Republican, James Watson Webb assured Seward that there was "no *cause* for doubting. It is only a question of time. . . . And I tell you, and stake my judgment upon it entirely, that nothing has, or can occur . . . to shake my convictions in regard to the result." The next day, Congressman Eldridge Spaulding telegraphed Seward: "Your friends are firm and confident that you will be nominated after a few ballots." And on the morning of the 18th, just before the balloting was set to begin, William Evarts, chairman of the New York delegation, sent an optimistic message: "All right. Everything indicates your nomination today sure." The dream that had powered Seward and Weed for three decades seemed within reach at last.

• • •

WHILE FRIENDS AND SUPPORTERS gathered about Seward on the morning of the 18th, Ohio's governor, Salmon Chase, awaited the balloting results in characteristic solitude. History records no visitors that day to the majestic Gothic mansion bristling with towers, turrets, and chimneys at the corner of State and Sixth Streets in Columbus, Ohio, where the handsome fifty-two-year-old widower lived with his two daughters, nineteen-year-old Kate and her half sister, eleven-year-old Nettie.

There are no reports of crowds gathering spontaneously in the streets as the hours passed, though preparations had been made for a great celebration that evening should Ohio's favorite son receive the nomination he passionately believed he had a right to expect. Brass bands stood at the ready. Fireworks had been purchased, and a dray procured to drag an enormous cannon to the statehouse, where its thunder might roll over the city once the hoped-for results were revealed. Until that announcement, the citizens of Columbus apparently went about their business, in keeping with the reserved, even austere, demeanor of their governor.

Chase stood over six feet in height. His wide shoulders, massive chest, and dignified bearing all contributed to Carl Schurz's assessment that Chase "looked as you would wish a statesman to look." One reporter observed that "he is one of the finest specimens of a perfect man that we have ever seen; a large, well formed head, set upon a frame of herculean proportions," with "an eye of unrivaled splendor and brilliancy." Yet where Lincoln's features became more warm and compelling as one drew near him, the closer one studied Chase's good-looking face, the more one noticed the unattractive droop of the lid of his right eye, creating "an arresting duality, as if two men, rather than one, looked out upon the world."

Fully aware of the positive first impression he created, Chase dressed with meticulous care. In contrast to Seward or Lincoln, who were known to greet visitors clad in slippers with their shirttails hanging out, the dignified Chase was rarely seen without a waistcoat. Nor was he willing to wear his glasses in public, though he was so nearsighted that he would often pass friends on the street without displaying the slightest recognition.

An intensely religious man of unbending routine, Chase likely began that day, as he began every day, gathering his two daughters and all the members of his household staff around him for a solemn reading of Scripture. The morning meal done, he and his elder daughter, Kate, would repair to the library to read and discuss the morning papers, searching together for signs that people across the country regarded Chase as highly as he regarded himself—signs that would bolster their hope for the Republican nomination.

During his years as governor, he kept to a rigid schedule, setting out at the same time each morning for the three-block walk to the statehouse, which was usually his only exercise of the day. Never late for appointments, he had no patience with the sin of tardiness, which robbed precious minutes of life from the person who was kept waiting. On those evenings when he had no public functions to attend, he would sequester himself in his library at home to answer letters, consult the statute books, memorize lines of poetry, study a foreign language, or practice the jokes that, however hard he tried, he could never gracefully deliver.

On the rare nights when he indulged in a game of backgammon or chess with Kate, he would invariably return to work at his fastidiously arranged drop-leaf desk, where everything was always in its "proper place" with not a single pen or piece of paper out of order. There he would sit for hours, long after every window on his street was dark, recording his thoughts in the introspective diary he had kept since he was twenty years old. Then, as the candle began to sink, he would turn to his Bible to close the day as it had begun, with prayer.

Unlike Seward's Auburn estate, which he and Frances had furnished over the decades with objects that marked different stages of their lives, Chase had filled his palatial house with exquisite carpets, carved parlor chairs, elegant mirrors, and rich draperies that important people of his time *ought* to display to prove their eminence to the world at large. He had moved frequently during his life, and this Columbus dwelling was the first home he had really tried to make his own. Yet everything was chosen for effect: even the dogs, it was said, seemed "designed and posed."

Columbus was a bustling capital city in 1860, with a population of just under twenty thousand and a reputation for gracious living and hospitable entertainment. The city's early settlers had hailed largely from New England, Pennsylvania, and Virginia, but in recent decades German and Irish immigrants had moved in, along with a thousand free blacks who lived primarily in the Long Street district near the Irish settlement. It was a time of steady growth and prosperity. Spacious blocks with wide shade trees were laid out in the heart of the city, where, the writer William Dean Howells recalled, beautiful young women, dressed in great hoopskirts, floated by "as silken balloons walking in the streets." Fashionable districts developed along High and State Streets, and a new Capitol, nearly as big as the United States Capitol, opened its doors in January 1857. Built in Greek Revival style, with tall Doric columns defining each of the entrances and a large cupola on top, the magnificent structure, which housed the governor's office as well as the legislative chambers, was proclaimed to be "the greatest State capitol building" in the country.

Unlike Seward, who frequently attended theater, loved reading novels, and found nothing more agreeable than an evening of cards, fine cigars, and a bottle of port, Chase neither drank nor smoked. He considered both theater and novels a foolish waste of time and recoiled from all games of chance, believing that they unwholesomely excited the mind. Nor was he likely to regale his friends with intricate stories told for pure fun, as did Lincoln. As one contemporary noted, "he seldom told a story without spoiling it." Even those who knew him well, except perhaps his beloved Kate, rarely recalled his laughing aloud.

Kate Chase, beautiful and ambitious, filled the emotional void in her father's heart created by the almost incomprehensible loss of three wives, all having died at a young age, including Kate's mother when Kate was five years old. Left on his own, Chase had molded and shaped his brilliant daughter, watching over her growth and cultivation with a boundless ardor. When she was seven, he sent her to an expensive boarding school in Gramercy Park, New York, where she remained for ten years, studying Latin, French, history, and the classics, in addition to elocution, deportment, and the social graces. "In a few years you will necessarily go into society," he had told her when she was thirteen. "I desire that you may be qualified to ornament any society in our own country or elsewhere into which I may have occasion to take you. It is for this reason that I care more for your improvement in your studies, the cultivation of your manners, and the establishment of your moral & religious principles, than for anything else."

After Kate graduated from boarding school and returned to Columbus, she blossomed as Ohio's first lady. Her father's ambitions and dreams became the ruling passions of her life. She gradually made herself absolutely essential to him, helping with his correspondence, editing his speeches, discussing political strategy, entertaining his friends and colleagues. While other girls her age focused on the social calendar of balls and soirées, she concentrated all her energies on furthering her father's political career. "She did everything in her power," her biographers suggest, "to fill the gaps in his life so that he would not in his loneliness seek another Mrs. Chase." She sat beside him at lyceum lectures and political debates. She presided over his dinners and receptions. She became his surrogate wife.

Though Chase treated his sweet, unassuming younger daughter, Janette (Nettie), with warmth and affection, his love for Kate was powerfully intertwined with his desire for political advancement. He had cultivated her in his own image, and she possessed an ease of conversation far more relaxed than his own. Now he could depend on her to assist him every step along the way as, day after day, year after year, he moved steadily toward his goal of becoming president. From the moment when the high office appeared possible to Chase, with his stunning election in 1855 as the first Republican governor of a major state, it had become the consuming passion of both father and daughter that he reach the White House—a passion that would endure even after the Civil War was over. Seward was no less ambitious, but he was far more at ease with diverse people, and more capable of discarding the burdens of office at the end of the day.

Yet if Chase was somewhat priggish and more self-righteous than Seward, he was more inflexibly attached to his guiding principles, which, for more than a quarter of a century, had encompassed an unflagging commitment to the cause of the black man. Whereas the more accommodating Seward could have been a successful politician in almost any age, Chase functioned best in an era when dramatic moral issues prevailed. The slavery debate of the antebellum period allowed Chase to argue his antislavery principles in biblical terms of right and wrong. Chase was actually more radical than Seward on the slavery issue, but because his speeches were not studded with memorable turns of phrase, his positions were not as notorious in the country at large, and, therefore, not as damaging in more moderate circles.

"There may have been abler statesmen than Chase, and there certainly were more agreeable companions," his biographer Albert Hart has asserted, "but none of them contributed so much to the stock of American political ideas as he." In his study of the origins of the Republican Party, William Gienapp underscores this judgment. "In the long run," he concludes, referring both to Chase's intellectual leadership of the antislavery movement and to his organizational abilities, "no individual made a more significant contribution to the formation of the Republican party than did Chase."

And no individual felt he *deserved* the presidency as a natural result of his past contributions more than Chase himself. Writing to his longtime friend the abolitionist Gamaliel Bailey, he claimed: "A very large body of the people—embracing not a few who would hardly vote for any man other than myself as a Republican nominee—seem to desire that I shall be a candidate in 1860. No effort of mine, and so far as I know none of my immediate personal friends has produced this feeling. It seems to be of spontaneous growth."

A vivid testimony to the power of the governor's wishful thinking is provided by Carl Schurz, Seward's avid supporter, who was invited to stay with Chase while lecturing in Ohio in March 1860. "I arrived early in the morning," Schurz recalled in his memoirs, "and was, to my great surprise, received at the uncomfortable hour by the Governor himself, and taken to the breakfast room." Kate entered, greeted him, "and then let herself down upon her chair with the graceful lightness of a bird that, folding its wings, perches upon the branch of a tree. . . . She had something imperial in the pose of the head, and all her movements possessed an exquisite natural charm. No wonder that she came to be admired as a great beauty and broke many hearts."

The conversation, in which "Miss Kate took a lively and remarkably intelligent part, soon turned upon politics," as Chase revealed to Schurz with surprising candor his "ardent desire to be President of the United States." Aware that Schurz would be a delegate at the convention, Chase sounded him on his own candidacy. "It would have given me a moment of sincerest happiness could I have answered that question with a note of encouragement, for nothing could have appeared to me more legitimate than the high ambition of that man," Schurz recalled. Chagrined, he nonetheless felt compelled to give an honest judgment, predicting that if the delegates were willing to nominate "an advanced anti-slavery man," they would take Seward before Chase.

Chase was taken aback, "as if he had heard something unexpected." A look of sadness came over his face. Quickly he regained control and proceeded to deliver a powerful brief demonstrating why he, rather than Seward, deserved to be considered the true leader of the antislavery forces. Schurz remained unconvinced, but he listened politely, certain that he had never before met a public man with such a serious case of "presidential fever," to the extent of "honestly believing that he owed it to the country and that the country owed it to him that he should be President." For his part, Chase remained hopeful that by his own unwavering self-confidence he had cast a spell on Schurz. The following day, Chase told his friend Robert Hosea about the visit, suggesting that in the hours they spent together Schurz had seemed to alter his opinion of Chase's chance at winning, making it "desirable to have him brought in contact with our best men." Despite Chase's best efforts Schurz remained loyal to Seward.

In the weeks before the convention, the Chase candidacy received almost daily encouragement in the *Ohio State Journal*, the Republican newspaper in Columbus. "No man in the country is more worthy, no one is more competent," the *Journal* declared. By "steady devotion to the principles of popular freedom, through a long political career," he "has won the confidence and attachment of the people in regions far beyond the State."

Certain that his cause would ultimately triumph, Chase refused to engage in the practical methods by which nominations are won. He had virtually no campaign. He had not conciliated his many enemies in Ohio itself, and as a result, he alone among the candidates would not come to the convention with the united support of his own state. Remaining in his Columbus mansion with Kate by his side, he preferred to make inroads by reminding his supporters in dozens of letters that he was the best man for the job. Listening only to what he wanted to hear, discounting troubling signs, Chase believed that "if the most cherished wishes of the people could prevail," he would be the nominee.

"Now is the time," one supporter told him. "You will ride triumphantly on the topmost wave." On the eve of the convention, he remained buoyant. "There is reason to hope," he told James Briggs, a lawyer from Cleveland—reason to hope that he and Kate would soon take their place as the president and first lady of the United States.

• • •

JUDGE EDWARD BATES awaited news from the convention at Grape Hill, his large country estate four miles from the city of St. Louis. Julia Coalter, his wife of thirty-seven years, was by his side. She was an attractive, sturdy woman who had borne him seventeen children, eight of whom survived to adulthood. Their extended family of six sons, two daughters, and nearly a dozen grandchildren remained unusually close. As the children married and raised families of their own, they continued to consider Grape Hill their primary home.

The judge's orderly life was steeped in solid rituals based on the seasons, the land, and his beloved family. He bathed in cold water every morning. A supper bell called him to eat every night. In the first week of April, he "substituted cotton for wollen socks, and a single breasted satin waistcoat for a double-breasted velvet." In July and August, he would monitor the progress of his potatoes, cabbage, squash, beets, and sweet corn. In the fall he would harvest his grape arbors. On New Year's Day, the Bates family followed an old country custom whereby the women remained home all day greeting visitors, while the men rode together from one house or farm to the next, paying calls on friends.

At sixty-six, Bates was among the oldest and best-loved citizens of St. Louis. In 1814, when he first ventured to the thriving city, it was a small fur trading village with a scattering of primitive cabins and a single ramshackle church. Four decades later, St. Louis boasted a population of 160,000 residents, and its infrastructure had boomed to include multiple churches, an extensive private and public educational system, numerous hospitals, and a variety of cultural facilities. The ever-increasing prosperity of the city, writes a historian of St. Louis, "led to the building of massive, ornate private homes equipped with libraries, ballrooms, conservatories, European paintings and sculpture."

Over the years, Bates had held a variety of respected offices—delegate to the convention that had drafted the first constitution of the state, member of the state legislature, representative to the U.S. congress, and judge of the St. Louis Land Court. His ambitions for political success, however, had been gradually displaced by love for his wife and large family. Though he had been asked repeatedly during the previous twenty years since his withdrawal from public life to run or once again accept high government posts, he consistently declined the offers.

Described by the portrait artist Alban Jasper Conant as "the quaintest looking character that walked the streets," Bates still wore "the old-fashioned Quaker clothes that had never varied in cut since he left his Virginia birthplace as a youth of twenty." He stood five feet seven inches tall, with a strong chin, heavy brows, thick hair that remained black until the end of his life, and a full white beard. In later years, Lincoln noted the striking contrast between Bates's black hair and white beard and teasingly suggested it was because Bates talked more than he thought, using "his chin more than his head." Julia Bates was also plain in her dress, "unaffected by the crinolines and other extravagances of the day, preferring a clinging skirt, a deep-pointed fichu called a Van Dyck, and a close-fitting little bonnet."

"How happy is my lot!" Bates recorded in his diary in the 1850s. "Blessed with a wife & children who spontaneously do all they can to make me comfortable, anticipating my wishes, even in the little matter of personal convenience, as if their happiness wholly depended on mine. O! it is a pleasure to work for such a family, to enjoy with them the blessings that God so freely gives." He found his legal work rewarding and intellectually stimulating, reveled in his position as an elder in the Presbyterian Church, and loved nothing more than to while away the long winter nights in his treasured library.

In contrast to Seward, whose restless energy found insufficient outlet in the bosom of his family, and to Chase, plagued all his days by unattained ambition, Bates experienced a passionate joy in the present, content to call himself "a very domestic, home, man." He had come briefly to national attention in 1847, when he delivered a spellbinding speech at the great River and Harbor Convention in Chicago, organized to protest President Polk's veto of a Whig-sponsored bill to provide federal appropriations for the internal improvement of rivers and harbors, especially needed in the fast-growing West. For a short time after the convention, newspapers across the country heralded Bates as a leading prospect for high political office, but he refused to take the bait. Thus, as the 1860 election neared, he assumed that, like his youth and early manhood, his old ambitions for political office had long since passed him by.

In this assumption, he was mistaken. Thirteen months before the Chicago convention, at a dinner hosted by Missouri congressman Frank Blair, Bates was approached to run for president by a formidable political group spearheaded by Frank's father, Francis Preston Blair, Sr. At sixty-six, the elder Blair had been a powerful player in Washington for decades. A Democrat most of his life, he had arrived in Washington from Kentucky during Andrew Jackson's first presidential term to publish the Democratic organ, the *Globe* newspaper. Blair soon became one of Jackson's most trusted advisers, a member of the famous "kitchen cabinet." Meetings were often held in the "Blair House," the stately brick mansion opposite the White House where Blair lived with his wife and four children. (Still known as the Blair House, the elegant dwelling is now owned by the government, serving as the president's official guesthouse.) To the lonely Jackson, whose wife had recently died, the Blairs became a surrogate family. The three Blair boys—James, Montgomery, and Frank Junior—had the run of the

White House, while Elizabeth, the only girl, actually lived in the family quarters for months at a time and Jackson doted on her as if she were his own child. Indeed, decades later, when Jackson neared death, he called Elizabeth to his home in Tennessee and gave her his wife's wedding ring, which he had worn on his watch chain from the day of her death.

Blair Senior had broken with the Democrats after the Mexican War over the extension of slavery into the territories. Although born and bred in the South, and still a slaveowner himself, he had become convinced that slavery must not be extended beyond where it already existed. He was one of the first important political figures to call for the founding of the Republican Party. At a Christmas dinner on his country estate in Silver Spring, Maryland, in 1855, he instigated plans for the first Republican Convention in Philadelphia that following summer.

Over the years, Blair's Silver Spring estate, just across the District of Columbia boundary, had become a natural gathering place for politicians and journalists. The house was situated amid hundreds of rolling acres surrounded by orchards, brooks, even a series of grottoes. From the "Big Gate" at the entrance, the carriage roadway passed through a forest of pine and poplar, opening to reveal a long driveway winding between two rows of chestnut trees and over a rustic bridge to the main house. In the years ahead, the Blairs' Silver Spring estate would become one of Lincoln's favorite places to relax.

The group that Blair convened included his two accomplished sons, Montgomery and Frank; an Indiana congressman, Schuyler Colfax, who would later become vice president under Ulysses Grant; and Charles Gibson, one of Bates's oldest friends in Missouri. Montgomery Blair, tall, thin, and scholarly, had graduated from West Point before studying law and moving to Missouri. In the 1850s he had returned to Washington to be closer to his parents. He took up residence in his family's city mansion on Pennsylvania Avenue. In the nation's capital, Monty Blair developed a successful legal practice and achieved national fame when he represented the slave Dred Scott in his bid for freedom.

Monty's charismatic younger brother Frank, recently elected to Congress, was a natural politician. Strikingly good-looking, with reddish-brown hair, a long red mustache, high cheekbones, and bright gray eyes, Frank was the one on whom the Blair family's burning ambitions rested. Both his father and older brother harbored dreams that Frank would one day become president. But in 1860, Frank was only in his thirties, and in the meantime, the Blair family turned its powerful gaze on Edward Bates.

The Blairs had settled on the widely respected judge, a longtime Whig and former slaveholder who had emancipated his slaves and become a

Free-Soiler, as the ideal candidate for a conservative national ticket opposed to both the radical abolitionists in the North and the proslavery fanatics in the South. Though he had never officially joined the Republican Party, Bates held fast to the cardinal principle of Republicanism: that slavery must be restricted to the states where it already existed, and that it must be prevented from expanding into the territories.

As a man of the West and a peacemaker by nature, Bates was just the person, Blair Senior believed, to unite old-line Whigs, antislavery Democrats, and liberal nativists in a victorious fight against the Southern Democratic slaveocracy. The fact that Bates had receded from the political scene for decades was an advantage, leaving him untainted by the contentious battles of the fifties. He alone, his supporters believed, could quell the threats of secession and civil war and return the nation to peace, progress, and prosperity.

Unsurprisingly, Bates was initially reluctant to allow his name to be put forward as a candidate for president. "I feel, tho' in perfect bodily health, an indolence and indecision not common with me," he conceded in July 1859. "The cause, I fear, is the mixing up of my name in Politics. . . . A large section of the Republican party, who think that Mr. Seward's nomination would ensure defeat, are anxious to take me up, thinking that I could carry the Whigs and Americans generally. . . . I must try to resist the temptation, and not allow my thoughts to be drawn off from the common channels of business and domestic cares. Ambition is a passion, at once strong and insidious, and is very apt to cheet a man out of his happiness and his true respectability of character."

Gradually, however, as letters and newspaper editorials advocating his candidacy crowded in upon him, a desire for the highest office in the land took command of his nature. The office to which he heard the call was not, as he had once disdained, "a mere seat in Congress as a subaltern member," but the presidency of the United States. Six months after the would-be kingmakers had approached him, Frank Blair, Jr., noted approvingly that "the mania has bitten old Bates very seriously," and predicted he would "play out more boldly for it than he has heretofore done."

By the dawn of the new year, 1860, thoughts of the White House monopolized the entries Bates penned in his diary, crowding out his previous observations on the phases of the moon and the state of his garden. "My nomination for the Presidency, which at first struck me with mere wonder, has become familiar, and now I begin to think my prospects very fair," he recorded on January 9, 1860. "Circumstances seem to be remarkably concurrent in my favor, and there is now great probability that the Opposition of all classes will unite upon me: And that will be equivalent to election. . . .

Can it be reserved for me to defeat and put down that corrupt and dangerous party [the Democratic Party]? Truly, if I can do my country that much good, I will rejoice in the belief that I have not lived in vain."

In the weeks that followed, his days were increasingly taken up with politics. Though he did not enjoy formal dinner parties, preferring intimate suppers with his family and a few close friends, Bates now spent more time than ever before entertaining political friends, educators, and newspaper editors. Although still tending to his garden, he immersed himself in periodicals on politics, economics, and public affairs. He felt he should prepare himself intellectually for the task of presidential leadership by reading historical accounts of Europe's most powerful monarchs, as well as theoretical works on government. He sought guidance for his role as chief executive in Carlyle's *Frederick the Great* and Adam Smith's *Wealth of Nations*. Evenings once devoted to family were now committed to public speeches and correspondence with supporters. Politics had fastened a powerful hold upon him, disrupting his previous existence.

The chance for his nomination depended, as was true for Chase and Lincoln as well, on Seward's failure to achieve a first ballot victory at the convention. "I have many strong assurances that I stand second," Bates confided in his diary, "first in the Northwest and in some states in New England, second in New York, Pa." To be sure, there were pockets of opposition, particularly among the more passionate Republicans, who argued that the party must nominate one of its own, and among the German-Americans, who recalled that Bates had endorsed Millard Fillmore when he ran for president on the anti-immigrant American Party four years earlier. As the convention approached, however, his supporters were increasingly optimistic.

"There is no question," the *New York Tribune* predicted, "as there has been none for these three months past, that [Bates] will have more votes in the Convention than any other candidate presented by those who think it wiser to nominate a man of moderate and conservative antecedents." As the delegates gathered in Chicago, Francis Blair, Sr., prophesied that Bates would triumph in Chicago.

Though Bates acknowledged he had never officially joined the Republican Party, he understood that many Republicans, including "some of the most moderate and patriotic" men, believed that his nomination "would tend to soften the tone of the Republican party, without any abandonment of its principles," thus winning "the friendship and support of many, especially in the border States." His chances of success looked good. How strangely it had all turned out, for surely he understood that he had followed an unusual public path, a path that had curved swiftly upward when he was young, then leveled off, even sloped downward for many years. But now, as he positioned himself to reenter politics, he sighted what appeared to be a relatively clear trail all the way to the very top.

• • •

On that morning of May 18, 1860, Bates's chief objective was simply to stop Seward on the first ballot. Chase, too, had his eye on the front-runner, while Seward worried about Chase. Bates had become convinced that the convention would turn to him as the only real moderate. Neither Seward nor Chase nor Bates seriously considered Lincoln an obstacle to their great ambition.

Lincoln was not a complete unknown to his rivals. By 1860, his path had crossed with each of them in different ways. Seward had met Lincoln twelve years before at a political meeting. The two shared lodging that night, and Seward encouraged Lincoln to clarify and intensify his moderate position on slavery. Lincoln had met Bates briefly, and had sat in the audience in 1847 when Bates delivered his mesmerizing speech at the River and Harbor Convention. Chase had campaigned for Lincoln and the Republicans in Illinois in 1858, though the two men had never met.

There was little to lead one to suppose that Abraham Lincoln, nervously rambling the streets of Springfield that May morning, who scarcely had a national reputation, certainly nothing to equal any of the other three, who had served but a single term in Congress, twice lost bids for the Senate, and had no administrative experience whatsoever, would become the greatest historical figure of the nineteenth century.

CHAPTER 2

THE "LONGING TO RISE"

ABRAHAM LINCOLN, William Henry Seward, Salmon Chase, and Edward Bates were members of a restless generation of Americans, destined to leave behind the eighteenth-century world of their fathers. Bates, the oldest, was born when George Washington was still president; Seward and Chase during Jefferson's administration; Lincoln shortly before James Madison took over. Thousands of miles separate their birthplaces in Virginia, New York, New Hampshire, and Kentucky. Nonetheless, social and economic forces shaped their paths with marked similarities. Despite striking differences in station, talent, and temperament, all four aspirants for the Republican nomination left home, journeyed west, studied law, dedicated themselves to public service, joined the Whig Party, developed a reputation for oratorical eloquence, and became staunch opponents of the spread of slavery.

It was a country for young men. "We find ourselves," the twenty-eight-year-old Lincoln told the Young Men's Lyceum of Springfield, "in the peaceful possession, of the fairest portion of the earth, as regards extent of territory, fertility of soil, and salubrity of climate." The founding fathers had crafted a government more favorable to liberty "than any of which the history of former times tells us." Now it was up to their children to preserve and expand the great experiment.

The years following the Revolution fostered the belief that the only barriers to success were discipline and the extent of one's talents. "When both the privileges and the disqualifications of class have been abolished and men have shattered the bonds which once held them immobile," marveled the French visitor Alexis de Tocqueville, "the idea of progress comes naturally into each man's mind; the desire to rise swells in every heart at once, and all men want to quit their former social position. Ambition becomes a universal feeling."

The same observation that horrified Mrs. Frances Trollope on a visit to

America, that "any man's son may become the equal of any other man's son," propelled thousands of young men to break away from the small towns and limited opportunities their fathers had known. These ambitious youngsters ventured forth to test their luck in new careers as merchants, manufacturers, teachers, and lawyers. In the process, hundreds of new towns and cities were born, and with the rapid expansion of roads, bridges, and canals, a modern market economy emerged. Vast new lands and possibilities were opened when the Louisiana Purchase doubled the extent of America's territorial holdings overnight.

The newly liberated Americans crossed the Appalachian Mountains, which had separated the original colonies from the unsettled West. "Americans are always moving on," wrote Stephen Vincent Benét. "The stream uncrossed, the promise still untried/The metal sleeping in the mountainside." In the South, pioneers moved through the Gulf States toward the Mississippi River, extending cotton cultivation and slavery as they went. In the North, the movement west from New England and the mid-Atlantic brought settlers who created a patchwork of family farms and planted the seeds of thriving cities.

Bates traveled farthest, eight hundred miles from his home state of Virginia across Kentucky, Indiana, and Illinois to the young city of St. Louis in the newly established territory of Missouri. Chase made the arduous journey from New Hampshire to Cincinnati, Ohio, a burgeoning city recently carved from a forest rich with wild game. Seward left his family in eastern New York for the growing city of Auburn in the western part of the state. Lincoln traveled from Kentucky to Indiana, and then on to Illinois, where he would become a flatboatman, merchant, surveyor, and postmaster before studying law.

"Every American is eaten up with longing to rise," Tocqueville wrote. These four men, and thousands more, were not searching for a mythical pot of gold at the edge of the western rainbow, but for a place where their dreams and efforts would carve them a place in a fast-changing society.

• • •

OF THE CONTENDERS, William Henry Seward enjoyed the most privileged childhood. Blessed with a sanguine temperament that seemingly left him free from inner turmoil, he launched himself into every endeavor with unbounded vitality—whether competing for honors in school, playing cards with his classmates, imbibing good food and wine, or absorbing the pleasures of travel.

Henry Seward, as he would be called, was born on May 16, 1801. The fourth of six children, he grew up in the hill country of Orange County,

New York, in the village of Florida, about twenty-five miles from West Point. His father, Samuel Seward, had accumulated "a considerable fortune" through his various employments as physician, magistrate, judge, merchant, land speculator, and member of the New York state legislature. His mother, Mary Jennings Seward, was renowned in the community for her warmth, good sense, and kindly manner.

Affectionate and outgoing, with red hair and intelligent blue eyes, Henry was singled out among his brothers for a college education, "then regarded, by every family," he later wrote, "as a privilege so high and so costly that not more than one son could expect it." His "destined preferment," as he called it, led him at the age of nine to a preparatory academy in the village of Goshen, and then back to his own town when a new academy opened its doors. His day of study began, he recalled, "at five in the morning, and closed at nine at night." The regime imposed by the schoolmaster was rigorous. When young Henry faltered in his translations of Caesar or failed to decipher lines of Virgil's poetry, he was relegated to a seat on the floor "with the classic in one hand and the dictionary in the other." Although sometimes the pressure was "more than [he] could bear," he persisted, knowing that his father would never accept failure.

After the isolated hours consumed by books, Henry delighted in the sociability of winter evenings, when, he recalled, "the visit of a neighbor brought out the apples, nuts, and cider, and I was indulged with a respite from study, and listened to conversation, which generally turned upon politics or religion!" His pleasure in these social gatherings left Seward with a lifelong memory and appetite. Years later, when he established his own home, he filled evenings with a continuous flow of guests, always providing abundant food, drink, and conversation.

The Sewards, like other well-to-do families in the area, owned slaves. As a small child, Henry spent much of his time in the slave quarters, comprised of the kitchen and the garret above it. Basking in the warmth of the fireplace and the aroma of the turkeys and chickens roasting on the spit, he savored the "loquacious" and "affectionate" company of the garret's residents. They provided a welcome respite from the "severe decorum" of his parents' parlor on the other side of the house. As he grew older, however, he found it difficult to accept the diminished status of these slave friends, whose lives were so different from his own.

Although his father, an exception in the village, permitted his slaves to join his own children in the local schoolhouse, Henry puzzled over why "no other black children went there." More disturbing still, he discovered that one of his companions, a slave child his own age who belonged to a neighboring family, was regularly whipped. After one severe beating, the boy ran away. "He was pursued and brought back," Seward recalled, and was forced to wear "an iron yoke around his neck, which exposed him to contempt and ridicule," until he finally "found means to break the collar, and fled forever." Seward later would credit this early unease and personal awareness of the slaves' plight for his resolve to fight against slavery.

The youthful Seward was not alone in his budding dislike for slavery. In the years after the Revolutionary War, the state legislatures in eleven Northern states passed abolition laws. Some states banned slavery outright within their boundaries; others provided for a system of gradual emancipation, decreeing that all slaves born after a certain date would be granted freedom when they attained adulthood. The slaves Seward knew as a child belonged to this transitional generation. By 1827, slavery would be fully eradicated in New York. While Northern legislatures were eliminating the institution, however, slavery had become increasingly important to the economic life of the cotton-growing South.

At fifteen, Seward enrolled in upstate New York's prestigious Union College. His first sight of the steamboat that carried him up the Hudson was one he would never forget. Invented only a decade earlier, the steamboat seemed to him "a magnificent palace . . . a prodigy of power." His first glimpse of Albany, then a rural village with a population of twelve thousand, thrilled him—"so vast, so splendid, so imposing." Throughout his life, Seward retained an awe of the new technologies and inventions that fostered the industrial development of his rapidly expanding country.

At Union, Seward's open, affable nature made him dozens of friends. Upon his arrival, he later confessed, "I cherished in my secret thoughts aspirations to become . . . the valedictorian of my class." When he realized that his competitors for the honor seemed isolated from the social life of the school, he wondered if the prize was worth the cost. His ambitions were revitalized, however, when the president of Union announced that the Phi Beta Kappa Society "had determined to establish a fourth branch at Union College," with membership conferred on the top scholars at the end of junior year. There were then only three active branches of Phi Beta Kappa—at Harvard, Yale, and Dartmouth. To gain admission, Seward realized, would place him in the company of "all the eminent philosophers, scholars, and statesmen of the country."

He made a pact with his roommate whereby the two "rose at three o'clock in the morning, cooked and spread our own meals, washed our own dishes, and spent the whole time which we could save from prayers and recitations, and the table, in severe study, in which we unreservedly and constantly aided each other." Years later, his jovial self-confidence intact, Seward wrote: "Need I say that we entered the great society without encountering the deadly blackball?"

Seward began his senior year in good spirits. Without sacrificing his popularity with classmates, he was poised to graduate as valedictorian. But his prideful character temporarily derailed him. Strapped by the stingy allowance his father provided, he had fallen into debt with various creditors in Schenectady. The bills, mostly to tailors, were not large, but his father's refusal to pay spurred a rash decision to leave college for good, so that he might work to support himself. "I could not submit to the shame of credit impaired," he later wrote. Without notifying his parents, he accompanied a classmate to Georgia, where he found a good job teaching school. When his father discovered Henry's whereabouts, he "implored [him] to return," mingling promises of additional funds with threats that he would pursue the trustees of the school "with the utmost rigor of the law . . . if they should continue to harbor the delinquent."

If his father's threats increased his determination to stay, a letter from his mother, revealing "a broken heart," prompted Seward's return to New York. The following fall, after working off his debt that summer, he resumed his studies at Union. "Matters prosper in my favor," he wrote to a friend in January 1820, "and I have so far been inferior to none in my own opinion." He was back on track to become valedictorian, and his election as graduation speaker seemed likely. If denied the honor, he told his friend, "his soul would disdain to sit in the hearing of some, and listen to some whom he considers beneath even his notice." His goals were realized. He graduated first in his class and was unanimously elected by classmates and faculty to be Union College's commencement orator in June 1820.

From his honored place at Union College, Seward glided smoothly into the profession of law. In an era when "reading the law" under the guidance of an established attorney was the principal means of becoming a lawyer, he walked directly from his graduation ceremony to the law office of a distinguished Goshen lawyer, and then "was received as a student" in the New York City office of John Anthon, author of a widely known book on the legal practice. Not only did Seward have two eminent mentors, he also gained access to the "New York Forum," a society of ambitious law students who held mock trials and prosecutions to hone their professional skills before public audiences.

Accustomed to winning the highest honors, Seward was initially chagrined to discover that his legal arguments failed to bring the loudest applause. His confidence as a writer faltered until a fellow law student, whose orations "always carried away the audience," insisted that the problem was not Henry's compositions, which were, in fact, far superior to his own, but his husky voice, which a congenital inflammation in the throat rendered "incapable of free intonation." To prove this point, Seward's friend offered to exchange compositions, letting Seward read one of his while he read one of Seward's. Seward recalled that he read his friend's address "as well as I could, but it did not take at all. He followed me with my speech, and I think Broadway overheard the clamorous applause which arose on that occasion in Washington Hall."

During his stay in New York, Seward formed an intimate friendship with a bookish young man, David Berdan, who had graduated from Union the year after him. Seward believed that Berdan possessed "a genius of the highest order." He had read more extensively than anyone Seward knew and excelled as a scholar in the classics. "The domains of History, Eloquence, Poetry, Fiction & Song," Seward marveled, "were all subservient to his command." Berdan had entered into the study of law at the same office as Seward, but soon discovered that his vocation lay in writing, not law.

Together, the two young men attended the theater, read poetry, discussed books, and chased after women. Convinced that Berdan would become a celebrated writer, Seward stood in awe of his friend's talent and dedication. All such grand expectations and prospects were crushed when Berdan, still in his twenties, was "seized with a bleeding at the lungs" while sojourning in Europe. He continued traveling, but when his tuberculosis worsened, he booked his passage home, in "the hope that he might die in his native land." The illness took his life before the ship reached New York. His body was buried at sea. Seward was devastated, later telling his wife that he had loved Berdan as "never again" could he "love in this world."

Such intimate male attachments, as Seward's with Berdan, or, as we shall see, Lincoln's with Joshua Speed and Chase's with Edwin Stanton, were "a common feature of the social landscape" in nineteenth-century America, the historian E. Anthony Rotundo points out. The family-focused and community-centered life led by most men in the colonial era was transformed at the dawn of the new century into an individual and career-oriented existence. As the young men of Seward and Lincoln's generation left the familiarity of their small communities and traveled to seek employment in fast-growing, anonymous cities or in distant territories, they often felt unbearably lonely. In the absence of parents and siblings, they turned to one another for support, sharing thoughts and emotions so completely that their intimate friendships developed the qualities of passionate romances.

After passing the bar examination, Seward explored the western part of the state, seeking the perfect law office from which to launch an illustrious career. He found what he wanted in Auburn when Judge Elijah Miller offered him a junior partnership in his thriving firm. Seward quickly assumed responsibility for most of the legal work passing through the office, earning the senior partner's trust and respect. The fifty-two-year-old judge was a widower who shared with his daughters—Lazette and Frances—the grandest residence in Auburn. It seemed to follow naturally that, less than two years later, Seward should woo and win Miller's twenty-year-old daughter, the beautiful, sensitive Frances. The judge insisted, as a condition of consent to the marriage, that the young couple join his household, which included his mother and unmarried sister.

Thus, at twenty-three, Seward found himself the tenant of the elegant country mansion where he and Frances would live for the rest of their lives. With a brilliant marriage and excellent prospects in his chosen profession, he could look ahead with confidence. To the end of his long life, he gazed optimistically to the future, believing that he and his countrymen were steadily advancing along a road toward increased knowledge, achievement, prosperity, and moral development.

• • •

SALMON PORTLAND CHASE, in contrast to the ever buoyant Seward, possessed a restless soul incapable of finding satisfaction in his considerable achievements. He was forever brooding on a station in life not yet reached, recording at each turning point in his life his regret at not capitalizing on the opportunities given to him.

He was born in the rolling hills of Cornish, New Hampshire, in 1808, the eighth of eleven children. His ancestors had lived in the surrounding country for three generations, becoming pillars of the community. Chase would remember that "the neighboring folk used to say" of the substantial Chase homestead that "in that yellow house more brains were born than in any other house in New England." Three of his father's brothers attended Dartmouth College. One became a distinguished lawyer, another a U.S. senator, and the third an Episcopalian bishop.

Salmon's father, Ithamar Chase, was a successful farmer, a justice of the peace, and a representative from his district to the New Hampshire council. He was "a good man," Chase recalled, a kind father and a loving husband to his young wife, Janette Ralston. He governed his large family without a single "angry word or violent e[x]clamation from his lips." Chase long remembered a day when he was playing a game of ninepins with his friends. His father interrupted, saying he needed his son's help in the field.

The boy hesitated. "Won't you come and help your father?" That was all that needed to be said. "Only a look. . . . All my reluctance vanished and I went with a right good will. He ruled by kind words & kind looks."

Young Salmon, like Seward, demonstrated an unusual intellectual precocity. His father singled him out to receive a better education "than that given to his other children." The boy thrived in the atmosphere of high expectations. "I was . . . ambitious to be at the head of my class," he recalled. During the summer months, his elder sister, Abigail, a schoolteacher in Cornish, kept him hard at work studying Latin grammar. If he failed to grasp his lessons, he would retreat to the garden and stay there by himself until he could successfully read the designated passages. At Sunday school, he strove to memorize more Bible verses than anyone else in his class, "once repeating accurately almost an entire gospel, in a single recitation." Eager to display his capacity, Chase would boast to adults that he enjoyed studying volumes of ancient history and perusing the plays of Shakespeare "for the entertainment they afforded."

While he was considered "quite a prodigy" in his written work, Chase was uneasy reciting in public. In contrast to Lincoln, who loved nothing better than to entertain his childhood friends and fellow students with stories, sermons, or passages from books, the self-conscious Chase was terrified to speak before fellow students, having "little notion of what I had to do or of the way to do it." With his "hands dangling and head down," he looked as awkward as he felt.

From his very early days, Chase showed signs of the fierce, ingrained rectitude that would both fortify his battle against slavery and incur the enmity of many among his fellows. Baptized Episcopalian in a pious family, where the Lord's day of rest was strictly kept, the young boy needed only one Sunday scolding for "sliding down hill with some boys on the dry pine leaves" to know that he would never "transgress that way again." Nor did he argue when his mother forbade association with boys who used profane language: he himself found it shocking that anyone would swear. Another indelible childhood memory made him abhor intemperance. He had stumbled upon the dead body of a drunken man in the street, his "face forward" in a pool of water "not deep enough to reach his ears," but sufficient, in his extreme state of intoxication, to drown him. The parish priest had delivered sermons on "the evils of intemperance," but, as Chase observed, "what sermon could rival in eloquence that awful spectacle of the dead drunkard—helplessly perishing where the slightest remnant of sense or strength would have sufficed to save."

When Chase was seven years old, his father made a bold business move. The War of 1812 had put a halt to glass imports from Europe, creating a pressing demand for new supplies. Sensing opportunity, Ithamar Chase liquidated his assets in Cornish to invest in a glass factory in the village of Keene. His wife had inherited some property there, including a fourteen-room tavern house. Chase moved his family into one section of the tavern and opened the rest to the public. While a curious and loquacious child like the young Lincoln might have enjoyed the convivial entertainments of a tavern, the reticent Salmon found the move from his country estate in Cornish unsettling. And for his father, the relocation proved calamitous. With the end of the war, tariff duties on foreign goods were reduced and glass imports saturated the market. The glass factory failed, sending him into bankruptcy.

The Chase family was unable to recover. Business failure led to humiliation in the community and, eventually, to loss of the family home. Ithamar Chase succumbed to a fatal stroke at the age of fifty-three, when Salmon was nine. "He lingered some days," Chase recalled. "He could not speak to us, and we stood mute and sobbing. Soon all was over. We had no father . . . the light was gone out from our home."

Left with heavy debts and meager resources, Janette Chase was forced to assume the burden of housing, educating, and providing for her numerous children on her own. Only by moving into cheap lodgings, and scrimping "almost to suffering," was she able to let Salmon, her brightest and most promising child, continue his studies at the local academy, fulfilling her promise to his "ever lamented and deceased father." When she could no longer make ends meet, she was forced to parcel her children out among relatives. Salmon was sent to study under the tutelage of his father's brother, the Episcopal bishop Philander Chase, who presided over a boys' school in Worthington in the newly formed state of Ohio. In addition to his work as an educator, Philander Chase was responsible for a sizable parish, and owned a farm that provided food and dairy products for the student body. Young Chase, in return for milking cows and driving them to pasture, building fires, and hauling wood, would be given room and board, and a classical and religious education.

In 1819, at the age of twelve, the boy traveled westward, first by wagon through Vermont and New York, then by steamboat across Lake Erie to Cleveland, a tiny lakeside settlement of a few hundred residents. There Salmon was stranded until a group of travelers passed through en route to Worthington. In the company of strangers, the child made his way on foot and horseback through a hundred miles of virgin forest to reach his uncle's home.

The bishop was an imposing figure, brilliant, ambitious, and hardworking. His faith, Chase observed, "was not passive but active. If any thing was to be done he felt that he must do it; and that, if he put forth all his energy, he might safely & cheerfully leave the event to Divine Providence." Certainty gave him an unbending zeal. He was "often very harsh & severe," recalled Chase, and "among us boys he was almost and sometimes, indeed, quite tyrannical." The most insignificant deviation from the daily regimen of prayer and study was met with a fearful combination of physical flogging and biblical precept.

"My memories of Worthington on the whole are not pleasant," Chase said of the time he spent with his domineering uncle. "There were some pleasant rambles—some pleasant incidents—some pleasant associates: but the disagreeable largely predominated. I used to count the days and wish I could get home or go somewhere else and get a living by work." One incident long remained in Chase's memory. As punishment for some infraction of the daily rules, he was ordered to bring in a large stack of wood before daybreak. He completed the task but complained to a fellow student that his uncle was "a darned old tyrant." Upon hearing these words, the bishop allowed no one to speak to the boy and forbade him to speak until he confessed and apologized. Days later, Chase finally recanted, and the sentence was revoked. "Even now," Chase said, telling the story decades later, "I almost wish I had not."

When the bishop was made president of Cincinnati College, Chase accompanied his uncle to Cincinnati. At thirteen, he was enrolled as a freshman at the college. The course of study was not difficult, leaving boys time to indulge in "a good deal of mischief & fun." Salmon Chase was not among them. "I had little or nothing to do with these sports," he recalled. "I had the chores to do at home, & when I had time I gave it to reading." Even Chase's sympathetic biographer Robert Warden observed that his "life might have been happier" had he "studied less and had more fun!" These early years witnessed the development of the rigid, self-denying habits that, throughout his life, prevented Chase from fully enjoying the companionship of others.

When Chase turned fifteen, his uncle left for England to secure funding for the new theological seminary that would become Kenyon College. At last, Chase was allowed to return to his mother's home in Keene, New Hampshire, where he planned to teach while preparing for admittance to Dartmouth College. His first position lasted only weeks, however. Employing the harsh methods of his uncle rather than the gentle precepts of his father, he administered corporal punishment to discipline his students. When irate parents complained, he was dismissed.

When Chase made his application to Dartmouth, he found that his schooling in Ohio, though filled with misery, had prepared him to enter as a third-year student. At Dartmouth, for the first time, he seemed to relax. Though he graduated with distinction and a Phi Beta Kappa key, he began to enjoy the camaraderie of college life, forging two lifelong friendships with Charles Cleveland, an intellectual classmate who would become a classics professor, and Hamilton Smith, who would become a well-to-do businessman.

No sooner had he completed his studies than he berated himself for squandering the opportunity: "Especially do I regret that I spent so much of my time in reading novels and other light works," he told a younger student. "They may impart a little brilliancy to the imagination but at length, like an intoxicating draught, they enfeeble and deaden the powers of thought and action." With dramatic flair, the teenage Chase then added: "My life seems to me to have been wasted." While Seward joyfully devoured the works of Dickens and Scott, Chase found no room for fiction in his Spartan intellectual life. After finishing the new novel by Edward Bulwer-Lytton, the author of *The Last Days of Pompeii*, he conceded that "the author is doubtless a gifted being—but he has prostituted God's noblest gifts to the vilest purposes."

The years after his graduation found nineteen-year-old Chase in Washington, D.C., where he eventually established a successful school for boys that attracted the sons of the cabinet members in the administration of John Quincy Adams, as well as the son of Senator Henry Clay. Once again, instead of taking pleasure in his position, he felt his talents went unappreciated. There were distinct classes of society in Washington, Chase told Hamilton Smith. The first, to which he aspired, included the high government officials; the second, to which he was relegated, included teachers and physicians; and the third mechanics and artisans. There was, of course, a still lower class comprised of slaves and laborers. The problem with teaching, he observed, was that any "drunken, miserable dog who could thre'd the mazes of the Alphabet" could set himself up as a teacher, bringing the "profession of teachers into utter contempt." Chase was tormented by the lowly figure he cut in the glittering whirl of Washington life. "I have always thought," he confessed, "that Providence intended me as the instrument of effecting something more than falls to the lot of all men to achieve."

Though this thirst to excel and to distinguish himself had been instilled in Chase early on by his parents, and painfully reinforced by the years with Philander Chase, such sleepless ambition was inflamed by the dynamic American society in the 1820s. Visitors from Europe, the historian Joyce Appleby writes, "saw the novelty of a society directed almost entirely by the ambitious dreams that had been unleashed after the Revolution in the heated imagination of thousands of people, most of them poor and young."

Casting about for a career befitting the high estimation in which he held his own talents, Chase wrote to an older brother in 1825 for advice about the different professions. He was contemplating the study of law, perhaps inspired by his acquaintance with Attorney General William Wirt, the father of two of his pupils. Wirt was among the most distinguished figures in Washington, a respected lawyer as well as a literary scholar. He had served as U.S. Attorney General under President James Monroe and had been kept in office by John Quincy Adams. His popular biography of the patriot and lawyer Patrick Henry had made a small name for him in American letters.

A warmhearted, generous man, Wirt welcomed his sons' teenage instructor into his family circle, inviting the lonely Chase to the small dinner parties, private dances, and luxurious levees attended by Washington's elite. At the Wirt household, filled with music and lively conversation, Chase found a respite from the constant pressure he felt to read and study in order to stay ahead of his students. More than three decades later, in the midst of the Civil War, Chase could still summon up vivid details of the "many happy hours" he spent with the Wirt family. "Among women Mrs. [Elizabeth] Wirt had few equals," he recalled. Particularly stamped in his memory was an evening in the garden when Elizabeth Wirt stood beside him, "under the clusters of the multiflora which clambered all over the garden portico of the house and pointed out . . . the stars."

Though supportive and eager to mentor the ambitious and talented young man, the Wirts delicately acknowledged—or so Chase felt—the social gulf that divided Chase from their family. Any attempt on the young teacher's part to move beyond friendship with any one of their four beautiful daughters was, he thought, discouraged. Since he was surrounded by the tantalizing fruits of professional success and social eminence in the Wirt family's parlor, it is no wonder that a career in law beckoned. His brother Alexander warned him that of all the professions, law entailed the most strenuous course of preparation: success required mastery of "thousands of volumes" from "centuries long past," including works of science, the arts, and both ancient and contemporary history. "In fine, you must become a universal scholar." Despite the fact that this description was not an accurate portrait of the course most law students of the day embarked upon, typically, Chase took it to heart, imposing a severe discipline upon himself to rise before daybreak to begin his monumental task of study. Insecurity and ambition combined, as ever, to fuel his efforts. "Day and night must be witness to the assiduity of my labours," he vowed in his diary;

"knowledge may yet be gained and golden reputation. . . . Future scenes of triumph may yet be mine."

Wirt allowed Salmon to read law in his office and offered encouragement. "*You* will be a distinguished writer," he assured Chase. "I am *sure* of it—You have all the sensibility, talent and enthusiasm essential to success in that walk." The young man wrote breathlessly to Wirt in return, "God [prospering] my exertions, I will imitate your example." As part of his self-designed course of preparation, Chase diligently took notes in the galleries of the House and Senate, practiced his elocution by becoming a member of Washington's Blackstone debating club, and read tirelessly while continuing his duties as a full-time teacher. After hearing the great Daniel Webster speak before the Supreme Court, "his voice deep and sonorous; and his sentiments high and often sublime," he promised himself that if "any degree of industry would enable me to reach his height, how day and night should testify of my toils."

Neither his opportunities nor his impressive discipline yielded Chase much in the way of satisfaction. Rather than savoring his progress, he excoriated himself for not achieving enough. "I feel humbled and mortified," he wrote in his diary, as the year 1829 drew to a close, "by the conviction that the Creator has gifted me with intelligence almost in vain. I am almost twenty two and have as yet attained but the threshold of knowledge. . . . The night has seldom found me much advanced beyond the station I occupied in the morning. . . . I almost despair of ever making any figure in the world." Fear of failure, perhaps intensified by the conviction that his father's failure had precipitated his death and the devastation of his family, would operate throughout Chase's life as a catalyst to his powerful ambition. Even as he scourged himself, he continued to believe that there was still hope, that if he could "once more resolve to struggle earnestly for the prize of well-doing," he would succeed.

As Seward had done, Chase compressed into two years the three-year course of study typically followed by college-educated law students. When the twenty-two-year-old presented himself for examination at the bar in Washington, D.C., in 1829, the presiding judge expressed a wish that Chase "study another year" before attempting to pass. "Please," Chase begged, "I have made all my arrangements to go to the Western country & practice law." The judge, who knew Chase by reputation and was aware of his connection with the distinguished William Wirt, relented and ordered that Chase be sworn in at the bar. Chase had decided to abandon Washington's crowded professional terrain for the open vista and fresh opportunities afforded by the growing state of Ohio.

"I would rather be *first* in Cincinnati than first in Baltimore, twenty years hence," Chase immodestly confessed to Charles Cleveland. "As I have ever been first at school and college . . . I shall strive to be first wherever I may be." Cincinnati had become a booming city in 1830, one of the West's largest. Less than two decades earlier, when the state was founded, much of Ohio "was covered by the primeval forest." Chase knew the prospects for a young lawyer would be good in the rapidly developing region, but could not help feeling, as he had upon his arrival in Washington, like "a stranger and an adventurer."

Despite past achievements, Chase suffered from crippling episodes of shyness, exacerbated by his shame over a minor speech defect that lent an unusual tone to his voice. "I wish I was as sure of your *elocution* as I am of everything else," William Wirt cautioned. "Your voice is a little nasal as well as guttural, and your articulation stiff, laborious and thick. . . . I would not mention these things if they were incurable—but they are not, as Demosthenes has proved—and it is only necessary for you to know the fact, to provide the remedy." In addition to the humiliation he felt over his speaking voice, Salmon Chase was tormented by his own name. He fervently wished to change its "awkward, *fishy*" sound to something more elegant. "How wd. this name do (Spencer de Cheyce or Spencer Payne Cheyce)," he inquired of Cleveland. "Perhaps you will laugh at this but I assure you I have suffered no little inconvenience."

Bent on a meteoric rise in this new city, Chase redoubled his resolve to work. "I made this resolution today," he wrote in his diary soon after settling in. "I will try to excel in all things." Pondering the goals he had set for his new life in the West, Chase wrote: "I was fully aware that I must pass thro' a long period of probation. . . . That many obstacles were to be overcome, many difficulties to be surmounted ere I could hope to reach the steep where Fame's proud temple shines," complete with "deserved honor, eminent usefulness and a 'crown of glory.' "

Nonetheless, he had made a good beginning. After struggling for several years to secure enough legal business to support himself, he developed a lucrative practice, representing various business interests and serving as counsel for several large Cincinnati banks. At the same time, following Benjamin Franklin's advice for continual self-improvement, he founded a popular lecture series in Cincinnati, joined a temperance society, undertook the massive project of collecting Ohio's scattered statutes into three published volumes, tried his hand at poetry, and wrote numerous articles for publication in various magazines. To maintain these multiple pursuits, he would often arise at 4 a.m. and occasionally allowed himself to work on Sundays, though he berated himself whenever he did so.

The more successful Chase became, the more his pious family fretted over his relentless desire for earthly success and distinction. "I confess I almost tremble for you," his elder sister Abigail wrote him when he was twenty-four years old, "as I observe your desire to distinguish yourself and apparent devotedness to those pursuits whose interests terminate in this life." If his sister hoped that a warm family life would replace his ambition with love, her hopes were brutally crushed by the fates that brought him to love and lose three young wives.

His first, Catherine "Kitty" Garniss—a warm, outgoing, attractive young woman whom he loved passionately—died in 1835 from complications of childbirth after eighteen months of marriage. She was only twenty-three. Her death was "so overwhelming, so unexpected," he told his friend Cleveland, that he could barely function. "I wish you could have known her," he wrote. "She was universally beloved by her acquaintances. . . . She was gifted with unusual intellectual power. . . . And now I feel a loneliness the more dreadful, from the intimacy of the connexion which has been severed."

His grief was compounded by guilt, for he was away on business in Philadelphia when Kitty died, having been assured by her doctor that she would recover. "Oh how I accused myself of folly and wickedness in leaving her when yet sick," he confided in his diary, "how I mourned that the prospect of a little addition to my reputation . . . should have tempted me away."

Chase arrived home to find his front door wreathed in black crepe, a customary sign "that death was within." There "in our nuptial chamber, in her coffin, lay my sweet wife," Chase wrote, "little changed in features—but oh! the look of life was gone. . . . Nothing was left but clay." For months afterward, he berated himself, believing that "the dreadful calamity might have been averted, had I been at home to watch over her & care for her." Learning that the doctors had bled her so profusely that she lost consciousness shortly before she died, he delved into textbooks on medicine and midwifery that persuaded him that, had she been treated differently, she need not have died.

Worst of all, Chase feared that Kitty had died without affirming her faith. He had not pushed her firmly enough toward God. "Oh if I had not contented myself with a few conversations on the subject of religion," he lamented in his diary, "if I had incessantly followed her with kind & earnest persuasion . . . she might have been before her death enrolled among the professed followers of the Lamb. But I procrastinated and now she is gone."

His young wife's death shadowed all the days of his life. He was haunted by the vision that when he himself reached "the bar of God," he would meet her "as an accusing spirit," blaming him for her damnation. His guilt rekindled his religious commitment, producing a "second conversion," a renewed determination never to let his fierce ambition supersede his religious duties.

The child upon whom all his affections then centered, named Catherine in honor of her dead mother, lived only five years. Her death in 1840 during an epidemic of scarlet fever devastated Chase. Losing one's only child, he told Charles Cleveland, was "one of the heaviest calamities which human experience can know." Little Catherine, he said, had "lent wings to many delightful moments . . . I fondly looked forward to the time when her increasing attainments and strength would fit her at once for the superintendence of my household & to be my own counsellor and friend." Asking for his friend's prayers, he concluded with the thought that "no language can describe the desolation of my heart."

Eventually, Chase fell in love and married again. The young woman, Eliza Ann Smith, had been a good friend of his first wife. Eliza was only twenty when she gave birth to a daughter, Kate, named in memory of both his first wife and his first daughter. For a few short years, Chase found happiness in a warm marriage sustained by a deep religious bond. It would not last, for after the birth and death of a second daughter, Eliza was diagnosed with tuberculosis, which took her life at the age of twenty-five. "I feel as if my heart was broken," Chase admitted to Cleveland after he placed Eliza's body in the tomb. "I write weeping. I cannot restrain my tears. . . . I have no wife, my little Kate has no mother, and we are desolate."

The following year, Chase married Sarah Belle Ludlow, whose well-to-do father was a leader in Cincinnati society. Belle gave birth to two daughters, Nettie and Zoe. Zoe died at twelve months; two years later, her mother followed her into the grave. Though Chase was only forty-four years old, he would never marry again. "What a vale of misery this world is," he lamented some years later when his favorite sister, Hannah, suffered a fatal heart attack at the dining room table. "To me it has been emphatically so. Death has pursued me incessantly ever since I was twenty-five. . . . Sometimes I feel as if I could give up—as if I *must* give up. And then after all I rise & press on."

• • •

LIKE SALMON CHASE, Edward Bates left the East Coast as a young man, intending, he said, "to go West and grow up with the country." The youngest of twelve children, he was born on a plantation called Belmont, not far from Richmond, Virginia. His father, Thomas Fleming Bates, was a member of the landed gentry with an honored position in his community. Educated in England, the elder Bates was a planter and merchant who owned dozens of slaves and counted Thomas Jefferson and James Madison among his friends. His mother, Caroline Woodson Bates, was of old Virginia stock.

These aristocratic Southerners, recalled Bates's old friend Charles Gibson, were "as distinctly a class as any of the nobility of Western Europe." Modeled on an ideal of English manorial life, they placed greater value on family, hospitality, land, and honor than on commercial success or monetary wealth. Writing nostalgically of this antebellum period, Bates's grandson Onward Bates claimed that life after the Civil War never approached the "enjoyable living" of those leisurely days, when "the visitor to one of these homesteads was sure of a genial welcome from white and black," when "the negroes adopted the names and held all things in common with their masters, including their virtues and their manners."

Life for the Bates family was comfortable and secure until the Revolutionary War, when Thomas Bates, a practicing Quaker, set aside his pacifist principles to take up arms against the British. He and his family were proud of his service in the Continental Army. The flintlock musket he carried was handed down to the next generations with the silver-plated inscription: "Thomas F. Bates, whig of the revolution, fought for liberty and independence with this gun. His descendants keep it to defend what he helped to win." His decision to join the military, however, cost him dearly. Upon returning home, he was ostracized from the Quaker meetinghouse and never recovered from the debts incurred by the family estate while he was away fighting. Though he still owned extensive property, he struggled thenceforth to meet the needs of his seven sons and five daughters.

Like Seward and Chase, young Edward revealed an early aptitude for study. Though schools in Goochland County were few, Edward was taught to read and write by his father and, by the age of eight, showed a talent for poetry. Edward was only eleven when his father's death brought an abrupt end to family life at Belmont. Left in straitened circumstances, his mother, like Chase's, sent the children to live with various relatives. Edward spent two years with his older brother Fleming Bates, in Northumberland, Virginia, before settling into the home of a scholarly cousin, Benjamin Bates, in Hanover, Maryland. There, under his cousin's tutelage, he acquired a solid foundation in the fields of mathematics, history, botany, and astronomy. Still, he missed the bustle and companionship of his numerous siblings, and pined for his family's Belmont estate. At fourteen, he entered Charlotte Hall, a private academy in Maryland where he studied literature and the classics in preparation for enrollment at Princeton.

He never did attend Princeton. It is said that he sustained an injury that forced him to end his studies at Charlotte Hall. Returning to Belmont, he enlisted in the Virginia militia during the War of 1812, armed with his father's old flintlock musket. In 1814, at the age of twenty-one, he joined the flood of settlers into Missouri Territory, lured by the vast potential west of the Appalachian Mountains, lately opened by the Louisiana Purchase. Over the next three decades, the population of this western region would explode at three times the rate of the original thirteen states. From his home in Virginia, Bates set out alone on the arduous journey that would take him across Kentucky, Illinois, and Indiana to the Missouri Territory, "too young to think much of the perils which he might encounter," he later mused, "the West being then the scene of many Indian outrages."

Young Bates could not have chosen a better moment to move westward. President Jefferson had appointed Bates's older brother Frederick secretary of the new Missouri Territory. When Edward arrived in the frontier outpost of St. Louis, Missouri was seven years away from statehood. Bates saw no buildings or homes along the riverbank, only battered canoes and flatboats chafing at their moorings. Some 2,500 villagers dwelt predominantly in primitive cabins or single-story wooden houses. When he walked down Third Street to the Market, he recalled, "all was in commotion: a stranger had come from the States! He was 'feted' and followed by young and old, the girls looking at him as one of his own town lasses, in Virginia, would have regarded an elk or a buffalo!"

With help from his brother, Bates secured a position reading law with Rufus Easton, a distinguished frontier lawyer who had served as a territorial judge and delegate to Congress. "After years of family and personal insecurity," Bates's biographer Marvin Cain writes, "he at last had a stable situation through which he could achieve the ambition that burned brightly in him." Mentored by his older brother Frederick, the lawyer Easton, and a close circle of St. Louis colleagues, Bates, too, passed his bar examination after two years of study and instantly plunged into practice. Lawyers were in high demand on the rapidly settling frontier.

The economic and professional prospects were so promising in St. Louis that the Bates brothers determined to bring the rest of their family there. Edward returned to Virginia to sell his father's estate, auction off any family slaves he would not transport to Missouri, and arrange to escort his mother and his older sister Margaret on the long overland journey. "The slaves sold pretty well," he boasted to Frederick, "a young woman at $537 and a boy child 5 years old at $290!" As for the land, he expected to realize about $20,000, which would allow the family to relocate west "quite full-handed."

Edward's attempts to settle family affairs in Virginia dragged on, complicated by the death of his brother Tarleton, a fervent Jeffersonian, killed in a duel with a Federalist. "I am ashamed to say I am still in Goochland," he wrote Frederick in June 1818, nearly a year after he had left St. Louis; it is "my misfortune rather than my fault for I am the greatest sufferer by the delay." Finally, with his female relatives ensconced in a carriage and more than twenty slaves following on horseback and on foot, the little party set forth on an exasperating, difficult expedition. "In those days," one of Bates's friends later recalled, "there were no boats on the Western rivers, and no roads in the country." To cross the wilds of Illinois and Indiana, a guide was necessary. The slow pace caused Bates to worry that Frederick would think him "a lazy or squandering fellow." He explained that if accompanied only by his family, he could have reached St. Louis "in a tenth part of the time & with 1/4 of the trouble and expense—the slaves have been the greatest objects of my embarrassment." The journey did have benefits, he reported: "Mother & Sister are more active, more healthy & more cheerful than when they started. They bear the fatigues of hot dry traveling surprisingly." And once they reached St. Louis, Bates assured his brother, he would "make up in comfort & satisfaction for the great suspense and anxiety I must have occasioned you."

As he again settled into the practice of law in St. Louis, the twenty-five-year-old Bates fully appreciated the advantages gained by his older brother's prominence in the community. In a fulsome letter, he expressed fervent gratitude to his "friend and benefactor," realizing that Fred's "public reputation" as well as his "private wealth & influence" would greatly enhance his own standing. His brother also introduced him to the leading figures of St. Louis—including the famed explorer William Clark, now governor of the Missouri Territory; Thomas Hart Benton, editor of the *Missouri Enquirer*; and David Barton, speaker of the territorial legislature and the guiding hand behind Missouri's drive for statehood. Before long, he found himself in a partnership with Joshua Barton, the younger brother of David Barton. Together, the two well-connected young men began to build a lucrative practice representing the interests of influential businessmen and landholders.

• • •

ABRAHAM LINCOLN faced obstacles unimaginable to the other candidates for the Republican nomination. In sharp contrast to the comfortable lifestyle the Seward family enjoyed, and the secure early childhoods of Chase and Bates before their fathers died, Lincoln's road to success was longer, more tortuous, and far less likely.

Born on February 12, 1809, in a log cabin on an isolated farm in the slave state of Kentucky, Abraham had an older sister, Sarah, who died in childbirth when he was nineteen, and a younger brother who died in infancy. His father, Thomas, had never learned to read and, according to Lincoln, never did "more in the way of writing than to bunglingly sign his own name." As a six-year-old boy, young Thomas had watched when a Shawnee raiding party murdered his father. This violent death, Lincoln later suggested, coupled with the "very narrow circumstances" of his mother, left Thomas "a wandering laboring boy," growing up "litterally without education." He was working as a rough carpenter and hired hand when he married Nancy Hanks, a quiet, intelligent young woman of uncertain ancestry.

In the years following Abraham's birth, the Lincolns moved from one dirt farm to another in Kentucky, Indiana, and Illinois. On each of these farms, Thomas cleared only enough land for his family's use. Lack of ambition joined with insufficient access to a market for surplus goods to trap Thomas in relentless poverty.

In later life, Lincoln neither romanticized nor sentimentalized the difficult circumstances of his childhood. When asked in 1860 by his campaign biographer, John Locke Scripps, to share the details of his early days, he hesitated. "Why Scripps, it is a great piece of folly to attempt to make anything out of my early life. It can all be condensed into a single sentence . . . you will find in Gray's Elegy: 'The short and simple annals of the poor.' "

The traces of Nancy Hanks in history are few and fragmentary. A childhood friend and neighbor of Lincoln's, Nathaniel Grigsby, reported that Mrs. Lincoln "was a woman Know(n) for the Extraordinary Strength of her mind among the family and all who knew her: she was superior to her husband in Every way. She was a brilliant woman." Nancy's first cousin Dennis Hanks, a childhood friend of Abraham's, recalled that Mrs. Lincoln "read the good Bible to [Abe]—taught him to read and to spell—taught him sweetness & benevolence as well." She was described as "beyond all doubt an intellectual woman"; said to possess "Remarkable" perception; to be "very smart" and "naturally Strong minded."

Much later, Lincoln, alluding to the possibility that his mother had come from distinguished stock, told his friend William Herndon: "All that I am or hope ever to be I get from my mother, God bless her."

In the early autumn of 1818, when Abraham was nine, Nancy Lincoln contracted what was known as "milk sickness"—a fatal ailment whose victims suffered dizziness, nausea, and an irregular heartbeat before slipping into a coma. The disease first struck Thomas and Elizabeth Sparrow, Nancy Lincoln's aunt and uncle, who had joined the Lincolns in Indiana the previous winter. The Sparrows had parented Nancy since she was a child and served as grandparents to young Lincoln. The deadly illness took the lives of the Sparrows in rapid succession, and then, before a fortnight had passed, Lincoln's mother became gravely ill. "I am going away from you, Abraham," she reportedly told her young son shortly before she died, "and I shall not return."

In an era when men were fortunate to reach forty-five, and a staggering number of women died in childbirth, the death of a parent was commonplace. Of the four rivals, Seward alone kept parents into his adulthood. Chase was only eight when he lost his father. Bates was eleven. Both of their lives, like Lincoln's, were molded by loss.

The impact of the loss depended upon each man's temperament and the unique circumstances of his family. The death of Chase's father forced young Salmon to exchange the warm support of a comfortable home for the rigid boarding school of a domineering uncle, a man who bestowed or withdrew approval and affection on the basis of performance. An insatiable need for acknowledgment and the trappings of success thenceforth marked Chase's personality. Carl Schurz perceived this aspect of Chase's temperament when he commented that, despite all the high honors Chase eventually achieved, he was never satisfied. "He restlessly looked beyond for the will-of-the-wisp, which deceitfully danced before his gaze."

For Edward Bates, whose family of twelve was scattered by his father's death, the loss seems to have engendered a lifelong urge to protect and provide for his own family circle in ways his father never could. To his wife and eight surviving children, he dedicated his best energies, even at the cost of political ambition, for his happiness depended on his ability to give joy and comfort to his family.

While the early death of a parent had a transforming impact on each of these men, the loss of Lincoln's mother had a uniquely shattering impact on his family's tenuous stability. In the months following her death, his father journeyed from Indiana to Kentucky to bring back a new wife, abandoning his two children to a place Lincoln later described as "a wild region," where "the panther's scream, filled the night with fear and bears preyed on the swine." While Thomas was away, Lincoln's twelve-year-old sister, Sarah, did the cooking and tried to care for both her brother and her mother's cousin Dennis Hanks. Sarah Lincoln was much like her brother, a "quick minded woman" with a "good humored laugh" who could put anyone at ease. But the lonely months of living without adult supervision must have been difficult. When Sarah Bush Johnston, Lincoln's new stepmother, returned with Thomas, she found the abandoned children living like animals, "wild—ragged and dirty." Only after they were soaped, washed, and dressed did they seem to her "more human."

Within a decade, Lincoln would suffer another shattering loss when his sister Sarah died giving birth. A relative recalled that when Lincoln was told of her death, he "sat down on a log and hid his face in his hands while the tears rolled down through his long bony fingers. Those present turned away in pity and left him to his grief." He had lost the two women he had loved. "From then on," a neighbor said, "he was alone in the world you might say."

Years later, Lincoln wrote a letter of condolence to Fanny McCullough, a young girl who had lost her father in the Civil War. "It is with deep grief that I learn of the death of your kind and brave Father; and, especially, that it is affecting your young heart beyond what is common in such cases. In this sad world of ours, sorrow comes to all; and, to the young, it comes with bitterest agony, because it takes them unawares. The older have learned to ever expect it."

Lincoln's early intimacy with tragic loss reinforced a melancholy temperament. Yet his familiarity with pain and personal disappointment imbued him with a strength and understanding of human frailty unavailable to a man of Seward's buoyant disposition. Moreover, Lincoln, unlike the brooding Chase, possessed a life-affirming humor and a profound resilience that lightened his despair and fortified his will.

Even as a child, Lincoln dreamed heroic dreams. From the outset he was cognizant of a destiny far beyond that of his unlettered father and hardscrabble childhood. "He was different from those around him," the historian Douglas Wilson writes. "He knew he was unusually gifted and had great potential." To the eyes of his schoolmates, Lincoln was "clearly exceptional," Lincoln biographer David Donald observes, "and he carried away from his brief schooling the self-confidence of a man who has never met his intellectual equal." His mind and ambition, his childhood friend Nathaniel Grigsby recalled, "soared above us. He naturally assumed the leadership of the boys. He read & thoroughly read his books whilst we played. Hence he was above us and became our guide and leader."

If Lincoln's developing self-confidence was fostered initially by his mother's love and approval, it was later sustained by his stepmother, who came to love him as if he were her own child. Early on, Sarah Bush Lincoln recognized that Abraham was "a Boy of uncommon natural Talents." Though uneducated herself, she did all she could to encourage him to read, learn, and grow. "His mind & mine—what little I had seemed to run together—move in the same channel," she later said. "Abe never gave me a cross word or look and never refused in fact, or Even in appearance, to do any thing I requested him. I never gave him a cross word in all my life. He was Kind to Every body and Every thing and always accommodate[d] others if he could—would do so willingly if he could." Young Lincoln's self-assurance was enhanced by his physical size and strength, qualities that were valued highly on the frontier. "He was a strong, athletic boy," one friend related, "good-natured, and ready to out-run, out-jump and out-wrestle or out-lift anybody in the neighborhood."

In their early years, each of his rivals shared a similar awareness of unusual talents, but Lincoln faced much longer odds to realize his ambitions. His voyage would require a Herculean feat of self-creation. Perhaps the best evidence of his exceptional nature, as well as the genesis of his great gift for storytelling, is manifest in the eagerness with which, even at six or seven, he listened to the stories the adults exchanged as they sat by his father's fireplace at night. Knob Creek farm, where Lincoln lived from the age of two until seven, stood along the old Cumberland Trail that stretched from Nashville to Louisville. Caravans of pioneers passed by each day heading toward the Northwest—farmers, peddlers, preachers, each with a tale to tell.

Night after night, Thomas Lincoln would swap tales with visitors and neighbors while his young son sat transfixed in the corner. In these sociable settings, Thomas was in his element. A born storyteller, he possessed a quick wit, a talent for mimicry, and an uncanny memory for exceptional stories. These qualities would prove his greatest bequest to his son. Young Abe listened so intently to these stories, crafted from experiences of everyday life, that the words became embedded in his memory. Nothing was more upsetting to him, he recalled decades later, nothing made him angrier, than his inability to comprehend everything that was told.

After listening to adults chatter through the evening, he would spend, he said, "no small part of the night walking up and down, and trying to make out what was the exact meaning of some of their, to me, dark sayings." Unable to sleep, he would reformulate the conversations until, as he recalled, "I had put it in language plain enough, as I thought, for any boy I knew to comprehend." The following day, having translated the stories into words and ideas that his friends could grasp, he would climb onto the tree stump or log that served as an impromptu stage and mesmerize his own circle of young listeners. He had discovered the pride and pleasure an attentive audience could bestow. This great storytelling talent and oratorical skill would eventually constitute his stock-in-trade throughout both his legal and political careers. The passion for rendering experience into powerful language remained with Lincoln throughout his life.

The only schools in rural Kentucky and Indiana were subscription schools, requiring families to pay a tuition. Even when frontier families could afford the expense, their children did not always receive much education. "No qualification was ever required of a teacher," Lincoln recalled, "beyond '*readin, writin, and cipherin,*' to the Rule of Three. If a straggler supposed to understand latin, happened to sojourn in the neighborhood, he was looked upon as a wizzard." Allowed to attend school only "by littles" between stints of farmwork, "the aggregate of all his schooling," Lincoln admitted years later, "did not amount to one year." He had never even set foot "inside of a college or academy building" until he acquired his license to practice law. What he had in the way of education, he lamented, he had to pick up on his own.

Books became his academy, his college. The printed word united his mind with the great minds of generations past. Relatives and neighbors recalled that he scoured the countryside for books and read every volume "he could lay his hands on." At a time when ownership of books remained "a luxury for those Americans living outside the purview of the middle class," gaining access to reading material proved difficult. When Lincoln obtained copies of the King James Bible, John Bunyan's *Pilgrim's Progress, Aesop's Fables*, and William Scott's *Lessons in Elocution*, he could not contain his excitement. Holding *Pilgrim's Progress* in his hands, "his eyes sparkled, and that day he could not eat, and that night he could not sleep."

When printing was first invented, Lincoln would later write, "the great mass of men . . . were utterly unconscious, that their *conditions*, or their *minds* were capable of improvement." To liberate "the mind from this false and under estimate of itself, is the great task which printing came into the world to perform." He was, of course, also speaking of himself, of the transforming liberation of a young boy unlocking the miraculous mysteries of language, discovering a world of possibilities in the small log cabin on the frontier that he later called "as unpoetical as any spot of the earth."

"There is no Frigate like a Book," wrote Emily Dickinson, "to take us Lands away." Though the young Lincoln never left the frontier, would never leave America, he traveled with Byron's *Childe Harold* to Spain and Portugal, the Middle East and Italy; accompanied Robert Burns to Edinburgh; and followed the English kings into battle with Shakespeare. As he explored the wonders of literature and the history of the country, the young Lincoln, already conscious of his own power, developed ambitions far beyond the expectations of his family and neighbors. It was through literature that he was able to transcend his surroundings.

He read and reread the Bible and *Aesop's Fables* so many times that years later he could recite whole passages and entire stories from memory. Through Scott's *Lessons in Elocution*, he first encountered selections from Shakespeare's plays, inspiring a love for the great dramatist's writings long before he ever saw a play. He borrowed a volume of the *Revised Statutes of*

Indiana from the local constable, a work that contained the Declaration of Independence, the Constitution, and the Northwest Ordinance of 1787—documents that would become foundation stones of his philosophical and political thought.

Everywhere he went, Lincoln carried a book with him. He thumbed through page after page while his horse rested at the end of a long row of planting. Whenever he could escape work, he would lie with his head against a tree and read. Though he acquired only a handful of volumes, they were seminal works of the English language. Reading the Bible and Shakespeare over and over implanted rhythms and poetry that would come to fruition in those works of his maturity that made Abraham Lincoln our only poet-president. With remarkable energy and tenacity he quarried the thoughts and ideas that he wanted to remember. "When he came across a passage that Struck him," his stepmother recalled, "he would write it down on boards if he had no paper," and "when the board would get too black he would shave it off with a drawing knife and go on again." Then once he obtained paper, he would rewrite it and keep it in a scrapbook so that it could be memorized. Words thus became precious to him, never, as with Seward, to be lightly or indiscriminately used.

The volumes to feed Lincoln's intellectual hunger did not come cheaply. The story is often recounted of the time he borrowed Parson Weems's *Life of George Washington* from Josiah Crawford, a well-to-do farmer who lived sixteen miles away. Thrilled by this celebrated account of the first president's life, he took the book to his loft at night, where, by the light of a tallow candle, or if tallow was scarce, by a grease lamp made from hickory bark gathered in the woods, he read as long as he could stay awake, placing the book on a makeshift shelf between the cabin logs so he could retrieve it at daybreak. During a severe rainstorm one night, the book was badly soiled and the covers warped. Lincoln went to Crawford's house, explained what had happened, and offered to work off the value of the book. Crawford calculated the value of two full days' work pulling corn, which Lincoln considered an unfair reimbursement. Nevertheless, he straightway set to work and kept on until "there was not a corn blade left on a stalk." Then, having paid his debt, Lincoln wrote poems and songs lampooning "Josiah blowing his bugle"—Crawford's large nose. Thus Crawford, in return for loaning Lincoln a book and then exorbitantly penalizing him, won a permanent, if unflattering, place in American history.

A lucid, inquisitive, and extraordinarily dogged mind was Lincoln's native endowment. Already he possessed a vivid sensibility for the beauty of the English language. Often reading aloud, he was attracted to the sound of language along with its meaning—its music and rhythms. He found this in poetry, and to the end of his life would recite poems, often lengthy passages, from memory. He seemed especially drawn to poetry that spoke of our doomed mortality and the transience of earthly achievements. For clearly Lincoln, this acolyte of pure reason and remorseless logic, was also a romantic. All three of Lincoln's rivals shared his early love of books, but none had as difficult a task securing them or finding the leisure to read. In the household of his classically educated father, Seward had only to pick a book from well-stocked shelves, while both local academies he attended and Union College maintained substantial collections of books on history, logic, rhetoric, philosophy, chemistry, grammar, and geography. Chase, likewise, had access to libraries, at his uncle's boys' school in Worthington and at Dartmouth College. And while books were not plentiful where Bates grew up, he had the luxury of his scholarly relative's home, where he could peruse at will an extensive collection.

The distance between the educational advantages Lincoln's rivals enjoyed and the hardships he endured was rendered even greater by the cultural resistance Lincoln faced once his penchant for reading became known. In the pioneer world of rural Kentucky and Indiana, where physical labor was essential for survival and mental exertion was rarely considered a legitimate form of work, Lincoln's book hunger was regarded as odd and indolent. Nor would his community understand the thoughts and emotions stirred by his reading; there were few to talk to about the most important and deeply experienced activities of his mind.

While Lincoln's stepmother took "particular Care not to disturb him—would let him read on and on till [he] quit of his own accord," his father needed help with the tiresome chores of felling trees, digging up stumps, splitting rails, plowing, weeding, and planting. When he found his son in the field reading a book or, worse still, distracting fellow workers with tales or passages from one of his books, he would angrily halt the activity so work could continue. The boy's endeavors to better himself often incurred the resentment of his father, who occasionally destroyed his books and may have physically abused him.

Lincoln's relationship with his father grew strained, particularly when his last chance for schooling was foreclosed by his father's decision to hire him out. He labored for various neighbors butchering hogs, digging wells, and clearing land in order to satisfy a debt the family had incurred. Such conflict between father and son was played out in thousands of homes as the "self-made" men in Lincoln's generation sought to pursue ambitions beyond the cramped lives of their fathers.

The same "longing to rise" that carried Seward away from the Hudson

Valley brought Chase to the infant state of Ohio, and sent Bates to the Missouri Territory propelled Lincoln from Indiana to New Salem, Illinois. At twenty-two, he departed his family home with all his meager possessions bundled on his shoulder. New Salem was a budding town, with twenty-five families, three general stores, a tavern, a blacksmith shop, a cooper shop, and a tannery. Working simply to "keep body and soul together" as a flatboatman, clerk, merchant, postmaster, and surveyor, he engaged in a systematic regimen of self-improvement. He mastered the principles of English grammar at night when the store was closed. He carried Shakespeare's plays and books of poetry when he walked along the streets. Seated in the local post office, he devoured newspapers. He studied geometry and trigonometry while learning the art of surveying. And then, at the age of twenty-five, he decided to study law.

In a time when young men were apprenticed to practicing lawyers while they read the law, Lincoln, by his own account, "studied with nobody." Borrowing law books from a friend, he set about on his own to gain the requisite knowledge and skills. He buried himself in the dog-eared pages of Blackstone's *Commentaries;* he unearthed the thoughts in Chitty's *Pleadings;* he analyzed precepts in Greenleaf's *Evidence* and Story's *Equity Jurisprudence.* After a long day at one of his various jobs, he would read far into the night. A steadfast purpose sustained him.

Few of his colleagues experienced so solitary or steep a climb to professional proficiency. The years Seward and Chase spent in college eased the transition into legal study by exposing them to history, classical languages, and scientific reasoning. What is more, Lincoln had no outlet for discourse, no mentor such as Seward found in the distinguished author of *The Practice.* Nor did Lincoln have the social advantages Chase enjoyed by reading law with the celebrated William Wirt or the connections Bates derived from Rufus Easton.

What Lincoln lacked in preparation and guidance, he made up for with his daunting concentration, phenomenal memory, acute reasoning faculties, and interpretive penetration. Though untutored in the sciences and the classics, he was able to read and reread his books until he understood them fully. "Get the books, and read and study them," he told a law student seeking advice in 1855. It did not matter, he continued, whether the reading be done in a small town or a large city, by oneself or in the company of others. "The *books*, and your *capacity* for understanding them, are just the same in all places. . . . Always bear in mind that your own resolution to succeed, is more important than any other one thing."

• • •

I am Anne Rutledge who sleep beneath these weeds,
Beloved in life of Abraham Lincoln,
Wedded to him, not through union,
But through separation.
Bloom forever, O Republic,
From the dust of my bosom!
—Edgar Lee Masters, *Spoon River Anthology*

At New Salem, Lincoln would take his law books into the woods and stretch out on a "wooded knoll" to read. On these forays he was likely accompanied by Ann Rutledge, whose father owned Rutledge's Tavern, where Lincoln boarded from time to time.

Ann Rutledge was, to our knowledge, Lincoln's first and perhaps most passionate love. Years after her death, he reportedly divulged his feelings for her to an old friend, Isaac Cogdal. When Cogdal asked whether he had been in love, Lincoln replied, "it is true—true indeed . . . she was a handsome girl—would have made a good loving wife . . . I did honestly—& truly love the girl & think often—often of her now."

Not a single piece of correspondence has been uncovered to document the particulars of their relationship. It must be pieced together from the recollections of neighbors and friends in the small, closely knit community of New Salem. Ann was a few years younger than Lincoln, had "Eyes blue large, & Expressive," auburn hair, and a beautiful face. "She was beloved by Every body." Her intellect was said to be "quick—Sharp—deep & philosophic as well as brilliant." New Salem resident William Greene believed "she was a woman worthy of Lincoln's love." What began as a friendship between Ann and Abraham turned at some point into romance. They shared an understanding, according to friends, that they would marry after Ann completed her studies at the Female Academy at Jacksonville.

Ann was only twenty-two in the summer of 1835. While New Salem sweltered through one of the hottest summers in the history of the state, a deadly fever, possibly typhoid, spread through the town. Ann, as well as several of Lincoln's friends, perished in the epidemic. After Ann's death, Abraham seemed "*indifferent*, to transpiring Events," one neighbor recalled, "had but Little to say, but would take his gun and wander off in the woods by him self." Elizabeth Abell, a New Salem neighbor who had become a surrogate mother to Lincoln, claimed she had "never seen a man mourn for a companion more than he did." His melancholy deepened on dark and gloomy days, for he could never "be reconcile[d]," he said, "to have the snow—rains and storms to beat on her grave." Acquaintances feared he had become "temporarily deranged," and that unless he pulled himself together, "reason would desert her throne."

Lincoln himself admitted that he ran "off the track" a little after Ann's death. He had now lost the three women to whom he was closest—his mother, his sister, and Ann. Reflecting on a visit to his childhood home in Indiana some years later, he wrote a mournful poem.

I hear the loved survivors tell
How naught from death could save,
Till every sound appears a knell,
And every spot a grave.

He "was not crazy," maintained Elizabeth Abell. He was simply very sad. "Only people who are capable of loving strongly," Leo Tolstoy wrote, "can also suffer great sorrow; but this same necessity of loving serves to counteract their grief and heal them."

Had Lincoln, like Chase, lived in a large city when Ann died, he might have concealed his grief behind closed doors. In the small community of New Salem, there was no place to hide—except perhaps the woods toward which he gravitated. Moreover, as he brooded over Ann's death, he could find no consolation in the prospect of a reunion in the hereafter. When his New Salem friend and neighbor Mrs. Samuel Hill asked him whether he believed in a future realm, he answered no. "I'm afraid there isn't," he replied sorrowfully. "It isn't a pleasant thing to think that when we die that is the last of us." Though later statements make reference to an omnipotent God or supreme power, there is no mention in any published document, the historian Robert Bruce observes—except in one ambiguous letter to his dying father—of any "faith in life after death." To the end of his life, he was haunted by the finality of death and the evanescence of earthly accomplishments.

Lincoln's inability to take refuge in the concept of a Christian heaven sets him apart from Chase and Bates. While Chase admitted that his "heart was broken" when he buried his second wife, Eliza Smith, he was convinced that "all is not dark. The cloud is fringed with light." Unlike his first wife, Kitty, Eliza had died "trusting in Jesus." He could therefore picture her in heaven, waiting for him to join her in eternal companionship.

Sharing the faith that gave solace to Chase, Bates was certain when his nine-year-old daughter, Edwa, died that she had been called by God "to a higher world & to higher enjoyment." In the child's last hours, he related, she "talked with calmness, and apparently without alarm, of her approaching death. She did not fear to die, still the only reason she gave for not wishing to die, was that she would rather stay with her mother."

Seward shared Lincoln's doubt that any posthumous reunion beckoned. When his wife and precious twenty-one-year-old daughter, Fanny, died within sixteen months of each other, he was devastated. "I ought to be able to rejoice that [Fanny] was withdrawn from me to be reunited with [her mother] the pure and blessed spirit that formed her own," he told a friend. "But, unfortunately I am not spiritual enough to find support in these reflections."

If Lincoln, like Seward, confronted the loss of loved ones without prospect of finding them in the afterlife to assuage the loss, one begins to comprehend the weight of his sorrow when Ann died. Nonetheless, he completed his study of law and received his law license and the offer to become a partner with John Stuart, the friend whose law books he had borrowed.

• • •

IN APRIL 1837, twenty months after Ann Rutledge's death, Lincoln left New Salem for Springfield, Illinois, then a community of about fifteen hundred people. There he planned to embark upon what he termed his "experiment" in law. With no place to stay and no money to buy provisions, he wandered into the general store in the town square. He asked the young proprietor, Joshua Speed, how much it would cost to buy "the furniture for a single bed. The mattress, blankets, sheets, coverlid, and pillow." Speed estimated the cost at seventeen dollars, which Lincoln agreed was "perhaps cheap enough," though he lacked the funds to cover that amount. He asked if Speed might advance him credit until Christmastime, when, if his venture with law worked out, he would pay in full. "If I fail in this," added Lincoln abjectly, "I do not know that I can ever pay you."

Speed surveyed the tall, discomfited figure before him. "I never saw a sadder face," he recalled thinking at the time. Though the two men had never met, Speed had heard Lincoln speak a year earlier and came away deeply impressed. Decades later, he could still recite Lincoln's concluding words. Turning to Lincoln, Speed said: "You seem to be so much pained at contracting so small a debt, I think I can suggest a plan by which you can avoid the debt and at the same time attain your end. I have a large room with a double bed upstairs, which you are very welcome to share with me." Lincoln reacted quickly to Speed's unexpected offer. Racing upstairs to deposit his bags in the loft, he came clattering down again, his face entirely transformed. "Beaming with pleasure he exclaimed, 'Well, Speed, I am moved!' "

Five years younger than Lincoln, the handsome, blue-eyed Speed had been raised in a gracious mansion on his family's prosperous plantation, cultivated by more than seventy slaves. He had received an excellent education in the best Kentucky schools and at St. Joseph's College at Bardstown. While he could have remained at home, enjoying a life of ease, he determined to make his way west with the tide of his restless generation. Arriving in Springfield when he was twenty-one, he had invested in real estate and become the proprietor of the town's general store.

Lincoln and Speed shared the same room for nearly four years, sleeping in the same double bed. Over time, the two young men developed a close relationship, talking nightly of their hopes and their prospects, their mutual love of poetry and politics, their anxieties about women. They attended political meetings and forums together, went to dances and parties, relaxed with long rides in the countryside.

Emerging from a childhood and young adulthood marked by isolation and loneliness, Lincoln discovered in Joshua Speed a companion with whom he could share his inner life. They had similar dispositions, both possessing an ambitious impulse to improve themselves and rise in the world. No longer a boy but not yet an established adult, Lincoln ended years of emotional deprivation and intellectual solitude by building his first and deepest friendship with Speed. Openly acknowledging the strength of this attachment, the two pledged themselves to a lifelong bond of friendship. Those who knew Lincoln well pointed to Speed as his "most intimate friend," the only person to whom he ever disclosed his secret thoughts. "You know my desire to befriend you is everlasting," Lincoln assured Speed, "that I will never cease, while I know how to do any thing."

Some have suggested that there may have been a sexual relationship between Lincoln and Speed. Their intimacy, however, like the relationship between Seward and Berdan and, as we shall see, between Chase and Stanton, is more an index to an era when close male friendships, accompanied by open expressions of affection and passion, were familiar and socially acceptable. Nor can sharing a bed be considered evidence of an erotic involvement. It was common practice in an era when private quarters were a rare luxury, when males regularly slept in the same bed as children and continued to do so in academies, boardinghouses, and overcrowded hotels. The room above Speed's store functioned as a sort of dormitory, with two other young men living there part of the time as well as Lincoln and Speed. The attorneys of the Eighth Circuit in Illinois where Lincoln would travel regularly shared beds—with the exception of Judge David Davis, whose immense girth left no room for a companion. As the historian Donald Yacovone writes in his study of the fiercely expressed love and devotion among several abolitionist leaders in the same era, the "preoccupation with elemental sex" reveals more about later centuries "than about the nineteenth."

If it is hard to delineate the exact nature of Lincoln's relationship with Speed, it is clear that this intimate friendship came at a critical juncture in his young life, as he struggled to define himself in a new city, away from home and family. Here in Springfield he would carry forward the twin careers that would occupy most of his life: law and politics. His accomplishments in escaping the confines of his barren, death-battered childhood and his relentless self-education required luck, a stunning audacity, and a breadth of intelligence that was only beginning to reveal itself.

CHAPTER 3

THE LURE OF POLITICS

IN THE ONLY COUNTRY founded on the principle that men should and could govern themselves, where self-government dominated every level of human association from the smallest village to the nation's capital, it was natural that politics should be a consuming, almost universal concern.

"Scarcely have you descended on the soil of America," wrote Alexis de Tocqueville in the year Lincoln was serving his first term in the state legislature, "when you find yourself in the midst of a sort of tumult; a confused clamor is raised on all sides; a thousand voices come to your ear at the same time, each of them expressing some social needs. Around you everything moves: here, the people of one neighborhood have gathered to learn if a church ought to be built; there, they are working on the choice of a representative; farther on, the deputies of a district are going to town in all haste in order to decide about some local improvements; in another place, the farmers of a village abandon their furrows to go discuss the plan of a road or a school."

"Citizens assemble with the sole goal of declaring that they disapprove of the course of government," Tocqueville wrote. "To meddle in the government of society and to speak about it is the greatest business and, so to speak, the only pleasure that an American knows. . . . An American does not know how to converse, but he discusses; he does not discourse, but he holds forth. He always speaks to you as to an assembly."

In an illustration from Noah Webster's *Elementary Spelling Book,* widely read in Lincoln's generation, a man strikes a heroic pose as he stands on a wooden barrel, speaking to a crowd of enthralled listeners. Behind him the Stars and Stripes wave proudly, while a poster bearing the image of the national eagle connotes the bravery and patriotism of the orator. "Who can wonder," Ralph Waldo Emerson asked, at the lure of politics, "for our ambitious young men, when the highest bribes of society are at the feet of the successful orator? He has his audience at his devotion. All other fames must hush before his."

For many ambitious young men in the nineteenth century, politics proved the chosen arena for advancement. Politics attracted Bates in Missouri, Seward in upstate New York, Lincoln in Illinois, and Chase in Ohio.

• • •

THE OLDEST OF THE FOUR, Edward Bates was the first drawn into politics during the 1820 crusade for Missouri's statehood. As the petition was debated in the U.S. Congress, an argument arose as to whether the constitutional protection for slavery in the original states applied to the newly acquired territories. An antislavery representative from New York introduced an amendment requiring Missouri first to agree to emancipate all children of slaves on their twenty-first birthday. The so-called "lawyer faction," including Edward Bates, vehemently opposed an antislavery restriction as the price of admission to the Union. Bates argued that it violated the Constitution by imposing a qualification on a state beyond providing "a republican form of government," as guaranteed by the Constitution.

To Northerners who hoped containment in the South would lead inevitably to the end of slavery, its introduction into the new territories aroused fear that it would now infiltrate the West and, thereby, the nation's future. For Southerners invested in slave labor, Northern opposition to Missouri's admission as a slave state posed a serious threat to their way of life. At the height of the struggle, Southern leaders declared their intent to secede from the Union; many Northerners seemed willing to let them go. "This momentous question," Jefferson wrote at the time, "like a fire bell in the night, awakened and filled me with terror. I considered it at once as the knell of the Union."

The Senate ultimately stripped the bill of the antislavery amendment, bringing Missouri into the Union as a slave state under the famous Missouri Compromise of 1820. Fashioned by Kentucky senator Henry Clay, who earned the nickname the "*Great Pacificator*," the Compromise simultaneously admitted Maine as a free state and prohibited slavery in all the remaining Louisiana Purchase territory north of the latitude 36°30'. That line ran across the southern border of Missouri, making Missouri itself an exception to the new division.

Later that spring, Bates campaigned successfully for a place among the forty-one delegates chosen to write the new state's constitution. Though younger than most of the delegates, he "emerged as one of the principal authors of the constitution." When the time came to select candidates for state offices, the "lawyer faction" received the lion's share. David Barton and Thomas Benton were sent to Washington as Missouri's first senators, and Edward Bates became the state's first attorney general; his partner, Joshua Barton, became the first secretary of state. Two years later, Bates won a seat in the Missouri House, and two years after that, Frederick Bates was elected governor of the state.

This inner circle did not remain united for long, for tensions developed between Senators Barton and Benton. Barton's followers were primarily merchants and landowners, while Benton gradually aligned himself with the agrarian disciples of Jacksonian democracy. A tragic duel made the split irrevocable. In the course of his legal practice, Bates's partner, Joshua Barton, found proof of corruption in the office of Benton's friend and ally, Missouri's land surveyor-general, William Rector. Rector challenged Barton to a duel in which Barton was killed. Bates was devastated by the loss of his friend. He and David Barton went public with Joshua Barton's indictment implicating Benton as well as Rector. They demanded an investigation from U.S. Attorney General William Wirt, Chase's mentor and friend. The investigation sustained most of the charges and resulted in President Monroe's dismissal of Rector. The affair came to an end, but the rift between Barton and Benton never healed.

Proponents of Barton, including Bates, eventually coalesced into the Whig Party, while the Bentonites became Democrats. The Whigs favored public support for internal improvements designed to foster business in a new market economy. Their progressive agenda included protective tariffs, and a national banking system to develop and strengthen the resources of the country. The Democrats, with their base of power in the agrarian South, resisted these measures, appealing instead to the interests of the common man against the bankers, the lawyers, and the merchants.

Despite his immersion in the whirlpool of Missouri politics, an event occurred in 1823 that altered Bates's life and forever shifted his focus—he fell in love with and married Julia Coalter. Thereafter, home and family domesticity eclipsed politics as the signal pleasure of his life. His first child, named Joshua Barton Bates in honor of his slain partner, was born in 1824. Over the next twenty-five years, sixteen more children were born.

When Julia was young, family friend John Darby recalled, she was "a most beautiful woman." She came from a distinguished South Carolina family that settled in Missouri when she was a child. Her father was a wealthy man, having invested successfully in land. The husband of one of her sisters became governor of South Carolina. Another sister was married to the chancellor of the state of Missouri. A third sister married Hamilton Rowan Gamble, who served as a justice on Missouri's supreme court and wrote a dissenting opinion in the *Dred Scott* case. Despite these connections, Julia had little interest in politics. Her attentions were fully focused on her family. Her surviving letters, unlike those of Frances Seward, said nothing about the issues of the day, concentrating instead on her children's activities, their eating habits, their games, their broken bones. Her entire being, Darby observed, "was calculated to impart happiness around the domestic circle."

She succeeded in this beyond ordinary measure, providing Edward with what their friends uniformly described as an ideal home life. The enticements of public office gradually diminished in his contented eyes. When he sought and won a seat in the U.S. Congress in 1826, three years after his marriage, his pleasure in the victory was dimmed by the necessity of leaving home and hearth. Even short absences from Julia proved painful for him. "I have never found it so difficult to keep up my spirits," he confessed to her at one point when she had gone to visit friends for several days. "Indeed, ever since you left me, I have felt a painful consciousness of being alone. At court I can do well enough, but when I come home, to bed or board, I feel so utterly solitary, that I can enjoy neither eating nor sleeping. I mention these things not because it is either proper or becoming to feel them, but because they are novel to me. I never before had such a restless, dissatisfied, indefinable feeling; and never wish to have it again."

Disquiet returned a hundredfold when he departed on the lonely journey to take up his congressional seat in Washington, leaving his pregnant wife and small son at home. Writing from various taverns and boardinghouses along the way, he confessed that he was in "something of a melancholy and melting mood." There was a "magic" in her loveliness, which left him "like a schoolboy lover" in the absence of his "dear Julia." Now, after only a few weeks away, he was moved to cry, "a plague upon the vanity of petty ambition! Were I great enough to sway the destinies of the nation, the meed of ambition might be worth the sacrifice which it requires; but a mere seat in Congress as a subaltern member, is a contemptible price for the happiness which we enjoy with each other. It was always your opinion, & now I feel it to be true."

His spirits revived somewhat when he settled into a comfortable Washington boardinghouse and took his seat in Congress alongside David Crockett, James Polk, and Henry Clay. Though Bates seldom went out to parties, preferring to spend his nights reading and writing to his wife, he was thrilled, he told Julia, to spend a private evening with Henry Clay. "That man grows upon me more and more, every time I see him," he wrote. "There is an intuitive perception about him, that seems to see & understand at a glance, and a winning fascination in his manners that will suffer none to be his enemies who associate with him."

The main issues that confronted Bates during his congressional term concerned the disposition of western lands, internal improvements, and the tariff. On each of these issues, Senators Benton and Barton were antagonists. Benton had introduced a bill under which the federal government would make its lands available to settlers at a price so low that it was almost free. Cheap land, he argued, would bridle the rampant speculation that profited the few over the many. Barton countered with the claim that such cheap land would depress the entire Western economy. Bates sided with Barton, voting against the popular bill.

During the dispute over public lands, Bates published a pamphlet denouncing Benton that so angered "Old Bullion," as he was known, that the two men did not speak for nearly a quarter of a century. "My piece is burning into his reputation," Bates told Julia, "like aquafortis upon iron—the mark can never be effaced." Beyond his open quarrel with Benton, Bates got along well with his colleagues. His natural warmth and easy manner created respect and affection. Night sessions he found particularly amusing and intriguing, despite the "roaring disorder" of people "hawking, coughing, thumping with their canes & kicking about spit boxes." The hall, suffused with candlelight from members' desks, and from the massive chandelier suspended from the domed ceiling, "exhibit[ed] a most magnificent appearance."

Nonetheless, these few moments of pleasure could not compensate for missing the birth of his first daughter, Nancy. "As yet I only know that *she is*," he lamented, "I long to know *how* she is—*what* she is—who she is like . . . whether she has black eyes or gray—a long nose or a pug—a wide mouth or a narrow one—and above all, whether she has a pretty foot," for without a pretty foot, like her mother's, he predicted, she could never make "a *fine* woman."

"Oh! How I long to see & press you to my bosom," he told Julia, "if it were but for a moment. Sometimes, I almost realize the vision—I see you with such vivid and impassioned precision, that the very form developing is in my eye." In letter after letter, the physical immediacy of their relationship becomes clear. Responding to Julia's admission of her own downcast spirits, he wrote: "O, that I could kiss the tear from that cheek whose cheerful brightness is my sunshine."

Still, public life enticed him, and at the behest of his friends and supporters, Bates agreed to run for a second term. Despite his great personal popularity, he lost his bid for reelection in the wake of the great Jacksonian landslide that gave Benton and the Democrats complete control of Missouri politics. During the last days of his term, the usually soft-spoken Bates got into a heated argument with Congressman George McDuffie of South Carolina on the floor of the House. McDuffie ridiculed him personally, and Bates impulsively challenged the South Carolinian to a duel. Fortunately, McDuffie declined, agreeing to apologize for his offensive language. Years later, reflecting on the Southern "Code" of dueling, Bates's friend Charles Gibson maintained that as wicked as the code was, the vulgar public behavior following the demise of the practice was worse still. "The code preserved a dignity, justice and decorum that have since been lost," he argued, "to the great detriment of the professions, the public and the government. The present generation will think me barbarous but I believe that some lives lost in protecting the tone of the bar and the press, on which the Republic itself so largely depends, are well spent."

As the thirty-six-year-old Bates packed up his documents and books to return home, he assured Julia that he was genuinely relieved to have lost. While he loved his friends "as much as any man," he wrote, "for happiness I look alone to the bosom of my own family." Not a day passed, he happily reported, that he did not "divide and subdivide" his time by making plans for their future. He meant first of all "to take & maintain a station in the front rank" of his profession, so that he could provide for his family all the "various little comforts & amusements we have often talked over & wished we possessed."

Months and years slipped by, and Bates remained true to his word. Though he served two terms in the state legislature, where he was regarded as "the ablest and most eloquent member of that body," he decided in 1835 to devote his full attention to his flourishing law practice, rather than run for reelection. Throughout the prime of his life, therefore, Bates found his chief gratification in home and family.

His charming diary, faithfully recorded for more than three decades, provides a vivid testament to his domestic preoccupations. While ruminations upon ambition, success, and power are ubiquitous in Chase's introspective diary, Bates focused on the details of everyday life, the comings and goings of his children, the progress of his garden, and the social events in his beloved St. Louis. His interest in history, he once observed, lay less in the usual records of wars and dynasties than in the more neglected areas of domestic laws, morals, and social manners.

The smallest details of his children's lives fascinated him. When Ben, his fourteenth child, was born, he noted the "curious fact" that the child had a birthmark on the right side of his belly resembling a frog. Attempting to explain "one of the Mysteries in which God has shrouded nature," he recalled that a few weeks before the child was born, while his wife lay on the bed reading, she was unpleasantly startled by the sudden appearance of a tree frog. At the time, "she was lying on her left side, with her right hand resting on her body above the hip," Bates noted, "and in the corresponding part of the child's body is the distinct mark of the frog."

Faith in the powers of God irradiates the pages of his diary. His son Julian, a "bad stammerer from his childhood"—the family had begun to fear that "he was incurable"—miraculously began one day to speak without the slightest hesitation. "A new faculty," Bates recorded, "is given to one who seemed to have been cut off from one of the chief blessings of humanity." In return for this restoration to speech, Bates hoped that his son would eventually "qualify himself to preach the Gospel," for he had "never seen in any youth a more devoted piety." Sadly, the "miracle" did not last long; within six months Julian was stuttering again.

On rare occasions when his wife left to visit relatives, Bates mourned her absence from the home where she was both "Mistress & Queen." He reminded himself that he must not "begrudge her the short respite" from the innumerable tasks of caring for a large family. Giving birth to seventeen children in thirty-two years, Julia was pregnant throughout nearly all her childbearing years. Savoring the warmth of his family circle, Bates felt the loss of each child who grew up and moved away. "This day," he noted in 1851, "my son Barton, with his family—wife and one child—moved into his new house. . . . He has lived with us ever since his marriage in March 1849. This is a serious diminution of our household, being worried that, as our children are fast growing up, & will soon scatter about, in search of their own futures, we may soon expect to have but a little family in a large house."

The diaries Bates kept also reveal a deep commitment to his home city of St. Louis. Every year, on April 29, he marked the anniversary of his first arrival in the town. As the years passed, he witnessed "mighty changes in population, locomotion, commerce and the arts," which made St. Louis the jewel of the great Mississippi Valley and would, he predicted, eventually make it "the ruling city of the continent." His entries proudly record the first gas illumination of the streets, the transmission of the first telegraph between St. Louis and the eastern cities, and the first day that a railroad train moved west of the Mississippi.

Bates witnessed a great fire in 1849 that reduced the commercial section of the city to rubble and endured a cholera epidemic that same year that killed more than a hundred each day, hearses rolling through the muddy streets from morning till night. In one week alone, he recorded, the total deaths numbered nearly a thousand. His own family pulled through "in perfect health," in part, he believed, because they rejected the general opinion of avoiding fruits and vegetables. He agonized over the medical ignorance about the origin of the disease or its remedy. "No two of them agree with each other, and no one agrees with himself two weeks at a time." As the epidemic worsened, scores of families left the city in fear of contagion, but Bates refused to do so. To a friend who had offered sanctuary on his plantation outside of the city, he explained: "I am one of the oldest of the American inhabitants, have a good share of public respect & confidence, and consequently, some influence with the people. I hold it to be a sacred duty, that admits of no compromise, to stand my ground and be ready to do & to bear my part. . . . I should be ashamed to leave St. Louis under existing circumstances. . . . It would be an abandonment of a known duty."

Beyond commentary on his family and his city, Bates filled the pages of his diary with observations of the changing seasons, the progress of his flowers, and the phases of the moon. He celebrated the first crocus each year, his elm trees shedding seed, oaks in full tassel, tulips in their prime. So vivid are his descriptions of his garden that the reader can almost hear the rustling leaves of fall, or "the frogs . . . croaking, in full chorus" that filled the spring nights. With an acute eye he observed that plants change color with age. Meticulously noting variation and difference, he never felt that he was repeating the same patterns of activity year after year. He was a contented man.

However, he never fully abandoned his interest in politics. His passion for the development of the West led him to a major role in the River and Harbor Convention called in the late 1840s to protest President Polk's veto of the Whig-sponsored internal improvements bill. The assembly is said to have been "the largest Convention ever gathered in the United States prior to the Civil War." More than 5,000 accredited delegates and countless other spectators joined Chicago's 16,000 inhabitants, filling every conceivable room in every hotel, boardinghouse, and private dwelling. Desperate visitors to the overcrowded city even sought places to sleep aboard boats in Chicago's harbor.

Former and future governors, congressmen, and senators were there, including Tom Corwin from Ohio, Thurlow Weed and *New York Tribune* editor Horace Greeley from New York, and Schuyler Colfax of Indiana, who was chosen to serve as secretary of the convention. New York was also represented by Democrat David Dudley Field, designated to present Polk's arguments against federal appropriations for internal improvements in the states. Also in attendance, Greeley wrote, was "Hon. Abraham Lincoln, a tall specimen of an Illinoian, just elected to Congress from the only Whig District in the State." It was Lincoln's first mention in a paper of national repute.

"No one who saw [Lincoln] can forget his personal appearance at that time," one delegate recalled years later. "Tall, angular and awkward, he had on a short-waisted, thin swallow-tail coat, a short vest of same material, thin pantaloons, scarcely coming down to his ankles, a straw hat and a pair of brogans with woolen socks."

On the first day, Edward Bates was chosen president of the convention, much to his "deep astonishment," given the presence of so many eminent delegates. "If notice had been given me of any intention to nominate me for the presidency of the Convention, I should have shrunk from it with dread & repressed the attempt," Bates confided to his diary. He was apprehensive that party politics would render the convention unsuccessful and that he would then bear the brunt of responsibility for its failure. Yet so skillfully and impartially did he conduct the proceedings and so eloquently did he make the case for internal improvements and development of the inland waterways that he "leaped at one bound into national prominence." On a much smaller scale, Lincoln impressed the audience with his clever rebuttal of the arguments against public support for internal improvements advanced by Democrat Field.

At the close of the convention, Bates delivered the final speech. No complete record of this speech was made, for once Bates began speaking, the reporters, Weed confessed, were "too intent and absorbed as listeners, to think of Reporting." "No account that can now be given will do it justice," Horace Greeley wrote in the *New York Tribune* the following week. In clear, compelling language, Bates described the country poised at a dangerous crossroad "between sectional disruption and unbounded prosperity." He called on the various regions of the nation to speak in "voices of moderation and compromise, for only by statesmanlike concession could problems of slavery and territorial acquisition be solved so the nation could move on to material greatness." While he was speaking, Weed reported, "he was interrupted continually by cheer upon cheer; and at its close, the air rung with shout after shout, from the thousands in attendance." Overwhelmed by the reaction, Bates considered the speech "the crowning act" of his life, received as he "never knew a speech received before."

"The immense assembly," Bates noted in his diary, "seemed absolutely mesmerized—their bodies and hearts & minds subjected to my will, and answering to my every thought & sentiment with the speed and exactness of electricity. And when I ceased to speak there was one loud, long and spontaneous burst of sympathy & joyous gratification, the like of which I never expect to witness again."

Bates acknowledged when he returned home that his vanity had been "flattered," his "pride of character stimulated in a manner & a degree far beyond what I thought could ever reach me in this life-long retirement to which I have withdrawn." The experience was "more full of public honor & private gratification than any passage of my life . . . those three days at Chicago have given me a fairer representation & a higher standing in the nation, than I could have hoped to attain by years of labor & anxiety in either house of Congress."

With that single speech, Bates had become a prominent national figure, his name heralded in papers across the country as a leading prospect for high public office once the Whigs were returned to power. "The nation cannot afford to be deprived of so much integrity, talent, and patriotism," Weed concluded at the end of a long, flattering piece calling on Bates to reenter political life.

While Bates initially basked in such acclaim, within weeks of the convention's close, he convinced himself he no longer craved what he later called "the glittering bauble" of political success. Declining Weed's appeal that he return to public life, he wrote the editor a pensive letter. Once, he revealed to Weed, he had entertained such "noble aspirations" to make his mind "the mind of other men." But these desires were now gone, his "habits formed and stiffened to the standard of professional and domestic life." Consequently, there was "no office in the gift of prince or people" that he would accept. His refusal, he explained, was "the natural result" of his social position, his domestic relations, and his responsibilities to his large family.

• • •

SEWARD WAS NEXT to enter public life, realizing after several uninspired years of practicing law that he "had no ambition for its honors." Though resigned to his profession "with so much cheerfulness that [his] disinclination was never suspected," he found himself perusing newspapers and magazines at every free moment, while scrutinizing his law books only when he needed them for a case. He was discovering, he said, that "politics was the important and engrossing business of the country."

Fate provided an introduction to Thurlow Weed, the man who would secure his entry into the political world and facilitate his rise to prominence. Seward was on an excursion to Niagara Falls with Frances, her father, and his parents when the wheel of their stagecoach broke off, throwing the passengers into a swampy ravine. A tall, powerfully built man with deep-set blue eyes appeared and helped everyone to safety. He introduced himself as Thurlow Weed, editor of a Rochester newspaper, which "he printed chiefly with his own hand." That encounter sparked a friendship that would shape the destinies of both men.

Four years Seward's senior, Thurlow Weed could see at a glance that his new acquaintance was an educated young man belonging to the best society. Weed himself had grown up in poverty, his father frequently imprisoned for debt, his family forced to move from one upstate location to another. Apprenticed in a blacksmith's shop at eight years old, with only a few years of formal schooling behind him, he had fought to educate himself. He had walked miles to borrow books, studying history and devouring newspapers by firelight. A classic example of a self-made man, he no sooner identified an obstacle to his progress than he worked with discipline to counteract it. Concerned that he lacked a native facility for remembering names and appointments, and believing that "a politician who sees a man once should remember him forever," Weed consciously trained his memory. He spent fifteen minutes every night telling his wife, Catherine, everything that had happened to him that day, everyone he had met, the exact words spoken. The nightly mnemonics worked, for Weed soon became known as a man with a phenomenal recall. Gifted with abundant energy, shrewd intelligence, and a warm personality, he managed to carve out a brilliant career as printer, editor, writer, publisher, and, eventually, as powerful political boss, familiarly known as "the Dictator."

Weed undoubtedly sensed in the younger Seward an instinct for power and a fascination with politics that matched his own. In an era when political parties were in flux, Weed and Seward gravitated toward the proponents of a new infrastructure for the country, by deepening waterways and creating a new network of roads and rails. Such measures, Seward believed, along with a national banking system and protective tariffs, would enable the nation to "strengthen its foundations, increase its numbers, develop its resources, and extend its dominion." Eventually, those in favor of "the American system," as it came to be called, coalesced behind Henry Clay's Whig Party.

Weed's star rose rapidly in New York when, with Seward's help, he launched the *Albany Evening Journal*, first published in March 1830. The influential *Journal*, which eventually became the party organ for the Whigs (and later, for the Republicans), gave Weed a powerful base from which he would brilliantly shape public opinion for nearly four decades. Through his newspapers, Weed engineered Seward's first chance for political office. In September 1830, Seward secured the nomination for a seat in the state senate from the seventh district. That November, with Weed managing every step of the campaign, Seward won a historic victory as the youngest member to enter the New York Senate. He was twenty-nine.

Albany had nearly doubled in size since Seward had first seen it, but it was still a small town of 24,000 inhabitants. Originally settled by the Dutch, the state's capital boasted a stately array of brick mansions that belonged to wealthy merchant princes. The year before Seward's arrival, ground had been broken for the country's "first steam-powered railroad." This sixteen-mile track connecting Albany with Schenectady was "the first link in an eventual nationwide web of tracks."

The legislature consisted of 32 senators and 128 representatives, most of whom boarded in either the Eagle Tavern on South Market Street or around the corner on State Street, at Bemont's Hotel. Such close quarters, while congenial to politicians, were ill suited to families—especially those, like Seward's, with small children. Consequently, Seward decided to attend the four-month winter session alone.

"Weed is very much with me, and I enjoy his warmth of feeling," Seward confided to Frances after he had settled into Bemont's, describing his friend as "one of the greatest politicians of the age . . . the magician whose wand controls and directs" the party. Despite Weed's eminence, Seward proudly noted, he "sits down, stretches one of his long legs out to rest on my coal-box, I cross my own, and, puffing the smoke of our cigars into each other's faces, we talk of everything, and everybody, except politics." They enjoyed a mutual love of the theater and a passion for the novels of Charles Dickens and Walter Scott. Their shared ambition, for each other and their country, became a common bond that would keep their friendship alive until the end of their days.

Seward's gregarious nature was in perfect harmony with the clublike atmosphere of the boardinghouses, where colleagues took their daily meals together and spent evenings in one another's quarters gathered by the fire. "My room is a thoroughfare," he told Frances. Early in the session, he befriended an older colleague, Albert Haller Tracy, a senator from Buffalo who had served three terms in the U.S. Congress and had once been touted as a candidate for vice president. In recent years, however, a series of debilitating illnesses had stalled Tracy's political ambitions and "crushed all his aspirings." In Seward, perhaps, he found a young man who could fulfill the dreams he had once held dear. "I believe Henry tells him everything that passes in his mind," Frances Seward wrote to her sister, Lazette. "He and Henry appear equally in love with each other."

"It shames my manhood that I am so attached to you," Tracy confessed to Seward after several days' absence from Albany. "It is a foolish fondness from which no good can come." His friendship with another colleague, Tracy explained, was "just right, it fills my heart exactly, but yours crowds it producing a kind of girlish impatience which one can neither dispose of nor comfortably endure . . . every day and almost every hour since [leaving] I have suffered a womanish longing to see you. But all this is too ridiculous for the subject matter of a letter between two grave Senators, and I'll leave unsaid three fourths of what I have been dreaming on since I left Albany."

Seward at first reciprocated Tracy's feelings, professing a "rapturous joy" in discovering that his friend shared the "feelings which I had become half ashamed for their effeminancy to confess I possessed." In time, however, Tracy's intensity began to wear on the relationship. When Seward did not immediately respond to one of his letters, Tracy penned a petulant note. "My feelings confined in narrow channels have outstripped yours which naturally are more diffused—I was foolish enough to make an almost exclusive attachment the measure for one which is . . . divided with many."

Tracy's ardor would fuel an intense rivalry with Thurlow Weed. "Weed has never been to see us since Tracy came," Frances told her sister during a visit to Albany. "I am sorry for this although I can hardly account for it." Confronted with the need to choose, Seward turned to Weed, not Tracy, for vital collaboration. Although Tracy continued a cordial association with Seward, he harbored a smoldering resentment over Seward's increasing closeness to Weed. "Love—cruel tyrant as he is," Tracy reminded Seward, "has made reciprocity both the bond and aliment of our most hallowed affections." Absent that reciprocity, Tracy warned, it would be impossible to sustain the glorious friendship that they had once enjoyed.

A strange turn in Tracy's affections likely resulted from his mounting sense of distance from Seward. He transferred his unrequited love from Henry to Frances, who also was feeling distant from her husband. Though still deeply in love after ten years of marriage, Frances worried that her husband's passion for politics and worldly achievement surpassed his love for his family. She mourned "losing my influence over a heart I once thought so entirely my own," increasingly apprehensive that she and her husband were "differently constituted."

In 1832, Seward convinced Frances to accompany him to Albany for the legislative session that ran from January to March. Their quarters on the first floor of Bemont's Hotel were just below those taken by Tracy and his wife, Harriet. The two couples would often spend evenings or weekends together, and Tracy often tagged along with Henry and Frances when his wife was on one of her frequent trips to their home in Buffalo. He joined them on walks, shopping trips, and excursions with the children. "He is a singular being," Frances confided to Lazette. "He certainly knows more than any man I ever was acquainted with." His conversation, she marveled, "reminds me of a book of synonyms. He hardly ever makes use of the same words to express ideas that have a shade of difference."

Capitalizing on Frances's hunger for companionship, Tracy insinuated himself into the private emotional world she once shared only with her husband. He spoke with her freely about his quarrels with his wife. He invited her into his sitting room to read poetry and study French. They talked about their battles with ill health. "I believe at present he could convince me that a chameleon was blue, green or black just as he should choose," Frances admitted to Lazette. Following one extended absence, Frances announced unabashedly that she was "very glad to see him as I love him very much." Though there is no indication that Frances and Tracy ever shared a physical relationship, they had entered into something that was considered, in the subtle realm of Victorian social mores, almost as shameful and inappropriate—a private emotional intimacy.

The following summer, Seward left his wife and family in Auburn to accompany his father on a three-month voyage to Europe. While his aging father's need for companionship provided a rationale for the sojourn, Seward relished the opportunity to see foreign lands and observe new cultures. Father and son traveled extensively through England, Ireland, Holland, Switzerland, Italy, and France. "What a romance was this journey that I was making!" Seward recalled years later. Everywhere he went, however, his thoughts returned to America and his faith in his country's unique future.

"It is not until one visits old, oppressed, suffering Europe, that he can appreciate his own government," he observed, "that he realizes the fearful responsibility of the American people to the nations of the whole earth, to carry successfully through the experiment . . . that men are capable of self-government." He hungrily sought out American newspapers in library reading rooms, noting with regret ubiquitous reports of "malicious political warfare."

While Lincoln, Chase, and Bates would never visit the Old World, Seward, at the age of thirty-two, mingled comfortably with members of Parliament and received invitations to elegant receptions and dinner parties throughout Europe. In France, Seward spent a long weekend visiting with the Revolutionary War hero General Lafayette at his home, La Grange.

In Seward's absence, Frances corresponded frequently with Tracy. When Judge Miller noticed a letter in an unknown hand awaiting Frances on the mantelpiece, he demanded to see it. Frances did not know what to do, she explained to her sister. "I handed it to him and he very deliberately commenced breaking the seal for the purpose of reading it. My first impulse was to jump up and snatch the letter from his hand, which I did and then apologized by saying I would prefer reading it myself first. He appeared very much astonished that I should be so unreasonable."

As Tracy's letters multiplied, the deeply religious Frances began to contemplate the perilous shift in their friendship. Mortified in front of Henry, now returned from Europe, she proffered the letters, asking him to determine if Tracy was endeavoring to break their marital peace. At first Seward refused to read them, unwilling to impute such dishonorable intentions to Tracy. When a further letter arrived that caused Frances to collapse in tears, believing herself dishonored in both Tracy's and her husband's eyes, Seward resolved to confront him.

The next time the two men met in Albany, however, Seward made no mention of the delicate situation. Nor did he bring it up in the following months, for his attention was increasingly consumed by politics. Four years in the state senate had proved Seward an eloquent voice for reform. He had denounced imprisonment for debt, urged separate prisons for men and women, and pushed for internal improvements, all the while maintaining friendly relations on both sides of the aisle. It was time, Weed believed, to push his protégé toward higher office.

At the September 1834 convention in Utica, New York, Weed convinced members of the newly organized Whig Party that the young, energetic Seward would wage the best campaign for governor against the heavily favored Democrats. Seward was thrilled. Needing all the support he could gather, he did not want to risk alienating the influential Albert Tracy. Promises he had made to his wife could wait.

Brimming with high expectations in his upstart race, Seward eagerly embraced the Whig platform that promised to deliver for the nation something of the progress he had achieved for himself. Despite Weed's caution that he faced an uphill battle, his native optimism would not be dampened. The campaign, complete with slogans and songs, was a lively affair. To counter charges that the boyish, red-haired Seward was too young for high office, the Whigs offered a gallery of historical figures who had achieved greatness in their youth, including Charlemagne, Napoleon, Lafayette, Mozart, Newton, and, of course, Whig leader Henry Clay himself. Seward anticipated victory until the final votes were tallied over a three-day period in November 1834.

Defeat shook the usually buoyant Seward to the core. He began to reevaluate his present life, his marriage, and his future. Obliged to return to Albany that December for the final session of the state senate, where he was a lame duck, he fell into an uncharacteristic state of melancholy. Unable to sleep, Seward feared that his consuming ambition, which had kept him away from his wife and children for months, had jeopardized his marriage.

"What a demon is this ambition," he lamented from Albany, baring his soul in a long, emotional letter to his wife. Ambition had led him to stray, he now realized, "in thought, purpose, communion and sympathy from the only being who purely loves me." He confessed that he had thought her love only "an incident" among his many passions, when, in truth, it was "the chief good" of his life. This realization, he feared, had come too late "to win back" her love: "I banished you from my heart. I made it so desolate, so destitute of sympathy for you, of everything which you ought to have found there, that you could no longer dwell in it, and when the wretched T. [Tracy] took advantage of my madness and offered sympathies, and feelings and love such as I [never did], and your expelled heart was half won by his falsehoods. . . . God be praised for the escape of both of us from that fearful peril. . . . Loved, injured and angel spirit, receive this homage of my first return to reason and truth—say to me that understanding my own feelings, yours are not crushed."

Failing to receive an immediate reply from Frances, Seward tossed in his bed. He felt cold, clammy, and feverish. For the first time, the possibility occurred to him that his wife might have fallen out of love, and he was horrified. "I am growing womanish in fears," he admitted in a second heartfelt letter. "Tell me in your own dear way that I am loved and cherished in your heart as I used to be when I better deserved so happy a lot."

Finally, Seward received the answer he longed to hear. "You reproach yourself dear Henry with too much severity," Frances wrote. "Never in those times when I have wept the most bitterly over the decay of my young dreams . . . have I thought you otherwise than good and kind. . . . When I realized most forcibly that 'love is the whole history of woman and but an episode in the life of man' . . . even then I imputed it not to you as a fault but reproached myself for wishing to exact a return for affections which I felt were too intense." She assured him that "the love of another" could never bring her "consolation"—God had kept her "in the right path."

By return mail Seward pledged that he desired nothing but to return home, to share the family duties and read by the fireside on the long winter nights, "to live for you and for our dear boys," to be "a partner in your thoughts and cares and feelings." With Frances to support him, Seward promised to renew his Episcopal faith and attempt to find his way to God. He was "count[ing] with eagerness," he concluded, "the hours which intervene between this period and the time when that life will commence."

As Seward took leave of the many friends he had made in his four years in Albany, he decided against confronting Tracy. The day before his scheduled departure, however, a curious letter from his old friend provoked an immediate response. The letter opened with halcyon recollections of the early days of their acquaintance, when Tracy still possessed "golden dreams, of a devoted, peculiar friendship. How much I suffered," he wrote, "when I was first awakened to the perception that these were only dreams. . . . For this you are no way responsible. You loved me as much as you could . . . but it was less far less than I hoped." He explained that "this pain, this disappointment is my excuse for the capriciousness, and too frequent unkindness which I have displayed towards you."

In an emotional reply, Seward explained that Tracy misunderstood completely the nature of the "alienation" that had befallen them. "Availing yourself of the relation existing between us," Seward charged, "you did with or without premeditated purpose what as a man of honor you ought not to have done—pursued a course of conduct which but for the virtue and firmness of the being dearest to me" would have destroyed his entire family. Seward related his initial reluctance to read the letters Frances had surrendered to him; and his conclusion, after reading them, that Tracy "had failed to do me the injury you recklessly contemplated.

"Thenceforth Tracy," he wrote, "you lost that magic influence you once possessed over me. . . . You still have my respect as a man of eminent talents and of much virtue but you can never again be the friend of my secret thoughts. I part without anger, but without affection." Even at this heavy moment, Seward remained the consummate politician, unwilling to burn his bridges completely.

If Seward believed the crisis with Frances had forever muted the voice of his public ambitions with a contented domesticity, he was mistaken. No sooner had he returned to Auburn than he admitted to a friend: "It is seldom that persons who enjoy intervals of public life are happy in their periods of seclusion." Within days, he was writing to Weed, pleading with his old friend and mentor to "keep me informed upon political matters, and take care that I do not so far get absorbed in professional occupation, that you will cease to care for me as a politician."

In the summer of 1835, seeking distraction from the tedium of his legal practice, the thirty-four-year-old Seward organized a family expedition to the South. He and Frances occupied the backseat of a horse-drawn carriage, while their five-year-old son, Fred, sat up front with the coachman, former slave William Johnson. Their elder son, Gus, remained at home with his grandfather. Seward, as always, was thrilled by the journey. "When I travel," he explained, "I banish care and thought and reflection." Over a three-month period, the little party traveled through Pennsylvania and Virginia, stopping at the nation's capital on their way back. While their letters home extolled the warmth and generous hospitality extended to them by Southerners all along their route, their firsthand encounter with the consequences of slavery profoundly affected their attitudes toward the South.

At the time of their journey, three decades of immigration, commercial enterprise, and industrial production had invigorated Northern society, creating thriving cities and towns. The historian Kenneth Stampp well describes how the North of this period "teemed with bustling, restless men and women who believed passionately in 'progress' and equated it with growth and change; the air was filled with the excitement of intellectual ferment and with the schemes of entrepreneurs; and the land was honeycombed with societies aiming at nothing less than the total reform of mankind."

Yet, crossing into Virginia, the Sewards entered a world virtually unchanged since 1800. "We no longer passed frequent farm-houses, taverns, and shops," Henry wrote as the family carriage wound its way through Virginia's Allegheny Mountains, "but our rough road conducted us . . . [past] low log-huts, the habitations of slaves." They rarely encountered other travelers, finding instead "a waste, broken tract of land, with here and there an old, decaying habitation." Seward lamented: "How deeply the curse of slavery is set upon this venerated and storied region of the old dominion. Of all the countries I have seen France only whose energies have for forty years been expended in war and whose population has been more decimated by the sword is as much decayed as Virginia."

The poverty, neglect, and stagnation Seward surveyed seemed to pervade both the landscape and its inhabitants. Slavery trapped a large portion of the Southern population, preventing upward mobility. Illiteracy rates were high, access to education difficult. While a small planter aristocracy grew rich from holdings in land and slaves, the static Southern economy did not support the creation of a sizable middle class.

While Seward focused on the economic and political depredations of slavery, Frances responded to the human plight of the enslaved men, women, and children she encountered along the journey. "We are told that we see slavery here in its mildest form," she wrote her sister. But "disguise thyself as thou wilt, still, slavery, thou art a bitter draught." She could not stop thinking of the "wrongs of this injured race."

One day Frances stopped the carriage to converse with an old blind slave woman, who was at work "turning the ponderous wheel of a machine" in a yard. The work was hard, but she had to do something, she explained, "and this is all I can do now, I am so old." When Frances asked about her family, she revealed that her husband and all her children had been sold long ago to different owners and she had never heard from any of them again. This sad encounter left a lasting impression on Frances. She recorded the interview in detail, and later read it out loud to family and friends in Auburn.

A few days afterward, the Sewards came across a group of slave children chained together on the road outside of Richmond. Henry described the sorrowful scene: "Ten naked little boys, between six and twelve years old, tied together, two and two, by their wrists, were all fastened to a long rope, and followed by a tall, gaunt white man, who, with his long lash, whipped up the sad and weary little procession, drove it to the horse-trough to drink, and thence to a shed, where they lay down on the ground and sobbed and moaned themselves to sleep." The children had been purchased from different plantations that day and were on their way to be auctioned off at Richmond.

Frances could not endure to continue the journey. "Sick of slavery and the South," she wrote in her diary; "the evil effects constantly coming before me and marring everything." She begged her husband to cancel the rest of their tour, and he complied. Instead of continuing south to Richmond, they "turned their horses' heads northward and homeward." For decades afterward, indelible images of Southern poverty and the misery of enslaved blacks would strengthen Seward's hostility to slavery and mold Frances's powerful social conscience.

• • •

WHEN SEWARD RETURNED to Auburn, a lucrative opportunity beckoned. The Holland Land Company, which held more than three hundred thousand acres of undeveloped land in western New York, was searching for a manager to parcel the land and negotiate contracts and deeds with prospective settlers. The company offered Seward a multiyear contract with an annual salary of $5,000 plus a share in the profits. Though accepting the position meant he would reside for months at a time in Chautauqua County, more than a hundred miles from his family and home in Auburn, Seward did not hesitate.

He took a leave from his law firm and rented a five-bedroom house in Westfield, "more beautiful than you can have an idea," hopeful that his wife and family would join him during the summer months. In the meantime, he invited Weed's seventeen-year-old daughter, Harriet, to keep Frances company in Auburn, and to help with the two boys and their new baby girl, Cornelia, born in August 1836.

Seward soon found the land-developing business more engaging than law. The six young clerks he hired quickly became a surrogate domestic circle, though he assured Frances in his nightly letters that he missed her and his children terribly. Once more he reiterated how he yearned for the day when they would read aloud to each other by the fire. He had just finished and enjoyed three of Scott's Waverley novels, but "there are a thousand things in them, as in Shakespeare, that one may enjoy more and much longer if one has somebody to converse with while dwelling upon them." His children pined for him and the vibrant life his presence brought to the household. More than a half century later, his son Fred "so vividly remembered" one particular evening when his father read aloud from the works of Scott and Burns that he realized "it must have been a rare event."

Life in Westfield, meanwhile, settled into a pleasant routine. So long as Seward kept intact the image of his happy home in Auburn, he could fully immerse himself in new adventure elsewhere. His serenity was shattered when his little girl contracted smallpox and died in January 1837. Returning home for three weeks, he begged Frances, who had plunged into depression, to come back with him to Westfield. She refused to leave her two boys and "did not think it would be quite right to take them both from their Grandpa."

Back in Westfield, Seward wrote anxiously to Frances that the "lightness that was in all my heart when I thought of you and your sanctuary, and those who surrounded you there, was the main constituent of my cheerfulness." But now "I imagine you sitting alone, drooping, desponding, and unhappy; and, when I think of you in this condition, I cannot resist the sorrow that swells within me. If I could be with you, to lure you away to more active pursuits, to varied study, or more cheerful thoughts, I might save you for yourself, for your children, for myself."

The following summer, Frances was finally persuaded to join him in Westfield. In an exultant letter to Weed, Seward expressed his contentment. "Well, I am here for once, enjoying the reality of dreams," he wrote. "I read much, I ride some, and stroll more along the lake-shore. My wife and children are enjoying a measure of health which enables them to participate in these pleasures." He lacked but one thing to complete his happiness: "If you were here," he told Weed, "we would enjoy pleasures that would have seduced Cicero and his philosophic friends from Tusculum."

While Frances enjoyed her summer, she was unable to share her husband's great contentment. Returning to Auburn in September, she told Harriet Weed she had "found Westfield a very pleasant little village . . . but it was not my *home* and you can very well understand that I am more happy to be here—There is a sort of satisfaction, melancholy it is, in being once more in the room where my darling babe lived and died—in looking over her little wardrobe—in talking with those who missed and loved her."

By the fall of 1837, an economic slump had spread westward to Chautauqua County. This "panic" of 1837 brought widespread misery in its wake—bankrupt businesses, high unemployment, a run on banks, plummeting real estate values, escalating poverty. "I am almost in despair," Seward wrote home. "I have to dismiss three clerks; they all seem near to me as children, and are almost as helpless."

Once again, fortune smiled upon Seward in uncanny fashion. Because Democrats were blamed for the depression, the shrinking economy enlarged his party's political prospects. In the elections that fall, the Whigs swept the state. "There is such a buzz of 'glorious Whig victories' ringing in my ears," Seward wrote Weed, "that I hardly have time to think." Replying from Albany, where he was back in control, Weed was jubilant. "I have been two days endeavoring to snatch a moment for communion with you, to whom my heart always turns in joy or grief. . . . It is a great triumph—an overwhelming revolution. May that Providence which has given us deliverance, give us also wisdom to turn our power into healthful channels."

In the months that followed, Seward and Weed worked together to broaden the Whig Party beyond its base of merchants, industrialists, and prosperous farmers. Hoping to appeal to the masses of workingmen, who had generally voted Democratic since Andrew Jackson's day, Weed raised money for a new partisan weekly. Horace Greeley was chosen editor for the fledgling journal. The slight, rumpled-looking, nearsighted young Greeley occupied a garret in New York where he had edited a small magazine called *The New Yorker.* The new partisan weekly became an instant success, eventually evolving into the powerful *New York Tribune.* For nearly a quarter of a century, Weed, Seward, and Greeley collaborated to build support first for the Whigs and, later on, for the Republicans. For much of that time, the three were like brothers. If they often quarreled among themselves, they presented a united front to the world.

In the summer of 1838, Weed believed the time was right for Seward's second bid to become governor. At the Whig convention that September, "the Dictator" was everywhere, persuading one delegate after another that Seward was the strongest possible choice to top the ticket. To bolster his case, he distributed statistics from the 1834 gubernatorial race showing that, despite the Whigs' loss, Seward had claimed more votes than all the other Whig candidates. Weed's magic worked: his protégé received the nomination on the fourth ballot. "Well, Seward, we are again embarked upon a 'sea of difficulties,' and must go earnestly to work." In fact, most of the work was left to Weed, since it was thought improper in those days for candidates to stump on their own. And Weed did his job well. When the votes were counted, the thirty-seven-year-old Seward was the overwhelming victor.

Seward was thrilled to be back in the thick of things. "God bless Thurlow Weed!" he exulted. "I owe this result to him." Within a week of the election, however, Seward's nerve began to fail. "It is a fearful post I have coveted," he confided to his mentor. "I shudder at my own temerity, and have lost confidence in my ability to manage my own private affairs." Frances, pregnant with their third son, Will, had suffered weeks of illness and was nervous about the move to Albany. Confessing that he did not "know how to keep a house alone," he wondered if he could instead take up rooms at the Eagle Tavern.

Weed arrived in Auburn and immediately took charge. He secured a mansion with a full-time staff for the governor to rent, and convinced Frances to join her husband. The yellow brick house, Seward's son Fred recalled, "was in all respects well adapted for an official residence." Set on four acres, it contained a suite of parlors, a ballroom, a spacious dining room, and a library in one wing, with a suite of family rooms in another. While Seward combed through books on history and philosophy, preparing what proved to be a brilliant inaugural message to the legislature, Weed stocked the residence with wine and food, chose Seward's inaugural outfit, and met with hundreds of office seekers, eventually selecting every member of the governor's cabinet. Seward believed "it was [his] duty to receive, not make a cabinet."

During the transition period, Seward's impulsive remarks often aggravated the ever-cautious Weed. "Your letter admonishes me to a habit of caution that I cannot conveniently adopt," Seward replied. "I love to write what I think and feel as it comes up." Nonetheless, Seward generally deferred to Weed, recognizing a superior strategic prudence and experience. "I had no idea that dictators were such amiable creatures," he told Weed, no doubt provoking the approval of his proud mentor. "There were never two men in politics who worked together or understood each other better," Weed wrote years later in his memoir. "Neither controlled the other. . . . One did not always lead, and the other follow. They were friends, in the best, the rarest, and highest sense."

In later years, Seward told the story of a carriage ride he took from Albany shortly after his election. He had struck up a lively conversation with the coachman, who eventually asked him who he was. When Seward replied that he was governor of New York, the coachman laughed in disbelief. Seward said they had only to consult the proprietor of the next tavern along the road to confirm the truth. When they reached the tavern, Seward went in and asked, "Am I the Governor of the State of New York or not?" The man did not hesitate. "No, certainly not!" "Who is, then?" queried Seward. "Why . . . Thurlow Weed!" the man replied.

The youthful governor's inaugural address on New Year's Day, 1839, laid out an ambitious agenda: a vast expansion of the public school system (including better schools for the black population), the promotion of canals and railways, the creation of a more humane system for the treatment of the insane, and the abolition of imprisonment for debt. His vision of an ever-expanding economy, built on free labor, widespread public education, and technological progress, offered a categorical rejection of the economic and cultural malaise he had witnessed on his Southern trip in 1835.

"Our race is ordained to reach, on this continent, a higher standard of social perfection than it has ever yet attained; and that hence will proceed the spirit which shall renovate the world," he proclaimed to the New York legislature in the year of his election. If the energy, ingenuity, and ambitions of Northern free labor were "sustained by a wise and magnanimous policy on our part," Seward promised, "our state, within twenty years, will have no desert places—her commercial ascendancy will fear no rivalry, and a hundred cities will enable her to renew the boast of ancient Crete."

Looking once more to broaden the appeal of the Whig Party, Seward advocated measures to attract the Irish and German Catholic immigrants who formed the backbone of the state Democratic Party. He called on his fellow Americans to welcome them with "all the sympathy which their misfortunes at home, their condition as strangers here, and their devotion to liberty, ought to excite." He argued that America owed all the benefits of citizenship to these new arrivals, who helped power the engine of

Northern expansion. In particular, he proposed to reform the school system, where the virulently anti-Catholic curriculum frightened immigrants away, dooming vast numbers to illiteracy, poverty, and vice. To get these children off the streets and provide them with opportunities to advance, Seward hoped to divert some part of the public school funds to support parochial schools where children could receive instruction from members of their own faith.

Seward's school proposal provoked a violent reaction among nativist Protestants. They accused him of plotting "to overthrow republican institutions" by undoing the separation of church and state. Handbills charged that Seward was "in league with the Pope" and schemed to throw Protestant children into the hands of priests. In the end, the legislature passed a compromise plan that simply expanded the public school system. But the nativists, whose strength would grow dramatically in the decades ahead, never forgave Seward. Indeed, their opposition would eventually prove a fatal stumbling block to Seward's hopes for the presidential nomination in 1860.

If Seward's progressive policies on education and immigration made him an influential and controversial figure in New York State, his defiant stand against slavery in the "Virginia Case" brought him into national prominence in the late 1830s and early 1840s. In September 1839, a vessel sailing from Norfolk, Virginia, to New York was found to have carried a fugitive slave. The slave was returned to his master in Virginia in compliance with Article IV, Section 2, of the U.S. Constitution that persons held to service or labor in one state escaping into another should be delivered up to the owner. When Virginia also demanded the arrest and surrender of three free black seamen who had allegedly conspired to hide the slave on the vessel, the New York governor refused.

In a statement that brought condemnation throughout the South, Seward argued that the seamen were charged with a crime that New York State did not recognize: people were not property, and therefore no crime had been committed. On the contrary, "the universal sentiment of civilized nations" considered helping a slave escape from bondage "not only innocent, but humane and praiseworthy."

As controversy over the fate of the three sailors was prolonged, the Commonwealth of Virginia enacted a series of retaliatory measures to damage the commerce of New York, calling upon other Southern states to pass resolutions denouncing Seward and the state of New York for "intermeddling" with their time-honored "domestic institutions." Democratic periodicals in the North warned that the governor's stance would compromise highly profitable New York trade connections with Virginia and other slave states. Seward was branded "a bigoted New England fanatic." This only emboldened Seward's resolve to press the issue. He spurred the Whig-dominated state legislature to pass a series of antislavery laws affirming the rights of black citizens against seizure by Southern agents, guaranteeing a trial by jury for any person so apprehended, and prohibiting New York police officers and jails from involvement in the apprehension of fugitive slaves.

Such divisive incidents—the "new irritation" foreseen by Jefferson in 1820—widened the schism between North and South. Though few slaves actually escaped to the North each year—an estimated one or two hundred out of the millions held in bondage—the issue exacerbated rancor on both sides. In the North, William Lloyd Garrison's newspaper, the *Liberator*, called for immediate emancipation and racial equality, denouncing slavery as sinful and inhumane, advocating "all actions, even in defiance of the Constitution," to bring an end to *"The Empire of Satan."* Such scathing criticisms moved Southern leaders to equally fierce defenses. They proclaimed slavery a "positive good" rather than a mere necessity, of immense benefit to whites and blacks alike. As discord between North and South escalated, many Northerners turned against the abolitionists. Fear that the movement would destroy the Union incited attacks on abolitionist printers in the North and West. Presses were burned, editors threatened with death should their campaign persist.

In 1840, Seward was reelected governor, but by a significantly smaller margin. His dwindling support was blamed on the parochial school controversy, the protracted fight with Virginia, and a waning enthusiasm for social reform. Horace Greeley editorialized that Seward would "henceforth be honored more for the three thousand votes he has lost, considering the causes, than for all he has received in his life." Nonetheless, Seward decided not to run a third time: "All that can now be worthy of my ambition," he explained to a friend, "is to leave the State better for my having been here, and to entitle myself to a favorable judgment in its history."

Throughout the dispute with the state of Virginia, and every other controversy that threatened Seward's highly successful tenure, Weed had proved a staunch ally and friend, answering critics in the legislature, publishing editorials in the *Albany Evening Journal*, ever sustaining Seward's spirits. "What am I to deserve such friendship and affection?" Seward asked him in 1842 as his second term drew to its close. "Without your aid how hopeless would have been my prospect of reaching the elevation from which I am descending. How could I have sustained myself there . . . how could I have secured the joyous reflections of this hour, what would have been my prospect of future life, but for the confidence I so undenyingly reposed on your affection?"

Returning to Auburn, Seward resumed his law practice, concentrating now on lucrative patent cases. He found that his fight with Virginia had endeared him to antislavery men throughout the North. Members of the new Liberty Party bandied about his name in their search for a presidential candidate in 1844. Organized in 1840, the Liberty Party was born of frustration with the failure of either major party to deal head-on with slavery. The abrogation of slavery was their primary goal. Though flattered by the attention, Seward could not yet conceive of leaving the Whig Party.

Meanwhile, he continued to speak out on behalf of black citizens. In March 1846, a terrifying massacre took place in Seward's hometown. A twenty-three-year-old black man named William Freeman, recently released from prison after serving five years for a crime it was later determined he did not commit, entered the home of John Van Nest, a wealthy farmer and friend of Seward's. Armed with two knives, he killed Van Nest, his pregnant wife, their small child, and Mrs. Van Nest's mother. When he was caught within hours, Freeman immediately confessed. He exhibited no remorse and laughed uncontrollably as he spoke. The sheriff hauled him away, barely reaching the jail ahead of an enraged mob intent upon lynching him. "I trust in the mercy of God that I shall never again be a witness to such an outburst of the spirit of vengeance as I saw while they were carrying the murderer past our door," Frances Seward told her husband, who was in Albany at the time. "Fortunately, the law triumphed."

Frances recognized at once an "incomprehensible" aspect to the entire affair, and she was correct. Investigation revealed a history of insanity in Freeman's family. Moreover, Freeman had suffered a series of floggings in jail that had left him deaf and deranged. When the trial opened, no lawyer was willing to take Freeman's case. The citizens of Auburn had threatened violence against any member of the bar who dared to defend the cold-blooded murderer. When the court asked, "Will anyone defend this man?" a "death-like stillness pervaded the crowded room," until Seward rose, his voice strong with emotion, and said, "May it please the court, *I shall remain counsel for the prisoner until his death*!"

Seward's friends and family, including Thurlow Weed and Judge Miller, roundly criticized Seward for his decision. Only Frances stood proudly by her husband during the outburst that followed, assuring her sister that "he will do what is right. He will not close his eyes and know that a great wrong is perpetrated." To her son Gus she noted that "there are few men in America who would have sacrificed so much for the cause of humanity—he has his reward in a quiet conscience and a peaceful mind." Though her house and children were her entire world, she never flinched when retaliation against Seward's decision threatened her family. She remained steadfast throughout. Then in her early forties, she was a handsome woman, despite the hard, drawn look imparted by ill health. Over the years she had grown intellectually with her husband, sharing his passion for reading, his reformer's spirit, and his deep hatred of slavery. Defying her father and her neighbors, she sat in the courtroom each day, her quiet bearing lending strength to her husband.

Seward spent weeks investigating the case, interviewing Freeman's family, and summoning five doctors who testified to the prisoner's extreme state of mental illness. In his summation, he pleaded with the jury not to be influenced by the color of the accused man's skin. "He is still your brother, and mine. . . . Hold him then to be a man." Seward continued, "I am not the prisoner's lawyer . . . I am the lawyer for society, for mankind, shocked beyond the power of expression, at the scene I have witnessed here of trying a maniac as a malefactor." He argued that Freeman's conduct was "unexplainable on any principle of *sanity*," and begged the jury not to seek the death sentence. Commit him to an asylum for the term of his natural life, Seward urged: "there is not a *white* man or *white* woman who would not have been dismissed long since from the perils of such a prosecution."

There was never any doubt that the local jury would return a guilty verdict. "In due time, gentlemen of the jury," Seward concluded, "when I shall have paid the debt of nature, my remains will rest here in your midst, with those of my kindred and neighbors. It is very possible they may be unhonored, neglected, spurned! But, perhaps years hence, when the passion and excitement which now agitate this community shall have passed away, some wandering stranger, some lone exile, some Indian, some negro, may erect over them a humble stone, and thereon this epitaph, 'He was Faithful!' " More than a century afterward, visitors to Seward's grave at the Fort Hill Cemetery in Auburn would find those very words engraved on his tombstone.

While Seward endured the hostility of his hometown, his defense of Freeman became famous throughout the country. His stirring summation was printed in dozens of newspapers and reprinted in pamphlet form for still wider distribution. Salmon Chase, himself a leading proponent of the black man's cause, conceded to his abolitionist friend Lewis Tappan that he esteemed Seward as "one of the very first public men of our country. Who but himself would have done what he did for that poor wretch Freeman?" His willingness to represent Freeman, Chase continued, "considering his own personal position & the circumstances, was magnanimous in the highest degree."

So in the mid-1840s, as Seward settled back into private life in Auburn, his optimism about the future remained intact. He had established a national reputation based upon principle and a vision of national progress. He trusted that when his progressive principles once more gained favor with the masses, he would return to public life.

• • •

ABRAHAM LINCOLN, like Seward and Bates, was drawn to politics in his early years. At the age of twenty-three, after only six months in New Salem, Illinois, he decided to run for the state legislature from Sangamon County. While it must have seemed next to impossible that a new settler who had just arrived in town with no family connections and little formal education could compete for office, his belief in himself and awareness of his superior intellectual abilities proved to be powerful motivators. Both his ambition and his uncertainty are manifest in the March 1832 statement formally announcing his candidacy on an essentially Whig platform that called for internal improvements, public education, and laws against usury: "Every man is said to have his peculiar ambition," he wrote. "I have no other so great as that of being truly esteemed of my fellow men, by rendering myself worthy of their esteem. How far I shall succeed in gratifying this ambition, is yet to be developed."

Lincoln already possessed the lifelong dream he would restate many times in the years that followed—the desire to prove himself worthy, to be held in great regard, to win the veneration and respect of his fellow citizens. "I am young and unknown to many of you," he continued. "I was born and have ever remained in the most humble walks of life. I have no wealthy or popular relations to recommend me. My case is thrown exclusively upon the independent voters of this county, and if elected they will have conferred a favor upon me, for which I shall be unremitting in my labors to compensate. But if the good people in their wisdom shall see fit to keep me in the background, I have been too familiar with disappointments to be very much chagrined." At the same time he made it clear that this try would not be his last, telling voters that only after being defeated "some 5 or 6 times" would he feel disgraced and "never to try it again."

His campaign was interrupted when he joined the militia to fight against the Sac and Fox Indians in what became known as the Black Hawk War. Mustered out after three months, he returned home shortly before the election. Not surprisingly, when the votes were tallied, the little-known Lincoln had lost the election. Despite his defeat, he took pride that in his own small town of New Salem, where he "made friends everywhere he went," he had received 277 of the 300 votes cast. This astonishing level of support was attributed to his good nature and the remarkable gift for telling stories that had made him a favorite of the men who gathered each night in the general store to share opinions and gossip. "This was the only time," Lincoln later asserted, that he "was ever beaten on a direct vote of the people." Two years later, he ran for the seat a second time. By then he had widened his set of acquaintances beyond New Salem and won easily, capturing the first of four successive terms in the state legislature. Until he joined the new Republican Party, Lincoln would remain a steadfast Whig—as were Seward, Bates, and, for a brief moment, Chase.

Lincoln's four successful campaigns for the legislature were conducted across a sparsely populated frontier county the size of Rhode Island. Young Lincoln was "always the centre of the circle where ever he was," wrote Robert Wilson, a political colleague. "His Stories . . . were fresh and Sparkling. never tinctured with malevolence." Though his face, in repose, revealed nothing "marked or Striking," when animated by a story, "Several wrinkles would diverge from the inner corners of his eyes, and extend down and diagonally across his nose, his eyes would Sparkle, all terminating in an unrestrained Laugh in which every one present willing or unwilling were compelled to take part." This rapid illumination of Lincoln's features in conversation would be observed by countless others throughout his entire life, drawing many into his orbit.

During the campaigns, candidates journeyed on horseback across "entirely unoccupied" prairies, speaking at country stores and small villages. "The Speaking would begin in the forenoon," Wilson recalled, "the candidates Speaking alternately until all who could Speak had his turn, generally consuming the whole afternoon." Nor were the contests limited to speeches on public issues. At Mr. Kyle's store, west of Springfield, a group of Democrats made a wager. " 'See here Lincoln, if you can throw this Cannon ball further than we Can, We'll vote for you.' Lincoln picked up the large Cannon ball—felt it—swung it around—and around and said, 'Well, boys if thats all I have to do I'll get your votes.' " He then proceeded to swing the cannonball "four or Six feet further than any one Could throw it."

When he moved to Springfield in 1837, Lincoln began to attract the circle of friends and admirers who would play a decisive role in his political ascent. While he worked during the day to build his law practice, evenings would find him in the center of Springfield's young men, gathered around a fire in Speed's store to read newspapers, gossip, and engage in philosophical debates. "They came there," Speed recalled, "because they were sure to find Lincoln," who never failed to entertain with his remarkable stories.

"It was a sort of social club," Speed observed. Whigs and Democrats alike gathered to discuss the events of the day. Among the members of this "club" were three future U.S. senators: Stephen Douglas, who would become Lincoln's principal rival; Edward Baker, who would introduce him at his first inaugural and become one of the first casualties of the Civil War; and Orville Browning, who would assist his fight for the presidential nomination.

Throughout his eight years in the state legislature, Lincoln proved an extraordinarily shrewd grassroots politician, working to enlist voter support in the precincts for his party's candidates. While Seward could concentrate on giving voice to the party platform, relying on Weed to build poll lists and carry voters to the polls, Lincoln engaged in every aspect of the political process, from the most visionary to the most mundane. His experience taught him what every party boss has understood through the ages: the practical machinery of the party organization—the distribution of ballots, the checklists, the rounding up of voters—was as crucial as the broad ideology laid out in the platform. The same intimate involvement in campaign organization that he displayed in these early years would characterize all of Lincoln's future campaigns.

His 1840 campaign plan divided the party organization into three levels of command. The county captain was "to procure from the poll-books a separate list for each Precinct" of everyone who had previously voted the Whig slate. The list would then be divided by each precinct captain "into Sections of ten who reside most convenient to each other." The captain of each section would then be responsible to "see each man of his Section face to face, and procure his pledge . . . [to] vote as early on the day as possible."

That same year, Lincoln and four Whig colleagues, including Joshua Speed, published a circular directed at the presidential campaign of William Henry Harrison. "Our intention is to organize the whole State, so that every Whig can be brought to the polls." To this end, the publication outlined a plan whereby each county would be divided into small districts, each responsible for making "a perfect list" of all their voters, designating which names were likely from past behavior to vote with the Whigs and which were doubtful. Committees in each district would then "keep a *constant watch* on the *doubtful voters*, and from time to time have them *talked to* by those *in whom they have the most confidence*." These committees were to submit monthly progress reports to the central state committee, ensuring an accurate survey of voters in each county before election day. Party workers could then be dispatched to round up the right voters and get them to the polls to support the Whig Party. In setting forth his campaign plan, as meticulously structured as any modern effort to "get out the vote," Lincoln did not neglect the necessity of fund-raising, asking each county to send *"fifty or one hundred dollars"* to subscribe to a newspaper "devoted exclusively to the *great cause* in which we are engaged."

• • •

LINCOLN LIKENED his politics to an "old womans dance"—"Short & Sweet." He stood for three simple ideas: a national bank, a protective tariff, and a system for internal improvements. A state legislator could do little to promote a national bank or raise tariffs, but internal improvements, which then usually meant the improvement of roads, rivers, harbors, and railways, were largely a local matter. Many Whigs, Seward and Bates among them, spoke of improving waterways, but Lincoln had actually worked on a flatboat to bring meat and grain down the Mississippi to New Orleans; he had a flatboatman's knowledge of the hazards posed by debris and logs while navigating the Sangamon River. Nor would he ever forget the thrill of receiving his first dollar for transporting two gentlemen on his flatboat from the riverbank to their steamer, which was anchored "in the middle of the river." The experience of earning two half dollars in a single day made the world seem "wider and fairer," giving him confidence in the future.

Lincoln knew firsthand the deprivations, the marginal livelihood of the subsistence farmer unable to bring produce to market without dependable roads. He had been paid the meager wages of the hired hand. Primitive roads, clogged waterways, lack of rail connections, inadequate schools—such were not merely issues to Lincoln, but hurdles he had worked all his life to overcome in order to earn an ampler share of freedom. These "improvements" to the infrastructure would enable thousands of farming families to emerge from the kind of poverty in which the Lincoln family had been trapped, and would permit new cities and towns to flourish.

Lincoln's dedication to internal improvements and economic development was given strength, nourishment, and power, so the historian Gabor Boritt persuasively argues, by his passionate commitment "to the ideal that all men should receive a full, good, and ever increasing reward for their labors so they might have the opportunity to rise in life." Economic development provided the basis, Lincoln said much later, that would allow every American "an unfettered start, and a fair chance, in the race of life." To Lincoln's mind, the fundamental test of a democracy was its capacity to "elevate the condition of men, to lift artificial weights from all shoulders, to clear the paths of laudable pursuit for all." A real democracy would be a meritocracy where those born in the lower ranks could rise as far as their natural talents and discipline might take them.

Young Lincoln's great ambition in the 1830s, he told Joshua Speed, was to be the "DeWitt Clinton of Illinois." The pioneering New York governor had opened opportunities for all New Yorkers and left a permanent imprint on his state when he persuaded the legislature to support the Erie Canal project. In the Illinois legislature, Lincoln hoped to leave a similar imprint by way of an ambitious program of internal improvements.

During these same years, the young state legislator made his first public statement on slavery. The rise of abolitionism in the North and the actions of governors, such as Seward, who refused to fully respect fugitive slave provisions in the Constitution, led legislatures in both South and North to pass resolutions that censured abolitionism and confirmed the constitutional right to slavery. In conservative Illinois, populated by many citizens of Southern birth, the general assembly fell in line. By the lopsided vote of 77–6, the assembly resolved that "we highly disapprove of the formation of abolition societies," hold "sacred" the "right of property in slaves," and believe that "the General Government cannot abolish slavery in the District of Columbia, against the consent of the citizens."

Lincoln was among the six dissenting voices. With one other colleague who had also voted against the resolution, he issued a formal protest. This protest did not endorse abolitionism, for Lincoln believed then, as later, that the Constitution did not give Congress the power to interfere with slavery in the states where it was already established. Instead, resisting the tide of public opinion in Illinois, Lincoln proclaimed that "the institution of slavery is founded on both injustice and bad policy," and affirmed the constitutional power of Congress to abolish slavery in areas under federal control, such as the District of Columbia, though he recommended "that that power ought not to be exercised unless at the request of the people of said District."

Lincoln always believed, he later said, that "if slavery is not wrong, nothing is wrong," and he could not remember when he did not "so think, and feel." Though he was born in the slave state of Kentucky, his parents had been antislavery. Their opposition had led them to change religious congregations, and eventually, they had moved to the free state of Indiana "partly on account of slavery." Decades later, in his short autobiography written for the 1860 presidential campaign, Lincoln would describe his protest in the Illinois legislature as one that "briefly defined his position on the slavery question; and so far as it goes, it was then the same that it is now."

In these early years, however, Lincoln paid the slavery issue less attention than Seward or Chase, believing that so long as slavery could be restricted to places where it already existed, it would gradually become extinct. He did not share Chase's professional and personal aversion to slaveowners and did not hesitate to take whatever clients came his way. In the course of his practice, Lincoln defended both slaveowners and fugitive slaves. While he hated to see fugitive slaves hunted down, he publicly criticized the governor of Maine when he, like Seward, refused to give up two men who had aided a fugitive slave from Georgia. For Lincoln, the constitutional requirements for the return of fugitive slaves could not be evaded.

Lincoln's dreams of becoming the DeWitt Clinton of Illinois collapsed when a sustained recession hit the state in 1837. Public sentiment turned against the costly and still-unfinished internal improvements system. For months, Lincoln fervently defended the system against the rising tide of criticism, likening the abandonment of the canal to "stopping a skift in the middle of a river—if it was not going up, it *would* go down." Although his arguments fell on deaf ears, he refused to give ground, abiding by his father's old maxim: "If you make a bad bargain, *hug* it the tighter." His unwillingness to abandon the policies he had championed became self-destructive stubbornness. By 1840, the fourth year of recession, the mood in the legislature was set against continuing these projects. With funds no longer forthcoming, the improvements system collapsed. The state bank was forced to liquidate. Land values fell precipitously, and new pioneers were deterred from emigrating to Illinois.

As a vocal proponent of the system that had aggravated the state's fiscal catastrophe, Lincoln received a significant share of the blame. Though he managed to win a fourth term in 1840, he polled the least number of votes among the victorious candidates, his poorest showing since his first election. Belief in himself and his progressive agenda shaken, he resolved to retire from the legislature after his term was completed.

• • •

THIS FAILURE of Lincoln's political ambition coincided with a series of crises in his personal life. Despite his humor, intellectual passion, and oratorical eloquence, he had always been awkward and self-conscious in the presence of women. "He was not very fond of girls," his stepmother remembered. His gangly appearance and uncouth behavior did little to recommend him to the ladies. "He would burst into a ball," recalled a friend, "with his big heavy Conestoga boots on, and exclaim aloud—'Oh—boys, how clean those girls look.' " This was undoubtedly not the compliment the girls were looking for. Lincoln's friend Henry Whitney provides a comic recollection of leaving Lincoln alone with some women at a social gathering and returning to discover him "as demoralized and ill at ease as a bashful country boy. He would put his arms behind him, and bring them to the front again, as if trying to hide them, and he tried apparently but in vain to get his long legs out of sight." His female friendships were confined mostly to older, safely married women.

Never at ease talking with women, Lincoln found writing to them equally awkward, "a business which I do not understand." In Stephen Vincent Benét's epic poem *John Brown's Body*, Lincoln expresses his difficulties with the fairer sex.

. . . when the genius of the water moves,
And that's the woman's genius, I'm at sea
In every sense and meaning of the word,
With nothing but old patience for my chart,
And patience doesn't always please a woman.

His awkwardness did not imply a lack of sexual desire. "Lincoln had terribly strong passions for women—could scarcely keep his hands off them," said his law partner, William Herndon, who added that his "honor and a strong will . . . enabled him to put out the fires of his terrible passion." Judge David Davis, Lincoln's companion on the circuit, agreed with this assessment, noting that "his Conscience Kept him from seduction—this saved many—many a woman." Before his marriage Lincoln enjoyed close relations with young women and almost certainly found outlets for his sexual urges among the prostitutes who were readily available on the frontier.

A year after Ann Rutledge's death, Lincoln courted Mary Owens, the sister of his friend Mrs. Elizabeth Abell. Mary Owens was said to be "handsome," with dark blue eyes and "much vivacity." Well educated, she hailed from a comfortably affluent family in Kentucky and was noted as "a good conversationalist and a splendid reader."

Lincoln had met Miss Owens several years earlier when she visited her sister for a month in New Salem. In the aftermath of Ann Rutledge's death, Elizabeth Abell told Lincoln she thought the young pair would make a good match and proposed going to Kentucky to bring her sister back. Lincoln was "confoundedly well pleased" with the idea. He remembered that she was likable, smart, and a good companion, although somewhat "oversize."

When the twenty-eight-year-old Mary Owens returned to Illinois, however, a disturbing transformation had taken place. "She now appeared," he later wrote, with perhaps some exaggeration, "a fair match for Falstaff," with a "want of teeth, weather-beaten appearance," and a size unattainable in "less than thirtyfive or forty years." He tried in vain to persuade himself "that the mind was much more to be valued than the person." He attempted "to imagine she was handsome, which, but for her unfortunate corpulency, was actually true." He conjured up ways he "might procrastinate the evil day" when he had to make good on his promise of marriage, but finally felt honor-bound to keep his word.

His proposal, written on May 7, 1837, may well be one of the most curiously unappealing ever penned. "This thing of living in Springfield is rather a dull business after all," he observed of the dismal life she might share. "I am afraid you would not be satisfied. There is a great deal of flourishing about in carriages here, which it would be your doom to see without shareing in it. You would have to be poor without the means of hiding your poverty. Do you believe you could bear that patiently? . . . What I have said I will most positively abide by, provided you wish it. My opinion is that you had better not do it. You have not been accustomed to hardship, and it may be more severe than you now immagine. Yours, &c.—Lincoln."

Not surprisingly, Mary Owens turned him down. Her rejection prompted Lincoln to write a humorous, self-deprecating letter to his friend Eliza Browning, Orville Browning's wife. He acknowledged that he was "mortified almost beyond endurance" to think that "she whom I had taught myself to believe no body else would have, had actually rejected me with all my fancied greatness; and to cap the whole, I then, for the first time, began to suspect that I was really a little in love with her." He resolved "never again to think of marrying; and for this reason; I can never be satisfied with any one who would be block-head enough to have me."

Despite his disclaimer, eighteen months later, the thirty-one-year-old Lincoln became engaged to the lively and intelligent Mary Todd. The Edwards mansion on the hill, where Mary had come to stay with her sister, Elizabeth, was the center of Springfield society. Lincoln was among the many young men who gathered in the Edwards parlor, where the girls, dressed in the latest fashion, shared food, drink, and merry conversation.

To their friends and relatives, Mary and Abe seemed "the exact reverse" of each other—"physically, temperamentally, emotionally." She was short and voluptuous, her ample bosom accentuated by stays; he was uncommonly tall and cadaverous. While Mary possessed an open, passionate, and impulsive nature, "her face an index to every passing emotion," he was, even Mary admitted, a self-controlled man. What "he felt most deeply," Mary observed, "he expressed, the least." She was in her element at social gatherings, "the very creature of excitement." Vivacious and talkative, she was capable of making "a Bishop forget his prayers." While Lincoln's good nature made him "a welcome guest everywhere," one Springfield woman recalled, "he rarely danced," much preferring a position amid the men he could entertain effortlessly with his amusing stories.

For all their differences, the couple had much in common. Lincoln had always been attracted to intelligent women, and Mary was a woman of intellectual gifts who had earned "the highest marks" in school and taken home "the biggest prizes." Endowed with an excellent memory, a quick wit, and a voracious appetite for learning, she shared Lincoln's love for discussing books and poetry. Like Lincoln, she could recite substantial passages of poetry from memory, and they shared a love of Robert Burns. Indeed, four years after Lincoln's death, Mary journeyed to the poet's birthplace in Scotland, where, recalling one of her favorite poems about a lost love, she "sighed over poor 'Highland Mary's' grave."

Also, like Lincoln, she was fascinated by politics, having grown up in a political household. Among her happiest childhood memories were the sparkling dinner parties at her elegant brick house in Lexington, hosted by her father, Robert Todd, a Whig loyalist who had served in both the Kentucky House and Senate. At these sumptuous feasts, Lincoln's idol Henry Clay was a frequent guest, along with members of Congress, cabinet members, governors, and foreign ministers. Mesmerized by their discussions, Mary became, her sisters recalled, "a violent little Whig," convinced that she was "destined to be the wife of some future President."

Undoubtedly, Mary told Lincoln of her many personal contacts with Clay, including how she once proudly rode her new pony to the statesman's house. And she shared with him a vital interest in the political struggles of the day. "I suppose like the rest of us *Whigs*," she wrote a close friend in 1840, "you have been rejoicing in the recent election of Gen [William Henry] Harrison, a cause that has excited such deep interest in the nation and one of such vital importance to our prosperity—This fall I became quite a *politician*, rather an unladylike profession, yet at such a *crisis*, whose heart could remain untouched while the energies of all were called in question?" Lincoln was deeply engaged at the same time in "the *great cause*" of electing the "Old hero."

Beyond their love of poetry and politics, Mary and Abraham had both lost their mothers at an early age. Mary was only six when her thirty-one-year-old mother, Eliza Parker Todd, died giving birth to her seventh child. Eliza's death, unlike the death of Nancy Hanks, did not disrupt the physical stability of the household. The Todd slaves continued to cook the meals, care for the children, fetch the wood, bank the fires, and drive the carriages as they had always done. If Lincoln was fortunate in his father's choice of a second wife, however, Mary's loss was aggravated by her father's remarriage. Elizabeth Humphreys, a severe stepmother with cold blue eyes, gave birth to nine additional children, openly preferring her brood of Todds to the original clan. From the moment her stepmother moved in, Mary later recalled, her childhood turned "desolate." Henceforth, she lamented, her only real home was the boarding school to which she was exiled at the age of fourteen.

This estrangement, combined with a family history of mental instability and a tendency toward severe migraines, produced in Mary what one friend described as "an emotional temperament much like an April day, sunning all over with laughter one moment, the next crying as though her heart would break." She could be affectionate, generous, and optimistic one day; vengeful, depressed, and irritable the next. In the colloquial language of her friends, she was "either in the garret or cellar." In either mood, she needed attention, something the self-contained Lincoln was not always able to provide.

As their courtship proceeded, the very qualities that had first attracted the couple to each other may have become sources of conflict. Initially drawn to Mary by her ability to command any gathering with her intense energy, Lincoln may well have determined that this reflected a tiresome and compulsive need. Mary may have come to define Lincoln's patience and objectivity as aloofness and inconsiderateness. We know only that at some point in the winter of 1840–41, as they approached marriage, a break occurred in their relationship.

While the inner lives of men and women living long ago are never easy to recover, the difficulty is compounded here by the absence of intimate letters between Mary and Abraham. Seward, Chase, and Bates disclosed their deepest feelings in their diaries and letters, but not a single letter survives from the days of the Lincolns' courtship, and only a precious few remain from the years of their marriage. While the emotional lives of Lincoln's rivals still seem alive to us more than a century and a half after their deaths, the truth about Lincoln's courtship is harder to recapture. Inevitably, in the vacuum created by the absence of documents, gossip and speculation flourish.

Mary may have precipitated the break, influenced by the objections of her sister, Elizabeth, and her brother-in-law, Ninian Edwards, who believed she was marrying beneath her. Elizabeth warned Mary that she did not think that "Mr. L. & [she] were Suitable to Each other." The couple considered that Mary and Abraham's "natures, mind—Education—raising

&c were So different they Could not live happy as husband & wife." Mary had other suitors, including Edwin Webb, a well-to-do widower; Stephen Douglas, the up-and-coming Democratic politician; and, as Mary wrote her friend, Mercy Ann Levering, "an agreeable lawyer & grandson of *Patrick Henry—what an honor!*" Still, she insisted, "I love him not, & my hand will never be given, where my heart is not." With several good men to choose from, Mary may have decided she needed time to think through her family's pointed reservations about Lincoln.

Far more likely, Lincoln's own misgivings prompted a retreat from this second engagement. Though physically attracted to Mary, he seemed to question the strength of his love for her as he approached a final commitment. Joshua Speed recalled that "in the winter of 40 & 41," Lincoln "was very unhappy about his engagement to [Mary]—Not being entirely satisfied that his *heart* was going with his hand." Speed's choice of the same phrase that Mary used suggests that it must have been a common expression to indicate an embrace of marriage without the proper romantic feelings. "How much [Lincoln] suffered," Speed recalled, "none Know so well as myself—He disclosed his whole heart to me."

Recent scholarship has suggested that Lincoln's change of heart was influenced by his affection for Ninian Edwards's cousin Matilda Edwards, who had come to spend the winter in Springfield. "A lovelier girl I never saw," Mary herself conceded upon first meeting Matilda. Orville Browning traced Lincoln's "aberration of mind" to the predicament in which he found himself: "engaged to Miss Todd, and in love with Miss Edwards, and his conscience troubled him dreadfully for the supposed injustice he had done, and the supposed violation of his word." While there is no evidence that Lincoln ever made his feelings known to Matilda, Browning's observation is supported by an acquaintance's letter describing the complicated situation. Though Lincoln was committed to Mary, Springfield resident Jane Bell observed, he could "never bear to leave Miss Edward's side in company." He thought her so perfect that if "he had it in his power he would not have one feature in her face altered." His indiscreet behavior drew criticism from his friends, Bell claimed, who "thought he was acting very wrong and very imprudently and told him so and he went crazy on the strength of it."

Possibly, Lincoln's infatuation with Matilda was merely a distraction from the anxiety surrounding his impending marriage to Mary. According to Elizabeth Edwards, Lincoln was apprehensive about "his ability and Capacity to please and support a wife," and doubtful about the institution of marriage itself. He likely feared that a wife and family would undermine his concentration and purpose. He would be responsible for the life and happiness of a woman accustomed to wealth and luxury; he would be unable to read late into the nights, pursuing new knowledge and the mastery of law and politics.

His fear that marriage might hinder his career was a common one. The uncertainties of establishing a legal practice in the new-market economy of the mid-nineteenth century caused many young lawyers to delay wedlock, driving up the marriage age. The Harvard law professor Joseph Story is famously quoted as saying that the law "is a jealous mistress, and requires a long and constant courtship." What applied to the law applied still more to politics. For Lincoln, struggling to establish himself in both, marriage must have presented pitfalls for his enormous ambitions.

Lincoln drafted a letter to Mary ending the engagement. He asked Speed to deliver it, but Speed refused, warning that he should talk to her instead, for "once put your words in writing and they Stand as a living & eternal Monument against you." Lincoln did go to see Mary and, according to Speed, told her that he did not love her. As soon as she began to weep, he lost his nerve. "To tell you the truth Speed, it was too much for me. I found the tears trickling down my own cheeks. I caught her in my arms and kissed her." The engagement was temporarily renewed, and Lincoln was forced into another meeting to sever the engagement. This second confrontation left him devastated—both because he had hurt Mary and because he had long held his "ability to keep [his] resolves when they are made . . . as the only, or at least the chief, gem of [his] character."

• • •

DURING THIS GRIM WINTER, sorrows came to Lincoln "not single spies/But in battalions." Joshua Speed announced his intention to return in a few months' time to his family's plantation in Louisville, Kentucky. Speed's father had died, and he felt responsible for his grieving mother. On January 1, 1841, he sold his interest in the general store where he had lived and worked for seven years. Speed's departure would bring an end to the pleasant evenings around the fireplace, where the young men of Springfield had gathered to discuss politics. More discouraging for Lincoln, Speed's departure meant the loss of the one friend to whom he had opened his heart in free and easy communion. "I shall be verry lonesome without you," Lincoln told Speed. "How miserably things seem to be arranged in this world. If we have no friends, we have no pleasure; and if we have them, we are sure to lose them, and be doubly pained by the loss."

The awkward dissolution of his engagement to Mary and the anticipated loss of his best friend combined with the collapse of the internal improvement projects and the consequent damage to his reputation to induce a state of mourning that deepened for weeks. He stopped attending the legislature and withdrew from the lively social life he had enjoyed. His friends worried that he was suicidal. According to Speed, "Lincoln went Crazy—had to remove razors from his room—take away all Knives and other such dangerous things—&c—it was terrible." He was "delirious to the extent of not knowing what he was doing," Orville Browning recalled, and for a period of time was incapable of talking coherently. "Poor L!" James Conkling wrote to his future wife, Mercy Ann Levering; "he is reduced and emaciated in appearance and seems scarcely to possess strength enough to speak above a whisper. His case at present is truly deplorable."

In Lincoln's time, this combination of symptoms—feelings of hopelessness and listlessness, thoughts of death and suicide—was called hypochondriasis ("the hypo") or "the vapours." Its source was thought to be in the hypochondria, that portion of the abdomen which was then considered the seat of emotions, containing the liver, gallbladder, and spleen. Treatment for the liver and digestive system was recommended.

"I have, within the last few days, been making a most discreditable exhibition of myself in the way of hypochondriaism," Lincoln confessed to his law partner and friend John Stuart on January 20, 1841. Desperately, he sought a post office job for Dr. Anson Henry, who would leave Springfield if the job did not materialize. His presence, Lincoln told Stuart, was "necessary to my existence."

Three days later, Lincoln wrote Stuart again. "I am now the most miserable man living. If what I feel were equally distributed to the whole human family, there would not be one cheerful face on the earth. Whether I shall ever be better I can not tell; I awfully forebode I shall not. To remain as I am is impossible; I must die or be better, it appears to me."

Hoping medical treatment might assuage his sorrow, Lincoln consulted not only Dr. Henry but Dr. Daniel Drake at the medical college in Cincinnati; Drake was perhaps the most eminent medical scientist in the West. Lincoln described his condition at length in a letter and asked for counsel. The doctor wisely replied that he could not offer a diagnosis for Lincoln "without a personal interview."

Throughout the nadir of Lincoln's depression, Speed stayed at his friend's side. In a conversation both men would remember as long as they lived, Speed warned Lincoln that if he did not rally, he would most certainly die. Lincoln replied that he was more than willing to die, but that he had "done nothing to make any human being remember that he had lived, and that to connect his name with the events transpiring in his day and generation and so impress himself upon them as to link his name with something that would redound to the interest of his fellow man was what he desired to live for."

Even in this moment of despair, the strength of Lincoln's desire to engrave his name in history carried him forward. Like the ancient Greeks, Lincoln seemed to believe that "ideas of a person's worth are tied to the way others, both contemporaries and future generations, perceive him." Unable to find comfort in the idea of a literal afterlife in heaven, he found consolation in the conviction that in the memories of others, some part of us remains alive. "To see memory as the essence of life came naturally to Lincoln," Robert Bruce observes, for he was a man who "seemed to live most intensely through the process of thought, the expression of thought, and the exchange of thought with others." Indeed, in a poem inspired by a visit to his childhood home, Lincoln emphasized the centrality of memory, which he described as "thou midway world/'Twixt Earth and paradise."

Fueled by his resilience, conviction, and strength of will, Lincoln gradually recovered from his depression. He understood, he told Speed later, that in times of anxiety it is critical to "avoid being *idle,*" that *"business and conversation of friends"* were necessary to give the mind "rest from that *intensity* of thought, which will some times wear the sweetest idea threadbare and turn it to the bitterness of death." He returned to his law practice and his duties in the legislature, resuming his work on behalf of the Whig Party. That summer of 1841, he remedied the absence of good conversation and intimate friendship with a monthlong visit to Speed in Kentucky. The following February, he delivered an eloquent address to a temperance society in Springfield. This speech not only revealed a man in full command of his powers; it illustrated Lincoln's masterful approach to leadership: he counseled temperance advocates that if they continued to denounce the dram seller and the drinker in "thundering tones of anathema and denunciation," nothing would be accomplished. Far better to employ the approach of "erring man to an erring brother," guided by the old adage that a "drop of honey catches more flies than a gallon of gall."

Mental health, contemporary psychiatrists tell us, consists of the ability to adapt to the inevitable stresses and misfortunes of life. It does not mean freedom from anxiety and depression, but only the ability to cope with these afflictions in a healthy way. "An outstanding feature of successful adaptation," writes George Vaillant, "is that it leaves the way open for future growth." Of course, Abraham Lincoln's capacity for growth would prove enormous.

In the same month that he delivered his temperance address, Lincoln reported to Speed that he was "quite clear of the hypo" and "even better than I was along in the fall." So long as he remained unsure of his feelings, however, he kept himself apart from Mary. During the long months of their separation, Mary missed him tremendously. In a letter to a friend she lamented that she had been "much alone of late," having not seen Lincoln "in the gay world for months."

She whimsically considered taking up Lyman Trumbull—a former beau of her friend Mercy Ann—a Democrat who was then serving as secretary of state for Illinois. "I feel much disposed in your absence, to lay in my *claims*, as he is talented & agreeable & sometimes *countenances* me," she told Mercy Ann. But in fact, she had no serious desire to take up with someone else, so long as Lincoln remained a possibility. Her patience paid off. During the summer of 1842, after the couple had gone nearly eighteen months without personal contact, mutual friends conspired to bring Mary and Abraham back together.

This time around, thanks in part to the wise counsel Lincoln had provided Speed regarding his friend's tortured love affair with a young woman he had met in Kentucky, Lincoln recognized in his own forebodings "the worst sort of nonsense." Learning that Speed was plagued with doubts following his betrothal to Fanny Henning, Lincoln labored to convince him that he truly loved the young woman. The problem, he told Speed, was simply an unrealistic expectation of what love was supposed to be like. Speaking of himself as well, Lincoln rhapsodized: "It is the peculiar misfortune of both you and me, to dream dreams of Elysium far exceeding all that any thing earthly can realize." Indeed, Lincoln mused, had he understood his own muddled courtship as well as he understood Speed's, he might have "sailed through clear."

His doubts about marriage beginning to fade, he searched for final reassurance from his newly married friend. " 'Are you now, in *feeling* as well as in *judgement*, glad you are married as you are?' From any body but me, this would be an impudent question not to be tolerated; but I know you will pardon it in me. Please answer it quickly as I feel impatient to know." Assured that his closest friend had survived the ordeal of marriage and was, in fact, very happy, Lincoln summoned the courage to renew his commitment to Mary.

On the evening of November 4, 1842, before a small group of friends and relatives in the parlor of the Edwards mansion, Abraham Lincoln and Mary Todd were married. "Nothing new here," Lincoln wrote a friend a week later, "except my marrying, which to me, is a matter of profound wonder." Three days short of nine months after the marriage, a son,

Robert Todd, was born to the Lincolns, to be followed three years later by a second son, Edward.

• • •

LOOKING BACK to the winter of Lincoln's discontent, there is little doubt that he suffered what would later be called an incapacitating depression. While biographers have rightly looked to the twin losses of Mary Todd and Joshua Speed to explain Lincoln's descent into depression, less attention has been paid to the blow he must have suffered with the seeming disintegration of the political dreams that had sustained him for so many years. Manifestations of despair after Ann Rutledge's death had been awful to endure, but this episode was compounded by the shadow of a damaged reputation and diminished hope for the future.

Conscious of his superior powers and the extraordinary reach of his mind and sensibilities, Lincoln had feared from his earliest days that these qualities would never find fulfillment or bring him recognition among his fellows. Periodically, when the distance between his lofty ambition and the reality of his circumstances seemed unbridgeable, he was engulfed by tremendous sadness. If he rarely spoke of his inner feelings, he often expressed emotions through the poetry he admired. Gray's "Elegy," which Lincoln quoted in his small autobiography to explain his attitude toward his childhood poverty, asserts that "Full many a flower is born to blush unseen/And waste its sweetness on the desert air." The poet laments a dead young villager of immense but untapped talent. "Here rests his head upon the lap of earth/A youth to fortune and to fame unknown/Fair Science frowned not on his humble birth/And Melancholy marked him for her own." Lincoln's life had been a continuing struggle to escape such a destiny. In that troubling winter of 1841, he must have felt, at least for the moment, that his long struggle had been fruitless.

Some students of Lincoln have suggested that he suffered from chronic depression. One confusion in making this designation is the interchangeable use of the terms "sadness," "melancholy," and "depression." To be sure, Lincoln was a melancholy man. "His melancholy dript from him as he walked," said his law partner, William Herndon, an observation echoed by dozens of others. "No element of Mr. Lincoln's character was so marked, obvious and ingrained as his mysterious and profound melancholy," recalled Henry Whitney. "This melancholy was stamped on him while in the period of his gestation. It was part of his nature and could no more be shaken off than he could part with his brains."

At times Lincoln's melancholy signaled a withdrawal to the solitude of thought. As a child, he would retreat from others to read. In later life, he would work a problem through in private—whether a proof of Euclidean geometry or the meaning of the Declaration of Independence. Only when he had resolved the problems and issues in his own mind did he display the results of his private meditations. It is little wonder that others saw these withdrawals as evidence of melancholy. Furthermore, the very contours of Lincoln's face in repose lent him a sorrowful aspect. One observer remarked that "his face was about the saddest I ever looked upon." Another contemporary described his face as "slightly wrinkled about the brows, but not from trouble. It was intense, constant thought that planted the wrinkles there."

Unlike depression, melancholy does not have a specific cause. It is an aspect of temperament, perhaps genetically based. One may emerge from the hypo, as Lincoln did, but melancholy is an indelible part of one's nature. Lincoln understood this: "a tendency to melancholly," he told Joshua's sister, Mary, "is a misfortune not a fault."

"Melancholy," writes the modern novelist Thomas Pynchon, "is a far richer and more complex ailment than simple depression. There is a generous amplitude of possibility, chances for productive behavior, even what may be identified as a sense of humor." And, as everyone connected with Lincoln testified, he was an extraordinarily funny man. "When he first came among us," wrote a Springfield friend, "his wit & humor boiled over." When he told his humorous stories, Henry Whitney marveled, "he emerged from his cave of gloom and came back, like one awakened from sleep, to the world in which he lived, again." His storytelling, Speed believed, was "necessary to his very existence—Most men who have been great students such as he was in their hours of idleness have taken to the bottle, to cards or dice—He had no fondness for any of these—Hence he sought relaxation in anecdotes." Lincoln himself recognized that humor was an essential aspect of his temperament. He laughed, he explained, so he did not weep. He saw laughter as the "joyous, universal evergreen of life." His stories were intended "to whistle off sadness."

Modern psychiatry regards humor as probably the most mature and healthy means of adapting to melancholy. "Humor, like hope, permits one to focus upon and to bear what is too terrible to be borne," writes George Valliant. "Humor can be marvelously therapeutic," adds another observer. "It can deflate without destroying; it can instruct while it entertains; it saves us from our pretensions; and it provides an outlet for feeling that expressed another way would be corrosive."

The melancholy stamped on Lincoln's nature derived in large part from an acute sensitivity to the pains and injustices he perceived in the world. He was uncommonly tenderhearted. He once stopped and tracked back half a mile to rescue a pig caught in a mire—not because he loved the pig, recollected a friend, "just to take a pain out of his own mind." When his schoolmates tortured turtles by placing hot coals on their backs to see them wriggle, he told them "it was wrong." He refused to hunt animals, which ran counter to frontier mores. After he had broken with Mary, he wrote that the only thing that kept him from happiness was "the never-absent idea" that he had caused Mary to suffer.

Lincoln's abhorrence of hurting another was born of more than simple compassion. He possessed extraordinary empathy—the gift or curse of putting himself in the place of another, to experience what they were feeling, to understand their motives and desires. The philosopher Adam Smith described this faculty: "By the imagination we place ourselves in his situation . . . we enter as it were into his body and become in some measure him." This capacity Smith saw as "the source of our fellow-feeling for the misery of others . . . by changing places in fancy with the sufferer . . . we come either to conceive or to be affected by what he feels." In a world environed by cruelty and injustice, Lincoln's remarkable empathy was inevitably a source of pain. His sensibilities were not only acute, they were raw. "With his wealth of sympathy, his conscience, and his unflinching sense of justice, he was predestined to sorrow," observed Helen Nicolay, whose father would become Lincoln's private secretary.

Though Lincoln's empathy was at the root of his melancholy, it would prove an enormous asset to his political career. "His crowning gift of political diagnosis," suggested Nicolay, "was due to his sympathy . . . which gave him the power to forecast with uncanny accuracy what his opponents were likely to do." She described how, after listening to his colleagues talk at a Whig Party caucus, Lincoln would cast off his shawl, rise from his chair, and say: "From your talk, I gather the Democrats will do so and so . . . I should do so and so to checkmate them." He proceeded to outline all "the moves for days ahead; making them all so plain that his listeners wondered why they had not seen it that way themselves." Such capacity to intuit the inward feelings and intentions of others would be manifest throughout his career.

• • •

LINCOLN'S FEARS that marriage might hinder his ambitions proved unfounded. He and Mary eventually settled in a comfortable frame house at the corner of Eighth and Jackson, within easy walking distance of his law office. For the first time, he enjoyed the security and warmth of a family circle, without neglecting his devotion to reading, studying, traveling on the legal circuit, and cultivating politics. While the marriage was tumultuous at times, it provided Lincoln with a protected harbor from which he could come and go as he pleased while he continued his lifelong quest to become an educated person.

The adjustment to married life was harder for Mary than for her husband. Raised in a Southern mansion attended by slaves, she had never had to cook a meal, scrub the floor, chop wood, or pump water from the well. Nor, while living with her sister in the finest house in Springfield, had she ever worried about money, or hesitated before inviting friends for dinner parties and receptions. Now she was confronted with the innumerable chores of running a household when the money Lincoln earned barely covered living expenses. Though Lincoln helped with the marketing and the dishes and insisted, even in the leanest years of his practice, that she hire a maid to help with the children, most household tasks fell on Mary's shoulders.

Certainly such "hardships" were not shared by the wives of Lincoln's later rivals. When Julia Coalter married Edward Bates, her husband had upward of twenty slaves to nurse the children, clean the house, plant the vegetables, cook the meals, and drive the carriages. After Bates emancipated his slaves in the 1850s, several remained with the family as freedmen and women, while additional servants were found among the Irish and German immigrants in St. Louis. For Frances Seward, there was never a time when she was left alone to handle household chores. When she and Seward agreed to live in her father's Auburn estate, she inherited the faithful servants who had worked in the big house for decades. As governor, Seward was supplied with an experienced staff of household servants; while in Washington, he maintained a live-in staff to accommodate and entertain the endless stream of guests at dinner parties and receptions. When Frances suffered from migraine headaches, she could take to her bed without worrying that the domestic work would be left undone.

It was not simply Mary's relative poverty that made her early married life difficult. Both she and Lincoln had essentially detached themselves from their previous lives, cutting themselves off from parents and relatives and thereby creating a domestic lifestyle closer to the "nuclear family" of a later age than the extended family still common in the mid-nineteenth century. When Lincoln was away, Mary was left alone to deal with her terror of thunderstorms, her worries over the children's illnesses, and her spells of depression. Too proud to let her Springfield sisters know the difficulties she faced in these early years—particularly after the disapproval they had voiced over her choice of husband—Mary struggled stoically and proudly on her own.

Once again, her isolation stands in stark contrast to the familial support enjoyed by Frances Seward and Julia Bates. Frances could depend on the companionship not only of her widowed father but of three generations of women living in the same household—her favorite aunt, Cornelia; her sister and closest friend, Lazette, who spent months at a time in the Auburn house; and her beloved daughter, Fanny. Likewise, Julia Bates was surrounded by her children, several of whom continued to live with the family even after they married; and by her parents; her sisters; her brothers; and her husband's mother, all of whom lived nearby.

If Mary's solitary life with her husband brought hardship, the birth of two sons within the first forty months of their marriage brought great happiness. Both boys were high-spirited, intelligent, and dearly loved by their parents. In later years, Mary proudly noted that Lincoln was "the kindest—most tender and loving husband & father in the world. . . . Said to me always when I asked him for any thing—You know what you want—go and get it. He never asked me if it was necessary."

He was, by all accounts, a gentle and indulgent father who regularly took the boys on walks around the neighborhood, played with them in the house, and brought them to his office while he worked. While Herndon believed that Lincoln was too indulgent, that the children "litterally ran over him," leaving him "powerless to withstand their importunities," Lincoln maintained that children should be allowed to grow up without a battery of rules and restrictions. "It is my pleasure that my children are free—happy and unrestrained by paternal tyrrany," Mary recalled his saying. "Love is the chain whereby to lock a child to its parent."

• • •

WHEN, AT LAST, Illinois began to emerge from recession, Lincoln's hopes for a future in politics revived. "Now if you should hear any one say that Lincoln don't want to go to Congress," he wrote a friend three months after his marriage, "tell him . . . he is mistaken." His objective was the Seventh Congressional District—including Sangamon County—where the Whigs had a majority in a state that was otherwise solidly Democratic.

Lincoln's first goal was to win the endorsement of the Sangamon County Convention, which would appoint delegates to the congressional district nominating convention. The convention system had just been adopted by the Whigs to unify party members in the general election. "That 'union is strength' is a truth that has been known, illustrated and declared, in various ways and forms in all ages of the world," said Lincoln in support of the new system, pointing out that "he whose wisdom surpasses that of all philosophers, has declared that 'a house divided against itself cannot stand.' " Much later, of course, he would famously widen the application of this same biblical phrase beyond Sangamon County Whigs to the nation as a whole.

Lincoln's adversary in his home county was Edward Baker, a close friend after whom he named his second-born son. Despite a vigorous campaign, Lincoln fell short by a narrow margin. "We had a meeting of the whigs of the county here on last monday to appoint delegates to a district convention," Lincoln reported to Speed, "and Baker beat me & got the delegation instructed to go for him." Having been chosen a delegate himself, Lincoln ruefully remarked, "I shall be 'fixed' a good deal like a fellow who is made groomsman to the man what has cut him out, and is marrying his own dear 'gal.' "

Though bound not to oppose Baker in his own county, Lincoln still harbored a lingering hope that he might be nominated by another county, explaining to a friend in neighboring Menard County that his defeat in Sangamon was partially explained by his marriage into the Todd/Edwards clan. "It would astonish if not amuse, the older citizens of your County who twelve years ago knew me a strange[r], friendless, uneducated, penniless boy, working on a flat boat . . . to learn that I have been put down here as the candidate of pride, wealth, and arristocratic family distinction."

At the district convention in Pekin, the nomination went neither to Lincoln nor to Baker but to another young lawyer, John Hardin. At this convention, Lincoln successfully introduced a resolution that Baker would be the next candidate for the U.S. Congress, hoping to establish the idea of rotating terms that would later redound to his benefit. Baker was duly elected two years later, but when his term came to an end, Hardin wanted to return to Congress and was unwilling to yield to Lincoln.

Lincoln left nothing to chance in the contest that followed, seeking to prevent Whig papers from supporting Hardin, pressuring friends to influence neutrals in his favor. He asked friends to share the names of those who were against him. He sent letters to influential Whigs in every precinct. He planned "a quiet trip" through several counties, though he warned his friends, "Dont speak of this, or let it relax any of your vigilance."

His message remained the same throughout the campaign. Hardin and Baker had already served their terms in Congress, and now it was his turn. "That Hardin is talented, energetic, usually generous and magnanimous," he wrote a supporter, "I have, before this, affirmed to you, and do not now deny. You know that my only argument is that 'turn about is fair play.' " He wrote a long letter to Hardin, recalling the old understanding, but insisting that if he were "not, (in services done the party, and in capacity to serve in future) near enough your equal, when added to the fact of your having had a turn, to entitle me to the nomination, I scorn it on any and all other grounds."

Thoroughly outmaneuvered, Hardin withdrew from the contest. Lincoln was nominated, then easily elected to Congress, where the stage had already been set for the debate over the extension of slavery that would dominate the decade to come.

• • •

SALMON CHASE TRAVELED a different road to power than his three rivals. For many years he stayed clear of elective politics. "I am not a politician," he told a friend. "I feel disgusted with party strife and am greatly chagrined on seeing the means to which both parties resort to gain their ends."

The train of events that led Chase into the political world began in 1836, when James G. Birney, an Ohio abolitionist, began publishing the antislavery weekly *Philanthropist*, in Cincinnati. The paper's publication created consternation among Cincinnati's leading merchants and bankers, most of whom had substantial ties to the Southern plantation market. Adjacent to Kentucky, the state of Ohio depended on trade relations with its slaveholding neighbor to sustain a thriving economy. Birney himself had been a wealthy slaveowner in Kentucky before becoming an abolitionist. As soon as distribution of the *Philanthropist* commenced, a group of white community leaders, including many of the merchants Chase represented, attempted to close Birney down. When peaceful pressure failed, the group turned to violence.

On a hot summer night in July 1836, an organized mob broke into the shop where the abolitionist weekly was printed, dismantled the press, and tore up the edition that was about to be circulated. Refusing to be driven out, Birney continued to publish. Two weeks later, the mob returned. This time they succeeded in tearing apart the entire office. They threw tables and other equipment from the second-story window and then, to the cheers of the crowd, shoved out the printing press. While the mayor gazed on approvingly and the police were conspicuously absent, the press was hauled through the streets to the river. After it sank, the crowd began to shout for action against Birney himself, calling for the publisher to be tarred and feathered.

Though Chase had yet to take a public stand on the issue of abolition, he was appalled by the violence. Hearing of the mob's intention to raid the Franklin House where Birney was thought to reside, he raced to the hotel to warn the publisher. As the mob surged forward, Chase braced his arms against the door frame, blocking the hotel's entrance with his body. Six feet two, with broad shoulders, a massive chest, and a determined set to his jaw, Chase gave the rioters pause. The crowd demanded to know who he was. "Salmon P. Chase," the young lawyer replied. "You will pay for your actions," a frustrated member of the mob told him. "I [can] be found at any time," Chase said. "His voice and commanding presence caught the mood of the mob at just the right time," his biographer observes. The hour was late and the mob backed off.

The dramatic encounter had a profound effect on Chase. He became a hero in the antislavery community and began to see his future in a different way. In the years that followed, he became a leader in the effort to protect antislavery activists and their organizations. "No man of his time," the historian Albert Hart argues, "had a stronger conception of the moral issues" involved in the antislavery movement; "none showed greater courage and resolution." His passionate awakening to the antislavery cause was not surprising, given his receptiveness to religious arguments in favor of emancipation and equality. As time went by, however, Chase could not separate his own ambition from the cause he championed. The most calculating decisions designed to forward his political career were justified by advancement of the cause. His personal defeats would be regarded as setbacks for freedom itself. "By dedicating himself to moral activism," the historian Stephen Mazlish argues, "Chase could join his passion for personal advancement to the demands of his religious convictions. . . . 'Fame's proud temple' could be his and he need feel no guilt in its pursuit."

In 1837, a year after he had faced down the anti-Birney mob, Chase once more lent his support to the abolitionist publisher. He undertook the defense of a light-skinned young slave named Matilda, brought to Ohio on a business trip by a Missouri planter who was both her master and her natural father. While in Ohio, encountering black men and women in a free society, she begged her father to grant her liberty. When he refused, she took matters into her own hand, seeking refuge in Cincinnati's black community until her father returned to Missouri. She eventually secured employment in Birney's house, where she remained until she was discovered by a slave catcher and brought before a judge to be remanded to Missouri under the Fugitive Slave Law enacted by Congress in 1793 to enforce the constitutional provision requiring that slaves escaping from one state to another "be delivered up" to their original owners.

Perhaps Chase could have argued successfully that Matilda was not a fugitive from Missouri, since she had been brought into Ohio by her father. Rather, he chose to make a fundamental assault on the applicability of the Fugitive Slave Law to the free state of Ohio. He argued that as soon as Matilda stepped into Ohio, she acquired the legal right to freedom guaranteed by the Northwest Ordinance of 1787, which forbade the introduction of slavery into the vast Northwest Territory later occupied by the states of Ohio, Indiana, Illinois, and Michigan. To many opponents of slavery in later years, including Abraham Lincoln, the Ordinance of 1787 became, like the Declaration of Independence, a sacred document expressing the intent of the founding fathers to confine slavery within the boundaries of the existing states, prohibiting forever its future spread.

"Every settler within the territory, by the very act of settlement, became a party to this compact," Chase argued, "forever entitled to the benefit of its provisions." These provisions, he maintained, "are the birthright of the people of Ohio. It is their glorious distinction, that the genuine principles of American liberty are imbedded, as it were, in their very soil, and mingled with their very atmosphere. . . . Wherever [slavery] exists at all, it exists only in virtue of positive law . . . [and] can have no existence beyond the territorial limits of the state which sanctions it." The right to hold a person in bondage "vanishes when the master and the slave meet together" in a place, like Ohio, "where positive law interdicts slavery."

The conservative judge, as expected, ruled against Chase. The next day, Matilda was forcibly removed to the South and returned to slavery. The philosophical and legal arguments Chase had advanced, however, were considered so important by the antislavery community that they were printed in pamphlet form and distributed throughout the nation.

Publication of his arguments in the *Matilda* case brought Chase immediate acclaim in Northern intellectual circles. By anchoring his arguments firmly in history and law, he opened an antislavery approach that differed from the tactics of the allies of Garrison, who eschewed political organization, dismissed the founding fathers, and considered the Constitution "a covenant with death, an agreement with hell," because it condoned slavery. Where the Garrisonians called for a moral crusade to awaken the sleeping conscience of the nation, Chase targeted a political audience, hopeful that abolition could be achieved through politics, government, and the courts.

The time had come, Chase decided, to try for public office. Though he had not been active in party politics, he sought a nomination from the Whig Party to the state senate. To his disappointment, he was rebuffed as an abolitionist. Three years later, he tried again, seeking the Whig nomination for the Cincinnati City Council. Although he succeeded in gaining office, he was defeated for reelection after a single term, largely due to his position on temperance, which had led him to unpopular votes denying liquor licenses to city establishments.

Surveying the political landscape, Chase was unable to see a future for himself as either a Democrat or a Whig. Both parties, he wrote, submitted to the South upon the "*vital* question of slavery." Consequently, in 1841, he joined the fledgling Liberty Party, which was struggling to establish a solid base of support. The previous year, James Birney, since moved to New York to head the American Anti-Slavery Society, had gained the party's nomination for president. Unknown beyond abolitionist circles, Birney garnered only 7,000 votes.

Through the 1840s, Chase sought to guide the Liberty Party to a more moderate image so that it could gain wider appeal. Working closely with Gamaliel Bailey, Birney's astute successor at the *Philanthropist*, Chase persuaded the Ohio Liberty Party to adopt a resolution that explicitly renounced any intention "to interfere with slavery in the states where it exists." Concurring with Lincoln, Bates, and a number of progressive Whigs, they pledged to focus only on those areas where slavery was present "without constitutional warrant"—in the District of Columbia, on the high seas, in the new territories. At the same time, Chase encouraged his fellow party members to consider reaching outside their ranks to find a presidential candidate who could command a larger vote than the radical Birney, who, as Chase said, "has seen so little of public service."

In an 1842 letter to Joshua Giddings, the abolitionist congressman from Ohio's Western Reserve, Chase suggested that if John Quincy Adams or William Henry Seward "would accept the nomination, great additional strength might be gained for the party." He had no idea whether either man would accept, but ranked Governor Seward, "for his age," as "one of the first statesmen in the country," while former president Adams was "perhaps, the very first."

Though he had never met Seward, Chase opened an intriguing correspondence with the governor, in which they freely debated the role of third parties. Seward expressed his belief that "there can be only two permanent parties." In his view, the Democratic Party, with its strong base in the South, would always be the party of slavery, while the Whig Party would champion the antislavery banner, "more or less," depending "on the advancement of the public mind and the intentness with which it can be fixed on the question of Slavery." Seward conceded that while he was disheartened by the Whig Party's current "lukewarmness on the Subject of Slavery," he had no choice but to stay with the party he loved, and to hope for a more advanced position in the future. "To abandon a party and friends to whom I owe so much, whose confidence I do in some degree possess," he wrote, "would be criminal, and not more criminal than unwise."

Chase saw the situation differently. Though originally "*educated in the Whig school,*" with Whiggish views of the tariff, banking, and government, he had never considered party loyalty among his defining characteristics. Nor had he experienced the camaraderie of fellow party loyalists that Seward enjoyed when he and his colleagues boarded together in Albany during the lengthy legislative sessions. For Chase, the decision to leave the Whigs for the Liberty Party was not the momentous separation that it would have been for Seward.

Chase clearly understood that so long as the Liberty Party remained a "one idea" party, it would never attract majority support. Risking the displeasure of his abolitionist friends, who wanted no diminution of their principles, he envisioned a gradual movement of the Liberty Party toward one of the major parties. His efforts revealed a practical side to his principled stance, but old acquaintances in Ohio were troubled by his decision to set his sights on the more powerful Democratic Party, where he had a greater chance of statewide success than with the Whigs.

In his bid to cultivate Democratic leaders, Chase shifted his positions on the tariff and the banking system to align himself with the Democrats, though he insisted that the economic policies of either party were insignificant compared to the issue of slavery. For the moment, since neither major party would take a resolute stand on slavery, he remained with the Liberty Party, attending conventions, drawing up resolutions, and searching for candidates.

In the years that followed, in part because the free city of Cincinnati was a natural destination for runaways crossing the Ohio River from the slave state of Kentucky, a number of fugitive slave cases ended up in the Cincinnati courts. Chase volunteered his services in many such cases. The eloquent power of his arguments soon earned him the honorary title "Attorney General for the Negro." In the famous case that inspired Harriet Beecher Stowe's good-hearted John Van Trompe in *Uncle Tom's Cabin*, Chase represented John Van Zandt, an old farmer who had moved from Kentucky to Ohio so that he might live in a free state.

On an April night in 1842, Van Zandt was returning from the Cincinnati market to his home twenty miles north. On the road, he encountered a group of slaves who had crossed the river from Kentucky. "Moved by sympathy," Chase would argue, the farmer "undertook to convey them in his wagon to Lebanon or Springfield." En route, two slave catchers accosted the wagon. They captured the slaves and returned them to their Kentucky owner, receiving a $450 bounty for their efforts.

The owner then brought suit against Van Zandt for "harboring and concealing" the slaves, in violation of the 1793 Fugitive Slave Act. Chase "very willingly" agreed to represent the elderly farmer, who faced substantial penalties if found guilty. Chase's defense of Van Zandt transcended the particulars of the *Matilda* case, directly challenging the constitutionality of the Fugitive Slave Law. That law, he maintained, deprived fugitives of life and liberty without due process of law. "Under the constitution," he declared, "all the inhabitants of the United States are, without exception, persons,—persons, it may be, not free, persons, held to service . . . but still, persons," and therefore possessed of every right guaranteed under the Constitution and Declaration of Independence.

"What is a slave?" he asked. "A slave is a person held, as property, by legalized force, against natural right. . . . The very moment a slave passes beyond the jurisdiction of the state, in which he is held as such, he ceases to be a slave; not because any law or regulation of the state which he enters confers freedom upon him, but because he *continues* to be a man and *leaves behind* him the law of force, which made him a slave." Chase depicted slavery as "a creature of state law" and not a national institution. He argued that any slave state created after 1787, the year the Northwest Ordinance became law, existed in violation of the Constitution and the wishes of the founding fathers.

As most observers expected, the Cincinnati court refused to accept Chase's argument. Van Zandt was found guilty. As Chase left the courtroom, according to Harriet Beecher Stowe, then a Cincinnati resident, one of the judges reflected on the unpopularity of professed abolitionists: "There goes a young man who has *ruined* himself to-day."

Far from ruining his prospects, the *Van Zandt* case added considerable luster to Chase's national reputation. Appealing the decision to the U.S. Supreme Court, Chase enlisted Seward's help as co-counsel. The case moved slowly through the docket, affording the two men time to craft their written arguments. Chase presented the constitutional arguments, while Seward dealt with the technical ones. Though the Southern-dominated court wasted little time in affirming the lower court's ruling, the constitutional arguments Chase outlined became pillars of antislavery party doctrine.

Chase acknowledged that "poor old Van Zandt" was never able to recover from the loss and the damages inflicted upon him. Still, he believed that "even though my poor old client be sacrificed, the great cause of humanity will be a gainer." He had his 108-page argument reprinted in pamphlet form for wide distribution, and was delighted with the positive response it provoked. Antislavery activist Charles Sumner wrote from Massachusetts that "the question under the Ordinance of 1787 was novel" and might well "rally a *political* movement." President John Quincy

Adams's son, Charles Francis, extolled Chase, as did New Hampshire's Senator John Hale. Nothing gave him more satisfaction, than the praise he received from Seward, who expressed fervent hope that the "chaste and beautiful eloquence" of Chase's brief would be forever "preserved for the benefit of the cause of Freedom and for [Chase's] own fame." The fact that the case brought a personal and intellectual contact with Seward, Chase told abolitionist Lewis Tappan, proved "one of the gratifications, and one of the greatest too," of all his efforts.

Politicians were not alone in recognizing Chase's commitment. In gratitude for public service "in behalf of the oppressed" and his "eloquent advocacy of the rights of man," the black pastor of the Baker Street Church collected donations from his parishioners. In an emotional ceremony on May 6, 1845, attended by a large black congregation, Chase was honored with a beautifully engraved sterling silver pitcher. Presenting the gift on behalf of "the Colored People of Cincinnati," the Reverend A. J. Gordon told the enthusiastic gathering that "whenever the friendless objects of slaveholding cupidity" struggled to find freedom, they found in Chase "a firm, zealous and devoted friend." He assured Chase that his deeds on behalf of fugitive slaves and the black race would be "engraven on the tablets of our hearts . . . as long as memory retains her seat." Reverend Gordon avowed that when Chase was finally "called from [his] earthly labors," he would be ushered into paradise by God Himself, with the words "Well done thou good and faithful servant, enter into the joys of thy Lord. For inasmuch as you did it unto the least of these my brethren, you did it unto me!"

Chase was profoundly moved by the ceremony. Accepting the engraved pitcher, which he treasured the rest of his life, he pledged to continue his fight for freedom until "the colored man and white man are equal before the law." In his own state of Ohio, he lamented, various legal provisions known as the Black Laws excluded free blacks from public schools, the witness box, and the voting booth. These exclusions, he asserted (two years before Seward would make a similar argument), were clear infringements of the Constitution. "True Democracy makes no enquiry about the color of the skin, or the place of nativity," he ardently claimed. "Wherever it sees a man, it recognizes a being endowed by his Creator with original inalienable rights."

Laws denying black children public school education, while simultaneously requiring that their parents pay school taxes, were reprehensible, he argued. More unjust, blacks were banned from the witness box in all cases where either party was white. This exclusion exposed the black population "to every species of violence and outrage" from whites who felt secure from punishment so long as they committed their crimes only in the presence of black witnesses. "Every law on the statute book so wrong and mean that it cannot be executed, or felt, if executed, to be oppressive and unjust," averred Chase, "tends to the overthrow of all law, by separating in the minds of the people, the idea of law from the idea of right. . . .

"For myself," Chase concluded, "I am ready to renew my pledge—and I will venture to speak also in behalf of my co-workers,—that we go straight on, without faltering or wavering, until every vestige of oppression shall be erased from the statute book:—until the sun in all his journey from the utmost eastern horizon, through the mid-heaven, till he sinks beyond the western mountains into his ocean bed, shall not behold, in all our broad and glorious land, the foot print of a single slave." A tremendous round of applause was followed by an emotional rendition of the hymn "America." With a benediction, the exercises were brought to a close.

• • •

CHASE, UNLIKE SEWARD and Lincoln, did not make friends easily. A contemporary reporter observed that he knew "little of human nature," and that while "profoundly versed in man, he was profoundly ignorant of men." His abstractedness often lent an air of preoccupation, aggravated by his extreme nearsightedness. Both prevented him from gauging the reactions of others. Furthermore, his natural reserve, piety, temperance, and lack of humor made for uneasy relationships. Even his stately proportions and fastidious dress worked against social intimacy.

Despite his difficulty in making friends and instilling personal loyalties, Chase did form one significant relationship during the decade of the forties. His bond with Edwin M. Stanton would have important consequences during the Civil War, when the two men would serve together in Lincoln's cabinet. Six years younger than Chase, Stanton was a brilliant young lawyer from Steubenville, Ohio. He had been active in Democratic politics from his earliest days. A short, stout man, with thick brows and intense black eyes hidden behind steel-rimmed glasses, Stanton had grown up in a Quaker family dedicated to abolition. He later told the story that "when he was a boy his father had—like the father of Hannibal against Rome—made him swear eternal hostility to slavery."

When Chase and Stanton first met in Columbus in the early 1840s, each was dealing with appalling personal loss, for death had pursued Stanton much as it had pursued Chase. In the five-year span from 1841 to 1846, Stanton had lost his only daughter, Lucy; his young wife, Mary; and his only brother, Darwin. Confronting a similar reign of grief at almost the same time, Chase found in Stanton a solace and friendship more intense than if they had met at a different juncture in their lives.

In the summer of 1846, Stanton spent several days with Chase at his Cincinnati home. The wide-ranging conversations they enjoyed left a lasting impression on Stanton. "Since our pleasant intercourse together last summer," Stanton wrote Chase, "no living person has been oftener in my mind;—waking or sleeping,—for, more than once, I have dreamed of being with you. The strength of my regard and affection for you, I can, thus, tell more freely than were we face to face."

More than sorrow bound Chase and Stanton together. At the time of their acquaintance in the mid-1840s, both men were trying to find a footing in quick-shifting political currents. Chase had already taken his stand with the Liberty Party. Stanton, though intrigued by the newly formed party, remained a loyal Democrat. Over the course of many hours, in conversation and then by letter, they debated the merits of the new Liberty Party. Responding to Chase's worry about the narrowness of the party's platform, Stanton cited examples of single ideas that had achieved great triumphs: most notably, "Taxation & Representation," the slogan that guided the American Revolution. "I go for one idea in party," he wrote, "and in friendship my one idea is strong & sincere love for you." With Chase, Stanton felt free to criticize the Democratic Party, which had gravely disappointed him in a recent election when its candidate for governor came out in favor of the discriminatory Black Laws.

Chase tried to involve Stanton in the *Van Zandt* appeal, but Stanton declined, fearing he had neither the "physical nor intellectual strength sufficient to engage in the cause. Events of the past summer have broken my spirits, crushed my hopes, and without energy or purpose in life, I feel indifferent to the present, careless of the future." Chase apparently did not reply to this letter. "Many weeks have gone by," Stanton wrote in January 1847, "but your voice reaches me no more. Why is it? The question arises, as I move slowly & disappointed from the post office each day."

The correspondence picked up again in the spring, when Chase sent Stanton his argument in the *Van Zandt* case. "Rejoicing, as I do, to call you friend," Stanton wrote after reading through the lengthy document, "it gives me pleasure to acknowledge its intellectual merit." Rather than discuss it in writing, he hoped that he and Chase could soon meet and "spend two or three days" together. "I want to hear from you," Stanton concluded, "and so may as well confess it at once & throw myself upon your mercy."

They finally met in Cincinnati in July, but the visit was too abbreviated to satisfy Stanton. The desire for his friend's company had been lodged in his heart for so long, Stanton explained to Chase upon returning home to Steubenville, that the visit, while enjoyable, had left him ungratified. In the months that followed, however, they saw each other on a number of occasions and opened their hearts in correspondence. After receiving a particularly affectionate letter from Chase, Stanton fervently replied that it "filled my heart with joy; to be loved by you, and be told that you value my love is a gratification beyond my power to express." He went on to downplay reports Chase had heard that he had developed a "magnetic attraction" for a new woman. "I wish it were so," he admitted. "To love, and to be loved, is a necessary condition of my happiness . . . I have met with no one that exercises upon me the least attraction beyond the general qualities of the sex."

In the meantime, his friendship with Chase, and his memories of their time together, sustained him. "Allow me my dear friend again this evening to enter your study—you know I like it better than the parlor even without fire—but the fire is blazing there—let me take you by the hand throw my arm around you, say I love you, & bid you farewell."

As their friendship grew, Chase urged Stanton to involve himself more deeply in the struggle against slavery. He promised Stanton, who remained a Democrat, that he would join his campaign should he run for governor. But Stanton, who was now supporting his brother's family as well as his own, did not feel he could make the financial sacrifice. "How much I regret that your voice is not to be heard," a disappointed Chase wrote. "We have but a short life to live here my dear friend. But let us make it long by noble deeds. You have great gifts of God, energy, enthusiasm, talent, utterance. And now a great cause demands you."

Stanton's inability to commit himself more fully to the antislavery crusade cast a shadow on his relationship with Chase. When Stanton failed to attend a Democratic convention in Columbus where antislavery issues were on the agenda, Chase chastised him for placing personal interests above political duties. "Why—why are you not here?" Chase lamented. "If I had foreseen you would not attend the Convention, I am certain I should not have left home." Stanton's reply expressed hurt at the censure in Chase's letter, explaining that it was not merely private concerns that kept him away but a collision of obligations. "The practice of law," he conceded, "furnishes employment for all my time and faculties. . . . Such to be sure is not the condition that dreams of early love pictured for my manhood—but in the field of life some as sentinels must perform the lonely round while others enjoy the social festivity of the camp."

For Stanton, more than for Chase, the importance of the friendship exceeded political events and even personal ambition. "While public honors affords gratification," Stanton wrote, "such friendship as yours is to me of inestimable value." With sadness, he conceded that he was "well aware that public duties, the increasing pressure of private affairs as age advances, domestic vicissitudes and the inclination of the heart must cool the fervor of friendship among men." Still, he hoped that he and Chase might someday stand side by side in the struggle against slavery.

So as 1847 drew to a close, the four men who would contend for the 1860 presidential nomination were deeply and actively involved in the political, social, and economic issues that would define the growing nation. Each embraced a different position along the spectrum of growing opposition to slavery. Yet while Seward, Chase, and Bates had each developed a national renown, few beyond Illinois knew of the raw-boned young congressman coming to the nation's capital for the first time in his life.

CHAPTER 4

"PLUNDER & CONQUEST"

WASHINGTON WAS A CITY in progress when the Lincolns arrived at the wooden railroad station in December 1847 for the opening of the congressional session. The cornerstone of the Washington Monument would not be laid until the following summer. Cobblestoned Pennsylvania Avenue was one of only two paved streets. Not yet fitted with its familiar high dome, the Capitol stood on a hill that boasted "a full view of the cities of Washington, Georgetown, and Alexandria, and the varied and forest-clad hills in Maryland and Virginia." In the backs of most houses, recalled one of Lincoln's colleagues, "stood pig-styes, cow-sheds, and pens for the gangs of unyoked geese. During the day the animals and fowls roamed at will in lordly insolence, singly or in herds and flocks, through the streets and over the fields."

Nevertheless, with forty thousand inhabitants (including several thousand slaves), the capital was a metropolis compared to little Springfield. It was filled with the landmarks and memorials of the history that so captivated the Lincolns. Some of the most illustrious personages of the age still walked the halls of Congress—John Quincy Adams tirelessly battling on behalf of antislavery petitions; the eloquent Daniel Webster, whose words, Lincoln believed, would outlive the age; John Calhoun, the acknowledged spokesman for the South, who had already led one effort at rebellion. These titans who had shaped the history of the past decades were joined by those who would play leading roles in the great drama to unfold—Jefferson Davis and Alexander Stephens, future president and vice president of the Confederacy; Stephen Douglas, Lincoln's great rival; and Robert Barnwell Rhett, agitator of rebellion.

The Lincolns took up residence in Mrs. Spriggs's Boarding House on Capitol Hill, on the site of the present Library of Congress. Soon a favorite among his fellow boarders, Lincoln was always ready with a story or anecdote to entertain, persuade, or defuse argument. Samuel Busey, a young doctor who took his meals at the boardinghouse, recalled that whenever Lincoln was about to tell a story, "he would lay down his knife and fork, place his elbows upon the table, rest his face between his hands, and begin with the words 'that reminds me,' and proceed. Everybody prepared for the explosions sure to follow."

For recreation, Lincoln took up bowling with his fellow boarders. Though a clumsy bowler, according to Dr. Busey, Lincoln "played the game with great zest and spirit" and "accepted success and defeat with like good nature and humor." When word spread "that he was in the alley there would assemble numbers of people to witness the fun which was anticipated by those who knew of his fund of anecdotes and jokes." As ever, his quick wit and droll geniality provided a source of "merriment" for everyone around him.

While Lincoln attended meetings and congressional sessions, Mary was largely confined to the single room she shared with her husband and two small children—Robert, now five, and Eddie, two, whose often boisterous antics and excited running through the corridors did not endear Mary to her fellow boarders. None of the other congressmen in their boardinghouse were accompanied by wives. Indeed, most of the legislators in the city had left their families behind. Without female friends, Mary was compelled to spend most of the day alone with the children. Furthermore, the mores of the day forbade her to attend social gatherings and parties without her continually occupied husband. After a few months, by mutual consent, Mary and the children left Washington. Unable to return to their Springfield home, which was rented out for the congressional term, she took the children to her father's elegant house in Lexington, Kentucky, beginning what would be the longest continuous separation from her husband in their twenty-three-year marriage.

• • •

EIGHTEEN MONTHS before Abraham Lincoln arrived in Washington, history had taken an irrevocable turn when Democratic president James Polk ordered American troops to occupy disputed territory between the borders of the United States and Mexico. Relations between Mexico and the United States had been strained for decades as quarrels over boundary lines simmered. Announcing that Mexico had fired upon American soldiers on American soil, Polk called on Congress not to declare war but to recognize that a state of war already existed.

The onset of war with Mexico aroused the patriotic spirit of the American people, who regarded the war as "a romantic venture in a distant and exotic land." The Congress called for 50,000 men, but within weeks, 300,000 volunteers had poured into recruiting centers. Lincoln's former rival, John Hardin, was "the first to enlist" in Illinois. He would be elected colonel of his regiment and would die a hero's death at the Battle of Buena Vista. Edward Baker, still retaining his seat in Congress, would raise a regiment and, "with drums rolling and fifes shrilling," would lead his troops "through flag-bedecked streets crowded with cheering thousands, amid the weeping farewells of women, the encouraging God-speeds of men."

From the start, many leading Whigs questioned both the constitutionality and the justice of the war. "It is a fact," Lincoln would later say, "that the United States Army, in marching to the Rio Grande, marched into a peaceful Mexican settlement, and frightened the inhabitants away from their homes and their growing crops." By the time Lincoln took his congressional oath, the combat had come to an end. The peace treaty had only to be signed, on terms spectacularly advantageous for the victorious United States. At this point, Lincoln conceded, it would have been easier to remain silent about the questionable origins of the war. The Democrats, however, would "not let the whigs be *silent.*" When Congress reconvened, they immediately introduced resolutions blaming the war on Mexican aggression, thereby demanding that Congress endorse "the original justice of the war on the part of the President."

On December 13, less than two weeks after his arrival in Washington, Lincoln wrote his law partner, William Herndon: "As you are all so anxious for me to distinguish myself, I have concluded to do so, before long." Nine days later, he introduced a resolution calling on President Polk to inform the House "whether the particular spot of soil on which the blood of our *citizens* was so shed" belonged to Mexico or to the United States. He challenged the president to present evidence that "Mexico herself became the aggressor by invading *our soil* in hostile array."

The president, not surprisingly, did not respond to the unknown freshman congressman whose hasty reach for distinction earned him only the derisive nickname "spotty Lincoln." A few weeks later, Lincoln voted with his Whig brethren on a resolution introduced by Massachusetts congressman George Ashmun, which stated that the war had been "unnecessarily and unconstitutionally" initiated by the president.

The following week, on January 12, 1848, Lincoln defended his spot resolutions and his vote on the Ashmun resolution in a major speech. He claimed that he would happily reverse his vote if the president could prove that first blood was shed on American soil; but since he "*can* not, or *will* not do this," he suspected that the entire matter was, "from beginning to end, the sheerest deception." Having provoked both countries into war, Lincoln charged, the president had hoped "to escape scrutiny, by fixing the public gaze upon the exceeding brightness of military glory . . . that serpent's eye, that charms to destroy." He went on to liken the president's war message to "the half insane mumbling of a fever-dream." Perhaps recalling the turtles tormented with hot coals by his boyhood friends, Lincoln employed the bizarre simile of the president's confused mind "running hither and thither, like some tortured creature, on a burning surface, finding no position, on which it can settle down, and be at ease."

This maiden effort was not the tone of reasoned debate that later characterized Lincoln's public statements. Nor did it obey his oft-expressed belief that a leader should endeavor to transform, yet heed, public opinion. Compelling as Lincoln's criticisms might have been, they fell flat at a time when the majority of Americans were delighted with the outcome of the war. The Democratic *Illinois State Register* charged that Lincoln had disgraced his district with his "treasonable assault upon President Polk," claimed that "henceforth" he would be known as "Benedict Arnold," and predicted that he would enjoy only a single term. Lincoln sought to clarify his position, arguing that although he had challenged the instigation of the war, he had never voted against supplies for the soldiers. To accept Polk's position without question, he claimed, was to "allow the President to invade a neighboring nation . . . *whenever he may choose to say* he deems it necessary."

Even the loyal Herndon feared that Lincoln's antiwar stance would destroy his political future. "I saw that Lincoln would ruin himself," Herndon later explained. "I wrote to him on the subject again and again." Herndon was right to worry, for as it turned out, Lincoln's quest for distinction had managed only to infuriate the Democrats, worry fainthearted Whigs, and lose support in Illinois, where the war was extremely popular. A prominent Chicago politician, Justin Butterfield, asked if he was against the Mexican War, replied: "no, I opposed one War [the War of 1812]. That was enough for me. I am now perpetually in favor of war, pestilence and famine." In the years ahead, Lincoln would write frequent letters defending his position. If he had hoped for reelection to Congress, however, despite the unofficial agreement with his colleagues that he would serve only one term, his prospects rapidly evaporated in the fever of war. Indeed, when Stephen Logan, the Whig nominee to replace him, was defeated, his loss was blamed on Lincoln.

As Seward understood better than Lincoln, Manifest Destiny was in the air. "Our population," Seward predicted, "is destined to roll its resistless waves to the icy barriers of the north, and to encounter Oriental civilization on the shores of the Pacific." Though he wasn't in favor of the war,

Seward's political astuteness told him it was a mistake to argue against it. He warned that he did "not expect to see the Whig party successful in overthrowing an Administration carrying on a war in which the Whig party and its statesmen are found apologizing for our national adversaries."

Back in Ohio, Salmon Chase told the abolitionist Gerrit Smith that he "would not have engaged in" the war, but in public he muted his opposition. For Chase was caught in a political dilemma. On the one hand, his antislavery allies in the Liberty Party were strongly against the war. If he wanted a seat in the U.S. Senate, however, he would need the support of Ohio Democrats, a task that would not be made easier by assaulting a Democratic president.

Of the four future presidential rivals, only Edward Bates matched the vehemence of Lincoln's opposition. He charged Polk with "gross & palpable lying," arguing that the true object of the war was "plunder & conquest." Bates said he was ashamed of his Whig brethren who voted for the war, "actuated by a narrow & groveling policy, and a selfish fear of injuring their own popularity, & injuriously affecting the coming Presidential election." To Bates, the war was part of a conspiracy to extend the reach of slavery—a belief he shared with many other Whigs, though not with Lincoln, who argued it was simply "a war of conquest brought into existence to catch votes."

Whether or not it was begun to extend slavery, the war brought the issue of slavery expansion to the forefront. While the early battles were still raging, a little-known congressman from Pennsylvania, David Wilmot, had penned a historic amendment to a war appropriations bill providing that "neither slavery nor involuntary servitude shall ever exist in any part of said territory" acquired from Mexico—lands that would eventually comprise California, Nevada, Utah, Arizona, and New Mexico. This Wilmot Proviso was repeatedly passed in the House and repeatedly blocked in the Southern-dominated Senate. Its status became a battleground in the conflict between North and South. The issue of slavery in the territories would become *the* defining issue in the years that followed.

Seward, Chase, and Lincoln all favored the ban on slavery from entering the territories acquired from Mexico. Even before the Wilmot Proviso had been introduced, Lincoln positioned himself against the expansion of slavery, a position he would hold for the rest of his career, arguing that while the Constitution protected slavery in the states where it already existed, "we should never knowingly lend ourselves directly or indirectly, to prevent that slavery from dying a natural death—to find new places for it to live in, when it can no longer exist in the old."

In Missouri, Bates also supported the Wilmot Proviso, though for different reasons. Bates considered the problem of extending slavery into these new lands a practical rather than a moral question. If Southerners brought their slaves into the West in large numbers, he feared that migration of free whites would come to a halt, thereby precluding growth and progress in the region. More important, he worried that the agitation over the slavery issue, which he blamed equally on Northern abolitionists and Southern extremists, would pull the country apart.

Bates had reason to fear so. South Carolina's John Calhoun led the vocal opposition to the Proviso, denouncing it as an unconstitutional act that would deny Southerners the right to move freely "with their property" into commonly held American territory. Moreover, if slavery were banned from the new territories, free states would join the Union and skew the balance of power. The South, already losing ground in the House of Representatives to the more populous North, would lose its historic strength in the Senate as well. Southern interests would be subject to the dictates of an increasingly hostile North. This was a future the South would never accept. "The madmen of the North and North West," editorialized the *Richmond Enquirer*, "have, we fear, cast the die, and numbered the days of this glorious Union." Thus the debate over the war became a conflict over slavery and a threat to the Union itself.

• • •

DURING THIS PERIOD of great political stress and turmoil, Lincoln came to sorely miss the companionship of his wife and the presence of his children. The couple's correspondence from this time gives us nearly all the direct evidence we have of their relationship. Almost all other information must be gleaned from outside observers, some of whom regarded Mary with extreme hostility or believed that she was unworthy of her husband.

"When you were here," Lincoln wrote Mary on April 16, 1848, "I thought you hindered me some in attending to business; but now, having nothing but business—no variety—it has grown exceedingly tasteless to me . . . I hate to stay in this old room by myself." He recounted with pride that he had gone shopping for the children, and told her how he enjoyed her letters. He was pleased to hear that, for the first springtime since he had known her, she had been "free from head-ache." Then he added teasingly, "I am afraid you will get so well, and fat, and young, as to be wanting to marry again."

"My dear Husband," Mary answered, writing on a Saturday night after the children were asleep. "How much, I wish instead of writing, *we* were together this evening, I feel very sad away from you." She described the children and their doings, and coyly needled that Mr. Webb, who had unsuccessfully sought her hand in their Springfield days, was coming to Shelbyville, Kentucky. "I must go down about that time & carry on quite a flirtation, you know *we*, always had a *penchant* that way." In closing, she reassured him: "Do not fear the children, have forgotten you. . . . Even E(ddy's) eyes brighten at the mention of your name—My love to all."

Lincoln quickly responded: "The leading matter in your letter, is your wish to return to this side of the Mountains. Will you be a *good girl* in all things, if I consent?" Most likely, he was referring here to the problems Mary had experienced with the other boarders, and her unhappiness about the amount of work he had to do. Assuming that she had already affirmatively answered his question, he continued: "Then come along, and that as *soon* as possible. Having got the idea in my head, I shall be impatient till I see you." These letters are replete with gossip about their acquaintances in Washington and Springfield, detailed news of the children, some mention of Lincoln's political activities, gentle teasing, and expressions of longing, both for companionship and, by implication, for intimacy. In the fall of 1848, Mary and the children returned to Washington.

In June of that year, Lincoln joined his fellow Whigs in Philadelphia, where they nominated Mexican War hero General Zachary Taylor for president, hoping that military glory could work its magic once more, as it had for George Washington, Andrew Jackson, and William Henry Harrison. "I am in favor of Gen: Taylor," Lincoln wrote, "because I am satisfied we can elect him . . . and that we can not elect any other whig." He explained to Herndon that the nomination of Taylor would strike the Democrats "on the blind side. It turns the war thunder against them. The war is now to them, the gallows of Haman, which they built for us, and on which they are doomed to be hanged themselves."

Seward was not happy with his party's choice of Taylor, a slaveholder with no political affiliation. Even worse was the selection of his rival New Yorker Millard Fillmore for vice president. Nor did he like the party's gauzy platform, which avoided any discussion of important national issues, including the divisive Wilmot Proviso. He said that he would "very willingly" throw his support "in favor of a different candidate if it could be seen that it would hasten the triumph of Universal Freedom." Thurlow Weed, desiring above all to win, insisted that Taylor was fundamentally a nationalist who would protect Northern interests better than the Democratic candidate, Lewis Cass of Michigan. Cass was considered a "doughface"—a Northern man with Southern principles. Moreover, the Democratic platform explicitly opposed Wilmot's attempt to introduce the slavery issue into congressional deliberations. Finally, Seward, like

Lincoln and Bates, supported Taylor, in the hope that his candidacy would allow the minority Whigs to attract Northern Democrats and independent voters, and thereby widen their base.

Chase, once again, pursued a different strategy. With the question of slavery in the territories at the forefront of national politics, he believed the time had come for a broad Northern party that would unite Liberty men with antislavery Democrats and "conscience" Whigs. He joined together with others, including Charles Sumner of Massachusetts, to convene an antislavery party convention in Buffalo, in August 1848. Ten thousand men answered the call. The spirited gathering elected Chase president of the convention and placed him in charge of drafting a platform for the new party, the Free Soil Party.

During the deliberations, a Buffalo delegate wrote to Bates asking if his name could be entered as a candidate for the vice presidency. That Bates would even be considered illustrates the fluidity of parties at this juncture, for even though he opposed slavery's expansion, he himself remained a slaveowner, his belief in the inferiority of the black race reflecting his Southern upbringing. In contrast to Seward and Chase, he supported Northern codes that prevented blacks from voting, sitting on juries, or holding office. When one of his female slaves escaped to Canada, he had been incredulous. "Poor foolish thing," he wrote in his diary. "She will never be as well off as she was in our house." She had left behind three daughters, whom he promptly sold, "determined at once to be no longer plagued with them."

Not surprisingly, Bates declined the Free Soil nomination. While he endorsed the party's "true doctrine" that "Congress ought never to establish slavery where they did not find it," he did not believe that this sole principle could sustain a national party. Even if offered the chance to be president, he claimed, he would never agree to "join a sectional, geographical party."

After several days of deliberation, the Buffalo convention nominated former president Martin Van Buren for president and Charles Francis Adams for vice president. Following the motto suggested by Chase of "Free Soil, Free Speech, Free Labor and Free Men," the party pledged to "prohibit slavery extension" to the territories, setting in motion a hard-fought three-way contest.

In September 1848, with Congress in recess, Lincoln made his first foray into presidential politics, campaigning for Zachary Taylor throughout the Northeast. Arriving uninvited in Worcester, Massachusetts, he was happy to oblige the chairman of a Whig gathering who found himself without a speaker. Reporting on Lincoln's impromptu speech, the Boston

Daily Advertiser observed that the tall congressman had "an intellectual face, showing a searching mind, and a cool judgment," and that he carried "the audience with him in his able arguments and brilliant illustrations." When he finished, "the audience gave three enthusiastic cheers for Illinois, and three more for the eloquent Whig member from that State."

During this campaign swing, at a great Whig rally at the Tremont Temple in Boston, Seward and Lincoln met for the first time. Lincoln later acknowledged that his meeting with Seward that night "had probably made a stronger impression on his memory than it had on Governor Seward's."

Both men were seated on the same platform in the spacious hall that served Boston as a religious and a secular meeting place. Seward, as the star attraction, spoke first, monopolizing most of the evening. Whereas most Whig speakers concentrated on internal improvements, the tariff, and public lands, Seward focused on slavery. He defended Taylor as a good man, trustworthy to support the Whigs' determination to prevent slavery from expanding into those territories acquired by the Mexican War, though he hoped "the time will come, and that not far distant, when the citizens of the whole country, as well as Massachusetts, will select for their leader a freeman of the north, in preference to a slaveholder." Gaining momentum, Seward predicted the "time will soon arrive when further demonstrations will be made against the institution of slavery," eventually moving public conscience to liberate all the nation's slaves.

The hour was late when Lincoln was introduced, but he captivated his audience with what the *Boston Courier* described as "a most forcible and convincing speech," which scored a series of capital "hits" against both Democrat Cass and Free-Soiler Van Buren, whom he nicknamed the "artful dodger" of Kinderhook, referring to his frequent shifts of party and position. He concluded "amidst repeated rounds of deafening applause." Recalling Lincoln's "rambling, story-telling" speech more than two decades later, Seward agreed that it put "the audience in good humor," but he pointedly noted that it avoided "any extended discussion of the slavery question."

The next night, Seward and Lincoln shared the same room in a Worcester hotel. "We spent the greater part of the night talking," Seward remembered years later, "I insisting that the time had come for sharp definition of opinion and boldness of utterance." Listening with "a thoughtful air," Lincoln said: "I reckon you are right. We have got to deal with this slavery question, and got to give much more attention to it hereafter than we have been doing." While Lincoln had consistently voted for the Wilmot Proviso, he had not delivered a single speech on the issue of slavery or initiated anything to promote the issue. As the conversation drew to a close and the two men went to sleep side by side, they must have presented a comical image—the one nearly half a foot longer and a decade younger; Seward's disorderly mass of straw-colored hair on the pillow beside Lincoln's wiry shock of black hair.

Years later, as president, Lincoln recalled his trip to Massachusetts. "I went with hay seed in my hair to learn deportment in the most cultivated State in the Union." He recalled in vivid detail a dinner at the governor's house—"a superb dinner; by far the finest I ever saw in my life. And the great men who were there, too! Why, I can tell you just how they were arranged at table," whereupon he proceeded to do just that.

The Whigs triumphed at the polls that November, bringing Zachary Taylor to the White House. It was to be the last national victory for the Whigs, who, four years later, divided on the slavery issue, would win only four states. To Chase's delight, Free-Soiler Martin Van Buren polled more than 10 percent of the vote among the Northern electorate—enough to prove that antislavery had become a force in national politics. Indeed, in several Northern states, including New York, the votes for Van Buren that otherwise might have gone to the Democrats spelled victory for the Whigs.

When Lincoln returned to Congress for the rump session, influenced, perhaps, by his encounter with Seward, he drafted a proposal for the gradual emancipation of slaves in the nation's capital, pending approval by the District's voters. Similar proposals had been attempted before, but Lincoln now added several elements. He included provisions to compensate owners for the full value of the slaves with government funds and to allow government officials from slaveholding states to bring their servants while on government business. Finally, to mitigate the fears of Southern slaveholders in surrounding states, he added a provision requiring District authorities "to provide active and efficient means to arrest, and deliver up to their owners, all fugitive slaves escaping into said District." It was this last provision that prompted abolitionist Wendell Phillips to castigate him as "that slave hound from Illinois."

Through long and careful conversations with dozens of fellow Whigs, Lincoln thought he had devised a reasonable compromise that could gain the support of both moderates in the South and the strong antislavery wing in the North. Yet, once the proposal was distributed, Lincoln found that his support had evaporated. Increasingly bitter divisiveness had eclipsed any possibility of compromise. Zealous antislavery men objected to both the fugitive slave provision and the idea of compensating owners in any way, while Southerners argued that abolishing slavery in the District would open the door to abolishing slavery in the country at large. Disappointed but realistic in his appraisal of the situation, Lincoln never introduced his bill. "Finding that I was abandoned by my former backers and having little personal influence," he said, "I *dropped* the matter knowing it was useless to prosecute the business at that time."

His congressional term ending in March 1849, Lincoln campaigned vigorously for a presidential appointment as Commissioner of the Land Office—the highest office that would go to Illinois. On the strength of his services to the Taylor campaign, he believed he deserved the position. As commissioner, he would be responsible for deciding how to distribute all the public lands in the state. The office was awarded to another. It was just as well that Abraham Lincoln was not appointed. His strengths were those of the public leader, not the bureaucratic manager. "If I have one vice," he later quipped, "and I can call it nothing else,—it is not to be able to say no!" He then smiled and added: "Thank God for not making me a woman, but if He had, I suppose He would have made me just as ugly as He did, and no one would ever have tempted me."

Before he returned to Springfield, the former flatboatman applied to patent a method of lifting boats over shoals and bars by means of inflatable "buoyant chambers." Unfortunately, no analogous device existed to refloat a political career run aground. His securely Whig congressional district had turned Democratic, a shift many Whigs blamed on Lincoln's criticisms of the war. He was out of office, with little immediate prospect of return. Assessing his brief congressional tenure, there was little to celebrate. His term, John Nicolay wrote, "added practically nothing to his reputation." He had been a diligent congressman, making nearly all the roll calls and serving his party faithfully, but his efforts to distinguish himself—to make a mark—had failed.

All these disappointments notwithstanding, Lincoln had forged relationships and impressed men who would contribute significantly to his future success, including Caleb Smith of Indiana and Joshua Giddings of Ohio, Westerners whose political careers were similar to his.

Born in Boston, Caleb Smith had migrated west as a young man, ending up in Indiana, where he read law, was admitted to the bar, and entered politics as a Whig. He was a "handsome, trimly-built man," with a "smooth oval face." Despite a lisp, his power on the stump was celebrated far and wide. It was said that he could make you "feel the blood tingling through your veins to your finger ends and all the way up your spine." Indeed, one contemporary observer considered Smith a more compelling public speaker than Lincoln. Later, at the 1860 Republican Convention, Smith would help swing the Indiana delegation to Lincoln, a move that would lay the foundation for Lincoln's presidential nomination.

Joshua Giddings had faced obstacles as formidable as Lincoln. He had left his family and small farming community in Ashtabula County, Ohio, to study law in the town of Canfield, Ohio. His decision stunned his friends and neighbors. "He had lived with them from childhood, and toiled with them in the fields," his son-in-law, George Julian, observed. "He had never enjoyed the means of obtaining even a common-school education, and they regarded his course as the effect of a vain desire to defeat the designs of Providence, according to which they believed that people born in humble life should be content with their lot." Fourteen years older than Lincoln, Giddings was first elected to Congress in 1838. Reelected continuously after that, he threw himself at once into John Quincy Adams's valiant struggle over the right of Congress to receive antislavery petitions. While Giddings was decidedly more militant on the slavery issue than Lincoln, the two became close friends. Boarding together at Mrs. Spriggs's house in Carroll Row on Capitol Hill, they shared hundreds of meals, conversations, and stories. So much did Giddings like and respect Lincoln that seven years later, in 1855, when Lincoln ran for the Senate, Giddings proclaimed that he "would walk clear to Illinois" to help elect him.

Among Lincoln's Whig colleagues was Alexander Stephens of Georgia, later vice president of the Confederate states. Transfixed by Stephens's eloquent speaking style, Lincoln wrote a friend that "a little slim, pale-faced, consumptive man . . . has just concluded the very best speech, of an hour's length, I ever heard. My old, withered, dry eyes, are full of tears yet." (Lincoln was not yet forty.) Many years later, the classically educated Stephens recalled: "Mr. Lincoln was careful as to his manners, awkward in his speech, but was possessed of a very strong, clear and vigorous mind. He always attracted the riveted attention of the House when he spoke; his manner of speech as well as thought was original . . . his anecdotes were always exceedingly apt and pointed, and socially he always kept his company in a roar of laughter."

Lincoln's ability to win the respect of others, to earn their trust and even devotion, would prove essential in his rise to power. There was something mysterious in his persona that led countless men, even old adversaries, to feel bound to him in admiration.

• • •

TAKING UP HIS LAW PRACTICE once more, Lincoln began to feel, he later remarked, that he "was losing interest in politics." The likely reality was that his position on the Mexican War had temporarily closed the door to political office. Furthermore, this withdrawal from office was never complete. He worked to secure political posts for fellow Illinoisans, and joined in a call for a convention to reorganize the Whig Party. Through his lengthy eulogies for several Whig leaders, he spoke out on national issues, referring to slavery as "the one *great* question of the day." And he never missed an opportunity to criticize Stephen Douglas, now a leading national figure.

In the interim, he resolved to work at the law with "greater earnestness." His Springfield practice flourished, providing a steady income. Mary was able to enlarge their home, hire additional help with the household chores, and entertain more freely. These years should have been happy ones for Mary, but death intervened to crush her spirits. In the summer after Lincoln returned from Washington, Mary's father died during a cholera epidemic. He was only fifty-eight at the time, still vigorous and actively involved in politics; in fact, he was running for a seat in the Kentucky Senate when he succumbed to the epidemic. Six months later, Eliza Parker, Mary's beloved maternal grandmother, died in Lexington. To this grandmother, the six-year-old Mary had turned for love and consolation when her mother died.

February 1, 1850, brought Mary's most terrible loss: the death of her second son, three-year-old Eddie, from pulmonary tuberculosis. That destiny had branded her for misery became her conviction. For seven weeks, Mary had worked to arrest the high fever and racking cough that accompanied the relentless disease. Despite her ministrations, Eddie declined until he fell into unconsciousness and died early on the morning of the 1st. Neighbors recalled hearing Mary's inconsolable weeping. For days, she remained in her bed, refusing to eat, unable to stop crying. Only Lincoln, though despairing himself, was able to reach her. "Eat, Mary," he begged her, "for we must live."

Finally, Mary found some solace in long conversations with the pastor of the First Presbyterian Church, James Smith, who had conducted the funeral service for Eddie. So comforting was the pastor's faith in an eternal life after death that Mary was moved to join his congregation and renew her religious faith. A grateful Lincoln rented a family pew at the First Presbyterian and occasionally accompanied Mary to church, though he remained unable to share her thought that Eddie awaited their reunion in some afterlife.

Though Mary became pregnant again a month after Eddie's death, giving birth to a third son, William Wallace, in December 1850, and a fourth son, Thomas, in April 1853, Eddie's death left an indelible scar on her psyche—deepening her mood swings, magnifying her weaknesses, and increasing her fears. Tales of her erratic behavior began to circulate, stories of "hysterical outbursts" against her husband, rumors that she chased him through the yard with a knife, drove him from the house with a broomstick, smashed his head with a chunk of wood. Though the outbursts generally subsided as swiftly as they had begun, her instability and violent episodes unquestionably caused great upheavals in the family life.

When Mary fell into one of these moods, Lincoln developed what one neighbor called "a protective deafness," which doubtless exasperated her fury. Instead of engaging Mary directly, he would lose himself in thought, quietly leave the room, or take the children for a walk. If the discord continued, he would head to the state library or his office, where he would occasionally remain through the night until the emotional storm had ceased.

Had his marriage been happier, Lincoln's friends believed, he would have been satisfied as a country lawyer. Had he married "a woman of more angelic temperament," Springfield lawyer Milton Hay speculated, "he, doubtless, would have remained at home more and been less inclined to mingle with people outside."

Though a tranquil domestic union might have made Lincoln a happier man, the supposition that he would have been a contented homebody, like Edward Bates, belies everything we know of Lincoln's fierce ambition and extraordinary drive—an ambition that drove him to devour books in every spare moment, memorize his father's stories in order to captivate his friends, study law late into the night after a full day's work, and run for office at the age of twenty-three. Indeed, long before his political career even took shape, he had been determined to win the veneration of his fellow men by "rendering [himself] worthy" of their esteem.

Even as Lincoln focused his attention on the law, he was simply waiting for events to turn, waiting for the right time to reenter public life.

• • •

IF LINCOLN'S AMBITIONS appeared to have stalled, the careers of Seward and Chase gathered new momentum. Zachary Taylor's triumph at the polls created a Whig majority in the New York state legislature for the first time in many years. Because U.S. senators at the time were elected by state legislatures rather than by popular vote, Thurlow Weed focused his magic on the legislature to propel Seward into the U.S. Senate. His task was complicated by the division of the state's Whig Party into two distinct factions. Millard Fillmore, bolstered by his election as vice president, led the conservative wing, composed of merchants, capitalists, and cotton manufacturers who preferred to defuse the slavery issue. Weed and Seward represented the liberal wing.

Weed's difficulties were compounded when New York papers reported a fiery speech Seward delivered in Cleveland, putting him at odds with the more moderate stance of the new administration. "There are two antagonistical elements of society in America," Seward had proclaimed, "freedom and slavery. Freedom is in harmony with our system of government and with the spirit of the age, and is therefore passive and quiescent. Slavery is in conflict with that system, with justice, and with humanity, and is therefore organized, defensive, active, and perpetually aggressive." Free labor, he said, demands universal suffrage and the widespread "diffusion of knowledge." The slave-based system, by contrast "cherishes ignorance because it is the only security for oppression." Sectional conflict, Seward warned, would inevitably arise from these two intrinsically different economic systems, which were producing dangerously divergent cultures, values, and assumptions.

Seward stood before his Cleveland audience and called for the abolition of the black codes that prevented blacks from voting, sitting on juries, or holding office in Ohio. Slavery, he conceded, was once the sin of all the states. "We in New York are guilty of slavery still, by withholding the right of suffrage from the race we have emancipated. You in Ohio are guilty in the same way, by a system of black-laws still more aristocratic and odious." Seward's support that day for the black vote, black presence on juries, and black officeholding was startlingly radical for a mainstream politician. Even a full decade later, during his debates with Stephen Douglas, Abraham Lincoln would maintain that he had never been in favor "of making voters or jurors of negroes, nor of qualifying them to hold office, nor to intermarry."

Although the difference in their positions was due largely to the contrasting political environments of the more progressive New York and the conservative, Southern-leaning Illinois, Seward was more willing than Lincoln to employ language designed to ignite the emotions of particular crowds, tailoring his rhetoric to suit the convictions of his immediate audience. Knowing that his audience in the Western Reserve was likely far more progressive than many Eastern audiences, Seward ventured further toward abolitionism than he had in the past. Even so, the *Cleveland Plain Dealer* charged, Seward fell short of the antislavery zeal that put the Reserve a decade ahead of the East Coast.

Nor did Seward stop with his condemnation of the Black Laws, he proceeded to deliver a powerful attack against the Fugitive Slave Law, written, he claimed, in violation of divine law. He brought his speech to a close with a stirring appeal intended to rouse his audience to act. " 'Can nothing be done for freedom because the public conscience is inert?' Yes, much can be done—everything can be done. Slavery can be limited to its present bounds, it can be ameliorated, it *can* be and *must* be abolished and you and I can and must do it."

Seward's speech worried Weed. Though he agreed that slavery was "a political crime and a national curse—a great moral and political evil," he predicted that "this question of slavery, when it becomes a matter of political controversy, will shake, if not unsettle, the foundations of our Government. It is too fearful, and too mighty, in all its bearings and consequences, to be recklessly mixed up in our partisan conflicts."

At a time when professed abolitionists remained an unpopular minority, subjected in some Northern cities to physical assault, Weed warned Seward that his provocative language would place him in the same camp with extremist figures such as William Lloyd Garrison and Wendell Phillips. Seward weighed Weed's concerns, acknowledging that the emancipation issue had not fully "ripened." In the weeks that followed, he muted his stridency on slavery, allowing Weed the space necessary to carry his protégé to the next level. Weed ingratiated Seward with the legislators one by one. He rounded up the liberals and assured the moderates that when Seward talked about slavery, he "wanted to level society up, not down." Furthermore, he promised the Taylor administration that Seward would loyally follow the moderate party line. Despite the split in the party and Fillmore's rising star, Weed managed to corral a majority and send his friend Seward to the Senate.

"Probably no man ever yet appeared for the first time in Congress so widely known and so warmly appreciated," declared the *New York Tribune* after his election. Seward arrived with an aura of celebrity, even notoriety. Yet Weed proved correct when he anticipated that Seward's radical speech in Cleveland would come back to haunt him. Not long after the young New Yorker was sworn into the Senate, a Southern senator rose from his seat and read aloud the peroration in which Seward told his audience that slavery "can and must be abolished." It was said that "a shudder" ran through the chamber. "If we ever find you in Georgia," one letter writer warned Seward, "you will forfeit your odious neck."

• • •

SALMON CHASE'S BID for success through a viable antislavery party came to fruition in 1849. Thirteen Free-Soilers had been elected to the seventy-two-member Ohio state legislature, which would choose the next U.S. senator. Neither the Whigs nor the Democrats had a controlling majority, which gave the tiny Free Soil bloc enormous leverage. Though many assumed that former Whig Joshua Giddings, who had championed the antislavery cause in Congress for more than a decade, had earned the right to be considered the front-runner, Chase managed to gain the seat for himself. Ironically, his winning tactics in pursuit of this goal would shadow his career and ultimately bring him the lasting enmity of many important figures in his own state.

Most of the Free-Soilers were former Whigs who would not vote with the Democrats. They favored Giddings. Two independents, meanwhile, vacillated: Dr. Norton Townshend, once a Democrat, who had been a member of the Liberty Party; and John F. Morse, formerly a "conscience Whig." The decisions of these two men would prove pivotal. Working behind the scenes, Chase drafted a deal with Samuel Medary, the boss of the Democratic Party in Ohio. If Chase delivered Townshend and Morse to the Democrats, Medary would see to it that Chase became the new U.S. senator. In addition, the Democrats would vote to repeal the Black Laws, a condition Morse insisted upon before he would agree to the deal. In return, the Democrats would have the House speakership and control of the extensive patronage that office enjoyed. For Medary, control of the state was far more important than naming a senator.

Chase worked ceaselessly to deliver Townshend and Morse to the Democrats. While Giddings remained in Washington, Chase journeyed to Columbus and took a room at the Neil House close to the state Capitol so he could attend Free Soil caucuses at night and negotiate with individual Democrats during the day. He planted articles in key newspapers, praising not only himself but Townshend and Morse. He lent money to more than one paper, and when the needs of the Free Soil weekly, the Columbus *Daily Standard*, exceeded his means, he reassured its editor: "After the Senatorial Election, whether the choice falls on me or another, I can act more efficiently, and you may rely on me." He advanced money to the *Standard* and later agreed to a loan but refused to take a mortgage on the newspaper as security because he did not want his name publicly connected, "which could not be avoided in case of a mortgage to myself."

Knowing that Morse was introducing a bill to establish separate schools for blacks, Chase enlisted the editor of the *Standard* to help get it passed. "It is really important," he urged, "and if it can be got through with the help of democratic votes, will do a great deal of good to the cause generally & our friend Morse especially." Certainly, it would do a great deal of good for the career of Salmon Chase, who sanctimoniously told Morse that the only consideration in determining the next senator should be ability to best advance the cause: "Every thing, but sacrifice of principle, for the Cause, and nothing for men except as instruments of the Cause." Advancement of self and advancement of the cause were intertwined in Chase's mind. In Chase's mind, both were served when Morse and Townshend voted with the Democrats to organize the legislature and the victorious Medary swung his new Democratic majority to Chase for senator.

The unusual circumstances of Chase's election provoked negative comment in the press. "Every act of his was subsidiary to his own ambition," charged the *Ohio State Journal:* "He talked of the interests of Free Soil, he *meant* His Own." This judgment by a hostile paper was perhaps unduly harsh, for the deal with the Democrats did indeed end up promoting the Free Soil cause. As Medary had promised, the Democrats voted to repeal the hated Black Laws. And when Chase reached the Senate, he would become a stalwart leader in the antislavery cause.

Nonetheless, fallout from Chase's Senate election eventually found its way into the widely circulated pages of Horace Greeley's *New York Tribune.* Editorializing on the machinations involved, Greeley declared that he did "not see how men who desire to maintain a decent reputation can countenance or profit by it." Indeed, the suspicions and mistrust engendered by the peculiar circumstances of the Senate election would never be wholly erased. "It lost to him at once and forever the confidence of every Whig of middle age in Ohio," a fellow politician observed. "Its shadow never wholly dispelled, always fell upon him, and hovered near and darkened his pathway at the critical places in his political after life." The Whigs, and their later counterparts, the Republicans, would deny Chase the united support of the Ohio delegation so vital to his hopes for the presidential nomination in 1860. And Chase, for his part, would never forgive them.

Showing little intuitive sense of how others might view his maneuvering, Chase failed to appreciate that with each party shift, he betrayed old associates and made lifelong enemies. Certainly, his willingness to sever bonds and forge new alliances, though at times courageous and visionary, was out of step with the political custom of the times.

Though troubled by the criticism attending his election, Chase was thrilled with his victory. So was Charles Sumner, who would join Chase two years later in the Senate by way of a similar alliance between Free-Soilers and independent Democrats in Massachusetts. "I can hardly believe it," Sumner wrote. "It does seem to me that this is 'the beginning of the end.' Your election must influence all the Great West. Still more your presence in the Senate will give an unprecedented impulse to the discussion of our cause."

When Chase took his seat in the handsome Senate chamber in March 1849, nearly twenty years had elapsed since his early days as a poor teacher living on the margins of the city's social whirl. Now, as a renowned political organizer, prominent lawyer, and fabled antislavery crusader, Chase could claim a place in the first tier of Washington society. William Wirt would have been proud. For a brief moment, Chase's relentless need "to be first wherever I may be" was sated.

As the 1840s drew to a close, William Henry Seward and Salmon P. Chase had moved toward the summit of political power in the United States Senate. Edward Bates, though spending most of his days at his country home with his ever-growing family, had become a widely respected national figure, considered a top prospect for a variety of high political posts. Abraham Lincoln, by contrast, was practicing law, regaling his fellow lawyers on the circuit with an endless stream of anecdotes, and reflecting with silent absorption on the great issues of the day.

▪ POLITICAL MAP OF THE

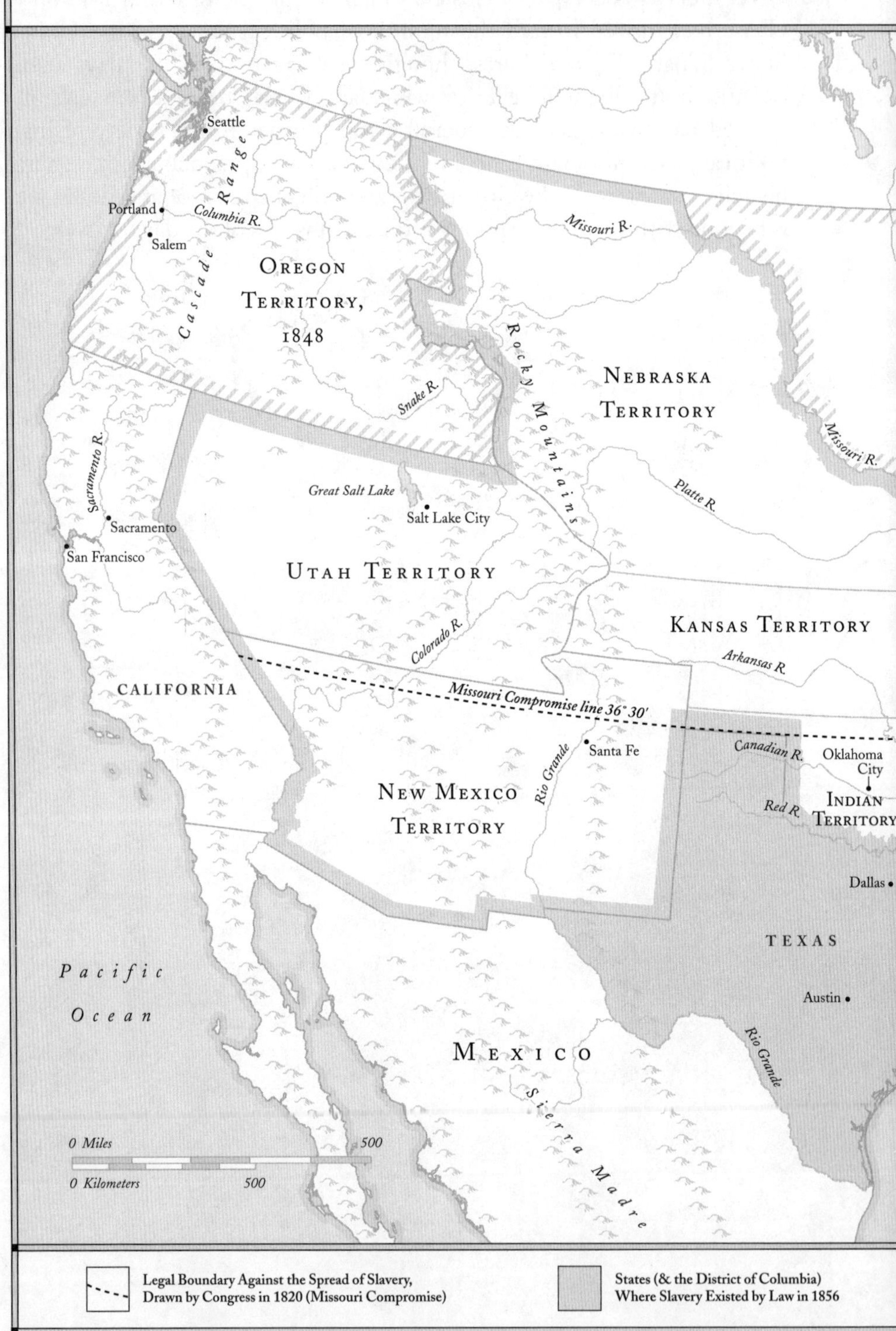
Seattle
Cascade Range
Portland
Salem
Columbia R.
OREGON TERRITORY, 1848
Missouri R.
Rocky Mountains
NEBRASKA TERRITORY
Missouri R.
Snake R.
Platte R.
Sacramento R.
Great Salt Lake
Salt Lake City
Sacramento
San Francisco
UTAH TERRITORY
KANSAS TERRITORY
Colorado R.
Arkansas R.
CALIFORNIA
Missouri Compromise line 36° 30′
Santa Fe
Rio Grande
Canadian R.
Oklahoma City
INDIAN TERRITORY
Red R.
NEW MEXICO TERRITORY
Dallas
TEXAS
Pacific Ocean
Austin
Rio Grande
MEXICO
Sierra Madre
0 Miles
500
0 Kilometers
500
Legal Boundary Against the Spread of Slavery, Drawn by Congress in 1820 (Missouri Compromise)
States (& the District of Columbia) Where Slavery Existed by Law in 1856

United States, circa 1856

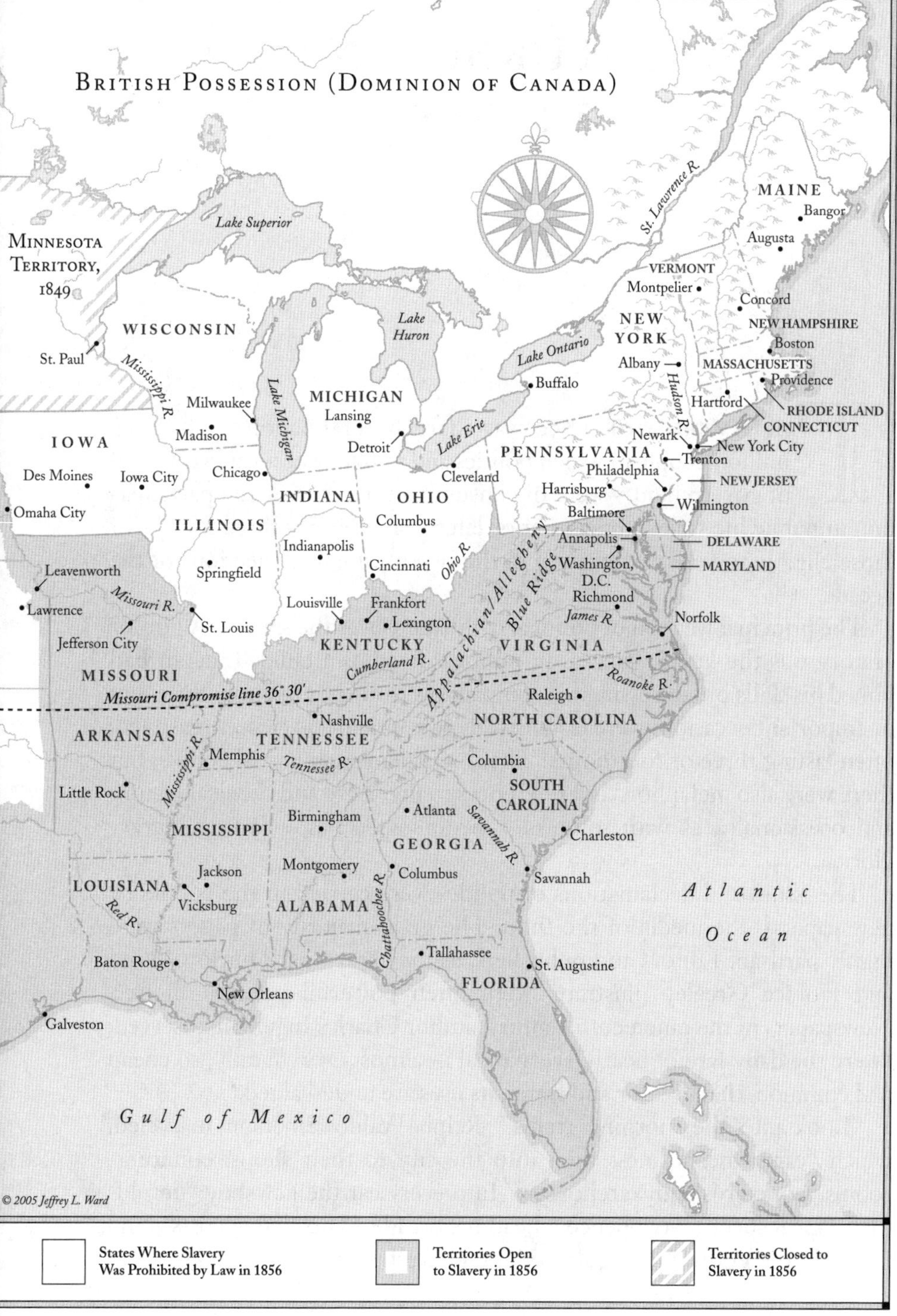
British Possession (Dominion of Canada)
Minnesota Territory, 1849
Lake Superior
Lake Huron
Lake Michigan
Lake Ontario
Lake Erie
St. Lawrence R.
MAINE
Bangor
Augusta
VERMONT
Montpelier
NEW YORK
Albany
Hudson R.
Concord
NEW HAMPSHIRE
Boston
MASSACHUSETTS
Providence
Hartford
RHODE ISLAND
CONNECTICUT
Newark
New York City
Trenton
NEW JERSEY
WISCONSIN
St. Paul
Mississippi R.
Milwaukee
Madison
MICHIGAN
Lansing
Detroit
Buffalo
IOWA
Des Moines
Iowa City
Omaha City
Chicago
INDIANA
OHIO
Cleveland
PENNSYLVANIA
Philadelphia
Harrisburg
Wilmington
Baltimore
Annapolis
DELAWARE
Washington, D.C.
MARYLAND
ILLINOIS
Columbus
Indianapolis
Springfield
Cincinnati
Ohio R.
Appalachian/Allegheny
Blue Ridge
Richmond
James R.
Norfolk
Leavenworth
Lawrence
Missouri R.
St. Louis
Louisville
Frankfort
Lexington
Jefferson City
KENTUCKY
VIRGINIA
Cumberland R.
MISSOURI
Missouri Compromise line 36° 30′
Roanoke R.
Raleigh
Nashville
NORTH CAROLINA
ARKANSAS
TENNESSEE
Memphis
Tennessee R.
Columbia
SOUTH CAROLINA
Little Rock
Atlanta
Savannah R.
Birmingham
MISSISSIPPI
Charleston
GEORGIA
Jackson
Montgomery
Columbus
Savannah
LOUISIANA
Vicksburg
ALABAMA
Red R.
Chattahoochee R.
Tallahassee
Baton Rouge
St. Augustine
FLORIDA
New Orleans
Galveston
Atlantic Ocean
Gulf of Mexico
© 2005 Jeffrey L. Ward
States Where Slavery Was Prohibited by Law in 1856
Territories Open to Slavery in 1856
Territories Closed to Slavery in 1856

CHAPTER 5

THE TURBULENT FIFTIES

The America of 1850 was a largely rural nation of about 23 million people in which politics and public issues—at every level of government—were of consuming interest. Citizen participation in public life far exceeded that of later years. Nearly three fourths of those eligible to vote participated in the two presidential elections of the decade.

The principal weapon of political combatants was the speech. A gift for oratory was the key to success in politics. Even as a child, Lincoln had honed his skills by addressing his companions from a tree stump. Speeches on important occasions were exhaustively researched and closely reasoned, often lasting three or four hours. There was demagoguery, of course, but there were also metaphors and references to literature and classical history and occasionally, as with some of Lincoln's speeches, a lasting literary glory.

The issues and declamations of politics were carried to the people by newspapers—the media of the time. The great majority of papers were highly partisan. Editors and publishers, as the careers of Thurlow Weed and Horace Greeley illustrate, were often powerful political figures. Newspapers in the nineteenth century, author Charles Ingersoll observed, "were the daily fare of nearly every meal in almost every family; so cheap and common, that, like air and water, its uses are undervalued."

"Look into the morning trains," Ralph Waldo Emerson marveled, which "carry the business men into the city to their shops, counting-rooms, workyards and warehouses." Into every car the newsboy "unfolds his magical sheets,—twopence a head his bread of knowledge costs—and instantly the entire rectangular assembly, fresh from their breakfast, are bending as one man to their second breakfast." A European tourist was amazed at the central role newspapers played in the life of the new nation. "You meet newspaper readers everywhere; and in the evening the whole city knows what lay twenty-four hours ago on newswriters' desks. . . . The few who cannot read can hear news discussed or read aloud in ale- and-oyster houses."

Seventeen years before the decade had begun, President Andrew Jackson had prophesied: "The nullifiers in the south intend to blow up a storm on the slave question . . . be assured these men would do any act to destroy this union and form a southern confederacy bounded, north, by the Potomac river."

And now the storm had come.

The slavery issue had been a source of division between North and South from the beginning of the nation. That difference was embodied in the Constitution itself, which provided that a slave would be counted as three fifths of a person for purposes of congressional representation and which imposed an obligation to surrender fugitive slaves to their lawful masters. Although slavery was not named in the Constitution, it was, as antislavery Congressman John Quincy Adams said, "written in the bond," which meant that he, like everyone else, must "faithfully perform its obligations."

The constitutional compromise that protected slavery in states where it already existed did not apply to newly acquired territories. Thus, every expansion of the nation reignited the divisive issue. The Missouri Compromise had provided a temporary solution for nearly three decades, but when Congress was called upon to decide the fate of the new territories acquired in the Mexican War, the stage was set for the renewal of the national debate. "If by your legislation you seek to drive us from the territories of California and New Mexico, purchased by the common blood and treasure of the whole people," Robert Toombs of Georgia warned, *"I am for disunion."* Mississippi called for a convention of Southern states to meet in Nashville for the defense of Southern rights.

The issue of slavery could no longer be put aside. It would dominate the debates in Congress. As Thomas Hart Benton once colorfully observed: "We read in Holy Writ, that a certain people were cursed by the plague of frogs, and that the plague was everywhere! You could not look upon the table but there were frogs, you could not sit down at the banquet but there were frogs, you could not go to the bridal couch and lift the sheets but there were frogs!" A similar affliction infested national discourse as every other topic was subsumed by slavery. "We can see nothing, touch nothing, have no measures proposed, without having this pestilence thrust before us. Here it is, this black question, forever on the table, on the nuptial couch, everywhere!"

Of course, slavery was not the only issue that divided the sections. The South opposed protective tariffs designed to foster Northern manufacturing and fought against using the national resources for internal improvements in Northern transportation. But issues like these, however hard fought, were subject to political accommodation. Slavery was not. "We must concern ourselves with what is, and slavery exists," said John Randolph of Virginia early in the century. Slavery "is to us a question of life and death." By the 1850s, Randolph's observation had come to fruition. The "peculiar institution" now permeated every aspect of Southern society—economically, politically, and socially. For a minority in the North, on the other hand, slavery represented a profoundly disturbing moral issue. For many more Northerners, the expansion of slavery into the territories threatened the triumph of the free labor movement. Events of the 1850s would put these "antagonistical elements" on a collision course.

"It is a great mistake," warned John Calhoun in 1850, "to suppose that disunion can be effected by a single blow. The cords which bind these States together in one common Union are far too numerous and powerful for that. Disunion must be the work of time. It is only through a long process . . . that the cords can be snapped until the whole fabric falls asunder. Already the agitation of the slavery question has snapped some of the most important." If these common cords continue to rupture, he predicted, "nothing will be left to hold the States together except force."

The spiritual cords of union—the great religious denominations—had already been fractured along sectional lines. The national political parties, the political cords of union, would be next, splintered in the struggle between those who wished to extend slavery and those who resisted its expansion. Early in the decade the national Whig Party, hopelessly divided on slavery, would begin to diminish and then disappear as a national force. The national Democratic Party, beset by defections from Free Soil Democrats, would steadily lose ground, fragmenting beyond repair by the end of the decade.

The ties that bound the Union were not simply institutions but a less tangible sense of nationhood—shared pride in the achievements of the revolutionary generation, a sense of mutual interests and common aspirations for the future. The chronicle of the 1850s is, at bottom, a narrative of the increasing strain placed upon these cords, their gradual fraying, and their final rupture. Abraham Lincoln would correctly prophesy that a house divided against itself could not stand. By the end of the decade, as Calhoun had warned, only force would be left to sustain the Union.

Was this outcome inevitable? It is not a question that can be answered in the abstract. We must begin with the historical realities and ask if the same actors with the same convictions, emotions, and passions could have behaved differently. Possibly, but all we can know for certain is that they felt what they felt, believed as they believed, and did as they would do. And so they moved the country inexorably toward Civil War.

• • •

As the 31st Congress opened, the rancorous discord boiled to the surface. All eyes turned to the seventy-three-year-old Henry Clay, who, Lincoln later said, was "regarded by all, as *the* man for a crisis." Henry Clay had saved the Union once before. Now, thirty years after the Missouri Compromise, the Congress and nation looked to him once again. Already Clay suffered from the tuberculosis that would take his life two years later. He could not even manage the stairs leading up to the Senate chamber. Nonetheless, when he took the floor to introduce the cluster of resolutions that would become known as the Compromise of 1850, he mustered, the *New York Tribune* marveled, "the spirit and the fire of youth."

He began by admitting he had never been "so anxious" facing his colleagues, for he believed the country stood "at the edge of the precipice." He beseeched his colleagues to halt "before the fearful and disastrous leap is taken in the yawning abyss below, which will inevitably lead to certain and irretrievable destruction." He prophesied that dissolution would bring a war "so furious, so bloody, so implacable and so exterminating" that it would be marked forever in the pages of history. To avoid catastrophe, a compromise must be reached.

His first resolution called for admitting the state of California immediately, leaving the decision regarding the status of slavery within its borders to California's new state legislature. As it was widely known that a majority of Californians wished to prohibit slavery entirely, this resolution favored the North. He then proposed dividing the remainder of the Mexican accession into two territories, New Mexico and Utah, with no restrictions on slavery—a provision that favored the South. He called for an end to the slave trade within the boundaries of the national capital, but called on Congress to strengthen the old Fugitive Slave Law of 1793 to facilitate the recapture of runaway slaves. Fugitives would be denied a jury trial, commissioners would adjudicate claims, and federal marshals would be empowered to draft citizens to hunt down escapees.

Clay recognized that the compromise resolutions demanded far greater concessions from the North than he had asked from the slave states, but he appealed to the North to sustain the Union. Northern objections to slavery were based on ideology and sentiment, rather than on the Southern concerns with property, social intercourse, habit, safety, and life itself. The North had nothing tangible to lose. Finally, he implored God that "if the direful and sad event of the dissolution of the Union shall happen, I may not survive to behold the sad and heart-rending spectacle." This prayer was answered. He died two years later, nearly a decade before the Civil War began.

Frances Seward was in the overcrowded gallery on February 5, 1850, when Henry Clay rose from his desk to speak. She had come to Washington to help her husband get settled in a spacious three-story brick house on the north side of F Street. "He *is* a charming orator," Frances confessed to her sister. "I have never heard but one more impressive speaker—and that is *our* Henry (don't say this to anybody)." But Clay was mistaken, she claimed, if he believed the wound between North and South could be sutured by his persuasive charm. Though he might make "doughfaces out of half the Congress," his arguments had not convinced her. Most upsetting was Clay's claim that "Northern men were only activated by policy and party spirits. Now if Henry Clay has lived to be 70 years old and still thinks slavery is opposed only from such motives I can only say he knows much less of human nature than I supposed."

Four weeks later, the galleries were once again filled to hear South Carolina's John Calhoun speak. Although unsteady in his walk and enveloped in flannels to ward off the chill of pneumonia that had plagued him all winter, the sixty-seven-year-old arch defender of states' rights appeared in the Senate with the text of the speech he intended to deliver. He rose with great difficulty from his chair and then, recognizing that he was too weak to speak, handed his remarks to his friend Senator James Mason of Virginia to read.

The speech was an uncompromising diatribe against the North. Calhoun warned that secession was the sole option unless the North conceded the Southern right to bring slavery into every section of the new territories, stopped agitating the slave question, and consented to a constitutional provision restoring the balance of power between the two regions. Making much the same argument he had utilized in the early debates surrounding the Wilmot Proviso, he warned that additional free states would tilt the power in the Senate, as well as in the House of Representatives, and destroy "the equilibrium between the two sections in the Government, as it stood when the constitution was ratified." This final address to the Senate concluded, Calhoun retired to his boardinghouse, where he would die before the month was out.

Daniel Webster of Massachusetts, the third of the "great triumvirate"(as Clay, Calhoun, and Webster were called), was scheduled to speak on the 7th of March. The Senate chamber was "crammed" with more men and women, a Washington newspaper reported, than on any previous occasion. Anticipation soared with the rumor that Webster had decided, against the fervent hopes of his overwhelmingly antislavery constituents, to support Clay's Southern-leaning compromise. Frances Seward was watching when the senator rose.

"I wish to speak to-day, not as a Massachusetts man, nor as a northern man, but as an American," Webster began. "I speak to-day for the preservation of the Union. 'Hear me for my cause.' " He proceeded to stun many in the North by castigating abolitionists, vowing never to support the Wilmot Proviso, and coming out in favor of every one of Clay's resolutions—including the provision to strengthen the hateful Fugitive Slave Law. Many in New England found Webster's new stand particularly abhorrent. "Mr Webster has deliberately taken out his name from all the files of honour," Ralph Waldo Emerson wrote. "He has undone all that he spent his years in doing."

Frances found the speech greatly disappointing. The word *"compromise,"* she told her sister, "is becoming hateful to me." Acknowledging that Webster was "a forcible speaker," particularly when he extolled the Union, she found him "much less eloquent than Henry Clay because his heart is decidedly colder—people must have feeling themselves to touch others." Despite such criticisms, the speech won nationwide approval from moderates who desperately wanted a peaceful settlement of the situation. A few antislavery Whigs expressed a fear that Seward might hesitate when the time came to deliver his own speech, scheduled three days later. "How little they know his nature," Frances wrote. "Every concession of Mr. Webster to Southern principles only makes Henry advocate more strongly the cause which he thinks just."

Frances was right. Antislavery advocates had no need to worry about her husband. For weeks, Seward had been working hard on his maiden address to the Senate, delivered on March 11, 1850. He had talked at length with Weed and rehearsed various drafts before Frances. The Capitol of the 1850s offered no private office space, so Seward wrote at home, rising early in the morning and working long past the midnight hour.

As he began his Senate oration, Seward spoke somewhat hesitantly. Reading from his manuscript without dramatic gestures, he quoted Machiavelli, Montesquieu, and the ancient philosophers in a voice so low that it seemed he was talking to himself rather than addressing the chamber and the galleries. His words were so powerful, however, that Webster was riveted; while John Calhoun, attending one of his final sessions in the chamber, was "restless at first" but "soon sat still."

Seward began by maintaining flatly that he was opposed to compromise, "in any and all the forms in which it has been proposed." He refused to strengthen the Fugitive Slave Law. "We are not slaveholders. We cannot . . . be either true Christians or real freemen," he continued, "if we impose on another a chain that we defy all human power to fasten on ourselves." He declared that a ban on the slave trade in the District was insufficient: slavery itself must be abolished in the capital. Finally, staunchly affirming the Wilmot Proviso, he refused to accept the introduction of slavery anywhere in the new territories.

As he moved into the second hour of his speech, his conviction gave him ease and confidence. Step by step, he laid the foundation for the "higher law" doctrine that would be forever associated with his name. Not only did the Constitution bind the American people to goals incompatible with slavery, he asserted, "but there is a higher law than the Constitution, which regulates our authority over the domain, and devotes it to the same noble purposes. The territory is a part . . . of the common heritage of mankind, bestowed upon them by the Creator of the universe. We are his stewards."

With this single speech, his first national address, Seward became the principal antislavery voice in the Senate. Tens of thousands of copies of the speech were printed and distributed throughout the North. The *New York Tribune* predicted that it would awaken the nation, that his words would "live longer, be read with a more hearty admiration, and exert a more potential and pervading influence on the National mind and character than any other speech of the Session."

• • •

ARRIVING ON THE NATIONAL SCENE at this same dramatic moment, Chase expected to take a leading role in the fight. He, too, labored over his speech for weeks, poring through old statute books and exchanging ideas with fellow crusader Charles Sumner. The bond between Chase and Sumner would continue to grow through the years, providing both men with emotional support in the face of the condemnation they suffered due to their strong antislavery views. "I find no man so congenial to me as yourself," Chase confided in Sumner. For his part, Sumner considered Chase "a tower of strength" whose election to the Senate would "confirm the irresolute, quicken the indolent and confound the trimmers."

"I cannot disguise the deep interest with which I watch your movements," Sumner wrote Chase shortly before he was to give his speech. "I count confidently upon an exposition of our cause which will toll throughout the country." When Chase took the floor on March 26, for the first part of his five-hour address, however, Seward had already delivered the celebrated address that outlined most of the positions Chase intended to take and had instantly made the fiery New Yorker the foremost national voice among the antislavery forces.

Nor did Chase possess Seward's compelling speaking style. If, over the years, constant practice had improved his range and delivery, he was unable to eradicate the slight lisp that remained from his boyhood days. Although his arguments were thoughtful and well reasoned, the chamber emptied long before he finished speaking. Writing home, he admitted great disappointment with the result, which was "infinitely below my own standards . . . and fell below those of my friends who expected much."

"You know I am not a rousing speaker at best," he conceded in a letter to a friend. He wanted it understood, however, that the speech was delivered "under very great disadvantages": the first chapter of the celebrated Benton-Foote confrontation, "which so engaged the attention of everybody," occurred on the very same day, so that "I had hardly any chance of attention, and in fact, received not much."

Chase was referring to a dramatic argument that broke out on the Senate floor between Senator Thomas Hart Benton of Missouri and Senator Henry Foote of Mississippi. Benton had called Foote a coward, leading Foote to recall an earlier histrionic incident when Benton himself had behaved in cowardly fashion. In response to this personal attack, Benton rose from his chair and rushed forward menacingly. Foote retreated behind a desk and then drew and cocked a pistol. "I disdain to carry arms!" Benton shouted. "Let him fire! . . . Stand out of the way, and let the assassin fire!" The melodrama was finally brought to a peaceful close when Foote was persuaded to hand over his pistol to a fellow senator and Benton returned to his chair.

Chase's disappointment over his failure was compounded by Sumner's praise for Seward's compelling maiden effort, which, Sumner told Chase, had filled him with gratitude. "Seward is with us," Sumner exulted. "You mistake when you say 'Seward is with us,' " Chase replied, with a heat not unmixed with resentment. While Seward "holds many of our Anti Slavery opinions," he continued, his loyalty to the Whig Party made him untrustworthy. "I have never been able to establish much sympathy between us," he explained in a follow-up letter. "He is too much of a politician for me."

Over the course of the previous decade, Seward and Chase had maintained a dialogue on the most effective methods to promote the antislavery cause. Despite their divergent views on whether or not to join a third party, Chase had always held Seward in the highest esteem and looked forward to working with him on antislavery issues in the Senate.

The alteration in his attitude was likely spurred by jealousy, an emotion the introspective Chase begrudged in others yet could never subdue in himself. "I made this resolution today," he had confided in his diary when he was twenty-three years old. "I will try to excel in all things yet if I am excelled, without fault of mine, I will not be mortified. I will not withhold from any one the praise which I think his due; nor will I allow myself to envy another's praise or to feel jealousy when I hear him praised. May God help me to keep it." His best intentions, however, could not assuage the invidious envy that possessed him at the realization that, given an identical opportunity, Seward had emerged the acclaimed leader of the antislavery forces. A rift developed between the two men that would last long into the Lincoln administration, with far-reaching consequences for the country.

Even as Seward basked in the applause of the antislavery community, however, he found himself excoriated in both Southern editorials and conservative papers throughout the North. "Senator Seward is against all compromise," the *New York Herald* observed, "so are the negroes of New York. . . . [His] views are those of the extreme fanatics of the North, looking forward to the utter destruction of the institutions of the South." Seward was initially untroubled by such criticism from expected sources and remained convinced he had "spoken words that will tell when I am dead." Frances had never been prouder of her husband. When she looked at him, she told her sister, she felt almost overwhelmed by her love and respect for him.

Such elation was soon tempered by a disquieting letter from Weed, who feared that Seward had overreached when enunciating a "higher law" than the Constitution. Though Weed had seen earlier versions, he had not read the final draft. "Your speech . . . sent me to bed with a heavy heart," Weed confessed to Seward. "A restless night and an anxious day have not relieved my apprehensions." Weed's criticism distressed Seward, who recognized that his mentor's political instincts were usually better than his own. Indeed, the implications of Weed's critical letter left Seward sunk in "despondency . . . covered with sorrow and shame," apprehensive that he had jeopardized not only his own career but that of his mentor as well.

Seward's status was further shaken when President Zachary Taylor, who had admitted both Weed and Seward to his inner circle, developed a fatal gastronomical illness after attending Fourth of July festivities on the grounds of the unfinished Washington Monument. Taylor's sudden death brought Seward's conservative rival, Millard Fillmore, into the presidency.

With Fillmore in the White House, the antislavery contingent had no prospect of stopping the Compromise. Under the skillful leadership of Illinois senator Stephen Douglas, Clay's omnibus bill was broken up into a series of separate pieces of legislation, which passed in both the House and Senate in September.

The Compromise of 1850 seemed to end the crisis. Stephen Douglas regarded the bill as a "final settlement," urging his colleagues on both sides to "stop the debate, and drop the subject." Upon its passage, the leading hotels in the capital were illuminated and a salute of one hundred guns was sounded. Serenaders, accompanied by a large crowd of spectators, honored Clay, Webster, and Douglas, singing "Hail Columbia" and "The Star-Spangled Banner" under the windows of their residences. "The joy of everyone seemed unbounded," the *New York Tribune* noted. The Southern-leaning Lewis Cass exulted: "The crisis is passed—the cloud is gone." While the nation hailed the Compromise, however, a Georgia editor warned prophetically: "The elements of that contest are yet all alive and they are destined yet to outlive the Government. There is a feud between the North and the South which may be smothered, but never overcome."

• • •

IN SPRINGFIELD, tracing the unfolding drama in the newspapers, Abraham Lincoln appeared to be satisfied that a peaceful solution had been reached. While he was unhappy about the provision bolstering the Fugitive Slave Law, he understood, he later said, that "devotion to the Union rightfully inclined men to yield somewhat, in points where nothing could have so inclined them." Rejecting Seward's concept of a "higher law," he preferred to rest his own opposition to slavery in the Constitution and the Declaration of Independence.

During the relative calm that followed the passage of the Compromise, Lincoln rode the legal circuit, a pursuit that proved congenial to his personality as well as his finances. He relished the convivial life he shared with the lawyers who battled one another fiercely during the day, only to gather as friends in the taverns at night. The arrival of the judge and lawyers generally created a stir in each town on their circuit. Villagers traveled from miles around, anticipating the courtroom drama as hundreds of small cases were tried, ranging from disputed wills, divorce, and bastardy proceedings to slander and libel suits, from patent challenges and collection of debts to murder and robbery.

"The local belles came in to see and be seen," fellow circuit rider Henry Whitney recalled, "and the court house, from 'early morn till dewy eve,' and the tavern from dewy eve to early morn, were replete with bustle, business, energy, hilarity, novelty, irony, sarcasm, excitement and eloquence." In some villages, the boardinghouses were clean and comfortable and the food was excellent; in others, there were "plenty of bedbugs" and the dirt was "half an inch thick." The lawyers generally slept two to a bed, with three or four beds in a room. While most of the traveling bar regularly bemoaned the living conditions, Lincoln savored the rollicking life on the circuit.

He was singularly good at his work, earning the respect and admiration of his fellow lawyers. Several of these associates became great friends and supporters, among them Circuit Judge David Davis. In letters to his wife, Sarah, Davis spoke not only of Lincoln's exceptional skill in addressing juries but of his "warm-hearted" nature and his "exceeding honesty & fairness." Davis had come to Illinois from Maryland when he was twenty-one, after graduating from Kenyon College and New Haven Law School. In his late twenties he was elected to the state legislature and considered a career in politics, but his wife, whom he loved "too well to thwart her views," was vehemently opposed. Instead, he ran for circuit judge, a position that offered the camaraderie of the circuit six months a year, yet enabled him to devote sufficient energy to business ventures that he eventually accumulated a substantial fortune.

The evolution of a warm and intimate friendship with Lincoln is evident in the judge's letters home. The two men took lazy strolls along the river, shared accommodations in various villages, read books in common, and enjoyed long conversations on the rides from one county to the next. No lawyer on the circuit was better loved than Lincoln, a fellow lawyer recalled. "He arrogated to himself no superiority over anyone—not even the most obscure member of the bar. . . . He was remarkably gentle with young lawyers. . . . No young lawyer ever practised in the courts with Mr. Lincoln who did not in all his after life have a regard for him akin to personal affection."

At mealtimes, all those with an interest in the various cases at hand would eat together at the same long table. Judge Davis would preside, surrounded by the lawyers, the members of the jury, the witnesses, the bailiffs, and the prisoners out on bail. Once the meal was done, everyone would gather before the blazing fire or in Judge Davis's quarters to talk, drink, smoke, and share stories. Though Lincoln did not drink, smoke tobacco, use profane language, or engage in games of chance, he never condescended to those who did. On the contrary, when he had addressed the Springfield Temperance Society at the height of the temperance crusade, he had insisted that "such of us as have never fallen victims, have been spared more from the absence of appetite, than from any mental or moral superiority over those who have."

No sooner had everyone settled in than the call would come for Lincoln to take center stage. Standing with his back to the fire, he juggled one tale after another, Herndon recalled, keeping his audience "in full laugh till near daylight." His "eyes would sparkle with fun," one old-timer remembered, "and when he had reached the point in his narrative which invariably evoked the laughter of the crowd, nobody's enjoyment was greater than his."

One of Lincoln's favorite anecdotes sprang from the early days just after the Revolution. Shortly after the peace was signed, the story began, the Revolutionary War hero Ethan Allen "had occasion to visit England," where he was subjected to considerable teasing banter. The British would make "fun of the Americans and General Washington in particular and one day they got a picture of General Washington" and displayed it prominently in the outhouse so Mr. Allen could not miss it. When he made no mention of it, they finally asked him if he had seen the Washington picture. Mr. Allen said, "he thought that it was a very appropriate [place] for an Englishman to Keep it. Why they asked, for said Mr. Allen there is Nothing that Will Make an Englishman Shit So quick as the Sight of Genl Washington."

Another story, relayed years later by John Usher, centered on a man "who had a great veneration for Revolutionary relics." Learning that an old woman still possessed a dress that "she had worn in the Revolutionary War," he traveled to her house and asked to see it. She took the dress from a bureau and handed it to him. He was so excited that he brought the dress to his lips and kissed it. "The practical old lady rather resented such foolishness over an old piece of wearing apparel and she said: 'Stranger if you want to kiss something old you had better kiss my ass. It is sixteen years older than that dress.' "

But Lincoln's stories provided more than mere amusement. Drawn from his own experiences and the curiosities reported by others, they frequently provided maxims or proverbs that usefully connected to the lives of his listeners. Lincoln possessed an extraordinary ability to convey practical wisdom in the form of humorous tales his listeners could remember and repeat. This process of repetition is central to the oral tradition; indeed, Walter Benjamin in his essay on the storyteller's art suggests that repetition "is the nature of the web in which the gift of storytelling is cradled."

"Would we do nothing but listen to Lincoln's stories?" Whitney was asked. "Oh! yes, we frequently talked philosophy, politics, political economy, metaphysics and men; in short, our subjects of conversation ranged through the universe of thought and experience." Years later, Whitney recalled a lengthy discussion about George Washington. The question for debate was whether the first president was perfect, or whether, being human, he was fallible. According to Whitney, Lincoln thought there was merit in retaining the notion of a Washington without blemish that they had all been taught as children. "It makes human nature better to believe that one human being was perfect," Lincoln argued, "that human perfection is possible."

When the court closed on Saturday afternoons, most of the lawyers traveled home to rejoin their families, returning on Sunday night or Monday morning. Davis later recalled that Lincoln was the exception to the rule, often remaining on the circuit throughout the weekend. At first they all "wondered at it," Davis said; but they "soon learned to account for his strange disinclination to go home"—while "most of us had pleasant, inviting homes" to return to, Lincoln did not. With the traveling bar, Lincoln was "as happy as *he* could be . . . and happy no other place." Herndon agreed, arguing that Lincoln stayed on the circuit as long as he could because "his home was *Hell*. . . . Absence from home was his *Heaven.*"

Such withering commentary on Lincoln's marriage and home life was made years afterward, when both Davis and Herndon had developed a deep hostility to Mary. The letters Davis wrote to Sarah at the time reveal quite a different story. "Lincoln speaks very affectionately of his wife & children," Davis told Sarah in 1851. On other occasions, Davis described a letter Lincoln had received from Mary reporting nursing troubles with Willie, and a conversation in which Lincoln had confided that both he and Mary were hoping for a girl before Tad was born. Nothing in these letters hint that Davis detected marital discord in the Lincoln home.

The specter of some domestic hell is not necessary to justify Lincoln's devotion to his law career. Life on the circuit provided Lincoln the time and space he needed to remedy the "want of education" he regretted all his life. During his nights and weekends on the circuit, in the absence of domestic interruptions, he taught himself geometry, carefully working out propositions and theorems until he could proudly claim that he had "nearly mastered the Six-books of Euclid." His first law partner, John Stuart, recalled that "he read hard works—was philosophical—logical—mathematical—never read generally."

Herndon describes finding him one day "so deeply absorbed in study he scarcely looked up when I entered." Surrounded by "a quantity of blank paper, large heavy sheets, a compass, a rule, numerous pencils, several bottles of ink of various colors, and a profusion of stationery," Lincoln was apparently "struggling with a calculation of some magnitude, for scattered about were sheet after sheet of paper covered with an unusual array of figures." When Herndon inquired what he was doing, he announced "that he was trying to solve the difficult problem of squaring the circle." To this insoluble task posed by the ancients over four thousand years earlier, he devoted "the better part of the succeeding two days . . . almost to the point of exhaustion."

In addition to geometry, Lincoln's solitary researches allowed him to study the astronomy, political economy, and philosophy that his fellow lawyers had learned in college. "Life was to him a school," fellow circuit rider Leonard Swett observed, "and he was always studying and mastering every subject which came before him."

Lincoln's time on the circuit was certainly difficult for Mary; his long absences from home were "one of the greatest hardships" of their marriage. For Lincoln, circuit life was invaluable. Beyond the congeniality of boardinghouse life and the opportunity to continue his lifelong education, these travels provided the chance to walk the streets in dozens of small towns, eat at local taverns in remote corners of the state, and gain a firsthand knowledge of the desires, fears, and hopes of thousands of ordinary people in Illinois—the people who would become his loyal base of support in the years ahead when the time came to return to his first love: politics.`

• • •

WHILE LINCOLN was productively engaged on the circuit, Seward was dispirited by what he perceived as a reactionary turn in the country's mood. "If I muzzle not my mouth on the subject of slavery," he wrote Frances, "I shall be set down as a disturber, seeking to disturb the Whig Administration and derange the Whig party." Responding to the public mood, he muted his strident voice on slavery and turned his attention to the less controversial issues of education, internal improvements, and foreign policy. Progress on emancipation, he endeavored to convince himself, could come only with the gradual enlightenment of the American public. When both Henry Clay and Daniel Webster died in 1852, he delivered such glowing eulogies on the Senate floor that his more radical friends took offense. "They cannot see," Seward complained to Frances, "how much of the misery of human life is derived from the indulgence of wrath!"

The idealistic Frances accepted her husband's rationale for the eulogies but could not countenance his reluctance to resist the reactionary zeal that enveloped the country after the Compromise. When it appeared that the 1852 Whig Convention was on the verge of endorsing the Compromise in an attempt to create a moderate platform for its presidential candidate, General Winfield Scott, Frances begged her husband to come home. "I do not wish you to be held responsible for the doings of that Convention if they are to endorse the Compromise in any manner or degree," she wrote. "It will be a sad disappointment to men who are true to liberty."

Nor did she spare him whenever she detected a blatantly conciliatory tone in his speeches or writings. While she conceded that "worldly wisdom certainly does impel a person to 'swim with the tide'—and if they can judge unerringly which way the tide runs, may bring them to port," she continued to argue for "a more elevated course" that would "reconcile one to struggling against the current if necessary."

In Charles Sumner, Frances found a politician who consistently chose the elevated course she favored, even though he was often isolated as a result. Sumner, a bachelor, who, like Chase, was said to look like a statesman, with imperious, well-chiseled features, would often dine with the Sewards when Frances was in town. When she returned to Auburn, they kept up a rich correspondence. Sumner valued her unflagging confidence particularly during his early days in the Senate when his unyielding position on slavery provoked anger and ridicule. Though his attempt to repeal the Fugitive Slave Act in August 1852 garnered only 4 votes in the Senate, not including Seward's—who, like other antislavery men, refused to support it on the grounds that it would torpedo Scott's chances for the presidency—Frances stood loyally by her friend. "This fearless defense of Freedom must silence those cavilers who doubted your sincerity," she wrote. "It is a noble plea for a righteous cause."

That November, when the Southerners' candidate, Franklin Pierce, crushed Scott in what Northern Whigs considered "a Waterloo defeat," Frances fell into a state of despair. Her confidence in the mainstream political system gone, she was tempted, she told her husband, to join the abolitionists. Seward persuaded her to hold back, arguing that it would do "more harm than good" if the Seward name were attached to the abolitionist cause.

Try as he might, Seward could not persuade Frances to stay with him for more than a few months at a time in Washington. Her decision to remain in upstate New York, especially in the wretched summer months, was not unusual, but even when the weather began to cool as autumn set in, Frances remained in Auburn. "Would that I were nearer to you," he lamented from Washington on his fifty-fourth birthday; but he accepted that his "widened spheres of obligation and duty" prevented him from realizing his wishes.

Had Frances Seward enjoyed good health, the course of their marriage might have been different; everywhere Seward went he rented sumptuous homes, hopeful that she and the children might join him. Burdened with a fragile constitution, Frances was increasingly debilitated by a wide range of nervous disorders: nausea, temporary blindness, insomnia, migraines, mysterious pains in her muscles and joints, crying spells, and sustained bouts of depression. A flashing light, a bumpy carriage ride, or a piercing sound was often sufficient to send her to bed. As her health deteriorated, she found it more and more difficult to leave her "sanctuary" in Auburn, where she was attended by her solicitous extended family.

Doctors could not pinpoint the physical origin of the various ailments that conspired to leave Frances a semi-invalid. A brilliant woman, Frances once speculated whether the "various nervous afflictions & morbid habits of thought" that plagued so many women she knew had their origin in the frustrations of an educated woman's life in the mid-nineteenth century. Among her papers is a draft of an unpublished essay on the plight of women: "To share in any kind of household work is to demean herself, and she would be thought mad, to run, leap, or engage in active sports." She was permitted to dance all night in ballrooms, but it "would be deemed unwomanly" and "imprudent" for her to race with her children "on the common, or to search the cliff for flowers." Reflecting on "the number of invalids that exist among women exempted from Labour," she suggested that the "want of fitting employment—real purpose in their life" was responsible.

Seward himself recognized that his marriage was built upon contradictions. "There you are at home all your life-long. It is too cold to travel in winter and home is too pleasant in summer to be foresaken. The children cannot go abroad and must not be left at home. Here I am, on the contrary, roving for instruction when at leisure, and driven abroad continually by my occupation. How strange a thing it is that we can never enjoy each others cares and pleasures, except at intervals."

The Sewards' relationship was sustained chiefly through the long, loving letters they wrote to each other day after day, year after year. In her letters, which number in the thousands, Frances described the progress of the garden and the antics of the children. She offered advice on political matters, critiqued his speeches, and expressed her passionate opinions about slavery. She encouraged his idealism, pressing him repeatedly to consider what *should* be done rather than what *could* be done. In his letters, he analyzed the personalities of his colleagues, confessed his fears, discussed his reactions to the books he was reading, and told her repeatedly how he loved her "above every other thing in the world." He conjured images of the moon, whose "silver rays" they shared as they each sat in their separate homes "writing the lines" that would cross in the mail. He recollected pleasures of home, where the children played in the smoke from his cigar, and husband and wife were engaged in free and open conversation, so different from the talk of politicians.

Yet in the end, it was the talk of politicians he craved. As a result, the Sewards, to a far greater extent than the Lincolns, spent much of their married life apart.

• • •

CHASE, TOO, found himself in a dispirited state in the months that followed the Compromise. "Clouds and darkness are upon us at present," he wrote Sumner. "The Slaveholders have succeeded beyond their wildest hopes twelve months ago." It seemed as if, temporarily at least, the wind had been taken out of the sails of the antislavery movement.

Moreover, Chase was isolated in the Senate, the regular Democratic Party having shut him out of committee work and political meetings. Nor could he rely on the camaraderie of the Free-Soilers, who believed he had sacrificed them to achieve his position. With time heavy on his hands, he spent hours writing to Kate at her boarding school in New York, where she had been sent when his third wife, Belle, contracted the tuberculosis that took her life.

The long years away from home must have been bleak and often difficult for the motherless child. Located at Madison Avenue and Forty-ninth Street, Miss Haines's School held the girls to a strict routine. They rose at 6 a.m. to study for an hour and a half before breakfast and prayers. A brisk walk outside, with no skipping permitted, preceded classes in literature, French, Latin, English grammar, science, elocution, piano, and dancing. At midafternoon, they were taken out once again for an hour-long walk. In the evenings, they attended study hall, where, "without [the teacher's] permission," one student recalled, "we could hardly breathe." Only on weekends, when they attended recitals or the theater, was the routine relaxed.

Living ten months a year under such regimented circumstances, Kate yearned to see the one person she loved: her father. Though he wrote hundreds of letters to her, his correspondence lacked the playful warmth of Seward's notes to his own children. In cold, didactic fashion, Chase alternately praised and upbraided her, instructing her in the art of letter writing and admonishing her to cultivate good habits. If her letters were well written, he critiqued her penmanship. If the penmanship was good, he criticized her flat style of expression. If both met his standards, he complained that she had waited too long to write.

"Your last letter . . . was quite well written," he told her when she was ten years old. "I should be glad, however, to have you describe more of what you see and do every day. Can't you tell me all about your schoolmates one by one. . . . Take pains, use your eyes, reflect." "I wish you could put a little more life into your letters." Four years later, he was still urging improvement. "Your nice letter, my darling child, came yesterday," he wrote, "but I must say that it had rather a sleepy air. The words seemed occasionally chosen and arranged under the influence of the drowsy God."

"It will be a great advantage to you to cultivate a *noticing habit,*" he advised. "Accustom yourself to talk of what you see and to write details, and in a conversational, & even narrative style. There is the greatest possible difference in charm between the same narrative told by one person and by another. . . . No doubt a large part of this difference is to be ascribed to constitutional differences of temperament, but any intelligent person can greatly increase facility of apprehension & expression by careful self culture." The ascetic refrain of Chase's instruction to Kate is that an effort of will can surmount most obstacles and self-denial can lead to its own gratifications: "I know you do not like writing. . . . You can overcome if you will. . . . I dislike for example to bathe myself all over with cold water in the morning especially when the thermometer is so low as at present: but I find I can when I determine to do so overcome my feeling of dislike and even substitute a certain pleasurable sensation."

In his efforts to discipline and educate his daughter, Chase did not spare Kate his own morbid thoughts about death. "Remember, my dear child, that the eye of a Holy God is upon you all the time, and that not an act or word or thought is unnoticed by Him. Remember too, that you may die soon. . . . Already eleven years of your life are passed. You may not live another eleven years. . . . How short then is this life! And how earnest ought to be our preparation for another!" To illustrate his point, he described the death of a little girl just Kate's age, the daughter of a fellow senator. The Monday before her death, he had seen her in the capital, "strong, robust, active, intelligent; the very impersonation of life and health. A week after and she had gone from earth. What a lesson was here. Lay it to heart, dear Katie, and may God give you grace."

If Kate's school reports were unfavorable, Chase refused to allow her to return home for vacation. "I am sorry that you feel so lonely," he told her one summer. "I wish I could feel it safe to allow you to visit more freely, but your conversations with Miss Haines have made known to you the reasons why." He urged her to understand: "you have it in your power greatly to promote my happiness by your good conduct, and greatly to destroy my comfort and peace by ill conduct."

More often she excelled, relying on her nearly encyclopedic memory and hard work to please her exacting father. If unsparing in his criticism, he was extravagant in his praise. "To an affectionate father" nothing was more gratifying, he told her—not even the thought that he might someday "be made President"—than "a beloved child, improving in intelligence, in manners, in physical development, and giving promise of a rich and delightful future."

He rewarded her with invitations to Washington, visits she vividly recalled years later. "I knew Clay, Webster and Calhoun," she proudly told a reporter when she was in her fifties. As a small girl, she was particularly impressed by Clay, so tall that "he had to unwind himself to get up." At ease with children, Clay "made much of me and I liked him." Daniel Webster appeared to Kate an "ideal of how a statesman ought to look," the very words later used to describe her father. "He seldom laughed, yet he was very kind and he used to send me his speeches. I don't suppose he thought I would read them, but he wanted to compliment me and show that he remembered me and I know that I felt very proud when I saw Daniel Webster's frank upon pieces of mail which came to me at the New York school."

Of all her father's Senate colleagues, Charles Sumner was her favorite, as he was of Frances Seward. "He was warm-hearted and sensitive," Kate recalled. "He was full of anecdotes and was a brilliant talker." When Sumner, in turn, spoke well of little Kate, Chase was overjoyed. "You cannot think, my precious child, how much pleasure it gives me to hear you praised."

Buoyant at such moments with satisfied expectations, Chase shared with her intimate chronicles of his life in Washington, long descriptions of the protocol followed when a senator visited the president in his office, detailed accounts of dinners at the White House, amusing reports of late-night sessions in the Senate chamber, when all too many of his colleagues "have visited the refectory a little too often, and are not as sober as they should be."

"The sun shines warm and clear," he wrote one beautiful June day. "The wind stirs the trees and fans the earth. I sit in my room and hear the rustle of branches; the merry twitter and song of the birds; the chirp of insects." "I should like to have you with me and we should take a ramble together."

Not surprisingly, Kate cherished the prospect of living in the nation's capital, accompanying her father wherever he went, assisting him in his daily tasks. Chase understood her desire and was careful to assuage her fear that he might remarry and deprive her of her rightful place by his side. Describing a visit to the Elliotts, a Quaker family with two remarkable daughters, he confessed that "Miss Lizzie is the best looking of them all, and is really a very superior woman, with a great deal of sense and a great deal of heart. You need not however be alarmed for me, for a gentleman in New York is said to be her accepted lover, and I look only for *friends* among ladies as I do among gentlemen."

• • •

OF THE FOUR future presidential candidates, Edward Bates was the only one who supported the Compromise wholeheartedly. At last, with what he called the "African mania" finally subdued, he felt the American people might focus their energies once more on the vast economic opportunities provided by the ever-expanding frontier.

With equal ire, he denounced both "the lovers of free negroes in the North & the lovers of slave negroes in the South," believing that the argument over slavery was simply "a struggle among politicians for sectional supremacy," with radicals like Seward and Chase in the North, and Calhoun and Toombs in the South, exploiting the issue for personal ambition.

He specifically condemned Seward's *"higher law"* supposition invoked to invalidate the Fugitive Slave Law, arguing that "in Civil government, such as we have, there can be no law *higher* than the Constitution and the Statutes. And he would set himself above these, claiming some transcendental authority for his disobedience, must be, as I deliberately think, either a Canting hypocrite, a presumptuous fool, or an arbitrary designing knave."

He exhibited similar scorn for Calhoun, who would shatter "the world's best hope of freedom for the white man, because he is not allowed to have his own wayward will about negro slaves! . . . Poor man, he is greatly to be pitied! . . . It is truly a melancholy spectacle to behold his sun going down behind a cloud so black."

In the early fifties, Bates still believed that the West could refrain from taking sides, trusting that "if we stood aloof from the quarrel & pressed the even tenor of our way, for the public good, both of those factions would soon sink to the level of their intrinsic insignificance." His hopes would quickly prove futile, for the settlement was destined to last only four years.

• • •

"A HUMAN BEING," the novelist Thomas Mann observed, "lives out not only his personal life as an individual, but also, consciously or subconsciously, the lives of his epoch and his contemporaries . . . if the times, themselves, despite all their hustle and bustle," do not provide opportunity, he continued, "the situation will have a crippling effect."

More than a decade earlier, speaking to the Springfield Young Men's Lyceum, Lincoln had expressed his concern that his generation had been left a meager yield after the "field of glory" was harvested by the founding fathers. They were a "forest of giant oaks," he said, who faced the "task (and nobly they performed it) to possess themselves, and through themselves, us, of this goodly land," and to build "upon its hills and its valleys, a political edifice of liberty and equal rights." Their destinies were "*inseparably* linked" with the experiment of providing the world, "a practical demonstration" of "*the capability of a people to govern themselves.* If they succeeded, they were to be immortalized; their names were to be transferred to counties and cities, and rivers and mountains; and to be revered and sung, and toasted through all time."

Because their experiment succeeded, Lincoln observed, thousands "won their deathless names in making it so." What was left for the men of his generation to accomplish? There was no shortage of good men "whose ambition would aspire to nothing beyond a seat in Congress, a gubernatorial or a presidential chair; but *such belong not to the family of the lion, or the tribe of the eagle.*" Such modest aspirations, he argued, would never satisfy men of "towering genius" who scorned "a beaten path."

In 1854, the wheel of history turned. A train of events that mobilized the antislavery North resulted in the formation of the Republican Party and ultimately provided Lincoln's generation with a challenge equal to or surpassing that of the founding fathers. The sequence began when settlers in Kansas and Nebraska called upon Congress to grant them territorial status, raising once again the contentious question of extending slavery into the territories. As chairman of the Committee on Territories, Illinois senator Stephen Douglas introduced a bill that appeared to provide an easy solution to the problem by allowing the settlers themselves the "popular sovereignty" to decide if they wished to become free or slave states. This solution proved anything but simple. Since both Kansas and Nebraska lay north of the old 36° 30' line, the passage of the Kansas-Nebraska Act would mean that the Missouri Compromise was null and void, opening the possibility of slavery to land long since guaranteed to freedom.

The debate over the Kansas-Nebraska Act opened against increased antislavery sentiment in the North. Enforcement of the fugitive slave provisions contained in the Compromise of 1850 had aroused Northern ire. Near riots erupted when slaveholders tried to recapture runaway slaves who had settled in Boston and New York. Ralph Waldo Emerson expressed a common sentiment among Northerners: "I had never in my life up to this time suffered from the Slave Institution. Slavery in Virginia or Carolina was like Slavery in Africa or the Feejees, for me. There was an old fugitive law, but it had become, or was fast becoming a dead letter, and, by the genius and laws of Massachusetts, inoperative. The new Bill made it operative, required me to hunt slaves, and it found citizens in Massachusetts willing to act as judges and captors. Moreover, it discloses the secret of the new times, that Slavery was no longer mendicant, but was becoming aggressive and dangerous."

Northern sentiment had been inflamed further by the publication of Harriet Beecher Stowe's *Uncle Tom's Cabin.* Less than a year after its publication in March 1852, more than three hundred thousand copies of the novel had sold in the United States, a sales rate rivaled only by the Bible. Abolitionist leader Frederick Douglass later likened it to "a flash" that lit "a million camp fires in front of the embattled hosts of slavery," awakening such powerful compassion for the slave and indignation against slavery that many previously unconcerned Americans were transformed into advocates for the antislavery cause.

Until the introduction of the Kansas-Nebraska Act, there was no signal point around which the antislavery advocates could rally. As the Senate debate opened, Northerners were stirred into action "in greater numbers than ever," the historian Don Fehrenbacher has written, fighting "with all the fierceness of an army defending its homeland against invasion."

Passions in the South were equally aroused. To Southerners, the issue of Kansas was not merely an issue of slavery, but whether they, who had helped create and enlarge the nation with their "blood and treasure," would be entitled to share in the territories held in common by the entire country. "The day may come," said Governor Thomas Bragg of North Carolina, "when our Northern brethren will discover that the Southern States intend to be equals in the Union, or independent out of it!"

This time Salmon Chase assumed the leadership of the antislavery forces. Seward understood that the bill was "a mighty subject" that "required research and meditation," but he was distracted by a multitude of issues and the demands of Washington's social life. With "the street door bell [ringing] every five minutes," the popular New Yorker was unable to find the time to construct a great speech or to marshal the opposition. Consequently, while Seward's speeches against the Nebraska bill were simply "essays against slavery," Stephen Douglas later said, "Chase of Ohio was the leader."

Chase, along with Sumner and Ohio congressman Joshua Giddings, conceived the idea of reaching beyond the Senate to the country at large with an open "Appeal of the Independent Democrats in Congress to the People of the United States." The "Appeal" was originally printed in *The National Era,* the abolitionist newspaper that had first serialized *Uncle*

Tom's Cabin. Deemed by historians "one of the most effective pieces of political propaganda ever produced," the Appeal was reprinted in pamphlet form to organize opposition to the Kansas-Nebraska Act.

"We arraign this bill as a gross violation of a sacred pledge," the Appeal began, charging that a rapacious proslavery conspiracy was determined to subvert the old Missouri compact, which forever had excluded slavery in all the territory acquired from France in the Louisiana Purchase. Passage of the Nebraska Act would mean that "this immense region, occupying the very heart" of the continent, would, in "flagrant disregard" of a "sacred faith," be transformed into "a dreary region of despotism, inhabited by masters and slaves." The manifesto urged citizens to protest by any means available. Its authors promised to call on their constituents "to come to the rescue of the country from the domination of slavery . . . for the cause of human freedom is the cause of God."

"Chase's greatest opportunity had at last come to him," his biographer Albert Hart observes, "for in the Kansas-Nebraska debate he was able to concentrate all the previous experience of his life." By the time he rose to speak on the Senate floor on February 3, 1854, the country was aroused and prepared for a great battle. "By far the most numerous audience of the season listened to Mr. Chase's speech," the *New York Times* reported. "The galleries and lobbies were densely crowded an hour before the debate began, and the ladies even crowded into and took possession of, one-half the lobby seats on the floor of the Senate."

In the course of the heated debate, Chase accused Douglas of sponsoring the bill to aid his quest for the presidency, an allegation that brought the Illinois senator to such a "high pitch of wrath" that he countered, accusing Chase of entering the Senate by a corrupt bargain. "Do you say I came here by a corrupt bargain?" Chase demanded to know. "I said the man who charged me with having brought in this bill as a bid for the Presidency did come here by a corrupt bargain," Douglas replied. "Did you mean me? If so, I mean you."

Seated beside his friend, Sumner watched with rapturous attention as Chase refuted Douglas's claim that the concept of "popular sovereignty" would provide a final settlement of all territorial questions. On the contrary, Chase predicted, "this discussion will hasten the inevitable reorganization of parties." Moreover, he asked, "What kind of popular sovereignty is that which allows one portion of the people to enslave another portion? Is that the doctrine of equal rights? . . . No, sir, no! There can be no real democracy which does not fully maintain the rights of man, as man."

At midnight, Douglas began his concluding speech, which lasted nearly four hours. At one point, Seward interrupted to ask for an explanation of something Douglas had said. "Ah," Douglas retorted, "you can't crawl behind that free nigger dodge." In reply, Seward said: "Douglas, no man will ever be President of the United States who spells 'negro' with two gs."

"Midnight passed and the cock crew, and daylight broke before the vote was taken," the *New York Tribune* reported. The all-night session was marked by "great confusion, hard words between various Senators and intense excitement in which the galleries participated." Many of the senators were observed to be "beastly drunk," their grandiloquence further inflated by "too frequent visits to one of the ante-chambers of the Senate room."

When the Senate majority cast its votes in favor of the bill at 5 a.m. on the morning of March 4, the antislavery minority was crushed. "The Senate is emasculated," Senator Benton exclaimed. As Chase and Sumner descended the sweeping steps of the Capitol, a distant cannonade signaled passage of the bill. "They celebrate a present victory," Chase said, "but the echoes they awake will never rest until slavery itself shall die."

"Be assured, be assured, gentlemen," *New York Tribune* reporter James Pike warned the Southerners, that "you are sowing the wind and you will reap the whirlwind. . . . No man can stand in the North in that day of reckoning who plants himself on the ground of sustaining the repeal of the Missouri Compromise. . . . [Here is] the opening of a great drama that . . . inaugurates the era of a geographical division of political parties. It draws the line between North and South. It pits face to face the two opposing forces of slavery and freedom."

In the weeks that followed, mass protest meetings spread like wildfire throughout the North, fueled by the enormous reach of the daily newspaper. "The tremendous storm sweeping the North seemed to gather new force every week," writes the historian Allan Nevins. Resolutions against the law were signed by tens of thousands in Connecticut, New Hampshire, Ohio, Indiana, Iowa, Massachusetts, and Pennsylvania. In New York, the *Tribune* reported, two thousand protesters marched up Broadway, "led by a band of music, and brilliant with torches and banners." On college campuses and village squares, in town halls and county fairgrounds, people gathered to make their voices heard.

• • •

LINCOLN WAS RIDING the circuit in the backcountry of Illinois when the news reached him of the passage of the Kansas-Nebraska Act. A fellow lawyer, T. Lyle Dickey, sharing a room with Lincoln, reported that "he sat on the edge of his bed and discussed the political situation far into the night." At dawn, he was still "sitting up in bed, deeply absorbed in thought." He told his companion—"I tell you, Dickey, this nation cannot exist half-slave and half-free."

Lincoln later affirmed that the successful passage of the bill roused him "as he had never been before." It permanently recast his views on slavery. He could no longer maintain that slavery was on course to ultimate extinction. The repeal of the Missouri Compromise persuaded him that unless the North mobilized into action against the proslavery forces, free society itself was in peril. The Nebraska Act "took us by surprise," Lincoln later said. "We were thunderstruck and stunned." The fight to stem the spread of slavery would become the great purpose Lincoln had been seeking.

Before speaking out against the Nebraska Act, Lincoln spent many hours in the State Library, studying present and past congressional debates so that he could reach back into the stream of American history and tell a clear, reasoned, and compelling tale. He would express no opinion on anything, Herndon observed, until he knew his subject "inside and outside, upside and downside." Lincoln told Joshua Speed, "I am slow to learn and slow to forget that which I have learned. My mind is like a piece of steel, very hard to scratch any thing on it and almost impossible after you get it there to rub it out."

Lincoln delivered his first great antislavery speech in Springfield at the annual State Fair before a crowd of thousands on October 4, 1854. Farmers and their families had journeyed to the capital from all over the state, filling every hotel room, tavern, and boardinghouse. Billed as the largest agricultural fair in the history of the state, the exhibition featured the most advanced farm implements and heavy machinery, including a "world-renowned" plow. Residents took pride in what was considered the finest display of livestock ever assembled in one place. Games and amusements, music and refreshments were provided from morning until night, ensuring, as one reporter wrote, that "a jolly good time ensued."

The previous day, Lincoln had heard Stephen Douglas hold forth for three hours before the same audience. Douglas, stunned by the widespread hostility in northern Illinois to his seminal role in passing the controversial Kansas-Nebraska Act, had chosen the State Fair as the best forum for a vigorous defense of the bill. Rain forced the event into the house of representatives chamber, but the change of venue didn't diminish the impact of Douglas's speech. Sharpening arguments he had made in the Senate, Douglas emphasized that his bill rested on the unassailable principle of self-government, allowing the people themselves to decide whether or not to allow slavery into their own territorial lands.

The expressive face of "the Little Giant," as the short, stocky Douglas was called, was matched by his stentorian voice. "He had a large head, surmounted by an abundant mane," one reporter observed, "which gave him the appearance of a lion prepared to roar or crush his prey." In the midst of speaking, he would "cast away his cravat" and undo the buttons on his coat, captivating his audience with "the air and aspect of a half-naked pugilist." "He was frequently interrupted by cheers and hearty demonstrations of applause," the *Peoria Daily Press* reported, "thus showing that a large majority of the meeting was with him." When he finished, Lincoln jumped up and announced to the crowd that a rebuttal would be delivered the following day.

The next afternoon, with Douglas seated in the front row, Lincoln faced most likely the largest audience of his life. He appeared "awkward" at first, in his shirtsleeves with no collar. "He began in a slow and hesitating manner," the reporter Horace White noted. Yet, minutes into his speech, "it was evident that he had mastered his subject, that he knew what he was going to say, and that he knew he was right." White was only twenty at the time but was aware even then, he said, that he was hearing "one of the world's masterpieces of argumentative power and moral grandeur." Sixty years later, that conviction remained. The initial impression was "overwhelming," White told an audience in 1914, "and it has lost nothing by the lapse of time."

Although Lincoln's voice was "thin, high-pitched," White observed, it had "much carrying power" and "could be heard a long distance in spite of the bustle and tumult of the crowd." As Lincoln hit his stride, "his words began to come faster." Gesturing with his "body and head rather than with his arms," he grew "very impassioned" and "seemed transfigured" by the strength of his words. "Then the inspiration that possessed him took possession of his hearers also. His speaking went to the heart because it came from the heart. I have heard celebrated orators who could start thunders of applause without changing any man's opinion. Mr. Lincoln's eloquence was of the higher type, which produced conviction in others because of the conviction of the speaker himself."

While Douglas simply asserted his points as self-evident, Lincoln embedded his argument in a narrative history, transporting his listeners back to their roots as a people, to the founding of the nation—a story that still retained its power to arouse strong emotion and thoughtful attention. Many of his arguments were familiar to those who had followed the Senate debate and had read Chase's masterly "Appeal"; but the structure of the speech was so "clear and logical," the *Illinois Daily Journal* observed, the arrangement of facts so "methodical," that the overall effect was strikingly original and "most effective."

At the State Fair, and twelve nights later, by torchlight in Peoria, where the debate over the Kansas-Nebraska Act was repeated, Lincoln presented his carefully "connected view" for better than three hours. In order to make his argument, Lincoln decided to begin with nothing less than an account of our common history, the powerful narrative of how slavery grew with our country, how its growth and expansion had been carefully contained by the founding fathers, and how on this fall night in 1854 the great story they were being told—the story of the Union—had come to such an impasse that the exemplary meaning, indeed, the continued existence of the story, hung in the balance.

For the first time in his public life, his remarkable array of gifts as historian, storyteller, and teacher combined with a lucid, relentless, yet always accessible logic. Instead of the ornate language so familiar to men like Webster, Lincoln used irony and humor, laced with workaday, homespun images to build an eloquent tower of logic. The proslavery argument that a vote for the Wilmot Proviso threatened the stability of the entire Union was reduced to absurdity by analogy—"because I may have refused to build an addition to my house, I thereby have decided to destroy the existing house!" Such flashes of figurative language were always available to Lincoln to drive home a point, gracefully educating while entertaining—in a word, *communicating* an enormously complicated issue with wit, simplicity, and a massive power of moral persuasion.

At the time the Constitution was adopted, Lincoln pointed out, "the plain unmistakable spirit of that age, towards slavery, was hostility to the *principle*, and toleration, *only by necessity*," since slavery was already woven into the fabric of American society. Noting that neither the word "slave" nor "slavery" was ever mentioned in the Constitution, Lincoln claimed that the framers concealed it, "just as an afflicted man hides away a wen or a cancer, which he dares not cut out at once, lest he bleed to death; with the promise, nevertheless, that the cutting may begin at the end of a given time." As additional evidence of the framers' intent, Lincoln brought his audience even further back, to the moment when Virginia ceded its vast northwestern territory to the United States with the understanding that slavery would be forever prohibited from the new territory, thus creating a "happy home" for "teeming millions" of free people, with "no slave amongst them." In recent years, he said, slavery had seemed to be gradually on the wane until the fateful Nebraska law transformed it into "a sacred right," putting it "on the high road to extension and perpetuity"; giving it "a pat on its back," saying, " 'Go, and God speed you.' "

Douglas had argued that Northern politicians were simply manufacturing a crisis, that Kansas and Nebraska were destined, in any event, to become free states because the soil and climate in both regions were inhospitable to the cultivation of staple crops. Labeling this argument "a *lullaby*," Lincoln exhibited a map demonstrating that five of the present slave states had similar climates to Kansas and Nebraska, and that the census returns for 1850 showed these states held one fourth of all the slaves in the nation.

Finally, as the greatest bulwark against the Nebraska Act and the concept of "popular sovereignty," Lincoln invoked the Declaration of Independence. He considered the Nebraska Act simply a legal term for the perpetuation and expansion of slavery and, as such, nothing less than the possible death knell of the Union and the meaning of America. "The doctrine of self government is right—absolutely and eternally right," he argued, but to use it, as Douglas proposed, to extend slavery perverted its very meaning. "No man is good enough to govern another man, *without that other's consent.* I say this is the leading principle—the sheet anchor of American republicanism." If the Negro was a man, which Lincoln claimed he most assuredly was, then it was "a total destruction of self-government" to propose that he be governed by a master without his consent. Allowing slavery to spread forced the American people into an open war with the Declaration of Independence, depriving "our republican example of its just influence in the world."

By appealing to the moral and philosophical foundation work of the nation, Lincoln hoped to provide common ground on which good men in both the North and the South could stand. "I am not now combating the argument of *necessity*, arising from the fact that the blacks are already amongst us; but I am combating what is set up as *moral* argument for allowing them to be taken where they have never yet been." Unlike the majority of antislavery orators, who denounced the South and castigated slaveowners as corrupt and un-Christian, Lincoln pointedly denied fundamental differences between Northerners and Southerners. He argued that "they are just what we would be in their situation. If slavery did not now exist amongst them, they would not introduce it. If it did now exist amongst us, we should not instantly give it up. . . . When it is said that the institution exists; and that it is very difficult to get rid of it, in any satisfactory way, I can understand and appreciate the saying. I surely will not blame them for not doing what I should not know how to do myself." And, finally, "when they remind us of their constitutional rights, I acknowledge them . . . and I would give them any legislation for the reclaiming of their fugitives."

Rather than upbraid slaveowners, Lincoln sought to comprehend their position through empathy. More than a decade earlier, he had employed a similar approach when he advised temperance advocates to refrain from denouncing drinkers in "thundering tones of anathema and denunciation," for denunciation would inevitably be met with denunciation, "crimination with crimination, and anathema with anathema." In a passage directed at abolitionists as well as temperance reformers, he had observed that it was the nature of man, when told that he should be "shunned and despised," and condemned as the author "of all the vice and misery and crime in the land," to "retreat within himself, close all the avenues to his head and his heart."

Though the cause be "naked truth itself, transformed to the heaviest lance, harder than steel," the sanctimonious reformer could no more pierce the heart of the drinker or the slaveowner than "penetrate the hard shell of a tortoise with a rye straw. Such is man, and so *must* he be understood by those who would lead him." In order to "win a man to your cause," Lincoln explained, you must first reach his heart, "the great high road to his reason." This, he concluded, was the only road to victory—to that glorious day "when there shall be neither a slave nor a drunkard on the earth."

Building on his rhetorical advice, Lincoln tried to place himself in the shoes of the slaveowner to reason his way through the sectional impasse, by asking Southerners to let their own hearts and history reveal that they, too, recognized the basic humanity of the black man. Never appealing like Seward to a "higher law," or resorting to Chase's "natural right" derived from "the code of heaven," Lincoln staked his argument in reality. He confronted Southerners with the contradictions surrounding the legal status of blacks that existed in their own laws and social practices.

In 1820, he reminded them, they had "joined the north, almost unanimously, in declaring the African slave trade piracy, and in annexing to it the punishment of death." In so doing, they must have understood that selling slaves was wrong, for they never thought of hanging men for selling horses, buffaloes, or bears. Likewise, though forced to do business with the domestic slave dealer, they did not "recognize him as a friend, or even as an honest man. . . . Now why is this?" he asked. "You do not so treat the man who deals in corn, cattle or tobacco." Finally, he observed, over four hundred thousand free blacks in the United States had been liberated at "vast pecuniary sacrifices" by white owners who understood something about the human rights of Negroes. "In all these cases it is your sense of justice, and human sympathy, continually telling you" that the slave is a man who cannot be considered "mere merchandise."

As he wound to a close, Lincoln implored his audience to re-adopt the Declaration of Independence and "return [slavery] to the position our fathers gave it; and there let it rest in peace." This accomplishment, he pledged, would save the Union, and "succeeding millions of free happy people, the world over, shall rise up, and call us blessed, to the latest generations." When he finished, the enthusiastic audience broke out in "deafening applause." Even the editors of the Democratic paper felt "compelled" to say that they had "never read or heard a stronger anti-Nebraska speech."

From that moment on, propelled by a renewed sense of purpose, Lincoln dedicated the major part of his energies to the antislavery movement. Conservative and contemplative by temperament, he embraced new positions warily. Once he committed himself, however, as he did in the mid-fifties to the antislavery cause, he demonstrated singular tenacity and authenticity of feeling. Ambition and conviction united, "as my two eyes make one in sight," as Robert Frost wrote, to give Lincoln both a political future and a cause worthy of his era.

CHAPTER 6

THE GATHERING STORM

As 1854 gave way to 1855, Abraham Lincoln's long-dormant dream of high political office was reawakened, now infused with a new sense of purpose by the passage of the Nebraska Act. He won a seat in the Illinois State Assembly, then promptly declared himself a candidate for the U.S. Senate. In the Illinois state elections the previous fall, the loose coalition of antislavery Whigs and independent Democrats had gained a narrow majority over the Douglas Democrats in the legislature. The victory was "mainly attributed" to Lincoln's leadership, observed state legislator Joseph Gillespie. With the new legislature set to convene in late January to choose the next U.S. senator from Illinois, Lincoln was "the first choice" of the overwhelming majority of anti-Nebraska members. His lifelong dream of achieving high political office seemed about to be realized at last.

On January 20, 1855, however, the worst blizzard in more than two decades isolated Springfield from the rest of the state, preventing a quorum from assembling in the state legislature. Immense snowdrifts cut off trains coming in from the North, and mail was halted for more than a week. While Springfield's children relished "the merry sleigh bells" jingling through the snow, the "pulsation of business" was "nearly extinct." Finally, the weather improved sufficiently for the legislature to convene.

On Thursday morning, February 8, long before the balloting opened at three o'clock, the Capitol was "a beehive of activity." Representatives caucused and whispered in every corner. The anti-Nebraska caucus, composed mainly of Whigs, voted, as expected, to support Lincoln, but a small group of five anti-Nebraska Democrats was ominously absent. The Douglas Democrats, meanwhile, had decided to support the incumbent senator, James Shields, on the early ballots. If Shields's campaign faltered, due to his outspoken endorsement of the Nebraska bill, they had devised a plan to switch their support to the popular Democratic governor, Joel Matteson, who had not taken an open position on the bill. In this way, the Democrats believed, they might win over some members of the anti-Nebraska caucus.

By noon, the "lobby and the galleries of the Hall of the House of Representatives began to fill with senators, representatives and their guests." Notable among the ladies in the gallery were Mary Todd Lincoln and her friend Julia Jayne Trumbull, wife of Democrat Lyman Trumbull, who had recently been elected to Congress on an anti-Nebraska platform. The wife and daughter of Governor Matteson were also in attendance. Some weeks earlier, Lincoln had bought a stack of small notebooks to record, with Mary's help, all hundred members of the two houses, identifying the party affiliation of each, as well as his stance on the Nebraska bill. Their calculations gave reason to hope, but the situation was complicated. To reach a majority of 51 votes, Lincoln would have to hold together the fragile coalition comprised of former rivals in the Whig and Democratic camps who had only recently joined hands against the Nebraska bill.

Led by the governor, the senators marched into the House chamber at the appointed hour. When all were sworn in, the balloting began. On the first ballot, Lincoln received 45 votes, against 41 for the Douglas Democrat, James Shields, and 5 for Congressman Lyman Trumbull. The five anti-Nebraska Democrats who voted for Trumbull were led by Norman Judd of Chicago. They had no personal animosity toward Lincoln, but "having been elected as Democrats . . . they could not sustain themselves at home," they claimed, if they voted for a Whig for senator.

In the ballots that followed, as daylight gave way to gaslights in the great hall, Lincoln reached a high point of 47 votes, only 4 shy of victory.

Nonetheless, the little Trumbull coalition refused to budge, denying Lincoln the necessary majority. Finally, after nine ballots, Lincoln concluded that unless his supporters shifted to Trumbull, the Douglas Democrats, who had, as expected, switched their allegiance to Matteson, would choose the next senator.

Unwilling to sacrifice all the hard work of the antislavery coalition, Lincoln advised his floor manager, Stephen Logan, to drop him for Trumbull. Logan refused at first, protesting the injustice of the candidate with the much larger vote giving in to the candidate with the smaller vote. Lincoln was adamant, insisting that if his name remained on the ballot, "you will lose both Trumbull and myself and I think the cause in this case is to be preferred to men."

When Logan rose to speak, the tension in the chamber was so great that the "spectators scarcely breathed." In a sad voice, he announced that it was "the purpose of the remaining Whigs to decide the contest." Obeying his directions, Lincoln's supporters switched their votes to Trumbull, giving him the 51 votes needed for victory. Lincoln's friends were inconsolable, believing that this was "perhaps his last chance for that high position." Logan put his hands over his face and began to cry, while Davis stormily announced that had he been in Lincoln's situation, "he never would have consented to the 47 men being controlled by the 5."

In public, Lincoln expressed no hard feelings toward either Trumbull or Judd. He deliberately showed up at Trumbull's victory party, with a smile on his face and a warm handshake for the victor. Consoled that the Nebraska men were "worse whipped" than he, Lincoln insisted that Matteson's defeat "gives me more pleasure than my own gives me pain. . . . On the whole, it is perhaps as well for our general cause that Trumbull is elected."

Lincoln's magnanimity served him well. While Seward and Chase would lose friends in victory—Seward by neglecting at the height of his success his old friend Horace Greeley, and Chase by not understanding the lingering resentments that followed in the wake of his 1849 Senate victory—Lincoln, in defeat, gained friends. Neither Trumbull nor Judd would ever forget Lincoln's generous behavior. Indeed, both men would assist him in his bid for the U.S. Senate in 1858, and Judd would play a critical role in his run for the presidency in 1860.

Mary Lincoln was unable to be so gracious. Convinced that Trumbull had acted with "cold, selfish, treachery," she never spoke another word to Trumbull's wife, Julia, who had been a bridesmaid at her wedding and one of her closest friends. Though intermediaries tried in succeeding years to bring the two women together, the ruptured friendship never healed. Neither could Mary forgive Norman Judd for his role in supporting Trumbull. Though Judd, along with Davis, would do more than anyone else to assure Lincoln's nomination at the Chicago convention, Mary did everything she could to blackball him from a cabinet post after her husband's election.

Despite the dignity of Lincoln's public demeanor, he privately suffered a brutal disappointment, describing the ordeal as an "agony." Though he had engineered Trumbull's victory for the sake of the anti-Nebraska cause, it was difficult to accept the manner of his loss. "He could bear defeat inflicted by his enemies with a pretty good grace," he told his friend Gillespie, "but it was hard to be wounded in the house of his friends." After all the hard work, the interminable nights and weekends on the hustings, the conversations with fellow politicians, the hours spent writing letters to garner support, after so many years of patient waiting and hopefulness, he seemed as far from realizing his ambition as ever. Fate seemed to take a curious delight in finding new ways to shatter his dreams.

• • •

IN THE SUMMER OF 1855, disappointment piled upon disappointment. Six months after his loss to Trumbull, Lincoln's involvement in a celebrated law case forced him to recognize that his legal reputation, secure as it might have been in frontier Illinois, carried little weight among the preeminent lawyers in the country.

The story began that June with the arrival in Springfield of Peter Watson, a young associate in the distinguished Philadelphia firm headed by George Harding, a nationally renowned patent specialist. Harding had been hired by the John Manny Company of Rockford, Illinois, to defend its mechanical reaping machine against a patent infringement charge brought by Cyrus McCormick, the original inventor of the reaper. *McCormick v. Manny*, better known as the "Reaper" suit, was considered an important test case, pitting two outstanding patent lawyers, Edward Dickerson of New York and former Attorney General Reverdy Johnson for McCormick, against Harding for Manny. Since the case was to be tried before a judge in Chicago, Harding decided to engage a local lawyer who "understood the judge and had his confidence," though, from his Eastern perspective, he condescendingly expressed doubt he could find a lawyer in Illinois "who would be of real assistance" in arguing the case.

Watson was sent to Springfield to see if Abraham Lincoln, whose name had been recommended, was the right man for the position. His initial impression was not positive. Neither the small frame house on Eighth Street nor Lincoln's appearance at the door with "neither coat nor vest" indicated a lawyer of sufficient standing for a case of this magnitude. After talking with Lincoln, however, Watson decided he might be "rather effective" after all. He paid Lincoln a retainer and arranged a substantial fee when the work was completed. Lincoln was thrilled with both the fee and the opportunity to test himself with the renowned Reverdy Johnson. He began working on the legal arguments for the case, understanding that Harding would present the scientific arguments.

Not long after Watson's Springfield visit, Harding received word that the case had been transferred from Chicago to Cincinnati. The change of venue to Ohio "removed the one object" for employing Lincoln, allowing Harding to team up with the man he had wanted in the first place—the brilliant Edwin Stanton. Unaware of the changed situation, Lincoln continued to develop his case. "At our interview here in June," he wrote Watson in late July, "I understood you to say you would send me copies of the Bill and Answer . . . and also of depositions . . . I have had nothing from you since. However, I attended the U.S. Court at Chicago, and while there, got copies . . . I write this particularly to urge you to forward on to me the additional evidence as fast as you can. During August, and the remainder of this month, I can devote some time to the case, and, of course, I want all the material that can be had. During my day at Chicago, I went out to Rockford, and spent half a day, examining and studying Manny's Machine."

Though Lincoln never heard from Watson, he pieced together what he needed and in late September set out for Cincinnati with a lengthy brief in his hands. Arriving at the Burnet House where all the lawyers were lodged, he encountered Harding and Stanton as they left for the court. Years later, Harding could still recall the shock of his first sight of the "tall, rawly boned, ungainly back woodsman, with coarse, ill-fitting clothing, his trousers hardly reaching his ankles, holding in his hands a blue cotton umbrella with a ball on the end of the handle." Lincoln introduced himself and proposed, "Let's go up in a gang." At this point, Stanton drew Harding aside and whispered, "Why did you bring that d——d long armed Ape here . . . he does not know any thing and can do you no good." With that, Stanton and Harding turned from Lincoln and continued to court on their own.

In the days that followed, Stanton "managed to make it plain to Lincoln" that he was expected to remove himself from the case. Lincoln did withdraw, though he remained in Cincinnati to hear the arguments. Harding never opened Lincoln's manuscript, "so sure that it would be only trash." Throughout that week, though Lincoln ate at the same hotel, Harding and Stanton never asked him to join them for a meal, or accompany them to or from court. When Judge John McLean hosted a dinner for the lawyers on both sides, Lincoln was not invited.

The hearing continued for a week. The sophisticated arguments were "a revelation" to Lincoln, recalled Ralph Emerson, one of Manny's partners. So intrigued was he by Stanton's speech, in particular, that he stood in "rapt attention . . . drinking in his words." Never before, Emerson realized, had Lincoln "seen anything so finished and elaborated, and so thoroughly prepared." When the hearing was over, Lincoln told Emerson that he was going home "to study law." Emerson did not understand at first what Lincoln meant by this, but Lincoln explained. "For any rough-and-tumble case (and a pretty good one, too), I am enough for any man we have out in that country; but these college-trained men are coming West. They have had all the advantages of a life-long training in the law, plenty of time to study and everything, perhaps, to fit them. Soon they will be in Illinois . . . and when they appear I will be ready."

As Lincoln prepared to leave Cincinnati, he went to say goodbye to William Dickson, one of the few people who had shown him kindness that week. "You have made my stay here most agreeable, and I am a thousand times obliged to you," Lincoln told Dickson's wife, "but in reply to your request for me to come again I must say to you I never expect to be in Cincinnati again. I have nothing against the city, but things have so happened here as to make it undesirable for me ever to return here."

After returning to Springfield, Lincoln received a check in the mail for the balance of his fee. He returned it, saying he had not earned it, never having made any argument. When Watson sent the check a second time, Lincoln cashed it.

Unimaginable as it might seem, after Stanton's bearish behavior, at their next encounter six years later, Lincoln would offer Stanton "the most powerful civilian post within his gift"—the post of secretary of war. Lincoln's choice of Stanton would reveal, as would his subsequent dealings with Trumbull and Judd, a singular ability to transcend personal vendetta, humiliation, or bitterness. As for Stanton, despite his initial contempt for the "long armed Ape," he would not only accept the offer but come to respect and love Lincoln more than any person outside of his immediate family.

Stanton's surly condescension toward Lincoln must be considered in the context of his anxiety over the Reaper trial, which had assumed crucial importance for him. Ever since the death of his father when he was only thirteen, Stanton had been obsessed with financial security. Until his father, a successful physician, died from apoplexy at the age of forty, young

Edwin had led a pampered existence in Steubenville, Ohio, surrounded by a loving family in a stately, two-story brick house with a large yard and fruitful garden. Taught to read when he was only three years old, the precocious child had ready access to his father's large collection of books and received an excellent education at the Old Academy in Steubenville. But when his father died, leaving no estate, Edwin was forced to leave school to help support his widowed mother and three younger siblings. First came the forced sale of the house, then the sale of his father's library, and finally, the necessity to move to much smaller quarters. Apprenticed to a bookseller, Stanton read books in every spare moment he could find and spent his evenings preparing for entrance to nearby Kenyon College, headed by Chase's uncle Philander. An excellent student, he enjoyed two happy years at Kenyon before his family's scarce resources required that he return to work, this time in a Columbus bookstore.

The following year, Stanton returned to Steubenville and secured an apprenticeship in a law office, where he simultaneously studied law and helped his mother with the younger children. In later years, his adoring sister Pamphila recalled Stanton's critical role in anchoring the entire family, tenderly nursing his ailing mother, sending his brother Darwin to Harvard Medical School, and encouraging his younger sisters to memorize dozens of poems by Byron and Whittier, all the while reading Plutarch's *Lives* and other works of history. Success in the law came quickly, the result of an intuitive mind, a prodigious capacity for work, and a forceful courtroom manner.

When he fell in love with Mary Lamson, he enjoyed what he much later called the "happiest hours of his life." A marvelously intellectual young woman, Mary shared his passion for reading and study, coupled with a feminist determination that women could "*regenerate the world*" if only they were rightly educated. When their marriage produced a daughter, Lucy, and a son, Edwin Junior, Stanton had every reason to believe that fortune was smiling on him. His sister Pamphila later recalled that her brother seemed perpetually "bright and cheery." As his practice grew, he had the means not only to take care of his own family but to provide for his mother and younger siblings as well.

Stanton looked upon Mary as his life companion. They both loved history, literature, and poetry. Together, they read Gibbon, Carlisle, Macaulay, Madame de Staël, Samuel Johnson, Bancroft, and Byron. "We years ago were lovers," he wrote her after the children were born. "We are now parents; a new relation has taken place. The love of our offspring has opened up fresh fountains of love for each other. We look forward now to life, not for ourselves only, but for our children. I loved you for your beauty, and grace and loveliness of your person. I love you now for the richness and surpassing excellence of your mind. One love has not taken the place of the other, but both stand side by side. I love you now with a fervor and truth of affection which speech cannot express."

His happiness was short-lived: his daughter Lucy died after an attack of scarlet fever; three years later, in March, 1844, his beloved Mary developed a fatal bilious fever and died at the age of twenty-nine. Stanton was so brokenhearted, his grief "verged on insanity." Before he would allow her burial, he had a seamstress fashion a wedding dress for her. "She is my bride and shall be dressed and buried like a bride." After the funeral, he could not bring himself to work for months. Since he was involved in almost every case that came before the court in Jefferson County, Ohio, no court was held that spring. For months, he laid out Mary's nightcap and gown on her pillow. His sister, Pamphila, who had come to stay with him, would never forget the horror of the long nights when, "with lamp in hand," he searched for Mary through every room of the house, "with sobs and tears streaming from his eyes," screaming over and over, "Where is Mary?"

Stanton's responsibilities to his family eventually brought him back to his law practice, but he could not let go of his sorrow. Fearful that his son, then only two years old, would have no memories of the mother he had lost, he spent his nights writing a letter of over a hundred pages to the boy. He described his romance with Mary from its earliest days and included extracts from all the letters they had exchanged over the years. His words were penned with an unsteady hand, he confessed, with "tears obscuring his vision" and an "anguish of heart" driving him periodically from his chair. He would have preferred to wait until the boy was older and better able to understand; "but time, care, sickness, and the vicissitudes of life, wear out and efface the impression of the mind. Besides life is uncertain. I may be called from you. . . . You might live and die without knowing of the affection your father and mother bore for you, and for each other."

Stanton's miseries multiplied when his younger brother, Darwin, who completed his studies at Harvard Medical School, developed a high fever that impaired his brain. Unhinged by his acute illness, the young doctor, who was married with three small children, took a sharp lance-head and punctured his throat. "He bled to death in a few moments," a family friend recalled. His mother watched helplessly as "the blood spouted up to the ceiling." Neighbors were sent to fetch Edwin, who lived nearby. When he witnessed the aftermath of the gruesome spectacle, he reportedly "lost self-control and wandered off into the woods without his hat or coat." Fearful that he, too, might commit suicide, neighbors pursued, restrained, and escorted him home, where they took turns watching over him.

This horrific train of events transformed Stanton's spirit. His natural ebullience faded. "Where formerly he met everybody with hearty and cheerful greeting," said a friend, "he now moved about in silence and gloom, with head bowed and hands clasped behind." Though he remained a tender father to his son and a loving brother to his younger sisters, he became increasingly aggressive in court, intimidating witnesses unnecessarily, antagonizing fellow lawyers, exhibiting rude and irascible behavior.

He derived his only satisfaction from his growing reputation and his increasing wealth, which allowed him to care for his son, his widowed mother, his sisters, and his dead brother's wife and children. The Reaper case was the biggest case of his career, "the most important Patent cause that has ever been tried," he told a friend, "and more time, labor, money and brains have been expended in getting it ready for argument, than any other Patent case ever has had bestowed upon it." If all went well, it would open doors for Stanton at the highest level of his profession.

When he arrived at the Burnet House, he discovered that Harding "had been unwell for several days" and might not be in a position to go to court. Terrified that in addition to the legal argument he had fully prepared, he might now have to present the "scientific part of the case to which [he] had given no attention," Stanton stayed up all night in preparation. He was greatly relieved when Harding recovered, but anxiety and lack of sleep compounded the irascibility that had marked his demeanor since the multiple deaths in his family.

Beyond the breaking pressures of the case, Stanton had become involved in a turbulent courtship. The young woman, Ellen Hutchison, the daughter of a wealthy Pittsburgh businessman, was the first woman who had attracted his interest since the death of his wife more than a decade earlier. Tall, blond, and blue-eyed, Ellen was, by Stanton's description, "radiant with beauty and intellect." While Stanton was smitten with Ellen immediately, she was slow to respond to his affections. She still suffered from a romantic disappointment that had left her heart in "agony" and convinced her that she could not love again.

Stanton understood, he told her, that "the trouble of early love fell like a killing frost upon the tree of your life," but he was confident that "enough life still remains to put forth fresh blossoms." Despite his encouragement, Ellen was vexed by some of the qualities others noted in Stanton: his obsessive concentration on work, his impatience and lack of humor, and, most worrisome, "his careless[ness] and indifferen[ce] to the feelings of all."

Addressing these concerns, Stanton admitted that "there is so much of the hard and repulsive in my—(I will not say nature, for that I think is soft and tender) but in the temper and habit of life generated by adverse circumstances, that great love only can bear with and overlook." If the last decade of his life had been different, he assured her, if he had been "blessed with the companionship of a woman whose love would have pointed out and kindly corrected my errors, I would have escaped the fault you condemn."

After the successful conclusion of the Reaper trial, Ellen was finally persuaded to marry Edwin on June 25, 1856. Happier years followed for Stanton. The Manny patent was sustained not only by the Cincinnati court but by the U.S. Supreme Court on appeal. With this huge victory behind him, Stanton moved his practice to Washington, D.C., where he argued important cases before the Supreme Court, achieved substantial financial security, and built a brick mansion for his new wife.

• • •

As Lincoln's own hopes were repeatedly frustrated, he wistfully watched the progress of others, in particular, Stephen Douglas, his great rival with whom he had often debated around the fire of Speed's general store. "Twenty-two years ago Judge Douglas and I first became acquainted," he confided in a private fragment later discovered in his papers. "We were both young then; he a trifle younger than I. Even then, we were both ambitious; I, perhaps, quite as much so as he. With *me* the race of ambition has been a failure—a flat failure; with *him* it has been one of splendid success. His name fills the nation; and is not unknown, even, in foreign lands. I affect no contempt for the high eminence he has reached. So reached, that the oppressed of my species, might have shared with me in the elevation, I would rather stand on that eminence, than wear the richest crown that ever pressed a monarch's brow."

At this juncture, some have suggested, Lincoln was sustained by his wife's unflagging belief that a glorious destiny awaited him. "She had the fire, will and ambition," his law partner John Stuart observed. When Mary was young and still being courted by many beaux, she had told a friend who had taken an old, wealthy husband, "I would rather marry a good man—a man of mind—with a hope and bright prospects ahead for position—fame and power than to marry all the houses—gold and bones in the world." Stephen Douglas, who had been among her suitors, she considered "a very little, *little* giant, by the side of my tall Kentuckian, and intellectually my husband towers above Douglas just as he does physically." Quite simply, in Mary's mind, her husband had "no equal in the United States."

In an era when, as Mary herself admitted, it was "unladylike" to be so interested in politics, she avidly supported her husband's political ambitions at every stage. Although she undoubtedly fortified his will at difficult moments, however, Lincoln's quest for public recognition and influence was so consuming, it is unlikely he would have abandoned his dreams, whatever the circumstances.

• • •

ONCE AGAIN, at a moment when Lincoln's career appeared to have come to a halt, Seward and Chase were moving forward. Chase's leadership during the political uprising in the North that followed the passage of the Nebraska Act had proved, in the words of Carl Schurz, to be "the first bugle call for the formation of a new party." Under the pressure of mounting sectional division, both national parties—the Whigs and the Democrats—had begun to fray. The Whig Party—the party of Clay and Webster, Lincoln, Seward, and Bates—had been the first to decline as "conscience Whigs," opposed to slavery, split from "cotton Whigs," who desired an accommodation with slavery. In the 1852 election, the divided Whig Party had been buried in a Democratic landslide. But the passage of the Nebraska Act brought serious defections in the Democratic Party as well, as Northerners unwilling to sanction the extension of slavery looked for a new home, leaving the party in control of the Southern Democrats.

The political upheaval was enormously complicated by the emergence of the Know Nothing Party, which had formed in reaction to an unprecedented flood of immigration in the 1840s and 1850s. In 1845, about 20 million people inhabited the United States. During the next decade, nearly 3 million immigrants arrived, mainly from Ireland and Germany. This largely Catholic influx descended on a country that was mostly native-born Protestant, anti-Catholic in sympathy. The Know Nothings fought to delay citizenship for the new immigrants and bar them from voting. In the early 1850s, they won elections in several cities, swept to statewide victory in Massachusetts, and gained surprising ground in New York. Newspapers and preachers assaulted "popery"; there were bloody anti-Catholic riots in several Northern cities.

Lincoln had nothing but disdain for the discriminatory beliefs of the Know Nothings. "How can any one who abhors the oppression of negroes, be in favor of degrading classes of white people?" he queried his friend Joshua Speed. "Our progress in degeneracy appears to me to be pretty rapid. As a nation, we began by declaring that *'all men are created equal.'* We now practically read it 'all men are created equal, *except negroes.'* When the Know-Nothings get control, it will read 'all men are created equal, except negroes, *and foreigners, and catholics.*' When it comes to this I should prefer emigrating to some country where they make no pretence of loving liberty—to Russia, for instance."

But this party, too, was soon to founder on the issue of slavery. Many Northern Know Nothings were also antislavery, and finally the anti-Nebraska cause proved more compelling, of more import, than resistance to foreign immigration. The split between the party's Northern and Southern factions would diminish its strength, though the nativist feelings that had fueled its birth would continue to influence the political climate even after the party itself collapsed and died.

With the Whigs disappearing and the Democrats under Southern domination, all those opposed to the extension of slavery found their new home in what eventually became the Republican Party, comprised of "conscience Whigs," "independent Democrats," and antislavery Know Nothings. In state after state, new coalitions with different names came into being—the Fusion Party, the People's Party, the Anti-Nebraska Party. In Ripon, Wisconsin, an 1854 gathering of antislavery men proposed the name "Republican Party," and other state conventions soon followed suit.

In Illinois, Lincoln held back, still hoping that the Whig Party could become the antislavery party. In New York, Seward hesitated as well, finding it difficult to sever friendships and relationships built over three decades. Salmon Chase, however, was unhindered by past loyalties. He was ready to commit himself wholeheartedly to the task of forging a new party under the Republican banner. He had always been willing to move on when new political arrangements offered richer prospects for himself and the cause. Beginning as a Whig, he had joined the Liberty Party. He had abandoned that party for the Free-Soilers and then had gone to the Senate as an independent Democrat. Now, with his Senate term coming to an end, and with little chance of being nominated by the Democrats for a second term, he was happy to become a Republican.

In Ohio, as in New York and Illinois, the new movement was complicated by the strength of nativist sentiment. A delicate balance would be required to court the old Know Nothings without forfeiting support in the immigrant German-American community, which was passionate in its hatred of slavery. Chase accomplished this feat by running for governor on a Republican platform endorsing no specific Know Nothing proposals, but including eight Know Nothing candidates for all the important offices on the statewide ticket.

It was a hard-fought canvass, and the indefatigable Chase left nothing to chance. Traveling by railroad, horseback, hand car, canoe, and open wagon, he spoke at fifty-seven different places in forty-nine counties.

Campaigning in the sparsely settled sections of Ohio proved to be an adventure. To reach the town of Delphos, he wrote Kate, he was driven along the railroad tracks "on a hand car" operated by two men who "placed themselves at the cranks." Though the stars provided light, "it was rather dangerous for who could tell but we might meet a train or perhaps another hand car."

Chase's strenuous work paid off, making him the first Republican governor of a major state. "The anxiety of the last few days is over," Sumner wrote from Boston. "At last I breathe freely!" Reading the news under the telegraphic band at breakfast, the Massachusetts senator could barely contain his excitement, predicting that his friend's victory would do more than anything else for the antislavery cause.

In New York, Seward faced a more difficult challenge than Chase in trying to placate the Know Nothings, who had never forgiven his proposal to extend state funds to Catholic schools. Indeed, they were determined to defeat Seward for reelection to the Senate in 1855. Facing the enmity of both the Know Nothings and the proslavery "cotton Whigs," he concluded that he could not risk moving to a new, untested party.

Seward's only hope for reelection lay in Weed's ability to cobble together an antislavery majority from among the various discordant elements in the state legislature. In the weeks before the legislature was set to convene, Weed entertained the members in alphabetical groups, angling for every possible vote, including a few Know Nothings who might put their antislavery principles above their anti-Catholic sentiments. At one of these lavish dinners, the story is told, three or four Know Nothings on a special tour of Weed's house confronted a portrait of Weed's good friend New York's bishop John Hughes. The stratagem would be doomed if the identity of the man in the portrait was known, so they were told that it was George Washington in his Continental robes, presented to Weed's father by Washington himself!

Working without rest, Weed somehow stitched together enough votes to reelect Seward to a second term in the Senate. "I snatch a minute from the pressure of solicitations of lobby men, and congratulations of newly-made friends, to express, not so much my deep, and deepened gratitude to you," Seward wrote Weed, "as my amazement at the magnitude and complexity of the dangers through which you have conducted our shattered bark." In Auburn, a great celebration followed the news of Seward's reelection. "I have never known such a season of rejoicing," Frances happily reported to her son Augustus. "They are firing 700 cannons here—a salute of 300 was given in Albany as soon as the vote was made known."

Once Seward was securely positioned for six additional years in the

Senate, he and Weed were liberated to join the Republican Party. Two state conventions, one Whig, one Republican, were convened in Syracuse in late September 1855. When Seward was asked by a friend which to attend, he replied that it didn't matter. Delegates would enter through two doors, but exit through one. The Whig delegates assembled first and adopted a strong antislavery platform. Then, led by Weed, they marched into the adjoining hall, where the Republicans greeted them with thunderous applause. From the remnants of dissolving parties, a new Republican Party had been born in the state of New York.

"I am so happy that you and I are at last on the same platform and in the same political pew," Sumner told Seward. That October, Seward announced his allegiance to the Republican Party in a rousing speech that traced the history of the growth of the slave power, illustrating the constant march to acquire new slave states and thereby ensure for slaveholders the balance of power in the Congress. "What, then, is wanted?" he asked. "Nothing but organization." The task before the new Republican Party was to consolidate its strength until it gained control of the Congress and secured the power to forbid the extension of slavery in the territories.

• • •

IN EARLY 1856, Lincoln decided that Illinois should follow New York and Ohio in organizing the various anti-Nebraska elements into the new Republican Party. Through his efforts, the call went out for an anti-Nebraska state convention to be held on May 29, 1856. Lincoln proceeded carefully in the weeks leading to the convention, recognizing the complexities of reconciling the disparate opponents of the Nebraska bill into a unified party. Despite the success of Weed and Chase in their respective states, Lincoln worried that the convention call would attract only the more radical elements of the coalition, providing too narrow a base for a viable new party.

Dramatic events in Kansas helped rally support for Lincoln's cause. A guerrilla war had broken out between Northern emigrants desiring to make Kansas a free state under the "popular sovereignty" provision of the Nebraska Act, and so-called "border ruffians," who crossed the river from Missouri and cast illicit votes to make Kansas a slave state. During the debate over the Nebraska Act, Seward had told the slave states that the North would "engage in competition for the virgin soil of Kansas, and God give the victory to the side which is stronger in numbers as it is in right." In the South, the *Charleston Mercury* responded: "When the North presents a sectional issue, and tenders battle upon it, she must meet it, or abide all the consequences of a victory easily won, by a remorseless and eager foe." As the violence spiraled, "Bleeding Kansas" became a new rallying cry for the antislavery forces. Kansas was not merely a contest between settlers but a war between North and South.

Moderate antislavery sentiment was further aroused when shocking news from Washington reached Illinois the week before the convention. On the Senate floor, South Carolina's Preston Brooks had savagely bludgeoned Charles Sumner in return for Sumner's incendiary antislavery speech. Sumner had begun unremarkably enough, presenting familiar arguments, laced with literary and historical references, against admitting Kansas as a slave state. The mood of the Senate chamber instantly shifted, however, when Sumner launched into a vituperative attack directed particularly against two of his fellow senators, Stephen Douglas of Illinois and Andrew Butler of South Carolina. He likened Butler to the aging, feeble Don Quixote, who imagined himself "a chivalrous knight," sentimentally devoted to his beloved "harlot, Slavery . . . who, though ugly to others, is always lovely to him." Riding forth by Butler's side, Douglas was "the squire of Slavery, its very Sancho Panza, ready to do all its humiliating offices."

In the days before delivering the speech, Sumner had read a draft to Frances Seward. She strongly advised him to remove the personal attacks, including a reference to Butler's slight paralysis that slurred his speech. In this instance Sumner did not heed her advice; when he finished speaking, Senator Lewis Cass of Michigan characterized the speech as "the most un-American and unpatriotic that ever grated on the ears of the members of this high body—as I hope never to hear again here or elsewhere."

Two days later, Butler's young cousin Congressman Preston Brooks entered the Senate chamber armed with a heavy cane. Walking up to Sumner, who was writing at his desk, Brooks reportedly said, "You have libelled South Carolina and my relative, and I have come to punish you." Before Sumner could speak, Brooks brought the cane down upon his head, cudgeling him repeatedly as Sumner futilely tried to rise from his desk. Covered with blood, Sumner fell unconscious and was carried from the floor.

News of the brutal assault, which left Sumner with severe injuries to his brain and spinal cord and kept him out of the Senate for three years, galvanized antislavery sentiment in the North. "Knots of men" on street corners pronounced it "a gross outrage on an American Senator and on freedom of speech," reported the *Boston Daily Evening Transcript.* Even the moderate supporters of the Nebraska bill "expressed themselves as never so much aroused before by the slave power." Mass public meetings, so crowded that thousands were unable to gain entrance, convened in cities and towns to protest the caning. Truly to "*see* the slave aggression," one of

Sumner's supporters wrote, the North had first to see "one of its best men Butchered in Congress." Other antislavery men had been assaulted, the *New York Tribune* observed, "but the knocking-down and beating to bloody blindness and unconsciousness of an American Senator while writing at his desk in the Senate Chamber is a novel illustration of the ferocious Southern spirit." The beating reached into the people's hearts and minds, which political events rarely touch, the historian William Gienapp has argued. It "proved a powerful stimulus in driving moderates and conservatives into the Republican party."

If Sumner became a hero in the North, Brooks was equally lionized in the South, where the press almost universally applauded the assault. The *Richmond Enquirer* spoke for many when it pronounced the act "good in conception, better in execution, and best of all in consequence." Celebratory gatherings were held everywhere, and in Columbia, South Carolina, the governor presented Brooks with a silver goblet and walking stick in honor of his good work.

More ominous still was the reaction of the distinguished *Richmond Whig*, a professed opponent of extremism on sectional issues. "*We are rejoiced at this,*" the *Whig* proclaimed. "The only regret we feel is, that Mr. Brooks did not employ a horsewhip or a cowhide upon his slanderous back, instead of a cane. *We trust the ball may be kept in motion. Seward and others should catch it next.*" The *Petersburg [Virginia] Intelligencer* sounded a similar theme. "If thrashing is the only remedy by which the foul conduct of the Abolitionists can be controlled . . . *it will be very well to give Seward a double dose at least every other day* until it operates freely on his political bowels . . . his adroit demagoguism and damnable doctrines are infinitely more dangerous to the country than the coarse blackguardism of the perjured wretch, Sumner." The antipodal reactions of North and South, David Donald notes, made it "apparent that something dangerous was happening to the American Union when the two sections no longer spoke the same language, but employed rival sets of clichés to describe the Brooks-Sumner affair."

With emotions running high in Illinois, "all shades of antislavery opinion" flocked to the Bloomington convention—"old-line Whigs, bolting Democrats, Free-Soilers, Know Nothings, and abolitionists." Lincoln's fears were put to rest. Every faction seemed willing to concede something to create a party that all could stand behind.

The adopted platform united disparate factions on the issue of slavery extension without giving in to the bigoted views of the Know Nothings. Lincoln then delivered a powerful speech, full of "fire and energy and force," that further fortified the jarring factions into a united front. "That is the greatest speech ever made in Illinois," state auditor Jesse Dubois said, "and puts Lincoln on the track for the presidency." So enthralled were those in the audience that reporters cast aside their pens so as to concentrate on what Lincoln said, and the unrecorded speech has become known to history as the famous "Lost Speech." Lincoln was now the acknowledged leader of the new Republican Party in Illinois.

• • •

BY THE LATE SPRING of 1856, branches of the Republican Party had already been organized in at least twenty-two states and the District of Columbia, a remarkable beginning for a new party, giving hope to the leaders that this time, with the Whig Party all but dissolved and the Democratic Party split in two, they stood a solid chance in the presidential election. On June 17, when energized Republicans assembled in Philadelphia for their first national convention, both Seward and Chase had their hearts set on the nomination.

In Republican circles, Chase's gubernatorial election had earned him such tremendous prestige that he was convinced he was destined for the presidency. Writing to a friend just ten days after his Ohio victory, Chase suggested that his success in uniting liberal nativists with antislavery German-Americans demonstrated the key to Republican victory in the future. Where Republicans challenged the Know Nothing Party, as they did in Massachusetts, they found defeat. Chase seemed to feel that he was now entitled to the Republican presidential nomination in 1856.

Chase had journeyed to Francis Blair's country home in Maryland the previous December for the legendary Christmas conclave called to organize the Republican Party on a national basis. Francis Blair, the patriarch of the Blair family, wielded great power in party politics because of his old ties to the Democratic Party and his newfound antislavery views. Chase arrived to find Sumner in attendance, along with his old friend Gamaliel Bailey, the abolitionist editor of *The National Era;* New York congressman Preston King; and Massachusetts politician Nathaniel Banks. Seward had been invited, but, uncertain of how he would proceed on a national scale, he had sent Blair a note "approving of his activity, but declining his invitation." After an elegant dinner, served, ironically, by Blair's household slaves, the group sat down to discuss the future of the Republican Party.

At Chase's suggestion, the gathering agreed to hold an organizational meeting the following month in Pittsburgh. Inevitably, the conversation turned to potential candidates for the upcoming presidential election. Blair's suggestion of John Charles Frémont, the celebrated explorer who had played a central role in the conquest of California during the Mexican

War, met with general approval. The discussion undoubtedly disappointed Chase, who believed up to the moment of Frémont's nomination at the Philadelphia convention on June 19 that "if the unvarnished wishes of the people" prevailed, he would be chosen.

Chase's certainty was insufficient to mobilize the wrangling elements at the convention in support of his candidacy. Not only had he neglected to appoint a manager, but he failed to unite his own state behind him on the first ballot. The questionable deals he had made to secure his Senate seat eight years earlier had created permanent enemies within his home state. "I know that if Ohio had united on you instead of dividing her votes between [John] McLean & Fremont & you," Chase's friend Hiram Barney wrote, "your nomination would have been a matter of necessity; or if a tithe of the pains which were taken to urge Fremont had been employed for your nomination, it would have been accomplished."

Before the convention met, Seward had greater reason for hope than Chase, for clearly, he was the first choice of Republican voters and politicians. Weed kept him from running, however, insisting that the party was not yet sufficiently organized to win a national election. Better to wait four years than to be tarred with failure.

While the Republican Convention was in progress, Lincoln was staying at the American House in Urbana, Illinois, attending court. He was in high spirits, recalled Henry Whitney, having engaged in one of the practical jokes of which he was so fond. He had hidden the loud and annoying gong that summoned his fellow boarders to dinner. When the loss was discovered, Whitney entered the dining room and saw Lincoln sitting "awkwardly in a chair tilted up after his fashion, looking amused, silly and guilty." When Judge Davis told him he must put it back, Lincoln took the gong from its hiding place and returned it, "after which he bounded up the stairs, two steps at a time."

Within a day or two, the merry prankster received word that in the balloting for vice president, he had received 110 votes, second only to the eventual nominee, William Dayton of New Jersey. "Davis and I were greatly excited," Whitney recalled. Lincoln did not take it seriously at first, remarking only that "there's another great man in Massachusetts named Lincoln, and I reckon it's him." His casual response aside, it is probable that this unexpected event stimulated Lincoln's aspiration for higher office.

Unlike Seward, Chase, and Lincoln in 1856, Edward Bates refused to desert the divided and much-diminished Whig Party. While he joined with Republicans in vigorous opposition to the Kansas-Nebraska Act and the repeal of the sacred Missouri Compromise, he feared that the Republican focus on slavery would lead to an irreparable divide between North and South. After some indecision, he agreed to preside over the shrunken Whig National Convention of July 1856. The Whigs gathered in Baltimore and ultimately decided to support Millard Fillmore for president. Fillmore ran as a member of the American Party (a more palatable title for the old Know Nothing Party) on a platform that denounced both Republicans and Democrats for agitating the slavery issue at the risk of the nation's peace.

Though not a fanatical nativist, Bates considered the American Party, with its emphasis on issues other than slavery and a support base drawn from all sections of the country, the best hope for preserving the Union. "I am neither North nor South," he said in a final plea before the convention, "I repudiate political geography. . . . I am a man believing in making laws and then whether the law is exactly to my liking or not, enforcing it—whether it be to catch a runaway slave and bring him back to his master or to quell a riot in a disordered territory."

The general election resulted in a three-way race between the Republican Frémont, the Southern-leaning Democrat James Buchanan, and American Party candidate Millard Fillmore. When the votes were counted, Weed's advice to Seward proved correct. Though the Republican Party showed considerable strength throughout the North in its first national effort, winning eleven states, the South threw its strength behind Democrat James Buchanan, who emerged the victor. In addition to his overwhelming strength in the South, Buchanan captured four Northern states—Illinois, Indiana, Pennsylvania, and New Jersey—the states destined to be the battleground in the 1860 election. Fillmore and the American Party captured only tiny Maryland.

• • •

AS THE DAY of Buchanan's inauguration approached, the Supreme Court was drafting a decision in the case of *Dred Scott v. Sandford*, which had originated in Missouri eleven years earlier. Scott, a slave, was suing for his freedom on the grounds that his master, an army doctor, had removed him for several years to military bases in both the free state of Illinois and the Wisconsin Territory before returning to the slave state of Missouri. The case wound its way through state and federal courts until it finally reached the Supreme Court for argument in 1856, with Francis Blair's son, Montgomery, representing Dred Scott and the celebrated Reverdy Johnson from the slave state of Maryland representing Scott's owners. The court was headed by Chief Justice Roger Taney of Maryland, "an uncompromising supporter of the South and slavery and an implacable foe of racial equality, the Republican Party, and the antislavery movement."

Seward was among the thousands of spectators gathered at the Capitol on March 4, 1857, to witness James Buchanan's inauguration. "Bright skies and a deliciously bland atmosphere" relieved the blustery weather of the previous two days. In his inaugural address, Buchanan conceded that a "difference of opinion" had arisen over the question of extending slavery into the territories. However, this vital question, which had figured in the formation of the Republican Party, was not a political issue, he claimed, but "a judicial question, which legitimately belongs to the Supreme Court of the United States." A decision in the *Dred Scott* case bearing on this very issue was pending before that august body. To that decision, Buchanan pledged: "I shall cheerfully submit, whatever this may be." All evidence suggests that Buchanan was already aware of the substance of the decision.

Two days later, on March 6, the historic decision was read by the seventy-nine-year-old Taney in the old Supreme Court chamber, one flight below the Senate. The 7–2 decision was breathtaking in its scope and consequences. The Court ruled that blacks "are not included, and were not intended to be included, under the word 'citizens' in the Constitution." Therefore, Scott had no standing in federal court. This should have decided the case, but Taney went further. Neither the Declaration of Independence nor the Constitution had been intended to apply to blacks, he said. Blacks were "so far inferior that they had no rights which the white man was bound to respect." But the Chief Justice did not stop even there; he went on to say that Congress had exceeded its authority when it forbade slavery in the territories by such legislation as the Missouri Compromise, for slaves were private property protected by the Constitution. In other words, the Missouri Compromise was unconstitutional. The act itself, of course, had already been repealed by the Nebraska Act, meaning that the Court was pronouncing on an issue that was not before it.

One of the justices later asserted that Taney had "become convinced that it was practicable for the Court to quiet all agitation on the question of slavery in the territories by affirming that Congress had no constitutional power to prohibit its introduction." But the fierce sectional conflict of the age, the question that had given birth to the Republican Party, could not be quieted by a divided judicial fiat. The *Dred Scott* case, Supreme Court Justice Felix Frankfurter later said, was "one of the Court's great self-inflicted wounds."

Initially, the decision appeared to be a stunning victory for the South. For more than a decade, the *Richmond Enquirer* proclaimed, antislavery forces had claimed for the federal government the right of prescribing the boundaries of slavery in the territories. Now the territorial prize for which the two sides had "often wrestled in the halls of Congress, has been awarded at last, by the proper umpire, to those who have justly won it." The decision of the Supreme Court, "the accredited interpreter of the Constitution and arbiter of disagreements between the several States," the *Enquirer* continued, has destroyed "*the foundation* of the theory upon which their warfare has been waged against the institutions of the South." Antislavery men were staggered, the *Enquirer* claimed, left "nonplused and bewildered, confounded and confused."

"Sheer blasphemy," Republicans responded. The ruling was "entitled to just so much moral weight as would be the judgment of a majority of those congregated in any Washington bar-room." The *New York Tribune* argued that the Supreme Court had forfeited its stature as "an impartial judicial body," and predicted that its attempt to derail the Republican Party, which had come so close to victory in the previous presidential election, would fail. "Judge Taney can do many things," Frederick Douglass observed, "but he cannot . . . change the essential nature of things—making evil good, and good, evil." Frances Seward hoped that the blatantly unethical decision would galvanize the national will of the North. It "has aroused many to the encroachments of the slave power," she happily reported to Sumner.

The furor broke yet another bond of union by involving the Supreme Court, the common guarantor of both North and South, in sectional conflict. Dred Scott was sold to a Mr. Taylor Blow, who promptly freed him. He would die within a year, a free man whose name would leave a deeper mark on American history than those of the justices who had consigned him to slavery.

Speaking in Springfield, Lincoln attacked the decision in characteristic fashion, not by castigating the Court but by meticulously exposing flaws of logic. The Chief Justice, Lincoln said, "insists at great length that negroes were no part of the people who made, or for whom was made, the Declaration of Independence, or the Constitution." Yet in at least five states, black voters acted on the ratification of the Constitution and were among the "We the People" by whom the Constitution was ordained and established. The founders, he acknowledged, did not "declare all men equal *in all respects*. They did not mean to say all were equal in color, size, intellect, moral developments, or social capacity." But they did declare all men "equal in 'certain inalienable rights, among which are life, liberty, and the pursuit of happiness.' . . . They meant simply to declare the *right*, so the *enforcement* of it might follow as fast as circumstances should permit."

• • •

Seward, too, would condemn the *Dred Scott* decision in a sensational oration on the Senate floor, accusing the administration of having engaged in a corrupt conspiracy with the Supreme Court. "The day of inauguration came," Seward said. The innocent crowd gathered for the ceremony were "unaware of the import of the whisperings carried on between the President and the Chief Justice." While the Chief Justice looked on and the members of the Senate watched in silence, Seward continued, President Buchanan proclaimed his complete support for the forthcoming, and supposedly yet unknown, Supreme Court ruling on the status of blacks under the Constitution. When "the pageant ended," Seward cried scornfully, "the judges, without even exchanging their silken robes for courtiers' gowns, paid their salutations to the President, in the Executive palace. Doubtlessly the President received them as graciously as Charles I did the judges who had, at his instance, subverted the statutes of English liberty."

While Seward's charges were echoed and acclaimed throughout the North, they provoked a violent reaction in the South and within the administration. President Buchanan was so enraged by the conspiracy charge that he forbade Seward access to the White House. Chief Justice Taney was even more infuriated, declaring later that if Seward had become president in 1861, he would "have refused to administer to him the official oath, and thereby proclaim to the nation that he would not administer that oath to such a man."

Six months later, Seward delivered another provocative speech that, like the "higher law" speech, would be indelibly linked to his name. Catering to the emotions of an ardent Republican gathering overflowing in Corinthian Hall in Rochester, New York, Seward argued that the United States was divided by two "incompatible" political and economic systems, which had developed divergent cultures, values, and assumptions. The free labor system had uneasily coexisted with slave labor, he observed, until recent advances in transportation, communication, and commerce increasingly brought the two "into closer contact." A catastrophic "collision" was inevitable. "Shall I tell you what this collision means?" he asked his audience. "They who think that it is accidental, unnecessary, the work of interested or fanatical agitators, and therefore ephemeral, mistake the case altogether. It is an *irrepressible conflict* between opposing and enduring forces, and it means that the United States must and will, sooner or later, become either entirely a slaveholding nation, or entirely a free-labor nation."

Frances Seward was thrilled with her husband's speech, believing its radical tone completely warranted by the increasingly aggressive stance of the South. Indeed, for all those fighting against slavery, the words "irrepressible conflict" provided a mighty battle cry. Seward had defined the sectional conflict as driven by fundamental differences rather than the machinations of extremists who exaggerated discord for their own political ends. He had taken his stand on an issue, Kenneth Stampp suggests, "that troubled the politicians of his generation as it has since troubled American historians: Was the conflict that ultimately culminated in the Civil War *repressible* or *irrepressible*?"

The speech produced an uproar in opposition papers. The Albany *Atlas and Argus* claimed that Seward was no longer content with restricting slavery to its present domain, but threatening to end slavery in South Carolina and Georgia. With this speech, the *New York Herald* claimed, Seward had thrown off his mask to reveal a "more repulsive abolitionist, because a more dangerous one, than Beecher, Garrison or [Massachusetts minister Theodore] Rev. Dr. Parker."

Seward, in fact, was not an abolitionist. He had long maintained that slavery in the states where it already existed was beyond the reach of national power. When he told of a nation without slavery, he referred to long-run historical forces and the inevitable triumph of an urbanizing, industrializing society. To Southerners, however, Seward seemed to be threatening the forced extinction of slavery and the permanent subjugation of the South. Seward, the historian William Gienapp suggests, "never comprehended fully the power of his words." He failed to anticipate the impact that such radical phrases as "higher law" and "irrepressible conflict" would have on the moderate image he wished to project. Long after the incendiary words had been spoken, Seward conceded that "if heaven would forgive him for stringing together two high sounding words, he would never do it again."

Ironically, while Seward was applauded in the antislavery North for his radical rhetoric, he was by temperament fundamentally conciliatory, eager to use his charisma and good-natured manner to unify the nation and find a peaceful solution to the sectional crisis. From his earliest days in politics, Seward had trusted the warmth and power of his personality to bridge any divide, so long as he could deal one-on-one with his adversaries. When his first election to the Senate was greeted with "alarm and apprehension" throughout the South, he remained placid. Although his positions on immigration, public education, the protective tariff, internal improvements, and above all, slavery made him a symbol of everything the South abhorred about the North, Seward's confidence was unshaken. "This general impression only amuses me," he wrote, "for I think that I shall prove as gentle a lion as he who played that part before the Duke, in the 'Midsummer Night's Dream.' "

He remained true to his resolve. "Those who assailed him with a view to personal controversy were disturbed by continual failures to provoke his anger," a contemporary recalled. The story was told and retold of a Southern senator who delivered an abusive speech against Seward, labeling him "an infidel and a traitor." When the senator resumed his seat, "heated and shaken with the fierce frenzy" of his own ire, Seward walked over to his chair and "sympathetically offered him a pinch of snuff."

Within the Washington community, Seward's extravagant dinner parties were legendary, attended by Northerners and Southerners alike. No one showed greater acumen in reconciling the most contentious politicians in a relaxing evening atmosphere. Throughout the 1850s, the New Yorker used such dinners to maintain cordial relations with everyone, from Jefferson Davis of Mississippi and John Crittenden of Kentucky to Charles Sumner and Charles Francis Adams of Massachusetts. Seward was a superb master of ceremonies, putting all at ease with his amiable disposition. Though an inveterate storyteller himself, he would draw the company into lively conversations ranging from literature and science to theater and history.

A woman who was present at one of these feasts recalled that seventeen courses were served, beginning with turtle soup. The plates were changed with each serving of fish, meat, asparagus, sweetbreads, quail, duck, terrapin, ice cream, and "beautiful pyramids of iced fruits, oranges, french kisses." By each place setting there stood wineglasses, "five in number, of different size, form and color, indicating the different wines to be served." After dinner, coffee was served to the women in the parlor while the men gathered in the study to enjoy after-dinner liqueurs, and cigars ordered specially from Cuba. Through these Bacchanalian feasts, "by the juice of the grape, and even certain distillations from peaches and corn," Seward endeavored, one reporter suggested, "to give his guests good cheer, and whether they are from the North or South, keep them in the bonds of good fellowship. Strange rumors have often crept out from Washington and startled the people, to the effect, that fire-eaters have been known to visit the house of the great New Yorker, and come away mellow with the oil of gladness, purple with the essence of the fruit of the wine."

Seward's social engagements did not lessen when Congress was out of session. The summer after the *Dred Scott* decision was handed down, he invited Francis Blair, Sr., and his wife, Eliza, to accompany him on a trip through Canada. Joining the party were Seward's son Fred and Fred's young wife, Anna. Though he understood that the Blairs were far more conservative than he, Seward trusted that his charm would win their support for the nomination in 1860.

The "voyage of discovery," as Blair later described the trip, took the travelers through Niagara Falls, Toronto, and the Thousand Islands to the coast of Labrador. The sprightly Blairs, who seemed far younger than their years, enjoyed the adventure thoroughly. In an exuberant letter of thanks, Blair told Seward he was the "very best traveling companion," who not only made every stop "doubly interesting" by his gifts as a storyteller, but had taken pains to remove all the hardships of the voyage, providing secure sleeping arrangements, a comfortable fishing boat that traversed rough waters without inducing seasickness, and elegant meals. It was a trip they would never forget. But when the time came for hard decisions, the Blair family would back the man more closely aligned with their political views—Edward Bates.

• • •

WHILE SEWARD WAS A NATURAL in social situations, Governor Chase struggled through the dinners and receptions he organized to further his political ambitions, possessing none of Seward's social grace. Chase's greatest resource was his seventeen-year-old daughter, Kate, who flourished in her role as her father's hostess. "At an age when most girls are shy and lanky," the *Cincinnati Enquirer* noted, "she stepped forth into the world an accomplished young woman, able to cross swords with the brightest intellects of the nation."

A child less strong-willed and high-spirited than Kate might have been crushed by the vicissitudes of her father's demanding love, which he bestowed or denied depending on her performance. In her case, however, the unremitting stress on good habits, fine manners, and hard work paid off. By the time she returned to Columbus, she had acquired an excellent education, a proficiency in several languages, an ability to converse with anyone, and, her biographer observes, "a scientific knowledge of politics that no woman, and few men, have ever surpassed."

Tall and willowy, Kate was celebrated far and wide as one of the most captivating women of her age. "Her complexion was marvellously delicate," a contemporary recalled, "her hair a wonderful color like the ripe corn-tassel in full sunlight. Her teeth were perfect. Poets sang then, and still sing, to the turn of her beautiful neck and the regal carriage of her head." Friends and acquaintances were struck by the extraordinary similarity in looks between the handsome Chase and his stunning daughter. Indeed, when they made an entrance, a hush invariably fell over the room, as if a king and his queen stood in the doorway.

Kate's return to Columbus prompted her father to settle in a house of his own. Devastated by the loss of three young wives, Chase had never summoned the energy to buy and furnish a home, shuttling instead between rented homes, boardinghouses, and hotel suites. Now, with both Kate and Nettie at home, he bought the stately Gothic mansion on Sixth Street, leaving most of the decorating decisions to Kate. He sent her to Cincinnati to select the wallpaper, carpets, draperies, and sideboards. "I feel I am trusting a good deal to the judgment of a girl of 17," Chase told her, "but I am confident I may safely trust yours" . . . "you have capacity and will do very well."

Assuming the role of Ohio's first lady, Kate wrote out the invitations and oversaw arrangements for scores of receptions, soirées, and dinners. "I knew all of the great men of my time," she later recalled. "I was thrown upon my own resources at a very early age." William Dean Howells, working then as a cub reporter in Columbus, never forgot his invitation to an elegant Thanksgiving party at the governor's house. It was his first dinner "in society," the first time he had seen individual plates placed before guests "by a shining black butler, instead of being passed from hand to hand among them." After dinner, the company was invited to a game of charades, which promised mortification for the shy young Howells. Kate immediately allayed his fears, he gratefully recalled, by "the raillery glancing through the deep lashes of her brown eyes which were very beautiful." Kate's dynamic grace and intellect made her the most interesting woman in any gathering, as well as a critical force behind her father's drive for the presidency.

While Kate projected a mature poise, she was yet a spirited young girl with a rebellious streak. Her craving for excitement and glamour led to a tryst with a wealthy young man who had recently married the daughter of a well-known Ohio journalist. The dashing figure reportedly "began his attentions by little civilities, then mild flirtations," building familiarity to take Kate for carriage rides and call on her in the Governor's Mansion. When Chase learned of these encounters, he banished Kate's admirer from the house. Nonetheless, the young couple continued meeting, signaling each other with handkerchiefs from the window. One day Chase apparently arrived home unexpectedly, to find the "enamored Benedict" in his drawing room. Chase used his horsewhip to put an end to the relationship.

Kate once again settled into her role as her father's helpmate, working with him side by side as he set his sights on a presidential run in 1860. Like Seward and Lincoln, Chase regarded the *Dred Scott* decision as part of a conspiracy aimed at free institutions, which only a Republican victory could stop. He had offered his services to Scott's defenders, but in the end had not taken part in the case. His true service to the nation, he believed, could best be served in the White House. "I find that many are beginning to talk about the election of 1860," he wrote his friend Charles Cleveland in November 1857, "and not a few are again urging my name. . . . Some imagine that I can combine more strength than any other man."

• • •

WHILE SEWARD AND CHASE eyed the presidency, Lincoln prepared for another bid for the U.S. Senate. As chief architect of the Republican Party in his state, Lincoln had first claim to run against Stephen Douglas in 1858. Recognizing the sacrifice he had made three years earlier to ensure Trumbull's election, hundreds of party workers stood ready to do everything they could to ensure that this time Lincoln had every chance to realize his dream. In addition to David Davis, Leonard Swett, and Billy Herndon, stalwart friends in 1855, he could count on Norman Judd, whose refusal to abandon Trumbull had contributed mightily to his earlier defeat.

Once again fate threatened to disrupt his plans as events in Kansas took an ominous turn. Although an overwhelming majority of the settlers were opposed to slavery and wanted to join the Union as a free state, a rump group of proslavery forces met in Lecompton, drafted a proslavery constitution, and applied for statehood. The Buchanan administration, hoping to appease Southern mainstays of the Democratic Party, endorsed the Lecompton Constitution, calling on Congress to admit Kansas as a slave state. A new wave of outrage swept the North.

At this juncture, Stephen Douglas stunned the political world by breaking with his fellow Democrats. In an acrimonious session with President Buchanan, he told him he would not support the Lecompton Constitution. The man who had led the Democratic fight for the Nebraska Act was now siding with the Republicans in open opposition to his own administration. "My objection to the Lecompton constitution did not consist in the fact that it made Kansas a slave State," he later explained. He cared not whether slavery was voted up or down; but the decision "was not the act and deed of the people of Kansas, and did not embody their will." To Douglas, the clash with the Buchanan administration must have seemed unavoidable. Support for Lecompton would have betrayed his own doctrine of "popular sovereignty," on which he had staked his political future, and seriously diminished his chances for reelection to the Senate from Illinois.

With Douglas on their side, Republicans were thrilled, believing they now had a chance to keep Kansas from entering the Union as a slave state.

"What can equal the caprices of politics?" Seward queried his wife the day after Douglas made his dramatic announcement. Throughout the entire decade, Seward explained, "the triumph of slavery . . . could not have occurred but for the accession to it of Stephen A. Douglas, the representative of the West." His defection, Seward exulted, was "a great day for freedom and justice." Old party enmities were forgotten as Eastern Republicans rushed to embrace Douglas as an ally in the fight against slavery. In the *Tribune*, Horace Greeley called on Illinois Republicans to cross party lines and endorse Douglas for senator in the upcoming race.

Lincoln at once understood the catastrophic implications for his own political prospects. Furthermore, knowing Douglas as he did, Lincoln believed that his "break" with the administration was but a temporary squabble over the facts of the situation in Kansas, rather than a change of heart on principle. Once the Kansas matter was settled, Lincoln suspected, Douglas would resume his long-standing alliance with the proslavery Democrats. In the meantime, duped Republican voters would have reelected Douglas, destroyed the Republican Party in Illinois, and ceded their voice in the Senate to a fundamentally proslavery politician.

Everywhere he went, lamented Lincoln, he was "accosted by friends" asking if he had read Douglas's speech. "In every instance the question is accompanied with an anxious inquiring stare, which asks, quite as plainly as words could, 'Can't you go for Douglas now?' Like boys who have set a bird-trap, they are watching to see if the birds are picking at the bait and likely to go under."

"What does the New-York Tribune mean by it's constant eulogising, and admiring, and magnifying [of] Douglas?" Lincoln demanded of Trumbull. "Have they concluded that the republican cause, generally, can be best promoted by sacraficing us here in Illinois?" Even in his bleakest moods, Lincoln characteristically refused to attribute petty motives to Greeley, whom he considered "incapable of corruption." While he recognized that Greeley would rather "see Douglas reelected over me or any other republican," it was not because Greeley conspired with Douglas, but because "he thinks Douglas' superior position, reputation, experience, and *ability*, if you please, would more than compensate for his lack of a pure republican position." Lincoln felt much the same about Seward's enthusiasm for Douglas's reversal, despite the hazard it posed to his own chances.

To Lincoln's immense relief, the interference of the Eastern Republicans only served to strengthen the determination of his friends and supporters. At hastily called conventions all over the state, resolutions were passed declaring that "Abraham Lincoln is the first and only choice of the

Republicans of Illinois for the United States Senate." In an unprecedented move, since the ultimate decision would be made by the state legislature elected that fall, a statewide Republican convention in Springfield was called in June to officially nominate Lincoln for senator. "Lincoln's rise from relative obscurity to a presidential nomination," Don Fehrenbacher has convincingly argued, "includes no more decisive date than June 16, 1858," when the convention met in Springfield and enthusiastically endorsed Lincoln as its "first and only choice . . . for the United States Senate, as the successor of Stephen A. Douglas."

"A house divided against itself cannot stand," Lincoln said, echoing the Gospels of Mark and Matthew, as he began his now famous acceptance speech at Springfield. Straightaway, he set forth an instantly accessible image of the Union as a house in danger of collapse under the relentless pressure of the slavery issue. "I believe this government cannot endure, permanently half *slave* and half *free*," he continued. "I do not expect the house to *fall*—but I *do* expect it will cease to be divided. It will become *all* one thing, or *all* the other."

Supporters and opponents alike believed that with his image of a house that could not "endure, permanently half *slave* and half *free*," Lincoln had abandoned the moderate approach of his Peoria speech four years earlier in favor of more militant action. His argument, however, remained essentially unchanged: slavery had seemed on the road to gradual extinction until the fateful passage of the Nebraska bill gave it new momentum. His call for action was no more radical than before—to "arrest the further spread" of slavery and "place it where the public mind shall rest in the belief" that it was back where the framers intended it, "in course of ultimate extinction." The true change since the Peoria speech was not in Lincoln's stance but in the designs of proslavery Democrats, who, he charged, had cunningly erected a new proslavery edifice to destroy the framers' house of democracy.

Lincoln deftly illustrated what he, like Seward, considered a plot to overthrow the Constitution. Whereas Seward cited the days of the English king, Charles I, with an oblique reference to the Roman emperor Nero, to present a tableau of a tyrant's coronation, Lincoln delineated the conspiracy with an everyday metaphor. "When we see a lot of framed timbers, different portions of which we know have been gotten out at different times and places by different workmen—Stephen, Franklin, Roger and James, for instance," Lincoln explained, "and when we see these timbers joined together, and see they exactly make the frame of a house . . . all the lengths and proportions of the different pieces exactly adapted to their respective places . . . we find it impossible to not *believe* that Stephen and Franklin and Roger and James all understood one another from the beginning, and all worked upon a common *plan* or *draft* drawn up before the first lick was struck." With these timbers in place, Lincoln warned, only one other "nice little niche" needed to be "filled with another Supreme Court decision," declaring that the constitutional protection of private property prevented states as well as territories from excluding slavery from their limits. Then, in one fell swoop, all laws outlawing slavery in the Northern states would be invalidated.

If "the point of this rather elaborate [house] metaphor seems obscure today," the historian James McPherson observes, "Lincoln's audience knew exactly what he was talking about." The four conniving Democratic carpenters were Stephen Douglas, architect of the lamentable Nebraska law and vocal defender of the *Dred Scott* decision; Franklin Pierce, the outgoing president who had used his last annual message to underscore the "*weight* and *authority*" of Supreme Court decisions even before the Court had completed its deliberations in the *Dred Scott* case; Roger Taney, the Chief Justice who had authored the revolutionary decision; and James Buchanan, the incoming president who had strongly urged compliance with the Supreme Court decision a full two days before the opinion was made public. Working together, these four men had put slavery on a path to "become alike lawful in *all* the States, *old* as well as *new—North* as well as *South.*"

Reminding his audience that Douglas had always been among the foremost carpenters in the Democratic plan to nationalize slavery, Lincoln made it clear that the Republican cause must be "intrusted to, and conducted by its own undoubted friends—those whose hands are free, whose hearts are in the work" of shoring up the frame first raised by the founding fathers. While Douglas might be "a very *great* man," and the "largest of *us* are very small ones," he had consistently used his influence to distort the framers' intentions regarding slavery, exhibiting a moral indifference to slavery itself. "Clearly, he is not *now* with us," Lincoln stated, "he does not *pretend* to be—he does not *promise* to *ever* be."

The image of America as an unfinished house in danger of collapse worked brilliantly because it provided a ringing challenge to the Republican audience, a call for action to throw out the conspiring carpenters, unseat the Democratic Party, and recapture control of the nation's building blocks—the laws that had wisely prevented the spread of slavery. Only then, Lincoln claimed, with the public mind secure in the belief that slavery was once more on a course to eventual extinction, would the people in all sections of the country live together peaceably in the great house their forefathers had built.

In the campaign that followed, Douglas would strenuously deny that he had ever conspired with Taney and Buchanan before the *Dred Scott* decision. "What if Judge Douglas never did talk with Chief Justice Taney and the President," replied Lincoln. "It can only show that he was *used* by conspirators, and was not a *leader* of them." This charge reflected his agreement with Seward and Chase that—whether there was an explicit conspiracy—there was a mutual intent by the slave power to extend slavery. Edward Bates also feared that Southern radicals "planned to seize control of the federal government and nationalize slavery."

• • •

SO THE STAGE WAS SET for a titanic battle, arguably the most famous Senate fight in American history, a clash that would make Lincoln a national figure and propel him to the presidency while it would, at the same time, undermine Douglas's support in the South and further fracture the Democratic Party.

In keeping with political strategy followed to this day, Lincoln, the challenger, asked Douglas to campaign with him so they could debate the issues. The incumbent, Douglas, who boasted a national reputation and deep pockets, had little to gain from debating Lincoln and initially refused the challenge, but eventually felt compelled to participate in the seven face-to-face debates known to history as the Lincoln-Douglas Debates.

In the course of the campaign, both men covered over 4,000 miles within Illinois, delivering hundreds of speeches. The northern part of the state was Republican territory. In the southern counties, populated largely by migrants from the South, the proslavery sentiment dominated. The election would be decided in the central section of Illinois, where the debates became the centerpiece of the struggle. With marching bands, parades, fireworks, banners, flags, and picnics, the debates brought tens of thousands of people together with "all the devoted attention," one historian has noted, "that many later Americans would reserve for athletic contests."

Attending the debate in Quincy, the young Republican leader Carl Schurz recounted how "the country people began to stream into town for the great meeting, some singly, on foot or on horseback, or small parties of men and women, and even children, in buggies or farm wagons; while others were marshaled in solemn procession from outlying towns or districts. . . . It was indeed the whole American people that listened to those debates," continued Schurz, later remarking that "the spectacle reminded one of those lays of ancient times telling us of two armies in battle array, standing still to see their two principal champions fight out the contested

1

Abraham Lincoln photographed at age forty-eight in Chicago on February 28, 1857. The lawyer's political star had begun to rise at last. A year later, accepting his party's nomination for U.S. senator, he would utter the famous words "A house divided against itself cannot stand."

2

Mary Todd Lincoln, shown here at twenty-eight, after four years of marriage. Upon their first meeting, Lincoln told Mary: "I want to dance with you in the worst way." And, Mary laughingly told her cousin later that night, "he certainly did."

3

The Lincolns were indulgent parents, believing that "love is the chain whereby to lock a child to its parent." Robert was the eldest *(above)*, followed by Willie *(left)* and Tad *(right)*. Another son, Eddie, died of tuberculosis in 1850 at the age of three.

4

5

When William H. Seward, shown here at age forty-three *(left)*, married Frances Miller *(right)*, the daughter of a wealthy judge, in 1824, he acquired wealth, professional connections, and the stately mansion in Auburn, New York *(below)*, that would become his lifelong home.

9

Possessed of a powerful intellect and strong moral convictions, Frances Seward *(above)* served as her husband's political conscience. Young Fanny Seward, shown with her father, adored her mother but idolized her father, thinking him one of the greatest men in the country.

10

11

12

"A vale of misery" descended upon Salmon P. Chase *(above left and below)* after he lost three wives, including Catherine *(above right)* and Sarah Bella *(below)*, in slightly over a decade.

13

14

Chase thereafter sought companionship with political friends such as Edwin M. Stanton *(above)*, whose own life had been marred by family tragedy. Only when he became governor of Ohio did Chase settle into a home of his own in Columbus *(below)*.

15

16 

 17

Julia Bates *(above left and below)* provided Edward Bates *(above right)* with what their friends uniformly described as an ideal home life. Through four decades of married life and the birth of seventeen children their intimacy remained strong.

18

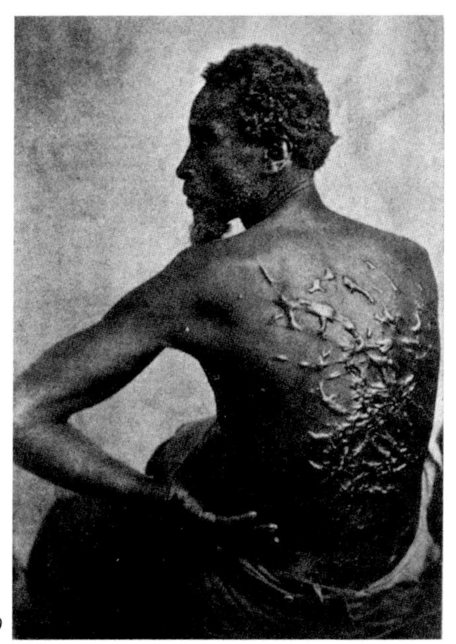

19

20

In the 1850s, Northern sentiment was inflamed by the publication of *Uncle Tom's Cabin*, with its disturbing scenes of slavery's violence *(left)*, and by the landmark *Dred Scott* decision. Scott *(right)* had sued for his freedom, but the Supreme Court, led by Roger B. Taney *(below)*, decreed that he "had no rights which the white man was bound to respect."

21

22

Lincoln's gift for making and keeping friends, such as Joshua Speed *(above)* and David Davis *(below)*, played a critical role in both his personal happiness and professional advancement.

23

24

25

Lincoln forged lasting friendships while riding the "circuit" with fellow lawyers, including William Herndon *(left)* and Ward Lamon *(right)*. In these convivial settings *(below)*, Lincoln's never-ending stream of stories made him the center of attention, while he, in turn, gained firsthand knowledge of the voters throughout Illinois.

26

27

28

Neither Lyman Trumbull *(left)* nor Norman Judd *(right)* would ever forget Lincoln's magnanimity when conceding defeat in his 1855 bid for the Senate. Both men would help Lincoln at the 1860 Republican National Convention in Chicago *(below)*.

29

THE REPUBLICAN WIGWAM AT CHICAGO.

30 

 31

Thurlow Weed *(right)* failed to win the Republican nomination for his protégé, William Seward. An act of betrayal by Horace Greeley *(left)*, who bore an old political grudge against Seward, contributed to the defeat. Editorial humor of the day cast Seward in the role of an assassinated Julius Caesar and depicted Greeley as a vengeful Brutus *(below)*.

32 

33

"A profound stillness fell upon the Wigwam" *(above)* as the results of the crucial third ballot hung in the balance. Seward awaited the news from Chicago in the garden of his Auburn home *(below)*.

34

35

Residents of Springfield congregated before Lincoln's home for a campaign rally after his unexpected capture of the Republican nomination over Seward, Chase, and Bates.

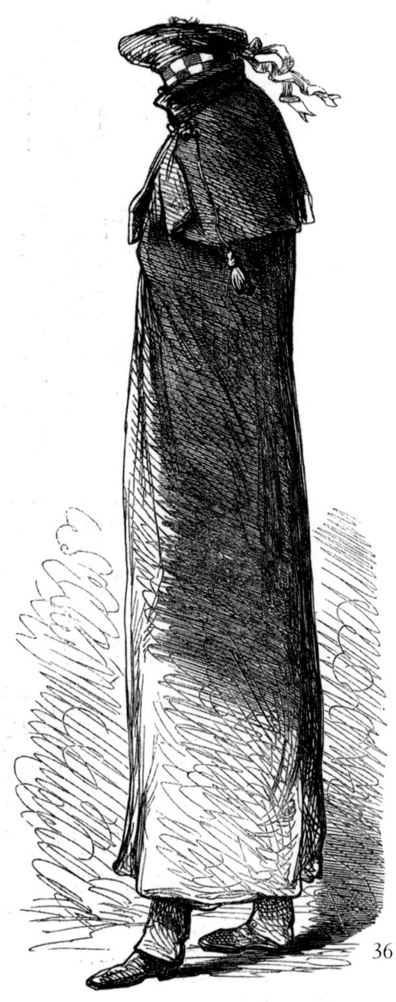

36

Assassination threats prompted President-elect Lincoln to enter Washington at the crack of dawn. A scurrilous rumor that he had disguised himself in a Scotch plaid cap and military cloak circulated widely in the media, causing him much embarrassment.

cause between the lines in single combat." The debates, said Lincoln in Quincy, "were the successive acts of a drama . . . to be enacted not merely in the face of audiences like this, but in the face of the nation."

"On the whole," Schurz observed, "the Democratic displays were much more elaborate and gorgeous than those of the Republicans, and it was said that Douglas had plenty of money to spend for such things. He himself also traveled in what was called in those days 'great style,' with a secretary and servants and a numerous escort of somewhat loud companions, moving from place to place by special train with cars specially decorated for the occasion, all of which contrasted strongly with Lincoln's extreme modest simplicity."

Each debate followed the same rules. The first contestant spoke for an hour, followed by a one-and-a-half-hour response, after which the man who had gone first would deliver a half-hour rebuttal. The huge crowds were riveted for the full three hours, often interjecting comments, cheering for their champion, bemoaning the jabs of his opponent. Newspaper stenographers worked diligently to take down every word, and their transcripts were swiftly dispatched throughout the country.

"No more striking contrast could have been imagined than that between those two men as they appeared upon the platform," one observer wrote. "By the side of Lincoln's tall, lank, and ungainly form, Douglas stood almost like a dwarf, very short of stature, but square-shouldered and broad-chested, a massive head upon a strong neck, the very embodiment of force, combativeness, and staying power."

The highly partisan papers concocted contradictory pictures of crowd response and outcome. At the end of the first debate, the Republican Chicago *Press and Tribune* reported that "when Mr. Lincoln walked down from the platform, he was seized by the multitude and borne off on their shoulders, in the center of a crowd of five thousand shouting Republicans, with a band of music in front." Observing the same occasion, the Democratic *Chicago Times* claimed that when it was over, Douglas's "excoriation of Lincoln" had been so successful and "so severe, that the republicans hung their heads in shame."

The people of Illinois had followed the careers of Douglas and, to a lesser extent, Lincoln for nearly a quarter of a century as they represented opposing parties in the State House, in Congress, and on the campaign trail. Indeed, in the opening debate at Ottawa, Douglas spoke of his first acquaintance with Lincoln when they were "both comparatively boys, and both struggling with poverty in a strange land," when Lincoln was "just as good at telling an anecdote as now. He could beat any of the boys wrestling, or running a foot race, in pitching quoits or tossing a copper, could ruin more liquor than all the boys of the town together, and the dignity and impartiality with which he presided at a horse race or fist fight, excited the admiration and won the praise of everybody," as well as the lifelong epithet "Honest Abe."

The amiable tone was laced with innuendo as Douglas described Lincoln's climb from "flourishing grocery-keeper" (meaning that Lincoln sold liquor, a curious charge from the notoriously hard-drinking Douglas) to the state legislature, where they had served together in 1836, till Lincoln was "submerged . . . for some years," turning up again in Congress, where he "in the Senate . . . was glad to welcome my old friend," for he had neither friends nor companions. "He distinguished himself by his opposition to the Mexican war, taking the side of the common enemy against his own country; and when he returned home he found that the indignation of the people followed him everywhere, and he was again submerged or obliged to retire into private life, forgotten by his former friends. He came up again in 1854, just in time to make this Abolition or Black Republican platform, in company with Giddings, Lovejoy, Chase, and Fred Douglass for the Republican party to stand upon." With this, the crowd broke into laughter, shouting: "Hit him again."

Lincoln readily conceded that Douglas was far better known than he. As he outlined the advantages of Douglas's stature, however, his audience laughed with glee. "All the anxious politicians of his party," Lincoln told a crowd at Springfield, "have been looking upon him as certainly, at no distant day, to be the President of the United States. They have seen in his round, jolly, fruitful face, postoffices, landoffices, marshalships, and cabinet appointments, chargeships and foreign missions, bursting and sprouting out in wonderful exuberance ready to be laid hold of by their greedy hands." When the cheers and laughter drawn forth by this comical image subsided, Lincoln went on, "Nobody has ever expected me to be President. In my poor, lean, lank face, nobody has ever seen that any cabbages were sprouting out. These are disadvantages all, taken together, that the Republicans labor under. *We* have to fight this battle upon principle and upon principle, alone."

Douglas asserted that Lincoln dare not repeat his antislavery principles in the southern counties of Illinois. "The very notice that I was going to take him down to Egypt made him tremble in the knees so that he had to be carried from the platform. He laid up seven days, and in the meantime held a consultation with his political physicians." Lincoln promptly responded, "Well, I know that sickness altogether furnishes a subject for philosophical contemplation, and I have been treating it in that way, and I have really come to the conclusion (for I can reconcile it no other way), that the Judge is crazy." There was "not a word of truth" to the claim that he had ever had to be carried prostrate from a platform, although he had been hoisted aloft by enthusiastic supporters. "I don't know how to meet that sort of thing. I don't want to call him a liar, yet, if I come square up to the truth, I do not know what else it is." Amid cheers and laughter, Lincoln closed: "I suppose my time is nearly out, and if it is not, I will give up and let the Judge set my knees to trembling—if he can."

Throughout the debates, Lincoln carried a small notebook that contained clippings relevant to the questions of the day sent to him by his law partner, William Herndon, along with the opening lines of his own "House Divided" speech and the paragraph of the Declaration of Independence proclaiming that "all men are created equal, that they are endowed by their Creator with certain unalienable Rights, that among these are Life, Liberty and the pursuit of Happiness." It was on the meaning of the Declaration that battle lines were drawn.

As Lincoln repeatedly said in many forums, slavery was a violation of the Declaration's "majestic interpretation of the economy of the Universe," allowed by the founders because it was already among us, but placed by them in the course of ultimate extinction. Although unfulfilled in the present, the Declaration's promise of equality was "a beacon to guide" not only "the whole race of man then living" but "their children and their children's children, and the countless myriads who should inhabit the earth in other ages."

For Douglas, the crux of the controversy was the right of self-government, the principle that the people in each territory and each state should decide for themselves whether to introduce or exclude slavery. "I care more for the great principle of self-government, the right of the people to rule, than I do for all the negroes in Christendom."

Lincoln agreed that "the doctrine of self government is right—absolutely and eternally right," but argued that "it has no just application" to slavery. "When the white man governs himself," he asserted, "that is self-government; but when he governs himself, and also governs *another* man, that is *more* than self-government—that is despotism. If the negro is a *man*, why then my ancient faith teaches me that 'all men are created equal'; and that there can be no moral right in connection with one man's making a slave of another."

While it did not matter to Douglas what the people of Kansas decided, so long as they had the right to decide, for Lincoln, the substance of the decision was crucial. "The difference between the Republican and the Democratic parties on the leading issue of this contest," declared Lincoln, "is, that the former consider slavery a moral, social and political wrong, while the latter *do not* consider it either a moral, social or political wrong; and the action of each . . . is squared to meet these views."

• • •

DOUGLAS UNDERSTOOD from the outset that his primary goal, more important than debating or defining his own position, was to cast Lincoln as a radical, bent on abolishing all distinctions between the races. The question of black equality—in the modern sense—was not controversial in Illinois, or in the nation as a whole. Almost every white man was against it, even most abolitionists. Douglas was certain that no candidate who professed a belief in the social or political equality of blacks and whites could possibly carry Illinois, where a long-standing set of Black Laws prevented blacks from voting, holding political office, giving testimony against whites, and sitting on juries.

At every forum, therefore, Douglas missed no opportunity to portray Lincoln as a Negro-loving agitator bent on debasing white society. "If you desire negro citizenship," Douglas baited his audience, "if you desire them to vote on an equality with yourselves, and to make them eligible to office, to serve on juries, and to adjudge your rights, then support Mr. Lincoln and the Black Republican party." The crowd responded as Douglas hoped: "Never, never." Cheers nearly drowned out his voice as he shouted his opinion that "the signers of the Declaration of Independence had no reference to negroes at all when they declared all men to be created equal. They did not mean negro, nor the savage Indians, nor the Fejee Islanders, nor any other barbarous race. They were speaking of white men. . . . I hold that this government was established . . . for the benefit of white men and their posterity forever, and should be administered by white men, and none others." Cries of "that's the truth" erupted from the agitated throng amid raucous applause.

In response, Lincoln avowed that he had "no purpose to introduce political and social equality between the white and the black races." He had never been in favor "of making voters or jurors of negroes, nor of qualifying them to hold office, nor to intermarry." He acknowledged "a physical difference between the two" that would "probably forever forbid their living together upon the footing of perfect equality." But "notwithstanding all this," he said, taking direct aim at the Supreme Court's decision in the *Dred Scott* case, "there is no reason in the world why the negro is not entitled to all the natural rights enumerated in the Declaration of Independence. . . . I agree with Judge Douglas he is not my equal in many respects—certainly not in color, perhaps not in moral and intellectual endowment. But in the right to eat the bread, without leave of anybody else, which his own hand earns, he is my equal and the equal of Judge Douglas, and the equal of every living man."

It is instructive, political philosopher Harry Jaffa perceptively notes, that the only unequivocal statement of white supremacy Lincoln ever made was as to "color"—the assertion of an obvious difference. Had he advocated political and social equality for blacks, he unquestionably would have lost the election in a state where the legislature not only supported the discriminatory Black Laws but had gone even further by passing a special law making it a criminal offense to bring into the boundaries of Illinois "a person having in him one-fourth negro blood, whether free or slave." And this same law essentially barred blacks and mulattos from entering the state to take up residence.

Nonetheless, Lincoln's implied support for the Black Laws stands in contrast to the bolder positions adopted by both Seward and Chase. Chase had long since adopted a liberal stance on race far in advance of the general public, and had been instrumental in removing some but not all of Ohio's discriminatory Black Laws. Seward, too, had spoken out vehemently against the Black Laws, and in favor of black suffrage, coming from the more progressive state of New York.

However, neither Seward nor Chase advocated full social and political equality for blacks. "Seward did not believe," his biographer concludes, "that the black man in America was the equal of the white, or that he was capable of assimilation as were the Irish and German immigrants. But he did believe that the Negro was a man, and as such deserved and should have all the privileges of the whites." Nor did Salmon Chase think that "the two races could live together." He told Frederick Douglass that he thought "separation was in everyone's best interests." He believed that blacks would find "happier homes in other lands." So long as they were here, however, he championed measures to fight discrimination.

These statements of Seward and Chase, coming from the leaders of the antislavery cause, reveal that racism, the belief in white supremacy, was deeply embedded in the entire country. It is only in this context that the statements of Lincoln and his contemporaries can be judged.

Less than two decades earlier, Alexis de Tocqueville, who was deeply opposed to slavery and believed emancipation to be inevitable, had written: "The most dreadful of all the evils that threaten the future of the United States arises from the presence of blacks on its soil." Even in the states where slavery had been eradicated and where suffrage had been granted, he observed, countless obstacles had been placed in the way of the black man. "If he presents himself to vote, he runs a risk to his life. Oppressed, he can complain, but he finds only whites among his judges. . . .

His son is excluded from the school where the descendants of Europeans come to be instructed. In theaters he cannot buy for the price of gold the right to be placed at the side of one who was his master; in hospitals he lies apart. The black is permitted to beseech the same God as whites, but not to pray to him at the same altar. He has his own priests and churches. One does not close the doors of Heaven to him; yet inequality hardly stops at the boundary of the other world. When the Negro is no longer, his bones are cast to one side, and the difference of conditions is still found even in the equality of death." Even when abolition should come, Tocqueville predicted, Americans would "have still to destroy three prejudices much more intangible and more tenacious than it: the prejudice of the master, the prejudice of race, and finally the prejudice of the white."

The dilemma faced by advocates of emancipation was the place of free blacks in American society. The opposition to assimilation was almost universal. Blacks were already barred from entering the borders of many free states. Confronting such barriers, what "in the name of humanity," Henry Clay asked, "is to become of them—where are they to go?"

"My first impulse," Lincoln had said before, "would be to free all the slaves, and send them to Liberia,—to their own native land." Lincoln had long supported the same implausible plan endorsed by Edward Bates and Henry Clay, the notion of compensating slaveowners and returning freed slaves to their homeland. Without such a program, "colonizers" argued, Southern whites would never accept the idea of emancipation. Still, Lincoln took note of the staggering administrative and economic difficulties. More than 3 million blacks lived in the South, representing 35 percent of the entire Southern population. The overwhelming majority had no desire to go to Africa, and only a few spokesmen, not including Lincoln, advocated forced deportation. They were here to stay.

"What then?" Lincoln asked. "Free them all, and keep them among us as underlings? Is it quite certain that this betters their condition?" But once freed, could they be made "politically and socially, our equals? My own feelings will not admit of this; and if mine would, we well know that those of the great mass of white people will not. Whether this feeling accords with justice and sound judgment, is not the sole question. . . . A universal feeling, whether well or ill-founded, can not be safely disregarded."

Lincoln understood that the greatest challenge for a leader in a democratic society is to educate public opinion. "With public sentiment, nothing can fail; without it nothing can succeed," he said. "Consequently he who moulds public sentiment, goes deeper than he who enacts statutes or pronounces decisions." This statement goes to the heart of his disagreement with Douglas; when such an influential leader as Mary's "Little

Giant" insisted that blacks were not included in the Declaration, he was molding public opinion and bending history in the wrong direction. "He is blowing out the moral lights around us," Lincoln warned, borrowing a phrase from his hero Henry Clay, "eradicating the light of reason and the love of liberty in this American people."

Lincoln's goal was to rekindle those very beacons, constantly affirming the revolutionary promises made in the Declaration. When the authors of the Declaration spoke of equality, Lincoln insisted, "they did not mean to assert the obvious untruth, that all were then actually enjoying that equality. . . . They meant to set up a standard maxim for free society, which should be familiar to all, and revered by all; constantly looked to, constantly labored for, and even though never perfectly attained, constantly approximated, and thereby constantly spreading and deepening its influence, and augmenting the happiness and value of life to all people of all colors everywhere."

He hoped to "penetrate the human soul" until, as he said, "all this quibbling about this man and the other man—this race and that race and the other race being inferior" could be discarded, until all Americans could "unite as one people throughout this land," providing true meaning to the phrase "all men are created equal." His comments on race here and throughout the debates reveal a brooding quality, as if he was thinking aloud, balancing a realistic appraisal of the present with a cautious eye toward progress in the future.

History demonstrates that Lincoln and his contemporaries were not overestimating the depth of racial bigotry in America. A century would pass before legal apartheid was outlawed in the South, before separate schools were deemed unconstitutional, before blacks were finally guaranteed the right to vote. Moreover, each of these steps toward what Frederick Douglass called the "practical recognition of our Equality" met with fierce white resistance and were made possible only by the struggles of blacks themselves, forcing the issue upon largely hostile or indifferent whites.

There is no way to penetrate Lincoln's personal feelings about race. There is, however, the fact that armies of scholars, meticulously investigating every aspect of his life, have failed to find a single act of racial bigotry on his part. Even more telling is the observation of Frederick Douglass, who would become a frequent public critic of Lincoln's during his presidency, that of all the men he had met, Lincoln was "the first great man that I talked with in the United States freely, who in no single instance reminded me of the difference between himself and myself, of the difference of color." This remark takes on additional meaning when one realizes that Douglass had met dozens of celebrated abolitionists, including Wendell

Phillips, William Lloyd Garrison, and Salmon Chase. Apparently, Douglass never felt with any of them, as he did with Lincoln, an "entire freedom from popular prejudice against the colored race."

• • •

THE SEVENTH AND LAST debate took place at Alton, a town on the Mississippi River in southwest Illinois, before an audience Lincoln described as "having strong sympathies southward by relationship, place of birth, and so on." By the middle of the day, the "whole town" was "alive and stirring with large masses of human beings." Gustave Koerner, a leader of the German-Americans, was among the throng that came to witness the show. "More than a thousand Douglas men," Koerner wrote, "had chartered a boat to attend the Alton meeting," while Lincoln "had come quietly down from Springfield with his wife that morning, unobserved. . . . He was soon surrounded by a crowd of Republicans; but there was no parade or fuss, while Douglas, about noon, made his pompous entry, and soon afterwards the boat from St. Louis landed at the wharf, heralded by the firing of guns and the strains of martial music." When Koerner reached Lincoln's hotel, he found him seated in the lobby. No sooner had they said hello than Lincoln suggested that they go together to "see Mary." Apparently, Mary was "rather dispirited" about his chances for victory, and Lincoln hoped that Koerner would lift her mood. Koerner told Mary that he was "certain" the Republicans would carry the state in the popular vote, "and tolerably certain of our carrying the Legislature."

Although there was little new in the Alton debate, Koerner believed that Lincoln's speech included "some of the finest passages of all the speeches he ever made." The "real issue," Lincoln argued, the issue that would continue long after the "tongues of Judge Douglas and myself shall be silent," was "the eternal struggle between . . . right and wrong"; the "common right of humanity" set against "the divine right of kings. . . .

"It is the same spirit that says, 'You work and toil and earn bread, and I'll eat it.' No matter in what shape it comes, whether from the mouth of a king who seeks to bestride the people of his own nation and live by the fruit of their labor, or from one race of men as an apology for enslaving another race, it is the same tyrannical principle." With this, Lincoln took his seat, Douglas made his concluding remarks, and the great debates came to an end.

In this race, as in all others, Lincoln was his own political manager. He drew up for his supporters a detailed battle plan, examining every district in the state and listing those he regarded as lost, those "we take to ourselves," and those "to be struggled for." Between his speeches, he drafted letters of instruction to key supporters, telling Koerner, for example, "We are in great danger in Madison. It is said half the Americans are going for Douglas. . . . Nothing must be left undone. Elsewhere things look reasonably well. Please write me."

Though Eastern Republicans stayed out of the race, Chase came to Illinois to stump for the Republican ticket. He believed that Lincoln was a man who could be trusted on the antislavery issue, while at the same time he recognized that the prairie lawyer could be helpful to him in the upcoming presidential convention. More clearly than Seward or Greeley, Chase saw from the start that Douglas would never truly stand with the antislavery forces. For eight days, traveling to Chicago, Galena, Warren, Rockford, and Mendota, Chase spoke to thousands on behalf of Lincoln and the Republican ticket in Illinois—a gesture Lincoln would not forget.

It was a dreary day, November 2, 1858, when the voters of Illinois went to the polls. The names of Lincoln and Douglas did not appear on the ballots, since the state legislature would choose the next senator. That evening, Lincoln anxiously awaited the returns with his friends in the telegraph office. Once again, he would be sorely disappointed. Though the Republicans had won the popular vote, the Democrats had retained control of the state legislature, thereby ensuring Douglas's reelection. Lincoln's supporters were disconsolate and angry, blaming an unfair apportionment scheme. Koerner charged that "by the gerrymandering the State seven hundred Democratic votes were equal to one thousand Republican votes." Republicans in Illinois bewailed the lack of support from Eastern Republicans and bitterly resented a last-minute intervention by the respected Whig leader and Kentucky senator John Crittenden, who had penned a series of highly publicized letters to Illinois, urging old Whigs and American supporters to vote for Douglas to repay his Lecompton stance. "Thousands of Whigs dropped us just on the eve of the election, through the influence of Crittenden," Herndon complained.

Two days later, still feeling the sting of his defeat, Lincoln wrote Crittenden. He suppressed his justifiable resentment, exhibiting as he had with Greeley, and earlier with Trumbull and Judd, a magnanimity rare in the world of politics. "The emotions of defeat, at the close of a struggle in which I felt more than a merely selfish interest, and to which defeat the use of your name contributed largely, are fresh upon me," he told Crittenden, "but, even in this mood, I can not for a moment suspect you of anything dishonorable."

Yet this defeat left Lincoln far less disheartened than his loss four years earlier. He had won the vote of the people. The ambition he had outlined in his very first public address at the age of twenty-three—to render himself worthy of his fellow citizens' esteem—had been realized.

"I am glad I made the late race," he wrote his Springfield friend Dr. Anson Henry on November 19. "It gave me a hearing on the great and durable question of the age, which I could have had in no other way. . . . I believe I have made some marks which will tell for the cause of civil liberty long after I am gone." That cause, he vowed to Henry Ashbury, "must not be surrendered at the end of *one*, or even, one *hundred* defeats." There was no reason for despondency, he told another friend, Dr. Charles Ray, who continued to brood over Lincoln's defeat. "You will soon feel better. Another 'blow-up' is coming; and we shall have fun again."

CHAPTER 7

COUNTDOWN TO THE NOMINATION

As 1859 opened, Lincoln remained guardedly optimistic about the future, knowing he had run a solid campaign for the Senate and made a good name for himself. Well aware that he had only an outside chance at the presidential nomination in 1860, he nevertheless worked to build his reputation nationally. He was always careful to conceal his ambitions. Whenever he was asked about the upcoming election, he would speak with well-modulated enthusiasm of other candidates. Yet all his actions were consistent with a cautious and politically skillful pursuit of the nomination. Indeed, no other period in his pre-presidential life better illustrates his consummate abilities as a politician.

Unlike Seward, he had no experienced political manager to guide his efforts. He would have to rely on himself, as he had from his early days on the frontier and throughout his career as shopkeeper, lawyer, and politician. A month earlier, Jesse Fell, secretary of the Illinois Republican state central committee, had expressed his "decided impression" in a letter to Lincoln that Lincoln's tremendous fight against Douglas had given him a national platform. If the details of his early life and his "efforts on the slavery question" could be "sufficiently brought before the people," he could be made "a formidable, if not a successful candidate for the presidency." Skeptical, Lincoln noted that Seward and Chase and others were "so much better known." With an equivocal modesty, he asked: "Is it not, as a matter of justice, due to such men, who have carried this movement forward to its present status, in spite of fearful opposition, personal abuse, and hard names? I really think so." As for a campaign biography, he curtly answered, "there is nothing in my early history that would interest you or anybody else."

Although refusing to confuse flattery with fact, he recognized nonetheless that Fell's argument had force. Lincoln's gradually evolving political strategy began with an awareness that while each of his three rivals had first claim on a substantial number of delegates, if he could position himself as the second choice of those who supported each of the others, he might pick up votes if one or another of the top candidates faltered.

As a dark horse, he knew it was important not to reveal his intentions too early, so as to minimize the possibility of opponents mobilizing against him. On April 16, 1859, when the Republican editor of the *Rock Island Register* proposed to call on other editors to make "a simultaneous announcement of your name for the Presidency," Lincoln replied: "I certainly am flattered, and gratified, that some partial friends think of me in that connection; but I really think it best for our cause that no concerted effort, such as you suggest, should be made." He added that he "must, in candor, say I do not think myself fit for the Presidency." By "fit," the self-confident Lincoln meant only to suggest that he did not necessarily have the credentials or experience appropriate to the office, not that he lacked the ability. It was important that any efforts on his behalf be squelched until the timing was right. And Lincoln, as would be evidenced throughout his presidency, was a master of timing.

• • •

WHILE LINCOLN MOVED CAREFULLY, step by step, Seward, Chase, and even Bates had grown so eager for the presidential nomination that they made a number of costly errors as they headed down the final stretch.

In the crucial months before the nomination, Seward, at Weed's rare misguided suggestion, took an extended tour of Europe. Certain that Seward had the nomination locked up so long as he refrained from the radical statements that frightened more moderate elements of the party, Weed recommended that his protégé remove himself from the increasingly contentious debate at home by traveling overseas for eight months. "All our discreet friends unite in sending me out of the country to spend the recess of Congress," Seward joked.

Fourteen-year-old Fanny Seward, at home with her mother, was desolate at the prospect of an eight-month separation from her father. In the days before his ship was set to sail from New York, she could think of nothing else, she confided in her diary, but his approaching departure. An intelligent, plain girl, Fanny had been encouraged from an early age to read broadly and to write. Beyond her daily journal, she tried her hand at poetry and plays, determined, she once vowed, never to marry, so that she could live at home and devote herself to a literary career. While extremely close to her mother, a relationship she described as " 'my affinity' with whom I *think* instead of speak," she idolized her father. The night before he left for Europe, she could barely contain her tears.

In Europe, Seward was entertained by politicians and royalty alike, who assumed that he would be the next president. He met with Queen Victoria, Lord Palmerston, William Gladstone, King Victor Emmanuel of Italy, King Leopold I of Belgium, and Pope Pius IX. Moving from one dazzling social occasion to the next, Seward was ebullient. His letters home revealed the great pleasure he took in his sojourn, which carried him to Egypt and the Holy Land. Yet in the countdown to the presidential nomination, eight months was a critical absence.

Upon his return to Washington for the new congressional session that began after the New Year in 1860, Seward took Weed's advice and prepared a major address. Designed to reassure Northern conservatives and moderate Southerners that he was a man who could be trusted to hold the Union together, the speech was to be delivered on the Senate floor on February 29, 1860. The reporter Henry Stanton later recalled that Seward showed it to him beforehand and asked him to write it up for the *New York Tribune*, with an accompanying description of the scene in the Senate chamber as he was speaking. "The description was elaborate," Stanton claimed, "the Senator himself suggesting some of the nicer touches, and every line of it was written and on its way to New York before Mr. Seward had uttered a word in the Senate Chamber." Seward was in "buoyant spirits," assuring Stanton that with this speech they would "go down to posterity together."

Frances Seward was less enthusiastic, perhaps fearing that her husband would bend too far to placate the moderates. "I wish it were over," she told her son Will on the morning of the speech. Fanny, however, seated in the gallery directly opposite her father, was thrilled to witness the great event. "The whole house of Reps were there," she gushed, "the galleries soon filled, alike with those of North and South, ladies and gentlemen, even the doorways were filled." When the three-hour speech started, Fanny recorded, "no Republican member left his seat . . . the house was very still." Everyone understood that this speech could influence the Republican nomination.

Seward took as his theme the enduring quality of the national compact. Though he maintained his principled opposition to slavery, he softened his tone, referring to the slave states as "capital States," while the free states became the "labor States." His language remained tranquil throughout, with no trace of the inflammatory phrases that had characterized his great speeches in the past. It seemed, one historian observed, that " 'the irrepressible conflict' between slavery and freedom had graciously given way to the somewhat repressible conflict of the political aspirants."

Departing from the bold assertions of his Rochester speech, Seward now claimed that "differences of opinion, even on the subject of slavery, with us are political, not social or personal differences. There is not one disunionist or disloyalist among us all. . . . We have never been more patient, and never loved the representatives of other sections more, than now. . . . The people of the North are not enemies but friends and brethren of the South, faithful and true as in the days when death has dealt his arrows promiscuously among them on the common battle-fields of freedom."

The Republican Party in the North, he pledged, did not "seek to force, or even to intrude, our system" upon the South. "You are sovereign on the subject of slavery within your own borders." The debate revolved only around the expansion of slavery in new and future states. Retreating from the larger vision of the nation's future manifest destiny in some of his earlier speeches, he promised that Republicans did not harbor any ulterior motive "to introduce negro equality" in the nation at large.

Seward's powerful conclusion—an altered form of which would appear in Lincoln's inaugural address—was an impassioned testimony to the Union. The nation could never be sundered, for its bonds were not simply "the written compact," or even the radiating network of roads, train tracks, trade routes, and telegraph lines that facilitated "commerce and social intercourse." Rather, Seward urged his audience to conceive of the strongest bonds holding the Union together as "the millions of fibers of millions of contented, happy human hearts," linked by affection and hope to their democratic government, "the first, the last, and the only such one that has ever existed, which takes equal heed always of their wants."

The speech produced deafening applause in the galleries and widespread praise in the press. Reprinted in pamphlet form, more than half a million copies were circulated throughout the country. Some, of course, considered Seward's tone too conciliatory, lacking the principle and fire of his previous addresses. That speech "*killed Seward with me forever,*" the abolitionist Cassius Clay reportedly said. Charles Sumner wrote to a friend that "as an intellectual effort," Seward's oration was "most eminent," but that there was "one passage"—perhaps the one disclaiming any intention to support black equality—which he "regretted, & [Seward's] wife agrees with me."

Nevertheless, Seward's goal had not been to rally the faithful but to disarm the opposition and placate uneasy moderates. "From the stand-point of Radical Abolitionism, it would be very easy to criticize," Frederick Douglass observed in his monthly paper, but "it is a masterly and triumphant effort. It will reassure the timid wing of his party, which has been rendered a little nervous by recent clamors against him, by its coolness of temper and conservatism of manner. . . . We think that Mr. Seward's prospects for the Chicago nomination will be essentially brightened by the wide circulation of this speech." Seward, he concluded, was "the ablest man of his party," and "as a matter of party justice," he deserved the nomination.

"I hear of ultra old Whigs in Boston who say they are ready to take up Mr. Seward upon his recent speech," a Massachusetts delegate told Weed. "All the New England delegates, save Connecticut's, will be equally satisfactory." And in Ohio, Salmon Chase admitted that there "seems to be at present a considerable set toward Seward." Seward himself believed that the speech had been a great success, the final step in his long journey to the presidency.

In the heady weeks that followed, Weed assured him that everything was in readiness for a victory at the convention. By trading legislative charters to build city railroads for campaign contributions, Weed had assembled what one observer called "oceans of money," a campaign chest worth several hundred thousand dollars.

As the convention approached, overconfidence reigned in the Seward camp and poor judgment set in. Despite Weed's generally keen political intuition, he failed to anticipate the damage Seward would suffer as a consequence of a rift with Horace Greeley. Over the years, Greeley had voiced a longing for political office, for both the monetary compensation it would provide and the prestige it promised. On several occasions, Greeley later claimed, he had made this desire clear to Seward and Weed. They never took his political aspirations seriously, believing that his strength and usefulness lay in writing, not in practical politics and public office. Greeley had written a plaintive letter to Seward in the autumn of 1854, in which he catalogued a long list of grievances and announced the dissolution of the political firm of Seward, Weed, & Greeley. He recalled the work he had done to secure Seward's first victory as governor, only to discover that jobs had been dispensed "worth $3000 to $20,000 per year to your friends and compatriots, and I returned to my garret and my crust, and my desperate battle with pecuniary obligations." With the exception of a single term in Congress, Greeley charged, Weed had never given him a chance to be nominated for any office. Despite hundreds of suggestions that he run for governor in the most recent election, Weed had refused to support the possibility, claiming that his candidacy would hurt Seward's chances for the Senate. But the most humiliating moment had come, Greeley revealed, when Weed handed the nomination for lieutenant governor that year to Henry Raymond, editor of the *New York Times*, the *Tribune*'s archrival.

Seward was distressed to read Greeley's letter, which he characterized as "full of sharp, pricking thorns," but he mistakenly assumed that Greeley's pique was temporary, akin to the anger, he said, that one of his sons might display if denied the chance to go to the circus or a dancing party. After showing it to his wife, Seward cast the letter aside. Frances read it more accurately. Recognizing the "mortal offense" Greeley had taken, she saved the letter, preserving a record of the tangled web of emotions that led Greeley in 1860 to abandon one of his oldest friends in favor of Edward Bates, a man he barely knew.

Week after week, through his columns in the *Tribune*, Greeley laid the groundwork for the nomination of Bates. Seward's supporters were incensed when he subtly began to sabotage the New Yorker's campaign. Henry Raymond remarked that Greeley "insinuated, rather than openly uttered, exaggerations of local prejudice and animosity against him; hints that parties and men hostile to him and to the Republican organization must be conciliated and their support secured; and a new-born zeal for nationalizing the party by consulting the slave-holding states in regard to the nomination." The influence of the *Tribune* was substantial, and with each passing day, enthusiasm for Bates's candidacy grew.

At some point that spring, Weed had a long talk with Greeley and came away with the mistaken conviction that Greeley was "all right," that despite his editorial support for Bates, he would not play a major role at the convention. The conversation mistakenly satisfied Weed that ties of old friendship would keep Greeley from taking an active role against Seward once the convention began.

Overconfidence also played a role in Weed's failure to meet with Pennsylvania's powerful political boss, Simon Cameron, before the convention opened. In mid-March, Cameron told Seward that he wanted to see Weed in either Washington or Philadelphia "at any time" convenient to Weed. Seward relayed the message to his mentor, but Weed, certain that Cameron would deliver Pennsylvania to Seward by the second ballot, as he thought he had promised, never managed to make the trip.

Weed's faith in Cameron was due partly to Seward's report of a special visit he had made to Cameron's estate, Lochiel, near Harrisburg, Pennsylvania. Shortly before leaving for Europe the previous spring, Seward had spent a day with Cameron and had returned certain that Cameron was pledged to his candidacy. "He took me to his home, told me all was right," Seward told Weed. "He was for me, and Pa. would be. It might want to cast a first ballot for him or might not. . . . He brought the whole legislature of both parties to see me—feasted them gloriously and they were in the main so free, so generous as to embarrass me." Reports of this lavish reception persuaded reporters and politicians alike that a deal had been brokered.

In the months that followed, even as gossip spread that Cameron did not have control of his entire delegation, Weed continued to believe that the Pennsylvania boss, so like himself in many ways, would do whatever was necessary to fulfill his pledge and deliver his state. After all, to Cameron was attributed the oft-quoted definition: "an honest politician is one who, when he is bought, stays bought."

Cameron had been quicker than Weed to exploit the lucrative potential of politics. Through contracts with canal companies, railroads, and banks, he amassed "so much money," he later boasted, that he might have become "the richest man in Pennsylvania" had he not pursued elective office. Unlike Weed, who remained behind the scenes, Cameron secured for himself two terms in the U.S. Senate; in 1844 and again in 1855. He began his political life as a Democrat but became frustrated by Democratic positions on slavery and, more important, on the tariff, which was his "legislative child." In 1855, he was instrumental in establishing Pennsylvania's Republican Party, initially called the People's Party.

At the People's Party state convention in February 1860, Cameron received the expected favorite-son nod for the presidency, but Andrew Curtin, a magnetic young politician who was challenging Cameron for control in the state, was nominated for governor. Though Cameron received a majority vote at the convention, a substantial number of district delegates remained to be chosen, eventually producing a split between the rival forces of Cameron and Curtin. Curtin was uncommitted to any candidate when the Republican Convention opened, yet it was known that he questioned Seward's electability. Seward's name on the ticket might hamstring his own election, for the anti-Catholic Know Nothings, who still exerted considerable power in Pennsylvania, had never forgiven Seward for his liberalism toward immigrants and his controversial support for parochial education. Boss Cameron might have been able to resolve these obstacles with Boss Weed in private conversation before the convention. Since that meeting never took place, Weed was left to navigate the countervailing forces of the Pennsylvania state delegation without Cameron's guidance.

• • •

SEWARD'S LEISURELY SOJOURN abroad afforded Chase the opportunity to actively secure pledges and workers for his nomination. Never the most astute of politicians, Chase made curiously little use of the precious months of 1859 to better his chances. Sure of the power and depth of his support, he once again, as in 1856, assumed he would somehow gain the nomination without much personal intervention. News to the contrary Chase dismissed out of hand, even when the intelligence came from his close friend Gamaliel Bailey.

Bailey and Chase had become acquainted in Cincinnati when Bailey was editing *The Philanthropist.* Later on, when Bailey became publisher of *The National Era* and moved his family to Washington, they warmly welcomed the lonely Chase into their home. When the Senate was in session, Chase lived for months at a time at their house, forming friendships with Bailey's wife, Margaret, and the entire Bailey clan. On Saturday evenings, the Baileys' home became "a salon in European tradition," replete with dinner and the word games at which Chase excelled.

Throughout their long friendship, Bailey had always been frank with Chase, castigating him in 1856 for his temporizing attitude toward the "detestable" Know Nothings. Nonetheless, Bailey remained loyal and supportive of his old friend, assuring him on numerous occasions that he would rather see him "in the presidential chair than any other man." Yet, as Bailey assessed the temper of the country in early 1859, conversing with many people, "observing the signs of the times and the phases of public opinion," he concluded in a long, candid letter to Chase that he thought it best to support Seward in 1860. The time for Chase would come again four years later.

"He and you are the two most prominent representative men of the party," Bailey wrote on January 16, 1859, "but he is older than you." His friends believe it is "*now or never*" with him, "to postpone him now is to postpone him forever . . . you are in the prime of life and have the promise of continuing so—you have not attained your full stature or *status—he has*—every year adds to your strength, and in 1864, you will be stronger than in 1860. . . . To be urgent now against the settled feeling of Seward's numerous friends, would provoke unpleasant and damaging discords, and tend hereafter to weaken your position." Bailey suspected that Chase might disagree with his recommendation, but "I know you will not question my integrity or my friendship."

"I do not doubt your friendship," Chase testily replied, "but I do think that if our situations were reversed I should take a different method of showing mine for you. . . . The suggestion 'now or never' [with regard to Seward] is babyish . . . how ridiculous . . . but to sum up all in brief . . . let me say it cannot change my position. I have no right to do so. . . . A very large body of the people—embracing not a few who would hardly vote for any man other than myself as a Republican nominee—seem to desire that I shall be a candidate in 1860. No effort of mine, and as far as I know none of my immediate personal friends has produced this feeling. It seems to be of spontaneous growth."

Bailey responded that he presumed Chase's characterization of the "now or never" position of Seward's supporters as "babyish" was "a slip of your pen. . . . It may be erroneous, groundless, but . . . it is entitled to consideration. It has reference not only to age, & health, but other matters. . . . Governor Seward will be fifty-nine in May, 1860. . . . Should another be nominated, and elected, the chances would be in favor of a renomination—which would postpone the Governor eight years—until he should be sixty-seven, in the shadow of seventy. . . . You are still growing [Chase had just turned fifty-one]—you are still increasing in reputation—four years hence . . . your chances of nomination & election to the Presidency would be greater than they are now." Bailey assured Chase that he would never work against him. "All I desired was to apprise you, as a friend."

Deluded by flattery, Chase preferred the unrealistic projections of New York's Hiram Barney, who thought his strength in New York State was growing so rapidly that it was possible he might receive New York's vote on the first ballot. So heroic was his self-conception, Chase believed that doubtful supporters would flock to his side once they understood the central role he had played as the guardian of the antislavery tradition and father of the Republican Party.

Failing once again to appoint a campaign manager, Chase had no one to bargain and maneuver for him, no one to promise government posts in return for votes. He rejected an appeal from a New Hampshire supporter who proposed to build a state organization. He never capitalized on the initial support of powerful Chicago *Press and Tribune* editor Joseph Medill. He turned down an invitation to speak at Cooper Union in a lecture series organized by his supporters as a forum for candidates other than Seward. Refusing even to consider that his own state might deny him a united vote on the first ballot, he failed to confirm that every delegate appointed to the convention was pledged to vote for him. Indeed, his sole contribution to his own campaign was a series of letters to various supporters and journalists around the country, reminding them that he was the best man for the job.

Frustrated supporters tried to shake him into more concerted action. "I now begin to fear that Seward will get a majority of the delegates from Maryland," Chase's loyal backer James Ashley warned. "He and his friends *work—work*. They not only work—but *he works*." The willful Chase was blind to troubling signs, convinced that if the delegates voted their conscience, he would ultimately prevail.

"I shall have nobody to push or act for me at Chicago," Chase boasted to Benjamin Eggleston, a delegate from Cincinnati, "except the Ohio delegation who will, I doubt not, faithfully represent the Republicans of the State." While a large majority of the Ohio state delegation indeed supported Chase, Senator Ben Wade had his own devoted followers. "The Ohio delegation does not seem to be anywhere as yet," delegate Erastus Hopkins warned. Heedless, Chase remained positive that the entire Ohio delegation would come around, given everything he had done and sacrificed for his state. To support any other candidate would put one "in a position no man of honor or sensibility would care to occupy."

A month before the convention, Kate convinced her father that a journey to Washington would shore up his support among various congressmen and senators. Lodging at the Willard Hotel, they made the rounds of receptions and dinners. Seward was very kind to them, Chase admitted to his friend James Briggs. The genial New Yorker hosted a dinner party in their honor at which "all sides were pretty fairly represented" and "there was a good deal of joking." The next evening, former Ohio congressman John Gurley organized a party to honor both Chase and Ohio's new governor, William Dennison. Seward was invited to join the Ohio gathering, which included former Whig leader Tom Corwin and Senator Ben Wade.

Writing home after the dinner, Seward joshingly noted that he "found much comfort" in the discovery that Ohio was home to at least three candidates for the presidency, "all eminent and excellent men, but each preferring anybody out of Ohio, to his two rivals within." While Seward immediately intuited signals that Ben Wade, in particular, coveted the nomination, Chase remained oblivious, refusing to believe that Ohio would not back its most deserving son. On the Chases' last evening in Washington, the Blairs threw them a lavish party at their country estate in Silver Spring.

As usual, Kate left a deep impression on everyone. Seward afterward told Frances that she was quite "a young lady, pleasant and well-cultivated." Chase wrote Nettie how pleased he was that many showed "attention to Katie," and many were "kind to me." He returned home convinced that his trip had accomplished a great deal. "Everybody seems to like me and to feel a very gratifying degree of confidence in me," he reported to a Cincinnati friend. Confusing hospitality with hard allegiance, he told one of his supporters that "a great change seemed to come over men's minds while I was in Washington."

• • •

THE BEGINNING of the pre-presidential year found the backers of Edward Bates more active in the pursuit of his nomination than the candidate himself. While Bates would gradually warm to the idea, he found himself, as always, conflicted about plunging into politics. Without the encouragement of the powerful Blairs, it is unlikely that he would have put his name forward. Once he agreed to stand, he was confronted with a political dilemma. His strength lay among old Whigs and nativists concentrated in the border states, and conservatives in the North and Northwest. To have a genuine chance for the nomination, he would have to prove himself acceptable to moderate Republicans as well.

Had he used the months prior to the nomination to travel to the very different states of Illinois, Indiana, Massachusetts, Connecticut, or Maryland, he might have acquainted himself with the wide range of views that comprised the new party. But he never left his home state, preferring to rely on intelligence received from colleagues and supporters who came to visit him. Not only did he keep to Missouri, he rarely left his beloved home, noting in his diary when he was forced to stay overnight in St. Louis that it was "the first that I have slept in town for about two years." Four decades of marriage had not diminished his bond with Julia.

Secluding himself at home, Bates never developed a clear understanding of the varied constituencies that had to be aligned, a deficit that resulted in a number of missteps. While his distance from the fierce arguments of the fifties was considered beneficial to his candidacy, his long absence from politics made him less familiar with the savage polarization created by the slavery issue. In late February 1859, he answered the request of the Whig Committee of New York for his "views and opinions on the politics of the country." The New York Whigs had passed a resolution calling for an end to agitation of "the Negro question" so that the country might focus on "topics of general importance," such as economic development and internal improvements, that would unite rather than fracture the nation. In his letter, which was published nationwide, Bates declared that he had always considered "the Negro question" to be "a pestilent question, the agitation of which has never done good to any party, section or class, and never can do good, unless it be accounted good to stir up the angry passions of men, and exasperate the unreasoning jealousy of sections." He believed that those who continued to press the issue, "after the sorrowful experience of the last few years," must be motivated by "personal ambition or sectional prejudice."

Lauded by Whigs and nativists, the letter provoked widespread criticism in Republican circles. Schuyler Colfax, who backed Bates for president, warned him that his comments "denouncing the agitation of the negro question" sounded like "a denunciation of the Rep[ublica]n party, and would turn many against [him]." Bates disagreed. "If my letter had been universally acceptable to the Republicans, that fact alone might have destroyed my prospects in two frontier slave states, Md. and Mo., and so I would have no streng[t]h at all but the Republican party," where Seward and Chase, he knew, were far better positioned. Maryland congressman Henry Winter Davis, the leading member of the American Party in the House, confirmed Bates's views, advising him that he was poised to secure majority approval and should not attempt to further define his views—"write no more public letters—let well enough alone."

As the new year opened, Bates believed his chances were growing "brighter every day." Supporters in the key battleground states of Indiana and Pennsylvania assured him that large percentages of the delegates appointed to the Chicago convention were "made up of 'Bates men.' " A visitor from Illinois told him that much "good feeling" existed in the southern part of the state, "but first (on a point of State pride,) they must support Lincoln." This was the first time in his daily entries that Bates so much as mentioned Lincoln's name as a presidential aspirant. In Illinois, Lincoln was keenly aware of Bates, answering an inquiring letter about how Illinois regarded the various candidates by saying that Bates "would be the best man for the South of our State, and the worst for the North of it," while Seward was "the very best candidate we could have for the North of Illinois, and the very *worst* for the South of it." With amusing self-serving logic, Lincoln suggested that neither Bates nor Seward could command a majority vote in Illinois.

On the last day of February 1860, the very day of Seward's conciliatory speech in the Senate, a great Opposition Convention comprised of Whigs and Americans met in Jefferson City, Missouri, and "enthusiastically" endorsed Bates for president. Two weeks later, Bates received a second endorsement from the Republican state convention in St. Louis. The Missouri Republicans, however, were in a carping mood, particularly the German-American contingent, which threatened to block the endorsement, still troubled by Bates's open support for the nativist party in 1856. To satisfy both the more ardent Republicans and the German-American community, Frank Blair suggested that Bates agree to outline his positions in answer to a questionnaire drawn up by the German-American press.

The questionnaire posed a difficult problem for Bates. He had to assuage the doubts of Republicans who felt, like editor Joseph Medill of Chicago, that it was better to be "beaten with a representative man" who placed himself squarely on the Republican platform than to "triumph with a 'Union-saver' " and "sink into the quicksands." However, if he moved too far to the left to satisfy the passionate Republicans, he would risk his natural base among the old Whigs and Americans. Though once noted for his deft touch in harmonizing opposing forces, Bates plunged into his answers without calculating the consequences.

Asked to render his opinions on the extension of slavery into the territories, he announced that Congress had the power to decide the issue, a position that directly contradicted the *Dred Scott* decision. He felt, moreover, that "the spirit and the policy of the Government ought to be against its extension." He advocated equal constitutional rights for all citizens, native-born or naturalized, claiming to endorse "no distinctions among Americans citizens," and adding that the "Government is bound to protect all the citizens in the enjoyment of all their rights every where." Beyond this, he favored colonizing former slaves in Africa and Central America, a Homestead Act, a Pacific Railroad, and the admission of Kansas as a free state.

His statement met with approval in traditional Republican enclaves in the Northeast and Northwest, but in the border states, where his advantage was supposed to reside, it proved disastrous. The *Lexington [Missouri] Express* wrote that the published letter came "as a clap of thunder from a clear sky," placing Bates so blatantly in the Black Republican camp that he should no longer expect support from the more conservative border states. By subscribing to every article of the Republican creed, the *Louisville Journal* complained, Bates became "just as good or bad a Republican as Seward, Chase or Lincoln is. . . . He has by a single blow severed every tie of confidence or sympathy which connected him with the Southern Conservatives." Only four years earlier, the *Memphis Bulletin* observed, Bates had denounced Black Republicans as "agitators," labeling them "dangerous enemies to the peace of our Union." Now he had become one of them. Bates himself recognized the backlash his letter had created, lamenting "the simultaneous abandonment of me by a good many papers" in the border states.

The attempt to pacify the anxious German-Americans had diminished his hold on what should have been his natural base, without bringing a commensurate number of Republicans to his side. Though the Bates camp maintained faith that their man was bound to win the nomination, Bates confided in his diary that "knowing the fickleness of popular favor, and on what small things great events depend, I shall take care not so to set my heart upon the glittering bauble, as to be mortified or made at all unhappy by a failure."

• • •

NOT HINDERED by the hubris, delusions, and inconsistencies that plagued his three chief rivals, Abraham Lincoln gained steady ground through a combination of hard work, skill, and luck. While Seward and Bates felt compelled in the final months to reposition themselves toward the center of the party, Lincoln never changed his basic stance. He could remain where he had always been, "neither on the left wing nor the right, but very close to dead center," as Don Fehrenbacher writes. From the time he had first spoken out against the extension of slavery into the territories in the wake of the Kansas-Nebraska Act, Lincoln had insisted that while the spread of slavery must be "fairly headed off," he had no wish "to interfere with slavery" where it already existed. So long as the institution was contained, which Lincoln considered a sacred pledge, it was "in course of ultimate extinction." This position represented perfectly the views of the moderate majority in the Republican Party.

Though a successful bid for the nomination remained unlikely, a viable candidacy was no longer an impossible dream. Slowly and methodically, Lincoln set out to improve his long odds. He arranged to publish his debates with Douglas in a book that was read widely by Republicans. As more and more people became familiar with him through the newspaper stories of the debates, invitations to speak at Republican gatherings began to pour in. Not yet an avowed candidate, Lincoln delivered nearly two dozen speeches in Iowa, Ohio, Wisconsin, Indiana, and Kansas in the four months between August and December 1859.

While Seward was still touring Europe and the Middle East, Lincoln was introducing himself to tens of thousands of Westerners. "I think it is a mistake," a leading New Yorker wrote Lincoln, "that Senator Seward is not on his own battlefield, instead of being in Egypt surveying the route of an old Underground Rail Road, over which Moses took, one day, a whole nation, from bondage into Liberty." Lincoln capitalized on Seward's absence. The crowds that greeted him grew with every stop along the way. Most of his audiences had never laid eyes on him, and he invariably forged an indelible impression. Once he began speaking, the *Janesville Gazette* reported, "the high order of [his] intellect" left a permanent impact upon his listeners, who would remember his "tall, gaunt form" and "his points and his hits" for "many a day."

Speaking not as a candidate but as an advocate for the Republican cause, Lincoln sharpened his attacks on the Democrats and, in particular, on the party's front-runner, Stephen Douglas, who preceded him at many of the same locations. "Douglasism," he wrote Chase, "is all which now stands in the way of an early and complete success of Republicanism." In this way, ironically, Douglas's national reputation continually increased the attention paid to Lincoln.

Perhaps Lincoln's most rewarding stop was Cincinnati, which he had vowed never again to visit after the humiliating Reaper trial. This time, he was "greeted with the thunder of cannon, the strains of martial music, and the joyous plaudits of thousands of citizens thronging the streets." He arrived at the Burnet House and was put up "in princely style," delighted to find that the most prominent of Cincinnati's residents were vying to meet the "rising star."

Lincoln addressed the Southern threats that the election of a Republican president would divide the Union, directing his remarks particularly to the many Kentuckians who had crossed the Ohio River to listen to him. "Will you make war upon us and kill us all? Why, gentlemen, I think you are as gallant and as brave men as live; that you can fight as bravely in a good cause, man for man, as any other people living . . . but, man for man, you are not better than we are, and there are not so many of you as there are of us. You will never make much of a hand at whipping us. If we were fewer in numbers than you, I think that you could whip us; if we were equal it would likely be a drawn battle; but being inferior in numbers, you will make nothing by attempting to master us." The next day, his speech was described in the *Cincinnati Gazette* "as an effort remarkable for its clear statement, powerful argument and massive common sense," and possessed of "such dignity and power as to have impressed some of our ablest lawyers with the conclusion that it was superior to any political effort they had ever heard."

Lincoln's crowded schedule allowed him no time to accept Joshua Speed's invitation to visit him in Kentucky for the opening of the national racecourse, "when," his old friend promised, "we expect to have some of the best horses in America to compete for the purses. In addition we think we can show the prettiest women," adding, "if you are not too old to enjoy either the speed of the horses or the beauty of the women come." If his speaking tour caused Lincoln to forgo speedy horses and beautiful women, it greatly increased his stature among western Republicans. "Your visit to Ohio has excited an extensive interest in your favor," former congressman Samuel Galloway told him. "We must take some man not hitherto corrupted with the discussion upon Candidates. Your name has been again and again mentioned. . . . I am candid to say you are my choice."

Rapidly becoming a national spokesman for the fledgling Republican Party, Lincoln sought to preserve the unity of the still-fragile coalition. He wished, he wrote Schuyler Colfax, "to hedge against divisions in the Republican ranks." An anti-immigrant movement in Massachusetts "failed to see that tilting against foreigners would ruin us in the whole North-West," while attempts in both Ohio and New Hampshire to thwart enforcement of the Fugitive Slave Law might "utterly overwhelm us in Illinois with the charge of enmity to the constitution itself. . . . In a word, in every locality we should look beyond our noses; and at least say *nothing* on points where it is probable we shall disagree."

Colfax appreciated Lincoln's "kind & timely note," which underscored the need to enlist in the Republican cause "men of all shades & gradations of opinion from the Conservative . . . to the bold radical." To be victorious in 1860, he wrote, "we must either win this Conservative sentiment, with its kindred sympathizers, represented under the title of North Americans, Old Line Whigs &c, to our banners" without alienating the radicals, "or by repelling them must go into the contest looking for defeat." In this cause of unity, Colfax assured Lincoln, "your counsel carries great weight . . . there is no political letter that falls from your pen, which is not copied throughout the Union." Lincoln's ability to bridge these divisions would prove of vital importance to his campaign.

On October 16, 1859, as Lincoln prepared for a trip to Kansas, the remaining bonds of union were strained almost to the point of rupture when the white abolitionist John Brown came to Virginia, in the words of Stephen Vincent Benét, "with foolish pikes/And a pack of desperate boys to shadow the sun." Brown and his band of thirteen white men and five blacks seized the federal arsenal at Harpers Ferry with a bold but ill-conceived plan of provoking a slave insurrection. The arsenal was swiftly recaptured and Brown taken prisoner by a federal force under the command of Colonel Robert E. Lee, accompanied by Lieutenant J. E. B. Stuart.

Brown was tried and sentenced to death. "I am waiting the hour of my public *murder* with great composure of mind, & cheerfulness," Brown wrote his family, "feeling the strongest assurance that in no other possible way could I be used to so much advance the cause of God; & of humanity." In the month between the sentence and his hanging, the dignity and courage of his conduct and the eloquence of his statements and letters made John Brown a martyr/hero to many in the antislavery North. His death, when it came, was mourned by public assemblies throughout the Northern states. "Church bells tolled," the historian David Potter writes, "black bunting was hung out, minute guns were fired, prayer meetings assembled, and memorial resolutions were adopted."

Brown's motivations, psychological profile, and strategy would be probed by historians, poets, and novelists for generations. The immediate impact of the intrepid raid, which "sent a shiver of fear to the inmost fiber of every white man, woman, and child" in the South, was unmistakable.

While antislavery fervor in the North was intensified, Southern solidarity and rhetoric reached a new level of zealotry. "Harper's Ferry," wrote the *Richmond Enquirer*, "coupled with the expression of Northern sentiment in support . . . have shaken and disrupted all regard for the Union; and there are but few men who do not look to a certain and not distant day when dissolution must ensue." The raid at Harpers Ferry, one historian notes, was "like a great meteor disclosing in its lurid flash the width and depth of that abyss," which cut the nation in two. Herman Melville, in his poem "The Portent," would use the same metaphor, calling "Weird John Brown/ The meteor of the war"—the tail of his long beard trailing out from under the executioner's cap.

Throughout the South, heightened fear of slave insurrection led to severe restrictions on the expression of antislavery sentiments. "I do not exaggerate in designating the present state of affairs in the Southern country as a reign of terror," the British consul in Charleston wrote. "Persons are torn away from their residences and pursuits . . . letters are opened at the Post Offices; discussion upon slavery is entirely prohibited under penalty of expulsion. . . . The Northern merchants and Travellers are leaving in great numbers." In Norfolk, Virginia, the *St. Louis News* reported, a grand jury indicted a merchant "for seditious language, because he declared that John Brown was a good man, fighting in a good cause."

Leading Southern politicians were quick to indict the Republican Party and, by extension, the entire North. The Tennessee legislature resolved that the raiders at Harpers Ferry were "the natural fruits of this treasonable 'irrepressible conflict' doctrine, put forth by the great head of the Black Republican party, and echoed by his subordinates." A man representing "one hundred gentlemen" published a circular that offered a $50,000 reward *"for the head of William H. Seward,"* along with the considerably smaller sum of $25 for the heads of a long list of "traitors," including Sumner, Greeley, Giddings, and Colfax. Lincoln was not included in the list of enemies.

Democratic papers in the North joined in, targeting Seward for special condemnation. "The first overt act in the great drama of national disruption which has been plotted by that demagogue, Wm. H. Seward, has just closed at Harper's Ferry," the *New York Herald* charged. "No reasoning mind can fail to trace cause and effect between the bloody and brutal manifesto of William H. Seward [the "irrepressible conflict" speech a year earlier] . . . and the terrible scenes of violence, rapine and death, that have been enacted at the confluence of the Potomac and the Shenandoah."

Republicans, naturally, countered Democratic attempts to implicate their party. Seward himself stated that although Brown was a sympathetic figure, his execution was "necessary and just." Weed's *Albany Evening Journal* also took a decided stance against the futile raid, deeming Brown's men guilty of treason for "seeking to plunge a peaceful community into the horrors of a servile insurrection." They "justly deserve, universal condemnation."

In Missouri, Bates concluded that "the wild extravagance and utter futility of his plan" proved that Brown was "a madman." He discussed the incident at length with his young friend Lieutenant J. E. B. Stuart, who had come to stay at Grape Hill for several days with his wife, Flora, his child, and two free black servants. "He tells me a good deal about 'Old Brown,' " Bates wrote in his diary. "He was at his capture—and has his [dagger]."

For Chase, the situation presented particular problems. Though he publicly denounced Brown's violation of law and order, his younger daughter, Nettie, later conceded that "for a household accustomed to revere as friends of the family such men as Sumner, Garrison, Wendell Phillips, Whittier, and Longfellow," it was impossible not to sympathize with "the truly good old man who was about to die for others." She and her friends built a small fort in the conservatory and "raised a flag on which was painted . . . defiantly 'Freedom forever; slavery never.' " When friends warned Chase that such open support of Brown could not be countenanced, he had to explain to his daughter that "a great wrong" could not be righted "in the way poor old John Brown had attempted to do." The little fort was dismantled.

At the time of Brown's execution on December 2, 1859, Lincoln was back on the campaign trail, telling an audience in Leavenworth, Kansas, that "the attempt to identify the Republican party with the John Brown business was an electioneering dodge." He wisely sought the middle ground between the statements of radical Republicans, like Emerson, who believed that Brown's execution would "make the gallows as glorious as the cross," and conservative Republicans, who denounced Brown for his demented, traitorous scheme. He acknowledged that Brown had displayed "great courage" and "rare unselfishness." Nonetheless, he concluded, "that cannot excuse violence, bloodshed, and treason. It could avail him nothing that he might think himself right."

• • •

WHEN HE RETURNED from his canvassing, Lincoln focused on the approaching meeting of the Republican National Committee, to be held on December 21, 1859, at the Astor House in New York. Committee members from nearly all the free states were gathered to decide where the Republican Convention would be held. Supporters of Seward, Chase, and

Bates argued in turn that the convention should be placed in New York, Ohio, or Missouri. Though Lincoln had not yet committed himself publicly to run for the nomination, he wrote to Norman Judd, a member of the selection committee, to press the claims of Illinois, to satisfy friends who "attach more consequence" to the location than either he or Judd had originally done.

Judd waited patiently as the claims of Buffalo, Cleveland, Cincinnati, St. Louis, Indianapolis, and Harrisburg were put forth. When no agreement could be reached, he shrewdly suggested Chicago as "good neutral ground where everyone would have an even chance." Although Lincoln was known to most of the committee members at this point, none considered him a serious candidate for the presidency. Judd "carefully kept 'Old Abe' out of sight," observed Henry Whitney, "and the delegates failed to see any personal bearing the place of meeting was to have on the nomination." The choice finally narrowed down to St. Louis and Chicago. Judd "promised that the members of the Convention and all outsiders of the Republican faith should have a hospitable reception," that sufficient accommodations would be provided "for feeding and lodging the large crowd," and that "a hall for deliberation should be furnished free." Ultimately, Chicago beat St. Louis by a single vote.

Once Chicago was selected, Judd, a railway lawyer, persuaded the railroad companies to provide "a cheap excursion rate from all parts of the State," so that lack of funds would not keep Lincoln supporters from attending the convention. Concealed from his rivals, Lincoln had taken an important step toward the nomination.

So confident were Seward's friends about his chances that they had no problem with the Chicago selection. "I like the place & the tenor of the call," New York editor John Bigelow wrote Seward at the time. "I do not see how either could be bettered, nor how it is possible to take exception to it." But Charles Gibson, Bates's friend and supporter, was not so sanguine; he recognized that it was a blow to the Bates candidacy. "Had the convention been held in St. Louis," Gibson later wrote, "Lincoln would not have been the nominee."

As Lincoln's candidacy became a real prospect, he attended to the request made by Jesse Fell a year earlier for a short history of his life to be published and distributed. After warning Fell that "there is not much of it, for the reason, I suppose, that there is not much of me," Lincoln detailed, without a hint of self-pity, the facts of his early life, growing up in "a wild region, with many bears and other wild animals still in the woods."

"If any thing be made out of it, I wish it to be modest," Lincoln told Fell. "Of course it must not appear to have been written by myself." This simple sketch written in his own hand would be used later in Republican efforts to romanticize Lincoln's humble beginnings.

• • •

LINCOLN'S HOPES for making himself better known outside the West received an immense boost when he received the invitation from Chase supporter James Briggs to speak as part of a lecture series in Brooklyn. The lecture was eventually scheduled for February 27, 1860. Chase, as we saw, had declined the opportunity to speak in the same series, despite word that its organizers were men seeking an alternative to Seward. Upon his arrival in New York, Lincoln sought out Henry Bowen, editor of the antislavery *New York Independent*, who had helped arrange the event. "His clothes were travel-stained and he looked tired and woe-begone," Bowen recalled. "In this first view of him, there came to me the disheartening and appalling thought of the great throng which I had been so instrumental in inducing to come." But Bowen's initial impression of Lincoln softened after Lincoln admitted that the long journey had worn him out, and said, "if you have no objection I will lie down on your lounge here and you can tell me about the arrangements for Monday night."

At the Astor House, Lincoln met Mayson Brayman, a fellow lawyer who had lived in Springfield for some years before returning to his native New York. "Well, B. how have you fared since you left Illinois?" Lincoln asked. "I have made one hundred thousand dollars and lost all," Brayman ruefully replied; "how is it with you, Mr. Lincoln?"

"Oh, very well," Lincoln said. "I have the cottage at Springfield and about $8,000 in money. If they make me Vice-President with Seward, as some say they will, I hope I shall be able to increase it to $20,000, and that is as much as a man ought to want." Lincoln's sights, however, were not trained on the vice presidency, and politics, not riches, were his object.

That February afternoon, Lincoln paid a visit to the studio of the photographer Mathew Brady on Broadway. When Brady was posing him, he urged Lincoln to hike up his shirt collar. Lincoln quipped that Brady wanted "to shorten [his] neck." The resulting three-quarter-length portrait shows the fifty-one-year-old Lincoln standing before a pillar, the fingers of his left hand spread over a book. Prominent cheekbones cast marked shadows across his clean-shaven face. The delicate long bow of his upper lip contrasts with the full lower lip, and the deep-set gaze is steady and melancholy. This photograph, circulated widely in engravings and lithographs in the Northeast, was the first arresting image many would see of Abraham Lincoln.

Nearly fifteen hundred people came to hear "this western man" speak in the great hall at Cooper Union. He had bought a new black suit for the occasion, but it was badly wrinkled from the trip. An observer noticed that "one of the legs of his trousers was up about two inches above his shoe; his hair was disheveled and stuck out like rooster's feathers; his coat was altogether too large for him in the back, his arms much longer than his sleeves." Yet once he began to speak, people were captivated by his earnest and powerful delivery.

Lincoln had labored to craft his address for many weeks, extensively researching the attitudes of the founding fathers toward slavery. He took as the text for his discourse a speech in which Senator Douglas had said of slavery: *"Our fathers, when they framed the Government under which we live, understood this question just as well, and even better, than we do now."* Fully endorsing this statement, Lincoln examined the beliefs and actions of the founders, concluding that they had marked slavery *"as an evil not to be extended, but to be tolerated and protected only because of and so far as its actual presence among us makes that toleration and protection a necessity."*

In the preceding months, tensions between North and South had continued to escalate, with each section joining in a "hue and cry" against the other. The troubling scenario that Lincoln had observed nearly two decades earlier, during the battle over temperance, had come to pass. Denunciation was being met by denunciation, "crimination with crimination, and anathema with anathema." To have expected either side to respond differently once the rhetoric had heated up, Lincoln warned during that earlier battle, "was to expect a reversal of human nature, which is God's decree, and never can be reversed."

At Cooper Union, as he had done in his celebrated Peoria speech six years earlier, Lincoln attempted to cut through the rancor of the embattled factions by speaking directly to the Southern people. While his faith in Southern responsiveness had seriously dimmed by this time, he hoped the fear and animosity of slaveholders might be assuaged if they understood that the Republicans desired only a return to the "old policy of the fathers," so "the peace of the old times" could once more be established. Denying charges of sectionalism, he said Republicans were the true conservatives, adhering "to the old and tried, against the new and untried."

Turning to his fellow Republicans, he entreated, *"let us do nothing through passion and ill temper. Even though the southern people will not so much as listen to us, let us calmly consider their demands, and yield to them if, in our deliberate view of our duty, we possibly can."* Though the approach was moderate, Lincoln spoke with such passion and certainty about the unifying principle of the Republican Party—never to allow slavery "to spread into the National Territories, and to overrun us here in these Free States"—

that even the most radical Republicans in the audience were captivated. When he came to the dramatic ending pledge—"LET US HAVE FAITH THAT RIGHT MAKES MIGHT, AND IN THAT FAITH, LET US, TO THE END, DARE TO DO OUR DUTY AS WE UNDERSTAND IT"—the audience erupted in thunderous applause.

After Lincoln spoke, several of the event organizers took the platform. Chase supporter James Briggs predicted that "one of three gentlemen will be our standard bearer"—William Henry Seward, Salmon Chase, or "the gallant son of Kentucky, who was reared in Illinois, and whom you have heard tonight." Lincoln's still-unannounced candidacy had taken an enormous step forward.

"When I came out of the hall," one member of the audience said, "my face glowing with an excitement and my frame all aquiver, a friend, with his eyes aglow, asked me what I thought of Abe Lincoln, the rail-splitter. I said, 'He's the greatest man since St. Paul.' "

Once the speech was reported in the papers, Lincoln was in demand across New England. He answered as many requests as possible, undertaking an exhausting tour of New Hampshire, Rhode Island, and Connecticut, repeating and modifying the arguments of his Cooper Union address. He was forced to decline invitations from outside New England but hoped "to visit New-Jersey & Pa. before the fall elections."

Writing to Mary from Exeter Academy in New Hampshire, where their son Robert was completing a preparatory year before entering Harvard College, Lincoln admitted that the Cooper Union speech, "being within my calculation before I started, went off passably well and gave me no trouble whatever. The difficulty was to make nine others, before reading audiences who had already seen all my ideas in print."

In Hartford, Connecticut, on March 5, Lincoln first met Gideon Welles, an editorial writer for the *Hartford Evening Press* who would become his secretary of the navy. Arriving by train in the afternoon, Lincoln had several hours to spare before his speech that evening. He walked up Asylum Street to the bookstore of Brown & Gross, where he encountered the fifty-eight-year-old Welles, a peculiar-looking man with a curly wig perched on his outsize head, and a flowing white beard. Welles had attended Norwich University and studied the law but then devoted himself to writing, leaving the legal profession at twenty-four to take charge of the Democratic *Hartford Times*. A strong supporter of Andrew Jackson, Welles had represented his town of Glastonbury in the state legislature for eight years. He remained a loyal Democrat until the mid-fifties, when he became troubled by his affiliation to "the party of the Southern slaveocracy."

Like many antislavery Democrats, he joined the Republican Party, though he still held fast to the frugal fiscal policies of the Democrats.

With the convention only two months away, Welles had settled on Chase, whom he had met four years earlier while visiting Cincinnati. While Welles held less radical views on slavery, he was comforted by Chase's similar sentiments regarding government spending and states' rights. Seward, by contrast, frightened Welles. For years, the former Whig and the former Democrat had been at loggerheads over government spending; Welles was convinced that Seward belonged "to the New York school of very expensive rulers." Moreover, Welles was appalled by Seward's talk of a "higher law" than the Constitution and his predictions of an "irrepressible conflict." He was ready to support any candidate but Seward, despite the fact that Seward was the most popular among the Republicans.

That afternoon, Lincoln and Welles spent several hours conversing on a bench in the front of the store. Welles had read accounts of Lincoln's debates with Douglas and had noted the extravagant reviews of his Cooper Union speech. There is no record of their conversation that day, but the prairie lawyer left a strong imprint on Welles, who watched that evening as he delivered a two-hour speech before an overflowing crowd at City Hall.

Though he retained much of his Cooper Union speech, Lincoln developed a new metaphor in Hartford to perfectly illustrate his distinction between accepting slavery where it already existed while doing everything possible to curtail its spread. Testing his image in Hartford, he would refine it further in subsequent speeches. "If I saw a venomous snake crawling in the road," Lincoln began, "any man would say I might seize the nearest stick and kill it; but if I found that snake in bed with my children, that would be another question. I might hurt the children more than the snake, and it might bite them. . . . But if there was a bed newly made up, to which the children were to be taken, and it was proposed to take a batch of young snakes and put them there with them, I take it no man would say there was any question how I ought to decide! . . . The new Territories are the newly made bed to which our children are to go, and it lies with the nation to say whether they shall have snakes mixed up with them or not."

The snake metaphor acknowledged the constitutional protection of slavery where it legally existed, while harnessing the protective instincts of parents to safeguard future generations from the venomous expansion of slavery. This homely vision of the territories as beds for American children exemplified what James Russell Lowell described as Lincoln's ability to speak "as if the people were listening to their own thinking out loud." When Seward reached for a metaphor to dramatize the same danger, he warned that if slavery were allowed into Kansas, his countrymen would have "introduced the Trojan horse" into the new territory. Even if most of his classically trained fellow senators immediately grasped his intent, the Trojan horse image carried neither the instant accessibility of Lincoln's snake-in-the-bed story nor its memorable originality.

The morning after his City Hall speech, Lincoln met with Welles again in the office of the *Hartford Evening Press.* When they parted after an hour of discussion, Welles was favorably impressed. "This orator and lawyer has been caricatured. He is not Apollo, but he is not Caliban," he wrote in the next edition of his paper. "He is [in] every way large, brain included, but his countenance shows intellect, generosity, great good nature, and keen discrimination. . . . He is an effective speaker, because he is earnest, strong, honest, simple in style, and clear as crystal in his logic."

Preparing to return to Springfield, Lincoln had accomplished more than he ever could have anticipated. No longer the distant frontiersman, he had made a name in the East. His possible candidacy was now widely discussed. "I have been sufficiently astonished at my success in the West," Lincoln told a Yale professor who had praised his speech highly. "But I had no thought of any marked success at the East, and least of all that I should draw out such commendations from literary and learned men." When James Briggs told him, "I think your chance for being the next President is equal to that of any man in the country," Lincoln responded, "When I was East several gentlemen made about the same remarks to me that you did to-day about the Presidency; they thought my chances were about equal to the best."

Now there was work to be done at home. A successful bid would require the complete support of the Illinois delegation. To accomplish this, Lincoln would need to bridge the often rancorous divisions within the Republican ranks, a task that would demand all his ample and subtle political skills.

At the end of January 1859, Lyman Trumbull, concerned that the increasingly popular Lincoln might contest his reelection to the Senate, had apprised him of an article "said to have been prepared by Col. John Wentworth," the Republican mayor of Chicago, "the object of which evidently is, to stir up bad feeling between Republicans who were formerly Whigs, & those who were Democrats." The piece suggested bad faith on the Democrats' part, singling out Norman Judd and Trumbull himself, in 1855, and again in 1858, when Lincoln ran a second time against Douglas. "Any effort to put enmity between you and me," Lincoln reassured Trumbull, "is as idle as the wind . . . the republicans generally, coming from the old democratic ranks, were as sincerely anxious for my success in the late contest, as I myself. . . . And I beg to assure you, beyond all possible cavil, that you can scarcely be more anxious to be sustained two years hence than I am that you shall be so sustained. I can not conceive it possible for me to be a rival of yours.

"A word now for your own special benefit," Lincoln warned in a follow-up note. "You better write no letters which can possibly be distorted into opposition, or quasi opposition to me. There are men on the constant watch for such things out of which to prejudice my peculiar friends against you. While I have no more suspicion of you than I have of my best friend living, I am kept in a constant struggle against suggestions of this sort."

It would require more effort to defuse the increasingly bitter feud between Norman Judd and John Wentworth. In public forums, Wentworth would drag out past wrongs, continuing to accuse Judd and his former Democratic allies of conspiring to defeat Lincoln in 1855, of "bungling" Lincoln's campaign in 1858, and of working now "to advance Trumbull as a presidential candidate, at Lincoln's expense."

Lincoln hastened to reassure Judd, who hoped to run for governor, that the "vague charge that you played me false last year, I believe to be false and outrageous." In 1855, "you did vote for Trumbull against me; and, although I think, and have said a thousand times, that was no injustice to me, I cannot change the fact, nor compel people to cease speaking of it. Ever since that matter occurred, I have constantly labored, as I believe you know, to have all recollection of it dropped." Finally, "as to the charge of your intriguing for Trumbull against me, I believe as little of that as any other charge." If such charges were made, Lincoln promised, they would not "go uncontradicted."

The controversy erupted into public view when Judd brought a libel suit against Wentworth, who tried to retain Lincoln as his counsel, claiming that the "very reason that you may assign for declining my offer is the very one that urges me to write you. You are friendly to us both. I prefer to put myself in the hands of mutual friends rather than . . . in the hands of those who have a deep interest in keeping up a quarrel." Of course, Lincoln had no intention of entangling himself in such explosive litigation, but he did help to mediate the altercation. The dispute was resolved without a court fight. Consequently, both Wentworth and Judd remained close to Lincoln and would support his efforts to control the Illinois delegation.

"I am not in a position where it would hurt much for me to not be nominated on the national ticket; but I am where it would hurt some for me to not get the Illinois delegation," Lincoln wrote Judd, knowing that the former Democrat had influence with the Chicago *Press and Tribune*, which covered the northern part of the state. "Can you not help me a little in this matter, in your end of the vineyard?" A week later, the *Tribune* published a resounding editorial on behalf of Lincoln's candidacy. "You saw what the Tribune said about you," Judd said to Lincoln. "Was it satisfactory?"

On May 10, 1860, the Illinois state Republicans assembled in Decatur. Buoyed by the noisy enthusiasm his candidacy elicited at the state convention, Lincoln nonetheless recognized that some of the delegates chosen to go to the national convention, though liking him, probably favored Seward or Bates. To head off possible desertions, Lincoln's friends introduced a resolution on the second day of the meeting: "That Abraham Lincoln is the choice of the Republican party of Illinois for the Presidency, and the delegates from this State are instructed to use all honorable means to secure his nomination by the Chicago Convention, and to vote as a unit for him."

With the Republican National Convention set to begin the following week, Lincoln could rest easy in the knowledge that he had used his time well. Though he often claimed to be a fatalist, declaring that "what is to be will be, and no prayers of ours can reverse the decree," his diligence and shrewd strategy in the months prior to the convention belied his claim. More than all his opponents combined, the country lawyer and local politician had toiled skillfully to increase his chances to become the Republican nominee for president.

CHAPTER 8

SHOWDOWN IN CHICAGO

FORTY THOUSAND VISITORS descended upon Chicago in the middle of May 1860, drawn by the festive excitement surrounding the Republican National Convention. Dozens of trains, mechanical marvels of the age, carried the delegates and supporters of America's youngest political party to America's fastest-growing city. All along the routes, as trains roared past the Niagara, up across the majestic Ohio River, and troubled the air of the western frontier, crowds gathered at every bunting-draped station, sounding their enthusiasm for the Republican cause with brass bands and volleys of cannon fire. Even at crossroads, reporters observed, "small groups were assembled to lend their countenances to the occasion, and from farm houses the ladies waved their kerchiefs, and farmers in the fields swung their hats."

Of all the trains bound for Chicago, none attracted more attention than the one that began its journey at the Suspension Bridge in Buffalo, New York, and swept to Chicago in an astonishing record time of sixteen hours. The unprecedented speed of the massive train was said to amaze every passenger. A reporter recalled that "when 'a mile a minute' was accomplished, the 'boldest held his breath,' and the timid ones trembled in their boots." Every seat was occupied: in addition to delegates, the train carried dozens of newspapermen, professional applauders, henchmen, office seekers, and prizefighters hired "to keep the peace," recalled one young passenger, "for in those hot days men's opinions often cost them broken heads." Amenities included a carload of "such refreshments," one reporter noted, "as lead inevitably to the conclusion that the majority of delegates are among the opponents" of temperance laws.

With boosterish pride, young Chicago was determined to show its best face to the world during the convention. Chicago's growth in previous decades had been "almost ridiculous," a contemporary magazine suggested. Indeed, "growth is much too slow a word," an English visitor marveled to describe the explosion Chicago had experienced since an 1830 guidebook depicted "a military post and fur station," with wolves prowling the streets at night, and a meager population of twelve families who would bunk together in the town's well-defended fort for safety each winter. Thirty years later, Chicago boasted a population of more than a hundred thousand, and the distinction of being "the first grain market in the world," surpassing not only Odessa, "the great grain market of Russia, but all of Europe." It had supplanted St. Louis as the chief marketplace for the vast herds of cattle that grazed the northwest prairies, and had become "the first lumber-market in the world." Newcomers to the bustling city were dazzled by its "miles of wharves crowded with shipping . . . long lines of stately warehouses," and "crowds of men busy in the active pursuit of trade." Only recently, its streets had been raised from the mud and water by a bold decision to elevate every building and roadway to a level of twelve feet above Lake Michigan.

"Our city has been chosen, here to throw to the winds the broad banner of Republicanism," the *Press and Tribune* proclaimed, "and here to name the leader who shall lead all our hosts to victory." Lavish preparations were made to give the arriving trains a reception to remember. Chicagoans who lived on Michigan Avenue were asked to illuminate their houses. "A most magically beautiful effect was the result," one reporter noted, "the lights flashing back from and multiplied countlessly in the waters of the Lake shore basin." Thousands of spectators lined the shore of the lake, and as the trains moved along the pier, "half minute guns were fired by the Chicago Light Artillery, and rockets shot off from the foot of Jackson Street." No one present, the reporter observed, would forget the effect of "artillery pealing, the flight of the rockets, the gleaming windows from the entire residence front of our city, the vast depot edifice filled with the eager crowd."

Hotels and boardinghouse proprietors had spent weeks sprucing up their establishments; private citizens were asked to open their homes; and restaurants promised hearty meals at low prices. The most popular luncheon in town included a glass of four-year-old ale and a ham sandwich for ten cents. As packed trains continued to steam into the thronged city, the number of eager Republican visitors on Chicago's streets climbed to forty thousand.

"I thought the city was crowded yesterday," one amazed reporter exclaimed on the day before the convention was set to open, "but it was as loose and comfortable as a last year's shoe beside the wedging and packing of today. The streets are full, and appear very like conduits leading off the overflowings of the hotels, where huge crowds are constantly pouring out as if they were spouted up from below in some popular eruption."

Even billiard rooms were enlisted to accommodate the staggering crowds. At a certain hour each evening, the games were brought to an abrupt halt as mattresses were laid across the tables to create beds for the sleepy visitors. Looking in on one such establishment at midnight, a reporter saw 130 people stretched out on billiard tables "with a zest, from the fatigues of the day, that would have excited the sympathy of the most unfeeling bosom."

"The city is thronged with Republicans," wrote the *Chicago Evening Journal*. "Republicans from the woods of Maine and the green valleys of all New England; Republicans from the Golden Gate and the old plantation, Republicans from everywhere. What seems a brilliant festival is but the rallying for a battle. It is an army with banners!" Amid "this murmur of the multitude, thought reverts to a time long past," the *Journal* reminded readers, "when a single car and one small chamber could have conveyed them all," when the antislavery principle that "now blossoms white over the land was deemed the vision of enthusiasts, ridiculed, shunned and condemned."

By 1860, the Republican Party had clearly become the dominant force in Northern politics. Its growth and momentum had absorbed two parties, the Whigs and the Know Nothings, and ruptured a third—the Democratic Party. If this new party could carry three of the four conservative Northern states it had lost in 1856—Illinois, Indiana, Pennsylvania, and New Jersey—it could win the presidency. These battleground states lay along the southern tier of the North; they all bordered on slave states; they would play a decisive role in choosing a nominee.

• • •

In the early hours of Wednesday, May 16, the streets surrounding the newly built convention hall swarmed with excited citizens "who crowded around the doors and windows, congregated upon the bridge, sat on the curb stones, and, in fine, used every available inch of standing room." When the big doors of the Wigwam—"so called," it was said, "because the chiefs of the Republican party were to meet there"—were finally opened to the assembled multitude, thousands of ticket holders raced forward to fill the center seats and the more exclusive side galleries, where gentlemen were allowed only if accompanied by a lady. Desperate men had scoured the streets for women—schoolgirls, washerwomen, painted ladies—anyone wearing a skirt and willing to be their date for the afternoon. Within minutes, every seat and nook of the Wigwam was occupied as ten thousand party members waited expectantly for the proceedings to begin.

Exactly at noon, New York's governor Edwin Morgan, chairman of the Republican National Committee, lowered his gavel, and the convention officially began. In his opening address, Morgan told the cheering crowd that "no body of men of equal number was ever clothed with greater responsibility than those now within the hearing of my voice. . . . Let me then invoke you to act in a spirit of harmony, that by the dignity, the wisdom and the patriotism displayed here you may be enabled to enlist the hearts of the people, and to strengthen them in [their] faith."

The work of the convention began. In the course of the first two days, credential battles were settled, and an inclusive platform, keyed to Northern interests, was enthusiastically adopted. While opposition to the extension of slavery remained as central as it had been in 1856, the 1860 platform also called for a Homestead Act, a protective tariff, a railroad to the Pacific, protection for naturalized citizens, and government support for harbor and river improvements—a far broader range of issues designed to attract a larger base.

After much debate, the delegates rejected a provision requiring a two-thirds vote to secure the nomination. Their decision that a simple majority was sufficient to nominate appeared to be a victory for Seward. Coming into Chicago as the best known of all the contenders, he already had nearly a majority of pledges. "The great body of ardent Republicans all over the country," James Pike observed, "desired to elevate to the Presidency the man who had begun so early and had labored so long in behalf of their cardinal doctrines." Indeed, when business came to a close at the end of the second day, a move was made to proceed directly to the presidential balloting. Had votes been cast at that moment, many believe, Seward would have emerged the victor. Instead, the secretary of the convention informed the delegates that the papers necessary for keeping the tally had not yet been prepared, and they adjourned until ten o'clock the next morning.

For those concerned that Seward was too radical on slavery and too liberal on immigration to win battleground states—Indiana, Illinois, New Jersey, and Pennsylvania—the central question was whether the opposition could be unified behind one man. A Committee of Twelve was formed by the prominent representatives of the four critical states to see if a consensus could be reached. By 10 p.m., twelve hours before the balloting was set to begin, no one had been agreed upon. "The time had been consumed in talking," a member of the opposition committee lamented, as each delegation argued stubbornly for its favorite son.

Shortly before midnight, Horace Greeley visited the committee to see if any agreement had been reached. Having surprised Weed by gaining entrance to the convention by representing Oregon as a proxy, Greeley planned to promote Bates and defeat Seward. Disappointed to learn that no agreement had been reached, Greeley sent a telegraph to the *Tribune*, concluding that since the opposition "cannot concentrate on any candidate," Seward "will be nominated." Murat Halstead of the *Cincinnati Commercial* telegraphed the same message to his paper at the same time, reporting that "every one of the forty thousand men in attendance upon the Chicago Convention will testify that at midnight of Thursday–Friday night, the universal impression was that Seward's success was certain." In the rooms shared by the New York delegation, great cheers were heard. "Three hundred bottles of champagne are said to have been cracked," reported Halstead; "it flowed freely as water."

Still, the night was young, the battle only just begun.

• • •

As THE HOURS PASSED, Weed must have sensed growing opposition among politicians in the conservative battleground states, many of whom feared that supporting Seward's candidacy would hurt their own chances in state elections. However, he never altered his original strategy: before each delegation, he simply asserted that in this perilous time, Seward was, without question, the best man for the job. His love and devotion to his friend of more than thirty years blinded him to the inner dynamics at work since the convention began, the serious doubts that were surfacing about Seward's availability, which meant, bluntly, his ability to win.

"Four years ago we went to Philadelphia to name our candidate," Weed told one delegation after another, "and we made one of the most inexcusable blunders. . . . We nominated a man who had no qualification for the position of Chief Magistrate. . . . We were defeated as we probably deserved to be. . . . We are facing a crisis; there are troublous times ahead of us. . . . What this country will demand as its chief executive for the next four years is a man of the highest order of executive ability, a man of real statesmanlike qualities, well known to the Country, and of large experience in national affairs. No other class of men ought to be considered at this time. We think we have in Mr. Seward just the qualities the Country will need. . . . We expect to nominate him . . . and to go before the Country full of courage and confidence."

No sooner did Weed leave each chamber than Horace Greeley came in and addressed the delegates: "I suppose they are telling you that Seward is the be all and the end all of our existence as a party, our great statesman, our profound philosopher, our pillar of cloud by day, our pillar of fire by night, but I want to tell you boys that in spite of all this you couldn't elect Seward if you could nominate him. You must remember as things stand today we are a sectional party. We have no strength outside the North, practically we must have the entire North with us if we hope to win. . . .

He cannot carry New Jersey, Pennsylvania, Indiana, or Iowa, and I will bring to you representative men from each of these states who will confirm what I say." Greeley proceeded to do just that, one delegate recalled, introducing Governor Samuel Kirkwood of Iowa, and gubernatorial candidates Andrew Curtin of Pennsylvania and Henry Lane of Indiana, "each of whom confirmed what Greeley had said."

"I know my people well," Pennsylvania's Henry Lane argued. "In the south half of my State a good proportion of my people have come from Slave States. . . . They will not tolerate slavery in Indiana or in our free territories but they will not oppose it where it is. . . . They are afraid Seward would be influenced by that abolition element of the East and make war on slavery where it is."

Greeley's spearheading of the anti-Seward forces was all the more credible because few were aware of his estrangement from Seward. Delegates accepted his arguments as those of a friend who simply feared Seward would not bring their party the presidency. "While professing so high a regard for Mr. Seward," one reporter later recognized, "there was rankling in the bosom of Greeley a hatred of the great statesman as bitter as that ever entertained by the most implacable of his political enemies. The feeling had been pent up for years, gathering strength and fury for an occasion when a final explosion could be had with effect. The occasion was afforded at Chicago. The match was lit—the combustible material was ignited, the explosion came. . . . Horace Greeley had his revenge."

Nor was Seward the only target of the late-night gatherings. Gustave Koerner, the leader of the German-Americans—an important component of the Republican constituency in the West—had never forgiven Bates for supporting Fillmore's Know Nothing Party in 1856. In his memoirs, Koerner described rushing into a crowded meeting of delegates from Pennsylvania and Indiana. Frank Blair was just finishing an eloquent speech for Bates when Koerner took the floor. "In all candor," he said, "if Bates [is] nominated," even if he were to win his home state of Missouri, which was doubtful, "the German Republicans in the other States would never vote for him; I for one would not, and I would advise my countrymen to the same effect."

Bates was further handicapped by the fact that he never really represented the middle of the party, however much the Blairs and Greeley tried to position him there. He was much too conservative for liberal Republicans, who might welcome him into their party but would never accord him chief command of an army in which he had never officially enlisted. At the same time, the letter he had written to prove his credentials to the Republicans had diminished the previous enthusiasm of conservatives and former Know Nothings.

Nor was all going well for Salmon Chase. Besides Seward, Chase was the most renowned Republican aspirant. Though more zealously committed to the black man than Seward, Chase was not hampered by Seward's radical reputation; his words had not become emblazoned on the banner of the antislavery movement. In contrast to Seward's reputation as a liberal spender, which hurt in battleground states, he was an economic conservative. And, unlike Seward, he had never openly attacked the Know Nothings.

Moreover, as the third largest delegation at the convention, Ohio wielded substantial power. "If united," observed Halstead, "it would have a formidable influence and might throw the casting votes between candidates, holding the balance of power between the East and the West." But Ohio would not unite behind Chase, as some delegates held out for Ben Wade or Judge McLean. The many enemies Chase had made and failed to conciliate over the years came back to haunt him at this critical juncture. Any hope of persuading McLean to turn over his votes had been lost long before as a consequence of his manipulations to gain his Senate seat. Chase, McLean remarked, "is selfish, beyond any other man. And I know from the bargain he has made in being elected to the Senate, he is ready to make any bargain to promote his interest."

"There was no unity of action, no determination of purpose," one Chase supporter later lamented; there was "a weakness in the spinal column in the Ohio delegation at Chicago, most pitiable to behold." Ohio's inability to settle firmly on Chase, another delegate told him, proved catastrophic. "If the Ohio delegation had been true . . . you would have been nominated. . . . I mingled freely with many of the delegations—they stood ready as a second choice . . . to give you their votes—would have done so if Ohio had . . . [been] relied upon."

Nor had Chase learned from his mistakes four years earlier. Once again, he failed to appoint a set of trusted managers who could guide his campaign, answer objections, cajole wavering delegates, and, at the right moment, make promises to buoy supporters and strengthen wills. "There are lots of good feeling afloat here for you," one of Chase's friends told him, "but there is no set of men in earnest for you . . . I think the hardest kind of death to die is that occasioned by indecisive, or lukewarm friends."

• • •

MEANWHILE, THROUGHOUT this night of a thousand knives, the opposition to Seward grew more vociferous, even frantic. "Men gather in little groups," observed Halstead, "and with their arms about each other, and chatter and whisper as if the fate of the country depended upon their immediate delivery of the mighty political secrets with which their imaginations are big." Rumors multiplied with each passing hour; "things of incalculable moment are communicated to you confidentially, at intervals of five minutes."

The rumor was deliberately circulated "that the Republican candidates for governor in Indiana, Illinois and Pennsylvania would resign if Seward were nominated." No one challenged Seward's ability; no one questioned his credentials as statesman of the party. He was opposed simply because it was thought he would damage the prospects of the Republican Party and hurt Republican candidates in local elections. Still, Halstead admiringly observed: "Amid all these cries of distress, the Sewardites are true as steel to their champion, and they will cling to 'Old Irrepressible,' as they call him, until the last gun is fired and the big bell rings."

All along, the main question among the gathering ranks of the "stop Seward" movement had been whether the opposition would be able to concentrate its strength on a single alternative, or be crippled by its own divisions.

For this eventuality, Lincoln had long prepared. Though he understood he could not positively count on the unanimous support of any delegation beyond Illinois, he knew he had earned widespread respect and admiration throughout the North. "You know how it is in Ohio," he wrote a friend from the Buckeye State two weeks before the convention. "I am certainly not the first choice there; and yet I have not heard that any one makes any positive objection to me. It is just so everywhere so far as I can perceive. Everywhere, except in Illinois, and possibly Indiana, one or another is prefered to me, but there is no positive objection."

To reach his goal of becoming everyone's second choice, Lincoln was careful not to disparage any other candidate. Nor was it in his nature to do so. His committed team of workers—including Judge David Davis, Leonard Swett, Norman Judd, and Stephen Logan—understood this, resolving from the start "to antagonize no one." They did not need to, for Greeley and candidates for governor in the doubtful states had that task well in hand. Nor, as Kenneth Stampp writes, did they need to win support based upon Lincoln's "relative ability compared with other candidates. . . . Their appeal was based on availability and expediency; they urged the delegates to nominate the man who could win."

"No men ever worked as our boys did," Swett later claimed. "I did not, the whole week I was there, sleep two hours a night." Although some of Lincoln's men had political ambitions of their own, Henry Whitney observed, "Most of them worked *con amore*, chiefly from love of the man, his lofty moral tone, his pure political morality." Working in his "typically methodical way," Davis designated specific tasks to each member of his team. Maine's Leonard Swett was charged with making inroads in the Maine delegation. Samuel Parks, a native Vermonter, was dispatched to the delegation of the Green Mountain State. In the spring elections in New England, the Republicans had suffered setbacks, leading Lincoln to observe that the election result would be seen as "a drawback upon the prospects of Gov. Seward," opening the door for one of his rivals. Stephen Logan and Richard Yates were given Kentucky, while Ward Lamon was assigned his home state of Virginia. In each of these states, the Lincoln men worked to pick off individual delegates to keep Seward from sweeping the field on the first ballot.

"It all worked to a charm," boasted Swett. "The first State approached was Indiana." Even before the convention had opened, Lincoln got word that "the whole of Indiana might not be difficult to get" and had urged Davis to concentrate on the Hoosier State. Though Indiana contained twenty thousand or more former Know Nothings who likely preferred Bates, the Indiana politicians were fearful that Bates was not strong enough to challenge Seward for the nomination. And if Seward headed the ticket, gubernational candidate Henry Lane never tired of warning, the radical image he projected and his unpopularity with the Know Nothings would jeopardize the entire state ticket.

Claims have been made that Davis made a deal with Indiana's chairman, Caleb Smith, to bring him into the cabinet in return for Indiana's vote. No deal was needed, however; Smith had admired Lincoln since their days in Congress and had agreed, even before the balloting, to second Lincoln's nomination. The Indiana delegates' decision to back Lincoln on the first ballot was more likely a practical decision based on the best interests of their own state.

By securing Indiana's pledge, the Lincoln men gained a decided advantage in the Committee of Twelve, which had remained deadlocked at midnight in its attempts to agree on a common candidate to oppose Seward—prompting Greeley and Halstead to predict a Seward victory. As the committee members continued to talk in the early-morning hours, someone proposed a straw vote to determine the opposition candidate with the greatest strength. In this impromptu poll, since Lincoln already had the support of both Illinois and Indiana, two of the four key states, he emerged as the strongest candidate. According to one committee member, "Mr. Dudley of New Jersey then proposed that for the general good of the party," Pennsylvania should give up its favorite son after the first ballot, as would New Jersey. The proposition was generally agreed upon, but Pennsylvania required further negotiations to ratify the agreement.

According to Henry Whitney, Davis had previously sent a telegram to Lincoln informing him that if Cameron were promised a space in the cabinet, Pennsylvania might be procured. Lincoln scribbled his answer in the margin of a newspaper, which an emissary carried to the convention. "*Make no contracts that will bind me.*" When the message arrived, Whitney writes, "Everybody was mad, of course. Here were men working night and day to place him on the highest mountain peak of fame, and he pulling back all he knew how. What was to be done? The bluff Dubois said: 'Damn Lincoln!' The polished Swett said, in mellifluous accents: 'I am very sure if Lincoln was aware of the necessities . . .' The critical Logan expectorated viciously, and said: 'The main difficulty with Lincoln is . . .' Herndon ventured: 'Now, friend, I'll answer that.' But Davis cut the Gordian knot by brushing all aside with: 'Lincoln ain't here, and don't know what we have to meet, so we will go ahead, as if we hadn't heard from him, and he must ratify it.' "

Moreover, Davis undoubtedly understood that other candidates were making pledges of their own. The Blairs had supposedly promised Cassius Clay the post of secretary of war if he would endorse Bates. And doubtless Weed could promise not only cabinet posts but the "oceans of money" he had accumulated for the Republican cause. Nonetheless, Davis's biographer concludes that no direct pledge was ever made to Cameron. Davis promised only that he would "get every member of the Illinois delegation to recommend Cameron's appointment," which the Cameron men mistook for a guaranteed pledge.

Whether or not explicit deals were made, the Lincoln men worked hard to convince Cameron's contingent that Pennsylvania would be treated generously if Lincoln received their votes. "My assurance to them," Swett later wrote Lincoln, was that despite the fact that Pennsylvania had not supported Lincoln from the start, "they should be placed upon the same footing as if originally they had been your friends. Now, of course, it is unpleasant for me to write all this *stuff* and for you to read it. Of course I have never feared you would unintentionally do anything unfair towards these men. I only write to suggest the very delicate situation I am placed towards them so that you might cultivate them as much as possible."

By adding the votes of Indiana, Pennsylvania, and New Jersey, three of the four doubtful states, to those of Illinois, Davis and Swett had achieved what many considered impossible: they had made possible the nomination of Abraham Lincoln.

• • •

As THE DAY of the balloting dawned, the Seward men, confident of victory, gathered at the Richmond House for a celebratory march to the convention hall. "A thousand strong," Murat Halstead observed, and accompanied by a "magnificent band, which was brilliantly uniformed—epaulets shining on their shoulders," they prolonged "their march a little too far." Upon reaching the Wigwam, they were dismayed to find that some of their number could not get in—Lincoln's partisans had manufactured duplicate tickets the evening before and had filed into the hall as soon as the doors opened.

Recognizing that "it was part of the Seward plan to carry the Convention" by bringing more supporters to Chicago than any other candidate, Lincoln's managers had mustered friends and supporters from all over the state. The nominations became the initial test of strength. New York's William Evarts was the first to rise, asking the convention to place Seward's name in nomination. His words were met "by a deafening shout." The applause was "loud and long," as supporters continued to stand, waving handkerchiefs in frenzied excitement. Lincoln's man, Leonard Swett, confessed that the level of enthusiasm "appalled us a little."

Nonetheless, Lincoln's contingent was ready when Norman Judd placed the name of Illinois's favorite son in nomination. "If Mr. Seward's name drew forth thunders of applause," one reporter noted, "what can be said of the enthusiastic reception of [Lincoln's] name. . . . The audience, like a wild colt with [a] bit between his teeth, rose above all cry of order, and again and again the irrepressible applause broke forth and resounded far and wide." To Seward's supporters, this "tremendous applause" was "the first distinct impression in Lincoln's favor." Though Chase and Bates were also nominated to loud applause, the responses were "cold when compared" to the receptions for Seward and Lincoln.

When the seconding nominations proceeded, the "trial of lungs" intensified. Determined to win the battle, Seward's adherents rallied when Austin Blair of Michigan rose to second his nomination. "The shouting was absolutely frantic," Halstead reported. "No Comanches, no panthers ever struck a higher note, or gave screams with more infernal intensity." Once again, the Lincoln men rose to the challenge. When Indiana's Caleb Smith seconded Lincoln's nomination, "five thousand people at once" jumped to their feet, Leonard Swett reported. "A thousand steam whistles, ten acres of hotel gongs . . . might have mingled in the scene unnoticed." A voice rose from the crowd: "Abe Lincoln has it by the sound, let us ballot!" The efforts of Lincoln's men to corral more supporters had paid off.

"This was not the most deliberate way of nominating a President," Swett later confessed, but "it had its weight."

The convention finally settled down and the balloting began. Two hundred thirty-three votes would decide the Republican presidential nomination. The roll call opened with the New England states, which had been considered solidly for Seward. In fact, a surprising number of votes went for Lincoln, as well as a scattering for Chase. Lincoln's journey through New England after the Cooper Union speech had apparently won over a number of delegates. As expected, New York gave its full 70 votes to Seward, allowing him to leap far ahead. The Seward men relaxed until Virginia, which had also been considered solid for Seward, split its 22 votes between Seward and Lincoln. Chase had assumed that Ohio, which came next, would give him its full 46 votes, but the delegation was divided in its vote, giving 34 to Chase and the remaining 12 to Lincoln and McLean. Perhaps the greatest surprise was Indiana, which Bates had assumed was his territory; instead, Lincoln gathered all 26 votes. "This solid vote was a startler," reported Halstead, "and the keen little eyes of Henry S. Lane glittered as it was given."

At the end of the first ballot, the tally stood: Seward 173½; Lincoln 102; Chase 49; Bates 48. The Bates managers were downhearted to realize, as the historian Marvin Cain writes, that "no pivotal state had gone for Bates, and the sought-after votes of the Iowa, Kentucky, Minnesota and Ohio delegations had not been delivered." Disappointment was equally evident in the faces of the Chase men, for they were keenly aware that the division within the Ohio delegation was probably fatal. Lincoln's camp was exhilarated, for with his total of 102 votes, Lincoln had emerged as the clear-cut alternative to Seward. Although taken aback by the unexpected defections, Weed still hoped that Seward would win on the second ballot. The 48 votes Cameron had supposedly promised from Pennsylvania would put Seward within striking distance of the victory number of 233.

The second ballot revealed a crucial shift in Lincoln's favor. In New England he picked up 17 more votes, while Delaware switched its 6 votes from Bates to Lincoln. Then came the biggest surprise of all, "startling the vast auditorium like a clap of thunder": Pennsylvania announced 44 votes for Lincoln, boosting his total to 181, only 3½ votes behind Seward's new total of 184½. Chase and Bates both lost ground on the second ballot, essentially removing them from contention. The race had narrowed to Seward and Lincoln.

Tension in the Wigwam mounted. The spectators sat on the edge of their seats as the third ballot began. Lincoln gained 4 additional votes from Massachusetts and 4 from Pennsylvania, also adding 15 votes from Ohio.

His total reached 231½, only 1½ votes shy of victory. "There was a pause," Halstead recorded. "In about ten ticks of a watch," David K. Cartter of Ohio stood and announced the switch of 4 votes from Chase to Lincoln. "A profound stillness fell upon the Wigwam," one eyewitness wrote. Then the Lincoln supporters "rose to their feet applauding rapturously, the ladies waving their handkerchiefs, the men waving and throwing up their hats by thousands, cheering again and again."

For the Sewardites, the defeat was devastating. "Great men wept like boys," one New Yorker observed, "faces drawn, white and aged as if ten years had passed in that one night of struggle." Everyone looked to Thurlow Weed, but there was no solace he could give. The work of his lifetime had ended in defeat, and he, too, could not restrain his tears. His failure to serve his country by making his good friend president, Weed later acknowledged, was "the great disappointment of his life."

All across the chamber, representatives rose, clamoring to change their votes so that Lincoln could achieve a unanimous victory. Their emotional tone revealed that the defeated Seward still had a great hold on their hearts. When Michigan shifted its votes to Lincoln, Austin Blair confessed that his state was laying down "her first, best loved candidate . . . with some bleeding of the heart, with some quivering in the veins; but she does not fear that the fame of Seward will suffer," for his story will be "written, and read, and beloved long after the temporary excitement of this day has passed away, and when Presidents are themselves forgotten." In similar fashion, Carl Schurz of Wisconsin predicted that Seward's ambition would be fulfilled "with the success of the cause which was the dream of his youth," and that his name would "remain in history, an instance of the highest merit uncrowned with the highest honor."

The most poignant moment came when New York's chairman, William Evarts, stood up. "Mounting a table, with grief manifest in his countenance, his hands clenched nervously," he delivered a powerful tribute to Seward: "Gentlemen, it was from Governor Seward that most of us learned to love Republican principles and the Republican party." He finally requested that New York shift its votes to Lincoln. So moving was his speech, one reporter noted, that "the spectator could not fail to be impressed with the idea that a man who could have such a friend must be a noble man indeed."

Once the vote was made unanimous, the celebration began in earnest. A man stationed on the roof of the Wigwam shouted the news of Lincoln's nomination, along with that of Hannibal Hamlin of Maine for vice president, to the thousands waiting on the street. Cannons were fired and "between 20,000 and 30,000 outside were yelling and shouting at once." The festivities continued through the night. "The Press and Tribune building," one of the paper's reporters wrote, "was illuminated from 'turret to foundation,' by the brilliant glare of a thousand lights which blazed from windows and doors." Shouldering the symbolic fence rails that Lincoln had supposedly split, Republicans paraded through the streets to the music of a dozen bands.

• • •

SEWARD RECEIVED THE NEWS of his loss while sitting with friends in his country garden at Auburn. A rider on a swift horse had waited at the telegraph office to dash through the crowded streets the moment a telegram arrived. When the totals of the first ballot came in, the messenger had galloped to Seward's house and handed the telegram to him. When the news of Seward's large lead was repeated to guests at his house and to the crowds on the street, great cheers went up. When the totals of the second ballot came in, Seward retained his optimism. "I shall be nominated on the next ballot," he predicted to the boisterous audience on the lawn, and a great cheer resounded from the streets. Long, anxious moments followed. When no further news arrived, Seward "rightly [judged] that . . . there was no news that friends would love to bring." Finally, the unwelcome telegram announcing Lincoln's nomination on the third ballot arrived. Seward turned "as pale as ashes." He understood at once, as did his supporters, his son Fred would remember, "that it was no ordinary political defeat, to be retrieved in some subsequent campaign. It was . . . final and irrevocable."

"The sad tidings crept through the vast concourse," one reporter noted. "The flags were furled, the cannon was rolled away, and Cayuga county went home with a clouded brow." Later that night, writing in his diary in Washington, Charles Francis Adams could not stop thinking of his defeated friend, "of his sanguine expectations, of his long services, of his large and comprehensive philosophy, and of his great ambition—all now merged for a time in a deep abyss of disappointment. He has too much of alloy in his composition to rise above it. Few men can."

Yet "he took the blow as a champion should," his biographer notes, putting on "a brave front before his family and the world." In her diary, sixteen-year-old Fanny Seward noted simply that "Father told Mother and I in three words, Abraham Lincoln nominated. His friends feel much distress—he alone has a smile—he takes it with philosophical and unselfish coolness." Informed that the editor of the local evening paper could find no one in the disconsolate town willing to write and comment on the news announcing Lincoln and Hamlin's nominations, Seward took up his own pen. "No truer or firmer defenders of the Republican faith could have been found in the Union," he graciously stated, "than the distinguished and esteemed citizens on whom the honors of the nomination have fallen."

Before he retired that night, Seward wrote to Weed: "You have my unbounded gratitude for this last, as for the whole life of efforts in my behalf. I wish that I was sure that your sense of the disappointment is as light as my own." A week later, in a public letter, Seward pledged his support to the Republican ticket and said he hoped his friends who had "labored so long" by his side would not allow their "sense of disappointment . . . to hinder or delay . . . the progress of that cause."

Beneath his graceful facade, Seward was angry, hurt, and humiliated. "It was only some months later," the biographer Glyndon Van Deusen writes, "when the shock had worn off and hope of a sort had revived, that he could say half ruefully, half whimsically, how fortunate it was that he did not keep a diary, for if he had there would be a record of all his cursing and swearing" when the news arrived.

If Seward managed to project a willed equanimity, Chase could not hide his bitterness at his defeat, nor his fury at the Ohio delegation that had failed to support him unanimously. "When I remember what New York did for Seward, what Illinois did for Lincoln and what Missouri did for Bates," Chase told a friend, "and remember also that neither of these gentlemen ever spent a fourth part—if indeed a tithe of the time labor and means for the Republican Party in their respective states that I have spent for our party in Ohio; & then reflect on the action of the Ohio delegation in Chicago towards me; I confess I have little heart to write or think about it. . . . I must say that had [Senator Ben Wade] received the same expression from Ohio which was given to me, and had I been in his place, I would have suffered my arm to be wrenched from my body, before I would have allowed my name to be brought into competition with his."

For years, Chase was racked by the thought that had Ohio remained loyal, he would have won the nomination. Even in a congratulatory letter to Lincoln, he could not refrain from citing his own situation. Supposing that the "adhesion of the Illinois delegation" yielded Lincoln "a higher gratification" even than "the nomination itself," Chase confessed that the perfidy of his own delegation was unbearable. "In this . . . I am quite sure you must participate," he sounded Lincoln, "for I err greatly in my estimate of your magnanimity, if you do not condemn as I do the conduct of delegates, from whatever state, who disregard . . . the clearly expressed preference of their own State Convention." Lincoln responded graciously without taking the bait.

Carl Schurz contemplated Chase's torment in the dark hours following the nomination. "While the victory of Mr. Lincoln was being announced to the outside world," he wrote, "my thoughts involuntarily turned to Chase, who, I imagined, sat in a quiet office room at Columbus with a telegraph near by clicking the news from Chicago. . . . Not even his own State had given him its full strength. No doubt he had hoped, and hoped, and hoped against hope . . . and now came this disastrous, crushing, humiliating defeat. I saw that magnificent man before me, writhing with the agony of his disappointment, and I sympathized with him most profoundly."

As the news of Chase's defeat filtered into the streets of Columbus, the dray readied to haul the cannon to the corner of Third and State streets, to announce his victory with a roar of thunder, was used instead to honor Lincoln's nomination. After the short "melancholy ceremony" was concluded, the dray hauled the cannon back to its shed, and the city went to sleep.

Bates accepted defeat with the composure that had marked his character from the outset. "As for me, I was surprised, I own, but not at all mortified, at the result at Chicago," he wrote Greeley. "I had no claim—literally none—upon the Republicans as a party, and no right to expect their party honors; and I shall cherish, with enduring gratitude, the recollection of the generous confidence with which many of their very best men have honored me. So far from feeling beaten and depressed, I have cause rather for joy and exultation; for, by the good opinion of certain eminent Republicans, I have gained much in standing and reputation before the country—more, I think, than any mere private man I have ever known."

In his private journal, however, Bates admitted to a sense of irritation. "Some of my friends who attended the Convention assure me that the nomination of Mr. Lincoln took every body by surprise: That it was brought about by accident or trick, by which my pledged friends had to vote against me. . . . The thing was well planned and boldly executed. A few Germans—Schurz of Wisconsin and Koerner of Illinois, with their truculent boldness, scared the timid men of Indiana into submission. Koerner went before the Indiana Delegation and assured them that if Bates were nominated, the *Germans* would bolt!"

The platform, he continued, "is exclusive and defiant, not attracting but repelling assistance from without. . . . It lugs in the lofty generalities of the Declaration of Independence, for no practical object that I can see, but needlessly exposing the party to the specious charge of favoring negro equality. . . . I think they will soon be convinced, if they are not already, that they have committed a fatal blunder—They have denationalized their Party; weakened it in the free states, and destroyed its hopeful beginnings in the border slave states."

While the melancholy spirit of defeated expectations settled upon the streets of Auburn, Columbus, and St. Louis, Springfield was euphoric. The legendary moment when Lincoln learned of his nomination has spawned many versions over the years. Some claim Lincoln was standing in a shop, purchasing some items that Mary had requested, when cheers were heard from the telegraph office, followed by the shouts of a boy rushing through the crowd: "Mr. Lincoln, Mr. Lincoln, you are nominated." Others maintain that he was talking with friends in the office of the *Illinois State Journal* when he received the news. Handed the scrap of paper that reported his victory, he "looked at it long and silently, not heeding the noisy exultation of all around." Shaking hands with everyone in the room, he remarked quietly, "I knew this would come when I saw the second ballot." Leaving the *Journal* office, Lincoln plunged into a crowd of well-wishers on the street. "My friends," he said, "I am glad to receive your congratulations, and as there is a little woman down on Eighth street who will be glad to hear the news, you must excuse me until I inform her." When he reached his home, Ida Tarbell reports, he found that Mary "already knew that the honor which for twenty years and more she had believed and stoutly declared her husband deserved . . . at last had come."

The tumult in Springfield that evening was recorded by a young journalist, John Hay, who would later become Lincoln's aide. He reported that "the hearty western populace burst forth in the wildest manifestations of joy . . . Lincoln banners, decked in every style of rude splendor, fluttered in the high west wind." The church bells tolled. Thousands assembled in the rotunda of the Capitol for a festive celebration replete with victory speeches. When the meeting adjourned, the happy throngs converged on Lincoln's house. His appearance at the door was "the signal for immense cheering." Modestly, Lincoln insisted that "he did not suppose the honor of such a visit was intended particularly for himself as a private citizen but rather as the representative to a great party."

• • •

FOR GENERATIONS, people have weighed and debated the factors that led to Lincoln's surprising victory. Many have agreed with the verdict of Murat Halstead, who wrote that "the fact of the Convention was the defeat of Seward rather than the nomination of Lincoln." Seward himself seemed to accept this analysis. When asked years later why Lincoln had won, he said: "The leader of a political party in a country like ours is so exposed that his enemies become as numerous and formidable as his friends." Abraham Lincoln, by contrast, "comparatively unknown, had not to contend with the animosities generally marshaled against a leader."

There is truth to this argument, but it tells only part of the story, for the question remains: why was Lincoln the beneficiary of Seward's downfall rather than Chase or Bates?

Some have pointed to luck, to the fact that Lincoln lived in a battleground state the Republicans needed to win, and to the fact that the convention was held in Chicago, where the strength of local support could add weight to his candidacy. "Had the Convention been held at any other place," Koerner admitted, "Lincoln would not have been nominated."

Others have argued that he was positioned perfectly in the center of the party. He was less radical than Seward or Chase, but less conservative than Bates. He was less offensive than Seward to the Know Nothings, but more acceptable than Bates to the German-Americans.

Still others have argued that Lincoln's team in Chicago played the game better than anyone else, conceiving the best strategy and cleverly using the leverage of promises to the best advantage. Without doubt, the Lincoln men, under the skillful leadership of David Davis, performed brilliantly.

Chance, positioning, and managerial strategy—all played a role in Lincoln's victory. Still, if we consider the comparative resources each contender brought to the race—their range of political skills, their emotional, intellectual, and moral qualities, their rhetorical abilities, and their determination and willingness to work hard—it is clear that when opportunity beckoned, Lincoln was the best prepared to answer the call. His nomination, finally, was the result of his character and his life experiences—these separated him from his rivals and provided him with advantages unrecognized at the time.

Having risen to power with fewer privileges than any of his rivals, Lincoln was more accustomed to rely upon himself to shape events. From beginning to end, he took the greatest control of the process leading up to the nomination. While Seward, at Weed's suggestion, spent eight months wandering Europe and the Middle East to escape dissension at home, Lincoln earned the goodwill and respect of tens of thousands with a strenuous speaking tour that left a positive imprint on Republicans in five crucial Midwestern states. While Chase unwisely declined his invitation to speak at the lecture series in New York at Cooper Union, Lincoln accepted with alacrity, recognizing the critical importance of making a good impression in Seward's home territory. In addition, Chase refused invitations to travel to New England and shore up his support. Ironically, despite repeated pledges in his diary to do anything necessary to achieve honor and fame, Chase showed a lack of resolution in the final weeks before the convention.

When ardent Republicans heard Lincoln speak, they knew that if their beloved Seward could not win, they had in the eloquent orator from Illinois a man of considerable capacity whom they could trust, one who would hold fast on the central issue that had forged the party—the fight against extending slavery into the territories. Though Lincoln had entered the antislavery struggle later than Seward or Chase, his speeches possessed unmatched power, conviction, clarity, and moral strength.

At the same time, his native caution and precision with language—he rarely said more than he was sure about, rarely pandered to his various audiences—gave Lincoln great advantages over his rivals, each of whom tried to reposition himself in the months before the convention. Seward disappointed liberal Republicans when he tried to soften his fiery rhetoric to placate moderates. Bates infuriated conservatives with his strongly worded public letter. And Chase fooled no one when he tried to shift his position on the tariff at the last moment. Lincoln remained consistent throughout.

Nor, as the Chicago *Press and Tribune* pointed out, was "his avoidance of extremes" simply "the result of ambition which measures words or regulates acts." It was, more accurately, "the natural consequence of an equable nature and a mental constitution that is never off its balance."

In his years of travel on the circuit through central Illinois, engaging people in taverns, on street corners, and in shops, Lincoln had developed a keen sense of what people felt, thought, needed, and wanted. Seward, too, had an instinctive feeling for people, but too many years in Washington had dulled those instincts. Like Lincoln, Chase had spent many months traveling throughout his home state, but his haughty demeanor prevented him from truly connecting with the farmers, clerks, and bartenders he met along the way. Bates, meanwhile, had isolated himself for so long from the hurly-burly of the political world that his once natural political savvy was diminished.

It was Lincoln's political intuition, not blind luck, that secured the convention site in Chicago. To be sure, the fact that Lincoln was "comparatively unknown" aided Norman Judd in landing the venue in Illinois. However, it was part of Lincoln's strategy to hold his name back as long as possible and to "give no offence to others—leave them in a mood to come to us, if they shall be compelled to give up their first love." It was Lincoln who first suggested to Judd that it might be important to secure Chicago. And it was Lincoln who first pointed out to his managers that Indiana might be won. Indeed, his guidance and determination were evident at every step along the way to the nomination.

Lincoln, like Seward, had developed a cadre of lifelong friends who were willing to do anything in their power to ensure his nomination. But unlike Seward, he had not made enemies or aroused envy along the way. It is hard to imagine Lincoln letting Greeley's resentment smolder for years as Seward did. On the contrary, he took pains to reestablish rapport with Judd and Trumbull after they had defeated him in his first run for the Senate. His ability to rise above defeat and create friendships with previous opponents was never shared by Chase, who was unable to forgive those who crossed him. And though Bates had a warm circle of friends in St. Louis, most of them were not politicians. His campaign at the convention was managed by a group of men who barely knew him. Without burning personal loyalty, they had simply picked him as a potential winner, dropping him with equal ease when the path to his nomination proved bumpy.

Finally, Lincoln's profound and elevated sense of ambition—"an ambition," Fehrenbacher observes, "notably free of pettiness, malice, and overindulgence," shared little common ground with Chase's blatant obsession with office, Seward's tendency toward opportunism, or the ambivalent ambition that led Bates to withdraw from public office. Though Lincoln desired success as fiercely as any of his rivals, he did not allow his quest for office to consume the kindness and openheartedness with which he treated supporters and rivals alike, nor alter his steady commitment to the antislavery cause.

In the end, though the men who nominated Abraham Lincoln in Chicago may not have recognized all these qualities, they chose the best man for the supreme challenge looming over the nation.

CHAPTER 9

"A MAN KNOWS HIS OWN NAME"

THE NEWS THAT Lincoln had defeated Seward came as a shock to much of the country, especially to the Eastern Republican establishment. On Capitol Hill, word of Lincoln's nomination "was received with general incredulity," conceded Charles Francis Adams, "until by repeated announcements from different quarters it appeared that he had carried the day by a union of all the anti-Seward elements. . . . The House was in such a state of confusion that it was clear no business would be done, so we adjourned."

Since people were unaware of the skill with which he had crafted his victory, Lincoln was viewed as merely the accidental candidate of the consolidated anti-Seward forces. Still an obscure figure, he was referred to by half the journals representing his own party as "Abram" rather than "Abraham." Pointing out that when Lincoln had visited the Historical Library at Hartford the previous March, he signed the visitors' book as "Abraham Lincoln," the Democratic *New York Herald* caustically noted that "it is but fair to presume that a man knows his own name." Lincoln wrote to George Ashmun, the Republican chairman of the acceptance committee: "It seems as if the question whether my first name is 'Abraham' or 'Abram' will never be settled. It is *'Abraham.'* "

Exulting in Lincoln's lack of national experience, Democratic newspapers had a field day ridiculing his biography. He is "a third rate Western lawyer," the *Herald* gloated. "The conduct of the republican party in this nomination is a remarkable indication of a small intellect, growing smaller." Rejecting Seward and Chase, "who are statesmen and able men," the *Herald* continued, "they take up a fourth rate lecturer, who cannot speak good grammar," and whose speeches are "illiterate compositions . . . interlarded with coarse and clumsy jokes." Not content to deride his intellect, hostile publications focused on his appearance. "Lincoln is the leanest, lankest, most ungainly mass of legs, arms and hatchet-face ever strung upon a single frame. He has most unwarrantably abused the privilege which all politicians have of being ugly."

More violent attacks appeared in the *Charleston Mercury*, which scornfully asked: "After him what decent white man would be President?" Seward, the paper insisted, had been "thrust aside" because he "lacked the necessary nerve to carry through measures of Southern subjugation." Lincoln, on the other hand, was "the *beau ideal* of a relentless, dogged, freesoil border-ruffian." He was "an illiterate partizan," claimed the influential *Richmond Enquirer*, "possessed only of his inveterate hatred of slavery and his openly avowed predilections for negro equality."

The venom of such attacks reflected the growing discord and apprehension among Southern Democrats. As Lincoln prepared for the election campaign, his prospects of victory had been enhanced considerably by the splintering of the Democratic Party, which was now the only party with supporters in both the North and South. Meeting in Charleston, South Carolina, before Lincoln's nomination, the Democratic National Convention had ended in chaos. A majority of delegates, comprised of Stephen Douglas's supporters, had presented a platform designed to paper over the slavery issue. Unfortunately for Douglas, the time when the slavery issue could be veiled had passed. Recent events, including the *Dred Scott* decision and the raid on Harpers Ferry by John Brown had hardened the position of many Southern leaders. The moderate positions acceptable in the past were rejected by radical Southern politicians who now condemned all compromise, demanding complete freedom to bring slaves into all the territories and explicit congressional protection for those slaves. They dismissed the doctrine of "popular sovereignty," once widely acceptable, as an abandonment of Southern principle.

When the convention approved the moderate Douglas platform, the representatives from Alabama walked out, followed first by Mississippi and then the other Southern states. As the Mississippi delegation rose to walk out, one incensed delegate climbed on a chair for a rousing farewell speech, predicting that "in less than sixty days there would be a United South." With this, observer Murat Halstead recorded, "the South Carolinians cheered loud and long," the applause mounting as each state bolted. That night, "there was a Fourth of July feeling in Charleston. . . . There was no mistaking the public sentiment of the city. It was overwhelmingly and enthusiastically in favor of the seceders."

Unable to secure a two-thirds vote for any nominee, the deadlocked Charleston convention was forced to reconvene in Baltimore after Lincoln had been nominated by the Republicans. There Douglas would finally receive the nomination he had long pursued. It was too late, however, to reassemble the pieces of the last national party. The positions of the Northern and Southern Democrats were now irreconcilable, shattered by the same forces that had destroyed the Whigs and the Know Nothings.

With Douglas the Democratic nominee, Southern seceders reconvened to nominate John C. Breckinridge of Kentucky, a staunch believer that slavery could not constitutionally be excluded from the territories. North Carolina–born senator Joseph Lane was chosen as the vice presidential nominee. To complicate matters further, the new Constitutional Union Party, composed of old-line Whigs and remnant Know Nothings, held its own convention, nominating John Bell of Tennessee and Edward Everett of Massachusetts on a platform rooted in the illusory hope that the dissolution of the Union could be avoided by ignoring the slavery question altogether.

"The great democratic organization has finally burst into pieces," Charles Francis Adams rejoiced in a diary entry of June 23, "and the two sections have respectively nominated candidates of their own." Two weeks later, Lincoln informed a friend that he figured "the chances were more than equal, that we could have beaten the Democracy *united.* Divided, as it is, it's chance appears very slim." Nonetheless, he cautioned, "great is Democracy in resources; and it may yet give it's fortunes a turn."

While the Democrats were splintering, a committee came to Springfield to notify Lincoln formally of his nomination. "Mr. Lincoln received us in the parlor of his modest frame house," wrote Carl Schurz, Seward's avid supporter and a leading spokesman for the German-Americans. In the "rather bare-looking room," Lincoln "stood, tall and ungainly in his black suit of apparently new but ill-fitting clothes, his long tawny neck emerging gauntly from his turn-down collar, his melancholy eyes sunken deep in his haggard face." Ashmun spoke for the committee, and Lincoln "responded with a few appropriate, earnest, and well-shaped sentences." Afterward, everyone relaxed into a more general conversation, "partly of a jovial kind, in which the hearty simplicity of Lincoln's nature shone out." As the committee members left, Mr. Kelley of Pennsylvania remarked to Schurz: "Well, we might have done a more brilliant thing, but we could hardly have done a better thing." Still, Schurz acknowledged, other members of the committee "could not quite conceal their misgivings as to how this single-minded man, this child of nature, would bear himself in the contact with the great world."

Another visitor, Thurlow Weed, detected an unexpected sophistication and political acumen in Lincoln. Still nursing wounds from Seward's defeat, Weed traveled to Springfield at the invitation of Swett and Davis shortly after the convention. The two master politicians analyzed "the prospects of success, assuming that all or nearly all the slave States would be against [them]," determining which states "were safe without effort . . . which required attention," and which "were sure to be vigorously contested." Lincoln exhibited, Weed later wrote, "so much good sense, such intuitive knowledge of human nature, and such familiarity with the virtues and infirmities of politicians, that I became impressed very favorably with his fitness for the duties which he was not unlikely to be called upon to discharge." Weed departed, ready to "go to work with a will."

As Weed and Lincoln plotted election strategy, it must have been apparent to both men that there would, in actuality, be two elections. In the free states, the contest would pit Lincoln against Douglas, while the Southern Democrat, Breckinridge, would battle border-state Bell for the slave states. Douglas, once the defender of Southern principles, the author of the infamous Kansas-Nebraska Act, was, by 1860, reviled throughout the South as a traitor or closet abolitionist. "Now what difference is it to the people whether Lincoln or Douglas shall be elected?" one Southern newspaper asked. "The same ends are sought by each, and we do not see any reason to choose between them."

A Lincoln victory would require at least 152 electoral votes. Anything short of a majority would throw the election into the turbulent chamber of the House of Representatives, which might well prove unable to elect anyone. The choice of vice president would be left to the Southern-dominated Senate, which might well elect Joseph Lane, Breckinridge's running mate, to occupy the vacant presidential chair. Lincoln, therefore, would have to capture virtually the entire North, including those states that had voted for the Democrat Buchanan in the last election.

In three of these "must win" states—Indiana, Pennsylvania, and Ohio—Douglas had considerable strength, especially in their southern counties, populated largely by settlers from the South. Although slavery was an issue everywhere, it was not always the dominant concern. Pennsylvanians were more interested in tariff protection, while voters in Indiana, Ohio, and elsewhere in the Northwest wanted free land for settlers and internal improvements to expand commerce there. In addition, remnants of the anti-immigrant American Party lingered everywhere. The antislavery vote would undoubtedly go Republican, but that alone could not build a majority among such diverse constituencies.

• • •

Lincoln's first task was to secure his hold on the Republican Party by conciliating and enlisting those who had fought him for the nomination—Chase, Seward, and Bates.

Chase was first approached to speak on behalf of Lincoln in the form of "*a mere printed circular.*" He felt, he later admitted, "not a little hurt & [his] first impulse was not to reply at all." Then a personal letter from Lincoln arrived. Ignoring newspaper reports that Chase was "much chagrined and much dissatisfied with the nomination of so obscure a man as Mr. Abe Lincoln," Lincoln graciously chose to construe Chase's formal congratulatory letter as a symbol of his willingness to help. "Holding myself the humblest of all whose names were before the convention," Lincoln wrote Chase, "I feel in especial need of the assistance of all; and I am glad—very glad—of the indication that you stand ready." His ego soothed, Chase spoke at numerous Republican gatherings in Ohio, Indiana, and Michigan during the weeks that followed. Though he harbored a lasting bitterness toward the Ohio delegation, he affirmed his hopes for the nation, arguing "first, that the Republican party is an inevitable party; secondly, that it grows out of the circumstances of the country; thirdly, that it proposes no measure which can be injurious to the true interests of the people."

The formation of the Constitutional Union Party had made the support of Edward Bates vital to Lincoln. The party had enlisted many of the Missouri statesman's old Whig supporters, and included many old Know Nothings. To engage the elder statesman's support, Lincoln's old friend Orville Browning called on Bates at his St. Louis home. Browning was in the best position to persuade Bates to help the Republican cause, since he had supported Bates's presidential bid until the Illinois delegation, of which he was a member, had pledged itself to Lincoln. During their conversation, Bates "declined to take the stump" but promised to pen a public letter supporting Lincoln, even though he was aware, he said later, that in doing so, he would "probably give offense to some members of the *Constitutional Union party.*"

True to his word, Bates produced a letter for Browning to publish in which he praised Lincoln lavishly, positioned him as a conservative, and affirmed his own determination to support the Republican ticket. "I give my opinion freely in favor of Mr. Lincoln," Bates wrote. "I consider Mr. Lincoln a sound, safe, national man. He could not be sectional if he tried. His birth, his education, the habits of his life, and his geographical position, compel him to be national." What was more, Bates continued, Lincoln had "earned a high reputation for truth, courage, candor, morals and ability so that, as a man, he is most trustworthy. And in this particular, he is more entitled to our esteem [than] some other men, his equals, who had far better opportunities and aids in early life." Later in the campaign Bates wrote of Lincoln: "His character is marked by a happy mixture of amiability and courage; and while I expect him to be as mild as Fillmore, I equally expect him to be as firm as Jackson."

While Lincoln worked to enlist the cooperation of all his rivals, he knew that the active support of William Henry Seward would be pivotal to his campaign. Seward's following among Republicans had brought him to the edge of nomination. His reverberant phrase making—"irrepressible conflict," "higher law than the Constitution"—though too flammable for some, had emblazoned the banners and helped define the Republican cause. The 35 electoral votes in his home state of New York might well prove the key to victory. And for Lincoln it did not bode well that Seward had returned to New York in the wake of the convention to find many of his supporters disillusioned and dispirited by the prospect of any other candidate.

"The campaign started heavily," Kansas delegate Addison Procter recalled. "Enthusiasm was lacking and conditions were getting more and more desperate." Hoping to organize a Lincoln Club in Kansas, Procter approached one of the state's most respected Republicans and asked him to preside. The man vehemently refused: "You fellows knew at Chicago what this country is facing. . . . You knew that it will take the very best ability we can produce to pull us through. You knew that above everything else, these times demanded a statesman and you have gone and given us a *rail splitter*. No, I will not preside or attend."

"My personal feelings have been so much disturbed by the result at Chicago," Charles Sumner wrote, "that I cannot yet appreciate it as a public act." There is but "one & only one thing consoles me," Michigan Republican George Pomeroy told Seward—"our chance of being defeated this time and *your* sure chance of a nomination in '64." Treasury agent William Mellen of Ohio expressed his disbelief to Frances Seward that Abraham Lincoln was presented as "the suitable man for the Presidency. The rail-candidate forsooth! I confess to a disposition to *rail* at him, & much more at the Convention for its self-stultification. . . . What is to be feared is the utter disintegration of the Republican party as a consequence of this abandonment of principle for mere expediency."

Though Seward had pledged his support to the Republican ticket in a public letter, he was so dejected in the aftermath of his defeat that he considered resigning immediately from the Senate. Without the onerous demands of the congressional session, he could remain in Auburn, surrounded by his loving family and consoling friends. "When I went out to market this morning," he told one friend, "I had the rare experience of a man walking about town, after he is dead, and hearing what people would say of him. I confess I was unprepared for so much real grief, as I heard expressed at every corner."

But he understood that a decision to resign would look petulant and would, as his friend Israel Washburn warned, "give the malignants" an opportunity to damage him further. In the end, he determined to return to Washington in late May to complete his Senate term. The journey back to Capitol Hill "in the character of a leader deposed by [his] own party" was agonizing for him, however, as he admitted in a long letter to Frances. "I arrived here on Tuesday night. Preston King, with a carriage, met me at the depot, and conveyed me to my home. It seemed sad and mournful." Even the pictures hanging on the wall, "Dr. Nott's benevolent face, Lord Napier's complacent one, Jefferson's benignant one, and Lady Napier's loving one, seemed all like pictures of the dead." When he reached the Senate, "good men came through the day to see me. . . . Their eyes fill with tears. . . . They console themselves with the vain hope of a day of 'vindication;' and my letters all talk of the same thing. But they awaken no response in my heart." His only solace, he told her, was the realization that "responsibility has passed away from me, and that the shadow of it grows shorter every day."

Frances was delighted at the thought of her husband's permanent return to their Auburn home when his Senate term ended the following March. "You have earned the right to a peaceful old age," she assured him; "35 years of the best part of a mans life is all that his country can reasonably claim." This was not the time, however, for Seward to fade contentedly from public life. Weed's report of his visit with Lincoln perhaps roused Seward's own resolve. To withdraw from this fight would be an abdication of his fierce political ambition and his belief in the Republican cause.

In the weeks that followed the convention, Seward was overwhelmed with speaking requests from dozens of Republican committees throughout the North. "Your services are more necessary to the cause than they ever were," Charles Francis Adams wrote. "And your own reputation will gain more of permanency from the becoming manner with which you meet this disappointment, than it would from all the brilliancy of the highest success."

"I am content to quit with the political world, when it proposes to quit with me," Seward told Weed in late June. "But I am not insensible to the claims of a million of friends, nor indifferent to the opinion of mankind. All that seems to me clear, just now, is that it would not be wise to rush in at the beginning of the canvass, and so seem, most falsely, to fear that I shall be forgotten. Later in the canvass, it may be seen that I am wanted for the public interest." So he delayed, while entreaties to join streamed in, finally committing himself to an electioneering tour in nine states in late August and early September. The announcement that Seward "was about to take the platform and open the campaign for Lincoln," Addison Procter recalled, "was our first gleam of sunshine from out of the depths of discouragement."

• • •

WHILE SEWARD PREPARED for his grand tour, Lincoln remained in Springfield. In deference to political tradition and to his own judgment that further public statements could only damage his prospects, he decided against a personal speaking tour. Recognizing that his cluttered law office could not accommodate the flood of visitors eager to see him, he moved his headquarters to the governor's reception room at the State House.

Initially, Lincoln's sole assistant was John Nicolay, a twenty-eight-year-old German-American immigrant who had worked for three years as a clerk in the secretary of state's office. Lincoln had often visited the serious-minded Nicolay when searching out the latest election figures maintained in the office. After the convention, Lincoln had asked Nicolay to be his private secretary, "a call to service," Nicolay's daughter, Helen, later noted, "that lasted until his hair grew white and the powers of life ran down."

With Nicolay's help, Lincoln answered letters, received hundreds, perhaps thousands, of visitors from all parts of the North, talked with politicians, and contributed to a short campaign biography that sold more than a million copies. From his impromptu headquarters at the State House, Lincoln would engineer many aspects of his campaign. The telegraph wires allowed for fairly swift communication to political battlegrounds. Confidential messages were sent by mail, carried by personal emissaries, and given to political visitors. Most of these meetings are lost to history, but those that were recorded reveal Lincoln as a skillful politician, formulating and guiding his own campaign strategy.

"He sat down beside me on the sofa," wrote a correspondent from Utica, New York, "and commenced talking about political affairs in my own State with a knowledge of details which surprised me. I found that he was more conversant with some of our party performances in Oneida County than I could have desired." He "can not only discuss ably the great democratic principle of our Government," wrote a newspaperman from Missouri, "but at the same time tell how to navigate a vessel, maul a rail, or even to dress a deer-skin." Each correspondent's impression was quickly forwarded to the newspapers, the principal conduits between candidates and the public.

To counter the savage caricatures of Lincoln in Democratic papers as semiliterate, ignorant, an uncultured buffoon, homely, and awkward, Republican journalists were dispatched to Springfield to write positive stories about Lincoln, his educated wife, Mary, and their dignified home. Newspapers that had supported Seward swiftly transferred their allegiance to the new leader of the Republican Party, and utilized every occasion to extol their candidate and attack the opposition.

Lincoln and his team doubtless controlled the "line" out of Springfield that reverberated in Republican papers across the nation. After spending an evening at the Lincoln home, the correspondent from the *Utica Morning Herald* reported that "an air of quiet refinement pervaded the place. You would have known instantly that she who presided over that modest household was a true type of the American lady." As for Lincoln, "he has all the marks of a mind that scans closely, canvasses thoroughly, concludes deliberately, and holds to such conclusions unflinchingly."

"Ten thousand inquiries will be made as to the looks, the habits, tastes and other characteristics of Honest Old Abe," the Chicago *Press and Tribune* wrote. "We anticipate a few of them. . . . Always clean, he is never fashionable; he is careless but not slovenly. . . . In his personal habits, Mr. Lincoln is as simple as a child . . . his food is plain and nutritious. He never drinks intoxicating liquors of any sort. . . . He is not addicted to tobacco. . . . If Mr. Lincoln is elected President, he will carry but little that is ornamental to the White House. The country must accept his sincerity, his ability and his honesty, in the mould in which they are cast. He will not be able to make as polite a bow as Frank Pierce, but he will not commence anew the agitation of the Slavery question by recommending to Congress any Kansas-Nebraska bills. He may not preside at the Presidential dinners with the ease and grace which distinguish the 'venerable public functionary,' Mr. Buchanan; but he will not create the necessity" for a congressional committee to investigate corruption in his administration.

The visiting correspondents from Republican papers had nothing but praise for Mary. "Whatever of awkwardness may be ascribed to her husband, there is none of it in her," a journalist from the *New York Evening Post* wrote. "She converses with freedom and grace, and is thoroughly *au fait* in all the little amenities of society." Frequent mention was made of her distinguished Kentucky relatives, her sophisticated education, her ladylike courtesy, her ability to speak French fluently, her son's enrollment in Harvard College, and her membership in the Presbyterian Church. Mrs. Lincoln is "a very handsome woman, with a vivacious and graceful manner," another reporter observed; "an interesting and often sparkling talker."

Reporters were fascinated by the contrast between a cultured woman from a refined background and the self-made rough-hewn Lincoln. Party leaders began to cultivate the legend of Lincoln that would permeate the entire campaign and, indeed, evolve into the present day. He was depicted as "a Man of the People," an appealing political title after the rustic Andrew Jackson first supplanted the Eastern elites who had occupied the presidency for the forty years from Washington through John Quincy Adams.

The log cabin was emblematic of the dignity of honest, common, impoverished origins ever since William Henry Harrison had been triumphantly dubbed the "log-cabin, hard-cider" candidate twenty years earlier. Harrison had merely been posed in front of a log cabin. Lincoln had actually been born in one. One Republican worker wrote: "It has also afforded me sincere pleasure to think of Mr. Lincoln taking possession of the White House; he, who was once the inmate of the log cabin—were he the pampered, effeminated child of fortune, no such pleasing emotions would be inspired." Answering the charge that Lincoln would be a "nullity," the *New York Tribune* suggested that a "man who by his own genius and force of character has raised himself from being a penniless and uneducated flat boatman on the Wabash River to the position Mr. Lincoln now occupies is not likely to be a nullity anywhere."

This aura of the Western man, the man of the prairie, had been reinforced during the Chicago convention, when Republicans paraded through the streets carrying the rails Lincoln had supposedly split. Although Lincoln—Honest Abe—was careful not to verify that any particular rail had been his handiwork, in one interview he held a rail aloft and said: "here is a stick I received a day or two since from Josiah Crawford. . . . He writes me that it is a part of one of the rails that I cut for him in 1825."

Lincoln was aware that being "a Man of the People" was an advantage, especially in the raw and growing Western states critical to the election of a Republican candidate. Prior to the campaign, he had reinforced this politically potent image with descriptions of his poor schooling, years of poverty, and manual labor. Although his grim beginnings held no fascination for him, Lincoln was astute enough to capitalize upon this invaluable political asset.

From the outset, he decided that "it would be both imprudent, and contrary to the reasonable expectation of friends for me to write, or speak anything upon doctrinal points now. Besides this, my published speeches contain nearly all I could willingly say." When his friend Leonard Swett asked his approval of a letter expressing the candidate's sentiments, Lincoln replied, "Your letter, written to go to N.Y. is . . . substantially right." However, he advised, "Burn this, not that there is any thing wrong in it; but because it is best not to be known that I write at all." He recognized that anything he said would be scanned scrupulously for partisan purposes. The slightest departure from the printed record would be distorted by friends as well as enemies. Even his simple reiteration of a previous position might, in the midst of a campaign, give it new emphasis. He preferred to point simply to the party platform that he had endorsed. His few lapses justified his fears. A facetious comment to a Democratic reporter that "he would like to go into Kentucky to discuss issues but was afraid of being lynched" was made into a campaign issue.

Underlying this policy of self-restraint was another important but unvoiced political reality: Lincoln had to maintain the cohesion of the new Republican Party, a coalition of old Democrats, former Whigs, and members of the nativist American Party. Informing a Jewish friend that he had never entered a Know Nothing lodge, as accused by Democrats, he cautioned that "our adversaries think they can gain a point, if they could force me to openly deny this charge, by which some degree of offence would be given to the Americans. For this reason, it must not publicly appear that I am paying any attention to the charge." Although Lincoln himself had disavowed any sympathy with the nativists, and had actually invested in a German paper, many Republicans remained hostile to immigrants, and their support was essential.

Lincoln knew this election would not be determined by a single issue. While opposition to slavery extension had led to the creation of the Republican Party and dominated the national debate, in many places other issues took precedence. In Pennsylvania, the leading iron producer in the nation, and in New Jersey, the desire for a protective tariff was stronger than hostility to slavery. In the West, especially among immigrant groups, multitudes hoped for homestead legislation providing free or cheap land to new settlers, many of whom had been hard hit by the Panic of 1857. "Land for the Landless" was the battle cry. And when, in the midst of the campaign, President Buchanan vetoed a mild Homestead Act, many in Indiana and throughout the West turned to Lincoln. All of these issues had been carefully addressed in the Republican Party platform. Had the election been fought on the single issue of slavery, it is likely that Lincoln would have lost.

• • •

WHILE LINCOLN KEPT a strategic silence in Springfield, Seward stepped forward to speak on public issues and provide the drama and excitement of the campaign. Traveling by train, steamboat, and carriage with an entourage (which included Fanny and her friend Ellen Perry; Charles Francis Adams and his son, Charles Junior; along with a contingent of politicians), Seward opened his tour in Michigan. From there, he proceeded west to Wisconsin and Minnesota, south to Iowa and Kansas, and east to Illinois and Ohio.

At every stop, Seward was met with "cannons, brass bands, and processions of torch-bearing 'Wide Awakes' "—young Republicans dressed in striking oilcloth capes and caps—who generated enthusiasm for the party. They created a circus atmosphere at Republican rallies, surrounding the perimeter of crowds and marching in meandering, illuminated processions. One such march took several hours to pass the Lincoln house in Springfield. "Viewed from an elevated position, it wound its sinuous track over a length of two miles, seeming, in its blazing lights and glittering uniforms, like a beautiful serpent of fire," wrote John Hay. "The companies . . . ignited vast quantities of Roman candles, and as the drilled battalions moved steadily on, canopied and crowded with a hissing and bursting blaze of fiery splendor . . . the enthusiasm of the people broke out in wild cheerings." Other candidates mustered marching clubs, but with less success. One group of Douglas partisans designated themselves the "Choloroformers," ready and able to "put the Wide Awakes to sleep."

Fifty thousand people gathered to hear Seward speak in Detroit, and the fervor only increased as his tour moved west. Thousands waited past midnight for the arrival of his train in Kalamazoo, and when he disembarked, crowds followed him along the streets to the place where he would sleep that night. The next day, thousands more assembled on the village green to enjoy a brilliant "procession of young men and women on horseback, all well mounted, children with banners, men with carts and wagons," that preceded the formal speeches. Still craving more, the crowd followed the entourage back to the train station, where Seward appeared at the window to speak again. To the discomfort of the elder Charles Francis Adams, Seward suggested that he, too, stick his head out of the window for some final words. "All of this reminded me of a menagerie," Adams confessed in his diary, "where each of the beasts, beginning with the lion, is passed in review before a gaping crowd."

In St. Paul, Minnesota, a correspondent reported, Seward's arrival was "a day ever memorable in the political history of our State." Early in the morning, the streets were "alive with people—the pioneer, the backwoodsman, the trapper, the hunter, the trader from the Red River," all of them standing in wonder as a "magnificent Lincoln and Hamlin pole" was raised. A procession of bands and carriages heralded the arrival of Seward, who spoke for nearly two hours on the front steps of the Capitol.

Reporters marveled at Seward's ability to make every speech seem spontaneous and vital, "without repetition of former utterances," surpassing "the ordinary stump speech in fervency . . . literary quality, elevation of thought, and great enthusiasm on the part of the auditors." It often appeared "the whole population of the surrounding country had turned out to greet him," one correspondent noted. "Gov. Seward, you are doing more for Lincoln's election than any hundred men in the United States," a judge on board the Mississippi boat told him. "Well, I ought to," Seward replied.

Charles Francis Adams, Jr., who was twenty-five at the time, could not figure "where, when, or how" Seward was able to prepare "the really remarkable speeches he delivered in rapid succession," for "the consumption of liquors and cigars" during the journey was excessive. "When it came to drinking, Seward was, for a man of sixty, a free liver; and at times his brandy-and-water would excite him, and set his tongue going with dangerous volubility; but I never saw him more affected than that—never approaching drunkenness. He simply liked the stimulus." Amazingly, Adams remarked, despite Seward's drinking, his capacity for work was unimpaired.

Young Adams was mesmerized by Seward, whom he considered the most "delightful traveling companion" imaginable. "The early morning sun shone on Seward, wrapped in a strange and indescribable Syrian cashmere cloak, and my humble self, puffing our morning cigars," Adams recorded in his diary after an overnight journey by rail to Quincy, Illinois. The two smokers had adjourned to the baggage car, "having rendered ourselves," in Seward's words, " 'independent on this tobacco question.' "

Seward's grand tour received extensive coverage, complete with excerpts from his speeches, in newspapers across the land. From Maine, Israel Washburn wrote that he was astonished at the "integrity & versatility" of the speeches. He considered the speech in Detroit "the most perfect & philosophical—the St. Paul the broadest, the Dubuque the warmest, the Chicago the most practical & effective . . . but, of all the speeches . . . I like the short one at Madison—it seems to me to be the most comprehensive & complete, the grandest & highest."

At home in Auburn, Frances Seward received dozens of letters praising her husband's performance. "I am sure you must be most happy," Seward's old friend Richard Blatchford wrote. "He has shown throughout a depth of power, eloquence & resonance of thought and mind, which we here who know him so well, are not a little taken a-back by." Sumner told

Frances that as he read each speech, he "marveled more & more. I know nothing like such a succession of speeches by any American." Frances took pride in her husband's accomplishments but simultaneously recognized that his great success had eclipsed the possibility he would soon retire to private life in Auburn. "Yes Henry is very popular now," she wrote Sumner. "He is monopolized by the public and I am at last—resigned—Is that the word."

On October 1, en route to Chicago, Seward's train made a brief stop in Springfield. "There was a rush into and about the windows of the car in which Mr. Seward was seated," observed a correspondent. Lincoln and Trumbull had waited with the crowd and came aboard to pay their respects. Lincoln "was a revelation," young Adams recorded in his diary. "There he was, tall, shambling, plain and good-natured. He seemed shy to a degree, and very awkward in manner; as if he felt out of place, and had a realizing sense that properly the positions should be reversed. Seward too appeared constrained." Adams undoubtedly ascribed his own feelings to Lincoln, who most likely did not feel "out of place" at all.

This was the first time Lincoln and Seward had met since the evening they spent together in Massachusetts in 1848. "Twelve years ago you told me that this cause would be successful," Lincoln told him, referring to the antislavery crusade, "and ever since I have believed that it would be."

During their conversation, Lincoln asked Seward if he would be willing in his upcoming Chicago speech to address a certain problematic subject: John Wentworth, now the mayor of Chicago, was continually making references to an argument the party was trying to avoid—that a Republican win would bring an eventual end to slavery altogether. Knowing Wentworth was set to introduce Seward, Lincoln asked the New Yorker to reassure the audience that Republicans "would not interfere with slavery where it already existed." Seward readily agreed and made it clear in his speech that Republicans were not attacking slavery in the South, that securing freedom for the territories need not interrupt ordinary intercourse with the South. In distancing themselves from Northern abolitionists, the Lincoln team was far more concerned with reassuring Northern conservatives than with conciliating the South.

Seward's tour came to a triumphant close on October 6. His train pulled into Auburn, where a "noisy throng" gave him a warm welcome home. "Seward, in fact, never appeared so well as at home," young Adams observed. "He walked the streets exchanging greetings with everyone." His responses were "all genuine, the relations were kindly, unaffected, neighborly." Seward's return created "an impression of individuality approaching greatness." It was a journey Adams would never forget.

Although Lincoln himself made no public statements or speeches, he labored constantly on his campaign and fully justified Weed's appraisal of his political acumen. He strove to hold his coalition together, while disrupting efforts of his opponents to unite on fusion tickets. He sent emissaries to his supporters with instructions to solve campaign problems and heal divisions. Indirectly, he sought to clarify his position on important issues without breaking his vow of silence. He rigorously abstained from making patronage commitments. Responding to Senator Trumbull's suggestion that he make some pledges in New York, Lincoln replied, "Remembering that Peter denied his Lord with an oath, after most solemnly protesting that he never would, I will not swear I will make no committals; but I do think I will not."

Despite the unremitting, consuming labor of organizing his campaign, Lincoln somehow found time to write a humorous fictional dialogue between Breckinridge and Douglas. He also answered many of the endless letters he received, writing personal, unpretentious replies to supporters and well-wishers of every kind. An author wishing to dedicate his new legal work to Lincoln was answered: "I give the leave, begging only that the inscription may be in modest terms, not representing me as a man of great learning, or a very extraordinary one in any respect." In mid-October, he replied to eleven-year-old Grace Bedell, who had recommended that he grow a beard, "for your face is so thin" and "all the ladies like whiskers." After lamenting the fact that he had no daughter of his own, he wondered: "As to the whiskers, having never worn any, do you not think people would call it a piece of silly affection if I were to begin it now?" Nonetheless, he proceeded to grow a beard. By January 1861, John Hay would pen a witty couplet: "Election news Abe's hirsute fancy warrant—Apparent hair becomes heir apparent."

Recognizing that much of the positive news he received from friends was biased, Lincoln implored his supporters to give straightforward accounts of his prospects in each state. He worried about reports from Maine, New York, and Chicago, and brooded over the lack of solid information from Pennsylvania. His political objectives in the Keystone State were to establish his soundness on the tariff issue and heal the ominous divisions between the followers of Cameron and Curtin, the gubernatorial candidate. Lincoln always understood the importance of what he described as "the dry, and irksome labor" of building organizations to get out the vote, while most politicians preferred "parades, and shows, and monster meetings."

He enthusiastically supported Carl Schurz's "excellent plan" for mobilizing the German-American vote, and assured Schurz that "your having supported Gov. Seward, in preference to myself in the convention, is not even remembered by me for any practical purpose . . . to the extent of our limited acquaintance, no man stands nearer my heart than yourself." A large part of the German-American vote would go to Lincoln, aiding his victories in the Northwest.

Although concerned with progress in all the Northern states, he focused his attention primarily on the critical West. He urged Caleb Smith to do his utmost in Indiana, believing that nothing would affect the November results in Illinois more strongly than the momentum provided by an Indiana victory in the October state elections. In July, he sent Nicolay to an Indiana supporter who wished to prevent a Bell ticket from being placed on the ballot. "Ascertain what he wants," Lincoln instructed Nicolay. "On what subjects he would converse with me. And the particulars if he will give them. Is an interview indispensable? Tell him my motto is 'Fairness to all,' but commit me to nothing."

Having pledged to make no new statement on public issues, Lincoln had surrogates present excerpts from his previous speeches to reinforce his positions. He had Judge Davis show Cameron selections of pro-tariff speeches he had made in the 1840s, and then cautioned Cameron: "Before this reaches you, my very good friend, Judge Davis, will have called upon you, and, perhaps, shown you the 'scraps.' . . . Nothing about these, must get into the news-papers." This tone reveals Lincoln's keen awareness that notes from unpublished thirteen-year-old speeches stretched his vow of silence, but he hoped the assurances they provided would corral Cameron's powerful influence in Pennsylvania. Cameron replied that he was pleased by the content of Lincoln's earlier writings.

To a correspondent who sought his intervention in the discord between Cameron and Curtin, Lincoln replied: "I am slow to listen to criminations among friends, and never expouse their quarrels on either side . . . allow by-gones to be by-gones, and look to the present & future only." Yet at the same time, he informed Leonard Swett, who was preparing a trip to Pennsylvania, that he was very concerned about former congressman Joseph Casey's disclosures that the Cameron faction lacked confidence in the Pennsylvania Central Committee, controlled by Curtin. "Write Mr. Casey," Lincoln urged, "suggest to him that great caution and delicacy of action, is necessary in that matter." Meanwhile, Republican money flowed into Pennsylvania. "After all," wrote Republican National Committeeman John Goodrich of Massachusetts, "Pennsylvania is the Sebastopol we must take."

Lincoln turned his political attention to every state where his campaign experienced difficulty. Hearing that two Republican seats might be lost in Maine's September elections, he told his vice presidential mate, Hannibal Hamlin, that "such a result . . . would, I fear, put us on the down-hill track, lose us the State elections in Pennsylvania and Indiana, and probably ruin us on the main turn in November. You must not allow it." In August, troubled by a letter received from Rhode Island "intimating that Douglas is inlisting some rich men there, who know how to use money, and that it is endangering the State," Lincoln asked Rhode Island's senator James Simmons, "How is this? Please write me." In the end, the September elections in New England favored the Republicans, preparing the way for the great October contests in the West.

Lincoln was not alone in his assessment that the October state elections in Indiana and Pennsylvania would prove critical to the fortunes of the Republican Party. On the eve of the state elections, Judge Davis told his son that "tomorrow is the most important day in the history of the Country." Lincoln's camp was elated by the positive results as large Republican majorities piled up in both states. When Judge Davis first heard the exciting news, Ward Lamon reported back to Lincoln, "he was trying an important criminal case, which terminated in his Kicking over the Clerk's desk, turned a double somersault and adjourned court until after the presidential Election." If the three-hundred-pound Davis actually performed such a stunt, it was a miracle second only to Lincoln's nomination. But there was no question that Davis was thrilled. "We are all in the highest glee on acct of the elections," he wrote his wife, Sarah. "Mr. Lincoln will evidently be the next Pres't." That Saturday night, Davis traveled to Springfield to celebrate with the Lincolns, Trumbull, and Governor Corwin. "I never was better entertained," he rejoiced, though he confessed that Mary was still "not to my liking." She appears to be "in high feather," he continued. "I am in hopes that she will not give her husband any trouble."

Mary reveled in her newfound celebrity. She delighted in the crowds of visitors coming to her house, the artists pleading to paint her husband's portrait, the prominent politicians waiting for the chance to converse with the presidential nominee. With pride, and perhaps a shade of spite toward the man who had so often bested her husband, she noted that a reception for Stephen Douglas in Springfield had attracted only thirty people when hundreds were expected. "This rather looks as if his greatness had passed away," she commented to a friend.

Still, Mary remained terribly anxious that ultimate success might once again prove elusive. "You used to be worried, that I took politics so cooly," she confessed to her friend Hannah Shearer; "you would not do so, were you to see me now. Whenever I *have time*, to think, my mind is sufficiently exercised for my comfort . . . I scarcely know, how I would bear up, under defeat. I trust that we will not have the trial."

For weeks, Stephen Douglas had been barnstorming the country, having decided immediately after his nomination to defy custom. Disregarding criticism that his unbecoming behavior diminished the "high office of the presidency . . . to the level of a county clerkship," he stumped the country, from the New England states to the Northwest, from the border states to the South, becoming "the first presidential candidate in American history to make a nationwide tour in person."

Douglas was in Cedar Rapids, Iowa, when he heard the news of the Republican victories in Indiana and Pennsylvania, which destroyed any hope he might have had for victory. "Mr. Lincoln is the next President," he declared. "We must try to save the Union. I will go South." It was a courageous move, his "finest hour," according to Allan Nevins. Exhausted from his nonstop weeks of campaigning, Douglas faced one hostile audience after another as he moved into the Deep South. No longer hoping to gain support for his candidacy, he campaigned for the survival of the Union. "I believe there is a conspiracy on foot to break up this Union," he warned an audience in Montgomery, Alabama. "It is the duty of every good citizen to frustrate the scheme . . . if Lincoln is elected, he must be inaugurated."

Douglas understood what the Republicans failed to see—that Southerners were serious in their threats to secede from the Union if Lincoln won the election. "The cardinal error of the Republicans," Nevins writes, was their failure to deal candidly with "the now imminent danger of secession." Their dismissal of the looming possibility of secession was in part, but only in part, a deliberate tactic to ignore the threat so that voters would not be scared away from the Republican ticket. Beyond that, they simply did not believe that the threat was serious. After all, the South had made similar threats intermittently for the past forty years. Charles Francis Adams, Jr., later admitted, "we all dwelt in a fool's Paradise." Though Northern Republicans had undoubtedly seen the threatening editorials in Southern newspapers, they continued to believe, as Lincoln told a journalist friend, that the movement was simply "a sort of political game of bluff, gotten up by politicians, and meant solely to frighten the North."

In mid-August, Lincoln assured one of his supporters, John Fry, that "people of the South have too much of good sense, and good temper, to attempt the ruin of the government." Many in the South were equally skeptical. A Tennessee editor later admitted that "the cry of disunion had been raised so often that few had taken it seriously during the campaign. Evidently the 'Northern sectionalists' had believed it to be 'all talk' . . . while most intelligent Southerners had assumed that it was 'an idle menace, made to sway Northern sentiment.' "

Bates likewise shrugged off Southern threats as the desperation of belligerent politicians, while Seward openly scorned the taunts of secession: "they cry out that they will tear the Union to pieces . . . 'Who's afraid?' Nobody's afraid." His audience echoed: "Nobody!" Among Lincoln's colleagues, only Frank Blair, Jr., recognized that the distortions of Lincoln's speeches in the Southern papers and the "misrepresentations" of extremists who intimated the Republicans intended an attack on the South had created "a large and influential class who are even now ready to apply the torch which will light the fires of civil discord." Still, Blair believed, these extremists would not succeed and "this glorious Union" would not "be sundered in consequence of the triumph of our party." Even John Breckinridge, the South's standard-bearer, sought to distance himself from Southern extremists. His sole campaign speech refuted charges that he favored splitting up the Union.

The realization that the "irrepressible conflict" might prove more than rhetoric came too late. The divided house would indeed fall. These phrases, intended by Seward and Lincoln as historical prophecies, were perceived by many in the South as threats—imminent and meant to be answered.

With the October elections, the campaign had gained decisive momentum, but it was not yet over. With four candidates dividing the vote, Lincoln would have to capture New York's pivotal 35 electoral votes to win an electoral majority and avoid throwing the election into the House. He relied on Thurlow Weed to manage the campaign in New York, but continued to seek other perspectives and intelligence. "I have a good deal of news from New-York," Lincoln told former congressman John Pettit, "but, of course, it is from *friends*, and is one-sided. . . . It would seem that assurances to this point could not be better than I have. And yet it *may* be delusive."

The Empire State posed unique problems for Republicans. New York was home to large numbers of traditionally Democratic Irish immigrants who were unfriendly to the antislavery cause. In addition, New York City contained an influential class of merchants and manufacturers who viewed Republicanism as a threat to their commercial relations with the South. If these groups united against Lincoln, and if, as the Douglas people believed, Seward's partisans remained unreconciled to Lincoln's nomination, New York could easily be lost.

Lincoln recognized these complications from the outset, warning Weed in August that "there will be the most extraordinary effort ever made, to carry New-York for Douglas." He feared that Douglas was "managing the Bell-element with great adroitness," and might well obtain a fusion of the two forces, thereby keeping the state from the Republicans. Less worried than Lincoln, Weed nonetheless left nothing to chance. He wrote to Seward in late October from the Astor House in New York City: "Can you afford to make a *soothing* speech in this city? . . . A speech in the spirit that you delivered last in the Senate, showing that it is the business of Republicans and the mission of the Republican Party to preserve the Union . . . that there is not an aggressive Plank in the Republican Platform. . . . I think it would finish the work." Seward agreed to come to New York at once. His speech, even in this Democratic stronghold, was punctuated by wild applause, and when he finished, "the whole audience broke forth into the most tumultuous cheering."

• • •

ON ELECTION DAY, November 6, 1860, the citizens of Springfield were awakened at sunrise by cannonade and rousing band music "to stir whatever sluggish spirits there might be among the populace." Lincoln spent the morning in his quarters at the State House, receiving and entertaining visitors. Samuel Weed of the *New York Times* long remembered the atmosphere in the room that morning. Lincoln "was chatting with three or four friends as calmly and as amiably as if he had started on a picnic." Tipping his armchair backward to prop his long legs atop the woodstove, he made such detailed inquiry into all the local races that "one would have concluded that the District Attorneyship of a county of Illinois was of far more importance than the Presidency."

Lincoln had originally declined to vote himself, believing that "the candidate for a Presidential office ought not to vote for his own electors," but Herndon insisted that if he cut off the presidential electors at the top, he could still vote for all the state and local offices. Warming to the idea, Lincoln headed over at about three o'clock to the polling place at the courthouse. His appearance drew a large crowd, "who welcomed him with immense cheering, and followed him in dense numbers along the hall and up stairs into the Court room," where he was hailed with another wild "burst of enthusiasm."

At five, he headed home to have supper with Mary and the boys, returning to the State House at seven, accompanied by Judge Davis and a few friends. An immense crowd followed him into the Capitol, leading one supporter to suggest that he ask everyone but his closest friends to withdraw. "He said he had never done such a thing in his life, and wouldn't commence now." When the polls had closed, the first dispatches began to filter into the telegraph office. A correspondent from the *Missouri Democrat* noted that throughout the evening, "Lincoln was calm and collected as ever in his life, but there was a nervous twitch on his countenance when the messenger from the telegraphic offices entered that revealed an anxiety within that no coolness from without could repress." The first dispatch, indicating a strong Republican win in Decatur, Illinois, was "borne into the Assembly hall as a trophy of victory, to be read to the crowd," who responded with great shouts of joy. Though the early returns were incomplete, it was observed that Lincoln "seemed to understand their bearing on the general result in the State and commented upon every return by way of comparison with previous elections."

By nine o'clock, as tallies were relayed from distant states, Lincoln, Davis, and a few friends gathered at the telegraph office for immediate access to the returns. While Lincoln reclined on a sofa, the telegraph tapped out good news all around. New England, the Northwest, Indiana, and Pennsylvania had all come into the Republican camp. When ten o'clock arrived, however, with no word from New York, Lincoln grew fretful. "The news would come quick enough if it was good," he told his cohorts that "and if bad, he was not in any hurry to hear it."

Finally, at 11:30, a message came from New York. "We have made steady gains everywhere throughout the State, but the city returns are not sufficiently forward to make us sure of the result, although we are quite sanguine a great victory has been won." The dispatch produced tremendous cheers. Minutes later, Lyman Trumbull came running into the room: "Uncle Abe, you're the next President, and I know it." Lincoln was still uncertain, for if the Democrats piled up huge majorities in New York City, the Republican votes in the rest of the state could be offset. "Not too fast, my friends," he said. "Not too fast, it may not be over yet."

At midnight, Lincoln attended a "victory" supper prepared by the Republican ladies. While everyone else was in high spirits, assured of victory, Lincoln remained anxious about New York. Too often in the past his dreams had collapsed at the last moment. Without New York's 35 electoral votes, his total of 145 electoral votes would be 7 short of a majority.

Lincoln's concerns proved groundless, for Thurlow Weed's unparalleled organization had been at work since dawn, rounding up Republican voters in every precinct. "Don't wait until the last hour," Weed had instructed his workers. "Consider every man a 'delinquent' who doesn't vote before 10 o'clock." He left his organization plenty of time to prod, push, and, if necessary, carry voters to the polls.

Soon after midnight, the returns from New York and Brooklyn came in, revealing that Democratic control of New York City was not enough to counter the Republican vote throughout the state. Celebrations could begin in earnest, for Lincoln's victory was accomplished.

Church bells began to ring. Cheers for "Old Abe" resounded through the streets. Lincoln was jubilant, admitting that he was "a very happy man . . . who could help being so under such circumstances?" Pocketing the final dispatch, he headed home to tell Mary, who had been waiting anxiously all day. "Mary, Mary," he cried out, *"we are elected!"*

CHAPTER 10

"AN INTENSIFIED CROSSWORD PUZZLE"

BY THE TIME LINCOLN got to bed, it was two o'clock. He was exhausted but could not sleep. "The excitement which had kept him up through the campaign had passed away," he later recalled to Gideon Welles, "and he was oppressed with the load of responsibility that was upon him." Outside his windows, he could hear the citizens of Springfield partying in the streets, laughing, singing, and marching until they could carry on no longer. With the arrival of dawn, they finally dispersed to their homes.

Undoubtedly, Lincoln shared the elation of his neighbors. From his earliest days in politics, he had craved the opportunity to accomplish important deeds that would benefit his fellows. In modern parlance, he wanted to make a difference and now he had the opportunity to do so. Yet, keenly aware of both the fractious nature of the youthful Republican Party and the ominous threats from the South, he understood that his country was entering a most perilous time.

"I began at once to feel that I needed support," he noted later; "others to share with me the burden." As the exhausted townsfolk shuffled back to their homes and the city sank "into its usual quietness," Lincoln began to compose his official family—the core of his administration. "This was on Wednesday morning," he revealed, "and before the sun went down, I had made up my Cabinet. It was almost the same as I finally selected."

On a blank card he wrote the names of the seven men he wanted. At the center of his list stood his chief rivals for the nomination—Seward, Chase, and Bates. The list also included Montgomery Blair, Gideon Welles, and Norman Judd, all former Democrats, as well as William Dayton of New Jersey, a former Whig. While several months would pass before the cabinet was assembled, subjecting Lincoln to intense pressures from all sides, he resolved that day to surround himself with the strongest men from every faction of the new Republican Party—former Whigs, Free-Soilers, and antislavery Democrats.

The stillness of this first day that allowed Lincoln to contemplate the formulation of his ideal cabinet proved to be the calm before the storm. Soon, "the mad scramble" for the lesser positions began. With letters of recommendation stuffed in their pockets and fervent hopes in their hearts, hordes of office seekers descended on Springfield. Some arrived with "muddy boots and hickory shirts," while others were dressed in their finest linen and woolens. All were graciously welcomed by Lincoln.

He decided to hold two receptions a day, the first in the morning, the second in the late afternoon. The receptions were held in the Governor's Room in the State House, a chamber far too small for the constant crush of visitors pushing their way through the narrow doorway, guided by Lincoln's "clear voice and often ringing laughter." *New York Tribune* correspondent Henry Villard, although initially skeptical of Lincoln's qualifications to be president, observed that the president-elect "showed remarkable tact" with every caller. Listening patiently to each applicant, Lincoln revealed a quick-witted "adaptation to individual characteristics and peculiarities. He never evaded a proper question, or failed to give a fit answer." What most impressed Villard was Lincoln's remarkable ability to tell a humorous story or deliver an appropriate anecdote "to explain a meaning or enforce a point, the aptness of which was always perfect."

While the opposition papers derided Lincoln's penchant for telling stories, imagining that he babbled on from the moment he awakened—at mealtimes, on the street, in his office, in stores, even in his sleep (with Mary beside him in her nightcap)—the perceptive Villard understood that the president-elect's perpetual supply of stories "helped many times to heal wounded feelings and mitigate disappointments." Everyone Lincoln dealt with, Villard concluded, agreed that "he is the very embodiment of good temper and affability. They will all concede that he has a kind word, an encouraging smile, a humorous remark for nearly everyone that seeks his presence, and that but few, if any, emerge from his reception room without being strongly and favorably impressed with his general disposition."

At this juncture, Lincoln was sorely in need of a second assistant. Nicolay recommended twenty-two-year-old John Hay, the young journalist and Brown University graduate who had become actively involved in the campaign and had written pro-Lincoln columns for the *Missouri Democrat.* Nicolay had originally met Hay in private school. When Nicolay asked his boyhood friend to help with the overflowing correspondence, the gregarious young man was delighted. Though Hay was preparing for the bar in the Springfield office of his uncle Milton Hay, he was passionate about literature. On Class Day at Brown, he had delivered a poem that was remembered for years afterward. He had hoped quixotically to make his living as a poet upon graduation, but had reluctantly settled for a career in law. He leaped at the chance to work in the White House.

For Mary, Willie, and Tad, it was an exciting time. At night, after the formal receptions were over, visitors, sketch artists, and friends flocked to their home. Mary flourished in her role as hostess, while the boys regaled visitors with laughter and stories of their own. The ardent political conversations of celebrated men surely reminded Mary of childhood evenings when her father entertained congressmen and senators, including Henry Clay, in the parlor of his Kentucky mansion. To be sure, there were unpleasant moments, as when mud was tracked into the house, or when callers would point to Mary and boisterously ask: "Is that the old woman?" But Mary seemed to take it all in stride. Her delight in victory overshadowed such small aggravations.

Even as the Lincolns entertained their colorful parade of callers, the president-elect never lost sight of the intricate task he faced in building a cabinet that would preserve the integrity of the Republican Party in the North, while providing the fairest possible representation from the South. To help with his deliberations, he asked Hannibal Hamlin, his vice president–elect, to meet him in Chicago. Once the arrangements were made, he invited his old friend Joshua Speed to join him, and suggested that he bring his wife, Fanny, to keep Mary company. Traveling by train with a small party of journalists and friends, the Lincolns took up quarters at the Tremont House, which had lodged Davis and Swett six months earlier when they managed the unexpected nomination.

Although Hamlin had been a senator when Lincoln was in the House, this was the first time they would meet. Hamlin recalled listening to a speech Lincoln delivered that "was so full of good humor and sharp points" that the entire chamber "was convulsed with laughter." Born in Maine the same year as Lincoln, Hamlin was a tall, powerfully built man with a swarthy complexion. He had entered politics as a Jacksonian Democrat at a young age, serving first in the Maine state legislature, then in the U.S. House of Representatives, and finally in the Senate.

The two men began their discussions in Lincoln's room in the Tremont House, but news of their meeting soon brought "a great throng of visitors," necessitating a public reception and a round of dinners. The following day, however, their dialogue resumed privately at a friend's house, where Lincoln made clear his determination to create "a compact body" by drawing his former rivals into "his official household." Hamlin apparently agreed with this notion, and the conversation turned to selecting a representative from New England. Lincoln's original choice, Gideon Welles, was mentioned, along with Nathaniel Banks and Charles Francis Adams, Jr. Hamlin objected to Banks but agreed to look into the availability and feasibility of both Adams and Welles.

Amid the flood of political aspirants and tactical discussions, Lincoln must have coveted his time with Speed. He arranged for Fanny to visit with Mary so that he might speak with his old friend in private. Speed later recalled that Lincoln "threw himself on the bed" and said: "Speed what are your pecuniary Conditions—are you rich, or poor." Understanding the import of the question, Speed replied: "I think I know what you wish. I'll Speak Candidly to you—My pecuniary Conditions are good—I do not think you have any office within your gift that I can afford to take." Though Speed's resolve never wavered, the two friends would maintain contact during the war, and Speed would play an important role in keeping Kentucky in the Union.

While Lincoln was preoccupied with selecting his cabinet, Mary had a splendid time. She visited the scene of her husband's triumph at the Wigwam, toured the Custom House and the Post Office, and maintained her poise and charm at the large public reception accorded the president-elect and his wife.

Returning home, Lincoln corresponded with a wide range of politicians and listened carefully to their suggestions for his cabinet. In the end, however, he alone would solve what Nicolay's daughter, Helen, later described as "an intensified crossword puzzle in which party loyalty and service, personal fitness, geographical location and a dozen other factors have to be taken into account and made to harmonize."

From the start, Lincoln determined to give the highest place to Seward, "in view of his ability, his integrity, and his commanding influence." The presidency now unavailable, Seward never questioned that he deserved the premier post as secretary of state. Not only had he been the overwhelming favorite for the nomination, but he had vigorously campaigned for Lincoln in the general election and had helped to bring the critical state of New York to Lincoln's side.

"*Of course,* Mr. Lincoln will offer you the chief place in his Cabinet," Charles Francis Adams wrote Seward. "I trust no considerations will deter you from accepting it. . . . I know of no such faith existing in the competency of any other person." From Pennsylvania, Simon Cameron tendered a similar prediction. "You will be offered the State Dept. within a few days and you *must not* refuse it. The whole victory achieved by the labor of so many years, will be lost if you run away now. My whole ambition is to see you in the Presidency."

Lincoln agreed wholeheartedly with the presumption that Seward deserved first consideration. Seward, however, harbored more elaborate ambitions. While Lincoln desired a cabinet that stitched together the various factions of the Republican Party, Seward believed the cabinet should be dominated by former Whigs like himself. The Whig Party had provided nearly two thirds of Lincoln's total vote. Lesser posts could be given to the leading representatives of the other factions, but the former Whigs, Seward believed, deserved all the top prizes. Furthermore, Seward intended, with Weed's help, to have a major role in choosing the remaining cabinet members, thus acquiring a position in the new government more commanding than that of Lincoln himself.

To set this in motion, Thurlow Weed invited Lincoln shortly after the election to join him at Seward's home in Auburn so the three men might deliberate about the cabinet. As precedent, he invoked the journey of President-elect William Harrison to Lexington, Kentucky, in 1841 to confer with his rival Henry Clay. Lincoln wisely declined. When Weed suggested meeting in a more neutral setting, Lincoln again declined. While more than willing to consult with Weed and Seward on his cabinet selections, Lincoln wanted it known that the ultimate decisions would emanate from Springfield and would be his alone.

Lincoln's careful maneuvering with Weed did not indicate any hesitation to make Seward his secretary of state. On the contrary, Lincoln responded testily to a warning from a conservative Kentucky judge that "if obnoxious men like Seward, Cassius M. Clay, &c were put in the Cabinet," the citizens of Kentucky might feel compelled to follow South Carolina in its call for a secession convention. "In what speech," Lincoln asked, had Seward or any prominent Republican "ever spoken menacingly of the South?" The problem was not what the Republicans said or believed but the manner in which Southerners "persistently bespotted and bespattered every northern man by their misrepresentations to rob them of what strength they might otherwise have."

In fact, after newspapers had speculated that Seward had no interest in a cabinet post, and that, even if he did, Lincoln did not want to offer him one, Lincoln resolved to act quickly. Early in December, he directed Hamlin to ascertain Seward's state of mind. When Hamlin approached Seward's friend Preston King, King suggested that the vice president–elect should deal directly with Seward. Knowing this would be equivalent "to a tender of a place," Hamlin again sought Lincoln's instructions.

Lincoln concluded the time had come to make the offer official. In reply to Hamlin, he enclosed two letters for Seward and directed Hamlin, after consulting with Trumbull in Washington, to deliver them to Seward "at once." On the afternoon of December 10, after the Senate had adjourned, Hamlin caught up with Seward on the street. Reaching the Washington House on the corner of Third Street and Pennsylvania Avenue where Hamlin was staying, the vice president–elect invited Seward in to talk. Asked if he would, in truth, reject the position of secretary of state, Seward was guarded. "If that is what you have come to talk to me about, Hamlin, we might as well stop here," he replied. "I don't want the place, and if I did, I have reason to know that I could not get it; therefore let us have no more talk about it."

"Very well," Hamlin said, "but before you express yourself to others as plainly as you have done to me, let me present you with this letter from Mr. Lincoln." Seward "trembled" and appeared "nervous" as he took the first letter, dated December 8, which contained the formal invitation. "With your permission," Lincoln wrote, "I shall, at the proper time, nominate you to the Senate, for confirmation, as Secretary of State, for the United States. Please let me hear from you at your own earliest convenience."

At first, Seward said little, perhaps suspecting this was the pro forma offer that the papers had predicted all along. Moments later, he opened the second letter, labeled private and confidential, which was brilliantly designed to soothe Seward's ego. "Rumors have got into the newspapers," Lincoln wrote, "to the effect that the Department, named above, would be tendered you, as a compliment, and with the expectation that you would decline it. I beg you to be assured that I have said nothing to justify these rumors. On the contrary, it has been my purpose, from the day of the nomination at Chicago, to assign you, by your leave, this place in the administration. . . . I now offer you the place, in the hope that you will accept it, and with the belief that your position in the public eye, your integrity, ability, learning, and great experience, all combine to render it an appointment pre-eminently fit to be made."

His face "pale with excitement," Seward grasped Hamlin's hand. "This is remarkable, Mr. Hamlin; I will consider the matter, and, in accordance with Mr. Lincoln's request, give him my decision at the earliest practicable moment." Three days later, on December 13, Seward wrote Lincoln a gracious note, explaining that it was an honor to have received the offer, but that he needed "a little time" to think about whether he had "the qualifications and temper of a minister, and whether it is in such a capacity that my friends would prefer that I should act if I am to continue at all in the public service." He wished, he said, that he could confer directly with Lincoln on these questions, but he did not see how such a meeting "could prudently be held under existing circumstances." While there was little doubt that Seward desired the post, he still wished to test the extent of his influence in selecting congenial (pro-Seward) colleagues.

• • •

After tendering the offer to Seward, Lincoln turned his attention to Bates. Through Frank Blair, arrangements were made for Bates to visit Lincoln in Springfield on December 15. Arriving the evening before, Bates took a room at the Chenery House, where he encountered John Nicolay the next morning at breakfast. Nicolay was somewhat taken aback by the elder statesman's appearance. "He is not of impressive exterior; his hair is grey, and his beard quite white," Nicolay recorded, "and his face shows all the marks of age quite strongly." Nonetheless, he found "his flow of words in conversation" to be "very genial and easy." After breakfast, Bates walked over to Lincoln's room at the State House. Since Lincoln had not yet arrived, Nicolay gave Bates the morning paper and hastened to Lincoln's house to inform him that Bates was waiting. Shortly, the two former Whigs settled down for what Bates described as a "free conversation—till interrupted by a crowd" of callers. In order to speak privately, Lincoln suggested that they adjourn to Bates's room in the hotel, where they spent much of the afternoon together.

Lincoln took little time in assuring Bates that "from the time of his nomination, his determination was, in case of success, to invite [him] into the Cabinet." In fact, Bates proudly noted in his diary, Lincoln told him that he deemed his participation in his administration "necessary to its complete success." Lincoln acknowledged that several of Bates's friends had urged his appointment as secretary of state, but he believed he "should offer that place to Mr. Seward," not only "as a matter of duty to the party, and to Mr. Sewards many and strong friends," but also because "it accorded perfectly with his own personal inclinations." However, "he had not yet communicated with Mr. Seward, and did not know whether he would accept the appointment—as there had been some doubts expressed about his doing so." While Lincoln may have deliberately chosen the word "communicated" to allow Bates the belief he was the first approached, he actually meant that Seward had not yet responded affirmatively to his letter. Bates understood it to mean that he was the first man to whom Lincoln had spoken about a cabinet position. Lincoln explained that although he could not offer Bates the premier slot as secretary of state, he could extend "what he supposed would be most congenial, and for which he was certainly in every way qualified, viz: the Attorney Generalship."

Bates told Lincoln that if "peace and order prevailed in the country," he would decline the honor much as he had refused the post of secretary of war under President Fillmore in 1850. Only two months earlier, acknowledging in his diary that "everybody expects Mr. Lincoln to offer me one of his Departments," he had vowed to decline the position. "My pecuniary circumstances (barely competent) and my settled domestic habits make it very undesirable for me to be in high office with low pay—it subjects a man to great temptations to live above his income, and thus become dishonest; and if he have the courage to live economically, it subjects his family to ridicule."

With the country "in trouble and danger," however, he "felt it his duty to sacrifice his personal inclinations, and if he could, to contribute his labor and influence to the restoration of peace in, and the preservation of his country." Lincoln knew he had his man, either for U.S. Attorney General, or, if Seward should decline, for secretary of state. When Bates suggested several days later that "a good effect might be produced on the public mind—especially in the border slave States" by leaking the news of his offer, Lincoln agreed. "Let a little editorial appear in the Missouri Democrat," he wrote Bates, revealing that he had accepted a place in the cabinet, though "it is not yet definitely settled which Department." The announcement of Bates's appointment received positive marks almost everywhere. Indeed, the appointment of Bates would require the least maneuvering of all Lincoln's selections.

Meanwhile, after receiving Lincoln's offer, Seward consulted Weed, as he had at every critical juncture in his long career. Weed had already established a strong working relationship with Leonard Swett, who had assured him after the election that "we all feel that New York and the friends of Seward have acted nobly. . . . We should be exceedingly glad to know your wishes and your views, and to serve you in any way in our power." Weed now contacted Swett to secure an invitation to discuss Seward's thoughts on the design of the cabinet with Lincoln. "Mr. Lincoln would be very glad to see you," Swett informed Weed on December 10. "He asks me to tell you so. . . . Mr. Lincoln wants your advice about his Cabinet, and the general policy of his administration."

With Weed en route to Illinois, Seward wrote to inform Lincoln of his conversations with Weed, who would convey his "present unsettled view of the subject upon which you so kindly wrote me a few days ago." Weed arrived in Springfield on December 20. For weeks, reporters representing New York papers had been scanning the guest lists of the local Springfield hotels for signatures of any of their fellow New Yorkers. They were about to conclude that the Eastern establishment was deliberately shunning Lincoln when they uncovered the name of Thurlow Weed on the register at the Chenery House: "The renowned chief of the Albany lobby—the maker and destroyer of political fortunes—the unrivaled party manager—the once almighty Weed," a newspaper in Rochester noted, has "migrated towards the rising sun!"

Lincoln and Weed settled down opposite each other in Lincoln's parlor, with Swett and Davis in attendance. Swett would never forget the image of the two men, who "took to each other" so strongly, both "remarkable in stature and appearance," with "rough, strongly marked features," both having "risen by their own exertions from humble relations to the control of a nation." Despite their mutual respect, Lincoln's resolve regarding his cabinet choices undoubtedly dismayed Weed, who had assumed that he and Seward would have a critical role in the composition of the entire body. To Lincoln's appointment of Bates, Weed did not object; neither did he complain when the conversation turned to Caleb Smith of Indiana and Simon Cameron. Though Cameron was a former Democrat, Weed understood that Pennsylvania deserved an appointment. Besides, Cameron was a practical man, a politician after his own heart. When mention was made, however, of Salmon Chase, Gideon Welles, and Montgomery Blair—all former Democrats, all unfriendly to Seward—Weed "made strong opposition."

Chase, Weed argued, was an abolitionist. Welles and his Democratic colleagues in Connecticut had been thorns in the side of Weed and Seward for years. To Welles, "more than any one, perhaps, Weed attributed the defeat of Mr. Seward at Chicago," for the Connecticut delegation was "unanimously opposed to Mr. Seward" and set the tone for other New England states. Far better than Welles, Weed recommended, would be Charles Francis Adams or George Ashmun, both former Whigs and good friends of both Seward and Weed. Lincoln somewhat disingenuously claimed that since Hamlin was from New England, where so much shipping was located, the vice president–elect had been designated to choose the New England representative for the Navy Department. Since Hamlin had chosen Welles, "the only question was as to whether he [Welles] was unfit personally." In fact, Hamlin and Lincoln had discussed various men for the post, including Welles. Hamlin preferred Charles Francis Adams, but Lincoln wanted the former Democrat Welles to help balance the Whig members of his cabinet. Indeed, several years later, in a conversation with Welles, Lincoln claimed that his mind was "fixed" on Welles from the start. Though his choice was "confirmed" by Hamlin and others, recalled Lincoln, "the selection was my own, and not theirs."

Understanding that Lincoln would not be swayed from Welles, Weed playfully suggested a fanciful alternative for secretary of the navy. The president-elect could purchase "an attractive figure-head, to be adorned with an elaborate wig and luxuriant whiskers, and transfer it from the prow of a ship to the entrance of the Navy Department," which would be "quite as serviceable as his secretary, and less expensive." Lincoln immediately appreciated the humor in the resemblance between Weed's image of a wigged, bewhiskered figurehead and Father Neptune, as he would later call Welles. He reckoned, however, he needed "a live secretary of the navy."

Next, Lincoln brought up the name of Montgomery Blair. "Has he been suggested by any one except his father, Francis P. Blair, Sr.?" Weed mocked. The question prompted from Lincoln an amusing anecdote that made it all too clear to Weed that Blair was Lincoln's choice. Still, Weed argued that Lincoln would eventually regret his selection. Lincoln explained that he needed a representative from the border states. Montgomery's appointment would ensure support both in Maryland and through his brother, Frank, in Missouri. Weed suggested instead John Gilmer of North Carolina, a loyal Union man. Lincoln knew Gilmer and liked him, but doubted if any Southerner would accept a post. Nonetheless, he conceded that if Gilmer were contacted and agreed, and if "there was no doubt of his fidelity, he would appoint him."

As the conversation was drawing to an end, Weed pointed out that the inclusion of Chase, Cameron, Welles, and Blair in the cabinet along with Seward, Bates, and Smith would give the Democrats a majority, slighting the Whigs who made up the major portion of the Republican Party. "You seem to forget," Lincoln replied, "that *I* expect to be there; and counting me as one, you see how nicely the cabinet would be balanced and ballasted."

Weed returned to Albany convinced that Lincoln was "capable in the largest sense of the term." In the *Albany Evening Journal*, he wrote: "his mind is at once philosophical and practical. He sees all who go there, hears all they have to say, talks freely with everybody, reads whatever is written to him; but thinks and acts by himself and for himself."

While publicly praising Lincoln's independence, Weed was privately so chagrined by the complexion of the cabinet that he was no longer certain Seward should accept. "In one aspect *all* is gone," Weed wrote Seward on Christmas Day, likely indicating Welles, "nor do I know how much can be saved in the other," probably referring to Blair.

The following evening, Seward sent a note to Charles Francis Adams, asking him to call in the morning. With a tone of sorrow in his voice, Seward told Adams he had imagined that when Lincoln offered him the premier position in the cabinet, he "would have consulted him upon the selection of the colleagues with whom he was to act"; but Weed had returned from Springfield empty-handed. He had hoped Adams would be awarded the Treasury, but the likely choice of Welles would fill New England's quota, closing the door on Adams. "This was not such a Cabinet," Seward confided to Adams, "as he had hoped to see, and it placed him in great embarrassment what to do. If he declined, could he assign the true reasons for it, which was the want of support in it? If he accepted, what a task he had before him!" Adams replied that "in this moment of great difficulty and danger, there was no alternative for him but acceptance." This is probably what Seward wanted to hear all along, after he had expressed his distress at not being able to bring his friend Adams along.

The next day, Seward wrote to Lincoln that "after due reflection and with much self distrust," he had "concluded; that if I should be nominated to the Senate . . . it would be my duty to accept." That evening, he wrote to his wife, "I have advised Mr. L. that I will not decline. It is inevitable. I will try to save freedom and my country." Frances was not surprised by her husband's acceptance. Though she wanted him to close the curtain on his political career and come home to his family in Auburn, when huge worshipful crowds met his whirlwind summer tour for Lincoln, she had foreseen that his driving ambition would never be satisfied in tranquil Auburn. Nor was she surprised by his grandiose claim that he would try to save freedom and his country. She often saw her man with a clearer eye than he saw himself.

• • •

WITH ACCEPTANCES from Seward and Bates in hand, Lincoln turned his attention to his third rival, Salmon Chase. Knowing that Chase would never accept a subordinate position, Lincoln had slated him for the Treasury Department. As soon as he received Seward's written acceptance, he wrote to Chase: "In these troublous times, I would [much] like a conference with you. Please visit me here at once." The pieces of the puzzle were beginning to fall into place.

But Lincoln's plans for Chase were temporarily waylaid by intense pressure for the appointment of Pennsylvania's Simon Cameron as secretary of the treasury. Exactly what promises Swett and Davis had made to Cameron's men at the convention for their switch to Lincoln on the second ballot went unrecorded. We know from Swett's letter to Lincoln, however, that he had given his word to the Cameron men that "they should be placed upon the same footing as if originally they had been your friends." The lobbying for Cameron began days after Lincoln's election with a deluge of letters "from very strong and unexpected quarters." Lincoln had understood from the start the importance of satisfying Pennsylvania. Initially, he had hoped Pennsylvania would accept New Jersey's William Dayton, who, like Cameron, was a staunch protectionist. As testimonials to Cameron poured in, however, Lincoln dispatched Swett to Harrisburg to invite Cameron to Springfield.

"The unexpected arrival of [Cameron] was somewhat of a stunner," Henry Villard confessed, "not only to your correspondent but to a majority of the political schemers and intriguants in Springfield." Considering Lincoln's "well known rigid adherence to honesty," it seemed impossible to Villard that Honest Abe would besmirch his cabinet with someone of Cameron's unsavory reputation. For years, charges of bribery and bad dealings with the Winnebago Indians had sullied Cameron's name. However compromised his reputation, the campaign on the Pennsylvanian's behalf was organized with great skill and effectiveness.

As soon as Cameron reached the Chenery House on December 30, he sent a note to Lincoln. "Shall I have the honor of waiting on you,—or will you do me the favor to call here?" Lincoln told him to come to his office, where they spoke for several hours. The conversation continued that evening at the Chenery House. Their talks were candid and enjoyable, for even those opposed to Cameron acknowledged his winning personality, shrewd understanding of politics, and repertoire of intriguing stories. At the end of the interview, Lincoln told Cameron he would appoint him to the cabinet, as either secretary of the treasury or secretary of war. The wily Cameron asked Lincoln to put the offer in writing, which Lincoln somewhat impulsively did, on the promise that it remain confidential. Unfortunately, when Cameron returned home, he brandished the offer among his friends like "an exuberant school boy."

As word of the probable appointment leaked out, opposition flared. "There is an odor about Mr. C. which would be very detrimental to your administration," Trumbull warned Lincoln in a letter that probably reached Springfield shortly after Cameron left. "Not a Senator I have spoken with, thinks well of such an appointment." Then, on January 3, 1861, Alexander McClure, representing one of Pennsylvania's anti-Cameron factions, came to Springfield carrying papers that purportedly revealed Cameron's lack of moral fitness, particularly inappropriate for stewardship of the Treasury. Recognizing that he had acted too hastily, Lincoln sent a private note to Cameron on January 3: "Since seeing you things have developed which make it impossible for me to take you into the cabinet. You will say this comes of an interview with McClure; and this is partly, but not wholly true. The more potent matter is wholly outside of Pennsylvania." To save face, Lincoln suggested that Cameron decline the appointment, in which case Lincoln would "not object to its being known that it was tendered you."

Hopeful that Cameron would cooperate, Lincoln looked forward to his meeting with Chase, who arrived in Springfield on Friday, January 4, "travel-stained and weary after two days on the cramped, stuffy cars of the four different railroads he took from Columbus." Ever meticulous about his appearance, Chase barely had time to wash up before being notified that Lincoln was downstairs in the lobby of the Chenery House. Though discomfited by the awkwardness of their introduction, Chase was immediately disarmed by Lincoln's warm expression of thanks for Chase's support in 1858 during his failed Senate campaign against Douglas.

Lincoln then directly addressed the point of the meeting. "I have done with you," he said, "what I would not perhaps have ventured to do with any other man in the country—sent for you to ask you whether you will accept the appointment of Secretary of the Treasury, without, however, being exactly prepared to offer it to you." The problem, Lincoln explained, would be garnering acceptance for Chase's appointment in Pennsylvania, a prospect complicated by the unresolved Cameron situation and by Chase's previous support for free trade that had enraged industrial Pennsylvania. Lincoln's straightforward manner impressed Chase, even as it irritated him. "I frankly said to him that I desired no position & could not easily reconcile myself to the acceptance of a subordinate one; but should gladly give to his admn., as a Senator, all the support which a sincere friend . . . could give." [Chase had once again been elected to the U.S. Senate by the Ohio legislature.]

As the interview continued, however, Chase began to relax. Lincoln explained that had Seward declined the State Department, he would have "without hesitation" offered it to Chase, certain that Seward and Chase deserved the two top positions in his cabinet. His dignity restored, Chase promised to consider the contingent Treasury offer "under the advice of friends." He and Lincoln continued their discussion on Saturday, and Chase attended Sunday church with the Lincoln family.

After this long weekend meeting, Lincoln considered Chase's inclusion in the cabinet essential. But what of Cameron, who had refused to withdraw from consideration? Early that Sunday morning, Lincoln walked over to the Chenery House, where Gustave Koerner was still in bed. Lincoln rounded up Judd and returned to Koerner's room. Speaking in an agitated voice, Lincoln said: "I am in a quandary. Pennsylvania is entitled to a cabinet office." He had received "hundreds of letters, and the cry is 'Cameron, Cameron!' . . . The Pennsylvania people say: 'If you leave out Cameron you disgrace him.' " Nonetheless, he had his mind "already fixed on Chase, Seward and Bates, my competitors at the convention." Koerner and Judd expressed themselves strongly against Cameron but were unable to solve Lincoln's dilemma.

By Monday morning, as Chase left for Columbus, Lincoln had reached a tentative solution. He would not offer Cameron the Treasury but would hold open the possibility of another post. "It seems to me not only highly proper, but a *necessity*," he confided in Trumbull that day, "that Gov. Chase shall take [the Treasury]. His ability, firmness, and purity of character, produce the propriety." As for the necessity, his name alone would reconcile the merchant class in New York who had long opposed Seward. "But then comes the danger that the protectionists of Pennsylvania will be dissatisfied; and, to clear this difficulty, Gen. C. must be brought to co-operate." The solution was to persuade him to take the lesser position of the War Department.

Moving carefully, Lincoln wrote a conciliatory letter to Cameron, admitting that his first letter was written "under great anxiety," and begging him to understand that he "intended no offence." He promised that if he made a cabinet appointment for Pennsylvania before he arrived in the capital, he would not do so without talking to Cameron, "and giving all the weight to your views and wishes which I consistently can."

Uncertain about Lincoln's complex plans, Chase left Springfield with some ambivalence. Although he had to admit that his conversations with Lincoln "were entirely free & unreserved," he had not been given the firm offer he coveted, even as he claimed a preference to remain in the Senate. On the train back to Ohio, he penned notes urging several friends to visit

Lincoln and support his case. "What is done must be done quickly & done judiciously," he told Hiram Barney, "with the concurrence of our best men & by a deputation to Springfield."

Chase's friends appealed to Lincoln, but the trouble occasioned by his impulsive letter to Cameron had convinced Lincoln to make no more official offers until he reached Washington in late February. Uncertainty left Chase increasingly agitated. "I think that in allowing my name to be *under consideration* . . . and to be tossed about in men's mouths and in the press as that of a competitor for a seat which I don't want, I have done all that any friends can reasonably ask of me," he wrote Elizabeth Pike. "And it is my purpose by a note to Mr. Lincoln within the present week to put my veto on any further *consideration* of it. If he had thought fit to tender me the Treasury Department with the same considerate respect which was manifested toward Mr. Seward and Mr. Bates I might have felt under a pretty strong obligation to defer to the judgment of friends and accept it." In the end, Chase never did send a note requesting Lincoln to withdraw his name from further cabinet consideration. His desire for position and glory, as Lincoln shrewdly guessed, would allow Lincoln alone to determine the time and place of his appointment.

• • •

WHILE LINCOLN WAS PREOCCUPIED with the construction of his official family, the country was tearing itself apart. On December 20, 1860, the same day that Lincoln met with Thurlow Weed, South Carolina held a state convention in the wake of the Republican victory and passed an ordinance to secede from the Union. The vote was unanimous. Throughout the Deep South, such "a snowballing process" began that over the next six weeks, six additional states followed suit—Mississippi, Louisiana, Florida, Alabama, Georgia, Texas.

For Southern radicals, a correspondent for the *Charleston Courier* observed, Lincoln's victory opened the door to the goal "desired by all true hearted Southerners, viz: a Southern Confederacy." The night after the election, the citizens of Charleston had turned out in droves for a torchlight parade featuring an effigy of Lincoln, with a placard in its hand reading: "Abe Lincoln, First President Northern Confederacy." Two slaves hoisted the figure to a scaffold, where it was set afire and "speedily consumed amid the cheers of the multitude."

As the various secession ordinances made clear, the election of a "Black Republican" was merely the final injury in a long list of grievances against the North. These documents cited attempts to exclude slaveholders from the new territories; failure to enforce the Fugitive Slave Act; continued agitation of the slavery question that held Southerners up to contempt and mockery; and the fear of insurrection provoked by the John Brown raid.

Though Southern newspapers had long threatened that secession would follow fast upon a Lincoln victory, the rapidity and vehemence of the secession movement took many in the North, including President Buchanan, by surprise. The bachelor president was attending a young friend's wedding reception when he heard news of South Carolina's secession. A sudden disturbance heralded the entrance of South Carolina congressman Lawrence Keitt. Flourishing his state's secession ordinance over his head, he shouted: "Thank God! Oh, thank God! . . . I feel like a boy let out from school." When Buchanan absorbed the news, he "looked stunned, fell back, and grasped the arms of his chair." No longer able to enjoy the festivities, he left immediately.

For Lincoln, who would not take office until March 4, it was a time of mounting anxiety and frustration. He strongly believed, he told John Nicolay, that the government possessed "both the authority and the power to maintain its own integrity," but there was little he could do until he held the reins of power. While he was "indefatigable in his efforts to arrive at the fullest comprehension of the present situation of public affairs," relying not simply on the newspapers he devoured but on "faithful researches for precedents, analogies, authorities, etc.," it was hard to stand by while his country was disintegrating. He declared at one point that he would be willing to reduce his own life span by "a period of years" equal to the anxious months separating his election and the inauguration.

Besieged with requests to say something conciliatory, Lincoln refused to take "a position towards the South which might be considered a sort of an apology for his election." He was determined to stand behind the Republican platform, believing that any attempt to soften his position would dishearten his supporters in the North without producing any beneficial impact on the South. When asked by the editor of a Democratic paper in Missouri to make a soothing public statement that would keep Missouri in the Union, Lincoln replied: "I could say nothing which I have not already said, and which is in print and accessible to the public. Please pardon me for suggesting that if the papers, like yours, which heretofore have persistently garbled, and misrepresented what I have said, will now fully and fairly place it before their readers, there can be no further misunderstanding. . . . I am not at liberty to shift my ground—that is out of the question. . . . The secessionists, *per se* believing they had alarmed me, would clamor all the louder."

As panic began to affect the stock market and the business community in the North, Lincoln reluctantly agreed to insert an authorized passage in a speech Trumbull was scheduled to make in Chicago. He simply repeated that once he assumed power, "each and all of the States will be left in as complete control of their own affairs respectively, and at as perfect liberty to choose, and employ, their own means of protecting property, and preserving peace and order within their respective limits, as they have ever been under any administration."

Just as Lincoln had predicted, however, the speech had no positive impact. "On the contrary," he wrote the *New York Times*'s Henry Raymond, "the Boston Courier, and its' class, hold me responsible for the speech, and endeavor to inflame the North with the belief that it foreshadows an abandonment of Republican ground by the incoming administration; while the Washington Constitution, and its' class hold the same speech up to the South as an open declaration of war against them." The South, he claimed, "has eyes but does not see, and ears but does not hear."

Although increasingly infuriated by Southern misrepresentations of his positions, Lincoln confined expression of his anger to private letters. Upon hearing from the *New York Times*'s Henry Raymond that one of his correspondents, a wealthy Mississippi gentleman named William Smedes, had justified the state's "blaze of passion" for secession on the grounds that Lincoln was "pledged to the ultimate extinction of slavery, holds the black man to be the equal of the white, & stigmatizes our whole people as immoral & unchristian," Lincoln issued a blistering reply. As evidence, Smedes had cited an "infamous" speech Lincoln had purportedly given on the occasion when Chase was presented with his silver pitcher by the free blacks of Cincinnati. For such a speech, Smedes proclaimed, he would "regard death by a stroke of lightning to Mr. Lincoln as but a just punishment from an offended deity."

"What a very mad-man your correspondent, Smedes is," Lincoln replied, countering that he "was never in a meeting of negroes in [his] life; and never saw a pitcher presented by anybody to anybody." Moreover, he went on, "Mr. Lincoln is not pledged to the ultimate extinctincton of slavery; does not hold the black man to be the equal of the white, unqualifiedly as Mr. S. states it; and never did stigmatize their white people as immoral & unchristian."

However justifiable Lincoln's anger at what he rightly called a "forgery out and out," his response reveals the gulf still separating him from Chase on the issue of race. Although Lincoln's views on racial equality reflected the majority position in the North, Chase regarded his call at the pitcher ceremony to eradicate the Black Laws one of the proudest moments of his life.

• • •

WHILE OUTRAGED BY the South's willful distortions of his positions, Lincoln was far more troubled by the growing rancor splitting his own party. Conciliators believed that with the proper compromises, the eight remaining slaveholding states could be kept in the Union, hoping that without expansion, the secession movement would ultimately die out. Hard-liners, meanwhile, ranged from those who thought compromise would only embolden the South to extremists who believed that military force alone would bring the South back to the Union fold. As president-elect, Lincoln had to balance two emerging poles of the Republican Party, a task made all the more difficult by the over 700 miles that separated Springfield from Washington.

Yet, almost unnoticed, Lincoln managed through a series of complex and subtle maneuvers to keep the Republican Party intact through the "Great Secession Winter." Whatever conciliatory measures he might consider, Lincoln was adamant, he told Trumbull, that there must be "no compromise on the question of *extending* slavery. If there be, all our labor is lost, and, ere long, must be done again. . . . Stand firm. The tug has to come, & better now, than any time hereafter." If the door were opened to slavery in any of the new territories, Lincoln feared that the South would eventually try to annex Cuba or invade Mexico, thereby restarting the long struggle.

Though Lincoln remained inflexible on the territorial question, he was willing, he told Seward, to compromise on "fugitive slaves, District of Columbia, slave trade among the slave states, and whatever springs of necessity from the fact that the institution is amongst us." Knowing that two parallel committees in the House and Senate were set to address the sectional crisis, Lincoln relayed a confidential message to Seward that he had drafted three short resolutions. He instructed Seward to introduce these proposals in the Senate Committee of Thirteen without indicating they issued from Springfield. The first resolved that "the Constitution should never be altered so as to authorize Congress to abolish or interfere with slavery in the states." The second would amend the Fugitive Slave Law "by granting a jury trial to the fugitive." The third recommended that all state personal liberty laws in opposition to the Fugitive Slave Law be repealed.

Seward agreed to introduce Lincoln's resolutions without revealing their source, though he was of the opinion that they would do nothing to stop the secession movement. The best option, he told Lincoln, was to focus on keeping the border states in the Union, though he feared "nothing could *certainly* restrain them" short of adopting the series of proposals authored by Kentucky's John Crittenden. The Crittenden Compromise, among other provisions, offered to extend the Missouri Compromise line to the Pacific, thereby initiating the very extension of slavery into the territories Lincoln had pledged to prevent.

Lincoln's clear resolve never to accept any measure extending slavery prevented the wavering Seward and other like-minded Republicans from backing the Crittenden Compromise. As one Southern state after another withdrew from the Union, Seward came to believe that only conciliation could save the Union. With Lincoln's iron hand guiding the way in this matter, however, Seward conceded that there was not "the slightest" chance that the Republican side would adopt the Compromise. Still, Seward retained his characteristic optimism, assuring Lincoln that with the passage of time, "sedition will be growing weaker and Loyalty stronger."

Events soon eclipsed the slender hope that time would bring about a peaceful solution to the sectional crisis. There were three federal forts in South Carolina: Fort Moultrie, under the command of Major Robert Anderson; Fort Sumter; and Castle Pinckney. South Carolina announced that all three were in its domain and that three commissioners of the new "republic" had been named to negotiate the matter with the Buchanan administration. "From the first," John Nicolay reported, it was apparent that "the Carolinians intended somehow to get possession of these fortifications, as it was the only means by which they could make any serious resistance to the federal government."

In late December, a rumor reached Springfield that Buchanan had instructed Major Anderson "to surrender Fort Moultrie if it is attacked." When Lincoln heard the news, he told Nicolay: "If that is true they ought to hang him!" Straightaway, he sent a message to General Scott through his friend Congressman Washburne, to be prepared at the time of the inauguration "to either *hold*, or *retake*, the forts, as the case may require."

In fact, the ever-vacillating Buchanan had not decided to surrender the forts. The issue produced an open rift in his already compromised cabinet. Treasury Secretary Howell Cobb of Georgia had resigned and departed for his native state, but several secessionists remained, "vying . . . for Buchanan's ear" with staunch Unionists Secretary of State Jeremiah Black and Postmaster General Joseph Holt. In the midst of the cabinet crisis, Black prevailed on Buchanan to offer the attorney generalship to his good friend Edwin Stanton, who was still practicing law in Washington. Black also pressured Stanton to accept the post, adding a third ally to bolster Buchanan's will. While Buchanan waffled over the proper course of action, Anderson preempted his decision on the night of December 26, 1860, by deciding to move his troops from Fort Moultrie to the less vulnerable Fort

Sumter. The next day, South Carolina took possession of the abandoned Fort Moultrie as well as Castle Pinckney.

Under the influence of Black, Holt, and Stanton, Buchanan agreed to send reinforcements to Anderson at Sumter. In early January, the same day that Lincoln met with Chase in Springfield, an unarmed merchant vessel, the *Star of the West*, headed for Charleston Harbor equipped with men and supplies. The mission failed when the weaponless vessel was fired upon by shore batteries. The *Star of the West* turned back immediately and headed north.

These dramatic events created what Seward called "a feverish excitement" in Washington. No one felt more apprehensive than the newest member of Buchanan's cabinet, Edwin Stanton. Thoroughly loyal to the Union, excitable and suspicious by nature, he became convinced that secessionists planned to seize the nation's capital and prevent Lincoln's inauguration. From his position inside the government, Stanton feared that "every department in Washington then contained numerous traitors and spies." He discovered that the army had been deployed in far-flung places and that treasonous officers had shifted arms and guns from arsenals in the North to various places in the South. If Maryland and Virginia could be provoked into secession, Stanton believed secessionists would be in a position to take Washington. With the essentially defenseless capital captured, they would possess "the *symbols* of government, the seals and the treaties—the treasuries & the apparent right to control the army & the navy." Stanton was driven to distraction when President Buchanan could not "*be made to believe*, the existence of this danger," and would not credit the treasonous plot, which, Stanton feared, would include an attempt to assassinate Lincoln before his inauguration.

At this juncture, his co-biographers report, Stanton "came to a momentous decision: he decided to throw party fealty and cabinet secrecy to the winds and to work behind the President's back." With the White House paralyzed and the Democratic Party at loggerheads, he determined that "Congress and its Republican leaders were the last hope for a strong policy, the last place for him to turn." Stanton knew that becoming an informer violated his oath of office, but concluded that his oath to support the Constitution was paramount.

Seeking the most powerful conduit for his information, Stanton chose Seward. Knowing they could not openly communicate, fearful that secessionists lurking on every corner would report the meetings in newspapers, Stanton prevailed on Peter Watson—the same Watson who had initially interviewed Lincoln for the Reaper trial—to act as his middleman. Almost every evening, Watson would call on Seward at his home to deliver oral and written messages from Stanton. Watson would then return to Stanton with Seward's responses. "The question what either of us could or ought to do at the time for the public welfare was discussed and settled," Seward later recalled.

The first meeting between Seward and Watson likely took place on December 29, prompting the flurry of private letters that Seward penned late that night. "At length I have gotten a position in which I can see what is going on in the Councils of the President," Seward wrote Lincoln. "It pains me to learn that things are even worse than is understood. . . . A plot is forming to seize the Capitol on or before the 4th of March. . . . Believe that I know what I write. In point of fact the responsibilities of your administration must begin before the time arrives. I therefore renew the suggestion of your coming here earlier than you otherwise would. . . . I trust that by this time you will be able to know your correspondent without his signature, which for prudence is omitted." That same evening, Seward confided in Frances that "treason is all around and amongst us," and warned Weed, whose presence in Washington he would welcome, that a plot to seize the government had "abettors near the President."

Seward assumed that Stanton was communicating with him alone. In fact, the cunning Stanton secretly spread word of the danger to several other Republicans, including Charles Sumner, Salmon Chase, and Congressman Henry Dawes. "By early disclosure," Dawes later wrote, Stanton was able to thwart some of the attempts by treasonous officers to turn supplies and arms over to "the enemies of their country." Increasingly paranoid, Stanton invited Sumner to his office and then led him through a half-dozen different rooms before feeling safe to talk for a few minutes. Arrangements were made for papers to be "found and read by the light of the street lamp at night, and then returned to the place of deposit."

Unaware of these other communications, Seward assumed it was on his shoulders to save the Union, that he "held the key to all discontent." After his appointment as secretary of state was made public on January 10, 1861, when he "came to be regarded somewhat extensively as a person representing the incoming administration and the Republican party," the pressure of his position was immense. "By common consent," Seward's admirer Henry Adams later wrote, "all eyes were turned on him, and he was overwhelmed by entreaties from men in all sections of the country to do something to save the Union." As members of Congress, the cabinet, and hundreds of nervous citizens approached him "with prayers and tears," Seward became "virtually the ruler of the country." Or so he thought.

Intuiting that the country needed a clear, strong Republican voice, Seward announced that he would deliver a major speech in the Senate on January 12. "Never in the history of the American Congress has there been witnessed so intense an anxiety to hear a speech as that which preceded the delivery of Mr. Seward's," a reporter for the Chicago *Tribune* wrote. "What gave so much interest and weight to the Senator's words, was the belief that it was equivalent to a speech from Lincoln himself."

"The families of nearly all the Senators and Cabinet officers were present," another correspondent reported, and the crush to get in was so great that "extravagant prices were offered to the various doorkeepers to obtain admission." As Seward began to speak, senators on both sides of the aisle sat in rapt attention, including Mississippi's Jefferson Davis, who would soon resign the Senate to become the president of the Southern Confederacy. "No man was as usual engaged in writing letters, no one called for pages, no one answered messages," a witness observed, "and every ear in the vast assembly was strained to catch his every word."

Seward's chief purpose was "to set forth the advantages, the necessities to the Union to the people . . . and the vast calamities to them and to the world which its destruction would involve." He warned that disunion would give rise to a state of "perpetual civil war," for neither side would tolerate an imbalance of strength or power. Opportunistic foreign nations would then move in, preying on the bickering factions. "When once the guardian angel has taken flight," he predicted, "everything is lost."

Listening from the packed galleries, a Boston reporter confessed that it was "difficult to restrain oneself from tears, when at the allusion of Seward to the great men of the country now dead and gone, and at his vivid portrayal of the horrors and evils of dissolution and civil war, we saw the venerable Senator Crittenden, who sat directly in front of Seward, shedding tears, and finally, overcome by his feelings, cover his face with his handkerchief."

As he moved into the second hour of his speech, Seward offered the concessions he hoped might stem the tide of secession. He endeavored "to meet prejudice with conciliation, exaction with concession which surrenders no principle, and violence with the right hand of peace." He began with Lincoln's resolutions calling for a constitutional amendment to prevent any future Congress from interfering with slavery where it already existed and suggesting a repeal of all personal liberty laws in opposition to the Fugitive Slave Law. He then added several resolutions of his own, including the prospect of a Constitutional Convention "when the eccentric movements of secession and disunion shall have ended" to consider additional changes to the Constitution. When, after nearly two hours, he concluded his emotional remarks, the galleries erupted in thunderous applause.

As Seward no doubt anticipated, his speech had little impact on the seven states of the Deep South, where the secession movement continued its course. The following week, five Southern senators, including Jefferson Davis, rose to deliver farewell speeches to their colleagues before resigning their seats and heading south. Davis delivered the most wrenching farewell. Unable to sleep for days, he appeared "inexpressibly sad," very ill, and "in a state of mind bordering on despair."

"I am sure I feel no hostility to you, Senators from the North," he began. "I am sure there is not one of you, whatever sharp discussion there may have been between us, to whom I cannot now say, in the presence of my God, I wish you well." The friendships forged over the years were not easily discarded. Seward himself had visited Davis every day during a painful illness several years earlier, when it seemed that Davis might lose his eyesight. Seated by Davis's side, Seward would recount all the speeches delivered that day by both Democrats and Republicans. The ever-genial Seward told how at one point, "Your man outtalked ours, you would have liked it, but I didn't." The families of the senators likewise suffered as Southerners prepared for departure. Old Man Blair's daughter, Elizabeth Blair Lee, and Varina Davis had been close friends for years. "Mrs Jef asked me if I was going down south to fight her," Elizabeth told her husband, Phil. "I told her no. I would kiss & hug her too tight to let her break any *bonds* between us."

As the senators from the seceded states packed up their belongings to return to their hometowns, it was clear that a "regime had ended in Washington." The mansions of the old Southern aristocracy were closed; the clothes, papers, china, rugs, and furniture that embellished their lives were stowed in heavy trunks and crates to be conveyed by steamers to their Southern plantations.

Seward understood the momentum in the Deep South. His words and hopes that winter were directed at the border states. His "great wish," young Henry Adams observed, "was to gain time," to give the Union men in the border states "some sign of good-will; something, no matter what, with which they could go home and deny the charges of the disunionists." In this respect, he seemed to succeed.

"As an indication of the *spirit* in which the Administration of Mr. Lincoln will be conducted," a *New York Times* editorial concluded, the speech "must convince every candid man that its predominant and paramount aim will be to perpetuate the Union,—that it will consult, with scrupulous care, the interests, the principles, and the sentiments of every section." While none of the concessions would recall the seceded states back into the Union, "many are sanguine in the hope that its wide diffusion through the border Slave States will stay the tide of secession."

During the tumultuous time from Lincoln's election in November 1860 to his inauguration in March 1861, Seward "fought," Henry Adams judged, "a fight which might go down to history as one of the wonders of statesmanship." In the weeks that followed, "the Union men in the South took new courage." In the critical state of Virginia, the Union party prevailed. Its members defeated the secessionists by a large margin, and proposed a Peace Convention to be held in Washington with the implied promise that no further action would be taken until the convention had completed its work. Days later, Tennessee and Missouri followed suit. "Secession has run its course," the New York diarist George Templeton Strong happily noted, betraying the false optimism throughout the North.

Seward was in the best of spirits after the speech, believing, as he told his wife, that without surrendering his principles, he had gained time "for the new Administration to organize and for the frenzy of passion to subside." Unfortunately, hard-liners read Seward's speech differently. Charles Sumner, Thaddeus Stevens, and Salmon Chase were outraged by his conciliatory tone in the face of what they considered treason on the part of the secessionist states. Animosity toward Seward was planted in the hearts of the more radical Republicans that would haunt him for the rest of his life. "I deplore S[eward]'s speech," Sumner wrote to a friend. He "read me his speech 4 days before its delivery. When he came to his propositions, I protested, with my whole soul—for the sake of our cause . . . & his own good name, & I supplicated him to say no such thing."

Thaddeus Stevens, the fiery abolitionist congressman from Pennsylvania, was beside himself. Writing to Chase, who had already spoken out against the adoption of any compromise measure, Stevens warned that if Lincoln "seeks to purchase peace by concession, and ignoring platforms, *á la mode* Seward, I shall give up the fight, being too old for another seven (or thirty) years war."

The speech was particularly disappointing to those, like Carl Schurz, who had long considered Seward the leader of the great antislavery cause. "What do you think of Seward, my child?" Schurz asked his wife. "The mighty is fallen. He bows before the slave power. He has trodden the way of compromise and concession, and I do not see where he can take his stand on this back track. . . . That is hard. We believed in him so firmly and were so affectionately attached to him. This is the time that tries men's souls, and many probably will be found wanting."

In the heated atmosphere of Washington, the realization that members of his own party had lost faith in him took a heavy toll on Seward. Visiting the Capitol after the speech, Charles Francis Adams, Jr., was stunned by Seward's altered appearance since their journey together on the campaign train the previous September. "There he was, the same small, thin, sallow man, with the pale, wrinkled, strongly marked face—plain and imperturbable—the thick, guttural voice and the everlasting cigar. Yet it was immediately apparent that his winter's cares had told on him, for he looked thin and worn, and ten years older than when I had left him at Auburn."

While his conciliatory address cost him the esteem of many longtime supporters, Seward still believed that offering his hand in peace in the attempt to prevent a civil war was the right judgment. His wife, Frances, profoundly disagreed. The final speech had reached her in Auburn by telegraph hours after it was delivered. She wrote her husband a blistering letter. "Eloquent as your speech was it fails to meet the entire approval of those who love you best," she began. "You are in danger of taking the path which led Daniel Webster to an unhonored grave ten years ago. Compromises based on the idea that the preservation of the Union is more important than the liberty of nearly 4,000,000 human beings cannot be right. The alteration of the Constitution to perpetuate slavery—the enforcement of a law to recapture a poor, suffering fugitive . . . these compromises cannot be approved by God or supported by good men. . . .

"No one can dread war more than I do," she continued; "for 16 years I have prayed earnestly that our son might be spared the misfortune of raising his hand against his fellow man—yet I could not to day assent to the perpetuation or extension of slavery to prevent war. I say this in no spirit of unkindness . . . but I must obey the admonitions of conscience which impel me to warn you of your dangers."

Stung deeply by her denunciation, Seward admitted that "I am not surprised that you do not like the 'concessions' in my speech. You will soon enough come to see that they are not compromises, but explanations, to disarm the enemies of Truth, Freedom, and Union, of their most effective weapons."

Perhaps no one understood Seward's painful position better than his oldest friend, Thurlow Weed. Weed loved the speech. "It will do to live and die by and with," he said. Still, he realized that Seward had opened himself to continuing attack. "In the cars, most of the night," Weed wrote, "I was thinking of the ordeal you are to pass. It is to be [a] great trial of Wisdom and Temper; in Wisdom you will not fail; but of our Tempers, at sixty, we are not so sure. . . . You had both once, and they made you strong. How much more you need them now when hemmed in and hedged in by envy, jealousies and hatreds."

Seward retained his equanimity amid the onslaught due largely to his belief that Lincoln not only endorsed but had covertly orchestrated his actions, for Lincoln himself had confidentially suggested several of the compromises that Seward had offered. Furthermore, in a private letter, Lincoln encouraged him: "Your recent speech is well received here; and, I think, is doing good all over the country." Meeting in the Capitol with Charles Francis Adams a few weeks after the speech, Seward confided that "he had heard from Mr. Lincoln, who approved his course, but was so badgered at Springfield that he felt compelled to keep uncommitted on it at present."

The president-elect was engaged in a more intricate game of political engineering than Seward realized. While undoubtedly pleased that Seward's conciliatory tone had produced a calming effect on the border states, Lincoln knew that if he personally called for compromise, he would lose the support of an important wing of the Republican Party. Instead, he maintained firmness through silence while Seward absorbed the backlash for what might prove an advantageous posture of conciliation.

When Carl Schurz visited Lincoln in Springfield after Seward's speech, Lincoln told the idealistic young man that "Seward made all his speeches without consulting him," a technically accurate if undeniably misleading statement. "[Lincoln] is a whole man," Schurz assured his wife, "firm as a stone wall and clear as crystal. . . . He himself will not hear of concessions and compromises, and says so openly."

In the end, though Lincoln's role was not fully recognized at the time, he was the one who kept his fractious party together when an open rupture might easily have destroyed his administration before it could even begin. By privately endorsing Seward's spirit of compromise while projecting an unyielding public image, President-elect Lincoln retained an astonishing degree of control over an increasingly chaotic and potentially devastating situation.

CHAPTER II

"I AM NOW PUBLIC PROPERTY"

As THE CONFUSION and turmoil of secession swept Washington, the Lincolns made final preparations for their departure from Springfield. In early January 1861, Mary journeyed to New York, both to spend time with her son Robert, whom she had been "*wild* to see" since he had left for the East Coast a year earlier, and to shop for a wardrobe befitting a first lady. Staying at the Astor Hotel, she was fêted by merchants eager to sell her fancy bonnets, richly textured shawls, kid gloves, and bolts of the finest antique silk for fashionable dresses. The store owners happily extended her credit, encouraging an extravagant spree, the first of many. After years of making do on a limited budget, this woman who was raised in a wealthy household took great pleasure in acquiring everything she wanted, even to the point of outspending her wealthier sisters.

"Buying was an intoxication with her," her biographer Ruth Randall writes, "it became an utterly irrational thing, an obsession." Mary's desire for elegant clothes reflected more than vanity, however. She was undoubtedly aware of the whispering comments about her plain looks and her husband's lack of breeding: "Could he, with any honor, fill the Presidential Chair?" one guest at an elegant restaurant was overhead saying. "Would his western gaucherie disgrace the Nation?" Her fighting spirit stimulated, she was determined to show the world that the civility of the West was more than equal to that of the East.

Entranced by her experience in New York, Mary stayed three extra days without notifying her husband, who plunged vainly through sleet and snow three nights running to meet her train. When she did return, Mary was in the best of spirits, as was her handsome, well-dressed son, whose "outward appearance" was said to present "a striking contrast to the loose, careless, awkward rigging of his Presidential father."

The Lincolns decided to rent out their house on Eighth Street, selling some of the furnishings and putting the rest into storage. Before packing their belongings, however, they held a farewell levee in the twin parlors of their home. Mary was in her element as she graciously welcomed a crowd of seven hundred Springfield friends. It was, Villard commented, "the most brilliant affair of the kind witnessed here in many years."

Mary was thrilled by the attention and relished the lavish gifts presented by office seekers. Nonetheless, she became increasingly apprehensive about her husband. Shortly before she left for New York, she received an unwelcome present from South Carolina—a painting depicting Lincoln "with a rope around his neck, his feet chained and his body adorned with tar and feathers." For Mary, terrified of thunderstorms and fearing death with every illness, the gruesome painting undoubtedly left her cold with foreboding.

For Lincoln, the hours of his remaining Springfield days must have seemed too short. The never-ending procession of office seekers and the hard work of packing left little time or space for the most important task of all—the composition of his inaugural address. Unable to concentrate either in his home or in the governor's office, he sought places to isolate himself and be undisturbed. For several precious hours each morning, he wrote and honed the words that were awaited anxiously by both the conciliators and the non-compromisers alike.

As the time for departure drew near, Lincoln appeared "unusually grave and reflective," saddened by the prospect of "parting with this scene of joys and sorrows during the last thirty years and the large circle of old and faithful friends." He journeyed to Farmington for an emotional farewell to his beloved stepmother, Sarah, and to visit his father's grave. Returning home, he called on Billy Herndon, his law partner for sixteen years. He wanted to assure Herndon that his election would only interrupt their partnership in the firm. "If I live I'm coming back some time, and then we'll go right on practising law as if nothing had ever happened."

The day of February 11 was damp and biting as Lincoln, accompanied by family and friends, headed for the Western Railroad Depot. The circuitous twelve-day trip to Washington, D.C., would permit contact with tens of thousands of citizens. He had packed his own trunk, tied it with a rope, and inscribed it simply: "A. Lincoln, White House, Washington, D.C." His oldest son, Robert, would accompany his father on the entire trip, while Mary and the two younger boys would join them the following day.

Arriving at the train station, Lincoln discovered that more than a thousand people had gathered to bid him farewell. He stood in the waiting room, shaking hands with each of his friends. "His face was pale, and quivered with emotion so deep as to render him almost unable to utter a single word," a reporter for the *New York Herald* noted. Just before 8 a.m., Lincoln was escorted to the platform of his private car. He took off his hat, requested silence, and began to speak: "My friends—No one, not in my situation, can appreciate my feeling of sadness at this parting. To this place, and the kindness of these people, I owe every thing. Here I have lived a quarter of a century, and have passed from a young to an old man. Here my children have been born, and one is buried. I now leave, not knowing when, or whether ever, I may return, with a task before me greater than that which rested upon Washington. . . . I hope in your prayers you will commend me, I bid you an affectionate farewell."

Many eyes, including Lincoln's, were filled with tears as he delivered his short but moving remarks. "As he turned to enter the cars three cheers were given," the *Herald* reporter observed, "and a few seconds afterwards the train moved slowly out of the sight of the silent gathering." Lincoln would never return to Springfield.

Neither the luxurious presidential car, decorated with dark furniture, crimson curtains, and a rich tapestry carpet, nor the colorful flags and streamers swaying from its paneled exterior could lift the solemn mood of the president-elect. For most of the ride to the first major stop in Indianapolis, Villard noted, Lincoln "sat alone and depressed" in his private car, "forsaken by his usual hilarious good spirits."

Lincoln understood that his country faced a perilous situation, perhaps the most perilous in its history. That same morning, Jefferson Davis was beginning a journey of his own. He had bade farewell to his wife, children, and slaves, heading for the Confederacy's new capital at Montgomery, Alabama. To the cheers of thousands and the rousing strains of the "Marseillaise," he would be inaugurated president of the new Confederacy. Alexander Stephens, Lincoln's old colleague from Congress, would be sworn in as his vice president.

Lincoln's spirits began to revive somewhat as he witnessed the friendly crowds lined up all along the way, buoyed by "the cheers, the cannon, and the general intensity of welcome." When he reached Indianapolis, thirty-four guns sounded before he alighted to face a wildly enthusiastic crowd of more than twenty thousand people. They lined the streets, waving flags and banners as he made his way to the Bates House, where he was scheduled to spend the night. Knowing that here in Indianapolis, he was expected to deliver his first public speech since election, he had carefully crafted its language before leaving Springfield.

From the balcony of the Bates House, he delivered a direct, powerful talk, one of the few substantive speeches he would make during the long journey. He began by illustrating the word "coercion." If an army marched into South Carolina without the prior consent of its people, that would admittedly constitute "coercion." But would it be coercion, he asked, "if the Government, for instance, but simply insists upon holding its own forts, or retaking those forts which belong to it?" If such acts were considered coercion, he continued, then "the Union, as a family relation, would not be anything like a regular marriage at all, but only as a sort of free-love arrangement." His words provoked loud cheers, sustained applause, and hearty laughter. The speech was considered a great success.

As the train rolled into Cincinnati the next day, John Hay noted that Lincoln had "shaken off the despondency which was noticed during the first day's journey, and now, as his friends say, looks and talks like himself. Good humor, wit and geniality are so prominently associated with him in the minds of those who know him familiarly, that to see him in a melancholy frame of mind, is much as seeing Reeve or Liston in high tragedy would have been." (Reeve and Liston were celebrated comic actors in Shakespeare's plays.) It is interesting to note that Hay considered Lincoln's despondency an aberration rather than the rule.

The following day, as Lincoln was fêted in the state Capitol at Columbus, Ohio, he received a telegram that the electors had met in Washington to count the votes and make his election official. For weeks, Seward and Stanton had worried that secessionists would choose this day to besiege the capital and prevent the electors from meeting. The day, Lincoln learned, had passed peacefully. "The votes have been counted," Seward's son Fred reported to his wife, Anna, "and the Capital is not attacked. Gen. Scott had his troops all under arms, out of sight but ready, with guns loaded, horses harnessed and matches lighted so that they could take the field at a moments notice. But there was no enemy."

Seward himself was immensely relieved to "have passed the 13th safely," believing, he wrote home, that "each day brings the people apparently nearer to the tone and temper, and even to the policy I have indicated. . . . I am, at last, out of direct responsibility. I have brought the ship off the sands, and am ready to resign the helm into the hands of the Captain whom the people have chosen." Despite his stated intentions, Seward would make one later effort to resume the helm.

In Columbus, a great celebration followed news of the official counting of the votes. In the late afternoon, Lincoln was presented at a "full evening dress" reception at Governor Dennison's home for members of the legislature; following dinner, he attended a lavish military ball, where it was said that he danced with Chase's lovely daughter, Kate, much to the irritation of Mary. The image of Lincoln dancing with the twenty-year-old beauty, tall, slim, and captivating, was spoken of in hushed tones for many years afterward. In fact, the charismatic young belle could not have danced with Lincoln that evening, for she was absent from the city when the Lincolns arrived. In an interview with a reporter more than three decades later, Kate maintained that "Mrs. Lincoln was piqued that I did not remain at Columbus to see her, and I have always felt that this was the chief reason why she did not like me at Washington."

For the rest of the trip, as the train wended its way through Pennsylvania, New York, and New Jersey, Lincoln said little to elaborate his position. Never comfortable with extemporaneous speech, he was forced to speak at dozens of stops along the way. He was determined not to foreshadow his inaugural address or to disturb the tenuous calm that seemed to have descended upon the country. He chose, therefore, to say little or nothing, projecting an optimistic tone that belied the seriousness of the situation. Lincoln repeatedly ignored conflicting statements in both his own "House Divided" speech and Seward's "Irrepressible Conflict" speech, assuring his audiences that "there is really no crisis except an *artificial one!* . . . I repeat it, then—*there is no crisis* excepting such a one as may be gotten up at any time by designing politicians. My advice, then, under such circumstances, is to keep cool. If the great American people will only keep their temper, on both sides of the line, the troubles will come to an end."

Throughout his journey, Lincoln endeavored to avoid any suggestion that might inflame or be used to destabilize the country before he could assume power. He simply acknowledged the cheers of the crowds, relying upon his good humor to divert attention from serious political discussion. In Ashtabula, Ohio, he playfully answered calls for Mrs. Lincoln by suggesting that "he should hardly hope to induce her to appear, as he had always found it very difficult to make her do what she did not want to." In Westfield, New York, he kissed Grace Bedell, the little girl who had encouraged him to grow a beard.

For Mary and the boys, the trip was "a continuous carnival," with "rounds of cheers, salvos of artillery, flags, banners, handkerchiefs, enthusiastic gatherings—in short, all the accessories of a grand popular ovation." Every glimpse of Mary or the children through the windows drew wild applause, as did the image of her smoothing her husband's ruffled hair and giving him a kiss before they disembarked in New York City.

To those who listened attentively for any revelation of the incoming administration's intentions, the speeches were a great disappointment. In his diary, Charles Francis Adams lamented that Lincoln's remarks on his journey toward Washington "are rapidly reducing the estimate put upon him. I am much afraid that in this lottery we may have drawn a blank. . . . They betray a person unconscious of his own position as well as of the nature of the contest around him. Good natured, kindly, honest, but frivolous and uncertain."

In fact, Lincoln was not oblivious to the abyss that could easily open beneath his feet. While he "observed the utmost caution of utterance and reticence of declaration," John Nicolay noted, "the shades of meaning in his carefully chosen sentences were enough to show how alive he was to the trials and dangers confronting his administration." In Trenton, for example, while he asserted that "the man does not live who is more devoted to peace than I am," he recognized that it might "be necessary to put the foot down firmly." At this point, Hay noted, he "lifted his foot lightly, and pressed it with a quick, but not violent, gesture upon the floor." The audience erupted with such sustained applause that for several minutes Lincoln was unable to continue his remarks.

Lincoln again revealed his strength of will in his short address at the Astor Hotel in New York City. While he opened with a conciliatory tone, promising that he would never of his own volition "consent to the destruction of this Union," he qualified his promise with "unless it were to be that thing for which the Union itself was made." Two days later, speaking in Independence Hall in Philadelphia, he clarified what he meant by those portentous words. Moved by a keen awareness that he was speaking in the hall where the Declaration of Independence was adopted, he asserted that he had "never had a feeling politically that did not spring from the sentiments embodied in the Declaration. . . . It was not the mere matter of the separation of the colonies from the mother land; but something in that Declaration" that provided "hope to the world for all future time. It was that which gave promise that in due time the weights should be lifted from the shoulders of all men, and that *all* should have an equal chance." If the Union could "be saved upon that basis," he would be among "the happiest men in the world"; but if it "cannot be saved without giving up that principle," he maintained, he "would rather be assassinated on this spot than to surrender it."

Lincoln's ominous mention of assassination may have been prompted by the previous day's report of a plot to kill him during his scheduled stop in Baltimore, a city rampant with Southern sympathizers. Lincoln first received word of the plot through the detective Allan Pinkerton, responsible for guarding him on the trip, who advised him to leave Philadelphia at once and pass through Baltimore on a night train ahead of schedule to confound the conspirators. "This," according to Ward Lamon, who accompanied Lincoln on the trip, "he flatly refused to do. He had engagements with the people, he said, to raise a flag over Independence Hall in the morning, and to exhibit himself at Harrisburg in the afternoon."

That same afternoon, Seward's son Fred was in the Senate gallery when a page summoned him to speak with his father at once. Meeting in the lobby, Seward handed Fred a note from General Winfield Scott carrying a similar warning of trouble in Baltimore. "I want you to go by the first train," Seward directed his son. "Find Mr. Lincoln, wherever he is. Let no one else know your errand." Fred immediately boarded a train and arrived at the Continental Hotel in Philadelphia, where Lincoln was staying, after ten that night.

"I found Chestnut street crowded with people, gay with lights, and echoing with music and hurrahs," Fred recalled. Lincoln was encircled by people, and Fred was forced to wait several hours to deliver his message. "After a few words of friendly greeting with inquiries about my father and matters in Washington," Fred remembered, "he sat down by the table under the gas-light to peruse the letter I had brought." After a few moments, Lincoln spoke: "If different persons, not knowing of each other's work, have been pursuing separate clews that led to the same result, why then it shows there may be something in it. But if this is only the same story, filtered through two channels, and reaching me in two ways, then that don't make it any stronger. Don't you see?" Then, Fred related, "noticing that I looked disappointed at his reluctance to regard the warning, he said kindly: 'You need not think I will not consider it well. I shall think it over carefully, and try to decide it right; and I will let you know in the morning.' "

The next morning, Lincoln agreed to leave Philadelphia for Washington on the night train as soon as his engagement in Harrisburg was completed. Pinkerton insisted, against Mary's judgment, that she and the boys should remain behind and travel to Washington in the afternoon as scheduled. Wearing a felt hat in place of his familiar stovepipe, Lincoln secretly boarded a special car on the night train, accompanied by Ward Lamon and Detective Pinkerton. All other trains were to be "side-tracked" until Lincoln's had passed. All the telegraph wires were to be cut between Harrisburg and Washington until it was clear that Lincoln had arrived in the capital. At 3:30 a.m., the train passed through Baltimore without mishap and proceeded straight to Washington. "At six o'clock," a relieved Lamon recalled, "the dome of the Capitol came in sight."

It was an inauspicious beginning for the new president. Though he arrived safely, critics, including Edwin Stanton, spoke maliciously of the manner in which Lincoln had "crept into Washington." A scurrilous rumor spread that he had entered the train in a Scotch plaid cap, Scottish kilts, and a long military cloak. "It's to be hoped that the conspiracy can be proved beyond cavil," wrote George Templeton Strong in his diary. "If it cannot be made manifest and indisputable, this surreptitious nocturnal dodging or sneaking of the President-elect into his capital city, under cloud of night, will be used to damage his moral position and throw ridicule on his Administration." Lincoln regretted ever heeding General Scott and Detective Pinkerton.

The question of Lincoln's accommodations in Washington for the ten days until his inauguration had been debated for weeks. In early December, Montgomery Blair had issued the Lincolns an invitation to stay at the Blair House on Pennsylvania Avenue, offering the very room "Genl Jackson intended to occupy after leaving the White house," and insisting that the Blairs "would be delighted for you to begin where he left." In the meantime, Senator Trumbull and Congressman Washburne had rented a private house for the Lincolns several blocks from the White House. When Lincoln had passed through Albany on his roundabout tour, however, Weed strongly objected. He advised Lincoln that he was "now public property, and ought to be where he can be reached by the people until he is inaugurated."

Lincoln agreed. "The truth is, I suppose I am now public property; and a public inn is the place where people can have access to me." A suite of rooms was reserved at the celebrated Willard Hotel, which stood at the corner of 14th Street and Pennsylvania Avenue, within sight of the White House.

• • •

SEWARD AND ILLINOIS CONGRESSMAN WASHBURNE were appointed to greet Lincoln and escort him to the Willard. Accounts vary, however, as to whether Seward was actually there to meet the train. He wrote his wife that "the President-elect arrived *incog.* at six this morning. I met him at the depot." Nevertheless, Washburne later claimed that Seward had overslept and arrived at the Willard two minutes after Lincoln, "much out of breath and somewhat chagrined to think he had not been up in season to be at the depot on the arrival of the train."

What is certain is that Seward greeted the president-elect with "a virtuoso performance," attempting to control his every movement and make himself indispensable to the relative newcomer. The two men breakfasted together that morning in the Willard, choosing from an elaborate menu of "fried oysters, steak and onions, blanc mange and *pâté de foie gras.*" Then, after breakfast, Seward escorted Lincoln to the White House to meet with President Buchanan and his cabinet. Lincoln's surprise call disconcerted Harriet Lane, Buchanan's niece, who had brilliantly performed the role of hostess for her bachelor uncle. The appearance of Buchanan's successor signaled the end of her days in the White House. Afterward, she had few kind words to say about the new couple who would occupy her former home. She likened Lincoln to the "tall awkward Irishman who waits on the door," but insisted that the doorman was "the best looking." About Mary, Harriet claimed, she had heard only that she "is awfully *western*, loud & unrefined."

From the White House, Seward shepherded Lincoln to see General Scott. An inch taller than Lincoln and twice his weight, the old hero of the Mexican War was now scarcely able to walk. After the conversation with Scott, Seward and Lincoln drove together for an hour through the streets of Washington. Pressing issues, particularly the still-unfinished cabinet, required immediate attention. Months earlier, Lincoln had promised Weed and Seward that if John Gilmer of North Carolina would accept a seat, he would offer him a position. Seward considered the inclusion of a Unionist Southerner vital in retaining the border states, and Lincoln also considered Gilmer the best choice due to his "*living* position in the South." Gilmer had failed to respond to Lincoln's invitation to visit him in Springfield, however, and Seward had been unable to secure a positive reply.

Simon Cameron remained a candidate whom Seward considered a necessary ingredient in the cabinet. Five weeks earlier, Seward had warned Lincoln that "to grieve as well as disrespect [Cameron] would produce great embarrassment. . . . I should dread exceedingly the army of Cameron's friends in hostility." In fact, after much painful deliberation, Lincoln had decided to offer Cameron a place. During his train trip through Pennsylvania, he had met with a delegation of Cameron supporters who assured him they were authorized to speak for Governor Curtin and Alexander McClure. All the charges against Cameron had been withdrawn, they told Lincoln; the state now stood strongly behind him. Apparently the fear that Pennsylvania might have no representation in the administration had brought warring factions to agree on Cameron. Telling the delegation that "the information relieved him greatly," Lincoln remained unwilling to make his decision until he reached Washington. The problem was that Cameron still insisted on the Treasury position, which Lincoln had resolved to give to Chase. Only when Cameron realized he was not in a position to dictate what he wanted did he grudgingly accept the War Department.

When his carriage ride with Seward ended, Lincoln rested for an hour in his suite before receiving his old adversary Stephen Douglas at two-thirty. Then, while Seward went to the train station to greet Mary, he welcomed the Blairs, Francis Senior and Montgomery. "The Blairs," Hay wrote in his diary, "have to an unusual degree the spirit of a clan. Their family is a close corporation. . . . They have a way of going with a rush for anything they undertake." Lincoln understood all this, but he liked and trusted the old man and knew that he needed former Democrats and hard-liners to counterbalance Seward.

The Blairs had been appalled by Seward's conciliatory speech. Old Man Blair warned Lincoln that Seward's compromises resembled Mr. Buchanan's approach and would only invite more aggression from the South. Indeed, the Blairs so violently championed their hard-line position that they effectively advocated war. Monty contended that so long as the Southerners continued to believe "that one Southern man is equal to half a dozen Yankees," they would never submit to anything without a "decisive defeat" on the field. "It will show the Southern people that they wholly mistake the quality of the men they are taught by demagogues to despise." Only as magnanimous victors could Northerners afford to conciliate. Beyond Seward's premature willingness to compromise, Francis Blair, Sr., cautioned that the New Yorker would prove a perpetual thorn in Lincoln's side. "In your cabinet his restless vanity & ambition would do nothing but mischief. He would set himself up as a rival . . . & make an influence to supplant all aspirants for the succession."

While Lincoln generally respected the opinions of Old Man Blair, he had long since determined that he needed Seward for the premier post in his administration. He also hoped, however, to include Monty Blair in his cabinet. While the availability of a true Southerner would have left no room for the border-state Blair, the attempt to enlist Gilmer had apparently failed. Lincoln was prepared to offer Monty a position, most likely as U.S. Postmaster General.

As Lincoln was conversing with the Blairs, Seward made his way through the large crowd at the train depot. Unaware that Lincoln had arrived earlier that day, the throng had gathered to welcome him on the special four o'clock train. When the train finally arrived, one reporter noted, "four carriages were driven up to the rear car, from which Mr. Seward soon emerged with Mrs. Lincoln" and her sons. Once it became clear that the president-elect was not aboard, the assembled citizens began to voice their dismay. "The rain was pouring down in torrents, there was no escape, and the crowd indulged in one or two jokes, a little whistling, and considerable swearing." This was not the welcome Mary had expected. Leaning upon

Seward's arm as she alighted at the Willard, she was anxious. She had distrusted Seward from the start, fearing that he would be a continuing rival to her husband; now she was forced to depend on him during her less than triumphant entry into the city that would be her new home.

That evening Lincoln visited Seward's home for a dinner hosted by Fred's wife, Anna, who served as mistress of the household while Frances remained in Auburn to complete some ongoing work on her home. Although Frances would visit several times a year, she never made Washington her home, leaving all the social duties to her husband, son, and daughter-in-law.

Lincoln returned to the Willard for a nine o'clock reception with the members of the Peace Convention, called by Virginia to attempt a compromise before Congress adjourned on March 4. As the convention members from both South and North assembled, one of the delegates, Lucius Chittenden, representing Vermont, called upon Lincoln in his suite to brief him on the workings of the convention. Chittenden knew that many of the Southern delegates had come simply "to scoff" or "to nourish their contempt for the 'rail-splitter.' " He could not imagine how Lincoln, who had traveled for ten days and "just escaped a conspiracy against his life," could face a gathering in which so many were openly hostile. Yet Lincoln's "wonderful vivacity surprised every spectator," Chittenden marveled. "He spoke apparently without premeditation, with a singular ease of manner and facility of expression."

Representing Ohio was Salmon Chase, whom Lincoln had not seen since their meeting in Springfield. Still uncertain whether he would have a place in the cabinet, Chase stiffly assumed the responsibility of introducing Lincoln to the members of the delegation. Lincoln, Chittenden recalled, "had some apt observation for each person ready the moment he heard his name." The introductions complete, a lively discussion ensued.

In the end, the Peace Convention produced no proposal that could command a majority in Congress, indicating that the time for compromise had passed. That evening at the Willard, however, the delegates had gotten a revelatory glimpse of the president-elect. "He has been both misjudged and misunderstood by the Southern people," William Rives of Virginia said. "They have looked upon him as an ignorant, self-willed man, incapable of independent judgment, full of prejudices, willing to be used as a tool by more able men. This is all wrong. He will be the head of his administration, and he will do his own thinking." Judge Thomas Ruffin of North Carolina considered Lincoln's unwillingness to make concessions on the territorial issue a great "misfortune," but was relieved to hear of his hearty support of the Constitution.

The next morning, a "clear and blustering" day with "a wind that sweeps over this city with mighty power," Seward escorted Lincoln to St. John's Episcopal Church; then, returning to Seward's house, they conferred for two hours. "Governor Seward, there is one part of my work that I shall have to leave largely to you," Lincoln said. "I shall have to depend upon you for taking care of these matters of foreign affairs, of which I know so little, and with which I reckon you are familiar." At some point that morning, Lincoln handed Seward a draft of his inaugural address and asked for his suggestions.

The following day, Seward and Lincoln made an informal visit to the House and the Senate. Senators from all parties congregated to greet Lincoln. Even firebrand Southerners who refused to acknowledge his presence were consumed with curiosity. Virginia's James Mason, one reporter noted, "affected *nonchalance* and pretended to be writing, but for the life of him he could not help looking askance, from time to time; and it may be doubted if what he wrote could be translated into plain English."

One reporter commented that Lincoln's "face has not yet become familiar enough to be popularly recognized here," so "he passed to and from the Capitol yesterday without catching the attention of the multitude." His informal visit, the *New York Times* noted, was "without a precedent. His illustrious predecessors . . . deemed it incompatible with the stately dignity of the Executive of the Union, to visit the coordinate departments of the Government. Clearly, the Railsplitter has, in following the dictates of his own feelings, rightly interpreted the proprieties of his position."

In the days ahead, Lincoln confirmed two more positions for his cabinet. He chose Caleb Smith, his old Whig colleague, over Schuyler Colfax for the Department of the Interior, despite widespread support for Colfax. In a gracious letter to Colfax, he explained: "I had partly made up my mind in favor of Mr. Smith—not conclusively of course—before your name was mentioned in that connection. When you were brought forward I said 'Colfax is a young man—is already in position—is running a brilliant career, and is sure of a bright future in any event. With Smith, it is now or never.' I considered either abundantly competent, and decided on the ground I have stated." Mentioning that Colfax had not supported him during his Senate campaign against Douglas, Lincoln begged him to "not do me the injustice to suppose, for a moment, that I remembered any thing against you in malice."

At one point, Norman Judd had been in consideration for a cabinet appointment, but the opposition to him in Illinois from Lincoln's campaign manager, David Davis, and a host of others was very strong. Mary Lincoln herself had written to Davis as an ally in the cause against Judd, charging that "*Judd* would cause trouble & dissatisfaction, & if Wall Street testifies correctly, his business transactions, have not always borne inspection." Mary, unlike her husband, was unable to forgive Judd's role in Trumbull's victory over Lincoln in 1855. In the end, Lincoln decided he alone would provide sufficient representation for his state of Illinois. Instead, he offered Judd a ministry post in Berlin, which was more agreeable to Judd's wife, Adeline.

For weeks, the newspapers had been reporting that Gideon Welles was the most likely candidate from New England. Though bitterly opposed by Seward and Weed, Welles had the full confidence of the more hard-line members of the party. Nonetheless, Welles was "in an agony of suspense during that last week in February," as he waited in Hartford for positive word. When his son Edgar eagerly wrote from Yale that he would love to accompany his father to Washington for the inauguration, Welles replied: "It is by no means certain, my son, that I shall go myself . . . if not invited [by Lincoln] I shall not go at all."

Finally, on March 1, Welles received a telegram from Vice President–elect Hannibal Hamlin in Washington: "I desire to see you here forthwith." In his hurry to catch the train the next day, he discovered he had left his toiletries behind. More disconcerting, he arrived at the Willard to find the corridors so crowded that his trunks were temporarily mislaid, forcing him to remain in his rumpled clothes. Fortunately, Lincoln was dining elsewhere that evening, and a meeting was called for the following day. Lincoln offered him the navy portfolio.

With hard-liners Blair and Welles on board to balance Cameron and Bates, Lincoln still faced a difficult problem. He had resolved from the start to bring both Seward and Chase into his cabinet, but as the inauguration approached, each man's supporters violently opposed the appointment of the other. "The struggle for Cabinet portfolios waxes warmer, hourly," the *Evening Star* reported on March 1. Seward's delegation met with Lincoln on March 2, claiming that Chase would make the cabinet untenable for Seward. Hoping Lincoln would agree to forsake Chase, they were dismayed when, instead, Lincoln countered that although he still preferred a cabinet with both men, he might consider offering State to William Dayton and giving Seward the ministry to Great Britain.

After receiving the report of his friends, and beleaguered by the strength of the opposition to him, Seward sent a note to Lincoln asking to withdraw his earlier acceptance of the State portfolio. Lincoln waited two days to answer. "I can't afford to let Seward take the first trick," he told Nicolay. Nonetheless, his gracious manner again soothed a troubled situation. In his reply to Seward's withdrawal note, he wrote: "It is the subject of most painful solicitude with me; and I feel constrained to beg that you will countermand the withdrawal. The public interest, I think, demands that you should; and my personal feelings are deeply inlisted in the same direction."

Never genuinely desiring to withdraw, but hoping to pressure Lincoln to drop Chase, Seward rescinded his decision and accepted. In a letter to Frances, the New Yorker portrayed his waffling reversals in the most honorable light: "The President is determined that he will have a compound Cabinet; and that it shall be peaceful, and even permanent. I was at one time on the point of refusing—nay, I did refuse, for a time to hazard myself in the experiment. But a distracted country appeared before me; and I withdrew from that position. I believe I can endure as much as any one; and may be that I can endure enough to make the experiment successful. At all events I did not dare to go home, or to England, and leave the country to chance."

All that remained was for Lincoln to secure Chase's acceptance. He had not exchanged a single word with Chase about the appointment since his arrival in Washington. Now, without consulting the proud Ohioan, Lincoln sent Chase's nomination as treasury secretary to the Senate. Chase was on the Senate floor when a number of his colleagues came over to congratulate him. "Ever conscious of his own importance and overly sensitive to matters of protocol," he promptly called on the president to express his anger and his decision to decline the appointment. In the course of their ensuing conversation, Chase later recalled, Lincoln "referred to the embarrassment my declination would occasion him." Chase promised to consider the matter further, and, as Lincoln hoped, he "finally yielded."

In the end, Lincoln had unerringly read the character of Chase and slyly called Seward's bluff. Through all the countervailing pressures, he had achieved the cabinet he wanted from the outset—a mixture of former Whigs and Democrats, a combination of conciliators and hard-liners. He would be the head of his own administration, the master of the most unusual cabinet in the history of the country.

His opponents had been certain that Lincoln would fail in this first test of leadership. "The construction of a Cabinet," one editorial advised, "like the courting of a shrewd girl, belongs to a branch of the fine arts with which the new Executive is not acquainted. There are certain little tricks which go far beyond the arts familiar to the stump, and the cross-road tavern, whose comprehension requires a delicacy of thought and subtlety of perception, secured only by experience."

In fact, as John Nicolay later wrote, Lincoln's "first decision was one of great courage and self-reliance." Each of his rivals was "sure to feel that the wrong man had been nominated." A less confident man might have surrounded himself with personal supporters who would never question his authority. James Buchanan, for example, had deliberately chosen men who thought as he did. Buchanan believed, Allan Nevins writes, that a president "who tried to conciliate opposing elements by placing determined agents of each in his official family would find that he had simply strengthened discord, and had deepened party divisions." While it was possible that his team of rivals would devour one another, Lincoln determined that "he must risk the dangers of faction to overcome the dangers of rebellion."

Later, Joseph Medill of the *Chicago Tribune* asked Lincoln why he had chosen a cabinet comprised of enemies and opponents. He particularly questioned the president's selection of the three men who had been his chief rivals for the Republican nomination, each of whom was still smarting from the loss.

Lincoln's answer was simple, straightforward, and shrewd. "We needed the strongest men of the party in the Cabinet. We needed to hold our own people together. I had looked the party over and concluded that these were the very strongest men. Then I had no right to deprive the country of their services."

Seward, Chase, Bates—they were indeed strong men. But in the end, it was the prairie lawyer from Springfield who would emerge as the strongest of them all.

PART II

MASTER AMONG MEN

In this composite, Lincoln has taken over Seward's central position in the Republican Party, becoming the clear leader of a most unusual team of rivals.

Second Floor of Lincoln White House

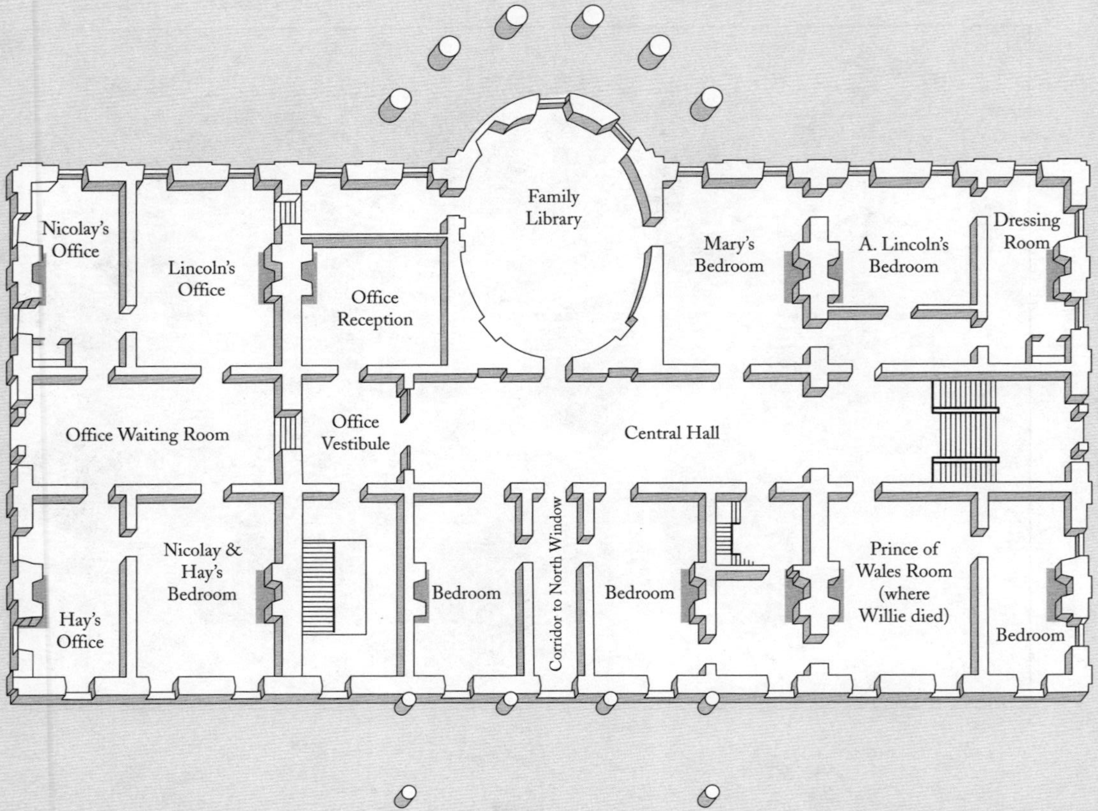

Family Library

Nicolay's Office

Lincoln's Office

Office Reception

Mary's Bedroom

A. Lincoln's Bedroom

Dressing Room

Office Waiting Room

Office Vestibule

Central Hall

Nicolay & Hay's Bedroom

Bedroom

Corridor to North Window

Bedroom

Prince of Wales Room (where Willie died)

Hay's Office

Bedroom

CHAPTER 12

"MYSTIC CHORDS OF MEMORY"

ON THE NIGHT BEFORE her husband's March 4 inauguration, Mary Lincoln was unable to sleep. She stood by her window in the Willard Hotel and watched strangers swarming in the darkened streets below. Though all the major hotels had laid out mattresses and cots in every conceivable open space, filling parlors, reception rooms, and lobbies, thousands were still left to wander the streets and wait for the great day to dawn.

Lincoln rose before sunrise to look over the inaugural address he had been crafting in his peculiar fashion. According to Nicolay, "Lincoln often resorted to the process of cumulative thought." He would reduce complex ideas to paragraphs and sentences, and then days or weeks later return to the same passage and polish it further "to elaborate or to conclude his point or argument." While Seward or Chase would consult countless books, drawing from ancient to modern history to illustrate and refine their arguments, Lincoln built the armature of his inaugural out of four documents: the Constitution, Andrew Jackson's nullification proclamation, Daniel Webster's memorable "Liberty and Union Forever" speech, and Clay's address to the Senate arguing for the Compromise of 1850.

Lincoln faced a dual challenge in this long-awaited speech, his first significant public address since his election. It was imperative that he convey his staunch resolution to defend the Union and to carry out his responsibilities as president, while at the same time mitigating the anxieties of the Southern states. Finding the balance between force and conciliation was not easy, and his early draft tilted more toward the forceful side. Among the first people to see the draft was Orville Browning. Browning had intended to accompany Lincoln on the train from Springfield to Washington, but finding "such a crowd of hangers on gathering about him," he decided to end the journey in Indianapolis. Before Browning left, Lincoln handed him a copy of his draft.

Browning focused on one imprudent passage that he feared would be seen in the South as a direct "threat, or menace," and would prove "irritating even in the border states." Lincoln had pledged: "All the power at my disposal will be used to reclaim the public property and places which have fallen; to hold, occupy and possess these, and all other property and places belonging to the government. . . ." Browning suggested he delete the promise to reclaim what had already fallen, such as Fort Moultrie or Castle Pinckney, limiting himself to "hold, occupy, and possess" what was still in Union hands. "In any conflict which may ensue between the government and the seceding States," Browning argued, "it is very important that the traitors shall be the aggressors, and that they be kept constantly and palpably in the wrong." Though in a number of private conversations during the long secession winter Lincoln had expressed his determination to take back the fallen properties, he accepted Browning's argument and took out the promise to reclaim places that the seceding states had already taken.

Of all who read the draft, it was Seward who had the largest impact on Lincoln's inaugural address. Seward had read the initial draft with a heavy heart. Though he believed Lincoln's argument for the perpetuity of the Union was "strong and conclusive," he felt that the bellicose tone of the text would render useless all the hard work, all the risks taken during the previous weeks to stop the secession movement from expanding. Working on the draft for hours, seated in his favorite swivel chair, Seward wrote a long, thoughtful letter to Lincoln that contained scores of revisions. Taken together, his suggested changes softened the tone of the draft, made it more conciliatory toward the South.

Lincoln's text had opened on a forceful note, pledging himself "bound by duty . . . upon the plainest grounds of good faith" to abide by the Chicago platform, without "liberty to shift his position." Since many seceders considered the Chicago platform one of the touchstones of their withdrawal from the Union, this was clearly a provocative beginning. Even Bates had lambasted the Chicago platform as "exclusive and defiant . . . needlessly exposing the party to the specious charge of favoring negro equality." Seward argued that unless Lincoln eliminated his words pledging strict adherence to the platform, he would "give such advantages to the Disunionists that Virginia and Maryland will secede, and we shall within ninety, perhaps within sixty, days be obliged to fight the South for this capital. . . . In that case the dismemberment of the republic would date from the inauguration of a Republican Administration." Lincoln agreed to delete the reference to the Chicago platform entirely.

Seward also criticized Lincoln's pledge to reclaim fallen properties and to hold those still belonging to the government. He suggested that the text refer more "ambiguously" to "the exercise of power." Lincoln had already planned to change the text as Browning advised, so he ignored this overly compromising suggestion and retained his pledge to "hold, occupy and possess" the properties still belonging to the federal government, including Fort Sumter.

Seward's revisions are evident in nearly every paragraph. He qualified some, removed rough edges in others. Where Lincoln had referred to the secession ordinances and the acts of violence as "treasonable," Seward substituted the less accusatory "revolutionary." With the *Dred Scott* decision in mind, Lincoln warned against turning the "government over to the despotism of the few men [life officers] composing the court." Seward deleted the word "despotism" and elevated the Court to read "that eminent tribunal."

Lincoln had decried the idea of an amendment to the Constitution to ensure that Congress could never interfere with slavery in the states where it already existed. "I am, rather, for the old ship," he had written, "and the chart of the old pilots." Lincoln's stance put Seward in a difficult position; at Lincoln's behest, he had introduced the controversial resolution that called for the amendment in the first place. Lincoln's reversal now would leave Seward exposed. Treading carefully, Seward suggested that Lincoln acknowledge a diversity of opinion surrounding the proposed amendment, and that his own views would only "aggravate the dispute." As it happened,

Lincoln went further than Seward had suggested. In the early hours of the night before the inauguration, Congress, in its final session, had passed the proposed amendment "to the effect that the federal government, shall never interfere with the domestic institutions of the States." In light of this action, Lincoln reversed his position yet again. He revised his passage to say that since Congress had proposed the amendment, and since he believed "such a provision to now be implied constitutional law, I have no objection to its being made express, and irrevocable."

Seward's greatest contribution to the tone and substance of the inaugural address was in its conclusion. Lincoln's finale threw down the gauntlet to the South: "With *you*, and not with *me*, is the solemn question of 'Shall it be peace, or a sword?' " Seward recommended a very different closing, designed "to meet and remove prejudice and passion in the South, and despondency and fear in the East. Some words of affection—some of calm and cheerful confidence." He suggested two alternate endings. Lincoln drew upon Seward's language to create his immortal coda.

Seward suggested: "I close. We are not we must not be aliens or enemies but fellow countrymen and brethren. Although passion has strained our bonds of affection too hardly they must not, I am sure they will not be broken. The mystic chords which proceeding from so many battle fields and so many patriot graves pass through all the hearts and all the hearths in this broad continent of ours will yet again harmonize in their ancient music when breathed upon by the guardian angel of the nation."

Lincoln proceeded to recast and sharpen Seward's patriotic sentiments into a concise and powerful poetry: "I am loth to close. We are not enemies, but friends. We must not be enemies. Though passion may have strained, it must not break our bonds of affection. The mystic chords of memory, stretching from every battle-field, and patriot grave, to every living heart and hearthstone, all over this broad land, will yet swell the chorus of the Union, when again touched, as surely they will be, by the better angels of our nature." Most significant, Seward's "guardian angel" breathes down on the nation from above; Lincoln's "better angels" are inherent in our nature as a people.

• • •

AFTER PLACING HIS FINISHING TOUCHES on the final draft, Lincoln read the speech to his family. Then he asked to be left alone. Several blocks away, Seward had finished reading the morning newspapers and was getting ready to go to the Capitol when a chorus of voices outside attracted his attention. Hundreds of devoted followers were assembled in front of his house. Moved by the spirit of the serenade, Seward spoke to them with emotion. "I have been a representative of my native State in the Senate for twelve years, and there is no living being who can look in my face and say that in all that time I have not done my duty toward all—the high and the low, the rich and the poor, the bond and the free."

Perhaps this show of popular support softened the wrenching realization that his chance had come and gone. When a congressman argued with him that a certain politician would be disappointed if he didn't get an appointment in the new administration, Seward lost his composure: "Disappointment! You speak to me of disappointment. To me, who was justly entitled to the Republican nomination for the presidency, and who had to stand aside and see it given to a little Illinois lawyer!"

As the clock struck noon, President Buchanan arrived at the Willard to escort the president-elect to the ceremony. Lincoln, only fifty-two, tall and energetic in his shiny new black suit and stovepipe hat, presented a striking contrast to the short and thickset Buchanan, nearly seventy, who had a sorrowful expression on his aged face. As they moved arm in arm toward the open carriage, the Marine Band played "Hail to the Chief." The carriage made its way up Pennsylvania Avenue, while cheering crowds and hundreds of dignitaries mingled uneasily with the hundreds of troops put in place by General Scott to guard against an attempted assassination. Sharpshooters looked down from windows and rooftops. Cavalry were placed strategically throughout the entire route.

Along the way, an ominous sound was heard. "A sharp, cracking, rasping sort of detonation, at regular intervals of perhaps three seconds" set everyone's nerves on edge, the Washington *Evening Star* reported. The perplexed police finally identified the sound as issuing from the New England delegation. They wore their customary "pegged" shoes, with heavy soles designed for the ice and snow of the north country. In the more temperate climate of Washington, the "heat and dryness of the atmosphere" had apparently "shrunk the peg timber in the foot-gear excessively, occasioning a general squeaking with every movement, swelling in the aggregate" when the delegation marched in step.

As the day brightened, Washington, according to one foreign observer, "assume[d] an almost idyllic garb." Though the city "displayed an unfinished aspect"—with the monument to President Washington still only one third of its intended height, the new Capitol dome two years away from completion, and most of the streets unpaved—the numerous trees and gardens were very pleasing, creating the feel of "a large rural village."

The appearance of Lincoln on the square platform constructed out from the east portico of the Capitol was met with loud cheers from more than thirty thousand spectators. Mary sat behind her husband, their three sons beside her. In the front row, along with Lincoln, sat President Buchanan, Senator Douglas, and Chief Justice Taney, three of the four men Lincoln had portrayed in his "House Divided" speech as conspiring carpenters intent on destroying the original house the framers had designed and built.

Lincoln's old friend Edward Baker, who had moved to Oregon and won a seat in the Senate, introduced the president-elect. Lincoln made his way to the little table from which he was meant to speak. Noting Lincoln's uncertainty as to where to place his stovepipe hat, Senator Douglas reached over, took the hat, and placed it on his own lap. Then Lincoln began. His clear high voice, trained in the outdoor venues of the Western states, could be heard from the far reaches of the crowd.

Having dropped his opening pledge of strict fealty to the Chicago platform, Lincoln moved immediately to calm the anxieties of the Southern people, quoting an earlier speech in which he had promised that he had "no purpose, directly or indirectly, to interfere with the institution of slavery in the States where it exists. I believe I have no lawful right to do so, and I have no inclination to do so." He turned then to the controversial Fugitive Slave Law, repeating his tenet that while "safeguards" should be put in place to ensure that free men were not illegally seized, the U.S. Constitution required that the slaves "shall be delivered upon claim of the party to whom such service or labor may be due." Although he understood that the Fugitive Slave Law offended "the moral sense" of many people in the North, he felt compelled, under the Constitution, to enforce it.

Lincoln went on to make his powerful case for continued federal authority over what he insisted, "in view of the Constitution and the laws," was an "unbroken" Union. While "there needs to be no bloodshed," he intended to execute the laws, "to hold, occupy, and possess the property, and places belonging to the government, and to collect the duties and imposts; but beyond what may be necessary for these objects, there will be no invasion—no using of force against, or among the people anywhere. . . .

"Physically speaking, we cannot separate," Lincoln declared, prophetically adding: "Suppose you go to war, you cannot fight always; and when, after much loss on both sides, and no gain on either, you cease fighting, the identical old questions, as to terms of intercourse, are again upon you. . . .

"In *your* hands, my dissatisfied fellow countrymen, and not in *mine*, is the momentous issue of civil war. The government will not assail *you*. You can have no conflict, without being yourselves the aggressors."

He closed with the lyrical assurance that "the mystic chords of memory . . . will yet swell the chorus of the Union, when again touched, as surely as they will be, by the better angels of our nature."

At the end of the address, Chief Justice Taney walked slowly to the table. The Bible was opened, and Abraham Lincoln was sworn in as the sixteenth President of the United States.

• • •

"THE MANSION was in a perfect state of readiness" when the Lincolns arrived, Mary's cousin Elizabeth Grimsley observed. "A competent chef, with efficient butler and waiters, under the direction of the accomplished Miss Harriet Lane, had an elegant dinner prepared." As Buchanan bade farewell, he said to Lincoln, "If you are as happy, my dear sir, on entering the house as I am in leaving it and returning home, you are the happiest man in this country." After some hasty unpacking, the Lincolns dressed for the Inaugural Ball, held in the rear of the City Hall, in a room referred to as the Muslim Palace of Aladdin "because of the abundance of white draperies trimmed with blue used in its decoration." Brightened by five enormous chandeliers, the room accommodated two thousand people, though the hooped crinolines worn by the women took up a good deal of space. Seward was there with his daughter-in-law Anna. Chase was accompanied by the lovely Kate. Still, this night Mary shone as the brightest star. "Dressed all in blue, with a necklace and bracelets of gold and pearls," she danced the quadrille with her old beau Stephen Douglas and remained at the ball for several hours after the departure of her exhausted husband.

While the party was still in full swing, word of Lincoln's inaugural speech was making its way across the country, carried by telegraph and printed in dozens of evening newspapers. In Auburn, Frances and Fanny waited in suspense throughout the night for the paper to arrive. Finally, Fanny heard a sound downstairs and raced to find out the news. "What an inappreciable relief," Fanny wrote in her diary when she read that the ceremony went off without violence. "For months I have felt constant anxiety for Father's safety—& of course joined in the fears so often expressed that Lincoln would never see the 5th of March." The news traveled more slowly west of St. Joseph, Missouri, where the telegraph lines stopped. Dozens of pony express riders, traveling in relays, carried the text of the address to the Pacific Coast. They did their job well. In a record time of "seven days and seventeen hours," Lincoln's words could be read in Sacramento, California.

Reactions to his speech varied widely, depending on the political persuasion of the commentators. Republican papers lauded the address as "grand and admirable in every respect," and "convincing in argument, concise and pithy in manner." It was "eminently conciliatory," the *Philadelphia Bulletin* observed, extolling the president's "determination to secure the rights of the whole country, of every State under the Constitution." The *Commercial Advertiser* of New York claimed that the inaugural was "the work of Mr. Lincoln's own pen and hand, unaltered by any to whom he confided its contents."

In Northern Democratic papers, the tone was less charitable. A "wretchedly botched and unstatesmanlike paper," the *Hartford Times* opined. "It is he that is the nullifier," the Albany *Atlas and Argus* raged. "It is he that defies the will of the majority. It is he that initiates Civil War." Not surprisingly, negative reactions were stronger in the South. The *Richmond Enquirer* argued that the address was "couched in the cool, unimpassioned, deliberate language of the fanatic . . . pursuing the promptings of fanaticism even to the dismemberment of the Government with the horrors of civil war." In ominous language, the Wilmington, North Carolina, *Herald* warned that the citizens of America "might as well open their eyes to the solemn fact that war is inevitable."

But beneath the blustery commentary in the majority of Southern papers, the historian Benjamin Thomas notes, the address "won some favorable comment in the all-important loyal slave states" of Virginia and North Carolina. This was the audience Seward had targeted when he told Lincoln to soften the tone of his speech. Indeed, Seward was greatly relieved, not only because he realized many of his suggestions had been adopted, but because Lincoln's conciliatory stance had given him cover with his critics in Congress. He could now leave the Senate, he told his wife, "without getting any bones broken," content with having provided a foundation "on which an Administration can stand."

Likewise, Charles Francis Adams, Sr., felt that a great burden had been lifted from his shoulders when Lincoln accepted the controversial amendment that prevented Congress from ever interfering with slavery. Having sponsored the amendment in the House, to the great dismay of the hard-liners, Adams now felt that he had "been fully justified in the face of the country by the head of the nation as well as of the Republican party. . . . Thus ends this most trying period of our history. . . . I should be fortunate if I closed my political career now. I have gained all that I can for myself and I shall never have such another opportunity to benefit my country."

Of the reactions to the inaugural speech, perhaps the most portentous came from within the Republican Party itself. Radicals and abolitionists were disheartened by what they considered an appeasing tone. The news of Lincoln's election had initially provided some desperately needed hope to the black abolitionist Frederick Douglass.

The dramatic life of the former slave who became an eloquent orator and writer was well known in the North. He had been owned by several cruel slaveholders, but his second master's kindly wife had taught him to read. When the master found out, he stopped the instruction immediately, warning his wife that "it was unlawful, as well as unsafe, to teach a slave to read . . . there would be no keeping him. It would forever unfit him to be a slave. . . . It would make him . . . discontented and unhappy." These words proved prescient. Young Douglass soon felt that "learning to read had been a curse rather than a blessing. It had given me a view of my wretched condition, without the remedy." He fervently wished that he were dead or perhaps an animal—"Any thing, no matter what, to get rid of thinking!" Only the faraway hope of escaping to freedom kept him alive. While waiting six years for his chance, he surreptitiously learned to write.

At the age of twenty, Douglass managed to escape from Maryland to New York, eventually becoming a lecturer with the Massachusetts Anti-Slavery Society, headed by William Lloyd Garrison. His autobiography made him a celebrity in antislavery circles, allowing him to edit his own monthly paper in Rochester, New York. Throughout all his writings, the historian David Blight argues, there was "no more pervasive theme in Douglass' thought than the simple sustenance of *hope* in a better future for blacks in America."

Douglass believed that the election of a Republican president foretold a rupture in the power of the slaveocracy. "It has taught the North its strength, and shown the South its weakness. More important still, it has demonstrated the possibility of electing, if not an Abolitionist, at least an *anti-slavery reputation* to the Presidency." But when Douglass read the inaugural, beginning with Lincoln's declaration that he had "no lawful power to interfere with slavery in the States," and worse still, no "*inclination*" to do so, he found little reason for optimism. More insufferable was Lincoln's readiness to catch fugitive slaves, "to shoot them down if they rise against their oppressors, and to prohibit the Federal Government *irrevocably* from interfering for their deliverance." The whole tone of the speech, Douglass claimed, revealed Lincoln's compulsion to grovel "before the foul and withering curse of slavery. Some thought we had in Mr. Lincoln the nerve and decision of an Oliver Cromwell; but the result shows that we merely have a continuation of the Pierces and Buchanans."

• • •

THE WHITE HOUSE FAMILY QUARTERS were then confined to the west end of the second floor. Lincoln chose a small bedroom with a large dressing room on the southwest side. Mary took the more spacious room adjacent to her husband's, while Willie and Tad occupied a bedroom across the hall. Beyond the ample sleeping quarters, there was only one other private space—an oval room, filled with bookcases, that Mary turned into the family's library. At the east end of the same floor was a sleeping chamber shared by Nicolay and Hay and a small, narrow workspace that opened onto the president's simply furnished office. The rest of the mansion was largely open to the public. In the first few weeks, Seward reported to his wife, "the grounds, halls, stairways, closets" were overrun with hundreds of people, standing in long winding lines and waving their letters of introduction in desperate hope of securing a job.

For Willie and Tad, now ten and almost eight, respectively, the early days in the White House were filled with great adventures. They ran from floor to floor, inspecting every room. They talked with everyone along the way, "from Edward, the door keeper, Stackpole, the messenger, to the maids and scullions." Willie was "a noble, beautiful boy," Elizabeth Grimsley observed, "of great mental activity, unusual intelligence, wonderful memory, methodical, frank and loving, a counterpart of his father, save that he was handsome." Willie spent hours memorizing railroad timetables and would entertain his friends by conducting "an imaginary train from Chicago to New York with perfect precision" and dramatic flair. He was an avid reader, a budding writer, and generally sweet-tempered, all reminiscent of his father.

Tad, to whom Willie was devoted, bore greater resemblance to his mother. Healthy and high-spirited, he had a blazing temper, which disappeared as quickly as it came. He was a "merry, spontaneous fellow, bubbling over with innocent fun, whose laugh rang through the house, when not moved to tears." Irrepressible and undisciplined, never hesitant to interrupt his father in the midst of a cabinet meeting, he was "the life, as also the worry of the household." A speech impediment made it hard for anyone outside his family to understand his words, but he never stopped talking. He had, John Hay recalled, "a very bad opinion of books and no opinion of discipline."

The boys harried the staff at the executive mansion, racing through the hallways, playing advocate for the most anguished office seekers, organizing little plays in the garret, and setting off all the servants' bells at the same time. Fearing that her boys would grow lonely and isolated, Mary found them two lively companions in twelve-year-old Horatio Nelson "Bud" Taft and his eight-year-old brother, Halsey, nicknamed "Holly."

Together with their older sister, Julia, who later wrote a small book recording their adventures in the White House, the Taft children quickly formed a tight circle with Willie and Tad. "If there was any motto or slogan of the White House during the early years," Julia recalled, "it was this: 'Let the children have a good time.' "

Mary, too, seemed happy at first, surrounded by friends and relatives, who stayed on for weeks after the inauguration. Her confidence that she could handle the demands of first lady was buoyed by the great success of the first evening levee on the Friday after they moved in. Seward had proposed that he would lead off the social season from his own mansion, but Mary immediately took exception. Like her husband, Mary had no desire "to let Seward take the first trick." She insisted that the new administration's first official entertainment take place at the White House. Though she had little time to prepare, she arranged an unforgettable event. "For over two hours," Nicolay wrote his fiancée, Therena, "the crowd poured in as rapidly as the door would admit them, and many climbed in at the windows." The president and first lady shook hands with as many of the five thousand "well dressed and well behaved" guests as they could. Even the blue-blood Charles Francis Adams was impressed by Mary's poise, though he found Lincoln to be wholly ignorant of formal "social courtesy." Nonetheless, according to Nicolay, the levee "was voted by all the 'oldest inhabitants' to have been the most successful one ever known here."

Mary was thrilled. "This is certainly a very charming spot," she wrote her friend Hannah Shearer several weeks later, "& I have formed many delightful acquaintances. Every evening our *blue room*, is filled with the elite of the land, last eve, we had about 40 to call in, to see us *ladies*, from Vice. P. Breckinridge down. . . . I am beginning to feel so perfectly at home, and enjoy every thing so much. The conservatory attached to this house is so delightful." Scarcely concealing her pride at having outdone her older sister Elizabeth, she told Hannah that Elizabeth had so enjoyed herself at the festivities that she "cannot settle down at home, since she has been here."

• • •

A "LIGHT AND CAPRICIOUS" SLEEPER, Lincoln generally awakened early in the morning. Before breakfast he liked to exercise, often by walking around the spacious White House grounds. After a simple meal, usually a single egg and a cup of coffee, he made his way down the corridor to his office, where on cool days a fire blazed in the white marble fireplace with a big brass fender. His worktable stood between two tall windows that faced the south lawn, affording a panorama of the incomplete Washington

Monument, the red-roofed Smithsonian, and the Potomac River. An armchair nearby allowed him to read in comfort, his long legs stretched before him or crossed one over the other.

In the center of the chamber, which doubled as the Cabinet Room, stood a long oak table around which the members arranged themselves in order of precedence. Old maps hung on the wall, and over the mantel, a portrait of President Andrew Jackson. A few sofas and an assortment of chairs completed the furnishings. The musty smell of tobacco, lodged in the draperies from the heavy cigar smoke of the previous president and the new secretary of state, conveyed the atmosphere of the traditional men's club.

When Lincoln entered his office on the first morning after his inauguration, he was confronted with profoundly disturbing news. On his desk, "the very first thing placed in his hands" was a letter from Major Anderson at Fort Sumter. The communication estimated, Lincoln later recalled, "that their provisions would be exhausted before an expedition could be sent to their relief." The letter carried General Winfield Scott's endorsement: "I now see no alternative but a surrender."

The immediacy of this crisis posed great difficulties for Lincoln. His revised inaugural had no longer contained a promise to "reclaim" fallen properties, but Lincoln had most definitely pledged to "hold, occupy and possess" all properties still in Federal hands. No symbol of Federal authority was more important than Fort Sumter. Ever since Major Anderson, in the dead of night on December 26, had surreptitiously moved his troops from Fort Moultrie to the better-protected Sumter, he had become a romantic hero in the North. Surrender of his garrison would be humiliating. Still, the president felt bound by his vow to his "dissatisfied fellow countrymen" that the new "government will not assail *you.* You can have no conflict, without being yourselves the aggressors."

The president needed time to think, but scarcely had a moment "to eat or sleep" amid the crush of office seekers. Hundreds, perhaps thousands, pressed in as soon as the doors were opened, ignoring the barriers set up to keep them in line. As Lincoln moved throughout the house to take his lunch—which was generally limited to bread, fruit, and milk—"he had literally to run the gantlet through the crowds." Each aspirant had a story to tell, a reason why a clerkship in Washington or a job in their local post office or customs house would allow their family to survive. Time and again, Lincoln was faulted for wasting his energies. "You will wear yourself out," Senator Henry Wilson of Massachusetts warned. "They don't want much," Lincoln replied, "they get but little, and I must see them."

Such openheartedness indicated incompetence to many, or, worse, a sign of terrible weakness. He "has no conception of his situation," Sumner told Adams. "He is ignorant, and must have help," Adams agreed, citing Seward as "our only security now." The *New York Times* reproved Lincoln repeatedly, writing disdainfully that he "owes a higher duty to the country . . . than to fritter away the priceless opportunities of the Presidency in listening to the appeals of competing office-hunters." Seward, too, was critical. "The President proposes to do all his work," he wrote home. "Of course he takes that business up, first, which is pressed upon him most."

Somehow Lincoln managed, despite the chaos, to focus upon the crisis at Sumter. Late at night, he would sit in the library, clothed in his "long-skirted faded dressing-gown, belted around his waist," his large leather Bible beside him. He liked to read and think in "his big chair by the window," observed Julia Taft, "in his stocking feet with one long leg crossed over the other, the unshod foot slowly waving back and forth, as if in time to some inaudible music."

Unwilling to accept Scott's assumption that Sumter must be evacuated, Lincoln penned a note to the old general, asking for more specifics. Exactly how long could Anderson hold out? What would it take to resupply him and to reinforce Sumter? Scott's reply laid out a bleak prospect indeed. With the government of South Carolina now preventing the garrison from resupplying in Charleston, Anderson could hold out, Scott estimated, for only twenty-six days. It would require "six to eight months" to assemble the "fleet of war vessels & transports, 5,000 additional regular troops & 20,000 volunteers" necessary to resupply and reinforce the garrison.

Rumors spread that Sumter would soon be surrendered, but Lincoln "was disinclined to hasty action," Welles recorded in his diary, "and wished time for the Administration to get in working order and its policy to be understood." Repeatedly, he called his cabinet into session to discuss the situation. He met with Francis Blair, who, like his son, Monty, believed passionately that the surrender of Sumter "was virtually a surrender of the Union unless under irresistible force—that compounding with treason was treason to the Govt."

At Monty Blair's suggestion, Lincoln met with his brother-in-law, Gustavus Fox, a former navy officer who had developed an ingenious plan for relief by sea. Bread and supplies could be loaded onto two sturdy tugboats, shadowed by a large steamer conveying troops ready to fire if the tugs were opposed. Intrigued, Lincoln asked Fox to present his plan; and the next day, March 15, the cabinet gathered around the long table to discuss the stratagem. Lincoln seldom took his seat, pacing up and down as he spoke. After the meeting, he sent a memo to each of the members, asking for a written response to the following question: "Assuming it to be possible to now provision Fort-Sumpter, under all the circumstances, is it wise to attempt it?"

Seward, who had exerted himself in the previous months trying to mollify the Union's remaining slave states, found the idea of provisioning Sumter and sending troops to South Carolina detestable. From his suite in the old State Department, a two-story brick building containing only thirty-two rooms, Seward drafted his reply, while his son Frederick, who had been confirmed by the Senate as assistant secretary of state, handled the crowds downstairs. In his lengthy reply to the president, Seward reiterated that without the conciliation measures that had solidified the Unionist sentiment in the South, Virginia, North Carolina, Arkansas, and the border states would have joined the Confederacy. The attempt to supply Fort Sumter with armed forces would inevitably provoke the remaining slave states to secede and launch a civil war—that "most disastrous and deplorable of national calamities." Far better, Seward advised, to assume a defensive position, leaving "the necessity for action" in the hands of "those who seek to dismember and subvert this Union. . . . In that case, we should have the spirit of the country and the approval of mankind on our side." His emphatic negative reply probably reached Lincoln within minutes, for the State Department was adjacent to the northern wing of the Treasury Department and connected by a short pathway to the White House.

Chase did not return his answer until the following day, repairing that evening to his suite at the Willard Hotel. Considering his hard-line credentials, Chase returned a surprisingly evasive and equivocal reply: "If the attempt will so inflame civil war as to involve an immediate necessity for the enlistment of armies and the expenditure of millions I cannot advise it." Better, he later explained, to consider "the organization of actual government by the seven seceded states *as an accomplished revolution*—accomplished through the complicity of the late admn.—& letting that confederacy try its experiment." Still, he concluded in his answer to Lincoln, "it seems to me highly improbable" that war will result. "I return, therefore, an affirmative answer."

Every other cabinet officer save Blair rejected the possibility of sustaining Fort Sumter. Bates argued that he was loath "to do any act which may have the semblance, before the world of beginning a civil war." Cameron contended that even if Fox's plan should succeed, which he considered doubtful, the surrender of the fort would remain "an inevitable necessity." Thus, "the sooner it be done, the better." Welles, writing from his second-floor suite in the Navy Department on 17th Street, reasoned that since the "impression has gone abroad that Sumter is to be evacuated and the shock caused by that announcement has done its work," it would only cause further damage to follow "a course that would provoke hostilities." And if it did not succeed, "failure would be attended with untold disaster." In like fashion, Interior Secretary Caleb Smith concluded that while the plan might succeed, "it would not be wise under all the circumstances."

Only Montgomery Blair delivered an unconditional yes, arguing that "every new conquest made by the rebels strengthens their hands at home and their claim to recognition as an independent people abroad." So long as the rebels could claim *"that the Northern men are deficient in the courage necessary to maintain the Government,"* the secession momentum would continue. Just as President Jackson stopped the attempted secession of South Carolina in 1833 by making it clear that punishment would follow, so Lincoln must now take "measures which will inspire respect for the power of the Government and the firmness of those who administer it."

In the end, five cabinet members strongly opposed the resupply and reinforcement of Sumter; one remained ambiguous; one was in favor.

• • •

IN THE DAYS THAT FOLLOWED the cabinet vote, Lincoln appeared to waver. Weed later insisted that on at least three occasions, the president said if he could keep Virginia in the Union, he would give up Sumter. Seward urged that so long as Fort Pickens in Florida remained in Union hands, Sumter's evacuation would matter little. Pickens was fully provisioned and, situated in Pensacola Bay, would be easier than Sumter to defend. Orders had already been issued to reinforce the garrison. However, Lincoln felt that the surrender of Sumter would be "utterly ruinous . . . that, at home, it would discourage the friends of the Union, embolden its adversaries, and go far to insure to the latter, a recognition abroad."

Desiring more information, Lincoln sent Fox to talk directly to Major Anderson and determine exactly how long his supplies would last. Through the intervention of an old friend who was close to the governor of South Carolina, Fox received permission to enter Sumter and meet with Anderson. If his men went on half-rations, Anderson told him, he could last until April 15. At the same time, Lincoln sent Stephen Hurlbut, whom he had known well in Springfield, to Charleston. Hurlbut had grown up in Charleston, and his sister still lived there. Speaking privately to old friends, he could test Seward's assumption that Unionist sentiment throughout the South would continue to strengthen so long as the government refrained from any provocative action or perceived aggression. Hurlbut spent two days in his native city. He returned with "no hesitation in reporting as unquestionable" that Unionist sentiment in both city and state was dead, "that separate nationality is a fixed fact."

While Lincoln was learning more about the facts of the situation, his cabinet colleagues were engaged in a series of petty feuds. Chase considered Smith "a cypher" and Bates "a humdrum lawyer." Seward was furious when Chase and Bates insisted on two appointments in his own district and stated that would be "humiliating" to him. "I would sooner attack either of those gentlemen in the open street," Seward indignantly wrote Lincoln, "than consent to oppose any local appointment they might desire to make in their respective states." From his Treasury Department office overlooking the White House grounds, Chase complained to Lincoln that Seward would "certainly have no cause to congratulate himself if he persists in denying the only favor he *can* show me." Blair Senior, echoing the sentiment of his son, grumbled to Chase that all the best missions abroad had been given to Seward's old Whig friends. "I believe our Republican Party will not endure, unless there is a fusion of the Whig & Democratic element," he noted ruefully.

While the cabinet members squabbled over patronage, they united in their resentment of Seward's preeminent position. They were irritated that he was the one who called the cabinet into session, and the time he spent with Lincoln inspired jealousy. Finally, with Chase as their "spokesman," they requested that cabinet meetings be held at regular times. Lincoln agreed, designating Tuesdays and Fridays at noon.

Still, Seward was recognized as the man who had the president's ear. William Russell of *The Times* in London capitalized on this intimacy when he first arrived in Washington. Russell was then forty-one, a spectacled, lively, rotund Englishman whose sparkling reports from the Crimean War had made him a celebrity in London. At a dinner party on March 26, he was fascinated by Seward, "a subtle, quick man, rejoicing in power . . . fond of badinage, bursting with the importance of state mysteries." The next day, Seward arranged for Russell to slip into a White House reception for the Italian minister. Russell recalled that Lincoln "put out his hand in a very friendly manner, and said, 'Mr. Russell, I am very glad to make your acquaintance, and to see you in this country. The London *Times* is one of the greatest powers in the world—in fact, I don't know anything which has much more power—except perhaps the Mississippi.' "

Russell attended the Lincolns' first state dinner that evening. Arriving at the White House, he noted that Mary "was already seated to receive her guests." He found her features "plain, her nose and mouth of an ordinary type, and her manners and appearance homely, stiffened, however, by the consciousness that her position requires her to be something more than plain Mrs. Lincoln, the wife of the Illinois lawyer; she is profuse in the introduction of the word 'sir' in every sentence."

Once acquainted with all the cabinet officers and the various guests, Russell rated Chase, with his "fine forehead" and his "face indicating energy and power," as "one of the most intelligent and distinguished persons in the whole assemblage." He was particularly taken with Kate Chase, whom he described as "very attractive, agreeable, and sprightly." Kate was in her element, talking "easily, with a low melodious voice . . . her head tilted slightly upward, a faint, almost disdainful smile upon her face, as if she were a titled English lady posing in a formal garden for Gainsborough or Reynolds." As her father's hostess, Kate stood fourth in official Washington society. Her only real rival was Mrs. Lincoln, since neither Ellen Hamlin nor Frances Seward had any desire for social aggrandizement. "In reality, there was no one in Washington to compare with Kate Chase," one of Kate's intimate friends later told the *Cincinnati Enquirer*. "She was the queen of society. Men showered adulation upon her and went on their knees to her. I have never seen a woman who has so much personal charm and magnetism." The possibly apocryphal story spread of Kate's introduction to Mary that night. "I shall be glad to see you any time, Miss Chase," Mary said. Kate replied: "Mrs. Lincoln, I shall be glad to have *you* call on *me* at any time." Though Mary would later manifest intense jealousy of Kate, it is doubtful that Kate's remark spoiled her pleasure that glittering evening.

At the formal dinner, "there was a Babel of small talk," Russell observed, "except when there was an attentive silence caused by one of the President's stories . . . for which he is famous." As he reeled off one humorous anecdote after another, no one could have guessed that earlier that day, Lincoln had received devastating news from General Scott. In a written memorandum, Scott had advised that it was now unlikely, "according to recent information from the South, whether the voluntary evacuation of Fort Sumter alone would have a decisive effect upon the States now wavering between adherence to the Union and secession." Fort Pickens would also have to be abandoned, Scott argued, in order to "give confidence to the eight remaining slave-holding States."

Shortly before the state dinner ended, Lincoln called his cabinet colleagues aside and asked them to follow him into a different room. Montgomery Blair would long remember Lincoln's agitation as he revealed the contents of Scott's report. "A very oppressive silence succeeded," Blair recalled, interrupted only by his own angry retort that Scott was playing "politician and not General," a comment directed at Seward's influence with Scott. Like his son, Blair Senior had long believed that Lincoln should have announced the reinforcement of Sumter at the time of his inauguration and he blamed Seward for Lincoln's "timid temporizing policy." It was Andrew Jackson's motto, he reminded, that "if you temporize, you are lost."

• • •

THAT NIGHT, Lincoln was unable to sleep. The time for musing and assessment was at an end. He must make the decision between a surrender that might compromise the honor of the North and tear it apart, or a reinforcement that might carry the country into civil war. Later he confessed to Browning, "of all the trials I have had since I came here, none begin to compare with those I had between the inauguration and the fall of Fort Sumpter. They were so great that could I have anticipated them, I would not have believed it possible to survive them."

At noon the next day, the cabinet convened. Lincoln presented all the intelligence he had gathered, including Fox's report on Major Anderson's situation and Hurlbut's conclusion that Unionism was essentially dead in South Carolina. Once more the members were asked to submit their opinions in writing. This time, shaped no doubt by Lincoln's presentation and General Scott's disturbing memo, the majority opinion—with only Seward and Smith clearly dissenting—advised that both Sumter and Pickens should be resupplied and reinforced.

Evidence suggests that Lincoln had reached a decision before the cabinet met, for he had already requested that Fox send a list of the "ships, men, and supplies he would need for his expedition." Several hours after the cabinet adjourned, he also implemented a drastic restructuring of his daily schedule. Much as he wanted to give office seekers their due, he needed time and space to consider the grave problems facing the country. He ordered Nicolay to limit visiting hours from 10 a.m. to 3 p.m., ending the hectic burden of twelve-hour days that Nicolay knew "would be impossible to sustain for a great length of time."

For Seward, Lincoln's decision to reinforce Sumter was shattering. He was in his house on the evening of March 29 when George Harrington, assistant secretary of the treasury, knocked at the door. Harrington had just left the White House, where Welles, Blair, and Fox had met with Lincoln, and "it was finally determined, with the President's approval to reinforce Fort Sumter."

"Thunder, George! What are you talking about?" Seward asked. "It cannot be." When Harrington repeated his news, Seward was irate. "I want no more at this time of the Administration which may be defeated. We are not yet in a position to go to war." Seward's success in getting Lincoln to soften the tone of his inaugural address, coupled with the cabinet vote on March 15, decisively echoing his own advice to evacuate Sumter, had left him with the mistaken conviction that he was the power behind a weak president.

Flattering letters from the South had compounded Seward's erroneous assumption. Frederick Roberts in North Carolina assured him that everyone was looking to him for "a peaceful adjustment of the difficulties." While Lincoln, the letter continued, was considered throughout the state as "a 3rd rate man," Seward was looked upon as "the Hector or Atlas of not only his Cabinet, but the giant intellect of the whole north." Another admirer swore that "Unionists look to yourself, and only to you Sir, as a member of the Cabinet—*to save the country*." With these judgments of both the president's failings and his own stature, Seward wholeheartedly agreed. He confided to Adams that Lincoln had "no conception of his situation—much absorption in the details of office dispensation, but little application to great ideas." Adams needed little convincing. Despite accepting the high-ranking appointment as minister to Great Britain, he remained dismissive of Lincoln, writing in his diary: "The man is not equal to the hour." The only hope, he repeatedly wrote, lay in the secretary of state's influence with the president.

For weeks, Seward had acted under "two supreme illusions": first, that he was in reality the man in charge; and second, that Southerners would be appeased by the abandonment of Sumter and would eventually return to the Union. He had risked his good name on his conviction that Lincoln would follow his advice and surrender Sumter. Three commissioners had been sent to Washington by the Confederacy to negotiate, among other issues, the question of the forts. Lincoln, however, had refused to allow any dealings with them on the grounds that direct communication would legitimize the seceded states. Stifled, Seward had resorted to an indirect link through Alabama's John Campbell, who had remained on the Supreme Court despite the secession of his state. After the March 15 cabinet meeting, Seward, believing that his vote to evacuate would soon be confirmed by Lincoln, had sent a message that Campbell relayed to the commissioners, who reported to the Confederacy's capital, then located in Montgomery, Alabama: Sumter "would be evacuated in the next five days."

Desperate to save his own honor and prevent the country from drifting into war, while the administration established no clear-cut policy, Seward composed an extraordinary memo that would become the source of great criticism and controversy. During the afternoon of April 1, Fred Seward recalled, his father wrote "Some thoughts for the President's consideration." Since his "handwriting was almost illegible," he asked Fred to copy it over and bring it personally to Lincoln, not allowing it "to be filed, or to pass into the hands of any clerk."

"We are at the end of a month's Administration, and yet without a policy either domestic or foreign," the contentious memo began. Seward proceeded to reiterate his argument for abandoning Fort Sumter, placing new emphasis on reinforcing Fort Pickens. He asserted that focusing on Fort Pickens rather than on Sumter would allow Lincoln to retain "the symbolism of Federal authority" with far less provocation. Seward's mistake was not the diabolical plot that some critics later charged, but a grave misreading of the situation and a grave misunderstanding of Lincoln.

Seward continued under the heading of "For Foreign Nations," suggesting that Lincoln deflect attention from the domestic crisis by demanding that Spain and France explain their meddling in the Western Hemisphere and that Great Britain, Canada, and Russia account for their threats to intervene in the American crisis. If the explanations of any country proved unsatisfactory, war should be declared. In fact, some such explanations were eventually demanded, convincing European leaders to be more careful in their response to the American situation. It was Seward's wilder proposal of declaring war, if necessary, that would arouse the harsh rebuke of biographers and historians.

Nor did Seward's overreaching end there. The previous February, Seward had informed a German diplomat "that there was no great difference between an elected president of the United States and an hereditary monarch." Neither truly ran things. "The actual direction of public affairs belongs to the leader of the ruling party." Seward had conceived of himself as a prime minister, with Lincoln the figurehead. Testing this presumptuous notion, Seward closed with the idea that "whatever policy we adopt, there must be an energetic prosecution of it. . . . Either the President must do it himself . . . or DEVOLVE it on some member of his Cabinet. . . . It is not in my especial province. But I neither seek to evade nor assume responsibility." As Nicolay later wrote, "had Mr. Lincoln been an envious or a resentful man, he could not have wished for a better occasion to put a rival under his feet." Seward's effrontery easily could have provoked a swift dismissal. Yet, as happened so often, Lincoln showed an "unselfish magnanimity," which was "the central marvel of the whole affair."

The president immediately dashed off a reply to Seward that he would never send, probably preferring to respond in person. Buried in Lincoln's papers, the document was not unearthed until decades later, as Nicolay and Hay labored on their massive Lincoln biography. Lincoln's response was short but pointed. Concerning the assertion that the administration was "without a policy," Lincoln reminded Seward of his inaugural pledge that "the power confided to me will be used to hold, occupy, and possess the property and places belonging to the government." This was the "exact domestic policy" that Seward called for, "with the single exception, that it does not propose to abandon Fort Sumpter." As for the charge that the administration lacked a foreign policy, "we have been preparing circulars, and instructions to ministers . . . without even a suggestion that we had no foreign policy." The idea of engineering a foreign war to reunify the country did not even rate a response.

Lincoln responded most emphatically to Seward's suggestion that perhaps the secretary of state was needed to design and pursue a vigorous policy where the president had not. In unmistakable language, Lincoln wrote: "I remark that if this must be done, *I* must do it."

Undaunted, Seward worked furiously to complete his plans for reinforcing Fort Pickens, hopeful that Lincoln might change his mind before the Fox expedition to Fort Sumter was launched. The previous day, he had sent an urgent summons to Captain Montgomery Meigs to come to his house. Recognizing that time was short, Seward requested Meigs "to put down upon paper an estimate & project for relieving & holding Fort Pickens" and "to bring it to the Presidents before 4 p.m." Lincoln was happy to receive the army captain's report, though in his mind, reinforcing Pickens did not mean choosing between the two garrisons. "Tell [Scott]," the president said, "that I wish this thing done & not to let it fail unless he can show that I have refused him something he asked for as necessary. I depend upon you gentlemen to push this thing through."

Lincoln was cautioned by Seward that the army's expedition to Pickens should be kept from naval authorities, given the number of navy men who were openly disloyal to the Union. Lincoln signed orders on April 1 to Andrew Foote, the commandant of the Navy Yard in Brooklyn, to "fit out the *Powhatan* without delay" for a secret mission to Pensacola under the command of Lieutenant David Porter. The *Powhatan* was the U.S. Navy's most powerful warship. "Under no circumstances" should "the fact that she is fitting out" be disclosed to the Navy Department, Lincoln emphasized. Both Navy Secretary Welles and Captain Fox, whose plans for the relief of Sumter depended on the *Powhatan*, remained unaware of the secret orders. With its mighty guns and three hundred sailors, the *Powhatan* was supposed to play an essential role in backing up the tugboats carrying supplies to Sumter.

Lincoln had failed to peruse the orders carefully and inadvertently assigned the *Powhatan* simultaneously to both Pickens and Sumter. In the confusion of the first weeks, it was not unusual for Lincoln to sign documents from Seward without reading them. Fred Seward later recalled that when he brought papers over to the White House for signature, Lincoln would say: "Your father says this is all right, does he? Well, I guess he knows. Where do I put my name?"

Still ignorant of the mix-up, Welles wrote to Samuel Mercer, the current commander of the *Powhatan*, on April 5, instructing him to "leave New York with the Powhatan in time to be off Charleston bar" by the morning of the 11th. If the supply boats were permitted to land at Fort Sumter, he should return to New York at once. If their entry was opposed, then the *Powhatan* and its support ships should be used "to open the way." Should the "peaceable" supply mission fail, "a reinforcement of the garrison" should be attempted by "disposing of your force," as needed. The orders from Welles to Mercer were read to the president that same day and authorized.

The next day, Lincoln drafted a letter for Cameron to send through a messenger to the governor of South Carolina: "I am directed by the President of the United States to notify you to expect an attempt will be made, to supply Fort-Sumpter with provisions only; and that, if such attempt be not resisted, no effort to throw in men, arms, or ammunition, will be made without further notice." Lincoln had devised a means to separate the peaceful supply mission from the more controversial issue of reinforcement, forging, at least for the record, a final alternative to war.

While Lincoln's strategy was creative, its execution was fatally bungled. Learning that the Pickens expedition was "embarrassed by conflicting orders from the Secretary of the Navy," Captain Meigs had telegraphed Seward for an explanation. Placed in an awkward situation, Seward knew he would have to reveal the secret Pickens mission to Welles. Sometime after 11 p.m., Seward and Fred took a short walk to the Willard to talk with Welles. Earlier that evening, Welles, assuming that the *Powhatan* and its accompanying ships had already set sail for Sumter, had congratulated himself on accomplishing so much in such a short time.

Seward showed Welles the telegram, explaining that it must relate to the *Powhatan*, which was now under command of David Porter and on its way to Pensacola. Welles insisted that was impossible. The *Powhatan* was "the flagship" of the mission to Sumter. They decided to consult the president at once. Though midnight was approaching, Lincoln was still awake. Upon hearing the problem, he "looked first at one and then the other, and declared there was some mistake." Once the error was clear, he told Seward to send Porter a telegram, ordering him to "return the Powhatan to Mercer without delay," so that the Sumter expedition could proceed. Seward tried to champion the Pickens expedition, but Lincoln "was imperative," insisting that the telegram go out that night.

To the astonishment of Welles, Lincoln "took upon himself the whole blame—said it was carelessness, heedlessness on his part—he ought to have been more careful and attentive." In fact, Welles continued, Lincoln "often declared that he, and not his Cabinet, was in fault for errors imputed to them." Seward reluctantly sent the telegram; but Porter had already set sail for Florida. A fast ship was dispatched to catch up with the *Powhatan*, but when Porter read the telegram, bearing Seward's signature instead of the president's, he continued to Florida, on the assumption that the previous order signed by the president had priority.

When Gustavus Fox reached Charleston, he spent hours futilely searching for the *Powhatan*, having no clue the vessel had been misrouted. Nor did he know that Confederate authorities in Montgomery had intercepted his plans and ordered the commander in Charleston, Brigadier General Pierre Beauregard, to attack the fort before the *Powhatan* and Union convoy were due to arrive. At 3:30 a.m. on April 12, Beauregard sent a note to Anderson announcing his intent to commence firing in one hour. Anderson's small garrison of sixty men returned fire but were quickly overwhelmed by the Confederate force of nine thousand. They had no chance, Fox lamented, without the *Powhatan*'s men, howitzers, and "fighting launches." Abner Doubleday, an officer on Anderson's staff, recalled that "the conflagration was terrible and disastrous. . . . One-fifth of the fort was on fire, and the wind drove the smoke in dense masses into the angle where we had all taken refuge."

Thirty-four hours after the fighting began, Major Anderson surrendered. In a gesture that forever endeared him to the North, he brought his men together and fired a dignified fifty-round salute to the shredded American flag before hauling it down and leaving the fort. Incredibly, only one Union soldier died, the result of an accidental explosion of gunpowder during the salute to the flag. Beauregard, who had been taught by Anderson at West Point and had great respect for him, waited until Anderson had departed before entering the fort, as "it would be an unhonorable thing . . . to be present at the humiliation of his friend."

Captain Fox was inconsolable. Convinced that his mission would have been successful with the missing *Powhatan*, he believed that for a failure that was not his fault, he had lost his "reputation with the general public." Lincoln, once more, assumed the blame, assuring him that "by an accident, for which you were in no wise responsible, and possibly I, to some extent was, you were deprived of a war vessel with her men, which you deemed of great importance to the enterprize. I most cheerfully and truly declare that the failure of the undertaking has not lowered you a particle, while the qualities you developed in the effort, have greatly heightened you, in my estimation.

"You and I," he continued, "both anticipated that the cause of the country would be advanced by making the attempt to provision Fort-Sumpter, even if it should fail; and it is no small consolation now to feel that our anticipation is justified by the result."

Critics later claimed that Lincoln had maneuvered the South into beginning the war. In fact, he had simply followed his inaugural pledge that he would "hold" the properties belonging to the government, "but beyond what may be necessary" to accomplish this, "there will be no invasion—no using of force." Fort Sumter could not be held without food and supplies. Had Lincoln chosen to abandon the fort, he would have violated his pledge to the North. Had he used force in any way other than to "hold" government properties, he would have breached his promise to the South.

The Confederates had fired the first shot. A war had begun that no one imagined would last four years and cost greater than six hundred thousand lives—more than the cumulative total of all our other wars, from the Revolution to Iraq. The devastation and sacrifice would reach into every community, into almost every family, in a nation of 31.5 million. In proportion to today's population, the number of deaths would exceed five million.

CHAPTER 13

"THE BALL HAS OPENED"

NEWS OF THE CONFEDERATE ATTACK on Fort Sumter spread throughout the North that weekend. Walt Whitman recalled hearing the shouts of newsboys after he emerged from an opera on 14th Street and was strolling down Broadway late Saturday night. At the Metropolitan Hotel, "where the great lamps were still brightly blazing," the news was read to a crowd of thirty or forty suddenly gathered round. More than twenty years later, he could "almost see them there now, under the lamps at midnight again."

The "firing on the flag" produced a "volcanic upheaval" in the North, Whitman observed, "which at once substantially settled the question of disunion." The *National Intelligencer* spoke for many Northerners: "Our people now, one and all, are determined to sustain the Government and demand a vigorous prosecution of the war inaugurated by the disunionists. All sympathy with them is dead."

The fevered excitement in the North was mirrored in the South. "The ball has opened," a dispatch from Charleston, South Carolina, began. "The excitement in the community is indescribable. With the very first boom of the guns thousands rushed from their beds to the harbor front, and all day every available place has been thronged by ladies and gentlemen, viewing the spectacle through their glasses."

On Sunday, Lincoln returned from church and immediately called his cabinet into session. He had decided to issue a proclamation to the North, calling out state militias and fixing a time for Congress to reconvene. The number of volunteer soldiers to be requested came under debate. Some wanted 100,000, others 50,000; Lincoln settled on 75,000. The timing of the congressional session also posed a difficult question. While the executive branch needed Congress to raise armies and authorize spending, Lincoln was advised that "to wait for 'many men of many minds' to shape a war policy would be to invite disaster." Seward was particularly adamant on this point, believing that "history tells us that kings who call extra parliaments lose their heads." Lincoln and his cabinet set the Fourth of July as the date for Congress to reconvene, relying on "their patriotism to sanction the war measures taken prior to that time by the Executive."

John Nicolay made a copy of the president's proclamation and delivered it to the secretary of state, who stamped the great seal and sent it for publication the following day. That afternoon, Lincoln took a carriage ride with his boys and Nicolay, trying for a moment to distract himself from the increasingly onerous events. Upon his return, he welcomed his old rival Stephen Douglas for a private meeting of several hours. Douglas was not well; a lifetime of alcohol and frenetic activity had taken its toll. In two months' time, he would be dead. Nevertheless, he offered his solid support to Lincoln, afterward publicly declaring himself ready "to sustain the President in the exercise of his constitutional functions to preserve the Union, and maintain the Government." His statement proved tremendously helpful in mobilizing Democratic support. "In this hour of trial it becomes the duty of every patriotic citizen to sustain the General Government," one Douglas paper began. Another urged "every man to lay aside his party bias . . . give up small prejudices and go in, heart and hand, to put down treason and traitors."

"The response to the Proclamation at the North," Fred Seward recalled, "was all or more than could be anticipated. Every Governor of a free State promptly promised that his quota should be forthcoming. An enthusiastic outburst of patriotic feeling—an 'uprising of the North' in town and country—was reported by telegraph." Northern newspapers described massive rallies, with bands blaring and volunteers marching in support of the Union. Old party lines seemed to have evaporated. "We begin to look like a United North," George Templeton Strong recorded in his diary, prophesying that the Democratic *New York Herald* would soon "denounce Jefferson Davis as it denounced Lincoln a week ago."

The enthusiastic solidarity of the North dangerously underestimated the strength and determination of the South. Seward predicted that the war would be over in sixty days. John Hay expressed the condescending wish that it would "be bloody and short, in pity to the maniac South. They are weak, ignorant, bankrupt in money and credit. Their army is a vast mob, insubordinate and hungry. . . . What is before them but defeat, poverty, dissensions, insurrections and ruin."

Ominous signals from the South soon deflated these facile forecasts. North Carolina, Tennessee, and Kentucky refused to send troops "for the wicked purpose of subduing [their] sister Southern States." Then, on April 17, citing the president's call to arms, the vital state of Virginia seceded from the Union. The historian James Randall would designate this act "one of the most fateful events in American history." News of Virginia's decision provoked jubilation throughout the South. "We never saw our population so much excited as it was yesterday afternoon, when the glorious news spread all over town as wildfire, that Virginia, the 'Mother of Presidents,' had seceded at last," the New Orleans *Daily Picayune* reported. "Citizens on the sidewalks, were shaking each other by the hand, our office was overcrowded, the boys were running to and fro, unable to restrain their delight, and now and then venting their enthusiasm by giving a hearty hurrah."

In their excitement, Southerners fell victim to the same hectic misjudgment that plagued the North, overstating their own chances as they underestimated their opponent's will. "And now we are eight!" the *Picayune* exulted, predicting they would soon be fifteen when all the remaining slave states followed Virginia's lead. In fact, the Old Dominion's action prodded only three more states to join the Confederacy—North Carolina, Arkansas, and Tennessee. For many agonizing months, however, Lincoln would remain apprehensive about the border states of Maryland, Missouri, and Kentucky.

The day after Virginia seceded, Francis Blair, Sr., invited Colonel Robert E. Lee to his yellow house on Pennsylvania Avenue. A graduate of West Point, the fifty-four-year-old Lee had served in the Mexican War, held the post of superintendent at West Point, and commanded the forces that captured John Brown at Harpers Ferry. General Scott regarded him as "the very best soldier I ever saw in the field." Lincoln had designated Blair to tender Lee the highest-ranking military position within the president's power to proffer.

"I come to you on the part of President Lincoln," Blair began, "to ask whether any inducement that he can offer will prevail on you to take command of the Union army?" Lee responded "as candidly and as courteously" as he could: "Mr. Blair, I look upon secession as anarchy. If I owned the four millions of slaves in the South I would sacrifice them all to the Union; but how can I draw my sword upon Virginia, my native state?"

When the meeting ended, Lee called upon old General Scott to discuss the dilemma further. Then he returned to his Arlington home to think. Two days later, he contacted Scott to tender his resignation from the U.S. Army. "It would have been presented at once," Lee explained, "but for the struggle it has cost me to separate myself from a service to which I have devoted all the best years of my life & all the ability I possessed. During the whole of that time, more than 30 years, I have experienced nothing but kindness from my superiors, & the most cordial friendship from my companions. . . . I shall carry with me to the grave the most grateful recollections of your kind consideration, & your name & fame will always be dear to me."

That same day, a distraught Lee wrote to his sister: "Now we are in a state of war which will yield to nothing." Though he could apprehend "no necessity for this state of things, and would have forborne and pleaded to the end for redress of grievances, real or supposed," he was unable, he explained, "to raise my hand against my relatives, my children, my home. I have, therefore, resigned my commission in the Army, and save in defense of my native State (with the sincere hope that my poor services may never be needed) I hope I may never be called upon to draw my sword." Shortly thereafter, Lee was designated commander of the Virginia state forces.

While Lee wrestled with the grim personal consequences of his decision, Lincoln's brother-in-law Benjamin Hardin Helm confronted a painful decision of his own. Helm, a native of Kentucky and a graduate of West Point, had married Mary's half sister Emilie in 1856. While conducting business in Springfield, he had stayed with the Lincolns. According to his daughter Katherine, he and Lincoln "formed a friendship which was more like the affection of brothers than the ordinary liking of men." Two weeks after Sumter, Lincoln brought Helm, a staunch "Southern-rights Democrat," into his office. "Ben, here is something for you," Lincoln said, placing a sealed envelope in his hands. "Think it over and let me know what you will do." The letter offered Helm the rank of major and the prestigious position of paymaster in the Union Army. That afternoon, Helm encountered Lee, whose face betrayed his anxiety. "Are you not feeling well, Colonel Lee?" Helm asked. "Well in body but not in mind," Lee replied. "In the prime of life I quit a service in which were all my hopes and expectations in this world." Helm showed Lee Lincoln's offer and asked for advice, saying, "I have no doubt of his kindly intentions. But he cannot control the elements. There must be a great war." Lee was "too much disturbed" to render advice, urging Helm to "do as your conscience and your honor bid."

That night, Emilie Helm later recalled, her husband was unable to sleep. The next day, he returned to the White House. "I am going home," he told Lincoln. "I will answer you from there. The position you offer me is beyond what I had expected, even in my most hopeful dreams. You have been very generous to me, Mr. Lincoln, generous beyond anything I have ever known. I had no claim upon you, for I opposed your candidacy, and did what I could to prevent your election. . . . Don't let this offer be made public yet. I will send you my answer in a few days." When Helm reached Kentucky and spoke with General Simon Bolivar Buckner and his friends, he realized he must decline Lincoln's offer and "cast his destinies with his native southland." The time spent in drafting his reply to Lincoln proved to be, he told a friend, "the most painful hour of his life." Soon after, he received a commission in the Confederate Army, where he eventually became a brigadier general.

• • •

EACH DAY BROUGHT NEW conflicts and decisions as Lincoln struggled to stabilize the beleaguered Union. In a contentious cabinet meeting, Seward argued that a blockade of Southern ports should be instituted at once. Recognized by the law of nations, the blockade would grant the Union the power to search and seize vessels. Gideon Welles countered that to proclaim a blockade would mistakenly acknowledge that the Union was engaged in a war with the South and encourage foreign powers to extend belligerent rights to the Confederacy. Better to simply close the ports against the insurrection and use the policing powers of municipal law to seize entering or exiting ships. The cabinet split down the middle. Chase, Blair, and Bates backed Welles, while Smith and Cameron sided with Seward. Lincoln concluded that Seward's position was stronger and issued his formal blockade proclamation on April 19. Welles, despite his initial hesitation, would execute the blockade with great energy and skill.

The commencement of war found Welles and the Navy Department in a grave situation. Southerners, who had made up the majority of navy officers in peacetime, resigned in droves every day. Treason was rampant.

Early in April, Lincoln had graciously attended a wedding celebration for the daughter of Captain Frank Buchanan, the commandant of the Navy Yard in Washington, D.C. Two weeks later, expecting that his home state of Maryland "would soon secede and join the Confederacy," Buchanan resigned his commission, vowing that he would "not take any part in the defence of this Yard from this date."

Meanwhile, the secession of Virginia jeopardized the Norfolk Navy Yard. With its strategic location, immense dry dock, great supply of cannons and guns, and premier vessel, the *Merrimac*, the Norfolk yard was indispensable to both sides. Welles had encouraged Lincoln to reinforce the yard before Sumter fell, but Lincoln had resisted any action that would provoke Virginia. This decision would seriously compromise the Union's naval strength. By the time Welles received orders to send troops to Norfolk, it was too late. The Confederates had secured control of the Navy Yard. The calamitous news, Charles Francis Adams recorded in his diary, sent him into a state of "extreme uneasiness" about the future of the Union. "We the children of the third and fourth generations are doomed to pay the penalties of the compromises made by the first."

The first casualties of the war came on April 19, 1861, the same day the blockade was announced. When the Sixth Massachusetts Regiment reached Baltimore by rail en route to defend Washington, the men were attacked by a secessionist mob. "The scene while the troops were changing cars was indescribably fearful," the Baltimore *Sun* reported. The enraged crowd, branding the troops "nigger thieves," assaulted them with knives and revolvers. Four soldiers and nine civilians were killed. As George Templeton Strong noted in his diary: "It's a notable coincidence that the first blood in this great struggle is drawn by Massachusetts men on the anniversary" of the battles of Lexington and Concord that touched off the Revolutionary War.

The president immediately summoned the mayor of Baltimore and the governor of Maryland to the White House. Still hoping to keep Maryland in the Union, Lincoln agreed to "make no point of bringing [further troops] *through* Baltimore" where strident secessionists were concentrated, but insisted that the troops must be allowed to go "*around* Baltimore." Shortly after midnight, an angry committee of delegates from Baltimore arrived at the White House to confront Lincoln. John Hay took them to see Cameron, but kept them from the president until morning. The delegation demanded that troops be kept not only out of Baltimore but out of the entire state of Maryland. Lincoln adamantly refused to comply. "I must have troops to defend this Capital," he replied. "Geographically it lies surrounded by the soil of Maryland. . . . Our men are not moles, and can't dig under the earth; they are not birds, and can't fly through the air. There is no way but to march across, and that they must do."

The day the war claimed its first casualties was also the day when "the censorship of the press was exercised for the first time at the telegraph office," a veteran journalist recalled. "When correspondents wished to telegraph the lists of the dead and wounded of the Massachusetts Sixth they found a squad of the National Rifles in possession of the office, with orders to permit the transmission of no messages." Infuriated, the correspondents rode to Seward's house to complain. The secretary of state argued that if they sent "accounts of the killed and wounded," they "would only influence public sentiment, and be an obstacle in the path of reconciliation." The issue became moot when reporters learned that secessionists had cut all the telegraph wires in Baltimore and demolished all the railroad bridges surrounding the city. Washington was isolated from all communication with the North.

For the next week, with wires cut and mails stopped, the residents of Washington lived in a state of constant fear. Visitors abandoned the great hotels. Stores closed. Windows and doors were barricaded. "Literally," Villard noted, "it was as though the government of a great nation had been suddenly removed to an island in mid-ocean in a state of entire isolation." Anxious citizens crowded the train station every day, hopeful to greet an influx of the Northern troops needed to protect the vulnerable city. Rumors spread quickly. Across the Potomac, the campfires of the Confederate soldiers were visible. It appeared they were ready to lay siege to Washington. Waiting for the attack, War Secretary Cameron slept in his office. "Here we were in this city," Nicolay wrote his fiancée, "in charge of all the public buildings, property and archives, with only about 2000 *reliable* men to defend it."

Elsewhere in the North, anxiety was nearly as great. "No despatches from Washington," Strong reported from New York. "People talked darkly of its being attacked before our reinforcements come to the rescue, and everyone said we must not be surprised by news that Lincoln and Seward and all the Administration are prisoners." Kate and Nettie Chase were in New York visiting Chase's wealthy friend Hiram Barney, who had received the powerful post of collector of customs in New York. Reflecting a general fear that the "rebels are at Washington or near it," Barney insisted that the girls stay in New York until the capital was out of danger. For Kate, so passionately attached to her father, these were difficult hours. "I can see that K. is anxious for her father," Barney wrote Chase; "it may be seen in many ways—in spite of her efforts to be calm & conceal it." Kate leaped at the chance to accompany Major Robert Anderson, who had just arrived in New York from Fort Sumter and was heading to Washington to report to the president.

The little party made its way to Philadelphia and then caught a steamer from Perryville to Annapolis, bypassing the blocked railroad tracks in Baltimore. En route, however, they were approached by an enemy vessel, which fired a warning shot. Fearing that the Confederates had intelligence that Anderson was on board and were intending to capture him, the captain placed a cannon in position and "crowded on steam." While Kate and Nettie remained below with the hatches closed, the steamer churned ahead, eventually gaining enough ground that its adversary "ran up a black flag, changed her course, and was soon out of sight." From Annapolis, they reached Washington and were reunited with their relieved father.

These "were terrible days of suspense" for the Seward family in Auburn as well. Young Will Seward, now twenty-two, made nightly forays to the local telegraph office, hoping in vain for news from his father. In daily letters, Frances entreated her husband to let her join him. "It is hard to be so far from you when your life is in danger," she pleaded. No reply came to her appeal.

In public, Lincoln maintained his calm, but the growing desperation of the government's position filled him with dread. Late one night, after "a day of gloom and doubt," John Hay saw him staring out the window in futile expectation of the troops promised by various Northern states, including New York, Rhode Island, and Pennsylvania. "Why don't they come!" he asked. "Why don't they come!" The next day, visiting the injured men of the Massachusetts Sixth, he was heard to say: "I don't believe there is any North. The Seventh Regiment [from New York] is a myth. R. Island is not known in our geography any longer. *You* [Massachusetts men] are the only Northern realities."

For days, the rioting in Baltimore continued. Fears multiplied that the Maryland legislature, which had convened in Annapolis, was intending to vote for secession. The cabinet debated whether the president should bring in the army "to arrest, or disperse the members of that body." Lincoln decided that "it would *not* be justifiable." It was a wise determination, for in the end, though secessionist mobs continued to disrupt the peace of Maryland for weeks, the state never joined the Confederacy, and eventually became, as Lincoln predicted, "the first of the redeemed."

Receiving word that the mobs intended to destroy the train tracks between Annapolis and Philadelphia in order to prevent the long-awaited troops from reaching the beleaguered capital, Lincoln made a controversial decision. If resistance along the military line between Washington and Philadelphia made it "necessary to suspend the writ of Habeas Corpus for the public safety," Lincoln authorized General Scott to do so. In Lincoln's words, General Scott could "arrest, and detain, without resort to the ordinary processes and forms of law, such individuals as he might deem dangerous to the public safety." Seward later claimed that he had urged a wavering Lincoln to take this step, convincing him that "perdition was the sure penalty of further hesitation." There may be truth in this, for Seward was initially put in charge of administering the program.

Lincoln had not issued a sweeping order but a directive confined to this single route. Still, by rescinding the basic constitutional protection against arbitrary arrest, he aroused the wrath of Chief Justice Taney, who was on circuit duty in Maryland at the time. Ruling in favor of one of the prisoners, John Merryman, Taney blasted Lincoln and maintained that only Congress could suspend the writ.

Attorney General Bates, though reluctant to oppose Taney, upheld Lincoln's suspension. Over a period of weeks, he drafted a twenty-six-page opinion, arguing that "in a time like the present, when the very existence of the Nation is assailed, by a great and dangerous insurrection, the President has the lawful discretionary power to arrest and hold in custody, persons known to have criminal intercourse with the insurgents."

Lincoln later defended his decision in his first message to Congress. As chief executive, he was responsible for ensuring "that the laws be faithfully executed." An insurrection "in nearly one-third of the States" had subverted the "whole of the laws . . . are all the laws, *but one*, to go unexecuted, and the government itself go to pieces, lest that one be violated?" His logic was unanswerable, but as Supreme Court Justice Thurgood Marshall argued in another context many years later, the "grave threats to liberty often come in times of urgency, when constitutional rights seem too extravagant to endure." Welles seemed to understand the complex balancing act, correctly predicting to his wife that the "government will, doubtless, be stronger after the conflict is over than it ever has been, and there will be less liberty."

Finally, after a week of mounting uneasiness, the Seventh Regiment of New York arrived in Washington. The *New York Times* reported that the "steps and balconies of the hotels, the windows of the private houses, the doorways of the stores, and even the roofs of many houses were crowded with men, women and children, shouting, and waving handkerchiefs and flags." In the days that followed, more regiments arrived. Mary and her friends watched the regimental parades from a window in the mansion. The presence of the troops considerably lightened Lincoln's mood. He blithely told John Hay that in addition to assuring the safety of the capital, he would eventually "go down to Charleston and pay her the little debt we are owing her." Hay was so happy to hear these words that he "felt like letting off an Illinois yell."

Frances Seward was greatly relieved when she received a letter from her husband confirming that more than eight thousand troops were in Washington. He did not, however, grant her request to join him there. His daughter-in-law, Anna, had almost completed decorating their new house on Lafayette Square. The carpets were down, and hundreds of books already lined the library shelves. They would move in at the end of April. Unlike Frances, Anna loved the bustle of Seward's life. "For six or eight nights we had visitors at all hours," she cheerfully reported. Perhaps Seward, anticipating the trials such a hectic environment would cause his wife, deemed it better for her to stay in their tranquil house in Auburn.

Furthermore, he knew they would argue about the purpose of the war. Frances, unlike her husband, had already decided that the principal goal was to end slavery. She recognized that the war might last years and entail "immense sacrifice of human life," but the eradication of slavery justified it all. "The true, strong, glorious North is at last fairly roused," she wrote her husband, "the enthusiasm of the people—high & low rich & poor . . . all enlisted at last in the cause of human rights. No concession from the South now will avail to stem the torrent.—No compromise will be made with slavery of black or white. God has heard the prayer of the oppressed and a fearful retribution awaits the oppressors."

In her all-embracing vision of the war, Frances stood at this point in opposition not only to her husband but to most of the cabinet and a substantial majority of Northerners. Still certain it would be a quick war with an easy reconciliation, Seward told a friend, "there would be no serious fighting after all; the South would collapse and everything be serenely adjusted." Bates wanted a limited war so as "to disturb as little as possible the accustomed occupations of the people," including Southern slaveholding. Blair agreed, counseling Lincoln that it would be a "fatal error" if the contest became "one between the whole people of the South and the people of the North."

To Lincoln's mind, the battle to save the Union contained an even larger purpose than ending slavery, which was after all sanctioned by the very Constitution he was sworn to uphold. "I consider the central idea pervading this struggle," he told Hay in early May, "is the necessity that is upon us, of proving that popular government is not an absurdity. We must settle this question now, whether in a free government the minority have the right to break up the government whenever they choose. If we fail it will go far to prove the incapability of the people to govern themselves."

The philosopher John Stuart Mill shared Lincoln's spacious understanding of the sectional crisis, predicting that a Southern victory "would give courage to the enemies of progress and damp the spirits of its friends all over the civilized world." From the opposite point of view, a member of the British nobility expressed the hope that with "the dissolution of the Union," men would "live to see an aristocracy established in America."

In his Farewell Address, George Washington had given voice to this transcendent idea of Union. "It is of infinite moment," George Washington said, "that you should properly estimate the immense value of your national union to your collective and individual happiness; that you should cherish a cordial, habitual, and immovable attachment to it; accustoming yourselves to think and speak of it as of the palladium of your political safety and prosperity." Foreseeing the potential for dissension, Washington advised vigilance against "the first dawning of every attempt to alienate any portion of our country from the rest or to enfeeble the sacred ties which now link together the various parts."

It was this mystical idea of popular government and democracy that propelled Abraham Lincoln to call forth the thousands of soldiers who would rise up to defend the sacred Union created by the Founding Fathers.

• • •

IN THE DAYS BEFORE the troops arrived, rumors spread that the White House would be targeted for a direct attack. Late one evening, an agitated visitor arrived to inform the president that "a mortar battery has been planted on the Virginia heights commanding the town." John Hay recorded in his diary that he "had to do some very dexterous lying to calm the awakened fears of Mrs. Lincoln in regard to the assassination suspicion." Only when troops appeared in force was she able to relax. "Thousands of soldiers are guarding us," she wrote a friend in Springfield, "and if there is safety in numbers, we have every reason, to feel secure." Mary's cousin Elizabeth Grimsley was equally relieved. "The intense excitement has blown over," she told a friend. "Washington is very quiet and pleasant. We enjoy the beautiful drives around the city."

With little understanding of the peril threatening the city and their well-being, Willie and Tad found the period of Washington's isolation exhilarating. Tad boasted at Sunday School that he had no fear of the "plug-uglies," as the rowdy secessionists in Baltimore were called. "You ought to see the fort we've got on the roof of our house. Let 'em come. Willie and I are ready for 'em." Though the fort consisted of only "a small log" symbolizing a cannon and several decommissioned rifles, the Lincoln boys developed elaborate plans to defend the White House from the roof. And they loved visiting the troops quartered in the East Room of the White House and in the Capitol, where Hay noted the contrast "between the grey haired dignity" that had previously prevailed in the Senate and the young soldiers, "scattered over the desks chairs and galleries some loafing, many writing letters, slowly and with plough hardened hands."

The Taft boys and their sixteen-year-old sister, Julia, were now almost daily guests at the White House. Like Willie, Bud was "rather pale and languid, not very robust," but a "pretty good" student. Holly, as described by his father, Judge Taft, resembled Tad—"all motion and activity, never idle, impatient of restraint, quick to learn when he *tries*, impetuous, all 'go ahead.' " In Bud and Holly, Willie and Tad each found a best friend. Julia, meanwhile, formed a friendship with Mary Lincoln. For the rest of her life, Julia retained warm memories of both the first lady and the president. "More than once," she recalled, Mary had said to her: "I wish I had a little girl like you, Julia." Mary even shared her memories of the death of her son Edward, and they "wept together." In the evenings, when the president unwound in the family sitting room, the four boys would beg him to tell a story. Julia long remembered the scene, as the president launched into one of his amusing tales: "Tad perched precariously on the back of the big chair, Willie on one knee, Bud on the other, both leaning against him," while Holly sat "on the arm of the chair."

As a proper young lady, Julia was appalled by some of the boys' antics. She refused to join in when she found the four of them sitting on the president, attempting to pin him to the floor. She was embarrassed when they interrupted cabinet meetings to invite members and the president to attend one of their theatrical performances in the attic. Though Lincoln himself never seemed to mind, taking great pleasure in their fun, Julia felt she was responsible for curbing their youthful exuberance. Sometimes Willie would help to restore order. He was, Julia wrote, "the most lovable boy" she had ever known, "bright, sensible, sweet-tempered and gentle-mannered." More often he would simply retreat to his mother's room, where he loved to read poetry and write verses.

Despite Julia's great affection for Mary, she was stunned by the first lady's overbearing need to get "what she wanted when she wanted it," regardless of how others might be hurt or inconvenienced. A curious example of such behavior took place when Julia's mother attended a White House concert, decked out in one of her fashionable bonnets. When Mary greeted her, she looked closely at the beautiful purple strings on the bonnet and then took Mrs. Taft aside. Watching the scene, Julia was "puzzled at the look of amazement" on her mother's face, not fathoming why she "should look so surprised at a passing compliment." It turned out that

Mary's milliner had created a purple-trimmed bonnet but lacked sufficient purple ribbon for the strings. Mary hoped to acquire Mrs. Taft's purple strings!

Few recognized the insecurity behind Mary's outlandish behavior, the terrible needs behind the ostentation and apparent abrasiveness. While initially thrilled to move into the White House, Mary soon found herself in the compromising situation of having one full brother, three half brothers, and three brothers-in-law in the Confederate Army. From the start, she was not fully trusted in the North. As the wife of President Lincoln, she was vilified in the South. As a Westerner, she did not meet the standards of Eastern society. Feeling pressure on all sides, she was determined to present herself as an accomplished and sophisticated woman; in short, the most elegant and admired lady in Washington.

Driven by the need to prove herself to society, Mary Lincoln became obsessed with recasting her own image and renovating that of her new home, the White House. Unattended for years, the White House had come to look like "an old and unsuccessful hotel." Elizabeth Grimsley was stunned to find that "the family apartments were in a deplorably shabby condition as to furniture, (which looked as if it has been brought in by the first President)." The public rooms, too, were in poor shape, with threadbare, tobacco-stained rugs, torn curtains, and broken chairs.

The sorry condition of the White House provided the energetic Mary with a worthy ambition. She would restore the people's home to its former elegance as a symbol of her husband's strength and the Union's power. In another era, this ambition might have been applauded, but in the midst of a civil war, it was regarded as frivolous.

In the middle of May, Mary went on a shopping trip to Philadelphia and New York, taking along her cousin Elizabeth Grimsley and William Wood, the commissioner of public buildings. Having discovered that each president was allotted a $20,000 allowance to maintain the White House, she bought new furniture, elegant curtains, and expensive carpets for the public rooms to replace their worn predecessors. For the state guest room, she purchased what later became known as the "Lincoln bed," an eight-foot-long rosewood bedstead with an ornate headboard carved with "exotic birds, grapevines and clusters of grapes." Again, merchants at the clothing stores were more than willing to extend the first lady credit. The press exaggerated her shopping spree, claiming she had purchased thousands of dollars of merchandise in stores she had never even visited. Exaggeration notwithstanding, when she returned to Washington, the bills added up. She received a $7,500 invoice for curtain materials and trimmings, and owed $900 for a new carriage. And the redecorating process to make the nation's house a fit emblem for the country and for herself had just begun.

Never one to be outdone, Kate Chase was hard at work decorating her father's new home—a large three-story brick mansion at Sixth and E Street NW. Though the secretary of the treasury worried constantly about money, he understood the importance of having an elegant home with expansive public rooms appropriate for entertaining senators, congressmen, diplomats, and generals. In the years ahead, he intended to gather friends and associates who would be ready to back him when the time came for the next presidential election. The lease on the house came to $1,200 a year; when the furnishing costs were added on, Chase found himself in debt. Unable to sell off his Cincinnati and Columbus properties in the depressed real estate market that prevailed in Ohio, he was forced to borrow $10,000 from his old friend Hiram Barney. It must have been painfully awkward for the straitlaced model of probity to request the loan, particularly since Barney, as collector of customs in New York, was technically his subordinate. Nevertheless, Chase persuaded himself that a person in his position, who had given so much to the public for so many years, deserved to live in a distinguished home.

So, like Mary Lincoln, Kate traveled to New York and Philadelphia to purchase carpets, draperies, and furniture. The house, complete with six servants, would prove perfect for entertaining, although Chase later complained that the distance from the White House, in comparison with Seward's new lodgings at Lafayette Square, denied him an equal intimacy with the president. He apparently never considered that Lincoln might simply find Seward more lively and amiable company.

None of her father's social demeanor or leaden eminence hindered Kate. As the mistress of his Washington household, she managed "in a single season" to be "as much at home in the society of the national capital as if she had lived there for a lifetime." Dozens of young men paid court to her. A contemporary reporter noted that "no other maiden in Washington had more suitors at her feet." Yet, he continued, "it was early noticed that among all the young men who flocked to the Chase home, and who were eager to obey her slightest nod, there was not one who seemed to obtain even the remotest hold upon her affections"—until Rhode Island's young governor, William Sprague, came to Washington and drew her attention.

Kate had first met the fabulously wealthy Sprague, whose family owned one of the largest textile manufacturing establishments in the country, the previous September in Cleveland. Sprague had come to Ohio at the head of an official delegation to dedicate a statue of Rhode Island native Commodore Oliver Perry, which was to be placed in the public square. Introduced at the festive ball that followed the ceremony, the two immediately hit it off. "For the rest of the evening," one observer recalled, "whenever we saw one of them we were pretty sure to see the other."

For his part, Sprague would never forget his first sight of Kate, "dressed in that celebrated dress," when "you became my gaze and the gaze of all observers, and you left the house taking with you my admiration and my appreciation, but more than all my *pulsations*. I remember well how I was possessed that night and the following day." Years later, he assured her he could "recall the sensation better than if it was yesterday."

Ten years Kate's senior, William Sprague had assumed responsibility for the family business at an early age. When William was thirteen, his father, Amasa Sprague, was shot down on the street as he walked home from his cotton mill one evening. The elder Sprague had been involved in a nasty fight over the renewal of a liquor license. The owner of the gin mill shut down by Sprague was arrested and hanged for the murder. Control of the company passed to William's uncle, who determined that young William should cut short his education to learn the business from the bottom up. "I was thrust into the counting-room, performing its lowest drudgeries, raising myself to all of its highest positions," he later recalled. When his uncle died of typhoid fever, William, at twenty-six, took over.

As the largest employer in Rhode Island, with more than ten thousand workers, young Sprague wielded enormous political influence. He capitalized on his resources when he ran for governor in 1860 and won on the Democratic ticket, spending over $100,000 of his own money. After the attack on Fort Sumter, Sprague organized the First Rhode Island Regiment, providing the state with "a loan of one hundred thousand dollars to outfit the troops," while his brother supplied the artillery battery with ninety-six horses. When the lavishly supplied volunteer regiment arrived in the threatened capital, the men were received as heroes. On April 29, the regiment was officially sworn in before the president and General Scott after a dress parade from its headquarters at the Patent Office to the White House. "The entire street was filled with spectators from Seventh to Ninth street," the *Evening Star* reported, "and many were the complimentary remarks made by the multitude upon the general appearance and movements of the regiment."

All the members of the cabinet were present at the ceremony, joining in the rousing greeting for the resplendent troops. Though Sprague stood only five feet six inches tall, his military uniform and his "yellow-plumed hat" undoubtedly increased his stature. John Hay commented after meeting the young man with brown wavy hair, gray eyes, and a thin mustache that while he appeared at first "a small, insignificant youth, who bought his place," he "is certainly all right now. He is very proud of his Company of its wealth and social standing." Hay, too, was impressed by the number of eminent young men in Sprague's regiment. "When men like these leave their horses, their women and their wine, harden their hands, eat crackers for dinner, wear a shirt for a week and never black their shoes,—all for a principle, it is hard to set any bounds to the possibilities of such an army." Washingtonians nicknamed the First Rhode Island "the millionaires' regiment" and dubbed Sprague the most eligible bachelor in the city.

It was only a matter of days before Sprague called on Kate. Unlike earlier tentative suitors, intimidated perhaps by Kate's beauty and brains, Sprague moved confidently to establish a place in her heart, becoming "the first, the only man," she said afterward, "that had found a lodgment there." Years later, writing to Kate, Sprague vividly recalled their earlier courtship days. "Do you remember the hesitating kiss I stole, and the glowing, blushing face that responded to the touch. I well remember it all. The step forward from the Cleveland meeting, and the enhanced poetical sensation, for it was poetry, if there ever is such in life."

For Kate, who acknowledged that she was "accustomed to command and be obeyed, to wish and be anticipated," Sprague's cocksure attitude must have presented a welcome challenge. In the weeks that followed, the young couple saw each other frequently. By summer's end, Nettie Chase told Kate that she liked Sprague "very much" and hoped the two would marry. Nettie's hopes were put on hold, however, as the war continued to escalate, changing the course of countless lives throughout the fractured nation.

The tragedies of war came home to the Lincolns with the death of Elmer Ellsworth on May 24, 1861. Young Ellsworth had read law in Lincoln's office and had become so close to the family that he made the journey from Springfield to Washington with them, catching the measles from Willie and Tad along the way. Once in the capital, Ellsworth joined the war effort by organizing a group of New York firemen into a Zouave unit, distinguished by their exotic and colorful uniforms. After Virginia seceded from the Union, Ellsworth's Zouaves were among the first troops to cross the Potomac River into Alexandria, a town counting ardent secessionists among its residents, including the proprietor of the Marshall House. Spying a Confederate flag waving above the hotel, Ellsworth dashed up to the roof to confiscate it. Having captured the flag, Ellsworth met the armed hotel manager, secessionist James Jackson, on his way down the stairs. Jackson killed Ellsworth on the spot, only to be shot by Ellsworth's men.

Ellsworth's death, as one of the first casualties of the war, was national news and mourned across the country. The bereaved president wrote a personal note of condolence to Ellsworth's parents, praising the young man whose body lay in state in the East Room. Nicolay confessed that he had been "quite unable to keep the tears out of my eyes" whenever he thought of Ellsworth. After the funeral, Mary was presented with the bloodied flag for which Ellsworth had given his life; but the horrified first lady, not wanting to be reminded of the sad event, quickly had it packed away.

• • •

WITH MORE THAN ENOUGH TROUBLES to occupy him at home, Lincoln faced a tangled situation abroad. A member of the British Parliament had introduced a resolution urging England to accord the Southern Confederacy belligerent status. If passed, the resolution would give Confederate ships the same rights in neutral ports enjoyed by Federal ships. Britain's textile economy depended on cotton furnished by Southern plantations. Unless the British broke the Union blockade to ensure a continuing supply of cotton, the great textile mills in Manchester and Leeds would be forced to cut back or come to a halt. Merchants would lose money, and thousands of workers would lose their jobs.

Seward feared that England would back the South simply to feed its own factories. While the "younger branch of the British stock" might support freedom, he told his wife, the aristocrats, concerned more with economics than morality, would become "the ally of the traitors." To prevent this from happening, he was "trying to get a bold remonstrance through the Cabinet, before it is too late." He hoped not only to halt further thoughts of recognition of the Confederacy but to ensure that the British would respect the Union blockade and refuse, even informally, to meet with the three Southern commissioners who had been sent to London to negotiate for the Confederacy. To achieve these goals, Seward was willing to wage war. "God damn 'em, I'll give 'em hell," he told Sumner, thrusting his foot in the air as he spoke.

On May 21, Seward brought Lincoln a surly letter drafted for Charles Francis Adams to read verbatim to Lord John Russell, Britain's foreign secretary. Lincoln recognized immediately that the tone was too abrasive for a diplomatic communication. While decisive action might be necessary to prevent Britain from any form of overt sympathy with the South, Lincoln had no intention of fighting two wars at once. All his life, he had taken care not to send letters written in anger. Now, to mitigate the harshness of the draft, he altered the tone of the letter at numerous points. Where Seward had claimed that the president was "surprised and grieved" that no protest had been made against unofficial meetings with the Southern commissioners, Lincoln wrote simply that the "President regrets." Where Seward threatened that "no one of these proceedings [informal or formal recognition, or breaking the blockade] will be borne," Lincoln shifted the phrase to "will *pass unnoticed.*"

Most important, where Seward had indicated that the letter be read directly to the British foreign secretary, Lincoln insisted that it serve merely for Adams's guidance and should not *"be read, or shown to any one."* Still, the central message remained clear: a warning to Britain that if the vexing issues were not resolved, and Britain decided "to fraternize with our domestic enemy," then a war between the United States and Britain "may ensue," caused by "the action of Great Britain, not our own." In that event, Britain would forever lose "the sympathies and the affections of the only nation on whose sympathies and affections she has a natural claim."

Thus, a threatening message that might have embroiled the Union in two wars at the same time became instead the basis for a hard-line policy that effectively interrupted British momentum toward recognizing the Confederacy. Furthermore, France, whose ministers had promised to act in concert with Britain, followed suit. This was a critical victory for the Union, preventing for the time being the recognition that would have conferred legitimacy on the Confederacy in the eyes of the world, weakened Northern morale, and accorded "currency to Southern bonds."

History would later give Secretary of State Seward high marks for his role in preventing Britain and France from intervening in the war. He is considered by some to have been "the ablest American diplomatist of the century." But here, as was so often the case, Lincoln's unseen hand had shaped critical policy. Only three months earlier, the frontier lawyer had confessed to Seward that he knew little of foreign affairs. His revisions of the dispatch, however, exhibit the sophisticated prowess of a veteran statesman: he had analyzed a complex situation and sought the least provocative way to neutralize a potential enemy while making crystal-clear his country's position.

Seward was slowly but inevitably coming to appreciate Lincoln's remarkable abilities. "It is due to the President to say, that his magnanimity is almost superhuman," he told his wife in mid-May. "His confidence and sympathy increase every day." As Lincoln began to trust his own abilities, Seward became more confident in him. In early June, he told Frances: "Executive skill and vigor are rare qualities. The President is the best of us; but he needs constant and assiduous cooperation." Though the feisty New Yorker would continue to debate numerous issues with Lincoln in the years ahead, exactly as Lincoln had hoped and needed him to do, Seward would become his most faithful ally in the cabinet. He committed himself "to his chief," Nicolay and Hay observed, "not only without reserve, but with a sincere and devoted personal attachment."

Seward's mortification at not having received his party's nomination in 1860 never fully abated, but he no longer felt compelled to belittle Lincoln to ease his pain. He settled into his position as secretary of state, and his optimistic and gregarious nature reasserted itself. Once more, his elaborate parties and receptions became the talk of Washington. Five days after the dispatch was sent, Seward hosted "a brilliant assemblage" at his new home. All the rooms were full, with dancing in one, drinks in another, and good conversation all around. Seward was "in excellent spirits," moving easily among cabinet members, military officers, diplomats, and senators. Even white-haired Secretary Welles, who, it was mockingly remarked, should have died, "to all intents and purposes, twenty years ago," was having such a good time that he seemed "good for, at least, twenty years more."

• • •

LINCOLN LOOKED TO CHASE for guidance on the complex problem of financing a war at a time when the government was heavily in debt. The economic Panic of 1857, corruption in the Buchanan administration, and the partial dismemberment of the Union had taken a massive toll on the government coffers. With Congress not in session to authorize new tariffs and taxes, Chase was forced to rely on government loans to sustain war expenditures. Banks held back at first, demanding higher interest rates than the government could afford to pay, but eventually, Chase cobbled together enough revenue to meet expenses until Congress convened.

Chase later noted proudly that in the early days of the war, Lincoln relied on him to carry out functions that ordinarily belonged to the War Department. According to Chase, he assumed "the principal charge" of preventing the key border states of Kentucky, Missouri, and Tennessee from falling into secessionist hands. He authorized a loyal state senator from Kentucky to muster twenty companies. He drew up the orders that allowed Andrew Johnson, the only senator from a Confederate state who remained loyal to the Union, "to raise regiments in Tennessee." He believed himself instrumental in keeping Kentucky and Missouri in the Union, seriously underestimating Lincoln's critical role.

Indeed, Chase would never cease to underestimate Lincoln, nor to resent the fact that he had lost the presidency to a man he considered his inferior. In late April, he presumptuously sent Lincoln a *New York Times* article highly derogatory of the administration. "The President and the Cabinet at Washington are far behind the people," the *Times* argued.

"They are like a person just aroused from sleep, and in a state of dreamy half-consciousness." This charge, Chase informed Lincoln, "has too much truth in it." Lincoln did not reply, well understanding Chase's implacable yearning for the presidency. But for now he needed the Ohioan's enormous talents and total cooperation.

Cameron, meanwhile, found the task of running the War Department unbearable. Unable to manage his vast responsibilities, he turned to both Seward and Chase for help. "Oh, it was a terrible time," Cameron remembered years later. "We were entirely unprepared for such a conflict, and for the moment, at least, absolutely without even the simplest instruments with which to engage in war. We had no guns, and even if we had, they would have been of but little use, for we had no ammunition to put in them—no powder, no saltpetre, no bullets, no anything." The demands placed on the War Department in the early days of the war were indeed excruciating. Not only were weapons in short supply, but uniforms, blankets, horses, medical supplies, food, and everything necessary to outfit the vast numbers of volunteer soldiers arriving daily in Washington were unobtainable. It would have taken thousands of personnel to handle the varied functions of the quartermaster's department, the ordnance office, the engineering department, the medical office, and the pay department. Yet, in 1861, the entire War Department consisted of fewer than two hundred people, including clerks, messengers, and watchmen. As Cameron lamented afterward: "I was certainly not in a place to be envied."

Lincoln later explained that with "so large a number of disloyal persons" infiltrating every department, the government could not rely on official agents to manage contracts for manufacturing the weapons and supplies necessary to maintain a fighting force. With the cabinet's unanimous consent, he directed Chase to dispense millions of dollars to a small number of trusted private individuals to negotiate and sign contracts that would mobilize the military. Acting "without compensation," the majority of these men did their utmost under the circumstances. A few, including Alexander Cummings, one of Cameron's lieutenants, would bring shame to the War Department.

• • •

AS SPRING GAVE WAY to the stifling heat of a Washington summer, Lincoln began work on the message he would deliver to Congress when the House and Senate assembled in special session on July 4. Needing time to think, he placed an "embargo" on all office seekers, "so strict" that they were not even allowed entry into the White House. As he labored in his newfound quiet, congressmen and senators gathered at Willard's and Brown's hotels, exchanging greetings and trading stories. They all anticipated, one reporter stated, that they would "soon ascertain the exact intentions of the Administration, through the medium of the President's message."

Lincoln worked long hours on the text, shifting words, condensing, deleting sentences. Even Senator Orville Browning, his old friend from Illinois who had come to see him, was told he was busy, but Lincoln overheard Browning talking and sent for him. It was after 9 p.m. on July 3, and he had just that moment finished writing. "He said he wished to read it to me, and did so," Browning recorded in his diary. "It is an able state paper and will fully meet the expectations of the Country."

Lincoln did not personally deliver his address on Capitol Hill. President Thomas Jefferson had denounced presidential appearances before Congress, considering them a monarchical remnant of the English system where kings personally opened parliamentary sessions. Since Jefferson, presidents had submitted their written messages to be read by a clerk. Yet, if the practice lacked theatricality, Lincoln's arguments against secession and for the necessity of executive action in the midst of rebellion left an indelible impression. He traced the history of the struggle and called on Congress to "give the legal means for making this contest a short, and a decisive one."

He asked for "at least four hundred thousand men, and four hundred millions of dollars . . . a less sum per head, than was the debt of our revolution." A "right result, at this time, will be worth more to the world, than ten times the men, and ten times the money," he assured Congress. For "this issue embraces more than the fate of these United States. It presents to the whole family of man, the question, whether a constitutional republic, or a democracy—a government of the people, by the same people—can, or cannot, maintain its territorial integrity, against its own domestic foes. . . .

"This is essentially a People's contest," the president asserted. "On the side of the Union, it is a struggle for maintaining in the world, that form, and substance of government, whose leading object is, to elevate the condition of men—to lift artificial weights from all shoulders—to clear the paths of laudable pursuit for all—to afford all, an unfettered start, and a fair chance, in the race of life." As evidence of the capacity of free institutions to better the "condition" of the people, "beyond any example in the world," he cited the regiments of the Union Army, in which "there is scarcely one, from which could not be selected, a President, a Cabinet, a Congress, and perhaps a Court, abundantly competent to administer the government itself."

Northern newspapers generally praised the message, though some failed to appreciate the rigor of Lincoln's appeal and the clear grace of his language. "In spite of obvious faults in style," the *New York Times* correspondent conceded, "I venture to say it will add to the popularity of the Rail-splitter. It is evidently the production of an honest, clear-headed and straightforward man; and its direct and forcible logic and quaint style of illustration will cause it to be read with peculiar pleasure by the masses of the people." More important, the Congress responded with alacrity. Its members authorized more money and an even larger mobilization of troops than the president had requested. In addition, they provided retroactive authority for nearly all of Lincoln's executive actions taken before they convened, remaining silent only on his suspension of habeas corpus. With the Southern Democrats gone, the Republicans had a substantial majority. And, for the moment, Northern Democrats also acceded, their dislike of Republicans overshadowed by patriotic fervor.

Not everyone was pleased. Abolitionists and radical Republicans found the message disheartening. "No mention is, at all, made of slavery," Frederick Douglass lamented. "Any one reading that document, with no previous knowledge of the United States, would never dream from anything there written that we have a slaveholding war waged upon the Government . . . while all here know that *that* is the vital and animating motive of the rebellion."

Radicals tended to blame Seward for Lincoln's reluctance to emphasize the role of slavery. "We have an honest President," Wendell Phillips, the abolitionist editor, proclaimed before a celebratory crowd on the Fourth of July, "but, distrusting the strength of the popular feeling behind him, he listens overmuch to Seward." Men like Phillips, Thaddeus Stevens, and Charles Sumner could never forgive Seward for apparently lowering the antislavery banner he had once carried so triumphantly. Seward was accustomed to criticism, however, and while he had the president beside him, he remained secure in his position.

Meanwhile, the events of the war itself began to reshape the old order in ways few realized. At Fort Monroe, at the tip of the peninsula in Virginia, a bold decision by General Benjamin Butler proved a harbinger of things to come. One night, three fugitive slaves arrived at the fort after escaping from the Confederate battery that their master had ordered them to help build. When an agent of their owner demanded their return, Butler refused. The rebels were using slaves in the field to support their troops, Butler argued. The slaves were therefore contraband of war, and the federal government was no longer obliged to surrender them to their masters.

Coming from Butler, a conservative Democrat from Massachusetts who had run for governor on the Breckinridge ticket in 1860, the decision delighted Republican stalwarts who had previously objected to Butler's high position. Butler himself would soon be equally delighted by Lincoln's magnanimity in making him a brigadier general. "I will accept the commission," Butler gratefully told Lincoln, but "there is one thing I must say to you, as we don't know each other: That as a Democrat I opposed your election, and did all I could for your opponent; but I shall do no political act, and loyally support your administration as long as I hold your commission; and when I find any act that I cannot support I shall bring the commission back at once, and return it to you."

Lincoln replied, "That is frank, that is fair. But I want to add one thing: When you see me doing anything that for the good of the country ought not to be done, come and tell me so, and why you think so, and then perhaps you won't have any chance to resign your commission." Had Butler known Lincoln, he would have been less astonished. The president commissioned officers with the same eye toward coalition building that he displayed in constructing his cabinet.

Butler's order was approved by both Lincoln and Cameron, and eventually, the Congress passed a confiscation law ending the rights of masters over fugitive slaves utilized to support the Confederate troops. Even conservative Monty Blair applauded Butler. "You were right when you declared *secession* niggers contraband of war," he told his fellow Democrat. "The Secessionists have used them to do all their fortifying."

Blair's approval of Butler's measure as an act of war did not mean that he advocated emancipation. On the contrary, he advised Butler to "improve the code by restricting its operations to working people, leaving the Secessionists to take care of the non working classes." The Union should provide safe harbor only to the "pick of the lot," the strong-bodied slaves who were helping the rebels in the field. Women and children and other "unproductive laborers" should be left for their Southern masters to house and feed.

Lincoln, as usual, was slowly formulating his own position on the slavery question. He told Blair that Butler's action raised "a very important subject . . . one requiring some thought in view of the numbers of negroes we were likely to have on hand in virtue of this new doctrine." Indeed, in the weeks that followed, hundreds of courageous slaves worked their way into Union lines. The situation worried Lincoln; at this juncture, he still favored compensated emancipation and voluntary colonization, allowing blacks who wished to do so to return to their original homeland in Africa. Most important, he knew that any hint of total, direct emancipation would alienate the border states, whose continued loyalty was essential for victory, and would shatter the Republicans' fragile alliance with Northern Democrats.

By shying from emancipation in these early months of the war, Lincoln aligned himself with the majority of the Northern people, the Republican Congress, and the whole of his cabinet. Two weeks into its session, the House passed a resolution declaring that the purpose of the war was "to preserve the Union," not to eliminate slavery. Even Chase, the most fervent antislavery man in the cabinet, agreed that at this time the "sword" of total abolition should be left "in the sheath." If the conflict were drawn out, however, he told the historian John Motley, if "we find it much more difficult and expensive in blood and treasure to put it down than we anticipated," then the sword would be drawn. "We do not wish this, we deplore it, because of the vast confiscation of property, and of the servile insurrections, too horrible to contemplate, which would follow. We wish the Constitution and Union as it is, with slavery, as a municipal institution, existing till such time as each State in its wisdom thinks fit to mitigate or abolish it . . . but if the issue be distinctly presented—death to the American Republic or death to slavery, slavery *must die.*"

• • •

BY MID-JULY, the outcry in the North for some form of significant action against the rebels reached fever pitch. "Forward to Richmond!" blared the headline in the *New York Tribune.* Senator Trumbull introduced a resolution calling for "the immediate movement of the troops, and the occupation of Richmond before the 20th July," the date set for the Confederate Congress to convene. General Scott hesitated, believing the army still unprepared for a major offensive, but Lincoln feared that without action, the morale of both the troops and the general public would diminish. European leaders would interpret Northern inaction as a faltering resolve in the Union.

General Irvin McDowell, a brigadier general from Ohio, devised a plan to engage the rebel forces under command of General Beauregard at Manassas, twenty-six miles southwest of Washington. It was an intelligent plan. Many Northerners had come to see Manassas as "a terrible, unknown, mysterious something . . . filled by countless thousands of the most ferocious warriors," poised to attack Washington, D.C. "Foreigners do not understand," Bates confided to a friend, "why we should allow a hostile army to remain so long almost in sight of the Capitol, if we were able to drive them off." With 30,000 Union troops at his disposal, McDowell could overrun Beauregard's forces so long as Union general Robert Patterson prevented the 9,000 Confederate troops under General Joseph Johnston at

Winchester, Virginia, from joining Beauregard. On June 29, Lincoln and his cabinet approved McDowell's plan.

The Battle of Bull Run, as it later became known in the North, began in the early-morning hours of Sunday, July 21. As the "roar of the artillery" reached the White House, Elizabeth Grimsley recalled, "the excitement grew intense." As far away as the Blair estate in Silver Spring, Monty's sister, Elizabeth, took a walk in the woods to "stop the *roar* in [her] ears," but the sound of the guns only increased. As soldiers on both sides of the battlefield were discovering the gruesome carnage of war, hundreds of Washingtonians hastily prepared picnic baskets filled with bread and wine. They raced to the hill at Centreville and the fields below to witness what most presumed would be an easy victory for the North. Senators, congressmen, government employees, and their families peered through opera glasses to survey the battlefield. After "an unusually heavy discharge," the British journalist William Russell overheard one woman exclaim: "That is splendid. Oh, my! Is not that first-rate? I guess we will be in Richmond this time to-morrow."

While Lincoln attended church, the Union troops pressed forward, forcing the rebels farther south into the woods. At midday, news of what seemed a complete Union victory reached Lincoln and the members of his cabinet at the telegraph office in the War Department. In the crowded space that housed the telegraph instruments, operators found it hard to focus on their responsibilities. Each new dispatch, the *New York Times* noted, was posted and read aloud to hundreds of people gathered in front of the Willard Hotel. The jubilant throng "cheered vehemently, and seemed fairly intoxicated with joy."

Even as the crowds celebrated in the streets, the fiercest stage of the fighting was just beginning. The Confederates refused to give up, rallied by the steadfast General Thomas Jackson. "There is Jackson with his Virginians, standing like a stone wall," General Barnard Bee reportedly shouted to inspire his troops, and both Confederate and Union soldiers thereafter referred to Jackson as "Stonewall" Jackson. The two sides fought valiantly in the blazing sun as the line of battle shifted back and forth. At 3 p.m., Lincoln was in the telegraph office studying the maps on the wall and waiting anxiously for the updated bulletins, which arrived in fifteen-minute intervals. The telegraph line stretched only as far as the Fairfax Court House. News from the battlefront farther south was relayed to Fairfax by a troupe of mounted couriers established by the young Andrew Carnegie, who then worked with the U.S. Military Telegraph Corps. Noting some confusion in the battlefield reports, Lincoln crossed over to General Scott's headquarters, "a small three-storied brick house" jammed with officers and clerks. Waking Scott from a nap, Lincoln expressed his concern. Scott, Nicolay reported, simply confirmed "his confidence in a successful result, and composed himself for another nap when the President left."

Succeeding dispatches became uniformly positive, conveying assurances that the Confederate lines had broken. At about 4:30, the telegraph operator proclaimed that "the Union Army had achieved a glorious victory." Lincoln decided to take his usual carriage ride, accompanied by Tad, Willie, and Secretary Bates. As they rode together to the Navy Yard to talk with John A. Dahlgren, one of Lincoln's favorite naval officers, Bates confided his anxiety for his son, Coalter, who was soon to be sent into battle. When young Coalter departed to join his regiment, Bates wrote, it was "the first time he ever left home." The carriage ride came to a close with Bates feeling a new intimacy with his president.

As Lincoln relaxed with Bates in his carriage, the tide of battle turned against the Union. Confederate general Johnston's forces had escaped General Patterson's grasp, and by midafternoon, nine thousand fresh Confederate troops arrived to reinforce Beauregard. McDowell had no reserve troops left. "A sudden swoop, and a body of [Confederate] cavalry rushed down upon our columns," Edmund Stedman reported from the battlefield. "They came from the woods . . . and infantry poured out behind them."

Exhausted Union infantrymen, including Sprague's First Rhode Island Regiment, broke ranks. An uncontrolled retreat toward Washington began, further confused by the panicked flight of horrified spectators. Indeed, an acquaintance of Chase's who had witnessed the battle "never stopped until he reached New-York." Young Stedman was appalled by the raging scene: "Army wagons, sutlers' teams, and private carriages, choked the passage, tumbling against each other, amid clouds of dust, and sickening sights and sounds." Muskets and small arms were discarded along the way. Wounded soldiers pled for help. Horses, running free, exacerbated the human stampede.

The shocking news reached Washington in Lincoln's absence. "General McDowell's army in full retreat through Centerville," the dispatch read; "the day is lost. Save Washington and the remnants of the Army." Seward grabbed the telegram and ran to the White House. With "a terribly frightened and excited look" on his face, he asked Nicolay for the latest news. Lincoln's secretary read him an earlier exultant dispatch. "Tell no one. That is not so. The battle is lost," Seward revealed. "Find the President and tell him to come immediately to Gen. Scott's."

When Lincoln returned, his young aides relayed Seward's message.

"He listened in silence," they later reported, "without the slightest change of feature or expression, and walked away to army headquarters." He remained there with Scott and his cabinet until a telegram from McDowell verified the loss. Immediate reinforcements were summoned to defend the capital. With no further recourse, the disconsolate team dispersed.

"Oh what a sad long weary day has this sabbath been," Elizabeth Blair told her husband. For Simon Cameron, the day brought a sharper personal grief. His brother James, in the service of Colonel William Sherman's brigade, was among the nearly nine hundred soldiers killed. "I loved my brother," Cameron wrote Chase, "as only the poor and lonely can love those with whom they have toiled & struggled up the rugged hill of life's success—but he died bravely in the discharge of his duty."

Seward stayed up past midnight composing a letter to Frances. "Every thing is being done that mortal man can do. Scott is grieved and disappointed. . . . What went out an army is surging back toward Washington as a disorganized mob. They fought well, did nobly, and apparently had gained the day, when some unreasonable alarm started a retreat. If the officers had experience and the men discipline, they could be rallied, and could be marched clear back to the field."

Lincoln returned to the White House, where he watched the returning soldiers straggle down the street, listened to the mournful sounds of ambulances, and sat for hours with various senators and congressmen who had witnessed the battle from the hill. Early the following morning, with rain pouring down, General Scott arrived, urging Mary to take the children to the North until Washington was deemed safe from capture. Elizabeth Grimsley recollected the exchange as Mary turned to her husband: "Will you go with us?" she asked. "Most assuredly I will not leave at this juncture," he replied. "Then I will not leave you at this juncture," she answered with finality.

Lincoln did not sleep that dreadful night. Finding his only comfort in forward motion, he began drafting a memo incorporating the painful lessons of Bull Run into a coherent future military policy. Understanding that the disorder of the newly formed troops had contributed to the debacle, he called for the forces to "be constantly drilled, disciplined and instructed." Furthermore, when he learned that soldiers preparing to end their three months of service had led the retreat, Lincoln proposed to let all those short-termers "who decline to enter the longer service, be discharged as rapidly as circumstances will permit." Anticipating European reactions to the defeat, he determined to move "with all possible despatch" to make the blockade operative. That night, a telegram was also sent to General George McClellan in western Virginia with orders to come to

Washington and take command of the Army of the Potomac. Lincoln then devised a strategy consisting of three advances: a second stand at Manassas; a move down the Mississippi toward Memphis; and a drive from Cincinnati to East Tennessee.

"If there were nothing else of Abraham Lincoln for history to stamp him with," Walt Whitman reflected, "it is enough to send him with his wreath to the memory of all future time, that he endured that hour, that day, bitterer than gall—indeed a crucifixion day—that it did not conquer him—that he unflinchingly stemmed it, and resolved to lift himself and the Union out of it."

Recriminations were plentiful. The Democratic *New York Herald* placed responsibility on "a weak, inharmonious and inefficient Cabinet." General Patterson was blamed for failing to keep Johnston's troops from joining Beauregard. "Two weeks ago," Chase self-righteously complained to a friend, "I urged the sending of Fremont to this command; and had it been done we should now have been rejoicing over a great victory." Still, the historian James Rawley concludes that "public censure touched too lightly on Lincoln," who should have held back the assault until the troops were ready.

"The sun rises, but shines not," Whitman wrote of the dismal day after the defeat. Rain continued to fall as the defeated troops flooded into Washington. From his window at Willard's, Russell observed these bedraggled soldiers. "Some had neither great-coats nor shoes, others were covered with blankets." Nettie Chase recalled being "awakened in the gray dawn by the heavy, unwonted, rumbling of laden wagons passing along the street below." Thinking at first they were bound for market, she was sickened to realize they were filled with wounded soldiers heading for the hospital nearby. To relieve the crowded hospital wards, Chase opened his spacious home to nearly a dozen wounded men. Bishop McIlvaine, a friend visiting from Ohio who happened to be staying with Chase at the time, tended to the sick and dying. Nettie recalled the bishop's uneasiness when one of the wounded men cursed loudly with each pain. "Just let me swear a bit," the young man entreated the stunned bishop, "it helps me stand the hurting."

"The dreadful disaster of Sunday can scarcely be mentioned," Stanton wrote to former president Buchanan five days after Bull Run. "The imbecility of this Administration culminated in that catastrophe," he pronounced with a sycophantic nod to his former boss, calling the fiasco "the result of Lincoln's 'running the machine' for five months. . . . The capture of Washington seems now to be inevitable—during the whole of Monday and Tuesday it might have been taken without any resistance. . . . Even now I doubt whether any serious opposition to the entrance of the Confederate forces could be offered."

Historians have long pondered the reluctance of the Confederates to capitalize on their victory by attacking Washington. Jefferson Davis later cited "an overweening confidence" after the initial victory that led to lax decisions. General Johnston observed that hundreds of volunteers, believing the war already won, simply left their regiments and returned home to "exhibit the trophies picked up on the field." Other soldiers melted into the countryside, accompanying wounded comrades to faraway hospitals. Perhaps the most straightforward explanation of both the dismal Union retreat and the Confederate failure to march into Washington is manifest in the plain assessment Nancy Bates posted to her young niece Hester: "Well we fought all day Sunday. Our men were so tired that they had to come away from Manassa I expect that the others were very tired too or they would have followed our men."

While Lincoln brooded in private, confiding in Browning that he was "very melancholy," he maintained a stoic public image. He refrained from answering Horace Greeley's acerbic letter, written in "black despair" after the *Tribune* editor had endured a week without sleep. "You are not considered a great man," Greeley charged, adding that if the Confederacy could not be defeated, Lincoln should "not fear to sacrifice [himself] to [his] country." Despite a blizzard of such indictments, Lincoln listened patiently to reports from the field of what went wrong. He told humorous stories to provide relief. And in the days that followed, with Seward by his side, he visited a number of regiments, raising spirits at every stop along the way.

At Fort Corcoran, on the Virginia side of the Potomac, he asked Colonel William T. Sherman if he could address the troops. Sherman was delighted, though he asked Lincoln to "discourage all cheering." After the boasts that preceded Bull Run, he explained, "what we needed were cool, thoughtful, hard-fighting soldiers—no more hurrahing, no more humbug." Lincoln agreed, proceeding to deliver what Sherman considered "one of the neatest, best, and most feeling addresses" he had ever heard. Lincoln commented on the lost battle but emphasized "the high duties that still devolved on us, and the brighter days yet to come." At various points, "the soldiers began to cheer, but [Lincoln] promptly checked them, saying: 'Don't cheer, boys. I confess I rather like it myself, but Colonel Sherman here says it is not military; and I guess we had better defer to his opinion.' "

The president closed his graceful speech with a pledge to provide the troops with all they needed, and even encouraged them to call on him "personally in case they were wronged." One aggrieved officer took him at his word, revealing that, as a three-month volunteer, he had tried to leave, but Sherman had "threatened to shoot" him. In a "stage-whisper," Lincoln counseled the officer: "Well, if I were you, and he threatened to shoot, I would not trust him, for I believe he would do it." The response produced gales of laughter among the men while upholding Sherman's discipline.

Northern public opinion reflected Lincoln's firm resolve. Republican newspapers across the land reported a "renewed patriotism," bringing thousands of volunteers to sign up for three years. "Let no loyal man be discouraged by the reverse," the *Chicago Tribune* proclaimed. "Like the great Antaeas, who, when thrown to the ground, gathered strength from the contact with mother earth and arose refreshed and stronger than before, to renew the contest, so of the Sons of Liberty; the loss of this battle will only nerve them to greater efforts." Several papers compared the Bull Run disaster to George Washington's early defeats in the Revolutionary War, which eventually resulted in triumph at Yorktown. "The spirit of the people is now thoroughly aroused," the *New York Times* announced, "and, what is equally important, it has been chastened and moderated by the stern lessons of experience."

With the stunning reversal and rout at Bull Run, however, Northern delusions of easy triumph dissolved. "It is pretty evident now that we have underrated the strength, the resources and the temper of the enemy," the *Times* conceded. "And we have been blind, moreover, to the extraordinary nature of the country over which the contest is to be waged,—and to its wonderful facilities for defence." Yet the harrowing lessons of Bull Run generated a perverse confidence that the North could "take comfort" in already knowing the worst that could happen. It was unimaginable in the anxious chaos following the first major battle of the Civil War that far worse was yet to come.

CHAPTER 14

"I DO NOT INTEND TO BE SACRIFICED"

"NOTHING BUT A PATENT PILL was ever so suddenly famous," it was said of George B. McClellan when he arrived in Washington on July 27, 1861, to take command of the Army of the Potomac. "That dear old domestic bird, the Public," an essayist later wrote, "was sure she had brooded out an eagle-chick at last." Among the Union's youngest generals at thirty-four, the handsome, athletic McClellan seemed to warrant the acclaim and great expectation. He was the scion of a distinguished Philadelphia family. His father graduated from Yale College and the University of Pennsylvania Medical School. His mother was elegant and genteel. Educated in excellent schools, including West Point, McClellan had served on the staff of General Scott in the Mexican War.

Most important, to a public looking for deliverance, he had recently defeated a guerrilla band in western Virginia, handing the North its only victory, albeit a small one.

To the nerve-worn residents of Washington, McClellan seemed "the man on horseback," just the leader to mold the disorganized Union troops into a disciplined army capable of returning to Manassas and defeating the enemy. Within days of his arrival, one diarist noted, Washington itself had assumed "a more martial look." Hotel bars no longer overflowed with drunken soldiers, nor did troops wander the city late at night in search of lodgings. The young general seemed able to mystically project his own self-confidence onto the demoralized troops, restoring their faith in themselves and their hope for the future. "You have no idea how the men brighten up now, when I go among them—I can see every eye glisten," he wrote proudly to his wife, Mary Ellen. "Yesterday they nearly pulled me to pieces in one regt. You never heard such yelling."

Lincoln hoped that between Scott's seasoned wisdom as general-in-chief and McClellan's vitality and force, he would finally have a powerfully effective team. From the start, however, McClellan viewed Scott as "the great obstacle" to both his own ambition for sole authority and to his larger strategy in the war. Less than two weeks after assuming command of the Army of the Potomac, McClellan questioned Scott's belief that the rush of reinforcements to Washington had secured the capital. In a letter to General Scott, which he copied to the president, he argued that his army was "entirely insufficient for the emergency," for "the enemy has at least 100,000 men in our front." Scott was furious that his judgment had been called into question, correctly insisting that McClellan was grossly exaggerating the opposition forces. It would not be the last of the imperious general's miscalculations.

Lincoln temporarily defused the animosity by asking McClellan to withdraw his offending letter, but the discord between the two generals continued to escalate. Scott wanted to employ "concentric pressure" on the rebels in different theaters of war. McClellan declared that only with an overwhelming force concentrated on Virginia could he put an end to hostilities. All other engagements he considered secondary, dispersing resources needed to "crush the rebels in one campaign."

In his almost daily letters to his wife, McClellan recognized that his disagreements with Scott might "result in a mortal enmity on his part against me." Justifying his unwillingness to make peace with Scott, he referred frequently to his sense of destiny. It was his conviction that "God has placed a great work in my hands." He felt that "by some strange operation of magic" he had "become *the* power of the land" and if "the people call upon me to save the country—I *must* save it & cannot respect anything that is in the way." McClellan told her that he received "letter after letter" begging him to assume the presidency or become a dictator. While he would eschew the presidency, he would "cheerfully take the Dictatorship & agree to lay down my life when the country is saved."

Frustrated by the lack of response to his constant calls for more troops and equipment, McClellan insisted that Scott was "a perfect imbecile," a "*dotard,*" even possibly "a *traitor.*" Refusing to acknowledge that the dispute represented an honest clash of opinions, McClellan insisted that the root of contention with Scott was the veteran's "eternal jealousy of all who acquire any distinction."

As the row between the two men intensified, McClellan decided to ignore Scott's communications, though the chain of command required that he inform his superior officer of his position and the number of troops at his disposal. Scott was indignant. "The remedy by arrest and trial before a Court Martial, would probably, soon cure the evil," Scott told Secretary of War Cameron, but he feared a public conflict "would be highly encouraging to the enemies, and depressing to the friends of the Union. Hence my long forbearance." Instead, he proposed that as soon as the president could make other arrangements, he himself would gladly retire, "being, as I am, unable to ride in the saddle, or to walk, by reason of dropsy in my feet and legs, and paralysis in the small of the back."

For two months, Lincoln tried to restore harmony between his commanders. He spent many hours at General Scott's headquarters, listening to the old warrior and attempting to mollify him. He made frequent visits to McClellan's headquarters, situated in a luxurious house at the corner of Lafayette Square, not far from Seward's new home. The upstairs rooms were reserved for McClellan's private use. The parlors downstairs were occupied by the telegraph office, with dozens of staff "smoking, reading the papers, and writing." Sometimes McClellan welcomed Lincoln's visits; on other occasions, he felt them a waste of time: "I have just been interrupted here by the Presdt & Secty Seward who had nothing very particular to say, except some stories to tell." Observers noted with consternation that McClellan often kept Lincoln waiting in the downstairs room, "together with other common mortals." British reporter William Russell began to pity the president, who would call only to be told that the general was "lying down, very much fatigued." Nonetheless, so long as he believed in McClellan's positive influence on the army, Lincoln tolerated such flagrant breaches of protocol.

The first public dissatisfaction with McClellan's performance began to emerge as the autumn leaves began to fall. While Washingtonians delighted in his magnificent reviews of more than fifty thousand troops marching in straight columns to the sounds of hundred-gun salutes, with "not a mistake made, not a hitch," they grew restive with the failure of the troops to leave camp. Undeterred, McClellan insisted to his wife that he would not move until he was certain that he was completely ready to take on the enemy. "A long time must yet elapse before I can do this, & I expect all the newspapers to abuse me for delay—but I will not mind that."

Radical Republicans who had initially applauded McClellan's appointment began to turn on him when they learned he had issued "a slave-catching order" requiring commanders to return fugitive slaves to their masters. McClellan repeatedly emphasized that he was "fighting to preserve the integrity of the Union & the power of the Govt," and that to achieve that overriding goal, the country could not "afford to raise up the negro question." Coming under attack, he sought cover from his Democratic friends. "Help me to dodge the nigger," he entreated Samuel Barlow of New York, "we want nothing to do with him."

At the first whiff of censure, McClellan shifted blame onto any other shoulder but his own—onto Scott's failure to muster necessary resources, onto the incompetence of the cabinet, "some of the greatest geese . . . I have ever seen—enough to tax the patience of Job." He considered Seward "a meddling, officious, incompetent little puppy," Welles "weaker than the most garrulous old woman," and Bates "an old fool." He was disgusted by the "rascality of Cameron," and though he commended Monty Blair's courage, he did not "altogether fancy him!" Only Chase was spared his scorn, perhaps because the treasury secretary had sent a flattering letter before McClellan was called to Washington in which he claimed that he was the one responsible for the general's promotion to major general.

Impatience with McClellan mounted when one of his divisions suffered a crushing defeat at a small engagement on October 21, 1861. Having learned that the rebels had pulled back some of their troops from Leesburg, Virginia, McClellan ordered General Charles P. Stone to mount "a slight demonstration on your part" in order "to move them." Stone assumed that he would have the help of a neighboring division, which McClellan had ordered back to Washington without informing Stone. Colonel Edward Baker, Lincoln's close friend from Illinois, was killed in action, along with forty-nine of his men when the Confederates trapped them at the river's edge at Ball's Bluff. Many more were seriously wounded, including the young Oliver Wendell Holmes, Jr., who was brought to Chase's spacious home to recover.

Baker was mourned by the entire Lincoln family. Lincoln later told the journalist Noah Brooks that "the death of his beloved Baker smote upon him like a whirlwind from a desert." The day before Baker was killed, the two old friends had talked together on the White House grounds. A passing officer recalled the poignant scene: "Mr. Lincoln sat on the ground leaning against a tree; Colonel Baker was lying prone on the ground his head supported by his clasped hands. The trees and the lawns were gorgeous in purple and crimson and scarlet, like the curtains of God's tabernacle." Not far away, ten-year-old Willie "was tossing the fallen leaves about in childish grace and abandon." When the time came for Baker to take his leave, he shook Lincoln's hand and then took Willie into his arms and kissed him.

Twenty-four hours later, Captain Thomas Eckert, in charge of the telegraph office at McClellan's headquarters, received word of Baker's death and the defeat at Ball's Bluff. Instructed to deliver all military telegrams directly to McClellan, Eckert searched for the commanding general. Finding him at the White House talking with Lincoln, he handed the general the wire and withdrew. McClellan chose not to reveal its contents to the president. Afterward, when Lincoln dropped in at the telegraph office to get the latest news from the front, he discovered the dispatch. A correspondent seated in the outer room observed Lincoln's reaction. He walked "with bowed head, and tears rolling down his furrowed cheeks, his face pale and wan, his heart heaving with emotion." He stumbled through the room and "almost fell as he stepped into the street."

Mary was similarly distraught. She had named her second son, Edward, in honor of Edward Baker. Now both her child and his dear namesake were lost. Willie and Tad, who had likewise adored Baker, were heartbroken. For Willie, much like his father, writing provided some measure of solace. He composed a small poem, "On the Death of Colonel Edward Baker," which was published in the *National Republican*. After two stanzas recalling Baker's patriotic life and celebrated oratorical skills, he wrote:

No squeamish notions filled his breast,
The Union *was his theme.*
"No surrender and no compromise,"
His day thought and night's dream.

His country has her *part to play,*
To'rds those he has left behind,
His widow and his children all,—
She must always keep in mind.

The child's homage to a cherished friend reflected a depressingly common circumstance as the war left mounting casualties and desolation in its wake. Ten-year-old Willie's words would be echoed in his father's memorable plea in the Second Inaugural Address, when he urged the nation "to care for him who shall have borne the battle, and for his widow, and his orphan."

McClellan straightaway denied responsibility for the defeat at Ball's Bluff, characteristically insisting that the "disaster was caused by errors committed" by the leaders at the front. "The whole thing took place some 40 miles from here without my orders or knowledge," he told his wife; "it was entirely unauthorized by me & I am in no manner responsible for it." The person "*directly* to blame," McClellan said, was Colonel Baker, who had exceeded General Stone's orders by crossing the river. Rumors then began to spread that Stone himself would be court-martialed.

When frustrated congressional leaders, many of whom were longtime friends of Baker, decried the defeat at Ball's Bluff and the general stagnation of the Union troops, the president defended McClellan. When these same leaders approached McClellan, he unleashed a diatribe against Scott, accusing him of placing obstacles at every step along his way. The congressional delegation left, vowing to remove Scott. "You may have heard from the papers etc of the small row that is going on just now between Genl Scott & myself," McClellan wrote his wife, "in which the vox populi is coming out strongly on my side. . . . I hear that off[icer]s & men all declare that they will fight under no one but 'our George,' as the scamps have taken it into their heads to call me."

On November 1, Lincoln regretfully accepted the veteran's request for retirement. The newspapers released General Scott's resignation letter along with Lincoln's heartfelt reply. The president extolled Scott's "long and brilliant career," stating that Americans would hear the news of his departure from active service "with sadness and deep emotion." At the same time, Lincoln designated McClellan to succeed Scott as general-in-chief of the Union Army.

Two days later, his objective accomplished, McClellan confessed to conflicted emotions when he accompanied Scott to the railroad station for his departure from Washington. "I saw there the end of a long, active & ambitious life," he wrote his wife, "the end of the career of the first soldier of his nation—& it was a feeble old man scarce able to walk—hardly any one there to see him off but his successor." The truth, as the newspapers reported, was that a large crowd had assembled at the depot, despite the train's leaving at 5 a.m. in a drenching rain. All the members of Scott's staff were there, along with McClellan's complete staff and a cavalry escort. Secretaries Chase and Cameron had come to join the general on his journey to Harrisburg. Moreover, "quite a number of citizens" had gathered to pay their respects, belying the ignominious farewell that McClellan depicted. Once again, the young Napoleon erred in his calculations.

As winter approached, public discontent with the inaction of the Union Army intensified. "I do not intend to be sacrificed," the new general-in-chief wrote his wife. Now that McClellan could no longer blame Scott for his troubles, he shifted his censure to Lincoln for denying him the means to confront the rebel forces in Virginia, whose numbers, he insisted, were at least three times his own. In letters home, he complained about Lincoln's constant intrusions, which forced him to hide out at the home of fellow Democrat Edwin Stanton, "to dodge all enemies in shape of 'browsing' Presdt etc." He reported a visit to the White House one Sunday after tea, where he found "the *original gorrilla,*" as he had taken to describing the president. "What a specimen to be at the head of our affairs now!" he ranted. "I went to Seward's, where I found the 'Gorilla' again, & was of course much edified by his anecdotes—ever apropos, & ever unworthy of one holding his high position."

On Wednesday night, November 13, Lincoln went with Seward and Hay to McClellan's house. Told that the general was at a wedding, the three waited in the parlor for an hour. When McClellan arrived home, the porter told him the president was waiting, but McClellan passed by the parlor room and climbed the stairs to his private quarters. After another half hour, Lincoln again sent word that he was waiting, only to be informed that the general had gone to sleep. Young John Hay was enraged. "I wish here to record what I consider a portent of evil to come," he wrote in his diary, recounting what he considered an inexcusable "insolence of epaulettes," the first indicator "of the threatened supremacy of the military authorities." To Hay's surprise, Lincoln "seemed not to have noticed it specially, saying it was better at this time not to be making points of etiquette & personal dignity." He would hold McClellan's horse, he once said, if a victory could be achieved.

Though Lincoln, the consummate pragmatist, did not express anger at McClellan's rebuff, his aides fumed at every instance of such arrogance. Lincoln's secretary, William Stoddard, described the infuriating delay when he accompanied Lincoln to McClellan's anteroom. "A minute passes, then another, and then another, and with every tick of the clock upon the mantel your blood warms nearer and nearer its boiling-point. Your face feels hot and your fingers tingle, as you look at the man, sitting so patiently over there . . . and you try to master your rebellious consciousness." As time went by, Lincoln visited the haughty general less frequently.

If he wanted to talk with McClellan, he sent a summons for him to appear at the White House.

• • •

DURING THESE TENSE DAYS, Mary tried to distract her husband. If old friends were in town, she would invite them to breakfast and dispatch a message to his office, calling the president to join the gathering. Initially irritated to be taken from his work, Lincoln would grudgingly sit down and begin exchanging stories. His "mouth would relax, his eye brighten, and his whole face lighten," Elizabeth Grimsley recalled, "and we would be launched into a sea of laughter." Mary had also introduced a therapeutic "daily drive," insisting that the two of them, and sometimes the children, take an hour-long carriage ride at the end of the afternoon, to absorb "the fresh air, which he so much needed."

More than most previous first ladies, Mary enjoyed entertaining. She had never lost her taste for politics. On many nights, while her husband worked late in his office, the first lady held soirées in the Blue Room, to which she invited a mostly male circle of guests. Her frequent visitors included Daniel Sickles, the New York congressman who recently had murdered the son of the composer of "The Star-Spangled Banner," Philip Barton Key, who was having an affair with Sickles's wife. Defended by a team of lawyers including Edwin Stanton, Sickles had been found innocent by reason of "temporary insanity."

Another flamboyant figure at Mary's salons was Henry Wikoff, who had published an account of his picaresque adventures in Europe. He had been a spy for Britain and had spent time in jail for kidnapping and seducing a young woman. Mary enjoyed people with scandalous backgrounds, and delighted in the lively conversation, which ranged from "love, law, literature, and war" to "gossip of courts and cabinets, of the *boudoir* and the *salon*, of commerce and the Church, of the peer and the pauper, of Dickens and Thackeray."

While Mary charmed guests in her evening salons, she gained respect for the energy and aplomb with which she hosted the traditional White House receptions for the public. She believed that these social gatherings helped to sustain morale. Most important, her husband was proud of both her social skills and her appearance. "My wife is as handsome as when she was a girl," he said at one White House levee, "and I a poor nobody then, fell in love with her and once more, have never fallen out."

When Prince Napoleon, the cousin of Napoleon Bonaparte III, visited Washington in early August, Mary organized an elaborate dinner party. She found the task of entertaining much simpler than it had been in

Springfield days. "We only have to give our orders for the dinner, and *dress* in proper season," she wrote her friend Hannah Shearer. Having learned French when she was young, she conversed easily with the prince. It was a "beautiful dinner," Lizzie Grimsley recalled, "beautifully served, gay conversation in which the French tongue predominated." Two days later, her interest in French literature apparently renewed, Mary requested Volume 9 of the *Oeuvres de Victor Hugo* from the Library of Congress.

Nor did Mary Lincoln confine her abundant energies to social ventures. A month after the French dinner, she strenuously pressured her husband on a matter of state—the pending execution of William Scott. A soldier from Vermont, Scott had fallen asleep during picket duty. His dereliction of duty had occurred during the predawn hours of his second straight night of standing guard. As the story was told, he had volunteered the first night to replace a sick friend, and then was called to duty the next night on his own. According to Lizzie Grimsley, the severity of the soldier's sentence distressed both Tad and his mother. "Think," Tad entreated, "if it was your own little boy who was just tired after fighting, and marching all day, that he could not keep awake, much as he tried to." Mary joined in, begging her husband to show mercy to the young soldier. The situation was not easy for Lincoln. While he understood the human circumstances that led to the soldier's lapse, he also recognized that his intervention might undermine military discipline. In the end, Mary's arguments apparently swayed him.

The day before the scheduled execution, Lincoln walked over to McClellan's office and asked him to issue a pardon, "suggesting," the general recollected, "that I could give as a reason in the order that it was by request of the 'Lady President.' " Vermont senator Lucius Chittenden, who had also interceded on young Scott's behalf, apologized for the imposition, recognizing "that it was asking too much of the President" to intervene "in behalf of a private soldier." Lincoln put Chittenden's mind at ease, assuring him that "Scott's life is as valuable to him as that of any person in the land. You remember the remark of a Scotchman about the head of a nobleman who was decapitated. 'It was a small matter of a head, but it was valuable to him, poor fellow, for it was the only one he had.' "

The renovation of the White House and its surrounding landscape engaged Mary throughout the summer and fall of 1861. She raved to a friend that she had "the most beautiful flowers & grounds imaginable, and company & excitement enough, to turn a wiser head than my own." Yet with each passing month, she spent less time with her husband, whose every hour was preoccupied with the war. Though he still took the afternoon drives she had prescribed, he often invited Seward along so the two men could talk. In late August, when Seward's wife and daughter arrived in

Washington to spend several weeks, Lincoln took them for drives nearly every afternoon. Frances took an immediate liking to the president, whom she described as "a plain unassuming farmer—not awkward or ungainly," who talked with equal ease about "the war & the crops." Fanny was captivated. "I liked him very much," she recorded in her diary. She was especially delighted when the president showed her the kittens her father had given to Willie and Tad and told her that "they climb all over him."

During these pleasant interludes with the Seward family, Lincoln stopped to visit the various encampments in the surrounding countryside. Halting the carriages, he and Seward would talk with the soldiers. A veteran reporter who had watched every president since Jackson wrote that he had never seen anyone go through the routine of handshaking with the "*abandon* of President Lincoln. He goes it with both hands, and hand over hand, very much as a sailor would climb a rope." The affable Seward was equally at ease. Fanny took particular delight in watching them greet troops from the 23rd Pennsylvania Regiment. "With one impulse" the men cheered Lincoln's appearance so loudly that the horses were "somewhat startled"; then they "began cheering for 'Secretary Seward' passing his name from mouth to mouth." Fanny proudly confided in her diary that "I love to remember all Father says and does."

Frances Seward was happy to be reunited with her husband for the first extended period in almost a year, but she found the frantic pace of wartime Washington life enervating. Nor did she feel at home in the "palatial" house her husband had taken on Lafayette Square. In a letter to her sister, she wistfully confessed that Henry was never "more pleased with a home—it accommodates itself marvelously to his tastes & habits—such as they are at this day." She praised Fred and Anna, who were so "gifted in making their surroundings . . . tasteful & attractive." But it was a home designed for the three of them—her husband, son, and daughter-in-law—not for her. It perfectly fitted the constant round of entertaining that Seward so enjoyed. And Anna was far better suited to the role of hostess than Frances—confined to her bed by migraines for several days every week—could ever hope to be.

As she readied herself to return to Auburn, Frances was concerned that she had not yet called on Mary Lincoln. The first lady had just come back from a three-week vacation in upstate New York and Long Branch, New Jersey, and Frances felt it her duty to visit, "especially as I went to see her husband." On the Monday before Frances was due to leave, word came that Mary would receive her and her family that evening. After dinner, John Nicolay arrived to escort the Sewards to the White House. The little group included Henry, Frances, Fred, Anna, and Fanny, as well as Seward's youngest son, Will, and his new bride, Jenny. They were shown into the Blue Parlor by Edward, the Irish doorkeeper who had worked in the White House for nearly two decades. "Edward drew a chair for Mrs. L.," Fanny recalled, and then arranged the chairs for the rest of the party, before leaving to inform Mary that her guests had arrived. "Well there we sat," Fanny recorded, until "after a lapse of some time the usher came and said Mrs. Lincoln begged to be excused, she was *very* much engaged."

"The truth," Fanny wrote, "was probably that she did not want to see Mother—else why not give general direction to the doorkeeper to let no one in? It was certainly very rude to have us all seated first." Referring to Mary's celebrated salons, Fanny archly added that it was "the only time on record that she ever refused to see company in the evening." In fact, Mary detested Seward and had most likely contrived to snub the entire Seward family. From the outset, she had resisted Seward's appointment to the cabinet, fearing that his celebrity would outshine her husband's. "If things should go on all right," she warned, "the credit would go to *Seward*—if they went wrong—the blame would fall upon my husband." Contrary to Mary's suspicions, it was Seward who received much of the censure incurred by the administration, as his fellow cabinet members tended to blame him more than Lincoln for whatever displeased them. Long after Seward had come to respect Lincoln's authority, however, many observers, including Mary, mistakenly assumed that the secretary of state was the mastermind of the administration. "It makes me mad to see you sit still and let that hypocrite, Seward, twine you around his finger as if you were a skein of thread," Mary fumed to her husband.

Furthermore, Mary resented the long evenings Lincoln spent at Seward's Lafayette Square mansion rather than remaining home with her. Warmed by Seward's fireplace and gregarious personality, Lincoln could unwind. Though he himself neither drank nor smoked, he happily watched Seward light up a Havana cigar and pour a glass of brandy. And while Lincoln rarely swore, he found Seward's colorful cursing amusing. On one occasion, as Lincoln and Seward were en route to review the troops, the driver lost control of his team and began swearing with gusto. "My friend, are you an Episcopalian?" Lincoln asked. The teamster replied that he was, in fact, a Methodist. "Oh, excuse me," Lincoln said with a laugh. "I thought you must be an Episcopalian for you swear just like Secretary Seward, and he's a churchwarden!"

Lincoln and Seward talked of many things besides the war. They debated the historical legacies of Henry Clay, Daniel Webster, and John Quincy Adams. Seward argued that neither Clay's nor Webster's would live "a tithe as long as J. Q. Adams." Lincoln disagreed, believing that

"Webster will be read for ever." They explored the concept of "personal courage." When Lincoln spoke admiringly of the intensity of a particular soldier's desire to take on the enemy in person, Seward disagreed. "He had always acted on the opposite principle, admitting you are scared and assuming that the enemy is." They traded stories and teased each other.

One night when John Hay was also present, another guest brought up the Chicago convention. Hay feared that reminding Seward of his loss was in "very bad taste," but Lincoln used the remark to tell a humorous story about 1860. At one point, he related, the mayor of Chicago, John Wentworth, had feared that Lincoln was oblivious to shifting opinion in Illinois. "I tell you what," Wentworth advised, referring to Thurlow Weed. "You must do like Seward does—get a feller to run you." Both Lincoln and Seward found the story "vastly amusing."

Lincoln's buoyant mood plummeted an hour or so later that evening when he received General Thomas W. Sherman's request for more troops before his advance upon Port Royal, South Carolina. Frustrated by repeated calls from every general for reinforcements, he told Seward he would refuse Sherman's request and would telegraph him to say he didn't have "much hope of his expedition anyway." Now it was Seward's turn to moderate the president's reply, much as Lincoln had softened Seward's language in the famous May 21 dispatch. "No," Seward replied, "you wont say discouraging things to a man going off with his life in his hand." Lincoln rejected Sherman's request for more troops but expressed no pessimism about the mission.

The long evenings of camaraderie at Seward's, where interesting guests wandered in and out, probably rekindled memories of Lincoln's convivial days on the circuit, when he and his fellow lawyers gathered together before the log fire to talk, drink, and share stories. Between official meetings and private get-togethers, Lincoln spent more time with Seward in the first year of his presidency than with anyone else, including his family. It was not therefore surprising that the possessive Mary felt rancor toward Seward and his family.

• • •

WHILE LINCOLN ENDURED complaints about the lack of forward movement in the East, he was forced to confront an equally thorny situation in the West, where the fighting between secessionists and Unionists in Missouri threatened to erupt into civil war. Though a majority of the state supported the Union, the new governor, Claiborne Jackson, commanded a sizable number of secessionists intent upon bringing the state into the Confederacy. Missouri initially succeeded in thwarting the rebel guerrillas, largely through the combined efforts of Frank Blair, who had left Congress to become a colonel, and his good friend, General Nathaniel Lyon. They had prevented rebel troops from seizing the St. Louis arsenal, and ingeniously captured Fort Jackson, where the Confederate troops were headquartered. Lyon had entered the rebel camp on a scouting mission, disguised as the familiar figure of Frank's mother-in-law, a well-respected old lady in St. Louis. He wore a dress and shawl, with a "thickly veiled sunbonnet," to hide his red beard. Hidden in his egg basket were revolvers in case he was recognized. The following day, with knowledge of the camp and seven thousand troops, Lyon marched in and took the fort.

In spite of these early successes, daring rebel raids soon destroyed bridges, roads, and property, and threw the state into a panic. To take charge of this perilous situation and command the entire Department of the West, Lincoln appointed General John C. Frémont, the dashing hero whose exploits in 1847 in the liberation of California from Mexico had earned him the first Republican nomination for president in 1856. Lincoln later recalled that it was upon the "earnest solicitation" and united advocacy of the powerful Blair family that he made Frémont a major general and sent him to Missouri.

Frémont's appointment was initially greeted with enthusiasm. "He is just such a person as Western men will idolize and follow through every danger to death or victory," John Hay wrote. "He is upright, brave, generous, enterprising, learned and eminently practical." Frémont's staunch antislavery principles found favor among the German-Americans who comprised a large portion of the St. Louis population. "There was a sort of romantic halo about him," Gustave Koerner recalled. His name alone had "a magical influence," inducing thousands of volunteers from the Western states to join the Union Army.

Within weeks of Frémont's arrival, however, stories filtered back to Washington of "recklessness in expenditures." Tales circulated that the Frémonts had set themselves up in a $6,000 mansion, where bodyguards deterred unwanted visitors, including Hamilton Gamble, the former Unionist governor of Missouri and brother-in-law of Edward Bates. Some worried that Frémont, like McClellan, had chosen to stay in the city to prepare for a move against the rebels rather than join his troops in the field. These unsettling rumors were followed by the shocking news of General Lyon's death in a struggle at Wilson's Creek on August 10. Weeks later, the Union forces suffered another devastating defeat when they were forced to surrender Lexington to the rebels. Among Missouri's loyalists morale plummeted.

In late August, realizing he must act before the situation deteriorated further, Frémont issued a bold proclamation. Without consulting Lincoln, he declared martial law throughout the state, giving the military the authority to try and, if warranted, shoot any rebels within Union lines who were found "with arms in their hands." Union troops were directed to confiscate all property, including slaves, of all persons "who shall be directly proven to have taken an active part with their enemies in the field." These slaves, Frémont proclaimed, "are hereby declared freemen." Frémont's policy far exceeded the Confiscation Act passed by the Congress earlier that month, which applied only to slaves supporting Confederate troops and did not spell out their future status.

Lincoln learned of Frémont's proclamation by reading it in the newspapers along with the rest of the nation. With this announcement, Frémont had unilaterally recast the struggle to preserve the Union as a war against slavery, a shift that the president believed would lead Kentucky and the border states to join the Confederacy. Lincoln wrote a private letter to Frémont, expressing his "anxiety" on two points: "First, should you shoot a man, according to the proclamation, the Confederates would very certainly shoot our best man in their hands in retaliation; and so, man for man, indefinitely." Even more troubling, he saw "great danger" in "liberating slaves of traiterous owners," a move that would certainly "alarm our Southern Union friends, and turn them against us—perhaps ruin our rather fair prospect for Kentucky. Allow me therefore to ask, that you will as of your own motion, modify that paragraph so as to conform" to the recent Confiscation Act of Congress. Lincoln was anxious that Frémont change the language of his own accord, so that the president would not be officially forced to override him. He understood that if the controversy became public, radical Republicans, whose loyalty was crucial to his governing coalition, might side with Frémont rather than with him.

Moreover, as Lincoln later explained to Orville Browning, "Fremont's proclamation, as to confiscation of property, and the liberation of slaves, is *purely political*, and not within the range of *military* law, or necessity." As chief executive, he could not allow a general in the field to determine the "permanent future condition" of slaves. Seward fully supported Lincoln on principle as well as policy. "The trouble with Fremont was, that he acted without authority from the President," Seward later maintained. "The President could permit no subordinate to assume a responsibility which belonged only to himself."

Lincoln's fears about the reaction to Frémont's proclamation in the border states were justified. Within days, frantic letters reached Washington from Unionists in Kentucky. Joshua Speed wrote to Lincoln that Frémont's proclamation had left him "unable to eat or sleep—It will crush out every vestige of a union party in the state—I perhaps & a few others will be left alone." He reminded his old friend that there were "from 180 to 200000 slaves" in Kentucky, of whom only 20,000 belonged to rebels. "So fixed is public sentiment in this state against freeing negroes & allowing negroes to be emancipated & remain among us," he continued, "that you had as well attack the freedom of worship in the north or the right of a parent to teach his child to read—as to wage war in a slave state on such a principle."

Meanwhile, events in Missouri took a strange turn. On September 1, the same day that Frémont made his proclamation public, Colonel Frank Blair penned a long letter to his brother, Montgomery, that would lead to the colonel's arrest and imprisonment two weeks later. "I know that you and I are both in some sort responsible for Fremonts appointment," he admitted, but "my decided opinion is that he should be relieved of his command." Blair was not reacting to the proclamation, as was assumed by contemporaries and historians alike. On the contrary, he told Monty he agreed with the proclamation, believing that stringent measures, including the liberation of slaves, were necessary to dispel the illusions of impunity the marauding bands of rebel guerrillas seemed to harbor. He wished only that the proclamation had been issued earlier, when Frémont "had the power to enforce it & the enemy no power to retaliate."

But since Frémont had taken command, Frank told his brother, the situation in Missouri had grown increasingly desperate. Through "gross & inexcusable negligence," the rebels had accumulated a substantial following. "Oh! for one hour of our dead Lyon," he lamented, adding that many now ascribed Lyon's death to Frémont's failure to reinforce him. Moreover, in the camps around St. Louis, there was "an active want of discipline" reminiscent of the disorganization in Washington that led to Bull Run. If his brother had information absolving Frémont, Frank continued, if the government knew more of Frémont's plans than he, then Montgomery should "burn this paper and say that I am an *alarmist*"; but at this moment, his faith was shaken "to the very foundations."

Monty Blair showed his brother's frank letter to Lincoln and added a letter of his own. He asserted that he himself had reluctantly concluded that Frémont must be dismissed. He acknowledged that he had sponsored Frémont at the start, having enjoyed a warm friendship with the celebrated explorer, "but being now satisfied of my mistake duty requires that I should frankly admit it and ask that it may be promptly corrected." Like Frank, he took no issue with the proclamation, believing a show of strength was necessary. Frémont's removal, he concluded, was "required by public interests."

Hearing similar testimony from other sources in Missouri, Lincoln sent General Meigs and Montgomery Blair on September 10 to talk with Frémont and "look into the affair." At this point, the president still had not received confirmation from Frémont that he would modify the proclamation as requested.

That evening, Frémont's spirited wife, Jessie, the daughter of former senator Thomas Benton, arrived in Washington after a three-day trip on a dusty, cramped train to hand-deliver Frémont's delayed response. She sent Lincoln a card asking when she could see him and received the peremptory response: "A. Lincoln. Now." Straightaway, Jessie left her room at the Willard in the wrinkled dress she had worn during her sweltering trip. As she later reported, when the president came into the room, he "bowed slightly" but did not speak. Nor did he offer her a seat. She handed him her husband's letter, which he read standing. To Lincoln's fury and dismay, Frémont had refused his private request to modify the proclamation, insisting that the president must publicly order him to do so. "If I were to retract of my own accord," the general argued, "it would imply that I myself thought it wrong and that I had acted without the reflection which the gravity of the point demanded. But I did not do so."

When Lincoln remarked that Frémont clearly knew what was expected of him, Jessie implied that Lincoln did not understand the complex situation in Missouri. Nor did he appreciate that unless the war became one of emancipation, European powers were more than likely to recognize the Confederacy. "You are quite a female politician," Lincoln remarked. He later recalled that Jessie Frémont had "taxed me so violently with many things that I had to exercise all the awkward tact I have to avoid quarelling with her. . . . She more than once intimated that if Gen Fremont should conclude to try conclusions with me he could set up for himself." As Jessie left, she asked Lincoln when she might return to receive his reply. He told her he would send for her when he was ready.

The next morning, Lincoln wrote his reply. This time, he issued "an open order" to Frémont to revise his proclamation to conform to the provisions of the Confiscation Act. Rather than allow Jessie to hand-deliver it, he sent it to be mailed. In keeping with Frémont's own tactics, he made the reply public before Frémont would receive it.

While Jessie waited vainly at the Willard for word from Lincoln, Francis Blair, Sr., visited her room. "He had always been fond of me," Jessie recalled, "I had been like a child in their family; but Mr. Blair was now very angry." He told her that she and her husband had made a great mistake in incurring the enmity of the president. Talking too freely over a two-hour period, the elder Blair revealed that Frank had sent a letter to Monty describing the situation in Missouri, and that the president had sent Monty to St. Louis to "examine into that Department."

Jessie was infuriated, assuming that Frank's letter had precipitated the investigation. She "threatened the old man that Fremont should hold Frank personally responsible expecting that she could make [him] quail at the thought of losing the son of whom [he] is most proud in a duel with a skilled duellist." Blair Senior told her "that the Blairs did not shrink from responsibility." Frank's sister, Lizzie, who, like the rest of the family, adored her high-spirited brother, believed her father had been "most incautious" in discussing Frank's letter with Jessie, rightly fearing that the Frémonts would retaliate.

Meanwhile, Meigs and Monty Blair had assessed affairs in Missouri and were heading home. Meigs had come to the clear conclusion that Frémont was not fit to command the Department of the West. "The rebels are killing and ravaging the Unionmen throughout the state," he wrote; "great distress and alarm prevail; In St. Louis the leading people of the state complain that they cannot see him; he does not encourage the men to form regiments for defence." Monty Blair agreed. After what he described to Lincoln as "a full & plain talk with Fremont," he claimed that the general "Seems Stupefied & almost unconscious, & is doing absolutely nothing." Rumors circulated that Frémont was an opium-eater. "No time is to be lost, & no mans feelings should be consulted," Blair concluded.

The day after Monty Blair and Meigs departed for Washington, Frémont imprisoned Frank Blair, claiming that the letter he had written his brother on September 1 was an act of insubordination. By criticizing his commanding officer "with a view of effecting his removal," Frank was guilty of conduct "unbecoming an officer and a gentleman."

Frémont and Jessie had concluded that the Blairs had betrayed them. Monty interceded, writing a conciliatory letter to Frémont that led to Frank's release from jail. Frank insisted on fighting the charges, however, and was soon arrested again. Opinion in Missouri was equally divided between Frank Blair and General Frémont, each intent on destroying the other. General Scott had finally stepped in, ordering a suspension of Frank's arrest and postponing the trial, which would never take place. But the quarrel between the two old allies would have serious consequences in the years ahead.

Lincoln's public abrogation of Frémont's proclamation produced a sigh of relief in the border states but, as Lincoln had apprehended, it profoundly disappointed radical Republicans and abolitionists. Only days earlier, Frances Seward had happily asked her sister, "Were you not pleased with Fremont's proclamation?" Now Lincoln had once again dashed her hopes. In Chicago, Joseph Medill lamented that Lincoln's letter "has cast a funeral gloom over our patriotic city. . . . It comes upon us like a killing June frost—which destroys the comming harvest. It is a *step backwards.*" Senator Ben Wade blamed Lincoln's "poor white trash" background for his revolting decision, while Frederick Douglass despaired: "Many blunders have been committed by the Government at Washington during this war, but this, we think, is the largest of them all."

While radicals hoping to make emancipation the war's focus rallied behind Frémont, his antislavery credentials could not compensate for his flagrant mismanagement of the Department of the West. On September 18, Monty Blair and Meigs delivered their negative report to the cabinet. Still, Lincoln hesitated. The president "is determined to let Fremont have a chance to win the State of Missouri," the frustrated postmaster general told Francis Blair, Sr. Bates, too, was irritated by the president's lack of resolution. With much of his large family still in Missouri, Bates had followed the state's troubles closely. He had spoken against Frémont on numerous occasions in the cabinet, certain that Frémont was doing "more damage to our cause than half a dozen of the ablest generals of the enemy can do." Having assured Unionist friends in his home state that Frémont's removal was imminent, Bates felt "distressed & mortified" by the president's inaction.

Anxious about Missouri's troubles and anguished by the illness of his wife, Julia, who had suffered a slight paralytic stroke, Bates uncharacteristically lashed out at Lincoln. "Immense mischief is caused by his lack of vim," he wrote his brother-in-law, the former governor of Missouri; "he has no will, no power to command—He makes no body afraid of him. And hence discipline is relaxed, & stupid inanity takes the place of action."

Frank Blair was more scathing in his criticisms of Lincoln and his cabinet. "I think God has made up his mind to ruin this nation," he wrote his brother Monty. "The only way to save it is to kick that pack of old women who compose the Cabinet into the sea. I never since I was born imagined that such a lot of poltroons & apes could be gathered together from the four quarters of the Globe as Old Abe has succeeded in bringing together in his Cabinet." His anger was focused on Seward and Cameron, and indirectly, of course, on Lincoln himself.

In fact, Lincoln had already dispatched Secretary of War Simon Cameron, accompanied by Adjutant General Lorenzo Thomas, to St. Louis to examine the situation once more and deliver, at his discretion, "a letter directing [Frémont] to surrender his command to the officer next below him." When Cameron arrived in St. Louis, he talked with Brigadier General Samuel R. Curtis, who "spoke very freely of [Frémont's] qualities and conduct" and warned the secretary of war that Missouri's safety could be guaranteed only by the termination of Frémont's command. Upon receiving the letter of dismissal, Frémont "was very much mortified." He told Cameron that "he was now in pursuit of the enemy, whom he believed were now within his reach, and that to recall him at this moment would not only destroy him, but render his whole expenditure useless." Cameron was swayed to withhold the order until he returned to Washington and talked with the president.

By this point, Lincoln had little doubt that Frémont should be discharged. In addition to the impressions of Meigs, Monty Blair, and Cameron, he had received a blistering report from Adjutant General Thomas detailing the sorry "constitution of Fremont's army, its defective equipment and arming, its confusion and imbecility, its lack of transportation," a catalogue of items leading to the unassailable conclusion that "its head is wholly incompetent and unsafe to be instructed with its management." Yet Lincoln still "yielded to delay," Bates angrily confided in his diary, holding Seward responsible when the president hesitated a few days longer. "The President still hangs in painful and mortyfying doubt," Bates wrote. "And if we persist in this sort of impotent indecision, we are very likely to share his fate—and, worse than all, *deserve it.*"

The Attorney General's impatience was understandable, but Lincoln's reasoning behind the delay was far shrewder than Bates realized. Two days after Bates made his angry entry, Lincoln dispatched his friend Leonard Swett to hand-carry a removal order to Frémont. Before Swett reached St. Louis, however, the War Department released the damning report of Adjutant General Thomas to the press. Published on October 31, the detailed report was considered by the *New York Times* "the most remarkable document that has seen the light since the beginning of the present war." So damning were the revelations about Frémont, the *Times* continued, that it was mystifying why the Lincoln administration had allowed their publication.

In fact, the decision to publicize the report was both calculated and canny. By the time the message was delivered to Frémont, the public had been primed with powerful arguments for his dismissal. Had Lincoln acted earlier, people might have concluded that Frémont was sacrificed to the Blairs or, worse still, cashiered because of his proclamation emancipating the slaves. By leaking the facts in the report, Lincoln had adroitly prepared public opinion to support his decision.

When Swett reached Missouri, he wisely anticipated that Frémont would suspect his mission and refuse him entry into camp. So he gave the dismissal order to an army captain, who disguised himself as a farmer.

With the document sewed into the lining of his coat, the messenger reached Frémont in person shortly after dawn on November 1, the same day that General Scott's resignation was announced. When Frémont opened the order, the captain recalled, a "frown came over his brow, and he slammed the paper down on the table and exclaimed, 'Sir, how did you get admission into my lines?' "

By November 2, when the news was made public, the general reaction was that Lincoln was "justified" in his decision. Frémont no longer had "apologists or defenders" in Washington, the correspondent for the *New York Times* wrote; "the evidences of his unfitness for command have naturally so accumulated here—the headquarters of the army—that no defence of him is possible." The *Philadelphia Inquirer* agreed. "Slowly and reluctantly we are forced to the conviction that General Fremont is unequal to the command of the Western army. The report of Adjutant-General Thomas, which we publish this morning, settles the question in our judgment." In an unusually pro-administration editorial, the Democratic *New York Herald* noted with approval that while "Lincoln is not the man to deal unjustly or ungenerously with any public officer," his firing of Frémont "had become a public necessity, to which the President could no longer shut his eyes; and this tells the whole story."

Even Chase had to admit that Lincoln had handled the tangled situation admirably. "I am thoroughly persuaded," he wrote a friend, "that in all he has done [concerning] Gen. F. the Prest. has been guided by a true sense of publ[ic] duty."

• • •

ONE WEEK AFTER the resignation of General Scott and the dismissal of General Frémont, the administration faced a pressing new dilemma. Seward had received word that the Confederacy had dispatched two prominent Southerners, James Mason and John Slidell, to England to argue its case for formal recognition. Seward hoped to intercept the Confederate ship carrying the two former senators, but they had escaped the Union blockade in Charleston and reached Cuba, where they boarded the *Trent*, a British mail ship. On November 8, Union captain Charles Wilkes, in command of an armed sloop, encountered the *Trent*. Acting without official orders, he fired a shot across the bow and then proceeded to search the vessel. When Mason and Slidell were found, they were courteously escorted back to the Union sloop *San Jacinto* and taken to prison at Fort Warren in Boston. The British ship was allowed to continue its journey.

Captain Wilkes became a national hero to a North desperate for good news. "We do not believe the American heart ever thrilled with more genuine delight than it did yesterday, at the intelligence of the capture of Messrs. Slidell and Mason," the *New York Times* reported. "If we were to search the whole of Rebeldom, no persons so justly obnoxious to the North, could have been found." Wilkes was fêted at Faneuil Hall in Boston, and a great banquet was given in his honor. Cameron appeared before a throng of happy Washingtonians and led "three cheers for Captain Wilkes." Bates recorded "great and general satisfaction" in his diary, while Chase reportedly said he regretted only that the captain had not gone one step further and seized the British ship.

Lincoln, too, seemed pleased at first. In a letter to Edward Everett, he spoke happily of "the items of news coming in last week," first the Union victory at Port Royal, and "then the capture of Mason & Slidell!" His gratification was soon mingled with anxiety, however, when Britain's furious reaction to the incident became known. It took nearly three weeks for news of Mason and Slidell's capture to reach London, but, as *The Times* reported, the "intelligence spread with wonderful rapidity." The complex situation was promptly reduced to a slogan: "Outrage on the British flag—the Southern Commissioners Forcibly Removed From a British Mail Steamer." The London press fulminated against the incident as an explicit violation of the law of nations, demanding "reparation and apology." Fabricated details of the capture depicted a brutal removal of the Southern commissioners.

Looking to give the supposed transgression a face, the British press focused upon Seward. Though the secretary of state told British officials confidentially that Wilkes had "acted without any instructions from the Government," thereby sparing the government "the embarrassment which might have resulted if the act had been specially directed by us," he decided not to speak publicly on the matter. The first public response should come from the British government, Seward maintained. Seward's silence troubled Thurlow Weed, whom Seward had sent to Europe as an unofficial representative. In one of his daily letters to Washington, Weed warned his oldest friend that "if the taking of the rebels from under the protection of the British flag was intended, and is avowed, and maintained, *it means war.*" Newspapers reported that steamers in every dockyard were being equipped with troops and supplies, ready to leave at the government's order. The press continued "fanning the popular flame by promising to clear the sea of the American navy in a month; acknowledge the Southern Confederacy; and, by breaking the blockade, letting out cotton, and letting in British manufactures." Secessionists in Europe, Weed reported, were "certainly jubilant."

Moreover, Weed anxiously wrote, word circulated in "high places" that

Seward hoped "to provoke a war with England for the purpose of getting Canada." Animosity toward Seward was widespread, he continued, "how created or why, I know not. It has been skillfully worked. I was told yesterday, repeatedly, that I ought to write the President demanding your dismissal."

Agitated by the vituperative attacks by the British press, Seward burst into Lincoln's office on Sunday afternoon, December 15. Orville Browning, who was taking tea with the president at the time, dismissed Seward's worries, insisting that England would not do "so foolish a thing" as to declare war. Lincoln was not so sure. He recalled a ferocious bulldog in his hometown. While neighbors convinced themselves that they had nothing to fear, one wise man observed: "I know the bulldog will not bite. You know he will not bite, but does the bulldog know he will not bite?"

The American press hounded Seward with questions about the affair, but both he and Lord Lyons, the British minister to Washington, remained silent as they awaited the official British response. On December 19, nearly six weeks after the initial incident, "Her Majesty's Government" finally declared the seizure of the envoys from the British ship "an affront to the national honor," which could be restored only if the prisoners were freed and returned to "British protection." In addition, Britain demanded "a suitable apology for the aggression." If the United States did not agree within a few days, Lyons and the entire British delegation were to pack up and return to Britain. Lyons carried the document to the secretary of state's office, where he discussed the inflamed situation with Seward. Before presenting the document formally, he agreed to leave a copy so that the secretary and the president might have more time to consider their response. "You will perhaps be surprised to find Mr. Seward on the side of peace," Lord Lyons wrote to the British foreign minister.

Fred Seward recalled that his father shut himself off from all visitors and "devoted one entire day" to drafting a reply. The astute secretary understood the dilemma perfectly. As a practical matter, the United States could not afford to go to war with Britain. "With England as an auxiliary to rebellion," Weed had forewarned, "we are 'crushed out.' " It was necessary that the government release the prisoners and allow them to continue their journey to England. Yet, overwhelming popular support in the North for the seizure of the rebels had to be taken into consideration. "They can never be given up," one newspaper protested. "The country would never forgive any man who should propose such a surrender." Lincoln himself, though resolved to avoid war with England, was reportedly unhappy about submitting to the British demands, which many considered humiliating.

Seward composed an ingenious response, arguing that while Captain

Wilkes had acted lawfully in searching the *Trent*, the legality of seizing contraband prisoners should have been decided by an American Prize Court. He recognized, he wrote, that he appeared to be taking "the British side" of the dispute "against my own country," but he was "really defending and maintaining, not an exclusively British interest, but an old, honored, and cherished American cause." The principle of referring such disputes to a legal tribunal, he reminded Britain, had been established nearly six decades earlier by Secretary of State James Madison when Britain had seized contraband from American ships in similar fashion. To "deny the justice" of the present British claim would be to "reverse and forever abandon" the very rationale upon which the United States had proudly stood in those earlier disputes. Therefore, in defense of "principles confessedly American," the government would "cheerfully" free the prisoners and turn them over to Lord Lyons.

Seward presented his arguments in an extraordinary cabinet session on Christmas morning. The discussion continued for four hours. "There was great reluctance on the part of some of the members of the cabinet—and even the President himself" to accept Seward's argument, Bates recorded. They feared "the displeasure of our own people—lest they should accuse us of timidly truckling to the power of England." The prospect of returning the prisoners was "gall and wormwood" to Chase. "Rather than consent to the liberation of these men," he wrote, "I would sacrifice everything I possess." Only Monty Blair, the consummate realist, stood firmly with Seward at the start. At Lincoln's invitation, Charles Sumner joined the session. As chairman of the Committee on Foreign Relations, he had conferred with Lincoln frequently during the crisis, asserting that the government should not risk war with England. Sumner had read letters from two respected London officials to Lincoln and Seward, revealing that Britain did not want war and that "if the present dispute were settled amicably Britain would not interfere further in the North's problems." The presentations by Seward and Sumner gained some support; but the cabinet, unable to reach a conclusion, decided to meet again the following day to hear Seward present a new draft.

As the meeting adjourned, Lincoln turned to his secretary of state. "Governor Seward, you will go on, of course, preparing your answer, which, as I understand it, will state the reasons why they [the prisoners] ought to be given up. Now I have a mind to try my hand at stating the reasons why they ought *not* to be given up. We will compare the points on each side."

Seward finished his twenty-six-page dispatch that night and read it to Chase at his house the next morning before the cabinet convened. After brooding through the night, Chase had concluded that Seward was right. "I am consoled by the reflection that while nothing but severest retribution is due to them, the surrender under existing circumstances, is but simply doing right," he recorded in his diary.

When the cabinet met the following day, Seward presented his final draft. Though disturbed by the prospect of surrendering the prisoners, the members were relieved that no apology had been rendered and, as Seward boasted, "a great point was gained for our Government." The dispatch was unanimously adopted. After the meeting, Seward asked Lincoln why he had not presented "an argument for the other side?" With a smile, Lincoln replied, "I found I could not make an argument that would satisfy my own mind, and that proved to me your ground was the right one."

The following night, Seward hosted a dinner party to which he invited Senators Crittenden and Conkling and their wives, Orville Browning, Charles Sumner, Preston King, and English novelist Anthony Trollope, whom Fanny described as "a great homely, red, stupid faced Englishman, with a disgusting beard of iron grey." The conversation at dinner was lively and contentious. Kentucky's Crittenden became enraged when Seward pronounced John Brown "a hero." Fanny was upset when Crittenden criticized Florence Nightingale, the celebrated British nurse of the Crimean War, saying, "he thought it a very unwomanly thing for a gentle lady to go into a hospital of wounded men." Fanny saved her retort for her diary. "That was enough of you, Mr. C. if I hadn't seen you at the table turn your head an[d] spit on the floor cloth." After dinner, Seward took the men into the cloakroom, where he read his *Trent* dispatch. The listeners generally commended Seward's handling of the crisis, though at the end of the reading, Crittenden "swore vehemently." Everyone assumed the public would be infuriated by the decision and that the publication of the dispatch would "doom [Seward] to unpopularity."

In the end, the public greeted the dispatch with relief, not anger. Compared to the prospect of fighting both a civil war and a foreign war at the same time, the release of the two prisoners seemed inconsequential. "The general acquiescence in this concession is a good sign," George Templeton Strong observed. "It looks like willingness to pass over affronts that touch the democracy in its tenderest point for the sake of concentrating all our national energies on the trampling out of domestic treason."

Lincoln himself finally recognized both the diplomatic logic and the absolute necessity of giving up the prisoners. And he was willing to admit that, in this case, his secretary of state had pursued the right course all along—a characteristic response that Fred Seward fully appreciated. "Presidents and Kings are not apt to see flaws in their own arguments," he wrote, "but fortunately for the Union, it had a President, at this critical juncture, who combined a logical intellect with an unselfish heart."

• • •

WITH THE RETURN OF CONGRESS for the winter session, the pace of social life in Washington quickened. "Houses are being fitted for winter gayeties, rich dresses and laughing faces pass on every side," reported *Iowa State Register* columnist Mrs. Cara Kasson, wife of the assistant postmaster general, who wrote under the pseudonym of "Miriam." The city is "thronged with strangers, every nook and corner is occupied with . . . lookers-on at this swiftly-moving Panorama of life in the Capital."

The crowds who streamed into the White House receptions that winter found a mansion transformed by Mary Lincoln's tireless efforts. Peeling walls had been stripped and covered with elegant Parisian wallpaper. New sets of china adorned the tables. Magnificent new rugs replaced their threadbare predecessors. Even one of Mary's severest critics, Mary Clemmer Ames, grudgingly admitted that the new rugs were magnificent. She considered the velvet one in the East Room the "most exquisite carpet ever" to cover the historic floor. "Its ground was of pale sea green, and in effect looked as if [the] ocean, in gleaming and transparent waves, were tossing roses at your feet." A California journalist praised the finished product highly: "The President's house has once more assumed the appearance of comfort and comparative beauty."

The historian George Bancroft reported favorably to his wife about a visit with the first lady, who was able with equal charm to discuss her plans for the "elegant fitting up of Mr. Lincoln's room" and to "discourse eloquently" on a recent military review. Bancroft "came home entranced." Mary "is better in manners and in spirit than we have generally heard: is friendly and not in the least arrogant."

As the bills came in, however, Mary discovered that she had overspent the $20,000 allowance by more than $6,800. Afraid to inform her husband, she inveigled John Watt, the White House groundskeeper, to inflate his expense accounts and funnel the extra money over to her. She had replaced her first Commissioner of Public Buildings after he refused to pay for an elaborate White House dinner from the manure account. She exchanged her patronage influence for reduced bills, and accepted gifts from wealthy donors. At one point, she asked John Hay to turn over the White House stationery fund for her use, and later to pay her as the White House steward. "I told her to kiss mine," Hay jokingly informed Nicolay. "Was I right?" Mary was irate when Hay denied her requests. She tried to have him fired, forever losing his goodwill. "The devil is abroad, having great wrath," he confided to Nicolay. "His daughter, the Hell-Cat . . . is in 'a state of mind' about the Steward's salary."

Despite her finagling, Mary found herself in trouble shortly before the New Year when more bills arrived with no money left in the account. She had no recourse but to tell her husband what had happened and to beg him to ask for an additional appropriation. To bolster her case, she asked Benjamin French, the new Commissioner of Public Buildings, to speak with her husband. French caught up with the president shortly after he returned home from a memorial service in the Senate for Edward Baker. The juxtaposition between the moving eulogies for his old friend and the unpleasant topic of decorating bills provoked in Lincoln an unusual display of anger.

The president was "inexorable," French recalled; "he said it would stink in the land to have it said that an appropriation of $20,000 for furnishing the house had been overrun by the President when the poor freezing soldiers could not have blankets, & he *swore* he would never approve the bills for *flub dubs for that damned old house!*" Moreover, Lincoln angrily pointed out, the place was "furnished well enough when they came—better than any house *they* had ever lived in—& rather than put his name to such a bill he would pay it out of his own pocket!"

French was nonetheless determined to aid Mary's cause. He liked her "better and better the more I see of her," he admitted, "and think she is an admirable woman. She bears herself, in every particular, like a lady and, say what they may about her, I will defend her." He succeeded in convincing a friendly congressman to hide a deficiency appropriation in a complex list of military appropriations. The crisis was resolved, at least temporarily, until Mary's continued spending produced another round of bills.

Mary was not alone in her worries about money. In the fall of 1861, Kate spent several weeks in Philadelphia and New York on a mission to purchase new furnishings for her father's mansion. Merchants gladly extended lines of credit for Kate as they had for Mary, creating great anxiety in her father's mind. "I need hardly caution you to avoid extravagance, as it is going to be hard work to make both ends meet here; and if any circumstances should compel me to resign before long my expences shall have far exceeded my income. It does seem a little hard that one who has so much & such important work to do as I have had for the past twelve years should all the time have to pay such a large part of his own expences."

The sense of injustice Chase felt in having to bear the burdens of public life lured him into a questionable relationship with a wealthy Philadelphia banker, Jay Cooke, who had been granted a lucrative contract from the Treasury Department for the sale of government bonds. Perceiving both

Chase's financial strain and his aggrieved pride, Cooke began to send valuable gifts to the Chase household, including an elegant open carriage for Kate and a set of bookcases for the parlor. As the relationship warmed, Chase borrowed money from Cooke, and eventually, Cooke took it upon himself to set up his own investment account for Chase. "I will take great pains to lay aside occasionally some choice 'tid bits' managing the investments for you and not bothering your head with them." If all went well, Cooke hoped, the profit earned would make up "the deficiency" between Chase's salary and his expenses, "for it is a shame that you should go 'behind hand' working as you do." In the smooth Philadelphia banker, the Chases had found what Mary Lincoln unsuccessfully sought—a reliable source to fund the high cost of being a leader of society in wartime Washington.

• • •

By the end of 1861, Lincoln realized that he had made a serious mistake in placing Simon Cameron at the head of the War Department. For many decades, Cameron had maintained his power base in Pennsylvania through the skillful use of patronage to reward loyalists and punish opponents. Unfortunately, the expertise of a wily political boss proved inadequate to the tremendous administrative challenge of leading the War Department in the midst of a civil war. A central system of civilian command was essential to construct a machine capable of providing strategy, supplies, logistics, and training for an army that had grown from 16,000 in March to 670,000 in December. Careful record keeping was indispensable when contracts worth millions had to be negotiated for rifles, cannons, horses, uniforms, food, and blankets.

As Lincoln confided to Nicolay, Cameron was "incapable either of organizing details or conceiving and advising general plans." His primitive filing system consisted mainly of scribbled notes. According to Ohio congressman Albert Riddle, when Cameron was asked about the progress of a particular matter, "he would look about, find a scrap of paper, borrow your pencil, make a note, put the paper in one pocket of his trousers and your pencil in the other."

The war was less than two months old when detailed accusations of corruption and inefficiency in the War Department began to surface in newspapers. In July, the Congress appointed a committee to investigate charges that middlemen had made off with scandalous profits on contracts for unworkable pistols and carbines, blind horses, and knapsacks that disintegrated when it rained. Though Cameron was not charged with pocketing the money himself, several of his political cronies had grown rich, vast public funds had been wasted, and the lives of Union soldiers had been jeopardized. As the charges multiplied, Republican newspapers began to call for his resignation, lest the entire administration become tainted by the scandal. "It is better to lose a mortified finger of the right hand at once," the *New York Times* declared, "than to cherish it till the arm is full of disease, and the whole system threatened with dissolution."

Determined to protect his position, Cameron sought to ingratiate himself with the increasingly powerful radical Republicans in Congress, led by Massachusetts's Charles Sumner, Ohio's Ben Wade, Indiana's George Julian, and Maine's William Fessenden. Though known as a conservative on the issue of slavery, Cameron began by degrees to embrace the radicals' contention that the central purpose of the war was to bring the institution of human bondage to an end. While he had allied himself initially with Seward, Cameron turned increasingly to Chase, the single cabinet member at the time not only in favor of allowing fugitive slaves to stay within Union lines but also of enlisting and arming them. "*We* agreed," Chase later recalled, "that the necessity of arming them was inevitable; but we were alone in that opinion."

Acting without Lincoln's approval, Cameron publicly endorsed the position of an army colonel who had sanctioned seizing slaves and using them for military service as one step in a more general policy of deploying "extremist measures against the rebels, even to their absolute ruin." In cabinet sessions and at private dinners, he instigated heated arguments with Bates, Blair, and Smith, who fiercely assailed his position. Cameron maintained that black soldiers would add an essential weapon in the quest for victory. Blair claimed that Cameron was riding the "nigger hobby" for his own political advantage.

The situation came to a head in early December. Each department customarily presented an annual report to the president as he prepared his own yearly message. While drafting the War Department report, the war secretary resolved to officially advocate arming slaves who came into Union lines. Well aware that he would ignite controversy, Cameron read his draft to a series of friends, most of whom urged him to keep silent on the contentious issue.

At this point, Cameron recalled, "I sought out another counsellor,—one of broad views, great courage, and of tremendous earnestness. It was Edwin Stanton." Cameron had called on Stanton during the summer and fall for legal advice on various contracts. This matter, however, was more delicate. Stanton "read the report carefully," according to Cameron, and "gave it his unequivocal and hearty support." In fact, he suggested his own provocative logic, which served to strengthen the argument for arming slaves: "It is clearly a right of the Government to arm slaves when it may become necessary," the addition read, "as it is to take gunpowder from the enemy."

It remains unclear whether Stanton offered his deliberately incendiary advice to encourage the war secretary openly to defy Lincoln, hoping that if Cameron were dismissed, he, Stanton, might be called upon to replace him. Perhaps he was "an abolitionist at heart," simply waiting for the right moment to reveal his honest convictions. He had, after all, given his boyhood pledge to his father that he would fight slavery until the end of his life, and had expressed similar sentiments to Chase in the bloom of their friendship in Ohio. More significant, Charles Sumner considered Stanton "my *personal* friend," who "goes as far [as] I do in directing the war against Slavery." Yet when Stanton talked with fellow Democrats during this same period of time, including McClellan and his former cabinet colleague Jeremiah Black, he expressed decidedly more conservative views on the issue of slavery. Whatever Stanton's purpose, his approval emboldened Cameron, who sent out advance copies of his report to a number of newspapers before submitting it to the president.

When the government printer brought the War Department report to the president for approval, Lincoln discovered the inflammatory paragraph. "This will never do!" he said. "Gen. Cameron must take no such responsibility. That is a question which belongs exclusively to me!" He deleted the paragraph and issued orders to seize every copy already sent. While Lincoln understood that the slaves coming into Union hands "must be provided for in some way," he did not believe, he later wrote, that he possessed the constitutional authority to liberate and arm them. The only way that such actions, "otherwise unconstitutional, might become lawful," was if those measures were deemed "indispensable" for "the preservation of the nation," and therefore for "the preservation of the constitution" itself. At this juncture, he was not convinced that arming seized slaves was "an indispensable necessity." Moreover, he was undeniably aware that such a measure at this time would alienate the moderate majority of his coalition.

Lincoln informed Cameron of his action at the next cabinet meeting, emphasizing, as he had with Frémont, that any decision regarding the future of slavery rested with the president, not with a subordinate official. Although Cameron immediately conceded and agreed to delete the vetoed language, he complained that his excised recommendation was no different from the suggestion Welles had made in his annual report. "This was the moment that Welles dreaded most," his biographer observed. Like the secretary of war, the secretary of the navy had felt compelled to make some provision for fugitive slaves who "have sought our ships for refuge and protection." In such cases, Welles declared, the slaves "should be cared for and employed" by either the navy or the army (depending on which branch had greater need), and "if no employment could be found for them in the public service, they should be allowed to proceed freely and peaceably, without restraint, to seek a livelihood."

Certain that he, too, would be commanded to revise his report, Welles resolved that he would resign before doing so. But to his bewilderment, Lincoln allowed the navy report to be printed without change. Shrewdly, Lincoln had recognized at once the political difference between the two situations: the army occupied territory in the border states, while the navy did not. Allowing blacks to find employment on naval ships or in surrounding harbors on the coast was fundamentally different from providing weapons to blacks in the slave states of Kentucky or Missouri, whose continued loyalty was critical to the Union. Lincoln still believed that such a step would drive the loyal citizens of these states into the Confederacy.

In fact, the president had developed his own policy for the increasing numbers of fugitive slaves who had come into Union lines. As members of Congress gathered on Capitol Hill for the opening of the winter session, he outlined his ideas in his annual message. He recognized, he wrote, that under the Confiscation Act, when Union armies secured territory where slaves had been used by their masters "for insurrectionary purposes," the legal rights of the slaveholders were "forfeited"; slaves "thus liberated" had to be "provided for in some way." He was hopeful that some of the loyal border states might soon "pass similar enactments." If such actions were taken, Lincoln recommended that the Congress compensate the states for each freed slave.

Lincoln still believed that both classes of freed slaves should be colonized on a purely voluntary basis, "at some place, or places, in a climate congenial to them. It might be well to consider, too,—whether the free colored people already in the United States could not, so far as individuals may desire, be included in such colonization."

So long as Lincoln remained hopeful that the Union could be restored before the conflict "degenerate[d] into a violent and remorseless revolutionary struggle," he was unwilling, he said, to sanction "radical and extreme measures" regarding slavery. Despite this assertion, he closed his message with a graceful and irrefutable argument against the continuation of slavery in a democratic society, the very essence of which opened "the way to all," granted "hope to all," and advanced the "condition of all." In this "just, and generous, and prosperous system," he reasoned, "labor is prior to, and independent of, capital." Then, reflecting upon the vicissitudes of his own experience, Lincoln added: "The prudent, penniless beginner in the world, labors for wages awhile, saves a surplus with which to buy tools or land for himself; then labors on his own account another while, and at length hires another new beginner to help him." Clearly, this upward mobility, the possibility of self-realization so central to the idea of America, was closed to the slave unless and until he became a free man.

Abolitionists condemned Lincoln's message. "Away with the unstatesmanlike scheme of Colonization, thrust so unfortunately into the face of the nation at this juncture!" the abolitionist Worthington G. Snethen wrote Chase. "Let the sword make a nation of four millions of black men free, and let them be free, as free as the white man." Frederick Douglass was so outraged both by the idea of colonizing freed slaves, and by the president's refusal to enlist blacks into the army, that he was close to losing all faith in Lincoln. The president did not understand that the black man was an American with no desire to live elsewhere; "his attachment to the place of his birth is stronger than iron." Moreover, why such fearful concern about the destiny of the freed slave? "Give him wages for his work, and let hunger pinch him if he don't work," Douglass declared. "He is used to [work], and is not afraid of it. His hands are already hardened by toil, and he has no dreams of ever getting a living by any other means than by hard work."

Since the beginning of the war, Douglass had avowed that nothing would terrify the South like the vision of thousands of former slaves wielding weapons on behalf of the Union Army. "One black regiment alone would be, in such a war, the full equal of two white ones. The very fact of color in this case would be more terrible than powder and balls." Predicting that a "lenient war" would be "a lengthy war and therefore the worst kind of war," Douglass contended that the survival of the nation depended upon enlisting the "slaves and free colored people" into the army. In a speech in Philadelphia, he proclaimed: "We are striking the guilty rebels with our soft, white hand, when we should be striking with the iron hand of the black man, which we keep chained behind us. We have been catching slaves, instead of arming them. . . . We pay more attention to the advice of the half-rebel State of Kentucky, than to any suggestion coming from the loyal North."

While the radical press criticized Lincoln's message, moderate and conservative Republicans lauded his tact. "It appeals to the judgment,—the solid convictions of the people, rather than their resentments or their impatient hopes and aspirations," the *New York Times* concluded, and as "the moderate men compose nine-tenths of the population of the country, the message will doubtless meet with popularity." Even the normally critical

New York Tribune conceded that the "country and the world will not fail to mark the contrast" between the magnanimity of Lincoln's message and a recent "truculent" address by Jefferson Davis. Though Davis was "commonly presumed the abler of the two" statesmen, and "certainly the better grammarian," the *Tribune* observed, the address of the Confederate chief was "boastful, defiant, and savage," whereas Lincoln "breathes not an unkind impulse" and "deals in no railing accusations."

CHAPTER 15

"MY BOY IS GONE"

THE LINCOLNS HOSTED the traditional New Year's Day reception to mark the advent of 1862. The day was "unusually beautiful," the *New York Times* reported, "the sky being clear and bright, and the air soft and balmy, more like May than January." Frances Seward, who had joined her husband for the holidays, found the festive atmosphere reassuring. "For the first time since we have been here," she told her sister, "the carriages are rolling along the streets as they used to do in old times." Bates, too, was braced by the glorious day. "All the world was out," he noted. Thousands of citizens streamed into the White House when the gates were opened at noon. The Marine Band played as members of the public shook hands with the president and first lady. They mingled with Supreme Court justices, senators, congressmen, foreign ministers, military officers, and cabinet officials. At long last, Fanny met the first lady, whom she described as "a compact little woman with a full round face," wearing "a black silk, or brocade, with purple clusters in it—and some appropriate velvet head arrangement."

Though Lincoln cordially greeted every guest, he was under great pressure. In the ninth month of the war, tales of corruption and mismanagement in the War Department combined with lack of progress on the battlefield to prevent Chase from raising the funds the Treasury needed to keep the war effort afloat. As public impatience mounted, Lincoln feared that "the bottom" was "out of the tub." While the disgruntled public might focus on various members of the military and the cabinet, the president knew that he would ultimately be held responsible for the choices of his administration. "If the new year shall be only the continuation of the faults, the mistakes, and the incapacities prevailing during 1861," diarist Count Gurowski warned, "then the worst is to be expected."

Lincoln had been so reticent during the summer and fall, when Cameron was first criticized for his lax administration and questionable contracts, that Seward questioned whether the president was sufficiently attentive to the unsavory situation. Then, one night in January, the secretary of state recalled, "there was a ring at my door-bell." The president entered, seated himself on the sofa, "and abruptly commenced talking about the condition of the War Department. He soon made it apparent that he had all along observed and known as much about it as any of us . . . his mind was now settled, and he had come to consult me about a successor to Mr. Cameron."

Choosing the right successor to Cameron was vital. Lincoln's initial preferences may have included Joseph Holt, Buchanan's war secretary who had crucially supported the Union during the secession crisis, or West Point graduate Montgomery Blair. According to Welles, Blair "had exhibited great intelligence, knowledge of military men, sagacity and sound judgment" during cabinet discussions. Instead of either man, in a decision that would prove most significant to the course of the war, Lincoln selected Edwin Stanton, the gruff lawyer who had humiliated him in Cincinnati six years earlier and whose disparaging remarks about his presidency were well known in Washington circles.

Washington insiders attributed the choice to the combined influence of Seward and Chase. These two rivals rarely agreed on policy or principle, but each had his own reasons for advocating Stanton. Seward would never forget Stanton's contribution as his informant during the last weeks of the

Buchanan tenure. The intelligence provided by Stanton had helped root out traitors and keep Washington safe from capture. It had also fortified Seward's role as the central figure in the critical juncture between Lincoln's election and inauguration. Chase's far more intimate friendship with Stanton had grown from their earlier days in Ohio when Stanton had assured Chase that "to be loved by you, and be told that you value my love is a gratification beyond my power to express." Equally important, Chase believed that Stanton would be a steadfast ally in the struggle against slavery.

Lincoln had his own recollections of Stanton, not all of which were negative. He had watched Stanton at work on the Reaper trial and had been impressed instantly by the powerful reasoning of Stanton's arguments, the passion of his delivery, and the unparalleled energy he had devoted to the case. "He puts his whole soul into any cause he espouses," one observer noted. "If you ever saw Stanton before a jury," you would see that "he toils for his client with as much industry as if his case was his own . . . as if his own life depended upon the issue." Energy and force were desperately needed to galvanize the War Department, and Stanton had both in abundance.

On Saturday, January 11, the president sent an uncharacteristically brusque letter to Cameron. In light of the fact that the war secretary had previously "expressed a desire for a change of position," he wrote, "I can now gratify you, consistently with my view of the public interest," by "nominating you to the Senate, next monday, as minister to Russia." After receiving the dismissal letter on Sunday, Cameron is said to have wept. "This is not a political affair," he insisted, "it means personal degradation."

After dinner that night, Cameron went to see Chase. They apparently talked over the troubled situation and decided to enlist Seward's help. Chase drove Cameron back to Willard's and then went alone to Seward's house. As planned, Cameron came in soon after, brandishing the president's letter, which, he said, was "intended as a dismissal, and, therefore, discourteous." Cameron was finally convinced "to retain the letter till morning, and then go and see the President." Later that night, Chase confided in his diary: "I fear Mr. Seward may think Cameron's coming into his house pre-arranged, and that I was not dealing frankly." As usual, however, so long as the high-minded Chase was certain that he had "acted right, and with just deference to all concerned," he was able to rationalize his machinations.

The next day, presumably briefed by Seward and Chase, Lincoln agreed to withdraw his terse letter and substitute a warm note indicating that Cameron had initiated the departure. Since the desirable post at St. Petersburg was vacant, the president would happily "gratify" Cameron's desire.

"Should you accept it, you will bear with you the assurance of my undiminished confidence, of my affectionate esteem, and of my sure expectation that . . . you will be able to render services to your country, not less important than those you could render at home." He also asked Cameron to recommend a successor. Cameron expressed his fervent opinion that his fellow Pennsylvanian Stanton was the best man for the job. In fact, Lincoln had already made his decision, but Cameron left believing he was responsible for Stanton's selection. In the end, each of the three men—Seward, Chase, and Cameron—assumed he was instrumental in Lincoln's appointment of the new secretary of war.

After settling matters with Cameron, Lincoln asked George Harding, whom he had made head of the Patent Office, to bring his old law partner Stanton to the White House. Stanton was then forty-seven, though the grizzled brown hair and beard made him look older, as did the glasses that hid his bright brown eyes. Harding was afraid that disagreeable recollections from the Reaper trial would cast a pall on the meeting. Both Lincoln and Stanton seemed to have put the past behind them, however, leaving Harding "the most embarrassed of the three."

The urgency of the situation left Stanton little time to deliberate. He consulted his wife, Ellen, who, according to her mother, "objected to his acceptance." The move to the War Department would substantially diminish the lifestyle of the Stanton family, slashing a legal income of over $50,000 a year to $8,000. Stanton, too, tormented all his life by fears of insolvency, must have been concerned about the drastic diminution of income. Nevertheless, he could not refuse to serve as secretary of war in the midst of a great civil war. And if he served with distinction, his life, however short in years, might be made "long by noble deeds," as Chase had once prophesied. He accepted the post, on the condition that he could retain Peter Watson, his old friend and assistant on the Reaper trial, "to take care of the contracts," for he realized he would "be swamped at once" without Watson's aid.

The announcement of Cameron's resignation and Stanton's appointment took the majority of the cabinet by surprise. "Strange," Bates confided in his diary, that "not a hint of all this" was discussed at the cabinet council the previous Friday, "and stranger still," the president had sent for no one but Seward over the weekend. Welles heard the dramatic news from Monty Blair, whom he met on the street. Neither one of them, Welles confessed, had been "taken into Lincoln's confidence." Indeed, Welles had never even met Stanton. Stanton's nomination dismayed radical Republicans on Capitol Hill. The powerful William Fessenden, fearful that Stanton's Democratic heritage would incline him toward a soft policy on both slavery and the South, worked to delay the Senate confirmation until he ascertained more about Stanton's position. He conferred with Chase, who assured Fessenden that "he, Secretary Chase, was responsible for Mr. Stanton's selection," and that he would arrange a meeting that very evening between the Maine senator and Stanton. Seward's role in the selection was not publicized, allowing the radicals to assume that Chase, their man in the cabinet, was the chief architect of the appointment. After a lengthy conversation with Stanton, Fessenden told Chase that he was thoroughly convinced that Stanton was "just the man we want." The senator was delighted to find that he and Buchanan's former Attorney General concurred "on every point," including "the conduct of the war" and "the negro question." The Senate confirmed Stanton's nomination the next day.

News of Stanton's replacement for Cameron met with widespread approval. The public generally assumed that Cameron had retired voluntarily. "Not only was the *press* completely taken by surprise," Seward told his wife, "but with all its fertility of conjecture, not one newspaper has conceived the real cause." Cameron's reputation was preserved until the House Committee on Contracts published its 1,100-page report in February 1862, detailing the extensive corruption in the War Department that had led to the purchase of malfunctioning weapons, diseased horses, and rotten food. According to one newspaper report, the committee "resolved to advise the immediate passage of a bill to punish with death any person who commits a fraud upon the Government, whereby a soldier is bodily injured, as for instance in the sale of unsound provisions." Though Cameron was never charged with personal liability, the House voted to censure him for conduct "highly injurious to the public service."

Cameron was devastated, knowing that he would never recover from the scandal. Lincoln, however, made a great personal effort to assuage his pain and humiliation. He wrote a long public letter to Congress, explaining that the unfortunate contracts were spawned by the emergency situation facing the government in the immediate aftermath of Fort Sumter. Lincoln declared that he and his entire cabinet "were at least equally responsible with [Cameron] for whatever error, wrong, or fault was committed."

Cameron would never forget this generous act. Filled with gratitude and admiration, he would become, Nicolay and Hay observed, "one of the most intimate and devoted of Lincoln's personal friends." He appreciated the courage it took for Lincoln to share the blame at a time when everyone else had deserted him. Most other men in Lincoln's situation, Cameron wrote, "would have permitted an innocent man to suffer rather than incur responsibility." Lincoln was not like most other men, as each cabinet member, including the new war secretary, would soon come to understand.

On his first day in office, the energetic, hardworking Stanton instituted "an entirely new *régime*" in the War Department. Cameron's department had been so inundated by office seekers and politicians that officials had little time to answer letters or file telegraphs they received. As a result, requests for military supplies were often delayed for weeks. Stanton decreed that "letters and written communications will be attended to the first thing in the morning when they are received, and will have precedence over all other business." While Cameron had welcomed congressmen and senators every day but Sunday, Stanton announced that the War Department would be closed to all business unrelated to military matters from Tuesdays through Fridays. Congressmen and senators would be received on Saturdays; the general public on Mondays.

Stanton quickly removed many of Cameron's people and surrounded himself with men much like himself, full of passion, devotion, and drive. He made it clear from the beginning that he would not tolerate unmerited requests for even the smallest job. The day after he took office, Stanton later recalled, he met with a man he instinctively judged to be "one of those indescribable half loafers, half gentlemen," who carried with him "a card from Mrs. Lincoln, asking that the man be made a commissary." Stanton was furious. He ripped up the note and sent the man away. The very next day, the man returned with an official request from Mary that he be given the appointment. Stanton did not budge, dismissing the job seeker once again. That afternoon, Stanton called on Mrs. Lincoln. He told her that "in the midst of a great war for national existence," his "first duty is to the people" and his "next duty is to protect your husband's honor, and your own." If he appointed unqualified men simply to return favors, it would "strike at the very root of all confidence." Mary understood his argument completely. "Mr. Stanton you are right," she told him, "and I will never ask you for anything again." True to her word, Stanton affirmed, "she never did."

Under Stanton's altered regime, the War Department opened early in the morning and the gas lamps remained lit late into the night. "As his carriage turned from Pennsylvania Avenue into Seventeenth Street," one of his clerks recalled, "the door-keeper on watch would put his head inside and cry, in a low, warning tone, 'The Secretary!' The word was passed along and around till the whole building was traversed by it, and for a minute or two there was a shuffling of feet and a noise of opening and shutting of doors, as the stragglers and loungers everywhere fled to their stations."

Stanton kept his meetings brief and pointed. He was "fluent without wordiness," George Templeton Strong wrote, "and above all, earnest, warm-hearted, and large-hearted." His tireless work style invigorated his colleagues. "Persons at a distance," a correspondent in the capital city wrote, "cannot well realize what a revolution has been wrought in Washington by the change of the head of the War Department. The very atmosphere of the city breathes of change; the streets, the hotels, the halls of Congress speak it."

After nearly a year of disappointment with Cameron, Lincoln had found in Stanton the leader the War Department needed.

• • •

EARLY IN FEBRUARY 1862, Mary Lincoln pioneered a new form of entertainment at the White House. Instead of the traditional public receptions, which allowed anyone to walk in off the street, or the expensive state dinners, designed for only a small number, she sent out some five hundred invitations for an evening ball to be held at the White House on February 5. Since the party was not open to the public, an invitation became a mark of prestige in Washington society. Those who were not on the original list, according to Nicolay, "sought, and almost begged their invitations."

Mary prepared for her gala with great enthusiasm. She arranged for the Marine Band to play in the corridor and brought in a famous New York catering firm to serve the midnight supper. She had her black seamstress, Elizabeth Keckley, create a beautiful white satin gown with black trimming, a long train, and a low-cut neckline that instantly attracted Lincoln's eye. He laughingly suggested that "if some of that tail was nearer the head, it would be in better style."

Meanwhile, Willie and Tad had settled into a happy routine. They worked with their tutor in the mornings and played with the two Taft boys in the afternoons and evenings, either at the White House or at the Taft home. Judge Taft became "much attached" to both Lincoln boys. He believed that Willie "had more judgment and foresight than any boy of his age that [he had] ever known." The four boys built a cabin on the mansion's flat roof, which was protectively encircled by "a high stone Ballistrade." They named their makeshift fortification the "Ship of State," and equipped it with a spyglass that enabled them to watch the movement of boats on the Potomac and troops on the shore. They invited guests to theatrical performances in the attic. Riding the pony given Willie as a gift became another favorite pastime. In mid-January, when Robert came home on vacation from Harvard College, the family was complete.

Then, a few days before Mary's grand party, Willie came down with a fever. Illness had been prevalent in Washington that January, as snow was followed by sleet and rain that left the ground covered with a thick layer of foul-smelling mud. Smallpox and typhoid fever had taken many lives. "There is a good deal of alarm in the City on account of the prevalence of the Small pox," Judge Taft recorded in his diary. "There are cases of it in almost every Street in the City."

Illness had struck the Stantons, the Sewards, and the Chases. Stanton's youngest son, James, had become critically ill after a smallpox vaccination caused "a dreadful eruption" on all parts of the baby boy's body. The illness continued for six weeks, during which time he was "not expected to live." In this same period, Fanny Seward, who had gone to Philadelphia with her mother, contracted what was first suspected to be smallpox but was probably typhoid. Her "burning fever," back pains, and "ulcerated" throat lasted for nearly two weeks. Seward left Washington in alarm to be with Fanny, one of the few departures from his work during the entire war. Nettie Chase was also seriously ill, having contracted scarlet fever on her way to boarding school in Pennsylvania.

Mary thought it best to cancel the party because of Willie's illness, but Lincoln hesitated, since the invitations had already been sent out. He called in Dr. Robert Stone, who was considered "the dean of the Washington medical community." After examining Willie, the renowned doctor concluded that the boy was "in no immediate danger" and "that there was every reason for an early recovery." Relieved by the diagnosis, the Lincolns decided to hold the ball.

The carriages began arriving at the brilliantly lit White House around 9 p.m. All the Washington elite were present—the cabinet members and their wives, generals and their high staff, the members of the diplomatic corps, senators and congressmen, lawyers and businessmen. McClellan, in dress uniform, attracted much attention, as did the new secretary of war. The Green, Red, and Blue parlors were open for inspection, along with the East Room, where the Lincolns received their guests. Society reporters commented on both the "exquisite taste with which the White House has been refitted under Mrs. Lincoln's directions" and the magnificence of the women's attire. The "violet-eyed" Kate Chase was singled out, as usual. "She wore a dress of mauve-colored silk, without ornament," one reporter wrote admiringly. "On her small, classically-shaped head a simple wreath of minute white flowers mingled with the blond waves of her sunny hair, which was arranged in a Grecian knot behind."

At midnight, the crowd began to move toward the closed dining room. During a slight delay occasioned by a steward who had temporarily misplaced the key, someone exclaimed, "I am in favor of a forward movement," and everyone laughed, including General McClellan. The doors were thrown open to reveal a sumptuous banquet, which was to be served with excellent wine and champagne. "The brilliance of the scene could not dispel the sadness that rested upon the face of Mrs. Lincoln," Elizabeth Keckley, the seamstress who had become a close confidante, recalled. "During the evening she came up-stairs several times, and stood by the bedside of the suffering boy."

Despite Mary's worry and watchfulness, the ball was a triumph. "Those who were here," Nicolay told his fiancée, "will be forever happy in the recollection of the favor enjoyed, because their vanity has been tickled with the thought that they have attained something which others have not." Although there was some caviling about "frivolity, hilarity and gluttony, while hundreds of sick and suffering soldiers" were "within plain sight," reviews in the capital city were overwhelmingly favorable. The Washington *Evening Star* pronounced the event "a brilliant spectacle," while *Leslie's Illustrated Newspaper* described Mary as "our fair 'Republican Queen,' " garbed in a "lustrous white satin robe" and black and white headdress "in perfect keeping with her regal style of beauty."

The success of the White House ball was followed by two Union victories in Tennessee, the captures of Fort Henry on the Tennessee River and Fort Donelson on the Cumberland. These twin victories shifted the defensive struggle in the West to an offensive war and brought national recognition to a new hero: General Ulysses S. Grant. A West Point graduate whose weakness for alcohol had contributed to his resignation from the army eight years earlier, Grant was struggling to support his family as a leather salesman in Galena, Illinois, when the Civil War began. He volunteered to serve immediately, and was put in charge of a regiment in Missouri. From the start, Grant understood that a southward movement from Missouri was essential, but he was unable to persuade General Henry Halleck, Frémont's successor, to authorize the move. Hearing rumors that the unkempt, bewhiskered Grant still drank too much, Halleck was unwilling to trust him with an important mission. Finally, on February 1, after the navy's Admiral Andrew Foote agreed to a joint army-navy expedition, Halleck gave the go-ahead for Grant "to take and hold Fort Henry."

Grant and Foote set out at once. The navy gunboats opened a blistering attack, forcing the retreat of 2,500 rebel troops to the more heavily reinforced Fort Donelson, twelve miles away. The remaining troops surrendered. "Fort Henry is ours," Grant telegraphed Halleck in the terse, straightforward style that would become his trademark. "I shall take and destroy Fort Donelson on the 8th." Though a severe rainstorm delayed the eastward march to Donelson, Grant remained confident. Writing to his sister, he assured her that her "plain brother however has, as yet, had no reason to feel himself unequal to the task." This was not a boast, he said, but "a presentiment" that proved accurate a few days later when he surrounded the rebel forces at Fort Donelson and began his successful assault. After many had died, the Confederate commander, Kentucky native General Simon Buckner, proposed a cease-fire "and appointment of commissioners to settle terms of capitulation." On February 16, Grant telegraphed back the historic words that would define both his character and career: "No terms except unconditional and immediate surrender can be accepted." Buckner and fifteen thousand Confederate soldiers were taken prisoner.

More than a thousand troops on both sides were killed and three times that number wounded. It was "a most bloody fight," a young Union soldier told his father, so devastating to his company that despite the victory, he remained "sad, lonely and down-hearted." Only seven of the eighty-five men in his unit survived, but "the flag was brought through."

The North was jubilant upon receiving news of Grant's triumph at Donelson, the first substantial Union victory in the war. Hundred-gun salutes were fired in celebrations across the land. The capital city was "quite wild with Excitement." In the Senate, "the gallery rose *en masse* and gave three enthusiastic cheers." Elaborate plans were made to illuminate the capital's public buildings in joint celebration of the double victory and George Washington's birthday.

The day after Grant's victory at Donelson, the president signed papers promoting him to major general. Lincoln had been following the Western general since he had read the gracious proclamation Grant issued when he had marched into Paducah, Kentucky, the previous fall. "I have come among you, not as an enemy," he told the Kentuckians, "but as your friend and fellow-citizen." Reports that "Grant had taken the field with only a spare shirt, a hair brush, and a tooth brush" made comparisons between "Western hardihood" and McClellan's "Eastern luxury" inevitable; it was well known that "six immense four-horse wagons" had arrived at McClellan's door to carry his clothes and other items to the front.

Fort Donelson's capture provided the Union with a strategic foothold in the South. After a ghastly battle at Shiloh two months later left twenty thousand casualties on both sides, the Union would go on to secure Memphis and the entire state of Tennessee. These victories would soon be followed by the capture of New Orleans.

• • •

THE COUNTRY'S EXULTATION at Grant's victory at Donelson found no echo in the White House. Willie's condition had grown steadily worse since the White House ball, and Tad, too, had become ill. It is believed that both boys had contracted typhoid fever, likely caused by the unsanitary conditions in Washington. The White House drew its water supply from the Potomac River, along the banks of which tens of thousands of troops without proper latrines were stationed. Perhaps because his constitution had been weakened by his earlier bout with scarlet fever, Willie was affected by the bacterial infection more severely than his brother Tad. He "grew weaker and more shadow-like" as the debilitating symptoms of his illness took their toll—high fever, diarrhea, painful cramps, internal hemorrhage, vomiting, profound exhaustion, delirium.

Tending to both boys, Mary "almost wore herself out with watching," Commissioner French observed. She canceled the customary Saturday receptions and levees. For Lincoln, too, it was an agonizing period. Nicolay reported that the president gave "pretty much all his attention" to his sons, but the grim business of conducting the war could not be avoided.

Slipping in and out of consciousness, Willie would call for his friend Bud Taft, who sat by his bedside day and night. Late one evening, seeing Bud at his son's side, Lincoln "laid his arm across Bud's shoulder and stroked Willie's hair." Turning to Bud, he said quietly, "You ought to go to bed, Bud," but Bud refused to leave, saying, "If I go he will call for me." Returning later, Lincoln "picked up Bud, who had fallen asleep, and carried him tenderly to bed."

As news of the boy's critical condition spread through Washington, most of the celebratory illuminations were canceled. The *Evening Star* wrote that "the President and Mrs. Lincoln have deep sympathy in this community in this hour of their affliction." Though work continued in the offices of the White House, staffers walked slowly down the corridors "as if they did not wish to make a noise." Lincoln's secretary, William Stoddard, recalled the question on everyone's lips: "Is there no hope? Not any. So the doctors say."

At 5 p.m. on Thursday, February 20, Willie died. Minutes later, Lincoln burst into Nicolay's office. "Well, Nicolay," he said, "my boy is gone—he is actually gone!" He began to sob. According to Elizabeth Keckley, when Lincoln came back into the room after Willie's body had been washed and dressed, he "buried his head in his hands, and his tall frame was convulsed with emotion." Though Keckley had observed Lincoln more intimately than most, she "did not dream that his rugged nature could be so moved."

Mary Lincoln was "inconsolable," Keckley recorded. "The pale face of her dead boy threw her into convulsions." She had frequently said of her blue-eyed, handsome son that "if spared by Providence, [he] would be the hope and stay of her old age." She took to her bed with no way to sleep or ease her grief.

Meanwhile, Tad was now critically ill. With Mary in no condition to care for him, Lincoln sought help. He sent his carriage to the Brownings, who came at once and spent the night at Tad's bedside. He asked Gideon Welles's young wife, Mary Jane, to sit with the boy. Julia Bates, recovered from her stroke, also watched over him. Clearly, Tad required professional care around the clock. Lincoln turned to Dorothea Dix, the tireless crusader who had been appointed by the secretary of war as Superintendent of Women Nurses. She was a powerful woman with set ideas, among them the belief that women's corsets had a baneful effect on their health. She would routinely lecture young women on the subject. One girl refused to listen, insisting that she would rather "be dead than so out of fashion." To this, Dix rejoined, "My dear . . . if you continue to lace as tightly as you do now, you will not long have the privilege of choice. You will be *both* dead and out of fashion."

Asked to recommend a nurse, Dix chose Rebecca Pomroy, a young widow who had worked on typhoid wards in two Washington hospitals. Introducing Nurse Pomroy to Lincoln, Dix assured the president that she had "more confidence" in her than any other nurse, even those twice her age. Lincoln took Pomroy's hand and smiled, saying: "Well, all I want to say is, let her turn right in."

While Willie's body lay in the Green Room and Mary remained in bed under sedation, Nurse Pomroy tended Tad. Whenever possible, the president brought his work into Tad's room and sat with his son, who was "tossing with typhoid." Always curious and compassionate about other people's lives, Lincoln asked the new nurse about her family. She explained that she was a widow and had lost two children. Her one remaining child was in the army. Hearing her painful story, he began to cry, both for her and for his own stricken family. "This is the hardest trial of my life," he said. "Why is it? Oh, why is it?" Several times during the long nights Tad would awaken and call for his father. "The moment [the president] heard Taddie's voice he was at his side," unmindful of the picture he presented in his dressing gown and slippers.

On the Sunday after Willie's death, Lincoln drove with Browning to Oak Hill Cemetery in Georgetown to inspect the vault where his son's body would lie until his final burial in Springfield. The funeral service was scheduled for 2 p.m. in the East Room the following day. Though scores of people were invited, Mary asked Mrs. Taft to "keep the boys home the day of the funeral; it makes me feel worse to see them." Nonetheless, without consulting his distraught wife, Lincoln "sent for Bud to see Willie before he was put in the casket." "He lay with his eyes closed," the essayist Nathaniel Parker Willis recalled, "his brown hair parted as we had known it—pale in the slumber of death; but otherwise unchanged, for he was dressed as if for the evening." At noontime, the president, the first lady, and Robert entered the Green Room to bid farewell to Willie before the casket was closed. Commissioner French was told that the Lincolns wanted "no spectator of their last sad moments in that house with their dead child," and that Mary was so overcome she could not attend the East Room service.

Congress had adjourned so that members could attend the service. Many of those present had attended the ball just nineteen days earlier—the vice president, the cabinet, the diplomatic corps, General McClellan and his staff. As the funeral guests filed in, a frightful storm arose. Heavy rain and high winds uprooted trees, destroyed a church, and tore the roofs off many houses. After the service was concluded, a long line of carriages made its way through the tempest to the cemetery chapel where Willie was laid to rest temporarily inside the vault. Lincoln, who had so agonized whenever the stormy weather had pelted the grave of his first love, Ann Rutledge, perhaps found some solace that his son's body was now sheltered from the rain and howling wind.

In the weeks that followed, Lincoln worried about Mary, who remained in her bed, unable to cope with daily life. Though Tad eventually recovered, Mary found it difficult to endure his company, which only intensified her sense of Willie's absence. Nor could she bear to see Bud and Holly Taft. She never invited them back to the White House, leaving Tad utterly isolated. Understanding the situation, the president tried to keep his son by his side, often carrying the boy to his own bed at night.

Mary seemed to find some small comfort in her conversations with Rebecca Pomroy and Mary Jane Welles. The latter, who spent many nights keeping vigil at Tad's bedside, had lost five children of her own and could relate to Mary's sorrow. In her talks with Mrs. Pomroy, Mary tried to understand how the widow could bear to nurse the children of strangers after the devastation of her own family. Mary knew that she should surrender to God's will, but found she could not. Looking back on Willie's bout with scarlet fever two years earlier, she concluded that he was spared only "to try us & wean us from a world, whose chains were fastening around us," but "when the blow came," she was still "unprepared" to face it. "Our home is very beautiful," she wrote a friend three months after Willie's death, "the world still smiles & pays homage, yet the charm is dispelled—everything appears a mockery, the idolised one, is not with us."

Indeed, the luxury and vanity in which she had indulged herself now seemed to taunt her. She plunged deeper into guilt and grief, speculating that God had struck Willie down as punishment for her overweening pride in her family's exalted status. "I had become, so wrapped up in the world, so devoted to our own political advancement that I thought of little else," she acknowledged. She knew it was a sin to think thus, but she believed that God must have "foresaken" her in taking away "so lovely a child."

Nor could she fully accept the comfort Mary Jane Welles found in the belief that her children awaited her in heaven. If only she had faith that Willie was "far happier" in an afterlife than he had been "when on earth," Mary suggested to Mary Jane, she might accept his loss. Although in later years she would come to trust that "*Death*, is only a blessed transition" to a place "where there are no more partings & and *no more* tears shed," her faith at this juncture was not strong enough to provide solace.

Crippled by her sadness, Mary was drawn to the relief offered by the spiritualist world. Through Elizabeth Keckley, she was introduced to a celebrated medium who helped her, said Mary, pierce the "veil" that "separates us, from the 'loved & lost.' " During several séances, some conducted at the White House, she believed she was able to see Willie. Spiritualism would reach epic proportions during the Civil War, fueled perhaps by the overwhelming casualties. Mediums could offer comfort to the bereaved, assuring them "the spirits of the dead do not pass from this earth, but remain here amongst us unseen." One contemporary commented that it seemed as if "one heard of nothing but of spirits and of mediums. All tables and other furniture seemed to have become alive." Some mediums communicated by producing rapping or knocking sounds; others made tables tip and sway; still others channeled voices of the dead. Whatever method they used, one scholar of the movement observes, they "offered tangible evidence that the most refractory barrier on earth, the barrier of death, could be transcended by the power of sympathy."

Mary's occasional glimpses of Willie provided only temporary relief. His death had left her "an altered woman," Keckley observed. "The mere mention of Willie's name would excite her emotion, and any trifling memento that recalled him would move her to tears." She was unable to look at his picture. She sent all his toys and clothes away. She refused to enter the guest room in which he died or the Green Room in which he was laid out.

Outwardly, the president appeared to cope with Willie's death better than his wife. He had important work to engage him every hour of the day. He was surrounded by dozens of officials who needed him to discuss plans, make decisions, and communicate them. Yet, despite his relentless duties, he suffered an excruciating sense of loss. On the Thursday after his son died, and for several Thursdays thereafter, he closed himself off in the Green Room and gave way to his terrible grief. "That blow overwhelmed me," he told a White House visitor; "it showed me my weakness as I had never felt it before."

Like Mary, Lincoln longed for Willie's presence, a longing fulfilled not through mediums but in his active dream life. Three months after Willie's death, while reading aloud a passage from Shakespeare's *King John* in which Constance grieves over the death of her son, Lincoln paused; he turned to a nearby army officer and said: "Did you ever dream of some lost friend, and feel that you were having a sweet communion with him, and yet have a consciousness that it was not a reality? . . . That is the way I dream of my lost boy Willie."

While Mary could not tolerate to see physical reminders of Willie, Lincoln cherished mementos of his son. He placed a picture Willie had painted on his mantelpiece so he could show it to visitors and tell stories about his beloved child. One Sunday after church, he invited Browning to the library to show him a scrapbook he had just found in which Willie kept dates of various battles and programs from important events. Maintaining vivid consciousness of his dead child was essential for a man who believed that the dead live on only in the minds of the living. Ten months later, when he wrote young Fanny McCullough shortly after her father's battlefield death, he closed with the consolation of remembrance. In time, he promised her, "the memory of your dear Father, instead of an agony, will yet be a sad sweet feeling in your heart, of a purer, and holier sort than you have known before."

Now, more than ever before, Lincoln was able to identify in a profound and personal way with the sorrows of families who had lost their loved ones in the war.

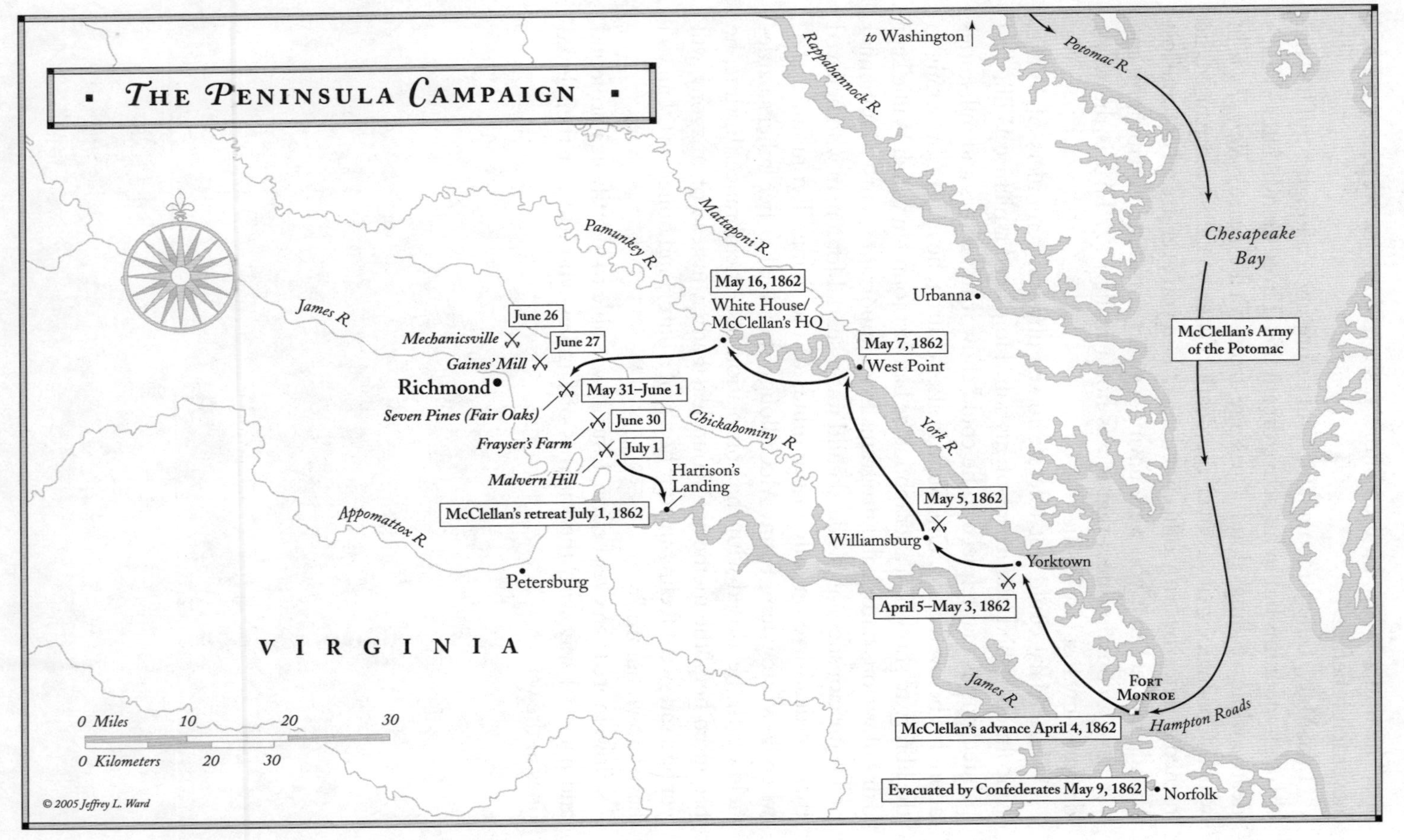
The Peninsula Campaign
to Washington
Potomac R.
Rappahannock R.
Chesapeake Bay
McClellan's Army of the Potomac
Urbanna
Mattaponi R.
Pamunkey R.
May 16, 1862
White House/ McClellan's HQ
May 7, 1862
West Point
York R.
James R.
June 26
Mechanicsville
June 27
Gaines' Mill
Richmond
May 31–June 1
Seven Pines (Fair Oaks)
June 30
Frayser's Farm
July 1
Malvern Hill
Chickahominy R.
Harrison's Landing
McClellan's retreat July 1, 1862
Appomattox R.
Petersburg
May 5, 1862
Williamsburg
Yorktown
April 5–May 3, 1862
VIRGINIA
James R.
Fort Monroe
Hampton Roads
McClellan's advance April 4, 1862
Evacuated by Confederates May 9, 1862
Norfolk
0 Miles 10 20 30
0 Kilometers 20 30
© 2005 Jeffrey L. Ward

CHAPTER 16

"HE WAS SIMPLY OUT-GENERALED"

Two days after Willie's death, General McClellan sent a private note expressing his heartfelt sympathy for the "sad calamity" that had overtaken the Lincoln family. "You have been a kind true friend to me," the general told the president, "your confidence has upheld me when I should otherwise have felt weak." Then, referring to the capture of Forts Henry and Donelson in the West as "an auspicious commencement" of his own forward campaign in the East, he beseeched Lincoln not to "allow military affairs to give [him] one moment's trouble," for "nothing shall be left undone" in pursuit of victory.

McClellan's assurances of forward movement provided Lincoln little comfort. The general had made similar promises for many months, while the great Army of the Potomac sat idle. Criticism of the general, previously confined to newspapers, found a powerful voice in the newly created Congressional Joint Committee on the Conduct of the War. Dominated by radicals from both houses, including Ben Wade, Michigan's Zachariah Chandler, and Indiana's George Julian, the committee detested McClellan both for his failure to prosecute the war vigorously and for his conservative views on slavery. From late December to mid-January, McClellan had remained in bed with typhoid. Suspicious that the general was using his illness as a cover for his continuing inaction, the committee held a contentious meeting with Lincoln and his cabinet. During the session, Congressman Julian recorded, it became disturbingly clear "that neither the President nor his advisers seemed to have any definite information . . . of General McClellan's plans."

More astonishing, according to Julian, "Lincoln himself did not think he had any *right* to know, but that, as he was not a military man, it was his duty to defer to General McClellan." Bates strenuously objected to

Lincoln's deferential stance, urging him repeatedly to "organize a *Staff* of his own, and assume to be in fact, what he is in law," the commander in chief, with a duty to "command the commanders." This opinion, voiced by the conservative, trustworthy Bates, struck Lincoln forcefully. He borrowed General Halleck's book on military strategy from the Library of Congress and told Browning a few days later that "he was thinking of taking the field himself."

Though his statement may not have reflected a literal intention, Lincoln had clearly resolved that he must energize the army at once. "The bottom is out of the tub," he confided in General Meigs, repeating a favorite phrase. The nearly bankrupt Treasury could no longer sustain the enormous expense of providing food, clothing, and shelter for hundreds of thousands of immobile soldiers. Without some forward progress, Chase told the president, he would get no additional funds from a discontented public. Meigs suggested that Lincoln convene a war council with his other generals to formulate a decisive course of action. Receiving news of this, McClellan suddenly recovered sufficiently to attend the meeting on the following day. Still reluctant to expose his plans, McClellan told Meigs that the president "can't keep a secret, he will tell them to Tadd."

Finally, Lincoln lost his vaunted patience. On January 27, 1862, he issued his famous General War Order No. 1, setting February 22 as "the day for a general movement of the Land and Naval forces of the United States against the insurgent forces." Lincoln correctly believed that, given the North's superior numbers, they should attack several rebel positions at the same time. The order prompted McClellan to submit his plans for a roundabout movement that developed into the Peninsula Campaign. The plan called for the troops to move by ship down the Potomac River to the Chesapeake Bay, with a turn into Urbanna on the south shore of the Rappahannock River. From there McClellan planned to march southwest to Richmond.

Lincoln, backed by Stanton and several generals, including McDowell, proposed a different strategy. Troops would march overland through nearby Manassas, pushing the rebel army farther and farther back toward Richmond, "destroying him by superior force." This straightforward approach would shield Washington, keeping the Union Army between the capital and the Confederates. Under McClellan's circuitous plan, it was feared that the Confederates might willingly sacrifice Richmond to capture Washington. If the South occupied the seat of the Union, foreign recognition of the Confederacy would undoubtedly follow. In the end, Lincoln reluctantly acquiesced to the Peninsula plan, but not before imposing a written order requiring that a sufficient force be left "in, and about Washington," to keep the capital safe from attack.

February 22, the date designated for the advance, arrived and went with Lincoln deeply preoccupied by Willie's death and Tad's grievous illness. A disheartened Stanton noted that "there was no more sign of movement on the Potomac than there had been for three months before." When he first took his cabinet position, Stanton later explained, he "was, and for months had been the sincere and devoted friend of General McClellan," but he had quickly grown disenchanted. After less than two weeks as secretary of war, he told a friend that "while men are striving nobly in the West, the champagne and oysters on the Potomac must be stopped." Stanton's remark alluded to the sumptuous dinners McClellan hosted each evening for nearly two dozen guests, many of whom were prominent figures in Washington's Southern-leaning society.

Stanton was further disgruntled when McClellan kept him waiting on a number of occasions. Unlike Lincoln, the proud war secretary did not ignore the arrogance of the general in chief. After one particularly galling experience, when he had been forced to wait for an hour after stopping by McClellan's headquarters on his way to the War Department, Stanton angrily announced: "That will be the last time General McClellan will give either myself or the President the waiting snub." A few weeks later, Stanton delivered orders to transfer the telegraph office from McClellan's headquarters to a room adjoining his office in the War Department. Dispatches from the miraculous new system that connected Washington with army officials, camps, and forts throughout the entire North would no longer be funneled through McClellan. McClellan was furious, considering the transfer "his humiliation." He had, indeed, lost significant influence, for the adjacent telegraph office not only allowed Stanton to exercise control over all military communications, but ensured that Lincoln would now spend many daily hours with his war secretary rather than his general in chief.

Still, McClellan had powerful allies in the cabinet, including the influential Montgomery Blair. The Democratic press largely credited the "young Napoleon" for the victories at Forts Henry and Donelson, as if Grant and the troops were merely puppets with McClellan pulling the strings from Washington. Stanton noted satirically that the image portrayed in the papers of a heroic McClellan, seated at the telegraph office, "organizing victory, and by sublime military combinations capturing Fort Donelson *six hours after* Grant and Smith had taken it," was "a picture worthy of *Punch.*"

As it turned out, the victories in the West increased the pressure on McClellan to act. At last, on the weekend of March 8, the massive Army of the Potomac prepared to break camp. Anticipating the move, the Confederates began to pull their batteries back from Manassas to the banks of the Rappahannock. Hearing reports of the fallback, McClellan led his armies on a short foray to catch the remaining troops. But once there, he found to his great embarrassment that the entire Confederate force had already departed with their tents, supplies, and weapons. Still more humiliating, the supposedly impregnable fortifications that had deterred him for months turned out to be simply wooden logs painted black to resemble cannons. Had McClellan attacked anytime in the previous months, he would have had superiority in numbers and weapons.

The "Quaker gun" affair, as the stage-prop guns were called, provoked the wrath of radicals. "We shall be the scorn of the world," Senator Fessenden wrote his wife. "It is no longer doubtful that General McClellan is utterly unfit for his position. . . . And yet the President will keep him in command." The embarrassing situation should have been expected, Fessenden lamented, for "we went in for a railsplitter, and we have got one." Echoing Fessenden's dismay, the Committee on the Conduct of the War demanded McClellan's resignation. When Lincoln asked who they proposed to replace McClellan, one of the committee members growled, "Anybody." Lincoln's reply was swift. "*Anybody* will do for you, but not for me. I must have *somebody.*"

Lincoln was convinced that something had to be done. On March 11, he issued a war order that relieved McClellan from his post as general in chief but left him in charge of the Army of the Potomac. Lincoln gave Halleck command of the Department of the Mississippi and, in a move that delighted the radicals, reinstated Frémont to take charge of a newly created Mountain Department. The post of general in chief was not filled, leaving Lincoln and Stanton to determine overall strategy. McClellan later recalled that he "learned through the public newspapers that [he] was displaced." Claiming that "no one in authority had ever expressed to [him] the slightest disapprobation," he was infuriated. Lincoln sent Ohio's Governor Dennison to his camp to assure him that this was not a demotion. The president, Dennison explained, simply wanted General McClellan to focus his full energies on the all-important Army of the Potomac, whose actions would most likely determine the result of the war.

Lincoln anticipated that his postmaster general, Monty Blair, would stridently oppose McClellan's removal from high command. The conservative Blair family were staunch McClellan supporters, a loyalty that would continue in the months ahead. Referring to his radical detractors,

Francis Blair, Sr., warned the general "not to let the Carpet Knights in Congress," who would sacrifice anyone's blood but their own, "hurry or worry him into doing anything." Meanwhile, Washington gossip spread that Monty Blair was openly berating his fellow cabinet colleague Stanton for his failure to support McClellan. While conservatives vilified Stanton, radicals upbraided the Blairs as "preservers of slavery" for defending the inert McClellan at Stanton's expense.

Already troubled by McClellan's loss of central control, the powerful Blair family was enraged by Lincoln's decision to reinstall Frémont in a position of command. Monty Blair privately considered Frémont's appointment "unpalatable" and warned his father that it would be "mortifying to Frank," who had been humiliated by his arrest and imprisonment by Frémont. Lizzie Blair told her husband it was "urged by Chase—& Stanton who has his revenges, too," and that her brother Frank felt it intensely. Only four days earlier, with the backing of Democrats and conservative Republicans, Frank Blair had delivered a blistering attack against Frémont on the floor of the House. Frémont had come to Washington at the request of the Committee on the Conduct of the War. For weeks, radicals on the committee had pressured Lincoln to give "the Emancipator," as they called Frémont, a second chance. Congressman Schuyler Colfax eloquently defended their position when he rose to the floor immediately after Frank Blair to deliver a scorching point-by-point repudiation of Blair's address.

The bitter public quarrel between the Blairs and Frémont must have given Lincoln pause as he considered reinstating Frémont. Though the appointment would thrill the radicals, it might cost him the allegiance of the Blairs and thereby destroy the delicate balance he had worked to foster between the conservatives and the radicals. As it happened, a magnanimous gesture by Lincoln just six days before Frémont's appointment played an important role in resolving the complex situation.

On March 5, Monty Blair had come to the White House in great distress. The *New York Tribune* had just published a private letter that he had written to Frémont the previous summer before the family feud had begun. In the letter, furnished by Frémont to the press in an attempt to embarrass Blair, the postmaster general had complained that Lincoln's past affiliations had brought "him naturally not only to incline to the feeble policy of Whigs, but to give his confidence to such advisers. It costs me a great deal of labor to get anything done because of the inclination of mind on the part of the President."

Elizabeth Blair described her brother's meeting with Lincoln in a note to her husband. "Brother just took the letter up to the P. & asked him to read it." Lincoln refused, "saying he did not intend to read it," as it was published for that very purpose. Monty acknowledged "it was a foolish letter" that he deeply regretted. "It is due to you," he told the president, "to make some amends by resigning my place. . . . I leave the whole thing to you & will do exactly as you wish." The president had no desire to exact retribution or remove Blair. "Forget it," he said, "& never mention or think of it again."

A grateful Monty Blair immediately came to Lincoln's defense regarding the Frémont appointment. Although he had not been consulted about the decision and realized his family would consider it a blatant affront to Frank, he told his father that he understood Lincoln's need to arrest "the spread of factions in the country & prevent divisions at this time," and for that reason, he thought "very well of it." The conservative *New York Times* agreed, approving Frémont's appointment as a necessary "concession to this craving for unity" and "the value of united counsels." In his conduct of the war, the *Times* observed, Lincoln believed "tenaciously" in the "necessity of perfect unity of popular opinion and action" in the North.

More than any other cabinet member, Seward appreciated Lincoln's peerless skill in balancing factions both within his administration and in the country at large. While radicals considered Seward a conservative influence on the president, in truth, he and the president were engaged in the same task of finding a middle position between the two extremes—the radical Republicans, who believed that freeing the slaves should be the primary goal of the war, and the conservative Democrats, who resisted any change in the status of the slaves and fought solely for the restoration of the Union. "Somebody must be in a position to mollify and moderate," Seward told Weed. "That is the task of the P. and the S. of S." In another letter to his old friend, Seward expressed great confidence in Lincoln. "The President is wise and practical," he wrote. His trust in Lincoln was complete, inspiring faith in the eventual success of the Union cause.

From the outside, however, Seward was viewed by radicals as a malevolent influence on Lincoln. Count Gurowski despaired at Seward's supposed ties with McClellan, Blair, and their allies in the conservative press. "Oh! Mr. Seward, Mr. Seward," he queried, "why is your name to be recorded among the most ardent supporters of [McClellan's] *strategy?*" In fact, already by the middle of March, Seward had lost his early faith in McClellan and wondered why Lincoln did not strip him of command. In a private conversation with a friend, Seward scorned McClellan's inflated estimates of enemy strength, suggesting that the Union troops from New York State alone probably outnumbered all the Confederate forces in northern Virginia! Nonetheless, he refrained from airing his doubts in public.

In the wake of the "Quaker gun" affair, Lincoln's confidence in McClellan had also eroded. While acknowledging that the general was a great "engineer," Lincoln noted drolly that "he seems to have a special talent for developing a '*stationary*' engine." The more he studied the general, he confided to Browning, the more he realized that when "the hour for action approached he became nervous and oppressed with the responsibility and hesitated to meet the crisis." For this reason, Lincoln had "given him peremptory orders to move." Finally, twenty-four hours before Lincoln's deadline, McClellan's massive army of nearly a quarter of a million men left the base camps around Washington and headed toward the Potomac, where more than four hundred ships had gathered to carry them to Fort Monroe in Hampton Roads, Virginia. Parading to the refrains of regimental bands, with rifles on their shoulders and new equipment on their backs, the high-spirited, well-disciplined troops presented a sight, one diarist noted, such as "the eye of man has seldom seen." Before the army set sail, McClellan delivered an emotional address. "I will bring you now face to face with the rebels," he told his beloved troops, "ever bear in mind that my fate is linked with yours. . . . I am to watch over you as a parent over his children, and you know that your General loves you from the depths of his heart."

When most of the force had reached Fort Monroe, Stanton later recalled, "information was given to me by various persons that there was great reason to fear that no adequate force had been left to defend the Capital," despite Lincoln's "explicit order that Washington should, by the judgment of *all* the commanders of Army corps, be left entirely secure." Stanton referred the matter to Lorenzo Thomas, the adjutant general, who, after surveying the circumstance, concluded that the president's order had most definitely *not* been obeyed. McClellan had left behind "less than 20,000 raw recruits with not a single organized brigade," a force utterly incapable of defending Washington from sudden attack. Enraged, Stanton carried the damning report to the president at midnight. Lincoln promptly withdrew General McDowell's 1st Corps from McClellan's command so that Washington would be protected. That withdrawal, Stanton later recalled, "provoked [McClellan's] wrath, and the wrath of his friends."

With immense forces still at his disposal, McClellan advanced from Fort Monroe to the outskirts of Yorktown, roughly fifty miles from Richmond. Once again, mistakenly insisting that the rebel force outnumbered his, McClellan kept his army in a state of perpetual preparation. His engineers spent precious weeks constructing earthworks so his big guns could quash rebel defenses before the infantry assault. On April 6, Lincoln telegraphed McClellan: "You now have over one hundred thousand troops. . . . I think you better break the enemies' line from York-town to Warwick River, at once. They will probably use *time*, as advantageously as you can." The following day, McClellan scorned the president's admonition, informing his wife that if Lincoln wanted the enemy line broken, "he had better come & do it himself."

Still, McClellan persisted in his baffling inaction. He notified Stanton that "the enemy batteries are stronger" than anticipated. Stanton was livid: "You were sent on purpose to *take* strong batteries," he reminded McClellan. Later that day, Lincoln telegraphed the general, warning that further delay would only allow the enemy to summon reinforcements from other theaters. "It is indispensable to *you* that you strike a blow," Lincoln advised his commander on April 9. "The country will not fail to note—is now noting—that the present hesitation to move upon an intrenched enemy, is but the story of Manassas repeated. I beg to assure you that I have never written you, or spoken to you, in greater kindness of feeling than now. . . . *But you must act.*"

Two more weeks passed without any sign of movement. "Do not misunderstand the apparent inaction here," McClellan wired Lincoln; "not a day, not an hour has been lost, works have been constructed that may almost be called gigantic—roads built through swamps & difficult ravines, material brought up, batteries built." In another letter to his wife, he rationalized his continuing delay with the dubious contention that the more troops the enemy gathered in Yorktown, "the more decisive the results will be." A few days later, McClellan formulated yet another justification for postponement, arguing that he had been "compelled to change plans & become cautious" without McDowell's 1st Corps that had been taken from him to protect Washington. This left him "unexpectedly weakened & with a powerful enemy strongly entrenched in my front." Therefore, he was not "answerable for the delay of victory."

As it happened, Confederate general Joe Johnston, after keeping McClellan at bay for a month with substantially inferior numbers, had decided in early May to withdraw twelve miles up the peninsula toward Richmond. Hearing that a fallback was under way, McClellan finally moved on Yorktown to discover that, in a repeat of his experience at Manassas, the rebels were gone. Though he tried to claim the rebel retreat as a great bloodless victory, the public was unconvinced, and the question remained: why had he kept idle for a month? Had he moved on Yorktown with his greater numbers, he could have done serious damage to the rebel army. In the meantime, just as Lincoln had forewarned, the long delay had allowed the rebels to bring additional forces from various theaters into the peninsula, where, under General Johnston's command, they prepared for a counteroffensive.

• • •

ANXIETY SURROUNDING the impending battle did little to curtail the spring social season in Washington. If anything, the pace of social life accelerated, as Washingtonians sought relaxation and entertainment in the traditional round of calls, receptions, soirées, musicales, and dinners. Once the air turned "soft and balmy," the *National Republican* reported, the public squares came alive with "crowds of visitors, who either tread its graveled walks, or seat themselves beneath the trees," listening to the songs of birds and the joyful shouts of children rolling "their hoops over the ground."

Mary remained in mourning for Willie, however, and the traditional spring receptions in the White House were canceled, along with the Marine Band concerts on the lawn. In the social vacuum, Kate Chase took command of the Washington social scene, making her a powerful asset to her father. Her intermittent romance with the Rhode Island–based Sprague did not diminish her signal commitment to her father, whose household she managed with matchless style.

Her social supremacy derived in part from her striking appearance, enhanced by the simple but elegant wardrobe assembled during her many trips to New York in pursuit of furnishings for her father's mansion. She was "more of a professional beauty than had at that time ever been seen in America," noted Mary Adams French, the wife of the famed sculptor Daniel Chester French, "with a beauty and a regal carriage which we called 'queenly,' but which no real queen ever has." In an era when "the universal art of being slim had not been discovered," Mrs. French continued, the "tall and slim" Kate seemed otherworldly. She had "an unusually long white neck, and a slow and deliberate way of turning it when she glanced around her. Wherever she appeared, people dropped back in order to watch her." Fanny Villard, wife of the journalist Henry Villard, was one of many who looked with awe on Kate: "I a simple young home body from New England never before had seen so beautiful and brilliant a creature as Kate Chase; and it seemed to me then that nothing could blight her perfection."

And yet Kate's grace and beauty accounted for only a small part of her social success. Her emergence as the foremost lady of Washington society resulted as much from hard work and meticulous planning as from her natural assets. She met each morning with her household servants, giving detailed instructions for the day's activities. Continuing the ritual she had established in Columbus, she and her father hosted regular breakfast parties for out-of-town guests. Her correspondence reveals the elaborate preparations these affairs entailed. A letter to her father's friend, the Philadelphia banker Jay Cooke, requests that he "stop at Van Zant's where you find the best fruit and have a basketful of the best and *prettiest* grapes, pears, oranges, apples etc. sent me by Adams Express . . . so that they may arrive here without fail early Tuesday morning." She regretted the imposition, but she "could not think of anyone who would do it quite so well," and was "especially anxious" to make this "an attractive and agreeable occasion."

In addition to these early-morning breakfasts, Kate presided over weekly receptions known as "Cabinet calling" days. Every Monday, a contemporary Washingtonian wrote, "the wives of the Cabinet officers receive their friends; also Mrs. McClellan is at home on this same day." Through the late morning and early afternoon, regardless of rain, mud, or snow, the ladies of Washington made the rounds, visiting in turn each cabinet member's home. "First to Mrs. Seward's," columnist Cara Kasson reported, where Anna Seward officiated in the absence of Frances. A black doorman delivered their card to yet another servant, "who places it in the silver-card receiver, at the same moment ushering us in (names clearly pronounced), to the presence of Mrs. Seward." Greetings were exchanged and refreshments served, before proceeding to the next reception at Mrs. Caleb Smith's. There they found "an elegantly set table, salads and all good things." After visiting Mrs. Welles, who always entertained "in her friendly manner," the ladies would "take a glass of wine at Mrs. Blair's, admire the queenly dignity of Miss Chase, enjoy a delightful talk with the kindly family of Mrs. Bates, and then drive on to pay our respects to Mrs. McClellan and Mrs. Stanton."

While Kate hosted the weekly cabinet receptions with elegance and grace, she devoted her greatest efforts to the celebrated candlelight dinners she held each Wednesday evening. With exacting care, she drew up the guest lists, prepared the menus, and arranged seating. With her father occupying the head of the table, she would help maintain lively, entertaining conversation from her place at the other end. After dinner, a band would play and dancing would begin. "Diplomats and statesmen felt it an honor to be her guests, and men of letters found that they needed their keenest wits to be her match in conversation," one reporter noted. "Her drawing-room was a salon, and it has been paralleled only in the ante-revolutionary days of the French monarchy, when women ruled the empire of the Bourbons."

Over time, the Chase home increasingly became a forum for critics of the Lincoln administration. In the relaxed atmosphere of Kate's private dinner parties, William Fessenden could freely condemn Lincoln's reluctance to confront the emancipation question. The members of the Committee on the Conduct of the War could censure General McClellan more harshly than public statement would safely allow. Over coffee and dessert in the parlor, the women could spread disdainful gossip about Mary Lincoln. Kate clearly understood the role that "parlor politics" could play in cementing alliances and consolidating power in furtherance of her father's irrepressible political ambitions. She was determined to create nothing less than a "rival court" to the White House that could help catapult Chase to the presidency. In the spring of 1862, she reigned supreme.

The most compelling conversations in the Chase drawing room that balmy spring swirled around the proclamation of General David Hunter, an old friend of Lincoln's who commanded the Department of the South, which encompassed South Carolina, Georgia, and Florida. In early May, acting without prior approval from the White House, Hunter had issued an official order declaring "forever free" all slaves in the three states under his jurisdiction. Chase's circle was exultant, for Hunter's proclamation went beyond even General Frémont's attempt of the previous August. "It seems to me of the highest importance," Chase wrote to Lincoln, "that this order not be revoked. . . . It will be cordially approved, I am sure, by more than nine tenths of the people on whom you must rely for support of your Administration." Lincoln's reply to Chase was swift and blunt: "No commanding general shall do such a thing, upon *my* responsibility, without consulting me."

By repudiating Hunter's proclamation, Lincoln understood that he would give "dissatisfaction, if not offence, to many whose support the country can not afford to lose." He firmly believed, however, that any such proclamation must come from the commander in chief, not from a general in the field. "Gen. Hunter is an honest man," Lincoln told a delegation after officially revoking Hunter's order. "He was, and I hope, still is, my friend. . . . He expected more good, and less harm from the measure, than I could believe would follow."

While Seward and Stanton supported Lincoln's decision, Chase publicly disagreed. In conversations with Sumner and others, he openly denounced Lincoln's action, fanning talk "among the more advanced members" of the Republican Party about Lincoln's "pusillanimity." Chase's defiance earned him plaudits from the *New York Tribune*, "all the more warmly appreciated," Chase told Horace Greeley, given the influential editor's "earlier unfavorable judgments" of his public career. Chase maintained to Greeley that he had "not been so sorely tried by anything here—though I have seen a great deal in the shape of irregularity, assumptions beyond law, extravagance, & deference to generals and reactionists which I could not approve,—as by the nullifying of Hunter's proclamation." Rumors began to surface that the controversy would cause an open rupture in the cabinet and precipitate Chase's departure. Still, so long as Lincoln believed Chase was the right man for the Treasury, he had no intention of requesting his resignation. As for Chase, so long as he could garner radical support by publicly opposing Lincoln on this critical issue, he would productively remain in the cabinet until the time was right to make a break.

• • •

IN THE FIRST WEEK OF MAY, Lincoln resolved to end months of frustration with McClellan by personally visiting Fort Monroe. Stanton had suggested that a presidential journey to the tip of the Peninsula might finally spur McClellan to act. On the evening of Monday, May 5, the president arrived at the Navy Yard and boarded the *Miami*, a five-gun Treasury cutter, accompanied by Stanton, Chase, and General Egbert Viele. "The cabin," Viele recalled, "was neat and cozy. A center table, buffet and washstand, with four berths, two on each side, and some comfortable chairs, constituted its chief appointments." Since the *Miami* was a Treasury ship, Chase "seemed to feel that we were his guests," General Viele observed. The treasury secretary even brought his own butler to serve meals, and "treated us as if we were in his own house."

Both Chase and Stanton began the twenty-seven-hour journey anxious about all the work they had left behind. As the hours passed by, however, they warmed to Lincoln's high-spirited discourse and began to relax. General Viele marveled how Lincoln was always the center of the circle gathered on the quarterdeck, keeping everyone engrossed for hours as he recited passages from Shakespeare, "page after page of Browning and whole cantos of Byron." Talking much of the day, he interspersed stories and anecdotes from his "inexhaustible stock." Many, as usual, were directly applicable to a point made in conversation, but some were simply jokes that set Lincoln laughing louder than all the combined listeners. One of his favorite anecdotes told of a schoolboy "called up by the teacher to be disciplined. 'Hold out your hand!' A paw of the most surprising description was extended, more remarkable for its filthiness than anything else." The schoolmaster was so stunned that he said, " 'Now, if there were such another dirty thing in the room, I would let you off.' *'There it is,'* quoth the unmoved culprit, drawing *the other hand* from behind his back."

While the presidential party lounged on the deck, Lincoln playfully demonstrated that in "muscular power he was one in a thousand," possessing "the strength of a giant." He picked up an ax and "held it at arm's length at the extremity of the [handle] with his thumb and forefinger, continuing to hold it there for a number of minutes. The most powerful sailors on board tried in vain to imitate him."

After the Tuesday luncheon table was cleared, the president and his advisers pored over maps and analyzed the army positions in and around Virginia. Union forces at Fort Monroe occupied the northern shore of Hampton Roads, which connected the Chesapeake to three rivers. Confederate forces on the southern shore still held Norfolk and the Navy Yard. Two months earlier, the rebels had used this strategic foothold to great advantage by sending the powerful nine-gun *Merrimac*, a scuttled Union ship that they had raised and covered with iron plates, into a series of devastating engagements. In the space of five hours, the ironclad had managed to sink, capture, and incapacitate three ships and two Union frigates.

The news had terrified government officials, who feared that the invincible *Merrimac* might sail up the Potomac to attack Washington or even continue on to New York. "It is a disgrace to the country that the rebels, without resources, have built a vessel with which we cannot cope," General Meigs had grumbled. An emergency cabinet meeting was convened, during which Stanton unfairly faulted Welles for the disaster. His attack was so personal, according to Welles's biographer, that the navy secretary "found it very difficult for a time even to be civil in [Stanton's] presence."

In fact, the navy had been more than adequately prepared to deal with the *Merrimac*. The very next day, the *Monitor*, a strange ironclad vessel resembling a "cheese box on a raft," engaged the *Merrimac* in battle. Though the little *Monitor* seemed "a pigmy to a giant," it proved far more maneuverable. Commanded by Lieutenant John L. Worden, who directed two large guns from a revolving turret, the *Monitor* fought the *Merrimac* to a draw and sent the Confederate vessel back to the harbor. When Stanton learned that Worden might lose one eye as a result of the struggle, he said: "Then we will fill the other with diamonds."

To Herman Melville, as to many others, the battle of the two ironclads marked the beginning of a new epoch in warfare. "The ringing of those plates on plates/Still ringeth round the world," he wrote. "War yet shall be, but warriors/Are now but operatives."

As the president and his advisers huddled over maps of Fort Monroe, Norfolk, and the surrounding area, they could not understand why McClellan had not ordered an attack on Norfolk immediately after his occupation of Yorktown. The Confederate retreat up the Peninsula had left the city and the Navy Yard vulnerable. Though the *Monitor* had held its own against the

Merrimac, there was no assurance that this feat would be repeated. If Norfolk were captured, perhaps the *Merrimac* could be captured as well. With McClellan and his troops about twenty miles away, Lincoln and his little group came to a decision of their own. If General John E. Wool, commander of Fort Monroe, had sufficient forces at his disposal, an *immediate* attack should be made on Norfolk. Disconcerted by the prospect, the seventy-eight-year-old General Wool insisted on consulting Commodore Louis Goldsborough, since the navy's warships would have to immobilize the Confederate batteries before any troops could be safely landed.

In the black of night, the *Miami* could not easily pull aside the *Minnesota*, Goldsborough's flagship, so Lincoln's party climbed into a tugboat and approached the port side of the *Minnesota.* The steps leading up to the deck were very "narrow," Chase wrote, "with the guiding ropes on either hand, hardly visible in the darkness. It seemed to me *very* high and a little fearsome. But etiquette required the President to go first and he went. Etiquette required the Secretary of the Treasury to follow." Stanton, climbing immediately behind Chase, must have overcome even greater trepidation, for an accident when he was younger had left one leg permanently damaged and he suffered, besides, from frequent attacks of vertigo. Fortunately, they all made it aboard without mishap. Though Lincoln was probably unfamiliar with Commodore Goldsborough, Chase had known him for several decades—the distinguished naval officer had won the hand of William Wirt's daughter, Elizabeth, at a time when Chase had not been deemed an appropriate suitor.

Goldsborough approved the idea of attack in theory, but feared that so long as the *Merrimac* was still a factor, it was too risky to carry troops across the water. Lincoln disagreed, and orders were given to begin shelling the Confederate batteries. Before long, "a smoke curled up over the woods," Chase recalled, "and each man, almost, said to the other, 'There comes the *Merrimac*,' and, sure enough, it was the *Merrimac.*" However, upon spying the *Monitor*, accompanied by a second powerful ship, "the great rebel terror paused—then turned back." The next day, Lincoln, Chase, and Stanton each personally surveyed the shoreline to determine the best landing place for the troops. Under a full moon, Lincoln went ashore in a rowboat. He walked on enemy soil and then returned to the *Miami.* Once the best spot was chosen, Chase pushed for an immediate attack, worried that McClellan might appear and delay the attack. The next night, the convoys headed for shore.

They discovered that the rebels had decided to evacuate Norfolk and scuttle the *Merrimac* to keep it out of Union hands soon after the shelling began. As the Union troops moved uncontested into the city, Chase, accompanying Generals Wool and Viele, heard the soldiers shouting "cheer after cheer." In the city center, they were met by a delegation of civilian authorities who formally surrendered Norfolk to General Viele. The general remained in City Hall as military governor of the region.

It was after midnight when Chase and General Wool finally returned to the *Miami.* Lincoln and Stanton, after waiting nervously all evening for their return, had just retired to their rooms. "The night was very warm," Lincoln recalled, "the moon shining brightly,—and, too restless to sleep, I threw off my clothes and sat for some time by the table, reading." Hearing a knock at Stanton's door, which was directly below his own, he guessed that "the missing men" had come back at last. Minutes later, Chase and General Wool came to Lincoln's room. Eschewing ceremony, Wool happily announced: "Norfolk is ours!" Stanton, who had "burst in, just out of bed, clad in a long nightgown," was so jubilant over the news that "he rushed at the General, whom he hugged most affectionately, fairly lifting him from the floor in his delight." Lincoln recognized that the scene "must have been a comical one," with Stanton clad in a nightgown that "nearly swept the floor" and he himself having just undressed. Nevertheless, they "were all too greatly excited to take much note of mere appearances." Beside the capture of Norfolk, the destruction of the fearsome *Merrimac* would open the supply lines from Washington to the peninsula.

When the triumphant trio returned to Washington, reporters noted that Stanton was "conveyed home seriously ill." Physicians feared at first that he was suffering from one of the bouts of vertigo that immobilized him for days at a time. He soon recovered, however, and enjoyed the sweetness of victory in what the Civil War historian Shelby Foote has called "one of the strangest small-scale campaigns in American military history."

Unusually buoyant, Chase expressed greater admiration for the president than he ever had before or ever would again. "So has ended a brilliant week's campaign of the President," Chase wrote, "for I think it quite certain that if he had not come down, Norfolk would still have been in possession of the enemy, and the *Merrimac*, as grim and defiant and as much a terror as ever. The whole coast is now virtually ours."

Not surprisingly, McClellan refused to credit the president for the return of Norfolk to the Union. "Norfolk is in our possession," he flatly declared to his wife; "the result of my movements."

• • •

THE DAY AFTER Lincoln's triumphant return, Navy Secretary Welles invited Seward, Bates, and their families to join him and his wife for a six-day cruise along the coast of Virginia, now cleared of rebel forces and the menacing *Merrimac*. "We had two pilots and thirteen sailors," Fred Seward informed his mother. "Wormley and his cook and waiters, two howitzers, and two dozen muskets, coal and provisions for a week, field glasses and maps." The armed navy steamer took them to Norfolk and the Gosport Navy Yard, where they viewed the ruins of the *Merrimac*. They proceeded up York River to McClellan's new headquarters at West Point, thirty miles from Richmond. The cabinet colleagues enjoyed an easy camaraderie as the steamer moved from one river to the next. They consumed hearty meals, sang patriotic songs to the music of a navy band, and joked with one another. When Seward discovered that rats had eaten a tie and socks belonging to Bates, he composed a humorous poem, complete with sketches, to commemorate the occasion.

By day, they went ashore and wandered through the seaboard towns now in possession of the Union armies. "Virginia is sad to look upon," Seward wrote to his wife, "not merely the rebellion, but society itself, is falling into ruin. Slaves are deserting the homes intrusted to them by their masters, who have gone into the Southern armies or are fleeing before ours. There is universal stagnation, and sullenness prevails everywhere." Like Lincoln, Seward was always sensitive to the devastation of war. Despite his satisfaction at the recent Union successes that had subdued this part of Virginia, he was disquieted by the bleakness he encountered. "We saw war, not in its holiday garb," he told Fanny, "but in its stern and fearful aspect. We saw the desolation that follows, and the terror that precedes its march."

The steamer reached McClellan's camp at about 3 p.m. on May 13. Approaching the shore, Fred Seward was amazed to find that "a clearing in the woods" had been "suddenly transformed into a great city of a hundred thousand people, by the advent of McClellan's Army and its supporting fleet." McClellan escorted the party ashore, where they reviewed thousands of his troops and discussed the general's plans.

Though McClellan considered such visits "a nuisance," he convinced his official guests that, if properly reinforced, he would soon prevail in a decisive fight "this side of Richmond," which would be "one of the great historic battles of the world." McClellan's high-spirited, well-disciplined troops and the gigantic size of the operation were impressive to all. "At night," Fred Seward observed, "the long lines of lights on the shore, the shipping and bustle in the river made it almost impossible to believe we were not in the harbor of Philadelphia or New York."

After the meeting with McClellan, Seward advised Lincoln by telegraph that McDowell's forces should be sent to the York River to reinforce McClellan "as soon as possible." Lincoln and Stanton agreed. McDowell was ordered to move his entire force from the vicinity of Washington to the peninsula. For weeks, McClellan's Democratic supporters had publicly criticized the president and secretary of war for retaining McDowell's force out of irrational fear for Washington. Yet now that McClellan stood to have his demands met, he told Lincoln that he wouldn't receive McDowell's men unless it was clear that he would have absolute authority over them. McClellan considered McDowell a radical on the issue of slavery and despised him personally, calling him an "animal" in a letter to his wife. Lincoln assured McClellan by telegraph that he was in command.

The day after Lincoln ordered McDowell to prepare for the move south, he made an impromptu visit, accompanied by Stanton and Dahlgren, to McDowell's headquarters at Fredericksburg. The trip was arranged so suddenly that Captain Dahlgren had no chance to bring food or beds aboard the steamboat that was to carry them to Aquia Landing. Despite the makeshift accommodations, Lincoln relaxed at once, reading aloud from the works of a contemporary poet, Fitz-Greene Halleck, then considered "the American Byron." Lincoln chose that night to read *Marco Bozzaris*, a lengthy poem celebrating the death of a Greek hero in the war against Turkey. Lincoln was drawn to the poet's vision of a lasting greatness, of deeds that would resound throughout history. Because of such achievements in life, both Greece, in which "there is no prouder grave," and the mother "who gave thee birth," can speak "of thy doom without a sigh":

For thou art Freedom's now, and Fame's;
One of the few, the immortal names,
That were not born to die.

When Lincoln and his party reached Aquia Creek shortly after dawn, they were driven to McDowell's camp in what Dahlgren described as "a common baggage car, with camp-stools for the party." McDowell was eager to show the little group his army's accomplishments in having rebuilt bridges and repaired telegraph lines, creating a direct link between Washington and Fredericksburg. The general was particularly proud of a new trestle bridge that spanned a creek and deep ravine at a height of a hundred feet. Though "there was nothing but a single plank for us to walk on," Dahlgren recalled, Lincoln impulsively said: "Let us walk over." So the president, followed by McDowell, and then poor Stanton, understandably fearful of heights, and finally Dahlgren, began the hazardous journey. "About half-way," Dahlgren wrote, "the Secretary said he was dizzy and feared he would fall. So he stopped, unable to proceed. I managed to step by him, and took his hand, thus leading him over, when in fact my own head was somewhat confused by the giddy height."

After breakfast, the president and McDowell mounted horses and spent the day inspecting the troops. Enduring a hot sun without the protection of a hat, Lincoln reviewed "one division after another, all in fine order, the men cheering tremendously." After a simple meal, the presidential party returned to Aquia Creek, departing for Washington sometime after 10 p.m. Lincoln "was in good spirits," according to Dahlgren. Once again, he read poetry aloud, and they all retired to their makeshift beds. Before falling asleep, Stanton confided to Dahlgren that "he did not think much of McDowell!"

Troublesome news reached Washington the following day that General Stonewall Jackson had been sent to attack Union forces in the Shenandoah Valley, hoping to prevent McDowell from moving south. The goal was realized. After Jackson attacked Front Royal, forcing General Banks to hastily retreat north to Winchester, the president telegraphed McClellan: "I have been compelled to suspend Gen. McDowell's movement to join you." He followed up with a telegram explaining that with Jackson chasing Banks farther and farther north, Washington was again endangered. "Stripped bare, as we are here, it will be all we can do to prevent [the enemy] crossing the Potomac at Harper's Ferry, or above. . . . If McDowell's force was now beyond our reach, we should be utterly helpless." Moreover, while Jackson and his forces made their way north, Lincoln reasoned, Richmond must be vulnerable. "I think the time is near when you must either attack Richmond or give up the job and come to the defence of Washington. Let me hear from you instantly."

McClellan replied at 5 p.m.: "Independently of it the time is very near when I shall attack Richmond." He then haughtily informed his wife that he had "just finished [his] reply to his Excellency," and complained, "it is perfectly sickening to deal with such people & you may rest assured that I will lose as little time as possible in breaking off all connection with them—I get more sick of them every day—for every day brings with it only additional proofs of their hypocrisy, knavery & folly."

James McPherson concludes that "Lincoln's diversion of McDowell's corps to chase Jackson was probably a strategic error—perhaps even the colossal blunder that McClellan considered it." For as soon as Jackson had managed to divert the Union forces bound for Richmond, he turned back southward to join in the defense of the Confederate capital. Still, McPherson adds, "even if McDowell's corps had joined McClellan as planned, the latter's previous record offered little reason to believe that he would have moved with speed and boldness to capture Richmond."

In the end, though McClellan had advanced to a position only four miles from Richmond by the end of May, he still refused to take the initiative, and his troops were surprised by a Confederate attack at Fair Oaks. Though the battle was inconclusive and the rebels suffered heavier losses than the Union, McClellan was so devastated by the toll of nearly five thousand Union dead and wounded that he lost whatever momentum he had created. "McClellan keeps sending word that he will attack Richmond very soon,—but every day brings some new excuse," reported Christopher Wolcott, Stanton's brother-in-law, now assistant secretary of war. The rain, a legitimate excuse during the first ten days of June, had stopped five days earlier. Nevertheless, Wolcott noted, "he has not stirred."

McClellan's catalogue of gripes and concerns was endless. There were bridges to be built, bad roads, regiments to be reorganized. When Lincoln eventually ordered McDowell to reinforce him, the general continued to protest that "if I cannot fully control all his [McDowell's] troops I want none of them, but would prefer to fight the battle with what I have and let others be responsible for the results." Finally, he confided in his wife, "utmost prudence" was essential. "I must not unnecessarily risk my life—for the fate of my army depends upon me & they all know it."

McClellan's chronic delays allowed General Lee to take the initiative once again. During the last week in June, the Confederates launched a brutal attack on Union forces that became known as the Seven Days Battles. The bloody series of engagements on the plains and in the swamps and forests surrounding the Chickahominy River left 1,734 Federals dead, 8,066 wounded, and 6,055 missing or captured. At the end of the first day's fighting, McClellan telegraphed Stanton to warn that he was up against "vastly superior odds." He calculated that the rebels had 200,000 troops when in fact they had fewer than half that figure. He would carry on without the reinforcements he had repeatedly requested, but, he continued, if his "great inferiority in numbers" caused "a disaster the responsibility cannot be thrown on my shoulders—it must rest where it belongs." Irked, Lincoln replied that McClellan's talk of responsibility "pains me very much. I give you all I can . . . while you continue, ungenerously I think, to assume that I could give you more if I would."

As the fighting intensified in the days that followed, neither McClellan nor Lincoln was able to sleep. Success alternated between the two forces during the first two days. Then, on June 27, the Confederates scored a critical victory at Gaines' Mill, forcing McClellan to retreat. "I now know the full history of the day," McClellan telegraphed Stanton shortly after midnight. "I have lost this battle because my force was too small. I again repeat that I am not responsible for this." The president "is wrong in regarding me as ungenerous when I said that my force was too weak. I merely intimated a truth which to-day has been too plainly proved." Finally, he vindictively added: "If I save this Army now, I tell you plainly that I owe no thanks to you or to any other persons in Washington. You have done your best to sacrifice this army." When the supervisor of telegrams at the War Department read this defiant message, he was so appalled by the insubordinate tone and the extraordinary charge against the government that he directed his staff to strike the last sentence before relaying it to Stanton.

Even the revised telegram conveyed the accusation that would be leveled by McClellan and his supporters for years to come: victory would have been achieved but for the government's failure to reinforce an overpowered McClellan. Even after the defeat at Gaines' Mill, however, McClellan's troops remained a strong and resilient force. In the days that followed, they fought hard and well, inflicting more than five thousand casualties at Malvern Hill while suffering only half that number. In truth, McClellan was psychologically defeated. "He was simply out-generaled," Christopher Wolcott concluded. Instead of counterattacking, he continued to retreat from Richmond until his exhausted troops reached a safe position eight miles down the James at Harrison's Landing. Equally depleted, Lee's troops returned to Richmond, and the Peninsula Campaign came to an end. The Confederates had successfully secured their capital and gained an important strategic victory. It would take nearly three more years and hundreds of thousands more deaths for the Union forces to come as close to Richmond as they had been in May and June 1862.

CHAPTER 17

"WE ARE IN THE DEPTHS"

THE DEFEAT ON THE Peninsula devastated Northern morale. "We are in the depths just now," George Templeton Strong admitted on July 14, 1862, "permeated by disgust, saturated with gloomy thinking." In Washington, columnist Cara Kasson observed the frustration written on every face, manifesting an anxiety greater than the aftermath of Bull Run, "for the present repulse is more momentous." Count Gurowski agreed, calling the Fourth of July holiday "the gloomiest since the birth of this republic. Never was the country so low." Even the normally stoical John Nicolay confided to his fiancée, Therena, that "the past has been a very blue week. . . . I don't think I have ever heard more croaking since the war began."

For the irrepressibly optimistic Seward, who had fervently hoped the capture of Richmond might signal an end to the war, the turn of events was shattering. "It is a startling sight to see the mind of a great people, saddened, angered, soured, all at once," he confided to Fanny, who was in Auburn with her mother for the summer. "If I should let a shade of this popular despondency fall upon a dispatch, or even rest upon my own countenance," he realized, "there would be black despair throughout the whole country." He begged her for letters detailing daily life at home—the flowers in bloom and the hatching of eggs—anything but war and defeat. "They bring no alarm, no remonstrances, no complaints, and no reproaches," he explained. "They are the only letters which come to me, free from excitement. . . . Write to me then cheerfully, as you are wont to do, of boys and girls and dogs and horses, and birds that sing, and stars that shine and never weep, and be blessed for all your days, for thus helping to sustain a spirit."

Chase was equally shaken and despondent. "Since the rebellion broke out I have never been so sad," he told a friend. "We ought [to have] won a victory and taken Richmond." Furthermore, Kate, who had gone to Ohio to visit her grandmother, was not in Washington to console him. "The house seemed very dull after you were gone," he told her in one of many long letters cataloguing the events of that summer. He described his sojourn to see General McDowell, who had been knocked unconscious by a bad fall from his horse; told her of an unusual cabinet meeting, a pleasant dinner party at Seward's with the Stantons and the Welles, a meeting with Jay Cooke, and a visit from Bishop McIlvaine. He queried her about her summer clothes, her lace veil, and a diamond she had ordered. In addition to commonplace matters, he provided her with confidential military intelligence about the Peninsula Campaign, delineating the flow of the Chickahominy and the position of the various divisions so she could visualize the course of the battle.

Kate was thrilled by her father's lengthy epistles, which she interpreted as "a mark of love and confidence." Her appreciation, he replied, was "more than ample reward for the time & trouble of writing." She must trust that she would always have his love and that he would continue to "confide greatly in [her] on many points." He was pleased, as well, with the quality of her letters, which finally seemed to meet his exacting standards. "All your letters have come and all have been good—some very good."

However, Kate's letters that summer concealed her unhappiness over the troubled course of her romance with William Sprague. The young couple had been close to an engagement before Sprague received some nasty letters retelling and likely embellishing the story of Kate's dalliance with the young married man in Columbus who had become obsessed with her when she was sixteen. Though Sprague was guilty of far greater indiscretions himself, having fathered a child during his twenties, it seems he was so taken aback by the rumors of Kate's behavior that he broke off the relationship. "Then came the blank," he later recalled. "Wherever there is day there must be night. In some countries the day is almost constant, but the night cometh. So with us it came."

Kate, unaccustomed to defeat and ignorant of Sprague's reasons for ending the courtship, was plunged into dejection. Sensing that something was wrong, Chase told Kate that if anything disappointed him, it was her failure to disclose her deepest personal concerns, to confide in him as he confided in her. "My confidence will be entire when you entirely give me yours and when I . . . am made by your acts & words to feel that nothing is held back from me which a father should know of the thoughts, sentiments & acts of a daughter. Cannot this entire confidence be given me? You will, I am sure be happier and so will I."

Hoping to raise her spirits, Chase arranged for Kate and Nettie to visit the McDowells' country home, Buttermilk Farm, in upstate New York. The quiet routine of country life did not suit Kate, who craved distraction from her sorrows. Mrs. McDowell, observing that Kate's "health and spirit" were suffering, kindly agreed to let her accompany friends to Saratoga in search of a more active social life. "Trust nothing I have said will alarm you," she assured Chase upon Kate's departure; but he, of course, could not help fretting over his beloved daughter.

Even more than Chase or Seward, Edwin Stanton was afflicted with troubles in the summer of '62. "The first necessity of every community after a disaster, is a *scapegoat*," the *New York Times* noted. "It is an immense relief to find some one upon whom can be fastened all the sins of a whole people, and who can then be sent into the wilderness, to be heard of no more." In the secretary of war, disgruntled Northerners found their scapegoat. "Journals of all sorts," the *Times* reported, "demand his instant removal."

The drumbeat began with McClellan, who told anyone who would listen that Stanton was to blame for the Peninsula defeat. "So you want to know how I feel about Stanton, & what I think of him now?" he wrote Mary Ellen in July. "I think that he is the most unmitigated scoundrel I ever knew, heard or read of; I think that . . . had he lived in the time of the Saviour, Judas Iscariot would have remained a respected member of the fraternity of the Apostles & that the magnificent treachery & rascality of E. M. Stanton would have caused Judas to have raised his arms in holy horror & unaffected wonder." A week later, McClellan wrote that he had "*the proof that the Secy reads all my private telegrams."* In fact, he took pleasure in the thought that "if he has read my private letters to you also his ears must have tingled somewhat." Nor did his suspicions stop him from reiterating his loathing for the former friend whom he now considered "the most depraved hypocrite & villain."

Democrats, unwilling to fault McClellan, were the loudest in their denunciations of Stanton. Spearheaded by the Blairs, conservatives charged that Stanton had abandoned both his Democratic heritage and his old friendship with McClellan. Two navy officers, speaking with Samuel Phillips Lee, Elizabeth Blair's husband, claimed "there had been treachery at the bottom of our Richmond reverse," spurred by "Stanton's political opposition to McClellan." Democrat John Astor could not refrain from cursing at the mere mention of Stanton's name. "He for one believes," Strong reported, "that Stanton willfully withheld reinforcements from McClellan lest he should make himself too important, politically, by a signal victory." Sanitary Commission member Frederick Law Olmsted expressed similar emotions. "If we could help to hang Stanton by resigning and posting him as a liar, hypocrite and knave," he wrote, "I think we should render the country a far greater service that we can in any other way."

The *New York Times* promised not to engage in the "very fierce crusade" against Stanton, but begged the president, "if we are to have a new Secretary of War, to give us a Soldier—one who knows what war is and how it is to be carried on. . . . If Mr. Stanton is to be removed, the country will be reassured, and the public interest greatly promoted, by making Gen. McClellan his successor. Even those who cavil at his leadership in the field, do not question his mastery of the art of war." As the weeks went by, and the pressure to replace him mounted, Stanton must have wondered how long Lincoln would continue to support him.

Beyond the distracting personal attacks, Stanton was tormented by the long lines of ambulances that rolled into the city each morning carrying the injured and the dead from the peninsula. All his life, Stanton had been unnerved in the presence of death. Now he was surrounded by it at every turn. Sometimes he took it upon himself to deliver the news to stricken families. Mary Ellet Cabell, whose father, Colonel Charles Ellet, was fatally wounded in Memphis, long recalled the moment when Stanton appeared at her family's home in Georgetown to tell of Ellet's heroism during the battle. "I have heard that this powerful War Minister was harsh and unfeeling; but I can never forget the tenderness of his manner" as he delivered the news with "tears to his eyes."

Stanton's own family was touched by death as well. In early July, his youngest son, James, entered the final stage of the smallpox precipitated by an inoculation six months earlier. The Stantons had planned to spend the Fourth of July holiday on a cruise with General Meigs and his family, but their child's illness occupied Ellen Stanton night and day. On July 5, a messenger called on Stanton in the War Department to report that "the baby was dying." He immediately began the three-mile drive to the country house where his family was staying for the summer. The child clung to life for several days, finally succumbing on July 10. For Stanton, who loved his children passionately, the death was devastating, particularly bitter in light of the overwhelming pressures at work that had kept him from his family for many weeks. Under the weight of public censure and private tragedy, his own health began to suffer.

• • •

While his cabinet reeled in the aftermath of the Peninsula defeat, Lincoln was faced with the grim knowledge that the ultimate authority had been his alone. Nonetheless, as Whitman had observed following the debacle at Bull Run, Lincoln refused to surrender to the gloom of defeat: "He unflinchingly stemm'd it, and resolv'd to lift himself and the Union out of it." While the battle was still ongoing, Lincoln had found time to write a letter to a young cadet at West Point, the son of Mary's cousin Ann Todd Campbell. The boy was miserable at the academy and his mother was worried. "Allow me to assure you it is a perfect certainty that you will, very soon, feel better—quite happy—if you only stick to the resolution you have taken to procure a military education. I am older than you, have felt badly myself, and *know*, what I tell you is true. Adhere to your purpose and you will soon feel as well as you ever did. On the contrary, if you falter, and give up, you will lose the power of keeping any resolution, and will regret it all your life." The boy stayed at West Point, graduating in 1866.

Now, in the wake of the Peninsula battle, confronted with public discontent, diminishing loan subscriptions and renewed threats that Britain would recognize the Confederacy, Lincoln demonstrated that his own purpose remained fixed. He decided to call for a major expansion of the army. Two months earlier, Stanton, assuming that victory would soon be achieved, had made the colossal mistake of shutting down recruiting offices. To call for more troops now on the heels of defeat, Lincoln realized, might well create "a general panic." But the troops were essential. Seward devised an excellent solution. He journeyed to New York, where a conference of Union governors was taking place. After consulting privately with the governors and securing their agreement, he drafted a circular that they would endorse *asking* the president to call for three hundred thousand additional troops. The president would be responding to a patriotic appeal rather than initiating a call on his own.

While Seward worked out the details from his suite at the Astor House, he was kept abreast of the military situation by telegrams from Lincoln. Fearing that their recruiting efforts might prove insufficient, Seward telegraphed Stanton for permission to promise each new recruit an advance of twenty-five dollars. The money "is of vital importance," he wrote. "We fail without it." Stanton hesitated at first. "The existing law does not authorize an advance," he replied. But finally, trusting Seward's judgment, he decided to make the allocation on his own responsibility.

That summer, Seward traveled throughout the North to help build up the Union Army. He set a precedent within his own department by entreating all those between eighteen and forty-five to volunteer, pledging that their positions would be waiting for them when they returned. A large percentage answered Seward's call. In Auburn, the Sewards' twenty-year-old-son, William Junior, was appointed secretary of the war committee responsible for raising a regiment in upstate New York. A half century later, William remembered "the Mass Meetings held in all the principal towns," the fervent appeals for volunteers, the quickened response once the government announced that unfilled quotas would by met by a draft. New recruits "filled the hotels and many private houses, occupied the upper floors of the business blocks, leaned against the fences, sat upon the curb stone," he recalled. They came on foot and in horse-drawn wagons. "The spectacle was so novel and inspiring that our citizens gave them a perfect ovation as they passed, canons were fired—bells rung and flags displayed from almost every house on the line of march."

Young William Seward had no intention of recruiting others without volunteering himself. His decision to enlist aroused trepidation in the Seward household, for William's new wife, Jenny, was expecting their first child in September. Jenny assured her husband that she would "be able to pass through her troubles," but she worried that his departure might jeopardize his mother's fragile health. In fact, although Frances had been heartbroken years before when Gus, now an army paymaster in Washington, had joined the Mexican War, her passionate feelings against slavery now outweighed her maternal anxiety. "As it is obvious all men are needed I made no objection," Frances told Fred.

While the call was out for fresh reserves, Lincoln decided to make a personal visit to bolster the morale of the weary troops who had fought the hard battles on the Peninsula. Accompanied by Assistant Secretary of War Peter Watson and Congressman Frank Blair, he left Washington aboard the *Ariel* early on the morning of July 8, 1862, beginning the twelve-hour journey to McClellan's new headquarters at Harrison's Landing on the James River. "The day had been intensely hot," an army correspondent noted, the temperature climbing to over 100 degrees. Even soldiers who lay in the shade of the trees found small respite from the "almost overpowering" heat. By 6 p.m., however, when General McClellan and his staff met the president at Harrison's Landing, the setting sun had yielded to a pleasant, moonlit evening.

News of the president's arrival spread quickly through the camp. Soldiers in the vicinity let out great cheers whenever they glimpsed him "sitting and smiling serenely on the after deck of the vessel." Lincoln's calm visage, however, masked his deep anxiety about McClellan and the progress of the war.

Equally troubled, the defeated McClellan had spent the hours before Lincoln's arrival drafting what he termed a "strong frank letter" delineating changes necessary to win the war. "If he acts upon it the country will be saved," he told his wife. McClellan handed the letter to Lincoln, who read it as the two sat together on the deck. Known to history as the "Harrison's Landing" letter, the document imperiously outlined for the president what the policy and aims of the war should be. "The time has come when the government must determine upon a civil and military policy," McClellan brazenly began, warning that without a clear-cut policy defining the nature of the war, "our cause will be lost." Somewhat resembling in attitude Seward's April 1 memo of fifteen months earlier, the presumptuous memo was even more astonishing in tone, as it came from a military officer.

"It should not be at all a war upon population," McClellan proclaimed, and all efforts must be made to protect "private property and unarmed persons." In effect, slave property must be respected, for if a radical approach to slavery were adopted, the "present armies" would "rapidly disintegrate." To carry out this conservative policy, the president would need "a Commander-in-Chief of the Army—one who possesses your confidence." While he did not specifically request that position for himself, McClellan made it clear that he was more than willing to retake the central command.

To McClellan's disappointment and disgust, Lincoln "made no comments upon [the letter], merely saying, when he had finished it, that he was obliged to me for it." Clearly, the president did not remain silent because he failed to grasp the political significance of the general's propositions. In the days that followed, his actions would manifest his rejection of the general's political advice. For the moment, however, Lincoln had come to see and support the troops, not to debate policy with his general.

For three hours, the president reviewed one division after another, riding slowly along the long lines of cheering soldiers. He was relieved to find the army in such high spirits after the bloody weeklong battle, which had decimated their ranks, leaving 1,734 dead and 8,066 wounded. "Mr. Lincoln rode at the right of Gen. McClellan," an army correspondent reported, "holding with one hand the reins which checked a spirited horse, and with the other a large-sized stove-pipe hat" that he repeatedly tipped to acknowledge the cheers of the troops. His attempts to coordinate the reins and doff his tall hat were not entirely successful. His legs almost became "entangled with those of the horse he rode . . . while his arms were apparently liable to similar mishap." One soldier admitted in a letter home that he had to lower his cap over his face "to cover a smile that overmastered" him at the "ludicrous sight." Still, he added, the troops loved Lincoln. "His benignant smile as he passed on was a real reflection of his honest, kindly heart; but deeper, under the surface of that marked and not all uncomely face, were the unmistakable signs of care and anxiety. . . . In fact, his popularity in the army is and has been universal."

As Lincoln approached each division, the "successive booming of salutes made known his progress," until finally, "his tall figure, like Saul of old," came into view, provoking wild applause. The tonic of the president's unexpected visit to the enervated regiments was instantaneous. As Lincoln reviewed the "thinned ranks of some of the divisions" and came upon regimental colors "torn almost to shreds by the balls of the enemy," the *Times* noted, he "more than once exhibited much emotion," affording the fatigued soldiers "the assurance of the nation's hearty sympathy with their struggle."

Returning to the steamer, Lincoln conferred again with McClellan. Making no mention of McClellan's letter, which remained in his pocket, he set sail for Washington the next morning. "On the way up the Potomac," the *New York Herald* reported, "the boat was aground for several hours on the Kettle Shoals, and the whole party, including the President, availed themselves of the opportunity to take a bath and swim in the river."

The visit invigorated the spirits of all who accompanied Lincoln. Frank Blair's sister Elizabeth noted that "Frank was as heart sick as man could be when he went off to the Army but he & the President came back greatly cheered." Despite Lincoln's enthusiasm for the mettle of the soldiers, however, his opinion of General McClellan had not improved. Less than forty-eight hours after his return, he summoned General Henry Halleck to Washington to assume the post of general in chief that McClellan had hoped would be his. Halleck's victories in the West, largely due to Grant, had made him a logical choice for the post. Known as "Old Brains," he had written several books on military strategy that were widely respected.

Even before McClellan heard the news, he suspected an unwelcome turn of events. "I do not know what paltry trick the administration will play next," he wrote his wife on the day after Lincoln's visit. "I did not like the Presdt's manner—it seemed that of a man about to do something of which he was much ashamed. A few days will however show, & I do not much care what the result will be. I feel that I have already done enough to prove in history that I am a General."

Although Halleck's appointment met with widespread approval, the clamor for further changes was undiminished. Radicals called for McClellan's dismissal, while conservatives continued their assault on Stanton. The arguments on both sides were heated. In a hotel lobby, Senator Chandler of Michigan called McClellan a "liar and coward," provoking a friend of McClellan's to angrily counter: "It is you who are the liar and the coward." The charges against Stanton were equally caustic, portraying him as brusque, domineering, and unbearably unpleasant to work with. Nonetheless, Lincoln was determined, as Browning advised, to "make up his mind calmly [and] deliberately," to "adhere firmly to his own opinions, and neither to be bullied or cajoled out of them."

In fact, not once during the vicious public onslaught against the secretary of war did Lincoln's support for Stanton waver. During the hours he had spent each day awaiting battlefront news in the telegraph office, Lincoln had taken his own measure of his high-strung, passionate secretary of war. He concluded that Stanton's vigorous, hard-driving style was precisely what was needed at this critical juncture. As one War Department employee said of Stanton, "much of his seeming harshness to and neglect of individuals" could be explained by the "concentration and intensity of his mind on the single object of crushing the rebellion."

And, as always, the president refused to let a subordinate take the blame for his own decisions. He insisted to Browning "that all that Stanton had done in regard to the army had been authorized by him the President." Three weeks later, Lincoln publicly defended the beleaguered Stanton before an immense Union meeting on the Capitol steps. All the government departments had closed down at one o'clock so that everyone could attend. Commissioner French believed he had "never seen more persons assembled in front of the Capitol except at an inauguration, which it very much resembled." Lincoln sat on the flag-draped platform with the members of his cabinet, including Chase, Blair, and Bates, as "the ringing of bells, the firing of cannon, and music from the Marine Band" heralded the speakers.

After a speech by Treasury Registrar Lucius Chittenden, Lincoln turned to Chase, who sat beside him. " 'Well! Hadn't I better say a few words and get rid of myself?' Hardly waiting for an answer, he advanced at once to the stand."

"I believe there is no precedent for my appearing before you on this occasion," he affably began, "but it is also true that there is no precedent for your being here yourselves." Reminding his audience that he was reluctant to speak unless he might "produce some good by it," Lincoln declared that something needed to be said, and it was "not likely to be better said by some one else," for it was *"a matter in which we have heard some other persons blamed for what I did myself."* Addressing the charge that Stanton had withheld troops from McClellan, he explained that every possible soldier available had been sent to the general. "The Secretary of War *is not to blame for not giving when he had none to give."* As the applause began to mount, he continued, *"I believe he is a brave and able man,* and I stand here, as justice requires me to do, *to take upon myself what has been charged on the Secretary of War."*

French was profoundly moved by Lincoln's speech. "He is one of the best men God ever created," he asserted. Chase, too, was impressed by the "originality and sagacity" of the address. "His frank, genial, generous face and direct simplicity of bearing, took all hearts." The great rally concluded to the strains of "Yankee Doodle Dandy" and a salute of sixty-eight guns, two for each state in the Union. Reported fully in every newspaper, Lincoln's defense of his beleaguered secretary brought the campaign against Stanton to an end.

• • •

AS THE SUMMER PROGRESSED, Lincoln and his family found some respite from the pressure and grief that had seemed so relentless throughout the cruel spring. At last, Mary's intense depression began to lift. Reporters noted that she had begun riding with her husband once more in the late afternoons. On Sundays, she returned to Dr. Gurley's church, though a parishioner seated behind her observed that "she was so hid behind her immense black veil—and very deep black flounces—that one could scarcely tell she was there."

Commissioner French reported that "she seemed to be in excellent spirits" as she prepared to take up residence for the summer at the Soldiers' Home, situated on almost 300 acres in the hills three miles north of the city. Created in the 1850s as a retirement community for disabled veterans, the Soldiers' Home consisted of a main building that could accommodate 150 boarders, an infirmary, a dining hall, and administrative offices. The property also encompassed a number of spacious cottages, including the two-story brick house where the Lincoln family would stay. Known as the Anderson Cottage, it had served as a country residence for George Riggs, founder of the Riggs Bank, before the federal government purchased the property.

Buchanan had been the first president to summer at the Soldiers' Home, where the cooling breeze brought relief from the oppressive heat of the city. Surrounded by abundant flowers, shrubs, and trees, it seemed almost "an earthly paradise," one visitor recalled. The beautiful gravel walks and winding carriage ways, all of which were open to the public, had become a choice destination for Washingtonians out for weekend rides in their carriages. Another visitor in the summer of 1862 claimed he had seen nothing in the capital more charming than "this quiet and beautiful retreat," from which "we look down upon the city and see the whole at a glance"—the Capitol dome, "huge, grand, gloomy, ragged and unfinished, like the war now waging for its preservation," the Potomac River, "stretching away plainly visible for twelve miles, Alexandria, Arlington, Georgetown, and the long line of forts that bristle along the hills."

At Mary's urging, Lincoln agreed to settle in with his family for the summer, riding his horse the three miles to the White House each morning and returning at night. "We are truly delighted, with this retreat," Mary wrote her friend Fanny Eames, "the drives & walks around here are delightful, & each day, brings its visitors. Then too, our boy Robert [home from Harvard], is with us, whom you may remember. We consider it a 'pleasant time' for us, when his vacations, roll around, he is very companionable, and I shall dread when he has to return to Cambridge." For Tad, whose companionship and daily routine had been obliterated by the death of his brother and the banishment of the Taft boys, the Soldiers' Home was a godsend. His lively, cheerful disposition earned him the affection of the soldiers assigned to guard his father. They dubbed him a "3rd Lieutenant," allowing him to join in their drills during the day and their meals around the campfire at night.

In the evenings, the Lincolns could entertain guests on the wide porch overlooking the grounds or in a formal parlor illuminated by gas lamps. Relaxing in his slippers, Lincoln was fond of reciting poetry or reading aloud from favorite authors. Though intermittent cannonfire was audible in the distance, the idyllic retreat provided precious privacy and space for conversation among family and friends. For Lincoln, the historian Matthew Pinsker observes, the soldiers assigned to his security detail "helped him recreate some of the spirit of fraternity that he had once enjoyed as a younger politician and circuit-riding attorney in Illinois."

It was during this restorative summer that Mary formed what one newspaper termed a "daily habit of visiting the hospitals in the District." The hospitals became her refuge, allowing her a few hours of reprieve from her private grief. "But for these humane employments," a friend who often accompanied her to the hospital wards recalled her saying, "her heart would have broken when she lost her child." It is clear in the recollections of Walt Whitman, who worked as a nurse in the hospital wards, that the harrowing experience made one's "little cares and difficulties" disappear "into nothing." After ministering each day to the hundreds of young men who had endured ghastly wounds, submitted to amputations without anesthesia, and often died without the comfort of family or friends, Whitman wrote, "nothing of ordinary misfortune seems as it used to."

In the days after the Peninsula Campaign, the *New York Daily Tribune* reported, the numbers of sick and wounded pouring into the city were enough "to form an immense army." Every morning, steamers arrived at the Sixth Street Wharf carrying hundreds of injured soldiers, many "horribly wounded." As crowds gathered around, the soldiers disembarked, some carried on stretchers, others stumbling along on crudely made crutches. Ambulances stood by, ready to transport them to the dozen or more hastily outfitted hospitals that had sprung up in various parts of the capital.

In the effort to meet the soaring demand for hospital space, the federal government had embarked on a massive project of converting hotels, churches, clubs, school buildings, and private residences into military hospitals. The old Union Hotel, where congressmen and senators had boarded during earlier administrations, became the Union Hotel Hospital. A visitor noted that "the rooms in which the politicians of the old school used to sit and sup their wine" were now crowded with patients lying on cots. Louisa May Alcott, who worked there as a nurse, observed that "many of the doors still bore their old names; some not so inappropriate as might be imagined, for my ward was in truth a *ball-room*, if gunshot wounds could christen it." The Braddock House, where it was said that "General George Washington held his Councils of War," was also pressed into service, with some of the same old chairs and desks.

The second floor of the Patent Office, under the guidance of Interior Secretary Caleb Smith's wife, Elizabeth, was likewise transformed into a hospital ward accommodating hundreds of patients. It presented "a curious scene," Whitman noted, with rows of "sick, badly wounded and dying soldiers" lying between "high and ponderous glass cases, crowded with models in miniature of every kind of utensil, machine or invention." In addition, "a great long double row" of cots ran "up and down through the middle of the hall," with extra beds placed in the gallery. Especially "at night, when lit up," the impromptu ward presented a bizarre spectacle with its "glass cases, the beds, the sick, thc gallery above and the marble pavement under foot."

In mid-June, the Methodist Episcopal Church on 20th Street offered its chapel for conversion to a hospital. Five days later, government carpenters and mechanics were hard at work covering pews with timbers to support a new floor upon which hundreds of beds would be placed. As in other church hospitals, the pulpit and assorted furnishings were safely stored under the floor, while the basement was turned into a laboratory and kitchen. Taken together, these makeshift government hospitals accommodated more than three thousand patients, still only a fraction of the beds that would be needed in the months and years ahead.

In preparation for her hospital visits, Mary filled her carriage with baskets of fruit, food, and fresh flowers. She cleaned out the strawberries in the White House garden and procured a donation from a wealthy merchant, impressed by "the quiet and unostentatious manner" of her ministrations, for $300 worth of lemons and oranges, so necessary to prevent scurvy. For hours, she would distribute the fruit and delicacies, placing fresh flowers on the pillows of wounded men to mask the pervasive stench of disinfectant and decay.

She sat by the side of lonely soldiers, talked with them about their experiences, read to them, and helped them write letters to their families at home. One wounded soldier discovered the identity of the kindly woman who had written to his mother explaining that he had been "quite sick," but was recovering, only after Mary's letter had reached his home with the first lady's signature.

For the soldiers, the need to communicate with their families was tantamount to their need to survive. Alcott told the story of a valiant soldier named John, a young man of "commanding stature," with a handsome face and "the serenest eyes" she had ever seen. A ball had pierced his left lung, making it almost impossible for him to breathe. Although the doctors deemed his condition hopeless, he clung to life for days, hoping to hear from home. "Unsubdued by pain," he never uttered a complaint, "tranquilly [observing] what went on about him." When he died, "many came to see him," paying respect to the quiet courage that had impressed both the hospital staff and his fellow soldiers. While Louisa May Alcott stood by his bed, the ward master handed her a letter from John's mother that had arrived the night before, "just an hour too late to gladden the eyes that had longed and looked for it so eagerly."

The emotional narratives of Whitman and Alcott testify to the enormous fortitude demanded by hospital work. Whitman told his mother that while he kept "singularly cool" during the days, he would "feel sick and actually tremble" at night, recalling the "deaths, operations, sickening wounds (perhaps full of maggots)," and the "heap of feet, arms, legs" that lay beneath a tree on some hospital grounds. Alcott confessed that she found it difficult to keep from weeping at "the sight of several stretchers, each with its legless, armless, or desperately wounded occupant" coming into her ward. Workers and visitors were also exposed to contagion, as soldiers with typhoid lay side by side with patients dying of pneumonia or diphtheria. The thirty-year-old Alcott developed a severe case of typhoid after only two months and was forced to return to her home in Concord, Massachusetts.

Watching the countless young men suffer and die around her, Mary must have found it difficult to dwell solely upon the loss of her own child. "Death itself has lost all its terrors," Whitman wrote. "I have seen so many cases in which it was so welcome and such a relief." Yet somehow the triumphs of life, humor, and love were also evident amid the horrors of the hospitals. One soldier, whose body "was so blackened and burned by a powder explosion that some one remarked, 'There is not much use bringing him in,' " showed such a fierce determination to live that he eventually recovered. Another youth, who had lost one leg and was soon to lose an arm, amazed onlookers when he joked about his condition, imagining the "scramble there'll be for arms and legs, when we old boys come out of our graves, on the Judgment Day." In ward after ward, recovering patients even organized impromptu bands to entertain their fellow bedmates with music and song.

Observing Mary as she departed for her regular round of hospital visits, William Stoddard wondered why she didn't publicize her efforts. "If she were worldly wise she would carry newspaper correspondents, from two to five, of both sexes, every time she went, and she would have them take shorthand notes of what she says to the sick soldiers and of what the sick soldiers say to her." This, more than anything, he surmised, would "sweeten the contents of many journals" that had frequently derided the first lady's receptions and redecorating projects. The *New York Independent* had been particularly relentless in its attacks on Mary. "While her sister-women scraped lint, sewed bandages, and put on nurses' caps," Mary Clemmer Ames wrote, "the wife of its President spent her time in rolling to and fro between Washington and New York, intent on extravagant purchases for herself and the White House."

Yet Mary continued her hospital trips without any publicity. Some physicians objected to further interruption in an already chaotic situation, while others thought it improper for ladies to associate with common soldiers in various states of undress. Under such circumstances, Mary decided to carry on her work discreetly.

So it happened that while newspapers regularly praised the work of other society women, referring to Mrs. Caleb Smith as "our ever-bountiful benefactress & friend," and to Mrs. Stephen Douglas, who had converted her mansion into a hospital, as "an angel of mercy," Mary Lincoln received scant credit for her steadfast attempts to comfort Union casualties. She found something more gratifying than public acknowledgment. For in the hours she spent with these soldiers she must have sensed their unwavering belief in her husband and in the Union for which they fought. Such a faith was not readily found elsewhere—not in the cabinet, the Congress, the press, or the social circles of the city.

• • •

WHILE WASHINGTON SWELTERED through the long, hot summer, Lincoln made the momentous decision on emancipation that would define both his presidency and the course of the Civil War.

The great question of what to do about slavery had provoked increasingly bitter debates on Capitol Hill for many months. Back in March, as foreshadowed in a message to Congress, Lincoln had asked the legislature to pass a joint resolution providing federal aid to any state willing to adopt a plan for the gradual abolition of slavery. The resolution called upon states to stipulate that all slaves within their borders would be freed upon attaining a certain age or specify a date after which slavery would no longer be allowed. Lincoln had calculated that "less than one half-day's cost of this war would pay for all the slaves in Delaware at four hundred dollars per head," and that eighty-seven days' expenses would buy all the slaves in all the other border states combined. He believed that nothing would bring the rebellion to an end faster than a commitment by the border slave states "to surrender on fair terms their own interest in Slavery rather than see the Union dissolved." If the rebels were deprived of hope that these states might join the Confederacy, they would lose heart.

The proposal depended upon approval by the border-state representatives, who would have to promote the plan in their state legislatures. Except for Frank Blair, however, who had long advocated compensated emancipation coupled with colonization, they refused to endorse the proposal. Even when Lincoln personally renewed his plea to them on July 12, they argued that "emancipation in any form" would lengthen, not shorten, the war; it "would further consolidate the spirit of rebellion in the seceded states and fan the spirit of secession among loyal slaveholders in the Border

States." They insisted that the measure would unjustly punish those who remained loyal to the Union, forcing them to relinquish their slaves while the rebellious states retained theirs. They would face an uproar among their own citizens, and the proposal would cost far more than the federal government could pay.

Meanwhile, the Republican majority in Congress, freed from the domination of the Southern bloc, began to push their own agenda on slavery. In April, Congress passed a bill providing for the compensated emancipation of slaves in the District of Columbia. The bill met Lincoln's wholehearted approval, for he had "never doubted the constitutional authority of congress to abolish slavery" in areas that fell under the jurisdiction of the federal government, and, indeed, Lincoln had drafted his own proposal to free slaves in the District when he had been in Congress fourteen years earlier. Frederick Douglass was ecstatic. "I trust I am not dreaming," he wrote Charles Sumner, "but the events taking place seem like a dream." As slaves in the District gained their freedom, slaveholders in surrounding Maryland and northern Virginia, fearful that their own slaves would grow restive, began selling them to owners farther south.

Francis Blair, Sr., who had already assured his slaves that they could "go when they wished," proudly affirmed that "all but one declined the privilege," electing to stay on as servants at Silver Springs, where they lived together in their own "quarters" that resembled those on Southern plantations. One servant, Henry, declared he "was used to quality all his days" and wanted to remain with the Blairs for the rest of his life. Nanny, another servant, agreed. She was "well off," had no thought of moving on, but was "delighted that her children are free."

The situation became more complex when the radical bloc in Congress began to address slavery in the seceded Southern states where it already existed and was protected by the Constitution. In July, despite the vehement protests of Democrats and conservative Republicans, the radical majority passed a new confiscation bill. Broader than the bill passed the previous year, which had limited the federal government to confiscating and freeing only those fugitive slaves employed by rebels in the field, the new act emancipated all slaves of persons engaged in rebellion, regardless of involvement in military affairs. The bill was ill considered, providing no workable means of enforcement and no procedure to determine whether the owner of a slave crossing Union lines was actually engaged in insurrection. "It was," the historian Mark Neely writes, "a dead letter from the start." But it stirred the hearts of all those, like Charles Sumner, who believed that slavery was a "disturbing influence which, so long as it exists, will keep this land a volcano, ever ready to break anew."

It was rumored in Washington that Lincoln would veto the controversial bill. Indeed, Browning carried a copy of it to the White House as soon as it passed, pleading with Lincoln to veto it. If approved, he warned, "our friends" in the border states "could no longer sustain themselves there." The bill would "form the basis upon which the democratic party would again rally, and reorganize an opposition to the administration." Lincoln's decision, Browning insisted, would "determine whether he was to control the abolitionists and radicals, or whether they were to control him." The key moment had arrived when "the tide in his affairs had come and he ought to take it at its flood."

Chase presented the diametrically opposed prediction, which maintained that if Lincoln vetoed the bill, it "will be an end of him." The Republican majority in Congress would break ranks with the administration, and Lincoln would be openly castigated on the floor. Worried that he, too, might be tainted by a presidential veto, Chase told his friends to spread word that he had not been consulted, "nor so far as he knew [had] a single member of his cabinet" been involved. While he would willingly answer for his actions as treasury secretary, Chase refused to take the blame "for other people's blunders or errors of policy."

Rumors that Lincoln would veto the bill proved incorrect. The next morning, Browning found the president working in his library. He "looked weary, care-worn and troubled," Browning noted, "and there was a cadence of deep sadness in his voice." The president had made his decision, which he knew would distress his friend. Still, before signing the bill that would become known as the Second Confiscation Act, Lincoln listed his objections in writing and obtained a revised bill that made it more likely to pass constitutional muster.

As was customary on the last day of the session, the president traveled to the Capitol, stationing himself in the vice president's office, where he signed the spate of bills rushed through in the final days of the term. It had been an extraordinarily productive session. Relieved of Southern opposition, the Republican majority was able to pass three historic bills that had been stalled for years: the Homestead Act, which promised 160 acres of free public land largely in the West to settlers who agreed to reside on the property for five years or more; the Morrill Act, providing public lands to states for the establishment of land-grant colleges; and the Pacific Railroad Act, which made the construction of a transcontinental railroad possible. The 37th Congress also laid the economic foundation for the Union war effort with the Legal Tender bill, which created a paper money known as "greenbacks." A comprehensive tax bill was also enacted, establishing the Internal Revenue Bureau in the Department of the Treasury and levying a federal income tax for the first time in American history.

At that time, the far-reaching impact of this epoch-making home front legislation was overshadowed by the continuing slavery controversy, which preoccupied both sides of the aisle. Referring to the endless hours the Republican stalwarts spent rehashing the issue, Seward jokingly told foreign diplomats over dinner that "he had lately begun to realize the value of a Cromwell," and sometimes longed for "a Coup d'etat for our Congress." As the summer progressed, his level of frustration with Congress grew. "I ask Congress to authorize a draft," he complained to Frances. "They fall into altercation about letting slaves fight and work. Every day is a day lost, and every day lost is a hazard to the whole country. What if I should say, that I concede all they want about negroes? . . . One party has gained another partisan; the country has lost one advocate."

Within the cabinet as well as on Capitol Hill, the rancor over slavery infected every discourse. The debates had grown "so bitter," according to Seward, that personal and even official relationships among members were ruptured, leading to "a prolonged discontinuance of Cabinet meetings." Though Tuesdays and Fridays were still designated for sessions, each secretary remained in his department unless a messenger arrived to confirm that a meeting would be held. Seward recalled that when these general discussions were still taking place, Lincoln had listened intently but had not taken "an active part in them." For Lincoln, the problem of slavery was not an abstract issue. While he concurred with the most passionate abolitionists that slavery was "a moral, a social and a political wrong," as president, he could not ignore the constitutional protection of the institution where it already existed.

The devastating reverses on the Peninsula, which made it clear that extraordinary means were necessary to save the Union, gave Lincoln an opening to deal more directly with slavery. Daily reports from the battlefields illuminated the innumerable uses to which slaves were put by the Confederacy. They dug trenches and built fortifications for the army. They were brought into camps to serve as teamsters, cooks, and hospital attendants, so that soldiers were freed to fight in the fields. They labored on the home front, tilling fields, raising crops, and picking cotton, so their masters could go to war without fearing that their families would go hungry. If the rebels were divested of their slaves, who would then be free to join the Union forces, the North could gain a decided advantage. Seen in this light, emancipation could be considered a military necessity, a legitimate exercise of the president's constitutional war powers. The border states had refused his idea of compensated emancipation as a voluntary first step, insisting that any such action should be initiated in the slave states. A historic decision was taking shape in Lincoln's mind.

Lincoln revealed his preliminary thinking to Seward and Welles in the early hours of Sunday, July 13, as they rode together in the president's carriage to the funeral of Stanton's infant son. The journey to Oak Hill Cemetery, where Stanton's child was to be buried, must have evoked painful memories of Willie, whose body remained there in the private vault awaiting final interment in Springfield. Despite such personal torment, the country's peril demanded Lincoln's complete concentration. During the journey, Welles recorded in his diary, the president informed them that he was considering "emancipating the slaves by proclamation in case the Rebels did not cease to persist in their war." He said that he had "dwelt earnestly on the gravity, importance, and delicacy" of the subject and had "come to the conclusion that it was a military necessity absolutely essential for the salvation of the Union, that we must free the slaves or be ourselves subdued." Thus, the constitutional protection of slavery could and would be overridden by the constitutionally sanctioned war powers of the president.

This was, Welles clearly recognized, "a new departure for the President, for until this time, in all our previous interviews . . . he had been prompt and emphatic in denouncing any interference by the General Government with the subject." The normally talkative Seward said merely that the "subject involved consequences so vast and momentous that he should wish to bestow on it mature reflection before giving a decisive answer," though he was inclined to think it "justifiable."

So the matter rested until Monday morning, July 21, when messengers were dispatched across Washington with notices of a special cabinet meeting to be held at 10 a.m. "It has been so long since any consultation has been held that it struck me as a novelty," Chase wrote in his diary. Earlier that day, Chase had shared breakfast in his home with Count Gurowski, whose acute frustration with Lincoln's hesitancy regarding emancipation had been evident for many months. In Gurowski's mind, Seward was the primary obstacle to progress, while Chase represented the best hope for spurring Lincoln forward. An inveterate gossip, Gurowski related to Chase the story of Seward's comments on Cromwell and the Congress, which, he claimed, had been received with marked disapproval by the diplomats in attendance.

When the cabinet convened, all members save the postmaster general were in attendance. Montgomery Blair was in Maryland, where he had recently built an elegant country estate, Falkland, in Silver Spring near his parents' estate. For this special meeting, the cabinet was summoned to the second-floor library rather than the president's official office. There, surrounded by the curved bookshelves that Mary had recently filled with splendidly bound sets of Shakespeare and Sir Walter Scott's novels, the president began with an admission that he was "profoundly concerned at the present aspect of affairs, and had determined to take some definitive steps in respect to military action and slavery." The members listened as Lincoln read several orders he was contemplating. One would authorize Union generals in Confederate territory to appropriate any property necessary to sustain themselves in the field; another would sanction the payment of wages to blacks brought into the army's employ. Taken together, these orders signaled a more vigorous prosecution of the war. When the discussion moved to address the possible arming of those blacks in the army's employ, Stanton and Chase were in favor. Lincoln, Chase recorded, was "not prepared to decide the question."

When the preliminary discussions had run long, the president scheduled another cabinet session the following day, July 22, to reveal his primary purpose in calling the meeting. This second session was likely held in Lincoln's office, as depicted in Francis Carpenter's famous painting, *First Reading of the Emancipation Proclamation.* There, surrounded by evidence of the ever-expanding war, with battlefield maps everywhere—rolled in standing racks, placed in folios on the floor, and reclining up against the walls—the conversation from the previous day continued.

The desultory talk abruptly ended when Lincoln took the floor and announced he had called them together in order to read the preliminary draft of an emancipation proclamation. He understood the "differences in the Cabinet on the slavery question" and welcomed their suggestions after they heard what he had to say; but he wanted them to know that he "had resolved upon this step, and had not called them together to ask their advice." Then, removing two foolscap sheets from his pocket and adjusting his glasses on his nose, he began to read what amounted to a legal brief for emancipation based on the chief executive's powers as commander in chief.

His draft proclamation set January 1, 1863, little more than five months away, as the date on which all slaves within states still in rebellion against the Union would be declared free, "thenceforward, and forever." It required no cumbersome enforcement proceedings. Though it did not cover the roughly 425,000 slaves in the loyal border states—where, without the use of his war powers, no constitutional authority justified his action—the proclamation was shocking in scope. In a single stroke, it superseded legislation on slavery and property rights that had guided policy in eleven states for nearly three quarters of a century. Three and a half million blacks who had lived enslaved for generations were promised freedom. It was a daring move, Welles later said, "fraught with consequences, immediate and remote, such as human foresight could not penetrate."

The cabinet listened in silence. With the exception of Seward and Welles, to whom the president had intimated his intentions the previous week, the members were startled by the boldness of Lincoln's proclamation. Only Stanton and, surprisingly, Bates declared themselves in favor of "its immediate promulgation." Stanton instantly grasped the military value of the proclamation. Having spent more time than any of his colleagues contemplating the logistical problems facing the army, he understood the tremendous advantage to be gained if the massive workforce of slaves could be transferred from the Confederacy to the Union. Equally important, he had developed a passionate belief in the justice of emancipation.

Bates, as one of the more conservative members of the cabinet, surprised his colleagues with his enthusiastic approval of the proclamation. He had previously registered disapproval of the more limited emancipation measures attempted by the military and had expressed grave misgivings about the confiscation legislation. His sudden support of this far more radical step can be traced, in part, to the terrible division that slavery and the war had wrought upon his family.

In a scenario common to many border-state homes torn by divided loyalties, the Bates brothers had joined opposing sides in the war. Twenty-eight-year-old Fleming Bates had enlisted in the Confederate Army and was serving under Major General Sterling Price. Fleming faced the prospect of going into battle against any of four brothers. His older brother Julian, a surgeon, had been made a colonel in the Missouri militia. His younger brother Coalter was with the Army of the Potomac and would fight at Antietam, Fredericksburg, Chancellorsville, and Gettysburg. Another brother, Richard, was clerking for his father but would soon join the Union navy; while the family's youngest son, Charles Woodson, was a cadet at West Point. For Bates, who valued his family above all else, nothing could be more heartbreaking than the possibility of his sons facing one another on the battlefield. He had long favored gradual emancipation, but if the president's proclamation could bring the war to a speedier conclusion, he would give it his "very decided approval."

Bates based his approval, however, on the condition that the freed slaves would be deported to someplace in Central America or Africa. Unlike Lincoln, who insisted that any emigration must be voluntary, Bates believed it should be mandatory. Bates "was fully convinced," Welles later recalled, "that the two races could not live and thrive in social proximity." He believed that assimilation was impossible without amalgamation, and that amalgamation would inevitably bring "degradation and demoralization to the white race." Although he conceded that "among our colored people who have been long free, there are many who are intelligent and well advanced in arts and knowledge," he could not imagine former slaves, "fresh from the plantations of the South, where they have been long degraded by the total abolition of the family relation, shrouded in artificial darkness, and studiously kept in ignorance," living on an equal footing with whites. Far better for everyone, he argued, if the government established treaties granting aid to foreign governments willing to accept and settle freed slaves. He was hopeful that such treaties would "provide for the just and humane treatment of the emigrants—e.g. ensuring an honest livelihood by their own industry . . . and guaranteeing to them 'their liberty, property and the religion which they profess.' "

Gideon Welles remained silent after Lincoln presented his proclamation. He later admitted that the prospect of emancipation involved such unpredictable results, "carrying with it a revolution of the social, civil, and industrial habits and condition of society in all the slave States," that he was oppressed by the "solemnity and weight" of the decision. He feared that, far from shortening the war, emancipation would generate an "energy of desperation on the part of the slave-owners" and "intensify the struggle." Yet, while he privately questioned the "extreme exercise of war powers" involved, Welles held his tongue and later loyally supported Lincoln.

Caleb Smith kept silent as well, though he, too, had serious reservations. John Usher, the assistant secretary of the Interior Department, later recalled Smith telling him that if Lincoln issued the proclamation, he would "resign and go home and attack the administration."

The division of sentiment within the cabinet was manifest as Blair, Chase, and Seward spoke. Arriving late, after Lincoln's announcement that he had already resolved to issue the proclamation, Blair spoke up vigorously in opposition and asked to file his objections. While he supported the idea of compensated, gradual emancipation linked to colonization, he feared that the president's radical proclamation would cause such an outcry among conservatives and Democrats that Republicans would lose the fall elections. More important, it would "put in jeopardy the patriotic element in the border States, already severely tried," and "would, as soon as it reached them, be likely to carry over those States to the secessionists." Lincoln replied that while he had considered these dangers, he had tried for months to get the border states "to move in this matter, convinced in his own mind that it was their true interest to do so, but his labors were in vain." The time had come to move ahead. He would, however, willingly let Blair file his written objections.

Perhaps the most astonishing response came from Salmon Chase. No cabinet member had more vehemently promoted emancipation, and none could match his lifelong commitment to the abolitionist cause. Yet when faced with a presidential initiative that, he admitted, went "beyond anything I have recommended," he recoiled. According to Stanton's notes, Chase argued that it was "a measure of great danger—and would lead to universal emancipation." He feared that widespread disorder would engulf the South, leading to "depredation and massacre on the one hand, and support to the insurrection on the other." Chase recommended a quieter, more incremental approach, "allowing Generals to organize and arm the slaves" and "directing the Commanders of Departments to proclaim emancipation within their Districts as soon as practicable." Still, since he considered the proclamation better than no action at all, he would support it.

Although Chase's argument that the army might better control the pace of emancipation was legitimate, it is difficult not to suspect personal considerations behind his failure to wholeheartedly endorse the president's proclamation. Chase had seen his bright hopes for the presidency vanish in 1856 and 1860. No president since Andrew Jackson had been reelected, and the next election was only two years away. Chase's strongest claim to beat Lincoln for the nomination in 1864 lay with the unswerving support he had earned among the growing circle of radical Republicans frustrated by Lincoln's slowness on the slavery issue. The bold proclamation threatened to undercut Chase's potential candidacy, for, as Welles astutely recognized, it "placed the President in advance of [Chase] on a path which was his specialty."

Stanton feared that Chase's arguments would deter Lincoln from issuing his proclamation, letting the "golden moment" slip away. Should this come to pass, Stanton's brother-in-law, Christopher Wolcott, wrote, then "Chase must be held responsible for delaying or defeating the greatest act of justice, statesmanship, and civilization, of the last four thousand years." Lincoln later maintained, however, that not a single argument had been presented that he "had not already fully anticipated and settled in [his] own mind, until Secretary Seward spoke."

William Henry Seward's mode of intricate analysis produced a characteristically complex reaction to the proclamation. After the others had spoken, he expressed his worry that the proclamation might provoke a racial war in the South so disruptive to cotton that the ruling classes in England and France would intervene to protect their economic interests. As secretary of state, Seward was particularly sensitive to the threat of European intervention. Curiously, despite his greater access to intelligence from abroad, Seward failed to grasp what Lincoln intuitively understood: that once the Union truly committed itself to emancipation, the masses in Europe, who regarded slavery as an evil demanding eradication, would not be easily maneuvered into supporting the South.

Beyond his worries about intervention, Seward had little faith in the efficacy of proclamations that he considered nothing more than paper without the muscle of the advancing Union Army to enforce them. "The public mind seizes quickly upon theoretical schemes for relief," he pointedly told Frances, who had long yearned for a presidential proclamation against slavery, "but is slow in the adoption of the practical means necessary to give them effect." Seward's position, in fact, was nearly identical to that held by Chase. His preference, he said, "would have been to confiscate all rebel property, including slaves, as fast as the territory was conquered." Only an immediate military presence could assure escaped slaves of protection. Yet Seward's practical focus underestimated the proclamation's power to unleash the moral fervor of the North and keep the Republican Party united by making freedom for the slaves an avowed objective of the war.

Despite his concerns about the effect of the proclamation, Seward had no thought of opposing it. Once Lincoln had made up his mind, Seward was steadfast in his loyalty to him. He demurred only on the issue of timing. "Mr. President," he said, "I approve of the proclamation, but I question the expediency of its issue at this juncture. The depression of the public mind, consequent upon our repeated reverses, is so great that I fear . . . it may be viewed as the last measure of an exhausted government, a cry for help . . . our last *shriek*, on the retreat." Better to wait, he grandiloquently suggested, "until the eagle of victory takes his flight," and buoyed by military success, "hang your proclamation about his neck." Seward's argument was reinforced later that day by Thurlow Weed, who met with Lincoln on a visit to Washington.

"The wisdom of the view of the Secretary of State struck me with very great force," Lincoln later told the artist Francis Carpenter. "It was an aspect of the case that, in all my thought upon the subject, I had entirely overlooked. The result was that I put the draft of the proclamation aside, as you do your sketch for a picture, waiting for a victory."

• • •

AS JULY GAVE WAY TO AUGUST, however, Lincoln's thoughts never strayed from his proclamation. Repeatedly, he returned to edit his draft, "touching it up here and there, anxiously watching the progress of events." Having resolved to present it for publication upon the first military success, he set out to educate public opinion, to prepare the ground for its acceptance. Lincoln had long believed, as we have seen, that "with public sentiment, nothing can fail; without it nothing can succeed." He understood that one of the principal stumbling blocks in the way of emancipation was the pervasive fear shared by whites in both the North and the South that the two races could never coexist peacefully in a free society. He thought that a plan for the voluntary emigration of freed slaves would allay some of these fears, fostering wider acceptance of his proclamation.

On August 14, Lincoln invited a delegation of freed slaves to a conference at the White House, hoping to inspire their cooperation in educating fellow blacks on the benefits of colonization. "You and we are different races," he began. "We have between us a broader difference than exists between almost any other two races." Lincoln acknowledged that with slavery, the black race had endured "the greatest wrong inflicted on any people." Still, he continued, "when you cease to be slaves, you are yet far removed from being placed on an equality with the white race. You are cut off from many of the advantages which the other race enjoy. The aspiration of men is to enjoy equality with the best when free, but on this broad continent, not a single man of your race is made the equal of a single man of ours." Meanwhile, the evil consequences of slavery upon the white race were manifest in a calamitous civil war that found them "cutting one another's throats." Far "better for us both, therefore, to be separated," Lincoln reasoned, informing the delegates that "a sum of money had been appropriated by Congress, and placed at his disposition" to aid in establishing a colony somewhere in Central America. He needed a contingent of intelligent, educated blacks, such as the men present, to promote the opportunity among their own people.

A discussion followed and the meeting came to a close. "We were entirely hostile to the movement until all the advantages were so ably brought to our views by you," the delegation chief wrote Lincoln two days later, promising to consult with prominent blacks in Philadelphia, New York, and Boston who he hoped would "join heartily in Sustaining Such a movement." His hope was misplaced. The black leaders responded swiftly with widespread antipathy to the proposal. As the *Liberator* eloquently argued, the nation's 4 million slaves "are as much the natives of the country as any of their oppressors. Here they were born; here, by every consideration of justice and humanity, they are entitled to live; and here it is for them to die in the course of nature." One might "as well attempt to roll back Niagara to its source, or to cast the Allegheny mountains into the sea, as to think of driving or enticing them out of the country." How pathetic, the *Liberator* noted, that the president of a country "sufficiently capacious to contain the present population of the globe," a nation that "proudly boasts of being the refuge of the oppressed of all nations," should consider exiling "the entire colored population . . . to a distant shore."

Reports of Lincoln's dialogue with the black delegation provoked Frederick Douglass to his most caustic assault yet on the president. While acknowledging that this was the first time blacks had been invited for a hearing at the White House, he accused Lincoln of making "ridiculous" comments showing a "pride of race and blood" and a "contempt for negroes." The president "ought to know," Douglass argued, "that negro hatred and prejudice of color are neither original nor invincible vices, but merely the offshoots of that root of all crimes and evils—slavery. If the colored people instead of having been stolen and forcibly brought to the United States had come as free immigrants, like the German and the Irish, never thought of as suitable objects of property, they never would have become the objects of aversion and bitter persecution."

Lincoln's remarkable empathy had singularly failed him in this initial approach to the impending consequences of emancipation. Though he had tried to put himself in the place of blacks and suggest what *he* thought was best for them, his lack of contact with the black community left him unaware of their deep attachment to their country and sense of outrage at the thought of removal. In time, Lincoln's friendship with Frederick Douglass and personal contact with hundreds of black soldiers willing to give up their lives for their freedom would create a deeper understanding of his black countrymen that would allow him to cast off forever his thoughts of colonization.

Even as he addressed the black delegation that August, Lincoln may not have been convinced that colonization was a feasible option. He recognized, however, that the mere suggestion of the plan might provide the "drop of honey" to make the prospect of emancipation more palatable. Chase would accept no such concession. "How much better would be a manly protest against prejudice against color!—and a wise effort to give freemen homes in America!" he wrote in his diary after reading Lincoln's colonization discussion. Count Gurowski was even harsher in his condemnation, characterizing Lincoln's talk of racial incompatibility as cheap "clap-trap," revealing a disturbing "display of ignorance or of humbug, or perhaps of both," unworthy of a president.

The most sensational criticism, however, came from Horace Greeley. He published an open letter to the president in the *New York Tribune* on August 20, which he entitled "The Prayer of Twenty Millions." Claiming to speak for his vast readership, he decried the policy Lincoln seemed "to be pursuing with regard to the slaves," which, "unduly influenced by the counsels . . . of certain fossil politicians hailing from the Border Slave States," failed to recognize that "all attempts to put down the Rebellion and at the same time uphold its inciting cause [slavery] are preposterous and futile."

Lincoln decided to reply to Greeley's letter, seizing the opportunity to begin instructing the public on the vital link between emancipation and military necessity. "As to the policy I 'seem to be pursuing' as you say, I have not meant to leave anyone in doubt," he began. "My paramount object in this struggle *is* to save the Union, and is *not* either to save or to destroy slavery. If I could save the Union without freeing *any* slave I would do it, and if I could save it by freeing *all* the slaves I would do it; and if I could save it by freeing some and leaving others alone I would also do that. What I do about slavery, and the colored race, I do because it helps to save the Union; and what I forbear, I forbear because I do *not* believe it would help to save the Union. I shall do *less* whenever I shall believe what I am doing hurts the cause, and I shall do *more* whenever I shall believe doing more will help the cause."

Having already decided upon emancipation, Lincoln hoped that his letter would soften the public impact of what he knew would be a controversial proclamation. Abolitionists, unaware that Lincoln had already committed himself to a path that would "do *more*" than even they had hoped, were infuriated by his response. "I am sorry the President answered Mr. Greeley," Frances Seward complained to her husband; "his letter hardly does him justice . . . he gives the impression that the mere keeping together a number of states is more important than human freedom."

Seward had argued this very issue with his zealous wife for many months. At home in June, he had apparently suggested that the preservation of republican institutions must supersede the immediate abolition of slavery. Though he had fought slavery all his life, Seward hesitated when faced with the possibility that moving too precipitously toward abolition might destroy the republic itself and all that it stood for on the stage of world history. He had no doubt that slavery would eventually be brought to an end. Indeed, he believed the future of slavery had been "killed years ago" by the progress of civilization. "But suppose, for one moment," he later explained, "the Republic destroyed. With it is bound up not alone the destiny of a race, but the best hopes of all mankind. With its overthrow the sun of liberty, like the Hebrew dial, would be set back indefinitely. The magnitude of such a calamity is beyond our calculation. The salvation of the nation is, then, of vastly more consequence than the destruction of slavery."

Frances profoundly disagreed with this balancing equation, asserting there could be no "truly republican" institutions with slavery intact—"they are incompatible." Sometime during that long, anxious summer, she recorded her exhortations in a note to her husband. "Whatever may be the principles in the determination of the President in this matter," she wrote, "you owe it to yourself & your children & your country & to God to make your record clear." If the president refused to act on slavery, "it would be far better for you to resign your place tomorrow than by continuing there seem to give countenance to a great moral evil."

Frances had no intimation that Lincoln's views on the relationship between emancipation and republican institutions had already evolved beyond those of her husband. For despite the continued criticism of his inaction on slavery, Lincoln kept his proclamation concealed until victory could offer the propitious moment. Everything depended on the success of his army.

CHAPTER 18

"MY WORD IS OUT"

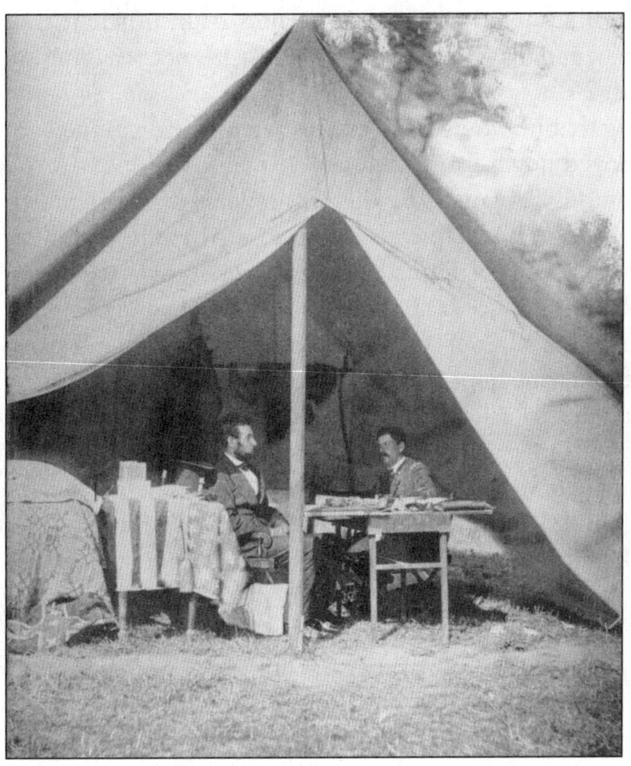

LINCOLN PINNED HIS HOPES for the victory that would allow him to issue his Emancipation Proclamation on the newly assembled Army of Virginia, headed by General John Pope. In the Western theater, Pope had demonstrated the aggression McClellan lacked. Early August 1862, Halleck ordered McClellan to withdraw his entire army by steamship from Harrison's Landing to Aquia Creek and Alexandria, thus ending the Peninsula Campaign. Once there, McClellan was to rendezvous with Pope, who would be pushing south from Manassas toward Richmond along the interior route Lincoln had initially favored.

Joined together, the two armies would substantially outnumber General Lee's forces.

But McClellan stalled, fearing that Pope would be placed in charge of the merged army. He argued ferociously against the move, warning Halleck it would "prove disastrous in the extreme." His only hope, he confided to his wife, was that he might "induce the enemy to attack" before he reached Washington and was relieved of his command. After delaying for ten days with strategic protests and claims of insufficient transports, he grudgingly began his withdrawal on August 14, not reaching Aquia Creek until August 24.

Realizing that he would be overpowered by the combined armies, General Lee moved north from Richmond to engage Pope before McClellan reached him. By August 18, the Confederate forces, under Generals Stonewall Jackson and James Longstreet, had come within striking distance of Pope. Only the Rappahannock River, midway between Washington and Richmond, separated the two forces. From the security of the northern riverbank, Pope waited in vain for McClellan's troops to reinforce what everyone hoped would be a major offensive.

Lee capitalized brilliantly on McClellan's delay. Leaving Longstreet's forces in front of Pope, he sent Jackson behind Pope's lines to capture the Union's supply base at Manassas Junction and then assemble in the woods near the old Bull Run battlefield. In a state of confusion, Pope left the Rappahannock and headed north, where he would encounter the combined forces of Lee, Longstreet, and Jackson. "What is the stake?" Seward wrote Frances. "They say that it is nothing less than this capital; and, as many think, the *cause also.*" While soldiers on both sides waited for the fighting to begin, a comet appeared in the northern sky. Lincoln, so familiar with Shakespeare, doubtless recalled Calpurnia's ominous warning to Caesar: "When beggars die there are no comets seen/The heavens themselves blaze forth the death of princes."

Although McClellan agreed to send two corps to Pope, he continued to delay, awaiting word on his own status as commander. If his troops were integrated into Pope's army, he told his wife on August 24, he would "try for a leave of absence!" Everything would change, however, if "Pope is beaten, in which case they may want me to save Washn again."

The Second Battle of Bull Run began in earnest on Friday, August 29. When the wind blew from the west, "the smell of the gunpowder was quite perceptible," the *Evening Star* reported, and the "distant thunder" of cannonfire was plainly audible throughout Washington. Crowds gathered on street corners and huddled in the great hotels. In the absence of reliable information from the front, rumors flew. At one moment, newsboys announced that "Stonewall Jackson was captured with 16,000 of his men." Minutes later, it was said that Jackson had crushed Pope and was heading north to capture Washington. Stories of victory and defeat for each side "alternated in about equal proportions."

These were disquieting days for the president. The manager of the War Department telegraph office recalled that Lincoln spent long hours in the crowded second-floor suite awaiting bulletins from the front, "prepared to stay all night, if necessary." He wired various generals, including McClellan, who had set up his headquarters at Alexandria, requesting news from Manassas. McClellan responded immediately, providing advice rather than information. The president now had only two options, McClellan counseled. Either he must "concentrate all our available forces to open communication with Pope," or he should "leave Pope to get out of his scrape & at once use all our means to make the capital perfectly safe."

On Saturday morning, John Hay met the president at the Soldiers' Home and rode with him to the White House. During the ride, Lincoln "was very outspoken in regard to McClellan's present conduct," saying that "it really seemed to him that McC wanted Pope defeated." He was particularly incensed, Lincoln told Hay, by McClellan's advice to "leave Pope to get out of his own scrape."

Lincoln's condemnation was mild, however, compared to the rage Stanton directed toward the general he now considered a traitor. McClellan's delay in bringing his troops to Pope's defense prompted the secretary of war to approach General Halleck for an official report. He asked Halleck to specify the exact date upon which McClellan had received orders to withdraw from the James, and to render an opinion as to whether the order was obeyed with a promptness commensurate with national safety. Halleck replied that the order given on August 3 "was not obeyed with the promptness I expected and the national safety, in my opinion, required."

Armed with Halleck's report, Stanton took Chase into his confidence. The two old friends decided that McClellan must be removed at once, and that they would have to force Lincoln's hand. Agreeing that verbal arguments with Lincoln were "like throwing water on a duck's back," they decided that "a more decisive expression must be made and that in writing." Stanton volunteered to draft a remonstrance against McClellan, to be signed, if possible, by a majority of the cabinet. They would present it to Lincoln with the inference that General McClellan's continued command would lead to the resignation of some cabinet members, and even the dissolution of the administration. Meanwhile, Stanton and Chase journeyed to Bates's F Street home, hoping to enlist his support. Finding that he was out, they left word for him to call on Chase the following morning.

When Bates stopped by the Treasury office early Saturday morning, Chase was delighted to learn that he was in full agreement regarding McClellan. "Never before was there such a grand army, composed of truly excellent materials, and yet," Bates complained, "so poorly commanded." To his mind, McClellan had "but one of the three Roman requisites for a general, he is young. I fear not brave, and surely not fortunate." Moreover, Bates agreed with Chase and Stanton that "unless there be very soon a change for the better, we [the administration] must sink into contempt." Certain now that Bates was a staunch ally in the cause of McClellan's dismissal, Chase proceeded to the War Department, where Stanton had completed a first draft of the letter.

The scathing document, written in Stanton's distinctive back-sloping script with words added and erased, declared that the undersigned were "unwilling to be accessory to the waste of natural resources, the protraction of the war, the destruction of our armies, and the imperiling of the Union which we believe must result from the continuance of George B. McClellan in command." It charged McClellan with willful "disobedience to superior orders," which had "imperiled the army commanded by General Pope." Chase made several suggestions for changes, affixed his signature above Stanton's, and promised to bring it to Bates, Smith, and Welles.

Having long since lost faith in McClellan, Smith was persuaded immediately to add his signature. Climbing the narrow stairs to the navy secretary's second-floor office later that afternoon, Chase reached him just as he was preparing to leave for the day. After reading the document, Welles assured Chase that he believed McClellan's "withdrawal from any command was demanded," but he "did not choose to denounce McC. for incapacity or declare him a traitor," as the document seemed to proclaim. Even when Chase repeated the damning facts of McClellan's fatal delay in moving to reinforce Pope, Welles hesitated. He pointedly asked whether Blair had seen the document. Chase replied that his "turn had not come." At that very moment, while Welles still held the document, Blair walked in. Sensing Chase's alarm, Welles kept the paper close to his chest until Blair departed only a few minutes later. With the postmaster general out of earshot, Chase entreated Welles not to mention the document to Blair or anyone else.

While Chase was performing his part in the intrigue, Stanton had invited Lincoln and Hay to his K Street home for an impromptu dinner. No clear information on the course of the battle was yet available, though preliminary reports suggested that Pope had gained the advantage. "A pleasant little dinner," Hay recorded, "and a pretty wife as white and cold and motionless as marble, whose rare smiles seemed to pain her." In conversation with Lincoln, Stanton was "unqualifiedly severe upon McClellan," charging that "nothing but foul play could lose us this battle & that it rested with McC. and his friends." Both Stanton and Lincoln expressed their strong belief in General Pope.

After dinner, the president and Hay went to army headquarters, where General Halleck appeared "quiet and somewhat confident" about the direction of what he considered "the greatest battle of the Century." Proceeding to Stanton's office, they found he had dispatched "a vast army of Volunteer Nurses out to the field" to help care for the sick and wounded. "Every thing seemed to be going well," Hay reported, "& we went to bed expecting glad tidings at sunrise."

For Stanton, however, much work was in store that evening. If Pope managed to win without McClellan's aid, it would only strengthen the argument for the young Napoleon's ouster. When Welles stopped by to get an update from the front, he found Stanton with Smith. Stanton launched into a long diatribe against McClellan, reaching back to the winter doldrums, the "Quaker gun" affair, and the blunders on the Peninsula. When Smith left, Welles recalled, Stanton lowered his voice to a whisper. He had previously learned from Chase that Welles had refused to sign the document. Welles explained that while he, by and large, agreed that McClellan must be removed, he "disliked the method and manner of proceeding." It seemed "discourteous and disrespectful to the President." The president, he declared, "had called us around him as friends and advisers to counsel and consult . . . not to enter into combinations against him."

Agitated, Stanton exclaimed that "he knew of no particular obligations he was under to the President who had called him to a difficult position and imposed upon him labors and responsibilities which no man could carry, and which were greatly increased by fastening upon him a commander who was constantly striving to embarrass him. . . . He could not and would not submit to a continuance of this state of things." Welles sympathized but was highly reluctant to join what seemed a cabal against the president.

The next morning, bleak news from the battlefield discredited the optimistic reports of the previous day. Pope's army had been crushed. John Hay recorded in his diary that at "about Eight oclock the President came to my room as I was dressing and calling me out said, 'Well John we are whipped again, I am afraid.' " Once again, as in the aftermath of the First Battle of Bull Run, Washington braced for attack. As rumors spread that General Jackson was crossing the Potomac at Georgetown, thousands of frightened residents began to flee the city. Soldiers straggled in from the front with tales of a demoralized army and units unwilling to fight under

Pope. The losses were immense—out of 65,000 men, the Federals had suffered 16,000 casualties. Momentum now clearly belonged to the Confederacy. At the end of June, the *New York Times* pointed out, "Jeff. Davis, from his chamber at Richmond, listened to the thunder of the cannon of hostile armies battling before his capital." At the end of August, "Lincoln, from the White House, heard the deep peals of the artillery of the contending hosts which, having now changed location, are struggling for supremacy before the National Capital."

The devastating defeat put the president in an untenable position. The more he contemplated McClellan's delay in sending his troops to Pope, the angrier he became. Yet there was no time to indulge in anger while Washington itself was threatened and he sorely needed the best forces at his disposal. He still believed McClellan was best equipped to reorganize the demoralized troops. During his inspection tours at Fort Monroe and Harrison's Landing, Lincoln had witnessed the soldiers' devotion to their commander. "There is no man in the army who can man these fortifications and lick these troops of ours into shape half as well as he," Lincoln told Hay. "Unquestionably he has acted badly toward Pope! He wanted him to fail. That is unpardonable. But he is too useful just now to sacrifice." When Halleck recommended restoring McClellan's command over both the Army of Virginia and the Army of the Potomac, Lincoln agreed.

In ignorance of Lincoln's deliberations, the cabinet vigorously pursued their machinations to oust McClellan. Bates rewrote the protest to soften its tone. Stanton, Chase, Smith, and Bates signed the new document, which Chase again presented to Welles on Monday, September 1. Welles agreed that the new draft was "an improvement," but still disliked the idea of "combining to influence or control the President." Chase admitted that the course of action "was unusual, but the case was unusual." They had to impress upon Lincoln that "the Administration must be broken up, or McC. dismissed." Furthermore, Chase told Welles that "McClellan ought to be shot, and should, were he President, be brought to a summary punishment." Welles granted that McClellan "was not a fighting general," and that "some recent acts indicate delinquencies of a more serious character." While he would not sign the demand, he told the "disappointed" Chase, he would speak up with "no hesitation" at the cabinet meeting the next day to tell Lincoln that he agreed McClellan should go. Accordingly, Stanton and Chase resolved to withhold their confrontation with Lincoln until the following day.

All the cabinet members, save Seward, gathered at noon on Tuesday the 2nd. The secretary of state had departed for Auburn the previous week for a long-awaited vacation. Welles, perpetually suspicious of Seward, believed "there was design in his absence," certain he had left town to avoid the messy controversy over McClellan. More likely, personal considerations dictated the timing of Seward's journey. Jenny was expecting his first grandchild any day. Will was scheduled to leave with his regiment as soon as the baby was born. And Frances's favorite aunt, Clara, was dying. When he heard about the defeat at Bull Run, however, he cut his vacation short. He was on his way back to Washington as the cabinet meeting convened.

The session had barely begun when the president was called out for a brief interval. In his absence, Stanton took the floor. Speaking "in a suppressed voice, trembling with excitement," he informed his colleagues that "McClellan had been ordered to take command of the forces in Washington." The members were stunned. Lincoln returned shortly and explained his decision, which he had communicated to McClellan at 7 a.m. that morning. "McClellan knows this whole ground," Lincoln said, and "can be trusted to act on the defensive." He knew all too well that McClellan had the "slows," but maintained that there was "no better organizer." Events, he believed, would justify his judgment.

In the general discussion that followed, Welles recorded in his diary, "there was a more disturbed and desponding feeling" than he had ever witnessed in any cabinet meeting. Lincoln was "extremely distressed," as were Stanton and Chase. Chase predicted that "it would prove a national calamity," while Stanton, recognizing that the protest was a dead letter, returned to the War Department "in the condition of a drooping leaf." The episode produced an estrangement between Stanton and Lincoln that persisted for weeks.

Lincoln was deeply troubled by the knowledge that his cabinet opposed him on a question of such vital importance. According to Bates, he "seemed wrung by the bitterest anguish—said he felt almost ready to hang himself." The cabinet debacle regarding McClellan, Pope's defeat, and the gruesome, protracted war itself pressed upon him with an appalling weight, leading him to meditate. "In great contests," he wrote in a fragment found among his pages, "each party claims to act in accordance with the will of God. Both *may* be, and one *must* be wrong. God can not be *for*, and *against* the same thing at the same time. In the present civil war it is quite possible that God's purpose is something different from the purpose of either party," and that God had willed "that it shall not end yet."

Lincoln's distress may have been assuaged somewhat by Seward's return to Washington. Lincoln could speak more frankly with his secretary than with any other member of his cabinet. Reaching the capital on the evening of September 3, Seward drove immediately to the Soldiers' Home. Unfortunately, Fred Seward wrote, "there were visitors, whose presence prevented private talk."

"Governor," Lincoln proposed, "I'll get in and ride with you a while." For the next few hours, the two friends drove along the winding carriage ways, "while Seward detailed what he had found at the North, and the President in turn narrated the military events and Cabinet conferences during his absence."

Seward may have revealed to Lincoln the sad, world-wise reflections he expressed to John Hay two days later. "What is the use of growing old?" he asked. "You learn something of men and things but never until too late to use it." Referring to the antagonism between McClellan and Pope that had contributed to the disaster at Bull Run, Seward admitted that he had "only just now found out what military jealousy is. . . . It had never occurred to [him] that any jealousy could prevent these generals from acting for their common fame and the welfare of the country." As an old seasoned politician, perhaps, he reflected, he "should have known it."

Though Seward was temporarily unnerved by the events at Bull Run, he remained confident that the North would ultimately prevail—a contagious confidence that must have bolstered Lincoln's spirits. Whenever faced with desolating prospects, Seward turned to history for guidance and comfort. Recalling the difficult days of the Revolutionary War before independence "enables me," he once said, "to cherish and preserve hopefulness." Moreover, unlike his colleagues in the cabinet, Seward did not question that Lincoln possessed the prudence, wisdom, and magnanimity needed to carry the country "safely through the sea of revolution." Seward's ability to empathize with Lincoln's unenviable position must have afforded Lincoln some real measure of comfort. Unlike Stanton and Chase, Seward clearly understood that a president had to work with the tools at his disposal. At this moment, McClellan was one of those tools.

Meanwhile, McClellan smugly returned to his old headquarters on the corner next to Seward's house. "Again I have been called upon to save the country," he wrote his wife. "It makes my heart bleed to see the poor shattered remnants of my noble Army of the Potomac, poor fellows! and to see how they love me even now. I hear them calling out to me as I ride among them—'George—don't leave us again!' 'They *shan't* take you away from us again.' "

McClellan had been restored to command for only two days when Lee, emboldened by his twin victories on the Peninsula and at Bull Run, crossed the Potomac to begin an invasion of Maryland. The Confederate commander mistakenly assumed that the residents of the slave state would rise up in support of his army. In fact, the Marylanders greeted the rebel army with disdain and reserved their enthusiastic welcome for McClellan's bluecoats, clapping and waving flags as the Federal troops marched through their countryside to engage Lee in battle. When the two armies met, McClellan had another distinct advantage. General Lee's battle plans had been discovered. A careless courier had used the orders to wrap three cigars and left them behind.

On September 17, the Battle of Antietam began. "We are in the midst of the most terrible battle of the age," McClellan wrote Mary Ellen in midafternoon as the fighting raged. By day's end, 6,000 soldiers on both sides were dead and an additional 17,000 had been wounded, a staggering total four times the number of Americans who would lose their lives on D-day during World War II. In the end, the Union Army prevailed, forcing Lee to retreat. "Our victory was complete," McClellan joyfully reported. "I feel some little pride in having with a beaten and demoralized army defeated Lee so utterly, & saved the North so completely."

Lincoln was thrilled by initial reports that indicated Lee's army might be destroyed. Subsequent telegrams, however, revealed that McClellan, flush with victory, had failed to pursue the retreating rebels and allowed Lee to cross the Potomac into Virginia, where he could regroup and replenish men and supplies.

Still, Antietam was a sorely needed victory for the demoralized North. "At last our Generals in the field seem to have risen to the grandeur of the National crisis," the *New York Times* noted. "Sept. 17, 1862, will, we predict, hereafter be looked upon as an epoch in the history of the rebellion, from which will date the inauguration of its downfall."

The statement would prove prescient for reasons the *Times* could not have surmised. The victory, incomplete as it was, was the long-awaited event that provided Lincoln the occasion to announce his plans to issue an Emancipation Proclamation the following January. On September 22, he convened a cabinet meeting to reveal his decision. As Chase and Stanton settled on his right and the others sat down on his left, Lincoln attempted to lighten the mood with a reading from the Maine humorist Charles Farrar Browne. Seward alone readily appreciated the diversion, laughing uproariously along with Lincoln at the antics of Artemus Ward. Chase assumed a forced smile, while Stanton's face betrayed impatience and irritation.

Once his humorous story was done, Lincoln took on "a graver tone," reminding his colleagues of the emancipation order he had drafted and read to them earlier. He told them that when Lee's army was in Maryland, he had decided "as soon as it should be driven out" of the state, he would issue his proclamation. "I said nothing to any one; but I made the promise to myself, and (hesitating a little) to my Maker." While Lincoln rarely acknowledged the influence of faith or religious beliefs, "there were occasions when, uncertain how to proceed," remarked Gideon Welles, "he had in this way submitted the disposal of the subject to a Higher Power, and abided by what seemed the Supreme Will." The president made clear he was not seeking "advice about the main matter," for he had already considered their views before reaching his decision; but he would welcome any suggestions on language. Lincoln then began to read the document that he had revised slightly in recent weeks to strengthen the rationale of military necessity.

Stanton "made a very emphatic speech sustaining the measure," and Blair reiterated his concerns about the border states and the fall elections, though in the end he filed no objection. Seward alone suggested a substantive change. Wouldn't it be stronger, he asked, if the government promised not only to recognize but to "maintain" the freedom of the former slaves, leaving "out all reference to the act being sustained during the incumbency of the present President"? Lincoln answered that he had thought about this, but "it was not my way to promise what I was not entirely *sure* that I could perform." When Seward "insisted that we ought to take this ground," Lincoln agreed, striking the limiting reference to the present administration.

The preliminary proclamation, published the following day, brought a large crowd of cheering serenaders to the White House. Though it would not take effect until Lincoln issued the final proclamation on January 1, 1863, giving the rebellious states one last chance to return to the Union, it had changed the course of the war. "I can only trust in God I have made no mistake," Lincoln told well-wishers from an upstairs window. "It is now for the country and the world to pass judgment on it." He then called attention to the brave soldiers in the field. While he might be "environed with difficulties" as president, these were "scarcely so great as the difficulties of those who, upon the battle field, are endeavoring to purchase with their blood and their lives the future happiness and prosperity of this country. Let us never forget them."

The serenaders proceeded to Chase's house at Sixth and E, where the large crowd listened "in a glorious humor" as Chase spoke. Afterward, an excited group, including Bates and "a few old fogies," remained inside, drinking wine. "They all seemed to feel a sort of new and exhilarated life," John Hay observed. "They gleefully and merrily called each other and themselves abolitionists, and seemed to enjoy the novel sensation of appropriating that horrible name."

Many radicals, including Count Gurowski and William Fessenden, remained wary of Lincoln. Gurowski complained that the proclamation was written "in the meanest and the most dry routine style; not a word to evoke a generous thrill," while Fessenden remarked that it "did not and could not affect the status of a single negro." Nevertheless, Frederick Douglass, whose criticism of Lincoln had been implacable, understood the revolutionary impact of the proclamation. "We shout for joy that we live to record this righteous decree," he wrote in his *Monthly.* Anticipating the powerful opposition it would encounter, he asked: "Will it lead the President to reconsider and retract." "No," he concluded, "Abraham Lincoln, will take no step backward." Intuitively grasping Lincoln's character, though they were not yet personally acquainted, Douglass explained that "Abraham Lincoln may be slow . . . but Abraham Lincoln is not the man to reconsider, retract and contradict words and purposes solemnly proclaimed over his official signature. . . . If he has taught us to confide in nothing else, he has taught us to confide in his word." Lincoln confirmed this assessment when he told Massachusetts congressman George Boutwell, "My word is out to these people, and I can't take it back."

Opposition came from the expected sources: conservatives feared the proclamation would "render eternal the hatred between the two sections," while Democrats predicted it would demoralize the army. Needless to say, an outcry arose in the South. The *Richmond Enquirer* charged Lincoln with inciting an insurrection that would inevitably lead, as with Nat Turner's uprising, to slaves being hunted down "like wild beasts" and killed. "Cheerful and happy now, he plots their death," the paper accused. None of this surprised Lincoln. Analyzing the range of editorial opinion, he "said he had studied the matter so long that he knew more about it than they did." When Vice President Hannibal Hamlin wrote that the proclamation would "be enthusiastically approved and sustained" and would "stand as the great act of the age," Lincoln replied that "while commendation in newspapers and by distinguished individuals is all that a vain man could wish, the stocks have declined, and troops come forward more slowly than ever. This, looked soberly in the face, is not very satisfactory."

• • •

As McClellan rested his troops in the vicinity of Antietam, he pondered his situation. Convinced that his military reputation had been fully restored by the recent victory, he believed it was his prerogative to insist that "Stanton must leave & that Halleck must restore my old place to me." If these two demands were not met, he told his wife, he would resign his commission. Furthermore, he could not bear the idea of fighting for "such an accursed doctrine" as the Emancipation Proclamation, which he considered an "infamous" call for "a servile insurrection." Indignant, McClellan drafted a letter of protest to Lincoln, declaring himself in opposition. After old friends, including Monty Blair and his father, warned him that it would be ruinous not to submit to the president's policy, he ultimately decided not to send the letter.

McClellan had overestimated his newfound clout. Though Stanton and Chase were so discouraged by the general's apparently unassailable position that they both considered resigning, Lincoln had made another private decision. If McClellan did not mobilize in pursuit of General Lee, which, as September gave way to October, he showed no sign of doing, he would be relieved from duty.

Hoping that a personal visit would inspire McClellan to action, Lincoln journeyed by train to the general's headquarters early in October. Though Halleck, fearing danger, opposed the idea, Lincoln was determined to "slip off . . . and see my soldiers." As always, he was fortified by his interactions with the troops. As the regiments presented arms to the beating of drums, the president, accompanied by McClellan, slowly rode by, lifting his hat. "The review was a splendid affair throughout," one correspondent noted. "The troops, notwithstanding their long marches and hard fighting, presented a fine appearance, for which they were highly complimented. The President indulged in a number of humorous anecdotes, which greatly amused the company."

Sharing McClellan's quarters for meals and occupying the adjoining tent at night, Lincoln quietly but candidly prompted his general to discard his "over-cautiousness" and plan for future movement. While McClellan conceded in a letter to his wife that Lincoln "was very affable" and "very kind personally," he rightly suspected that the "real purpose of his visit is to push me into a premature advance into Virginia."

Lincoln headed back to Washington on Saturday afternoon in high spirits, encouraged by the good condition of the troops. His train stopped at the tiny town of Frederick along the way, where he was greeted by a large crowd of cheering citizens, eager to demonstrate Maryland's loyalty to the Union. Called upon to speak, Lincoln replied cheerfully that "if I were as I have been most of my life, I might perhaps, talk amusing to you for half an hour," but as president, "every word is so closely noted" that he must avoid any "trivial" remarks. Nevertheless, before the train pulled away, he delivered a brief, eloquent speech from the platform of his car, thanking soldiers and citizens alike for their fidelity to the Union's cause. "May our children and our children's children to a thousand generations," he said in closing, "continue to enjoy the benefits conferred upon us by a united country, and have cause yet to rejoice under those glorious institutions bequeathed us by Washington and his compeers."

To ensure that McClellan would not misconstrue their conversations, Lincoln had Halleck telegraph him the following Monday that "the President directs that you cross the Potomac and give battle to the enemy or drive him south. Your army must move now while the roads are good." Weeks went by, however, and McClellan found all manner of excuses for inaction—lack of supplies, lack of shoes, tired horses. At this last excuse, Lincoln could no longer contain his irritation. "Will you pardon me for asking what the horses of your army have done since the battle of Antietam that fatigue anything?"

"Our war on rebellion languishes," a frustrated George Templeton Strong wrote on October 23. "McClellan's repose is doubtless majestic, but if a couchant lion postpone his spring too long, people will begin wondering whether he is not a stuffed specimen after all." The army's inaction combined with conservative resentment against the Emancipation Proclamation to produce what Seward called an "ill wind" of discontent when voters headed to the polls for the midterm November elections. The results were devastating to the administration. Though Republicans retained a slight majority in Congress, the so-called "Peace Democrats," who favored a compromise that would tolerate slavery, gained critical offices in Illinois, New York, Pennsylvania, Ohio, and Indiana. Asked how he felt about the Republican losses, Lincoln said: "Somewhat like that boy in Kentucky, who stubbed his toe while running to see his sweetheart. The boy said he was too big to cry, and far too badly hurt to laugh."

The following day, with the midterm elections behind him, Lincoln relieved McClellan of his command of the Army of the Potomac. Though the young Napoleon had finally crossed the Potomac, he had immediately stalled again. "I began to fear he was playing false—that he did not want to hurt the enemy," Lincoln told Hay. "I saw how he could intercept the enemy on the way to Richmond. I determined to make that the test. If he let them get away I would remove him. He did so & I relieved him."

McClellan received the telegram in his tent at 11 p.m., in the company of the man Lincoln had chosen to succeed him: General Ambrose Burnside. Known as a fighting general, Burnside had commanded a corps under McClellan on the Peninsula and at Antietam. "Poor Burn feels dreadfully, almost crazy," McClellan told his wife. "Of course I was much surprised," he admitted, but "not a muscle quivered nor was the slightest expression of feeling visible on my face."

"More than a hundred thousand soldiers are in great grief to-night," the correspondent for the *National Intelligencer* reported as General McClellan bade farewell to his staff and his troops. With all his officers assembled around a large fire in front of his tent, he raised a glass of wine. "Here's to the Army of the Potomac," he proposed. "And to its old commander," one of his officers added. "Tears were shed in profusion," both at the final toast and when McClellan rode past the lines of his troops. "In parting from you," he told them, "I cannot express the love and gratitude I bear for you. As an Army you have grown up under my care. . . . The glory you have achieved, our mutual perils & fatigues, the graves of our comrades fallen in battle & by disease, the broken forms of those whom wounds & sickness have disabled—the strongest associations which can exist among men, unite us still by an indissoluble tie."

Lincoln's choice of Burnside proved unfortunate. Though he was charismatic, honest, and industrious, he lacked the intelligence and confidence to lead a great army. He was said to possess "ten times as much *heart* as he has *head.*" On December 13, against Lincoln's advice, the new commander led about 122,000 troops across the Rappahannock to Fredericksburg, where General Lee waited on the heavily fortified high ground. Caught in a trap, the Union forces suffered 13,000 casualties, more than twice the Confederate losses, and were forced into a humiliating withdrawal.

Lincoln tried to mitigate the impact of the defeat, issuing a public letter of commendation to the troops: "The courage with which you, in an open field, maintained the contest against an entrenched foe . . . [shows] that you possess all the qualities of a great army, which will yet give victory to the cause of the country and of popular government." Even as he did the "awful arithmetic" of the relative losses, Lincoln realized, as he told William Stoddard, "that if the same battle were to be fought over again, every day, through a week of days, with the same relative results, the army under Lee would be wiped out to its last man, the Army of the Potomac would still be a mighty host, the war would be over, the Confederacy gone."

• • •

THE TRAIN OF RECRIMINATIONS that followed the Fredericksburg defeat led to a crisis for the administration that left Lincoln "more depressed," he said, "than by any event of [his] life." Radical Republicans on Capitol Hill began to insist that unless a more vigorous prosecution of the war were adopted, conservative demands for a compromise peace would multiply and the Union would be restored with slavery intact. The midterm elections, they argued, demonstrated growing public dissatisfaction with current tactics—the writing, clearly, was on the wall.

On the afternoon of Tuesday, December 16, all the Republican senators caucused in the high-ceilinged Senate reception room, hoping to devise a unified response to the disastrous situation. Without sweeping changes in the administration, they agreed, "the country was ruined and the cause was lost." Hesitant to publicly attack Lincoln in the midst of war, they focused their fury on the man they considered the malevolent power behind the throne—William Henry Seward. For months, Chase had claimed "there was a back stairs & malign influence which controlled the President, and overruled all the decisions of the cabinet," a hardly veiled reference to Seward. In private letters that had quickly become public knowledge, Chase had repeatedly griped about Lincoln's failure to consult the cabinet "on matters concerning the salvation of the country," intimating that his own councils would have averted the misfortunes now facing the country and the party.

In Republican circles, word spread that Seward was a "paralizing influence on the army and the President." He was rumored to be the "President *de facto*," responsible for the long delay in dismissing McClellan that led to stagnation and loss on the battlefield. Seward was said to have hindered Lincoln's intention to make the war a crusade for emancipation, and was deemed responsible for the resurgence of the conservatives in the midterm elections. In sum, Seward's insidious presence "kept a sponge saturated with chloroform to Uncle Abe's nose."

In the minds of the majority of the Republicans gathered together in the reception room that December afternoon, these rumors had congealed into facts. As one senator after another rose to speak of Seward's "controlling influence upon the mind of the President," Ben Wade suggested that they "should go in a body and demand of the President the dismissal of Mr Seward." Duty dictated that they exercise their constitutional power, as William Fessenden professed, to demand "that measures should be taken to make the Cabinet a unity and to remove from it any one who did not coincide heartily with our views in relation to the war." As the rhetoric grew more heated, Senator James W. Grimes of Iowa introduced a resolution proclaiming "a want of confidence in the Secretary of State" and concluding that "he ought to be removed from the Cabinet."

Fessenden asked for a vote, which clearly indicated that an overwhelming majority of the thirty-one senators were in favor. Seward's friend New York senator Preston King objected that the resolution was not only "hasty and unwise" but also "unjust to Mr. Seward, as it was predicated on mere rumors." Several others agreed. Orville Browning argued that he "had no evidence the charges were true," and therefore could not vote for the resolution. Moreover, this "was not the proper course of proceeding" and would likely provoke a "war between Congress and the President, and the knowledge of this antagonism would injure our cause greatly." Recognizing that "without entire unanimity our action would not only be without force but productive of evil," Fessenden agreed to adjourn until the following afternoon to "give time for reflection."

Though the proceedings were to be kept secret, Preston King felt compelled to acquaint Seward with the situation. That evening, he went to Seward's house. Finding his old colleague in the library, he sat down beside him and told him all that had transpired. Seward listened quietly and then said, "They may do as they please about me, but they shall not put the President in a false position on my account." Asking for pen and paper, he wrote out his resignation as secretary of state and asked his son Fred and King to deliver it to the White House.

Lincoln scanned the resignation "with a face full of pain and surprise, saying 'What does this mean?' " After listening to Senator King's description of the overwrought emotions that had created "a thirst for a victim," Lincoln walked over to Seward's house. The meeting was painful for both men. Masking his anguish, Seward told Lincoln that "it would be a relief to be freed from official cares." Lincoln replied: "Ah, yes, Governor, that will do very well for you, but I am like the starling in [Laurence] Sterne's story, 'I can't get out.' "

Lincoln straightaway understood that he was the true target of the radicals' wrath. "They wish to get rid of me, and I am sometimes half disposed to gratify them," he told Browning two days later. He described the chatter setting forth Seward's controlling influence over him as "a lie, an absurd lie," that one "could not impose upon a child." Seward was the one man in the cabinet Lincoln trusted completely, the only one who fully appreciated his unusual strengths as a leader, and the only one he could call an intimate friend. Still, he could scarcely afford to antagonize the Republican senators so essential to his governing coalition. He had to think through his options. He had to learn more about the dynamics of the situation.

Seward was greatly "disappointed," Welles sensed, "that the President did not promptly refuse to consider his resignation." The hesitation compounded the pain of the unexpected assault from his old colleagues on the Hill, leaving him noticeably "wounded, mortified, and chagrined." Fortunately, Frances had journeyed to Washington the week before to look after their son Will, who had contracted typhoid fever in his army camp six miles from the capital. Fanny, who had just turned eighteen, remained in Auburn with Jenny and the baby. The two women were due to leave Auburn for Washington a few days later to join the family for Christmas.

As Fanny and Jenny were packing their things, Fred sent a hurried telegram to Fanny: "Do not come at present." Fred, too, had offered his resignation as assistant secretary of state, and Frances followed his telegram with a letter telling Fanny that her father "thought he could best serve his country at present by resigning," and that they were all leaving shortly for Auburn. Disconcerted by her father's abrupt departure, Fanny worried greatly. "It seemed to me that if he were to leave," she noted in her diary, "the distracted state of affairs would prey upon his spirits all the more. I had a vague fear that he would come home ill, and longed to see him with my own eyes, safe. Spent a restless & uncomfortable night."

In some ways, Seward had exacerbated his own situation. His gratuitous comments about the radicals had made him enemies on Capitol Hill. Charles Sumner was particularly offended by a careless remark in one of the secretary's dispatches to London, suggesting that the mind-set of the men in Congress was not so different from that of the Confederates. Furthermore, it is not unlikely that Seward's pridefulness had led him occasionally to make immodest claims regarding his influence in the administration. Yet, despite such indiscretions, he was steadfast and loyal to the president. Having relinquished his own future ambitions, he had fought tirelessly to advance the fortunes of his chief and serve the country he loved.

When the Republican senators convened again Wednesday afternoon, Ira Harris of New York offered a substitute resolution that received unanimous approval. Rather than name Seward directly as the intended target, the resolution stated simply that "the public confidence in the present administration would be increased by a reconstruction of the Cabinet." When fears arose that Chase might lose his position as well, the resolution was amended to call for a "partial reconstruction of the Cabinet." Senator John Sherman of Ohio expressed doubt that any change in the cabinet would have an effect, since Lincoln "had neither dignity, order, nor firmness." Still, believing that they must take action, the caucus selected a Committee of Nine to call on the president and present the resolution. A meeting was set for 7 p.m. Thursday night, December 18.

Orville Browning came to the White House to see Lincoln shortly before the meeting began. "I saw in a moment that he was in distress," Browning recorded in his diary, "that more than usual trouble was pressing upon him." When Lincoln asked, "What do these men want?," Browning bluntly replied that they were "exceedingly violent towards the administration," and that the resolution adopted "was the gentlest thing that could be done." Furthermore, although Seward was "the especial object of their hostility," they were "very bitter" toward the president as well. Lincoln admitted that he had been enormously upset since receiving word about the caucus proceedings. "I can hardly see a ray of hope," he confided to Browning.

Concealing his distress, Lincoln greeted the Committee of Nine with his accustomed civility, affording them ample opportunity to speak their minds during a three-hour session. Jacob Collamer of Vermont opened the proceedings with a recitation of their primary contention that a president's cabinet council should jointly endorse principles and policy, "that all important public measures and appointments should be the result of their combined wisdom and deliberation." Since this was hardly the current state of affairs, the cabinet should be reconstructed to "secure to the country unity of purpose and action." In the conversation that followed, the senators argued that the prosecution of the war had been left too long "in the hands of bitter and malignant Democrats," like McClellan and Halleck, while the antislavery generals, like Frémont and Hunter, "had been disgraced."

This grim arraignment was attributed to Seward's domination of policy and his "lukewarmness in the conduct of the war." While the Republican senators professed belief in the president's honesty, Lincoln later said, "they seemed to think that when he had in him any good purposes, Mr. S[eward] contrived *to suck them out of him unperceived.*" Lincoln worked to defuse the anger and tension. He confessed that the movement against Seward "shocked and grieved him," maintaining that while his cabinet had been at loggerheads on certain issues, "there had never been serious disagreements." Rumors that Seward exercised some perfidious influence in opposition to the majority of the cabinet were simply not true. On the contrary, the cabinet had acted with great accord on most matters. Indeed, in his most trying days, "he had been sustained and consoled" by their "mutual and unselfish confidence and zeal." As the conversation continued, Lincoln seemed to sense that the committee members were "earnest and sad—not malicious nor passionate." He "expressed his satisfaction with the tone and temper" of the conversation, promised to examine the prepared paper with care, and left them with the feeling that he was "pleased with the interview."

Aware that "he must work it out by himself" with no adviser to consult, Lincoln "thought deeply on the matter." By morning, he had devised a plan of action. He sent notices to all of his cabinet members except Seward, requesting a special meeting at 10:30 a.m. When all were seated around the familiar oak table, Lincoln asked them to keep secret what he had to say. He informed them of Seward's letter of resignation, told them about his meeting with the Committee of Nine, and read aloud the paper the committee members had presented to him. He reiterated the statements he had made to the committee, emphasizing how his compound cabinet had worked together "harmoniously, whatever had been their previous party feelings," and that during the "overwhelming troubles of the country, which had borne heavily upon him," he had counted on their loyalty and "good feeling." He "could not afford to lose" any of them and declared that it would not be "possible for him to go on with a total abandonment of old friends."

Knowing that, when personally confronted, the cabinet members would profess they had worked well together, Lincoln proposed a joint session later that evening with the cabinet and the Committee of Nine. Presumably, they would disabuse the senators of their notions of disunity and discord in the cabinet. Chase was panicked at the thought of the joint meeting, since tales of the malfunctioning cabinet had originated largely with his own statements to the senators. Chase argued vehemently against the joint meeting, but when everyone else agreed, he was forced to acquiesce.

On the evening of December 19, when the members of the Committee of Nine arrived at the White House, Lincoln began the unusual session by reading the resolutions of the senators and inviting a candid discussion of the issues raised. He acknowledged that cabinet meetings had not been as regular as he might have liked, given the terrible time pressures that faced his administration. Nonetheless, he believed that "most questions of importance had received a reasonable consideration," and that "all had acquiesced in measures when once decided." He went on to defend Seward against the committee's charge that he had "improperly interfered" with decisions and had not been "earnest in the prosecution of the war." He specifically cited Seward's full concurrence in the Emancipation Proclamation.

The senators renewed their demand that "the whole Cabinet" must "consider and decide great questions," with no one individual directing the "whole Executive action." They noted with approval that John Quincy Adams adhered to the majority vote of his cabinet even when he disagreed with them. In like fashion, "they wanted united counsels, combined wisdom, and energetic action."

Blair followed with a long argument that "sustained the President and dissented most decidedly from the idea of a plural Executive." Though he "had differed much with Mr. Seward," he nonetheless "believed him as earnest as any one in the war; thought it would be injurious to the public service to have him leave the Cabinet, and that the Senate had better not meddle with matters of that kind." Bates expressed wholehearted agreement with Blair, as did Welles. As he contemplated the discussion, Welles wrote the next day, he realized that while he had likewise differed with Seward on numerous occasions, Seward's faults were "venial." Moreover, "no party or faction should be permitted to dictate to the President in regard to his Cabinet."

The course of the conversation had seriously compromised Chase's position. He noted irritably, recalled Fessenden, that "he should not have come here had he known that he was to be arraigned before a committee of the Senate," but he felt compelled to uphold Lincoln and his colleagues. Stating equivocally that he wished the cabinet had more fully considered every measure, Chase endorsed the president's statement that there had been accord on most measures. He grudgingly admitted that "no member had opposed a measure after it had once been decided on." As for the Emancipation Proclamation, Chase conceded that Seward had suggested amendments that substantially strengthened it. Neither Stanton nor Smith said a word.

After nearly five hours of open conversation, sensing he was making headway, Lincoln asked each of the senators if he still desired to see Seward resign his position. Though four, including Lyman Trumbull, reaffirmed their original position, the others had changed their minds. When the meeting adjourned at 1 a.m., the senators suspected that no change in the cabinet would be made.

The disappointed senators now turned their wrath upon Chase, whose duplicitous behavior infuriated them. When Collamer was asked how Chase could have presented such a different face when confronted in the meeting, the Vermont senator answered succinctly, "He lied." Lincoln agreed that Chase had been disingenuous, but not on that night. On the contrary, after months of spreading false stories about Seward and the cabinet, Chase had finally been compelled to tell the truth! Lincoln's political dexterity had enabled him to calm the crisis and expose the duplicity of his secretary of the treasury.

The next day, Welles paid an early call on the president. He said that he had "pondered the events" of the previous night and concluded that it would be a grievous mistake for Lincoln to accept Seward's resignation. The senators' presumption in their criticisms of Seward, "real or imaginary," was "inappropriate and wrong." In order to "maintain the rights and independence of the Executive," Lincoln must reject the senator's attempts to interfere with internal cabinet matters. Welles hoped that Seward would not press Lincoln to accept his resignation. Delighted by these comments, Lincoln asked Welles to talk with Seward.

Welles went at once to Seward's house, where he found Stanton conversing with the secretary of state. While Stanton had probably joined

Chase in airing his frustrations, most particularly when McClellan was restored to command, he had come to see the necessity for solidarity. The cabinet, he said, was like a window. "Suppose you allowed it to be understood that passers-by might knock out one pane of glass—just one at a time—how long do you think any panes would be left in it?"

When Stanton departed, Welles told Seward that he had advised the president not to accept his resignation. This "greatly pleased" Seward, who had been distraught over the whole episode. In short order, another visitor knocked on Seward's door and Monty Blair entered, also to object to the idea of Seward's resignation. So Lincoln had brought the cabinet to rally around one of their own. Like family members who would fault one another within the confines of their own household while fiercely rejecting external criticism, the cabinet put aside its quarrel with Seward, based largely on jealousy over his intimacy with Lincoln, to resist the interference of outsiders.

Still, Lincoln's troubles were not over. The news of Seward's offer of resignation had produced widespread comment, particularly among radicals who hoped that his departure would signal a first step toward a reconstructed cabinet purged of conservative influences. To refuse Seward's offer now that its tender was public knowledge would be interpreted as a slap against the radicals. The delicate balance Lincoln had struggled to maintain in his cabinet would be damaged.

Ironically, Salmon Chase unwittingly provided a perfect solution to Lincoln's difficulty. When Welles returned to Lincoln's office after speaking with Seward, he found Chase and Stanton waiting to see the president. Humiliated after the previous night, Chase had decided to hand in his own resignation. Word had already leaked out that he had been instrumental in the movement to remove Seward "for the purpose of obtaining and maintaining control in the cabinet." Were he to remain after Seward's departure, he told a friend, he would face the hostility of Seward's many friends. Yet a public offer to join Seward in resigning would put the onus on Lincoln to request Chase's continued service and "relieve him from imputations of Seward's friends and clear his future course of difficulties."

Discovering Chase, Stanton, and Welles in his office, Lincoln invited them all to sit with him before the fire. Chase said he "had been painfully affected by the meeting," which had come as "a total surprise" to him. He informed the president he had written out his resignation. "Where is it?" Lincoln asked, "his eye lighting up for a moment." When Chase said he had brought it with him, Lincoln leaped up, exclaiming, "Let me have it." Stretching out to snatch it, Lincoln pulled the paper from Chase, who now seemed "reluctant" to let it go. With "an air of satisfaction spread over his countenance," Lincoln said, "This . . . cuts the Gordian knot." As he began reading the note, he added, "I can dispose of this subject now without difficulty."

Chase gave Welles a "perplexed" look, suggesting he was not pleased that his colleague was a witness to this upsetting encounter. At this point, Stanton also offered to submit his resignation. "I don't want yours," Lincoln immediately replied. Then, indicating Chase's letter, he added, "This . . . is all I want—this relieves me—my way is clear—the trouble is ended. I will detain neither of you longer."

As soon as they left, Lincoln wrote a letter to both Seward and Chase, acknowledging that he had received their resignations, but that "after most anxious consideration," he had determined that the "public interest" required both men to remain in office. "I therefore have to request that you will resume the duties of your Departments respectively," he concluded. Welles immediately fathomed Lincoln's insistence on keeping the two rivals close despite their animosity: "Seward comforts him,—Chase he deems a necessity." By retaining both men, Lincoln kept the balance in his cabinet. When Senator Ira Harris called on him shortly after he had received Chase's resignation, Lincoln was in a buoyant mood. "Yes, Judge," he said, employing a metaphor shaped by his rural childhood, "I can ride on now, I've got a pumpkin in each end of my bag!"

Seward responded to Lincoln with alacrity. "I have cheerfully resumed the functions of this Department in obedience to your command," he replied. That afternoon, a relieved Fanny received a telegram from Fred instructing her and Jenny to "come as soon as possible" to Washington. Chase, meanwhile, had far more difficulty in determining how to respond. His first reaction was to draft a letter refusing Lincoln's wish. "Will you allow me to say," he wrote, "that something you *said* or looked, when I handed you my resignation this morning, made on my mind the impression, that, having received the resignations of both Gov. Seward and myself, you felt you could relieve yourself from trouble by declining to accept either and that the feeling was one of gratification." He then went on to express the opinion that he and Seward could "both better serve you and the country, at this time, as private citizens, than in your cabinet." When Chase received a note from Seward announcing his decision to resume his duties, however, he felt compelled to follow suit. While letting Lincoln know that his original desire to resign remained unchanged, Chase promised that he would do Lincoln's bidding and return to the Treasury.

At the next cabinet meeting, Welles noted, "Seward was feeling very happy," while "Chase was pale, and said he was ill, had been for weeks." Seward magnanimously invited Chase to dine with his family on Christmas Eve. Having achieved what Nicolay termed "a triumph over those who attempted to drive him out," Seward hoped that he and Chase could now make their peace. Though Chase declined the invitation, he sent a gracious note begging that his "unwilling absence" be excused, for he was "too really sick . . . to venture upon his hospitality."

For Lincoln, the most serious governmental crisis of his presidency had ended in victory. He had treated the senators with dignity and respect and, in the process, had protected the integrity and autonomy of his cabinet. He had defended the executive against a legislative attempt to dictate who should constitute the president's political family. He had saved his friend Seward from an unjust attack that was really directed at him, and, simultaneously, solidified his own position as master of both factions in his cabinet.

Mary Lincoln did not share her husband's gratification in the outcome. She told Elizabeth Blair that "she regretted the making up of the family quarrel—that there was not a member of the Cabinet who did not stab her husband & the Country daily," with the exception of Monty Blair. Her protective suspicions were reaffirmed during a visit to a Georgetown spiritualist on New Year's Eve. Mrs. Laury's revelations combined comforting communications from Willie with political commentary on affairs of the day. In particular, the spiritualist warned "that the cabinet were all the enemies of the President, working for themselves, and that they would have to be dismissed, and others called to his aid before he had success."

Lincoln listened patiently to Mary's concerns, but he knew that he had now balanced his team of rivals and consolidated his leadership. "I do not now see how it could have been done better," he told Hay. "I am sure it was right. If I had yielded to that storm & dismissed Seward the thing would all have slumped over one way & we should have been left with a scanty handful of supporters. When Chase gave in his resignation I saw that the game was in my own hands & I put it through."

The happy resolution of the crisis provided an upbeat ending to a very difficult year.

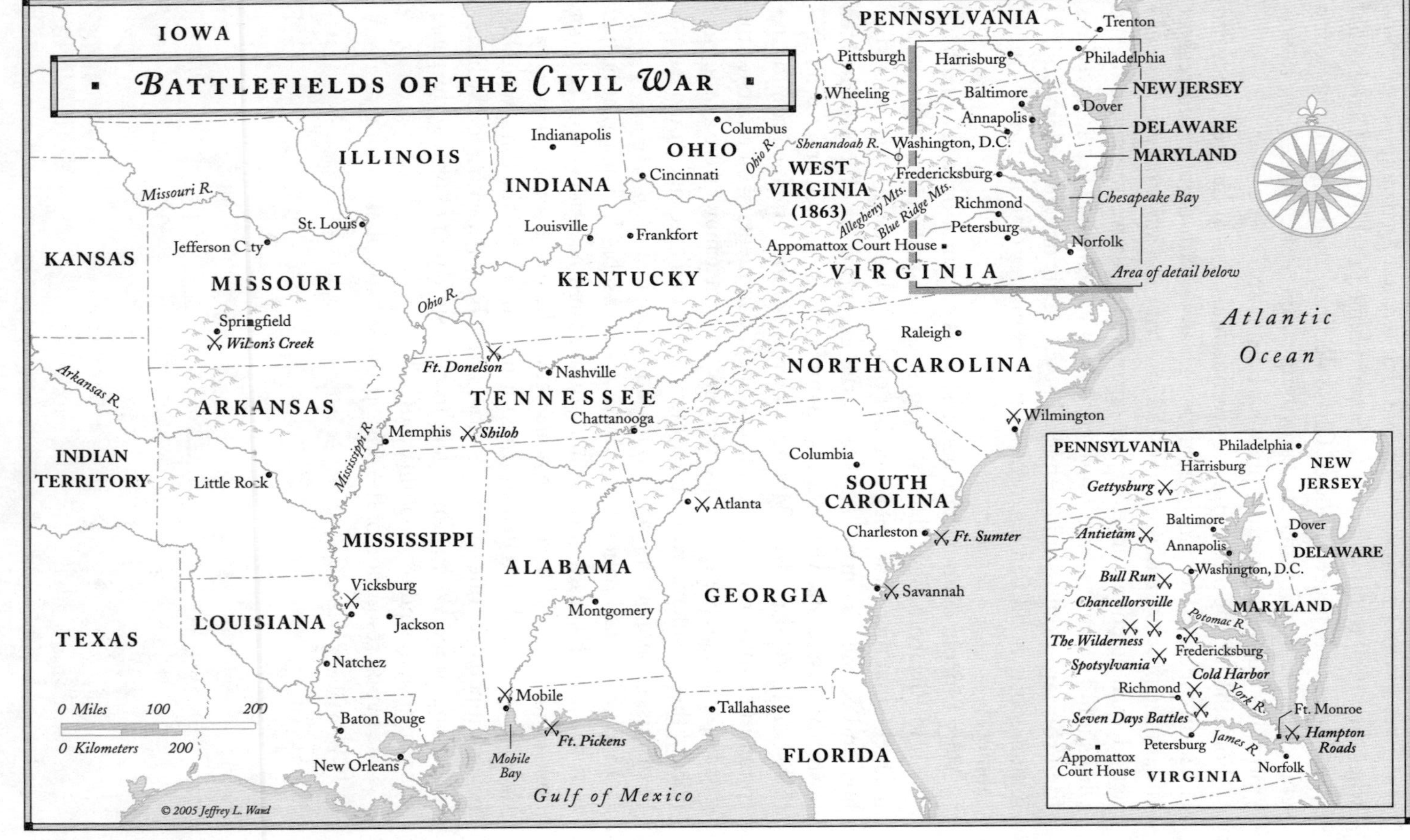

Battlefields of the Civil War
IOWA
KANSAS
MISSOURI
ILLINOIS
INDIANA
OHIO
KENTUCKY
PENNSYLVANIA
WEST VIRGINIA (1863)
VIRGINIA
NORTH CAROLINA
SOUTH CAROLINA
TENNESSEE
ARKANSAS
INDIAN TERRITORY
TEXAS
LOUISIANA
MISSISSIPPI
ALABAMA
GEORGIA
FLORIDA
NEW JERSEY
DELAWARE
MARYLAND
Trenton
Philadelphia
Harrisburg
Pittsburgh
Wheeling
Baltimore
Dover
Annapolis
Washington, D.C.
Shenandoah R.
Fredericksburg
Chesapeake Bay
Allegheny Mts.
Blue Ridge Mts.
Richmond
Petersburg
Norfolk
Appomattox Court House
Area of detail below
Atlantic Ocean
Columbus
Indianapolis
Cincinnati
Ohio R.
Missouri R.
St. Louis
Jefferson City
Louisville
Frankfort
Springfield
Wilson's Creek
Ohio R.
Ft. Donelson
Nashville
Arkansas R.
Memphis
Shiloh
Chattanooga
Raleigh
Wilmington
Mississippi R.
Little Rock
Columbia
Atlanta
Charleston
Ft. Sumter
Savannah
Vicksburg
Jackson
Montgomery
Natchez
Mobile
Tallahassee
Baton Rouge
Ft. Pickens
Mobile Bay
New Orleans
Gulf of Mexico
0 Miles 100 200
0 Kilometers 200
© 2005 Jeffrey L. Ward
PENNSYLVANIA
Philadelphia
Harrisburg
NEW JERSEY
Gettysburg
Baltimore
Dover
Antietam
Annapolis
DELAWARE
Bull Run
Washington, D.C.
Chancellorsville
MARYLAND
Potomac R.
The Wilderness
Fredericksburg
Spotsylvania
Cold Harbor
Richmond
York R.
Ft. Monroe
Seven Days Battles
Hampton Roads
James R.
Petersburg
Appomattox Court House
VIRGINIA
Norfolk

CHAPTER 19

"FIRE IN THE REAR"

As the first day of January 1863 approached, the public evinced a "general air of doubt" regarding the president's intention to follow through on his September pledge to issue his Emancipation Proclamation on New Year's Day. "Will Lincoln's backbone carry him through?" a skeptical George Templeton Strong asked. "Nobody knows."

The cynics were wrong. Despite repeated warnings that the issuance of the proclamation would have harmful consequences for the Union's cause, Lincoln never considered retracting his pledge. As Frederick Douglass had perceived, once the president staked himself to a forward position, he did not give up ground. The final proclamation deviated from the preliminary document in one major respect. The document still proclaimed that "all persons held as slaves" within states and parts of states still in rebellion "are, and henceforward shall be free"; but Lincoln, for the first time, officially authorized the recruitment of blacks into the armed forces. Stanton and Chase had advocated this step for many months, yet Lincoln, knowing that it would provoke serious disaffection in his governing coalition, had hesitated. Now, as the public began to comprehend the massive manpower necessary to fight a prolonged war, he believed the timing was right.

The cabinet members suggested a few changes that Lincoln cheerfully adopted, most notably Chase's proposal to conclude the legalistic document with a flourish, invoking "the considerate judgment of mankind, and the gracious favor of Almighty God . . . upon this act."

On the morning he would deliver the historic proclamation, Lincoln rose early after a fitful sleep. He walked over to his office to make final revisions and sent the document by messenger to the State Department, where it was put into legal form. He then met with General Burnside, who had readied his army for "another expedition against the rebels along the Rappahannock," only to be restrained by the president. Lincoln explained that several of Burnside's division commanders had made forceful objections to the new plan. Troubled by the realization that he had lost the confidence of his officers, Burnside offered to resign. Lincoln managed to assuage the discord temporarily, but three weeks later, he would replace Burnside with "Fighting Joe" Hooker. A West Point graduate who had fought in the Mexican War, Hooker had served under McClellan in the Peninsula Campaign and at Antietam.

Seward returned from the State Department with the formally copied proclamation shortly before 11 a.m. Lincoln read it over once more and made ready to sign it when he noticed a technical error in the format. The document had to be returned to the State Department for correction. Since the traditional New Year's reception was about to begin, the signing would have to be delayed until midafternoon.

The first hour of the three-hour reception was reserved for Washington officials—diplomats, senators, representatives, justices, and high officers in the armed forces. All the cabinet members and their families were there, with the exception of Caleb Smith, who had recently resigned his Department of Interior post to become a district judge in Indiana. Young Fanny Seward anxiously anticipated the occasion, for she had just passed her eighteenth birthday and this was her "coming out" day. Outfitted in blue silk with a white hat and an ivory fan, Fanny was thrilled when the president and first lady remembered her. Between the "full court dress" of the diplomatic corps and the dazzling costumes of the ladies, "the scene," Fanny recalled, was "very brilliant." She recorded in her diary that Mary "wore a rich dress of black velvet, with lozenge formed trimming on the waist," but she was especially captivated by Kate Chase, "looking like a fairy queen" in her lace dress: "Oh how pretty she is."

At noon, the cabinet members left to prepare for their own receptions and the gates to the White House were opened to the general public. The immense and disorderly crowd surged into the mansion at the cost of torn coattails and lost bonnets. The journalist Noah Brooks was relieved when he finally reached the Blue Room, where a single line formed to shake the president's hand. He had recently noted how Lincoln's appearance had "grievously altered from the happy-faced Springfield lawyer" he had first met in 1856. "His hair is grizzled, his gait more stooping, his countenance sallow, and there is a sunken, deathly look about the large, cavernous eyes." Nonetheless, the president greeted every visitor with a smile and a kind remark, "his blessed old pump handle working steadily" to ensure that his "People's Levee" would be a success. Benjamin French, standing beside Mary during the first part of the public reception, noted her doleful appearance. "Oh Mr. French," she said, "how much we have passed through since last we stood here." This was the first reception since Willie's death, and Mary was "too much overcome by her feelings to remain until it ended."

After mingling with the crowd, Noah Brooks took his California friends "a-calling" at the homes of various cabinet members. It was a beautiful, sunny day, and the streets were jammed with carriages. At Chase's mansion, they were greeted by a "young gentleman of color who had a double row of silver plated buttons from his throat to his toes." Handing their "pasteboards" to the doorkeeper, they were brought into the crowded parlor, where they shook hands with the secretary and his "very beautiful" daughter. Chase was "gentlemanly in his manners," Brooks noted, "though he has a painful way of holding his head straight, which leads one to fancy that his shirt collar cuts his ears." Their next stop was Seward's Lafayette Square house, where Brooks's eye, initially drawn to the elegant furnishings in the upstairs parlor, came to rest on "the prodigious nose" of the secretary, who greeted each visitor "with all of his matchless *suaviter in modo.*"

Of all the receptions that day, the Stantons' was the most elaborate. Brooks was overwhelmed by the abundant supply of "oysters, salads, game pastries, fruits, cake, wines . . . arranged with a most gorgeous display of china, glass, and silver." Remarking on Stanton's "little, aristocratic wife," Ellen, Brooks wondered if her lavish style was depleting the fortune Stanton had accumulated during his years as a lawyer. His observation was perceptive: while Stanton's salary had been reduced markedly by his decision to leave private practice, Ellen continued to spend money as though large retainers were still coming in. Yet Stanton refused to puncture Ellen's dreams, even as his rapidly diminishing wealth stirred old worries about bankruptcy.

At 2 p.m., Lincoln, wearily finished with his own reception, returned to his office. Seward and Fred soon joined him, carrying the corrected proclamation in a large portfolio. Not wishing to delay any longer, Lincoln commenced the signing. As the parchment was unrolled before him, he "took a pen, dipped it in ink, moved his hand to the place for the signature," but then, his hand trembling, he stopped and put the pen down.

"I never, in my life, felt more certain that I was doing right, than I do in signing this paper," he said. "If my name ever goes into history it will be for this act, and my whole soul is in it." His arm was "stiff and numb" from shaking hands for three hours, however. "If my hand trembles when I sign the Proclamation," Lincoln said, "all who examine the document hereafter will say, 'He hesitated.' " So the president waited a moment and then took up the pen once more, "slowly and carefully" writing his name. "The signature proved to be unusually bold, clear, and firm, even for him," Fred

Seward recalled, "and a laugh followed, at his apprehensions." The secretary of state added his own name and carried it back to the State Department, where the great seal of the United States was affixed before copies were sent out to the press.

In cities and towns all across the North, people had anxiously waited for word of Lincoln's action. Count Gurowski was in despair as the day dragged on without confirmation that the proclamation had been signed. "Has Lincoln played false to humanity?" he wondered. At Tremont Temple in Boston, where snow covered the ground, an audience of three thousand had gathered since morning, anticipating "the first flash of the electric wires." Frederick Douglass was there, along with two other antislavery leaders, John S. Rock and Anna Dickinson. At the nearby Music Hall, another expectant crowd had formed, including the eminent authors Henry Wadsworth Longfellow, Ralph Waldo Emerson, John Greenleaf Whittier, Harriet Beecher Stowe, and Oliver Wendell Holmes. "Every moment of waiting chilled our hopes, and strengthened our fears," Douglass recalled. "A line of messengers" connected the telegraph office with the platform at Tremont Temple, and although the time was passed with speeches, as it reached nine and then ten o'clock without any word, "a visible shadow" fell upon the crowd.

"On the side of doubt," Douglass recalled, "it was said that Mr. Lincoln's kindly nature [toward the South] might cause him to relent at the last moment." It was rumored that Mary Lincoln, "coming from an old slaveholding family," might have stayed his hand, persuading him to "give the slaveholders one other chance." These speculations, which "had absolutely no foundation," hurt Mary "to the quick," her niece Katherine noted. In fact, Mary had rushed a photograph of her husband to Sumner's abolitionist friend Harvard president Josiah Quincy, hoping it would "reach him, by the 1st of Jan" to mark the joyous occasion.

Finally, at roughly 10 p.m., when the anxiety at Tremont Temple "was becoming agony," a man raced through the crowd. "It is coming! It is on the wires!!" Douglass would long remember the "wild and grand" reaction, the shouts of "joy and gladness," the audible sobs and visible tears. The happy crowd celebrated with music and song, dispersing at dawn. A similar elation poured forth in the Music Hall. "It was a sublime moment," Quincy's daughter, Eliza, wrote Mary; "the thought of the millions upon millions of human beings whose happiness was to be affected & freedom secured by the words of President Lincoln, was almost overwhelming. . . . I wish you & the President could have enjoyed it with us, here."

In Washington, a crowd of serenaders gathered at the White House to applaud Lincoln's action. The president came to the window and silently bowed to the crowd. The signed proclamation rendered words unnecessary. While its immediate effects were limited, since it applied only to enslaved blacks behind rebel lines, the Emancipation Proclamation changed forever the relationship of the national government to slavery. Where slavery had been protected by the national government, it was now "under its ban." The armed forces that had returned fugitive slaves to bondage would be employed in securing their freedom. "Whatever partial reverses may attend its progress," the *Boston Daily Evening Transcript* predicted, "Slavery from this hour ceases to be a political power in the country . . . such a righteous revolution as it inaugurates never goes backward." Ohio congressman-elect James Garfield agreed, though he retained a low opinion of Lincoln, doubtless shaped by his close friendship with Chase. "Strange phenomenon in the world's history," he wrote, "when a second-rate Illinois lawyer is the instrument to utter words which shall form an epoch memorable in all future ages."

Lincoln did not need any such confirmation of the historic nature of the edict. "Fellow-citizens," he had said in his annual message in December, "*we* cannot escape history. We of this Congress and this administration, will be remembered in spite of ourselves. No personal significance, or insignificance, can spare one or another of us. The fiery trial through which we pass, will light us down, in honor or dishonor, to the latest generation."

When Joshua Speed next came to visit, Lincoln reminded his old friend of the suicidal depression he had suffered two decades earlier, and of his disclosure that he would gladly die but that he "had done nothing to make any human being remember that he had lived." Now, indicating his Emancipation Proclamation, he declared: "I believe that in this measure . . . my fondest hopes will be realized."

• • •

GRAVE QUESTIONS REMAINED: Had Lincoln chosen the right moment to issue his revolutionary edict? Would the Union cause be helped or hindered? Even Republican papers worried that the edict would create "discord in the North and concord in the South," strengthening "the spirit of the rebellion" while it diminished "the spirit of the nation." Lincoln's most intimate counselor, Seward, repeatedly warned that the situation demanded "union and harmony, in order to save the country from destruction."

All his life, Lincoln had exhibited an exceptionally sensitive grasp of the limits set by public opinion. As a politician, he had an intuitive sense of when to hold fast, when to wait, and when to lead. "It is my conviction," Lincoln later said, "that, had the proclamation been issued even six months earlier than it was, public sentiment would not have sustained it." If the question of "*slavery and quiet*" as opposed to war and abolition had been placed before the American people in a vote at the time of Fort Sumter, Walt Whitman wrote, the former "would have triumphantly carried the day in a majority of the Northern States—in the large cities, leading off with New York and Philadelphia, by tremendous majorities." In other words, the North would not fight to end slavery, but it would and did fight to preserve the Union. Lincoln had known this and realized that any assault on slavery would have to await a change in public attitudes.

The proposition to enlist blacks in the armed forces had required a similar period of preparation. "A man watches his pear-tree day after day, impatient for the ripening of the fruit," Lincoln explained. "Let him attempt to *force* the process, and he may spoil both fruit and tree. But let him patiently *wait*, and the ripe pear at length falls into his lap!" He had watched "this great revolution in public sentiment slowly but *surely* progressing." He saw this gradual shift in newspaper editorials, in conversations with people throughout the North, and in the views expressed by the troops during his own visits to the field. He had witnessed the subtle changes in the opinions of his cabinet colleagues, even those who represented the more conservative points of view. Although he knew that opposition would still be fierce, he believed it was no longer "strong enough to defeat the purpose."

Events soon tested Lincoln's belief. In the weeks that followed the issuance of the proclamation, the tenuous coalition of Democrats and Republicans that had supported the war showed signs of disintegration. In New York, the newly elected Democratic governor Horatio Seymour denounced emancipation in his inaugural message. In Kentucky, Governor James Robinson recommended that the state legislature reject the proclamation. Heavily Democratic legislatures in Illinois and Indiana threatened to sever ties with abolitionist New England and ally their states with the states of the lower Mississippi in order to end the war with slavery intact. "Every Democratic paper in Indiana is teeming with abuse of New England," Indiana governor Oliver Morton warned Stanton. "They allege that New England has brought upon us the War by a fanatical crusade against Slavery." As reports filtered into the White House, John Nicolay feared that "under the subterfuge of opposing the Emancipation Proclamation," a portion of the Democratic Party was "really organizing to oppose the War."

The "fire in the rear," in Lincoln's phrase, was fed by the lack of military progress. Heavy rains in January followed by a succession of snowstorms in February and March forced the demoralized Army of the Potomac into winter quarters on the north side of the Rappahannock. Nature conspired against Grant's Army of the Tennessee as well. Between February and March, four different attempts to capture Vicksburg failed, preventing the Union from gaining control of the Mississippi River. "This winter is, indeed, the Valley Forge of the war," one officer wrote.

In the Congress, the Peace Democrats, popularly known as Copperheads, thought war measures had strayed too far from simply repressing the rebellion and restoring the Union as it had been, and thus vigorously opposed legislation to reform the banking system, emancipate the slaves, and curtail civil liberties. They especially railed against the conscription law, which authorized provost marshals in every congressional district to enroll men between twenty and forty-five for a term of three years. As the March 4 date of adjournment neared, they engaged in a variety of tactics to suppress votes on all of these key measures. They hid out in the House lobbies and cloakrooms during quorum calls, attached unacceptable amendments onto each of the bills, and kept the Senate up day and night with filibusters.

In the House, Copperhead Clement Vallandigham, a lame duck congressman from Ohio, took the lead. He delivered a series of violent antiwar speeches that attracted national attention. As he warmed to his theme, Noah Brooks observed, his face "fearfully changed," his agreeable smile gave way to "a vindictive, ghastly grin," his smooth voice rose "higher and higher" until it reached a piercing shriek that echoed through the chamber. "Ought this war to continue?" Vallandigham thundered, depicting a war purportedly waged to defend the Union, now become "a war for the negro." He answered: "no—not a day, not an hour." The time had come for the soldiers on both sides to go home. Let the Northwest and the Old South come together in compromise. If New England did not want to remain in a Union with slavery intact, then let her go.

In the Senate, Willard Saulsbury of Delaware took to the floor to prevent a vote sustaining the administration on the suspension of habeas corpus. He could hardly keep his footing during a liquor-fueled harangue, while he inveighed against the president "in language fit only for a drunken fishwife," calling him "an imbecile" and claiming that he was "the weakest man ever placed in a high office." Called to order by Vice President Hamlin, he refused to take his seat. When the sergeant at arms approached to take Saulsbury into custody, he pulled out his revolver. "Damn you," he said, pointing the pistol at the sergeant's head, "if you touch me I'll shoot you dead." The wild scene continued for some time before Saulsbury was removed from the Senate floor.

The brouhaha on Capitol Hill troubled Lincoln less than repeated reports of growing disaffection in the army. Admiral Foote claimed that the proclamation was having a "baneful" impact on the troops, "damping their zeal and ardor, and producing discontent at the idea of fighting only for the negro." Orville Browning, who considered the proclamation a fatal mistake, warned Lincoln that recruiting new volunteers would be nearly impossible and that "an attempt to draft would probably be made the occasion of resistance to the government." Browning had talked with some friends upon their return from the front, where they had "conversed with a great many soldiers, all of whom expressed the greatest dissatisfaction, saying they had been deceived—that the[y] volunteered to fight for the Country, and had they known it was to be converted into a war for the negro they would not have enlisted. They think that scarcely one of the 200,000 whose term of service is soon to expire will re enlist."

Patiently, Lincoln weathered criticisms from Browning and a host of others. He listened carefully when David Davis, who, more than anyone, had helped engineer his victory at the Chicago convention and whom he had recently appointed to the Supreme Court, warned him about "the alarming condition of things." Yet when Davis told Lincoln to alter his policy of emancipation "as the only means of saving the Country," Lincoln told him it was "a fixed thing." And when Browning raised the specter that "the democrats would soon begin to clamor for compromise," Lincoln replied that if they moved toward concessions, "the people would leave them." Through the worst days of discord and division, Lincoln never lost his confidence that he understood the will and desires of the people.

"The resources, advantages, and powers of the American people are very great," he wrote the workingmen of London when they congratulated him on emancipation, "and they have, consequently, succeeded to equally great responsibilities. It seems to have devolved upon them to test whether a government, established on the principles of human freedom, can be maintained."

While his anxious friends observed only the rancor on Capitol Hill, Lincoln noted that before Congress adjourned on March 4, the people's representatives had passed every single one of the administration's war-related bills. They had supported the vital banking and currency legislation that would provide the financial foundation for a long and costly war, as well as the conscription bill, called by the *New York Times* "the grandest pledge yet given that our Government means to prevail."

Moreover, with Lincoln's blessings, monster mass rallies in city after city throughout the North were organized to express popular support for the war against the defeatism of the Copperheads. In New York, the *Times* reported, the "largest popular gathering ever held in this City" thronged

Madison Square to hear General Scott speak and to "cheer with hearty voice each testimony of fealty to the land of the free and the home of the brave." In Washington, Lincoln and his cabinet attended a giant Union rally at the Capitol, hailed as "the greatest popular demonstration ever known in Washington." A journalist noted that while Lincoln was dressed more plainly than the others on the platform, with "no sign of watch chain, white bosom or color . . . he wore on his breast, an immense jewel, the value of which I can form no estimate." She was speaking of little Tad, snuggled against his father's chest. Though he occasionally grew restless during the long speeches and jumped off his father's lap to wander along the platform, Tad quickly returned to the security of his father's embrace.

Scheduled for early April, the congressional and state elections in Connecticut, Rhode Island, and New Hampshire would be a test case in the battle for the heart of the North. Lincoln sent a telegram to Thurlow Weed at the Astor House in New York, requesting that he take the first train to Washington. Weed arrived the next morning, had breakfast with Seward, and met with Lincoln at the White House. "Mr. Weed, we are in a tight place," Lincoln explained. "Money for legitimate purposes is needed immediately; but there is no appropriation from which it can be lawfully taken. I didn't know how to raise it, and so I sent for you." The amount needed was $15,000. Weed returned to New York on the next train. Before the night had ended, "the Dictator" had persuaded fifteen New Yorkers to contribute $1,000 each. Although Weed later claimed that he was ignorant of the purpose of the secret fund, it is most likely, as Welles speculated, that it helped finance a plan worked out between Seward and Lincoln "to influence the New Hampshire and Connecticut elections."

It was money well spent. Voters in both states defeated the Copperhead candidates by clear majorities, ensuring that the great war measures would be sustained in the next House of Representatives. The results were "a stunning blow to the Copperheads," the *New York Times* noted. The surprising triumph "puts the Administration safely round the cape, and insures it clear seas to the end." John Hay reveled in the thought that the elections had "frightened" and "disheartened" the rebels and their sympathizers, who had expected war weariness to depress voter sentiment. "I rejoiced with my whole heart in your loyal victory," Stanton told an administration supporter in Connecticut. "It was in my judgement the most important election held since the War commenced."

"The feeling of the country is I think every day becoming more hopeful and buoyant," Nicolay told his fiancée, "a very healthy reaction against Copperheadism becoming everywhere manifest." Noah Brooks detected a similar shift in mood. "The glamour which the insidious enemies of the

Union had for a while cast over the minds of the people of the North is disappearing," he noted. The Copperheads "find that they have gone too fast and too far" in talking of a compromise peace, "and they have brought upon themselves the denunciations" of Republicans and loyal "War Democrats" alike.

This was precisely what Lincoln had anticipated in the dark days of January when he told Browning that "the people" would never sustain the Copperheads' call for peace on any terms. He had let the reaction against the defeatist propositions grow, then worked to mobilize the renewed Union spirit.

• • •

AMID THE CLAMOROUS OPPOSITION in Congress, the continued threats of intervention from abroad, and the stalemate in the war, Lincoln remained remarkably calm, good-natured, and self-controlled. While Chase confessed to an unremitting anxiety and Stanton suffered from repeated bouts of exhaustion, Lincoln found numerous ways to sustain his spirits. No matter how brutally trying his days, he still found time in the evenings to call at Seward's house, where he was assured of good conversation and much-needed relaxation.

Seward appreciated Lincoln's original mind and his keen wit. Fanny told of an intimate evening in their parlor when Lincoln engaged the entire family with an amusing tale about young women during the War of 1812 who made belts with engraved mottoes to give their lovers departing for battle. When one young girl suggested "Liberty or Death!," her soldier protested that the phrase was "rather strong." Couldn't she make it "Liberty or *be crippled*" instead? Although Seward laughed as uproariously as Lincoln, it is certain that neither Chase nor the serious-minded Stanton would have enjoyed such broad humor. Nor would either have approved of the grim levity of Lincoln's response to a gentleman who had waited for weeks to receive a pass to Richmond. "Well," said Lincoln, "I would be very happy to oblige you, if my passes were respected: but the fact is, sir, I have, within the past two years, given passes to two hundred and fifty thousand men to go to Richmond, and not one has got there yet."

Like Lincoln, Seward usually possessed a profound self-assurance that enabled him to withstand an endless, savage barrage of criticism. Noah Brooks noted that he was unfailingly cheerful, "smoking cigars always, ruffled or excited never, astute, keen to perceive a joke, appreciative of a good thing, and fond of 'good victuals.' " Newsmen loved to hear Seward's stories and he loved to tell them. At one dinner party, he talked nonstop from five-thirty to eleven o'clock. What left the deeper impression upon his listeners, however, was Seward's unconditional love for Lincoln, whom he praised "without limitation" as "the best and wisest man he [had] ever known."

On the nights he did not spend with Seward, Lincoln found welcome diversion in the telegraph office, where he could stretch his legs, rest his feet on the table, and enjoy the company of the young telegraph operators. He sought out Captains Dahlgren and Fox, whose conversation always cheered him. Describing a pleasant evening in Captain Fox's room, Dahlgren remarked that "Abe was in good humor, and at leaving said, 'Well I will go home; I had no business here; but, as the lawyer said, I had none anywhere else.' "

Occasionally, late at night, Lincoln would rouse John Hay. Seated on the edge of his young aide's bed, or calling him into the office, the president would read aloud favorite passages ranging from Shakespeare to the humorist Thomas Hood. Hay recorded one occasion, "a little after midnight," when Lincoln, with amused gusto, read a portion of Hood, "utterly unconscious that he with his short shirt hanging about his long legs & setting out behind like the tail feathers of an enormous ostrich was infinitely funnier than anything in the book he was laughing at. What a man it is! Occupied all day with matters of vast moment . . . he yet has such a wealth of simple bonhommie & good fellow ship that he gets out of bed & perambulates the house in his shirt to find us that we may share with him the fun of one of poor Hoods queer little conceits."

Lincoln's evening rambles suggest that Mary's continuing depression over Willie precluded easy relaxation at home. "Only those, who have passed through such bereavements, can realize, how the heart bleeds," Mary admitted to Mary Jane Welles. Yet despite the desolation that still tormented her, Mary had gamely resumed her duties as first lady, telling Benjamin French that she felt responsible to "receive the world at large" and would endeavor "to bear up" under her sorrow. French, in turn, marveled at the "affable and pleasant" demeanor the first lady regularly displayed in public. "The skeleton," he noted, "is always kept out of sight."

As the anniversary of Willie's death approached, Robert came down from Harvard to spend a few weeks with his family. Encountering him at a number of parties, Fanny Seward found him to be a delightful young man, "much shorter than his father," with "a good, strong face," though not an especially handsome one. "I talked some time with him. He is ready and easy in conversation—having, I fancy, considerable humor in his composition."

With the official mourning period behind them, the Lincolns resumed the weekly public receptions they both enjoyed despite the exhausting rounds of handshaking. In gratitude to Rebecca Pomroy, the nurse who had cared for Tad after Willie died, Mary arranged for all the nurses, officers, and soldiers at Pomroy's hospital to attend a grand White House reception in early March. Mrs. Pomroy instructed the soldiers "to provide themselves with clean white gloves, and to look their best." The White House that night was "brilliantly lighted and decorated with flowers in the greatest profusion." Pomroy was certain that her soldiers would remember this night, declaring that if they survived the war, "they will tell their children's children" of their enchanting evening at the White House.

The abolitionist Jane Grey Swisshelm had initially been reluctant to join her friends at one of these Saturday receptions. She had no interest in meeting Mary Lincoln after the tales suggesting the first lady's sympathy with the Confederate cause. Yet when she was actually introduced to Mary, she realized at once that the stories were slanderous gossip. "When I came to Mrs. Lincoln, she did not catch the name at first, and asked to hear it again, then repeated it, and a sudden glow of pleasure lit her face, as she held out her hand and said how very glad she was to see me. I objected to giving her my hand because my black glove would soil her white one; but she said: 'Then I shall preserve the glove to remember a great pleasure, for I have long wished to see you.' " Over time, as the two women developed a close friendship, Swisshelm came to believe that Mary was "more staunch even than her husband in opposition to the Rebellion and its cause."

In February, Mary was delighted and surprised by Lincoln's impulsive agreement to attend a séance in Georgetown featuring a celebrated medium, Nettie Colburn. The good-looking young woman's sessions attracted many distinguished people, including Joshua Speed, who described Nettie and a fellow medium to Lincoln as "very choice spirits, themselves. It will I am sure be some relief from the tedious round of office seekers to see two such agreeable ladies." When the president and first lady arrived, the host said: "Welcome, Mr. Lincoln . . . you were expected." Lincoln stopped short. "Expected! *Why, it is only five minutes since I knew that I was coming.*" The guests settled into chairs for the presentation, which, according to the Philadelphia banker S. P. Kase, included a piano that "began to move up and down in accord with the rise and fall of the music." Intrigued by the mechanics behind such spectacles, Lincoln told one of the soldiers present to sit on the piano to weigh it down. When it continued to move, the president himself "stepped to the end of the piano and added his weight to that of the soldiers." When the rise and fall of the piano persisted, Lincoln "resumed his seat in one of the large horse hair easy chairs of the day."

At this juncture, Nettie Colburn entered the room, and Lincoln addressed her cheerfully: "Well, Miss Nettie, do you think you have anything to say to me to-night?" There is no evidence that Lincoln believed in spiritualism. On the contrary, after hearing the mysterious clicking sounds in the presence of another medium the previous summer, he had asked the head of the Smithsonian, Joseph Henry, to discover how the noises were produced. Henry interviewed the medium, Lord Colchester, who, unsurprisingly, revealed nothing. Not long afterward, Henry happened to be seated on a train beside a young man who revealed that he manufactured telegraphic devices for spiritualists. Placed around the biceps, the instrument produced telegraphic clicks when the medium stretched his muscle. Asked if he had sold one to Lord Colchester, the young man said yes. Lincoln was reportedly "pleased to learn the secret."

Lincoln's lack of belief did not prevent him, however, from enjoying the evening's entertainment. Nettie was an accomplished actress, ably mimicking the booming baritone of Daniel Webster or the frail voice of an Indian maiden. She spoke for an hour, channeling one voice and then another as she related historical episodes from the landing of the Pilgrims to the current war. Her oration, which carried a passionate abolitionist message, seemed to S. P. Kase "the grandest" he had ever heard. When the spirits left her, she departed as abruptly as she had arrived. All was silent for a while, then "the President turned in his seat, threw his long right leg over the arm of his chair," and exclaimed, "Was not this wonderful?" He seemed to have viewed Nettie's performance with the same pleasure he derived from the theater—respite from the cares of the day.

• • •

CHASE, UNLIKE LINCOLN, was never able to forgo his statesmanlike persona and simply enjoy conversations and lighter amusements. He was inclined to let things fester, brooding over perceived slights and restlessly calculating the effect of every incident on his own standing. Weeks after the cabinet crisis had been resolved, he questioned his own decision to stay on board. "I have neither love nor taste for the position I occupy," he told Horace Greeley, "and have only two great regrets connected with it—one, that I ever took it; the other, that having resigned it I yielded to the counsels of those who said I must resume it."

Chase became physically ill during the tumultuous debate on Capitol Hill over his banking bill, terrified that the measures necessary to finance the war would not make it through. When the bills passed and the new greenbacks were ready for distribution, he momentarily basked in the knowledge that the Treasury was full for the first time since the war began.

He was also pleased by the fact that his own handsome face would appear in the left-hand corner of every dollar bill. He had deliberately chosen to place his picture on the ubiquitous one-dollar bill rather than a bill of a higher denomination, knowing that his image would thus reach the greatest number of people. His mood quickly darkened when he contemplated his own strained finances, however, and feared that his personal investments with Jay Cooke and his brother, Henry, might be misconstrued. Their virtual monopoly over the government bond business was beginning to attract negative newspaper comment, though they had succeeded brilliantly in selling the war bonds to the public.

The stormy and irascible secretary of war also seemed unable to relax or distract himself from the incessant pressures of his office. Stanton's clerk, Charles Benjamin, recalled that "a word or a gesture would set [Stanton] aflame in an instant. He would dash the glasses before his eyes far up on his forehead, as though they pained or obstructed his vision; the muscles of his face would become agitated, and his voice would tremble and grow intense, without elevation." Though "the storm would pass away as quickly as it came," and though Stanton would quickly make amends to victims of his ill humor, the employees in the War Department, while respecting Stanton greatly, never loved him as Lincoln's aides loved their president.

Stanton also lacked Lincoln's ability to put grudges behind him. When asked why he disliked the Sanitary Commission, which had done so much to promote healthy conditions in the army camps, Stanton replied that the commission had persuaded the president and the Senate to appoint a surgeon general against his vigorous objections. "I'm not used to being beaten, and don't like it," he said, "and therefore I am hostile to the Commission." In fact, Stanton admitted, he "detested it."

Those who worked with Stanton attributed his "nervous irritability" to the combination of overwork and poor health. At times, his asthma became so severe that he collapsed in "violent fits of strangulation." Still, he refused to take a break. When doctors pleaded with him to get some rest and exercise, he insisted that he wanted only to be kept alive until the war ended and then, and only then, would he consent to seek rest. Though he loved good conversation and had built his large house in order to gather interesting people around his table, he stayed in the War Department day and night, rarely enjoying the convivial evenings that replenished Seward and Lincoln or that Kate provided for Chase. And while he enjoyed reading novels, with a special preference for Dickens, Stanton seldom found the time to unwind with a book. Instead, one of his clerks recalled, when he wanted "an hour's rest," he would lock his door, lie on his couch, and peruse English periodicals sympathetic to the Confederate cause, endeavoring to better understand the British attitude to the war.

Unlike Seward, who had promptly brought Fred into the State Department and relished the professional and personal support of his own son, Stanton had no family member or intimate friend to rely upon for daily counsel. Except for the initial appointment of his brother-in-law Christopher Wolcott as assistant secretary of war, Stanton refused to bring any of his relatives into his department. When Senator Ben Wade recommended an appointment for Stanton's capable cousin William, the secretary angrily declared that no relative would have any "office in his gift" so long as he remained at his post. John Hay went so far as to remark that he "would rather make the tour of a small-pox hospital" than be forced to ask Stanton for a favor. Even when Stanton's own son, Edwin Junior, wanted to serve as his private secretary after graduating from Kenyon, Stanton refused to bend. Only after months of unpaid labor for an assistant secretary did the boy receive his father's consent to an official appointment.

Stanton rarely returned to Steubenville during the war. During the winter of 1862, Christopher Wolcott had become seriously ill. When he died in April 1863, Stanton and his son boarded a special train to join Stanton's sister for the funeral in Ohio. Pamphila's conviction that her husband had died from overwork must have made Stanton's attempts at consolation difficult. Though he tried to relax on his old home ground, revisit the places he had loved, Stanton returned to Washington more exhausted than restored.

As the pressure on all the key administration officials mounted, Lincoln, with the hardest task of all, maintained the most generous and even-tempered disposition. Even he, however, was sorely tried on occasion. After recommending that the War Department utilize the services of a meteorologist, Francis Capen, Lincoln was exasperated when none of Capen's presumably scientific predictions proved correct. "It seems to me Mr. Capen knows nothing about the weather, in advance," Lincoln wrote three days after Capen had assured him it would not rain for five or six days. "It is raining now & has been for ten hours. I can not spare any more time to Mr. Capen." He was more irritated when warring factions in Missouri refused to reconcile. He informed the recalcitrant groups that their continuing feud was "very painful" for him. "I have been tormented with it beyond endurance for months, by both sides. Neither side pays the least respect to my appeals to your reason. I am now compelled to take hold of the case."

But Lincoln refused to let resentments rankle. Discovering that a hastily written note to General Franz Sigel had upset the general, he swiftly followed up with another. "I was a little cross," he told Sigel, "I ask pardon. If I do get up a little temper I have no sufficient time to keep it up." Such gestures on Lincoln's part repaired injured feelings that might have escalated into lasting animosity.

The story is told of an army colonel who rode out to the Soldiers' Home, hopeful of securing Lincoln's aid in recovering the body of his wife, who had died in a steamboat accident. His brief period of relaxation interrupted, Lincoln listened to the colonel's tale but offered no help. "Am I to have no rest? Is there no hour or spot when or where I may escape this constant call? Why do you follow me out here with such business as this?" The disheartened colonel returned to his hotel in Washington. The following morning, Lincoln appeared at his door. "I was a brute last night," Lincoln said, offering to help the colonel in any way possible.

Republican stalwart Carl Schurz relates an equally remarkable encounter in the wake of an unpleasant written exchange that initially seemed to threaten his friendship with Lincoln. Discouraged by the lack of progress in the war, Schurz had blamed Lincoln's misguided appointment of Democrats "whose hearts" were not fully "in the struggle" to top positions in the field. Lincoln had responded testily, telling Schurz that he obviously wanted men with "heart in it." The question was "who is to be the judge of hearts, or of 'heart in it?' If I must discard my own judgment, and take yours, I must also take that of others; and by the time I should reject all I should be advised to reject, I should have none left, Republicans or others—not even yourself." Schurz, at the army camp in Centreville, Virginia, where he led the Third Division of the 11th Corps, detected in Lincoln's long reply "an undertone of impatience, of irritation, unusual with him." Though he had been encouraged by the president to correspond freely, he feared that his letter had transgressed.

Several days later, a messenger arrived at Schurz's encampment with an invitation from Lincoln "to come to see him as soon as my duties would permit." Obtaining permission to leave that same day, Schurz reached the White House at seven the next morning. He found Lincoln upstairs in his comfortable armchair, clad in his slippers. "He greeted me cordially as of old and bade me pull up a chair and sit by his side. Then he brought his large hand with a slap down on my knee and said with a smile: 'Now tell me, young man, whether you really think that I am as poor a fellow as you have made me out in your letter!' " Flustered, Schurz hesitantly explained the reason behind his tirade. Lincoln listened patiently and then delineated his own situation, explaining that his terse reply had been provoked by a hailstorm of criticism that had been pelting down on him. "Then, slapping my knee again, he broke out in a loud laugh and exclaimed: 'Didn't I give it to you hard in my letter? Didn't I? But it didn't hurt, did it? I did not mean to, and therefore I wanted you to come so quickly.' " Lincoln and Schurz talked for an hour, at the end of which Schurz asked whether his letters were still welcome. " 'Why, certainly,' he answered; 'write me whenever the spirit moves you.' We parted as better friends than ever."

• • •

To CELEBRATE Tad's tenth birthday on Saturday, April 4, Mary Lincoln proposed a family excursion by steamer and train to the Army of the Potomac headquarters in Falmouth, Virginia. Delighted by the chance to escape from Washington, Lincoln organized a small traveling party, including his old Illinois friend Dr. Anson Henry, Noah Brooks, and, at Henry's suggestion, Edward Bates. Dr. Henry had maintained a friendship with Bates over the years and considered him "one of the purest and best men in the world." Bates agreed to the foray, hoping to visit his son Coalter, who was with Hooker's army; as it happened, Coalter had just left to pay a final visit to the family in Washington before the expected spring battles began.

The little party left the White House in the midst of a furious blizzard. Gale winds blew clouds of dust and snow in all directions as they boarded the steamer *Carrie Martin* at sunset. They headed south past Alexandria and Mount Vernon, where, according to the custom of the river, a bell tolled a salute in honor of George Washington. The steamer was due to reach the army supply depot at Aquia Creek that evening, but the escalating storm required them to cast anchor in a protected cove for the night. Undeterred by the falling snow and the howling winds that drove everyone else to the warm comfort of the cabin, Tad remained on deck with his fishing line, determined to provide food for supper. Racing in to announce every bite to his parents, Tad finally caught a small fish that, much to his delight, was added to the dinner menu. Brooks marveled at the simplicity of the scene, watching "the chief magistrate of this mighty nation" relax with family and friends, "telling stories" and conversing in "a free and easy way," with no servant standing by and no guard on deck. Had the rebels known their whereabouts, Brooks mused, they "might have gobbled up the entire party without firing a shot."

The snowstorm was "at its height" when the *Carrie Martin* pulled into the busy dock at Aquia Creek, where, on Easter morning, the presidential party boarded a special train for Falmouth Station. Along the way, with "snow piled in huge drifts" and "the wind whistling fiercely over the hills," they passed one army camp after another. Each encampment along the thirty miles had hundreds of campfires surrounded by tents, fortifications, and stockades. Disembarking at Falmouth Station, they were taken by closed carriage over rough roads to Hooker's headquarters a half mile away. Situated about three miles from the Rappahannock, the headquarters resembled a small city, complete with telegraph office, printing establishment, bakery, post office, and accommodations for more than 133,000 soldiers.

General Hooker, tall and broad-shouldered, awaited them in front of his tent, which stood at the end of a wide street flanked with officers' tents on both sides. He greeted the party of six and beckoned them into his comfortable quarters, furnished with a large fireplace, two beds, chairs for the entire party, and a long table covered with papers and books.

Lincoln liked and respected Hooker. When he had tendered him command of the Army of the Potomac ten weeks earlier, he had sent along a remarkable letter of advice. "I believe you to be a brave and a skillful soldier," the letter began. "You have confidence in yourself, which is valuable, if not an indispensable quality. You are ambitious, which, within reasonable bounds, does good rather than harm. But I think that during Gen. Burnside's command of the Army, you have taken counsel of your ambition, and thwarted him as much as you could, in which you did a great wrong to the country, and to a most meritorious and honorable brother officer." Lincoln continued with an admonition about Hooker's recent comments suggesting the need for a dictator to assume command of "both the Army and the Government." He informed Hooker that "it was not *for* this, but in spite of it, that I have given you the command. Only those generals who gain successes, can set up dictators. What I now ask of you is military success, and I will risk the dictatorship." The president closed with shrewd words of guidance: "Beware of rashness, but with energy, and sleepless vigilance, go forward, and give us victories." Aside from the wisdom of the advice, the letter clearly manifests Lincoln's growing confidence in his own powers.

Hooker took the advice in stride. In fact, he was so moved by the kindhearted tone of the letter that over the next few days he read it aloud to various people, including Noah Brooks and Dr. Henry, who thought it should be printed in gold letters. "That is just such a letter as a father might write to his son," Hooker fervently told Brooks as the young journalist sat with him before a fire in his tent. "It is a beautiful letter," Hooker continued, "and, although I think he was harder on me than I deserved, I will say that I love the man who wrote it."

Reporters noted Mary's curiosity about every aspect of camp life; they commented on her simple attire and speculated that this was her first experience sleeping in a tent. In fact, the first couple's tent was far more elaborately outfitted than an ordinary one. It boasted a plank floor, a stove, and beds especially constructed for the occasion, complete with real sheets, blankets, and pillowcases. As the days went by, the weariness that had marked Mary's face upon arrival began to fade, and "the change seemed pleasant to her." Brooks reported badinage between husband and wife occasioned by a photograph of a Confederate officer with an inscription on the back: "A rebellious rebel." Mary suggested that this meant he "was a rebel against the rebel government." Lincoln smiled, countering that perhaps the officer "wanted everybody to know that he was not only a rebel, but a rebel of rebels—'a double-dyed-in-the-wool sort of rebel.' "

Stormy weather postponed the first grand review from Sunday to Monday afternoon, leaving the president and first lady free to talk at length with the members of Hooker's staff. The irrepressible Tad, meanwhile, inspected every facility in the compound, zealously racing from one place to another. A reporter present at the meetings with Hooker's officers and aides noted that "Lincoln was in unusual good humor," lightening the atmosphere "by his sociability and shafts of wit."

The roar of artillery at noon the next day signaled the start of the cavalry review. With General Hooker by his side, Lincoln rode along serried ranks that stretched for miles over the rolling hills. The soldiers cheered and shouted when they saw the president and cheered even louder when they saw Master Tad Lincoln bravely attempting to keep up, "clinging to the saddle of his pony as tenaciously as the best man among them," his gray cloak flapping "like a flag or banneret."

The boy's "short legs stuck straight out from his saddle," Brooks noted, "and sometimes there was danger that his steed, by a sudden turn in the rough road, would throw him off like a bolt from a catapult." Much to the relief of onlookers, Tad made it through "safe and sound," his reckless riding steadied by a young orderly who remained faithfully by his side. "And thereby hangs a tale," noted a *New York Herald* reporter. The orderly was a thirteen-year-old boy, Gustave Shuman, who had left home when the war began to accompany the New Jersey Brigade. General Philip Kearny had made him his bugler. The boy rode in front of the troops throughout the Peninsula Campaign. When General Kearny was killed in the late summer of 1862, the new commander, Daniel Sickles, retained the boy as bugler. So, though not much older than the president's son, Gustave was a hardened veteran, quite capable of containing the impulsive Tad. Reporters noted that from that first review on, the two boys became inseparable, roaming about the camp like brothers.

Over the next few hours, tens of thousands of troops passed in front of the president and first lady, sweeping one after another "like waves at sea." From atop the little knoll on which the Lincolns were stationed, the endless tiers provided a majestic vista. When the sun came out, one reporter observed, "the sunbeams danced on the rifles and bayonets, and lingered in the folds of the banners." At the review of the infantry and artillery, artists sketched the spectacle of sixty thousand men, "their arms shining in the distance and their bayonets bristling like a forest on the horizon as they disappeared far away."

Lincoln so enjoyed mingling with the men—who appeared amazingly healthy and lavishly outfitted with new uniforms, arms, and equipment—that he extended his visit until Friday. After one review, someone remarked that the regulars could be easily distinguished from the volunteers, for "the former stood rigidly in their places without moving their heads an inch as he rode by, while the latter almost invariably turned their heads to get a glimpse of him." Quick to defend the volunteers, Lincoln replied, "I don't care how much my soldiers turn their heads, if they don't turn their backs."

During a break from the reviews, several members of the presidential party, including Noah Brooks, journeyed down to the Rappahannock for a glimpse of the rebel camps across the river. With the naked eye, they could see the houses and steeples of Fredericksburg. The wooded hills and the renowned plain that had become "a slaughter pen for so many men" in the December battle were also clearly visible. Binoculars allowed a view of the ridge on which thousands of unmarked graves had been dug. Beyond the ridge, smoke rose from the rebel camps with elaborate earthworks, a myriad of white tents, and the flag of stars and bars. At the shoreline, the Union pickets paced their rounds mirrored by rebel sentries across the narrow river. Honoring the "tacit understanding" that sentries would not fire at each other, they bandied comments across the water, hailing each other as "Secesh" or "Yank," and conversing "as amiably as though belonging to friendly armies." At one point, Brooks noted, a Confederate officer "came down to the water's edge, doubtless to see if Uncle Abraham was of our party. Failing to see him, he bowed politely and retired."

Both sides knew that as soon as the weather cleared, the brutal fighting would resume. "It was a saddening thought," Brooks remarked after one impressive review, "that so many of the gallant men whose hearts beat high as they rode past must, in the course of events, be numbered with the slain before many days shall pass." Yet despite the awareness that a major engagement was not far off, "all enjoyed the present after a certain grim fashion and deferred any anxiety for the morrow until that period should arrive." Before he departed, Lincoln issued one final directive to Hooker and his second in command, General Darius Couch. "Gentlemen, in your next battle *put in all your men.*"

Tremendously heartened by the splendid condition of the army and the high spirits and reception of the troops, Lincoln boarded the *Carrie Martin* at sunset on Friday for the return trip to Washington. The *Herald* noted that he "received a salute from all the vessels in port and locomotives on shore, whistles being blown, bells run, and flags displayed."

• • •

LINCOLN RETURNED to the White House to find Blair enraged with Stanton, Welles feuding with Seward, and Chase threatening once again to resign. The Blairs, father and son, were defending James S. Pleasants, a Union man from Maryland who was related to Confederate John Key. Key had sought refuge at Pleasants's house, begging food and shelter. Reluctantly, the loyal Marylander had allowed him to stay at his home. Stanton insisted that such treason deserved the gallows. "The skirmish was sharp & long," Elizabeth Blair told her husband, but finally, the president commuted the sentence to imprisonment. Furthermore, when Lincoln learned of the man's poor health, he agreed, at the Blairs' request, to reduce the sentence. All of this left Stanton "very bitter."

The quarrel between Seward and Welles concerned an English ship captured in neutral waters by a blockade runner. Suspecting that the cargo aboard was meant for the Confederacy, the Union Navy sent the *Peterhoff* to New York for disposition by a prize court. Long-standing tradition dictated that the ship's mail be opened by the court to determine the true destination of the vessel and its cargo. The controversy had aroused strong protest from Britain regarding the sanctity of its mails. Seward, wanting to avoid British intervention at all cost, had agreed to surrender the mails unopened. Furious, Welles claimed that surrender was in violation of international law and would set a terrible precedent. Moreover, Seward had no basis meddling in this issue, since jurisdiction belonged to the Navy Department.

For days, as the unresolved matter led to rumors of war with England, the two colleagues argued the case before Lincoln. They visited him late at night armed with letters explaining their positions, argued in cabinet council, and solicited allies. Sumner backed Welles in the fray, maintaining that England would never go to war over this issue. The president, however, concurred with Seward that at this juncture good relations with England must supersede the legal questions surrounding the mails. Sumner left much disgruntled, considering Lincoln "very ignorant" about the precedents involved. Welles agreed, blaming Seward for "daily, and almost hourly wailing in [Lincoln's] ears the calamities of a war with England," thus diverting the president "from the real question." Montgomery Blair also sided with Welles, telling him after a cabinet meeting that Seward "knows less of public law and of administrative duties than any man who ever held a seat in the Cabinet." In the end, as Seward had advised, the president determined that the mails would be returned unopened to the British government.

Chase's disaffection also weighed heavily on Lincoln that spring. For the third time in five months, Chase threatened to resign his position in the Treasury. His first resignation during the cabinet crisis had been repeated in March when Lincoln, bowing to pressure from a Connecticut senator, had decided not to renominate one of Chase's appointees for collector of internal revenue in Hartford. Livid, Chase informed the president that unless his authority over his own appointments could be established, he could not continue in the cabinet: "I feel that I cannot be useful to you or the country in my present position." Lincoln managed once again to placate Chase, only to receive another threat in short order. This squabble was provoked by Lincoln's removal of one of Chase's appointees in the Puget Sound district who had been accused of speculating in land. Enraged that he was not consulted, Chase argued that he could not function in his department if decisions were made "not only without my concurrence, but without my knowledge." If the president could not respect his authority, Chase wrote, "I will, unhesitatingly, relieve you from all embarrassment so far as I am concerned by tendering you my resignation."

Understanding that "Chase's feelings were hurt," Lincoln set about once again to sooth his ruffled pride. That evening, he later recounted, he called at Chase's house with the resignation in hand. Placing his long arms on Chase's shoulders, he said: "Chase, here is a paper with which I wish to have nothing to do; take it back, and be reasonable." He then explained why he had felt compelled to make the decision, which had taken place in Chase's absence from the city, and promised his touchy secretary that he would have complete authority to name the removed appointee's successor. "I had to plead with him a long time, but I finally succeeded," Lincoln happily noted.

Though irritated by Chase's haughty yet fundamentally insecure nature, Lincoln recognized the superlative accomplishments of his treasury secretary. In the two months since Congress had adjourned, Chase had sold more than $45 million in bonds, and the demand for the bonds was steadily increasing. "Never before did the finances of any nation, in the midst of a great war, work so admirably as do ours," the *New York Times* noted in a laudatory article on Chase. Even as Lincoln deferred to Chase, however, he placed his prickly secretary's third resignation letter on file for future reference.

Monty Blair, meanwhile, resented Chase and showed little respect for his remaining colleagues. He considered Seward "an unprincipled liar" and Stanton "a great scoundrel." In fact, Blair thought the entire cabinet save Welles, and perhaps Bates, whom he liked but did not consider a stalwart ally, should be replaced, and that his father, "the ablest and best informed politician in America," should become Lincoln's "private counsellor." And so one personal struggle succeeded another, complicating the president's job, absorbing his energies.

Lincoln's uneasiness about his warring cabinet colleagues paled in comparison, however, to his disquietude about the impending movements of the Army of the Potomac. On April 13, 1863, three days after Lincoln returned from his trip, Hooker took the first step in what would become known as the Battle of Chancellorsville. He dispatched ten thousand cavalrymen under General George Stoneman to head south and insert themselves between Lee's army and Richmond. With the Confederate supply lines to Richmond severed, Hooker intended to cross the Rappahannock, draw the enemy away from Fredericksburg, and engage him in battle. Heavy rains and impassable roads delayed the advance, but finally, during the last week of April, Hooker's men began crossing the river.

For Lincoln and his cabinet, anxious days followed. "We have been in a terrible suspense here," Nicolay wrote his fiancée on Monday, May 4. Fighting had begun, but there was no "definite information" on the battle's progress. Welles joined Lincoln in the War Department to wait for news that did not come. Bates was particularly tense, knowing that his son John Coalter was with Hooker "in the most active and dangerous service." Lincoln admitted to Francis Blair, Sr., that nobody seemed to know what was going on. Welles found it odd that "no reliable intelligence" was reaching them, correctly surmising that this boded ill. "In the absence of news the President strives to feel encouraged and to inspire others," he wrote, "but I can perceive he has doubts and misgivings, though he does not express them."

"While I am anxious, please do not suppose I am impatient, or waste a moment's thought on me, to your own hindrance, or discomfort," Lincoln had written Hooker at the outset of the campaign. Even when disturbing fragments filtered in, Lincoln refused to pressure Hooker. "God bless you, and all with you. I know you will do your best," he wired his general on the morning of May 6. "Waste no time unnecessarily, to gratify our curiosity with despatches."

At 3 p.m. that afternoon, the suspense ended with an unwelcome telegram from Hooker's chief of staff. The Union forces had been defeated. The army had retreated to its original position on the north side of the Rappahannock, and seventeen thousand Union soldiers were dead, wounded, or missing. Hooker's second in command, General Darius Couch, later claimed that Hooker was simply "outgeneraled" by Lee. Assuming that Lee would "fall back without risking battle," Fighting Joe was "demoralized" by the fierceness of the Confederate attack. Had he committed all his troops, as Lincoln had directed him to do, the course of the battle might have been different. By immediately assuming a defensive stance, however, Hooker gave the initiative to Lee and never regained his footing. An injury sustained on the battlefield further dulled Hooker's perceptions. Though his subordinates wanted to press the battle, he issued the order to retreat.

Noah Brooks was with Lincoln when the news came. "I shall never forget that picture of despair," he later wrote. "Had a thunderbolt fallen upon the President he could not have been more overwhelmed." His beloved army, so healthy and spirited weeks earlier, had been "driven back, torn and bleeding, to our starting point, where the heart-sickening delay, the long and tedious work of reorganizing a decimated and demoralized army would again commence." Observing the president's "ashen" face, Brooks "vaguely took in the thought" that his complexion "almost exactly" matched the French gray wallpaper in the room. "Clasping his hands behind his back, he walked up and down the room, saying, 'My God! my God! What will the country say! What will the country say!' "

The news traveled fast. The president informed Senator Sumner, who rushed to tell Welles. "Lost, lost, all is lost!" Sumner exclaimed, lifting both hands as he entered the navy secretary's office. Welles went to the War Department, where Seward was with Stanton. "I asked Stanton if he knew where Hooker was. He answered curtly, No. I looked at him sharply, and I have no doubt with some incredulity, for he, after a moment's pause, said he is on this side of the river, but I know not where." As the afternoon wore on and endless casualty lists began streaming in, Stanton could no longer hide his despair. "This is the darkest day of the war," he lamented. At the Willard Hotel, Brooks observed, secessionists suddenly "sprang to new life and animation and with smiling faces and ill-suppressed joy" moved openly through the gloomy crowds.

Within the hour of receiving the news, Lincoln ordered a carriage to drive him to the Navy Yard. Accompanied by General Halleck, he boarded a steamer bound for Hooker's headquarters, a grim counterpoint to his joyous April visit. Once again, Lincoln found some redemption in the resolute determination of his troops. "All accounts agree," one reporter wrote from army headquarters, "that the troops on the Rappahannock came out of their late bloody fight game to the backbone." Though "fresh from all the horrors of the battlefield, with ranks decimated, and almost exhausted with exposure and fatigue," they remained "undaunted and erect, composed and ready to turn on the instant and follow their leaders back into the fray."

Moreover, while the Confederates had lost 4,000 fewer men, their casualty list of 13,000 represented a larger percentage of their total forces. In addition, they had lost one of their greatest generals: Thomas "Stonewall" Jackson. Returning from a reconnaissance mission, Jackson had been mistaken for an enemy and was fired upon by some of his own men. His left arm was amputated in a nearby field hospital, but he died of pneumonia eight days later. The South went into mourning. "Since the death of Washington," the *Richmond Whig* proclaimed, "no similar event has so profoundly and sorrowfully impressed the people of Virginia as the death of Jackson."

Lincoln remained at army headquarters for only a few hours. Before leaving, he handed Hooker a letter expressing confidence in the continuing campaign. "If possible," the president wrote, "I would be very glad of another movement early enough to give us some benefit from the fact of the enemies communications being broken, but neither for this reason or any other, do I wish anything done in desperation or rashness." Lincoln made it clear that he stood ready to assist Hooker in the development of a new plan of action. As he had done so many times before, Lincoln withstood the storm of defeat by replacing anguish over an unchangeable past with hope in an uncharted future.

CHAPTER 20

"THE TYCOON IS IN FINE WHACK"

No sooner had Lincoln returned from his May 7 visit to the troops than he was confronted by a colossal political uproar over the arrest and imprisonment of former Ohio congressman Clement Vallandigham on the charge of treason.

The arrest was ordered by General Burnside, who had assumed command of the Department of the Ohio after his replacement by Hooker. Responding to tumultuous peace demonstrations where speakers openly advocated the defeat of the Union's cause, Burnside issued General Orders No. 38, proclaiming that "the habit of declaring sympathy for the enemy will not be allowed in this department." All persons committing "treason, expressed or implied," would be arrested and tried by a military court. In deliberate defiance, Vallandigham incited a large crowd to a frenzy with his passionate denunciations of a failed war. This demagogue of defeat railed that the conflict would end only if soldiers deserted en masse and the people acted to "hurl King Lincoln from his throne."

After reading a transcript of Vallandigham's remarks, Burnside sent his soldiers to arrest him at his home in the middle of the night. "The door resisted the efforts of the soldiers," a local journalist wrote, "and Vallandigham flourished a revolver at the window, and fired two or three shots," but the soldiers made their entry through a side entrance. With unprecedented speed, a military tribunal found him guilty and sentenced him to prison for the remainder of the war. His application for a writ of habeas corpus was denied. When the *Chicago Times* exacerbated the incident with its incendiary coverage, Burnside, on his own authority, shut the paper down.

Learning of these events in the morning newspaper, Lincoln found himself in a difficult position. While he later admitted that the news of the arrest brought him pain, he felt compelled to uphold Burnside. Nonetheless, he anticipated the damaging political fallout. Criticism came not only from Copperheads and Democrats but from loyal Republicans. Thurlow Weed deplored the arrest. Senator Trumbull warned Browning that if such arbitrary arrests continued, "the civil tribunals will be completely subordinated to the military, and the government overthrown." A friend of Seward cautioned him that "by a large and honest portion of the community," the arrest was considered an "invasion of a great principle—the right of free speech," and that it might well precipitate civil war within the loyal states. Seward agreed. Indeed, in a moment of rare accord, every member of the cabinet united in opposition to the Vallandigham arrest.

Lincoln, searching for compromise, publicly supported Vallandigham's arrest but commuted the sentence to banishment within the Confederate lines. There, it was playfully remarked, his Copperhead body could go "where his heart already was." The *New York Times* recorded "general satisfaction" at the solution, which "so happily meets the difficulties of the case—avoiding the possibility of making him a martyr, and yet effectually destroying his power for evil." Escorted by Union cavalry holding a flag of truce, Vallandigham was removed to Tennessee. In an act that further diminished his reputation, he quickly escaped to Canada. Meanwhile, Stanton revoked Burnside's suspension of the *Chicago Times* and informed local officials that they were not to suppress newspapers.

Thus, Lincoln was able to maintain his support for General Burnside while minimizing any violation of civil liberties necessitated by war. Asked months later by a radical to "suppress the infamous 'Chicago Times,' " Lincoln told her, "I fear you do not fully comprehend the danger of abridging the *liberties* of the people. Nothing but the very sternest necessity can ever justify it. A government had better go to the very extreme of toleration, than to do aught that could be construed into an interference with, or to jeopardize in any degree, the common rights of its citizens."

After he dealt with Vallandigham, Lincoln's next priority was to comfort Burnside. Upon hearing that the entire cabinet had opposed his action, the general had offered to resign. Lincoln not only refused the resignation but insisted that while "the cabinet regretted the necessity" of the arrest, once it was done, "all were for seeing you through with it."

Finally, knowing that the public would ultimately be the judge of the administration's actions on the home front, Lincoln began drafting a document that would put the complex matter of military arrests into perspective. He had contemplated the subject for months, but his delineation of his ideas assumed new urgency with the public outrage at the arrest of Vallandigham. "Often an idea about it would occur to me which seemed to have force and make perfect answer to some of the things that were said and written about my actions," he later told a visitor. "I never let one of those ideas escape me, but wrote it on a scrap of paper." Now he would have to cobble those scraps into a cogent argument that the American public would accept.

Furthermore, Lincoln needed the proper forum in which to present his ideas. It came in late May, when a meeting of New York Democrats passed a set of resolutions condemning his military arrests as unconstitutional. Lincoln's extensive response to the Democratic resolutions took "less time than any other of like importance" because he had already "studied it from every side." In early June, the president read his draft to the cabinet. "It has vigor and ability," a delighted Welles noted. Blair advised the president to emphasize that "we are Struggling against a Conspiracy to put down popular Govt." Blair realized that Lincoln had often reiterated this theme, but as Thomas Hart Benton used to say, the "ding dong" proved to be "the best figure in Rhetoric."

The finished letter, addressed to New York Democrat Erastus Corning, was released to the *New York Tribune* on June 12. Conceding that in ordinary times, military arrests would be unconstitutional, Lincoln reminded his critics that the Constitution specifically provided for the suspension of the writ of habeas corpus "in cases of Rebellion or Invasion." He went on to say that Vallandigham was not arrested for his criticism of the administration but "because he was laboring, with some effect, to prevent the raising of troops, to encourage desertions from the army, and to leave the rebellion without an adequate military force to suppress it."

Pointing out that "long experience has shown that armies can not be maintained unless desertion shall be punished by the severe penalty of death," Lincoln posed a question that was soon echoed by supporters everywhere: "Must I shoot a simple-minded soldier boy who deserts, while I must not touch a hair of a wiley agitator who induces him to desert? This is none the less injurious when effected by getting a father, or brother, or friend, into a public meeting, and there working upon his feelings, till he is persuaded to write the soldier boy, that he is fighting in a bad cause, for a wicked administration of a contemptable government, too weak to arrest and punish him if he shall desert."

The president's letter garnered extravagant praise throughout the North. "It is full, candid, clear and conclusive," the *New York Times* affirmed. Even Democrats were impressed. While Edward Everett told Lincoln he would not have advocated Vallandigham's arrest, he considered the president's "defence of the step complete." Supporters were thrilled. "It is a grand document, strong, plain, simple, without one sparkle of tinsel ornament," Stoddard enthused, "yet dignified as becomes the ruler of a great people when the nation is listening to what he says. It should be printed in every Northern paper, and read by every citizen." In fact, Lincoln took every step to ensure that his words would shape public opinion. Printed in a great variety of formats, the letter eventually reached an astonishing 10 million people in their homes and workplaces, on isolated farms and in the cities. And as the American people absorbed the logic of Lincoln's argument, popular sentiment began to shift.

• • •

WITH THE APPROACH OF SUMMER, the tempers of the cabinet ministers grew shorter. Welles noted with disapproval that Stanton attended only half the cabinet meetings and said little when present. "Not unfrequently he has a private conference with the President in the corner of the room, or with Seward in the library," griped Welles. Seward, too, would turn up when a session commenced, speak privately with the president, then leave his son, Fred Seward, to represent his department. Stanton, who claimed he would never raise "any important question, when an assistant is present," was infuriated. Blair, frustrated by the superior access granted Seward and Stanton, often lingered after cabinet meetings in hopes of a private word with Lincoln.

"At such a time as this, it would seem there should be free, full and constant intercourse and interchange of views," fumed Welles. Bates, also discontented, agreed. "There is now no mutual confidence among the members of the Govt.—and really no such thing as a C.[abinet] C.[ouncil]," he grumbled. "The more ambitious members, who seek to control—Seward—Chase—Stanton—never start their projects in C. C. but try *first* to commit the Prest., and then, if possible, secure the *apparent* consent of the members." Chase found the lack of collective deliberation demeaning. "But how idle it seems to me to speculate on Military affairs!" he complained to David Dudley Field. "The President consults only Stanton & Halleck in the management of the War. I look on from the outside and, as well as I can, furnish the means." If he were president, Chase assured Congressman Garfield, surely he "would have a system of information which should at least keep my Secretary of the Treasury advised of every thing of importance."

More strongly than Chase, Blair decried the lack of more formal meetings, attributing the cabinet's failings to the machinations of Seward and Stanton. They had also been responsible, he believed, for Lincoln's unwillingness to replace Halleck, whom Blair despised, and restore McClellan. In Blair's mind, both Seward and Chase were "scheming for the succession. Stanton would cut the President's throat if he could." Blair's hatred for Stanton was so virulent that he refused to set foot in the War Department, the primary source of military information. Talking with Welles one evening at the depot, Blair admitted that Lincoln's behavior puzzled him. "Strange, strange," he exclaimed, "that the President who has sterling ability should give himself over so completely to Stanton and Seward."

Certainly, Lincoln was not oblivious to the infighting of his colleagues. He remained firmly convinced, however, that so long as each continued to do his own job well, no changes need be made. Moreover, he had no desire for contentious cabinet discussions on tactical matters, preferring to rely on the trusted counsel of Seward and Stanton. Still, he understood the resentment this provoked in neglected members of his administration; and through many small acts of generosity, he managed to keep the respect and affection of his disgruntled colleagues.

Recognizing Blair's desire for more personal influence, Lincoln kept his door open to both Monty and his father. Monty Blair, despite his frustrations, was ultimately loyal and had accomplished marvels as postmaster general, utterly transforming a primitive postal system without letter carriers, mailboxes on streets, or free delivery. Modernizing the postal service was particularly important for the soldiers, who relied on letters, newspapers, and magazines from home to sustain morale. To this end, Blair created a special system of army post offices, complete with army postmasters and stamp agents. His innovations provided the means for soldiers to send mail without postage so long as the recipient paid three cents on delivery of each letter. Even when foul weather and muddy roads made the delivery of mails to the army camps nearly impossible, inordinate efforts allowed the mail to get through.

Lincoln was also careful to reserve time for private conversation with Welles. He would often catch up with his "Neptune" on the pathway leading from the White House to the War and Navy Departments or call him aside as they awaited news in the telegraph office. In his written correspondence, the president was equally thoughtful. When he felt compelled to issue Welles an order regarding the instructions of naval officers at neutral ports, he assured Welles that "it is not intended to be insinuated that you have been remiss in the performance of the arduous and responsible duties of your Department, which I take pleasure in affirming has, in your hands, been conducted with admirable success."

So, in the end, the feuding cabinet members, with the exception of Chase, remained loyal to their president, who met rivalry and irritability with kindness and defused their tensions with humor. A particularly bitter argument arose between Chase and Monty Blair when Blair claimed that the Fugitive Slave Law still applied in loyal states and should be employed to return a runaway to his owner; Chase demanded instead that the slave be placed into military service. Lincoln mediated the dispute, assuring them both that this very issue had long bedeviled him. "It reminded him," Welles recorded in his diary, "of a man in Illinois who was in debt and terribly annoyed by a pressing creditor, until finally the debtor assumed to be crazy whenever the creditor broached the subject. I, said the President, have on more than one occasion, in this room when beset by extremists on this question, been compelled to appear to be very mad."

During another tense session, Lincoln cited the work of the humorist Orpheus C. Kerr, which he especially relished, even though it often lampooned him and the members of the cabinet. "Now the hits that are given to you, Mr. Welles or to Chase I can enjoy, but I dare say they may have disgusted you while I was laughing at them. So *vice versa* as regards myself."

• • •

WHILE WORKING TO SUSTAIN the spirits of his cabinet, Lincoln also tried to soothe the incessant bickering and occasional resentment among his generals. Learning that William Rosecrans, headquartered in Nashville, had taken umbrage at a note he had sent, Lincoln replied at once. "In no case have I intended to censure you, or to question your ability," he wrote. "I frequently make mistakes myself, in the many things I am compelled to do hastily." He had merely intended to express concern over Rosecrans's action regarding a particular colonel. And when Lincoln felt compelled to remove General Samuel Curtis from command in Missouri, he assured him that his removal was necessary only "to somehow break up the state of things in Missouri," where Governor Gamble headed one quarreling faction and Curtis another. "I did not mean to cast any censure upon you, nor to indorse any of the charges made against you by others. With me the presumption is still in your favor that you are honest, capable, faithful, and patriotic."

Despite Lincoln's diplomacy, the quarrels in Missouri continued, eliciting a note from Governor Gamble complaining that the language in one of Lincoln's published letters had been "grossly offensive" to him. When Hay presented the note to Lincoln, he was told "to put it away." Lincoln explained to Gamble that as he was "trying to preserve [his] own temper, by avoiding irritants, so far as practicable," he had decided not to read what his secretary had described as a "*cross*" letter. Having made his point, Lincoln assured the wounded Gamble: "I was totally unconscious of any malice, or disrespect towards you, or of using any expression which should offend you."

Lincoln's patience had its limits, however. When Major General Robert H. Milroy railed about "the blind unreasoning hatred" of Halleck that he claimed had supposedly led to his suspension from command, Lincoln was unyielding. "I have scarcely seen anything from you at any time, that did not contain imputations against your superiors," Lincoln replied. "You have constantly urged the idea that you were persecuted because you did not come from West-Point, and you repeat it in these letters. This, my dear general, is I fear, the rock on which you have split."

Likewise, when Rosecrans grumbled that his request for a predated commission to secure a higher rank had been denied, Lincoln was unsympathetic: "Truth to speak, I do not appreciate this matter of rank on paper, as you officers do. The world will not forget that you fought the battle of 'Stone River' and it will never care a fig whether you rank Gen. Grant on paper, or he so, ranks you."

As he was forced to deal with quarreling generals on almost every front, it is little wonder that Lincoln developed such respect and admiration for Ulysses S. Grant. Steadily and uncomplainingly, Grant had advanced toward Vicksburg, the Confederate stronghold whose capture would give the Union control of the Mississippi River and split the Confederacy. By the middle of May, after five successive victories, Grant had come within striking distance of Vicksburg. After two direct assaults against John Pemberton's forces failed on May 19 and May 22, he settled into a siege designed to starve the Confederates out.

"Whether Gen. Grant shall or shall not consummate the capture of Vicksburg," Lincoln wrote a friend on May 26, "his campaign from the beginning of this month up to the twenty second day of it, is one of the most brilliant in the world." During the troubling weeks with Hooker's army in the East, news from Grant's army in the West had sustained Lincoln. In March, Stanton had sent Charles Dana, the newspaperman who would later become assistant secretary of war, to observe General Grant and report on his movements. Dana had developed a powerful respect for Grant that was evident in his long, detailed dispatches. Lincoln's own estimation of his general steadily increased as reports revealed a terse man of character and action. Requesting that General Banks join forces with him in the final drive to open the Mississippi, Grant assured Banks that he "would gladly serve under him as his superior in rank or simply cooperate with him for the benefit of the common cause if he should prefer that course."

Despite his growing regard for Grant, there were instances that required Lincoln to intervene with his most successful general. In a misguided effort to stop peddlers from illegally profiteering in cotton in areas penetrated by Union armies, Grant had issued an order expelling "the

Jews, as a class," from his department. The discriminatory order, which contained no provision for individual hearings or trials, forced all Jewish people to depart within twenty-four hours, leaving horses, carriages, and other valuables behind.

When a delegation of Jewish leaders approached Lincoln, it was clear that he was not fully informed about the matter. He responded to their plight with a biblical allusion: "And so the children of Israel were driven from the happy land of Canaan?" The delegation leader answered: "Yes, and that is why we have come unto Father Abraham's bosom, asking protection." Lincoln replied quickly: "And this protection they shall have at once." He took his pen and wrote a note to Halleck, ordering immediate cancellation of the order. Halleck reluctantly complied after assuring Grant that "the President has no objection to your expelling traitors and Jew peddlers, which, I suppose, was the object of your order; but, as it in terms proscribed an entire religious class, some of whom are fighting in our ranks, the President deemed it necessary to revoke it."

Lincoln was also confronted by continuing rumors of Grant's relapse into excessive drinking. Tales of drunkenness were not confined to Grant. Elizabeth Blair heard that during the Battle of Chancellorsville, Hooker "was drunk all the time," while Bates was told that "General H.[alleck] was a confirmed *opium-eater*," a habit that contributed to his "watery eyes" and "bloated" appearance. In Grant's case, the gossip reached Lincoln by way of the puritanical Chase, who had received a letter from Murat Halstead. The respected journalist warned Chase that Grant was "most of the time more than half drunk, and much of the time idiotically drunk."

In fact, Lincoln and Stanton had already heard similar complaints. After dispatching investigators to look into General Grant's behavior, however, they had concluded that his drinking did not affect his unmatched ability to plan, execute, and win battles. A memorable story circulated that when a delegation brought further rumors of Grant's drinking to the president, Lincoln declared that if he could find the brand of whiskey Grant used, he would promptly distribute it to the rest of his generals!

• • •

WHILE THE SIEGE of VICKSBURG tightened in the West, a deceptive quiet settled on the Rappahannock. After visiting Hooker's headquarters in mid-May, Senators Wade and Chandler told Lincoln that the pickets on both sides of the river had resumed "their old pastime of bandying wit and repartee . . . 'I say Yank,' shouted over one of the Rebels, 'where is fightin' Joe Hooker, now?' 'Oh, he's gone to Stonewall Jackson's funeral,' shouted 'Yank' in reply."

During this interlude on the Eastern front, Seward accompanied Frances and Fanny back to Auburn, where they were planning to spend the summer. For a few precious days, he entertained old friends, caught up on his reading, and tended his garden. The sole trying event was the decision to fell a favorite old poplar tree that had grown unsound. Frances could not bear to be present as it was cut, certain that she "should feel every stroke of the axe." Once it was over, however, she could relax in the beautiful garden she had sorely missed during her prolonged stay in Washington. On June 1, when Seward boarded the train to return to the capital, Fanny wrote that their home seemed "very lonely" without him.

No sooner had Seward departed Auburn than Frances and Fanny began hearing troubling rumors that Lee intended to invade Washington, Maryland, or Pennsylvania. "We have again been anxious about Washington," Fanny told her father. "Although I don't consider myself a protection, Washington seems safer to me when I am there." Reassuring his daughter, Seward noted that during his stay in Auburn, he, too, had remained "in constant uneasiness" over all manner of rumors that proved groundless upon his return to the capital. "Certainly the last thing that any one here thinks of, now-a-days, is an invasion of Washington."

On Monday, June 8, Mary and Tad left the capital for a two-week vacation in Philadelphia, where they took a suite at the Continental Hotel. After they had gone, Welles spoke with Lincoln about a "delicate" matter concerning Mary. In the aftermath of Willie's death the previous year, she had canceled the weekly Marine Band summer concerts on the White House lawn. Welles warned that if the public were deprived of the entertainment for yet another season, the "grumbling and discontent" of the previous summer would only increase. Lincoln hesitated at first. Willie had loved the weekly concerts with their picniclike festivities, but "Mrs. L. would not consent, certainly not until after the 4th of July." When Welles persisted, Lincoln finally agreed to let him do whatever he "thought best." That night, most likely unsettled by the conversation about Willie, Lincoln had a nightmare about Tad's recently acquired revolver. "Think you better put 'Tad's' pistol away," he wired Mary the next morning. "I had an ugly dream about him."

In the days that followed, reports that Lee's army was heading north through the Shenandoah Valley to invade Maryland and Pennsylvania multiplied. On June 15, Seward sent a telegram to his son Will, suggesting he had better cut short his leave to return to his regiment in Washington. "Oh! what a disappointment!" Fanny lamented. Will had just arrived in Auburn for a twenty-day sojourn with both his own family and Jenny's. Many plans would be canceled, including "a double family pic-nic to the

Lake." Writing to Frances that same day, Seward sought to set her mind at ease. Though it now seemed certain that Lee had crossed the Rappahannock, she must "not infer that there is any increase of danger for any of us in this change." On the contrary, "the near approach of battles toward us brings disadvantages to the enemy, and adds to our strength."

In similar fashion, Lincoln reassured Mary when a headline in a Northern paper blared: *"Invasion! Rebel Forces in Maryland and Pennsylvania."* "It is a matter of choice with yourself whether you come home," he told her. "I do not think the raid into Pennsylvania amounts to anything at all." When each day brought reports of further Confederate advances, however, Mary decided to rejoin her husband in Washington.

"The country, now, is in a blaze of excitement," Benjamin French recorded on June 18. "Some of the Rebel troops have crossed into the upper part of Pennsylvania, & the North is wide awake." While Welles worried that "something of a panic pervades the city," Lincoln remained quietly confident that the Union troops, fighting on home ground, would achieve the signal victory so long denied. Capitalizing on the intense patriotism inspired by the invasion, he called out a hundred thousand troops from the militias in Pennsylvania, Maryland, Ohio, and the new state of West Virginia.

"I should think this constant toil and moil would kill him," French marveled, yet the resilient president seemed "in excellent spirits." Inspired by Lincoln's steadfast nature, French added, "the more I see of him the more I am convinced of his superlative goodness, truth, kindness & Patriotism."

In the tense atmosphere of Washington, the committee charged with planning the Fourth of July celebrations considered suspending their preparations. "Don't you stop!" Mary Lincoln ordered White House secretary William Stoddard, promising to personally help make the anniversary celebrations a success. Reflecting her husband's unruffled confidence, she assured Stoddard of her husband's certainty that "the crisis has come and that all the chances are on our side. This move of Lee's is all he could ask for."

Lincoln's primary concern was that Hooker would again be "outgeneraled" by Lee. His worry escalated in the last weeks of June when he "observed in Hooker the same failings that were witnessed in McClellan after the Battle of Antietam. A want of alacrity to obey, and a greedy call for more troops which could not, and ought not to be taken from other points." When Hooker delivered a prickly telegram asking to be relieved of command, Lincoln and Stanton replaced him with General George Meade, who had participated in the Peninsula Campaign, Second Bull Run, and Chancellorsville. The surprising move distressed Chase. He had long championed Hooker and had recently returned from spending the day with him in the field. When Lincoln informed his cabinet that the change was already accomplished, Welles noted that "Chase was disturbed more than he cared should appear." The following day, Chase wrote to Kate, who was in New York. "You must have been greatly astonished for the relieving of General Hooker; but your astonishment cannot have exceeded mine."

• • •

THREE DAYS LATER, in Pennsylvania, the three-day Battle of Gettysburg began. "The turning point of the whole war seems to be crowding itself into the present," wrote John Nicolay. "It seems almost impossible to wait for the result. Hours become days and days become months in such a suspense." If Lee achieved victory at Gettysburg, he could move on to Philadelphia, Baltimore, and Washington. His aura of invincibility might, it was feared, eventually lead the British and French to recognize the independence of the Confederacy and bring the war to an end.

Telegraph service from the front was "poor and desultory," according to operator David Bates. Lincoln remained a constant fixture in the telegraph office, resting fitfully on the couch. At intervals, Stanton, Seward, Welles, and Senators Sumner and Chandler drifted in and out. Senator Chandler would "never forget the painful anxiety of those few days when the fate of the nation seemed to hang in the balance; nor the restless solicitude of Mr. Lincoln, as he paced up and down the room, reading dispatches, soliloquizing, and often stopping to trace the map which hung on the wall." Sketched on the map were the generals and places that would later be engraved in history: James Longstreet and George Pickett, Winfield Hancock and Joshua Chamberlain, Little Round Top and Cemetery Ridge.

After inconclusive fighting on the first day, a dispatch from Meade on Thursday night, July 2, reported that "after one of the severest contests of the war," the rebels had been "repulsed at all points." Still, given recent reversals and the protracted uncertainty in the present, everyone held their breath. As of 9 p.m. the following night, the *New York Times* reported, "no reliable advices have been received here from the Pennsylvania battlefield. It is generally felt that this is the crisis of the war. Intense anxiety prevails." At midnight, a messenger handed Welles a telegram from a Connecticut editor named Byington, who had left the battlefield a few hours earlier and reported that "everything looked hopeful." Welles assured Lincoln that Byington was "reliable," but the hours of uncertainty continued until shortly after dawn, July 4, when a telegram from Meade reported that the battle had been successfully concluded. The rebels were withdrawing after severe losses. Casualties were later calculated at 28,000, nearly a third of Lee's army.

General Abner Doubleday described the tenacious fighting, which cost 23,000 Union casualties, "as being the most desperate which ever took place in the world." He told a reporter that "nothing can picture the horrors of the battlefield around the ruined city of Gettysburg. Each house, church, hovel, and barn is filled with the wounded of both armies. The ground is covered with the dead."

On the morning of the Fourth of July, Lincoln issued a celebratory press release that was carried by telegram across the country. For young Fanny Seward, waiting anxiously in Auburn, the day had started as "the gloomiest Fourth" she had ever known. "No public demonstration here—No ringing of bells." Everything changed in the late afternoon when the "extra" arrived, carrying the tidings of victory. Fireworks were set off to glorify simultaneously the country's independence and the long-awaited victory.

In New York City, George Templeton Strong exulted in the colorful newspaper accounts of Lee's retreat. "The results of this victory are priceless," he wrote. "Government is strengthened four-fold at home and abroad. Gold one hundred and thirty-eight today, and government securities rising. Copperheads are palsied and dumb for the moment at least."

Triumphant news from Vicksburg followed on the heels of victory at Gettysburg. Grant's forty-six-day siege had finally forced Pemberton to surrender his starving troops. Welles had received the first tiding that Vicksburg had surrendered to Grant in a dispatch from Admiral David Porter. The bespectacled, "slightly fossilized" Welles hurried to the White House, dispatch in hand. Reaching the room where Lincoln was talking with Chase and several others, Welles reportedly "executed a double shuffle and threw up his hat by way of showing that he was the bearer of glad tidings." Lincoln affirmed that "he never before nor afterward saw Mr. Welles so thoroughly excited as he was then."

The elated president "caught my hand," recorded Welles, "and throwing his arm around me, exclaimed: 'what can we do for the Secretary of the Navy for this glorious intelligence—He is always giving us good news. I cannot, in words, tell you my joy over this result. It is great, Mr. Welles, it is great!' " With the fall of Vicksburg, as Lincoln later said, "The Father of Waters again goes unvexed to the sea."

Dana described the surrender in a telegram to Stanton the next day. "The rebel troops marched out and stacked arms in front of their works while Genl. Pemberton appeared for a moment with his staff upon the parapet of the central post. . . . No troops remain outside—everything quiet here. Grant entered the city at 11 o'clock and was rec'd by Pemberton," whom he treated with great "courtesy & dignity." Dana estimated the number of prisoners, for whom rations were being distributed, to be about thirty thousand.

Lincoln expressed his joyful appreciation to Grant in a remarkable letter. "I write this now as a grateful acknowledgment for the almost inestimable service you have done the country," he began. He conceded that while he had approved most of the general's maneuvers during the long struggle, he had harbored misgivings over Grant's decision to turn "Northward East of the Big Black" instead of joining General Banks. "I now wish to make the personal acknowledgment that you were right, and I was wrong."

Word of Vicksburg's surrender unleashed wild celebrations throughout the North. In Washington, a large crowd, led by the 34th Massachusetts Regimental Band, formed at the National Hotel and marched to the White House to congratulate the president. Lincoln appeared before the cheering multitude, revealing the preliminary thoughts that would coalesce in his historic Gettysburg Address. "How long is it—eighty odd years—since on the Fourth of July for the first time in the history of the world a nation, by its representatives, assembled and declared as a self-evident truth that 'all men are created equal.' " He went on to recall the signal events that had shared the anniversary of the nation's birth, beginning with the twin deaths of Thomas Jefferson and John Adams on July 4, and ending with the Union's twin victories at Gettysburg and Vicksburg on the same day. "Gentlemen," the president declared, "this is a glorious theme, and the occasion for a speech, but I am not prepared to make one worthy of the occasion." Instead, he spoke of the "praise due to the many brave officers and soldiers who have fought in the cause of the Union."

The band played some patriotic airs, and the crowd pressed on to the War Department, where Stanton paid generous tribute to General Grant. Although several more speeches followed and songs were played, the people had not exhausted their euphoria. Marching to Lafayette Square, they joined another throng at Seward's house, cheering for the secretary to appear. The indefatigable Seward happily obliged, delivering a long, animated speech tracing the conflict from its troubled early days to its recent triumphs, which, he assured them, foretold "the beginning of the end."

The following day, little work was accomplished in the offices of government. In every building, Noah Brooks reported, the official bulletins were read "over and over again," producing "cheer upon cheer from the crowds of officers and clerks." On the streets, "Union men were shaking hands wherever they met, like friends after a long absence," while the Copperheads had "retired to their holes like evil beasts at sunrise."

The joyous occasion was marred for the Lincolns by a serious carriage accident that took place on the second day of the Gettysburg battle. As Rebecca Pomroy related the events, the Lincolns were returning to the White House from the Soldiers' Home. Lincoln was riding on horseback while Mary followed behind in their carriage. The night before, presumably targeting the president, an unknown assailant had removed the screws fastening the driver's seat to the body of the carriage. When the vehicle began to descend from a winding hill, the seat came loose, throwing the driver to the ground. Unable to restrain the runaway horses, Mary tried to leap from the carriage. She landed on her back, hitting her head against a sharp stone. The wound was dressed at a nearby hospital, but a dangerous infection set in that kept her incapacitated for several weeks. With the Battle of Gettysburg in full swing, Lincoln was unable to minister to Mary's needs. He brought Mrs. Pomroy to the Soldiers' Home to nurse his wife round the clock. Robert Lincoln believed that his mother "never quite recovered from the effects of her fall," which exacerbated the debilitating headaches that she already endured.

• • •

In the wake of the triumphs at Gettysburg and Vicksburg, Lincoln anticipated a quick end to the rebellion. General Meade, he told Halleck, had only to "complete his work, so gloriously prosecuted thus far, by the literal or substantial destruction of Lee's army." In the days that followed, both Halleck and Lincoln urged Meade to go after Lee, to attack him vigorously, to capture his army before he could escape into Virginia. Robert Lincoln later said that his father had sent explicit orders to Meade "directing him to attack Lee's army with all his force immediately, and that if he was successful in the attack, he might destroy the order, but if he was unsuccessful he might preserve it for his vindication." The order has never been found. If Meade did receive it, he nonetheless failed to move against Lee. As the days passed, Lincoln began "to grow anxious and impatient."

Lincoln's worst fears were realized on July 14, when he received a dispatch from Meade reporting that Lee's army had escaped his grasp by successfully crossing the Potomac at Williamsport, Maryland, into Virginia. At the cabinet meeting that day, Stanton was reluctant to share the news, though his face clearly revealed that he "was disturbed, disconcerted." Welles recorded that, when asked directly if Lee had escaped, "Stanton said abruptly and curtly he knew nothing of Lee's crossing. '*I do,*' said the President emphatically, with a look of painful rebuke to Stanton." Lincoln revealed what he had learned and suggested that the cabinet meeting be adjourned. "Probably none of us were in a right frame of mind for deliberation," Welles wrote. Certainly, he added, the president "was not."

Lincoln caught up with Welles as his navy secretary was leaving and walked with him across the lawn. His sorrow that Lee had once again managed to escape was palpable. "On only one or two occasions have I ever seen the President so troubled, so dejected and discouraged," Welles wrote. "Our Army held the war in the hollow of their hand & they would not close it," Lincoln said later. "We had gone through all the labor of tilling & planting an enormous crop & when it was ripe we did not harvest it."

Later that afternoon, Lincoln wrote a frank letter to General Meade. While expressing his profound gratitude for "the magnificent success" at Gettysburg, he acknowledged that he was "distressed immeasurably" by "the magnitude of the misfortune involved in Lee's escape. He was within your easy grasp, and to have closed upon him would, in connection with our other late successes, have ended the war. As it is, the war will be prolonged indefinitely." Before sending the letter, which he knew would leave Meade disconsolate, Lincoln held back, as he often did when he was upset or angry, waiting for his emotions to settle. In the end, he placed the letter in an envelope inscribed: "To Gen. Meade, never sent, or signed."

Lincoln later told Connecticut congressman Henry C. Deming that Meade's failure to attack Lee after Gettysburg was one of three occasions when "better management upon the part of the commanding general might have terminated the war." The other two command failures he attributed to McClellan during the Peninsula Campaign and Hooker at Chancellorsville. Still, he acknowledged, "I do not know that I could have given any different orders had I been with them myself. I have not fully made up my mind how I should behave when minie-balls were whistling, and those great oblong shells shrieking in my ear. I might run away."

Troubling events in New York City soon diverted the nation's attention. For weeks, authorities had worried about the potential for violence on July 11. On that date, the names of all the men eligible for the first draft in American history would be placed in a giant wheel and drawn randomly until the prescribed quota was filled. The unpopular idea of coercing men to become soldiers had provided traction for Copperhead politicians. Speaking on July 4, Governor Seymour had told an immense crowd that the federal government had exceeded its constitutional authority by forcing men into an "ungodly conflict" waged on behalf of the black man. The antagonistic *Daily News*, read by the majority of working-class Irish, claimed that the purpose of the draft was to "kill off Democrats."

A provision in the Conscription Act that allowed a draftee to either pay $300 or provide a substitute provoked further discontent. Both Stanton and Lincoln had objected to this feature of the bill, but Congress had insisted. Opponents of the draft gained powerful ammunition that this was "a rich man's war and a poor man's fight." Still, the first day of the draft proceeded peacefully, leaving the city woefully unprepared for the violent uprising that accompanied the spinning of the wheel on the second day. "Scarcely had two dozen names been called," the *New York Times* reported, "when a crowd, numbering perhaps 500," stormed the building "with clubs, stones, brickbats and other missiles." Entering through the broken windows, they stoned the drafting officers, smashed the giant wheel, shredded the lists and records, and then set the building on fire.

Returning to the street, the mob, composed mainly of poor Irish immigrants, turned its vengeance against anyone it encountered. "It seemed to be an understood thing," the *Times* reporter noted, "that the negroes should be attacked wherever found, whether they offered any provocation or not. As soon as one of these unfortunate people was spied, whether on a cart, a railroad car, or in the street, he was immediately set upon by a crowd of men and boys." Terror unfolded as the rioters beat their victims to death and then strung their bodies on trees. An orphanage for black children was burned to the ground, hundreds of stores were looted, and dozens of policemen lost their lives. More than a thousand people were killed or wounded.

The riots continued unchecked for five days, becoming "the all engrossing topic of conversation" in Washington. The inability of the authorities to restore law and order prompted Chase to announce his desire to "have the power for a week." The mob violence finally ended when a regiment of soldiers, returning from Pennsylvania, entered the city. Although some advised Lincoln to suspend the draft indefinitely, he insisted that it go forward.

The turmoil in New York created foreboding throughout the North as other cities prepared to commence their own drafts. In the days preceding Auburn's draft on July 23, Frances Seward lived "in daily apprehension of a riot." In frequent letters to her husband, she reported that Copperheads were spreading "malicious stories" blaming Seward's "higher law" for the riots in New York. Tensions in Auburn escalated when several Irishmen fought with blacks, resisted arrest, and threatened to destroy the Seward home. Frances awoke one morning to find that a large rock had been thrown into the room where she regularly sat to read. After discovering the damage, she advised her daughter-in-law to remove anything she considered valuable. "So that afternoon," Jenny recalled, "I took my husband's photograph down to my mother's house, it being, to my mind, the most valuable thing that I possessed."

From Washington, Seward sought to placate his wife. "Do not give yourself a thought about the house. There will hardly be any body desperate enough to do you personal harm, and if the country, in its unwonted state of excitement, will destroy our home, the sacrifice will be a small one for our country, and not without benefit." Frances persevered, retaining her calm during these difficult days, as she had done years before during the trial of William Freeman. "As to personal injury," she told her husband, "I fear more for the poor colored people than for others—They cannot protect themselves and few persons are willing to assist them."

On the morning of Auburn's draft, Frances reported to her son Fred that while everyone was "somewhat anxious," she was feeling "more secure" since the local citizenry had organized a volunteer police force. The *New York Times* reported the successful results of the efforts in Auburn. "The best of order was observed and the best spirit was manifested" by the two thousand citizens who had gathered to witness the draft. As local officials addressed patriotic speeches to the crowd, the drafted men cheered for "The Union," "Old Abe," "The Draft," and "Our recent victories."

Even before such reassuring accounts reached him, Seward had predicted that the disturbances in New York, like a "thunder shower," would "clear the political skies, of the storms" that the Copperheads had been "gathering up a long time." His words proved prescient, for when the loss of life and property was tallied in the wake of the New York riots, public opinion turned against Governor Seymour. His incendiary Fourth of July speech was seen by many as a direct "incitement to the people to resist the government." John Hay learned from a visiting New Yorker that Seymour was "in a terrible state of nervous excitement," precipitated "both by the terrible reminiscence of the riots" and the virulent condemnation by the press for his handling of the situation. The news that Seymour had "lost ground immensely with a large number of the best men" engendered great satisfaction in the Lincoln administration. And when the draft was eventually resumed in New York City, everything went smoothly.

"The nation is great, brave, and generous," Seward confidently told Frances. "All will go on well, and though not without the hindrance of faction at every step, yet it will go through to the right and just end. How differently the nation has acted, thus far in the crisis, from what it did in 1850 to 1860!"

Within twenty-four distressing hours, the president had learned of both Lee's escape and the disgraceful riots in New York. Nonetheless, he was able to shake off his gloom within a matter of days. On Sunday morning, July 19, Hay reported that the "President was in very good humour." He had written a humorous verse mocking the "pomp, and mighty swell" with which Lee had gone forth to "sack Phil-del." While he remained fully cognizant of the consequences of Lee's escape, he had willed himself to reconsider his outlook on General Meade and the Battle of Gettysburg. "A few days having passed," he assured one of Meade's commanding generals, "I am now profoundly grateful for what was done, without criticism for what was not done. Gen. Meade has my confidence as a brave and skillful officer, and a true man."

Oddly enough, Lincoln's good spirits that Sunday morning were due in part to the six straight hours he had spent with Hay the previous day reviewing one hundred courts-martial. Whereas the young secretary was "in a state of entire collapse" after the ordeal, Lincoln found relief and renewed vigor as he exercised the power to pardon. As they went through the cases, Hay marveled "at the eagerness with which the President caught at any fact which would justify him in saving the life of a condemned soldier."

Confronted with soldiers who had been sentenced to death for cowardice, Lincoln typically reduced the sentence to imprisonment or hard labor. "It would frighten the poor devils too terribly, to shoot them," he said. One case involved a private who was sentenced to be shot for desertion though he had later re-enlisted. Lincoln simply proposed, "Let him fight instead of shooting him." Lincoln acknowledged to General John Eaton that some of his officers believed he employed the pardoning power "with so much freedom as to demoralize the army and destroy the discipline." Although "officers only see the force of military discipline," he explained, he tried to comprehend it from the vantage of individual soldiers—a picket so exhausted that "sleep steals upon him unawares," a family man who overstayed his leave, a young boy "overcome by a physical fear greater than his will." He liked to tell of a soldier who, when asked why he had run away, said: "Well, Captain, it was not my fault. I have got just as brave a heart as Julius [Caesar] but these legs of mine will always run away with me when the battle begins."

Rather than fearing that he had overused his pardoning power, Lincoln feared he had made too little use of it. He could not bear the sound of gunshot on the days when deserters were executed. Only "where meanness or cruelty were shown" did he exhibit no clemency.

Yet even as he plowed through one court-martial after another, Lincoln's humor remained intact. At one point, he was handed the case of a captain charged with "looking thro keyholes & over transoms at a lady undressing." He laughingly suggested that the captain "be elevated to the peerage" so that he could be accorded the appropriate title "Count Peeper."

• • •

THE SUMMER OF 1863 brought the hottest weather Washington had suffered in many years. "Men and horses dropping dead in the streets every day," Hay reported to Nicolay, who had escaped to the Rocky Mountains. "The garments cling to the skin," one resident observed, "shirt collars are laid low; moisture oozes from every object, standing in clammy exudation upon iron, marble, wood, and human flesh; the air is pervaded with a faint odor as of withered bouquets and dead mint juleps, and the warm steam of a home washing day is over everything."

Stanton found the "hot, dusty weather, the most disagreeable" he had ever experienced. "Burning sun all day, sultry at night." Ellen Stanton had escaped with her children for the summer, leaving her husband alone in Washington. Writing to her at a mountain retreat in Bedford, Pennsylvania, Stanton acknowledged that "all is silent and lonely, but there is consolation in knowing that you and the children are free from the oppressive heat and discomfort of Washington."

"Nearly everybody except the members of the unfortunate Can't-get-away Club has gone to the seaside or countryside," Noah Brooks reported. "Truly the season is one of languor, lassitude, and laziness," and even "the reporters have nearly all followed the example of better men and have likewise skeddadled from the heat."

As soon as Mary felt well enough to travel, she, too, fled the capital with both Tad and Robert, commencing a two-month sojourn in New York, Philadelphia, and the White and Green Mountains. The cool breezes of New Hampshire and Vermont would prove beneficial to young Tad, whose health remained fragile, while the lure of a resort hotel in the mountains kept Robert by her side through most of August. A correspondent who caught up with her at "Tiptop," Mount Washington, was delighted with her "very easy, agreeable" manner and her "very fair, cheerful, smiling face."

Only a dozen short telegrams between the Lincolns remain from that summer. In these brief communications, Lincoln talked about the heat, shared news of the Kentucky elections, and asked her to let "dear Tad" know that his nanny goat had run away and left his father "in distress about it." Only in mid-September, as the time drew near for Mary's return, did Lincoln admit that he had missed her, repeating in two separate telegrams his eagerness to be reunited with her and with Tad. Mary understood that he was "not *given* to letter writing," and so long as she was assured of his good health, she remained content.

The Lincolns' undemonstrative communications stand in marked contrast to the effusive letters the Sewards exchanged all summer, openly sharing their feelings about the family, the war, and the country. "I wish I could gain from some other source the confidence with which you inspire me when I am with you," Frances told her husband. "I need it in these disastrous times. . . . The loyalty of the people is now to be put to the test." Seward urged her to be calm and confident: "Every day since the war broke out we have drawn on the people for a thousand men, and they have gone to the field." To her husband, Frances acknowledged that while the country rejoiced over the victories at Gettysburg and Vicksburg, she despaired when she "read the lists of killed & wounded." Only with Frances could the stalwart Seward reveal his own distress, confusion, and exhaustion.

While Lincoln spent hours writing letters to keep generals and politicians on an even keel, he apparently never found the solace Seward and Chase took in their extensive family correspondence. Nor did his wife and children write regularly. Tad, a slow learner, may not have developed the skill to easily compose letters. Robert, then entering his junior year at Harvard, surely was capable of penning descriptions of his days in the mountains. Very different in temperament, Lincoln and his eldest son never seemed to develop a close relationship. During Robert's childhood, Lincoln had been absent for months at a time, traveling the circuits of both politics and law. At sixteen, Robert entered boarding school in New Hampshire, and he was a student at Harvard when his father became president. "Thenceforth," Robert noted sadly, "any great intimacy between us became impossible. I scarcely even had ten minutes quiet talk with him during his Presidency, on account of his constant devotion to business."

For Lincoln, it was enough to know that his wife and sons were happily ensconced at the Equinox House in Manchester, Vermont, then considered "a primary summer resort," providing access to fishing, nature walks, gardens, swimming holes, concerts, croquet, archery, and excellent dining facilities. During the visit, Mary climbed a mountain, socialized with General Doubleday and his wife, and enjoyed the clear, refreshing air.

• • •

KATE CHASE WOULD REMEMBER the summer of 1863 less for its record-breaking heat than for her rekindled romance with William Sprague, elected earlier in the year to the U.S. Senate. When the young millionaire came to Washington to take his seat, he called on Kate, and their troubled past was soon forgotten. "We did again join hands, and again join fortunes," Sprague later said. In early May, Sprague invited Kate to visit his estate in Providence, Rhode Island, so that she would meet his family and see his immense manufacturing company. Running at full tilt, the company's 10,000 employees could turn out "35,000 pieces of print-cloth" weekly, with the 280,000 spindles and 28 printing machines in the factories. "I want to show you how to make calico from cotton," he told Kate. "You are a statesman's daughter, will doubtless be a statesman's wife, and who if not you, should know how things are done, not how only they are undone or destroyed."

Shortly after they returned to Washington, Sprague asked Chase for Kate's hand in marriage. "The Gov and Miss Kate have consented to take me into their fold," Sprague proudly reported to a friend in New York. Sprague's adoration for Kate is clear from the flood of letters he wrote during the first months of their engagement. "The business which takes my time, my attention, my heart, my all," he wrote, "is of a certain young lady who has become so entwined in every pulsation, that my former self has lost its identity." Without her, he confessed, his life seemed "a wilderness, a blank." He kept her miniature by his side and waited for her return letters "as a drowning man [seizing] at anything to sustain him." A five-day separation seemed "an age" to him, so "strong a hold" had she gained upon his heart. Even when they were both in Washington, he sent her loving notes from his room at the Willard Hotel. "I am my darling up & in sympathy with the sunshine," he wrote early one morning. And another morning, "I hope my darling you are up feeling fresh and happy. Knowing that you are so is happiness to me. I kiss you good morning and adieu."

Kate's attachment to Sprague, however, did not indicate a readiness to leave her father. Nor was Chase, despite his claims, prepared to relinquish his hold on Kate. The impending marriage set in motion a curious series of machinations as to where the young couple should reside. Still harboring the illusory hope that closer proximity to Lincoln would beget greater influence, Chase opened the discussion by suggesting that Kate and William "take the house just as it is and let me find a place suited to my purpose nearer the Presidents." He assured Sprague that he was not among those fathers "who wish to retain the love & duty of daughters even in larger measure that they are given to their husbands." On the contrary, he wrote, "I want to have Katie honor & love you with an honor & love far exceeding any due to me."

Kate, however, was not persuaded by such protestations. She thought her father would be lost without her daily devotions and her consummate grace in orchestrating his social life. Under her supervision, the parties at the Chase mansion had become legendary. "Probably no woman in American history has had as brilliant a social career," one journalist observed of Kate. "Even the achievements of Dolly Madison pale into insignificance compared with her successes." Fanny Seward considered herself lucky to receive an invitation to one of Kate's parties. "Scarcely a person there whom it was not a pleasure to meet," she bubbled. "I don't know whether it was Miss Chase being so charming herself that made the party pass so pleasantly, but I think so sweet a presence must have lent a charm to the whole."

Unwilling to abandon her role in forwarding Chase's dreams, Kate persuaded William that they should all reside under the same roof. Approaching her father, she insisted that both she and William desired a united household. Though Chase had undoubtedly longed for this very arrangement, he made a show of reluctantly abandoning his "idea of taking a house or apartment near the Presidents" to suit their wishes. "Life is short and uncertain and I am not willing to do anything which will grieve my children," he wrote. "So I yield the point." They agreed that Chase would continue to pay the rent and the servants while William would cover the food and entertainment, assume half the stable expenses, and renovate the house to suit the needs of both a senator and a cabinet official.

Recognizing "the delicate link which has so long united father & daughter," Sprague wisely decided to "respect and honor" their relationship. "I am not afraid that the tenacious affection of a daughter will detract from that she owes to one she accepts for her life companion," he wrote Kate. "I am not so silly as not to see & feel that it is a surer garuantee of a more permanent and enduring love." While he bristled at the discovery that Kate allowed her father to read all of Sprague's letters to her, he was gratified by the praise his writing drew from the ever critical Chase. "Katie showed me yesterday your letters to her," Chase told William, "and I cannot refrain from telling you how much they delighted me." Making no mention of misspellings or grammatical mistakes, as he usually did with Kate and Nettie, Chase assured Sprague that the "manly affection breathed in them satisfied me that I had not given my daughter to one [who] did not fully appreciate her, or to whom she could not give the full wealth of her affections."

For Chase, William's desire to assume "as much of the pecuniary burden as possible" was timely, indeed. The engagement allowed him to divest himself of his financial ties to the Cooke brothers, whose private loans and gifts had assisted him over the years. Recent months had brought mounting criticism over the virtual monopoly the Cookes enjoyed in the lucrative sale of Treasury bonds, but Chase had not felt free to dispense with the arrangement. On June 1, however, he informed Jay Cooke that his compensation for the sale of the bonds would henceforth be reduced. "I have a duty to the country to perform," he sanctimoniously wrote, "which forbids me to pay rates which will not be approved by all right-minded men." The following day, he returned a check for $4,200 that he had received from Cooke as profit on the sale of a stock that he had not paid for. "In order to be able to render most efficient service to our country it is essential for me to *be* right as well as *seem* right & to *seem* right as well as *be* right."

Late in July, Chase joined Kate and Nettie for a few days' vacation in Rhode Island, where Sprague had secured rooms near the shore at South Pier. With a carriage provided by Sprague and good dining in the resort hotels on Narragansett Bay, the hardworking secretary relaxed for the first time in months. Leaving the girls at the seashore, he returned to Washington on August 7. Alone in the big house, he complained to Nettie that his only companion was their dog, Nellie, who "comes to see me every evening after dinner and puts her nose up in my face in a sort of sympathetic way." A sullen irritability is evident in his letters to both girls that summer. He chastised Nettie for her "somewhat ragged looking letter," pointing out how much her carelessness pained him, and he reprimanded Kate for failing to inform him when she borrowed money for the vacation expenses.

In his loneliness, Chase resumed a warm correspondence with Charlotte Eastman, the widow of a former congressman. Handsome and intelligent, she had enjoyed a sporadic friendship with Chase over the years. When the relationship had promised to develop into a romance, however, Kate had disapproved, going "so far as to intercept her letters." Chase had been unwilling to defy his daughter. Now, in Kate's absence, the two wrote to each other again. With inviting detail, Mrs. Eastman described her house on the Massachusetts seashore. She evinced little hope that Chase would join her, however. She suspected that her letters gave him "little satisfaction, as they can do but nothing to advance the object for which it seems to me you live for—Now shall I be frank? and perhaps offend you and tell you I am jealous! and of whom and what, of your Ambition and through that of yourself; for dont Ambition make the worshipper the God of his own idolatry?"

"What a sweet letter you have sent me," Chase replied from his desk at the Treasury. "I have read and reread it. What a charming picture you draw of the old house. . . . It made [me] half feel myself with you & quite wish to be. . . . I am so sorry that you & Katie—one so dear to me as a friend and the other as a daughter don't exactly *jee*." As for her remarks on his ambition, he acknowledged that he was, in fact, driven in ways that sometimes led him to neglect "duties of friendship & charity." She should understand, however, that he would always "try to direct my ambition to public ends and in honorable ways." It would amuse her to know, he concluded, how many times he had been interrupted while writing this letter, which he had to bring to a close in order to attend to the president.

While the heat enervated most of official Washington, Lincoln thrived on the long days, the relative freedom from office seekers, and the lack of family interference with his work. "The Tycoon is in fine whack," John Hay reported on August 7. "I have rarely seen him more serene & busy. He is managing this war, the draft, foreign relations, and planning a reconstruction of the Union, all at once. I never knew with what tyrannous authority he rules the Cabinet, till now. The most important things he decides & there is no cavil. I am growing more and more firmly convinced that the good of the country absolutely demands that he should be kept where he is till this thing is over. There is no man in the country, so wise so gentle and so firm. I believe the hand of God placed him where he is."

With Mary out of town, Lincoln found John Hay a ready companion. Smart, energetic, and amusing, the twenty-five-year-old Hay had become far more intimately connected to the president than his own eldest son. Their conversation moved easily from linguistics to reconstruction, from Shakespeare to Artemus Ward. Hay had a good sense of humor and, according to William Stoddard, could "tell a story better than most boys of his age." Stoddard long recalled an occasion when he and Nicolay were rocked with laughter at one of Hay's humorous tales. Hearing the noise, Lincoln came to the door. "His feet had made no sound in coming over from his room, or our own racket had drowned any foot-fall, but here was the President." If the young secretaries feared that Lincoln would chastise them for the interruption, he quickly dissipated their concern. He sat down in a chair and demanded that Hay repeat his tale. When the story was done, "down came the President's foot from across his knee, with a heavy stamp on the floor, and out through the hall went an uproarious peal of fun."

On Sunday, August 9, Hay accompanied the president to Alexander Gardner's photo studio at the corner of Seventh and D streets. The pictures taken that day do not reflect what Hay characterized as the president's "very good spirits." Rigidly posed, with one hand on a book and the other at his waist, Lincoln was forced to endure the lengthy process of the photograph, which almost invariably produced a grim, unsmiling portrait. Subjects would be required to sit absolutely still while the photographer removed the cap from the lens to expose the picture. "Don't move a muscle!" the subject would be told, for the slightest twitch would blur the image. Moreover, since "contrived grinning in photographs had not yet become obligatory," many faces, like Lincoln's, took on a melancholy cast.

Lincoln retained his high spirits through much of the summer, buoyed by the thought that "the rebel power is at last beginning to disintegrate." In his diary, Hay described a number of pleasant outings, including an evening journey to the Observatory. They viewed the moon and the star Arcturus through a newly installed telescope before driving out to the Soldiers' Home, where Lincoln read Shakespeare to Hay—"the end of Henry VI and the beginning of Richard III till my heavy eye-lids caught his considerate notice & he sent me to bed."

The route Lincoln traveled to and from the Soldiers' Home took him down Vermont Avenue past the lodgings of Walt Whitman. "I see the President almost every day," Whitman wrote. "None of the artists or pictures has caught the deep, though subtle and indirect expression of this man's face. There is something else there. One of the great portrait painters of two or three centuries ago is needed." Whitman proudly noted that "we have got so that we exchange bows, and very cordial ones. Sometimes the President goes and comes in an open barouche. The cavalry always accompany him, with drawn sabers. Often I notice as he goes out evenings—and sometimes in the morning, when he returns early—he turns off and halts at the large and handsome residence of the Secretary of War, on K Street."

All summer, Stanton harbored hopes that he and Lincoln might escape to the mountains of Pennsylvania. "The President and I have been arranging to make a trip to Bedford," he told Ellen, "but something always turns up to keep him or me in Washington. He is so eager for it that I expect we shall accomplish it before the season is over." In fact, though Stanton finally joined his wife during the first week of September, Lincoln journeyed no farther that summer than the Soldiers' Home.

The president was rarely alone, however. In addition to Hay and Stanton, he could rely on Seward for good companionship. John Hay witnessed a typically wide-ranging conversation between them as the three rode to the Capitol on August 13 to view a sculptural work, *The Progress of Civilization*, recently installed in the eastern pediment of the north wing of the Capitol. The conversation opened on the topic of slavery, slipped back to the time of the Masons and anti-Masons, then turned to the Mexican War. Both Seward and Lincoln agreed that "one fundamental principle of politics is to be always on the side of your country in a war. It kills any party to oppose a war." As, indeed, Lincoln knew from his own experience in opposing the Mexican War.

The following day, Seward left for a two-week tour of upstate New York with foreign ministers, including those from England, France, Spain, Germany, and Russia. Seward had engineered the trip to counter the impression abroad that the lengthy war was starting to exhaust the resources of the North. With Seward as their guide, members of the diplomatic corps journeyed up the Hudson, stopping in Albany, Schenectady, and Cooperstown. They sailed on the Finger Lakes, visited Niagara Falls, and spent the night in Auburn, where they were joined by Seward's neighbors and friends for a picnic on the lake.

"All seemed to be enjoying themselves very much," Frances noted. Seward, extroverted as always, provided a sparkling commentary, excellent food, abundant drink, and good cheer. After months of tense wrangling over the status of the Confederacy, the European ministers saw a different side of Seward and enjoyed his easy camaraderie. "When one comes really to know him," Lord Lyons reported to Lord Russell, "one is surprised to find much to esteem and even to like in him."

More important, the tour allowed the skeptical ministers to witness the boundless resources of the North. "Hundreds of factories with whirring wheels," Fred Seward wrote, "thousands of acres of golden harvest fields, miles of railway trains, laden with freight, busy fleets on rivers, lakes and canals"—all presaged the inevitable triumph of the Union. This clear perception of the Union's strength contributed to the successful resolution of a troubling controversy with Great Britain and France. Since the previous autumn, the administration had been bedeviled by knowledge that the Confederacy had contracts with European shipbuilders for armored vessels vastly superior to anything in the Union fleet. For months, Seward had coupled diplomatic efforts with strident warnings of war should the ironclads leave Europe. Not until September, several weeks after the diplomatic tour, did he receive trustworthy assurances from the governments of England and France that the rams would not be delivered.

With Seward in upstate New York, Stanton in the mountains of Pennsylvania, Nicolay out west, and Hay setting out for a week's vacation in Long Branch, New Jersey, Lincoln was left in relative solitude. "The White House," Stoddard noted, "is deserted, save by our faithful and untiring Chief Magistrate, who, alone of all our public men, is *always* at his post." Notwithstanding, Stoddard observed, "he looks less careworn and emaciated than in the spring, as if, living only for his country, he found his own vigor keeping pace with the returning health of the nation."

CHAPTER 21

"I FEEL TROUBLE IN THE AIR"

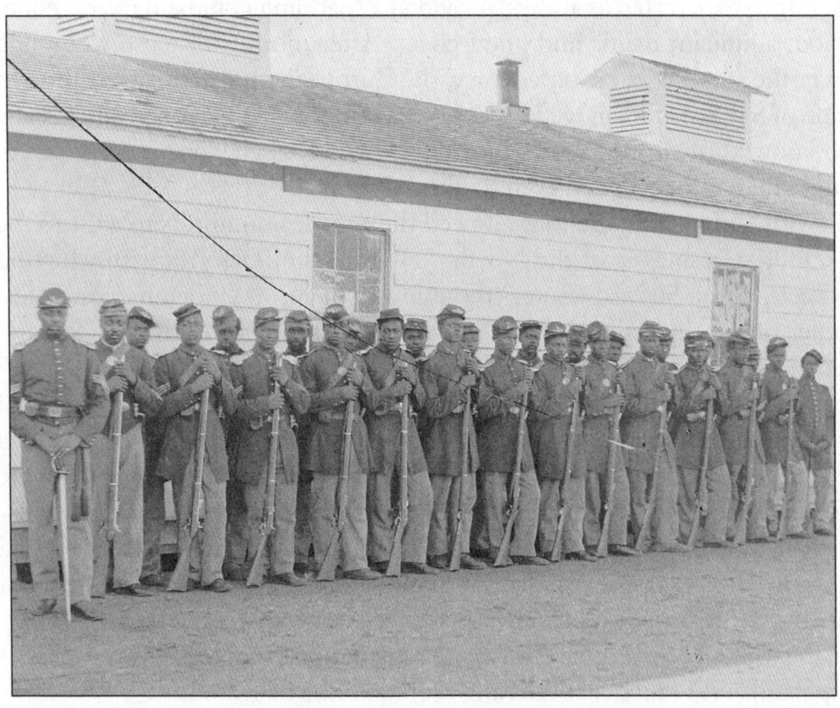

THE SUMMER OF 1863 marked a crucial transformation in the Union war effort—the organization and deployment of black regiments that would eventually amount to 180,000 soldiers, a substantial proportion of eligible black males. The struggle to open the door for black recruits had finally ended when Lincoln's Emancipation Proclamation flatly declared that blacks would "be received into the armed service of the United States." Three weeks later, Stanton authorized Massachusetts governor John Andrew to raise two regiments of black troops. Since Massachusetts had only a small black population, Andrew called on Major George L. Stearns to head a recruitment effort that would reach into New York and other Northern states. Stearns approached Frederick Douglass for help.

Douglass was overjoyed. He had long believed that the war would not be won so long as the North refused "to employ the black man's arm in suppressing the rebels." He wrote stirring appeals in his *Monthly* magazine and traveled throughout the North, speaking at large meetings in Albany, Syracuse, Buffalo, Philadelphia, and many other cities, offering a dozen answers to the question: "Why should a colored man enlist?" Nothing, he assured them, would more clearly legitimize their call for equal citizenship: "You will stand more erect, walk more assured, feel more at ease, and be less liable to insult than you ever were before. He who fights the battles of America may claim America as his country—and have that claim respected."

The black soldiers who initially answered Douglass's call became part of the famed 54th Massachusetts Regiment. Captained by Robert Gould Shaw, the son of wealthy Boston abolitionists, this first black regiment from the North included two of Frederick Douglass's own sons, Charles and Lewis. On May 28, thousands of Bostonians poured into the streets cheering the men as they marched past the State House and the Common. At the parade ground, they were reviewed by the governor and various high-ranking military officials. "No single regiment has attracted larger crowds," the *Boston Daily Evening Transcript* reported. "Ladies lined the balconies and windows of the houses," waving their handkerchiefs as the brass band led the proud regiment to the parade ground.

Frederick Douglass attended the ceremonies, proudly extolling the "manly bearing" and "admirable marching" of the men he had worked hard to recruit. After bidding his sons farewell, he returned to the task of recruiting with renewed zeal.

Lincoln was in full accord with this drive to build black regiments. Though he had initially resisted proposals to arm blacks, he was now totally dedicated. He urged Banks, Hunter, and Grant to speed the enlisting process and implored Governor Andrew Johnson of Tennessee to raise black troops. "The colored population is the great *available* and yet *unavailed* of, force for restoring the Union," Lincoln wrote. "The bare sight of fifty thousand armed, and drilled black soldiers on the banks of the Mississippi, would end the rebellion at once." Chase, who had argued more strongly than any other cabinet member for black soldiers, took great satisfaction in Lincoln's newfound commitment. "The President is now thoroughly in earnest in this business," he wrote a friend, "& sees it much as I saw it nearly two years ago."

In his efforts to recruit black soldiers, Douglass encountered a series of obstacles forged by white prejudice: black soldiers received less pay than white soldiers, they were denied the enlistment bounty, and they were not allowed to be commissioned as officers. Still, Douglass insisted, "this is no time for hesitation. . . . Once let the black man get upon his person the brass letters, U.S.; let him get an eagle on his button, and a musket on his shoulder, and bullets in his pocket," he told a mass audience in Philadelphia, "and there is no power on the earth or under the earth which can deny that he has earned the right of citizenship in the United States. I say again, this is our chance, and woe betide us if we fail to embrace it."

When the newly organized black troops went into battle—at Port Hudson, Milliken's Bend, and Fort Wagner—they earned great respect from white soldiers and civilians alike for their "bravery and steadiness." If captured, however, they ran the risk of losing their freedom or their lives, for the Confederate Congress had passed an ordinance "dooming to death or slavery every negro taken in arms, and every white officer who commands negro troops."

As word of the unique dangers they faced spread through the black community, Douglass found that the size and enthusiasm of his audiences were swiftly diminishing, as was the number of black enlistments. He blamed Lincoln for not speaking out against the Confederate ordinance. "What has Mr. Lincoln to say about this slavery and murder? What has he said?—Not one word. In the hearing of the nation he is as silent as an oyster on the whole subject." The time for patience with the president had come and gone, he argued. Until he "shall interpose his power to prevent these atrocious assassinations of negro soldiers, the civilized world will hold him equally with Jefferson Davis responsible for them."

Lincoln's failure to speak out and protect the Union's black soldiers convinced Douglass that he could no longer persuade men to enlist in good conscience. "When I plead for recruits, I want to do it with my heart, without qualification," he explained to Major Stearns. "I cannot do that now. The impression settles upon me that colored men have much overrated the enlightenment, justice and generosity of our rulers at Washington."

In fact, Lincoln was already formulating a response. During the last week of July 1863, he asked Halleck to prepare an Order of Retaliation, which was issued on July 30. The order made clear that "the law of nations and the usages and customs of war as carried on by civilized powers, permit no distinction as to color in the treatment of prisoners of war." The Confederate ordinance represented "a relapse into barbarism" that required action on the part of the Union. "It is therefore ordered that for every soldier of the United States killed in violation of the laws of war, a rebel soldier shall be executed; and for every one enslaved by the enemy or sold into slavery, a rebel soldier shall be placed at hard labor."

The order was "well-written," the antagonistic Count Gurowski conceded, "but like all Mr. Lincoln's acts it is done almost too late, only when the poor President was so cornered by events, that shifting and escape became impossible." Douglass agreed but acknowledged that the president, "being a man of action," might have been waiting "for a case in which he should be required to act."

Although the retaliatory order alleviated one major concern, Douglass feared that the lack of "fair play" in the handling of black enrollees would continue to hamper recruiting. Major Stearns suggested that Douglass should go to Washington and explain the situation to the president. Having never visited the nation's capital, Douglass experienced an inexpressible "tumult of feeling" when he entered the White House. "I could not know what kind of a reception would be accorded me. I might be told to go home and mind my business. . . . Or I might be refused an interview altogether."

Finding a large crowd in the hallway, Douglass expected to wait hours before gaining an audience with the president. Minutes after presenting his card, however, he was called into the office. "I was never more quickly or more completely put at ease in the presence of a great man than in that of Abraham Lincoln," he later recalled. The president was seated in a chair when Douglass entered the room, "surrounded by a multitude of books and papers, his feet and legs were extended in front of his chair. On my approach he slowly drew his feet in from the different parts of the room into which they had strayed, and he began to rise." As Lincoln extended his hand in greeting, Douglass hesitantly began to introduce himself. "I know who you are, Mr. Douglass," Lincoln said. "Mr. Seward has told me all about you. Sit down. I am glad to see you." Lincoln's warmth put Douglass instantly at ease. Douglass later maintained that he had "never seen a more transparent countenance." He could tell "at a glance the justice of the popular estimate of the President['s] qualities expressed in the prefix *'honest'* to the name of Abraham Lincoln."

Douglass laid before the president the discriminatory measures that were frustrating his recruiting efforts. "Mr. Lincoln listened with earnest attention and with very apparent sympathy," he recalled. "Upon my ceasing to speak [he] proceeded with an earnestness and fluency of which I had not suspected him." Lincoln first recognized the indisputable justice of the demand for equal pay. When Congress passed the bill for black soldiers, he explained, it "seemed a necessary concession to smooth the way to their employment at all as soldiers," but he promised that "in the end they shall have the same pay as white soldiers." As for the absence of black officers, Lincoln assured Douglass that "he would sign any commission to colored soldiers whom his Secretary of War should commend to him."

Douglass was particularly impressed by Lincoln's justification for delaying the retaliatory order until the public mind was prepared for it. Had he acted earlier, Lincoln said, before the recent battles "in which negroes had distinguished themselves for bravery and general good conduct," he was certain that "such was the state of public popular prejudice that an outcry would have been raised against the measure. It would be said—Ah! we thought it would come to this. White men were to be killed for negroes." In fact, he confessed to grave misgivings that, "once begun, there was no telling where it would end; that if he could get hold of the Confederate soldiers who had been guilty [of killing black prisoners] he could easily retaliate, but the thought of hanging men for a crime perpetrated by others was revolting to his feelings." While Douglass disagreed, believing the order essential, he respected the "humane spirit" that prompted Lincoln's concerns.

Before they parted, Lincoln told Douglass that he had read a recent speech in which the fiery orator had lambasted "the tardy, hesitating and vacillating policy of the President of the United States." Though he conceded that he might move with frustrating deliberation on large issues, he disputed the accusation of vacillation. "I think it cannot be shown that when I have once taken a position, I have ever retreated from it." Douglass would never forget his first meeting with Lincoln, during which he felt "as though I could . . . put my hand on his shoulder."

Later that same day, Douglass met with Stanton. "The manner of no two men could be more widely different," he observed. "His first glance was that of a man who says: 'Well, what do you want? I have no time to waste upon you or anybody else.' " Nonetheless, once Douglass began to outline much the same issues he had addressed with the president, "contempt and suspicion and brusqueness had all disappeared from his face," and Stanton, too, promised "that justice would ultimately be done." Indeed, Stanton had already implored Congress to remove the discriminatory wage and bounty provisions, which it would eventually do. Impressed by Douglass, Stanton promised to make him an assistant adjutant general assigned to Lorenzo Thomas, then charged with recruiting black soldiers in the Mississippi Valley. The War Department followed up with an offer of a $100-a-month salary plus subsistence and transportation, but the commission was not included. Douglass declined: "I knew too much of

37

President Abraham Lincoln,
photographed by Mathew Brady in 1862.

38

Lincoln's office in the White House *(above)* doubled as the cabinet's meeting room. Late at night, he liked to relax and share stories with his two secretaries, John Nicolay *(below left)* and John Hay *(below right)*, who became almost like sons to him.

39

40

41

Seventy-five-year-old General Winfield Scott *(below)*, veteran of the War of 1812 and the Mexican War, commanded the U.S. Army when Lincoln took office. Shown here with the cabinet *(above)*, Scott suffered from a variety of ailments that limited his active role in military planning.

42

43

Even during the Civil War, ordinary people had nearly unlimited access to the White House. Volunteer troops bivouacked in the East Room in May 1861 *(above)*, while large public receptions *(below)* attracted a "living tide of humanity" who poured in to shake hands with the president and first lady.

44

45 

 46

In February 1862, while Mary Lincoln *(left)* hosted a triumphant reception downstairs, her twelve-year-old son, Willie, lay dying upstairs. After Mary fell into a depression *(right)*, Lincoln was left to care for their youngest son, Tad *(below)*, who was equally devastated by Willie's death.

47 

48

49

When Seward became secretary of state *(left)*, he installed his son Fred as his second in command *(above, far right)* and settled his close-knit family, including Augustus *(below, standing)*, Fred *(left)*, Fanny *(right)*, and Fred's wife, Anna *(foreground)*, into an elegant mansion on Lafayette Square.

50

51

Treasury Secretary Salmon Chase *(above)* craved the presidency with every fiber of his being, an ambition shared by his beautiful daughter Kate *(below left, and seated, right)*. Rumors circulated that her 1863 marriage to William Sprague *(below, right)* "was a coldly calculated plan to secure the Sprague millions" to finance her father's 1864 campaign.

52

53

54 

 55

When his first war secretary, Simon Cameron *(left)*, resigned under fire, Lincoln called on Edwin M. Stanton *(right)*, who overcame his initial contempt for the president to embrace a deep friendship. The Lincoln and Stanton families spent their summers together at the Soldiers' Home *(below)*.

56

Francis P. Blair and his wife, Eliza *(middle)*, presided over a political dynasty that included their sons, Postmaster General Montgomery Blair *(bottom right)* and Union general Frank *(bottom left)*. Daughter Elizabeth's *(top right)* voluminous letters to her husband, Captain Samuel P. Lee *(top left)*, left a vivid record of life in Washington during the Civil War.

62

In addition to their cabinet duties, both Navy Secretary Gideon Welles *(above)* and Attorney General Edward Bates *(below)* kept detailed diaries that recorded the inner workings of the Lincoln administration.

63

64

In letters to his wife, Mary Ellen *(right)*, General George B. McClellan regularly derided Lincoln, his cabinet, and most of the hierarchy in the Union army, while crediting himself with every success. Admirers hailed him as a young Napoleon *(below)*.

65

66

67

Lincoln went through a succession of generals, including Ambrose E. Burnside *(below left)* and Joseph Hooker *(below right)*, before he found a winning team in Ulysses S. Grant *(above left)* and William T. Sherman *(above right)*.

68

69

70

71

Antislavery leader Frederick Douglass *(left)* and Senator Charles Sumner *(right)* urged Lincoln to bring blacks into the Union army. Ultimately, almost two hundred thousand black men served, including this young soldier *(below)*.

72

73

Lincoln took more than a dozen trips to the front, both to consult with his generals and to inspire the troops *(above)*. Scenes of the dead littered on the battlefield *(below)* tore at his heart.

74

Lincoln and his son Tad walked through the Confederate capital of Richmond on April 4, 1865. Freed slaves crowded the streets, shouting, "Glory! Hallelujah!" when Lincoln came into view.

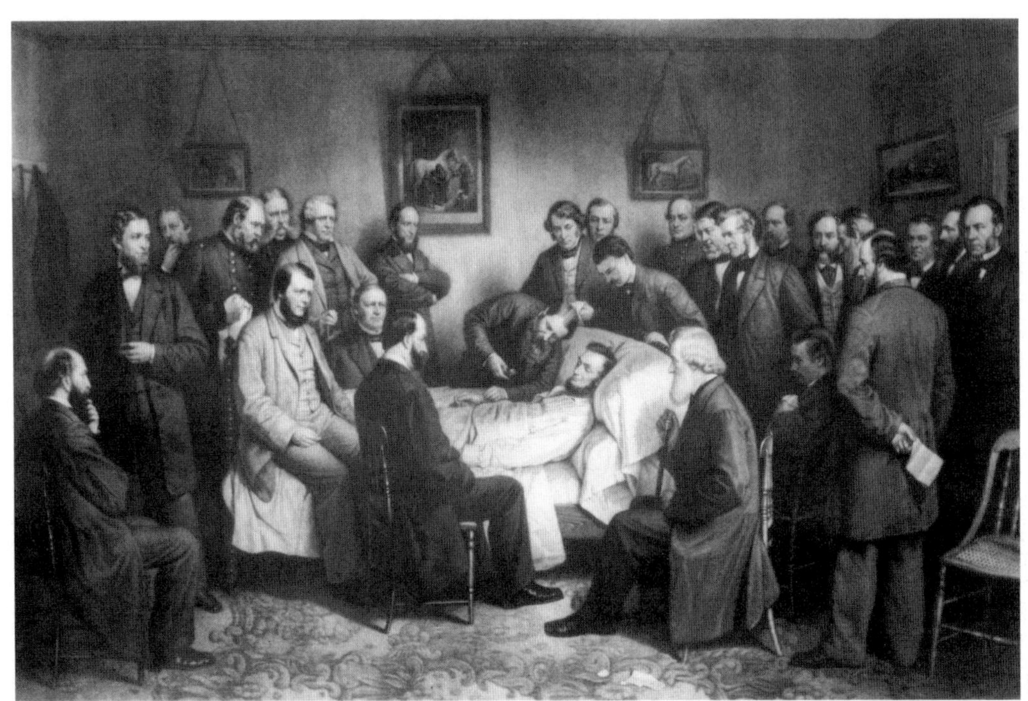

76

As Lincoln lay dying in the Petersen boardinghouse, he was surrounded by family, members of his cabinet, congressmen, senators, and military officials. When Lincoln died at 7:22 A.M. on April 15, 1865, Stanton proclaimed: "Now he belongs to the ages."

camp life and the value of shoulder straps in the army to go into the service without some visible mark of my rank."

Douglass and Lincoln had established a relationship that would prove important for both men in the weeks and months ahead. In subsequent speeches, Douglass frequently commented on his gracious reception at the White House. "Perhaps you may like to know how the President of the United States received a black man at the White House," he would say. "I will tell you how he received me—just as you have seen one gentleman receive another." As the crowd erupted into "great applause," he continued, "I tell you I felt big there!"

• • •

In the relative quiet that followed, Lincoln immersed himself in the task of composing another public letter. This letter was addressed to James Conkling, the old Springfield friend in whose office he had anxiously awaited news from Chicago during the Republican nominating convention. As a leading Illinois Republican, Conkling had invited Lincoln to attend a mass meeting in Springfield on September 3, organized to rally loyal Unionists in a show of strength against the Copperhead influence, which remained strong in the Northwest. Union victories at Gettysburg and Vicksburg had created a deceptive feeling that peace was close at hand. False rumors circulated that Lincoln had received and rejected several viable peace proposals. It was essential to derail these damaging stories and halt Copperhead momentum in its tracks. While he doubtless would have been received with adoration in his hometown, Lincoln decided to remain in Washington and compose a comprehensive letter for Conkling to read at the meeting and then have printed for mass distribution.

After completing an early draft, Lincoln searched out someone to listen as he read it aloud. It was a Sunday night, and the mansion was nearly vacant. Entering the library, the president was delighted to find William Stoddard. "Ah! I'm glad you're here," Lincoln said. "Come over into my room." Stoddard followed him into his office. "Sit down," Lincoln urged. "What I want is an audience. Nothing sounds the same when there isn't anybody to hear it and find fault with it." Stoddard expressed doubt that he would be inclined to criticize the president's words. "Yes, you will," Lincoln good-humoredly replied. "Everybody else will. It's just what I want you to do." Then, taking the sheets of foolscap paper from the end of the cabinet table on which he had been writing, he began to read.

Warming to the task, Lincoln allowed his voice to rise and fall as if he were speaking to an audience of thousands. When he finished, he asked

Stoddard's impression. Stoddard's sole objection was to fault Lincoln's metaphor—"Uncle Sam's web-feet"—for the navy gunboats that plied the rivers and bayous. "I never saw a web-footed gunboat in all my life," Stoddard said. "They're a queer kind of duck." Lincoln laughed. "Some of 'em did get ashore, though. I'll leave it in, now I know how it's going to sound." Then, thanking Stoddard, he bade him good night.

The address was designed to curb the "deceptive and groundless" rumors that Lincoln had secretly rejected peace proposals. If any legitimate propositions should be received, he pledged, they would not be kept a secret from the people he was elected to serve. "But, to be plain," he went on, "you are dissatisfied with me about the negro. . . . You dislike the emancipation proclamation; and, perhaps, would have it retracted." On this point there would be no compromise: "it can not be retracted, any more than the dead can be brought to life," for "the promise being made, must be kept." Furthermore, black soldiers had become so integral to the war effort that "some of the commanders of our armies in the field who have given us our most important successes, believe the emancipation policy, and the use of colored troops, constitute the heaviest blow yet dealt to the rebellion. . . .

"Peace does not appear so distant as it did," Lincoln concluded. "And then, there will be some black men who can remember that, with silent tongue, and clenched teeth, and steady eye, and well-poised bayonet, they have helped mankind on to this great consummation; while, I fear, there will be some white ones, unable to forget that, with malignant heart, and deceitful speech, they have strove to hinder it."

Lincoln continued to refine his letter over the next ten days, stealing what time he could from his public duties. He finally sent it, accompanied with a personal note to Conkling: "You are one of the best public readers. I have but one suggestion. Read it very slowly." An immense crowd was expected, drawn "from the farm and the workshop," the local newspaper reported, "from the office and the counting-room," to prove to the Copperheads that behind the soldiers already in the field were "hundreds of thousands more who are willing to offer their services whenever the country calls."

Confident in his final composition, Lincoln anticipated a positive reception on September 3 when it would be read to the crowd and then given to newspapers for publication the following day. When he awoke on the morning of the mass meeting, however, he was furious to see a truncated version of his letter printed in the Washington *Daily Chronicle*. Lincoln immediately complained to the editor, John Forney. Don't blame us, Forney explained to Lincoln, we got it from the Associated Press, and it's in daily newspapers around the country. Provoked, Lincoln telegraphed

Conkling in Springfield. "I am mortified this morning to find the letter to you, botched up, in the Eastern papers, telegraphed from Chicago. How did this happen?"

Hearing nothing that day from Conkling, Lincoln remained testy. When a petitioner tried to solicit his help in securing property for a Memphis woman whose husband was in the Confederate Army, the president uncharacteristically replied that he had "neither the means nor time" to consider the request and that "the impropriety of bringing such cases to me, is obvious to any one."

The following morning, a message arrived from Conkling. Apparently, he had telegraphed the letter in advance, with "strict injunctions not to permit it to be published before the meeting or make any improper use of it." He was "mortified" that someone had broken faith, but trusted that "no prejudicial results have been experienced as the whole Letter was published the next day."

In fact, the publication of the entire letter received excellent reviews. "Disclaiming the arts of the diplomatist, the cunning of the politician, and the graces of rhetoric, he comes straight to the points he wants to discuss," praised the *New York Daily Tribune.* "The most consummate rhetorician never used language more pat to the purpose," the *New York Times* declared, "and still there is not a word in the letter not familiar to the plainest plowman." While "felicity of speech" was usually linked to "high culture," the *Times* continued, Lincoln, "in his own independent, and perhaps we might say very peculiar, way," exhibits a "felicity of speech far surpassing" stylistic preference. He possesses a far more valuable "felicity of thought," which "invariably gets at the needed truth of the time," hitting "the very nail of all others which needs driving." The *Philadelphia Inquirer* had regarded Lincoln's unconventional habit of writing public letters with skepticism, but granted that his recent letters, including this one, "have dispelled the doubt. If he is as felicitous in the future, we hope he will continue to write."

"His last letter is a great thing," Hay told Nicolay a few days later. "Some hideously bad rhetoric—some indecorums that are infamous—yet the whole letter takes its solid place in history, as a great utterance of a great man. The whole Cabinet could not have tinkered up a letter which could have been compared with it. He can snake a sophism out of its hole, better than all the trained logicians of all schools."

In its fulsome praise of the letter to Conkling, the *New York Times* also commended a long line of Lincoln's writings, including his inaugural, the letters to McClellan made public by the congressional Committee on the Conduct of the War, and his published letters to Greeley and Corning, which revealed "the same fitness to the occasion, and the same effectiveness in its own direction." Taken together, these remarkable documents had made Lincoln "the most popular man in the Republic. All the denunciations and all the arts of demagogues are perfectly powerless to wean the people from their faith in him."

"I know the people want him," Hay wrote to Nicolay, looking forward to the next election. "There is no mistaking that fact. But politicians are strong yet & he is not their 'kind of a cat.' I hope God wont see fit to scourge us for our sins by any one of the two or three most prominent candidates on the ground."

• • •

BY THE MIDDLE of September 1863, all the members of Lincoln's cabinet had returned from their summer sojourns. Seward came back invigorated by his trip through the lake region with the diplomatic corps. Bates was back from Missouri in time to celebrate his seventieth birthday, grateful that his long life had "been crowned with many blessings, and, comparatively few crosses." He noted with pride that, as a public figure, he had achieved a reputation "for knowledge and probity, quite as good as I deserve." Stanton, too, had enjoyed a much-needed vacation with his family in the mountains of Pennsylvania. Chase, in characteristic fashion, had allowed himself scant respite from work, leaving his daughters at the seashore and then peevishly awaiting their return. Welles was gratified to return from his ten-day visit to the Navy Yards, noting in his diary that all his colleagues seemed "glad to see me,—none more so than the President, who cordially and earnestly greeted me. I have been less absent than any other member and was therefore perhaps more missed." Lincoln himself still enjoyed leisurely nights at the Soldiers' Home and looked forward to Mary's homecoming from the Green Mountains.

Grim news from Tennessee deflated the genial, relaxed mood of the president and his cabinet. After the victories at Gettysburg and Vicksburg, Lincoln and Stanton had hoped that General Rosecrans, with the Army of the Cumberland, could deliver the "finishing blow to the rebellion." He was positioned to push the enemy from Chattanooga and Knoxville, Tennessee, with an eye to advancing on Georgia. However, after Rosecrans delivered "a great and bloodless victory at Chattanooga" as the enemy fled from the city before advancing troops, the Confederates regrouped and "unexpectedly appeared in force, on the south bank of [the] Chicamauga." A furious battle commenced on Saturday, September 19. Within thirty-six hours, the telegrams from the field indicated a stunning Confederate victory. "Chicamauga is as fatal a name in our history as Bull

Run," Dana wired Stanton. Union casualties totaled sixteen thousand men. "We have met with a serious disaster," Rosecrans acknowledged. "Enemy overwhelmed us, drove our right, pierced our center and scattered troops there."

Lincoln told Welles that the dispatches reached him "at the Soldiers' Home shortly after he got asleep, and so disturbed him that he had no more rest, but arose and came to the city and passed the remainder of the night awake and watchful." At daybreak, the president wandered into Hay's room, where, seated on the bed, he broke the news to his young aide. "Well, Rosecrans has been whipped, as I feared. I have feared it for several days. I believe I feel trouble in the air before it comes."

Later that same day, perhaps hoping that the presence of his family might lift his spirits, Lincoln telegraphed Mary. "The air is so clear and cool, and apparently healthy, that I would be glad for you to come. Nothing very particular, but I would be glad [to] see you and Tad." Mary responded immediately, saying she was "anxious to return home" and had already made plans to do so.

As further reports filtered in, the fallout of the battle proved "less unfavorable than was feared," a relieved Chase noted. General George Thomas's corps had held its ground, and the rebels had lost even more troops than the Federals. Chattanooga "still remains in our hands," Charles Dana wired to Stanton and, with reinforcements of twenty to thirty thousand troops "can be held by this army for from fifteen to twenty days." Without the additional troops, however, the outnumbered Federals would have to abandon Chattanooga or face another potentially disastrous battle. Everything hinged on whether this massive movement of troops would reach Tennessee in time. Shortly before midnight on Wednesday, Stanton came up with a bold idea that required the president's approval.

Unwilling to waste the remainder of the night, Stanton dispatched messengers to bring Lincoln, Halleck, Seward, and Chase to a secret meeting in his office. Chase had just retired for the night when the courier rang his bell. "The Secretary of War desires that you will come to the Department immediately & has sent a carriage for you," he announced. Chase "hastily rose & dressed," terrified that the enemy had captured Rosecrans and his entire army. John Hay was sent to the Soldiers' Home to summon Lincoln, who, like Chase, was already in bed. As Lincoln rose to dress, "he was considerably disturbed," saying that "it was the first time Stanton had ever sent for him." Guided by the light of the moon, Lincoln and Hay then rode back to the War Department.

When the five men were assembled around the table, the austere Stanton said: "I have invited this meeting because I am thoroughly convinced that something must be done & done immediately." He proceeded to outline an audacious proposal to remove twenty thousand men from General Meade's Army of the Potomac to Nashville and Chattanooga under General Hooker's command. The plan struck both Halleck and Lincoln as dangerous and impractical. Halleck protested that it would take at least forty days to reach Tennessee. The troops would arrive too late, and Meade would be left vulnerable on the Rappahannock. The president agreed. "Why," he quipped, "you cant get one corps into Washington in the time you fix for reaching Nashville." A humorous anecdote he employed to illustrate his point "greatly annoyed" Stanton, who remarked that "the danger was too imminent & the occasion [too] serious for jokes." He said that "he had fully considered the question of practicability & should not have submitted his proposition had he not fully satisfied himself" as to its feasibility.

After further discussion, Chase suggested taking a break for the refreshments Stanton had prepared. "On returning," Chase recalled, "Mr. Seward took up the subject & supported Mr. Stantons proposition with excellent arguments." Chase believed that Seward's support for the proposal was instrumental. Sensing his advantage, Stanton immediately sent an orderly to find Colonel D. C. McCallum, director of the Department of Military Railroads. Stanton had briefed McCallum earlier in the evening and directed him to prepare an estimate of the time necessary to transfer the troops by rail if all available trains were put at his disposal. When McCallum entered, Lincoln described the proposition and asked him to estimate how long it would take to achieve the goal. Without disclosing that he had received prior notice to consider the matter, McCallum asked for a moment to "make a few figures." Seated at a desk with timetables spread before him, he worked for some time while the room remained silent. Finally, he stood up and said: "I can complete it in seven days."

"Good!" Stanton exclaimed, turning contemptuously to Halleck. "I told you so! I knew it could be done! Forty days! Forty days indeed, when the life of the nation is at stake!" He then addressed McCallum: "Go ahead; begin now." At this point, Lincoln interrupted. "I have not yet given my consent," he reminded the secretary of war. "Colonel McCallum, are you sure about this?" Lincoln asked. "There must be no mistake." When McCallum said he would "pledge [his] life to accomplish it inside of seven days," Lincoln was satisfied. "Mr. Secretary, you are the captain. Give the necessary orders and I will approve them."

Relentlessly, Stanton worked for more than forty-eight hours straight, commandeering trains for military use, telegraphing railroad managers along the route, determining the various gauges of the tracks. He acquired the provisions necessary for soldiers and horses to travel straight across the Alleghenies into East Tennessee without a stop to resupply.

The first train left Washington at 5 p.m. on September 25, with departures every hour until 23,000 men and 1,100 horses, 9 batteries, and hundreds of wagons, tents, and supplies arrived in Tennessee ready to join Rosecrans in defense of Chattanooga. Monitoring reports from every station along the way, Stanton refused to go home. When exhaustion overtook him, he would collapse on his couch for a few hours, a cologne-moistened handkerchief tied around his forehead. Only when it became clear that the movement would succeed within the promised seven days did he agree to leave his post. "It was an extraordinary feat of logistics," James McPherson writes, "the longest and fastest movement of such a large body of troops before the twentieth century."

The immediate peril was past, but Dana's reports in the following weeks indicated that the rebels had cut off supply routes into Chattanooga and that the troops had lost confidence in Rosecrans. Lincoln and Stanton decided that the time had come for a change in command. Stanton telegraphed Grant to leave Cairo, Illinois, for Louisville, Kentucky, where he would "meet an officer of the War Department" and receive new instructions. When Grant reached Indianapolis, he discovered that the War Department officer was Stanton himself. This was the first meeting between the two men.

Stanton presented Grant with a choice between two orders. Both offered him command of a new "Military Division of the Mississippi" encompassing the Departments of the Cumberland, the Ohio, and the Tennessee. The first left the departmental commanders in place. Grant chose the second order, which replaced Rosecrans with Thomas. Stanton spent a day with Grant discussing the overall military situation before the general departed for Chattanooga. There, under his leadership, the Federals eventually drove the rebels from Tennessee after a stunning victory at Missionary Ridge.

In his memoirs, Grant credits Stanton for playing an important role in saving Chattanooga. The unprecedented troop movement prevented a retreat that, Grant acknowledged, "would have been a terrible disaster." Chase, too, lauded Stanton. "The country does not know how much it owes Edwin M. Stanton for that nights work."

It was this indomitable drive that Lincoln had sought when he put aside any resentment at the humiliation Stanton had inflicted years earlier in Cincinnati. The bluntness and single-minded intensity behind Stanton's brusque dismissal of Lincoln at that first acquaintance were the qualities the president valued in his secretary of war—whom he would affectionately call his "Mars."

Those who observed the improbable pair in the little room adjoining the telegraph office noted the "esteem and affection" that characterized their relationship. "It was an interesting and a pleasant sight," clerk Charles Benjamin recalled, "that of Mr. Lincoln seated with one long leg crossed upon the other, his head a little peaked and his face lit up by the animation of talking or listening, while Mr. Stanton would stand sidewise to him, with one hand resting lightly on the high back of the chair in the brief intervals of that everlasting occupation of wiping his spectacles." Should Lincoln rise from the writing desk that Stanton arranged for him, "the picturesqueness of the scene" would give way to laughter, for "the striking differences in height and girth at once suggested the two *gendarmes* in the French comic opera."

"No two men were ever more utterly and irreconcilably unlike," Stanton's private secretary, A. E. Johnson, observed. "The secretiveness which Lincoln wholly lacked, Stanton had in marked degree; the charity which Stanton could not feel, coursed from every pore in Lincoln. Lincoln was for giving a wayward subordinate seventy times seven chances to repair his errors; Stanton was for either forcing him to obey or cutting off his head without more ado. Lincoln was as calm and unruffled as the summer sea in moments of the gravest peril; Stanton would lash himself into a fury over the same condition of things. Stanton would take hardships with a groan; Lincoln would find a funny story to fit them. Stanton was all dignity and sternness, Lincoln all simplicity and good nature . . . yet no two men ever did or could work better in harness. They supplemented each other's nature, and they fully recognized the fact that they were a necessity to each other."

Johnson believed that "in dealing with the public, Lincoln's heart was greater than his head, while Stanton's head was greater than his heart." The antithetical styles are typified in the story of a congressman who had received Lincoln's authorization for the War Department's aid in a project. When Stanton refused to honor the order, the disappointed petitioner returned to Lincoln, telling him that Stanton had not only countermanded the order but had called the president a damned fool for issuing it. "Did Stanton say I was a d——d fool?" Lincoln asked. "He did, sir," the congressman replied, "and repeated it." Smiling, the president remarked: "If Stanton said I was a d——d fool, then I must be one, for he is nearly always right, and generally says what he means. I will step over and see him."

As Stanton came to know and understand Lincoln, his initial disdain turned to admiration. When George Harding, his old partner in the Reaper trial, assumed that Stanton was the author of the "remarkable passages" in one of Lincoln's messages, Stanton set him straight. "Lincoln wrote it—every word of it; and he is capable of more than that, Harding, no men were ever so deceived as we at Cincinnati."

"Few war ministers have had such real personal affection and respect for their king or president as Mr. Stanton had for Mr. Lincoln," a contemporary observed. Both had suffered great personal losses, and both were haunted all their days by thoughts of mortality and death. When Stanton was eighteen, a cholera epidemic had spread through the Midwest. Victims were buried as quickly as possible in an effort to contain the plague. Learning that a young friend had been buried within hours of falling ill, Stanton panicked, fearing that "she had been buried alive while in a faint." He raced to the grave, where, with the help of a medical student friend, he exhumed her body to determine if she was truly dead. Contact with the body led to his own infection and near death from cholera. When his beloved wife, Mary, died ten years later, he insisted on including her wedding ring, valuable pieces of her jewelry, and some of his correspondence in her casket. He spent hours at her gravesite, and when he could not be there, he sent an employee to stand guard.

That Lincoln was also preoccupied with death is clear from the themes of many of his favorite poems that addressed the ephemeral nature of life and reflected his own painful acquaintance with death. He particularly cherished "Mortality," by William Knox, and transcribed a copy for the Stantons.

Oh! Why should the spirit of mortal be proud?
Like a swift-fleeting meteor, a fast-flying cloud,
A flash of lightning, a break of the wave,
He passeth from life to his rest in the grave.

He could recite from memory "The Last Leaf," by Oliver Wendell Holmes, and once claimed to the painter Francis Carpenter that "for pure pathos" there was "nothing finer . . . in the English language" than the six-line stanza:

The mossy marbles rest
On lips that he has prest
In their bloom,
And the names he loved to hear
Have been carved for many a year
On the tomb.

Yet, beyond sharing a romantic and philosophical preoccupation with death, the commander in chief and the secretary of war shared the harrowing knowledge that their choices resulted in sending hundreds of thousands of young men to their graves. Stanton's Quaker background made the strain particularly unbearable. As a young man, he had written a passionate essay decrying society's exaltation of war. "Why is it," he asked, that military generals "are praised and honored instead of being punished as malefactors?" After all, the work of war is "the making of widows and orphans—the plundering of towns and villages—the exterminating & spoiling of all, making the earth a slaughterhouse." Though governments might argue war's necessity to achieve certain objectives, "how much better might they accomplish their ends by some other means? But if generals are useful so are butchers, and who will say that because a butcher is useful he should be honored?"

Three decades after writing this, Stanton found himself responsible for an army of more than 2 million men. "There could be no greater madness," he reasoned, "than for a man to encounter what I do for anything less than motives that overleap time and look forward to eternity." Lincoln, too, found the horrific scope of the burden hard to fathom. "Doesn't it strike you as queer that I, who couldn't cut the head off of a chicken, and who was sick at the sight of blood, should be cast into the middle of a great war, with blood flowing all about me?"

Like Stanton, the president tried to console himself that the Civil War, however terrible, represented a divine will at work in human affairs. The previous year, he had granted an audience to a group of Quakers, including Eliza Gurney. "If I had had my way," he reportedly said during the meeting, "this war would never have been commenced; if I had been allowed my way this war would have been ended before this, but we find it still continues; and we must believe that He permits it for some wise purpose of his own, mysterious and unknown to us; and though with our limited understandings we may not be able to comprehend it, yet we cannot but believe, that He who made the world still governs it."

He understood the terrible conflict suffered by the Friends, he wrote Mrs. Gurney later. "On principle, and faith, opposed to both war and oppression, they can only practically oppose oppression by war." Their support and their prayers, even as they endured their own "very great trial," would never be forgotten. "Meanwhile," he continued, "we must work earnestly in the best light He gives us, trusting that so working still conduces to the great ends He ordains. Surely He intends some great good to follow this mighty convulsion, which no mortal could make, and no mortal could stay."

• • •

As THE FRIENDSHIP between Stanton and Lincoln deepened, Chase, who had been Stanton's most intimate companion, was increasingly marginalized. Chase maintained a warm relationship with the secretary of war, however. Stanton still wrote affectionate notes to him. "I return your knife which by some means found its way into my pocket," Stanton had written Chase the previous winter. "Let me add that, 'if you love me like I love you no knife can cut our love in two.' " A year later, Stanton would ask Chase to stand as godfather to his newborn child. Nevertheless, the balance of power between the two men had shifted. Stanton was now a happily married man with four children. The overworked secretary of war no longer begrudged the lack of time Chase was able to spend with him. On the contrary, it was Chase who now had to pay court to Stanton. Deprived of access to vital military decisions, Chase was forced to rely on the war secretary for the latest intelligence. Stanton had once yearned to spend entire evenings in Chase's study; now Chase was lucky to obtain a private conversation with his old friend when he joined the crowd that gathered in the telegraph office at the end of the working day.

"It is painful for one to be so near the springs of action and yet unable to touch them," Chase admitted to an acquaintance. "It is almost like the nightmare in oppressiveness, and worse because there is no illusion. I can only counsel; and that without any certainty of being understood, or, if understood, of being able to obtain concurrence, or, even after concurrence, action."

Chase's frustration with his position was alleviated only by his dreams of future glory, by his dogged hope that he, rather than Lincoln, would be the Republican nominee in 1864. In an era when single-term presidencies were the rule, he believed that if he could outflank Lincoln on Reconstruction—an issue most dear to radical Republicans—he could capture the nomination. The recent victories at Gettysburg and Vicksburg had created an illusion in the North that the end of the war was at hand. Questions of how the rebel states should be brought back into the Union began to dominate discussions in the halls of Congress, at dinner parties, in newspaper editorials, and in the smoke-filled bar of the Willard Hotel.

The issue divided the Republican Party. Radicals insisted that only those who had never displayed even indirect support for the Confederacy should be allowed to vote in the redeemed states. Lawyers and teachers who had not been staunch Unionists should not be allowed to resume their professions. Slavery should be immediately abolished without compensation, and newly freed blacks should be allowed to vote in some cases. Conservative Republicans preferred compensated emancipation and a lenient definition of who should gain suffrage. They argued that in every Southern state, a silent majority of non-slaveholders had been dragged into secession by the wealthy plantation owners. It would be unjust to exclude them in the new order so long as they would take an oath to uphold both the Union and emancipation.

It was assumed in political circles that Lincoln would be the "standard-bearer for the Conservatives," while Chase would be "the champion of the Radicals." The state elections in the fall would presumably serve as the opening round of the presidential race. It was expected that Chase would aggressively promote the candidacies of fellow radicals, who, in turn, would be indebted to him the following year. While Chase's desire for the presidency was no less worthy a pursuit than Lincoln's, Noah Brooks observed, Chase's decision to pursue that ambition from within the president's cabinet rather than resign his seat and openly proclaim his campaign struck many as disingenuous.

Chase's strategy was to approach potential supporters without expressly acknowledging that he would run. Late at night in his study, he wrote hundreds of letters to local officials, congressional leaders, generals, and journalists, citing the failures of the Lincoln administration. "I should fear nothing," he wrote the editor of the *Cincinnati Gazette*, "if we had An *Administration* in the first sense of the word guided by a bold, resolute, farseeing, & active mind, guided by an honest, earnest heart. But this we have not. Oh! for energy & economy in the management of the War."

A similar style prevailed in all of his letters. After detailing the flaws in Lincoln's leadership, Chase would suggest the differences that would characterize his own presidency. He denied that he coveted the position, but said he would accept the burden if pressed by his countrymen. "If I were myself controlled merely by personal sentiments I should prefer the reelection of Mr. Lincoln," Chase explained, but "I think that a man of different qualities from those the President has will be needed for the next four years. I am not anxious to be regarded as that man; but I am quite willing to refer that question to the decision of those who agree in thinking that some such man should be had."

As in 1860, Chase took great pains to cultivate the press, not recognizing that it was too early to extract binding commitments. He was thrilled by Horace Greeley's letter in late September, telling him that he knew no one "better qualified for President than yourself, nor one whom I should more cordially support." Chase apparently discounted Greeley's closing caveat that in six months, events might dictate the need to concentrate on another candidate. Similarly, while Chase elicited assurance from Hiram

Barney, the head of the New York Custom House, that he was his "first choice for the presidency," Barney insisted on deciding only when the time came "whether yourself, the President, or some other person should receive it."

Lincoln was fully aware of what Chase was doing. Governor Dennison alerted him that Chase was "working like a beaver," and Seward cautioned that several organizations were "fixing to control delegate appointments for Mr. Chase." Ohio congressman Samuel Cox warned the White House that Chase had tied up "nearly the whole strength of the New England States." A Pennsylvanian politician informed the White House that Chase had so ardently campaigned for his support that he could see the "Presidency glaring out of both eyes." John Hay learned that Chase had called on the New York journalist Theodore Tilton, working "all a summer's day" to maneuver the influential *Independent* to his side.

Whereas Lincoln's loyal young secretary was disturbed by "Chase's mad hunt after the Presidency," Lincoln was amused. Chase's incessant presidential ambitions reminded him of the time when he was "plowing corn on a Kentucky farm" with a lazy horse that suddenly sped forward energetically to "the end of the furrow." Upon reaching the horse, he discovered "an enormous chin-fly fastened upon him, and knocked him off," not wanting "the old horse bitten in that way." His companion said that it was a mistake to knock it off, for "that's all that made him go."

"Now," Lincoln concluded, "if Mr. [Chase] has a presidential chin-fly biting him, I'm not going to knock him off, if it will only make his department go." Lincoln agreed that his secretary's tactics were in "very bad taste," and "was sorry the thing had begun, for though the matter did not annoy him his friends insisted that it ought to." Lincoln's friends could not understand why the president continued to approve appointments for avid Chase supporters who were known to be "hostile to the President's interests." Lincoln merely asserted that he would rather let "Chase have his own way in these sneaking tricks than getting into a snarl with him by refusing him what he asks." Moreover, he had no thought of dismissing Chase while he was hard at work raising the resources needed to support the immense Union Army.

Lincoln's response to Chase was neither artless nor naive. His old friend Leonard Swett maintained that there never was a greater mistake than the impression that Lincoln was a "frank, guileless, unsophisticated man." In fact, "he handled and moved man *remotely* as we do pieces upon a chessboard." Nor did Lincoln's posture toward Chase imply a tepid desire for a second term. Swett was correct in supposing that Lincoln "was much more eager for it, than he was for the first one." The Union, emancipation, his reputation, his honor, and his legacy—all depended on the outcome of the ongoing war. But he recognized it was safer to keep Chase as a dubious ally within the administration rather that to cut him loose to mount a full-blown campaign. Meanwhile, so long as Chase remained in the cabinet, Lincoln insisted on treating him with respect and dignity.

That Chase was disconcerted by Lincoln's warmth is evident in a letter he wrote to James Watson Webb, the former editor who was now the American minister to Brazil. After criticizing Lincoln's "disjointed method of administration" and admitting that he had "been often tempted to retire," Chase acknowledged that "the President has always treated me with such personal kindness and has always manifested such fairness and integrity of purpose, that I have not found myself free to throw up my trust. . . . So I still work on."

Lincoln told a worried Hay that he had "all along clearly seen [Chase's] plan of strengthening himself. Whenever he [sees] that an important matter is troubling me, if I am compelled to decide it in a way to give offense to a man of some influence he always ranges himself in opposition to me and persuades the victim that he has been hardly dealt by and that he (C.) would have arranged it very differently. It was so with Gen. Fremont—with Genl. Hunter when I annulled his hasty proclamation—with Gen. Butler when he was recalled from New Orleans." Recognizing the truth of Lincoln's words, Hay speculated that "Chase would try to make capital out of this Rosecrans business," though Lincoln had simply relieved the general from command of the Department of the Tennessee at Grant's request. Lincoln drolly replied: "I suppose he will, like the bluebottle fly, lay his eggs in every rotten spot he can find."

In late September, as the rift within Missouri's Republican Party threatened to erupt into open warfare, Chase continued his divisive plotting. Lincoln sought to keep radicals and conservatives united against the rebels. Chase aligned himself with the radicals. The struggle centered on Reconstruction. Since the Emancipation Proclamation did not extend to the loyal border states, the people of Missouri were left to determine the fate of slavery independently in their state. The conservatives, led by Frank Blair and Bates's brother-in-law Governor Hamilton Gamble, were in favor of a gradual emancipation that provided protection to slaveholders during a transitional period. Radical leaders such as B. Gratz Brown, Charles Drake, and Henry Blow favored changes in the state constitution that would immediately extinguish slavery.

So flammable had the dispute become that Governor Gamble worried the radicals intended to overthrow the elected state government. For their part, the radicals had come to believe that General John M. Schofield, the military commander of Missouri whom Lincoln had put in place as a neutral figure, had become a conservative partisan. He was accused of abusing his authority by arresting leading radicals and suppressing radical papers under the guise of military necessity.

On September 30, a delegation of radicals led by Charles Drake journeyed to Washington to demand Schofield's removal. The night before the scheduled meeting, Lincoln talked with Hay about the tense situation. He acknowledged Hay's argument that "the Radicals would carry the State and it would be well not to alienate them." Moreover, he believed that "these Radical men have in them the stuff which must save the state and on which we must mainly rely." They would never abandon the cause of emancipation, "while the Conservatives, in casting about for votes to carry through their plans, are tempted to affiliate with those whose record is not clear." If he had to choose, Lincoln told his aide, "if one side *must* be crushed out & the other cherished," he would "side with the Radicals." On another occasion, he had expressed this affinity more strongly, stating that "they are nearer to me than the other side, in thought and sentiment, though bitterly hostile personally." While they might be "the unhandiest devils in the world to deal with . . . their faces are set Zionwards."

Nevertheless, Lincoln refused to be coerced into choosing one faction or the other, and resented the radicals' demand that he treat Gamble, Frank Blair, and the conservatives "as copperheads and enemies to the Govt." rather than as mere political opponents. "This is simply monstrous," Lincoln declared, to denounce men who had courageously upheld the Union in the early days, when that affiliation threatened not only their political futures but their very lives. By contrast, the delegation's vociferous leader, Charles Drake, was originally a Southern-leaning Democrat who had delighted in railing against Black Republicans. "Not that he objected to penitent rebels being radical: he was glad of it: but fair play: let not the pot make injurious reference to the black base of the kettle: he was in favor of short statutes of limitations." Welles understood Lincoln's dilemma. "So intense and fierce" were these radicals, he wrote in his diary, that they might well "inflict greater injury—on those Republicans . . . who do not conform to their extreme radical and fanatical views than on the Rebels in the field." Such vindictiveness, he lamented, was "among the saddest features of the times."

Lincoln assured Hay that if the radicals could "show that Schofield has done anything wrong & has interfered to their disadvantage with State politics," he would consider their case. But if Schofield had "incurred their ill will by refusing to take sides with them," then it would be an entirely different matter. Indeed: "I cannot do anything contrary to my convictions to please these men, earnest and powerful as they may be."

No sooner had the delegates settled themselves at the Willard Hotel than they received an invitation to spend the evening at Chase's home. When Bates learned of the invitation, he told Gamble he was "surprised and mortified" that Chase had extended his hand to those men he considered mortal enemies, and "still more surprised" when Chase invited him as well. He immediately declined. "I refuse flatly to hold social, friendly intercourse with men, who daily denounce me and all my friends, as traitors." Gamble replied that Bates should hardly be shocked by Chase's willingness to entertain "these ~~dogs~~ persons," for "Mr. Chase is the author of our troubles here." His "criminal ambition" for the presidency had led him to incite the struggle, and he would undoubtedly have the support of every radical paper in the state if he were to decide to run against Lincoln.

The president's meeting with the Missourians lasted over two hours. Drake read his list of demands "as pompously as if it were full of matter instead of wind," noted John Hay. Lincoln listened attentively, allowing his critics to enumerate their grievances. He knew well that these men would be important in the coming presidential canvass, but felt their call for Schofield's dismissal was misguided. He explained his position clearly, calmly, and forcefully, both at the meeting that day and in a letter drafted a few days later. While he acknowledged their version of the turmoil facing Missouri, he was not convinced that Schofield was "responsible for that suffering and wrong." On the contrary, he suggested, all the troubles they described could be explained by the fact that during a civil war, confusion abounds: "Deception breeds and thrives. Confidence dies, and universal suspicion reigns." Until he received evidence that Schofield had used his powers arbitrarily for or against a particular faction, he could not, in good conscience, remove him from command. That evidence had not been provided.

"The President never appeared to better advantage in the world," Hay noted proudly in his diary. "Though He knows how immense is the danger to himself from the unreasoning anger of that committee, he never cringed to them for an instant. He stood where he thought he was right and crushed them with his candid logic." Lincoln emerged from the meeting "in a good humor," Bates observed. "Some of them he said, were not as bad as he supposed." Yet, while clarifying the fact that "whoever commands in Missouri, or elsewhere" was responsible to him, "and not to either radicals or conservatives," Lincoln once again moved to defuse the situation without alienating vital constituents. On the day the radicals left town, he wrote to remind Schofield that his authority to "arrest individuals, and suppress assemblies, or newspapers" was limited only to those who were "working *palpable* injury to the Military."

Indeed, several months later, when Lincoln became convinced that Schofield was actually leaning toward the conservatives instead of using "his influence to harmonize the conflicting elements," he decided to replace him with Rosecrans, a man long favored by the radicals. But even then, he engineered the transfer in a manner that protected Schofield's good name, while preserving his own presidential authority to determine when and where to change his commanders.

At this juncture, Frank Blair seriously aggravated matters. That October, returning to Missouri after heroic duty with Grant and Sherman at Vicksburg, the soldier-politician escalated the dissension with an explosive speech. Before an overflowing crowd at Mercantile Library Hall in St. Louis, he proclaimed his firm opposition to every one of the radicals' Reconstruction ideas. Condemning their call for the immediate emancipation of Missouri's slaves, he insisted that no action should be taken until the war was won. He argued that Missourians should focus solely on supporting the Union, deferring all issues regarding slavery. He warned that if the radicals gained control, the country would "degenerate into a revolution like that which afflicted France." They would set themselves up as "judges, witnesses and executioners alike." They would send to the guillotine "men who come back grimed all over with powder from our battle fields" but who happen to disagree with them on Reconstruction.

Blair then turned his ire on Chase, fully aware that the treasury secretary was hoping to ride the radicals' support to the White House. Loyalty to Lincoln and hatred for Chase combined to produce a vitriolic rant in which Blair accused the secretary of manipulating Treasury regulations that governed the cotton trade between North and South to benefit his radical friends and prevent conservative merchants, who "were among the first men to come forward and clothe and arm the troops," from receiving the cotton they desperately needed. As a friendly audience roared its approval, Blair accused Chase of using his cabinet post to create a political machine designed to unseat Lincoln in the next election. In sum, the treasury secretary was a traitor and blackguard indistinguishable from Jefferson Davis himself.

Blair's speech outraged the radicals, who promptly denounced *him* as a Copperhead and a traitor. The *Liberator* criticized his vindictive language, observing that "his style of address does him no honor, and will not advance the ideas of public policy which he advocates." Even his sister, Elizabeth, remarked that he could "not let even a great man set his small dogs on him without kicking the dog & giving his master some share of his resentment."

Lincoln was dismayed by the whole affair, realizing that Frank, whom he liked a great deal, had seriously compromised his future. He wrote a letter to Monty, offering advice as if the tempestuous Frank "were my brother instead of yours." He warned that by "a misunderstanding," Frank was "in danger of being permanently separated from those with whom only he can ever have a real sympathy—the sincere opponents of slavery." By allowing himself to be provoked into personal attacks, he could end up exiled from "the house of his own building. He is young yet. He has abundant talent—quite enough to occupy all his time, without devoting any to temper." If Frank decided to resume his seat in the House when the new Congress assembled, he should bear this in mind. Otherwise, he would "serve both the country and himself more profitably" by returning to the military, where his recent promotion to corps commander proved that he was "rising in military skill and usefulness."

Lincoln's counsel to Frank was echoed in a gentle letter of reprimand to another young man whose intemperate words had made him vulnerable. Captain James Cutts, Jr., had been court-martialed for using "unbecoming language" in addressing a superior officer and for publicly derogating his superior's accomplishments to the point where a duel almost took place. Young Cutts was the brother of Adele Cutts, Stephen Douglas's second wife. In remitting the sentence, Lincoln wrote, "You have too much of life yet before you, and have shown too much of promise as an officer, for your future to be lightly surrendered." He tried to impart some of the measured outlook that had served him so well: "No man resolved to make the most of himself, can spare time for personal contention. Still less can he afford to take all the consequences, including the vitiating of his temper, and the loss of self-control. Yield larger things to which you can show no more than equal right; and yield lesser ones, though clearly your own. Better give your path to a dog, than be bitten by him in contesting for the right. Even killing the dog would not cure the bite."

Frank Blair's battle against Chase in Missouri was carried forward by Monty Blair in Maryland, where a similar struggle over Reconstruction had arisen. Chase again intervened, lending his support to the radical Henry Winter Davis as a candidate for Congress. Davis was a proponent of immediate uncompensated emancipation and rigorous standards for defining eligibility to vote. Monty voiced his opposition at Rockville in early October, flaying the radicals' program, and arguing that the "ultra-abolitionists" were as despotic as the old slaveocrats. If they succeeded in their draconian measures toward the rebel states, he warned, it would be "fatal to republican institutions." He excoriated Sumner's proposition that the rebel states had forfeited their rights to equal participation in the Union by committing suicide by secession. Although Blair's speech met with approval from his partisan audience, it aroused deep hostility in Congress. Fifty congressmen signed a petition calling on Lincoln to remove Blair from his cabinet.

Once again, Lincoln was forced to balance the interests of contentious factions. Many assumed incorrectly that Blair was speaking for the White House. In fact, Lincoln refused to support Blair's candidate against Winter Davis, insisting that a Union convention had nominated Davis and it "would be mean to do anything against him." In the end, the president's most vital objective for Maryland was realized in the election—a dramatic Republican victory over the Copperheads, ensuring that the former slave state stood firmly behind the Union's cause. Noah Brooks attended a mass rally in Baltimore to celebrate the triumph of Winter Davis and the entire Republican ticket. As he surveyed the festive banners proclaiming: "Slavery is dead," he marveled at the thought that not long before, the state "was almost coaxed into open rebellion against the government, in simulated defense of slavery." The enthusiastic crowd signaled that "a great and momentous revolution" had occurred in the hearts and minds of the people. "Do we dream," marveled Brooks, "or do we actually hear with our own ears loyal Marylanders making speeches in favor of immediate emancipation and a loyal crowd of Baltimoreans applauding to the echo the most radical utterances."

Chase was a featured speaker at the celebration, and, according to Brooks, "his simple words of sympathy and cheer for the struggling sons of freedom in Maryland were received with wildest enthusiasm." The complete triumph of the emancipationists was read as a sharp rebuke to Monty Blair and his "fossil theories." Chase was elated, telling Greeley that he attached "a great deal of importance" to the occasion, for it suggested "the time is ripe" for a "great unconditional Union Party, with *Emancipation as a Cardinal principle*"—a party with Salmon Chase, presumably, at its head.

Worried that Lincoln's adversaries were successfully eclipsing him by appealing to the "radical element," Leonard Swett recommended that the president call for a constitutional amendment abolishing slavery. "I told him if he took that stand, it was an outside position and no one could maintain himself upon any measure more radical," Swett recalled, "and if he failed to take the position, his rivals would." Lincoln, too, could see the "time coming" for a constitutional amendment, and then whoever "stands in its way, will be run over by it"; but the country was not yet ready. The "discordant elements" of the great coalition still had to be held together to ensure victory in the war. Moreover, he objected, "I have never done an official act with a view to promote my own personal aggrandizement, and I don't like to begin now."

Herein, Swett concluded, lay the secret to Lincoln's gifted leadership. "It was by ignoring men, and ignoring all small causes, but by closely calculating the tendencies of events and the great forces which were producing logical results." John Forney of the Washington *Daily Chronicle* observed the same intuitive judgment and timing, arguing that Lincoln was "the most truly progressive man of the age, because he always moves in conjunction with propitious circumstances, not waiting to be dragged by the force of events or wasting strength in premature struggles with them."

CHAPTER 22

"STILL IN WILD WATER"

As the fall 1863 elections in the crucial states of Ohio and Pennsylvania approached, Lincoln was visibly unsettled. Recalling the disastrous midterm elections of the previous autumn, he confided to Welles in October that his anxiety was greater than during his presidential race in 1860.

If the antiwar Democrats had gained ground since the previous year, it would signal that Northern support for the war was crumbling. Such results would dispirit the army and invigorate rebel morale. While recent battlefield victories augured well for Republican chances, the divisive issues of civil liberties, slavery, and Reconstruction threatened to erode support in many places. Civil liberties was also a divisive issue in the Confederacy, which had suspended habeas corpus, imposed martial law, and instituted conscription. The former Confederate secretary of state Robert Toombs accused "that scoundrel Jeff Davis" of pursuing "an illegal and unconstitutional course" that "outraged justice" and brought a "tide of despotism" upon the South. People in both North and South were becoming increasingly restive.

Lincoln was particularly concerned about Ohio, where Democrats had chosen Copperhead Clement Vallandigham as their gubernatorial candidate against the pro-Union John Brough. Conducting his campaign from exile in Canada, Vallandigham was running on a platform condemning the war as a failure and calling for "peace at any price"—even if slavery was maintained and the Union divided. Lincoln was disheartened that the historic Democratic Party had selected "a man [such] as Vallandigham" for "their representative man." Whatever votes he received would be "a discredit to the country."

In Pennsylvania, the Democrats were running George Woodward, an archly conservative judge, against Republican governor Andrew Curtin. Though not as incendiary as Vallandigham's, Woodward's opinions were well known. "Slavery," he had once said, "was intended as a special blessing to the people of the United States." The contest tightened when the Woodward campaign received a welcome letter of support from George McClellan, written from his residence in New Jersey. If he were voting in Pennsylvania, McClellan wrote, he would "give to Judge Woodward my voice & my vote."

Lincoln, however, had learned from the bitter election of the previous year and took steps to ensure better results. Any government clerk from Ohio or Pennsylvania who wanted to go home to vote was given a fifteen-day leave and provided with a free railroad pass for the trip. Recognizing that the absence of the army vote had been devastating to Republicans in 1862, the president also arranged for soldiers in the field to receive furloughs to return home to vote.

A week before the election, Chase called on Lincoln with a suggestion. If the president granted him a leave of absence from the Treasury, he, like his clerks, would go home to vote the Union ticket. Lincoln had no doubt that Chase would use the campaign trip to bolster his own drive for the presidency. Nevertheless, Chase's presence in Ohio might well help the Union ticket.

To ensure publicity, Chase invited the journalist Whitelaw Reid to accompany him on the train to Columbus and write regular dispatches for the *Cincinnati Gazette* and the Associated Press as they traveled around the state. Advance word of the train's arrival was circulated, and an enormous crowd greeted Chase in Columbus at 2 a.m. The delighted secretary was met with "prolonged cheering, and shouts of 'Hurrah for our old Governor,' 'How are you, old Greenbacks?' 'Glad to see you home again.' " Chase indicated his gratitude for this "most unexpected welcome," and proceeded to give a speech that ostensibly praised the president as a man who "is honestly and earnestly doing his best," even though the war was not being prosecuted "so fast as it ought." With a different leader, he hinted, "some mistakes might have been avoided—some misfortunes averted."

At each stop in his swing through Ohio, Chase encountered huge crowds of supporters. "I come not to speak, but to vote," he insisted, before launching into a series of self-promoting speeches laced with subtle denigration of Lincoln. Military bands followed him through the streets, creating a festival-like atmosphere. In Cincinnati, a long procession and a military escort accompanied Chase, seated in a carriage drawn by six white horses, to the Burnet House, the site of Lincoln's unpleasant encounter with Stanton during the Reaper trial. From the balcony of the elegant hotel, he delivered a few words, followed by a lengthy address that evening before a packed audience at Mozart Hall. With slavery and Reconstruction as his themes, he once again covertly criticized the president. He acknowledged that the Emancipation Proclamation was "the great feature of the war," without which "we could not achieve success," but hastened to add that "it would have been even more right, had it been earlier, and without exceptions."

Lincoln had calculated correctly by giving Chase permission for the trip. His tour helped draw record numbers of pro-Union supporters to the polls. In public squares lit by bonfires and torchlights, the former governor called upon his fellow Ohioans to regard the election as "the day of trial for our Country. All eyes turn to Ohio." On the Monday before the voting, he begged his audiences "to remember that to-morrow is the most important of all the three hundred and sixty-five days in the year."

On Election Day, Lincoln took up his usual post in the crowded telegraph office. By midnight, everything indicated good results in both Ohio and Pennsylvania. Still, the president refused to retire until he was certain. At 1:20 a.m., a welcome telegram arrived from Chase: "The victory is complete, beyond all hopes." Chase predicted that Brough's margin over Vallandigham would be at least 50,000, and would rise higher still when the soldiers' vote was counted. By 5 a.m., Brough's margin had widened to 100,000. "*Glory to God in the highest,*" Lincoln wired to the victorious governor-elect. "*Ohio has saved the Nation.*" The results from Pennsylvania, where Governor Curtin defeated his antiwar challenger, produced another jubilant outburst in the telegraph office. "All honor to the Keystone State!" Stanton wired to John Forney. In July, he wrote, the state "drove rebel invaders from her soil; and, now, in October, she has again rallied for the Union, and overwhelmed the foe at the ballot-box."

When Welles called on the president to congratulate him, he found him "in good spirits." Republicans had crushed Copperheads in the two bellwether states, boding well for the congressional elections the following month. Chase had been instrumental in achieving these signal victories. If his journey home to Ohio had also advanced the secretary's presidential aspirations, so be it. Lincoln understood Chase's thirst for the presidency. "No man knows what *that gnawing* is till he has had it," he said. Should Chase become president, he told Hay, "all right. I hope we may never have a worse man."

Lincoln might "shut his eyes" to Chase's stratagems so long as Chase remained a good secretary, but members of his cabinet possessed less tolerance. "I'm afraid Mr. Chase's head is turned by his eagerness in pursuit of the presidency," Bates recorded in his diary. "That visit to the west is generally understood as [his] opening campaign." Perusing newspaper accounts of Chase's speeches, the Attorney General noted derisively that his colleague had attributed "the salvation of the country to his own *admirable financial system*"—much as Cicero had sworn, "By the immortal Gods, I have saved my country." Chase ought to have focused solely on his cabinet position, Bates observed, but "it is of the nature of ambition to grow prurient, and run off with its victim." Like Bates, Welles believed that Chase's presidential aspirations had "warped" his judgment, leading him to divisively exploit the Reconstruction issue to consolidate the radical wing of the party behind him. Yet these critiques were moderate compared to the scathing indictments the Blairs poured forth in daily correspondence to their friends.

Chase remained oblivious to the ire of his colleagues. He had found the trip immensely gratifying. "I little imagined the reception that awaited me," he proudly told a friend. "Such appreciation & such manifestation of warm personal esteem—moved me deeply." Chase apparently never considered that he owed a good part of his tremendous reception to the president he represented and to the victories of the Union armies at Gettysburg and Vicksburg. All personal praise and flattering letters he accepted as his just due. "The late election in this City & State, to you, more than to any other living man was a personal triumph," he was told by James Baker, stationed in St. Louis. "I feel hopeful now for you in the contest of '64." After a few more fawning remarks, Baker proceeded to request a job as a collector, explaining that months "in the saddle" had produced a bad case of hemorrhoids, leaving him unfit for active duty.

Chase also basked in the extravagant praise from the radical press. "To him, more than any other man in the cabinet," the *Liberator* wrote, "are we indebted for the Presidents' proclamation, and the other executive acts which have struck the diabolical system of slavery." The *Liberator* supposed Chase's victory over Seward's influence had finally allowed the proclamation to be issued. "If in any one month of Mr. Seward's administration, he had chosen strenuously to urge upon Abraham Lincoln the abolition of slavery throughout the country on the ground that the conflict *is* irrepressible," the *Liberator* maintained, then "the war would have ended in our victory within six months thereafter." The public should carefully consider "whether a vote for old Abe will not choose Seward to be again acting President."

• • •

No one understood better than Seward the absurdity of the claim that he was the acting president. By the fall of 1863, he had both accepted and respected Lincoln's consummate control of his cabinet, and the relationship between the two men "had grown very close and unreserved," Fred Seward observed. "Thrown into daily companionship, they found, not only cordial accord in most of their political opinions but a trait in common not shared by all their contemporaries. That was their disposition to take a genial, philosophical view of human nature, and of national destiny." Such intimate cooperation benefited not only both men but the country at large.

"As they sat together by the fireside, or in the carriage," Seward's son continued, "the conversation between them, however it began, always drifted back into the same channel—the progress of the great national struggle. Both loved humor, and however trite the theme, Lincoln always found some quaint illustration from his western life, and Seward some case in point, in his long public career, that gave it new light."

Fred Seward recounted the events of one morning in October 1863 when his father called on Lincoln. "They say, Mr. President, that we are stealing away the rights of the States. So I have come to-day to advise you, that there is another State right I think we ought to steal." Raising his head from his pile of papers, Lincoln asked, "Well, Governor, what do you want to steal now?" Seward replied, "The right to name Thanksgiving Day!" He explained that at present, Thanksgiving was celebrated on different days at the discretion of each state's governor. Why not make it a national holiday? Lincoln immediately responded that he supposed a president "had as good a right to thank God as a Governor."

Seward then presented Lincoln with a proclamation that invited citizens "in every part of the United States," at sea, or abroad, "to set apart and observe the last Thursday of November" to give thanks to "our beneficent Father." The proclamation also commended to God's care "all those who have become widows, orphans, mourners or sufferers," and called on Him "to heal the wounds of the nation" and restore it to "peace, harmony, tranquillity and Union." These sentiments would reappear in Lincoln's second inaugural, where once again, as with Seward's "mystic chords" in his First Inaugural Address, Lincoln would transform Seward's language into a powerfully resonant poetry.

Their mutual faith in each other helped sustain both Lincoln and Seward through the continuing attacks of radicals and conservatives. Under political fire, both men remained remarkably calm. Lincoln told Nicolay that before his meeting with the Missouri radicals, Seward had asked him to prepare his response without saying "a word to him on the subject," lest anyone claim he had influenced the president on the controversial matter. Despite their precautions, said Lincoln, Wendell Phillips gave a passionate speech decrying the White House response and stating "that Seward had written the whole of that letter."

As the November congressional elections approached, both men hoped that the North would overwhelmingly support the administration, the Union, and the war. They knew that these elections would set the stage for the presidential contest the following year. In one of their fireside conversations, Seward assured Lincoln that his own hopes for the presidency were "all past and ended." He desired only that Lincoln be his "own successor," for when the rebels "find the people reaffirming their decision to have you President, I think the rebellion will collapse."

Two days before the November 3 elections, Seward left for Auburn. He had worried for weeks about the condition of his son Will, who had returned home on convalescent leave after contracting typhoid in the army. Will suffered fever and terrible stomach pains. As the illness progressed, he had to be carried from his bed to a chair where he could sit up for only short periods of time. The elections offered Seward a chance to attend to his son and rally support among New York voters as well.

Lincoln, too, was concerned about young Will, whom he had come to like and respect. The previous spring, he had ordered Will, then stationed with the army in Virginia, to report to the White House for a special assignment. As Will later recalled, the road to the capital was "exceedingly muddy" that day. He appeared at the president's door "covered with mud" and looking "more like a tramp than a soldier." He was "well known to the old porter at the door," however, and was quickly ushered into the president's library. Lincoln greeted him warmly, handing him a secret dispatch for delivery to General Banks in Louisiana. He would have to travel through "hostile" areas, Lincoln warned, so he would "have to take the chances of riding alone." The dispatch was "of great importance and must not fall into the enemy's hands," so he should commit it to memory. Will left that night and delivered his intelligence safely.

Seward arrived at home to find Will in stable condition. On election eve, he delivered a speech to the citizens of Auburn. He began with the sanguine prediction that the rebellion "will perish . . . and slavery will perish with it." While his optimism might provoke criticism in some quarters, he explained, "as in religion, so in politics, it is faith, and not despondency, that overcomes mountains and scales the heavens." His faith, he predicted, would be confirmed by the Unionist triumph in the coming elections. "The object of this election," he said, "is the object of the war. It is to make Abraham Lincoln President *de facto*" in the South as he is in the North.

"There can be no peace and quiet, until Abraham Lincoln is President of the whole United States." Then, arousing the wrath of radicals, Seward extended his hand to the South, saying, "I am willing that the prodigal son shall return. The doors, as far as I am concerned, shall always be open to him."

As the voters went to the polls on Tuesday, Lincoln telegraphed Seward. "How is your son?" he inquired. "Thanks. William is better," Seward replied. "Our friends reckon on (25,000) majority in the state." New York did even better than that, reversing the losses of the previous year to give a 30,000 majority to the administration. In every state with the exception of New Jersey, Seward reported, "the Copperhead spirit is crushed and humbled."

• • •

A FESTIVE ATMOSPHERE enveloped the nation's capital after the elections as official Washington prepared for the social event of the decade: the wedding of Kate Chase and William Sprague. Fifty guests, including the president, the entire cabinet, and selected congressmen, senators, and generals, were invited to the wedding ceremony on Thursday evening, November 12, in the parlor of the Chase mansion. Five hundred additional invitations had been delivered for the reception immediately following the exchange of vows.

For weeks, the newspapers were filled with gossip about the wedding. It was said that Sprague had given Kate a diamond tiara worth $50,000. Women readers relished details "about the bridal *trousseau*—the robes, the pearls, the diamonds, the lace, the silver, and all the magnificent gifts of this Millionaire Wedding." Curiosity seekers noted the arrival of eminent guests at the Willard Hotel. The spectacle offered a brief respite from the endless sorrows of the war—the casualty reports, the scenes of suffering in the hospitals, the rumors of impending military engagements.

For Salmon Chase, the imminent marriage brought a welter of conflicting emotions. Writing frankly to Sprague thirteen days before the wedding, he acknowledged that he was beginning "to realize how changed every thing will be when she is gone." His life had long been occupied with "the solicitous care" of his beloved daughter, who had "constantly become more thoughtful, more affectionate, more loving; and, at this hour, is dearer than ever." Though they would share the same Washington household, Chase understood that he would no longer enjoy Kate's undivided attention. By return mail, Sprague reassured Chase that he fully appreciated their "high & holy relation" and would "never be happier than when contributing to continue the same relations between father & daughter—

that has heretofore existed." Referring most likely to his drinking problem, Sprague admitted that in the past he had "neglected both mind & body," but promised henceforth to take care of himself, and "with good health and a proper exercise of the talent God has been pleased to give me, I hope to do something usefull for my day and generation."

Those close to Kate remarked that her emotions ran high as the marriage drew near. John Hay recounted that she cried "like a baby" just weeks before the wedding when he took her to see Maggie Mitchell in *The Pearl of Savoy*. The play revolves around the romantic travails of Marie, a peasant girl whose innocent love for a peasant boy is thwarted by a lecherous aristocrat determined to possess the lovely young girl. Through the wealthy suitor's machinations, Marie's family stand to lose their farm unless she gives herself to him. Torn between her devotion to her noble father and her love for the young peasant boy, Marie goes mad. Perhaps Kate shed so many tears over the melodrama because she identified with the tormented heroine's devotion to her father.

Over the years, as the Cinderella match would culminate in tragedy and poverty for Kate, journalists and historians have subjected Kate's feelings for Sprague to considerable analysis. Many have speculated that her decision to marry "was a coldly calculated plan to secure the Sprague millions," thereby to advance the "two great passions in her life—her father and politics." It was said that "in her eyes all other men sank into insignificance when compared with her father," and that no one else had "even the remotest hold upon her affections." Her marriage to Sprague would relieve her father from further financial worries and provide abundant means for an all-out presidential campaign in 1864.

Even journalists at the time noted that outside of his fortune, Sprague possessed few attractive qualities. Having left school early for the cotton mill, he was "wholly innocent of even an approximate understanding of the arts or sciences, polite or vulgar literature." Furthermore, he was "small, thin and unprepossessing in appearance." Still, if he was not physically attractive, the *Brooklyn Daily Eagle* noted, "pecuniarily, he is—several millions." And, as Gideon Welles recorded in his diary, "Miss Kate has talents and ambition sufficient for both."

Henry Adams was among those who deemed Kate's marriage a sacrifice for her father. He spoke of her as Jephthah's daughter, referring to the biblical warrior who promised God that if he gained success in battle, "whatsoever" greeted him at his victorious return would be sacrificed as "a burnt offering." Jephthah arrived home triumphant and was greeted at his door by his daughter, his only child. As the anguished father prepared the sacrificial pyre, his daughter comforted him with assurances that she accepted her fate, for a promise made to God could not be broken.

The sacrificial nature of this scenario is belied by Kate's own words, later confided to her diary as the fifth anniversary of her wedding approached. Thinking back to the night before her marriage, she wrote: "Memory has been busy with the hopes and dreams on a calm moonlight night five years ago of a woman, then in the full flush of social influence and triumph whose career had been curiously independent and successful, surrounded by some kind friends and many more ready to flatter and do her homage, accustomed to command and be obeyed, to wish and be anticipated, successful beyond any right or dessert of her own to claim, and yet stood ready, without a sigh of regret, to lay all these and more upon the altar of her love in exchange for a more earnest and truer life: one long dream of happiness and love."

She remembered spending that evening praying that she might fill her role of loving wife "to completeness," that she "might become, his companion, friend and advocate, that he might be in a word—a husband satisfied. All there is of love and beauty, nobleness & gentleness were woven with this fair dream & I believed no future brighter than that our united lives spread open before us." When folded in William's "loving arms," she continued, "oh the sense of ineffable rest, joy & completeness." She felt like "a child, in security and trust. A lover won, a protector found, a husband to be cherished. . . . Not a reserve in my heart, not a hidden corner he might not scan, the first, the only man that had found a lodgment there."

In the hours before the nuptials began, "a large crowd of all sexes, ages and conditions" gathered around the Chase mansion to watch the procession of guests. The eager crowd was "very good-natured," the Washington *Daily Chronicle* reported, exchanging congenial remarks as the occupants of the long line of carriages stepped down and proceeded inside. One by one the cabinet secretaries arrived; all but Monty Blair, who refused to attend, though his eighty-year-old father thoroughly enjoyed himself and was "quite the belle of the occasion." The entrance of Lord Lyons and the French minister Count Henri Mercier attracted attention, as did the arrivals of Generals Halleck, McDowell, and Robert C. Schenck.

"Much anxiety was manifested for the appearance of President Lincoln," the *Chronicle* reported. At 8:30 p.m., minutes before the ceremony was scheduled to start, Lincoln pulled up in his carriage, unescorted, and without Mrs. Lincoln by his side. As Mary later said, she refused to "bow in reverence" to the twin "Gods, *Chase & daughter.*" Predictably, Mary's absence at the wedding was noticed by the press. Noah Brooks later reported that Lincoln "stayed two and half hours 'to take the cuss off' the meagerness of the presidential party."

All eyes were on Kate, however, as she descended the staircase in "a gorgeous white velvet dress, with an extended train, and upon her head wore a rich lace veil," encircled by her new pearl and diamond tiara. As the wedding party approached the Episcopal bishop of Rhode Island, the Marine Band played a march composed specifically for the occasion. When the vows were completed, "Chase was the first to kiss the newly made wife." A lavish meal was served, followed by dancing in the dining room, which lasted until midnight.

John Hay thought it "a very brilliant" affair, noting that Kate "had lost all her old severity & formal stiffness of manner, & seemed to think she had *arrived.*" The young couple left the next morning for New York, where their presence at the Fifth Avenue Hotel drew crowds of women eager to see the young bride in person, having followed all the details of her wedding in the papers.

Marriage did not diminish the regular flow of letters between father and daughter. "Your letter—so full of sweet words and good thoughts—came yesterday," Chase wrote Kate less than a week after the wedding, "and I need not tell you how welcome it was." His new son-in-law, to Chase's delight, also proved to be a good correspondent. "My heart is full of love for you both," Chase replied to Sprague, "and I rejoice as I never expected to rejoice in the prospects of happiness opening before both of you. I feared some inequalities of temper—some too great love of the world, either of its possessions or its shows—something I hardly know about. But I find that you each trust the other fully . . . and above all that you both look to God for his blessing & guidance."

Chase expressed but a single qualm: "I fear that Katie may be a little too anxious about my political future. She must not be so." He insisted to Sprague that nothing could be "so uncertain as the political future of any man: and especially as the future which must be determined by popular preferences founded quite as much on sentiment as on reason." While he suggested to his new son-in-law that the country needed a leader other than Lincoln, Chase ingenuously asserted that he would never allow himself "to be drawn into any hostile or unfriendly position as to Mr. Lincoln. His course towards me has always been so fair & kind; his progress towards entire agreement with me on the great question of slavery has been so constant, though rather slower than I wished for; and his general character is so marked by traits which command respect & affection; that I can never consent to anything, which he himself could or should consider as incompatible with perfect honor & good faith."

• • •

AT A TUESDAY CABINET MEETING shortly after Kate's wedding, Lincoln informed his colleagues that he would leave for Gettysburg that Thursday, November 19, 1863. He had been asked to say a few words to consecrate the cemetery grounds set aside so that the Union soldiers who had been interred near the battlefield and hospitals the previous July could be "properly buried." Edward Everett, the noted orator and former president of Harvard, was scheduled to give the main address, after which the president would speak. Lincoln told his cabinet that he hoped they would accompany him to the dedication. Seward, Blair, and John Usher readily agreed, but the other members feared they could not spare the time from their duties, particularly since their annual reports to Congress were due in a couple of weeks.

Lincoln was uneasy about the trip. He had been "extremely busy," he told Ward Lamon, and had not been able to carve out the solitary time he needed to compose his address. He "greatly feared he would not be able to acquit himself with credit, much less to fill the measure of public expectation." Stanton had arranged a special train for the presidential party to depart on the morning of the dedication and return home around midnight that same day. Lincoln, however, rescheduled it to leave on Wednesday. "I do not wish to so go that by the slightest accident we fail entirely," he explained, "and, at the best, the whole to be a mere breathless running of the gauntlet." Perhaps he also hoped that an early departure from the White House would allow him more time to work on his address.

The day before setting out, Lincoln told a friend he had "found time to write about half of his speech." Various accounts suggest that he labored over the speech during the four-hour trip. One young man, peering through the window when the train was temporarily stopped at Hanover Junction, distinctly recalled the president at work on some document, "the top of his high hat serving as a makeshift desk." Others swear that he jotted notes on an envelope as the train roared along. Nicolay, who was there, insists that he wrote nothing during the trip, choosing instead to relax and engage his fellow riders with good conversation and humorous stories.

When Lincoln arrived at Gettysburg, he was escorted to the home of David Wills, the event organizer, where he would spend the night along with Governor Andrew Curtin and Edward Everett. "All the hotels as well as the private houses were filled to overflowing," the *New York Times* reported. "People from all parts of the country seem to have taken this opportunity to pay a visit to the battle-fields which are hereafter to make the name of Gettysburgh immortal."

After supper, while Lincoln settled himself in his room to complete his draft, a crowd gathered in front of the house to serenade him. He came to the door to thank them, but said he would make no remarks for the simple reason that "I have no speech to make. In my position it is somewhat important that I should not say any foolish things." His reluctance elicited the snide comment from a member of the audience: "If you can help it." Lincoln's swift rejoinder delighted the crowd. "It very often happens that the only way to help it is to say nothing at all."

Returning to his room, Lincoln sent a servant downstairs to fetch a few additional sheets of paper. A telegram arrived from Stanton with welcome news. Tad had been ill when Lincoln left that morning. The boy's condition had frightened Mary, but now the report that Tad was better eased Lincoln's mind, allowing him to focus on his speech. He went over each line, revising the ending, which was not yet satisfactory.

Meanwhile, the crowd surged over to Robert Harper's house on the public square, where Seward was staying. Seward responded to the serenade with a heartfelt speech, concluding with thanks to the Almighty "for the hope that this is the last fratricidal war which will fall upon this country—the richest, the broadest, the most beautiful, and capable of a great destiny, that has ever been given to any part of the human race." Afterward, inside the house, the convivial secretary held sway for hours in such a lucid manner that Benjamin French, a fellow boarder, averred he had "seldom, if ever, met with a man whose mind is under such perfect discipline, and is so full of original and striking matter as Secretary Seward's. His conversation, no matter on what subject, is worthy of being written down and preserved, and if he had a Boswell to write, as Boswell did of Johnson, one of the most interesting and useful books of the age might be produced from the conversations and sayings of William H. Seward. He is one of the greatest men of this generation."

Sometime after 11 p.m., Lincoln came downstairs, the pages of his speech in his hands. He wanted to talk with Seward, perhaps to share his draft with the colleague whose judgment he most respected and trusted. He walked over to the Harper house and remained there with Seward for about an hour before returning to his room and retiring. The huge, boisterous crowd on the public square, however, did not retire so easily. "They sang, & hallooed, and cheered," French recalled. Listening from his window, he heard a full chorus of the popular refrain "We are coming Father Abraham, three hundred thousand more."

After breakfast the next morning, Lincoln made his final revisions, carefully folded the speech, and placed it in his coat pocket. Mounting a chestnut horse, he joined the procession to the cemetery. He was accompanied by nine governors, members of Congress, foreign ministers, military officials, and the three cabinet officers. Marine lieutenant Henry Clay Cochrane recalled that Seward, riding to Lincoln's right, was "entirely unconscious" that his trousers had pulled up above his shoes, revealing "homemade gray socks" unbefitting the occasion.

An audience of roughly nine thousand stretched away from the platform in a half circle. Lincoln was seated in the front row between Everett and Seward. For two hours, Everett delivered his memorized address, superbly recounting the various battles that had taken place over the three dramatic days. Lincoln reportedly "leaned from one side to the other and crossed his legs, turning his eyes full upon the speaker. Somewhat later he again shifted his position and rested his chin in the palm of his right hand." Another member of the audience remembered Lincoln removing his speech and glancing over it before returning it to his pocket.

French lauded Everett's speech, believing it "could not be surpassed by mortal man." Several correspondents were less enthusiastic. "Seldom has a man talked so long and said so little," wrote the editor of the *Philadelphia Age*. "He gave us plenty of words, but no heart. . . . He talked like a historian, or an encyclopaedist, or an essayist, but not like an orator."

As Everett started back to his seat, Lincoln stood to clasp his hand and warmly congratulate him. George Gitt, a fifteen-year-old who had stationed himself beneath the speaker's stand, later remembered that the "flutter and motion of the crowd ceased the moment the President was on his feet. Such was the quiet that his footfalls, I remember very distinctly, woke echoes, and with the creaking of the boards, it was as if some one were walking through the hallways of an empty house."

Lincoln put on his steel-rimmed spectacles and glanced down at his pages. Though he had had but a brief time to prepare the address, he had devoted intense thought to his chosen theme for nearly a decade. As Garry Wills observes in his classic study of the address: "He had spent a good part of the 1850s repeatedly relating all the most sensitive issues of the day to the Declaration's supreme principle." During the debates with Stephen Douglas, Lincoln had frequently reminded his audiences of the far-reaching promises contained in the Declaration of Independence. Someday, he said, "all this quibbling about . . . this race and that race and the other race being inferior" would be eliminated, giving truth to the phrase "all men are created equal."

Twenty months before the Emancipation Proclamation, the president had told Hay that "the central idea pervading this struggle is the necessity that is upon us, of proving that popular government is not an absurdity," predicting that "if we fail it will go far to prove the incapability of the people to govern themselves." Now tens of thousands had died in pursuit of that purpose. At Gettysburg, he would express that same conviction in far more concise and eloquent terms.

"Four score and seven years ago," he began,

> our fathers brought forth upon this continent, a new nation, conceived in Liberty, and dedicated to the proposition that all men are created equal.
>
> Now we are engaged in a great civil war, testing whether that nation, or any nation so conceived, and so dedicated, can long endure. We are met on a great battle-field of that war. We have come to dedicate a portion of that field, as a final resting place for those who here gave their lives, that that nation might live. It is altogether fitting and proper that we should do this.
>
> But, in a larger sense, we can not dedicate—we can not consecrate—we can not hallow—this ground. The brave men, living and dead, who struggled here, have consecrated it, far above our poor power to add or detract. The world will little note, nor long remember, what we say here, but it can never forget what they did here. It is for us, the living, rather, to be dedicated here to the unfinished work which they who fought here, have, thus far, so nobly advanced. It is rather for us to be here dedicated to the great task remaining before us—that from these honored dead we take increased devotion to that cause for which they here gave the last full measure of devotion—that we here highly resolve that these dead shall not have died in vain—that this nation, under God, shall have a new birth of freedom—and that, government of the people, by the people, for the people, shall not perish from the earth.

When Lincoln finished, "the assemblage stood motionless and silent," according to the awestruck George Gitt. "The extreme brevity of the address together with its abrupt close had so astonished the hearers that they stood transfixed. Had not Lincoln turned and moved toward his chair, the audience would very likely have remained voiceless for several moments more. Finally there came applause." Lincoln may have initially interpreted the audience's surprise as disapproval. As soon as he finished, he turned to Ward Lamon. "Lamon, that speech won't *scour*! It is a flat failure, and the people are disappointed." Edward Everett knew better, and expressed his wonder and respect the following day. "I should be glad," he wrote Lincoln, "if I could flatter myself that I came as near to the central idea of the occasion, in two hours, as you did in two minutes."

Lincoln had translated the story of his country and the meaning of the war into words and ideas accessible to every American. The child who would sleeplessly rework his father's yarns into tales comprehensible to any boy had forged for his country an ideal of its past, present, and future that would be recited and memorized by students forever.

• • •

LINCOLN RETURNED FROM GETTYSBURG to find a vexing letter from Zachariah Chandler, the radical Michigan senator who had made a fortune in dry goods and real estate before entering politics. Chandler had been a thorn in Lincoln's side, constantly criticizing his conduct of the war, his reliance on overly cautious, conservative generals, and his tardiness on emancipation. "Your president is unstable as water," Chandler had warned Trumbull the previous September. "For God & country's sake, send some-one to stay with [him] who will controll & hold him."

Now, without having seen a word of the president's upcoming message to Congress, which Lincoln had only begun drafting, Chandler was anticipating a disaster. Having read in the press that Thurlow Weed and New York governor Edwin Morgan had come to the White House to urge a "bold conservative" stance in the message, Chandler warned the president that if he acquiesced, he would jeopardize all the gains made in the fall elections. The president must realize that in each of the victorious states, radical platforms had carried the day. He could be the "master of the Situation," Chandler patronizingly suggested, only if he could "*Stand firm*" against the influences of men like Weed, Seward, and Blair. "They are a millstone about Your neck." If he dropped them, "they are politically ended for ever." The success of the radical canvass proved that. "Conservatives and Traitors are buried together, for Gods sake dont exhume their remains in Your Message. They will smell worse than Lazarus did after he had been buried three days."

Ordinarily, Lincoln would have shelved Chandler's arrogant letter until his temper cooled. This time, however, he did not stifle his anger. Apparently, Chandler had struck a nerve by insinuating that Lincoln did not know his own mind. Although the president listened to the opinions of many, he took pride in arriving at his own decisions in his own way. Nor would he countenance Chandler's slanderous assertion that men like Seward, Weed, and Blair deserved the dishonorable grave of traitors.

"My dear Sir," Lincoln began his cold reply. "I have seen Gov. [Edwin D.] Morgan and Thurlow Weed, separately, but not together, within the last ten days; but neither of them mentioned the forthcoming message, or said anything, so far as I can remember, which brought the thought of the

Message to my mind. I am very glad the elections this autumn have gone favorably, and that I have not, by native depravity, or under evil influences, done anything bad enough to prevent the good result. I hope to 'stand firm' enough not to go backward, and yet not go forward fast enough to wreck the country's cause."

Lincoln's impatience with Chandler may have been aggravated by the fact that he was coming down with a mild case of smallpox. The illness would last for several weeks and fray his self-restraint, yet it left his humor intact. "Yes, it is a bad disease, but it has its advantages," he told some visitors. "For the first time since I have been in office, I have something now to *give* to everybody that calls." The enforced bedrest that attended his sickness allowed Lincoln the quiet he needed to complete his message to Congress. The pause in his frenetic life proved helpful as he laid out his own views on the knotty problem of Reconstruction, which he considered "the greatest question ever presented to practical statesmanship."

Most everyone assumed, Noah Brooks wrote, "that the President would either ignore reconstruction altogether," as the conservatives suggested, or follow the radicals' advice and "give an elaborate and decisive program." No one predicted "such an original message," which cleverly mollified both wings of his divided party. John Hay was present when the message was read. "I never have seen such an effect produced by a public document," he recorded in his diary that night. "Chandler was delighted, Sumner was beaming, while at the other political pole [James] Dixon and Reverdy Johnson said it was highly satisfactory."

Radicals were thrilled with the stipulation that before the president would pardon any rebel or restore the rights of property, he must not only swear allegiance to the Union but also accept emancipation. To abandon the laws and proclamations promising freedom to the slaves would be "a cruel and an astounding breach of faith," Lincoln said, adding that "while I remain in my present position I shall not attempt to retract or modify the emancipation proclamation; nor shall I return to slavery any person who is free by the terms of that proclamation, or by any of the acts of Congress." By this statement, Sumner enthused, "He makes Emancipation the corner-stone of reconstruction." The Missouri radical Henry Blow agreed. Though he recently had castigated Lincoln, he now lauded him. "God bless Old Abe," he said. "I am one of the Radicals who have always believed in the President."

Once again the radicals' doubts about Lincoln's firmness on slavery had proved unfounded. Early in August, he had written a letter to Nathaniel Banks, the general in charge of occupied Louisiana, delineating his thoughts on Reconstruction and emancipation. While not desiring to dictate to the Creole state, Lincoln "would be glad for her to make a new Constitution recognizing the emancipation proclamation, and adopting emancipation in those parts of the state to which the proclamation does not apply. And while she is at it, I think it would not be objectionable for her to adopt some practical system by which the two races could gradually live themselves out of their old relation to each other, and both come out better prepared for the new. Education for young blacks should be included in the plan."

Agreeing that no rebellious state could be reconstructed without emancipation, Lincoln still refused to tolerate the radicals' desire to punish the South. He offered full pardons to all those who took the oath, excepting those who had served at high levels in the Confederate government or the army. When the number of loyal men taking the oath reached 10 percent of the votes cast in the 1860 election, they could "re-establish a State government" recognized by the United States. The names and boundaries of the states would remain as they were.

Conservatives hailed the 10 percent plan, believing it effectively destroyed Sumner's scheme to consider the defeated states as territories that Congress could rename and reorganize as it wished. Nevertheless, Sumner told a fellow radical that Lincoln's "theory is identical with ours," for he, too, required Reconstruction before the "subverted" rebel states could rejoin the Union, "although he adopts a different nomenclature."

In presenting his 10 percent plan, Lincoln assured members of Congress that it was not fixed in stone. He would listen to their ideas as the process evolved. He hoped simply to give the Southern states "a rallying point," bringing them "to act sooner than they otherwise would." He recognized that it would devastate Confederate morale to see Southern citizens declare their fealty to the Union and their support for emancipation.

Though the happy accord would not last long, Lincoln had succeeded for the moment in uniting the Republican Party. When the Blairs, Sumner, and the Missouri radicals "are alike agreed to accept" the president's message, Brooks observed, "we may well conclude that the political millennium has well-nigh come, or that the author of the message is one of the most sagacious men of modern times." The president, announced Congressman Francis Kellogg of Michigan, "is the great man of the century. There is none like him in the world. He sees more widely and more clearly than anybody."

Lincoln's old friend Norman Judd called on the president the evening of the annual address. He speculated that, given the radical tone of the document, Blair and Bates "must walk the plank." On the contrary, Lincoln assured him, both "acquiesced in it without objection. The only member of the Cabinet who objected to it was Mr. Chase."

Chase had obstinately demanded a requirement for states to prove their "sincerity" by changing their constitutions to perpetuate emancipation. This legitimate objection had the felicitous effect of allowing Chase to stay in front of Lincoln on Reconstruction in order to cement his standing in radical circles. While Republicans of all stripes praised the message, Chase expressed disappointment. Writing to the abolitionist Henry Ward Beecher, he said he had tried but failed to get Lincoln to make it "more positive and less qualified. . . . But I suppose I must use Touchstone's philosophy & be thankful for skim milk when cream is not to be had."

• • •

LINCOLN APPROACHED the Christmas season in high spirits. As he said in his annual message, he detected a more hopeful mood in the country after the "dark and doubtful days" following the Emancipation Proclamation. The fall elections had been "highly encouraging"; the rebels had been defeated in a series of recent battles; and the opening round in the debate over Reconstruction had gone surprisingly well.

Early in December, Lincoln translated his rhetoric about forgiveness and reconciliation into action when he invited his sister-in-law, Emilie Helm, to stay at the White House. Emilie's husband, Ben, had disappointed Lincoln in the early days of the war by taking a commission in the Confederate Army instead of Lincoln's offer of the Union Army paymaster's position. Helm was fatally wounded in Tennessee at the Battle of Chickamauga, where he commanded the First Kentucky Brigade. Judge Davis saw Lincoln shortly after he received the news of Helm's death. "I never saw Mr. Lincoln more moved than when he heard that his young brother-in-law, Ben Hardin Helm, scarcely thirty-two years of age, had been killed," Davis said. "I saw how grief-stricken he was . . . so I closed the door and left him alone."

Emilie had been living with her young daughter in Selma, Alabama, when she learned that her wounded husband had been taken to Atlanta. She reached the hospital minutes too late. Alone in Atlanta, she had no desire to return to Selma, where she had moved only for its proximity to her husband's post. Now she desperately wanted to see her mother in Kentucky. Confederate general Braxton Bragg unsuccessfully sought through Grant to secure a pass for her through Union lines. Helm's father then wrote to Betsy Todd, Mary's stepmother, in Lexington, Kentucky. "I am totally at a loss to know how to begin. Could you or one of your daughters write to Mrs. Lincoln and through her secure a pass?"

Four days later, Lincoln personally issued a pass allowing Mrs. Todd "to go south and bring her daughter . . . with her children, North to Kentucky." When Emilie arrived at Fort Monroe, however, the officials demanded that she take the oath of allegiance to the United States. Unable to contemplate such a momentous step so soon after her husband's death in the Confederate cause, she refused. The officials sent a telegram to the president, explaining the dilemma. They received a prompt directive: "Send her to me."

After weeks of uncertainty, the young widow was received at the White House by the president and first lady "with the warmest affection." The three of them, Emilie wrote in her diary, were "all too grief-stricken at first for speech." The Lincolns had lost Willie, Emilie had lost her husband, and the two sisters had lost three brothers in the Confederate Army—Sam Todd at Shiloh, David Todd from wounds at Vicksburg, and little Alexander, Mary's favorite baby brother, at Baton Rouge.

Families rent apart by the Civil War abounded in border states such as Missouri or Kentucky, the ancestral home of the Todds. The reality of "brother fighting brother" lent an intimate horror to the idea of a nation divided. "Often the boundaries separating people of opposing loyalties," the historian John Shaffer writes, "were nothing more than the property line between two farms, or a table over which members of the same family argued and ultimately chose sides."

That night, as Mary and Emilie dined alone, they carefully avoided mention of the war, which "comes between us," Emilie acknowledged, "like a barrier of granite closing our lips." They talked instead of old times and of old friends. Emilie marveled at Mary's "fine tact," which allowed her to "so quickly turn a dangerous subject into other channels." In the days that followed, Mary did her utmost to deflect her sister's mind from her sorrow. She gave her the Prince of Wales guest room, took her for long carriage rides, made sure Emilie's little daughter was entertained, and sat with her at night in the drawing room before the light and warmth of a blazing fire.

Emilie's visit provided solace for both sisters. One night after Emilie had gone to her room, Mary knocked on the door, intending to share an experience that she could not readily discuss with others. She wanted Emilie to know that in her own grief over Willie's death, she now was comforted by the belief that his spirit was still present. "He comes to me every night," she told Emilie, "with the same sweet, adorable smile he has always had; he does not always come alone; little Eddie is sometimes with him and twice he has come with our brother Alec, he tells me he loves his Uncle Alec and is with him most of the time."

The vision of spiritual harmony between Willie and Alec seemed to promise a day when the Todd family would again be united, and the devastating divisions between North and South would be dissolved by history. Then Mary herself would no longer be "the scape-goat" for both sides. "You cannot dream of the comfort this gives me," she told her sister, speaking "with a thrill in her voice" that Emilie would long remember.

Sadly for Mary, her reconciliation with her Confederate sister had some troubling consequences. Lincoln had tried to keep Emilie's visit a secret, knowing that it would give rise to intense criticism at a time when Northerners were still punished for fraternizing with the enemy. On December 14, he confided her presence to Browning but cautioned that "he did not wish it known." When two of Mary's friends, General Daniel Sickles and Senator Ira Harris, called on her one night, however, Mary let down her guard and invited Emilie to join them. Both men were loyal to Lincoln and had been regulars at Mary's drawing room salons. Lincoln had personally attended Sickles when Sickles returned to Washington after losing a leg at Gettysburg. Sickles had been in severe pain at the time, but Lincoln's cheerful presence at his bedside had helped to restore his spirits. Mary also considered Harris a special friend, recalling years later how he invariably brightened her drawing room with his merriment.

Still, neither Sickles nor Harris could tolerate the presence of a traitor in the home of the commander in chief. Emilie recorded the events in her diary. No sooner had she entered the room than Senator Harris turned to her, a triumphant tone in his voice. "Well, we have whipped the rebels at Chattanooga and I hear, madam, that the scoundrels ran like scared rabbits." Emilie replied, "It was the example, Senator Harris, that you set them at Bull Run and Manassas."

The conversation degenerated rapidly. Mary's face "turned white as death" when Senator Harris asked why Robert Lincoln had not joined the army. "If fault there be, it is mine," Mary replied. "I have insisted that he should stay in college a little longer." She did not state her underlying terror that she would lose another son. "I have only one son and he is fighting for his country," Harris countered. "And, Madam," he said, turning to Emilie, "If I had twenty sons they should all be fighting the rebels."

"And if I had twenty sons," Emilie coldly replied, "they should all be opposing yours." This brought the evening to an abrupt close. Emilie fled the room with Mary close behind. The sisters threw their arms around each other and wept. The hot-tempered General Sickles insisted on reporting directly to Lincoln on what had happened. John Stuart, who was present, recalled that after Lincoln heard the tale, his "eyes twinkled," and he told the general, "The child has a tongue like the rest of the Todds."

Lincoln's remark apparently infuriated Sickles, who said "in a loud, dictatorial voice, slapping the table with his hand, 'You should not have that rebel in your house.' "

"Excuse me, General Sickles," Lincoln replied, "my wife and I are in the habit of choosing our own guests. We do not need from our friends either advice or assistance in the matter."

The nasty confrontation in the Red Room prompted Emilie to leave, despite the protestations of Lincoln and Mary. "Oh, Emilie," Mary lamented, "will we ever awake from this hideous nightmare?"

• • •

LINCOLN REFUSED TO LET the unpleasant experience destroy his good humor. As Emilie and Mary said their goodbyes, he took Nicolay and Hay to Ford's Theatre to see James Hackett play Falstaff in *Henry IV.* Afterward, he engaged his aides in a lively conversation about the play. The next day, at the regular Tuesday cabinet meeting, Welles found him "in fine spirits." Eager for distraction, Lincoln returned to Ford's Theatre two days later for *The Merry Wives of Windsor.* The following evening, he "was greeted with loud applause" at Willard's Hall as he arrived for a lecture on Russia by the diplomat Bayard Taylor.

The next week, Lincoln related a peculiarly pleasant dream. He was at a party, he told Hay, and overheard one of the guests say of him, "He is a very common-looking man." In the dream, he relished his reply: "The Lord prefers Common-looking people that is the reason he makes so many of them." His dreamed response still amused him as he recalled it the next day.

The holiday season found most of the cabinet in cheerful spirits as well. Seward entertained the members of the visiting Russian fleet in his usual lavish style: a four-course meal, served with an unlimited supply of the best wine. As the ladies took tea in the parlor, the men adjourned to the sitting room, where Fred Seward recalled that "the conversation would often be continued for two or three hours in a cloud of smoke."

Edward Bates, too, had reason to be gladdened. Though he remained despondent over the defection of his son Fleming to the Confederate Army, the rest of his large brood were doing well. Coalter had fought at Chancellorsville and Gettysburg, and remained on General Meade's staff. Woodson would soon graduate from West Point. Barton and Julian were both in Missouri, where Barton was a judge of the state Supreme Court and Julian a surgeon in the Missouri militia. His two daughters lived with the family at home. Even Dick, his troubled eighth child, who had struggled with alcoholism, seemed to be improving.

Of all the causes for holiday thanksgiving, Bates was most grateful for his wife's complete return to health after her stroke. After forty years of marriage, he still believed that "no man has been more blessed." He was proud to make the rare claim that "in all that time," Julia had never committed "an unkind act" toward him, nor spoken a disparaging word against him. On Christmas Day, he attended a funeral for the wife of one of his closest friends. The couple had been married for more than half a century. "I know not how he can bear the loss of such a companion," he wrote, speaking for himself as well as for his friend. "I am prepared to see him sink rapidly and die soon."

Christmas Day found Welles rejoicing at his son Edgar's return from Kenyon College, though holiday festivities immediately brought back memories of the children he had lost. "The glad faces and loving childish voices that cheered our household with 'Merry Christmas' in years gone by are silent on earth forever." His mood was lightened, however, by the situation in the country. "The year closes more satisfactorily than it commenced," he wrote; "the heart of the nation is sounder and its hopes brighter." Although the president still faced "trying circumstances," Welles predicted that his leadership would "be better appreciated in the future than now."

The Stantons' domestic life had brightened with the birth of a new baby girl, Bessie, eleven months after the death of their infant son, James. As Ellen prepared for the baptismal celebration, Stanton spent Christmas visiting wounded soldiers. He shared with the men his renewed faith that "when the next anniversary of the day you are now celebrating occurs, this war will be ended, and you will have returned to your homes and your firesides. When you shall have so returned, you will be considered as honored guests of the nation."

Lincoln invited Stanton to accompany him "down the river" to visit the Union prison camp at Point Lookout, Maryland. He had heard that a significant number of the rebel prisoners had expressed willingness to take the oath of allegiance to the United States, and swear acceptance of emancipation in return for a full presidential pardon. The general in charge of the prison confirmed this hopeful intelligence when Lincoln and Stanton arrived, prompting Stanton to make plans for carrying Lincoln's "10% plan" into the Deep South, where it might spur further disaffection in Confederate strongholds.

As 1863 drew to a close, even the carping Count Gurowski had to admit that the Union's position had improved. "Oh! dying year! you will record that the American people increased its sacrifices in proportion to its dangers; that blood, time, and money were cheerfully thrown into the balance against treason—inside and outside. And brighter hopes dawn." The surly count remained unwilling to acknowledge the president's role in the improved situation, but other former critics revealed a new appreciation of Lincoln. Charles Francis Adams, the American minister to Britain, had been unimpressed by his first encounter with Lincoln in 1861, describing him as "a tall, illfavored man, with little grace of manner or polish of appearance." After several awkward meetings, the haughty Adams had concluded that Lincoln did not belong to the same "sphere of civilization" as the rest of official Washington. The first six months of the administration further confirmed this low estimation. Adams saw in Lincoln no "heroic qualities" whatsoever and was convinced that he was "not equal to the gravity of his position." But by the end of 1863, Adams had drastically altered his assessment.

At a festive dinner for loyal Americans in St. James's Hall in London, Adams delivered an eloquent speech praising Lincoln's leadership. He reminded his listeners of the dire situation the new president had faced arriving in Washington when "the edifice of Government seemed crumbling around him." Treachery reigned in every department. Traitors at Treasury had undermined the country's credit, the foreign service was replete with secessionists, and both the army and the navy had to be completely rebuilt. Few believed that this novice, who "came to his post with less of practical experience in the Government than any individual," was equal to the task. Nevertheless, the past three years had seen treason excised from the government; European nations had come to look upon the North with respect; the Treasury was flush with funds to support the armed forces; the army had grown to "half a million men," and the navy was now "respected upon every sea in all parts of the globe." All this had been accomplished, Adams acknowledged, with a remnant tinge of condescension, not because Lincoln possessed "any superior genius" but because he, "from the beginning to the end, impressed upon the people the conviction of his honesty and fidelity to one great purpose."

James Russell Lowell, a Harvard professor considered the "foremost American man of letters in his time," revealed a more incisive view of Lincoln's qualities. In a long article for the *North American Review*, which Lincoln read with pleasure, Lowell traced the progress of the Lincoln administration. "Never did a President enter upon office with less means at his command," he began. "All that was known of him was that he was a good stump-speaker, nominated for his *availability*,—that is, because he had no history." For many months, Lowell observed, the untried president seemed too hesitant—on military engagements, on emancipation, on recruiting black troops. Increasingly, it was becoming evident that this Abraham Lincoln was "a character of marked individuality and capacity for affairs." In a democratic nation, Lowell added, "where the rough and ready understanding of the people is sure at last to be the controlling power, a profound common-sense is the best genius for statesmanship." Lincoln had demonstrated a perfectly calibrated touch for public sentiment and impeccable timing in his introduction of new measures. While some thought he had delayed his decision on emancipation too long, he undoubtedly had a "sure-footed understanding" of the American people. Similarly, when the first black regiments were formed, many feared that "something terrible" would happen, "but the earth stood firm."

"Mr. Lincoln's perilous task has been to carry a rather shackly raft through the rapids, making fast the unrulier logs as he could snatch opportunity," concluded Lowell, "and the country is to be congratulated that he did not think it his duty to run straight at all hazards, but cautiously to assure himself with his setting-pole where the main current was, and keep steadily to that."

Despite the remarkable transformations of the previous three years, Lowell understood that the raft was "still in wild water." So, of course, did Lincoln. The president recommended the Lowell piece to Gideon Welles, telling him it presented a "very excellent" discussion of the administration's policy, but that it "gave him over-much credit."

CHAPTER 23

"THERE'S A MAN IN IT!"

NEW YEAR'S DAY, 1864, dawned "fearfully cold and windy," Noah Brooks recorded, and "the morning newspaper and the milkman were alike snapped up by the nipping frosts." Eventually, a bright sun scattered the clouds, and a mood of good cheer enveloped the city as the *National Republican* headlined the long list of Union victories during the previous year—"Murfreesboro, Vicksburg, Morris Island, Gettysburg, Port Hudson, Chattanooga, Knoxville."

"History does not furnish a year's victories by the armies of any country in any war that will excel these," the *National Republican* boasted. "We have a right to be somewhat gay and festive here at the national metropolis. No one wishes to deny that we have had a rebellious storm, and that the political horizon is still somewhat muggy; but our gallant old ship of State, with

Abraham Lincoln at the helm, has weathered the gale." William Stoddard echoed these sentiments in a published dispatch. "The instinct of all, rather than the reasoning, teaches us, as it has the rest of the country, that once and for all the danger is over."

At 10 a.m., official Washington began arriving at the White House for the traditional New Year's reception. At noon, when the gates opened to the general public, eight thousand people streamed in—"a human kaleidescope, constantly changing," of "diplomats and dragoons, exquisites from the Atlantic cities and hardy backwoodsmen, contented contractors and shoddy swindlers, ingenious patentees and persevering petitioners."

Lincoln considered his meetings with the general public his "*public-opinion baths.*" They "serve to renew in me a clearer and more vivid image of that great popular assemblage out of which I sprung," he told a visitor, "and though they may not be pleasant in all their particulars, the effect, as a whole, is renovating and invigorating to my perceptions of responsibility and duty."

"European democrats go into ecstasies over so palpable a sign of our universal equality," Stoddard noted, while "European aristocrats, attaches of legations, tourists, and the like, turn up their noses somewhat scornfully at so singularly American a custom." Visitors noted that Lincoln "appeared to be in excellent health and spirits, and whatever perplexities his generals may give him, he possesses the happy faculty of leaving them in his office upstairs, when he comes down to receive the salutations of the people. His clear eyes beamed with good humor, and he not only cordially returned the pressure of each offered hand, but generally said a pleasant word or two." Noah Brooks noted that Mary Lincoln "never looked better," having replaced her black "mourning garb" with a rich purple velvet dress.

"We seem to have reached a new stage in the war," Fred Seward wrote home. "Gayety has become as epidemic in Washington this winter, as gloom was last winter. There is a lull in political discussions; and people are inclined to eat, drink, and be merry. The newspapers can furnish nothing more interesting to their readers, than accounts of parties, balls and theaters, like so many Court Journals. Questions of etiquette are debated with gravity. People talk of 'society,' who never before knew or cared about it."

The winter social calendar followed a prescribed order. The president's receptions were on Tuesday evenings, the first lady's matinées on Saturday afternoons, the soirées of the Speaker of the House on Friday nights. No cards of invitation were required for these events. Since the president and speaker held their offices at the will of the people, their homes were open to the public at large. In contrast, invitations were necessary, and highly coveted, for the elegant parties at the dwellings of cabinet officers. Access to the drawing rooms of Seward and Chase were prized most of all.

Social columnists attributed the legendary success of the parties held by the secretary of state to both his genial wit and the "grace and elegance" of his daughter-in-law, Anna, "who with such rare art groups those of congenial tastes, and makes all truly 'at home.' " For young belles, there was added mystique in the presence of the diplomatic corps, which held out the titillating prospect of attracting a titled foreigner. For those fascinated by fashion and etiquette, nothing compared to the impeccable manners and gorgeous dress of the diplomats, bespangled with ribbons and garters denoting different orders of knighthood. "Who wonders that the House of Gov. Seward is a favorite resort," one columnist asked, "and who that enjoys his hospitality does not wish that he might be Secretary of State forever, and be 'at home' once a week."

At the Chase mansion, Kate Sprague continued to be the "observed of all observers." Whether dressed in blue brocade, gray, or simple black, she impressed congressmen, senators, and generals alike with her interest in politics and familiarity with military affairs. Holding court at the entrance, she had an appropriate greeting for every guest. Benjamin French thought her "one of the most lovable women" he had ever seen. Noah Brooks was likewise smitten, at once recognizing the delightful contrast to her "frosty" father, who "looked uncomfortable and generally bothered" at these affairs. Chase's nearsightedness had grown so extreme that he was unable to recognize anyone without "a very close examination." Nevertheless, he still refused to wear glasses.

The Washington elite preferred the fancy dinner parties at the Seward and Chase mansions to the public levees at the White House, where bonnets were crushed and cloaks occasionally stolen in the chaos. During the winter, Mary found it necessary to put durable brown coverings over her elegant French carpets to protect them from the muddy tramp of the "human tide" that poured in to shake hands with the president. Many visitors were ill dressed and bedraggled, as after a long dusty ride, and some still carried their carpetbags. The elegant furnishings that Mary had so lovingly and expensively put in place took a beating. Brooks noted that "the lace curtains, heavy cords, tassels, and damask drapery have suffered considerably this season from the hands of relic-hunting vandals who actually clip off small bits of the precious stuff to carry home as mementoes." Desperate to preserve their experience, some even lifted the brown covering and cut out pieces of the French carpet "as large as a man's hand."

For Mary, who relished her position as first lady, it was galling to read in the papers that Seward, not she, would inaugurate "the fashionable 'season.' " He was to host an exclusive party for the visiting members of the National Academy of Science, along with "the heads of the foreign Legations, the Cabinet, the Justices of the Supreme Court, the presiding officers of the two Houses of Congress and the Committees on Foreign Relations, with their families." That same week, the *New York Herald* noted, the White House reception was "not so largely attended as usual." Benjamin French, who was Mary's customary escort at public functions, saw that she was "disappointed." The Sewards hosted three more receptions in January 1864, accounted the "grandest," "most elegant," and "most brilliant" affairs of the season, with guest lists including barons, counts, lords, ladies, and young Robert Lincoln, home for vacation.

Mary's wounded pride increased her feelings of resentment toward Seward. She continued to begrudge the intimacy he shared with her husband, the many nights Lincoln chose to spend with Seward instead of her. Fred Seward records a pleasant evening that January when Lincoln walked over to Seward's with John Hay to share a humorous language guidebook, *English as She is Spoke.* "As John Hay read aloud its queer inverted sentences, Lincoln and Seward laughed heartily, their minds finding a brief but welcome relief from care." Though Seward had long since ceased to be a political threat to her husband, Mary could not relinquish her suspicions. She told their family friend Anson Henry that Seward and his friends were behind the various "scandalous reports in circulation about her." Dr. Henry dismissed her fears, saying that the nasty rumors probably originated in "the Treasury Department," for he had "traced many of them" to Chase's friends and supporters.

Indeed, by early 1864, Chase's presidential ambitions were widely known and frequently discussed in political circles. Mary's anger toward Chase grew "very bitter," Elizabeth Keckley recalled: she "warned Mr. Lincoln not to trust him," but Lincoln continued to insist that Chase was "a patriot." As Mary planned for her first state dinner of the year, traditionally held for the members of the cabinet, justices of the Supreme Court, and their families, she decided to take matters into her own hands. She perused the guest list compiled by John Nicolay, and crossed out the names of Kate Chase and William Sprague. Certain the "snub" would become public and reflect badly on Lincoln, Nicolay appealed to his boss to reinstate the Spragues. Lincoln immediately agreed, sending Mary into a rage.

"There soon arose such a rampage as the House hasn't seen for a year," Nicolay confided to an absent Hay, "and I am again taboo. How the thing is to end is yet as dark a problem as the Schleswig-Holstein difficulty." Mary directed her wrath toward Nicolay, banishing him from the dinner and eschewing his customary help with the arrangements. "Things ran on thus till the afternoon of the dinner," Nicolay reported, when Mary "backed down, requested my presence and assistance—apologizing, and explaining that the affair had worried her so she hadn't slept for a night or two."

The dinner "was pleasant," Welles recorded in his diary. "A little stiff and awkward on the part of the some of the guests [perhaps referring to Chase], but passed off very well." Welles, however, was unable to share the capital's renewed delight in parties, receptions, and fairs. It all seemed inappropriate, "like merry-making at a funeral," he wrote his son Edgar.

Not every occasion was merely a frivolous distraction. The hosts and partygoers did not forget the imperiled men in the armed forces. Where once "the old secession or semi-secesh element" reigned in Washington society, injured soldiers and sailors became the stars of every occasion. Admiral Dahlgren's twenty-one-year-old son, Ulric, had lost a leg at Gettysburg. When he appeared at a Washington party, he was surrounded by pretty girls. They stayed by his side all night, refusing to dance, in tribute to the handsome colonel who had been known as an expert waltzer.

In late January, Copperhead congressman Fernando Wood of New York, who had often and bitterly denounced the Republican administration and the war, threw a great party to which he invited Republicans as well as fellow Democrats. Republicans were expected to stay away, but many actually attended, as did "Abolitionists of the most ultra stripe." Stoddard found it "one of the charming features of life in Washington" that "political animosities" were not carried "into social life," that people who publicly savaged one another could still be "commendably cordial and friendly in all personal intercourse."

In keeping with that tradition, Mary Lincoln sent a bouquet of flowers to Mrs. Wood. The Woods exaggerated the courtesy by placing cards that read: "Compliments of Mrs. A. Lincoln" beside all the many flower vases, making it appear that Mary had supplied the entire array. Newspapers played up the story, citing the supposedly lavish display as evidence of Mary's Southern sympathies. Stung by the criticism, Mary wrote her influential friend General Sickles: "I am pleased to announce to you my entire innocence. . . . With the exception of two political public receptions, they [the Woods] have not entered the [White] house—all of my, friends, who know my detestation of disloyal persons will discredit the rumor—You know me too well to believe it."

Still, slander against the president and first lady continued to fill the columns of opposition papers. In December, when Emilie Todd Helm had come through Union lines after her husband's death, she had been accompanied north by another sister, Martha Todd White. After Emilie left the White House, Lincoln issued a pass to Martha, allowing her to return to the Confederacy. Such passes were not unusual, but the false story spread that Lincoln, presumably at his wife's request, had granted a special permit allowing Martha to bring her bags through without inspection. Some opposition papers claimed that she was, in fact, a Confederate spy and had used her privilege to smuggle contraband through Union lines. It was bruited that when she arrived at Fort Monroe and was told to open her trunks, she waved the president's permit in General Butler's face, defiantly proclaiming: "Here (pushing it under their noses) here is the positive order of your master."

Ordinarily, Lincoln took little heed of scurrilous rumors, but in this case, he directed Nicolay to ascertain the facts from General Butler. Butler replied that the smuggling story was spurious. Mrs. White's bags had undergone the usual search. Nothing untoward had been found. Nicolay used Butler's letter to document a public rebuttal of the fraudulent story. Butler was surprised that the White House would even bother to respond to something so "silly," but after the Wood affair had cast doubt on his wife's loyalty, Lincoln may have wanted to nip the new round of rumors in the bud. Nor did he want his soldiers to think that he would ever facilitate the Confederacy's access to contraband items that might sustain the rebel cause.

It is scarcely surprising that Lincoln not long afterward showed little patience when his old friend Orville Browning requested a favor for a loyal Unionist who owned a cotton plantation in Mississippi. When the Union Army overran her home and took her slaves, she had fallen into poverty. She asked if the government could provide her an equal number of Negroes whom she would pay to work her farm. Lincoln "became very much excited," according to Browning, and "said with great vehemence he had rather take a rope and hang himself than to do it." When Browning argued for "some sort of remuneration" for the lost property, Lincoln countered that "she had lost no property—that her slaves were free when they were taken." Puzzled by Lincoln's sharp reaction, Browning "left him in no very good humor."

As was usually the case with Lincoln's rare episodes of pique, other strains had contributed to the sharp rejoinder. Earlier that day, he had visited the sickbed of Illinois congressman Owen Lovejoy, whom he considered "the best friend [he] had in Congress." The fifty-three-year-old Lovejoy was suffering from a debilitating liver and kidney ailment that would soon take his life. Lincoln was distraught over Lovejoy's misery and seemed to internalize the grim prospects facing his friend. "This war is eating my life out," he told the dying Lovejoy. "I have a strong impression that I shall not live to see the end."

On the night of February 10, a fire alarm rang in the White House. Smoke was seen issuing from the president's private stables, which stood between the mansion and the Treasury building, and Lincoln raced to the scene. "When he reached the boxwood hedge that served as an enclosure to the stables," a member of his bodyguard, Robert McBride, recalled, "he sprang over it like a deer." Learning that the horses were still inside, Lincoln, "with his own hands burst open the stable door." It was immediately apparent that the fast-moving fire, the work of an arsonist, prevented any hope of rescue. "Notwithstanding this," McBride observed, "he would apparently have tried to enter the burning building had not those standing near caught and restrained him."

Six horses burned to death that night. When McBride returned to the White House, he found Lincoln in tears. Ten-year-old Tad "explained his father's emotion": one of the ponies had belonged to his brother, Willie. A coachman who had been fired by Mary that morning was charged with setting the fire. The following day, Lincoln had collected himself and moved forward. He called Commissioner French to his office and instructed him to consult contractors, estimate the cost, and "bring the matter to the attention of Congress to-day, if possible, that measures might be taken to have it rebuilt."

• • •

LINCOLN'S GIFT FOR MANAGING men was never more apparent than during the presidential boomlet for Chase that peaked in the winter months of 1864. While Chase's supporters prematurely showed their hand, Lincoln, according to the Pennsylvania politician Alexander McClure, "carefully veiled his keen and sometimes bitter resentment against Chase, and waited the fullness of time when he could by some fortuitous circumstance remove Chase as a competitor, or by some shrewd manipulation of politics make him a hopeless one."

The game had begun in earnest early in January. Friends of Chase, including Jay and Henry Cooke, contributed thousands of dollars to the publisher of the *American Exchange and Review*, a small Philadelphia magazine, so he would print a flattering biographical sketch of the treasury secretary. Chase's friend William Orton warned him that "no matter how able or 'faithful' the biography may be," its publication in a "seedy" magazine with a reputation for selling its space to whomever could pay enough would be seen "as a flimsy political trick." Orton's note elicited no direct reply, but at some point the president had apparently questioned the involvement of the Cooke brothers, who were still official agents for selling government bonds. The president's questions elicited a long, emotional letter from Chase.

Chase opened his letter with the assertion that his actions, as always, proceeded from the purest of motives. He claimed he had "never, consciously & deliberately, injured one fellow man." He had been told that the publisher intended to print a series of sketches about prominent figures, starting with him. "How could I object?" Treasury business so occupied him that he had paid no further attention to the matter. "What Mr. H. D. Cooke did about the unfortunate biography was done of his own accord without any prompting from me," Chase insisted. Had Cooke or his brother sought his consent, he would have stopped them. "Not that any wrong was intended or done; but because the act was subject to misconstruction. . . . You will pardon me if I write as one somewhat moved. It makes me hate public life when I realize how powerless are the most faithful labors and the most upright conduct to protect any man from carping envy or malignant denunciations."

Embarrassment over the circumstances surrounding the *Exchange and Review* piece did not stop Chase from writing twenty-five long letters that winter to the Boston writer John Trowbridge. His missives were designed to provide the foundation for a small inspirational book about his life, *The Ferry-Boy and the Financier.* An excerpt appeared that spring in the *Atlantic Monthly.* These letters were but a small part of a massive campaign to extol his own virtues at Lincoln's expense. From early morning until late at night, Chase toiled to maintain his stream of correspondence with friends and supporters. "So far," he told a friend in Cincinnati, "I think I have made few mistakes. Indeed, on looking back over the whole ground with an earnest desire to detect error and correct it, I am not able to see where, if I had to do my work all over again, I could in any matter do materially otherwise than I have."

With Kate married and Nettie away at school, Chase resumed his sporadic correspondence with Charlotte Eastman. "I think of you constantly," he assured her, "and—if any feeling is left in me—with the sincerest affection. . . . How I wish you were here in our house—in this little library room—and that we could talk, instead of this writing by myself, while you are—where?" Such romantic inclinations were probably never consummated. Similarly, though he enjoyed the company of Susan Walker, an educated "bluestocking" from Cincinnati, the relationship never seemed to deepen. "*I wish* you could come to Washington," he wrote Miss Walker in late January, "though I could probably see so little of you that it would be difficult to tell which would be greater, the pleasure of seeing you, or the sensation of not seeing you enough." Though Chase obviously admired both Eastman and Walker, his intense focus on his ambition for the presidency kept him from ever making the time to unbend in their company.

The second push in Chase's race for the presidential nomination opened with the public announcement of a "Chase for President" committee. The committee, headed by Kansas senator Samuel Pomeroy and a successful railroad agent, James Winchell, was another enterprise backed by Jay Cooke. In this case, however, Chase's son-in-law, William Sprague, contributed the largest share of the funds. Pomeroy and Winchell were both committed abolitionists who believed Chase would best protect the rights of blacks. Their appearance of altruistic principle was compromised by the fact that they stood to benefit financially if Chase released funds for the construction of the Kansas-Pacific Railroad in which both held a large interest.

Lincoln's old friend Judge David Davis was incensed that Chase was "eating a man's bread and stabbing him at the same time." Chase, unsurprisingly, viewed things differently. Since one-term presidencies had become the rule, Chase felt justified in presenting himself as an alternative. While the committee was being organized, Chase busied himself lining up support in Ohio, determined to avoid the humiliation he had suffered in 1860, when his own state had withheld its support.

Optimistic that he might defeat Lincoln, Chase told his old law partner Flamen Ball that he was immensely "gratified" by the newly formed committee and the quality of the people supporting his candidacy, for they tended to be "men of great weight." Much would depend on the Buckeye State, for "if Ohio should express a preference for any other person, I would not allow my name to be used." Should all go well, Chase believed he would put up a good fight against the president, for, sad to say, the prairie lawyer was simply not up to the job. "If to his kindliness of spirit and good sense he joined strong will and energetic action, there would be little left to wish for in him. As it is, I think that he will be likely to close his first term with more honor than he will the second, should he be reelected."

Nor did Chase confine his criticisms of Lincoln to conversation and correspondence with trusted friends. Speaking with Gideon Welles early in February, he "lamented the want of energy and force by the President, which he said paralyzed everything." Disregarding Welles's silence, he went on to suggest that the president's "weakness was crushing" the nation. When Welles still "did not respond to this distinct feeler," Chase finally let the matter drop. Chase was equally indiscreet with Bates, seeming not to recognize that while the Attorney General occasionally criticized the president, he "immeasurably" preferred him to any other candidate.

Lincoln seemed unfazed by the machinations surrounding the race. Welles reported with delight an exchange with a "fair plump lady" who appeared in the hallway just before a cabinet meeting. She said she lived in Iowa and had come to get a look at the president. Hearing her story, Lincoln invited her into his office. "Well, in the matter of looking at one another," said he with a smile and a chuckle, "I have altogether the advantage."

In February, the Pomeroy Committee distributed a confidential circular to one hundred leading Republicans throughout the North. Intended to mobilize support for Chase, the circular opened with a slashing critique of the president, claiming that "even were the reelection of Mr. Lincoln desirable, it is practically impossible," given the widespread opposition. Furthermore, "should he be reelected, his manifest tendency toward compromises and temporary expedients of policy will become stronger during a second term than it has been in the first." The war would "continue to languish," the country would be bankrupted, and "the dignity of the nation" would suffer. Therefore, in order to win the war, establish the peace, and "vindicate the honor of the republic," it was essential that Republicans unite in nominating the one man with "more of the qualities needed in a President, during the next four years, than are combined in any other available candidate"—Salmon P. Chase.

When the Pomeroy circular was leaked to the press, it created a political explosion. Lincoln's friends were furious, while Democrats celebrated the open division in Republican ranks. "No sensible man here is in doubt that Chase was privy to this," David Davis told a friend. "They did not expect that it wd see the light so soon. . . . I wd dismiss him [from] the cabinet if it killed me."

In a state of panic, Chase sent Lincoln a letter in which he claimed he "had no knowledge" of the circular until it was printed in the *Constitutional Union* on February 20. Though he had been approached by friends to use his name in the coming election, he had not been consulted about the formation of the Pomeroy Committee and was unfamiliar with its members. "You are not responsible for acts not your own," he reminded Lincoln, "nor will you hold me responsible except for what I do or say myself." Yet, he proclaimed, "if there is anything in my action or position which, in your judgment, will prejudice the public interest under my charge I beg you to say so. I do not wish to administer the Treasury Department one day without your entire confidence."

It is unlikely that Lincoln believed Chase's protestations of innocence. Indeed, a decade later, the circular's author, James Winchell, testified that Chase had been fully informed about everything and had personally affirmed "that the arraignment of the Administration made in the circular was one which he thoroughly indorsed, and would sustain." Still, Lincoln restrained his anger and carefully gauged his response, taking a dispassionate view of the situation. He understood the political landscape, he assured Bates. There was a number of malcontents within his own party who "would strike him at once, if they durst; but they fear that the blow would be ineffectual, and so, they would fall under his power, as *beaten enemies.*" So long as he remained confident that he had the public's support, he could afford to let the game play out a little longer. Keeping Chase in suspense, Lincoln simply acknowledged receipt of the letter and promised to "answer a little more fully when I can find time to do so." Then he sat back to measure the reaction of the people to the circular.

It did not take long. The morning it was printed, Welles correctly predicted: "Its recoil will be more dangerous I apprehend than its projectile. That is, it will damage Chase more than Lincoln." Even papers friendly to Chase lamented the circular's publication. "It is unworthy of the cause," the *New York Times* proclaimed. "We protest against the spirit of this movement." Four days later, Nicolay happily informed his fiancée, Therena, that the effect of the circular had been the opposite of what its authors intended, for "it has stirred up all Mr. Lincoln's friends to active exertion," seriously diminishing Chase's prospects. In state after state, Republicans met and passed unanimous resolutions in favor of Lincoln's renomination. Even in Pomeroy's home state of Kansas, a counter-circular was distributed among Republicans that denounced the efforts to carry the state for Chase and rallied support for Lincoln.

Noting the "long list" of state legislatures that had come out for Lincoln, the *Times* acknowledged that the "universality of popular sentiment in favor of Mr. Lincoln's reelection, is one of the most remarkable developments of the time. . . . The faith of the people in the sound judgment and honest purpose of Mr. Lincoln is as tenacious as if it were a veritable instinct. Nothing can overcome it or seriously weaken it. This power of attracting and holding popular confidence springs only from a rare combination of qualities. Very few public men in American history have possessed it in an equal degree with Abraham Lincoln." *Harper's Weekly* agreed. In an editorial endorsing the president's reelection, it claimed that "among all the prominent men in our history from the beginning none have ever shown the power of understanding the popular mind so accurately as Mr. Lincoln." In moving gradually toward emancipation, as he had done, the *Harper's* editor observed, Lincoln understood that in a democracy, "every step he took must seem wise to the great public mind." Thus, he had wisely nullified the premature proclamations issued by Frémont and Hunter, waiting until "the blood of sons and brothers and friends would wash clear a thousand eyes that had been blinded." In his grudging fashion, even Lincoln's critic Count Gurowski acknowledged the president's hold on the people's affections. "The masses are taken in by Lincoln's *apparent* simplicity and good-naturedness, by his awkwardness, by his vulgar jokes, and, in the people's belief, the great shifter is earnest and honest."

The fatal blow to the Chase campaign came again in Ohio, as it had four years before. Although Chase's friends in the Union caucus of the state legislature had previously blocked attempts to endorse Lincoln's re-election, the publication of the Pomeroy circular, a Chase ally conceded, "brought matters to a crisis. . . . It arrayed at once men agt each other who had been party friends always; & finally produced a perfect convulsion in the party." The end result was the unanimous passage of a resolution in favor of Lincoln. "As matters now stand here, with so many states already declared for Lincoln," Chase's friend Cleveland attorney Richard Parsons warned, "prolonging a contest that will in the end array our 'house against itself,' & bring no good to our party at last, seems to me one of the gravest character."

Perceiving this turn of events, Lincoln decided the time was right to answer Chase's letter. He informed Chase that the circular had not surprised him, for he "had knowledge of Mr. Pomeroy's Committee," and of its "secret issues" and "secret agents," for a number of weeks. However, he did not intend to hold Chase responsible. "I fully concur with you that neither of us can be justly held responsible for what our respective friends may do without our instigation or countenance; and I assure you, as you have assured me, that no assault has been made upon you by my instigation, or with my countenance." As to whether Chase should remain as treasury secretary, Lincoln would decide based solely on "my judgement of the public service." For the present, he wrote, "I do not perceive occasion for a change."

A few days later, Chase withdrew his presidential bid. In a public letter to an influential state senator in Ohio, he reminded his fellow Ohioans that he had determined to withdraw from the race if he did not gain the support of his home state. With the legislature's support of Lincoln, "it becomes my duty therefore,—and I count it more a privilege than a duty,—to ask that no further consideration be given to my name."

Trying as ever to explain his action as an unselfish move, Chase told his daughter Nettie that he had withdrawn from the race, though "a good many of the best and most earnest men of the country desired to make me a candidate," because "it was becoming daily more & more clear that the continuance of my name before the people would produce serious discords in the Union organization and might endanger the success of the measures & the establishment of the principles I thought most indispensable to the welfare of the country." Attorney General Bates suggested a less patriotic explanation: "It proves only that the *present* prospects of Mr. Lincoln are too good to be openly resisted."

Discipline and keen insight had once again served Lincoln most effectively. By regulating his emotions and resisting the impulse to strike back at Chase when the circular first became known, he gained time for his friends to mobilize the massive latent support for his candidacy. Chase's aspirations were crushed without Lincoln's direct intrusion. He had known all along that his treasury secretary was no innocent, but by seeming to accept Chase's word, he allowed the secretary to retain some measure of his dignity while the country retained his services in the cabinet. Lincoln himself would determine the appropriate time for Chase's departure.

• • •

LINCOLN'S ABILITY TO RETAIN his emotional balance in such difficult situations was rooted in an acute self-awareness and an enormous capacity to dispel anxiety in constructive ways. In the most difficult moments of his presidency, nothing provided Lincoln greater respite and renewal than to immerse himself in a play at either Grover's or Ford's. Leonard Grover estimated that Lincoln had visited his theater "more than a hundred times" during his four years as president. He was most frequently accompanied by Seward, who shared Lincoln's passion for drama and was an old friend of Mr. Grover's. But his three young assistants, Nicolay, Hay, and Stoddard, also joined him on occasion, as did Noah Brooks, Mary, and Tad. On many nights, Lincoln came by himself, delighted at the chance to sink into his seat as the gaslights dimmed and the action on the stage began.

"It gave him an hour or two of freedom from care and worry," observed Brooks, "and what was better, freedom from the interruption of office-seekers and politicians. He was on such terms with the managers of two of the theaters that he could go in privately by the stage door, and slip into the stage boxes without being seen by the audience." More than anything else, Stoddard remarked how "the drama by drawing his mind into other channels of thought, afforded him the most entire relief." At a performance of *Henry IV: Part One*, Stoddard noted how thoroughly Lincoln enjoyed himself. "He has forgotten the war. He has forgotten Congress. He is out of politics. He is living in Prince Hal's time."

It is not surprising that the theater offered ideal refreshment for a man who regularly employed storytelling to ease tensions. The theater held all the elements of a perfect escape. Enthralled by the live drama, the costumes and scenery, the stagecraft, and the rhetorical extravagances, he was transported into a realm far from the troubling events that filled the rest of his waking hours.

In the mid-nineteenth century, developments with gaslight had vastly improved the experience of theatergoers. Managers had learned "to dim or brighten illumination" by manipulating the valves that fed the gas to the jets. A setting sun, a full moon, or a misty evening could be achieved by placing "colored glass mantles" over the lamps. Technicians stationed above the balcony could illuminate individual actors as they made their entrance onto the stage.

"To envision nineteenth-century theater audiences correctly," the cultural historian Lawrence Levine suggests, "one might do well to visit a contemporary sporting event in which the spectators not only are similarly heterogeneous but are also . . . more than an audience; they are participants who can enter into the action on the field, who feel a sense of immediacy and at times even of control, who articulate their opinions and feelings vocally and unmistakably." Though different classes occupied different areas of the theater—the wealthy in the first-tier boxes, the working class in the orchestra, and the poor in the balcony—the entire audience shared a fairly intimate space. Indeed, Frances Trollope complained that in American theaters she encountered men without jackets, their sleeves rolled to their elbows, and their breath smelling of "onions and whiskey." Though Lincoln was seated in his presidential box, he could still enjoy the communal experience, which allowed him to feel the pulse of the people, much as he had done when he traveled the circuit in his early days.

The years surrounding the Civil War have been called the golden age of American acting. During those years, one historian claims, "the American theatre was blessed with a galaxy of performers who have never been excelled"—including Edwin Forrest, John McCullough, Edwin Booth, Laura Keene, and Charlotte Cushman. It was said of Miss Cushman, who was lionized in both Europe and America for her role as Lady Macbeth, that "she was not a great actress merely, but she was a great woman." She had a magnetic personality and "when she came upon the stage she filled it with . . . the brilliant vitality of her presence." A liberated woman, far ahead of her time, she had lovers but never married. Her work was her chief passion.

Seward and Miss Cushman had met in the 1850s and become great friends. Whenever she was in Washington, she stayed at the Seward home.

The celebrated actress forged a close relationship with young Fanny, who idolized her. Miss Cushman offered a glimpse of the vital and independent life Fanny hoped to lead someday, if her dream to become a writer came true. "Imagine me," Fanny wrote her mother after one of Miss Cushman's visits, "full of the old literary fervor and anxious to be at work, to try hard—& at the same time 'learn to labor, & to wait' I mean, improve in the work which I cannot choose but take . . . I am full of hope that I may yet make my life worth the living and be of some use in the world."

In honor of the star guest, Seward organized a series of dinner parties, inviting members of foreign legations and cabinet colleagues. For her part, Miss Cushman regarded Seward as "the greatest man this country ever produced." Fanny believed that Cushman understood her noble father better than almost anyone outside their family.

Fred Seward recalled that Lincoln made his way to their house almost every night while Miss Cushman visited. Seward had introduced Cushman to the president in the summer of 1861. She had hoped to ask Lincoln for help in obtaining a West Point appointment for a young friend, but the scintillating conversation distracted her from the purpose of her visit. And Lincoln was undoubtedly riveted by the celebrated actress of his beloved Shakespeare.

Unlike Seward, who had been attending theater since he was a young man, Lincoln had seen very few live performances until he came to Washington. So excited was he by his first sight of Falstaff on the stage that he wrote the actor, James Hackett: "Perhaps the best compliment I can pay is to say, as I truly can, I am very anxious to see it again." Although he had not read all of Shakespeare's plays, he told Hackett that he had studied some of them "perhaps as frequently as any unprofessional reader. Among the latter are Lear, Richard Third, Henry Eighth, Hamlet, and especially Macbeth. I think nothing equals Macbeth. It is wonderful. Unlike you gentlemen of the profession, I think the soliloquy in Hamlet commencing 'O, my offence is rank' surpasses that commencing, 'To be, or not to be.' But pardon this small attempt at criticism." When Hackett shared the president's letter with friends, it unfortunately made its way into opposition newspapers. Lincoln was promptly ridiculed for his attempt to render dramatic judgments. An embarrassed Hackett apologized to Lincoln, who urged him to have "no uneasiness on the subject." He was not "shocked by the newspaper comments," for all his life he had "endured a great deal of ridicule without much malice."

The histories and tragedies of Shakespeare that Lincoln loved most dealt with themes that would resonate to a president in the midst of civil war: political intrigue, the burdens of power, the nature of ambition, the relationship of leaders to those they governed. The plays illuminated with stark beauty the dire consequences of civil strife, the evils wrought by jealousy and disloyalty, the emotions evoked by the death of a child, the sundering of family ties or love of country.

Congressman William D. Kelley of Pennsylvania recalled bringing the actor John McDonough to the White House on a stormy night. Lincoln had relished McDonough's performance as Edgar in *King Lear* and was delighted to meet him. For his part, McDonough was "an intensely partisan Democrat, and had accepted the theory that Mr. Lincoln was a mere buffoon." His attitude changed after spending four hours discussing Shakespeare with the president. Lincoln was eager to know why certain scenes were left out of productions. He was fascinated by the different ways that classic lines could be delivered. He lifted his "well-thumbed volume" of Shakespeare from the shelf, reading aloud some passages, repeating others from memory. When the clock approached midnight, Kelley stood up to go, chagrined to have kept the president so long. Lincoln swiftly assured his guests that he had "not enjoyed such a season of literary recreation" in many months. The evening had provided an immensely "pleasant interval" from his work.

Of all the remarkable stage actors in this golden time, none surpassed Edwin Booth, son of the celebrated tragedian Junius Booth and elder brother to Lincoln's future assassin, John Wilkes Booth. "Edwin Booth has done more for the stage in America than any other man," wrote a drama critic in the 1860s. The soulful young actor captivated audiences everywhere with the naturalness of his performances and his conversational tone, which stood in contrast to the bombastic, stylized performances of the older generation.

In late February and early March 1864, Edwin Booth came to Grover's Theatre for a three-week engagement, delivering one masterly performance after another. Lincoln and Seward attended the theater night after night. They saw Booth in the title roles of Hamlet and Richard III. They applauded his performance as Brutus in *Julius Caesar* and as Shylock in *The Merchant of Venice*.

On Friday evening, March 11, Booth came to dinner at the Sewards'. Twenty-year-old Fanny Seward could barely contain her excitement. She had seen every one of his performances and had been transfixed by his "magnificent dark eyes." At dinner, Seward presumed to ask Booth if he might advise the thespian how "his acting might be improved." According to Fanny, Booth "accepted Father's criticisms very gracefully—often saying he had felt those defects himself." Seward focused particularly on

Booth's performance in Bulwer-Lytton's *Richelieu*, where he thought he had made the crafty cardinal "too old and infirm." Long identified as the power behind the throne himself, Seward perhaps wanted a younger, more vibrant characterization for Richelieu. When Seward told Booth he thought his performance as Shylock was perfect, Booth disagreed, saying he "had a painful sense of something wanting—could compare it to nothing else but the want of body in wine."

Detained at the White House, Lincoln missed the enjoyable interchange with Booth. A few days earlier, anticipating Booth's Hamlet, Lincoln had talked about the play with Francis Carpenter, the young artist who was at work on his picture depicting the first reading of the Emancipation Proclamation. In the course of the conversation, Lincoln recited from memory his favorite passage, the king's soliloquy after the murder of Hamlet's father, "with a feeling and appreciation unsurpassed by anything I ever witnessed upon the stage."

What struck Carpenter most forcefully was Lincoln's ability to appreciate tragedy and comedy with equal intensity. He could, in one sitting, bring tears to a visitor's eyes with a sensitive rendering from *Richard III* and moments later induce riotous laughter with a comic tall tale. His "laugh," Carpenter observed, "stood by itself. The 'neigh' of a wild horse on his native prairie is not more undisguised and hearty." Lincoln's ability to commingle joy with sorrow seemed to Carpenter a trait the president shared with his favorite playwright. "It has been well said," Carpenter noted, "that 'the spirit which held the woe of "Lear," and the tragedy of "Hamlet," would have broken, had it not also had the humor of the "Merry Wives of Windsor," and the merriment of "Midsummer Night's Dream." ' "

No other cabinet member went to the theater as regularly as Lincoln and Seward. Chase and Bates considered it a foolish waste of time, perhaps even a "Satanic diversion," while Stanton came only once to Grover's playhouse, with the sole intention of buttonholing Lincoln about some pressing matter. Seated with Lincoln in his box, Grover had been startled when Stanton arrived a half hour late, sidled up to Lincoln, and engaged him in a long conversation. Lincoln listened attentively but kept his eyes on the stage. Frustrated, Stanton "grasped Mr. Lincoln by the lapel of his coat, slowly pulled him round face to face, and continued the conversation. Mr. Lincoln responded to this brusque act with all the smiling geniality that one might bestow on a similar act from a favorite child, but soon again turned his eyes to the stage." Finally, Stanton despaired utterly of conducting his business. He "arose, said good night, and withdrew."

According to Grover, Tad loved the theater as much as his father. John

Hay noted that Tad would laugh "enormously whenever he saw his father's eye twinkle, though not seeing clearly why." Often escorted to Grover's by his tutor, Tad "felt at home and frequently came alone to the rehearsals, which he watched with rapt interest. He made the acquaintance of the stage attachés, who liked him and gave him complete liberty of action." Tad would help them move scenery, and on one occasion, he actually appeared in a play. For the lonely boy, who broke down in tears when the appearance of Julia Taft at a White House reception recalled his happier days with Willie and the Taft boys, the camaraderie of the playhouse must have been immensely comforting.

• • •

ULYSSES S. GRANT, the hero of Vicksburg and Chattanooga, arrived in the nation's capital on March 8, 1864, to take command of all the Union armies. A grateful Congress had revived the grade of lieutenant general, not held since George Washington, and Lincoln had nominated Grant to receive the honored rank. With Grant's promotion, Halleck became chief of staff, and Sherman assumed Grant's old command of the Western armies.

Grant's entrance into Washington was consistent with his image as an unpretentious man of action, the polar opposite of McClellan. He walked into the Willard Hotel at dusk, accompanied only by his teenage son, Fred. Unrecognized by the desk clerk, he was told that nothing was available except a small room on the top floor. The situation was remedied only when the embarrassed clerk looked at the signature in the register—U. S. Grant and son, Galena, Illinois—and immediately switched the accommodations. After freshening up, Grant took his son to the dining room at the lobby level. His slim build, "stooping shoulders, mild blue eyes, and light brown hair and whiskers" attracted little notice until someone began pointing at his table. Suddenly, "there was a shout of welcome from all present, an immense cheer going up from the crowd," who banged their fists on the tops of the tables until he finally stood up and took a bow.

After readying his son for bed, Grant walked over to the White House, where a large crowd had gathered for the president's weekly reception. Horace Porter, a young colonel who would later become Grant's aide-de-camp, was standing near Lincoln in the Blue Room when "a sudden commotion near the entrance to the room attracted general attention." The cause was the appearance of General Grant, "walking along modestly with the rest of the crowd toward Mr. Lincoln." Meeting Grant for the first time, Lincoln's face lit up with a broad smile. Not waiting for his visitor to reach him, the president "advanced rapidly two or three steps," taking Grant by the hand. "Why, here is General Grant! Well, this is a great pleasure."

Porter was struck by the physical contrast between the two men. From his uncommon height, the president "looked down with beaming countenance" upon Grant, who stood eight inches shorter. The collar on Lincoln's evening dress was "a size too large," his necktie "awkwardly tied." He seemed to Porter "more of a Hercules than an Adonis." Yet Porter noted the "merry twinkle" in his gray eyes and "a tone of familiarity" that instantly set people at ease. Watching the two men together, Welles, who was also present, was slightly disconcerted by Grant's demeanor, remarking on his lack of soldierly presence, "a degree of awkwardness."

After talking with Grant, Lincoln referred him to Seward, knowing that his gregarious secretary could best help the general navigate the crowds of admirers shouting his name and rapidly descending upon him. So frantic was the cheering throng to draw near the conquering hero that "laces were torn, crinoline mashed, and things were generally much mixed." Seward rapidly maneuvered Grant into the East Room, where he persuaded the general to stand on a sofa so that everyone could see his face. "He blushed like a girl," the *New York Herald* correspondent noted. "The handshaking brought streams of perspiration down his forehead and over his face." Grant later remarked that the reception was "his warmest campaign during the war."

The president was delighted by the crowd's embrace of Grant. He willingly ceded to the unassuming general his own customary place of honor, fully aware that the path to victory was wide enough, as Porter phrased it, for the two of them to "walk it abreast." Lincoln's reception of Grant might have been more calculated if he had thought the general intended to compete for the presidency, but he had ascertained from a trustworthy source that Grant wanted nothing more than to successfully complete his mission to end the war. "My son, you will never know how gratifying that is to me," Lincoln had told J. Russell Jones, the emissary who carried a letter from Grant affirming that not only did he have no desire for the presidency but he fully supported "keeping Mr. Lincoln in the presidential chair."

After mingling with the excited crowd for an hour, the indefatigable Seward and the exhausted general made their way back to Lincoln, who was waiting with Stanton in the drawing room. They talked over the details of the ceremony the next day, when Grant would be given his commission. To help him prepare his response, Lincoln handed the general a copy of the remarks he would deliver before Grant was expected to speak. Returning to his room at the Willard, Grant wrote out his statement in pencil on a half sheet of paper. When the time came the following afternoon to speak, he seemed, according to Nicolay, "quite embarrassed by the occasion, and finding his own writing so very difficult to read," he stumbled through his speech.

After the ceremony, Lincoln and Grant went upstairs to talk in private. Lincoln explained that while "procrastination on the part of commanders" had led him in the past to issue military orders from the White House, "all he wanted or had ever wanted was some one who would take the responsibility and act," leaving to him the task of mobilizing "all the power of the government" to provide whatever assistance was needed.

On Thursday, Grant journeyed by rail to the headquarters of the Army of the Potomac to consult with General Meade. Upon Grant's return, Lincoln informed him that Mrs. Lincoln was planning a dinner in his honor that Saturday. When Grant begged off, arguing that he wanted to get back to the field as soon as possible, Lincoln laughingly said: "But we can't excuse you. It would be the play of 'Hamlet' with *Hamlet* left out." Still, Grant insisted. "I appreciate fully the honor," he said, "but—time is very precious just now—and—really, Mr. President, I believe I have had enough of the '*show*' business!"

Grant's visit to Washington that March solidified his image as a man of the people. The public had already heard stories of his aversion to what Congressman Elihu Washburne called the "trappings and paraphernalia so common to many military men." While the bill to establish the new rank of lieutenant general was being debated in Washington, Washburne recounted spending six days on the road with Grant, who "took with him neither a horse nor an orderly nor a servant nor a camp-chest nor an overcoat nor a blanket nor even a clean shirt." Carrying only a toothbrush, "he fared like the commonest soldier in his command, partaking of his rations and sleeping upon the ground with no covering except the canopy of heaven." Noting his preference for pork and beans, the *New York Times* speculated that caterers who had previously served "the delicate palates" of officers were "in spasms." Everything Grant did during his four-day stay in Washington, from his unheralded entrance to his early departure, "was done exactly right," the historian William McFeely concludes. "He was consummately modest and quietly confident; the image held for the rest of his political career—and beyond, into history."

• • •

THE SPRING OF 1864 was "unusually backward," Bates recorded in his diary. Trees that normally blossomed in early April did not "put out their leaves" until the end of the month. To those waiting anxiously for the army's spring campaign to begin, it seemed that the "stormy and inclement" weather, which brought "torrents" of rain day after day, was nature's attempt to forestall the inevitable bloodshed. Stoddard speculated that Grant was detained by the same "old enemy" that had stymied McClellan, obstructed Burnside, and allowed Lee to escape after Gettysburg: "the red mud of the Old Dominion."

Lincoln remained convinced that in Ulysses S. Grant he had finally found the commander he needed. At a White House reception in late March, held in the midst of "the toughest snowstorm" of the year, Benjamin French reported that the president was "as full of fun and story as ever I saw him." Three weeks later, on another stormy day, Lincoln was still "as pleasant and funny as could be," entertaining an immense crowd of visitors at his Saturday levee. The following Sunday, he strolled into John Hay's room, "picked up a paper and read the Richmond Examiners recent attack on Jeff. Davis. It amused him. 'Why,' said he 'the Examiner seems abt. as fond of Jeff as the World is of me.' "

That Jefferson Davis was under attack in his own house was not surprising. In the spring of 1864, the Confederacy was "a beleaguered nation," in James Randall's words. "Finances were shaky; currency was unsound; the foreign outlook was never bright." Though rebel convictions remained remarkably steady, there was "real suffering among the people." A letter intended to be sent overseas fell into the hands of a *New York Times* correspondent. The writer, a Virginian, acknowledged the harsh impact of the blockade and rampant inflation upon daily life. "Refined and graceful ladies, who have been used to drink Chambertin, and to eat the rich beef and mutton . . . are reduced to such a state that they know not tea nor coffee, and are glad to put up daily with a slice or two of the coarsest bacon." Furthermore, the "mass of misery" increased exponentially "as one goes down in the social scale." Food riots had broken out in Richmond and Atlanta, and clothing was in such short supply that shops were vandalized.

Davis's health gradually succumbed to the strain; his innate despondency deepened. Friends noticed a withdrawn air about him, and his evening rides were often companionless. Only the company of his wife, Varina, and his family let him truly relax and replenish his energies. Much like Lincoln, he spoiled his children, letting them interrupt grave cabinet meetings and enjoying their games.

Tragedy struck the Davis household on the last day of April 1864.

Varina Davis had left five-year-old Joseph and his seven-year-old brother, Jeff Junior, for a few moments while she brought lunch to her husband in his second-floor office. Little Joe had climbed onto the balcony railing and lost his balance. He died when his head hit the brick pavement below. His parents were inconsolable. It was said that Varina's screams could be heard for hours, while Davis isolated himself on the top floor. The "tramp" of his feet pacing up and down, recalled the diarist Mary Chesnut, wife of Confederate general James Chesnut, produced an eerie echo in the drawing room below. The relentless pace of the war allowed little time for mourning, for Davis understood, as did Lincoln, that it was only a matter of days before the spring campaign would begin.

By the first week of May, William Stoddard observed, Washington was filled with an "oppressive sense of something coming," almost like the "pause and hush before the coming of the hurricane." Although the trees were finally "full of buds and blossoms" and "a few adventurous birds" had begun to sing, "the day had no spring sunshine in it, nor any temptations to make music," for everyone knew that ominous events were imminent. While confidence in Grant remained high, many people, Nicolay conceded, were "beginning to feel superstitious" about his prospects, since previous spring campaigns had "so generally been failures."

Aware that communications would be sporadic once Lieutenant General Grant launched his assault on Lee, Lincoln wrote him a letter that Hay described as "full of kindness & dignity at once." He conveyed his "entire satisfaction with what you have done," and promised that "if there is anything wanting which is within my power to give," it would be provided. Grant graciously replied that he had thus far "been astonished at the readiness with which every thing asked for has been yielded." The final line of Grant's letter illustrated the profound difference between his character and McClellan's. "Should my success be less than I desire, and expect, the least I can say is, the fault is not with you."

Lincoln had heartily approved Grant's plan to move in three directions at once: the Army of the Potomac would strike Lee head-on, forcing him to retreat south toward Richmond; Sherman would move through Georgia from west to east, with the aim of capturing Atlanta; Butler, meanwhile, would move northeast against Richmond from the James River. "This concerted movement," Lincoln reminded Hay, was what he had wanted all along, "so as to bring into action to our advantage our great superiority in numbers." Still, on the eve of battle, Lincoln felt great "solicitude" for his lieutenant general, telling Browning that while he had complete confidence in Grant, he feared that "Lee would select his own ground, and await an attack, which would give him great advantages."

Lincoln's fears proved prescient. As Grant moved south, Lee awaited him in an area just west of Fredericksburg known as the Wilderness—an unforgiving maze of craggy ravines and slippery bogs, dense with vines and thorn bushes. The gloomy terrain provided cover for Lee's earthworks and prevented Grant's superb artillery from being used: it effectively negated the Union's superiority of numbers. Nonetheless, Grant pushed relentlessly south to Spotsylvania and Cold Harbor, slightly northeast of Richmond, engaging Lee in a hideous struggle. Men on both sides had to climb over the dead and dying, "lying in some places in piles three and four deep." Grant's biographer calls the campaign "a nightmare of inhumanity," resulting in 86,000 Union and Confederate casualties in the space of seven weeks. "The world has never seen so bloody and so protracted a battle as the one being fought," Grant told his wife at the end of the first nine days, "and I hope never will again." He later admitted in his memoirs that he "always regretted that the last assault at Cold Harbor was ever made."

Grant buried the dead and sent the wounded to Washington, where they arrived by the thousands. Noah Brooks recorded the heartbreaking scene as steamers reached the city wharves, carrying the "shattered wrecks" of brave soldiers. "Long trains of ambulances are in waiting, and the suffering heroes are tenderly handled and brought out upon stretchers, though with some of them even the lightest touch is torture and pain." The ghastly scene, repeated day after day, was hard for Washingtonians to bear. Judge Taft was present at the wharves one morning when three thousand wounded soldiers disembarked, "some with their heads bound up and some with their arms in a Sling," others limping along. As each steamer landed, crowds gathered around, hoping to recognize in "a maimed and battle-stained form, once so proud and manly," a husband, son, or brother. Elizabeth Blair fled the city, admitting that "the lines [of] ambulances & the moans of their poor suffering men were too much for my nerves."

"The carnage has been unexampled," a depressed Bates lamented in his diary. Even the optimistic Seward acknowledged in his European circular that "it seems to myself like exaggeration, when I find, that, in describing conflict after conflict, in this energetic campaign, I am required always to say of the last one, that it was the severest battle of the war." The immense tension in the War Department, where the cabinet colleagues gathered each night to await the latest news, made it impossible to carry out ordinary business. "The intense anxiety is oppressive," Welles conceded, "and almost unfits the mind for mental activity." John Nicolay wrote to Therena that he was "more nervous and anxious" during these weeks than he had been "for a year previous." Still, he added, "if my own anxiety is so great, what must be [the president's] solicitude, after waiting through three long, weary years of doubt and disaster."

There were, indeed, nights when Lincoln did not sleep. One of these nights, Francis Carpenter "met him, clad in a long morning wrapper, pacing back and forth . . . his hands behind him, great black rings under his eyes, his head bent forward upon his breast." There were moments when he was overwhelmed with sorrow at the appalling loss of life. As the leader of his cabinet and the leader of his country, however, he understood the need to remain collected and project hope and confidence to his colleagues and his people. Between anxious hours at the War Department awaiting news from the front, Lincoln made time to get to the theater, attend a public lecture on Gettysburg, and see an opera. "People may think strange of it," he explained, "but I *must* have some relief from this terrible anxiety, or it will kill me."

Schuyler Colfax came to visit one Sunday during the Battle of the Wilderness. "I saw [Lincoln] walk up and down the Executive Chamber, his long arms behind his back, his dark features contracted still more with gloom; and as he looked up, I thought his face the saddest one I had ever seen." But, Colfax added, "he quickly recovered," and suddenly spoke of Grant with such confidence that "hope beamed on his face." An hour later, greeting a delegation of congressional visitors, he managed to tell "story after story," which hid "his saddened heart from their keen and anxious scrutiny."

Lincoln never lost faith in Grant. He realized that whereas "any other General" would have retreated after sustaining such terrible losses, Grant somehow retained "the dogged pertinacity . . . that wins." Lincoln hugged and kissed a young reporter on the forehead who arrived at the White House with a verbal message from the general that said, "there is to be no turning back." His spirits rose further when he read the words in Grant's famous dispatch on May 11: "I propose to fight it out on this line if it takes all summer." When a visitor asked one day about the prospects of the army under Grant, Lincoln's face lit up "with that peculiar smile which he always puts on when about to tell a good story." The question, he said, "reminds me of a little anecdote about the automaton chessplayer, which many years ago astonished the world by its skill in that game. After a while the automaton was challenged by a celebrated player, who, to his great chagrin, was beaten twice by the machine. At the end of the second game, the player, significantly pointing his finger at the automaton, exclaimed in a very decided tone. *'There's a man in it!'* " That, he explained, referring to Grant, was "the secret" to the army's fortunes.

• • •

In early June, when the Republican Convention was set to open in Baltimore, Salmon Chase grew restless. Though he had withdrawn his name from the race the previous March, he still retained the hope that events might turn in his favor. Thurlow Weed had repeatedly warned the president that Chase's withdrawal was simply a "shrewd dodge" that would allow him "to turn up again with more strength than ever." The well-informed political boss had compiled a long list of Treasury employees who were devoting all their energies to the Chase campaign. More troubling still, Weed had heard from myriad sources that corrupt Treasury agents were exchanging army supplies for Confederate cotton in violation of the congressional law that forbade any trade between the free and slave states without an express permit from the Treasury. Weed believed that Chase's son-in-law, Sprague, was a beneficiary of one of these schemes. He could not fathom Lincoln's refusal to fire Chase, predicting that if the president "goes into the canvass with this mill-stone tied to him, he will inevitably sink."

Meanwhile, the smoldering feud between Chase and the Blairs erupted into full public view. With the army in winter quarters the previous January, Frank Blair had resigned his commission and retaken his seat in Congress. He intended to return to Sherman's command in time for the march to Atlanta, but first, he had a score to settle with Chase. A Chase partisan had publicly accused Blair of swindling the government by charging $8,000 for a personal shipment of liquor and tobacco. Blair knew the document in question was spurious and suspected that it had been forged in the Treasury Department. He asked a congressional committee to investigate the matter. The resulting report fully exonerated Blair. The accusing document was, indeed, a forgery penned by a Treasury agent. Although there was no suggestion of Chase's personal involvement, Blair waited for the issuance of the committee's report before rising to speak on the floor.

Addressing a packed audience the day before his scheduled departure for Sherman's army, he began by calmly summarizing the report's findings. His self-control swiftly vanished, however, as he turned his anger on Chase. "These dogs have been set on me by their master, and since I have whipped them back into their kennel I mean to hold their master responsible for this outrage and not the curs who have been set upon me." Speaker Colfax admonished Blair to stick to the committee report, but Blair's supporters insisted that he be allowed to continue. He accused Chase of corruption, treachery against Lincoln, lack of patriotism, and sordid ambition for the presidency.

Elizabeth Blair, present in the galleries, believed the speech "a complete triumph" in the short run but worried about its livid tone. "Anger is the poorest of counselors," she conceded, "& revenge is suicide." She was right to worry, for the speech inflamed the ongoing war between Chase and Blair that would end by damaging both men. Chase's friends reacted quickly, labeling the accusations against the treasury secretary "mendacious slanders."

Gideon Welles considered the speech "violent and injudicious" and feared that it would ultimately hurt the president. The wise navy secretary was dismayed by the continuing feud between Chase and the Blairs, believing both sides shared the blame. "Chase is deficient in magnanimity and generosity. The Blairs have both, but they have strong resentments. Warfare with them is open, bold and unsparing. With Chase it is silent, persistent, but regulated with discretion."

Chase was told about the speech later that night as he boarded a train to the Sanitary Fair in Baltimore. His friend Congressman Albert Riddle joined him in his private car. "He was alone," Riddle recalled, "and in a frightful rage, and controlled himself with difficulty while he explained the cause. The recital in a hoarse, constrained voice, seemed to rekindle his anger and aggravate his intensity. The spacious car fairly trembled under his feet." Chase felt certain that "all this, including the speech, had been done with the cordial approval of the President." Ohio congressman James Garfield agreed with this assessment. He considered Frank Blair Lincoln's "creature," sent to the House for the "special purpose" of destroying Chase's reputation. With this accomplished, Garfield charged, Lincoln would simply renew Blair's commission and return him to the front, "thus ratifying all he said and did while here." Chase told Riddle that unless Lincoln repudiated Blair, he would feel honor-bound once again to tender his resignation.

Riddle and another friend of Chase's, Rufus Spalding, called on the president. They warned him that "Chase's abrupt resignation now would be equal in its effects to a severe set-back of the army under Grant." Explaining that the coincidence of Blair's vicious speech and the president's renewal of his commission "seemed as if planned for dramatic effect, as parts of a conspiracy against a most important member of the Cabinet," they demanded to know if Lincoln had known ahead of time the nature of Blair's remarks.

Lincoln had prepared well for the encounter. The last thing he wanted was for Chase to resign on a point of honor. The rift between the radicals and conservatives in the Republican Party might then become irreparable. He gave the visitors his usual undivided attention. When they finished, Riddle recalled, "he arose, came round, and with great cordiality took each of us by the hand and evinced the greatest satisfaction at our presence." Then, taking up a stack of papers on his desk, he inquired if either of them had seen his letter to Chase two months earlier when the secretary had offered to resign over his implication in the humiliating Pomeroy circular. Determining that Riddle had not, Lincoln read aloud the lines where he concurred with Chase that neither of them should be "held responsible for what our respective friends may do without our instigation or countenance."

He explained that while he had great respect for Frank Blair, he "was annoyed and mortified by the speech." He had, in fact, warned Blair against "pursuing a personal warfare." As soon as he heard of Blair's rant, Lincoln knew that "*another beehive was kicked over*" and considered canceling "the orders restoring him to the army and assigning him to command." After assessing how much General Sherman valued Frank's services, however, he had decided to let the orders stand.

In making his case, Riddle recalled, Lincoln "was plain, sincere, and most impressive." Riddle and Spalding were "perfectly satisfied" and assured Lincoln that Chase would be, too. Once again, Lincoln had sutured a potentially dangerous wound within his administration and his party.

• • •

IT WAS A WARM DAY on June 7, 1864, when Republicans gathered in Baltimore to choose their candidates for president and vice president. Noah Brooks was moved by the sight of the people's representatives gathering "in the midst of a civil war and in the actual din of battle" to perform the most precious function of democracy. The Democrats would also meet that summer, though they delayed their convention until the end of August to give themselves a better chance to react to the latest events on the battlefield.

As the delegates from twenty-five states flocked to the Republican Convention, which was relabeled the National Union Convention, Lincoln's renomination was assured. So certain was the outcome that David Davis, who had been instrumental in guiding Lincoln to the nomination four years earlier, chose not to attend. He had originally planned to go, he told Lincoln, "but since the New York & Ohio Conventions, the necessity for doing so is foreclosed—I have kept count of all the States that have instructed, & you must be nominated by acclamation—if there had been a speck of opposition, I wd have gone to Baltimore—But the opposition is so utterly beaten, that the fight is not even interesting, and the services of no one is necessary." In Judge Davis's stead, Lincoln sent John Nicolay as his personal emissary to the convention.

Even Horace Greeley, while holding out for an alternative, acknowledged that the president had earned an honored place in the hearts of his fellow Americans. "The People think of him by night & by day & pray for him & their *hearts* are where they have made so heavy investments." Long before the convention opened its doors, the official nominating committee said, "popular instinct had plainly indicated [Lincoln] as its candidate," and the work of the convention was simply to register "the popular will." While politicians in Washington may have entertained other prospects, Brooks observed, "the country at large really thought of no name but Lincoln's."

There were, of course, some pockets of resistance. At the end of May, several hundred malcontents had gathered in Cleveland's Chapin Hall to nominate John Frémont for president on a third-party ticket. Frémont had never forgiven Lincoln for relieving him of command in 1861. Though he had eventually been offered another commission, he had refused upon learning that he would report to another general. His supporters were a mix of radicals, abolitionists, disappointed office seekers, and Copperheads. They hoped to split the Republican Party with a platform calling for a constitutional amendment ending slavery. They demanded that Congress, rather than the president, take the lead on Reconstruction, and pressed for the "confiscation of the lands of the rebels, and their distribution among the soldiers."

Lincoln had been in the telegraph office when reports of the Frémont convention came over the wires. Hearing that the attendance was a mere four hundred of the expected thousands, he was reminded of a passage in the Bible. Opening his Bible to I Samuel 22:2, he read aloud: "And every one that was in distress, and every one that was in debt, and every one that was discontented, gathered themselves unto him; and he became a captain over them: and there were with him about four hundred men."

The night before the Baltimore convention, Lincoln talked with Noah Brooks. When Brooks observed that his "renomination was an absolute certainty," Lincoln "cheerfully conceded that point without any false modesty." Understanding that there were several candidates for vice president, including the incumbent Hannibal Hamlin, New York's Daniel Dickinson, and Tennessee's military governor, Andrew Johnson, Lincoln declined to express his preference. He did say, however, that "he hoped that the convention would declare in favor of the constitutional amendment abolishing slavery," and he asked Brooks to report back to him all "the odd bits of gossip" that a good reporter would pick up.

As expected, the convention was initially confronted with two contesting delegations from Missouri: an anti-Blair radical delegation pledged to vote for Grant as a means of expressing displeasure with Lincoln, and a pro-Blair conservative delegation pledged to Lincoln. With the president's approval, the radical delegation was seated. Lincoln understood the importance, as one delegate put it, of integrating "all the elements of the Republican party—including the impracticables, the Pharisees, the better-than-thou declaimers, the long-haired men and the short-haired women." Moreover, the radicals had tacitly agreed that they would switch their votes to Lincoln after the first ballot, making the president's nomination unanimous.

Nothing better indicated the nation's transformation since the Chicago convention four years earlier than the tumultuous applause that greeted the third resolution of the platform: "*Resolved*, That as Slavery was the cause, and now constitutes the strength, of this Rebellion . . . [we] demand its utter and complete extirpation from the soil of the Republic." While upholding the president's proclamation, which "aimed a death-blow at this gigantic evil," the resolution continued: "we are in favor, furthermore," of a constitutional amendment to "forever prohibit the existence of slavery" in the United States.

Resounding applause also greeted the resolution thanking soldiers and sailors, "who have periled their lives in defense of their country"; but the crowd's greatest demonstration was reserved for the resolution endorsing Lincoln's leadership. "The enthusiasm was terrific," Brooks noted, "the convention breaking out into yells and cheers unbounded as soon as the beloved name of Lincoln was spoken." The only discordant note was the passage of a radical plank aimed at conservative Montgomery Blair, calling for "a purge of any cabinet member" who failed to support the platform in full. "Harmony was restored" when the roll call nominating Lincoln was completed, at which point, the *National Republican* noted, "the audience rose *en masse*, and such an enthusiastic demonstration was scarcely ever paralleled. Men waved their hands and hats, and ladies, in the galleries, their kerchiefs," while the band played "The Star-Spangled Banner."

The next order of business was the nomination of a vice president. Though Thurlow Weed was not a delegate, his towering presence played a central role in the selection of Andrew Johnson. Always alive to the interests of his oldest friend, Seward, Weed at once understood that if New

York's Daniel Dickinson received the vice presidential nod, Seward might not retain his position as secretary of state. An unwritten rule dictated that two significant posts could not be allotted to a single state. Weed had initially supported Hamlin but soon saw that the growing sentiment for a War Democrat would result in the nomination of either Dickinson or Johnson. He placed the Weed-Seward machine behind the victorious Johnson.

The results of the convention were routed through the telegraph office at the War Department. It was "Stanton's theory," his secretary explained, that "*everything* concerned his own Department," and he had centralized into his office "the whole telegraphic system of the United States." Lincoln was present in the late afternoon when a clerk handed him a dispatch reporting Johnson's nomination. Having not yet heard his own nomination confirmed, Lincoln was startled. "What! do they nominate a Vice-President before they do a President?" Is that not putting "the cart before the horse"? The embarrassed operator explained that the dispatch about the president's nomination had come in several hours earlier, while Lincoln was at lunch, and had been sent directly to the White House. "It is all right," replied Lincoln. "I shall probably find it on my return."

The following day, a committee appointed by the delegates arrived at the White House to officially notify Lincoln of his nomination. In response to their laudatory statement, Lincoln said he did not assume that the convention had found him to be "the best man in the country; but I am reminded, in this connection, of a story of an old Dutch farmer, who remarked to a companion once that 'it was not best to swap horses when crossing streams.' " Later that night, when the Ohio delegation came to serenade him at the White House, he humbly directed their attention to the soldiers in the field. "What we want, still more than Baltimore conventions or presidential elections, is success under Gen. Grant," he said. "I propose that you help me to close up what I am now saying with three rousing cheers for Gen. Grant and the officers and soldiers under his command."

A visitor to the White House at this time told Lincoln that "nothing could defeat him but Grant's *capture of Richmond*, to be followed by [the general's] nomination at Chicago"—where the Democratic Convention was scheduled to take place later that summer. "Well," said Lincoln, "I feel very much like the man who said he didn't want to die particularly, but if he had got to die, that was precisely the disease he would like to die of."

CHAPTER 24

"ATLANTA IS OURS"

UNION HOPES FOR imminent victory faded as the spring of 1864 gave way to summer. "Our troops have suffered much and accomplished but little," Gideon Welles recorded in his diary on June 20. "The immense slaughter of our brave men chills and sickens us all." Unable to dislodge Lee's troops, who displayed what the White House secretary William Stoddard called an awe-inspiring "steady courage," Grant settled in for a siege at Petersburg. Meanwhile, Sherman was encountering tough resistance as he moved slowly through Georgia.

Daily reports of the brutal battles in Virginia and Georgia provoked a particular dread in the Sewards, the Blairs, the Bates, and the Welleses, all of whom had loved ones at the front. For the Sewards, whose youngest son, William, nearly lost his life at Cold Harbor, there were many sleepless nights. "I cannot yet bring myself to the contemplation of your death or of your suffering as others have done," Frances Seward told Will, though she considered that he was "fighting for a holy cause" in a "righteous" conflict, unlike the Mexican War, which she had vigorously opposed when her older son, Augustus, had been in the army.

Elizabeth Blair had become "so nervous" with her husband in the navy and her brother Frank moving toward Atlanta with Sherman that she "quake[d] all night with terror." Even her normally cheerful father was perpetually "grave & anxious," certain that if Frank were taken prisoner, the Confederates "would be as eager to kill him physically—as the Radicals are politically." Bates feared for his twenty-one-year-old son, Coalter, who was with General Meade and the Army of the Potomac, and Welles was pained "beyond what I can describe" when his eighteen-year-old son, Thomas, departed "with boyish pride and enthusiasm" to join General Grant. "It was uncertain whether we should ever meet again," he recorded in his diary, "and if we do he may be mutilated, and a ruined man." His anxiety left Welles "sad, and unfit for any labor." The painful apprehension within the administration mirrored the fears experienced in hundreds of thousands of homes throughout the country.

Lincoln knew the ravages of this most bloody war had touched every town and household of America. The time had come to revive the oppressed spirits of the people. In mid-June, he found the perfect forum for a public speech when he journeyed to the Great Central Fair in Philadelphia, designed to benefit the Sanitary Commission. Thousands of citizens had come from the surrounding area to enjoy the collections of art, statuary, and flowers, the zoological garden, restaurants, raffles, and games that covered a two-mile concourse and were said to offer "miracles as many as Faust saw in his journey through the world of magic."

At seven o'clock on the morning of June 16, Lincoln, Mary, and Tad left for Philadelphia by train. Word of their journey had spread. At every depot along the way, cheering crowds gathered for a glimpse of the first family. Arriving before noon, they were escorted in an open carriage up Broad Street to Chestnut Street and the Continental Hotel. The streets were "lined with citizens" and the windows "crowded with ladies waving their handkerchiefs." The unbounded ardor and spontaneous applause was such, one reporter noted, "as has not been heard for many a day in Philadelphia." Lincoln declined to speak at the hotel or at the fairgrounds that afternoon, preferring to wait until the dinner that evening. Perhaps he knew that his remarks, which he had carefully drafted, would be recorded more accurately in that setting.

"War, at the best, is terrible, and this war of ours, in its magnitude and in its duration, is one of the most terrible," he began. "It has destroyed property, and ruined homes; it has produced a national debt and taxation unprecedented. . . . It has carried mourning to almost every home, until it can almost be said that the 'heavens are hung in black.' " Nonetheless, he reminded his listeners, "We accepted this war for an object, a worthy object, and the war will end when that object is attained. Under God, I hope it never will until that time." The force of his words and the unshakable determination they embodied instantly uplifted and emboldened his audience.

A few days later, in order to stem his own "intense anxiety" about the stalemate in Virginia, Lincoln decided to visit Grant at his headquarters at City Point. Welles strongly disapproved of the decision. "He can do no good," he predicted. "It can hardly be otherwise than to do harm, even if no accident befalls him. Better for him and the country that he should remain at his post here." The navy secretary failed to understand the importance of these trips to Lincoln, who needed the contact with the troops to lift his own spirits so that he, in turn, could better buoy the spirits of those around him.

Accompanied by Tad and Assistant Navy Secretary Gustavus Fox, Lincoln left the Washington Navy Yard aboard the river steamer *Baltimore* in the early evening of June 20. The journey to City Point, which was about 180 miles farther south by water than Aquia Creek, took more than sixteen hours. Horace Porter, Grant's aide-de-camp, recalled that when the steamer arrived at the wharf, Lincoln "came down from the upper deck . . . and reaching out his long, angular arm, he wrung General Grant's hand vigorously, and held it in his for some time," as he expressed great appreciation for all that Grant had been through since they last met in Washington. Introduced to the members of Grant's staff, the president "had for each one a cordial greeting and a pleasant word. There was a kindliness in his tone and a hearty manner of expression which went far to captivate all who met him."

Over a "plain and substantial" lunch, typical of "the hero of Vicksburg," noted the *Herald* correspondent, Lincoln conversed entertainingly and delivered "three capital jokes" that provoked hilarity. When the meal was finished, Grant suggested a ride to the front ten miles away. Porter noted that Lincoln made an odd appearance on his horse as his "trousers gradually worked up above his ankles, and gave him the appearance of a country farmer riding into town wearing his Sunday clothes." The sight "bordered upon the grotesque," but the troops he passed along the way "were so lost in admiration of the man that the humorous aspect did not seem to strike them . . . cheers broke forth from all the commands, and enthusiastic shouts and even words of familiar greeting met him on all sides."

Reaching the front, the president took "a long and lingering look" at the sights of Petersburg, where Lee's armies were gathered behind formidable earthworks. On the return trip, they passed a brigade of black soldiers, who rushed forward to greet the president, "screaming, yelling, shouting: 'Hurrah for the Liberator; Hurrah for the President.' " Their "spontaneous outburst" moved Lincoln to tears, "and his voice was so broken by emotion" that he could hardly reply.

That evening, Porter recalled, as Lincoln sat for hours with General Grant and his staff, "we had an opportunity of appreciating his charm as a talker, and hearing some of the stories for which he had become celebrated." The young aide-de-camp observed what so many others had seen before, that Lincoln "did not tell a story merely for the sake of the anecdote, but to point a moral or clench a fact." Seated on "a low camp-chair," with his long legs wrapped around each other "as if in an effort to get them out of the way," he used his arms to accompany his words and "joined heartily with the listeners in the laugh which followed." Discussion of a new form of gunpowder prompted a story of two competing powder merchants in Springfield. The sight of a newly patented artillery trace led to the recitation of a line from a poem: "Sorrow had fled, but left her traces there." Reference to the electoral college brought forth the quaint observation that "the Electoral College is the only one where they choose their own masters." When the convivial evening came to a close, the president walked with Porter to his tent, taking a peek inside, "from curiosity, doubtless, to see how the officers were quartered," before returning to his stateroom on the *Baltimore*.

The next morning, "in excellent spirits," Lincoln steamed up the James River with Grant to visit General Butler and Admiral Samuel Phillips Lee, Elizabeth Blair's husband. Talking with Butler about Grant, he observed that "When Grant once gets possession of a place, he holds on to it as if he had inherited it." After lunch, it was time to return to Washington. On taking leave, General Grant took Lincoln aside, assuring him with a rousing pledge that the president would repeat and cite in the weeks ahead: "You will never hear of me farther from Richmond than now, till I have taken it. I am just as sure of going into Richmond as I am of any future event. It may take a long summer day, but I will go in."

On the morning of June 23, John Hay reported that Lincoln returned to the White House "sunburnt and fagged but still refreshed and cheered. He found the army in fine health good position and good spirits." The next day, at the regular Friday cabinet meeting, the skeptical Welles conceded that the trip to the front had "done him good, physically, and strengthened him mentally in confidence in the General and army." And of signal importance, Lincoln could now better project his own renewed hope to the anxious public, lauding Grant's "extraordinary qualities as a commander" to one reporter, and speaking to another "of the condition of army matters in the very highest terms of confidence."

Acutely aware of his own emotional needs, Lincoln had chosen exactly the right time to review the troops, for his conversations with Grant and his interactions with the soldiers sustained and inspired him during the troubling days ahead. "Having hope," writes Daniel Goleman in his study of emotional intelligence, "means that one will not give in to overwhelming anxiety, a defeatist attitude, or depression in the face of difficult challenges or setbacks." Hope is "more than the sunny view that everything will turn out all right"; it is "believing you have the will and the way to accomplish your goals." More clearly than his colleagues, Lincoln understood that numerous setbacks were inevitable before the war could be brought to a close. Yet in the end, he firmly believed the North would prevail. "We are today further ahead than I thought one year and a half ago we should be," he told Noah Brooks that June, "and yet there are plenty of people who believe that the war is about to be substantially closed. As God is my judge I shall be satisfied if we are over with the fight in Virginia within a year."

• • •

BY THE LAST WEEK of June, the forbearance Lincoln had long shown toward his ambitious secretary of the treasury was finally exhausted. The dramatic upheaval in the cabinet began when John Cisco, assistant treasurer of New York, announced his resignation. Cisco had held the prestigious post through three different administrations and was well respected by all factions. Lincoln was anxious that his replacement satisfy both wings of New York's Republican Party. For several months, the president had been bombarded by complaints from friends in New York, including Thurlow Weed and Senator Edwin Morgan, that Chase was filling all the customs house positions with his own partisans—former Democrats who were now radical Republicans supporting Chase's own presidential hopes.

Sensitive to Weed's concerns, Lincoln told Chase to consult with Senator Morgan and ensure that his selection was satisfactory to all sides. Chase discussed the matter with the powerful New York senator but then proceeded, over Morgan's strong objection, to send Lincoln a formal nomination for Maunsell Field. A Democratic journalist with ties to New York society, Field was serving as third assistant secretary of the treasury, a post

Chase had designed especially to compensate Field for the access he had provided Chase to the inner circles of New York literary and social life. The appointment was stunning, recalled the treasury registrar, Lucius Chittenden, for Field "had no financial or political standing, and his natural abilities were of a literary rather than an executive character."

Undeterred, Chase apparently assumed that his own services were so indispensable that Lincoln would sanction a controversial nominee rather than risk a messy squabble when the financial health of the nation was at stake. Chase awoke the morning after sending the Field nomination to the White House and cheerfully undertook his daily reading of the Bible, which on that summer morning included a letter St. Paul sent to the Ephesians imploring them to "Stand therefore, having your loins girt about with truth, and having on the breastplate of righteousness." When he reached the department, however, he found a disturbing note from the president on his desk. "I can not, without much embarrassment, make this appointment," Lincoln informed him, "principally because of Senator Morgan's very firm opposition to it." It would "really oblige" him, he said, if Chase and Senator Morgan could agree on another nominee.

Still confident that he could change the president's mind, Chase wrote an immediate request for a personal interview. When Lincoln did not respond, Chase decided to resolve the difficulty on his own. He telegraphed Cisco in New York and pleaded with him to withdraw his resignation and stay on for another three months. Before obtaining Cisco's answer, he received Lincoln's reply to his interview request. "The difficulty," wrote Lincoln, "does not, in the main part, lie within the range of a conversation between you and me." Lincoln went on to explain the criticism he had faced in the previous months over treasury appointments in New York, and noted that to disregard Morgan's judgment in this instance might trigger "open revolt."

Cisco's agreement to stay on should have ended the matter; but Chase, peeved at Lincoln's refusal to meet in person and bent on reestablishing his authority over his own appointments, could not rest. He decided to chasten the president with what was essentially his fourth letter of resignation, certain it would again be rejected. He began his letter by enclosing Cisco's telegram withdrawing his resignation, which, he acknowledged, "relieves the present difficulty." But then he went on: "I cannot help feeling that my position here is not altogether agreeable to you; and it is certainly too full of embarrassment and difficulty and painful responsibility to allow in me the least desire to retain it. I think it my duty therefore to enclose to you my resignation."

Lincoln was seated at his desk in his office, he later recalled, when a messenger handed him a letter from the Treasury Department. "I opened it, recognized Chase's handwriting, read the first sentence, and inferred from its tenor that this matter was in the way of satisfactory adjustment. I was truly glad of this, and, laying the envelope with its inclosure down upon the desk, went on talking. People were coming and going all the time till three o'clock, and I forgot all about Chase's letter. At that hour it occurred to me that I would go down stairs and get a bit of lunch. My wife happened to be away, and they had failed to call me at the usual time [Mary was in Massachusetts for Robert's graduation from Harvard]. While I was sitting alone at table my thoughts reverted to Chase's letter, and I determined to answer it just as soon as I should go up stairs again.

"Well, as soon as I was back here, I took pen and paper and prepared to write, but then it occurred to me that I might as well read the letter before I answered it. I took it out of the envelope for that purpose, and, as I did so, another inclosure fell from it upon the floor. I picked it up, read it, and said to myself, '*Halloo, this is a horse of another color!*' It was his resignation. I put my pen into my mouth, and *grit my teeth* upon it. I did not long reflect."

Lincoln quickly perceived that Chase was essentially saying: "You have been acting very badly. Unless you say you are sorry, & ask me to stay & agree that I shall be absolute and that you shall have nothing, no matter how you beg for it, I will go." This presumption the president could not and would not countenance. He took his pen from his mouth and began to write.

"Your resignation of the office of Secretary of the Treasury," he tersely opened, "is accepted. Of all I have said in commendation of your ability and fidelity, I have nothing to unsay; and yet you and I have reached a point of mutual embarrassment in our official relation which it seems can not be overcome, or longer sustained, consistently with the public service."

Early the next morning, Lincoln called John Hay into his office and asked him to deliver the news of Chase's resignation to the Senate as soon as it convened, along with his recommendation of former Ohio governor David Tod as his successor. "It is a big fish," he said. "I thought I could not stand it any longer." Though worried that the president was making a costly mistake, the loyal Hay proceeded to the Capitol, reaching the Senate just as the chaplain recited the opening prayer.

Still ignorant of the president's letter, Chase went about his daily business, anticipating Lincoln's penitent request for him to continue his duties. Perhaps Lincoln would personally visit his office, put his arm around him, and again tell him how much he was needed. After breakfast, Chase went to his office, where he received word that Senator Fessenden of Maine wanted to see him immediately at the Capitol. Riding in his carriage, he surmised that the chairman of the Finance Committee wanted to discuss the various financial bills currently before him. In the midst of his conversation with Fessenden, a messenger arrived to tell the senator of David Tod's nomination. "Have you resigned?" the distraught Fessenden asked. "I am called to the Senate & told that the President has sent in the nomination of your successor." Stunned, Chase explained that he had indeed sent in his resignation, but did not know that it had been accepted.

Returning at once to the department, Chase found the letter from Lincoln. Reaching the part where Lincoln spoke of "mutual embarrassment" in their relations, Chase was dumbfounded. "I had found a good deal of embarrassment from him," he recorded in his diary that night, "but what he had found from me I could not imagine, unless it has been created by my unwillingness to have offices distributed by spoils or benefits with more regard to the claims of divisions, factions, cliques and individuals, than to fitness of selection." Blinded by self-righteousness and donning what Nicolay and Hay termed "his full armor of noble sentiments," Chase refused to see that in choosing the inexperienced Field, he, not the president, was filling an office on the basis of faction rather than fitness.

The startling news spread quickly on Capitol Hill. "The Senators were struck dumb with amazement," Noah Brooks reported. The members of the Senate Finance Committee convened an emergency meeting and decided to go as a body to the White House to lodge a vehement protest. "Fessenden was frightened," Lincoln later told Hay; "Conness [of California] was mad." Lincoln listened patiently to their concerns about losing Chase at this perilous time and their doubts about Tod as a viable successor. Then, reaching into his desk, he pulled out Chase's previous letters of resignation and read them aloud to his visitors, along with the gracious replies that had kept Chase in the cabinet each time. Moreover, though he agreed that "Mr. Chase had a full right to indulge in his ambition to be President," he suggested that the indiscretions of Chase's friends had so complicated matters that the two of them "disliked to meet each other" in person. In fact, in recent weeks, Chase had declined to attend most of the regular cabinet meetings. The situation had become "unendurable," Lincoln concluded, this most recent controversy being simply "the last straw." Though the committee left dissatisfied, they at least departed with a true picture of the long history behind the final break.

Chase's friend Massachusetts congressman Samuel Hooper came in to see the president later that afternoon. He said he felt "very nervous & cut up" by Chase's departure. Treasury Registrar Lucius Chittenden was equally distraught, telling Lincoln that the loss of Chase was "worse than another Bull Run defeat," for there was not a single man in the country who could replace him. "I will tell you," Lincoln said, "how it is with Chase. It is the easiest thing in the world for a man to fall into a bad habit. Chase has fallen into two bad habits. . . . He thinks he has become indispensable to the country. . . . He also thinks he ought to be President; he has no doubt whatever about that." These two unfortunate tendencies, Lincoln explained, had made Chase "irritable, uncomfortable, so that he is never perfectly happy unless he is thoroughly miserable."

At this point, according to Chittenden, Lincoln paused. "And yet there is not a man in the Union who would make as good a chief justice as Chase," he continued, "and, if I have the opportunity, I will make him Chief Justice of the United States." Chittenden concluded that this extraordinary want of vindictiveness toward someone who had caused him such grief proved that Lincoln "must move upon a higher plane and be influenced by loftier motives than any man" he had ever known. Yet while Lincoln did indeed possess unusual magnanimity, he was also a shrewd politician. He mentioned the chief justiceship to Chittenden knowing that when Chase learned of it, the prospect might dampen his public opposition. Lincoln made a similar remark to Congressman Hooper. In a relaxed conversation, he expressed his "esteem" for the secretary and his sincere "regret" that the two of them had become so "awkward" and "constrained" when they got together. When Hooper relayed these comments to his friend, Chase was moved, suggesting that "had any such expressions of good will" been tendered before his resignation, he might have acted differently. Unfortunately, it was too late.

The news of Chase's resignation was met with dismay and regret in the country. He was "the great magician of the treasury," the *Chicago Tribune* wrote; "his name will be handed down to history as the greatest financier of his century." Greeley's *Tribune* went even further, claiming that "Mr. Chase is one of the very few great men left in public life since the almost simultaneous decease of Messrs. Clay, Webster and Calhoun."

Choosing a worthy successor was vital, and it was not clear that David Tod was up to the task. Any concerns Lincoln might have had about his hasty choice were alleviated, however, when he received a telegram from the former governor declining the post for reasons of health. According to Francis Carpenter, Lincoln "laid awake some hours, canvassing in his mind the merits of various public men." By morning, he had found the ideal solution, a candidate so perfect he should have considered him from the start: William Pitt Fessenden. "*First,*" he told Hay the next morning, "he knows the ropes thoroughly: as Chairman of the Senate Committee on Finance he knows as much of this special subject as Mr. Chase. *2nd* he is a man possessing a national reputation and the confidence of the country.

3d He is a radical—without the petulant and vicious fretfulness of many radicals."

In a far better humor, Lincoln handed Hay his official nomination of Fessenden to carry to the Senate. When Hay told him that Fessenden was in the reception room waiting to see him, Lincoln said: "Send him in & go at once to the Senate." Understanding that Fessenden might be reluctant, and perhaps remembering that three years earlier he had sent in Chase's nomination before securing his acceptance, the president hoped that a fait accompli would once again move the process forward.

Lincoln greeted Fessenden warmly and listened politely for a few minutes as the senator suggested a few names for the vacant Treasury post. Smiling, Lincoln finally interrupted and told Fessenden there was no need to continue. He had found his man, and the nomination of Fessenden was already en route to the Senate. "You must withdraw it, I cannot accept," Fessenden cried out, jumping to his feet. He explained that his health was not good, and he was certain that the pressures of the new job would kill him. "If you decline," Lincoln said, "you must do it in open day: for I shall not recall the nomination." Fessenden left with a promise that he would think on it further, though his acceptance was doubtful.

Returning to the Senate, Fessenden discovered that his colleagues had unanimously approved his nomination. Encircled by the warmth of their good wishes and congratulations, he began to waver. "Telegrams came pouring in from all quarters," he later recalled, insisting that he accept for the good of the nation, that he was an inspired choice for the critical post. It was both the most rewarding and "the most miserable" day of his life, for he still feared that the duties of the post would be his death. "Very well," the always blunt Stanton told him, "you cannot die better than in trying to save your country."

As he was driven to the White House the next morning, however, Fessenden carried with him a letter declining the nomination. It took all of the president's persuasive powers to change his mind. "He said the crisis was such as demanded any sacrifice, even life itself," Fessenden recalled, "that Providence had never deserted him or the country, and that his choice of me was a special proof that Providence would not desert him. All this and more." In the end, Fessenden felt he "could not decline but at the risk of danger to the country."

Fessenden's appointment received universal praise. "He is a man of undoubted financial ability, and of unsurpassed personal integrity," the *Chicago Tribune* wrote, reflecting the sentiment of many Northern papers. Radicals felt he was one of their own, while conservatives applauded his intelligence and experience. "He is honest," Elizabeth Blair told her husband, "& as Mrs Jeff [Davis] once said the ablest of all the Republican Senators." The business world, long familiar with his work on the Senate Finance Committee, breathed a sigh of relief. "I am the most popular man in my country," Fessenden wryly noted several days after his acceptance.

"So my official life closes," Chase recorded in his diary on the last day of June. Sadness pervades the entry, written when the oppressive heat of Washington was such, observed Bates, that "even the trees in the streets are wilting." Chase believed he had "laid broad foundations" to secure financial support for the troops, but he knew the job was still unfinished. From this point on, he would not have any real influence.

If Chase had hoped his resignation would produce consternation and regret among his cabinet colleagues, he was disappointed. On the night his departure was announced, Blair and Bates called on Welles to talk over the startling event. While they were all surprised, none was sorry to see him go. "I look upon it as a blessing," Welles said. On numerous occasions Welles had confided doubts about Chase's character to his diary, observing that he lacked "the courage and candor to admit his errors," and that "his jokes are always clumsy—he is destitute of wit." Bates greeted Chase's retirement with "a vague feeling of relief from a burden, and a hope of better things," observing that Chase's relations with his fellow cabinet ministers had long since failed "to be cordial." And Monty Blair, whose family regarded Chase as a mortal enemy, was thrilled. Old Man Blair happily informed Frank that Chase had "dropped off at last like a rotten pear unexpectedly to himself & every body else." Seward, unlike his other colleagues, expressed no personal pleasure in Chase's demise. He simply informed Frances of his relief that the "Cabinet crisis" did not engender a "severe shock" in the country. He traced the origin of the present upheaval back to "the first day of the Administration," when, against his advice, Lincoln had created his compound cabinet.

As Chase prepared to leave Washington, he noted sadly that Stanton, "warm & cordial as ever," was the only former colleague who came to see him "—no other Head of Dept. has called on me since my resignation." If Chase believed the powerful war secretary might feel the slightest compulsion to resign his own place in solidarity with his old friend, however, he was mistaken.

In his misery, Chase searched for reasons why Lincoln had so abruptly accepted his resignation. His answers betray an unwillingness to take the slightest responsibility for his own missteps. "I can see but one reason," he wrote, "that I am too earnest, too antislavery, &, say, too radical to make him willing to have me connected with the Admn., just as my opinion that he is not earnest enough; not antislavery enough; not radical enough,—but goes naturally with those hostile to me." As his melancholy deepened, he generated another explanation that displayed the obtuseness that had always proved his undoing as a politician. "The root of the matter," he told his friend Whitelaw Reid, "was a difficulty of temperament. The truth is that I have never been able to make a joke out of this war."

To Kate, who remained at the Sprague mansion in Narragansett through the summer, he confessed that he was "oppressed" by anxiety. "You know how much I have endured rather than run counter to those friends who have insisted that I should remain in my place." He should have resigned earlier, he told her, right after Frank Blair's attack. Then he might have departed while heroically defending the radicals against the conservatives, but now "I am reproached with having left my post in the hour of danger." And though "the crushing load is off my shoulders," there is the regret that "I cannot finish what I began."

Chase's gloom was mirrored by the distress of his daughter, whose marriage to William Sprague was in trouble. Kate had seemed to hold "the balance of power" throughout the courtship, yet William now believed he had a right to control his high-spirited wife. Though he had made her responsible for redecorating his several multimillion-dollar households, he angrily rebuked her in private and in public for exorbitant spending. "Can it be," she later lamented in her diary, "that he would keep this hateful thought of my dependence ever before me, forcing me to believe that every dollar given or expended upon his home is begrudged?" She worried that, "reared in a pinched, prejudiced narrow atmosphere," with the thought of the "insatiable Moloch—money" always before him, he had vested in it "all the power when after all it is only a tributary. . . . My father was, in comparison with my husband, a poor man, but he felt himself rich when he was enabled to bestow a benefit upon the needy or a pleasure upon those he loved & a treasure laid up in his home was money well invested."

Though she was proud of her new husband's "worldly success" as both a senator and businessman, she had hoped to be a partner in all his endeavors, as she had been with her father. She "would gladly follow all his interests with sympathy & encouragement," she wrote, "but I cannot make them mine for his effort would seem to be to show me that I have no part in them." In fact, he rebuffed her when she tried to talk of business or politics, complaining in public that she had "different ideas & ways of life, from his own."

Most hurtful of all, Sprague had started drinking again. He would lash out at her when drunk, provoking bitter arguments that would take days to resolve. Kate could not restrain herself from replying to his insults with "harsh and cruel words" of her own. When sober, Sprague would vow reform, pledging "to fill & occupy his place, in the home circle he has created . . . as well as the position he has secured for himself in the world." These resolves were short-lived, and Kate began to fear that he did not seriously contemplate a worthy future, that his only thought was "to slip through these obligations in life" with the least effort possible. "God forgive me," she later confessed, "that I had so often wished that I had found in my husband a man of more intellectual resources, even with far less material wealth."

Though she acknowledged occasionally loathing her husband, she also believed that "few men were loved" as much as she loved him. Perhaps she, too, was at fault. "My hopes were too high," she confessed. "Proud, passionate and intolerant, I had never learned to submit." Chase witnessed a fight between the young couple at Narragansett but mistakenly interpreted the problem as a simple "misunderstanding" that time and patience would make right. His hopes seemed justified a few weeks later when he learned that Kate was pregnant with her first child.

• • •

THE GOODWILL ENGENDERED among congressional radicals by Lincoln's appointment of Fessenden was swiftly eroded by his refusal to sign the punitive Reconstruction bill that passed the Congress in the final hours of July 2, 1864, before it adjourned for the summer. Sponsored by Ben Wade and Henry Winter Davis, the bill laid down a rigid formula for bringing the seceded states back into the Union. The process differed in significant ways from the more lenient plan Lincoln had announced the previous December. Lincoln had proposed to rehabilitate individual states as quickly as possible, hoping their return would deflate Southern morale and thereby shorten the war. The Wade-Davis bill, in contrast, postponed any attempts at Reconstruction until all fighting had ceased. It required that a majority of a state's citizens, not simply 10 percent, take an oath of allegiance to the Constitution before the process could begin. In addition, suffrage would be denied to all those who had held civil or military office in the Confederacy and who could not prove they had borne arms involuntarily. Finally, the bill imposed emancipation by congressional fiat where Lincoln believed that such a step overstepped constitutional authority and instead proposed a constitutional amendment to ensure that slavery could never return.

Rather than veto the bill outright, Lincoln exercised a little-known provision called the pocket veto, according to which unsigned bills still on the president's desk when Congress adjourns do not become law. In a written proclamation, he explained that while he would not protest if any individual state adopted the plan outlined in the bill, he did not think it wise to require every state to adhere to a single, inflexible system. Talking with Noah Brooks, he likened the Wade-Davis bill to the infamous bed designed by the tyrant Procrustes. "If the captive was too short to fill the bedstead, he was stretched by main force until he was long enough; and if he was too long, he was chopped off to fit the bedstead."

Lincoln understood that he would be politically damaged if the radicals "choose to make a point upon this." Nevertheless, he told John Hay, "I must keep some consciousness of being somewhere near right: I must keep some standard of principle fixed within myself." He would rely on this conviction in the days ahead when Wade and Davis published a bitter manifesto against him. He was not surprised by their anger at the suppression of their bill, but he was stung by their vitriolic tone and their suggestion that his veto had been prompted by crass electoral concerns. "To be wounded in the house of one's friends," he told Brooks, "is perhaps the most grievous affliction that can befall a man," the same sentiment he had expressed when he lost his first Senate race in 1855. Now personal sorrow was compounded by the realization that radical opposition might divide the Republican Party, undoing the unity he had struggled to maintain through the turbulent years of his presidency.

During the first week of July, rumors spread that a rebel force of undetermined strength was moving north through the Shenandoah Valley toward Washington. The rumors alarmed Elizabeth Blair, who feared that the Confederate troops would come through Silver Spring, Maryland, exposing both her parents' home and that of her brother Monty to direct danger. She cautioned her father, but his mind was elsewhere. For weeks he and Monty had been planning a hunting and fishing trip to the Pennsylvania mountains, and he was eager to get started. In a letter to Frank on July 4, the seventy-three-year-old Blair happily anticipated the two-week vacation. Two grandsons were coming along; their grandfather hoped "to give them a taste for woodcraft and to amuse & invigorate them." Meanwhile, the womenfolk were heading to Cape May. "Your mother & I enjoy our young progeny's happiness as our own," Blair told his son, "& look on it as a prolongation of our enjoyment of the earth, through a remote future."

Elizabeth's admonitions concerned Monty at first, but after the War Department erroneously told him that the Confederate force had been stopped at Harpers Ferry, he and his father set off for the Pennsylvania countryside. Unable to prevent their departure, Elizabeth tried to convince her mother to remove the silver and other valuables to their city home before leaving for Cape May. Eliza Blair refused, telling her daughter "she would not have the house pulled to pieces."

Elizabeth Blair's fears proved justified. Grant's decision to move south of Richmond and attack Petersburg from the rear had inspired Lee to send General Jubal Early and fifteen thousand troops north, hoping to catch Washington unawares. If a panic like that which prevailed at the time of Bull Run could be induced, Grant might have to withdraw some of his troops from Virginia. For several weeks, Early's movements remained undetected, and on July 5 he crossed the Potomac into Maryland. At this point, only miscellaneous troops under the command of General Lew Wallace, later to become famous as the author of *Ben Hur*, barred the path to the nation's capital. Wallace understood that with only half as many men as Early, he could not push the enemy back, but hoped he might hinder Early's progress while Washington prepared itself for attack.

The two sides met at Monocacy River on July 9. Young Will Seward, a colonel now, participated in the fierce engagement. "The battle lasted most of the day," he proudly recalled years later, "and every inch of the ground was hotly contested, until our men were finally overwhelmed by superior numbers." During the fighting, Will's horse was shot from under him, hurling the young colonel to the ground and breaking his leg. Encircled by rebels when he fell, Will was assumed to have been captured.

Secretary Seward spent a tense night at the War Department waiting for news of his son. He had just returned home after midnight when Stanton appeared with a discouraging report from General Wallace that Will had been wounded and taken prisoner. "None of us slept much the rest of the night," Fred Seward recalled, and in the morning, "it was arranged that Augustus should go over in the first train to Baltimore to make inquiries." At 3 p.m., Augustus telegraphed more hopeful news. Though Will's injury was confirmed, he had not been captured. "God be praised for the safety of our boy," Frances exclaimed. "With the help of one of his men," Will somehow "reached a piece of woods; where mounting a mule, and using his pocket-handkerchief for a bridle, he succeeded, after a painful ride of many miles during the night, in rejoining the forces."

The routing of the Federals at Monocacy gave Early an unobstructed path to Washington. As the rebel troops ranged through the countryside, they destroyed railroad tracks, stores, mills, and houses, much as the Union men under David Hunter had done in Virginia. Reaching Silver Spring, they came upon Monty's Falkland mansion. Blair's carpenter reported that the troops had immediately "commenced the work of wholesale destruction, battering the doors, robbing all the bookcases, breaking or carrying off all the chinaware, and ransacking the house from top to bottom." The next night, they torched the house, leaving only a "blackened ruin."

At the nearby home of Monty's father, the patriarch, the soldiers scattered papers, documents, and books. They rummaged through the wine cellar and the bedrooms, littering the lawn with furniture and clothing. Elizabeth Blair was told that "one man dressed in Betty's riding habit, pants & all—another in Fathers red velvet wrapper." Still others donned assorted coats and uniforms, dancing with "great frolic" on the lawn.

The "perfect saturnalia" that Elizabeth decried was brought to an immediate halt when Generals Jubal Early and John Breckinridge arrived. Cursing the marauding soldiers, Breckinridge made them return stolen items. He retrieved the scattered papers and documents and sent them away for safekeeping. He asked Early to station a guard on the grounds to preserve the trees, grapery, shrubs, horses, and crops.

When Early inquired why he would "fret about one house when we have lost so much by this proceeding," Breckinridge replied that "this place is the only one I felt was a home to me on this side of the Mts." He explained that some years earlier, during a difficult period in his life, the old gentleman had taken him in, providing a "place of refuge & of rest." A neighbor told Blair Senior that Breckinridge "made more fuss" about preserving the house and its possessions "than if they had belonged to Jeff Davis."

When the older Blairs eventually returned home, they found a note on the mantel: "a confederate officer, for himself & all his comrades, regrets exceedingly that damage & pilfering was committed in this house. . . . Especially we regret that Ladies property has been disturbed." In this manner, Elizabeth marveled, "bread cast upon the waters came back to us."

The time the Confederates lost during the Battle of Monocacy and the frolic at Silver Spring allowed Washington to mobilize its defenses. In his initial panic, Stanton had sent his secretary to take his bonds and gold from a War Department safe and place them under his mattress at home. He took heart from Lincoln's calm demeanor, however, and thereafter, the two worked together as one during the crisis. They telegraphed Grant, who put his highly respected Sixth Corps on a fast route to the capital. They called up the militia, supplied government clerks with muskets, and ordered "all convalescents capable of defending the forts and rifle-pits" to report for duty.

Throughout the tense days, Lincoln remained "in a pleasant and confident humor," observed John Hay, not seeming to be "in the least concerned about the safety of Washington. With him the only concern seems to be whether we can bag or destroy this force in our front." Welles noted approvingly that Stanton "exhibits none of the alarm and fright I have seen in him on former occasions." As nervous farmers with homes in the Confederate path poured into Washington, the president and the war secretary drove together through the streets in a open carriage, "to *show* the *people*," one resident thought, "that *they* were not *frightened*." Such calm evinced by the administration had a salutary effect, allowing the residents of Washington, who had despaired in the wake of Bull Run, a measure of solace. Some "could even appreciate," as Fred Seward noted, "the grim humour of their predicament, in being thus suddenly attacked from the north, after having sent their available troops to the south."

By the time the Capitol dome was visible to the rebel force, the opportunity for a successful attack had receded. "Before even the first brigade of the leading division was brought into line," General Early later acknowledged, "a cloud of dust from the direction of Washington" revealed that Grant's reinforcements had arrived. Furthermore, inspection of the Union fortifications revealed them "to be exceedingly strong . . . with a tier of lower works in front of each pierced for an immense number of guns." Stretching "as far as the eye could reach," the earthworks appeared in many places to be "impregnable."

Still, Early refused to withdraw. He was determined to show the North how close he had come and sent a small force to engage the Union troops at Fort Stevens, about five miles from the White House. The skirmishing continued for several days, during which time Lincoln witnessed the action from a parapet, accompanied by Mary on one occasion, by Seward and Welles on another. The tall president's presence in the line of fire made a vivid impression upon those who were there. "The President evinced a remarkable coolness and disregard of danger," recalled General Horatio G. Wright. Even after a surgeon standing by his side was shot, "he still maintained his ground till I told him I should have to remove him forcibly. The absurdity of the idea of sending off the President under guard seemed to amuse Lincoln, but in consideration of my earnestness in the matter, he agreed to compromise by sitting behind the parapet instead of standing upon it."

Still, Lincoln would periodically stand, provoking concern on the part of a young captain who shouted, "Get down, you fool!" Years later, the captain, Oliver Wendell Holmes, Jr., son of the poet whom Lincoln greatly admired and himself to become a distinguished Supreme Court justice, would recall this unusual incident. For the normally sedentary Gideon Welles, to witness live action "was exciting and wild," until the sight of dead soldiers carried away on stretchers instantly sobered his mind. "In times gone by I had passed over these roads little anticipating scenes like this, and a few years hence they will scarcely be believed to have occurred."

Having made his point, Early retired as swiftly and mysteriously as he had come, leaving behind a spate of recriminations. The misguided command signals in Washington that allowed him to escape constituted "an egregious blunder," acknowledged Stanton's aide, Charles Dana. Blame was generally attributed to General Halleck, though Welles knew that in the eyes of the public, the entire administration appeared "contemptible."

Mary Lincoln, sensing her husband's profound disappointment that the rebels had escaped, turned on Stanton during a conversation at the Soldiers' Home. "Mrs. Lincoln," Stanton remarked with rare levity, "I intend to have a full-length portrait of you painted, standing on the ramparts at Fort Stevens overlooking the fight!"

"That is very well," Mary replied, "and I can assure you of one thing, Mr. Secretary, if I had had a few *ladies* with me the Rebels would not have been permitted to get away as they did!"

Mary was not alone in her indignation. The sight of his ruined home provoked Monty Blair into openly defiant rants against the command structure in Washington directed by Halleck. His diatribes were reported to Halleck, who immediately wrote a furious letter to Stanton. "I am informed by an officer of rank," he began, "that the Hon. M. Blair, Post Master Genl, in speaking of the burning of his house in Maryland, this morning said, in effect, that 'the officers in command about Washington are poltroons; that there were not more than five hundred rebels on the Silver Spring road and we had a million of men in arms; that it was a disgrace.' " On behalf of those officers "who have devoted their time and energies night and day, and have periled their lives," Halleck demanded to know whether "such wholesale denouncement & accusation by a member of the cabinet receives the sanction and approbation of the President of the United States. If so the names of the officers accused should be stricken from the rolls of the Army; if not, it is due to the honor of the accused that the slanderer should be dismissed from the cabinet."

Stanton sent the letter to Lincoln, who replied the same day. "Whether the remarks were really made I do not know; nor do I suppose such knowledge is necessary to a correct response. If they were made I do *not* approve them; and yet, under the circumstances, I would not dismiss a member of the Cabinet thereof. I do not consider what may have been hastily said in a moment of vexation at so severe a loss, is sufficient ground for so grave a step." Moreover, he concluded, "I propose continuing to be myself the judge as to when a member of the Cabinet shall be dismissed." Then, to further underscore his authority in the matter, Lincoln composed a note to his cabinet colleagues, stating categorically that only he would decide when the time had come to let one of them go. "It would greatly pain me to discover any of you endeavoring to procure anothers removal, or, in any way to prejudice him before the public. Such endeavor would be a wrong to me; and much worse, a wrong to the country. My wish is that on this subject, no remark be made, nor question asked, by any of you, here or elsewhere, now or hereafter."

Lincoln's restrained reaction was validated by Blair's conduct once the shock of seeing his gutted homestead wore off. Learning that Ben Butler had torched a Confederate officer's house in retaliation for the burning of Falkland, Monty implored the general to avoid any more like actions. "If we allow the military to invade the rights of private property on any other grounds than those recognized by civilized warfare," he cautioned, "there will soon cease to be any security whatever for the rights of civilians on either side." When friends offered to raise funds for him to rebuild, he graciously declined their help. "The loss is a very great one to me it is true," but it did not compare "to the losses suffered by the unknown millions in this great struggle for the life of the nation. Could I consent to have my house rebuilt by friends, whilst my neighbor a poor old blacksmith is unrelieved[?]" Monty Blair had confirmed Lincoln's faith in him as a man and as a responsible public figure. The postmaster general would retain his post until Lincoln himself decided it was time for him to go.

• • •

"THE MONTH OF AUGUST does not open cheerfully," Noah Brooks reported. The steady progression of unfavorable events—the shocking slaughter at Petersburg, the raid on Washington, and the failure to capture Jubal Early's troops—had created a mood of widespread despondency throughout the North. In addition, the president's mid-July call for five hundred thousand additional volunteers had disturbed many Republicans, who feared negative repercussions on the fall elections. Lincoln himself acknowledged the "dissatisfaction" with his new recruiting effort but emphasized that "the men were needed, and must be had, and that should he fall in consequence, he would at least have the satisfaction of going down with the colors flying."

Meanwhile, dispatches from Grant revealed a continuing stalemate in the siege against Petersburg. An ingenious attempt by a regiment of former coal miners to mine under the Confederate earthworks and blow a hole in the enemy lines had resulted in a spectacular tragedy instead. In the confusion after the explosion, Union soldiers advanced into the 32-foot-deep crater itself, rather than circle around it, and had become trapped.

"Piled on top of each other like frightened sheep," they were easy targets for slaughter. By day's end, Grant had lost nearly four thousand men. "It was the saddest affair I have witnessed in the war," Grant wired Halleck. "Such opportunity for carrying fortifications I have never seen and do not expect again to have."

The appalling event left Gideon Welles in a depressed state, "less however from the result, bad as it is, than from an awakening apprehension that Grant is not equal to the position assigned him. . . . A blight and sadness comes over me like a dark shadow when I dwell on the subject, a melancholy feeling of the past, a foreboding of the future." Edward Bates shared his colleague's despair. In his diary he admitted feeling heartsick when he contemplated "the obstinate errors and persistent blunders of certain of our generals."

Unlike Welles or Bates, Lincoln refused to let the incident shake his faith in Grant. The day after the Battle of the Crater, he met with Grant at Fort Monroe, where the two men looked resolutely toward the future. Grant had received intelligence that the hard-riding Early had once again crossed the Potomac, spreading fear and devastation in Chambersburg, Pennsylvania. He dispatched General Philip Sheridan, one of his best commanders, to the Shenandoah Valley with instructions to find Early "and follow him to the death. Wherever the enemy goes let our troops go also." Lincoln, as determined as Grant to take the battle directly to the enemy without respite, replied: "This, I think, is exactly right."

A few days later, Commissioner French enjoyed "a long and very pleasant talk" with Lincoln. "He said we must be patient, all would come out right—that he did not expect Sherman to take Atlanta in a day, nor that Grant could walk right into Richmond,—but that we should have them both in time." Lincoln's confidence was not now shared by the country. The ongoing disasters had combined to create "much wretchedness and great humiliation in the land," a doleful Welles noted. "The People are wild for Peace," Thurlow Weed cautioned Seward.

Even before this train of events, Horace Greeley had taken it upon himself to counsel Lincoln. Greeley had received word that *"two Ambassadors"* representing Jefferson Davis had come to Niagara Falls in Canada *"with full & complete powers for a peace."* Urging the president to meet with them immediately, he reminded Lincoln that "our bleeding, bankrupt, almost dying country also longs for peace—shudders at the prospect of fresh conscriptions, of further wholesale devastations, and of new rivers of human blood. And a wide-spread conviction that the Government . . . [is] not anxious for Peace, and do not improve proffered opportunities to achieve it, is doing great harm."

Though fairly certain that the so-called "ambassadors" had not been authorized by Jefferson Davis, Lincoln nonetheless discussed the matter with Seward and commissioned Horace Greeley to go to Niagara Falls. If the Confederate envoys were genuinely carrying legitimate propositions for peace, Greeley should offer them "safe conduct" and escort them to Washington. In addition, Lincoln dispatched John Hay to join Greeley at Niagara Falls and deliver a handwritten, confidential note to the envoys. "To Whom it may concern," the note read. "Any proposition which embraces the restoration of peace, the integrity of the whole Union, and the abandonment of slavery . . . will be met by liberal terms on other substantial and collateral points."

As Lincoln suspected, the two envoys had "no credentials whatever" and could offer no assurances that Jefferson Davis was ready to stop the war. He hoped the failed mission would demonstrate to Greeley and others the absurdity of the claims that *he* was the one preventing peace. Unfortunately, his intention backfired when the Confederate envoys sent Lincoln's confidential letter to the newspapers, falsely proclaiming that Lincoln's inadmissible demand for abolition had torpedoed the negotiations. Democratic newspapers embellished the story, accusing Lincoln of continuing the war for the sole purpose of freeing the slaves.

Leading Republicans were also upset by the president's "To Whom it may concern" letter. Looking simply for restoration of the Union, Thurlow Weed complained, the people "are told that the President will only listen to terms of Peace on condition Slavery be 'abandoned.' " Deeply disheartened, Weed and other leading Republicans became convinced that their party would be defeated in November. Weed journeyed to Washington during the first week in August and told Lincoln "that his re-election was an impossibility." Leonard Swett felt compelled to inform his friend of a growing movement to "call a convention and supplant him." A date for the new convention had been set for September 22 in Cincinnati, three weeks after the Democratic Convention. Swett warned Lincoln that a "most alarming depression" had overtaken his erstwhile supporters, and that unless something were done "to stem the tide," the situation was hopeless.

Dissatisfaction was rife inside the cabinet as well. Both Gideon Welles and Montgomery Blair were mystified by Lincoln's decision to "impose conditions" that were "inadmissible" by their very nature. Knowing that only Seward and Fessenden had been privy to his plan, Welles questioned the president's right "to assume this unfortunate attitude without consulting his Cabinet."

Henry Raymond, editor of the *New York Times* and chairman of the Republican National Party, added to Lincoln's woes. "I am in active correspondence with your staunchest friends in every state and from them all I hear but one report," wrote Raymond in late August. "The tide is setting strongly against us." Raymond went on to predict that if the election were held immediately, Lincoln would be beaten in Illinois, Pennsylvania, and Indiana. Raymond ascribed two causes for "this great reaction in public sentiment,—the want of military successes, and the impression in some minds, the fear and suspicion in others" that the Confederates were ready for reunion and peace, but for the absolute demand that slavery be abandoned. He recognized the inaccuracy of this perception but argued that it could "only be expelled by some authoritative act, at once bold enough to fix attention." He recommended sending a commissioner to meet with Jefferson Davis *"to make distinct proffers of peace . . . on the sole Condition of acknowledging the supremacy of the Constitution,"* leaving all remaining issues to be settled later.

Lincoln's response to these extraordinary pressures reveals much about his character. "I confess that I desire to be re-elected," he told Thaddeus Stevens and Simon Cameron that August. "I have the common pride of humanity to wish my past four years administration endorsed; and besides I honestly believe that I can better serve the nation in its need and peril than any new man could possibly do. I want to finish this job of putting down the rebellion, and restoring peace and prosperity to the country."

Yet he forthrightly faced the likelihood of defeat and resolved to do his utmost in the remaining months both to win the war on the North's terms and to bring as many slaves as possible into Union lines before newly elected Democratic leaders could shut the door forever. In the third week of August, Lincoln asked all cabinet members to sign—without having read—a memorandum committing the administration to devote all its powers and energies to help bring the war to a successful conclusion. The presumption was that no Democrat would be able to resist the immense pressure for an immediate compromise peace. Slavery would thus be allowed to remain in the South, and even independence might be sanctioned.

"This morning, as for some days past," the blind memo began, "it seems exceedingly probable that this Administration will not be re-elected. Then it will be my duty to so co-operate with the President elect, as to save the Union between the election and the inauguration; as he will have secured his election on such ground that he can not possibly save it afterwards."

In these same weeks, Colonel John Eaton recalled, Lincoln "was considering every possible means by which the Negro could be secured in his freedom." He knew that Eaton had come into contact with thousands of slaves who had escaped as the Union troops advanced. Tens of thousands more remained in the South. Lincoln asked Eaton if he thought Frederick Douglass "could be induced to come to see him" and discuss how these slaves could be brought into freedom. Eaton was aware that Douglass had recently criticized the president vehemently, denouncing the administration's insufficient retaliatory measures against the Confederacy for its blatant refusal to treat captured black soldiers as prisoners of war. He also knew, however, that Douglass respected Lincoln and was certain that he would lend his hand.

Douglass met with the president on August 19. In an open conversation that Douglass later recounted, Lincoln candidly acknowledged his fear that the "mad cry" for peace might bring a premature end to the war, "which would leave still in slavery all who had not come within our lines." He had thought the publication of his Emancipation Proclamation would stimulate an exodus from the South, but, he lamented, "the slaves are not coming so rapidly and so numerously to us as I had hoped." Douglass suggested that "the slaveholders knew how to keep such things from their slaves, and probably very few knew of his proclamation." Hearing this, Lincoln proposed that the federal government might underwrite an organized "band of scouts, composed of colored men, whose business should be somewhat after the original plan of John Brown, to go into the rebel states, beyond the lines of our Armies, and carry the news of emancipation, and urge the slaves to come within our boundaries." Douglass promised to confer with leaders in the black community on the possibility of such a plan.

There was yet another subject Lincoln wanted to discuss with Douglass. Three days earlier, Wisconsin's former governor Alexander Randall had hand-delivered a heartfelt letter from Charles Robinson, the editor of a Democratic paper in Wisconsin. "I am a War Democrat," Robinson began. "I have sustained your Administration. . . . It was alleged that because I and my friends sustained the Emancipation measure, we had become abolitionized. We replied that we regarded the freeing of the negroes as sound war policy, in that the depriving the South of its laborers weakened the strength of the Rebellion. That was a good argument, and was accepted by a great many men who would have listened to no other. It was solid ground on which we could stand, and still maintain our position as Democrats." Now the Niagara Falls declaration that "no steps can be taken towards peace, from any quarter, unless accompanied with an abandonment of slavery," left him with "no ground to stand upon." He was not writing "for the purpose of finding fault . . . but with the hope that you may suggest some interpretation of it, as well as make it tenable ground on which we War Democrats may stand."

Lincoln shared a draft of his reply with Douglass and requested his advice on whether or not to send it. "To me it seems plain," the draft began, "that saying reunion and abandonment of slavery would be considered, if offered, is not saying that nothing *else* or *less* would be considered." Having written these evasive words, however, he at once emphasized that as a "matter of morals" and a "matter of policy," it would be ruinous to recant the promise of freedom contained in his proclamation "as it seems you would have me to do. . . . For such a work, another would have to be found." Nonetheless, he acknowledged that if the rebels agreed to "cease fighting & consent to reunion" so long as they could keep their slaves, he would be powerless to continue the war for the sole purpose of abolition. The people would not support such a war; their congressional representatives would cut off supplies. All such figuring was irrelevant, in any case, for "no one who can control the rebel armies has made the offer supposed."

Douglass saw clearly that Lincoln was trying "to make manifest his want of power to do the thing which his enemies and pretended friends professed to be afraid he would do." Regardless of his personal convictions, he seemed to be saying, he "could not carry on the war for the abolition of slavery. The country would not sustain such a war, and [he] could do nothing without the support of Congress." Douglass emphatically urged Lincoln not to send the letter. "It would be given a broader meaning than you intend to convey; it would be taken as a complete surrender of your anti-slavery policy, and do you serious damage."

After listening carefully to the impassioned advice of Douglass, Lincoln turned the conversation to other topics. While they were talking, a messenger informed Lincoln that the governor of Connecticut wished for an audience. "Tell Governor Buckingham to wait, I want to have a long talk with my friend Douglass," Lincoln instructed. Douglass could barely "suppress his excitement" when he encountered John Eaton later that day. "He treated me as a man; he did not let me feel for a moment that there was any difference in the color of our skins! The President is a most remarkable man. I am satisfied now that he is doing all that circumstances will permit him to do." Eaton believed that Douglass "had seen the situation for the first time as it appeared to Mr. Lincoln's eyes." For his part, Lincoln told Eaton that "considering the conditions from which Douglass rose, and the position to which he had attained, he was . . . one of the most meritorious men in America."

That same night, perhaps buoyed by his conversation with Douglass, Lincoln invited Governor Randall and Judge Joseph Mills to the Soldiers' Home for a further discussion of the Robinson letter. "The President was free & animated in conversation," Mills recorded in his diary. "I was astonished at his elasticity of spirits." Lincoln admitted from the outset that he could not help "but feel that the weal or woe of this great nation will be decided in the approaching canvas." This was not "personal vanity, or ambition," but rather a firm belief that the Democrats' strategy of mollifying the South with a promise to renounce abolition as a condition for peace would "result in the dismemberment of the Union." He pointed out that there were "between 1 & 200 thousand black men now in the service of the Union." If the promise of freedom were rescinded, these men would rightly give up their arms. "Abandon all the posts now possessed by black men surrender all these advantages to the enemy, & we would be compelled to abandon the war in 3 weeks."

Lincoln's tone grew more fervent as he continued, as if he were arguing with himself against sending the reply to Robinson. "There have been men who have proposed to me to return to slavery the black warriors of Port Hudson & Olustee to their masters to conciliate the South. I should be damned in time & in eternity for so doing." Those who accused him of "carrying on this war for the sole purpose of abolition" must understand that "no human power can subdue this rebellion without using the Emancipation lever. . . . Let them prove by the history of this war, that we can restore the Union without it."

Mills, who had been initially skeptical of Lincoln, was overwhelmed by "his transparent honesty" and the depth of his convictions. "As I heard a vindication of his policy from his own lips, I could not but feel that his mind grew in stature like his body, & that I stood in the presence of the great guiding intellect of the age." His confidence in the justice of the Union cause "could not but inspire me with confidence." The visitors stood to leave, but Lincoln entreated them to stay so that he might entertain them with a mix of stories, jokes, and "reminiscences of the past."

His momentary ambivalence over a peace compromise put to rest by his own logic, Lincoln permanently shelved the draft of his letter to Robinson. Nor did he accede to Raymond's suggestion that he dispatch a commissioner to Richmond and sound out Jefferson Davis's conditions for peace. He played with the idea for a few days, even drafting a letter allowing Raymond to proceed to Richmond with authority to say that "upon the restoration of the Union and the national authority, the war shall cease at once, all remaining questions [including slavery] to be left for adjustment by peaceful modes." But he soon discarded the idea. The Raymond letter, like the reply to Robinson, was placed in an envelope and "slept undisturbed" for over two decades until unearthed by Nicolay and Hay when writing their biography of Lincoln.

Through these difficult days that Nicolay deemed "a sort of political Bull Run," Lincoln was sustained most of all by his "ever present and companionable" secretary of state. Mary and Tad had once again escaped the summer heat, spending August and early September in Manchester, Vermont. Seward had hoped to get away but did not feel he should leave Lincoln in this trying period, when "one difficulty no sooner passes away than another arises." His presence buoyed Lincoln, for he never lost faith that all would be well. While Seward agreed that "the signs of discontent and faction are very numerous and very painful," he refused to panic, believing that "any considerable success would cause them all to disappear." So long as ordinary people retained their faith in the cause, a faith evidenced by new enlistments in the army, Seward remained "firm and hopeful," convinced that Lincoln would see the country through.

Stanton provided additional reassurance to the beleaguered president. The relationship among Lincoln, Seward, and Stanton had strengthened over the years. Welles observed that "the two S's" had developed "an understanding" enabling them to act in concert supporting the president. Though Stanton lacked the genial temperament that won both Lincoln and Seward countless friends, he believed passionately in both the Union and the soldiers who were risking their lives to support it. Though he regularly argued with Lincoln over minor matters and peremptorily dismissed favor seekers from his office, the sight of a disabled soldier would command his immediate attention. In the mind of this brilliant, irascible man, there could be no peace without submission by the South.

On August 25, Lincoln invited Raymond to the White House and explained why, after careful consideration, he had decided that sending a commissioner to Richmond "would be utter ruination." Raymond was already in Washington, chairing a meeting of the Republican National Committee. The committee members charged with organizing support for Lincoln in the upcoming election had been so dubious about his chances that, as yet, they had done nothing to mobilize the party.

John Nicolay believed the president's meeting with Raymond and his colleagues could prove "the turning-point in our crisis." As the group gathered that morning, Nicolay wrote to John Hay, who was visiting his family in Illinois, "If the President can infect R. and his committee with some of his own patience and pluck, we are saved." If the committee members were unmoved after talking with Lincoln, however, hope for the election would fade.

Nicolay was relieved to see that Lincoln had invited Seward, Stanton, and Fessenden, "the stronger half of the Cabinet," to join the meeting. The results exceeded Nicolay's fondest hopes. In a memo written that same day, Nicolay delightedly noted that the president and his cabinet colleagues had managed to convince Raymond "that to follow his plan of sending a commission to Richmond would be worse than losing the Presidential contest—it would be ignominiously surrendering it in advance." Nicolay was convinced that the meeting had done "great good." The president's iron will impressed the committee members. They returned home "encouraged and cheered," with renewed belief that the election could be salvaged.

Two days later, a revealing item appeared in Raymond's *New York Times.* Noting that the members of the Republican National Committee would remain in Washington for another day to complete their plans for the presidential canvass, the *Times* declared: "Every member is deeply impressed with the belief that Mr. Lincoln will be reelected; and regards the political situation as most hopeful and satisfactory for the Union party."

Even before the approaching military success in Atlanta, which would transform the public mood, Lincoln had alleviated his own discouragement by refocusing his intense commitment to the twin goals of Union and freedom. He gave voice to these ideals in late August with an emotional address to the men of an Ohio regiment returning home to their families. "I happen temporarily to occupy this big White House," he said. "I am a living witness that any one of your children may look to come here as my father's child has. It is in order that each of you may have through this free government which we have enjoyed, an open field and a fair chance for your industry, enterprise and intelligence; that you may all have equal privileges in the race of life, with all its desirable human aspirations. It is for this the struggle should be maintained, that we may not lose our birthright. . . . The nation is worth fighting for, to secure such an inestimable jewel."

• • •

THE PRESIDENT'S REELECTION CAMPAIGN received a significant boost when the long-delayed Democratic Convention finally met on August 29, 1864. Until this moment, when a candidate would be chosen and a platform written, Nicolay wrote, anxious Republicans had imagined "giants in the airy and unsubstantial shadows of the opposition." Brooks, who had traveled to Chicago to cover the convention, agreed. He attributed the despondent mood that had overtaken Republicans in July and August to the fact that "we have had nothing to solidify and compact us; a platform and candidate from here will materially change all this."

Although Democrats had cheerfully capitalized all summer long on dissensions within the Republican camp, their own party was rent by the anger between War Democrats who supported a continuation of the war until reunion (though not abolition) was assured and Peace Democrats, who called for an immediate armistice at any cost. "They have a peace leg and a war leg," *New York Herald* editor James Gordon Bennett noted, "but, like a stork by a frog pond, they are as yet undecided which to rest upon." When the convention opened, Noah Brooks reported, it seemed as if the Peace Democrats had the upper hand. "It was noticeable that peace men and measures and sentiments were applauded to the echo, while patriotic utterances, what few there were, received no response from the crowd." The playing of "Dixie" was cheered, while Union tunes were met with virtual silence.

Though the peace wing commanded the emotions at the convention hall, it was generally assumed that War Democrat George McClellan would be the nominee. "His partisans are united and have plenty of money," Brooks observed, "while his opponents are divided as to their own choice." The peace wing, led by New York governor Horatio Seymour, Congressman Fernando Wood, and former congressman Clement Vallandigham, who had returned from his exile in Canada, floated several possible names but with no consensus. As a result, when the balloting began, McClellan easily won.

If McClellan's victory "was expected," George Templeton Strong confided to his diary, "the baseness of the platform on which he is to run was unexpected. Jefferson Davis might have drawn it. The word 'rebel' does not occur in it. It contemplates surrender and abasement." Pressed upon the party by the peace contingent, the platform declared that "after four years of failure to restore the Union by the experiment of war," the time had come to "demand that immediate efforts be made for a cessation of hostilities." Strong predicted that if McClellan agreed to represent this dishonorable platform, "he condemns his name to infamy." Indeed, it was rumored that he would "decline a nomination on such terms." For Democrats, the capitulation called for in their platform proved to be exceedingly ill timed.

Three days later came the stunning news that Atlanta had fallen. "Atlanta is ours, and fairly won," Sherman wired Washington on September 3. This joyous news, which followed on the heels of Admiral David

Farragut's capture of Mobile Bay, Alabama, prompted Lincoln to order that one hundred guns be fired in Washington and a dozen other cities to celebrate the victories. Jubilant headlines filled Northern newspapers. "Atlanta is ours," the *New York Times* repeated. "The foundries, furnaces, rolling-mills, machine-shops, laboratories and railroad repair-shops; the factories of cannon and small arms; of powder, cartridges and percussion caps; of gun carriages, wagons, ambulances, harnesses, shoes and clothing, which have been accumulated at Atlanta, are ours now"—although, unbeknownst to the *Times*, the departing Confederates had set fire to nearly "everything of military value." Still, George Templeton Strong instantly understood the importance of Atlanta's fall. "Glorious news this morning," he exulted, "it is (coming at this political crisis) the greatest event of the war."

Seward received the news from the War Department while seated in his library in Auburn, where he had finally escaped for a few days to see his family. He had barely finished reading Stanton's telegram before a crowd gathered at his house to celebrate. As the news spread, the crowd swelled until it spilled over to the park adjoining his residence. "Flags were hoisted in all parts of the city," a local correspondent reported, "all the bells commenced ringing, and a salvo of one hundred guns was fired." At the request of the spirited assemblage, which included "several hundred volunteers, who were waiting to be mustered in," Seward delivered a spontaneous talk that lasted more than an hour.

Seward's extemporaneous words were considered by one reporter present to be "one of his most impressive and effective speeches." He remarked that the twin victories should help inspire the three hundred thousand more men—"volunteers, if you will, drafted men if we must"—necessary "to end the war." He paid homage not only to the sailors and soldiers but to "the wisdom and the energy of the war Administration," pointing out that "Farragut's fleet did not make itself, nor did he make it. It was prepared by the Secretary of the Navy. And he that shall record the history of this war impartially will write that, since the days of Carnot [the military organizer of the French Revolution], no man has organized war with ability equal to that of Stanton." Seward ended with a moving tribute to his friend and president, telling the crowd that nothing was more important than Lincoln's reelection. "If we do this, the rebellion will perish and leave no root." The crowd roared its approval.

When Gideon Welles read Seward's speech, with its generous praise for the Navy Department, he professed himself delighted. "For a man of not very compact thought . . . often loose in the expressions of his ideas," Seward had set forth an argument, Welles believed, that would serve as "the keynote" of the upcoming campaign. Welles understood that Atlanta's fall would wreak havoc on the plans of his old party, the Democrats. "This intelligence will not be gratifying to the zealous partisans who have just sent out a peace platform, and declared the war a failure. . . . There is a fatuity in nominating a general and warrior in time of war on a peace platform."

McClellan, meanwhile, remained secluded at his home in Orange, New Jersey. He found himself under tremendous pressure from both factions of his divided party as he tried to draft his letter of acceptance. War Democrats warned that unless he repudiated the peace platform, his candidacy would be stillborn. Peace Democrats threatened that if he wavered on the proposed armistice, they might "withdraw their support." He went through six drafts before he finally delivered his letter to the Democratic Nominating Committee at midnight on September 8.

He began with a nod to the peace wing. Had the war been conducted for the sole purpose of preserving the Union, McClellan argued, "the work of reconciliation would have been easy, and we might have reaped the benefits of our many victories on land and sea." Were he in power, he would "exhaust all the resources of statesmanship" to yield peace. This said, he went on to disavow aspects of the strident demand for peace at any cost, insisting that hostilities would not end without the restoration of the Union. "I could not look in the face of my gallant comrades of the Army and Navy, who have survived so many bloody battles, and tell them that their labors, and the sacrifice of so many of our slain and wounded brethren had been in vain." The peace men were furious but had no alternative candidate. The stage was set for the fall election.

The fall of Atlanta produced a remarkable transformation in the mood of Republicans. "We are going to win the Presidential election," Lincoln's longtime critic Theodore Tilton wrote Nicolay. "All divisions are going to be healed. I have never seen such a sudden lighting up of public mind as since the late victory at Atlanta. This great event, following the Chicago platform—a most villainous political manifesto known to American history!—has secured a sudden unanimity for Mr. Lincoln." Even he, "never having been a partisan for Mr. Lincoln's re-election, but the reverse," was intending to advise everyone he knew "to unite on Mr. Lincoln."

Leonard Swett, who only weeks before had warned Lincoln that his reelection looked doubtful, believed that God had given the Union its glorious victory to make the floundering ship of state "right itself, as a ship in a storm does after a great wave has nearly capsized it." Relieved, Thurlow Weed informed Seward that with military success, the "conspiracy against Mr. Lincoln collapsed."

The changed public mood took Salmon Chase by surprise. He had spent the summer traveling through New England, meeting with abolitionist friends, including Ralph Waldo Emerson, Massachusetts governor John Andrew, the writer Richard Henry Dana, Jr., and Congressman Samuel Hooper. He had maintained contact with organizers of the secret meetings being held to pursue the possibility of a new convention to draft an alternative to Lincoln. He had done his best, according to Gideon Welles, "to weaken the President and impair confidence in him . . . expressing his discontent, not in public speeches but in social intercourse down East." Now that support for Lincoln had revived, Welles observed, Chase "is beginning to realize that the issue is made up, and no new leaders are to be brought forward, and he will now support Lincoln."

Deciding to return to Washington to offer his services to Lincoln, Chase stopped en route in New York. There, he had an unsettling conversation with a "gentleman who thought Lincoln very wise—if more radical would have offended conservatives—if more conservative the radicals." Would this, Chase asked himself, be the "judgment of history?"

When he reached the capital, Chase called on Fessenden, who told him the president would like to see him. News of their meeting spread quickly. "Mr. Chase had a long confab in his visit to the President yesterday after abusing him every where at the north," Elizabeth Blair told her husband. Two days later, Chase accompanied Stanton to the Soldiers' Home, where he once again spoke with Lincoln. "I have seen the President twice since I have been here," Chase told Kate. "Both times third persons were present & there was nothing like private conversation. His manner was evidently intended to be cordial & so were his words: and I hear of nothing but good will from him."

Graciousness did not satisfy Chase, however. He wanted the president to be more "demonstrative" toward him after an absence of two months. Chase still acknowledged no responsibility for sundering their relationship, believing it was he who had been "wronged and hurt" by the events surrounding his resignation. "I never desired any thing else than his complete success," Chase insisted, "and never indulged a personal feeling incompatible with absolute fidelity to his Administration."

Proud of his own magnanimity, Chase professed a "conviction that the cause I love & the general public interests will be best promoted by his election, and I have resolved to join my efforts to those of almost the whole body of my friends in securing it."

In the weeks that followed, Chase remained true to his word. He traveled by train, boat, and horseback to Ohio, Kentucky, Pennsylvania, Michigan, Illinois, and Missouri, delivering dozens of speeches in support of Lincoln's reelection before overflowing crowds. Meanwhile, the state elections in Vermont and Maine revealed larger Union majorities than the previous year. After the Vermont election, Nicolay wrote a cheery letter to Therena: "Three weeks ago, our friends everywhere were despondent, almost to the point of giving up the contest in despair. Now they are hopeful, jubilant, hard at work and confident of success."

More good news greeted Republicans on September 19, when Philip Sheridan, having finally caught up with Jubal Early in the Shenandoah Valley, fought a brutal but successful battle that destroyed more than a quarter of Early's army. The "shouting of Clerks" could be heard in every government department when the news became known. "This will do much to encourage and stimulate all Union loving men," Welles recorded in his diary.

• • •

MILITARY SUCCESS MAY have substantially cleared Lincoln's road to victory, but a serious obstacle remained in the form of John Frémont's candidacy. Time and again, a divided party had lost elections when a third-party candidate swayed the final result. To ensure party unity, Lincoln needed the support of the radicals. His task was made difficult by the dissatisfaction of men like Wade and Davis over his conciliatory policy on Reconstruction. In addition, the radicals objected to the continuing presence of Montgomery Blair in the cabinet while Chase had been allowed to resign.

Blair was aware that he had become the target of the radicals' wrath. When the Baltimore convention passed its resolution essentially calling for his dismissal, he had offered his resignation to Lincoln. Later that summer, his father had repeated Monty's offer during a visit with Lincoln at the Soldiers' Home. He assured Lincoln that to heal the party, Monty "would very willingly be a martyr to the Radical phrenzy or jealousy, that would feed on the Blairs, if that would help." At the time, Lincoln had declined to take action, saying that "he did not think it good policy to sacrifice a true friend to a false one or an avowed enemy." But the pressure to remove Blair continued to build. Henry Wilson warned Lincoln in early September that "tens of thousands of men will be lost to you or will give a reluctant vote on account of the Blairs."

The feud between the Blairs and the radicals had rendered cabinet life increasingly unbearable. Monty Blair detested Stanton. He believed the war secretary was in league with Wade and Davis against both the Blair family and the president. He spoke publicly of Stanton with what John Hay considered "unbecoming harshness," calling him "a liar" and "a thief." When these intemperate words reached Stanton, he refused to sit in cabinet meetings if Blair was present. In mid-August, Welles observed that the two embittered colleagues had not "interchanged words for weeks."

Lincoln had no patience for such personal contention. He had warned his cabinet members in July to refrain from criticizing one another in public. He decided that when the opportunity arose, he would take Monty Blair up on his offer to resign. That moment arose when Michigan senator Zachariah Chandler informed him that Blair's resignation would elicit the support of Wade and Davis for Lincoln's reelection. Chandler later asserted that the radical senator and congressman were only part of a larger bargain that included Frémont's agreement to withdraw his candidacy if Blair were removed. Historians have debated the extent of Chandler's influence on Frémont. By September, the Pathfinder had no hope of winning in any case and realized that his reputation would be sullied if he stayed in the race.

Two facts are clear: On September 22, Frémont announced his withdrawal from the race. Then, on the morning of September 23, Lincoln sent a letter to Monty's office asking for his resignation. "You have generously said to me more than once," he began, "that whenever your resignation could be a relief to me, it was at my disposal. The time has come. You very well know that this proceeds from no dissatisfaction of mine with you personally or officially. Your uniform kindness has been unsurpassed by that of any friend." Moreover, "in the three years and a half during which you have administered the General Post-Office, I remember no single complaint against you in connection therewith."

Despite his offer to resign, Blair was surprised to find the dismissal letter on his desk. Later that morning, he encountered Welles and Bates coming out of the White House. "I suppose you are both aware that my head is decapitated," he told them. "I am no longer a member of the Cabinet." Welles was so stunned that he asked Blair to repeat himself, at which point Blair took the letter from his pocket and read it aloud to his two colleagues. Blair said "he had no doubt he was a peace-offering to Frémont and his friends." Welles was uncertain, telling Blair that while "pacifying the partisans of Frémont might have been brought into consideration . . . the President would never have yielded to that." Welles thought it more likely that Blair had been sacrificed to restore balance to the cabinet after Chase's resignation. Chase's partisans clearly "felt wounded" that their man was gone while his assailant remained. The removal of Blair would allow Lincoln to "reconcile all parties, and rid the Administration of irritating bickerings." Lincoln chose the former governor of Ohio, William Dennison, to succeed Blair.

Welles was saddened by Blair's departure. "In parting with Blair,"

Welles recorded in his diary, "the President parts with a true friend, and he leaves no adviser so able sagacious. Honest, truthful and sincere, he has been wise, discriminating and correct." In the days that followed, Welles came to view "the removal of Montgomery from our counsels as the greatest misfortune that had befallen the Cabinet." Bates was equally distressed. Though he did not consider himself so intimate with Blair, he respected his straight-speaking colleague and believed Lincoln had erred in making a bargain for Wade and Davis. "I think Mr. Lincoln could have been elected without them and in spite of them. In that event, the Country might have been governed, free from their *malign influences.*"

Although Blair was hurt by a dismissal that he felt was "an unnecessary mortification," he remained certain, he told his wife, that Lincoln had acted "from the best motives" and that "it is for the best all around." His father wholeheartedly agreed. "In my opinion it is all for the best," he told Frank, no doubt worried that his fiery son would make some regrettable public remark. The patriarch suggested that Monty himself had "pressed this matter" by intimating to Frémont's friends that he would resign if Frémont withdrew. In the end, the senior Blair concluded, "if it tends to give a greater certainty of the defeat of McClellan, which I look upon as the salvation of the Republic, it is well. . . . I hope you will concur with the views I have taken. The true interests of the Country require the reelection of Lincoln."

Frank eventually did concur with his father, though, like his brother, he at first found it "somewhat mortifying to reflect that this triumph has been given to those who are equally the enemies of the President & 'the Blairs.' " On the other hand, he was certain that "a failure to re-elect Mr. Lincoln would be the greatest disaster that could befall the country and the sacrifice made by [Monty] to avert this is so incomparably small that I felt it would not cost him a penny to make."

Elizabeth Blair, hearing the noble sentiments of the men, believed that she and Monty's wife, Minna, were "more hurt than anybody else." As far as Monty's loyal sister was concerned, Lincoln should have stuck with his "first view—of the poor policy of sacrificing his friends to his enemies." She was impressed, however, by her brother's "fine manly bearing," which he illustrated repeatedly in the days ahead as he took to the stump on behalf of Abraham Lincoln. Speaking to large conservative gatherings, Monty insisted that the request for his resignation had not proceeded from any unkindness on Lincoln's part. On the contrary, the president "has at least the support of those who are nearer to me than all other people on this earth. I retired by the recommendation of my own father to the President."

John Hay returned from Illinois just at the time of Blair's resignation. He noted that Blair was behaving "very handsomely and is doing his utmost" to reelect Lincoln. Monty would never forget that Lincoln had stood by him after the mortifying publication of his private letter to Frémont three years earlier, which contained passages demeaning the president. He knew that his father had never been turned away when he requested a private audience with Lincoln, and that his sister, Elizabeth, was always welcome at the White House. His entire family would forever appreciate Lincoln's support for Frank during his continuing battle with the radicals in Congress. Indeed, Lincoln's countless acts of generosity and kindness had cemented a powerful connection with the close-knit Blair family that even Monty's forced resignation could not break. In the end, Lincoln gained the withdrawal of Frémont and the backing of the radicals without losing the affection and support of the conservative and powerful Blairs.

• • •

BOTH REPUBLICANS AND DEMOCRATS considered the state elections in Ohio, Pennsylvania, and Indiana on October 11 harbingers of the presidential election in November. Not only would the results reveal public sentiment, but the party that gained the governor's offices in those states would have "a grand central rallying point" for its partisans. That evening, Lincoln made his customary visit to the telegraph office in the War Department to read the dispatches as they came over the wire. Stanton was there, as was his assistant secretary, Charles Dana, and Thomas Eckert, chief of the telegraph office. Early reports from Cincinnati and Philadelphia looked hopeful, but reliable figures were unbearably slow in coming.

To defuse the tension, Dana recalled, Lincoln took from his pocket "a thin yellow-covered pamphlet" containing the latest writings of the humorist Petroleum V. Nasby. "He would read a page or a story, pause to con[sider] a new election telegram, and then open the book again and go ahead with a new passage." John Hay, who had accompanied Lincoln, found the selections "immensely amusing" and mistakenly thought Stanton felt the same way. During a break in the readings, however, the solemn war secretary signaled Dana to follow him into the adjoining room. "I shall never forget," Dana later recalled, "the fire of his indignation at what seemed to him to be mere nonsense." Stanton found it incomprehensible that "when the safety of the Republic was thus at issue, when the control of an empire was to be determined by a few figures brought in by the telegraph, the leader, the man most deeply concerned, not merely for himself but for his country, could turn aside to read such balderdash and to laugh at such frivolous jests." Stanton never would understand the indispensable role that laughter played in sustaining Lincoln's spirits in difficult times.

As the night wore on, the news from Ohio and Indiana proved better than anyone expected. The Republicans in Ohio gained twelve congressional seats, and the state provided a fifty-thousand-vote Republican majority. In Indiana, the Republican candidate for governor, Oliver Morton, won by a large margin, and Republicans captured eight of the eleven congressional seats.

The results in Pennsylvania were less decisive. Sometime after midnight, Lincoln sent a telegram to Simon Cameron. "Am leaving office to go home," he wrote. "How does it stand now?" No answer was received from Cameron, which seemed "ominous" to Hay. It turned out that the margin was so close that neither party could declare victory. Only when the absentee soldier vote was tallied in the days ahead could the Republicans claim a slight margin.

Welles observed that "Seward was quite exultant over the elections—feels strong and self gratified. Says this Administration is wise, energetic, faithful and able beyond any of its predecessors. That it has gone through trials which none of them has ever known." Lincoln, characteristically, reacted with more caution than his debonair colleague. Though delighted by Ohio and Indiana, he found the close vote in Pennsylvania sobering.

Two nights after the state elections, appearing "unusually weary," Lincoln returned to the telegraph office in the War Department to calculate the probability of his election in November. Taking a blank sheet of telegraph paper, he made two neat columns. The one on the left represented his estimate of the electoral votes McClellan would win; the one on the right tabulated the states he thought would be his. The cipher operator David Homer Bates noted that he wrote "slowly and deliberately, stopping at times in thoughtful mood to look out of the window for a moment or two, and then resuming his writing." The president guessed he would lose both New York and Pennsylvania, which meant his best hope was to squeak through by a total of only 3 electoral votes: 117 to 114. If these calculations were correct, he lamented, "the moral effect of his triumph would be broken and his power to prosecute the war and make peace would be greatly impaired."

During the anxious four-week period that stretched between the state and presidential elections, Lincoln received the heartening news that voters in Maryland had ratified a new constitution officially terminating slavery in their state. The margin had been perilously close, with the absentee soldier vote making the difference. "Most heartily do I congratulate you, and Maryland, and the nation, and the world, upon the event," Lincoln told a group of serenaders. Speaking that same day with Noah Brooks, he said: "I had rather have Maryland upon that issue than have a State twice its size upon the Presidential issue; it cleans up a piece of ground." Brooks admired the "frank homeliness" of Lincoln's choice of words: "Any one who has ever had to do with 'cleaning up' a piece of ground, digging out vicious roots and demolishing old stumps, can appreciate the homely simile applied to Maryland, where slavery has just been cleaned up effectually."

It was clear to both parties that the absentee vote could prove critical in the presidential election. Democrats, remembering the fanatical devotion McClellan had inspired among his men, believed their man would receive an overwhelming majority of the soldier vote. "We are as certain of two-thirds of that vote for General McClellan as that the sun shines," the Democratic publisher Manton Marble jauntily predicted.

Lincoln thought differently. He trusted the bond he had developed with his soldiers during his many trips to the front. After every defeat, he had joined them, riding slowly along their lines, boosting their spirits. He had wandered companionably through their encampments, fascinated by the smallest details of camp life. Sitting with the wounded in hospital tents, he had taken their hands and wished them well. The humorous stories he had told clusters of soldiers had been retold to hundreds more. The historian William Davis estimates that "a quarter-million or more had had some glimpse of him on their own." In addition, word of his pardons to soldiers who had fallen asleep on picket duty or exhibited fear in the midst of battle had spread through the ranks. Most important of all, through his eloquent speeches and public letters he had given profound meaning to the struggle for which they were risking their lives.

Provisions for soldiers to cast absentee ballots in the field had recently been introduced in thirteen states. Four other states allowed soldiers to vote by proxy, placing their ballots in a sealed envelope to be sent or carried for deposit in their hometowns. In several crucial states, however, soldiers still had to be in their hometowns on Election Day to cast their ballots. In an attempt to remedy this situation before the October state elections, Lincoln had wired General Sherman about Indiana, "whose soldiers cannot vote in the field. Any thing you can safely do to let her soldiers, or any part of them, go home and vote at the State election, will be greatly in point." He emphasized that "this is, in no sense, an order," but merely a request.

Stanton followed up, making certain that furloughs were liberally granted wherever possible. "All the power and influence of the War Department . . . was employed to secure the re-election of Mr. Lincoln,"

Charles Dana later asserted. When Thurlow Weed alerted the White House that among the sailors "on Gun Boats along the Mississippi," there were "several thousand" New Yorkers ready to vote if the government could provide a steamer to reach them and gather their ballots, Lincoln asked Welles to put a navy boat "at the disposal of the New York commission to gather votes."

As the election drew close, Lincoln told a visitor: "I would rather be defeated with the soldier vote behind me than to be elected without it." It is likely that McClellan shared Lincoln's sentiment. The election would tell which man had won the hearts and minds of the more than 850,000 men who were fighting for the Union.

• • •

ON ELECTION DAY, November 8, 1864, the *New York Times* editorialized that "before this morning's sun sets, the destinies of this republic, so far as depends on human agency, are to be settled for weal or for woe." To elect Lincoln was to choose "war, tremendous and terrible, yet ushering in at the end every national security and glory." To choose McClellan was to choose "the mocking shadow of a peace . . . sure to rob us of our birthright, and to entail upon our children a dissevered Union and ceaseless strife."

In Washington, it was "dark and rainy." Arriving at the White House about noon, Noah Brooks was surprised to find the president "entirely alone." Seward and Usher had gone home to vote, as had William Dennison, Blair's replacement as postmaster general. This would be the tenth time Seward had cast a presidential ballot in Auburn; he had voted in more than half of the nineteen presidential elections since the beginning of the country. Fessenden was in New York working out the details of a new government loan, while Stanton was at home with a fever. Lincoln could not vote that day, for Illinois required voters to be present in the state.

Lincoln felt no need to conceal his anxiety from Brooks. "I am just enough of a politician to know that there was not much doubt about the result of the Baltimore convention; but about this thing I am very far from being certain. I wish I were certain." Brooks remained with Lincoln through most of the afternoon, noting that the president "found it difficult to put his mind on any of the routine work of his office." The only respite he found was in telling a humorous story about Tad, whose pet turkey apparently roamed at will among the Pennsylvania soldiers quartered at the White House. When the day had come for the Bucktail soldiers to cast their absentee ballots before their state's commission, Tad had excitedly rushed into his father's office so they could watch the voting from the window. Teasing his son, Lincoln had asked if the turkey, too, intended to vote. Tad's clever reply delighted his father. "No," he said. "He is not of age." Brooks noted that Lincoln so "dearly loved the boy" that "for days thereafter he took pride in relating this anecdote illustrative of Tad's quick-wittedness."

As the clock struck seven, the president, accompanied by John Hay, walked over to the telegraph office to begin the long vigil. "It is a little singular," Lincoln remarked to Hay, "that I who am not a vindictive man, should have always been before the people for election in canvasses marked for their bitterness." The lights of the War Department, bursting with dozens of orderlies and clerks, provided a welcome contrast to the murky night.

The muddy grounds had caused Thomas Eckert to fall on his face, which, "of course," Hay noted, "reminded the Tycoon" of a story. "For such an awkward fellow," Lincoln began, "I am pretty sure-footed. It used to take a pretty dextrous man to throw me. I remember, the evening of the day in 1858, that decided the contest for the Senate between Mr. Douglas and myself, was something like this, dark, rainy & gloomy. I had been reading the returns, and had ascertained that we had lost the Legislature and started to go home. The path had been worn hog-backed & was slippering. My foot slipped from under me, knocking the other one out of the way, but I recovered myself & lit square: and I said to myself, '*It's a slip and not a fall.*' " Even at the time Lincoln had understood that his defeat for the Senate was "a slip and not a fall." Little could he then have imagined, however, that on another dreary night six years later, he would be waiting to hear if he had been elected to a second presidential term.

The early returns were positive, revealing larger Republican majorities than in the state elections. Lincoln asked to have the good news carried to Mary at the White House. "She is more anxious than I," he commented. Shortly afterward, Welles and Fox arrived. Fox was thrilled to hear that Winter Davis had been defeated in Maryland. "You have more of that feeling of personal resentment than I," Lincoln said. "A man has not time to spend half his life in quarrels. If any man ceases to attack me, I never remember the past against him."

The returns, including those from Pennsylvania, continued to be promising, though New York, with its large number of traditionally Democratic Irish immigrants, remained in doubt. By the hour of midnight, however, when a supper of fried oysters was served, Lincoln's victory was assured, though his lopsided electoral college win would not be known for several days. In the end, he would win all but three states—New Jersey, Delaware, and Kentucky—giving him 212 electoral votes against McClellan's 21. The popular vote was closer; the two candidates were separated by about 400,000 votes. Nonetheless, the results were far better than Lincoln had predicted. The Republican/Union Party had gained thirty-seven seats in Congress and placed twelve governors in office. It had also seized control of most of the state legislatures with the power to name the next round of U.S. senators.

It was after 2 a.m. when Lincoln left the telegraph office. The rain had stopped, and along Pennsylvania Avenue, an impromptu crowd had gathered, "singing 'The Battle Cry of Freedom' at the tops of their voices." As he went to sleep that night, Lincoln carried with him the knowledge, as Brooks put it, that "the verdict of the people was likely to be so full, clear, and unmistakable that there could be no dispute," thereby affording him the chance to continue the war until both liberty and Union were secured.

Most impressive, the soldier vote had swung overwhelmingly in his favor. In the armies of the West, he won eight out of ten votes, and even in McClellan's Army of the Potomac, Lincoln earned the votes of seven out of every ten soldiers. Many of these soldiers still admired McClellan but could not countenance the defeatist Democratic platform or the fact that the Confederacy was obviously hoping the young Napoleon would win. But there was something else, something Democrats had failed to understand. Over the years, Lincoln had inspired an almost mystical devotion among his troops. "The men had come to regard Mr. Lincoln with sentiments of veneration and love," noted an Illinois corporal. "To them he really was 'Father Abraham,' with all that the term implied." By supporting Lincoln, the soldiers understood that they were voting to prolong the war, but they voted with their hearts for the president they loved and the cause that he embodied.

CHAPTER 25

"A SACRED EFFORT"

On Thursday night, November 10, 1864, an immense crowd, "gay with banners and resplendent with lanterns," gathered on the White House lawn to congratulate the president on his reelection. "Martial music, the cheers of people, and the roar of cannon, shook the sky." When the joyful throng demanded his appearance, Lincoln spoke to the crowd from a second-floor window. Acknowledging that the recent canvass had been marred by "undesirable strife," he nonetheless felt it had "demonstrated that a people's government can sustain a national election, in the midst of a great civil war. Until now it has not been known to the world that this was a possibility."

When Lincoln drew his little speech to a close, the revelers moved on to Seward's Lafayette Square home. They found the secretary of state, who had just returned from Auburn, "in an exceedingly jocose frame of mind." He predicted that the time was near when "we will all come together again . . . when the stars and stripes wave over Richmond," and "you will have to look mighty sharp to find a man who was a secessionist, or an aider of the rebellion." He recollected that when he was a boy in the early 1800s, his parents had told of "the vast number of tories" who opposed the government during the American revolution; yet, thirty years later, "there was not a tory to be found in the whole United States."

Seward's good humor infected the crowd, who responded with cheers and laughter. In closing, he observed that the night was young. "I advise you to go and see Mr. Fessenden, for if he gets discouraged we shall all come to grief; also be good enough to poke up Mr. Stanton; he needs poking up, for he has been seriously sick, I hear, for several days past. You cannot do better also than to call upon my excellent friend Gideon Welles, and ask him if he cannot make the blockade off Wilmington more stringent, so that I shall not need to have so much trouble with my foreign relations."

Seward's playful remarks about his colleagues reflected the improved atmosphere in the cabinet now that Chase and Blair were gone. Both men had symbolized the animosity between radicals and conservatives in the country at large; their clashing emotions had long reverberated through the cabinet. The periodic jealousy Welles felt over the superior access Seward and Stanton enjoyed with the president had been intensified a hundredfold so long as Blair was there to fuel the flames. Likewise, when Stanton was angry with Lincoln over pardons or appointments, Chase had eagerly lent an approving ear to his complaints. Never initiated into this contentious drama, Fessenden and Dennison brought cooperation and amity to the cabinet. Strife abated, and Welles even acknowledged that his relations with Seward had grown more "amicable" and that Stanton was sounding more reasonable and less radical regarding Reconstruction.

Rumormongers had speculated that Lincoln would now want to replace his entire cabinet. It was positively asserted that Seward would give way to Charles Francis Adams, that General Butler would replace Stanton, and that Welles and Bates had outlived their usefulness. It was surmised that Lincoln would prefer more controllable colleagues. The busy, hypothetical cabinetmakers did not understand that Lincoln had no wish to disturb the rhythm of his relationships with his colleagues, which, to his mind, worked exceedingly well.

Lincoln's friendship with Seward had deepened with each passing year. "His confidence in Seward is great," observed Welles that autumn. Seward "spends more or less of every day with the President." On subjects "of the gravest importance," Seward was the president's "only confidant and adviser." Whenever Lincoln bounced an idea off Seward, he received straightforward advice. When a plan to foster Union sentiment in the South through confidential government purchase of a controlling share in a number of failing Southern newspapers was presented to Lincoln, he turned to Seward for advice. "It seems to me very judicious and wise," Seward responded. It would provide a forum for Union men to help sway the opinion of fellow Southerners. If government funds were not readily available, he suggested that Thurlow Weed "might find money by contribution."

Though some still considered the talkative New Yorker the "power behind the throne," Seward had long since understood that Lincoln was the master. "There is but one vote in the Cabinet," asserted Seward, "and that is cast by the President." Two days after the election, Seward told a crowd of supporters, "Henceforth all men will come to see him, as you and I have seen him. . . . Abraham Lincoln will take his place with Washington and Franklin, and Jefferson, and Adams, and Jackson, among the benefactors of the country and of the human race."

Lincoln's partnership with his volatile secretary of war, though not as intimate and leisurely, was equally effective. Stanton was only fifty in the fall of 1864, but he "looked older," his clerk Benjamin recalled, "by reason of the abundant tinging of his originally brown hair and beard with iron-gray." The war had taken a toll on his constitution, already weakened by the lifelong struggle with asthma that caused periodic "fits of strangulation." The illness that kept him in bed on election eve lasted for nearly three weeks. For a time it seemed he would not rally. His doctor begged him to take a leave of absence from his post. "Barnes," Stanton replied, "keep me alive till this rebellion is over, and then I will take a rest . . . a long one, perhaps." In a letter to Chase written shortly after Lincoln's reelection, he acknowledged that his health could be restored only by "absolute rest and relief from labor and care," though nothing could keep him from his post until he had brought the soldiers home in peace.

By late November, Stanton was back working fifteen-hour days at his stand-up desk, directing his subordinates with a steely determination. The complex relationship between the president and his secretary of war was not easy to comprehend. At times it seemed as if Stanton controlled the president; at other times it was clear that Lincoln was the dominant force in dictating policy. In fact, there was an unwritten code between the two powerful men: "Each could veto the other's acts, but Lincoln was to rule when he felt it necessary."

Lincoln used his veto over Stanton sparingly, as two of his congressional friends learned to their dismay. Having obtained the president's assent to a military appointment for one of their constituents, they carried the endorsed application to Stanton. Stanton flatly refused to consider it. "The position is of high importance," Stanton explained. "I have in mind a man of suitable experience and capacity to fill it." When informed that Lincoln wanted this man, Stanton bellowed, "I do not care what the President wants; the country wants the very best it can get. I am serving the country . . . regardless of individuals."

The two congressmen walked back to the White House, assuming the president would override his secretary, but Lincoln refused: "Gentlemen, it is my duty to submit. I cannot add to Mr. Stanton's troubles. His position is one of the most difficult in the world. Thousands in the army blame him because they are not promoted and other thousands out of the army blame him because they are not appointed. The pressure upon him is immeasurable and unending. He is the rock on the beach of our national ocean against which the breakers dash and roar, dash and roar without ceasing. He fights back the angry waters and prevents them from undermining and overwhelming the land. Gentlemen, I do not see how he survives, why he is not crushed and torn to pieces. Without him I should be destroyed. He performs his task superhumanly. Now do not mind this matter, for Mr. Stanton is right and I cannot wrongly interfere with him."

At the same time, Lincoln expected Stanton to be aware of the special burdens he faced as president. For weeks, Lincoln wrote Stanton, he had been pressed by relatives of "prisoners of war in our custody, whose homes are within our lines, and who wish . . . to take the oath and be discharged." He believed that "taking the oath" was an act of honor, that "none of them will again go to the rebellion," though he acknowledged that "the rebellion again coming to them, a considerable per centage of them, probably not a majority, would rejoin it." With "a cautious discrimination," however, "the number so discharged would not be large enough to do any considerable mischief." Moreover, looking forward to the day when the two sides would once again be united, he thought the government "should avoid planting and cultivating too many thorns in the bosom of society." With all these considerations in mind, it would provide "relief from an intolerable pressure" if he could have Stanton's "cheerful assent to the discharge of those names I may send, which I will only do with circumspection." Stanton replied the following day: "Your order for the discharge of any prisoners of war, will be cheerfully & promptly obeyed."

Lincoln's liberal use of his pardoning power created the greatest tension between the two men. Stanton felt compelled to protect military discipline by exacting proper punishment for desertions or derelictions of duty, while Lincoln looked for any "good excuse for saving a man's life." When he found one, he said, "I go to bed happy as I think how joyous the signing of my name will make him and his family and his friends."

Stanton would not allow himself such leniency. A clerk recalled finding Stanton one night in his office, "the mother, wife, and children of a soldier who had been condemned to be shot as a deserter, on their knees before him pleading for the life of their loved one. He listened standing, in cold and austere silence, and at the end of their heart-breaking sobs and prayers answered briefly that the man must die. The crushed and despairing little family left and Mr. Stanton turned, apparently unmoved, and walked into his private room." The clerk thought Stanton an unfeeling tyrant, until he discovered him moments later, "leaning over a desk, his face buried in his hands and his heavy frame shaking with sobs. 'God help me to do my duty; God help me to do my duty!' he was repeating in a low wail of anguish." On such occasions, when Stanton felt he could not afford to set a precedent, he must have been secretly relieved that the president had the ultimate authority.

When Stanton thought he was right, however, he tenaciously pursued his purpose. When a group of Pennsylvania politicians received the president's assent for discharging some prisoners of war in their district who were willing to take the oath and join the Union army fighting Indians in the West, Stanton flatly refused to execute the order. The order specified that the discharged prisoners would receive a bounty and be credited against Pennsylvania's draft quota, thus reducing the number of troops required of the Keystone State. "Mr. President, I cannot do it," he asserted. "The order is an improper one, and I cannot execute it." Lincoln was equally firm in his reply: "Mr. Secretary, it will have to be done." And so it was.

When the order was publicized, a storm of criticism descended upon Stanton. To give a bounty to soldiers who were already in government custody seemed wasteful and wrong, as did counting the discharged prisoners against the quota that Pennsylvania, like every other state, was required to supply. Lincoln learned that Grant, too, was unhappy and blamed Stanton. "I send this," Lincoln promptly wrote Grant, "to do justice to the Secretary of War." He then explained that he had responded to the idea "upon pressing application . . . and the thing went so far before it came to the knowledge of the Secretary of War that in my judgment it could not be abandoned without greater evil than would follow it's going through. I did not know, at the time, that you had protested against that class of thing being done; and I now say that while this particular job must be completed, no other of the sort, will be authorized, without an understanding with you, if at all. The Secretary of War is wholly free of any part in this blunder."

In this instance, Stanton was transparently blameless, but Lincoln protected his volatile secretary even when criticism was justified, when "his firmness degenerated, at times, into sheer obstinacy; his enthusiasm, into intolerance; his strength of will, into arrogance." Even the equitable George Templeton Strong acknowledged that it was "hard to vote for sustaining an Administration of which Stanton is a member. He is a ruffian."

Implacable and abrasive as Stanton could be, his scrupulous honesty, energy, and determination were invaluable to Lincoln. When one caller complained bitterly about Stanton's bearish style, Lincoln stopped him cold: "Go home my friend, and read attentively the tenth verse of the thirtieth chapter of Proverbs!" The verse reads as follows: "Accuse not a servant to his master, lest he curse thee, and then be found guilty." When people speculated about cabinet changes after his reelection, Lincoln made it clear that Stanton would not be leaving. "Folks come up here and tell me that there are a great many men in the country who have all Stanton's excellent qualities without his defects," he commented. "All I have to say is, I have n't met 'em! I don't know 'em!"

Nor did Lincoln consider dismissing his "Neptune," Gideon Welles. Reserved by nature, Welles did not enjoy the easy camaraderie with Lincoln that Seward did. The discreet New Englander looked askance at the curious pleasure both Lincoln and Seward took in talking with "the little newsmongers" and hearing "all the political gossip." And he was often vexed by the odd intimacy between Lincoln and Stanton. Unlike Chase, however, he confined his complaints to his diary and remained totally loyal to the president whose natural sagacity he greatly admired.

Moreover, Lincoln recognized that Welles had accomplished a Herculean task—he had built a navy almost from scratch, utterly revamping a department initially paralyzed by subversion and strife. Even the normally critical *Times* of London was forced to concede the extraordinary growth of the American navy under the leadership of Gideon Welles. When Welles took office, there were only 76 vessels flying the American flag; four years later, there were 671. The number of seamen had increased from 7,600 to 51,000. In the span of only four years, the American navy had become "a first class power."

A shrewd judge of character, Welles had assembled an excellent team, including his dynamic assistant secretary, Gustavus Vasa Fox, and the industrious commandant of the Navy Yard, John Dahlgren. Welles had opposed the blockade but, once overruled, had enforced it with determination and skill. He had fought Lincoln on the admission of West Virginia as a state and the suspension of the writ of habeas corpus, but he had never publicly vented his objections.

With Seward, Stanton, and Welles secure in their cabinet places, the resignation of Edward Bates provided the only opening for change in the immediate aftermath of the election. The seventy-one-year-old Bates had contemplated resigning the previous spring, after suffering through a winter of chronic illness. In May, his son Barton had pleaded with him to return to St. Louis. "The situation of affairs is such that you are not required to sacrifice your health and comfort for any good which you may possibly do," urged Barton. "As to pecuniary matters, I know well that you have but little to fall back on . . . for the present at least make your home at my house & Julian's, going from one to the other as suits your convenience. . . . You've done your share of work anyhow, & it is time the youngsters were working for you. If you had nothing at all, Julian and I could continue to take good care of you and Ma and the girls; & you know that we would do it as cheerfully as you ever worked for us, and we would greatly prefer to do it rather than you should be wearing yourself out as now with labor and cares unsuited to your age."

The prospect of going home to children and grandchildren was attractive, especially to Julia Bates, whose wishes remained paramount with her husband after forty-one years of marriage. On their anniversary in late May, Bates happily noted that "our mutual affection is as warm, and our mutual confidence far stronger, than in the first week of marriage. This is god's blessing."

However, during the dark period that preceded the fall of Atlanta, when Bates believed "the fate of the nation hung, in doubt & gloom," he did not feel he could leave his post. Nor did he wish to depart until Lincoln's reelection was assured. "Now, on the contrary," he wrote to Lincoln on November 24, 1864, "the affairs of the Government display a brighter aspect; and to you, as head & leader of the Government all the honor & good fortune that we hoped for, has come. And it seems to me, under these altered circumstances, that the time has come, when I may, without dereliction of duty, ask leave to retire to private life."

Bates went on to express his profound gratitude to Lincoln "not only for your good opinion which led to my appointment, but also for your uniform & unvarying courtesy & kindness during the whole time in which we have been associated in the public service. The memory of that kindness & personal favor, I shall bear with me into private life, and hope to retain in my heart, as long as I live."

Bates had served his president and his country faithfully. In his first months as Attorney General, though he had been uncomfortable confronting Justice Taney on the issue of arbitrary arrests, he had composed an elaborate opinion justifying Lincoln's suspension of the writ of habeas corpus. When McClellan had refused to divulge his plans in early 1862, Bates had urged Lincoln to assume control of his commanders, advising him that the authority of the presidency stood above that of his generals, even on military matters. When the president read his first draft of the Emancipation Proclamation to the cabinet in July 1862, Bates had been one of the first to speak favorably. Though Bates never fully escaped from the racial prejudices formed in his early years—he continued to believe until the end of his life that emancipation should be accompanied by colonization—his ideas had evolved to the point where he supported some very progressive measures. When asked in 1864 to deliver a legal opinion on the controversial question of the unequal pay scale for black soldiers, he declared "unhesitatingly" that "persons of color" who were performing in the field the same duties as their white counterparts should receive "the same pay, bounty, and clothing."

Abolitionists applauded this opinion along with an earlier one declaring blacks to be citizens of the United States. The citizenship issue had arisen when a commercial schooner plying the coastal trade was detained because its captain was a black man. The *Dred Scott* decision had declared that blacks were not citizens, and naval law required one to be a citizen to command a ship flying the American flag. When the question was put to him, Bates carefully researched definitions of citizenship dating back to Greek and Roman times. After much consideration, he concluded that place of birth, not color of skin, determined citizenship. The *Dred Scott* decision was wrong; free blacks were citizens of the United States.

Bates's decision did not cover the status of slaves, nor did it suggest that citizenship implied the right of suffrage or the right to sit on juries. Nonetheless, as a local Washington paper noted at the time of his resignation: "Though esteemed by many as more conservative than the majority of his countrymen at the present day, Mr. Bates has given opinions involving the rights of the colored race which have been quite abreast with the times, and which will henceforth stand as landmarks of constitutional interpretation."

From their first acquaintance, the relationship between Bates and Lincoln had been marked by warmth and cordiality. On occasion, Bates's diary reveals frustration with Lincoln's loose management style, which left the administration with "no system—no unity—no accountability—no subordination." He believed Lincoln relied too heavily on Seward and Stanton. He could not fathom why the disloyal Chase had been kept in place for so long or why General Butler was not fired when complaints arose about his arbitrary arrests in Norfolk. In fact, Bates confided in his diary, his "chief fear" was "the President's easy good nature."

Nonetheless, by the end of his tenure as Attorney General, Bates had formed a more spacious understanding of the president's unique leadership style. While troubled at the start by Lincoln's "never-failing fund of anecdote," he had come to realize that storytelling played a central role in the president's ability to communicate with the public. "The character of the President's mind is such," Bates remarked, "that his thought habitually takes on this form of illustration, by which the point he wishes to enforce is invariably brought home with a strength and clearness impossible in hours of abstract argument.

"Mr. Lincoln," Bates told Francis Carpenter, "comes very near being a perfect man, according to my ideal of manhood. He lacks but one thing . . . the element of *will.* I have sometimes told him, for instance, that he was unfit to be intrusted with the pardoning power. Why, if a man comes to him with a touching story, his judgment is almost certain to be affected by it. Should the applicant be a *woman*, a wife, a mother, or a sister,—in nine cases out of ten, her tears, if nothing else, are sure to prevail."

As Bates prepared to leave Washington, each of his colleagues stopped to say goodbye, in contrast to the lonely leave-taking endured by Salmon Chase. Stanton was "especially civil," Bates noted. "Told me to write to my sons, in the army and assure them that he would [do] any thing for them that they would expect me to do." Bates joined Seward, Welles, and Usher in the president's office for a "pleasant" farewell. The departing Attorney General was once again touched by the president's "affable and kind" manner.

Bates left his colleagues and staff "with regret," but with the knowledge that his life was forever connected with the history of his country. Because Lincoln had chosen him as his Attorney General, Edward Bates had been able to "leave a trail which might make known/That I once lived—when I am gone."

To replace Bates, Lincoln felt he had to find a man from one of the border states. "My Cabinet has *shrunk up* North, and I must find a Southern man," he explained to a colleague. "I suppose if the twelve Apostles were to be chosen nowadays the shrieks of locality would have to be heeded." His first choice was Judge Advocate General Joseph Holt. The native Kentuckian had been one of the trio of cabinet members, together with Edwin Stanton and Jeremiah Black, who had stiffened Buchanan's will to resist secession. Lincoln liked and respected Judge Holt, having worked closely with him on court-martial cases. Holt declined the offer, however, recommending instead his fellow Kentuckian James Speed, the older brother of

Lincoln's great friend Joshua. "I can recall no public man in the State of *uncompromising loyalty*," Holt told Lincoln, "who unites in the same degree, the qualifications of professional attainments, fervent devotion to the union, & to the principles of your administration, & spotless points of personal character."

Lincoln followed Holt's recommendation that very day, sending a telegram to Speed. "I appoint you to be Attorney General. Please come on at once." Though taken by surprise, Speed was honored to accept: "Will leave tomorrow for Washington."

James Speed would prove to be an excellent choice. Over the years, he had arrived at a radical position on slavery. The previous spring, he and his brother, Joshua, had been instrumental in forming a new liberal party in conservative Kentucky, the Unconditional Union Party, which supported Lincoln's reelection and emancipation. "I am a thorough Constitutional Abolitionist," James Speed had declared during the fall campaign, meaning he, like Lincoln, was "for abolishing Slavery under the War Power of the National Constitution, and then clinching it by a Constitutional amendment prohibiting it everywhere forever." Though unable to swing the state for Lincoln, the Unconditionalists remained hopeful that they might eventually direct Kentucky's future. "We are less now but true," James Speed had written Lincoln after the election.

To those unfamiliar with the Louisville lawyer, Lincoln explained that Speed was "a man I know well, though not so well as I know his brother Joshua. That, however, is not strange, for I slept with Joshua for four years, and I suppose I ought to know him well." Lincoln's ease in referring to his sleeping arrangement with Joshua Speed is further evidence that theirs was not a sexual relationship. Had it been, historian David Donald suggests, the president would not have spoken of it "so freely and publicly."

"You will find," Lincoln predicted as James Speed set out for Washington, "he is one of those well-poised men, not too common here, who are not spoiled by a big office."

• • •

THE EASE WITH WHICH LINCOLN filled the post of Attorney General was not replicated when Roger Taney's death in mid-October left vacant the seat of Chief Justice of the Supreme Court. Though Lincoln had initially planned to offer Salmon Chase the position, he discovered that three of his most loyal cabinet members—Edwin Stanton, Edward Bates, and Montgomery Blair—desired the honored post for themselves. He decided to postpone his choice until after the election.

Stanton's claim seemed the most compelling. The Chief Justiceship was the only position, observed a longtime friend, "Stanton ever desired." His brilliant legal career had brought him to argue numerous cases before the Supreme Court. Lifetime tenure would secure his family's finances, which had diminished seriously during the war. His unstable health might be restored with the pressures of the war office removed. "You have been wearing out your life in the service of your country & have fulfilled the duties of your very responsible & laborious office with unexampled ability," wrote his friend the Supreme Court justice Robert Grier. Though Grier himself was an obvious choice to fill Taney's position, he believed Stanton deserved the honor. "It would give me the greatest pleasure and satisfaction," he wrote Stanton, "to have you preside on our bench. . . . I think the Pres owes it to you."

Ellen Stanton, doubtless acting at her husband's behest, invited Orville Browning to their house one Sunday night when Stanton was at City Point. "She expressed to me a great desire to have her husband appointed Chief Justice," Browning recorded in his diary, "and wished me to see the President upon the subject. I fear Mr Chase's appointment, and am anxious to prevent it. Mr Stanton is an able lawyer, learned in his profession, and fond of it, of great application, and capacity of endurance in labor—I think a just man—honest and upright, and incapable of corruption, and I, therefore, think would be an appointment most fit to be made. I will see the President upon the subject tomorrow."

Methodist bishop Matthew Simpson also called on Lincoln to urge Stanton's appointment "on the grounds of his fitness, and as a reward for his services and labors." Lincoln "listened attentively" and then, "throwing his leg over a chair, and running his hands through his hair," responded with heartfelt emotion: "Bishop, I believe every word you have said. But where can I get a man to take Secretary Stanton's place? Tell me that, and I will do it."

Like Lincoln, General Grant worried about losing Stanton's indispensable talents in the War Department. At City Point, he urged the secretary to stay at his post. The strain of the situation likely contributed to Stanton's ongoing illness that fall. In the end, Stanton informed Lincoln through a friend that he should no longer be considered "among candidates." He "felt that the completion of the work he had in hand," his sister Pamphila recalled, "was nearer to his heart, and a far higher ambition."

A heartfelt note from Henry Ward Beecher helped to dispel Stanton's disappointment at relinquishing his ambition. "The country cannot spare your services from your present place," wrote the celebrated minister, "or I could wish that you might redeem Taney's place and restore to that Court, the honor and trust of Marshall's day. . . . I regard your administration of the War Department, from whatever point it is viewed, as one of the greatest features of this grand time. Your energy vitalizing industry, and fidelity, but above all, *Your moral vision* . . . are just as sure to give your name honor and fame. . . . If you were to die to-morrow you have done enough for your own fame already."

In an emotional reply, Stanton told Beecher that he was deeply moved by his generous remarks. "Often, in dark hours, you have come before me, and I have longed to hear your voice, feeling that above all other men you could cheer, strengthen, guide, and uphold me in this great battle, where, by God's providence, it has fallen upon me to hold a post and perform a duty beyond my own strength. But being a stranger I had no right to claim your confidence or ask for help. . . . Now, my dear Sir, your voice has reached me, and your hand is stretched forth as to a friend. . . . Already my heart feels renewed strength and is inspired with fresh hope."

Montgomery Blair desired the post of Chief Justice even more fervently than Stanton. He had gracefully acceded to Lincoln's request for his resignation, but the high appointment would certainly compensate for the remnant wound. His distinguished career as a lawyer had been defined by his eloquent representation of the slave Dred Scott in the case that had forever cast a blight on Justice Taney's name. Monty had powerful backers, including Seward, Weed, and Welles, all of whom vastly preferred him to Chase. Welles told Lincoln that, of all the candidates, Blair "best conformed to these requirements—that the President knew the man, his ability, his truthfulness, honesty and courage." Lincoln "expressed his concurrence . . . and spoke kindly and complimentarily of Mr. Blair but did not in any way commit himself, nor did I expect or suppose he would."

Lincoln understood that the appointment mattered greatly, not only to Monty but to his father, who had taken his son's forced resignation as a personal blow. A week after Taney died, the elder Blair wrote Lincoln an impassioned plea: "I beg you to indulge me with a little conference with you on paper about a thing which as involving a good deal of egotism, I am ashamed to talk about face to face." He went on to describe the Blairs' enduring loyalty to both the Union and the president. "Now I come," he pressed, "to what I hope you will consider another & higher opportunity of serving you & the Republic by carrying your political principles & the support of your policy expressed in relation to the reconstruction of the Union & the support of the freedman's proclamation, into the Supreme Court. I think Montgomery's unswerving support of your administration in all its aspects coupled with his unfaltering attachment to you personally fits him to be your representative man at the head of that Bench."

When Mary Lincoln warned Old Man Blair that "Chase and his friends are besieging my Husband for the Chief-Justiceship," Blair discarded his embarrassment and requested a personal interview. Lincoln listened graciously as Monty's father suggested that his son "had been tried as a Judge and not found wanting, that his practice in the West had made him conversant with our land law, Spanish law, as well as the common and civil law in which his university studies had grounded him, that his practice in the Supreme Court brought him into the circle of commercial and constitutional questions. That, besides on political issues he sustained him [the President] in every thing," and "when Chase and every other member of [the] Cabinet declined to make war for Sumter, Montgomery stood by him."

Lincoln agreed that Monty would admirably acquit himself as Chief Justice, but he was also aware that the nomination would produce a storm of criticism from his many enemies in the Congress. He had no desire to provoke unnecessary animosity among the radicals, who probably held sufficient power to deny confirmation. Nor did Lincoln trust where Monty Blair's conservative philosophy would lead on issues surrounding Reconstruction and the integration of the country's new black citizens.

The same objections most likely applied to Edward Bates. Believing the post would be "a crowning and retiring honor," Bates had "personally solicited" Lincoln to consider his name. "If not overborne by others," Lincoln told Bates, he would happily consider him for the post, but "Chase was turning every stone, to get it, and several others were urged, from different quarters." Hearing this, Bates declared himself "happy in the feeling that the failure to get the place, will be no painful disappointment for my mind is made up to private life."

In the end, Lincoln returned to his first impulse upon learning of Roger Taney's illness—Salmon P. Chase. "Of Mr. Chase's ability and of his soundness on the general issues of the war there is, of course, no question," he told Chase's friend Henry Wilson. "I have only one doubt about his appointment. He is a man of unbounded ambition, and has been working all his life to become President. That he can never be; and I fear that if I make him chief-justice he will simply become more restless and uneasy and neglect the place in his strife and intrigue to make himself President. If I were sure that he would go on the bench and give up his aspirations and do nothing but make himself a great judge, I would not hesitate a moment." He made a similar comment when Schuyler Colfax gave his word that Chase "would dedicate the remainder of his life to the Bench."

When supporters of other candidates reminded the president of Chase's myriad intrigues against him, Lincoln responded, "Now, I know meaner things about Governor Chase than any of those men can tell me," but "we have stood together in the time of trial, and I should despise myself if I allowed personal differences to affect my judgment of his fitness for the office."

Chase remained in Ohio throughout this tumult, confident that the nomination would be his. Oblivious to Stanton's own hopes, he told the war secretary two days after Taney's death that "within the last three or four months I have been assured that it was the Presidents intention, to offer the place to me in case of a vacancy. I think I should accept it if offered: for I am weary of political life & work." However, when weeks passed with no word from the president, Chase anxiously decided to come to Washington. Fessenden and Sumner assured him that the appointment would be made as soon as the elections were over, but Lincoln waited until December 6 to announce his choice.

That morning, Chase's friend John Alley of Massachusetts had called on the president. "I have something to tell you that will make you happy," Lincoln announced. "I have just sent Mr. Chase word that he is to be appointed Chief-Justice, and you are the first man I have told of it." Alley enthusiastically replied, "Mr. President, this is an exhibition of magnanimity and patriotism that could hardly be expected of any one. After what he has said against your administration, which has undoubtedly been reported to you, it was hardly to be expected that you would bestow the most important office within your gift on such a man."

"To have done otherwise I should have been recreant to my convictions of duty to the Republican party and to the country," Lincoln answered. "As to his talk about me, I do not mind that. Chase is, on the whole, a pretty good fellow and a very able man. His only trouble is that he has 'the White House fever' a little too bad, but I hope this may cure him and that he will be satisfied."

Lincoln later told Senator Chandler that personally he "would rather have swallowed his buckhorn chair than to have nominated Chase," but the decision was right for the country. "Probably no other man than Lincoln," Nicolay wrote to Therena, "would have had, in this age of the world, the degree of magnanimity to thus forgive and exalt a rival who had so deeply and so unjustifiably intrigued against him. It is however only another most marked illustration of the greatness of the President."

Chase got the official word from Kate when he arrived home that night. He immediately sat down to write the president. "I cannot sleep before I thank [you] for this mark of your confidence. . . . Be assured that I prize your confidence & good will more than nomination or office."

On December 15, the Supreme Court was "overflowing with an immense throng of dignitaries of various degrees, ladies, congressmen, foreign ministers, and others who wished to view the simple but impressive ceremony of swearing in the chief judicial officer of the republic." Kate Sprague and her sister, Nettie, were there, "gorgeously dressed," according to Noah Brooks. Secretary Seward was also present, along with Nathaniel Banks, Ben Wade, Reverdy Johnson, and Charles Sumner, whose "handsome features plainly showed his inward glow of gratification." At the usher's solemn announcement, everyone stood as the robed justices entered the room. The senior justice, James W. Wayne, administered the oath, which Chase "read in a clear but tremulous voice." When he finished, Chase "lifted his right hand, looked upward to the beautiful dome of the court-room, and with deep feeling added, 'So help me God.' "

"I hope the President may have no occasion to regret his selection," Gideon Welles confided in his diary, sharing Lincoln's apprehension that Chase would "use the place for political advancement and thereby endanger confidence in the court." Still, Lincoln believed the risk worth taking. He trusted that Chase would help secure the rights of the black man, for which he had fought throughout his career, a belief that outweighed concerns about Chase's restless temperament.

Chase quickly justified Lincoln's confidence in this regard. Within hours of Chase's accession to the Court, John Rock, a black lawyer from Massachusetts, wrote a hopeful letter to Charles Sumner. Rock had been seeking to practice before the Supreme Court for over a year, but his efforts had been denied on the basis of his race. "We now have a great and good man for our Chief Justice, and with him I think my color will not be a bar to my admission," he wrote. Sumner immediately contacted Chase, who was delighted to pursue the cause of opening the Court to its first black barrister.

Six weeks later, Sumner stood before the Supreme Court as Rock's sponsor: "May it please the Court, I move that John S. Rock, a member of the Supreme Court of the State of Massachusetts, be admitted to practice as a member of this Court." Then, with Chase's assent, Rock stepped forward for the oath that would allow him to practice before the highest court in the land. "This event," *Harper's Weekly* observed, represented an "extraordinary reversal" of the decision in the *Dred Scott* case. Rock's admission, *Harper's* predicted, would "be regarded by the future historian as a remarkable indication of the revolution which is going on in the sentiment of a great people."

• • •

MARY LINCOLN TOOK special satisfaction in her husband's reelection. The White House "has been quite a *Mecca* of late," she wrote to her friend Mercy Conkling. "We are surrounded, at all times, by a great deal of company," and "it has been gratifying, from all quarters, to receive so many kind & congratulatory letters, so fraught, with good feeling."

Mary's pleasure in her husband's victory reflected more than simple pride. During the fall election, she had been terrified that his defeat might signal merchants in New York and Philadelphia—to whom she still owed substantial sums—to call in her debt. "I owe altogether about twenty-seven thousand dollars," she confided in Elizabeth Keckley. "Mr. Lincoln has but little idea of the expense of a woman's wardrobe. He glances at my rich dresses, and is happy in the belief that the few hundred dollars that I obtain from him supply all my wants. I must dress in costly materials. The people scrutinize every article that I wear with critical curiosity. The very fact of having grown up in the West, subjects me to more searching observation. To keep up appearances, I must have money—more than Mr. Lincoln can spare for me. He is too honest to make a penny outside of his salary; consequently I had, and still have, no alternative but to run in debt."

Although padded bills and attempts to trade upon her White House influence exposed her to serious scandal, Mary could not curtail her excessive spending habits. "Here is the carriage of Mrs Lincoln before a dry goods Store," Judge Taft noted four weeks after the election, "her footman has gone into the Store. The Clerk is just going out to the carriage (where Mrs L is waiting) with some pieces of goods for her to choose from. I should rather think that she would have a better chance at the goods if she was to go into the Store but then she *might* get jostled and gazed at and that too would be doing just as the common people do. The footman holds the carriage door open. The driver sits on the box and hold[s] the horses. Mrs L. thumbs the goods and asks a great many questions."

A week later, Mary journeyed to Philadelphia for another shopping trip. Not long afterward, she visited New York, where she purchased a new dress, expensive furs, and "300 pairs of kid gloves." When the items she purchased did not measure up to her expectations, her manic sprees quickly gave way to depression and anger. "I can neither wear, or settle with you, for my bonnet without different inside flowers," she threatened a milliner in New York. "I cannot retain or wear the bonnet, as it is—I am certainly taught a lesson, by your acting thus."

Mary's self-conscious attention to the details of her bonnet was not entirely misplaced. Newspaper reports of her evening receptions invariably commented on every piece of her apparel. At the first White House levee of the new winter season, the *National Republican* noted that she "was charmingly and elegantly attired . . . dressed in a rich, plain white silk, with heavy black lace flounce and black lace shawl, and upon her head was a coronet of white and purple flowers—a most tasteful decoration." Her outfit at a state dinner a few weeks later drew equal praise. "Mrs. Lincoln was tastefully attired in a heavy black and white spotted silk, elegantly trimmed with black lace, her headdress and rich set of jewelry harmonizing throughout."

The new season brought new rules of etiquette for visitors at public receptions at the White House: "Overcoats, hats, caps, bonnets, shawls, cloaks &c. should be deposited in the several ante-rooms provided for that purpose, and where they will be in charge of proper persons for safe-keeping." The new arrangement pleased the Washington social elite, who began returning to the open receptions they had shunned. A reporter for the *National Republican* noted on the part of all the guests "a more general observance of the proprieties of dress and demeanor," which seemed to suggest "increasing respect for the President, his family and themselves."

Mary also took great pride in her informal Blue Room receptions, which continued to draw distinguished visitors. She was particularly gratified by the regular appearance of Charles Sumner. The handsome senator, though in his early fifties, was considered one of the most eligible bachelors in Washington. "*I* was pleased," Mary later recalled, "knowing he visited no other lady—His time was so immersed in his business—and that cold & haughty looking man to the world—would insist upon my telling him all the news, & we would have such frequent and delightful conversations & often late in the evening—My darling husband would join us & they would laugh together, like *two* school boys."

However, the prestige and pleasure of her second term as first lady could not assuage Mary's lingering grief over the loss of Willie. Over two years after her son's death, it was still difficult for her to enter the library, which had been one of his favorite rooms. Her "darling Boy!"—"the idolized child, of the household"—was never far from her mind. "I have sometimes feared," she admitted to a friend, "that the *deep waters*, through which we have passed would overwhelm me." In the absence of her gentle son, "*The World*, has lost so much, of its charm. My position, requires my presence, where my heart is *so far* from being."

After Willie's death, Mary had been determined not to allow her oldest son, Robert, to risk his life in the army. But after his graduation from Harvard, she could no longer detain him. In January 1865, Lincoln wrote to General Grant: "Please read and answer this letter as though I was not President, but only a friend. My son, now in his twenty second year, having graduated at Harvard, wishes to see something of the war before it ends. I do not wish to put him in the ranks, nor yet to give him a commission, to which those who have already served long, are better entitled, and better qualified to hold. Could he, without embarrassment to you, or detriment to the service, go into your Military family with some nominal rank, I, and not the public, furnishing his necessary means? If no, say so without the least hesitation, because I am as anxious, and as deeply interested, that you shall not be encumbered."

Grant replied two days later. "I will be most happy to have him in my Military family," he wrote. He suggested that the rank of captain would be most appropriate. So Robert's wish to join the army was granted. Stationed at Grant's headquarters, Robert "soon became exceedingly popular," Horace Porter recalled. "He was always ready to perform his share of hard work, and never expected to be treated differently from any other officer on account of his being the son of the Chief Executive of the nation."

• • •

IN THE FIRST DAYS OF 1865, Gideon Welles was preoccupied with thoughts of "passing time and accumulating years." His wistful contemplation was shared by Salmon Chase. On the first of January, the Chief Justice's last surviving sister, Helen, was buried in Ohio. Of ten siblings, only Chase and his brother Edward, both in their mid-fifties, remained alive. Chase wrote to Lincoln explaining that the death of his sister precluded his attendance at the traditional New Year's reception. "Without your note of to-day," Lincoln promptly replied, "I should have felt assured that some sufficient reason had detained you. Allow me to condole with you in the sad bereavement."

One of the guests at the White House reception noted "a great contrast between this 'New Years' and any previous one for the past three years, four years ago there was a solemn stillness, a burthensome weight hanging upon the minds of all, a fearful foreboding of Evil, a dread of the future. It was but little better *three* years or *two* years ago. . . . Even one year ago we could scarcely see any light. Today all are in good spirits."

The stunning success of Sherman's March to the Sea, which had ended with the capture of Savannah just prior to Christmas, was largely responsible for the ebullience that prevailed in Washington. "Our joy was irrepressible," recalled Assistant Treasury Secretary Hugh McCulloch, "because it was an assurance that the days of the Confederacy were numbered." The president had initially been "*anxious*, if not fearful," about Sherman's plan to abandon his supply lines and trust that his men could forage for necessary food and provisions along the way. The day after Christmas, Lincoln recalled his skepticism in a gracious note to Sherman: "The honor is all yours; for I believe none of us went farther than to acquiesce."

Sherman's March to the Sea proved devastating to Southern property and countryside. Frank Blair, whose troops played a major role in the historic march, rationalized the indiscriminate destruction in a letter to his father: "We have destroyed nearly four hundred miles of Railroad, severing the western from the Eastern part of the Confederacy, and we have burned millions of dollars worth of cotton which is the only thing that enables them to maintain credit abroad & to purchase arms & munitions of war & we have actually 'gobbled' up enough provisions to have fed Lee's army for six months." Though the military gains justified the march in the minds of Union soldiers, the memory of its terrible impact on civilian lives haunts the South to this day.

In his congratulatory note to Sherman, Lincoln also paid tribute to General George Thomas, who had defeated John Bell Hood's forces at Nashville ten days earlier. News of the two victories, Lincoln wrote, brought "those who sat in darkness, to see a great light." The telegram announcing Thomas's victory had been carried to Stanton in the middle of the night. "Hurrah," Stanton cried as he hurriedly dressed and rushed to the White House with Thomas Eckert, the chief of the telegraph office. Eckert would long remember the delight on Lincoln's face when he heard the news. Standing at the top of the stairs "in his night-dress, with a lighted candle in his hand," the tall president created an arresting tableau.

The fall of Fort Fisher, which guarded the port of Wilmington, North Carolina, followed in mid-January. Headlines trumpeted the "Combined Work of the Army and Navy!," which had gained the capture of the fort and its seventy-two large-caliber guns. "This glorious work," hailed the *National Republican*, "closes the port of Wilmington, and shuts off supplies to the rebels from abroad." Gideon Welles was ecstatic, recording that at the cabinet meeting that morning, "there was a very pleasant feeling. Seward thought there was little now for the Navy to do. . . . The President was happy." The defeat was shattering to Southern logistics and morale. Confederate vice president Alexander Stephens considered the fall of Fort Fisher "one of the greatest disasters which had befallen our Cause from the beginning of the war—not excepting the loss of Vicksburg or Atlanta." With nearly every other port closed by the naval blockade, the closing of Wilmington signaled "the complete shutting out of the Confederate States from all intercourse by sea with Foreign Countries," bringing an end to the exchange of cotton for vitally needed munitions and supplies.

Stanton was in Savannah, Georgia, for a conference with Sherman when "the rebel flag of Fort Fisher was delivered to [him]." Eager to see the battleground, he journeyed to North Carolina, where he spent the night with General Rufus Saxton and his wife. When he arrived, he warned his hosts that "fatigue would compel him to retire early," but, relaxing before the fire, surrounded by a collection of books, he revived. "Ah, here are old friends," he said, picking up a volume of Macauley's poetry from the table. He asked Mrs. Saxton to read "Horatius at the Bridge," which he followed with "The Battle of Ivry." Midnight found him still seated by the fire, "repeating snatches of poetry." During his stay, Mrs. Saxton noted, "the Titan War Secretary was replaced by the genial companion, the man of letters, the lover of nature—the *real* Stanton." For a few hours, Stanton allowed himself the distraction and the levity he had often decried in Lincoln.

Stanton had journeyed south to confer with Sherman, concerned by reports of the general's hostile behavior toward the black refugees who were arriving by the thousands into his lines. It was said that Sherman opposed their employment as soldiers, drove them from his camp even when they were starving, and manifested toward them "an almost *criminal* dislike." Sherman countered that the movement of his military columns was hindered "by the crowds of helpless negroes that flock after our armies . . . clogging my roads, and eating up our substance." Military success, he felt, had to take precedence over treatment of the Negroes.

In his conversations with Stanton, however, Sherman agreed to issue "Special Field Orders, No. 15," a temporary plan to allocate "a plot of not more than forty acres of tillable ground" to help settle the tide of freed slaves along the coast of Georgia and on the neighboring islands. Stanton returned home feeling more at ease about the situation. In the weeks that followed, Congress followed up by creating a Freedmen's Bureau with authority to distribute lands and provide assistance to displaced refugees throughout the South.

• • •

NOTHING ON THE HOME FRONT in January engaged Lincoln with greater urgency than the passage of the Thirteenth Amendment, abolishing slavery. He had long feared that his Emancipation Proclamation would be discarded once the war came to an end. "A question might be raised whether the proclamation was legally valid," he said. "It might be added that it only aided those who came into our lines . . . or that it would have no effect upon the children of the slaves born hereafter." Passage of a constitutional amendment eradicating slavery once and for all would be "a King's cure for all the evils."

The previous spring, the Thirteenth Amendment had passed in the Senate by two thirds but failed to garner the necessary two-thirds vote in the House, where Republicans had voted aye and Democrats nay along nearly unanimous party lines. In his annual message in December, Lincoln had urged Congress to reconsider the measure. He acknowledged that he was asking the same body to debate the same question, but he hoped the intervening election had altered the situation. Republican gains in November ensured that if he called a special session after March 4, the amendment would pass. Since it was "only a question of *time*," how much better it would be if this Congress could complete the job, if Democrats as well as Republicans could be brought to support its passage in a show of bipartisan unity.

Congressman James M. Ashley of Ohio reintroduced the measure into the House on January 6, 1865. Lincoln set to work at once to sway the votes of moderate Democrats and border-state Unionists. He invited individual House members to his office, dealing gracefully and effectively with each one. "I have sent for you as an old whig friend," he told Missouri's James Rollins, "that I might make an appeal to you to vote for this amendment. It is going to be very close, a few votes one way or the other will decide it." He emphasized the importance of sending a signal to the South that the border states could no longer be relied upon to uphold slavery. This would "bring the war," he predicted, "rapidly to a close." When Rollins agreed to support the amendment, Lincoln jumped from his chair and grasped the congressman's hands, expressing his profound gratitude. The two old Whigs then discussed the leanings of the various members of the Missouri delegation, determining which members might be persuaded. "Tell them of my anxiety to have the measure pass," Lincoln urged, "and let me know the prospect of the border state vote."

He assigned two of his allies in the House to deliver the votes of two wavering members. When they asked how to proceed, he said, "I am President of the United States, clothed with great power. The abolition of slavery by constitutional provision settles the fate, for all coming time, not only of the millions now in bondage, but of unborn millions to come—a measure of such importance that *those two votes must be procured.* I leave it to you to determine how it shall be done; but remember that I am President of the United States, clothed with immense power, and I expect you to procure those votes." It was clear to his emissaries that his powers extended to plum assignments, pardons, campaign contributions, and government jobs for relatives and friends of faithful members. Brooklyn Democrat Moses F. Odell agreed to change his vote; when the session ended, he was given the lucrative post of navy agent in New York. Elizabeth Blair noted that her father had successfully joined in the lobbying effort, persuading several members.

Ashley learned that the Camden & Amboy Railroad could secure the vote of two New Jersey Democrats if Senator Sumner could be convinced to postpone a bill he had introduced to end the monopoly the railroad enjoyed. Unable to move Sumner, Ashley asked Lincoln to intervene. Lincoln regretfully replied that he could "do nothing with Mr. Sumner in these matters," and feared if he tried, Sumner "would be all the more resolute."

As the vote neared, pressure intensified. The leader of the opposition was McClellan's running mate, Democrat George Pendleton of Ohio. "Though he had been defeated in the election," observed Senator James Blaine, "he returned to the House with increased prestige among his own political associates." Democrats who considered changing their vote were made to understand that dire consequences would follow if they failed to maintain the party line on an issue compromising the sanctity of states' rights and effecting a fundamental shift in the Constitution.

Both sides knew that the outcome would be decided by the thinnest of margins. "We are like whalers," Lincoln observed, "who have been long on a chase: we have at last got the harpoon into the monster, but we must now look how we steer, or with one 'flop' of his tail he will send us all into eternity." On the morning of the scheduled vote, Ashley feared that the entire effort would collapse. Rumors circulated that Confederate Peace Commissioners were on the way to Washington or had already arrived in the capital. "If it is true," Ashley urgently wrote to the president, "I fear we shall [lose] the bill." The Democratic leadership would prevail upon wavering party members, arguing that the amendment would lead the commissioners to abort the peace talks. "Please authorize me to contradict it, if not true," Ashley entreated.

"So far as I know," Lincoln promptly replied, "there are no peace Commissioners in the City, or likely to be in it." Ashley later learned that Lincoln, in fact, had been informed that three Peace Commissioners were en route to Fort Monroe, but he could honestly, if insincerely, claim that no commissioners were *in* the capital city. Without this cunning evasion, Ashley believed, "the proposed amendment would have failed."

As the debate opened, Ashley acknowledged that "never before, and certain I am that never again, will I be seized with so strong a desire to give utterance to the thoughts and emotions which throbbed my heart and brain." The amendment's passage would signal "the complete triumph of a cause, which at the beginning of my political life I had not hoped to live long enough to see."

Ashley recalled, "Every available foot of space, both in the galleries and on the floor of the House, was crowded at an early hour, and many hundred could not get within hearing." Chief Justice Chase and the members of the Supreme Court were present, along with Seward, Fessenden, and

Dennison representing the cabinet. Dozens of senators had come to witness the historic debate, as had members of most foreign ministries.

Ashley wisely decided to yield his time to the small band of Democrats who would support the amendment but needed to justify their shift to constituents. He called first on Archibald McAllister. The Pennsylvania congressman explained that he had changed his mind when he saw that the only way to achieve peace was to destroy "the corner-stone of the Southern Confederacy." His remarks brought forth applause from the galleries, as did those of his colleague Alexander Coffroth. "If by my action to-day I dig my political grave," the congressman from Somerset County proclaimed, "I will descend into it without a murmur."

After every Democrat who wanted to speak had been heard, the voting began. "Hundreds of tally sheets had been distributed on the floor and in the galleries," Ashley recorded. It appeared at first that the amendment had fallen two or three votes short of the requisite two-thirds margin. The floor was in tumult when Speaker Colfax stood to announce the final tally. His voice shaking, he said, "On the passage of the Joint Resolution to amend the Constitution of the United States the ayes have 119, the noes 56. The constitutional majority of two thirds having voted in the affirmative, the Joint Resolution has passed." Without the five Democrats who had changed their votes, the amendment would have lost.

"For a moment there was a pause of utter silence," Noah Brooks reported, "as if the voices of the dense mass of spectators were choked by strong emotion. Then there was an explosion, a storm of cheers, the like of which probably no Congress of the United States ever heard before."

"Before the members left their seats," Congressman Arnold recalled, "the roar of artillery from Capitol Hill announced to the people of Washington that the amendment had passed." Ashley brought to the War Department a list of all those who had voted in favor. Stanton ordered three additional batteries to "fire one hundred guns with their heaviest charges" while he slowly read each name aloud, proclaiming, "History will embalm them in great honor."

Lincoln's friends raced to the White House to share the news. "The passage of the resolution," recalled Arnold, "filled his heart with joy. He saw in it the complete consummation of his own great work, the emancipation proclamation." The following evening, Lincoln spoke to celebrants gathered at the White House. "The occasion was one of congratulation to the country and to the whole world," he said. "But there is a task yet before us—to go forward and consummate by the votes of the States that which Congress so nobly began." The audience responded with cheers. "They will do it" was the confident cry. And, indeed, the legislatures in twenty states acted almost immediately. Before the year 1865 was out, the requisite three quarters had spoken putting a dramatic end to the slavery issue that had disturbed the nation's tranquillity from its earliest days.

No praise must have been more welcome to Lincoln than that of his old critic, the fiery abolitionist William Lloyd Garrison. "And to whom is the country more immediately indebted for this vital and saving amendment of the Constitution than, perhaps, to any other man?" Garrison asked a cheering crowd at the Boston Music Hall. "I believe I may confidently answer—to the humble railsplitter of Illinois—to the Presidential chain-breaker for millions of the oppressed—to Abraham Lincoln!"

• • •

THE STORY OF the Peace Commissioners, whose presence had almost derailed the vote on the new amendment, had begun with Francis Preston Blair. Lincoln's reelection had convinced the old editor that another attempt at peace might be successful. Lincoln remained unconvinced that talks at this juncture would be effective, but Blair was so anxious to try that Lincoln gave him a pass for Richmond. It was understood, however, that he was proceeding on his own, without authority to speak for the president.

After leaving Lincoln, Blair wrote two letters to Jefferson Davis. The first, designed for public consumption, requested simply "the privilege of visiting Richmond" to inquire about the papers Blair had lost when General Early's troops took possession of his Silver Spring house. The second revealed that his "main purpose" in coming was to discuss "the state of the affairs of our country." He promised to "unbosom [his] heart frankly & without reserve," hopeful that some good might result.

On January 11, 1865, the seventy-three-year-old Blair arrived in Richmond, where he was greeted warmly by numerous old friends. Jefferson Davis's wife, Varina, "threw her arms around him" and said, "Oh you Rascal, I am overjoyed to see you." Seated with President Davis in the library of the Confederate White House, Blair conceded his proposal "might be the dreams of an old man," but he was confident of Davis's "practical good sense" and "utmost frankness." He reminded Davis of his own deep attachment to the South. "Every drop" of his own blood and his children's sprang from "a Southern source." Davis responded with equal warmth, assuring Blair that he "would never forget" the many "kindnesses" exhibited by the Blairs toward the Davis family, and that "even when dying they would be remembered in his prayers."

Blair presented his proposal, which would essentially postpone the war between the North and the South while the armies allied against the

French, who had invaded Mexico and installed a puppet regime in violation of the Monroe Doctrine. Davis agreed that nothing would better heal the raw emotions on both sides "than to see the arms of our countrymen from the North and the South united in a war upon a Foreign Power." The specifics of this improbable and unauthorized plan, reminiscent of Seward's proposal four years earlier, were not discussed, though Davis agreed to send Peace Commissioners to Washington "with a view to secure peace to the two Countries."

Though tired from his arduous journey back to Washington by carriage, train, and steamer, Blair rushed to the White House and delivered the Davis letter to the president. Lincoln consulted Stanton, who pointedly noted: "There are not two countries . . . and there never will be two countries. Tell Davis that if you treat for peace, it will be for this one country; negotiations on any other basis are impossible." Lincoln immediately agreed. "You may say to him," Lincoln directed Blair, "that I have constantly been, am now, and shall continue, ready to receive any agent . . . with the view of securing peace to the people of our one common country."

Blair returned straightaway to Richmond with Lincoln's response, and Davis called a cabinet meeting at his home to discuss his next move. His advisers recognized the irreconcilable conflict between the concepts of "two countries" and "one common country," but the insistent clamor for peace had convinced Davis to send three commissioners to Fort Monroe—Vice President Alexander Stephens, former United States senator R. M. T. Hunter, and former Supreme Court Justice John A. Campbell.

On Sunday, January 29, a flag of truce flown at Petersburg announced the arrival of the commissioners. "By common consent all picket firing was suspended," the *New York Herald* reported, "and the lines of both armies presented the appearance of a gala day." Viewed as "harbingers of peace," the three gentlemen elicited "prolonged and enthusiastic" applause from both sides, revealing the depth of the soldiers' desire to end the fighting and return to their families and homes. One reporter noted that when rival songs were played by Southern and Northern bands—"Dixie" and "Yankee Doodle Dandy"—each side responded only to its own patriotic air, "but when the band struck up 'Home Sweet Home,' the opposing camps forgot their hostility, and united in vociferous tribute to the common sentiment."

A Union colonel escorted the commissioners to Grant's headquarters at City Point. "It was night when we arrived," Alexander Stephens later recalled. "There was nothing in [Grant's] appearance or surroundings which indicated his official rank. There were neither guards nor aids about him. . . . I was instantly struck with the great simplicity and perfect naturalness of his manners, and the entire absence of everything like affectation, show, or even the usual military air or *mien* of men in his position. He was plainly attired, sitting in a log-cabin, busily writing on a small table, by a Kerosene lamp. . . . His conversation was easy and fluent, without the least effort or restraint." After talking for a while, Grant escorted them to the steamship *Mary Martin*, where he had arranged "comfortable quarters" for his three distinguished visitors. Though Grant was not authorized to discuss the peace mission itself, Stephens got the impression that he was very anxious for "the return of peace and harmony throughout the country."

Meanwhile, at Lincoln's request, Seward headed south to meet with the commissioners. "You will make known to them that three things are indispensable," Lincoln wrote: "The restoration of the national authority. . . . No receding, by the Executive of the United States on the Slavery question. . . . No cessation of hostilities short of an end of the war." If these three conditions were accepted, he was to tell them that all other propositions would be met with "a spirit of sincere liberality." After riding the train to Annapolis, Seward boarded Grant's flagship, the *River Queen*, and proceeded to Fort Monroe.

Before Seward could interview the commissioners, word reached Lincoln that President Davis had instructed them to negotiate peace for *two* countries. The president felt he had no choice but to recall Seward, until an urgent telegram from Grant changed his mind. Grant was "convinced," he had written to Stanton, after talking with the three men "that their intentions are good," and he believed that "their going back without any expression from any one in authority will have a bad influence." Given the complexity of the situation, Grant wished that the president could meet with them personally. "Induced by a despatch of Gen. Grant," Lincoln promptly telegraphed Seward and Grant, "Say to the gentlemen I will meet them personally at Fortress-Monroe, as soon as I can get there."

Accompanied by a single valet and an overnight bag, the president left Washington two hours later on a train headed to Annapolis. There, the steamer *Thomas Collyer*, "supposed to be the fastest in the world," stood ready to take him to Fort Monroe. "Upon getting out of the bay," noted a *Herald* correspondent who had boarded the vessel before the president arrived, "we encountered large fields of ice, through which we passed slowly." The steamer finally arrived at Fort Monroe a little past ten that evening, and Lincoln joined Seward on the *River Queen*.

The four-hour meeting, known as the Hampton Roads Conference, took place the next day in the saloon of the *River Queen*, which had been lashed to the *Mary Martin* the night before and "gaily decked out with a superabundance of streamers and flags." After everyone was introduced, Stephens opened the conversation with warm memories of his days as Lincoln's congressional colleague nearly two decades earlier. The president "responded in a cheerful and cordial manner," Stephens recalled, "as if the remembrance of those times . . . had awakened in him a train of agreeable reflections." They talked for several minutes of old acquaintances before Stephens asked, "Well, Mr. President, is there no way of putting an end to the present trouble, and bringing about a restoration of the general good feeling and harmony *then* existing between the different States and Sections of the country?"

The conversation that followed, Seward later wrote, "was altogether informal. There was no attendance of secretaries, clerks, or other witnesses. Nothing was written or read." The only other person who entered the room was the "steward, who came in occasionally to see if anything was wanted, and to bring in water, cigars, and other refreshments."

In reply to the question posed by Stephens, Lincoln attested that "there was but one way that he knew of, and that was, for those who were resisting the laws of the Union to cease that resistance." Stephens countered with the hope for a temporary solution that would integrate their respective armies to fight the French "until the passions on both sides might cool."

"I suppose you refer to something Mr. Blair has said," Lincoln replied. "Now it is proper to state at the beginning, that whatever he said was of his own accord. . . . The restoration of the Union is a *sine qua non* with me." There could be no substantive talk of an armistice or postponement until "the resistance ceased and the National Authority was recognized." Attempting to circumvent this declaration, Hunter recalled that Charles I of England had entered repeatedly into arrangements with his adversaries despite ongoing hostilities. "I do not profess to be posted in history," Lincoln answered. "On all such matters I will turn you over to Seward. All I distinctly recollect about the case of Charles I, is, that he lost his head in the end."

Judge Campbell then turned the conversation to the question of "how restoration was to take place, supposing that the Confederate States were consenting to it." This opened a discussion of slavery, which Seward addressed by reciting verbatim from Lincoln's annual address in which he had said that he would not "attempt to retract or modify the Emancipation Proclamation, nor . . . return to slavery any person who is free by the terms of that Proclamation." Moreover, Seward said, he felt obliged to inform the commissioners that Congress had just passed a constitutional amendment banning slavery throughout the entire United States.

They had clearly reached an impasse, but the conversation continued in an amicable tone. Lincoln let the commissioners know that "he would be willing to be taxed to remunerate the Southern people for their slaves." He was fairly confident "the people of the North" would sustain him with "an appropriation as high as Four Hundred Millions of Dollars for this purpose." On the question of some sort of postponement of hostilities prior to the end of the war, Lincoln was immovable. The conference drew to a close without agreement on any issue.

Before any outcome was made public, the radicals had worked themselves into "a fury of rage," certain that the president "was about to give up the political fruits which had been already gathered from the long and exhausting military struggle." Fearing Lincoln would turn his back on emancipation, Thaddeus Stevens excoriated him on the floor of the House. In the Senate, "the leading members of the Committee on the Conduct of the War" roundly castigated the very idea of the conference, predicting that "we shall be sold out, and that the Peace we shall obtain, if any we do, will dishonor us." Both branches passed a resolution calling for a full report on the proceedings. Even Stanton worried that the president's kindheartedness "might lead him to make some admission which the astute Southerners would wilfully misconstrue and twist to serve their purpose."

Lincoln's report on the conference, complete with the telegrams and documents preceding it, was "read amidst a breathless silence in the hall, every member being in his seat. A low gush of satisfaction broke out when the phrase 'one common country' was read in the Blair letter, and an involuntary burst followed the annunciation of the three conditions of peace, given to Seward." Noah Brooks observed that "as the reading of the message and documents went on, the change which took place in the moral atmosphere of the hall of the House was obvious. The appearance of grave intentness passed away, and members smilingly exchanged glances as they began to appreciate Lincoln's sagacious plan for unmasking the craftiness of the rebel leaders." When the presentation was done, "there was an instant and irrepressible storm of applause . . . it was like a burst of refreshing rain after a long and heartbreaking drought." Representatives vied with one another to praise the president. Even Thaddeus Stevens "paid a high tribute to the sagacity, wisdom, and patriotism of President Lincoln."

"Indeed," *Harper's Weekly* observed, "nothing but the foolish assumption of four years ago, that Mr. Lincoln was unfit for his office," could explain the fatuous predictions that he would "flinch and falter" before the Southern delegates. "If there is any man in the country who comprehends the scope of the war more fully than the President, who is he? . . . We venture to say that there is no man in our history who has shown a more felicitous combination of temperament, conviction, and ability to grapple with a complication like that in which this country is involved than Abraham Lincoln."

Jefferson Davis pragmatically employed the failed conference to incite greater effort on the battlefield, pledging that "he would be willing to yield up everything he had on earth" before acceding to Northern demands. He predicted that before another year had passed, the South would be able to secure peace on its own terms, with separation and slavery intact. "I can have no 'common country' with the Yankees," he announced. "My life is bound up in the Confederacy; and, if any man supposes that, under any circumstances, I can be an agent of reconstruction of the Union, he has mistaken every element of my nature!"

Still, Lincoln did not relinquish hope that he might somehow bring the war to an honorable end before tens of thousands more young men had to die. Following his Hampton Roads suggestion of compensated emancipation, he drafted a proposal that Congress empower him "to pay four hundred millions of dollars" to the Southern states, distributed according to "their respective slave populations." The first half would be paid if "all resistance to the national authority" came to an end by April 1; the second half would be allocated if the Thirteenth Amendment were ratified by July 1. At that point, with the armed rebellion at an end, the Union restored, and slavery eradicated, "all political offences will be pardoned" and "all property, except slaves, liable to confiscation or forfeiture, will be released." Furthermore, "liberality will be recommended to congress upon all points not lying within executive control."

The proposition met with unanimous disapproval from the cabinet, all of whom were present except Seward. "The earnest desire of the President to conciliate and effect peace was manifest," Welles recorded, "but there may be such a thing as so overdoing as to cause a distrust or adverse feeling." Usher believed that the radicals in Congress "would make it the occasion of a violent assault on the President." Stanton had long maintained that it was unnecessary and wasteful to talk about compensation for slaves already freed by the Emancipation Proclamation. Fessenden declared "that the only way to effectually end the war was by force of arms, and that until the war was thus ended no proposition to pay money would come from us."

Lincoln pointed out that the sum he proposed was simply the cost of continuing the war for another one or two hundred days, "to say nothing of the lives lost and property destroyed." Still, the cabinet was adamant. "You are all against me," Lincoln said, his voice filled with sadness. "His heart was so fully enlisted in behalf of such a plan that he would have followed it if only a single member of his Cabinet had supported him," Usher thought. Had Seward been there, Usher mused, "he would probably have approved the measure." Without a trace of support among his colleagues at the table, Lincoln felt compelled to forsake his proposition, which, in any event, as Jefferson Davis had made clear, was unacceptable to the Confederacy. So the war would continue until the South capitulated.

• • •

MEANWHILE, THE WAR FRONT continued to generate good news for the Union. After capturing Savannah, Sherman had headed north to Columbia, reaching the state capital of South Carolina on February 17. Columbia's fall led to the evacuation of Charleston. Stanton ordered "a national salute" fired from "every fort arsenal and army headquarters of the United States, in honor of the restoration of the flag of the Union upon Fort Sumter." In Washington, the *National Republican* noted, "the flash and smoke were visible from the tops of buildings on the avenue, and the thunder of the guns was heard in all parts of the city." That evening, Lincoln was in "cheerful" spirits as he relaxed with Seward, Welles, and General Hooker in his office. "General H. thinks it the brightest day in four years," Welles recorded in his diary.

The following day, however, Browning found Lincoln "more depressed" than he had seen him in the four years of his presidency. His low spirits were probably caused by the pending execution of John Yates Beall, a former Confederate captain who had been tried and found guilty as a spy. In the fall of 1864, when Confederate agents based in Canada were pursuing plots to disrupt the draft and influence the elections, Beall had led a team of raiders in a daring and elaborate scheme to commandeer Union ships in the Great Lakes area, destroy railroad lines, and liberate Confederate prisoners in Ohio. The commander of the army in New York State, General John A. Dix, was unyielding in his belief that Beall must be executed as an example to others.

But Beall came from a prominent Virginia family, and a wide array of supporters petitioned Lincoln for clemency, including Orville Browning, Monty Blair, eight dozen congressmen, and six United States senators. They argued that Beall was acting as a commissioned officer in the Confederate army and should not be treated as "a robber, brigand, and pirate." The case troubled Lincoln greatly, but he felt compelled to support General Dix. "I had to stand firm," he told an acquaintance a few weeks later, "and I even had to turn away his poor sister when she came and begged for his life, and let him be executed, and he was executed, and I can't get the distress out of my mind yet."

The week before his second inaugural on March 4, Lincoln announced that he would "not receive callers (except members of the Cabinet) for any purpose whatever, between the hours of three and seven o'clock p.m." He needed solitude to work on his inaugural speech. "The hopeful condition of the Union cause" had brought thousands of visitors to Washington, the *National Republican* reported. They were anxious not only to partake of the inaugural revelries but to share in the general elation that pervaded the capital. The city was so overcrowded that the parlors of all the leading hotels "were occupied by ladies and gentlemen, sitting up all night because no beds could be found for them."

Frederick Douglass decided to join "in the grand procession of citizens from all parts of the country." Blacks had been excluded from previous inaugural festivities, but with soldiers of both races "mingling their blood," it seemed to him that "it was not too great an assumption for a colored man to offer his congratulations to the President with those of other citizens." The evening before the inauguration, he visited Chase's Sixth Street home. There, he later recalled, he helped Kate "in placing over her honored father's shoulders the new robe then being made in which he was to administer the oath to the reelected President." As he looked at the new Chief Justice, Douglass recollected the "early anti-slavery days" of their first acquaintance. Chase had "welcomed [him] to his home and his table when to do so was a strange thing."

The steady rain on the morning of March 4 did not dampen the spirits of the estimated fifty thousand citizens gathered at the Capitol to witness the inauguration. Invited guests poured into the Senate chamber for the first part of the ceremony, which included a farewell address by the outgoing vice president, Hannibal Hamlin, and the swearing in of Andrew Johnson. Shortly before noon, a stir in the galleries revealed the arrival of the "notables"—generals, governors, the justices of the Supreme Court, the cabinet members, led by Seward, and finally, the president himself, whose chair was positioned in the middle of the front row. Mary Lincoln was seated in the Diplomatic Gallery, surrounded by members of the foreign ministries. "One ambassador was so stiff with gold lace," Noah Brooks observed, "that he could not sit down except with great difficulty and had to unbutton before he could get his feet on the floor."

After Hamlin delivered a graceful farewell address, Andrew Johnson rose to take the oath. His face was "extraordinarily red," his balance precarious. He appeared to observers to be "in a state of manifest intoxication." For twenty long minutes, he spoke incoherently, repeatedly declaring his plebeian background and his pride that such a humble man "could rise from the ranks, under the Constitution, to the proud position of the second place in the gift of the people." Pivoting to face the Supreme Court justices, he reminded them that they also derived their "power from the people." Then he spoke to the members of the cabinet, insisting they, too, were "creature[s]" of the people. He addressed each secretary by name—Mr. Seward, Mr. Stanton, and down the ranks—until he reached Gideon Welles, whose name he could not remember. Seemingly nonplused, he turned to someone near him and loudly inquired, "What's the name of the Secretary of the Navy?" Continuing his tirade, he ignored Hamlin's pointed reminder that "the hour for the inauguration ceremony had passed."

The crowd stirred uneasily, and the men on the dais tried with varying success to conceal their dismay. "Stanton looked like a petrified man," Noah Brooks observed. "All this is in wretched bad taste," Speed whispered to Welles. "The man is certainly deranged." Welles whispered to Stanton that "Johnson is either drunk or crazy." Dennison, the new postmaster general, "was red and white by turns," while Justice Samuel Nelson's jaw "dropped clean down in blank horror." Seward and Lincoln alone appeared unruffled. Seward remained as "serene as summer," charitably suggesting to Welles that Johnson's performance was a by-product of "emotion on returning and revisiting the Senate." Lincoln listened in silence, "patiently waiting" for the harangue to end, his eyes shut so that no one could discern his discomfort. "You need not be scared," he said a few days later; Johnson had "made a bad slip" but was not "a drunkard."

When Johnson finished at last, the audience proceeded outside to the east front of the Capitol for the inaugural ceremony. As the president appeared on the platform, observed Noah Brooks, "the sun, which had been obscured all day, burst forth in its unclouded meridian splendor and flooded the spectacle with glory and light." It seemed to many, including the superstitious Lincoln, an auspicious omen, as did the appearance of the newly completed Capitol dome, topped with the statue of Freedom.

If the spirited crowd expected a speech exalting recent Union victories, they were disappointed. In keeping with his lifelong tendency to consider all sides of a troubled situation, Lincoln urged a more sympathetic understanding of the nation's alienated citizens in the South. There were no unbridgeable differences, he insisted: "Both read the same Bible, and pray to the same God; and each invokes His aid against the other. It may seem strange that any men should dare to ask a just God's assistance in wringing their bread from the sweat of other men's faces; but let us judge not that we be not judged. The prayers of both could not be answered; that of neither has been answered fully. The Almighty has His own purposes."

In his Springfield speech a decade earlier, Lincoln had maintained that he could not condemn the South for an inability to end slavery when he himself knew of no easy solution. Now the president suggested that God had given "to both North and South, this terrible war" as punishment for their shared sin of slavery. Speaking with "the eloquence of the prophets," he continued, "Fondly do we hope—fervently do we pray—that this mighty scourge of war may speedily pass away. Yet, if God wills that it continue, until all the wealth piled by the bond-man's two hundred and fifty years of unrequited toil shall be sunk, and until every drop of blood drawn with the lash, shall be paid by another drawn with the sword, as was said three thousand years ago, so still it must be said 'the judgments of the Lord, are true and righteous altogether.' "

Drawing upon the rare wisdom of a temperament that consistently displayed uncommon magnanimity toward those who opposed him, he then issued his historic plea to his fellow countrymen: "With malice toward none; with charity for all; with firmness in the right, as God gives us to see the right, let us strive on to finish the work we are in; to bind up the nation's wounds; to care for him who shall have borne the battle, and for his widow, and his orphan—to do all which may achieve and cherish a just, and a lasting peace, among ourselves, and with all nations."

More than any of his other speeches, the Second Inaugural fused spiritual faith with politics. While Lincoln might have questioned the higher force that shaped human ends, "as he became involved in matters of the gravest importance," his friend Leonard Swett observed, "a feeling of religious reverence, and belief in God—his justice and overruling power—increased upon him." If his devotion were determined by his lack of "faith in ceremonials and forms," or by his failure "to observe the Sabath very scrupulously," Swett added, "he would fall far short of the standard." However, if he were judged "by the higher rule of purity of conduct, of honesty of motive, of unyielding fidelity to the right," or by his powerful belief "in the great laws of truth, the rigid discharge of duty, his accountability to God," then he was undoubtedly "full of natural religion," for "he believed in God as much as the most approved Church member."

His address completed, the president turned to Chief Justice Salmon Chase, who administered the oath of office. The crowd cheered loudly, the artillery fired a round of salutes, the band played, and the peaceful ceremony drew to a close.

That evening the gates of the White House were opened for a public reception attended by "the largest crowd that has been here yet," according to Nicolay. The president was reported to be "in excellent spirits" as he tirelessly shook the hands of the more than five thousand people who came to show their respect and affection. "It was a grand ovation of *the People* to their President," Commissioner French observed, and Mary vowed "to remain till morning, rather than have the door closed on a single visitor." French estimated that Lincoln shook hands "at the rate of 100 every 4 minutes."

Frederick Douglass would always remember the events of that evening. "On reaching the door, two policemen stationed there took me rudely by the arm and ordered me to stand back, for their directions were to admit no persons of my color." Douglass assured the officers "there must be some mistake, for no such order could have emanated from President Lincoln; and that if he knew I was at the door he would desire my admission." His assumption was later confirmed when he discovered there were "no orders from Mr. Lincoln, or from any one else. They were simply complying with an old custom." The impasse continued for a few moments, until Douglass recognized a gentleman going in and asked him to tell the president that he was unable to gain entry. Minutes later, the word came back to admit Douglass. "I walked into the spacious East Room, amid a scene of elegance such as in this country I had never before witnessed."

Douglass had no difficulty spotting Lincoln, who stood "like a mountain pine high above the others," he recalled, "in his grand simplicity, and home-like beauty. Recognizing me, even before I reached him, he exclaimed, so that all around could hear him, 'Here comes my friend Douglass.' Taking me by the hand, he said, 'I am glad to see you. I saw you in the crowd to-day, listening to my inaugural address; how did you like it?' " Douglass was embarrassed to detain the president in conversation when there were "thousands waiting to shake hands," but Lincoln insisted. "You must stop a little, Douglass; there is no man in the country whose opinion I value more than yours. I want to know what you think of it?"

For a moment these two remarkable men stood together amid the sea of faces. Lincoln knew that Douglass would speak his mind, just as he always had. "Mr. Lincoln," Douglass said finally, "that was a sacred effort." Lincoln's face lit up with delight. "I am glad you liked it!" he replied.

A few days later, Lincoln provided his own assessment to Thurlow Weed, predicting that the address would "wear as well as—perhaps better than—any thing" he had written, though he did not believe it would be "immediately popular. Men are not flattered by being shown that there has been a difference of purpose between the Almighty and them." Just as Lincoln surmised, the speech drew criticism from several quarters. The Democratic *New York World* faulted Lincoln for his "substitution of religion for statesmanship," while the *Tribune* charged that the stern biblical overtones would impede any chance for peace.

Many others, however, recognized the historic weight of the address.

"That rail-splitting lawyer is one of the wonders of the day," Charles Francis Adams, Jr., wrote to his father in London. "The inaugural strikes me in its grand simplicity and directness as being for all time the historical keynote of this war." The London *Spectator*, previously critical of Lincoln, agreed with young Adams, judging the address as "by far the noblest which any American President has yet uttered to an American Congress."

Praise for the speech mingled with praise for Lincoln himself. The *Spectator* suggested that it was "divine inspiration, or providence" that brought the Republican Convention in 1860 to choose Lincoln the "village lawyer" over Seward. Congressman Isaac Arnold overheard a conversation between a celebrated minister and an unidentified New York statesman, who one historian suggests was likely William Henry Seward himself. "The President's inaugural is the finest state paper in all history," the minister declared. "Yes," the New Yorker answered, "and as Washington's name grows brighter with time, so it will be with Lincoln's. A century from to-day that inaugural will be read as one of the most sublime utterances ever spoken by man. Washington is the great man of the era of the Revolution. So will Lincoln be of this, but Lincoln will reach the higher position in history."

Perhaps the most surprising contemporaneous evaluation of Lincoln's leadership appeared in the extreme secessionist paper the *Charleston Mercury*. "He has called around him in counsel," the *Mercury* marveled, "the ablest and most earnest men of his country. Where he has lacked in individual ability, learning, experience or statesmanship, he has sought it, and found it. . . . Force, energy, brains, earnestness, he has collected around him in every department." Were he not a "blackguard" and "an unscrupulous knave in the end," the *Mercury* concluded, "he would undoubtedly command our respect as a ruler. . . . We turn our eyes to Richmond, and the contrast is appalling, sickening to the heart."

The editors of the *Mercury* would have been even more astonished if they had an inkling of the truth recognized by those closer to Lincoln: his political genius was not simply his ability to gather the best men of the country around him, but to impress upon them his own purpose, perception, and resolution at every juncture. With respect to Lincoln's cabinet, Charles Dana observed, "it was always plain that he was the master and they were the subordinates. They constantly had to yield to his will, and if he ever yielded to them it was because they convinced him that the course they advised was judicious and appropriate."

CHAPTER 26

THE FINAL WEEKS

As Lincoln began his second term, "he was in mind, body, and nerves a very different man," John Hay observed, "from the one who had taken the oath in 1861. He continued always the same kindly, genial, and cordial spirit he had been at first; but the boisterous laughter became less frequent year by year; the eye grew veiled by constant meditation on momentous subjects; the air of reserve and detachment from his surroundings increased."

Four years of relentless strain had touched Lincoln's spirit and his countenance. The aged, wearied face in the life-mask cast by Clark Mills in the spring of 1865 barely resembled the mold Leonard Volk had taken five years earlier. In 1860, noted John Hay, "the large mobile mouth is ready to speak, to shout, or laugh; the bold, curved nose is broad and substantial, with spreading nostrils; it is a face full of life, of energy, of vivid aspiration." The second life-mask, with its lined brow and cavernous cheeks, has "a look as of one on whom sorrow and care had done their worst . . . the whole expression is of unspeakable sadness and all-sufficing strength."

That inner strength had sustained Lincoln all his life. But his four years as president had immeasurably enhanced his self-confidence. Despite the appalling pressures he had faced from his very first day in office, he had never lost faith in himself. In fact, he was the one who had sustained the spirits of those around him time and again, gently guiding his colleagues with good humor, energy, and steady purpose. He had learned from early mistakes, transcended the jealousy of rivals, and his insight into men and events had deepened with each passing year. Though "a tired spot" remained within that no rest or relaxation could restore, he was ready for the arduous tasks of the next four years.

Settling into his daily routine after the inauguration, Lincoln was determined to avoid the thousands of office seekers who again descended "like Egyptian locusts" upon Washington. "The bare thought of going through again what I did the first year here, would *crush* me," he confessed. In the first months of his presidency, he had been disparaged for allowing office seekers to accost him at all hours, consuming his energy and disrupting his concentration. Nicolay and Hay had tried to get him to be more methodical, to close his door to outsiders for longer periods, but at the time he had insisted that "they don't want much; they get but little, and I must see them." Experience had finally taught him that he must set priorities and concentrate on the vital questions of war and Reconstruction confronting his administration. "I think now that I will not remove a single man, except for delinquency," he told New Hampshire senator Clark. "To remove a man is very easy," he commented to another visitor, "but when I go to fill his place, there are *twenty* applicants, and of these I must make *nineteen* enemies."

With two classes of office seekers, however, he was prepared to take a personal interest—artists and disabled veterans. He expressed to Seward his hope that consul positions could be offered to "facilitate artists a little [in] their profession," mentioning in particular a poet and a sculptor he wished to help. To General Scott, who was working with the Sanitary Commission to find government jobs for disabled veterans, Lincoln emphasized that the Commission should "at all times be ready to recognize the paramount claims of the soldiers of the nation, in the disposition of public trusts."

With his cabinet, he was satisfied. The only change he made after the inauguration was to replace treasury secretary William Pitt Fessenden with the banker Hugh McCulloch. When he had assumed the post the previous summer, Fessenden had been assured that he could leave once the finances of the country were in good shape. By the spring of 1865, the Treasury was stable, and when Maine reelected him to the Senate for a term to begin on March 4, Fessenden felt free to resign.

Lincoln was sorry to lose his brilliant, hardworking secretary. Fessenden, too, "parted from the President with regret." During his tenure at the Treasury, his initial critical attitude toward Lincoln had been transformed into warm admiration. "I desire gratefully to acknowledge the kindness and consideration with which you have invariably treated me," he wrote to the president, "and to assure you that in retiring I carry with me great and increased respect for your personal character and for the ability which has marked your administration." Noting that the "prolonged struggle for national life" was finally nearing a successful conclusion, he went on, "no one can claim to have so largely contributed as the chosen chief magistrate of this great people."

Hugh McCulloch was entirely familiar with Treasury operations, having served as comptroller of the currency. When Lincoln first approached him, however, he was nervous about accepting the position. "I should be glad to comply with your wishes," he told Lincoln, "if I did not distrust my ability to do what will be required of the Secretary of the Treasury." Lincoln cheerfully replied, "I will be responsible for that, and so I reckon we will consider the matter settled." McCulloch would remain at his post for four years and was "never sorry" that he had acceded to Lincoln's wishes. The only other cabinet change Lincoln anticipated was in the Department of the Interior, where, in several months' time, he intended to replace Usher with Senator James Harlan of Iowa.

The time had also come for John Nicolay and John Hay to move on. The two secretaries had served Lincoln exceptionally well, introducing a systematic order into the president's vast correspondence and drafting replies to the great majority of letters he received. In their small offices on the second floor of the White House, they had served as gatekeepers, tactfully holding back the crush of senators, congressmen, generals, diplomats, and office seekers endeavoring to gain access to the president. John Hay was particularly adept at keeping the throngs entertained. "No one could be in his presence, even for a few moments," Hay's college roommate recalled, "without falling under the spell which his conversation and companionship invariably cast upon all who came within his influence."

Lincoln had increased their responsibilities with each passing year. In 1864, Nicolay functioned as the "unofficial manager of Lincoln's reelection campaign" and was dispatched as his personal emissary to ease tensions in Missouri and New York. Hay was chosen to accompany Greeley to

Canada, to carry sensitive messages back and forth to Capitol Hill, and to enroll Confederate voters under Lincoln's plan for the reconstruction of Florida.

More essential to Lincoln than the duties they so faithfully discharged was the camaraderie the young assistants provided him. They were part of his family, like sons during the troubled days and nights of his first term. They would listen spellbound when he recited Shakespeare or told another tale from his endless store. Throughout their years in the White House, they offered Lincoln conversation, undivided loyalty, and love. They were awake late at night when he could not sleep, up early in the morning to share the latest news, offering the lonely president round-the-clock companionship.

At the outset, Hay had been dumbfounded by the haphazard administrative style of the man he nicknamed "the Ancient" or "the Tycoon." Something of an intellectual snob, the young college graduate had betrayed early on a hint of condescension toward his self-taught boss. Proximity to the president soon altered his opinion. He had come to believe by 1863 that "the hand of God" had put the prairie lawyer in the White House. If the "patent leather kid glove set" did not yet appreciate this giant of a man, it was because they "know no more of him than an owl does of a comet, blazing into his blinking eyes."

By the spring of 1865, Nicolay, soon to marry Therena Bates, was contemplating the purchase of a newspaper in Washington or Baltimore, while Hay wanted time for his studies and his active social life, too long constrained by fourteen-hour workdays. While they would both miss Lincoln, they were glad to escape the constant struggles with Mary—the "Hellcat," as they irreverently called her—who still resented their claims on her husband's attention. Indeed, soon after Lincoln's reelection, Mary had enlisted the help of Dr. Anson Henry in an effort to replace Nicolay with the journalist Noah Brooks. Nicolay had apparently tried to talk with Lincoln about his problems with Mary, but the president had refused any such discussion.

Seward found worthy alternatives for both Nicolay and Hay. When the consulate in Paris opened up in March, he recommended Nicolay for the job. The president agreed, understanding the significance of the opportunity for his loyal assistant. "So important an appointment has rarely been conferred on one so young," the *National Republican* commented when the Senate confirmed Nicolay without a dissenting vote. Nicolay was thrilled. The position paid five thousand dollars a year, allowing him to start married life on solid ground.

Once Nicolay was confirmed, Seward turned his attentions to Hay, with whom he had become especially close over the years. Many nights Hay had wandered over to Seward's house, where he was certain to find a good meal, vivid conversation, and a warm welcome. Moreover, in watching Seward and Lincoln together, Hay had recognized that the secretary of state had been the first cabinet member to recognize Lincoln's "personal preeminence."

In mid-March, Seward arranged for Hay to receive an appointment as secretary of the legation in Paris. "It was entirely unsolicited and unexpected," Hay told his brother Charles. "It is a pleasant and honorable way of leaving my present post which I should have left in any event very soon." He had thought of returning to Warsaw, Illinois, but Paris, France, was far more exciting. Hay planned to stay at the White House for another month or so, until arrangements were completed for Noah Brooks to assume his duties. Then he and Nicolay would sail for Europe to begin their new adventures. "It will be exceedingly pleasant," Nicolay said, "for both of us, to be there at the same time."

Spring seemed to revive the spirits of Mary Lincoln, who invariably sank into depression each February, with the anniversary of Willie's death. "We are having charming weather," she wrote to her friend Abram Wakeman on March 20. "We went to the Opera on Saturday eve; Mr Sumner accompanied us—we had a very gay little time. Mr S when he throws off his heavy manner, as he often does, can make himself very very agreeable. Last evening, he again joined our little coterie & tomorrow eve,—we all go again to hear 'Robin Adair,' sung in 'La Dame Blanche' by Habelmann. This is always the pleasant time to me in W. springtime, some few of the most pleasant Senators families remain until June, & all ceremony, with each other is laid aside." A few days later, she wrote a note to Sumner, telling him that she would be sending along a copy of Louis Napoleon's manuscript on Julius Caesar, which she had just received from the State Department and knew he would want to read. "In the coming summer," she promised, "I shall peruse it myself, for I have so sadly neglected the little French, I fancied so familiar to me."

Like his mother, Tad Lincoln possessed "an emotional temperament much like an April day, sunning all over with laughter one moment, the next crying as though [his] heart would break." The painter Francis Carpenter recounted an incident when photographers from Brady's studio set up their equipment in an unoccupied room that Tad had turned into a little theater. Taking "great offence at the occupation of his room without his consent," Tad locked the door and hid the key, preventing the photographers from retrieving their chemicals and supplies. Carpenter pleaded with Tad to unlock the door, but he refused. Finally, the president had to intervene. He left his office and returned a few minutes later with the key. Though Tad "was violently excited when I went to him," Lincoln told Carpenter, "I said, 'Tad, do you know you are making your father a great deal of trouble?' He burst into tears, instantly giving me up the key."

Most of the time, however, Tad was "so full of life and vigor," recalled John Hay, "so bubbling over with health and high spirits, that he kept the house alive with his pranks and his fantastic enterprises." From dawn to dusk, "you could hear his shrill pipe resounding through the dreary corridors of the Executive residence . . . and when the President laid down his weary pen toward midnight, he generally found his infant goblin asleep under his table or roasting his curly head by the open fire-place; and the tall chief would pick up the child and trudge off to bed with the drowsy little burden on his shoulder, stooping under the doors and dodging the chandeliers."

Though Tad never developed a love of books, and "felt he could not waste time in learning to spell," he had a clever, intuitive mind and was a good judge of character. "He treated flatterers and office-seekers with a curious coolness and contempt," marveled Hay, "but he often espoused the cause of some poor widow or tattered soldier, whom he found waiting in the ante-rooms." His enterprising nature and natural shrewdness would augur well for him once his schooling was completed. With all his heart, Lincoln loved his "little sprite."

• • •

IN LATE MARCH, Lincoln, Mary, and Tad journeyed to City Point to visit General Grant. For Lincoln, the eighteen-day sojourn was his longest break from Washington in four years. Grant had issued the invitation at the suggestion of his wife, Julia, who had been struck by constant newspaper reports of "the exhausted appearance of the President." Grant worried at first about the propriety of issuing an invitation when the president could visit without waiting "to be asked," but on March 20, he wrote a note to Lincoln: "Can you not visit City Point for a day or two? I would like very much to see you and I think the rest would do you good."

Delighted with the idea, Lincoln asked the Navy Department to make arrangements for a ship to carry him south. Assistant Secretary Fox was not happy to be assigned the task, for he believed "the President was incurring great risk in making the journey." To minimize danger, he ordered John Barnes, commander of the *Bat*, a fast-moving gunboat, to report to the Washington Navy Yard at once. Work immediately commenced on the interior of the armed ship to make alterations necessary "to insure the personal comfort of the President as long as he desired to make the *Bat* his home." To discuss the meals and amenities Lincoln might require, Fox brought Barnes to the White House. Lincoln told Barnes "he wanted no luxuries but only plain, simple food and ordinary comfort—that what was good for me would be good enough for him." Barnes returned to the Navy Yard to supervise the changes.

The next morning, Lincoln summoned Barnes back to the White House. Embarrassed at the thought that workers had stayed up all night to make alterations that might now require additional work, Lincoln explained apologetically that "Mrs. Lincoln had decided that she would accompany him to City Point, and could the *Bat* accommodate her and her maid servant." Barnes was, "in sailor's phrase, taken 'all aback,' " knowing that the austere gunboat "was in no respect adapted to the private life of womankind, nor could she be made so." He returned to the Navy Yard, where "the alterations to the *Bat* were stopped and the steamer *River Queen* was chartered." The change of plans was particularly upsetting to Fox, who "expressed great regret that the determination of Mrs. Lincoln to accompany the President" had forced the shift to "an unarmed, fragile, river-boat, so easily assailed and so vulnerable." He directed Barnes to follow Lincoln's steamer in the *Bat*, but still could not shake his anxiety. Though aware of the danger, Lincoln remained relaxed and cheerful, talking about the problems of accommodating womenfolk at sea "in very funny terms."

The presidential party, which included army captain Charles B. Penrose, Tad and Mary Lincoln, Mary's maid, and Lincoln's bodyguard, W. H. Crook, departed from the Arsenal Wharf at Sixth Street at 1 p.m. on Thursday, March 23. Stanton had been laid up for several days, but against Ellen's advice, he took a carriage to see Lincoln off, arriving minutes after the *River Queen*'s departure. Anxious about the president's safety, Stanton panicked an hour later when "a hurricane swept over the city." The "terrific squalls of winds, accompanied by thunder and lightning, did considerable damage here," the *Herald*'s Washington correspondent reported. "The roof of a factory on Sixth street was blown off into the street and fell upon a hack, crushing the horses and its driver." In some neighborhoods, trees were felled and houses destroyed, "while down the river the steamboats and sailing craft were dashed about with great violence." Leaving his bed once again, Stanton went to the War Department and telegraphed Lincoln at 8:45 p.m. "I hope you have reached Point Lookout safely notwithstanding the furious gale that came on soon after you started. . . . Please let me hear from you at Point Lookout."

Lincoln, meanwhile, was enjoying himself immensely. While Tad raced around the ship, investigating every nook and befriending members of the crew, Lincoln remained on deck, watching "the city until he could see it no more." Once inside, he listened with relish to the adventures of the *River Queen*'s captain, who had chased blockade runners early in the war. "It was nearly midnight when he went to bed," Crook recalled.

Crook, who shared a stateroom with Tad, was "startled out of a sound sleep" by Mary Lincoln. "It is growing colder," she explained, "and I came in to see if my little boy has covers enough on him." Later that night, Crook was awakened by the steamer passing through rough waters, which felt as if it were "slowly climbing up one side of a hill and then rushing down the other." The next morning, still feeling seasick, Crook noted that the turbulent passage had apparently not disturbed Lincoln. On the contrary, the president looked rested, claimed to be "feeling splendidly," and did "full justice to the delicious fish" served at breakfast.

Mary would nostalgically recall her husband's fine humor during this last trip to City Point. "Feeling *so encouraged*" the war "was near its close," and relieved from the daily burdens of his office, "he freely gave vent to his cheerfulness," to such an extent that "he was almost boyish, in his mirth & reminded me, of his original nature, what I had always remembered of him, in our own home—free from care, surrounded by those he loved so well."

Crook recalled that "it was after dark on the 24th" when the *River Queen* reached City Point. He would long remember the beauty of the scene that stretched before him, "the many-colored lights of the boats in the harbor and the lights of the town straggling up the high bluffs of the shore, crowned by the lights from Grant's headquarters at the top."

Newly minted captain Robert Lincoln escorted General and Mrs. Grant to call on the president shortly after he arrived. "Our gracious President met us at the gangplank," Julia Grant recalled, "greeted the General most heartily, and, giving me his arm, conducted us to where Mrs. Lincoln was awaiting." Leaving the two women together, the men went into the president's room for a short consultation, "at the end of which," reported Crook, "Mr. Lincoln appeared particularly happy," reassured by Grant's estimation that the conflict was nearing an end. After the Grants left, Lincoln and Mary, appearing "in very good spirits," talked late into the night.

While the Lincolns were breakfasting the next day on the lower deck, Robert came by to report that the review planned for that morning would have to be postponed. Rebels had initiated an attack on Fort Stedman, only eight miles away. With Grant and Sherman closing in upon him, Lee had decided to abandon Petersburg and move his army south to North Carolina, hoping to join General Joseph Johnston and prevent Sherman from joining Grant. Abandoning Petersburg meant losing Richmond, but it was the only way to save his army. The attack on Fort Stedman, intended to open an escape route, took the Federals by surprise. Nonetheless, within hours, Grant's men succeeded in retaking the fort and restoring the original line.

After breakfast, Lincoln walked up the bluff to Grant's headquarters, where plans were made for a visit to the front. As the presidential party passed by the battle sites, it became clear that the engagement had been more serious than first realized. "The ground immediately about us was still strewn with dead and wounded men," recalled Barnes. The Confederates had suffered nearly five thousand casualties; the Federals over two thousand. Burial parties were already at work as ambulances transported the wounded to the hospital and surgeons attended those still lying in the field. When a long line of captured Confederate soldiers passed by, "Lincoln remarked upon their sad and unhappy condition . . . his whole face showing sympathetic feeling for the suffering about him." On the return trip, he commented "that he had seen enough of the horrors of war, that he hoped this was the beginning of the end, and that there would be no more bloodshed or ruin of homes."

"I am here within five miles of the scene of this morning's action," Lincoln telegraphed Stanton from Meade's headquarters in the field. "I have seen the prisoners myself and they look like there might be the number Meade states—1600." Unsettled by Lincoln's proximity to the front, Stanton replied, "I hope you will remember Gen. Harrison's advice to his men at Tippecanoe, that they 'can see as well a little further off.' " But for the soldiers in the field who greeted him with heartfelt cheers, Lincoln's presence at the scene revealed that "he was not afraid to show himself among them, and willing to share their dangers here, as often, far away, he had shared the joy of their triumphs."

Seated at the campfire that night, Lincoln seemed to Horace Porter much more "grave and his language much more serious than usual." Undoubtedly, the grisly images of the dead and wounded were not easily dismissed. As the night wore on, the president rallied and "entertained the general-in-chief and several members of the staff by talking in a most interesting manner about public affairs, and illustrating the subjects mentioned with his incomparable anecdotes." Toward the end of the evening, Grant asked, "Mr. President, did you at any time doubt the final success of the cause?" "Never for a moment," Lincoln replied.

Grant then turned the conversation to the *Trent* affair. According to Grant, Seward had given "a very interesting account" of the tangled questions involved during his visit the previous summer. " 'Yes,' said the President; 'Seward studied up all the works ever written on international law, and came to cabinet meetings loaded to the muzzle with the subject. We gave due consideration to the case, but at that critical period of the war it was soon decided to deliver up the prisoners. It was a pretty bitter pill to swallow, but I contented myself with believing that England's triumph in the matter would be short-lived, and that after ending our war successfully we would be so powerful that we could call her to account for all the embarrassments she had inflicted upon us."

Lincoln continued, "I felt a good deal like the sick man in Illinois who was told he probably had n't many days longer to live, and he ought to make his peace with any enemies he might have. He said the man he hated worst of all was a fellow named Brown, in the next village. . . . So Brown was sent for, and when he came the sick man began to say, in a voice as meek as Moses's, that he wanted to die at peace with all his fellow-creatures, and he hoped he and Brown could now shake hands and bury all their enmity. The scene was becoming altogether too pathetic for Brown, who had to get out his handkerchief and wipe the gathering tears from his eyes. . . . After a parting that would have softened the heart of a grindstone, Brown had about reached the room door when the sick man rose up on his elbow and called out to him: 'But see here, Brown; if I should happen to get well, mind, that old grudge stands.' So I thought that if this nation should happen to get well we might want that old grudge against England to stand." Everyone laughed heartily, and the pleasant evening drew to a close.

On Sunday morning, the *River Queen* carried the presidential party downriver to where Admiral Porter's naval flotilla awaited them, "ranged in double line, dressed with flags, the crews on deck cheering." As each vessel passed by, reported Barnes, Lincoln "waved his high hat as if saluting old friends in his native town, and seemed as happy as a schoolboy." After lunch aboard Porter's flagship, the *River Queen* sailed to Aiken's Landing. There, arrangements were made for Lincoln to ride on horseback with Grant to General Ord's encampment four miles away while Mary Lincoln and Julia Grant followed in an ambulance. "The President was in high spirits," observed Barnes, "laughing and chatting first to General Grant and then to General Ord as they rode forward through the woods and over the swamps." Reaching the parade ground ahead of the ladies, they decided to begin the review without them, since the troops had been waiting for hours and had missed their midday meal. General Ord's wife, Mary, asked if "it was proper for her to accompany the cavalcade" without Mrs. Lincoln and Mrs. Grant. "Of course," she was told. "Come along!"

Meanwhile, the ambulance carrying the women had encountered great discomfort due to the corduroyed road, which jounced them into the air each time a log was struck. Concerned that the agonizingly slow pace would make them late for the review, Mary ordered the driver to go faster. This only made things worse, for the first "jolt lifted the party clear off the seats," striking their heads on the top of the wagon. Mary "now insisted on getting out and walking," recalled Horace Porter, who had been assigned to escort the ladies, "but as the mud was nearly hub-deep, Mrs. Grant and I persuaded her that we had better stick to the wagon as our only ark of refuge."

When Mary finally reached the parade grounds and saw the attractive Mrs. Ord riding beside her husband in the place of honor that should have been her own, she erupted in an embarrassing tirade against Mrs. Ord, calling her "vile names in the presence of a crowd of officers." Mrs. Ord, according to one observer, "burst into tears and inquired what she had done, but Mrs. Lincoln refused to be appeased, and stormed till she was tired. Mrs. Grant tried to stand by her friend, and everybody was shocked and horrified."

That evening Mary continued her harangue at dinner, manifestly aggrieving her husband, whose attitude toward her, marveled Captain Barnes, "was always that of the most affectionate solicitude, so marked, so gentle and unaffected that no one could see them together without being impressed by it." Knowing his wife would awake the next morning humiliated by such a public display of temper, Lincoln had no desire to exacerbate the situation. Perhaps, as Mary's biographer suggests, the blow in the wagon that Mary suffered to her head had initiated a migraine headache, spurring the irrational outburst of wrath. Whether from illness or mortification, she remained sequestered in her stateroom for the next few days.

At this time, General Sherman was on his way to City Point. His army had stopped in Goldsboro, North Carolina, to resupply, leaving him several days to visit Grant and discuss plans for the final push. When Sherman arrived, he and Grant eagerly greeted each other, "their hands locked in a cordial grasp." To Horace Porter, "their encounter was more like that of two school-boys coming together after a vacation than the meeting of the chief actors in a great war tragedy." After talking for an hour, they walked down to the wharf and joined the president on the *River Queen.* Lincoln greeted Sherman "with a warmth of manner and expression" that the general would long remember, and initiated "a lively conversation," intently questioning Sherman about his march from Savannah to Goldsboro.

The talk darkened as Sherman and Grant agreed that "one more bloody battle was likely to occur before the close of the war." They believed Lee's only option now was to retreat to the Carolinas. There, joining forces with

Johnston, he would stage a desperate attack against either Sherman or Grant. "Must more blood be shed?" Lincoln asked. "Cannot this last bloody battle be avoided?" That was not in their hands, the generals explained. All would depend upon the actions taken by Robert E. Lee.

The next morning, March 28, Sherman and Grant, accompanied this time by Admiral Porter, returned to the *River Queen* for a long talk with Lincoln in the upper saloon. With the war drawing to a close, Sherman inquired of Lincoln: "What was to be done with the rebel armies when defeated? And what should be done with the political leaders, such as Jeff. Davis, etc.?" Lincoln replied that "all he wanted of us was to defeat the opposing armies, and to get the men composing the Confederate armies back to their homes, at work on their farms and in their shops." He wanted no retaliation or retribution. "Let them have their horses to plow with, and, if you like, their guns to shoot crows with. I want no one punished; treat them liberally all round. We want those people to return to their allegiance to the Union and submit to the laws."

Regarding Jefferson Davis and his top political leaders, Lincoln privately wished they could somehow "escape the country," though he could not say this in public. "As usual," Sherman recalled, "he illustrated his meaning by a story: 'A man once had taken the total-abstinence pledge. When visiting a friend, he was invited to take a drink, but declined, on the score of his pledge; when his friend suggested lemonade, [the man] accepted. In preparing the lemonade, the friend pointed to the brandy-bottle, and said the lemonade would be more palatable if he were to pour in a little brandy; when his guest said, if he could do so "unbeknown" to him, he would not object.' " Sherman grasped the point immediately. "Mr. Lincoln wanted Davis to escape, 'unbeknown' to him."

Later that afternoon, Sherman left City Point to return to his troops and prepare for the expected battle. Saying goodbye to the president, he "was more than ever impressed by his kindly nature, his deep and earnest sympathy with the afflictions of the whole people," and his "absolute faith in the courage, manliness, and integrity of the armies in the field." To be sure, "his face was care-worn and haggard; but, the moment he began to talk, his face lightened up, his tall form, as it were, unfolded, and he was the very impersonation of good-humor and fellowship." A decade later, Sherman remained convinced of Lincoln's unparalleled leadership. "Of all the men I ever met, he seemed to possess more of the elements of greatness, combined with goodness, than any other."

Lincoln walked to the railroad station early the next morning to bid farewell to Grant, who was heading to the front for what they hoped would be the final offensive against Lee. Oppressed by thoughts of the expected battle, "Lincoln looked more serious than at any other time since he had visited headquarters," recalled Horace Porter; "the lines in his face seemed deeper, and the rings under his eyes were of a darker hue." As the train pulled away from the platform, Grant and his party tipped their hats in honor of the president. Returning the salute, his "voice broken by an emotion he could ill conceal," Lincoln said: "Good-by, gentlemen, God bless you all!"

As Grant was leaving City Point, Seward was heading south to join Lincoln. "I think the President must have telegraphed for him," Welles surmised, "and if so I came to the conclusion that efforts are again being made for peace. I am by no means certain that this irregular proceeding and importunity on the part of the Executive is the wisest course." The *Tribune* concurred: "We presume no person of even average sagacity has imagined that the President of the United States had gone down to the front at such a time as this in quest merely of pleasure, or leisure or health even." That he hoped to "bring peace with him on his return," the editorial suggested, was "too palpable to be doubted."

Though Lincoln clearly would have loved "to bring peace with him on his return," he went to City Point with no intention of engaging in further negotiations. He had, in fact, sought a "change of air & rest," as well as the chance "to escape the unceasing and relentless pressure of visitors." More important, he wanted to underscore his directive that Grant should converse with Lee only with regard to capitulation or solely military concerns. Grant was "not to decide, discuss, or confer upon any political question. Such questions the President holds in his own hands." Lincoln wished to ensure that his lenient policy toward the rebels would not be undercut by a punitive agenda.

He knew that work was accumulating on his desk as his second week of absence from Washington began, but he was not yet ready to return. "I begin to feel that I ought to be at home," he telegraphed Stanton on March 30, "and yet I dislike to leave without seeing nearer to the end of General Grant's present movement. He has now been out since yesterday morning. . . . Last night at 10.15, when it was dark as a rainy night without a moon could be, a furious cannonade, soon joined in by a heavy musketry-fire, opened near Petersburg and lasted about two hours. The sound was very distinct here, as also were the flashes of guns upon the clouds. It seemed to me a great battle, but the older hands here scarcely noticed it, and, sure enough, this morning it was found that very little had been done." Stanton replied promptly, "I hope you will stay to see it out, or for a few days at least. I have strong faith that your presence will have great influence in inducing exertions that will bring Richmond; compared to that no other duty can weigh a feather. . . . A pause by the army now would do harm; if you are on the ground there will be no pause. All well here."

Seward, who had most likely come to keep Lincoln company, remained only two days. On April 1, he accompanied Mary back to Washington. The Lincolns had apparently decided that, after her public outburst, she would be better off in the White House, away from prying reporters. Moreover, Lincoln had related to her a dream in which the White House had caught fire, and Mary wanted to assure herself that all was well. Once she was aboard the steamer heading north, her spirits lifted abruptly. Fellow passenger Carl Schurz talked with her on the voyage. She "was overwhelmingly charming to me," he wrote to his wife. "She chided me for not visiting her, overpowered me with invitations, and finally had me driven to my hotel in her own state carriage. I learned more state secrets in a few hours than I could otherwise in a year. . . . She is an astounding person."

All that day, Lincoln haunted the telegraph office at City Point, anxiously awaiting news from Grant. Returning to the *River Queen*, he could see "the flash of the cannon" in the distance, signaling that the battle for Petersburg had begun. "Almost all night he walked up and down the deck," Crook recalled, "pausing now and then to listen or to look out into the darkness to see if he could see anything. I have never seen such suffering in the face of any man as was in his that night."

The battle was intense, but by early morning, the Federals had broken through Petersburg's outer lines of defense and had almost reached General Lee's headquarters at the Turnbull House. Realizing he could no longer hold on, Lee ordered his troops to withdraw from both Petersburg and Richmond. That evening Lincoln received the news that Grant had "Petersburg completely enveloped from river below to river above," and had taken "about 12,000 prisoners." Grant invited the president to visit him in Petersburg the following day.

Earlier that day, Lincoln had moved from the luxurious *River Queen* to the compact *Malvern*, Admiral Porter's flagship. Concerned by the cramped quarters, Porter had offered Lincoln his bed, "but he positively declined it," Porter recalled, choosing instead "the smallest kind of a room, six feet long by four and a half feet wide." The next morning he insisted he had "slept well," but teasingly remarked that "you can't put a long blade into a short scabbard." Realizing that the president's six-foot-four frame must have overhung the bed considerably, Porter got carpenters to knock down the wall, increasing the size of both the room and the bed. When Lincoln awoke the next morning, he announced with delight that "a greater miracle than ever happened last night; I shrank six inches in length and about a foot sideways."

To reach Grant, who was waiting in "a comfortable-looking brick house with a yard in front" on Market Street in Petersburg, Lincoln had to ride over the battlefields, littered with dead and dying soldiers. Years later, his bodyguard could recall the sight of "one man with a bullet-hole through his forehead, and another with both arms shot away." As Lincoln absorbed the sorrowful scene, Crook noticed that his "face settled into its old lines of sadness." By the time he reached Grant, he had recovered himself. Grant's aide Horace Porter watched as Lincoln "dismounted in the street, and came in through the front gate with long and rapid strides, his face beaming with delight. He seized General Grant's hand as the general stepped forward to greet him, and stood shaking it for some time." Lincoln showed such elation that Porter doubted whether he had "ever experienced a happier moment in his life."

Lincoln and his lieutenant general conferred for about an hour and a half on the piazza in front of the house while curious citizens strolled by. Though no word had arrived yet from Richmond, Grant surmised that, with the fall of Petersburg, Lee had no choice but to evacuate the capital and move west along the Danville Road, hoping to escape to North Carolina, in which case the Federals would attempt to "get ahead of him and cut him off." Grant had hoped to receive word of Richmond's fall while still in the president's company, but when no message arrived, he felt compelled to join his troops in the field.

Lincoln was back at City Point when news reached him that Union troops commanded by General Weitzel had now occupied Richmond. "Thank God that I have lived to see this!" he remarked to Admiral Porter. "It seems to me that I have been dreaming a horrid dream for four years, and now the nightmare is gone."

For Jefferson Davis and the Confederate government, the nightmare was just beginning. Twenty-four hours earlier, the Confederate president had received the devastating news of Lee's evacuation plans. Seated in his customary pew at St. Paul's Church for the Sunday service, Davis had received "a telegram announcing that General Lee could not hold his position longer than till night, and warning [him] that we must leave Richmond, as the army would commence retreating that evening."

"Thereupon," an attendant at the service noted, Davis "instantly arose, and walked hurriedly down the aisle, beneath the questionings of all eyes in the house." Summoning his cabinet to an emergency session, he made preparations for a special train to carry the leading officials and important government papers south and west to Danville, where a new capital could be established. As word of the evacuation of the troops spread, the citizenry panicked, and a general exodus began. In the tumult, a small fire, deliberately set to destroy the tobacco warehouses before the Federals arrived, raged out of control, burning "nearly everything between Main street and the river for about three-quarters of a mile." All the public buildings in its path, including the offices of the Richmond *Examiner* and the *Inquirer*, were destroyed, leaving only the Customhouse and the Spotswood Hotel.

The news of Richmond's capture on April 3, 1865, reached the War Department in Washington shortly before noon. When over the wire came the words "Here is the first message for you in four years from Richmond," the telegraph operator leaped from his seat and shouted from the window, "Richmond has fallen." The news quickly "spread by a thousand mouths," and "almost by magic the streets were crowded with hosts of people, talking, laughing, hurrahing, and shouting in the fullness of their joy." A *Herald* reporter noted that many "wept as children" while "men embraced and kissed each other upon the streets; friends who had been estranged for years shook hands and renewed their vows of friendship."

Gathering at the War Department, the crowd called for Stanton, who had not left his post for several nights. "As he stood upon the steps to speak," recalled his aide A. E. Johnson, "he trembled like a leaf, and his voice showed his emotion." He began by expressing "gratitude to Almighty God for his deliverance of the nation," then called for thanks "to the President, to the Army and Navy, to the great commanders by sea and land, to the gallant officers and men who have periled their lives upon the battle-field, and drenched the soil with their blood." Stanton was "so overcome by emotion that he could not speak continuously," but when he finished, the crowd roared its approval.

Seward, who had been at the War Department awaiting news of Richmond's fall, was urged to speak next. Clearly understanding that the moment belonged to Stanton, he kept his remarks short and humorous. He was beginning to think that it was time for a change in the cabinet, he began. "Why I started to go to 'the front' the other day, and when I got to City Point they told me it was at Hatcher's Run, and when I got there I was told it was not there but somewhere else, and when I get back I am told by the Secretary that it is at Petersburg; but before I can realize that, I am told again that it is at Richmond, and west of that. Now I leave you to judge what I ought to think of such a Secretary of War as this." The crowd erupted in "loud and lusty" cheers, and a "beaming" Stanton led them in a chorus of "The Star-Spangled Banner."

Newspapers raced to issue special editions. "The demand seemed inexhaustible," the *Star* reported, "and almost beyond the power of our lightning press to supply." One hundred *Herald* couriers, "as fleet on foot and as breathless with enthusiasm as Malice with his fiery cross," raced to distribute papers in every section of the city. EXTRA! GLORIOUS! FALL OF RICHMOND! read the headlines, adding that black troops were among the first to enter the city. For anyone who missed the cries of the newsboys, the sound of eight hundred guns, fired at Stanton's order, marked the signal triumph.

That night, with bands playing in the streets, candles sparkling in the windows of government buildings, and flags flying from every housetop, Seward joined a group of guests for dinner at Stanton's house. The evening's joy was diminished only by the anxiety Stanton and Seward shared for Lincoln's safety. Earlier that day, Seward had talked with James Speed about his fear that "if there were to be assassinations, now was the time." With the fall of Richmond, Seward told Speed, "the Southern people would feel as though the world had come to an end." At such moments, history suggested, desperate men might be prompted to take desperate action, and "the President, being the most marked man on the Federal side, was the most liable to attack." Aware that Mary had invited Speed to join her two days later on a return trip to City Point, Seward begged him to "warn the President of the danger."

Stanton, who worried constantly about the president's safety, needed no reminders that the situation was more hazardous than ever. He had tried to keep Lincoln from going to Petersburg, asking him "to consider whether you ought to expose the nation to the consequence of any disaster to yourself," and pointing out that while generals must run such risks "in the line of their duty," political leaders were not "in the same condition." Lincoln was already back from Petersburg when he received Stanton's telegram. He thanked the secretary for his concern and promised to "take care of [himself]," while simultaneously announcing his intended departure for Richmond the next day.

At 8 a.m. on Tuesday morning, April 4, Lincoln set forth on his historic journey to Richmond. When the *Malvern* reached the channel approaching the city, its passage was blocked by "wreckage of all sorts," including "dead horses, broken ordnance, wrecked boats," and floating torpedoes. They were forced to transfer to the captain's barge, which was towed in behind a little tug manned by marines. When the tug went aground, the president's arrival was left to the rowing skills of a dozen sailors. The situation was unnerving to Crook. "On either side," he recalled, "we passed so close to torpedoes that we could have put out our hands and touched them."

"Here we were in a solitary boat," Admiral Porter remembered, "after having set out with a number of vessels flying flags at every mast-head, hoping to enter the conquered capital in a manner befitting the rank of the

President of the United States." Lincoln was not disturbed in the slightest. The situation reminded him, he cheerfully noted, of a man who had approached him seeking a high position as a consulate minister: "Finding he could not get that, he came down to some more modest position. Finally he asked to be made a tide-waiter. When he saw he could not get that, he asked me for an old pair of trousers. But it is well to be humble."

No sooner had the presidential party reached the landing than Lincoln was surrounded by a small group of black laborers shouting, "Bress de Lord! . . . dere is de great Messiah! . . . Glory, Hallelujah!" First one and then several others fell on their knees. "Don't kneel to me," Lincoln said, his voice full of emotion, "that is not right. You must kneel to God only, and thank him for the liberty you will hereafter enjoy." The men stood up, joined hands, and began to sing a hymn. The streets, which had been "entirely deserted," became "suddenly alive" with crowds of black people "tumbling and shouting, from over the hills and from the water-side."

An ever-growing crowd trailed Lincoln as he walked up the street. "It was a warm day," Admiral Porter noted, and Lincoln, whose tall figure "overtopped every man there," was easily visible. From the windows of the houses along the two-mile route, hundreds of white faces looked on with curiosity at the lanky figure, "walking with his usual long, careless stride, and looking about with an interested air and taking in everything."

Lincoln's bodyguard was relieved when they finally reached the safety of General Weitzel's headquarters, for he thought he had glimpsed a figure in Confederate uniform pointing a gun at Lincoln from a window along the route. Weitzel and his officers had occupied the stucco mansion that Jefferson Davis had abandoned only two days earlier. Captain Barnes recalled that when Lincoln walked into the "comfortably furnished" office of the Confederate president, he crossed the room "to the easy chair and sank down in it." To all present, it seemed "a supreme moment," but Lincoln betrayed no sense of exaltation or triumph. His first words, softly spoken, were simply to ask for a glass of water. The water was promptly supplied, along with a bottle of whiskey. An old black servant still at his post told them that "Mrs. Davis had ordered him to have the house in good condition for the Yankees."

Lincoln had already toured the mansion, seeming "interested in everything," and had met with the members of General Weitzel's staff, when the Confederate assistant secretary of war, John Campbell, arrived to see him. Lincoln welcomed Campbell, whom he had met two months earlier at the Hampton Roads Conference. While the details of their conversation were later disputed, it appears that Lincoln, still fearing that Lee might engage in a final battle, agreed to allow the Virginia legislature to convene, on the understanding that they would repeal the order of secession and remove the state's troops from the war.

Riding through the city that afternoon in an open carriage, the president and his entourage found the Confederate statehouse "in dreadful disorder, signs of a sudden and unexpected flight; members' tables were upset, bales of Confederate scrip were lying about the floor, and many official documents of some value were scattered about." When they finally returned to the flagship, both Admiral Porter and William Crook were greatly relieved. Having worried all day about Lincoln's safety, Crook later wrote that it was "nothing short of miraculous that some attempt on [Lincoln's] life was not made. It is to the everlasting glory of the South that he was permitted to come and go in peace."

As Lincoln rested on the *Malvern* that night, all the public buildings in the nation's capital were illuminated by order of the secretary of state. "The city was all alight with rockets, fireworks, and illuminations of every description," observed Noah Brooks, "the streets being one blaze of glory." It seemed "the entire population of Washington" had poured into the streets to share in the triumph and view the brilliant spectacle produced by "thousands of lighted candles."

Though Seward joined in the glorious celebrations, he continued to fret. The following day he told Welles that he had secured a revenue cutter to take him to Richmond with some important papers that required the president's immediate attention. "He is filled with anxiety to see the President," Welles recorded in his diary, "and these schemes are his apology."

Minutes after taking leave of Welles, Seward nearly lost his life in a carriage accident. Fanny and her friend Mary Titus had come to the Department to join her father and brother Fred for their "customary" afternoon ride. As the horses moved up Vermont Avenue, the coachman stopped to close the carriage door, which had not been properly latched. Before he could return to his seat, the horses bolted, "swinging the driver by the reins as one would swing a cat by the tail." Both Fred and Seward jumped out, hoping they could stop the runaway horses. Fred was not hurt, but Seward caught his heel on the carriage as he jumped, and landed "violently upon the pavement," causing him to lose consciousness.

"The horses tore along," Fanny recorded in her diary, and "we seemed to be whirling on to certain destruction." At an alley, they "turned. We brushed against a tree," and headed straight toward the corner of a house, where she feared she would be "crushed to death." Fortunately, a passing soldier got control of the reins and brought an end to the terrifying ride. Rushing back to the place where her father had fallen, Fanny was horrified to find his broken body, "blood streaming from his mouth." At first she feared he was dead.

For two hours after he was carried to his home, Seward remained unconscious. When he came to at last, he was delirious with pain, having suffered a broken jaw and a badly dislocated shoulder. Doctors arrived, and Fanny could hear his agonized cries through the bedroom door. When she was finally allowed to see him, "he was so disfigured by bruises . . . that he had scarcely a trace of resemblance to himself."

Hearing the news, Stanton rushed to Seward's bedside, where, Fanny recalled, he "was like a woman in the sickroom." He ministered carefully to his friend, perhaps remembering childhood days when he had accompanied his father on sick calls. He "wiped his lips" where the blood had caked, "spoke gently to him," and remained by his side for hours. Returning to the War Department, Stanton sent Lincoln a telegram at City Point: "Mr Seward was thrown from his carriage his shoulder bone at the head of the joint broken off, his head and face much bruised and he is in my opinion dangerously injured. I think your presence here is needed."

Receiving the message shortly before midnight, Lincoln advised Grant that Seward's accident necessitated his return to Washington. Meanwhile, Mary and her invited guests, including James Speed, Elizabeth Keckley, Charles Sumner, Senator Harlan, and the Marquis de Chambrun, were steaming toward City Point. At dawn the next morning, Mary sent a telegram to Stanton: "If Mr Seward is not too severely injured—cannot the President, remain until we arrive at City Point." By this time the surgeon general had determined that Seward had suffered no internal injuries. Stanton informed Mary that there was "no objection to the President remaining at City Point." A few hours later, he sent word to Lincoln that Seward was recovering. "I have seen him and read him all the news. . . . His mind is clear and spirits good."

When Mary's party arrived at noon on April 6, Lincoln brought them into the drawing room of the *River Queen* and relayed the latest bulletins, all positive, from Grant. "His whole appearance, pose, and bearing had marvelously changed," Senator Harlan noted. "He was, in fact, transfigured. That indescribable sadness which had previously seemed to be an adamantine element of his very being had been suddenly changed for an equally indescribable expression of serene joy, as if conscious that the great purpose of his life had been attained." Nonetheless, the marquis marveled, "it was impossible to detect in him the slightest feeling of pride, much less of vanity."

While the visitors went off to Richmond, Lincoln remained at City

Point to await further word from Grant. Welcome news soon arrived—a copy of a telegram from Sheridan, reporting a successful engagement with Lee's retreating armies that had resulted in the capture of "several thousand prisoners," including a half-dozen generals. "If the thing is pressed," Sheridan predicted, "I think Lee will surrender." Lincoln rejoined: "Let the *thing* be pressed."

That evening Julia Grant, accompanied by Lincoln's old friend E. B. Washburne, joined the Lincoln party on the *River Queen*. The conversation turned on what should be done with Jefferson Davis if he were apprehended. "Don't allow him to escape the law," one of the group said, "he must be hung." At once Lincoln interjected: "Let us judge not, that we be not judged."

On Saturday morning, Lincoln and his guests visited Petersburg. At a certain spot, the marquis recalled, "he gave orders to stop the carriage." On his previous visit, Lincoln had noticed a "very tall and beautiful" oak tree that he wanted to examine more closely. "He admired the strength of its trunk, the vigorous development of branches," which reminded him of "the great oaks" in the Western forests. He halted the carriage again when they passed "an old country graveyard" where trees shaded a carpet of spring flowers. Turning to his wife, Lincoln said, "Mary, you are younger than I. You will survive me. When I am gone, lay my remains in some quiet place like this." On the train ride back to City Point, Lincoln observed a turtle "basking in the warm sunshine on the wayside." He asked that the train be stopped so that the turtle could be brought into the car. "The movements of the ungainly little animal seemed to delight him," Elizabeth Keckley recalled. He and Tad shared "a happy laugh" all the way back to the wharf.

Such distractions could not forestall the afternoon's grim task. Lincoln visited injured soldiers at City Point, moving "from one bed to another," the marquis recalled, "saying a friendly word to each wounded man, or at least giving him a handshake." At one bed, he held the hand of a twenty-four-year-old captain who had been cited for bravery. "The dying man half-opened his eyes; a faint smile passed over his lips. It was then that his pulse ceased beating." Lincoln remained among the wounded for five hours and returned to the steamer depleted. "There has been war enough," he said when the marquis inquired about troubles with France over Mexico, "during my second term there will be no more fighting."

That evening, as the *River Queen* prepared to return to Washington, Grant's officers and staff came to say farewell. Lincoln had hoped to remain at City Point until Lee's surrender, but he felt he should visit Seward. "As the twilight shadows deepened the lamps were lighted, and the boat was brilliantly illuminated," Elizabeth Keckley recalled, "it looked like an enchanted floating palace." When the military band came aboard, Lincoln asked them to play "La Marseillaise" in honor of the Marquis de Chambrun.

As the *River Queen* steamed toward Washington on Sunday, "the conversation," Chambrun recalled, "dwelt upon literary subjects." Holding "a beautiful quarto copy of Shakespeare in his hands," Lincoln read several passages from *Macbeth*, including the king's pained tribute to the murdered Duncan:

> *Duncan is in his grave;*
> *After life's fitful fever he sleeps well.*
> *Treason has done his worst; nor steel, nor poison,*
> *Malice domestic, foreign levy, nothing,*
> *Can touch him further.*

Lincoln read the lines slowly, marveling "how true a description of the murderer that one was; when, the dark deed achieved, its tortured perpetrator came to envy the sleep of his victim," and when he finished, "he read over again the same scene." Lincoln's ominous selection prompted James Speed to deliver Seward's warning about the increased threat upon his life. "He stopped me at once," Speed recalled, "saying, he had rather be dead than to live in continual dread." Moreover, he considered it essential "that the people know I come among them without fear."

Early that evening, the steamer passed by Mount Vernon, prompting Chambrun to say to Lincoln, "Mount Vernon and Springfield, the memories of Washington and your own, those of the revolutionary and civil wars; these are the spots and names America shall one day equally honor." The remark brought a dreamy smile to Lincoln's face. "Springfield!" he said. "How happy, four years hence, will I be to return there in peace and tranquility."

Years later, Chambrun remained intrigued by Lincoln's temperament. On first impression, he "left with you with a sort of impression of vague and deep sadness." Yet he "was quite humorous," often telling hilarious stories and laughing uproariously. "But all of a sudden he would retire within himself; then he would close his eyes, and all his features would at once bespeak a kind of sadness as indescribable as it was deep. After a while, as though it were by an effort of his will, he would shake off this mysterious weight under which he seemed bowed; his generous and open disposition would again reappear."

Lincoln's bodyguard, William Crook, believed he understood something of the shifting moods that mystified the French aristocrat. He had observed that Lincoln seemed to absorb the horrors of the war into himself. In the course of the two-week trip, Crook had witnessed Lincoln's "agony when the thunder of the cannon told him that men were being cut down like grass." He had seen the anguish on the president's face when he came within "sight of the poor, torn bodies of the dead and dying on the field of Petersburg." He discerned his "painful sympathy with the forlorn rebel prisoners," and his profound distress at "the revelation of the devastation of a noble people in ruined Richmond." In each instance, Lincoln had internalized the pain of those around him—the wounded soldiers, the captured prisoners, the defeated Southerners. Little wonder that he was overwhelmed at times by a profound sadness that even his own resilient temperament could not dispel.

• • •

DIRECTLY UPON HIS RETURN to Washington, Lincoln went to Seward's bedside. "It was in the evening," Fred Seward recalled, "the gas-lights were turned down low, and the house was still, every one moving softly, and speaking in whispers." His father had taken a turn for the worse. A high fever had developed, and "grave apprehensions were entertained, by his medical attendants, that his system would not survive the injuries and the shock." Frances had hurried down from Auburn to find her husband in a more serious state than she had imagined, his face "so marred and swollen and discolored that one can hardly persuade themselves of his identity; his voice so changed; utterance almost entirely prevented by the broken jaw and the swollen tongue. It makes my heart ache to look at him." His mind was "perfectly clear," however, and he remained, as always, "patient and uncomplaining."

"The extreme sensitiveness of the wounded arm," Fred recalled, "made even the touch of the bed clothing intolerable. To keep it free from their contact, he was lying on the edge of the bed, farthest from the door." When Lincoln entered the room, he walked over to the far side of the bed and sat down near the bandaged patient. "You are back from Richmond?" Seward queried in a halting, scarcely audible voice. "Yes," Lincoln replied, "and I think we are near the end, at last." To continue the conversation more intimately, Lincoln stretched out on the bed. Supporting his head with his hand, Lincoln lay side by side with Seward, as they had done at the time of their first meeting in Massachusetts many years before. When Fanny came in to sit down, Lincoln somehow managed to unfold his long arm and bring it "around the foot of the bed, to shake hands in his cordial way." He related the details of his trip to Richmond, where he had "worked as hard" at the task of shaking seven thousand hands as he had when he sawed wood, "& seemed," Fanny thought, "much satisfied at the labor."

Finally, when he saw that Seward had fallen into a much-needed sleep, Lincoln quietly got up and left the room. Drained by Seward's grievous condition, Lincoln revived when Stanton burst into the White House bearing a telegram from Grant: "General Lee surrendered the Army of Northern Virginia this afternoon upon terms proposed by myself." It was later said that "the President hugged him with joy" upon hearing the news, and then went immediately to tell Mary.

Although it was close to 10 p.m., Stanton knew that Seward would want to be awakened for this news. "God bless you," Seward said when Stanton read the telegram. This was the third time Stanton had come to see Seward that Sunday. "Don't try to speak," Stanton said. "You have made me cry for the first time in my life," Seward replied.

• • •

BOTH GRANT AND LEE had acquitted themselves admirably at the courtly surrender ceremony that afternoon at the Appomattox Court House. "One general, magnanimous in victory," historian Jay Winik writes, "the other, gracious and equally dignified in defeat." Two days earlier, Grant had sent a note to Lee asking him to surrender. In light of "the result of the last week," Grant wrote, he hoped that Lee understood "the hopelessness of further resistance" and would choose to prevent "any further effusion of blood." At first Lee refused to accept the futility of his cause, contemplating one last attempt to escape. But Sunday morning, with his troops almost completely surrounded, Lee sent word to Grant that he was ready to surrender.

As the distinguished silver-haired general dressed for the historic meeting, his biographer writes, he "put on his handsomest sword and his sash of deep, red silk." Thinking it likely he would be imprisoned before day's end, he told General William Pendleton, "I must make my best appearance." He need not have worried, for Grant was determined to follow Lincoln's lenient guidelines. The terms of surrender allowed Confederate officers, after relinquishing their arms and artillery, "to return to their homes, not to be disturbed by the United States authority," on the condition that they never "take up arms" against the Union "until properly exchanged."

As Grant continued to work out the terms, he later recalled, "the thought occurred to me that the officers had their own private horses and effects, which were important to them, but of no value to us; also that it would be an unnecessary humiliation to call upon them to deliver their side arms." He therefore added a provision allowing officers to take their sidearms, as well as their private horses and baggage. This permission, Lee observed, "would have a happy effect upon his army." Before the two men parted, Lee mentioned that "his army was in a very bad condition for want of food." Grant responded immediately, promising to send rations for twenty-five thousand men.

As Lee rode back to his headquarters, word of the surrender spread through the Confederate lines. He tried to speak to his men, but "tears came into his eyes," and he could manage to say only "Men, we have fought the war together, and I have done the best I could for you." If Lee had trouble expressing his grief and pride, his soldiers showed no such reservations. In an overwhelming display of respect and devotion, they spontaneously arranged themselves on "each side of the road to greet him as he passed, and two solid walls of men were formed along the whole distance." When their cheers brought tears to Lee's eyes, they, too, began to weep. "Each group began in the same way, with cheers, and ended in the same way, with sobs, all along the route to his quarters." One soldier spoke for all: "I love you just as well as ever, General Lee!"

At dawn the next day, Noah Brooks heard "a great boom." The reverberation of a five-hundred-gun salute "startled the misty air of Washington, shaking the very earth, and breaking the windows of houses about Lafayette Square." The morning newspapers would carry the details, but "this was Secretary Stanton's way of telling the people that the Army of Northern Virginia had at last laid down its arms."

"The nation seems delirious with joy," noted Welles. "Guns are firing, bells ringing, flags flying, men laughing, children cheering—all, all jubilant. This surrender of the great Rebel captain and the most formidable and reliable army of the Secessionists virtually terminates the Rebellion." A spontaneous holiday was announced in all departments. Employees poured into the streets.

An exuberant crowd of several thousand gathered at the White House. "The bands played, the howitzers belched forth their thunder, and the people cheered," reported the *National Intelligencer.* Despite shouted demands for him to speak, Lincoln hesitated. He was planning a speech for the following evening and did not want to "dribble it all out" before he completed his thoughts. If he said something mistaken, it would make its way into print, and a person in his position, he modestly said, "ought at least try not to make mistakes." Still, the crowd was so insistent that the president finally appeared at the second-story window, where he "was received in the most enthusiastic manner, the people waving their hats, swinging their umbrellas, and the ladies waving their handkerchiefs."

When the assembly quieted down, Lincoln acknowledged their euphoria with a smile of his own. "I am very greatly rejoiced to find that an occasion has occurred so pleasurable that the people cannot restrain themselves." These words drew even wilder cheers. Lincoln then announced a special request for the band. "I have always thought 'Dixie' one of the best tunes I have ever heard," he began. "Our adversaries over the way attempted to appropriate it, but I insisted yesterday that we fairly captured it." This was followed by tumultuous applause. "I presented the question to the Attorney General, and he gave it as his legal opinion that it is our lawful prize. I now request the band to favor me with its performance." In requesting the patriotic song of the South, Lincoln believed that "it is good to show the rebels that with us they will be free to hear it again." The band followed "Dixie" with "Yankee Doodle," and "the crowd went off in high good-humor."

"If possible," Mary wrote, "this is a happier day, than last Monday," when the news of Richmond's capture had reached Washington. Her exhilaration was evident in a note she wrote to Charles Sumner the next morning, inviting him and the marquis to join her in a carriage ride around the city to see the grand illumination and to hear the president speak. "It does not appear to me," she wrote, "that this *womanly* curiosity will be undignified or indiscreet, qu'en pensez vous?"

Illuminated once again, the city was spectacular to behold. The windows of every government building were ablaze with candles and lanterns, and the lights of the newly completed Capitol dome were visible for miles around. "Bonfires blazed in many parts of the city, and rockets were fired" in ongoing celebrations. Knowing the president was going to address the public, Stanton put his men to work decorating the front of the War Department "with flags, corps badges and evergreens."

When Lincoln came to a second-story window on the north side of the White House, "he carried a roll of manuscript in his hand." He had explained to Noah Brooks that "this was a precaution" against colloquial expressions that might offend men such as Charles Sumner, who had objected previously to phrases such as "the rebels turned tail and ran" or "sugar-coated pill." At the sight of the president, the immense crowd's enthusiasm was loosed in "wave after wave of applause," requiring him to stand still for some time until the din subsided.

"The speech," Noah Brooks observed, "was longer than most people had expected, and of a different character." Instead of simply celebrating the moment, Lincoln wanted to address the national debate surrounding the reintroduction of the Southern states into the Union, "the greatest question," he still believed, "ever presented to practical statesmanship."

He acknowledged that in Louisiana, where the process had already begun, some were disappointed that, in the new state constitution, "the elective franchise is not given to the colored man." He felt the right of suffrage should be extended to blacks—to those who were literate and those "who serve our cause as soldiers." On the other hand, the new Louisiana constitution contained a number of remarkable provisions. It emancipated all the slaves within the state and provided "the benefit of public schools equally to black and white." The state legislature, which had already revealed its good intentions by ratifying the Thirteenth Amendment, was empowered specifically "to confer the elective franchise upon the colored man." Were they to cast out the hard work already achieved, Lincoln asked rhetorically, or trust that this was the start of a process that would eventually produce "a complete success"? Relying on a simple, rustic image to convey the complex question, he wondered if "we shall sooner have the fowl by hatching the egg than by smashing it?"

In the crowd that evening was Confederate sympathizer John Wilkes Booth. The younger brother of the famed Shakespearian actor Edwin Booth, whose performances Lincoln so admired, Wilkes had also acquired popularity as an actor. Unlike his older brother, who supported the Union, John Wilkes "had spent the most formative years of his youth in the South" and had developed an abiding passion for the rebels' cause. In recent months, this passion had become a full-blown obsessive hatred for the North. Since the previous summer, he and a small group of conspirators had evolved a plan to kidnap Lincoln and bring him to Richmond, where he could be exchanged for rebel prisoners of war. The capture of Richmond and the surrender of Lee rendered the plan useless, but Booth was not ready to yield. "Our cause being almost lost," he wrote in his diary, "something decisive and great must be done."

Two other conspirators were with Booth in the crowd—drugstore clerk David Herold and former Confederate soldier Lewis Powell, also known as Lewis Payne. When Lincoln spoke of his desire to extend suffrage to blacks, Booth turned to Powell. "That means nigger citizenship. That is the last speech he will ever make," he said. He pleaded with Powell to shoot Lincoln then and there. When Powell demurred, Booth proclaimed, "By God, I'll put him through."

Curiously, Lincoln had recently experienced a dream that carried ominous intimations. "There seemed to be a death-like stillness about me," Lincoln purportedly told Ward Lamon. "Then I heard subdued sobs, as if a number of people were weeping. . . . I went from room to room; no living person was in sight, but the same mournful sounds of distress met me as I passed along. . . . Determined to find the cause of a state of things so mysterious and so shocking, I kept on until I arrived at the East Room, which I entered. There I met with a sickening surprise. Before me was a catafalque, on which rested a corpse wrapped in funeral vestments. Around it were stationed soldiers who were acting as guards; and there was a throng of people, some gazing mournfully upon the corpse, whose face was covered, others weeping pitifully. 'Who is dead in the White House?' I demanded of one of the soldiers. 'The President,' was his answer; 'he was killed by an assassin!' "

Lamon also described what he claimed was the president's attempt to evade the dire portent of the dream. "Don't you see how it will turn out?" Lincoln comforted Lamon. "In this dream, it was not me but some other fellow that was killed. . . . Well, let it go. I think the Lord in His own good time and way will work this out all right. God knows what is best." Historian Don Fehrenbacher is persuasive that Lamon's chronology is confused, which casts doubt on the veracity of the entire story. Yet Lincoln's penchant for portentous dreams and his tendency to relate them to others were remarked on by many of his intimate acquaintances.

While radicals, including Sumner and Chase, believed that universal suffrage should be mandated, rebel leaders should be punished, and the federal government should assume control of the seceded states, "a large majority of the people" approved of Lincoln's speech. "Reunion," according to Noah Brooks, "was then the foremost thought in the minds of men."

Lincoln's support for the quickly assembled imperfect governments in Louisiana and elsewhere drew further criticism from radicals. He believed "there must be courts, and law, and order, or society would be broken up, the disbanded armies would turn into robber bands and guerillas." That same belief had informed his conversations with Judge Campbell in Richmond and his conditional permission for the old Virginia legislature to assemble. At the time of their meeting, five days before Lee's surrender, Lincoln had hoped the Virginians would vote to take back the order of secession and remove Virginia's troops from the war. He also felt that it was sound policy to let "the prominent and influential men of their respective counties . . . come together and undo their own work."

Lincoln's cabinet strongly disagreed with the idea of letting the rebel legislature assemble for any reason. In Seward's absence, Stanton assumed center stage, telling Lincoln "that to place such powers in the Virginia legislature would be giving away the scepter of the conqueror; that it would transfer the result of victory of our arms from the field to the very legislatures which four years before had said, 'give us war'; that it would put the Government in the hands of its enemies; that it would surely bring trouble with Congress." Stanton insisted that "any effort to reorganize the Government should be under Federal authority solely, treating the rebel organizations and government as absolutely null and void."

Attorney General Speed expressed his accord with Stanton's assessment in the meeting and, afterward, privately with Lincoln. The president confessed to Welles that the opposition of Speed and Stanton troubled him tremendously. Welles provided no relief. He, too, "doubted the policy of convening a Rebel legislature," and predicted that, "once convened, they would with their hostile feelings be inclined perhaps, to conspire against us." Lincoln still disagreed, maintaining that if "prominent Virginians" were to come together, they would "turn themselves and their neighbors into good Union men." Nonetheless, Welles said, "as we had all taken a different view he had perhaps made a mistake, and was ready to correct it if he had."

Lincoln's thinking was further influenced by a telegram from Campbell to General Weitzel, which suggested that Campbell was indeed assuming more powers for the legislature than he and Lincoln had originally discussed. In the late afternoon of April 12, Lincoln walked over to the War Department to confer again with Stanton. Stanton's clerk A. E. Johnson recalled that Lincoln sat on the sofa and listened intently while Stanton, "full of feeling," reiterated his passionate opposition to allowing the legislature to convene, warning that "the fate of the emancipated millions" would be left in the hands of untrustworthy men, that "being once assembled, its deliberations could not be confined to any specific acts."

Finally, Lincoln stood up and walked over to Stanton's desk, where he wrote what would be the final telegram issued under his name from the War Department. He directed General Weitzel to withdraw the original permission for the legislature to convene. "Do not now allow them to assemble; but if any have come, allow them safe-return to their homes." Stanton was pleased, believing "*that* . . . was exactly right."

On Thursday, April 13, Grant journeyed to Washington, where Stanton had planned a celebration in his honor. "As we reached our destination that bright morning in our boat," Julia Grant recalled, "every gun in and near Washington burst forth—and such a salvo!—all the bells rang out merry greetings, and the city was literally swathed in flags and bunting." Grant went to see the president while Julia, at the Willard Hotel, received "calls of congratulations all day." Later in the afternoon, she and Ellen Stanton joined their husbands at the War Department. There, Julia recalled, "Stanton was in his happiest mood, showing me many stands of arms, flags, and, among other things, a stump of a large tree perforated on all sides by bullets, taken from the field of Shiloh." He enthusiastically detailed plans for the illumination of his department that night, and "facetiously remarked: 'They are going to illuminate at the Navy Department, I know, for they sent and borrowed two or three boxes of candles from my department.' "

For the first time since Willie's death, Mary Lincoln seemed positively carefree. She had received a delightful note from her husband the day before, only "a few lines," but "playfully & tenderly worded, notifying, the hour, of the day, *he* would drive with me!" She wrote a number of letters, all brimming with vitality. "We are rejoicing beyond expression, over our great and glorious victories," she told James Bennett. To her friend Abram Wakeman, she described in detail the "charming time" she had enjoyed at City Point. "I wish very much you had been with us, even our stately dignified Mr Sumner acknowledged himself transformed, into a lad of sixteen." She told Sumner that her new volume of *Julius Caesar* had arrived, and she invited him to join her that evening at the White House for a visit with General Grant.

• • •

Good Friday, April 14, 1865, was surely one of Lincoln's happiest days. The morning began with a leisurely breakfast in the company of his son Robert, just arrived in Washington. "Well, my son, you have returned safely from the front," Lincoln said. "The war is now closed, and we soon will live in peace with the brave men that have been fighting against us." He urged Robert to "lay aside" his army uniform and finish his education, perhaps in preparation for a law career. As the father imparted his advice, Elizabeth Keckley observed, "his face was more cheerful than [she] had seen it for a long while."

At 11 a.m., Grant arrived at the White House to attend the regularly scheduled Friday cabinet meeting. He had hoped for word that Johnston's army, the last substantial rebel force remaining, had surrendered to Sherman, but no news had yet arrived. Lincoln told Grant not to worry. He predicted that the tidings would come soon, "for he had last night the usual dream which he had preceding nearly every great and important event of the War." Welles asked him to describe the dream. Turning toward him, Lincoln said it involved the navy secretary's "element, the water—that he seemed to be in some singular, indescribable vessel, and that he was moving with great rapidity towards an indefinite shore; that he had this dream preceding Sumter, Bull Run, Antietam, Gettysburg, Stone River, Vicksburg, Wilmington, etc." Grant remarked that not all those great events had been victories, but Lincoln remained hopeful that this time this event would be favorable.

The complexities of reestablishing law and order in the Southern states dominated the conversation. A few days earlier, Stanton had drafted a plan for imposing a temporary military government on Virginia and North Carolina, until the restoration of civilian rule. "Lincoln alluded to the paper," Stanton later recalled, "went into his room, brought it out, and asked me to read it." A general discussion revealed that most of the cabinet concurred, although Welles and Dennison objected to the idea of undoing state boundaries by uniting two different states into a single military department. Recognizing the validity of this objection, Lincoln asked Stanton to revise his plan to make it applicable to two separate states.

Lincoln said that "he thought it providential that this great rebellion was crushed just as Congress had adjourned," since he and the cabinet were more likely to "accomplish more without them than with them" regarding Reconstruction. He noted that "there were men in Congress who, if their motives were good, were nevertheless impracticable, and who possessed feelings of hate and vindictiveness in which he did not sympathize and could not participate. He hoped there would be no persecution, no bloody work, after the war was over."

As for the rebel leaders, Lincoln reiterated his resolve to perpetrate no further violence: "None need expect he would take any part in hanging or killing those men, even the worst of them." While their continued presence on American soil might prove troublesome, he preferred to "frighten them out of the country, open the gates, let down the bars, scare them off." To illustrate his point, he shook "his hands as if scaring sheep," and said, "Enough lives have been sacrificed. We must extinguish our resentments if we expect harmony and union."

After the cabinet meeting, Stanton and Speed descended the stairs together. "Didn't our Chief look grand today?" Stanton asked. Years later, Speed held fast "to the memory of Lincoln's personal appearance" that day, "with cleanly-shaved face, well-brushed clothing and neatly-combed hair and whiskers," a marked contrast to his usual rumpled aspect. Stanton later wrote that Lincoln seemed "more cheerful and happy" than at any previous cabinet meeting, thrilled by "the near prospect of firm and durable peace at home and abroad." Throughout the discussion, Stanton recalled, Lincoln "spoke very kindly of General Lee and others of the Confederacy," exhibiting "in marked degree the kindness and humanity of his disposition, and the tender and forgiving spirit that so eminently distinguished him."

Later that day, Lincoln put into practice his liberal policy toward the rebel leaders. Intelligence had reached Stanton at the War Department that "a conspicuous secessionist," Jacob Thompson, was en route to Portland, Maine, where a steamer awaited to take him to England. Operating from Canada, Thompson had organized a series of troublesome raids across the border that left Stanton with little sympathy for the Confederate marauder. Upon reading the telegram, Stanton did not hesitate a moment. "Arrest him!" he ordered Assistant Secretary Dana. As Dana was leaving the room, however, Stanton called him back. "No, wait; better to go over and see the President."

Dana found Lincoln in his office. "Halloo, Dana!" Lincoln greeted him. "What's up?" Dana described the situation, explaining that Stanton wanted to arrest Thompson but thought he should first "refer the question" to Lincoln. "Well," said Lincoln, "no, I rather think not. When you have got an elephant by the hind leg, and he's trying to run away, it's best to let him run."

Mary Lincoln's memories of her husband's infectious happiness that day match the recollections of his inner circle. She had never seen him so "cheerful," she told Francis Carpenter, "his manner was even playful. At three o'clock, in the afternoon, he drove out with me in the open carriage, in starting, I asked him, if any one, should accompany us, he immediately replied—'No—I prefer to ride by ourselves to day.' During the drive he was so gay, that I said to him, laughingly, 'Dear Husband, you almost startle me by your great cheerfulness,' he replied, 'and well I may feel so, Mary, I consider *this day*, the war, has come to a close—and then added, 'We must *both*, be more cheerful in the future—between the war & the loss of our darling Willie—we have both, been very miserable.' "

As the carriage rolled toward the Navy Yard, Mary recalled, "he spoke of his old Springfield home, and recollections of his early days, his little brown cottage, the law office, the court room, the green bag for his briefs and law papers, his adventures when riding the circuit." They had traveled an unimaginable distance together since their first dance in Springfield a quarter of a century earlier. Over the years, they had supported each other, irritated each other, shared a love of family, politics, poetry, and drama. Mary's descent into depression after Willie's death had added immeasurably to Lincoln's burdens, and the terrible pressures of the war had further distorted their relationship. His intense focus on his presidential responsibilities had often left her feeling abandoned and resentful. Now, with the war coming to an end and time bringing solace to their grief, the Lincolns could plan for a happier future. They hoped to travel someday—to Europe and the Holy Land, over the Rockies to California, then back home to Illinois, where their life together had begun.

As the carriage neared the White House, Lincoln saw that a group of old friends, including Illinois governor Richard Oglesby, were just leaving. "Come back, boys, come back," he told them, relishing the relaxing company of friends. They remained for some time, Governor Oglesby recalled. "Lincoln got to reading some humorous book; I think it was by 'John Phoenix.' They kept sending for him to come to dinner. He promised each time to go, but would continue reading the book. Finally he got a sort of peremptory order that he must come to dinner at once."

The early dinner was necessary, for the Lincolns had plans to see Laura Keene in *Our American Cousin* at Ford's Theatre that evening. After supper, the president met with Noah Brooks, Massachusetts congressman George Ashmun, and Speaker Colfax, who was soon to depart for California. "How I would rejoice to make that trip!" Lincoln told Colfax, "but public duties chain me down here, and I can only envy you its pleasures." The president invited Colfax to join him at the theater that night, but Colfax had too many commitments.

To Noah Brooks, Lincoln had never seemed "more hopeful and buoyant concerning the condition of the country. . . . He was full of fun and anecdotes, feeling especially jubilant at the prospect before us." His parting words, Brooks recalled, focused on the country's economic future. "Grant thinks that we can reduce the cost of the army establishment at least a half million a day, which, with the reduction of expenditures of the Navy, will soon bring down our national debt to something like decent proportions, and bring our national paper up to a par, or nearly so with gold."

Speaker Colfax was among several people who declined the Lincolns' invitation to the theater that evening. The morning edition of the *National Republican* had announced that the Grants would join the Lincolns in the president's box that night, but Julia Grant had her heart set on visiting their children in New Jersey, so Grant asked to be excused. The Stantons also declined. Stanton, like Chase, considered the theater a foolish diversion and, more important, a dangerous one. He had fought a losing battle for months to keep the president from such public places, and he felt that his presence would only sanction an unnecessary hazard. Earlier that day, "unwilling to encourage the theater project," Stanton had refused to let his chief telegrapher, Thomas Eckert, accept Lincoln's invitation, even though the president had teasingly requested him for his uncommon strength—he had been known to "break a poker over his arm" and could serve as a bodyguard.

It was after eight when the Lincolns entered their carriage to drive to the theater. "I suppose it's time to go," Lincoln told Colfax, "though I would rather stay." While nothing had provided greater diversion during the bitter nights of his presidency than the theater, Lincoln required no escape on this happy night. Still, he had made a commitment. "It has been advertised that we will be there," he told his bodyguard, Crook, who had the night off, "and I cannot disappoint the people." Clara Harris—the daughter of Mary's friend Senator Ira Harris—and her fiancé, Major Henry Rathbone, joined the Lincolns in their carriage.

• • •

As the Lincolns rode to Ford's Theatre on 10th Street, John Wilkes Booth and three conspirators were a block away at the Herndon House. Booth had devised a plan that called for the simultaneous assassinations of President Lincoln, Secretary of State Seward, and Vice President Johnson. Having learned that morning of Lincoln's plan to attend the theater, he had decided that this night would provide their best opportunity. The powerfully built Lewis Powell, accompanied by David Herold, was assigned to kill Seward at his Lafayette Square home. Meanwhile, the carriage maker George Atzerodt was to shoot the vice president in his suite at the Kirkwood Hotel. Booth, whose familiarity with the stagehands would ensure access, would assassinate the president.

Just as Brutus had been honored for slaying the tyrant Julius Caesar, Booth believed he would be exalted for killing an even "greater tyrant." Assassinating Lincoln would not be enough. "Booth knew," his biographer observes, "that in the end, the Brutus conspiracy was foiled by Marc Antony, whose famous oration made outlaws of the assassins and a martyr of Caesar." William Henry Seward, Lincoln's Mark Antony, must not live. Finally, to throw the entire North into disarray, the vice president must die as well. The triple assassinations were set for 10:15 p.m.

• • •

Still bedridden, Seward had enjoyed his best day since his nearly fatal carriage accident nine days earlier. Fanny Seward noted in her diary that he had slept well the previous night and had taken "solid food for the first time." In the afternoon, he had "listened with a look of pleasure to the narrative of the events of the Cabinet meeting," which Fred, as assistant secretary, had attended in his father's stead. Later in the afternoon, he had listened to Fanny's reading of "Enoch Arden" and remarked on how much he enjoyed it.

The three-story house was full of people. The entire family, except Will and Jenny, were there—Frances, Augustus, Fred, Anna, and Fanny. In addition to the half-dozen household servants and the State Department messenger rooming on the third floor, two soldiers had been assigned by Stanton to stay with Seward. In the early evening, Edwin Stanton had stopped by to check on his friend and colleague. He stayed for a while, chatting with other visitors until martial music in the air reminded him that War Department employees had planned on serenading him that night at his home six blocks away.

After all the guests left, "the quiet arrangements for the night" began. To ensure that Seward was never left alone, the family members had taken turns sitting by his bed. That night Fanny was scheduled to stay with him until 11 p.m., when her brother Gus would relieve her. George Robinson, one of the soldiers whom Stanton had detailed to the household, was standing by. Shortly after 10 p.m., Fanny noticed that her father was falling asleep. She closed the pages of the *Legends of Charlemagne*, turned down the gas lamps, and took a seat on the opposite side of the bed.

Fred Seward later wrote that "there seemed nothing unusual in the occurrence, when a tall, well dressed, but unknown man presented himself" at the door. Powell told the servant who answered the bell that he had some medicine for Mr. Seward and had been instructed by his physician to deliver it in person. "I told him he could not go up," the servant later testified, "that if he would give me the medicine, I would tell Mr. Seward how to take it." Powell was so insistent that the boy stepped aside. When he reached the landing, Fred Seward stopped him. "My father is asleep; give me the medicine and the directions; I will take them to him." Powell argued that he must deliver it in person, but Fred refused.

At this point, Fred recalled, the intruder "stood apparently irresolute." He began to head down the stairs, then "suddenly turning again, he sprang up and forward, having drawn a Navy revolver, which he levelled, with a muttered oath, at my head, and pulled the trigger." This was the last memory Fred would have of that night. The pistol misfired, but Powell brought it down so savagely that Fred's skull was crushed in two places, exposing his brain and rendering him unconscious.

Hearing the disturbance, Private Robinson ran to the door from Seward's bedside. The moment the door was opened, Powell rushed inside, brandishing his now broken pistol in one hand and a large knife in the other. He slashed Robinson in the forehead with his knife, knocking him "partially down," and headed toward Seward. Fanny ran beside Powell, begging him not to kill her father. When Seward heard the word "kill," he awakened, affording him "one glimpse of the assassin's face bending over" before the large bowie knife plunged into his neck and face, severing his cheek so badly that "the flap hung loose on his neck." Oddly, he would later recall that his only impressions were what a fine-looking man Powell was and "what handsome cloth that overcoat is made of."

Fanny's screams brought her brother Gus into the room as Powell advanced again upon Seward, who had been knocked to the floor by the force of the blows. Gus and the injured Robinson managed to pull Powell away, but not before he struck Robinson again and slashed Gus on the forehead and the right hand. When Gus ran for his pistol, Powell bolted down the stairs, stabbing Emerick Hansell, the young State Department messenger, in the back before he bolted out the door and fled through the city streets.

The clamor had roused the entire household. Anna sent the servant to fetch Dr. Verdi, while Private Robinson, though bleeding from his head and shoulders, lifted Seward onto the bed and instructed Fanny about "staunching the blood with clothes & water." Still fearing that another assassin might be hiding in the house, Frances and Anna checked the attic while Fanny searched the rooms on the parlor floor.

Dr. Verdi would never forget his first sight of Seward that night. "He looked like an exsanguinated corpse. In approaching him my feet went deep in blood. Blood was streaming from an extensive gash in his swollen cheek; the cheek was now laid open." So "frightful" was the wound and "so great was the loss of blood" that Verdi assumed the jugular vein must have been cut. Miraculously, it was not. Further examination revealed that the knife had been deflected by the metal contraption holding Seward's broken jaw in place. In bizarre fashion, the carriage accident had saved his life.

"I had hardly sponged his face from the bloody stains and replaced the flap," Verdi recalled, "when Mrs. Seward, with an intense look, called me to her. 'Come and see Frederick,' said she." Not understanding, he followed Frances to the next room, where he "found Frederick bleeding profusely from the head." Fred's appearance was so "ghastly" and his wounds so large that Verdi feared he would not live, but with the application of "cold water pledgets," he was able to stanch the bleeding temporarily.

Once Fred was stabilized, Frances drew Dr. Verdi into another room on the same floor. "For Heaven's sake, Mrs. Seward," asked the befuddled doctor, "what does all this mean?" Verdi found Gus lying on the bed with stab wounds on his hand and forehead, but assured Frances that he would recover. Frances barely had time to absorb these words of comfort before entreating Dr. Verdi to see Private Robinson. "I ceased wondering," Verdi recalled, "my mind became as if paralyzed; mechanically I followed her and examined Mr. Robinson. He had four or five cuts on his shoulders."

"Any more?" Verdi asked, though not imagining the carnage could go on. "Yes," Frances answered, "one more." She led him to Mr. Hansell, "piteously groaning on the bed." Stripping off the young man's clothes, Verdi "found a deep gash just above the small of the back, near the spine."

"And all this," Verdi thought, "the work of one man—yes, of one man!"

• • •

IN PREPARING FOR the attack on the vice president, George Atzerodt had taken a room at the Kirkwood Hotel, where Johnson was staying. At 10:15, he was supposed to ring the bell of Suite 68, enter the room by force, find his target, and murder him. When first informed that the original plan to kidnap the president had shifted to a triple assassination, he had balked. "I won't do it," he had insisted. "I enlisted to abduct the President of the United States, not to kill." He had eventually agreed to help, but fifteen minutes before the appointed moment, seated at the bar of the Kirkwood House, he changed his mind, left the hotel, and never returned.

• • •

JOHN WILKES BOOTH had left little to chance in his plot to kill the president. Though already well acquainted with the layout of Ford's Theatre, Booth had attended a dress rehearsal the day before to better rehearse his scheme for shooting Lincoln in the state box and then escaping into the alley beside the theater. That morning he had again visited the theater to collect his mail, chatting amiably in the front lobby with the theater owner's brother, Harry Ford. Booth had already taken his place inside the theater when the Lincolns arrived.

The play had started as the presidential party entered the flag-draped box in the dress circle. The notes of "Hail to the Chief" brought the audience to their feet, applauding wildly and craning to see the president. Lincoln responded "with a smile and bow" before taking his seat in a comfortable armchair at the center of the box, with Mary by his side. Clara Harris was seated at the opposite end of the box, while Henry Rathbone occupied a small sofa on her left. Observing the president and first lady, one theatergoer noticed that she "rested her hand on his knee much of the time, and often called his attention to some humorous situation on the stage." Mary herself later recalled that as she snuggled ever closer to her husband, she had whispered, "What will Miss Harris think of my hanging on to you so?" He had looked at her and smiled. "She wont think any thing about it."

During the performance, the White House footman delivered a message to the president. At about twelve minutes after ten, the impeccably dressed John Wilkes Booth presented his calling card to the footman and gained admittance to the box. Once inside, he raised his pistol, pointed it at the back of the president's head, and fired.

As Lincoln slumped forward, Henry Rathbone attempted to grab the intruder. Booth pulled out his knife, slashed Rathbone in the chest, and managed to leap from the box onto the stage fifteen feet below. "As he jumped," one eyewitness recalled, "one of the spurs on his riding-boots caught in the folds of the flag draped over the front, and caused him to fall partly on his hands and knees as he struck the stage." Another onlooker observed that "he was suffering great pain," but, "making a desperate effort, he struggled up." Raising "his shining dagger in the air, which reflected the light as though it had been a diamond," he shouted the now historic words of the Virginia state motto—"Sic semper tyrannis" (Thus always to tyrants)—and ran from the stage.

Until the screams broke forth from the president's box, many in the audience thought the dramatic moment was part of the play. Then they saw Mary Lincoln frantically waving. "They have shot the President!" she cried. "They have shot the President!" Charles Leale, a young doctor seated near the presidential box, was the first to respond. "When I reached the President," he recalled, "he was almost dead, his eyes were closed." Unable at first to locate the wound, he stripped away Lincoln's coat and collar. Examining the base of the skull, he discovered "the perfectly smooth opening made by the ball." Using his finger "as a probe" to remove "the coagula which was firmly matted with the hair," he released the flow of blood, relieving somewhat the pressure on Lincoln's brain. Another doctor, Charles Sabin Taft, Julia Taft's half brother, soon arrived, and the decision was made to remove the president from the crowded box to a room in the Petersen boardinghouse across the street.

By this time, people had massed in the street. The word began to spread that assassins had attacked not only Lincoln but Seward as well. Joseph Sterling, a young clerk in the War Department, rushed to inform Stanton of the calamity. On his way, he encountered his roommate, J. G. Johnson, who joined him on the terrible errand. "When Johnson and I reached Stanton's residence," Sterling recalled, "I was breathless," so when Stanton's son Edwin Jr. opened the door, Johnson was the one to speak. "We have come," Johnson said, "to tell your father that President Lincoln has been shot." Young Stanton hurried to his father, who had been undressing for bed. When the war secretary came to the door, Sterling recalled, "he fairly shouted at me in his heavy tones: 'Mr. Sterling what news is this you bring?' " Sterling told him that both Lincoln and Seward had been assassinated. Desperately hoping this news was mere rumor, Stanton remained calm and skeptical. "Oh, that can't be so," he said, "that can't be so!" But when another clerk arrived at the door to describe the attack on Seward, Stanton had his carriage brought around at once, and against the appeals of his wife, who feared that he, too, might be a target, he headed for Seward's house at Lafayette Square.

The news reached Gideon Welles almost simultaneously. He had already gone to bed when his wife reported someone at the door. "I arose at once," Welles recorded in his diary, "and raised a window, when my messenger, James called to me that Mr. Lincoln the President had been shot," and that Seward and his son had been assassinated. Welles thought the story "very incoherent and improbable," but the messenger assured him that he had already been to Seward's house to check its veracity before coming to see his boss. Also ignoring his wife's protests, Welles dressed and set forth in the foggy night for the Seward house on the other side of the square.

Upon reaching Seward's house, Welles and Stanton were shocked at what they found. Blood was everywhere—on "the white wood work of the entry," on the stairs, on the dresses of the women, on the floor of the bedroom. Seward's bed, Welles recalled, "was saturated with blood. The Secretary was lying on his back, the upper part of his head covered by a cloth, which extended down over his eyes." Welles questioned Dr. Verdi in a whisper, but Stanton was unable to mute his stentorian voice until the doctor asked for quiet. After looking in on Fred's unconscious form, the two men walked together down the stairs. In the lower hall, they exchanged what information they had regarding the president. Welles thought they should go to the White House, but Stanton believed Lincoln was still at the theater. Army quartermaster general Meigs, who had just come to the door, implored them not to go to 10th Street, where thousands of people had gathered. When they insisted, he decided to join them.

Twelve blocks away, in his home at Sixth and E streets, Chief Justice Chase had already retired for the night. Earlier that afternoon, he had taken a carriage ride with Nettie, intending to stop at the White House to remonstrate with Lincoln over his too lenient approach to Reconstruction and his failure to demand universal suffrage. At the last minute, "uncertain how [Lincoln] would take it," Chase had decided to wait until the following day.

He was fast asleep when a servant knocked on his bedroom door. There was a gentleman downstairs, the servant said, who claimed "the President had been shot." The caller was a Treasury employee who had actually witnessed the shooting "by a man who leaped from the box upon the stage & escaped by the rear." Chase hoped "he might be mistaken," but in short order, three more callers arrived. Each "confirmed what I had been told & added that Secretary Seward had also been assassinated, and that guards were being placed around the houses of all the prominent officials, under the apprehension that the plot had a wide range. My first impulse was to rise immediately & go to the President . . . but reflecting that I could not possibly be of any service and should probably be in the way of those who could, I resolved to wait for morning & further intelligence. In a little while the guard came—for it was supposed that I was one of the destined victims—and their heavy tramp-tramp was heard under my window all night. . . . It was a night of horrors."

When Stanton and Welles arrived at the crammed room in the Petersen boardinghouse, they found that Lincoln had been placed diagonally across a bed to accommodate his long frame. Stripped of his shirt, "his large arms," Welles noted, "were of a size which one would scarce have expected from his spare appearance." His devastating wound, the doctors reported with awe, "would have killed most men instantly, or in a very few minutes. But Mr. Lincoln had so *much vitality*" that he continued to struggle against the inevitable end.

Mary spent most of the endless night weeping in an adjoining parlor, where several women friends tried vainly to comfort her. "About once an hour," Welles noted, she "would repair to the bedside of her dying husband and with lamentation and tears remain until overcome by emotion." She could only rotely repeat the question "Why didn't he shoot me? Why didn't he shoot me?" Though everyone in the room knew the president was dying, Mary was not told, out of fear that she would collapse. Whenever she came into the room, Dr. Taft recalled, "clean napkins were laid over the crimson stains on the pillow."

Early on, Mary sent a messenger for Robert, who had remained at home that night in the company of John Hay. He had already turned in when the White House doorkeeper came to his room. "Something happened to the President," Thomas Pendel told Robert, "you had better go down to the theater and see what it is." Robert asked Pendel to get Hay. Reaching Hay's room, Pendel told him, "Captain Lincoln wants to see you at once. The President has been shot." Pendel recalled that when Hay heard the news, "he turned deathly pale, the color entirely leaving his cheeks." The two young men jumped in a carriage, picking up Senator Sumner along the way.

Mary was torn over whether to summon Tad, but was apparently persuaded that the emotional boy would be devastated if he saw his father's condition. Tad and his tutor had gone that night to Grover's Theatre to see *Aladdin.* The theater had been decorated with patriotic emblems, and a poem commemorating Fort Sumter's recapture was read aloud between the acts. An eyewitness recalled that the audience was "enjoying the spectacle of Aladdin" when the theater manager came forward, "as pale as a ghost." A look of "mortal agony" contorted his face as he announced to the stunned audience that the president had been shot at Ford's Theatre.

In the midst of the pandemonium that followed, Tad was seen running "like a young deer, shrieking in agony."

"Poor little Tad," Pendel recalled, returned to the White House in tears. "O Tom Pen! Tom Pen!" Tad wailed. "They have killed Papa dead. They've killed Papa dead!" Pendel carried the little boy into Lincoln's bedroom. Turning down the bedcovers, he helped Tad undress and finally got him to lie down. "I covered him up and laid down beside him, put my arm around him, and talked to him until he fell into a sound sleep."

By midnight the entire cabinet, with the exception of Seward, had gathered in the small room at the Petersen boardinghouse. An eyewitness noted that Robert Lincoln "bore himself with great firmness, and constantly endeavored to assuage the grief of his mother by telling her to put her trust in God." Despite his brave attempts to console others, he was sometimes "entirely overcome" and "would retire into the hall and give vent to most heartrending lamentations." Almost no one was able to contain his grief that night, for as one witness observed, "there was not a soul present that did not love the president."

To Edwin Stanton fell the onerous task of alerting the generals, taking the testimony of witnesses at the theater, and orchestrating the search for the assassins. "While evidently swayed by the great shock which held us all under its paralyzing influence," Colonel A. F. Rockwell noted, "he was not only master of himself but unmistakably the dominating power over all. Indeed, the members of the cabinet, much as children might to their father, instinctively deferred to him in all things."

Throughout the night, Stanton dictated numerous dispatches, which were carried to the War Department telegraph office by a relay team of messengers positioned nearby. "Each messenger," Stanton's secretary recalled, "after handing a dispatch to the next, would run back to his post to wait for the next." The first telegram went to General Grant, requesting his immediate presence in Washington. "The President was assassinated at Ford's Theater at 10.30 to-night and cannot live. . . . Secretary Seward and his son Frederick were also assassinated at their residence and are in a dangerous condition." The dispatch reached Grant in the Bloodgood Hotel, where he was taking supper. He "dropped his head," Horace Porter recalled, "and sat in perfect silence." Noticing that he had turned "very pale," Julia Grant guessed that bad news had arrived and asked him to read the telegram aloud. "First prepare yourself for the most painful and startling news that could be received," he warned. As he made plans to return to Washington, he told Julia that the tidings filled him "with the gloomiest apprehension. The President was inclined to be kind and magnanimous, and his death at this time is an irreparable loss to the South, which now needs so much both his tenderness and magnanimity."

At 1 a.m., Stanton telegraphed the chief of police in New York, telling him to "send here immediately three or four of your best detectives." Half an hour later, he notified General Dix, "The wound is mortal. The President has been insensible ever since it was inflicted, and is now dying." Three hours later, he updated Dix: "The President continues insensible and is sinking." Early eyewitness accounts, Stanton revealed, suggested "that two assassins were engaged in the horrible crime, Wilkes Booth being the one that shot the President."

Shortly after dawn, Mary entered the room for the last time. "The death-struggle had begun," Welles recorded. "As she entered the chamber and saw how the beloved features were distorted, she fell fainting to the floor." Restoratives were given, and Mary was assisted back to the sofa in the parlor, never again to see her husband alive.

No sooner had "the town clocks struck seven," one observer recalled, than "the character of the President's breathing changed. It became faint and low. At intervals it altogether ceased, until we thought him dead. And then it would be again resumed." Lincoln's nine-hour struggle had reached its final moments. "Let us pray," Reverend Phineas D. Gurley said, and everyone present knelt.

At 7:22 a.m., April 15, 1865, Abraham Lincoln was pronounced dead. Stanton's concise tribute from his deathbed still echoes. "Now he belongs to the ages."

When Mary was told that he was gone, she piteously demanded, "Oh, why did you not tell me that he was dying." Her moans could be heard throughout the house. Finally, with Robert's help, she was taken to her carriage, which had waited in front of the house through the long night.

Until the moment of Lincoln's death, Stanton's "coolness and self-possession" had seemed "remarkable" to those around him. Now he could not stop the tears that streamed down his cheeks. In the days that followed, even as he worked tirelessly to secure the city and catch the conspirators, "Stanton's grief was uncontrollable," recalled Horace Porter, "and at the mention of Mr. Lincoln's name he would break down and weep bitterly."

While Stanton's raw grief surprised those who had seen only his gruff exterior, John Hay understood. "Not everyone knows, as I do," he wrote Stanton, "how close you stood to our lost leader, how he loved you and trusted you, and how vain were all the efforts to shake that trust and confidence, not lightly given & never withdrawn. All this will be known some time of course, to his honor and yours."

Salmon Chase was up at dawn. Soldiers had guarded him through the "night of horrors," and he was ready to join his colleagues at Lincoln's side. As he reached 10th Street, however, he encountered Assistant Treasury Secretary Maunsell Field. "Is he dead?" Chase asked. "Yes," Field replied, noting that Chase's "eyes were bloodshot, and his entire face was distorted." The Chief Justice had arrived too late, the president was already dead, and his colleagues had dispersed. Uncertain what to do next, Chase walked to Seward's house. Guards had been stationed to prevent entry, but Chase was recognized and allowed into the lower hall. There, doctors told him that Seward "had partially recovered" and, though still in critical condition, "might live—but that Mr. Frederick Seward's case was hopeless."

Chase headed toward the Kirkwood Hotel to call on the man who represented the future: the soon-to-be president, Andrew Johnson. In Johnson's suite, he encountered his old enemies Montgomery Blair and his father. He took Old Man Blair's hand and "with tearful eyes said 'Mr. Blair I hope that from this day there will cease all anger & bitterness between us.' " The old gentleman responded with equal warmth and kindness.

Perhaps more than any of Lincoln's colleagues, the Southern-born Blairs understood that the assassination was a calamity for the South. "Those of southern sympathies know now they have lost a friend willing— & more powerful to protect & serve them than they can now ever hope to find again," Elizabeth Blair remarked to her husband in a letter later that day. "Their grief is as honest as that of any one of our side." An editorial in the *Richmond Whig* expressed similar sentiments, observing that with Lincoln's death, "the heaviest blow which has ever fallen upon the people of the South has descended."

In distant St. Louis, where his son Barton had found him a new house with a large garden and a comfortable study, Edward Bates was shaken by "the astounding news" that reached him by telegram. In his diary, he remarked that beyond the "calamity which the nation has sustained, my private feelings are deeply moved by the sudden murder of my chief, with and under whom I have served the country, through many difficult and trying scenes, and always with mutual sentiments of respect and friendship. I mourn his fall, both for the country and for myself."

News of Lincoln's death was withheld from Seward. The doctors feared that he could not sustain the shock. On Easter Sunday, however, as he looked out the window toward Lafayette Park, he noticed the War Department flag at half-mast. "He gazed awhile," Noah Brooks reported, "then, turning to his attendant," he announced, "The President is dead." The attendant tried to deny it, but Seward knew with grim certainty. "If he had been alive he would have been the first to call on me," he said, "but he has not been here, nor has he sent to know how I am, and there's the flag at halfmast." He lay back on the bed, "the great tears coursing down his gashed cheeks, and the dreadful truth sinking into his mind." His good friend, his captain and chief, was dead.

"The history of governments," John Hay later observed, "affords few instances of an official connection hallowed by a friendship so absolute and sincere as that which existed between these two magnanimous spirits. Lincoln had snatched away from Seward at Chicago the prize of a laborious life-time, when it seemed within his grasp. Yet Seward was the first man named in his Cabinet and the first who acknowledged his personal preeminence. . . . From the beginning of the Administration to that dark and terrible hour when they were both struck down by the hand of murderous treason, there was no shadow of jealousy or doubt ever disturbed their mutual confidence and regard."

• • •

FLAGS REMAINED AT HALF-STAFF in the nation's capital until the last week of May, when citizens from all over the country came to Washington to witness "the farewell march" of nearly two hundred thousand Union soldiers who would soon disband and return to their homes. Stanton had orchestrated the two-day pageant as a final tribute to the brave men who had fought on battlefields from Antietam to Fredericksburg, Gettysburg to Vicksburg, Atlanta to the sea. "Never in the history of Washington," reported Noah Brooks, "had there been such an enormous influx of visitors as at that time. For weeks there had been so vast a volume of applications for accommodations at the hotels and boarding-houses that every available nook and corner had been taken."

Schools and government buildings were closed for the occasion. Reviewing stands had been built all along Pennsylvania Avenue, "from the Capitol to the White House." A covered platform had been erected to seat President Andrew Johnson, General Grant, and an assortment of dignitaries. The weather was beautiful on both days: "The air was bright, clear, and invigorating."

The first day was dedicated to the Army of the Potomac. Hour after hour the troops filed past in review—the cavalry, the mounted artillery, the infantry, the engineering brigades—each with their distinctive uniforms and badges, accompanied by "the clatter of hoofs, the clank of sabers, and the shrill call of bugles." It was, Gideon Welles marveled, a "magnificent and imposing spectacle."

"You see in these armies," Stanton predicted, "the foundation of our

Republic—our future railway managers, congressmen, bank presidents, senators, manufacturers, judges, governors, and diplomats; yes, and not less than half a dozen presidents." (He was very nearly right, for five of the next seven presidents would be Civil War veterans: Ulysses S. Grant, Rutherford B. Hayes, James Garfield, Benjamin Harrison, and William McKinley.)

Over a quarter of a century earlier, in 1838, young Abraham Lincoln had spoken with fervor of the veterans of the Revolutionary War, who were by then mostly gone, the fabled scenes of their great struggle for American independence growing "more and more dim by the lapse of time." In that war, "nearly every adult male had been a participant," he said, "in the form of a husband, a father, a son or a brother," until "a *living history was* to be found in every family." Such he had said was no longer true for his generation.

Now a new "living history" had been forged in the families of nearly three million Union soldiers who had fought to create what their matured leader had called "a new birth of freedom" to ensure that "government of the people, by the people, for the people, shall not perish from the earth." The soldiers marching down Pennsylvania Avenue that warm spring day knew they had accomplished something that would change their lives and their nation forever.

The second day belonged to the Army of the West, marching with solemn dignity behind General Sherman. "The streets were filled with people to see the pageant," Sherman recalled. "When I reached the Treasury-building, and looked back, the sight was simply magnificent. The column was compact, and the glittering muskets looked like a solid mass of steel, moving with the regularity of a pendulum."

When Sherman came to the corner of Lafayette Square, someone pointed to an upper window of a brick house where Seward, still too feeble to walk on his own, had been carried to witness the parade. "I moved in that direction and took off my hat to Mr. Seward," Sherman recalled. "He recognized the salute, returned it, and then we rode on steadily past the President, saluting with our swords."

All of Washington was present, Gideon Welles sadly noted—congressmen, senators, justices, diplomats, governors, military officers, the members of the cabinet, fathers and sons, mothers and daughters. "But Abraham Lincoln was not there. All felt this." None felt that absence more keenly than the members of his cabinet, the remarkable group of rivals whom Lincoln had brought into his official family. They had fiercely opposed one another and often contested their chief on important questions, but, as Seward later remarked, "a Cabinet which should agree at once on every such question would be no better or safer than one counsellor." By calling these men to his side, Lincoln had afforded them an opportunity to exercise their talents to the fullest and to share in the labor and the glory of the struggle that would reunite and transform their country and secure their own places in posterity.

• • •

"I HAVE NO DOUBT that Lincoln will be the conspicuous figure of the war," predicted Ulysses S. Grant. "He was incontestably the greatest man I ever knew."

The poet Walt Whitman felt much the same. "I have more than once fancied to myself," Whitman wrote in 1888, "the time when the present century has closed, and a new one open'd, and the men and deeds of that contest have become somewhat vague and mythical." He fancied that at some commemoration of those earlier days, an "ancient soldier" would sit surrounded by a group of young men whose eyes and "eager questions" would betray their sense of wonder. "What! have you seen Abraham Lincoln—and heard him speak—and touch'd his hand?" Though conceding that the future might decide differently about the prairie president, Whitman had no trouble speaking for his own generation: "Abraham Lincoln seems to me the grandest figure yet, on all the crowded canvas of the Nineteenth Century."

Even Whitman might have been amazed by the scope of Lincoln's legacy by the time the new century arrived. In 1908, in a wild and remote area of the North Caucasus, Leo Tolstoy, the greatest writer of the age, was the guest of a tribal chief "living far away from civilized life in the mountains." Gathering his family and neighbors, the chief asked Tolstoy to tell stories about the famous men of history. Tolstoy told how he entertained the eager crowd for hours with tales of Alexander, Caesar, Frederick the Great, and Napoleon. When he was winding to a close, the chief stood and said, "But you have not told us a syllable about the greatest general and greatest ruler of the world. We want to know something about him. He was a hero. He spoke with a voice of thunder; he laughed like the sunrise and his deeds were strong as the rock. . . . His name was Lincoln and the country in which he lived is called America, which is so far away that if a youth should journey to reach it he would be an old man when he arrived. Tell us of that man."

"I looked at them," Tolstoy recalled, "and saw their faces all aglow, while their eyes were burning. I saw that those rude barbarians were really interested in a man whose name and deeds had already become a legend." He told them everything he knew about Lincoln's "home life and youth . . . his habits, his influence upon the people and his physical strength." When he finished, they were so grateful for the story that they presented him with "a wonderful Arabian horse." The next morning, as Tolstoy prepared to leave, they asked if he could possibly acquire for them a picture of Lincoln. Thinking that he might find one at a friend's house in the neighboring town, Tolstoy asked one of the riders to accompany him. "I was successful in getting a large photograph from my friend," recalled Tolstoy. As he handed it to the rider, he noted that the man's hand trembled as he took it. "He gazed for several minutes silently, like one in a reverent prayer, his eyes filled with tears."

Tolstoy went on to observe, "This little incident proves how largely the name of Lincoln is worshipped throughout the world and how legendary his personality has become. Now, why was Lincoln so great that he overshadows all other national heroes? He really was not a great general like Napoleon or Washington; he was not such a skilful statesman as Gladstone or Frederick the Great; but his supremacy expresses itself altogether in his peculiar moral power and in the greatness of his character.

"Washington was a typical American. Napoleon was a typical Frenchman, but Lincoln was a humanitarian as broad as the world. He was bigger than his country—bigger than all the Presidents together.

"We are still too near to his greatness," Tolstoy concluded, "but after a few centuries more our posterity will find him considerably bigger than we do. His genius is still too strong and too powerful for the common understanding, just as the sun is too hot when its light beams directly on us."

• • •

"EVERY MAN IS SAID to have his peculiar ambition," the twenty-three-year-old Abraham Lincoln had written in his open letter to the people of Sangamon County during his first bid for public office in the Illinois state legislature. "Whether it be true or not, I can say for one that I have no other [ambition] so great as that of being truly esteemed of my fellow men, by rendering myself worthy of their esteem. How far I shall succeed in gratifying this ambition, is yet to be developed."

The ambition to establish a reputation worthy of the esteem of his fellows so that his story could be told after his death had carried Lincoln through his bleak childhood, his laborious efforts to educate himself, his string of political failures, and a depression so profound that he declared himself more than willing to die, except that "he had done nothing to make any human being remember that he had lived." An indomitable sense of purpose had sustained him through the disintegration of the Union and through the darkest months of the war, when he was called upon again and again to rally his disheartened countrymen, soothe the animosity of his generals, and mediate among members of his often contentious administration.

His conviction that we are one nation, indivisible, "conceived in Liberty, and dedicated to the proposition that all men are created equal," led to the rebirth of a union free of slavery. And he expressed this conviction in a language of enduring clarity and beauty, exhibiting a literary genius to match his political genius.

With his death, Abraham Lincoln had come to seem the embodiment of his own words—"With malice toward none; with charity for all"—voiced in his second inaugural to lay out the visionary pathway to a reconstructed union. The deathless name he sought from the start had grown far beyond Sangamon County and Illinois, reached across the truly United States, until his legacy, as Stanton had surmised at the moment of his death, belonged not only to America but to the ages—to be revered and sung throughout all time.

EPILOGUE

AGAINST ALL ODDS, Seward and his son Frederick eventually recovered from their frightful injuries, but the "night of horrors" took its ultimate toll on Frances Seward. Six weeks afterward, convinced that she had taken on the afflictions of her loved ones through "vicarious suffering," she collapsed and died. Her funeral in Auburn was said to have brought together "the largest assemblage that ever attended the funeral of a woman in America." In the months that followed, Fanny remained at her father's side, trying to compensate for her departed mother until she herself fell desperately ill from tuberculosis. When she died two months short of her twenty-second birthday, Seward was inconsolable. "Truly it may be said," the *Washington Republican* noted, "that the assassin's blows passed by the father and son and fell fatally on the mother and daughter."

Seward remained secretary of state throughout President Andrew Johnson's term. While his attempts to mediate Johnson's bitter struggles with the radicals in Congress failed, he took great pride in what was originally lampooned as "Seward's Folly"—the purchase of Alaska. After retiring from public office, he spent his last years traveling. With Fred and Anna, he embarked on an eight-month journey to Alaska, California, and Mexico. Returning to Auburn, he immediately made plans for a trip around the world, visiting Japan, China, India, Egypt, Greece, Turkey, and France. He died peacefully in 1872 at the age of seventy-one, surrounded by his family. When his daughter-in-law Jenny asked if he had any deathbed advice to impart, he said simply: "Love one another." Thurlow Weed, who served as a pallbearer, wept openly as the body of his oldest friend was lowered into the grave.

Stanton's remaining days in the cabinet were acrimonious. His sympathy with the congressional radicals on Reconstruction brought him into open conflict with the president, who asked for his resignation. Refusing to honor Johnson's request even after he was handed a removal order, Stanton "barricaded himself" in his office for weeks, taking his meals in the department and sleeping on his couch. He argued that his dismissal violated the Tenure of Office Act, recently passed by congressional radicals over the president's veto, which required Senate consent for the removal of any cabinet officer. Johnson's disregard for the Tenure of Office Act became one of the articles of impeachment lodged against him in 1868. When the impeachment failed by one vote in the Senate, Stanton finally submitted his resignation.

Although exhausted by the ordeal, Stanton had little time to rest. His fortune had been depleted during his tenure in the cabinet. After returning to the practice of law, he was overjoyed when President Grant nominated him to the Supreme Court, the "only office" he had ever desired to hold, in December 1869. His happiness was short-lived. Three days later, as his family gathered for the Christmas holidays, he suffered a severe asthma attack, lapsed into unconsciousness, and died. He had just turned fifty-five. "I know that it is useless to say anything," Robert Todd Lincoln wrote to Stanton's son Edwin, Jr., "and yet when I recall the kindness of your father to me, when my father was lying dead and I felt utterly desperate, hardly able to realize the truth, I am as little able to keep my eyes from filling with tears as he was then."

Edward Bates spent his remaining years with his close-knit family, reunited with his son Fleming, whom he had welcomed home from the Confederate Army once the war ended. When Bates died in 1869 at the age of seventy-six, he was revered as much for his character as for his public accomplishments. Above all, one eulogist noted, "it was in his social and domestic relations that his character shown brightest; it was as a husband, as a father and a friend that he has endeared himself to others by ties which death cannot sever."

After presiding over the impeachment trial of Andrew Johnson, Salmon Chase turned his addicted gaze to the 1868 presidential race, his hopes resting with the Democrats after Grant had secured the Republican nomination. With Kate serving as his campaign manager, he had his name placed before the delegates, but when Ohio announced for New York's Horace Seymour, Chase's candidacy was doomed. Once more, his home state had derailed his ambitions. Four years later, still hoping for the presidential nod, he switched his allegiance to the Liberal Republican Party. Again the nomination eluded him, going instead to Horace Greeley. His physical condition weakened by a heart attack and a stroke, Chase fell into depression, confiding to a friend that he was "too much of an invalid to be more than a cipher. Sometimes I feel as if I were dead." Death came on May 7, 1873, with Kate and Nettie by his side. He was sixty-five.

After her father's death, Kate saw her marriage to Sprague fall apart. An affair with New York senator Roscoe Conkling ended in scandal when Sprague, finding the couple together at his Narragansett mansion, went after Conkling with a shotgun. Following a violent argument during which

Sprague tried to throw Kate from a bedroom window, she sued for divorce. She returned to Washington, where she died in poverty at fifty-eight.

The Blairs returned to the Democratic Party. Though Frank Blair was selected as Seymour's vice presidential candidate in 1868, his intemperate denunciations of opponents cut short what might have been a promising political future. He died from a fall in his house in 1875 at the age of fifty-four. Old Man Blair outlived his son by one year, maintaining "his physical vigor, his mental faculties and his sprightliness of disposition" until his death at eighty-five. Montgomery served as counsel to Democrat Samuel Tilden in the disputed election of 1876, which Republican Rutherford B. Hayes eventually won. Blair was writing a biography of Andrew Jackson when he died in 1883 at the age of seventy.

Gideon Welles supported Andrew Johnson during the impeachment trial, remaining in the cabinet until 1868. Returning to Connecticut, he wrote a series of historical essays and was among the first to depict Lincoln as "a towering figure, coping admirably with herculean tasks." His perceptive diary, which he edited in his last years, remains one of the most valuable sources on the dynamics within the Lincoln administration. Welles was seventy-five when he died from a streptococcus infection in 1878.

John Nicolay and John Hay remained friends until the end of their lives, coauthoring a massive ten-volume study of Lincoln based on his then-unpublished papers. Nicolay was at work on an abridged version of their study when he died in 1901 at sixty-nine. Hay served as secretary of state under Presidents William McKinley and Theodore Roosevelt. Shortly before he died from a blood clot at the age of sixty-six in 1905, he dreamed that he had returned "to the White House to report to the President who turned out to be Mr. Lincoln. He was very kind and considerate, and sympathetic about my illness. . . . He gave me two unimportant letters to answer. I was pleased that this slight order was within my power to obey." Forty years after the assassination of his beloved chief, Hay awoke with an "overpowering melancholy."

Mary Lincoln never recovered from her husband's death. After returning to Illinois, she confided to Elizabeth Blair Lee that "each morning, on awakening, from my troubled slumbers, the utter impossibility of living another day, so wretched, appears to me, as an impossibility." Were it not for her "precious Tad," she told her boy's tutor, she "would gladly welcome death."

Mother and son were nearly inseparable. Tad journeyed with Mary to Europe, demonstrating what John Hay described as "a thoughtful devotion and tenderness beyond his years." Not long after returning to America, Tad suffered what doctors termed "compression of the heart." He died two months later at eighteen. "The modest and cordial young fellow who passed through New York a few weeks ago with his mother will never be known outside the circle of his mourning friends," commented John Hay in a touching obituary written for the *New York Tribune*. "But 'little Tad' will be remembered as long as any live who bore a personal share in the great movements whose center for four years was Washington. He was so full of life and vigor—so bubbling over with health and high spirits, that he kept the house alive with his pranks and his fantastic enterprises."

Mary's misery was compounded by her ever-consuming worries over money. "It is very hard to deal with one who is sane on all subjects but one," Robert confided in Mary Harlan, the young woman who would become his wife. "You could hardly believe it possible, but my mother protests to me that she is in actual want and nothing I can do or say will convince her to the contrary." Her increasingly erratic behavior persuaded Robert to commit her to a state hospital for the insane where she remained for four months until she was released to the care of her sister Elizabeth in Springfield. The episode permanently estranged Mary from her only remaining child. After a final trip to Europe, she lived her remaining years as a virtual recluse in the Edwards mansion, where, in happier days, she and Abraham Lincoln had met and married. She was sixty-three in 1882 when her oft-stated longing for death was fulfilled at last.

ACKNOWLEDGMENTS

ANYONE WRITING on Abraham Lincoln stands on the shoulders of a monumental body of work, including classic volumes by some of our country's finest historians. I am immensely grateful to the many Lincoln scholars who generously welcomed me into their field, sharing sources, discussing ideas, inviting me to their homes, reading parts of my manuscript, and offering access to their rare collections of Lincolniana. They include David Herbert Donald, Douglas L. Wilson, Thomas F. Schwartz, Frank J. Williams, Harold Holzer, John R. Sellers, Virginia Laas, Michael A. Burlingame, Gabor S. Boritt, James O. Hall, Harold M. Hyman, Philip B. Kunhardt III, Peter W. Kuhnhardt, and Louise Taper.

In the course of the last ten years, I have been guided in my search for primary materials by superb staffs at thirty different libraries. I especially wish to thank the remarkably generous Thomas F. Schwartz, Kim Matthew Bauer, Mary Michals, and John Marruffo at the Abraham Lincoln Presidential Library and Museum in Springfield, Illinois.

I owe thanks as well to the following: in California, John Rhodehamel and the staff of the Huntington Library. In Illinois, the Chicago Historical Society; the Newberry Library; the University of Chicago's Special Collections Research Center and Harper Memorial Library; Daniel Weinberg and the Abraham Lincoln Book Shop. In Indiana, the Lincoln Museum. In Iowa, the State Historical Society of Iowa and the University of Iowa Library. In Kentucky, the Eastern Kentucky University Archives. In Louisiana, Judy Bolton and the staff of the Louisiana and Lower Mississippi Valley Collections of the Louisiana State University Library. In Maryland, the Maryland Historical Society.

In Massachusetts, the Boston Public Library's Rare Book and Manuscript Collections; the Concord Public Library; Harvard University's Government Documents and Microfilm Collection, the Houghton Library, the Arthur and Elizabeth Schlesinger Library on the History of Women in America, and Widener Library; and the Massachusetts Historical Society. In Missouri, Dennis Northcott and the staff of the Missouri Historical Society; the St. Louis Art Museum; and the State Historical Society of Missouri. In New Jersey, Don C. Skemer and Anna Lee Pauls at Princeton University's Department of Rare Books and Special Collections.

In New York, the New York State Library; Betty Mae Lewis and Peter A. Wisbey of the Seward House, Auburn; Mary M. Huth and the staff of the University of Rochester Library's Department of Rare Books and Special Collections. In Ohio, the Cincinnati Historical Society; John Haas and the staff of the Ohio Historical Society; the Ohio State House; and the Western Reserve Historical Society. In Pennsylvania, the Dauphin County Historical Society and the Historical Society of Pennsylvania. In Rhode Island, Mary-Jo Kline and Ann Morgan Dodge of Brown University's John Hay Library. In Virginia, the Virginia Historical Society. In Washington, D.C., John Sellers, Clark Evans, and the staff of the Library of Congress; Michael Musick and the staff of the National Archives and Records Administration; James C. Hewes at the Willard Hotel; and the staff at the Blair House. And last, Michael Burlingame, who is for all Lincoln scholars a library unto himself, generously sharing his unparalled knowledge of Lincoln while writing his own monumental Lincoln biography.

I owe an immense debt once again to my great friend and indefatigable assistant, Linda Vandegrift, who has worked at my side on all my projects for the past twenty years.

I am grateful to Nora Titone (currently writing what I am certain will be an extraordinary biography of Edwin Booth, actor and brother to Lincoln's assassin), who did research at Harvard University and in Illinois, the Land of Lincoln. Through our many discussions, she provided invaluable insights into the social, intellectual, and literary milieu of nineteenth-century America.

In Washington, Dr. Michelle Krowl, a brilliant Civil War historian who has published numerous scholarly articles and teaches at Northern Virginia Community College, displayed remarkable energy, intuition, and intelligence in digging through archives and checking source materials at both the Library of Congress and the National Archives.

There are many others who read portions of the manuscript and helped in various ways, including Judith Arnold, Beth Laski, Erik Owens, Louisa Thomas, Chad Callaghan, Michael Goodwin, Lindsay Hosmer, J. Wayne Lee, Phyllis Grann, John Logan, Paul Webb, Kathleen Krowl, Brad Gernand, Karen Needles, and John Hill, and all our good friends at our two favorite watering holes in Concord, Massachusetts—Serafina Ristorante and Walden Grille. To Michael Kushakji, who came to our house day and night when our computers failed, I owe a special debt.

As always, I am grateful to my supportive and enthusiastic literary agent, Binky Urban, and to the men and women at Simon & Schuster who have become almost like family after more than twenty-five years of collaboration: David Rosenthal, Carolyn Reidy, Irene Kheradi, Jackie Seow,

George Turianski, Linda Dingler, Ellen Sasahara, Lisa Healy, Victoria Meyer, and Elizabeth Hayes. For a superb job in copyediting the manuscript, I thank Ann Adelman and Emily Beth Thomas. I owe a special thanks to Roger Labrie, who displayed extraordinary grace under pressure while shepherding the book to meet various deadlines in the final stages.

I have long depended on my incomparable editor, Alice E. Mayhew, but never did her massive contributions weigh more heavily than on this book. No editor has a more profound knowledge of Abraham Lincoln. No editor could have given me better advice from start to finish on structure, tone, and language. She is the absolute best in her profession. I shall be forever grateful to her.

Finally, I owe more than I can ever express to my husband, Richard Goodwin, to whom this book is dedicated. He read and edited every single page, from the earliest drafts to the finished product. His passion for the subject of Abraham Lincoln matches my own. I argued with him, debated with him, and ended up usually following his advice. He has thought as deeply about Lincoln as anyone. This book is his creation as much as mine.

Concord, Massachusetts
July 2005

NOTES

Abbreviations Used in the Notes:

AL	Abraham Lincoln
CS	Charles Sumner
EB	Edward Bates
EBL	Elizabeth Blair Lee
EMS	Edwin M. Stanton
FAS	Frances A. (Miller) Seward
FB	Francis Preston ("Frank") Blair, Jr.
FPB	Francis Preston Blair, Sr.
FS	Frances A. ("Fanny") Seward
FWS	Frederick W. Seward
GBM	George B. McClellan
GW	Gideon Welles
JGN	John G. Nicolay
JH	John Hay
JWW	Jesse W. Weik
KCS	Kate Chase Sprague
LW	Lazette M. (Miller) Worden
MB	Montgomery Blair
MEM	Mary Ellen McClellan
MTL	Mary Todd Lincoln
SPC	Salmon P. Chase
SPL	Samuel Phillips Lee
TB	Therena Bates
TW	Thurlow Weed
USG	Ulysses S. Grant
WHH	William H. Herndon
WHS	William H. Seward
CW	*Collected Works of Abraham Lincoln*
HI	*Herndon's Informants*
NR	*National Republican*, Washington, D.C.
NYH	*New York Herald*, New York, N.Y.
NYT	*New York Times*, New York, N.Y.
NYTrib	*New York Tribune*, New York, N.Y.
OR	*The War of the Rebellion: A Compilation of the Official Records of the Union and Confederate Armies* (128 vols., Washington, D.C.: Government Printing Office, 1880–1901)
Star	*Evening Star*, Washington, D.C.

Chase Papers	*The Salmon P. Chase Papers: Microfilm Edition*, ed. John Niven (Frederick, Md.: University Publications of America, 1987)
Lincoln Papers	Papers of Abraham Lincoln, Manuscript Division, Library of Congress. Available at *Abraham Lincoln Papers at the Library of Congress*, Manuscript Division (Washington, D.C.: American Memory Project, [2000–01]), http://memory.loc.gov/ammem/alhtml/alhome.html
Nicolay Papers	Papers of John G. Nicolay, Manuscript Division, Library of Congress
Seward Papers	*The Papers of William H. Seward* (Woodbridge, Conn.: Research Publications, 1983
Welles Papers	Papers of Gideon Welles, Manuscript Division, Library of Congress

NOTE TO READERS: When quoting from primary documents, original spelling and grammar have been kept.

INTRODUCTION

Page

xv "there is little . . . of Abraham Lincoln": Frederick Douglass, "Oration in Memory of Abraham Lincoln," April 14, 1876, in *Frederick Douglass: Selected Speeches and Writings*, ed. Philip S. Foner, abridged by Yuval Taylor (Chicago: Lawrence Hill Books, 1999), pp. 620–21.

xvi "comparatively unknown . . . such anxious times": Ralph Waldo Emerson, "Abraham Lincoln," in *Miscellanies* (Cambridge, Mass.: Riverside Press, 1904), pp. 330–31.

xvi "very near . . . perfect man": EB, quoted in F. B. Carpenter, *Six Months at the White House with Abraham Lincoln* (New York: Hurd and Houghton, 1866), p. 68.

xix "field of glory": AL, "Address Before the Young Men's Lyceum of Springfield, Illinois," January 27, 1838, in *CW*, I, p. 113.

xix "a new birth of freedom": AL, "Address Delivered at the Dedication of the Cemetery at Gettysburg, November 19, 1863; Edward Everett Copy," in *CW*, VII, p. 21.

CHAPTER 1: FOUR MEN WAITING

Page

5 Lincoln was up early: Henry B. Rankin, *Personal Recollections of Abraham Lincoln* (New York and London: G. P. Putnam's Sons, 1916), p. 187.

5 Chenery House: Paul M. Angle, *"Here I Have Lived": A History of Lincoln's Springfield, 1821–1865* (Springfield, Ill.: Abraham Lincoln Association, 1935), p. 175.

5 Springfield businesses: See advertisements in *Illinois State Journal*, Springfield, Ill., May 18, 1860.

5 first ballot was not due to be called until 10 a.m.: *Press and Tribune*, Chicago, May 19, 1860; *Star*, May 19, 1860.

5 visibly "nervous, fidgety . . . excited": Christopher C. Brown interview, 1865–1866, in Douglas L. Wilson and Rodney O. Davis, eds., *Herndon's Informants: Letters, Interviews, and Statements About Abraham Lincoln* (Urbana and Chicago: University of Illinois Press, 1998), p. 438 [hereafter *HI*].

5 the untidy office: William H. Herndon and Jesse W. Weik, *Herndon's Life of Lincoln*, introduction and notes by Paul M. Angle, new introduction by Henry Steele Commager (Cleveland, Ohio: World Publishing Co., 1942; New York: Da Capo Press, 1983), pp. 254–55.

5 The editorial room: Paul Angle, *Lincoln in Springfield: A Guide to the Places in Springfield which were Associated with the Life of Abraham Lincoln* (Springfield, Ill.: Lincoln Centennial Association, 1927), p. 2.

6 a "complimentary" gesture: Entry of May 19, 1860, in Edward Bates, *The Diary of Edward Bates, 1859–1866*, ed. Howard K. Beale. Vol. IV of the Annual Report of the American Historical Association for the Year 1930 (Washington, D.C.: Government Printing Office, 1933), p. 130.

6 the town clock: *Illinois State Journal*, Springfield, Ill., January 17, 1860.

6 James Conkling: Clinton L. Conkling, "How Mr. Lincoln Received the News of His First Nomination," *Transactions of the Illinois State Historical Society* (1909), p. 64.

6 his singular way of walking . . . needed oiling: Herndon and Weik, *Herndon's Life of Lincoln*, p. 471.

6 "His legs . . . a hard day's work": William E. Doster, *Lincoln and Episodes of the Civil War* (New York and London: G. P. Putnam's Sons, 1915), p. 15.

6 His features . . . "as belong to a handsome man": *Press and Tribune*, Chicago, May 23, 1860.

6 "so overspread with sadness . . . capital of Illinois": Horace White, *Abraham Lincoln in 1854: An Address delivered before the Illinois State Historical Society, at its 9th Annual Meeting at Springfield, Illinois, Jan. 30, 1908* (Springfield, Ill.: Illinois State Historical Society, 1908), p. 19.

6 "this expression . . . true friendship": Ibid.

6 "his winning manner . . . and gentleness": *NYTrib*, November 10, 1860.

7 "you cease to think . . . awkward": *Utica Morning Herald*, reprinted in *NYTrib*, July 9, 1860.

7 "on a borrowed horse . . . a few clothes": Joshua F. Speed, *Reminiscences of Abraham Lincoln and Notes of a Visit to California* (Louisville, Ky.: John P. Morton & Co., 1884), p. 21.

7 population of Springfield: Harry E. Pratt, *Lincoln's Springfield* (Springfield, Ill.: Abraham Lincoln Association, 1938), p. 2; Octavia Roberts, *Lincoln in Illinois* (Boston: Houghton Mifflin, 1918), p. 94.

7 number of hotels, saloons, etc.: C.S. Williams, comp., *Williams' Springfield Directory City Guide, and Business Mirror, for 1860–61. To Which is Appended a List of Post Offices in the United States and Territories, Corrected up to Date* (Springfield, Ill.: Johnson & Bradford, 1860).

7 "the belle of the town": "Lincoln and Mary Todd," [c. 1880s], reel 11, Herndon-Weik Collection of Lincolniana, Manuscript Division, Library of Congress [hereafter Herndon-Weik Collection, DLC].

7 Mary's education: Ruth Painter Randall, *Mary Lincoln: Biography of a Marriage* (Boston: Little, Brown, 1953), pp. 23, 25, 27, 28; Jean H. Baker, *Mary Todd Lincoln: A Biography* (New York and London: W. W. Norton & Co., 1987), pp. 37–42, 44–45.

7 "I want to dance . . . he certainly did": Katherine Helm, *The True Story of Mary, Wife of Lincoln* (New York and London: Harper & Bros., 1928), p. 74.

7 children born, and one buried in Springfield: AL, "Farewell Address at Springfield, Illinois," February 11,

1861, in *The Collected Works of Lincoln*, Vol. IV, ed. Roy P. Basler (8 vols., New Brunswick, N.J.: Rutgers University Press, 1953), p. 190.

7 "two-story" . . . no garden: *New York Evening Post*, reprinted in *Albany Evening Journal*, May 24, 1860 (quote); *Utica Morning Herald*, reprinted in *NYTrib*, July 9, 1860; Frances Todd Wallace interview, [1865–1866], in *HI*, p. 486.

7 "The adornments . . . chastely appropriate": *Utica Morning Herald*, reprinted in *NYTrib*, July 9, 1860.

7 "the customary little table": Carl Schurz, *The Reminiscences of Carl Schurz. Vol. II: 1852–1863* (New York: McClure Co., 1907), p. 188.

7 "Everything tended to represent . . . showy display": *Springfield [Mass.] Republican*, May 23, 1860.

8 "moving heaven & Earth": David Davis and Jesse K. Dubois to AL, May 15, 1860, Lincoln Papers.

8 "a big brain and a big heart": Mrs. John A. Logan, quoted by Allan Nevins in foreword to Willard L. King, *Lincoln's Manager: David Davis* (Cambridge, Mass.: Harvard University Press, 1960), p. xi.

8 Norman Judd: Ibid., pp. 128–29.

8 he knew Lincoln "as intimately": Leonard Swett, quoted in Osborn H. Oldroyd, *Lincoln's Campaign, or The Political Revolution of 1860* (Chicago: Laird & Lee, 1896), p. 70.

8 the "circuit": Henry Clay Whitney, *Life on the Circuit with Lincoln*, introduction and notes by Paul M. Angle (Caldwell, Idaho: The Caxon Printers, 1940), pp. 61–88; see "Travelling on the Circuit," chapter 15 in Ida M. Tarbell, *The Life of Abraham Lincoln*, Vol. I (New York: S. S. McClure Co., 1895; New York: The Macmillan Company, 1917), pp. 241–56.

8 Lincoln . . . the center of attention: Henry C. Whitney, *Lincoln the Citizen. Vol. I of A Life of Lincoln* (1892; New York: Baker & Taylor Co., 1908), pp. 190–91; William H. Herndon, *A Letter from William H. Herndon to Isaac N. Arnold Relating to Abraham Lincoln, His Wife, and Their Life in Springfield* (privately printed, 1937).

8 crowds of villagers: Francis Fisher Browne, *The Every-Day Life of Abraham Lincoln* (New York: N. D. Thompson Publishing Co., 1886; Lincoln, Nebr., and London: University of Nebraska Press, 1995), p. 158.

8 emboldened his quest for office: David Herbert Donald, *Lincoln* (New York: Simon & Schuster, 1995), p. 106.

8 "broke down . . . mutual trust": Robert H. Wiebe, "Lincoln's Fraternal Democracy," in John L. Thomas, ed., *Abraham Lincoln and the American Political Tradition* (Amherst: University of Massachusetts Press, 1986), p. 19.

8 disparate elements of . . . Republican Party: Theodore Clarke Smith, *The Liberty and Free Soil Parties in the Old Northwest. Harvard Historical Studies*, Vol. VI (New York: Longmans, Green & Co., 1897; New York: Russell & Russell, 1967), p. 1; William Lee Miller, *Lincoln's Virtues: An Ethical Biography* (New York: Alfred A. Knopf, 2002), p. 317.

9 "Of *strange, discordant* . . . fought the battle through": AL, "A House Divided": Speech at Springfield, Illinois, June 16, 1858, in *CW*, II, p. 468.

9 when speech-making prowess: Lawrence W. Levine, *Highbrow / Lowbrow: The Emergence of Cultural Hierarchy in America* (Cambridge, Mass.: Harvard University Press, 1988), p. 36.

9 "from sun-up til sun-down": Christine Ann Fidler, "Young Limbs of the Law: Law Students, Legal Education and the Occupational Culture of Attorneys, 1820–1860." Ph.D. diss., University of California, Berkeley, 1996, p. 165.

9 attendance at Cooper Union speech: Benjamin P. Thomas, *Abraham Lincoln: A Biography* (New York: Alfred A. Knopf, 1952), p. 202.

9 "one of the happiest . . . New York audience": *NYTrib*, February 28, 1860.

9 state convention at Decatur: *Press and Tribune*, Chicago, May 11, 1860; Don E. Fehrenbacher, *Prelude to Greatness: Lincoln in the 1850s* (Stanford, Calif.: Stanford University Press, 1962), p. 148.

9 "the Rail Candidate for President": *NYH*, May 24, 1860.

9 "with no clogs . . . rights of the South": *Press and Tribune*, Chicago, May 15, 1860. The *Press and Tribune* became the *Tribune* on October 25, 1860.

9 "new in the field . . . very great many": AL to Sam Galloway, March 24, 1860, in *CW*, IV, p. 34.

10 "in a mood to come . . . their first love": Ibid.

10 "We are laboring . . . for any result": Nathan M. Knapp to AL, May 14, 1860, Lincoln Papers.

10 "Am very hopeful . . . be Excited": David Davis to AL, May 17, 1860, Lincoln Papers.

10 Lincoln stretched . . . "and practice law": Conkling, "How Mr. Lincoln Received the News," *Transactions* (1909), pp. 64–65.

11 Seward typically rose: Frederick W. Seward, *William H. Seward: An Autobiography from 1801 to 1834, with a Memoir of His Life, and Selections from His Letters, 1831–1846* (New York: D. Appleton & Co., 1877), p. 658 [hereafter Seward, *An Autobiography*]; Frederick W. Seward, *Seward at Washington, as Senator and Secretary of State. A Memoir of His Life, with Selections from His Letters, 1846–1861* (New York: Derby & Miller, 1891), p. 203.

11 description of Seward mansion: Interview with Betty Mae Lewis, curator of Seward House, Auburn, N.Y., 1999 [hereafter Lewis interview]; *The Seward House* (Auburn, N.Y.: The Foundation Historical Association, 1955); *NYH*, August 27, 1860.

11 Seward's interest in gardening: Seward, *An Autobiography*, pp. 368, 657–58.

11 "a lover's interest": WHS to [TW?], April 12, 1835, in ibid., p. 257.

11 "came in to the table . . . that was exhausted": Ibid., pp. 658, 461, 481; Lewis interview.

12 "The cannoneers . . . joyful news": *Auburn Democrat*, reprinted in the *Atlas and Argus*, Albany, N.Y., May 28, 1860.

12 weather conditions: WHS to FAS, December 17, 1834, reel 112, Seward Papers; Patricia C. Johnson, "Sensi-

tivity and Civil War: The Selected Diaries and Papers, 1858–1866, of Frances Adeline [Fanny] Seward." Ph.D. diss, University of Rochester, 1963, pp. 1–2.

12 Visitors had come . . . Weedsport to the north: Henry B. Stanton, *Random Recollections*, 3rd edn. (New York: Harper & Bros., 1887), p. 215.

12 Local restaurants had stocked up: *NYH*, August 27, 1860; *Auburn Democrat*, reprinted in the *Atlas and Argus*, Albany, N.Y., May 28, 1860.

12 the vigorous senator: See Glyndon G. Van Deusen, *William Henry Seward* (New York: Oxford University Press, 1967), pp. 255–57, 263.

12 *New York Herald* . . . "dauntless and intrepid": *NYH*, August 27, 1860.

12 slender frame . . . "most glorious original": Henry Adams to Charles Francis Adams, Jr., December 9, 1860, in *Letters of Henry Adams (1858–1891)*, Vol. I., ed. Worthington Chauncey Ford (Boston and New York: Houghton Mifflin, 1930), p. 63.

12 physical description of Seward: John M. Taylor, *William Henry Seward: Lincoln's Right Hand* (New York: HarperCollins, 1991), p. 17; Burton J. Hendrick, *Lincoln's War Cabinet* (Boston, Little, Brown, 1946), p. 8; Johnson, "Sensitivity and Civil War," pp. 11, 56–57; Frederic Bancroft, *The Life of William H. Seward*, Vol. I (New York: Harper & Bros., 1899; Gloucester, Mass.: Peter Smith, 1967), p. 184.

13 "school-boy elasticity . . . slashing swagger": Murat Halstead, *Three Against Lincoln: Murat Halstead Reports the Caucuses of 1860*, ed. William B. Hesseltine (Baton Rouge: Louisiana State University Press, 1960), p. 120.

13 Every room . . . by Washington Irving: Lewis interview; *The Seward House*, pp. 5–6, 12, 16, 23, 26; Seward, *An Autobiography*, pp. 440, 677; Susan Sutton Smith, "Mr. Seward's Home," *University of Rochester Library Bulletin* 31 (Autumn 1978), pp. 69–93.

13 "the honor in question . . . of its principles": *National Intelligencer*, Washington, D.C., May 19, 1860.

13 "No press has opposed . . . leadership of the man": *Atlas and Argus*, Albany, N.Y., May 19, 1860.

13 valedictory speech to the Senate: Bancroft, *The Life of William H. Seward*, Vol. I, p. 522; Van Deusen, *William Henry Seward*, p. 222; entry for May 13, 1860, Diary of Charles Francis Adams, reel 75, *microfilms of The Adams Papers owned by the Adams Manuscript Trust and deposited in the Massachusetts Historical Society*, Part I (Boston: Massachusetts Historical Society, 1954) [hereafter Charles Francis Adams diary].

13 love of Auburn: Seward, *An Autobiography*, p. 744.

13 "free to act . . . to die": *Auburn Journal*, December 31, 1859, reprinted in *Albany Evening Journal*, Albany, N.Y., January 3, 1860.

14 Auburn in the 1860s: Johnson, "Sensitivity and Civil War," pp. 2–3.

14 Seward had arrived . . . Cayuga County: Van Deusen, *William Henry Seward*, pp. 6–7.

14 description of Frances: Ibid., p. 10; Taylor, *William Henry Seward*, pp. 18–19.

14 death of Cornelia: Van Deusen, *William Henry Seward*, p. 37.

14 slow to take up the Republican banner: Clarence Edward Macartney, *Lincoln and His Cabinet* (New York and London: Charles Scribner's Sons, 1931), pp. 94–95.

14 "would inspire a cow . . . language": Henry Adams to Charles Francis Adams, Jr., December 9, 1860, *Letters of Henry Adams (1858–1891)*, Vol. I, p. 62.

14 the "leader of the political . . . pass-words of our combatants": Schurz, *Reminiscences*, Vol. II, pp. 173–74.

15 his exuberant personality . . . yellow pantaloons: Hendrick, *Lincoln's War Cabinet*, p. 8; Johnson, "Sensitivity and Civil War," p. 57.

15 an aura of inevitability: Halstead, *Three Against Lincoln*, p. 120.

15 "Men might love . . . ignore him": Glyndon G. Van Deusen, "Thurlow Weed: A Character Study," *American Historical Review* XLIX (April 1944), p. 427.

15 "as a hen does its chicks": Hendrick, *Lincoln's War Cabinet*, p. 17.

15 an exceptional team: Richard L. Watson, Jr., "Thurlow Weed, Political Boss," *New York History* 22 (October 1941), p. 415.

15 "Seward is Weed": WHS, quoted in Gideon Welles, *Lincoln and Seward Remarks Upon the Memorial Address of Chas. Francis Adams, on the Late Wm. H. Seward* . . . (New York: Sheldon & Co., 1874), p. 23.

15 Weed certainly understood . . . created jealousy: Van Deusen, *William Henry Seward*, pp. 216, 222–23.

16 Weed believed . . . emerge the victor: TW to WHS, May 20, 1860, reel 59, Seward Papers.

16 Members . . . confirmed Weed's assessment: Mary King Clark, "Lincoln's Nomination As Seen By a Young Girl from New York," *Putnam's Magazine* 5 (February 1909), pp. 536–37.

16 "no *cause* for doubting . . . to the result": James Watson Webb to WHS, May 16, 1860, reel 59, Seward Papers.

16 "Your friends . . . a few ballots": Elbridge Gerry Spaulding to WHS, May 17, 1860, reel 59, Seward Papers.

16 "All right . . . today sure": Telegram from Preston King, William M. Evarts, and Richard M. Blatchford to WHS, May 18, 1860, reel 59, Seward Papers.

16 Gothic mansion . . . State and Sixth Streets: "History of the Chase House," article in the Central Ohio Buildings File, Local History Room, Columbus Metropolitan Library, Columbus, Ohio; William Dean Howells, *Years of My Youth* (New York and London: Harper & Bros., 1916; 1917), p. 153.

16 Brass bands . . . were revealed: *Daily Ohio Statesman*, Columbus, Ohio, May 19, 1860.

17 Chase's height, physical description: Albert Bushnell Hart, *Salmon P. Chase*, introduction by G. S. Boritt. *American Statesmen Series* (Boston: Houghton Mifflin, 1899; New York and London: Chelsea House, 1980), p. 415; Hendrick, *Lincoln's War Cabinet*, p. 32.

17 "looked . . . statesman to look": Schurz, *Reminiscences*, Vol. II, p. 34.

17 "he is one of . . . splendor and brilliancy": *Troy [N.Y.] Times*, October 18, 1860, quoted in *Columbus Gazette*, November 2, 1860.

17 "an arresting duality . . . the world": Thomas Graham Belden and Marva Robins Belden, *So Fell the Angels* (Boston: Little, Brown, 1956), p. 4.

17 dressed with meticulous care: Hart, *Salmon P. Chase*, p. 415.

17 so nearsighted: John Niven, *Salmon P. Chase: A Biography* (New York and Oxford: Oxford University Press, 1995), pp. 79, 173, 193.

17 man of unbending routine: Virginia Tatnall Peacock, *Famous American Belles of the Nineteenth Century* (1900; Freeport, N.Y.: Books for Libraries Press, 1970), p. 211; Demarest Lloyd, "The Home-Life of Salmon Portland Chase," *Atlantic Monthly* 32 (November 1873), pp. 528, 530–31, 536, 538; Niven, *Salmon P. Chase*, pp. 203–05; J. W. Schuckers, *The Life and Public Services of Salmon Portland Chase, United States Senator and Governor of Ohio; Secretary of the Treasury, and Chief-Justice of the United States* (New York: D. Appleton & Co., 1874), p. 595; Schurz, *Reminiscences*, Vol. II, pp. 169–70.

17 On the rare nights: Lloyd, "Home-Life of Salmon Portland Chase," *Atlantic Monthly*, pp. 529 (quote), 531; Peacock, *Famous American Belles of the Nineteenth Century*, pp. 211–12; Ishbel Ross, *Proud Kate: Portrait of an Ambitious Woman* (New York: Harper & Bros., 1953), p. 37.

18 items in Chase home: SPC to KCS, December 3, 4, 5, and 6, 1857, reel 11, Chase Papers.

18 dogs . . . "designed and posed": Doster, *Lincoln and Episodes of the Civil War*, p. 173.

18 description of Columbus in 1860: Howells, *Years of My Youth*, pp. 134, 169, 181 (quote); Francis Phelps Weisenburger, *Columbus during the Civil War* (n.p.: Ohio State University Press for the Ohio Historical Society, 1963), pp. 3–4.

18 new Capitol building: Henry Howe, *Historical Collections of Ohio*, Vol. I, Ohio Centennial Edition (Norwalk, Ohio: Laning Printing Co., 1896), p. 621 (quote); Writers' Program of the Works Projects Administration, comps., *The Ohio Guide*, sponsored by Ohio State Archaeological and Historical Society (New York: Oxford University Press, 1940; 1948), pp. 251, 254.

18 contrast between Seward and Chase: Hendrick, *Lincoln's War Cabinet*, p. 36; Johnson, "Sensitivity and Civil War," pp. 58–59.

18 recoiled from all games of chance: SPC to KCS, September 15, 1854, reel 10, Chase Papers; Lloyd, "Home-Life of Salmon Portland Chase," *Atlantic Monthly*, pp. 529, 531.

18 "he seldom . . . without spoiling it": Lloyd, "Home-Life of Salmon Portland Chase," *Atlantic Monthly*, p. 536.

18 Kate's education: Belden and Belden, *So Fell the Angels*, p. 15; Ross, *Proud Kate*, pp. 19–22, 34.

19 "In a few years . . . anything else": SPC to KCS, December 20, 1853, reel 9, Chase Papers.

19 absolutely essential: Belden and Belden, *So Fell the Angels*, pp. 16, 18, 21–22; Niven, *Salmon P. Chase*, pp. 202–03.

19 "She did everything . . . another Mrs. Chase": Belden and Belden, *So Fell the Angels*, p. 22.

19 Chase treated his . . . younger daughter: Peacock, *Famous American Belles of the Nineteenth Century*, p. 207.

19 Chase was actually more radical than Seward: Hart, *Salmon P. Chase*, pp. 423, 429.

20 "There may have been . . . ideas as he": Ibid., p. 434.

20 "In the long run . . . than did Chase": William E. Gienapp, *The Origins of the Republican Party, 1852–1856* (New York and Oxford: Oxford University Press, 1987), p. 192.

20 "A very large body . . . spontaneous growth": SPC to Gamaliel Bailey, January 24, 1859, reel 12, Chase Papers.

20 "I arrived early . . . he should be President": Schurz, *Reminiscences*, Vol. II, pp. 169–72.

21 "desirable . . . our best men": SPC to Robert Hosea, March 18, 1860, reel 13, Chase Papers.

21 "No man . . . more competent": *Ohio State Journal*, Columbus, Ohio, March 12, 1860.

21 "steady devotion . . . beyond the State": Ibid., May 21, 1860.

21 refused to engage in the practical methods: Niven, *Salmon P. Chase*, pp. 214–17; Hart, *Salmon P. Chase*, p. 428.

21 "if the most cherished . . . could prevail": SPC to Edward S. Hamlin, June 12, 1856, reel 11, Chase Papers.

21 "Now is the time . . . topmost wave": Calvin Ellis Stowe to SPC, March 30, 1858, reel 12, Chase Papers.

21 "There is reason to hope": SPC to James A Briggs, from Wheeling, Va., May 8, 1860, reel 13, Chase Papers.

21 Judge Edward Bates awaited: Marvin R. Cain, *Lincoln's Attorney General: Edward Bates of Missouri* (Columbia, Mo.: University of Missouri Press, 1965), p. 115.

21 Grape Hill: Entry of September 28, 1859, Orville H. Browning, *The Diary of Orville Hickman Browning. Vol. I: 1850–1864*, ed. Theodore Calvin Pease and James G. Randall. *Collections of the Illinois State Historical Library*, Volume XX (Springfield, Ill.: Illinois State Historical Library, 1925), p. 380; Cain, *Lincoln's Attorney General*, p. 59.

21 general information on Bates family: Introduction, *The Diary of Edward Bates, 1859–1866*, pp. xv–xvi; *Missouri Republican*, St. Louis, Mo., March 26, 1869.

22 The judge's orderly life: EB to Julia Bates, January 1, 1835; January 5, 1828; November 7, 1827; Edward Bates Papers, 1778–1872, mss 1 B3184a, Virginia Historical Society, Richmond, Va. [hereafter Bates Papers, ViHi]; entry for April 9, 1860, in *The Diary of Edward Bates, 1859–1866*, p. 120 (quote).

22 description of St. Louis: "Lecture of Edward Bates," *St. Louis Weekly Reveille*, February 24, 1845, typescript copy, St. Louis History Collection, Missouri Historical Society, St. Louis, Mo. [hereafter MoSHi]; William C. Winter, *The Civil War in St. Louis: A Guided Tour* (St. Louis, Mo.: Missouri Historical Society, 1995), p. 3; James Neal Primm, *Lion of the Valley: St. Louis, Missouri, 1764–1980*, 3rd edn. (St. Louis: Missouri Historical Society Press, 1998), pp. 192, 182 (quote).

22 "the quaintest looking . . . youth of twenty": Alban Jasper Conant, "A Visit to Washington in 1861–62," *Metropolitan Magazine* XXXIII (June 1910), p. 313.

22 descriptions of Bates: Hendrick, *Lincoln's War Cabinet*, pp. 46–47; Cain, *Lincoln's Attorney General*, pp. 1, 64.

22 Lincoln noted the striking . . . "more than his head": AL quoted in Hendrick, *Lincoln's War Cabinet*, p. 46.

23 "unaffected by . . . little bonnet": Conant, "A Visit to Washington in 1861–62," *Metropolitan Magazine*, p. 313.

23 "How happy is my lot! . . . so freely gives": Edward Bates diary, November 27, 1851, Edward Bates Papers, Missouri Historical Society, St. Louis, Mo. [hereafter Bates diary].
23 "a very domestic, home, man": Ibid., May 2, 1852.
23 speech at the River and Harbor Convention: "Bates, Edward," *Dictionary of American Biography. Vol. I: Abbe-Brazer*, ed. Allen Johnson (New York: Charles Scribner's Sons, 1927; 1957), p. 48; James Shaw, "A Neglected Episode in the Life of Abraham Lincoln," *Transactions of the Illinois State Historical Society*, no. 29 of the Illinois State Historical Library (1922), pp. 52, 54.
23 as the 1860 election neared: Cain, *Lincoln's Attorney General*, pp. 95–96.
23 dinner at Frank Blair's home: Entry of April 27, 1859, in *The Diary of Edward Bates, 1859–1866*, p. 11; Reinhard H. Luthin, *The First Lincoln Campaign* (Cambridge, Mass.: Harvard University Press, 1944; Gloucester, Mass.: Peter Smith, 1964), pp. 54–55.
23 Blair family details: See Elbert B. Smith, *Francis Preston Blair* (New York: Free Press/Macmillan Publishing Co., 1980), pp. 172–73; William Ernest Smith, *The Francis Preston Blair Family in Politics*, Vol. I (New York: The Macmillan Company, 1933), pp. 185–88, 189–91; Hendrick, *Lincoln's War Cabinet*, pp. 61–69, 388; *Washington Post*, September 14, 1906; *Star*, September 14, 1906; Virginia Jeans Laas, ed., *Wartime Washington: The Civil War Letters of Elizabeth Blair Lee* (Chicago: University of Illinois Press, 1991), pp. 1, 2; William E. Parrish, *Frank Blair: Lincoln's Conservative* (Columbia, Mo., and London: University of Missouri Press, 1998). Francis P. Blair, owner, slave schedule for 5th District, Montgomery County, Maryland, Eighth Census of the United States, 1860 (National Archives Microfilm Publication M653, reel 485), Records of the Bureau of the Census, Record Group [RG] 29, National Archives and Records Administration, Washington, D.C. [hereafter DNA]. Blair owned fifteen slaves in 1860.
24 had settled on the widely respected judge: *Lincoln's Attorney General*, pp. 84–86, 91–92; Primm, *Lion of the Valley*, p. 230; Smith, *Francis Preston Blair*, p. 257; Smith, *The Francis Preston Blair Family in Politics*, Vol. I, pp. 461–62.
25 "I feel . . . of character": Entry of July 5, 1859, in *The Diary of Edward Bates, 1859–1866*, pp. 29–30.
25 "a mere seat . . . member": EB to Julia Coalter Bates, November 7, 1827, Bates Papers, ViHi.
25 "the mania . . . heretofore done": FB, quoted in Parrish, *Frank Blair*, p. 81.
25 "My nomination . . . in vain": Entry of January 9, 1860, in *The Diary of Edward Bates, 1859–1866*, pp. 89–90.
26 days were increasingly . . . first ballot victory: Cain, *Lincoln's Attorney General*, pp. 93, 94, 107.
26 "I have many strong . . . in New York, Pa.": Entry of December 1, 1859, in *The Diary of Edward Bates, 1859–1866*, pp. 71–72.
26 pockets of opposition . . . German-Americans: Cain, *Lincoln's Attorney General*, pp. 103, 106.
26 "There is no question . . . conservative antecedents": *NYTrib*, May 15, 1860.
26 Bates would triumph in Chicago: Cain, *Lincoln's Attorney General*, p. 110.
26 "some of the most moderate and patriotic": EB, *Letter of Hon. Edward Bates, of Missouri, Indorsing Mr. Lincoln, and Giving His Reasons for Supporting the Chicago Nominees* (Washington, D.C.: Printed at the Congressional Globe Office, 1860).
26 "would tend to soften . . . in the border States": Ibid.

CHAPTER 2: THE "LONGING TO RISE"

Page

28 "We find ourselves . . . times tells us": AL, "Address Before the Young Men's Lyceum of Springfield, Illinois," January 27, 1838, in *CW*, I, p. 108.
28 "When both the . . . universal feeling": Alexis de Tocqueville, *Democracy in America*, ed. J. P. Mayer, trans. George Lawrence (New York: Harper & Row, 1966; 1988), p. 629.
29 "any man's son . . . any other man's son": Frances M. Trollope, *Domestic Manners of the Americans* (London: Whittaker, Treacher, & Co., 1832; Barre, Mass.: Imprint Society, 1969), p. 93.
29 thousands of young men to break away: Joyce Appleby, *Inheriting the Revolution: The First Generation of Americans* (Cambridge, Mass., and London: Belknap Press of Harvard University Press, 2000), p. 88.
29 the Louisiana Purchase: See Robert Wiebe, *The Opening of American Society: From the Adoption of the Constitution to the Eve of Disunion* (New York: Alfred A. Knopf, 1984), pp. 131–32; "Louisiana Purchase," in *The Reader's Companion to American History*, ed. Eric Foner and John A. Garraty (Boston: Houghton Mifflin, 1991), p. 682.
29 "Americans are always moving . . . the mountainside": Stephen Vincent Benét, *Western Star* (New York: Farrar & Rinehart, 1943), pp. 3, 7–8.
29 In the South . . . thriving cities: Thomas Dublin, "Internal Migration," in *The Reader's Companion to American History*, ed. Foner and Garraty, pp. 564–65.
29 "Every American . . . to rise": de Tocqueville, *Democracy in America*, ed. Mayer, p. 627.
29 born on May 16, 1801: Van Deusen, *William Henry Seward*, p. 3.
30 Samuel Seward: Seward, *An Autobiography*, pp. 19–20; Bancroft, *The Life of William H. Seward*, Vol. I, pp. 1–2; Taylor, *William Henry Seward*, p. 12.
30 "a considerable . . . destined preferment": Seward, *An Autobiography*, pp. 20, 21.
30 Seward's early education: Ibid., pp. 20, 22; "Biographical Memoir of William H. Seward," *The Works of William H. Seward*, Vol. I, ed. George E. Baker (5 vols., New York: J. S. Redfield, 1853; New York: AMS Press, 1972), pp. xvi–xvii.
30 "at five in the morning . . . politics or religion!": Seward, *An Autobiography*, pp. 21, 22.

30 Seward slaves: Ibid., p. 27. The Sewards still owned seven slaves in 1820. See entry for Samuel S. Seward, Warwick, Orange County, N.Y., Fourth Census of the United States, 1820 (National Archives Microfilm Publication M33, reel 64), RG 29, DNA.
30 "loquacious" . . . to fight against slavery: Seward, *An Autobiography*, pp. 27–28.
31 status of slavery in the North after the Revolution: Winthrop D. Jordan, *White Over Black: American Attitudes Toward the Negro, 1550–1812* (New York: W. W. Norton & Co., 1977), p. 345; Leon F. Litwack, *North of Slavery: The Negro in the Free States, 1790–1860* (Chicago and London: University of Chicago Press, 1961), pp. 3, 6.
31 slavery eliminated in New York by 1827: Taylor, *William Henry Seward*, p. 14.
31 enrolled in . . . Union College: Van Deusen, *William Henry Seward*, p. 4.
31 "a magnificent . . . so imposing": Seward, *An Autobiography*, p. 29.
31 "I cherished . . . of my class": Ibid., p. 31.
31 "had determined . . . at Union College": Ibid., p. 35.
31 "all the eminent . . . a broken heart": Ibid., pp. 35, 36–43.
32 "Matters prosper . . . even his notice": WHS to Daniel Jessup, Jr., January 24, 1820, reel 1, Seward Papers.
32 "was received as a student . . . in Washington Hall": Seward, *An Autobiography*, pp. 47–48.
33 friendship with . . . David Berdan: "David Berdan," Eulogy read before the Adelphic Society of Union College, July 21, 1828, and published in *The Knickerbocker Magazine* (December 1839), in *The Works of William H. Seward*, Vol. III, pp. 117–27; WHS to the President of the Adelphic Society, Union College, draft copy, September 3, 1827, reel 1, Seward Papers; Taylor, *William Henry Seward*, p. 18.
33 "a genius of the highest order" . . . Seward was devastated: WHS to the President of the Adelphic Society, Union College, draft copy, September 3, 1827, reel 1, Seward Papers.
33 "never again . . . in this world": FAS to WHS, February 15, 1831, reel 113, Seward Papers.
33 "a common feature" . . . passionate romances: E. Anthony Rotundo, *American Manhood: Transformations in Masculinity from the Revolution to the Modern Era* (New York: Basic Books/HarperCollins, 1993), pp. 3, 76 (quote), 86.
34 Relationship with Judge Miller: "Biographical Memoir of William H. Seward," *Works of William H. Seward*, Vol. I, p. xxi.
34 marriage to Frances Miller . . . The judge insisted: Seward, *An Autobiography*, p. 62.
34 Chase's ancestors: Niven, *Salmon P. Chase*, pp. 5–7, 21; Schuckers, *The Life and Public Services of Salmon Portland Chase*, p. 3; Robert B. Warden, *An Account of the Private Life and Public Services of Salmon Portland Chase* (Cincinnati: Wilstach, Baldwin & Co., 1874), pp. 22–27.
34 "the neighboring folk . . . in New England": SPC to John T. Trowbridge, December 27, 1863, reel 30, Chase Papers.
34 "a good man": SPC to Trowbridge, January 19, 1864, reel 31, Chase Papers.
34 "angry word . . . from his lips": SPC to Trowbridge, December 27, 1863, reel 30, Chase Papers.
34 Chase long remembered . . . "& kind looks": SPC to Trowbridge, January 19, 1864, reel 31, Chase Papers.
35 "I was . . . ambitious . . . of my class": SPC to Trowbridge, December 27, 1863, reel 30, Chase Papers.
35 taught by elder sister: Warden, *Private Life and Public Services*, p. 36.
35 retreat to the garden . . . designated passages: SPC to Trowbridge, January 19, 1864, reel 31, Chase Papers.
35 "once repeating . . . a single recitation": Biographical sketch of Salmon P. Chase, quoted in Warden, *Private Life and Public Services*, p. 39.
35 "for the entertainment they afforded": Warden, *Private Life and Public Services*, p. 38.
35 "quite a prodigy . . . and head down": SPC to Trowbridge, January 21, 1864, reel 31, Chase Papers.
35 "sliding down hill" . . . would swear: SPC to Trowbridge, December 27, 1863, reel 30, Chase Papers.
35 made him abhor intemperance: Warden, *Private Life and Public Services*, p. 63.
35 "face forward . . . sufficed to save": SPC to Trowbridge, January 21, 1864, reel 31, Chase Papers.
36 Ithamar's glass venture and financial ruin: SPC to Trowbridge, January 19, 1864, reel 31, Chase Papers; Niven, *Salmon P. Chase*, pp. 7–8.
36 Ithamar Chase's fatal stroke: Niven, *Salmon P. Chase*, p. 8.
36 "He lingered . . . our home": SPC to Trowbridge, January 19, 1864, reel 31, Chase Papers.
36 "almost to suffering": SPC to Trowbridge, February 1, 1864, reel 31, Chase Papers.
36 "ever lamented and deceased father": Janette Ralston Chase to SPC, August 14, 1824, [filed as 1824–1825 correspondence], reel 4, Chase Papers.
36 Salmon sent to Philander Chase: SPC to Trowbridge, January 21 and 31, 1864, reel 31, Chase Papers; Arthur Meier Schlesinger, "Salmon Portland Chase: Undergraduate and Pedagogue," *Ohio Archaeological and Historical Quarterly* [hereafter *OAHQ*] 28 (April 1919), pp. 120–21.
36 Salmon's journey to Worthington: SPC to Trowbridge, January 23, 1864, reel 31, Chase Papers; Niven, *Salmon P. Chase*, pp. 9–11.
36 "was not passive . . . quite tyrannical": SPC to Trowbridge, January 25, 1864, reel 31, Chase Papers.
37 "My memories . . . wish I had not": SPC to Trowbridge, January 27, 1864, reel 31, Chase Papers.
37 Cincinnati College . . . "gave it to reading": SPC to Trowbridge, January 31, 1864, typescript copy, reel 31, Chase Papers.
37 his "life might have been . . . more fun!": Warden, *Private Life and Public Services*, p. 94.
37 first teaching position . . . dismissed: Niven, *Salmon P. Chase*, p. 17.
38 At Dartmouth: Ibid., pp. 18–19; Frederick J. Blue, *Salmon P. Chase: A Life in Politics* (Kent, Ohio, and London: Kent State University Press, 1987), pp. 6–7.
38 two lifelong friendships: Niven, *Salmon P. Chase*, p. 97.

38 "Especially do I . . . have been wasted": SPC to Thomas Sparhawk, July 8, 1827, reel 4, Chase Papers.
38 "the author is doubtless . . . vilest purposes": Entry for September 22, 1829, SPC diary, reel 40, Chase Papers. The editors of the published edition of the Salmon P. Chase Papers identify the author of the novel as Edward Bulwer-Lytton. See note 65 for entry of September 22, 1829, *The Salmon P. Chase Papers*. Vol. I: *Journals, 1829–1872*, ed. John Niven (Kent, Ohio, and London: Kent State University Press, 1993), p. 24 [hereafter *Chase Papers*, Vol. I].
38 established a successful school: SPC to Trowbridge, February 10, 1864, reel 31, Chase Papers; Schlesinger, "Salmon Portland Chase," *OAHQ* (1919), pp. 132–33, 143.
38 distinct classes of society . . . "utter contempt": SPC to Hamilton Smith, May 31, 1827, reel 4, Chase Papers.
38 "I have always thought . . . to achieve": SPC to Hamilton Smith, April 7, 1829, reel 4, Chase Papers.
38 "saw the novelty . . . poor and young": Appleby, *Inheriting the Revolution*, p. 7.
39 wrote to an older brother in 1825 for advice: Alexander R. Chase to SPC, November 4, 1825, reel 4, Chase Papers.
39 Attorney General William Wirt: Warden, *Private Life and Public Services*, pp. 124–25, 175; Fidler, "Young Limbs of the Law," pp. 245, 276. See also Michael L. Oberg, "Wirt, William," *American National Biography*, Vol. XXIII, ed. John A. Garraty and Mark C. Carnes, American Council of Learned Societies (New York and Oxford: Oxford University Press, 1999), pp. 675–76.
39 Wirt welcomed: Entries of January 10, 29, 30, 1829; February 9, 1829; April 8, 20, 1829; *Chase Papers*, Vol. I, pp. 5–9, 13–14; Schuckers, *The Life and Public Services of Salmon Portland Chase*, p. 29.
39 to read and study . . . his students: SPC to Trowbridge, February 13, 1864, reel 31, Chase Papers.
39 "many happy hours . . . the stars": SPC to Trowbridge, February 10, 1864, in *The Salmon P. Chase Papers*. Vol. IV: *Correspondence, April 1863–1864*, ed. John Niven (Kent, Ohio, and London: Kent State University Press, 1997), p. 283.
39 the social gulf . . . discouraged: Elizabeth Goldsborough to Robert Warden, quoted in Warden, *Private Life and Public Services*, p. 126; Niven, *Salmon P. Chase*, pp. 23, 40.
39 "thousands . . . universal scholar": Alexander R. Chase to SPC, November 4, 1825, reel 4, Chase Papers.
39 "Day and night . . . my labours": Entry for March 1, 1830, *Chase Papers*, Vol. I, p. 45.
40 "knowledge may yet . . . be mine": Entry for January 13, 1829, ibid., p. 6.
40 "*You* will be . . . in that walk": William Wirt to SPC, May 4, 1829, reel 4, Chase Papers.
40 "God [prospering] . . . your example": SPC to William Wirt, June 16, 1829, reel 4, Chase Papers.
40 self-designed course of preparation: Niven, *Salmon P. Chase*, pp. 23, 26.
40 "his voice deep . . . of my toils": Entry for February 14, 1829, diary, reel 1, Papers of Salmon P. Chase, Manuscript Division, Library of Congress [hereafter Chase Papers, DLC].
40 "I feel humbled . . . of well-doing": Entry for December 31, 1829, diary, reel 1, Chase Papers, LC.
40 Chase before the bar, 1829: William Cranch, quoted in Niven, *Salmon P. Chase*, p. 27.
40 "study another year" . . . sworn in at the bar: SPC, "Admission to the Bar," June 30, 1853, reel 32, Chase Papers, DLC.
40 "I would rather . . . wherever I may be": SPC to Charles D. Cleveland, February 8, 1830, reel 4, Chase Papers.
41 Cincinnati in 1830: Hart, *Salmon P. Chase*, pp. 13–16.
41 "was covered by the primeval forest": SPC, "On the Dedication of a New State House, January 6, 1857," reel 41, Chase Papers.
41 "a stranger and an adventurer": Entry for September 1, 1830, *Chase Papers*, Vol. I, p. 53.
41 shyness, speech defect: Niven, *Salmon P. Chase*, p. 31.
41 "I wish I was . . . provide the remedy": William Wirt to SPC, May 4, 1829, reel 4, Chase Papers.
41 "awkward, *fishy* . . . little inconvenience": SPC to Charles D. Cleveland, February 8, 1830, reel 4, Chase Papers.
41 "I made this resolution . . . excel in all things": Entry for April 29, 1831, *Chase Papers*, Vol. I, p. 57.
41 "I was fully . . . a 'crown of glory' ": Entry for March 1, 1830, ibid., p. 45.
41 founded a popular lecture series . . . berated himself: Entry for February 8, 1834, diary, reel 40, Chase Papers; Niven, *Salmon P. Chase*, pp. 32, 34–38; Mary Merwin Phelps, *Kate Chase, Dominant Daughter: The Life Story of a Brilliant Woman and Her Famous Father* (New York: Thomas Y. Crowell, 1935), pp. 12, 35.
42 "I confess . . . terminate in this life": Abigail Chase Colby to SPC, April 21, 1832, reel 4, Chase Papers.
42 death of Catherine Garniss Chase: Entries for November 21 and December 1, 1835, *Chase Papers*, Vol. I, pp. 87, 92–93.
42 "so overwhelming . . . has been severed": SPC to Charles D. Cleveland, April 6, 1836, reel 5, Chase Papers.
42 "Oh how I accused . . . tempted me away": Entry for December 25, 1835, *Chase Papers*, Vol. I, p. 94.
42 "that death was within . . . left but clay": Entry for December 1, 1835, ibid., pp. 93–94.
42 "the dreadful calamity . . . care for her": SPC to Charles D. Cleveland, April 6, 1836, reel 5, Chase Papers.
42 doctors had bled her so profusely: Entry for December 26, 1835, *Chase Papers*, Vol. I, p. 96.
42 he delved into textbooks: Entry for December 28, 1835, ibid., p. 99.
42 "Oh if I had not . . . now she is gone": Entry for December 27, 1835, ibid., pp. 97–98.
42 "the bar of God . . . an accusing spirit": Entry for December 28, 1835, ibid., p. 99.
43 a "second conversion": Stephen E. Maizlish, "Salmon P. Chase: The Roots of Ambition and the Origins of Reform," *Journal of the Early Republic* 18 (Spring 1998), p. 62.
43 death of daughter Catherine: Blue, *Salmon P. Chase*, p. 35; Warden, *Private Life and Public Services*, p. 286; Niven, *Salmon P. Chase*, p. 72.
43 "one of the . . . desolation of my heart": SPC to Charles D. Cleveland, February 7, 1840, reel 5, Chase Papers.
43 marriage to Eliza; birth of Kate: Blue, *Salmon P. Chase*, pp. 25–26; Warden, *Private Life and Public Services*, pp. 290–91, 295, 296, 301, 302.

43 "I feel as if . . . we are desolate": SPC to Charles D. Cleveland, October 1, 1845, reel 6, Chase Papers.
43 Marriage to Belle; death of wife and daughter: Blue, *Salmon P. Chase*, p. 74; Warden, *Private Life and Public Services*, pp. 311–12.
43 "What a vale . . . I rise & press on": SPC to CS, January 28, 1850, reel 8, Chase Papers (quote); Niven, *Salmon P. Chase*, p. 135.
43 "to go West and grow up with the country": William F. Switzler, "Lincoln's Attorney General: Edward Bates, One of Missouri's Greatest Citizens—His Career as a Lawyer, Farmer and Statesman," reprinted in Onward Bates, *Bates, et al., of Virginia and Missouri* (Chicago: P. F. Pettibone, 1914), p. 26.
43 His father, Thomas Fleming Bates: For general information on Bates's family and early years, see Cain, *Lincoln's Attorney General*, pp. 1–3, 5; "Bates, Edward," *DAB*, Vol. I, p. 48; James M. McPherson, "Bates, Edward," *American National Biography*, Vol. II, ed. John A. Garraty and Mark C. Carnes, American Council of Learned Societies (New York and Oxford: Oxford University Press, 1999), p. 329; Introduction, *The Diary of Edward Bates, 1859–1866*, p. xi; Bates, *Bates, et al., of Virginia and Missouri*, p. 22; "Death of Edward Bates," *Missouri Republican*, St. Louis, Mo., March 26, 1869; Elie Weeks, "Belmont," *Goochland County Historical Society Magazine* 12 (1980), pp. 36–49; EB to C. I. Walker, February 10, 1859, reprinted in *Collections of the Pioneer Society of the State of Michigan Together with Reports of County Pioneer Societies*, Vol. VIII, 2nd edn. (1886; Lansing, Mich.: Wynkoop Hallenbeck Crawford Co., 1907), pp. 563–64.
44 "as distinctly . . . Western Europe": Charles Gibson, *The Autobiography of Charles Gibson*, ed. E. R. Gibson, 1899, Charles Gibson Papers, Missouri Historical Society, St. Louis, Mo. [hereafter Gibson Papers, MoSHi].
44 English manorial life . . . monetary wealth: James Truslow Adams, *America's Tragedy* (New York and London: Charles Scribner's Sons, 1934), pp. 87–88.
44 "enjoyable living . . . and their manners": Bates, *Bates, et al., of Virginia and Missouri*, p. 20.
44 The flintlock musket . . . "helped to win": Ibid., p. 22.
45 lured by the vast potential . . . Louisiana Purchase: Wiebe, *The Opening of American Society*, pp. 131–32.
45 Over the next three decades: James M. McPherson, *Battle Cry of Freedom: The Civil War Era* (New York: Oxford University Press, 1988; New York: Ballantine Books, 1989), p. 42.
45 "too young . . . a buffalo!": "Lecture by Edward Bates," St. Louis *Weekly Reveille*, February 24, 1845, St. Louis History Collection, MoSHi.
45 "After years of family . . . burned brightly in him": Cain, *Lincoln's Attorney General*, p. 5.
45 passed his bar examination . . . the rest of their family there: EB to Frederick Bates, September 29, 1817; October 13, 1817; June 15, 1818; July 19, 1818; Bates Papers, MoSHi; Cain, *Lincoln's Attorney General*, p. 7.
45 "The slaves sold . . . at $290!": EB to Frederick Bates, September 21, 1817, Bates Papers, MoSHi.
45 expected to realize . . . "full-handed": EB to Frederick Bates, September 29, 1817, Bates Papers, MoSHi.
46 death of his brother Tarleton . . . "by the delay": Cain, *Lincoln's Attorney General*, p. 6; EB to Frederick Bates, June 15, 1818, Bates Papers, MoSHi (quote).
46 "In those days . . . in the country": Samuel T. Glover, "Addresses by the Members of the St. Louis Bar on the Death of Edward Bates," *Minutes of the St. Louis Bar Association* (1869), Bates Papers, MoSHi.
46 "a lazy or squandering fellow": EB to Frederick Bates, July 19, 1818, Bates Papers, MoSHi.
46 if accompanied only by his family: EB to Frederick Bates, September 29, 1817, Bates Papers, MoSHi.
46 "in a tenth part of the time . . . my embarrassment": EB to Frederick Bates, June 15, 1818, Bates Papers, MoSHi.
46 "Mother & Sister . . . occasioned you": EB to Frederick Bates, July 19, 1818, Bates Papers, MoSHi.
46 "friend and benefactor . . . wealth & influence": EB to Frederick Bates, October 13, 1817, Bates Papers, MoSHi.
46 introduced him to the leading figures: Cain, *Lincoln's Attorney General*, p. 4.
46 a partnership with Joshua Barton: Ibid., p. 7.
47 "more in the way . . . his own name": AL, "Autobiography Written for John L. Scripps," [c. June 1860], in *CW*, IV, p. 61 [hereafter "Scripps autobiography"].
47 Thomas had watched: A. H. Chapman statement, ante September 8, 1865, in *HI*, p. 95; Donald, *Lincoln*, p. 21.
47 "very narrow circumstances . . . without education": AL, "Scripps autobiography," in *CW*, IV, p. 61.
47 Nancy Hanks: Dennis F. Hanks to WHH, June 13, 1865, and John Hanks interview, May 25, 1865, in *HI*, pp. 5, 37; Benjamin P. Thomas, *Abraham Lincoln: A Biography* (New York: Alfred A. Knopf, 1952), p. 6. On Nancy Hanks's ancestry, see Paul H. Verduin, "New Evidence Suggest Lincoln's Mother Born in Richmond County, Virginia, Giving Credibility to Planter-Grandfather Legend," *Northern Neck of Virginia Historical Magazine* XXXVIII (December 1988), pp. 4, 354–89.
47 Thomas in relentless poverty: Thomas, *Abraham Lincoln*, p. 5; Kenneth J. Winkle, *The Young Eagle: The Rise of Abraham Lincoln* (Dallas: Taylor Trade Publishing, 2001), p. 13.
47 "Why Scripps, it is . . . 'annals of the poor' ": John L. Scripps to WHH, June 24, 1865, in *HI*, p. 57.
47 "was a woman . . . a brilliant woman": Nathaniel Grigsby interview, September 12, 1865, in ibid., p. 113.
47 "read the good . . . benevolence as well": Dennis F. Hanks to WHH (interview), June 13, 1865, in ibid., p. 40.
47 "beyond all doubt an intellectual woman": John Hanks interview, [1865–1866], in ibid., p. 454.
47 "Remarkable" perception: Dennis F. Hanks to WHH, [December 1865?], in ibid., p. 149.
47 "very smart . . . naturally Strong minded": William Wood interview, September 15, 1865, in ibid., p. 124.
47 "All that I am . . . God bless her": AL, comment to WHH, quoted in Michael Burlingame, *The Inner World of Abraham Lincoln* (Urbana and Chicago: University of Illinois Press, 1994), p. 42.
47 "milk sickness": Philip D. Jordan, "The Death of Nancy Hanks Lincoln," *Indiana Magazine of History* XL (June 1944), pp. 103–10.
47 Thomas and Elizabeth Sparrow: Thomas, *Abraham Lincoln*, pp. 10–11.
48 "I am going away . . . return": Nancy Lincoln, quoted in Robert Bruce, "The Riddle of Death," in Gabor

Boritt, ed., *The Lincoln Enigma: The Changing Faces of an American Icon* (Oxford and New York: Oxford University Press, 2001), p. 132.
48 average life expectancy: Appleby, *Inheriting the Revolution*, p. 63.
48 "He restlessly looked . . . before his gaze": Schurz, *Reminiscences*, Vol. II, p. 187.
48 had a uniquely shattering impact: Bruce, "The Riddle of Death," in *The Lincoln Enigma*, p. 132.
48 "a wild region": AL, "Autobiography written for Jesse W. Fell," December 20, 1859, in *CW*, III, p. 511.
48 "the panther's . . . on the swine": "The Bear Hunt," [September 6, 1846?], in *CW*, I, p. 386.
48 Sarah, did the cooking . . . Dennis Hanks: Dennis F. Hanks to WHH (interview), June 13, 1865, in *HI*, p. 40.
48 a "quick minded woman . . . laugh": Nathaniel Grigsby interview, September 12, 1865, in ibid., p. 113.
48 "wild—ragged and dirty": Dennis F. Hanks to WHH, June 13, 1865, in ibid., p. 41.
48 soaped . . . "more human": Sarah Bush Lincoln interview, September 8, 1865, in ibid., p. 106.
49 "sat down . . . to his grief": Redmond Grigsby, quoted in Burlingame, *The Inner World of Abraham Lincoln*, p. 95.
49 "From then on . . . you might say": John W. Lamar, quoted in ibid.
49 "It is with deep grief . . . ever expect it": AL to Fanny McCullough, December 23, 1862, in *CW*, VI, pp. 16–17.
49 "He was different . . . great potential": Douglas L. Wilson, "Young Man Lincoln," in *The Lincoln Enigma*, p. 35.
49 "clearly exceptional . . . intellectual equal": Donald, *Lincoln*, p. 32.
49 "soared above us . . . guide and leader": Nathaniel Grigsby interview, September 12, 1865, in *HI*, p. 114.
49 "a Boy of uncommon natural Talents": A. H. Chapman statement, ante September 8, 1865, in ibid., p. 99.
49 "His mind & mine . . . if he could": Sarah Bush Lincoln interview, September 8, 1865, in ibid., pp. 108, 107.
50 "He was a strong . . . neighborhood": Leonard Swett, "Lincoln's Story of His Own Life," in *Reminiscences of Abraham Lincoln by Distinguished Men of His Time*, ed. Allen Thorndike Rice (1885; New York and London: Harper & Bros., 1909), p. 71.
50 his great gift for storytelling . . . fireplace at night: Sarah Bush Lincoln interview, September 8, 1865, in *HI*, p. 107; John Hanks interview, [1865–1866], in ibid., p. 454.
50 along the old Cumberland Trail: Thomas, *Abraham Lincoln*, p. 7.
50 Thomas Lincoln would swap tales: Dennis F. Hanks to WHH, June 13, 1865, in *HI*, p. 37.
50 Young Abe listened . . . in his memory: Sarah Bush Lincoln interview, September 8, 1865, in ibid., p. 107.
50 Nothing was more upsetting . . . that was told: Rev. J. P. Gulliver article in *New York Independent*, September 1, 1864, quoted in F. B. Carpenter, *Six Months at the White House with Abraham Lincoln* (New York: Hurd & Houghton, 1866), p. 312.
50 "no small part . . . to comprehend": AL, quoted in ibid., pp. 312–13.
50 having translated the stories . . . young listeners: Dennis F. Hanks to WHH, June 13, 1865, and Dennis F. Hanks interview, September 8, 1865, in *HI*, pp. 42, 104; Sarah Bush Lincoln interview, September 8, 1865, in ibid., p. 107.
50 subscription schools: Donald, *Lincoln*, p. 29.
51 "No qualification . . . wizzard": AL, "Autobiography written for Jesse W. Fell," December 20, 1859, in *CW*, III, p. 511.
51 "by littles" . . . pick up on his own: AL, "Scripps autobiography," in *CW*, IV, p. 62.
51 "he could lay his hands on": Dennis F. Hanks to WHH, June 13, 1865, in *HI*, p. 41; Sarah Bush Lincoln interview, September 8, 1865, in ibid., p. 107; John S. Houghland interview, September 17, 1865, in ibid., p. 130.
51 "a luxury . . . the middle class": Fidler, "Young Limbs of the Law," p. 249.
51 obtained copies of: Thomas, *Abraham Lincoln*, p. 15; Nathaniel Grigsby interview, September 12, 1865, in *HI*, p. 112; Charles B. Strozier, *Lincoln's Quest for Union: Public and Private Meanings* (New York: Basic Books, 1982), p. 231.
51 "his eyes sparkled . . . could not sleep": David Herbert Donald, *Lincoln Reconsidered: Essays on the Civil War Era*, 3rd edn. (New York: Alfred A. Knopf, 1956; New York: Vintage Books, 2001), pp. 67–68.
51 "the great mass . . . to perform": AL, "Second Lecture on Discoveries and Inventions," [February 11, 1859], in *CW*, III, pp. 362–63.
51 "as unpoetical . . . of the earth": AL to Andrew Johnston, April 18, 1846, in *CW*, I, p. 378.
51 "There is no Frigate . . . Lands away": Emily Dickinson, "There is no Frigate like a Book," *The Complete Poems of Emily Dickinson*, ed. Thomas H. Johnson (Boston: Little, Brown, 1960), p. 553.
51 the *Revised Statutes* . . . and political thought: Helen Nicolay, *Personal Traits of Abraham Lincoln* (New York: Century Co., 1912), pp. 66–68.
52 Everywhere he went: Nathaniel Grigsby interview, September 12, 1865, in *HI*, p. 113.
52 "When he came across" . . . memorized: Sarah Bush Lincoln interview, September 8, 1865, in ibid., p. 107.
52 The story is often recounted . . . "on a stalk": Oliver C. Terry to JWW, July 1888, in ibid., p. 662.
52 Lincoln wrote poems . . . Crawford's large nose: Dennis F. Hanks to WHH, June 13, 1865, in ibid., p. 41; A. H. Chapman statement, ante September 8, 1865, in ibid., p. 101.
52 "Josiah blowing his bugle": AL, "Chronicles of Reuben," as paraphrased in Herndon and Weik, *Herndon's Life of Lincoln*, p. 47.
53 Seward had only to pick: Seward, *An Autobiography*, pp. 19–22, 31–35.
53 regarded as odd and indolent: Herndon and Weik, *Herndon's Life of Lincoln*, p. 38; Dennis Hanks interview, September 8, 1865, in *HI*, p. 104.
53 "particular Care . . . of his own accord": Sarah Bush Lincoln interview, September 8, 1865, in ibid., p. 108.
53 When he found . . . could continue: Matilda Johnston Moore interview, September 8, 1865, in ibid., p. 110.
53 destroyed his books . . . abused him: Burlingame, *The Inner World of Abraham Lincoln*, pp. 38–39.

53 father's decision to hire him out: Swett, "Lincoln's Story of His Own Life," in *Reminiscences of Abraham Lincoln*, ed. Rice, p. 70.
53 the "self-made" men in Lincoln's generation: Appleby, *Inheriting the Revolution*, p. 231; Wiebe, *The Opening of American Society*, p. 271.
53 The same "longing to rise": de Tocqueville, *Democracy in America*, p. 627.
54 departed . . . bundled on his shoulder: Swett, "Lincoln's Story of His Own Life," in *Reminiscences of Abraham Lincoln*, ed. Rice, pp. 71–72.
54 New Salem was a budding town: Benjamin P. Thomas, *Lincoln's New Salem* (Springfield, Ill.: Abraham Lincoln Association, 1934; 1947), p. 15.
54 to "keep body and soul together": AL, "Scripps autobiography," in *CW*, IV, p. 65.
54 Lincoln in New Salem: Thomas, *Lincoln's New Salem*, pp. 41–77; Mentor Graham to WHH, May 29, 1865, in *HI*, pp. 9–10; Wilson, *Honor's Voice*, pp. 59–67.
54 "studied with nobody": AL, "Scripps autobiography," in *CW*, IV, p. 65.
54 He buried himself . . . *Equity Jurisprudence:* Donald, *Lincoln*, p. 55; Thomas, *Abraham Lincoln*, p. 43.
54 able to read and reread his books . . . "any other one thing": AL to Isham Reavis, November 5, 1855, in *CW*, II, p. 327.
55 *"I am Anne Rutledge* . . . : Edgar Lee Masters, "Anne Rutledge," in *Spoon River Anthology* (New York: The Macmillan Company, 1914; 1916), p. 220.
55 Lincoln would take . . . "wooded knoll" to read: W. D. Howells, "Life of Abraham Lincoln," in *Lives and Speeches of Abraham Lincoln and Hannibal Hamlin* (New York: W. A. Townsend & Co., and Columbus, Ohio: Follett, Foster & Co., 1860), p. 31.
55 "it is true . . . of her now": Isaac Cogdal interview, 1865–1866, in *HI*, p. 440.
55 "Eyes blue large, & Expressive," auburn hair: Mentor Graham interview, April 2, 1866, in ibid., p. 242.
55 "She was beloved by Every body": Ibid., p. 243.
55 "quick . . . worthy of Lincoln's love": William G. Greene to WHH (interview), May 30, 1865, in ibid., p. 21.
55 that they would marry . . . at Jacksonville: Thomas, *Lincoln's New Salem*, p. 82; Tarbell, *The Life of Abraham Lincoln*, Vol. I, p. 119.
55 details of Ann's death: Rankin, *Personal Recollections of Abraham Lincoln*, pp. 73–74.
55 *"indifferent* . . . woods by him self": Henry McHenry to WHH, January 8, 1866, in *HI*, p. 155.
55 "never seen a man . . . he did": Elizabeth Abell to WHH, February 15, 1867, in ibid., p. 557.
55 "be reconcile[d] . . . temporarily deranged": William G. Greene interview, May 30, 1865, in ibid., p. 21.
56 "reason would desert her throne": Robert B. Rutledge to WHH, ca. November 1, 1866, in ibid., p. 383.
56 he ran "off the track": Isaac Cogdal interview, [1865–1866], in ibid., p. 440.
56 *"I hear the loved survivors tell* . . .": AL to Andrew Johnston, April 18, 1846, in *CW*, I, p. 379.
56 "was not crazy": Elizabeth Abell to WHH, February 15, 1867, in *HI*, p. 557.
56 "Only people . . . and heal them": Leo Tolstoy, *Childhood, Boyhood, Youth*, quoted in George E. Vaillant, *The Wisdom of the Ego* (Cambridge, Mass., and London: Harvard University Press, 1993), p. 358.
56 "I'm afraid . . . last of us": AL to Mrs. Samuel Hill, quoted in Wilson, *Honor's Voice*, p. 83.
56 of any "faith in life after death": Bruce, "The Riddle of Death," in *The Lincoln Enigma*, pp. 137–39. Lincoln wrote to his stepbrother that were his father to die soon, Thomas Lincoln would have a "joyous [meeting] with many loved ones gone before; and where [the rest] of us, through the help of God, hope ere-long [to join] them." AL to John D. Johnston, January 12, 1851, in *CW*, II, p. 97.
56 his "heart was broken" . . . eternal companionship: SPC to Charles D. Cleveland, October 1, 1845, reel 6, Chase Papers.
56 "to a higher world . . . with her mother": Bates diary, November 15, 1846.
57 "I ought to be able . . . in these reflections": WHS to Charlotte S. Cushman, January 7, 1867, Vol. 13, The Papers of Charlotte S. Cushman, Manuscript Division, Library of Congress.
57 his "experiment . . . never saw a sadder face": Speed, *Reminiscences of Abraham Lincoln*, p. 21.
57 Speed had heard Lincoln speak: Ibid., pp. 17–18; Joshua F. Speed statement, 1865–1866, in *HI*, p. 477.
57 "You seem to be . . . 'I am moved!' ": Speed, *Reminiscences of Abraham Lincoln*, pp. 21–22.
57 description of Joshua Speed: See ibid., pp. 3–14; Robert L. Kincaid, *Joshua Fry Speed: Lincoln's Most Intimate Friend*, reprinted from *The Filson Club History Quarterly* 17 (Louisville, Ky.: Filson Club, 1943; Harrogate, Tenn.: Department of Lincolniana, Lincoln Memorial University, 1943), pp. 10–11.
58 Lincoln and Speed shared: For the relationship between Lincoln and Speed, see Speed, *Reminiscences of Abraham Lincoln;* Kincaid, *Joshua Fry Speed*, pp. 13–14.
58 as his "most intimate friend": Kincaid, *Joshua Fry Speed*, pp. 10, 33 n2.
58 "You know my desire . . . to do any thing": AL to Joshua F. Speed, February 13, 1842, in *CW*, I, p. 269.
58 Some have suggested: C. A. Tripp, *The Intimate World of Abraham Lincoln*, ed. Lewis Gannett (New York: Free Press, 2005), pp. 126–29.
58 sharing a bed: Rotundo, *American Manhood*, pp. 84–85; Strozier, *Lincoln's Quest for Union*, p. 43.
58 The room above Speed's store: Michael Burlingame, "A Respectful Dissent," Afterword I, in Tripp, *The Intimate World of Abraham Lincoln*, p. 228.
58 attorneys of the Eighth Circuit . . . for a companion: Whitney, *Life on the Circuit with Lincoln*, pp. 63, 72.
58 the "preoccupation . . . the nineteenth": Donald Yacovone, "Abolitionists and the 'Language of Fraternal Love,' " in *Meanings for Manhood: Constructions of Masculinity in Victorian America*, ed. Mark C. Carnes and Clyde Griffen (Chicago: University of Chicago Press, 1990), p. 94.

CHAPTER 3: THE LURE OF POLITICS

Page

60 "Scarcely have you . . . as to an assembly": Alexis de Tocqueville, *Democracy in America*, ed. and trans. Harvey C. Mansfield and Delba Winthrop (Chicago and London: University of Chicago Press, 2000), p. 232.
61 Noah Webster's *Elementary Spelling Book:* Fidler, "Young Limbs of the Law," pp. 175–76.
61 "Who can wonder . . . hush before his": Ralph Waldo Emerson, "Eloquence," in *The Works of Ralph Waldo Emerson: Society and Solitude*, Vol. VI, Fireside Edition (Boston and New York: n.p., 1870; 1898), p. 65.
61 Bates was the first . . . "form of government": Cain, *Lincoln's Attorney General*, pp. 8–9, 11 (quotes pp. 9, 11); Appleby, *Inheriting the Revolution*, p. 247.
62 "This momentous question . . . of the Union": Thomas Jefferson to John Holmes, April 22, 1820, *The Works of Thomas Jefferson*, Vol. XII, Federal Edition, ed. Paul Leicester Ford (New York and London: G. P. Putnam's Sons/The Knickerbocker Press, 1905), p. 158.
62 Missouri Compromise: "Missouri Compromise," in *The Reader's Companion to American History*, ed. Foner and Garraty, p. 737.
62 "*Great Pacificator*": Stephen Douglas, quoted by AL, "Speech at Peoria, Illinois," October 16, 1854, in *CW*, II, p. 251.
62 "emerged as one" . . . candidates for state offices: Cain, *Lincoln's Attorney General*, pp. 14–15 (quote p. 14).
62 tensions developed between Senators Barton and Benton: Cain, *Lincoln's Attorney General*, pp. 19–22.
62 The Whigs favored public support: See Michael F. Holt, *The Rise and Fall of the American Whig Party: Jacksonian Politics and the Onset of the Civil War* (New York: Oxford University Press, 1999), pp. 27, 64, 66–70.
63 "a most beautiful woman": John F. Darby, "Mrs. Julia Bates, Widow of the Late Ed. Bates, Esq. For the Republican," reprinted in Bates, *Bates, et al., of Virginia and Missouri*, p. 31.
63 Julia's South Carolina family: Ibid., pp. 31–32.
63 Her surviving letters: Julia Davenport Bates to Caroline Hatcher Bates, April 10, 1850; Julia Davenport Bates to Onward Bates, July 24, 1855, February 14, 1861, Bates Papers, MoSHi.
63 "was calculated . . . domestic circle": Darby, "Mrs. Julia Bates," reprinted in Bates, *Bates, et al., of Virginia and Missouri*, p. 31.
63 When he sought and won a seat: Cain, *Lincoln's Attorney General*, pp. 26–27.
63 "I have never . . . to have it again": EB to Julia Bates, April 11, 1825, Bates Papers, ViHi.
63 Bates's lonely journey to Washington: EB to Julia Bates, November 7, 1827, Bates Papers, ViHi.
63 "something of a melancholy . . . mood": EB to Julia Bates, November 7, 1827, Bates Papers, ViHi.
64 "magic . . . feel it to be true": EB to Julia Bates, November 7, 1827, Bates Papers, ViHi.
64 life in Washington: EB to Julia Bates, January 5 and 22, February 25, March 17, 1828, December 4, 1829, Bates Papers, ViHi.
64 "That man grows . . . associate with him": EB to Julia Bates, February 25, 1828, Bates Papers, ViHi.
64 The main issues that confronted Bates: EB to Julia Bates, March 17, 1828, Bates Papers, ViHi; Cain, *Lincoln's Attorney General*, pp. 28–32.
64 Benton and Barton were antagonists: Cain, *Lincoln's Attorney General*, pp. 28–29.
64 Bates published a pamphlet: EB, *Edward Bates Against Thomas H. Benton* (St. Louis: Charless & Paschall, 1828).
64 "My piece is . . . never be effaced": EB to Julia Bates, December 4, 1829, Bates Papers, ViHi.
64 "roaring disorder . . . magnificent appearance": EB to Julia Bates, February 23, 1829, Bates Papers, ViHi.
64 "As yet I only . . . is in my eye": EB to Julia Bates, January 5, 1828, Bates Papers, ViHi.
65 "O, that I could . . . my sunshine": EB to Julia Bates, February 25, 1828, Bates Papers, ViHi.
65 he lost his bid for reelection: EB to Julia Bates, December 4, 1829, Bates Papers, ViHi.
65 got into a heated argument: Cain, *Lincoln's Attorney General*, pp. 38–39.
65 "The code preserved . . . are well spent": Charles Gibson, *The Autobiography of Charles Gibson*, ed. E. R. Gibson, 1899, Gibson Papers, MoSHi.
65 "as much as any man . . . we possessed": EB to Julia Bates, December 4, 1829, Bates Papers, ViHi.
65 two terms in the state legislature: "Bates, Edward," *DAB*, Vol. I, p. 48.
65 "the ablest . . . of that body": Switzler, "Lincoln's Attorney General," reprinted in Bates, *Bates, et al., of Virginia and Missouri*, p. 27.
65 he decided in 1835: Cain, *Lincoln's Attorney General*, pp. 53, 55, 58.
66 the "curious fact . . . of the frog": Bates diary, September 17, 1847.
66 "bad stammerer . . . more devoted piety": Bates diary, December 15, 1849.
66 "Mistress & Queen": Bates diary, July 10, 1851.
66 "begrudge her the short respite": Bates diary, April 23, 1848.
66 "This day . . . in a large house": Bates diary, November 15, 1851.
67 Every year, on April 29: See, for example, entry for April 29, 1859, in *The Diary of Edward Bates*, 1859–1866, p. 13.
67 "mighty changes . . . of the continent": Entry for April 29, 1859, in ibid.
67 His entries proudly record: Bates diary, November 7, 1847; December 20, 1847; December 9, 1852.
67 a great fire . . . cholera epidemic: Bates diary, May 18; June 14–28; July 1–11, 1849.
67 "in perfect health" . . . fruits and vegetables: Bates diary, July 19, 1849.
67 medical ignorance . . . "two weeks at a time": Bates diary, June 21, 1849.
67 "I am one . . . of a known duty": EB to R. B. Frayser, June 1849, Bates Papers, MoSHi.
67 Bates filled the pages of his diary: Bates diary, May 21, 1847; May 22, 1847; November 22, 1847; December 10, 1847; March 13, 1848; May 6, 1848; March 11, 1849; March 29, 1851 (quote).

67 "the largest Convention . . . the Civil War": Floyd A. McNeil, "Lincoln's Attorney General; Edward Bates," Ph.D. diss., State University of Iowa, 1934, p. 155.
67 5,000 accredited delegates . . . David Dudley Field: Shaw, "A Neglected Episode in the Life of Abraham Lincoln," *Transactions* (1922), p. 54; Albert J. Beveridge, *Abraham Lincoln, 1809–1858,* Vol. II (Boston and New York: Houghton Mifflin/Riverside Press, 1928), pp. 89–90.
68 "Hon. Abraham . . . in the State": *NYTrib,* July 14, 1847.
68 "No one who saw . . . with woolen socks": E. B. Washburne, "Political Life in Illinois," in *Reminiscences of Abraham Lincoln,* ed. Rice, p. 92.
68 "deep astonishment" . . . responsibility for its failure: Bates diary, July 5, 1847.
68 "leaped at one bound . . . prominence": Switzler, "Lincoln's Attorney General," reprinted in Bates, *Bates, et al., of Virginia and Missouri,* p. 28.
68 Lincoln impressed . . . Democrat Field: *Beveridge, Abraham Lincoln, 1809–1859,* Vol. II, p. 91.
68 "too intent . . . of Reporting": *Albany Evening Journal,* July 23, 1847.
68 "No account . . . do it justice": *NYTrib,* July 15, 1847.
68 "between sectional disruption . . . material greatness": Cain, *Lincoln's Attorney General,* p. 63.
69 "he was interrupted . . . in attendance": TW, quoted in Bates, *Bates, et al., of Virginia and Missouri,* p. 30.
69 "the crowning act . . . either house of Congress": Bates diary, July 5, 1847.
69 "The nation cannot . . . and patriotism": *Albany Evening Journal,* July 23, 1847.
69 "the glittering bauble": Entry for February 28, 1860, *The Diary of Edward Bates, 1859–1866,* p. 106.
69 "noble aspirations . . . natural result": EB to TW, August 9, 1847, reprinted in *Albany Evening Journal,* January 11, 1861.
69 "had no ambition . . . business of the country": Seward, *An Autobiography,* pp. 52, 53.
70 Seward and Weed meet: See ibid., pp. 55–56; Thurlow Weed, *Autobiography of Thurlow Weed,* ed. Harriet A. Weed (Boston: Houghton Mifflin, 1883), p. 139.
70 "he printed . . . his own hand": Seward, *An Autobiography,* p. 56.
70 details of Weed's early life: *Autobiography of Thurlow Weed,* ed. Weed; Thurlow Weed Barnes, *Memoir of Thurlow Weed* (Boston: Houghton Mifflin, 1884).
70 He had walked miles: *Autobiography of Thurlow Weed,* ed. Weed, pp. 12–13.
70 "a politician who sees . . . him forever": Barnes, *Memoir of Thurlow Weed,* pp. 26–27.
70 Such measures . . . "extend its dominion": Seward, *An Autobiography,* p. 54.
71 the *Albany Evening Journal: Autobiography of Thurlow Weed,* ed. Weed, pp. 360–62.
71 Weed engineered . . . from the seventh district: Seward, *An Autobiography,* p. 80.
71 the youngest member to enter: Taylor, *William Henry Seward,* p. 24.
71 Albany still a small town: John J. McEneny, *Albany: Capital City on the Hudson* (Sun Valley, Calif.: American Historical Press, 1998), p. 76.
71 description of Albany: "Albany Fifty Years Ago," *Harper's New Monthly Magazine* 14 (March 1857), pp. 451–63.
71 "first steam-powered . . . web of tracks": McEneny, *Albany,* pp. 16 (quote), 98.
71 The legislature . . . Bemont's Hotel: Seward, *An Autobiography,* pp. 80–81; Frederick W. Seward, *Reminiscences of a War-Time Statesman and Diplomat, 1830–1915* (New York and London: G. P. Putnam's Sons, 1916), p. 2; Taylor, *William Henry Seward,* p. 24.
71 Seward attends alone: Seward, *An Autobiography,* p. 80.
71 "Weed is . . . warmth of feeling": WHS to FAS, January 12, 1831, in ibid., p. 166.
71 "one of the greatest . . . except politics": WHS to FAS, February 6, 1831, in ibid., pp. 179–80.
71 Weed and Seward's mutual interests: Van Deusen, *William Henry Seward,* p. 17; Taylor, *William Henry Seward,* p. 25.
71 "My room is a thoroughfare": WHS to FAS, February 16, 1831, in Seward, *An Autobiography,* p. 182.
72 Albert Haller Tracy: Van Deusen, *William Henry Seward,* p. 17; "Tracy, Albert Haller, 1793–1859," *Biographical Directory of the United States Congress,* http://bioguide.congress.gov (accessed December 2003).
72 "crushed . . . passes in his mind": FAS to LW, March 12, 1832, reel 118, Seward Papers.
72 "He and Henry . . . love with each other": FAS to LW, March 4, 1832, reel 118, Seward Papers.
72 "It shames my . . . since I left Albany": Albert H. Tracy to WHS, February 7, 1831, reel 1, Seward Papers.
72 Seward at first reciprocated: FAS to LW, March 12, 1832, reel 118, Seward Papers.
72 a "rapturous joy . . . I possessed": WHS to Albert H. Tracy, February 11, 1831, typescript copy, Albert Haller Tracy Papers, New York State Library, Albany, New York [hereafter Tracy Papers].
72 "My feelings . . . divided with many": Albert H. Tracy to WHS, June 12, 1832, reel 1, Seward Papers.
72 "Weed has never . . . account for it": FAS to LW, March [?] 1832, reel 118, Seward Papers (quote); FAS to LW, April 5, 1832, reel 118, Seward Papers.
72 "Love—cruel tyrant . . . hallowed affections": Albert H. Tracy to WHS, September 24, 1832, reel 1, Seward Papers.
72 He transferred his unrequited love: FAS to LW, March [?] and September 27, 1832, reel 118, Seward Papers; WHS to FAS, November 28, 1834, reel 112, Seward Papers.
73 "losing my influence . . . differently constituted": FAS to WHS, December 5, 1834, reel 113, Seward Papers.
73 relationship between Tracys and Sewards: FAS to LW, March 12, 24, and undated March, April 9, 1832, reel 118, Seward Papers.
73 "He is a singular . . . shade of difference": FAS to LW, March 12, 1832, reel 118, Seward Papers.
73 "I believe at present . . . should choose": FAS to LW, March [?] 1832, reel 118, Seward Papers.
73 "very glad . . . very much": FAS to LW, November 17, 1833, reel 118, Seward Papers.
73 private emotional intimacy: See Karen Lystra, *Searching the Heart: Women, Men and Romantic Love in Victorian America* (New York: Oxford University Press, 1989), pp. 31–33.

73 a three-month voyage to Europe: Seward, *An Autobiography*, pp. 104–41.
73 "What a romance . . . malicious political warfare": Ibid., pp. 116, 128.
74 spent a long weekend visiting: Ibid., pp. 134–40.
74 When Judge Miller . . . "be so unreasonable": FAS to LW, September 27, 1833, reel 118, Seward Papers.
74 she proffered the letters: WHS to Albert Tracy, quoted in WHS to FAS, December 29, 1834, reel 112, Seward Papers.
74 Seward's first run for governor: Glyndon G. Van Deusen, *Thurlow Weed: Wizard of the Lobby* (Boston: Little, Brown, 1947), pp. 87–89; Taylor, *William Henry Seward*, pp. 35–36.
75 Whigs offered a gallery . . . Henry Clay himself: Seward, *An Autobiography*, p. 238. This same campaign tactic was adopted by the youthful John F. Kennedy in his campaign for the presidency in 1960.
75 Defeat shook . . . jeopardized his marriage: WHS to FAS, November 24 and 28, 1834, reel 112, Seward Papers; Van Deusen, *William Henry Seward*, pp. 28, 33–34.
75 "What a demon . . . are not crushed": WHS to FAS, November 28, 1834, reel 112, Seward Papers.
75 "I am growing womanish . . . happy a lot": WHS to FAS, December 5, 1834, reel 112, Seward Papers.
75 "You reproach yourself . . . the right path": FAS to WHS, December 5, 1834, reel 113, Seward Papers.
76 Seward pledged: WHS to FAS, December 15 and 29, 1834, reel 112, Seward Papers.
76 "to live for you . . . dear boys": WHS to FAS, December 29, 1834, reel 112, Seward Papers.
76 "a partner in . . . cares and feelings": WHS to FAS, December 1, 1834, reel 112, Seward Papers.
76 "count[ing] with eagerness . . . life will commence": WHS to FAS, December 29, 1834, reel 112, Seward Papers.
76 "golden dreams . . . displayed towards you": Albert Tracy to WHS, December 29, 1834, reel 3, Seward Papers.
76 "alienation . . . but without affection": WHS to Albert Tracy, quoted in Seward to FAS, December 29, 1834, reel 112, Seward Papers.
76 If Seward believed: WHS to TW, January 18, 1835, in Seward, *An Autobiography*, p. 249; WHS to unknown recipient, June 1, 1836, in ibid., p. 300.
76 "It is seldom . . . periods of seclusion": WHS to Alvah Hunt, January 25, 1843, quoted in Van Deusen, *William Henry Seward*, p. 99.
77 "keep me informed . . . as a politician": WHS to TW, January 1835, in Seward, *An Autobiography*, p. 249.
77 family expedition to the South: Taylor, *William Henry Seward*, p. 37; Seward, *Reminiscences of a War-Time Statesman and Diplomat*, p. 9.
77 "When I travel . . . and reflection": WHS to Albert H. Tracy, June 23, 1831, Tracy Papers.
77 their letters home extolled: Seward, *An Autobiography*, pp. 272–73; Seward, *Reminiscences of a War-Time Statesman and Diplomat*, pp. 12–13.
77 "teemed with . . . reform of mankind": Introduction to "The Conflict of Cultures," in *The Causes of the Civil War*, 3rd edn., ed. Kenneth M. Stampp (Englewood Cliffs, N.J.: Prentice-Hall, 1959; New York: Touchstone Books, 1991), p. 201.
77 a world virtually unchanged: James M. McPherson, "Modernization and Sectionalism," in ibid., p. 104.
77 "We no longer passed . . . of slaves": Entry for June 12, 1835, WHS journal, quoted in Seward, *An Autobiography*, p. 267.
77 "a waste . . . decaying habitation": Entry for June 12, 1835, WHS journal, in ibid., p. 267.
77 "How deeply . . . decayed as Virginia": WHS to Albert H. Tracy, June 25, 1835, Tracy Papers.
77 Slavery trapped . . . a sizable middle class: McPherson, "Modernization and Sectionalism," in *The Causes of the Civil War*, ed. Stampp, pp. 104–05.
78 "We are told that . . . this injured race": FAS to LW, quoted in Seward, *An Autobiography*, p. 272.
78 "turning the ponderous" . . . any of them again: Seward, *Reminiscences of a War-Time Statesman and Diplomat*, pp. 14–15.
78 "Ten naked little boys . . . themselves to sleep": Seward, *An Autobiography*, p. 271.
78 "Sick of slavery and the South": Entry for June 13, 1835, FAS, "Diary of Trip through Pennsylvania, Virginia, and Maryland, 1835," reel 197, Seward Papers.
78 "the evil effects . . . marring everything": Entry of June 17, 1835, FAS, "Diary of Trip through Pennsylvania, Virginia, and Maryland, 1835," reel 197, Seward Papers.
78 "turned their horses' . . . homeward": Seward, *An Autobiography*, p. 272.
78 indelible images . . . social conscience: Entry for June 15, 1835, WHS journal in Seward, *An Autobiography*, p. 268; FAS to LW, January 15, 1853, reel 119, Seward Papers; WHS, "Speech in Cleveland, Ohio on the Election of 1848," *Works of William H. Seward*, Vol. III, pp. 295–96.
78 a lucrative opportunity . . . Seward did not hesitate: Van Deusen, *William Henry Seward*, pp. 38–39.
79 "more beautiful" . . . invited Weed's seventeen-year-old daughter: WHS to Harriet Weed, September 8, 1836, Thurlow Weed Papers, Department of Rare Books & Special Collections, University of Rochester Library, Rochester, N.Y. [hereafter Weed Papers].
79 "there are a thousand . . . upon them": WHS to FAS, December 21, 1836, in Seward, *An Autobiography*, p. 321.
79 "so vividly remembered . . . a rare event": Seward, *An Autobiography*, p. 162.
79 death of Cornelia from smallpox: Seward, *An Autobiography*, p. 323.
79 "did not think it . . . from their Grandpa": FAS to Harriet Weed, February 9, 1837, Weed Papers.
79 "lightness that was . . . for myself": WHS to FAS, February 12, 1837, in Seward, *An Autobiography*, p. 325.
79 Frances and the boys come to Westfield: Seward, *An Autobiography*, pp. 334–35.
80 "Well, I am here . . . from Tusculum": WHS to TW, July 10, 1837, in ibid., p. 336.
80 "found Westfield . . . missed and loved her": FAS to Harriet Weed, September 6, 1837, Weed Papers.
80 "I am almost in despair . . . almost as helpless": WHS to [FAS], December 17, 1837, in Seward, *An Autobiography*, p. 354.

80 "There is such . . . time to think": WHS to [TW], undated, in ibid., p. 344.
80 "I have been two . . . healthful channels": TW to WHS, November 11, 1837, quoted in Van Deusen, *Thurlow Weed*, p. 95.
80 Weed raised money . . . powerful *New York Tribune: Autobiography of Thurlow Weed*, ed. Weed, pp. 466–67; Seward, *Reminiscences of a War-Time Statesman and Diplomat*, pp. 45, 88.
81 1838 gubernatorial campaign: Van Deusen, *William Henry Seward*, pp. 49–52.
81 received the nomination on the fourth ballot: Seward, *An Autobiography*, p. 373; Van Deusen, *Thurlow Weed*, p. 100.
81 "Well, Seward . . . earnestly to work": TW to WHS, September 15, 1838, reel 5, Seward Papers.
81 the overwhelming victor: Seward, *An Autobiography*, p. 378.
81 "God bless . . . result to him": WHS, quoted in J. C. Derby, *Fifty Years Among Authors, Books and Publishers* (New York: G.W. Carleton & Co., 1884), p. 58.
81 "It is a fearful post . . . a house alone": WHS to TW, November 11, 1838, hereafter Weed Papers.
81 Weed arrived . . . inaugural outfit: WHS to TW, November 28, 1838, Weed Papers; Seward, *An Autobiography*, pp. 381–82 (quote p. 382); Van Deusen, *Thurlow Weed*, p. 102.
81 "it was [his] . . . a cabinet": WHS to Hiram Ketchum, February 15, 1839, reel 8, Seward Papers.
81 "Your letter . . . as it comes up": WHS to [TW], November 23, 1837, in Seward, *An Autobiography*, p. 345.
82 "I had no idea . . . amiable creatures": WHS to TW, December 14, 1838, in ibid., p. 381.
82 "There were never two . . . highest sense": Barnes, *Memoir of Thurlow Weed*, p. 262.
82 told the story of a carriage ride: Seward, *An Autobiography*, p. 395.
82 an ambitious agenda . . . imprisonment for debt: WHS, "Annual Message to the Legislature, January 1, 1839," *The Works of William H. Seward*, Vol. II, pp. 183–211; Seward, *An Autobiography*, pp. 386–87.
82 "Our race is ordained" . . . the engine of Northern expansion: WHS, "Annual Message, 1839," *Works of William H. Seward*, Vol. II, pp. 197–99.
83 to support parochial schools: Ibid., p. 199; WHS, "Annual Message to the Legislature, January 7, 1840," p. 215.
83 "to overthrow republican" . . . the hands of priests: Seward, *An Autobiography*, p. 462.
83 "Virginia Case" . . . governor refused: WHS, "Biographical Memoir of William H. Seward," *Works of William H. Seward*, Vol. I, pp. lxiii–lxvi.
83 "the universal sentiment . . . praiseworthy": George E. Baker, ed., *Life of William H. Seward, with Selections from His Works* (New York: J. S. Redfield, 1855), p. 85.
83 "intermeddling . . . New England fanatic": Seward, *An Autobiography*, pp. 463, 464.
84 This only emboldened Seward's resolve: Ibid., pp. 463–64, 510–11.
84 the "new irritation": Thomas Jefferson to John Holmes, April 22, 1820, in *The Works of Thomas Jefferson*, Vol. XII, ed. Ford, p. 158.
84 number of slaves who escaped to the North: Don E. Fehrenbacher, "The Wilmot Proviso and the Mid-Century Crisis," in Fehrenbacher, *The South and Three Sectional Crises* (Baton Rouge: Louisiana State University Press, 1980), p. 33.
84 "all actions . . . Constitution": William H. Pease and Jane H. Pease, ed. *The Antislavery Argument* (Indianapolis: Bobbs-Merrill, 1965), p. xxx.
84 *"The Empire of Satan"*: Henry Mayer, *All on Fire: William Lloyd Garrison and the Abolition of Slavery* (New York: St. Martin's Press, 1998), p. 188.
84 They proclaimed slavery a "positive good": John C. Calhoun, *Remarks of Mr. Calhoun of South Carolina, on the Reception of Abolition Petitions, delivered in the Senate of the United States, February 1837*, reprinted in Robert C. Byrd, *The Senate, 1789–1989*. Vol. III: *Classic Speeches, 1830–1993*, Bicentennial Edition, ed. Wendy Wolff (Washington, D.C.: Government Printing Office, 1994), p. 177.
84 incited attacks on abolitionist printers: Niven, *Salmon P. Chase*, pp. 47–48.
84 Seward reelected but with a reduced margin: Seward, *An Autobiography*, p. 506.
84 "henceforth be . . . in his life": Horace Greeley article, *Log Cabin*, in ibid., p. 510.
84 "All that can . . . in its history": WHS to Christopher Morgan, [June?] 1841, in ibid., p. 547.
84 "What am I . . . on your affection?": WHS to TW, December 31, 1842, quoted in Barnes, *Memoir of Thurlow Weed*, p. 98.
85 the new Liberty Party: "Liberty Party," in *The Reader's Companion to American History*, ed. Foner and Garraty, p. 657; Taylor, *William Henry Seward*, p. 59.
85 story of black man named William Freeman: Baker, ed., *Life of William H. Seward*, pp. 99–113; "Defence of William Freeman," *Works of William H. Seward*, Vol. I, pp. 409–75.
85 "I trust in the mercy . . . incomprehensible": FAS to WHS, March 1846, in Seward, *An Autobiography*, pp. 787, 786.
85 insanity . . . floggings in jail: Seward, *An Autobiography*, p. 812.
85 "Will anyone defend . . . *until his death*!": Baker, ed., *Life of William H. Seward*, pp. 104, 106.
85 roundly criticized Seward for his decision: WHS to TW, May 29, 1846, quoted in Seward, *An Autobiography*, p. 810.
85 Only Frances stood proudly: Van Deusen, *William Henry Seward*, p. 97.
85 "he will do . . . wrong is perpetrated": FAS to LW, July 1, 1846, reel 119, Seward Papers.
85 "there are few men . . . a peaceful mind": FAS to Augustus Seward, July 19, 1846, reel 114, Seward Papers.
86 she sat in the courtroom: FAS to LW, January–February 1850, reel 119, Seward Papers.
86 summoning five doctors: Seward, *An Autobiography*, pp. 811, 813.
86 "He is still your brother . . . be a man": "Defence of William Freeman," *Works of William H. Seward*, Vol. I, p. 417.

86 "I am not . . . malefactor": Ibid., pp. 414–15.
86 "unexplainable on any principle of *sanity*": WHS to TW, May 29, 1846, in Seward, *An Autobiography*, p. 810.
86 "there is not . . . such a prosecution": "Defence of William Freeman," *Works of William H. Seward*, Vol. I, p. 419.
86 "In due time . . . 'He was Faithful!' ": WHS, quoted in Seward, *An Autobiography*, p. 822.
86 While Seward endured . . . still wider distribution: Seward, *Seward at Washington . . . 1846–1861*, pp. 29, 32, 46.
86 "one of the very first . . . the highest degree": SPC to Lewis Tappan, March 18, 1847, reel 6, Chase Papers.
87 Lincoln's run for legislature from Sangamon County: Thomas, *Abraham Lincoln*, pp. 28–29, 34–35.
87 "Every man . . . very much chagrined": AL, "Communication to the People of Sangamo County," March 9, 1832, in *CW*, I, pp. 8–9.
87 only after being defeated . . . "to try it again": J. Rowan Herndon to WHH, May 28, 1865, in *HI*, p. 7.
87 Lincoln had lost the election: AL, "Communication to the People of Sangamo County," March 9, 1832, in *CW*, I, p. 5n.
87 "made friends everywhere he went": "Conversation with Hon. J. T. Stuart June 23 1875," quoted in John G. Nicolay, *An Oral History of Abraham Lincoln: John G. Nicolay's Interviews and Essays*, ed. Michael Burlingame (Carbondale and Edwardsville: Southern Illinois University Press, 1996), p. 10.
88 "This was the only time . . . of the people": AL, "Scripps autobiography," in *CW*, IV, p. 64.
88 Two years later . . . in the state legislature: Thomas, *Abraham Lincoln*, p. 41.
88 frontier county . . . "consuming the whole afternoon": Robert L. Wilson to WHH, February 10, 1866, in *HI*, pp. 201–02.
88 At Mr. Kyle's store . . . "one Could throw it": Andrew S. Kirk interview, March 7, 1887, in ibid., pp. 602–03.
88 "They came there . . . social club": Speed, *Reminiscences of Abraham Lincoln*, p. 23.
89 Lincoln proved . . . grassroots politician: Thomas, *Abraham Lincoln*, pp. 58, 63, 79.
89 three levels of command . . . "day as possible": "Lincoln's Plan of Campaign in 1840" [c. January 1840], in *CW*, I, p. 180.
89 "Our intention . . . which we are engaged": "Campaign Circular from Whig Committee," January [31?], 1840, in ibid., pp. 201–03. See also "Lincoln's Plan of Campaign in 1840" [c. January 1840], in ibid., pp. 180–81.
90 Lincoln likened . . . internal improvements: James A. Herndon to WHH, May 29, 1865, in *HI*, p. 16.
90 Lincoln had actually . . . "wider and fairer": Carpenter, *Six Months at the White House*, pp. 97–98 (quote p. 97).
90 "to the ideal . . . rise in life": G. S. Boritt, *Lincoln and the Economics of the American Dream* (Memphis, Tenn.: Memphis State University Press, 1978), p. ix.
90 "an unfettered start . . . pursuit for all": AL, "Message to Congress in Special Session," July 4, 1861, in *CW*, IV, p. 438.
91 "DeWitt Clinton of Illinois": Herndon and Weik, *Herndon's Life of Lincoln*, p. 140.
91 "we highly disapprove . . . of the citizens": Resolutions by the General Assembly of the State of Illinois, quoted in note 2 of "Protest in Illinois Legislature on Slavery," March 3, 1837, in *CW*, I, p. 75.
91 he issued a formal protest . . . "people of said District": "Protest in Illinois Legislature on Slavery," March 3, 1837, in ibid., p. 75. Daniel Stone of Springfield co-authored the protest with Lincoln.
91 "if slavery . . . so think, and feel": AL to Albert G. Hodges, April 4, 1864, draft copy, Lincoln Papers.
91 "partly on account . . . that it is now": AL, "Scripps autobiography," in *CW*, IV, pp. 61, 65.
92 In these early years . . . gradually become extinct: For an example of Lincoln stating that he believed slavery would gradually become extinct, see AL, "Speech at Greenville, Illinois," September 13, 1858, in *CW*, III, p. 96.
92 Lincoln defended both slaveowners and fugitive slaves: Donald, *Lincoln*, p. 104.
92 the constitutional requirements . . . could not be evaded: Burlingame, *The Inner World of Abraham Lincoln*, p. 28.
92 a sustained recession . . . sentiment turned: Donald, *Lincoln*, pp. 61–62; Boritt, *Lincoln and the Economics of the American Dream*, p. 28.
92 "stopping a skift . . . go down": AL, "Remarks in the Illinois Legislature Concerning the Illinois and Michigan Canal," January 22, 23, 1840, in *CW*, I, p. 196.
92 "If you make . . . the tighter": AL to Joshua F. Speed, February 25, 1842, in ibid., p. 280 (quote); Boritt, *Lincoln and the Economics of the American Dream*, p. 30.
92 was forced to liquidate . . . deterred from emigrating: *King, Lincoln's Manager*, p. 40.
92 to win a fourth term . . . term was completed: Thomas, *Abraham Lincoln*, p. 77; entry for August 3, 1840, *Lincoln Day by Day: A Chronology, 1809–1865*. Vol. I, ed. Earl Schenck Miers (Washington, D.C.: Lincoln Sesquicentennial Commission, 1960; Dayton, Ohio: Morningside, 1991), p. 142.
92 "He was not very fond of girls": Sarah Bush Lincoln interview, September 8, 1865, in *HI*, p. 108.
92 "He would burst . . . 'clean those girls look' ": AL, quoted in William H. Herndon, "Analysis of the Character of Abraham Lincoln," *Abraham Lincoln Quarterly* I (September 1941), p. 367.
93 "as demoralized . . . out of sight": Whitney, *Life on the Circuit with Lincoln*, p. 59.
93 "a business which I do not understand": AL to Mrs. M. J. Green, September 22, 1860, in *CW*, IV, p. 118.
93 ". . . *when the genius of*": Stephen Vincent Benét, *John Brown's Body* (New York: Henry Holt & Co., 1927; 1990), p. 189.
93 "Lincoln had . . . his terrible passion": WHH to JWW, January 23, 1890, reel 10, Herndon-Weik Collection, DLC.
93 "his Conscience . . . many a woman": David Davis interview, September 20, 1866, in *HI*, p. 350.
93 "handsome . . . much vivacity": Esther Sumners Bale interview, [1866], in ibid., p. 527 (first quote); Nancy G. Vineyard to JWW, February 4, 1887, in ibid., p. 601 (second quote).

93 "a good conversationalist . . . splendid reader": Benjamin R. Vineyard to JWW, March 14, 1887, in ibid., p. 610.
93 would make a good match . . . honor-bound to keep his word: AL to Mrs. Orville H. Browning, April 1, 1838, in *CW*, I, pp. 117–19.
94 "This thing of living . . . Yours, &c.—Lincoln": AL to Mary S. Owens, May 7, 1837, in ibid., pp. 78–79.
94 "mortified almost beyond . . . enough to have me": AL to Mrs. Orville H. Browning, April 1, 1838, in ibid., p. 119.
94 The Edwards mansion . . . drink, and merry conversation: Randall, *Mary Lincoln*, p. 5.
94 "the exact reverse": Herndon and Weik, *Herndon's Life of Lincoln*, p. 165.
94 "physically, temperamentally, emotionally": Rankin, *Personal Recollections of Abraham Lincoln*, p. 160.
94 "her face an . . . passing emotion": Elizabeth Humphreys Norris to Emilie Todd Helm, September 28, 1895, quoted in Randall, *Mary Lincoln*, p. 24.
94 a self-controlled man: Elizabeth and Ninian W. Edwards interview, July 27, 1887, in *HI*, p. 623; MTL to Josiah G. Holland, December 4, 1865, in Justin G. Turner and Linda Levitt Turner, *Mary Todd Lincoln: Her Life and Letters* (New York: Knopf, 1972; New York: Fromm International, 1987), p. 293.
94 "he felt most deeply . . . the least": MTL to Josiah G. Holland, December 4, 1865, in ibid., p. 293.
95 "the very creature of excitement": James C. Conkling to Mercy Ann Levering, September 21, 1840, quoted in ibid., pp. 10–11.
95 "a Bishop forget his prayers": Ninian W. Edwards, quoted in Helm, *The True Story of Mary*, p. 81.
95 "a welcome guest everywhere . . . rarely danced": Tarbell, *The Life of Abraham Lincoln*, Vol. I (New York: Doubleday & McClure Co., 1900), p. 171.
95 "the highest marks . . . the biggest prizes": Helm, *The True Story of Mary*, p. 52.
95 Mary journeyed to . . . " 'Mary's' grave": MTL to Rhoda White, August 30, 1869, in Turner and Turner, *Mary Todd Lincoln*, p. 516.
95 Mary's life in Lexington: See chapters 1–3 in Baker, *Mary Todd Lincoln*.
95 "a violent little Whig": Helm, *The True Story of Mary*, p. 41.
95 "destined to be . . . future President": Elizabeth Todd Edward interview, 1865–1866, in *HI*, p. 443.
95 proudly rode her new pony: Helm, *The True Story of Mary*, pp. 1–2.
95 "I suppose like the rest . . . called in question?": MTL to Mercy Ann Levering, December [15?], 1840, in Turner and Turner, *Mary Todd Lincoln*, p. 21.
95 "the *great cause*": "Campaign Circular from Whig Committee," January [31?], 1840, in *CW*, 1, p. 202.
95 "Old hero": "Communication to the Readers of *The Old Soldier*," February 28, 1840, in ibid., p. 204.
95 death of Mary's mother; father's remarriage: See Baker, *Mary Todd Lincoln*, pp. 20, 22, 24, 28–30.
96 turned "desolate": MTL to Eliza Stuart Steele, May 23, 1871, in Turner and Turner, *Mary Todd Lincoln*, p. 588.
96 her only real home: MTL to Elizabeth Keckley, October 29, 1867, in ibid., p. 447.
96 "an emotional . . . heart would break": Mrs. Woodrow, quoted in Helm, *The True Story of Mary*, p. 32.
96 "either in the garret or cellar": Orville H. Browning, quoted in Nicolay, *An Oral History of Abraham Lincoln*, p. 1.
96 Mary may have precipitated: Abner Y. Ellis to WHH, March 24, 1866, in *HI*, p. 238; Stephen B. Oates, *With Malice Toward None: The Life of Abraham Lincoln* (New York: New American Library Penguin Books, 1977; 1978), p. 60.
96 Elizabeth warned . . . "husband & wife": Elizabeth Todd Edwards interview, 1865–1866, in *HI*, pp. 443, 444.
97 Mary had other suitors: MTL to Mercy Ann Levering, July 23 and December [15?], 1840, in Turner and Turner, *Mary Todd Lincoln*, pp. 18, 20; Baker, *Mary Todd Lincoln*, pp. 84–85.
97 "an agreeable . . . my heart is not": MTL to Mercy Ann Levering, July 23, 1840, in Turner and Turner, *Mary Todd Lincoln*, p. 18.
97 Far more likely, Lincoln's own misgivings: Tarbell, *The Life of Abraham Lincoln*, Vol. I, p. 173; Donald, *Lincoln*, pp. 86–87; Paul M. Angle, Appendix, in Carl Sandburg and Paul M. Angle, *Mary Lincoln, Wife and Widow* (New York: Harcourt, Brace & World, 1932; 1960), p. 331.
97 "in the winter . . . whole heart to me": Joshua F. Speed to WHH, November 30, 1866, in *HI*, p. 430.
97 Lincoln's change of heart . . . Matilda Edwards: Douglas L. Wilson, "Abraham Lincoln and 'That Fatal First of January,' " in Douglas L. Wilson, *Lincoln before Washington: New Perspectives on the Illinois Years* (Urbana and Chicago: University of Illinois Press, 1997), pp. 99–125.
97 "A lovelier girl I never saw": MTL to Mercy Ann Levering, December [15?], 1840, in Turner and Turner, *Mary Todd Lincoln*, p. 20.
97 "aberration of mind . . . violation of his word": Browning, quoted in Nicolay, *An Oral History of Abraham Lincoln*, p. 1.
97 no evidence that Lincoln ever made his feelings known: Elizabeth Todd and Ninian W. Edwards interviews, September 22, 1865, [1865–1866], July 27, 1887, in *HI*, pp. 133, 444, 623.
97 "never bear to leave . . . the strength of it": Jane Bell quoted in Wilson, "Abraham Lincoln and 'That Fatal First of January,' " in Wilson, *Lincoln before Washington*, p. 110.
97 "his ability and Capacity . . . support a wife": Elizabeth Todd Edwards interview, 1865–1866, in *HI*, p. 443.
98 driving up the marriage age: Fidler, "Young Limbs of the Law," pp. 266–67.
98 "is a jealous mistress . . . constant courtship": Joseph Story, "The Value and Importance of Legal Studies. A Discourse Pronounced at the Inauguration of the Author as Dane Professor of Law in Harvard University, August 25, 1829," in *The Miscellaneous Writings of Joseph Story*, ed. William W. Story. *Da Capo Press Reprints in American Constitutional and Legal History*, gen. ed. Leonard W. Levy (Boston, 1852; New York: Da Capo Press, 1972), p. 523.

98 Lincoln drafted a letter . . . lost his nerve: Joshua F. Speed interview, 1865–1866, in *HI*, pp. 475, 477.
98 "To tell you the truth . . . kissed her": AL, quoted in Herndon and Weik, *Herndon's Life of Lincoln*, p. 169.
98 This second confrontation: Wilson, "Abraham Lincoln and 'That Fatal First of January,' " in Wilson, *Lincoln before Washington*, pp. 103, 112.
98 "ability to keep . . . gem of [his] character": AL to Joshua F. Speed, July 4, 1842, in *CW*, I, p. 289.
98 "not single spies . . . battalions": William Shakespeare, "Hamlet," act 4, scene 5, *William Shakespeare Tragedies, Volume 1. Everyman's Library* (New York and Toronto: Alfred A. Knopf, 1992), p. 105.
98 details of Speed leaving Springfield: Kincaid, *Joshua Fry Speed*, p. 15.
98 Speed's departure would bring: James Conkling to Mercy Ann Levering, January 24, 1841, and Levering to Conkling, February 7, 1841, quoted in Wilson, "Abraham Lincoln and 'That Fatal First of January,' " in Wilson, *Lincoln before Washington*, p. 117; Burlingame, *The Inner World of Abraham Lincoln*, p. 100.
98 "I shall be verry . . . pained by the loss": AL to Joshua F. Speed, February 25, 1842, in *CW*, I, p. 281.
99 worried that he was suicidal: James H. Matheny interview, May 3, 1866, in *HI*, p. 251; Speed, *Reminiscences of Abraham Lincoln*, p. 39.
99 "Lincoln went Crazy . . . it was terrible": Joshua F. Speed interview, [1865–1866], in *HI*, p. 474.
99 "delirious to the extent . . . he was doing": Browning, quoted in Nicolay, *An Oral History of Abraham Lincoln*, p. 2.
99 "Poor L! . . . truly deplorable": James Conkling to Mercy Ann Levering, January 24, 1841, quoted in Wilson, "Abraham Lincoln and 'That Fatal First of January,' " in Wilson, *Lincoln Before Washington*, p. 117.
99 was called hypochondriasis: See J. S. Forsyth, *The New London Medical and Surgical Dictionary* (London: Sherwood, Gilbert & Piper, 1826), p. 379; Robley Dunglison, M.D., *A New Dictionary of Medical Science and Literature, Containing a Concise Account of the Various Subjects and Terms; with the Synonymes in Different Languages; and Formulæ for Various Officinal and Empirical Preparations*, Vol. I (Boston: Charles Bowen, 1833), p. 508; German E. Berrios, "Hypochondriasis: History of the Concept," in Vladan Starcevic and Don R. Lipsitt, eds., *Hypochondriasis: Modern Perspectives on an Ancient Malady* (New York: Oxford University Press, 2001), pp. 3–20.
99 "I have, within . . . to my existence": AL to John T. Stuart, January 20, 1841, in *CW*, I, p. 228. Dr. Henry did not receive the postmastership of Springfield.
99 "I am now the most . . . it appears to me: AL to John T. Stuart, January 23, 1841, in ibid., p. 229.
99 Hoping medical treatment . . . "without a personal interview": Joshua F. Speed to WHH, November 30, 1866, in *HI*, p. 431.
99 the nadir of Lincoln's depression . . . most certainly die: Speed, *Reminiscences of Abraham Lincoln*, p. 39.
99 "done nothing . . . desired to live for": Joshua F. Speed to WHH, February 7, 1866, in *HI*, p. 197.
100 "ideas of a person's . . . perceive him": William G. Thalmann, *The Odyssey: An Epic of Return. Twayne's Masterwork Studies*, No. 100 (New York: Twayne Publishers, 1992), p. 39.
100 "To see memory . . . thought with others": Bruce, "The Riddle of Death," in *The Lincoln Enigma*, p. 141.
100 "thou midway world . . . and paradise": AL to Andrew Johnston, April 18, 1846, in *CW*, I, p. 378.
100 critical to "avoid being *idle*": AL to Joshua F. Speed, February 13, 1842, in ibid., p. 269.
100 "*business and conversation* . . . bitterness of death": AL to Joshua F. Speed, [January 3?, 1842], in ibid., p. 265.
100 he delivered an eloquent address . . . "than a gallon of gall": AL, "Temperance Address. An Address, Delivered before the Springfield Washington Temperance Society," February 22, 1842, in ibid., p. 273.
100 "An outstanding . . . future growth": George E. Vaillant, *Adaptation to Life* (Boston: Little, Brown, 1977), p. 27.
101 "quite clear of the hypo . . . in the fall": AL to Joshua F. Speed, February 3, 1842, in *CW*, I, p. 268.
101 "much alone of late . . . *countenances* me": MTL to Mercy Ann Levering, June 1841, in Turner and Turner, *Mary Todd Lincoln*, pp. 25, 27.
101 mutual friends conspired: Baker, *Mary Todd Lincoln*, p. 93.
101 "worse sort . . . can realize": AL to Joshua F. Speed, February 25, 1842, in *CW*, I, p. 280. For correspondence between Lincoln and Speed discussing Speed's doubts during courtship of Fanny Henning, see AL to Speed, [January 3?], February 3, and February 13, 1842, in ibid., pp. 265–70.
101 "sailed through clear": AL to Joshua F. Speed, July 4, 1842, in ibid., p. 289.
101 " 'Are you now' . . . impatient to know": AL to Joshua F. Speed, October 5, 1842, in ibid., p. 303.
101 and was, in fact, very happy: AL to Joshua F. Speed, March 27, 1842, in ibid., p. 282.
101 description of the wedding: Baker, *Mary Todd Lincoln*, pp. 97–98; Helm, *The True Story of Mary*, pp. 93–95.
101 "Nothing new here . . . of profound wonder": AL to Samuel D. Marshall, November 11, 1842, in *CW*, I, p. 305.
102 "Full many a flower": Thomas Gray, "Elegy Written in a Country Churchyard," in *The Norton Anthology of Poetry*, 3rd edn., ed. Alexander W. Allison, et al. (New York: W. W. Norton, 1983), pp. 249–50.
102 "His melancholy . . . as he walked": Herndon, "Analysis of the Character," *ALQ* (1941), p. 359.
102 "No element . . . profound melancholy": Whitney, *Life on the Circuit with Lincoln*, p. 146.
102 "This melancholy . . . with his brains": Henry C. Whitney to WHH, June 23, 1887, in *HI*, p. 616.
103 "his face was . . . ever looked upon": Joseph Wilson Fifer, quoted in Rufus Rockwell Wilson, *Intimate Memories of Lincoln* (Elmira, N.Y.: Primavera Press, 1945), p. 155.
103 "slightly wrinkled . . . the wrinkles there": William Calkins, "The First of the Lincoln and Douglas Debates," quoted in ibid., pp. 169–70.
103 melancholy does not have: See Jerome Kagan, *Galen's Prophecy: Temperament in Human Nature*, with the collaboration of Nancy Snidman, Doreen Arcus, and J. Steven Reznick (New York: Basic Books, 1994), pp. 7–8.
103 "a tendency to . . . not a fault": AL to Mary Speed, September 27, 1841, in *CW*, I, p. 261.
103 "Melancholy . . . a sense of humor": Thomas Pynchon, introduction to *The Teachings of Don B.: Satires, Parodies, Fables, Illustrated Stories, and Plays of Donald Barthelme*, ed. Kim Herzinger (New York: Turtle Bay Books, Random House, 1992), p. xviii.

103 "When he first came . . . boiled over": James H. Matheny interview, November 1866, in *HI*, p. 432.
103 "he emerged . . . he lived, again": Whitney, *Life on the Circuit with Lincoln*, p. 147.
103 "necessary to his . . . relaxation in anecdotes": Joshua F. Speed to WHH, December 6, 1866, in *HI*, p. 499.
103 He laughed, he explained: Whitney, *Life on the Circuit with Lincoln*, p. 148.
103 "joyous, universal evergreen of life": AL, quoted in Nicolay, *Personal Traits of Abraham Lincoln*, p. 16.
103 "to whistle off sadness": David Davis interview, September 20, 1866, in *HI*, pp. 348, 350.
103 "Humor, like hope . . . to be borne": George E. Vaillant, *The Wisdom of the Ego*, p. 73.
103 "Humor can be marvelously . . . corrosive": Unnamed source, quoted in ibid., p. 73.
103 to rescue a pig . . . "his own mind": AL, quoted in Nicolay, *Personal Traits of Abraham Lincoln*, p. 81.
104 tortured turtles . . . "it was wrong": Nathaniel Grigsby interview, September 12, 1865, in *HI*, p. 112.
104 He refused to hunt animals: Miller, *Lincoln's Virtues*, pp. 26–27.
104 "the never-absent idea": AL to Joshua F. Speed, March 27, 1842, in *CW*, I, p. 282.
104 "By the imagination . . . what he feels": Adam Smith, *The Theory of Moral Sentiments* (London: A. Millar, 1759; facsimile, New York: Garland Publishing, 1971), pp. 2–3.
104 "With his wealth . . . that way themselves": Nicolay, *Personal Traits of Abraham Lincoln*, pp. 213, 77, 78.
104 marriage was tumultuous . . . was harder for Mary: *With Malice Toward None*, pp. 69–70; Strozier, *Lincoln's Quest for Union*, p. 119; Baker, *Mary Todd Lincoln*, pp. 105–10.
105 Lincoln helped with the marketing and the dishes: Burlingame, *The Inner World of Abraham Lincoln*, p. 279.
105 Julia Bates's early marriage: Darby, "Mrs. Julia Bates" in Bates, *Bates, et al., of Virginia and Missouri*, n.p.; EB to Frederick Bates, June 15 and July 19, 1818, quoted in ibid.
105 Frances Seward spared household chores: Seward, *An Autobiography*, pp. 62, 382, 466; Patricia C. Johnson, " 'I Could Not be Well or Happy at Home . . . When Called to the Councils of My Country': Politics and the Seward Family," *University of Rochester Library Bulletin* 31 [hereafter *URLB*] (Autumn 1978), pp. 42, 47, 49.
105 Lincolns detached from respective families: Baker, *Mary Todd Lincoln*, pp. 105–07, 111–12.
105 When Lincoln was away: Ibid., pp. 108–09.
105 Frances's family surrounded her: Johnson, "I Could Not be Well or Happy at Home," *URLB*, p. 42.
106 Julia Bates's family in St. Louis: Bates, *Bates, et al., of Virginia and Missouri*, n.p.
106 "the kindest . . . was necessary": MTL interview, September 1866, in *HI*, p. 357.
106 a gentle and indulgent father: Herndon and Weik, *Herndon's Life of Lincoln*, p. 344. See also " 'Unrestrained by Parental Tyranny': Lincoln and His Sons," chapter 3 in Burlingame, *The Inner World of Abraham Lincoln*, pp. 57–72.
106 "litterally ran over . . . their importunities": Joseph Gillespie to WHH, January 31, 1866, in *HI*, p. 181.
106 "It is my pleasure . . . child to its parent": AL, quoted in MTL interview, September 1866, in ibid., p. 357.
106 "Now if you should . . . he is mistaken": AL to Richard S. Thomas, February 14, 1843, in *CW*, I, p. 307.
106 "That 'union is strength' . . . 'cannot stand' ": "Campaign Circular from Whig Committee," March 4, 1843, in ibid., p. 315.
107 "We had a meeting . . . own dear 'gal' ": AL to Joshua F. Speed, March 24, 1843, in ibid., p. 319.
107 his defeat in Sangamon . . . "family distinction": AL to Martin S. Morris, March 26, 1843, in ibid., p. 320.
107 in Pekin . . . idea of rotating terms: AL, "Resolution Adopted at Whig Convention at Pekin, Illinois," May 1, 1843, in ibid., p. 322.
107 Lincoln left nothing to chance: Thomas, *Abraham Lincoln*, p. 105.
107 He asked friends to share . . . every precinct: Beveridge, *Abraham Lincoln, 1809–1858*, Vol. II, pp. 74–75.
107 "a quiet trip . . . vigilance": AL to Benjamin F. James, January 14, 1846, in *CW*, I, p. 354.
107 "That Hardin is talented . . . 'is fair play' ": AL to Robert Boal, January 7, 1846, in ibid., p. 353.
108 "not . . . all other grounds": AL to John J. Hardin, February 7, 1846, in ibid., p. 364.
108 "I am not a politician . . . their ends": SPC to Charles D. Cleveland, August 29, 1840, reel 5, Chase Papers.
108 James G. Birney: See Betty Fladeland, *James Gillespie Birney: Slaveholder to Abolitionist* (Ithaca, N.Y.: Cornell University Press, 1955), esp. pp. 129–36.
108 a group of white community leaders: Niven, *Salmon P. Chase*, p. 47.
108 On a hot summer night . . . continued to publish: Fladeland, *James Gillespie Birney*, pp. 136–37; Blue, *Salmon P. Chase*, p. 29.
108 the mob returned . . . tarred and feathered: Fladeland, *James Gillespie Birney*, pp. 140–41.
108 he raced to the hotel . . . "at any time": SPC, quoted in Niven, *Salmon P. Chase*, p. 48.
109 "His voice and commanding . . . right time": Ibid.
109 "No man . . . courage and resolution": Hart, *Salmon P. Chase*, p. 435.
109 "By dedicating himself . . . in its pursuit": Maizlish, "Salmon P. Chase," *JER* (1998), p. 62.
109 background of the *Matilda* case: Niven, *Salmon P. Chase*, pp. 50–51; Hart, *Salmon P. Chase*, pp. 73–74; Schuckers, *The Life and Public Services of Salmon Portland Chase*, pp. 41–44.
110 "Every settler . . . interdicts slavery": SPC, *Speech of Salmon P. Chase in the Case of the Colored Woman, Matilda: Who was Brought Before the Court of Common Pleas of Hamilton County, Ohio, by Writ of Habeas Corpus, March 11, 1837* (Cincinnati: Pugh & Dodd, 1837), pp. 29, 30, 8.
110 they were printed in pamphlet form: SPC, *Speech of Salmon P. Chase in the Case of the Colored Woman, Matilda.*
110 Chase versus the Garrisonians: Hart, *Salmon P. Chase*, pp. 50, 55–56, 65.
110 "a covenant with . . . agreement with hell": Quoted in James Brewer Stewart, *William Lloyd Garrison and the Challenge of Emancipation.* American Biographical History Series (Arlington Heights, Ill.: Harlan Davidson, 1992), p. 164.
110 Chase decided, to try for public office . . . city establishments: Niven, *Salmon P. Chase*, pp. 57–59.
111 the "*vital* question of slavery": SPC to Charles D. Cleveland, August 29, 1840, reel 5, Chase Papers.
111 Chase and the Liberty Party: Niven, *Salmon P. Chase*, pp. 67–70; Eric Foner, *Free Soil, Free Labor, Free Men:*

The Ideology of the Republican Party before the Civil War (New York: Oxford University Press, 1970), pp. 78–81. See also "Liberty Party," in *The Reader's Companion to American History*, ed. Foner and Garraty, p. 657.

111 "to interfere . . . where it exists": "Proceedings and Resolutions of the Ohio Liberty Convention," *Philanthropist*, December 29, 1841, quoted in Niven, *Salmon P. Chase*, p. 68.

111 "without constitutional warrant": SPC to Gerrit Smith, May 14, 1842, reel 5, Chase Papers.

111 "has seen so little . . . the very first": SPC to Joshua R. Giddings, January 21, 1842, reel 5, Chase Papers.

111 "there can be only . . . criminal than unwise": WHS to SPC, August 4, 1845, reel 6, Chase Papers.

112 *"educated in the Whig school"* . . . defining characteristics: SPC to Lyman Hall, August 6, 1849, quoted in Warden, *Private Life and Public Services*, p. 331.

112 decision to leave . . . for Seward: Gienapp, *The Origins of the Republican Party*, p. 7.

112 "one idea" . . . than with the Whigs: Niven, *Salmon P. Chase*, pp. 62 (quote), 67, 88, 90–91.

112 Chase shifted his positions: Hendrick, *Lincoln's War Cabinet*, p. 40.

112 Cincinnati was a natural destination: de Tocqueville, *Democracy in America*, p. 345.

112 "Attorney General for the Negro": Donnal V. Smith, "Salmon P. Chase and the Election of 1860," *OAHQ* 39 (July 1930), p. 515.

112 represented John Van Zandt: See Hart, *Salmon P. Chase*, pp. 75–78; Schuckers, *The Life and Public Services of Salmon Portland Chase*, pp. 53–66; Niven, *Salmon P. Chase*, pp. 76–83.

112 "Moved by sympathy . . . very willingly": SPC to Trowbridge, March 18, 1864, reel 32, Chase Papers.

113 "Under the constitution . . . which made him a slave": SPC, *Reclamation of Fugitives from Service: An Argument for the Defendant, Submitted to the Supreme Court of the United States, at the December Term, 1846, in the Case of Wharton Jones vs. John Vanzandt* (Cincinnati: R. P. Donogh & Co., 1847), pp. 82–84.

113 "a creature of state law": Chase, *Reclamation of Fugitives from Service*, p. 81.

113 "There goes . . . himself to-day": Unnamed judge in Van Zandt trial quoted in *Life and Letters of Harriet Beecher Stowe*, ed. Annie Fields (Boston: Houghton Mifflin, 1897; Detroit: Gale Research Co., 1970), p. 145.

113 Chase enlisted Seward's help as co-counsel: WHS, *In the Supreme Court of the United States: John Van Zandt, ad sectum Wharton Jones: Argument for the Defendant* (Albany, N.Y.: Weed & Parsons, 1847); Seward, *Seward at Washington . . . 1846–1861*, pp. 39–40; Niven, *Salmon P. Chase*, p. 83.

113 "poor old Van Zandt . . . be a gainer": SPC to CS, April 24, 1847, reel 6, Chase Papers (quote); SPC to Trowbridge, March 18, 1864, reel 32, Chase Papers.

113 argument reprinted in pamphlet form: See SPC, *Reclamation of Fugitives from Service.*

113 "the question . . . a *political* movement": CS to SPC, March 12, 1847, reel 6, Chase Papers.

114 Adams and Hale: Charles Francis Adams to SPC, March 4, 1847, reel 6, Chase Papers; SPC to John P. Hale, May 12, 1847, reel 6, Chase Papers.

114 "chaste and beautiful . . . own fame": WHS to SPC, February 18, 1847, reel 6, Chase Papers.

114 "one of the gratifications . . . greatest too": SPC to Lewis Tappan, March 18, 1847, reel 6, Chase Papers.

114 In gratitude . . . sterling silver pitcher: For a description of the event, see *The Address and Reply on the Presentation of a Testimonial to S. P. Chase, by the Colored People of Cincinnati* (Cincinnati, Ohio: Henry W. Derby & Co., 1845); Niven, *Salmon P. Chase*, pp. 85–86.

114 "whenever the friendless . . . unto me!": "Mr. Gordon's Address," in *The Address and Reply on the Presentation of a Testimonial to S. P. Chase*, pp. 12–13, 18.

114 Chase's reply: "Reply of Mr. Chase," in ibid., pp. 19–35.

115 did not make friends easily: Niven, *Salmon P. Chase*, p. 130.

115 "little of human nature": Lloyd, "Home-Life of Salmon Portland Chase," *Atlantic Monthly*, p. 534.

115 "profoundly versed . . . of men": Whitelaw Reid, *Ohio in the War*, paraphrased in Warden, *Private Life and Public Services*, p. 244.

115 Edwin M. Stanton: Frank Abial Flower, *Edwin McMasters Stanton: The Autocrat of Rebellion, Emancipation, and Reconstruction* (Akron, Ohio: Saalfield Publishing Co., 1905), p. 24; Belden and Belden, *So Fell the Angels*, p. 77; Henry Wilson, "Jeremiah S. Black and Edwin M. Stanton," *Atlantic Monthly* 26 (October 1870), pp. 469–70.

115 "when he was a boy . . . to slavery": William Thaw, quoted in Flower, *Edwin McMasters Stanton*, p. 25.

115 death had pursued Stanton: Pamphila Stanton Wolcott, "Edwin M. Stanton: A Biographical Sketch," Ohio Historical Society, Columbus, Ohio; EMS, "Mary Lamson, Wife of Edwin M. Stanton, and their infant daughter Lucy," Edwin M. Stanton Manuscript, Mss. 1648, Louisiana and Lower Mississippi Valley Collections, Louisiana State University Libraries, Baton Rouge, La.

116 "Since our pleasant . . . face to face": EMS to SPC, November 30, 1846, reel 6, Chase Papers.

116 "Taxation . . . sincere love for you": EMS to SPC, August 1846, reel 6, Chase Papers.

116 Stanton felt free . . . "careless of the future": EMS to SPC, November 30, 1846, reel 6, Chase Papers.

116 "Many weeks . . . post office each day": EMS to SPC, January 5, 1847, reel 6, Chase Papers.

116 "Rejoicing, as I do . . . upon your mercy": EMS to SPC, March 11, 1847, reel 6, Chase Papers.

117 "filled my heart . . . bid you farewell": EMS to SPC, December 2, 1847, reel 6, Chase Papers.

117 "How much I regret . . . not have left home": SPC to EMS, January 9, 1848, reel 1, Papers of Edwin M. Stanton, Manuscript Division, Library of Congress [hereafter Stanton Papers, DLC].

117 "The practice of law . . . of the camp": EMS to SPC, May 27, 1849, reel 7, Chase Papers.

117 "While public honors . . . inestimable value": EMS to SPC, May 27, 1849, reel 7, Chase Papers.

117 "well aware . . . among men": EMS to SPC, June 28, 1850, reel 8, Chase Papers.

CHAPTER 4: "PLUNDER & CONQUEST"

Page

119 Washington was a city in progress: Beveridge, *Abraham Lincoln, 1809–1858,* Vol. II, pp. 101–03.
119 "a full view . . . and Virginia": William Q. Force, "Picture of Washington and its Vicinity for 1850," Washington, D.C., p. 49.
119 "stood pig-styes . . . over the fields": Samuel C. Busey, M.D., *Personal Reminiscences and Recollections of Forty-Six Years' Membership in the Medical Society of the District of Columbia, and Residence in this City, with Biographical Sketches of Many of the Deceased Members* (Washington, D.C.: [Philadelphia: Dornan, Printer], 1895), pp. 64–65.
119 population of Washington: Beveridge, *Abraham Lincoln, 1809–1858,* Vol. II, p. 102.
119 Webster . . . would outlive the age: "12 October 1861, Saturday," in John Hay, *Inside Lincoln's White House: The Complete Civil War Diary of John Hay,* ed. Michael Burlingame and John R. Turner Ettlinger (Carbondale and Edwardsville: Southern Illinois University Press, 1997), p. 26.
119 Jefferson Davis . . . Rhett, agitator of rebellion: Robert C. Byrd, *The Senate, 1789–1989,* Vol. I: *Addresses on the History of the United States Senate,* Bicentennial Edition, ed. Mary Sharon Hall (Washington, D.C.: Government Printing Office, 1988), p. 182.
120 "he would lay down . . . merriment": Busey, *Personal Reminiscences,* pp. 25, 27.
120 Mary in Washington: Randall, *Mary Lincoln,* pp. 107–08; Baker, *Mary Todd Lincoln,* pp. 136–40.
120 background of the Mexican War: Robert W. Johannsen, "Mexican War," in *The Reader's Companion to American History,* ed. Foner and Garraty, pp. 722–24: McPherson, *Battle Cry of Freedom,* pp. 47, 49–50.
120 "a romantic . . . exotic land": Johannsen, "Mexican War," in *The Reader's Companion to American History,* ed. Foner and Garraty, p. 723.
121 John Hardin, was . . . "God-speeds of men": Beveridge, *Abraham Lincoln, 1809–1858,* Vol. II, pp. 79–80.
121 "It is a fact . . . growing crops": AL to John M. Peck, May 21, 1848, in *CW,* I, p. 473.
121 combat ended, peace treaty: Johannsen, "Mexican War," in *The Reader's Companion to American History,* ed. Foner and Garraty, p. 723.
121 "not let the whigs be *silent*": AL to Usher F. Linder, March 22, 1848, in *CW,* I, p. 457.
121 "the original justice . . . of the President": AL, "Speech in United States House of Representatives: The War with Mexico," January 12, 1848, in ibid., p. 432.
121 "As you are . . . before long": AL to WHH, December 13, 1847, in ibid., p. 420.
121 "whether the particular . . . hostile array": AL, " 'Spot' Resolutions in the United States House of Representatives," December 22, 1847, in ibid., p. 421.
121 "spotty Lincoln": Beveridge, *Abraham Lincoln, 1809–1858,* Vol. II, p. 135.
121 "unnecessarily . . . be at ease": AL, "Speech in United States House of Representatives: The War with Mexico," January 12, 1848, in *CW,* I, pp. 432, 433, 439–41.
122 "treasonable assault" . . . only a single term: *Illinois State Register,* March 10, 1848, quoted in Beveridge, *Abraham Lincoln, 1809–1858,* Vol. II, p. 135.
122 to "allow the President . . . deems it necessary": AL to WHH, February 15, 1848, in *CW,* I, p. 451.
122 "I saw that Lincoln . . . and again": WHH to JWW, February 11, 1887, reel 10, Herndon-Weik Collection, DLC.
122 only to infuriate the Democrats . . . fainthearted Whigs: Donald, *Lincoln,* pp. 124–25.
122 "no . . . pestilence and famine": AL, quoting Justin Butterfield in entry for August 13, 1863, in Hay, *Inside Lincoln's White House,* p. 73.
122 "Our population . . . shores of the Pacific": WHS, 1846, quoted in Seward, *An Autobiography,* p. 791.
123 "not expect . . . national adversaries": WHS to unknown recipient, May 28, 1846, in ibid., p. 809.
123 "would not have engaged in": SPC to Gerrit Smith, September 1, 1846, reel 6, Chase Papers.
123 "gross . . . plunder & conquest": Bates diary, March 13, 1848.
123 ashamed of his Whig . . . "Presidential election": Bates diary, March 14, 1848.
123 "a war of conquest . . . to catch votes": *Delaware State Journal,* June 13, 1848, quoted as "Speech at Wilmington, Delaware, June 10, 1848," in *CW,* I, p. 476.
123 David Wilmot . . . Senate: "Wilmot Proviso," in *The Reader's Companion to American History,* ed. Foner and Garraty, p. 1155; David M. Potter, *The Impending Crisis, 1848–1861,* completed and ed. Don E. Fehrenbacher. New American Nation Series (New York: Harper & Row, 1976), pp. 21–23 (quote p. 21).
123 Lincoln positioned himself . . . "exist in the old": AL to Williamson Durley, October 3, 1845, in *CW,* I, p. 348.
124 Bates considered the problem . . . pull the country apart: Cain, *Lincoln's Attorney General,* pp. 59–60, 66.
124 John Calhoun led the . . . American territory: John C. Calhoun, February 19, 1847, *Congressional Globe,* 29th Cong., 2nd sess., pp. 453–55 (quote p. 455).
124 "The madmen of the North . . . glorious Union": *Richmond [Va.] Enquirer,* February 18, 1847.
124 "When you were . . . marry again": AL to MTL, April 16, 1848, in *CW,* I, pp. 465–66.
124 "My dear Husband . . . love to all": MTL to AL, May 1848, in Turner and Turner, *Mary Todd Lincoln,* pp. 36–38.
125 "The leading matter . . . till I see you": AL to MTL, June 12, 1848, in *CW,* I, p. 477.
125 "I am in favor . . . elect any other whig": AL to Thomas S. Flournoy, February 17, 1848, in ibid., p. 452.
125 "on the blind side . . . hanged themselves": AL to WHH, June 12, 1848, in ibid., p. 477.
125 "very willingly . . . Universal Freedom": WHS to SPC, June 12, 1848, reel 6, Chase Papers.
125 a "doughface": Anonymous, *A Bake-Pan for Dough-Faces* (Burlington, Vt.: Chauncey Goodrich, 1854), p. 1; Byrd, *The Senate, 1789–1989,* Vol. I, pp. 206–07.

126 the Free Soil Convention in Buffalo, 1848: See Foner, *Free Soil. Free Labor, Free Men*, p. 125; Blue, *Salmon P. Chase*, pp. 61–66.

126 asking if his name . . . vice presidency: Bates diary, August 5, 1848.

126 remained a slaveowner: Entry for Edward Bates, Dardenne, St. Charles County, Missouri, Sixth Census of the United States, 1840 (National Archives Microfilm Publication M704, reel 230), RG 29, DNA. According to Bates's entry in the 1840s federal census, there were nine slaves in the Bates household. By 1860, the servants and farmhands employed by Bates seem to have been exclusively Irish. Entry for Edward Bates, Carondelet, St. Louis Township, St. Louis County, Missouri, Eighth Census of the United States, 1860 (National Archives Microfilm Publication M653, reel 656), RG 29, DNA.

126 his belief in the inferiority of the black race: Hendrick, *Lincoln's War Cabinet*, p. 46.

126 one of his female slaves escaped . . . "plagued with them": Bates diary, April 15, 1848.

126 Bates declined . . . "geographical party": Bates diary, August 5, 1848.

126 "Free Soil, Free Speech": SPC to Thomas Bolton, December 1, 1848, reel 7, Chase Papers.

126 to "prohibit slavery extension": Smith, *The Liberty and Free Soil Parties in the Old Northwest*, p. 140.

126 Arriving uninvited . . . without a speaker: Beveridge, *Abraham Lincoln, 1809–1858*, Vol. II, pp. 171–72.

127 "an intellectual face . . . from that State": Boston *Daily Advertiser*, September 14, 1848, reprinted as "Speech at Worcester, Massachusetts," September 12, 1848, in *CW*, II, pp. 1–2, 5.

127 Whig rally at the Tremont Temple; Seward and Lincoln meet: James Schouler, "Abraham Lincoln at Tremont Temple in 1848," *Massachusetts Historical Society Proceedings, October, 1908–June, 1909* XLII (1909), pp. 70–83.

127 "had probably . . . Governor Seward's": AL, quoted in Seward, *Seward at Washington . . . 1846–1861*, p. 80.

127 "the time will come . . . institution of slavery": WHS, "Whig Mass Meeting, Boston, October 15, 1848," *Works of William H. Seward*, Vol. III, pp. 289, 288.

127 "a most forcible . . . applause": *Boston Courier*, September 23, 1848.

127 "rambling, story-telling . . . boldness of utterance": F. B. Carpenter, "A Day with Governor Seward at Auburn," July 1870, reel 196, Seward Papers.

127 "a thoughtful air": Seward, *Seward at Washington . . . 1846–1861*, p. 80.

127 "I reckon . . . have been doing": AL, quoted in ibid., p. 80.

127 voted for the Wilmot Proviso . . . single speech on the issue: Thomas, *Abraham Lincoln*, pp. 126–27.

128 "I went with . . . State in the Union": Edward L. Pierce to JWW, February 12, 1890, in *HI*, p. 697.

128 "a superb dinner . . . arranged at table": Governor Henry J. Gardner statement, [February–May 1890], enclosure in Edward L. Pierce to WHH, May 27, 1890, in *HI*, p. 699.

128 election results, 1848: Congressional Quarterly, *Presidential Elections Since 1789* (Washington, D.C.: Congressional Quarterly, 1991), p. 106.

128 who, four years later . . . only four states: Allan Nevins, *Ordeal of the Union*. Vol. II: *A House Dividing, 1852–1857* (New York and London: Charles Scribner's Sons, 1947), p. 36.

128 he drafted a proposal: AL, "Remarks and Resolution Introduced in United States House of Representatives Concerning Abolition of Slavery in the District of Columbia," January 10, 1849, in *CW*, II, pp. 20–22 (quote p. 21).

128 "that slave hound from Illinois": Wendell Phillips, quoted in Beveridge, *Abraham Lincoln, 1809–1858*, Vol. II, p. 185.

128 once the proposal was distributed . . . never introduced his bill: Donald, *Lincoln*, pp. 136–37.

129 "Finding that I was . . . at that time": AL, quoted in James Q. Howard, Biographical Notes, May 1860, Lincoln Papers.

129 campaigned vigorously . . . Commissioner of the Land Office: Thomas, *Abraham Lincoln*, p. 129. See also Lincoln's correspondence from May to July 1849 in *CW*, II, pp. 51–55, 57–58.

129 "If I have one vice . . . tempted me": AL, quoted in Egbert L. Viele, "A Trip with Lincoln, Chase, and Stanton," *Scribners Monthly* 16 (October 1878), p. 818.

129 applied to patent . . . "buoyant chambers": AL, "Application for Patent on an Improved Method of Lifting Vessels over Shoals," March 10, 1849, in *CW*, II, p. 32.

129 "added practically . . . his reputation": John G. Nicolay, *A Short Life of Abraham Lincoln. Condensed from Nicolay & Hay's Abraham Lincoln: A History* (New York: Century Co., 1902), p. 77.

129 Caleb Smith of Indiana: John P. Usher, *President Lincoln's Cabinet, with a Foreword and a Sketch of the Life of the Author by Nelson H. Loomis* (Omaha, Nebr.: n.p., 1925); Louis J. Bailey, "Caleb Blood Smith," *Indiana Magazine of History* 29 (September 1933), pp. 213–39; *Indianapolis Daily Journal*, January 9, 1864.

129 "handsome, trimly-built man": C. P. Ferguson, quoted in Bailey, "Caleb Blood Smith," *Indiana Magazine of History* (1933), p. 237.

129 "smooth oval face": John Coburn, quoted in ibid., p. 236.

129 "feel the blood . . . up your spine": Usher, *President Lincoln's Cabinet*, p. 17.

129 Smith a more compelling public speaker: Macartney, *Lincoln and His Cabinet*, p. 49; Bailey, "Caleb Blood Smith," *Indiana Magazine of History* (1933), pp. 237–39.

129 Joshua Giddings: James Brewer Stewart, *Joshua R. Giddings and the Tactics of Radical Politics* (Cleveland: Case Western Reserve University Press, 1970); George W. Julian, *The Life of Joshua R. Giddings* (Chicago: A. C. McClurg & Co., 1892).

130 "He had lived . . . with their lot": Julian, *The Life of Joshua R. Giddings*, p. 21.

130 "would walk clear to Illinois": Elihu B. Wasburne to AL, December 26, 1854, Lincoln Papers.

130 "a little slim . . . full of tears yet": AL to WHH, February 2, 1848, in *CW*, I, p. 448.

130 "Mr. Lincoln was careful . . . roar of laughter": Alexander Stephens recollection, in Osborn H. Oldroyd, comp., *The Lincoln Memorial: Album-Immortelles* (New York: G. W. Carleton & Co., 1882), p. 241.

130 "was losing interest in politics": AL, "Autobiography Written for Jesse W. Fell," December 20, 1859, in *CW,* III, p. 512.
131 "the one *great* question of the day": AL, "Eulogy on Zachary Taylor," July 25, 1850, in *CW,* II, p. 89.
131 with "greater earnestness": AL, "Scripps autobiography," in *CW,* IV, p. 67.
131 deaths of Mary's father, grandmother, and Eddie: Randall, *Mary Lincoln*, pp. 139–41; Baker, *Mary Todd Lincoln*, pp. 125–28; Donald, *Lincoln*, p. 153.
131 That destiny had branded her: Baker, *Mary Todd Lincoln*, p. 128.
131 Mary's inconsolable weeping: Ibid., p. 126.
131 "Eat, Mary . . . for we must live": AL, quoted in Randall, *Mary Lincoln*, p. 141.
131 found some solace . . . rented a family pew: Ibid., pp. 143–44.
131 Eddie's death left an indelible scar: See Baker, *Mary Todd Lincoln*, pp. 125–29.
131 "hysterical outbursts": Burlingame, *The Inner World of Abraham Lincoln*, p. 296.
131 chased him through the yard: Stephen Whitehurst interview, 1885–1889, in *HI*, p. 722; WHH to JWW, January 23, 1886, reel 9, Herndon-Weik Collection, DLC.
132 drove him from the house: Mrs. Hillary Gobin to Alfred J. Beveridge, May 17, 1923, container 288, Papers of Alfred J. Beveridge, Manuscript Division, Library of Congress [hereafter Beveridge Papers, DLC].
132 smashed his head with a chunk of wood: Margaret Ryan interview, October 27, 1886, in *HI*, p. 597; WHH to JWW, January 23, 1886, reel 9, Herndon-Weik Collection, DLC.
132 "a protective deafness": J. P. McEvoy, quoted in Randall, *Mary Lincoln*, p. 121.
132 quietly leave the room . . . for a walk: James Gourley interview, 1865–1866, in *HI*, p. 453.
132 If the discord continued . . . storm had ceased: Thomas, *Abraham Lincoln*, p. 91.
132 "a woman of more angelic . . . people outside": Milton Hay interview, c. 1883–1888, in *HI*, p. 729.
132 "rendering [himself] worthy": AL, "Communication to the People of Sangamo County," March 9, 1832, in *CW,* I, p. 8.
132 Weed's campaign for Senate seat for Seward: Van Deusen, *William Henry Seward*, pp. 110–11; Van Deusen, *Thurlow Weed*, pp. 165–66.
133 "There are two . . . and odious": WHS, "The Election of 1848, Cleveland, Ohio, October 26, 1848," *Works of William H. Seward*, Vol. III, pp. 291–302.
133 "of making voters . . . to intermarry": AL's speech, "Fourth Debate with Stephen A. Douglas at Charleston, Illinois," September 18, 1858, in *CW,* III, p. 145.
133 radicalism of the Western Reserve: Smith, *The Liberty and Free Soil Parties in the Old Northwest*, pp. 13–14, 31–32, 128.
133 the *Cleveland Plain Dealer* charged: *Cleveland Plain Dealer*, October 27, 1848.
133 " 'Can nothing' . . . can and must do it": WHS, "The Election of 1848," *Works of William H. Seward*, Vol. III, p. 301.
134 "a political crime . . . political evil": TW, quoted in Van Deusen, *Thurlow Weed*, p. 90.
134 "this question of slavery . . . partisan conflicts": TW, *Albany Evening Journal*, 1836, in Seward, *An Autobiography*, p. 319.
134 his provocative language: WHS to TW, March 31, 1850, Weed Papers; Holman Hamilton, *Zachary Taylor: Soldier in the White House*, Vol. II (New York: Bobbs-Merrill, 1951), pp. 321–22.
134 not fully "ripened": WHS to unknown recipient, May 28, 1846, in Seward, *An Autobiography*, p. 809.
134 "wanted to level society up, not down": Van Deusen, *Thurlow Weed*, p. 166.
134 "Probably no man . . . warmly appreciated": *NYTrib*, quoted in Van Deusen, *William Henry Seward*, p. 113.
134 a Southern senator . . . "a shudder": Seward, *Seward at Washington . . . 1846–1861*, p. 119.
134 "If we ever find . . . your odious neck": "Georgia Savannah" to WHS, January 22, 1850, in ibid., p. 130.
134 balance of power in the Ohio legislature: [Albert G. Riddle], "The Election of Salmon P. Chase to the Senate, February 22, 1849," *The Republic* 4 (March 1875), p. 180; Schuckers, *The Life and Public Services of Salmon Portland Chase*, p. 91.
135 Dr. Norton Townshend and John F. Morse: See Niven, *Salmon P. Chase*, p. 118; Schuckers, *The Life and Public Services of Salmon Portland Chase*, pp. 91–92.
135 drafted a deal . . . extensive patronage: SPC to Sarah Bella D. L. Chase, December 20, 1848, reel 7, Chase Papers; Hart, *Salmon P. Chase*, pp. 104–09, 112.
135 Chase journeyed to Columbus . . . money to more than one paper: Niven, *Salmon P. Chase*, pp. 117–19, 121.
135 "After the Senatorial Election . . . rely on me": SPC to Edward S. Hamlin, January 17, 1849 (erroneously dated 1848), reel 7, Chase Papers.
135 advanced money to . . . "mortgage to myself": SPC to Stanley Matthews (copybook version), February 26, 1849, reel 7, Chase Papers.
135 "It is really important . . . Morse especially": SPC to Edward S. Hamlin, January 17, 1849 (erroneously dated 1848), reel 7, Chase Papers.
135 "Every thing . . . of the Cause": SPC to John F. Morse, January 19, [1849], reel 7, Chase Papers. The recipient's name does not appear on the letter itself, but he has been identified as John F. Morse. See Vol. II of Niven, ed., the *Salmon P. Chase papers*, pp. 216–19.
136 "Every act . . . *meant* His Own": *Ohio State Journal*, quoted in Blue, *Salmon P. Chase*, p. 72.
136 voted to repeal the hated Black Laws: Noah Brooks, *Statesmen* (New York: Charles Scribner's Sons, 1904), p. 158.
136 "not see how . . . or profit by it": Horace Greeley to SPC, April 16, 1852, reel 9, Chase Papers.
136 "It lost to him . . . his political after life": Riddle, "The Election of Salmon P. Chase," *Republic* (1875), p. 183.

136 Certainly, his willingness to sever . . . custom of the times: Ibid., p. 183; Blue, *Salmon P. Chase*, p. 90; Niven, *Salmon P. Chase*, pp. 146–47.
136 "I can hardly . . . of our cause": CS to SPC, February 27, 1849, reel 7, Chase Papers.
136 "to be first wherever I may be": SPC to Charles D. Cleveland, February 8, 1830, reel 4, Chase Papers.

CHAPTER 5: THE TURBULENT FIFTIES

Page

140 population: "Area and Population of the United States: 1790–1970," series A 1–5, in U.S. Bureau of the Census, *Historical Statistics of the United States, Colonial Times to 1970*, Bicentennial Edition, Part 1 (Washington, D.C.: Government Printing Office, 1975), p. 8.
140 Nearly three fourths . . . participated: "Voter Participation in Presidential Elections, 1824–1928," available at infoplease website, www.infoplease.com/ipa/A0877659.html (accessed July 2005).
140 "were the daily fare . . . are undervalued": Charles Ingersoll, quoted in Appleby, *Inheriting the Revolution*, p. 102.
140 "Look into the morning . . . second breakfast": Ralph Waldo Emerson, "The Fugitive Slave Law," reprinted in *The Portable Emerson*, new ed., ed. Carl Bode, with Malcolm Cowley (New York: Penguin Books, 1981), p. 542.
141 "You meet . . . ale- and oyster-houses": Ludwig Gall, quoted in Appleby, *Inheriting the Revolution*, pp. 102–3.
141 "The nullifiers . . . Potomac river": Andrew Jackson, quoted in Marquis James, *Andrew Jackson: Portrait of a President* (New York: Grosset & Dunlap, 1937), p. 324.
141 three fifths of a person . . . lawful masters: U.S. Constitution, Section I, Article II, and Section IV, Article II.
141 "written in the bond . . . its obligations": John Quincy Adams, quoted in Potter, *The Impending Crisis, 1848–1861*, p. 47.
141 "If by your legislation . . . *for disunion*": Robert Toombs, debate in the House of Representatives, December 13, 1849, *Congressional Globe*, 31st Cong., 1st sess., p. 28.
141 Mississippi called for a convention: Potter, *The Impending Crisis, 1848–1861*, pp. 88, 94, 104.
141 "We read . . . nuptial couch, everywhere!": Thomas Hart Benton, May 31, 1848, *Appendix to the Congressional Globe*, 30th Cong., 1st sess., p. 686.
142 "We must concern . . . of life and death": John Randolph, quoted in Margaret L. Coit, *John C. Calhoun: American Portrait* (Atlanta, Ga.: Cherokee Publishing Co., 1990), p. 166.
142 "antagonistical elements": WHS, "The Election of 1848, Cleveland, Ohio, October 26, 1848," *Works of William H. Seward*, Vol. III, p. 295.
142 "It is a great mistake . . . except force": John C. Calhoun, "The Compromise," March 4, 1850, *Congressional Globe*, 31st Cong., 1st sess., p. 453.
143 All eyes turned to . . . Henry Clay: Robert V. Remini, *Henry Clay: Statesman for the Union* (New York and London: W. W. Norton & Co., 1991), pp. 730–38.
143 "regarded by all . . . man for a crisis": AL, "Eulogy on Henry Clay," July 6, 1852, in *CW*, II, p. 129.
143 "the spirit and the fire of youth": James S. Pike, "Mr. Clay's Speech," May 20, 1850, from the *NYTrib*, reprinted in James S. Pike, *First Blows of the Civil War: The Ten Years of Preliminary Conflict in the United States* (New York: American News Company, 1879), p. 72.
143 Henry Clay speech, resolutions: "Compromise Resolutions. Speech of Mr. Clay, of Kentucky, in the Senate of the United States, February 5 and 6, 1850," *Appendix to the Congressional Globe*, 31st Cong., 1st sess., pp. 115–27 (quotes pp. 115, 127).
143 denied a jury trial . . . hunt down escapees: Potter, *The Impending Crisis, 1848–1861*, pp. 130–31.
144 "if the direful . . . heart-rending spectacle": "Compromise Resolutions. Speech of Mr. Clay," *Appendix to the Congressional Globe*, p. 127.
144 Frances Seward in the gallery: FAS to LW, February 10, 1850, reel 119, Seward Papers.
144 F Street house in Washington: Van Deusen, *William Henry Seward*, p. 118; Seward, *Seward at Washington . . . 1846–1861*, p. 111. The house was located on the north side of F Street, NW, between Sixth and Seventh Streets.
144 "He *is* a charming . . . I supposed": FAS to LW, February 10, 1850, reel 119, Seward Papers.
144 John Calhoun in the Senate: Pike, "Speeches of Webster and Calhoun," from the *Portland Advertiser*, March 9, 1850, in Pike, *First Blows of the Civil War*, p. 15; Ben: Perley Poore, *Perley's Reminiscences of Sixty Years in the National Metropolis*, Vol. I (Philadelphia, 1886; New York: AMS Press, 1971), p. 365.
144 Calhoun's speech read by Mason: John C. Calhoun, "The Compromise," March 4, 1850, *Congressional Globe*, 31st Cong., 1st sess., pp. 451–55.
145 the "great triumvirate": Richard N. Current, "Webster, Daniel," in *The Reader's Companion to American History*, ed. Foner and Garraty, p. 1139.
145 "crammed" . . . previous occasion: *National Intelligencer*, Washington, D.C., March 8, 1850.
145 the rumor that Webster . . . was watching: FAS to LW, March 10, 1850, reel 119, Seward Papers.
145 "I wish to speak": "Compromise Resolutions. Speech of Mr. Webster, of Massachusetts, in the Senate, March 7, 1850," *Appendix to the Congressional Globe*, 31st Cong., 1st sess., pp. 269–76 (quote p. 269).
145 "Mr Webster has deliberately . . . years in doing": Journal BO, p. 217, in *The Journals and Miscellaneous Notebooks of Ralph Waldo Emerson*, Vol. XI: *1848–1851*, ed. A. W. Plumstead and William H. Gilman (Cambridge, Mass., and London: Belknap Press of Harvard University Press, 1975), pp. 347–48.
145 Frances Seward on Webster's speech: FAS to LW, March 10, 1850, reel 119, Seward Papers.

145 speech won nationwide approval from moderates: Robert V. Remini, *Daniel Webster: The Man and His Time* (New York and London: W. W. Norton & Co., 1997), pp. 674–75.
145 "How little they know . . . he thinks just": FAS to LW, March 10, 1850, reel 119, Seward Papers.
145 Antislavery advocates had no need: Hendrick, *Lincoln's War Cabinet*, p. 23.
145 He had talked at length . . . before Frances: FAS to WHS, July 8, 1850, reel 114, Seward Papers; Seward, *An Autobiography*, p. 703; Van Deusen, *Thurlow Weed*, p. 175.
145 description of Seward's speaking style: Van Deusen, *William Henry Seward*, p. 122; Bancroft, *The Life of William H. Seward*, Vol. I, pp. 190–91.
145 he quoted Machiavelli: Pike, "Governor Seward's Speech," March 12, 1850, from the *Boston Courier*, in Pike, *First Blows of the Civil War*, p. 18.
146 Webster was riveted . . . "sat still": Holman Hamilton, *Zachary Taylor: Soldier in the White House*, Vol. II (Indianapolis: Bobbs-Merrill, 1951; Norwalk, Conn.: Easton Press, 1989), p. 316.
146 content of Seward's speech: WHS, "California, Union, and Freedom. Speech of William H. Seward, of New York, in the Senate, March 11, 1850," *Appendix to the Congressional Globe*, 31st Cong., 1st sess., pp. 260–69 (quotes pp. 262, 263, and 265).
146 With this single speech: Van Deusen, *William Henry Seward*, p. 128.
146 Tens of thousands of copies: WHS to TW, March 22 and 31, 1850, in Seward, *Seward at Washington . . . 1846–1861*, p. 129.
146 "live longer . . . of the Session": *NYTrib*, March 19, 1850.
146 Chase prepares with Sumner: CS to SPC, February 19, March 22 and 23, 1850, reel 8, Chase Papers.
146 "I find no man . . . yourself": SPC to CS, September 15, 1849, reel 8, Chase Papers.
146 "a tower of strength": CS to SPC, February 7, 1849, reel 7, Chase Papers.
146 "confirm the irresolute . . . confound the trimmers": CS to SPC, February 7, 1849, reel 7, Chase Papers.
146 "I cannot disguise . . . throughout the country": CS to SPC, March 22, 1850, reel 8, Chase Papers.
147 Chase's speech: SPC, "Union and Freedom, Without Compromise. Speech of Mr. Chase, of Ohio, in the Senate, March 26–27, 1850," *Appendix to the Congressional Globe*, 31st Cong., 1st sess., pp. 468–80.
147 Chase's speaking style: Blue, *Salmon P. Chase*, p. 102; Warden, *Private Life and Public Services*, p. 340.
147 "infinitely below . . . who expected much": SPC to Sarah Bella Chase, March 27, 1850, reel 8, Chase Papers.
147 "You know . . . received not much": SPC to Stanley Matthews, May 6, 1850, reel 8, Chase Papers.
147 Benton-Foote argument: William Nisbet Chambers, *Old Bullion Benton, Senator from the New West: Thomas Hart Benton, 1782–1858* (Boston: Little, Brown, 1956), pp. 360–62; Henry S. Foote, *Casket of Reminiscences* (Washington, D.C.: Chronicle Publishing, 1874), pp. 338–39; March 26–27, April 2, and April 17, 1850, in *Congressional Globe*, 31st Cong., 1st sess., pp. 602–04, 609–10, 762–63.
147 "I disdain to carry . . . the assassin fire!": Thomas Hart Benton, quoted in *Congressional Globe*, 31st Cong., 1st sess., p. 762.
147 Sumner's praise . . . "Seward is with us": CS to SPC, April 10, 1850, reel 8, Chase Papers.
147 "You mistake . . . Anti Slavery opinions": SPC to CS, April 13, 1850, reel 8, Chase Papers.
147 "I have never been . . . a politician for me": SPC to CS, December 14, 1850, reel 9, Chase Papers.
148 relationship between Chase and Seward: WHS to SPC, October 2 and 22, 1843; August 4, 1845; reels 5, 6, Chase Papers.
148 "I made this resolution . . . me to keep it": Entry for April 29, 1831, *Chase Papers*, Vol. I, pp. 57–58.
148 reaction to Seward's "Higher Law" speech: Seward, *Seward at Washington . . . 1846–1861*, pp. 128, 130; FAS to LW, March 19 and March 21, 1850, reel 119, Seward Papers; Van Deusen, *William Henry Seward*, pp. 124–27.
148 "Senator Seward is against . . . the South": *NYH*, March 13, 1850.
148 Seward was initially untroubled: Seward, *Seward at Washington . . . 1846–1861*, pp. 120–21.
148 "spoken words . . . when I am dead": WHS to TW, March 31, 1850, in ibid., p. 129.
148 When she looked at him: FAS to LW, undated letter, in ibid., p. 120.
148 "Your speech . . . relieved my apprehensions": TW to WHS, March 14, 1850, reel 36, Seward Papers.
148 "despondency . . . shame": WHS to TW, March 31, 1850, Weed Papers.
148 death of Taylor, succession of Fillmore: Hamilton, *Zachary Taylor*, Vol. II (1951 ed.), pp. 388–94.
149 Under the skillful leadership . . . omnibus bill was broken up: Potter, *The Impending Crisis, 1848–1861*, pp. 109–12; Johannsen, *Stephen A. Douglas*, pp. 294–96.
149 Douglas regarded . . . "drop the subject": Stephen Douglas, quoted in Potter, *The Impending Crisis, 1848–1861*, p. 121.
149 Upon its passage: *NYH*, September 8, 9, and 10, 1850.
149 "The joy of everyone seemed unbounded": *NYTrib*, September 10, 1850.
149 "The crisis is passed—the cloud is gone": Lewis Cass quoted in *NYH*, September 10, 1850.
149 "The elements . . . but never overcome": *Columbus [Ga.] Sentinel*, reprinted in *Charleston [S.C.] Mercury*, January 23, 1851.
149 "devotion to . . . inclined them": AL, "Speech at Peoria, Illinois," October 16, 1854, in *CW*, II, p. 253.
149 Rejecting Seward's concept . . .: AL, "Endorsement on the Margin of the *Missouri Democrat*," [May 17, 1860], in *CW*, IV, p. 50.
149 He relished the convivial life: Strozier, *Lincoln's Quest for Union*, p. 144.
149 "The local belles . . . and eloquence": Whitney, *Life on the Circuit with Lincoln*, p. 63.
150 "plenty of bedbugs": David Davis to Sarah Davis, May 1, 1851, quoted in King, *Lincoln's Manager*, p. 77.
150 "half an inch thick": David Davis to Sarah Davis, April 24, 1851, David Davis Papers, Abraham Lincoln Presidential Library and Museum, Springfield, Ill. [hereafter Davis Papers, ALPLM].
150 slept two to a bed . . . in a room: Whitney, *Life on the Circuit with Lincoln*, p. 62.
150 David Davis: See King, *Lincoln's Manager*, esp. pp. 9–13, 17, 61.

150 "warm-hearted" nature: David Davis to Sarah Davis, November 3, 1851, Davis Papers, ALPLM.
150 "exceeding honesty & fairness": David Davis to Sarah Davis, March 23, 1851, Davis Papers, ALPLM.
150 "too well to thwart her views": David Davis, quoted in King, *Lincoln's Manager*, p. 42.
150 the judge's letters about Lincoln: David Davis to Sarah Davis, May 3 and October 20, 1851, Davis Papers, ALPLM.
150 "He arrogated . . . personal affection": Unidentified lawyer, quoted in Tarbell, *The Life of Abraham Lincoln*, Vol. I, p. 247.
150 At mealtimes . . . prisoners out on bail: Whitney, *Life on the Circuit with Lincoln*, pp. 63, 72.
150 "such of us . . . those who have": AL, "Temperance Address delivered before the Springfield Washington Temperance Society," February 22, 1842, in *CW*, I, p. 278.
151 "in full laugh till near daylight": WHH to "Mr. N.," February 4, 1874, *Grandview [Ind.] Monitor*, March 15, 1934, quoted in Burlingame, *The Inner World of Abraham Lincoln*, p. 18 n67.
151 "eyes would sparkle . . . than his": Jonathan Birch, "A Student Who Was Aided by Mr. Lincoln," in Wilson, *Intimate Memories of Lincoln*, p. 105.
151 Ethan Allen/George Washington story: Abner Y. Ellis statement, January 23, 1866, in *HI*, p. 174.
151 "who had a great . . . 'than that dress' ": John Usher interview with George Alfred Townsend, December 25, 1878, scrapbook, Papers of George Alfred Townsend, Manuscript Division, Library of Congress.
151 "is the nature . . . is cradled": Walter Benjamin, "The Storyteller," in *Illuminations*, ed. Hannah Arendt, trans. Harry Zohn (New York: Harcourt, Brace & World, 1968; New York: Schocken Books, 1969), p. 91.
151 "Would we do . . . thought and experience": Whitney, *Life on the Circuit with Lincoln*, p. 66.
152 "It makes human nature . . . is possible": AL on George Washington, quoted in ibid., p. 67.
152 When the court closed . . . throughout the weekend: Jesse W. Weik, *The Real Lincoln: A Portrait* (Boston and New York: Houghton Mifflin, 1923), p. 90.
152 "wondered at it . . . pleasant, inviting homes": David Davis, quoted in Herndon and Weik, *Herndon's Life of Lincoln*, p. 249.
152 "as happy as . . . no other place": David Davis interview, September 20, 1866, in *HI*, p. 349.
152 "his home was *Hell* . . . *Heaven*": WHH, *A Letter from William H. Herndon to Isaac N. Arnold*, n.p.
152 "Lincoln speaks very . . . children": David Davis to Sarah Davis, November 3, 1851, quoted in King, *Lincoln's Manager*, p. 85.
152 Davis described a letter . . . Tad was born: David Davis to Sarah Davis, May 17, 1852, and September 18, 1853, Davis Papers, ALPLM; King, *Lincoln's Manager*, pp. 74, 84.
152 remedy the "want of education": Donald, *Lincoln Reconsidered*, p. 71.
152 "nearly mastered . . . Euclid": AL, "Scripps autobiography," in *CW*, IV, p. 62.
152 "he read hard works . . . read generally": John T. Stuart interview, December 20, 1866, in *HI*, p. 519.
152 "so deeply absorbed . . . point of exhaustion": WHH, in Weik, *The Real Lincoln*, p. 240.
153 "Life was to him . . . came before him": Swett, "Lincoln's Story of His Own Life," in *Reminiscences of Abraham Lincoln*, ed. Rice, p. 79.
153 "one of the greatest hardships": Randall, *Mary Lincoln*, p. 79.
153 circuit life was invaluable: Thomas, *Abraham Lincoln*, p. 94; White, *Abraham Lincoln in 1854*, p. 20; Strozier, *Lincoln's Quest for Union*, p. 144.
153 "If I muzzle not . . . the Whig party": WHS to FAS, July 21, 1850, in Seward, *Seward at Washington . . . 1846–1861*, p. 148.
153 Seward's eulogies to Clay and Webster: WHS, "Henry Clay" and "Daniel Webster," in *Works of William H. Seward*, Vol. III, pp. 104–16.
153 "They cannot see . . . of wrath!": WHS to unidentified recipient [FAS?], 1852, in Seward, *Seward at Washington . . . 1846–1861*, p. 194.
153 "I do not wish you . . . true to liberty": FAS to WHS, June 13, [1852], reel 114, Seward Papers.
154 "worldly wisdom . . . current if necessary": FAS to WHS, July 20, 1856, reel 114, Seward Papers.
154 "This fearless defense . . . righteous cause": FAS to CS, September 18, 1852, reel 9, The Papers of Charles Sumner, Chadwyck-Healey microfilm edition [hereafter Sumner Papers].
154 "a Waterloo defeat": Seward, *Seward at Washington . . . 1846–1861*, p. 196.
154 she was tempted . . . "more harm than good": FAS to LW, January 15, 1854, reel 119, Seward Papers.
154 "Would that I were . . . obligation and duty": WHS to FAS, May 16, 1855, quoted in Seward, *Seward at Washington . . . 1846–1861*, p. 251.
154 everywhere Seward went . . . join him: Johnson, "I Could Not be Well or Happy at Home," *URLB* (1978), p. 48.
155 Frances's health problems: FAS to LW, January 2, February 7, 1832; August 31, 1833, reel 118, Seward Papers; FAS, "Diary of Trip through Pennsylvania, Virginia, and Maryland, 1835," reel 197, and FAS, MSS Fragment on Illness, 1865, Seward Papers; entries for December 28, 1858, and March 16, 1859, FS diary, reel 198, Seward Papers; Johnson, "Sensitivity and Civil War," pp. 23–27.
155 her "sanctuary": WHS to FAS, February 12, 1837, in Seward, *An Autobiography*, p. 325.
155 Doctors could not pinpoint: Johnson, "I Could Not be Well or Happy at Home," URLB (1978), pp. 46–47.
155 the "various . . . purpose in their life": FAS, "Womans Mission, Westminster, 1850," reel 197, Seward Papers.
155 "There you are . . . pleasures, except at intervals": WHS to [FAS], June 13, 1847, in Seward, *Seward at Washington . . . 1846–1861*, p. 51.
155 The Sewards' relationship was sustained: Seward, *An Autobiography*, p. 162; Johnson, "I Could Not be Well or Happy at Home," *URLB* (1978), p. 53.
155 "above every other thing in the world": WHS to FAS, August 22, 1834, reel 112, Seward Papers.
155 whose "silver rays" . . . in the mail: WHS to FAS, January 27, 1831, in Seward, *An Autobiography*, p. 173.

155 played in the smoke from his cigar: WHS to FAS, January 15, 1831, in ibid., p. 168.
156 "Clouds and darkness . . . twelve months ago": SPC to CS, September 8, 1850, reel 7, Sumner Papers.
156 isolated in the Senate . . . achieve his position: Niven, *Salmon P. Chase*, pp. 142, 146–47.
156 routine at Miss Haines's School: Julia Newberry, *Julia Newberry's Diary*, intro. Margaret Ayer Barnes and Janet Ayer Fairbank (New York: W. W. Norton & Co., 1933), pp. 35–36: Phelps, *Kate Chase, Dominant Daughter*, pp. 74–75; Alice Hunt Sokoloff, *Kate Chase for the Defense* (New York: Dodd, Mead, 1971), pp. 28–29.
156 "without . . . we could hardly breathe": Newberry, *Julia Newberry's Diary*, p. 36.
156 correspondence between Chase and Kate: Niven, *Salmon P. Chase*, p. 201. Examples of loving but critical letters to KCS: July 22, August 23, September 5, 1850; January 15, March 2, April 19, August 30, September 10, 1851; January 23, 1853; May 27, 1855; April 30, 1859.
156 "Your last letter . . . use your eyes, reflect": SPC to KCS, January 15, 1851, reel 9, Chase Papers.
157 "I wish . . . into your letters": SPC to KCS, January 22, 1851, reel 9, Chase Papers.
157 "Your nice letter . . . drowsy God": SPC to KCS, June 21, 1855, reel 10, Chase Papers.
157 "It will be a . . . pleasurable sensation": SPC to KCS, February 8, 1855, reel 10, Chase Papers.
157 "Remember . . . preparation for another!": SPC to KCS, December 5, 1851, reel 9, Chase Papers.
157 "strong, robust . . . give you grace": SPC to KCS, June 15, 1852, reel 9, Chase Papers.
157 "I am sorry . . . to you the reasons why": SPC to KCS, August 10, 1852, reel 9, Chase Papers.
157 "you have it . . . by ill conduct": SPC to KCS, January 23, 1853, reel 9, Chase Papers.
157 "To an affectionate father . . . delightful future": SPC to KCS, March 27, 1855, reel 10, Chase Papers.
158 "be made President": SPC to KCS, February 21, 1852, reel 9, Chase Papers.
158 "I knew Clay . . . and was a brilliant talker": "Kate Chase in 1893," undated newspaper clipping from the *Star*, "Sprague, Kate Chase" vertical file, Washingtoniana Division, Martin Luther King, Jr. Memorial Library, Washington, D.C. [hereafter KCS vertical file, DWP].
158 "You cannot think . . . hear you praised": SPC to KCS, January 8, 1855, reel 10, Chase Papers.
158 "have visited . . . as they should be": SPC to KCS, August 27, 1852, reel 9, Chase Papers.
158 "The sun shines . . . the chirp of insects": SPC to KCS, June 15, 1852, reel 9, Chase Papers.
158 "I should like . . . a ramble together": SPC to KCS, April 3, 1852, reel 9, Chase Papers.
158 Chase understood her desire: Hart, *Salmon P. Chase*, p. 419.
158 "Miss Lizzie . . . among gentlemen": SPC to KCS, August 4, 1853, reel 9, Chase Papers.
159 the "African mania": Bates diary, January 1, 1850.
159 "lovers of free . . . in the South": Bates diary, January 1, 1850.
159 "a struggle among . . . sectional supremacy": Bates diary, May 31, 1851.
159 radicals . . . personal ambition: Hendrick, *Lincoln's War Cabinet*, p. 46.
159 "in Civil government . . . arbitrary designing knave": Bates diary, July 4, 1851.
159 "the world's best hope . . . so black": Bates diary, March 6, 1850.
159 "if we stood aloof . . . insignificance": Bates diary, November 27, 1850.
159 "A human being . . . crippling effect": Thomas Mann, *The Magic Mountain*, trans. John E. Woods (New York: Alfred A. Knopf, 1999), p. 31.
159 speech at Young Men's Lyceum: AL, "Address Before the Young Men's Lyceum of Springfield, Illinois," January 27, 1838, in *CW*, I, pp. 108–15, esp. 108, 113–14.
160 A train of events . . . grant them territorial status: Henry V. Jaffa, *Crisis of the House Divided: An Interpretation of the Issues in the Lincoln-Douglas Debates* (Chicago: University of Chicago Press, 1982), pp. 104–05; Fehrenbacher, *The South and Three Sectional Crises*, pp. 49, 56–57.
160 Kansas-Nebraska Act: See "Kansas-Nebraska Act," in *The Reader's Companion to American History*, ed. Foner and Garraty, p. 609.
160 Enforcement . . . in Boston and New York: Allan Nevins, *Ordeal of the Union*. Vol. I: *Fruits of Manifest Destiny, 1847–1852* (New York and London: Charles Scribner's Sons, 1947), pp. 387–88.
160 "I had never . . . aggressive and dangerous": Ralph Waldo Emerson, "The Fugitive Slave Law," reprinted in *The Portable Emerson*, pp. 547–48.
161 *Uncle Tom's Cabin*: See Thomas F. Gossett, *Uncle Tom's Cabin and American Culture* (Dallas: Southern Methodist University Press, 1985), pp. 164, 183–84.
161 "a flash . . . hosts of slavery": Frederick Douglass, quoted in ibid., p. 172.
161 "in greater numbers . . . against invasion": Fehrenbacher, *Prelude to Greatness*, p. 23.
161 "blood and treasure": Fehrenbacher, "The Wilmot Proviso and the Mid-Century Crisis" in Fehrenbacher, *The South and Three Sectional Crises*, p. 35.
161 "The day may come . . . out of it!": Thomas Bragg, quoted in Avery O. Craven, *The Growth of Southern Nationalism, 1848–1861*. Vol. VI: *A History of the South* (Baton Rouge: Louisiana State University Press, 1953; 1984), p. 204.
161 "a mighty subject . . . every five minutes": WHS to [FAS?], February 12, 1854, in Seward, *Seward at Washington . . . 1846–1861*, p. 219.
161 "essays against slavery . . . was the leader": Stephen Douglas, quoted in Hart, *Salmon P. Chase*, p. 134.
162 "one of the most effective . . . ever produced": Blue, *Salmon P. Chase*, p. 93 (quote); Gienapp, *The Origins of the Republican Party*, p. 72.
162 "We arraign . . . cause of God": SPC, et al., *Appeal of the Independent Democrats in Congress, to the People of the United States. Shall Slavery be Permitted in Nebraska?* (Washington, D.C.: Towers' Printers, 1854).
162 "Chase's greatest . . . experience of his life": Hart, *Salmon P. Chase*, p. 134.
162 "By far the most . . . of the Senate": *NYT*, February 6, 1854.
162 "high pitch of wrath . . . a corrupt bargain": Pike, "Night Scenes in the Passage of the Nebraska Bill," March 4, 1854, from *NYTrib*, in Pike, *First Blows of the Civil War*, pp. 217–18 (quote p. 217).

162 "I said the man . . . I mean you": *NYTrib*, March 6, 1854.
162 "this discussion . . . man, as man": SPC, "Maintain Plighted Faith. Speech of Hon. S. P. Chase, of Ohio, in the Senate, February 3, 1854," *Appendix to the Congressional Globe*, 33rd Cong., 1st sess., p. 140.
163 "Ah . . . 'negro' with two gs": *NYTrib*, March 7, 1854 (first quote); Carl Sandburg, *Abraham Lincoln: The War Years*, Vol. I (4 vols., New York: Harcourt, Brace & Co., 1939), p. 144 (second quote).
163 "Midnight passed . . . was taken": Pike, "Night Scenes in the Passage of the Nebraska Bill," March 4, 1854, from *NYTrib*, in Pike, *First Blows of the Civil War*, p. 216.
163 The all-night session: Johannsen, *Stephen A. Douglas*, p. 432.
163 by "great confusion . . . galleries participated": *NYTrib*, March 4, 1854.
163 "beastly drunk . . . the Senate room": Ibid.
163 "The Senate is emasculated": Thomas Hart Benton, quoted by Pike, "Night Scenes in the Passage of the Nebraska Bill," March 4, 1854, from *NYTrib*, in Pike, *First Blows of the Civil War*, p. 220.
163 a distant cannonade: Niven, *Salmon P. Chase*, p. 152.
163 "They celebrate . . . itself shall die": Schuckers, *The Life and Public Services of Salmon Portland Chase*, p. 156.
163 "Be assured . . . forces of slavery and freedom": Pike, "A Warning," April 1854, from *NYTrib*, in Pike, *First Blows of the Civil War*, pp. 222–23.
163 "The tremendous storm . . . every week": Nevins, *Ordeal of the Union*. Vol. II: *A House Dividing*, p. 125.
163 Resolutions: *NYTrib*, March 6 and 10, 1854.
163 "led by a band . . . torches and banners": *NYTrib*, March 6, 1854.
163 "he sat on the edge . . . half-slave and half-free": T. Lyle Dickey, paraphrased in Frederick Trevor Hill, *Lincoln the Lawyer* (New York: Century Co, 1906), p. 264.
164 "as he had never been before": AL, "Scripps autobiography," in *CW*, IV, p. 67 (quote); Miller, *Lincoln's Virtues*, pp. 232–34, 238–39.
164 "took us by . . . and stunned": AL, "Speech at Peoria, Illinois," October 16, 1854, in *CW*, II, p. 282.
164 spent many hours in the State Library: *Illinois State Register*, quoted in Donald, *Lincoln*, p. 173.
164 "inside and . . . downside": Herndon and Weik, *Herndon's Life of Lincoln*, p. 478.
164 "I am slow . . . to rub it out": Joshua F. Speed to WHH, December 6, 1866, in *HI*, p. 499.
164 at the annual State Fair: *Illinois State Journal*, October 5, 1854; *Peoria Daily Press*, October 9, 1854; *Illinois State Register*, October 6, 1854.
164 a "world-renowned" plow: *Peoria Daily Press*, October 9, 1854.
164 "a jolly good time ensued": Ibid.
164 Douglas at the State Fair: Thomas, *Abraham Lincoln*, pp. 147–48; Oates, *With Malice Toward None*, p. 124.
164 "He had a large . . . crush his prey": Horace White, *The Lincoln and Douglas Debates: An Address Before the Chicago Historical Society, February 17, 1914* (Chicago: University of Chicago Press, 1914), pp. 7–8.
165 "cast away . . . a half-naked pugilist": John Quincy Adams diary, quoted in William Gardner, *Life of Stephen A. Douglas* (Boston: Roxburgh Press, 1905), p. 20.
165 "He was frequently . . . with him": *Peoria Daily Press*, October 7, 1854.
165 Lincoln announced rebuttal the following day: Thomas, *Abraham Lincoln*, p. 148.
165 Douglas seated in the front row: White, *Abraham Lincoln in 1854*, p. 12.
165 largest audience: Donald, *Lincoln*, p. 174.
165 "awkward . . . knew he was right": White, *Abraham Lincoln in 1854*, p. 10.
165 "one of the world's . . . lapse of time": White, *The Lincoln and Douglas Debates*, p. 12.
165 "thin, high-pitched . . . of the speaker himself": White, *Abraham Lincoln in 1854*, p. 10.
165 Lincoln embedded his argument: AL, "Speech at Peoria Illinois," October 16, 1854, in *CW*, II, pp. 247–83.
165 so "clear and logical . . . most effective": *Illinois Daily Journal*, October 5, 1854.
166 "connected view . . . reclaiming of their fugitives": AL, "Speech at Peoria Illinois," October 16, 1854, in *CW*, II, pp. 248–75. The text of Lincoln's speech in Springfield on October 4, 1854, is no longer extant, but as the editors of *The Collected Works of Abraham Lincoln* have noted, the speech Lincoln delivered in Peoria on October 16, 1854, "is much the same speech." In the absence of a verbatim transcription of the Springfield speech, Lincoln's words from the October 16, 1854, Peoria one have been substituted. See footnote 1 to "Speech at Springfield, Illinois," *CW*, II, p. 240.
168 "thundering tones . . . drunkard on the earth": AL, "Temperance Address. An Address, Delivered before the Springfield Washington Temperance Society," February 22, 1842, in *CW*, I, pp. 273, 279.
168 "joined the north . . . to the latest generations": AL, "Speech at Peoria Illinois," October 16, 1854, in *CW*, II, pp. 264–76.
169 "deafening applause . . . anti-Nebraska speech": *Peoria Daily Press*, October 7, 1854.
169 Once he committed . . . authenticity of feeling: Miller, *Lincoln's Virtues*, p. 14; Donald, *Lincoln*, p. 270.
169 "as my two eyes make one in sight": Robert Frost, "Two Tramps in Mudtime," *The Poetry of Robert Frost: The Collected Poems*, ed. Edward Connery Lathem (New York: Henry Holt & Co., 1969; 1979), p. 277.

CHAPTER 6: THE GATHERING STORM

Page

170 "mainly attributed . . . the first choice": Joseph Gillespie to WHH, January 31, 1866, in *HI*, p. 182.
171 the worst blizzard in more than two decades: Entries for January 20–28, 1855, in *Lincoln Day by Day: A Chronology, 1809–1865*. Vol. II: *1848–1860*, ed. Earl Schenck Miers (Washington, D.C.: Lincoln Sesquicen-

tennial Commission, 1960; Dayton, Ohio: Morningside, 1991), pp. 136–37 [hereafter *Lincoln Day by Day*, Vol. II]; articles in the *Illinois Daily Journal*, Springfield, Ill., January 23–February 8, 1855.

171 "the merry sleigh bells . . . nearly extinct": *Illinois Daily Journal*, January 24, 27, and 30, 1855.

171 "a beehive of activity": *Daily Alton Telegraph*, February 12, 1855, quoted in Mark M. Krug, *Lyman Trumbull, Conservative Radical* (New York and London: A. S. Barnes & Co., and Thomas Yoseloff, 1965), p. 98.

171 "lobby and the galleries . . . and their guests": Krug, *Lyman Trumbull*, p. 98.

171 ladies in the gallery: Ibid.; White, *Abraham Lincoln in 1854*, p. 17.

171 bought a stack of small notebooks: Entry for January 1, 1855, *Lincoln Day by Day*, Vol. II, p. 136; "List of Members of the Illinois Legislature in 1855," [January 1, 1855?], in *CW*, II, pp. 296–98.

171 To reach a majority . . . fragile coalition: Miller, *Lincoln's Virtues*, p. 303.

171 On the first ballot: AL to Elihu B. Washburne, February 9, 1855, in *CW*, II, p. 304.

171 five anti-Nebraska . . . "at home": Joseph Gillespie to WHH, September 19, 1866, in *HI*, p. 344.

172 Trumbull story: AL to Elihu B. Washburne, February 9, 1855, in *CW*, II, pp. 304–06; Joseph Gillespie to WHH, January 31, 1866, and September 19, 1866, in *HI*, pp. 182–83, 344–45.

172 "you will lose both . . . to men": Joseph Gillespie to WHH, January 31, 1866, in *HI*, p. 183.

172 "spectators scarcely . . . the contest": John G. Nicolay and John Hay, *Abraham Lincoln: A History*, Vol. I (New York: Century Co., 1917), p. 390.

172 "perhaps his last . . . high position": Joseph Gillespie to WHH, January 31, 1866, in *HI*, p. 182.

172 Logan put his hands: Oates, *With Malice Toward None*, p. 130.

172 "he never would . . . by the 5": David Davis, quoted in AL to Elihu B. Washburne, February 9, 1855, *CW*, II, p. 306.

172 at Trumbull's victory party: Albert J. Beveridge, *Abraham Lincoln, 1809–1858*, Vol. III (Boston and New York: Houghton Mifflin, The Riverside Press, 1928), p. 287; White, *Abraham Lincoln in 1854*, p. 19.

172 "worse whipped . . . Trumbull is elected": AL to Elihu B. Washburne, February 9, 1855, Lincoln Papers.

172 Lincoln, in defeat, gained friends: Donald, *Lincoln*, p. 185.

172 "cold, selfish, treachery": MTL to Leonard Swett, January 12, 1867, in Turner and Turner, *Mary Todd Lincoln*, p. 406.

172 never spoke another word: Beveridge, *Abraham Lincoln, 1809–1858*, Vol. III, p. 286; Miller, *Lincoln's Virtues*, p. 312.

172 intermediaries tried . . . never healed: Burlingame, *The Inner World of Abraham Lincoln*, p. 310; Strozier, *Lincoln's Quest for Union*, p. 76.

173 to blackball him: MTL to David Davis, January 17, 1861, in Turner and Turner, *Mary Todd Lincoln*, p.71; entry for December 3, 1865, *Diary of Gideon Welles: Secretary of the Navy Under Lincoln and Johnson*. Vol. II: *April 1, 1864–December 31, 1866*, ed. Howard K. Beale (New York: W.W. Norton & Company, Inc., 1960), p. 390 [hereafter Welles diary, Vol. II].

173 an "agony": AL to Elihu B. Washburne, February 9, 1855, in *CW*, II, p. 304.

173 "He could bear . . . his friends": Joseph Gillespie, quoted in Donald, *Lincoln*, p. 184.

173 celebrated law case: Unless otherwise noted, information and quotations related to the Reaper case have been derived from Robert H. Parkinson to Albert J. Beveridge, May 28, 1923, container 292, Beveridge Papers, DLC.

173 Peter Watson: Beveridge, *Abraham Lincoln, 1809–1858*, Vol. II, p. 280.

174 "At our interview . . . Manny's machine": AL to Peter H. Watson, July 23, 1855, in *CW*, II, pp. 314–15.

174 "Why did you bring . . . no good": WHH to JWW, January 6, 1887, reel 10, Herndon-Weik Collection, DLC.

175 "rapt attention": Ralph and Adaline Emerson, *Mr. & Mrs. Ralph Emerson's Personal Recollections of Abraham Lincoln* (Rockford, Ill.: Wilson Brothers Co., 1909), p. 7.

175 "drinking in his words": Flower, *Edwin McMasters Stanton*, p. 63.

175 "to study law": Emerson, *Emerson's Personal Recollections*, p. 7.

175 "For any rough- . . . will be ready": Flower, *Edwin McMasters Stanton*, p. 63.

175 "You have made . . . to return here": AL, quoted in W. M. Dickson, "Abraham Lincoln in Cincinnati," *Harper's New Monthly Magazine* 69 (June 1884), p. 62.

175 "the most powerful . . . his gift": Miller, *Lincoln's Virtues*, p. 425.

175 despite his initial contempt . . . respect and love Lincoln: Lewis Hutchison Stanton to unknown correspondent, January 4, 1930, quoted in the appendix to Gideon Townsend Stanton, ed., "Edwin M. Stanton: A Personal Portrait as revealed in letters addressed to his wife Ellen Hutchison during his voyage to and sojourn in San Francisco . . . and including letters covering the period 1854 to 1869," undated, typed manuscript, Edwin M. Stanton Manuscript, Mss. 1648, Louisiana and Lower Mississippi Valley Collections, LSU Libraries, Baton Rouge, La. [hereafter Gideon Stanton, ed., "Edwin M. Stanton"]; Thomas, *Abraham Lincoln*, p. 382.

175 the "long armed Ape": WHH to JWW, January 6, 1887, reel 10, Herndon-Weik Collection, DLC.

175 Stanton's comfortable childhood . . . and other works of history: Wolcott, "Edwin M. Stanton," esp. pp. 20–21, 24, 28, 30, 38, 39, 40, 66–67.

176 the "happiest hours of his life": Flower, *Edwin McMasters Stanton*, p. 37.

176 *"regenerate the world":* Mary Lamson Stanton to EMS, December 13, 1843, quoted in Wolcott, "Edwin M. Stanton," p. 108.

176 Mary Lamson and children: EMS, "Mary Lamson, Wife of Edwin M. Stanton"; Flower, *Edwin McMasters Stanton*, pp. 30, 32, 36–37, 38.

176 "bright and cheery": Wolcott, "Edwin M. Stanton," p. 63.

176 Stanton looked upon . . . and Byron: EMS to Edwin L. Stanton, quoted in Wolcott, "Edwin M. Stanton," p. 113.

176 "We years ago . . . cannot express": EMS to Mary Lamson Stanton, December 16, 1842, EMS, "Mary Lamson, Wife of Edwin M. Stanton."
177 deaths of Lucy and Mary: EMS, "Mary Lamson, Wife of Edwin M. Stanton"; Wolcott, "Edwin M. Stanton," pp. 72, 99; Flower, *Edwin McMasters Stanton*, pp. 38, 44.
177 "verged on insanity": Benjamin P. Thomas and Harold M. Hyman, *Stanton: The Life and Times of Lincoln's Secretary of War* (New York: Alfred A. Knopf, 1962), p. 35.
177 "She is my bride" . . . held that spring: Flower, *Edwin McMasters Stanton*, p. 39.
177 "with lamp in hand . . . Where is Mary?": Wolcott, "Edwin M. Stanton," p. 100.
177 Stanton's responsibilities . . . go of his sorrow: Thomas and Hyman, *Stanton*, pp. 35–36.
177 a letter of over a hundred pages: EMS, "Mary Lamson, Wife of Edwin M. Stanton."
177 "tears obscuring his vision": Gideon Stanton, ed., "Edwin M. Stanton."
177 "anguish of heart": EMS, "Mary Lamson, Wife of Edwin M. Stanton."
177 "but time, care . . . for each other": Ibid.
177 developed a high fever: Thomas and Hyman, *Stanton*, p. 40.
177 "He bled . . . few moments": Alfred Taylor, quoted in Flower, *Edwin McMasters Stanton*, p. 45.
177 His mother watched: Ibid.
177 "the blood spouted . . . ceiling": Thomas and Hyman, *Stanton*, p. 41.
177 Neighbors were sent . . . watching over him: Alfred Taylor, quoted in Flower, *Edwin McMasters Stanton*, p. 45.
178 "Where formerly . . . clasped behind": Mrs. Davison Filson, quoted in ibid., p. 40.
178 Stanton's change of personality in court: Ibid., p. 34.
178 "the most important" . . . He was greatly relieved: EMS to Ellen Hutchison, September 25, 1855, Stanton Papers, Donated Historical Materials, formerly Record Group 200, National Archives and Records Administration, Washington, D.C. [hereafter Stanton Papers, DNA] (quote); Dickson, "Abraham Lincoln in Cincinnati," *Harper's* (1884), p. 62.
178 Ellen Hutchison: See Flower, *Edwin McMasters Stanton*, p. 66.
178 "radiant with beauty and intellect": EMS to Ellen Hutchison, October 10, 1854, Stanton Papers, DNA.
178 in "agony": EMS to Ellen Hutchison, October 28, 1854, Stanton Papers, DNA.
178 "the trouble . . . fresh blossoms": EMS to Ellen Hutchison, October 10, 1854, Stanton Papers, DNA.
178 Ellen was vexed: EMS to Ellen Hutchison, May 21, 1855, and undated letter, Stanton Papers, DNA.
178 "his careless[ness] . . . feelings of all": EMS to Ellen Hutchison, undated, Stanton Papers, DNA.
179 "there is so much . . . overlook": EMS to Ellen Hutchison, May 21, 1855, Stanton Papers, DNA.
179 "blessed with . . . you condemn": EMS to Ellen Hutchison, undated, Stanton Papers, DNA.
179 to marry Edwin on June 25, 1856: EMS to Ellen Hutchison, June 25, 1856, Stanton Papers, DNA.
179 Happier years followed: Gideon Stanton, ed., "Edwin M. Stanton."
179 to Washington . . . a brick mansion: Flower, *Edwin McMasters Stanton*, p. 79.
179 "Twenty-two . . . a monarch's brow": AL, "Fragment on Stephen A. Douglas," [December 1856?], in *CW*, II, pp. 382–83.
179 "She had . . . ambition": John T. Stuart interview, late June 1865, in *HI*, p. 63.
179 "I would rather . . . in the world": MTL, quoted in Elizabeth Todd Edwards interview, 1865–1866, in *HI*, p. 444.
179 "a very little . . . does physically": Helm, *The True Story of Mary*, p. 140.
179 "no equal in the United States": MTL, quoted in ibid., p. 144.
180 "unladylike": MTL to Mercy Ann Levering, December [15?], 1840, in Turner and Turner, *Mary Todd Lincoln*, p. 21.
180 "the first bugle call . . . a new party": Schurz, *Reminiscences*, Vol. II, p. 34.
180 upheaval complicated by the emergence of the Know Nothings: McPherson, *Battle Cry of Freedom*, pp. 142–43; Eugene H. Roseboom, "Salmon P. Chase and the Know Nothings," *Mississippi Valley Historical Review* 25 (December 1938), pp. 335–50.
180 the Know Nothing Party . . . "popery": Potter, *The Impending Crisis, 1848–1861*, pp. 240–52 (quote p. 242); McPherson, *Battle Cry of Freedom*, p. 32.
180 "How can any one . . . Russia, for instance": AL to Joshua F. Speed, August 24, 1855, in *CW*, II, p. 323.
181 Republican Party, comprised of . . . over three decades: Gienapp, *The Origins of the Republican Party*, pp. 114–17, 123–24, 224–25; Potter, *The Impending Crisis, 1848–1861*, pp. 247, 249; McPherson, *Battle Cry of Freedom*, p. 127.
181 Chase . . . unhindered by past loyalties: Riddle, "The Election of Salmon P. Chase," *Republic* (1875), p. 183; Hendrick, *Lincoln's War Cabinet*, p. 33.
181 Chase accomplished . . . statewide ticket: Niven, *Salmon P. Chase*, pp. 157–58, 171: Gienapp, *The Origins of the Republican Party*, pp. 192–203.
181 Chase's campaign for governor: SPC to James S. Pike, October 18, 1855, and SPC to CS, October 15, 1855, reel 10, Chase Papers; Gienapp, *The Origins of the Republican Party*, pp. 200–01.
182 "on a hand car . . . another hand car": SPC to KCS, September 30, 1855, reel 10, Chase Papers.
182 "The anxiety . . . breathe freely!": CS to SPC, October 11, 1855, reel 10, Chase Papers.
182 Seward faced a more difficult challenge: Gienapp, *The Origins of the Republican Party*, pp. 223–25.
182 lavish dinners . . . bishop John Hughes: Hugh Hastings letter, reprinted in Barnes, *Memoir of Thurlow Weed*, pp. 232–33.
182 Working without rest . . . in the Senate: Taylor, *William Henry Seward*, p. 96.
182 "I snatch . . . shattered bark": WHS to TW, February 7, 1855, quoted in Seward, *Seward at Washington . . . 1846–1861*, p. 245.

182 "I have never . . . was made known": FAS to Augustus Seward, February 7, 1855, reel 115, Seward Papers.
183 liberated to join . . . in the state of New York: Gienapp, *The Origins of the Republican Party*, pp. 224–27.
183 "I am so happy. . . . political pew": CS to WHS, October 15, 1855, reel 49, Seward Papers.
183 Seward's October speech: WHS, "The Advent of the Republican Party, Albany, October 12, 1855," in *The Works of William H. Seward*, Vol. IV, ed. George E. Baker (Boston: Houghton Mifflin, 1884; New York: AMS Press, 1972), pp. 225–40 (quote p. 237).
183 organizing the various . . . Republican Party: Donald, *Lincoln*, pp. 189–91.
183 guerrilla war had broken out: Potter, *The Impending Crisis, 1848–1861*, pp. 199–215.
183 "engage in competition . . . in right": WHS, remarks in "The Nebraska and Kansas Bill," May 25, 1854, *Appendix to the Congressional Globe*, 33rd Cong., 1st sess., p. 769.
183 "When the North . . . eager foe": *Charleston Mercury*, June 21, 1854, quoted in Craven, *The Growth of Southern Nationalism*, p. 204.
184 assault on Sumner by Preston Brooks: David Donald, *Charles Sumner and the Coming of the Civil War*, collector's edition (New York: Alfred A. Knopf, 1960; Norwalk, Conn.: Easton Press, 1987), pp. 294–95; William E. Gienapp, "The Crime Against Sumner: The Caning of Charles Sumner and the Rise of the Republican Party," *Civil War History* 25 (September 1979), pp. 218–45.
184 Sumner's speech: CS, "Kansas Affairs. Speech of Hon. C. Sumner, of Massachusetts, in the Senate, May 19–20, 1856," *Appendix to the Congressional Globe*, 34th Cong., 1st sess., pp. 529–44.
184 laced with literary and historical references: Donald, *Charles Sumner and the Coming of the Civil War*, pp. 281–82.
184 "a chivalrous knight . . . humiliating offices": CS, "Kansas Affairs," *Appendix to the Congressional Globe*, 34th Cong., 1st sess., pp. 530–31.
184 advised him to remove the personal attacks: William H. Seward, Jr., "Youthful Recollections," p. 13, folder 36, Box 120, William Henry Seward Papers, Department of Rare Books & Special Collections, University of Rochester Library [hereafter Seward Papers, NRU], Rochester, N.Y.
184 "the most un-American . . . or elsewhere": Response by Lewis Cass to CS's speech, May 20, 1856, *Appendix the Congressional Globe*, 34th Cong., 1st sess., p. 544.
184 Preston Brooks's attack on Sumner: See *Boston Pilot*, May 31, 1856; *NYT*, May 23, 1856; Donald, *Charles Sumner and the Coming of the Civil War*, pp. 294–97.
184 "You have libelled . . . come to punish you": *Boston Pilot*, May 31, 1856.
184 "Knots of men . . . by the slave power": *Boston Daily Evening Transcript*, May 29, 1856.
184 Mass public meetings: Donald, *Charles Sumner and the Coming of the Civil War*, pp. 300–01.
184 "*see* the slave aggression . . . in Congress": F. A. Sumner to CS, June 24, 1856, quoted in Gienapp, "The Crime Against Sumner," *CWH* (1979), p. 230.
185 "but the knocking-down . . . Southern spirit": *NYTrib*, May 24, 1856.
185 "proved a . . . Republican party": Gienapp, "The Crime Against Sumner," *CWH* (1979), p. 239.
185 Sumner hero in North, Brooks in South: Ibid., pp. 221, 222–23; Donald, *Charles Sumner and the Coming of the Civil War*, pp. 297–99, 304–07.
185 "good in conception . . . in consequence": *Richmond Enquirer*, June 3, 1856, quoted in Gienapp, "The Crime Against Sumner," *CWH* (1979), p. 222.
185 presented Brooks . . . and walking stick: *Columbia [S.C.] Carolinian*, reprinted in *Charleston Daily Courier*, May 28, 1856.
185 "*We are rejoiced . . . catch it next*": *Richmond Whig*, quoted in *NYT*, May 26, 1856.
185 "If thrashing is . . . wretch, Sumner": *Petersburg [Va.] Intelligencer*, quoted in *NYT*, May 29, 1856.
185 "apparent that . . . Brooks-Sumner affair": Donald, *Charles Sumner and the Coming of the Civil War*, p. 309.
185 "all shades . . . and abolitionists": Thomas, *Abraham Lincoln*, p. 165.
185 "fire and energy and force": Herndon and Weik, *Herndon's Life of Lincoln*, p. 313.
185 "That is the greatest . . . the presidency": Jesse K. Dubois, quoted in Weik, *The Real Lincoln*, p. 257.
186 "Lost Speech": Speech at Bloomington, Illinois, May 29, 1856, report in the Alton *Weekly Courier*, June 5, 1856, in *CW*, II, p. 341; Oates, *With Malice Toward None*, pp. 136–37.
186 By the late spring of 1856: Republican National Convention, *One Hundred Years Ago: Proceedings of the First Republican Nominating Convention, Philadelphia, 1856* (n.p.: n.p., 1956); Gienapp, *The Origins of the Republican Party*, pp. 334–45.
186 both Seward and Chase . . . the nomination: Van Deusen, *William Henry Seward*, pp. 174, 176; SPC to Hiram Barney, June 6, 1856, reel 11, Chase Papers.
186 gubernatorial election . . . nomination in 1856: Reinhard H. Luthin, "Salmon P. Chase's Political Career Before the Civil War," *Mississippi Valley Historical Review* 29 (March 1943), p. 525; SPC to Kinsley S. Bingham, October 19, 1855, reel 10, Chase Papers.
186 meeting at Blair home: Smith, *The Francis Preston Blair Family in Politics*, Vol. I, pp. 323–24; Niven, *Salmon P. Chase*, p. 178; Gienapp, *The Origins of the Republican Party*, pp. 250–51.
186 "approving . . . invitation": WHS to TW, December 31, 1855, quoted in Seward, *Seward at Washington . . . 1846–1861*, p. 264.
186 turned to potential candidates: Niven, *Salmon P. Chase*, pp. 178–79.
187 "if the unvarnished . . . people": SPC to Edward Hamlin, June 12, 1856, reel 11, Chase Papers.
187 neglected to appoint a manager . . . failed to unite: Hiram Barney to SPC, June 21, 1856, reel 11, Chase Papers; entry for June 1856, SPC diary, 1845–1859, reel 1, Chase Papers, DLC; Luthin, "Salmon P. Chase's Political Career Before the Civil War," *MVHR* (1943), p. 526.
187 "I know that if . . . been accomplished": Hiram Barney to SPC, June 21, 1856, reel 11, Chase Papers.

187 Seward had greater reason . . . Weed kept him from running: WHS to FAS, June 14 and 17, 1856, quoted in Seward, *Seward at Washington . . . 1846–1861*, pp. 277–78; Van Deusen, *William Henry Seward*, pp. 174, 176–77; Macartney, *Lincoln and His Cabinet*, p. 95; Gienapp, *The Origins of the Republican Party*, pp. 310, 339.
187 Lincoln was staying . . . "two steps at a time": Whitney, *Life on the Circuit with Lincoln*, pp. 94–95 (quote p. 95).
187 110 votes for vice president: Republican National Convention, *One Hundred Years Ago*, p. 67.
187 "Davis and I . . . reckon it's him": Whitney, *Life on the Circuit with Lincoln*, p. 96.
187 Bates refused . . . Whig National Convention: Cain, *Lincoln's Attorney General*, pp. 85, 86–88.
188 American Party . . . preserving the Union: Ibid., p. 82.
188 "I am neither . . . disordered territory": EB before the Whig National Convention in Baltimore, July 1856, quoted in ibid., p. 88.
188 results of 1856 presidential election: Congressional Quarterly, *Presidential Elections Since 1789*, p. 181.
188 *Dred Scott* case: Paul Finkelman, *Dred Scott v. Sandford: A Brief History with Documents. The Bedford Series in History and Culture* (Boston and New York: Bedford Books, 1997); Don E. Fehrenbacher, *The Dred Scott Case: Its Significance in American Law and Politics* (New York: Oxford University Press, 1978).
188 "an uncompromising . . . antislavery movement": Finkelman, *Dred Scott v. Sandford*, p. 29.
189 "Bright skies . . . bland atmosphere": *Star*, March 4, 1857.
189 Buchanan inaugural address: James Buchanan, "Inaugural Address, March 4, 1857," in *The Works of James Buchanan, Comprising His Speeches, State Papers, and Private Correspondence*. Vol. X: *1856–1860*, ed. John Bassett Moore (Philadelphia and London: J. B. Lippincott Co., 1910), p. 106.
189 "are not included . . . bound to respect": Roger B. Taney, opinion quoted in Finkelman, *Dred Scott v. Sandford*, pp. 35–36.
189 did not stop even there . . . was not before it: Potter, *The Impending Crisis, 1848–1861*, pp. 276–79.
189 "become convinced . . . its introduction": Justice Benjamin R. Curtis, quoted in ibid., p. 279 n24.
189 "one of the Court's . . . wounds": Opinion of Felix Frankfurter, in conversation with law clerk Richard N. Goodwin, as told to the author.
190 "often wrestled in the halls . . . justly won it": *Richmond Enquirer*, March 10, 1857.
190 "the accredited interpreter . . . and confused": *Richmond Enquirer*, March 13, 1857.
190 "Sheer blasphemy": Congressman John F. Potter, quoted in Kenneth M. Stampp, *America in 1857: A Nation on the Brink* (New York and Oxford: Oxford University Press, 1990), p. 104.
190 "entitled to just . . . Washington bar-room": *NYTrib*, March 7, 1857.
190 "an impartial judicial body" . . . would fail: Pike, "Decision of the Supreme Court," March 8, 1857, from the *NYTrib*, reprinted in Pike, *First Blows of the Civil War*, pp. 368–69 (quote p. 368).
190 "Judge Taney . . . good, evil": Frederick Douglass, "The *Dred Scott* Decision: Speech at New York, on the Occasion of the Anniversary of the American Abolition Society, May 11, 1857," reprinted in Finkelman, *Dred Scott v. Sandford*, p. 174.
190 "has aroused" . . . reported to Sumner: FAS to CS, April 23, 1857, reel 15, Sumner Papers.
190 Dred Scott was sold . . . to slavery: Potter, *The Impending Crisis, 1848–1861*, p. 290.
190 Speaking in Springfield . . . "circumstances should permit": AL, "Speech at Springfield, Illinois," June 16, 1857, in *CW*, II, pp. 398–410 (quotes p. 403, 405, 406).
191 "The day of inauguration . . . English liberty": WHS, "Kansas-Lecompton Constitution," March 3, 1858, Senate, *Congressional Globe*, 35th Cong., 1st sess., p. 941.
191 reaction to Seward speech . . . access to the White House: Van Deusen, *William Henry Seward*, p. 190.
191 "have refused . . . to such a man": Samuel Tyler, *Memoir of Roger Brooke Taney* (Baltimore, 1872; New York: Da Capo Press, 1970), p. 391.
191 Seward's Rochester, New York, speech: WHS, "The Irrepressible Conflict, Rochester, October 25, 1858," in *Works of William H. Seward*, Vol. IV, pp. 289–302 (quotes pp. 291, 292; italics added).
191 Frances Seward . . . stance of the South: FAS to CS, January 4, 1859, reel 17, Sumner Papers.
192 "that troubled . . . *irrepressible*?": Kenneth M. Stampp, "The Irrepressible Conflict," in Stampp, *The Imperiled Union: Essays on the Background of the Civil War* (New York: Oxford University Press, 1980; 1981), p. 191.
192 uproar in opposition papers: *Atlas and Argus*, Albany, N.Y., October 28, 1858.
192 "more repulsive . . . Rev. Dr. Parker": *NYH*, October 28, 1858.
192 "never comprehended . . . words": Gienapp, *The Origins of the Republican Party*, p. 191.
192 "if heaven . . . do it again": WHS, quoted in Van Deusen, *William Henry Seward*, p. 194.
192 conciliatory . . . with his adversaries: David M. Potter, *Lincoln and His Party in the Secession Crisis* (New Haven, Conn.: Yale University Press, 1942), pp. 25–26.
192 "alarm and apprehension": WHS to FAS, February 9, 1849, quoted in Seward, *Seward at Washington . . . 1846–1861*, p. 98.
192 "This general impression . . . 'Night's Dream' ": WHS to FAS, February 9, 1849, quoted in ibid., p. 98.
193 "Those who assailed . . . pinch of snuff": *Albany Evening Journal*, May 19, 1890.
193 Seward's extravagant dinner parties: *Columbus [Ohio] Gazette*, April 6, 1860 (quotes); Van Deusen, *William Henry Seward*, pp. 257–58.
193 a trip through Canada: Seward, *Seward at Washington . . . 1846–1861*, pp. 301–22; Van Deusen, *William Henry Seward*, p. 183.
194 "voyage of discovery": FPB to WHS, October 5, 1857, quoted in Seward, *Seward at Washington . . . 1846–1861*, p. 324.
194 "very best traveling" . . . elegant meals: FPB to WHS, November 1, 1857, quoted in ibid., p. 326.
194 "At an age . . . of the nation": *Cincinnati Enquirer*, August 6, 1899.
194 "a scientific knowledge . . . surpassed": Peacock, *Famous American Belles of the Nineteenth Century*, p. 214.

194 "Her complexion . . . of her head": Sara A. Pryor, *Reminiscences of Peace and War.* Revised and enlarged ed. (New York: The Macmillan Company, 1905), pp. 75–76.
195 Gothic mansion on Sixth Street: Niven, *Salmon P. Chase*, pp. 200, 201, 204; SPC to KCS, December 3, 4, 5, and 6, 1857, reel 11, Chase Papers.
195 "I feel I am . . . trust yours": SPC to KCS, December 5, 1857, reel 11, Chase Papers.
195 "you have capacity and will do very well": SPC to KCS, December 4, 1857, reel 11, Chase Papers.
195 role of Ohio's first lady: Ross, *Proud Kate*, pp. 32–33, 36–37.
195 "I knew all . . . very early age": "Kate Chase in 1893," undated newspaper clipping from the *Star*, KCS vertical file, DCPL.
195 first dinner "in society . . . very beautiful": Howells, *Years of My Youth*, pp. 154–55.
195 led to a tryst . . . end to the relationship: *Columbus Special* to the *Chicago Times*, reprinted in *Cincinnati Enquirer*, August 13, 1879.
196 "I find that . . . any other man": SPC to Charles D. Cleveland, November 3, 1857, reel 11, Chase Papers.
196 met in Lecompton . . . applied for statehood: Potter, *The Impending Crisis, 1848–1861*, pp. 300, 306–07, 313–15, 318–20, 322–25.
196 now siding with the Republicans: Potter, *The Impending Crisis, 1848–1861*, pp. 316, 318, 320–21.
196 "My objection . . . a slave State": Stephen A. Douglas's speech, "Third Debate with Stephen A. Douglas at Jonesboro, Illinois," September 15, 1858, in *CW*, III, p. 115.
196 He cared not . . . voted up or down: AL on Stephen Douglas, in "A House Divided": Speech at Springfield, Illinois, June 16, 1858, in *CW*, II, p. 463.
196 "was not the act . . . embody their will": Stephen A. Douglas's speech, "Third Debate with Stephen A. Douglas at Jonesboro, Illinois," September 15, 1858, in *CW*, III, p. 115.
197 "What can . . . freedom and justice": WHS to [FAS?], December 10, 1857, quoted in Seward, *Seward at Washington . . . 1846–1861*, p. 330.
197 Greeley called on Illinois Republicans: Fehrenbacher, *Prelude to Greatness*, p. 61.
197 Lincoln at once . . . destroyed the Republican Party: AL to Elihu B. Washburne, May 27, 1858, in *CW*, II, p. 455; AL to SPC, April 30, 1859, in *CW*, III, p. 378; Donald, *Lincoln*, pp. 204, 208.
197 "accosted by friends . . . to go under": AL, "Fragment of a Speech," [c. May 18, 1858], in *CW*, II, p. 448.
197 "What does . . . here in Illinois?": AL to Lyman Trumbull, December 28, 1857, in ibid., p. 430.
197 "incapable of . . . pure republican position": AL to Charles L. Wilson, June 1, 1858, in ibid., p. 457.
197 interference of the Eastern Republicans: *Illinois Daily Journal*, Springfield, Ill., June 16, 1858; Fehrenbacher, *Prelude to Greatness*, pp. 62–63.
197 "Abraham Lincoln . . . United States Senate": Thomas, *Abraham Lincoln*, p. 179.
198 a statewide Republican convention . . . "Stephen A. Douglas": Fehrenbacher, *Prelude to Greatness*, pp. 63, 48 (quote p. 48).
198 "A house divided . . . another Supreme Court decision": AL, "A House Divided": Speech at Springfield, Illinois, June 16, 1858, in *CW*, II, pp. 461, 465–67. "A House Divided" appears in the Bible in Matthew 12:25; Mark 3:24.
199 If "the point . . . talking about": James M. McPherson, "How Lincoln Won the War with Metaphors," Eighth Annual R. Gerald McMurtry Lecture, 1985, reprinted in James M. McPherson, *Abraham Lincoln and the Second American Revolution* (New York and Oxford: Oxford University Press, 1991), p. 104.
199 "*weight* and *authority* . . . not *promise* to *ever* be": AL, "A House Divided": Speech at Springfield, Illinois, June 16, 1858, in *CW*, II, pp. 462–63, 467–68.
200 "What if Judge" . . . to extend slavery: AL's reply, "First Debate with Stephen A. Douglas at Ottawa, Illinois," August 21, 1858, in *CW*, III, pp. 22, 20 (quote p. 22).
200 "planned to seize . . . nationalize slavery": Cain, *Lincoln's Attorney General*, p. 77.
200 Lincoln, the challenger, asked Douglas: *The Lincoln-Douglas Debates: The First Complete, Unexpurgated Text*, ed. Harold Holzer (New York: HarperCollins, 1993), pp. 2–6.
200 both men covered over 4,000 miles: Ibid., p. 20.
200 marching bands . . . picnics: Baringer, *Lincoln's Rise to Power*, pp. 21–22, 24–25, 28, 30–31, 33–34, 37.
200 "all the devoted . . . for athletic contests": Fehrenbacher, *Prelude to Greatness*, p. 15.
200 "the country people . . . lines in single combat": Schurz, *Reminiscences*, Vol. II, pp. 92, 88.
201 "were the successive . . . of the nation": AL's speech, "Sixth Debate with Stephen A. Douglas, at Quincy, Illinois," October 13, 1858, in *CW*, III, pp. 252–53.
201 "On the whole . . . extreme modest simplicity": Schurz, *Reminiscences*, Vol. II, p. 92.
201 followed the same rules . . . Newspaper stenographers: *The Lincoln-Douglas Debates*, ed. Holzer, pp. 4, 9.
201 "No more striking . . . and staying power": Schurz, *Reminiscences*, Vol. II, p. 94.
201 The highly partisan papers: See *The Lincoln-Douglas Debates*, ed. Holzer, pp. 7–8.
201 "when Mr. Lincoln . . . music in front": *Press and Tribune*, Chicago, following Ottawa debate, quoted in *The Lincoln-Douglas Debates*, ed. Holzer, p. 85.
201 "excoriation of Lincoln . . . in shame": *Chicago Times*, in ibid.
201 "both comparatively . . . Hit him again": Stephen Douglas's speech, "First Debate with Stephen A. Douglas at Ottawa, Illinois," August 21, 1858, in *CW*, III, pp. 5–6.
202 conceded that Douglas . . . "upon principle, alone": AL, "Speech at Springfield, Illinois," July 17, 1858, in *CW*, II, p. 506.
202 "The very notice . . . political physicians": Stephen Douglas, quoted in *NYTrib*, included in AL's reply, "Third Joint Debate at Jonesboro," September 15, 1858, in *The Lincoln-Douglas Debates*, ed. Holzer, p. 173.

202 "Well, I know . . . if he can": AL's reply, "Third Joint Debate at Jonesboro," September 15, 1858, in ibid., pp. 173, 175.
203 a small notebook . . . "pursuit of Happiness": Ibid., p. 17. Quotation from paragraph two of the Declaration of Independence (1776).
203 "majestic interpretation . . . in other ages": AL, "Speech at Lewistown, Illinois," August 17, 1858, quoted in *Press and Tribune*, Chicago, August 21, 1858, in *CW*, II, p. 546.
203 "I care more . . . in Christendom": Stephen Douglas's reply, "Seventh and Last Debate with Stephen A. Douglas at Alton, Illinois," October 15, 1858, in *CW*, III, p. 322.
203 "the doctrine . . . a slave of another": AL, "Speech at Peoria, Illinois," October 16, 1854, in *CW*, II, pp. 265–66.
203 "The difference between . . . these views": AL, "Speech at Edwardsville, Illinois," September 11, 1858, in *CW*, III, p. 92.
204 set of Black Laws . . . on juries: Leon F. Litwack, *North of Slavery: The Negro in the Free States, 1790–1860* (Chicago and London: University of Chicago Press, 1961), pp. 93, 278.
204 "If you desire . . . Never, never": Stephen Douglas's speech, "First Debate with Stephen A. Douglas at Ottawa, Illinois," August 21, 1858, in *CW*, III, p. 9.
204 "the signers . . . that's the truth": Stephen A. Douglas's speech, "Seventh and Last Debate with Stephen A. Douglas at Alton, Illinois," October 15, 1858, in ibid., p. 296.
204 "no purpose . . . the black races": AL's reply, "First Debate with Stephen A. Douglas at Ottawa, Illinois," August 21, 1858, in ibid., p. 16.
204 "of making voters . . . nor to intermarry": AL's speech, "Fourth Debate with Stephen A. Douglas at Charleston, Illinois," September 18, 1858, in ibid., p. 145.
204 "a physical difference . . . of every living man": AL's reply, "First Debate with Stephen A. Douglas at Ottawa, Illinois," August 21, 1858, in ibid., p. 16.
205 only unequivocal statement: Harry Jaffa, *Crisis of the House Divided*, pp. 382–84.
205 passing a special law . . . "whether free or slave": Koerner, *Memoirs of Gustave Koerner*, Vol. II, p. 30.
205 "Seward did not . . . of the whites": Van Deusen, *William Henry Seward*, p. 94.
205 "the two races . . . in other lands": Blue, *Salmon P. Chase*, pp. 83, 84; SPC, quoted in ibid.
205 "The most dreadful . . . prejudice of the white": de Tocqueville, *Democracy in America*, ed. Mansfield and Winthrop, pp. 326, 329, 328.
206 "in the name of . . . to go?": Henry Clay, quoted in Nevins, *Ordeal of the Union*. Vol. I: *Fruits of Manifest Destiny*, p. 515.
206 "My first impulse . . . native land": AL, "Speech at Peoria, Illinois," October 16, 1854, in *CW*, II, p. 255.
206 More than 3 million: Craven, *The Growth of Southern Nationalism*, p. 12.
206 "What then? . . . safely disregarded": AL, quoting his 1854 Peoria speech in his reply, "First Debate with Stephen A. Douglas at Ottawa, Illinois," August 21, 1858, in *CW*, III, p. 15.
206 "With public sentiment . . . this American people": AL's reply, "First Debate with Stephen A. Douglas at Ottawa, Illinois," August 21, 1858, in ibid., pp. 27, 29.
207 "they did not mean . . . all colors everywhere": AL, "Speech at Springfield, Illinois," June 26, 1857, in *CW*, II, p. 406.
207 "penetrate the human soul": AL's reply, "First Debate with Stephen A. Douglas at Ottawa, Illinois," August 21, 1858, in *CW*, III, p. 29.
207 "all this quibbling . . . men are created equal": AL, "Speech at Chicago, Illinois," July 10, 1858, quoted by Stephen Douglas in his reply, "Sixth Debate with Stephen A. Douglas at Quincy, Illinois," October 13, 1858, in ibid., p. 263.
207 "practical recognition of our Equality": Frederick Douglass, quoted in David W. Blight, *Frederick Douglass' Civil War: Keeping Faith in Jubilee* (Baton Rouge and London: Louisiana State University Press, 1989), p. 16.
207 "the first great man . . . the colored race": Frederick Douglass, "Lincoln and the Colored Troops," in *Reminiscences of Abraham Lincoln*, ed. Rice, p. 323.
208 "having strong sympathies . . . and so on": AL's reply, "Seventh and Last Debate with Stephen A. Douglas at Alton, Illinois," October 15, 1858, in *CW*, III, p. 300.
208 "whole town . . . human beings": Eyewitness at Alton debate, quoted in *The Lincoln-Douglas Debates*, ed. Holzer, p. 322.
208 "More than a thousand . . . he ever made": Koerner, *Memoirs of Gustave Koerner*, Vol. II, pp. 66–68.
208 The "real issue . . . same tyrannical principle": AL's reply, "Seventh and Last Debate with Stephen A. Douglas at Alton, Illinois," October 15, 1858, in *CW*, III, p. 315.
208 He drew up . . . "to be struggled for": AL, "1858 Campaign Strategy," [July? 1858], in *CW*, II, pp. 476–81 (quote p. 479).
209 "We are in . . . must be left undone": AL to Gustave P. Koerner, July 25, 1858, in ibid., p. 524.
209 Chase came to Illinois: Niven, *Salmon P. Chase*, p. 210; Blue, *Salmon P. Chase*, pp. 118–19.
209 a gesture Lincoln would not forget: AL to SPC, April 30, 1859, in *CW*, III, p. 378; AL to Samuel Galloway, March 24, 1860, in *CW*, IV, p. 34.
209 a dreary day, November 2, 1858: *Illinois State Journal*, Springfield, Ill., November 3, 1858.
209 Lincoln anxiously awaited the returns: Baringer, *Lincoln's Rise to Power*, p. 43; Oates, *With Malice Toward None*, p. 173.
209 "by the gerrymandering . . . Republican votes": Koerner, *Memoirs of Gustave Koerner*, Vol. II, p. 68.
209 John Crittenden: Fehrenbacher, *Prelude to Greatness*, p. 118.
209 "Thousands of Whigs . . . influence of Crittenden": WHH to Theodore Parker, November 8, 1858, quoted in Baringer, *Lincoln's Rise to Power*, p. 49.

209 "The emotions of defeat . . . anything dishonorable": AL to John J. Crittenden, November 4, 1858, in *CW,* III, pp. 335–36.
210 "I am glad . . . after I am gone": AL to Anson G. Henry, November 19, 1858, in ibid., p. 339.
210 "must not be surrendered . . . *hundred* defeats": AL to Henry Asbury, November 19, 1858, in ibid., p. 339.
210 "You will soon . . . have fun again": AL to Charles H. Ray, November 20, 1858, in ibid., p. 342.

CHAPTER 7: COUNTDOWN TO THE NOMINATION

Page
211 "decided impression . . . candidate for the presidency": Jesse W. Fell, quoted in Oldroyd, comp., *The Lincoln Memorial,* p. 474.
211 "so much better known . . . you or anybody else": AL, quoted by Jesse W. Fell, quoted in ibid., pp. 474, 476.
212 when the Republican editor . . . "for the Presidency": Thomas J. Pickett to AL, April 13, 1859, Lincoln Papers.
212 "I certainly am . . . fit for the Presidency": AL to Thomas J. Pickett, April 16, 1859, in *CW,* III, p. 377.
212 Certain that Seward . . . overseas for eight months: Luthin, *First Lincoln Campaign,* p. 31.
212 "All our discreet friends . . . recess of Congress": WHS to George W. Patterson, April 6, 1859, quoted in Van Deusen, *William Henry Seward,* p. 196.
212 Fanny Seward desolate . . . approaching departure: April 1859 entries, Frances (Fanny) Adeline Seward diary, reel 198, Seward Papers [hereafter Fanny Seward diary, Seward Papers].
212 description of Fanny Seward, literary pursuits: Johnson, "Sensitivity and Civil War," pp. 27, 76–78, 83–84.
212 " 'my affinity' . . . instead of speak": Fanny Seward, quoted in ibid., p. 55.
213 Seward in Europe: Seward, *Seward at Washington . . . 1846–1861,* pp. 362–436.
213 prepared a major address: Taylor, *William Henry Seward,* pp. 115–16.
213 Henry Stanton later . . . "posterity together": Stanton, *Random Recollections,* pp. 212–13.
213 "I wish it were over": FAS to William H. Seward, Jr., February 29, 1860, reel 115, Seward Papers.
213 Fanny . . . seated in the gallery: Entry for February 29, 1860, Fanny Seward diary, Seward Papers.
213 "The whole house . . . was very still": Entry for February 29, 1860, Fanny Seward diary, Seward Papers.
213 Seward took as his theme: WHS, February 29, 1860, *Congressional Globe,* 36th Cong., 1st sess., pp. 910–14.
213 " 'the irrepressible conflict' . . . the political aspirants": Bancroft, *The Life of William H. Seward,* Vol. I, p. 519.
214 "differences of opinion . . . always of their wants": WHS, February 29, 1860, *Congressional Globe,* 36th Cong., 1st sess., pp. 912–14.
214 produced deafening applause: Entry for February 29, 1860, Fanny Seward diary, Seward Papers; Baringer, *Lincoln's Rise to Power,* pp. 197, 198; Van Deusen, *William Henry Seward,* p. 220.
214 half a million copies were circulated: Van Deusen, *William Henry Seward,* p. 219.
214 "*killed Seward with me forever*": Cassius Marcellus Clay, *The Life of Cassius Marcellus Clay. Memoirs, Writings, and Speeches, Showing His Conduct in the Overthrow of American Slavery, the Salvation of the Union, and the Restoration of the Autonomy of the United States* (n.p.: J. Fletcher Brennan & Co., 1886; New York: Negro Universities Press/Greenwood Publishing Corp., 1969), pp. 242–43.
214 "as an intellectual . . . agrees with me": CS to Duchess Elizabeth Argyll, March 2, 1860, reel 74, Sumner Papers.
214 "From the stand-point . . . matter of party justice": Frederick Douglass, "Mr. Seward's Great Speech," *Douglass' Monthly* (April 1860).
215 "I hear of ultra . . . equally satisfactory": Samuel Bowles to TW, March 5, 1860, quoted in Barnes, *Memoir of Thurlow Weed,* p. 260.
215 "seems to be . . . set toward Seward": Bancroft, *The Life of William H. Seward,* Vol. I, p. 519.
215 Weed assured him that everything was in readiness: TW to WHS, May 2, 6, and 8, 1860, reel 59, Seward Papers.
215 "oceans of money": Halstead, *Three Against Lincoln,* p. 162.
215 a longing for political office: Glyndon G. Van Deusen, *Horace Greeley: Nineteenth-Century Crusader,* (Philadelphia: University of Pennsylvania Press, 1953), pp. 116–17, 185–86; Thurlow Weed, "Recollections of Horace Greeley," *Galaxy* 15 (March 1873), pp. 379–80.
215 Greeley's plaintive letter to Seward: Horace Greeley to WHS, November 11, 1854, reel 48, Seward Papers.
216 "full of sharp, pricking thorns": WHS to TW, November 12, 1854, quoted in Seward, *Seward at Washington . . . 1846–1861,* p. 239.
216 mistakenly assumed . . . "mortal offense": Carpenter, "A Day with Governor Seward," Seward Papers.
216 "insinuated . . . to the nomination": Henry Raymond, quoted in Barnes, *Memoir of Thurlow Weed,* p. 274.
216 Weed had a long talk with Greeley . . . "all right": WHS to home, Seward, *Seward at Washington . . . 1846–1861,* p. 395.
216 Weed's failure to meet . . . Seward relayed the message: WHS to TW, March 15, 1860, quoted in Barnes, *Memoir of Thurlow Weed,* p. 261.
216 Seward's visit to Lochiel: WHS to TW, April 11, 1859, Weed Papers; Lee F. Crippen, *Simon Cameron, Antebellum,* The American Scene: Comments and Commentators series (Oxford, Ohio, 1942; New York: Da Capo Press, 1972), p. 209.
216 "He took me . . . to embarrass me": WHS to TW, April 11, 1859, Weed Papers.

217 "an honest politician . . . stays bought": Simon Cameron, quoted in Macartney, *Lincoln and His Cabinet*, p. 46.
217 "so much money . . . man in Pennsylvania": *NYT*, June 3, 1878.
217 Cameron's political offices: Macartney, *Lincoln and His Cabinet*, p. 26.
217 his "legislative child": Hendrick, *Lincoln's War Cabinet*, p. 53.
217 People's Party state convention: Crippen, *Simon Cameron, Ante-bellum Years*, pp. 201, 205.
217 Andrew Curtin . . . challenging Cameron: Hendrick, *Lincoln's War Cabinet*, pp. 55–56.
218 Chase and the Baileys . . . "in European tradition": Niven, *Salmon P. Chase*, pp. 61, 123, 140–41 (quote p. 140).
218 "detestable" Know Nothings: Gamaliel Bailey to SPC, November 27, 1855, reel 10, Chase Papers.
218 "in the presidential . . . other man": Gamaliel Bailey to SPC, June 26, 1855, reel 10, Chase Papers.
218 "observing the signs . . . integrity or my friendship": Gamaliel Bailey to SPC, January 16, 1859, reel 12, Chase Papers.
218 "I do not doubt . . . spontaneous growth": SPC to Gamaliel Bailey, January 24, 1859, reel 12, Chase Papers.
219 "a slip of your pen . . . as a friend": Gamaliel Bailey to SPC, January 30, 1859, reel 12, Chase Papers.
219 preferred the unrealistic . . . on the first ballot: Hiram Barney to SPC, November 10, 1859, reel 13, Chase Papers.
219 Failing once again to appoint: Donnal V. Smith, "Salmon P. Chase and the Election of 1860," *OAHQ* 39 (July 1930), p. 520.
219 He rejected an appeal from a New Hampshire supporter: Amos Tuck to SPC, March 14, 1860, reel 13, Chase Papers.
219 He never capitalized . . . a series of letters: Reinhard H. Luthin, "Pennsylvania and Lincoln's Rise to the Presidency," *Pennsylvania Magazine of History and Biography* 67 (January 1943), p. 66; SPC to Hiram Barney, September 22, 1860, reel 13, Chase Papers; Smith, "Salmon P. Chase and the Election of 1860," *OAHQ* (1930), pp. 520–21; Luthin, "Salmon P. Chase's Political Career Before the Civil War," *MVHR* (1943), p. 531.
219 "I now begin . . . but *he works*": James M. Ashley to SPC, April 5, 1860, reel 13, Chase Papers.
220 "I shall have nobody . . . of the State": SPC to Benjamin Eggleston, May 10, 1860, reel 13, Chase Papers.
220 "The Ohio delegation . . . as yet": Erastus Hopkins to SPC, May 17, 1860, reel 13, Chase Papers.
220 "in a position . . . to occupy": SPC to Benjamin R. Cowen, May 14, 1860, reel 13, Chase Papers.
220 Kate convinced her father: Ross, *Proud Kate*, p. 42.
220 Seward was very kind . . . "good deal of joking": SPC to James A. Briggs, April 27, 1860, reel 13, Chase Papers (quote); WHS to FAS, April 27, 1860, quoted in Seward, *Seward at Washington . . . 1846–1861*, p. 447.
220 organized a party . . . "two rivals within": WHS to FAS, April 28, 1860, quoted in Seward, *Seward at Washington . . . 1846–1861*, p. 447.
220 the Blairs threw . . . "well-cultivated": WHS to FAS, April 29, 1860, quoted in ibid., p. 448.
220 "attention to Katie . . . kind to me": SPC to Janet Chase Hoyt, May 4, 1860, reel 13, Chase Papers.
220 "Everybody seems . . . confidence in me": SPC to James A. Briggs, April 27, 1860, reel 13, Chase Papers.
220 "a great change . . . I was in Washington": SPC to James A. Briggs, May 8, 1860, reel 13, Chase Papers.
221 But he never left his home state . . . to visit him: See entries from January to May 1860 in *The Diary of Edward Bates, 1859–1866;* Cain, *Lincoln's Attorney General*, p. 95.
221 "the first . . . two years": Entry for February 22, 1860, in *The Diary of Edward Bates, 1859–1866*, p. 101.
221 his distance from the fierce arguments of the fifties: Introduction, ibid., p. xii.
221 his "views and opinions . . . of the country": Entry for April 20, 1859, in ibid., p. 1.
221 The New York Whigs . . . "sectional prejudice": EB to Whig Committee of New York, February 24, 1859, reprinted in entry for April 20, 1859, in ibid., pp. 1–9 (quotes pp. 1–2).
222 "denouncing . . . the Republican party": Entry for April 27, 1859, in ibid., p. 12.
222 confirmed Bates's . . . "well enough alone": Entry for December 17, 1859, in ibid., pp. 78–79.
222 "brighter every day": Note of February 2, 1860, added to entry for January 28, 1860, in ibid., p. 94.
222 "made up of 'Bates men' ": Entries for February 25 and March 1, 1860, in ibid., pp. 102 (quote), 107.
222 "good feeling . . . support Lincoln": Entry for April 26, 1860, in ibid., p. 122.
222 "would be the best . . . the South of it": AL to Richard M. Corwine, April 6, 1860, in *CW*, IV, p. 36.
222 endorsements by conventions: Entries for March 1 and March 13, 1860, in *The Diary of Edward Bates, 1859–1866*, pp. 106, 108 (quote p. 106).
222 the German-American contingent . . . party in 1856: Reinhard H. Luthin, "Organizing the Republican Party in the 'Border-Slave' Regions: Edward Bates's Presidential Candidacy in 1860," *Missouri Historical Review* 38 (January 1944), pp. 149–50.
222 Blair suggested a questionnaire: Parrish, *Frank Blair*, p. 82.
222 "beaten with . . . into the quicksands": Joseph Medill, quoted in O. J. Hollister, *Life of Schuyler Colfax* (New York and London: Funk & Wagnalls, 1886), p. 147.
223 Bates's response to questionnaire: EB to Committee of the Missouri Republican Convention, March 17, 1860, reprinted in *The Diary of Edward Bates, 1859–1866*, pp. 111–14.
223 responses to Bates's statement: See Cain, *Lincoln's Attorney General*, pp. 104–05.
223 "as a clap . . . a clear sky": *Lexington [Mo.] Express*, reprinted in *Daily Missouri Republican*, St. Louis, Mo., April 5, 1860.
223 "just as good . . . the Southern Conservatives": *Louisville [Ky.] Journal*, extracted in the *[Indianapolis] Daily Journal*, quoted in Luthin, "Organizing the Republican Party in the 'Border-Slave' Regions," *MHR* (1944), p. 151.
223 "agitators . . . peace of our Union": *Memphis Bulletin*, reprinted in *Missouri Republican*, St. Louis, Mo., March 31, 1860.
223 Bates himself . . . "a good many papers": Entry of April 7, 1860, in *The Diary of Edward Bates, 1859–1866*, p. 118.
223 "knowing the fickleness . . . a failure": Entry of February 28, 1860, in ibid., pp. 105–06.
224 "neither on the left . . . dead center": Fehrenbacher, *Prelude to Greatness*, p. 147.

224 "fairly headed off . . . of ultimate extinction": AL to John L. Scripps, June 23, 1858, in *CW*, II, p. 471.
224 He arranged to publish: Baringer, *Lincoln's Rise to Power*, pp. 128, 137, 171; Donald, *Lincoln*, p. 237.
224 nearly two dozen speeches: Fehrenbacher, *Prelude to Greatness*, pp. 143–44; Baringer, *Lincoln's Rise to Power*, chapter 3.
224 "I think it is . . . into Liberty": James A. Briggs to AL, November 1, 1859, Lincoln Papers.
224 The crowds that greeted . . . "many a day": *Janesville Gazette*, quoted in Baringer, *Lincoln's Rise to Power*, pp. 110–11 (quote p. 110).
224 "Douglasism . . . of Republicanism": AL to SPC, September 21, 1859, in *CW*, III, p. 471.
225 stop was Cincinnati: Baringer, *Lincoln's Rise to Power*, pp. 103–07.
225 "greeted with . . . rising star": Dickson, "Abraham Lincoln in Cincinnati," *Harper's New Monthly* (1884), p. 65.
225 Lincoln's speech in Cincinnati: AL, "Speech at Cincinnati, Ohio," September 17, 1859, in *CW*, III, p. 454.
225 "as an effort . . . had ever heard": *Cincinnati Gazette*, reprinted in *Illinois State Journal*, Springfield, Ill., October 7, 1859.
225 Lincoln's crowded schedule . . . "the women come": Joshua F. Speed to AL, September 22, 1859, Lincoln Papers.
225 "Your visit to Ohio . . . in your favor": Samuel Galloway to AL, October 13, 1859, Lincoln Papers.
225 "We must take . . . are my choice": Samuel Galloway to AL, July 23, 1859, Lincoln Papers.
225 "to hedge against . . . we shall disagree": AL to Schuyler Colfax, July 6, 1859, in *CW*, III, pp. 390–91.
226 Colfax appreciated . . . "throughout the Union": Schuyler Colfax to AL, July 14, 1859, Lincoln Papers.
226 "with foolish pikes": Stephen Vincent Benét, *John Brown's Body* (New York: Henry Holt & Co., 1927; 1955), p. 52.
226 John Brown at Harpers Ferry: See chapter 19 of Stephen B. Oates, *To Purge This Land with Blood: A Biography of John Brown* (New York: Harper & Row, 1970), pp. 290–306.
226 "I am waiting . . . & of humanity": John Brown to his family, November 30, 1859, quoted in Oswald Garrison Villard, *John Brown, 1800–1859: A Biography Fifty Years After* (Boston and New York: Houghton Mifflin, 1910), p. 551.
226 the dignity . . . eloquence of his statements: Villard, *John Brown, 1800–1859*, pp. 538–39.
226 His death . . . "resolutions were adopted": Potter, *The Impending Crisis, 1848–1861*, p. 378.
226 "sent a shiver of fear . . . woman, and child": *Press and Tribune*, Chicago, October 22, 1859.
227 "Harper's Ferry . . . dissolution must ensue": *Richmond Enquirer*, November 25, 1859.
227 "like a great . . . that abyss": Craven, *The Growth of Southern Nationalism*, p. 309.
227 "Weird John Brown": Herman Melville, "The Portent," in *Battle-Pieces and Aspects of the War*, reprinted in *The Poems of Herman Melville*, rev. edn., ed. Douglas Robillard (Kent, Ohio, and London: Kent State University Press, 2000), p. 53.
227 "I do not exaggerate . . . in great numbers": Robert Bunch, December 9, 1859, quoted in Laura A. White, "The South in the 1850's as Seen by British Consuls," *Journal of Southern History* I (February 1935), p. 44.
227 "for seditious . . . in a good cause": Editor's description of *St. Louis News* article of November 23, 1859, pasted in entry of November 23, 1859, in *The Diary of Edward Bates, 1859–1866*, p. 65.
227 "the natural fruits . . . his subordinates": *Charleston [S.C.] Mercury*, December 16, 1859.
227 "one hundred gentlemen" . . . and Colfax: Advertisement by "Richmond," quoted in Seward, *Seward at Washington . . . 1846–1861*, p. 440.
227 "The first overt act . . . the Shenandoah": *NYH*, October 19, 1859.
228 "necessary and just": WHS, "The State of the Country," February 29, 1860, in *Works of William H. Seward*, Vol. IV, p. 637.
228 "seeking to plunge . . . universal condemnation": *Albany Evening Journal*, October 19, 1859.
228 "the wild extravagance . . . a madman": Entry of October 25, 1859, in *The Diary of Edward Bates, 1859–1866*, pp. 50–51.
228 He discussed the incident . . . "his [dagger]": Entry of November 21, 1859, in ibid., p. 63.
228 "for a household . . . attempted to do": Janet Chase Hoyt, "A Woman's Memories. Salmon P. Chase's Home Life," *NYTrib*, February 15, 1891.
228 Lincoln was back on the campaign trail: Baringer, *Lincoln's Rise to Power*, p. 124; entry for December 2, 1859, *Lincoln Day by Day*, Vol. II, pp. 266–67.
228 "the attempt . . . electioneering dodge": "Second Speech at Leavenworth, Kansas," December 5, 1859, synopsis of speech printed in the *Leavenworth Times*, December 6, 1859, in *CW*, III, p. 503.
228 "make the gallows . . . the cross": Ralph Waldo Emerson, "Courage," November 7, 1859, lecture in Boston, as reported by the *NYTrib*, quoted in John McAleer, *Ralph Waldo Emerson: Days of Encounter* (Boston and Toronto: Little, Brown, 1984), p. 532.
228 "great courage" . . . "rare unselfishness": Elwood *Free Press* on AL, "Speech at Elwood, Kansas," December 1 [November 30?], 1859, in *CW*, III, p. 496.
228 "that cannot . . . think himself right": AL, "Speech at Leavenworth, Kansas," December 3, 1859, in ibid., p. 502.
228 Republican National Committee at Astor House: Luthin, *The First Lincoln Campaign*, pp. 20–21.
229 "attach more consequence": AL to Norman B. Judd, December 14, 1859, in *CW*, III, p. 509.
229 "good neutral ground . . . an even chance": Archie Jones, "The 1860 Republican Convention," transcript of Chicago station WAAF radio broadcast, May 16, 1960, Chicago Historical Society, Chicago, Ill.
229 "carefully kept . . . on the nomination": Whitney, *Lincoln the Citizen*, Vol. I, p. 285.
229 "promised that . . . furnished free": *Press and Tribune*, Chicago, December 27, 1859.
229 Chicago beat St. Louis by a single vote: Luthin, *The First Lincoln Campaign*, p. 21.

229 "a cheap excursion . . . of the State": Whitney, *Lincoln the Citizen*, Vol. I, p. 285.
229 "I like the place . . . take exception to it": John Bigelow to WHS, January 18, 1860, reel 59, Seward Papers.
229 "Had the convention . . . been the nominee": Charles Gibson, "Edward Bates," *Missouri Historical Society Collections* II (January 1900), p. 55.
229 "there is not . . . not much of me": AL to Jesse W. Fell, December 20, 1859, in *CW*, III, p. 511.
229 "a wild region . . . in the woods": AL, "Autobiography by Abraham Lincoln, enclosed with Lincoln to Jesse W. Fell," December 20, 1859, in ibid., p. 511.
229 "If any thing . . . written by myself": AL to Jesse W. Fell, December 20, 1859, in ibid., p. 511.
230 he received an invitation: James A. Briggs to AL, October 12, 1859, Lincoln Papers; Harold Holzer, *Lincoln at Cooper Union: The Speech That Made Abraham Lincoln President* (New York: Simon & Schuster, 2004), p. 10.
230 "His clothes were travel-stained . . . for Monday night": Henry C. Bowen, paraphrased in Henry B. Rankin, *Intimate Character Sketches of Abraham Lincoln* (Philadelphia and London: J. B. Lippincott Co., 1924), pp. 179–80.
230 "Well, B. . . . as a man ought to want": "Recollections of Mr. McCormick," in Wilson, *Intimate Memories of Lincoln*, p. 251 (quote); Holzer, *Lincoln at Cooper Union*, p. 86. Holzer identifies "B." as Mayson Brayman.
230 Lincoln paid a visit . . . "shorten [his] neck": AL, quoted in James D. Horan, *Mathew Brady: Historian with a Camera* (New York: Crown Publishers, 1955), p. 31. For portrait, see plate 93 in Horan.
230 weather and attendance: Thomas, *Abraham Lincoln*, p. 202; Holzer, *Lincoln at Cooper Union*, pp. 103, 303 n55.
230 "this western man": Rankin, *Intimate Character Sketches of Abraham Lincoln*, p. 173.
231 Lincoln's appearance: Herndon and Weik, *Herndon's Life of Lincoln*, p. 369.
231 "one of the legs . . . longer than his sleeves": Russell H. Conwell, "Personal Glimpses of Celebrated Men and Women," quoted in Wayne Whipple, *The Story-Life of Lincoln. A Biography Composed of Five Hundred True Stories Told by Abraham Lincoln and His Friends* (Philadelphia: J. C. Winston Co., 1908), p. 308.
231 had labored to craft his address: Rankin, *Intimate Character Sketches of Abraham Lincoln*, pp. 174–75; Holzer, *Lincoln at Cooper Union*, pp. 50–53.
231 *"Our fathers . . . protection a necessity"*: AL, "Address at Cooper Institute, New York City," February 27, 1860, in *CW*, III, pp. 522, 535.
231 a "hue and cry . . . never can be reversed": AL, "Temperance Address delivered before the Springfield Washington Temperance Society," February 22, 1842, in *CW*, I, p. 273.
231 Cooper Union speech: AL, "Address at Cooper Institute, New York City," February 27, 1860, in *CW*, III, pp. 522–50, esp. 537, 538, 547, 550.
232 erupted in thunderous applause: Baringer, *Lincoln's Rise to Power*, pp. 158–59.
232 Briggs predicted . . . "have heard tonight": James Briggs, quoted in Holzer, *Lincoln at Cooper Union*, p. 147.
232 "When I came out . . . 'since St. Paul' ": Unknown observer, quoted in ibid., p. 146.
232 undertaking an exhausting tour: See copies of Lincoln's speeches in Rhode Island and New Hampshire, in *CW*, III, pp. 550–54, and speeches in Connecticut, *CW*, IV, pp. 2–30; Holzer, *Lincoln at Cooper Union*, pp. 176–77.
232 He was forced to decline . . . "before the fall elections": AL to Isaac Pomeroy, March 3, 1860, in *CW*, III, p. 554.
232 "being within my calculation . . . ideas in print": AL to MTL, March 4, 1860, in ibid., p. 555.
232 Lincoln first met Gideon Welles: J. Doyle DeWitt, *Lincoln in Hartford* (privately printed: n.d.), p. 5; John Niven, *Gideon Welles: Lincoln's Secretary of the Navy* (New York: Oxford University Press, 1973), pp. 287, 289.
232 Gideon Welles's appearance and career: John T. Morse, Introduction, *Diary of Gideon Welles: Secretary of the Navy Under Lincoln and Johnson*, Vol. I: *1861–March 30, 1864* (Boston and New York: Houghton Mifflin/The Riverside Press, 1911), pp. xvii–xxi; Richard S. West, Jr., *Gideon Welles: Lincoln's Navy Department* (Indianapolis and New York: Bobbs-Merrill, 1943).
232 "the party of the Southern slaveocracy": Morse, Introduction, *Diary of Gideon Welles* (1911 edn.), p. xix.
233 had settled on Chase . . . "very expensive rulers": West, *Gideon Welles*, pp. 78–79, 81 (quote p. 78).
233 Lincoln and Welles spent several hours: DeWitt, *Lincoln in Hartford*, p. 5; Niven, *Gideon Welles*, p. 289.
233 the Hartford speech: AL, "Speech at New Haven, Connecticut," March 6, 1860, in *CW*, IV, p. 18.
233 "as if the people . . . out loud": James Russell Lowell, "Abraham Lincoln," in *The Writings of James Russell Lowell*, Vol. V, *Political Essays* (Boston: Houghton Mifflin, 1892), p. 208.
234 "introduced the Trojan horse": WHS, "Admission of Kansas. Speech of Hon. W. H. Seward, of New York, In the Senate, April 9, 1856," *Appendix to the Congressional Globe*, 34th Cong., 1st sess., p. 405.
234 Lincoln met with Welles again: "The Career of Gideon Welles," typescript manuscript draft, Henry B. Learned Papers, reel 36, Welles Papers; Hendrick, *Lincoln's War Cabinet*, p. 78.
234 "This orator . . . in his logic": GW's editorial in *Hartford Evening Press*, quoted in West, *Gideon Welles*, p. 81.
234 "I have been sufficiently . . . and learned men": Rev. J. P. Gulliver article in *New York Independent*, September 1, 1864, quoted in Carpenter, *Six Months at the White House*, p. 311.
234 "I think your chance . . . man in the country": James A. Briggs, "Narrative of James A. Briggs, Esq.," *New York Evening Post*, August 16, 1867, reprinted in *An Authentic Account of Hon. Abraham Lincoln, Being Invited to give an Address in Cooper Institute, N.Y., February 27, 1860* (Putnam, Conn.: privately printed, 1915), n.p.
234 "When I was East . . . to the best": AL, quoted in Briggs, "Narrative of James A. Briggs, Esq."
234 At the end of January 1859: Lyman Trumbull to AL, January 29, 1859, Lincoln Papers.
234 "Any effort . . . a rival of yours": AL to Lyman Trumbull, February 3, 1859, in *CW*, III, pp. 355–56.
235 "A word now . . . suggestions of this sort": AL to Lyman Trumbull, April 29, 1860, in *CW*, IV, p. 46.
235 Lincoln's effort to defuse . . . Judd and Wentworth: Don E. Fehrenbacher, *Chicago Giant: A Biography of "Long John" Wentworth* (Madison, Wisc.: American History Research Center, 1957), pp. 163, 169–74.
235 Wentworth would drag out . . . "at Lincoln's expense": Note 1, accompanying transcript of AL to Norman B. Judd, December 9, 1859, Lincoln Papers (quote); Fehrenbacher, *Chicago Giant*, pp. 169–70.

235 Lincoln hastened to reassure . . . "go uncontradicted": AL to Norman B. Judd, December 9, 1859, in *CW*, III, p. 505.
235 Judd brought a libel suit . . . tried to retain Lincoln: See note 1 provided with John Wentworth to AL, November 28, 1859, Lincoln Papers; Fehrenbacher, *Chicago Giant*, pp. 170–72.
235 "very reason . . . keeping up a quarrel": John Wentworth to AL, December 21, 1859, Lincoln Papers.
235 he did help to mediate: Don E. Fehrenbacher, "The Judd-Wentworth Feud," *Journal of the Illinois State Historical Society* XLV (Autumn 1952), pp. 203, 204.
235 "I am not . . . end of the vineyard?": AL to Norman B. Judd, February 9, 1860, in *CW*, III, p. 517.
236 a resounding editorial: See Baringer, *Lincoln's Rise to Power*, pp. 148–50.
236 "You saw what . . . Was it satisfactory?": Norman B. Judd to AL, February 21, 1860, Lincoln Papers.
236 "That Abraham Lincoln . . . a unit for him": Baringer, *Lincoln's Rise to Power*, p. 186.
236 "what is to be . . . reverse the decree": MTL interview, September 1866, in *HI*, p. 360 n4.

CHAPTER 8: SHOWDOWN IN CHICAGO

Page

237 Forty thousand visitors: Tarbell, *The Life of Abraham Lincoln*, Vol. I, p. 344: *Buffalo Morning Express*, May 16, 1860, David Davis Papers, Chicago Historical Society, Chicago, Ill. [hereafter Davis Papers, ICHi].
237 trains . . . carried the delegates: Baringer, *Lincoln's Rise to Power*, p. 212.
237 youngest political party . . . fastest-growing city: Jones, "The 1860 Republican Convention."
237 crowds gathered . . . "swung their hats": *Press and Tribune*, Chicago, May 15, 1860.
237 the one that began its journey: *Press and Tribune*, Chicago, May 12, 1860.
237 "when 'a mile a minute' . . . in their boots": *Press and Tribune*, Chicago, May 16, 1860.
237 prizefighters hired "to keep the peace . . . broken heads": Clark, "Lincoln's Nomination As Seen By a Young Girl," *Putnam's*, p. 537.
237 "such refreshments . . . among the opponents": *Buffalo Morning Express*, May 15, 1860, Davis Papers, ICHi.
237 "almost ridiculous": Anonymous writer, quoted in *As Others See Chicago: Impressions of Visitors, 1673–1933*, ed. Bessie Louise Pierce (Chicago: University of Chicago Press, 1933), p. 151.
237 "growth is . . . a word": James Stirling, quoted in ibid., p. 123.
238 "a military post and fur station": *A Guide to the City of Chicago* (Chicago: Zell & Co., 1868), pp. 32–33.
238 population of more than a hundred thousand: Thomas, *Abraham Lincoln*, p. 207.
238 "the first grain . . . all of Europe": *A Strangers' and Tourists' Guide to the City of Chicago* (Chicago: Relig. Philo. Pub. Assoc., 1866), p. 24.
238 "the first lumber-market in the world": Anonymous writer, quoted in *As Others See Chicago*, p. 151.
238 "miles of wharves . . . pursuit of trade": *A Strangers' and Tourists' Guide to the City of Chicago*, p. 19.
238 a bold decision to elevate every building: Anonymous writer, quoted in *As Others See Chicago*, pp. 157–58.
238 "Our city has been chosen" . . . Lavish preparations: *Press and Tribune*, Chicago, May 12, 1860.
238 "A most magically . . . the eager crowd": *Press and Tribune*, Chicago, May 15, 1860.
238 Accommodations, restaurants: Baringer, *Lincoln's Rise to Power*, pp. 212–13; *Press and Tribune*, Chicago, May 9, 14, and 17, 1860.
238 The most popular luncheon: *Chicago Daily Evening Journal*, May 15, 1860, Davis Papers, ICHi.
238 As packed trains continued . . . to forty thousand: *Buffalo Morning Express*, May 15, 1860, Davis Papers, ALPLM; Baringer, *Lincoln's Rise to Power*, p. 222.
238 "I thought . . . some popular eruption": *Daily [Ind.] Journal*, May 17, 1860, Davis Papers, ICHi.
239 "with a zest . . . unfeeling bosom": *Press and Tribune*, Chicago, May 17, 1860.
239 "The city is thronged . . . shunned and condemned": *Chicago Daily Evening Journal*, May 15, 1860.
239 If this new party . . . the presidency: Luthin, *The First Lincoln Campaign*, p. 140.
239 "who crowded . . . standing room": *Chicago Daily Evening Journal*, May 16, 1860, Davis Papers, ICHi.
239 When the big doors . . . date for the afternoon: Halstead, *Three Against Lincoln*, pp. 147–48; Baringer, *Lincoln's Rise to Power*, pp. 246–47; Jones, "The 1860 Republican Convention"; Clark, "Lincoln's Nomination As Seen By a Young Girl," *Putnam's*, p. 537 (quote).
239 Exactly at noon . . . officially began: *Press and Tribune*, Chicago, May 17, 1860.
240 "no body of men . . . in [their] faith": Governor Morgan, quoted in Oldroyd, *Lincoln's Campaign*, pp. 27–28; *Press and Tribune*, Chicago, May 17, 1860.
240 an inclusive platform . . . a two-thirds vote: Halstead, *Three Against Lincoln*, pp. 156–58, 159.
240 "The great body . . . cardinal doctrines": Pike, "Mr. Seward's Defeat," May 20, 1860, from *NYTrib*, reprinted in Pike, *First Blows of the Civil War*, p. 517.
240 a move was made to proceed: Halstead, *Three Against Lincoln*, pp. 158, 159, 161; *Press and Tribune*, Chicago, May 18, 1860.
240 A Committee of Twelve . . . "consumed in talking": Charles P. Smith, "The Nomination of Lincoln," undated pamphlet from the Collections of the New Jersey State Library, Archives & History Division, Trenton, N.J., copy in Davis Papers, ICHi.
240 Greeley at convention: Van Deusen, *Horace Greeley*, pp. 245–48; Smith, "The Nomination of Lincoln."
241 "cannot concentrate . . . will be nominated": May 17 telegram from Horace Greeley, reprinted in *NYTrib*, May 18, 1860.
241 "every one of the . . . freely as water": Halstead, *Three Against Lincoln*, pp. 160–61.
241 "Four years ago . . . courage and confidence": TW, quoted in Addison G. Procter, *Lincoln and the Convention of*

1860: An Address Before the Chicago Historical Society, April 4, 1918 (Chicago: Chicago Historical Society, 1918), pp. 6–7.
241 "I suppose . . . confirm what I say": Horace Greeley, quoted in Procter, *Lincoln and the Convention of 1860*, p. 8.
242 "each of whom . . . Greeley had said": Ibid.
242 "I know my people well . . . slavery where it is": Henry Lane, quoted in ibid., pp. 12–13.
242 few were aware of his estrangement: Henry J. Raymond, quoted in Barnes, *Memoir of Thurlow Weed*, p. 274.
242 "While professing so high . . . had his revenge": *Auburn [N.Y.] Daily Advertiser*, May 31, 1860.
242 "In all candor . . . to the same effect": Koerner, *Memoirs of Gustave Koerner*, Vol. II, pp. 88–89.
242 He was much too conservative . . . officially enlisted: *Missouri Republican*, St. Louis, Mo., May 19, 1860; Potter, *The Impending Crisis, 1848–1861*, p. 427.
243 "If united . . . and the West": Halstead, *Three Against Lincoln*, p. 148.
243 Any hope of persuading . . . "promote his interest": John McLean, quoted in Luthin, *The First Lincoln Campaign*, p. 146.
243 "There was no unity . . . pitiable to behold": Statement of Willard Warner, paraphrased in *Columbus [Ohio] Gazette*, May 25, 1860.
243 "If the Ohio delegation . . . [been] relied upon": Francis M. Wright to SPC, May 21, 1860, reel 13, Chase Papers.
243 "There are lots . . . lukewarm friends": Erastus Hopkins to SPC, May 17, 1860, reel 13, Chase Papers.
243 "Men gather . . . the big bell rings": Halstead, *Three Against Lincoln*, pp. 143, 163, 149–50.
244 "You know how . . . no positive objection": AL to Richard M. Corwine, May 2, 1860, in *CW*, IV, p. 47.
244 "to antagonize no one": King, *Lincoln's Manager*, p. 136.
244 "relative ability . . . man who could win": Stampp, "The Republican National Convention of 1860," in Stampp, *The Imperiled Union*, p. 160.
244 "No men ever worked . . . two hours a night": Leonard Swett to Josiah Drummond, May 27, 1860, Davis Papers, ALPLM.
245 "Most of them . . . political morality": Whitney, *Lincoln the Citizen*, Vol. 1, p. 266.
245 "typically methodical way": King, *Lincoln's Manager*, p. 135 (quote); see also p. 136, and chapter 11 generally.
245 "a drawback . . . Gov. Seward": AL, quoted in Luthin, *The First Lincoln Campaign*, p. 145.
245 "It all worked . . . was Indiana": Leonard Swett to Josiah H. Drummond, May 27, 1860, quoted in Oldroyd, *Lincoln's Campaign*, p. 71.
245 "the whole of Indiana . . . to get": AL to Richard M. Corwine, May 2, 1860, in *CW*, IV, p. 47 (quote); AL to Cyrus M. Allen, May 1, 1860, in ibid., p. 46.
245 Claims have been made . . . Caleb Smith: Baringer, *Lincoln's Rise to Power*, pp. 214–15.
245 No deal was needed: Donald, *Lincoln*, p. 249.
245 Indiana . . . to back Lincoln: John D. Defrees to Schuyler Colfax, quoted in Hollister, *Life of Schuyler Colfax*, p. 148.
245 Committee of Twelve . . . "general good of the party": Smith, "The Nomination of Lincoln," Davis Papers, ICHi.
246 Davis had previously . . . might be procured: Whitney, *Lincoln the Citizen*, Vol. I, p. 289.
246 "*Make no . . . bind me*": AL, Endorsement on the Margin of the *Missouri Democrat*, May 17, 1860, in *CW*, IV, p. 50.
246 "Everybody was mad . . . 'he must ratify it' ": Whitney, *Lincoln the Citizen*, Vol. I, p. 289.
246 The Blairs had supposedly promised: Clay, *The Life of Cassius Marcellus Clay*, pp. 244–46; Luthin, *The First Lincoln Campaign*, p. 68.
246 "oceans of money": Halstead, *Three Against Lincoln*, p. 162.
246 "get every member . . . appointment": King, *Lincoln's Manager*, p. 140.
246 "My assurance to them . . . as much as possible": Leonard Swett to AL, May 20, 1860, Davis Papers, ALPLM.
247 for a celebratory march . . . "a little too far": Halstead, *Three Against Lincoln*, p. 164.
247 had manufactured duplicate tickets: Luthin, *The First Lincoln Campaign*, pp. 160–61.
247 "it was part of . . . the Convention": Swett to Drummond, May 27, 1860, quoted in Oldroyd, *Lincoln's Campaign*, p. 72.
247 friends and supporters from all over the state: Luthin, *The First Lincoln Campaign*, pp. 160–61.
247 "by a deafening shout": Swett to Drummond, May 27, 1860, quoted in Oldroyd, *Lincoln's Campaign*, p. 72.
247 "loud and long": *Albany Evening Journal*, May 18, 1860.
247 "appalled us a little": Swett to Drummond, May 27, 1860, quoted in Oldroyd, *Lincoln's Campaign*, p. 72.
247 "If Mr. Seward's name . . . far and wide": *NYT*, May 21, 1860.
247 "tremendous applause . . . Lincoln's favor": Henry Raymond article, quoted in Barnes, *Memoir of Thurlow Weed*, p. 276.
247 "cold when compared": *NYT*, May 21, 1860.
247 "trial of lungs": *Albany Evening Journal*, May 18, 1860; *NYH*, May 19, 1860; *NYT*, May 19, 1860.
247 "The shouting was . . . infernal intensity": Halstead, *Three Against Lincoln*, p. 165.
247 "five thousand . . . the scene unnoticed": Swett to Drummond, May 27, 1860, quoted in Oldroyd, *Lincoln's Campaign*, p. 72.
247 "Abe Lincoln . . . let us ballot!": *NYH*, May 19, 1860; *Buffalo Commercial Advertiser*, May 19, 1860, Davis Papers, ICHi.
248 "This was not . . . it had its weight": Swett to Drummond, May 27, 1860, quoted in Oldroyd, *Lincoln's Campaign*, pp. 72–73.
248 results of the first ballot: Halstead, *Three Against Lincoln*, p. 167.
248 "This solid vote . . . it was given": Ibid., p. 166.

248 "no pivotal state . . . been delivered": Cain, *Lincoln's Attorney General*, p. 112.
248 results of the second ballot: Halstead, *Three Against Lincoln*, p. 169.
248 "startling . . . of thunder": Barnes, *Memoir of Thurlow Weed*, p. 264.
248 results of the third ballot: Halstead, *Three Against Lincoln*, p. 170.
249 "There was a pause . . . ticks of a watch": Ibid., p. 171.
249 "A profound stillness fell upon the Wigwam": Unidentified spectator, quoted in Allan Nevins, *Ordeal of the Union*. Vol. II: *The Emergence of Lincoln, part II, Prologue to Civil War, 1857–1861*, new introduction by James M. McPherson (New York: Collier Books, Macmillan Publishing Co., 1992), p. 260.
249 "rose to their feet . . . and again": *Press and Tribune*, Chicago, May 19, 1860.
249 "Great men . . . night of struggle": Clark, "Lincoln's Nomination As Seen By a Young Girl," *Putnam's*, p. 538.
249 he, too, could not restrain his tears: Taylor, *William Henry Seward*, p. 9.
249 "the great disappointment of his life": *Chicago Tribune*, July 14, 1878.
249 "her first . . . are themselves forgotten": Austin Blair, quoted in *Albany Evening Journal*, May 23, 1860, in Halstead, *Three Against Lincoln*, p. 173; Baringer, *Lincoln's Rise to Power*, p. 292; Carl Schurz "Speeches at the Chicago Convention," quoted in *Works of William H. Seward*, Vol. IV, p. 682.
249 "with the success . . . highest honor": Carl Schurz, "Speeches at the Chicago Convention," quoted in *Works of William H. Seward*, Vol. IV, p. 682.
249 "Mounting a table . . . clenched nervously": *NYT*, May 21, 1860.
249 "Gentlemen . . . Republican party: *Buffalo Commercial Advertiser*, May 19, 1860, Davis Papers, ICHi.
249 "the spectator . . . noble man indeed": *NYT*, May 21, 1860.
249 A man stationed on the roof . . . Cannons were fired: Halstead, *Three Against Lincoln*, pp. 171–72.
249 "between 20,000 . . . shouting at once": *Buffalo Commercial Advertiser*, May 19, 1860, Davis Papers, ICHi.
250 "The Press and Tribune . . . windows and doors": *Press and Tribune*, Chicago, May 19, 1860.
250 Seward received the news . . . "on the next ballot": Stanton, *Random Recollections*, pp. 215–16 (quote p. 216).
250 "rightly [judged] that . . . to bring": Seward, *Seward at Washington . . . 1846–1861*, p. 452.
250 turned "as pale as ashes": Stanton, *Random Recollections*, p. 216.
250 "that it was no ordinary . . . and irrevocable": Seward, *Seward at Washington . . . 1846–1861*, p. 452.
250 "The sad tidings . . . clouded brow": Stanton, *Random Recollections*, p. 216.
250 "of his sanguine . . . Few men can": Entry for May 19, 1860, Charles Francis Adams diary, reel 75.
250 "he took the blow . . . family and the world": Van Deusen, *William Henry Seward*, pp. 228, 229.
250 "Father told Mother . . . unselfish coolness": Entry for May 18, 1860, Fanny Seward diary, Seward Papers.
251 "No truer . . . nomination have fallen": WHS for the *Auburn Daily Advertiser*, in "Biographical Memoir of William H. Seward," *Works of William H. Seward*, Vol. IV, p. 79.
251 "You have my . . . light as my own": WHS to TW, May 18, 1860, quoted in Barnes, *Memoir of Thurlow Weed*, p. 270; WHS to TW, May 18, 1860, quoted in Seward, *Seward at Washington . . . 1846–1861*, p. 453.
251 in a public letter . . . "progress of that cause": WHS to the New York Republican Central Committee, quoted in Seward, *Seward at Washington . . . 1846–1861*, p. 454.
251 "It was only some months . . . cursing and swearing": Van Deusen, *William Henry Seward*, p. 229.
251 "When I remember . . . competition with his": SPC to Robert Hosea, June 5, 1860, reel 13, Chase Papers.
251 For years, Chase was racked: Blue, *Salmon P. Chase*, p. 126.
251 "adhesion of the . . . own State Convention": SPC to AL, misdated as May 17, 1860, Lincoln Papers.
251 Lincoln responded graciously: AL to SPC, May 26, 1860, in *CW*, IV, p. 53.
252 "While the victory . . . most profoundly": Schurz, *Reminiscences*, Vol. II, pp. 186–87.
252 "melancholy ceremony": *Daily Ohio Statesman*, Columbus, Ohio, May 19, 1860.
252 "As for me . . . I have ever known": EB to Horace Greeley, quoted in Hollister, *Life of Schuyler Colfax*, p. 148.
252 "Some of my friends . . . border slave states": Entry of May 19, 1860, in *The Diary of Edward Bates, 1859–1866*, pp. 129, 130–31.
253 Some claim . . . Others maintain: See Conkling, "How Mr. Lincoln Received the News," *Transactions* (1909), p. 65; Tarbell, *The Life of Abraham Lincoln*, Vol. I, p. 358; *Illinois State Register*, February 13, 1903.
253 "Mr. Lincoln . . . you are nominated": quoted in Tarbell, *The Life of Abraham Lincoln*, Vol. I, p. 358
253 office of the *Illinois State Journal*: Charles S. Zane interview, 1865–1866, in *HI*, p. 492; *Press and Tribune*, Chicago, May 22, 1860.
253 he "looked at it . . . all around": *Chicago Journal* correspondent, quoted in *Cincinnati Daily Commercial*, May 25, 1860.
253 "I knew . . . second ballot": AL, quoted in Donald, *Lincoln*, p. 250.
253 "My friends . . . at last had come": quoted in Tarbell, *The Life of Abraham Lincoln*, Vol. I, p. 358.
253 "the hearty western" . . . rotunda of the Capitol: "Ecarte" [John Hay], *Providence [R.I.] Journal*, May 26, 1860, reprinted in *Lincoln's Journalist: John Hay's Anonymous Writings for the Press, 1860–1864*, ed. Michael Burlingame (Carbondale and Edwardsville: Southern Illinois University Press, 1998), p. 1.
253 "the signal for immense . . . a great party": *Missouri Republican*, May 20, 1860.
253 "the fact of . . . of Lincoln": Halstead, *Three Against Lincoln*, p. 176.
253 "The leader of . . . against a leader": T. S. Verdi, "The Assassination of the Sewards," *The Republic* 1 (July 1873), pp. 289–90.
254 Some have pointed to luck . . . held in Chicago: See Fehrenbacher, *Prelude to Greatness*, p. 5; Alexander McClure, quoted in Taylor, *William Henry Seward*, p. 10.
254 "Had the Convention . . . nominated": Koerner, *Memoirs of Gustave Koerner*, Vol. II, p. 80.
254 Lincoln's team in Chicago played the game: Potter, *The Impending Crisis, 1848–1861*, pp. 427–28; Stampp, "The Republican National Convention of 1860," in Stampp, *The Imperiled Union*, pp. 155, 157–58.

254 Lincoln was the best prepared: Fehrenbacher, *Prelude to Greatness*, p. 2.
255 speeches possessed unmatched . . . moral strength: Miller, *Lincoln's Virtues*, pp. 397–401.
255 "his avoidance of extremes . . . off its balance": *Press and Tribune*, Chicago, May 16, 1860.
255 "comparatively unknown": Verdi, "The Assassination of the Sewards," *The Republic* (1873), p. 290.
255 "give no offence . . . their first love": AL to Samuel Galloway, March 24, 1860, in *CW*, IV, p. 34.
255 he had not made enemies: *Illinois State Journal*, Springfield, Ill., March 23, 1860.
256 "an ambition . . . overindulgence": Fehrenbacher, *Prelude to Greatness*, p. 161.

CHAPTER 9: "A MAN KNOWS HIS OWN NAME"

Page

257 "was received . . . so we adjourned": Entry for May 18, 1860, Charles Francis Adams diary, reel 75.
257 journals . . . "Abraham": *NYT*, May 21, 1860.
257 "it is but fair . . . his own name": *NYH*, June 5, 1860.
257 "It seems as if . . . '*Abraham*' ": AL to George Ashmun, June 4, 1860, in *CW*, IV, p. 68.
257 "a third rate Western . . . clumsy jokes": *NYH*, May 19, 1860.
258 "Lincoln is the leanest . . . being ugly": *Houston Telegraph*, quoted in *NYTrib*, June 12, 1860.
258 "After him . . . be President?": *Charleston [S.C.] Mercury*, June 9, 1860, quoted in Emerson David Fite, *The First Presidential Campaign*, (New York: The Macmillan Company, 1911), p. 210.
258 "thrust aside . . . freesoil border-ruffian": *Charleston Mercury*, October 15, 1860.
258 "an illiterate partizan . . . negro equality": *Richmond Enquirer*, May 22, 1860.
258 Democratic National Convention in Charleston: See "The Charleston Convention," chapter 1 in Halstead, *Three Against Lincoln*, pp. 3–10.
258 "in less than sixty . . . of the seceders": Ibid., pp. 84, 87.
258 Baltimore convention: For a full discussion of the Democratic Convention that nominated Douglas, see "The National Democratic Convention at Baltimore," chapter 6 in ibid., pp. 185–264.
259 Breckinridge/Lane; Bell/Everett: For a discussion of the conventions that nominated Breckinridge and Bell, see "Institute Hall ('Seceders') Convention" and "The Constitutional Democratic Convention," respectively, chapters 7 and 2, in ibid., pp. 265–77, 111–17.
259 "The great democratic . . . of their own": Entry for June 23, 1860, Charles Francis Adams diary, reel 75.
259 "the chances were . . . fortunes a turn": AL to Anson G. Henry, July 4, 1860, in *CW*, IV, p. 82.
259 "Mr. Lincoln received . . . the great world": Schurz, *Reminiscences*, Vol. II, pp. 187–88.
260 "the prospects of . . . work with a will": *Autobiography of Thurlow Weed*, ed. Weed, p. 603.
260 apparent to both . . . Lincoln against Douglas: In Pennsylvania, the sole exception, Douglas would finish third to Lincoln and Breckinridge.
260 "Now what difference . . . between them": *Montgomery [Ala.] Daily Mail*, July 6, 1860, quoted in Craven, *The Growth of Southern Nationalism*, p. 342.
260 A Lincoln victory . . . such diverse constituencies: For an analysis of the multifaceted campaign in the North, see Luthin, *The First Lincoln Campaign*, passim; Miller, *Lincoln's Virtues*, pp. 465–67.
261 "*a mere printed circular* . . . not to reply at all": SPC to Lyman Trumbull, November 12, 1860, reel 14, Chase Papers.
261 "much chagrined . . . Mr. Abe Lincoln": *Journal of Commerce*, reprinted in *NYTrib*, June 27, 1860.
261 "Holding myself . . . stand ready": AL to SPC, May 26, 1860, in *CW*, IV, p. 53.
261 "first, that . . . of the people": *NYTrib*, October 25, 1860.
261 Browning called on Bates: Entry for May 31, 1860, in *The Diary of Edward Bates, 1859–1866*, p. 132; Cain, *Lincoln's Attorney General*, p. 115.
261 "declined to take the stump": Entry for May 31, 1860, in *The Diary of Edward Bates, 1859–1866*, p. 132.
261 "probably give offense . . . *Union party*": Entry for September 20, 1860, in ibid., p. 145.
261 "I give my opinion . . . in early life": EB, *Letter of Hon. Edward Bates, of Missouri, Indorsing Mr. Lincoln, and Giving His Reasons for Supporting the Chicago Nominees* (Washington, D.C.: Congressional Globe Office, 1860); EB to O. H. Browning, June 11, 1860, reprinted in "Political: Letter of Judge Bates, pledging his support to the Republican ticket," *NYT*, supplement, June 23, 1860.
262 "His character is . . . firm as Jackson": EB to Wyndham Robertson, November 3, 1860, quoted in Cain, *Lincoln's Attorney General*, p. 120.
262 "The campaign started . . . preside or attend": Procter, *Lincoln and the Convention of 1860*, p. 16.
262 "My personal feelings . . . a public act": CS to WHS, May 20, 1860, reel 59, Seward Papers.
262 "one & only one . . . nomination in '64": George Pomeroy to WHS, May 21, 1860, reel 59, Seward Papers.
262 "the suitable man . . . for mere expediency": William Mellen to FAS, May 21, 1860, reel 59, Seward Papers.
262 considered resigning immediately from the Senate: Van Deusen, *William Henry Seward*, p. 229.
262 "When I went out . . . at every corner": Seward, *Seward at Washington . . . 1846–1861*, pp. 453–54.
263 "give the malignants": Israel Washburn to WHS, May 19, 1860, reel 59, Seward Papers.
263 "in the character . . . response in my heart": WHS to FAS, May 30, 1860, quoted in Seward, *Seward at Washington . . . 1846–1861*, pp. 454–56.
263 "responsibility . . . shorter every day": WHS to home, June 13, 1860, quoted in ibid., p. 458.
263 "You have earned . . . reasonably claim": FAS to WHS, May 30, 1860, reel 114, Seward Papers.
263 "Your services . . . highest success": Charles Francis Adams to WHS, May 22, 1860, reel 59, Seward Papers.

263 "I am content . . . the public interest": WHS to TW, June 26, 1860, quoted in Seward, *Seward at Washington . . . 1846–1861*, p. 459.
264 "was about to take . . . depths of discouragement": Procter, *Lincoln and the Convention of 1860*, p. 16.
264 John Nicolay . . . "life ran down": Helen Nicolay, *Lincoln's Secretary: A Biography of John G. Nicolay* (New York: Longmans, Green & Co., 1949; Westport, Conn.: Greenwood Press, 1971), pp. vii (quote), 27, 34, 36.
264 "He sat down . . . could have desired": *Utica Morning Herald*, reprinted in *NYTrib*, July 9, 1860.
264 "can not only discuss . . . dress a deer-skin": *Missouri Democrat*, reprinted in *NYTrib*, September 29, 1860.
265 "an air of quiet . . . unflinchingly": *Utica Morning Herald*, reprinted in *NYTrib*, July 9, 1860.
265 "Ten thousand inquiries . . . create the necessity": *Press and Tribune*, Chicago, May 23, 1860.
265 "Whatever of awkwardness . . . of society": *New York Evening Post*, reprinted in *Albany Evening Journal*, May 24, 1860.
266 "a very handsome . . . sparkling talker": *Ohio State Journal*, Columbus, Ohio, May 29, 1860.
266 "a Man of the People": *NYTrib*, May 26, 1860, quoted in Nevins, *Ordeal of the Union*. Vol. II: *The Emergence of Lincoln, part II, Prologue to Civil War, 1857–1861*, p. 274.
266 "log-cabin, hard-cider": Samuel Eliot Morison and Henry Steele Commager, *The Growth of the American Republic*, 4th edn. (New York: Oxford University Press, 1930; 1950), p. 556.
266 "It has also afforded . . . be inspired": Ryland Fletcher, quoted in Luthin, *The First Lincoln Campaign*, p. 169.
266 a "nullity . . . a nullity anywhere": Quoted in Tarbell, *The Life of Abraham Lincoln*, Vol. I, p. 365.
266 "here is a stick . . . in 1825": *NYH*, October 20, 1860.
266 "it would be both . . . willingly say": AL to T. Apolion Cheney, August 14, 1860, in *CW*, IV, p. 93.
267 "Your letter . . . I write at all": AL to Leonard Swett, May 30, 1860, in *CW*, IV, p. 57.
267 "he would like . . . of being lynched": Luthin, *The First Lincoln Campaign*, p. 170.
267 the cohesion of the new Republican Party: Ibid., pp. 21–22.
267 "our adversaries . . . to the charge": AL to Abraham Jonas, July 21, 1860, in *CW*, IV, p. 86.
267 this election would not be determined . . . carefully addressed in the Republican Party platform: Luthin, *The First Lincoln Campaign*, pp. 13 (quote), 148–53.
268 an entourage: Seward, *Seward at Washington . . . 1846–1861*, p. 461; Van Deusen, *William Henry Seward*, pp. 232–33.
268 "cannons . . . 'Wide Awakes' ": Seward, *Seward at Washington . . . 1846–1861*, p. 461; Oldroyd, *Lincoln's Campaign*, pp. 104–07.
268 "Viewed from . . . in wild cheerings": "Springfield Correspondence, 9 August 1860," in Hay, *Lincoln's Journalist*, p. 6.
268 the "Chloroformers": Luthin, *The First Lincoln Campaign*, p. 174.
268 "procession of young men . . . carts and wagons": Entry for September 8, 1860, Charles Francis Adams diary, reel 75.
268 "All of this reminded . . . a gaping crowd": Ibid.
268 In St. Paul, Minnesota . . . steps of the Capitol: *Press and Tribune*, Chicago, September 24, 1860.
269 "without repetition . . . of the auditors": Fite, *The First Presidential Campaign*, p. 213.
269 "the whole population . . . Well, I ought to": Supplement to *NYT*, September 29, 1860.
269 "where, when . . . 'this tobacco question' ": Charles Francis Adams, Jr., *Charles Francis Adams, 1835–1915: An Autobiography, with a Memorial Address Delivered November 17, 1915, by Henry Cabot Lodge* (Boston and New York: Houghton Mifflin, 1916), pp. 61–62.
269 "integrity . . . grandest & highest": Israel Washburn, Jr., to WHS, November 14, 1860, reel 60, Seward Papers.
269 "I am sure . . . taken a-back by": Richard Blatchford to FAS, October 3, 1860, reel 60, Seward Papers.
270 "marveled more & more . . . by any American": CS to FAS, October 10, 1860, reel 60, Seward Papers.
270 "Yes Henry is . . . Is that the word": FAS to CS, September 5, 1860, reel 20, Sumner Papers.
270 "There was a rush . . . Seward was seated": *NYH*, October 2, 1860.
270 "was a revelation . . . out of place": Adams, Jr., *Charles Francis Adams, 1835–1915*, pp. 61, 64 (quote).
270 "Twelve years ago . . . believed that it would be": *NYH*, October 2, 1860.
270 Lincoln asked . . . "it already existed": King, *Lincoln's Manager*, p. 157.
270 Seward readily agreed . . . intercourse with the South: *NYT*, September 27, 1860; Van Deusen, *William Henry Seward*, p. 233.
270 "noisy throng . . . approaching greatness": Adams, Jr., *Charles Francis Adams, 1835–1915*, pp. 67–68.
271 "Remembering that Peter . . . I will not": AL to Lyman Trumbull, June 5, 1860, in *CW*, IV, p. 71.
271 a humorous fictional dialogue: AL, "Dialogue between Stephen A. Douglas and John C. Breckinridge," September 29, 1860, in ibid., pp. 123–24.
271 "I give the leave . . . in any respect": AL to William D. Kelley, October 13, 1860, in ibid., p. 127.
271 "for your face . . . like whiskers": Grace Bedell to AL, October 15, 1860, in ibid., p. 130.
271 "As to the whiskers . . . begin it now?": AL to Grace Bedell, October 19, 1860, in ibid., p. 129.
271 "Election news . . . heir apparent": "Springfield Correspondence, 7 January 1861," in Hay, *Lincoln's Journalist*, p. 17.
271 biased . . . prospects in each state: AL to John Pettit, September 14, 1860, in *CW*, IV, p. 115.
271 "the dry, and irksome . . . monster meetings": AL to Henry Wilson, September 1, 1860, in ibid., p. 109.
271 Schurz's "excellent plan . . . than yourself": AL to Carl Schurz, June 18, 1860, in ibid., p. 78.
272 He urged Caleb Smith . . . an Indiana victory: AL to Caleb Smith, [July 23], 1860, in ibid., pp. 87–88.
272 "Ascertain . . . commit me to nothing": AL, "Instructions for John G. Nicolay," [c. July 16, 1860], in ibid., p. 83.

272 "Before this reaches . . . into the news-papers": AL to Simon Cameron, August 6, 1860, in ibid., p. 91.
272 Cameron replied . . . writings: Simon Cameron to AL, August 1, 1860, Lincoln Papers.
272 "I am slow . . . present & future only": AL to John M. Pomeroy, August 31, 1860, in *CW*, IV, p. 103.
272 "Write Mr. Casey . . . in that matter": AL to Leonard Swett, July 16, 1860, in ibid., p. 84.
272 "After all . . . Sebastopol we must take": John Z. Goodrich, quoted in Luthin, *The First Lincoln Campaign*, p. 205.
273 "such a result . . . must not allow it": AL to Hannibal Hamlin, September 4, 1860, in *CW*, IV, p. 110.
273 "intimating that Douglas . . . Please write me": AL to James F. Simmons, August 17, 1860, in ibid., p. 97.
273 "tomorrow is . . . of the Country": David Davis, quoted in King, *Lincoln's Manager*, p. 158.
273 "he was trying . . . the presidential Election": Ward Hill Lamon to AL, October 10, 1860, Lincoln Papers.
273 "We are all in . . . be the next Pres't": David Davis to Sarah Davis, October 12, 1860, Davis Papers, ALPLM.
273 "I never was better . . . any trouble": David Davis to Sarah Davis, October 15, 1860, Davis Papers, ALPLM.
273 With pride . . . "have the trial": MTL to Hannah Shearer, October 20, 1860, in Turner and Turner, *Mary Todd Lincoln*, p. 66.
274 Douglas had been barnstorming . . . to the South: Johannsen, *Stephen A. Douglas*, pp. 778–81, 786–97 (quote p. 781).
274 "the first presidential . . . in person": Paul F. Boller, Jr., *Presidential Campaigns* (New York and Oxford: Oxford University Press, 1984), p. 101.
274 "Mr. Lincoln is the next . . . I will go South": Stephen A. Douglas, quoted in Johannsen, *Stephen A. Douglas*, pp. 797–98.
274 "finest hour": Nevins, *Ordeal of the Union*. Vol. II: *The Emergence of Lincoln, part II, Prologue to Civil War, 1857–1861*, p. 290.
274 "I believe there is . . . must be inaugurated": Stephen A. Douglas, quoted in Johannsen, *Stephen A. Douglas*, p. 800.
274 "The cardinal error . . . danger of secession": Nevins, *Ordeal of the Union*. Vol. II: *The Emergence of Lincoln, part II, Prologue to Civil War, 1857–1861*, p. 305.
274 "we all dwelt in a fool's Paradise": Adams, Jr., *Charles Francis Adams, 1835–1915*, p. 69.
274 "a sort of political . . . frighten the North": Donn Piatt, *Memories of the Men Who Saved the Union* (New York and Chicago: Belford, Clarke & Co., 1887), p. 30.
274 "people of the South . . . of the government": AL to John B. Fry, August 15, 1860, in *CW*, IV, p. 95.
274 "the cry of disunion . . . 'sway Northern sentiment' ": Nashville *Union and American*, November 11, 1860, quoted and paraphrased in Craven, *The Growth of Southern Nationalism*, pp. 352–53.
275 shrugged . . . belligerent politicians: *Press and Tribune*, Chicago, October 3, 1860.
275 "they cry out . . . Nobody!": WHS, "Political Equality the National Idea, Saint Paul, September 18, 1860," in *Works of William H. Seward*, Vol. IV, p. 344.
275 "misrepresentations . . . triumph of our party": FB, et al., to AL, October 31, 1860, Lincoln Papers.
275 Even John Breckinridge . . . splitting up the Union: Craven, *The Growth of Southern Nationalism*, p. 341.
275 "I have a good deal of news . . . it *may* be delusive": AL to John Pettit, September 14, 1860, in *CW*, IV, p. 115.
275 "there will be the most . . . great adroitness": AL to TW, August 17, 1860, in ibid., pp. 97–98.
276 "Can you afford . . . finish the work": TW to WHS, October 25, 1860, reel 60, Seward Papers.
276 "the whole audience . . . tumultuous cheering": *NYTrib*, November 3, 1860.
276 "to stir whatever . . . the populace": *NYTrib*, November 10, 1860.
276 "was chatting . . . than the Presidency": Samuel R. Weed, "Hearing the Returns with Mr. Lincoln," *New York Times Magazine*, February 14, 1932, p. 8.
276 "the candidate . . . for his own electors": William H. Herndon and Jesse W. Weik, *Herndon's Lincoln: The True Story of a Great Life*, Vol. III (Springfield, Ill.: Herndon's Lincoln Publishing Co., 1888), p. 467.
276 "who welcomed him . . . the Court room": [JGN to TB?], November 6, 1860, container 2, Nicolay Papers.
276 wild "burst of enthusiasm": *NYTrib*, November 10, 1860.
276 "He said he had . . . read to the crowd": *Missouri Democrat*, reprinted in *Cincinnati Daily Commercial*, November 9, 1860.
277 "seemed to understand . . . with previous elections": Weed, "Hearing the Returns with Mr. Lincoln," *NYT Magazine*, p. 8.
277 gathered at the telegraph office: *Missouri Democrat*, reprinted in *Cincinnati Daily Commercial*, November 9, 1860.
277 "The news would come . . . any hurry to hear it": Weed, "Hearing the Returns with Mr. Lincoln," *NYT Magazine*, p. 9.
277 "We have made steady . . . victory has been won": Simeon Draper, quoted in ibid.
277 "Uncle Abe . . . I know it": Lyman Trumbull, quoted in ibid.
277 "Not too fast . . . may not be over yet": Ibid.
277 a "victory" supper: Oates, *With Malice Toward None*, p. 206.
277 "Don't wait . . . before 10 o'clock": TW, quoted in Luthin, *The First Lincoln Campaign*, p. 218.
278 "a very happy man . . . such circumstances?": AL, quoted by Henry C. Bowen, *Recollections*, p. 31, reprinted in Whipple, *The Story-Life of Lincoln*, p. 345.
278 "Mary . . . *we are elected!*": Henry C. Bowen, "Recollections of Abraham Lincoln," *The Independent*, April 4, 1895, p. 4.

CHAPTER 10: "AN INTENSIFIED CROSSWORD PUZZLE"

Page

279 "The excitement . . . was upon him": GW to Isaac N. Arnold, November 27, 1872, folder 1, Isaac Newton Arnold Papers, Chicago Historical Society.

279 the citizens of Springfield . . . to their homes: William E. Baringer, *A House Dividing: Lincoln as President Elect* (Springfield, Ill.: Abraham Lincoln Association, 1945), p. 6.

280 "I began at once . . . the burden": Entry for August 15, 1862, *Diary of Gideon Welles: Secretary of the Navy Under Lincoln and Johnson.* Vol. I: *1861–March 30, 1864,* ed. Howard K. Beale (New York: W. W. Norton, 1960), p. 82.

280 "into its usual quietness": JGN to TB, November 11, 1860, container 2, Nicolay Papers.

280 "This was on . . . finally selected": Entry for August 15, 1862, *Welles diary,* Vol. I (1960 edn.), p. 82.

280 On a blank card . . . a former Whig: Enclosure in Kinsley S. Bingham, Solomon Foot, and Zachariah Chandler to AL, January 21, 1861, Lincoln Papers; Donald, *Lincoln,* pp. 261–62.

280 "the mad scramble": Harry J. Carman and Reinhard H. Luthin, *Lincoln and the Patronage* (New York: Columbia University Press, 1943; Gloucester, Mass.: Peter Smith, 1964), p. 3.

280 "muddy boots . . . often ringing laughter": Henry Villard, *Lincoln on the Eve of '61: A Journalist's Story,* ed. Harold G. and Oswald Garrison Villard (New York: A. A. Knopf, 1941; Westport, Conn.: Greenwood Press, 1974), pp. 15, 13.

280 "showed remarkable tact . . . always perfect": Henry Villard, *Memoirs of Henry Villard, Journalist and Financier, 1835–1900.* Vol. I: *1835–1862* (Boston and New York: Houghton Mifflin, 1904; New York: Da Capo Press, 1969), pp. 142, 143.

281 Lincoln's penchant for telling stories: *New York Daily News,* reprinted in *Daily Ohio Statesman,* Columbus, Ohio, November 20, 1860.

281 "helped many times . . . disappointments": Villard, *Memoirs of Henry Villard,* Vol. I, p. 147.

281 "he is the very . . . general disposition": Villard, *Lincoln on the Eve of '61,* pp. 39–40.

281 John Hay: William Roscoe Thayer, *The Life and Letters of John Hay,* Vol. I (Boston and New York: Houghton Mifflin, 1915), pp. 19, 48–49, 52–53, 68–69, 74, 82, 87; Villard, *Memoirs of Henry Villard,* Vol. I, p. 141.

281 For Mary . . . exciting time: Baker, *Mary Todd Lincoln,* p. 165.

281 "Is that the old woman": Villard, *Lincoln on the Eve of '61,* p. 20.

281 he asked Hannibal Hamlin . . . to meet him in Chicago: AL to Hannibal Hamlin, November 8, 1860, in *CW,* IV, p. 136.

281 he invited his old friend: AL to Joshua F. Speed, November 19, 1860, in ibid., p. 141.

282 "was so full of good humor . . . with laughter": Charles Eugene Hamlin, *The Life and Times of Hannibal Hamlin.* Vol. II. American History and Culture in the Nineteenth Century series (Cambridge, Mass.: Riverside Press, 1899; Port Washington, N.Y., and London: Kennikat Press, 1971), p. 367.

282 biographical information on Hamlin: See William A. Robinson, "Hamlin, Hannibal," in *Dictionary of American Biography,* Vol. IV, ed. Allen Johnson and Dumas Malone (New York: Charles Scribner's Sons, 1931; 1960), pp. 196–99; H. Draper Hunt, *Hannibal Hamlin of Maine: Lincoln's First Vice-President* (Syracuse, N.Y.: Syracuse University Press, 1969).

282 two men began . . . of both Adams and Welles: Hamlin, *The Life and Times of Hannibal Hamlin,* Vol. II, pp. 368–70 (quotes p. 368).

282 "threw himself . . . can afford to take": Joshua F. Speed interview, [1865–1866], in *HI,* p. 475.

282 Mary had a splendid time: *NYH,* November 23 and 24, 1860.

283 "an intensified crossword . . . to harmonize": Helen Nicolay, "Lincoln's Cabinet," *Abraham Lincoln Quarterly* 5 (March 1949), p. 258.

283 "in view of . . . influence": JGN memorandum, December 15, 1860, container 2, Nicolay Papers.

283 Seward never questioned: Miller, *Lincoln's Virtues,* p. 12.

283 "*Of course* . . . any other person": Charles Francis Adams to WHS, November 11, 1860, reel 60, Seward Papers.

283 "You will be offered . . . in the Presidency": Simon Cameron to WHS, November 13, 1860, reel 60, Seward Papers.

283 The Whig Party had provided: Hendrick, *Lincoln's War Cabinet,* p. 79.

283 Thurlow Weed invited Lincoln . . . Lincoln wisely declined: Entry of December 3, 1865, *Welles diary,* Vol. II, pp. 388–89; Hendrick, *Lincoln's War Cabinet,* pp. 93–94.

284 "if obnoxious men . . . otherwise have": JGN to [TB?], November 16, 1860, container 2, Nicolay Papers.

284 he directed Hamlin . . . Lincoln's instructions: Hannibal Hamlin to AL, December 4, 1860, Lincoln Papers.

284 In reply to Hamlin . . . "at once": AL to Hannibal Hamlin, December 8, 1860, in *CW,* IV, p. 147.

284 Hamlin caught up . . . contained the formal invitation: Hamlin, *The Life and Times of Hannibal Hamlin,* Vol. II, p. 372 (quote); "Alphabetical List of Senators and Representatives, with Their Residences in Washington," in William H. Boyd, *Boyd's Washington and Georgetown Directory* (Washington, D.C.: Taylor & Maury, 1860), p. 230.

284 "trembled . . . nervous": Entry for December 3, 1865, *Welles diary,* Vol. II, p. 389.

284 "With your permission . . . fit to be made": AL to WHS, December 8, 1860, in *CW,* IV, p. 148.

285 "pale with excitement . . . practicable moment": Hamlin, *The Life and Times of Hannibal Hamlin,* Vol. II, pp. 372–73.

285 "a little time . . . under existing circumstances": WHS to AL, December 13, 1860, Lincoln Papers.

285 Bates in Springfield: Entry for December 15, 1860, in *Lincoln Day by Day,* Vol. II, p. 301; Cain, *Lincoln's Attorney General,* p. 122.

285 he encountered John Nicolay . . . "genial and easy": JGN memorandum, December 15, 1860, container 2, Nicolay Papers.
285 Bates walked over . . . the afternoon together: Entry for December 16, 1860, in *The Diary of Edward Bates, 1859–1866*, p. 164 (quote); JGN memorandum, December 15, 1860, container 2, Nicolay Papers.
285 "from the time . . . its complete success": Entry for December 16, 1860, in *The Diary of Edward Bates, 1859–1866*, p. 164.
286 "should offer . . . the Attorney Generalship": JGN memorandum, December 15, 1860, container 2, Nicolay Papers.
286 "peace and order" . . . under President Fillmore: Entry for December 16, 1860, in *The Diary of Edward Bates, 1859–1866*, p. 165.
286 "everybody expects . . . family to ridicule": Entry for October 13, 1860, in ibid., p. 153.
286 "in trouble and danger . . . of his country": JGN memorandum, December 15, 1860, container 2, Nicolay Papers.
286 "a good effect . . . border slave States": EB to AL, December 18, 1860, Lincoln Papers.
286 "Let a little . . . which Department": AL to EB, December 18, 1860, in *CW*, IV, p. 154.
287 "we all feel . . . way in our power": Leonard Swett to TW, November 26, 1860, reprinted in Barnes, *Memoir of Thurlow Weed*, p. 301.
287 "Mr. Lincoln . . . his administration": Swett to TW, December 10, 1860, reprinted in ibid., pp. 301–02.
287 "present unsettled . . . a few days ago": WHS to AL, December 16, 1860, Lincoln Papers.
287 Weed arrived in Springfield: Entry for December 20, 1860, *Lincoln Day by Day*, Vol. II, p. 302.
287 uncovered . . . "the rising sun!": Newspaper clipping, Rochester, N.Y., Weed Papers.
287 "took to each other . . . of a nation": Swett to TW, reprinted in Barnes, *Memoir of Thurlow Weed*, pp. 294–95.
287 conversation between Weed and Lincoln: *Autobiography of Thurlow Weed*, ed. Weed, pp. 606–11; Swett, quoted in Barnes, *Memoir of Thurlow Weed*, pp. 293–94; see also *Chicago Tribune*, July 14, 1878.
287 "made strong opposition": Swett to TW, reprinted in Barnes, *Memoir of Thurlow Weed*, p. 294.
287 "more than any one . . . to Mr. Seward": GW to Isaac N. Arnold, November 27, 1872, folder 1, Isaac Newton Arnold Papers, Chicago Historical Society, Chicago, Ill.
288 Far better than Welles: Entry for December 27, 1860, Charles Francis Adams diary, reel 76; *NYTrib*, June 25, 1877.
288 disingenuously claimed . . . "unfit personally": Swett to TW, reprinted in Barnes, *Memoir of Thurlow Weed*, p. 294.
288 Hamlin preferred: Hamlin, *The Life and Times of Hannibal Hamlin*, Vol. II, p. 375.
288 Lincoln claimed . . . "and not theirs": Entry for August 15, 1862, *Welles diary*, Vol. I (1960 edn.), p. 82.
288 "an attractive figure-head . . . secretary of the navy": *Autobiography of Thurlow Weed*, ed. Weed, p. 611.
288 "Has he been . . . Blair, Sr.?": Ibid., p. 607.
288 regret his selection . . . "he would appoint him": Swett to TW, reprinted in Barnes, *Memoir of Thurlow Weed*, p. 294.
288 "You seem to forget . . . and ballasted": *Autobiography of Thurlow Weed*, ed. Weed, p. 610.
289 "capable in the . . . for himself": TW in *Albany Evening Journal*, quoted in Van Deusen, *Thurlow Weed*, p. 261.
289 "In one aspect . . . in the other": TW to WHS, December 25, 1860, reel 60, Seward Papers.
289 he had imagined . . . "for him but acceptance": Entry for December 27, 1860, Charles Francis Adams diary, reel 76.
289 "after due reflection . . . to accept": WHS to AL, December 28, 1860, Lincoln Papers.
289 "I have advised . . . freedom and my country": WHS to FAS, December 1860, quoted in Seward, *Seward at Washington . . . 1846–1861*, p. 487.
290 "In these troublous . . . here at once": AL to SPC, December 31, 1860, in *CW*, IV, p. 168.
290 "they should be placed . . . been your friends": Swett to AL, May 20, 1860, Davis Papers, ALPLM.
290 "from very strong and unexpected quarters": AL to Hannibal Hamlin, November 27, 1860, in *CW*, IV, p. 145.
290 Cameron to Springfield: Carman and Luthin, *Lincoln and the Patronage*, p. 25.
290 "The unexpected arrival" . . . unsavory reputation: Villard, *Lincoln on the Eve of '61*, pp. 45–46 (quotes p. 45).
290 reached the Chenery House: Entry for December 30, 1860, *Lincoln Day by Day*, Vol. II, p. 304.
290 "Shall I have the honor . . . to call here?": Simon Cameron to AL, December 30, 1860, Lincoln Papers.
290 conversation between Lincoln and Cameron: Carman and Luthin, *Lincoln and the Patronage*, pp. 25–26.
291 "an exuberant school boy": Erwin Stanley Bradley, *Simon Cameron, Lincoln's Secretary of War: A Political Biography* (Philadelphia: University of Pennsylvania Press, 1966), p. 168.
291 "There is an odor . . . such an appointment": Lyman Trumbull to AL, December 31, 1860, Lincoln Papers.
291 "Since seeing you . . . tendered you": AL to Simon Cameron, January 3, 1861, in *CW*, IV, pp. 169–70.
291 "travel-stained . . . from Columbus": Niven, *Salmon P. Chase*, p. 222 (quote); entry for January 4, 1861, *Lincoln Day by Day*, Vol. II, p. 3.
291 meeting between Lincoln and Chase . . . "offer it to you": Schuckers, *The Life and Public Services of Salmon Portland Chase*, p. 201.
291 "I frankly said . . . could give": SPC to George Opdyke, January 9, 1861, reel 14, Chase Papers.
292 "without hesitation . . . the advice of friends": SPC to George Opdyke, January 9, 1861, reel 14, Chase Papers.
292 Chase attended Sunday church: Entry for January 6, 1861, *Lincoln Day by Day: A Chronology, 1809–1865*. Vol. III: *1861–1865*, ed. Earl Schenck Miers (Washington, D.C.: Lincoln Sesquicentennial Commission, 1960; Dayton, Ohio: Morningside, 1991), p. 4.
292 Lincoln meets with Koerner and Judd: Entry for January 6, 1861, ibid., pp. 3–4.
292 "I am in a quandary . . . at the convention": Koerner, *Memoirs of Gustave Koerner*, Vol. II, p. 114.
292 "It seems to me . . . brought to co-operate": AL to Lyman Trumbull, January 7, 1861, in *CW*, IV, p. 171.

292 "under great anxiety . . . I consistently can": AL to Simon Cameron, January 13, 1861, in ibid., p. 174.
292 "were entirely free & unreserved": SPC to James S. Pike, January 10, 1861, reel 14, Chase Papers.
293 "What is done . . . to Springfield": SPC to Hiram Barney, January 8, 1861, reel 14, Chase Papers.
293 had convinced Lincoln . . . official offers: Oates, *With Malice Toward None*, p. 220.
293 "I think that in allowing . . . and accept it": SPC to Elizabeth Ellicott Pike, January 27, 1861, reel 14, Chase Papers.
293 "a snowballing process": Elbert B. Smith, *The Presidency of James Buchanan* (Lawrence: University Press of Kansas, 1975), p. 138.
293 "desired by all . . . of the multitude": *Charleston Courier*, quoted in *Richmond Enquirer*, November 16, 1860.
293 the election of a . . . the John Brown raid: Smith, *The Presidency of James Buchanan*, pp. 129–32.
294 The bachelor president . . . "let out from school": Sara Pryor, *Reminiscences of Peace and War*, rev. and enlarged edn. (New York: The Macmillan Company, 1904; New York: Grosset & Dunlap, 1905; 1908), pp. 110–11 (quotes p. 111).
294 "looked stunned . . . of his chair": Entry for December 20, 1860, in E. B. Long, *The Civil War Day by Day: An Almanac, 1861–1865* (Garden City, N.Y.: Doubleday, 1971), p. 13.
294 "both the authority . . . integrity": [JGN to TB?], November 15, 1860, container 2, Nicolay Papers.
294 "indefatigable . . . authorities, etc.": Villard, *Lincoln on the Eve of '61*, p. 37.
294 willing to reduce . . . "a period of years": AL, quoted in Helm, *The True Story of Mary*, p. 161.
294 "a position towards . . . for his election": Koerner, *Memoirs of Gustave Koerner*, Vol. II, p. 105.
294 He was determined to stand . . . impact on the South: Donald, *Lincoln*, p. 260.
294 "I could say nothing . . . clamor all the louder": AL to Nathaniel P. Paschall, November 16, 1860, in *CW*, IV, pp. 139–40.
295 "each and all of the States . . . any administration": AL, "Passage Written for Lyman Trumbull's Speech at Springfield, Illinois," November 20, 1860, in ibid., p. 141.
295 "On the contrary . . . war against them": AL to Henry J. Raymond, November 28, 1860, in ibid., p. 146.
295 "has eyes . . . does not hear": AL, quoted in Oates, *With Malice Toward None*, p. 213.
295 "blaze of passion . . . offended deity": William Smedes to Henry J. Raymond, December 8, 1860, enclosed in Raymond to AL, December 14, 1860, Lincoln Papers.
295 "What a very mad-man . . . forgery out and out": AL to Henry J. Raymond, December 18, 1860, in *CW*, IV, p. 156.
296 the "Great Secession Winter": See Henry Adams, *The Great Secession Winter of 1860–61 and Other Essays*, ed. George Hochfield (New York: Sagamore Press, 1958).
296 "no compromise . . . any time hereafter": AL to Lyman Trumbull, December 10, 1860, in *CW*, IV, pp. 149–50.
296 "fugitive slaves . . . amongst us": AL to WHS, February 1, 1861, in ibid., p. 183.
296 "the Constitution should" . . . Fugitive Slave Law be repealed: Footnote to AL, "Resolutions Drawn up for Republican Members of Senate Committee of Thirteen," [December 20, 1860], in ibid., p. 157n.
296 Seward agreed . . . John Crittenden: WHS to AL, December 26, 1860, Lincoln Papers.
297 The Crittenden Compromise: Potter, *The Impending Crisis, 1848–1861*, pp. 531–32.
297 "the slightest . . . Loyalty stronger": WHS to AL, December 26, 1860, Lincoln Papers.
297 three federal forts . . . all three were in its domain: Entry for December 22, 1860, in Long, *The Civil War Day by Day*, p. 14.
297 three commissioners . . . Buchanan administration: Thomas and Hyman, *Stanton*, p. 95.
297 "From the first . . . the federal government": JGN to TB, December 30, 1860, container 2, Nicolay Papers.
297 "to surrender . . . hang him!": JGN to [TB?], December 22, 1860, container 2, Nicolay Papers.
297 "to either *hold* . . . may require": AL to Elihu B. Washburne, December 21, 1860, in *CW*, IV, p. 159.
297 "vying" . . . bolster Buchanan's will: Thomas and Hyman, *Stanton*, pp. 91, 93 (quote).
297 Anderson preempted . . . Castle Pinckney: Entries for December 26 and 27, 1860, in Long, *The Civil War Day by Day*, pp. 15–16.
298 Buchanan agreed . . . and headed north: Entries for January 2, 5, 8, and 9, 1861, in Long, *The Civil War Day by Day*, pp. 21–24; entries for January 4 and 5, 1860, *Lincoln Day by Day*, Vol. III, p. 3.
298 "a feverish excitement": WHS to AL, December 28, 1860, Lincoln Papers.
298 Edwin Stanton . . . "traitors and spies": Edwin L. Stanton, quoted in George C. Gorham, *Life and Public Services of Edwin M. Stanton*, Vol. I (2 vols., Boston and New York: Houghton Mifflin and The Riverside Press, 1899), p. 168.
298 If Maryland and Virginia . . ."& the navy": Stephen H. Phillips to Horace Gray, January 31, 1861, Papers of Horace Gray, Manuscript Division, Library of Congress.
298 "*be made to believe* . . . this danger": EMS to SPC, January 23, 1861, reel 14, Chase Papers.
298 "came to a momentous . . . for him to turn": Thomas and Hyman, *Stanton*, pp. 98 (first quote), 99 (second quote), 100.
298 Watson would call . . . "discussed and settled": Henry Wilson, "Jeremiah S. Black and Edwin M. Stanton," *Atlantic Monthly* 26 (October 1870), p. 465.
299 "At length I have gotten . . . prudence is omitted": WHS to AL, December 29, 1860, Lincoln Papers.
299 "treason is all around and amongst us": WHS to FAS, December 29, 1860, quoted in Seward, *Seward at Washington . . . 1846–1861*, p. 488.
299 "abettors near the President": WHS to TW, December 29, 1860, quoted in ibid., p. 487.
299 Stanton secretly spread word: Thomas and Hyman, *Stanton*, pp. 108, 110, 111; Henry Wilson, "Edwin M. Stanton," *Atlantic Monthly* 25 (February 1870), p. 237.
299 "By early disclosure . . . enemies of their country": Henry L. Dawes, "Washington the Winter Before the War," *Atlantic Monthly* 72 (August 1893), p. 163.

299 Stanton invited Sumner to his office: Thomas and Hyman, *Stanton*, p. 111; Wilson, "Jeremiah S. Black and Edwin M. Stanton," *Atlantic Monthly* (1870), p. 466.
299 "found and read . . . place of deposit": Dawes, "Washington the Winter Before the War," *Atlantic Monthly* (1893), p. 163.
299 "held the key to all discontent": "Two Manuscripts of Gideon Welles," ed. Muriel Bernitt, *New England Quarterly* XI (September 1938), p. 589.
299 "came to be regarded . . . Republican party": Wilson, "Jeremiah S. Black and Edwin M. Stanton," *Atlantic Monthly* (1870), p. 465.
299 "By common consent . . . ruler of the country": Adams, *The Great Secession Winter*, p. 22.
300 "Never in the history . . . from Lincoln himself": *Chicago Tribune*, January 17, 1861.
300 "The families of nearly" . . . Jefferson Davis: *NYTrib*, January 19, 1861.
300 "No man was . . . his every word": *Boston Atlas and Bee*, reprinted *Cincinnati Commercial*, January 20, 1861.
300 "to set forth . . . destruction would involve": *NYT*, January 14, 1861.
300 of "perpetual civil war . . . everything is lost": WHS, January 12, 1861, *Congressional Globe*, 36th Cong., 2nd sess., p. 342.
300 "difficult to restrain . . . his handkerchief": *Boston Atlas and Bee*, reprinted *Cincinnati Commercial*, January 20, 1861.
300 "to meet prejudice . . . shall have ended": WHS, January 12, 1861, *Congressional Globe*, 36th Cong., 2nd sess., pp. 343–44.
301 five Southern senators: See farewell remarks of Senators Yulee, Mallory, Clay, Fitzpatrick, and Davis, January 21, 1861, *Congressional Globe*, 36th Cong., 2nd sess., pp. 484–87; entry for January 21, 1861, in Long, *The Civil War Day by Day*, pp. 28–29.
301 "inexpressibly sad": William C. Davis, *Jefferson Davis: The Man and His Hour* (New York: HarperCollins, 1991), pp. 295–96 (quote p. 296).
301 "in a state . . . on despair": *NYT*, January 23, 1861.
301 "I am sure . . . wish you well": Farewell remarks of Jefferson Davis, January 21, 1861, *Congressional Globe*, 36th Cong., 2nd sess., p. 487.
301 Seward himself had visited . . . Democrats and Republicans: Davis, *Jefferson Davis*, p. 261.
301 "Your man outtalked . . . but I didn't": Ishbel Ross, *First Lady of the South: The Life of Mrs. Jefferson Davis* (New York: Harper & Bros., 1958), p. 85.
301 "Mrs Jef asked me . . . *bonds* between us": EBL to SPL, December 17, 1860, in ed. Laas, *Wartime Washington*, p. 18.
301 packed up their belongings . . . "ended in Washington": Margaret Leech, *Reveille in Washington, 1860–1865* (New York: Harper & Row, 1941; New York: Carroll & Graf, 1991), p. 31.
301 His "great wish . . . of the disunionists": Adams, *The Great Secession Winter*, pp. 13, 14.
301 "As an indication . . . of every section": *NYT*, January 14, 1861.
301 "many are sanguine . . . tide of secession": *NYT*, January 16, 1861.
302 "fought . . . took new courage": Adams, *The Great Secession Winter*, p. 23.
302 "Secession has run its course": Entry for February 20, 1861, *Diary of George Templeton Strong. Vol. III: The Civil War, 1860–1865*, ed. Allan Nevins and Milton Halsey Thomas (New York: Macmillan Publishing Co., 1952), p. 100.
302 "for the new Administration . . . to subside": WHS to FAS, January 23, 1861, quoted in Seward, *Seward at Washington . . . 1846–1861*, p. 497.
302 "I deplore S[eward]'s speech": CS to John Jay, January 17, 1861, reel 74, Sumner Papers.
302 "read me his speech . . . no such thing": CS to Samuel Gridley Howe, January 17, 1861, reel 64, Sumner Papers.
302 "seeks to purchase peace . . . years war": Thaddeus Stevens to SPC, February 3, 1861, reel 14, Chase Papers.
302 "What do you think . . . be found wanting": Carl Schurz to his wife, February 4, 1861, in Carl Schurz, *Intimate Letters of Carl Schurz, 1841–1869*, trans. and ed. Joseph Schafer, orig. published as Vol. XXX of the *Collections* of the State Historical Society of Wisconsin, 1928 (New York: Da Capo Press, 1970), pp. 242–43.
303 "There he was . . . left him at Auburn": Adams, Jr., *Charles Francis Adams, 1835–1915*, p. 79.
303 "Eloquent as your speech . . . of your dangers": FAS to WHS, January 19, 1861, reel 14, Seward Papers.
303 "I am not surprised . . . most effective weapons": WHS to FAS, quoted in Seward, *Seward at Washington . . . 1846–1861*, pp. 496–97.
303 "It will do . . . by and with": TW to WHS, January 19, 1861, reel 61, Seward Papers.
303 "In the cars . . . jealousies and hatreds": TW to WHS, February 14, 1861, reel 61, Seward Papers.
304 "Your recent speech . . . over the country": AL to WHS, January 19, 1861, in *CW*, IV, p. 176.
304 "he had heard from . . . on it at present": Entry of February 5, 1861, Charles Francis Adams diary, reel 76.
304 "Seward made all . . . says so openly": Carl Schurz to his wife, February 9, 1861, in Schurz, *Intimate Letters of Carl Schurz, 1841–1869*, p. 247.

CHAPTER 11: "I AM NOW PUBLIC PROPERTY"

Page

305 Mary journeyed to New York: Turner and Turner, *Mary Todd Lincoln*, p. 69; Randall, *Mary Lincoln*, pp. 192–94.
305 "*wild* to see": MTL to Adeline Judd, June 13, 1860, in Turner and Turner, *Mary Todd Lincoln*, p. 64.

305 fêted by merchants . . . "an obsession": Randall, *Mary Lincoln*, p. 192.
305 "Could he . . . disgrace the Nation?": Elizabeth Todd Grimsley, "Six Months in the White House," *Journal of the Illinois State Historical Society* XIX (October 1926–January 1927), p. 44.
305 "outward appearance . . . Presidential father": Entries for January 23–25, 1861, *Lincoln Day by Day*, Vol. III, p. 7; Villard, *Lincoln on the Eve of '61*, p. 55 (quote).
306 decided to rent out their house: Turner and Turner, *Mary Todd Lincoln*, p. 72.
306 "the most brilliant . . . in many years": Entry for February 6, 1861, *Lincoln Day by Day*, Vol. III, p. 9; Villard, *Lincoln on the Eve of '61*, p. 63 (quote).
306 "with a rope around . . . tar and feathers": Villard, *Lincoln on the Eve of '61*, pp. 52–53.
306 he sought places to isolate himself: WHH, quoted in Miller, *Lincoln's Virtues*, p. 442; Villard, *Lincoln on the Eve of '61*, pp. 57–58.
306 "unusually grave . . . old and faithful friends": Villard, *Lincoln on the Eve of '61*, p. 64.
306 farewell to his beloved stepmother . . . father's grave: Ibid., pp. 55–56.
306 "If I live . . . nothing had ever happened": AL, quoted in Donald, *Lincoln*, p. 272.
306 packed his own trunk . . . "Washington, D.C.": Weik, *The Real Lincoln*, p. 307.
307 "His face was pale . . . a single word": Villard, *Lincoln on the Eve of '61*, p. 71.
307 "My friends . . . an affectionate farewell": AL, "Farewell Address at Springfield, Illinois [A. Version]," February 11, 1861, in *CW*, IV, p. 190.
307 "As he turned . . . the silent gathering": *NYH*, February 12, 1861.
307 the luxurious presidential car . . . president-elect: Randall, *Mary Lincoln*, p. 202.
307 "sat alone and depressed": Villard, *Lincoln on the Eve of '61*, p. 73.
307 "forsaken . . . hilarious good spirits": "Indianapolis Correspondence, 11 February 1861," in Hay, *Lincoln's Journalist*, p. 24.
307 Jefferson Davis was beginning: Entries for February 11 and 18, 1861, in Long, *The Civil War Day by Day*, pp. 35–36, 38–39; Davis, *Jefferson Davis*, pp. 304–07; *The Papers of Jefferson Davis*. Vol. VII: *1861*, ed. Lynda Lasswell Crist and Mary Seaton Dix (Baton Rouge and London: Louisiana State University Press, 1992), p. 46.
307 Lincoln's spirits began to revive . . . thirty-four guns: Villard, *Lincoln on the Eve of '61*, pp. 76, 77.
307 "the cheers" . . . before leaving Springfield: "Indianapolis Correspondence, 11 February 1861," in Hay, *Lincoln's Journalist*, pp. 25 (quote), 27.
307 a direct, powerful talk . . . "free-love arrangement": AL, "Speech from the Balcony of the Bates House at Indianapolis, Indiana," February 11, 1861, in *CW*, IV, p. 195.
308 "shaken off . . . tragedy would have been": "Cincinnati Correspondence, 12 February 1861," in Hay, *Lincoln's Journalist*, p. 28.
308 fêted in the state Capitol . . . his election official: Entry for February 13, 1861, *Lincoln Day by Day*, Vol. III, p. 13.
308 "The votes have been . . . was no enemy": FWS to Anna (Wharton) Seward, February 14, 1861, reel 116, Seward Papers.
308 "have passed the 13th . . . people have chosen": WHS to home, quoted in Seward, *Seward at Washington . . . 1846–1861*, p. 505.
308 "full evening dress" . . . lavish military ball: Entry for February 13, 1861, *Lincoln Day by Day*, Vol. III, p. 13.
308 he danced with Chase's lovely daughter: This story was told to the author by a tour guide at the Ohio State House during a visit to Columbus, Ohio, in 1998.
309 "Mrs. Lincoln was piqued . . . at Washington": "Kate Chase in 1893," *Star* clipping, KCS vertical file, DWP.
309 Never comfortable with extemporaneous speech: Harold Holzer, "Avoid Saying 'Foolish Things': The Legacy of Lincoln's Impromptu Oratory," in *"We Cannot Escape History": Lincoln and the Last Best Hope of Earth*, ed. James M. McPherson (Urbana: University of Illinois Press, 1995), pp. 105–21.
309 "there is really . . . will come to an end": AL, "Speech at Pittsburgh, Pennsylvania," February 15, 1861, in *CW*, IV, p. 211.
309 "he should hardly . . . did not want to": AL, "Remarks at Ashtabula, Ohio," February 16, 1861, in ibid, p. 218.
309 he kissed Grace Bedell: Entry for February 16, 1861, *Lincoln Day by Day*, Vol. III, p. 14.
309 "a continuous carnival . . . grand popular ovation": "Indianapolis Correspondence, 11 February 1861," in Hay, *Lincoln's Journalist*, p. 23.
309 Every glimpse of Mary: Entry for February 19, 1861, *Lincoln Day by Day*, Vol. III, p. 18.
310 "are rapidly reducing . . . frivolous and uncertain": Entries for February 16 and 20, 1861, Charles Francis Adams diary, reel 76.
310 "observed the utmost . . . his administration": Nicolay, *A Short Life of Abraham Lincoln*, p. 170.
310 "the man does not . . . the foot down firmly": AL, "Address to the New Jersey General Assembly at Trenton, New Jersey," February 21, 1861, in *CW*, IV, p. 237.
310 "lifted his foot" . . . continue his remarks: "Philadelphia Correspondence, 21 February 1861," in Hay, *Lincoln's Journalist*, p. 40.
310 "consent to . . . Union itself was made": AL, "Reply to Mayor Fernando Wood at New York City," February 20, 1861, in *CW*, IV, p. 233.
310 "never had a feeling . . . to surrender it": AL, "Speech in Independence Hall, Philadelphia, Pennsylvania," February 22, 1861, in ibid., p. 240.
310 the Baltimore plot: See Isaac H. [*sic*] Arnold, "Plot to Assassinate Abraham Lincoln," *Harper's New Monthly Magazine* 37 (June 1868), pp. 123–28.
310 "This . . . in the afternoon": Ward Hill Lamon, *Recollections of Abraham Lincoln, 1847–1865*, ed. Dorothy Lamon Teillard (n.p.: A. C. McClurg & Co., 1895; 1911; Lincoln, Nebr., and London: University of Nebraska Press, 1994), p. 39.

311 Fred was in the Senate gallery . . . " 'let you know in the morning' ": Seward, *Seward at Washington . . . 1846–1861*, pp. 509–10.
311 Pinkerton insisted . . . in the afternoon as scheduled: Turner and Turner, *Mary Todd Lincoln*, p. 78.
311 "side-tracked . . . Capitol came in sight": Lamon, *Recollections of Abraham Lincoln*, pp. 40, 45.
311 had "crept into Washington": EMS, quoted in Helen Nicolay, *Our Capital on the Potomac* (New York and London: Century Co., 1924), p. 358.
311 A scurrilous rumor spread . . . a long military cloak: Thomas, *Abraham Lincoln*, p. 244.
312 "It's to be hoped . . . on his Administration": Entry for February 23, 1861, *Diary of George Templeton Strong*, Vol. III, p. 102.
312 "Genl Jackson . . . where he left": MB to AL, December 8, 1860, Lincoln Papers.
312 had rented a private house: Lamon, *Recollections of Abraham Lincoln*, p. 34; Leech, *Reveille in Washington*, p. 36.
312 "now public property . . . he is inaugurated": TW, quoted in Lamon, *Recollections of Abraham Lincoln*, p. 34.
312 "The truth is . . . have access to me": Ibid., p. 35.
312 "the President-elect . . . met him at the depot": Seward, *Seward at Washington . . . 1846–1861*, p. 511.
312 "much out of breath . . . arrival of the train": "Seward and Lincoln: The Washington Depot Episode," *University of Rochester Library Bulletin* (Spring 1965), p. 33.
312 "a virtuoso performance": Daniel W. Crofts, "Secession Winter: William Henry Seward and the Decision for War," *New York History* 65 (July 1984), p. 248.
313 breakfasted together . . . *"pâté de foie gras"*: Leech, *Reveille in Washington*, p. 8.
313 "tall awkward Irishman . . . loud & unrefined": Harriet Lane to unknown recipient, February 24, 1861, reel 3, Papers of James Buchanan and Harriet Lane Johnston, Manuscript Division, Library of Congress.
313 Seward shepherded Lincoln . . . conversation with Scott: *Star*, February 23 and 25, 1861.
313 Lincoln had promised Weed and Seward: Crofts, "Secession Winter," *New York History* (1984), p. 248.
313 "*living* position in the South": AL to WHS, January 12, 1861, in *CW*, IV, p. 173.
313 "to grieve . . . in hostility": WHS to AL, January 15, 1861, Lincoln Papers.
313 he had met with a delegation . . . he reached Washington: Baringer, *A House Dividing*, pp. 289–90 (quote p. 289); James Millikin to Simon Cameron, February 22, 1861, in *Concerning Mr. Lincoln: In Which Abraham Lincoln is Pictured as he Appeared to Letter Writers of His Time*, comp. Harry E. Pratt (Springfield, Ill.: Abraham Lincoln Association, 1944), pp. 57–60; Titian J. Coffey to Simon Cameron, February 22, 1861, in ibid., pp. 60–63.
314 Lincoln rested . . . his old adversary: Entry for February 23, 1861, *Lincoln Day by Day*, Vol. III, p. 21; Sandburg, *Abraham Lincoln: The War Years*, Vol. I, p. 90; *Star*, February 25, 1861.
314 "The Blairs . . . they undertake": AL, quoted in "[9 December 1863, Wednesday]," in Hay, *Inside Lincoln's White House*, p. 123.
314 Blairs had been appalled . . . aggression from the South: FPB to AL, January 14, 1861, Lincoln Papers.
314 "that one Southern man . . . to despise": MB to Gustavus V. Fox, January 31, 1861, reprinted in *Confidential Correspondence of Gustavus Vasa Fox, Assistant Secretary of the Navy, 1861–1865*, Vol. I, ed. Robert Means Thompson and Richard Wainwright, orig. published as Vols. IX–X of the *Publications* of the Naval History Society, 1920 (Freeport, N.Y.: Books for Libraries Press, 1972), pp. 4–5.
314 "In your cabinet . . . for the succession": FPB to AL, January 14, 1861, Lincoln Papers.
314 "four carriages . . . considerable swearing": *Star*, Washington, D.C., February 25, 1861.
315 Seward's home for a dinner: Entry for February 23, 1861, *Lincoln Day by Day*, Vol. III, p. 21; Van Deusen, *William Henry Seward*, pp. 265–68.
315 members of the Peace Convention: Entry for February 23, 1861, *Lincoln Day by Day*, Vol. III, p. 21.
315 "to scoff . . . facility of expression": Lucius E. Chittenden, *Recollections of Lincoln and His Administration* (New York: Harper & Bros., 1891), pp. 71, 72.
315 Chase stiffly assumed: Niven, *Salmon P. Chase*, p. 236.
315 "had some apt . . . his name": Chittenden, *Recollections of Lincoln*, p. 72.
315 "He has been both . . . misfortune": William Rives and Thomas Ruffin, both quoted in ibid., p. 77.
316 "clear and blustering . . . with mighty power": Entry for February 24, 1861, Charles Francis Adams diary, reel 76.
316 "Governor Seward . . . you are familiar": Seward, *Reminiscences of a War-Time Statesman and Diplomat*, p. 147.
316 Seward and Lincoln made an informal visit: Entry for February 25, 1861, *Lincoln Day by Day*, Vol. III, p. 22.
316 "affected *nonchalance* . . . plain English": *NYT*, February 27, 1861.
316 "face has not yet . . . of the multitude": *Star*, February 26, 1861.
316 "without a precedent . . . proprieties of his position": *NYT*, February 27, 1861.
316 "I had partly . . . against you in malice": AL to Schuyler Colfax, March 8, 1861, in *CW*, IV, p. 278.
316 opposition to Norman Judd; offered ministry post in Berlin: See King, *Lincoln's Manager*, pp. 170–72.
317 "*Judd* . . . borne inspection": MTL to David Davis, January 17, 1861, in Turner and Turner, *Mary Todd Lincoln*, p. 71.
317 "in an agony . . . in February": Niven, *Gideon Welles*, p. 321.
317 "It is by no means . . . not go at all": GW to Edgar T. Welles, February 27, 1861, reel 18, Welles Papers.
317 "I desire to see you here forthwith": Hannibal Hamlin to GW, February 28, 1861, quoted in Niven, *Gideon Welles*, p. 321.
317 In his hurry to catch the train . . . the navy portfolio: Niven, *Gideon Welles*, pp. 321–22.
317 "The struggle for Cabinet . . . hourly": *Star*, March 1, 1861.
317 conflict over Chase and Seward: Niven, *Salmon P. Chase*, p. 237.
317 Seward sent a note to Lincoln: Entry for March 2, 1861, *Lincoln Day by Day*, Vol. III, p. 23.

317 "I can't afford . . . the first trick": John G. Nicolay and John Hay, *Abraham Lincoln: A History*, Vol. III (New York: Century Co., 1917), p. 371.
317 "It is the subject . . . the same direction": AL to WHS, March 4, 1861, in *CW*, IV, p. 273.
318 "The President . . . the country to chance": WHS to FAS, March 8, 1861, quoted in Seward, *Seward at Washington . . . 1846–1861*, p. 518.
318 Lincoln sent Chase's nomination . . . to the Senate: Entries for March 3, 5, and 6, 1861, *Lincoln Day by Day*, Vol. III, pp. 24, 26; Niven, *Salmon P. Chase*, p. 234.
318 "Ever conscious . . . of protocol": Niven, *Salmon P. Chase*, p. 238.
318 "referred to the . . . finally yielded": SPC to Trowbridge, quoted in Schuckers, *The Life and Public Services of Salmon Portland Chase*, p. 207.
318 "The construction of . . . only by experience": *The States and Union*, Washington, D.C., February 26, 1861.
318 Lincoln's "first decision . . . been nominated": "Campaign of 1860 & Journey to Washington," container 9, Nicolay Papers.
319 James Buchanan . . . "deepened party divisions": Allan Nevins, *Ordeal of the Union. Vol. II: The Emergence of Lincoln, part I: Douglas, Buchanan, and Party Chaos, 1857–1859*, new introduction by James M. McPherson (New York: 1978; New York: Collier Books, Macmillan Publishing Co., 1992), p. 67.
319 "he must risk . . . dangers of rebellion": "Campaign of 1860 & Journey to Washington," container 9, Nicolay Papers.
319 asked Lincoln why . . . "of their services": Joseph Medill, quoted in H. I. Cleveland, "Booming the First American President: A Talk with Abraham Lincoln's Friend, the Late Joseph Medill," *Saturday Evening Post* 172, August 5, 1899, p. 85.
319 For further analysis of the making of the cabinet, see Phillip Shaw Paludan, *The Presidency of Abraham Lincoln* (n.p.: University Press of Kansas, 1994), pp. 21–45.

CHAPTER 12: "MYSTIC CHORDS OF MEMORY"

Page

323 Mary the night before the inaugural: Helm, *The True Story of Mary*, p. 168.
323 strangers swarming . . . streets below: *Star*, March 4, 1861.
323 "Lincoln often resorted . . . or argument": JGN, "Some Incidents in Lincoln's Journey from Springfield to Washington," in Nicolay, *An Oral History of Abraham Lincoln*, p. 107.
324 out of four documents: Herndon and Weik, *Herndon's Life of Lincoln*, p. 386.
324 "such a crowd . . . about him": Orville H. Browning, quoted in Nicolay, *An Oral History of Abraham Lincoln*, p. 6.
324 Browning focused on one imprudent passage: WHS to AL, February 24, 1861, quoted in Nicolay and Hay, *Abraham Lincoln*, Vol. III, p. 322.
324 "threat, or menace . . . palpably in the wrong": Orville H. Browning to AL, February 17, 1861, Lincoln Papers.
324 "strong and conclusive": WHS to AL, February 24, 1861, quoted in Nicolay and Hay, *Abraham Lincoln*, Vol. III, p. 321.
325 "bound by duty . . . shift his position": AL, "First Inaugural Address—First Edition and Revisions," January 1861, in *CW*, IV, p. 250.
325 "exclusive and defiant . . . negro equality": Entry for May 19, 1860, in *The Diary of Edward Bates, 1859–1866*, p. 129.
325 "give such advantages . . . exercise of power": WHS to AL, February 24, 1861, quoted in Nicolay and Hay, *Abraham Lincoln*, Vol. III, pp. 320, 321.
325 "treasonable" . . . would only "aggravate the dispute": AL, "First Inaugural Address—First Edition and Revisions," January 1861, in *CW*, IV, pp. 253 n32, 257 n67, 260, 260 n85.
326 "to the effect . . . and irrevocable": AL, "First Inaugural Address—Final Text," March 4, 1861, in ibid., p. 270.
326 "With *you* . . . 'or a sword?' ": AL, "First Inaugural Address—First Edition and Revisions," January 1861, in ibid., p. 261.
326 "to meet . . . cheerful confidence": WHS to AL, February 24, 1861, quoted in Nicolay and Hay, *Abraham Lincoln*, Vol. III, p. 321.
326 "I close . . . angel of the nation": WHS revision, in AL, "First Inaugural Address—First Edition and Revisions," January 1861, in *CW*, IV, pp. 261–62 n99.
326 "I am loth . . . angels of our nature": AL, "First Inaugural Address—Final Text," March 4, 1861, in ibid., p. 271.
326 Lincoln read the speech . . . left alone: Randall, *Mary Lincoln*, p. 208.
326 the morning newspapers . . . of his house: Seward, *Seward at Washington . . . 1846–1861*, p. 515.
327 "I have been . . . and the free": L. A. Gobright, *Recollection of Men and Things at Washington, During the Third of a Century* (Philadelphia: Claxton, Remsen & Haffelfinger, 1869), p. 291.
327 "Disappointment! . . . little Illinois lawyer!": Schurz, *Reminiscences*, Vol. II, pp. 221–22.
327 As the clock . . . "Hail to the Chief": Stanley Kimmel, *Mr. Lincoln's Washington* (New York: Coward-McCann, 1957), p. 23; Browne, *The Every-Day Life of Abraham Lincoln*, pp. 402–03.
327 cheering crowds . . . throughout the entire route: Julia Taft Bayne, *Tad Lincoln's Father* (Boston: Little, Brown, 1931), pp. 17–18; "The Diary of a Public Man, part III," *North American Review* 129 (October 1879), p. 382.
327 "A sharp, cracking . . . in the aggregate": *Star*, March 4, 1861.

327 "assume[d] an almost idyllic . . . large rural village": Edna M. Colman, *Seventy-five Years of White House Gossip: From Washington to Lincoln* (Garden City, N.Y.: Doubleday, Page & Co., 1926), pp. 279–81 (first and third quotes attributed by Colman to foreign observer J. G. Kohl).

327 platform seating; Baker . . . introduced the president-elect: *NYT,* March 5, 1861; Grimsley, "Six Months in the White House," *JISHS*, pp. 45–46.

328 Douglas reached over . . . his own lap: "The Diary of a Public Man, part III," *NAR* (1879), p. 383; Grimsley, "Six Months in the White House," *JISHS*, p. 46.

328 outdoor venues of the Western states: *NYT,* March 5, 1861; Leech, *Reveille in Washington*, p. 44.

328 "no purpose . . . better angels of our nature": AL, "First Inaugural Address—Final Text," March 4, 1861, in *CW,* IV, pp. 263–66, 269, 271.

329 "The Mansion . . . dinner prepared": Grimsley, "Six Months in the White House," *JISHS*, p. 46.

329 "If you are as happy . . . this country": James Buchanan, quoted in Sandburg, *Abraham Lincoln: The War Years*, Vol. I, pp. 137–38.

329 hasty unpacking . . . dressed for the Inaugural Ball: Randall, *Mary Lincoln*, p. 209.

329 Inaugural Ball: *NYH*, March 6, 1861; *NYT,* March 6, 1861; Colman, *Seventy-five Years of White House Gossip*, p. 268.

329 "because of . . . in its decoration": Colman, *Seventy-five Years of White House Gossip*, p. 268.

329 Brightened by . . . good deal of space: *NYH*, March 6, 1861.

329 "Dressed all in blue . . . and pearls": Leech, *Reveille in Washington*, p. 46.

329 she danced the quadrille . . . her exhausted husband: *Star,* March 5, 1861; Leech, *Reveille in Washington*, p. 46.

329 "What an inappreciable . . . 5th of March": Entry for March 4, 1861, Fanny Seward diary, Seward Papers.

329 "seven days and seventeen hours": Sandburg, *Abraham Lincoln: The War Years*, Vol. I, p. 140.

330 "grand . . . in every respect": *NYTrib*, March 7, 1861.

330 "convincing . . . manner": *New York Evening Post*, reprinted in *NYTrib*, March 7, 1861.

330 "eminently . . . under the Constitution": *Philadelphia Bulletin*, reprinted in *NYTrib*, March 7, 1861.

330 "the work . . . its contents": *Commercial Advertiser,* N.Y., reprinted in *NYTrib*, March 7, 1861.

330 "wretchedly . . . unstatesmanlike paper": *Hartford Times*, reprinted in *NYTrib*, March 7, 1861.

330 "It is he . . . Civil War": *Atlas and Argus*, Albany, N.Y., quoted in *Albany Evening Journal*, March 5, 1861.

330 "couched in the cool . . . civil war": *Richmond Enquirer,* reprinted in *NYTrib*, March 7, 1861.

330 "might as well . . . inevitable": *Herald*, Wilmington, N.C., quoted in *Star,* March 7, 1861.

330 "won some favorable . . . slave states": Thomas, *Abraham Lincoln*, p. 248.

330 "without getting . . . can stand": WHS to FAS, March 8, 1861, quoted in Seward, *Seward at Washington . . . 1846–1861*, p. 518.

330 "been fully justified . . . my country": Entry for March 4, 1861, Charles Francis Adams diary, reel 76.

330 Radicals . . . considered an appeasing tone: T. Harry Williams, *Lincoln and the Radicals* (Madison: University of Wisconsin Press, 1941), p. 22.

331 Frederick Douglass . . . cruel slaveholders: Frederick Douglass, *Narrative of the Life of Frederick Douglass, an American Slave*, introduction by Houston A. Baker, Jr. (The Anti-Slavery Office, 1845; New York: Penguin Books, 1986), chapters I–X.

331 "it was unlawful . . . rid of thinking!": Ibid., pp. 78 (first quote), 84 (second and third quotes).

331 "no more pervasive . . . in America": Blight, *Frederick Douglass' Civil War,* p. 3.

331 "It has taught . . . the Presidency": *Douglass' Monthly* (December 1860).

331 "no lawful power . . . Pierces and Buchanans": *Douglass' Monthly* (April 1861).

332 White House family quarters: William Seale, *The President's House: A History*, Vol. I (Washington, D.C.: White House Historical Association/National Geographic Society, 1986) pp. 366, 368, 377, 379–80, illustration 41.

332 "the grounds . . . closets": WHS to home, March 16, 1861, quoted in Seward, *Seward at Washington . . . 1846–1861*, p. 530.

332 hundreds of people . . . securing a job: Seward, *Reminiscences of a War-Time Statesman and Diplomat*, p. 147; William O. Stoddard, *Inside the White House in War Times: Memoirs and Reports of Lincoln's Secretary*, ed. Michael Burlingame (Lincoln and London: University of Nebraska Press, 2000), p. 5.

332 "from Edward . . . that he was handsome": Grimsley, "Six Months in the White House," *JISHS*, pp. 47, 48.

332 memorizing railroad timetables . . . "perfect precision": John Hay, "Life in the White House in the Time of Lincoln," *Century* 41 (November 1890), p. 35.

332 Tad . . . "worry of the household": Grimsley, "Six Months in the White House," *JISHS*, pp. 48–49.

332 A speech impediment: Bayne, *Tad Lincoln's Father,* p. 8; Hay, "Life in the White House in the Time of Lincoln," *Century* (1890), p. 35.

332 "a very bad . . . discipline": *NYTrib*, July 17, 1871.

332 The boys harried the staff: Stoddard, *Inside the White House in War Times*, pp. 26–27; *NYTrib*, July 17, 1871; Bayne, *Tad Lincoln's Father,* pp. 102–06.

333 "If there was . . . a good time": Bayne, *Tad Lincoln's Father,* p. 107.

333 Seward had proposed: Grimsley, "Six Months in the White House," *JISHS*, p. 49.

333 "For over two hours . . . at the windows": JGN to TB, March 10, 1861, container 2, Nicolay Papers.

333 "well dressed . . . social courtesy": Entry for March 8, 1861, reel 76, Charles Francis Adams diary.

333 "was voted by . . . ever known here": JGN to TB, March 10, 1861, container 2, Nicolay Papers.

333 "This is certainly . . . she has been here": MTL to Hannah Shearer, March [28, 1861], in Turner and Turner, *Mary Todd Lincoln*, p. 82.

333 "light and capricious" . . . morning schedule: Hay, "Life in the White House in the Time of Lincoln," *Century* (1890), p. 34.

333 white marble fireplace . . . a panorama: Browne, *The Every-Day Life of Abraham Lincoln*, p. 416.
333 description of the Cabinet Room: Seale, *The President's House*, Vol. I, pp. 364, 367; Isaac Arnold, quoted in Browne, *The Every-Day Life of Abraham Lincoln*, p. 416.
334 "the very first . . . in his hands": Entry for July 3, 1861, in Browning, *The Diary of Orville Hickman Browning*, Vol. I, p. 476.
334 "that their provisions . . . their relief": Memorandum, July 3, 1861, quoted in John G. Nicolay, *With Lincoln in the White House: Letters, Memoranda, and Other Writings of John G. Nicolay, 1860–1865*, ed. Michael Burlingame (Carbondale and Edwardsville: Southern Illinois University Press, 2000), p. 47.
334 "I now see . . . surrender": Joseph Holt and Winfield Scott to AL, March 5, 1861, Lincoln Papers.
334 to "reclaim . . . yourselves the aggressors": AL, "First Inaugural Address—First Edition and Revisions," January 1861, in *CW*, IV, p. 254 (first and second quotes); AL, "First Inaugural Address—Final Text," March 4, 1861, in ibid., p. 271 (third and fourth quotes).
334 "to eat or sleep": AL, quoted in Villard, *Memoirs of Henry Villard*, Vol. I, p. 156.
334 "he had literally . . . I must see them": Hay, "Life in the White House in the Time of Lincoln," *Century* (1890), pp. 34, 33.
335 "has no conception . . . security now": Entry for March 10, 1861, Charles Francis Adams diary, reel 76.
335 "owes a higher . . . office-hunters": *NYT*, April 4, 1861.
335 "The President proposes . . . upon him most": WHS to home, March 16, 1861, quoted in Seward, *Seward at Washington . . . 1846–1861*, p. 530.
335 "long-skirted . . . around his waist": Browne, *The Every-Day Life of Abraham Lincoln*, p. 418.
335 his large leather Bible . . . "inaudible music": Bayne, *Tad Lincoln's Father*, pp. 32–33.
335 Lincoln penned a note: AL to Winfield Scott, March 9, 1861, in *CW*, IV, p. 279.
335 Scott's reply . . . "20,000 volunteers": Winfield Scott to AL, March 11, 1861, Lincoln Papers.
335 "was disinclined . . . to be understood": *Welles diary*, Vol. I (1960 edn.), p. 6.
335 "was virtually . . . irresistible force": FPB to MB, March 12, 1861, Lincoln Papers.
335 Fox's ingenious plan: "Result of G.V. Fox's Plan for Reinforcing Fort Sumpter; In His Own Writing," in *Confidential Correspondence of Gustavus Vasa Fox*, pp. 38–39; West, *Gideon Welles*, p. 98.
335 pacing up and down as he spoke: Helen Nicolay, "Lincoln's Cabinet," *Abraham Lincoln Quarterly* 5 (March 1949), p. 274.
336 "Assuming it to be . . . to attempt it?": AL to WHS, March 15, 1861, in *CW*, IV, p. 284.
336 description of the State Department: Charles Lanman, *Bohn's Hand-Book of Washington* (Washington, D.C.: Casimir Bohn, 1856), p. 35; Robert Mills, *Guide to the National Executive Offices and the Capitol of the United States* (Washington, D.C.: Peter Force Printer, 1841), published work 5007, reel 14, *The Papers of Robert Mills, 1781–1855*, ed. Pamela Scott, Scholarly Resources, microfilm edn.
336 Frederick . . . assistant secretary of state: WHS to FAS, March 8, 1861, in Seward, *Seward at Washington . . . 1846–1861*, p. 518.
336 Seward reiterated . . . emphatic negative reply: WHS to AL, March 15, 1861, Lincoln Papers.
336 "If the attempt . . . cannot advise it": SPC to AL, March 16, 1861, Lincoln Papers.
336 "the organization of . . . its experiment": SPC to Alphonso Taft, April 28, 1861, reel 15, Chase Papers.
336 "it seems to me . . . affirmative answer": SPC to AL, March 16, 1861, Lincoln Papers.
336 "to do any act . . . a civil war": Entry for March 16, 1861, in *The Diary of Edward Bates, 1859–1866*, p. 179.
336 "an inevitable . . . the better": Simon Cameron to AL, March 16, 1861, Lincoln Papers.
337 "impression has gone . . . untold disaster": GW to AL, March 15, 1861, Lincoln Papers.
337 "it would not . . . circumstances": Caleb B. Smith to AL, March 16, 1861, Lincoln Papers.
337 "every new conquest . . . those who administer it": MB to AL, March 15, 1861, Lincoln Papers.
337 if he could keep Virginia . . . give up Sumter: Thomas, *Abraham Lincoln*, pp. 251–52; Van Deusen, *William Henry Seward*, p. 278.
337 "utterly ruinous . . . recognition abroad": AL, "Message to Congress in Special Session," July 4, 1861, in *CW*, IV, p. 424.
337 Lincoln sent Fox to talk directly: Nicolay and Hay, *Abraham Lincoln*, Vol. III, p. 389.
337 half-rations . . . until April 15: Ari Hoogenboom, "Gustavus Fox and the Relief of Fort Sumter," *Civil War History* 9 (December 1963), p. 386.
337 Lincoln sent Stephen Hurlbut . . . "a fixed fact": Nicolay and Hay, *Abraham Lincoln*, Vol. III, pp. 390–91 (quote p. 391).
338 "a cypher . . . a humdrum lawyer": Niven, *Salmon P. Chase*, p. 244.
338 "humiliating . . . their respective states": WHS to AL, March 28, 1861, Lincoln Papers.
338 "certainly have . . . show me": SPC to AL, March 28, 1861, Lincoln Papers.
338 "I believe . . . Whig & Democratic element": FPB to SPC, March 26, 1861, reel 14, Chase Papers.
338 cabinet meetings set for Tuesdays and Fridays: Niven, *Salmon P. Chase*, p. 247 (quote); *Welles diary*, Vol. I, (1960 edn.), pp. 7–8.
338 William Russell: Leech, *Reveille in Washington*, p. 51.
338 "a subtle, quick . . . state mysteries": Entry for March 26, 1861, in William Howard Russell, *My Diary North and South* (Boston: T. O. H. P. Burnham, 1863), p. 34.
338 "put out his hand . . . 'the Mississippi' ": Entry for March 27, 1861, in ibid., p. 39.
338 "was already seated . . . agreeable, and sprightly": Ibid., pp. 41–42.
339 "easily . . . or Reynolds": Belden and Belden, *So Fell the Angels*, pp. 5–6.
339 "In reality . . . charm and magnetism": Mrs. Charles Walker, quoted in *Cincinnati Enquirer*, August 1, 1899.
339 "I shall be glad . . . *me* at any time": *Cincinnati Enquirer*, August 1, 1899; Belden and Belden, *So Fell the Angels*, p. 4 (italics from Belden and Belden).

339 "there was a Babel . . . he is famous": Entry for March 28, 1861, in Russell, *My Diary North and South*, pp. 43, 44.
339 "according to recent . . . slave-holding States": Nicolay and Hay, *Abraham Lincoln*, Vol. III, p. 394.
339 "A very oppressive silence . . . not General": MB to GW, May 17, 1873, reel 25, Welles Papers.
340 "timid temporizing . . . you are lost": FPB, Sr., to Martin Van Buren, May 1, 1861, reel 34, Papers of Martin Van Buren, Manuscript Division, Library of Congress.
340 Lincoln was unable to sleep: Nicolay and Hay, *Abraham Lincoln*, Vol. III, p. 395.
340 "of all the trials . . . to survive them": Memorandum, July 3, 1861, quoted in Nicolay, *With Lincoln in the White House*, p. 46.
340 Lincoln presented . . . "for his expedition": Nicolay and Hay, *Abraham Lincoln*, Vol. III, pp. 429–33 (quote p. 433).
340 "would be impossible . . . of time": JGN to TB, March 31, 1861, container 2, Nicolay Papers.
340 "it was finally . . . to go to war": George Harrington, "President Lincoln and His Cabinet: Inside Glimpses," undated, unpublished manuscript, George R. Harrington Papers, Missouri Historical Society, St. Louis, Mo.
341 "a peaceful . . . of the whole north": Frederick L. Roberts to WHS, March 18, 1861, reel 62, Seward Papers.
341 "Unionists . . . *save the country*": Benjamin Ogle Tayloe to WHS, April 3, 1861, reel 63, Seward Papers.
341 "no conception . . . equal to the hour": Entries for March 28 (first quote) and March 31, 1861, Charles Francis Adams diary, reel 76.
341 "two supreme illusions": Frederic Bancroft, "Seward's Proposition of April 1, 1861, For a Foreign War and a Dictatorship," *Harper's New Monthly Magazine* 99 (October 1899), p. 791.
341 Three commissioners . . . resorted to an indirect link: Thomas, *Abraham Lincoln*, pp. 250–51.
341 "would be evacuated . . . next five days": Ellsworth D. Draper and Joshua L. Rosenbloom, "Secession C: Fort Sumter: The Near Fiasco," p. 9, Case Study, Lincoln and Fort Sumter, Kennedy School of Government, Harvard University, 1983, author's collection.
341 "Some thoughts for the President's consideration": WHS to AL, April 1, 1861, Lincoln Papers.
341 "handwriting . . . hands of any clerk": Seward, *Reminiscences of a War-Time Statesman and Diplomat*, p. 149.
342 "We are . . . domestic or foreign": WHS to AL, "Some thoughts for the President's consideration," April 1, 1861, Lincoln Papers.
342 "the symbolism of Federal authority": Draper and Rosenbloom, "Secession C: Fort Sumter," p. 11.
342 under the heading of "For Foreign Nations": Norman B. Ferris, "Lincoln and Seward in Civil War Diplomacy: Their Relationship at the Outset Reexamined," *Journal of the Abraham Lincoln Association* 12 (1991), pp. 25–26.
342 "that there was no . . . the ruling party": WHS, quoted by Rudolf Schleiden, quoted in Richard N. Current, "Comment," *JALA* (1991), p. 45.
342 "whatever policy . . . assume responsibility": WHS to AL, "Some thoughts for the President's consideration," April 1, 1861, Lincoln Papers.
342 "had Mr. Lincoln . . . the whole affair": Nicolay, *A Short Life of Abraham Lincoln*, pp. 186, 187.
342 dashed off a reply . . . to respond in person: Donald, *Lincoln*, p. 290.
342 "without a policy . . . *I* must do it": AL to WHS, April 1, 1861, in *CW*, IV, pp. 316–17.
343 "to put down . . . this thing through": Entry for March 31, 1861, private journal of Montgomery Meigs (copy), container 13, Nicolay Papers.
343 "fit out the *Powhatan* . . . she is fitting out": AL to Andrew H. Foote, April 1, 1861, in *CW*, IV, p. 314.
343 three hundred sailors: Fox to MB, April 17, 1861, in *Confidential Correspondence of Gustavus Vasa Fox*, p. 33; "Result of G.V. Fox's Plan for Reinforcing Fort Sumpter; In His Own Writing," reprinted in ibid., p. 39.
343 assigned the *Powhatan* simultaneously to both Pickens and Sumpter: "Result of G.V. Fox's Plan for Reinforcing Fort Sumpter" p. 40; Fox to his wife [Virginia Woodbury Fox], May 2, 1861, ibid., pp. 42–43.
344 "Your father says . . . put my name?": Seward, *Reminiscences of a War-Time Statesman and Diplomat*, p. 148.
344 "leave New York . . . disposing of your force": *Welles diary*, Vol. I (1960 edn.), pp. 22–23.
344 "I am directed . . . without further notice": Simon Cameron to Robert S. Chew, April 6, 1861, in *CW*, IV, p. 323.
344 Lincoln had devised a means: Don E. Fehrenbacher, "Lincoln's Wartime Leadership: The First Hundred Days," *Journal of the Abraham Lincoln Association* 9 (1987), esp. p. 7.
344 "embarrassed by . . . errors imputed to them": *Welles diary*, Vol. I (1960 edn.), pp. 23–25.
345 Porter had already set sail . . . had priority: Hoogenboom, "Gustavus Fox and the Relief of Fort Sumter," *CWH* (1963), p. 392.
345 Fox reached Charleston . . . futilely searching: Fox to MB, April 17, 1861, in *Confidential Correspondence of Gustavus Vasa Fox*, p. 32.
345 At 3:30 a.m. . . . in one hour: James Chesnut, Jr., and Stephen D. Lee to Robert Anderson, April 12, 1861, enclosure 5 of Robert Anderson to Lorenzo Thomas, April 19, 1861, *OR*, Ser. 1, Vol. I, p. 14.
345 Anderson's small garrison . . . "fighting launches": Fox to MB, April 17, 1861, in *Confidential Correspondence of Gustavus Vasa Fox*, pp. 32–34 (quote p. 33).
345 "the conflagration . . . taken refuge": Abner Doubleday, *Reminiscences of Forts Sumter and Moultrie in 1860–'61* (New York: Harper & Bros., 1876), p. 157.
345 Thirty-four hours after . . . surrendered: Robert Anderson to Simon Cameron, April 18, 1860, *OR*, Ser. 1, Vol. I, p. 12.
345 a dignified fifty-round salute: Entry of April 14, 1861, *Diary of Edmund Ruffin*, Vol. I, ed. William Kauffmann Scarborough (Baton Rouge: Louisiana State University Press, 1972), p. 599; Robert Anderson to Simon Cameron, April 18, 1860, *OR*, Ser. 1, Vol. I, p. 12.

345 only one Union soldier: David S. Heidler and Jeanne T. Heidler, "Fort Sumter, Bombardment of 12–14 April 1861," in *Encyclopedia of the American Civil War: A Political, Social, and Military History*, ed. David S. Heidler and Jeanne T. Heidler (New York and London: W. W. Norton, 2000), p. 760. Another soldier was mortally wounded in the explosion.

345 "it would be . . . of his friend": Hamilton Basso, *Beauregard: The Great Creole* (New York and London: Charles Scribner's Sons, 1933), p. 84.

345 Convinced that . . . "the general public": "Result of G.V. Fox's Plan for Reinforcing Fort Sumpter," in *Confidential Correspondence of Gustavus Vasa Fox*, p. 41.

345 "by an accident . . . justified by the result": AL to Gustavus V. Fox, in *CW*, IV, pp. 350–51.

346 "but beyond . . . no using of force": AL, "First Inaugural Address—Final Text," March 4, 1861, in ibid., p. 266.

346 fatalities: "The Price in Blood: Casualties in the Civil War," www.civilwarhome/casualties.htm., accessed July 2005.

CHAPTER 13: "THE BALL HAS OPENED"

Page

347 "where the great lamps . . . question of disunion": Walt Whitman, *Specimen Days, The Complete Prose Works of Walt Whitman*, Vol. I (New York: G. P. Putnam's Sons, 1902), pp. 28–30.

347 "Our people now . . . is dead": *Daily National Intelligencer*, Washington, D.C., April 15, 1861.

348 "The ball has opened . . . their glasses": *NYT*, April 13, 1861.

348 cabinet session . . . "to invite disaster": Seward, *Reminiscences of a War-Time Statesman and Diplomat*, p. 152.

348 "history tells us . . . lose their heads": WHS, quoted in entry for March 26, 1861, in Russell, *My Diary North and South*, p. 35.

348 set the Fourth of July . . . "by the Executive": Seward, *Reminiscences of a War-Time Statesman and Diplomat*, p. 152.

348 Nicolay made a copy: JGN to TB, April 14, 1861, container 2, Nicolay Papers.

348 stamped the great seal . . . following day: Seward, *Reminiscences of a War-Time Statesman and Diplomat*, p. 152.

348 Lincoln took a carriage ride: JGN to TB, April 14, 1861, container 2, Nicolay Papers.

348 he welcomed his old rival . . . would be dead: Sandburg, *Abraham Lincoln: The War Years*, Vol. I, p. 213; entry for June 3, 1861, in Long, *The Civil War Day by Day*, p. 82.

348 his solid support . . . "maintain the Government": *Daily Morning Chronicle*, Washington, D.C., October 16, 1864.

348 "In this hour . . . treason and traitors": *New York Leader* (first quote) and *Boston Herald* (second quote), reprinted in *NYTrib*, April 15, 1861.

348 "The response . . . by telegraph": Seward, *Reminiscences of a War-Time Statesman and Diplomat*, p. 153.

349 "We begin to look . . . a week ago": Entry for April 15, 1861, *Diary of George Templeton Strong*, Vol. III, pp. 120–21.

349 Seward predicted . . . in sixty days: Carpenter, "A Day with Governor Seward," Seward Papers.

349 "be bloody . . . and ruin": "Washington Correspondence, 16 April 1861," in Hay, *Lincoln's Journalist*, p. 58.

349 "for the wicked . . . Southern States": Governor of Kentucky (Beriah Magoffin), quoted in Seward, *Reminiscences of a War-Time Statesman and Diplomat*, p. 154.

349 Virginia seceded from the Union: Long, *The Civil War Day by Day*, p. 60.

349 "one of the most . . . history": J. G. Randall, *Lincoln the President*. Vol. I: *Springfield to Gettysburg, part I* (New York: Dodd, Mead & Co., 1946–55; New York: Da Capo Press, 1997), p. 357.

349 "We never saw" . . . soon be fifteen: *Daily Picayune*, New Orleans, April 19, 1861, morning edition (first and second quote), afternoon edition (third quote).

350 "the very best . . . in the field": General Winfield Scott, quoted in *The Wartime Papers of R. E. Lee*, ed. Clifford Dowdey and Louis H. Manarin (Boston: Little, Brown, for the Virginia Civil War Commission, 1961), p. 3.

350 Lincoln had designated Blair: Robert E. Lee to Reverdy Johnson, February 25, 1868, in *Wartime Papers of R. E. Lee*, p. 4.

350 "I come to you . . . the Union army?": FPB, quoted in William Ernest Smith, *The Francis Preston Blair Family in Politics*, Vol. II (New York: The Macmillan Company, 1933), p. 17.

350 "as candidly and as courteously": Lee to Johnson, February 25, 1868, in *Wartime Papers of R. E. Lee*, p. 4.

350 "Mr. Blair . . . my native state?": R. E. Lee, quoted in *National Intelligencer*, Washington, D.C., August 9, 1866.

350 Lee called upon old General Scott: Lee to Johnson, February 25, 1868, in *Wartime Papers of R. E. Lee*, p. 4

350 he contacted Scott . . . "be dear to me": Lee to Scott, April 20, 1861, in ibid., pp. 8–9 (quotes p. 9).

350 "Now we are in . . . draw my sword": Lee to Anne Marshall, April 20, 1861, in ibid., pp. 9–10.

350 Lee was designated . . . Virginia state forces: Ibid., pp. 3, 4, 5.

350 Benjamin Hardin Helm: "Helm, Benjamin Hardin (1831–1863)," in Stewart Sifakis, *Who Was Who in the Confederacy* (New York: Facts on File, 1988), p. 125.

350 While conducting business . . . "liking of men": Helm, *The True Story of Mary*, p. 127.

350 "Southern-rights Democrat": Ibid., pp. 128, 183.

350 "Ben, here is . . . your honor bid": *Daily Picayune*, New Orleans, March 14, 1897 (quotes); AL to Simon Cameron, April 16, 1861, in *CW*, IV, p. 335.

351 Helm unable to sleep . . . "hour of his life": *Daily Picayune*, New Orleans, March 14, 1897.

351 a Commission in the Confederate Army: "Helm, Benjamin Hardin," in Sifakis, *Who Was Who in the Confederacy*, p. 125.

351 Seward argued . . . seize vessels: Ivan Musicant, *Divided Waters: The Naval History of the Civil War* (New York: HarperCollins, 1995), pp. 51–52.
351 Welles countered . . . exiting ships: Niven, *Gideon Welles*, p. 356; Musicant, *Divided Waters*, p. 51.
351 The cabinet split down the middle: Niven, *Gideon Welles*, p. 356.
351 formal blockade proclamation: AL, "Proclamation of a Blockade," April 19, 1861, in *CW*, IV, pp. 338–39.
351 Welles and the Navy Department: Robert V. Bruce, *Lincoln and the Tools of War* (Indianapolis and New York: Bobbs-Merrill, 1956), pp. 6, 16; Musicant, *Divided Waters*, pp. 41–43.
352 a wedding celebration: Grimsley, "Six Months in the White House," *JISHS*, p. 51; Bruce, *Lincoln and the Tools of War*, p. 9.
352 "would soon secede . . . Confederacy": Craig L. Symonds, "Buchanan, Franklin," in *Encyclopedia of the American Civil War*, ed. Heidler and Heidler, p. 303.
352 Buchanan resigned . . . "from this date": Bruce, *Lincoln and the Tools of War*, p. 16 (quote); "Buchanan, Franklin (1800–1874)," in Sifakis, *Who Was Who in the Confederacy*, p. 40.
352 the Norfolk Navy Yard: Musicant, *Divided Waters*, pp. 28–29.
352 "extreme uneasiness . . . made by the first": Entry for April 18, 1861, Charles Francis Adams diary, reel 76.
352 "The scene . . . indescribably fearful": *Sun*, Baltimore, Md., April 20, 1861.
352 The enraged crowd . . . knives and revolvers: John G. Nicolay and John Hay, *Abraham Lincoln: A History*, Vol. IV (New York: Century Co., 1917), p. 115 (quote); *Sun*, Baltimore, Md., April 20, 1861.
352 "It's a notable . . . the anniversary": Entry for April 19, 1861, *Diary of George Templeton Strong*, Vol. III, p. 126.
352 "make no point . . . *around* Baltimore": AL to Thomas H. Hicks and George W. Brown, April 20, 1861, in *CW*, IV, p. 340.
352 an angry committee of delegates: Entry for April 22, 1861, in *Lincoln Day by Day*, Vol. III, p. 37.
352 "I must have troops . . . that they must do": AL, "Reply to Baltimore Committee," April 22, 1861, in *CW*, IV, pp. 341–42.
353 "the censorship" . . . bridges surrounding the city: Ben: Perley Poore, *Perley's Reminiscences of Sixty Years in the National Metropolis*, Vol. II (Philadelphia, 1886; New York, AMS Press, 1971), pp. 78–79.
353 "Literally . . . entire isolation": Villard, *Memoirs of Henry Villard*, Vol. I, p. 167.
353 Cameron slept in his office: Leech, *Reveille in Washington*, p. 61.
353 "Here we were . . . to defend it": JGN to TB, April 26, 1861, container 2, Nicolay Papers.
353 "No despatches . . . are prisoners": Entry for April 20, 1861, *Diary of George Templeton Strong*, Vol. III, p. 127.
353 "rebels are at . . . calm & conceal it": Hiram Barney to SPC, April 21, 1861, reel 15, Chase Papers.
354 to accompany Major Robert Anderson . . . with their relieved father: Janet Chase Hoyt, "A Woman's Memories," *NYTrib*, April 5, 1891.
354 These "were terrible days of suspense" . . . let her join him: Entry for May 19, 1861, Fanny Seward diary, Seward Papers.
354 "It is hard . . . life is in danger": FAS to WHS, April [27? 1861], reel 114, Seward Papers.
354 "a day of gloom and doubt": "24 April 1861, Wednesday," in Hay, *Inside Lincoln's White House*, p. 11.
354 staring out the window . . . "Why don't they come!": Nicolay and Hay, *Abraham Lincoln*, Vol. IV, p. 152.
354 "I don't believe . . . Northern realities": "24 April 1861, Wednesday," in Hay, *Inside Lincoln's White House*, p. 11.
354 "to arrest . . . *not* be justifiable": AL to Winfield Scott, April 25, 1861, in *CW*, IV, p. 344.
354 "the first of the redeemed": "1 May 1861, Wednesday," in Hay, *Inside Lincoln's White House*, p. 16.
355 If resistance along . . . "for the public safety": AL to Winfield Scott, April 27, 1861, in *CW*, IV, p. 347.
355 "arrest, and detain . . . to the public safety": AL, "Message to Congress in Special Session," July 4, 1861, in ibid., p. 429.
355 Seward later claimed . . . "further hesitation": Carpenter, "A Day with Governor Seward," Seward Papers.
355 Taney blasted Lincoln: Hon. Sherrill Halbert, "The Suspension of the Writ of Habeas Corpus by President Lincoln," *American Journal of Legal History* 2 (April 1958), pp. 97–100.
355 Bates, though reluctant to oppose Taney: Cain, *Lincoln's Attorney General*, pp. 145, 147.
355 "in a time . . . the insurgents": EB to AL, July 5, 1861, Lincoln Papers.
355 As chief executive . . . "one be violated?": AL, "Message to Congress in Special Session," July 4, 1861, in *CW*, IV, p. 430.
355 "grave threats . . . extravagant to endure": Justice Thurgood Marshall, dissenting opinion in *Skinner v. Railway Labor Executives' Association*, 489 U.S. 602 (1989), text available through Legal Information Institute website, Cornell Law School, www.law.cornell.edu (accessed June 2003).
355 "government will . . . be less liberty": GW to Mary Jane Welles, May 5, 1861 (transcript), reel 19, Welles Papers.
355 "steps and balconies" . . . Mary and her friends watched: *NYT*, May 1, 1861.
355 "go down to Charleston . . . an Illinois yell": "25 April 1861, Thursday," in Hay, *Inside Lincoln's White House*, p. 11.
356 more than eight thousand troops were in Washington: WHS to FAS, April 26, 1861, quoted in Seward, *Seward at Washington . . . 1846–1861*, p. 559.
356 He did not, however, grant her request: FAS to WHS, April [27? 1861], reel 114, Seward Papers.
356 almost completed . . . "at all hours": Anna Wharton Seward to FAS, April 28, 1861, reel 116, Seward Papers.
356 "immense sacrifice . . . awaits the oppressors": FAS to WHS, April [28? 1861], reel 114, Seward Papers.
356 "there would be . . . serenely adjusted": Conversation between WHS and Charles King, reported in entry of May 20, 1861, *Diary of George Templeton Strong*, Vol. III, p. 144.
356 "to disturb as little . . . of the people": Entry of April 15, 1861, in *The Diary of Edward Bates, 1859–1866*, p. 183.
356 a "fatal error . . . of the North": MB to AL, May 16, 1861, Lincoln Papers.
356 "I consider . . . to govern themselves": "7 May, Tuesday," in Hay, *Inside Lincoln's White House*, p. 20.

356 John Stuart Mill . . . "the civilized world": John Stuart Mill, quoted in McPherson, *Battle Cry of Freedom*, p. 550.
357 "the dissolution . . . established in America": The Earl of Shrewsbury, quoted in ibid., p. 551.
357 "It is of infinite . . . the various parts": George Washington, "Farewell Address," September 17, 1796, in *A Compilation of the Messages and Papers of the Presidents*, Vol. I (New York: Bureau of National Literature, Inc., 1897), p. 207.
357 "a mortar battery . . . assassination suspicion": "19 April 1861, Friday," in Hay, *Inside Lincoln's White House*, pp. 2–3.
357 "Thousands of soldiers . . . to feel secure": MTL to Mrs. Samuel H. Melvin, April 27, 1861, in Turner and Turner, *Mary Todd Lincoln*, p. 86.
357 "The intense . . . around the city": Elizabeth Grimsley to Mrs. John T. Stuart, April 29, 1861, quoted in *Concerning Mr. Lincoln*, comp. Pratt, p. 77.
357 Tad boasted . . . from the roof: Bayne, *Tad Lincoln's Father*, pp. 68–69 (quotes p. 68).
358 "between the grey haired . . . plough hardened hands": "20 April 1861, Saturday," in Hay, *Inside Lincoln's White House*, p. 4.
358 "rather pale . . . all 'go ahead' ": Entry for January 13, 1862, *The Diary of Horatio Nelson Taft, 1861–1865*, available through "Washington During the Civil War: The Diary of Horatio Nelson Taft, 1861–1865," American Memory, Library of Congress, http://memory.loc.gov [hereafter Taft diary].
358 "More than once . . . arm of the chair": Bayne, *Tad Lincoln's Father*, pp. 35, 108.
358 Julia was appalled: Ibid., pp. 101, 102–06, 109–10.
358 "the most lovable . . . gentle-mannered": Ibid., p. 8.
358 retreat to his mother's room . . . write verses: Turner and Turner, *Mary Todd Lincoln*, p. 120.
358 "what she wanted when she wanted it": Bayne, *Tad Lincoln's Father*, p. 49.
358 A curious example . . . purple strings!: Ibid., pp. 43–48 (quotes p. 45).
359 brothers and brothers-in-law: Randall, *Mary Lincoln*, p. 294; Ishbel Ross, *The President's Wife: Mary Todd Lincoln, A Biography* (New York: G. P. Putnam's Sons, 1973), p. 144.
359 the White House . . . "unsuccessful hotel": Stoddard, *Inside the White House in War Times*, p. 26.
359 "the family apartments . . . (first President)": Grimsley, "Six Months in the White House," *JISHS*, p. 47.
359 went on a shopping trip: See entries for May 10–22, 1861, in *Lincoln Day by Day*, Vol. III, pp. 41–43.
359 $20,000 allowance to maintain the White House: Seale, *The President's House*, Vol. I, p. 382.
359 state guest room . . . "clusters of grapes": Betty C. Monkman, *The White House: Its Historic Furnishings and First Families* (New York: Abbeville Press, 2000), p. 125.
359 The press exaggerated . . . never even visited: Grimsley, "Six Months in the White House," *JISHS*, pp. 58–59.
359 the bills added up: Entries for May 13, 21, 24, and 29, 1861, in *Lincoln Day by Day*, Vol. III, pp. 41, 43–45.
360 Kate Chase was hard at work . . . to borrow $10,000: Ross, *Proud Kate*, p. 62; SPC to Henry Carrington, April 16, 1861, reel 15, Chase Papers.
360 Chase later complained . . . with the president: Belden and Belden, *So Fell the Angels*, p. 94.
360 "in a single season" . . . William Sprague: William Perrine, "The Dashing Kate Chase and Her Great Ambition," *Ladies' Home Journal* XVIII (June 1901), p. 11.
360 Kate had first met . . . "see the other": Richard Parsons, quoted in *Ohio State Journal*, Columbus, Ohio, August 4, 1899.
361 Sprague would never forget . . . "it was yesterday": William Sprague to KCS, May 27, 1866, William and Catherine Chase Sprague Papers, 1850–1900, MS 79.17, Manuscript Division, Special Collections Department, Brown University Library, Providence, Rhode Island [hereafter Sprague Papers].
361 William Sprague: Peg A. Lamphier, *Kate Chase and William Sprague: Politics and Gender in a Civil War Marriage* (Lincoln: University of Nebraska Press, 2003), pp. 27–28.
361 "I was thrust . . . highest positions": William Sprague, quoted in Lamphier, *Kate Chase and William Sprague*, p. 32.
361 As the largest employer . . . of his own money: "The Rhode Island Spragues," unknown newspaper clipping, December 5, 1883, in KCS vertical file, DWP.
361 "a loan . . . the troops": Belden and Belden, *So Fell the Angels*, p. 42; ninety-six horses, Lamphier, *Kate Chase and William Sprague*, p. 39.
361 On April 29 . . . "movements of the regiment": *Star*, April 29, 1861.
361 physical description of Sprague: Belden and Belden, *So Fell the Angels*, p. 42.
361 "a small . . . wealth and social standing": "26 April 1861, Friday," in Hay, *Inside Lincoln's White House*, p. 12.
362 "When men like . . . such an army": "30 April 1861, Tuesday," in ibid., p. 14.
362 "the first, the only . . . lodgment there": Entry for November 11, 1868, KCS diary, Sprague Papers.
362 "Do you remember . . . such in life": William Sprague to KCS, May 27, 1866, Sprague Papers.
362 "accustomed to . . . be anticipated": Entry for November 11, 1868, KCS diary, Sprague Papers.
362 Nettie Chase told Kate . . . would marry: KCS to Janet Chase Hoyt, September 29, 1861, reel 17, Chase Papers.
362 Elmer Ellsworth: Brian D. McKnight, "Ellsworth, Elmer Ephraim," in *Encyclopedia of the American Civil War*, ed. Heidler and Heidler, p. 647: Turner and Turner, *Mary Todd Lincoln*, p. 92.
362 wrote a personal note of condolence: AL to Ephrain D. and Phoebe Ellsworth, May 25, 1861, in *CW*, IV, pp. 385–86.
363 "quite unable . . . out of my eyes": JGN to TB, May 25, 1861, container 2, Nicolay Papers.
363 Mary was presented . . . packed away: Bayne, *Tad Lincoln's Father*, p. 39.
363 a resolution . . . belligerent status: Entry for May 6, 1861, in Long, *The Civil War Day by Day*, pp. 70–71; Norman A. Graebner, "Northern Diplomacy and European Neutrality," in *Why the North Won the Civil War*, ed.

David Donald (Baton Rouge: Louisiana State University Press, 1960; New York and London: Collier Books, Macmillan Publishing Co., 1962), p. 60.

363 "younger branch . . . is too late": WHS to FAS, May 17, 1861, quoted in Seward, *Seward at Washington . . . 1846–1861*, pp. 575–76.

363 "God damn 'em, I'll give 'em hell": Van Deusen, *William Henry Seward*, p. 298.

363 On May 21 . . . two wars at once: Jay Monaghan, *Diplomat in Carpet Slippers: Abraham Lincoln Deals with Foreign Affairs* (Indianapolis and New York: Bobbs-Merrill, 1945), p. 114; Allen Thorndike Rice, "A Famous Diplomatic Dispatch," *North American Review* 142 (April 1886), pp. 402–11.

363 "surprised and grieved . . . she has a natural claim": AL, "Revision of William H. Seward to Charles Francis Adams," May 21, 1861, in *CW*, IV, pp. 377–78, 379 n14, 380.

364 the basis for a hard-line policy: Todd Anthony Rosa, "Diplomacy, U.S.A." in *Encyclopedia of the American Civil War*, ed. Heidler and Heidler, p. 602.

364 "currency to Southern bonds": WHS to TW, May 23, 1861, quoted in Seward, *Seward at Washington . . . 1846–1861*, p. 576.

364 "the ablest American" . . . his country's position: Rice, "A Famous Diplomatic Dispatch," *NAR* 142 (1886), pp. 402–3, 404 (quote).

364 "It is due to . . . every day": WHS to FAS, May 17, 1861, quoted in Seward, *Seward at Washington . . . 1846–1861*, p. 575.

364 "Executive skill . . . assiduous cooperation": WHS to FAS, June 5, 1861, quoted in ibid., p. 590.

365 "to his chief . . . personal attachment": Nicolay and Hay, *Abraham Lincoln*, Vol. IV, p. 449.

365 "a brilliant assemblage . . . twenty years more": *NYT*, May 22, 1861.

365 forced to rely on government loans: Blue, *Salmon P. Chase*, pp. 143–46.

365 functions . . . belonged to the War Department: Niven, *Salmon P. Chase*, pp. 253–54; Bradley, *Simon Cameron*, pp. 177–78.

365 "the principal charge . . . regiments in Tennessee": SPC to Trowbridge, March 21, 1864, reel 32, Chase Papers.

365 "The President . . . half-consciousness": *NYT*, April 23, 1861, enclosed with SPC to AL, April 25, 1861, Lincoln Papers.

366 "has too much truth in it": SPC to AL, April 25, 1861, Lincoln Papers.

366 "Oh, it was a terrible time . . . no anything": *NYT*, June 3, 1878.

366 weapons in short supply . . . messengers, and watchmen: A. Howard Meneely, *The War Department, 1861: A Study in Mobilization and Administration* (New York: Columbia University Press, 1928), pp. 25–26, 106–11.

366 "I was . . . to be envied": *NYT*, June 3, 1878.

366 "so large . . . without compensation": AL, "To the Senate and House of Representatives," May 26, 1862, in *CW*, V, p. 242.

366 Alexander Cummings: Bradley, *Simon Cameron*, pp. 196–97.

366 "embargo" on . . . "so strict": *NYT*, June 22, 1861.

366 congressmen and senators . . . "President's message": *NYT*, July 4, 1861.

367 Senator Orville Browning . . . "of the Country": Entry for July 3, 1861, in Browning, *The Diary of Orville Hickman Browning*, Vol. I, p. 475.

367 Jefferson had denounced: "From Time to Time: History of the State of the Union," The White House, www.whitehouse.gov/stateoftheunion/history.html (accessed July 2003); "History of the State of the Union," National Archives and Records Administration, http://clinton4.nara.gov/WH/SOTU00/history/address.html (accessed July 2003).

367 had submitted their written messages: Entry for July 5, 1861, in Russell, *My Diary North and South*, p. 388.

367 "give the legal means . . . the government itself": AL, "Message to Congress in Special Session," July 4, 1861, in *CW*, IV, pp. 426, 431–32, 437, 438.

368 "In spite of . . . masses of the people": *NYT*, July 7, 1861.

368 Congress responded . . . patriotic fervor: Nicolay and Hay, *Abraham Lincoln*, Vol. IV, pp. 370, 375–76, 382–83.

368 "No mention is . . . of the rebellion": *Douglass' Monthly* (August 1861).

368 "We have an honest . . . to Seward": *NYT*, July 7, 1861.

368 Benjamin Butler . . . therefore contraband of war: Benjamin F. Butler to Winfield Scott, May 24, 1861, *OR*, Ser. 1, Vol. II, pp. 649–50; Edward L. Pierce, "The Contrabands at Fortress Monroe," *Atlantic Monthly* 8 (November 1861), pp. 627–28.

369 "I will accept . . . resign your commission": Benjamin F. Butler, *Butler's Book: Autobiography and Personal Reminiscences of Major-General Benjamin F. Butler* (Boston: A. M. Thayer & Co., 1892), p. 242.

369 Butler's order . . . a confiscation law: Endorsements by Winfield Scott and Simon Cameron, in Benjamin F. Butler to Winfield Scott, May 24, 1861, *OR*, Ser. 1, Vol. II, p. 652; Simon Cameron to Benjamin F. Butler, May 30, 1861, container 5, Papers of Benjamin F. Butler, Manuscript Division, Library of Congress [hereafter Butler Papers]; John Syrett, "Confiscation Acts (6 August 1861 and 17 July 1862)," in *Encyclopedia of the American Civil War*, ed. Heidler and Heidler, pp. 477–79.

369 "You were right . . . this new doctrine": MB to Benjamin F. Butler, May 29, 1861, container 5, Butler Papers.

369 hundreds of courageous slaves: Pierce, "The Contrabands at Fortress Monroe," *Atlantic Monthly* (1861), pp. 628, 630.

370 Two weeks into . . . not to eliminate slavery: Entry for July 22, 1861, in Long, *The Civil War Day by Day*, p. 100.

370 "sword . . . slavery *must die*": John Lothrop Motley to his wife, June 23, 1861, in *The Correspondence of John Lothrop Motley*, Vol. I, ed. George William Curtis (New York: Harper & Bros., 1889), p. 390.

370 "Forward to Richmond!": *NYTrib*, June 26, 1861.

370 "the immediate movement . . . 20th July": Entry for July 11, 1861, in Browning, *The Diary of Orville Hickman Browning*, Vol. I, p. 479.
370 General Scott hesitated . . . public would diminish: James A. Rawley, *Turning Points of the Civil War* (Lincoln: University of Nebraska Press, 1966), pp. 52–53.
370 McDowell's plan: John G. Nicolay, *The Outbreak of Rebellion. Campaigns of the Civil War*, new introduction by Mark E. Neeley, Jr. (New York: Charles Scribner's Sons, 1881; New York: Da Capo Press, 1995), p. 173.
370 "a terrible . . . ferocious warriors": Entry for August 1861, in Adam Gurowski, *Diary from March 4, 1861 to November 12, 1862*. Burt Franklin: Research & Source Works #229 (Boston, 1862; New York: Burt Franklin, 1968), pp. 78–79.
370 "Foreigners . . . drive them off": EB to James O. Broadhead, July 13, 1861, James Overton Broadhead Papers, Missouri Historical Society, St. Louis, Mo. [hereafter Broadhead Papers, MoSHi].
370 troop strengths: Rawley, *Turning Points of the Civil War*, p. 54.
371 On June 29 . . . approved McDowell's plan: Nicolay, *Outbreak of Rebellion*, p. 173.
371 The Battle of Bull Run: Many battles of the Civil War came to be known by different names within the Union and the Confederacy. The first battle at Manassas Junction, for example, would be known as the Battle of Bull Run in the North and the Battle of Manassas in the South. As James M. McPherson explains, "In each case but one (Shiloh) the Confederates named the battle after the town that served as their base, while the Union forces chose the landmark nearest to the fighting or to their own lines, usually a river or stream." In the case of Shiloh, the Confederates named the battle for a nearby church, McPherson, *Battle Cry of Freedom*, p. 346 n7.
371 "roar of the artillery . . . grew intense": Grimsley, "Six Months in the White House," *JISHS*, p. 65.
371 "stop the *roar* in [her] ears": EBL to SPL, July 21, 1861, in *Wartime Washington*, ed. Laas, p. 65.
371 "an unusually heavy . . . this time to-morrow": Entry for July 21, 1861, in Russell, *My Diary North and South*, p. 449.
371 In the crowded space . . . responsibilities: David Homer Bates, *Lincoln in the Telegraph Office: Recollections of the United States Military Telegraph Corps during the Civil War*, introduction by James A. Rawley (New York: Century Co., 1907; Lincoln and London: University of Nebraska Press, 1995), p. 87.
371 and read aloud . . . "with joy": *NYT*, July 22, 1861 (quote); *NYT*, July 26, 1861.
371 "There is Jackson . . . like a stone wall": Poore, *Perley's Reminiscences*, Vol. II, p. 85.
371 At 3 p.m. . . . fifteen-minute intervals: Entry for July 21, 1861, in *Lincoln Day by Day*, Vol. III, p. 55.
371 The telegraph line . . . Telegraph Corps: Bates, *Lincoln in the Telegraph Office*, p. 88.
371 "a small three-storied" . . . description of headquarters: Entry for July 19, 1861, in Russell, *My Diary North and South*, p. 431.
372 "his confidence . . . President left": JGN to TB, July 21, 1861, container 2, Nicolay Papers.
372 "the Union Army . . . victory": Seward, *Seward at Washington . . . 1846–1861*, p. 598.
372 Bates confided his anxiety: Cain, *Lincoln's Attorney General*, p. 153; entry for July 21, 1861, in *Lincoln Day by Day*, Vol. III, p. 55.
372 "the first time he ever left home": Entry for July 5, 1861, in *The Diary of Edward Bates, 1859–1866*, p. 188.
372 a new intimacy with his president: Cain, *Lincoln's Attorney General*, p. 153.
372 "A sudden swoop . . . behind them": Edmund C. Stedman, *The Battle of Bull Run* (New York: Rudd & Carleton, 1861), p. 32.
372 "never stopped . . . New-York": Janet Chase Hoyt, "A Woman's Memories," *NYTrib*, June 7, 1891.
372 "Army wagons . . . sights and sounds": Stedman, *The Battle of Bull Run*, p. 35.
372 "General McDowell's . . . of the Army": Seward, *Seward at Washington . . . 1846–1861*, p. 598.
372 "a terribly frightened . . . to Gen. Scott's": JGN to TB, July 21, 1861, container 2, Nicolay Papers.
373 "He listened in silence . . . army headquarters": Nicolay and Hay, *Abraham Lincoln*, Vol. IV, pp. 353–54.
373 "Oh what a sad . . . sabbath been": EBL to SPL, July 21, 1861, in *Wartime Washington*, ed. Laas, p. 65.
373 death of James Cameron: "Cameron, James (?–1861)," in Stewart Sifakis, *Who Was Who in the Union* (New York: Facts on File, 1988), p. 63; Nicolay, *Outbreak of Rebellion*, p. 214.
373 "I loved my brother . . . of his duty": Simon Cameron to SPC, July 21, 1861, reel 16, Chase Papers.
373 "Every thing . . . to the field": WHS to family, July 1861, quoted in Seward, *Seward at Washington . . . 1846–1861*, pp. 598–99.
373 the returning soldiers . . . "at this juncture": Grimsley, "Six Months in the White House," *JISHS*, pp. 66–67 (quotes p. 67).
373 Lincoln did not sleep . . . future military policy: Nicolay and Hay, *Abraham Lincoln*, Vol. IV, p. 368.
373 "be constantly drilled" . . . the blockade operative: AL, "Memoranda of Military Policy Suggested by the Bull Run Defeat," July 23, 1861, in *CW*, IV, p. 457.
373 a telegram was also sent: Lorenzo Thomas to George B. McClellan, July 22, 1861, *OR*, Ser. 1, Vol. II, p. 753; entry for July 22, 1861, in *Lincoln Day by Day*, Vol. III, p. 56.
374 devised a strategy . . . East Tennessee: AL, "Memoranda of Military Policy Suggested by the Bull Run Defeat," July 27, 1861, in *CW*, IV, pp. 457–58.
374 "If there were . . . Union out of it": Walt Whitman, *Specimen Days* (Philadelphia: Rees Welch Co., 1882; Philadelphia: David McKay, 1892; Boston: D. R. Godine, 1971), p. 13.
374 "a weak . . . inefficient Cabinet": *NYH*, July 27, 1861.
374 "Two weeks ago . . . a great victory": SPC to William P. Mellen, July 23, 1861, reel 16, Chase Papers.
374 "public censure . . . on Lincoln": Rawley, *Turning Points of the Civil War*, p. 56.
374 "The sun rises, but shines not": Whitman, *Specimen Days* (1971 edn.), p. 12.
374 "Some had neither . . . blankets": Entry for July 22, 1861, in Russell, *My Diary North and South*, p. 467.
374 "awakened in the . . . stand the hurting": Janet Chase Hoyt, "A Woman's Memories," *NYTrib*, June 7, 1891.
374 "The dreadful disaster . . . could be offered": EMS to James Buchanan, July 26, 1861, reprinted in "A Page of

Political Correspondence. Unpublished Letters of Mr. Stanton to Mr. Buchanan," *North American Review* 129 (November 1879), pp. 482–83.

375 "an overweening confidence": Jefferson Davis, *The Rise and Fall of the Confederate Government*, Vol. I (1881; Richmond, Va.: Garrett & Massie, 1938; New York: Da Capo Press, 1990), p. 330.

375 General Johnston observed . . . faraway hospitals: Joseph E. Johnson, quoted in Nicolay, *Outbreak of Rebellion*, p. 211.

375 "Well we fought . . . our men": Nancy Bates to Hester Bates, July 25, 1861, Bates Papers, MoSHi.

375 "very melancholy": Entry of July 28, 1861, in Browning, *The Diary of Orville Hickman Browning*, Vol. I, p. 489.

375 "black despair . . . to [his] country": Horace Greeley to AL, July 29, 1861, Lincoln Papers.

375 He told humorous stories: Browne, *The Every-Day Life of Abraham Lincoln*, pp. 448–49.

375 "discourage all . . . I believe he would do it": William Tecumseh Sherman, *Memoirs of General W. T. Sherman*, (New York: D. Appleton and Company, 1875; New York: Penguin Books, 2000), pp. 175–76.

376 a "renewed patriotism": *NYT*, July 23, 1861.

376 "Let no loyal . . . greater efforts": *Chicago Tribune*, July 23, 1861.

376 Several papers compared: *Chicago Tribune*, July 23, 1861; *NYTrib*, reprinted in *Star*, July 27, 1861.

376 "The spirit of . . . facilities for defence": *NYT*, July 26, 1861.

376 could "take comfort": *Philadelphia Inquirer*, July 25, 1861.

CHAPTER 14: "I DO NOT INTEND TO BE SACRIFICED"

Page

377 "Nothing but a patent . . . at last": James Russell Lowell, "General McClellan's Report (1864)," in *The Writings of James Russell Lowell.* Vol. V: *Political Essays* (Cambridge, Mass.: The Riverside Press, 1871; 1890), pp. 94, 99.

377 when he arrived . . . Army of the Potomac: Entry for July 27, 1861, in Long, *The Civil War Day by Day*, p. 101.

377 Among the Union's . . . the Mexican War: See chapter 1 of Stephen W. Sears, *George B. McClellan: The Young Napoleon* (New York: Ticknor & Fields, 1988).

378 defeated a guerrilla band: Sears, *George B. McClellan*, p. 80.

378 "the man on horseback": Entry for July 27, 1861, in Russell, *My Diary North and South*, p. 480.

378 "a more martial look": Entry for July 1861, in Gurowski, *Diary from March 4, 1861 to November 12, 1862*, p. 76.

378 drunken soldiers . . . troops wander the city: Entry for July 27, 1861, in Russell, *My Diary North and South*, p. 479; *Star*, July 31, 1861.

378 "You have no idea . . . such yelling": GBM to MEM, [September 11, 1861], in *The Civil War Papers of George B. McClellan, Selected Correspondence, 1861–1865*, ed. Stephen W. Sears (New York: Ticknor & Fields, 1989), p. 98.

378 "the great obstacle": GBM to MEM, August 9, 1861, in ibid., 81.

378 "entirely insufficient . . . in our front": GBM to Winfield Scott, August 8, 1861, in ibid., p. 80.

378 Scott was furious . . . opposition forces: Winfield Scott to Simon Cameron, August 9, 1861, Lincoln Papers.

378 It would not be . . . miscalculations: Sears, *George B. McClellan*, pp. 103, 109.

378 discord . . . continued to escalate: GBM to AL, August 10, 1861, in *Civil War Papers of George B. McClellan*, p. 82; GBM to MEM, September 27, 1861, in ibid., pp. 103–04.

378 "concentric pressure": Sears, *George B. McClellan*, p. 98.

378 "crush . . . in one campaign": GBM to MEM, August 2, 1861, in *Civil War Papers of George B. McClellan*, p. 74.

378 "result . . . in my hands": GBM to MEM, August 9, 1861, in ibid., pp. 81–82.

378 "by some strange . . . of the land": GBM to MEM, July 27, 1861, in ibid., p. 70.

378 "the people call . . . country is saved": GBM to MEM, August 9, 1861, in ibid., pp. 81–82.

379 Scott was "a perfect imbecile . . . a *traitor*": GBM to MEM, August 8, 1861, in ibid., p. 81.

379 "eternal jealousy . . . distinction": GBM to MEM, October 6, 1861, in ibid., p. 106.

379 "The remedy . . . small of the back": Winfield Scott to Simon Cameron (copy), October 4, 1861, reel 1, Stanton Papers, DLC.

379 McClellan's headquarters: Entry for September 2, 1861, in Russell, *My Diary North and South*, pp. 520–21; Sears, *George B. McClellan*, p. 100.

379 "smoking . . . writing": Entry for September 2, 1861, in Russell, *My Diary North and South*, p. 520.

379 "I have just been . . . stories to tell": GBM to MEM, October 16, 1861, in *Civil War Papers of George B. McClellan*, p. 107.

379 "together . . . mortals": Entry for November 1861, in Gurowski, *Diary from March 4, 1861 to November 12, 1862*, p. 123.

379 "lying down, very much fatigued": Brigadier Van Vliet, quoted in entry for October 9, 1861, in Russell, *My Diary North and South*, p. 552.

380 magnificent reviews of more than fifty thousand troops: *Frank Leslie's Illustrated Newspaper*, October 5, 1861; JGN to TB, November 21, 1861, container 2, Nicolay Papers.

380 "not a mistake . . . a hitch": GBM to MEM, November 20, 1861, in *Civil War Papers of George B. McClellan*, p. 137.

380 "A long time . . . not mind that": GBM to MEM, October 6, 1861, in ibid., p. 106.

380 "a slave-catching order" . . . their masters: Entry for September 1861, in Gurowski, *Diary from March 4, 1861 to November 12, 1862*, p. 95.

380 "fighting to preserve . . . to do with him": GBM to Samuel L. M. Barlow, November 8, 1861, in *Civil War Papers of George B. McClellan*, p. 128.
380 "some of the greatest . . . of Job": GBM to MEM, October 10, 1861, in ibid., p. 106.
380 "a meddling . . . old woman": GBM to MEM, October 11, 1861, in ibid., pp. 106–07.
380 "an old fool . . . altogether fancy him!": GBM to MEM, October 31, 1861, in ibid., p. 114.
380 a flattering letter . . . promotion to major general: SPC to GBM, July 7, 1861, quoted in Schuckers, *The Life and Public Services of Salmon Portland Chase*, p. 427.
380 engagement at Ball's Bluff: Entry for October 21, 1861, in Long, *The Civil War Day by Day*, p. 129.
380 "a slight demonstration . . . move them": GMB to Charles P. Stone, October 20, 1861, quoted in note 2 of GBM to Stone, October 21, 1861, in *Civil War Papers of George B. McClellan*, p. 109.
380 casualties at Ball's Bluff: "Return of casualties in the Union forces in the engagement at Ball's Bluff, Virginia, October 21, 1861," *OR*, Ser. 1, Vol. V, p. 308.
380 Oliver Wendell Holmes, Jr. . . . home to recover: SPC to KCS, July 28, 1865, reel 35, Chase Papers.
381 "the death . . . a desert": Noah Brooks, "Recollections of Abraham Lincoln," *Harper's New Monthly Magazine* 31 (July 1865), p. 228.
381 "Mr. Lincoln sat" . . . and kissed him: Benjamin Rush Cowen, *Abraham Lincoln: An Appreciation by One Who Knew Him* (Cincinnati, Ohio: Robert Clarke Co., 1909), pp. 29–30.
381 Eckert . . . received word: Bates, *Lincoln in the Telegraph Office*, pp. 95–96.
381 "with bowed head . . . into the street": Charles Carleton Coffin, "Lincoln's First Nomination and His Visit to Richmond in 1865," in *Reminiscences of Abraham Lincoln*, ed. Rice (1909 edn.), p. 176.
381 Mary was similarly distraught: Entry for October 22, 1861, in Russell, *My Diary North and South*, p. 558.
381 Willie and Tad . . . were heartbroken: Helm, *The True Story of Mary*, p. 191.
381 "On the Death of Colonel Edward Baker": *NR*, November 4, 1861.
382 "to care for him . . . his orphan": AL, "Second Inaugural Address," March 4, 1865, in *CW*, VIII, p. 333.
382 "disaster . . . committed": GBM to Division Commanders, Army of the Potomac, October 24, 1861, in *Civil War Papers of George B. McClellan*, p. 111.
382 "The whole thing . . . *directly* to blame": GBM to MEM, October 25, 1861, in ibid., p. 111.
382 the president defended McClellan: Entry for October 26, 1861, in Hay, *Inside Lincoln's White House*, p. 28.
382 unleashed a diatribe . . . to remove Scott: GBM to MEM, October 26, 1861, in *Civil War Papers of George B. McClellan*, p. 112; Sears, *George B. McClellan*, p. 123.
382 "You may have . . . heads to call me": GBM to MEM, October 30, 1861, in *Civil War Papers of George B. McClellan*, p. 112.
382 "long and brilliant . . . deep emotion": AL, "Order Retiring Winfield Scott from Command," November 1, 1861, in *CW*, V, p. 10.
382 Lincoln designated McClellan: AL to GBM, November 1, 1861, in ibid., pp. 9–10.
382 "I saw there . . . his successor": GBM to MEM, November 3, 1861, in *Civil War Papers of George B. McClellan*, pp. 123–24.
382 All the members . . . on his journey: *Star*, November 2, 1861; Charles Winslow Elliott, *Winfield Scott: The Soldier and the Man*. American Military Experience Series (New York: Arno Press, 1979), p. 743.
383 "quite a number of citizens": *NYH*, November 4, 1861.
383 the young Napoleon: Sears, *George B. McClellan*, p. xi.
383 "I do not intend to be sacrificed": GBM to MEM, October 31, 1861, in *Civil War Papers of George B. McClellan*, p. 113.
383 to confront the rebel forces: GBM to Simon Cameron, October 31, 1861, in ibid., pp. 114–19; GBM to MEM, August 16, 1861, in ibid., p. 85.
383 "to dodge . . . Presdt etc.": GBM to MEM, October 31, 1861, in ibid., p. 113.
383 "the *original* . . . his high position": GBM to MEM, November 17, 1861, in ibid., pp. 135–36.
383 "I wish here to record . . . personal dignity": Entry for November 13, 1861, in Hay, *Inside Lincoln's White House*, p. 32.
383 He would hold . . . could be achieved: Henry Ketcham, *The Life of Abraham Lincoln* (New York: A. L. Burt, 1901), p. 291.
383 "A minute passes . . . rebellious consciousness": Stoddard, *Inside the White House in War Times*, p. 63.
384 His "mouth would relax . . . sea of laughter": Grimsley, "Six Months in the White House," *JISHS*, p. 55.
384 "daily drive . . . so much needed": Ibid.
384 soirées in the Blue Room: Turner and Turner, *Mary Todd Lincoln*, pp. 96–97, 98; MTL to Hannah Shearer, October 6, 1861, ibid., p. 108; Baker, *Mary Todd Lincoln*, p. 231.
384 Daniel Sickles . . . "temporary insanity": Thomas and Hyman, *Stanton*, pp. 83–85.
384 Henry Wikoff . . . "and Thackeray": John W. Forney, *Anecdotes of Public Men*, Vol. I (New York: Harper & Bros., 1873; New York: Da Capo Press, 1970), pp. 366–71 (quote p. 367).
384 "My wife . . . never fallen out": AL, quoted in Baker, *Mary Todd Lincoln*, p. 196.
384 When Prince Napoleon . . . visited: Entry for August 3, 1861, in *Lincoln Day by Day*, Vol. III, p. 58.
385 "We only have . . . proper season": MTL to Hannah Shearer, August 1, 1861, in Turner and Turner, *Mary Todd Lincoln*, p. 96.
385 "beautiful dinner . . . predominated": Grimsley, "Six Months in the White House," *JISHS*, p. 70.
385 Mary requested Volume 9: Entry for August 5, 1861, in *Lincoln Day by Day*, Vol. III, p. 59.
385 William Scott: Court-martial of Private William Scott, Co. K, 3rd Vermont Infantry, case file OO-209, Court-Martial Case Files, 1809–1894, entry 15, Records of the Office of the Judge Advocate General (Army), RG 153, DNA; *NYT*, September 10, 1861.

385 As the story was told: See L. E. Chittenden, *Recollections of President Lincoln and His Administration* (New York and London: Harper & Bros., 1901), p. 267.
385 "Think . . . much as he tried to": Grimsley, "Six Months in the White House," *JISHS*, p. 71.
385 Lincoln walked over . . . " 'Lady President' ": George B. McClellan, *McClellan's Own Story* (New York: Charles L. Webster & Co., 1887), p. 91 (quote); entry for September 8, 1861, in *Lincoln Day by Day*, Vol. III, p. 65.
385 "that it was asking . . . 'only one he had' ": Chittenden, *Recollections of President Lincoln* (1901 edn.), p. 273.
385 "the most beautiful . . . my own": MTL to Hannah Shearer, July 11, 1861, Turner and Turner, *Mary Todd Lincoln*, p. 94.
385 drives with the Sewards: See entries for September 1, 3, and 6, 1861, Fanny Seward diary, Seward Papers, for examples of afternoons spent driving with Sewards; FAS to LW, [August 1861], reel 119, Seward Papers.
386 "a plain . . . & the crops": FAS to LW, [July 1861?], reel 119, Seward Papers.
386 "I liked him . . . all over him": Entry for September 1, 1861, Fanny Seward diary, Seward Papers.
386 "*abandon* of . . . climb a rope": *NYT*, June 17, 1861.
386 "With one impulse . . . mouth to mouth": Entry for September 6, 1861, Fanny Seward diary, Seward Papers.
386 "I love . . . and does": Entry for September 9, 1861, Fanny Seward diary, Seward Papers.
386 "palatial . . . tasteful & attractive": FAS to LW, [July 1861?], reel 119, Seward Papers.
386 confined to her bed by migraines: See FAS to LW, [August 1861], reel 119, Seward Papers; " 'I have supped full on horrors,' from Fanny Seward's Diary," ed. Patricia Carley Johnson, *American Heritage* X (October 1959), p. 62.
386 vacation in upstate New York and Long Branch: Entry for August 14, 1861, in *Lincoln Day by Day*, Vol. III, p. 60.
386 "especially as . . . her husband": FAS to LW, [July 1861?], reel 119, Seward Papers.
386 word came . . . "company in the evening": Entry for September 9, 1861, Fanny Seward diary, Seward Papers.
387 "If things . . . my husband": MTL, quoted in George B. Lincoln to GW, April 25, 1874, quoted in "New Light on the Seward-Welles-Lincoln Controversy," *Lincoln Lore* 1718 (April 1981), p. 3.
387 "It makes me . . . skein of thread": MTL, quoted in Elizabeth Keckley, *Behind the Scenes. Or, Thirty Years a Slave, and Four Years in the White House.* The Schomburg Library of Nineteenth-Century Black Women Writers Series (New York: G. W. Carleton & Co., 1868; New York: Oxford University Press, 1988), p. 131.
387 the long evenings Lincoln spent at Seward's: Hendrick, *Lincoln's War Cabinet*, p. 186.
387 "My friend . . . churchwarden!": Wilson, *Intimate Memories of Lincoln*, p. 422.
387 "a tithe . . . read for ever": Entry for October 12, 1861, in Hay, *Inside Lincoln's White House*, p. 26.
387 "personal courage . . . the enemy is": Entry for October 10, 1861, in ibid., p. 25.
388 brought up the Chicago convention . . . "his life in his hand": Entry for October 17, 1861, in ibid., pp. 26, 27.
388 probably rekindled memories . . . on the circuit: Taylor, *William Henry Seward*, p. 188.
388 the fighting . . . in Missouri: See Nicolay and Hay, *Abraham Lincoln*, Vol. IV, chapter 11, esp. pp. 206–11; Thomas L. Snead, "The First Year of the War in Missouri," in *Battles and Leaders of the Civil War*, Vol. I, *Part I*, Grant-Lee edition (New York: Century Co., 1887–88; Harrisburg, Penn.: Archive Society, 1991), pp. 262–65.
389 Frank Blair . . . General Nathaniel Lyon: Snead, "The First Year of the War in Missouri," *Battles and Leaders of the Civil War*, Vol. I, Pt. 1, pp. 264–68; Williams, *Lincoln and the Radicals*, p. 39; "Missouri for the Union," in Parrish, *Frank Blair*.
389 "thickly veiled" . . . revolvers: Snead, "The First Year of the War in Missouri," *Battles and Leaders of the Civil War*, Vol. I, Pt. 1, p. 265 (quote); see also Franklin A. Dick, "Memorandum of Matters in Missouri," Papers of F. A. Dick, Miscellaneous Manuscripts Collection, Manuscript Division, Library of Congress.
389 the "earnest solicitation": Entry for December 9, 1863, in Hay, *Inside Lincoln's White House*, p. 123.
389 "He is just . . . eminently practical": "Editorial, 3 August 1861," in Hay, *Lincoln's Journalist*, p. 84.
389 "There was . . . magical influence": Koerner, *Memoirs of Gustave Koerner*, Vol. II, p. 162.
389 "recklessness in expenditures": JGN, memorandum of September 17, 1861, container 2, Nicolay Papers.
389 Tales circulated . . . unwanted visitors: Ibid.; FB to Governor Dennison, September 19, 1861, quoted in Smith, *The Francis Preston Blair Family in Politics*, Vol. II, pp. 79–80.
389 Frémont . . . had chosen to stay: Lorenzo Thomas to Simon Cameron, October 21, 1861, in *OR*, Ser. 1, Vol. III, p. 543; Parrish, *Frank Blair*, p. 116.
389 General Lyon's death . . . devastating defeat: Entries for August 10 and September 20, 1861, in Long, *The Civil War Day by Day*, pp. 107, 120.
390 Frémont issued a bold proclamation . . . "declared freemen": Proclamation of John C. Frémont, August 30, 1861, in *OR*, Ser. 1, Vol. III, pp. 466–67 (quotes p. 467).
390 far exceeded . . . their future status: Joseph Holt to AL, September 12, 1861, Lincoln Papers.
390 Lincoln learned of . . . a private letter to Frémont: Nicolay and Hay, *Abraham Lincoln*, Vol. IV, pp. 416, 417–18.
390 unilaterally recast . . . war against slavery: Benjamin Quarles, *Lincoln and the Negro* (New York: Oxford University Press, 1962; repr. New York: Da Capo Press, 1990), p. 71.
390 has "anxiety . . . so as to conform": AL to John C. Frémont, September 2, 1861, in *CW*, IV, p. 506.
390 "Fremont's proclamation . . . future condition": AL to Orville H. Browning, September 22, 1861, in ibid., p. 531.
390 "The trouble . . . only to himself": Carpenter, "A Day with Governor Seward," Seward Papers.
390 "unable to eat . . . on such a principle": Joshua Speed to AL, September 3, 1861, Lincoln Papers.
391 "I know that you . . . to the very foundations": FB to MB, September 1, 1861, Lincoln Papers.
391 he himself had reluctantly concluded: Williams, *Lincoln and the Radicals*, pp. 48–49.
391 "but being . . . public interests": MB to AL, September 4, 1861, Lincoln Papers.

392 General Meigs and Montgomery Blair . . . "look into the affair": JGN, memorandum of September 17, 1861, container 2, Nicolay Papers; entry for September 10 to September 18, 1861, extracts from diary of Montgomery C. Meigs, container 13, Nicolay Papers.
392 Jessie . . . arrived in Washington: "The Lincoln Interview: Excerpt from 'Great Events,' " in *The Letters of Jessie Benton Frémont*, ed. Pamela Herr and Mary Lee Spence (Urbana and Chicago: University of Illinois Press, 1993), pp. 264–65.
392 "If I were . . . I did not do so": John C. Frémont to AL, September 8, 1861, Lincoln Papers.
392 "You are quite a female politician": "The Lincoln Interview," *Letters of Jessie Benton Frémont*, p. 266.
392 "taxed me . . . for himself": Entry for December 9, 1863, in Hay, *Inside Lincoln's White House*, p. 123.
392 she asked Lincoln . . . when he was ready: "The Lincoln Interview," *Letters of Jessie Benton Frémont*, p. 266.
392 Lincoln wrote . . . "an open order": AL to John C. Frémont, September 11, 1861, in *CW*, IV, pp. 517–18.
392 he sent it to be mailed: Jessie Benton Frémont to AL, September 12, 1861, in *Letters of Jessie Benton Frémont*, p. 271 n1.
392 "He had always . . . now very angry": "The Lincoln Interview," *Letters of Jessie Benton Frémont*, p. 267.
392 the elder Blair revealed: Jessie B. Frémont to AL, September 12, 1861, Lincoln Papers.
393 "examine into that Department": AL to Jessie B. Frémont, September 12, 1861, draft copy, Lincoln Papers.
393 "threatened the old man . . . from responsibility": MB to W. O. Barlett, September 26, 1861, copy, reel 21, Blair Family Papers, Manuscript Division, Library of Congress [hereafter Blair Family Papers, DLC].
393 "most incautious": EBL to SPL, October 7, 1861, in *Wartime Washington*, ed. Laas, p. 83.
393 "The rebels . . . for defence": Entry for September 10 to September 18, 1861, extracts from diary of Montgomery C. Meigs, container 13, Nicolay Papers.
393 "a full & plain . . . should be consulted": MB to AL, September 14, 1861, Lincoln Papers.
393 Rumors circulated: Entry for December 28, 1861, in *The Diary of Edward Bates, 1859–1866*, p. 217; EBL to SPL, October 19, 1861, in *Wartime Washington*, ed. Laas, pp. 88, 90 n2.
393 "with a view . . . removal": *NYT*, September 17, 1861.
393 "unbecoming . . . gentleman": Smith, *The Francis Preston Blair Family in Politics*, Vol. II, p. 78.
393 Monty interceded: MB to John C. Frémont, September 20, 1861, copy, reel 21, Blair Family Papers, DLC.
393 the trial, which would never take place: MB to FPB, October 1, 1861, box 7, folder 6, Blair-Lee Papers, Dept. of Rare Books and Special Collections, Princeton University Library [hereafter Blair-Lee Papers, NjP-SC].
393 "Were you not . . . proclamation?": FAS to LW, [c. September 4, 1861], quoted in Seward, *Seward at Washington . . . 1846–1861*, p. 612.
394 "has cast . . . *step backwards*": Joseph Medill to SPC, September 15, 1861, reel 17, Chase Papers.
394 "poor white trash": Benjamin F. Wade to Zachariah Chandler, September 23, 1861, reel 1, Papers of Zachariah Chandler, Manuscript Division, Library of Congress.
394 "Many blunders . . . them all": *Douglass' Monthly* (October 1861), pp. 530–31.
394 Blair and Meigs delivered: Entry for September 18, 1861, in *Lincoln Day by Day*, Vol. III, p. 67.
394 "is determined . . . Missouri": MB to FPB, October 1, 1861, box 7, folder 6, Blair-Lee Papers, NjP-SC.
394 "more damage . . . can do": EB to SPC, September 11, 1861, reel 17, Chase Papers.
394 "distressed & mortified": EB to James O. Broadhead, September 28, 1861, Broadhead Papers, MoSHi.
394 "Immense mischief . . . place of action": EB to Hamilton Gamble, October 3, 1861, Hamilton Rowan Gamble Papers, Missouri Historical Society, St. Louis, Mo. [hereafter Gamble Papers, MoShi].
394 "I think God . . . in his Cabinet": FB to MB, October 7, 1861, quoted in Smith, *The Francis Preston Blair Family in Politics*, Vol. II, pp. 83–84.
394 "a letter directing . . . and conduct": Simon Cameron to AL, October 12, 1861, Lincoln Papers.
395 "was very much mortified" . . . talked with the president: Simon Cameron to AL, October 14, 1861, Lincoln Papers.
395 "constitution . . . with its management": *NYT*, October 31, 1861. For the report, see Lorenzo Thomas to Simon Cameron, October 21, 1861, in *OR*, Ser. 1, Vol. III, pp. 540–49.
395 "yielded to delay . . . *deserve it*": Entry of October 22, 1861, in *The Diary of Edward Bates, 1859–1866*, pp. 198–99.
395 Lincoln dispatched . . . Swett: Entry for October 24, 1861, in *Lincoln Day by Day*, Vol. III, p. 73.
395 "the most remarkable" . . . publication: *NYT*, October 31, 1861.
395 When Swett reached Missouri: Leonard Swett to AL, November 9, 1861, Lincoln Papers.
396 "frown came over . . . 'my lines?' ": General T. I. McKenny, quoted in Ida M. Tarbell, *The Life of Abraham Lincoln*, Vol. III, Sangamon Edition (4 vols., n.p.: S. S. McClure Co., 1895; New York: Lincoln History Society, 1924), pp. 122–25 (quote p. 124).
396 "justified . . . is possible": *NYT*, November 7, 1861.
396 "Slowly . . . our judgment": *Philadelphia Inquirer*, October 31, 1861.
396 "Lincoln . . . the whole story": *NYH*, November 7, 1861.
396 "I am . . . publ[ic] duty": SPC to Richard Smith, November 11, 1861, reel 18, Chase Papers.
396 the Confederacy had dispatched . . . Mason and Slidell: Van Deusen, *William Henry Seward*, p. 308.
396 Charles Wilkes . . . Fort Warren in Boston: *NYT*, November 17 and 19, 1861.
396 "We do not believe . . . been found": *NYT*, November 17, 1861.
397 Wilkes was fêted . . . a great banquet: *NYT*, November 26 and 27, 1861.
397 "three cheers . . . Wilkes": Smith, *Francis Preston Blair*, p. 315.
397 "great and general satisfaction": Entry for November 16, 1861, in *The Diary of Edward Bates, 1859–1866*, p. 202.
397 Chase reportedly . . . seized the British ship: *NYT*, November 19, 1861.
397 "the items . . . Mason & Slidell!": AL to Edward Everett, November 18, 1861, in *CW*, V, p. 26.

397 "intelligence . . . Mail Steamer": *The Times* (London), quoted in the *NYT,* December 13, 1861.
397 "reparation and apology": *Morning Post* (London), quoted in the *NYT,* December 14, 1861.
397 Fabricated details: Charles Francis Adams to Henry Adams, December 19, 1861, *A Cycle of Adams Letters, 1861–1865,* Vol. I, ed. Worthington Chauncey Ford (Boston and New York: Houghton Mifflin, 1920), p. 86.
397 "acted without . . . directed by us": WHS to Charles Francis Adams, undated, quoted in Frederick W. Seward, *Seward at Washington, as Senator and Secretary of State. A Memoir of His Life, with Selections from His Letters, 1861–1872* (New York: Derby & Miller, 1891), p. 21.
397 The first public response should come from the British government: WHS to Charles Francis Adams, undated, quoted in ibid., p. 24.
397 "if the taking . . . *it means war*": TW to WHS, December 2, 1861, quoted in ibid., pp. 27, 28 (quote).
397 "fanning the popular flame . . . manufactures": *NYT,* December 16, 1861.
397 "certainly jubilant": TW to WHS, December 5, 1861, quoted in Seward, *Seward at Washington . . . 1861–1872,* p. 28.
397 in "high places": TW to WHS, December 6, 1861, quoted in ibid., p. 29.
398 "to provoke . . . getting Canada": TW to WHS, December 2, 1861, quoted in ibid., p. 27.
398 "how created . . . your dismissal": TW to WHS, December 6, 1861, quoted in ibid., p. 29.
398 Seward burst . . . "so foolish a thing": Entry for December 15, 1861, in Browning, *The Diary of Orville Hickman Browning,* Vol. I, p. 515.
398 "I know . . . will not bite?": AL, quoted in Monaghan, *Diplomat in Carpet Slippers,* p. 187.
398 both he and Lord Lyons . . . remained silent: Seward, *Seward at Washington . . . 1861–1872,* p. 187; Lord Thomas Newton, *Lord Lyons: A Record of British Diplomacy,* Vol. I (New York: Longmans, Green, & Co., 1913), p. 55.
398 "Her Majesty's . . . for the aggression": Earl Russell to Lord Lyons, November 30, 1861, quoted in John G. Nicolay and John Hay, *Abraham Lincoln: A History,* Vol. V (New York: Century Co., 1917), pp. 29–30. While the letter was dated November 30, it did not arrive in Washington until December 19, 1861.
398 If the United States . . . return to Britain: Ibid., p. 30; Newton, *Lord Lyons,* p. 62.
398 Lyons carried the document . . . consider their response: Seward, *Seward at Washington . . . 1861–1872,* p. 24.
398 "You will perhaps . . . side of peace": Newton, *Lord Lyons,* p. 69.
398 "devoted one entire day": Seward, *Seward at Washington . . . 1861–1872,* p. 24.
398 "With England . . . 'crushed out' ": TW to WHS, December 10, 1861, quoted in ibid., p. 30.
398 "They can never . . . such a surrender": Quoted in ibid., p. 24.
398 Lincoln himself . . . considered humiliating: Hendrick, *Lincoln's War Cabinet,* p. 205.
399 "the British side . . . cheerfully": WHS to Lord Lyons, December 26, 1861, in *The Works of William H. Seward,* Vol. V, ed. George E. Baker (Boston: Houghton Mifflin, 1884; New York: AMS Press, 1972), pp. 295–309 (quotes pp. 307–09).
399 "There was great . . . power of England": Entry for December 25, 1861, in *The Diary of Edward Bates, 1859–1866,* p. 216.
399 "gall and wormwood . . . I possess": Entry for December 25, 1861, in *Chase Papers,* Vol. I, p. 320.
399 Only Monty Blair . . . with Seward: Hendrick, *Lincoln's War Cabinet,* p. 206.
399 Charles Sumner . . . "the North's problems": Monaghan, *Diplomat in Carpet Slippers,* p. 191.
399 "Governor Seward . . . on each side": Seward, *Seward at Washington . . . 1861–1872,* p. 25.
399 Seward finished . . . read it to Chase: Monaghan, *Diplomat in Carpet Slippers,* p. 191; entry for December 26, 1861, Fanny Seward diary, Seward Papers.
400 "I am consoled . . . simply doing right": Entry for December 25, 1861, in *Chase Papers,* Vol. I, p. 320.
400 "a great point . . . Government": Carpenter, "A Day with Governor Seward," Seward Papers.
400 "an argument . . . the right one": Seward, *Seward at Washington . . . 1861–1872,* p. 26.
400 Seward hosted a dinner party: Entry for December 27, 1861, in Browning, *The Diary of Orville Hickman Browning,* Vol. I, p. 519; entry for December 27, 1861, Fanny Seward diary, Seward Papers.
400 "a great homely . . . iron grey": Entry for December 27, 1861, Fanny Seward diary, Seward Papers.
400 The conversation at dinner . . . "on the floor cloth": Ibid.
400 "swore vehemently": Entry for December 27, 1861, in Browning, *The Diary of Orville Hickman Browning,* Vol. I, p. 519.
400 "doom [Seward] to unpopularity": Seward, *Seward at Washington . . . 1861–1872,* p. 26.
400 "The general . . . domestic treason": Entry for December 29, 1861, *Diary of George Templeton Strong,* Vol. III, p. 198.
400 "Presidents and Kings . . . unselfish heart": Seward, *Seward at Washington . . . 1861–1872,* p. 26.
401 "Houses are being . . . life in the Capital": "Miriam," *Iowa State Register,* Des Moines, November 13, 1861.
401 a mansion transformed: Randall, *Mary Lincoln,* pp. 258–63, 266; Monkman, *The White House,* pp. 123–33.
401 the new rugs . . . "roses at your feet": Mary Clemmer Ames, *Ten Years in Washington. Life and Scenes in the National Capital, as a Woman Sees Them* (Hartford, Conn.: A. D. Worthington & Co., 1871), p. 171.
401 "The President's . . . comparative beauty": *Daily Alta California,* May 12, 1862, quoted in Monkman, *The White House,* p. 132.
401 "elegant fitting up . . . in the least arrogant": George Bancroft to his wife, December 12 and 14, 1862, in M. A. DeWolfe Howe, *The Life and Letters of George Bancroft,* Vol. II (New York: Charles Scribner's Sons, 1908), pp. 144–45.
401 she had overspent . . . extra money over to her: Baker, *Mary Todd Lincoln,* pp. 187, 191.
401 She had replaced . . . the manure account: Entry for November 3, 1861, in *William Howard Russell's Civil War: Private Diary and Letters, 1861–1862,* ed. Martin Crawford (Athens, Ga., and London: University of Georgia Press, 1992), p. 162.

401 She exchanged her patronage . . . wealthy donors: For a general discussion of MTL's financial finagling, see Michael Burlingame, "Mary Todd Lincoln's Unethical Conduct as First Lady," appendix 2 in *At Lincoln's Side: John Hay's Civil War Correspondence and Selected Writings*, ed. Michael Burlingame (Carbondale and Edwardsville: Southern Illinois University Press, 2000).
401 she asked John Hay . . . "the Steward's salary": JH to JGN, April 4 and 5, 1862, in ibid., pp. 19–20.
402 She had no recourse . . . to speak with her husband: Entry for December 16, 1861, in Benjamin Brown French, *Witness to the Young Republic: A Yankee's Journal, 1828–1870*, ed. Donald B. Cole and John J. McDonough (Hanover, N.H., and London: University Press of New England, 1989), p. 382.
402 after he returned home . . . Edward Baker: *NR*, December 14, 1861.
402 "inexorable . . . his own pocket!": Entry for December 16, 1861, in French, *Witness to the Young Republic*, p. 382.
402 "better and better . . . will defend her": Entry for December 22, 1861, in ibid., p. 383.
402 hide a deficiency appropriation: Baker, *Mary Todd Lincoln*, p. 190.
402 "I need hardly . . . his own expences": SPC to KCS, October 25, 1861, reel 17, Chase Papers.
402 a questionable relationship . . . investment account for Chase: Belden and Belden, *So Fell the Angels*, pp. 36–37.
403 "I will take . . . working as you do": Jay Cooke to SPC, quoted in ibid., p. 37.
403 growth in size of the Union army: Simon Cameron to AL, December 1, 1861, *OR*, Ser. 3, Vol. I pp. 669, 700.
403 "incapable . . . general plans": "A Private Paper. Conversation with the President, October 2d, 1861," memorandum, container 2, Nicolay Papers.
403 "he would look . . . in the other": Albert Gallatin Riddle, *Recollection of War Times: Reminiscences of Men and Events in Washington, 1860–1865* (New York and London: G. P. Putman's Sons, 1895), p. 180.
403 accusations of corruption . . . in the War Department: *NYT*, July 3 and 9, and August 28, 1861.
403 Congress appointed . . . Cameron was not charged: Thomas, *Abraham Lincoln*, p. 293; Macartney, *Lincoln and His Cabinet*, pp. 35–36; Hendrick, *Lincoln's War Cabinet*, pp. 222–23.
404 "It is better . . . with dissolution": *NYT*, July 7, 1861.
404 Cameron sought . . . Republicans: Williams, *Lincoln and the Radicals*, p. 59.
404 "*We* agreed . . . in that opinion": SPC to Trowbridge, March 31, 1844, quoted in Schuckers, *The Life and Public Services of Salmon Portland Chase*, p. 420.
404 "extremist measures . . . absolute ruin": *National Intelligencer*, Washington, D.C., November 14, 1861.
404 heated arguments with Bates, Blair, and Smith: Entry for November 20, 1862, in *The Diary of Edward Bates, 1859–1866*, p. 203; Niven, *Gideon Welles*, p. 392.
404 Cameron maintained . . . "nigger hobby": MB, paraphrased in entry of September 12, 1862, *Welles diary*, Vol. I (1960 edn.), p. 127 (quote); Bradley, *Simon Cameron*, p. 203.
404 Each department customarily presented: Nicolay and Hay, *Abraham Lincoln*, Vol. V, p. 125.
404 Cameron read his draft: Henry Wilson, "Edwin M. Stanton," *Atlantic Monthly* 25 (February 1870), p. 238; Bradley, *Simon Cameron*, p. 203.
404 "I sought out . . . Edwin Stanton": Simon Cameron, quoted in Henry Wilson, "Jeremiah S. Black and Edwin M. Stanton," *Atlantic Monthly* 26 (October 1870), p. 470.
404 "read the report . . . hearty support": Ibid.
404 he suggested his own provocative logic: Bradley, *Simon Cameron*, p. 203; Thomas and Hyman, *Stanton*, p. 134 n7.
405 "It is clearly a right . . . from the enemy": "From the Report of the Secretary of War, Dec. 1, 1861," in Edward McPherson, *The Political History of the United States of America, During the Great Rebellion, 1861–1865*, 2nd edn. (Washington, D.C.: Philp & Solomons, 1865; New York: Da Capo Press, 1972), p. 249 (quote). For the official version of the annual report of the secretary of war sent to Congress, see *OR*, Ser. 3, Vol. I, pp. 698–708 (esp. p. 708).
405 It remains unclear: See Thomas and Hyman, *Stanton*, pp. 134–35; Hendrick, *Lincoln's War Cabinet*, pp. 236–37, 260.
405 "an abolitionist at heart": Jeremiah S. Black, "Senator Wilson and Edwin M. Stanton," *Galaxy* 9 (June 1870), p. 822.
405 his boyhood pledge to his father: Flower, *Edwin McMasters Stanton*, p. 25.
405 "my *personal* friend . . . war against Slavery": CS to Francis Lieber, December 19, 1861, reel 64, Summer Papers.
405 when Stanton talked with fellow Democrats: Thomas and Hyman, *Stanton*, p. 135.
405 his approval emboldened Cameron . . . to the president: Flower, *Edwin McMasters Stanton*, p. 116.
405 "This will never do!" . . . copy already sent: AL, quoted in Carpenter, *Six Months at the White House*, p. 136.
405 "must be provided for in some way": AL, "Annual Message to Congress," December 3, 1861, in *CW*, V, p. 48.
405 "otherwise unconstitutional . . . necessity": AL to Albert G. Hodges, April 4, 1864, in *CW*, VII, pp. 281–82.
405 Lincoln informed Cameron . . . the vetoed language: Nicolay and Hay, *Abraham Lincoln*, Vol. V, p. 127.
405 he complained . . . "dreaded most": Niven, *Gideon Welles*, pp. 394–95 (quote p. 395).
406 "have sought our ships . . . a livelihood": *NYT*, December 4, 1861, p. 3.
406 Welles resolved that . . . into the Confederacy: Niven, *Gideon Welles*, p. 395.
406 he outlined his ideas . . . "new beginner to help him": AL, "Annual Message to Congress," December 3, 1861, in *CW*, V, pp. 48, 49, 52.
407 "Away with . . . free as the white man": Worthington G. Snethen to SPC, December 10, 1861, reel 18, Chase Papers.
407 "his attachment . . . than iron": "The Claims of the Negro Ethnologically Considered: An Address Delivered in Hudson, Ohio, on 12 July 1854," *The Frederick Douglass Papers, Series One: Speeches, Debates, and Interviews.* Vol. II: *1847–54*, ed. John W. Blassingame (New Haven and London: Yale University Press, 1982), p. 524.
407 "Give him wages . . . by hard work": *Douglass' Monthly* (January 1862), p. 579.

407 "One black regiment . . . free colored people": *Douglass' Monthly* (May 1861), p. 451.
407 "We are striking . . . the loyal North": Frederick Douglass, "The Reasons for Our Troubles," ed. Philip S. Foner, *The Life and Writings of Frederick Douglass.* Vol. III: *The Civil War, 1861–1865* (New York: International Publishers, 1952), p. 204.
407 "It appeals to the judgment . . . aspirations": *NYT Supplement*, December 4, 1861.
407 "the moderate men . . . with popularity": Ibid.
408 "country and the world . . . railing accusations": *NYTrib*, December 4, 1861.

CHAPTER 15: "MY BOY IS GONE"

Page
409 "unusually beautiful . . . than January": *NYT Supplement*, January 3, 1862.
409 "For the first time . . . in old times": FAS to LW, January 1, 1862, reel 119, Seward Papers.
409 "All the world" . . . opened at noon: Entry for January 1, 1862, in *The Diary of Edward Bates, 1859–1866*, p. 221.
409 The Marine Band . . . cabinet officials: Poore, *Perley's Reminiscences*, Vol. II, pp. 105–06; *NYT Supplement*, January 3, 1862.
410 "a compact little . . . head arrangement": Entry for January 1, 1862, Fanny Seward diary, Seward Papers.
410 Lincoln cordially greeted every guest: Leech, *Reveille in Washington*, pp. 122–23.
410 "the bottom . . . out of the tub": AL, quoted in Montgomery C. Meigs, "General M. C. Meigs on the Conduct of the Civil War," *American Historical Review* 26 (January 1921), p. 292.
410 "If the new year . . . to be expected": Entry for January 1862, in Gurowski, *Diary from March 4, 1861 to November 12, 1862*, p. 137.
410 Seward questioned whether . . . "to Mr. Cameron": Maunsell B. Field, *Memories of Many Men and of Some Women: Being Personal Recollections of Emperors, Kings, Queens, Princes, Presidents, Statesmen, Authors, and Artists, at Home and Abroad, During the Last Thirty Years* (New York: Harper & Bros., 1874), pp. 266–67.
410 Lincoln's initial preferences . . . Joseph Holt: Flower, *Edwin McMasters Stanton*, p. 116.
410 West Point graduate Montgomery Blair . . . "sound judgment": Gideon Welles, "Narrative of Events," in "Three Manuscripts of Gideon Welles," comp. A. Howard Meneely, *American Historical Review* 31 (April 1926), p. 491.
410 Seward would never forget: Wilson, "Jeremiah S. Black and Edwin M. Stanton," *Atlantic Monthly* (1870), p. 465.
411 "to be loved . . . power to express": EMS to SPC, December 2, 1847, reel 6, Chase Papers.
411 "He puts his whole . . . upon the issue": *Philadelphia Press*, January 20, 1862.
411 an uncharacteristically brusque letter: Memorandum of conversation between SPC and J. W. Schuckers, January 22, 1871, Papers of Jacob William Schuckers, Manuscript Division, Library of Congress.
411 "expressed a desire . . . minister to Russia": AL to Simon Cameron, January 11, 1862, reel 8, Papers of Simon Cameron, Manuscript Division, Library of Congress [hereafter Cameron Papers, DLC].
411 to have wept . . . "personal degradation": Recollection of Alexander McClure, in Hendrick, *Lincoln's War Cabinet*, p. 234.
411 Chase drove Cameron . . . "to all concerned": Entry for January 12, 1862, *Chase Papers*, Vol. I, pp. 325–26.
411 Lincoln agreed to withdraw his terse letter: A. K. McClure, *Abraham Lincoln and Men of War-Times: Some Personal Recollections of War and Politics During the Lincoln Administration*, 4th edn. (Philadelphia: Times Publishing Co., 1892; Lincoln and London: University of Nebraska Press, 1996), p. 165.
411 "gratify . . . could render at home": AL to Simon Cameron, January 11, 1862, reel 8, Cameron Papers, DLC. For Cameron's resignation letter, see Simon Cameron to AL, January 11, 1862, Lincoln Papers.
412 Cameron expressed his fervent opinion: Simon Cameron to Frank A. Flower, March 6, 1887, reel 16, Cameron Papers, DLC.
412 Lincoln asked George Harding . . . "of the three": Charles F. Benjamin, quoted in Thomas and Hyman, *Stanton*, p. 136.
412 Ellen . . . "objected to his acceptance": Wolcott, "Edwin M. Stanton," p. 153.
412 diminish the lifestyle of the Stanton family: Thomas and Hyman, *Stanton*, p. 137.
412 "long by noble deeds": SPC to EMS, January 9, 1848, reel 6, Chase Papers.
412 He accepted the post . . . "swamped at once": Wolcott, "Edwin M. Stanton," p. 154.
412 "Strange" . . . no one but Seward: Entry for January 13, 1862, in *The Diary of Edward Bates, 1859–1866*, p. 226.
412 Welles heard . . . "Lincoln's confidence": Welles, "Narrative of Events," *AHR* (1926), p. 488; Hendrick, *Lincoln's War Cabinet*, p. 234 (quote).
412 Welles had never even met Stanton: *Welles diary*, Vol. I (1960 edn.), p. 54.
412 Stanton's nomination . . . he would arrange a meeting: Francis Fessenden, *Life and Public Services of William Pitt Fessenden*, Vol. I (Boston and New York: Houghton Mifflin, 1907), p. 230.
413 After a lengthy . . . "the negro question": William Pitt Fessenden, quoted in ibid., p. 231.
413 "Not only was . . . the real cause": WHS to home, January 15, 1862, in Seward, *Seward at Washington . . . 1861–1872*, p. 46.
413 the House Committee . . . rotten food: *NYT*, February 6, 1862.
413 "resolved to advise . . . unsound provisions": *Frank Leslie's Illustrated Newspaper*, February 1, 1862.

413 "highly injurious to the public service": House resolution of April 30, 1862, quoted in AL, "To the Senate and House of Representatives," May 26, 1862, in *CW,* V, p. 243.
413 He wrote a long public letter . . . "was committed": AL, "To the Senate and House of Representatives," May 26, 1862, in ibid., p. 243.
413 "one of the most intimate . . . personal friends": Nicolay and Hay, *Abraham Lincoln,* Vol. V, p. 130.
413 Most other men . . . "incur responsibility": Simon Cameron to AL, June 26, 1862, Lincoln Papers.
414 "an entirely new *régime*" . . . removed many of Cameron's people: *NYT,* January 23, 1862.
414 The day after . . . "she never did": EMS, quoted in *Boston Daily Evening Transcript,* January 7, 1870.
414 "As his carriage . . . to their stations": Charles F. Benjamin, "Recollections of Secretary Edwin M. Stanton," *Century* 33 (March 1887), p. 761.
414 "fluent without . . . and large-hearted": Entry for January 29, 1862, *Diary of George Templeton Strong,* Vol. III, p. 203.
415 "Persons at a distance . . . Congress speak it": *NYT,* January 25, 1862.
415 Instead of the traditional . . . an evening ball: Keckley, *Behind the Scenes,* pp. 95–96; *Frank Leslie's Illustrated Newspaper,* February 22, 1862.
415 some five hundred invitations: *Frank Leslie's Illustrated Newspaper,* February 22, 1862.
415 "sought . . . their invitations": JGN to TB, February 6, 1862, container 2, Nicolay Papers.
415 Marine Band . . . midnight supper: Poore, *Perley's Reminiscences,* Vol. II, pp. 116, 119.
415 white satin gown . . . "in better style": Keckley, *Behind the Scenes,* p. 101.
415 "much attached . . . ever known": Entry for February 20, 1862, Taft diary.
415 built a cabin . . . troops on the shore: Entry for January 11, 1862, Taft diary (quote); Bayne, *Tad Lincoln's Father,* p. 177.
415 performances in the attic: Bayne, *Tad Lincoln's Father,* pp. 102, 106.
415 the pony . . . favorite pastime: Keckley, *Behind the Scenes,* p. 98; entries for January 26 and 27, 1862, Taft diary.
415 weather conditions in January: See January 1862 entries in Taft diary.
416 "There is a good deal . . . in the City": Entry for January 8, 1862, Taft diary.
416 "a dreadful eruption . . . expected to live": EMS to Oella Wright, March 24, 1862, in Wolcott, "Edwin M. Stanton," p. 155.
416 "burning fever . . . ulcerated" throat: FAS to LW, February 2, 1862, reel 119, Seward Papers.
416 Seward left Washington: WHS to AL, February 6, 1862, Lincoln Papers.
416 Nettie Chase . . . contracted scarlet fever: SPC to KCS, January 10, 1862, reel 18, Chase Papers.
416 Mary thought it best . . . been sent out: Keckley, *Behind the Scenes,* p. 100.
416 "the dean . . . medical community": Baker, *Mary Todd Lincoln,* p. 209.
416 "in no immediate . . . an early recovery": Keckley, *Behind the Scenes,* p. 100.
416 The carriages . . . received their guests: Poore, *Perley's Reminiscences,* Vol. II, pp. 115–18; *Frank Leslie's Illustrated Newspaper,* February 22, 1862.
416 "exquisite taste . . . a Grecian knot behind": *Frank Leslie's Illustrated Newspaper,* February 22, 1862.
416 At midnight . . . including General McClellan: "Lincoln's First Levee," *Journal of the Illinois State Historical Society* 11 (October 1918), p. 389; Poore, *Perley's Reminiscences,* Vol. II, pp. 119–20 (quote).
417 "The brilliance . . . the suffering boy": Keckley, *Behind the Scenes,* p. 102.
417 "Those who were here . . . others have not": JGN to TB, February 6, 1862, container 2, Nicolay Papers.
417 "frivolity, hilarity . . . within plain sight": *Jeffersonian Democrat,* reprinted in *The Liberator,* February 28, 1862.
417 "a brilliant spectacle": *Star,* February 6, 1862.
417 "our fair 'Republican Queen' . . . of beauty": *Frank Leslie's Illustrated Newspaper,* February 22, 1862.
417 General Ulysses S. Grant: On Ulysess S. Grant's careers prior to the Civil War, see chapters 2–5 of William S. McFeely, *Grant: A Biography* (New York and London: W. W. Norton, 1982).
417 Grant understood . . . an important mission: Ibid., pp. 96–97.
417 "to take and hold Fort Henry": H. W. Halleck to USG, January 30, 1862, *OR,* Ser. 1, Vol. VII, p. 121.
417 Grant and Foote . . . Fort Donelson: McPherson, *Battle Cry of Freedom,* p. 396; Nicolay and Hay, *Abraham Lincoln,* Vol. V, pp. 120–22.
417 "Fort Henry is ours . . . on the 8th": USG to H. W. Halleck, February 6, 1862, *OR,* Ser. 1, Vol. VII, p. 124.
417 Though a severe rainstorm: Ulysses S. Grant, *Personal Memoirs of U.S. Grant* (New York: C. L. Webster, 1885; New York: Modern Library, 1999), p. 152.
417 "plain brother . . . a presentiment": USG to Mary Grant, February 9, 1862, *The Papers of Ulysses S. Grant.* Vol. IV: *January 8–March 31, 1862,* ed. John Y. Simon (Carbondale and Edwardsville: Southern Illinois University Press, 1972), p. 180.
418 Buckner, proposed a cease-fire . . . "can be accepted": USG to Simon B. Buckner, February 16, 1862, enclosure 3 of USG to G. W. Cullum, February 16, 1862, in *OR,* Ser. 1, Vol. VII, p. 161.
418 Buckner . . . taken prisoner: USG to General G. W. Cullum, February 16, 1862, *OR,* Ser. 1, Vol. VII, p. 159.
418 More than a thousand troops: McPherson, *Battle Cry of Freedom,* p. 401.
418 "a most bloody . . . brought through": Captain L. D. Waddell to William Coventry H. Wadell, quoted in *NYT,* February 26, 1862.
418 Hundred-gun salutes: *NYT,* February 18, 1862.
418 "quite wild with Excitement": Entry for February 15, 1862, Taft diary.
418 "the gallery rose . . . enthusiastic cheers": *NYT,* February 18, 1862.
418 to illuminate the capital's public buildings . . . Washington's birthday: *NYH,* February 21, 1862.
418 promoting him to major general: Entry for February 17, 1862, in *Lincoln Day by Day,* Vol. III, p. 95.

418 Lincoln had been following: Sandburg, *Abraham Lincoln: The War Years*, Vol. I, p. 462.
418 "I have come among you . . . fellow-citizen": USG, "Proclamation, to the Citizens of Paducah!" September 6, 1861, *The Papers of Ulysses S. Grant.* Vol. II: *April–September 1861*, ed. John Y. Simon (Carbondale and Edwardsville: Southern Illinois University Press, 1969), p. 194.
418 "Grant had taken the field" . . . items to the front: Isaac N. Arnold, *The Life of Abraham Lincoln* (Chicago: Jansen, McClurg, & Co., 1885), p. 281.
418 Fort Donelson's capture . . . capture of New Orleans: For more on events from the surrender of Fort Donelson to the capture of New Orleans, see McPherson, *Battle Cry of Freedom*, pp. 402–20.
418 It is believed that both boys . . . typhoid fever: Baker, *Mary Todd Lincoln*, p. 208: Seale, *The President's House*, Vol. I, p. 379.
419 Willie was affected . . . more severely: MTL to Julia Ann Sprigg, May 29, 1862, in Turner and Turner, *Mary Todd Lincoln*, p. 128; Milton H. Shutes, "Mortality of the Five Lincoln Boys," *Lincoln Herald* 57 (Spring–Summer 1955), p. 4.
419 "grew weaker . . . shadow-like": Keckley, *Behind the Scenes*, p. 98.
419 symptoms of his illness: "Typhus, Typhoid, and Relapsing Fevers," *Encyclopaedia Britannica*, Vol. XXIII, ed. Day Otis Kellogg (30 vols., New York and Chicago: The Werner Company, 1898), pp. 678–79.
419 "almost wore . . . with watching": Benjamin B. French to Henry F. French, February 27, 1862, reel 5, Papers of Benjamin B. French Family, Manuscript Division, Library of Congress [hereafter French Family Papers, DLC].
419 She canceled the customary: Unknown Washington newspaper, quoted in Helm, *The True Story of Mary*, p. 197.
419 "pretty much all his attention": JGN to TB, February 11, 1862, container 2, Nicolay Papers.
419 Willie would call for . . . "tenderly to bed": Bayne, *Tad Lincoln's Father*, pp. 199–200.
419 celebratory illuminations were canceled: Entry for February 23, 1862, in French, *Witness to the Young Republic*, p. 388; Benjamin B. French to Henry F. French, February 27, 1862, reel 5, French Family Papers, DLC.
419 "the President . . . of their affliction": *Star*, February 18, 1862.
419 "as if they did . . . So the doctors say": Stoddard, *Inside the White House in War Times*, p. 66.
419 on Thursday, February 20, Willie died: Entry for February 20, 1862, in *Lincoln Day by Day*, Vol. III, p. 96.
419 "Well, Nicolay . . . actually gone!": Entry for February 20, 1862, notebook, February–March 1862, container 1, Nicolay Papers.
419 "buried his head . . . of her old age": Keckley, *Behind the Scenes*, pp. 103, 104.
419 She took to her bed . . . ease her grief: Rebecca R. Pomroy to "Mary," March 27, 1862, Rebecca R. Pomroy Letters, Schlesinger Library, Radcliffe College [hereafter Pomroy Letters].
420 He sent his carriage to the Brownings . . . Tad's bedside: Entries for February 20 and 21, 1862, in Browning, *The Diary of Orville Hickman Browning*, Vol. I, p. 530.
420 He asked . . . Mary Jane, to sit with the boy: Niven, *Gideon Welles*, pp. 442–43.
420 Julia Bates . . . also watched over him: Entry for February 22, 1862, in *The Diary of Edward Bates, 1859–1866*, p. 236.
420 Lincoln turned to Dorothea Dix: Anna L. Boyden, *Echoes from Hospital and White House: A Record of Mrs. Rebecca R. Pomroy's Experience in War-times* (Boston: D. Lothrop & Co., 1884), p. 52.
420 a powerful woman . . . "out of fashion": Dorothy Clarke Wilson, *Stranger and Traveler: The Story of Dorothea Dix, American Reformer* (Boston: Little, Brown, 1975), p. 256.
420 Dix chose Rebecca Pomroy . . . "turn right in": Pomroy to "Mary," March 27, 1862, Pomroy Letters.
420 Willie's body lay . . . "Oh, why is it?": AL, quoted in Boyden, *Echoes from Hospital and White House*, pp. 54–56 (quotes pp. 54, 56).
420 Tad would awaken . . . gown and slippers: Pomroy to "Mary," March 27, 1862, Pomroy Letters.
420 Lincoln drove with Browning to Oak Hill Cemetery: Entry for February 23, 1862, in Browning, *The Diary of Orville Hickman Browning*, Vol. I, p. 531.
420 The funeral service . . . in the East Room: *National Intelligencer*, Washington, D.C., February 25, 1862; *Star*, February 24, 1862.
420 "keep the boys . . . in the casket": Bayne, *Tad Lincoln's Father*, p. 200.
420 "He lay with his eyes . . . for the evening": Nathaniel Parker Willis, quoted in Keckley, *Behind the Scenes*, p. 108.
421 "no spectator" . . . the East Room service: Entry for March 2, 1862, in French, *Witness to the Young Republic*, p. 389.
421 Congress had adjourned: *Star*, February 24, 1862; *National Intelligencer*, Washington, D.C., February 25, 1862; entry for February 24, 1862, in Browning, *The Diary of Orville Hickman Browning*, Vol. I, p. 531.
421 a frightful storm arose: Benjamin B. French to Henry F. French, February 27, 1862, reel 5, French Family Papers, DLC; *Star*, February 25, 1862.
421 stormy weather . . . the grave: William G. Greene interview, May 30, 1865, in *HI*, p. 21.
421 Mary found it difficult to endure: Elizabeth Todd Edwards to Julia Edwards Baker, quoted in Randall, *Mary Lincoln*, p. 287.
421 She never invited them back to the White House: Bayne, *Tad Lincoln's Father*, p. 200.
421 In her talks with Mrs. Pomroy . . . her own family: Boyden, *Echoes from Hospital and White House*, pp. 58–59.
421 she should surrender to God's will: Baker, *Mary Todd Lincoln*, p. 214.
421 "to try us . . . is not with us": MTL to Julia Ann Sprigg, May 29, 1862, in Turner and Turner, *Mary Todd Lincoln*, p. 128.
421 speculating that God . . . "of little else": MTL to Hannah Shearer, November 20, 1864, in ibid., p. 189.
422 "foresaken . . . so lovely a child": MTL to Mrs. Charles Eames, July 26, 1862, in ibid., p. 131.

422 "far happier . . . when on earth": MTL to Mary Jane Welles, February 21, 1863, in ibid., p. 147.
422 "*Death* . . . blessed transition": MTL to CS, July 4, 1865, in ibid., p. 256.
422 "where there are . . . *no more* tears shed": MTL to Mary Jane Welles, July 11, 1865, in ibid., p. 257.
422 Through Elizabeth Keckley . . . celebrated medium: Baker, *Mary Todd Lincoln*, p. 219.
422 the "veil . . . the 'loved & lost' ": MTL to CS, July 4, 1865, in Turner and Turner, *Mary Todd Lincoln*, p. 256.
422 "the spirits of the dead . . . have become alive": Princess Felix Salm-Salm, *Ten Years of My Life* (Detroit: Belford Bros., 1877), pp. 59, 60.
422 "offered tangible . . . power of sympathy": Robert S. Cox, *Body and Soul: A Sympathetic History of American Spiritualism* (Charlottesville and London: University of Virginia Press, 2003), p. 85.
422 "an altered woman" . . . look at his picture: Keckley, *Behind the Scenes*, p. 116.
422 She sent all his toys . . . was laid out: Ibid., pp. 116–17; Baker, *Mary Todd Lincoln*, pp. 210, 213.
422 On the Thursday . . . his terrible grief: Stoddard, *Inside the White House in War Times*, p. 67.
422 "That blow . . . never felt it before": AL, quoted by Rev. Willets, in Carpenter, *Six Months at the White House*, pp. 187–88.
423 Three months after . . . "my lost boy Willie": AL, quoted in Le Grand B. Cannon, *Personal Reminiscences of the Rebellion, 1861–1866*. Black Heritage Library Collection (1895; Freeport, N.Y.: Books For Libraries Press, 1971), p. 174; the quotation from *King John* is in Act III, scene IV.
423 Lincoln cherished mementos . . . and tell stories: Randall, *Mary Lincoln*, pp. 291–92.
423 he invited Browning . . . important events: Entry for June 22, 1862, in Browning, *The Diary of Orville Hickman Browning*, Vol. I, p. 553.
423 "the memory . . . you have known before": AL to Fanny McCullough, December 23, 1862, in *CW*, VI, p. 17.

CHAPTER 16: "HE WAS SIMPLY OUT-GENERALED"

Page

425 the "sad calamity . . . be left undone": GBM to AL, February 22, 1862, Lincoln Papers.
425 McClellan's assurances . . . contentious meeting: Williams, *Lincoln and the Radicals*, pp. 77–84; Bruce Tap, "Joint Committee on the Conduct of the War (1861–1865)," in *Encyclopedia of the American Civil War*, ed. Heidler and Heidler, p. 1086.
425 "that neither . . . defer to General McClellan": George W. Julian, *Political Recollections, 1840 to 1872* (Chicago: Jansen, McClurg & Co., 1884), p. 201.
425 Bates strenuously objected . . . "commanders": Entry for January 10, 1862, in *The Diary of Edward Bates, 1859–1866*, pp. 223–24.
426 He borrowed General Halleck's book: Entry for January 8, 1862, in *Lincoln Day by Day*, Vol. III, p. 88.
426 "he was thinking . . . himself": Entry for January 12, 1862, in Browning, *The Diary of Orville Hickman Browning*, Vol. I, p. 523.
426 "The bottom is out of the tub": AL, quoted in Meigs, "General M. C. Meigs on the Conduct of the Civil War," *AHR* 26 (1921), p. 292.
426 The nearly bankrupt Treasury . . . meeting on the following day: Ibid.
426 "can't keep a . . . to Tadd": GBM, quoted in ibid., p. 293.
426 General War Order No. 1: AL, "President's General War Order No. 1," January 27, 1862, in *CW*, V, p. 111.
426 Lincoln correctly believed . . . at the same time: Entry for January 12, 1862, in Browning, *The Diary of Orville Hickman Browning*, Vol. I, p. 523.
426 the Peninsula Campaign: See Stephen W. Sears, *To the Gates of Richmond: The Peninsula Campaign* (New York: Ticknor & Fields, 1992).
426 proposed a different strategy . . . "superior force": EMS to Heman Dyer, May 18, 1862, reel 3, Stanton Papers, DLC.
426 it was feared that the Confederates: AL to GBM, February 3, 1862, Lincoln Papers. On McClellan's plans see GBM to EMS, January 31, 1862, Lincoln Papers.
426 Lincoln reluctantly . . . safe from attack: AL, "President's General War Order No. 3," March 8, 1862, in *CW*, V, p. 151.
427 "there was no more" . . . grown disenchanted: EMS to Heman Dyer, May 18, 1862, reel 3, Stanton Papers, DLC.
427 "while men are striving . . . must be stopped": EMS to Charles A. Dana, January 24, 1862, quoted in Charles A. Dana, *Recollections of the Civil War: With the Leaders at Washington and in the Field in the Sixties* (New York: D. Appleton & Co., 1898), p. 5.
427 Stanton's remark . . . society: Flower, *Edwin McMasters Stanton*, pp. 125–26.
427 "That will be . . . the waiting snub": EMS, quoted in Albert E. H. Johnson, "Reminiscences of the Hon. Edwin M. Stanton, Secretary of War," *Records of the Columbia Historical Society* 13 (1910), p. 73.
427 delivered orders to transfer . . . "his humiliation": Flower, *Edwin McMasters Stanton*, p. 216 (quote); Johnson, "Reminiscences of the Hon. Edwin M. Stanton," *RCHS* (1910), pp. 73–74.
427 The Democratic press . . . "worthy of *Punch*": EMS to Charles A. Dana, February 23, 1862, quoted in Flower, *Edwin McMasters Stanton*, p. 131.
428 on the weekend of March 8 . . . supplies, and weapons: Sears, *George B. McClellan*, pp. 163–64; Sears, *To the Gates of Richmond*, pp. 14, 16–17.
428 "We shall be the . . . we have got one": William P. Fessenden to family, March 15, 1862, quoted in Fessenden, *Life and Public Services of William Pitt Fessenden*, Vol. I, p. 261.

428 *"Anybody . . . must have somebody"*: "Conversation with Vice President Wilson, Nov. 16, 1875," container 10, Nicolay Papers.
428 On March 11 . . . Mountain Department: AL, "President's War Order No. 3," March 11, 1862, in *CW,* V, p. 155.
428 "learned through the" . . . the result of the war: McClellan, *McClellan's Own Story,* pp. 224–26.
429 "not to let . . . doing anything": EBL to SPL, April 12, 1862, *Wartime Washington,* ed. Laas, p. 127 (quote); FPB to GBM, April 12, 1862, reel 20, Papers of George B. McClellan, Sr., Manuscript Division, Library of Congress [hereafter McClellan Papers, DLC].
429 Washington gossip . . . to support McClellan: CS to John Andrew, April 27, 1862, in *The Selected Letters of Charles Sumner,* Vol. II, ed. Beverly Wilson Palmer (Boston: Northeastern University Press, 1990), p. 112.
429 "preservers of slavery": Entry for February 1862, in Gurowski, *Diary from March 4, 1861 to November 12, 1862,* p. 157.
429 Monty Blair privately . . . "mortifying to Frank": MB to FPB, March 12, 1862, box 7, folder 6, Blair-Lee Papers, NjP-SC.
429 "urged by Chase" . . . felt it intensely: EBL to SPL, March 11, [1862], in *Wartime Washington,* ed. Laas, p. 109.
429 Frank Blair had delivered . . . of Blair's address: Smith, *The Francis Preston Blair Family in Politics,* Vol. II, pp. 87–89; Williams, *Lincoln and the Radicals,* pp. 105–09.
429 The *New York Tribune* . . . "of the President": MB to John C. Frémont, August 24, 1861, quoted in *NYTrib,* March 4, 1862.
429 "Brother just took . . . think of it again": EBL to SPL, March 6, 1862, in *Wartime Washington,* ed. Laas, pp. 105–06.
430 A grateful Monty Blair . . . "very well of it": MB to FPB, March 12, 1862, box 7, folder 6, Blair-Lee Papers, NjP-SC.
430 approving Frémont's appointment . . . "opinion and action": *NYT,* March 13, 1862.
430 Seward appreciated . . . at large: Seward, *Seward at Washington . . . 1861–1872,* pp. 50–51.
430 "Somebody must be . . . the S. of S.": WHS to TW, April 25, 1862, quoted in ibid., p. 88.
430 "The President . . . and practical": WHS to TW, April 1, 1862, quoted in ibid., p. 81.
430 Count Gurowski despaired . . . *"strategy?"*: Entry for February 1862, in Gurowski, *Diary from March 4, 1861 to November 12, 1862,* pp. 156, 226–27, 171 (quote).
430 by the middle of March . . . him of command: Allan Nevins, *The War for the Union.* Vol. II: *War Becomes Revolution, 1862–1863* (1960; New York: Konecky & Konecky, undated reprint), p. 44.
430 Seward scorned . . . northern Virginia!: WHS, paraphrased in letter from Sam Ward to S. L. M. Barlow, March 27, 1862, in ibid.
431 While acknowledging . . . " *'stationary'* engine": Carpenter, *Six Months at the White House,* p. 255.
431 he confided to Browning . . . "orders to move": Entry for April 2, 1862, in Browning, *The Diary of Orville Hickman Browning,* Vol. I, pp. 537–38.
431 twenty-four hours before . . . to Fort Monroe: Sears, *To the Gates of Richmond,* p. xi; Sears, *George B. McClellan,* p. 168.
431 presented a sight . . . "seldom seen": Entry for March 16, 1862, in French, *Witness to the Young Republic,* p. 391.
431 "I will bring you . . . of his heart": GBM to the Soldiers of the Army of the Potomac, March 14, 1862, quoted in *NYT,* March 16, 1862.
431 "information . . . defend the Capital": EMS to Heman Dyer, May 18, 1862, reel 3, Stanton Papers, DLC.
431 "explicit order . . . entirely secure": AL to GBM, April 9, 1862, in *CW,* V, p. 184.
431 Stanton referred . . . "wrath of his friends": EMS to Heman Dyer, May 18, 1862, reel 3, Stanton Papers, DLC.
431 McClellan advanced . . . constructing earthworks: Sears, *To the Gates of Richmond,* pp. 36–62; Todd Anthony Rosa, "Peninsula Campaign," in *Encyclopedia of the American Civil War,* ed. Heidler and Heidler, p. 1483.
432 "You now have . . . as you can": AL to GBM, April 6, 1862, in *CW,* V, p. 182.
432 "he had better come & do it himself": GBM to MEM, April 8, [1862], in *Civil War Papers of George B. McClellan,* p. 234.
432 "the enemy . . . strong batteries": GBM and EMS paraphrased in entry of April 9, 1862, in *The Diary of Edward Bates, 1859–1866,* p. 249.
432 "It is indispensable . . . *But you must act*": AL to GBM, April 9, 1862, in *CW,* V, p. 185.
432 "Do not misunderstand . . . batteries built": GBM to AL, April 23, 1862, Lincoln Papers.
432 "the more decisive the results will be": GBM to MEM, April 19, [1862], in *Civil War Papers of George B. McClellan,* p. 243.
432 "compelled to change . . . delay of victory": GBM to EMS, [c. April 27, 1862], in ibid., pp. 248–49.
432 Joe Johnston . . . damage to the rebel army: Sears, *To the Gates of Richmond,* pp. 68, 62; GBM to EMS, May 4, 1862, in *Civil War Papers of George B. McClellan,* p. 254.
433 the long delay . . . a counteroffensive: McPherson, *Battle Cry of Freedom,* p. 455.
433 the spring social season . . . "over the ground": *NR,* April 4, 1862.
433 Mary remained in mourning . . . on the lawn: Commissioner B. B. French to Colonel John Harris, Commandant U.S. Marine Corps, June 12, 1862, p. 134, Vol. 14, Letters Sent by the Commissioner of Public Buildings, Vols. 12, 14 (July 2, 1855–June 9, 1865), reel 7, Records of the District of Columbia Commissioners and of the Offices Concerned with Public Buildings, 1791–1867 (National Archives Microfilm Publication M371), Records of the Office of Public Buildings and Public Parks of the National Capital, RG 42, DNA.
433 "more of a . . . in order to watch her": Mrs. Daniel Chester (Mary) French, *Memories of a Sculptor's Wife* (Boston and New York: Houghton Mifflin, 1928), pp. 147–48.
433 "I a simple . . . her perfection": Fanny Garrison Villard, quoted in Phelps, *Kate Chase, Dominant Daughter,* p. 279.

434 Kate's daily schedule, breakfasts and parties: Ross, *Proud Kate*, p. 78; Phelps, *Kate Chase, Dominant Daughter*, p. 112.
434 "stop at Van Zant's . . . and agreeable occasion": KCS to Jay Cooke, quoted in Ross, *Proud Kate*, p. 94.
434 "Cabinet calling . . . and Mrs. Stanton": "Miriam," February 19, 1862, *Iowa State Register*, Des Moines, quoted in Mrs. John A. Kasson, "An Iowa Woman in Washington, D.C., 1861–1865," *Iowa Journal of History* 52 (January 1954), pp. 66–67.
434 While Kate hosted . . . lively, entertaining conversation: Phelps, *Kate Chase, Dominant Daughter*, pp. 111–12.
434 "Diplomats and statesmen . . . the Bourbons": *Washington Post*, August 1, 1899.
435 the Chase home . . . a forum: Ross, *Proud Kate*, pp. 78, 93.
435 "parlor politics": For more on Washington women using entertaining for political purposes see Catherine Allgor, *Parlor Politics: In Which the Ladies of Washington Help Build a City and a Government* (Charlottesville and London: University Press of Virginia, 2000).
435 a "rival court": Belden and Belden, *So Fell the Angels*, p. 33.
435 the proclamation of General David Hunter: General Orders No. 11, May 9, 1862, quoted in AL, "Proclamation Revoking General Hunter's Order of Military Emancipation of May 9, 1862," May 19, 1862, in *CW*, V, p. 222.
435 "It seems to me . . . your Administration": SPC to AL, May 16, 1862, Lincoln Papers.
435 "No commanding general . . . consulting me": AL to SPC, [May 17, 1862], in *CW*, V, p. 219.
435 "dissatisfaction . . . believe would follow": AL, "Appeal to Border State Representatives to Favor Compensated Emancipation," July 12, 1862, in ibid., p. 318.
435 "among the more advanced . . . pusillanimity": Carl Schurz to AL, May 19, 1862, Lincoln Papers.
435 "all the more warmly . . . of Hunter's proclamation": SPC to Horace Greeley, May 21, 1862, reel 20, Chase Papers.
436 Rumors began to surface: *NYT*, May 20, 1862.
436 "The cabin" . . . his "inexhaustible stock": Viele, "A Trip with Lincoln, Chase, and Stanton," *Scribners Monthly* (1878), pp. 813–14.
436 "called up by . . . behind his back": Entry for April 19, 1862, in Madeline Vinton Dahlgren, *Memoir of John A. Dahlgren, Rear-Admiral United States Navy* (Boston: James R. Osgood & Co., 1882), p. 364 n2.
437 "muscular power . . . in vain to imitate him": Viele, "A Trip with Lincoln, Chase, and Stanton," *Scribners Monthly* (1878), pp. 815–16.
437 pored over maps . . . around Virginia: Ibid., p. 815; William E. Baringer, "On Enemy Soil: President Lincoln's Norfolk Campaign," *Abraham Lincoln Quarterly* 7 (March 1952), p. 6.
437 Union forces at Fort Monroe: "Map of Hampton Roads and Adjacent Shore," in John Taylor Wood, "The First Fight of Iron-Clads," in *Battles and Leaders of the Civil War*, Vol. I, Part 2, p. 699. The mouths of the James, Nansemond, and Elizabeth rivers all converge at Hampton Roads.
437 *Merrimac* . . . devastating engagements: Gene A. Smith, "*Monitor* versus *Virginia* (8 March 1862)," in *Encyclopedia of the American Civil War*, ed. Heidler and Heidler, p. 1348. Although the Confederates had rechristened the ironclad the CSS *Virginia*, the vessel continued to be known by its previous name, the *Merrimac.*
437 "It is a disgrace . . . cannot cope": Montgomery C. Meigs, quoted in Gorham, *Life and Public Services of Edwin M. Stanton*, Vol. I, p. 371.
437 An emergency cabinet meeting . . . "presence": Niven, *Gideon Welles*, p. 403.
437 *Monitor* . . . "cheese box on a raft": Entry for October 10, 1862, in French, *Witness to the Young Republic*, p. 412.
437 "a pigmy to a giant": *NYT*, March 14, 1862 (quote); *NYT*, March 11, 1862.
437 When Stanton learned . . . "with diamonds": *NYT*, March 16, 1862.
437 "The ringing of those plates": Herman Melville, "A Utilitarian View of the *Monitor's* Fight," in *The Works of Herman Melville*, Vol. XVI (London: Constable & Co., 1924), pp. 44, 45.
437 huddled over maps . . . Navy Yard vulnerable: Baringer, "On Enemy Soil," *ALQ* 7 (1952), p. 8; Shelby Foote, *The Civil War: A Narrative*. Vol. I: *Fort Sumter to Perryville* (New York: Random House, 1958; New York: Vintage Books, 1986), p. 414.
438 Lincoln and his little group . . . "Treasury to follow": SPC to Janet Chase Hoyt, May 7, 1862, reel 20, Chase Papers.
438 one leg permanently damaged: Wolcott, "Edwin M. Stanton," p. 131.
438 Goldsborough approved . . . across the water: Foote, *The Civil War*, Vol. I, p. 414.
438 "a smoke curled . . . turned back": SPC to Janet Chase Hoyt, May 8, 1862, quoted in Warden, *Private Life and Public Services*, p. 428.
438 each personally surveyed . . . delay the attack: SPC to Janet Chase Hoyt, May 11, 1862, reel 20, Chase Papers; Baringer, "On Enemy Soil," *ALQ* (1952), pp. 15–18.
438 Chase, accompanying . . . of the region: SPC to Janet Chase Hoyt, May 11, 1862, reel 20, Chase Papers.
439 "The night was very . . . of mere appearances": Carpenter, *Six Months at the White House*, pp. 104–05.
439 reporters noted . . . bouts of vertigo: *Philadelphia Inquirer*, May 13, 1862.
439 "one of the strangest . . . military history": Foote, *The Civil War*, Vol. I, p. 413.
439 "So has ended . . . now virtually ours": SPC to Janet Chase Hoyt, May 11, 1862, reel 20, Chase Papers.
439 "Norfolk . . . my movements": GBM to MEM, May 10, [1862], in *Civil War Papers of George B. McClellan*, p. 262.
439 Welles invited . . . "field glasses and maps": FWS to FAS, undated letter, quoted in Seward, *Seward at Washington . . . 1861–1872*, p. 89.
440 enjoyed an easy camaraderie . . . with one another: Mary Jane Welles to Edgar T. Welles, May 19, 1862, typescript, reel 34, Welles Papers.
440 Seward . . . composed a humorous poem: Entry for May 19, 1862, in Dahlgren, *Memoir of John A. Dahlgren*, p. 368.

440 "Virginia is sad . . . everywhere": WHS to FAS, May 19, 1862, quoted in Seward, *Seward at Washington . . . 1861–1872*, p. 94.
440 "We saw war . . . precedes its march": WHS to FAS, undated letter, quoted in ibid., p. 93.
440 The steamer reached McClellan's camp . . . "its supporting fleet": FWS to FAS, undated letter, quoted in ibid., p. 89.
440 "a nuisance": GBM to MEM, May 15, [1862], in *Civil War Papers of George B. McClellan*, p. 267.
440 he convinced . . . "this side of Richmond": WHS to AL, May 14, 1862, Lincoln Papers.
440 "one of the great . . . of the world": GBM to MEM, May 22, [1862], in *Civil War Papers of George B. McClellan*, p. 274.
440 "At night . . . or New York": FWS to FAS, undated letter, quoted in Seward, *Seward at Washington . . . 1861–1872*, p. 89.
440 Seward advised Lincoln . . . "as soon as possible": WHS to AL, May 14, 1862, Lincoln Papers.
440 McDowell was ordered: AL to Irvin McDowell, [May 17, 1862], in *CW*, V, pp. 219–20.
441 McClellan stood . . . "animal": GBM to MEM, [June 9, 1862], in *Civil War Papers of George B. McClellan*, p. 293.
441 an impromptu visit . . . *Marco Bozzaris*: Entry for May 22, [1862], in Dahlgren, *Memoir of John A. Dahlgren*, pp. 368, 368 n1; John W. M. Hallock, *The American Byron: Homosexuality and the Fall of Fitz-Greene Halleck* (Madison: University of Wisconsin Press, 2000), pp. 96–98; Fitz-Greene Halleck, "Marco Bozzaris," in *Yale Book of American Verse*, ed. Thomas R. Lounsbury (New Haven, Conn.: Yale University Press, 1912), pp. 12–13.
441 "a common baggage . . . think much of McDowell!": Entry for May 23, 1862, in Dahlgren, *Memoir of John A. Dahlgren*, pp. 369–70.
442 General Stonewall Jackson had been sent: McPherson, *Battle Cry of Freedom*, pp. 455–57.
442 "I have been compelled . . . to join you": AL to GBM, May 24, 1862, in *CW*, V, p. 232.
442 "Stripped bare . . . from you instantly": AL to GBM, May 25, 1862, in ibid., pp. 236–37.
442 "Independently . . . shall attack Richmond": GBM to AL, May 25, 1862, Lincoln Papers.
442 "just finished . . . knavery & folly": GBM to MEM, May 25, [1862], in *Civil War Papers of George B. McClellan*, p. 275.
442 "Lincoln's diversion . . . to capture Richmond": McPherson, *Battle Cry of Freedom*, p. 460.
443 Confederate attack at Fair Oaks: Sears, *To the Gates of Richmond*, pp. 111–45, 147, 149; Sears, *George B. McClellan*, p. 196.
443 "McClellan keeps sending . . . has not stirred": Christopher Wolcott to Pamphila Stanton Wolcott, June 11, 1862, in Wolcott, "Edwin M. Stanton," p. 156 (first quote); Wolcott to Wolcott, June 22, 1862, ibid., p. 157a (second quote).
443 bridges to be built: Sears, *To the Gates of Richmond*, p. 158.
443 "if I cannot fully . . . for the results": GBM to EMS, June 16, 1862, reel 3, Stanton Papers, DLC.
443 "utmost prudence . . . all know it": GBM to MEM, June 22, [1862], in *Civil War Papers of George B. McClellan*, p. 305.
443 allowed General Lee to take the initiative: Sears, *To the Gates of Richmond*, p. 151.
443 the Seven Days Battles: For a detailed description of the Seven Days Battles, see Sears, *To the Gates of Richmond*, pp. 181–336.
443 Federals dead, wounded, and missing: Ibid., pp. 344–45.
443 "vastly superior . . . where it belongs": GBM to EMS, June 25, [1862], in *Civil War Papers of George B. McClellan*, pp. 309–10.
443 "pains me . . . if I would": AL to GBM, June 26, 1862, in *CW*, V, p. 286.
443 neither McClellan nor Lincoln was able to sleep: Entry for July 5, 1862, in Dahlgren, *Memoir of John A. Dahlgren*, p. 375; Sears, *George B. McClellan*, p. 209.
443 Gaines' Mill . . . McClellan to retreat: Sears, *To the Gates of Richmond*, pp. 213–50; Sears, *George B. McClellan*, p. 212.
443 "I now know . . . sacrifice this army": GBM to EMS, June 28, 1862, *OR*, Ser. 1, Vol. XI, p. 61.
444 When the supervisor of telegrams . . . it to Stanton: Bates, *Lincoln in the Telegraph Office*, pp. 109–10.
444 McClellan's troops remained a strong: McPherson, *Battle Cry of Freedom*, p. 468.
444 Malvern Hill: Sears, *To the Gates of Richmond*, pp. 308–36.
444 "He was simply out-generaled": Christopher Wolcott to Pamphila Stanton Wolcott, July 2, 1862, in Wolcott, "Edwin M. Stanton," p. 157a.
444 he continued to retreat: McPherson, *Battle Cry of Freedom*, p. 470; Sears, *To the Gates of Richmond*, p. 338.

CHAPTER 17: "WE ARE IN THE DEPTHS"

Page

445 "We are in the . . . gloomy thinking": Entry for July 14, 1862, *Diary of George Templeton Strong*, Vol. III, p. 241.
445 manifesting an anxiety . . . "more momentous": *Iowa State Register*, Des Moines, July 16, 1862.
445 "the gloomiest . . . so low": Entry for July 4, 1862, in Gurowski, *Diary from March 4, 1861 to November 12, 1862*, p. 235.
445 "the past has been . . . the war began": JGN to TB, July 13, 1862, container 2, Nicolay Papers.
446 "It is a startling . . . sustain a spirit": WHS to FS, August 2, 1862, in Seward, *Seward at Washington . . . 1861–1872*, pp. 120–21.

446 "Since the rebellion . . . taken Richmond": SPC to Richard C. Parsons, July 20, 1862, reel 21, Chase Papers.
446 "The house seemed . . . you were gone": SPC to KCS, June 24, 1862, reel 21, Chase Papers.
446 many long letters: SPC to KCS, June 24, 25, 29, and 30, July 1, 2 and 4, 1862, reel 21, Chase Papers.
446 "a mark of love and . . . on many points": SPC to KCS, July 6, 1862, reel 21, Chase Papers.
446 "All your letters . . . very good": SPC to KCS, July 4, 1862, reel 21, Chase Papers.
446 concealed her unhappiness . . . "So with us it came": William Sprague to KCS, May 27, 1866, Sprague Papers.
447 "My confidence . . . and so will I": SPC to KCS, July 6, 1862, reel 21, Chase Papers.
447 to visit the McDowells' . . . "will alarm you": Mrs. McDowell, quoted in Phelps, *Kate Chase, Dominant Daughter*, p. 121.
447 "The first necessity . . . of no more": *NYT*, July 7, 1862.
447 "Journals of all . . . instant removal": *NYT*, July 10, 1862.
447 "So you want . . . unaffected wonder": GBM to MEM, [July] 13, [1862], in *Civil War Papers of George B. McClellan*, pp. 354–55.
447 *"the proof* . . . hypocrite & villain": GBM to MEM, July 22, [1862], in ibid., p. 368.
448 "there had been . . . opposition to McClellan": SPL to EBL, July 6, 1862, box 230, folder 7, Blair-Lee Papers, NjP-SC.
448 John Astor . . . "by a signal victory": Entry for July 11, 1862, *Diary of George Templeton Strong*, Vol. III, p. 239.
448 "If we could help . . . any other way": Frederick Law Olmsted to "My Dear Doctor," July 13, 1862, reel 2, Papers of Frederick Law Olmsted, Manuscript Division, Library of Congress.
448 "very fierce crusade . . . the art of war": *NYT*, July 10, 1862.
448 Mary Ellet Cabell . . . "tears to his eyes": Mary Ellet Cabell, quoted in Flower, *Edwin McMasters Stanton*, p. 164.
449 "the baby was dying" . . . on July 10: Christopher Wolcott to Pamphila Stanton Wolcott, July 6, 1862, in Wolcott, "Edwin M. Stanton," p. 157b (quote); Gideon Welles, "The History of Emancipation," *Galaxy* 14 (December 1872), p. 842.
449 his own health began to suffer: Benjamin, "Recollections of Secretary Edwin M. Stanton," *Century* (1887), p. 759.
449 "He unflinchingly . . . out of it": Whitman, *Specimen Days* (1902 edn.), p. 36.
449 "Allow me to assure . . . all your life": AL to Quintin Campbell, June 28, 1862, in *CW*, V, p. 288.
449 Stanton . . . shutting down recruiting offices: Thomas and Hyman, *Stanton*, p. 201; Sears, *George B. McClellan*, p. 180.
449 "a general panic": AL to WHS, June 28, 1862, in *CW*, V, p. 292.
449 Seward devised an excellent solution: AL, "Call for Troops," June 30, 1862, in ibid., p. 294 n1.
450 Seward telegraphed . . . "We fail without it": WHS to EMS, July 1, 1862, *OR*, Ser. 3, Vol. II, p. 186.
450 "The existing law" . . . his own responsibility: EMS to WHS, July 1, 1862, *OR*, Ser. 3, Vol. II, pp. 186–87 (quote p. 186).
450 He set a precedent . . . answered Seward's call: *NR*, August 14, 1862.
450 William Junior . . . "line of march": William H. Seward, Jr., speech before members of the 9th New York Artillery, 1912, box 121, Seward Papers, NRU.
450 Will's enlistment . . . his mother's fragile health: William H. Seward, Jr., to WHS, July 17, 1862, reel 117, Seward Papers.
450 "As it is obvious . . . no objection": FAS to FWS, August 10, 1862, reel 115, Seward Papers.
450 to make a personal visit . . . at Harrison's Landing: *Sun*, Baltimore, Md., July 11, 1862.
451 "The day had" . . . to over 100 degrees: *NYT*, July 12, 1862 (quote); *NYH*, July 11, 1862.
451 the "almost overpowering" heat: GBM to MEM, July 8, [1862], in *Civil War Papers of George B. McClellan*, p. 346.
451 at Harrison's Landing . . . moonlit evening: *NYT*, July 12, 1862; *NYH*, July 11, 1862.
451 great cheers . . . "deck of the vessel": *NYT*, July 11, 1862.
451 "strong frank . . . will be saved": GBM to MEM, July 8, [1862], in *Civil War Papers of George B. McClellan*, p. 346.
451 the "Harrison's Landing" letter: GBM to AL, July 7, 1862, *OR*, Ser. 1, Vol. XI, pp. 73–74.
451 Lincoln "made no comments . . . to me for it": McClellan, *McClellan's Own Story*, p. 487.
452 the president reviewed . . . wounded: Sears, *To the Gates of Richmond*, pp. 344–45; *NYH*, July 11, 1862.
452 "Mr. Lincoln rode . . . stove-pipe hat": *NYT*, July 11, 1862.
452 "entangled . . . has been universal": Rev. Joseph H. Twichell, "Army Memories of Lincoln. A Chaplain's Reminiscences," *The Congregationalist and Christian World*, January 30, 1913, p. 154.
452 "successive booming . . . Saul of old": *NYH*, July 11, 1862.
452 "thinned ranks . . . with their struggle": *NYT*, July 12, 1862.
452 "On the way . . . swim in the river": *NYH*, July 11, 1862.
452 "Frank was . . . greatly cheered": EBL to SPL, July 18, 1862, in *Wartime Washington*, ed. Laas, p. 165 n8.
452 summoned General Henry Halleck . . . general in chief: AL, "Order Making Henry W. Halleck General-in-Chief," July 11, 1862, in *CW*, V, pp. 312–13.
452 Halleck's victories . . . widely respected: "Halleck, Henry Wager (1815–1872)," in Sifakis, *Who Was Who in the Union*, p. 172.
453 "I do not know . . . I am a General": GBM to MEM, [July] 10, [1862], in *Civil War Papers of George B. McClellan*, p. 348.
453 Senator Chandler of Michigan . . . "the coward": Entry for June 4, 1862, in *The Diary of Edward Bates, 1859–1866*, p. 260.

453 Lincoln was determined . . . "cajoled out of them": Entry for July 24, 1862, in Browning, *The Diary of Orville Hickman Browning*, Vol. I, p. 563.
453 "much of his . . . crushing the rebellion": Benjamin, "Recollections of Secretary Edwin M. Stanton," *Century* (1887), p. 765.
453 "that all that Stanton . . . the President": Entry for July 14, 1862, in Browning, *The Diary of Orville Hickman Browning*, Vol. I, p. 559.
453 All the government departments had closed down: *NR*, August 7, 1862.
453 "never seen more persons . . . resembled": Entry for August 10, 1862, in French, *Witness to the Young Republic*, p. 405.
453 "the ringing of bells . . . Marine Band": *NYT*, August 7, 1862.
454 " 'Well! Hadn't I' . . . once to the stand": Entry for August 6, 1862, *Chase Papers*, Vol. I, p. 360.
454 "I believe there . . . *the Secretary of War*": AL, "Address to Union Meeting at Washington," August 6, 1862, in *CW*, V, pp. 358–59.
454 "He is one of . . . ever created": Entry for August 10, 1862, in French, *Witness to the Young Republic*, p. 405.
454 "originality . . . took all hearts": Entry for August 6, 1862, *Chase Papers*, Vol. I, p. 360.
454 The great rally concluded . . . in the Union: *NR*, August 7, 1862.
454 she had begun riding: *NYT*, April 5, 1862.
454 "she was so hid . . . she was there": Mary Hay to Milton Hay, April 13, 1862, in *Concerning Mr. Lincoln*, comp. Pratt, p. 94.
454 "she seemed to be" . . . Soldiers' Home: Entry for June 16, 1862, in French, *Witness to the Young Republic*, p. 400.
454 Soldiers' Home: Matthew Pinsker, *Lincoln's Sanctuary: Abraham Lincoln and the Soldiers' Home* (Oxford and New York: Oxford University Press, 2003); National Park Service, U.S. Department of the Interior, *President Lincoln and Soldiers' Home National Monument*, Special Resource Draft Study (August 2002).
455 "an earthly paradise": Julia Wheelock Freeman, *The Boys in White; The Experience of a Hospital Agent in and Around Washington* (New York: Lange & Hillman, 1870), p. 171.
455 a choice destination for Washingtonians: Pinsker, *Lincoln's Sanctuary*, p. 12.
455 "this quiet and beautiful . . . along the hills": *Iowa State Register*, Des Moines, July 2, 1862.
455 At Mary's urging: Pinsker, *Lincoln's Sanctuary*, pp. 4–5.
455 "We are truly . . . to Cambridge": MTL to Mrs. Charles Eames, July 26, [1862], in Turner and Turner, *Mary Todd Lincoln*, p. 131.
455 For Tad . . . campfire at night: Pinsker, *Lincoln's Sanctuary*, p. 78.
455 the Lincolns could entertain . . . among family and friends: Ibid., pp. 9–10.
455 "helped him . . . attorney in Illinois": Ibid., pp. 15 (quote), 81–82.
456 "daily habit . . . in the District": *Saturday Evening Post*, June 21, 1862.
456 "But for these humane . . . lost her child": Mrs. E. F. Ellet, *The Court Circles of the Republic* (Hartford, Conn.: Hartford Publishing Co., 1869; New York: Arno Press, 1975), p. 526.
456 "little cares . . . into nothing": Walt Whitman to Louisa Whitman, December 29, 1862, in Walt Whitman, *The Wound Dresser: A Series of Letters Written from the Hospitals in Washington During the War of the Rebellion*, ed. Richard Maurice Bucke (Boston: Small, Maynard & Co., 1898; Folcroft, Penn.: Folcroft Library Editions, 1975), p. 48.
456 "nothing of ordinary . . . it used to": Walt Whitman to Louisa Whitman, August 25, 1863, in ibid., p. 104.
456 "to form an immense army": *NYTrib*, July 9, 1862.
456 steamers arrived . . . Ambulances stood by: *NR*, June 30, 1862.
456 a massive project of . . . military hospitals: see *NR*, June 17–23, 1862; *Iowa State Register*, Des Moines, July 9, 1862.
456 Union Hotel Hospital . . . "sup their wine": *NR*, January 9, 1862.
456 "many of the doors . . . could christen it": Louisa May Alcott, *Hospital Sketches* (New York: Sagamore Press, 1957), p. 59.
456 The Braddock House . . . old chairs and desks: Freeman, *The Boys in White*, p. 37.
456 the Patent Office . . . transformed into a hospital ward: *NR*, June 27 and September 2, 1862.
456 "a curious scene . . . pavement under foot": Walt Whitman, quoted in *NYT*, February 26, 1863.
457 the Methodist Episcopal Church on 20th Street: *NR*, June 18, 1862.
457 covering pews . . . laboratory and kitchen: *NR*, June 23, 1862.
457 more than three thousand patients: *NR*, April 11, 1862.
457 baskets of fruit . . . pillows of wounded men: *NYTrib*, August 13, 1862 (quote); Ellet, *The Court Circles of the Republic*, p. 526; AL to Hiram P. Barney, August 16, 1862, in *CW*, V, pp. 377–78.
457 One wounded soldier . . . signature: MTL to "Mrs. Agen," August 10, 1864, in Turner and Turner, *Mary Todd Lincoln*, p. 179.
457 of "commanding stature . . . for it so eagerly": Alcott, *Hospital Sketches*, pp. 89–92, 99–100, 103, 104.
458 "singularly cool . . . (full of maggots)": Walt Whitman to Louisa Whitman, October 6, 1863, in Whitman, *The Wound Dresser*, pp. 123–24.
458 "heap of feet" . . . hospital grounds: Walt Whitman to Louisa Whitman, December 29, 1862, in ibid., p. 48.
458 she found it difficult . . . "wounded occupant": Alcott, *Hospital Sketches*, p. 59.
458 "Death itself . . . such a relief": Walt Whitman to Louisa Whitman, August 25, 1863, in Whitman, *The Wound Dresser*, p. 104.
458 "was so blackened" . . . eventually recovered: Amanda Stearns to her sister, May 14, 1863, reprinted in Amanda Akin Stearns, *The Lady Nurse of Ward E* (New York: Baker & Taylor Co., 1909), pp. 25–26 (quote p. 25).
458 Another youth . . . "on the Judgment Day": Alcott, *Hospital Sketches*, pp. 62–63 (quote p. 63).

458 "If she were worldly wise . . . many journals": Stoddard, *Inside the White House in War Times*, p. 48.
458 "While her sister-women . . . the White House": Ames, *Ten Years in Washington*, p. 237.
458 Mary continued . . . work discreetly: *Chicago Tribune*, July 4, 1872; Mary Elizabeth Massey, *Bonnet Brigades* (New York: Alfred A. Knopf, 1966), p. 44.
459 "our ever-bountiful benefactress & friend": *NR*, December 27, 1861.
459 "an angel of mercy": *NR*, June 27, 1862.
459 Lincoln had asked the legislature: AL, "Message to Congress," March 6, 1862, in *CW*, V, pp. 144–46.
459 "less than one half-day's" . . . border states combined: AL to James A. McDougall, March 14, 1862, in *CW*, V, p. 160.
459 "to surrender . . . the Union dissolved": *NYT*, July 13, 1862.
459 If the rebels . . . lose heart: AL, "Message to Congress," March 6, 1862, in *CW*, V, p. 145.
459 "emancipation in any form . . . the Border States": Editors' note on majority reply to AL, "Appeal to Border State Representatives to Favor Compensated Emancipation," July 12, 1862, in ibid., p. 319 n1.
460 "never doubted . . . to abolish slavery": AL, "Message to Congress," April 16, 1862, in ibid., p. 192.
460 "I trust I am not . . . seem like a dream": Frederick Douglass to CS, April 8, 1862, reel 25, Sumner Papers.
460 As slaves in the District . . . "when they wished": Smith, *Francis Preston Blair*, p. 354.
460 "all but one . . . quarters": EBL to SPL, April 19, 1862, in *Wartime Washington*, ed. Laas, p. 130.
460 Henry . . . the rest of his life: Henry, quoted in Smith, *Francis Preston Blair*, p. 354.
460 Nanny . . . "children are free": EBL to SPL, April 19, 1862, in *Wartime Washington*, ed. Laas, p. 130.
460 a new confiscation bill: "An Act to suppress Insurrection, to punish Treason and Rebellion, to seize and confiscate the Property of Rebels, and for other Purposes," July 17, 1862, in *Statutes at Large, Treaties, and Proclamations of the United States of America*, Vol. 12 (Boston, 1863), pp. 589–92, available through "Chronology of Emancipation During the Civil War," *Freedmen and Southern Society Project*, University of Maryland, College Park, www.history.umd.edu/Freedmen/conact2.htm (accessed April 2004).
460 "It was . . . a dead letter from the start": "Confiscation Act of July 17, 1862," in Mark E. Neely, Jr., *The Abraham Lincoln Encyclopedia* (New York: McGraw-Hill, 1982), p. 68.
460 a "disturbing influence . . . to break anew": CS, quoted in James G. Blaine, *Twenty Years of Congress: From Lincoln to Garfield*, Vol. I (Norwich, Conn.: Henry Bill Publishing Co., 1884), p. 374.
461 "our friends . . . take it at its flood": Entry for July 14, 1862, in Browning, *The Diary of Orville Hickman Browning*, Vol. I, p. 558.
461 "will be an end . . . errors of policy": Henry Cooke to Jay Cooke, July 16, 1862, in Ellis Paxson Oberholtzer, *Jay Cooke: Financier of the Civil War* (Philadelphia: George W. Jacobs & Co., 1907), p. 199.
461 "looked weary . . . in his voice": Entry for July 15, 1862, in Browning, *The Diary of Orville Hickman Browning*, Vol. I, p. 560.
461 the president traveled . . . final days of the term: JGN to TB, July 18, 1862, container 2, Nicolay Papers.
461 an extraordinarily productive session: See Leonard P. Curry, *Blueprint for Modern America: Nonmilitary Legislation of the First Civil War Congress* (Nashville, Tenn.: Vanderbilt University Press, 1968), pp. 101–36, 147–48, 179–97, 244–52.
462 "he had lately begun . . . d'etat for our Congress": Entry for July 21, 1862, *Chase Papers*, Vol. I, p. 348.
462 "I ask Congress . . . lost one advocate": WHS to FAS, July 12, 1862, quoted in Seward, *Seward at Washington . . . 1861–1872*, pp. 115–16.
462 The debates had grown . . . "part in them": Field, *Memories of Many Men*, pp. 264–65.
462 "a moral . . . political wrong": AL, "Sixth Debate with Stephen A. Douglas, at Quincy, Illinois," October 13, 1858, in *CW*, III, p. 254.
462 uses to which slaves were put by the Confederacy: Welles, "History of Emancipation," *Galaxy* (1872), pp. 843, 844; Hendrick, *Lincoln's War Cabinet*, p. 355.
462 emancipation could be considered a military necessity: Welles, "History of Emancipation," *Galaxy* (1872), p. 850.
463 the funeral of Stanton's infant son: *Star*, July 11, 1862.
463 "emancipating the slaves . . . justifiable": Entry for c. July 1862, *Welles diary*, Vol. I (1960 edn.), pp. 70–71.
463 when messengers . . . by the diplomats in attendance: Entry for July 21, 1862, *Chase Papers*, Vol. I, p. 348.
463 all members save the postmaster: Welles, "History of Emancipation," *Galaxy* (1872), p. 844.
464 books in the library: MTL to Benjamin B. French, July 26, [1862], in Turner and Turner, *Mary Todd Lincoln*, pp. 129–30; Seale, *The President's House*, Vol. I, pp. 291–92, 380.
464 "profoundly concerned . . . and slavery": Entry for July 21, 1862, *Chase Papers*, Vol. I, p. 348.
464 Lincoln read several orders . . . "decide the question": Entry for July 21, 1862, ibid., pp. 348–49.
464 another cabinet session; Carpenter painting: Stoddard, *Inside the White House in War Times*, p. 11; entry for July 22, 1862, *Chase Papers*, Vol. I, p. 351.
464 Lincoln took the floor . . . "on the slavery question": Welles, "History of Emancipation," *Galaxy* (1872), p. 844.
464 "had resolved upon . . . their advice": Carpenter, *Six Months at the White House*, p. 21.
464 His draft proclamation . . . "and forever": AL, "Emancipation Proclamation—First Draft," [July 22, 1862], in *CW*, V, p. 337.
464 statistics on slaves in border states and Confederacy: These statistics are based on 1860 census data for the numbers of slaves living in the border slave states that remained in the Union, and the eleven slave states that formed the Confederacy.
465 "fraught with consequences . . . could not penetrate": Welles, "History of Emancipation," *Galaxy* (1872), p. 841.

465 the members were startled . . . "immediate promulgation": EMS memorandum, July 22, 1862, reel 3, Stanton Papers, DLC.
465 Bates's approval . . . cadet at West Point: Introduction, and entries for April 14, 1862, and November 30, 1863, in *The Diary of Edward Bates, 1859–1866*, pp. xv–xvi, 250, 319.
465 his "very decided . . . the white race": Welles, "History of Emancipation," *Galaxy* (1872), pp. 844–45.
466 "among our colored . . . 'which they profess' ": Entry for September 25, 1862, in *The Diary of Edward Bates, 1859–1866*, pp. 263–64.
466 Welles remained silent . . . "intensify the struggle": Memorandum from September 22, 1862, quoted in Welles, "History of Emancipation," *Galaxy* (1872), p. 848.
466 "extreme exercise of war powers": Entry for October 1, 1862, *Welles diary*, Vol. I (1960 edn.), p. 159.
466 Caleb Smith . . . "attack the administration": Usher, *President Lincoln's Cabinet*, p. 17.
466 Blair spoke up . . . "were in vain": Welles, "History of Emancipation," *Galaxy* (1872), p. 847.
467 "beyond anything . . . universal emancipation": EMS memorandum, July 22, 1862, reel 3, Stanton Papers, DLC.
467 "depredation and massacre . . . soon as practicable": Entry for July 22, 1862, *Chase Papers*, Vol. I, p. 351.
467 The bold proclamation . . . "was his specialty": Entry for August 22, 1863, *Welles diary*, Vol. I (1960 edn.), p. 415.
467 "golden moment . . . four thousand years": Christopher Wolcott to Pamphila Stanton Wolcott, July 27, 1862, in Wolcott, "Edwin M. Stanton," p. 158a.
467 Lincoln later maintained . . . "Seward spoke": Carpenter, *Six Months at the White House*, p. 21.
467 a racial war in the South . . . their economic interests: EMS memorandum, July 22, 1862, reel 3, Stanton Papers, DLC.
468 "The public mind . . . to give them effect": WHS to FAS, August 7, 1862, in Seward, *Seward at Washington . . . 1861–1872*, p. 121.
468 "would have been . . . territory was conquered": Carpenter, "A Day with Governor Seward," Seward Papers.
468 "Mr. President . . . *shriek*, on the retreat": WHS, quoted in Carpenter, *Six Months at the White House*, pp. 21–22.
468 "until the eagle . . . about his neck": Carpenter, "A Day with Governor Seward," Seward Papers.
468 Seward's argument . . . met with Lincoln: Francis B. Cutting to EMS, February 20, 1867, reel 11, Stanton Papers, DLC.
468 "The wisdom of . . . the progress of events": AL, quoted in Carpenter, *Six Months at the White House*, p. 22.
469 "with public sentiment . . . nothing can succeed": AL, "First Debate with Stephen A. Douglas at Ottawa, Illinois," August 21, 1858, in *CW*, III, p. 27.
469 On August 14 . . . opportunity among their own people: "Address on Colonization to a Deputation of Negroes," August 14, 1862, in *CW*, V, pp. 371–75.
469 "We were entirely hostile" . . . to the proposal: Edward M. Thomas to AL, August 16, 1862, Lincoln Papers.
469 "are as much the natives . . . to a distant shore": *Liberator*, August 22, 1862.
470 provoked Frederick Douglass: Christopher N. Breiseth, "Lincoln and Frederick Douglass: Another Debate," *Journal of the Illinois State Historical Society* 68, no. 1 (February 1975), pp. 14–15.
470 "ridiculous . . . and bitter persecution": *Douglass' Monthly* (September 1862).
470 the "drop of honey": AL, "Temperance Address," February 22, 1842, in *CW*, I, p. 273.
470 "How much better . . . homes in America!": Entry for August 15, 1862, *Chase Papers*, Vol. I, p. 362.
470 cheap "clap-trap . . . perhaps of both": Entry for August, 1862, in Gurowski, *Diary from March 4, 1861 to November 12, 1862*, pp. 251–52.
470 "The Prayer of Twenty Millions": *NYTrib*, August 20, 1862.
471 seizing the opportunity to begin instructing the public: *NYT*, August 24, 1862.
471 "As to the policy . . . will help the cause": AL to Horace Greeley, August 22, 1862, in *CW*, V, pp. 388–89.
471 "I am sorry . . . than human freedom": FAS to WHS, August 24, 1862, reel 114, Seward Papers.
471 "killed years ago . . . destruction of slavery": WHS, quoted in Carpenter, *Six Months at the White House*, pp. 72–73.
472 no "truly republican . . . a great moral evil": FAS, miscellaneous fragment, reel 197, Seward Papers.

CHAPTER 18: "MY WORD IS OUT"

Page

473 Halleck ordered McClellan . . . Alexandria: Henry W. Halleck to EMS, August 30, 1862, in *OR*, Ser. 1, Vol. XII, Part III, p. 739; John J. Hennessy, *Return to Bull Run: The Campaign and Battle of Second Manassas* (New York: Simon & Schuster, 1993), p. 10.
474 He argued ferociously . . . "disastrous in the extreme": GBM to Henry W. Halleck, August 4, 1862, in *Civil War Papers of George B. McClellan*, pp. 383–84 (quote p. 383).
474 His only hope . . . of his command: GBM to MEM, August 8, [1862], in ibid., p. 388.
474 After delaying . . . until August 24: GBM to Henry W. Halleck, August 12, [1862], in ibid., pp. 390–93; Henry W. Halleck to EMS, August 30, 1862, in *OR*, Ser. 1, Vol. XII, Part III, p. 739.
474 General Lee moved north . . . the combined forces of Lee, Longstreet, and Jackson: Hennessy, *Return to Bull Run*, pp. 50–51, 55, 92–93, 122–23, 136.

474 "What is the stake? . . . *cause also*": WHS to FAS[?], August 21, 1862, quoted in Seward, *Seward at Washington . . . 1861–1872*, p. 124.
474 a comet appeared in the northern sky: *NR*, August 27, 1862.
474 "When beggars die": William Shakespeare, *The Tragedy of Julius Caesar*, Act II, sc. 2.
474 Although McClellan agreed . . . "leave of absence!": Sears, *George B. McClellan*, pp. 252–56; GBM to MEM, August 24, [1862], in *Civil War Papers of George B. McClellan*, p. 404 (quote).
474 "Pope is beaten . . . Washn again": GBM to MEM, August 23, [1862], in *Civil War Papers of George B. McClellan*, p. 400.
474 "the smell of the gunpowder . . . perceptible": *Star*, August 30, 1862.
474 "distant thunder": *NR*, September 1, 1862.
474 gathered on street corners . . . rumors flew: Leech, *Reveille in Washington*, p. 188; entry for September 3, 1862, *Welles diary*, Vol. I (1960 edn.), p. 106.
475 "Stonewall Jackson . . . about equal proportions": *NR*, September 1, 1862.
475 "prepared to stay all night, if necessary": Bates, *Lincoln in the Telegraph Office*, p. 118.
475 He wired various generals . . . news from Manassas: AL to Ambrose Burnside, August 29, 1862, in *CW*, V, p. 398; Lincoln to Herman Haupt, August 29, 1862, in ibid., p. 399; Lincoln to GBM, August 29, 1862 in ibid.; Bates, *Lincoln in the Telegraph Office*, pp. 119–21.
475 The president now had . . . "perfectly safe": GBM to AL, August 29, 1862, Lincoln Papers.
475 John Hay met the president . . . "his own scrape": "[1 September 1862, Monday]," in Hay, *Inside Lincoln's White House*, pp. 36–37.
475 McClellan's delay . . . "my opinion, required": EMS to Henry W. Halleck, August 28, 1862, in *OR*, Ser. 1, Vol. XII, Part III, p. 706; Henry W. Halleck to EMS, August 30, 1862, in ibid., p. 739 (quote).
475 "like throwing water . . . that in writing": SPC, paraphrased in entry for September 1, 1862, *Welles diary*, Vol. I (1960 edn.), p. 102.
475 Stanton volunteered . . . agreement regarding McClellan: Entries for August 29–30, 1862, in *Chase Papers*, Vol. I, pp. 366–67.
476 "Never before . . . sink into contempt": EB to Hamilton Gamble, September 1, 1862, Bates Papers, MoSHi.
476 written in Stanton's distinctive back-sloping script: Entry for September 1, 1862, *Welles diary*, Vol. I (1960 edn.), p. 100.
476 "unwilling to be . . . commanded by General Pope": Flower, *Edwin McMasters Stanton*, pp. 176–77.
476 Smith was persuaded . . . to Blair or anyone else: Entry for August 31, 1862, *Welles diary*, Vol. I (1960 edn.), pp. 93–95. Howard Beale has identified some of the language included in the 1911 edition of Welles's published diary as having been added later to the original manuscript diary. See Beale's emendations in individual diary entries for subsequent changes made in Welles's diary.
476 Stanton had invited Lincoln . . . "glad tidings at sunrise": "[1 September 1862, Monday]," in Hay, *Inside Lincoln's White House*, p. 37.
477 When Welles stopped by . . . "disrespectful to the President": Entry for August 31, 1862, *Welles diary*, Vol. I (1960 edn.), pp. 95–98 (quotes pp. 97–98).
477 "had called us . . . against him": Entry for September 1, 1862, ibid., pp. 101–02.
477 "he knew of no particular" . . . cabal against the president: Entry for August 31, 1862, ibid., p. 98.
477 "about Eight oclock . . . 'I am afraid' ": "[1 September 1862, Monday]," in Hay, *Inside Lincoln's White House*, pp. 37–38.
477 As rumors spread . . . 16,000 casualties: "5 September 1862, Friday," in ibid., p. 38; FWS to WHS, September 1, 1862, quoted in Seward, *Seward at Washington . . . 1861–1872*, p. 126; McPherson, *Battle Cry of Freedom*, p. 532.
478 "Jeff. Davis . . . before the National Capital": *NYT*, August 31, 1862.
478 put the president in an untenable . . . angrier he became: "1 September 1862, Monday," in Hay, *Inside Lincoln's White House*, p. 37.
478 "There is no . . . now to sacrifice": AL, quoted in "5 September 1862, Friday," in ibid., pp. 38–39.
478 When Halleck recommended . . . Lincoln agreed: Entry for September 12, 1862, *Welles diary*, Vol. I (1960 edn.), p. 124; Sears, *George B. McClellan*, p. 260.
478 Bates rewrote the protest . . . he agreed McClellan should go: Entry for September 1, 1862, ibid., pp. 100–03 (quotes); entry for September 1, 1863, in *Chase Papers*, Vol. I, pp. 367–68.
478 gathered at noon . . . messy controversy over McClellan: Entry for September 2, 1862, in *Lincoln Day by Day*, Vol. III, p. 137; entry for September 2, 1862, *Welles diary*, Vol. I (1960 edn.), p. 104 (quote).
479 Jenny was expecting . . . Clara, was dying: Janet W. Seward, "Personal Experiences of the Civil War," box 132, Seward Papers, NRU; FAS to WHS, August 24, September 7, 1862, reel 114, Seward Papers; FAS to WHS, September 10, 1862, reel 116, Seward Papers.
479 When he heard . . . cut his vacation short: Seward, *Seward at Washington . . . 1861–1872*, p. 127.
479 the president was called out: Entry for September 2, 1862, *Welles diary*, Vol. I (1960 edn.), p. 104.
479 "in a suppressed voice . . . prove a national calamity": Ibid., pp. 104–05 (quotes); entry for September 2, 1862, in *Lincoln Day by Day*, Vol. III, p. 137.
479 Stanton, recognizing . . . "a drooping leaf": *Evening Post*, New York, July 13, 1891 (quote); Flower, *Edwin McMasters Stanton*, p. 179.
479 "seemed wrung . . . to hang himself": EB, quoted in footnote to AL, "Meditation on the Divine Will," [September 2, 1862?], in *CW*, V, p. 404 n1.
479 "In great contests . . . it shall not end yet": AL, "Meditation on the Divine Will," [September 2, 1862?], in ibid., pp. 403–04.

479 Seward drove immediately . . . "during his absence": Seward, *Seward at Washington . . . 1861–1872*, p. 127.
480 "What is the use . . . should have known it": WHS, quoted in "[Mid-September 1862?]," in Hay, *Inside Lincoln's White House*, p. 40.
480 Seward turned to history . . . "preserve hopefulness": WHS to FS, c. November 1862, quoted in Seward, *Seward at Washington . . . 1861–1872*, p. 144.
480 Seward did not question . . . "sea of revolution": WHS to FAS, September 20, 1862, quoted in ibid., p. 132.
480 a president had to work: "5 September 1862, Friday," in Hay, *Inside Lincoln's White House*, p. 38.
480 McClellan smugly returned to his old headquarters: FWS to WHS, September 3, 1862, quoted in Seward, *Seward at Washington . . . 1861–1872*, p. 127.
480 "Again I have . . . 'away from us again' ": GBM to MEM, September 5, [1862], in *Civil War Papers of George B. McClellan*, p. 435.
480 crossed the Potomac . . . three cigars: James M. McPherson, *Crossroads of Freedom: Antietam.* Pivotal Moments in American History Series (New York: Oxford University Press, 2002), pp. 98, 104–05, 107–08. For actual "Lost Orders," see "Special Orders, No. 191, Hd Qrs Army of Northern Va, Sept 9th 1862," reel 31, McClellan Papers, DLC.
480 the Marylanders greeted . . . their countryside: GBM to MEM, September 12 and 14, [1862], and GBM to AL, September 13, [1862], in *Civil War Papers of George B. McClellan*, pp. 450, 458, 453.
481 "We are in . . . battle of the age": GBM to MEM, [September] 17, [1862], in ibid., p. 468.
481 casualties higher than D-Day: McPherson, *Battle Cry of Freedom*, p. 544.
481 "Our victory was . . . so completely": GBM to MEM, September 20, [1862], in *Civil War Papers of George B. McClellan*, p. 473.
481 Lincoln was thrilled . . . and allowed Lee to cross: AL to GBM, September 15, 1862, *CW*, V, p. 426; GBM to Henry W. Halleck, September 19 and 20, 1862, in *Civil War Papers of George B. McClellan*, pp. 470, 475.
481 "At last our Generals . . . National crisis": *NYT*, September 18, 1862.
481 "Sept. 17 . . . of its downfall": *NYT*, September 20, 1862.
481 On September 22 . . . "a graver tone": Carpenter, *Six Months at the White House*, p. 24; entry for September 22, 1862, in *Chase Papers*, Vol. I, p. 393 (quote); EMS, quoted by Judge Hamilton Ward in interview in the *Lockport Journal*, May 21, 1893, reprinted in Whipple, *The Story-Life of Lincoln*, p. 421.
481 reminding his colleagues . . . "to my Maker": AL, quoted in entry for September 22, 1862, in *Chase Papers*, Vol. I, pp. 393–94.
482 "there were occasions . . . the Supreme Will": Welles, "History of Emancipation," *Galaxy* (1872), p. 847.
482 not seeking "advice" . . . suggestions on language: AL, paraphrased in entry for September 22, 1862, in *Chase Papers*, Vol. I, p. 394.
482 "made a very emphatic . . . the measure": Welles, "History of Emancipation," *Galaxy* (1872), p. 846.
482 Blair reiterated . . . the fall elections: Entry for September 22, 1862, in *Chase Papers*, Vol. I, p. 395.
482 "maintain . . . present President"?: WHS, quoted in entry for September 22, 1862, in ibid., p. 394.
482 "it was not my way . . . take this ground": AL, quoted in Carpenter, *Six Months at the White House*, pp. 23–24.
482 "I can only trust . . . never forget them": AL, "Reply to Serenade in Honor of Emancipation Proclamation," September 24, 1862, in *CW*, V, p. 438.
482 proceeded to Chase's house . . . "that horrible name": "[24 September 1862, Wednesday]," in Hay, *Inside Lincoln's White House*, p. 41 (quote); entry for September 24, 1862, in *Chase Papers*, Vol. I, p. 399; *NYT*, September 25, 1862.
483 "in the meanest . . . evoke a generous thrill": Entry for September 23, 1862, in Gurowski, *Diary from March 4, 1861 to November 12, 1862*, p. 278.
483 "did not . . . of a single negro": Fessenden, paraphrased in entry for November 28, 1862, in Browning, *The Diary of Orville Hickman Browning*, Vol. I, p. 587.
483 "We shout for joy . . . confide in his word": *Douglass' Monthly* (October 1862).
483 "My word is out . . . take it back": AL, quoted in George S. Boutwell, *Speeches and Papers Relating to the Rebellion and the Overthrow of Slavery* (Boston: Little, Brown, 1867), p. 362.
483 "render eternal . . . the two sections": *The Times* (London), quoted in *NYT*, September 30, 1862.
483 *Richmond Enquirer* charged . . . "plots their death": *Richmond Enquirer*, October 1, 1862, quoted in *Philadelphia Inquirer*, October 6, 1862.
483 "said he had studied . . . than they did": "[24 September 1862, Wednesday]," in Hay, *Inside Lincoln's White House*, p. 41.
483 "be enthusiastically . . . great act of the age": Hannibal Hamlin to AL, September 25, 1862, Lincoln Papers.
483 "while commendation . . . not very satisfactory": AL to Hannibal Hamlin, September 28, 1862, in *CW*, V, p. 444.
483 "Stanton must leave . . . old place to me": GBM to MEM, September 20, [1862], in *Civil War Papers of George B. McClellan*, p. 476.
483 he would resign . . . "a servile insurrection": GBM to MEM, September 25, [1862], in ibid., p. 481.
484 McClellan drafted a letter . . . not to send the letter: Sears, *George B. McClellan*, pp. 326–27.
484 Though Stanton and Chase . . . considered resigning: Entries for September 25 and October 3, 1862, *Welles diary*, Vol. I (1960 edn.), pp. 148–49, 160–61.
484 Lincoln had made . . . relieved from duty: AL, quoted in "25 September 1863, Sunday," in Hay, *Inside Lincoln's White House*, p. 232.
484 Lincoln journeyed . . . early in October: Entry for October 1, 1862, in *Lincoln Day by Day*, Vol. III, p. 143; John G. Nicolay and John Hay, *Abraham Lincoln: A History*, Vol. VI (New York: Century Co., 1917), p. 174.
484 Halleck, fearing . . . "see my soldiers": AL, quoted in "Lincoln Visits the Army of the Potomac," *Lincoln Lore*, no. 1277, September 28, 1953.

484 As the regiments . . . "greatly amused the company": *NYH*, October 5, 1862.
484 accommodations at Antietam: "Lincoln Visits the Army of the Potomac," *Lincoln Lore*, no. 1277, September 28, 1953.
484 his "over-cautiousness": AL to GBM, October 13, 1862, Lincoln Papers.
484 "was very affable . . . very kind personally": GBM to MEM, October 5, [1862], in *Civil War Papers of George B. McClellan*, p. 490.
484 "real purpose . . . advance into Virginia": GBM to MEM, October 2, [1862], in ibid., p. 488.
484 "if I were . . . trivial": AL, "Speech at Frederick, Maryland," October 4, 1862, in *CW*, V, p. 450.
484 "May our children . . . and his compeers": AL, "Second Speech at Frederick, Maryland," October 4, 1862, in ibid., p. 450.
485 Lincoln had Halleck telegraph . . . "roads are good": Henry W. Halleck to GBM, October 6, 1862, in *OR*, Ser. 1, Vol. XIX, Part II, p. 10.
485 found all manner of excuses: GBM to Henry W. Halleck, October 7, 9, 11, and 18, 1862, and GBM to AL, October 17 and 30, 1862, in *Civil War Papers of George B. McClellan*, pp. 493, 495, 499, 502, 516.
485 "Will you pardon me . . . fatigue anything?": AL to GBM, October [25], 1862, in *CW*, V, p. 474.
485 "Our war on rebellion . . . specimen after all": Entry for October 23, 1862, *Diary of George Templeton Strong*, Vol. III, p. 267.
485 an "ill wind" of discontent: WHS to FS, October 1862, quoted in Seward, *Seward at Washington . . . 1861–1872*, pp. 141, 142 (quote p. 141).
485 the midterm November elections . . . "hurt to laugh": Sears, *George B. McClellan*, p. 335; Hendrick, *Lincoln's War Cabinet*, p. 325; AL, quoted in Sandburg, *Abraham Lincoln: The War Years*, Vol. I, p. 611 (quote).
485 "I began . . . I relieved him": AL, quoted in "25 September 1863, Sunday," in Hay, *Inside Lincoln's White House*, p. 232.
485 McClellan received . . . "visible on my face": GBM to MEM, November 7, [1862], in *Civil War Papers of George B. McClellan*, p. 520.
485 "More than a hundred . . . shed in profusion": *National Intelligencer*, Washington, D.C., November 14, 1862.
486 "In parting . . . an indissoluble tie": GBM to the Army of the Potomac, November 7, 1862, in *Civil War Papers of George B. McClellan*, p. 521.
486 choice of Burnside proved unfortunate: Darius N. Couch, "Sumner's 'Right Grand Division,' " in *Battles and Leaders of the Civil War*, Vol. III, Pt. 1, p. 106; Schurz, *Reminiscences*, Vol. II, pp. 397–98.
486 "ten times . . . as he has *head*": Entry for January 1, 1863, Fanny Seward diary, Seward Papers.
486 Fredericksburg Campaign: McPherson, *Battle Cry of Freedom*, pp. 571–72; Spencer C. Tucker, "Fredericksburg, First Battle of," in *Encyclopedia of the American Civil War*, ed. Heidler and Heidler, pp. 774–79.
486 "The courage . . . popular government": AL, "Congratulations to the Army of the Potomac," December 22, 1862, in *CW*, VI, p. 13.
486 "awful arithmetic . . . Confederacy gone": AL, paraphrased in Stoddard, *Inside the White House in War Times*, p. 101.
486 "more depressed . . . [his] life": Entry for December 18, 1862, in Browning, *The Diary of Orville Hickman Browning*, Vol. I, p. 601.
487 Tuesday, December 16 . . . "cause was lost": Fessenden, *Life and Public Services of William Pitt Fessenden*, Vol. I, pp. 231–32 (quote p. 232).
487 Chase had claimed . . . "of the cabinet": Benjamin Wade, paraphrased in entry for December 16, 1862, in Browning, *The Diary of Orville Hickman Browning*, Vol. I, p. 597.
487 had repeatedly griped . . . "salvation of the country": SPC to John Sherman, September 20, 1862, reel 22, Chase Papers (quote); SPC to Zachariah Chandler, September 20, 1862, reel 1, Chandler Papers, DLC.
487 "paralizing influence . . . the President": Boston *Commonwealth*, December 6, 1862, quoted in David Donald, *Charles Sumner and the Rights of Man* (New York: Alfred A. Knopf, 1970), p. 87.
487 "President *de facto* . . . to Uncle Abe's nose": *Chicago Tribune*, quoted in Thomas, *Abraham Lincoln*, p. 352.
487 "controlling influence . . . of the President": Fessenden, *Life and Public Services of William Pitt Fessenden*, Vol. I, p. 232.
487 "should go in . . . dismissal of Mr Seward": Benjamin Wade, paraphrased in entry for December 16, 1862, in Browning, *The Diary of Orville Hickman Browning*, Vol. I, p. 597.
487 "that measures should . . . to the war": Fessenden, *Life and Public Services of William Pitt Fessenden*, Vol. I, p. 234.
487 "a want of confidence . . . from the Cabinet": Senator Grimes, paraphrased in ibid., p. 233.
487 Fessenden asked . . . "on mere rumors": Ibid., p. 235.
487 "had no evidence . . . our cause greatly": Entry for December 16, 1862, in Browning, *The Diary of Orville Hickman Browning*, Vol. I, pp. 597–98.
488 "without entire . . . productive of evil": Fessenden, *Life and Public Services of William Pitt Fessenden*, Vol. I, p. 236.
488 "give time for reflection": Entry for December 16, 1862, in Browning, *The Diary of Orville Hickman Browning*, Vol. I, p. 598.
488 Preston King felt . . . " 'I can't get out' ": Seward, *Seward at Washington . . . 1861–1872*, pp. 146–47 (quotes); entry for December 19, 1862, *Welles diary*, Vol. I (1960 edn.), p. 194.
488 "They wish to . . . impose upon a child": Entry for December 18, 1862, in Browning, *The Diary of Orville Hickman Browning*, Vol. I, p. 600.
488 "disappointed . . . and chagrined": Entry for December 20, 1862, *Welles diary*, Vol. I (1960 edn.), p. 201.
488 Frances had journeyed . . . family for Christmas: Entry for December 22, 1862, Fanny Seward diary, Seward Papers.

489 "Do not come . . . & uncomfortable night": Entry for c. December 18 and 20, 1862, Fanny Seward diary, Seward Papers.
489 Charles Sumner was particularly . . . of the Confederates: Fessenden, *Life and Public Services of William Pitt Fessenden*, Vol. I, p. 242.
489 Republican senators convened . . . December 18: Ibid., pp. 236–38.
489 "I saw in a moment . . . ray of hope": Entry for December 18, 1862, in Browning, *The Diary of Orville Hickman Browning*, Vol. I, p. 600.
490 during a three-hour session: Fessenden, *Life and Public Services of William Pitt Fessenden*, Vol. I, p. 242.
490 Jacob Collamer . . . "purpose and action": Committee of Nine paper, quoted in ibid., p. 239.
490 "in the hands . . . malignant Democrats: Benjamin Wade, paraphrased in ibid., p. 240.
490 "had been disgraced": Ibid., p. 241.
490 "lukewarmness . . . *of him unperceived*": Entry for December 19, 1862, in *The Diary of Edward Bates, 1859–1866*, p. 269.
490 "shocked and grieved . . . confidence and zeal": Entry for December 19, 1862, *Welles diary*, Vol. I (1960 edn.), p. 195.
490 "earnest and sad . . . nor passionate": Entry for December 19, 1862, in *The Diary of Edward Bates, 1859–1866*, p. 269.
490 "expressed his satisfaction . . . interview": Fessenden, *Life and Public Services of William Pitt Fessenden*, Vol. I, pp. 242–43.
490 "he must work it out . . . on the matter": "30 October 1863, Friday," in Hay, *Inside Lincoln's White House*, p. 104.
490 He sent notices . . . and "good feeling": Entry for December 19, 1862, *Welles diary*, Vol. I (1960 edn.), pp. 194–95.
491 "could not afford to lose": Entry for December 19, 1862, in *The Diary of Edward Bates, 1859–1866*, p. 269.
491 "possible for him" . . . was forced to acquiesce: Entry for December 19, 1862, *Welles diary*, Vol. I (1960 edn.), pp. 195–96 (quote p. 195).
491 Lincoln began . . . "a reasonable consideration": Entry for December 20, 1862, ibid., p. 196; Fessenden, *Life and Public Services of William Pitt Fessenden*, Vol. I, p. 243 (quote).
491 "all had acquiesced . . . once decided": Entry for December 20, 1862, *Welles diary*, Vol. I (1960 edn.), p. 196.
491 He went on to defend Seward . . . Emancipation Proclamation: Fessenden, *Life and Public Services of William Pitt Fessenden*, Vol. I, pp. 243–44, 245–46.
491 "the whole Cabinet . . . and energetic action": Entry for December 20, 1862, *Welles diary*, Vol. I (1960 edn.), pp. 196–97.
491 Blair followed . . . "plural Executive": Ibid., p. 197.
491 "had differed much . . . matters of that kind": MB, paraphrased in Fessenden, *Life and Public Services of William Pitt Fessenden*, Vol. I, p. 245.
491 Bates expressed . . . as did Welles: Entry for December 19, 1862, in *The Diary of Edward Bates, 1859–1866*, p. 270.
491 As he contemplated . . . "regard to his Cabinet": Entry for December 20, 1862, *Welles diary*, Vol. I (1960 edn.), p. 199.
492 "he should not have come" . . . that substantially strengthened it: SPC, paraphrased in Fessenden, *Life and Public Services of William Pitt Fessenden*, Vol. I, pp. 244, 246.
492 Neither Stanton nor Smith: Ibid., p. 249.
492 Lincoln asked each . . . would be made: Ibid., pp. 246–49; Nicolay and Hay, *Abraham Lincoln*, Vol. VI, p. 266.
492 When Collamer . . . "He lied": Jacob Collamer, quoted in entry for December 22, 1862, in Browning, *The Diary of Orville Hickman Browning*, Vol. I, p. 603.
492 Lincoln agreed . . . tell the truth!: AL, paraphrased by Robert Todd Lincoln, in Nicolay, *Personal Traits of Abraham Lincoln*, pp. 159–60.
492 Welles paid an early call . . . where he found Stanton: Entry for December 20, 1862, *Welles diary*, Vol. I (1960 edn.), pp. 199–200.
493 "Suppose you . . . be left in it?": EMS, quoted in Seward, *Seward at Washington . . . 1861–1872*, p. 147.
493 Welles told Seward . . . "greatly pleased": Entry for December 20, 1862, *Welles diary*, Vol. I (1960 edn.), p. 200.
493 Monty Blair entered . . . Seward's resignation: Seward, *Seward at Washington . . . 1861–1872*, p. 147.
493 When Welles returned . . . hand in his own resignation: Entry for December 20, 1862, *Welles diary*, Vol. I (1960 edn.), p. 201.
493 Word had already leaked . . . "course of difficulties": Henry Cooke to Jay Cooke, December 20, 1862, in Oberholtzer, *Jay Cooke*, pp. 224, 226 (quotes p. 226).
493 "had been painfully . . . neither of you longer": Entry for December 20, 1862, *Welles diary*, Vol. I (1960 edn.), pp. 201–02.
494 Lincoln wrote a letter . . . "your Departments respectively": AL to WHS and SPC, December 20, 1862, in *CW*, VI, p. 12.
494 "Seward comforts . . . deems a necessity": Entry for December 23, 1862, *Welles diary*, Vol. I (1960 edn.), p. 205.
494 "Yes, Judge . . . end of my bag!": AL, quoted in Seward, *Seward at Washington . . . 1861–1872*, p. 148.
494 "I have cheerfully . . . to your command": WHS to AL, December 21, 1862, Lincoln Papers.
494 "come as soon as possible": Entry for December 22, 1862, Fanny Seward diary, Seward Papers.
494 "Will you allow me . . . than in your cabinet": SPC to AL, December 20, 1862, Lincoln Papers.
494 When Chase received . . . return to the Treasury: SPC to AL, December 22, 1862, Lincoln Papers.
494 "Seward was feeling . . . had been for weeks": Entry for December 23, 1862, *Welles diary*, Vol. I (1960 edn.), p. 205.

494 Seward magnanimously invited . . . Christmas Eve: SPC to FWS, December 24, 1862, reel 24, Chase Papers.
495 "a triumph over . . . drive him out": JGN to TB, December 23, 1862, container 2, Nicolay Papers.
495 Chase declined . . . "his hospitality": SPC to FWS, December 24, 1862, reel 24, Chase Papers.
495 "she regretted" . . . exception of Monty Blair: EBL to SPL, January 14, [1863], in *Wartime Washington*, ed. Laas, p. 231.
495 a visit to a Georgetown spiritualist . . . "had success": Entry for January 1, 1863, in Browning, *The Diary of Orville Hickman Browning*, Vol. I, pp. 608–09.
495 "I do not now see . . . I put it through": "30 October 1863, Friday," in Hay, *Inside Lincoln's White House*, p. 104.

CHAPTER 19: "FIRE IN THE REAR"

Page

497 a "general air of doubt": *NYT,* December 27, 1862.
497 "Will Lincoln's . . . Nobody knows": Entry for December 30, 1862, *Diary of George Templeton Strong*, Vol. III, p. 284.
497 As Frederick Douglass . . . give up ground: *Douglass' Monthly* (October 1862).
497 The final proclamation . . . "upon this act": Allen C. Guelzo, *Lincoln's Emancipation Proclamation: The End of Slavery in America* (New York: Simon & Schuster, 2004), pp. 178–81, 254–60 (quotes p. 260); entry for December 31, 1862, *Welles diary*, Vol. I (1960 edn.), pp. 210–11.
497 On the morning . . . fitful sleep: Quarles, *Lincoln and the Negro*, p. 140; Guelzo, *Lincoln's Emancipation Proclamation*, p. 181.
497 He then met with General Burnside . . . offered to resign: *Conversations with Lincoln*, ed. Charles M. Segal (1961; New Brunswick, N.J., and London: Transaction Publishers, 2002), pp. 232–34 (quote p. 232); Donald, *Lincoln*, pp. 409–11.
498 he would replace Burnside with "Fighting Joe" Hooker: Entry for January 25, 1863, in *Lincoln Day by Day*, Vol. III, p. 165.
498 A West Point graduate . . . at Antietam: "Hooker, Joseph (1814–1879)," in Sifakis, *Who Was Who in the Union*, pp. 199–200.
498 Seward returned . . . for correction: Guelzo, *Lincoln's Emancipation Proclamation*, p. 181.
498 New Year's reception . . . "trimming on the waist": Entry for January 1, 1863, Fanny Seward diary, Seward Papers.
498 "looking like a fairy queen": EBL to SPL, January 1, 1863, in *Wartime Washington*, ed. Laas, p. 224.
498 "Oh how pretty she is": Entry for January 1, 1863, Fanny Seward diary, Seward Papers.
498 the gates to the White House . . . shake the president's hand: Noah Brooks, *Mr. Lincoln's Washington: Selections from the Writings of Noah Brooks, Civil War Correspondent*, ed. P. J. Staudenraus (South Brunswick, N.J.: Thomas Yoseloff, 1967), pp. 58–60.
498 "grievously altered . . . cavernous eyes": Ibid., p. 29.
498 "his blessed . . . People's Levee": Ibid., p. 60.
498 "Oh Mr. French . . . remain until it ended": Benjamin B. French, quoted in Randall, *Mary Lincoln*, p. 320.
499 At Chase's mansion . . . "china, glass, and silver": Brooks, *Mr. Lincoln's Washington*, pp. 61–62.
499 "little, aristocratic" . . . years as a lawyer: Ibid., p. 176.
499 Stanton's salary . . . Ellen's dreams: Thomas and Hyman, *Stanton*, p. 392.
499 At 2 p.m. . . . soon joined him: Guelzo, *Lincoln's Emancipation Proclamation*, p. 182.
499 he "took a pen" . . . put the pen down: Carpenter, *Six Months at the White House*, p. 269.
499 "I never . . . signing this paper": AL quoted in Seward, *Seward at Washington . . . 1861–1872*, p. 151.
499 "If my name . . . soul is in it": Carpenter, *Six Months at the White House*, p. 269.
499 "stiff and numb": Seward, *Seward at Washington . . . 1861–1872*, p. 151.
499 "If my hand trembles . . . 'He hesitated' ": Carpenter, *Six Months at the White House*, p. 269.
499 "slowly and carefully" . . . sent out to the press: Seward, *Seward at Washington . . . 1861–1872*, p. 151.
500 "Has Lincoln played false to humanity?": Entry for January 1, 1863, in Adam Gurowski, *Diary from November 18, 1862 to October 18, 1863.* Vol. II. Burt Franklin: Research & Source Works #229 (New York, 1864; New York: Burt Franklin, 1968), p. 61.
500 At Tremont Temple . . . Anna Dickinson: Frederick Douglass, *Life and Times of Frederick Douglass, Written by Himself* (1893 edn.), reprinted in *Frederick Douglass, Autobiographies.* Library of America Series (New York: Literary Classics of the United States, 1994) p. 790 (quote); *Boston Journal*, January 2, 1863; *Boston Transcript*, January 2, 1863.
500 At the nearby Music Hall . . . Oliver Wendell Holmes: *Boston Journal*, January 2, 1863; *Boston Post*, January 2, 1863; Quarles, *Lincoln and the Negro*, p. 143.
500 "Every moment . . . one other chance": Douglass, *Life and Times of Frederick Douglass*, p. 791.
500 "had absolutely no foundation . . . to the quick": Helm, *The True Story of Mary*, pp. 208–09.
500 Mary had rushed . . . the joyous occasion: MTL to CS, December 30, 1862, in Turner and Turner, *Mary Todd Lincoln*, p. 144.
500 "was becoming agony . . . joy and gladness": Douglass, *Life and Times of Frederick Douglass*, p. 791.
500 "It was a sublime . . . with us, here": Eliza S. Quincy to MTL, January 2, 1863, Lincoln Papers.
500 a crowd of serenaders . . . in securing their freedom: Guelzo, *Lincoln's Emancipation Proclamation*, p. 186; *NYT,* January 3, 1863 (quote).
501 "Whatever partial . . . goes backward": *Boston Daily Evening Transcript*, January 2, 1863.

501 "Strange phenomenon . . . in all future ages": James A. Garfield to Burke Hinsdale, January 6, 1863, quoted in Theodore Clarke Smith, *The Life and Letters of James Abram Garfield.* Vol. I: *1831–1877* (New Haven: Yale University Press, 1925), p. 266.
501 "Fellow-citizens . . . the latest generation": AL, "Annual Message to Congress," December 1, 1862, in *CW,* V, p. 537.
501 "had done nothing . . . will be realized": AL, paraphrased in Joshua F. Speed to WHH, February 7, 1866, in *HI,* p. 197.
501 "discord in the North . . . spirit of the nation": *Louisville Journal,* quoted in *Boston Post,* January 2, 1863.
501 "union and harmony . . . destruction": WHS to FS, September 1862, quoted in Seward, *Seward at Washington . . . 1861–1872,* p. 135.
501 "It is my conviction . . . sustained it": AL, quoted in Carpenter, *Six Months at the White House,* p. 77.
502 *"slavery and quiet . . .* by tremendous majorities": Walt Whitman, "Origins of Attempted Secession," *The Complete Prose Works of Walt Whitman,* Vol. II (New York: G. P. Putnam's Sons/The Knickerbocker Press, 1902), p. 155.
502 "A man watches . . . strong enough to defeat the purpose": AL, quoted in Carpenter, *Six Months at the White House,* p. 77.
502 Horatio Seymour denounced . . . inaugural message: Guelzo, *Lincoln's Emancipation Proclamation,* p. 187.
502 James Robinson recommended: *NYT,* January 10, 1863.
502 Democratic legislatures . . . "crusade against Slavery": Oliver P. Morton to EMS, February 9, 1863, reel 3, Stanton Papers, DLC.
502 "under the subterfuge . . . oppose the War": JGN to TB, January 11, 1863, container 2, Nicolay Papers.
502 The "fire in the rear": AL, quoted in CS to Francis Lieber, January 17, 1863, quoted in Edward L. Pierce, *Memoir and Letters of Charles Sumner.* Vol. IV: *1860–1874* (Boston: Roberts Brothers, 1893), p. 114.
502 Army of the Potomac into winter quarters . . . "Valley Forge of the war": McPherson, *Battle Cry of Freedom,* pp. 586–88, 590 (quote).
503 Copperheads: McPherson, *Battle Cry of Freedom,* pp. 493, 591, 593, 600; John C. Waugh, *Reelecting Lincoln: The Battle for the 1864 Presidency* (New York: Crown Publishers, 1997), p. 91.
503 "fearfully changed" . . . a piercing shriek: Brooks, *Mr. Lincoln's Washington,* pp. 105–06.
503 "Ought this war" . . . then let her go: Clement L. Vallandigham, "The Constitution—Peace—Reunion," January 14, 1863, *Appendix to the Congressional Globe,* 37th Cong., 3rd sess. pp. 55, 57–59 (quotes on p. 55).
503 The time had come . . . let her go: Brooks, *Mr. Lincoln's Washington,* p. 70.
503 Saulsbury . . . removed from the Senate floor: Ibid., pp. 87–88.
504 "baneful . . . only for the negro": Andrew H. Foote, paraphrased in entry for January 9, 1863, in Browning, *The Diary of Orville Hickman Browning,* Vol. I, p. 611.
504 Orville Browning, who considered . . . "the government": Entry for January 26, 1863, in ibid., p. 620.
504 "conversed with . . . will re enlist": Entry for January 29, 1863, in ibid., pp. 620–21 (quotes p. 621).
504 "the alarming condition . . . a fixed thing": Entry for January 19, 1863, in ibid., p. 616.
504 "the democrats would soon . . . leave them": Entry for January 26, 1863, in ibid., p. 620.
504 "The resources . . . can be maintained": AL, "To the Workingmen of London," February 2, 1863, in *CW,* VI, pp. 88–89.
504 the people's representatives had passed: See Curry, *Blueprint for Modern America.*
504 "the grandest pledge . . . means to prevail": *NYT,* February 20, 1863.
504 "largest popular gathering . . . home of the brave": *NYT,* April 21, 1863.
505 "the greatest popular . . . in Washington": *Daily Morning Chronicle,* Washington, D.C., April 1, 1863.
505 Lincoln was dressed . . . of his father's embrace: Jane Grey Swisshelm, quoted in *St. Cloud [Minn.] Democrat,* April 9, 1863, in Frank Klement, "Jane Grey Swisshelm and Lincoln: A Feminist Fusses and Frets," *Abraham Lincoln Quarterly* 6 (December 1950), pp. 235–36.
505 Lincoln sent a telegram to Thurlow Weed . . . "and so I sent for you": AL, quoted in Barnes, *Memoir of Thurlow Weed,* pp. 434–35.
505 The amount needed was $15,000: Ibid., p. 435; AL to TW, February 19, 1862, in *CW,* VI, pp. 112–13.
505 "to influence . . . Connecticut elections": Entry for February 10, 1863, *Welles diary,* Vol. I (1960 edn.), p. 235.
505 "a stunning blow to the Copperheads": *NYT,* April 8, 1863.
505 "puts the Administration . . . seas to the end": *NYT,* April 9, 1863.
505 "frightened" . . . depress voter sentiment: JH to Mrs. Charles Hay, April 23, 1863, in Hay, *At Lincoln's Side,* p. 38.
505 "I rejoiced . . . the War commenced": EMS to Isabella Beecher Hooker, May 6, 1863, in Wolcott, "Edwin M. Stanton," p. 160.
505 "The feeling of . . . everywhere manifest": JGN to TB, March 22, 1863, container 2, Nicolay Papers.
505 "The glamour . . . the denunciations": Brooks, *Mr. Lincoln's Washington,* p. 138.
506 when Lincoln engaged . . . *"be crippled":* Entry for January 17, 1863, Fanny Seward diary, Seward Papers.
506 "Well . . . not one has got there yet": AL, quoted in "Personal," *Daily Morning Chronicle,* Washington, D.C., May 2, 1863.
506 "smoking cigars . . . 'good victuals' ": Brooks, *Mr. Lincoln's Washington,* p. 175.
506 At one dinner party . . . "[had] ever known": Entry for January 28, 1863, *Diary of George Templeton Strong,* Vol. III, p. 292.
507 welcome diversion in the telegraph office: Bates, *Lincoln in the Telegraph Office,* pp. 41–42, 143, 190.
507 "Abe was in . . . 'none anywhere else' ": AL, quoted in entry for April 21, 1863, in Dahlgren, *Memoir of John A. Dahlgren,* p. 390.

507 "a little after midnight . . . queer little conceits": Entry for April 30, 1864, in Hay, *Inside Lincoln's White House*, p. 194.
507 "Only those . . . heart bleeds": MTL to Mary Janes Welles, February 21, 1863, reel 35, Welles Papers.
507 Mary had gamely resumed . . . "to bear up": MTL to Benjamin B. French, March 10, 1863, in Thomas F. Schwartz and Kim M. Bauer, "Unpublished Mary Todd Lincoln," *Journal of the Abraham Lincoln Association* 17 (Summer 1996), p. 5.
507 "affable and pleasant . . . out of sight": Entry for February 22, 1863, in French, *Witness to the Young Republic*, p. 417.
507 "much shorter . . . his composition": Entry for February 12, 1863, Fanny Seward diary, Seward Papers.
508 In gratitude to Rebecca Pomroy . . . "look their best": Boyden, *Echoes from Hospital and White House*, pp. 131–32.
508 "brilliantly lighted . . . children's children": Pomroy, quoted in ibid., pp. 132–33.
508 Swisshelm had initially . . . "and its cause": Jane Grey Swisshelm, *Half a Century* (Chicago: J. G. Swisshelm, 1880), pp. 236–37 (quotes p. 237).
508 Mary was delighted . . . Nettie Colburn: Nettie Colburn Maynard, *Was Abraham Lincoln a Spiritualist?, or Curious Revelations from the Life of a Trance Medium* (Philadelphia: Rufus C. Hartranft, 1891), p. 83.
508 "very choice spirits . . . agreeable ladies": Joshua F. Speed to AL, October 26, 1863, Lincoln Papers.
508 "Welcome, Mr. Lincoln . . . *I was coming*": Mr. Laurie and AL, quoted in Maynard, *Was Abraham Lincoln a Spiritualist?*, p. 83.
508 The guests settled into . . . "easy chairs of the day": S. P. Kase, quoted in J. J. Fitzgerrell, *Lincoln Was a Spiritualist* (Los Angeles: Austin Publishing Co., 1924), pp. 18–19.
509 "Well, Miss Nettie . . . say to me to-night?": Maynard, *Was Abraham Lincoln a Spiritualist?*, p. 85.
509 There is no evidence that Lincoln . . . "learn the secret": "Lord Colchester—Spirit Medium," *Lincoln Lore*, no. 1497 (November 1962), p. 4.
509 She spoke for an hour . . . "not this wonderful?": S. P. Kase, quoted in Fitzgerrell, *Lincoln Was a Spiritualist*, pp. 20–21.
509 "I have neither . . . I must resume it": SPC to Horace Greeley, January 28, 1863, reel 24, Chase Papers.
509 Chase became physically ill . . . make it through: SPC to Richard C. Parsons, February 16, 1863, reel 25, Chase Papers.
510 his own handsome face . . . every dollar bill: SPC, *"Going Home to Vote." Authentic Speeches of S. P. Chase, Secretary of the Treasury, During His Visit to Ohio, with His Speeches at Indianapolis, and at the Mass Meeting in Baltimore, October, 1863* (Washington, D.C.: W. H. Moore, 1863), p. 25; Brooks, *Mr. Lincoln's Washington*, p. 176.
510 his own strained finances . . . bonds to the public: SPC to Jay Cooke, June 2, 1863, reel 27, Chase Papers.
510 Charles Benjamin . . . quickly make amends: Benjamin, "Recollections of Secretary Edwin M. Stanton," *Century* (1887), p. 759.
510 asked why he disliked . . . "detested it": Entry for April 25, 1863, *Diary of George Templeton Strong*, Vol. III, p. 314.
510 "nervous irritability": E. D. Townsend, *Anecdotes of the Civil War in the United States* (New York: D. Appleton & Co., 1884), p. 136.
510 his asthma . . . consent to seek rest: Benjamin, "Recollections of Secretary Edwin M. Stanton," *Century* (1887), pp. 759–60.
510 he enjoyed reading . . . attitude to the war: Ibid., p. 766; Johnson, "Reminiscences of the Hon. Edwin M. Stanton," *RCHS* (1910), p. 80 (quote).
511 Stanton refused to bring . . . remained at his post: Wolcott, "Edwin M. Stanton," p. 161; Thomas and Hyman, *Stanton*, pp. 165–66.
511 "would rather make" . . . ask Stanton for a favor: JH to JGN, November 25, 1863, quoted in Hay, *At Lincoln's Side*, p. 69.
511 Even when Stanton's own son . . . an official appointment: Johnson, "Reminiscences of the Hon. Edwin M. Stanton," *RCHS* (1910), p. 92.
511 rarely returned to Steubenville . . . for the funeral in Ohio: *NYT*, April 14, 1863; Wolcott, "Edwin M. Stanton," p. 130a.
511 Pamphila's conviction . . . died from overwork: Wolcott, "Edwin M. Stanton," p. 159.
511 the War Department utilize the services . . . "to Mr. Capen": AL, "Memorandum Concerning Francis L. Capen's Weather Forecasts," April 28, 1863, in *CW*, VI, pp. 190–91.
511 warring factions in Missouri . . . "hold of the case": AL to Henry T. Blow, Charles D. Drake and Others, May 15, 1863, in ibid., p. 218.
512 hastily written note to General Franz Sigel . . . "keep it up": AL to Franz Sigel, February 5, 1863, in ibid., p. 93.
512 The story is told: AL, quoted in Pinsker, *Lincoln's Sanctuary*, pp. 52–53.
512 Carl Schurz laid the blame . . . "We parted as better friends than ever": Schurz, *Reminiscences*, Vol. II, pp. 393–96.
513 excursion to Falmouth: Noah Brooks, "A Boy in the White House," *St. Nicholas: An Illustrated Magazine for Young Folks* 10 (November 1882), p. 62; Brooks, *Mr. Lincoln's Washington*, pp. 147–64.
513 "one of the purest . . . in the world": Anson G. Henry to his wife, April 12, 1863, transcribed in "Another Hooker Letter," *Abraham Lincoln Quarterly* 2 (March 1942), pp. 10–11.
513 Bates agreed . . . spring battles began: Entry for April 4, 1863, in *The Diary of Edward Bates, 1859–1866*, p. 288.

513 weather conditions: *Sun*, Baltimore, Md., April 6, 1863; entry for April 4, 1863, in *The Diary of Edward Bates, 1859–1866*, p. 287; Brooks, *Mr. Lincoln's Washington*, p. 51.
513 the steamer *Carrie Martin* . . . of George Washington: Seward, *Reminiscences of a War-Time Statesman and Diplomat*, p. 185; Noah Brooks, *Washington, D.C., in Lincoln's Time*, ed. Herbert Mitgang (Chicago: Quadrangle Books, 1971; Athens, Ga., and London: University of Georgia Press, 1989), p. 51.
513 the escalating storm . . . to the dinner menu: Brooks, "A Boy in the White House," *St. Nicholas* (1882), p. 62.
513 "the chief magistrate . . . firing a shot": Brooks, *Mr. Lincoln's Washington*, pp. 148–49.
513 "at its height" . . . a special train: *Sun*, Baltimore, Md., April 7, 1863 (quote); Brooks, *Mr. Lincoln's Washington*, p. 149.
513 "snow piled in huge . . . over the hills": *NYH*, April 10, 1863 (quotes); Brooks, *Washington, D.C. in Lincoln's Time*, p. 52.
514 Hooker's headquarters . . . 133,000 soldiers: Brooks, *Mr. Lincoln's Washington*, pp. 150–51; Shelby Foote, *The Civil War: A Narrative. Vol. II: Fredericksburg to Meridian* (New York: Random House, 1963: New York: Vintage Books, 1986), p. 235.
514 General Hooker and his accommodations: Entry for April 27, 1863, Fanny Seward diary, Seward Papers; *NYH*, April 10, 1863; Brooks, *Mr. Lincoln's Washington*, p. 150.
514 "I believe you to be . . . give us victories": AL to Joseph Hooker, January 26, 1863, in *CW*, VI, pp. 78–79.
514 was so moved by . . . printed in gold letters: Anson G. Henry to his wife, April 12, 1863, transcribed in "Another Hooker Letter," *ALQ* 2 (1942), p. 11.
514 "That is just such . . . man who wrote it": Joseph Hooker, quoted in Brooks, *Washington, D.C. in Lincoln's Time*, p. 57.
514 Mary's curiosity . . . "pleasant to her": *NYH*, April 10, 1863 (quote); *Star*, April 7, 1863; Brooks, *Mr. Lincoln's Washington*, p. 150.
515 reported badinage between . . . " 'sort of rebel' ": Brooks, *Washington, D.C. in Lincoln's Time*, p. 59.
515 Stormy weather . . . "shafts of wit": Brooks, *Mr. Lincoln's Washington*, p. 150; *NYH*, April 10, 1863 (quote).
515 The roar of artillery . . . "among them": Brooks, *Washington, D.C., in Lincoln's Time*, p. 53; *NYH*, April 11, 1863; Brooks, *Mr. Lincoln's Washington*, p. 153 (quote).
515 his gray cloak . . . faithfully by his side: Brooks, "A Boy in the White House," *St. Nicholas* (1882), p. 62.
515 "And thereby hangs . . . folds of the banners": *NYH*, April 11, 1863.
516 At the review of the infantry . . . "far away": Brooks, *Mr. Lincoln's Washington*, pp. 154, 158–59 (quote).
516 he extended his visit: Ibid., p. 161.
516 "the former stood . . . turn their backs": *NYH*, April 10, 1863.
516 rebel camps across the river . . . stars and bars: Brooks, *Mr. Lincoln's Washington*, pp. 155–56.
516 Union pickets . . . "belonging to friendly armies": Seward, *Seward at Washington . . . 1861–1872*, p. 162 (first quote); *NYH*, April 10, 1863 (last quote).
516 a Confederate officer . . . "politely and retired": Brooks, *Mr. Lincoln's Washington*, p. 156.
516 "It was a saddening . . . should arrive": Ibid., pp. 153–54.
517 issued one final directive . . . *all your men*": AL, quoted in Couch, "Sumner's 'Right Grand Division,' " in *Battles and Leaders of the Civil War*, Vol. III, Pt. I, p. 120.
517 boarded the *Carrie Martin* . . . "flags displayed": *NYH*, April 12, 1863.
517 were defending James S. Pleasants . . . "very bitter": EBL to SPL, April 16, 1863, in *Wartime Washington*, ed. Laas, p. 259 (quotes); Court-martial file of James Snowden Pleasants, file MM-15, entry 15, RG 153, DNA; *Sun*, Baltimore, Md., April 9, 1863.
517 sent the *Peterhoff* . . . to the Navy Department: Van Deusen, *William Henry Seward*, pp. 350–51; Monaghan, *Diplomat in Carpet Slippers*, pp. 303–04.
517 led to rumors of . . . "from the real question": Entries for April 23–28, 1863, *Welles diary*, Vol. I (1960 edn.), pp. 285–87 (quotes p. 287).
518 Montgomery Blair also sided . . . "in the Cabinet": Entry for April 17, 1863, ibid., pp. 274–75 (quote p. 275).
518 "I feel that . . . my present position": SPC to AL, March 2, 1863, Lincoln Papers.
518 This squabble was provoked . . . "my resignation": SPC to AL, May 11, 1863, Lincoln Papers.
518 "Chase's feelings were hurt": AL to Anson G. Henry, May 13, 1863, in *CW*, VI, p. 215.
518 he called at Chase's . . . "I finally succeeded": Field, *Memories of Many Men*, p. 303.
518 $45 million in bonds . . . "as do ours": *NYT*, May 3, 1863.
519 he placed his prickly secretary's third resignation: Riddle, *Recollections of War Times*, p. 273.
519 Blair, meanwhile, resented Chase . . . "private counsellor": Entry for May 10, 1863, in *The Diary of Edward Bates, 1859–1866*, pp. 290–91.
519 the Battle of Chancellorsville: See Stephen W. Sears, *Chancellorsville* (Boston and New York: Houghton Mifflin, 1996); Stanley S. McGowen, "Chancellorsville, Battle of," in *Encyclopedia of the American Civil War*, ed. Heidler and Heidler, pp. 394–98; Foote, *The Civil War*, Vol. II, p. 263.
519 "We have been . . . definite information": JGN to TB, May 4, 1863, container 2, Nicolay Papers.
519 Welles joined Lincoln: Entry of May 4, 1863, *Welles diary*, Vol. I (1960 edn.), p. 291.
519 Bates was particularly tense . . . "dangerous service": Entry for May 5, 1863, in *The Diary of Edward Bates, 1859–1866*, p. 289.
519 Lincoln admitted . . . what was going on: EBL to SPL, May 4, 1863, in *Wartime Washington*, ed. Laas, p. 264.
519 "no reliable . . . does not express them": Entry for May 5, 1863, *Welles diary*, Vol. I (1960 edn.), pp. 292–93.
519 "While I am anxious . . . or discomfort": AL to Joseph Hooker, April 28, 1863, in *CW*, VI, pp. 189–90.
519 "God bless you . . . with despatches": AL to Joseph Hooker, 9:40 a.m. telegram, May 6, 1863, in ibid., p. 199.
520 an unwelcome telegram . . . the order to retreat: Joseph Hooker to AL, May 6, 1863, Lincoln Papers; Sears,

Chancellorsville, p. 492; Darius N. Couch, "The Chancellorsville Campaign," in *Battles and Leaders of the Civil War*, Vol. III, Pt. I, pp. 164 (first quote), 167, 169–71 (second and third quotes p. 171).
520 "I shall never forget . . . of despair": Brooks, *Washington, D.C., in Lincoln's Time*, p. 60.
520 "Had a thunderbolt . . . would again commence": Brooks, *Mr. Lincoln's Washington*, p. 179.
520 "ashen" face . . . " 'will the country say!' ": Brooks, *Washington, D.C., in Lincoln's Time*, p. 61.
520 The president informed Senator Sumner . . . "I know not where": Entry for May 6, 1863, *Welles diary*, Vol. I (1960 edn.), pp. 293–94.
520 "This is the darkest day of the war": JH paraphrasing EMS, quoted in *Lincoln's Third Secretary: The Memoirs of William O. Stoddard*, ed. William O. Stoddard, Jr. (New York: Exposition Press, 1955), p. 173.
520 At the Willard . . . bound for Hooker's headquarters: Brooks, *Mr. Lincoln's Washington*, p. 180.
521 "All accounts agree . . . back into the fray": *NYT*, May 12, 1863.
521 casualties at Chancellorsville: McPherson, *Battle Cry of Freedom*, p. 645; Sears, *Chancellorsville*, pp. 492, 501.
521 death of Stonewall Jackson: James I. Robertson, Jr., "Jackson, Thomas Jonathan," in *Encyclopedia of the American Civil War*, ed. Heidler and Heidler, p. 1065.
521 "Since the death . . . death of Jackson": *Richmond Whig*, May 12, 1863.
521 "If possible" . . . ready to assist Hooker: AL to Joseph Hooker, May 7, 1863, in *CW*, VI, p. 201.

CHAPTER 20: "THE TYCOON IS IN FINE WHACK"

Page
522 General Orders No. 38 . . . tried by a military court: "General Orders, No. 38," Department of the Ohio, April 13, 1863, in *OR*, Ser. 1, Vol. XXIII, Part II, p. 237.
522 "hurl King Lincoln from his throne": Clement L. Vallandigham speech, May 1, 1863, quoted in Fletcher Pratt, *Stanton: Lincoln's Secretary of War* (New York: W. W. Norton & Co., 1953), p. 289.
522 "The door resisted" . . . a side entrance: *Cincinnati Commercial*, quoted in *Star*, May 9, 1863.
522 found him guilty . . . habeas corpus was denied: Trial of Clement L. Vallandigham, enclosure in Ambrose E. Burnside to Henry W. Halleck, May 18, 1863, and General Orders, No. 68, Headquarters, Department of the Ohio, May 16, 1863, *OR*, Ser. 2, Vol. V, pp. 633–46; McPherson, *Battle Cry of Freedom*, p. 597.
522 the *Chicago Times* . . . the paper down: Entry for June 3, 1863, in Browning, *The Diary of Orville Hickman Browning*, Vol. I, p. 632.
522 While he later admitted . . . uphold Burnside: McPherson, *Battle Cry of Freedom*, p. 597; entry for June 3, 1863, *Welles diary*, Vol. I (1960 edn.), p. 321.
523 Thurlow Weed deplored the arrest: TW to John Bigelow, June 27, 1863, in John Bigelow, *Retrospective of an Active Life*. Vol. II: *1863–1865* (New York: Baker & Taylor Co., 1909), p. 23.
523 Senator Trumbull . . . "government overthrown": Entry for May 17, 1863, in Browning, *The Diary of Orville Hickman Browning*, Vol. I, p. 630.
523 "by a large and honest" . . . the loyal states: Nathaniel P. Tallmadge to WHS, May 24, 1863, Lincoln Papers.
523 Lincoln, searching . . . Confederate lines: Charles F. Howlett, "Vallandigham, Clement Laird," in *Encyclopedia of the American Civil War*, ed. Heidler and Heidler, p. 2012.
523 his Copperhead body . . . "where his heart already was": Schuyler Colfax to AL, June 13, 1863, Lincoln Papers.
523 "general satisfaction . . . power for evil": *NYT*, May 21, 1863.
523 Vallandigham was removed . . . escaped to Canada: McPherson, *Battle Cry of Freedom*, p. 597.
523 Stanton revoked . . . to suppress newspapers: EMS to Ambrose E. Burnside, June 1, 1863, in *OR*, Ser. 2, Vol. V, p. 724; General Orders, No. 91, Headquarters, Department of the Ohio, June 4, 1863, *OR*, Ser. 1, Vol. XXIII, Part II, p. 386.
523 "suppress the . . . of its citizens": Carpenter, *Six Months at the White House*, pp. 156–57.
523 Upon hearing . . . opposed his action: Ambrose E. Burnside to AL, May 29, 1863, Lincoln Papers.
523 Lincoln not only refused . . . "through with it": AL to Ambrose E. Burnside, May 29, 1863, in *CW*, VI, p. 237.
523 "Often an idea . . . from every side": James F. Wilson recollections, quoted in Carl Sandburg, *Abraham Lincoln: The War Years*, Vol. II (New York: Harcourt, Brace & Co., 1936; 1939), p. 308.
524 "It has vigor and ability": Entry of June 5, 1863, *Welles diary*, Vol. I (1960 edn.), p. 323.
524 "we are Struggling . . . in Rhetoric": MB to AL, June 6, 1863, Lincoln Papers.
524 The finished letter . . . "if he shall desert": AL to Erastus Corning and Others, [June 12,] 1863, in *CW*, VI, pp. 260–69 (quotes pp. 264, 266–67).
524 "It is full . . . and conclusive": *NYT*, June 15, 1863.
524 Edward Everett . . . "the step complete": Edward Everett to AL, June 16, 1863, Lincoln Papers.
524 "It is a grand document . . . every citizen": "The President's Letter," June 15, 1863, in William O. Stoddard, *Dispatches from Lincoln's White House: The Anonymous Civil War Journalism of Presidential Secretary William O. Stoddard*, ed. Michael Burlingame (Lincoln and London: University of Nebraska Press, 2002), p. 160.
525 Printed in a great variety . . . 10 million people: Donald, *Lincoln*, pp. 443–44.
525 Welles noted . . . "assistant is present": Entry for June 2, 1863, *Welles diary*, Vol. I (1960 edn.), pp. 319–20 (quote p. 320).
525 Blair, frustrated . . . word with Lincoln: Hendrick, *Lincoln's War Cabinet*, p. 387; entry for May 12, 1863, in *The Diary of Edward Bates, 1859–1866*, p. 292.
525 "At such a time . . . interchange of views": Entry for June 30, 1863, *Welles diary*, Vol. I (1960 edn.), p. 351.

525 "There is now . . . consent of the members": Entry for May 16, 1863, in *The Diary of Edward Bates, 1859–1866*, pp. 292–93.
525 "But how idle . . . furnish the means": SPC to David Dudley Field, June 30, 1863, reel 27, Chase Papers.
525 If he were president . . . "of importance": SPC to James A. Garfield, May 31, 1863, reel 12, Papers of James A. Garfield, Manuscript Division, Library of Congress [hereafter Garfield Papers, DLC].
525 Blair decried . . . of Seward and Stanton: Entry for June 23, 1863, *Welles diary*, Vol. I (1960 edn.), p. 340.
525 Lincoln's unwillingness . . . restore McClellan: Entry for June 26, 1863, ibid., p. 345.
525 In Blair's mind . . . "throat if he could": "19 July 1863, Sunday," in Hay, *Inside Lincoln's White House*, p. 65.
526 Blair's hatred for Stanton . . . military information: Entry for June 30, 1863, *Welles diary*, Vol. I (1960 edn.), p. 352.
526 "Strange, strange . . . Stanton and Seward": Entry for June 15, 1863, ibid., p. 329.
526 Recognizing Blair's desire . . . to get through: For a description of Blair's innovations with the postal service, see chapter 31 of Smith, *The Francis Preston Blair Family in Politics*, Vol. II, pp. 90–111.
526 catch up with his "Neptune" . . . telegraph office: Entry for July 14, 1863, *Welles diary*, Vol. I (1960 edn.), p. 370.
526 When he felt compelled . . . "admirable success": AL to GW, July 25, 1863, in *CW*, VI, p. 349.
526 A particularly bitter . . . "be very mad": AL, quoted in entry for May 26, 1863, *Welles diary*, Vol. I (1960 edn.), p. 313.
527 the humorist Orpheus Kerr . . . "as regards myself": Entry for June 17, 1863, ibid., p. 333.
527 William Rosecrans . . . "to do hastily": AL to William S. Rosecrans, May 20, 1863, in *CW*, VI, p. 224.
527 felt compelled to remove General Samuel Curtis . . . "faithful, and patriotic": AL to Samuel R. Curtis, June 8, 1863, in ibid., p. 253.
527 a note from Governor Gamble . . . "grossly offensive": Hamilton R. Gamble to AL, July 13, 1863, Lincoln Papers.
527 was told "to put it away": "23 July 1863, Thursday," in Hay, *Inside Lincoln's White House*, p. 66.
527 "trying to preserve . . . should offend you": AL to Hamilton R. Gamble, July 23, 1863, Lincoln Papers.
528 Milroy railed about "the . . . hatred" of Halleck: Robert H. Milroy to AL, June 28, 1863, Lincoln Papers. See also Robert H. Milroy to John P. Usher, June 28, 1863, Lincoln Papers.
528 "I have scarcely seen . . . you have split": AL to Robert H. Milroy, June 29, 1863, in *CW*, VI, p. 308.
528 "Truth to speak . . . so, ranks you": AL to William S. Rosecrans, March 17, 1863, in ibid., p. 139.
528 Grant had advanced . . . settled into a siege: Stanley S. McGowen, "Vicksburg Campaign (May–July 1863)," in *Encyclopedia of the American Civil War*, ed. Heidler and Heidler, pp. 2021–25.
528 "Whether Gen. Grant . . . brilliant in the world": AL to Isaac N. Arnold, May 26, 1863, in *CW*, VI, p. 230.
528 Stanton had sent Charles Dana . . . long, detailed dispatches: Bruce Catton, *Grant Moves South*. Vol. I: *1861–1863* (Boston: Little, Brown, 1960; 1988), pp. 388–89; Thomas and Hyman, *Stanton*, p. 267.
528 Requesting that General Banks . . . "should prefer that course": Charles A. Dana to EMS, May 26, 1863, reel 5, Stanton Papers, DLC.
528 In a misguided effort . . . other valuables behind: "General Orders, No. 11," Department of the Tennessee, December 17, 1862, in *OR*, Ser. 1, Vol. XVII, Part II, p. 424. See also USG to Christopher P. Wolcott, December 17, 1862, in ibid., pp. 421–22; D. Wolff & Bros, C. F. Kaskell, and J. W. Kaswell to AL, December 29, 1862, in ibid., p. 506; Bertram Wallace Korn, *American Jewry and the Civil War* (Philadelphia: Jewish Publication Society of America, 1951), pp. 122–23.
529 a delegation of Jewish leaders . . . "have at once": Leaders quoted in Korn, *American Jewry and the Civil War*, pp. 124–25.
529 wrote a note to Halleck: Ibid., p. 125.
529 after assuring Grant . . . "necessary to revoke it": Henry W. Halleck to USG, January 21, 1863, in *OR*, Ser. 1, Vol. XXIV, Part I, p. 9 (quote); Henry W. Halleck to USG, January 4, 1863, in *OR*, Ser. 1, Vol. XVII, Part II, p. 530; Circular, 13th Army Corps, Department of the Tennessee, January 7, 1863, in ibid., p. 544.
529 Elizabeth Blair heard . . . "all the time": EBL to SPL, May 8, 1863, in *Wartime Washington*, ed. Laas, p. 266.
529 Bates was told . . . "bloated" appearance: Entry for May 23, 1863, in *The Diary of Edward Bates, 1859–1866*, p. 293.
529 In Grant's case . . . "idiotically drunk": Murat Halstead to SPC, April 1, 1863, Lincoln Papers.
529 After dispatching investigators to look into: Catton, *Grant Moves South*, Vol. I, pp. 388–89; Jean Edward Smith, *Grant* (New York: Simon & Schuster, 2001), p. 231.
529 A memorable story . . . rest of his generals!: John Eaton, *Grant, Lincoln and the Freedmen: Reminiscences of the Civil War* (New York: Longmans, Green & Co., 1907; New York: Negro Universities Press, 1969), p. 90.
529 Wade and Chandler told Lincoln . . . "in reply": JGN to TB, May 17, 1863, container 2, Nicolay Papers.
530 Seward accompanied . . . his garden: See entries for May 1863, in Fanny Seward diary, Seward House, Auburn, New York.
530 favorite old poplar . . . "stroke of the axe": FAS to WHS, June 5, 1863, reel 114, Seward Papers.
530 Fanny wrote that . . . "very lonely": FS to WHS, June 7, 1863, reel 116, Seward Papers.
530 troubling rumors . . . "when I am there": FAS to WHS, June 5, 1863, reel 114, Seward Papers; FS to WHS, June 7, 1863, reel 116, Seward Papers (quote).
530 Seward noted . . . "an invasion of Washington": WHS to [FAS], June 11, 1863, in Seward, *Seward at Washington . . . 1861–1872*, p. 169.
530 Mary and Tad left . . . Continental Hotel: Entry for June 8, 1863, in *Lincoln Day by Day*, Vol. III, p. 188; MTL to John Meredith Read, June 16, [1863], in Turner and Turner, *Mary Todd Lincoln*, p. 152 n2.
530 Welles spoke with Lincoln . . . "thought best": Entry for June 8, 1863, *Welles diary*, Vol. I (1960 edn.), p. 325.

530 "Think you better . . . ugly dream about him": AL to MTL, June 9, 1863, in *CW,* VI, p. 256.
530 Seward sent a telegram . . . "pic-nic to the Lake": Entry for June 15, 1863, in Johnson, "Sensitivity and Civil War," p. 813.
531 Lee had crossed . . . "adds to our strength": WHS to [FAS], June 15, 1863, in Seward, *Seward at Washington . . . 1861–1872,* pp. 169–70.
531 *"Invasion! . . . in Maryland and Pennsylvania": NYT* headline, June 16, 1863.
531 "It is a matter of choice . . . anything at all": AL to MTL, June 16, 1863, in *CW,* VI, p. 283.
531 "The country, now . . . is wide awake": Entry for June 18, 1863, in French, *Witness to the Young Republic,* p. 423.
531 "something of a panic pervades the city": Entry for June 15, 1863, *Welles diary,* Vol. I (1960 edn.), p. 329.
531 he called out a hundred thousand troops: AL, "Proclamation Calling for 100,000 Militia," June 15, 1863, in *CW,* VI, p. 277.
531 "I should think . . . kindness & Patriotism": Entry for June 18, 1863, in French, *Witness to the Young Republic,* p. 424.
531 the committee charged with . . . "all he could ask for": Stoddard, *Inside the White House in War Times,* p. 117.
531 Lincoln's primary concern . . . "outgeneraled": Brooks, *Mr. Lincoln's Washington,* p. 196.
531 "observed in Hooker . . . taken from other points": Entry for June 28, 1863, *Welles diary,* Vol. I (1960 edn.), p. 348.
531 When Hooker delivered a prickly telegram: Joseph Hooker to Henry W. Halleck, June 27, 1863 (9:00 a.m.), in *OR,* Ser. 1, Vol. XXVII, Part I, p. 59; Hooker to Halleck, June 27, 1863 (3:00 p.m.), in ibid., p. 60; Halleck to Hooker, June 27, 1863 (8:00 p.m.), in ibid., p. 60.
531 Lincoln and Stanton replaced him: Henry W. Halleck to George G. Meade, June 27, 1863, in *OR,* Ser. 1, Vol. XXVII, Part I, p. 61; Meade to Halleck, June 28, 1863, in ibid., pp. 61–62; "Meade, George Gordon (1815–1872)," in Sifakis, *Who Was Who in the Union,* p. 266.
532 "Chase was disturbed . . . cared should appear": SPC to Joseph Hooker, June 20, 1863, quoted in Schuckers, *The Life and Public Services of Salmon Portland Chase,* p. 468; entry of June 28, 1863, *Welles diary,* Vol. I (1960 edn.), p. 348 (quote).
532 "You must have been . . . exceeded mine": SPC to KCS, June 29, 1863, reel 27, Chase Papers.
532 "The turning point . . . such a suspense": JGN to TB, July 5, 1863, container 3, Nicolay Papers.
532 "poor and desultory" . . . in the telegraph office: Bates, *Lincoln in the Telegraph Office,* p. 155.
532 Chandler would "never forget . . . on the wall": Zachariah Chandler, quoted in Browne, *The Every-Day Life of Abraham Lincoln,* pp. 597–98.
532 a dispatch from Meade . . . "at all points": George G. Meade to Henry W. Halleck, July 2, 1863 (8:00 p.m.), in *OR,* Ser. 1, Vol. XXVII, Part I, p. 72.
532 "no reliable advices . . . anxiety prevails": *NYT,* July 3, 1863.
532 a messenger handed . . . "reliable": Entry for July 4, 1863, *Welles diary,* Vol. I (1960 edn.), p. 357.
532 a telegram from Meade . . . after severe losses: George G. Meade to Henry W. Halleck, July 3, 1863, *OR,* Ser. 1, Vol. XXVII, Part I, pp. 74–75.
533 Casualties were later calculated: Richard A. Sauers, "Gettysburg, Battle of," in *Encyclopedia of the American Civil War,* ed. Heidler and Heidler, p. 836.
533 "as being the most . . . covered with the dead": McPherson, *Battle Cry of Freedom,* p. 664; Brooks, *Mr. Lincoln's Washington,* pp. 202, 203 (quotes).
533 a celebratory press release: AL, "Announcement of News From Gettysburg," July 4, 1863, in *CW,* VI, p. 314.
533 "the gloomiest Fourth" . . . Fireworks were set off: Entry for July 4, 1863, Fanny Seward diary, Seward Papers.
533 "The results . . . for the moment at least": Entry for July 6, 1863, *Diary of George Templeton Strong,* Vol. III, p. 330.
533 Grant's forty-six-day siege: McGowen, "Vicksburg Campaign (May–July 1863)," in *Encyclopedia of the American Civil War,* ed. Heidler and Heidler, p. 2026; Foote, *The Civil War,* Vol. II, p. 607.
533 Welles had received . . . dispatch in hand: Entry for July 7, 1863, *Welles diary,* Vol. I (1960 edn.), p. 364; Brooks, *Mr. Lincoln's Washington,* pp. 177 (quote), 201.
533 "executed a double . . . excited as he was then": Brooks, *Washington, D.C., in Lincoln's Time,* p. 82.
533 "caught my hand . . . 'it is great!' ": Entry for July 7, 1863, *Welles diary,* Vol. I (1960 edn.), p. 364.
533 "The Father . . . to the sea": AL to James C. Conkling, August 26, 1863, *CW,* VI, p. 409.
533 "The rebel troops" . . . about thirty thousand: Charles A. Dana to EMS, July 5, 1863, reel 5, Stanton Papers, DLC.
534 "I write this now . . . and I was wrong": AL to USG, July 13, 1863, in *CW,* VI, p. 326.
534 a large crowd . . . "the beginning of the end": *NYH,* July 8, 1863.
534 the official bulletins were read . . . "beasts at sunrise": Brooks, *Mr. Lincoln's Washington,* p. 201.
535 Mary's carriage accident: *Star,* July 2, 1863; *NYH,* July 11, 1863; Boyden, *Echoes from Hospital and White House,* pp. 143–44; Pinsker, *Lincoln's Sanctuary,* pp. 102–04, 105–06.
535 "never quite recovered . . . of her fall": Robert Todd Lincoln, quoted in Helm, *The True Story of Mary,* p. 250.
535 "complete his work . . . destruction of Lee's army": AL to Henry W. Halleck, [July 7, 1863], in *CW,* VI, p. 319.
535 both Halleck and Lincoln urged Meade: Henry W. Halleck to George G. Meade, July 8, 1863, *OR,* Ser. 1, Vol. XXVII, Part III, p. 605; note 1 of AL to Henry W. Halleck, [July 7, 1863], in *CW,* VI, p. 319.
535 Robert Lincoln later said . . . "his vindication": "[Robert Todd Lincoln's Reminiscences, Given 5 January 1885]," in Nicolay, *An Oral History of Abraham Lincoln,* pp. 88–89.
535 he nonetheless failed to move . . . "anxious and impatient": "13 July 1863, Monday," in Hay, *Inside Lincoln's White House,* p. 62.
535 he received a dispatch from Meade: "14 July 1863, Tuesday," in ibid., p. 62; Circular, Army of the Potomac,

July 14, 1863, in *OR*, Ser. 1, Vol. XXVII, Part III, p. 690; Sauers, "Gettysburg, Battle of," in *Encyclopedia of the American Civil War*, ed. Heidler and Heidler, p. 836.

535 Stanton was reluctant to share . . . president "was not": Entry for July 14, 1863, *Welles diary*, Vol. I (1960 edn.), p. 370.

536 Lincoln caught up . . . "and discouraged": Entry for July 14, 1863, ibid., p. 371.

536 "Our Army held . . . we did not harvest it": AL, quoted in "19 July 1863, Sunday," in Hay, *Inside Lincoln's White House*, pp. 64–65.

536 his profound gratitude . . . "never sent, or signed": AL to George G. Meade, July 14, 1863, Lincoln Papers.

536 Meade's failure to attack . . . "I might run away": Carpenter, *Six Months at the White House*, pp. 219–20.

536 the draft: Samantha Jane Gaul, "Conscription, U.S.A.," in *Encyclopedia of the American Civil War*, ed. Heidler and Heidler, p. 487.

536 Governor Seymour had told . . . the black man: Governor Horatio Seymour, quoted in John G. Nicolay and John Hay, *Abraham Lincoln: A History*, Vol. VII (New York: Century Co., 1917), p. 17.

536 *Daily News* . . . "kill off Democrats": *New York Daily News*, quoted in ibid., p. 18.

536 A provision in the Conscription Act: Gaul, "Conscription, U.S.A.," in *Encyclopedia of the American Civil War*, ed. Heidler and Heidler, p. 488.

537 "a rich man's war and a poor man's fight": Sandburg, *Abraham Lincoln: The War Years*, Vol. II, p. 362.

537 the first day of the draft proceeded: *NYT*, July 14, 1863; Nicolay and Hay, *Abraham Lincoln*, Vol. VII, p. 18.

537 "Scarcely had two dozen" . . . continued unchecked for five days: *NYT*, July 14, 1863 (quotes); *NYT*, July 16, 1863; Sandburg, *Abraham Lincoln: The War Years*, Vol. II, p. 360; Gaul, "Conscription, U.S.A." and "New York City Draft Riots (13–17 July 1863)," in *Encyclopedia of the American Civil War*, ed. Heidler and Heidler, pp. 488, 1414–15.

537 "the all engrossing topic of conversation": Brooks, *Mr. Lincoln's Washington*, p. 219.

537 "have the power for a week": SPC to William Sprague, July 14, 1863, reel 27, Chase Papers.

537 The mob violence finally ended . . . go forward: *NYT*, July 18, 1863.

537 Auburn's draft . . . "apprehension of a riot": FAS to Augustus Seward, July 20, 1863, reel 115, Seward Papers.

537 she reported that Copperheads . . . riots in New York: FAS to WHS, July 18, 1863, reel 114, Seward Papers.

537 several Irishmen fought . . . the Seward home: FAS to WHS, June 28, 1863, reel 114, Seward Papers; FAS to WHS, July 12, 1863, reel 114, Seward Papers; FAS to FWS, July 23, 1863, reel 115, Seward Papers.

537 Frances awoke one morning . . . "I possessed": Janet W. Seward, "Personal Experiences of the Civil War," Seward Papers, NRU.

538 "Do not give yourself . . . not without benefit": WHS to FAS, July 21, 1863, in Seward, *Seward at Washington . . . 1861–1872*, p. 177.

538 "As to personal injury . . . willing to assist them": FAS to WHS, July 18, 1863, reel 114, Seward Papers.

538 everyone was "somewhat" . . . police force: FAS to FWS, July 23, 1863, reel 115, Seward Papers.

538 "The best of order . . . Our recent victories": *NYT*, July 24, 1863.

538 Seward had predicted . . . "up a long time": WHS to [FAS], July 17, 1863, quoted in Seward, *Seward at Washington . . . 1861–1872*, p. 176.

538 "incitement . . . resist the government": FAS to WHS, July 15, 1863, reel 114, Seward Papers.

538 John Hay learned . . . handling of the situation: "25 July 1863, Saturday," in Hay, *Inside Lincoln's White House*, p. 67.

538 "lost ground . . . best men": John A. Dix to EMS, July 25, 1863, reel 5, Stanton Papers, DLC.

538 "The nation is great . . . in 1850 to 1860!": WHS to [FAS], July 25, 1863, quoted in Seward, *Seward at Washington . . . 1861–1872*, p. 177.

538 "President was in . . . sack Phil-del": "19 July 1863, Sunday," in Hay, *Inside Lincoln's White House*, pp. 64, 306 n80.

539 "A few days having passed . . . a true man": AL to Oliver O. Howard, July 21, 1863, in *CW*, VI, p. 341.

539 the six straight hours . . . power to pardon: JH to JGN, [July 19, 1863], in Hay, *At Lincoln's Side*, p. 45.

539 Hay marveled . . . "instead of shooting him": "18 July 1863, Saturday," in Hay, *Inside Lincoln's White House*, p. 64.

539 Lincoln acknowledged . . . "upon him unawares": Eaton, *Grant, Lincoln and the Freedmen*, p. 180.

539 "overcome by a physical . . . the battle begins": "Conversation with Hon. J. Holt, Washington Oct 29 1875," in Nicolay, *An Oral History of Abraham Lincoln*, p. 69.

539 Rather than fearing . . . deserters were executed: Eaton, *Grant, Lincoln and the Freedmen*, p. 180.

539 "where meanness or cruelty were shown": "18 July 1863, Saturday," in Hay, *Inside Lincoln's White House*, p. 64.

539 the case of a captain . . . "Count Peeper": "[July–August 1863]," in ibid., p. 76.

540 "Men and horses . . . every day": JH to JGN, August 13, 1863, in Hay, *At Lincoln's Side*, p. 50.

540 "The garments cling . . . is over everything": Brooks, *Mr. Lincoln's Washington*, p. 223.

540 "hot, dusty weather . . . discomfort of Washington": EMS to Ellen Stanton, August 25, 1863, quoted in Gideon Stanton, ed., "Edwin M. Stanton" (quotes); Pinsker, *Lincoln's Sanctuary*, pp. 116–17.

540 "Nearly everybody . . . skeddadled from the heat": Brooks, *Mr. Lincoln's Washington*, p. 223.

540 Mary fled the capital . . . through most of August: AL to MTL, August 8, 1863, Lincoln Papers; Turner and Turner, *Mary Todd Lincoln*, pp. 153–54.

540 A correspondent . . . "smiling face": *Boston Journal*, August 10, 1863.

540 Lincoln talked about the heat . . . "distress about it": AL to MTL, August 8, 1863, Lincoln Papers.

540 Only in mid-September . . . with her and with Tad: AL to MTL, September 21 and 22, 1863, in *CW*, VI, pp. 471, 474.

540 Mary understood . . . "to letter writing": MTL to AL, November 2, [1862], in Turner and Turner, *Mary Todd Lincoln*, p. 139.

541 "I wish I could gain . . . put to the test": FAS to WHS, June 17, 1863, reel 114, Seward Papers.
541 "Every day . . . gone to the field": WHS to [FAS], July 25, 1863, quoted in Seward, *Seward at Washington . . . 1861–1872*, p. 177.
541 she despaired when . . . "killed & wounded": FAS to WHS, July 5, 1863, reel 114, Seward Papers.
541 Only with Frances . . . exhaustion: WHS to FAS, June 8, 1863, reel 112, Seward Papers.
541 "Thenceforth . . . constant devotion to business": Robert Todd Lincoln to Dr. J. G. Holland, June 6, 1865, box 6, folder 37, William Barton Collection, Special Collections of the Regenstein Library at the University of Chicago.
541 the Equinox House . . . dining facilities: "From The Beginning," historical pamphlet, Equinox House, Manchester, Vt.
541 Mary climbed a mountain . . . Doubleday and his wife: Randall, *Mary Lincoln*, p. 229; *NYH*, September 1,1863.
541 "We did again . . . fortunes": William Sprague to KCS, May 27, 1866, Sprague Papers.
542 his immense manufacturing company . . . weekly: "The Rhode Island Spragues," December 5, 1883, unidentified newspaper, KCS vertical file, DWP.
542 "I want to show you . . . undone or destroyed": William Sprague to KCS, May 1, 1863, Sprague Papers.
542 "The Gov and Miss Kate . . . into their fold": William Sprague to Hiram Barney, May 18, 1863, Salmon Portland Chase Collection, Historical Society of Pennsylvania, Philadelphia [hereafter Chase Papers, Phi.].
542 "The business . . . lost its identity": William Sprague to KCS, June 16, 1863, Sprague Papers.
542 "a wilderness, a blank": William Sprague to KCS, July 1, 1863, Sprague Papers.
542 He kept her miniature . . . "strong a hold": William Sprague to KCS, June 3, 7 and 8, 1863, Sprague Papers (quotes from June 7 letter).
542 "I am my darling up . . . with the sunshine": William Sprague to KCS, May 21, 1863, Sprague Papers.
542 "I hope my darling . . . morning and adieu": William Sprague to KCS, June 1, 1863, Sprague Papers.
542 Chase opened the discussion . . . "any due to me": SPC to William Sprague, June 6, 1863, reel 27, Chase Papers.
542 "Probably no woman . . . her successes": *Washington Post*, August 1, 1899.
543 "Scarcely a person . . . lent a charm to the whole": FS to LW, February 1, 1863, reel 116, Seward Papers.
543 Kate persuaded William: William Sprague to SPC, May 31, 1863, reel 27, Chase Papers; William Sprague to KCS, June 12, 1863, Sprague Papers; SPC to William Sprague, July 14, 1863, reel 27, Chase Papers.
543 "idea of taking . . . So I yield the point": SPC to William Sprague, July 14, 1863, reel 27, Chase Papers.
543 Chase would continue . . . William would cover: SPC to William Sprague, July 14, 1863, reel 27, Chase Papers; William Sprague to KCS, July 22, 1863, Sprague Papers; Niven, *Salmon P. Chase*, p. 342.
543 "the delicate link . . . united father & daughter": William Sprague to SPC, November 4, 1863, reel 29, Chase Papers.
543 Sprague wisely decided . . . "enduring love": William Sprague to KCS, June 12, 1863, Sprague Papers.
543 "Katie showed me . . . full wealth of her affections": SPC to William Sprague, June 6, 1863, reel 27, Chase Papers.
543 "as much of the pecuniary burden as possible": William Sprague to SPC, May 31, 1863, reel 27, Chase Papers.
543 to divest himself: Belden and Belden, *So Fell the Angels*, pp. 84–85.
543 he informed Jay Cooke . . . "all right-minded men": SPC to Jay Cooke, June 1, 1863, reel 27, Chase Papers.
544 he returned a check . . . "as *be* right": SPC to Jay Cooke, June 2, 1863, reel 27, Chase Papers.
544 Chase joined Kate . . . returned to Washington: Lamphier, *Kate Chase and William Sprague*, p. 54.
544 his only companion . . . "sympathetic way": SPC to Janet Chase Hoyt, August 19, 1863, reel 28, Chase Papers (quote). See also note 2 to published edition of August 19 letter in *The Salmon P. Chase Papers*. Vol. IV: *Correspondence, April 1863–1864*, ed. John Niven (Kent, Ohio, and London: Kent State University Press, 1997), p. 106 n2.
544 He chastised Nettie . . . carelessness pained him: SPC to Janet Chase Hoyt, August 19, 1863, reel 28, Chase Papers.
544 he reprimanded Kate . . . vacation expenses: SPC to KCS, August 19, 1863, reel 28, Chase Papers.
544 a warm correspondence . . . "her letters": Belden and Belden, *So Fell the Angels*, pp. 88–89 (quote p. 89).
544 Mrs. Eastman described . . . "of his own idolatry?": Charlotte S. Eastman to SPC, July 19, 1863, reel 27, Chase Papers.
544 "What a sweet letter" . . . attend to the president: SPC to Charlotte S. Eastman, August 22, 1863, reel 28, Chase Papers.
545 "The Tycoon is in fine whack . . . where he is": JH to JGN, August 7, 1863, in Hay, *At Lincoln's Side*, p. 49.
545 Hay had a good sense of humor . . . "peal of fun": Stoddard, *Inside the White House in War Times*, pp. 93–94.
545 Hay accompanied the president: August 9, 1863, photograph of AL, in Philip B. Kunhardt, Jr., Philip B. Kunhardt III, and Peter W. Kunhardt, *Lincoln: An Illustrated Biography* (New York: Alfred A. Knopf, 1992), p. 216.
545 "very good spirits": "9 August 1863, Sunday," in Hay, *Inside Lincoln's White House*, p. 70.
545 Rigidly posed . . . unsmiling portrait: Kunhardt, et al., *Lincoln*, p. 216.
545 required to sit . . . "Don't move a muscle!": George Sullivan, *Mathew Brady: His Life and Photographs* (New York: Cobblehill Books, 1994), pp. 17–18 (quote p. 18).
545 "contrived grinning . . . become obligatory": James Mellon, ed., *The Face of Lincoln* (New York: Viking Press, 1979), pp. 13–14.
546 "the rebel power . . . to disintegrate": "9 August 1863, Sunday," in Hay, *Inside Lincoln's White House*, p. 70.
546 pleasant outings . . . "sent me to bed": "23 August 1863, Sunday," in ibid., pp. 75–76 (quote p. 76); *Washington Post*, August 3, 1924; Pinsker, *Lincoln's Sanctuary*, p. 115.

546 "I see the President . . . on K Street": Whitman, *Specimen Days* (1971 edn.), p. 26.
546 "The President and I . . . the season is over": EMS to Ellen Stanton, August 25, 1863, quoted in Gideon Stanton, ed., "Edwin M. Stanton."
546 Stanton finally joined his wife . . . the Soldiers' Home: Thomas and Hyman, *Stanton*, p. 284.
546 typically wide-ranging . . . "party to oppose a war": "13 August 1863, Thursday," in Hay, *Inside Lincoln's White House*, pp. 72–73 (quote); Pamela Scott and Antoinette J. Lee, *Buildings of the District of Columbia*. Buildings of the United States Series (New York and Oxford: Oxford University Press, 1993), pp. 119, 128; "*Progress of Civilization*," Architect of the Capitol website, www.aoc.gov/cc/art/pediments/prog_sen_r.htm (accessed November 2004).
546 tour of upstate New York . . . picnic on the lake: Philip Van Doren Stern, *When the Guns Roared: World Aspects of the American Civil War* (Garden City, N.Y.: Doubleday & Co., 1965), p. 230; Seward, *Seward at Washington . . . 1861–1872*, pp. 186–87.
547 "All seemed . . . themselves very much": FAS to Augustus Seward, August 27, 1863, reel 115, Seward Papers.
547 "When one comes really . . . to like in him": Lord Lyons to Lord Russell, quoted in Stern, *When the Guns Roared*, p. 231.
547 "Hundreds of factories . . . and canals": Seward, *Seward at Washington . . . 1861–1872*, p. 186.
547 European shipbuilders . . . not be delivered: Van Deusen, *William Henry Seward*, pp. 352–56, 361; entries for August 12, 29, September 18, 25, 1863, *Welles diary*, Vol. I (1960 edn.), pp. 399, 429, 435–37, 443.
547 "The White House . . . health of the nation": Dispatch of August 31, 1863, in Stoddard, *Dispatches from Lincoln's White House*, p. 166.

CHAPTER 21: "I FEEL TROUBLE IN THE AIR"

Page

548 180,000 soldiers . . . black males: Eric Foner, *Reconstruction: America's Unfinished Revolution, 1863–1877* (New York: Harper & Row, 1988; 1989), p. 8.
548 Emancipation Proclamation flatly declared . . . "United States": AL, "Emancipation Proclamation," January 1, 1863, in *CW*, VI, p. 30.
548 Stanton authorized . . . and other Northern states: Quarles, *Lincoln and the Negro*, p. 156; Dudley Taylor Cornish, *The Sable Arm: Black Troops in the Union Army, 1861–1865* (Lawrence: University Press of Kansas, 1956; 1987), p. 105.
549 the war would not be won . . . "suppressing the rebels": *Douglass' Monthly* (August 1862).
549 He wrote stirring appeals . . . many other cities: Blight, *Frederick Douglass' Civil War*, pp. 157–59.
549 "Why should a colored . . . that claim respected": *Douglass' Monthly* (April 1863).
549 thousands of Bostonians . . . high-ranking military officials: *Boston Daily Evening Transcript*, May 28, 1863.
549 "No single regiment . . . admirable marching": Ibid.
549 He urged Banks . . . the enlisting process: AL to Nathaniel P. Banks, March 29, 1863, in *CW*, VI, p. 154; AL to David Hunter, April 1, 1863, in ibid., p. 158; AL to USG, August 9, 1863, in ibid., p. 374.
549 "The colored population . . . rebellion at once": AL to Andrew Johnson, March 26, 1863, in ibid., pp. 149–50.
549 Chase . . . "nearly two years ago": SPC to James A. Garfield, May 31, 1863, reel 12, Garfield Papers, DLC.
550 a series of obstacles . . . losing their freedom or their lives: Benjamin Quarles, *Frederick Douglass*. Studies in American Negro Life Series (Associated Publishers, 1948; New York: Atheneum, 1970), pp. 209–10; Quarles, *Lincoln and the Negro*, pp. 167, 169, 173–74, 177.
550 "this is no time . . . to embrace it": *Douglass' Monthly* (August 1863).
550 they earned great respect . . . "bravery and steadiness": Cornish, *The Sable Arm*, pp. 142–43 (quote p. 143).
550 "dooming to death . . . negro troops": *NYTrib*, reprinted in *Liberator*, May 15, 1863.
550 As word of the unique . . . swiftly diminishing: James M. McPherson, *The Negro's Civil War: How American Blacks Felt and Acted During the War for Union* (New York: Pantheon Books, 1965; New York: Ballantine Books, 1991), pp. 176, 179.
550 "What has Mr. Lincoln . . . responsible for them": *Douglass' Monthly* (August 1863).
550 "When I plead . . . rulers at Washington": Frederick Douglass to Major G. L. Stearns, August 1, 1863, reprinted in ibid.
550 he asked Halleck . . . "placed at hard labor": AL, "Order of Retaliation," July 30, 1863, in *CW*, VI, p. 357.
551 The order was "well-written . . . became impossible": Entry for August 4, 1863, in Gurowski, *Diary from November 18, 1862 to October 18, 1863*, pp. 292–93.
551 Douglass agreed . . . "required to act": Douglass to Stearns, August 1, 1863, in *Douglass' Monthly* (August 1863).
551 the lack of "fair play" . . . to the president: Douglass, *Life and Times of Frederick Douglass*, pp. 784–85.
551 "tumult of feeling": Frederick Douglass, quoted in the *Washington Post*, February 13, 1888.
551 "I could not know . . . an interview altogether": Douglass, *Life and Times of Frederick Douglass*, p. 785.
551 a large crowd in the hallway . . . into the office: *Liberator*, January 29, 1864; Philip S. Foner, *Frederick Douglass* (New York: Citadel Press, 1950; repr. 1964), p. 216.
551 "I was never more . . . Abraham Lincoln": Douglass, *Life and Times of Frederick Douglass*, p. 785.
551 The president was seated . . . "began to rise": Douglass, "Lincoln and the Colored Troops," in *Reminiscences of Abraham Lincoln*, ed. Rice, p. 316.
551 Douglass hesitantly began . . . "glad to see you": Douglass, *Life and Times of Frederick Douglass*, p. 786.
551 Lincoln's warmth . . . "Abraham Lincoln": Frederick Douglass to George L. Stearns, August 12, 1863 (photo-

copy), container 53, Papers of Frederick Douglass, Manuscript Division, Library of Congress [hereafter Douglass Papers, DLC].

551 Douglass laid before . . . "very apparent sympathy": Douglass, "Lincoln and the Colored Troops," in *Reminiscences of Abraham Lincoln*, ed. Rice, p. 317.

551 "Upon my ceasing . . . not suspected him": Douglass to Stearns, August 12, 1863, Douglass Papers, DLC.

551 it "seemed a necessary . . . at all as soldiers": Douglass, *Life and Times of Frederick Douglass*, p. 787.

552 "in the end they shall . . . as white soldiers": AL quoted in Douglass, "Lincoln and the Colored Troops," in *Reminiscences of Abraham Lincoln*, ed. Rice, p. 318.

552 "he would sign . . . commend to him": Douglass, *Life and Times of Frederick Douglass*, p. 787.

552 Lincoln's justification . . . "killed for negroes": Douglass to Stearns, August 12, 1863, Douglass Papers, DLC.

552 "once begun . . . humane spirit": Douglass, *Life and Times of Frederick Douglass*, p. 787.

552 he had read a recent speech . . . "retreated from it": *Liberator*, January 29, 1864.

552 "as though I could . . . his shoulder": Douglass, "Lincoln and the Colored Troops," in *Reminiscences of Abraham Lincoln*, ed. Rice, p. 325.

552 "The manner of" . . . in the Mississippi Valley: Douglass, *Life and Times of Frederick Douglass*, pp. 787–88 (quote); Quarles, *Lincoln and the Negro*, pp. 168, 172.

552 The War Department followed up . . . commission was not included: Quarles, *Lincoln and the Negro*, p. 169.

552 "I knew too much . . . mark of my rank": Douglass, *Life and Times of Frederick Douglass*, p. 788.

553 "Perhaps you may like . . . I felt big there!": *Liberator*, January 29, 1864.

553 Conkling had invited . . . loyal Unionists: AL to James C. Conkling, August 26, 1863, in *CW*, VI, p. 406.

553 False rumors circulated: *NYT*, August 8 and 13, 1863.

553 "Ah! I'm glad" . . . he bade him good night: Stoddard, *Inside the White House in War Times*, pp. 129–30.

554 "deceptive and groundless . . . they have strove to hinder it": AL to James C. Conkling, August 26, 1863, in *CW*, VI, pp. 407–10.

554 Lincoln continued to refine . . . public duties: "23 August 1863, Sunday," in Hay, *Inside Lincoln's White House*, p. 76.

554 "You are one of the best . . . very slowly": AL to James C. Conkling, August 27, 1863, in *CW*, VI, p. 414.

554 An immense crowd . . . "the country calls": *Illinois State Journal*, Springfield, Ill., September 2, 1863.

554 he was furious to see . . . around the country: John W. Forney to AL, September 3, 1863, Lincoln Papers.

555 "I am mortified . . . How did this happen?": AL to James C. Conkling, September 3, 1863, in *CW*, VI, p. 430.

555 When a petitioner tried . . . "obvious to any one": AL to D. M. Leatherman, September 3, 1863, in ibid., p. 431.

555 a message arrived from Conkling . . . "the next day": James C. Conkling to AL, September 4, 1863, Lincoln Papers.

555 "Disclaiming the arts . . . wants to discuss": *NYTrib*, September 3, 1863.

555 "The most consummate . . . which needs driving": *NYT*, September 7, 1863.

555 The *Philadelphia Inquirer* . . . "continue to write": *Philadelphia Inquirer*, September 5, 1863.

555 "His last letter . . . logicians of all schools": JH to JGN, September 11, 1863, in Hay, *At Lincoln's Side*, p. 54.

555 the *New York Times* also commended . . . "their faith in him": *NYT*, September 7, 1863.

556 "I know the people . . . on the ground": JH to JGN, September 11, 1863, in Hay, *At Lincoln's Side*, p. 54.

556 Seward came back . . . the diplomatic corps: WHS to Charles Francis Adams, August 25, 1863, quoted in Seward, *Seward at Washington . . . 1861–1872*, p. 188.

556 to celebrate his seventieth . . . "good as I deserve": Entry for September 4, 1863, in *The Diary of Edward Bates, 1859–1866*, pp. 305–06.

556 his ten-day visit . . . "perhaps more missed": Entry for September 11, 1863, *Welles diary*, Vol. I (1960 edn.), p. 431.

556 Lincoln and Stanton had hoped . . . "blow to the rebellion": EMS to William S. Rosecrans, July 7, 1863, in *OR*, Ser. 1, Vol. XXIII, Part II, p. 518.

556 Rosecrans delivered . . . "victory at Chattanooga": JH to JGN, September 11, 1863, in Hay, *At Lincoln's Side*, p. 54.

556 "unexpectedly appeared . . . of [the] Chicamauga": Charles A. Dana to EMS, September 12, 1863, reel 5, Stanton Papers, DLC.

556 battle of Chickamauga: See Dave Powell, "Chickamauga, Battle of," in *Encyclopedia of the American Civil War*, ed. Heidler and Heidler, pp. 427–31.

556 "Chicamauga is as fatal . . . as Bull Run": Charles A. Dana to EMS, September 20, 1863, reel 6, Stanton Papers, DLC.

557 Union casualties: Entry for September 20, 1862, in Long, *The Civil War Day by Day*, p. 412.

557 "We have met with . . . scattered troops there": William S. Rosecrans to Henry W. Halleck, September 20, 1863, in *OR*, Ser. 1, Vol. XXX, Part I, pp. 142–43.

557 the dispatches reached him . . . "awake and watchful": Entry for September 21, 1863, *Welles diary*, Vol. I (1960 edn.), p. 438.

557 wandered into Hay's room . . . "air before it comes": "[27 September 1863, Sunday]," in Hay, *Inside Lincoln's White House*, p. 85.

557 Lincoln telegraphed Mary . . . "see you and Tad": AL to MTL, September 21, 1863, in *CW*, VI, p. 471.

557 Mary responded . . . plans to do so: MTL to AL, September 22, 1863, quoted in Helm, *The True Story of Mary*, p. 215.

557 proved "less unfavorable . . . feared": Entry for September 22, 1863, in *Chase Papers*, Vol. I, p. 449 (quote); Charles A. Dana to EMS, September 20, 1863, in *OR*, Ser. 1, Vol. XXX, Part I, p. 193.

557 Thomas's corps had held . . . than the Federals: Powell, "Chickamauga, Battle of," in *Encyclopedia of the American Civil War*, ed. Heidler and Heidler, p. 430.
557 "still remains in . . . to twenty days": Charles A. Dana to EMS, September 23, 1863, reel 6, Stanton Papers, DLC.
557 Stanton came up with . . . dispatched messengers: Flower, *Edwin McMasters Stanton*, p. 203.
557 Chase had just retired . . . and his entire army: Entry for September 23, 1863, in *Chase Papers*, Vol. I, p. 450.
557 John Hay was sent to the Soldiers' Home . . . back to the War Department: "[27 September 1863, Sunday]," in Hay, *Inside Lincoln's White House*, p. 86 (quotes); John G. Nicolay and John Hay, *Abraham Lincoln: A History*, Vol. VIII (New York: Century Co., 1917), p. 112.
557 "I have invited . . . serious for jokes": Entry for September 23, 1863, in *Chase Papers*, Vol. I, pp. 450–52 (quotes); Flower, *Edwin McMasters Stanton*, p. 203.
558 "he had fully considered . . . with excellent arguments": Entry for September 23, 1863, in *Chase Papers*, Vol. I, p. 452.
558 Stanton immediately sent an orderly . . . "make a few figures": W. H. Whiton recollections, quoted in Gorham, *Life and Public Services of Edwin M. Stanton*, Vol. I, pp. 123–24.
558 "I can complete . . . given my consent": McCallum, EMS, and AL, quoted in Flower, *Edwin McMasters Stanton*, p. 204.
558 "Colonel McCallum . . . I will approve them": AL, quoted in W. H. Whiton recollections, quoted in Gorham, *Life and Public Services of Edwin M. Stanton*, Vol. I, pp. 124–25.
558 Stanton worked . . . stop to resupply: EMS to J. T. Boyle, September 23, 1863, in *OR*, Ser. 1, Vol. XXIX, Part I, p. 147; EMS to R. P. Bowler, September 24, 1863, in ibid., p. 153; Daniel Butterfield to Oliver O. Howard, September 26, 1863, in ibid., p. 160; W. P. Smith to EMS, September 26, 1863, in ibid., p. 161; Flower, *Edwin McMasters Stanton*, pp. 204–06. For documentation of Stanton's efforts to move the 11th and 12th Army Corps to the Army of the Cumberland, see *OR*, Ser. 1, Vol. XXIX, Part 1, pp. 146–95.
559 The first train left Washington . . . arrived in Tennessee: W. P. Smith to EMS, September 26, 1863, in *OR*, Ser. 1, Vol. 29, Part I, p. 161; Flower, *Edwin McMasters Stanton*, pp. 205–06.
559 Monitoring reports . . . agree to leave his post: Flower, *Edwin McMasters Stanton*, pp. 205–07; W. P. Smith to EMS, September 26, 1863, in *OR*, Ser. 1, Vol. XXIX, Part I, p. 162.
559 "It was an extraordinary . . . the twentieth century": McPherson, *Battle Cry of Freedom*, p. 675.
559 Dana's reports . . . troops had lost confidence: Charles A. Dana to EMS, September 30, 1863, in *OR*, Ser. 1, Vol. XXX, Part I, p. 204.
559 Stanton telegraphed Grant . . . discussing the overall military situation: Grant, *Personal Memoirs of U.S. Grant*, pp. 315–16.
559 the general departed for Chattanooga . . . Lookout Mountain: Ibid., pp. 320–51; James H. Meredith, "Chattanooga Campaign" and "Lookout Mountain, Battle of," in *Encyclopedia of the American Civil War*, ed. Heidler and Heidler, pp. 411–15, 1216–18.
559 "would have been a terrible disaster": Grant, *Personal Memoirs of U.S. Grant*, p. 318.
559 "The country does . . . nights work": Entry for September 23, 1863, in *Chase Papers*, Vol. I, p. 453.
560 affectionately call his "Mars": Bates, *Lincoln in the Telegraph Office*, p. 400.
560 "esteem and affection . . . French comic opera": Benjamin, "Recollections of Secretary Edwin M. Stanton," *Century* (1887), pp. 768, 760–61.
560 "No two men were . . . a necessity to each other": *New York Evening Post*, July 13, 1891.
560 "in dealing with the public . . . than his heart": A. E. Johnson, opinion cited in Bates, *Lincoln in the Telegraph Office*, p. 389.
560 the story of a congressman . . . "step over and see him": Julian, *Political Recollections, 1840 to 1872*, pp. 211–12.
561 "remarkable passages . . . at Cincinnati": EMS, quoted in Parkinson to Beveridge, May 28, 1923, container 292, Beveridge Papers, DLC.
561 "Few war ministers . . . for Mr. Lincoln": "The Late Secretary Stanton," *Army and Navy Journal*, January 1, 1870, p. 309.
561 When Stanton was eighteen . . . near death from cholera: Wolcott, "Edwin M. Stanton," p. 36.
561 he insisted on including . . . to stand guard: Joseph Buchanan and William Stanton Buchanan, quoted in Flower, *Edwin McMasters Stanton*, pp. 39, 40.
561 *Oh! Why should the spirit* . . . : William Knox, "Mortality," quoted in Bruce, "The Riddle of Death," in *The Lincoln Enigma*, p. 135.
561 He could recite from memory . . . "in the English language": Carpenter, *Six Months at the White House*, p. 59.
561 *The mossy marbles rest*: Oliver Wendell Holmes, "The Last Leaf," in *The Poetical Works of Oliver Wendell Holmes*, Vol. I (Boston and New York: Houghton Mifflin, 1892), p. 4.
562 he had written . . . "he should be honored?": EMS, "Our Admiration of Military Character Unmerited," 1831, reel 1, Stanton Papers, DLC.
562 an army of more than 2 million men: Margaret E. Wagner, Gary W. Gallagher, and Paul Finkelman, eds., *The Library of Congress Civil War Desk Reference* (New York: Grand Central Press/Simon & Schuster, 2002), p. 376.
562 "There could be no greater . . . to eternity": EMS, quoted in Gideon Stanton, ed., "Edwin M. Stanton."
562 "Doesn't it strike you . . . flowing all about me?": AL quoted in Louis A. Warren, *Lincoln's Youth: Indiana Years, Seven to Twenty-one, 1816–1830* (New York: Appleton Century Crofts, 1959), p. 225 n29.
562 an audience to a group of Quakers: AL to Eliza P. Gurney, September 4, 1864, in *CW*, VII, p. 535.
562 "If I had had . . . still governs it": AL, quoted in Eliza P. Gurney, copy of interview with AL, [October 26, 1862], Lincoln Papers.
562 "On principle . . . no mortal could stay": AL to Eliza P. Gurney, September 4, 1864, in *CW*, VII, p. 535.

563 Stanton still wrote . . . " 'our love in two' ": EMS to SPC, March 7, 1863, Chase Papers, Phi.
563 Stanton would ask Chase to stand: EMS to SPC, December 30, 1863, reel 30, Chase Papers.
563 "It is painful . . . after concurrence, action": SPC to George Wilkes, August 27, 1863, reel 28, Chase Papers.
563 Radicals insisted . . . both the Union and emancipation: Foner, *Reconstruction*, pp. 35–50, 60–62.
564 "standard-bearer . . . of the Radicals": Brooks, *Mr. Lincoln's Washington*, p. 236.
564 Chase's desire . . . proclaim his campaign: Ibid., p. 237.
564 he wrote hundreds of letters . . . Lincoln administration: Hendrick, *Lincoln's War Cabinet*, p. 400.
564 "I should fear nothing . . . management of the War": SPC to Edward D. Mansfield, October 18, 1863, reel 29, Chase Papers.
564 "If I were myself . . . man should be had": SPC to William Sprague, November 26, 1863, reel 30, Chase Papers.
564 He was thrilled . . . on another candidate: Horace Greeley to SPC, September 29, 1863, reel 28, Chase Papers.
565 "first choice . . . should receive it": Edward Jordan to SPC, October 27, 1863, reel 29, Chase Papers.
565 Governor Dennison alerted him . . . "like a beaver": "17 October 1863, Saturday, New York," in Hay, *Inside Lincoln's White House*, p. 92.
565 Seward cautioned . . . "for Mr. Chase": TW note, quoted in "28 November 1863, Saturday," in ibid., p. 119.
565 Samuel Cox . . . "New England States": "24 December 1863, Thursday," in ibid., p. 132.
565 A Pennsylvanian politician . . . "out of both eyes": "25 October 1863, Sunday," in ibid., p. 100.
565 John Hay learned . . . *Independent* to his side: "28 November 1863, Saturday," in ibid., p. 120.
565 "Chase's mad hunt after the Presidency": "29 October 1863, Thursday," in ibid., p. 103.
565 "plowing corn . . . make his department go": "[July–August 1863]," in ibid., pp. 78, 313 n143.
565 Lincoln agreed . . . "very bad taste": AL, quoted in "18 October 1863, Sunday," in ibid., p. 93.
565 "was sorry . . . that it ought to": "29 October 1863, Thursday," in ibid., p. 103.
565 Lincoln's friends . . . "President's interests": Eaton, *Grant, Lincoln and the Freedmen*, p. 176.
565 let "Chase have . . . what he asks": "29 October 1863, Thursday," in Hay, *Inside Lincoln's White House*, p. 103.
565 a "frank, guileless . . . for the first one": Leonard Swett to WHH, January 17, 1866, in *HI*, pp. 168, 164.
566 After criticizing . . . "So I still work on": SPC to James Watson Webb, November 7, 1863, reel 29, Chase Papers.
566 "all along clearly . . . from New Orleans": AL, quoted in "18 October 1863, Sunday," in Hay, *Inside Lincoln's White House*, p. 93.
566 "Chase would try . . . spot he can find": "29 October 1863, Thursday," in ibid., p. 103.
566 the people of Missouri . . . extinguish slavery: AL to Charles D. Drake and Others, October 5, 1863, in *CW*, VI, pp. 499–504; Foner, *Reconstruction*, pp. 41–42.
566 Governor Gamble worried . . . a conservative partisan: Hamilton R. Gamble to AL, October 1, 1863, Lincoln Papers.
567 He was accused . . . guise of military necessity: AL to Charles D. Drake and Others, October 5, 1863, in *CW*, VI, p. 500; "Conversation with Hon. M. S. Wilkinson, May 22 1876," in Nicolay, *An Oral History of Abraham Lincoln*, pp. 59–60; Williams, *Lincoln and the Radicals*, p. 299.
567 a delegation of radicals . . . "not to alienate them": "29 September 1863, Tuesday," in Hay, *Inside Lincoln's White House*, pp. 88–89 (quote); Williams, *Lincoln and the Radicals*, p. 299.
567 "these Radical men . . . side with the Radicals": AL, paraphrased in "10 December 1863, Thursday," in Hay, *Inside Lincoln's White House*, p. 125.
567 "they are nearer . . . set Zionwards": AL, quoted in "28 October 1863, Wednesday," in ibid., p. 101.
567 resented the radicals' demand . . . "short statutes of limitations": "10 December 1863, Thursday," in ibid., p. 125.
567 "So intense and fierce . . . saddest features of the times": Entry for September 29, 1863, *Welles diary*, Vol. I (1960 edn.), p. 448.
567 "show that . . . powerful as they may be": AL, quoted in "29 September 1863, Tuesday," in Hay, *Inside Lincoln's White House*, pp. 88–89.
568 an invitation to spend the evening: EB to J. O. Broadhead, October 24, 1863, Broadhead Papers, MoSHi.
568 "surprised and mortified . . . as traitors": EB to Hamilton R. Gamble, October 10, 1863, Bates Papers, MoSHi (quote); entry for September 30, 1863, in *The Diary of Edward Bates, 1859–1866*, p. 308.
568 Bates should hardly be . . . if he were to decide to run against Lincoln: Hamilton R. Gamble to EB, October 17, 1863, Bates Papers, MoSHi.
568 meeting with the Missourians . . . "instead of wind": "30 September 1863, Wednesday," in Hay, *Inside Lincoln's White House*, p. 89.
568 Lincoln listened attentively . . . remove him from command: AL to Charles D. Drake and Others, October 5, 1863, in *CW*, VI, pp. 500 (quotes), 503.
568 "The President never . . . his candid logic": "30 September 1863, Wednesday," in Hay, *Inside Lincoln's White House*, pp. 89–90.
568 Lincoln emerged . . . "as he supposed": Entry for September 30, 1863, in *The Diary of Edward Bates, 1859–1866*, p. 308.
568 "whoever commands . . . or conservatives": AL to Charles D. Drake and Others, October 5, 1863, in *CW*, VI, p. 504.
569 he wrote to remind . . . "injury to the Military": AL to John M. Schofield, October 1, 1863, in ibid., p. 492.
569 leaning toward . . . "conflicting elements": "13 December 1863, Sunday," in Hay, *Inside Lincoln's White House*, p. 127.
569 he decided to replace him with Rosecrans: "Rosecrans, William Starke (1819–1898)," and "Schofield, John McAllister (1831–1906)," in Sifakis, *Who Was Who in the Union*, pp. 342, 355.

569 Before an overflowing crowd . . . Jefferson Davis himself: Speech by Frank Blair, reprinted in *Missouri Republican*, St. Louis, September 27, 1863.
569 The *Liberator* criticized . . . "which he advocates": *Roxbury Journal*, quoted in *Liberator*, October 16, 1863.
570 "not let even . . . share of his resentment": EBL to SPL, [October 24, 1863], in *Wartime Washington*, ed. Laas, p. 316.
570 He wrote a letter to Monty . . . "skill and usefulness": AL to MB, November 2, 1863, in *CW*, VI, p. 555.
570 a gentle letter of reprimand . . . "would not cure the bite": AL to James M. Cutts, Jr., October 26, 1863, in ibid., p. 538, and note.
570 Chase again intervened . . . eligibility to vote: Niven, *Salmon P. Chase*, p. 339.
570 voiced his opposition at Rockville: Speech of Montgomery Blair, reprinted in the *Star*, October 5, 1863.
571 it aroused deep hostility . . . Blair from his cabinet: Smith, *The Francis Preston Blair Family in Politics*, Vol. II, pp. 241–43, 248; Williams, *Lincoln and the Radicals*, pp. 298, 303.
571 Lincoln refused to support . . . "against him": "22 October 1863, Thursday," in Hay, *Inside Lincoln's White House*, p. 97.
571 Noah Brooks attended a mass rally . . . "utterances": Brooks, *Mr. Lincoln's Washington*, pp. 246–48.
571 Chase was a featured . . . his "fossil theories": Ibid., pp. 247–49.
571 Chase was elated . . . *"a Cardinal principle"*: SPC to Horace Greeley, October 31, 1863, reel 29, Chase Papers.
571 Worried that Lincoln's . . . "were producing logical results": Leonard Swett to WHH, January 17, 1866, in *HI*, pp. 164–65.
572 "the most truly progressive . . . struggles with them": John W. Forney, quoted in "31 December 1863, Thursday," in Hay, *Inside Lincoln's White House*, p. 135.

CHAPTER 22: "STILL IN WILD WATER"

Page

573 Lincoln was visibly unsettled . . . his presidential race: Entry for October 14, 1863, *Welles diary*, Vol. I (1960 edn.), p. 470.
573 Civil liberties was also . . . instituted conscription: William C. Davis, *Look Away! A History of the Confederate States of America* (New York: Free Press, 2002), pp. 174–76, 226.
573 Toombs accused . . . "tide of despotism": Burton J. Hendrick, *Statesmen of the Lost Cause: Jefferson Davis and His Cabinet* (New York: Literary Guild of America, 1939), p. 417.
573 concerned about Ohio: Waugh, *Reelecting Lincoln*, pp. 14–15.
573 Lincoln was disheartened . . . "to the country": Entry for October 14, 1863, *Welles diary*, Vol. I (1960 edn.), p. 470.
573 In Pennsylvania . . . "of the United States": McPherson, *Battle Cry of Freedom*, p. 685.
574 the Woodward campaign . . . "voice & my vote": GBM to Charles J. Biddle, October 12, 1863, in *Civil War Papers of George B. McClellan*, p. 559.
574 took steps to ensure . . . return home to vote: Waugh, *Reelecting Lincoln*, p. 16.
574 If the president granted . . . Union ticket: SPC, *"Going Home to Vote,"* p. 22; Niven, *Salmon P. Chase*, p. 336.
574 the journalist Whitelaw Reid: Niven, *Salmon P. Chase*, p. 336; Hendrick, *Lincoln's War Cabinet*, p. 401.
574 Chase in Columbus . . . "misfortunes averted": SPC, *"Going Home to Vote,"* p. 4.
574 "I come not to speak . . . and without exceptions": Ibid., pp. 5, 13.
575 In public squares . . . "turn to Ohio": *Daily Ohio State Journal*, Columbus, Ohio, October 13, 1863; SPC, *"Going Home to Vote,"* p. 8 (quote).
575 begged his audiences . . . "sixty-five days in the year": SPC, *"Going Home to Vote,"* p. 8.
575 Lincoln took up his usual post: Waugh, *Reelecting Lincoln*, p. 14.
575 a welcome telegram . . . was counted: SPC to AL, October 14, 1863, Lincoln Papers.
575 By 5 a.m. . . . to 100,000: Browne, *The Every-Day Life of Abraham Lincoln*, p. 603; Waugh, *Reelecting Lincoln*, p. 14.
575 *"Glory to God . . . saved the Nation"*: Browne, *The Every-Day Life of Abraham Lincoln*, p. 603.
575 "All honor . . . foe at the ballot-box": EMS to John W. Forney, *NYT*, October 15, 1863.
575 found him "in good spirits": Entry for October 14, 1863, *Welles diary*, Vol. I (1960 edn.), p. 470.
575 "No man knows . . . till he has had it": AL, quoted in James B. Fry, in *Reminiscences of Abraham Lincoln by Distinguished Men of His Time*, ed. Allen Thorndike Rice (New York: North American Publishing Co., 1886), p. 390.
575 "all right" . . . a good secretary: AL, quoted in "18 October 1863, Sunday," in Hay, *Inside Lincoln's White House*, p. 93.
576 "I'm afraid . . . of the presidency": Entry for October 17, 1863, in *The Diary of Edward Bates, 1859–1866*, p. 310.
576 "That visit to the west . . . saved my country": Entry for October 20, 1863, in ibid., p. 311.
576 "it is of the nature . . . with its victim": Edward Bates to James O. Broadhead, October 24, 1863, Broadhead Papers, MoSHi.
576 had "warped" . . . party behind him: Entry for August 22, 1863, *Welles diary*, Vol. I (1960 edn.), p. 413.
576 were moderate compared to the scathing indictments: See Smith, *The Francis Preston Blair Family in Politics*, Vol. II, pp. 234–37.

576 "I little imagined . . . me deeply": SPC to Edward D. Mansfield, October 18, 1863, reel 29, Chase Papers.
576 "The late election" . . . unfit for active duty: James H. Baker to SPC, November 7, 1863, reel 29, Chase Papers.
576 "To him, more than . . . system of slavery": *Liberator,* November 13, 1863.
576 *Liberator* maintained . . . "again acting President": *Liberator,* November 13, 1863.
577 the relationship between the two . . . "gave it new light": Seward, *Seward at Washington . . . 1861–1872,* p. 197.
577 "They say, Mr. President . . . as a Governor": WHS and AL, quoted in ibid., pp. 193–94.
577 a proclamation . . . "tranquillity and Union": AL, "Proclamation of Thanksgiving," October 3, 1863, in *CW,* VI, p. 497 (quote); Seward, *Seward at Washington . . . 1861–1872,* p. 194.
577 Lincoln told Nicolay . . . "whole of that letter": December 8, 1863 memorandum, container 3, Nicolay Papers.
578 Seward assured Lincoln . . . "will collapse": Seward, *Seward at Washington . . . 1861–1872,* p. 196.
578 Seward left for Auburn . . . short periods of time: See Seward family correspondence in October 1863 on reels 112, 114, and 115 of Seward Papers, and FAS to Anna (Wharton) Seward, November 17, 1863, reel 115, Seward Papers.
578 The previous spring . . . his intelligence safely: William H. Seward, Jr., "Reminiscences of Lincoln," *Magazine of History* 9 (February 1909), pp. 105–06.
578 he delivered a speech . . . "will perish with it": WHS, quoted in Williams, *Lincoln and the Radicals,* p. 301.
578 "as in religion . . . whole United States": WHS, quoted in Seward, *Seward at Washington . . . 1861–1872,* p. 195.
579 arousing the wrath . . . "always be open to him": WHS, quoted in Williams, *Lincoln and the Radicals,* p. 301.
579 Lincoln telegraphed . . . "How is your son?": AL to WHS, November 3, 1863, in *CW,* VI, p. 562.
579 "Thanks . . . majority in the state": WHS to AL, November 3, 1863, Lincoln Papers.
579 a 30,000 majority: Seward, *Seward at Washington . . . 1861–1872,* p. 195.
579 "the Copperhead . . . and humbled": "8 November 1863, Sunday," in Hay, *Inside Lincoln's White House,* p. 109.
579 invitations to the Chase-Sprague wedding: See Niven, *Salmon P. Chase,* p. 342.
579 a diamond tiara worth $50,000: Ibid., p. 343.
579 "about the bridal *trousseau* . . . Millionaire Wedding": *NYT,* November 18, 1863.
579 "to realize" . . . undivided attention: SPC to William Sprague, October 31, 1863, reel 29, Chase Papers.
579 Sprague reassured Chase . . . "and generation": William Sprague to SPC, November 4, 1863, reel 29, Chase Papers.
580 Hay recounted . . . *The Pearl of Savoy*: "22 October 1863, Thursday," in Hay, *Inside Lincoln's White House,* p. 98.
580 The play revolves . . . Marie goes mad: Gaetano Donizetti, *The Pearl of Savoy: A Domestic Drama in Five Acts. French's Standard Drama.* Acting Edition No. 337 (New York: S. French, [1864?]). *The Pearl of Savoy* was an adaptation of Donizetti's *Linda de Chamounix.*
580 "was a coldly calculated . . . father and politics": See J. P. Cullen, "Kate Chase: Petticoat Politician," *Civil War Times Illustrated* 2 (May 1963), p. 15.
580 "in her eyes . . . upon her affections": Perrine, "The Dashing Kate Chase," *Ladies' Home Journal* (1901), p. 11.
580 "wholly innocent . . . several millions": *Daily Eagle,* Brooklyn, N.Y., November 14, 1863.
580 "Miss Kate has . . . sufficient for both": Entry for May 19, 1863, *Welles diary,* Vol. I (1960 edn.), p. 306.
580 Henry Adams . . . as Jephthah's daughter: Ross, *Proud Kate,* p. 121. The tale of Jephthah's daughter is in Judges 11:30–40.
581 "Memory has been busy . . . found a lodgment there": KCS diary, November 11, 1868, Sprague Papers.
581 In the hours before . . . proceeded inside: *Daily Morning Chronicle,* Washington, D.C., November 13, 1863.
581 Monty Blair, who refused . . . "of the occasion": EBL to SPL, November 12, [1863], in *Wartime Washington,* ed. Laas, p. 319.
581 Lord Lyons . . . and Robert C. Schenck: *Daily Morning Chronicle,* Washington, D.C., November 13, 1863; Perrine, "The Dashing Kate Chase," *Ladies' Home Journal* (1901), pp. 11–12; "12 November 1863, Thursday," in Hay, *Inside Lincoln's White House,* p. 111.
581 "Much anxiety" . . . and without Mrs. Lincoln: *Daily Morning Chronicle,* Washington, D.C., November 13, 1863.
581 "bow in reverence . . . *Chase & daughter*": MTL to Simon Cameron, June 16, [1866], in Turner and Turner, *Mary Todd Lincoln,* p. 370.
581 Mary's absence . . . "presidential party": Brooks, *Mr. Lincoln's Washington,* pp. 260–61.
582 "a gorgeous white velvet" . . . specifically for the occasion: *Daily Morning Chronicle,* Washington, D.C., November 13, 1863 (quote); Brooks, *Mr. Lincoln's Washington,* p. 261; Ross, *Proud Kate,* p. 140.
582 "Chase was . . . newly made wife": Brooks, *Mr. Lincoln's Washington,* p. 261.
582 A lavish meal . . . midnight: *Daily Morning Chronicle,* Washington, D.C., November 13, 1863.
582 "a very brilliant . . . had *arrived*": "12 November 1863, Thursday," in Hay, *Inside Lincoln's White House,* p. 111.
582 The young couple left the next morning: *NYT,* November 18, 1863.
582 "Your letter . . . how welcome it was": SPC to KCS, November 18, 1863, reel 29, Chase Papers.
582 "My heart is full . . . perfect honor & good faith": SPC to William Sprague, November 26, 1863, reel 30, Chase Papers.
583 He had been asked . . . would speak: David Wills to AL, November 2, 1863, Lincoln Papers.
583 Lincoln told his cabinet . . . could not spare the time: Entry for December 1863, *Welles diary,* Vol. I (1960 edn.), p. 480; SPC to KCS, November 18, 1863, reel 29, Chase Papers; entry for November 19, 1863, in *The Diary of Edward Bates, 1859–1866,* p. 316.
583 "extremely busy . . . public expectation": Lamon, *Recollections of Abraham Lincoln,* p. 173.

583 Stanton had arranged . . . "the gauntlet": AL to EMS, [November 17, 1863], in *CW*, VII, p. 16 and note.
583 The day before . . . "half of his speech": James Speed quoted in John G. Nicolay, "Lincoln's Gettysburg Address," *Century* 47 (February 1894), p. 597.
583 Various accounts suggest . . . "a makeshift desk": George D. Gitt, quoted in Wilson, *Intimate Memories of Lincoln*, p. 476.
583 Others swear . . . on an envelope: See Garry Wills, *Lincoln at Gettysburg: The Words That Remade America* (New York: Simon & Schuster, 1992), p. 27.
583 Nicolay . . . and humorous stories: Nicolay, "Lincoln's Gettysburg Address," *Century* (1894), p. 601.
583 he was escorted . . . and Edward Everett: David Wills to AL, November 1, 1863, Lincoln Papers.
583 "All the hotels . . . of Gettysburgh immortal": *NYT*, November 21, 1863.
584 He came to the door . . . "say nothing at all": AL, "Remarks to Citizens of Gettysburg, Pennsylvania," November 18, 1863, in *CW*, VI, pp. 16–17.
584 Lincoln sent a servant: Frank L. Klement, "The Ten Who Sat in the Front Row on the Platform During the Dedication of the Soldiers' Cemetery at Gettysburg," *Lincoln Herald* 88 (Winter 1985), p. 108.
584 A telegram arrived . . . Tad was better: EMS to AL, November 18 and 19, 1863, Lincoln Papers.
584 the crowd surged over . . . "part of the human race": WHS, quoted in Seward, *Seward at Washington . . . 1861–1872*, p. 201 (quote); *NYT*, November 21, 1863.
584 the convivial secretary . . . "men of this generation": Entry for November 22, 1863, in French, *Witness to the Young Republic*, p. 434.
584 He wanted to talk . . . and retiring: Klement, "The Ten Who Sat," *Lincoln Herald* (1985), p. 108; Wills, *Lincoln at Gettysburg*, p. 31; entry for November 22, 1863, in French, *Witness to the Young Republic*, p. 434.
584 The huge, boisterous crowd . . . "thousand more": Entry for November 22, 1863, in French, *Witness to the Young Republic*, p. 434.
584 made his final revisions: Nicolay, "Lincoln's Gettysburg Address," *Century* (1894), pp. 601, 602.
584 a chestnut horse . . . three cabinet officers: Sandburg, *Abraham Lincoln: The War Years*, Vol. II, p. 466.
585 Seward, riding . . . "homemade gray socks": Henry Clay Cochrane, quoted in ibid.
585 An audience . . . between Everett and Seward: Klement, "The Ten Who Sat," *Lincoln Herald* (1985), p. 106.
585 "leaned from one side . . . of his right hand": Gitt, quoted in Wilson, *Intimate Memories of Lincoln*, p. 478.
585 Another member . . . to his pocket: Monaghan, *Diplomat in Carpet Slippers*, p. 341.
585 "could not be surpassed by mortal man": Entry for November 22, 1863, in French, *Witness to the Young Republic*, p. 435.
585 "Seldom has a man . . . not like an orator": Klement, "The Ten Who Sat," *Lincoln Herald* (1985), p. 108.
585 "flutter and motion . . . an empty house": Gitt, quoted in Wilson, *Intimate Memories of Lincoln*, p. 478.
585 steel-rimmed spectacles . . . at his pages: Sandburg, *Abraham Lincoln: The War Years*, Vol. II, p. 468.
585 "He had spent . . . supreme principle": Wills, *Lincoln at Gettysburg*, p. 120.
585 "all this quibbling . . . created equal": AL, "Speech at Chicago, Illinois," July 10, 1858, in *CW*, II, p. 501.
585 "the central idea . . . govern themselves": AL, quoted in "7 May 1861, Tuesday," in Hay, *Inside Lincoln's White House*, p. 20.
586 "Four score and seven . . . shall not perish from the earth": AL, "Address Delivered at the Dedication of the Cemetery at Gettysburg, November 19, 1863; Edward Everett Copy," in *CW*, VII, p. 21.
586 "the assemblage . . . there came applause": Gitt, quoted in Wilson, *Intimate Memories of Lincoln*, p. 479.
586 he turned to Ward Lamon . . . "disappointed": Lamon, *Recollections of Abraham Lincoln*, p. 173.
586 "I should be glad . . . in two minutes": Edward Everett to AL, November 20, 1863, Lincoln Papers.
587 Zachariah Chandler . . . tardiness on emancipation: Bruce Tap, "Chandler, Zachariah," in *Encyclopedia of the American Civil War*, ed. Heidler and Heidler, pp. 398–99.
587 "Your president . . . & hold him": Zachariah Chandler to Lyman Trumbull, quoted in Williams, *Lincoln and the Radicals*, p. 179.
587 Having read in the press . . . "buried three days": Zachariah Chandler to AL, November 15, 1863, Lincoln Papers.
587 "My dear Sir . . . wreck the country's cause": AL to Zachariah Chandler, November 20, 1863, in *CW*, VII, pp. 23–24.
588 a mild case of smallpox: Entry for December 2, 1863, in French, *Witness to the Young Republic*, p. 439; entry for December 1863, *Welles diary*, Vol. I (1960 edn.), p. 480.
588 "Yes, it is a bad . . . that calls": *NYT*, December 18, 1863.
588 "the greatest question . . . practical statesmanship": "31 July 1863, Friday," in Hay, *Inside Lincoln's White House*, p. 69.
588 everyone assumed . . . of his divided party: Brooks, *Mr. Lincoln's Washington*, p. 271.
588 John Hay was present . . . "highly satisfactory": "[9 December 1863, Wednesday]," in Hay, *Inside Lincoln's White House*, pp. 121–22.
588 Radicals were thrilled . . . "acts of Congress": AL, "Annual Message to Congress," December 8, 1863, in *CW*, VII, p. 51.
588 "He makes Emancipation . . . of reconstruction": CS to Orestes A. Brownson, December 27, 1863, in *Selected Letters of Charles Sumner*, Vol. II, p. 216.
588 "God bless Old Abe . . . in the President": "[9 December 1863, Wednesday]," in Hay, *Inside Lincoln's White House*, p. 122.
588 had written a letter to Nathaniel Banks . . . "included in the plan": AL to Nathaniel P. Banks, in *CW*, VI, p. 365.
589 He offered full pardons . . . remain as they were: AL, "Proclamation of Amnesty and Reconstruction," December 8, 1863, in *CW*, VII, pp. 54–56.

589 Conservatives hailed . . . as it wished: EBL to SPL, December 8, 1863, in *Wartime Washington*, ed. Laas, p. 325.
589 "theory is identical . . . different nomenclature": CS to Orestes A. Brownson, December 27, 1863, in *Selected Letters of Charles Sumner*, Vol. II, pp. 216–17.
589 Lincoln assured . . . "otherwise would": AL, "Annual Message to Congress," December 8, 1863, in *CW*, VII, p. 52.
589 would devastate Confederate morale: Foner, *Reconstruction*, pp. 36–37.
589 When the Blairs . . . "of modern times": Brooks, *Mr. Lincoln's Washington*, p. 273.
589 "is the great man . . . clearly than anybody": "[9 December 1863, Wednesday]," in Hay, *Inside Lincoln's White House*, p. 122.
589 Judd called . . . "was Mr. Chase": Norman Judd and AL, quoted in "[9 December 1863, Wednesday]," in Hay, *Inside Lincoln's White House*, p. 124.
590 Chase had obstinately . . . perpetuate emancipation: SPC to AL, November 25, 1863, Lincoln Papers.
590 "more positive . . . is not to be had": SPC to Henry Ward Beecher, December 26, 1863, reel 30, Chase Papers.
590 he detected a more hopeful . . . surprisingly well: AL, "Annual Message to Congress," December 8, 1863, in *CW*, VII, pp. 49–50.
590 invited his sister-in-law . . . "and left him alone": David Davis, quoted in *Daily Picayune*, New Orleans, March 14, 1897.
590 Emilie had been living . . . through Union lines: Helm, *The True Story of Mary*, p. 220.
590 "I am totally at a loss . . . secure a pass?": John L. Helm to Mrs. Robert S. Todd, October 11, 1863, quoted in ibid., p. 219.
591 Lincoln personally issued . . . "to Kentucky": AL to Lyman B. Todd, October 15, 1863, in *CW*, VII, p. 517.
591 When Emilie arrived . . . explaining the dilemma: Helm, *The True Story of Mary*, pp. 220–21.
591 "Send her to me": AL, quoted in ibid., p. 221.
591 was received at the White House . . . Confederate Army: Emilie Todd Helm diary [hereafter Helm diary], quoted in ibid., pp. 221–22.
591 "Often the boundaries . . . chose sides": John W. Shaffer, *Clash of Loyalties: A Border County in the Civil War* (Morgantown: West Virginia University Press, 2003), p. 2.
591 they carefully avoided mention . . . "into other channels": Helm diary, quoted in Helm, *The True Story of Mary*, p. 224.
591 Mary did her utmost: Helm diary, quoted in ibid., pp. 222–23.
591 "He comes to me . . . most of the time": MTL, quoted in Helm diary, in ibid., p. 227.
592 "the scape-goat . . . thrill in her voice": MTL, quoted in Helm diary, in ibid., pp. 225, 227.
592 he confided her presence . . . "it known": Entry for December 14, 1863, in Browning, *The Diary of Orville Hickman Browning*, Vol. I, p. 651.
592 invited Emilie to join them: Helm, *The True Story of Mary*, p. 228.
592 Lincoln had personally . . . restore his spirits: Edgcumb Pinchon, *Dan Sickles: Hero of Gettysburg and "Yankee King of Spain"* (Garden City, N.Y.: Doubleday, Doran & Co., 1945), pp. 203–04.
592 Mary also considered . . . merriment: MTL to Sally Orne, [December 12, 1869], in Turner and Turner, *Mary Todd Lincoln*, pp. 533–34.
592 Senator Harris turned . . . "and Manassas": Helm diary, quoted in Helm, *The True Story of Mary*, p. 229.
592 Mary's face "turned . . . assistance in the matter": Helm diary, quoted in ibid., pp. 227, 229–31.
593 prompted Emilie to leave: Helm diary, quoted in ibid., p. 231.
593 "Oh, Emilie . . . hideous nightmare?": MTL, quoted in Helm diary, ibid., p. 226.
593 he took Nicolay and Hay . . . about the play: "[18 December 1863]," in Hay, *Inside Lincoln's White House*, p. 128; *Daily Morning Chronicle*, Washington, D.C., December 19, 1863.
593 "in fine spirits": Entry for December 15, 1863, *Welles diary*, Vol. I (1960 edn.), p. 485.
593 returned to Ford's . . . Bayard Taylor: "[18 December 1863]," in Hay, *Inside Lincoln's White House*, p. 128; *Daily Morning Chronicle*, Washington, D.C., December 18 and 19, 1863.
593 a peculiarly pleasant dream . . . the next day: "23 December 1863," in Hay, *Inside Lincoln's White House*, p. 132.
593 Seward entertained . . . "cloud of smoke": Seward, *Seward at Washington . . . 1861–1872*, p. 206.
593 Bates's children: See introduction, entries for May 28; June 5 and 20; July 1; November 15, 22, 25, and 30; December 16, 19 and 22, 1863, *The Diary of Edward Bates, 1859–1866*, pp. xv–xvi, 294, 295, 299, 315, 319, 320–21, 323.
594 After forty years . . . word against him: Entry for September 4, 1863, in *The Diary of Edward Bates, 1859–1866*, p. 306.
594 he attended a funeral . . . "and die soon": Entry for December 25, 1863, in ibid., p. 324.
594 Edgar's return . . . "on earth forever": Entry for December 25, 1863, *Welles diary*, Vol. I (1960 edn.), p. 494.
594 "The year closes . . . the future than now": Entry for December 31, 1863, ibid., pp. 499–500.
594 the birth of a new baby girl . . . baptismal celebration: EMS to SPC, December 30, 1863, reel 30, Chase Papers.
594 He shared with the men . . . "guests of the nation": *NYT*, December 29, 1863.
594 Lincoln invited Stanton . . . Point Lookout: AL to EMS, December 26, 1863, in *CW*, VII, p. 95 (quote); *NYTrib*, December 29, 1863.
594 He had heard that . . . Confederate strongholds: Thomas and Hyman, *Stanton*, p. 309; "28 December 1863, Monday," in Hay, *Inside Lincoln's White House*, p. 134.
595 "Oh! dying year! . . . brighter hopes dawn": Entry for December 31, 1863, in Adam Gurowski, *Diary: 1863–'64–'65*, Vol. III. Burt Franklin: Research & Source Works #229 (Washington, D.C., 1866; New York: Burt Franklin, 1968), p. 57.

595 "a tall . . . polish of appearance": Entry for February 24, 1861, Charles Francis Adams diary, reel 76.
595 "sphere of civilization": Entry for March 8, 1861, Charles Francis Adams diary, reel 76.
595 no "heroic qualities": Entry for February 21, 1861, Charles Francis Adams diary, reel 76.
595 "not equal . . . of his position": Entry for August 16, 1861, Charles Francis Adams diary, reel 76.
595 At a festive dinner . . . "to one great purpose": Charles Francis Adams, quoted in *NR*, February 2, 1864.
595 "foremost American . . . in his time": "Lowell, James Russell," in *Dictionary of American Biography*, Vol. VI, ed. Dumas Malone (New York: Charles Scribner's Sons, 1933), p. 458.
595 "Never did a President . . . still in wild water": James Russell Lowell, "The President's Policy," *North American Review* 98 (January 1864), pp. 241–43, 249, 254–55.
596 "very excellent . . . over-much credit": Entry for January 5, 1864, *Welles diary*, Vol. I (1960 edn.), p. 504.

CHAPTER 23: "*THERE'S A MAN IN IT!*"

Page

597 New Year's Day . . . scattered the clouds: Brooks, *Mr. Lincoln's Washington*, pp. 273–74 (quote); *Star*, January 1, 1864; *NR*, January 2, 1864.
597 "Murfreesboro . . . excel these": *NR*, January 1, 1864.
597 "We have a right . . . weathered the gale": *NR*, January 13, 1864.
598 "The instinct of all . . . danger is over": Dispatch of January 18, 1864, in Stoddard, *Dispatches from Lincoln's White House*, p. 203.
598 the traditional New Year's reception: Entry for January 1, 1864, in *Lincoln Day by Day*, Vol. III, p. 231; dispatch of January 4, 1864, in Stoddard, *Dispatches from Lincoln's White House*, p. 199.
598 "a human kaleidescope . . . petitioners": *NR*, January 2, 1864.
598 "*public-opinion baths* . . . and duty": Carpenter, *Six Months at the White House*, pp. 281–82.
598 "European democrats . . . American a custom": Dispatch of January 4, 1864, in Stoddard, *Dispatches from Lincoln's White House*, p. 199.
598 Lincoln "appeared to be . . . word or two": *NR*, January 2, 1864.
598 Mary Lincoln "never looked better" . . . velvet dress: Brooks, *Mr. Lincoln's Washington*, pp. 274–75 (quote p. 275).
598 "We seem to have . . . cared about it": FWS, quoted in Seward, *Seward at Washington . . . 1861–1872*, p. 207.
598 The winter social calendar . . . of cabinet officers: *NR*, January 19, 1864.
599 "grace and elegance": *NR*, January 26, 1864.
599 "who with such . . . once a week": *NR*, January 16, 1864.
599 "observed of all observers": *NR*, January 2, 1864.
599 "one of the most lovable women": Entry for January 3, 1864, in French, *Witness to the Young Republic*, p. 443.
599 "frosty . . . a very close examination": Brooks, *Mr. Lincoln's Washington*, p. 275.
599 Mary found it necessary . . . "human tide": Stoddard, *Inside the White House in War Times*, p. 49; *NR*, January 2, 1864.
599 ill dressed . . . their carpetbags: *NR*, January 13, 1864.
599 "the lace curtains . . . as a man's hand": Brooks, *Mr. Lincoln's Washington*, p. 253 (quote); B. B. French to Charles R. Train, January 5, 1863, p. 181, Vol. 14, reel 7; French to John H. Rice, March 7, 1864, p. 313, Vol. 14, reel 7; French to Rice, June 16, 1864, pp. 375–76, Vol. 14, reel 7, M371, RG 42, DNA.
600 would inaugurate "the fashionable 'season' ": *NR*, January 6, 1864.
600 visiting members . . . "with their families": *NYT*, January 8, 1864.
600 "not so largely attended as usual": *NYH*, January 13, 1864.
600 she was "disappointed": Entry for January 14, 1864, in French, *Witness to the Young Republic*, p. 443.
600 The Sewards hosted . . . "most brilliant": *NR*, January 26, 1864 (first quote); *NR*, January 15, 1864 (second quote); *NYT*, January 26, 1864 (third quote); *Star*, January 26, 1864.
600 a pleasant evening . . . "relief from care": Seward, *Seward at Washington . . . 1861–1872*, p. 208.
600 Mary could not relinquish . . . and supporters: Anson G. Henry to Isaac Newton, April 21, 1864, Lincoln Papers.
600 Mary's anger . . . "a patriot": Keckley, *Behind the Scenes*, pp. 127–29 (quotes pp. 128, 129).
600 and crossed out . . . "Schleswig-Holstein difficulty": JGN to JH, January 18, 1864, in Nicolay, *With Lincoln in the White House*, p. 124.
600 directed her wrath . . . "night or two": JGN to JH, January 29, 1864, in ibid., p. 125.
601 dinner "was pleasant . . . off very well": Entry for January 22, 1864, *Welles diary*, Vol. I (1960 edn.), p. 512.
601 unable to share . . . "merry-making at a funeral": GW to Edgar T. Welles, February 14, 1864, reel 22, Welles Papers.
601 "the old secession" . . . stars of every occasion: Dispatch of February 6, 1864, in Stoddard, *Dispatches from Lincoln's White House*, pp. 206–07 (quote p. 206).
601 Ulric . . . expert waltzer: Stoddard, *Inside the White House in War Times*, p. 128.
601 Fernando Wood . . . "personal intercourse": Dispatch of February 1, 1864, in Stoddard, *Dispatches from Lincoln's White House*, p. 205.
601 Mary Lincoln sent . . . "to believe it": MTL to Daniel E. Sickles, February 6, 1864, in Turner and Turner, *Mary Todd Lincoln*, pp. 167–68; see also note 3 of MTL to Sickles.
601 when Emilie . . . Martha Todd White: See note 1 to JGN to Benjamin F. Butler, April 19, 1864, Lincoln Papers.

602 Lincoln issued a pass: On the subject of Martha Todd White's dealings with the Lincolns, see JGN to Butler, April 19, 1864; Butler to JGN, April 21, 1864, Lincoln Papers.
602 "Here . . . of your master": Undated newspaper article pasted in JGN to Butler, April 19, 1863, container 28, Butler Papers; newspaper reports of Martha Todd White's statements to General Butler, quoted in Butler to JGN, April 21, 1864, Lincoln Papers.
602 he directed Nicolay to ascertain the facts: JGN to Butler, April 19, 1863, container 28, Butler Papers.
602 Butler replied . . . untoward had been found: Butler to JGN, April 21, 1864, Lincoln Papers.
602 Nicolay used Butler's letter: JGN to Butler, April 28, 1864; JGN to Horace Greeley, April 25, 1864; Greeley to JGN, April 26, 1864, Lincoln Papers. For an example of rebuttal issued, see *NYTrib*, April 27, 1864.
602 Butler was surprised . . . so "silly": Butler to JGN, April 21, 1864, Lincoln Papers.
602 Nor did he want . . . sustain the rebel cause: O. Stewart to AL, April 27, 1864, Lincoln Papers.
602 Browning requested a favor . . . "very good humor": Entry for February 6, 1894, in Browning, *The Diary of Orville Hickman Browning*, Vol. I, p. 659.
602 he had visited . . . Owen Lovejoy: Entry for February 6, 1864, in *Lincoln Day by Day*, Vol. III, p. 238.
602 "the best friend [he] had in Congress": AL, quoted in Carpenter, *Six Months at the White House*, p. 18.
602 suffering from a debilitating liver and kidney ailment: *NYT*, March 28, 1864; Edward Magdol, *Owen Lovejoy: Abolitionist in Congress* (New Brunswick, N.J.: Rutgers University Press, 1967), pp. 400, 402–03.
602 "This war is eating . . . live to see the end": AL, quoted in Carpenter, *Six Months at the White House*, p. 17.
603 a fire alarm rang . . . his brother, Willie: Robert W. McBride, *Personal Recollections of Abraham Lincoln* (Indianapolis: Bobbs-Merrill, 1926), pp. 29–30, 44–46 (quotes pp. 44–45); *Star*, February 11, 1864; *Daily Morning Chronicle*, Washington, D.C., February 11, 1864.
603 A coachman . . . setting the fire: *Star*, February 11, 1864; JGN to JH, February 10, 1864, in Nicolay, *With Lincoln in the White House*, p. 126.
603 instructed him to consult . . . "have it rebuilt": Commissioner B. B. French to John H. Rice, February 11, 1863, pp. 295–96, Vol. 14, reel 7, M371, RG 42, DNA (quote); *Star*, February 11, 1864.
603 "carefully veiled . . . a hopeless one": McClure, *Abraham Lincoln and Men of War-Times*, p. 136.
603 Friends of Chase . . . biographical sketch: Niven, *Salmon P. Chase*, p. 358.
603 "no matter how . . . flimsy political trick": William Orton to SPC, January 6, 1864, in *Chase Papers*, Vol. IV, p. 247.
604 "malignant denunciations": SPC to AL, January 13, 1864, reel 30, Chase Papers.
604 twenty-five long letters . . . inspirational book: Chase's series of autobiographical letters to John T. Trowbridge began on December 27, 1863, and ended on March 22, 1864, see Chase Papers; [John T. Trowbridge], *The Ferry-Boy and the Financier, by a Contributor to the "Atlantic"* (Boston: Walker, Wise, & Co., 1864).
604 An excerpt appeared: J. T. Trowbridge, "The First Visit to Washington," *Atlantic Monthly* 13 (April 1864), pp. 448–57.
604 "So far . . . otherwise than I have": SPC to J. W. Hartwell, February 2, 1864, reel 31, Chase Papers.
604 "I think of you . . . you are—where?": SPC to Charlotte S. Eastman, February 1, 1864, reel 31, Chase Papers.
604 Susan Walker . . . "bluestocking": Niven, *Salmon P. Chase*, pp. 97 (quote), 203–04.
604 "*I wish* you could come . . . you enough": SPC to Susan Walker, January 23, 1864, reel 31, Chase Papers.
605 the public announcement . . . held a large interest: Niven, *Salmon P. Chase*, pp. 357, 359–60; Blue, *Salmon P. Chase*, p. 222.
605 "eating a man's bread . . . the same time": David Davis, quoted in King, *Lincoln's Manager*, p. 213.
605 Chase busied himself lining up support: Hart, *Salmon P. Chase*, pp. 309–10.
605 "gratified . . . should he be reelected": SPC to Flamen Ball, February 2, 1864, reel 31, Chase Papers.
605 "lamented the . . . distinct feeler": Entry for February 3, 1864, *Welles diary*, Vol. I (1960 edn.), pp. 520–21.
605 "immeasurably" . . . to any other candidate: Entry for March 22, 1864, in *The Diary of Edward Bates, 1859–1866*, p. 350.
606 "fair plump lady . . . altogether the advantage": Entry for February 19, 1864, *Welles diary*, Vol. I (1960 edn.), p. 528.
606 the Pomeroy Committee . . . "available candidate": "The Pomeroy Circular," quoted in Schuckers, *The Life and Public Services of Salmon Portland Chase*, pp. 499–500.
606 Pomeroy circular was leaked to the press: J. M. Winchell, quoted in *NYT*, September 15, 1874.
606 "No sensible man . . . if it killed me": David Davis, quoted in King, *Lincoln's Manager*, p. 215.
606 "had no knowledge . . . entire confidence": SPC to AL, February 22, 1864, Lincoln Papers.
606 the circular's author . . . "would sustain": J. M. Winchell, quoted in *NYT*, September 15, 1874.
607 He understood the political . . . "*enemies*": Entry for February 13, 1864, in *The Diary of Edward Bates, 1859–1866*, p. 333.
607 acknowledged receipt . . . "time to do so": AL to SPC, February 23, 1864, reel 31, Chase Papers.
607 "Its recoil . . . than Lincoln": Entry for February 22, 1864, *Welles diary*, Vol. I (1960 edn.), p. 529.
607 "It is unworthy . . . of this movement": *NYT*, February 24, 1864.
607 the effect of the circular . . . Chase's prospects: JGN to TB, February 28, 1864, container 3, Nicolay Papers.
607 In state after state . . . Lincoln's renomination: *NYT*, February 24, 1864; Fitz Henry Warren to TW, March 25, 1864, Lincoln Papers.
607 Pomeroy's home state . . . support for Lincoln: W. W. H. Lawrence to Abel C. Wilder and James H. Lane, February 15, 1864, Lincoln Papers.
607 the "long list . . . degree with Abraham Lincoln": *NYT*, February 29, 1864.
607 *Harper's Weekly* . . . "had been blinded": *Harper's Weekly*, March 5, 1864, p. 146.
608 "The masses . . . earnest and honest": Entry for January 3, 1864, in Gurowski, *Diary: 1863–'64–'65*, p. 60.
608 The fatal blow: Niven, *Salmon P. Chase*, p. 361.

608 "brought matters . . . of the gravest character": Richard C. Parsons to SPC, March 2, 1864, reel 32, Chase Papers.
608 to answer Chase's . . . "occasion for a change": AL to SPC, February 29, 1864, reel 31, Chase Papers.
608 In a public letter . . . "given to my name": SPC to James C. Hall, March 5, 1864, reel 32, Chase Papers.
608 Chase told his daughter . . . "welfare of the country": SPC to Janet Chase Hoyt, March 15, 1864, reel 32, Chase Papers.
609 "It proves only . . . openly resisted": Entry for March 9, 1864, in *The Diary of Edward Bates, 1859–1866*, p. 345.
609 Leonard Grover estimated . . . "a hundred times": Leonard Grover, "Lincoln's Interest in the Theater," *Century* 77 (April 1909), p. 944.
609 "It gave him . . . seen by the audience": Noah Brooks, "Personal Reminiscences of Lincoln," *Scribners Monthly* 15 (March 1878), p. 675.
609 "the drama . . . entire relief": Stoddard, *Inside the White House in War Times*, p. 191.
609 At a performance . . . "Hal's time": Ibid., p. 107.
610 developments with gaslight . . . onto the stage: Mary C. Henderson, "Scenography, Stagecraft, and Architecture in the American Theatre: Beginnings to 1870," in Don Wilmeth and Christopher Bigsby, eds., *The Cambridge History of American Theatre*. Vol. I: *Beginnings to 1870* (New York: Cambridge University Press, 1998), p. 415.
610 "To envision nineteenth-century . . . intimate space: Levine, *Highbrow / Lowbrow*, pp. 26, 24–25.
610 Frances Trollope complained . . . "and whiskey": Trollope, *Domestic Manners of the Americans*, p. 102.
610 The years surrounding . . . Charlotte Cushman: Garff B. Wilson, *Three Hundred Years of American Drama and Theatre: From Ye Bear and Ye Cubb to Hair* (Englewood Cliffs, N.J.: Prentice-Hall, 1973), p. 144.
610 "she was not . . . vitality of her presence": *NYTrib*, February 19, 1876.
610 Seward and Miss Cushman . . . at the Seward home: Van Deusen, *William Henry Seward*, p. 338.
611 a close relationship with young Fanny: See Fanny Seward diary, Seward Papers; FAS to CS, June 10, 1858, reel 17, Sumner Papers.
611 "Imagine me . . . use in the world": FS to FAS, February 11, 1864, reel 116, Seward Papers.
611 "the greatest man" . . . outside their family: Charlotte Cushman, quoted in entry for October 14, 1864, Fanny Seward diary, Seward Papers.
611 Lincoln made his way . . . purpose of her visit: Charlotte Cushman to [WHS], July 9, 1861, Lincoln Papers.
611 "Perhaps the best . . . at criticism": AL to James H. Hackett, August 17, 1863, in *CW*, VI, p. 392.
611 Hackett shared . . . "without much malice": On the dissemination of Lincoln's letter to Hackett, see note 1 to AL to James H. Hackett, August 17, 1863, in ibid., p. 393; James H. Hackett to AL, October 22, 1863, Lincoln Papers; AL to James H. Hackett, November 2, 1863, in *CW*, VI, pp. 558–59 (quote p. 558).
612 recalled bringing . . . "pleasant interval" from his work: William Kelley, in *Reminiscences of Abraham Lincoln*, ed. Rice (1886 edn.), pp. 264–67, 270.
612 "Edwin Booth has done . . . any other man": Lucia Gilbert Calhoun, "Edwin Booth," *Galaxy* 7 (January 1869), p. 85.
612 captivated audiences . . . generation: Richard Lockridge, *Darling of Misfortune: Edwin Booth, 1833–1893* (New York: Century Co., 1932; New York: Benjamin Blom, 1971), pp. 14, 24, 38–39, 56, 78–79, 81; *Harper's New Monthly Magazine* 22 (April 1861), p. 702; E. C. Stedman, "Edwin Booth," *Atlantic Monthly* 17 (May 1866), p. 589.
612 Lincoln and Seward attended . . . *Merchant of Venice*: Entries for February 19, 25, 26; March 2, 4, and 10, 1864, in *Lincoln Day by Day*, Vol. III, pp. 241–45; *NR*, March 3, 5, and 10, 1864; Grover, "Lincoln's Interest in the Theater," *Century* (1909), p. 946.
612 Booth came to dinner . . . "want of body in wine": Entry for March 1864, Fanny Seward diary, Seward Papers.
613 anticipating Booth's Hamlet . . . "upon the stage": Carpenter, *Six Months at the White House*, pp. 49–51 (quote p. 51).
613 "laugh . . . ' "Midsummer Night's Dream" ' ": Ibid., p. 150.
613 Chase and Bates considered . . . "Satanic diversion": Hendrick, *Lincoln's War Cabinet*, p. 10.
613 Stanton came only once . . . Tad loved the theater: Grover, "Lincoln's Interest in the Theater," *Century* (1909), pp. 946, 944–45.
614 Tad would laugh . . . "seeing clearly why": "24 April 1864, Sunday," in Hay, *Inside Lincoln's White House*, p. 188.
614 "felt at home" . . . actually appeared in a play: Grover, "Lincoln's Interest in the Theater," *Century* (1909), p. 945.
614 who broke down in tears . . . and the Taft boys: Bayne, *Tad Lincoln's Father*, p. 201.
614 arrived in the nation's capital: Brooks, *Mr. Lincoln's Washington*, p. 290.
614 Congress had revived . . . the Western armies: Smith, *Grant*, pp. 284, 286, 293, 294.
614 He walked into the Willard . . . the accommodations: Smith, *Grant*, p. 289, Brooks D. Simpson, *Ulysses S. Grant: Triumph Over Adversity, 1822–1865* (Boston and New York: Houghton Mifflin, 2000), pp. 258–59.
614 Grant took his son . . . and took a bow: Brooks, *Mr. Lincoln's Washington*, p. 290 (quotes); Smith, *Grant*, p. 289.
614 walked over to the White House . . . "a tone of familiarity": Horace Porter, *Campaigning with Grant* (New York: Century Co., 1897; New York: Konecky & Konecky, 1992), pp. 18–19.
615 "a degree of awkwardness": Entry for March 9, 1864, *Welles diary*, Vol. I (1960 edn.), p. 538.
615 Lincoln referred him to Seward: Smith, *Grant*, pp. 289–90; entry for March 9, 1864, *Welles diary*, Vol. I (1960 edn.), pp. 538–39.
615 "laces were torn . . . much mixed": Brooks, *Mr. Lincoln's Washington*, p. 290.
615 Seward rapidly maneuvered . . . see his face: Carpenter, *Six Months at the White House*, p. 56.
615 "He blushed . . . and over his face": *NYH*, March 12, 1864.
615 "his warmest campaign during the war": Carpenter, *Six Months at the White House*, p. 56.

615 The president . . . "walk it abreast": Porter, *Campaigning with Grant*, p. 20.
615 Grant wanted nothing more . . . "presidential chair": J. Russell Jones recollections, quoted in Tarbell, *Life of Abraham Lincoln*, Vol. II (1917 edn.), pp. 187–88.
615 made their way back . . . Grant wrote out his statement: Smith, *Grant*, p. 290; Memorandum, March 9, 1864, container 3, Nicolay Papers.
616 "quite embarrassed . . . difficult to read": Memorandum, March 9, 1864, container 3, Nicolay Papers.
616 went upstairs to talk . . . assistance was needed: Grant, *Personal Memoirs of U.S. Grant*, p. 370.
616 Grant journeyed . . . " '*show*' business!": Carpenter, *Six Months at the White House*, p. 57.
616 "trappings and . . . canopy of heaven": Elihu Washburne, quoted in Blaine, *Twenty Years of Congress*, p. 510.
616 his preference for pork . . . "in spasms": *NYT*, March 31, 1864.
616 "was done exactly . . . into history": McFeely, *Grant*, p. 152.
617 "unusually backward" . . . end of the month: Entry for May 1, 1864, in *The Diary of Edward Bates, 1859–1866*, p. 363.
617 "stormy and inclement . . . of the Old Dominion": Dispatch of April 11, 1864, in Stoddard, *Dispatches from Lincoln's White House*, p. 219.
617 "the toughest snowstorm . . . ever I saw him": Entry for March 23, 1864, in French, *Witness to the Young Republic*, p. 447.
617 "as pleasant and funny" . . . Saturday levee: Benjamin B. French to Pamela Prentiss French, April 10, 1864, transcription, reel 10, French Family Papers, DLC.
617 he strolled into John Hay's room . . ." 'is of me' ": "24 April 1864, Sunday," in Hay, *Inside Lincoln's White House*, p. 188.
617 "a beleaguered nation . . . was never bright": J. G. Randall, *The Civil War and Reconstruction* (1937; Boston: D. C. Heath & Co., 1953), pp. 670, 347.
617 "real suffering . . . in the social scale": *NYT*, July 7, 1864.
617 Food riots had broken out . . . vandalized: Randall, *The Civil War and Reconstruction*, p. 670; Emory M. Thomas, *The Confederate Nation, 1861–1865*. New American Nation Series (New York: Harper & Row, 1979), pp. 199–206.
617 Davis's health gradually . . . isolated himself: Davis, *Jefferson Davis*, pp. 539–40, 551–53.
618 The "tramp" of his feet: Entry for May 8, 1864, in Mary Chesnut, *Mary Chesnut's Civil War*, ed. C. Vann Woodward (New Haven: Yale University Press, 1981), p. 601.
618 Washington was filled . . . were imminent: Dispatch of May 2, 1864, in Stoddard, *Dispatches from Lincoln's White House*, p. 223.
618 "beginning to feel . . . generally been failures": JGN to TB, May 1, 1864, container 3, Nicolay Papers.
618 Lincoln wrote him a letter . . . "dignity at once": "30 April 1864, Saturday," in Hay, *Inside Lincoln's White House*, p. 192.
618 "entire satisfaction . . . power to give": AL to USG, April 30, 1864, in *CW*, VII, p. 324.
618 "been astonished . . . fault is not with you": USG to AL, May 1, 1864, Lincoln Papers.
618 the Army . . . from the James River: Michael Korda, *Ulysses S. Grant: The Unlikely Hero*. Eminent Lives Series (New York: HarperCollins, 2004), p. 97.
618 "This concerted movement . . . in numbers": "30 April 1864, Saturday," in Hay, *Inside Lincoln's White House*, p. 193.
618 great "solicitude . . . great advantages": Entry for May 1, 1864, in Browning, *The Diary of Orville Hickman Browning*, Vol. I, p. 668.
619 the Wilderness: E. M. Law, "From the Wilderness to Cold Harbor," in *Battles and Leaders of the Civil War*, Vol. IV, Pt. I, p. 122; McFeely, *Grant*, p. 167; Gordon C. Rhea, *The Battle of the Wilderness, May 5–6, 1864* (Baton Rouge and London: Louisiana State University Press, 1994), pp. 27, 51, 142, 163, 178, 193.
619 climb over the dead . . . "three and four deep": *NYT*, May 15, 1864.
619 "a nightmare of inhumanity": McFeely, *Grant*, p. 165.
619 86,000 Union and Confederate casualties: Table of casualties, Noah Andre Trudeau, *Bloody Roads South: The Wilderness to Cold Harbor, May–June 1864* (Boston: Little, Brown, 1989), p. 341.
619 "The world has never seen . . . never will again": USG to Julia Dent Grant, May 13, 1864, in *The Papers of Ulysses S. Grant*. Vol. X: *January 1–May 31, 1864*, ed. John Y. Simon (Carbondale and Edwardsville: Southern Illinois University Press, 1982), p. 444.
619 "always regretted . . . was ever made": Grant, *Personal Memoirs of U. S. Grant*, p. 462.
619 as steamers reached the city . . . "torture and pain": Brooks, *Mr. Lincoln's Washington*, pp. 320, 323 (quotes).
619 Judge Taft was present . . . others limping along: Entry for May 11, 1864, Taft diary.
619 As each steamer landed . . . "and manly": Brooks, *Mr. Lincoln's Washington*, p. 323.
619 Elizabeth Blair fled . . . "for my nerves": EBL to SPL, May 30, 1864, in *Wartime Washington*, ed. Laas, p. 386.
619 "The carnage has been unexampled": Entry for May 15, 1864, in *The Diary of Edward Bates, 1859–1866*, p. 366.
619 "it seems to myself . . . battle of the war": WHS, diplomatic circular of May 16, 1864, quoted in Seward, *Seward at Washington . . . 1861–1872*, p. 219.
619 "The intense anxiety . . . for mental activity": Entry for May 17, 1864, *Welles diary*, Vol. II, p. 33.
619 "more nervous and anxious . . . and disaster": JGN to TB, May 15, 1864, container 3, Nicolay Papers.
620 nights when Lincoln did not sleep: Entry for May 7, 1864, *Welles diary*, Vol. II, p. 25.
620 "met him . . . his breast": Carpenter, *Six Months at the White House*, p. 30.
620 made time . . . an opera: Grover, "Lincoln's Interest in the Theater," *Century* (1909), p. 947; entry for May 18, 1864, in *Lincoln Day by Day*, Vol. III, p. 259; Schuyler Colfax, *Life and Principles of Abraham Lincoln* (Philadelphia: Jas. B. Rodgers, 1865), p. 12.

620 "People may think . . . it will kill me": AL, quoted in Colfax, *Life and Principles of Abraham Lincoln*, p. 12.
620 "I saw [Lincoln] walk . . . and anxious scrutiny": Colfax in *Reminiscences of Abraham Lincoln*, ed. Rice (1886 edn.), pp. 337–38.
620 "any other General . . . that wins": "9 May 1864, Monday," in Hay, *Inside Lincoln's White House*, p. 195.
620 Lincoln hugged and kissed . . . "no turning back": Henry E. Wing, *When Lincoln Kissed Me: A Story of the Wilderness Campaign* (New York: Eaton & Mains, and Cincinnati: Jennings & Graham, 1913), pp. 12–13, 38–39.
620 "I propose to fight it out . . . all summer": USG to EMS, May 11, 1864, in *Papers of Ulysses S. Grant*, Vol. X, p. 422.
620 Lincoln's face lit up . . . "the secret" to the army's fortunes: *NYT*, May 18, 1864.
621 Chase grew restless . . . retained the hope: Niven, *Salmon P. Chase*, p. 364.
621 Weed had repeatedly warned . . . Treasury employees: JGN to AL, March 30, 1864; TW to AL, March 25, 1864; W. W. Williams to TW, March 25, 1864, Lincoln Papers.
621 corrupt Treasury agents . . . "inevitably sink": TW to FWS, June 2, 1864, reel 84, Seward Papers.
621 Frank Blair had resigned . . . Treasury agent: Leonard B. Wurthman, Jr., "Frank Blair: Lincoln's Congressional Spokesman," *Missouri Historical Review* LXIV (April 1970), pp. 278–79, 284–86; "Charges Against a Member," April 23, 1864, *Congressional Globe*, 38th Cong., 1st sess., pp. 1827–29; Parrish, *Frank Blair*, p. 192.
621 he began by calmly . . . for the presidency: FB remarks before the House of Representatives, April 23, 1864, *Congressional Globe*, 38th Cong., 1st sess., pp. 1828–32 (quote p. 1829).
622 Elizabeth Blair . . . "revenge is suicide": EBL to SPL, April 23 and June 13, 1864, in *Wartime Washington*, ed. Laas, pp. 369, 392.
622 "mendacious slanders": Thomas Heaton to SPC, April 29, 1864, reel 33, Chase Papers.
622 "violent and injudicious . . . with discretion": Entry for April 28, 1864, *Welles diary*, Vol. II, p. 20.
622 told about the speech . . . "approval of the President": Riddle, *Recollection of War Times*, pp. 267, 268.
622 He considered Frank Blair . . . "did while here": James A. Garfield to J. Harrison Rhodes, April 28, 1864, quoted in Smith, *The Life and Letters of James Abram Garfield*, Vol. I, p. 376.
622 Chase told Riddle . . . "perfectly satisfied": Riddle, *Recollection of War Times*, pp. 268, 270–76.
623 "in the midst . . . actual din of battle": Brooks, *Mr. Lincoln's Washington*, p. 325.
623 the National Union Convention: Ibid., pp. 332–33. According to Brooks, twenty-three states "were represented without contest," and the contested delegations of Missouri and Tennessee were allowed to vote. Unofficial representatives from Confederate states and the territories attended but were not included on the official roll.
623 David Davis . . . "no one is necessary": David Davis to AL, June 2, 1864, Lincoln Papers.
624 Horace Greeley . . . "so heavy investments": Horace Greeley, quoted in *Conversations with Lincoln*, ed. Segal, pp. 320–21.
624 "popular instinct . . . the popular will": William Dennison, et al., to AL, June 14, 1864, Lincoln Papers.
624 "the country at large . . . but Lincoln's": Brooks, *Washington, D.C., in Lincoln's Time*, p. 140.
624 gathered in Cleveland's: Waugh, *Reelecting Lincoln*, pp. 177–80.
624 with a platform . . . "among the soldiers": Resolutions of the "Radical Democracy" party platform, quoted in *NYT*, June 1, 1864.
624 in the telegraph office . . . "four hundred men": Bates, *Lincoln in the Telegraph Office*, pp. 194–95 (quote p. 195).
624 "renomination . . . the odd bits of gossip": Brooks, *Washington, D.C., in Lincoln's Time*, p. 141.
625 was initially confronted . . . "short-haired women": Clark E. Carr, quoted in Waugh, *Reelecting Lincoln*, p. 192.
625 the radicals had tacitly . . . unanimous: Ibid., pp. 195, 196.
625 the tumultuous applause . . . "defense of their country": "Platform of the Union National Convention," quoted in note 1 of AL, "Reply to the Committee Notifying Lincoln of His Renomination," June 9, 1864, in *CW*, VII, pp. 381–82.
625 "The enthusiasm . . . Lincoln was spoken": Brooks, *Mr. Lincoln's Washington*, p. 335.
625 "a purge of any" . . . platform in full: Sixth plank of Union Convention platform, paraphrased in Waugh, *Reelecting Lincoln*, p. 193.
625 "Harmony was . . . their kerchiefs": *NR*, June 9, 1864.
625 his towering presence . . . allotted to a single state: Waugh, *Reelecting Lincoln*, pp. 199–200; Brooks, *Mr. Lincoln's Washington*, p. 326.
626 Weed had initially supported . . . the victorious Johnson: Thomas, *Abraham Lincoln*, p. 429.
626 "Stanton's theory . . . the United States": Albert E. H. Johnson, quoted in *New York Evening Post*, July 13, 1891.
626 a clerk handed him a dispatch . . . "a President?": AL, quoted in Carpenter, *Six Months at the White House*, p. 163.
626 "the cart before the horse": *NR*, June 9, 1864.
626 The embarrassed operator . . . "on my return": AL, quoted in Carpenter, *Six Months at the White House*, p. 163.
626 a committee appointed . . . of his nomination: Ibid., p. 166; entry for June 9, 1864, in *Lincoln Day by Day*, Vol. III, p. 263.
626 did not assume . . ." 'when crossing streams' ": AL, "Reply to Delegation from the National Union League," June 9, 1864, in *CW*, VII, pp. 383–84 (quote p. 384).
626 the Ohio delegation . . . "under his command": AL, "Response to a Serenade by the Ohio Delegation," June 9, 1864, in ibid., p. 384.
626 "nothing could defeat . . . like to die of": *NYT*, June 13, 1864.

CHAPTER 24: "ATLANTA IS OURS"

Page

627 "Our troops have . . . but little": Entry for June 20, 1864, *Welles diary*, Vol. II, pp. 54–55.
627 "The immense slaughter . . . sickens us all": Entry for June 2, 1864, ibid., p. 44.
627 "steady courage": Dispatch of June 6, 1864, in Stoddard, *Dispatches from Lincoln's White House*, p. 234.
628 nearly lost his life at Cold Harbor: Janet W. Seward, "Personal Experiences of the Civil War," Seward Papers, NRU.
628 "I cannot yet . . . a holy cause": FAS to William H. Seward, Jr., May 20, 1864, reel 115, Seward Papers.
628 a "righteous" conflict . . . Mexican War: FAS to Augustus Seward, May 15, 1864, reel 115, Seward Papers.
628 "so nervous . . . all night with terror": EBL to SPL, June 19, [1864], in *Wartime Washington*, ed. Laas, p. 394.
628 "grave & anxious": EBL to SPL, June 21, 1864, in ibid., p. 395.
628 if Frank were taken . . . "are politically": EBL to SPL, June 22, 1864, in note 2 of EBL to SPL, June 21, 1864, in ibid., p. 396.
628 Welles was pained . . . "unfit for any labor": Entry for July 20, 1864, *Welles diary*, Vol. II, p. 82.
628 the Great Central Fair in Philadelphia: William Thompson, "Sanitary Fairs of the Civil War," *Civil War History* 4 (March 1958), p. 60; *NR*, June 16, 1864.
628 "miracles as many . . . world of magic": Unknown observer, quoted in Thompson, "Sanitary Fairs of the Civil War," *CWH* 4 (1958), p. 60.
628 Lincoln, Mary, and Tad left: Entry for June 16, 1864, in *Lincoln Day by Day*, Vol. III, p. 265.
628 they were escorted . . . "in Philadelphia": *NR*, June 16 and 17, 1864 (quote June 17).
629 "War, at the best . . . until that time": AL, "Speech at Great Central Sanitary Fair, Philadelphia, Pennsylvania," June 16, 1864, in *CW*, VII, pp. 394, 395.
629 his own "intense anxiety . . . his post here": Entry for June 20, 1864, *Welles diary*, Vol. II, p. 55.
629 Accompanied by Tad . . . of June 20: Entry for June 20, 1864, in *Lincoln Day by Day*, Vol. III, p. 266.
629 "came down from . . . all who met him": Porter, *Campaigning with Grant*, pp. 217, 218.
629 "plain and substantial . . . hero of Vicksburg": *NYH*, June 25, 1864.
629 Lincoln conversed . . . "three capital jokes": Sylvanus Cadwallader, *Three Years with Grant: As Recalled by War Correspondent Sylvanus Cadwallader*, ed. Benjamin P. Thomas (New York: Alfred A. Knopf, 1956), p. 232.
629 Grant suggested a ride . . . "met him on all sides": Porter, *Campaigning with Grant*, p. 218 (quote); *NR*, June 24, 1864.
630 "a long and lingering look": *NYH*, June 25, 1864.
630 passed a brigade . . . "spontaneous outburst": Cadwallader, *Three Years with Grant*, p. 233.
630 "and his voice . . . if he had inherited it": Porter, *Campaigning with Grant*, pp. 222–23.
630 General Grant took Lincoln aside . . . "but I will go in": USG, quoted in entry for June 26, 1864, in Browning, *The Diary of Orville Hickman Browning*, Vol. I, p. 673.
630 "sunburnt and . . . position and good spirits": "23 June 1864, Thursday," in Hay, *Inside Lincoln's White House*, p. 210.
630 regular Friday cabinet meeting . . . "the General and army": Entry for June 24, 1864, *Welles diary*, Vol. II, p. 58.
631 project his own renewed hope . . . "as a commander": *NYTrib*, June 25, 1864.
631 "of the condition . . . terms of confidence": *Philadelphia Inquirer*, June 25, 1864.
631 "Having hope . . . your goals": Daniel Goleman, *Emotional Intelligence* (New York: Bantam Books, 1995), p. 87. Goleman quotes C. R. Snyder in the third quote.
631 "We are today . . . within a year": Brooks, *Mr. Lincoln's Washington*, p. 343.
631 John Cisco . . . own presidential hopes: John G. Nicolay and John Hay, *Abraham Lincoln: A History*, Vol. IX (New York: Century Co., 1917), p. 91.
631 Lincoln told Chase . . . for Maunsell Field: SPC to AL, June 27, 1864, Lincoln Papers.
631 Field was serving . . . "executive character": Chittenden, *Recollections of President Lincoln* (1901 edn.), pp. 371, 374.
632 Chase awoke the morning after . . . to the Ephesians: Entry for June 28, 1864, in *Chase Papers*, Vol. I, pp. 465–66.
632 "Stand therefore . . . righteousness": Ephesians 6:14.
632 "I can not" . . . on another nominee: AL to SPC, June 28, 1864, in *CW*, VII, pp. 412–13.
632 Chase wrote an immediate request: SPC to AL, June 28, 1864, Lincoln Papers.
632 He telegraphed Cisco . . . three months: SPC to John J. Cisco, June 28, 1864, reel 34, Chase Papers; entry for June 28, 1864, in *Chase Papers*, Vol. I, p. 467.
632 "The difficulty . . . open revolt": AL to SPC, June 28, 1864, in *CW*, VII, pp. 413–14.
632 He began his letter . . . "my resignation": John J. Cisco to SPC, June 28, 1864; SPC to AL, June 29, 1864, Lincoln Papers.
633 "I opened it . . . I did not long reflect": AL, quoted in Field, *Memories of Many Men*, pp. 301–02.
633 "You have been acting . . . I will go": "30 June 1864, Thursday," in Hay, *Inside Lincoln's White House*, p. 213.
633 "Your resignation . . . with the public service": AL to SPC, June 30, 1864, in *CW*, VII, p. 419.
633 Lincoln called John Hay . . . the opening prayer: "30 June 1864, Thursday," in Hay, *Inside Lincoln's White House*, p. 212.
633 Lincoln's penitent request . . . he was needed: Field, *Memories of Many Men*, p. 303.
633 After breakfast . . . it had been accepted: *Chase Papers*, Vol. I, pp. 469–70 (quotes p. 470).
634 spoke of "mutual embarrassment": AL to SPC, June 30, 1864, in *CW*, VII, p. 419.
634 "I had found . . . fitness of selection": Entry for June 30, 1864, in *Chase Papers*, Vol. I, p. 470.

634 "his full armor of noble sentiments": Nicolay and Hay, *Abraham Lincoln*, Vol. IX, p. 84.
634 "The Senators were struck" . . . vehement protest: Brooks, *Washington, D.C., in Lincoln's Time*, p. 119.
634 "Fessenden was frightened . . . was mad": AL, quoted in "30 June 1864, Thursday," in Hay, *Inside Lincoln's White House*, p. 213.
634 Lincoln listened patiently . . . "meet each other": Brooks, *Washington, D.C., in Lincoln's Time*, pp. 119–120 (quotes p. 120).
634 Chase had declined to attend: Entry for June 24, 1864, *Welles diary*, Vol. II, p. 58.
634 "unendurable . . . the last straw": Brooks, *Washington, D.C., in Lincoln's Time*, pp. 120, 121.
634 "very nervous & cut up": "30 June 1864, Thursday," in Hay, *Inside Lincoln's White House*, p. 214.
634 Chittenden was equally . . . "thoroughly miserable": AL, quoted in Chittenden, *Recollections of President Lincoln* (1901 edn.), pp. 377–79 (quotes pp. 378–79).
635 Lincoln paused . . . "loftier motives than any man": Ibid., pp. 379–80.
635 a similar remark . . . "of good will": Entry for June 30, 1864, in *Chase Papers*, Vol. I, p. 471.
635 "the great magician . . . financier of his century": *Chicago Tribune*, July 3, 1864.
635 "Mr. Chase is . . . Webster and Calhoun": *NYTrib*, July 1, 1864.
635 he received a telegram . . . reasons of health: David Tod to AL, June 30, 1864, Lincoln Papers.
635 "laid awake . . . public men": Carpenter, *Six Months at the White House*, p. 182.
635 By morning . . . William Pitt Fessenden: Chittenden, *Recollections of President Lincoln* (1901 edn.), p. 381.
635 "*First* . . . of many radicals": "1 July 1864, Friday," in Hay, *Inside Lincoln's White House*, p. 216.
636 Lincoln handed Hay . . . "at once to the Senate": AL, quoted in "1 July 1864, Friday," in ibid., p. 215.
636 Lincoln greeted Fessenden . . . would kill him: William Pitt Fessenden, quoted in Fessenden, *Life and Public Services of William Pitt Fessenden*, Vol. I, pp. 315–16.
636 "If you decline . . . the nomination": AL, quoted in "1 July 1864, Friday," in Hay, *Inside Lincoln's White House*, p. 216.
636 "Telegrams came pouring . . . the most miserable": William Pitt Fessenden to his cousin, quoted in Fessenden, *Life and Public Services of William Pitt Fessenden*, Vol. I, p. 320.
636 "Very well . . . save your country": EMS, quoted in ibid., p. 321.
636 As he was driven . . . "danger to the country": William Pitt Fessenden to Justice Tenney, quoted in ibid., pp. 317–18.
636 "He is a man . . . personal integrity": *Chicago Tribune*, July 2, 1864.
636 "He is honest . . . Republican Senators": EBL to SPL, July 2, 1864, in *Wartime Washington*, ed. Laas, p. 398.
637 "I am the most popular man in my country": William Pitt Fessenden, quoted in Fessenden, *Life and Public Services of William Pitt Fessenden*, Vol. I, p. 326.
637 "So my official life closes": Entry for June 30, 1864, in *Chase Papers*, Vol. I, p. 471.
637 the oppressive heat of Washington . . . "are wilting": Entry for July 31, 1864, in *The Diary of Edward Bates, 1859–1866*, p. 392.
637 "laid broad foundations" . . . was still unfinished: Entry for June 30, 1864, in *Chase Papers*, Vol. I, p. 471.
637 Blair and Bates called . . . "as a blessing": Entry for June 30, 1864, *Welles diary*, Vol. II, pp. 62–63 (quote p. 63).
637 "the courage and candor to admit his errors": Entry for March 23, 1864, ibid., p. 545.
637 "his jokes are . . . destitute of wit": Entry for March 22, 1864, ibid., p. 545.
637 "a vague feeling . . . to be cordial": Entry for June 30, 1864, in *The Diary of Edward Bates, 1859–1866*, p. 381.
637 "dropped off . . . every body else": FPB to FB, July 4, 1864, quoted in Smith, *The Francis Preston Blair Family in Politics*, Vol. II, p. 271.
637 Seward, unlike . . . "first day of the Administration": WHS to FAS, [July] 2, 1864, quoted in Seward, *Seward at Washington . . . 1861–1872*, p. 230.
637 he noted sadly . . . "since my resignation": Entry for July 13, 1864, in *Chase Papers*, Vol. I, p. 479.
637 If Chase believed . . . he was mistaken: SPC to EMS, June 30, 1864, in Warden, *Private Life and Public Services*, p. 618.
637 Chase searched for reasons . . . "hostile to me": Entry for July 4, 1864, in *Chase Papers*, Vol. I, p. 476.
638 "The root . . . a joke out of this war": SPC to Whitelaw Reid, quoted in Albert Bushnell Hart, *Salmon P. Chase*. American Statesmen Series (Boston and New York: Houghton Mifflin, 1899), p. 318.
638 To Kate . . . "cannot finish what I began": SPC to KCS, July 3, 1864, reel 34, Chase Papers.
638 whose marriage to William . . . "the balance of power": Lamphier, *Kate Chase and William Sprague*, p. 78.
638 "Can it be . . . even with far less material wealth": Entry for November 4, 1868, KCS diary, Sprague Papers (quotes); Lamphier, *Kate Chase and William Sprague*, pp. 74, 84–85.
639 occasionally loathing . . . "learned to submit": Entry for November 11, 1868, KCS diary, Sprague Papers.
639 Chase witnessed a fight . . . her first child: Entry for September 9, 1864, in *Chase Papers*, Vol. I, p. 501 (quote); Belden and Belden, *So Fell the Angels*, pp. 135–36, 141.
639 The Wade-Davis bill: H. R. 244, 38th Cong., 1st sess. ("Wade-Davis Bill"), in *The Radical Republicans and Reconstruction, 1861–1870*, ed. Harold Hyman. American Heritage Series (Indianapolis and New York: Bobbs-Merrill, 1967), pp. 128–34.
639 In a written proclamation . . . single, inflexible system: AL, "Proclamation Concerning Reconstruction," July 8, 1864, in *CW*, VII, p. 433.
640 he likened the Wade-Davis . . . "fit the bedstead": Brooks, *Washington, D.C., in Lincoln's Time*, pp. 156–57.
640 Lincoln understood . . . "fixed within myself": "4 July 1864, Monday," in Hay, *Inside Lincoln's White House*, pp. 218–19.
640 Wade and Davis published . . . manifesto against him: "The Wade-Davis Manifesto, August 5, 1864," in *The Radical Republicans and Reconstruction, 1861–1870*, ed. Hyman, pp. 137–47.
640 He was not surprised by . . . "that can befall a man": Brooks, *Washington, D.C. in Lincoln's Time*, p. 156.

640 The rumors alarmed . . . eager to get started: EBL to SPL, July 6, 1864, in *Wartime Washington*, ed. Laas, p. 400.
640 In a letter to Frank . . . "a remote future": FPB to FB, July 4, 1864, quoted in Smith, *The Francis Preston Blair Family in Politics*, Vol. II, p. 272.
640 admonitions concerned Monty . . . the Pennsylvania countryside: EBL to SPL, July 6, 1864, in *Wartime Washington*, ed. Laas, p. 400.
640 tried to convince her mother . . . "pulled to pieces": EBL to SPL, July 14, 1864, in ibid., p. 403.
641 Grant's decision . . . General Lew Wallace: John Henry Cramer, *Lincoln Under Enemy Fire: The Complete Account of His Experiences During Early's Attack on Washington* (Baton Rouge: Louisiana State University Press, 1948), pp. 2–8.
641 Wallace understood . . . prepared itself for attack: Seward, *Seward at Washington . . . 1861–1872*, p. 231.
641 "The battle lasted . . . superior numbers": Seward, 9th N.Y. Artillery speech, 1912, Seward Papers, NRU.
641 Will's horse . . . have been captured: Seward, *Seward at Washington . . . 1861–1872*, pp. 244–45.
641 Seward spent a tense . . . he had not been captured: Letter to FAS, quoted in Seward, *Seward at Washington . . . 1861–1872*, p. 233 (quote); Lew Wallace to Henry W. Halleck, July 9, 1864, *OR*, Ser. 1, Vol. XXXVII, Part II, p. 145.
641 "God be praised for the safety of our boy": FAS to WHS, July 11, 1864, reel 114, Seward Papers.
641 "With the help . . . rejoining the forces": Seward, *Seward at Washington . . . 1861–1872*, pp. 231–32.
641 Falkland mansion . . . "top to bottom": Mr. Turton, quoted in *National Intelligencer*, reprinted from the *Daily Morning Chronicle*, Washington, D.C., July 16, 1864.
642 "blackened ruin": EBL to SPL, August 5, 1864, quoted in note 2 of EBL to SPL, July 16, 1864, in *Wartime Washington*, ed. Laas, p. 405.
642 the soldiers scattered papers . . . "great frolic" on the lawn: EBL to SPL, July 16 and 31, [1864], in ibid., pp. 404, 413 (quotes).
642 "perfect saturnalia": EBL to SPL, July 31, [1864], in ibid., p. 413.
642 Breckinridge made them . . . "side of the Mts.": EBL to SPL, July 16 and 31, [1864], in ibid., pp. 404, 413 (quote).
642 He explained . . . "refuge & of rest": EBL to SPL, July 16, [1864], in ibid., p. 405.
642 "made more fuss . . . came back to us": EBL to SPL, July 16, [1864], in ibid., pp. 404–05.
642 In his initial panic . . . during the crisis: Thomas and Hyman, *Stanton*, pp. 319–20.
642 "all convalescents . . . and rifle-pits": Henry W. Halleck to George Cadwalader, July 9, 1864, *OR*, Ser. 1, Vol. XXXVII, Part II, p. 153.
642 "in a pleasant and confident humor": "12 July 1864, Tuesday," in Hay, *Inside Lincoln's White House*, p. 222.
642 "in the least concerned . . . force in our front": "11 July 1864, Monday," in ibid., p. 221.
643 "exhibits none . . . on former occasions": Entry for July 11, 1864, *Welles diary*, Vol. II, p. 72.
643 drove together . . . "were not *frightened*": Entry for July 11, 1864, Taft diary.
643 allowing the residents of Washington . . . "troops to the south": Seward, *Reminiscences of a War-Time Statesman and Diplomat*, p. 246.
643 "Before even the first . . . direction of Washington": Jubal A. Early, "The Advance on Washington in 1864. Letter from General J. A. Early," *Southern Historical Society Papers*, Vol. IX, January–December 1881 (Richmond, Va.: Southern Historical Society; Wilmington, N.C.: Broadfood Publishing Co., Morningside Bookshop, 1990), p. 306.
643 "to be exceedingly . . . impregnable": Jubal Anderson Early, *War Memoirs: Autobiographical Sketch and Narrative of the War Between the States*, ed. Frank E. Vandiver. Civil War Centennial Series (Bloomington: Indiana University Press, 1960), p. 390.
643 at Fort Stevens: Benjamin Franklin Cooling, *Jubal Early's Raid on Washington, 1864* (Baltimore: Nautical & Aviation Publishing Co. of America, 1989), pp. 117–55.
643 "The President evinced . . . standing upon it": Cramer, *Lincoln Under Enemy Fire*, p. 30.
643 "Get down" . . . unusual incident: Oliver Wendell Holmes, Jr., quoted in ibid., p. 22.
643 "was exciting and wild . . . to have occurred": Entry for July 12, 1864, *Welles diary*, Vol. II, pp. 75–76.
644 "an egregious blunder": Charles A. Dana, *Recollections of the Civil War* (New York: Collier Books, 1963), p. 205.
644 Welles knew . . . appeared "contemptible": Entry for July 13, 1864, *Welles diary*, Vol. II, p. 76.
644 "Mrs. Lincoln . . . away as they did!": Carpenter, *Six Months at the White House*, pp. 301–02 (quote p. 302).
644 "I am informed . . . dismissed from the cabinet": Henry W. Halleck to EMS, July 13, 1864, Lincoln Papers.
644 "Whether the remarks . . . shall be dismissed": EMS to AL, July 14, 1864, Lincoln Papers; AL to EMS, July 14, 1864, in *CW*, VII, pp. 439–40 (quote).
645 "It would greatly pain . . . now or hereafter": AL, "Memorandum Read to Cabinet," [July 14?], 186[4], in *CW*, VII, p. 439.
645 Learning that Ben Butler . . . "civilians on either side": MB to Benjamin F. Butler, August 10, 1864, in *Private and Official Correspondence of Gen. Benjamin F. Butler During the Period of the Civil War*. Vol. V: *August 1864–March 1868* (Norwood, Mass.: Plimpton Press, 1917), p. 32 (quote); Cooling, *Jubal Early's Raid on Washington, 1864*, pp. 152–53.
645 "The loss is . . . is unrelieved[?]": MB to R. A. Sloane, July 21, 1864, reel 22, Blair Family Papers, DLC.
645 "The month of August" . . . throughout the North: Brooks, *Lincoln Observed, Civil War Dispatches of Noah Brooks*, ed. Michael Burlingame (Baltimore, Md., and London: Johns Hopkins University Press, 1998), p. 129.
645 mid-July call for five hundred thousand additional volunteers: *NYT*, July 19, 1864.
645 "dissatisfaction . . . with the colors flying": Ibid.
645 An ingenious attempt: See Dorothy L. Drinkard, "Crater, Battle of the (30 July 1864)," in *Encyclopedia of the American Civil War*, ed. Heidler and Heidler, p. 517; McPherson, *Battle Cry of Freedom*, pp. 758–60.

646 "Piled on top . . . frightened sheep": Brooks, *Lincoln Observed*, p. 130.
646 "It was the saddest . . . again to have": USG to Henry W. Halleck, August 1, 1864, *OR*, Ser. 1, Vol. XL, Part I, p. 17.
646 "less however from the result . . . of the future": Entry for August 2, 1864, *Welles diary*, Vol. II, p. 92.
646 he admitted feeling . . . "of our generals": Entry for August 1, 1864, in *The Diary of Edward Bates, 1859–1866*, p. 392.
646 he met with Grant at Fort Monroe: *NYH*, August 3, 1864.
646 dispatched General Philip Sheridan . . . "troops go also": USG to Henry W. Halleck, August 1, 1864, *OR*, Ser. 1, Vol. XXXVII, Part II, p. 558.
646 "This, I think, is exactly right": AL to USG, August 3, 1864, in *CW*, VII, p. 476.
646 "a long and very pleasant . . . both in time": Benjamin B. French to Henry F. French, August 9, 1864, typescript copy, reel 10, French Family Papers, DLC.
646 "much wretchedness . . . in the land": Entry for August 4, 1864, *Welles diary*, Vol. II, p. 93.
646 "The People are wild for Peace": TW to WHS, August 22, 1864, Lincoln Papers.
646 *"two Ambassadors . . . for a peace"*: William C. Jewett to Horace Greeley, July 5, 1864, Lincoln Papers.
646 Urging the president . . . "doing great harm": Horace Greeley to AL, July 7, 1864, Lincoln Papers.
647 commissioned Horace Greeley . . . escort them to Washington: AL to Horace Greeley, July 9, 1864, in *CW*, VII, p. 435.
647 dispatched John Hay to join Greeley: "[ca. 21 July 1864]," in Hay, *Inside Lincoln's White House*, pp. 224–25; "[after 22 July 1864]," in ibid., p. 228; entry for July 18, 1864, in *Lincoln Day by Day*, Vol. III, p. 273.
647 "To Whom it may concern . . . collateral points": AL, "To Whom It May Concern," July 18, 1864, in *CW*, VII, p. 451.
647 the two envoys . . . to stop the war: "[after 22 July 1864]," in Hay, *Inside Lincoln's White House*, p. 228.
647 He hoped the failed mission . . . of freeing the slaves: Eaton, *Grant, Lincoln and the Freedmen*, p. 176; Nicolay and Hay, *Abraham Lincoln*, Vol. IX, pp. 193–94.
647 "are told . . . an impossibility": TW to WHS, August 22, 1864, Lincoln Papers.
647 Swett felt compelled . . . situation was hopeless: Leonard Swett to his wife, September 8, 1864, quoted in Tarbell, *The Life of Abraham Lincoln*, Vol. II (—: S. S. McClure Co., 1895; New York Doubleday & McClure Co., 1900), p. 202.
647 were mystified . . . "his Cabinet": Entry of August 17, 1864, *Welles diary*, Vol. II, p. 109.
648 "I am in active . . . *of the Constitution*": Henry J. Raymond to AL, August 22, 1864, Lincoln Papers.
648 "I confess that I . . . prosperity to the country": "The Interview between Thad Stevens & Mr. Lincoln as related by Col R. M. Hoe," compiled by JGN, container 10, Nicolay Papers.
648 asked all cabinet members . . . a successful conclusion: "11 November 1864, Friday," in Hay, *Inside Lincoln's White House*, pp. 247–48.
648 "This morning . . . possibly save it afterwards": AL, "Memorandum Concerning His Probable Failure of Re-election," August 23, 1864, in *CW*, VII, p. 514.
648 "was considering" . . . would lend his hand: Eaton, *Grant, Lincoln and the Freedmen*, pp. 173–75 (quotes pp. 173, 175).
649 Douglass met with . . . "within our boundaries": Douglass, *Life and Times of Frederick Douglass*, pp. 796–97.
649 Douglass promised to confer: Frederick Douglass to AL, August 29, 1864, Lincoln Papers.
649 Randall had hand-delivered . . . "Democrats may stand": Charles D. Robinson to AL, August 7, 1864, Lincoln Papers.
650 Lincoln shared a draft: Frederick Douglass to Theodore Tilton, October 15, 1864, in *The Life and Writings of Frederick Douglass*, Vol. III, ed. Foner, p. 423.
650 "To me it seems . . . matter of policy": AL to Charles D. Robinson, [August] 1864, Lincoln Papers.
650 "as it seems you would . . . made the offer supposed": AL to Charles D. Robinson, August 17, 1864, Lincoln Papers.
650 Douglass saw clearly . . . "do you serious damage": Frederick Douglass to Theodore Tilton, October 15, 1864, in *The Life and Writings of Frederick Douglass*, Vol. III, ed. Foner, p. 423.
650 a messenger informed Lincoln . . . "my friend Douglass": AL, quoted in Douglass, "Lincoln and the Colored Troops," in *Reminiscences of Abraham Lincoln*, ed. Rice, p. 320.
650 "suppress his excitement . . . men in America": Eaton, *Grant, Lincoln and the Freedmen*, pp. 175, 176.
651 "The President was free . . . reminiscences of the past": "Interview with Alexander W. Randall and Joseph T. Mills," August 19, 1864, quoted from the diary of Joseph T. Mills, State Historical Society of Wisconsin, Madison, in *CW*, VII, pp. 506–08 (quotes); Pinsker, *Lincoln's Sanctuary*, p. 158.
651 Lincoln permanently shelved the draft: Note 1 of AL to Charles D. Robinson, August 17, 1864, in *CW*, VII, p. 501.
651 Raymond's suggestion . . . "by peaceful modes": AL to Henry J. Raymond, August 24, 1864, in ibid., p. 517.
652 "slept undisturbed" . . . biography of Lincoln: Nicolay and Hay, *Abraham Lincoln*, Vol. IX, p. 221.
652 "a sort of political Bull Run": JGN to TB, August 28, 1864, container 3, Nicolay Papers.
652 "ever present and companionable": Entry for August 19, 1864, *Welles diary*, Vol. II, p. 112.
652 Mary and Tad . . . Vermont: AL to MTL, August 31, September 8 and September 11, 1864, in *CW*, VII, p. 526, 544, 547.
652 but did not feel he should . . . "than another arises": WHS to FAS, August 27, 1864, quoted in Seward, *Seward at Washington . . . 1861–1872*, p. 241.
652 "the signs of discontent . . . all to disappear": WHS to home, August 16, 1864, quoted in ibid., p. 240.
652 "firm and hopeful": WHS to FAS, August 27, 1864, quoted in ibid., p. 241.

652 Welles observed . . . "an understanding": Entry for August 19, 1864, *Welles diary*, Vol. II, p. 112.
652 the sight of a disabled soldier: Benjamin, "Recollections of Secretary Edwin M. Stanton," *Century* (1887), p. 761.
652 Lincoln invited Raymond . . . "utter ruination": JGN to JH, August 25, 1864, in Nicolay, *With Lincoln in the White House*, p. 152.
652 chairing a meeting . . . mobilize the party: Leonard Swett to his wife, September 8, 1864, quoted in Tarbell, *The Life of Abraham Lincoln*, Vol. II (1900 edn.), pp. 202–03.
652 "the turning-point . . . we are saved": JGN to JH, August 25, 1864, in Nicolay, *With Lincoln in the White House*, p. 152.
653 Nicolay was relieved . . . "encouraged and cheered": JGN memoranda, quoted in Nicolay and Hay, *Abraham Lincoln*, Vol. IX, p. 221.
653 Noting that the members . . . "for the Union party": *NYT*, August 27, 1864.
653 "I happen temporarily . . . an inestimable jewel": AL, "Speech to One Hundred Sixty-sixth Ohio Regiment," August 22, 1864, in *CW*, VII, p. 512.
653 "giants in the . . . of the opposition": JGN to JH, August 25, 1864, in Nicolay, *With Lincoln in the White House*, p. 152.
654 "we have had nothing . . . change all this": Noah Brooks to JGN, August 29, 1864, Lincoln Papers.
654 "They have a peace . . . to rest upon": Waugh, *Reelecting Lincoln*, p. 89.
654 "It was noticeable" . . . virtual silence: Noah Brooks to JGN, August 29, 1864, Lincoln Papers.
654 "His partisans are united . . . their own choice": Brooks, *Mr. Lincoln's Washington*, p. 368.
654 "was expected . . . surrender and abasement": Entry for September 2, 1864, *Diary of George Templeton Strong*, Vol. III, p. 479.
654 the platform declared . . . "cessation of hostilities": "The Democratic National Platform of 1864 (August 29 1864)," in *Encyclopedia of the American Civil War*, ed. Heidler and Heidler, p. 2375.
654 Strong predicted . . . "on such terms": Entry for September 2, 1864, *Diary of George Templeton Strong*, Vol. III, p. 480.
654 "Atlanta is ours, and fairly won": William T. Sherman to Henry W. Halleck, September 3, 1864, *OR*, Ser. 1, Vol. XXXVIII, Part V, p. 777.
655 Lincoln to order that one hundred guns: AL, "Order for Celebration of Victories at Atlanta, Georgia, and Mobile, Alabama," September 3, 1864, in *CW*, VII, p. 532.
655 "Atlanta is ours . . . are ours now": *NYT*, September 5, 1864.
655 the departing Confederates . . . "of military value": McPherson, *Battle Cry of Freedom*, p. 774.
655 "Glorious news . . . event of the war": Entry for September 3, 1864, *Diary of George Templeton Strong*, Vol. III, pp. 480–81.
655 Seward received the news . . . at his house to celebrate: Seward, *Seward at Washington . . . 1861–1872*, p. 242.
655 the crowd swelled . . . "effective speeches": *NYT*, September 6, 1864.
655 the twin victories . . . "perish and leave no root": WHS, quoted in Seward, *Seward at Washington . . . 1861–1872*, pp. 242–44.
655 "For a man of not very" . . . the upcoming campaign: Entry for September 10, 1864, *Welles diary*, Vol. II, p. 140.
656 "This intelligence will . . . on a peace platform": Entry for September 3, 1864, ibid., pp. 135–36.
656 Peace Democrats threatened . . . "their support": Clement L. Vallandigham to GBM, September 4, 1864, reel 36, McClellan Papers, DLC.
656 six drafts . . . midnight on September 8: *Civil War Papers of George B. McClellan*, p. 588; GBM to MEM, [September 9, 1864], ibid., p. 597.
656 He began with a nod . . . "brethren had been in vain": GBM to the Democratic Nomination Committee, September 8, 1864, in *Civil War Papers of George B. McClellan*, pp. 595–96.
656 "We are going to win . . . unite on Mr. Lincoln": Theodore Tilton to JGN, September 6, 1864, Lincoln Papers.
656 believed that God . . . "nearly capsized it": Leonard Swett to his wife, September 8, 1864, quoted in Tarbell, *The Life of Abraham Lincoln*, Vol. II (1900 edn.), p. 203.
656 "conspiracy against Mr. Lincoln collapsed": TW to WHS, September 10, [1864], Lincoln Papers.
657 "to weaken the President . . . now support Lincoln": Entry for September 10, 1864, *Welles diary*, Vol. II, pp. 140–41.
657 Chase stopped en route . . . "judgment of history?": Entry for September 13, 1864, in *Chase Papers*, Vol. I, p. 502.
657 "Mr. Chase had a long . . . at the north": EBL to SPL, September 16, 1864, in *Wartime Washington*, ed. Laas, p. 429.
657 Chase accompanied Stanton . . . with Lincoln: Entry for September 16, 1864, in *Chase Papers*, Vol. I, pp. 503–04.
657 "I have been . . . demonstrative": SPC to KCS, September 17, 1864, reel 35, Chase Papers.
657 "wronged and hurt . . . fidelity to his Administration": Entry for September 17, 1864, in *Inside Lincoln's Cabinet: The Civil War Diaries of Salmon P. Chase*, ed. David Donald (New York: Longmans, Green, 1954), p. 255.
657 "conviction that . . . in securing it": SPC to KCS, September 17, 1864, reel 35, Chase Papers.
657 He traveled . . . before overflowing crowds: Entries for September 24–November 11, 1864, in *Chase Papers*, Vol. I, pp. 507–10.
658 the state elections . . . previous year: JGN to TB, September 11, 1864, container 3, Nicolay Papers; *NYT*, September 13, 1864.
658 "Three weeks ago . . . confident of success": JGN to TB, September 11, 1864, container 3, Nicolay Papers.

658 Philip Sheridan . . . of Early's army: McPherson, *Battle Cry of Freedom*, p. 777.
658 "shouting of Clerks" . . . news became known: Entry for September 20, 1864, in *Chase Papers*, Vol. I, p. 506.
658 "This will do much . . . loving men": Entry for September 20, 1864, *Welles diary*, Vol. II, p. 151.
658 Blair was aware . . . his resignation to Lincoln: MB to Mary Elizabeth Blair, September 23, 1864, quoted in Smith, *The Francis Preston Blair Family in Politics*, Vol. II, p. 288.
658 his father had repeated . . . "an avowed enemy": FPB to FB, quoted in EBL to SPL, September 24, [1864], in *Wartime Washington*, ed. Laas, p. 433.
658 Henry Wilson warned Lincoln . . . "account of the Blairs": Henry Wilson to AL, September 5, 1864, Lincoln Papers.
658 Monty Blair detested Stanton . . . "a thief": "26 September 1864, Monday," in Hay, *Inside Lincoln's White House*, p. 233.
659 "interchanged words for weeks": Entry for August 11, 1864, *Welles diary*, Vol. II, p. 102.
659 when the opportunity arose . . . stayed in the race: William Frank Zornow, *Lincoln & the Party Divided* (Norman: University of Oklahoma Press, 1954), pp. 144–47.
659 Frémont announced his withdrawal: *NYT*, September 23, 1864.
659 "You have generously . . . connection therewith": AL to MB, September 23, 1864, in *CW*, VIII, p. 18. For Blair's resignation letter, see MB to AL, September 23, 1864, Lincoln Papers.
659 Blair was surprised . . . "yielded to that": Entry for September 23, 1864, *Welles diary*, Vol. II, pp. 156–57.
659 Blair had been . . . "irritating bickerings": Addition to entry for September 23, 1864, ibid., p. 158 n1.
659 "In parting with Blair . . . discriminating and correct": Entry for September 23, 1864, ibid., p. 157.
660 "the removal of . . . befallen the Cabinet": Entry for September 27, 1864, ibid., p. 161.
660 did not consider . . . straight-speaking colleague: Entry for August 2, 1864, ibid., p. 93.
660 "I think Mr. Lincoln . . . *malign influences*": Entry for September 23, 1864, in *The Diary of Edward Bates, 1859–1866*, p. 413.
660 "an unnecessary mortification . . . best all around": MB to Mary Elizabeth Blair, September 23, 1864, quoted in Smith, *The Francis Preston Blair Family in Politics*, Vol. II, p. 288.
660 "In my opinion . . . the reelection of Lincoln": FPB to FB, quoted in EBL to SPL, September 24, [1864], in *Wartime Washington*, ed. Laas, p. 433.
660 "somewhat mortifying . . . a penny to make": FB to FPB, September 30, 1864, Lincoln Papers.
660 hearing the noble . . . "fine manly bearing": EBL to SPL, September 24, [1864], in *Wartime Washington*, ed. Laas, p. 434.
660 Monty insisted . . . "father to the President": MB, quoted in *Chicago Tribune*, October 1, 1864.
661 "very handsomely and is doing his utmost": "26 September 1864, Monday," in Hay, *Inside Lincoln's White House*, p. 233.
661 "a grand central rallying point": "11 October 1864, Tuesday," in Hay, *Inside Lincoln's White House*, p. 240.
661 Lincoln made his . . . chief of the telegraph office: Bates, *Lincoln in the Telegraph Office*, pp. 276–77; Charles A. Dana, "Lincoln and the War Department," *Reminiscences of Abraham Lincoln*, ed. Rice, p. 278.
661 Lincoln took from his pocket . . . "a new passage": Dana, "Lincoln and the War Department," in *Reminiscences of Abraham Lincoln*, ed. Rice (1909 edn.), p. 278. "Petroleum Vesuvius Nasby" was the pseudonym of David Ross Locke.
661 "immensely amusing": "11 October 1864, Tuesday," in Hay, *Inside Lincoln's White House*, p. 239.
661 "I shall never forget . . . such frivolous jests": Dana, "Lincoln and the War Department," in *Reminiscences of Abraham Lincoln*, ed. Rice (1909 edn.), pp. 278–79. Dana's recollection is that this episode occurred while Lincoln was waiting for the results of the November presidential election. Other sources, however, suggest that it probably occurred while a larger crowd waited in the telegraph office for results of the state elections in October. Given that Stanton was ill and remained at home during November elections, Dana has probably confused the two dates.
662 the news from Ohio . . . Republican majority: Waugh, *Reelecting Lincoln*, p. 335.
662 In Indiana . . . congressional seats: AL to USG, October 12, 1864, in *CW*, VIII, p. 45.
662 Lincoln sent a telegram . . . "does it stand now?": AL to Simon Cameron, October 11, 1864, in ibid., p. 43.
662 No answer was received . . . "ominous": "11 October 1864, Tuesday," in Hay, *Inside Lincoln's White House*, p. 240.
662 the margin was so close . . . claim a slight margin: Waugh, *Reelecting Lincoln*, p. 336.
662 "Seward was quite exultant . . . has ever known": Entry for October 13, 1864, *Welles diary*, Vol. II, p. 176.
662 Two nights after . . . 117 to 114: Bates, *Lincoln in the Telegraph Office*, pp. 277–79, 282.
662 "the moral effect . . . greatly impaired": McClure, *Abraham Lincoln and Men of War-Times*, p. 202.
662 voters in Maryland . . . making the difference: Waugh, *Reelecting Lincoln*, p. 354.
662 "Most heartily . . . upon the event": AL, "Response to a Serenade," October 19, 1864, in *CW*, VIII, p. 52.
663 "I had rather have . . . cleaned up effectually": AL, quoted in Brooks, *Lincoln Observed*, p. 138.
663 "We are as certain . . . the sun shines": *New York World*, October 14, 1864.
663 "a quarter-million" . . . deposit in their hometowns: William C. Davis, *Lincoln's Men: How President Lincoln became Father to an Army and a Nation* (New York: Free Press, 1999), pp. 214 (quote), 211.
663 had wired General Sherman . . . "no sense, an order": AL to William T. Sherman, September 19, 1864, in *CW*, VIII, p. 11.
663 Stanton followed up . . . "re-election of Mr. Lincoln": Dana, *Recollections of the Civil War* (1963 edn.), p. 227.
664 Weed alerted . . . New Yorkers ready to vote: TW to FWS, October 10, 1864, reel 85, Seward Papers.
664 Lincoln asked Welles . . . "to gather votes": Entry for October 11, 1864, *Welles diary*, Vol. II, p. 175.
664 "I would rather be . . . elected without it": Ida M. Tarbell, *A Reporter for Lincoln: Story of Henry E. Wing, Soldier and Newspaperman* (New York: The Macmillan Company, 1927), p. 70.

664 "before this morning's . . . ceaseless strife": *NYT,* November 8, 1864.
664 "dark and rainy . . . entirely alone": Brooks, *Washington, D.C., in Lincoln's Time,* p. 195.
664 the tenth time . . . beginning of the country: WHS, "Perseverance in War. Auburn, November 7, 1864," in *Works of William H. Seward,* Vol. V, p. 505.
664 Fessenden was in New York . . . with a fever: Brooks, *Washington, D.C., in Lincoln's Time,* p. 195; Brooks, *Mr. Lincoln's Washington,* p. 385.
664 "I am just enough . . . of Tad's quick-wittedness": Brooks, *Washington, D.C., in Lincoln's Time,* p. 196.
665 As the clock struck . . . a supper of fried oysters: "8 November 1864, Tuesday" in *Inside Lincoln's White House,* pp. 243–46.
665 Lincoln's victory was assured . . . separated by about 400,000 votes: Waugh, *Reelecting Lincoln,* p. 354.
666 the results were far better . . . of U.S. senators: Zornow, *Lincoln & the Party Divided,* p. 198.
666 It was after 2 a.m. . . . "tops of their voices": Pratt, *Stanton,* p. 391.
666 "the verdict of the people . . . no dispute": Brooks, *Washington, D.C., in Lincoln's Time,* p. 197.
666 the soldier vote . . . seven out of every ten soldiers: Waugh, *Reelecting Lincoln,* p. 354.
666 the Confederacy was obviously . . . Napoleon would win: Davis, *Lincoln's Men,* p. 210.
666 "The men had come . . . the term implied": Corporal Leander Stillwell, quoted in ibid., p. 226.

CHAPTER 25: "A SACRED EFFORT"

Page

667 immense crowd . . . second-floor window: Brooks, *Washington, D.C., in Lincoln's Time,* p. 200.
667 "undesirable strife . . . a possibility": AL, "Response to a Serenade," November 10, 1864, in *CW,* VIII, p. 101.
667 "in an exceedingly . . . frame of mind": Brooks, *Washington, D.C., in Lincoln's Time,* p. 200.
668 "we will all come . . . United States": WHS, "The Assurance of Victory," November 10, 1864, *Works of William H. Seward,* Vol. V, pp. 513–14.
668 "I advise you . . . my foreign relations": Brooks, *Washington, D.C., in Lincoln's Time,* pp. 200–01.
668 symbolized the animosity . . . the cabinet: William C. Harris, *Lincoln's Last Months* (Cambridge, Mass., and London: Belknap Press of Harvard University Press, 2004), p. 83.
668 Welles even acknowledged . . . "amicable": Entry for November 26, 1864, *Welles diary,* Vol. II, p. 185.
668 Stanton was sounding . . . Reconstruction: Entry for November 25, 1864, ibid., p. 179.
668 asserted that Seward . . . had outlived: *NYT,* November 29, 1864.
668 "His confidence in Seward is great": Entry for September 27, 1864, *Welles diary,* Vol. II, p. 160.
668 "spends more or less . . . the President": Entry for October 1, 1864, ibid., p. 166.
668 "of the gravest . . . and adviser": Entry for July 22, 1864, ibid., p. 84.
669 plan to foster . . . "by contribution": H. P. Livingston to AL, November 14, 1864, Lincoln Papers; AL to WHS, November 17, 1864, endorsement on Livingston to AL, ibid.; WHS to AL, November 17, 1864, endorsement on Livingston to AL, ibid. (quote).
669 Seward had long since . . . "by the President": Seward, *Seward at Washington . . . 1846–1861,* p. 528.
669 "Henceforth . . . of the human race": WHS, quoted in Seward, *Seward at Washington . . . 1861–1872,* p. 250.
669 "looked older . . . long one, perhaps": Benjamin, "Recollections of Secretary Edwin M. Stanton," *Century* (1887), pp. 758, 759–60.
669 letter to Chase . . . "labor and care": EMS to SPC, November 19, 1864, quoted in Thomas and Hyman, *Stanton,* p. 334.
669 unwritten code . . . "felt it necessary": Thomas and Hyman, *Stanton,* p. 390.
669 president's assent . . . "interfere with him": Flower, *Edwin McMasters Stanton,* pp. 369–70.
670 pressed by relatives . . . "circumspection": AL to EMS, March 18, 1864, in *CW,* VII, pp. 254–55.
670 Stanton replied . . . "promptly obeyed": EMS to AL, March 19, 1864, Lincoln Papers.
671 Lincoln looked . . . "his friends": Carpenter, *Six Months at the White House,* p. 172.
671 clerk recalled . . . "wail of anguish": William H. Whiton, quoted in Flower, *Edwin McMasters Stanton,* pp. 418–19.
671 group of Pennsylvania . . . "have to be done": EMS and AL, quoted in Thomas and Hyman, *Stanton,* p. 387.
671 "I send this . . . in this blunder": AL to USG, September 22, 1864, in *CW,* VIII, p. 17.
672 "his firmness . . . into arrogance": Alonzo Rothschild, *Lincoln, Master of Men: A Study in Character* (Boston and New York: Houghton Mifflin, 1906), p. 231.
672 "hard to vote . . . is a ruffian": Entry for September 17, 1864, in *Diary of George Templeton Strong,* Vol. III, p. 489.
672 "Go home . . . be found guilty": Carpenter, *Six Months at the White House,* p. 246.
672 "Folks come up . . . don't know 'em!": AL, quoted in Rothschild, *Lincoln, Master of Men,* p. 285.
672 discreet New Englander . . . "political gossip": Entry for August 31, 1864, *Welles diary,* Vol. II, p. 131.
672 *Times* of London . . . "first class power": *NR,* January 7, 1865.
673 Bates had contemplated . . . "to your age": Barton Bates to EB, May 13, 1864, Bates Papers, MoSHi.
673 prospect of going home . . . "god's blessing": Entry for May 29, 1864, *The Diary of Edward Bates, 1859–1866,* p. 371.
673 Bates believed . . . "as long as I live": EB to AL, November 24, 1864, Lincoln Papers.
673 first months as Attorney General . . . military matters: Entry for December 31, 1861, *The Diary of Edward Bates, 1859–1866,* pp. 218–19; entry for January 10, 1862, ibid., pp. 223–26.

674 deliver a legal opinion . . . "and clothing": EB to AL, July 14, 1864, *OR*, Ser. 3, Vol. IV, pp. 490–93 (quote p. 493).
674 Abolitionists applauded: Entry for May 26, 1864, *The Diary of Edward Bates, 1859–1866*, p. 371.
674 citizenship issue . . . of the United States: Frank J. Williams, "Attorney General Bates and Attorney President Lincoln," R. Gerald McMurtry Lecture, Lincoln Museum, Fort Wayne, Ind., September 23, 2000, author's collection; Cain, *Lincoln's Attorney General*, pp. 222–23.
674 "Though esteemed . . . constitutional interpretation": *Daily Morning Chronicle*, Washington, D.C., December 4, 1864, quoted in *The Diary of Edward Bates, 1859–1866*, p. 430.
674 reveals frustration . . . "no subordination": Entry for October 1, 1861, ibid., p. 196.
674 General Butler . . . arrests in Norfolk: Entry for August 4, 1864, ibid., pp. 393–94.
675 "chief fear . . . easy good nature": Entry for February 13, 1864, ibid., p. 334.
675 troubled at the start . . . "sure to prevail": EB, quoted in Carpenter, *Six Months at the White House*, pp. 68–69.
675 each of his colleagues . . . "affable and kind": Entry for December 2, 1864, *The Diary of Edward Bates, 1859–1866*, p. 429.
675 Bates left . . . "with regret": Entry for November 30, 1864, ibid., p. 428.
675 forever connected . . . "when I am gone": Poem, quoted in entry for October 13, 1864, ibid., p. 419.
675 "My Cabinet . . . would have to be heeded": AL, quoted in Titian J. Coffey, "Lincoln and the Cabinet," in *Reminiscences of Abraham Lincoln*, ed. Rice (1909 edn.), p. 197.
675 Holt declined the offer . . . "personal character": Joseph Holt to AL, December 1, 1864, Lincoln Papers.
676 "I appoint you . . . come on at once": AL to James Speed, in *CW*, VIII, p. 126.
676 "Will leave tomorrow for Washington": James Speed to AL, December 1, 1864, Lincoln Papers.
676 "I am a . . . everywhere forever": James Speed, quoted in Gary Lee Williams, "James and Joshua Speed: Lincoln's Kentucky Friends" (Ph.D. diss., Duke University, 1971), p. 137.
676 "We are less now but true": James Speed to AL, November 25, 1864, quoted in ibid., p. 138.
676 "a man I know . . . ought to know him well": AL, quoted in Coffey, "Lincoln and the Cabinet," in *Reminiscences of Abraham Lincoln*, ed. Rice (1909 edn.), p. 197.
676 Had it been . . . "freely and publicly": David Herbert Donald, *"We Are Lincoln Men": Abraham Lincoln and His Friends* (New York: Simon & Schuster, 2003), p. 38.
676 "You will find . . . by a big office": AL, quoted in Coffey, "Lincoln and the Cabinet," in *Reminiscences of Abraham Lincoln*, ed. Rice (1909 edn.), p. 197.
677 only position . . . "Stanton ever desired": Wolcott, "Edwin M. Stanton," p. 162.
677 "You have been wearing . . . owes it to you": Robert Grier to EMS, October 13, 1864, Stanton Papers, DLC.
677 Ellen Stanton . . . "subject tomorrow": Entry for October 16, 1864, in Browning, *The Diary of Orville Hickman Browning*, Vol. I, p. 687–88.
677 Matthew Simpson . . . "I will do it": AL, quoted in Gideon Stanton, ed., "Edwin M. Stanton."
677 Grant worried . . . stay at his post: Thomas and Hyman, *Stanton*, p. 337.
677 Stanton informed . . . "among candidates": Edwards Pierrepont to AL, November 24, 1864, Lincoln Papers.
677 He "felt that . . . higher ambition": Wolcott, "Edwin M. Stanton," p. 162.
677 "The country cannot . . . fame already": Henry Ward Beecher to EMS, November 30, 1864, quoted in ibid., p. 163.
678 "Often, in dark hours . . . fresh hope": EMS to Henry Ward Beecher, December 4, 1864, quoted in ibid., pp. 163–64.
678 Welles told Lincoln . . . "suppose he would": Entry for November 26, 1864, *Welles diary*, Vol. II, p. 182.
678 taken his son's . . . personal blow: Entry for September 27, 1864, ibid., p. 161.
678 "I beg you to indulge . . . of that Bench": FPB to AL, October 20, 1864, quoted in Smith, *The Francis Preston Blair Family in Politics*, Vol. II, pp. 298–99.
678 "Chase and his friends . . . Chief-Justiceship": MTL, quoted in "If All the Rest Oppose," in *Conversations with Lincoln*, ed. Segal, p. 360.
679 "had been tried . . . stood by him": FPB to John A. Andrew, quoted in ibid., p. 360.
679 "a crowning and retiring honor": Entry for November 22, 1864, *The Diary of Edward Bates, 1859–1866*, p. 428.
679 had "personally solicited": Entry for October 18, 1864, in Browning, *The Diary of Orville Hickman Browning*, Vol. I, p. 688.
679 "If not overborne . . . to private life": Entry for November 22, 1864, *The Diary of Edward Bates, 1859–1866*, pp. 427–28.
679 "Of Mr. Chase's . . . not hesitate a moment": AL, quoted in John G. Nicolay and John Hay, *Abraham Lincoln: A History*, Vol. IX (New York: Century Co., 1890), p. 394.
679 similar comment . . . "life to the Bench": Schuyler Colfax, quoted in Blue, *Salmon P. Chase*, p. 245.
679 "Now, I know . . . men can tell me": Noah Brooks, "Personal Reminiscences of Lincoln," *Scribner's Monthly* 15 (March 1878), p. 677.
679 "we have stood . . . fitness for the office": AL, quoted in Blue, *Salmon P. Chase*, pp. 244–45.
680 Oblivious to Stanton's . . . "life & work": SPC to EMS, October 13, 1864, *Chase Papers*, Vol. IV, p. 434.
680 "I have something . . . will be satisfied": AL and John B. Alley, quoted in John B. Alley, in *Reminiscences of Abraham Lincoln*, ed. Rice (1886 edn.), pp. 581–82.
680 Lincoln later told Senator Chandler . . . "nominated Chase": Entry for December 15, 1864, *Welles diary*, Vol. II, p. 196.
680 "Probably no other . . . of the President": JGN to TB, December 8, 1864, container 3, Nicolay Papers.
680 got the official word . . . "or office": SPC to AL, December 6, 1864, Lincoln Papers.
680 "overflowing with . . . 'So help me God' ": Brooks, *Washington, D.C., in Lincoln's Time*, pp. 175–76.

681 "I hope the President . . . in the court": Entry for December 6, 1864, *Welles diary*, Vol. II, p. 193.
681 Within hours . . . first black barrister: John S. Rock to CS, December 17, 1864, enclosed in CS to SPC, December 21, 1864, in *Selected Letters of Charles Sumner*, Vol. II, ed. Palmer, p. 259 n1 (quote); entry for January 21, 1865, *Chase Papers*, Vol. I, p. 519.
681 Sumner stood before . . . "of this Court": CS, quoted in Quarles, *Lincoln and the Negro*, p. 232.
681 Rock stepped forward . . . "of a great people": *Harper's Weekly*, February 25, 1865.
681 "has been quite . . . with good feeling": MTL to Mercy Levering Conkling, November 19, [1864], in Turner and Turner, *Mary Todd Lincoln*, p. 187.
682 she had been terrified . . . "run in debt": Keckley, *Behind the Scenes*, pp. 147, 149–50 (quotes).
682 exposed her . . . could not curtail: "Mary Todd Lincoln's Unethical Conduct as First Lady," appendix 2, in Hay, *At Lincoln's Side*, pp. 185–205.
682 "Here is the carriage . . . many questions": Entry for December 14, 1864, Taft diary.
682 new dress . . . "kid gloves": Entry for July 3, 1873, Browning diary, quoted in appendix 2, in Hay, *At Lincoln's Side*, p. 187.
682 "I can neither . . . your acting thus": MTL to Ruth Harris, December 28, [1864], in Turner and Turner, *Mary Todd Lincoln*, p. 196.
682 Newspaper reports . . . "tasteful decoration": *NR*, January 10, 1865.
683 "Mrs. Lincoln was . . . throughout": *NR*, February 17, 1865.
683 "Overcoats . . . for safe-keeping": *NR*, January 6, 1865.
683 "a more general . . . and themselves": *NR*, January 10, 1865.
683 "*I* was pleased . . . *two* school boys": MTL to Sally Orne, [December 12, 1869], quoted in Turner and Turner, *Mary Todd Lincoln*, p. 534.
683 lingering grief . . . favorite rooms: Entry for March 31, 1864, Benjamin B. French journal, reel 2, French Family Papers, DLC.
683 "darling Boy! . . . *far* from being": MTL to Hannah Shearer, November 20, 1864, in Turner and Turner, *Mary Todd Lincoln*, p. 189.
683 Lincoln wrote to General Grant . . . "encumbered": AL to USG, January 19, 1865, in *CW*, VIII, p. 223.
684 Grant replied . . . "Military family": USG to AL, January 21, 1865, Lincoln Papers.
684 Stationed at Grant's . . . "of the nation": Porter, *Campaigning with Grant*, pp. 388–89.
684 "passing time and accumulating years": Entry for January 1, 1865, *Welles diary*, Vol. II, p. 218.
684 last surviving . . . buried in Ohio: Entry for January 1, 1865, *Chase Papers*, Vol. I, p. 511.
684 Chase wrote to . . . New Year's reception: SPC to AL, January 2, 1865, Lincoln Papers.
684 "Without your note . . . bereavement": AL to SPC, January 2, 1865, in *CW*, VIII, p. 195.
684 "a great contrast . . . in good spirits": Entry for January 1, 1865, Taft diary.
684 "Our joy . . . Confederacy were numbered": Hugh McCullough, quoted in Thomas and Hyman, *Stanton*, p. 342.
684 "*anxious* . . . than to acquiesce": AL to William T. Sherman, December 26, 1864, in *CW*, VIII, p. 181.
685 "We have destroyed . . . for six months": FB to FPB, December 16, 1864, quoted in Smith, *The Francis Preston Blair Family in Politics*, Vol. II, p. 180.
685 also paid tribute . . . "great light": AL to William T. Sherman, December 26, 1864, in *CW*, VIII, p. 182.
685 telegram announcing . . . "candle in his hand": Bates, *Lincoln in the Telegraph Office*, pp. 316–17 (quotes p. 317).
685 Fort Fisher . . . "rebels from abroad": *NR*, January 17, 1865 (quote); *NR*, January 18, 1865.
685 at the cabinet . . . "President was happy": Entry for January 17, 1865, *Welles diary*, Vol. II, p. 227.
685 Stephens considered . . . "or Atlanta": Alexander H. Stephens, *A Constitutional View of the Late War Between the States*, Vol. II (Philadelphia: National Publishing Company, 1870), p. 619.
685 nearly every other . . . munitions and supplies: Ibid., p. 620.
685 was in Savannah . . . "delivered to [him]": EMS to AL, quoted in *NR*, January 18, 1865.
685 journeyed to North Carolina . . . "the *real* Stanton": Mrs. Rufus Saxton, quoted in Flower, *Edwin McMasters Stanton*, p. 420.
686 confer with Sherman . . . "*criminal* dislike": Sherman, *Memoirs of General W. T. Sherman*, pp. 604–07; Henry W. Halleck to William Sherman, December 30, 1865, *OR*, Ser. 1, Vol. XLIV, p. 836 (quote).
686 Sherman countered . . . "our substance": William T. Sherman to SPC, January 11, 1865, in *The Salmon P. Chase Papers*, Vol. 5: *Correspondence, 1865–1873*, ed. John Niven (Kent, Ohio, and London, England: Kent State University Press, 1998), pp. 6–7.
686 "Special Field Orders . . . tillable ground": Sherman, *Memoirs of General W. T. Sherman*, p. 609; Special Field Orders, No. 15, Headquarters, Military Division of the Mississippi, January 16, 1865, *OR*, Ser. I, Vol. XLVII, Part II, pp. 60–62.
686 Freedmen's Bureau . . . the South: Foner, *Reconstruction*, pp. 68–69.
686 "A question might . . . all the evils": AL, "Response to a Serenade," February 1, 1865, in *CW*, VIII, p. 254.
686 previous spring . . . party lines: "Thirteenth Amendment," in Neely, *The Abraham Lincoln Encyclopedia*, p. 308.
686 annual message . . . bipartisan unity: AL, "Annual Message to Congress," December 6, 1864, in *CW*, VIII, p. 149.
687 "I have sent for you . . . border state vote": AL, quoted by James S. Rollins, "The King's Cure-All for All Evils," in *Conversations with Lincoln*, ed. Segal, pp. 363–64.
687 assigned two . . . "procure those votes": AL, quoted in John B. Alley, in *Reminiscences of Abraham Lincoln*, ed. Rice (1886 edn.), pp. 585–86.
687 powers extended . . . in New York: "Thirteenth Amendment," in Neely, *The Abraham Lincoln Encyclopedia*, p. 308.

687 Elizabeth Blair noted . . . several members: EBL to SPL, January 31, 1865, in *Wartime Washington*, ed. Laas, p. 469.
687 Ashley learned . . . "the more resolute": AL, quoted in JGN memorandum, January 18, 1865, in Nicolay, *With Lincoln in the White House*, pp. 171, 257 n11.
688 leader of the . . . "political associates": Blaine, *Twenty Years of Congress*, p. 537.
688 Democrats who considered changing: Harris, *Lincoln's Last Months*, p. 128.
688 "We are like whalers . . . into eternity": AL, quoted in John G. Nicolay and John Hay, *Abraham Lincoln: A History*, Vol. X (New York: Century Co., 1890), p. 74.
688 Rumors circulated . . . "have failed": AL and James M. Ashley correspondence, quoted in James M. Ashley to WHH, November 23, 1866, in *HI*, pp. 413–14.
688 "never before . . . within hearing": *Address of Hon. J. M. Ashley, before the Ohio Society of New York*, February 19, 1899 (privately published), p. 21.
688 Chief Justice Chase . . . foreign ministries: Brooks, *Washington, D.C., in Lincoln's Time*, pp. 185–86; *Address of Hon. J. M. Ashley*, p. 21.
689 McAllister . . . "Southern Confederacy": Brooks, *Washington, D.C., in Lincoln's Time*, p. 186.
689 brought forth applause . . . "without a murmur": Alexander Coffroth, quoted in Carl Sandburg, *Abraham Lincoln: The War Years*, Vol. IV (New York: Harcourt, Brace & Company, 1939), p. 10.
689 "Hundreds of tally" . . . votes short: *Address of Hon. J. M. Ashley*, pp. 23–24.
689 Colfax stood . . . "Resolution has passed": Brooks, *Washington, D.C., in Lincoln's Time*, pp. 186–87.
689 five Democrats . . . would have lost: Harris, *Lincoln's Last Months*, p. 132.
689 "For a moment . . . ever heard before": Brooks, *Washington, D.C., in Lincoln's Time*, p. 187.
689 "Before the members . . . had passed": Arnold, *The Life of Abraham Lincoln*, p. 365.
689 Ashley brought . . . "great honor": EMS, quoted in Flower, *Edwin McMasters Stanton*, p. 190.
689 "The passage . . . emancipation proclamation": Arnold, *The Life of Abraham Lincoln*, pp. 365–66.
689 "The occasion was . . . They will do it": AL, "Response to a Serenade," February 1, 1865, in *CW*, VIII, p. 254.
689 legislatures in twenty . . . had spoken: "Thirteenth Amendment," in Neely, *The Abraham Lincoln Encyclopedia*, p. 308.
690 "And to whom . . . to Abraham Lincoln!": William Lloyd Garrison, quoted in Nicolay and Hay, *Abraham Lincoln*, Vol. X, p. 79n.
690 remained unconvinced . . . a pass: AL, pass for FPB, December 28, 1864, Lincoln Papers.
690 proceeding on . . . "without reserve": FPB to Jefferson Davis, December 30, 1864, Lincoln Papers.
690 arrived in Richmond . . . "around him": *NR*, January 19, 1865.
690 "Oh you Rascal . . . to see you": EBL to SPL, January 16, 1865, in *Wartime Washington*, ed. Laas, p. 463.
690 "might be the dreams . . . in his prayers": FPB, memorandum of conversation with Jefferson Davis [January 12, 1865], Lincoln Papers.
690 his proposal . . . allied against the French: FPB, address made to Jefferson Davis [January 12, 1865], Lincoln Papers.
691 Davis agreed . . . "a Foreign Power": FPB, memorandum of conversation with Jefferson Davis [January 12, 1865], Lincoln Papers.
691 Davis agreed to send . . . "two Countries": Jefferson Davis to FPB, January 12, 1865, Lincoln Papers.
691 Lincoln consulted . . . immediately agreed: EMS, quoted in Flower, *Edwin McMasters Stanton*, p. 257.
691 "You may say . . . one common country": AL to FPB, January 18, 1865, in *CW*, VIII, pp. 220–21.
691 Davis called a cabinet . . . Campbell: Davis, *Jefferson Davis*, p. 590.
691 flag of truce . . . the commissioners: *Philadelphia Inquirer*, February 3, 1865.
691 "By common consent . . . a gala day": *NYH*, February 4, 1865.
691 "harbingers of peace . . . common sentiment": *NR*, February 3, 1865.
691 "It was night . . . throughout the country": Stephens, *A Constitutional View of the Late War*, pp. 597–98.
692 Seward headed south . . . "sincere liberality": AL to WHS, January 31, 1865, in *CW*, VIII, p. 250.
692 "convinced" . . . meet with them personally: USG to EMS, February 1, 1865, Lincoln Papers.
692 "Induced by a despatch of Gen. Grant": AL to WHS, February 2, 1865, in *CW*, VIII, p. 256.
692 "Say to the gentlemen . . . can get there": AL to USG, February 2, 1865, in ibid.
692 a single valet . . . Annapolis: *NYH*, February 3, 1865.
692 "supposed to be" . . . little past ten: *NYH*, February 5, 1865.
692 Lincoln joined Seward . . . *River Queen*: *NYT*, February 6, 1865.
692 saloon of . . . "streamers and flags": Stephens, *A Constitutional View of the Late War*, p. 599; *NYT*, February 6, 1865 (quote).
693 Stephens opened . . . "Sections of the country?": Stephens, *A Constitutional View of the Late War*, p. 599.
693 "was altogether . . . was written or read": Seward, *Seward at Washington . . . 1861–1872*, p. 260.
693 "steward, who came" . . . agreement on any issue: Stephens, *A Constitutional View of the Late War*, pp. 619, 600–01, 612, 613, 609, 617.
694 radicals had worked . . . excoriated him: Brooks, *Washington, D.C., in Lincoln's Time*, p. 202.
694 "the leading members . . . will dishonor us": *NYT*, February 3, 1865.
694 Both branches . . . on the proceedings: Brooks, *Washington, D.C., in Lincoln's Time*, pp. 203–04.
694 Stanton worried . . . "serve their purpose": Bates, *Lincoln in the Telegraph Office*, p. 338.
694 Lincoln's report . . . "given to Seward": Brooks, *Lincoln Observed*, pp. 162–63.
694 "as the reading . . . President Lincoln": Brooks, *Washington, D.C., in Lincoln's Time*, pp. 207, 208.
694 "Indeed . . . than Abraham Lincoln": *Harper's Weekly*, February 25, 1865.

695 employed the failed . . . slavery intact: *Richmond Dispatch*, February 7, 1865, quoted in Nicolay and Hay, *Abraham Lincoln*, Vol. X, p. 130.
695 "I can have . . . element of my nature!": Jefferson Davis, quoted in *NR*, February 13, 1865.
695 drafted a proposal . . . "executive control": AL, "To the Senate and House of Representatives," February 5, 1865, in *CW*, VIII, pp. 260–61.
695 unanimous disapproval . . . "adverse feeling": Entry for February 6, 1865, *Welles diary*, Vol. II, p. 237.
695 Usher believed . . . "assault on the President": J. P. Usher, quoted in Nicolay, *An Oral History of Abraham Lincoln*, p. 66.
695 Stanton had long maintained . . . "compensation for slaves": Flower, *Edwin McMasters Stanton*, p. 258.
695 Fessenden declared . . . "come from us": William Pitt Fessenden, quoted in Francis Fessenden, *Life and Public Services of William Pitt Fessenden*, Vol. II (Boston and New York: Houghton, Mifflin, 1907), p. 8.
695 sum he proposed . . . "approved the measure": J. P. Usher, quoted in Nicolay, *An Oral History of Abraham Lincoln*, p. 66.
696 Sherman had headed north . . . on February 17: Entry for February 17, 1865, in Long, *The Civil War Day by Day*, pp. 639–40.
696 Stanton ordered . . . "parts of the city": *NR*, February 22, 1865.
696 "cheerful . . . brightest day in four years": Entry for February 22, 1865, *Welles Diary*, Vol. II, p. 245.
696 "more depressed" . . . in the four years: Entry for February 23, 1865, in *The Diary of Orville Hickman Browning*, Vol. II, 1865–1881, ed. Theodore Calvin Pease and James G. Randall; *Collections of the Illinois State Historical Library*, Vol. XXII (Springfield: Illinois State Historical Library, 1933), p. 8.
696 low spirits . . . "brigand, and pirate": Jonathan Truman Dorris, *Pardon and Amnesty Under Lincoln and Johnson: The Restoration of the Confederates to Their Rights and Privileges, 1861–1898* (Chapel Hill: University of North Carolina Press, 1953), pp. 76–78 (quote p. 77).
696 "I had to stand . . . out of my mind yet": Henry P. H. Bromwell, quoted in *Recollected Words of Abraham Lincoln*, ed. Don E. Fehrenbacher and Virginia Fehrenbacher (Stanford, Calif.: Stanford University Press, 1996), p. 41.
697 he would "not receive . . . seven o'clock p.m.": *NR*, March 2, 1865.
697 "The hopeful condition" . . . the capital: *NR*, March 1, 1865.
697 so overcrowded . . . "found for them": *NR*, March 3, 1865.
697 Douglass decided . . . "of other citizens": Douglass, *Life and Times of Frederick Douglass*, p. 803.
697 visited Chase's . . . "a strange thing": Ibid., pp. 799–800.
697 steady rain . . . foreign ministries: Brooks, *Washington, D.C., in Lincoln's Time*, pp. 210–11; Brooks, *Mr. Lincoln's Washington*, pp. 418, 420 (quote).
697 "One ambassador . . . feet on the floor": Brooks, *Mr. Lincoln's Washington*, p. 421.
697 Johnson rose . . . "extraordinarily red": Brooks, *Washington, D.C., in Lincoln's Time*, p. 211.
697 "in a state of manifest . . . a petrified man": Brooks, *Mr. Lincoln's Washington*, pp. 422, 423.
698 "All this is . . . drunk or crazy": Entry for March 4, 1865, *Welles diary*, Vol. II, p. 252.
698 Dennison . . . "serene as summer": Brooks, *Mr. Lincoln's Washington*, pp. 423–24.
698 "emotion on . . . revisiting the Senate": Entry for March 4, 1865, *Welles diary*, Vol. II, p. 252.
698 Lincoln listened . . . harangue to end: Brooks, *Mr. Lincoln's Washington*, p. 423.
698 his eyes shut: Marquis de Chambrun [Charles Adolphe Pineton], "Personal Recollections of Mr. Lincoln," *Scribner's* 13 (January 1893), p. 26.
698 "You need not . . . a drunkard": AL, as quoted by Hugh McCullough in *Recollected Words of Abraham Lincoln*, p. 320.
698 audience proceeded . . . "glory and light": Brooks, *Mr. Lincoln's Washington*, pp. 424, 425 (quote).
698 an auspicious omen . . . Freedom: Brooks, *Washington, D.C., in Lincoln's Time*, pp. 213, 20–21.
698 "Both read the same . . . this terrible war": AL, "Second Inaugural Address," March 4, 1865, in *CW*, VIII, p. 333. For a thorough discussion of Lincoln's Second Inaugural Address, see Ronald C. White, *Lincoln's Greatest Speech: The Second Inaugural* (New York: Simon & Schuster, 2002).
699 "the eloquence of the prophets": Chambrun, "Personal Recollections of Mr. Lincoln," *Scribner's*, p. 27.
699 "Fondly do we hope . . . with all nations": AL, "Second Inaugural Address," March 4, 1865, in *CW*, VIII, pp. 332–33.
699 "as he became . . . Church member": Leonard Swett to WHH, January 17, 1866, in *HI*, pp. 167–68.
699 crowd cheered . . . drew to a close: *Boston Daily Evening Transcript*, March 4, 1865.
699 "the largest crowd . . . been here yet": JGN to TB, March 5, 1865, container 3, Nicolay Papers.
699 president was . . . five thousand people: *Star*, March 6, 1865.
699 "It was a grand . . . every 4 minutes": Entry for March 5, 1865, in French, *Witness to the Young Republic*, p. 466.
700 "On reaching the door . . . you liked it!": Douglass, *Life and Times of Frederick Douglass*, pp. 803–04.
700 his own assessment . . . "Almighty and them": AL to TW, March 15, 1865, *CW*, VIII, p. 356.
700 *New York World* . . . "statesmanship": *New York World*, March 6, 1865, quoted in Harris, *Lincoln's Last Months*, p. 149.
700 *Tribune* charged . . . chance for peace: *NYTrib*, March 6, 1865, quoted in Harris, p. 150.
701 "That rail-splitting . . . keynote of this war": Charles Francis Adams, Jr., to Charles Francis Adams, Sr., quoted in Harris, *Lincoln's Last Months*, p. 148.
701 London *Spectator* . . . "village lawyer": London *Spectator*, March 25, 1865, quoted in *Lincoln As They Saw Him*, ed. Herbert Mitgang (New York and Toronto: Rinehart & Company, Inc., 1956), pp. 447, 446.
701 Arnold overheard . . . Seward himself: Harris, *Lincoln's Last Months*, p. 148.
701 "The President's . . . position in history": Arnold, *The Life of Abraham Lincoln*, pp. 404–05.

701 "He has called . . . sickening to the heart": *Charleston [S.C.] Mercury*, January 10, 1865, reprinted in *Liberator*, March 3, 1865.
701 "it was always plain . . . judicious and appropriate": Charles A. Dana, quoted in Hay, "Life in the White House in the Time of Lincoln," *Century* (1890), p. 36.

CHAPTER 26: THE FINAL WEEKS

Page

702 "he was in mind . . . all-sufficing strength": Hay, "Life in the White House in the Time of Lincoln," *Century* (1890), p. 37.
703 "a tired spot": Brooks, *Mr. Lincoln's Washington*, p. 161.
703 avoid the thousands . . . "Egyptian locusts": JGN to TB, March 5, 1865, in Nicolay, *With Lincoln in the White House*, p. 175.
703 "The bare thought . . . *crush* me": AL, quoted in Carpenter, *Six Months at the White House*, p. 276.
703 "they don't want . . . must see them": AL, quoted in Hay, "Life in the White House in the Time of Lincoln," *Century* (1890), p. 33.
703 "I think now . . . *nineteen* enemies": AL, quoted in Carpenter, *Six Months at the White House*, p. 276.
703 hope that consul . . . wished to help: AL to WHS, March 6, 1865, *CW*, VIII, p. 337.
703 "at all times . . . of public trusts": AL to Winfield Scott and others, March 1, 1865, *CW*, VIII, p. 327.
704 Fessenden had been assured . . . "with regret": Fessenden, *Life and Public Services of William Pitt Fessenden*, Vol. I, pp. 365, 367 (quote).
704 "I desire gratefully . . . this great people": William Pitt Fessenden to AL, quoted in Fessenden, *Life and Public Services of William Pitt Fessenden*, Vol. I, p. 366.
704 he was nervous . . . "never sorry": Hugh McCulloch, *Men and Measures of Half a Century: Sketches and Comments* (New York: Charles Scribner's Sons, 1888; 1900), pp. 193–94.
704 intended to replace Usher: "Usher, John Palmer," in Neely, *The Abraham Lincoln Encyclopedia*, p. 317.
704 Hay was particularly adept . . . "his influence": William Leete Stone, quoted by Michael Burlingame, in introduction to Hay, *Inside Lincoln's White House*, p. xiii.
704 Nicolay functioned . . . and New York: Donald, *"We Are Lincoln Men,"* p. 209.
704 Hay was chosen . . . reconstruction of Florida: "Hay, John Milton," in Neely, *The Abraham Lincoln Encyclopedia*, p. 149.
705 had come to believe . . . "the hand of God": JH to JGN, August 7, 1863, in Hay, *At Lincoln's Side*, p. 49 (quote); "Hay, John Milton," in Neely, *The Abraham Lincoln Encyclopedia*, p. 149.
705 If the "patent . . . blinking eyes": JH to WHH, September 5, 1866, in *HI*, p. 332.
705 contemplating the purchase of a newspaper: Nicolay, *Lincoln's Secretary*, p. 224.
705 Mary had enlisted . . . Noah Brooks: Anson G. Henry to his wife, March 13, 1865, in *Concerning Mr. Lincoln*, comp. Pratt, p. 117.
705 tried to talk . . . any such discussion: JGN to TB, quoted in Nicolay, *Lincoln's Secretary*, p. 223.
705 Seward found . . . dissenting vote: *NR*, quoted in ibid., p. 224.
705 position paid . . . start married life: JGN to TB, March 12, 1865, quoted in ibid., p. 225.
706 Hay had recognized . . . "personal preeminence": "Hay's Reminiscences of the Civil War," in Hay, *At Lincoln's Side*, p. 129.
706 arranged for Hay . . . for another month: JH to Charles Hay, March 31, 1865, in Hay, *At Lincoln's Side*, p. 103.
706 "It will be . . . at the same time": JGN to TB, quoted in Nicolay, *Lincoln's Secretary*, p. 227.
706 "We are having . . . laid aside": MTL to Abram Wakeman, March 20, [1865], in Turner and Turner, *Mary Todd Lincoln*, pp. 205–06.
706 note to Sumner . . . "familiar to me": MTL to CS, March 23, 1865, in ibid., p. 209.
706 "an emotional temperament . . . heart would break": Helm, *The True Story of Mary*, p. 32.
706 an incident . . . "giving me up the key": Carpenter, *Six Months at the White House*, pp. 91–92.
707 "so full of life . . . little sprite": *NYTrib*, July 17, 1871.
707 Grant had issued . . . "to be asked": *The Personal Memoirs of Julia Dent Grant (Mrs. Ulysses S. Grant)*, ed. John Y. Simon (New York: G. P. Putnam's Sons, 1975), p. 141.
707 "Can you not . . . would do you good": USG to AL, March 20, 1865, Lincoln Papers.
707 Fox was not happy . . . "making the journey": John S. Barnes, "With Lincoln from Washington to Richmond in 1865," Part 1, *Appleton's* 9 (June 1907), p. 519.
707 ordered John Barnes . . . "very funny terms": Ibid., pp. 517–20.
708 presidential party . . . Wharf at Sixth Street: Entry for March 23, 1865, in *Lincoln Day by Day*, Vol. III, p. 322.
708 Stanton had been laid up . . . minutes after: Thomas and Hyman, *Stanton*, p. 350.
708 "a hurricane swept over the city": *Star*, February 15, 1896.
708 "terrific squalls . . . and its driver": *NYH*, March 24, 1865.
708 "while down the river . . . great violence": *Star*, February 15, 1896.
708 Stanton went . . . "at Point Lookout": EMS to AL, March 23, 1865, Lincoln Papers.
708 Tad raced around . . . "delicious fish": William H. Crook, "Lincoln as I Knew Him," *Harper's Monthly* 115 (May/June 1907), p. 46.
709 "Feeling *so* . . . loved so well": MTL to Francis B. Carpenter, November 15, [1865], in Turner and Turner, *Mary Todd Lincoln*, p. 284.
709 "it was after . . . headquarters at the top": Crook, "Lincoln as I Knew Him," *Harper's Monthly* (1907), p. 46.

709 Robert Lincoln . . . "was awaiting": *Personal Memoirs of Julia Dent Grant*, p. 142.
709 men went into . . . talked late into the night: Crook, "Lincoln as I Knew Him," *Harper's Monthly* (1907), pp. 46, 47.
709 While the Lincolns . . . original line: Shelby Foote, *The Civil War: A Narrative*. Vol. III: *Red River to Appomattox* (New York: Random House, 1958; New York: Vintage Books, 1986), pp. 838, 840–45.
710 walked up the bluff . . . "ruin of homes": Barnes, "With Lincoln from Washington to Richmond in 1865," Part 1, *Appleton's* (1907), pp. 521–22.
710 "I am here . . . states—1600": AL to EMS, March 25, 1865, *CW*, VIII, p. 374.
710 Stanton replied . . . " 'further off' ": EMS to AL, March 25, 1865, Lincoln Papers.
710 Lincoln's presence . . . "of their triumphs": *NYH*, March 28, 1865.
710 Lincoln seemed . . . "anecdotes": Porter, *Campaigning with Grant*, p. 407.
710 "Mr. President . . . old grudge against England to stand": USG and AL, quoted in Porter, *Campaigning with Grant*, pp. 408–9.
711 Porter's naval flotilla . . . "Come along!": Barnes, "With Lincoln from Washington to Richmond in 1865," Part 1, *Appleton's* (1907), pp. 522–23.
711 ambulance carrying . . . "ark of refuge": Porter, *Campaigning with Grant*, pp. 413–14 (quotes p. 414).
712 saw the attractive . . . "shocked and horrified": Adam Badeau, quoted in Foote, *The Civil War*, Vol. III, p. 847.
712 "was always that . . . impressed by it": John S. Barnes, "With Lincoln from Washington to Richmond in 1865," Part II, *Appleton's* (1907), p. 743.
712 had no desire . . . irrational outburst: Randall, *Mary Lincoln*, pp. 372–74.
712 Sherman was on his way . . . final push: William T. Sherman to Isaac N. Arnold, November 28, 1872, in Arnold, *The Life of Abraham Lincoln*, p. 421.
712 "their hands locked" . . . *River Queen:* Porter, *Campaigning with Grant*, pp. 417–18, 419.
712 greeted Sherman . . . depend upon the actions: William T. Sherman to Isaac N. Arnold, November 28, 1872, in Arnold, *The Life of Abraham Lincoln*, pp. 421–22.
713 long talk with Lincoln . . . "their shops": Sherman, *Memoirs of General W. T. Sherman*, p. 682.
713 "Let them have . . . to the laws": AL, quoted in David D. Porter, *Incidents and Anecdotes of the Civil War* (New York: D. Appleton and Company, 1886), p. 314.
713 privately wished . . . "goodness, than any other": Sherman, *Memoirs of General W. T. Sherman*, pp. 682–83.
713 walked to the railroad . . . "bless you all!": AL, quoted in Porter, *Campaigning with Grant*, pp. 425–26.
714 "I think . . . the wisest course": Entry for March 30, 1865, *Welles diary*, Vol. II, p. 269.
714 "We presume . . . palpable to be doubted": *NYTrib*, March 30, 1865.
714 "change of air & rest": MTL to CS, March 23, 1865, in Turner and Turner, *Mary Todd Lincoln*, p. 209.
714 "to escape the . . . pressure of visitors": *Philadelphia Inquirer*, March 24, 1865.
714 underscore his directive . . . "own hands": EMS to USG, March 3, 1865, *CW*, VIII, pp. 330–31.
714 "I begin to feel . . . little had been done": AL to EMS, March 30, 1865, ibid., p. 377.
714 "I hope you will . . . All well here": EMS to AL, March 31, 1865, ibid., p. 378 n1.
715 accompanied Mary . . . was well: Entry for April 1, 1865, in *Lincoln Day by Day*, Vol. III, p. 324; Randall, *Mary Lincoln*, p. 374.
715 "overwhelmingly charming . . . astounding person": Carl Schurz to his wife, April 2, 1865, in Schurz, *Intimate Letters of Carl Schurz, 1841–1869*, pp. 326–27.
715 "the flash of the cannon . . . in his that night": *Through Five Administrations: Reminiscences of Colonel William H. Crook, Body-Guard to President Lincoln*, ed. Margarita Spalding Gerry (New York and London: Harper & Brothers, 1910), p. 47.
715 broken through Petersburg's . . . and Richmond: Foote, *The Civil War*, Vol. III, pp. 876–80.
715 Lincoln received . . . "12,000 prisoners": AL to MTL, April 2, 1865, *CW*, VIII, p. 384.
715 Lincoln had moved . . . "a foot sideways": AL, quoted in Porter, *Incidents and Anecdotes of the Civil War*, pp. 284–85.
716 "a comfortable . . . yard in front": Porter, *Campaigning with Grant*, p. 449.
716 battlefields, littered . . . "lines of sadness": *Through Five Administrations*, ed. Gerry, p. 48.
716 "dismounted in the street" . . . strolled by: Porter, *Campaigning with Grant*, pp. 450, 451.
716 Grant surmised . . . "and cut him off": Grant, *Personal Memoirs of U. S. Grant*, p. 559.
716 back at City Point . . . "nightmare is gone": AL, quoted in Porter, *Incidents and Anecdotes of the Civil War*, p. 294.
716 in his customary pew . . . "retreating that evening": Davis, *Jefferson Davis*, p. 603; Jefferson Davis to Varina Davis, quoted in Robert McElroy, *Jefferson Davis: The Unreal and the Real* (New York and London: Harper & Brothers, 1937; New York: Smithmark, 1995), p. 454 (quote).
716 "Thereupon . . . all eyes in the house": *NYTrib*, April 8, 1865.
716 Summoning his cabinet . . . west to Danville: Davis, *Jefferson Davis*, p. 604.
716 small fire . . . "three-quarters of a mile": Charles A. Dana to EMS, April 6, 1865, *OR*, Ser. 1, Vol. XLVI, Part III, p. 594.
717 All the public buildings . . . were destroyed: *NYTrib*, April 8, 1865.
717 leaving only . . . the Spotswood Hotel: Charles A. Dana to EMS, April 6, 1865, *OR*, Ser. 1, Vol. XLVI, Part III, p. 594.
717 "Here is . . . Richmond has fallen": Bates, *Lincoln in the Telegraph Office*, pp. 360–61.
717 "spread by a thousand mouths": *Star*, April 3, 1865.
717 "almost by magic . . . fullness of their joy": Brooks, *Washington, D.C., in Lincoln's Time*, p. 219.
717 "wept as children . . . vows of friendship": *NYH*, April 4, 1865.

717 crowd called for Stanton . . . "his emotion": *Star,* February 15, 1896.
717 "gratitude to Almighty . . . with their blood": EMS, quoted in Brooks, *Washington, D.C., in Lincoln's Time,* p. 220.
717 "so overcome by emotion . . . speak continuously": Ibid.
717 Seward . . . "Secretary of War as this": WHS, quoted in ibid., p. 221.
717 crowd erupted . . . "loud and lusty" cheers: *NR,* April 3, 1865.
717 "beaming" Stanton . . . "The Star Spangled Banner": *NYTrib,* April 4, 1865.
717 "The demand seemed . . . press to supply": *Star,* April 3, 1865.
717 One hundred *Herald* . . . section of the city: *NYH,* April 4, 1865.
718 EXTRA! . . . first to enter the city: *NR,* April 3, 1865.
718 eight hundred guns, fired at Stanton's order: Brooks, *Mr. Lincoln's Washington,* p. 431.
718 dinner at Stanton's house: Thomas and Hyman, *Stanton,* p. 353.
718 "if there were to be . . . of the danger": James Speed to Joseph H. Barrett, 1885 September 16, Lincoln Collection, Lincoln Miscellaneous Manuscripts, Box 9, Folder 66, Special Collections, Research Center, University of Chicago Library.
718 tried to keep Lincoln . . . "the same condition": EMS to AL, April 3, 1865, Lincoln Papers.
718 Lincoln was already . . . Richmond the next day: AL to EMS, April 3, 1865, *CW,* VIII, p. 385.
718 At 8 a.m. . . . historic journey to Richmond: Barnes, "With Lincoln from Washington to Richmond in 1865," Part II, *Appleton's* (1907), p. 746.
718 channel approaching . . . "and touched them": *Through Five Administrations,* ed. Gerry, pp. 51–52.
718 "Here we were . . . well to be humble": AL, quoted in Porter, *Incidents and Anecdotes of the Civil War,* pp. 294–95.
719 Lincoln was surrounded . . . "hereafter enjoy": Ibid., p. 295.
719 men stood up . . . "and from the water-side": Ibid., pp. 296–97.
719 crowd trailed Lincoln . . . easily visible: Ibid., p. 299.
719 "walking with his usual . . . in everything": Thomas Thatcher Graves, "The Occupation," Part II of "The Fall of Richmond," in *Battles and Leaders of the Civil War,* Vol. IV, Pt. II, p. 727 (quote); Porter, *Incidents and Anecdotes of the Civil War,* p. 299; *Through Five Administrations,* ed. Gerry, p. 53.
719 Lincoln's bodyguard . . . along the route: *Through Five Administrations,* ed. Gerry, p. 54.
719 occupied the stucco mansion . . . glass of water: Barnes, "With Lincoln from Washington to Richmond in 1865," Part II, *Appleton's* (1907), pp. 748–49.
719 bottle of whiskey . . . "condition for the Yankees": *Through Five Administrations,* ed. Gerry, p. 55.
719 toured the mansion . . . "interested in everything": Graves, "The Occupation," in *Battles and Leaders of the Civil War,* Vol. IV, Pt. II, p. 728.
719 met with the members . . . troops from the war: J. G. Randall and Richard N. Current, *Lincoln the President: The Last Full Measure,* originally published as Vol. 4 of *Lincoln the President* (New York: Dodd, Mead, 1955; Urbana: University of Illinois Press, 1991), pp. 353–56; AL to Godfrey Weitzel, April 6, 1865, *CW,* VIII, p. 389.
720 Confederate statehouse . . . greatly relieved: Porter, *Incidents and Anecdotes of the Civil War,* pp. 302–03.
720 "nothing short of miraculous . . . go in peace": *Through Five Administrations,* ed. Gerry, p. 54.
720 all the public buildings . . . "one blaze of glory": Brooks, *Mr. Lincoln's Washington,* p. 434.
720 "the entire population . . . of lighted candles": *NR,* April 5, 1865.
720 he told Welles . . . "schemes are his apology": Entry for April 5, 1865, *Welles diary,* Vol. II, p. 275.
720 Fanny and her friend . . . horses bolted: Seward, *Seward at Washington . . . 1861–1872,* p. 270 (quote); entry for April 5, 1865, in Johnson, "Sensitivity and Civil War," p. 867; *NR,* April 6, 1865.
720 "swinging the driver . . . a cat by the tail": *NR,* April 6, 1865.
720 Fred and Seward jumped . . . consciousness: Seward, *Seward at Washington . . . 1861–1872,* p. 270 (quote); entry for April 5, 1865, in Johnson, "Sensitivity and Civil War," pp. 867–68; Verdi, "The Assassination of the Sewards," *The Republic* (1873), p. 290.
720 "The horses tore" . . . his broken body: Entry for April 5, 1865, in Johnson, "Sensitivity and Civil War," pp. 867–68.
721 "blood streaming from his mouth": Verdi, "The Assassination of the Sewards," *The Republic* (1873), p. 290.
721 delirious with pain . . . his side for hours: Entry for April 5, 1865, in Johnson, "Sensitivity and Civil War," pp. 868, 869.
721 Stanton sent . . . "presence here is needed": EMS to AL, April 5, 1865, Lincoln Papers.
721 Lincoln advised Grant . . . return to Washington: AL to USG, April 6, 1865, *CW,* VIII, p. 388.
721 Mary and her invited . . . "arrive at City Point": MTL to EMS, April 6, 1865, in Turner and Turner, *Mary Todd Lincoln,* p. 214 (quote); Foote, *The Civil War,* Vol. III, p. 903; Keckley, *Behind the Scenes,* p. 163.
721 Stanton informed . . . "remaining at City Point": EMS to MTL, April 6, 1865, Lincoln Papers.
721 he sent word . . . "clear and spirits good": EMS to AL, April 6, 1865, Lincoln Papers.
721 Mary's party arrived . . . bulletins, all positive: Chambrun, "Personal Recollections of Mr. Lincoln," *Scribner's* (1893), p. 27.
721 "His whole appearance . . . had been attained": James Harlan, quoted in Foote, *The Civil War,* Vol. III, P874p. 903.
721 "it was impossible . . . much less of vanity": Chambrun, "Personal Recollections of Mr. Lincoln," *Scribner's* (1893), p. 28.
722 telegram from Sheridan . . . "Lee will surrender": Phil Sheridan to USG, quoted in AL to EMS, April 7, 1865, *CW,* VIII, p. 389.
722 "Let the *thing* be pressed": AL to USG, April 7, 1865, *CW,* VIII, p. 392.

722 Julia Grant . . . "that we be not judged": *Personal Memoirs of Julia Dent Grant*, p. 149; Chambrun, "Personal Recollections of Mr. Lincoln," *Scribner's* (1893), p. 33 (quote).
722 "he gave orders . . . the great oaks": Chambrun, "Personal Recollections of Mr. Lincoln," *Scribner's* (1893), p. 29 (quote); Keckley, *Behind the Scenes*, p. 169.
722 "an old country . . . quiet place like this": AL, quoted in Arnold, *The Life of Abraham Lincoln*, p. 435.
722 observed a turtle . . . shared "a happy laugh": Keckley, *Behind the Scenes*, p. 170.
722 visited injured soldiers . . . "no more fighting": Chambrun, "Personal Recollections of Mr. Lincoln," *Scribner's* (1893), pp. 30, 33–34.
722 came to say farewell . . . "floating palace": Keckley, *Behind the Scenes*, pp. 171–72.
723 asked them to play . . . "upon literary subjects": Chambrun, "Personal Recollections of Mr. Lincoln," *Scribner's* (1893), pp. 34, 35.
723 "a beautiful quarto . . . in his hands": Edward L. Pierce, *Memoir and Letters of Charles Sumner*, Vol. IV (London: Sampson Low, Marston and Co., 1893), p. 235.
723 passages from *Macbeth* . . . *touch him further*: William Shakespeare, *Macbeth*, Scene II, in *The Riverside Shakespeare*, 2nd edn., Vol. II (Boston and New York: Houghton Mifflin, 1997), p. 1373; Chambrun, "Personal Recollections of Mr. Lincoln," *Scribner's* (1893), p. 35.
723 "how true a description . . . the same scene": Chambrun, "Personal Recollections of Mr. Lincoln," *Scribner's* (1893), p. 35.
723 ominous selection . . . "in continual dread": Speed to Barrett, September 16, 1885, University of Chicago Library.
723 "that the people know . . . without fear": AL, quoted in Thomas and Hyman, *Stanton*, p. 395.
723 passed by Mount Vernon . . . "would again reappear": Chambrun, "Personal Recollections of Mr. Lincoln," *Scribner's* (1893), pp. 35, 32.
724 He had observed . . . "in ruined Richmond": *Through Five Administrations*, ed. Gerry, p. 59.
724 "It was in the evening . . . injuries and the shock": Seward, *Seward at Washington . . . 1861–1872*, pp. 271, 270.
724 his face "so marred . . . patient and uncomplaining": FAS to LW, quoted in ibid., p. 271.
724 "The extreme sensitiveness . . . from the door": Seward, ibid., p. 271.
724 Lincoln entered the room . . . "the end, at last": WHS and AL, quoted in ibid., p. 271.
724 stretched out . . . "satisfied at the labor": Seward, *Seward at Washington . . . 1861–1872*, p. 271; entry for April 9, 1865, in Johnson, "Sensitivity and Civil War," p. 872 (quotes).
725 saw that Seward . . . got up and left the room: Seward, *Seward at Washington . . . 1861–1872*, p. 272.
725 telegram from Grant . . . "proposed by myself": USG to EMS, April 9, 1865, *OR*, Ser. 1, Vol. XLVI, Part III, p. 663.
725 "the President hugged him with joy": *Star*, February 15, 1896.
725 close to 10 p.m. . . . "first time in my life": Entry for April 9, 1865, in Johnson, "Sensitivity and Civil War," p. 871.
725 Both Grant and Lee . . . "dignified in defeat": Jay Winik, *April 1865: The Month That Saved America* (New York: HarperCollins, 2001), p. 193.
725 Grant had sent a note . . . "effusion of blood": USG to Robert E. Lee, April 7, 1865, *OR*, Ser. 1, Vol. XLVI, Part III, p. 619.
725 Lee refused to accept . . . ready to surrender: McPherson, *Battle Cry of Freedom*, p. 848.
725 dressed for the historic . . . "deep, red silk": Douglas Southall Freeman, *R. E. Lee: A Biography*, Vol. IV (New York: Charles Scribner's Sons, 1936), p. 118.
725 imprisoned before . . . "my best appearance": Robert E. Lee, quoted in ibid., p. 118.
725 terms of surrender . . . "properly exchanged": USG to Robert E. Lee, April 9, 1865, quoted in Grant, *Personal Memoirs of U.S. Grant*, p. 581.
725 "the thought occurred to me" . . . twenty-five thousand men: Grant, *Personal Memoirs of U.S. Grant*, pp. 581–83.
726 tried to speak . . . "tears came into his eyes": Freeman, *R. E. Lee*, Vol. IV, p. 144.
726 "Men, we have fought . . . best I could for you": Robert E. Lee, quoted in ibid.
726 "each side of . . . as ever, General Lee!": Charles Blackford, quoted in ibid. pp. 146, 147.
726 "a great boom . . . laid down its arms": Brooks, *Washington, D.C., in Lincoln's Time*, p. 223.
726 "The nation seems . . . terminates the Rebellion": Entry for April 10, 1865, *Welles diary*, Vol. II, p. 278.
726 several thousand gathered . . . "people cheered": *National Intelligencer*, Washington, D.C., April 11, 1865, quoted in *CW*, VIII, p. 393 n1.
726 planning a speech . . . "dribble it all out": AL, "Response to Serenade," *National Intelligencer* version, April 10, 1865, *CW*, VIII, p. 393.
726 If he said something . . . "not to make mistakes": AL, "Response to Serenade," *NR* version, April 10, 1865, *CW*, VIII, p. 394.
726 finally appeared . . . "waving their handkerchiefs": *NR*, April 11, 1865.
727 "I am very greatly . . . with its performance": AL, "Response to Serenade," *National Intelligencer* version, April 10, 1865, *CW*, VIII, p. 393.
727 "it is good to show the rebels . . . hear it again": Chambrun, "Personal Recollections of Mr. Lincoln," *Scribner's* (1893), p. 34.
727 band followed "Dixie" . . . "in high good-humor": *Through Five Administrations*, ed. Gerry, p. 62 (quote); *National Intelligencer*, April 11, 1865, in *CW*, VIII, pp. 393–94 n1.
727 "If possible . . . than last Monday": MTL to CS, April 10, 1865, in Turner and Turner, *Mary Todd Lincoln*, p. 216.

727 exhilaration was evident . . . "qu'en pensez vous?": MTL to CS, April 11, 1865, in ibid., p. 217.
727 Illuminated once again . . . miles around: Brooks, *Washington, D.C., in Lincoln's Time*, p. 225.
727 "Bonfires blazed . . . rockets were fired": *NYTrib*, April 12, 1865.
727 decorating the front . . . "and evergreens": *Star*, February 15, 1896.
727 a second-story window . . . "of a different character": Brooks, *Washington, D.C., in Lincoln's Time*, pp. 226–27.
727 "the greatest question . . . practical statesmanship": "31 July 1863, Friday," in Hay, *Inside Lincoln's White House*, p. 69.
728 acknowledged that in Louisiana . . . "by smashing it?": AL, "Last Public Address," April 11, 1865, *CW*, VIII, pp. 403–04.
728 John Wilkes Booth . . . passion for the rebels' cause: Lockridge, *Darling of Misfortune*, p. 111.
728 evolved a plan to kidnap . . . not ready to yield: Michael W. Kauffman, *American Brutus: John Wilkes Booth and the Lincoln Conspiracies* (New York: Random House, 2004), pp. 134, 211–12.
728 "Our cause being almost . . . great must be done": Text of John Wilkes Booth diary, available through Abraham Lincoln research website, http://members/aol.com/RVSNorton1/Lincoln52.html (accessed May 2005).
728 Two other conspirators . . . "put him through": John Wilkes Booth, quoted in Donald, *Lincoln*, p. 588.
728 Curiously . . . "God knows what is best": Lamon, *Recollections of Abraham Lincoln*, pp. 116–18.
729 Fehrenbacher is persuasive . . . confused: Commentary on Lamon recollection, *Recollected Words of Abraham Lincoln*, ed. Fehrenbacher and Fehrenbacher, p. 293.
729 While radicals . . . control of the seceded states: Pierce, *Memoir and Letters of Charles Sumner*, Vol. IV, p. 236; SPC to AL, April 12, 1865, Lincoln Papers.
729 "a large majority of the people": *NYH*, quoted in Harris, *Lincoln's Last Months*, p. 216.
729 "Reunion . . . in the minds of men": Brooks, *Washington, D.C., in Lincoln's Time*, p. 228.
729 "there must be . . . robber bands and guerillas": Entry for April 13, 1865, *Welles diary*, Vol. II, p. 279.
729 Lincoln had hoped . . . "their own work": Ibid.
729 "that to place . . . bring trouble with Congress": A. E. H. Johnson, quoted in Flower, *Edwin McMasters Stanton*, p. 272.
729 Stanton insisted . . . "absolutely null and void": EMS, quoted in ibid., p. 271.
730 Speed expressed his accord . . . with Lincoln: Williams, "James and Joshua Speed," p. 148.
730 confessed to Welles . . . tremendously: Gideon Welles, "Lincoln and Johnson," *Galaxy* 13 (April 1872), p. 524.
730 "doubted the policy . . . correct it if he had": Entry for April 13, 1865, *Welles diary*, Vol. II, pp. 279–80.
730 telegram from Campbell . . . originally discussed: John A. Campbell to Godfrey Weitzel, April 7, 1865, *CW*, VIII, pp. 407–08 n1.
730 Lincoln walked over . . . "any specific acts": A. E. H. Johnson, quoted in Flower, *Edwin McMasters Stanton*, p. 272.
730 Lincoln stood up . . . "safe-return to their homes": AL to Godfrey Weitzel, April 12, 1865, *CW*, VIII, p. 407 (quote); EMS, in Flower, *Edwin McMasters Stanton*, p. 271.
730 "*that* . . . was exactly right": Ibid.
730 "As we reached . . . 'candles from my department' ": *Personal Memoirs of Julia Dent Grant*, pp. 153, 154.
731 received a delightful note . . . "drive with me!": MTL to Mary Jane Welles, July 11, 1865, in Turner and Turner, *Mary Todd Lincoln*, p. 257.
731 "We are rejoicing . . . glorious victories": MTL to James Gordon Bennett, [April 13, 1865], in ibid., p. 219.
731 "charming time . . . into a lad of sixteen": MTL to Abram Wakeman, April 13, [1865], in ibid., p. 220.
731 told Sumner . . . a visit with General Grant: MTL to CS, [April] 13, [1865], in ibid., p. 219.
731 "Well, my son . . . for a long while": Keckley, *Behind the Scenes*, pp. 137–38.
731 Grant arrived . . . this event would be favorable: Entry for April 14, 1865, *Welles diary*, Vol. II, pp. 282–83.
732 Stanton had drafted . . . "asked me to read it": EMS, quoted in Flower, *Edwin McMasters Stanton*, p. 301.
732 cabinet concurred . . . two separate states: Entry for April 14, 1865, *Welles diary*, Vol. II, p. 281; Nicolay and Hay, *Abraham Lincoln*, Vol. X (1890 edn.), p. 284.
732 "he thought it providential . . . harmony and union": Gideon Welles, "Lincoln and Johnson," *Galaxy* 13 (April 1872), p. 526.
732 "Didn't our Chief . . . hair and whiskers": Speed to Barrett, September 16, 1885, Lincoln Collection, University of Chicago Library.
732 Lincoln seemed "more cheerful . . . at home and abroad": EMS to Charles Francis Adams, April 15, 1865, Telegrams Sent by the Secretary of War, Vol. 185–186, December 27, 1864–April 20, 1865, Telegrams Collected by the Office of the Secretary of War (Bound) (National Archives Microfilm Publication M-473, reel 88), Records of the Office of the Secretary of War, RG 107, DNA.
732 "spoke very kindly . . . of the Confederacy": EMS to John A. Dix, April 15, 1865, *OR*, Ser. 1, Vol. XLVI, Part III, p. 780.
732 "in marked degree . . . distinguished him": EMS to Charles Francis Adams, April 15, 1865 (M-473, reel 88), RG 107, DNA.
732 "a conspicuous . . . best to let him run": Dana, *Recollection of the Civil War* (1996 edn.), pp. 273–74.
733 She had never seen . . . " 'been very miserable' ": MTL to Francis B. Carpenter, November 15, [1865], in Turner and Turner, *Mary Todd Lincoln*, pp. 284–85.
733 "he spoke of his old . . . riding the circuit": Arnold, *The Life of Abraham Lincoln*, pp. 429–30.
733 hoped to travel . . . back home to Illinois: MTL interview, [September 1866], in *HI*, p. 359; Randall, *Mary Lincoln*, p. 382.
733 group of old friends . . . "to dinner at once": Tarbell, *The Life of Abraham Lincoln*, Vol. II (1900 edn.), p. 235.
734 met with Noah Brooks . . . "its pleasures": AL, quoted in Hollister, *Life of Schuyler Colfax*, p. 252.
734 invited Colfax to join . . . that night: Ibid., p. 253.

734 "more hopeful . . . nearly so with gold": Brooks, *Mr. Lincoln's Washington*, p. 443.
734 *Republican* had announced . . . box that night: *NR*, April 14, 1865.
734 Julia Grant . . . asked to be excused: Grant, *Personal Memoirs of U. S. Grant*, p. 592; *Personal Memoirs of Julia Dent Grant*, p. 155.
734 The Stantons also declined: Thomas and Hyman, *Stanton*, p. 395.
734 "unwilling to encourage . . . poker over his arm": Bates, *Lincoln in the Telegraph Office*, p. 367.
734 "I suppose it's time . . . would rather stay": AL, quoted in Hollister, *Life of Schuyler Colfax*, p. 253.
734 "It has been advertised . . . disappoint the people": AL, quoted in *Through Five Administrations*, p. 67.
735 Booth had devised a plan . . . assassinate the president: Kauffman, *American Brutus*, pp. 212–15.
735 Booth believed he would be . . . "greater tyrant": Text of John Wilkes Booth diary, available through Abraham Lincoln research website, http://members/aol.com/RVSNorton1/Lincoln52.html (accessed May 2005).
735 "Booth knew . . . martyr of Caesar": Kauffman, *American Brutus*, p. 212.
735 slept well the previous . . . "for the first time": Entry for April 14, 1865, in Johnson, "Sensitivity and Civil War," p. 876.
735 "listened with a look . . . the Cabinet meeting": Seward, *Reminiscences of a War-Time Statesman and Diplomat*, p. 258.
735 Fanny's reading . . . how much he enjoyed it: Entry for April 14, 1865, in Johnson, "Sensitivity and Civil War," p. 876.
735 Stanton had stopped by . . . serenading him: Thomas and Hyman, *Stanton*, p. 396.
736 "quiet arrangements" . . . opposite side of the bed: Entry for April 14, 1865, in Johnson, "Sensitivity and Civil War," p. 877.
736 "there seemed nothing unusual . . . presented himself": Seward, *Reminiscences of a War-Time Statesman and Diplomat*, p. 258.
736 Powell told the servant . . . but Fred refused: Verdi, "The Assassination of the Sewards," *The Republic* (1873), p. 293.
736 "stood apparently irresolute . . . pulled the trigger": Seward, *Reminiscences of a War-Time Statesman and Diplomat*, p. 259.
736 last memory Fred would have . . . unconscious: *Cincinnati [Ohio] Commercial*, December 8, 1865.
736 Private Robinson . . . headed toward Seward: Charles F. Cooney, "Seward's Savior: George F. Robinson," *Lincoln Herald* (Fall 1973), p. 93.
736 begging him not to kill . . . "face bending over": Entry for April 14, 1865, in Johnson, "Sensitivity and Civil War," pp. 879–80.
736 large bowie knife . . . "loose on his neck": Verdi, "The Assassination of the Sewards," *The Republic* (1873), p. 291.
736 his only impressions . . . "overcoat is made of": WHS, quoted in *Cincinnati [Ohio] Commercial*, December 8, 1865.
736 Fanny's screams . . . the floor: Entry for April 14, 1865, in Johnson, "Sensitivity and Civil War," p. 880.
737 managed to pull Powell away . . . the right hand: Verdi, "The Assassination of the Sewards," *The Republic* (1873), p. 292.
737 Gus ran for his pistol . . . fled through the city: Seward, *Seward at Washington . . . 1861–1872*, p. 279.
737 lifted Seward onto the bed . . . rooms on the parlor floor: Entry for April 14, 1865, in Johnson, "Sensitivity and Civil War," pp. 882, 884.
737 "He looked like an . . . yes, of one man!": Verdi, "The Assassination of the Sewards," *The Republic* (1873), pp. 291–92.
738 Atzerodt had taken a room . . . "not to kill": Donald, *Lincoln*, p. 596.
738 seated at the bar . . . and never returned: Winik, *April 1865*, p. 226.
738 had attended a dress rehearsal . . . Harry Ford: Kauffman, *American Brutus*, pp. 214, 217.
738 play had started . . . "with a smile and bow": Charles A. Leale, M.D., to Benjamin F. Butler, July 20, 1867, container 43, Butler Papers, DLC.
738 armchair at the center . . . sofa on her left: "Major Rathbone's Affidavit," in J. E. Buckingham, Sr., *Reminiscences and Souvenirs of the Assassination of Abraham Lincoln* (Washington, D.C.: Rufus H. Darby, 1894), pp. 73, 75.
738 "rested her hand . . . situation on the stage": Charles Sabin Taft, "Abraham Lincoln's Last Hours," *Century* 45 (February 1893), p. 634.
738 later recalled . . . "think any thing about it": Randall, *Mary Lincoln*, p. 382.
738 footman delivered a message . . . and fired: Winik, *April 1865*, p. 223; Harris, *Lincoln's Last Months*, p. 224.
739 "As he jumped . . . struck the stage": Taft, "Abraham Lincoln's Last Hours," *Century* 45 (1893), p. 634.
739 "he was suffering . . . he struggled up": Annie F. F. Wright, "The Assassination of Abraham Lincoln," *Magazine of History* 9 (February 9, 1909), p. 114.
739 "his shining dagger . . . it had been a diamond": Leale to Butler, July 20, 1867, container 43, Butler Papers, DLC.
739 shouted . . . "Sic semper tyrannis": Wright, "The Assassination of Abraham Lincoln," *Magazine of History* (1909), p. 114.
739 saw Mary Lincoln . . . "shot the President!": Ibid.
739 Charles Leale . . . pressure on Lincoln's brain: Leale to Butler, July 20, 1867, container 43, Butler Papers, DLC.
739 Charles Sabin Taft . . . boardinghouse: Taft, "Abraham Lincoln's Last Hours," *Century* 45 (1893), p. 635.
739 Joseph Sterling . . . headed for Seward's house: Joseph A. Sterling, quoted in *Star*, April 14, 1918.
740 already gone to bed . . . set forth in the foggy night: Entry for April 14, 1865, *Welles diary*, Vol. II, pp. 283–84.

740 Blood was everywhere . . . floor of the bedroom: Entry for April 14, 1865, in Johnson, "Sensitivity and Civil War," p. 886.
740 "was saturated with blood" . . . he decided to join them: Entry for April 14, 1865, *Welles diary*, Vol. II, pp. 285–86 (quote p. 285).
740 Chase had already retired . . . "a night of horrors": Entries for April 14, 1865, *Chase Papers*, Vol. 1, pp. 528–29.
741 Lincoln had been placed . . . "spare appearance": Entry for April 14, 1865, *Welles diary*, Vol. II, p. 286.
741 "would have killed most men . . . *much vitality*": Entry for April 30, 1865, Taft diary.
741 Mary spent most . . . "overcome by emotion": Entry for April 14, 1865, *Welles diary*, Vol. II, p. 287.
741 "Why didn't he shoot me?" . . . not told, out of fear: Field, *Memories of Many Men*, p. 322.
741 "clean napkins . . . stains on the pillow": Taft, "Abraham Lincoln's Last Hours," *Century* 45 (1893), p. 635.
741 Robert, who had remained . . . "leaving his cheeks": Thomas F. Pendel, *Thirty-Six Years in the White House* (Washington, D.C.: Neale Publishing Company, 1902), pp. 42–43.
741 to summon Tad . . . his father's condition: Leale to Butler, July 20, 1867, container 43, Butler Papers, DLC.
741 Tad and his tutor . . . to see *Aladdin:* M. Helen Palmes Moss, "Lincoln and Wilkes Booth as Seen on the Day of the Assassination," *Century* LXXVII (April 1909), p. 951.
741 decorated with patriotic . . . "shrieking in agony": *NR*, April 15, 1865.
742 "Poor little Tad . . . fell into a sound sleep": Pendel, *Thirty-Six Years in the White House*, p. 44.
742 entire cabinet . . . "heartrending lamentations": *NYH*, April 16, 1865.
742 "there was not a soul . . . love the president": *Star*, February 15, 1896.
742 "While evidently swayed . . . in all things": A. F. Rockwell, quoted in Flower, *Edwin McMasters Stanton*, p. 283.
742 dictated numerous dispatches . . . "wait for the next": *Star*, February 15, 1896.
742 first telegram . . . "in a dangerous condition": Thomas T. Eckert to USG, April 14, 1865, *OR*, Ser. 1, Vol. XLVI, Part III, pp. 744–45.
742 reached Grant . . . "in perfect silence": Porter, *Campaigning with Grant*, p. 499.
742 he had turned "very pale": *Personal Memoirs of Julia Dent Grant*, p. 156.
742 Julia Grant guessed . . . "that could be received": Porter, *Campaigning with Grant*, pp. 499–500.
742 he told Julia . . . "tenderness and magnanimity": *Personal Memoirs of Julia Dent Grant*, p. 156.
743 At 1 a.m., Stanton telegraphed . . . "best detectives": EMS to John H. Kennedy, April 15, 1865, *OR*, Ser. 1, Vol. XLVI, Part III, p. 783.
743 "The wound is mortal . . . is now dying": EMS to John A. Dix, April 15, 1865, 1:30 a.m., *OR*, Ser. 1, Vol. XLVI, Part III, p. 780.
743 "The President continues . . . shot the President": Ibid., 4:10 a.m., p. 781.
743 Shortly after dawn . . . "death-struggle had begun": Entry for April 14, 1865, *Welles diary*, Vol. II, p. 288.
743 "As she entered" . . . sofa in the parlor: Taft, "Abraham Lincoln's Last Hours," *Century* 45 (1893), p. 635.
743 "the town clocks . . . be again resumed": Field, *Memories of Many Men*, p. 325.
743 "Let us pray" . . . everyone present knelt: Leale to Butler, July 20, 1867, container 43, Butler Papers, DLC.
743 At 7:22 a.m. . . . "belongs to the ages": Donald, *Lincoln*, p. 599. As David Donald notes, witnesses thought they heard several variations of Stanton's utterance, including "He belongs to the ages now," "He now belongs to the Ages," and "He is a man for the ages." Donald, *Lincoln*, p. 686, endnote for p. 599 beginning *"to the ages."*
743 "Oh, why did you not . . . he was dying": *NYH*, April 16, 1865.
743 moans could be heard . . . taken to her carriage: Taft, "Abraham Lincoln's Last Hours," *Century* 45 (1893), p. 636; Field, *Memories of Many Men*, p. 326.
743 Stanton's "coolness" . . . streamed down his cheeks: *NYH*, April 16, 1865.
743 "Stanton's grief . . . break down and weep bitterly": Porter, *Campaigning with Grant*, p. 501.
743 "Not everyone knows . . . his honor and yours": JH to EMS, July 26, 1865, in Hay, *At Lincoln's Side*, p. 106.
744 "Is he dead? . . . entire face was distorted": Field, *Memories of Many Men*, p. 327.
744 walked to Seward's house . . . Blair and his father: Entry for April 15, 1865, *Chase Papers*, Vol. I, pp. 529, 530.
744 "with tearful eyes . . . of our side": EBL to SPL, April 15, 1865, in *Wartime Washington*, ed. Laas, p. 495.
744 *Richmond Whig* . . . "South has descended": *Richmond Whig*, quoted in Robert S. Harper, *Lincoln and the Press* (New York: McGraw-Hill, 1951), p. 360.
744 St. Louis . . . comfortable study: Entry for January 27, 1865, *The Diary of Edward Bates, 1859–1866*, p. 443.
744 "the astounding news . . . country and for myself": Entry for April 15, 1865, in ibid., p. 473.
744 News of Lincoln's death . . . "sinking into his mind": Brooks, *Mr. Lincoln's Washington*, pp. 458–59 (quotes p. 459).
745 "The history of governments . . . confidence and regard": "Hay's Reminiscences of the Civil War," in Hay, *At Lincoln's Side*, pp. 128–29.
745 Flags remained . . . "the farewell march": Brooks, *Washington, D.C., in Lincoln's Time*, pp. 271 (quote), 273.
745 nearly two hundred thousand Union soldiers: Smith, *The Francis Preston Blair Family in Politics*, Vol. II, p. 185.
745 "Never in the history . . . shrill call of bugles": Brooks, *Washington, D.C., in Lincoln's Time*, pp. 272–74.
745 "magnificent and imposing spectacle": Entry for May 19, 1865, *Welles diary*, Vol. II, p. 310.
745 "You see in these . . . half a dozen presidents": EMS, quoted in Flower, *Edwin McMasters Stanton*, p. 288.
746 "more and more dim . . . found in every family": AL, "Address Before the Young Men's Lyceum of Springfield, Illinois," January 27, 1838, in *CW*, I, p. 115.
746 "a new birth of freedom . . . perish from the earth": AL, "Address Delivered at the Dedication of the Cemetery at Gettysburg," final text, November 19, 1863, in *CW*, VII, p. 23.
746 second day belonged . . . "with our swords": Sherman, *Memoirs of General W. T. Sherman*, p. 731.
746 All of Washington . . . "All felt this": Entry for April 19, 1865, *Welles diary*, Vol. II, p. 310.
746 "a Cabinet which should . . . than one counsellor": WHS, "The President and His Cabinet," October 20, 1865, *Works of William H. Seward*, Vol. V, p. 527.

747 "I have no doubt . . . greatest man I ever knew": Tribute by General Grant, in Browne, *The Every-Day Life of Abraham Lincoln*, p. 7.
747 "I have more than once . . . Nineteenth Century": Walt Whitman, "November Boughs," *The Complete Prose Works of Walt Whitman*, Vol. III (New York: G. P. Putnam's Sons, Knickerbocker Press, 1902), pp. 206–07.
747 Leo Tolstoy . . . "light beams directly on us": Leo Tolstoy, quoted in *The World*, New York, February 7, 1908.
748 "Every man is said . . . yet to be developed": AL, "Communication to the People of Sangamo County," March 9, 1832, in *CW*, I, p. 8.
748 "he had done nothing . . . that he had lived": AL, paraphrased in Joshua F. Speed to WHH, February 7, 1866, in *HI*, p. 197.
749 "conceived in Liberty . . . all men are created equal": AL, "Address Delivered at the Dedication of the Cemetery at Gettysburg, November 19, 1863; Edward Everett Copy," in *CW*, VII, p. 21.
749 "With malice toward none; with charity for all": AL, "Second Inaugural Address," March 4, 1865, *CW*, VIII, p. 333.

EPILOGUE

Page

751 "night of horrors": Entries for April 14, 1865, *Chase Papers*, Vol. I, p. 529.
751 "vicarious suffering": FAS, in "Miscellaneous Fragments in Mrs. Seward's Handwriting," reel 197, Seward Papers.
751 "the largest . . . woman in America": *New York Independent*, undated, in Seward family scrapbook, Seward House Foundation Historical Association, Inc., Library, Auburn, N.Y.
751 Fanny remained . . . tuberculosis: Taylor, *William Henry Seward*, p. 266.
751 Seward was inconsolable: Van Deusen, *William Henry Seward*, p. 417.
751 "Truly it may . . . mother and daughter": *Washington Republican*, undated, in Seward family scrapbook, Seward House.
751 attempts to mediate . . . radicals in Congress: Van Deusen, *William Henry Seward*, p. 452.
751 "Seward's Folly": Taylor, *William Henry Seward*, p. 278.
751 spent his last years traveling: Ibid., pp. 290–91, 292–94; *NYT*, October 11, 1872.
751 Jenny asked . . . "Love one another": Taylor, *William Henry Seward*, p. 296; Seward, *Seward at Washington . . . 1861–1872*, p. 508 (quote).
751 Thurlow Weed . . . wept openly: Taylor, *William Henry Seward*, p. 296.
751 Stanton's remaining . . . asked for his resignation: Pratt, *Stanton*, p. 452; Thomas and Hyman, *Stanton*, p. 583.
751 Refusing to honor . . . removal order: George C. Gorham, *Life and Public Services of Edwin M. Stanton*, Vol. II (Boston and New York: Houghton, Mifflin, Riverside Press, 1899), p. 444.
751 "barricaded himself": Pratt, *Stanton*, p. 452.
751 taking his meals in the department: Thomas and Hyman, *Stanton*, p. 595.
751 Tenure of Office Act: "Tenure of Office Act," in *The Reader's Companion to American History*, ed. Foner and Garraty, pp. 1,063–64.
752 impeachment failed . . . submitted his resignation: Thomas and Hyman, *Stanton*, p. 608.
752 Grant nominated him . . . "only office": Wolcott, "Edwin M. Stanton," p. 178.
752 short-lived . . . severe asthma attack: *Dictionary of American Biography*, Vol. IX, ed. Dumas Malone (New York: Charles Scribner's Sons, 1935; 1964), p. 520; Thomas and Hyman, *Stanton*, pp. 637–38; Christopher Bates, "Stanton, Edwin McMasters," in *Encyclopedia of the American Civil War*, ed. Heidler and Heidler, p. 1852.
752 "I know that it is . . . he was then": Robert Todd Lincoln to Edwin L. Stanton, quoted in Thomas and Hyman, *Stanton*, p. 638.
752 close-knit family . . . Confederate Army: Cain, *Lincoln's Attorney General*, p. 330.
752 "it was in his social . . . death cannot sever": Address by Colonel J. C. Broadhead, in "Addresses by the Members of the St. Louis Bar on the Death of Edward Bates," Bates Papers, MoSHi.
752 impeachment trial . . . resting with the Democrats: Blue, *Salmon P. Chase*, p. 285.
752 Kate serving . . . derailed his ambitions: *Dictionary of American Biography*, Vol. II, ed. Allen Johnson and Dumas Malone (New York: Charles Scribner's Sons, 1929; 1958), p. 33.
752 switched his allegiance . . . to Horace Greeley: Niven, *Salmon P. Chase*, pp. 447–48.
752 physical condition weakened . . . depression: Ibid., pp. 444, 448–49.
752 "too much of an invalid . . . I were dead": SPC to Richard C. Parsons, May 5, 1873, *Chase Papers*, Vol. V, p. 370.
752 Kate saw her marriage . . . died in poverty: Belden and Belden, *So Fell the Angels*, pp. 297–98, 306–10, 320, 326–27, 348.
753 Frank Blair . . . intemperate denunciations: *Dictionary of American Biography*, Vol. I, ed. Allen Johnson (New York: Charles Scribner's Sons, 1927; 1964), pp. 333–34.
753 died from a fall: *NYT*, July 10, 1875.
753 "his physical vigor . . . of disposition": *Sun*, Baltimore, Md., October 19, 1876.
753 Montgomery served . . . biography of Andrew Jackson: *Dictionary of American Biography*, Vol. I (1964 edn.), p. 340.
753 wrote a series . . . "herculean tasks": Niven, *Gideon Welles*, pp. 576–77 (quote p. 576).
753 perceptive diary . . . streptococcus infection: Ibid., pp. 578, 580.
753 remained friends . . . abridged version: Nicolay, *Lincoln's Secretary*, pp. 301, 342.

753 Shortly before he died . . . "overpowering melancholy": William Roscoe Thayer, *The Life and Letters of John Hay* (Boston and New York: Houghton Mifflin, 1929), pp. 405, 407.
753 "each morning . . . as an impossibility": MTL to EBL, August 25, 1865, in Turner and Turner, *Mary Todd Lincoln*, p. 268.
753 "precious Tad . . . gladly welcome death": MTL to Alexander Williamson, [May 26, 1867], in ibid., p. 422.
753 Tad journeyed . . . "beyond his years": *NYTrib*, July 17, 1871.
754 "compression of the heart": Turner and Turner, *Mary Todd Lincoln*, p. 585.
754 "The modest and cordial . . . fantastic enterprises": *NYTrib*, July 17, 1871.
754 "It is very hard . . . to the contrary": Robert Todd Lincoln to Mary Harlan, quoted in Helm, *The True Story of Mary*, p. 267.
754 erratic behavior . . . permanently estranged: Randall, *Mary Lincoln*, pp. 430–34.
754 virtual recluse . . . fulfilled at last: Ibid., pp. 442–43.

ILLUSTRATION CREDITS

Numbers in roman type refer to illustrations in the inserts; numbers in *italics* refer to book pages.

Chicago Historical Society: 1, 33, *702*

Abraham Lincoln Presidential Library & Museum: *xx–1*, 2, 3, 4, 5, 13, 19, 22, 23, 26, 29, 31, 32, 35, 36, 39, 44, 46, 47, 48, 49, 51, 55, 62, 63, 72, 73, 74, 76, *170*, *321*, *409*, *445*, *667*

Courtesy of the Department of Rare Books and Special Collections, University of Rochester Library: 6, 7, 9

Seward House, Auburn, New York: 8, 10, 34, 50

From the collection of Louise Taper: 11, 12

Ohio Historical Society: 14, 52

The Saint Louis Art Museum: *60*

Library of Congress: 15, 21, 24, 25, 27, 37, 41, 43, 56, 59, 64, 65, 68, 69, *347*, *377*, *548*

Missouri Historical Society: 16, 17, 18

Picture History: 20, 28, 30, 54, *473*

Western Reserve Historical Society, Cleveland, Ohio: 38

Brown University Library: 40

United States Army Military History Institute: 42

National Archives: 45, 53, 60, 61, 66, 67, 71, 75

Courtesy of J. Wayne Lee: 57, 58

National Portrait Gallery, Smithsonian Institution / Art Resource, New York: 70

Courtesy, American Antiquarian Society: *279*

Civil War Collection, Eastern Kentucky University Archives, Richmond, Kentucky: *323*

White House Historical Association (White House Collection): *597*, *627*

INDEX

DORIS KEARNS GOODWIN won the Pulitzer Prize in history for *No Ordinary Time.* She is also the author of the bestselling *Wait Till Next Year, The Fitzgeralds and the Kennedys,* and *Lyndon Johnson and the American Dream.* She lives in Concord, Massachusetts, with her husband, Richard Goodwin.